Collins
COBUILD
Student's
Dictionary
PLUS GRAMMAR

HarperCollins Publishers
Westerhill Road
Bishopbriggs
Glasgow
G64 2QT
Great Britain

Third Edition 2005

Latest Reprint 2006

© HarperCollins Publishers 1997, 2002, 2005

with CD-ROM
ISBN-13 978-0-00-718386-9
ISBN-10 0-00-718386-0

without CD-ROM
ISBN-13 978-0-00-720203-4
ISBN-10 0-00-720203-2

Hardback
ISBN-13 978-0-00-774468-8
ISBN-10 0-00-774468-4

Collins®, COBUILD® and Bank of English®
are registered trademarks of
HarperCollins Publishers Limited

www.collins.co.uk

A catalogue record for this book is available
from the British Library

Typeset by
Morton Word Processing Ltd, Scarborough
and Wordcraft, Glasgow

Printed and bound at
Thomson Press (India) Ltd

Acknowledgements
We would like to thank those authors and
publishers who kindly gave permission for
copyright material to be used in the Collins
Word Web. We would also like to thank
Times Newspapers Ltd for providing
valuable data.

CONTENTS

SECOND/THIRD EDITION

Founding Editor-in-Chief
John Sinclair

Publishing Director
Lorna Sinclair Knight

Editorial Director
Michela Clari

Managing Editor
Maree Airlie

Project Manager
Carol MacLeod

Lexicographers
Elizabeth Potter
Bob Grossmith

Editors
Maggie Seaton
Alison Macaulay

From the New Student's Dictionary

Publishing Director
Gwyneth Fox

Editorial Manager
Stephen Bullon

Senior Editors
Rosalind Combley
Michael Murphy
Christina Rammell
Laura Wedgeworth

Editors
Isabel Griffiths
Ceri Hewitt
Sean Lynch
Carole Murphy

Editorial Assistance
Catherine Brown

Computing Staff
Tim Lane

Design
Chi Leung

Practice Material
Bill Mascull

Usage Notes
John Williams

Secretarial Staff
Sue Crawley
Michelle Devereux

Production Manager
Gillian McNair

Illustrations
Anthony Boswell
Ela Bullon

From the Student's Grammar

Managing Editor
Gwyneth Fox

Senior Editor
Ramesh Krishnamurthy

Editor
Jenny Watson

Assistant Editors
Christina Rammell
Keith Stuart

Secretarial Staff
Sue Smith
Sue Crawley

Computing
Tim Lane Stephen Bullon
Zoe James

Illustrators
John Batten Clyde Pearson David Parkins
Gillian Martin Peter Schrank

And Annette Capel, Lorna Heaslip, Douglas Williamson

We would like to thank Dave Willis additionally for his valuable contributions to the grammar pages; Sylvia Chalker and Sue Inkster for their detailed comments and suggestions on the text; Annette Capel for writing the Key to the Exercises; Richard Fay and Paschalena Groutka for their part in the original drafting of the Units; Kirsty Haynes for secretarial assistance; Sue Inkster, Anthony Harvey, John Curtin, John Dyson, Tom Stableford, Bob Walker, David Evans, and Angus Oliver for their comments on the initial list of Units.

INTRODUCTION

A dictionary is probably the single most important reference book that a student of English can buy. This dictionary is especially important, because for many of its users it could be the first dictionary that they use which is written entirely in English.

Like all Collins COBUILD dictionaries, this new edition of the Student's Dictionary is based on the analysis of real language in use. Over the last few years, we have built up a huge electronic collection of text, both written and spoken, called Collins Word Web. At present, The Bank of English, part of Collins Word Web, stands at over 524 million words, and has been used as the basis of all Collins COBUILD dictionaries. It enables the dictionary writers at COBUILD to look at how the language works, and reveals the patterns and systems of the English language.

Because it is all held on computer, The Bank of English provides very fast and accurate access to all sorts of information about the language. One very significant area is word frequency. This information is absolutely vital in helping to prepare dictionary entries, both because it helps in the selection of words that are suitable for use in dictionary definitions, and because it provides a sensible list of words that need to be included and defined.

The words explained in this dictionary account for over 90% of the language that is written and spoken. That is because there is a relatively small number of words which are used over and over again, while there is a larger number of words which are not used very frequently. This dictionary concentrates on the words that occur over and over again, and the entries represent the language that students really do need to know and to use.

One of the primary purposes of a learner's dictionary such as this one is to provide information about those words that the user already 'knows', as well as to provide information that the user does not know. Many words have several uses and meanings, and we do not really 'know' a word until we are familiar with its full range of meaning and grammatical behaviour.

The entries provide a detailed account of the main uses and meanings of each word. Each of the word forms is listed at the start of each entry, along with information about variant spellings where they exist. Explanations are written in full sentences, and reflect typical grammatical behaviour as well as providing a clear description of meaning. And of course, the thousands of examples are taken directly from The Bank of English, showing typical patterns of use and grammatical structure. All of the information in this dictionary has been carefully chosen and presented in order to enable the student to write better English and also understand English better.

As well as continuing the traditions for which Collins COBUILD dictionaries have become known over the last 15 years, this new edition of the Student's Dictionary has a number of useful features. Colour has been used to help the entries stand out on a page, and enable users to find what they are looking for more quickly and easily.

Over 3,000 of the most frequent English words in the dictionary are clearly labelled with a star ✪. These have been identified by using the information on frequency provided by The Bank of English. There are also a number of usage notes throughout the text which supplement the information already provided in the dictionary entries. In many cases, these help to clarify the differences that exist between some items.

At the beginning of the book there is a guide to Using your Dictionary: this lists all the important features in the dictionary, and provides exercises to help the user become more proficient in dictionary use. We have also included reference pages which give essential phrases using time, date and numbers, information on punctuation symbols, and a full explanation of all grammatical labels. At the end of the dictionary text there are over 20 pages of illustrations providing essential vocabulary for a wide range of useful topics.

The final section of the dictionary comprises a clear, thorough **English Grammar Guide**, which explains the rules and principles of the English grammatical system using examples of real English from The Bank of English.

We believe that this dictionary will prove to be an indispensable reference tool for learners of English. As always, we welcome any comments that users may have about our books, so please contact us if you have any observations, criticisms, or questions.

You can contact us on our website at: http://www.collins.co.uk/cobuild
by email directly to: cobuild.collins@harpercollins.co.uk
or you can write to us at the following address:

Collins COBUILD
Westerhill Road
Bishopbriggs
Glasgow G64 2QT

GRAMMATICAL LABELS USED IN THE DICTIONARY

Introduction

Nearly all the words that are explained in this dictionary have grammar information given about them. For each word or meaning, its word class is shown in capital letters, just before the definition. Examples of word classes are N-COUNT, VERB, PRON and ADV. The sections below contain further information about each word class. You will find more detailed information about word classes in the English Grammar Guide at the back of the dictionary.

Verbs

VERB

A **verb** is a word which is used to say what someone or something does or what happens to them, or to give information about them.

eat: *We **ate** chips every night.*
lose: *My husband **lost** his job.*
sleep: *She **slept** till noon.*

PHR-VERB

A **phrasal verb** is a combination of a verb and an adverb (for example *catch up*) or a verb and a preposition (for example *call for*), which together have a particular meaning. Some phrasal verbs have both an adverb and a preposition (for example *add up to*).

catch up: *I stopped and waited for her to **catch up**.*
call for: *I shall **be calling for** you at seven o'clock.*
cut off: *He threatened to **cut** my hair **off**.*
add up to: *Profits can **add up to** millions of dollars.*

PASSIVE-VERB

A **passive verb** is a verb that is formed using a form of 'be' followed by the past participle of the main verb. Passive verbs focus on the person or thing that is affected by the action.

glue: *She **was glued** to the television.*
born: *My mother was 40 when I **was born**.*

LINK-VERB

A **link verb** is a verb such as 'be', 'become', 'feel', or 'seem'. These verbs connect the subject of a sentence to a complement. Most link verbs do not occur in the passive.

be: *He **was** the tallest in the room.*
feel: *We **felt** very happy.*
seem: *He **seemed** to like me.*

MODAL

A **modal verb** is a verb such as 'may', 'must', or 'would'.

can: ***Can** I help you?*
must: *I **must** leave fairly soon.*
shall: *I **shall** do what you suggest.*

Nouns

N-COUNT

Count nouns refer to things which can be counted, and they have both singular and plural forms. When a count noun is used in the singular, it must normally have a word such as 'a', 'an', 'the', or 'my' in front of it.

head: *She turned her **head** away from him.*
room: *Does the hotel have large **rooms**?*

N-UNCOUNT

Uncount nouns refer to things that are not normally counted or not considered to be individual items. Uncount nouns do not have a plural form, and are used with a singular verb.

help: *I need **help** with my homework.*
electricity: ***Electricity** is dangerous.*
bread: *Please buy some **bread** when you go to town.*

N-VAR

Variable nouns are uncount when they refer to something in general, and count nouns when they refer to a particular instance of something.

conversation: *I found her in* **conversation** *with Mrs Williams.*
I struck up a **conversation** *with him.*

Other variable nouns refer to substances. They are uncount when they refer to a mass of the substance, and count nouns when they refer to types or brands.

shampoo: *... a bottle of* **shampoo**.
... bubble baths, soaps, and **shampoos**.

N-SING

A **singular noun** is always singular and must have a word such as 'a', 'an', 'the', or 'my' in front of it.

sun: *The* **sun** *was shining.*
wash: *His grey socks were in the* **wash**.

N-PLURAL

A **plural noun** is always plural and is used with plural verbs.

clothes: *His* **clothes** *looked terribly dirty.*
expenses: *They have agreed to pay for travel and* **expenses**.

N-TITLE

A **title noun** is a noun that is used to refer to someone who has a particular role or position. Titles come before the name of the person and begin with a capital letter.

President: *He believes there probably was a conspiracy to kill* **President** *Kennedy in 1963.*
Sir: *...* **Sir** *Christopher Wren.*

N-VOC

A **vocative noun** is a noun that is used when speaking directly to someone or writing to them.

darling: *Thank you,* **darling**.
dad: *How do you feel,* **Dad**?

N-PROPER

A **proper noun** refers to one person, place, thing, or institution, and begins with a capital letter.

God: *He believes in* **God**.
Senate: *All of the president's cabinet appointments must be confirmed by the* **Senate**.

Adjectives

ADJ

An **adjective** is a word which is used to tell you more about a person or thing, such as their appearance, colour, size, or other qualities.

white: *She bought a loaf of* **white** *bread.*
angry: *I felt* **angry**.
blank: *He tore a* **blank** *page from his notebook.*

ADJ BEFORE N

This is used to mean an adjective that is normally used only in front of a noun. For example, you can talk about an *'indoor swimming pool'*, but you do not say 'The swimming pool was indoor'.

maximum: *We want the* **maximum** *number of people to attend.*
northern: *Matilda was born in* **northern** *Italy.*

ADJ AFTER LINK-V

This is used to mean an adjective that is normally used only after a link verb. For example, you can say *'She was glad'*, but you do not talk about *'a glad woman'*.

alone: *I want to be* **alone**.
sure: *I'm not quite* **sure**.

Adverbs

ADV

An **adverb** is a word that gives more information about when, how, where, or in what circumstances something happens.

tomorrow: *I'll see you **tomorrow**, all right?*
quickly: *He dressed **quickly**.*
home: *She wanted to go **home**.*

Other word classes

PHRASE

A **phrase** is a group of words which have a particular meaning when they are used together. This meaning is not always understandable from the separate parts.

in the bag: *It's **in the bag**. Unofficially, the job's yours.*
sit tight: ***Sit tight**, I'll be right back.*

PREP

A **preposition** is a word such as 'by', 'with', or 'from' which is always followed by a noun group or the '-ing' form of a verb.

near: *He stood **near** the door.*
of: *He had little chance **of** winning.*

PRON

A **pronoun** is used to refer to someone or something that has already been mentioned or whose identity is already known.

he: *My father is fat. **He** weighs over fifteen stone.*
them: *Did you give it to **them**?*
this: ***This** is what I wanted to say: it wasn't my idea.*
someone: *He has a reputation of being **someone** who is independent.*

CONJ

A **conjunction** is a word such as 'and', 'but', 'although', or 'nor', which is used to link two words or two clauses in a sentence.

since: *So much has changed in the sport **since** I was a teenager.*
before: *He phoned on Tuesday, just **before** you came.*

DET

A **determiner** is a word such as 'a', 'the', 'my', or 'every' which is used at the beginning of a noun group.

an: *We went to **an** art exhibition.*
the: ***The** man began to run towards **the** boy.*
every: *She spoke to **every** person at that party.*

CONVENTION

This is used to mean a word or fixed phrase which is used in conversation, for example when greeting someone, apologizing, or replying. Examples of conventions are 'hello', 'sorry', and 'I'm afraid'.

QUANT

A **quantifier** is a word or phrase like 'plenty' or 'a lot' which allows you to say in a general way how many there are of something, or how much there is of something. Quantifiers are often followed by 'of'.

all: *He was talking to **all** of us.*
enough: *They had **enough** cash for a one-way ticket.*
little: ***Little** is known about his childhood.*
whole: *We spent the **whole** summer in Italy.*

NUM

This is used to mean **number**.

eighteen: *He was employed by them for **eighteen** years.*
billion: *... 3 **billion** dollars.*

ORD

An **ordinal** is a number that is used like an adjective or an adverb.

hundredth: *The bank celebrates its **hundredth** anniversary in December.*
first: *There's no time for boyfriends, my career comes **first**.*

PREDET

A **predeterminer** is a word such as 'all' or 'half' which can come before a determiner.

all: *She's worked **all** her life.*
half: ***Half** the letter was in Swedish.*

EXCLAM

An **exclamation** is a word or phrase which is spoken suddenly, loudly, or with emphasis in order to express a strong emotion.

oh: *'**Oh**!' Kenny blinked. 'Has everyone gone?'*
gee: ***Gee**, it's hot.*

Some words and meanings have two word classes, and the definition and example sentences show how the word is used in those two word classes. For example:

control 2: VERB & N-UNCOUNT If you **control** a person or machine, or if you have **control** of them, you are able to make them do what you want them to do.

*I can't **control** what the judge says or what people think... He lost **control** of his car.*

behind 1: PREP & ADV

*I put one of the cushions **behind** his head... She led the way upstairs, with Terry following **behind**.*

USING YOUR DICTIONARY

Introduction

These study pages are designed to help you to get the most out of your dictionary. Each feature of the dictionary is described and explained, and there are exercises to help you develop your dictionary skills. The answers to all the exercises are given in the Answer Key on pages xviii-xix.

Entries and letter index

The main text of the dictionary is made up of entries from A to Z. An **entry** is a complete explanation of a word and all its meanings. For example, the first three entries on page 1 are 'a', 'aback', and 'abandon'. Entries are listed under the letter that they begin with. A **letter index** at the side of each page shows you the complete alphabet and highlights the first letter of all the entries on that page. On left-hand pages, the alphabet is shown in capital letters, on right-hand pages, it is shown in small letters.

Running heads

At the top of every page you will see a word. This word is called a **running head**. On left-hand pages, the running head is the same as the first complete entry on that page. For example, on page 2 the first complete entry is 'abnormality' and this is the running head at the top of the page. On right-hand pages, the running head is the same as the last entry beginning on that page. On page 3, for example, the running head is 'abundant', because that is the last entry which begins on the page.

Exercise 1

Put the words on the left between the appropriate running heads. The first one has been done for you as an example.

1	abroad	a	**among** .... Anglo
2	aerosol	b	**antique** .... appealing
3	ancestor	c	**adviser** .... against
4	any	d	**abolish** ....._abroad_..... accelerate
5	approval	e	**appear** .... aptitude

Entry order

In the alphabetical order of entries in the dictionary, spaces, hyphens, apostrophes, and accents do not count. For example, 'check-up' comes after 'checkpoint' and before 'cheek', and 'director general' comes after 'directorate' and before 'directory'. In the same way, abbreviations and entries beginning with capital letters are treated exactly like ordinary words, so 'DIY' comes between 'divulge' and 'dizzy', and 'Edwardian' comes between 'education' and 'eel'.

Exercise 2

Put these groups of words into alphabetical order, as you would find them in the dictionary.

1   egg, effortless, e.g., EFL, ego, effort

....

2   full-length, full-blown, full, full stop, full-size, full-scale

....

3   head teacher, head-on, headquarters, head start, head of state, headphones

....

4   philosophic, phase, PhD, phenomenon, phenomenal, philosopher

....

5   takeoff, takeout, takeover, takeaway, taker, taken, takings

....

Headwords and superheadwords

Every entry begins with a **headword**, starting in the left-hand margin of the column. All the headwords are printed in blue. Words which are closely related in meaning to the headword are also printed in blue and are preceded by a black diamond. Some entries are very long or have very different meanings and so have been divided up into two or more sub-sections, each indicated by a blue strip. These entries are called **superheadwords**.

Exercise 3

Look up the following superheadwords in the dictionary and find out how many sub-sections they are divided into.

1   can   4   mean ....

2   down   5   post ....

3   just ....

Inflected forms and alternative spellings

Inflected forms are the different grammatical forms that a word can have. Different forms are shown after the pronunciation. Verbs are shown with the 3rd person singular, the -ing form, the past tense and, where it is different from the past tense, the past participle. Adjectives and adverbs are shown with their comparative forms and nouns are shown with their plural forms.

Where a noun does not change its form in the plural, this information is also given, for example:

deer /dɪə/.
☑ **Deer** is both the singular and the plural form.

Where there are alternative spellings for the headword, these are given in blue before the pronunciation.

Where there is an American alternative or an alternative British spelling, the abbreviations AM or BRIT are used and the alternative is shown in blue, for example:

> ★ **colour** (AM **color**) /ˈkʌlə/ **colours, colouring, coloured.** [1] N-COUNT The **colour** of something is the appearance that it has as a result of reflecting light. Red, blue, and green are colours.

Exercise 4

Which headword would you look at to find the following words? The first one has been done as an example.

1 actresses ....*actress*........

2 clearer ....

3 denied ....

4 funneling, funneled ....

5 geese ....

6 minded ....

7 nooses ....

8 set ....

9 trekking ....

10 winded ....

Definitions, meanings and set structures

Definitions are written in full sentences using simple words and showing the common ways in which the headword is used. When there is more than one **meaning**, the different meanings are numbered. If a word or expression is used to show approval or disapproval, this information is also given in the definition.

Many words are used in particular grammatical patterns. The definitions show you these important patterns by highlighting these **set structures**.

For example, if you look at the entry for the verb 'agree', you can see that the preposition 'with' is also in bold to show that it is used with this verb.

> ★ **agree** /əˈgriː/ **agrees, agreeing, agreed.** [1] VERB If you **agree with** someone, you have the same opinion about something. *I agree with you entirely... We agreed that she was not to be told.*

Exercise 5

Look up the following words in the dictionary and find out which prepositions they are usually found with.

1 rely ....

2 belong ....

3 sympathize ....

4 fond ....

5 responsible ....

Exercise 6

Decide what is wrong with each of the following sentences by looking up the word printed in bold. Use the information given in the entry to write down the correct sentence.

1 He hasn't made his **homework**.

2 The Prime Minister did a **speech** to the journalists.

3 Sally **graduated** Edinburgh University in the summer.

4 He **asked** to me my name.

5 The price of petrol has **fallen** down.

Examples

The **examples** in italics following the definitions are all examples of real language taken from *The Bank of English*. They show typical contexts in which the word or expression is found and give more information about the grammatical patterns in which it most often occurs.

Exercise 7

Look up the examples for the words in bold to find:

1 typical members of an **entourage**

2 something that you can be **hooked** on

3 a word that can come after the adjective **lightning**

4 emotions that people are sometimes **overcome** by

5 an illness that **strikes people down**

Grammatical labels

Before a definition, there is a **grammatical label**. These labels are explained on pages vii-x. Where a word has more than one meaning, there is a grammatical label at the beginning of each numbered meaning.

Exercise 8

In each sentence below, there is a grammatical problem with the word in bold. Look at the dictionary entry for the word and use the grammatical labels and information on pages vii-x to correct the mistake.

1   He is very good **at** play the piano.

2   Jane is a very **fed-up** person.

3   If you want to be a professional footballer, you have to **practice** every day.

4   He gave me some useful **advices**.

5   Rachel is going on holiday. **Because** she needs a rest.

Style

Some words are used by particular groups of people or in particular contexts. This is shown in the dictionary by a label in square brackets and in small capitals after the definition.

Geographical labels: BRITISH
                                        AMERICAN

Style labels:

FORMAL	used in official situations such as politics and business
INFORMAL	used mainly in informal situations, conversations, and personal letters
WRITTEN	used mainly in writing rather than speech
SPOKEN	used mainly in speech rather than writing
DATED	no longer in common general use
LITERARY	used mainly in novels, poetry and other literature
TECHNICAL	used mainly when talking or writing about specialist subjects such as medicine or law
JOURNALISM	used mainly in newspapers, television, and radio
COMPUTING	used mainly when talking about computers

Exercise 9

Look at the following sentences. In each case say whether the word in bold is British or American English, using the dictionary to help you. Then write the equivalent in British or American English in the space provided.

Examples	British or American?	Equivalent?
1 There was a long **queue** of foreigners waiting to get through immigration.		
2 I watched a **subway** train coming into the station.		
3 I'll be wearing a red shirt and black **trousers**.		
4 I work every evening in a **petrol** station as a cashier.		
5 He walked down the **sidewalk** toward the car.		

Exercise 10

Look at the following sentences. In each one, the word in bold is informal. Use the dictionary to help you find a more formal word with a similar meaning.

1 The company was **upbeat** about its future.

2 I'll pay you back that two **quid** next week.

3 His eldest **kid** is in trouble at school.

4 I now share a flat with my best **mate**.

5 He walked up and grabbed the **guy** by the shoulder.

Pronunciation

In this dictionary, IPA symbols are used to show you how the word is pronounced. Look on the last page of the dictionary for explanations of these symbols.

In written English, the same sound can be shown by more than one letter or combination of letters. This can make spelling difficult in English.

Exercise 11

In each of the following sentences, there are at least 3 occurrences of one sound.

In each case:

i identify the sound and write its symbol in column 2;
ii in column 3, write the number of times this sound appears in the sentence;
iii in column 4 write down the different possible spellings of the sound;
iv in column 5, use the IPA chart to write an example of a word using each
    spelling in phonetic script;
v check your answers by looking up the words in the dictionary.
   The first one has been done for you as an example.

	IPA symbol	Number of occurrences	Possible spellings of this sound	Transcription
1 Fit children have a winning system.	/ɪ/	5	i y	/fɪt/ /ˈsɪstəm/
2 My friend said he went to bed wet.				
3 Can you guess if they've got a ghost?				
4 You choose if we use the shoe or the boot.				
5 It took an hour to queue in the chemist's on the corner.				

Usage notes

Usage notes give you extra information about words and meanings, for example
how to avoid common mistakes or when to use a related word. They appear in
blue shaded boxes after the entry or meaning they relate to. Look at the entry for
'cold' to find an example of a usage note.

Exercise 12

Use the usage notes to help you find the answers to the following questions, and
then say at which word you found the answer. The first one has been done for you.

1 In cooking, do Americans talk about 'grilling' meat?

> *No, they talk about 'broiling' it.   Cook*

2 Is it possible to say that you 'discuss about something with someone'?

3 Is it possible to pass an exam and fail it?

4 Does 'I have little money' mean the same as 'I have a little money'?

Answer Key

Exercise 1

1d, 2c, 3a, 4b, 5e

Exercise 2

1 effort, effortless, EFL, e.g., egg, ego
2 full, full-blown, full-length, full-scale, full-size, full-stop
3 head of state, head-on, headphones, headquarters, head start, head teacher
4 phase, PhD, phenomenal, phenomenon, philosopher, philosophic
5 takeaway, taken, takeoff, takeout, takeover, taker, takings

Exercise 3

1 can: 2
2 down: 3
3 just: 2
4 mean: 3
5 post: 3

Exercise 4

1 actress
2 clear
3 deny
4 funnel
5 goose
6 mind
7 noose
8 set
9 trek
10 wind

Exercise 5

1 rely **on**
2 belong **to**
3 sympathize **with**
4 fond **of**
5 responsible **for**

Exercise 6

1 'He hasn't **done** his homework' is the correct sentence. You can see from the definition that you 'do' homework, not 'make' it.
2 'The Prime Minister **gave** a speech' is correct. The fourth definition tells you that a speech is **given** to an audience.
3 'Sally graduated **from** Edinburgh University in the summer' is correct. If you look at the definition of 'graduate', you can see that it takes the preposition 'from'.
4 'He asked me my name' is correct. You can see from the definition that you 'ask someone something'. The preposition 'to' is not necessary.
5 'The price of petrol has fallen' is correct. The usage note at 'fall' tells you that people and structures can 'fall down', but prices 'fall'.

Exercise 7

1 personal assistant, hairdresser, bodyguard
2 a book
3 reflexes
4 fear and despair
5 heart attack

Exercise 8

1 'He is very good at **playing** the piano' is correct. The word 'at' is a preposition, and must therefore be followed by an -ing form of the verb here.

2 'Jane is very fed-up' is correct. 'Fed-up' is an adjective used after a link verb, not in front of a noun, so you cannot say 'a fed-up person'.

3 'If you want to be a professional footballer, you have to **practise** every day' is correct. You can see that 'practice' is a noun. The verb is spelled 'practise' in British English.

4 'He gave me some useful **advice**' is the correct sentence. You can see from the grammar label that the noun 'advice' is uncount, and so does not have a plural form.

5 'Rachel is going on holiday **because** she needs a rest' is correct. The word 'because' is a conjunction. You can see from the grammar notes that conjunctions are used to link two words or ideas in a sentence. The two ideas therefore need to be linked into **one** sentence here.

Exercise 9

1 British. The American equivalent is 'line'.

2 American. The British equivalent is 'underground'.

3 British. The American equivalent is 'pants'.

4 British. The American equivalent is 'gas'.

5 American. The British equivalent is 'pavement'.

Exercise 10

1	cheerful, optimistic	4	friend
2	pounds	5	man
3	child		

Exercise 11

1 /ɪ/; 5; 'i' and 'y'; /fɪt/, /'sɪstəm/

2 /e/; 5; 'ie', 'ai' and 'e'; /frend/, /sed/, /went/

3 /g/; 3; 'gu', 'g', 'gh'; /ges/, /gɒt/, /gəʊst/

4 /uː/; 5; 'ou', 'oo', 'u', 'oe'; /juː/, /tʃuːz/, /juːz/, /ʃuː/

5 /k/; 3; 'qu', 'ch', 'c'; /kjuː/, /'kemɪst/, /'kɔːnə/

Exercise 12

1 No, they talk about 'broiling' it; cook

2 No, you discuss something with someone; discuss

3 No, because if you pass, you succeed. You can 'take' or 'sit' an exam and fail it, though; exam

4 No, 'I have little money' means you have almost no money, or not enough money. 'I have a little money' means that you have some; little

GUIDE TO THE DICTIONARY ENTRIES

BANK OF ENGLISH® FREQUENT WORD

GEOGRAPHICAL LABELS

COLOUR HEADWORDS

AMERICAN FORMS

MEANING SPLITS

PHRASAL VERBS

CROSS REFERENCE TO EXTRA INFORMATION

GRAMMATICAL LABELS

PRONUNCIATION

DERIVED WORDS

EXAMPLES

colon /ˈkəʊlən/ colons. N-COUNT A **colon** is the punctuation mark (:). →See also Reference Page on Punctuation.

★ **colonel** /ˈkɜːnəl/ colonels. N-COUNT & N-TITLE A **colonel** is a senior military officer.

colonial /kəˈləʊniəl/. ADJ BEFORE N **Colonial** means relating to countries that are colonies, or to colonialism. ...independence from British colonial rule. ...the colonial civil service.

colonialism /kəˈləʊniəlɪzəm/. N-UNCOUNT **Colonialism** is the practice by which a powerful country directly controls less powerful countries. ...the residual effects of colonialism.

colonist /ˈkɒlənɪst/ colonists. N-COUNT **Colonists** are people who start a colony. ...the early American colonists.

colonize (BRIT also **colonise**) /ˈkɒlənaɪz/ colonizes, colonizing, colonized. VERB When large numbers of people or animals **colonize** a place, they go to live there and make it their home. The first British attempt to colonize Ireland was in the twelfth century... Toads are colonising the whole place. ◆ **colonization** N-UNCOUNT ...the European colonization of America.

colony /ˈkɒləni/ colonies. ☐1 N-COUNT A **colony** is a country which is controlled by a more powerful country. ☐2 N-COUNT A **colony** is a group of people or animals of a particular sort living together. ...an artists' colony. ...a seal colony.

color /ˈkʌlə/. See **colour**.

colorless /ˈkʌlələs/. See **colourless**.

colossal /kəˈlɒsəl/. ADJ Something that is **colossal** is very large. ...a colossal waste of money.

★ **colour** (AM **color**) /ˈkʌlə/ colours, colouring, coloured. ☐1 N-COUNT The **colour** of something is the appearance that it has as a result of reflecting light. Red, blue, and green are colours. 'What colour is the car?' – 'Red.'... Her silk dress was sky-blue, the colour of her eyes. ☐2 N-COUNT Someone's **colour** is the colour of their skin. People often use **colour** in this way to refer to a person's race. ...colour and ethnic origins were utterly irrelevant. ☐3 ADJ A **colour** television, film, or photograph shows things in all their colours, and not just in black and white. ...colour illustrations. ☐4 N-UNCOUNT **Colour** is a quality that makes something interesting or exciting. Check shirts add colour to a sober work suit. ☐5 VERB If something **colours** your opinion, it affects your opinion.

▶**colour in.** PHR-VERB If you **colour in** a drawing, you give it different colours using crayons or paints.

fantastic /fæn'tæstɪk/. **1** ADJ If you say that something is **fantastic**, you are emphasizing that you think it is very good. [INFORMAL] *I have a fantastic social life.* **2** ADJ BEFORE N You use **fantastic** to emphasize the size, amount, or degree of something. [INFORMAL] *...fantastic amounts of money.* ♦ **fantastically** ADV *...a fantastically expensive restaurant.* **3** ADJ You describe something as **fantastic** when it seems strange and wonderful or unlikely. *Unlikely and fantastic legends grew up around a great many figures.*

★ **fantasy** /'fæntəzi/ **fantasies.** **1** N-COUNT A **fantasy** is a situation or event that you think about and that you want to happen, especially one that is unlikely to happen. *...fantasies of romance and true love.* **2** N-VAR You can refer to a story or situation that someone creates from their imagination and that is not based on reality as **fantasy**. *...the words from a Disney fantasy.*

FAQ /fæk/ **FAQs.** **FAQ** is used especially on websites to refer to questions about computers and the Internet. **FAQ** is an abbreviation for 'frequently asked questions'. [COMPUTING]

★ **far** /fɑː/ **farther** (or **further**) **farthest** (or **furthest**).

> **Far** has two comparatives, **farther** and **further**, and two superlatives, **farthest** and **furthest**. **Farther** and **farthest** are used mainly in sense 1, and are dealt with here. **Further** and **furthest** are dealt with in separate entries.

1 ADV If one place, thing, or person is **far** away from another, there is a great distance between them. *...a nice little Italian restaurant not far from here... Both of my sisters moved even farther away from home... He had wandered to the far end of the room.* **2** ADV You use **far** in questions and statements about distances. *How far is it to Malcy?... How far can you throw?... She followed the tracks as far as the road.*

> **USAGE Far** is used in negative sentences and questions about distance, but not usually in affirmative sentences. If you want to state the distance of a particular place from where you are, you can say that it is that distance **away**. *...Durban, which is over 300 kilometres away.* If a place is very distant, you can say that it is **a long way away**, or that it is **a long way from** another place. *It is a long way from London... Anna was still a long way away.*

PUNCTUATION

● **full stop** (AM period)

A full stop is used at the end of a sentence, unless it is a question or an exclamation.

It's not your fault.
Cook the rice in salted water until just tender.

 question mark

If a sentence is a direct question, you put a question mark at the end.

Why did you do that?
He's certain to be elected, isn't he?

● **exclamation mark** (AM exclamation point)

You put an exclamation mark at the end of a sentence which expresses surprise, excitement, enthusiasm, or horror.

What an aroma! It's tremendous!
How awful!

comma

You put a comma between items on a list. The comma can be left out if the items are separated by 'and' or 'or'.

... a long, narrow, twisting corridor.
We ate fish, steak and fruit.

You put a comma after or in front of someone's name, nickname, or title.

Jenny, I'm sorry.
I love you, darling.
The reply was: 'Guilty, your Honour.'

You put a comma between the name of a place and the county, state, or country it is in.

She was born in Richmond, Surrey, in 1913.

You put a comma in front of an adjective which is separate from the main part of the sentence.

She nodded, speechless.

You put a comma at the end of a clause when it is followed by a subordinate clause starting with an -ing form.

The police told them all to leave the area, arresting those who refused.

You put a comma before a non-defining relative clause.

The only decent room is the living room, which is rather small.

You put a comma before a question tag.

You've noticed, haven't you?

• semi-colon
,

You use a semi-colon to separate clauses that are closely related, especially when they contrast with each other.

He knew everything about me; I knew nothing about his recent life.

• colon
•

You use a colon in front of a list or explanation, where the list or explanation follows and relates to the previous clause.

To be authentic these garments must be of natural materials: cotton, silk, wool, or leather.

, apostrophe

You use an apostrophe with 's' to show that a person or thing belongs to someone or something. When the noun is singular, the apostrophe is placed before the 's'.

... my friend's house.

When the noun is plural and formed with an 's', the apostrophe is placed after the 's'.

... friends' houses.

When the noun is plural and not formed with an 's', the apostrophe is placed before the 's'.

... children's clothing.

Note that you do not use an apostrophe in front of the 's' of the posessive pronouns 'yours', 'hers', 'ours', 'theirs', or 'its'.

You use an apostrophe in shortened forms of 'be', 'have', 'would', and 'not'.

I think I'd go crazy without the telly.	*I'm terribly sorry.*
I've got two brothers and two sisters.	*I can't see a thing.*

– hyphen

You use a hyphen to join together two words to make another word which is a combination of both things or ideas.

... a steel-framed coffee table.	*He was forty-three years old.*
... an anti-American demonstration.	*... super-fit athletes.*

You can also use a hyphen to split a word over two lines.

❝❞ quotation marks (or quotemarks or inverted commas)

You put quotation marks at the beginning and end of direct speech. You start direct speech with a capital letter and you end it with a full stop, a question mark, or an exclamation mark. You can use either single or double quotation marks.

'What happened?'

If you put something like 'he said' after the direct speech, you put a comma in front of the second inverted comma, not a full stop.

'We have to go home,' she told him.
'Yes, yes,' he replied. 'He'll be all right.'

TIMES AND DATES

Time

If you want to indicate the time on a clock or watch, you use the verb 'be'.

'What's the time now?' – *'**It's three thirty**.'*
'Can you tell me the time?' – *'**It's twenty-five past twelve**.'*
*The time **is six forty-five**.*
*It's **five to eight** and breakfast's **at eight o'clock**.*

Note that if it is clear what hour you are talking about, you do not need to add the hour after 'past' or 'to'.

'What time is it?' – *'**Twenty-five past**.'*
'What time's the morning break?' – *'I think it's **twenty-five to** or **twenty to**.'*

You also use these prepositions to indicate a specific time.

at	on	past	to

*I'll meet you **at seven o'clock**.*
*He mentioned it to me **on Friday**.*

You use these prepositions to relate events to a non-specific time.

after	before	by	during	following	over	prior to

*The match resumed **after lunch**.*
*She awoke **during the night**.*

Dates

There are several different ways of writing a date.

20 April	April 20	the twentieth of April
20th April	April 20th	

*He comes back **on the twentieth**.*   *I was born **in 1969**.*
*I was born **on December 15th 1983**.*   *It was built as recently as **the 1930s**.*

You can write a date entirely in figures. Note that in American English the month is given in front of the day.

15/12/98	15.12.98	12/15/98	12.15.98

Days of the week

Monday	Tuesday	Wednesday	Thursday	Friday	Saturday	Sunday

Here are the most common ways of talking about days of the week.

*Alice has asked us round **on Friday afternoon**.*
*They meet here **every Tuesday morning**.*
*He took a flight back home to the USA **last Thursday**.*
*Talks are likely to start **next Tuesday**.*

You can also use the following constructions:

*The restaurant is open **from Monday to Friday**.*
*We'll know the results **by Thursday**.*
*The committee meets **on the last Friday of the month**.*
*Eddie worked **on Saturdays**.*
*The first match is **two weeks on Sunday**.*

Months of the year

January	February	March	April	May	June
July	August	September	October	November	December

Here are the most common ways of talking about months.

*We always have snow **in January**.*
*His exhibition opens **on 5 February**.*
*I flew to Milan **in early March**.*
*Staff have been on strike **since last June**.*
*There's no telling what the voters will do **next November**.*

Seasons

spring	summer	autumn	winter

Here are the most common ways of talking about seasons.

***In winter** the nights are cold and long.*
*The final report is due out **next autumn**.*
*We met again **in the spring of 1977**.*

In American English 'fall' is often used instead of 'autumn'.

*He begins teaching **in the fall**.*

General phrases

There are many other ways of talking about times and dates more generally. The following 'timeline' may help you to work out the sequence of days.

the day before yesterday	yesterday	today	tomorrow	the day after tomorrow
Monday	Tuesday	Wednesday	Thursday	Friday

Here are some other common ways of talking about times and dates.

*I'll see you **tomorrow afternoon**.*
*He rang me **the night before last**.*
*I myself am going to Moscow **in a week's time**.*
***This time last year** they were completely unknown.*
*Susan came to visit me **six months ago**.*
***Last month** thousands watched as the hotel toppled over the cliff edge.*

TELLING THE TIME

Here are the most common ways of saying and writing the time.

four o'clock
four
4.00

nine o'clock
nine
9.00

twelve o'clock
twelve
12.00

four in the morning
4 a.m.

nine in the morning
9 a.m.

twelve
12 a.m.
midday
noon

four in the afternoon
4 p.m.

nine in the evening
9 p.m.

twelve (at night)
12 p.m.
midnight

half past eleven [BRITISH]
half eleven [BRITISH]
eleven thirty
11.30

(a) quarter past twelve [BRITISH]
12.15
(a) quarter after twelve
[AMERICAN]

twenty-five (minutes) past two
[BRITISH]
two twenty-five
2.25
twenty-five after two [AMERICAN]

(a) quarter to one [BRITISH]
twelve forty-five
12.45
(a) quarter of one [AMERICAN]

ten (minutes) to eight [BRITISH]
seven-fifty
7.50
ten of eight [AMERICAN]

The following examples show some ways of
expressing the time.

'What time is it?' – 'Four o'clock.'

'What time is it now?' – 'Three thirty.'

It was quarter of seven in the morning.

It's nearly ten after twelve.

Mary left at three and caught the bus.

*The students were ordered to vacate their halls of
residence by nine o'clock this morning.*

*She was free until three o'clock, when she had to
meet her parents back at the hotel.*

I'd been awake since four.

*'Have you had anything to eat?' – 'Not since one
o'clock yesterday.'*

I'll be watching the eleven o'clock news.

The flight to Cardiff takes exactly half an hour.

*It took her a quarter of an hour to find a parking
place.*

*The news service brings you updates every hour,
on the hour.*

I'm meeting Eleanor in an hour's time.

*We expect them to arrive in just over two hours
from now.*

In ten minutes there would be a train for Brighton.

*His destiny was going to be decided in the next
three minutes.*

GREETINGS AND GOODBYES

Meeting

The usual way of greeting someone is by saying **hello**. To greet someone more informally, you can say **hello there**, **hi**, or **hiya**.

After you have greeted someone, you often say their name, or ask how they are.

'Hello, it's only Molly.' – 'Oh, hello love.'
'Hello, Tina.' – 'Hello. How are you today?'
'Hiya Tommy. How are you doing?'

To greet someone at a particular time of day, you can use the expressions **good morning**, **good afternoon**, and **good evening**. **Good morning** is used before twelve o'clock midday. **Good afternoon** is used between midday and about six o'clock, and after that people say **good evening**. With people you know, these greetings are often abbreviated to **morning**, **afternoon**, and **evening**. Note that **good night** is usually only used to say goodbye to someone before you or they go to bed.

'Good morning, Mr Comerford, how are you this morning?'
'Good night, sleep well'

You can respond to a greeting or goodbye by repeating the expression that the other person has used, or with another appropriate expression.

'Hello Colin.' – 'Hello.'
'Hello Colin.' – Good evening, how are you?'

Parting

When two people part, they usually say **goodbye**, **bye**, or **bye bye**. People who know each other are more likely to say **bye** than **goodbye**. **Bye** or **bye bye** is not usually used in very formal situations. To say goodbye more informally, people use the expressions **see you** and **see you later**. They also sometimes say **take care**, **all the best**, and **so long**, or in British English, **cheerio** or **look after yourself**.

'See you later.' – 'Okay bye.'
'Cheerio – see you tonight.'

Polite greetings

To say hello or goodbye politely, people sometimes say **nice to see you**. In British English people also say **lovely to see you**, and in American English, **good to see you**.

If you have just met someone for the first time you can say **nice to meet you** or **nice to have met you**.

Thanks for coming along here. It was very nice to meet you.
'Hello, it's nice to see you. How are you?' – 'Nice to see you too, Mr Bates.'

⭐ **a** /ə, STRONG eɪ/ or **an** /ən, STRONG æn/.

✅ The form **an** is used in front of words that begin with vowel sounds.

1 DET You use **a** or **an** when you are referring to someone or something for the first time, or when you do not want to be specific. *Today you've got a new teacher... A waiter entered with a tray... He refused to work with an orchestra ever again.* **2** DET You can use **a** or **an** in front of nouns when the noun is followed by other words that describe it more fully. *...a happiness she had never believed possible.* **3** DET You can use **a** or **an** instead of the number 'one' in front of some numbers and measurements. *...a hundred miles.* **4** DET You use **a** or **an** in expressions such as **eight hours a day** to express a rate or ratio. *Prices start at £13.95 a metre.*

aback /ə'bæk/. PHRASE If you are **taken aback**, you are very surprised or shocked by something. *His resignation may have taken most people aback.*

⭐ **abandon** /ə'bændən/ **abandons, abandoning, abandoned.** **1** VERB If you **abandon** a thing, place, or person, you leave them permanently or for a long time. *His parents had abandoned him.*
♦ **abandoned** ADJ *...an abandoned village.*
♦ **abandonment** N-UNCOUNT *...her father's complete abandonment of her.* **2** VERB If you **abandon** an activity or idea, you stop doing it or thinking about it before it is finished. *He abandoned his studies after two years.*
♦ **abandonment** N-UNCOUNT *Rain forced the abandonment of the next day's competitions.*
3 N-UNCOUNT If you do something **with abandon**, you do it in a carefree way. *...smoking and drinking with abandon.*

abate /ə'beɪt/ **abates, abating, abated.** VERB When something **abates**, it becomes much less strong or widespread. [FORMAL] *...a crime wave that shows no sign of abating.*

abbey /'æbi/ **abbeys.** N-COUNT An **abbey** is a church with buildings attached to it in which monks or nuns live or used to live.

abbreviate /ə'briːvieɪt/ **abbreviates, abbreviating, abbreviated.** VERB If a word or a phrase **is abbreviated**, it is made shorter. *'Compact disc' is often abbreviated to 'CD'... He persuaded his son to abbreviate his first name to Alec.* ♦ **abbreviated** ADJ *...a very abbreviated description of the project.*

abbreviation /ə,briːvi'eɪʃən/ **abbreviations.** N-COUNT An **abbreviation** is a short form of a word or phrase. *The postal abbreviation for Kansas is KS.*

abdicate /'æbdɪkeɪt/ **abdicates, abdicating, abdicated.** **1** VERB If a king or queen **abdicates**, he or she resigns. *...when King Constantine was forced to abdicate the Greek throne.*

♦ **abdication** N-UNCOUNT *...the abdication of Edward VIII.* **2** VERB If you **abdicate** responsibility for something, you refuse to accept the responsibility for it any longer. *Their parents have abdicated their responsibilities.*
♦ **abdication** N-UNCOUNT *...an outrageous abdication of their duties.*

abdomen /'æbdəmən/ **abdomens.** N-COUNT Your **abdomen** is the part of your body below your chest where your stomach is. ♦ **abdominal** /æb'dɒmɪnəl/ ADJ BEFORE N *...the abdominal muscles.*

abduct /æb'dʌkt/ **abducts, abducting, abducted.** VERB If someone **is abducted**, he or she is taken away illegally. *He was charged with abducting a taxi driver.* ♦ **abduction, abductions** N-VAR *...the abduction of four black youths.*

aberration /,æbə'reɪʃən/ **aberrations.** N-VAR An **aberration** is an incident or way of behaving that is not normal. [FORMAL] *...whether today's coup attempt is a minor aberration on the road to democracy.*

abide /ə'baɪd/ **abides, abiding, abided.** PHRASE If you say that you **can't abide** someone or something, you are emphasizing that you dislike them intensely. *I can't abide people who can't make up their minds.*
▸ **abide by.** PHR-VERB If you **abide by** a law, agreement, or decision, you do what it says.

abiding /ə'baɪdɪŋ/. ADJ BEFORE N An **abiding** feeling or memory is one that you have for a very long time. *He also acquired an abiding interest in history.* ● See also **law-abiding**.

⭐ **ability** /ə'bɪlɪti/ **abilities.** N-VAR Your **ability** is the quality or skill that you have which makes it possible for you to do something. *Her drama teacher spotted her ability. ...his leadership abilities. ...the human ability to recognise complex sound patterns.*

abject /'æbdʒekt/. ADJ You use **abject** to emphasize that a situation or quality is shameful or depressing. *...abject poverty... This scheme was an abject failure.*

ablaze /ə'bleɪz/. ADJ AFTER LINK-V Something that is **ablaze** is burning fiercely. *Within seconds, curtains and woodwork were ablaze... Two houses were set ablaze.*

⭐ **able** /'eɪbəl/ **abler, ablest.** **1** PHRASE If someone or something **is able to** do something, they have the skills, freedom, or other means which make it possible for them to do it. *I was never able to play any sports.* **2** ADJ An **able** person is clever or good at doing something. ♦ **ably** /'eɪbli/ ADV *He was ably assisted by Robert James... She campaigns so ably for one-parent families.*

abnormal /æb'nɔːməl/. ADJ Someone or something that is **abnormal** is unusual or

A

exceptional in a way that is worrying. ...*an abnormal fear of strangers.* ◆ **abnormally** ADV ...*abnormally high levels of glucose.*

abnormality /ˌæbnɔːˈmælɪti/ **abnormalities.** N-VAR An **abnormality** is an unusual part or feature of something that is worrying or dangerous. ...*a genetic abnormality.*

aboard /əˈbɔːd/. PREP & ADV If you are **aboard** a ship or plane, you are on or in it. *No-one else was aboard the plane... It had taken two hours to load all the people aboard.*

abolish /əˈbɒlɪʃ/ **abolishes, abolishing, abolished.** VERB If someone in authority **abolishes** a practice or organization, they put an end to it. *Parliament voted to abolish the death penalty.* ◆ **abolition** /ˌæbəˈlɪʃən/ N-UNCOUNT ...*the total abolition of slavery.*

abominable /əˈbɒmɪnəbəl/. ADJ Something that is **abominable** is very unpleasant or very bad. *Their treatment of him was abominable. ...this abominable war.*

Aboriginal /ˌæbəˈrɪdʒɪnəl/ **Aboriginals.** N-COUNT An **Aboriginal** is a member of one of the tribes which were living in Australia when Europeans arrived. ...*health and housing for Aboriginals.* ...*Aboriginal art.*

Aborigine /ˌæbəˈrɪdʒɪni/ **Aborigines.** N-COUNT **Aborigine** means the same as **Aboriginal.** Some people consider **Aborigine** to be a racist word.

abort /əˈbɔːt/ **aborts, aborting, aborted.** [1] VERB If an unborn baby **is aborted**, the pregnancy is ended deliberately and the baby is not born alive. ...*the lover who walked out on her after she had aborted their child.* [2] VERB If you **abort** a process, plan, or activity, you stop it before it is finished. *The take-off was aborted.*

⭐ **abortion** /əˈbɔːʃən/ **abortions.** N-VAR An **abortion** is a medical operation in which a pregnancy is deliberately ended and the baby is not born alive. ...*the Vatican's teaching on abortion.*

abortive /əˈbɔːtɪv/. ADJ An **abortive** attempt or action is unsuccessful. ...*the abortive rebellion.*

abound /əˈbaʊnd/ **abounds, abounding, abounded.** VERB If things **abound**, or if a place **abounds with** things, there are very large numbers of them. [FORMAL] *Stories abound about when he was in charge... San Francisco abounds with lawyers.*

⭐ **about** /əˈbaʊt/. [1] PREP You use **about** to introduce who or what something relates to or concerns. *Helen's told me about you. ...advice about exercise... He felt helpless to do anything about it.* [2] PREP When you say that there is a particular quality **about** someone or something, you mean that they have this quality. *There was something special about her.* [3] ADV **About** in front of a number means approximately. *The child is about eight years old.* [4] ADV & PREP If someone or something moves **about**, they keep moving in different directions. *The kids ran about in the garden... From 1879 to 1888 he wandered about Germany.* [5] ADJ AFTER LINK-V If someone or something is **about**, they are present or available.

There's lots of money about. [6] PHRASE If you **are about to** do something, you are going to do it soon. *The film was about to start.* [7] ● **how about**: see **how.** ● **what about**: see **what.** ● **just about**: see **just.**

USAGE When you are talking about movement in no particular direction, you can use **around** and **round** as well as **about.** *It's so romantic up there, flying around in a small plane... I spent a couple of hours driving round Richmond... Police constables walk about with guns on their hips.*
When you are talking about something being generally present or available, you can use **around** or **about**, but not **round**, as adverbs. *There is a lot of talent around at the moment... There are not that many jobs about.*
Round has a lot of other meanings, as a noun, verb, and adjective which you can see at the entry for **round.** You cannot use **about** in these cases.

⭐ **above** /əˈbʌv/. [1] PREP & ADV If one thing is **above** another one, it is directly over it or higher than it. *He lifted his hands above his head. ...the flat above mine... A long scream sounded from somewhere above.* [2] ADV & N-SING & ADJ BEFORE N You use **above** in writing to refer to something that has already been mentioned. ...*the results described above... For additional information, contact any of the above... I may be reached at the above address.* [3] PREP & ADV If an amount or measurement is **above** a particular level, it is greater than that level. *The temperature crept up to just above 40 degrees. ...above average levels of rainfall. ...people of 18 years and above.* [4] PREP & ADV If someone is **above** you, they are in a position of authority over you. ...*the people above you in the positions of power... I had orders from above.* [5] PREP If someone thinks that they are **above** something, they think that they are too good or too important for it; used showing disapproval. *He would consider himself above such petty personal comments.* [6] PREP If someone is **above** criticism or suspicion, they cannot be criticized or suspected because of their good qualities or their position. *He was a respected academic and above suspicion.* [7] ● **over and above**: see **over.**

abrasive /əˈbreɪsɪv/. [1] ADJ If you describe someone's manner as **abrasive**, you think they are rude and unkind. *The abrasive style that prompted one member of Congress to describe him as a pit bull.* [2] ADJ An **abrasive** substance is rough and can be used to clean hard surfaces.

abreast /əˈbrest/. [1] ADV If people or things walk or move **abreast**, they are side by side. ...*they walked three abreast.* [2] PREP If you keep **abreast of** a subject, you know all the most recent facts about it. *He will be keeping abreast of the news.*

⭐ **abroad** /ə'brɔːd/. ADV If you go **abroad**, you go to a foreign country. *I would love to go abroad this year.*

abrupt /ə'brʌpt/. **1** ADJ An **abrupt** action is very sudden and often unpleasant. *Rosie's idyllic world came to an abrupt end when her parents' marriage broke up.* ♦ **abruptly** ADV *He stopped abruptly.* **2** ADJ Someone who is **abrupt** is rather rude and unfriendly. ♦ **abruptly** ADV *'Good night, then,' she said abruptly.*

⭐ **absence** /'æbsəns/ **absences**. **1** N-VAR Someone's **absence** from a place is the fact that they are not there. *...letters which had arrived for me in my absence. ...her husband's frequent absences.* **2** N-SING The **absence** of something is the fact that it is not there. *In the absence of a will, the courts decide who the guardian is.*

absent /'æbsənt/. **1** ADJ If someone or something is **absent from** a place or situation, they are not there. *He was absent from work for over 35 days.* **2** ADJ If someone appears **absent**, they are not paying attention. ♦ **absently** ADV *He nodded absently.*

absentee /ˌæbsən'tiː/ **absentees**. N-COUNT An **absentee** is a person who should be in a particular place but who is not there. *...absentees from work. ...absentee landlords.*

absent-'minded. ADJ An **absent-minded** person is very forgetful or does not pay attention to what they are doing. ♦ **absent-mindedly** ADV *He did it automatically, almost absent-mindedly.*

⭐ **absolute** /'æbsəluːt/ **absolutes**. **1** ADJ BEFORE N **Absolute** means total and complete. *...absolute beginners. ...the absolute proof that we needed... It's absolute nonsense.* **2** N-COUNT & ADJ BEFORE N **Absolutes** or **absolute** rules or principles are believed to be true or right for all situations.

⭐ **absolutely** /ˌæbsə'luːtli/. **1** ADV **Absolutely** means totally and completely. *Jill is absolutely right... It's an absolutely brilliant book... I absolutely refuse to get married.* **2** ADV **Absolutely** is an emphatic way of saying yes or agreeing with someone. **Absolutely not** is an emphatic way of saying no or disagreeing with someone. *'Was it worth it?'—'Absolutely.'... 'Did they approach you?'—'No, absolutely not.'*

absorb /əb'zɔːb/ **absorbs, absorbing, absorbed**. **1** VERB To **absorb** a substance means to soak it up or take it in. *Plants absorb carbon dioxide from the air... Refined sugars are absorbed into the bloodstream very quickly.* ♦ **absorption** /əb'zɔːpʃən/ N-UNCOUNT *...the absorption of iron from food.* **2** VERB If a group **is absorbed into** a larger group, it becomes part of the larger group. *The Colonial Office was absorbed into the Foreign Office. ...the ability of a bigger bank to absorb a smaller one.* ♦ **absorption** N-UNCOUNT *Two new camps were readied for the absorption of refugees.* **3** VERB If you **absorb** information, you

understand and remember it. *Too often he only absorbs half the information. ...to give employees time to absorb the bad news.* **4** VERB If something **absorbs** you, it interests you and gets all your attention. **5** VERB If something **absorbs** a force, it reduces its effect. *...shoes that are not designed to absorb the impact of running.*

absorbed /əb'zɔːbd/. ADJ AFTER LINK-V If you are **absorbed in** a person, activity, or subject, they get all your attention. *She was totally absorbed in her partner.*

absorbing /əb'zɔːbɪŋ/. ADJ An **absorbing** activity interests you a great deal and takes up all your attention. *...an absorbing hobby.*

absorption /əb'zɔːpʃən/. See **absorb**.

abstain /æb'steɪn/ **abstains, abstaining, abstained**. **1** VERB If you **abstain from** something you like doing, you deliberately do not do it. *Overeaters can't totally abstain from eating.* ♦ **abstention** /æb'stenʃən/ N-UNCOUNT *...abstention from alcohol.* **2** VERB If you **abstain** during a vote, you do not vote. ♦ **abstention, abstentions** N-VAR *The voting was twenty in favour, six against, and sixteen abstentions.*

abstinence /'æbstɪnəns/. N-UNCOUNT **Abstinence** is the practice of not having something you enjoy, often for health or religious reasons. *...lifelong abstinence from alcohol.*

abstract /'æbstrækt/ **abstracts**. **1** ADJ & PHRASE An **abstract** idea or way of thinking is based on general ideas rather than on particular things. You can also talk or think about something **in the abstract**. *Money was a commodity she never thought about except in the abstract.* **2** ADJ BEFORE N & N-COUNT **Abstract** art makes use of shapes and patterns rather than showing people or things as they actually are. An **abstract** is an abstract work of art. **3** N-COUNT An **abstract** of an article or speech is a short piece of writing that summarizes the main points.

abstraction /æb'strækʃən/ **abstractions**. N-COUNT An **abstraction** is a general idea rather than one relating to a specific thing. *Is it worth fighting a big war, in the name of an abstraction like sovereignty?*

absurd /æb'sɜːd/. ADJ & N-SING If you say that something is **absurd**, you think that it is ridiculous or does not make sense. **The absurd** is something that is absurd. *The thought of being a movie star was absurd to her. ...a highly developed sense of the absurd.* ♦ **absurdly** ADV *Prices were still absurdly low.* ♦ **absurdity** /æb'sɜːdɪti/ **absurdities** N-VAR *...the absurdity of all wars.*

abundance /ə'bʌndəns/. N-SING & PHRASE If there is an **abundance of** something, or if something is **in abundance**, there is a large quantity of it. *...an abundance of safe beaches... Food is in abundance.*

abundant /ə'bʌndənt/. ADJ Something that is **abundant** is present in large quantities. *...an abundant supply of energy.*

a
b
c
d
e
f
g
h
i
j
k
l
m
n
o
p
q
r
s
t
u
v
w
x
y
z

⭐ **abuse, abuses, abusing, abused;** noun /əˈbjuːs/, verb /əˈbjuːz/. [1] VERB & N-VAR If someone **is abused**, or if they are victims of **abuse**, they are treated cruelly and violently. ...*parents who feel they cannot cope or might abuse their children.* ...*human rights abuses.* [2] VERB & N-UNCOUNT You can say that someone **is abused** if rude and insulting things are said to them. **Abuse** is rude and insulting things that people say when they are angry. *He was verbally abused by other soldiers... I was left shouting abuse as the car sped off.* [3] VERB & N-UNCOUNT If you **abuse** something, you use it in a wrong way or for a bad purpose. **Abuse** of something is the use of it in this way. ...*how the rich and powerful can abuse their position.* ...*an abuse of power.* ...*alcohol abuse.*

abusive /əˈbjuːsɪv/. [1] ADJ **Abusive** language is extremely rude and insulting. ...*abusive language.* [2] ADJ Someone who is **abusive** is cruel and violent towards someone else. ...*her cruel and abusive husband.*

abysmal /əˈbɪzməl/. ADJ **Abysmal** means very bad or poor in quality. *My ignorance on the subject of drugs was abysmal.* ♦ **abysmally** ADV *Standards of hygiene are abysmally low.*

abyss /æˈbɪs/ **abysses.** [1] N-COUNT An **abyss** is a hole in the ground which is so deep that it is impossible to measure. *He crawled to peer over the edge of the abyss.* [2] N-COUNT You can refer to a frightening situation which could have terrible consequences as an **abyss**. [WRITTEN] ...*taking his country to the abyss of war.*

⭐ **academic** /ˌækəˈdemɪk/ **academics.** [1] ADJ BEFORE N **Academic** means relating to work done in schools, colleges, and universities, especially work which involves studying and reasoning rather than practical or technical skills. ...*the academic year... Their academic standards are high.* ♦ **academically** ADV *He is academically gifted.* [2] ADJ Someone who is **academic** is good at studying. [3] N-COUNT An **academic** is a member of a university or college who teaches or does research. [4] ADJ If you say that something is **academic**, you mean that it has no real relevance or effect. *If Andy had been fit it might have been a different story. But it's all academic now.*

academy /əˈkædəmi/ **academies.** N-COUNT A school or college specializing in a particular subject is sometimes called an **academy**. ...*the Royal Academy of Music.*

accelerate /əkˈseləreɪt/ **accelerates, accelerating, accelerated.** VERB When the rate or speed of something **accelerates**, it increases. *Growth will accelerate to about 4 per cent... We need to accelerate the pace of change... The car accelerated.* ♦ **acceleration** N-UNCOUNT ...*acceleration to 60 mph.*

accelerator /əkˈseləreɪtə/ **accelerators.** N-COUNT In a vehicle, the **accelerator** is the pedal you press to go faster.

accent /ˈæksənt/ **accents.** [1] N-COUNT Someone who speaks with a particular **accent** pronounces the words of a language in a way that indicates their country, region, or social class. ...*a slight American accent.* [2] N-COUNT An **accent** is a mark written above or below certain letters in some languages to show how they are pronounced. [3] N-SING If you put the **accent on** a particular feature of something, you give it special importance or emphasis.

accentuate /ækˈsentʃueɪt/ **accentuates, accentuating, accentuated.** VERB To **accentuate** something means to emphasize it or make it more noticeable. *His shaven head accentuates his large round face.*

⭐ **accept** /əkˈsept/ **accepts, accepting, accepted.** [1] VERB If you **accept** something that you have been offered, you say yes to it or agree to take it. *I accepted his offer of permanent employment... All those invited to next week's peace conference have accepted.* ♦ **acceptance** /əkˈseptəns/ N-UNCOUNT ...*acceptance of the invitation to Moscow.* [2] VERB If you **accept** a fact, you believe that it is true or valid. *He could never accept that he had been wrong... Her parents accepted her decision.* ♦ **acceptance** N-UNCOUNT ...*a theory that is steadily gaining acceptance.* [3] VERB To **accept** a difficult or unpleasant situation means to recognize that it cannot be changed. *Urban dwellers often accept noise as part of city life... We also accept that some marriages die.* ♦ **acceptance** N-UNCOUNT ...*his calm acceptance of whatever comes his way.* [4] VERB If you **accept** the blame or responsibility for something, you admit that you are responsible for it. [5] VERB When an organization or group **accepts** someone, they give them a job or allow them to join their group. *They refused to accept women as bus drivers... Stephen was accepted into the family.* ♦ **acceptance** N-UNCOUNT *Would he be popular enough to gain acceptance?* [6] See also **accepted.**

⭐ **acceptable** /əkˈseptəbəl/. [1] ADJ If a situation or action is **acceptable**, people generally approve of it or allow it to happen. *It is becoming more acceptable for women to drink... The air pollution exceeds acceptable levels.* ♦ **acceptability** N-UNCOUNT ...*increasing the social acceptability of divorce.* ♦ **acceptably** ADV *Teach children to behave acceptably.* [2] ADJ If something is **acceptable**, it is good enough or fairly good. *We've made an acceptable start.*

⭐ **accepted** /əkˈseptɪd/. ADJ **Accepted** ideas are agreed by most people to be correct or reasonable. *It was generally accepted that men disliked shopping.*

⭐ **access** /ˈækses/ **accesses, accessing, accessed.** [1] N-UNCOUNT If you have **access to** a building or other place, you are able or allowed to go into it. [FORMAL] ...*unlimited access to the swimming pool.* [2] N-UNCOUNT Your **access to** someone is the opportunity or right you have to see them. *His ex-partner denies him access to his children.* [3] VERB & N-UNCOUNT If you **access** information, or if you have **access to** it, you are able to see or get it. ...*to give patients right of access to their medical records.*

accessible /æk'sesɪbəl/ **1** ADJ If a place is **accessible**, you are able to reach it or get into it. ...*a low cupboard that's easily accessible.* ♦ **accessibility** /æk,sesɪ'bɪlɪti/ N-UNCOUNT ...*accessibility to the city centre.* **2** ADJ If something is **accessible to** people, they can easily use it or obtain it. ...*making computers truly accessible to people.* ♦ **accessibility** N-UNCOUNT ...*the cost, quality and accessibility of health care.*

accessory /æk'sesəri/ **accessories.** **1** N-COUNT **Accessories** are extra parts added to something to make it more efficient, useful, or decorative. ...*bathroom accessories.* **2** N-COUNT An **accessory to** a crime is someone who willingly helps the person who commits it, but does not take part in the crime itself. [TECHNICAL]

⭐ **accident** /'æksɪdənt/ **accidents.** **1** N-VAR An **accident** is an event which happens completely by chance. You can also say that something happens **by accident**. *Is it destiny that brings people together, or is it accident?... She discovered the problem by accident.* **2** N-COUNT An **accident** is something unpleasant that happens and that often causes injury or death. ...*a serious car accident.*

accidental /,æksɪ'dentəl/ ADJ An **accidental** event happens by chance or as the result of an accident. *The fire was accidental.* ♦ **accidentally** ADV *Names were accidentally erased from computer disks.*

acclaim /ə'kleɪm/ **acclaims, acclaiming, acclaimed.** VERB & N-UNCOUNT If someone or something **is acclaimed**, or wins **acclaim**, they are praised publicly and enthusiastically. [FORMAL] *She has been acclaimed for the TV dramas 'Prime Suspect' and 'Civvies'... He was acclaimed as England's greatest modern painter... Angela Bassett won critical acclaim for her excellent performance.* ♦ **acclaimed** ADJ ...*six highly acclaimed novels.*

acclimatize (BRIT also **acclimatise**) /ə'klaɪmətaɪz/ **acclimatizes, acclimatizing, acclimatized.** VERB When you **acclimatize** or **are acclimatized to** a new situation, place, or climate, you become used to it. *The athletes are acclimatising to the heat... He has left for St Louis early to acclimatise himself... It would take her two years to get acclimatized.*

accolade /'ækəleɪd/ **accolades.** N-COUNT An **accolade** is something that is done or said about someone which shows how much people admire them. [FORMAL] ...*the ultimate international accolade, the Nobel Peace Prize.*

accommodate /ə'kɒmədeɪt/ **accommodates, accommodating, accommodated.** **1** VERB If a building or space can **accommodate** someone or something, it has enough room for them. *The school in Poldown was not big enough to accommodate all the children.* **2** VERB To **accommodate** someone means to provide them with a place to stay. ...*a hotel built to* accommodate guests for the wedding. **3** VERB To **accommodate** someone means to help them. ...*the full-service beauty salon which accommodates both men and women.* ♦ **accommodating** ADJ *Lindi seemed a nice, accommodating girl.*

accommodation /ə,kɒmə'deɪʃən/ N-UNCOUNT **Accommodation** is used to refer to rooms or buildings where people live, stay, or work. *Travel and overnight accommodation are included.*

accompaniment /ə'kʌmpnimənt/ **accompaniments.** **1** N-UNCOUNT The **accompaniment** to a singer or instrument is the music that is played at the same time, forming a background to it. ...*a lively musical accompaniment.* **2** N-VAR An **accompaniment to** something is another thing that happens or exists at the same time, usually something that complements the first thing. *Eclairs make an ideal accompaniment to morning coffee... The procession wends its way through the streets to the accompaniment of wildly excited shouting.*

⭐ **accompany** /ə'kʌmpəni/ **accompanies, accompanying, accompanied.** **1** VERB If you **accompany** someone, you go somewhere with them. [FORMAL] *Children must be accompanied by an adult.* **2** VERB If one thing **accompanies** another, the two things happen or exist at the same time. ...*sauces that accompany chicken dishes.* **3** VERB When you **accompany** a singer or a musician, you play one part of a piece of music while they sing or play the main tune.

accomplice /ə'kʌmplɪs, AM ə'kɒm-/ **accomplices.** N-COUNT An **accomplice** is a person who helps to commit a crime.

accomplish /ə'kʌmplɪʃ, AM ə'kɒm-/ **accomplishes, accomplishing, accomplished.** VERB If you **accomplish** something, you succeed in doing it. *If we'd all work together, I think we could accomplish our goal.* ♦ **accomplishment** N-UNCOUNT ...*the accomplishment of his highly important mission.*

accomplished /ə'kʌmplɪʃt, AM ə'kɒm-/ ADJ If someone is **accomplished**, they are very good at something. ...*an accomplished linguist.*

accomplishment /ə'kʌmplɪʃmənt, AM ə'kɒm-/ **accomplishments.** **1** N-COUNT Your **accomplishments** are the things you have achieved or the things that you do well. [FORMAL] *The list of her accomplishments is staggering.* **2** See also **accomplish**.

⭐ **accord** /ə'kɔːd/ **accords, according, accorded.** **1** VERB If you **are accorded** a particular kind of treatment, people treat you in that way. [FORMAL] ...*the military honours accorded to all visiting heads of state.* **2** N-COUNT An **accord** between countries or groups of people is a formal agreement, for example to end a war. ...*the 1991 peace accords.*

PHRASES ● If one person, action, or fact is **in accord with** another, there is no conflict between them. You can also say that two people or things are **in accord**. [FORMAL] ● When you do something **of** your **own accord**, you do it freely and because you want to. If something happens **of** its **own accord**, it seems to happen automatically, without anybody making it happen. *He had left her of his own accord.*

accordance /əˈkɔːdəns/. PHRASE If something is done **in accordance with** a rule or system, it is done in the way that the rule or system says it should be done. *Act in accordance with the law.*

accordingly /əˈkɔːdɪŋli/. ADV You use **accordingly** to say that one thing happens as a result of another thing. *It is a difficult job and they should be paid accordingly.*

⭐ **acˈcording to**. ☐ PREP If something is true **according to** a particular person or book, that person or book claims that it is true. *Philip stayed at the hotel, according to Mr Hemming.* ② PREP If something is done **according to** a particular principle or plan, this principle or plan is used as the basis for the way it is done. *Things really did work out according to plan.*

⭐ **account** /əˈkaʊnt/ **accounts, accounting, accounted.** ☐ N-COUNT If you have an **account** with a bank, you leave money with the bank and withdraw it when you need it. *...a savings account.* ② N-COUNT In business, a regular customer of a company can be referred to as an **account**. *The marketing agency has won two Edinburgh accounts.* ③ N-COUNT **Accounts** are detailed records of all the money that a person or business receives and spends. *He kept detailed accounts.* ④ N-COUNT An **account** is a written or spoken report of something that has happened. *He gave a detailed account of what happened... He is, by all accounts, a superb teacher.*

PHRASES ● If someone **is called, held,** or **brought to account** for something they have done wrong, they are made to explain why they did it, and are often criticized or punished for it. ● If you **take** something **into account**, you consider it when you are thinking about a situation. ● If you tell someone not to do something **on** your **account**, you mean that they should do it only if they want to, and not because they think it will please you. *Don't leave on my account.* ● If you say that something should **on no account** be done, you are emphasizing that it should not be done under any circumstances. *When asked for your views about your current job, on no account must you be negative.*

▸**account for**. ☐ PHR-VERB If you can **account for** something, you can explain it or give the necessary information about it. *How do you account for the company's alarmingly high staff turnover?* ② PHR-VERB If something **accounts for** a particular proportion of a whole thing, it is what that proportion consists of. *Computers account for 5% of the country's commercial electricity consumption.*

accountable /əˈkaʊntəbəl/. ADJ If you are **accountable for** something that you do, you are responsible for it. *Public officials can finally be held accountable for their actions.* ♦ **accountability** N-UNCOUNT *...the system of local accountability for the police.*

accountancy /əˈkaʊntənsi/. N-UNCOUNT **Accountancy** is the work of keeping financial accounts.

accountant /əˈkaʊntənt/ **accountants.** N-COUNT An **accountant** is a person whose job is to keep financial accounts.

accumulate /əˈkjuːmjʊleɪt/ **accumulates, accumulating, accumulated.** VERB When you **accumulate** things or when they **accumulate**, they collect or are gathered over a period of time. *Chemicals can accumulate in processed foods.* ♦ **accumulation, accumulations** N-COUNT *...accumulation of wealth. ...accumulations of dirt.*

⭐ **accurate** /ˈækjʊrət/. ☐ ADJ Something that is **accurate** is correct to a detailed level. *This is the most accurate description of the killer to date... Quartz watches are very accurate.* ♦ **accuracy** N-UNCOUNT *...the accuracy of the story.* ♦ **accurately** ADV *The questions have been accurately recorded.* ② ADJ A person, device, or machine that is **accurate** is able to perform a task without making a mistake. *The rifle was extremely accurate.* ♦ **accuracy** N-UNCOUNT *Every bank pays close attention to the speed and accuracy of its staff.* ♦ **accurately** ADV *...shooting back accurately, aiming to kill.*

accusation /ˌækjʊˈzeɪʃən/ **accusations.** N-COUNT If you make an **accusation** against someone, you express the belief that they have done something wrong.

⭐ **accuse** /əˈkjuːz/ **accuses, accusing, accused.** VERB If you **accuse** someone **of** something, you say that you believe they did something wrong or dishonest. *He was accusing her of having an affair... Prosecutors had accused him of stealing about $26 million.*

accused /əˈkjuːzd/.

✅ **Accused** is both the singular and the plural form.

N-COUNT **The accused** refers to the person or people charged with a crime or on trial for it. *The accused is alleged to be a member of a right-wing gang... The accused are out on bail.*

accustom /əˈkʌstəm/ **accustoms, accustoming, accustomed.** VERB If you **accustom yourself to** something, you experience it or learn about it, so that it becomes familiar or natural. *...while his team accustoms itself to the pace of first division rugby... Shakespeare has accustomed us to a mixture of humor and tragedy in the same play.* ♦ **accustomed** ADJ AFTER LINK-V *He was accustomed to hard work.*

ace /eɪs/ **aces.** ☐ N-COUNT An **ace** is a playing card with a single symbol on it. *...the ace of hearts.* ② N-COUNT In tennis, an **ace** is a serve which is so good that the other player cannot return the ball.

ache /eɪk/ **aches, aching, ached.** ☐ VERB & N-COUNT If part of your body **aches**, or if you have an **ache**, you feel a steady, fairly strong pain. *He really was* *aching, tired, and hungry. ...an effective remedy for aches and pains.* [2] VERB If you **ache for** something or **ache to** do something, you want it very much. *She still ached for the lost intimacy and sexual contact of marriage. ...a country aching to get away from its past.*

⭐ **achieve** /ə'tʃiːv/ **achieves, achieving, achieved.** VERB If you **achieve** a particular aim or effect, you succeed in doing it or causing it to happen, usually after a lot of effort. *Achieving our goals makes us feel good.*

⭐ **achievement** /ə'tʃiːvmənt/ **achievements.** [1] N-COUNT An **achievement** is something which someone has succeeded in doing, especially after a lot of effort. [2] N-UNCOUNT **Achievement** is the process of achieving something. *It is only the achievement of these goals that will finally bring lasting peace.*

achiever /ə'tʃiːvə/ **achievers.** N-COUNT A high **achiever** is someone who is successful in their studies or their work, usually as a result of their efforts. A low **achiever** is someone who is unsuccessful.

⭐ **acid** /'æsɪd/ **acids.** [1] N-VAR An **acid** is a liquid or substance with a pH value of less than 7. Strong acids can damage your skin and clothes. *...citric acid... Acids in the stomach destroy the virus.* [2] ADJ An **acid** substance contains acid. *These shrubs must have an acid, lime-free soil.* [3] ADJ An **acid** fruit or drink has a sour or sharp taste. *These wines may taste rather hard and somewhat acid.* [4] ADJ An **acid** remark is unkind or critical.

acidic /ə'sɪdɪk/. ADJ Something that is **acidic** contains acid or has a pH value of less than 7.

acidity /æ'sɪdɪti/. N-UNCOUNT **Acidity** is the quality of having a pH value lower than 7.

,**acid 'rain.** N-UNCOUNT **Acid rain** is rain that damages plants, rivers, and buildings because it contains acid released into the atmosphere from factories and other industrial processes.

⭐ **acknowledge** /æk'nɒlɪdʒ/ **acknowledges, acknowledging, acknowledged.** [1] VERB If you **acknowledge** a fact, you accept that it is true. [FORMAL] *Naylor acknowledged, in a letter to the judge, that he was a drug addict... This is now acknowledged as an urgent national problem.* [2] VERB If you **acknowledge** someone, you show that you have seen and recognized them. *She never even acknowledged the man who opened the door.* [3] VERB If you **acknowledge** a message or letter, you tell the person who sent it that you have received it. *The army sent me a postcard acknowledging my request.*

acknowledgement (or **acknowledgment**) /æk'nɒlɪdʒmənt/ **acknowledgements.** [1] N-SING An **acknowledgement** of something is a statement or action that recognizes that it is true. *The President's resignation appears to be an acknowledgment that he has lost all hope.* [2] N-VAR If you receive an **acknowledgement** of something you have sent to someone, you are told officially that it has arrived. [3] N-PLURAL The

acknowledgements in a book are the parts in which the author thanks the people who have helped.

acne /'ækni/. N-UNCOUNT **Acne** is a skin disease which causes spots on the face and neck.

acorn /'eɪkɔːn/ **acorns.** N-COUNT An **acorn** is a pale oval nut that is the fruit of an oak tree.

acoustic /ə'kuːstɪk/ **acoustics.** [1] ADJ BEFORE N An **acoustic** guitar is not made louder by an electrical amplifier. [2] N-PLURAL The **acoustics** of a room are the structural features which determine how well you can hear sound in it. *The acoustics of the theatre are still superb.* [3] ADJ **Acoustic** means relating to sound or hearing. *...acoustic signals.*

acquaint /ə'kweɪnt/ **acquaints, acquainting, acquainted.** VERB If you **acquaint** someone **with** something, you tell them about it, so that they know it or become familiar with it. [FORMAL] *I want to acquaint myself with your abilities.*

acquaintance /ə'kweɪntəns/ **acquaintances.** [1] N-COUNT An **acquaintance** is someone who you have met but do not know particularly well. *Rose and Jim Gordon were old acquaintances.* [2] N-VAR If you have an **acquaintance with** someone, you have met them and you know them. *I struck up an acquaintance with a shopkeeper.* [3] N-SING Your **acquaintance with** a subject is your knowledge or experience of it. *They had little or no acquaintance with Chinese history.*

acquainted /ə'kweɪntɪd/. [1] ADJ AFTER LINK-V If you are **acquainted with** something, you know about it because you have learned it or experienced it. [FORMAL] *He was well acquainted with the literature of France.* [2] ADJ AFTER LINK-V If you are **acquainted with** someone, you know them but they are not a close friend. You can also say that two people are **acquainted**.

⭐ **acquire** /ə'kwaɪə/ **acquires, acquiring, acquired.** [1] VERB If you **acquire** something, you obtain it. *General Motors acquired a 50% stake in Saab.* [2] VERB If you **acquire** a skill or habit, you learn it or develop it. *He had acquired the habit of observing people... Salt is an acquired taste.*

⭐ **acquisition** /,ækwɪ'zɪʃən/ **acquisitions.** [1] N-COUNT An **acquisition** is something that you have obtained. *His latest acquisition is a 1928 Lancia.* [2] N-UNCOUNT The **acquisition** of something is the process of getting it or being given it. *...the acquisition of land by force.* [3] N-UNCOUNT The **acquisition** of a skill or habit is the process of learning it or developing it. *...language acquisition.*

acquit /ə'kwɪt/ **acquits, acquitting, acquitted.** [1] VERB If someone **is acquitted of** a crime, it is formally declared in court that they did not commit it. *Mr Ling was acquitted of disorderly behaviour... All the accused were acquitted.* [2] VERB If you **acquit yourself** in a particular way, other people feel that you behave in that way. [FORMAL] *Most officers and men acquitted themselves well.*

a
b
c
d
e
f
g
h
i
j
k
l
m
n
o
p
q
r
s
t
u
v
w
x
y
z

acquittal /ə'kwɪtəl/ **acquittals.** N-VAR The **acquittal** of someone who has been accused of a crime is a formal declaration that they are innocent. *The judge ordered their acquittal.*

⭐ **acre** /'eɪkə/ **acres.** N-COUNT An **acre** is a unit of area equal to 4,840 square yards or approximately 4,047 square metres.

acrimonious /ˌækrɪ'məʊniəs/ ADJ **Acrimonious** words or quarrels are bitter and angry. [FORMAL]

acronym /'ækrənɪm/ **acronyms.** N-COUNT An **acronym** is a word made of the initial letters of the words in a phrase, especially when this is the name of something. An example of an acronym is NATO.

⭐ **across** /ə'krɒs, AM ə'krɔːs/. [1] PREP & ADV If you go or look **across** somewhere, you go or look from one side of it to the other. *He watched Karl run across the street... He glanced across at his sleeping wife.* [2] PREP & ADV Something that is situated **across** a street, river, or area is on the other side of it, or stretches from one side to the other. *I saw you across the room... They parked across from the Castro Theatre. ...the floating bridge across Lake Washington.* [3] ADV **Across** is used to indicate the width of something. *This hand-decorated plate measures 30cm across.* [4] PREP When something happens **across** a place or organization, it happens equally everywhere within it. *The film opens across America on December 11.* ● **across the board**: see **board**.

acrylic /æ'krɪlɪk/. ADJ **Acrylic** material is man-made, and manufactured by a chemical process. *...new acrylic wigs.*

⭐ **act** /ækt/ **acts, acting, acted.** [1] VERB When you **act**, you do something for a particular purpose. *...when police acted to stop widespread looting... We have acted properly and responsibly in this case.* [2] N-COUNT An **act** is a single action or thing that someone does. *...the act of reading... My insurance excludes acts of sabotage.* [3] VERB If someone **acts** in a particular way, they behave in that way. *...a gang of youths who were acting suspiciously... He acted as if he hadn't heard.* [4] VERB If someone or something **acts as** a particular thing, they have that role or function. *He acted both as the ship's surgeon and as chaplain for the men.* [5] N-SING If you say that someone's behaviour is an **act**, you mean that it does not express their real feelings. [6] VERB If you **act** in a play or film, you have a part in it. *Every time I see her act I am filled with admiration.* [7] N-COUNT An **act** in a play, opera, or ballet is one of the main parts into which it is divided. [8] N-COUNT An **act** in a show is one of the short performances in the show. *...the best new comedy acts.* [9] N-COUNT An **Act** is a law passed by the government. *...the Tax Reform Act of 1986.*

acting /'æktɪŋ/. [1] N-UNCOUNT **Acting** is the activity or profession of performing in plays or films. *The acting was superb. ...her acting career.* [2] ADJ BEFORE N You use **acting** before the title of a job to indicate that someone is doing that job temporarily. *...the new acting President.*

⭐ **action** /'ækʃən/ **actions.** [1] N-UNCOUNT **Action** is doing something for a particular purpose. *She was anxious to avoid any action which might harm him.* [2] N-COUNT An **action** is something that you do on a particular occasion. *Peter had a reason for his action.* [3] N-SING The **action** refers to all the important and exciting things that are happening in a situation. *Hollywood is where the action is now.* [4] N-UNCOUNT **Action** is fighting in a war. *He'd been listed as missing in action.*
PHRASES ● If you **put** an idea or policy **into action**, you begin to use it. ● If someone is **out of action**, they are injured and cannot work. You can also say that something is **out of action**. *...the lifts went out of action.*

activate /'æktɪveɪt/ **activates, activating, activated.** VERB If a device or process **is activated**, something causes it to start working. *Video cameras can be activated by movement.*

⭐ **active** /'æktɪv/. [1] ADJ An **active** person is energetic and always busy. *Having an active youngster about the house can be quite wearing.* [2] ADJ If someone is **active** in an organization or cause, they are involved in it and work hard for it. *...an active member of the Conservative Party... He is active on Tyler's behalf.* ♦ **actively** ADV *They actively campaigned for the vote.* [3] ADJ BEFORE N **Active** is used to emphasize that someone is taking action in order to achieve something, rather than just waiting for it to happen. *They are taking active steps to reduce stress.* ♦ **actively** ADV *They have never been actively encouraged to take such risks.* [4] ADJ An **active** volcano has erupted recently.

⭐ **activist** /'æktɪvɪst/ **activists.** N-COUNT An **activist** is a person who works to bring about political or social changes. *...animal rights activists.*

⭐ **activity** /æk'tɪvɪti/ **activities.** [1] N-UNCOUNT **Activity** is a situation in which a lot of things are happening. *Other boats came and went in a flurry of activity.* [2] N-COUNT An **activity** is something that you spend time doing. *...outdoor activities.* [3] N-PLURAL The **activities** of a group are the things they do to achieve their aims. *...terrorist activities.*

⭐ **actor** /'æktə/ **actors.** N-COUNT An **actor** is someone whose job is acting in plays or films.

> **USAGE** Note that many women who act prefer to be called **actors** rather than **actresses**. *She wants to be an actor when she grows up.*

⭐ **actress** /'æktrəs/ **actresses.** N-COUNT An **actress** is a woman whose job is acting in plays or films.

⭐ **actual** /'æktʃʊəl/. [1] ADJ BEFORE N **Actual** is used to emphasize that you are referring to something real or genuine. *The actual number of AIDS victims is much higher than statistics reflect.* [2] ADJ BEFORE N You use **actual** to contrast the important aspect of something with a less important aspect. *The exercises in this chapter can guide you, but it will be up to you to do the actual work.* • **in actual fact**: see **fact**.

⭐ **actually** /'æktʃʊəli/. [1] ADV You use **actually** to indicate that a situation exists or that it is true. *I grew bored and actually fell asleep for a few minutes... Interest is only payable on the amount actually borrowed.* [2] ADV You use **actually** as a way of being more polite, especially when you are correcting or contradicting someone, advising them, or when you are introducing a new topic of conversation. *No, I'm not a student. I'm a doctor, actually... Well actually, John, I rang you for some advice.*

> **USAGE** Actual and **actually** are not used to refer to something which is happening now, at the present time. For this meaning, you need to use adjectives such as **current** or **present**, or adverbs such as **currently** or **now**. Actual and **actually** are used to emphasize what is true or genuine in a situation, often when this is surprising, or a contrast with what has just been said.

acumen /'ækjʊmen, AM ə'kju:mən/. N-UNCOUNT **Acumen** is the ability to make good judgments and quick decisions. *...business acumen.*

acupuncture /'ækjʊpʌŋktʃə/. N-UNCOUNT **Acupuncture** is the treatment of a person's illness or pain by sticking small needles into their body.

acute /ə'kju:t/. [1] ADJ An **acute** situation or feeling is very intense or unpleasant. *...a very acute infection.* ◆ **acutely** ADV *It was an acutely uncomfortable journey.* [2] ADJ If a person's or animal's senses are **acute**, they are sensitive and powerful. *Cats have very acute hearing.* ◆ **acutely** ADV *He was acutely aware of the odour of cooking oil.* [3] ADJ In geometry, an **acute** angle is less than 90°.

⭐ **ad** /æd/ **ads**. N-COUNT An **ad** is an advertisement. [INFORMAL]

AD /,eɪ 'di:/. You use **AD** in dates to indicate a number of years or centuries since the year in which Jesus Christ is believed to have been born. *...the Great Fire of 1136 AD.*

adamant /'ædəmənt/. ADJ If you are **adamant about** something, you are determined not to change your mind. *Sue was adamant about that job in Australia... The prime minister is adamant that he will not resign.* ◆ **adamantly** ADV *She adamantly refused to put the book back.*

adapt /ə'dæpt/ **adapts, adapting, adapted**. [1] VERB If you **adapt to** a new situation, you change your ideas or behaviour in order to deal with it. *MPs have quickly adapted themselves to the cameras.* [2] VERB If you **adapt** something, you change it to make it suitable for a new purpose or situation. *Shelves were built to adapt the library for use as an office.* [3] VERB If you **adapt** a book or play, you change it so that it can be made into a film or a television programme. *The scriptwriter helped him to adapt his novel for the screen.* [4] See also **adapted**.

adaptable /ə'dæptəbəl/. ADJ Someone or something that is **adaptable** is able to change or be changed in order to suit new situations. *Humans are infinitely adaptable. ...an adaptable piece of summer clothing.* ◆ **adaptability** N-UNCOUNT *...this adaptability which many animals do indeed show.*

adaptation /,ædæp'teɪʃən/ **adaptations**. [1] N-COUNT An **adaptation** of a story is a play or film based on it. *...his screen adaptation of Shakespeare's Henry the Fifth.* [2] N-UNCOUNT **Adaptation** is the act of changing something to make it suitable for a new purpose or situation. *Most living creatures are capable of adaptation.*

adapted /ə'dæptɪd/. ADJ AFTER LINK-V If something is **adapted to** a particular situation or purpose, it is especially suitable for it. *Plants are adapted to being short of water in summer.*

⭐ **add** /æd/ **adds, adding, added**. [1] VERB If you **add** one thing **to** another, you put it with the other thing, to complete or improve it. *Add the grated cheese to the sauce... He wants to add a huge sports complex to Binfield Manor.* [2] VERB & PHR-VERB If you **add** numbers or amounts, or **add** them **up**, you calculate their total. *Banks add all the interest and other charges together.* [3] VERB If one thing **adds to** another, it makes the other thing greater in degree or amount, or it gives it a particular quality. *Cheerful faces added to the general gaiety.* ◆ **added** ADJ BEFORE N *For added protection choose moisturising lipsticks with a sun screen.* [4] VERB If you **add** something when you are speaking, you say something more. *Hunt added his congratulations.*
▸**add in**. PHR-VERB If you **add in** something, you include it as a part of something else. *Once the vegetables start to cook add in a couple of tablespoons of water.*
▸**add on**. [1] PHR-VERB If something **is added on**, it is attached to or made part of something else. *The colour is either drab or garish and is obviously added on.* [2] PHR-VERB If you **add on** an extra item or amount to a list or total, you include it in the list or total. *Many loan application forms automatically add on insurance.*
▸**add up**. [1] See **add** 2. [2] PHR-VERB If facts or events do not **add up**, they make you confused about the true nature of the situation. *This charge of burglary just doesn't add up.* [3] PHR-VERB If small amounts of something **add up**, they gradually increase. *It's the little minor problems that add up.*
▸**add up to**. PHR-VERB If amounts **add up to** a particular total, they result in that total when they are put together. *Profits can add up to millions of dollars.*

addict /'ædɪkt/ **addicts**. [1] N-COUNT An **addict** is someone who cannot stop taking harmful drugs.

...*a drug* **addict**. **2** N-COUNT You can say that someone is an **addict**, when they like a particular activity very much. *She is a TV addict.*

addicted /əˈdɪktɪd/. **1** ADJ Someone who is **addicted to** a drug cannot stop taking it. *Many of the women are addicted to heroin.* **2** ADJ If you are **addicted to** something, you like it very much. *She had become addicted to golf.*

addiction /əˈdɪkʃən/ **addictions.** **1** N-VAR **Addiction** is the condition of being addicted to drugs. ...*drug addiction.* **2** N-VAR An **addiction to** something is a very strong desire or need for it. ...*his addiction to gambling.*

addictive /əˈdɪktɪv/. **1** ADJ If a drug is **addictive**, people who start taking it find that they cannot stop. *Cigarettes are highly addictive.* **2** ADJ Something that is **addictive** is so enjoyable that it makes you want to do it or have it a lot. *Video movie-making can become addictive.*

⭐ **addition** /əˈdɪʃən/ **additions.** **1** PHRASE You use **in addition** or **with the addition of** to mention another item connected with the subject you are discussing. *There's a postage and packing fee in addition to the repair charge.* **2** N-COUNT An **addition to** something is a thing which is added to it. ...*recent additions to the range of 4x4 cars.* ♦ **additional** ADJ *The US is sending additional troops to the region.* **3** N-UNCOUNT **Addition** is the process of calculating the total of two or more numbers.

additionally /əˈdɪʃənəli/. **1** ADV You use **additionally** to introduce an extra fact. [FORMAL] *All teachers are qualified to teach their native language. Additionally, we select our teachers for their engaging personalities.* **2** ADV **Additionally** is used to say that something happens to a greater extent than before. *The birds are additionally protected in the reserves at Birsay.*

additive /ˈædɪtɪv/ **additives.** N-COUNT An **additive** is a substance which is added to food by the manufacturer for a particular purpose, such as colouring it. ...*food additives.*

⭐ **address** /əˈdres, AM ˈædres/ **addresses, addressing, addressed.** **1** N-COUNT Your **address** is the number of the house, the name of the street, and the town where you live or work. *The address is 2025 Main Street, Northwest, Washington, DC, 20036.* **2** VERB If a letter **is addressed to** you, your name and address has been written on it. *Applications should be addressed to the business affairs editor.* **3** N-COUNT The **address** of a website is its location on the Internet, for example http://www.cobuild.collins.co.uk. *Internet addresses are also known as URLs.* **4** VERB & N-COUNT If you **address** a group of people or if you give an **address**, you give a speech to them. *He turned to address the multitude.* ...*an address to the American people.* **5** VERB If you **address** someone or **address** a remark to someone, you say something to them. *The two foreign ministers did not address each other directly.* **6** VERB If you **address** someone by a name or a title such as 'sir', you call them that name or title. *I heard him*

address her as darling. **7** VERB If you **address** a problem or if you **address yourself to** it, you try to understand it or deal with it. *Mr King sought to address those fears when he spoke at the meeting... Throughout the book we have addressed ourselves to the problem of ethics.*

adept /ˈædept/. ADJ Someone who is **adept at** something does it skilfully. *He's usually very adept at keeping his private life out of the media... He is an adept guitar player.*

⭐ **adequate** /ˈædɪkwət/. ADJ If something is **adequate**, there is enough of it or it is good enough for a particular purpose. ...*an amount adequate to purchase another house.* ♦ **adequacy** N-UNCOUNT ...*the adequacy of the diet.* ♦ **adequately** ADV *I speak the language adequately.*

adhere /ædˈhɪə/ **adheres, adhering, adhered.** **1** VERB If you **adhere to** a rule, you act in the way that it says you should. *All members of the association adhere to a strict code of practice.* ♦ **adherence** /ædˈhɪərəns/ N-UNCOUNT ...*strict adherence to the constitution.* **2** VERB If you **adhere to** an opinion or belief, you support or hold it. ...*those who adhered to more traditional views.* **3** VERB If a substance **adheres to** a surface or object, it sticks to it. [FORMAL] *Small particles adhere to the seed.*

adhesive /ædˈhiːsɪv/ **adhesives.** N-VAR & ADJ An **adhesive** or an **adhesive** substance is used to make things stick together. ...*adhesive tape.*

ad hoc /ˌæd ˈhɒk/. ADJ An **ad hoc** activity or organization is done or formed only when it becomes necessary, rather than being planned in advance. ...*on an ad hoc basis.* ...*ad hoc committees.*

adjacent /əˈdʒeɪsənt/. ADJ If two things are **adjacent**, they are next to each other. *He sat in an adjacent room.* ...*offices adjacent to the court.*

adjective /ˈædʒɪktɪv/ **adjectives.** N-COUNT In grammar, an **adjective** is a word such as 'big', 'dead', or 'financial' that describes a person or thing, or gives extra information about them. Adjectives usually come before nouns or after link verbs.

adjoin /əˈdʒɔɪn/ **adjoins, adjoining, adjoined.** VERB If one room, place, or object **adjoins** another, they are next to each other. [FORMAL] *We waited in an adjoining office.*

adjourn /əˈdʒɜːn/ **adjourns, adjourning, adjourned.** VERB If a meeting or trial **is adjourned** or if it **adjourns**, it is stopped for a short time. *The proceedings have now been adjourned until next week.* ♦ **adjournment** /əˈdʒɜːnmənt/ **adjournments** N-COUNT *The court ordered a four month adjournment.*

⭐ **adjust** /əˈdʒʌst/ **adjusts, adjusting, adjusted.** **1** VERB When you **adjust to** a new situation, you get used to it by changing your behaviour or your ideas. *I felt I had adjusted to the idea of being a mother very well... It has been hard to adjust.* ♦ **adjustment** /əˈdʒʌstmənt/ **adjustments** N-COUNT *He will have to make major adjustments* to his thinking. **2** VERB If you **adjust** something, you change it so that it is more effective or appropriate. *Panama has adjusted its tax and labour laws.* ♦ **adjustment**N-COUNT *Investment is up by 5.7% after adjustment for inflation.* **3** VERB If you **adjust** something, you correct or alter its position or setting. *You can manually adjust the camera.* ♦ **adjustment**N-COUNT *...a large workshop for repairs and adjustments.*

adjustable /ə'dʒʌstəbəl/. ADJ If something is **adjustable**, it can be changed to different positions or sizes. *The bags have adjustable shoulder straps... The seats are fully adjustable.*

administer /æd'mɪnɪstə/ **administers, administering, administered.** **1** VERB If someone **administers** something such as a country, the law, or a test, they take responsibility for organizing and supervising it. *The plan calls for the UN to administer the country until elections can be held.* **2** VERB If a doctor or a nurse **administers** a drug, they give it to a patient. [FORMAL]

⭐ **administration** /æd,mɪnɪ'streɪʃən/. **1** N-UNCOUNT **Administration** is the range of activities connected with organizing and supervising the way that an organization functions. *Too much time is spent on administration. ...business administration.* **2** N-SING The **administration** of a company or institution is the group of people who organize and supervise it. *They would like the college administration to exert more control.* **3** See note at **government**.

administrative /æd'mɪnɪstrətɪv, AM -streɪt-/. ADJ **Administrative** work involves organizing and supervising an organization. *...administrative costs.*

administrator /æd'mɪnɪstreɪtə/ **administrators.** N-COUNT An **administrator** is a person whose job involves helping to organize and supervise the way that an organization functions.

admirable /'ædmɪrəbəl/. ADJ An **admirable** quality or action deserves to be praised and admired. *He was, in many ways, a very admirable person.* ♦ **admirably**ADV *Peter had dealt admirably with the sudden questions.*

admiral /'ædmərəl/ **admirals.** N-COUNT & N-TITLE An **admiral** is a naval officer of the highest rank.

admiration /,ædmɪ'reɪʃən/. N-UNCOUNT **Admiration** is a feeling of great liking and respect. *I have always had the greatest admiration for him.*

⭐ **admire** /əd'maɪə/ **admires, admiring, admired.** **1** VERB If you **admire** someone or something, you like and respect them. *All those who knew him will admire him for his work.* ♦ **admirer, admirers** N-COUNT *He was an admirer of her grandfather's paintings.* **2** VERB If you **admire** someone or something, you look at them with pleasure. *We took time to stop and admire the view.*

admission /æd'mɪʃən/ **admissions.** **1** N-VAR If you gain **admission to** a place or organization, you are allowed to enter it or join it. *Students apply for admission to a particular college. ...increases in hospital admissions.* **2** N-UNCOUNT **Admission** or an **admission fee** is the amount of money you pay to enter a place such as a park or museum. **3** N-VAR An **admission** is a statement that something bad or embarrassing is true. *She wanted some admission of guilt from her father.*

⭐ **admit** /əd'mɪt/ **admits, admitting, admitted.** **1** VERB If you **admit** that something bad or embarrassing is true, you agree, often reluctantly, that it is true. *Up to two thirds of 14 to 16 year olds admit to buying drink illegally... None of these people will admit responsibility.* **2** VERB If someone **is admitted to** hospital, they are taken into hospital for treatment. **3** VERB If someone **is admitted to** a place or organization, they are allowed to enter it or join it. *He was admitted to university after the war... Journalists are rarely admitted to the region.*

admittedly /æd'mɪtɪdli/. ADV You use **admittedly** when you are saying something which weakens the force of your statement. *It's only a theory, admittedly, but the pieces fit together.*

adolescent /,ædə'lesənt/ **adolescents.** ADJ & N-COUNT **Adolescent** is used to describe young people who are no longer children but who have not yet become adults. An **adolescent** is a young person. *...an adolescent boy.* ♦ **adolescence** /,ædə'lesəns/ N-UNCOUNT *...children who have reached adolescence.*

⭐ **adopt** /ə'dɒpt/ **adopts, adopting, adopted.** **1** VERB If you **adopt** someone else's child, you take it into your own family and make it legally your own. *...an adopted child.* ♦ **adoption, adoptions** N-VAR *They gave their babies up for adoption.* **2** VERB If you **adopt** a new attitude or plan, you begin to have it. *Pupils should be helped to adopt a positive approach to the environment.* ♦ **adoption** N-UNCOUNT *...the adoption of Japanese management practices.*

adoptive /ə'dɒptɪv/. ADJ BEFORE N Someone's **adoptive** family is the family that adopted them. *He was brought up by adoptive parents in London.*

adorable /ə'dɔːrəbəl/. ADJ If you say that someone or something is **adorable**, you are emphasizing that they are very attractive and you feel great affection for them. *We had three adorable children.*

adore /ə'dɔː/ **adores, adoring, adored.** **1** VERB If you **adore** someone, you love and admire them. ♦ **adoration**N-UNCOUNT *He had been used to female adoration.* **2** VERB If you **adore** something, you like it very much. [INFORMAL] *My mother adores bananas.*

adoring /ə'dɔːrɪŋ/. ADJ An **adoring** person loves and admires someone else very much. ♦ **adoringly**ADV *She gazes adoringly at her husband.*

a
b
c
d
e
f
g
h
i
j
k
l
m
n
o
p
q
r
s
t
u
v
w
x
y
z

adorn /ə'dɔːn/ **adorns, adorning, adorned.** VERB If something **adorns** a place or an object, it makes it look more beautiful. *Several magnificent oil paintings adorn the walls.* ♦ **adornment** /ə'dɔːnmənt/ **adornments** N-VAR ...*a building without any adornment or decoration.*

adrenalin (or **adrenaline**) /ə'drenəlɪn/. N-UNCOUNT **Adrenalin** is a substance produced by your body which makes your heart beat faster and gives you more energy.

adrift /ə'drɪft/. [1] ADJ AFTER LINK-V If a boat is **adrift**, it is floating on the water without being controlled. *They were spotted after three hours adrift in a dinghy.* [2] ADJ AFTER LINK-V If something or someone has gone **adrift**, they no longer seem to have any purpose or direction. ...*a policy that has gone adrift.*

★ **adult** /'ædʌlt, AM ə'dʌlt/ **adults.** N-COUNT & ADJ BEFORE N An **adult** is a mature, fully developed person or animal. **Adult** means relating to the time when you are an adult, or typical of adults. ...*a pair of adult birds... I've lived most of my adult life in London.*

adultery /ə'dʌltəri/. N-COUNT If a married person commits **adultery**, they have sex with someone that they are not married to.

adulthood /'ædʌlthʊd, AM ə'dʌlt-/. N-UNCOUNT **Adulthood** is the state of being an adult. ...*children coming into adulthood.*

★ **advance** /æd'vɑːns, -'væns/ **advances, advancing, advanced.** [1] VERB & N-VAR To **advance** or to make an **advance** means to move forward, often in order to attack someone. *Rebel forces are advancing on the capital... The defences are intended to obstruct any advance by tanks.* [2] VERB & N-VAR If you **advance** or make an **advance** in something you are doing, you make progress in it. *Japan has advanced from a rural, feudal society to an urban, industrial power. ...the dramatic advances of the 1970s.* [3] VERB & N-COUNT If you **advance** someone a sum of money, or if you give them an **advance**, you give them money earlier than arranged. *The bank advanced $1.2 billion... She was paid a £100,000 advance for her next two novels.* [4] VERB To **advance** an event, or its time or date, means to bring it forward to an earlier time or date. *Too much protein in the diet may advance the ageing process.* [5] ADJ BEFORE N **Advance** booking or warning is done or given before an event happens. *The event received little advance publicity.* [6] PHRASE If you do something **in advance**, you do it before a particular date or event. If one thing happens or is done **in advance of** another, it happens or is done before the other thing. *I had asked everyone to submit questions in advance of the meeting.*

★ **advanced** /æd'vɑːnst, -'vænst/. [1] ADJ An **advanced** system, method, or design is modern and has been developed from an earlier version of the same thing. ...*the most advanced optical telescope in the world.* [2] ADJ A country that is **advanced** has reached a high level of industrial

or technological development. ...*the educational levels reached in other advanced countries.* [3] ADJ An **advanced** student has learned the basic facts of a subject and is doing more difficult work.

advancement /æd'vɑːnsmənt, -'væns-/. [1] N-UNCOUNT **Advancement** is promotion in your job, or to a higher social class. *He cared little for social advancement.* [2] N-UNCOUNT The **advancement** of something is the process of helping it to progress. ...*the advancement of education.*

★ **advantage** /æd'vɑːntɪdʒ, -'væn-/ **advantages.** [1] N-VAR An **advantage** is something that puts you in a better position than other people. **Advantage** is the state of being in a better position than others who are competing against you. *A good crowd will be a definite advantage to me and the rest of the team... Men have created a social and physical position of advantage for themselves.* [2] N-COUNT An **advantage** is a way in which one thing is better than another. *The great advantage of home-grown oranges is their magnificent flavour.* [3] PHRASE If you **take advantage of** something, you make good use of it while you can. *I intend to take full advantage of this trip to buy the things we need.* [4] PHRASE If someone **takes advantage of** you, they treat you unfairly for their own benefit. [5] PHRASE If you **use** something **to your advantage** or **turn** something **to your advantage**, you exploit it in order to benefit from it.

advantageous /,ædvən'teɪdʒəs/. ADJ Something that is **advantageous to** you is likely to benefit you. *Free exchange of goods was advantageous to all. ...very advantageous prices.*

advent /'ædvent/. N-UNCOUNT The **advent of** something is the fact of it starting or coming into existence. [FORMAL] ...*the advent of the computer.*

adventure /æd'ventʃə/ **adventures.** N-VAR An **adventure** is a series of events that you become involved in that are unusual, exciting, and perhaps dangerous. *I set off for a new adventure in the United States. ...a feeling of adventure.* ♦ **adventurer, adventurers** N-COUNT ...*a true adventurer's paradise.*

adventurous /æd'ventʃərəs/. ADJ An **adventurous** person is willing to take risks and eager to have new experiences. Something that is **adventurous** involves new things or ideas. *The menu seemed more adventurous before.*

adverb /'ædvɜːb/ **adverbs.** N-COUNT In grammar, an **adverb** is a word such as 'slowly' or 'very' which adds information about time, place, or manner.

adversary /'ædvəsəri, AM -seri/ **adversaries.** N-COUNT Your **adversary** is someone you are competing with or fighting against. ...*political adversaries.*

adverse /'ædvɜːs, AM æd'vɜːrs/. ADJ **Adverse** effects or conditions are unfavourable to you. *Stress can have an adverse effect on their health.*

♦ **adversely** ADV ...*countries adversely affected by the increase in the price of oil.*

adversity /æd'vɜːsɪti/. N-UNCOUNT **Adversity** is a very difficult situation. ...*ways in which people manage to enjoy life despite adversity.*

advert /'ædvɜːt/ **adverts.** N-COUNT An **advert** is the same as an **advertisement**. [INFORMAL]

⭐ **advertise** /'ædvətaɪz/ **advertises, advertising, advertised.** [1] VERB If you **advertise** something such as a product, event, or job, you tell people about it in newspapers, on television, or on posters. *Religious groups are currently not allowed to advertise on television.* ♦ **advertiser, advertisers** N-COUNT ...*campaigns by the advertiser in support of the film.* [2] VERB If you **advertise for** someone to do something for you, you place an advertisement for it in a newspaper, on television, or on a poster, saying that you need someone to do it. *We advertised for staff in a local newspaper.*

advertisement /æd'vɜːtɪsmənt, AM ˌædvə'taɪz-/ **advertisements.** N-COUNT An **advertisement** is an announcement in a newspaper, on television, or on a poster that tells people about a product, event, or job vacancy. ...*job advertisements.*

advertising /'ædvətaɪzɪŋ/. N-UNCOUNT **Advertising** is the business activity of encouraging people to buy products, go to events, or apply for jobs. ...*a ban on tobacco advertising.*

⭐ **advice** /æd'vaɪs/. N-UNCOUNT If you give someone **advice**, you tell them what you think they should do. *Take my advice and stay away from him!*

> **USAGE** Note that **advice** is only ever used as an uncount noun. You can say *a piece of advice* or *some advice*, but you cannot say 'an advice' or 'advices'.

ad'vice ˌline, advice lines. N-COUNT An **advice line** is a service that you can telephone in order to get advice about something.

advisable /æd'vaɪzəbəl/. ADJ AFTER LINK-V If you tell someone that it is **advisable to** do something, you are suggesting that they should do it, because it is sensible and likely to achieve the result they want. *It's always advisable to book for dinner at leading restaurants.*

⭐ **advise** /æd'vaɪz/ **advises, advising, advised.** [1] VERB If you **advise** someone **to** do something, you tell them what you think they should do. *Could you advise me how to use a telescope with a camera?* [2] VERB If you **advise** people **on** a particular subject, you give them help and information on it. ...*a new booklet advising on financial problems.* [3] VERB If you **advise** someone **of** a fact or situation, you tell them the fact or explain what the situation is. [FORMAL] *A counselor will advise you of your rights.*

⭐ **adviser** (or **advisor**) /æd'vaɪzə/ **advisers.** N-COUNT An **adviser** is an expert whose job is to advise people on a particular subject. ...*a university careers adviser.*

advisory /æd'vaɪzəri/. ADJ An **advisory** committee gives people help and information on a particular subject. ...*the advisory committee on the safety of nuclear installations.*

advocacy /'ædvəkəsi/. [1] N-SING Someone's **advocacy of** a particular action or plan is their act of recommending it publicly. [FORMAL] ...*the president's advocacy of higher taxes.* [2] N-UNCOUNT **Advocacy** is the way in which lawyers deal with cases in court. [FORMAL]

⭐ **advocate, advocates, advocating, advocated;** verb /'ædvəkeɪt/, noun /'ædvəkət/. [1] VERB & N-COUNT If you **advocate** a particular action or plan, or if you are an **advocate of** it, you support it publicly. [FORMAL] *Mr Williams is a conservative who advocates fewer government controls on business.* [2] N-COUNT An **advocate** is a lawyer who speaks in favour of someone or defends them in a court of law.

aerial /'eəriəl/ **aerials.** [1] ADJ BEFORE N You use **aerial** to talk about things which happen in the air or are done from the air, particularly from an aeroplane. ...*aerial photographs.* [2] N-COUNT In British English, an **aerial** is a piece of metal equipment that receives television or radio signals. The American word is **antenna**.

aerobics /eə'rəʊbɪks/ N-PLURAL **Aerobics** is a form of exercise which increases the amount of oxygen in your blood and strengthens your heart and lungs. **Aerobics** can take the singular or plural form of the verb. ...*an aerobics class.*

aeroplane /'eərəpleɪn/ **aeroplanes.** N-COUNT An **aeroplane** is a vehicle with wings and engines that enable it to fly through the air. The usual American word is **airplane**.

aerosol /'eərəsɒl, AM -sɔːl/ **aerosols.** N-COUNT An **aerosol** is a small container in which a liquid such as paint is kept under pressure. When you press a button, the liquid is forced out in a fine spray or foam.

aesthetic (or **esthetic**) /iːs'θetɪk, AM es-/. ADJ **Aesthetic** is used to talk about beauty or art, and people's appreciation of beautiful things. ...*products chosen for their aesthetic appeal.* ♦ **aesthetically** ADV ...*aesthetically pleasing furniture and carpets.*

affable /'æfəbəl/. ADJ **Affable** people are pleasant and friendly. ...*his gentle, affable nature.*

⭐ **affair** /ə'feə/ **affairs.** [1] N-COUNT You refer to an event as an **affair** when you are talking about it in a general way. *The government has mishandled the whole affair.* [2] N-PLURAL In politics and journalism, **affairs** is used to refer to a particular type of activity or to the activities in a particular place. ...*our foreign affairs correspondent.* ● See also **current affairs, state of affairs.** [3] N-PLURAL Your **affairs** are your personal concerns. *The unexpectedness of my father's death meant that*

a
b
c
d
e
f
g
h
i
j
k
l
m
n
o
p
q
r
s
t
u
v
w
x
y
z

his affairs were not entirely in order. **4** N-SING If you say that a decision or situation is someone's **affair**, you mean that other people should not interfere. *If you wish to make a fool of yourself, that is your affair.* **5** N-COUNT If two people who are not married to each other have an **affair**, they have a sexual relationship.

★ **affect** /ə'fekt/ **affects, affecting, affected.** **1** VERB When something **affects** someone or something, it influences them or causes them to change. *...decisions that would affect me for the rest of my life... More than seven million people have been affected by drought.* **2** VERB If a disease **affects** you, it makes you ill. *AIDS seems to affect men and women in equal numbers.*

affection /ə'fekʃən/ **affections.** **1** N-UNCOUNT If you regard someone or something with **affection**, you are fond of them. **2** N-PLURAL Your **affections** are your feelings of love or fondness for someone. *She had focused her affections on her father.*

affectionate /ə'fekʃənət/. ADJ If you are **affectionate**, you show your fondness for another person in your behaviour. *They were more affectionate towards the younger child.* ♦ **affectionately** ADV *He looked affectionately at his niece.*

affidavit /ˌæfɪ'deɪvɪt/ **affidavits.** N-COUNT An **affidavit** is a written statement which you swear is true and which may be used as evidence in a court of law.

affiliate, affiliates, affiliating, affiliated. **1** N-COUNT /ə'fɪliət/ An **affiliate** is an organization which is officially connected with another, larger organization or is a member of it. **2** VERB /ə,fɪli'eɪt/ If an organization **affiliates to** or **with** another larger organization, it forms a close connection with it or becomes a member of it. *...the United Nations and its affiliated organisations.* ♦ **affiliation, affiliations** N-COUNT *The group has no affiliation to any political party.*

affinity /ə'fɪnɪti/ **affinities.** **1** N-SING If you have an **affinity with** someone or something, you feel that you belong with them and understand them. *...fishermen who have a natural affinity for the water.* **2** N-COUNT If people or things have an **affinity with** each other, they are similar in some ways. *The festival has affinities with the Roman festival of Cybele.*

affirm /ə'fɜːm/ **affirms, affirming, affirmed.** **1** VERB If you **affirm** that something is true, you state firmly and publicly that it is true. [FORMAL] *...a speech in which he affirmed a commitment to lower taxes.* ♦ **affirmation** /ˌæfə'meɪʃən/ **affirmations** N-VAR *...affirmation that Mr Green was a man of courage.* **2** VERB If an event **affirms** something, it shows that it is true or exists. [FORMAL] ♦ **affirmation** N-UNCOUNT *...the youngsters' expression of violence, which he saw as the affirmation of their rebellion.*

affirmative /ə'fɜːmətɪv/. ADJ An **affirmative** word or gesture indicates that you agree with

someone or that the answer to a question is 'yes'. [FORMAL] *...an affirmative nod.*

afflict /ə'flɪkt/ **afflicts, afflicting, afflicted.** VERB If you **are afflicted with** something, it affects you badly. *Both people who died were afflicted with a rare genetic disease... Italy has been afflicted by political corruption for decades.*

affliction /ə'flɪkʃən/ **afflictions.** N-VAR An **affliction** is something which causes suffering. [FORMAL] *Baldness is an affliction that can ruin a young man's life.*

affluent /'æfluənt/. ADJ **Affluent** people have a lot of money. *...Philadelphia's affluent suburbs.* ♦ **affluence** N-UNCOUNT *The postwar era was one of new affluence for the working class.*

★ **afford** /ə'fɔːd/ **affords, affording, afforded.** **1** VERB If you cannot **afford** something, you do not have enough money to pay for it. *We can't afford to pay private fees.* **2** VERB If you cannot **afford to** do something or allow it to happen, you must not do it or you must prevent it from happening because it would be harmful or embarrassing to you. *We can't afford to wait... The country could not afford the luxury of an election.*

affordable /ə'fɔːdəbəl/. ADJ If something is **affordable**, people have enough money to buy it. *...affordable housing.* ♦ **affordability** N-UNCOUNT *...advertisements that emphasized affordability.*

affront /ə'frʌnt/ **affronts, affronting, affronted.** VERB & N-COUNT If something **affronts** you, or if it is an **affront to** you, it makes you feel insulted. *...results which would affront the good sense of right-thinking persons... It's an affront to human dignity to keep someone alive like this.*

afield /ə'fiːld/. **1** PHRASE **Further afield** or **farther afield** mean in places other than the nearest or most obvious one. *Lucerne is a good base for travelling further afield.* **2** PHRASE If people come from **far afield**, they come from a long way away.

afloat /ə'fləʊt/. **1** ADV When someone or something is **afloat**, they remain partly above the surface of water and do not sink. **2** ADV If a person or business manages to stay **afloat**, they have just enough money to pay their debts. *He and his family kept afloat by doing odd jobs.*

afoot /ə'fʊt/. ADJ AFTER LINK-V If something such as a plan is **afoot**, it is already happening or being planned, often secretly. *US workers claim plans are afoot to move work to Germany.*

aforementioned /ə'fɔːmenʃənd/. ADJ BEFORE N When you refer to **the aforementioned** person or subject, you mean the person or subject that has already been mentioned. [FORMAL]

★ **afraid** /ə'freɪd/. **1** ADJ AFTER LINK-V If you are **afraid of** someone or **afraid to** do something, you are frightened because you think that something horrible is going to happen. *I was afraid of the other boys.* **2** ADJ AFTER LINK-V If you are **afraid** that something unpleasant will happen, you are worried that it may happen. *The*

Government is afraid of losing the election. **3** ADJ AFTER LINK-V If you are **afraid for** someone else, you are worried that they are in danger. *She's afraid for her family in Somalia.* **4** CONVENTION When you want to disagree with someone or apologize to them in a polite way, you can say **'I'm afraid'**. *I'm afraid I can't agree with you on that John.*

afresh /ə'freʃ/. ADV If you do something **afresh**, you do it again in a different way.

⭐ **African** /'æfrɪkən/ **Africans.** **1** ADJ **African** means belonging or relating to the continent of Africa. *...African art.* **2** N-COUNT An **African** is someone who comes from Africa.

African-A'merican, African-Americans. N-COUNT & ADJ An **African-American** is an American whose family originally came from Africa. **African-American** means relating to African-Americans.

African-Cari'bbean, African-Caribbeans. N-COUNT & ADJ An **African-Caribbean** is someone from the Caribbean whose family originally came from Africa. **African-Caribbean** means relating to African-Caribbeans.

aft /ɑːft, æft/. ADV & ADJ BEFORE N If you go **aft** in a boat or plane, you go to the back of it. The **aft** end of a boat or plane is towards the back. *Clark shook hands with the pilot and walked aft. ...the aft cabin.*

⭐ **after** /'ɑːftə, 'æftə/.

> ✓ In addition to the uses below, **after** is used in phrasal verbs such as 'ask after' or 'look after'.

1 PREP & CONJ If something happens or is done **after** a particular event or date, it happens or is done during the period of time that follows it. → See Reference Page on Times and Dates. *I went for a walk after lunch... After completing and signing it, please return the form to us... She's leaving the day after tomorrow.* **2** PREP In American English, **after** is used when telling the time. → See Reference Page on Telling the Time. **3** PREP If you are **after** someone, you follow or chase them. *He would be smart enough to know the police were after him.* **4** PREP If you shout or stare **after** someone, you shout or stare at them as they move away from you. **5** PREP If you are **after** something, you are trying to get it. *I'm not after Rick's job.* **6** PREP To be named **after** someone or something means to be given the same name as them. *Phillimore Island is named after Sir Robert Phillimore.* **7** PREP You use **after** in order to give the most important aspect of something when comparing it with something else. *After Germany, America is Britain's second-biggest customer.* **8** CONVENTION If you say **'after you'** to someone, you mean you are being polite and allowing them to go in front of you. **9** **after all**: see **all**.

aftermath /'ɑːftəmɑːθ, 'æftəmæθ/. N-SING The **aftermath** of an important or serious event is the situation that results from it. *In the aftermath of*

the coup, the troops opened fire on the demonstrators.

⭐ **afternoon** /,ɑːftə'nuːn, ,æf-/ **afternoons.** N-COUNT The **afternoon** is the part of each day which begins at 12 o' clock lunchtime and ends at about six o'clock.

⭐ **afterwards** /'ɑːftəwədz, 'æf-/.

> ✓ The form **afterward** is also used, mainly in American English.

ADV If something is done or happens **afterwards**, it is done or happens later than a particular event or time that has already been described. *Shortly afterwards, police arrested four suspects... James was taken to hospital but died soon afterwards.*

⭐ **again** /ə'gen, ə'geɪn/. **1** ADV You use **again** to indicate that something happens a second time, or after it has already happened before. *He kissed her again... I don't ever want to go through anything like that again.* **2** PHRASE You can use **again and again** or **time and again** to emphasize that something happens many times. *Time and again political parties have failed to tackle this issue.* **3** ADV You use **again** to indicate that something has returned to the particular state or place that it used to be in. *She opened the door and closed it again.* **4** **every now and again**: see **now**.

⭐ **against** /ə'genst, ə'geɪnst/. **1** PREP If something is leaning or pressing **against** something else, it is touching it. *She leaned against him. ...the rain beating against the window panes.* **2** PREP & ADV If you are **against** an idea, policy, or system, you think it is wrong or stupid. *...a march to protest against job losses. ...12 votes in favour, 2 votes against.* **3** PREP If you take action **against** someone or something, you try to harm them. *...the crime of violence against women.* **4** PREP If you do something **against** someone's wishes, advice, or orders, you do it although they tell you not to. *He discharged himself from hospital against the advice of doctors.* **5** PREP If you compete **against** someone in a game, you try to beat them. *The tour will include games against the Australians.* **6** PREP If you do something to protect yourself **against** something unpleasant, you do something which will make its effects on you less serious. *This cream protects against damage from sunlight.* **7** PREP Something that is **against** the law is forbidden by law. **8** PREP & ADV The odds **against** something happening are the odds that it will not happen.

⭐ **age** /eɪdʒ/ **ages, ageing** (or **aging**), **aged.** **1** N-VAR Your **age** is the number of years that you have lived. *She has a nephew who is just ten years of age... At the age of sixteen he qualified for a place at the University.* **2** N-UNCOUNT **Age** is the state of being old. *This cologne, like wine, improves with age... At 67, he is showing signs of age.* **3** VERB When someone **ages**, they become or seem much older. *He seemed to have aged in the last few months... Worry had aged him.* ♦ **ageing** N-UNCOUNT *Inadequate fluid intake and poor diet all* contribute to ageing. **4** N-COUNT An **age** is a period in history. *We're living in the age of television. ...the Bronze Age.* **5** See also **aged**, **middle age**.

PHRASES • Someone who is **under age** is not legally old enough to do something. *Many of the drinkers in the town's pubs are under age. ...under age smoking.* • When someone **comes of age**, they legally become an adult.

aged. **1** ADJ/eɪdʒd/ You use **aged** followed by a number to say how old someone is. *They have a son aged five.* **2** ADJ BEFORE N & N-PLURAL /'eɪdʒɪd/ An **aged** person is very old. You can refer to people who are very old as **the aged**. *...his aged parents. ...a home for the aged.* **3** See also **middle-aged**.

⭐ **agency** /'eɪdʒənsi/ **agencies.** **1** N-COUNT An **agency** is a business which provides services for a person or another business. *...a dating agency. ...an advertising agency.* **2** N-COUNT An **agency** is an administrative organization run by a government. *...the Central Intelligence Agency.*

⭐ **agenda** /ə'dʒendə/ **agendas.** **1** N-COUNT An **agenda** is a list of items to be discussed at a meeting. *This is sure to be an item on the agenda next week.* **2** N-COUNT You can refer to the political issues which are important at a particular time as an **agenda**. *His speech today will set the agenda for Labour's general election campaign.*

⭐ **agent** /'eɪdʒənt/ **agents.** **1** N-COUNT An **agent** is someone who arranges work or business for someone else, especially actors or musicians. *You are buying direct, rather than through an agent.* • See also **estate agent**, **travel agent**. **2** N-COUNT An **agent** is someone who works for a country's secret service.

age of con'sent. N-SING The **age of consent** is the age at which a person can legally marry or agree to have a sexual relationship.

age-old. ADJ BEFORE N An **age-old** story, tradition, or problem has existed for a very long time.

aggravate /'æɡrəveɪt/ **aggravates, aggravating, aggravated.** **1** VERB If someone or something **aggravates** a situation, they make it worse. *Tipping the head may aggravate any neck injury.* **2** VERB If someone or something **aggravates** you, they make you annoyed. [INFORMAL] *It's been aggravating me for months.* ♦ **aggravating** ADJ *It's very aggravating to be so low on merchandise.* ♦ **aggravation, aggravations** N-VAR *The sounds were a constant aggravation.*

aggregate /'æɡrɪɡət/ **aggregates.** **1** N-COUNT & ADJ BEFORE N An **aggregate** or **aggregate** amount is an amount made up of several smaller amounts. *An aggregate of twelve hundred acres spread over four separate parks. ...an aggregate loss of £353 million.* **2** PHRASE If one team beats another team **on aggregate**, it wins by getting the higher total over a series of games. [BRITISH] *Raith Rovers lost 1-0 away to the Icelandic side, Akranes, but went through 3-2 on aggregate.*

aggression /ə'ɡreʃən/. N-UNCOUNT **Aggression** is angry or violent behaviour towards someone. *...an act of aggression.*

⭐ **aggressive** /ə'ɡresɪv/. **1** ADJ An **aggressive** person behaves angrily or violently towards other people. *Some children are much more aggressive than others. ...aggressive behaviour.* ♦ **aggressively** ADV *...rumours she always aggressively denies.* **2** ADJ If you are **aggressive** in your work or other activities, you behave in a forceful way because you are eager to succeed. *...a very aggressive and competitive executive.*

aggressor /ə'ɡresə/ **aggressors.** N-COUNT The **aggressor** is the person or country that starts a fight.

aggrieved /ə'ɡriːvd/. ADJ If you feel **aggrieved**, you feel upset and angry because of the way you have been treated.

aghast /ə'ɡɑːst, ə'ɡæst/. ADJ If you are **aghast**, you are filled with horror and surprise. [FORMAL]

agile /'ædʒaɪl, AM -dʒəl/. **1** ADJ Someone who is **agile** can move with surprising ease and speed. *He is very agile for a big man.* ♦ **agility** /ə'dʒɪlɪti/ N-UNCOUNT *He lacks Bruce's natural agility.* **2** ADJ If you have an **agile** mind, you think quickly and intelligently. ♦ **agility** N-UNCOUNT *...exercises in mental agility.*

agitate /'ædʒɪteɪt/ **agitates, agitating, agitated.** VERB If people **agitate for** something, they protest or take part in political activity in order to get it. *The women who worked in these mills had begun to agitate for better conditions.* ♦ **agitation** N-UNCOUNT *...continuing agitation against the decision.*

agitated /'ædʒɪteɪtɪd/. ADJ If someone is **agitated**, they are very worried or upset, and show this in their behaviour or voice. *Susan seemed agitated about something.*

agitation /ˌædʒɪ'teɪʃən/. N-UNCOUNT **Agitation** is worry. *Sheila lit a cigarette, trying to mask her agitation.* • See also **agitate**.

⭐ **ago** /ə'ɡəʊ/. ADV You use **ago** to refer to past time. For example, if something happened one year **ago**, it is one year since it happened. *She died long ago.*

> **USAGE** You only use **ago** when you are talking about a period of time measured back from the present. If you are talking about a period measured back from some earlier time, you use **before** or **previously**. *She had died a month before.*

agonize (BRIT also **agonise**) /'æɡənaɪz/ **agonizes, agonizing, agonized.** VERB If you **agonize over** something, you feel anxious and spend a long time thinking about it. *I agonize over what to give my wife for Christmas.*

agonizing (BRIT also **agonising**) /'æɡənaɪzɪŋ/. ADJ Something that is **agonizing** causes you to feel great physical or mental pain.

The wait was agonizing... It was an agonising decision.

agony /'ægəni/ **agonies.** N-VAR **Agony** is great physical or mental pain. *She called out in agony. ...the agonies of parenthood.*

⭐ **agree** /ə'griː/ **agrees, agreeing, agreed.** 1 VERB If you **agree with** someone, you have the same opinion about something. *I agree with you entirely... We agreed that she was not to be told.* 2 VERB If you **agree to** do something, you say that you will do it. *He agreed to meet me at my hotel.* 3 VERB If people **agree on** something or **agree** something, they all decide to have or do something. *We never agreed a date.* 4 VERB If you **agree with** an action or a suggestion, you approve of it. *The Cabinet agreed with his plan.* 5 VERB If two stories or totals **agree**, they are the same as each other. *His second statement agrees with facts as stated by the other witnesses.*

agreeable /ə'griːəbəl/. 1 ADJ If something or someone is **agreeable**, they are pleasant and people like them. *...an agreeable surprise... He had been a very agreeable guest.* 2 ADJ AFTER LINK-V If you are **agreeable** to something or if it is **agreeable to** you, you are willing to do it or to allow it. [FORMAL] *...a solution that would be agreeable to all.*

⭐ **agreement** /ə'griːmənt/ **agreements.** 1 N-COUNT An **agreement** is a decision that two or more people, groups, or countries have made together. *...a ceasefire agreement.* 2 N-UNCOUNT & PHRASE **Agreement** with someone means having the same opinion as they have. You can also say that you are **in agreement** with someone. *The unions had reached broad agreement on the resolution... Not all scholars are in agreement with her.*

⭐ **agriculture** /'ægrɪkʌltʃə/. N-UNCOUNT **Agriculture** is farming and the methods used to look after crops and animals. ♦ **agricultural** /ˌægrɪ'kʌltʃərəl/ ADJ *...agricultural research.*

aground /ə'graʊnd/. ADV If a ship or boat runs **aground**, it gets stuck on the ground in a shallow area of water.

⭐ **ahead** /ə'hed/. 1 ADV Something that is **ahead** is in front of you. If you look **ahead**, you look directly in front of you. *The road ahead was now blocked solid... Ahead, he saw the side railings of First Bridge... Brett looked straight ahead.* 2 ADV If you are **ahead** in your work or achievements, you have made more progress than you expected. *Children in small classes were 1.5 months ahead in reading.* 3 ADV If a person or a team is **ahead** in a competition, they are winning. *A goal would have put Dublin 6-1 ahead... Clinton was ahead in the polls.* 4 ADV If you go on **ahead**, you leave for a place before other people. *I'd have to send Tina on ahead with Rachael.* 5 ADV **Ahead** means in the future. *A much bigger battle is ahead for the president... Book ahead as the restaurant is very popular. ...the days ahead.*

⭐ **a'head of.** 1 PREP If someone or something is **ahead of** you, they are in front of you. *I saw a man in a blue jacket thirty metres ahead of me... She walked ahead of Helene up the steps.* 2 PREP If an event or period of time lies **ahead of** you, it is going to happen or come soon or in the future. *We have a very busy day ahead of us.* 3 PREP If something happens **ahead of** an event, it happens before that event. If something happens **ahead of** time, it happens earlier than was planned. *The Prime Minister was speaking ahead of today's meeting... The election was held six months ahead of schedule.* 4 PREP If one person is **ahead of** another, they have made more progress and are more advanced in what they are doing. *Henry generally stayed ahead of the others in the academic subjects.* 5 **ahead of** one's **time**: see **time**.

⭐ **aid** /eɪd/ **aids, aiding, aided.** 1 VERB & N-UNCOUNT To **aid** a person, country, or organization, or to give them **aid**, means to help them by giving them money, equipment, or services. *...American efforts to aid the refugees... They have already pledged billions of dollars in aid.* ♦ **-aided** *...state-aided schools.* 2 VERB & N-UNCOUNT To **aid** someone or to give them **aid** means to help or assist them. *...a software system to aid managers in advanced decision-making... He was forced to turn for aid to his former enemy.* 3 VERB & N-COUNT If something **aids** a process, it makes it easier or more likely to happen. An **aid** is something that makes things easier to do. *The export sector will continue to aid the economic recovery. ...slimming aids.* 4 See also **first aid**.

PHRASES ● If an activity or event is **in aid of** a particular cause, it raises money for that cause. *...a charity performance in aid of Great Ormond Street Children's Hospital.* ● If you come or go to someone's **aid**, you try to help them when they are in danger or difficulty. *Horrified neighbours rushed to his aid as he fell.*

aide /eɪd/ **aides.** N-COUNT An **aide** is an assistant to a person with an important job. *...a presidential aide.*

⭐ **AIDS** /eɪdz/. N-UNCOUNT **AIDS** is an illness which destroys the natural system of protection that the body has against disease. **AIDS** is an abbreviation for 'acquired immune deficiency syndrome'.

ailing /'eɪlɪŋ/. 1 ADJ If someone is **ailing**, they are ill and not getting better. 2 ADJ An **ailing** business is in difficulty and is becoming weaker.

ailment /'eɪlmənt/ **ailments.** N-COUNT An **ailment** is an illness, especially one that is not very serious.

⭐ **aim** /eɪm/ **aims, aiming, aimed.** 1 VERB If you **aim for** something or **aim** to do it, you plan or hope to achieve it. *He said he would aim for the 100 metres world record. ...an appeal which aims to raise funds for children with special needs.* 2 N-COUNT The **aim** of something that you do is the purpose for which you do it or the result that it is intended to achieve. *The aim of the festival is to increase awareness of Hindu culture.* 3 PASSIVE-VERB If an action or plan **is aimed at** achieving something, it is intended to achieve it.

a
b
c
d
e
f
g
h
i
j
k
l
m
n
o
p
q
r
s
t
u
v
w
x
y
z

The new measures are aimed at tightening existing sanctions. [4] VERB If your action **is aimed at** a particular person, you intend it to affect and influence them. *Much of cigarette advertising is aimed at women.* [5] VERB & N-SING If you **aim** a weapon **at** someone or something, you point it towards them before firing. Your **aim** is the act of pointing a weapon at a target or your ability to hit the target. *He was aiming the rifle at Wade.* [6] PHRASE If you **take aim at** someone or something, you point a loaded weapon at them.

aimless /'eɪmləs/. ADJ A person or activity that is **aimless** has no clear purpose or plan. *...several hours of aimless searching.* ♦ **aimlessly** ADV *I wandered around aimlessly.*

ain't /eɪnt/. **Ain't** is used in some dialects of English instead of 'am not', 'aren't', or 'isn't'. [SPOKEN]

⭐ **air** /eə/ **airs, airing, aired.** [1] N-UNCOUNT **Air** is the mixture of gases which forms the earth's atmosphere and which we breathe. *Keith opened the window and leaned out into the cold air.* [2] N-SING **The air** is the space around things or above the ground. *...firing their guns in the air.* [3] N-UNCOUNT **Air** is used to refer to travel in aircraft. *Amy had never travelled by air before. ...help towards the air fare.* [4] N-SING If someone or something has a particular **air**, they give this general impression. *...regarding him with an air of faint amusement... The meal gave the occasion an almost festive air.* [5] VERB If you **air** your opinions, you make them known to people. *Both sides agreed they had aired all their differences.* ♦ **airing** N-SING *Their views would at long last get an airing.* [6] VERB If you **air** a room, you let fresh air circulate around it. When you **air** clothes, you put them in a place where warm air can circulate around them, helping to dry them.

PHRASES ● If you do something to **clear the air**, you do it in order to get rid of any misunderstandings that there might be. *...an inquiry just to clear the air and settle the facts of the case.* ● If a person or programme is **on the air**, they are broadcasting or being broadcast on radio or television. *I was on the air for two hours... The show first went on the air in 1964.*

'air base (or **airbase**) **air bases.** N-COUNT An **air base** is a military airport.

airborne /'eəbɔːn/. ADJ **Airborne** means flying in the air or coming from the air. *The aircraft was soon airborne again. ...airborne troops.*

air-con'ditioned. ADJ If a room is **air-conditioned**, the air in it is kept cool and dry by means of a special machine.

air-con'ditioning (or **air conditioning**). N-UNCOUNT **Air-conditioning** is a method of providing buildings and vehicles with cool dry air.

⭐ **aircraft** /'eəkrɑːft, -kræft/.

✔ **Aircraft** is both the singular and the plural form.

N-COUNT An **aircraft** is a vehicle which can fly, for example an aeroplane or a helicopter.

airfield /'eəfiːld/ **airfields.** N-COUNT An **airfield** is a place where aircraft take off and land, usually small planes or military aircraft.

⭐ **'air force** (or **airforce**) **air forces.** N-COUNT An **air force** is the part of a country's military organization that is concerned with fighting in the air.

,air hostess, air hostesses. N-COUNT An **air hostess** is a woman whose job is to look after passengers in an aircraft. [BRITISH]

airlift /'eəlɪft/ **airlifts, airlifting, airlifted.** VERB & N-COUNT If people or goods **are airlifted** somewhere, they are carried by air, especially in a war or when land routes are closed. An **airlift** is an operation to do this. *The injured were airlifted to hospital in Prestwick. ...an airlift of food, medicines and blankets.*

⭐ **airline** /'eəlaɪn/ **airlines.** N-COUNT An **airline** is a company which provides regular services carrying people or goods in aeroplanes.

airliner /'eəlaɪnə/ **airliners.** N-COUNT An **airliner** is a large aeroplane used for carrying passengers.

airman /'eəmæn/ **airmen.** N-COUNT An **airman** is a man who serves in his country's air force.

airplane /'eəpleɪn/ **airplanes.** N-COUNT An **airplane** is the same as an **aeroplane**. [AMERICAN]

⭐ **airport** /'eəpɔːt/ **airports.** N-COUNT An **airport** is a place where aircraft land and take off, usually with a lot of buildings and facilities.

'air raid, air raids. N-COUNT An **air raid** is an attack in which military aircraft drop bombs on people or places.

airspace /'eəspeɪs/. N-UNCOUNT A country's **airspace** is the part of the sky that is over that country and is considered to belong to that country.

airtight /'eətaɪt/. ADJ If a container is **airtight**, its lid fits so tightly that no air can get in or out.

airwaves /'eəweɪvz/. N-PLURAL If someone says something **over the airwaves** or **on the airwaves**, they say it on the radio or television. [JOURNALISM]

airy /'eəri/. ADJ If a room or building is **airy**, it is large and has plenty of fresh air inside. *The bathroom has a light and airy feel.*

aisle /aɪl/ **aisles.** N-COUNT An **aisle** is a long narrow gap that people can walk along between rows of seats in a public building such as a church, or between rows of shelves in a supermarket.

aka. aka is an abbreviation for 'also known as'; it is used especially when referring to a nickname or stage name. *...Anna Mae Bullock, aka Tina Turner.*

akin /ə'kɪn/. ADJ AFTER LINK-V If one thing is **akin to** another, it is similar to it in some way. [FORMAL] *The journey will be more akin to air travel than to a conventional train.*

⭐ **alarm** /ə'lɑːm/ **alarms, alarming, alarmed.** [1] VERB & N-UNCOUNT If something **alarms** you, it makes you afraid or anxious that something unpleasant might happen. This feeling is called **alarm**. *We could not see what had alarmed him... She sat up in alarm.* ♦ **alarmed** ADJ *They should not be too alarmed by the press reports.* ♦ **alarming** ADJ *The statistics were even more alarming.* ♦ **alarmingly** ADV *...the alarmingly high rate of heart disease.* [2] N-COUNT An **alarm** is an automatic device that warns you of danger, for example by ringing a bell. *He heard the alarm go off.*

a'larm clock, alarm clocks. N-COUNT An **alarm clock** is a clock that you can set to make a noise so that it wakes you up at a particular time.

alas /ə'læs/. ADV **Alas** is used to express sadness or regret about something that has happened. [FORMAL] *Many wonderful people who are, alas, no longer here.*

albeit /ɔːl'biːɪt/. ADV You use **albeit** to introduce a fact or comment which reduces the force or significance of what you have just said. [FORMAL] *He has a majority, albeit a small one.*

★ **album** /'ælbəm/ **albums.** [1] N-COUNT An **album** is a CD, record, or cassette with music on it, usually several different tracks. *This new single is taken from their latest album.* [2] N-COUNT An **album** is a book in which you put things such as photographs or stamps that you have collected.

★ **alcohol** /'ælkəhɒl, AM -hɔːl/. [1] N-UNCOUNT Drinks that can make people drunk, such as beer, wine, and whisky, can be referred to as **alcohol**. [2] N-UNCOUNT **Alcohol** is a colourless liquid which is found in drinks such as beer, wine, and whisky. It is also used in products such as perfumes and cleaning fluids.

alcoholic /ˌælkə'hɒlɪk, AM -'hɔːl-/ **alcoholics.** [1] N-COUNT An **alcoholic** is someone who is addicted to alcohol. ♦ **alcoholism** /'ælkəhɒlɪzəm/ N-UNCOUNT *His sister died two years ago as a result of alcoholism.* [2] ADJ **Alcoholic** drinks contain alcohol.

ale /eɪl/ **ales.** N-VAR **Ale** is the same as **beer**.

★ **alert** /ə'lɜːt/ **alerts, alerting, alerted.** [1] ADJ If you are **alert**, you are paying full attention to things around you and are ready to deal with anything that might happen. *We all have to stay alert... He had been spotted by an alert neighbour.* ♦ **alertness** N-UNCOUNT *A doctor's alertness saved her son.* [2] ADJ AFTER LINK-V & VERB If you are **alert to** a problem, you are fully aware of it. You can also **alert** someone **to** a dangerous or unpleasant situation. *The bank is alert to the danger... He wanted to alert people to the activities of the group.* [3] N-COUNT An **alert** is a situation in which people prepare themselves for something dangerous that may happen soon. *...a security alert.* [4] PHRASE When soldiers, police, or other authorities are **on alert**, they are ready to deal with anything that may happen.

'A level, A levels. N-VAR **A levels** are British educational qualifications which schoolchildren take when they are about eighteen years old.

algae /'ældʒiː, 'ælgaɪ/. N-UNCOUNT **Algae** is a type of plant with no stems or leaves that grows in water or on damp surfaces.

algebra /'ældʒɪbrə/. N-UNCOUNT **Algebra** is a type of mathematics in which letters are used to represent quantities.

alias /'eɪliəs/ **aliases.** N-COUNT & PREP An **alias** is a false name, especially one used by a criminal or actor. *He was travelling under an alias. ...Richard Thorp, alias Alan Turner.*

alibi /'ælɪbaɪ/ **alibis.** N-COUNT If you have an **alibi**, you can prove that you were somewhere else when a crime was committed.

alien /'eɪliən/ **aliens.** [1] ADJ **Alien** is used to describe someone or something that belongs to a different country, race, group, or culture. This use is considered offensive by some people. *...alone in an alien culture.* [2] N-COUNT An **alien** is someone who is not a legal citizen of the country in which they live. [TECHNICAL] [3] ADJ AFTER LINK-V If something is **alien to** you, it is not the way you would normally feel or behave. *Such an attitude is alien to most businessmen.* [4] N-COUNT In science fiction, an **alien** is a creature from outer space.

alienate /'eɪliəneɪt/ **alienates, alienating, alienated.** [1] VERB If you **alienate** someone such as a friend, you cause them to lose their friendly relationship with you. *The government cannot afford to alienate either group.* [2] VERB If you **are alienated from** something, you are emotionally and intellectually separated from it. *Gambling was alienating me from anyone who'd ever loved me.* ♦ **alienated** ADJ *Most of these students also feel alienated from their parents.* ♦ **alienation** N-UNCOUNT *...her sense of alienation from the world.*

alight /ə'laɪt/ **alights, alighting, alighted.** [1] ADJ AFTER LINK-V If something is **alight**, it is burning. *Several buildings were set alight.* [2] ADJ AFTER LINK-V If you describe someone's face or expression as **alight**, you mean that it shows that they are feeling a strong emotion such as excitement or happiness. *Her eyes were alight with a girlish enjoyment of life.* [3] VERB When you **alight from** a train or bus, you get out of it after a journey. [FORMAL]

align /ə'laɪn/ **aligns, aligning, aligned.** [1] VERB If you **align yourself with** a particular group, you support their political aims. ♦ **alignment, alignments** N-VAR *He refused to compromise the church by a particular political alignment.* [2] VERB If objects **are aligned with** each other, they are placed in a precise position in relation to each other. *Keep the edge of the fabric aligned with the edge of the piping.* ♦ **alignment** N-UNCOUNT *...the alignment of the planets.*

alike /ə'laɪk/. [1] ADJ AFTER LINK-V & ADV If two or more people or things are **alike**, they are similar. *We looked very alike. ...their assumption that all men and women think alike.* [2] ADV You use **alike** after mentioning two or more people, groups, or things in order to emphasize that you are referring to both or all of them. *The techniques are being applied by big and small firms alike.*

⭐ **alive** /ə'laɪv/. **1** ADJ AFTER LINK-V If people or animals are **alive**, they are living. *They kept her alive on a life support machine.* **2** ADJ AFTER LINK-V If an activity, organization, or situation is **alive**, it continues to exist or to function. *The big factories are trying to stay alive by cutting costs.* **3** ADJ If you say that someone seems **alive**, you mean that they seem to be lively and to enjoy everything that they do. *I never expected to feel so alive in my life again.* **4** ADJ & PHRASE If a place is **alive with** something, a lot of people or things are there and it seems busy or exciting. You can say people, places, or events **come alive** when they start to be active or lively. *The forest had been alive with the sounds of squawking birds.*

⭐ **all** /ɔːl/. **1** QUANT You use **all** to indicate that you are referring to the whole of a group or thing or to everyone or everything of a particular kind. *He was talking to all of us... I'd spent all I had, every last penny... We all admire professionalism and dedication.*

> **USAGE** **All** is often used to mean the same as **whole** but when used in front of plurals, **all** and **whole** have different meanings. For example, if you say, '**All the buildings have been destroyed**', you mean that every building has been destroyed. If you say '**Whole buildings have been destroyed**', you mean that some buildings have been destroyed completely.

2 DET & PREDET You use **all** to refer to the whole of a period of time. *George had to cut grass all afternoon... She's worked all her life.* **3** PRON You use **all** to refer to a situation or to life in general. *All is silent on the island now.* **4** ADV You use **all** to emphasize the extent to which something happens or is true. *I got scared and I ran and left her all alone. ...universities all round the world.* **5** ADV **All** is used in expressions such as **all the more** or **all the better** to mean even more or even better than before. *The living room is decorated in pale colours that make it all the more airy.* **6** ADV You use **all** when you are talking about an equal score in a game. For example, if the score is three **all**, both players or teams have three points.

PHRASES ● You say **above all** to emphasize that the thing you are mentioning is the most important point. ● You use **after all** when introducing a statement which supports or helps explain something you have just said. *They know only too well that the stakes are high. After all, health care is a $900 billion industry.* ● You use **after all** when you are saying that something that you thought might not be true is in fact true. *There wasn't much wrong after all.* ● You use **all in all** to introduce a summary or generalization. *All in all, it appeared that a pretty depressing*

summer awaited Jones. ● You use **at all** to emphasize a negative or a question. *Robin never really liked him at all.* ● You use **for all** to say that a particular fact does not affect or contradict what you are saying, although it may seem to do so. *For all his shortcomings, he was kind and considerate.* ● **In all** means in total. *In all some 15 million people live in the selected areas.* ● You use **of all** to emphasize the words 'first' or 'last', or a superlative adjective or adverb. *First of all, answer these questions... Now she faces her toughest task of all.*

Allah /'ælə, 'ælɑː/. N-PROPER **Allah** is the name of God in Islam.

all-A'merican. ADJ BEFORE N If you describe someone as an **all-American** boy or girl, you mean that they seem to have all the typical qualities that are valued by ordinary Americans, such as patriotism and healthy good looks.

all-a'round. See **all-round**.

allay /ə'leɪ/ **allays, allaying, allayed.** VERB If you **allay** someone's fears or doubts, you stop them feeling afraid or doubtful. [FORMAL] *He did what he could to allay his wife's fears.*

⭐ **allegation** /,ælɪ'geɪʃən/ **allegations.** N-COUNT An **allegation** is a statement saying that someone has done something wrong. *...allegations of brutality and theft.*

allege /ə'ledʒ/ **alleges, alleging, alleged.** VERB If you **allege** that someone has done something wrong, you say it but do not prove it. [FORMAL] *The accused is alleged to have killed a man... It is alleged that the restaurant discriminated against black customers. ...protests at the alleged beatings.*
♦ **allegedly** ADV *His van allegedly struck them as they were crossing a street.*

allegiance /ə'liːdʒəns/ **allegiances.** N-VAR Your **allegiance** is your support for and loyalty to a group, person, or belief. *My allegiance to Kendall and his company ran deep.*

allergic /ə'lɜːdʒɪk/. ADJ If you are **allergic to** something, or have an **allergic** reaction to it, you become ill or get a rash when you eat it, smell it, or touch it.

allergy /'ælədʒi/ **allergies.** N-VAR If you have a particular **allergy**, you become ill or get a rash when you eat, smell, or touch something that does not normally make people ill. *Allergy to cats is one of the commonest causes of asthma. ...food allergies.*

alleviate /ə'liːvieɪt/ **alleviates, alleviating, alleviated.** VERB If you **alleviate** pain, suffering, or an unpleasant condition, you make it less intense or severe. *...the problem of alleviating mass poverty.*
♦ **alleviation** N-UNCOUNT *...the alleviation of the refugees' misery.*

alley /'æli/ **alleys.** N-COUNT An **alley** or **alleyway** is a narrow passage or street with buildings or walls on both sides.

⭐ **alliance** /ə'laɪəns/ **alliances.** N-VAR An **alliance** is a relationship in which different countries, political parties, or organizations work together for some purpose. You can also refer to the group that is formed in this way as an **alliance**. ...*a movement of professionals in alliance with progressive businessmen and politicians*.

⭐ **allied** /'ælaɪd, AM ə'laɪd/. ① ADJ BEFORE N **Allied** countries, political parties, or groups are united by a formal agreement. ...*forces from three allied nations*. ② ADJ If one thing or group is **allied to** another, the two things are related because they have particular qualities or characteristics in common. ...*lectures on subjects allied to health, beauty and fitness*. ...*doctors, and allied medical professionals*. ③ See also **ally**.

alligator /'ælɪɡeɪtə/**alligators**. N-COUNT An **alligator** is a large reptile with short legs, a long tail and very powerful jaws.

allocate /'æləkeɪt/**allocates, allocating, allocated**. VERB If one item or share of something is **allocated to** a particular person or **for** a particular purpose, it is given to that person or used for that purpose. *The budget allocated $7.3 billion for development programmes... Our plan is to allocate one member of staff to handle appointments*. ♦ **allocation** N-UNCOUNT ...*the allocation of land for new homes*.

allot /ə'lɒt/**allots, allotting, allotted**. VERB If something is **allotted to** someone, it is given to them as their share. *The seats are allotted to the candidates who have won the most votes... We were allotted half an hour to address the committee*. ♦ **allotment, allotments** N-COUNT ...*their full allotment of $300 million*.

allotment /ə'lɒtmənt/**allotments**. N-COUNT In Britain, an **allotment** is a small area of land which a person rents to grow vegetables on.

,**all-'out**. ADJ BEFORE N & ADV You use **all-out** to talk about actions that are carried out in a very energetic and determined way, using all the resources available. ...*an all-out effort to bring the fire under control... We will be going all out to ensure it doesn't happen again*.

⭐ **allow** /ə'laʊ/**allows, allowing, allowed**. ① VERB If someone is **allowed to** do something, it is all right for them to do it. *The children are not allowed to watch violent TV programmes*. ② VERB If you **are allowed** something, you are given permission to have it or are given it. *Gifts like chocolates or flowers are allowed... He should be allowed the occasional treat*. ③ VERB If you **allow** something **to** happen, you do not prevent it. *If the soil is allowed to dry out the tree could die*. ④ VERB If something **allows** a particular thing **to** happen, it makes it possible. *The money it saved allowed them to distribute aid more widely to others*. ⑤ VERB If you **allow** a length of time or an amount of something for a particular purpose, you include it in your planning. *Please allow 28 days for delivery*.

▶**allow for**. PHR-VERB If you **allow for** certain problems or expenses, you include some extra time or money in your planning so that you can deal with them if they occur. *You should allow for*

the possibility that taxes will be 15 to 20 per cent higher.

allowance /ə'laʊəns/**allowances**. ① N-COUNT An **allowance** is money that is given regularly to someone. ② PHRASE If you **make allowances for** certain circumstances in a situation, you take them into consideration when making your plans. *The raw exam results make no allowance for social background*. ③ PHRASE If you **make allowances for** someone who is behaving badly, you deal with them less severely than you would normally, usually because of a problem that they have. *You make allowances for your children when they are feeling ill*.

⭐ ,**all 'right** (or **alright**). ① ADJ AFTER LINK-V If you say that someone or something is **all right**, you mean that you find them satisfactory but not especially good. *Most of the teachers are all right... The red wine sauce was all right*. ② ADJ AFTER LINK-V If someone is **all right**, they are well or safe. *I'm all right now... Are you feeling all right?* ③ CONVENTION You say '**all right**' when you are agreeing to something. *'I think you should go now.'—'All right.'*

,**all-'round** (AM also **all-around**). ① ADJ BEFORE N An **all-round** person is good at a lot of different things. *He is a great all-round player*. ② ADJ BEFORE N **All-round** means doing or relating to all aspects of a job or activity... *an excellent all-round guide on how to shop for the very best foods*.

'**all-time**. ADJ **All-time** is used when you are comparing all the things of a particular type that there have ever been. ...*her all-time favourite film*.

allude /ə'lu:d/**alludes, alluding, alluded**. VERB If you **allude to** something, you mention it in an indirect way. [FORMAL] *She alluded to his absence in vague terms*.

allure /ə'ljʊə, AM ə'lʊr/. N-UNCOUNT The **allure** of something is a pleasing or exciting quality that it has. *Novels without stories have lost their allure for the young author*.

allusion /ə'lu:ʒən/**allusions**. N-VAR An **allusion to** something is an indirect or vague reference to it. *She made an allusion to the events in Los Angeles... His poetry is made up with many literary allusions*.

⭐ **ally, allies, allying, allied**. ① N-COUNT /'ælaɪ/ An **ally** is a country, organization, or person that helps and supports another. ...*the Western allies*. ② VERB /ə'laɪ/ If you **ally yourself** with someone, you support them. *Ten years later he allied himself with the British*. ● See also **allied**.

almighty /ɔːl'maɪti/. ① N-PROPER The **Almighty** is another name for God. ...*a hymn to the Almighty*. ② ADJ BEFORE N An **almighty** row, problem, or mistake is a very serious one. *Apparently they kicked up an almighty fuss*.

almond /'ɑːmənd/**almonds**. N-COUNT An **almond** is a kind of pale oval nut.

⭐ **almost** /'ɔːlməʊst/. ADV **Almost** means very nearly, but not completely. *The camps are now almost full... I stood up and almost fell*.

a
b
c
d
e
f
g
h
i
j
k
l
m
n
o
p
q
r
s
t
u
v
w
x
y
z

aloft /ə'lɒft, AM ə'lɔːft/. ADV Something that is **aloft** is in the air or off the ground. [LITERARY] *After the result was announced, Mr Peres was raised aloft by his supporters.*

★ **alone** /ə'ləʊn/. [1] ADJ AFTER LINK-V When you are **alone**, you are not with any other people. *She wanted to be alone.* [2] ADJ AFTER LINK-V A person who is **alone** is someone who has no family or friends. *Never in her life had she felt so alone, so abandoned.* [3] ADJ AFTER LINK-V If one person is **alone with** another, they are together, with nobody else present. *I couldn't imagine why he would want to be alone with me... We'll be alone together, quite like old times.* [4] ADV If you do something **alone**, you do it without help from other people. *He was working alone and did not have an accomplice.* [5] ADV You say that one person or thing **alone** does something when you are emphasizing that only one person or thing is involved. *The cost of the damage in Florida alone would amount to billions of dollars.* [6] to **leave** someone **alone**: see **leave**.

★ **along** /ə'lɒŋ, AM ə'lɔːŋ/. [1] PREP If you move or look **along** something, you move or look towards one end of it. *Newman walked along the street... The young man led Mark along a corridor... I looked along the length of the building.* [2] PREP & ADV If something is situated **along** a road, river, or corridor, it is situated in it or beside it. *Half the houses along the road were for sale... Two thirds of the way along, turn right and take the path across the park.* [3] ADV If something is going **along** in a particular way, it is progressing in that way. *Everything was coming along fine after all.* [4] ADV If you take someone **along** when you go somewhere, you take them with you. If someone comes **along**, they come to a particular place. *Some of the men would take their wives along... Bring along your friends and colleagues.*
PHRASES • You use **all along** to say that something has existed or been the case throughout a period of time. *She had been planning all along to leave Hungary.* • If you do something **along with** someone else, you both do it. • If you take one thing **along with** another, you take both things. *The baby's mother escaped along with two other children.*

★ **alongside** /ə,lɒŋ'saɪd, AM -,lɔːŋ-/. [1] PREP & ADV If something is **alongside** something else, it is next to it. *He crossed the street and walked alongside Central Park... I rode the bicycle and he ran alongside.* [2] PREP If people or systems work or exist **alongside** each other, they work or exist in the same place or in the same situation. *Volunteers work alongside local staff.*

aloof /ə'luːf/. [1] ADJ If you say that someone is **aloof**, you think they are not very friendly and that they try to keep away from other people. [2] ADJ AFTER LINK-V If you stay **aloof from** something, you do not become involved with it. *The Government is keeping aloof from the controversy.*

aloud /ə'laʊd/. ADV When you speak or read **aloud**, you speak so that other people can hear you. *When we were children, our father read aloud to us, usually after supper.*

alphabet /'ælfəbet/**alphabets**. N-COUNT The **alphabet** is the set of letters in a fixed order which is used for writing the words of a language.

alphabetical /,ælfə'betɪkəl/. ADJ BEFORE N **Alphabetical** means arranged according to the normal order of the letters in the alphabet. *...arranged in strict alphabetical order.*

alpine /'ælpaɪn/. ADJ **Alpine** means existing in or relating to mountains. *...alpine plants.*

★ **already** /ɔːl'redi/. [1] ADV If something has **already** happened, it has happened before the present time. *I have already started making baby clothes... They've spent nearly a billion dollars on it already... She says she already told the neighbors not to come over for a couple of days.*

> **USAGE** In British English, **already** and **yet** are usually used with the present perfect tense. *I have already started knitting baby clothes... Have they said sorry or not yet?* In American English, a past tense is commonly used. *She already told the neighbours not to come... I didn't get any sleep yet.* This usage is becoming more common in British English.

[2] ADV You use **already** to say that a situation exists at this present moment or that it exists at an earlier time than expected. You use **already** after the verb 'be' or an auxiliary verb, or before a verb if there is no auxiliary. *He was already late for his appointment with the Prime Minister... Is it five o'clock already?... Various insurance schemes already exist for this purpose.*

alright /,ɔːl'raɪt/. See **all right**.

★ **also** /'ɔːlsəʊ/. [1] ADV You use **also** when you are giving more information about a person or thing. *Furniture designer Linley, who also owns a nearby restaurant, employs up to 20 craftsmen... We've got a big table and also some stools and benches.* [2] ADV You can use **also** to say that the same fact applies to someone or something else. *The UN says six other civilians were also injured.*

> **USAGE** **Also** and **too** are similar in meaning. **Also** never comes at the end of a clause, whereas **too** usually comes at the end. *He was also an artist and lived at Compton... He's a singer and an actor too.*

altar /'ɔːltə/**altars**. N-COUNT An **altar** is a holy table in a church or temple.

★ **alter** /'ɔːltə/**alters, altering, altered**. VERB If something **alters**, or if you **alter** it, it changes. *Little had altered in the village... The government has altered the rules.* ◆ **alteration, alterations**

N-VAR *There were a few minor alterations to the cast.*

alternate, **alternates, alternating, alternated.** [1] VERB /ˈɔːltəneɪt/ When you **alternate between** two things, you regularly do or use one thing and then the other. *I alternated between feeling freezing cold and boiling hot.* [2] VERB When one thing **alternates** with another, the two things occur regularly, one after the other. *Her aggressive moods alternated with gentle or more co-operative states.* [3] ADJ BEFORE N /ɔːlˈtɜːnət/ **Alternate** actions, events, or processes regularly occur after each other. *They were streaked with alternate bands of colour.* ♦ **alternately** ADV *He lived alternately in Florence and Naples.* [4] ADJ BEFORE N If something happens on **alternate** days, it happens on one day, then happens on every second day after that. In the same way, something can happen in **alternate** weeks or years. *Some government offices open on alternate Saturdays.* [5] ADJ BEFORE N In American English, **alternate** is used to describe something that can exist or you can do instead of something else. The British word is **alternative**. *He also sent Congress an alternate version of the bill.* ♦ **alternately** ADV *Alternately, the coconut can be toasted under the broiler.*

⭐ **alternative** /ɔːlˈtɜːnətɪv/ **alternatives.** [1] N-COUNT & ADJ BEFORE N In British English, an **alternative** is something that can exist or you can do instead of something else. The American adjective is **alternate**. *How about natural gas? Is that an alternative?... There were alternative methods of travel available.* [2] ADJ BEFORE N **Alternative** is used to describe things which are different from traditional or established things of their kind. *...alternative medicine.*

alternatively /ɔːlˈtɜːnətɪvli/. ADV You use **alternatively** to introduce a suggestion or to mention something different from what has just been stated. *Allow about eight hours for the drive from Calais. Alternatively, you can fly to Brive.*

⭐ **although** /ɔːlˈðəʊ/. [1] CONJ You use **although** to introduce a statement which contrasts with something else that you are saying. *Although I was only six, I can remember seeing it on TV... Their system worked after a fashion, although no one was sure how.* [2] CONJ **Although** is used to introduce clauses that modify what is being said or that add further information. *Something about the man was familiar, although Hillsden could not immediately place him.*

altitude /ˈæltɪtjuːd, AM -tuːd/ **altitudes.** N-VAR If something is at a particular **altitude**, it is at that height above sea level. *As we lost altitude, the wind became stronger.*

alto /ˈæltəʊ/ **altos.** N-COUNT An **alto** is a woman with a low singing voice, or a man with a high singing voice.

⭐ **altogether** /ɔːltəˈɡeðə/. [1] ADV You use **altogether** to emphasize that something has stopped, been done, or finished completely. *His tour may have to be cancelled altogether.* [2] ADV

You use **altogether** in front of an adjective or adverb to emphasize that adjective or adverb. *This wine has an altogether stronger, more pronounced flavour... The choice of language is altogether different.* [3] ADV You use **altogether** to indicate that the amount you are mentioning is a total. *There were 11 of us altogether.*

altruism /ˈæltruːɪzəm/. N-UNCOUNT **Altruism** is unselfish concern for other people's happiness and welfare. ♦ **altruistic** ADJ *The company was not being entirely altruistic.*

aluminium /ˌæluːˈmɪniəm/ (AM **aluminum** /əˈluːmɪnəm/). N-UNCOUNT **Aluminium** is a lightweight metal used for making things such as cooking equipment and aircraft parts.

⭐ **always** /ˈɔːlweɪz/. [1] ADV If you **always** do something, you do it regularly, whenever a particular situation arises. *Always lock your garage... David always collects Alistair from school.* [2] ADV If you **always** do a particular thing, you do it all the time, continuously. *He has always been the family solicitor... He was always cheerful.* [3] ADV You use **always** in expressions such as **can always** or **could always** when you are making suggestions or giving advice. *I guess I can always ring Jean.*

am /əm, STRONG æm/. **Am** is the first person singular of the present tense of **be**.

a.m. /ˌeɪ ˈem/. **a.m.** after a number indicates that the number refers to a particular time between midnight and noon. → See Reference Page on Telling the Time. *Visitor Centre and shop open 9 a.m. – 5 p.m.*

amalgamate /əˈmælɡəmeɪt/ **amalgamates, amalgamating, amalgamated.** VERB When two or more organizations **amalgamate**, or when they **are amalgamated**, they become one large organization. *The firm has amalgamated with an American company.* ♦ **amalgamation** N-UNCOUNT *...an amalgamation of the two parties.*

amass /əˈmæs/ **amasses, amassing, amassed.** VERB If you **amass** something such as money, you gradually get a lot of it. *She has amassed a personal fortune of £8 million.*

⭐ **amateur** /ˈæmətə, AM -tʃɜːr/ **amateurs.** N-COUNT An **amateur** is someone who does a particular activity as a hobby, not as a job. *He was encouraged to continue racing for another year as an amateur. ...amateur dramatic productions.*

amaze /əˈmeɪz/ **amazes, amazing, amazed.** VERB If something **amazes** you, it surprises you very much. *He amazed us by his knowledge of Welsh history.* ♦ **amazed** ADJ *I was amazed to learn she was still writing her stories.*

amazement /əˈmeɪzmənt/. N-UNCOUNT **Amazement** is what you feel if you are very surprised by something. *Both men stared at her in amazement... To my amazement, Peterson disagreed.*

⭐ **amazing** /əˈmeɪzɪŋ/. ADJ If something is **amazing**, it is very surprising and makes you feel pleasure or admiration. *It's the most amazing*

a
b
c
d
e
f
g
h
i
j
k
l
m
n
o
p
q
r
s
t
u
v
w
x
y
z

thing to watch... It's amazing how people collect so much stuff. ♦ **amazingly** ADV She was an amazingly good cook.

⭐ **ambassador** /æm'bæsədə/ **ambassadors.** N-COUNT An **ambassador** is an important official living in a foreign country who represents the government of his or her own country.

amber /'æmbə/. ADJ Something that is **amber** in colour is orange or yellowish-brown.

ambience (or **ambiance**) /'æmbiəns/. N-SING The **ambience** of a place is its character and atmosphere. [LITERARY] The overall ambience of the room is cosy.

ambiguity /,æmbɪ'gjuːɪti/ **ambiguities.** N-VAR You say that there is **ambiguity** when something can be understood in more than one way.

ambiguous /æm'bɪgjʊəs/. ADJ Something that is **ambiguous** can be understood in more than one way. There had been a few ambiguous remarks. ♦ **ambiguously** ADV ...an ambiguously worded document.

⭐ **ambition** /æm'bɪʃən/ **ambitions.** **1** N-COUNT If you have an **ambition** to achieve something, you want very much to achieve it. His ambition is to sail round the world. **2** N-UNCOUNT **Ambition** is the desire to be successful, rich, or powerful. He is full of ambition and resolve.

ambitious /æm'bɪʃəs/. **1** ADJ Someone who is **ambitious** wants to be successful, rich, or powerful. **2** ADJ An **ambitious** idea or plan is on a large scale and needs a lot of work in order to be successful.

ambivalent /æm'bɪvələnt/. ADJ If you are **ambivalent about** something, you are not sure exactly what you think about it. She remained ambivalent about her marriage.

amble /'æmbəl/ **ambles, ambling, ambled.** VERB When you **amble** somewhere, you walk there slowly and in a relaxed manner. Slowly they ambled back to the car.

ambulance /'æmbjʊləns/ **ambulances.** N-COUNT An **ambulance** is a vehicle for taking people to and from hospital.

ambush /'æmbʊʃ/ **ambushes, ambushing, ambushed.** VERB & N-COUNT If people **ambush** their enemies, they attack them after hiding and waiting for them. The attack is called an **ambush**. The Guatemalan army says rebels ambushed and killed 10 patrolmen.

amen /ɑː'men, ,eɪ-/. CONVENTION **Amen** is said or sung by Christians at the end of a prayer.

amend /ə'mend/ **amends, amending, amended.** **1** VERB If you **amend** something that has been written or said, you change it. They voted unanimously to amend the constitution. **2** PHRASE If you **make amends** when you have harmed someone, you show you are sorry by doing something to please them. He wanted to make amends for causing their marriage to fail.

⭐ **amendment** /ə'mendmənt/ **amendments.** N-COUNT An **amendment** is a section that is added to a law or rule in order to change it.

amenity /ə'miːnɪti, AM -'men-/ **amenities.** N-COUNT **Amenities** are things such as shopping centres or sports facilities that are for people's convenience or enjoyment. The hotel amenities include health clubs, and conference facilities.

⭐ **American** /əm'erɪkən/ **Americans.** ADJ & N-COUNT **American** means belonging or relating to the United States of America. An **American** is someone who comes from the United States of America. ...the American economy.

A,merican 'football. See **football**.

amiable /'eɪmiəbəl/. ADJ Someone who is **amiable** is friendly and pleasant. ...an educated, amiable and decent man. ♦ **amiably** ADV We chatted amiably about old friends.

amicable /'æmɪkəbəl/. ADJ When people have an **amicable** relationship, they are pleasant to each other and solve their problems without quarrelling. Our discussions were amicable and productive. ...an amicable agreement. ♦ **amicably** ADV Mr Black divorced amicably from his wife.

⭐ **amid** /ə'mɪd/. **1** PREP If something happens **amid** other things, it happens while the other things are happening. [LITERARY] Amid the tumult, she jumped into her car. **2** PREP If something is **amid** other things, it is surrounded by them. [LITERARY] ...a tiny bungalow amid clusters of trees.

amidst /ə'mɪdst/. **Amidst** means the same as **amid**.

amiss /ə'mɪs/. ADJ AFTER LINK-V If you say that something is **amiss**, you mean there is something wrong.

ammonia /ə'məʊniə/. N-UNCOUNT **Ammonia** is a colourless liquid or gas with a strong sharp smell.

ammunition /,æmjʊ'nɪʃən/. **1** N-UNCOUNT **Ammunition** consists of bullets and rockets that are made to be fired from guns. **2** N-UNCOUNT If you use information as **ammunition**, you use it against someone. It helps to have details as ammunition.

amnesty /'æmnɪsti/ **amnesties.** **1** N-COUNT If a prisoner is granted an **amnesty**, they are officially pardoned. ...a general amnesty for political prisoners. **2** N-COUNT An **amnesty** is a period of time during which people can confess to a crime or give up weapons without being punished.

⭐ **among** /ə'mʌŋ/. **1** PREP A person or thing that is **among** a group of people or things is surrounded by them or is with them. They walked among the crowds. ...houses set among well-tended gardens... I was brought up among people who read and wrote a lot. **2** PREP If someone or something is **among** a group, they are a member of that group. A British man was among the people killed... Among his purchases were several books. **3** PREP If an opinion or situation exists **among** a group of people, they have it or experience it. If something happens **among** a group of people, they do it. ...concern among book and magazine retailers. ...when we discuss it among ourselves.

4 PREP If something is divided **among** three or more people, they all get a part of it.

amongst /ə'mʌŋst/. PREP **Amongst** means the same as **among**.

⭐ **amount** /ə'maʊnt/ **amounts, amounting, amounted.**
1 N-COUNT An **amount** of something is how much of it you have, need, or get. *He needs that amount of money to survive... I still do a certain amount of work.* **2** VERB If something **amounts to** a particular total, all the parts of it add up to that total. *The total rain and snowfall amounted to 50mm.* **3** PHRASE If you say that there are **any amount** of things or people, you mean that there are a lot of them. *There are any amount of clubs you could join.*
▸ **amount to.** PHR-VERB If you say that one thing **amounts to** something else, you mean that the first thing is the same as the second. *The banks have what amounts to a monopoly.*

amp /æmp/ **amps.** N-COUNT An **amp** is a unit which is used for measuring electric current. *...a 3 amp fuse.*

ample /'æmpəl/. ADJ If there is an **ample** amount of something, there is enough of it and some extra. *There'll be ample opportunity to relax. ...ample space for a good-sized kitchen.* ♦ **amply** ADV *Its 160 pages are amply illustrated.*

amplifier /'æmplɪfaɪə/ **amplifiers.** N-COUNT An **amplifier** is an electronic device in a radio or stereo system, which causes sounds or signals to become louder.

amplify /'æmplɪfaɪ/ **amplifies, amplifying, amplified.**
1 VERB To **amplify** a sound means to make it louder. *This landscape seemed to trap and amplify sounds.* ♦ **amplification** /ˌæmplɪfɪ'keɪʃən/ N-UNCOUNT *...an electronic amplification system.* **2** VERB To **amplify** an idea, feeling, or statement means to increase its strength or intensity. *Her anxiety about the world was amplifying her personal fears.*

amputate /'æmpjʊteɪt/ **amputates, amputating, amputated.** VERB If a surgeon **amputates** someone's arm or leg, he or she cuts it off in an operation. *He had to have one leg amputated.*
♦ **amputation, amputations** N-VAR *...the amputation of limbs.*

amuse /ə'mjuːz/ **amuses, amusing, amused.** **1** VERB If something **amuses** you, it makes you want to laugh or smile. *The thought seemed to amuse him.* **2** VERB If you **amuse yourself**, you do something in order to pass the time and not become bored. *I always invented stories to amuse myself... Archie kept us amused.*

amused /ə'mjuːzd/. ADJ If you are **amused** by something, it makes you want to laugh or smile.

He was amused to learn that he and O'Brien had similar ideas.

amusement /ə'mjuːzmənt/ **amusements.**
1 N-UNCOUNT **Amusement** is the feeling that you have when you think that something is funny. *He stopped and watched with amusement.* **2** N-UNCOUNT **Amusement** is the pleasure that you get from being entertained or from doing something interesting. *He wrote for the amusement of his friends.* **3** N-COUNT **Amusements** are ways of passing the time pleasantly. *People had very few amusements to choose from.*

amusing /ə'mjuːzɪŋ/. ADJ An **amusing** person or thing makes you laugh or smile. *...a capable and amusing companion.* ♦ **amusingly** ADV *It must be amusingly written.*

an /ən, STRONG æn/. DET **An** is used instead of 'a' in front of words that begin with vowel sounds.

anaemia (or **anemia**) /ə'niːmiə/. N-UNCOUNT **Anaemia** is a medical condition in which there are too few red cells in your blood, so that you feel tired and look pale. ♦ **anaemic** ADJ *Losing a lot of blood makes you tired and anaemic.*

anaesthetic (or **anesthetic**) /ˌænɪs'θetɪk/ **anaesthetics.** N-VAR **Anaesthetic** is a substance used to stop you feeling pain during an operation. *...while they are under the anaesthetic.*

anaesthetist (or **anesthetist**) /ə'niːsθətɪst/ **anaesthetists.** N-COUNT In British English, an **anaesthetist** is a doctor or nurse who gives anaesthetics to patients. The usual American word is **anesthesiologist**.

anal /'eɪnəl/. ADJ **Anal** means relating to the anus.

analogue /'ænəlɒg/.

✓ The spelling **analog** is used in American English, and also in British English for meaning 2.

1 ADJ An **analogue** watch or clock shows the time with two pointers called hands, rather than with a number display. Compare **digital**. **2** ADJ **Analogue** technology involves measuring, storing, or recording information by using physical quantities such as voltage. Compare **digital**.

analogy /ə'nælədʒi/ **analogies.** N-COUNT If you draw an **analogy** between two things, you show that they are similar. *...the analogy of looking for a needle in a haystack.* ♦ **analogous** /ə'næləgəs/ ADJ *Swimming has no event that is analogous to the 100 metres in athletics.*

analyse /'ænəlaɪz/. See **analyze**.

⭐ **analysis** /ə'nælɪsɪs/ **analyses** /ə'nælɪsiːz/.
1 N-VAR **Analysis** is the process of considering something or examining it in order to understand it or to find out what it consists of. *...a careful analysis of the situation... They collect blood samples for analysis.* **2** PHRASE You say **in the final analysis** or **in the last analysis** to indicate that the statement you are making is about the

basic facts of a situation. *Violence in the last analysis produces more violence.*

⭐ **analyst** /ˈænəlɪst/ **analysts.** **1** N-COUNT An **analyst** is a person whose job is to analyse a subject and give opinions about it. *...a political analyst.* **2** N-COUNT An **analyst** is someone who is trained to examine and treat people who have emotional problems. *My analyst has helped me not to feel guilty.*

analytic /ˌænəˈlɪtɪk/. ADJ **Analytic** means the same as **analytical.**

analytical /ˌænəˈlɪtɪkəl/. ADJ **Analytical** skills or methods involve the use of logical reasoning. *...your analytical and leadership skills.*

analyze (BRIT also **analyse**) /ˈænəlaɪz/ **analyzes, analyzing, analyzed.** VERB If you **analyze** something, you consider it or examine it in order to understand it or to find out what it consists of. *Analyze what is causing the stress in your life... They had their tablets analysed.*

anarchist /ˈænəkɪst/ **anarchists.** N-COUNT An **anarchist** is someone who believes the laws and power of governments should be replaced by people working together freely. ♦ **anarchism** N-UNCOUNT *...fervent political anarchism.*

anarchy /ˈænəki/. N-UNCOUNT **Anarchy** is a situation where nobody obeys rules or laws. *...an attempt to stop the country slipping into anarchy.* ♦ **anarchic** /æˈnɑːkɪk/ ADJ *...the near anarchic level of violence.*

anatomy /əˈnætəmi/ **anatomies.** N-VAR **Anatomy** is the study of the bodies of people or animals. The **anatomy** of a person or animal is the structure of their body. *...a professor of anatomy. ... the female anatomy.* ♦ **anatomical** /ˌænəˈtɒmɪkəl/ ADJ *...the minute anatomical differences between insects.*

ancestor /ˈænsestə/ **ancestors.** N-COUNT Your **ancestors** are the people from whom you are descended. *...our daily lives, so different from those of our ancestors.* ♦ **ancestral** /ænˈsestrəl/ ADJ *...the family's ancestral home.*

ancestry /ˈænsestri/ **ancestries.** N-COUNT Your **ancestry** consists of the people from whom you are descended. *...a family who could trace their ancestry back to the sixteenth century.*

anchor 1

anchor /ˈæŋkə/ **anchors, anchoring, anchored.** **1** N-COUNT An **anchor** is a heavy hooked object at the end of a chain that is dropped from a boat into the water to make the boat stay in one place. **2** VERB When a boat **anchors**, or when you **anchor** it, its anchor is dropped into the water to make it stay in one place. *We could anchor off the pier.* **3** VERB If you **anchor** an object, you fix it to something so that it will not move. *The roots anchor the plant in the earth.*

⭐ **ancient** /ˈeɪnʃənt/. ADJ **Ancient** means very old, or having existed for a long time. *...ancient Greece and Rome. ...ancient Jewish traditions.*

⭐ **and** /ənd, STRONG ænd/. **1** CONJ You use **and** to link two or more words, groups, or clauses. *She and Simon had already gone... I'm 53 and I'm very happy.* **2** CONJ You use **and** to link two identical words or phrases to emphasize their degree or to suggest that something continues or increases over a period of time. *We talked for hours and hours... Learning becomes more and more difficult.* **3** CONJ **And** links two statements about events which follow each other. *I waved goodbye and went down the stone harbour steps... I looked up and found her staring at me.* **4** CONJ You use **and** to link two statements when the second statement continues the point that has been made in the first statement. *You could only really tell the effects of the disease in the long term, and five years wasn't long enough... 'He used to be so handsome.'—'And now?'.* **5** CONJ **And** indicates that two numbers are to be added together. *What does two and two make?*

anecdote /ˈænɪkdəʊt/ **anecdotes.** N-COUNT An **anecdote** is a short entertaining account of something that has happened. *Pete was telling them an anecdote about his mother.* ♦ **anecdotal** /ˌænɪkˈdəʊtəl/ ADJ *...anecdotal accounts of journeys and encounters.*

anemia /əˈniːmiə/. See **anaemia.**

anemic /əˈniːmɪk/. See **anaemia.**

anesthetic /ˌænɪsˈθetɪk/. See **anaesthetic.**

anesthetist /əˈniːsθətɪst/. See **anaesthetist.**

anew /əˈnjuː, AM əˈnuː/. ADV If you do something **anew**, you do it again, often in a different way. [LITERARY] *She's ready to start anew.*

angel /ˈeɪndʒəl/ **angels.** **1** N-COUNT **Angels** are spiritual beings that some people believe are God's messengers and servants in heaven. **2** N-COUNT If you refer to someone as an **angel**, you mean that they are good, kind, and gentle. *Thank you a thousand times. You're an angel.*

angelic /ænˈdʒelɪk/. ADJ You can describe someone as **angelic** when they are very good, kind, and gentle. *...an angelic face.*

⭐ **anger** /ˈæŋgə/ **angers, angering, angered.** **1** N-UNCOUNT **Anger** is the strong emotion that you feel when you think someone has behaved in an unfair, cruel, or unacceptable way. *He cried with anger and frustration.* **2** VERB If someone or something **angers** you, they make you angry. *His coldness angered her.*

★ **angle** /ˈæŋɡəl/ **angles, angling, angled.** **1** N-COUNT If something is **at an angle**, it is leaning in a particular direction so that it is not straight, horizontal, or vertical. *The boat is now leaning at a 30 degree angle. ...brackets to adjust the steering wheel's angle.* **2** N-COUNT An **angle** is the direction from which you look at something. *Thanks to the angle at which he stood, he could just see the sunset.* **3** N-COUNT You can refer to a way of presenting something or thinking about it as a particular **angle**. *He was considering the idea from all angles.* **4** VERB If you are **angling for** something, you are trying to make someone offer it to you without asking for it directly. *It sounds very much as if he's just angling for sympathy.* **5** See also **right angle**.

angler /ˈæŋɡlə/ **anglers.** N-COUNT An **angler** is someone who fishes with a fishing rod as a hobby.

angling /ˈæŋɡlɪŋ/. N-UNCOUNT **Angling** is the activity of fishing with a fishing rod.

Anglo- /ˈæŋɡləʊ-/. **Anglo-** is added to adjectives indicating nationality to form adjectives describing something which involves relations between Britain and another country. *...his contribution to Anglo-American relations.*

★ **angry** /ˈæŋɡri/ **angrier, angriest.** ADJ When you are **angry**, you feel strong emotion about something that you consider unfair, cruel, or insulting. *She was angry at her husband. ...an angry mob.* ♦ **angrily** ADV *France and Italy reacted angrily to the decision.*

> **USAGE Angry** is normally used to talk about someone's mood or feelings on a particular occasion. If someone is often angry, you can describe them as **bad-tempered**. *She's a bad-tempered young lady.* If someone is very angry, you can describe them as **furious**. *Senior police officers are furious at the blunder.* If they are less angry, you can describe them as **annoyed** or **irritated**. *The Premier looked annoyed but calm. ...a man irritated by the barking of his neighbour's dog.* Typically, someone is **irritated** by something because it happens constantly or continually.

angst /æŋst/. N-UNCOUNT **Angst** is a feeling of anxiety and worry. *Many kids suffer from acne and angst.*

anguish /ˈæŋɡwɪʃ/. N-UNCOUNT **Anguish** is great mental or physical suffering. *For a few brief minutes we forgot the anxiety and anguish.*

anguished /ˈæŋɡwɪʃt/. ADJ **Anguished** means feeling or showing great mental or physical suffering. [WRITTEN] *She let out an anguished cry.*

angular /ˈæŋɡjʊlə/. ADJ **Angular** things have shapes that contain a lot of straight lines and sharp points. *She has a very angular face.*

★ **animal** /ˈænɪməl/ **animals.** **1** N-COUNT Any living creature other than a human being can be referred to as an **animal**. *He was attacked by wild animals.* → See pictures on pages 815 and 816. **2** N-COUNT An **animal** is any living thing that is not a plant, including people. *...members of the animal kingdom.* **3** ADJ **Animal** qualities or feelings relate to your physical nature and instincts rather than your mind. *...an animal panic to run and hide.* **4** N-COUNT If you say that someone is an **animal**, you find their behaviour disgusting or very unpleasant. *This man is an animal.*

animate /ˈænɪmət/. ADJ Something that is **animate** has life, in contrast to things like stones and machines which do not. *...all aspects of the material world, animate and inanimate.*

animated /ˈænɪmeɪtɪd/. **1** ADJ Someone or something that is **animated** is lively and interesting. *She was seen in animated conversation with the singer.* **2** ADJ BEFORE N An **animated** film is one in which puppets or drawings appear to move. *...Disney's animated film 'Lady and the Tramp.'*

animation /ˌænɪˈmeɪʃən/. **1** N-UNCOUNT **Animation** is the quality of being lively and interesting. *They both spoke with great animation.* **2** N-UNCOUNT **Animation** is the use of puppets or drawings that appear to move in films. *...traditional cartoon animation.*

animosity /ˌænɪˈmɒsɪti/ **animosities.** N-VAR **Animosity** is a feeling of strong dislike and anger. *The animosity between the two men grew.*

ankle /ˈæŋkəl/ **ankles.** N-COUNT Your **ankle** is the joint where your foot joins your leg. → See picture on page 822.

annex (or **annexe**) **annexes, annexing, annexed.** **1** N-COUNT /ˈæneks/ An **annex** is a building which is joined to or is next to a larger main building. **2** VERB /æˈneks/ If a country **annexes** another country or an area of land, it seizes it and takes control of it. *Rome annexed the Nabatean kingdom in 106 AD.* ♦ **annexation** N-UNCOUNT *...the annexation of occupied territories.*

annihilate /əˈnaɪɪleɪt/ **annihilates, annihilating, annihilated.** VERB If something **is annihilated**, it is destroyed completely. *The lava annihilates everything in its path.* ♦ **annihilation** N-UNCOUNT *Leaders fear the annihilation of their people.*

★ **anniversary** /ˌænɪˈvɜːsəri/ **anniversaries.** N-COUNT An **anniversary** is a date which is remembered or celebrated because a special event happened on that date in a previous year. *...their third wedding anniversary.*

★ **announce** /əˈnaʊns/ **announces, announcing, announced.** **1** VERB If you **announce** something, you tell people about it publicly or officially. *She was planning to announce her engagement... He will announce tonight that he is resigning.* **2** VERB If you **announce** something, you say it in a deliberate and rather aggressive way. *He announced that he was leaving... 'I'm having a bath and going to bed,' she announced.*

★ **announcement** /əˈnaʊnsmənt/ **announcements.**
1 N-COUNT An **announcement** is a public statement which gives information about something that has happened or that will happen. *...an announcement of a cut in the bank loan rate.* **2** N-SING The **announcement of** something is the act of telling people about it. *...the announcement of Jeanne's engagement.*

announcer /əˈnaʊnsə/ **announcers.** N-COUNT An **announcer** is someone who introduces programmes on radio or television.

annoy /əˈnɔɪ/ **annoys, annoying, annoyed.** VERB If someone **annoys** you, they make you fairly angry and impatient. *Try making a note of the things which annoy you... It annoyed me that I didn't have time to do more ironing.*

annoyance /əˈnɔɪəns/. N-UNCOUNT **Annoyance** is the feeling that you get when someone annoys you. *To her annoyance the stranger did not go away.*

annoyed /əˈnɔɪd/. ADJ If you are **annoyed**, you are fairly angry about something. *Eleanor was annoyed at having had to wait so long.* ● See note at **angry**.

annoying /əˈnɔɪɪŋ/. ADJ An **annoying** person or action makes you feel fairly angry and impatient. *It's very annoying when this happens.*

★ **annual** /ˈænjʊəl/. **1** ADJ BEFORE N **Annual** means happening or done once every year. *...our annual holiday.* ◆ **annually** ADV *Interest will be paid annually.* **2** ADJ BEFORE N **Annual** quantities or rates relate to a period of one year. *...annual sales of about $80 million.* ◆ **annually** ADV *El Salvador produces more than 100,000 tons of refined copper annually.*

annum /ˈænəm/. See **per annum.**

anomaly /əˈnɒməli/ **anomalies.** N-COUNT If something is an **anomaly**, it is different from what is normal or usual. [FORMAL]

anonymous /əˈnɒnɪməs/. **1** ADJ If you remain **anonymous** when you do something, you do not let people know that you were the person who did it. Something that is **anonymous** does not reveal who you are. *You can remain anonymous if you wish. ...anonymous phone calls.* ◆ **anonymously** ADV *Reports can be made anonymously.* ◆ **anonymity** /ˌænəˈnɪmɪti/ N-UNCOUNT *The official requested anonymity.* **2** ADJ Something that is **anonymous** has no interesting features. *...an anonymous holiday villa.*

anorak /ˈænəræk/ **anoraks.** N-COUNT An **anorak** is a warm waterproof jacket, usually with a hood.

anorexia /ˌænəˈreksiə/. N-UNCOUNT **Anorexia** or **anorexia nervosa** is an illness in which a person refuses to eat enough because they have an overwhelming fear of becoming fat.

★ **another** /əˈnʌðə/. **1** DET & PRON **Another** thing or person means one more in addition to those that already exist or are known about. *We're going to have another baby... Drink up, there's time for another.* **2** DET & PRON **Another** can be used to mean a different thing or person from the one just mentioned. *Her doctor referred her to another therapist... He said one thing and has done quite another.* **3** PHRASE You use **one another** to indicate that each member of a group does something to or for the other members. *...women learning to help themselves and one another.* **4** PHRASE If you talk about **one** thing **after another**, you are referring to a series of repeated or continuous events. *They kept going, destroying one store after another.*

★ **answer** /ˈɑːnsə, ˈæn-/ **answers, answering, answered.** **1** VERB When you **answer** someone who has asked you something, you say something back to them. *Just answer the question... 'When?' asked Alba, calmly. 'Tonight', answered Hunter.* **2** VERB If you **answer** a letter or advertisement, you write to the person who wrote it. *She answered an advert for a job.* **3** N-COUNT An **answer** is something that you say or write when you answer someone. *I wrote to him but I never had an answer back.* **4** VERB & N-COUNT When you **answer** the telephone, you pick it up when it rings. When you **answer** the door, you open it when you hear a knock or the bell. If no-one picks up the phone or opens the door, you can say there is no **answer**. *She answered her phone on the first ring.* **5** N-COUNT An **answer** to a problem is a possible solution to it. *Legislation is only part of the answer.* **6** VERB & N-COUNT When you **answer** a question in a test, or give an **answer** to it, you write or say something in an attempt to give the facts that are asked for. *She answered 81 questions... Simply marking an answer wrong will not help the pupil.*

▸**answer back.** PHR-VERB If someone, especially a child, **answers** you **back**, or if they **answer back**, they speak rudely to you when you speak to them. *She was beaten by teachers for answering back.*

▸**answer for.** PHR-VERB If you have to **answer for** something bad or wrong you have done, you are punished for it. *He must be made to answer for his terrible crimes.*

'answering machine, answering machines. N-COUNT An **answering machine** is a device which records telephone messages while you are out.

ant /ænt/ **ants.** N-COUNT **Ants** are small crawling insects that live in large groups. → See picture on page 824.

antagonism /ænˈtægənɪzəm/. N-UNCOUNT **Antagonism** is hatred or hostility. *...a history of antagonism between the two sides.*

antagonist /ænˈtægənɪst/ **antagonists.** N-COUNT Your **antagonist** is your opponent or enemy.

antagonize (BRIT also **antagonise**) /ænˈtægənaɪz/ **antagonizes, antagonizing, antagonized.** VERB If you **antagonize** someone, you make them feel hostile towards you. *Jordan does not wish to antagonise Saudi Arabia.*

antenna /æn'tenə/ **antennae** /æn'teniː/ or **antennas.**

☑ For meaning 2 the plural is usually **antennas**.

1 N-COUNT The **antennae** of an insect are the two long thin parts attached to its head that it uses to feel things with. 2 N-COUNT An **antenna** is a device that sends and receives television or radio signals.

anthem /'ænθəm/ **anthems.** N-COUNT An **anthem** is a song or hymn written for a special occasion. ...the Olympic anthem. ● See also **national anthem**.

anthology /æn'θɒlədʒi/ **anthologies.** N-COUNT An **anthology** is a collection of writings by different writers published together in one book.

anthropology /ˌænθrə'pɒlədʒi/. N-UNCOUNT **Anthropology** is the study of people, society, and culture. ◆ **anthropologist, anthropologists** N-COUNT ...an anthropologist who had been in China.

antibiotic /ˌæntibaɪ'ɒtɪk/ **antibiotics.** N-COUNT **Antibiotics** are drugs that are used in medicine to kill bacteria and to cure infections.

antibody /'ænti,bɒdi/ **antibodies.** N-COUNT **Antibodies** are substances which your body produces in order to fight diseases.

anticipate /æn'tɪsɪpeɪt/ **anticipates, anticipating, anticipated.** 1 VERB If you **anticipate** an event, you realize in advance that it may happen and you are prepared for it. We couldn't have anticipated the result of our campaigning. ◆ **anticipation** N-UNCOUNT They hoard food in anticipation of future shortages. 2 VERB If you **anticipate** a question, request, or need, you do what is necessary or required before the question, request, or need occurs. Do you expect your partner to anticipate your needs? 3 VERB If you **anticipate** something pleasant or exciting that is going to happen, you look forward to it with pleasure. ◆ **anticipation** N-UNCOUNT His eyes gleamed in anticipation.

anti-clockwise /ˌænti'klɒkwaɪz/. ADV & ADJ In British English, if something is moving **anti-clockwise**, it is moving in a circle in the opposite direction to the hands of a clock. The usual American word is **counterclockwise**.

antics /'æntɪks/. N-PLURAL **Antics** are funny, silly, or unusual ways of behaving.

antidote /'æntɪdəʊt/ **antidotes.** N-COUNT An **antidote** is a chemical substance that controls the effect of a poison.

antiquated /'æntɪkweɪtɪd/. ADJ **Antiquated** things seem very old or old-fashioned. Many factories are so antiquated they are not worth saving.

★ **antique** /æn'tiːk/ **antiques.** N-COUNT An **antique** is an old object which is valuable because of its beauty or rarity. ...antique silver jewellery.

antiquity /æn'tɪkwɪti/ **antiquities.** 1 N-UNCOUNT **Antiquity** is the distant past, especially the time of the ancient Egyptians, Greeks, and Romans. ...famous monuments of classical antiquity. 2 N-COUNT **Antiquities** are interesting old things, such as buildings and statues, that you can visit.

antiseptic /ˌænti'septɪk/ **antiseptics.** N-VAR **Antiseptic** is a substance that kills bacteria.

anti-'social. 1 ADJ **Anti-social** people are unwilling to meet and be friendly with other people. ...an anti-social loner. 2 ADJ **Anti-social** behaviour is annoying or upsetting to others.

anus /'eɪnəs/ **anuses.** N-COUNT A person's **anus** is the hole between their buttocks, from which faeces leave their body.

★ **anxiety** /æŋ'zaɪəti/ **anxieties.** N-VAR **Anxiety** is a feeling of nervousness or worry. Her voice was full of anxiety. ...anxieties about money.

★ **anxious** /'æŋkʃəs/. 1 ADJ AFTER LINK-V If you are **anxious to** do something or **anxious** that something should happen, you very much want to do it or want it to happen. I was anxious to get him here... He is anxious that there should be no delay. 2 ADJ If you are feeling **anxious**, you are worried about something. You can also use **anxious** to describe a time when someone feels anxious. She had become very anxious and alarmed... They had to wait 10 anxious days. ◆ **anxiously** ADV They waited anxiously for news.

★ **any** /'eni/. 1 QUANT You use **any** in negative statements to mean none of a particular thing. I never make any big decisions... You don't know any of my friends... The children needed new school clothes and Kim couldn't afford any. 2 ADV You can use **any** to emphasize a comparative adjective or adverb in a negative statement. I can't see things getting any easier. 3 QUANT You use **any** in questions and conditional clauses to ask if there is some of a particular thing or to suggest that there might be. Do you speak any foreign languages?... Do you use any of the following?... I'll be happy to answer any questions if there are any.

USAGE **Any** is mainly used in questions and negative sentences. You use **not any** instead of **some** in negative sentences. There isn't any money. You only use **some** in questions when you expect the answer yes. Did you buy some wine? Otherwise you say **any**. Did you buy any wine?

4 QUANT You use **any** in positive statements when you are referring to something or someone without saying exactly what, who, or which kind you mean. I'm prepared to take any advice. ...the biggest mistake any of them could remember... Clean the mussels and discard any that do not close. 5 PHRASE If something does not happen or is not true **any more** or **any longer**, it has stopped happening or is no longer true. I don't want to see her any more... I couldn't keep the tears hidden any longer.

A
B
C
D
E
F
G
H
I
J
K
L
M
N
O
P
Q
R
S
T
U
V
W
X
Y
Z

★ **anybody**/'enibɒdi/. See **anyone**.

> **USAGE Anybody** is mainly used in questions and negative sentences. You use **not anybody** instead of **somebody** in negative sentences. *There isn't anybody here.* You only use **somebody** in questions when you expect the answer yes. *Is somebody there?* Otherwise you say **anybody**. *Is anybody there?*

anyhow/'enihaʊ/. See **anyway**.

anymore/ˌeniˈmɔː/ (or **any more**). ADV If something does not happen or is not true **anymore**, it has stopped happening or is no longer true. Some people think this spelling is incorrect and prefer to use **any more**. *People are not interested in movies anymore.*

★ **anyone**/'eniwʌn/ (or **anybody**/'enibɒdi/). ① PRON You use **anyone** in negative statements to indicate that nobody is present or involved in an action. *You needn't talk to anyone if you don't want to... He was far too scared to tell anybody.* ② PRON You use **anyone** in questions and conditional clauses to ask or talk about someone who might be involved in a particular situation or action. *Did you tell anyone?... If anybody wants me, I'll be at the police station.* ③ PRON You use **anyone** before words which indicate the kind of person you are talking about. *It's not a job for anyone who is slow with numbers.* ④ PRON You use **anyone** to say that a particular thing would be true of any person out of a very large number of people. *Al Smith could make anybody laugh.*

> **USAGE** Do not confuse **anyone** with **any one**. **Anyone** always refers to people. In the phrase **any one**, 'one' is a pronoun or a determiner that can refer to either a person or a thing, depending on the context. It is often followed by the word **of**. *Parting from any one of you for a short time is hard... None of us stay in any one place for a very long time.* In these examples, **any one** is a more emphatic way of saying **any**.
> **Anyone** is mainly used in questions and negative sentences. You use **not anyone** instead of **someone** in negative sentences. *There isn't anyone here.* You only use **someone** in questions when you expect the answer yes. *Is someone there?* Otherwise you say **anyone**. *Is anyone there?*

anyplace/'enipleɪs/. **Anyplace** means the same as **anywhere**. [AMERICAN]

★ **anything**/'eniθɪŋ/. ① PRON You use **anything** in negative statements to say that nothing is present or an action or event does not happen.

She couldn't see or hear anything... I couldn't manage anything. ② PRON You use **anything** in questions and conditional clauses to ask or talk about whether something is present or happening. *Did you find anything? ...if there's anything I could do for him.* ③ PRON You use **anything** to emphasize that a particular thing could be true about any one of a very large number of things. *Anything could happen... He can have anything... anything from 25 to 40 litres of milk.* ④ PRON You use **anything** before words which indicate the kind of thing you are talking about. *She collects anything that has charm.* ⑤ PRON You use **anything** in expressions such as **anything near**, **anything close to**, and **anything like** to emphasize a statement that you are making. *...the only way he can live anything near a normal life.*

> **USAGE Anything** is mainly used in questions and negative sentences. You use **not anything** instead of **something** in negative sentences. *There isn't anything here.* You only use **something** in questions when you expect the answer yes. *Is something wrong?* Otherwise you say **anything**. *Is anything wrong?*

anytime/ˌeniˈtaɪm/. ADV You use **anytime** to mean at an unspecified point in time. *The college admits students anytime during the year... He can leave anytime he wants.*

★ **anyway**/'eniweɪ/ (or **anyhow**/'enihaʊ/). ① ADV You use **anyway** to indicate that a statement explains or supports a previous point. *I'm certain David's told you his business troubles. Anyway, it's no secret that he owes money.* ② ADV You use **anyway** to suggest that a statement is true or relevant in spite of other things that have been said. *I wasn't qualified to apply for the job really but I got it anyhow.* ③ ADV You use **anyway** to correct or modify a statement. *Ann doesn't want to have children. Not right now, anyway.* ④ ADV You use **anyway** to change the topic or return to a previous topic. *'I've got a terrible cold.'—'Have you? Oh dear. Anyway, so you're not going to go away this weekend?'.*

anyways/'eniweɪz/. ADV Some people use **anyways** instead of **anyway**. [AMERICAN]

★ **anywhere**/'eniweə/. ① ADV You use **anywhere** in negative statements, questions, and conditional clauses to refer to a place without saying exactly where you mean. *Did you try to get help from anywhere?... I haven't got anywhere to live.* ② ADV You use **anywhere** in positive statements to emphasize an expression that refers to a place or area. *...jokes that are so funny they always work anywhere... He'll meet you anywhere you want.* ③ ADV When you do not want to be exact, you use **anywhere** to refer to a particular range of things. *His shoes cost anywhere from $200 up.*

⭐ **apart** /əˈpɑːt/. **1** ADV When someone or something is positioned **apart from** a person or thing, they are some distance from them. *He was standing a bit apart from the rest of us... He was standing, feet apart... He tried in vain to keep the two dogs apart.* **2** ADV If two people are **apart**, they are no longer living together or spending time together. *Mum and Dad live apart.* **3** ADV If something comes **apart**, its parts separate from each other. *The handles of two of Ivanisevic's new rackets came apart.* **4** PREP You use **apart from** when you are giving an exception to a general statement. *The room was empty apart from one man seated beside the fire.* **5** PREP You use **apart from** to indicate that you are aware of one aspect of a situation, but that you are going to focus on another aspect. *The Queen remains above criticism, apart from the issue of her tax liability.*

⭐ **apartheid** /əˈpɑːthaɪt/. N-UNCOUNT **Apartheid** was a political system in South Africa in which people were divided into racial groups and kept apart by law.

⭐ **apartment** /əˈpɑːtmənt/. **apartments.** N-COUNT An **apartment** is a set of rooms for living in, usually on one floor of a large building. This word can be used in British and American English, although **flat** is the more commonly used word in Britain.

apathy /ˈæpəθi/. N-UNCOUNT **Apathy** is a state of mind in which you are not interested in or enthusiastic about anything. *...the political apathy of young Americans.* ♦ **apathetic** /ˌæpəˈθetɪk/ ADJ *The voters seem so apathetic about European issues.*

ape /eɪp/ **apes, aping, aped.** **1** N-COUNT **Apes** are animals such as chimpanzees or gorillas. **2** VERB If you **ape** someone's behaviour, you imitate it. *...French films which merely aped Hollywood.*

aperture /ˈæpətʃə/. **apertures.** N-COUNT An **aperture** is a narrow hole or gap, for example the opening in a camera through which light passes into it. [FORMAL] *Through the aperture he could clearly see daylight.*

apex /ˈeɪpeks/ **apexes.** **1** N-SING The **apex** of an organization or system is the highest and most important position in it. *At the apex of the party was its central committee.* **2** N-COUNT The **apex** of something such as a pyramid is its pointed top.

apiece /əˈpiːs/. ADV If people have a particular number of things **apiece**, they have that number each. *He and I had two fish apiece.*

apologetic /əˌpɒləˈdʒetɪk/. ADJ If you are **apologetic**, you show or say that you are sorry that you have hurt someone or caused trouble for them. *He sounded very apologetic about his activities.* ♦ **apologetically** ADV *Mary Ann smiled at her apologetically.*

apologize (BRIT also **apologise**) /əˈpɒlədʒaɪz/ **apologizes, apologizing, apologized.** VERB When you **apologize to** someone, you say that you are sorry that you have hurt them or caused trouble for them. You can say '**I apologize**' as a formal way of saying sorry. *He apologized to the people who had been affected... I apologize for being late.*

apology /əˈpɒlədʒi/ **apologies.** N-VAR An **apology** is something that you say or write in order to tell someone that you are sorry that you have hurt them or caused trouble for them. *I make no apologies for the way we played. ...a letter of apology.*

apostrophe /əˈpɒstrəfi/ **apostrophes.** N-COUNT An **apostrophe** is the mark ', written to indicate that one or more letters have been omitted from a word, as in 'isn't'. It is also added to nouns to form possessives, as in 'Mike's car'. → See Reference Page on Punctuation.

appal (AM **appall**) /əˈpɔːl/ **appals, appalling, appalled.** VERB If something **appals** you, it shocks you because it is so bad. *My wife now looks like her mother, which appals me.* ♦ **appalled** ADJ *I am absolutely appalled at what this man has done.*

appalling /əˈpɔːlɪŋ/. ADJ Something that is **appalling** is so bad that it shocks you. *They have been living under the most appalling conditions.* ♦ **appallingly** ADV *...an appallingly bad speech.*

apparatus /ˌæpəˈreɪtəs, -ˈræt-/ **apparatuses.** **1** N-VAR The **apparatus** of an organization or system is its structure and method of operation. *...the technical apparatus of management.* **2** N-UNCOUNT **Apparatus** is the equipment which is used to do a particular job or activity. *...firemen wearing breathing apparatus.*

⭐ **apparent** /əˈpærənt/. **1** ADJ BEFORE N An **apparent** situation seems to be the case, although you cannot be certain that it is. *The apparent failure of the mission is a serious blow.* **2** ADJ AFTER LINK-V If something is **apparent**, it is clear and obvious. *It was apparent that he had got very confused.*

⭐ **apparently** /əˈpærəntli/. ADV You use **apparently** to refer to something that seems to be the case although it may not be. *The news apparently came as a complete surprise.*

⭐ **appeal** /əˈpiːl/ **appeals, appealing, appealed.** **1** VERB & N-COUNT If you **appeal for** something that you need, or make an **appeal for** it, you make a serious and urgent request for it. *The UN has appealed for help from the international community. ...a last-minute appeal to him to call* off his trip. [2] VERB & N-COUNT If you **appeal to** someone in authority against a decision, or if you make an **appeal**, you formally ask them to change it. *The government has appealed against the court's decision... Maguire has appealed to the Supreme Court.* [3] VERB & N-UNCOUNT If something **appeals to** you, or if it has **appeal**, you find it attractive or interesting. *The idea appealed to him. ...tiny dolls with great appeal to young girls.*

appealing /əˈpiːlɪŋ/. ADJ Someone or something that is **appealing** is pleasing and attractive. *...a sense of humour that I found very appealing.*

★ **appear** /əˈpɪə/ **appears, appearing, appeared.** [1] LINK-VERB If you say that something **appears to** be the case or **appears to** have a certain quality, you mean that you have the impression that it is the case or that it has that quality. *He appeared to be depressed... The aircraft appears to have crashed... There appears to be no problem with your baby's breathing... He is anxious to appear a gentleman.* [2] VERB When something or someone **appears**, it becomes possible to see them or obtain them. *A woman appeared at the far end of the street. ...white flowers which appear in early summer... New diet books appear at a rate of nearly one a week.* [3] VERB When someone **appears** in a play, a show, or a television programme, they take part in it. [4] VERB When someone **appears** before a court of law, they go there to answer charges or to give information.

★ **appearance** /əˈpɪərəns/ **appearances.** [1] N-COUNT When someone makes an **appearance** at a public event or in a broadcast, they take part in it. *...the president's second public appearance. ...a brief appearance on television.* [2] N-SING The **appearance** of someone or something in a place is the fact of their arriving or becoming visible there. *...the welcome appearance of Cousin Fred... Flowering plants were making their first appearance.* [3] N-SING Your **appearance** is what you look like or how you present yourself. *She used to be so fussy about her appearance... It adds nothing to the value or appearance of the house.*

appease /əˈpiːz/ **appeases, appeasing, appeased.** VERB If you try to **appease** someone, you try to maintain a peaceful situation by giving them what they want; often used showing disapproval. *The government tried to appease discontented workers.* ♦ **appeasement** N-UNCOUNT *Appeasement didn't work with Hitler.*

appendix /əˈpendɪks/ **appendices** /əˈpendɪsiːz/. [1] N-COUNT Your **appendix** is a small tube inside your body at the end of your digestive system. [2] N-COUNT An **appendix** to a book is extra information that is placed at the end of it.

appetite /ˈæpɪtaɪt/ **appetites.** [1] N-VAR Your **appetite** is your desire to eat. *He has a healthy appetite. ...loss of appetite.* [2] N-COUNT If you have an **appetite for** something, you have a strong desire for it. *...his appetite for success.*

appetizing (BRIT also **appetising**) /ˈæpɪtaɪzɪŋ/. ADJ **Appetizing** food looks and smells nice, so that you want to eat it.

applaud /əˈplɔːd/ **applauds, applauding, applauded.** [1] VERB When a group of people **applaud**, they clap their hands to show that they have enjoyed a performance. *I didn't applaud him because it was a very bad speech.* [2] VERB When a person or their behaviour **is applauded**, people praise it. *He should be applauded for his courage... We applaud her determination.*

applause /əˈplɔːz/. N-UNCOUNT **Applause** is the noise made by a group of people clapping their hands to show approval. *They greeted him with thunderous applause.*

★ **apple** /ˈæpəl/ **apples.** N-VAR An **apple** is a round fruit with a smooth skin and firm white flesh. → See picture on page 821.

appliance /əˈplaɪəns/ **appliances.** N-COUNT An **appliance** is a device such as a vacuum cleaner that does a particular job in your home. *...electrical appliances.*

applicable /ˈæplɪkəbəl, əˈplɪkə-/. ADJ Something that is **applicable to** a particular situation is relevant to it. *...standards applicable to all police officers... One knows their name and also, where applicable, their professional post.*

applicant /ˈæplɪkənt/ **applicants.** N-COUNT An **applicant for** a job or position is someone who applies for it.

★ **application** /ˌæplɪˈkeɪʃən/ **applications.** [1] N-VAR An **application for** something such as a job or a place at a college is a formal written request to be given it. *His application for membership of the organisation was rejected... Tickets are available on application.* [2] N-VAR The **application** of a rule or piece of knowledge is the use of it in a particular situation. *...the practical application of the theory. ...artificial intelligence and its application to robotics.*

applied /əˈplaɪd/. ADJ An **applied** subject of study is practical rather than theoretical. *...applied research.*

★ **apply** /əˈplaɪ/ **applies, applying, applied.** [1] VERB If you **apply for** something or **to** do something, you write asking formally to be allowed to have it or do it. *I am continuing to apply for jobs... They may apply to join the organization.* [2] VERB If you **apply yourself to** something, you concentrate hard on it. *Faulks has applied himself to this task with considerable energy... They would have to apply their minds to many questions.* [3] VERB If something **applies to** a person or a situation, it is relevant to them. *The convention does not apply to us.* [4] VERB If you **apply** a rule or piece of knowledge, you use it in a situation or activity. *...applying the technology to practical business problems.* [5] VERB If you **apply** something **to** a surface, you put it onto the surface or rub it into it. [FORMAL] *Apply direct pressure to the wound... Applying the dye can be messy.*

★ **appoint** /əˈpɔɪnt/ **appoints, appointing, appointed.** VERB If you **appoint** someone to a job or post, you formally choose them for it. *The Prime Minister has appointed a civilian as defence minister.* ♦ **appointment** N-UNCOUNT ...*his appointment as foreign minister.*

appointed /ə'pɔɪntɪd/. ADJ BEFORE N If something happens at the **appointed** time, it happens at the time that was decided in advance. [FORMAL]

⭐ **appointment** /ə'pɔɪntmənt/ **appointments.** [1] N-COUNT An **appointment** is a job or position of responsibility. *Mr Fay is to take up an appointment as a researcher.* [2] N-VAR If you have an **appointment with** someone, you have arranged to see them at a particular time. If something can be done **by appointment**, you can make an appointment to do it. [3] See also **appoint**.

appraisal /ə'preɪzəl/ **appraisals.** N-VAR If you make an **appraisal of** something, you consider it carefully and form an opinion about it. ...*a calm appraisal of the situation.*

appraise /ə'preɪz/ **appraises, appraising, appraised.** VERB If you **appraise** something or someone, you consider them carefully and form an opinion about them. *I carefully appraised the situation.*

⭐ **appreciate** /ə'priːʃieɪt/ **appreciates, appreciating, appreciated.** [1] VERB If you **appreciate** something, you like it because you recognize its good qualities. *Anyone can appreciate our music.* ♦ **appreciation** N-UNCOUNT ...*children's understanding and appreciation of art.* [2] VERB If you **appreciate** a situation or problem, you understand it and know what it involves. *We appreciate how tough it is in business... You'll appreciate the reason for secrecy.* ♦ **appreciation** N-UNCOUNT *They lacked appreciation of social and political issues.* [3] VERB If you say that you **appreciate** something someone has done for you, you mean that you are grateful for it. *I'd appreciate it if you wouldn't mention it.* ♦ **appreciation** N-UNCOUNT ...*gifts presented to them in appreciation of their work.* [4] VERB If something **appreciates** over a period of time, its value increases. *Houses will always appreciate in value.* ♦ **appreciation** N-UNCOUNT ...*long-term price appreciation.*

appreciative /ə'priːʃətɪv/. ADJ If you are **appreciative**, you are grateful. *We have been very appreciative of their support.* ♦ **appreciatively** ADV *Michael smiled appreciatively.*

apprehension /ˌæprɪ'henʃən/ **apprehensions.** N-VAR **Apprehension** is a feeling of fear that something bad may happen. [FORMAL] ...*her apprehensions about the big risks she was taking.*

apprehensive /ˌæprɪ'hensɪv/. ADJ Someone who is **apprehensive** is afraid that something bad may happen.

apprentice /ə'prentɪs/ **apprentices.** N-COUNT An **apprentice** is a young person who works with someone in order to learn their skill.

apprenticeship /ə'prentɪsʃɪp/ **apprenticeships.** N-VAR Someone who has an **apprenticeship**

works for a fixed period of time for someone who teaches them a particular skill. **Apprenticeship** is the system of learning a skill like this. *He served an apprenticeship as an engineer.*

⭐ **approach** /ə'prəʊtʃ/ **approaches, approaching, approached.** [1] VERB & N-COUNT When someone **approaches**, they come nearer to you. You can also talk about their **approach**. *He didn't approach the front door at once. ...the approaching car... At their approach the little boy ran away.* [2] N-COUNT The **approach to** a place is the road or path that leads to it. *The path serves as an approach to the boat house.* [3] VERB & N-COUNT If you **approach** someone **about** something or if you make an **approach to** them, you speak to them because you want them to do something for you. *Chappel approached me about the job... Anna approached several builders.* [4] VERB & N-COUNT When you **approach** a situation in a particular way, you think about it or deal with it in that way. You can call this your **approach to** it. *The Bank has approached the issue in a practical way. ...different approaches to gathering information.* [5] VERB & N-SING As a future time or event **approaches**, or as you **approach** it, it gradually comes nearer. You can also talk about **the approach of** a future time or event. ...*the approaching crisis. ...the approach of crucial elections.* [6] VERB If something **approaches** a particular level or state, it almost reaches that level or state. ...*speeds approaching 200mph.*

⭐ **appropriate, appropriates, appropriating, appropriated.** [1] ADJ /ə'prəʊpriət/ Something that is **appropriate** is suitable or acceptable for a particular situation. ...*an outfit appropriate to the job... The teacher can then take appropriate action... It is appropriate that the exhibition should be sponsored by BMW.* ♦ **appropriately** ADV *Dress appropriately.* [2] VERB /ə'prəʊprieɪt/ If you **appropriate** something which does not belong to you, you take it for yourself. [FORMAL] *Several other newspapers have appropriated the idea.* ♦ **appropriation** N-UNCOUNT ...*illegal appropriation of land.*

⭐ **approval** /ə'pruːvəl/. [1] N-UNCOUNT If a plan or request gets someone's **approval**, they agree to it. *He gave his personal approval to the security arrangements. ...the royal seal of approval.* [2] N-UNCOUNT If someone has your **approval**, you like and admire them.

⭐ **approve** /ə'pruːv/ **approves, approving, approved.** [1] VERB If you **approve of** something or someone, you like them or think they are good. *Not everyone approves of the festival... You don't approve, do you?* [2] VERB If someone in authority **approves** a plan or idea, they formally agree to it.

approved /ə'pruːvd/. ADJ An **approved** method or person is generally or officially recommended or acceptable for a particular job. ...*tuition from an approved driving instructor.*

approving /əpr'uːvɪŋ/. ADJ An **approving** reaction shows support for something, or

a
b
c
d
e
f
g
h
i
j
k
l
m
n
o
p
q
r
s
t
u
v
w
x
y
z

satisfaction with it. ♦ **approvingly** ADV *He nodded approvingly.*

approximate, **approximates**, **approximating**, **approximated.** [1] ADJ /ə'prɒksɪmət/ **Approximate** quantities are close to the correct quantity, but are not exact. *The times are approximate only... Could you tell me its approximate age?* ♦ **approximately** ADV *The conservatory measures approximately 13ft x 16ft.* [2] VERB /ə'prɒksɪmeɪt/ If something **approximates to** something else, it is similar to it but not exactly the same. *Something approximating to a just outcome will be ensured.*

approximation /ə,prɒksɪ'meɪʃən/ **approximations.** N-COUNT An **approximation** is a fact, description, or calculation that is not exact. *This story is probably a good approximation to the truth.*

apricot /'eɪprɪkɒt/ **apricots.** N-COUNT An **apricot** is a small, soft, round fruit with yellow-orange flesh and a stone inside.

⭐ **April** /'eɪprɪl/. N-UNCOUNT **April** is the fourth month of the year. → See Reference Page on Times and Dates.

apron /'eɪprən/ **aprons.** N-COUNT An **apron** is a piece of clothing that you put on over the front of your clothes to prevent them from getting dirty.

apt /æpt/. [1] ADJ If someone is **apt** to behave in a particular way, they often behave in that way. *She was apt to raise her voice.* [2] ADJ **Apt** means suitable. ♦ **aptly** ADV *...the beach in the aptly named town of Oceanside.*

aptitude /'æptɪtjuːd, AM -tuːd/ **aptitudes.** N-VAR If you have an **aptitude for** something, you are able to learn it quickly and do it well. *Alan has no aptitude for music.*

aquatic /ə'kwætɪk/. ADJ **Aquatic** means existing or happening in water. *...aquatic plants.*

arable /'ærəbəl/. ADJ **Arable** farming involves growing crops rather than keeping animals. **Arable** land is land that is used for arable farming.

arbitrary /'ɑːbɪtri, AM -treri/. ADJ An **arbitrary** decision or action is not based on any principle or plan, and therefore may seem unfair. *...arbitrary arrests and detention without trial.* ♦ **arbitrarily** ADV *Prisoners-of-war are being arbitrarily killed.*

arbitrate /'ɑːbɪtreɪt/ **arbitrates, arbitrating, arbitrated.** VERB When someone **arbitrates** between two people who are in dispute, they consider all the facts and decide who is right. *The tribunal had been set up to arbitrate in the dispute.* ♦ **arbitration** N-UNCOUNT *Both sides hope to settle through arbitration.*

arc /ɑːk/ **arcs.** N-COUNT An **arc** is a smoothly curving line or movement.

arcade /ɑː'keɪd/ **arcades.** N-COUNT An **arcade** is a covered passageway where there are shops. *...a shopping arcade.*

arch /ɑːtʃ/ **arches, arching, arched.** [1] N-COUNT An **arch** is a structure which is made when two columns join at the top in a curve. *...railway arches.* [2] VERB If something **arches** or if you **arch** it, it forms a curved shape or line. *Don't arch your back.*

archaeology (or **archeology**) /,ɑːki'ɒlədʒi/. N-UNCOUNT **Archaeology** is the study of the past by examining the remains of things such as buildings and tools. ♦ **archaeological** /,ɑːkiə'lɒdʒɪkəl/ ADJ BEFORE N *...archaeological sites.* ♦ **archaeologist, archaeologists** N-COUNT *...archaeologists uncovering Mayan treasures.*

archaic /ɑː'keɪɪk/. ADJ **Archaic** means very old or very old-fashioned. *The existing law is archaic.*

archbishop /,ɑːtʃ'bɪʃəp/ **archbishops.** N-COUNT In the Roman Catholic church, and in some other churches, an **archbishop** is a bishop of the highest rank.

arched /ɑːtʃt/. See **arch.**

archeology /,ɑːki'ɒlədʒi/. See **archaeology.**

archetype /'ɑːkɪtaɪp/ **archetypes.** N-COUNT The **archetype** of a particular kind of person or thing is a perfect or typical example of it. ♦ **archetypal** ADJ *Cricket is the archetypal English game.*

architect /'ɑːkɪtekt/ **architects.** [1] N-COUNT An **architect** is a person who designs buildings. [2] N-COUNT The **architect of** an idea or event is the person who invented it or made it happen. *...the architect of Russia's economic reforms.*

architecture /'ɑːkɪtektʃə/. [1] N-UNCOUNT **Architecture** is the art of designing and constructing buildings. ♦ **architectural** /,ɑːkɪ'tektʃərəl/ ADJ *...architectural drawings.* ♦ **architecturally** ADV *...sites which are architecturally interesting.* [2] N-UNCOUNT The **architecture** of a building is the style in which it is constructed. *...a fine example of Moroccan architecture.*

archive /'ɑːkaɪv/ **archives.** N-COUNT **Archives** are collections of documents that contain information about the history of an organization or group of people. *...Soviet military archives.*

ardent /'ɑːdənt/. ADJ Someone who is **ardent** about something is very enthusiastic or passionate about it. *...ardent fans.* ♦ **ardently** ADV *Its electorate supports abortion rights.*

arduous /'ɑːdʒʊəs/. ADJ Something that is **arduous** is difficult and involves a lot of physical effort. *...a long, arduous journey.*

are /ə, STRONG ɑː/. **Are** is the plural and the second person singular of the present tense of **be. Are** is often abbreviated to **'re** after pronouns.

⭐ **area** /'eəriə/ **areas.** [1] N-COUNT An **area** is a particular part of a city, a country, or the world. *Half the French population still lived in rural areas.* [2] N-COUNT A particular **area** of a room or other place is a part that is used for a particular activity. *...Gatwick airport's luggage area.* [3] N-COUNT The **area** of a shape or piece of land is the amount that it covers, expressed as a measurement. *The islands cover a total area of 625.6 square kilometers.* [4] N-COUNT You can use **area** to refer to a particular subject or to a particular part of a general situation or activity. *...awards to the best writers in every area of the arts.*

arena /əˈriːnə/ **arenas.** [1] N-COUNT An **arena** is a place where public events such as concerts take place. *...a spectacular sports arena.* [2] N-COUNT You can refer to a particular field of activity, especially one where there is a lot of conflict, as an **arena**. *He entered the political arena in 1987.*

aren't /ɑːnt, AM ˈɑːrənt/. [1] **Aren't** is the usual spoken form of 'are not'. [2] **Aren't** is used instead of 'am not' in negative questions.

arguably /ˈɑːɡjʊəbli/. ADV You can use **arguably** when you are stating your opinion or belief, as a way of giving more authority to it. *We now have arguably the best bookshops in the world.*

★ **argue** /ˈɑːɡjuː/ **argues, arguing, argued.** [1] VERB If you **argue with** someone, you disagree with them about something, often angrily. *...arguing with patients about smoking... They argued about the cost of a taxi.* [2] VERB If you **argue** that something is true, you give the reasons why you think it is true. If you **argue for** or **against** an idea or policy, you state the reasons why you support or oppose it. *His lawyers are arguing that he is unfit to stand trial... The report argues against tax increases.*

★ **argument** /ˈɑːɡjʊmənt/ **arguments.** [1] N-COUNT If people have an **argument**, they disagree with each other, often angrily. *She got into an argument with one of the marchers.* [2] N-VAR An **argument** is a set of statements that you use to try to convince people that your opinion is correct. *There's a strong argument for lowering the price.*

arid /ˈærɪd/. ADJ **Arid** land is so dry that very few plants can grow on it.

★ **arise** /əˈraɪz/ **arises, arising, arose** /əˈrəʊz/, **arisen** /əˈrɪzən/. [1] VERB If a situation or problem **arises**, it begins to exist or people start to become aware of it. *Language problems arose when their families moved from England.* [2] VERB If something **arises from** a particular situation, or **arises out of** it, it is created or caused by the situation. *...claims for damages arising from the Piper Alpha disaster... The charges arise out of a fraud enquiry.*

aristocracy /ˌærɪˈstɒkrəsi/ **aristocracies.** N-COUNT The **aristocracy** is a class of people in some countries who have a high social rank and special titles.

aristocrat /ˈærɪstəkræt, əˈrɪst-/ **aristocrats.** N-COUNT An **aristocrat** is someone whose family has a high social rank, especially someone with a title. ♦ **aristocratic** ADJ *...aristocratic values.*

arithmetic /əˈrɪθmɪtɪk/. N-UNCOUNT **Arithmetic** is the part of mathematics that deals with adding, subtracting, multiplying, and dividing numbers.

★ **arm** /ɑːm/ **arms.** [1] N-COUNT Your **arms** are the parts of your body between your hands and your shoulders. → See picture on page 822. [2] N-COUNT The **arm** of a piece of clothing is the part of it that covers your arm. [3] N-COUNT The **arm** of a chair is the part on which you rest your arm. [4] N-PLURAL **Arms** are weapons, especially bombs and guns. *...nuclear arms reductions.* [5] VERB To **arm** someone with a weapon means to provide them with it. *She had armed herself with a loaded rifle... Governments have been reluctant to arm all police officers.* [6] PHRASE If something gives you **a shot in the arm**, it gives you help and encouragement when you need it very much.

armaments /ˈɑːməmənts/. N-PLURAL A particular country's **armaments** are its weapons and military equipment.

armchair /ˈɑːmtʃeə/ **armchairs.** N-COUNT An **armchair** is a comfortable chair with a support on each side for your arms.

★ **armed** /ɑːmd/. ADJ Someone who is **armed** is carrying a weapon. You can also use **armed** to describe crimes or conflicts involving weapons. *He may be armed. ...armed robbery.*

★ **armed 'forces.** N-PLURAL The **armed forces** or the **armed services** of a country are its army, navy, and air force.

armour (AM **armor**) /ˈɑːmə/. [1] N-UNCOUNT **Armour** is a metal covering that protects a military vehicle against attack. *...a warhead that can penetrate the armour of most tanks.* [2] N-UNCOUNT In former times, **armour** was the protective metal clothing worn by soldiers.

armoured (AM **armored**) /ˈɑːməd/. ADJ An **armoured** vehicle has a metal covering that protects it from gunfire and other missiles.

armoury (AM **armory**) /ˈɑːməri/ **armouries.** [1] N-COUNT An **armoury** is a place where weapons, bombs, and other military equipment are stored. You can also refer to all a country's weapons and military equipment as its **armoury**. [2] N-COUNT You can refer to a large number of things which someone can use to achieve a particular goal as their **armoury**. *...a large armoury of drugs for the treatment of mental illness.*

armpit /ˈɑːmpɪt/ **armpits.** N-COUNT Your **armpits** are the areas of your body under your arms where your arms join your shoulders. → See picture on page 822.

★ **army** /ˈɑːmi/ **armies.** [1] N-COUNT An **army** is a large organized group of people who are armed and trained to fight. [2] N-COUNT An **army of** people, animals, or things is a large number of them together. *...an army of volunteers.*

aroma /əˈrəʊmə/ **aromas.** N-COUNT An **aroma** is a strong pleasant smell. *...the wonderful aroma of freshly baked bread.*

aromatic /ˌærəˈmætɪk/. ADJ **Aromatic** plants, food, or oil has a strong pleasant smell.

arose /əˈrəʊz/. **Arose** is the past tense of **arise**.

around /ə'raʊnd/. **1** **Around** means the same as the preposition and adverb uses of **round**. **2** ADV & PREP If someone or something is **around**, they are near, present, or available. *The idea has been around for ages without catching on... Most people around here no longer care.* **3** ADV **Around** means approximately. *My salary was around £19,000... He expects the elections to be held around November.*

> **USAGE Around** and **round** are used in various ways as prepositions and adverbs, often as part of phrasal verbs. In most cases, you can use either word without any difference of meaning. In American English, **around** is much more common than **round**.
> When you are talking about movement in no particular direction, you can use **about** as well as **around** and **round**. *It's so romantic up there, flying around in a small plane... I spent a couple of hours driving round Richmond... Police constables walk about with guns on their hips.*
> When you are talking about something being generally present or available, you can use **around** or **about**, but not **round**, as adverbs. *There is a lot of talent around at the moment... There's not that many jobs about.*
> **Round** has a lot of other meanings, as a noun, verb, and adjective. You cannot use **around** in these cases.

arousal /ə'raʊzəl/. N-UNCOUNT If you are in a state of **arousal**, you are excited or alert.

arouse /ə'raʊz/ **arouses, arousing, aroused.** **1** VERB If something **arouses** a particular reaction or feeling in you, it causes you to have that reaction or feeling. *She had a knack of arousing strong emotions.* **2** ADJ To **arouse** someone means to make them feel sexually excited.

⭐ **arrange** /ə'reɪndʒ/ **arranges, arranging, arranged.** **1** VERB If you **arrange** something such as an event or meeting, you make the plans and preparations that are necessary for it to happen. *We arranged a social event once a year... I've arranged to see him on Friday morning... I will arrange for someone to take you.* **2** VERB If you **arrange** objects, you place them in a particular position. *She enjoys arranging dried flowers.*

⭐ **arrangement** /ə'reɪndʒmənt/ **arrangements.** **1** N-PLURAL **Arrangements** are plans and preparations which you make so that something can happen. *I must make all the arrangements for the burial.* **2** N-COUNT An **arrangement** of things is a group of them displayed in a particular way. *...imaginative flower arrangements.*

array /ə'reɪ/. N-COUNT An **array of** different things is a large number of them. *She experienced a bewildering array of emotions.*

arrears /ə'rɪəz/. N-PLURAL **Arrears** are amounts of money that someone owes. If someone is **in arrears with** regular payments, they have not paid them. *The arrears have been mounting in recent months.*

⭐ **arrest** /ə'rest/ **arrests, arresting, arrested.** VERB & N-VAR When the police **arrest** someone or make an **arrest**, they take them to a police station in order to decide whether they should be charged with an offence. *Police arrested five young men in connection with the attacks... Detectives placed him under arrest.*

⭐ **arrival** /ə'raɪvəl/ **arrivals.** **1** N-VAR Your **arrival** at a place is the act of arriving there. **2** N-SING If you talk about **the arrival of** something new, you are referring to the fact that it has begun to exist or become available. *...the arrival of modern technologies.* **3** N-COUNT An **arrival** is someone who has just arrived at a place. *Each day there are new arrivals in the camp.*

⭐ **arrive** /ə'raɪv/ **arrives, arriving, arrived.** **1** VERB When you **arrive** at a place, you reach it at the end of a journey. *Fresh groups of guests arrived... I've just arrived from England.* **2** VERB When something **arrives**, it is brought to you or it becomes available to you. *Your letter arrived yesterday.* **3** VERB When you **arrive at** an idea, decision, or conclusion, you reach it or decide on it. *The jury cannot arrive at a unanimous decision.*

arrogant /'ærəgənt/. ADJ If you say that someone is **arrogant**, you disapprove of them because they behave as if they are better than other people. ♦ **arrogance** N-UNCOUNT *The arrogance of those in power is quite blatant.* ♦ **arrogantly** ADV *The doctor arrogantly dismissed their cry for help.*

arrow /'ærəʊ/ **arrows.** **1** N-COUNT An **arrow** is a long, thin weapon with a sharp point at one end which is shot from a bow. → See picture on page 75. **2** N-COUNT An **arrow** is a written sign which points in a particular direction to indicate where something is.

arsenal /'ɑːsənəl/ **arsenals.** N-COUNT An **arsenal** is a large collection of weapons and military equipment. *...reductions in Britain's nuclear arsenal.*

arson /'ɑːsən/. N-UNCOUNT **Arson** is the crime of deliberately setting fire to a building or vehicle.

⭐ **art** /ɑːt/ **arts.** **1** N-UNCOUNT **Art** is paintings, drawings, and sculpture which are beautiful or which express an artist's ideas. **Art** is also the activity of creating these things. *...contemporary American art. ...an art class for children.* **2** N-VAR The **arts** are activities such as music, painting, literature, cinema, and dance. *...people working in the arts. ...the art of cinema.* **3** N-PLURAL At a university or college, **arts** are subjects such as history or languages in contrast to scientific subjects. *...arts and social science graduates.* **4** N-COUNT If you describe an activity as an **art**, you mean that it requires a lot of skill. *...the art of* *acting.* **5** See also **fine art, martial art, state-of-the-art, work of art.**

artefact (AM **artifact**) /ˈɑːtɪfækt/ **artefacts.**
N-COUNT An **artefact** is an ornament, tool, or other object made by a human being, especially one that has archaeological or cultural interest.

artery /ˈɑːtəri/ **arteries.** N-COUNT Your **arteries** are the tubes that carry blood from your heart to the rest of your body.

arthritis /ɑːˈθraɪtɪs/. N-UNCOUNT **Arthritis** is a condition in which the joints in someone's body are swollen and painful. ♦ **arthritic** /ɑːˈθrɪtɪk/ ADJ ...*arthritic hands.*

artichoke /ˈɑːtɪtʃəʊk/ **artichokes.** **1** N-VAR An **artichoke** or a **globe artichoke** is a round vegetable with thick green leaves arranged like the petals of a flower. **2** N-VAR An **artichoke** or a **Jerusalem artichoke** is a small, yellow-white vegetable similar to a potato.

★ **article** /ˈɑːtɪkəl/ **articles.** **1** N-COUNT An **article** is a piece of writing in a newspaper or magazine. **2** N-COUNT You can refer to objects as **articles of** some kind. [FORMAL] ...*articles of clothing.* **3** N-COUNT An **article of** a formal document is a section dealing with a particular point. ...*Article 50 of the UN charter.* **4** See also **definite article, indefinite article.**

articulate, articulates, articulating, articulated. **1** ADJ /ɑːˈtɪkjʊlət/ If you are **articulate**, you are able to express yourself well. ...*an articulate description.* **2** VERB /ɑːˈtɪkjʊleɪt/ When you **articulate** your ideas or feelings, you express them clearly in words. [FORMAL] *Encourage her to articulate her views.*

articulated /ɑːˈtɪkjʊleɪtɪd/. ADJ An **articulated** vehicle, especially a lorry, is made in two sections with a moving joint between them. [BRITISH]

artifact /ˈɑːtɪfækt/. See **artefact.**

artificial /ˌɑːtɪˈfɪʃəl/. **1** ADJ **Artificial** objects, materials, or situations do not occur naturally and are created by people. ...*artificial limbs.* ...*the artificial environment of an office.* ♦ **artificially** ADV ...*artificially sweetened lemonade.* ...*artificially high prices.* **2** ADJ If you describe someone's behaviour as **artificial**, you disapprove of them because they are pretending to have attitudes and feelings which they do not really have. ...*a fixed, artificial smile.*

artificial in'telligence. N-UNCOUNT **Artificial intelligence** is a type of computer technology concerned with making machines work in a similar way to the human mind. [COMPUTING]

artillery /ɑːˈtɪləri/. N-UNCOUNT & N-SING **Artillery** consists of large, powerful guns which are transported on wheels. **The artillery** is the section of the army which uses these guns.

★ **artist** /ˈɑːtɪst/ **artists.** **1** N-COUNT An **artist** is someone who draws, paints, or produces other works of art. **2** N-COUNT You can refer to a musician, actor, dancer, or other performer as an **artist.** ...*a popular artist who has sold millions of records.*

artistic /ɑːˈtɪstɪk/. **1** ADJ Someone who is **artistic** is good at drawing or painting, or arranging things in a beautiful way. *They encourage boys to be sensitive and artistic.* **2** ADJ **Artistic** means relating to art or artists. ...*the campaign for artistic freedom.* ♦ **artistically** ADV ...*artistically gifted children.*

artistry /ˈɑːtɪstri/. N-UNCOUNT **Artistry** is great skill. ...*his artistry as a cellist.*

★ **as** /əz, STRONG æz/. **1** CONJ If something happens **as** something else happens, it happens at the same time. *We shut the door behind us as we entered.* **2** PREP You use **as** when you are referring to the appearance or function of something. *I only told them that as a joke... He has worked as a diplomat.* **3** CONJ You use **as** when you are saying how something is done. *I'll behave toward them as I would like to be treated.* **4** PREP You use the structure **as...as** when you are comparing things, or emphasizing how large or small something is. *This was not as easy as we imagined. ...as many as eight thousand letters.* **5** CONJ You can use **as** to mean 'because'. *This is important as it sets the mood for the rest of the day.* **6** PREP You use **as** in expressions like **as a result** and **as a consequence** to indicate how two situations or events are related to each other. *Large shoals of fish are dying as a result of pollution in the oceans.* **7** CONJ You use **as if** and **as though** when you are comparing one situation to another. *He burst into a high-pitched laugh, as though he'd said something funny.* **8** PREP You use **as for** and **as to** to introduce a slightly different subject. *I feel that there's a lot of pressure put on policemen. And as for putting guns in their hands, I don't think that's a very good idea at all.* **9** PREP You use **as to** to indicate what something refers to. *They should make decisions as to whether the student needs more help.* **10** PREP If you say that something will happen **as of** or **as from** a particular date or time, you mean that it will happen from that time onwards. *She is to retire as from 1 October.*

asbestos /ˌæsˈbestɒs/. N-UNCOUNT **Asbestos** is a grey material which does not burn.

ascend /əˈsend/ **ascends, ascending, ascended.** **1** VERB If you **ascend** a hill or a staircase, you go up it. [WRITTEN] *Mrs Clayton had to hold Lizzie's hand as they ascended the steps... Then we ascend steeply through forests of rhododendron.* **2** VERB If something **ascends**, it leads or goes upwards. [WRITTEN] *They ascended 55,900 feet in their balloon... A number of staircases ascend from the cobbled streets.*

ascending /əˈsendɪŋ/. ADJ BEFORE N If a group of things is arranged in **ascending** order, each thing is greater in size, amount, or importance than the thing before it. *The batteries were lettered in ascending order of size.*

ascent /əˈsent/ **ascents.** N-COUNT An **ascent** is a steep upward slope, or a journey up a steep slope. ...*the first ascent of the world's highest peak.*

a
b
c
d
e
f
g
h
i
j
k
l
m
n
o
p
q
r
s
t
u
v
w
x
y
z

ascertain /ˌæsə'teɪn/ **ascertains, ascertaining, ascertained.** VERB If you **ascertain** the truth about something, you find out what it is. [FORMAL] *They had ascertained that he was not a spy... They were unable to ascertain the extent of the damage.*

ascribe /ə'skraɪb/ **ascribes, ascribing, ascribed.** VERB If you **ascribe** something **to** a person, thing, or event, you believe that they cause it or have it. [FORMAL] *They ascribe every setback to some kind of conspiracy. ...mystical characteristics which are sometimes ascribed to cats.*

ash /æʃ/ **ashes.** ① N-UNCOUNT & N-PLURAL **Ash** or **ashes** is the grey powder-like substance that is left after something is burnt. *He ordered their villages burned to ashes.* ② N-VAR An **ash** is a kind of tree. **Ash** is the wood of this tree.

ashamed /ə'ʃeɪmd/. ADJ AFTER LINK-V If someone is **ashamed** of something or someone, they feel embarrassed about it or guilty because of it. *I felt incredibly ashamed of myself for getting so angry... She was ashamed that she looked so shabby... Women are often ashamed to admit they are being abused.*

ashore /ə'ʃɔː/. ADV Something that comes **ashore** comes from the sea onto the shore. *Oil from the tanker has come ashore at two beaches in Devon.*

ashtray /'æʃtreɪ/ **ashtrays.** N-COUNT An **ashtray** is a small dish in which people put the ash from their cigarettes and cigars.

⭐ **Asian** /'eɪʃən, 'eɪʒən/ **Asians.** ① ADJ **Asian** means belonging or relating to Asia. *...Asian music.* ② N-COUNT An **Asian** is a person who comes from India, Pakistan, or some other part of Asia.

⭐ **aside** /ə'saɪd/. ① ADV If you move something **aside**, you move it to one side of you. If you move **aside**, you move to one side. *Sarah closed the book and laid it aside... He stood aside and allowed Hillsden to enter.* ② ADV If you take someone **aside**, you take them away from a group of people in order to talk to them in private. *An officer took us aside and told us everyone was okay.* ③ PREP **Aside from** means the same as **apart from**. [AMERICAN] *Does he look O.K., aside from his clothes?*

⭐ **ask** /ɑːsk, æsk/ **asks, asking, asked.** ① VERB If you **ask** someone something, you say something in the form of a question because you want some information. *'How is Frank?' he asked... I asked him his name... I wasn't the only one asking questions... She asked me if I'd enjoyed my dinner.* ② VERB If you **ask** someone **to** do something, you tell them that you want them to do it. If you **ask to** do something, you tell someone that you want to do it. *We had to ask him to leave... I asked to see the Director.* ③ VERB If you **ask for** something, you say that you would like it. If you **ask for** someone, you say that you want to see them or speak to them. *I decided to go to the next house and ask for food... There's a man at the gate asking for you.* ④ VERB If you **ask** someone's permission or forgiveness, you try to obtain it. *He asked*

permission to leave. ⑤ VERB If you **ask** someone somewhere, you invite them there. *Couldn't you ask Jon to the party?* ⑥ PHRASE You can say **'if you ask me'** to emphasize that you are stating your personal opinion. *He was too sarcastic for his own good, if you ask me.*

asleep /ə'sliːp/. ADJ AFTER LINK-V Someone who is **asleep** is sleeping. *He was asleep on Mum's bed.* PHRASES ● When you **fall asleep**, you start sleeping. *I was so tired I fell asleep.* ● Someone who is **fast asleep** or **sound asleep** is sleeping deeply.

asparagus /ə'spærəgəs/. N-UNCOUNT **Asparagus** is a vegetable with green shoots that you cook and eat.

⭐ **aspect** /'æspekt/ **aspects.** ① N-COUNT An **aspect** of something is one of the parts of its character or nature. *Climate and weather affect every aspect of our lives.* ② N-COUNT A room or a window with a particular **aspect** faces in that direction. [FORMAL] *The house had a south-west aspect.*

aspiration /ˌæspɪ'reɪʃən/ **aspirations.** N-VAR Someone's **aspirations** are their ambitions to achieve something. *The girl had aspirations to a movie career.*

aspire /ə'spaɪə/ **aspires, aspiring, aspired.** VERB If you **aspire to** something such as an important job, you have a strong desire to have it. *He aspired to a career in diplomacy.*

aspirin /'æspɪrɪn/ **aspirins.** N-VAR **Aspirin** is a mild drug which reduces pain and fever.

aspiring /ə'spaɪərɪŋ/. ADJ BEFORE N **Aspiring** describes someone who is trying to become successful in a particular career. *...aspiring young artists.*

ass /æs/ **asses.** ① N-COUNT An **ass** is the same as a **donkey**. [DATED] ② N-COUNT If you call someone an **ass**, you mean that they are behaving in a silly way. [INFORMAL]

assailant /ə'seɪlənt/ **assailants.** N-COUNT Someone's **assailant** is a person who has physically attacked them. [FORMAL]

assassin /ə'sæsɪn/ **assassins.** N-COUNT An **assassin** is a person who assassinates someone.

assassinate /ə'sæsɪneɪt/ **assassinates, assassinating, assassinated.** VERB If someone important **is assassinated**, they are murdered as a political act. *Robert Kennedy was assassinated in 1968.* ♦ **assassination, assassinations** N-VAR *...an assassination plot.* ● See note at **kill**.

⭐ **assault** /ə'sɔːlt/ **assaults, assaulting, assaulted.** ① VERB & N-VAR To **assault** someone means to attack them physically. An **assault on** a person is a physical attack on them. *The gang assaulted him with iron bars. ...a series of savage sexual assaults on women.* ② N-COUNT An **assault on** someone is a strong criticism of them. *...a fierce personal assault on John Major.* ③ N-COUNT An **assault** by an army is a strong attack made against an enemy.

assemble /ə'sembəl/ **assembles, assembling, assembled.** ① VERB When people **assemble**, or when someone **assembles** them, they come together in a group. ...*a convenient place for students to assemble between classes.* [2] VERB To **assemble** something means to fit the different parts of it together. *Workers were assembling planes.*

⭐ **assembly** /ə'sembli/ **assemblies.** [1] N-COUNT An **assembly** is a group of people gathered together for a particular purpose. ...*an assembly of party members from the Russian republic.* [2] N-VAR The **assembly** of a machine or device is the process of fitting its parts together.

as'sembly line, assembly lines. N-COUNT An **assembly line** is an arrangement of workers and machines in a factory where the product passes from one worker to another until it is finished.

assent /ə'sent/ **assents, assenting, assented.** [1] N-UNCOUNT If someone gives their **assent to** something, they formally agree to it. *He gave his assent to the proposed legislation.* [2] VERB To **assent to** something means to agree to it. [FORMAL] *They reluctantly assented to having their picture taken.*

assert /ə'sɜːt/ **asserts, asserting, asserted.** [1] VERB If you **assert** a fact or belief, you state it firmly. [FORMAL] *The company asserts that it won't be held responsible... He asserted his innocence.* ♦ **assertion, assertions** N-VAR *Police accepted his assertion that the men had threatened him.* [2] VERB If you **assert yourself** or **assert** your authority, you speak and act in a firm, forceful way. *He's speaking up and asserting himself.*

assertive /ə'sɜːtɪv/. ADJ Someone who is **assertive** speaks and acts in a firm, forceful way. *Assertive behaviour gets positive results.* ♦ **assertiveness** N-UNCOUNT ...*assertiveness training.*

⭐ **assess** /ə'ses/ **assesses, assessing, assessed.** VERB If you **assess** something or someone, you consider them carefully and make a judgement about their quality or value. *I looked around and assessed the situation; I was safe... You can ask the court to assess whether the bill is fair.* ♦ **assessment, assessments** N-VAR ...*the assessment of future senior managers.*

⭐ **asset** /'æset/ **assets.** [1] N-COUNT If something that you have is an **asset**, it is useful to you. *He's been a great asset to the company.* [2] N-PLURAL The **assets** of a company or a person are the things that they own.

assign /ə'saɪn/ **assigns, assigning, assigned.** [1] VERB If you **assign** a task or function **to** someone, you give it to them. *I would assign a topic to children which they would write about. ...when teachers assign homework.* [2] VERB If you **are assigned to** a place or group, you are sent to work in the place or with the group. *I was assigned to Troop A of the 10th Cavalry.*

assignment /ə'saɪnmənt/ **assignments.** N-VAR An **assignment** is a piece of work that you are given to do, as part of your job or studies. ...*written*

assignments and practical tests. ...a photographer on assignment for Life magazine.

assimilate /ə'sɪmɪleɪt/ **assimilates, assimilating, assimilated.** [1] VERB When immigrants **are assimilated into** a community, or when that community **assimilates** them, they become an accepted part of it. *His family tried to assimilate into the white and Hispanic communities... The Vietnamese are trying to assimilate themselves.* ♦ **assimilation** N-UNCOUNT ...*assimilation of minority ethnic groups.* [2] VERB If you **assimilate** new ideas, customs, or methods, you learn them and make use of them. ...*someone who assimilates facts well.* ♦ **assimilation** N-UNCOUNT ...*assimilation of knowledge.*

⭐ **assist** /ə'sɪst/ **assists, assisting, assisted.** VERB If someone or something **assists** you, they help you. [FORMAL] *The family decided to assist me with my chores. ...information to assist you in making the best selection.*

⭐ **assistance** /ə'sɪstəns/. N-UNCOUNT If you give someone **assistance**, you help them. Someone or something that is **of assistance** is helpful or useful. [FORMAL] *I would be grateful for any assistance.*

⭐ **assistant** /ə'sɪstənt/ **assistants.** [1] ADJ BEFORE N **Assistant** is used in front of titles or jobs to indicate a slightly lower rank. ...*the assistant secretary of defense.* [2] N-COUNT Someone's **assistant** is a person who helps them in their work. ...*a research assistant.* [3] N-COUNT An **assistant** is a person who sells things in a shop. ...*a sales assistant.*

⭐ **associate, associates, associating, associated.** [1] VERB /ə'səʊsieɪt/ If you **associate** one thing **with** another, the two are connected or you think of them as connected. *I associate her with feelings of well-being... Poverty is associated with old age.* [2] VERB If you **are associated with** an organization, cause, or point of view, you support it publicly. *I have no wish to associate myself with stupidity.* [3] VERB If you **associate with** a person or group of people, you spend a lot of time with them. *I began associating with different crowds of people.* [4] N-COUNT /ə'səʊsiət/ Your **associates** are your business colleagues.

⭐ **association** /ə,səʊsi'eɪʃən/ **associations.** [1] N-COUNT An **association** is an official group of people who have the same occupation, aim, or interest. ...*the British Astronomical Association.* [2] N-UNCOUNT Your **association with** a person, group, or organization is the connection that you have with them. If someone does something **in association with** someone else, they do it together. ...*his recently published biography written in association with Tony Cosier.* [3] N-COUNT If something has particular **associations** for you, it is connected in your mind with a particular memory or feeling. ...*a flood of unhappy associations.*

assorted /ə'sɔːtɪd/. ADJ A group of **assorted** things of a particular kind have different sizes, colours, or qualities. ...*paper in assorted sizes.*

a
b
c
d
e
f
g
h
i
j
k
l
m
n
o
p
q
r
s
t
u
v
w
x
y
z

A
B
C
D
E
F
G
H
I
J
K
L
M
N
O
P
Q
R
S
T
U
V
W
X
Y
Z

assortment /əˈsɔːtmənt/ **assortments.** N-COUNT An **assortment** is a group of similar things that have different sizes, colours, or qualities.

★ **assume** /əˈsjuːm, AM əˈsuːm/ **assumes, assuming, assumed.** [1] VERB If you **assume** that something is true, you suppose that it is true, sometimes wrongly. *I can safely assume the eggs will be fresh... Mistakes were assumed to be the fault of the commander.* [2] VERB If someone **assumes** power or responsibility, they take power or responsibility. *It is usually the woman who assumes overall care of the baby.* [3] VERB If you **assume** a particular expression, quality, or way of behaving, you start to look or behave in this way. *His face assumed a weary expression.*

assuming /əˈsjuːmɪŋ, AM -ˈsuːm-/ CONJ You use **assuming** or **assuming that** when you are supposing that something is true, so that you can think about what the consequences would be. *Assuming he's still alive, what is he doing now?*

★ **assumption** /əˈsʌmpʃən/ **assumptions.** N-COUNT If you make an **assumption**, you suppose that something is true, sometimes wrongly. *...their assumption that all men and women think alike.*

assurance /əˈʃʊərəns/ **assurances.** [1] N-VAR If you give someone an **assurance** about something, you say that it is the case, in order to make them less worried. *He gave written assurance that he would start work at once.* [2] N-UNCOUNT If you do something **with assurance**, you do it with confidence and certainty. *Masur led the orchestra with assurance.*

assure /əˈʃʊə/ **assures, assuring, assured.** [1] VERB If you **assure** someone that something is true or will happen, you tell them that it is the case, to make them less worried. *I can assure you that the animals are well cared for.* [2] VERB To **assure** someone **of** something means to make certain that they will get it. *The series is assured of success.*

★ **assured** /əˈʃʊəd/ ADJ Someone who is **assured** is very confident and relaxed. *It was an assured performance.*

asterisk /ˈæstərɪsk/ **asterisks.** N-COUNT An **asterisk** is the symbol ∗.

asthma /ˈæsmə, AM ˈæz-/ N-UNCOUNT **Asthma** is an illness which affects the chest and makes breathing difficult.

asthmatic /æsˈmætɪk, AM æz-/ N-COUNT & ADJ An **asthmatic** or someone who is **asthmatic** suffers from asthma.

astonish /əˈstɒnɪʃ/ **astonishes, astonishing, astonished.** VERB If someone or something **astonishes** you, they surprise you very much. ◆ **astonished** ADJ *I was shocked and astonished by his stupidity.*

astonishing /əˈstɒnɪʃɪŋ/ ADJ Something that is **astonishing** is very surprising. ◆ **astonishingly** ADV *...an astonishingly beautiful young woman.*

astonishment /əˈstɒnɪʃmənt/ N-UNCOUNT

Astonishment is a feeling of great surprise. *She looked at her husband in astonishment.*

astound /əˈstaʊnd/ **astounds, astounding, astounded.** VERB If something **astounds** you, you are amazed by it. ◆ **astounding** ADJ *...an astounding discovery.*

astray /əˈstreɪ/ PHRASES ● If you **are led astray** by someone or something, they make you behave badly or foolishly. *He was led astray by this older woman.* ● If something **goes astray**, it gets lost. *Many items of mail being sent to her have gone astray.*

astride /əˈstraɪd/ PREP If you sit or stand **astride** something, you sit or stand with one leg on each side of it. *...three youths who stood astride their bicycles.*

astrology /əˈstrɒlədʒi/ N-UNCOUNT **Astrology** is the study of the movements of the planets, sun, moon, and stars in the belief that they can influence people's lives. ◆ **astrologer,** astrologers N-COUNT *He consulted an astrologer.*

astronaut /ˈæstrənɔːt/ **astronauts.** N-COUNT An **astronaut** is a person who travels in a spacecraft.

astronomical /ˌæstrəˈnɒmɪkəl/ ADJ If you describe an amount as **astronomical**, you are emphasizing that it is very large. *The cost will be astronomical.*

astronomy /əˈstrɒnəmi/ N-UNCOUNT **Astronomy** is the scientific study of the stars, planets, and other natural objects in space. ◆ **astronomer,** astronomers N-COUNT *...an amateur astronomer.*

astute /əˈstjuːt, AM əˈstuːt/ ADJ Someone who is **astute** is clever and skilful at understanding behaviour and situations. *She was politically astute. ...astute business decisions.*

asylum /əˈsaɪləm/ **asylums.** [1] N-COUNT An **asylum** is a mental hospital. [2] N-UNCOUNT **Asylum** is protection given to foreigners who have left their own country for political reasons. *He applied for asylum in 1987.*

★ **at** /ət, STRONG æt/. [1] PREP You use **at** to say where something happens or is situated. *We had dinner at a restaurant. ...muscles at the back of the thigh... Graham was already at the door... I majored in psychology at Hunter College.* [2] PREP If you look **at** something or someone, you look towards them. If you direct something **at** someone, you direct it towards them. *He looked at Michael and laughed... They threw petrol bombs at the police.* [3] PREP You use **at** to say when something happens. → See Reference Page on Times and Dates. *We closed our offices at 2:00 p.m... He only sees her at Christmas.* [4] PREP You use **at** to express a rate, frequency, level, or price. *I drove back down the highway at normal speed... Oil prices were closing at $19.76 a barrel.* [5] PREP If you are working **at** something, you are dealing with it. If you are aiming **at** something, you are trying to achieve it. *She has worked hard at her marriage. ...a $1.04m grant aimed at improving student performance.* [6] PREP If something is done **at** someone's command or invitation, it is done as a result of it. *I visited Japan in 1987 at the invitation of the Foreign Minister.* **7** PREP You use **at** to say that someone or something is in a particular state or condition. *Their countries had been at war for nearly six weeks.* **8** PREP You use **at** to say how something is done. *...shots fired at random from a minibus... Mr Martin was taken out of his car at gunpoint.* **9** PREP If you are good **at** something, you do it well. If you are bad **at** something, you do it badly. **10** PREP If you are delighted, pleased, or appalled **at** something, that is the effect it has on you.

ate /et, eɪt/. **Ate** is the past tense of **eat**.

atheism /ˈeɪθiːzəm/. N-UNCOUNT **Atheism** is the belief that there is no God. ♦ **atheist** /ˈeɪθiːɪst/ **atheists** N-COUNT *...a confirmed atheist.*

⭐ **athlete** /ˈæθliːt/ **athletes**. N-COUNT An **athlete** is a person who takes part in athletics competitions.

athletic /æθˈletɪk/. **1** ADJ BEFORE N **Athletic** means relating to athletes and athletics. **2** ADJ An **athletic** person is fit, healthy, and active.

athletics /æθˈletɪks/. N-UNCOUNT **Athletics** consists of sports such as running, the high jump, and the javelin.

atlas /ˈætləs/ **atlases**. N-COUNT An **atlas** is a book of maps.

⭐ **atmosphere** /ˈætməsfɪə/ **atmospheres**. **1** N-COUNT A planet's **atmosphere** is the layer of air or other gas around it. ♦ **atmospheric** /ˌætməsˈferɪk/ ADJ *...atmospheric pressure.* **2** N-COUNT The **atmosphere** of a place is the air that you breathe there. *...the smoky atmosphere of the gaming room.* **3** N-SING The **atmosphere** of a place is the general impression that you get of it. *We try and provide a very homely atmosphere.*

atom /ˈætəm/ **atoms**. N-COUNT An **atom** is the smallest possible amount of a chemical element.

atomic /əˈtɒmɪk/. ADJ BEFORE N **Atomic** means relating to atoms or to the power produced by splitting atoms. *...atomic particles. ...an atomic bomb.*

atrocious /əˈtrəʊʃəs/. ADJ If you describe something as **atrocious**, you mean it is extremely bad or unpleasant. *The food here is atrocious. ...atrocious weather conditions.*

atrocity /əˈtrɒsɪti/ **atrocities**. N-VAR An **atrocity** is a very cruel, shocking action. *Rebel forces have committed atrocities against civilians.*

⭐ **attach** /əˈtætʃ/ **attaches, attaching, attached**. **1** VERB If you **attach** something **to** an object, you join it or fasten it to the object. *We attach labels to things before we file them away... Don't forget to attach the completed entry form.* **2** VERB If you **attach** a quality **to** something or someone, you consider that they have that quality. *We attach great importance to the food at all our hotels.* **3** VERB If you **attach** a file **to** a message that you send to someone, you send it with the message but separate from it. [COMPUTING]

attached /əˈtætʃt/. ADJ AFTER LINK-V If you are

attached to someone or something, you are very fond of them. *She is very attached to her family.*

attachment /əˈtætʃmənt/ **attachments**. **1** N-VAR An **attachment to** someone or something is a fondness for them. *Mother and child form a close attachment. ...a feeling of attachment to the land.* **2** N-COUNT An **attachment** is a device that can be fixed onto a machine in order to enable it to do different jobs. *...a close-up lens attachment for your camera.* **3** N-COUNT An **attachment** is an extra document that is added to another documents. **4** N-COUNT An **attachment** is a file which is attached separately to a message that you send to someone. [COMPUTING]

⭐ **attack** /əˈtæk/ **attacks, attacking, attacked**. **1** VERB & N-VAR To **attack** a person or place, or to launch an **attack on** them, means to try to hurt or damage them using physical violence. *I thought he was going to attack me... He commanded his troops to attack. ...a vicious attack on a black youth... The police came under attack.* ♦ **attacker, attackers** N-COUNT *She struggled with her attacker.* **2** N-COUNT An **attack of** an illness is a short period in which you suffer badly from it. *...an attack of asthma.* **3** VERB & N-VAR If you **attack** a person, belief, or idea, or if you launch an **attack on** them, you criticize them strongly. *The union has attacked the plan... He attacked greedy bosses for awarding themselves big rises. ...his response to attacks on his work.* **4** VERB If you **attack** a job or a problem, you start to deal with it in an energetic way. *Parents shouldn't attack the problem on their own.* **5** VERB In a game such as football, when players **attack**, they try to score. **6** See also **counter-attack, heart attack**.

attain /əˈteɪn/ **attains, attaining, attained**. VERB If you **attain** something, you gain it, often after a lot of effort. [FORMAL] *Jim is halfway to attaining his pilot's licence.* ♦ **attainment** N-UNCOUNT *...the attainment of independence.*

⭐ **attempt** /əˈtempt/ **attempts, attempting, attempted**. **1** VERB & N-COUNT If you **attempt to** do something or **attempt** it, or if you make an **attempt to** do it, you try to do it. *They are accused of attempting to murder British soldiers... He attempted a brave smile. ...a deliberate attempt to mislead people.* ♦ **attempted** ADJ BEFORE N *...a case of attempted murder.* **2** N-COUNT If someone makes an **attempt on** a person's life, they try to kill that person. *There were several attempts on her life.*

⭐ **attend** /əˈtend/ **attends, attending, attended**. **1** VERB If you **attend** a meeting or other event, you are present at it. [FORMAL] *Thousands of people attended the funeral... They had been invited but were not expected to attend.* ♦ **attendance** N-UNCOUNT *...his lack of attendance at classes.* **2** VERB If you **attend** an institution such as a school or church, you go to it regularly. [FORMAL] *They attended college together.* **3** VERB If you **attend to** something, you deal with it. *The staff will helpfully attend to your needs.*

a
b
c
d
e
f
g
h
i
j
k
l
m
n
o
p
q
r
s
t
u
v
w
x
y
z

attendance /ə'tendəns/ **attendances.** N-VAR The **attendance** at an event is the number of people who are present there. ...*falling church attendances.*

attendant /ə'tendənt/ **attendants.** [1] N-COUNT An **attendant** is someone whose job is to serve people, for example in a petrol station or a cloakroom. [2] ADJ You use **attendant** to describe something that results from or is connected to a thing already mentioned. ...*Mr Brady's victory, and all the attendant publicity.*

★ **attention** /ə'tenʃən/. [1] N-UNCOUNT If something has your **attention** or if you are **paying attention to** it, you have noticed it and are interested in it. *A gleam of light had attracted his attention... They have sought to draw world attention to human rights abuses... He never paid much attention to his audience.* [2] N-UNCOUNT If something needs **attention**, it needs care or action. *If you are badly burnt, seek medical attention.*

attentive /ə'tentɪv/. [1] ADJ If you are **attentive**, you watch or listen carefully. ...*an attentive audience.* ◆ **attentively** ADV *He listened attentively.* [2] ADJ Someone who is **attentive** is helpful and polite. *He is attentive to his wife.*

attest /ə'test/ **attests, attesting, attested.** VERB To **attest** something or to **attest to** it means to show that it is true. [FORMAL] *Police records attest to his long history of violence... I can attest that this approach is effective.*

attic /'ætɪk/ **attics.** N-COUNT An **attic** is a room at the top of a house, just below the roof.

★ **attitude** /'ætɪtjuːd/, AM -tuːd/ **attitudes.** N-VAR Your **attitude** to something is the way you think and feel about it. ...*the general change in attitude towards handicapped people. ...negative attitudes to work.*

★ **attorney** /ə'tɜːni/ **attorneys.** N-COUNT In American English, an **attorney** is a lawyer.

★ **attract** /ə'trækt/ **attracts, attracting, attracted.** [1] VERB If someone or something **attracts** you, they have qualities which make it easy for you to like or admire them. *The theory attracted him by its logic... What first attracted me to her was her incredible experience of life.* ◆ **attracted** ADJ *I wasn't deeply attracted to him.* [2] VERB If something **attracts** attention, publicity, or support, it gets it. *His country would also like to attract investment from private companies.* [3] VERB If something **attracts** people or animals, it has features that make them want to go to it. *The Cardiff Bay project is attracting many visitors.* [4] VERB If something magnetic **attracts** an object, it causes the object to move towards it.

attraction /ə'trækʃən/ **attractions.** [1] N-COUNT An **attraction** is a feature which makes something interesting or desirable. ...*America's top tourist attraction, Disney World... What's the attraction of trains and train books?* [2] N-UNCOUNT **Attraction** is

a feeling of liking someone. ...*our level of attraction to the opposite sex.*

★ **attractive** /ə'træktɪv/. [1] ADJ An **attractive** person or thing is pleasant to look at. *He was immensely attractive to women... The flat was small but attractive.* ◆ **attractiveness** N-UNCOUNT ...*the attractiveness of the region.* ● See note at **beautiful.** [2] ADJ You say that something is **attractive** when it seems desirable. *Making easy money has always been an attractive proposition.*

attribute, **attributes, attributing, attributed.** [1] VERB /ə'trɪbjuːt/ If you **attribute** something **to** a person, thing, or event, you believe that they cause it or have it. [FORMAL] *Women tend to attribute their success to luck... People were beginning to attribute superhuman qualities to him.* [2] VERB If a piece of writing or a remark is **attributed** to someone, people say that that person created it or said it. ...*a play attributed to William Shakespeare.* [3] N-COUNT /'ætrɪbjuːt/ An **attribute** is a quality or feature. *Cruelty is a normal attribute of human behaviour.*

aubergine /'əʊbəʒiːn/ **aubergines.** N-VAR An **aubergine** is a vegetable with a smooth purple skin.

auburn /'ɔːbən/. ADJ **Auburn** hair is reddish brown.

★ **auction** /'ɔːkʃən/ **auctions, auctioning, auctioned.** [1] N-VAR An **auction** is a sale where goods are sold to the person who offers the highest price. *Lord Salisbury bought the picture at auction.* [2] VERB If something **is auctioned**, it is sold in an auction. *We'll auction them for charity.*
▸ **auction off.** PHR-VERB If you **auction off** a number of things, you get rid of them all by selling them at an auction. *They're coming to auction off my farm.*

auctioneer /ˌɔːkʃə'nɪə/ **auctioneers.** N-COUNT An **auctioneer** is a person in charge of an auction.

audacious /ɔː'deɪʃəs/. ADJ Something or someone that is **audacious** is very daring and takes a lot of risks. ...*an audacious plan to win the presidency.* ◆ **audacity** /ɔː'dæsɪti/ N-UNCOUNT *He had the audacity to make a 200-1 bet on himself to win.*

audible /'ɔːdɪbəl/. ADJ An **audible** sound can be heard. ◆ **audibly** ADV *Hugh sighed audibly.*

★ **audience** /'ɔːdiəns/ **audiences.** [1] N-COUNT The **audience** is all the people who are watching or listening to a play, concert, film, or programme. *The entire audience broke into loud applause.* [2] N-COUNT You can use **audience** to refer to the people who read someone's books or hear about their ideas. ...*books that are accessible to a general audience.*

audio /'ɔːdiəʊ/. ADJ BEFORE N **Audio** equipment is used for recording and reproducing sound. ...*audio tapes.*

audit /'ɔːdɪt/ **audits, auditing, audited.** VERB & N-COUNT When an accountant **audits** an organization's accounts or conducts an **audit** on them, he or she examines them to make sure that they are correct. ♦ **auditor, auditors** N-COUNT ...*the group's internal auditors.*

audition /ɔːˈdɪʃən/ **auditions, auditioning, auditioned.** N-COUNT & VERB If someone does an **audition**, or if they **audition**, they give a short performance so that a director or conductor can decide if they are good enough to be in a play, film, or orchestra. You can also say that a director or conductor **auditions** someone. *He made a mess of his audition... She wrote to Paramount Studios and asked if they would audition her.*

auditorium /ˌɔːdɪˈtɔːriəm/ **auditoriums** (or **auditoria** /ˌɔːdɪˈtɔːriə/). N-COUNT In a theatre or concert hall, the **auditorium** is the part of the building where the audience sits.

augment /ɔːgˈment/ **augments, augmenting, augmented.** VERB To **augment** something means to make it larger by adding something to it. [FORMAL] ...*searching for a way to augment the family income.*

⭐ **August** /ˈɔːgəst/. N-UNCOUNT **August** is the eighth month of the year. → See Reference Page on Times and Dates.

⭐ **aunt** /ɑːnt, ænt/ **aunts.** N-COUNT Your **aunt** is the sister of your mother or father, or the wife of your uncle. ...*Aunt Vera.*

auntie (or **aunty**) /ˈɑːnti, ˈænti/ **aunties.** N-COUNT **Auntie** means the same as **aunt**. [INFORMAL]

au pair /ˌəʊ ˈpeə, AM -ˌɔː/ **au pairs.** N-COUNT An **au pair** is a young person who lives with a family in a foreign country in order to learn their language and help around the house.

aura /ˈɔːrə/ **auras.** N-COUNT An **aura** is a quality or feeling that appears to surround a person or place. *She had an aura of authority.*

aural /ˈɔːrəl, ˈaʊrəl/. ADJ **Aural** means related to the sense of hearing. ...*astonishing visual and aural effects.*

auspices /ˈɔːspɪsɪz/. PHRASE If something is done **under the auspices** of a person or organization or **under** someone's **auspices**, it is done with their support. [FORMAL] ...*a conference held in 1961 under British auspices.*

austere /ɔːˈstɪə/. ① ADJ Something that is **austere** is plain and not decorated. ♦ **austerity** /ɔːˈsterɪti/ N-UNCOUNT ...*the austerity of the priest's coat.* ② ADJ An **austere** person is strict and serious. ...*a rather austere, distant, somewhat cold person.* ③ ADJ An **austere** way of life is rather harsh, with no luxuries. *The life of the troops was still comparatively austere.* ♦ **austerity** N-UNCOUNT ...*the years of austerity which followed the war.*

authentic /ɔːˈθentɪk/. ADJ If something is **authentic**, it is genuine or accurate. ...*authentic Italian food.* ♦ **authenticity** /ˌɔːθenˈtɪsɪti/ N-UNCOUNT ...*factors that have cast doubt on the statue's authenticity.*

⭐ **author** /ˈɔːθə/ **authors.** ① N-COUNT The **author of** a piece of writing is the person who wrote it. ...*Rick Rogers, the author of the report.* ② N-COUNT

An **author** is a person whose occupation is writing books. *Tolstoy's my favourite author.*

authorise /ˈɔːθəraɪz/. See **authorize**.

authoritarian /ɔːˌθɒrɪˈteəriən, AM -ˈtɔːr-/ **authoritarians.** N-COUNT & ADJ An **authoritarian** or an **authoritarian** person wants to control other people rather than letting them decide things themselves; used showing disapproval. ...*authoritarian governments.*

authoritative /ɔːˈθɒrɪtətɪv, AM -ˈθɔːrɪteɪtɪv/. ① ADJ An **authoritative** statement or piece of writing is based on a complete knowledge of the subject. ...*the first authoritative study of polio.* ♦ **authoritatively** ADV *I can't speak authoritatively on that.* ② ADJ An **authoritative** person seems powerful and in control; used showing approval. ...*a calm and authoritative voice.*

⭐ **authority** /ɔːˈθɒrɪti, AM -ˈtɔːr-/ **authorities.** ① N-COUNT An **authority** is an official organization that has the power to make decisions. You can refer generally to these organizations, especially government ones, as **the authorities.** ...*the Health Education Authority.* ...*a pretext for the authorities to cancel the elections.* ② N-UNCOUNT If you have **authority to** do something, you have been given the power or permission to do it. *The judge had no authority to order a second trial... The bank changed my current account to a business account without my authority.* ③ N-COUNT Someone who is an **authority on** a subject knows a lot about it. ...*a world authority on heart-diseases.*

authorize (BRIT also **authorise**) /ˈɔːθəraɪz/ **authorizes, authorizing, authorized.** VERB If someone **authorizes** something, they give their official permission for it to happen. *Only the President could authorize the use of the atomic bomb... The police have been authorized to break up any large gatherings.* ♦ **authorization, authorizations** N-VAR *We didn't have authorization to go.*

autobiography /ˌɔːtəbaɪˈɒgrəfi/ **autobiographies.** N-COUNT Your **autobiography** is an account of your life, which you write yourself. ♦ **autobiographical** /ˌɔːtəbaɪəˈgræfɪkəl/ ADJ ...*a highly autobiographical novel.*

autograph /ˈɔːtəgrɑːf, -græf/ **autographs, autographing, autographed.** N-COUNT & VERB If a famous person puts their **autograph** on something, or if they **autograph** it, they write their signature on it for you. *They asked for his autograph. ...an autographed photo.*

automated /ˈɔːtəmeɪtɪd/. ADJ An **automated** factory, office, or process uses machines to do the work instead of people.

automation /ˌɔːtəˈmeɪʃən/ N-UNCOUNT **Automation** is the use of machines to do work instead of people. *In the last ten years automation has reduced the work force here by half.*

⭐ **automatic** /ˌɔːtəˈmætɪk/ **automatics.** ① ADJ & N-COUNT An **automatic** machine can keep running without someone operating its controls.

a
b
c
d
e
f
g
h
i
j
k
l
m
n
o
p
q
r
s
t
u
v
w
x
y
z

You can refer to an automatic gun, car, or washing machine as an **automatic**. *Modern trains have automatic doors... The weapons were automatics.* ♦ **automatically** ADV *...equipment to automatically bottle the wine.* [2] ADJ An **automatic** action is one that you do without thinking about it. *His response was automatic.* ♦ **automatically** ADV *He switched automatically into interview mode.* [3] ADJ If something such as an action or a punishment is **automatic**, it happens as the normal result of something else. *Israel offers automatic citizenship to all Jews who want it.* ♦ **automatically** ADV *Many loan application forms automatically add on insurance.*

automobile /'ɔːtəməbiːl, AM -məʊ'biːl/ **automobiles.** N-COUNT In American English, cars are sometimes called **automobiles**.

autonomy /ɔː'tɒnəmi/. N-UNCOUNT If a country, person, or group has **autonomy**, they control themselves rather than being controlled by others. *Activists stepped up their demands for local autonomy.* ♦ **autonomous** ADJ *...the autonomous regional government of Andalucia.*

autopsy /'ɔːtɒpsi/ **autopsies.** N-COUNT An **autopsy** is an examination of a dead body by a doctor in order to discover the cause of death.

⭐ **autumn** /'ɔːtəm/ **autumns.** N-VAR In British English, **autumn** is the season between summer and winter. The American word is **fall**. → See Reference Page on Times and Dates. *The best time to visit is in autumn... She died last autumn.*

auxiliary /ɔːg'zɪljəri, AM -ləri/ **auxiliaries.** [1] N-COUNT & ADJ BEFORE N An **auxiliary**, or an **auxiliary** staff member, is a person who is employed to assist other people, often in the health service or the armed forces. *...nursing auxiliaries.* [2] ADJ BEFORE N **Auxiliary** equipment is extra equipment that is available for use when necessary. *...auxiliary fuel tanks.* [3] N-COUNT In grammar, the **auxiliary verbs** are 'be', 'have', and 'do'. They are used with a main verb to form tenses, negatives and questions.

avail /ə'veɪl/. PHRASE If an action is **to no avail**, it does not achieve what you want. *His efforts were to no avail... Matt fought back but to little avail.*

⭐ **available** /ə'veɪləbəl/. [1] ADJ If something is **available**, you can use it or obtain it. *Breakfast is available to fishermen from 6 a.m... There are three small boats available for hire. ...the best available information.* ♦ **availability** N-UNCOUNT *...the easy availability of guns.* [2] ADJ AFTER LINK-V Someone who is **available** is free to talk to you or spend time with you. *Mr Leach is on holiday and was not available for comment.*

avalanche /'ævəlɑːntʃ, -læntʃ/ **avalanches.** [1] N-COUNT An **avalanche** is a large mass of snow or rock that falls down the side of a mountain. [2] N-SING You can refer to a large quantity of things that arrive or happen at the same time as

an **avalanche of** them. *The newcomer was greeted with an avalanche of publicity.*

avant-garde /ˌævɒn 'gɑːd/. ADJ **Avant-garde** theatre or writing is modern and experimental.

avenge /ə'vendʒ/ **avenges, avenging, avenged.** VERB If you **avenge** a wrong or harmful act, you hurt or punish the person who did it. [FORMAL] *He was trying to avenge the death of his friend.*

avenue /'ævɪnjuː, AM -nuː/ **avenues.** [1] N-COUNT An **avenue** is a wide road, with shops or houses on each side. *...the most expensive stores on Park Avenue.* [2] N-COUNT An **avenue** is a way of getting something done. *...potential avenues of investigation.*

⭐ **average** /'ævərɪdʒ/ **averages, averaging, averaged.** [1] N-COUNT & ADJ BEFORE N An **average**, or an **average** amount, is the result you get when you add several amounts together and divide the total by the number of amounts. *The boats remain at sea for an average of ten days... The average age was 63.* [2] PHRASE You say **on average** to indicate that a number is the average of several numbers. *Women are, on average, paid 25 per cent less than men.* [3] VERB To **average** a particular amount means to be that amount as an average over a period of time. *We averaged 42 miles per hour.* [4] ADJ & N-SING Something that is **average** or **the average** is normal in quality or amount for a particular group of things or people. *His first novel is much, much better than the average novel. ...what is found in an average British dustbin.*

aversion /ə'vɜːʃən, AM -ʒən/ **aversions.** N-VAR If you have an **aversion to** someone or something, you dislike them very much. [FORMAL] *I've always had an aversion to being part of a group.*

avert /ə'vɜːt/ **averts, averting, averted.** [1] VERB If you **avert** something unpleasant, you prevent it from happening. *Talks with the teachers' union have averted a strike.* [2] VERB If you **avert** your eyes, you look away from something.

aviary /'eɪvjəri/ **aviarys.** N-COUNT An **aviary** is a large cage in which birds are kept.

aviation /ˌeɪvi'eɪʃən/. N-UNCOUNT **Aviation** is the operation and production of aircraft.

avid /'ævɪd/. ADJ You use **avid** to describe someone who is very enthusiastic about something. *He's an avid reader.* ♦ **avidly** ADV *...a most entertaining magazine, which I read avidly each month.*

avocado /ˌævə'kɑːdəʊ/ **avocados.** N-VAR An **avocado** is a fruit in the shape of a pear with a dark green skin and a large stone inside it.

⭐ **avoid** /ə'vɔɪd/ **avoids, avoiding, avoided.** [1] VERB If you **avoid** something unpleasant that might happen, you take action in order to prevent it from happening. *...emergency action to avoid a disaster... Drink lots of water to avoid becoming dehydrated.* [2] VERB If you **avoid** doing something, you make a deliberate effort not to do it. *I avoid working in places which are too public... He fled to Costa Rica to avoid military* service. ♦ **avoidance** N-UNCOUNT ...*tips regarding health maintenance and stress avoidance.*

> **USAGE** When you try not to do something, you say that you **avoid doing it**, not that you 'avoid to do it'. *This leaflet tells you how to avoid getting ill.* If you want to suggest that you cannot stop yourself from doing something, you should use the expression **can't help**. *I'm sorry, I can't help being suspicious... Nobody liked her to cough, but she couldn't help it.*

3 VERB If you **avoid** someone or something, you try not to have contact with them. *She thought he was trying to avoid her.* **4** VERB If a person or vehicle **avoids** someone or something, they change the direction they are moving in, so that they do not hit them. *She dashed across the road to avoid an oncoming car.*

⭐ **await** /əˈweɪt/ **awaits, awaiting, awaited.** **1** VERB If you **await** someone or something, you wait for them. [FORMAL] *We awaited the arrival of the chairman.* **2** VERB Something that **awaits** you is going to happen to you in the future. [FORMAL] *A nasty surprise awaited them.*

awake /əˈweɪk/ **awakes, awaking, awoke, awoken.** **1** ADJ AFTER LINK-V If you are **awake**, you are not sleeping. If you are **wide awake**, you are fully awake. **2** VERB When you **awake**, or when something **awakes** you, you wake up. [LITERARY] *The sound of many voices awoke her.*

awaken /əˈweɪkən/ **awakens, awakening, awakened.** **1** VERB To **awaken** a feeling in a person means to cause them to have this feeling. [FORMAL] *...struggling to awaken people's interest in local issues.* ♦ **awakening, awakenings** N-COUNT ...*the awakening of national consciousness in people.* **2** VERB When you **awaken**, or when something **awakens** you, you wake up. [LITERARY]

⭐ **award** /əˈwɔːd/ **awards, awarding, awarded.** **1** N-COUNT An **award** is a prize or certificate you get for doing something well. ...*the Booker Prize, Britain's top award for fiction.* **2** VERB If you **are awarded** something, you get a prize or certificate for doing something well. *The Mayor awarded him a medal of merit.* **3** VERB If a judge or referee **awards** someone something, they decide that a sum of money should be given to the person. *A High Court judge had awarded him £6 million damages.* **4** N-COUNT An **award** is a sum of money that a judge or referee decides should be given to someone. ...*workmen's compensation awards.*

⭐ **aware** /əˈweə/ **1** ADJ AFTER LINK-V If you are **aware of** a fact or situation, you know about it. *Smokers are well aware of the dangers to their own health... We are aware that we might lose our jobs.* ♦ **awareness** N-UNCOUNT ...*general awareness about bullying.* **2** ADJ AFTER LINK-V If you are **aware of** something, you realize that it is present

or is happening because you hear it, see it, smell it, or feel it. *She was acutely aware of the noise of the city.* **3** ADJ AFTER LINK-V Someone who is **aware** notices events that are happening around them. *They are politically very aware.*

awash /əˈwɒʃ/ ADJ AFTER LINK-V If an area or a floor is **awash**, there is a lot of water on it. *Slum areas are awash with mud and sewage.*

⭐ **away** /əˈweɪ/ **1** ADV If you move **away from** a place, you move so that you are no longer there. If you are **away**, you are not in the usual place. *He walked away from his car... The waitress whipped the plate away... Jason was away on a business trip.* **2** ADV If you put something **away**, you put it in a safe place. *All her letters were carefully filed away... I have $100m hidden away.* **3** PREP & ADV If something is **away from** a person or place, it is at a distance from that person or place. *The two women were sitting as far away from each other as possible... The nearest river was four miles away.* ● See note at **far**. **4** ADJ BEFORE N & ADV When a sports team plays an **away** game, or when it plays **away**, it plays at its opponents' ground. **5** ADV You can use **away** to say that something slowly disappears, or changes so that it is no longer the same. *So much snow has already melted away... The Liberal Democrats' support fell away.* **6** ADV You use **away** to talk about future events. For example, if an event is a week away, it will happen in a week. **7** ADV **Away** is used to emphasize that an action is continuous or repeated. *He would often be working away on his word processor.* **8** **right away**: see **right**. ● **far and away**: see **far**.

awe /ɔː/ **awes, awed.** N-UNCOUNT & VERB **Awe** is the respect and amazement that you feel when you are faced with something wonderful and rather frightening. When you have this feeling you are **in awe of** it or **awed** by it. *She gazed in awe at the great stones... I am still awed by David's courage.*

awesome /ˈɔːsəm/ ADJ Something that is **awesome** is very impressive and often frightening. *The responsibility is awesome.*

⭐ **awful** /ˈɔːfʊl/ **1** ADJ If you say that something is **awful**, you mean that it is very bad. ...*the same awful jokes... Her injuries were massive. It was awful... I hardly slept at all and felt pretty awful.* **2** ADJ BEFORE N You can use **awful** to emphasize how large an amount or how long a time is. [INFORMAL] *I've got an awful lot of work to do.*

awfully /ˈɔːfʊli/ ADV You use **awfully** to emphasize how much of a quality someone or something has. [INFORMAL] *The caramel looks awfully good... I'm awfully sorry.*

awhile /əˈwaɪl/ ADV **Awhile** means for a short time. [AMERICAN] *He worked awhile as a pharmacist in Cincinnati.*

awkward /ˈɔːkwəd/ **1** ADJ An **awkward** situation is embarrassing and difficult to deal with. If you feel **awkward**, you feel embarrassed and shy. *It was a bit awkward for me. ...awkward*

A
B
C
D
E
F
G
H
I
J
K
L
M ★
N
O
P
Q
R
S
T
U
V
W
X
Y
Z

questions. ♦ **awkwardly** ADV *Awkwardly, we took our places.* [2] ADJ Something that is **awkward to** use or carry is difficult to use or carry because of its design. An **awkward** job is difficult to do. *It was small but heavy enough to make it awkward to carry.* ♦ **awkwardly** ADV *...an awkwardly shaped room.* [3] ADJ An **awkward** movement or position is uncomfortable or clumsy. *Amy made an awkward gesture with her hands.* ♦ **awkwardly** ADV *He fell awkwardly.* [4] ADJ Someone who is **awkward** deliberately causes problems for other people. *Don't be awkward.*

awoke /ə'wəʊk/. **Awoke** is the past tense of **awake**.

awoken /ə'wəʊkən/. **Awoken** is the past participle of **awake**.

axe (AM **ax**) /æks/ **axes, axing, axed.** [1] N-COUNT An **axe** is a tool used for chopping wood. It consists of a blade attached to the end of a long handle. → See picture on page 833. [2] VERB If someone's job or something such as a service or programme **is axed**, it is ended suddenly.

axis /'æksɪs/ **axes,** /'æksiːz/. [1] N-COUNT An **axis** is an imaginary line through the middle of something. *...the daily rotation of the earth upon its axis.* [2] N-COUNT An **axis** of a graph is one of the two lines on which the scales of measurement are marked.

B b

babble /'bæbəl/ **babbles, babbling, babbled.** VERB & N-SING If someone **babbles**, they talk in a confused or excited way. You can refer to people's voices as a **babble of** sound when they babble. *Momma babbled on and on. ...the high babble of voices.*

babe /beɪb/ **babes.** [1] N-VOC Some people use **babe** as an affectionate way of addressing someone. [INFORMAL] *I'm sorry, babe.* [2] N-COUNT A **babe** is the same as a **baby.** [DATED]

★ **baby** /'beɪbi/ **babies.** [1] N-COUNT A **baby** is a very young child that cannot yet walk or talk. [2] N-VOC & N-COUNT Some people use **baby** as an affectionate way of addressing someone. [INFORMAL] *He was confused, poor baby.*

babysit (or **baby-sit**) /'beɪbisɪt/ **babysits, babysitting, babysat.** VERB If you **babysit** for someone, you look after their children while they are out. *You can take it in turns to babysit.* ♦ **babysitter, babysitters** N-COUNT *It's difficult to find a good babysitter.*

bachelor /'bætʃələ/ **bachelors.** N-COUNT A **bachelor** is a man who has never married. *Benfield, a bachelor, enjoyed the respect of his colleagues.*

back 1 adverb uses

★ **back** /bæk/. [1] ADV If someone moves **back**, they move in the opposite direction to the one in which they are facing. *She stepped back from the door.* [2] ADV You use **back** to say that someone or something returns to a particular place or state. *I went back to bed... I'll be back as soon as I can... Denise hopes to be back at work soon.* [3] ADV If you give or put something **back**, you return it to the person who had it or to the place where it was before you took it. If you get or take something **back**, you then have it again after not having it for a while. *She handed the knife back... Put it back in the freezer... You'll get your money back.* [4] ADV You use **back** to indicate that you are talking or thinking about something that happened in the past. *The story starts back in 1950. ...that terrorist attack a few years back.*

[5] ADV If you do something **back,** you do to someone what they have done to you. *If the phone rings say you'll call back... Lee looked at Theodora. She stared back.* [6] ADV If someone or something is kept or situated **back** from a place, they are at a distance from it. *Keep back from the edge of the platform.* [7] PHRASE If someone moves **back and forth**, they repeatedly move in one direction and then in the opposite direction. *He paced back and forth.*

back 2 opposite of front; noun and adjective uses

★ **back** /bæk/ **backs.** [1] N-COUNT Your **back** is the part of your body from your neck to your waist that is on the opposite side to your chest. → See picture on page 822. [2] N-COUNT & ADJ BEFORE N The **back** or the **back** part of something is the part of it that is towards the rear or farthest from the front. *...the back of her neck. ...the index at the back of the book. ...the back door.* [3] N-COUNT The **back** of a chair is the part you lean against.
PHRASES • If you do something **behind** someone's **back**, you do it without them knowing about it. • If you **turn** your **back on** someone or something, you ignore them or refuse to help them. • If you are wearing something **back to front**, you are wearing it with the back of it on the front of your body.

back 3 verb uses

★ **back** /bæk/ **backs, backing, backed.** [1] VERB If a building **backs onto** something, the back of it faces in the direction of that thing or touches the edge of that thing. *...a ground floor flat which backs on to a busy street.* [2] VERB When you **back** a vehicle somewhere, or when it **backs** somewhere, it moves backwards. *He got into his car and backed out of the drive.* [3] VERB If you **back** a person or a course of action, you support them. *...a new witness to back his claim that he is a victim of mistaken identity.* [4] VERB If you **back** someone in a competition, you bet money that they will win. [5] See also **backing.**
▶**back away.** PHR-VERB If you **back away**, you

move away because you are nervous or frightened. *Jupe backed away from the door.*

▶**back down.** PHR-VERB If you **back down**, you withdraw a claim or demand that you made earlier.

▶**back off.** PHR-VERB If you **back off**, you move away in order to avoid problems or a fight.

▶**back out.** PHR-VERB If you **back out**, you decide not to do something that you previously agreed to do. *The Hungarians backed out of the project in 1989.*

▶**back up.** [1] PHR-VERB If someone or something **backs up** a statement, they supply evidence to show it is true. [2] PHR-VERB If you **back** someone **up**, you help and support them. [3] PHR-VERB If you **back up** a computer file, you make a copy of it which you can use if the original file is damaged or lost. [4] See also **back-up**.

backbench /ˈbækbentʃ/. ADJ BEFORE N A **backbench** MP is a Member of Parliament who is not a minister and who does not hold an official position in his or her political party. [BRITISH]

backbone /ˈbækbəʊn/. backbones. N-COUNT Your **backbone** is the column of small linked bones along the middle of your back.

backer /ˈbækə/. backers. N-COUNT A **backer** is someone who gives support or financial help to a person or project.

backfire /ˌbækˈfaɪə, AM -ˈfaɪr/. backfires, backfiring, backfired. [1] VERB If a plan **backfires**, it has the opposite result to the one that was intended. [2] VERB When a motor vehicle or its engine **backfires**, it produces an explosion in the exhaust pipe.

★ **background** /ˈbækɡraʊnd/. backgrounds. [1] N-COUNT Your **background** is the kind of family you come from and the kind of education you have had. *She came from a working-class Yorkshire background.* [2] N-COUNT The **background to** an event or situation consists of the facts that explain what caused it. *...the background to the current troubles...* [3] N-SING The **background** refers to things, shapes, colours, or sounds that are not the main ones and are often partly hidden by other things. *...the sound of applause in the background. ...white flowers on a green background. ...background music.*

★ **backing** /ˈbækɪŋ/. backings. [1] N-UNCOUNT **Backing** is money, resources, or support given to a person or organization. *Mr Bach set up his own consulting business with the backing of his old boss.* [2] N-VAR A **backing** is a layer of strong material that is put onto the back of something in order to protect or strengthen it.

backlash /ˈbæklæʃ/. N-SING A **backlash against** a tendency or recent development in society or politics is a sudden strong reaction against it. *...the backlash against working women.*

backlog /ˈbæklɒɡ, AM -lɔːɡ/. backlogs. N-COUNT A **backlog** is a number of things which have not yet been done, but which need to be done. *...a backlog of repairs and maintenance in schools.*

backside /ˌbækˈsaɪd/. backsides. N-COUNT Your **backside** is the part of your body that you sit on. [INFORMAL]

backstage /ˌbækˈsteɪdʒ/. ADV In a theatre, **backstage** refers to the areas behind the stage. *He went backstage and asked for her autograph.*

backstroke /ˈbækstrəʊk/. N-UNCOUNT **Backstroke** is a swimming stroke that you do lying on your back.

ˈ**back-up** (or **backup**) back-ups. [1] N-VAR **Back-up** consists of extra equipment, resources, or people that you can get help or support from if necessary. *Does the company have a 24-hour backup service?* [2] N-VAR If you have something such as a second set of plans as **back-up**, you have arranged for them to be available for use in case the first one does not work. *Computer users should make regular back-up copies.*

backward /ˈbækwəd/. backwards.

✔ In American English and in informal British English, **backward** is often used as an adverb instead of **backwards**.

[1] ADV & ADJ BEFORE N If you move or look **backwards**, you move or look in the direction that your back is facing. A **backward** movement or look is in the direction that your back is facing. *The diver flipped over backwards into the water... He took two steps backward. ...a backward glance.* [2] ADV If you do something **backwards**, you do it in the opposite way to the usual way. *He works backwards, building a house from the top downwards.* [3] ADJ A **backward** country or society does not have modern industries and machines; used showing disapproval. [4] PHRASE If someone or something moves **backwards and forwards**, they move repeatedly first in one direction and then in the opposite direction. *...people travelling backwards and forwards.*

backwater /ˈbækwɔːtə/. backwaters. N-COUNT A **backwater** is a place or an institution that is isolated from modern ideas or influences; used showing disapproval. *The city was a provincial backwater for more than seven centuries.*

backyard /ˌbækˈjɑːd/. backyards. N-COUNT A **backyard** is an area of land at the back of a house.

bacon /ˈbeɪkən/. N-UNCOUNT **Bacon** is salted or smoked meat taken from the back or sides of a pig.

bacteria /bækˈtɪəriə/. N-PLURAL **Bacteria** are very small organisms which can cause disease.
♦ **bacterial** ADJ BEFORE N *Cholera is a bacterial infection.*

★ **bad** /bæd/ **worse, worst.** [1] ADJ Something that is **bad** is unpleasant, harmful, or of poor quality. *...a bad day at work... The floods are described as the worst in nearly fifty years.* [2] ADJ You can say that something is **not bad** to mean that it is quite good or acceptable. *The wine wasn't bad.* [3] ADJ Someone who is **bad at** doing something is not very skilful at it. *Dad was really bad at getting to places on time... He was a bad driver.* [4] ADJ If you feel **bad** about something, you feel sorry or guilty about it. *I feel bad that he's doing most of the work.* **5** ADJ If you have a **bad** back, heart, leg, or eye, there is something wrong with it. **6** ADJ **Bad** language is language that contains rude or offensive words. **7** ADJ If you are in a **bad** mood, you are cross and behave unpleasantly to people. **8** PHRASE If you say **'too bad'**, you are indicating in a rather harsh way that nothing can be done to change the situation. *Too bad if you missed the bus.*

badge /bædʒ/ **badges.** N-COUNT A **badge** is a small piece of metal or cloth which you attach to your clothes for decoration.

badger /'bædʒə/ **badgers, badgering, badgered.** **1** N-COUNT A **badger** is a wild animal with a white head with two wide black stripes on it. → See picture on page 815. **2** VERB If you **badger** someone, you repeatedly tell them to do something or repeatedly ask them questions.

⭐ **badly** /'bædli/ **worse, worst.** **1** ADV If something is done **badly**, it is done with very little success or effect. *The project was badly managed.* **2** ADV **Badly** is used to say that something bad happens to a great degree. *...fires which badly damaged the prison's chapel... In all twelve people were badly injured... Low exam results will reflect badly on them.* **3** ADV If you need or want something

badly, you need or want it very much. **4** See also **worse, worst**.

badly 'off, worse off, worst off. ADJ If you are **badly off**, you are in a bad situation or condition, especially financially. *Surely you can't be that badly off... There are people much worse off than me, crippled, or in pain.*

badminton /'bædmɪntən/. N-UNCOUNT **Badminton** is a game played on a rectangular court by two or four players. They hit a feathered object called a shuttlecock across a high net.

bad-'tempered. ADJ Someone who is **bad-tempered** is not very cheerful and gets angry easily. *I became bad-tempered and tearful with my boyfriend.* ● See note at **angry**.

baffle /'bæfəl/ **baffles, baffling, baffled.** VERB If something **baffles** you, you cannot understand it or explain it. *Scientists are baffled by the find.* ◆ **baffling** ADJ *...a baffling array of wires.*

⭐ **bag** /bæg/ **bags.** **1** N-COUNT A **bag** is a container made of paper, plastic, or leather which is used to carry things. *...a clear polythene bag. ...a bag of sweets.* **2** N-PLURAL If you have **bags** under your eyes, you have folds of skin there, usually because you have not had enough sleep. **3** PHRASE If you say that something is **in the bag,** you mean that you are certain to get it or achieve it. [INFORMAL]

Bags

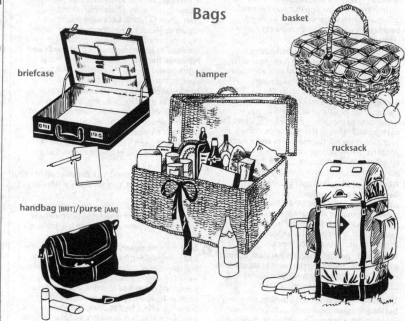

basket

briefcase

hamper

rucksack

handbag [BRIT]/purse [AM]

baggage /ˈbæɡɪdʒ/. [1] N-UNCOUNT Your **baggage** consists of the suitcases and bags that you take with you when you travel. [2] N-UNCOUNT You can use **baggage** to refer to someone's problems or prejudices. *He's carrying a lot of old emotional baggage.*

> **USAGE Baggage** is an uncount noun. You can have **a piece of baggage** or **some baggage** but you cannot have 'a baggage' or 'some baggages'.

baggy /ˈbæɡi/. ADJ **Baggy** clothes hang loosely on your body.

bail /beɪl/ **bails, bailing, bailed.**

> ☑ **Bail** is also spelled **bale** for meaning 2, and for meaning 1 of the phrasal verb.

[1] VERB & N-UNCOUNT If someone who is awaiting trial **is bailed**, or if they are released **on bail**, they are set free until they are due to appear in court, provided someone agrees to pay a sum of money if they fail to appear. *He was freed on bail pending an appeal.* [2] VERB If you **bail** water from a boat, you remove it using a container. *We kept her afloat for a couple of hours by bailing frantically.*
▶ **bail out.** [1] PHR-VERB If you **bail** someone **out**, you help them out of a difficult situation, often by giving them money. [2] PHR-VERB If you **bail** someone **out**, you pay bail on their behalf.

bailiff /ˈbeɪlɪf/ **bailiffs.** N-COUNT A **bailiff** is a law officer who makes sure that the decisions of a court are obeyed. [BRITISH]

bait /beɪt/ **baits, baiting, baited.** [1] N-UNCOUNT & VERB **Bait** is food which you put on a hook or in a trap in order to catch fish or animals. When you **bait** a hook or trap, you put bait on it. [2] N-UNCOUNT If someone or something is being used as **bait**, they are being used to tempt someone to do something. *He lured the youngsters by using his own children as bait.* [3] VERB If someone **baits** you, they deliberately try to make you angry by teasing them. *The defense lawyers may be able to bait him and get him to act aggressively.*

⭐ **bake** /beɪk/ **bakes, baking, baked.** [1] VERB When you **bake** food, or when it **bakes**, you cook it in the oven without any extra liquid or fat. *Bake the cake for 50 minutes. ...baked potatoes.* [2] VERB When you **bake**, you prepare and mix together ingredients to make cakes, biscuits, or bread. You then put them in the oven to cook. *Mary Rathbun loves to bake... How did you learn to bake cakes?* ♦ **baking** N-UNCOUNT *Christine describes her main activities as 'cooking, cleaning, ironing and baking'.* [3] See note at **cook**. ● See also **baking**.

baker /ˈbeɪkə/ **bakers.** N-COUNT A **baker** is a person whose job is to bake and sell bread and cakes. You also refer to the shop where bread and cakes are sold as a **baker** or a **baker's.**

bakery /ˈbeɪkəri/ **bakeries.** N-COUNT A **bakery** is a building where bread and cakes are baked, or the shop where they are sold.

baking /ˈbeɪkɪŋ/. ADJ & ADV You can use **baking** to describe weather or a place that is very hot indeed. *...a baking July day. ...the baking hot summer of 1969.*

⭐ **balance** /ˈbæləns/ **balances, balancing, balanced.** [1] VERB If something or someone **balances** somewhere, or if you **balance** them there, they remain steady and do not fall over. *I balanced on the ledge... She had balanced a glass on her chest.* [2] N-UNCOUNT **Balance** is the stability that someone or something has when they are balanced on something. *He lost his balance as his foot slipped on the ice.* [3] N-SING A **balance** is a situation or combination of things in which all the different parts are equal or correct in strength or importance. *...the ecological balance of the forest.* [4] VERB If you **balance** one thing **with** something different, or if one thing **balances with** another, each of the things has the same strength or importance. *...trying to balance his demanding career with the demands of his wife.* [5] VERB To **balance** a budget or **balance the books** means to make sure that the amount of money that is spent is not greater than the amount that is received. [6] N-COUNT The **balance** in your bank account is the amount of money in it. [7] N-SING The **balance** to be paid on something is the total amount of money which remains to be paid for it. *They were due to pay the balance on delivery.*
PHRASES ● If something is **in the balance,** its future is uncertain. ● You can say **on balance** to indicate that you are stating an opinion only after considering all the relevant facts or arguments. *On balance he agreed with Christine.*

balanced /ˈbælənst/. [1] ADJ A **balanced** account or report is fair and reasonable. [2] ADJ Something that is **balanced** is pleasing or beneficial because its different parts are in the correct proportions. *...a balanced diet.*

balcony /ˈbælkəni/ **balconies.** [1] N-COUNT A **balcony** is a platform on the outside of a building with a wall or railing around it. [2] N-COUNT The **balcony** in a theatre or cinema is an upstairs seating area.

bald /bɔːld/ **balder, baldest.** [1] ADJ Someone who is **bald** has little or no hair on the top of their head. ♦ **baldness** N-UNCOUNT *He wears a cap to cover a spot of baldness.* [2] ADJ A **bald** tyre has become worn down and it is no longer safe or legal to use. [3] ADJ BEFORE N A **bald** statement has no unnecessary words in it. ♦ **baldly** ADV *Phrased so baldly, the point seems obvious.*

balding /ˈbɔːldɪŋ/. ADJ A **balding** person is beginning to lose the hair on the top of their head.

bale /beɪl/ **bales, baling, baled.** [1] N-COUNT A **bale of** something such as hay or paper is a large quantity tied into a tight bundle. [2] VERB When hay or paper **is baled**, it is tied together in a tight bundle. [3] See also **bail.**

balk (or **baulk**) /bɔːlk, AM bɔːk/, **balks, balking, balked.** VERB If you **balk at** something, you are very reluctant to do it. *Even biology undergraduates may balk at animal experiments.*

⭐ **ball** /bɔːl/ **balls.** **1** N-COUNT A **ball** is a round object used in games such as football. **2** N-COUNT A **ball** is something that has a round shape. *Thomas screwed the letter up into a ball.* **3** N-COUNT The **ball of** your foot or the **ball of** your thumb is the rounded part where your toes join your foot or where your thumb joins your hand. **4** N-COUNT A **ball** is a large formal dance. PHRASES ● If you **are having a ball**, you are having a wonderful time. [INFORMAL] ● If you **start the ball rolling**, you start something happening.

ballad /'bæləd/ **ballads.** **1** N-COUNT A **ballad** is a slow, romantic, popular song. **2** N-COUNT A **ballad** is a long song or poem which tells a story using simple language.

ballet /'bæleɪ, AM bæ'leɪ/ **ballets.** **1** N-UNCOUNT **Ballet** is a type of artistic dancing with carefully planned movements. **2** N-COUNT A **ballet** is an artistic work performed by ballet dancers.

balloon /bə'luːn/ **balloons, ballooning, ballooned.** **1** N-COUNT A **balloon** is a small, thin, rubber bag that becomes larger when you blow air into it. **2** N-COUNT A **balloon** is a large strong bag filled with gas or hot air, which can carry passengers in a compartment underneath it. **3** VERB When something **balloons**, it quickly becomes bigger. *Her weight ballooned from 8 stone to 11 stone.*

⭐ **ballot** /'bælət/ **ballots, balloting, balloted.** **1** N-COUNT A **ballot** is a secret vote in which people select a candidate in an election, or express their opinion about something. **2** VERB If you **ballot** a group of people, you find out what they think about something by organizing a secret vote. *The union said they will ballot members on whether to strike.*

balm /bɑːm/ **balms.** N-VAR **Balm** is a sweet-smelling oil that is obtained from some tropical trees and is used to make ointments that heal wounds or lessen pain.

bamboo /bæm'buː/ **bamboos.** N-VAR **Bamboo** is a tall tropical plant with hard hollow stems.

⭐ **ban** /bæn/ **bans, banning, banned.** **1** VERB & N-COUNT To **ban** something or place a **ban on** it means to state officially that it must not be done, shown, or used. *Canada will ban smoking in all offices later this year... The General also lifted a ban on political parties.* **2** VERB If you **are banned from** doing something, you are officially prevented from doing it. *He was banned from driving for three years.*

banal /bə'nɑːl, -'næl/. ADJ If you describe something as **banal**, you mean that it is so ordinary that it is not at all effective or interesting. *...a banal conversation.* ◆ **banality** /bə'næliti/ N-UNCOUNT *...the sheer banality of colonial life.*

banana /bə'nɑːnə, -'næn-/ **bananas.** N-VAR A **banana** is a long curved fruit with a yellow skin. → See picture on page 821.

⭐ **band** /bænd/ **bands, banding, banded.** **1** N-COUNT A **band** is a group of musicians who play jazz, rock,

or pop music, or who play brass instruments together. **2** N-COUNT A **band of** people is a group of people who have joined together because they share an interest or belief. *...a band of rebels.* **3** N-COUNT A **band** is a flat narrow strip of cloth which you wear round your head or wrists, or round a piece of clothing. *...a black arm-band.* **4** N-COUNT A **band** is a strip or loop of metal or other strong material which strengthens something, or which holds several things together. **5** N-COUNT A **band** is a range of numbers or values within a system of measurement. *...a new tax band of 20p in the pound.*

▸ **band together.** PHR-VERB If people **band together,** they act as a group in order to try and achieve something.

bandage /'bændɪdʒ/ **bandages, bandaging, bandaged.** **1** N-COUNT A **bandage** is a long strip of cloth that is tied around a wounded part of someone's body in order to protect or support it. **2** VERB If you **bandage** a wound or part of someone's body, you tie a bandage round it. *...a man with a bandaged head.*

B&'B, B&Bs. See **bed and breakfast**.

bandit /'bændɪt/ **bandits.** N-COUNT A **bandit** is an armed robber.

bandwagon /'bændwægən/ **bandwagons.** N-COUNT If you say that someone has **jumped on the bandwagon,** you mean that they have become involved in an activity only because it has become fashionable. *Many conservative politicians have jumped on the anti-immigrant bandwagon.*

bandwidth /'bændwɪdθ/ **bandwidths.** N-VAR A **bandwidth** is the range of frequencies used for a particular telecommunications signal, radio transmission, or computer network.

bang /bæŋ/ **bangs, banging, banged.** **1** N-COUNT A **bang** is a sudden loud noise such as an explosion. **2** VERB If you **bang** something such as a door, or if it **bangs**, it closes suddenly with a loud noise. *The door banged shut behind them.* **3** VERB If you **bang on** something, or if you **bang** it, you hit it so that it makes a loud noise. *I banged on the wall... There is no point in shouting or banging the table... Daryl banged his fist on the desk.* **4** VERB & N-COUNT If you **bang** part of your body **against** something, you accidentally knock into it and hurt yourself. A **bang** is a knock or blow. *He hurried into the hall, banging his shin against a chair. ...a nasty bang on the head.*

banish /'bænɪʃ/ **banishers, banishing, banished.** **1** VERB If someone or something **is banished from** a place or activity, they are sent away from it and prevented from entering it. *John was banished from England.* **2** VERB If you **banish** something, you get rid of it. *... diseases like malaria that have been banished for centuries.*

⭐ **bank** /bæŋk/ **banks, banking, banked.** **1** N-COUNT A **bank** is a place where you can keep your money in an account. **2** N-COUNT You use **bank** to refer to a large amount of something, stored for use. For example, a blood **bank** is a store of blood. **3** N-COUNT The **banks** of a river, canal, or lake are the raised areas of ground along its edge. **4** N-COUNT A **bank** of ground is a raised area of it with a flat top and one or two sloping sides. *...a grassy bank.* **5** N-COUNT A **bank of** something is a long high row or mass of it. *...a bank of fog.* ▸**bank on.** PHR-VERB If you **bank on** something happening, you rely on it happening. *You might be able to get it altered – but don't bank on it.*

★ **banker** /'bæŋkə/ **bankers.** N-COUNT A **banker** is someone involved in banking at a senior level.

,**bank 'holiday, bank holidays.** N-COUNT A **bank holiday** is a public holiday. [BRITISH]

★ **banking** /'bæŋkɪŋ/ N-UNCOUNT **Banking** is the business activity of banks and similar institutions.

banknote (or **bank note**) /'bæŋknəʊt/ **banknotes.** N-COUNT A **banknote** is a piece of paper money. *...coins and banknotes.*

bankrupt /'bæŋkrʌpt/ **bankrupts, bankrupting, bankrupted.** **1** ADJ People or organizations that go **bankrupt** do not have enough money to pay their debts. *He was declared bankrupt after failing to pay a £114m loan guarantee.* **2** VERB To **bankrupt** a person or organization means to make them go bankrupt. *The cost of the court case bankrupted him.* **3** ADJ You use **bankrupt** to say that someone or something is completely without a particular quality. *He thinks that European civilisation is morally bankrupt.*

bankruptcy /'bæŋkrʌptsi/ **bankruptcies.** **1** N-UNCOUNT **Bankruptcy** is the state of being bankrupt. *Many established firms were facing bankruptcy.* **2** N-COUNT A **bankruptcy** is an instance of an organization or person going bankrupt.

banner /'bænə/ **banners.** N-COUNT A **banner** is a long strip of cloth with a message or slogan on it.

banquet /'bæŋkwɪt/ **banquets.** N-COUNT A **banquet** is a grand formal dinner.

banter /'bæntə/. N-UNCOUNT **Banter** is friendly teasing or joking talk.

baptism /'bæptɪzəm/ **baptisms.** N-VAR A **baptism** is a ceremony in which a person is baptized. *...adult baptism.*

baptize (BRIT also **baptise**) /bæp'taɪz/ **baptizes, baptizing, baptized.** VERB When someone **is baptized**, water is sprinkled on them or they are immersed in water as a sign that they have become a member of the Christian Church.

★ **bar** /bɑː/ **bars, barring, barred.** **1** N-COUNT A **bar** is a place where you can buy and drink alcoholic drinks. **2** N-COUNT A **bar** is a counter on which alcoholic drinks are served. *He leaned forward across the bar.* **3** N-COUNT A **bar** is a long, straight, rigid piece of metal. *...an iron bar.* **4** N-COUNT A **bar of** something is a roughly rectangular piece of it. *...a bar of soap.* **5** VERB If you **bar** someone from going somewhere or doing it, you prevent them from going there or doing it. *She stood in the doorway,*

barring his way out... *Amnesty workers have been barred from Sri Lanka since 1982.* **6** PREP You can use **bar** to mean 'except'. For example, all the work **bar** the washing means all the work except the washing. [FORMAL] **7** N-PROPER **The Bar** is used to refer to the profession of a barrister in England, or of any kind of lawyer in the United States. *Robert was planning to read for the Bar.* **8** N-COUNT In music, a **bar** is one of the several short parts of the same length into which a piece of music is divided. **9** See also **barring.**

PHRASES ● If someone is **behind bars**, they are in prison. ● You say that there are **no holds barred** when people are competing forcefully, without following any rules in their efforts to win.

barbaric /bɑː'bærɪk/. ADJ **Barbaric** behaviour is extremely cruel. *...the most barbaric form of execution still in existence today.* ♦ **barbarism** /'bɑːbərɪzəm/ N-UNCOUNT *...an act of barbarism.* ♦ **barbarity** /bɑː'bærɪti/ **barbarities** N-VAR *...the barbarities of the Nazi regime.*

barbecue /'bɑːbɪkjuː/ **barbecues, barbecuing, barbecued.** **1** N-COUNT A **barbecue** is a grill used to cook food outdoors. **2** N-COUNT A **barbecue** is an outdoor party at which people eat food cooked on a barbecue. **3** VERB If you **barbecue** food, you cook it on a barbecue. *Tuna can be grilled, fried or barbecued. ...barbecued chicken.*

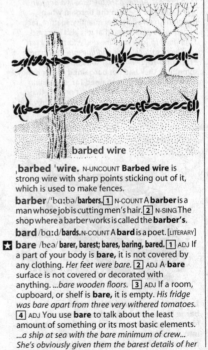

barbed wire

,**barbed 'wire.** N-UNCOUNT **Barbed wire** is strong wire with sharp points sticking out of it, which is used to make fences.

barber /'bɑːbə/ **barbers.** **1** N-COUNT A **barber** is a man whose job is cutting men's hair. **2** N-SING The shop where a barber works is called the **barber's.**

bard /bɑːd/ **bards.** N-COUNT A **bard** is a poet. [LITERARY]

★ **bare** /beə/ **barer, barest; bares, baring, bared.** **1** ADJ If a part of your body is **bare**, it is not covered by any clothing. *Her feet were bare.* **2** ADJ A **bare** surface is not covered or decorated with anything. *...bare wooden floors.* **3** ADJ If a room, cupboard, or shelf is **bare**, it is empty. *His fridge was bare apart from three very withered tomatoes.* **4** ADJ You use **bare** to talk about the least amount of something or its most basic elements. *...a ship at sea with the bare minimum of crew... She's obviously given them the barest details of her* *illness.* [5] VERB If you **bare** something, you uncover it and show it. [WRITTEN] *She bared her teeth like a dog.*

PHRASES ● If someone does something with their **bare hands**, they do it without using any weapons or tools. *...using their bare hands to reach the trapped miners.*

barefoot/'beəfʊt/. ADJ If you are **barefoot** or **barefooted**, you are wearing nothing on your feet.

⭐ **barely** /'beəli/. ADV You use **barely** to say that something is only just true or possible. *Anastasia could barely remember the ride to the hospital... The water had barely come to a simmer when she cracked four eggs into it.*

⭐ **bargain** /'bɑːgɪn/ **bargains, bargaining, bargained.** [1] VERB When people **bargain with** each other, they discuss what each of them will do, pay, or receive. *They prefer to bargain with individual clients... Shop in small local markets and don't be afraid to bargain.* ◆ **bargaining** N-UNCOUNT *The government has called for sensible pay bargaining.* [2] N-COUNT A **bargain** is a formal agreement on what two people will do, pay, or receive. *The treaty was based on a bargain between the French and German governments.* [3] N-COUNT A **bargain** is something which is good value for money, usually because it has been sold at a lower price than normal. *At this price the wine is a bargain.* [4] PHRASE You use **into the bargain** when mentioning an additional quantity, feature, fact, or action, to emphasize that it is also involved. *...designed to save you time and effort, and keep your work surfaces neat and tidy into the bargain.* ▸**bargain for.** PHR-VERB If someone gets something they had not **bargained for**, or if they get more than they **bargained for**, something happens that they did not expect or something happens to a much greater degree than they had expected.

barge

barge /bɑːdʒ/ **barges, barging, barged.** [1] N-COUNT A **barge** is a narrow boat with a flat bottom, used for carrying heavy loads. [2] VERB If you **barge into** a place or person, you rush into it or push past them in a rude or rough way. [INFORMAL] *He*

barged past her and sprang at Gillian... Students tried to barge into the buildings.

baritone /'bærɪtəʊn/ **baritones.** N-COUNT A **baritone** is a man with a fairly deep singing voice.

bark /bɑːk/ **barks, barking, barked.** [1] VERB & N-COUNT When a dog **barks** or gives a **bark**, it makes a short loud noise. *A small dog barked at a seagull.* [2] N-UNCOUNT **Bark** is the tough material that covers the outside of a tree.

barley /'bɑːli/. N-UNCOUNT **Barley** is a crop which has seeds that are used in the production of food, beer, and whisky.

barmaid /'bɑːmeɪd/ **barmaids.** N-COUNT In British English, a **barmaid** is a woman who serves drinks in a bar or pub. The American word is **bartender**.

barman /'bɑːmən/ **barmen.** N-COUNT In British English, a **barman** is a man who serves drinks in a bar or pub. The American word is **bartender**.

barn /bɑːn/ **barns.** N-COUNT A **barn** is a building on a farm in which crops or animal food are kept.

barometer /bə'rɒmɪtə/ **barometers.** N-COUNT A **barometer** is an instrument that measures air pressure and shows when the weather is changing. *The barometer was falling.*

baron/'bærən/**barons.** [1] N-COUNT & N-TITLE A **baron** is a man who is a member of the nobility. [2] N-COUNT You use **baron** to refer to someone who controls a large amount of an industry and who is therefore extremely powerful. *...drug barons.*

baroness /'bærənes/ **baronesses.** N-COUNT & N-TITLE A **baroness** is a woman who has the same rank as a baron, or who is the wife of a baron.

barracks /'bærəks/. N-COUNT A **barracks** is a building or group of buildings where members of the armed forces live.

barrage /'bærɑːʒ, AM bə'rɑːʒ/ **barrages.** [1] N-COUNT If you get a lot of questions or complaints about something, you can say that you are getting a **barrage of** them. *He was faced with a barrage of angry questions.* [2] N-COUNT A **barrage** is continuous firing on an area with a large number of artillery weapons such as heavy guns and tanks. *...a barrage of anti-aircraft fire.*

barrel [2]

barrel [1]

baseball

⭐ **barrel** /ˈbærəl/ **barrels.** ⓵ N-COUNT A **barrel** is a large round container for liquids or food. Barrels are usually wider in the middle than at the top or bottom. ...*oak barrels.* ⓶ N-COUNT The **barrel** of a gun is the long metal tube through which the bullet moves when the gun is fired. → See picture on page 52.

barren /ˈbærən/. ADJ **Barren** land has soil of such bad quality that plants cannot grow on it. ...*a bleak, barren desert.*

barricade /ˈbærɪkeɪd/ **barricades, barricading, barricaded.** ⓵ N-COUNT A **barricade** is a line of vehicles or other objects placed across a road or passage to stop people getting past. ⓶ VERB If people **barricade** a road or passage, they put something across it to stop other people reaching it. *The rioters barricaded streets with piles of blazing tyres.* ⓷ VERB If you **barricade yourself** inside a room or building, you put something heavy against the door so that other people cannot get in. *The students have barricaded themselves into their dormitory building.*

⭐ **barrier** /ˈbæriə/ **barriers.** ⓵ N-COUNT A **barrier** is a fence or wall that prevents people or things from moving from one area to another. ⓶ N-COUNT A **barrier** is something such as a law or policy that makes it difficult or impossible for something to happen. *Duties and taxes are the most obvious barrier to free trade.*

barring /ˈbɑːrɪŋ/. PREP You use **barring** to indicate that the person, thing, or event that you are mentioning is an exception to the point that you are making. *Barring accidents, I believe they will succeed.*

barrister /ˈbærɪstə/ **barristers.** N-COUNT A **barrister** is a lawyer who represents people in the higher courts of law. [BRITISH]

bartender /ˈbɑːtendə/ **bartenders.** N-COUNT In American English, a **bartender** is a person who serves drinks in a bar. The British word is **barman** or **barmaid.**

barter /ˈbɑːtə/ **barters, bartering, bartered.** VERB & N-UNCOUNT If you **barter** goods, you exchange them for other goods, rather than selling them. **Barter** is the act of exchanging goods in this way.

They have been bartering wheat for cotton and timber. ...the old barter system.

⭐ **base** /beɪs/ **bases, basing, based.** ⓵ N-COUNT The **base** of something is its lowest edge or part, or the part at which it is attached to something else. ...*a cake tin with a removable base.* ...*the base of the cliffs.* ⓶ N-COUNT A position or thing that is a **base** for something is one from which that thing can be developed or achieved. *The family base was crucial to my development.* ⓷ VERB If you **base** one thing on another thing, or if one thing **is based on** another, the first thing is developed from the second one. *He based his conclusions on the evidence... Three of the new products are based on traditional herbal medicines.* ⓸ N-COUNT & ADJ Your **base** is the main place where you work, stay, or live. If you **are based** in a particular place, that is the place where you live or do most of your work. *Her base was her home in Scotland... Both firms are based in Kent.* ⓹ N-VAR A military **base** is a place which part of an army, navy, or air force works from. ...*a British army base near Hanover.*

⭐ **baseball** /ˈbeɪsbɔːl/. N-UNCOUNT **Baseball** is a game played by two teams of nine players. Each player from one team hits a ball with a bat and then tries to run round all four bases before the other team can get the ball back.

basement /ˈbeɪsmənt/ **basements.** N-COUNT The **basement** of a building is an area partly or completely below ground level, with a room or rooms in it. ...*a damp basement flat.*

bases. ⓵ /ˈbeɪsɪz/ **Bases** is the plural and the third person singular of **base.** ⓶ /ˈbeɪsiːz/ **Bases** is the plural of **basis.**

bash /bæʃ/ **bashes, bashing, bashed.** ⓵ N-COUNT A **bash** is a party or celebration. [INFORMAL] ...*one of the biggest showbiz bashes of the year.* ⓶ VERB If you **bash** someone or something, you hit them hard in a rough way. *I bashed him on the head... Too many golfers try to bash the ball out of sand.*

⭐ **basic** /ˈbeɪsɪk/ **basics.** ⓵ ADJ & N-PLURAL You use **basic** or **the basics** to describe the most important or the simplest aspects of something. ...*access to justice is a basic right... Let's get down* to basics. ...*teaching the basics of reading, writing and arithmetic.* [2] ADJ **Basic** goods and services are very simple ones which every human being needs. ...*shortages of even the most basic foodstuffs.* ...*the basic needs of food and water.* [3] ADJ AFTER LINK-V An activity, situation, or plan that is **basic to** the achievement or success of something else is necessary for it. *There are certain ethical principles that are basic to all the great religions.* [4] ADJ You describe something as **basic** when it has only the most important features and no luxuries. ...*basic cooking and camping equipment.*

★ **basically** /ˈbeɪsɪkli/. ADV You use **basically** to indicate what the most important feature of something is, or to give a general description of something complicated. *He is basically healthy... There are basically three types of club... This gun is designed for one purpose – it's basically to kill people.*

basin /ˈbeɪsən/ **basins.** [1] N-COUNT A **basin** is a deep bowl that you use for holding liquids, or for mixing food in. [2] N-COUNT A **basin** is the same as a **washbasin.** [3] N-COUNT The **basin** of a large river is the area of land around it from which water and streams run down into it. ...*the Amazon basin.*

★ **basis** /ˈbeɪsɪs/ **bases** /ˈbeɪsiːz/. [1] N-COUNT The **basis** of something is the central and most important part of it, from which it can be developed. *Technical skill is a fundamental basis for most, if not all, great art.* [2] N-COUNT The **basis** for something is the thing that provides a reason for it. *The idea has its basis in fact.* [3] PHRASE If something happens or is done on a particular **basis**, it happens or is done in that way. *We're going to be meeting there on a regular basis... Most members work on a voluntary basis.*

bask /bɑːsk, bæsk/ **basks, basking, basked.** [1] VERB If you **bask in** the sunshine, you lie in it and enjoy its warmth. [2] VERB If you **bask in** someone's approval, favour, or admiration, you thoroughly enjoy it. *For now, though, the company can bask in its success.*

basket /ˈbɑːskɪt, ˈbæs-/ **baskets.** N-COUNT A **basket** is a container made of thin strips of cane woven together. → See picture on page 48.

basketball /ˈbɑːskɪtbɔːl, ˈbæs-/. N-UNCOUNT **Basketball** is a game in which two teams of five players each try to score points by throwing a large ball through a circular net fixed to a metal ring at each end of the court.

basketball

★ **bass** /beɪs/ **basses.** [1] N-COUNT A **bass** is a man with a deep singing voice. [2] ADJ BEFORE N A **bass** instrument has a range of notes of low pitch. ...*a bass guitar.*

bastion /ˈbæstɪən, AM -tʃən/ **bastions.** N-COUNT If you describe a system or organization as a **bastion of** a particular way of life, you mean that it is important and effective in defending that way of life. [LITERARY] ...*a town which had been a bastion of white prejudice.*

★ **bat** /bæt/ **bats, batting, batted.** [1] N-COUNT A **bat** is a specially shaped piece of wood that is used for hitting the ball in cricket, baseball, or table tennis. ...*a baseball bat.* [2] VERB When you **bat,** you have a turn at hitting the ball with a bat in cricket or baseball. *Penney also batted well to make 57.* [3] N-COUNT A **bat** is a small flying animal that looks like a mouse with wings. Bats fly at night.

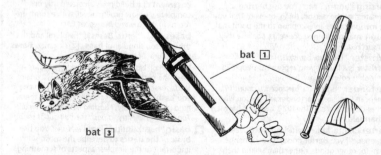

bat [1]

bat [3]

batch /bætʃ/ **batches.** N-COUNT A **batch of** things or people is a group of them, especially one that is dealt with at the same time. *Bread is baked in batches throughout the day. ...the current batch of trainee priests.*

⭐ **bath** /bɑːθ, bæθ/ **baths, bathing, bathed.** [1] N-COUNT In British English, a **bath** is a container which you fill with water and sit in while you wash your body. The American word is **bathtub.** [2] N-COUNT When you **have** a **bath** or **take** a **bath**, you wash your body while sitting in a bath filled with water. *I took a long hot bath.* [3] VERB & N-COUNT If you **bath** a child or other person, or if you give them a **bath**, you wash them in a bath. *Don't feel you have to bath your child every day.*

bathe /beɪð/ **bathes, bathing, bathed.** [1] VERB When you **bathe** in a sea, river, or lake, you swim or play there. [FORMAL, BRITISH] *The water's 45 degrees centigrade, it's so nice to bathe in.* ♦ **bathing** N-UNCOUNT *...bathing beaches.* [2] VERB When you **bathe,** you have a bath. [AMERICAN] *At least 60% of us now bathe or shower once a day.* [3] VERB When you **bathe** a wound, you wash it gently. *Bathe the infected area in a salt solution.* [4] VERB If a place **is bathed in** light, it is very bright. *I was led to a small room bathed in soft red light.*

⭐ **bathroom** /bɑːθruːm, bæθ-/ **bathrooms.** [1] N-COUNT A **bathroom** is a room in a house that contains a bath or shower, a washbasin, and sometimes a toilet. [2] N-SING In American English, a **bathroom** is a room in a house or public building that contains a toilet. The usual British word is **toilet.**

bathtub /bɑːθtʌb, bæθ-/ **bathtubs.** N-COUNT In American English, a **bathtub** is a container which you fill with water and sit in while you wash your body. The British word is **bath.**

baton /bætɒn, AM bəˈtɑːn/ **batons.** [1] N-COUNT A **baton** is a stick, for example one which is used by the conductor of an orchestra, or by athletes in a relay race. [2] N-COUNT A **baton** is a short heavy stick which is sometimes used as a weapon by the police.

batsman /bætsmən/ **batsmen.** N-COUNT In a game of cricket, the **batsman** is the person who is batting.

battalion /bəˈtæljən/ **battalions.** N-COUNT A **battalion** is a large group of soldiers consisting of three or more companies.

batter /bætə/ **batters, battering, battered.** [1] VERB To **batter** someone or something means to hit them many times. *...boys who witness fathers battering their mothers. ...battered wives... Batter the steaks flat.* [2] N-UNCOUNT **Batter** is a mixture of flour, eggs, and milk used to make pancakes.

battered /bætəd/. ADJ Something that is **battered** is old, worn, and damaged. *...a battered leather suitcase.*

battering /bætərɪŋ/ **batterings.** N-COUNT If something **takes** a **battering**, it suffers very badly as a result of a particular event or action. *We took an awful battering during the war.*

battery /bætəri/ **batteries.** [1] N-COUNT **Batteries** are the devices that you put in electrical items to provide the power that makes these devices work. [2] N-COUNT A **battery of** things, people, or events is a large number of them. *...a battery of journalists and television cameras.*

⭐ **battle** /bætəl/ **battles, battling, battled.** [1] N-VAR In a war, a **battle** is a fight between armies or between groups of ships or planes. *...a gun battle. ...men who die in battle.* [2] N-COUNT & VERB A **battle** is a conflict in which different people or groups compete for power or try to achieve opposite things. Opposing groups can also **battle with** one another. *...a major legal battle... 2,000 fans battled with riot police... The sides must battle again for a quarter-final place.* [3] VERB To **battle** means to try hard to be successful in spite of very difficult circumstances. *Doctors battled throughout the night to save her life... He is battling with a leg injury.* [4] PHRASE If one person or group **does battle with** another, they take part in a battle or contest against them.

battlefield /bætəlfiːld/ **battlefields.** N-COUNT A **battlefield** is a place where a battle is fought.

battleground /bætəlɡraʊnd/ **battlegrounds.** [1] N-COUNT A **battleground** is the same as a **battlefield.** [2] N-COUNT You can refer to a subject over which people disagree or compete as a **battleground.** *...the battleground of education.*

battleship /bætəlʃɪp/ **battleships.** N-COUNT A **battleship** is a very large, heavily armoured warship.

baulk /bɔːlk, AM bɔːk/. See **balk.**

bawl /bɔːl/ **bawls, bawling, bawled.** [1] VERB If you **bawl,** you shout or sing something loudly and harshly. *Laura and Peter were shouting and bawling at each other.* [2] VERB If a child **is bawling,** it is crying loudly. *...a bawling baby.*

⭐ **bay** /beɪ/ **bays, baying, bayed.** [1] N-COUNT A **bay** is a part of a coastline where the land curves inwards. *...San Francisco Bay.* [2] N-COUNT A **bay** is a partly enclosed area used for a particular purpose. *The car reversed into the loading bay.* [3] PHRASE If you **keep** something or someone **at bay,** or **hold** them **at bay,** you prevent them from reaching or affecting you. *Eating oranges keeps colds at bay.* [4] VERB If you say that a number of people **are baying for** something, you mean that they are shouting for something or demanding it angrily. *The referee ignored voices baying for a penalty.*

bayonet /beɪənət/ **bayonets.** N-COUNT A **bayonet** is a long sharp blade that can be fixed to the end of a rifle and used as a weapon.

bazaar /bəˈzɑː/ **bazaars.** [1] N-COUNT A **bazaar** is an area with many small shops and stalls, especially in the Middle East and India. [2] N-COUNT A **bazaar** is a sale to raise money for charity.

BC /ˌbiː ˈsiː/. You use **BC** in dates to indicate a number of years or centuries before the year in which Jesus Christ is believed to have been born. *...the fourth century BC.*

⭐ Bank of English® frequent word   For a full explanation of all grammatical labels, see pages vii–x

be /bɪ, STRONG biː/ **am, are, is, being, was, were, been.** **1** LINK-VERB You use **be** to introduce more information about the subject, such as its identity, nature, qualities, or position. *She's my mother... Cheney was in Madrid... He's still alive isn't he?* **2** LINK-VERB You use **be**, with 'it' as the subject, in clauses where you are describing something or giving your judgement of a situation. *Sometimes it is necessary to say no... It's nice having friends to chat to... It's a good idea to avoid refined food.* **3** LINK-VERB You use **be** as a link between a subject and a clause and in certain other clause structures, as exemplified below. *It was me she didn't like... Our greatest problem is convincing them.* **4** LINK-VERB You use **be** with 'there' in expressions like **there is** and **there are** to say that something exists or happens. *Clearly there is a problem here... There are very few cars on this street.*

★ **beach** /biːtʃ/ **beaches.** N-COUNT A **beach** is an area of sand or pebbles by the sea.

beacon /'biːkən/ **beacons.** N-COUNT A **beacon** is a light or a fire on a hill or tower, which acts as a signal or a warning.

bead /biːd/ **beads.** **1** N-COUNT **Beads** are small pieces of coloured glass, wood, or plastic with a hole through the middle which are used for jewellery or decoration. **2** N-COUNT A **bead of** liquid or moisture is a small drop of it. *...the beads of sweat on his forehead.*

beak /biːk/ **beaks.** N-COUNT A bird's **beak** is the hard curved or pointed part of its mouth.

beaker /'biːkə/ **beakers.** **1** N-COUNT A **beaker** is a plastic cup. **2** N-COUNT A **beaker** is a glass or plastic jar which is used in chemistry.

beam /biːm/ **beams, beaming, beamed.** **1** VERB If someone **is beaming**, they are smiling because they are happy. [WRITTEN] *The bartender was beaming at him.* **2** VERB If something such as radio signals or television pictures **are beamed** somewhere, or if they **beam** somewhere, they are sent there by means of electronic equipment. *Soon, CMTV will be beaming into British homes. ...beaming radio broadcasts to China.* **3** N-COUNT A **beam of** light is a line of light that shines from an object such as a torch or the sun. **4** VERB If something such as the sun or a lamp **beams down**, it sends light to a place and shines on it. *A sharp white spot-light beamed down on a small stage.* **5** N-COUNT A **beam** is a long thick bar of wood, metal, or concrete, especially one which is used to support the roof of a building. *...oak beams.*

★ **bean** /biːn/ **beans.** **1** N-COUNT **Beans** are the pods of a climbing plant, or the seeds that the pods contain, which are eaten as a vegetable. → See picture on page 836. **2** N-COUNT Beans such as coffee **beans** or cocoa **beans** are the seeds of a plant that is used in the production of coffee and chocolate.

★ **bear** /beə/ **bears, bearing, bore, borne.** **1** N-COUNT A **bear** is a large strong wild animal with thick fur

and sharp claws. **2** VERB If you **bear** something somewhere, you carry it there. [LITERARY] *They bore the oblong hardwood box into the kitchen.* **3** VERB If something **bears** the weight of something else, it supports the weight of that thing. *The ice was not thick enough to bear their weight.* **4** VERB If you **bear** something difficult, you accept it and are able to deal with it. *They will have to bear the misery of living in constant fear... He can't bear to talk about it.* **5** VERB If you **bear** someone a feeling such as love or hate, you feel that emotion towards them. [FORMAL] *She bore no ill will. If people didn't like her, too bad.* **6** PHRASE If you **bring** pressure or influence **to bear on** someone, you use it to try and persuade them to do something. *His companions brought pressure to bear on him, urging him to stop wasting money.* **7** to **bear the brunt of**: see brunt. ● to **bear in mind**: see mind.

▸**bear out.** PHR-VERB If something **bears** someone **out** or **bears out** what they are saying, it supports what they are saying. *Unhappily the facts do not wholly bear out the theory.*

▸**bear with.** PHR-VERB If you ask someone to **bear with** you, you are asking them to be patient. *Bear with me, Frank, just let me try to explain.*

bearable /'beərəbəl/. ADJ If something is **bearable**, you can accept it, although it is rather unpleasant. *...the small luxuries that made life bearable.*

beard /bɪəd/ **beards.** N-COUNT A man's **beard** is the hair that grows on his chin and cheeks.

bearded /'bɪədɪd/. ADJ A **bearded** man has a beard.

bearer /'beərə/ **bearers.** **1** N-COUNT The **bearer of** something such as a document or a piece of news is the person who has it in their possession, or the person who brings it to you. *Spanish identity documents state the bearer's profession... I hate to be the bearer of bad news.* **2** N-COUNT A **bearer** is a person who carries a stretcher or coffin.

★ **bearing** /'beərɪŋ/ **bearings.** **1** PHRASE If something **has a bearing on** a situation or event, it is relevant to it. *Diet has an important bearing on your general health.* **2** PHRASE If you **get** your **bearings** or **find** your **bearings**, you find out where you are or what you should do next. If you **lose** your **bearings**, you do not know where you are or what you should do next.

beast /biːst/ **beasts.** N-COUNT A **beast** is an animal, especially a large one. [LITERARY]

★ **beat** /biːt/ **beats, beating, beat, beaten.** **1** VERB To **beat** someone or something means to hit them very hard. *They were beaten to death with baseball bats... The rain was beating on the windowpanes.* ◆ **beating, beatings** N-COUNT *...prisoners showing signs of severe beatings. ...the beating of the rain.* **2** VERB & N-COUNT When your heart or pulse **beats**, it continually makes regular rhythmic movements. The **beat** of your heart or pulse is a single movement of it. *I felt my heart beating*

faster. ...more than 70 beats per minute.
♦ **beating** N-SING *...the beating of my heart.*
3 N-COUNT The **beat** of a piece of music is the main rhythm that it has. *...the thumping beat of rock music.* **4** VERB If you **beat** eggs, cream, or butter, you mix them thoroughly using a fork or whisk. **5** VERB To **beat** someone in a competition means to do better than them. *She was easily beaten into third place.* ♦ **beating** N-SING *The candidates the government liked took a beating.*
▸**beat down.** **1** PHR-VERB When the sun **beats down,** it is very hot and bright. **2** PHR-VERB When the rain **beats down,** it rains very hard. **3** PHR-VERB If you **beat down** a person who is selling something, you force them to accept a lower price for it.
▸**beat up.** PHR-VERB If someone **beats** a person **up,** they hit or kick the person many times.
⭐ **beautiful** /ˈbjuːtɪfʊl/. **1** ADJ **Beautiful** means attractive to look at. *...the most beautiful child on earth... New England is beautiful.* ♦ **beautifully** ADV *...a beautifully clear, sunny day.*

> **USAGE** When you are describing someone's appearance, you usually use **beautiful** and **pretty** to describe women, girls, and babies. **Beautiful** is a much stronger word than **pretty.** The equivalent word for a man is **handsome. Good-looking** and **attractive** can be used to describe people of either sex.

2 ADJ You can describe something that someone does as **beautiful** when they do it very skilfully. *...the finest and most beautiful display of bowling.* ♦ **beautifully** ADV *He writes beautifully.*
⭐ **beauty** /ˈbjuːti/**beauties. 1** N-UNCOUNT **Beauty** is the state or quality of being beautiful. *...an area of outstanding natural beauty. ...the idea of feminine beauty.* **2** N-COUNT A beautiful woman is sometimes described as a **beauty. 3** N-COUNT The **beauties of** something are its attractive qualities or features. [LITERARY] *...the beauties of the countryside.* **4** N-COUNT If you say that a particular feature is **the beauty of** something, you mean that this feature is what makes the thing so good. *That's the beauty of it. Any fool can make this.*
beaver /ˈbiːvə/ **beavers, beavering, beavered.** N-COUNT A **beaver** is a furry animal like a large rat with a big flat tail.
▸**beaver away.** PHR-VERB If you **are beavering away at** something, you are working very hard at it.
became /bɪˈkeɪm/. **Became** is the past tense of **become.**
⭐ **because** /bɪˈkʌz, bɪˈkɒz/. **1** CONJ You use **because** when stating the reason or explanation for something. *He is called Mitch, because his name is Mitchell... Maybe they just didn't want to ask too many questions, because they rented us a*

room without even asking to see our papers.
2 PREP If an event or situation occurs **because of** something, that thing is the reason or cause. *Many families break up because of a lack of money.*
beckon /ˈbekən/ **beckons, beckoning, beckoned.**
1 VERB If you **beckon to** someone, you signal to them to come to you. *He beckoned to the waiter... I beckoned her over.* **2** VERB If something **beckons,** it is so attractive that you want to become involved in it. *...the warm bars and restaurants which now beckoned.*
⭐ **become** /bɪˈkʌm/ **becomes, becoming, became.** **1** LINK-VERB If someone or something **becomes** a particular thing, they start being that thing. *He became a professional footballer... The wind became stronger.* **2** PHRASE If you wonder **what has become of** someone, you wonder where they are and what has happened to them.
⭐ **bed** /bed/ **beds. 1** N-VAR A **bed** is a piece of furniture that you lie on when you sleep. *We finally went to bed at about 4am... Sam and Robina put the children to bed.* **2** PHRASE To **go to bed with** someone means to have sex with them. **3** N-COUNT A flower **bed** is an area of earth in which you grow plants. **4** N-COUNT The sea **bed** or a river **bed** is the ground at the bottom of the sea or of a river.
ˌ**bed and** ˈ**breakfast.** N-UNCOUNT **Bed and breakfast** is a system of accommodation in a hotel or guest house in which you pay for a room for the night and for breakfast the following morning. The abbreviation **B&B** is also used.
bedclothes /ˈbedkləʊðz/. N-PLURAL **Bedclothes** are the sheets and covers which you put over you when you get into bed.
bedding /ˈbedɪŋ/. N-UNCOUNT **Bedding** consists of sheets, blankets, and other covers used on beds.
bedrock /ˈbedrɒk/. N-UNCOUNT The **bedrock of** something refers to all the principles, ideas, or facts on which it is based. *Trust is the bedrock of a relationship.*
⭐ **bedroom** /ˈbedruːm/ **bedrooms.** N-COUNT A **bedroom** is a room which is used for sleeping in.
bedside /ˈbedsaɪd/. **1** N-SING Your **bedside** is the area beside your bed. *He drew a chair up to the bedside and sat down.* **2** N-SING If you talk about being at someone's **bedside,** you are talking about being near them when they are ill in bed. *She was called to her brother's bedside.*
bee /biː/ **bees.** N-COUNT A **bee** is an insect with a yellow-and-black striped body that makes a buzzing noise as it flies. → See picture on page 824.
beef /biːf/. **beefs, beefing, beefed.** N-UNCOUNT **Beef** is the meat of a cow, bull, or ox.
▸**beef up.** PHR-VERB If you **beef** something **up,** you increase, strengthen, or improve it. *...a campaign to beef up security.*
been /bɪn, biːn/. **1 Been** is the past participle of **be. 2** VERB If you have **been** to a place, you

a
b
c
d
e
f
g
h
i
j
k
l
m
n
o
p
q
r
s
t
u
v
w
x
y
z

have gone to it or visited it. *He's already been to Tunisia.*

⭐ **beer** /bɪə/ **beers.** N-VAR **Beer** is a bitter alcoholic drink made from grain. A **beer** is a glass of beer. *Would you like a beer?*

beet /biːt/ **beets.** [1] N-UNCOUNT **Beet** is a root vegetable that is used as food for animals. [2] N-VAR In American English, **beets** are **beetroot.**

beetle /'biːtəl/ **beetles.** N-COUNT A **beetle** is an insect with a hard covering to its body. → See picture on page 824.

beetroot /'biːtruːt/ **beetroots.** N-VAR In British English, **beetroot** is a dark red root vegetable which can be cooked or pickled. The American word is **beets.**

befall /bɪ'fɔːl/ **befalls, befalling, befell** /bɪ'fel/, **befallen.** VERB If something bad or unlucky **befalls** you, it happens to you. [LITERARY] *...the disaster that befell the island of Flores.*

befit /bɪ'fɪt/ **befits, befitting, befitted.** VERB If something **befits** a person or thing, it is suitable or appropriate for them. *He writes beautifully, as befits a poet.*

⭐ **before** /bɪ'fɔː/. [1] PREP & CONJ & ADV If something happens **before** a time or event, it happens earlier than that time or event. → See Reference Page on Times and Dates. *My husband rarely comes to bed before 2 or 3am. ...Greenwich, where Mary lived before moving to Newtown... He phoned on Tuesday, just before you came... The war had ended only a month or so before.* [2] ADJ If something happened the day **before,** it happened during the previous day. *I'd been to a housewarming party the night before.* [3] ADV If someone has done something **before,** they have done it on a previous occasion. *'Have you been to York before?' ...conversation with people she has never met before.* [4] PREP If someone is **before** something, they are in front of it. [FORMAL] *They stopped before a large white villa.* [5] PREP When you have a task or difficult situation **before** you, you have to deal with it. *...the duty which lay before me.*

beforehand /bɪ'fɔːhænd/. ADV If you do something **beforehand,** you do it earlier than a particular event. *Make a list of your questions beforehand.*

befriend /bɪ'frend/ **befriends, befriending, befriended.** VERB If you **befriend** someone, you make friends with them.

beg /beɡ/ **begs, begging, begged.** [1] VERB If you **beg** someone **to** do something, you ask them anxiously or eagerly to do it. *I begged to be allowed to leave... We are not going to beg for help. ...weeping and begging forgiveness... 'Please leave,' I begged.* [2] VERB If someone is **begging,** they are asking people to give them food or money. *I was surrounded by people begging for food... She was living alone, begging food from neighbors.* [3] PHRASE If you say that something **begs** a particular **question,** you mean that it makes people want to ask that question. Some

people think this use is incorrect. *Hopewell's success begs the question: why aren't more companies doing the same?* [4] **I beg your pardon:** see **pardon.**

began /bɪ'ɡæn/. **Began** is the past tense of **begin.**

beggar /'beɡə/ **beggars.** N-COUNT A **beggar** is someone who lives by asking people for money or food.

⭐ **begin** /bɪ'ɡɪn/ **begins, beginning, began** /bɪ'ɡæn/, **begun** /bɪ'ɡʌn/. [1] VERB When someone or something **begins to** do something, they start doing it. *He stood up and began to move around the room... Snow began falling again... 'Professor Theron,' he began, 'I'm very pleased to see you.'* [2] VERB When something **begins** or when you **begin** it, it takes place from a particular time onwards. *The concert begins at 5 p.m... He had begun his career as a painter.* [3] PHRASE You use the phrase **to begin with** when you are talking about the first stage of a situation, event, or process, or to introduce the first of several things that you want to say. *To begin with, jobs in journalism were scarce... 'What do scientists you've spoken with think about that?'—'Well, to begin with, they doubt it's going to work.'*

beginner /bɪ'ɡɪnə/ **beginners.** N-COUNT A **beginner** is someone who has just started learning to do something and cannot do it well yet.

⭐ **beginning** /bɪ'ɡɪnɪŋ/ **beginnings.** N-COUNT The **beginning** of something is the first part of it. *This was the beginning of her recording career... She contacted me at the beginning of August... I had the beginnings of a headache.*

begun /bɪ'ɡʌn/. **Begun** is the past participle of **begin.**

⭐ **behalf** /bɪ'hɑːf, -'hæf/. PHRASE If you do something on someone's **behalf,** you do it as their representative. *She made an emotional public appeal on her son's behalf.*

⭐ **behave** /bɪ'heɪv/ **behaves, behaving, behaved.** [1] VERB The way that you **behave** is the way that you do and say things, and the things that you do and say. *He'd behaved badly.* [2] VERB If you **behave yourself,** you act in the way that people think is correct and proper. *You're going to behave and do what you're told... They were expected to behave themselves.*

⭐ **behaviour** (AM **behavior**) /bɪ'heɪvjə/ **behaviours.** N-VAR A person's **behaviour** is the way they behave. *...anti-social behaviour... Being over-expressive is a behaviour typical of people with no authority.*

behavioural (AM **behavioral**) /bɪ'heɪvjərəl/. ADJ BEFORE N **Behavioural** means relating to the behaviour of a person or animal, or to the study of their behaviour. *...infant behavioural patterns.*

⭐ **behind** /bɪ'haɪnd/ **behinds.** In addition to the uses shown below, **behind** is also used in phrasal verbs such as 'fall behind' and 'lie behind'.

1 PREP & ADV If someone or something is **behind** another person or thing, they are facing the back of that person or thing. *I put one of the cushions behind his head... They were parked behind the truck... She led the way upstairs, with Terry following behind.* **2** ADV If you stay **behind**, you remain in a place after other people have gone. **3** ADV If you leave something or someone **behind**, you do not take them with you when you go. **4** PREP When someone or something is **behind**, they are delayed or are making less progress than they should. *The train was seven minutes behind schedule.* **5** PREP The people or events **behind** a situation are the causes of it or the things that are responsible for it. *It is still not clear who was behind the killing.* **6** PREP If something or someone is **behind** you, they support and help you. *His family are completely behind him, whatever he decides.* **7** N-COUNT Your **behind** is the part of your body that you sit on. [INFORMAL] **8** to do something **behind** someone's **back**: see **back**. • **behind bars**: see **bar**. • **behind the scenes**: see **scene**.

⭐ **being** /'biːɪŋ/ **beings**. **1** **Being** is the present participle of **be**. **2** N-UNCOUNT **Being** is existence. Something that **comes into being** begins to exist. *The committee came into being in 1993.* **3** N-COUNT You can refer to any real or imaginary creature as a **being**. *...beings from outer space.*

belated /bɪˈleɪtɪd/. ADJ A **belated** action happens later than it should have done. *...John Hall's belated return to the international side.* ◆ **belatedly** ADV *People have belatedly become aware of how fragile the planet is.*

belch /beltʃ/ **belches, belching, belched**. **1** VERB & N-COUNT If someone **belches**, they make a sudden noise, called a **belch**, in their throat because air has risen up from their stomach. **2** VERB If an engine or factory **belches** smoke, or if smoke **belches from** it, large amounts of smoke come from it. *Clouds of steam started to belch from the engine.*

beleaguered /bɪˈliːgəd/. ADJ **Beleaguered** people or places are being attacked or criticized. [FORMAL] *...the beleaguered city of Vukovar.*

belie /bɪˈlaɪ/ **belies, belying, belied**. VERB If one thing **belies** another, it creates a false idea or image of someone or something. *...a man with energy that belies his years.*

⭐ **belief** /bɪˈliːf/ **beliefs**. N-VAR **Belief** is a feeling of certainty that something exists, is true, or is good. *...a belief in reincarnation.*

believable /bɪˈliːvəbəl/. ADJ Something that is **believable** makes you think that it could be true or real. *This book is full of believable characters.*

⭐ **believe** /bɪˈliːv/ **believes, believing, believed**. **1** VERB If you **believe** that something is true, you think that it is true. *Experts believe that the drought will be extensive.*

USAGE Note that when you are using the verb **believe** with a **that** clause in order to state a negative opinion or belief, you normally make **believe** negative, rather than the verb in the **that** clause. For instance, it is more usual to say *'He didn't believe she could do it'* than *'He believed she couldn't do it'*. The same pattern applies to other verbs with a similar meaning, such as **consider, suppose** and **think**. *I don't consider that you kept your promise... I don't suppose he ever saw it... I don't think he saw me.*

2 VERB If you **believe** someone, you accept that they are telling the truth. *He did not sound as if he believed her... Don't believe what you read in the papers.* **3** VERB If you **believe in** things such as God, fairies, or miracles, you are sure that they exist or happen. **4** VERB If you **believe in** a way of life or an idea, you think it is good or right. *He believed in marital fidelity.*

believer /bɪˈliːvə/ **believers**. **1** N-COUNT If you are a **believer in** something, you think that it is good or right. *Mum was a great believer in herbal medicines.* **2** N-COUNT A **believer** is someone who is sure that God exists or that the teachings of their religion are true.

bell **2**

bell **1**

⭐ **bell** /bel/ **bells**. **1** N-COUNT A **bell** is a device that makes a ringing sound which attracts people's attention. *I've been ringing the door bell.* **2** N-COUNT A **bell** is a hollow metal object with a loose piece hanging inside it that hits the sides and makes a sound. *...church bells.*

belligerent /bɪˈlɪdʒərənt/. ADJ A **belligerent** person is hostile and aggressive. ◆ **belligerence** N-UNCOUNT *He could be accused of passion, but never belligerence.*

bellow /'beləʊ/ **bellows, bellowing, bellowed**.

✓ In meaning 2, **bellows** is the singular and the plural form.

a
b
c
d
e
f
g
h
i
j
k
l
m
n
o
p
q
r
s
t
u
v
w
x
y
z

1 VERB & N-COUNT If someone **bellows**, they shout angrily in a loud deep voice. You call a sound like this a **bellow**. *'I didn't ask to be born!' she bellowed... The owner bellowed orders at the teenager... Alfred let out a bellow.* **2** N-COUNT A **bellows** is a device used for blowing air into a fire in order to make it burn more fiercely.

belly /'bɛli/ **bellies.** N-COUNT A person's or animal's **belly** is their stomach or abdomen.

⭐ **belong** /bɪ'lɒŋ/, AM -'lɔːŋ/ **belongs, belonging, belonged.** **1** VERB If something **belongs to** you, you own it. *At one time the jeep had belonged to the army... The handwriting belongs to a male.* **2** VERB If someone or something **belongs to** a particular group, they are a member of it. *I used to belong to a youth club.* **3** VERB If a person or thing **belongs in** a particular category, group, or place, they are of that category or group, or are usually found in that place. *The judges could not decide which category it belonged in.*

belongings /bɪ'lɒŋɪŋz, AM -'lɔːŋ-/. N-PLURAL Your **belongings** are the things that you own.

beloved /bɪ'lʌvɪd/.

✔ Also pronounced /bɪ'lʌvd/ when used after a noun or after the verb 'be'.

ADJ A **beloved** person, thing, or place is one that you feel great love or affection for. *He lost his beloved wife last year.*

⭐ **below** /bɪ'ləʊ/. **1** PREP & ADV If something is **below** something else, it is in a lower position. *To the west, the sun dipped below the horizon... The path runs below a long brick wall... Spread out below was a great crowd... Please write to me at the address below.* **2** PREP & ADV If something is **below** a particular amount or level, it is less than it. *Rainfall has been below average. ...temperatures at zero or below.* **3** **below par**: see **par**.

⭐ **belt** /bɛlt/ **belts, belting, belted.** **1** N-COUNT A **belt** is a strip of leather or cloth that you fasten round your waist. **2** N-COUNT A **belt** is a circular strip of rubber used in machines to drive moving parts or to move objects along. **3** N-COUNT A **belt** of land or sea is a long, narrow area of it that has some special feature. *Behind him was a belt of trees. ...Zambia's northern copper belt.* **4** VERB & N-COUNT If someone **belts** or gives you a **belt**, they hit you very hard. [INFORMAL] **5** See also **safety belt, conveyor belt.**

PHRASES ● If you have to **tighten** your **belt**, you must manage without things because you have less money than you used to have. ● If you have something **under** your **belt**, you have already achieved it or done it. *Colvin already has two albums under her belt.*

bemused /bɪ'mjuːzd/. ADJ If you are **bemused**, you look slightly puzzled or confused. *Mary looked at her with a bemused expression.*

bench /bɛntʃ/ **benches.** **1** N-COUNT A **bench** is a long seat of wood or metal. **2** N-COUNT A **bench** is a long narrow table in a factory, laboratory, or workshop. **3** N-SING In a court of law, **the bench** consists of the judge or magistrates. *Allgood served on the bench for more than 50 years.*

⭐ **bend** /bɛnd/ **bends, bending, bent** /bɛnt/. **1** VERB When you **bend**, you move the top part of your body downwards and forwards. *I bent over and kissed her cheek... She was bent over the sink.* **2** VERB When you **bend** a part of your body such as your arm or leg, or when it **bends**, you change its position so that it is no longer straight. *Stand up straight, then slightly bend one leg... As you walk faster, you will find the arms bend naturally.* ♦ **bent** ADJ *Keep your knees slightly bent.* **3** VERB When you **bend** something that is flat or straight, you use force to make it curved or angular. *Bend the bar into a horseshoe.* ♦ **bent** ADJ *...a length of bent wire.* **4** VERB When a road or river **bends**, it changes direction to form a curve or angle. *The road bent sharply to the left.* **5** N-COUNT A **bend** in a road, river, or pipe is a curved part in it. **6** VERB If someone **bends the rules**, they do something which is not allowed, either to gain an advantage or to help someone else. **7** See also **bent**. ● to **bend double**: see **double**.

⭐ **beneath** /bɪ'niːθ/. PREP & ADV Something that is **beneath** another thing is under it. *She could see the muscles of his shoulders beneath his T-shirt... Beneath the surface gaiety were traces of sadness... On a shelf beneath he spotted a photo album.*

benefactor /'bɛnɪfæktə/ **benefactors.** N-COUNT Your **benefactor** is a person who helps you by giving you money.

beneficial /ˌbɛnɪ'fɪʃəl/. ADJ Something that is **beneficial** helps people or improves their lives. *Wine in moderation is beneficial to health.*

beneficiary /ˌbɛnɪ'fɪʃəri, AM -ʃieri/ **beneficiaries.** N-COUNT Someone who is a **beneficiary of** something is helped by it. *The main beneficiaries of pension equality so far have been men.*

⭐ **benefit** /'bɛnɪfɪt/ **benefits, benefiting, benefited,** or **benefitting, benefitted.** **1** VERB & N-VAR If you **benefit from** something or if you **have the benefit of** it, it helps you or improves your life. *He hopes to benefit from the tax cuts. ...government programs benefiting children... Steve didn't have the benefit of a formal college education... I hope what I have written will be of benefit to someone else.* **2** N-UNCOUNT **Benefit** is money given by the government to people who are poor, ill, or unemployed. *...unemployment benefit.* **3** PHRASE If you give someone **the benefit of the doubt**, you accept what they say as true, because you cannot prove that it is not true.

benevolent /bɪ'nɛvələnt/. ADJ A **benevolent** person is kind, helpful, and tolerant. ♦ **benevolence** N-UNCOUNT *He chuckles often and radiates benevolence.*

benign /bɪ'naɪn/. **1** ADJ You use **benign** to describe someone who is kind, gentle, and harmless. *...a good-looking chap with a benign expression.* ♦ **benignly** ADV *I just smiled* benignly. [2] ADJ A **benign** disease or substance will not cause death or serious harm. [TECHNICAL]

bent /bent/. [1] **Bent** is the past tense and past participle of **bend**. [2] ADJ AFTER LINK-V If someone is **bent on** doing something, they are determined to do it. *They seem bent on destroying the city.* [3] N-SING If you have a **bent for** something, you have a natural ability to do it or a natural interest in it. ...*his bent for history.*

bequeath /bɪˈkwiːð/ **bequeaths, bequeathing, bequeathed.** VERB If you **bequeath** something **to** someone, you formally state that they should have it when you die, usually in your will. *Fields's will bequeathed them the sum of twenty thousand dollars... He bequeathed all his silver to his children.*

bereaved /bɪˈriːvd/. ADJ & N-PLURAL A **bereaved** person has a relative or close friend who has recently died. Bereaved people are sometimes called **the bereaved.** [FORMAL] *Mr Dinkins visited the bereaved family to offer comfort... He wanted to show his sympathy for the bereaved.*
♦ **bereavement** /bɪˈriːvmənt/ **bereavements** N-VAR ...*those who have suffered a bereavement.*

bereft /bɪˈreft/. ADJ If a person or thing is **bereft of** something, they no longer have it. [FORMAL] *The place seemed to be utterly bereft of human life... They were bereft of ideas.*

berry /ˈberi/ **berries.** N-COUNT **Berries** are small round fruit that grow on a bush or a tree.

berth /bɜːθ/ **berths, berthing, berthed.** [1] N-COUNT A **berth** is a space in a harbour where a ship stays for a period of time. [2] VERB When a ship **berths**, it sails into harbour and stops at the quay. *As soon as they berthed, the boxes of fish would be unloaded. ...the port where the ferry is berthed.* [3] N-COUNT A **berth** is a bed on a boat or train, or in a caravan.

beset /bɪˈset/ **besets, besetting, beset.** VERB If someone or something **is beset** by problems or fears, they have many problems or fears which affect them severely. ...*the problems now besetting the country.*

★ **beside** /bɪˈsaɪd/. [1] PREP Something that is **beside** something else is at the side of it or next to it. *Beside his plate was a pile of books... I moved from behind my desk to sit beside her.* [2] PHRASE If you are **beside yourself with** anger or excitement, you are extremely angry or excited. [3] **beside the point**: see **point**.

★ **besides** /bɪˈsaɪdz/. [1] PREP & ADV **Besides** or **beside** something means in addition to it. *I think she has many good qualities besides being very beautiful. ...the shortage of training, ill health and much else besides.* [2] ADV You use **besides** to make an additional point or give an additional reason. '*I don't need any help. Besides, I'm nearly finished.*'

besiege /bɪˈsiːdʒ/ **besieges, besieging, besieged.** [1] VERB If you **are besieged** by people, many people want something from you and continually

bother you. *She was constantly besieged by the press.* [2] VERB If soldiers **besiege** a place, they surround it and wait for the people in it to surrender.

★ **best** /best/. [1] **Best** is the superlative of **good**. [2] **Best** is the superlative of **well**. [3] N-SING Your **best** is the greatest effort or the highest achievement that you are capable of. *Miss Blockey was at her best when she played the piano.* [4] N-SING **The best** is used to refer to things of the highest quality or standard. *He'll have the best of care.* [5] ADV If you like something **best** or like it **the best,** you prefer it. *What music do you like best?... What was the role you loved the best?* [6] PHRASE You use **at best** to indicate that even if you describe something as favourably as possible, it is still not very good. *At best Nella would be an invalid; at worst she would die.* [7] PHRASE If you **make the best of** an unsatisfactory situation, you accept it and try to be cheerful about it. *He was determined to be cheerful and make the best of a bad job.* [8] **the best part of** something: see **part.** ● **the best of both worlds**: see **world.**

bestow /bɪˈstəʊ/ **bestows, bestowing, bestowed.** VERB To **bestow** something **on** someone means to give it to them. [FORMAL] *The Mayor bestowed medals on the police.*

best-'seller (or **bestseller**) **best-sellers.** N-COUNT A **best-seller** is a book of which a very large number of copies have been sold.

best-'selling (or **bestselling**). [1] ADJ BEFORE N A **best-selling** product is very popular and a large quantity of it has been sold. [2] ADJ BEFORE N A **best-selling** author is an author who has sold a very large number of copies of his or her book.

★ **bet** /bet/ **bets, betting, bet.** [1] VERB & N-COUNT If you **bet on** the result of a horse race, football match, or other event, or if you put a **bet on** it, you give someone a sum of money which they give you back with extra money if the result is what you predicted, or which they keep if it is not. *I bet £10 on a horse called Premonition... He bet them 500 pounds they would lose... He had already placed a bet on one of the horses.* ♦ **betting** N-UNCOUNT ...*off-course betting shops.* [2] PHRASE You say '**You bet**' or '**You bet your life**' as an emphatic way of saying 'yes' or of emphasizing a statement. [INFORMAL] '*It's settled, then?'—'You bet.*' [3] PHRASE If you use a phrase such as '**I bet**', '**I'll bet**', or '**you can bet**', you mean that you are sure something is true. *I bet you were good at games when you were at school.*

betray /bɪˈtreɪ/ **betrays, betraying, betrayed.** [1] VERB If you **betray** someone who trusts you, you do something which hurts and disappoints them. *When I tell someone I will not betray his confidence I keep my word.* [2] VERB If someone **betrays** their country or their comrades, they give information to an enemy, putting their country's security or their comrades' safety at risk. *He could never bring himself to betray his country.* [3] VERB If you

A
B
C
D
E
F
G
H
I
J
K
L
M
N
O
P
Q
R
S
T
U
V
W
X
Y
Z

betray your feelings or thoughts, you show them without intending to. *Jeremy's voice betrayed little emotion.*

betrayal /bɪ'treɪəl/ **betrayals.** N-VAR A **betrayal** is an action that betrays someone or something. *She felt that what she had done was a betrayal of Patrick.*

⭐ **better** /'betə/. [1] ADJ **Better** is the comparative of **good.** [2] ADV **Better** is the comparative of **well.** [3] ADV If you like one thing **better than** another, you like it more. *I always liked you better than Sandra... They liked it better when it rained.* [4] ADJ AFTER LINK-V If you are **better** after an illness or injury, you are less ill. If you feel **better**, you no longer feel so ill. ● See note at **recover.** [5] ADV You can tell someone that they **are better** doing one thing **than** another, or **it is better** doing one thing **than** another when you are advising them about what they should do. *You are better eating just a small snack than hurrying a main meal.* [6] PHRASE If you say that someone **had better** do something, you mean that they ought to do it. *I think we had better go home.* [7] PHRASE If someone **is better off**, they are in a more pleasant situation than before. *A baby or child is better off in its country of birth.* [8] PHRASE If something changes **for the better**, it improves. [9] PHRASE If something **gets the better of** you, you are unable to resist it. [10] **the better part of:** see **part.**

⭐ **between** /bɪ'twiːn/. [1] PREP & ADV If something is **between** two things or is **in between** them, it has one of the things on one side of it and the other thing on the other side. *There was a cigarette stuck between his lips. ...raised flower beds that have brick paths in between.* [2] PREP If people or things travel **between** two places, they travel regularly from one place to the other and back again. *I often travel between Britain, France and Germany.* [3] PREP A relationship, discussion, or difference **between** two people, groups, or things is one that involves them both or relates to them both. *...the relationship between patients and doctors.* [4] PREP If something stands **between** you and what you want, it prevents you from having it. [5] PREP If something is **between** or **in between** two amounts or ages, it is greater or older than the first one and smaller or younger than the second one. *A third of its population is aged between 18 and 30.* [6] PREP & ADV If something happens **between** or **in between** two times or events, it happens after the first time or event and before the second time. *The canal was built between 1793 and 1797. ...pain lasting a few minutes, with periods of calm in between.* [7] PREP If you must choose **between** two things, you must choose one thing or the other one. [8] PREP If people have a particular amount of something **between** them, this is the total amount that they have. *The three sites employ 12,500 people between them.* [9] PREP When something is divided or shared **between** people, they each

have a share of it. *All the tasks are shared between us.*

> **USAGE** If there are only two people or things, you should use **between**. If there are more than two people or things, you should use **among**. **Amongst** is slightly old-fashioned.

beverage /'bevərɪdʒ/ **beverages.** N-COUNT A **beverage** is a drink. [FORMAL] *...alcoholic beverages.*

beware /bɪ'weə/.

✔ **Beware** is only used as an imperative or infinitive. It does not have any other forms.

VERB If you tell someone to **beware of** a person or thing, you are warning them that the person or thing may harm them. *Beware of being too impatient with others... Motorists were warned to beware of slippery conditions.*

bewildered /bɪ'wɪldəd/. ADJ If you are **bewildered**, you are very confused and cannot understand something or decide what you should do. *Some shoppers looked bewildered by the sheer variety.* ♦ **bewildering** ADJ *The choice of excursions was bewildering.*

bewilderment /bɪ'wɪldəmənt/. N-UNCOUNT **Bewilderment** is the feeling of being bewildered. *He shook his head in bewilderment.*

bewitch /bɪ'wɪtʃ/ **bewitches, bewitching, bewitched.** VERB If someone or something **bewitches** you, you find them so attractive that you cannot think about anything else. *He is bewitched by Maya's beauty.* ♦ **bewitching** ADJ *...bewitching eyes.*

⭐ **beyond** /bɪ'jɒnd/. [1] PREP & ADV If something is **beyond** a place or barrier, it is on the other side of it. *They heard footsteps in the main room, beyond a door. ...a fabulous view out to the Strait of Georgia and the Rockies beyond.* [2] PREP & ADV If something extends **beyond** a particular thing, it affects or includes other things. If something happens **beyond** a particular time or date, it continues after that time or date has passed. *His interests extended beyond the fine arts to international politics and philosophy. ...through the 1990s and beyond.* [3] PREP If something is, for example, **beyond** understanding or **beyond** belief, it is so extreme in some way that it cannot be understood or believed. *By the year 2007, business computing will have changed beyond recognition.* [4] PREP If you say that something is **beyond** someone, you mean that they are incapable of dealing with it. *Any practical help would almost certainly be beyond him.*

bias /'baɪəs/ **biases.** [1] N-VAR **Bias** is prejudice against one group and favouritism towards another, which may badly affect someone's judgment. *...the bias in favour of new road schemes. ...allegations of bias against women.* [2] N-VAR **Bias** is a concern with or interest in one thing more than others. *The Department has a strong bias towards neuroscience.*

biased /ˈbaɪəst/. [1] ADJ AFTER LINK-V Someone or something that is **biased towards** one thing is more concerned with it than with other things. *University funding was tremendously biased towards scientists.* [2] ADJ If someone or something is **biased**, they show prejudice against one group and favouritism towards another, or are influenced so much by something that any judgment they make is likely to be unfair. *She claimed that judges were biased against women.*

bible /ˈbaɪbəl/ **bibles.** [1] N-PROPER **The Bible** is the sacred book of the Christian religion. ◆ **biblical** /ˈbɪblɪkəl/ ADJ *...a biblical story.* [2] N-COUNT A **bible** is a copy of the Bible.

bibliography /ˌbɪbliˈɒɡrəfi/ **bibliographies.** [1] N-COUNT A **bibliography** is a list of books on a particular subject. [2] N-COUNT A **bibliography** is a list of the books and articles referred to in a particular book.

bicker /ˈbɪkə/ **bickers, bickering, bickered.** VERB When people **bicker,** they quarrel about unimportant things. *They bickered endlessly.* ◆ **bickering** N-UNCOUNT *...political bickering.*

bicycle /ˈbaɪsɪkəl/ **bicycles.** N-COUNT A **bicycle** is a vehicle with two wheels which you ride by sitting on it and pushing two pedals with your feet. → See picture on page 817.

⭐ **bid** /bɪd/ **bids, bidding, bid.** [1] N-COUNT A **bid for** something or a **bid to** do something is an attempt to obtain it or do it. *...Sydney's successful bid for the 2000 Olympic Games... He may have changed his appearance in a bid to evade capture.* [2] N-COUNT & VERB If you make a **bid for** something or if you **bid for** it, you offer to pay a particular amount of money to buy it. *Hanson made an agreed takeover bid of £351 million.* ◆ **bidder,** **bidders** N-COUNT *The sale will be made to the highest bidder.*

> **USAGE Big**, **large**, and **great** are all used to talk about size. In general, **large** is more formal than **big**, and **great** is more formal than **large**.
> **Big** and **large** are normally used to describe objects. If you use **great** to describe an object, you are suggesting that it is impressive because of its size. *The great bird of prey was a dark smudge against the sun.*
> You can use **large** or **great**, but not **big**, to describe amounts. *He noticed a large amount of blood on the laundry floor... The coming of tourists in great numbers changes things.*
> **Great** is often used with nouns referring to things such as feelings or ideas. It is the only one of the three words that can be used in front of an uncount noun. *It gives me very great pleasure to welcome you.* Remember that **great** has several other meanings, when it does not refer to size, but to something that is remarkable, very good, or enjoyable.

⭐ **big** /bɪɡ/ **bigger, biggest.** [1] ADJ Something that is **big** is large in size or great in degree, extent, or importance. *Australia's a big country... Her husband was a big man. ...the big backlog of applications. ...one of the biggest companies in Italy... Her problem was just too big for her to tackle on her own.* [2] ADJ BEFORE N Children often refer to their older brother or sister as their **big** brother or sister. [INFORMAL] *I asked my big brother Peter what it meant.*

,big 'business. N-UNCOUNT Something that is **big business** has become an important commercial activity. *Sport has become big business.*

,big 'deal. [1] N-SING If you say that something is a **big deal**, you mean that it is important or significant. *Winning was such a big deal for the whole family.* [2] CONVENTION If you say **'big deal'** to someone, you mean that you are not impressed by something or someone that they consider important or impressive. [INFORMAL] *'You'll miss The Brady Bunch.' 'Big deal'.*

bigot /ˈbɪɡət/ **bigots.** N-COUNT If you describe someone as a **bigot**, you disapprove of them because they have strong unreasonable prejudices or opinions. *...a narrow-minded bigot.*

bigotry /ˈbɪɡətri/. N-UNCOUNT **Bigotry** is the fact of having or expressing strong unreasonable prejudices or opinions. *He deplored religious bigotry.*

⭐ **bike** /baɪk/ **bikes.** N-COUNT A **bike** is a bicycle or a motorcycle. [INFORMAL] → See pictures on page 817. *I used to ride a bike years ago. ...to encourage motorists to go by bike.*

bikini /bɪˈkiːni/ **bikinis.** N-COUNT A **bikini** is a two-piece swimming costume worn by women.

bilingual /ˌbaɪˈlɪŋɡwəl/. ADJ **Bilingual** means involving or using two languages. *...bilingual education. ...the Collins bilingual dictionaries... He is bilingual in an Asian language and English.*

⭐ **bill** /bɪl/ **bills, billing, billed.** [1] N-COUNT In British English, a **bill** is a written statement of money that you owe for goods or services. The American word is **check**. *He paid his bill for the newspapers. ...phone bills.* [2] N-SING In British English, **the bill** in a restaurant is a piece of paper on which the price of the meal you have just eaten is written and which you are given before you pay. The American word is **check**. [3] VERB If you **are billed for** something, you are given or sent a bill for it. *Are you going to bill me for this?* [4] N-COUNT In American English, a **bill** is a piece of paper money. The usual British word is **note**. [5] N-COUNT In parliament, a **bill** is a formal statement of a proposed new law that is discussed and then voted on. *...the toughest crime bill that Congress has passed in a decade.*

billboard /ˈbɪlbɔːd/ **billboards.** N-COUNT A **billboard** is a very large board on which posters are displayed.

a
b
c
d
e
f
g
h
i
j
k
l
m
n
o
p
q
r
s
t
u
v
w
x
y
z

billiards /'bɪljədz/.

✓ The form **billiard** is used as a modifier.

N-UNCOUNT **Billiards** is a game played on a large table, in which you use a long stick called a cue to hit small heavy balls against each each other or into pockets around the sides of the table. ...*a game of billiards.*

⭐ **billion** /'bɪljən/ **billions.** [1] NUM A **billion** is a thousand million. ...*3 billion dollars.* [2] QUANT You can use **billions** and **billion** to mean an extremely large amount. *They've sold billions of them... It must be worth billions.*

billionaire /ˌbɪljə'neə/ **billionaires.** N-COUNT A **billionaire** is an extremely rich person who has money or property worth at least a thousand million pounds or dollars.

billow /'bɪləʊ/ **billows, billowing, billowed.** VERB When something **billows**, it swells out and moves slowly in the wind. *Her pink dress billowed out around her... Dense smoke swirled and billowed.*

bin /bɪn/ **bins.** N-COUNT A **bin** is a container that you put rubbish in.

bind /baɪnd/ **binds, binding, bound.** [1] VERB If something **binds** people together, it makes them feel as if they are all part of the same group. ...*the social and political ties that bind the USA to Britain.* [2] VERB If you **are bound** by something such as a rule or agreement, you are forced or required to act in a certain way. *The authorities will be legally bound to arrest any suspects... The treaty binds them to respect their neighbour's independence.* [3] VERB If you **bind** something, you tie string or rope tightly round it. *Bind the ends of the cord together with thread.* [4] VERB When a book **is bound**, the pages are joined together and the cover is put on. [5] See also **bound**.

binding /'baɪndɪŋ/ **bindings.** [1] ADJ A **binding** agreement or decision must be obeyed or carried out. ...*a legally binding commitment... The panel's decisions are secret and not binding on the government.* [2] N-VAR The **binding** of a book is its cover. *Its books are noted for the quality of their paper and bindings.*

binge /bɪndʒ/ **binges, binging, binged.** N-COUNT & VERB If you go on a **binge**, or if you **binge**, you do too much of something, such as drinking alcohol or eating. [INFORMAL] *I binged on pizzas.*

bingo /'bɪŋgəʊ/. N-UNCOUNT **Bingo** is a game in which players aim to match the numbers that someone calls out with the numbers on a card that they have been given. *Do you play bingo?*

binoculars /bɪ'nɒkjʊləz/. N-PLURAL **Binoculars** consist of two small telescopes joined together side by side, which you look through in order to see things that are a long way away. You can also say **a pair of binoculars**.

biochemical /ˌbaɪəʊ'kemɪkəl/. ADJ BEFORE N **Biochemical** processes are the chemical processes that happen in living things.

biochemistry /ˌbaɪəʊ'kemɪstri/. N-UNCOUNT **Biochemistry** is the study of the chemical processes that happen in living things. ♦ **biochemist, biochemists** N-COUNT ...*a team of biochemists from Cambridge University.*

biographer /baɪ'ɒgrəfə/ **biographers.** N-COUNT Someone's **biographer** is a person who writes an account of their life.

biography /baɪ'ɒgrəfi/ **biographies.** N-COUNT A **biography** of a person is an account of their life, written by someone else. ♦ **biographical** /ˌbaɪə'græfɪkəl/ ADJ ...*a 14-minute biographical film.*

biological /ˌbaɪə'lɒdʒɪkəl/. [1] ADJ **Biological** is used to describe processes and states that occur in the bodies and cells of living things. ...*a natural biological response.* ♦ **biologically** ADV *Much of our behaviour is biologically determined.* [2] ADJ BEFORE N **Biological** studies are connected with research in biology. ...*biological sciences.* [3] ADJ **Biological** weapons and **biological** warfare involve the use of organisms which damage living things. ...*biological pest control.*

biology /baɪ'ɒlədʒi/. N-UNCOUNT **Biology** is the science concerned with the study of living things. ♦ **biologist, biologists** N-COUNT ...*biologists studying the fruit fly.*

biotechnology /ˌbaɪəʊtek'nɒlədʒi/. N-UNCOUNT **Biotechnology** is the use of living parts such as cells or bacteria in industry and medicine. [TECHNICAL]

birch /bɜːtʃ/ **birches.** N-VAR A **birch** is a tall tree with thin branches. **Birch** is the wood of this tree.

⭐ **bird** /bɜːd/ **birds.** N-COUNT A **bird** is a creature with feathers and wings.

Biro /'baɪərəʊ/ **Biros.** N-COUNT A **Biro** is a pen with a small metal ball at its tip. **Biro** is a trademark.

⭐ **birth** /bɜːθ/ **births.** [1] N-VAR When a baby is born, you refer to this event as its **birth**. When a woman **gives birth**, she produces a baby from her body. *The twins were separated at birth.* [2] N-UNCOUNT You can refer to the beginning or origin of something as its **birth**. ...*the birth of popular democracy.*

'birth control. N-UNCOUNT **Birth control** means planning whether to have children and using contraception to prevent unwanted pregnancy.

⭐ **birthday** /'bɜːθdeɪ, -di/ **birthdays.** N-COUNT Your **birthday** is the anniversary of the date on which you were born. ...*his 24th birthday... I'm getting a bike for my birthday... Happy Birthday!*

birthplace /'bɜːθpleɪs/ **birthplaces.** [1] N-COUNT Your **birthplace** is the place where you were born. [WRITTEN] [2] N-COUNT The **birthplace of** something is the place where it began or originated. ...*Athens, the birthplace of the ancient Olympics.*

'birth rate, birth rates. N-COUNT The **birth rate** is the number of babies born for every 1000 people during a particular period.

biscuit /'bɪskɪt/ **biscuits.** N-COUNT In British English, a **biscuit** is a small flat cake that is crisp and usually sweet. The usual American word is **cookie**.

bisexual /ˌbaɪˈsekʃuəl/ **bisexuals.** ADJ & N-COUNT A **bisexual** person or a **bisexual** is sexually attracted to both men and women.

bishop /ˈbɪʃəp/ **bishops.** N-COUNT A **bishop** is a clergyman of high rank.

bistro /ˈbiːstrəʊ/ **bistros.** N-COUNT A **bistro** is a small restaurant or bar.

★ **bit** /bɪt/ **bits.** [1] QUANT A **bit of** something is a small amount of it, or a small piece or part of it. [INFORMAL] ...a little bit of money. ...crumpled bits of paper... Now comes the really important bit. [2] PHRASE A **bit** means to a small extent or degree. [INFORMAL] This girl was a bit strange... I have a bit more to offer. [3] PHRASE You can use a **bit of** to make a statement less extreme. It's all a bit of a mess. [4] N-COUNT In computing, a **bit** is the smallest unit of information that is held in a computer's memory. [5] **Bit** is the past tense of **bite**.

PHRASES ● You can say that someone's behaviour is **a bit much** when you are annoyed about it. [INFORMAL] It seems to be a bit much to say, 'well we don't trust you to drink'. ● You say that one thing is **every bit as** good or interesting **as** another to emphasize that they are just as good or interesting as each other. My dinner jacket is every bit as good as his. ● If you do something **for a bit**, you do it for a short period of time. [INFORMAL] That should keep you busy for a bit. ● **Quite a bit** means a lot. [INFORMAL] He's quite a bit older than me.

bitch /bɪtʃ/ **bitches.** N-COUNT A **bitch** is a female dog.

★ **bite** /baɪt/ **bites, biting, bit, bitten.** [1] VERB & N-COUNT When a person or animal **bites** something, they use their teeth to cut into it or through it. A **bite** is an act of biting something. He bit into his sandwich... Llamas won't bite or kick... You cannot eat a bun in one bite. [2] VERB & N-COUNT If an insect or a snake **bites** you, it makes a mark or hole in your skin, called a **bite**. A poisonous snake bit his ankle... Try not to scratch insect bites.

> **USAGE** Note that animals, snakes and mosquitoes **bite** you, but wasps and bees **sting** you.

[3] VERB When an action or policy begins to **bite**, it begins to have a serious or harmful effect. The recession started biting deeply into British industry. [4] PHRASE If you **bite** your **lip**, or if you **bite** your **tongue**, you stop yourself from saying something that you want to say, because it would be wrong in the circumstances.

biting /ˈbaɪtɪŋ/. [1] ADJ A **biting** wind is extremely cold. [2] ADJ **Biting** criticism or wit is very harsh or unkind. This was the most biting criticism made against her.

bitten /ˈbɪtən/. **Bitten** is the past participle of **bite**.

★ **bitter** /ˈbɪtə/ **bitterest; bitters.** [1] ADJ In a **bitter** argument or conflict, people argue very angrily

or fight very fiercely. ...a bitter attack on the Government. [2] ADJ If someone is **bitter**, they feel angry and resentful. She is said to be very bitter about the way she was sacked. ♦ **bitterly** ADV ...bureaucrats who bitterly resented their loss of power. ♦ **bitterness** N-UNCOUNT She still feels bitterness towards him. [3] ADJ You can use **bitter** to emphasize feelings of disappointment. ♦ **bitterly** ADV I was bitterly disappointed to have lost. [4] ADJ A **bitter** wind or **bitter** weather is extremely cold. ♦ **bitterly** ADV It's bitterly cold here in Moscow. [5] ADJ A **bitter** taste is sharp, not sweet, and often slightly unpleasant. [6] N-VAR **Bitter** is a kind of British beer. ...a pint of bitter.

bizarre /bɪˈzɑː/. ADJ Something that is **bizarre** is very odd and strange. What a bizarre story! ♦ **bizarrely** ADV She dressed bizarrely.

★ **black** /blæk/ **blacker, blackest; blacks, blacking, blacked.** [1] ADJ & N-VAR Something that is **black** is of the darkest colour that there is. ...a flowing black gown... He was dressed all in black. ♦ **blackness** N-UNCOUNT ...the blackness of night. [2] ADJ & N-COUNT A **black** person belongs to a race of people with dark skins, especially a race from Africa. You can refer to black people as **blacks**, but some people find this use offensive. ...black musicians... I'm black and I'm proud to be black. [3] ADJ **Black** coffee or tea has no milk or cream added to it. I drink coffee black. [4] ADJ If you describe a situation as **black**, you are emphasizing that it is very bad indeed. ...one of the blackest days of his political career. [5] ADJ **Black** humour involves jokes about things that are sad or unpleasant. ...a black comedy. [6] VERB When a group **blacks** particular goods or people, it refuses to handle the goods or to have dealings with the people. The Union had blacked incoming goods at the London Docks.

▸**black out.** PHR-VERB If you **black out**, you lose consciousness for a short time. ● See also **blackout**.

ˌblack and ˈwhite. [1] ADJ & N-UNCOUNT In a **black and white** photograph or film, everything is shown in black, white, and grey. The pictures were in black and white. [2] PHRASE You say that something is **in black and white** when it has been written or printed, and not just spoken. He'd seen the proof in black and white.

blackberry /ˈblækbəri, AM -beri/ **blackberries.** N-COUNT A **blackberry** is a small dark purple fruit.

blackboard /ˈblækbɔːd/ **blackboards.** N-COUNT In British English, a **blackboard** is a dark-coloured board which teachers write on with chalk. The usual American word is **chalkboard**.

blackcurrant /ˌblækˈkʌrənt, AM -ˈkɜːrənt/ **blackcurrants.** N-COUNT **Blackcurrants** are very small, dark purple fruits that grow in bunches.

blacken /ˈblækən/ **blackens, blackening, blackened.** VERB To **blacken** something means to make it black or very dark in colour. Smoke from the wood fire has blackened the kitchen walls. ...his blackened teeth.

a
b
c
d
e
f
g
h
i
j
k
l
m
n
o
p
q
r
s
t
u
v
w
x
y
z

,**black 'eye**, **black eyes**. N-COUNT A **black eye** is a dark-coloured bruise around the eye. *Smith gave him a black eye.*

blackmail /'blækmeɪl/ **blackmails, blackmailing, blackmailed**. N-UNCOUNT & VERB **Blackmail** is the action of threatening to do something unpleasant to someone unless they do what you want them to do. If one person **blackmails** another person, they use blackmail against them. *She was a prime target for blackmail... He was trying to blackmail me into saying whatever he wanted.* ♦ **blackmailer, blackmailers** N-COUNT ...*a blackmailer who threatened to poison supermarket food.*

,**black 'market**, **black markets**. N-COUNT If something is bought or sold on the **black market**, it is bought or sold illegally. *There is a plentiful supply of guns on the black market.*

blackout /'blækaʊt/ **blackouts.** [1] N-COUNT A **blackout** is a period of time during a war in which the buildings in an area are made dark for safety reasons. *The last show had to be over before the blackout began.* [2] N-COUNT If you have a **blackout**, you temporarily lose consciousness.

blacksmith /'blæksmɪθ/ **blacksmiths.** N-COUNT A **blacksmith** is someone whose job is making things out of metal, for example horseshoes.

bladder /'blædə/ **bladders.** N-COUNT Your **bladder** is the part of your body where urine is held until it leaves your body.

blade /bleɪd/ **blades.** [1] N-COUNT The **blade** of a knife, axe, or saw is the sharp edge of it that is used for cutting. [2] N-COUNT The **blades** of a propeller are the parts that turn round.

⭐ **blame** /bleɪm/ **blames, blaming, blamed.** [1] VERB & PHRASE If you **blame** a person or thing **for** something bad, or if you think or say they are **to blame**, you think or say that they are responsible for it. *The commission is expected to blame the army for many of the atrocities... The police blamed the explosion on terrorists. ...who is to blame?* [2] N-UNCOUNT The **blame for** something bad that has happened is the responsibility for causing it or letting it happen. *I'm not going to take the blame for that.* [3] VERB If you say that you do not **blame** someone **for** doing something, you mean that it was a reasonable thing to do in the circumstances. *I do not blame them for trying to make some money.*

blanch /blɑːntʃ, blæntʃ/ **blanches, blanching, blanched.** VERB If you **blanch**, you suddenly become very pale. *She felt herself blanch at the unpleasant memories.*

bland /blænd/ **blander, blandest.** [1] ADJ If you describe someone or something as **bland**, you mean that they are dull and very ordinary. ...*a bland beige or tan carpet.* [2] ADJ **Bland** food has very little flavour. ...*bland kidney beans.*

blank /blæŋk/ **blanker, blankest.** [1] ADJ Something that is **blank** has nothing on it. ...*a blank page.* ...*blank cassettes.* [2] ADJ If you look **blank**, your face shows no feeling or understanding. *He gave her a blank look.* ♦ **blankly** ADV *She stared at him blankly.* [3] ADJ & N-SING If your mind or memory **goes blank** or if it is **a blank**, you cannot think of anything or remember anything. [4] See also **point-blank**.

blanket /'blæŋkɪt/ **blankets, blanketing, blanketed.** [1] N-COUNT A **blanket** is a large piece of thick cloth, especially one which you put on a bed to keep you warm. [2] N-SING & VERB If there is a **blanket of** something such as snow, or if snow **blankets** an area, it covers it. *Heavy cloud and rain blanketed the valley.* [3] ADJ You use **blanket** to describe something which affects or refers to every person or thing in a group. *There's already a blanket ban on foreign unskilled labour.*

blare /bleə/ **blares, blaring, blared.** VERB & N-SING When something such as a siren or radio **blares** or **blares out**, it makes a loud, unpleasant noise called a **blare**. *Music blared from the flat behind me. ...the blare of a radio through a thin wall.*

blasphemy /'blæsfəmi/ **blasphemies.** N-VAR You can describe something that shows disrespect for God or a religion as **blasphemy**. ♦ **blasphemous** /'blæsfəməs/ ADJ *The book was blasphemous, and offended Muslims worldwide.*

⭐ **blast** /blɑːst, blæst/ **blasts, blasting, blasted.** [1] N-COUNT A **blast** is a big explosion. *250 people were killed in the blast.* [2] VERB If people or things **blast** something, they destroy or damage it with a bomb or an explosion. *They're using dynamite to blast away rocks.* [3] N-COUNT A **blast of** air or wind, or a **blast of** a sound, is a sudden strong rush of it. *Blasts of cold air swept down from the mountains. ...the loud blast of a horn.* [4] VERB To **blast** someone means to shoot them with a gun. [JOURNALISM] *Suddenly all the men pull out pistols and begin blasting away.*

▸**blast off.** PHR-VERB When a space rocket **blasts off**, it leaves the ground at the start of its journey.

blatant /'bleɪtənt/. ADJ If you describe something you think is bad as **blatant**, you mean that, rather than hide it, those responsible actually seem to be making it obvious. ...*the most blatant discrimination. ...a blatant attempt to blackmail me.* ♦ **blatantly** ADV ...*a blatantly sexist question... Blatantly false assertions have gone unchallenged.*

blaze /bleɪz/ **blazes, blazing, blazed.** [1] VERB When a fire **blazes**, it burns strongly and brightly. ...*a blazing fire.* [2] N-COUNT A **blaze** is a large fire in which things are damaged. ...*a blaze which swept through a tower block.* [3] VERB Something that **blazes with** light or colour is extremely bright. [4] N-COUNT A **blaze of** light or colour is a large amount of it. [5] N-SING A **blaze of** publicity or attention is a great amount of it. *He wanted his presidency to end in a blaze of glory.* [6] PHRASE If someone **blazes a trail**, they discover or explore something new. *These surgeons have blazed the trail in the treatment of bomb victims.*

blazer /'bleɪzə/ **blazers.** N-COUNT A **blazer** is a kind of jacket.

blazing /'bleɪzɪŋ/. [1] ADJ BEFORE N You use **blazing** or **blazing hot** to describe the weather when it is very hot and sunny. ...*blazing hot summers.* [2] ADJ BEFORE N When people have a **blazing** row, they quarrel in a very noisy and excited way.

bleach /bliːtʃ/ **bleaches, bleaching, bleached.** [1] VERB To **bleach** material means to use a chemical to make it white or pale. The sun can also **bleach** things, especially someone's hair. *She bleached her hair blonde... They put cloth out to bleach in the sun.* [2] N-UNCOUNT **Bleach** is a chemical that is used to make cloth white, or to clean things thoroughly. ...*a solution of household bleach.*

bleak /bliːk/ **bleaker, bleakest.** [1] ADJ If a situation is **bleak**, it is bad, and seems unlikely to improve. *The immediate outlook remains bleak.* ♦ **bleakness** N-UNCOUNT ...*the continued bleakness of the American job market.* [2] ADJ If you describe something as **bleak**, you mean it looks cold or unpleasant. ...*bleak inner-city streets... The weather can be quite bleak on the coast.* [3] ADJ If someone looks or sounds **bleak**, they seem depressed or unfriendly. *Julian's face took on a bleak look.* ♦ **bleakly** ADV *'There is nothing left,' she says bleakly.*

bleed /bliːd/ **bleeds, bleeding, bled.** VERB When you **bleed**, you lose blood from your body as a result of injury or illness. *She's going to bleed to death... His head had struck the sink and was bleeding.* ♦ **bleeding** N-UNCOUNT ...*internal bleeding.*

blemish /'blemɪʃ/ **blemishes, blemishing, blemished.** [1] N-COUNT A **blemish** is a mark that spoils the appearance of something. *If there is the slightest blemish it is rejected.* [2] VERB & N-COUNT If something **blemishes** your reputation, or if it is a **blemish on** it, it spoils it. *He wasn't about to blemish that pristine record... These are minor blemishes on a remarkably smooth operation.*

blend /blend/ **blends, blending, blended.** [1] VERB & N-COUNT When you **blend** substances together, you mix them together so that they become one substance. A **blend** of substances is a mix of them. *Blend the butter with the sugar. ...a blend of spices.* [2] VERB When colours or sounds **blend**, they combine in a pleasing way. *Paint the walls and ceilings the same colour so they blend together.*
▶ **blend into** or **blend in.** PHR-VERB If something **blends into** the background or **blends in**, it is so similar to the background in appearance or sound that it is difficult to see or hear it separately. *The toad had changed its colour to blend in with its new environment.*

bless /bles/ **blesses, blessing, blessed.** [1] VERB When a priest **blesses** people or things, he or she asks for God's favour and protection for them. [2] PASSIVE-VERB If someone **is blessed with** a good quality or skill, they have it. *Both are blessed with an uncommon ability to fix things.* [3] PHRASE When people say **God bless** or **bless you** to someone, they are expressing their affection or thanks. *Bless you, you're so kind.*

blessed /'blesɪd/. ADJ BEFORE N You use **blessed** to describe something that you are thankful for or relieved about. *Rainy weather brings blessed relief to hay fever victims.* ♦ **blessedly** ADV *Most British election campaigns are blessedly brief.*

blessing /'blesɪŋ/ **blessings.** [1] N-COUNT A **blessing** is something good that you are thankful for. ...*the blessings of prosperity.* [2] N-COUNT If something is done **with** your **blessing**, you approve of it. [3] PHRASE If you say that a situation is a **mixed blessing**, you mean that it has disadvantages as well as advantages. ...*the mixed blessing of modern technology.*

blew /bluː/. **Blew** is the past tense of **blow**.

blight /blaɪt/ **blights, blighting, blighted.** [1] N-COUNT You can refer to something as a **blight** when it causes great difficulties or damage to something. *This discriminatory policy has really been a blight on America.* [2] VERB If something **blights** something else, it damages it. *An embarrassing blunder nearly blighted his career.*

★ **blind** /blaɪnd/ **blinds, blinding, blinded.** [1] ADJ & N-PLURAL Someone who is **blind** cannot see because their eyes are damaged. You can refer to people who are blind as **the blind**. ...*a blind person... He went blind.* ♦ **blindness** N-UNCOUNT *Early diagnosis and treatment can usually prevent blindness.* [2] VERB If something **blinds** you, you become unable to see, either for a short time or permanently. *The strong sunlight blinded him.* [3] ADJ AFTER LINK-V & VERB If you are **blind to** a fact or situation or if something **blinds** you **to** it, you take no notice of it or are unaware of it. *All the time I was blind to your suffering.* [4] ADJ If you describe someone's beliefs or actions as **blind**, you think that they do not question or think about what they are doing. ...*her blind faith in the wisdom of the Church.* [5] PHRASE If you say that someone **is turning a blind eye to** something bad or illegal, you mean that they are pretending not to notice that it is happening so that they will not have to do anything about it. *Teachers are turning a blind eye to pupils smoking at school.* [6] ADJ BEFORE N A **blind** corner is one that you cannot see round. [7] N-COUNT A **blind** is a roll of material which you pull down over a window to keep out the light.

blindfold /'blaɪndfəʊld/ **blindfolds, blindfolding, blindfolded.** [1] N-COUNT A **blindfold** is a strip of cloth that is tied over someone's eyes so that they cannot see. [2] VERB If you **blindfold** someone, you tie a blindfold over their eyes. *He had been blindfolded and his hands were tied.*

blinding /'blaɪndɪŋ/. ADJ A **blinding** light is extremely bright.

blindly /'blaɪndli/. [1] ADV If you do something **blindly**, you do it when you cannot see properly. *Lettie groped blindly for the glass.* [2] ADV You use **blindly** to say that someone does something without having enough information, or without thinking about it. *Don't just blindly follow what the banker says.*

blink /blɪŋk/ **blinks, blinking, blinked.** [1] VERB &
N-COUNT When you **blink** or when you give a
blink, you shut your eyes and very quickly open
them again. *She was blinking her eyes rapidly... He
kept giving quick blinks.* [2] VERB When a light
blinks, it flashes on and off. *A warning light
blinked on.*

bliss /blɪs/. N-UNCOUNT **Bliss** is a state of
complete happiness. *It was a scene of such
domestic bliss.*

blissful /'blɪsfʊl/. ADJ A **blissful** time or state is
a very happy one. *We spent a blissful week
together.* ✦ **blissfully** ADV *We're blissfully happy.*

blister /'blɪstə/ **blisters, blistering, blistered.**
[1] N-COUNT A **blister** is a painful swelling
containing clear liquid on the surface of your
skin. [2] VERB When your skin **blisters**, blisters
appear on it as a result of burning or rubbing. *The
affected skin turns red and may blister... The sap of
this plant blisters the skin.*

blistering /'blɪstərɪŋ/. [1] ADJ **Blistering** heat is
very great heat. *...a blistering summer day.* [2] ADJ
A **blistering** remark expresses great anger or
sarcasm. *...a blistering attack on his critics.*

blithe /blaɪð/. ADJ You use **blithe** to indicate
that something is done casually, without serious
thought. *...blithe disregard for best scientific
practice.* ✦ **blithely** ADV *Your editorial blithely
ignores the hard facts.*

blitz /blɪts/ **blitzes, blitzing, blitzed.** [1] VERB &
N-COUNT If a city or building **is blitzed** during a
war, bombs are dropped on it by enemy aircraft.
You can refer to an attack like this as a **blitz**.
[2] N-COUNT If you have a **blitz on** something, you
make a big effort to deal with it or to improve it.
[INFORMAL] *There is to be a blitz on incorrect
grammar.*

blizzard /'blɪzəd/ **blizzards.** N-COUNT A **blizzard** is
a storm in which snow falls heavily and there are
strong winds.

bloated /'bləʊtɪd/. ADJ Something that is
bloated is much larger than normal, usually
because it has a lot of liquid or gas inside it. *...the
bloated body of a dead bullock.*

blob /blɒb/ **blobs.** N-COUNT A **blob of** thick or
sticky liquid is a small amount of it. *...a blob of
cream.*

bloc /blɒk/ **blocs.** N-COUNT A **bloc** is a group of
countries who act together because they have
similar political aims and interests. *...the former
Soviet bloc.*

⭐ **block** /blɒk/ **blocks, blocking, blocked.** [1] N-COUNT A
block of flats or offices is a large building
containing them. *...blocks of council flats. ...a
white-painted apartment block.* [2] N-COUNT In a
town, a **block** is a group of buildings with streets
on all four sides. *She walked four blocks down
High Street.* [3] N-COUNT A **block of** a substance is
a large rectangular piece of it. [4] VERB To **block** a
road or channel means to put something across
or in it so that nothing can go through it or along
it. *Police blocked the entrance to Westminster
Bridge. ...a blocked drain.* [5] VERB If something
blocks your view, it prevents you from seeing
something by being between you and that thing.
...a row of trees that blocked his view. [6] VERB
When people **block** something, they do not
allow it to happen. *The country has tried to block
imports of various cheap foreign products.*
▸**block out.** PHR-VERB If you **block out** a
thought, you try not to think about it. *She accuses
me of having blocked out the past.*
▸**block up.** PHR-VERB If you **block** something **up**
or if it **blocks up**, it becomes completely blocked
so that nothing can get through it. *'Any holes in
the kitchen where the mice are getting
through?'—'I've blocked them up.'*

blockade /blɒ'keɪd/ **blockades, blockading,
blockaded.** N-COUNT & VERB A **blockade** is an action
that is taken to prevent goods from entering or
leaving a place. You can also say that people
blockade a place. *...a blockade of the harbour...
Warships are blockading the port.*

blockage /'blɒkɪdʒ/ **blockages.** N-COUNT A
blockage in a pipe or tunnel is something that is
blocking it. *...a fatal blockage in the lung.*

blockbuster /'blɒkbʌstə/ **blockbusters.** N-COUNT
A **blockbuster** is a very popular and successful
film or book. [INFORMAL]

bloke /bləʊk/ **blokes.** N-COUNT A **bloke** is a man.
[INFORMAL, BRITISH]

blonde (or **blond**) /blɒnd/ **blondes.** ADJ & N-COUNT
A **blonde** person or a **blonde** has pale yellow-
coloured hair. The form **blonde** is used to refer to
women, and **blond** to refer to men. *Do blondes
really have more fun?... The baby had blond curls.*

⭐ **blood** /blʌd/. [1] N-UNCOUNT **Blood** is the red
liquid that flows inside your body. [2] N-UNCOUNT
You can use **blood** to refer to the race or social
class of someone's parents or ancestors. *There
was Greek blood in his veins.*
PHRASES ● If something violent and cruel is done
in cold blood, it is done deliberately and in an
unemotional way. ● New people who are
introduced into an organization and whose fresh
ideas are likely to improve it are referred to as
new blood, fresh blood, or **young blood.**
*There's been a major reshuffle of the cabinet to
bring in new blood.* ● **own flesh and blood**: see
flesh.

'**blood pressure.** N-UNCOUNT Your **blood
pressure** is a measure of the force with which
blood is pumped around your body. *Your doctor
will monitor your blood pressure.*

bloodshed /'blʌdʃed/. N-UNCOUNT **Bloodshed** is
violence in which people are killed or wounded.
...rioting and bloodshed.

bloodstream /'blʌdstriːm/ **bloodstreams.**
N-COUNT Your **bloodstream** is your blood as it
flows around your body. *The disease releases
toxins into the bloodstream.*

'**blood test, blood tests.** N-COUNT A **blood test** is
a medical examination of a sample of your blood.

'blood vessel, blood vessels. N-COUNT **Blood vessels** are the narrow tubes through which your blood flows.

⭐ **bloody** /'blʌdi/ **bloodier, bloodiest.** [1] **Bloody** is a swear word. Some people use 'bloody' to emphasize what they are saying, especially when they are angry about something someone has said or done. [BRITISH] [2] ADJ A situation or event that is **bloody** is one in which there is a lot of violence and people are killed. ...the bloody riots of 1981.

bloom /bluːm/ **blooms, blooming, bloomed.** [1] N-COUNT A **bloom** is the flower on a plant. [2] PHRASE A plant or tree that is in **bloom** has flowers on it. [3] VERB When a plant or tree **blooms,** it produces flowers. When a flower **blooms,** the flower bud opens.

blossom /'blɒsəm/ **blossoms, blossoming, blossomed.** [1] N-VAR **Blossom** is the flowers that appear on a tree before the fruit. ...cherry blossom. [2] VERB When a tree **blossoms,** it produces blossom. [3] VERB If someone or something **blossoms,** they develop good, attractive, or successful qualities. What began as a local festival has blossomed into an international event.

blot /blɒt/ **blots, blotting, blotted.** N-COUNT A **blot** is a drop of liquid that has been spilled on a surface and has dried. ...an ink blot.
▶**blot out.** [1] PHR-VERB If one thing **blots out** another thing, it is in front of the other thing and prevents it from being seen. Clouds blotted out the sun. [2] PHR-VERB If you try to **blot out** a memory, you try to forget it. She's trying to blot out all memory of the incident.

blotch /blɒtʃ/ **blotches.** N-COUNT A **blotch** is a small area of colour, for example on someone's skin. His face was covered in red blotches.

blouse /blaʊz, AM blaʊs/ **blouses.** N-COUNT A **blouse** is a kind of shirt worn by girls or women.
→ See picture on page 819.

⭐ **blow** /bləʊ/ **blows, blowing, blew, blown.** [1] VERB When a wind or breeze **blows,** the air moves. A chill wind blew at the top of the hill. [2] VERB If the wind **blows** something somewhere, or if something **blows** there, it is moved there by the wind. The wind blew her hair back from her forehead... Sand blew in our eyes. [3] VERB If you **blow,** you send out a stream of air from your mouth. Danny blew on his fingers to warm them. [4] VERB When a whistle or horn **blows,** or when someone **blows** it, they make a sound by blowing into it. [5] VERB When you **blow** your **nose,** you force air out of it through your nostrils in order to clear it. [6] VERB To **blow** something **out, off,** or **away** means to violently remove or destroy it with an explosion. The can exploded, wrecking the kitchen and bathroom and blowing out windows... Rival gunmen blew the city to bits. [7] N-COUNT If someone receives a **blow,** they are hit by someone or something. He went off to hospital after a blow to the face. [8] N-COUNT A **blow** is something that happens which makes

you very disappointed or unhappy. It was a terrible blow when he was made redundant. [9] VERB If you **blow** a chance or an attempt to do something, you make a mistake which wastes the chance or causes the attempt to fail. [INFORMAL] / had probably blown my chances for this job... Oh you fool! You've blown it! [10] VERB If you **blow** a large amount of money, you spend it quickly on luxuries. [INFORMAL]
▶**blow out.** PHR-VERB If you **blow out** a flame or a candle, you blow at it so that it stops burning.
▶**blow over.** PHR-VERB If something such as trouble or an argument **blows over,** it comes to an end. Wait, and it'll all blow over.
▶**blow up.** [1] PHR-VERB If someone **blows** something **up,** or if it **blows up,** it is destroyed by an explosion. Their boat blew up. [2] PHR-VERB If you **blow up** something such as a balloon or a tyre, you fill it with air.

blown /bləʊn/. **Blown** is the past participle of **blow.**

bludgeon /'blʌdʒən/ **bludgeons, bludgeoning, bludgeoned.** VERB If someone **bludgeons** you **into** doing something, they make you do it by bullying or threatening you. Their approach simply bludgeons you into submission.

⭐ **blue** /bluː/ **bluer, bluest; blues.** [1] ADJ & N-VAR Something that is **blue** is the colour of the sky on a sunny day. [2] PHRASE Something that happens **out of the blue** happens suddenly and unexpectedly. Turner's resignation came out of the blue. [3] N-UNCOUNT **The blues** is a type of music which is similar to jazz, with a slow tempo and a strong rhythm.

blue-'collar. ADJ **Blue-collar** workers work in industry, doing physical work, rather than in offices.

blueprint /'bluːprɪnt/ **blueprints.** N-COUNT A **blueprint for** something is an original plan or description of how it is expected to work. ...his blueprint for the country's future.

bluff /blʌf/ **bluffs, bluffing, bluffed.** [1] N-VAR A **bluff** is an attempt to make someone believe that you will do something when you do not really intend to do it. The letter was a bluff. ...a game of bluff. [2] PHRASE If you **call** someone's **bluff,** you tell them to do what they have been threatening to do, because you are sure that they will not really do it. [3] VERB If you **bluff,** you try to make someone believe that you will do something although you do not really intend to do it, or that you know something when you really do not know it. Either side, or both, could be bluffing... He tried to bluff his way through another test.

blunder /'blʌndə/ **blunders, blundering, blundered.** [1] N-COUNT & VERB If you make a **blunder,** or if you **blunder,** you make a stupid mistake. It had been a monumental blunder to give him the assignment... The company admitted it had blundered. [2] VERB If you **blunder** somewhere, you move there in a clumsy way. He had blundered into the table.

a
b
c
d
e
f
g
h
i
j
k
l
m
n
o
p
q
r
s
t
u
v
w
x
y
z

blunt /blʌnt/ **blunter, bluntest; blunts, blunting, blunted.** [1] ADJ If you are **blunt**, you say exactly what you think without trying to be polite. *His blunt response surprised them.* ♦ **bluntly** ADV *'I don't believe you!' Jeanne said bluntly.* ♦ **bluntness** N-UNCOUNT *His bluntness got him into trouble.* [2] ADJ BEFORE N A **blunt** object has a rounded or flat end rather than a sharp one. *He had been battered to death with a blunt instrument.* [3] ADJ A **blunt** knife is no longer sharp and does not cut well. [4] VERB If something **blunts** an emotion or feeling, it weakens it. *Our appetite was blunted by the beer.*

blur /blɜː/ **blurs, blurring, blurred.** [1] N-COUNT A **blur** is a shape or area which you cannot see clearly because it has no distinct outline or because it is moving very fast. *Her face is a blur.* [2] VERB If an image **blurs**, or if it **is blurred**, it becomes a blur. *A dizziness overcame him, blurring his vision.* ♦ **blurred** ADJ *...slightly blurred images.* [3] VERB If something **blurs** a distinction between things, the differences between them are no longer clear. *Television is blurring the distinction between sport and show business.* ♦ **blurred** ADJ *Fiction and reality were increasingly blurred.*

blurt /blɜːt/ **blurts, blurting, blurted.**
▸ **blurt out.** PHR-VERB If you **blurt** something **out**, you say it suddenly, after trying hard to keep quiet or to keep it secret. *'You're mad,' the driver blurted out... Richard blurted out what was on his mind.*

blush /blʌʃ/ **blushes, blushing, blushed.** VERB & N-COUNT When you **blush**, or when a **blush** spreads over your face, your face becomes redder than usual because you are ashamed or embarrassed. *I felt myself blush... Ann accepted it with a blush.*

bluster /ˈblʌstə/ **blusters, blustering, blustered.** VERB & N-UNCOUNT If you say that someone is **blustering** or that what they say is **bluster**, you mean that they are speaking aggressively or proudly but without authority. *'That's lunacy,' he blustered... At the heart of Tom's bluster was a great shyness.*

boar /bɔː/.

✓ The plural is **boar** or **boars**.

[1] N-COUNT A **boar** or a **wild boar** is a wild pig. [2] N-COUNT A **boar** is a male pig.

⭐ **board** /bɔːd/ **boards, boarding, boarded.** [1] N-COUNT A **board** is a flat piece of wood, plastic, or cardboard which is used for a particular purpose. *...a chopping board. ...a chess board... They put down wooden boards, and laid new carpets on top.* [2] N-COUNT You can refer to a blackboard or a noticeboard as a **board**. *He wrote a few more notes on the board.* [3] N-COUNT The **board** of a company or organization is the group of people who control it. *...the board of directors. ...board meetings.* [4] VERB & PHRASE When you **board** a train, ship, or aircraft, or when you go **on board**, you get on it. *Are you ready to board?... There were four people on board the aircraft.* [5] N-UNCOUNT

Board is the food which is provided when you stay somewhere, for example in a hotel. *Free room and board are provided for all hotel staff.*
PHRASES ● If a policy or a situation applies **across the board**, it affects everything or everyone in a particular group. *...to increase salaries across the board.* ● If you **take on board** an idea or suggestion, you begin to accept it or take it into consideration. *I shall be hoping that the council will take that message on board.*
▸ **board up.** PHR-VERB If you **board up** a door or window, you fix pieces of wood over it so that it is covered up. *Half the shops are boarded up.*

'boarding school, boarding schools. N-VAR A **boarding school** is a school where the pupils live during the term. *Now she is away at boarding school.*

boardroom /ˈbɔːdruːm/ **boardrooms.** N-COUNT The **boardroom** is a room where the board of a company meets.

boast /bəʊst/ **boasts, boasting, boasted.** VERB & N-COUNT If someone **boasts about** something that they have done or that they own, they talk about it proudly in a way that other people may find irritating or offensive. A **boast** is what someone says when they boast. *Carol boasted about her costume... Furci boasted that he took part in killing them. ...her boast of being a great lover.*

⭐ **boat** /bəʊt/ **boats.** [1] N-COUNT A **boat** is something in which people can travel across water. *...a small fishing boat... The island may be reached by boat.* → See pictures on page 818. [2] N-COUNT You can refer to a passenger ship as a **boat**. *My father met me off the boat... It would be just his luck to miss the last boat.*
PHRASES ● If you say that someone **is rocking the boat**, you mean that they are upsetting a calm situation and causing trouble. ● If two or more people are **in the same boat**, they are in the same unpleasant situation. *She's in the same boat as me. She's unemployed herself.*

boating /ˈbəʊtɪŋ/. N-UNCOUNT **Boating** is travelling on a lake or river in a small boat for pleasure. *...a boating accident... I wanted to go boating.*

bob /bɒb/ **bobs, bobbing, bobbed.** VERB If something **bobs**, it moves up and down, like something does when it is floating on water. *The raft bobbed along... Huge balloons bobbed about in the sky above.*

bode /bəʊd/ **bodes, boding, boded.** VERB If something **bodes ill**, it makes you think that something bad will happen in the future. If something **bodes well**, it makes you think that something good will happen. [LITERARY] *The way the bill was passed bodes ill for democracy.*

bodily /ˈbɒdɪli/. [1] ADJ BEFORE N Your **bodily** needs and functions are the needs and functions of your body. [2] ADV You use **bodily** to indicate that an action involves the whole of someone's body. *I was hurled bodily to the deck.*

⭐ **body** /'bɒdi/ **bodies.** **1** N-COUNT Your **body** is all your physical parts, including your head, arms, and legs. → See pictures on pages 822 and 823. *My whole body hurt.* **2** N-COUNT You can refer to the main part of your **body**, excluding your arms, head, and legs, as your **body**. *Gently pull your leg toward your body.* **3** N-COUNT A **body** is a dead person's body. *Police later found a body.* **4** N-COUNT A **body** is an organized group of people who deal with something officially. *...public bodies such as local authorities.* **5** N-COUNT The **body** of a car or plane is its main part, excluding its engine, wheels, and wings.

bodyguard /'bɒdigɑːd/ **bodyguards.** N-COUNT Someone's **bodyguard** is the person or group of people employed to protect them.

'**body language.** N-UNCOUNT Your **body language** is the way you show your feelings or thoughts using the movements of your body.

bog /bɒg/ **bogs.** N-COUNT A **bog** is a wet muddy area of land.

,**bogged 'down.** ADJ If you are **bogged down** in something, it prevents you from making progress or getting something done. [INFORMAL] *Why get bogged down in legal details?*

boggle /'bɒgəl/ **boggles, boggling, boggled.** VERB If you say that the mind **boggles at** something, you mean that it is so strange or amazing that it is difficult to imagine or understand. [INFORMAL] *The mind boggles at how much work they have to do... The implications of this boggle the mind.*

bogus /'bəʊgəs/. ADJ If you describe something as **bogus**, you mean that it is not genuine. *...their bogus insurance claim.*

bohemian /bəʊ'hiːmiən/ **bohemians.** ADJ & N-COUNT You can describe someone as **bohemian**, or as a **bohemian**, if they are artistic and live in an unconventional way.

⭐ **boil** /bɔɪl/ **boils, boiling, boiled.** **1** VERB When a hot liquid **boils**, or when you **boil** it, bubbles appear in it and it starts to change into steam or vapour. *Boil the water in the saucepan. ...a large pan of boiling water.* **2** PHRASE When you **bring** a liquid **to the boil**, you heat it until it boils. **3** VERB When you **boil** a kettle, or when you put it on **to boil**, you heat the water inside it until it boils. *Marianne put the kettle on to boil.* **4** VERB When you **boil** food, or when you put it on **to boil**, you cook it in boiling water. *Boil the potatoes for 10 minutes.* ● See note at **cook**. **5** N-COUNT A **boil** is a red painful swelling on your skin.
▸**boil down to.** PHR-VERB If you say that a situation or problem **boils down to** a particular thing, you mean that this is the most important aspect of it. *It all boils down to money again.*
▸**boil over.** PHR-VERB When a liquid that is being heated **boils over**, it rises and flows over the edge of the container.

boiler /'bɔɪlə/ **boilers.** N-COUNT A **boiler** is a device which burns fuel to provide hot water.

boiling /'bɔɪlɪŋ/. ADJ Something that is **boiling**

or **boiling hot** is very hot. *It's boiling in here. ...boiling hot plates.* ● See note at **hot**.

boisterous /'bɔɪstərəs/. ADJ Someone who is **boisterous** is noisy, lively, and full of energy. *...a boisterous but good-natured crowd.*

bold /bəʊld/ **bolder, boldest.** **1** ADJ Someone who is **bold** is brave or confident. *I don't feel I'm being bold. ...bold economic reforms.* ◆ **boldly** ADV *You can and must act boldly... 'You should do it,' the girl said, boldly.* ◆ **boldness** N-UNCOUNT *...the boldness of his economic programme.* **2** ADJ **Bold** colours or designs are painted or drawn in a clear strong way. *...bold handwriting.*

bolster /'bəʊlstə/ **bolsters, bolstering, bolstered.** VERB If you **bolster** someone's confidence or courage, you make them more confident or more courageous. *...measures intended to bolster morale.*

bolt /bəʊlt/ **bolts, bolting, bolted.** **1** N-COUNT A **bolt** is a long metal object which screws into a nut and is used to fasten things together. → See picture on page 833. *...nuts and bolts that haven't been tightened up.* **2** VERB If you **bolt** one thing **to** another, you fasten them firmly together, using a bolt. *Bolt the components together. ...a wooden bench which was bolted to the floor.* **3** N-COUNT A **bolt** on a door or window is a metal bar that you slide across in order to fasten the door or window. *...the sound of a bolt being slowly and reluctantly slid open.* **4** VERB If you **bolt** a door or window, you slide the bolt across to fasten it. *Lock and bolt the kitchen door.* **5** VERB If a person or animal **bolts**, they suddenly start to run very fast, often because something has frightened them. *I made some excuse and bolted for the exit.*

⭐ **bomb** /bɒm/ **bombs, bombing, bombed.** **1** N-COUNT A **bomb** is a device which explodes, damaging a large area or killing people. **2** VERB When a place **is bombed**, it is attacked with bombs. *Airforce jets bombed the airport.* ◆ **bombing, bombings** N-VAR *...the bombing of Dresden.*

bombard /ˌbɒm'bɑːd/ **bombards, bombarding, bombarded.** **1** VERB If someone **bombards** you **with** something, they make you face a great deal of it. *We have been bombarded with requests for information... He began bombarding her with love letters.* **2** VERB When soldiers **bombard** a place, they attack it with continuous heavy gunfire or bombs. ◆ **bombardment** N-UNCOUNT *...the sound of heavy aerial bombardment.*

bomber /'bɒmə/ **bombers.** **1** N-COUNT A **bomber** is an aeroplane that drops bombs. **2** N-COUNT **Bombers** are people who plant bombs in public places.

bombshell /'bɒmʃel/ **bombshells.** N-COUNT A **bombshell** is a sudden piece of bad or unexpected news. *His resignation after thirteen years is a political bombshell.*

bonanza /bə'nænzə/ **bonanzas.** N-COUNT You can refer to a time or situation when people suddenly

a
b
c
d
e
f
g
h
i
j
k
l
m
n
o
p
q
r
s
t
u
v
w
x
y
z

become much richer as a **bonanza**. ...*a sales bonanza for computer makers.*

⭐ **bond** /bɒnd/ **bonds, bonding, bonded.** **1** N-COUNT A **bond** between people is a close link between them, for example feelings of love, or a special agreement. ...*the bond between mothers and babies... The republic is successfully breaking its bonds with Moscow.* **2** VERB When people **bond with** each other, they form a relationship based on love or shared experiences. *Belinda was having trouble bonding with the baby... We were bonded by years of mutual history.* **3** N-PLURAL **Bonds** are feelings, duties, or customs that force you to behave in a particular way. ...*the bonds of tradition.* **4** VERB When things **bond together**, they stick to each other or become joined in some way. *In graphite sheets, carbon atoms bond together in rings.* **5** N-COUNT A **bond** is a certificate issued by a government or company which shows that you have lent them money and that they will pay you interest.

bondage /'bɒndɪdʒ/. N-UNCOUNT **Bondage** is the condition of being a slave. [LITERARY] *Masters sometimes allowed slaves to buy their way out of bondage.*

⭐ **bone** /bəʊn/ **bones, boning, boned.** **1** N-VAR Your **bones** are the hard parts inside your body which together form your skeleton. *Stephen fractured a thigh bone... The body is made up primarily of bone, muscle, and fat.* **2** VERB If you **bone** a piece of meat or fish, you remove the bones from it before cooking it.

bonfire /'bɒnfaɪə/ **bonfires.** N-COUNT A **bonfire** is a fire built outdoors, usually to burn rubbish.

bonnet /'bɒnɪt/ **bonnets.** **1** N-COUNT In British English, the **bonnet** of a car is the metal cover over the engine at the front. The American word is **hood.** **2** N-COUNT A **bonnet** is a hat worn by babies which has ribbons that are tied under the chin.

bonus /'bəʊnəs/ **bonuses.** **1** N-COUNT A **bonus** is an amount of money that is added to someone's pay, usually because they have worked very hard. **2** N-COUNT A **bonus** is something good that you get in addition to something else, usually something which is unexpected. *When we qualified for both the finals it was an extra bonus.*

bony /'bəʊni/. ADJ If someone has, for example, a **bony** face or **bony** hands, their face or hands are too thin.

boo /buː/ **boos, booing, booed.** VERB & N-COUNT If you **boo** a speaker or performer, you shout 'boo' or make other loud sounds to indicate that you do not like them. The sounds you make are called **boos**. *He was booed off the stage... She was greeted with boos and hisses.* ♦ **booing** N-UNCOUNT *The stadium became a riot of booing and ill feeling.*

⭐ **book** /bʊk/ **books, booking, booked.** **1** N-COUNT A **book** consists of pieces of paper, usually with words printed on them, which are fastened together and fixed inside a cover of strong paper or cardboard. **2** N-COUNT A **book of** something such as stamps is a small number of them fastened together between thin cardboard or plastic covers. **3** N-PLURAL An organization's **books** are written records of money that has been spent and earned, or of the names of people who belong to it. *An accountant has gone over the books... Many of the people on our books are in the computing industry.* **4** VERB When you **book** something such as a hotel room or a ticket, you arrange to have it or use it at a particular time. [BRITISH] *I have booked a table in the nearby restaurant.* **5** PHRASE If a hotel, restaurant, or theatre is **fully booked, booked solid**, or **booked up**, it has no rooms, tables, or tickets left. ▶**book into** or **book in.** PHR-VERB In British English, when you **book into** a hotel or when you **book in**, you officially state that you have arrived to stay there, usually by signing your name in a register. The American term is **check in**.

bookcase /'bʊkkeɪs/ **bookcases.** N-COUNT A **bookcase** is a piece of furniture with shelves for books.

bookie /'bʊki/ **bookies.** N-COUNT A **bookie** is the same as a **bookmaker.** [INFORMAL]

booklet /'bʊklət/ **booklets.** N-COUNT A **booklet** is a small paperback book, containing information on a particular subject.

bookmaker /'bʊkmeɪkə/ **bookmakers.** N-COUNT A **bookmaker** is a person whose job is to take your money when you bet and to pay you money if you win.

bookmark /'bʊkmɑːk/ **bookmarks, bookmarking, bookmarked.** **1** N-COUNT A **bookmark** is a narrow piece of card or leather that you put between the pages of a book so that you can find a particular page easily. **2** N-COUNT A **bookmark** is the address of an Internet site that you put into a list on your computer so that you can return to it easily. [COMPUTING] **3** VERB If you **bookmark** an Internet site, you put it into a list on your computer so that you can return to it easily. [COMPUTING]

⭐ **boom** /buːm/ **booms, booming, boomed.** **1** N-COUNT & VERB If there is a **boom** in something such as the economy, or if it **is booming**, it increases or develops very quickly. ...*the 1980s property boom... Sales are booming.* **2** VERB & N-COUNT When something such as a cannon or someone's voice **booms** or **booms out**, it makes a loud, deep, echoing sound called a **boom**. *'Ladies,' boomed Helena, 'we all know why we're here tonight'... The stillness of the night was broken by the boom of a cannon.*

boon /buːn/ **boons.** N-COUNT You say that something is a **boon to** people or **for** people when it makes their life better or easier. *Fans that follow the games will provide a boon to local hotels.*

⭐ **boost** /buːst/ **boosts, boosting, boosted.** **1** VERB & N-COUNT If one thing **boosts** another, or if it gives it a **boost**, it causes the second thing to increase or be more successful. *The campaign had boosted sales... That would provide a tremendous boost to education.* **2** VERB & N-COUNT If something **boosts** your confidence or morale, or if it gives it a **boost**, it improves it. *It did give me a boost to win such a big event.*

⭐ **boot** /buːt/ **boots, booting, booted.** **1** N-COUNT **Boots** are strong heavy shoes that cover your whole foot and the lower part of your leg. → See picture on page 820. **2** VERB If you **boot** something such as a ball, you kick it hard. [INFORMAL] **3** N-COUNT In British English, the **boot** of a car is a covered space at the back or front that is used for luggage. The usual American word is **trunk**.

PHRASES ● If you **get the boot**, you are forced to leave your job. [INFORMAL] ● You can say **to boot** after the last item in a list of things in order to emphasize that particular thing. *He was a liar, a cheat and a bad businessman to boot.*

booth /buːð/ **booths.** **1** N-COUNT A **booth** is a small area separated from a larger public area by screens or thin walls where, for example, you can make a telephone call. **2** N-COUNT A **booth** is a small tent or stall, usually at a fair, in which you can buy goods or watch some entertainment.

booze /buːz/ **boozes, boozing, boozed.** **1** N-UNCOUNT **Booze** is alcoholic drink. [INFORMAL] **2** VERB When people **booze**, they drink a lot of alcohol. [INFORMAL] *...a load of drunken businessmen who had been boozing all afternoon.*

⭐ **border** /'bɔːdə/ **borders, bordering, bordered.** **1** N-COUNT The **border** between two countries is the dividing line between them. *They fled across the border.* **2** VERB If one thing **borders** another, it is next to it. *...the countries bordering the Mediterranean. ...miles of white sand beach bordered by palm trees.* **3** N-COUNT A **border** is a strip or band around the edge of something. *...a wall of plain tiles with a bright border.* **4** VERB When you say that something **borders on** a particular state, you mean that it has almost reached that state. *He admitted last night that his feelings bordered on despair.*

⭐ **bore** /bɔː/ **bores, boring, bored.** **1** VERB If someone or something **bores** you, you find them dull and uninteresting. *Dick bored him all the way through the meal.* **2** N-COUNT You describe someone as a **bore** when you think that they talk in a very uninteresting way. **3** N-SING You can describe a situation as **a bore** when you find it annoying or a nuisance. *It's a bore to be sick.* **4** VERB If you **bore** a hole in something, you make a deep round hole in it using a drilling tool. **5 Bore** is the past tense of **bear**.

bored /bɔːd/ ADJ If you are **bored**, you feel tired and impatient because you are not interested in something or because you have nothing to do. *I got bored with my job as a travel agent... I'm so bored.*

boredom /'bɔːdəm/ N-UNCOUNT **Boredom** is the state of being bored. *He had given up attending lectures out of sheer boredom.*

boring /'bɔːrɪŋ/ ADJ If you say that someone or something is **boring**, you think that they are very dull and uninteresting. *...a boring job.*

⭐ **born** /bɔːn/ **1** PASSIVE-VERB When a baby **is born**, it comes out of its mother's body. You can refer to a baby's parents by saying that he or she **is born of** or **born to** those people. *My mother was 40 when I was born... He was born of German parents and lived most of his life abroad.* **2** ADJ BEFORE N You use **born** to describe someone who has a natural ability to do a particular activity or job. For example, a **born** cook has a natural ability to cook well.

-born. **-born** is added to the name of a place or nationality to indicate where a person was born. *...the German-born photographer.*

borne /bɔːn/ **Borne** is the past participle of **bear**.

borough /'bʌrə, AM 'bɜːrəʊ/ **boroughs.** N-COUNT A **borough** is a town or district, which has its own council. *...the New York City borough of Queens.*

⭐ **borrow** /'bɒrəʊ/ **borrows, borrowing, borrowed.** VERB If you **borrow** something that belongs to someone else, you take it, usually with their permission, intending to return it. *Can I borrow a pen please?... He borrowed $200 from his wife.* ♦ **borrowing** N-UNCOUNT *Government borrowing is set to surge.*

borrower /'bɒrəʊə/ **borrowers.** N-COUNT A **borrower** is a person or organization that borrows money. *Most borrowers repay a fixed amount each month.*

bosom /'bʊzəm/ **bosoms.** **1** N-COUNT A woman's breasts are sometimes referred to as her **bosom** or her **bosoms**. [DATED] **2** N-SING If you are in **the bosom of** your family or **of** a community, you are among people who love and protect you. [LITERARY] *...after five long months away from the bosom of his family.* **3** ADJ BEFORE N A **bosom** friend is a very close friend. *...his bosom buddy.*

⭐ **boss** /bɒs/ **bosses, bossing, bossed.** **1** N-COUNT Your **boss** is the person in charge of the organization or department where you work. *He cannot stand his boss.* **2** PHRASE If you **are** your **own boss**, you work for yourself or do not have to ask other people for permission to do something. *I'm very much my own boss and no one interferes with what I do.* **3** VERB & PHR-VERB If someone **bosses** you, or if they **boss** you **around**, they keep telling you what to do. *We cannot boss them into doing more.*

bossy /'bɒsi/ ADJ A **bossy** person enjoys telling other people what to do; used showing disapproval. *...a rather bossy little girl.*

botany /'bɒtəni/ N-UNCOUNT **Botany** is the scientific study of plants. ♦ **botanical** ADJ BEFORE N *The area is of great botanical interest.* ♦ **botanist** /'bɒtənɪst/ **botanists** N-COUNT *He trained as a botanist.*

botch /bɒtʃ/ botches, botching, botched. VERB & PHR-VERB If you **botch** a piece of work, or if you **botch** it **up**, you do it badly or clumsily. [INFORMAL] *What if I botched it?... I hate having builders botch up repairs on my house.*

★ **both** /bəʊθ/. [1] QUANT You use **both** when you are referring to two people or things and saying that something is true about each of them. *Put both vegetables into a bowl... Both of us had tears in our eyes... Well, I'll leave you both then.* [2] CONJ You use the structure **both...and** when you are giving two facts or alternatives and emphasizing that each of them is true or possible. *Now, many women work both before and after having children.*

> **USAGE** Notice that all these sentences mean the same thing: 'Both boys have been ill', 'Both the boys have been ill', 'Both of the boys have been ill', 'The boys have both been ill'. You cannot say 'Both of boys have been ill'. When a pronoun is used, you can say 'Both of us have been ill'.

★ **bother** /ˈbɒðə/ bothers, bothering, bothered. [1] VERB If you do not **bother to** do something or if you do not **bother with** it, you do not do it, consider it, or use it because you think it is unnecessary or because you are too lazy. *Lots of people don't bother to go through a marriage ceremony... The papers didn't even bother reporting it... He does not bother with a helmet.* [2] PHRASE If you say that you **can't be bothered** to do something, you mean that you are not going to do it because you think it is unnecessary or because you are too lazy. *I just can't be bothered to look after the house.* [3] N-UNCOUNT **Bother** is trouble, fuss, or difficulty. *I usually buy sliced bread – it's less bother... Going to the police is a bother.* [4] VERB If something **bothers** you, it worries, annoys, or upsets you. *It bothered me that boys weren't interested in me... Never bother about other people's opinions.* ♦ **bothered** ADJ AFTER LINK-V *I was bothered about the blister on my hand.* [5] VERB If you **bother** someone, you talk to them or interrupt them when they are busy. *I just don't know why he bothers me with this kind of rubbish.*

★ **bottle** /ˈbɒtəl/ bottles, bottling, bottled. [1] N-COUNT A **bottle** is a glass or plastic container for keeping liquids in. *...two empty beer bottles... He had drunk half a bottle of whisky.* [2] VERB To **bottle** liquid means to put it into bottles after it has been made. *...equipment to automatically bottle the wine.* ♦ **bottled** ADJ *...bottled water.* ▶**bottle up.** PHR-VERB If you **bottle up** feelings, you do not express them or show them. *Tension in the home increases if you bottle things up... Be assertive rather than bottle up anger.*

★ **bottom** /ˈbɒtəm/ bottoms, bottoming, bottomed. [1] N-COUNT The **bottom** of something is the lowest part of it. *He sat at the bottom of the stairs. ...the bottom of page 8.* [2] ADJ BEFORE N The **bottom** thing in a series of things is the lowest

one. *...the bottom drawer. ...the bottom shelf.* [3] N-SING If someone is **bottom** or at **the bottom** in a survey, test, or league, their performance is worse than that of all the other people involved. *He was always bottom of the class.* [4] N-COUNT Your **bottom** is the part of your body that you sit on. → See picture on page 822. [5] PHRASE If you **get to the bottom of** something, you discover the real cause of it. *I have to get to the bottom of this mess.* ▶**bottom out.** PHR-VERB If a trend such as a fall in prices **bottoms out**, it stops getting worse or decreasing. *He expects the recession to bottom out.*

,**bottom 'line,** bottom lines. N-SING The **bottom line** in a decision or situation is the most important factor that you have to consider. *The bottom line is that it's not profitable.*

bought /bɔːt/. **Bought** is the past tense and past participle of **buy**.

boulder /ˈbəʊldə/ boulders. N-COUNT A **boulder** is a large rounded rock.

boulevard /ˈbuːləvɑːd, AM ˈbʊl-/ boulevards. N-COUNT A **boulevard** is a wide street in a city, usually with trees along each side. *...Lenton Boulevard.*

bounce /baʊns/ bounces, bouncing, bounced. [1] VERB & N-COUNT When something such as a ball **bounces**, or when you **bounce** it, it moves upwards or away immediately after hitting a surface. This movement is called a **bounce**. *...a falling pebble, bouncing down the eroded cliff... I bounced a ball against the house. ...two bounces of the ball.* [2] VERB If you **bounce** on something, you jump up and down on it repeatedly. *She lets us do anything, even bounce on our beds.* [3] VERB If something **bounces** or if something **bounces** it, it swings or moves up and down. *Her long black hair bounced as she walked... The wind was bouncing the branches of the big oak trees.* [4] VERB If a cheque **bounces** or if a bank **bounces** it, the bank refuses to accept it and pay out the money.

bouncer /ˈbaʊnsə/ bouncers. N-COUNT A **bouncer** is a man who is employed to prevent unwanted people from entering a nightclub or causing trouble in it.

bouncy /ˈbaʊnsi/. ADJ Someone or something that is **bouncy** is very lively and enthusiastic. *...good, bouncy pop songs... She was bouncy and full of energy.*

★ **bound** /baʊnd/ bounds, bounding, bounded. [1] **Bound** is the past tense and past participle of **bind**. [2] PHRASE If one thing is **bound up with** another, it is closely connected with it. *My fate was bound up with hers.* [3] PHRASE If something is **bound to** happen or be true, it is certain to happen or be true. *There are bound to be price increases next year... He's bound to know.* [4] ADJ AFTER LINK-V If a vehicle is **bound for** a particular place, it is travelling towards it. *The ship was bound for Italy.* [5] N-PLURAL **Bounds** are limits

bow 1

bow 3

arrow

bow 2

which restrict what can be done. *Visitors are kept firmly within bounds—no noise, no photographs.* [6] PHRASE If a place is **out of bounds**, people are not allowed to go there. [7] VERB When animals or people **bound**, they move quickly with large leaps. *He bounded up the steps.*

boundary /ˈbaʊndəri/ **boundaries.** N-COUNT The **boundary** of an area of land is an imaginary line that separates it from other areas. *...that disputed boundary between the two countries.*

bounty /ˈbaʊnti/ **bounties.** N-VAR You can refer to something that is provided in large amounts as **bounty.** [LITERARY] *...autumn's bounty of fruits, seeds and berries.*

bouquet /bəʊˈkeɪ, buː-/ **bouquets.** N-COUNT A **bouquet** is a bunch of flowers arranged in an attractive way. *...a bouquet of dried violets.*

bourgeois /ˈbʊəʒwɑː/. ADJ **Bourgeois** means typical of fairly rich middle-class people; used showing disapproval. *...his privileged bourgeois family.*

bout /baʊt/ **bouts.** [1] N-COUNT If you have a **bout** of something such as an illness, you have it for a short period. *...a severe bout of flu.* [2] N-COUNT A **bout of** activity is a short time during which it happens a great deal or in which you do it a great deal. *...the latest bout of violence.*

boutique /buːˈtiːk/ **boutiques.** N-COUNT A **boutique** is a small shop that sells fashionable clothes, shoes, or jewellery.

bow 1 bending or submitting

bow /baʊ/ **bows, bowing, bowed.** [1] VERB & N-COUNT When you **bow to** someone, or if you give them a **bow**, you briefly bend your body towards them as a formal way of greeting them or showing respect. *They bowed low to Louis and hastened out of his way... I gave a theatrical bow.* [2] VERB If you **bow** your head, you bend it downwards so that you are looking towards the ground. *He bowed his head, ashamed.* [3] VERB If you **bow to** pressure or **to** someone's wishes, you agree to do what they want you to do. *Some shops are bowing to consumer pressure and stocking organically grown vegetables.*

▶ **bow out.** PHR-VERB If you **bow out of** something, you stop taking part in it. *He would bow out of politics after the next election... He had bowed out gracefully.*

bow 2 objects

bow /baʊ/ **bows.** [1] N-COUNT A **bow** is a knot with two loops and two loose ends that is used in tying shoelaces and ribbons. *...a length of ribbon tied in a bow.* [2] N-COUNT A **bow** is a weapon for shooting arrows, consisting of a long curved piece of wood with a string attached to both its ends. [3] N-COUNT The **bow** of a violin or other stringed instrument is a long thin piece of wood with horse hair stretched along it, which you move across the strings of the instrument in order to play it.

bowed. [1] ADJ /bəʊd/ Something that is **bowed** is curved. *...an old lady with bowed legs.* [2] ADJ /baʊd/ If a person's body is **bowed**, it is bent forward. *Head bowed, she was listening or praying.*

bowel /baʊəl/ **bowels.** N-COUNT Your **bowels** are the tubes in your body through which digested food passes from your stomach to your anus.

★ **bowl** /bəʊl/ **bowls, bowling, bowled.** [1] N-COUNT A **bowl** is a circular container with a wide uncovered top that is used for mixing and serving food. → See picture on page 825. *...decorative wooden bowls. ...a bowl of soup.* [2] N-COUNT You can refer to the hollow rounded part of an object as its **bowl**. *...the toilet bowl.* [3] VERB In cricket, when a bowler **bowls**, they throw the ball down the pitch towards the batsman. [4] N-UNCOUNT **Bowls** is a game in which the players try to roll large wooden balls as near as possible to a small ball.

▶ **bowl over.** [1] PHR-VERB To **bowl** someone **over** means to push into them and make them fall to the ground. [2] PHR-VERB If you **are bowled over** by something, you are very impressed or surprised by it. *I was bowled over by the beauty of Cornwall.*

bowler /ˈbəʊlə/ **bowlers.** [1] N-COUNT In cricket, the **bowler** is the person who is bowling.

★ Bank of English® frequent word   For a full explanation of all grammatical labels, see pages vii-x

a
b
c
d
e
f
g
h
i
j
k
l
m
n
o
p
q
r
s
t
u
v
w
x
y
z

2 N-COUNT A **bowler** or a **bowler hat** is a round stiff hat with a narrow curved brim.

bowling /'bəʊlɪŋ/. N-UNCOUNT **Bowling** is a game in which you roll a heavy ball down a narrow track towards a group of wooden objects and try to knock down as many of them as possible. *I go bowling for relaxation.*

⭐ **box** /bɒks/ **boxes, boxing, boxed.** **1** N-COUNT A **box** is a square or rectangular container with stiff sides and sometimes a lid. *...a small wooden box. ...a box of chocolates.* **2** N-COUNT A **box** on a form is a square or rectangular space in which you have to write something. **3** N-COUNT In a theatre or at a sports ground, a **box** is a small enclosed area where a small number of people can sit to watch the performance or game. **4** VERB To **box** means to fight someone according to the rules of the sport of boxing. *At school I boxed and played rugby.* ◆ **boxer, boxers** N-COUNT *...a professional boxer.*
▶**box in.** PHR-VERB If you **are boxed in**, you are unable to move because you are surrounded by other people or cars. *The black cabs cut in front of them, trying to box them in.*

boxing /'bɒksɪŋ/. N-UNCOUNT **Boxing** is a sport in which two people wearing padded gloves fight, using only their hands.

'**box office, box offices.** **1** N-COUNT The **box office** in a theatre or cinema is the place where the tickets are sold. **2** N-SING People talk about the **box office** when they are referring to the success of a film or play in terms of the number of people who go to see it. *The movie looks set to be the biggest box office success of all time.*

⭐ **boy** /bɔɪ/ **boys.** **1** N-COUNT A **boy** is a male child. **2** N-COUNT You can refer to a young man as a **boy**, especially when talking about relationships between young men and women. *...the age when girls get interested in boys.*

'**boy band, boy bands.** N-COUNT A **boy band** is a band consisting of young men who sing popular music and dance.

boycott /'bɔɪkɒt/ **boycotts, boycotting, boycotted.** VERB & N-COUNT When people **boycott** a product they disapprove of, or organize a **boycott** against it, they refuse to buy it. People also **boycott** events and organizations by refusing to have anything to do with them. *The main opposition parties are boycotting the elections. ...the lifting of the economic boycott against Israel.*

boyfriend /'bɔɪfrend/ **boyfriends.** N-COUNT Someone's **boyfriend** is the man or boy with whom they are having a romantic or sexual relationship.

boyhood /'bɔɪhʊd/. N-UNCOUNT **Boyhood** is the period of a man's life during which he is a boy. *He has been a Derby County supporter since boyhood.*

boyish /'bɔɪɪʃ/. ADJ If you describe a man as **boyish**, you mean that his appearance or behaviour is like that of a boy, and you find this attractive. *...a boyish grin. ...a boyish enthusiasm for life.* ◆ **boyishly** ADV *John grinned boyishly.*

Br. Br. is a written abbreviation for **British**.

bra /brɑː/ **bras.** N-COUNT A **bra** is a piece of underwear that a woman wears to support her breasts.

brace /breɪs/ **braces, bracing, braced.** **1** VERB If you **brace yourself for** something unpleasant or difficult, you prepare yourself for it. *He braced himself for the icy plunge into the black water.* **2** VERB If you **brace yourself against** something, you press against it in order to steady yourself or to avoid falling. *Elaine braced herself against the dresser.* **3** N-COUNT A **brace** is a device attached to a person's leg to strengthen or support it. **4** N-COUNT A **brace** is a metal device fastened to a child's teeth to help them grow straight. **5** N-PLURAL In British English, **braces** are a pair of straps that you wear over your shoulders to prevent your trousers from falling down. The American word is **suspenders**.

bracelet /'breɪslɪt/ **bracelets.** N-COUNT A **bracelet** is a piece of jewellery that you wear round your wrist.

bracing /'breɪsɪŋ/. ADJ If you describe a place, climate, or activity as **bracing,** you mean that it makes you feel fit and full of energy.

bracket /'brækɪt/ **brackets.** **1** N-COUNT If you say that someone or something is in a particular **bracket,** you mean that they are within a particular range. *...a low income bracket.* **2** N-COUNT **Brackets** are pieces of metal, wood, or plastic that are fastened to a wall in order to support something such as a shelf. → See picture on page 329. **3** N-COUNT **Brackets** are a pair of written marks such as ( ) that you place round a word or sentence in order to indicate that you are giving extra information.

brag /bræg/ **brags, bragging, bragged.** VERB If someone **brags**, they talk very proudly about what they have done or what they own; used showing disapproval. *He's always bragging about his ability as a cricketer... The chairman never tires of bragging that he and Mr. McCormack are old friends.*

braid /breɪd/ **braids, braiding, braided.** **1** N-UNCOUNT **Braid** is a narrow piece of decorated cloth or twisted threads, used to decorate clothes or curtains. **2** VERB In American English, if you **braid** hair, you twist three or more lengths of it over and under each other to make one thick length. The usual British word is **plait**. **3** N-COUNT In American English, a **braid** is a length of hair which has been plaited and tied. The usual British word is **plait**.

⭐ **brain** /breɪn/ **brains.** **1** N-COUNT Your **brain** is the organ inside your head that controls your body's activities and enables you to think and to feel things. **2** N-COUNT Your **brain** is your mind and the way that you think. *Once you stop using your brain you soon go stale.* **3** N-COUNT If you say that someone has **brains** or a good **brain**, you mean that they are intelligent and have the ability to make good decisions. *You've got brains, you've got ideas, get on with it.* [4] N-COUNT The person who plans the activities of an organization can be referred to as **the brains** behind it. [INFORMAL] *Some investigators regarded her as the brains of the gang.*

brainchild /'breɪntʃaɪld/. N-SING The **brainchild** of a person is an idea or invention that they have thought up or created.

brake /breɪk/ **brakes, braking, braked.** [1] N-COUNT A vehicle's **brakes** are devices that make it go slower or stop. [2] VERB When the driver of a vehicle **brakes**, or when the vehicle **brakes**, the driver presses the vehicle's brake, to make it slow down or stop. *She braked sharply to avoid another car.*

bran /bræn/. N-UNCOUNT **Bran** consists of small brown flakes that are left when wheat grains have been used to make white flour.

⭐ **branch** /brɑːntʃ, bræntʃ/ **branches, branching, branched.** [1] N-COUNT The **branches** of a tree are the parts that grow out from its trunk. [2] N-COUNT A **branch** of a business or other organization is one of the offices, shops, or local groups which belong to it. *The local branch of Bank of America is handling the accounts.* [3] N-COUNT A **branch of** a subject is a part or type of it. *...a new branch of mathematics known as complexity theory.*
▸**branch off.** PHR-VERB A road or path that **branches off** from another one starts from it and goes in a slightly different direction. If you **branch off** somewhere, you change the direction in which you are going. *After a few miles, a small road branched off to the right.*
▸**branch out.** PHR-VERB If you **branch out**, you do something different from your normal activities or work. *...as telephone companies branch out into new information services.*

⭐ **brand** /brænd/ **brands, branding, branded.** [1] N-COUNT A **brand of** a product is the version made by one particular manufacturer. *...a brand of cigarette. ...a supermarket's own brand.* [2] VERB If someone **is branded** as something bad, many people decide that they are that thing. *The company has been branded racist by some of its own staff... They recently branded him a war criminal.* [3] VERB When someone **brands** an animal, they burn a permanent mark onto its skin in order to show who it belongs to.

brandish /'brændɪʃ/ **brandishes, brandishing, brandished.** VERB If you **brandish** something, especially a weapon, you hold it in a threatening way. *He appeared in the lounge brandishing a knife.*

'**brand name, brand names.** N-COUNT A product's **brand name** is the name the manufacturer gives it and under which it is sold.

,**brand-'new.** ADJ Something that is **brand-new** is completely new.

brandy /'brændi/ **brandies.** N-VAR **Brandy** is a strong alcoholic drink.

brash /bræʃ/ **brasher, brashest.** ADJ If you describe someone as **brash**, you disapprove of them because you think that they are aggressive and too confident. ◆ **brashly** ADV *...the young man who had brashly challenged his leadership.*
◆ **brashness** N-UNCOUNT *...a brashness bordering on arrogance.*

brass /brɑːs, bræs/. [1] N-UNCOUNT **Brass** is a yellow metal made from copper and zinc. *...shining brass buttons.* [2] N-PLURAL The **brass** is the section of an orchestra which consists of brass wind instruments such as trumpets and horns.

brat /bræt/ **brats.** N-COUNT If you call a child a **brat**, you disapprove of their bad or annoying behaviour.

bravado /brə'vɑːdəʊ/. N-UNCOUNT **Bravado** is an appearance of courage that someone shows in order to impress other people.

⭐ **brave** /breɪv/ **braver, bravest; braves, braving, braved.** [1] ADJ Someone who is **brave** is willing to do dangerous things, and does not show fear in difficult or dangerous situations. *...your mother's brave fight with the dread disease... He was not brave enough to report the loss of the documents.* ◆ **bravely** ADV *The enemy fought bravely.* [2] VERB If you **brave** a difficult or dangerous situation, you deliberately experience it, in order to achieve something. *Thousands have braved icy rain to demonstrate their support.* [3] PHRASE If you say that someone is **putting a brave face on** a difficult situation, you mean that they are pretending that they are happy or coping with a problem when they are not.

bravery /'breɪvəri/. N-UNCOUNT **Bravery** is brave behaviour or the quality of being brave.

brawl /brɔːl/ **brawls, brawling, brawled.** VERB & N-COUNT If people **brawl with** each other, or become involved in a **brawl**, they fight in a rough disorganized way. *He was suspended for a year from University after brawling with police.*

brazen /'breɪzən/. ADJ If you describe someone as **brazen**, you mean that they are very bold and do not care if other people think that they are behaving wrongly. *They have been more brazen about taking the law into their own hands.*
◆ **brazenly** ADV *Every taboo was brazenly violated in a spirit of reckless adventure.*

breach /briːtʃ/ **breaches, breaching, breached.** [1] N-VAR & VERB If there is a **breach of** an agreement or a law, or if you **breach** an agreement or a law, you break it. *His employer sued him for breach of contract.* [2] N-COUNT A **breach** in a relationship is a serious disagreement which often results in the relationship ending. *...a serious breach in relations between the two countries.* [3] VERB If someone or something **breaches** a barrier, they make an opening in it, usually leaving it weakened or destroyed. *The blast is thought to have breached a fire wall.* [4] N-COUNT A **breach** in a barrier is a wide gap in it. [5] VERB & N-COUNT If someone

a
b
c
d
e
f
g
h
i
j
k
l
m
n
o
p
q
r
s
t
u
v
w
x
y
z

breaches security or defences, or if there is a **breach** in security or defences, they manage to get through and attack an area that is heavily guarded and protected.

⭐ **bread** /bred/. N-UNCOUNT **Bread** is a food made from flour, water, and often yeast. The mixture is made into a soft dough and baked in an oven. ...*a loaf of bread.*

breadth /bretθ, AM bredθ/. ☐1 N-UNCOUNT The **breadth** of something is the distance between its two sides. *The breadth of the whole camp was 400 paces.* ☐2 N-UNCOUNT **Breadth** is the quality of consisting of or involving many different things. *Older people have a tremendous breadth of experience.*

breadwinner /'bredwɪnə/ **breadwinners.** N-COUNT In a family, the **breadwinner** is the person who earns the money that the family needs.

⭐ **break** /breɪk/ **breaks, breaking, broke, broken.** ☐1 VERB When an object **breaks** or when you **break** it, it suddenly separates into two or more pieces, often because it has been hit or dropped. *The plane broke into three pieces... He fell through the window, breaking the glass... Break the cauliflower into florets.* ☐2 VERB When a tool or a piece of machinery **breaks** or when you **break** it, it is damaged and no longer works. *He accused her of breaking the stereo. ...broken washing machines.* ☐3 VERB If you **break** a rule or agreement, you do something that the rule or agreement indicates you should not do. *We didn't know we were breaking the law. ...broken promises.* ☐4 VERB If you **break free** or **break loose**, you free yourself from something or escape from it. *She broke free by thrusting her elbow into his chest.* ☐5 VERB To **break** a difficult or unpleasant situation that has existed for some time means to end it suddenly. ...*to break the vicious circle between disadvantage and crime.* ☐6 VERB To **break** someone means to destroy their determination, their success, or their career. *He never let his jailers break him.* ☐7 N-COUNT & VERB If you have a **break** or if you **break**, you stop what you are doing and do something else or have a rest. *Do you want to have a little break?... They broke for lunch.* ☐8 VERB To **break** the force of something such as a blow or fall means to weaken its effect. *Here the trees might have broken his fall.* ☐9 VERB If you **break** a piece of bad news to someone, you tell it to them. *Then Louise broke the news that she was leaving me.* ☐10 N-COUNT A **break** is a lucky opportunity. [INFORMAL] *Her big break came when she appeared on network TV.* ☐11 VERB If you **break** a record, you beat the previous record for a particular achievement. ☐12 VERB When day or dawn **breaks**, it starts to grow light after the night has ended. ☐13 VERB When a wave **breaks**, it passes its highest point and turns downwards. ☐14 VERB If you **break** a secret code, you work out how to understand it. ☐15 VERB When a boy's voice **breaks**, it becomes permanently deeper. ☐16 See

also **broke, broken.** ☐17 to **break even**: see **even.**

▶**break down.** ☐1 PHR-VERB If a machine or a vehicle **breaks down**, it stops working. ☐2 PHR-VERB When a discussion, relationship, or system **breaks down**, it fails because of a problem or disagreement. *Talks with business leaders broke down last night.* ☐3 PHR-VERB If someone **breaks down**, they start crying. ☐4 PHR-VERB When a substance **breaks down** or when something **breaks it down**, it changes into a different form because of a chemical process. *The oil is attacked by naturally occurring microbes which break it down.* ☐5 PHR-VERB If you **break down** a door or barrier, you hit it so hard that it falls down. *His father failed to break the door down.* ☐6 See also **breakdown.**

▶**break in.** ☐1 PHR-VERB If someone **breaks in**, they get into a building by force. *Masked robbers broke in and made off with $8,000.* ● See also **break-in.** ☐2 PHR-VERB If you **break in on** someone's conversation, you interrupt them. *'She told you to stay here,' Mike broke in.*

▶**break into.** ☐1 PHR-VERB If someone **breaks into** a building, they get into it by force. ☐2 PHR-VERB You can use **break into** to indicate that someone suddenly starts doing something. *I feel as if I should break into song.* ☐3 PHR-VERB If you **break into** a new area of activity, you become involved in it. *She finally broke into films after an acclaimed stage career.*

▶**break off.** ☐1 PHR-VERB When part of something **breaks off** or when you **break** it **off**, it is snapped off or torn away. *Lee broke off a small piece of orange.* ☐2 PHR-VERB If you **break off** when you are doing or saying something, you suddenly stop doing it or saying it. *Llewelyn broke off in mid-sentence.* ☐3 PHR-VERB If you **break off** a relationship, you end it. ...*the courage to break it off with her.*

▶**break out.** ☐1 PHR-VERB If something such as a fight or disease **breaks out**, it begins suddenly. *He was 29 when war broke out.* ☐2 PHR-VERB If you **break out in** a rash or a sweat or if it **breaks out**, it appears on your skin.

▶**break through.** ☐1 PHR-VERB If you **break through** a barrier, you succeed in forcing your way through. *About fifteen inmates broke through onto the roof.* ☐2 See also **breakthrough.**

▶**break up.** ☐1 PHR-VERB When something **breaks up** or when you **break** it **up**, it separates or is divided into several smaller parts. *Break up the chocolate and melt it... He broke the bread up into chunks.* ☐2 PHR-VERB If you **break up with** your partner, you end your relationship with them. [INFORMAL] *My girlfriend had broken up with me... The marriage broke up.* ☐3 PHR-VERB If an activity **breaks up** or if you **break it up**, it is brought to an end. *Police used tear gas to break up a demonstration.* ☐4 PHR-VERB When schools or their pupils **break up**, the term ends and the pupils start their holidays. [BRITISH] ...*the last week before they break up.* ☐5 See also **break-up.**

breakaway /ˈbreɪkəweɪ/. ADJ BEFORE N A **breakaway** group is a group of people who have separated from a larger group. ...*Yugoslavia's breakaway republic of Croatia.*

breakdown /ˈbreɪkdaʊn/ **breakdowns.**
[1] N-COUNT The **breakdown** of a system, plan, or discussion is its failure or ending. ...*the breakdown of trade talks between the US and EU officials.*
[2] N-COUNT If you suffer a **breakdown**, you become so depressed that you cannot cope with life. *They often seem depressed and close to emotional breakdown.* ● See also **nervous breakdown.** [3] N-COUNT A **breakdown** of a car or piece of machinery is when it stops working. [4] N-COUNT A **breakdown** of something is a list of its separate parts. *The organisers were given a breakdown of the costs.*

⭐ **breakfast** /ˈbrekfəst/ **breakfasts.** N-VAR **Breakfast** is the first meal of the day, which is usually eaten early in the morning. *He likes two eggs for breakfast... I have breakfast at 9am.* ● See note at **meal.**

'**break-in, break-ins.** N-COUNT When there is a **break-in**, someone gets into a building by force.

'**breaking point.** N-UNCOUNT If something or someone has reached **breaking point**, they have so many problems that they may soon be unable to continue. *My nerves are almost at breaking point.*

breakneck /ˈbreɪknek/. ADJ BEFORE N Something that happens or travels at **breakneck** speed happens or travels very fast. *The company has expanded at a breakneck pace.*

breakout (or **break-out**) /ˈbreɪkaʊt/ **breakouts.** N-COUNT If there has been a **breakout**, someone has escaped from prison. *High Point prison had the highest number of breakouts of any jail.*

breakthrough /ˈbreɪkθruː/ **breakthroughs.** N-COUNT A **breakthrough** is an important development or achievement. *The company looks poised to make a significant breakthrough in China.*

'**break-up, break-ups.** N-COUNT The **break-up** of a group, relationship, or system is its end. ...*since the break-up of his marriage.*

⭐ **breast** /brest/ **breasts.** [1] N-COUNT A woman's **breasts** are the two soft round pieces of flesh on her chest that can produce milk to feed a baby. [2] N-COUNT A person's chest can be referred to as his or her **breast**. [LITERARY] *He struck his breast.* [3] N-COUNT A bird's **breast** is the front part of its body. [4] N-VAR A piece of **breast** is a piece of meat that is cut from the front of a bird or lamb. ...*grilled chicken breast.*

breaststroke /ˈbreststrəʊk/. N-UNCOUNT **Breaststroke** is a swimming stroke which you do lying on your front, and making circular movements with your arms and legs.

⭐ **breath** /breθ/ **breaths.** [1] N-VAR Your **breath** is the air which you take into and let out of your lungs when you breathe. *I could smell the whisky on his breath.* [2] N-VAR When you take a **breath**, you breathe in once. *He took a deep breath... He spoke for one and a half hours and barely paused for breath.*
PHRASES ● If you are **out of breath**, you are breathing very quickly and with difficulty because you have been doing something energetic. ● If you **hold your breath**, you make yourself stop breathing for a few moments. ● If you say something **under** your **breath**, you say it in a very quiet voice. ● If you describe something new or different as **a breath of fresh air**, you mean that you approve of it as it makes a situation or subject more interesting or exciting. *Her brisk treatment of an almost taboo subject was a breath of fresh air.* ● If you say that something **takes** your **breath away**, you mean that it is extremely beautiful or amazing. *I heard this song on the radio and it just took my breath away.*

breathalyze (BRIT also **breathalyse**) /ˈbreθəlaɪz/ **breathalyzes, breathalyzing, breathalyzed.** VERB If the driver of a car **is breathalyzed** by the police, they ask him or her to breathe into a special device in order to test whether he or she has drunk too much alcohol.

⭐ **breathe** /briːð/ **breathes, breathing, breathed.**
[1] VERB When people or animals **breathe**, they take air into their lungs and let it out again. *No American should have to drive out of town to breathe clean air... A thirteen year old girl is being treated after breathing in smoke.* ◆ **breathing** N-UNCOUNT *Her breathing became slow and heavy.* [2] VERB If someone says something very quietly, you can say that they **breathe** it. [LITERARY] *'You don't understand,' he breathed.* [3] VERB If someone **breathes** life, confidence, or excitement **into** something, they improve it by adding this quality. [WRITTEN]
▸ **breathe in.** PHR-VERB When you **breathe in**, you take some air into your lungs.
▸ **breathe out.** PHR-VERB When you **breathe out**, you send air out of your lungs through your nose or mouth.

breather /ˈbriːðə/ **breathers.** N-COUNT If you take a **breather**, you stop what you are doing for a short time and have a rest. [INFORMAL]

'**breathing space.** N-UNCOUNT A **breathing space** is a short period of time in which you can recover from one activity and prepare for a second one. *We hope that it will give us some breathing space.*

breathless /ˈbreθləs/. ADJ If you are **breathless**, you have difficulty in breathing properly, for example because you have been running. ◆ **breathlessly** ADV *'I'll go in,' he said breathlessly.* ◆ **breathlessness** N-UNCOUNT *Asthma causes wheezing and breathlessness.*

breathtaking (or **breath-taking**) /ˈbreθteɪkɪŋ/. ADJ If you say that something is **breathtaking,** you mean that it is extremely beautiful or amazing. *The house has breathtaking views from every room.* ◆ **breathtakingly** ADV ...*a breathtakingly simple gadget.*

breed /briːd/ **breeds, breeding, bred** /bred/.
[1] N-COUNT A **breed of** animal is a particular type of it. For example, terriers are a breed of dog.
[2] VERB If you **breed** animals or plants, you keep them for the purpose of producing more animals or plants. *He used to breed dogs for the police... New varieties of rose are bred each year.*
♦ **breeder, breeders** N-COUNT *...horse breeders.*
♦ **breeding** N-UNCOUNT *...selective breeding for better yields.* [3] VERB When animals **breed,** they mate and produce offspring. ♦ **breeding** N-UNCOUNT *...the breeding season.* [4] VERB If something **breeds** a situation or feeling, it causes it to develop. *If they are unemployed it's bound to breed resentment.* [5] PHRASE Someone who was **born and bred** in a particular place was born there and spent their childhood there. *...a Londoner born and bred.* [6] N-COUNT A particular **breed of** person is a type of person, with special qualities or skills. *...one of the new breed of British women squash players.*

breeze /briːz/ **breezes, breezing, breezed.** [1] N-COUNT A **breeze** is a gentle wind. *I imagined a breeze blowing against my face. ...a cool salty sea breeze.*
[2] VERB If you **breeze** into a place, you enter it in a casual and carefree way. *He was late, but eventually he breezed in.*

breezy /ˈbriːzi/. [1] ADJ Someone who is **breezy** behaves in a brisk, casual, cheerful, and confident way. *...his bright and breezy personality.* [2] ADJ When the weather is **breezy,** there is a fairly strong but pleasant wind blowing. *The day was breezy and warm.*

brethren /ˈbreðrɪn/. See **brother.**

brew /bruː/ **brews, brewing, brewed.** [1] VERB When you **brew** tea or coffee, you make it by pouring hot water over tea leaves or ground coffee.
[2] N-COUNT A **brew** is a pot of tea or coffee. It can also be a particular kind of tea or coffee. *...a mild herbal brew.* [3] VERB If someone **brews** beer, they make it. [4] VERB If an unpleasant situation **is brewing,** it is starting to develop. *A crisis was brewing.*

brewer /ˈbruːə/ **brewers.** N-COUNT A **brewer** is a person or company that makes beer.

brewery /ˈbruːəri/ **breweries.** N-COUNT A **brewery** is a place where beer is made.

bribe /braɪb/ **bribes, bribing, bribed.** N-COUNT & VERB If you are offered a **bribe** or if you **are bribed,** you are offered a sum of money or something valuable in order to persuade you to do something. *He was being investigated for receiving bribes... He bribed the workers to silence.*

bribery /ˈbraɪbəri/. N-UNCOUNT **Bribery** is the action of giving someone a bribe. *He was jailed on charges of bribery.*

brick /brɪk/ **bricks.** N-VAR **Bricks** are rectangular blocks of baked clay used for building walls. *...a huge brick building.*

bride /braɪd/ **brides.** N-COUNT A **bride** is a woman who is getting married or who has just got married. *The guests had crowded around the bride*

and groom. ♦ **bridal** ADJ BEFORE N *...a bridal shop.*

bridegroom /ˈbraɪdgruːm/ **bridegrooms.** N-COUNT A **bridegroom** is a man who is getting married.

bridesmaid /ˈbraɪdzmeɪd/ **bridesmaids.** N-COUNT A **bridesmaid** is a woman or a girl who accompanies a bride on her wedding day.

bridge /brɪdʒ/ **bridges.** [1] N-COUNT A **bridge** is a structure built over a river, road, or railway so that people or vehicles can cross from one side to the other. *I walked across the bridge.* [2] VERB & N-COUNT If something **bridges** the gap between two people or things, or if it acts as a **bridge** between them, it makes it easier for the differences or disagreements between them to be reduced or overcome. *It is unlikely that the two sides will be able to bridge their differences.*
[3] N-UNCOUNT **Bridge** is a card game for four players.

bridle /ˈbraɪdəl/ **bridles, bridling, bridled.** N-COUNT & VERB A **bridle** is a set of straps that is put around a horse's head and mouth so that the person riding or driving the horse can control it. When you **bridle** a horse, you put a bridle on it.

brief /briːf/ **briefer, briefest; briefs, briefing, briefed.** [1] ADJ Something that is **brief** lasts for only a short time. *She once made a brief appearance on television. ...a brief statement.* [2] ADJ AFTER LINK-V If you are **brief,** you say what you want to say in as few words as possible. *I hope to be brief and to the point.* [3] N-PLURAL Men's or women's underpants can be referred to as **briefs.** [4] VERB If someone **briefs** you, they give you information or instructions that you need. *The Prime Minister has been briefed by her parliamentary aides.*

briefcase /ˈbriːfkeɪs/ **briefcases.** N-COUNT A **briefcase** is a case for carrying documents. → See picture on page 48.

briefing /ˈbriːfɪŋ/ **briefings.** N-VAR A **briefing** is a meeting at which information or instructions are given to people. *They're holding a press briefing tomorrow.*

briefly /ˈbriːfli/. [1] ADV Something that happens **briefly** happens for a very short period of time. *He smiled briefly... The couple chatted briefly on the doorstep.* [2] ADV If you say something **briefly,** you use very few words or give very few details. *She told them briefly what had happened... Briefly, these are some of my main findings.*

brigade /brɪˈɡeɪd/ **brigades.** N-COUNT A **brigade** is one of the groups which an army is divided into.
● See also **fire brigade.**

brigadier /ˌbrɪɡəˈdɪə/ **brigadiers.** N-COUNT & N-TITLE A **brigadier** is an army officer of high rank.

bright /braɪt/ **brighter, brightest.** [1] ADJ A **bright** colour is strong and noticeable, and not dark. *...a bright red dress.* ♦ **brightly** ADV *...brightly coloured wallpaper.* [2] ADJ A **bright** light, object, or place is shining strongly or is full of light. *...a bright October day.* ♦ **brightly** ADV *...a warm,*

brightly lit room... The sun shone brightly.
♦ **brightness** N-UNCOUNT ...the brightness of each star. **3** ADJ **Bright** people or ideas are clever and original. Were you always fairly bright at school? **4** ADJ If someone looks or sounds **bright**, they look or sound cheerful. 'May I help you?' said a bright American voice. ♦ **brightly** ADV He smiled brightly. **5** ADJ If the future is **bright**, it is likely to be pleasant and successful. Both had successful careers and the future looked bright.

brighten /'braɪtən/ **brightens, brightening, brightened.** **1** VERB If you **brighten**, or if you **brighten up**, you suddenly look happier. They brightened up at the mention of departure. **2** VERB If someone or something **brightens** a situation, or if the situation **brightens**, it becomes more pleasant or favourable. Prospects for the industry may be brightening. **3** VERB & PHR-VERB If something **brightens** a place, or if it **brightens** it **up**, the place becomes brighter or lighter. It could do with a lick of paint to brighten up its premises.

⭐ **brilliant** /'brɪliənt/. **1** ADJ If you describe people or ideas as **brilliant**, you mean that they are extremely clever. He was a brilliant musician... She had a brilliant mind. ♦ **brilliantly** ADV ...a very high quality production, brilliantly written and acted. ♦ **brilliance** N-UNCOUNT ...his brilliance as a director. **2** ADJ You can say something is **brilliant** when it is very successful. ...his brilliant career... She knew he could have a brilliant future. **3** ADJ BEFORE N A **brilliant** light or colour is extremely bright. The woman had brilliant green eyes. ♦ **brilliantly** ADV ...brilliantly coloured flowers.

brim /brɪm/ **brims, brimming, brimmed.** **1** N-COUNT The **brim** of a hat is the wide part that sticks outwards at the bottom. **2** VERB If something **is brimming with** things of a particular kind, it is full of them. Her eyes were brimming with tears now.

⭐ **bring** /brɪŋ/ **brings, bringing, brought.** **1** VERB If you **bring** someone or something **with** you when you come to a place, they come with you or you have them with you. Remember to bring an apron... Someone went upstairs and brought down a huge kettle... Come to my party and bring a girl with you. **2** VERB If you **bring** something somewhere, you move it there. Reaching into her pocket, she brought out a cigarette... Her mother brought her hands up to her face... He poured a brandy for Dena and brought it to her. **3** VERB To **bring** something or someone to a place means to cause them to come to that place. I told you about what brought me here. **4** VERB To **bring** something or someone into a particular state or condition means to cause them to be in it. You can also say that something **brings** a particular feeling, situation, or quality. He brought the car to a stop... They have brought down income taxes... Her three children brought her joy. **5** VERB If you cannot **bring yourself to** do something, you

cannot make yourself do it. I just cannot bring myself to talk about it.

USAGE **Bring** and **take** are both used to talk about carrying something or accompanying someone somewhere, but **bring** is used to suggest movement towards the speaker and **take** is used to suggest movement away from the speaker. We could not bring it here because it is rather heavy... Anna took the book to bed with her. In the first sentence, bring suggests that we are coming to the same place as the speaker, that is, the speaker is here too. In the second sentence, took suggests that Anna moved away from the speaker when she went to bed, or alternatively that the speaker is merely reporting something that he or she was not involved in.
The difference between **bring** and **take** is equivalent to that between **come** and **go**. **Bring** and **come** suggest movement towards the speaker, while **take** and **go** suggest movement away.
Fetch suggests that someone goes away to get something and comes back with it. O'Leary went to fetch tickets and was soon back.

▶**bring about.** PHR-VERB To **bring** something **about** means to cause it to happen. ...the only way to bring about political change... That's what's brought it all about.
▶**bring along.** PHR-VERB If you **bring** someone or something **along**, you bring them with you when you come to a place. Dad brought a notebook along... Bring along your friends.
▶**bring back.** **1** PHR-VERB If something **brings back** a memory, it makes you start thinking about it. Your article brought back sad memories for me. **2** PHR-VERB When people **bring back** a fashion or practice that existed at an earlier time, they introduce it again. ...whether to bring back the death penalty.
▶**bring down.** PHR-VERB To **bring down** a government or ruler means to cause them to lose power. ...to bring down the government.
▶**bring forward.** **1** PHR-VERB To **bring forward** an event means to arrange for it to take place at an earlier time than had been planned. He had to bring forward an 11 o'clock meeting... We decided to bring the wedding forward. **2** PHR-VERB If you **bring forward** an argument or proposal, you state it so that people can consider it. The Government will bring forward proposals for legislation.
▶**bring in.** **1** PHR-VERB When an organization **brings in** a new law or system, they introduce it. The government brought in a controversial law. **2** PHR-VERB To **bring in** money means to earn it. [INFORMAL] I have three part-time jobs, which bring in about £14,000 a year.

a
b
c
d
e
f
g
h
i
j
k
l
m
n
o
p
q
r
s
t
u
v
w
x
y
z

▶ **bring off.** PHR-VERB If you **bring off** something difficult, you succeed in doing it. [INFORMAL] *They were about to bring off an even bigger coup... He thought his book would change society. But he didn't bring it off.*

▶ **bring out.** **1** PHR-VERB When a person or company **brings out** a new product, they produce it and sell it. *He's now brought out a book.* **2** PHR-VERB Something that **brings out** a particular kind of behaviour **in** you causes you to behave in that way. *A challenge brought out the best in him.*

▶ **bring up.** **1** PHR-VERB To **bring up** a child means to look after it until it is grown up. *She brought up four children... I bring my children up to be trusting, honest and helpful.* **2** PHR-VERB If you **bring up** a particular subject, you introduce it into a discussion or conversation. *Why are you bringing it up now?* **3** PHR-VERB If you **bring up** food, you vomit. [INFORMAL] *If I taste anything, I bring it up again directly.*

brink /brɪŋk/. N-SING If you are **on the brink of** something important, terrible, or exciting, you are just about to do it or experience it. *I was on the brink of poverty... He was driven to the brink of madness.*

brisk /brɪsk/ **brisker, briskest.** **1** ADJ A **brisk** action is done quickly and in an energetic way. *...a brisk walk.* ♦ **briskly** ADV *Eve walked briskly down the corridor.* **2** ADJ If someone's behaviour is **brisk**, they behave in a busy confident way which shows that they want to get things done quickly. *Her voice was brisk and professional.* ♦ **briskly** ADV *'Anyhow,' she added briskly, 'it's none of my business'.* **3** ADJ If the weather is **brisk**, it is cold and refreshing. *...a brisk winter's day.*

bristle /ˈbrɪsəl/ **bristles, bristling, bristled.** **1** N-COUNT **Bristles** are short thick hairs that feel hard and rough. **2** N-COUNT The **bristles** of a brush are the thick hairs attached to the handle. **3** VERB If the hair on your body **bristles**, it rises away from your skin because you are cold, frightened, or angry. *It makes the hairs at the nape of the neck bristle.* **4** VERB If you **bristle at** something, you react to it angrily. *He still bristles at the suggestion that he is arrogant.*

⭐ **British** /ˈbrɪtɪʃ/. **1** ADJ **British** means belonging or relating to Great Britain. *...the British government.* **2** N-PLURAL The **British** are the people who come from Great Britain.

Briton /ˈbrɪtən/ **Britons.** N-COUNT A **Briton** is a person who comes from Great Britain.

brittle /ˈbrɪtəl/. ADJ A **brittle** object or substance is hard but easily broken. *...the dry, brittle ends of the hair.*

broach /brəʊtʃ/ **broaches, broaching, broached.** VERB When you **broach** a subject, you mention it in order to start a discussion on it. *I broached the subject of her early life.*

⭐ **broad** /brɔːd/ **broader, broadest.** **1** ADJ Something that is **broad** is wide. *His shoulders were broad. ...the broad river.* **2** ADJ You use **broad** to describe something that involves many different things or people. *A broad range of issues was discussed.* **3** ADJ A **broad** description is general rather than detailed. *...a broad outline of the Society's development.* **4** ADJ BEFORE N A **broad** hint is a very obvious one. *They've been giving broad hints about what to expect.* **5** ADJ A **broad** accent is strong and noticeable. *He has a broad Yorkshire accent.*

broadband /ˈbrɔːdbænd/. N-UNCOUNT **Broadband** is a method of sending many electronic messages at the same time by using a wide range of frequencies.

⭐ **broadcast** /ˈbrɔːdkɑːst, -kæst/ **broadcasts, broadcasting, broadcasted** or **broadcast.** **1** N-COUNT A **broadcast** is something that you hear on the radio or see on television. *A broadcast of the speech was heard in San Francisco.* **2** VERB To **broadcast** a programme means to send it out by radio waves, so that it can be heard on the radio or seen on television. *The concert will be broadcast live on television.* ♦ **broadcasting** N-UNCOUNT *...the BBC Weather Service celebrated 70 years of broadcasting.*

broadcaster /ˈbrɔːdkɑːstə, -kæst-/ **broadcasters.** N-COUNT A **broadcaster** is someone who gives talks or takes part in discussions on radio or television.

broaden /ˈbrɔːdən/ **broadens, broadening, broadened.** **1** VERB When something **broadens**, it becomes wider. *The smile broadened to a grin... As we drove towards Chamdo, the river broadened.* **2** VERB If you **broaden** something, or if it **broadens**, you make it involve or affect more things or people. *We must broaden our appeal... The political spectrum has broadened.*

broadly /ˈbrɔːdli/. **1** ADV You use **broadly** to indicate that something is generally true. *The idea that software is capable of any task is broadly true.* **2** ADV You use **broadly** to say that something is true to a large extent. *The new law has been broadly welcomed.* **3** ADV If someone smiles **broadly**, their mouth is stretched very wide.

broad-'minded. ADJ Someone who is **broad-minded** does not disapprove of actions or attitudes that many other people disapprove of; used showing approval. *...a shrewd, broad-minded man of high intelligence.*

broccoli /ˈbrɒkəli/. N-UNCOUNT **Broccoli** is a vegetable with green stalks and green or purple flower buds. → See picture on page 836.

brochure /ˈbrəʊʃə, AM brəʊˈʃʊr/ **brochures.** N-COUNT A **brochure** is a booklet with pictures that gives you information about a product or service. *...holiday brochures.*

broil /brɔɪl/ **broils, broiling, broiled.** VERB In American English, if you **broil** food, you cook it using strong heat directly above or below it. The British word is **grill**. ● See note at **cook**.

broke /brəʊk/. **1 Broke** is the past tense of **break**. **2** ADJ If you are **broke**, you have no money. [INFORMAL] *He was broke when I married* *him.* **3** PHRASE If a company or person **goes broke**, they lose money and are unable to continue in business or to pay their debts.

broken /'brəʊkən/. **1** **Broken** is the past participle of **break**. **2** ADJ BEFORE N A **broken** line is not continuous but has gaps in it. **3** ADJ BEFORE N You use **broken** to describe a marriage that has ended in divorce, or a home in which the parents of the family are divorced, when you think this is a sad thing. *...children from broken homes.* **4** ADJ BEFORE N If someone talks in **broken** English or in **broken** French, for example, they speak slowly and make a lot of mistakes because they do not know the language very well.

⭐ **broker** /'brəʊkə/ **brokers, brokering, brokered.** **1** N-COUNT A **broker** is a person whose job is to buy and sell shares, foreign money, or goods for other people. **2** VERB If a country or government **brokers** an agreement, they try to negotiate or arrange it. *The United Nations brokered a peace in Mogadishu.*

bronze /brɒnz/ **bronzes.** **1** N-UNCOUNT **Bronze** is a yellowish-brown metal made from copper and tin. **2** N-COUNT A **bronze** is a sculpture made of bronze. *...a bronze of Napoleon on horseback.* **3** ADJ Something that is **bronze** is yellowish-brown in colour. *Her hair shone bronze and gold.*

,bronze 'medal, **bronze medals.** N-COUNT If you win a **bronze medal**, you come third in a competition, especially a sports contest, and are often given a medal made of bronze as a prize.

brooch /brəʊtʃ/ **brooches.** N-COUNT A **brooch** is a small piece of jewellery which can be pinned on a dress, blouse, or coat.

brood /bruːd/ **broods, brooding, brooded.** **1** N-COUNT A **brood** is a group of baby birds belonging to the same mother. **2** VERB If someone **broods over** or **about** something, they think about it a lot, seriously and often unhappily. *She constantly broods about her family.*

brooding /'bruːdɪŋ/. **1** ADJ **Brooding** is used to describe an atmosphere or feeling that causes you to feel disturbed or slightly afraid. [LITERARY] *...a heavy, brooding silence.* **2** ADJ If you describe someone's expression as **brooding**, you mean that they look as if they are thinking deeply about something. *...his dark, brooding eyes.*

brook /brʊk/ **brooks.** N-COUNT A **brook** is a small stream.

broom /bruːm/ **brooms.** N-COUNT A **broom** is a long-handled brush which is used to sweep the floor.

broth /brɒθ, AM brɔːθ/. N-UNCOUNT **Broth** is a kind of soup. It usually has vegetables or rice in it.

brothel /'brɒθəl/ **brothels.** N-COUNT A **brothel** is a building where men pay to have sex with prostitutes.

⭐ **brother** /'brʌðə/ **brothers.**

☑️ The old-fashioned form **brethren** is also used as the plural for meaning 2.

1 N-COUNT Your **brother** is a boy or a man who has the same parents as you. *...my younger brother.* ● See also **half-brother**.

> **USAGE** Note that there is no common English word that can refer to both a brother and a sister. You simply have to use both words. *She has 13 brothers and sisters.* The word **sibling** exists, but it is rare and very formal.

2 N-COUNT Some people describe a man as their **brother** when he belongs to the same group as them. *Sri Lankans share a common ancestry with their Indian brethren.* **3** N-TITLE **Brother** is a title given to a man who belongs to a religious institution such as a monastery. *...Brother Otto.*

brotherhood /'brʌðəhʊd/ **brotherhoods.** **1** N-UNCOUNT **Brotherhood** is the affection and loyalty that you feel for people who you have something in common with. *He believed in socialism and the brotherhood of man.* **2** N-COUNT A **brotherhood** is an organization whose members all have the same political aims and beliefs or the same job or profession.

'brother-in-law, **brothers-in-law.** N-COUNT Someone's **brother-in-law** is the brother of their husband or wife, or the man who is married to their sister.

brought /brɔːt/. **Brought** is the past tense and past participle of **bring**.

brow /braʊ/ **brows.** **1** N-COUNT Your **brow** is your forehead. *He wiped his brow with the back of his hand.* **2** N-COUNT Your **brows** are your eyebrows. **3** N-COUNT The **brow** of a hill is the top part of it.

⭐ **brown** /braʊn/ **browner, brownest; browns, browning, browned.** **1** ADJ & N-VAR Something that is **brown** is the colour of earth or wood. *...her deep brown eyes.* **2** ADJ You can describe a white-skinned person as **brown** when they have been sitting in the sun until their skin is darker than usual. *I don't want to be really brown, just have a nice light golden colour.* **3** VERB If someone **browns** in the sun or if the sun **browns** them, they become brown in colour. When food **browns** or when you **brown** food, you cook it, usually for a short time on a high flame. *...gorgeous females busy browning themselves... Cook for ten minutes until the sugar browns.*

browse /braʊz/ **browses, browsing, browsed.** **1** VERB & N-COUNT If you **browse** or have a **browse** in a shop, you look at things in a casual way, without intending to buy anything. *I stopped in several bookstores to browse... I'm just browsing around. ...a browse around the shops.* **2** VERB If you **browse through** a book or magazine, you look through it in a casual way. *...browsing through brochures.* **3** VERB If you **browse** on a computer, you search for information in files or on the Internet. [COMPUTING] *Allen spends an average of four hours a weekend browsing the Internet.*

browser /'braʊzə/ **browser.** 1 N-COUNT A **browser** is a piece of computer software that you use to search for information on the Internet. [COMPUTING] 2 N-COUNT A **browser** is someone who browses in a shop. ...*a casual browser.*

bruise /bruːz/ **bruises, bruising, bruised.** 1 N-COUNT A **bruise** is an injury which appears as a purple mark on your body. 2 VERB If you **bruise** a part of your body, a bruise appears on it, for example because something hits you. *I had only bruised my knee.* ♦ **bruised** ADJ ...*a badly bruised leg.*

brunt /brʌnt/. PHRASE If someone or something **bears the brunt** or **takes the brunt of** something unpleasant, they suffer the main part or force of it. *Young people are bearing the brunt of unemployment.*

⭐ **brush** /brʌʃ/ **brushes, brushing, brushed.** 1 N-COUNT A **brush** is an object with a large number of bristles fixed to it. You use brushes for painting, for cleaning things, and for tidying your hair. ...*a hair brush.* 2 VERB & N-SING When you **brush** something or when you give it a **brush**, you clean it or tidy it using a brush. ...*he brushed away the fine sawdust.* 3 VERB If you **brush** something somewhere, you remove it with quick light movements of your hands. *He brushed the snow off the windshield.* 4 VERB If one thing **brushes against** another or if you **brush** one thing **against** another, the first thing touches the second thing lightly while passing it. *Something brushed against her leg... She brushed her lips softly across Michael's cheek.*

▶ **brush aside** or **brush away.** PHR-VERB If you **brush aside** or **brush away** an idea, remark, or feeling, you refuse to consider it because you think it is not important or useful, even though it may be. *Perhaps you shouldn't brush the idea aside too hastily.*

▶ **brush up.** PHR-VERB If you **brush up** something or if you **brush up on** it, you practise it or improve your knowledge of it. *Eleanor spent much of the summer brushing up on her driving.*

brusque /brʌsk/. ADJ If you describe a person as **brusque**, you mean that they deal with people quickly and abruptly, without showing much consideration for their feelings. *The doctors are brusque and busy.* ♦ **brusquely** ADV *'It's only a sprain,' Paula said brusquely.*

,**brussels 'sprout** (or **Brussels sprout**) **brussels sprouts.** N-COUNT **Brussels sprouts** or **sprouts** are vegetables that look like tiny cabbages. → See picture on page 836.

brutal /'bruːtəl/. 1 ADJ A **brutal** act or person is cruel and violent. ...*the brutal suppression of anti-government protests.* ♦ **brutally** ADV *Her real parents had been brutally murdered.* 2 ADJ If someone expresses something unpleasant with **brutal** honesty or frankness, they express it in a clear and accurate way, without attempting to disguise or reduce its unpleasant effect. *She*

spoke with a brutal honesty. ♦ **brutally** ADV *The talks had been brutally frank.*

brutality /bruː'tælɪti/ **brutalities.** N-VAR **Brutality** is cruel and violent treatment or behaviour. A **brutality** is an instance of cruel and violent treatment or behaviour. ...*police brutality.* ...*the brutalities of civil war.*

brute /bruːt/ **brutes.** 1 N-COUNT If you call a man a **brute**, you mean that he is rough and insensitive. ...*a drunken brute.* 2 ADJ BEFORE N When you refer to **brute** strength or force, you are contrasting it with gentler methods or qualities. *He used brute force to take control.*

BSE /,biː es 'iː/. N-UNCOUNT **BSE** is a fatal disease which affects the nervous system of cattle. **BSE** is an abbreviation for 'bovine spongiform encephalopathy'.

BTW. **BTW** is the written abbreviation for 'by the way', mainly used in e-mail. [COMPUTING]

bubble /'bʌbəl/ **bubbles, bubbling, bubbled.** 1 N-COUNT **Bubbles** are small balls of air or gas in a liquid. ...*a bubble of gas.* 2 N-COUNT A **bubble** is a hollow delicate ball of soapy liquid floating in the air or standing on a surface. ...*soap bubbles.* 3 VERB When a liquid **bubbles**, bubbles move in it, for example because it is boiling or moving quickly. *The water bubbled to the surface.* 4 VERB If you **are bubbling with** a good feeling, you are full of it. *She was bubbling with excitement.*

bubbly /'bʌbli/ **bubblier, bubbliest.** 1 ADJ If something is **bubbly**, it has a lot of bubbles in it. ...*warm, bubbly water.* 2 N-UNCOUNT Champagne is sometimes called **bubbly**. [INFORMAL] 3 ADJ Someone who is **bubbly** is very lively and cheerful. ...*a bubbly girl who loves to laugh.*

buck /bʌk/ **bucks, bucking, bucked.** 1 N-COUNT A **buck** is a US or Australian dollar. [INFORMAL] *That would probably cost you about fifty bucks.* 2 PHRASE When someone makes **a fast buck** or makes **a quick buck**, they earn a lot of money quickly and easily, often by doing something which is considered to be dishonest. [INFORMAL] 3 N-COUNT A **buck** is the male of various animals, including the deer and rabbit. 4 VERB If a horse **bucks**, it jumps into the air wildly with all four feet off the ground. 5 PHRASE If you **pass the buck**, you refuse to accept responsibility for something. *David says the responsibility is Mr Smith's and it's no good trying to pass the buck.*

▶ **buck up.** 1 PHR-VERB If you **buck** someone **up** or if you **buck up** their spirits, you say or do something to make them more cheerful. [INFORMAL] 2 PHR-VERB If you tell someone to **buck up** or to **buck up** their ideas, you are telling them to start behaving in a more positive manner. [INFORMAL] *If we don't buck up we'll be in trouble.*

bucket /'bʌkɪt/ **buckets.** N-COUNT A **bucket** is a deep round metal or plastic container with a handle. ...*a blue bucket.* ...*a bucket of water.* → See picture on page 85.

bucket

buckle /'bʌkəl/ **buckles, buckling, buckled.**
1 N-COUNT & VERB A **buckle** is a piece of metal or plastic attached to one end of a belt or strap and used to fasten it. When you **buckle** a belt or strap, you fasten it with a buckle. → See picture on page 249. ...*a big silver belt buckle*... *He always buckles his seat belt.* **2** VERB If an object **buckles** or if something **buckles** it, it becomes bent as a result of severe heat or force. *A freak wave had buckled the deck.* **3** VERB If your legs **buckle,** they bend because they have become very weak. *His knees buckled and he fell backwards.*
▸**buckle down.** PHR-VERB If you **buckle down to** something, you start working seriously at it. *He has buckled down to work in the reserves... I just buckled down and got on with playing.*

bud /bʌd/ **buds, budding, budded. 1** N-COUNT A **bud** is a small pointed lump that appears on a tree or plant and develops into a leaf or flower. **2** VERB When a tree or plant **is budding,** buds are appearing on it or are beginning to open. **3** PHRASE To **nip** something **in the bud** means to stop it before it can develop very far. [INFORMAL] *It is important to recognize jealousy and to nip it in the bud before it gets out of hand.*

Buddhist /'bʊdɪst/ **Buddhists.** N-COUNT & ADJ **Buddhists** believe in a religion which teaches that the way to end suffering is by overcoming your desires. **Buddhist** means relating to this religion. *She has been a Buddhist since 1976. ...a Buddhist temple.* ♦ **Buddhism** N-UNCOUNT ...*the doctrine of Buddhism.*

budding /'bʌdɪŋ/. ADJ BEFORE N You use **budding** to describe someone who is just beginning to succeed or become interested in a certain activity. You also use **budding** to describe a situation that is just beginning. ...*a budding actress.* ...*our budding romance.*

buddy /'bʌdi/ **buddies. 1** N-COUNT A **buddy** is a close friend, usually a male friend of a man. [INFORMAL] *We became great buddies.* **2** N-VOC Men sometimes address other men as **buddy.** [AMERICAN, INFORMAL]

budge /bʌdʒ/ **budges, budging, budged. 1** VERB If someone will not **budge** on a matter, or if nothing will **budge** them, they refuse to change their mind or to compromise. *Both sides say they will not budge... No amount of prodding will budge him.* **2** VERB If someone or something will not

budge, or if you cannot **budge** them, they will not move. *Her mother refused to budge from London... I got a grip on the boat and pulled but I couldn't budge it.*

⭐ **budget** /'bʌdʒɪt/ **budgets, budgeting, budgeted.**
1 N-COUNT A **budget** is a plan showing how much money a person or organization has available and how it will be spent. The **budget for** something is the amount of money that a person, organization, or country has available to spend on it. *I do try and buy within my budget.* ...*this year's budget for AIDS prevention.* **2** VERB If you **budget** certain amounts of money for particular things, you decide that you can afford to spend those amounts on those things. *The movie is only budgeted at $10 million... I'm learning how to budget.* ♦ **budgeting** N-UNCOUNT ...*our budgeting for the current year.* **3** ADJ BEFORE N **Budget** is used to suggest that something is being sold cheaply. ...*a budget-priced CD.*

buff /bʌf/ **buffs, buffing, buffed. 1** N-COUNT You use **buff** to talk about people who know a lot about a particular subject. [INFORMAL] ...*an avid film buff.* **2** VERB If you **buff** the surface of something, you rub it with a piece of soft material in order to make it shine.

buffalo /'bʌfələʊ/.

✒ The plural is **buffalo** or **buffaloes.**

N-COUNT A **buffalo** is a wild animal like a large cow with long curved horns.

buffer /'bʌfə/ **buffers. 1** N-COUNT A **buffer** is something that prevents something else from being harmed. *Keep savings as a buffer against unexpected cash needs.* **2** N-COUNT The **buffers** on a train or at the end of a railway line are two metal discs on springs that reduce the shock when they are hit.

buffet, buffets, buffeting, buffeted. 1 N-COUNT /'bʌfeɪ, AM bʊ'feɪ/ A **buffet** is a café in a station. **2** N-COUNT A **buffet** is a meal of cold food at a special occasion. Guests usually help themselves to the food. **3** N-COUNT On a train, the **buffet** or the **buffet car** is the carriage where meals and snacks are sold. [BRITISH] **4** VERB /'bʌfɪt/ If something **is buffeted** by rough winds or seas, it is repeatedly struck or blown around by them. *Their plane had been severely buffeted by storms.*

bug /bʌg/ **bugs, bugging, bugged. 1** N-COUNT A **bug** is a tiny insect, especially one that causes damage. [INFORMAL] **2** N-COUNT A **bug** is a minor illness such as a cold. ...*a stomach bug... There was a bug going around.* **3** N-COUNT If there is a **bug** in a computer program, there is an error in it. [COMPUTING] **4** VERB If a place **is bugged,** tiny microphones are hidden there to secretly record what people are saying. **5** VERB If something or someone **bugs** you, they worry or annoy you. [INFORMAL] *I only did it to bug my parents. ...this little short guy who really bugged me.*

⭐ **build** /bɪld/ **builds, building, built** /bɪlt/. **1** VERB If you **build** a structure, you make it by joining

a
b
c
d
e
f
g
h
i
j
k
l
m
n
o
p
q
r
s
t
u
v
w
x
y
z

things together. *Developers are now proposing to build a hotel on the site... Workers at the plant build the F-16 jet fighter.* [2] VERB If you **build** something **into** a wall or object, you make it in such a way that it is in the wall or object, or is part of it. *The TV was built into the ceiling.* [3] VERB If people **build** an organization or a society, they gradually form it. *Their purpose is to build a fair society and a strong economy.* [4] VERB If you **build** an organization, system, or product **on** something, you base it on it. *...a firmer foundation of fact on which to build theories... Build on the qualities you are satisfied with.* [5] VERB If you **build** something **into** a policy, system, or product, you make it a part of it. *We have to build computers into the school curriculum.* [6] N-COUNT Your **build** is the shape that your bones and muscles give to your body. *He is of medium build.*
● See also **built**.

▶**build up.** [1] PHR-VERB If an amount of something **builds up**, or if you **build** it **up**, it gradually gets bigger as a result of more being added to it. *Slowly a thick layer of fat builds up on the pan's surface.* [2] PHR-VERB If you **build** someone **up**, you help them to feel stronger or more confident. [3] See also **build-up, built-up.**

builder /'bɪldə/ **builders.** N-COUNT A **builder** is a person whose job is to build or repair buildings.

⭐ **building** /'bɪldɪŋ/ **buildings.** N-COUNT A **building** is a structure with a roof and walls.

'building society, building societies. N-COUNT In Britain, a **building society** is a business in which people can invest their money, and which lends people money to buy houses.

'build-up (also **buildup** or **build up**) **build-ups.** [1] N-COUNT A **build-up** is a gradual increase in something. *There has been a build-up of troops on both sides of the border.* [2] N-COUNT The **build-up to** an event is the way that people talk about it a lot in the period immediately before it. *...the build-up to Christmas.*

built /bɪlt/ [1] **Built** is the past tense and past participle of **build.** [2] ADJ If you say that someone is **built** in a particular way, you are describing the kind of body they have. *He is heavily built.*

built-'in. ADJ BEFORE N **Built-in** features are included in something as an essential part of it. *...built-in cupboards in the bedrooms.*

'built-up. ADJ A **built-up** area is one where there are many buildings.

bulb /bʌlb/ **bulbs.** [1] N-COUNT A **bulb** is the glass part of an electric lamp which gives out light when electricity passes through it. [2] N-COUNT A **bulb** is an onion-shaped root that grows into a plant.

bulge /bʌldʒ/ **bulges, bulging, bulged.** [1] VERB If something **bulges,** it sticks out. *His eyes were bulging.* [2] VERB If something **is bulging with** things, it is very full of them. *She returned home with the car bulging with boxes. ...a bulging briefcase.* [3] N-COUNT A **bulge** is a lump on an

otherwise flat surface. *...those bulges on your hips and thighs.*

bulimia /buː'lɪmiə/. N-UNCOUNT **Bulimia** or **bulimia nervosa** is a mental illness in which a person eats very large amounts and then makes themselves vomit. ♦ **bulimic** /buː'lɪmɪk/ ADJ *Nobody knew I was bulimic.*

bulk /bʌlk/ **bulks.** [1] N-SING You can refer to the **bulk** of a person or thing when you want to indicate that they are very large and heavy. *Despite his bulk he moved lightly on his feet.* [2] QUANT **The bulk of** something is most of it. *They come from all over the world, though the bulk is from the Indian subcontinent.* [3] N-UNCOUNT If you buy or sell something **in bulk,** you buy or sell it in large quantities.

bulky /'bʌlki/ **bulkier, bulkiest.** ADJ Something that is **bulky** is large and heavy. *...a bulky grey sweater.*

bull /bʊl/ **bulls.** [1] N-COUNT A **bull** is a male animal of the cow family. → See picture on page 815. [2] N-COUNT Male elephants and whales are called **bulls.**

bulldog /'bʊldɒg, AM -dɔːg/ **bulldogs.** N-COUNT A **bulldog** is a type of dog with a large square head and powerful jaws.

bulldozer /'bʊldəʊzə/ **bulldozers.** N-COUNT A **bulldozer** is a large tractor with a broad metal blade at the front, used for moving earth or knocking down buildings. → See picture on page 834.

bullet /'bʊlɪt/ **bullets.** N-COUNT A **bullet** is a small piece of metal which is fired from a gun.

bulletin /'bʊlɪtɪn/ **bulletins.** [1] N-COUNT A **bulletin** is a short news report on radio or television. *...NBC's evening news bulletin.* [2] N-COUNT A **bulletin** is a regular newspaper or leaflet produced by a group or organization.

'bullet point, bullet points. N-COUNT A **bullet point** is one of a series of important items for discussion or action in a document, marked by a square or round symbol.

'bullet-proof (or **bulletproof**). ADJ Something that is **bullet-proof** is made of a strong material that bullets cannot pass through.

bullion /'bʊliən/. N-UNCOUNT **Bullion** is gold or silver in the form of bars.

bullock /'bʊlək/ **bullocks.** N-COUNT A **bullock** is a young bull that has been castrated.

bully /'bʊli/ **bullies, bullying, bullied.** [1] VERB & N-COUNT If someone **bullies** you, or if someone is a **bully,** they use their strength or power to hurt or frighten you. ♦ **bullying** N-UNCOUNT *...schoolchildren who were victims of bullying.* [2] VERB If someone **bullies** you **into** doing something, they make you do it by using force or threats. *She should never have bullied us into going.*

bum /bʌm/ **bums.** [1] N-COUNT A **bum** is a person who has no permanent home or job and who gets money by doing occasional work or by begging. [INFORMAL, AMERICAN] [2] N-COUNT Your **bum** is the part of your body which you sit on. [INFORMAL]

bump /bʌmp/ **bumps, bumping, bumped.** [1] VERB & N-COUNT If you **bump into** or **against** something, you accidentally hit it while you are moving. You can also talk about a **bump**. *The boat bumped against something... He bumped his head... Small children often cry after a minor bump.* [2] N-COUNT A **bump** is a minor swelling that you get on your body if you hit something or if something hits you. *He had a huge bump on his head.* [3] VERB If a vehicle **bumps over** a surface, it travels in a rough, bouncing way because the surface is very uneven. *We left the road, and again bumped over the mountainside.* [4] N-COUNT A **bump** on a road is a raised, uneven part.
▶ **bump into.** PHR-VERB If you **bump into** someone you know, you meet them by chance. [INFORMAL] *I bumped into a friend of yours today.*

bumper /bʌmpə/ **bumpers.** [1] N-COUNT **Bumpers** are bars at the front and back of a vehicle which protect it if it bumps into something. [2] ADJ BEFORE N A **bumper** crop or harvest is larger than usual.

bumpy /bʌmpi/ **bumpier, bumpiest.** [1] ADJ A **bumpy** road or path has a lot of bumps on it. [2] ADJ A **bumpy** journey is uncomfortable and rough. *...a hot and bumpy ride across the desert.*

bun /bʌn/ **buns.** [1] N-COUNT A **bun** is a small round cake. [2] N-COUNT If a woman has her hair in a **bun**, it is fastened into a round shape at the back of her head. → See picture on page 312.

⭐ **bunch** /bʌntʃ/ **bunches, bunching, bunched.** [1] N-COUNT A **bunch** of people or things is a group of them. *The players were a great bunch... We did a bunch of songs together.* [2] N-COUNT A **bunch** of flowers or fruit is a group of them held or tied together, or growing on the same stem.
▶ **bunch up** or **bunch together.** PHR-VERB If people or things **bunch up** or **bunch together**, they move close to each other so that they form a small tight group. *A cluster of Iraqi prisoners appeared, bunched together on a truck.*

bundle /bʌndəl/ **bundles, bundling, bundled.** [1] N-COUNT A **bundle** is a number of things tied together or wrapped in a cloth so that they can be carried or stored. *...a bundle of five pound notes. ...bundles of clothing.* [2] N-SING If you describe someone as, for example, a **bundle of** fun, you are emphasizing that they are full of fun. *Stan was a bundle of nerves.* [3] VERB If you **bundle** someone somewhere, you push them there in a rough and hurried way. *He was bundled into a car.*

bungalow

bungalow /bʌŋɡələʊ/ **bungalows.** N-COUNT A **bungalow** is a house with only one storey.

bungle /bʌŋɡəl/ **bungles, bungling, bungled.** VERB If you **bungle** something, you fail to do it properly, because you make mistakes or are clumsy. *Two prisoners bungled an escape bid.* ♦ **bungled** ADJ *...a bungled kidnap attempt.*

bunk /bʌŋk/ **bunks.** N-COUNT A **bunk** is a bed fixed to a wall, especially in a ship or caravan.

bunker /bʌŋkə/ **bunkers.** [1] N-COUNT A **bunker** is an underground shelter, built with strong walls to protect it against heavy gunfire and bombing. [2] N-COUNT A **bunker** is a container for coal or other fuel. [3] N-COUNT On a golf course, a **bunker** is a large hollow filled with sand that golfers must try and avoid.

bunny /bʌni/ **bunnies.** N-COUNT Small children call a rabbit a **bunny** or a **bunny rabbit**.

buoy /bɔɪ, AM 'buːi/ **buoys, buoying, buoyed.** N-COUNT A **buoy** is a floating object that shows ships and boats where they can go and warns them of danger.
▶ **buoy up.** PHR-VERB If someone in a difficult situation **is buoyed up** by something, it makes them feel more cheerful and optimistic. *They are buoyed up by a sense of hope.*

buoyant /bɔɪənt/. [1] ADJ If you are **buoyant**, you feel lively and cheerful. *He sounded buoyant once again.* ♦ **buoyancy** N-UNCOUNT *...a mood of buoyancy and optimism.* [2] ADJ Something that is **buoyant** floats on a liquid or in the air. ♦ **buoyancy** N-UNCOUNT *Air can be pumped into the diving suit to increase buoyancy.*

⭐ **burden** /bɜːdən/ **burdens, burdening, burdened.** [1] N-COUNT Something that is a **burden** causes you a lot of worry or hard work. *Her death will be an impossible burden on Paul.* [2] VERB If someone **burdens** you **with** something that is likely to worry you, they tell you about it. *We decided not to burden him with the news.* [3] N-COUNT A **burden** is a heavy load that is difficult to carry. [FORMAL]

burdened /bɜːdənd/. ADJ If you are **burdened with** something, it causes you a lot of worry or hard work. *Developing countries are already burdened with debt.*

bureau /bjʊərəʊ/ **bureaux** or **bureaus.** [1] N-COUNT A **bureau** is an office, organization, or government department that collects and distributes information. *...the Australian Bureau of Statistics.* [2] N-COUNT A **bureau** is a desk with drawers and a lid that opens to form a writing surface. [BRITISH]

bureaucracy /bjʊˈrɒkrəsi/ **bureaucracies.** [1] N-COUNT A **bureaucracy** is an administrative system operated by a large number of officials following rules and procedures. *State bureaucracies can tend to stifle enterprise.* [2] N-UNCOUNT **Bureaucracy** is all the rules and procedures followed by government departments and similar organizations; often

a b c d e f g h i j k l m n o p q r s t u v w x y z

used showing disapproval. *People usually complain about too much bureaucracy.*

bureaucrat /'bjʊərəkræt/ **bureaucrats.** N-COUNT A **bureaucrat** is an official who works in a bureaucracy, especially one who seems to follow rules and procedures too strictly.

bureaucratic /ˌbjʊərə'krætɪk/. ADJ **Bureaucratic** rules and procedures are complicated and can cause long delays. *The department has become a bureaucratic nightmare.*

bureaux /'bjʊərəʊz/. **Bureaux** is a plural of **bureau.**

burgeon /'bɜːdʒən/ **burgeons, burgeoning, burgeoned.** VERB If something **burgeons**, it grows or develops rapidly. [LITERARY] *...Japan's burgeoning satellite-TV industry.*

burger /'bɜːgə/ **burgers.** N-COUNT A **burger** is a flat round mass of minced meat or vegetables, which is grilled or fried.

burglar /'bɜːglə/ **burglars.** N-COUNT A **burglar** is a thief who breaks into houses and steals things.

burglary /'bɜːgləri/ **burglaries.** N-VAR If someone commits **burglary**, they enter a building by force and steal things. *He's been arrested for burglary... Basement flats are very vulnerable to burglaries.*

burgle /'bɜːgəl/ **burgles, burgling, burgled.** VERB In British English, if a house **is burgled**, someone breaks in and steals things. The usual American word is **burglarize**. *I found that my flat had been burgled.*

burial /'beriəl/ **burials.** N-VAR A **burial** is the ceremony that takes place when a dead body is put into a grave. *The priest prepared the body for burial.*

burly /'bɜːli/. ADJ A **burly** man has a broad body and strong muscles. *...a burly security guard.*

★ **burn** /bɜːn/ **burns, burning, burned** or **burnt.** [1] VERB If there is a fire or a flame somewhere, you say that there is a fire or flame **burning** there. *Fires were burning out of control.* [2] VERB If something **is burning**, it is on fire. *When I arrived one of the vehicles was still burning.* ♦ **burning** N-UNCOUNT *...a terrible smell of burning.* ♦ **burnt** ADJ *...the smell of burnt toast.* [3] VERB If you **burn** something, you destroy it with fire. *Protesters set cars on fire and burned a building.* [4] VERB & N-COUNT If you **burn yourself**, or if you suffer **burns**, you are injured by fire or by something very hot. *...the amount of time you can stay in the sun without burning... She suffered appalling burns to her back.* [5] VERB If you **are burning with** an emotion, you feel it very strongly. *Shannon was burning with impatience.*
▸ **burn down.** PHR-VERB If a building **burns down** or if someone **burns** it **down**, it is completely destroyed by fire. *Anarchists burnt down a restaurant.*

burner /'bɜːnə/ **burners.** N-COUNT A **burner** is a device which produces heat or a flame.

burning /'bɜːnɪŋ/. ADJ If something is extremely hot, you can say that it is **burning** or **burning hot**. *...the burning desert of Central Asia.*

burnt /bɜːnt/. **Burnt** is a past tense and past participle of **burn**.

burnt-'out (or **burned-out**). ADJ **Burnt-out** vehicles or buildings have been very badly damaged by fire.

burrow /'bʌrəʊ, AM 'bɜː-/ **burrows, burrowing, burrowed.** VERB & N-COUNT When an animal **burrows**, or digs a **burrow**, it digs a tunnel or hole in the ground.

★ **burst** /bɜːst/ **bursts, bursting, burst.** [1] VERB When something **bursts** or when you **burst** it, it suddenly splits open, and air or some other substance comes out. *A tyre burst... It is not a good idea to burst a blister.* [2] VERB If you **burst into** or **through** something, you suddenly go into it or through it with a lot of energy. *Gunmen burst into his home and opened fire.* [3] N-COUNT A **burst of** something is a sudden short period of it. *...a burst of gunfire.*
▸ **burst into.** PHR-VERB If you **burst into** tears or laughter, you suddenly begin to cry or laugh. ● to **burst into flames:** see **flame.**
▸ **burst out.** PHR-VERB If you **burst out** laughing or crying, you suddenly begin laughing or crying loudly.

bursting /'bɜːstɪŋ/. [1] ADJ AFTER LINK-V If a place is **bursting** with people or things, it is full of them. *The wardrobes were bursting with clothes.* [2] ADJ AFTER LINK-V If you are **bursting with** a feeling, you are full of it. *I was bursting with curiosity.* [3] ADJ If you are **bursting to** do something, you are very eager to do it. *She was bursting to tell everyone.*

★ **bury** /'beri/ **buries, burying, buried.** [1] VERB To **bury** something means to put it into a hole in the ground and cover it up, often in order to hide it. *...squirrels who bury nuts and seeds.* [2] VERB When a dead person **is buried**, their body is put into a grave and covered with earth. [3] VERB If you **are buried** under something that falls on top of you, you are completely covered and may not be able to get out. *...people buried under the collapsed buildings.* [4] VERB If you **bury yourself** in your work, you concentrate hard on it.

★ **bus** /bʌs/ **buses.** N-COUNT A **bus** is a large motor vehicle which carries passengers → See picture on page 835.

bush /bʊʃ/ **bushes.** [1] N-COUNT A **bush** is a plant which is like a very small tree. [2] N-SING The wild parts of some hot countries are referred to as **the bush**. *...the dense Mozambican bush.*

bushy /'bʊʃi/ **bushier, bushiest.** ADJ **Bushy** hair or fur grows very thickly. *...bushy eyebrows.*

busily /'bɪzɪli/. ADV If you do something **busily**, you do it in a very active way. *Her father was busily taking notes.*

★ **business** /'bɪznɪs/ **businesses.** [1] N-UNCOUNT **Business** is work relating to the production, buying, and selling of goods or services. *...young people seeking a career in business. ...Harvard Business School.* [2] N-COUNT A **business** is an organization which produces and sells goods or provides a service. ...*small businesses.*

3 N-UNCOUNT **Business** is used when talking about how many products or services a company is able to sell. ...*German companies would lose business... Business is booming.* **4** PHRASE If a shop or company goes **out of business**, it has to stop trading because it is not making enough money. **5** N-UNCOUNT You can use **business** to refer to any activity, situation, or series of events. *I've got some unfinished business to attend to.* **6** N-SING If you say that something is your **business,** you mean that it concerns you personally and that other people should not get involved in it. *If she doesn't want the police involved, that's her business... My marriage is none of your business, David.* **7** See also **big business**.

PHRASES • If you say that someone **has no business to** do something, you mean that they have no right to do it. *I had no business to be there at all.* • If someone **means business,** they are serious and determined about what they are doing. [INFORMAL]

businesslike /'bɪznəslaɪk/. ADJ Someone who is **businesslike** deals with things in an efficient way.

★ **businessman** /'bɪznɪsmæn/ **businessmen.** N-COUNT A **businessman** is a man who works in business.

businesswoman /'bɪznɪswʊmən/ **businesswomen.** N-COUNT A **businesswoman** is a woman who works in business.

busk /bʌsk/ **busks, busking, busked.** VERB People who **busk** play music or sing for money in public places. [BRITISH] ◆ **busking** N-UNCOUNT *Restrictions on busking have to be eased.* ◆ **busker, buskers** N-COUNT *He earned a living as a busker.*

bust /bʌst/ **busts, busting, busted.** **1** VERB When you **bust** something, you break it or damage it so badly that it cannot be used. [INFORMAL] *They will have to bust the door to get him out.* **2** PHRASE If a company **goes bust**, it loses so much money that it is forced to close down. [INFORMAL] **3** N-COUNT A **bust** is a statue of someone's head and shoulders. ...*a bronze bust of the Queen.* **4** N-COUNT You can refer to a woman's breasts as her **bust**. *Good posture also helps your bust look bigger.*

bustle /'bʌsəl/ **bustles, bustling, bustled.** **1** VERB If someone **bustles** somewhere, they move there in a hurried and determined way. *My mother bustled around the kitchen.* **2** VERB A place that **is bustling with** people or activity is full of people who are very busy or lively. *The harbour bustled with activity. ...the bustling market.* **3** N-UNCOUNT **Bustle** is busy noisy activity. *There was a good deal of cheerful bustle.*

'**bust-up, bust-ups.** N-COUNT If you have a **bust-up** with someone, you have a serious quarrel, often resulting in the end of a relationship. [INFORMAL]

★ **busy** /'bɪzi/ **busier, busiest; busies, busying, busied.** **1** ADJ If you are **busy,** you are working hard at

something, so that you are not free to do anything else. *They are busy preparing for a hectic day's activity... She would be too busy to come.* **2** VERB If you **busy yourself with** something, you occupy yourself by dealing with it. *He busied himself with the camera... She busied herself getting towels ready.* **3** ADJ A **busy** street or place is full of traffic and people moving about.

★ **but** /bət, STRONG bʌt/. **1** CONJ You use **but** to introduce something which contrasts with what you have just said. *'You said you'd stay till tomorrow.'—'I know, Bel, but I think I would rather go back.'* **2** CONJ You use **but** when you are adding something or changing the subject. *I still can't figure out why he did what he did – but anyway, he succeeded.* **3** CONJ You use **but** to link an excuse or apology with what you are about to say. *I'm sorry, but it's nothing to do with you.* **4** ADV **But** can mean 'only'. [FORMAL] *This is but one of the methods used.* **5** PREP **But** means 'except'. *He didn't speak anything but Greek.* **6** PHRASE You use **but for** to introduce the only factor that causes a particular thing not to happen or not to be completely true. ...*the small square below, empty but for a delivery van.*

butcher /'bʊtʃə/ **butchers, butchering, butchered.** **1** N-COUNT A **butcher** is a shopkeeper who sells meat. You can refer to a shop where meat is sold as a **butcher** or a **butcher's.** **2** VERB You say that someone **has butchered** people when they have killed a lot of them in a very cruel way, and you want to express your horror and disgust. *Guards butchered 1,350 prisoners.*

butler /'bʌtlə/ **butlers.** N-COUNT A **butler** is the chief male servant in the house of a wealthy family.

butt /bʌt/ **butts, butting, butted.** **1** N-COUNT The **butt** of a weapon is the thick end of its handle. **2** N-COUNT The **butt** of a cigarette or cigar is the small part that is left when you have finished smoking it. **3** N-COUNT A **butt** is a large barrel used for collecting or storing liquid. ...*a water butt.* **4** N-SING If you are **the butt of** teasing or criticism, people keep teasing you or criticizing you. *He is the butt of countless jokes.* **5** VERB If a person or animal **butts** you, they hit you with the top of their head. **6** N-COUNT Someone's **butt** is their bottom. [AMERICAN, INFORMAL]
▶ **butt in.** PHR-VERB If you **butt in,** you rudely join in a private conversation without being asked to. *'I should think not,' Sarah butted in.*

★ **butter** /'bʌtə/ **butters, buttering, buttered.** **1** N-UNCOUNT **Butter** is a yellowish substance made from cream which you spread on bread or use in cooking. **2** VERB When you **butter** bread, you spread butter on it.

butterfly /'bʌtəflaɪ/ **butterflies.** N-COUNT A **butterfly** is an insect with large colourful wings and a thin body. → See picture on page 824.

buttock /'bʌtək/ **buttocks.** N-COUNT Your **buttocks** are the two rounded fleshy parts of your body that you sit on.

★ Bank of English® frequent word   For a full explanation of all grammatical labels, see pages vii–x

button /'bʌtən/ **buttons, buttoning, buttoned.**
[1] N-COUNT **Buttons** are small hard objects sewn on to pieces of clothing, which you use to fasten the clothing. → See picture on page 249. [2] VERB & PHR-VERB If you **button** or **button up** a shirt, coat, or other piece of clothing, you fasten it by pushing its buttons through the buttonholes. *I buttoned up my mink coat.* [3] N-COUNT A **button** is a small object that you press in order to operate something. *He reached for the remote control and pressed the 'play' button.* [4] N-COUNT In American English, a **button** is a small piece of metal or plastic which you pin onto your clothes to show your support for someone or something. The British word is **badge**. *...campaign buttons.*
▸**button up.** See **button** 2.

buttonhole /'bʌtənhəʊl/ **buttonholes, buttonholing, buttonholed.** [1] N-COUNT A **buttonhole** is a hole that you push a button through in order to fasten a piece of clothing. → See picture on page 249. [2] N-COUNT A **buttonhole** is a flower that you wear on your lapel. [BRITISH] [3] VERB If you **buttonhole** someone, you stop them and make them listen to you.

buttress /'bʌtrəs/ **buttresses, buttressing, buttressed.** [1] N-COUNT **Buttresses** are supports, usually made of stone or brick, that support a wall. [2] VERB To **buttress** an argument or system means to give it support and strength. *As always, his argument is buttressed by facts and quotations.*

⭐ **buy** /baɪ/ **buys, buying, bought.** [1] VERB If you **buy** something, you obtain it by paying money for it. *He could not afford to buy a house... Lizzie bought herself a mountain bike... I'd like to buy him lunch.*
♦ **buyer, buyers** N-COUNT *Car buyers are more interested in safety.* [2] N-COUNT If something is a good **buy**, it is of good quality and not very expensive. *Good buys this week include broccoli, and tomatoes.* [3] VERB If you **buy** something such as time or freedom, you obtain it but only by offering or giving up something in return. *It was a risky operation, but might buy more time.*
▸**buy out.** PHR-VERB If you **buy** someone **out**, you buy their share of something that you previously owned together. *The bank had to pay to buy out most of the 200 former partners.*
▸**buy up.** PHR-VERB If you **buy up** land, property, or a commodity, you buy large amounts of it, or all that is available. *His officials were yesterday buying up vast stocks of corn.*
▸**buy into.** PHR-VERB If someone **buys into** a company or an organization, they buy part of it, often in order to gain some control of it.

buyout (or **buy-out**) /'baɪaʊt/ **buyouts.** N-COUNT A **buyout** is the buying of a company, especially by its managers or employees. *...a management buyout.*

buzz /bʌz/ **buzzes, buzzing, buzzed.** [1] N-SING A **buzz** is a continuous sound, like the sound of a bee when it is flying. *...the incessant buzz of insects. ...the buzz of a chainsaw. ...the excited buzz of conversation.* [2] VERB If something **buzzes**, it makes a long continuous sound, like a bee. *A fly buzzed on the window-pane... Helicopter gunships buzzed overhead.* [3] VERB If a place **is buzzing with** activity or conversation, there is a lot of activity or conversation there, especially because something important or exciting is about to happen. *The capital is buzzing with rumours. ...Hong Kong's buzzing, pulsating atmosphere.* [4] N-SING If a place or event has a **buzz**, it has a lively, interesting and modern atmosphere. *There's a buzz about Dublin.*

buzzer /'bʌzə/ **buzzers.** N-COUNT A **buzzer** is a device that makes a buzzing sound, for example in an alarm clock.

buzzword (or **buzz word**) /'bʌzwɜːd/ **buzzwords.** N-COUNT A **buzzword** is a word or expression that has become fashionable in a particular field. *Specialisation is the new buzzword.*

⭐ **by** /baɪ/. [1] PREP If something is done **by** a person or thing, that person or thing does it. *The boys had to be rescued by firemen... He was so fascinated by her beauty.* [2] PREP **By** is used to say how something is done. *...if you're travelling by car. ...dinners by candlelight... Make the sauce by boiling the cream... I'd like to pay by cheque.* [3] PREP If you say that a book, a piece of music, or a painting is **by** someone, you mean that they wrote it or created it. *...detective stories by American writers.* [4] PREP If you hold someone or something **by** a particular part of them, you hold that part. *He caught her by the shoulder.* [5] PREP & ADV Someone or something that is **by** something else is beside it and close to it. *...a rocking-chair by the window... Large numbers of security police stood by.* [6] PREP & ADV If a person or vehicle goes **by** you, it moves past without stopping. *A few cars passed close by me... A police patrol went by.* [7] PREP If something happens **by** a particular time, it happens at or before that time. → See Reference Page on Times and Dates. *By eight o'clock he had arrived.* [8] PREP Things that are made or sold **by** the million or **by** the dozen are made or sold in those quantities. *Parcels arrived by the dozen from America.* [9] PREP If something increases or decreases **by** a particular amount, that amount is gained or lost. *Violent crime has increased by 10 percent.* [10] PREP You use **by** in expressions such as 'day by day' to say that something happens gradually. [11] PREP If you are **by** yourself, you are alone. If you do something **by** yourself, you do it without any help.

⭐ **bye** /baɪ/. CONVENTION **'Bye'** and **'bye-bye'** are informal ways of saying goodbye. → See Reference Page on Greetings and Goodbyes.

'by-election, by-elections. N-COUNT A **by-election** is an election that is held to choose a new member of parliament when a member has resigned or died.

bygone /'baɪgɒn, AM -gɔːn/. ADJ BEFORE N **Bygone** means happening or existing a very long time ago. *...a bygone era. ...bygone generations.*

bypass /'baɪpɑːs, -pæs/ **bypasses, bypassing, bypassed.** [1] VERB If you **bypass** someone in authority, you avoid asking their permission to do something. ② N-COUNT A **bypass** is a main road which takes traffic round the edge of a town rather than through its centre. ③ VERB If you **bypass** a place, you go round it rather than through it. ④ N-COUNT A **bypass** is an operation in which the flow of blood is redirected so that it does not flow through a part of the heart which is diseased or blocked. ...*heart bypass surgery.*

by-product, by-products. N-COUNT A **by-product** is something which is made during the manufacture or processing of another product. *Glycerine is a by-product of soap-making.*

bystander /ˈbaɪstændə/ **bystanders.** N-COUNT A **bystander** is a person who sees something happen but does not take part in it.

byte /baɪt/ **bytes.** N-COUNT In computing, a **byte** is a unit of storage approximately equivalent to one printed character.

C c

cab /kæb/ **cabs.** ① N-COUNT A **cab** is a taxi. *She called a cab.* ② N-COUNT The **cab** of a lorry is the part in which the driver sits.

cabaret /ˈkæbəreɪ, AM -ˈreɪ/ **cabarets.** N-VAR **Cabaret** is live entertainment consisting of dancing, singing, or comedy acts that are performed in the evening in restaurants or nightclubs. *He began singing in bars and cabarets.* ...*a cabaret act.*

cabbage /ˈkæbɪdʒ/ **cabbages.** N-VAR A **cabbage** is a round vegetable with green leaves. → See picture on page 836.

cabin /ˈkæbɪn/ **cabins.** ① N-COUNT A **cabin** is a small room in a ship or boat, or one of the areas inside a plane. ...*the First Class cabin.* ② N-COUNT A **cabin** is a small wooden house.

★ **cabinet** /ˈkæbɪnɪt/ **cabinets.** ① N-COUNT A **cabinet** is a cupboard used for storing things such as medicines or alcoholic drinks or for displaying decorative things in. ...*a medicine cabinet.* ② N-COUNT The **Cabinet** is a group of the most senior ministers in a government. ● See note at **government**.

★ **cable** /ˈkeɪbəl/ **cables, cabled, cabling.** ① N-UNCOUNT **Cable** is used to refer to television systems in which the signals are sent along underground wires rather than by radio waves. *They ran commercials on cable systems across the country.* ② VERB If an area or building **is cabled**, cables and other equipment are put in place so that the people there can receive cable television. ③ N-VAR A **cable** is a thick wire, or a bundle of wires inside a rubber or plastic covering, which is used to carry electricity or electronic signals. ...*overhead power cables.*

cache /kæʃ/ **caches.** N-COUNT A **cache** is a quantity of things such as weapons that have been hidden.

cactus /ˈkæktəs/ **cactuses** (or **cacti** /ˈkæktaɪ/). N-COUNT A **cactus** is a desert plant with a thick stem, often with spikes.

cadet /kəˈdet/ **cadets.** N-COUNT A **cadet** is a young person who is being trained in the armed forces or police.

café /ˈkæfeɪ, AM kæˈfeɪ/ **cafés.** N-COUNT A **café** is a place where you can buy and have simple meals, snacks, and drinks.

USAGE In Britain, a **café** serves tea, coffee, soft drinks, and light meals, but not usually alcoholic drinks. If you want an alcoholic drink, you can go to a **pub**. In American English, a **pub** is more usually called a **bar**. Many pubs serve food, especially at lunchtime, but for a larger or more special meal, you might want to go to a **restaurant**.

cafeteria /ˌkæfɪˈtɪəriə/ **cafeterias.** N-COUNT A **cafeteria** is a self-service restaurant in a large shop or workplace.

caffeine /ˈkæfiːn, AM kæˈfiːn/. N-UNCOUNT **Caffeine** is a chemical substance found in coffee, tea, and cocoa, which makes your brain and body more active.

cage /keɪdʒ/ **cages.** N-COUNT A **cage** is a structure of wire or metal bars in which birds or animals are kept.

caged /keɪdʒd/. ADJ A **caged** bird or animal is inside a cage.

cajole /kəˈdʒəʊl/ **cajoles, cajoling, cajoled.** VERB If you **cajole** someone, you get them to do something after persuading them for some time. *He had cajoled Garland into doing the film.*

★ **cake** /keɪk/ **cakes.** ① N-VAR A **cake** is a sweet food made by baking a mixture of flour, eggs, sugar, and fat. ...*a piece of chocolate cake.* ② N-COUNT Food that is formed into flat round shapes before it is cooked can be referred to as **cakes**. ...*fish cakes.*

calamity /kəˈlæmɪti/ **calamities.** N-COUNT A **calamity** is an event that causes a great deal of damage or distress. [FORMAL] ...*the calamity of war.*

calcium /ˈkælsiəm/. N-UNCOUNT **Calcium** is a soft white element found in bones and teeth, and also in limestone, chalk, and marble.

calculate /ˈkælkjʊleɪt/ **calculates, calculating, calculated.** ① VERB If you **calculate** a number or amount, you work it out by doing some arithmetic. *We calculate that the average size farm in Lancaster County is 65 acres.* ◆ **calculation** /ˌkælkjʊˈleɪʃən/ **calculations** N-VAR *The machine does the calculations.* ② VERB If you **calculate** the effects of something, you consider what they will be. *I believe I am capable of calculating the political consequences accurately.* ◆ **calculation** N-VAR ...*political calculation.*

calculated /'kælkjʊleɪtɪd/. ADJ If something is **calculated**, it is deliberately planned to have a particular effect. *Everything she said seemed deliberately calculated to make him feel guilty. ...a calculated attempt to cover up her crime.*

calculating /'kælkjʊleɪtɪŋ/. ADJ If you describe someone as **calculating**, you disapprove of the fact that they deliberately plan to get what they want, often by harming other people. ...*a cool, calculating and clever criminal.* ◆ **calculation** /ˌkælkjʊ'leɪʃən/ N-UNCOUNT ...*cold, unspeakably cruel calculation.*

calculation. See **calculate, calculating.**

calculator /'kælkjʊleɪtə/ **calculators.** N-COUNT A **calculator** is a small electronic device used for doing mathematical calculations.

calendar /'kælɪndə/ **calendars.** ☐ N-COUNT A **calendar** is a chart or device which displays the date and the day of the week, and often the whole of a particular year. ☒ ADJ A **calendar** month is one of the twelve periods of time that a year is divided into. ☐ N-COUNT A **calendar** is a list of dates within a year that are important for a particular organization or activity. ...*one of the most popular fixtures in the racing calendar.*

calf /kɑːf, AM kæf/ **calves.** ☐ N-COUNT A **calf** is a young cow. ☒ N-COUNT The young of some animals, such as elephants, giraffes, and whales, are called **calves.** ☐ N-COUNT Your **calves** are the backs of your legs between your ankles and knees. → See picture on page 822.

calibre (AM **caliber**) /'kælɪbə/ **calibres.** ☐ N-UNCOUNT The **calibre of** someone or something is their qualities, abilities, or high standards. *The calibre of the teaching was very high.* ☒ N-COUNT The **calibre** of a gun is the width of the inside of its barrel. [TECHNICAL]

⭐ **call** /kɔːl/ **calls, calling, called.** ☐ VERB If you **call** someone or something **by** a particular name or title, you give them that name or title. *Everybody called each other by their surnames... There are two men called Buckley at the Home Office.* ☒ VERB If you **call** a person or situation something, that is how you describe them. *They called him a traitor... She calls me lazy.* ☐ VERB & PHR-VERB If you **call** something, or if you **call** it **out,** you say it in a loud voice. *I heard someone calling my name... The train stopped and a porter called out, 'Middlesbrough!'.* ☐ VERB & N-COUNT If you **call** someone, or make a telephone **call,** you telephone them. *He called me at my office... I think we should call the doctor... I made a phone call to the United States.* ☐ PHRASE If someone is **on call,** they are ready to go to work at any time if they are needed. ...*a doctor on call.* ☐ VERB If you **call** a meeting, you arrange for it to take place. ☐ VERB & N-COUNT If you **call** somewhere, or pay a **call** there, you make a short visit there. *A market*

researcher called at the house... He decided to pay a call on Tommy. ☒ N-COUNT If there is a **call for** something, someone demands that it should happen. ...*a call for all businessmen to work together.* ☐ to **call it a day:** see **day.**

▸**call back.** PHR-VERB If you **call** someone **back,** you telephone them again or in return for a telephone call that they have made to you.

▸**call for.** ☐ PHR-VERB If you **call for** someone or something, you go to collect them. *I shall be calling for you at seven o'clock.* ☒ PHR-VERB If you **call for** an action, you demand that it should happen. *They angrily called for Robinson's resignation.* ☐ PHR-VERB If something **calls for** a particular action or quality, it needs it. *Does the situation call for military intervention?*

▸**call in.** ☐ PHR-VERB If you **call** someone **in,** you ask them to come and help you or do something for you. *Call in an architect or surveyor to oversee the work.* ☒ PHR-VERB If you **call in** somewhere, you make a short visit there. *He just calls in occasionally.*

▸**call off.** PHR-VERB If you **call off** an event that has been planned, you cancel it. *The deal was called off.*

▸**call on** or **call upon.** ☐ PHR-VERB If you **call on** someone **to** do something, you say publicly that you want them to do it. *One of Kenya's leading churchmen has called on the government to resign.* ☒ PHR-VERB If you **call on** someone, you pay them a short visit.

▸**call out.** ☐ PHR-VERB If you **call** someone **out,** you order them to come to help, especially in an emergency. *Colombia has called out the army.* ☒ See also **call** 3.

▸**call up.** ☐ PHR-VERB If you **call** someone **up,** you telephone them. *When I'm in Pittsburgh, I call him up.* ☒ PHR-VERB If someone **is called up,** they are ordered to join the armed forces.

▸**call upon.** See **call on.**

¹**call centre** (AM **call center**) **call centres.** N-COUNT A **call centre** is an office where people work answering or making telephone calls for a company.

caller /'kɔːlə/ **callers.** ☐ N-COUNT A **caller** is a person who is making a telephone call. ☒ N-COUNT A **caller** is a person who comes to see you for a short visit.

callous /'kæləs/. ADJ A **callous** person or action is cruel and shows no concern for other people. ...*his callous disregard for human life.* ◆ **callously** ADV ...*callously ill-treating his wife.* ◆ **callousness** N-UNCOUNT ...*the callousness of Raymond's murder.*

⭐ **calm** /kɑːm/ **calmer, calmest; calms, calming, calmed.** ☐ ADJ & N-UNCOUNT A **calm** person does not show or feel any worry, anger, or excitement. You can refer to someone's feeling of **calm.** ...*a calm and diplomatic woman... Try to keep calm... He felt a sudden sense of calm.* ◆ **calmly** ADV *She speaks slowly and calmly.* ☒ N-UNCOUNT **Calm** is a state of being quiet and peaceful. ...*the rural calm of Grand Rapids, Michigan.* ☐ ADJ If the weather is

calm, there is little or no wind. If the sea is **calm**, the water is not moving very much. [4] VERB If you **calm** someone, you do something to make them less upset or excited. *Isabella had helped calm her fears.* ♦ **calming** ADJ *...a very calming effect on the mind.*
►**calm down.** PHR-VERB If you **calm down** or if someone **calms** you **down**, you become less upset or excited. *I'll try a herbal remedy to calm him down.*

calorie /'kæləri/ **calories.** N-COUNT A **calorie** is a unit of measurement for the energy value of food.

calves /kɑːvz, AM kævz/. **Calves** is the plural of **calf**.

camcorder /'kæmkɔːdə/ **camcorders.** N-COUNT A **camcorder** is a portable video camera.

came /keɪm/. **Came** is the past tense of **come**.

camel /'kæməl/ **camels.** N-COUNT A **camel** is a desert animal with one or two humps on its back. → See picture on page 816.

cameo /'kæmiəʊ/ **cameos.** [1] N-COUNT A **cameo** is a short descriptive piece of acting or writing. *...memorable cameos of Scottish history.* [2] N-COUNT A **cameo** is a brooch with a raised stone design on a flat stone of another colour.

⭐ **camera** /'kæmrə/ **cameras.** [1] N-COUNT A **camera** is a piece of equipment for taking photographs or for making a film. *...a video camera.* [2] PHRASE If someone or something is **on camera**, they are being filmed.

cameraman /'kæmrəmæn/ **cameramen.** N-COUNT A **cameraman** is a person who operates a television or film camera.

camouflage /'kæməflɑːʒ/ **camouflages, camouflaging, camouflaged.** [1] N-UNCOUNT **Camouflage** consists of things such as leaves, branches, or paint, used to make military forces difficult to see. *...a camouflage jacket.* [2] VERB When military forces **camouflage themselves** or their weapons, they use camouflage to make themselves or their weapons difficult to see. ♦ **camouflaged** ADJ *You won't see them from the air. They'd be very well camouflaged.* [3] N-UNCOUNT **Camouflage** is the way in which some animals are coloured and shaped to look as though they are part of their natural surroundings.

⭐ **camp** /kæmp/ **camps, camping, camped.** [1] N-VAR A **camp** is a place where people live or stay in tents or caravans. [2] VERB If you **camp** somewhere, you stay there in a tent or caravan. *We camped near the beach... For six months they camped out in a caravan in a meadow.* ♦ **camping** N-UNCOUNT *They recently went on a camping trip to Africa.* [3] N-COUNT A **camp** is a collection of buildings for people such as soldiers, refugees, or prisoners. *...refugee camps.* [4] N-COUNT You can use **camp** to refer to a group of people with a particular idea or belief. *The press release provoked furious protests from the Gore camp.*

⭐ **campaign** /ˌkæm'peɪn/ **campaigns, campaigning, campaigned.** N-COUNT & VERB A **campaign** is a

planned set of actions aimed at achieving a particular result. To **campaign** means to carry out a campaign. *...an advertising campaign to attract more people. ...a bombing campaign... They have been campaigning to improve the legal status of women.* ♦ **campaigner, campaigners** N-COUNT *...peace campaigners.*

camper /'kæmpə/ **campers.** [1] N-COUNT A **camper** is a person who goes camping. [2] N-COUNT A **camper** is a van equipped with beds and cooking equipment.

campsite /'kæmpsaɪt/ **campsites.** N-COUNT A **campsite** or a **camping site** is a place where people who are on holiday can stay in tents.

campus /'kæmpəs/ **campuses.** N-COUNT A **campus** is the area of land containing the main buildings of a college or university.

can 1 modal uses

⭐ **can** /kən, STRONG kæn/. [1] MODAL If you **can** do something, you have the ability or opportunity to do it. *I can take care of myself... See if you can find Karlov... You can't be with your baby all the time.* [2] MODAL If you **can** do something, you are allowed to do it. *You must buy the credit life insurance before you can buy the disability insurance... I can't tell you what he said.* [3] MODAL You use **can** to indicate that something is true sometimes or is true in some circumstances. *...long-term therapy that can last five years or more... Exercising alone can be boring.* [4] MODAL You use **cannot** or **can't** to state that you are certain that something is not true or will not happen. *She feels sure the person can't have been Douglas.* [5] MODAL You use **can** in order to make suggestions or requests, or to offer to do something. *You can always try the beer... Can I have a look at that?... Can I help you?*

can 2 container

can /kæn/ **cans, canning, canned.** [1] N-COUNT A **can** is a sealed metal container for food, drink, or paint. *...empty beer cans.* [2] VERB When food or drink **is canned**, it is put into a metal container and sealed.

canal /kə'næl/ **canals.** N-COUNT A **canal** is a long, narrow, man-made stretch of water.

⭐ **cancel** /'kænsəl/ **cancels, cancelling, cancelled** (AM **canceling, canceled**). [1] VERB If you **cancel** something that has been arranged, you stop it from happening. If you **cancel** an order for goods or services, you tell the person or organization supplying them that you no longer wish to receive them. *Many trains have been cancelled and a limited service is operating... There is normally no refund should a client choose to cancel.* ♦ **cancellation, cancellations** N-VAR *The cancellation of his visit has disappointed many people.* [2] VERB If someone in authority **cancels** a document or a debt, they officially declare that it is no longer valid or no longer legally exists. *...a government order cancelling his passport.* ♦ **cancellation** N-UNCOUNT *...cancellation of Third World debt.*

a
b
c
d
e
f
g
h
i
j
k
l
m
n
o
p
q
r
s
t
u
v
w
x
y
z

A
B
C
D
E
F
G
H
I
J
K
L
M
N
O
P
Q
R
S
T
U
V
W
X
Y
Z

▶ **cancel out.** PHR-VERB If one thing **cancels out** another thing, the two things have opposite effects which combine to produce no real effect. *Gary Bannister's goal was cancelled out by Chris Waddle's. ...cooling and heating effects seem to cancel each other out.*

⭐ **cancer** /ˈkænsə/ **cancers.** N-VAR **Cancer** is a serious illness in which abnormal body cells increase, producing growths. *Ninety per cent of lung cancers are caused by smoking.* ◆ **cancerous** ADJ *Nine out of ten lumps are not cancerous.*

candid /ˈkændɪd/. ADJ If you are **candid with** someone or **about** something, you speak honestly. *I haven't been completely candid with him. ...a candid interview.* ◆ **candidly** ADV *He has stopped taking heroin now, but admits candidly that he will always be a drug addict.*

candidacy /ˈkændɪdəsi/. N-UNCOUNT Someone's **candidacy** is their position of being a candidate in an election. *Today he is formally announcing his candidacy for President.*

⭐ **candidate** /ˈkændɪdeɪt/ **candidates.** 1 N-COUNT A **candidate** is someone who is being considered for a position, for example in an election or for a job. *...the Democratic candidate... He is a candidate for the office of Governor.* 2 N-COUNT A **candidate** is someone taking an examination. 3 N-COUNT A **candidate** is a person or thing regarded as suitable for a particular purpose, or as likely to be or do a particular thing. *The director looked like a candidate for a heart attack.*

candle /ˈkændəl/ **candles.** N-COUNT A **candle** is a stick of hard wax with a piece of string called a wick through the middle. You light the wick so the candle produces light.

candour (AM **candor**) /ˈkændə/. N-UNCOUNT **Candour** is the quality of speaking honestly and openly about things. *He covered a wide range of topics with unusual candour.*

candy /ˈkændi/ **candies.** N-VAR In American English, sweet foods such as toffees, chocolates, and mints are referred to as **candy**. The British word is **sweets**. *...a piece of candy.*

cane /keɪn/ **canes, caning, caned.** 1 N-UNCOUNT **Cane** is the long hollow stems of a plant such as bamboo. *...cane baskets and furniture.* 2 N-COUNT A **cane** is a long narrow stick. *He wore a grey suit and leaned heavily on his cane.* 3 VERB & N-SING When schoolchildren **were caned** or were given **the cane**, they were hit with a cane as a punishment. *...if you misbehaved you would get the cane.*

canine /ˈkeɪnaɪn/. ADJ **Canine** means relating to or resembling a dog.

canister /ˈkænɪstə/ **canisters.** N-COUNT A **canister** is a metal container.

cannabis /ˈkænəbɪs/. N-UNCOUNT **Cannabis** is a drug which some people smoke. It is illegal in many countries.

cannibal /ˈkænɪbəl/ **cannibals.** N-COUNT A **cannibal** is a person who eats human flesh.

◆ **cannibalism** /ˈkænɪbəlɪzəm/ N-UNCOUNT *...tales of cannibalism among the starving explorers.*

cannon /ˈkænən/.

✅ The plural is **cannon** or **cannons**.

1 N-COUNT A **cannon** is a large gun on wheels, formerly used in battles. 2 N-COUNT A **cannon** is a heavy automatic gun, especially one fired from an aircraft.

cannot /ˈkænɒt, kəˈnɒt/. **Cannot** is the negative form of **can**.

canoe /kəˈnuː/ **canoes.** N-COUNT A **canoe** is a small narrow boat that you row using a paddle.

canon /ˈkænən/ **canons.** N-COUNT A **canon** is one of the clergy on the staff of a cathedral.

canopy /ˈkænəpi/ **canopies.** N-COUNT A **canopy** is a decorated cover which hangs above something such as a bed or throne.

can't /kɑːnt, AM kænt/. **Can't** is the usual spoken form of **cannot**.

canteen /kænˈtiːn/ **canteens.** N-COUNT A **canteen** is a place in a factory, office, or shop where the workers can have meals.

canter /ˈkæntə/ **canters, cantering, cantered.** VERB & N-SING When a horse **canters** or when it moves **at a canter**, it moves at a speed between a gallop and a trot.

canvas /ˈkænvəs/ **canvases.** 1 N-UNCOUNT **Canvas** is strong heavy cloth used for making tents, sails, and bags. 2 N-VAR A **canvas** is a piece of canvas on which an oil painting is done, or the painting itself. *...canvases by masters like Carpaccio, Canaletto and Guardi.*

canvass /ˈkænvəs/ **canvasses, canvassing, canvassed.** 1 VERB If you **canvass for** a person or political party, you try to persuade people to vote for them. *I have gone around my community canvassing for the Labor Party.* 2 VERB If you **canvass** public opinion, you find out how people feel about something. *The poll canvassed the views of almost eighty economists.*

canyon /ˈkænjən/ **canyons.** N-COUNT A **canyon** is a long narrow valley with very steep sides.

⭐ **cap** /kæp/ **caps, capping, capped.** 1 N-COUNT A **cap** is a soft flat hat usually worn by men or boys. → See picture on page 819. 2 N-COUNT The **cap** of a bottle is its lid. 3 VERB You can say that the last event in a series of events **caps** the others. *The unrest capped a weekend of right-wing attacks on foreigners.*

⭐ **capable** /ˈkeɪpəbəl/. 1 ADJ AFTER LINK-V If you are **capable of** doing something, you are able to do it. *He had been hardly capable of standing up... I realised he was capable of murder.* ◆ **capability** /ˌkeɪpəˈbɪlɪti/ **capabilities** N-VAR *The standards set four years ago will be far below the athletes' capabilities now.* 2 ADJ Someone who is **capable** has the ability to do something well. *She's a very capable speaker.* ◆ **capably** ADV *It was all dealt with very capably.*

⭐ **capacity** /kəˈpæsɪti/ **capacities.** 1 N-UNCOUNT & ADJ BEFORE N The **capacity** of something is the maximum amount that it can hold or produce. A **capacity** crowd completely fills a theatre or stadium. *Each stadium had a seating capacity of about 50,000... The restaurant was packed to capacity. ...a feature which gave the vehicles a much greater fuel capacity.* [2] N-COUNT Your **capacity for** something is your ability to do it. *...our capacity for giving care, love and attention.* [3] N-COUNT If someone does something **in** a particular **capacity**, they do it as part of their duties. *He was visiting the territory in his capacity as an official.*

cape /keɪp/ **capes.** [1] N-COUNT A **cape** is a large piece of land that sticks out into the sea. [2] N-COUNT A **cape** is a short cloak.

⭐ **capital** /ˈkæpɪtəl/ **capitals.** [1] N-UNCOUNT **Capital** is a sum of money used to start or expand a business or invested to make more money. [2] N-COUNT The **capital** of a country is the city where its government meets. *...Kathmandu, the capital of Nepal.* [3] N-COUNT & ADJ BEFORE N A **capital** or a **capital letter** is the large form of a letter used at the beginning of sentences and names.

USAGE Note that you must always use a capital letter with days of the week, months of the year, and festivals. *...on Monday the 13th of January. ...at Christmas.* Names of seasons, however, usually begin with a small letter. *...in spring.* Capitals must also be used with the names of countries and other places, as well as with the adjectives and nouns derived from them, such as those which refer to their inhabitants or languages. *...in Portugal. ...the Swiss police... Thousands of Germans filled the streets of Berlin... He spoke fluent Arabic.*
→ See also the Reference Page on Punctuation.

---

[4] ADJ BEFORE N A **capital** offence is one that is punished by death.

capitalise /ˈkæpɪtəlaɪz/. See **capitalize**.

capitalism /ˈkæpɪtəlɪzəm/. N-UNCOUNT **Capitalism** is an economic and political system in which property, business, and industry are owned by private individuals and not by the state. ◆ **capitalist, capitalists** N-COUNT *...the industrialized capitalist countries. ...industrial capitalists.*

capitalize (BRIT also **capitalise**) /ˈkæpɪtəlaɪz/ **capitalizes, capitalizing, capitalized.** VERB If you **capitalize on** a situation, you use it to gain some advantage. *The rebels seem to be trying to capitalize on the public's discontent with the government.*

capital ˈpunishment. N-UNCOUNT **Capital punishment** is the legal killing of a person who has committed a serious crime.

capitulate /kəˈpɪtʃʊleɪt/ **capitulates, capitulating, capitulated.** VERB If you **capitulate**, you stop resisting and do what someone else wants you to do. *Cohen capitulated to virtually every demand.* ◆ **capitulation** N-UNCOUNT *Acceptance of the plan would mean capitulation.*

capsize /kæpˈsaɪz, AM ˈkæpsaɪz/ **capsizes, capsizing, capsized.** VERB If you **capsize** a boat or if it **capsizes**, it turns upside down in the water.

capsule /ˈkæpsjuːl, AM ˈkæpsəl/ **capsules.** [1] N-COUNT A **capsule** is a small container with powdered or liquid medicine inside, which you swallow. [2] N-COUNT The **capsule** of a spacecraft is the part in which the astronauts travel.

⭐ **captain** /ˈkæptɪn/ **captains, captaining, captained.** [1] N-COUNT & N-TITLE A **captain** is a military officer of middle rank. [2] N-COUNT The **captain** of an aeroplane or ship is the officer in charge of it. [3] N-COUNT The **captain** of a sports team is its leader. [4] VERB If you **captain** a ship or team, you are the captain of it. *The team was captained by celebrity Brian Kelley.*

captaincy /ˈkæptɪnsi/. N-UNCOUNT The **captaincy** of a team is the position of being captain. *Under his captaincy, Leeds lost twice to Rangers.*

⭐ **caption** /ˈkæpʃən/ **captions.** N-COUNT The **caption** of a picture consists of the words which are printed underneath.

captivate /ˈkæptɪveɪt/ **captivates, captivating, captivated.** VERB If you **are captivated** by someone or something, you find them fascinating and attractive. *For 40 years she has captivated the world with her radiant looks.* ◆ **captivating** ADJ *...her captivating smile.*

captive /ˈkæptɪv/ **captives.** [1] ADJ BEFORE N A **captive** animal or person is being kept in a particular place and is not allowed to escape. *...captive rats, mice, and monkeys.* [2] PHRASE If someone **takes** or **holds** you **captive**, they take or keep you as a prisoner. [3] N-COUNT A **captive** is a prisoner. [LITERARY]

captivity /kæpˈtɪvɪti/. N-UNCOUNT **Captivity** is the state of being kept as a captive. *The great majority of barn owls are reared in captivity.*

⭐ **capture** /ˈkæptʃə/ **captures, capturing, captured.** [1] VERB & N-UNCOUNT If you **capture** someone or something, you catch them or take possession of them, especially in a war, or after a chase. You can also talk about the **capture of** someone or something. *The guerrillas shot down one aeroplane and captured the pilot. ...the final battles which led to the army's capture of the town.* [2] VERB To **capture** something means to gain control of it. *In 1987, McDonald's captured 19 percent of all fast-food sales.* [3] VERB If someone **captures** the atmosphere or quality of something, they represent it successfully in pictures, music, or words. *...a portrait photographer poised to capture the moment.*

⭐ **car** /kɑː/ **cars.** [1] N-COUNT A **car** is a motor vehicle with room for a small number of passengers.

a
b
c
d
e
f
g
h
i
j
k
l
m
n
o
p
q
r
s
t
u
v
w
x
y
z

They arrived by car. [2] N-COUNT In American English, a **car** is one of the separate sections of a train that carries passengers. The usual British word is **carriage**. [3] N-COUNT In Britain, railway carriages are called **cars** when they are used for a particular purpose. ...*the dining car.*

caramel /'kærəmel/ **caramels.** [1] N-COUNT A **caramel** is a kind of toffee. [2] N-UNCOUNT **Caramel** is burnt sugar used for colouring and flavouring food.

carat /'kærət/ **carats.** [1] N-COUNT A **carat** is a unit equal to 0.2 grams used for measuring the weight of diamonds and other precious stones. ...*a huge eight-carat diamond.* [2] N-COUNT A **carat** is a unit for measuring the purity of gold. The purest gold is 24-carat gold. ...*a 14-carat gold fountain pen.*

caravan [1]

caravan /'kærəvæn/ **caravans.** [1] N-COUNT In British English, a **caravan** is a vehicle in which people live or spend their holidays. It is usually pulled by a car. The usual American word is **trailer**. ...*a caravan holiday in France.* [2] N-COUNT A **caravan** is a group of people and animals that travel together in deserts and other similar places. ...*a caravan of horses.*

'caravan site, caravan sites. N-COUNT In British English, a **caravan site** is an area of land where people can stay in a caravan on holiday, or where people live in caravans. The American term is **trailer park**.

carbohydrate /ˌkɑːbəʊˈhaɪdreɪt/ **carbohydrates.** N-VAR **Carbohydrates** are energy-giving substances found in foods such as sugar and bread.

⭐ **carbon** /'kɑːbən/. N-UNCOUNT **Carbon** is a chemical element that diamonds and coal are made of.

carbon dioxide /ˌkɑːbən daɪˈɒksaɪd/. N-UNCOUNT **Carbon dioxide** is a gas that animals and people breathe out.

carbon monoxide /ˌkɑːbən məˈnɒksaɪd/. N-UNCOUNT **Carbon monoxide** is a poisonous gas produced for example by cars.

carcass (or **carcase**) /'kɑːkəs/ **carcasses.** N-COUNT A **carcass** is the body of a dead animal.

⭐ **card** /kɑːd/ **cards.** [1] N-COUNT A **card** is a piece of stiff paper or thin cardboard on which something is written or printed. [2] N-UNCOUNT **Card** is strong stiff paper or thin cardboard. [3] N-COUNT A **card** is a piece of stiff paper with a picture and a

message which you send to someone on a special occasion. *She sends me a card on my birthday.* [4] N-COUNT **Cards** are thin pieces of cardboard decorated with numbers or pictures, used to play various games. ...*a pack of cards...* I taught Rachel how to play cards. [5] N-COUNT You can use **card** to refer to something that gives you an advantage in a particular situation. *This permitted Western manufacturers to play their strong cards: capital and technology.*

cardboard /'kɑːdbɔːd/. N-UNCOUNT **Cardboard** is thick stiff paper used to make boxes and other containers. ...*a thin cardboard folder.*

cardiac /'kɑːdiæk/. ADJ BEFORE N **Cardiac** means relating to the heart. [TECHNICAL] ...*a top cardiac surgeon.*

cardigan /'kɑːdɪgən/ **cardigans.** N-COUNT A **cardigan** is a knitted woollen garment that fastens at the front.

cardinal /'kɑːdnəl/ **cardinals.** [1] N-COUNT A **cardinal** is a priest of high rank in the Catholic church. [2] ADJ BEFORE N **Cardinal** means extremely important. [FORMAL] *One of the cardinal rules of movie reviewing is not to give away too much.*

⭐ **care** /keə/ **cares, caring, cared.** [1] VERB If you **care about** something, you are concerned about it or interested in it. ...*a company that cares about the environment...* I really didn't care whether he came or not. [2] VERB If you **care for** or **about** someone, you feel a lot of affection for them. *He still cared for me.* ...*people who are your friends, who care about you.* [3] VERB To **care to** do something or **care for** it means to want or choose to do it. [FORMAL] *He said he was off to the beach and would we care to join him...* Would you care for some orange juice? [4] VERB & N-UNCOUNT If you **care for** someone or something, or if you **take care of** them, you look after them and keep them in a good state or condition. *They hired a nurse to care for her...* There was no one else to take care of their children. ...*sensitive teeth which need special care.* [5] N-UNCOUNT Children who are **in care** are looked after by the state. ...*a home for children in care...* She was taken into care as a baby. [6] N-UNCOUNT If you do something **with care**, you do it with great attention to avoid mistakes or damage. *Condoms are an effective method of birth control if used with care...* We'd taken enormous care in choosing the location. [7] CONVENTION You can say **'Take care'** when saying goodbye to someone. [INFORMAL] → See Reference Page on Greetings and Goodbyes. [8] N-COUNT Your **cares** are your worries, anxieties, or fears. [9] See also **caring.**

⭐ **career** /kəˈrɪə/ **careers, careering, careered.** [1] N-COUNT A **career** is a job or profession. ...*a career in journalism.* ...*a political career.* [2] N-COUNT Your **career** is the part of your life that you spend working. *During his career, he wrote more than fifty plays.* [3] VERB If a person or vehicle **careers** somewhere, they move fast and in an uncontrolled way. *His car careered into a river.*

carefree /ˈkeəfriː/. ADJ A **carefree** person or period of time does not have any problems or responsibilities. *...carefree summers at the beach.*

⭐ **careful** /ˈkeəfʊl/. 1 ADJ If you are **careful**, you give serious attention to what you are doing in order to avoid damage or mistakes. *Be very careful with this stuff, it can be dangerous... We had to be very careful not to be seen.* ♦ **carefully** ADV *Drive carefully... He had chosen his words carefully.* 2 ADJ **Careful** work, thought, or examination is thorough and shows a concern for details. *The trip needs careful planning. ...keeping careful records.* ♦ **carefully** ADV *All her letters were carefully filed away.*

careless /ˈkeələs/. ADJ If you are **careless**, you do not pay enough attention to what you are doing, and so you make mistakes. *The company denied that it was careless about safety.* ♦ **carelessly** ADV *She was fined £100 for driving carelessly.* ♦ **carelessness** N-UNCOUNT *The fire had resulted from extreme carelessness.*

caress /kəˈres/ caresses, caressing, caressed. VERB & N-COUNT If you **caress** someone, you stroke them gently and affectionately. A **caress** is an act of caressing someone. *He was gently caressing her golden hair... She smoothed his forehead with a caress.*

caretaker /ˈkeəteɪkə/ caretakers. N-COUNT A **caretaker** is a person who looks after a large building such as a school or a block of flats.

cargo /ˈkɑːgəʊ/ cargoes. N-VAR The **cargo** of a ship or plane is the goods that it is carrying. *...a cargo of bananas. ...cargo planes.*

caricature /ˈkærɪkətʃʊə, AM -tʃər/ caricatures, caricaturing, caricatured. 1 N-VAR A **caricature** is a drawing or description of someone that exaggerates their appearance or behaviour. *...a caricature of Hitler with a devil's horns.* 2 VERB If you **caricature** someone, you draw or describe them in an exaggerated way in order to make people laugh. *...being caricatured as the proverbial American tourist.*

⭐ **caring** /ˈkeərɪŋ/. ADJ A **caring** person is affectionate, helpful, and sympathetic. *...a loving, caring husband.*

carnage /ˈkɑːnɪdʒ/. N-UNCOUNT **Carnage** is the violent killing of a lot of people. [LITERARY] *...his strategy for stopping the carnage.*

carnation /kɑːˈneɪʃən/ carnations. N-COUNT A **carnation** is a plant with white, pink, or red flowers.

carnival /ˈkɑːnɪvəl/ carnivals. N-COUNT A **carnival** is a public festival with music, processions, and dancing.

carol /ˈkærəl/ carols. N-COUNT **Carols** are Christian religious songs that are sung at Christmas.

'car park, car parks. N-COUNT In British English, a **car park** is an area or building where people can leave their cars. The American word is **parking lot**.

carpenter /ˈkɑːpɪntə/ carpenters. N-COUNT A **carpenter** is a person whose job is making and repairing wooden things.

carpet /ˈkɑːpɪt/ carpets. 1 N-COUNT A **carpet** is a thick covering for a floor or staircase, made of wool or a similar material. 2 N-COUNT A **carpet of** something is a layer of it covering the ground. *...the carpet of leaves in my yard.*

carpeted /ˈkɑːpɪtɪd/. 1 ADJ If a floor or room is **carpeted**, it has a carpet on the floor. *...the gray-carpeted dining room.* 2 ADJ If the ground is **carpeted with** something, there is a layer of it covering the ground. *The ground was thickly carpeted with pine needles.*

carriage /ˈkærɪdʒ/ carriages. 1 N-COUNT In British English, a **carriage** is one of the separate sections of a train that carries passengers. The usual American word is **car**. 2 N-COUNT A **carriage** is an old-fashioned vehicle pulled by horses.

carriageway /ˈkærɪdʒweɪ/ carriageways. N-COUNT A **carriageway** is one of the two sides of a motorway or major road. [BRITISH]

⭐ **carrier** /ˈkæriə/ carriers. 1 N-COUNT A **carrier** is a vehicle that is used for carrying people, especially soldiers, or things. *...armoured personnel carriers and tanks.* 2 N-COUNT A **carrier** is a passenger airline. *...Switzerland's national carrier, Swissair.* 3 N-COUNT A **carrier** or a **carrier bag** is a paper or plastic bag with handles. [BRITISH]

carrot /ˈkærət/ carrots. 1 N-VAR **Carrots** are long, thin, orange-coloured vegetables that grow under the ground. → See picture on page 836. 2 N-COUNT Something that is offered to people in order to persuade them to do something can be referred to as a **carrot**. *They will be set targets, with a carrot of extra cash and pay if they achieve them.*

⭐ **carry** /ˈkæri/ carries, carrying, carried. 1 VERB If you **carry** something, you take it with you, holding it so that it does not touch the ground. *He was carrying a briefcase... She carried her son to the car.* 2 VERB To **carry** something means to have it with you wherever you go. *He always carried a gun.* 3 VERB To **carry** someone or something means to take them somewhere. *...carrying a message of thanks to President Mubarak... The ship could carry seventy passengers.* 4 VERB If someone **is carrying** a disease, they are infected with it and can pass it on to other people. *...people carrying the AIDS virus.* 5 VERB If an action or situation **carries** a particular quality or consequence, it has it. *Exposure to the sun carries the risk of developing skin cancer. ...an offence which can carry the death penalty.* 6 VERB If you **carry** an idea or a method further, you use or develop it or apply it in new circumstances. *It's not such a new idea, but I carried it to extremes.* 7 VERB If a newspaper **carries** a picture or an article, it contains it. 8 VERB If a proposal or motion **is carried** in a debate, a majority of people vote in favour of it. 9 VERB If a sound **carries**, it can be heard a long way away. *He doubted if the sound would carry far.* 10 PHRASE If

A
B
C
D
E
F
G
H
I
J
K
L
M
N
O
P
Q
R
S
T
U
V
W
X
Y
Z

you **get carried away**, you are so eager or excited about something that you do something hasty or foolish.

▶**carry on.** ☐1☐ PHR-VERB If you **carry on** doing something, you continue to do it. *The assistant carried on talking.* ☐2☐ PHR-VERB If you **carry on** an activity, you take part in it. *They carried on a conversation through most of the morning.*

▶**carry out.** PHR-VERB If you **carry out** a threat, task, or instruction, you do it or act according to it. *The security forces carried out the arrests.*

▶**carry through.** PHR-VERB If you **carry** something **through**, you do it, often in spite of difficulties. *It would carry through its military operation to the very end.*

cart /kɑːt/ **carts, carting, carted.** ☐1☐ N-COUNT A **cart** is an old-fashioned wooden vehicle, usually pulled by an animal. → See picture on page 834. ☐2☐ VERB If you **cart** things somewhere, you carry or transport them there, often with difficulty. [INFORMAL] *He carted off the contents of the house.*

cartel /kɑː'tel/ **cartels.** N-COUNT A **cartel** is an association of companies or countries involved in the same industry who act together to control competition and prices.

cartilage /'kɑːtɪlɪdʒ/ N-UNCOUNT **Cartilage** is a strong flexible substance which surrounds the joints in your body.

carton /'kɑːtən/ **cartons.** ☐1☐ N-COUNT A **carton** is a plastic or cardboard container in which food or drink is sold. *...a carton of milk.* ☐2☐ N-COUNT A **carton** is a large strong cardboard box. [AMERICAN]

cartoon /kɑː'tuːn/ **cartoons.** ☐1☐ N-COUNT A **cartoon** is a humorous drawing in a newspaper or magazine. ☐2☐ N-COUNT A **cartoon** is a film in which all the characters and scenes are drawn rather than being real people or objects.

cartoonist /kɑː'tuːnɪst/ **cartoonists.** N-COUNT A **cartoonist** is a person whose job is to draw cartoons for newspapers and magazines.

cartridge /'kɑːtrɪdʒ/ **cartridges.** ☐1☐ N-COUNT In a gun, a **cartridge** is a tube containing a bullet and an explosive substance. ☐2☐ N-COUNT A **cartridge** is a part of a machine that can be easily removed and replaced when it is worn out or empty.

carve /kɑːv/ **carves, carving, carved.** ☐1☐ VERB If you **carve** an object, you cut it out of stone or wood. You **carve** wood or stone in order to make the object. *One of the prisoners has carved a beautiful wooden chess set.* ☐2☐ VERB If you **carve** writing or a design on an object, you cut it into the surface. *He carved his name on his desk.* ☐3☐ VERB If you **carve** meat, you cut slices from it. ☐4☐ VERB & PHR-VERB If you **carve** a career or a niche for yourself, or if you **carve out** a career or niche, you succeed in getting the career or the position that you want by your own efforts.

▶**carve up.** PHR-VERB If someone **carves** something **up**, they divide it into smaller areas or pieces; used showing disapproval.

carving /'kɑːvɪŋ/ **carvings.** ☐1☐ N-COUNT A **carving** is an object or design that has been cut out of

stone or wood. ☐2☐ N-UNCOUNT **Carving** is the act of carving objects or designs.

cascade /kæs'keɪd/ **cascades, cascading, cascaded.** ☐1☐ N-COUNT A **cascade of** something is a large amount of it. [LITERARY] *...a cascade of laughter.* ☐2☐ VERB When water **cascades**, it pours downwards very fast and in large quantities.

⭐ **case** /keɪs/ **cases.** ☐1☐ N-COUNT A **case** is a particular situation or instance, especially one that you are using as an example of something more general. *Suffering can have beneficial results and certainly I know that was true in my case... In extreme cases, insurance companies can prosecute.* ☐2☐ N-COUNT A **case** is a person that a professional such as a doctor is dealing with. *Child protection workers were meeting to discuss her case.* ☐3☐ N-COUNT A crime, or a trial that takes place after a crime, can be called a **case**. *...her connection with the kidnapping case. ...trying to determine the outcome of court cases.* ☐4☐ N-COUNT In an argument, the **case for** or **against** something consists of the facts and reasons used to support or oppose it. *He sat there while I made the case for his dismissal.* ☐5☐ N-COUNT A **case** is a container that is designed to hold or protect something. *...a black case for his spectacles. ...cases of liquor.* ☐6☐ N-COUNT A **case** is the same as a **suitcase**.
PHRASES ● You say **in any case** when you are adding another reason for something you have said or done. *The concert was booked out, and in any case, most of the people gathered in the square could not afford the price of a ticket.* ● You say **in case** to indicate that you have something or are doing something because a particular thing might happen or might have happened. *All exits must be kept clear in case of fire... I'm waiting for Mary, in case you're wondering... She carried her pills in her purse, just in case.* ● You say **in that case** or **in which case** to indicate that you are assuming that a previous statement is correct or true. *You may, of course, disagree, in which case, don't hesitate to let me know.* ● When you say that a job or task **is a case of** doing a particular thing, you mean that the job or task consists of doing that thing. *Every team has a weakness; it's just a case of finding it.*

case-'sensitive. ADJ If a word is **case-sensitive**, it must be written in a particular form, for example using all capital letters or all small letters, in order for the computer to recognize it. [COMPUTING]

'case study, case studies. N-COUNT A **case study** is a written account that gives detailed information about a person, group, or thing and their development over a period of time. *...a large case study of malaria in West African children.*

⭐ **cash** /kæʃ/ **cashes, cashing, cashed.** ☐1☐ N-UNCOUNT **Cash** is money, especially money in the form of notes and coins. *We were desperately short of cash. ...two thousand pounds in cash.* ☐2☐ VERB If you **cash** a cheque, you exchange it at a bank for the amount of money that it is worth.

▶ **cash in** PHR-VERB If someone **cashes in on** a situation, they use it to gain an advantage for themselves. *Local Conservatives have been accused of cashing in on racial tension in the area.*

cashier /kæ'ʃɪə/ **cashiers.** N-COUNT A **cashier** is the person that customers pay money to or get money from in a shop or bank.

cashmere /ˌkæʃ'mɪə, AM 'kæʒmɪr/. N-UNCOUNT **Cashmere** is a kind of very fine soft wool.

casino /kə'siːnəʊ/ **casinos.** N-COUNT A **casino** is a place where people play gambling games.

casserole /'kæsərəʊl/ **casseroles.** **1** N-VAR A **casserole** is a meal made by cooking food in liquid in an oven. *...lamb casserole.* **2** N-COUNT A **casserole** or **casserole dish** is a large heavy container with a lid used for cooking casseroles.

cassette /kə'set/ **cassettes.** N-COUNT A **cassette** is a small, flat, rectangular, plastic container with magnetic tape inside, which is used for recording and playing back sounds.

⭐ **cast** /kɑːst, kæst/ **casts, casting, cast.** **1** N-COUNT The **cast** of a play or film is all the people who act in it. In the singular **cast** may be followed by a singular or plural verb. *Most of the cast was amazed by the play's success.* **2** VERB To **cast** an actor means to choose them to act a particular role. *He was cast as a college professor.* **3** VERB If you **cast** something somewhere, you throw it there. [LITERARY] *He cast the stone away.* **4** VERB If you **cast** your eyes or **cast** a look somewhere, you look there. [WRITTEN] *He cast a stern glance at the two men.* **5** VERB If you **cast** doubt or suspicion on something, you make other people unsure about it. *New tests cast new doubt on the cause of the blast.* **6** VERB When you **cast** your vote in an election, you vote. **7** VERB To **cast** an object means to make it by pouring hot liquid metal into a container and leaving it until it becomes hard.

▶ **cast about** or **cast around.** PHR-VERB If you **cast about** or **cast around for** something, you try to find it. *She had been casting around for a good excuse.*

▶ **cast aside.** PHR-VERB If you **cast** someone or something **aside**, you get rid of them. *In America we seem to cast aside our elderly people.*

▶ **cast off.** PHR-VERB If you **cast** something **off**, you get rid of it or no longer use it. [WRITTEN] *...having cast off a grossly inefficient economic system.*

caste /kɑːst, kæst/ **castes.** N-VAR A **caste** is one of the social classes into which people in a Hindu society are divided. *India divides in many ways: by caste, religion, language, region.*

castigate /'kæstɪgeɪt/ **castigates, castigating, castigated.** VERB If you **castigate** someone, you scold or criticize them severely. [FORMAL]

'cast-iron. **1** ADJ **Cast-iron** objects are made of a special type of iron containing carbon. *...a cast-iron bath.* **2** ADJ A **cast-iron** excuse, guarantee, or solution is absolutely certain to be effective.

⭐ **castle** /'kɑːsəl, 'kæsəl/ **castles.** N-COUNT A **castle** is a large building with thick high walls, built by important people, such as kings, in former times, for protection during wars and battles.

castrate /kæ'streɪt, AM 'kæstreɪt/ **castrates, castrating, castrated.** VERB To **castrate** a male animal means to remove its testicles. ♦ **castration**, **castrations** N-VAR *...the castration of male farm animals.*

casual /'kæʒʊəl/. **1** ADJ If you are **casual**, you are relaxed and not very concerned about what is happening. ♦ **casually** ADV *'No need to hurry,' Ben said casually.* **2** ADJ BEFORE N Something that is **casual** happens by chance or without planning. *...a casual remark.* **3** ADJ BEFORE N **Casual** clothes are ones that you normally wear at home or on holiday, and not for formal occasions. ♦ **casually** ADV *They were smartly but casually dressed.* **4** ADJ BEFORE N **Casual** work is done for short periods and is not permanent. *...establishments which employ people on a casual basis.*

⭐ **casualty** /'kæʒʊəlti/ **casualties.** **1** N-COUNT A **casualty** is a person who is injured or killed in a war or in an accident. *The casualties on our side were frightful.* **2** N-COUNT A **casualty of** an event or situation is a person or a thing that has suffered badly as a result of it. *Small companies were early casualties of the recession.* **3** N-UNCOUNT **Casualty** is an informal name for the department of a hospital where people are taken for emergency treatment. [BRITISH]

⭐ **cat** /kæt/ **cats.** **1** N-COUNT A **cat** is a small furry animal with a tail, whiskers, and sharp claws. Cats are often kept as pets. → See picture on page 815. **2** N-COUNT **Cats** are a group of animals which includes lions, tigers, and domestic cats. **3** PHRASE In a fight or contest, if the stronger person or group **plays cat and mouse with** the other, they choose to defeat their opponent slowly, using skill and deceit, rather than force or violence.

catalogue (AM **catalog**) /'kætəlɒg/ **catalogues, cataloguing, catalogued.** **1** N-COUNT A **catalogue** is a list of things, such as the goods you can buy from a company, the objects in a museum, or the books in a library. **2** VERB To **catalogue** things means to make a list of them. **3** N-COUNT A **catalogue of** similar things, especially bad things, is a number of them happening one after another. *Mr Wills struggled to explain the catalogue of errors.*

catalyst /'kætəlɪst/ **catalysts.** **1** N-COUNT You can describe a person or thing as a **catalyst** when they cause a change or event to happen. *I think the report will serve as a catalyst to bring all of the parties together.* **2** N-COUNT In chemistry, a **catalyst** is a substance that causes a reaction to take place more quickly.

catapult /'kætəpʌlt/ **catapults, catapulting, catapulted.** **1** N-COUNT A **catapult** is a device for shooting small stones. It consists of a Y-shaped stick with a piece of elastic tied between the two

a
b
c
d
e
f
g
h
i
j
k
l
m
n
o
p
q
r
s
t
u
v
w
x
y
z

top parts. **2** VERB If someone or something **catapults** through the air, they move or are thrown very suddenly and violently through it. *His car catapulted off the kerb... Georgina was catapulted through the windscreen.*

cataract /'kætərækt/ **cataracts.** N-COUNT A **cataract** is a layer that has grown over a person's eye that prevents them from seeing properly.

catastrophe /kə'tæstrəfi/ **catastrophes.** N-COUNT A **catastrophe** is an unexpected event that causes great suffering or damage. *From all points of view, war would be a catastrophe.*

catastrophic /,kætə'strɒfɪk/. ADJ **Catastrophic** means extremely bad or serious, often causing great suffering or damage. *Even a small oil spill would be catastrophic. ...a catastrophic mistake.*

⭐ **catch** /kætʃ/ **catches, catching, caught.** **1** VERB If you **catch** a person or animal, you capture them. *Police say they are confident of catching the gunman. ...an animal caught in a trap.* **2** VERB If you **catch** an object which is moving through the air, you seize it with your hands. *I jumped up to catch the ball.* **3** VERB If something which is moving **catches** something else, it hits it. *He caught her on the side of her head with his other fist.* **4** VERB If something **catches** on or in an object, or if it **is caught** on or in it, it becomes trapped by it. *Her heel caught on a rusty bedspring.* **5** VERB If you **catch** a bus, train, or plane, you get on it to travel somewhere. **6** VERB If you **catch** someone doing something wrong, you discover them doing it. *He caught a youth breaking into a car... They caught him with $30,000 cash in a briefcase.* **7** PASSIVE-VERB If you **are caught** in a storm or other unpleasant situation, it happens when you cannot avoid its effects. *Visitors to the area were caught between police and the rioters.* **8** VERB If something **catches** your attention or your eye, you notice it or become interested in it. **9** VERB If you cannot **catch** what someone says, you cannot manage to hear it. *I do not believe I caught your name.* **10** VERB If you **catch** a cold or a disease, you become ill with it. **11** VERB If something **catches** the light, or if the light **catches** it, it reflects the light and looks bright or shiny. **12** N-COUNT A **catch** on a window or door is a device that fastens it. **13** N-SING A **catch** is a hidden problem or difficulty in a plan or course of action. *'It's your money. You deserve it.'—'What's the catch?'*

▸**catch on.** **1** PHR-VERB If you **catch on to** something, you understand it, or realize that it is happening. *I was slow to catch on to what she was trying to tell me.* **2** PHR-VERB If something **catches on**, it becomes popular. *Photography began to catch on as a respectable activity.*

▸**catch out.** PHR-VERB To **catch** someone **out** means to cause them to make a mistake that reveals that they are lying about something. *His clumsy attempts to catch her out had failed.*

▸**catch up.** **1** PHR-VERB If you **catch up with** someone, you reach them by walking faster than them. *I ran faster to catch up with him... I stopped and waited for her to catch up.* **2** PHR-VERB To **catch up with** someone means to reach the same standard or level that they have reached. *She'll soon catch up with the other students... The school is used by kids who want to catch up on English.* **3** PHR-VERB If you **catch up on** an activity that you have not had much time to do, you spend time doing it. *I was catching up on a bit of reading.* **4** PHR-VERB If you **are caught up in** something, you are involved in it, usually unwillingly. *...innocent people caught up in the fighting.*

▸**catch up with.** **1** PHR-VERB When people **catch up with** someone who has done something wrong, they succeed in finding them. **2** PHR-VERB If something **catches up with** you, you find yourself in an unpleasant situation which you have been able to avoid but which you are now forced to deal with. *His criminal past caught up with him.*

catchy /'kætʃi/ **catchier, catchiest.** ADJ A **catchy** tune, name, or phrase is attractive and easy to remember.

categorical /,kætɪ'ɡɒrɪkəl, AM -'ɡɔːr-/. ADJ If you are **categorical** about something, you state your views with certainty and firmness. *...his categorical denial of the charges.*
♦ **categorically** ADV *I categorically refused to leave.*

categorize (BRIT also **categorise**) /'kætɪɡəraɪz/ **categorizes, categorizing, categorized.** VERB If you **categorize** people or things, you say which set they belong to. *They categorized me as a rock 'n' roll player.* ♦ **categorization, categorizations** N-VAR *...the labeling and categorization of people in news reports.*

⭐ **category** /'kætɪɡri, AM -ɡɔːri/ **categories.** N-COUNT If people or things are divided into **categories**, they are divided into groups according to their qualities and characteristics. *The law covers four categories of experiments.*

cater /'keɪtə/ **caters, catering, catered.** VERB In British English, to **cater for** people means to provide them with the things they need. In American English, you **cater to** people. *...shops that cater for the needs of men.*

caterer /'keɪtərə/ **caterers.** N-COUNT A **caterer** is a person or a company that provides food in a particular place or on a special occasion.

catering /'keɪtərɪŋ/. N-UNCOUNT **Catering** is the activity or business of providing food for people. *...a catering company.*

caterpillar /'kætəpɪlə/ **caterpillars.** N-COUNT A **caterpillar** is a small worm-like animal that eventually develops into a butterfly or moth.

cathedral /kə'θiːdrəl/ **cathedrals.** N-COUNT A **cathedral** is a large important church which has a bishop in charge of it.

★ **Catholic** /'kæθlɪk/ **Catholics.** ADJ & N-COUNT The **Catholic** Church is the branch of the Christian Church that accepts the Pope as its leader. A **Catholic** is a member of the Catholic Church. ...*Catholic priests.* ...*a very devout Catholic.*
♦ **Catholicism** /kə'θɒlɪsɪzəm/ N-UNCOUNT ...*her conversion to Catholicism.*

cattle /'kætəl/. N-PLURAL **Cattle** are cows and bulls.

catwalk /'kætwɔːk/ **catwalks.** N-COUNT At a fashion show, the **catwalk** is a narrow platform that models walk along to display clothes.

caucus /'kɔːkəs/ **caucuses.** N-COUNT A **caucus** is an influential group of people within an organization who share similar aims and interests. [FORMAL] ...*the black caucus in the US Congress.*

caught /kɔːt/. **Caught** is the past tense and past participle of **catch**.

cauliflower /'kɒlɪflaʊə, AM 'kɔː-/ **cauliflowers.** N-VAR A **cauliflower** is a large, round, white vegetable surrounded by green leaves. → See picture on page 836.

★ **cause** /kɔːz/ **causes, causing, caused.** ① N-COUNT & VERB The **cause of** an event or the thing that **causes** it is the thing that makes it happen. *Oil pollution is the commonest cause of death for seabirds.* ...*the factors that caused prices to rise... They never really caused us problems.*
② N-UNCOUNT If you **have cause for** a particular feeling or action, you have good reasons for it. *It seems that you have cause for celebration.* ...*if you've ever had cause to be angry at a computer.*
③ N-COUNT A **cause** is an aim which a group of people supports or is fighting for. ...*present-day champions of the cause.*

caution /'kɔːʃən/ **cautions, cautioning, cautioned.** ① N-UNCOUNT **Caution** is great care taken in order to avoid danger. *Extreme caution should be exercised when buying part-worn tyres.* ② VERB & N-UNCOUNT If someone **cautions** you, or if they give you a **caution**, they warn you. *Tony cautioned against misrepresenting the situation... They cautioned that the process is long and difficult... One word of caution. It is not wise to become totally dependent on others.*

cautionary /'kɔːʃənri, AM -neri/. ADJ A **cautionary** story is intended to give a warning. ...*her cautionary tales of men.*

★ **cautious** /'kɔːʃəs/. ADJ A **cautious** person acts very carefully in order to avoid danger. *Employers may become overly cautious about taking on new staff.* ♦ **cautiously** ADV *David moved cautiously forward.*

cavalier /,kævə'lɪə/. ADJ If you describe a person as **cavalier**, you disapprove of them because you think that they do not consider other people's feelings or take account of the seriousness of a situation. *The Editor takes a cavalier attitude to the concept of fact checking.*

cavalry /'kævəlri/. N-SING The **cavalry** used to be the soldiers who rode horses in an army.

Nowadays, it is usually the soldiers who use armoured vehicles in an army.

★ **cave** /keɪv/ **caves, caving, caved.** N-COUNT A **cave** is a large hole in the side of a cliff or hill, or under the ground.
▶**cave in.** ① PHR-VERB When a roof or wall **caves in**, it collapses inwards. ② PHR-VERB If you **cave in**, you suddenly stop arguing or resisting. *The Government has caved in to pressure from property developers.*

cavern /'kævən/ **caverns.** N-COUNT A **cavern** is a large deep cave.

caviar (or **caviare**) /'kævɪɑː/ **caviars.** N-VAR **Caviar** is a food that consists of the salted eggs of a fish called the sturgeon.

cavity /'kævɪti/ **cavities.** N-COUNT A **cavity** is a small space or hole in something solid. ...*the decay that causes cavities in your teeth.*

cc /,siː 'siː/. **cc** is an abbreviation for 'cubic centimetres', used when referring to the volume or capacity of something. ...*1,500 cc sports cars.*

CCTV /,siː siː tiː 'viː/ N-UNCOUNT **CCTV** is an abbreviation for 'closed-circuit television'. ...*a CCTV camera... The girls were filmed on CCTV.*

★ **CD** /,siː 'diː/ **CDs.** N-COUNT A **CD** is a small shiny disc on which music or information is stored.

'CD burner, CD burners. N-COUNT A **CD burner** is the same as a **CD writer**.

'CD player, CD players. N-COUNT A **CD player** is a machine on which you can play CDs.

CD-ROM /,siː diː 'rɒm/ **CD-ROMs.** N-COUNT A **CD-ROM** is a disc which can be read by a computer, and on which a very large amount of data is stored. [COMPUTING]

'CD writer, CD writers. N-COUNT A **CD writer** is a piece of computer equipment that you use for copying data from a computer onto a CD. [COMPUTING]

★ **cease** /siːs/ **ceases, ceasing, ceased.** ① VERB If something **ceases**, it stops happening. [FORMAL] *At one o'clock the rain had ceased.* ② VERB To **cease to** do something means to stop doing it. [FORMAL] *He never ceases to amaze me... A small number of firms have ceased trading.*

★ **ceasefire** /'siːsfaɪə/ **ceasefires.** N-COUNT A **ceasefire** is an arrangement in which countries at war agree to stop fighting for a time.

cedar /'siːdə/ **cedars.** N-VAR A **cedar** is a kind of evergreen tree. **Cedar** is the wood of this tree.

cede /siːd/ **cedes, ceding, ceded.** VERB If someone in a position of authority **cedes** land or power to someone else, they let them have it. [FORMAL] *The General had promised to cede power by January.*

ceiling /'siːlɪŋ/ **ceilings.** ① N-COUNT A **ceiling** is the top inside surface of a room. ...*a small air vent in the ceiling.* ② N-COUNT A **ceiling** is an official upper limit on prices or wages. ...*an informal agreement to put a ceiling on salaries.*

★ **celebrate** /'selɪbreɪt/ **celebrates, celebrating, celebrated.** ① VERB If you **celebrate** something, you do something enjoyable because of a special

a b c d e f g h i j k l m n o p q r s t u v w x y z

A B C D E F G H I J K L M N O P Q R S T U V W X Y Z

occasion. *The England football team have been celebrating their victory... I was in a mood to celebrate.* ♦ **celebration, celebrations** N-VAR *Only a few people can find any cause for celebration. ...his eightieth birthday celebrations.* ② VERB When priests **celebrate** Holy Communion or Mass, they officially perform the actions and ceremonies that are involved.

celebrated /'selɪbreɪtɪd/. ADJ A **celebrated** person or thing is famous and much admired. *...his most celebrated film.*

celebrity /sɪ'lebrɪti/ **celebrities.** N-COUNT A **celebrity** is someone who is famous. *At the age of 30, Hersey suddenly became a celebrity.*

celery /'seləri/. N-UNCOUNT **Celery** is a vegetable with long pale green stalks. → See picture on page 836.

celestial /sɪ'lestiəl/. ADJ **Celestial** is used to describe things connected with heaven or the sky. [LITERARY]

celibate /'selɪbət/. ADJ Someone who is **celibate** does not marry or have sex. [FORMAL] ♦ **celibacy** N-UNCOUNT *...a monk who took the vow of celibacy.*

⭐ **cell** /sel/ **cells.** ① N-COUNT A **cell** is the smallest part of an animal or plant. All animals and plants are made up of millions of cells. ② N-COUNT A **cell** is a small room in which a prisoner is locked. *...police cells.*

cellar /'selə/ **cellars.** N-COUNT A **cellar** is a room underneath a building.

cello /'tʃeləʊ/ **cellos.** N-VAR A **cello** is a musical instrument that looks like a large violin. You hold it upright and play it sitting down. → See picture on page 827. ♦ **cellist, cellists** N-COUNT *...the world's greatest cellist.*

cellphone /'selfəʊn/ **cellphones.** N-COUNT A **cellphone** is a telephone that you can carry with you and use to make or receive calls wherever you are.

cellular /'seljʊlə/. ADJ **Cellular** means relating to the cells of animals or plants. *...molecular and cellular mechanisms.*

cellulite /'seljʊlaɪt/. N-UNCOUNT **Cellulite** is lumpy fat which people may get under their skin, especially on their thighs.

Celsius /'selsiəs/. ADJ **Celsius** is a scale for measuring temperature, in which water freezes at 0° and boils at 100°. Another word for this is 'centigrade'. *Night temperatures can drop below 15 degrees Celsius.* ● See note at **temperature**.

cement /sɪ'ment/ **cements, cementing, cemented.** ① N-UNCOUNT **Cement** is a grey powder which is mixed with sand and water in order to make concrete. ② VERB If things **are cemented** together, they are stuck or fastened together. *The lice eggs are cemented to the hairs on the scalp.* ③ VERB Something that **cements** a relationship or agreement makes it stronger. *Nothing cements a friendship between countries so much as trade.*

cemetery /'semətri, AM -teri/ **cemeteries.** N-COUNT

A **cemetery** is a place where dead people are buried.

censor /'sensə/ **censors, censoring, censored.** ① VERB If someone **censors** a letter or the media, they officially examine it and cut out any parts that they consider unacceptable. *Television companies tend to censor bad language in feature films.* ② N-COUNT A **censor** is a person who has been officially appointed to censor things.

censorship /'sensəʃɪp/. N-UNCOUNT When there is **censorship**, letters or the media are censored. *I am totally against censorship.*

censure /'senʃə/ **censures, censuring, censured.** VERB & N-UNCOUNT If someone **is censured** or if they attract **censure**, they are criticized strongly. [FORMAL] *I would not presume to censure Osborne for hating his mother. ...a controversial policy which has attracted international censure.*

census /'sensəs/ **censuses.** N-COUNT A **census** is an official survey of the population of a country.

cent /sent/ **cents.** N-COUNT A **cent** is a small unit of money in many countries, for example in the United States and Australia. ● See also **per cent.**

centenary /sen'tiːnəri, AM -'ten-/ **centenaries.** N-COUNT A **centenary** is the one hundredth anniversary of an event. [BRITISH] *...the centenary of the death of Lord Tennyson.*

center /'sentə/. See **centre.**

Centigrade /'sentɪɡreɪd/. ADJ **Centigrade** means the same as **Celsius**. *...daytime temperatures of up to forty degrees centigrade.* ● See note at **temperature.**

centimetre (AM **centimeter**) /'sentɪmiːtə/ **centimetres.** N-COUNT A **centimetre** is a unit of length equal to ten millimetres or one-hundredth of a metre.

⭐ **central** /'sentrəl/. ① ADJ BEFORE N A **central** group or organization makes all the important decisions for a larger organization or country. *...the central committee of the Cuban communist party.* ♦ **centrally** ADV *...a centrally planned economy.* ② ADJ Something that is **central** is in the middle of a place or area. *...central London.* ♦ **centrally** ADV *...a full-sized double bed centrally placed.* ③ ADJ The **central** person or thing in a particular situation is the most important one. *...a central part of their culture.*

central 'heating. N-UNCOUNT **Central heating** is a heating system in which water or air is heated and passed round a building through pipes and radiators.

centralize (BRIT also **centralise**) /'sentrəlaɪz/ **centralizes, centralizing, centralized.** VERB To **centralize** a country or organization means to create a system in which one central authority gives instructions to regional groups. *Multinational firms tended to centralize their operations.* ♦ **centralized** ADJ *...a centralized economy.* ♦ **centralization** N-UNCOUNT *...the centralization of political power.*

⭐ **centre** (AM **center**) /'sentə/ **centres, centring, centred.** ① N-COUNT The **centre** of something is the middle of it. ...*the centre of the room.* **2** N-COUNT A **centre** is a place where people have meetings, get help of some kind, or take part in a particular activity. ...*the medical centre.* ...*the National Exhibition Centre.* **3** N-COUNT If an area or town is a **centre** for an industry or activity, that industry or activity is very important there. *London is also the major international insurance centre.* **4** N-COUNT If something is **the centre of** attention or interest, people are giving it a lot of attention. *The centre of attraction was Pierre Auguste Renoir's oil painting.* **5** PASSIVE-VERB Someone or something that **is centred** in a particular place is based there. ...*the silk industry, which was centered in Valencia.* **6** VERB If something **centres on** or **is centred on** a particular thing or person, that thing or person is the main subject of attention. ...*a plan which centred on academic achievement... All his concerns were centred around himself rather than Rachel.* ◆ **-centred** ...*a child-centred approach to teaching.*

★ **century** /ˈsentʃəri/ **centuries.** **1** N-COUNT A **century** is a period of a hundred years that is used when stating a date. For example, the 19th century was the period from 1801 to 1900. **2** N-COUNT A **century** is any period of a hundred years.

ceramic /sɪˈræmɪk/ **ceramics.** **1** N-VAR **Ceramic** is clay that has been heated to a very high temperature so that it becomes hard. **2** N-COUNT **Ceramics** are ceramic ornaments or objects. **3** N-UNCOUNT **Ceramics** is the art of making ceramic objects.

cereal /ˈsɪəriəl/ **cereals.** **1** N-VAR **Cereal** is a food made from grain, usually mixed with milk and eaten for breakfast. **2** N-COUNT **Cereals** are plants such as wheat or rice that produce grain. ...*4 million hectares of cereal crops.*

cerebral /ˈserɪbrəl/ **1** ADJ **Cerebral** means relating to thought or reasoning rather than to emotions. [FORMAL] *Some think him too cerebral to win the support of voters.* **2** ADJ BEFORE N **Cerebral** means relating to the brain. [TECHNICAL] ...*a cerebral haemorrhage.*

ceremonial /ˌserɪˈməʊniəl/ ADJ BEFORE N Something that is **ceremonial** is used in a ceremony or relates to a ceremony. *He represented the nation on ceremonial occasions.*

★ **ceremony** /ˈserɪməni, AM -məʊni/ **ceremonies.** **1** N-COUNT A **ceremony** is a formal event such as a wedding or a coronation. **2** N-UNCOUNT **Ceremony** consists of the special things that are said and done on very formal occasions. ...*the pomp and ceremony of the Pope's visit.*

★ **certain** /ˈsɜːtən/ **1** ADJ If you are **certain of** or **about** something or if it is **certain**, you firmly believe it is true and have no doubt about it. *She's absolutely certain she's going to make it... It wasn't a balloon – I'm certain of that... The scheme is certain to meet opposition.* **2** ADJ You use **certain** to indicate that you are referring to one particular thing or person, without actually

saying exactly which it is. *There will be certain people who'll say 'I told you so!'... You owe a certain person a sum of money.*
   PHRASES ● If you know something **for certain**, you have no doubt about it. *She couldn't know what time he'd go, or even for certain that he'd go at all.* ● When you **make certain** that something happens, you take action to ensure that it happens. *He had made certain he hadn't shown his face.*

★ **certainly** /ˈsɜːtənli/ **1** ADV You can use **certainly** to emphasize what you are saying. *The public is certainly getting tired of hearing about it... Certainly, pets can help children develop friendship skills.* **2** ADV You use **certainly** when you are agreeing or disagreeing strongly with what someone has said. *'You keep out of their way don't you?'—'I certainly do.'... 'Perhaps it would be better if I withdrew altogether.'—'Certainly not!'*

certainty /ˈsɜːtənti/ **certainties.** **1** N-UNCOUNT **Certainty** is the state of having no doubts at all. *I have told them with absolute certainty there'll be no change of policy.* **2** N-COUNT **Certainties** are things that nobody has any doubts about. *In politics there are never any certainties.*

certificate /səˈtɪfɪkət/ **certificates.** N-COUNT A **certificate** is an official document which states that particular facts are true, or which you receive when you have successfully completed a course of study or training. ...*birth certificates.* ...*the Post-Graduate Certificate of Education.*

certify /ˈsɜːtɪfaɪ/ **certifies, certifying, certified.** **1** VERB If someone in an official position **certifies** something, they officially state that it is true or genuine. *The president certified that the project would receive at least $650m... The National Election Council is supposed to certify the results.* ◆ **certification** /ˌsɜːtɪfɪˈkeɪʃən/ **certifications** N-VAR ...*written certification that the relative is really ill.* **2** VERB If someone **is certified as** a particular kind of worker, they are given a certificate stating that they have successfully completed a course of training in their profession. *They wanted to get certified as divers.* ◆ **certification** N-UNCOUNT ...*training leading to the certification of their skill in a particular field.*

cervix /ˈsɜːvɪks/.

✔ The plural is **cervixes** or **cervices**.

N-COUNT The **cervix** is the entrance to the womb. [TECHNICAL] ◆ **cervical** /ˈsɜːvɪkəl, səˈvaɪkəl/ ADJ BEFORE N ...*cervical cancer.*

CFC /ˌsiː ef ˈsiː/ **CFCs.** N-COUNT **CFCs** are chemicals that are used in aerosols, refrigerators, and cooling systems, and in the manufacture of various plastics. **CFC** is an abbreviation for 'chlorofluorocarbon'.

★ **chain** /tʃeɪn/ **chains, chaining, chained.** **1** N-COUNT A **chain** consists of metal rings connected together in a line. *His open shirt revealed a fat gold chain.* **2** VERB If a person or thing **is chained to** something, they are fastened to it with a chain. *The dog was chained to the leg of the garden*

a
b
c
d
e
f
g
h
i
j
k
l
m
n
o
p
q
r
s
t
u
v
w
x
y
z

seat... *She chained her bike to the railings.*
3 N-COUNT A **chain of** things is a group of them arranged in a line. *...a chain of islands.* **4** N-COUNT A **chain** of shops or hotels is a number of them owned by the same company. *...a large supermarket chain.* **5** N-COUNT A **chain of** events is a series of them happening one after another.

⭐ **chair** /tʃeə/ **chairs, chairing, chaired. 1** N-COUNT A **chair** is a piece of furniture for one person to sit on, with a back and four legs. **2** N-COUNT At British universities, a **chair** is the post of professor. **3** VERB If you **chair** a meeting, you are the person in charge of it. *...a committee chaired by Dr Robert Song.* **4** N-COUNT The **chair** of a meeting is the chairperson.

⭐ **chairman** /ˈtʃeəmən/ **chairmen.** N-COUNT The **chairman** of a meeting or organization is the person in charge of it.

chairperson /ˈtʃeəpɜːsən/ **chairpersons.** N-COUNT The **chairperson** of a meeting or organization is the person in charge of it.

chairwoman /ˈtʃeəwʊmən/ **chairwomen.** N-COUNT The **chairwoman** of a meeting or organization is the woman in charge of it.

chalet /ˈʃæleɪ, AM ʃæˈleɪ/ **chalets.** N-COUNT A **chalet** is a small wooden house, especially in a mountain area or holiday camp.

chalk /tʃɔːk/ **chalks, chalking, chalked. 1** N-UNCOUNT **Chalk** is soft white rock. *...the highest chalk cliffs in Britain.* **2** N-COUNT **Chalk** refers to small pieces of chalk used for writing or drawing. *...coloured chalks.*
▸**chalk up.** PHR-VERB If you **chalk up** a success, you achieve it. *The team chalked up another victory.*

chalkboard /ˈtʃɔːkbɔːd/ **chalkboards.** N-COUNT In American English, a **chalkboard** is a dark-coloured board that you can write on with chalk. The British word is **blackboard**.

⭐ **challenge** /ˈtʃælɪndʒ/ **challenges, challenging, challenged. 1** N-VAR A **challenge** is something new and difficult which requires great effort and determination. *The new government's first challenge is the economy.* **2** PHRASE If someone **rises to the challenge**, they successfully act in response to a difficult situation. *They rose to the challenge of entertaining 80 schoolchildren.* **3** VERB & N-COUNT If you **challenge** someone or if you present them with a **challenge**, you invite them to fight or compete with you. *He left a note at the scene of the crime, challenging detectives to catch him... A third presidential candidate emerged to mount a serious challenge.* **4** VERB & N-VAR To **challenge** ideas or people means to question their truth, value, or authority. A **challenge** is an act of challenging someone or something. *Rose challenged him to come on stage and explain his opinions... The details are open to challenge. ...a direct challenge to the authority of the government.* **5** ADJ If you say that someone is **challenged** in a particular way, you mean that they have a disability in that area. **Challenged** is

often used for humorous effect, but is only used after an adverb for this meaning. *She ran off with an intellectually challenged ski instructor.*

challenger /ˈtʃælɪndʒə/ **challengers.** N-COUNT A **challenger** is someone who competes for a position or title. *...the sixth challenger for the 1995 Americas Cup.*

challenging /ˈtʃælɪndʒɪŋ/. **1** ADJ A **challenging** job or activity requires great effort and determination. *I'm ready to do all those things which are more challenging.* **2** ADJ **Challenging** behaviour seems to be inviting people to argue or compete. *Mona gave him a challenging look.*

⭐ **chamber** /ˈtʃeɪmbə/ **chambers. 1** N-COUNT A **chamber** is a large room that is used for formal meetings, or that is designed and equipped for a particular purpose. *...the Council chamber. ...a burial chamber.* **2** N-COUNT You can refer to a country's parliament or to one section of it as a **chamber**.

chamber of 'commerce, chambers of commerce. N-COUNT A **chamber of commerce** is a group of business people who work together to improve business and industry in their area.

champ /tʃæmp/ **champs.** N-COUNT A **champ** is the same as a **champion**. [INFORMAL]

champagne /ʃæmˈpeɪn/. N-UNCOUNT **Champagne** is an expensive French sparkling white wine. It is often drunk to celebrate something.

⭐ **champion** /ˈtʃæmpiən/ **champions, championing, championed. 1** N-COUNT A **champion** is someone who has won the first prize in a competition. *...a former Olympic champion. ...champion boxer Lennox Lewis.* **2** N-COUNT & VERB If you are a **champion of** a person, a cause or a principle, or if you **champion** them, you support or defend them. *He was once known as a champion of social reform... He passionately championed the poor.*

⭐ **championship** /ˈtʃæmpiənʃɪp/ **championships. 1** N-COUNT A **championship** is a competition to find the best player or team in a particular sport. *...the world chess championship.* **2** N-SING The **championship** refers to the title or status of being a sports champion. *He went on to take the championship.*

⭐ **chance** /tʃɑːns, tʃæns/ **chances, chancing, chanced. 1** N-VAR If there is a **chance of** something happening, it is possible that it will happen. *His chances of winning are slim... There seems little chance of the situation improving.* **2** N-SING If you have a **chance to** do something, you have the opportunity to do it. *All eligible people would get a chance to vote... I felt I had to give him a chance.* **3** N-UNCOUNT & ADJ BEFORE N Something that happens **by chance** was not planned. *He was found by chance on Tuesday by a relative. ...a chance meeting.*
PHRASES ● If you say that someone **stands a chance** of achieving something, you mean that they are likely to achieve it. If you say that they do not **stand a chance**, you mean that they

cannot possibly achieve it. ● When you **take a chance**, you try to do something although there is a large risk of danger or failure. *You take a chance on the weather if you holiday in the UK.*

chancellor /ˈtʃɑːnslə, ˈtʃæns-/ **chancellors.**
[1] N-TITLE In several European countries, **the Chancellor** is the head of government. *...Chancellor Schröder of Germany.* [2] N-COUNT The heads of British universities and some American universities are called **Chancellors**.

ˌChancellor of the Exˈchequer, **Chancellors of the Exchequer.** N-COUNT The **Chancellor of the Exchequer** or the **Chancellor** is the minister in the British government who makes decisions about finance and taxes.

chandelier /ˌʃændəˈlɪə/ **chandeliers.** N-COUNT A **chandelier** is an ornamental frame hanging from a ceiling, which holds a number of light bulbs or candles.

★ **change** /tʃeɪndʒ/ **changes, changing, changed.**
[1] N-VAR If there is a **change in** something, it becomes different. *...a change in US policy... What is needed is a change of attitude on the part of architects... Political change is on its way.* [2] VERB When something **changes** or when you **change** it, it becomes different. *She has now changed into a happy, self-confident woman... They should change the law to make it illegal to own replica weapons.* [3] PHRASE If you say that something **is a change** or **makes a change**, you mean that it is enjoyable because it is different from what you are used to. *A dinner party on a Spanish theme would certainly make a delicious change.* [4] PHRASE If you say that something is happening **for a change**, you mean that you are glad that it is happening because usually it does not. *Now let me ask you a question, for a change.* [5] VERB & N-COUNT To **change** something means to replace it with something new or different. A **change of** something is an act of replacing something. *All they did was change a fuse... A change of leadership alone will not be enough.* [6] VERB When you **change** your clothes, you take them off and put on different ones. *They had allowed her to shower and change... I changed into a tracksuit... I've got to get changed first.* ● See note at **wear**. [7] VERB When you **change** a baby or **change** its nappy, you take off its dirty nappy and put on a clean one. [8] VERB When you **change** buses or trains, you get off one and get on to another to continue your journey. [9] VERB When you **change** a bed or **change** the sheets, you take off the dirty sheets and put on clean ones. [10] N-UNCOUNT Your **change** is the money that you receive when you pay for something with more money than it costs. [11] N-UNCOUNT **Change** is coins, rather than notes.

▸**change over.** PHR-VERB If you **change over from** one thing **to** another, you stop doing one thing and start doing the other. *We are gradually changing over to a completely metric system.*

★ **channel** /ˈtʃænəl/ **channels, channelling, channelled** (AM **channeling, channeled**). [1] N-COUNT A **channel** is a wavelength on which television programmes are broadcast. *...movie channels.* [2] N-COUNT If something has been done through particular **channels**, a particular group of people have arranged for it to be done. *The President will contact other leaders either directly or through diplomatic channels.* [3] VERB If you **channel** money into something, you arrange for it to be used for that purpose. *...a system set up to channel funds to the poor countries.* [4] N-COUNT A **channel** is a passage along which water flows. *...a drainage channel.* [5] N-PROPER **The Channel** or **the English Channel** is the narrow area of water between England and France.

chant /tʃɑːnt, tʃænt/ **chants, chanting, chanted.**
[1] N-COUNT A **chant** is a word or group of words that is repeated over and over again. *...chants of 'four more years'.* [2] N-COUNT A **chant** is a religious song or prayer that is sung on only a few notes. *...a Gregorian chant.* [3] VERB If you **chant** something, you repeat the same words over and over again. *Demonstrators chanted slogans.* ◆ **chanting** N-UNCOUNT *A lot of the chanting was in support of the deputy Prime Minister.*

★ **chaos** /ˈkeɪɒs/ N-UNCOUNT **Chaos** is a state of complete disorder and confusion. *Their gigs often ended in chaos.*

chaotic /keɪˈɒtɪk/ ADJ If a situation is **chaotic**, it is in a state of disorder and confusion.

chap /tʃæp/ **chaps.** N-COUNT A **chap** is a man or boy. [BRITISH, INFORMAL]

chapel /ˈtʃæpəl/ **chapels.** [1] N-COUNT A **chapel** is part of a church which has its own altar and which is used for private prayer. [2] N-COUNT A **chapel** is a small church in a school, hospital, or prison.

chaplain /ˈtʃæplɪn/ **chaplains.** N-COUNT A **chaplain** is a member of the Christian clergy who does religious work in places such as hospitals, schools, or prisons.

chapped /tʃæpt/. ADJ If your skin is **chapped**, it is dry, cracked, and sore.

★ **chapter** /ˈtʃæptə/ **chapters.** [1] N-COUNT A **chapter** is one of the parts that a book is divided into. *Turn to Chapter 1.* [2] N-COUNT You can refer to a part of your life or a period in history as a **chapter**. [WRITTEN] *This had been a particularly difficult chapter in Lebanon's recent history.* [3] N-COUNT A **chapter** is a branch of a society, club, or union.

★ **character** /ˈkærɪktə/ **characters.** [1] N-COUNT The **character** of a person or place consists of all the qualities they have that make them distinct. *There is a negative side to his character... The character of this country has been formed by immigration.* [2] PHRASE If someone behaves **in character**, they behave in the way you expect them to. If they behave **out of character**, they do not behave as you expect. [3] N-VAR Someone's **character** is their reputation. *...her opponent's attack on her character. ...his previous good character.*

4 N-COUNT The **characters** in a film, book, or play are the people in it. **5** N-COUNT You can refer to a person as a **character**, especially when describing their qualities. *He's a very strange character.* **6** N-COUNT A **character** is a letter, number, or other symbol that is written or printed.

⭐ **characteristic** /ˌkærɪktəˈrɪstɪk/ **characteristics.**
1 N-COUNT A **characteristic** is a quality or feature that is typical of someone or something. *Genes determine the characteristics of every living thing.* **2** ADJ If something is **characteristic of** a person, thing, or place, it is typical of them. *Refusal to admit defeat was characteristic of Davis.*
♦ **characteristically** ADV *He replied in characteristically robust style.*

characterize (BRIT also **characterise**) /ˈkærɪktəraɪz/ **characterizes, characterizing, characterized.** **1** VERB If something **is characterized** by a particular feature or quality, that feature or quality is very evident in it. [FORMAL] *...the greed that characterized the 1980s.* **2** VERB If you **characterize** someone or something **as** a particular thing, you describe them as that thing. [FORMAL] *Both companies have characterized the relationship as friendly.*
♦ **characterization, characterizations** N-VAR *...his characterisation of other designers as 'thieves'.*

charade /ʃəˈrɑːd, AM -ˈreɪd/ **charades.** N-COUNT A **charade** is a pretence which is so obvious that nobody is deceived.

charcoal /ˈtʃɑːkəʊl/. N-UNCOUNT **Charcoal** is a black substance used as a fuel and for drawing, obtained by burning wood without much air.

⭐ **charge** /tʃɑːdʒ/ **charges, charging, charged.** **1** VERB If you **charge** someone an amount of money, you ask them to pay that amount for something. *Local nurseries charge £100 a week. ...the architect who charged us a fee of seven hundred pounds.* **2** N-COUNT A **charge** is an amount of money that you have to pay for a service. *We can arrange this for a small charge.* **3** PHRASE If something is **free of charge**, it does not cost anything. **4** N-COUNT A **charge** is a formal accusation that someone has committed a crime. *He may still face criminal charges.* **5** VERB When the police **charge** someone, they formally accuse them of having done something illegal. *Police have charged Mr Smith with murder.* **6** N-UNCOUNT If you have **charge of** or are **in charge of** something or someone, you have responsibility for them. *A few years ago Bacryl took charge of the company. ...the Swiss governess in charge of the smaller children.* **7** VERB If you **charge** towards someone or something, you move quickly and aggressively towards them. *He charged through the door to my mother's office.* **8** VERB To **charge** a battery means to pass an electrical current through it to make it more powerful or to make it last longer.

charisma /kəˈrɪzmə/. N-UNCOUNT If someone has **charisma**, they can attract, influence, and inspire people by their personal qualities.

♦ **charismatic** /ˌkærɪzˈmætɪk/ ADJ *...a charismatic politician.*

charitable /ˈtʃærɪtəbəl/. **1** ADJ Someone who is **charitable** is kind and tolerant. **2** ADJ BEFORE N A **charitable** organization or activity helps and supports people who are ill, disabled, or poor.

⭐ **charity** /ˈtʃærɪti/ **charities.** **1** N-COUNT A **charity** is an organization which raises money to help people who are ill, disabled, or poor. **2** N-UNCOUNT People who live on **charity** live on money or goods which are given to them because they are poor. *She wouldn't accept charity.* **3** N-UNCOUNT **Charity** is kindness and tolerance towards other people. *...acts of charity.*

charm /tʃɑːm/ **charms, charming, charmed.** **1** N-VAR **Charm** is the quality of being attractive and pleasant. *The 1937 Disney classic has lost none of its original charm.* **2** VERB If you **charm** someone, you please them by using your charm. *He charmed all of us.* **3** N-COUNT A **charm** is an action, saying, or object that is believed to have magic powers. *...a good luck charm.*

charming /ˈtʃɑːmɪŋ/. ADJ If someone or something is **charming**, they are very pleasant and attractive. *What a charming man! ...a charming little village.* ♦ **charmingly** ADV *Moira smiled charmingly.*

charred /tʃɑːd/. ADJ Something that is **charred** is black as a result of being badly burnt. *...charred wreckage.*

⭐ **chart** /tʃɑːt/ **charts, charting, charted.** **1** N-COUNT A **chart** is a diagram or graph which displays information. *Consult the chart on page 44 for the correct cooking times.* **2** N-COUNT A **chart** is a map of the sea or stars. **3** VERB If you **chart** the development or progress of something, you observe and record it carefully. *The book charts the history of four generations of the family.* **4** N-PLURAL **The charts** are the official lists that show which pop records have sold the most copies each week.

⭐ **charter** /ˈtʃɑːtə/ **charters, chartering, chartered.** **1** N-COUNT A **charter** is a formal document describing the rights, aims, or principles of an organization. *...the United Nations Charter.* **2** ADJ BEFORE N A **charter** plane or boat is hired for use by a particular person or group. *...charter flights to Spain.* **3** VERB If someone **charters** a plane or boat, they hire it for their own use. *He chartered a jet to fly her home.*

chartered /ˈtʃɑːtəd/. ADJ BEFORE N **Chartered** is used to show that someone such as an accountant or surveyor has formally qualified in their profession. [BRITISH]

⭐ **chase** /tʃeɪs/ **chases, chasing, chased.** **1** VERB & N-COUNT If you **chase** someone, you run after them or follow them in order to catch them or force them to leave a place. A **chase** is an act of chasing someone. *She chased the thief for 100 yards... Many farmers will then chase you off their land... He was reluctant to give up the chase.* **2** VERB If you **are chasing** something you want, such as work or money, you are trying hard to get it. *14 people are chasing every job. ...booksellers chasing after profits.*

chasm /ˈkæzəm/ **chasms.** ⒈ N-COUNT A **chasm** is a very deep crack in rock or ice. ⒉ N-COUNT If there is a **chasm** between two things or between two groups, there is a very large difference between them. *...the chasm that divides the worlds of university and industry.*

⭐ **chat** /tʃæt/ **chats, chatting, chatted.** VERB & N-COUNT When people **chat**, or when they have a **chat**, they talk in an informal and friendly way. *I was chatting to him the other day... We chatted about old times... I had a chat with John.*
▸**chat up.** PHR-VERB If you **chat** someone **up**, you talk to them in a friendly way because you are sexually attracted to them. [BRITISH, INFORMAL] *He'd spent most of that evening chatting up one of my friends.*

château (or **chateau**) /ˈʃætəʊ/ **châteaux** /ˈʃætəʊz/. N-COUNT A **château** is a large country house in France.

chatline /ˈtʃætlaɪn/ **chatlines.** N-COUNT People phone in to **chatlines** to have conversations with other people who have also phoned in.

'chat room, chat rooms. N-COUNT A **chat room** is a site on the Internet where people can exchange messages about a particular subject. [COMPUTING]

'chat show, chat shows. N-COUNT In British English, a **chat show** is a television or radio show in which an interviewer and his or her guests talk in a friendly informal way about different topics. The usual American expression is **talk show**.

chatter /ˈtʃætə/ **chatters, chattering, chattered.** ⒈ VERB & N-COUNT If you **chatter**, you talk quickly and continuously about unimportant things. **Chatter** is this kind of talk. *...chattering away in different languages... Erica was friendly and chattered about Andrew's children. ...idle chatter.* ⒉ VERB If your teeth **chatter**, they rattle together because you are cold.

chauffeur /ˈʃəʊfə, ʃəʊˈfɜː/ **chauffeurs, chauffeuring, chauffeured.** ⒈ N-COUNT A **chauffeur** is a person whose job is to drive and look after another person's car. ⒉ VERB If you **chauffeur** someone somewhere, you drive them there in a car, usually as part of your job. *It was certainly useful to have her there to chauffeur him around.*

chauvinism /ˈʃəʊvɪnɪzəm/. ⒈ N-UNCOUNT If you accuse a man of **chauvinism**, you are criticizing him because he believes that men are naturally better and more important than women. ♦ **chauvinist, chauvinists** N-COUNT *...the male chauvinist pig who wants women in the home.* ⒉ N-UNCOUNT **Chauvinism** is a strong and unreasonable belief that your own country is better and more important than other people's. ♦ **chauvinist** N-COUNT *...the emergence of extreme nationalist and chauvinist forces.*

⭐ **cheap** /tʃiːp/ **cheaper, cheapest.** ⒈ ADJ **Cheap** goods or services cost less money than usual or

than you expected. *Tickets are still unbelievably cheap.* ♦ **cheaply** ADV *...to help you to plan your holiday more cheaply.* ⒉ ADJ BEFORE N **Cheap** goods cost less money than similar products but their quality is poor. *...some cheap material. ...cheap clothes shops.* ⒊ ADJ BEFORE N **Cheap** remarks are unkind and unnecessary. *...accusing him of making cheap remarks.*

cheat /tʃiːt/ **cheats, cheating, cheated.** ⒈ VERB & N-COUNT If someone **cheats**, or if they are a **cheat**, they do not obey a set of rules which they should be obeying, for example in a game or exam. *Students may be tempted to cheat... His wife knew him to be a cheat and a liar.* ♦ **cheating** N-UNCOUNT *He was accused of cheating.* ⒉ VERB If someone **cheats** you **out of** something, they get it from you by behaving dishonestly. *...a deliberate effort to cheat them out of their pensions.* ⒊ PHRASE If you **feel cheated**, you feel that you have been let down or treated unfairly. *They may feel cheated when the actual holiday doesn't match their fantasies.*
▸**cheat on.** PHR-VERB If someone **cheats on** their husband, wife, or partner, they have a sexual relationship with another person. [INFORMAL]

⭐ **check** /tʃek/ **checks, checking, checked.** ⒈ VERB & N-COUNT If you **check** something, or if you make a **check on** it, you make sure that it is satisfactory, safe, or correct. *I think there is an age limit, but I'd have to check... She hadn't checked whether she had a clean ironed shirt... Stephen checked on her several times during the night. ...regular checks on his blood pressure.* ⒉ VERB To **check** something, usually something bad, means to stop it from continuing or spreading. *Sex education is also expected to help check the spread of AIDS.* ⒊ PHRASE If something or someone **is held** or **kept in check**, they are prevented from becoming too great or powerful. *Life on Earth will become unsustainable unless population growth is held in check.* ⒋ N-SING In American English, **the check** in a restaurant is a piece of paper on which the price of the meal you have just eaten is written and which you are given before you pay. The British word is **bill.** ⒌ N-COUNT A pattern of squares, usually of two colours, can be referred to as **checks** or a **check.** *...check trousers.* → See picture on page 829. ⒍ See also **cheque.**
▸**check in** or **check into.** ⒈ PHR-VERB When you **check into** a hotel or clinic, or when you **check in**, you arrive and go through the necessary procedures before staying there. *I'll tell them we'll check in tomorrow... He has checked into an alcohol treatment centre.* ⒉ PHR-VERB When you **check in** at an airport, you arrive and show your ticket before going on a flight. ♦ **check-in, check-ins.** N-COUNT *Ask at the check-in if families can board early.*
▸**check out.** ⒈ PHR-VERB When you **check out of** a hotel, you pay the bill and leave. ⒉ PHR-VERB If you **check** someone or something **out**, you find out about them. *The police had to check out the call.* ⒊ See also **checkout.**

►**check up.** PHR-VERB If you **check up on** someone or something, you find out information about them.

checked /tʃekt/. ADJ Something that is **checked** has a pattern of small squares, usually of two colours. ...*a checked shirt.*

checkout /'tʃekaʊt/ **checkouts.** N-COUNT In a supermarket, a **checkout** is a counter where you pay for your goods.

checkpoint /'tʃekpɔɪnt/ **checkpoints.** N-COUNT A **checkpoint** is a place where traffic has to stop and be checked.

'**check-up, check-ups.** N-COUNT A **check-up** is a routine examination by a doctor or dentist.

cheek /tʃiːk/ **cheeks.** [1] N-COUNT Your **cheeks** are the sides of your face below your eyes. → See picture on page 823. [2] N-SING You say that someone has a **cheek** when you are annoyed at something unacceptable they have done. [INFORMAL] *I'm amazed they had the cheek to ask.*

cheekbone /'tʃiːkbəʊn/ **cheekbones.** N-COUNT Your **cheekbones** are the two bones in your face just below your eyes.

cheeky /'tʃiːki/ **cheekier, cheekiest.** ADJ Someone who is **cheeky** is rude to someone they ought to respect, but often in a charming or amusing way. *The boy was cheeky and casual.* ...*a cheeky grin.*

⭐ **cheer** /tʃɪə/ **cheers, cheering, cheered.** [1] VERB & N-COUNT When people **cheer**, they shout loudly to show approval or encouragement. *Swiss fans cheered Jakob Hlasek during yesterday's match.* ...*a resounding cheer.* [2] VERB If you **are cheered** by something, it makes you feel happier. *He has been cheered by the hundreds of letters of support.* [3] CONVENTION People say '**Cheers**' just before they drink an alcoholic drink.

►**cheer on.** PHR-VERB If you **cheer** someone **on**, you shout loudly in order to encourage them. *500,000 spectators lined the course to cheer on the runners.*

►**cheer up.** PHR-VERB When you **cheer up**, you stop feeling depressed and become more cheerful. *I wrote that song just to cheer myself up... Cheer up, better times may be ahead.*

cheerful /'tʃɪəfʊl/. [1] ADJ A **cheerful** person is happy. *They are both very cheerful in spite of their colds.* ♦ **cheerfully** ADV *'We've come with good news,' Pat said cheerfully.* ♦ **cheerfulness** N-UNCOUNT ...*his unfailing cheerfulness.* [2] ADJ **Cheerful** things are pleasant and make you feel happy. *The nursery is bright and cheerful.*

cheery /'tʃɪəri/. ADJ **Cheery** means cheerful and happy. ♦ **cheerily** ADV *'Come on in,' she said cheerily.*

⭐ **cheese** /tʃiːz/ **cheeses.** N-VAR **Cheese** is a solid food made from milk.

chef /ʃef/ **chefs.** N-COUNT A **chef** is a cook in a restaurant or hotel.

⭐ **chemical** /'kemɪkəl/ **chemicals.** [1] ADJ BEFORE N **Chemical** means involving or resulting from a reaction between two or more substances, or

relating to the substances that something consists of. ...*chemical reactions.* ...*the chemical composition of the ocean.* ♦ **chemically** ADV ...*chemically treated foods.* [2] N-COUNT **Chemicals** are substances that are used in or made by a chemical process.

chemist /'kemɪst/ **chemists.** [1] N-COUNT In Britain, a **chemist** or a **chemist's** is a shop where medicines are sold or given out. You can also refer to the specially qualified person who prepares and sells the medicines in this shop as a **chemist**.

USAGE In British English, the usual way of referrring to a shop where medicines are sold or given out is **chemist** or **chemist's**. *She went into a chemist's and bought some aspirin.* **Pharmacy** is also used, but is not as common. In American English, the word **drugstore** is used, but this usually refers to a shop where you can buy drinks, snacks, and other items, as well as medicines. *At the drugstore I bought a Coke and the local papers.*

---

[2] N-COUNT A **chemist** is a person who studies chemistry.

chemistry /'kemɪstri/. N-UNCOUNT **Chemistry** is the scientific study of the characteristics and composition of substances.

cheque (AM **check**) /tʃek/ **cheques.** N-COUNT A **cheque** is a printed form on which you write an amount of money and say who it is to be paid to. Your bank then pays the money to that person from your account. *He wrote them a cheque for £10,000... I'd like to pay by cheque.*

cherish /'tʃerɪʃ/ **cherishes, cherishing, cherished.** [1] VERB If you **cherish** something such as a hope or a pleasant memory, you keep it in your mind for a long period of time. *The president will cherish the memory of this visit to Ohio.* ♦ **cherished** ADJ ...*the cherished dream of a world without wars.* [2] VERB If you **cherish** someone or something, you take good care of them because you love them. ♦ **cherished** ADJ BEFORE N ...*his most cherished possession.* [3] VERB If you **cherish** a right or a privilege, you regard it as important and try hard to keep it. *They cherish their independence.* ♦ **cherished** ADJ BEFORE N ...*some deeply cherished beliefs.*

cherry /'tʃeri/ **cherries.** [1] N-COUNT **Cherries** are small, round fruit with red or black skins. → See picture on page 821. [2] N-COUNT A **cherry** or a **cherry tree** is a tree that cherries grow on.

chess /tʃes/. N-UNCOUNT **Chess** is a game for two people played on a board with 64 black and white squares. Each player has 16 pieces including a King. The aim is to trap your opponent's King.

⭐ **chest** /tʃest/ **chests.** [1] N-COUNT Your **chest** is the top part of the front of your body. → See picture on page 822. *He was shot in the chest. ...mild chest pain.* [2] N-COUNT A **chest** is a large heavy box, used for storing things.

chestnut /'tʃesnʌt/ **chestnuts.** [1] N-COUNT A **chestnut** or **chestnut tree** is a tall tree with broad leaves. [2] N-COUNT The nuts that grow on chestnut trees are called **chestnuts.** [3] ADJ & N-VAR Something that is **chestnut** is dark reddish-brown. *...a woman with chestnut hair.*

chew /tʃuː/ **chews, chewing, chewed.** VERB When you **chew** food, you break it up with your teeth and make it easier to swallow. *He chewed on his toast... Polly took a bite, chewed and swallowed.*

chic /ʃiːk/. ADJ Something or someone that is **chic** is fashionable and sophisticated. *...very chic bars and restaurants.*

chick /tʃɪk/ **chicks.** N-COUNT A **chick** is a baby bird. → See picture on page 815.

★ **chicken** /'tʃɪkɪn/ **chickens, chickening, chickened.** [1] N-COUNT **Chickens** are birds which are kept on a farm for their eggs and their meat. [2] N-UNCOUNT **Chicken** is the meat of a chicken eaten for food.
▸ **chicken out.** PHR-VERB If someone **chickens out** of something, they do not do it because they are afraid. [INFORMAL] *I chickened out of producing the album myself.*

ꞌ**chick flick, chick flicks.** N-COUNT A **chick flick** is a romantic film that is not very serious and is intended to appeal to women.

chide /tʃaɪd/ **chides, chiding, chided.** VERB If you **chide** someone, you scold them. [DATED] *Cross chided himself for worrying.*

★ **chief** /tʃiːf/ **chiefs.** [1] N-COUNT The **chief** of an organization or department is its leader or the person in charge of it. *...the chief test pilot. ...the police chief.* [2] ADJ BEFORE N The **chief** cause, part, or member of something is the most important one. *The job went to one of his chief rivals.*

chiefly /'tʃiːfli/. ADV You use **chiefly** to indicate that a particular reason, emotion, method, or feature is the main or most important one. *The museum is hoped to be self-financing, chiefly through education... He painted chiefly portraits.*

chiffon /'ʃɪfɒn, AM ʃɪ'fɑːn/. N-UNCOUNT **Chiffon** is a kind of very thin silk or nylon cloth.

★ **child** /tʃaɪld/ **children.** [1] N-COUNT A **child** is a human being who is not yet an adult. *...when I was a child... It was only suitable for children.* [2] N-PLURAL Someone's **children** are their sons and daughters. *His children have left home.*

childbirth /'tʃaɪldbɜːθ/. N-UNCOUNT **Childbirth** is the act of giving birth to a child. *She died in childbirth.*

★ **childhood** /'tʃaɪldhʊd/ **childhoods.** N-VAR A person's **childhood** is the time when they are a child. *She had a happy childhood.*

childish /'tʃaɪldɪʃ/. [1] ADJ **Childish** means relating to or typical of a child. *...childish enthusiasm.* [2] ADJ If you describe someone, especially an adult, as **childish**, you mean their behaviour is silly and more like that of a child

than an adult. *...very childish behaviour.*
♦ **childishly** ADV *Such remarks were childishly simplistic.*

childless /'tʃaɪldləs/. ADJ Someone who is **childless** has no children.

childlike /'tʃaɪldlaɪk/. ADJ You describe someone as **childlike** when they seem like a child in their appearance or behaviour.

children /'tʃɪldrən/. **Children** is the plural of **child.**

chili /'tʃɪli/. See **chilli.**

chill /tʃɪl/ **chills, chilling, chilled.** [1] VERB To **chill** something means to make it cold. *Chill the cheesecake for two hours before serving... The wind chilled our wet bodies to the bone. ...a glass of chilled champagne.* [2] VERB & N-COUNT If something that you see, hear, or feel **chills** you, it frightens you. If something sends a **chill** through you, it gives you a sudden feeling of fear or anxiety. [WRITTEN] *Some films chill you to the marrow of your bones. ...a chill of fear.* ♦ **chilling** ADJ *...a chilling reminder of the destruction.* [3] N-COUNT A **chill** is a mild illness which can give you a slight fever.
▸ **chill out.** PHR-VERB If you **chill out**, you relax after doing something tiring or stressful. [INFORMAL] *...music to chill out to.*

chilli (or **chili**) /'tʃɪli/ **chillies.** N-COUNT **Chillies** are small red or green seed pods with a hot, spicy taste.

chilly /'tʃɪli/. [1] ADJ **Chilly** means uncomfortably cold. *It was a chilly afternoon... The house itself felt chilly.* [2] ADJ You say that relations between people are **chilly** or that a person's response is **chilly** when they are not at all friendly or enthusiastic. *The students received a very chilly welcome.*

chime /tʃaɪm/ **chimes, chiming, chimed.** [1] VERB When a bell or clock **chimes**, it makes ringing sounds. *The clock chimed three o'clock.* [2] N-COUNT A **chime** is a ringing sound made by a bell, especially when it is part of a clock.
▸ **chime in.** PHR-VERB If someone **chimes in**, they say something just after someone else has spoken. *'Why?' Pete asked impatiently.—'Yes, why?' Bob chimed in.*

chimney /'tʃɪmni/ **chimneys.** N-COUNT A **chimney** is a pipe above a fireplace or furnace through which smoke can go up into the air.

chimpanzee /ˌtʃɪmpæn'ziː/ **chimpanzees.** N-COUNT A **chimpanzee** is a kind of small African ape. → See picture on page 816.

chin /tʃɪn/ **chins.** N-COUNT Your **chin** is the part of your face below your mouth and above your neck. → See picture on page 823.

china /'tʃaɪnə/. [1] N-UNCOUNT **China** or **china clay** is a very thin clay used to make cups, plates, and ornaments. [2] N-UNCOUNT Cups, plates, and ornaments made of china are referred to as **china.** *Judy collects blue and white china.*

chink /tʃɪŋk/ **chinks, chinking, chinked.** [1] N-COUNT A **chink** is a very narrow opening. *...a chink in the*

a b c d e f g h i j k l m n o p q r s t u v w x y z

curtains. [2] VERB When objects **chink**, they touch each other, making a light ringing sound.

⭐ **chip** /tʃɪp/ **chips, chipping, chipped.** [1] N-COUNT In British English, **chips** are long thin pieces of fried potato eaten hot. The American expression is **French fries.** [2] N-COUNT In American English, **chips** or **potato chips** are very thin slices of potato that have been fried until they are hard and crunchy and that are eaten cold as a snack. The British word is **crisps.** [3] N-COUNT A silicon **chip** is a very small piece of silicon with electronic circuits on it. [4] VERB If you **chip** something, a small piece is broken off it. *A singer chipped a tooth on his microphone... Steel baths are lighter but chip easily.* ♦ **chipped** ADJ *...a chipped tooth.* → See picture on page 154. [5] N-COUNT A **chip** is a small piece of something, especially a piece which has been broken off something. *...chocolate chips. ...wood chips.* [6] PHRASE If you say that someone has **a chip on** their **shoulder**, you mean they behave aggressively, because they believe they have been treated unfairly. [INFORMAL]

▶**chip in.** PHR-VERB When a number of people **chip in**, each person gives some money so that they can pay for something together. [INFORMAL] *The brothers chip in money each month.*

chisel /'tʃɪzəl/ **chisels, chiselling, chiselled,** (AM **chiseling, chiseled**). [1] N-COUNT A **chisel** is a tool that has a long metal blade with a sharp edge at the end. It is used for cutting and shaping wood and stone. → See picture on page 833. [2] VERB If you **chisel** wood or stone, you cut and shape it using a chisel. *They chisel the stone to size.*

chlorine /'klɔːriːn/. N-UNCOUNT **Chlorine** is a gas that is used to disinfect water and to make cleaning products.

⭐ **chocolate** /'tʃɒklɪt, AM 'tʃɔːk-/ **chocolates.** [1] N-VAR **Chocolate** is a sweet food made from cocoa beans. [2] N-COUNT **Chocolates** are small sweets or nuts covered with a layer of chocolate. [3] N-UNCOUNT **Chocolate** or **hot chocolate** is a hot drink made from a powder containing chocolate.

⭐ **choice** /tʃɔɪs/ **choices; choicer, choicest.** [1] N-COUNT If there is a **choice** of things, there are several of them and you can choose the one you want. *It's available in a choice of colours... At lunchtime, there's a choice between the buffet or the set menu.* [2] N-COUNT Your **choice** is the thing or things that you choose. *His choice of words made Rodney angry. ...tickets to see the football team of your choice.* [3] PHRASE If you **have no choice but to** do something, or **have little choice but to** do it, you cannot avoid doing it. [4] N-COUNT The item **of choice** is the one that most people prefer. *The drink of choice seems to be vodka.* [5] ADJ BEFORE N **Choice** means of very high quality. [FORMAL] *...his choicest cuts of meat.*

choir /kwaɪə/ **choirs.** N-COUNT A **choir** is a group of people who sing together.

choke /tʃəʊk/ **chokes, choking, choked.** [1] VERB If you **choke on** something, it prevents you from breathing properly. *A small child could choke on the doll's hair... The girl choked to death after breathing in smoke... The parachute tangled round his body, almost choking him.* [2] VERB To **choke** someone means to squeeze their neck until they are dead. [3] VERB If a place **is choked with** things or people, it is full of them and they prevent movement in it. *The village's roads are choked with traffic... The gutters were choked by fallen leaves.* [4] N-COUNT A vehicle's **choke** is a device that reduces the amount of air going into the engine and makes it easier to start.

cholera /'kɒlərə/. N-UNCOUNT **Cholera** is a serious disease that affects your digestive organs.

cholesterol /kə'lestərɒl, AM -rɔːl/. N-UNCOUNT **Cholesterol** is a substance that exists in the fat, tissues, and blood of all animals. Too much cholesterol in the blood can cause heart disease.

⭐ **choose** /tʃuːz/ **chooses, choosing, chose, chosen.** [1] VERB If you **choose** someone or something from all the people or things that are available, you decide to have that person or thing. *They will be able to choose their own leaders... She chose a chair slightly behind her husband's.* [2] VERB If you **choose to** do something, you do it because you want to or because you feel that it is right. *The NRDC chose to inform the public about the risks.*

⭐ **chop** /tʃɒp/ **chops, chopping, chopped.** [1] VERB If you **chop** something, you cut it into pieces with a knife or axe. *Finely chop the onion.* [2] N-COUNT A **chop** is a small piece of meat cut from the ribs of a sheep or pig. *...lamb chops.*

▶**chop down.** PHR-VERB If you **chop down** a tree, you cut through its trunk with an axe so that it falls to the ground.

▶**chop off.** PHR-VERB To **chop off** something such as a part of someone's body means to cut it off. *They both chopped off their hair.*

▶**chop up.** PHR-VERB If you **chop** something **up**, you chop it into small pieces. *Chop up three firm tomatoes.*

chopper /'tʃɒpə/ **choppers.** N-COUNT A **chopper** is a helicopter. [INFORMAL]

choral /'kɔːrəl/. ADJ **Choral** music is sung by a choir.

chord /kɔːd/ **chords.** N-COUNT A **chord** is a number of musical notes played or sung together with a pleasing effect. *...the opening chords of 'Stairway to Heaven'.*

chore /tʃɔː/ **chores.** N-COUNT A **chore** is an unpleasant task. *Making pasta by hand with a rolling pin can be a real chore. ...household chores.*

choreograph /'kɒriəgrɑːf, AM 'kɔːriəgræf/ **choreographs, choreographing, choreographed.** VERB When someone **choreographs** a ballet or other dance, they invent the steps and movements and tell the dancers how to perform them. *...one of the first dance pieces to be choreographed by Morris.* ♦ **choreographer** /ˌkɒri'ɒgrəfə, AM ˌkɔː-/ **choreographers.** N-COUNT *...dancer and choreographer Rudolph Nureyev.*

choreography /ˌkɒriˈɒɡrəfi/, AM ˌkɔː-/. N-UNCOUNT **Choreography** is the inventing of steps and movements for ballets and other dances. ♦ **choreographic** /ˌkɒriəˈɡræfɪk/, AM ˌkɔː-/ ADJ ...*his choreographic work for The Birmingham Royal Ballet.*

chorus /ˈkɔːrəs/ **choruses, chorusing, chorused.** [1] N-COUNT A **chorus** is a large group of people who sing together. [2] N-COUNT The **chorus** of a song is the part which is repeated after each verse. [3] N-SING When there is a **chorus** of criticism, disapproval, or praise, that attitude is expressed by a lot of people at the same time. ...*the growing chorus of complaint.* [4] VERB When people **chorus** something, they say or sing it together. '*Hi,' they chorused.*

chose /tʃəʊz/. **Chose** is the past tense of **choose**.

chosen /ˈtʃəʊzən/. **Chosen** is the past participle of **choose**.

christen /ˈkrɪsən/ **christens, christening, christened.** [1] VERB When a baby **is christened**, he or she is given Christian names during a christening. *She was christened Susan.* [2] VERB You say that you **christen** a person, place, or object if you choose a name for them and start calling them by that name. ...*his car, which he had christened Lola.*

christening /ˈkrɪsənɪŋ/ **christenings.** N-COUNT A **christening** is a ceremony in which a baby is made a member of the Christian church and is given his or her Christian names.

⭐ **Christian** /ˈkrɪstʃən/ **Christians.** N-COUNT & ADJ A **Christian** or a **Christian** person follows the teachings of Jesus Christ. ...*the Christian Church.*

Christianity /ˌkrɪstiˈænɪti/. N-UNCOUNT **Christianity** is a religion based on the teachings of Jesus Christ.

'**Christian name, Christian names.** N-COUNT A person's **Christian name** is the name given to them when they were born or christened.

⭐ **Christmas** /ˈkrɪsməs/ **Christmases.** N-VAR **Christmas** is the period around the 25th of December when Christians celebrate the birth of Jesus Christ. *Merry Christmas.* ...*Christmases past.*

ˌChristmas '**Day.** N-UNCOUNT **Christmas Day** is the 25th of December.

ˌChristmas '**Eve.** N-UNCOUNT **Christmas Eve** is the 24th of December.

'**Christmas tree, Christmas trees.** N-COUNT A **Christmas tree** is a real or artificial fir tree, which people put in their houses at Christmas and decorate with lights and balls.

chrome /krəʊm/. N-UNCOUNT **Chrome** is a hard silver-coloured metal, used to coat other metals.

chromium /ˈkrəʊmiəm/. N-UNCOUNT **Chromium** is the same as chrome.

chromosome /ˈkrəʊməsəʊm/ **chromosomes.** N-COUNT A **chromosome** is a part of a cell in an animal or plant. It contains genes which determine what characteristics the animal or plant will have.

chronic /ˈkrɒnɪk/. [1] ADJ A **chronic** illness lasts for a very long time. ...*chronic depression.* ♦ **chronically** ADV *Most of them were chronically ill.* [2] ADJ A **chronic** situation is very severe and unpleasant. ...*chronic housing shortages.* ♦ **chronically** ADV *Counselling services are chronically underfunded.*

chronicle /ˈkrɒnɪkəl/ **chronicles, chronicling, chronicled.** [1] VERB If you **chronicle** a series of events, you describe them in the order in which they happened. *The book chronicles baseball's disgraceful incidents.* [2] N-COUNT A **chronicle** is an account or record of a series of events. ...*this vast chronicle of Napoleonic times.*

chronological /ˌkrɒnəˈlɒdʒɪkəl/. ADJ If things are described or shown in **chronological** order, they are described or shown in the order in which they happened. ...*chronological tables of China's history.* ♦ **chronologically** ADV *The exhibition is organised chronologically.*

chrysanthemum /krɪˈzænθɪməm/ **chrysanthemums.** N-COUNT A **chrysanthemum** is a large garden flower with many long, thin petals.

chubby /ˈtʃʌbi/. ADJ A **chubby** person is rather fat. ● See note at **fat.**

chuck /tʃʌk/ **chucks, chucking, chucked.** VERB When you **chuck** something somewhere, you throw it there in a casual way. [INFORMAL] *He screwed the paper up and chucked it in the bin.*
▸**chuck away** or **chuck out. PHR-VERB** If you **chuck** something **away** or **chuck** it **out**, you throw it away. [INFORMAL]

chuckle /ˈtʃʌkəl/ **chuckles, chuckling, chuckled.** VERB & N-COUNT When you **chuckle**, you laugh quietly. A quiet laugh is called a **chuckle**. *He gave a little chuckle.*

chug /tʃʌɡ/ **chugs, chugging, chugged.** VERB When a vehicle **chugs** somewhere, it goes there slowly with its engine making short thudding sounds. *The train chugs down the track.*

chum /tʃʌm/ **chums.** N-COUNT In British English, your **chums** are your friends. [INFORMAL] ...*his old chum Anthony.*

chunk /tʃʌŋk/ **chunks.** [1] N-COUNT A **chunk** of something is a thick solid piece of it. ...*chunks of ice.* [2] N-COUNT A **chunk of** something is a large amount or part of it. [INFORMAL] ...*a chunk of farmland near Gatwick Airport.*

chunky /ˈtʃʌŋki/. ADJ A **chunky** person or thing is large and heavy. ...*a chunky girl from California.* ...*a chunky sweater.*

⭐ **church** /tʃɜːtʃ/ **churches.** [1] N-VAR A **church** is a building in which Christians worship. *I didn't see you in church on Sunday.* [2] N-COUNT A **Church** is one of the groups of people within the Christian religion that have their own beliefs, clergy, and forms of worship. ...*the Catholic Church.*

churn /tʃɜːn/ **churns, churning, churned.** [1] N-COUNT A **churn** is a container used for making butter. [2] VERB & PHR-VERB If something **churns** mud, water, or dust, or **churns** it **up**, it moves it about violently. *Ferries churn the waters of Howe Sound.*

a
b
c
d
e
f
g
h
i
j
k
l
m
n
o
p
q
r
s
t
u
v
w
x
y
z

...*dust churned up by the passing trucks.* ③ VERB If you say that your stomach **is churning**, you mean that you feel sick. You can also say that something **churns** your stomach. *My stomach churned as I stood up.*
▸ **churn out.** PHR-VERB To **churn** something **out** means to produce large quantities of it very quickly. [INFORMAL] ...*those fantasy novels he churned out in the 1960s.*
▸ **churn up.** See **churn** 2.

chute /ʃuːt/ **chutes.** ① N-COUNT A **chute** is a steep narrow slope down which people or things can slide. ...*a laundry chute.* ② N-COUNT A **chute** is a parachute. [INFORMAL] *The chute failed to open.*

chutney /'tʃʌtni/ **chutneys.** N-VAR **Chutney** is a strong-tasting mixture of fruit, vinegar, sugar, and spices.

cider /'saɪdə/ **ciders.** N-VAR **Cider** is an alcoholic drink made from apples.

cigar /sɪ'gɑː/ **cigars.** N-COUNT **Cigars** are rolls of dried tobacco leaves which people smoke.

⭐ **cigarette** /ˌsɪgə'ret/ **cigarettes.** N-COUNT **Cigarettes** are small tubes of paper containing tobacco which people smoke.

cinder /'sɪndə/ **cinders.** N-COUNT **Cinders** are the pieces of blackened material that are left after wood or coal has burned.

⭐ **cinema** /'sɪnɪmɑː/ **cinemas.** ① N-COUNT In British English, a **cinema** is a place where people go to watch films. The American term is **movie theater** or **movie house.** ② N-UNCOUNT **Cinema** is the business and art of making films. ...*the greatest director in the history of cinema.* ♦ **cinematic** /ˌsɪnɪ'mætɪk/ ADJ ...*the cinematic industry.*

cinnamon /'sɪnəmən/. N-UNCOUNT **Cinnamon** is a spice used for flavouring sweet food.

circa /'sɜːkə/. PREP If you write **circa** in front of a year, you mean that the date is approximate. ...*circa 1850.*

⭐ **circle** /'sɜːkəl/ **circles, circling, circled.** ① N-COUNT A **circle** is a round shape. Every part of its edge is the same distance from the centre. → See picture on page 829. *The flag was red, with a large white circle in the center... Cut out 4 circles of pastry.* ② VERB To **circle** someone or something, or to **circle around** them, means to move around them in a circle. *I circled my living room half a dozen times... Emily kept circling around her mother... A police helicopter circled overhead.* ③ N-COUNT You can refer to a group of people as a **circle**. *He has a small circle of friends... It was common knowledge in financial circles.* ④ N-SING **The circle** in a theatre is an area of seats on the upper floor. ⑤ See also **vicious circle.**

⭐ **circuit** /'sɜːkɪt/ **circuits.** ① N-COUNT An electrical **circuit** is a complete route which an electric current can flow around. ● See also **closed-circuit.** ② N-COUNT A **circuit** is a series of places that are visited regularly by a person or group. ...*the Australian comedy circuit.* ③ N-COUNT A racing **circuit** is a track on which cars, motorbikes, or cycles race. [BRITISH] ④ N-COUNT A

circuit of a place or area is a journey all the way round it. [FORMAL] *She made a slow circuit of the room.*

circular /'sɜːkjʊlə/ **circulars.** ① ADJ Something that is **circular** is shaped like a circle. ...*a circular hole twelve feet wide.* ...*a circular motion.* ...*a long, circular route.* ② N-COUNT A **circular** is a letter or advertisement which is sent to a large number of people at the same time.

circulate /'sɜːkjʊleɪt/ **circulates, circulating, circulated.** ① VERB When something **circulates** or **is circulated**, it is passed round or spread among a group of people. *He has circulated a discussion document, asking for comments... Rumours began to circulate about his health.* ♦ **circulation** N-UNCOUNT ...*the circulation of leaflets aimed at discrediting both men.* ② VERB When something **circulates**, it moves easily and freely within a closed place or system. ...*a virus which circulates via the bloodstream.* ♦ **circulation** N-UNCOUNT ...*free circulation of goods.*

circulation /ˌsɜːkjʊ'leɪʃən/ **circulations.** ① N-COUNT The **circulation** of a newspaper or magazine is the number of copies sold each time it is produced. *The Daily News once had the highest circulation of any daily in the country.* ② N-SING Your **circulation** is the movement of blood around your body. ...*cold spots in the fingers caused by poor circulation.* ③ PHRASE If something such as money is **in circulation**, it is being used by the public. ...*America, with perhaps 180 million guns in circulation.* ④ See also **circulate.**

circumcise /'sɜːkəmsaɪz/ **circumcises, circumcising, circumcised.** VERB If a boy or man **is circumcised**, the loose skin at the end of his penis is cut off. ♦ **circumcision** /ˌsɜːkəm'sɪʒən/ N-UNCOUNT *Jews and Moslems practise circumcision for religious reasons.*

circumference /sə'kʌmfrəns/ **circumferences.** N-COUNT The **circumference** of a circle, place, or round object is the distance around its edge. *The island is 3.5 km in circumference.*

⭐ **circumstance** /'sɜːkəmstæns/ **circumstances.** ① N-COUNT **Circumstances** are the conditions which affect what happens in a particular situation. *60 percent favor abortion under certain circumstances... I wish we could have met under happier circumstances... Everton last night insisted they would not increase their offer under any circumstances.* ② PHRASE You can use **in the circumstances** or **under the circumstances** before or after a statement to indicate that you have considered the conditions affecting the situation before making the statement. *In the circumstances, Paisley's plans looked highly appropriate.* ③ N-PLURAL Your **circumstances** are the conditions of your life, especially the amount of money that you have. ...*help and support for the single mother, whatever her circumstances.*

circus /'sɜːkəs/ **circuses.** N-COUNT A **circus** is a travelling show performed in a large tent, with performers such as clowns and trained animals.

clamber

citation /saɪˈteɪʃən/ **citations.** [1] N-COUNT A **citation** is an official document or speech which praises a person for something brave or special that they have done. [2] N-COUNT A **citation** from a book or piece of writing is a quotation from it. [FORMAL]

⭐ **cite** /saɪt/ **cites, citing, cited.** VERB If you **cite** something, you quote it or mention it, especially as an example or proof of what you are saying. [FORMAL] *She cites a favourite poem by George Herbert... I am merely citing his reaction as typical of British industry.*

⭐ **citizen** /ˈsɪtɪzən/ **citizens.** [1] N-COUNT If someone is a **citizen** of a country, they are legally accepted as belonging to that country. *...American citizens living in Canada.* [2] N-COUNT The **citizens of** a town are the people who live there. *...the citizens of Buenos Aires.* [3] See also **senior citizen**.

citizenship /ˈsɪtɪzənʃɪp/. N-UNCOUNT If you have **citizenship** of a country, you are legally accepted as belonging to it.

citrus /ˈsɪtrəs/. ADJ BEFORE N A **citrus** fruit is a sharp-tasting fruit such as an orange, lemon, or grapefruit.

⭐ **city** /ˈsɪti/ **cities.** [1] N-COUNT A **city** is a large town. *...a busy city centre.* [2] N-PROPER **The City** is the part of London where many financial institutions have their main offices. *The City fears that profits could fall.*

civic /ˈsɪvɪk/. ADJ BEFORE N **Civic** means having an official status in a town. *...the businessmen and civic leaders of Manchester.*

⭐ **civil** /ˈsɪvəl/. [1] ADJ You use **civil** to describe things that relate to the people of a country, and their rights and activities, often in contrast with the armed forces. *...civil unrest. ...the US civil aviation industry. ...civil and political rights.* [2] ADJ A **civil** person is polite in a formal way, but not particularly friendly. [FORMAL] ♦ **civility** /sɪˈvɪlɪti/ **civilities** N-VAR *She treats the press with civility.*

⭐ **civilian** /sɪˈvɪliən/ **civilians.** N-COUNT A **civilian** is anyone who is not a member of the armed forces. *...the country's civilian population.*

civilization (BRIT also **civilisation**) /ˌsɪvɪlaɪˈzeɪʃən/ **civilizations.** [1] N-VAR A **civilization** is a human society with its own social organization and culture. *...the ancient civilizations of Central and Latin America.* [2] N-UNCOUNT **Civilization** is the state of having an advanced level of social organization and a comfortable way of life. *...our advanced state of civilisation.*

civilized (BRIT also **civilised**) /ˈsɪvɪlaɪzd/. [1] ADJ A **civilized** society has an advanced level of social organization. *I believed that in civilized countries, torture had ended long ago.* [2] ADJ If you describe a person or their behaviour as **civilized**, you mean that they are polite and reasonable.

⭐ **civil 'rights.** N-PLURAL **Civil rights** are the rights that people have to equal treatment and equal opportunities, whatever their race, sex, or religion.

civil 'servant, civil servants. N-COUNT A **civil servant** is a person who works in the Civil Service.

Civil 'Service. N-SING **The Civil Service** of a country consists of the government departments and the people who work in them.

⭐ **civil 'war, civil wars.** N-COUNT A **civil war** is a war which is fought between different groups of people living in the same country.

CJD /ˌsiː dʒeɪ ˈdiː/. N-UNCOUNT **CJD** is an incurable brain disease that affects human beings and is believed to be caused by eating beef from cows with BSE. **CJD** is an abbreviation of 'Creutzfeld Jacob disease'.

clad /klæd/. ADJ AFTER LINK-V If you are **clad in** particular clothes, you are wearing them. [LITERARY] *...the figure of a woman, clad in black.*

⭐ **claim** /kleɪm/ **claims, claiming, claimed.** [1] VERB & N-COUNT If someone **claims** that something is true, or if they make a **claim** that it is true, they say that it is true but they have not proved it and it may be false. *...a man claiming to be a journalist... He claims a 70 to 80 per cent success rate... He repeated his claim that the people of Trinidad and Tobago backed his action.* [2] VERB If someone **claims** responsibility, or **claims** the credit for something, they say that they are responsible for it. *He was too modest to claim the credit.* [3] VERB & N-COUNT If you **claim** something such as money, property, or land, or if you make a **claim for** it, you ask for it because you have a right to it. *Now they are returning to claim what was theirs. ...the office which has been dealing with their claim for benefit.* [4] VERB If a fight or disaster **claims** someone's life, they are killed in it. [WRITTEN] *Heart disease is the biggest killer, claiming 180,000 lives a year.* [5] N-COUNT If you have a **claim on** someone or their attention, you have a right to demand things from them or to demand their attention. *He was surrounded by people, all with claims on his attention.*

PHRASES ● Someone's **claim to fame** is something quite important or interesting that they have done or that is connected with them. *His claim to fame is that he climbed Mount Everest.* ● If you **lay claim to** something, you say that it is yours. [FORMAL] ● If you **stake** your **claim**, you show or say that you have a right to be something or to have something. *Jane is determined to stake her claim as an actress.*

claimant /ˈkleɪmənt/ **claimants.** N-COUNT A **claimant** is someone who has applied for something such as compensation, an insurance payment, or unemployment benefit which they think they are entitled to.

clam /klæm/ **clams.** N-COUNT A **clam** is a kind of shellfish.

clamber /ˈklæmbə/ **clambers, clambering, clambered.** VERB If you **clamber** somewhere, you climb there with difficulty. *They clambered up the stone walls.*

a
b
c
d
e
f
g
h
i
j
k
l
m
n
o
p
q
r
s
t
u
v
w
x
y
z

clamour (AM **clamor**) /'klæmə/ **clamours, clamouring, clamoured.** [1] VERB & N-UNCOUNT If people **are clamouring for** something, or if there is a **clamour for** it, people are demanding it noisily or angrily. [JOURNALISM] ...*competing parties clamouring for the attention of the voter.* ...*the clamour for his resignation.* [2] N-SING **Clamour** is used to describe the loud noise of a large group of people talking or shouting together. *She could hear a clamour in the road outside.*

clamp /klæmp/ **clamps, clamping, clamped.** [1] N-COUNT A **clamp** is a device that holds two things firmly together. [2] VERB When you **clamp** one thing **to** another, you fasten them together with a clamp. *Clamp the microphones to the pole.* [3] VERB To **clamp** something in a particular place means to put it there firmly and tightly. *He clamped his lips together.*

▶**clamp down.** PHR-VERB To **clamp down on** something means to stop it or control it. [JOURNALISM] *The authorities are now determined to clamp down on the media.*

clan /klæn/ **clans.** N-COUNT A **clan** is a group of families related to each other.

clandestine /klæn'destɪn/. ADJ Something that is **clandestine** is hidden or secret, and often illegal. [FORMAL] ...*their clandestine meetings.*

clap /klæp/ **claps, clapping, clapped.** [1] VERB & N-SING When you **clap**, you hit your hands together to express appreciation or attract attention. This action is called a **clap**. *Midge clapped her hands, calling them back to order... As long as the crowd give them a clap, they're quite happy.* [2] VERB If you **clap** an object or your hand onto something, you put it there quickly and firmly. *I clapped a hand over her mouth.* [3] N-COUNT A **clap of thunder** is a sudden and loud noise of thunder.

claret /'klærət/ **clarets.** N-VAR **Claret** is a type of red French wine.

clarify /'klærɪfaɪ/ **clarifies, clarifying, clarified.** VERB To **clarify** something means to make it easier to understand. *A bank spokesman was unable to clarify the situation.* ♦ **clarification** /ˌklærɪfɪ'keɪʃən/ N-UNCOUNT *The union has written to Zurich asking for clarification of the situation.*

clarinet /ˌklærɪ'net/ **clarinets.** N-COUNT A **clarinet** is a wind instrument with a single reed in its mouthpiece. → See picture on page 828.

clarity /'klærɪti/. N-UNCOUNT **Clarity** is the quality of being clear and easy to understand. ...*a fascinating book, written with clarity.*

★ **clash** /klæʃ/ **clashes, clashing, clashed.** [1] VERB & N-COUNT When people **clash**, or when they are involved in a **clash**, they disagree, argue, or fight with each other. ...*the two countries clashed over human rights.* ...*clashes between police in riot gear and demonstrators.* [2] VERB & N-COUNT Beliefs, ideas, or qualities that **clash** are very different from each other and are therefore opposed. You can also talk about a **clash** of these things. ...*policy decisions which clash with official company thinking.* ...*a clash of views.* [3] VERB If

one event **clashes with** another, they happen at the same time and so you cannot go to both of them. *His wedding clashed with a fixture... We'll go to both of them if the times don't clash.*

clasp /klɑːsp, klæsp/ **clasps, clasping, clasped.** [1] VERB & N-COUNT If you **clasp** someone or something, you hold them tightly. A **clasp** is an act of clasping someone or something. *She clasped the children to her... With one last clasp of his hand, she left him.* [2] N-COUNT A **clasp** is a small metal fastening.

★ **class** /klɑːs, klæs/ **classes, classing, classed.** [1] N-COUNT A **class** is a group of pupils or students who are taught together. [2] N-COUNT A **class** is a course of teaching in a particular subject. *He acquired a law degree by taking classes at night.* [3] N-UNCOUNT If you do something **in class**, you do it during a lesson in school. *There is lots of reading in class.* [4] N-VAR **Class** is used to refer to the division of people in a society according to their social status. ...*the British class structure.* ...*the relationship between social classes.* [5] N-COUNT A **class of** things is a group of them with similar characteristics. ...*the largest class of racing sailboats in the world.* [6] N-UNCOUNT If you say that someone has **class**, you mean that they are elegant and sophisticated. [7] VERB If someone or something **is classed as** a particular thing, they are considered as belonging to that group of things. *I would like to know why this film is classed as political.* [8] PHRASE If you say that someone is **in a class of** their **own**, you mean that they have more of a particular skill or quality than anyone else. [9] See also **middle class, upper class, working class.**

★ **classic** /'klæsɪk/ **classics.** [1] ADJ A **classic** example of something has all the features which you expect that kind of thing to have. *His first two goals were classic cases of being in the right place at the right time.* ♦ **classically** ADV *He's not classically handsome.* [2] ADJ BEFORE N & N-COUNT A **classic** piece of writing or film, or a **classic**, is a piece of writing or film of high quality that has become a standard against which similar things are judged. ...*a classic study of the American penal system.* ...*a film classic.* [3] N-UNCOUNT **Classics** is the study of ancient Greek and Roman civilizations, especially their languages, literature, and philosophy.

★ **classical** /'klæsɪkəl/. [1] ADJ You use **classical** to describe something that is traditional in form, style, or content. ...*classical, rock and jazz music.* ♦ **classically** ADV ...*classically trained dancers.* [2] ADJ **Classical** is used to describe things relating to ancient Greek or Roman civilization. ...*ancient Egypt and classical Greece.*

classified /'klæsɪfaɪd/. ADJ **Classified** information is officially secret. *The document was highly classified.*

classify /'klæsɪfaɪ/ **classifies, classifying, classified.** VERB To **classify** things means to divide them into groups or types so that things with similar characteristics are in the same group. *The coroner*

immediately classified his death as a suicide.
♦ **classification** /ˌklæsɪfɪˈkeɪʃən/ **classifications**
N-VAR ...*the classification of people into racial subtypes.*

classless /ˈklɑːsləs, ˈklæs-/. ADJ If politicians refer to a **classless** society, they mean a society in which people are not affected by differences in social status; used showing approval.

classmate /ˈklɑːsmeɪt, ˈklæs-/ **classmates.** N-COUNT Your **classmates** are students in the same class as you at school or college.

classroom /ˈklɑːsruːm, ˈklæs-/ **classrooms.** N-COUNT A **classroom** is a room in a school where lessons take place.

classy /ˈklɑːsi, ˈklæsi/ **classier, classiest.** ADJ If you describe someone or something as **classy**, you mean they are stylish and sophisticated. [INFORMAL] *They need classier brand names to sell upmarket cars.*

clatter /ˈklætə/ **clatters, clattering, clattered.** 1 VERB If you say that people or things **clatter** somewhere, you mean that they move there noisily. *He turned and clattered down the stairs.* 2 VERB & N-SING When something hard **clatters**, or when it makes a **clatter**, it makes repeated short noises as it hits against another hard thing. [LITERARY] *She set her cup down, and it clattered against the saucer. ...the clatter of a typewriter.*

clause /klɔːz/ **clauses.** 1 N-COUNT A **clause** is a section of a legal document. 2 N-COUNT In grammar, a **clause** is a group of words containing a verb.

claw /klɔː/ **claws, clawing, clawed.** 1 N-COUNT The **claws** of a bird or animal are the thin curved nails on its feet. 2 VERB When people or animals **claw** something, or when they **claw at** it, they damage it or try to get hold of it with their nails or claws. *His fingers clawed at Blake's wrist.*

clay /kleɪ/. N-UNCOUNT **Clay** is a type of earth that is soft when it is wet and hard when it is baked dry.

⭐ **clean** /kliːn/ **cleaner, cleanest; cleans, cleaning, cleaned.** 1 ADJ Something that is **clean** is free from dirt or unwanted marks. ...*the cleanest beach in Europe... Tiled kitchen floors are easy to keep clean.* 2 VERB & N-SING If you **clean** something, or if you give it a **clean**, you make it free from dirt and unwanted marks. *It took half an hour to clean the orange powder off the bath... Give the cooker a good clean.* ♦ **cleaning** N-UNCOUNT *I do the cleaning myself.* 3 ADJ If something such as a book, joke, or lifestyle is **clean**, it is not sexually immoral or offensive; used showing approval. ...*clean, wholesome, decent movies.* 4 ADJ If someone's reputation or record is **clean**, they have never done anything illegal or wrong. ...*a clean driving licence.* 5 ADJ BEFORE N If you make a **clean** break or start, you end a situation completely and start again in a different way. *Voters have chosen to make a clean break with their past.* 6 PHRASE If you **come clean about** something that you have been keeping secret, you admit it. [INFORMAL]

▶**clean out.** PHR-VERB If you **clean out** a cupboard or room, you clean and tidy it thoroughly.

▶**clean up.** PHR-VERB If you **clean up** something, you clean it thoroughly. *Many regional governments cleaned up their beaches.*

cleaner /ˈkliːnə/ **cleaners.** 1 N-COUNT A **cleaner** is someone who is employed to clean the rooms and furniture inside a building or someone whose job is to clean a particular type of thing. *He was a window cleaner.* 2 N-VAR A **cleaner** is a substance or device for cleaning things. ...*oven cleaner. ...an air cleaner.* 3 N-COUNT A **cleaner** or a **cleaner's** is a shop where things such as clothes are dry-cleaned. 4 See also **vacuum cleaner.**

cleanliness /ˈklenlɪnəs/. N-UNCOUNT **Cleanliness** is the degree to which people keep themselves and their surroundings clean. *Many of Britain's beaches fail to meet minimum standards of cleanliness.*

cleanse /klenz/ **cleanses, cleansing, cleansed.** 1 VERB To **cleanse** a person, place, or organization **of** something dirty, unpleasant, or evil means to make them free of it. ...*the safest way to cleanse your body of poisons.* 2 VERB If you **cleanse** your skin or a wound, you clean it.

cleanser /ˈklenzə/ **cleansers.** N-VAR A **cleanser** is a liquid or cream that you use for cleaning something, especially your skin.

⭐ **clear** /klɪə/ **clearer, clearest; clears, clearing, cleared.** 1 ADJ Something that is **clear** is easy to understand, see, or hear. ...*a pretty clear account of the sequence of events. ...television which transmits far clearer pictures.* ♦ **clearly** ADV *It was important for children to learn to express themselves clearly.* 2 ADJ Something that is **clear** is obvious. *It was a clear case of homicide... It became clear that I hadn't been able to convince Mike.* ♦ **clearly** ADV *Clearly, the police cannot break the law.* 3 ADJ If you are **clear about** something, you understand it completely. *She paused, trying to be clear about her feelings.* 4 ADJ If you have a **clear** mind or way of thinking, you are able to think sensibly and logically. *She needed a clear head to carry out her instructions.* ♦ **clearly** ADV *I can think clearly when I'm alone.* 5 ADJ If a substance is **clear**, it has no colour and you can see through it. ...*a clear glass panel. ...a clear gel.* 6 ADJ **Clear** skin or eyes look healthy. 7 ADJ If it is a **clear** day, there is no mist, rain, or cloud. 8 VERB When fog or mist **clears**, it gradually disappears. 9 ADJ If a surface or place is **clear**, it is free from obstructions or unwanted objects. *The runway is clear – go ahead and land.* 10 VERB When you **clear** a place, you remove unwanted things from it. *Firemen were still clearing rubble from apartments.* 11 ADJ If your conscience is **clear**, you do not feel guilty about anything. *I can look back on things with a clear conscience.* 12 ADJ AFTER LINK-V If one thing is **clear of** another, the two things are not touching. *He lifted him clear of the deck.* 13 VERB

a b c d e f g h i j k l m n o p q r s t u v w x y z

If an animal or person **clears** a fence, wall, or hedge, they jump over it without touching it. [14] VERB If a course of action **is cleared**, people in authority give permission for it to happen. *The helicopter was cleared for take-off.* [15] VERB If someone **is cleared** of a crime or mistake, they are proved to be not guilty of it. [16] See also **clearing**.

PHRASES ● If you **stay clear of** or **steer clear of** a person or place, you do not go near them. ● If someone is **in the clear**, they are free from blame, suspicion, or danger. [INFORMAL] *The Audit Commission said that the ministry was in the clear.* ● to **clear** your **throat**: see throat.

▸**clear away.** PHR-VERB When you **clear** things **away**, or when you **clear away**, you put away things that you have been using. *The waitress had cleared away the plates... Tania cooked, served, and cleared away.*

▸**clear off.** PHR-VERB If you tell someone to **clear off**, you are telling them in a rude way to go away. [INFORMAL]

▸**clear out.** [1] PHR-VERB If you tell someone to **clear out of** a place or to **clear out**, you are telling them rather rudely to leave the place. [INFORMAL] *'Clear out!' he bawled. 'Private property!'* [2] PHR-VERB If you **clear out** a cupboard or room, you tidy it and throw away unwanted things.

▸**clear up.** [1] PHR-VERB When you **clear up**, or when you **clear** a place **up**, you tidy a place and put things away. *I cleared up my room.* [2] PHR-VERB To **clear up** a problem, misunderstanding, or mystery means to settle it or find a satisfactory explanation for it. [3] PHR-VERB When bad weather **clears up**, it stops raining or being cloudy.

clearance /'klɪərəns/ **clearances.** [1] N-VAR **Clearance** is the removal of old or unwanted buildings, trees, or other things from an area. *The UN pledged to help supervise the clearance of mines.* [2] N-VAR If you get **clearance** to do or have something, you get official approval or permission to do or have it. *The plane had been given clearance to land.*

,**clear-**'**cut.** ADJ Something that is **clear-cut** is easy to understand and definite or distinct. *This was a clear-cut case of the original land owner being in the right.*

clearing /'klɪərɪŋ/ **clearings.** N-COUNT A **clearing** is a small area in a forest where there are no trees.

clench /klentʃ/ **clenches, clenching, clenched.** [1] VERB When you **clench** your **fist**, you curl your fingers up tightly, usually because you are very angry. *...angry protestors with clenched fists.* [2] VERB When you **clench** your **teeth**, you squeeze them together firmly, usually because you are angry or upset. *Slowly, he released his breath through clenched teeth.*

clergy /'klɜːdʒi/. N-PLURAL The **clergy** are the religious leaders of a particular group of believers. *...Catholic clergy.*

clergyman /'klɜːdʒimən/ **clergymen.** N-COUNT A **clergyman** is a male member of the clergy.

cleric /'klerɪk/ **clerics.** N-COUNT A **cleric** is a member of the clergy.

clerical /'klerɪkəl/. [1] ADJ BEFORE N **Clerical** jobs, skills, and workers are concerned with work that is done in an office. *...a clerical error.* [2] ADJ BEFORE N **Clerical** means relating to the clergy. *...Iran's clerical leadership.*

clerk /klɑːk, AM klɜːrk/ **clerks.** N-COUNT A **clerk** is a person who works in an office, bank, or law court and whose job is to look after records or accounts. *...an accounts clerk with a travel firm.*

⭐ **clever** /'klevə/ **cleverer, cleverest.** [1] ADJ A **clever** person is intelligent and able to understand things easily or to plan things well. *My sister was always a lot cleverer than I was.* ◆ **cleverly** ADV *He did this much more cleverly than I could have done.* ◆ **cleverness** N-UNCOUNT *He sat back, smiling complacently at his own cleverness.* [2] ADJ A **clever** idea, book, or invention is extremely effective and shows the skill of the people involved. *It is a clever and gripping novel. ...this clever new gadget.* ◆ **cleverly** ADV *...a cleverly designed swimsuit.*

cliché (or **cliche**) /'kliːʃeɪ, AM kliːˈʃeɪ/ **clichés.** N-COUNT A **cliché** is an idea or phrase which has been used so much that it is no longer interesting or effective; used showing disapproval. *It has become a cliche to describe Asia-Pacific as the world's most dynamic economic area.*

click /klɪk/ **clicks, clicking, clicked.** [1] VERB & N-COUNT If something **clicks**, or if you **click** it, it makes a short sharp sound, called a **click**. *He clicked off the radio... Blake clicked his fingers at a passing waiter. ...a click of a button.* [2] VERB & N-COUNT If you **click on** an area of a computer screen, you point the cursor at that area and press one of the buttons on the mouse in order to make something happen. This action is called a **click**. [COMPUTING] *Just click on the icon and you will go to a registration form... You can check your email with a click of your mouse.* [3] VERB When you suddenly understand something, you can say that it **has clicked**. [INFORMAL] *It suddenly clicked that this was fantastic fun.*

⭐ **client** /'klaɪənt/ **clients.** N-COUNT A **client** is someone for whom a professional person or organization is providing a service or doing some work. *The company required clients to pay substantial fees.*

clientele /ˌkliːɒnˈtel, ˌklaɪən-/. N-SING The **clientele** of a place or business are its customers or clients. *This pub had a mixed clientele.*

cliff /klɪf/ **cliffs.** N-COUNT A **cliff** is a high area of land with a very steep side, especially one next to the sea.

⭐ **climate** /ˈklaɪmət/ **climates.** ① N-VAR The **climate** of a place is the general weather conditions that are typical of it. *...the hot and humid climate of Cyprus.* ② N-COUNT You can use **climate** to refer to the atmosphere or situation somewhere. *...the existing climate of violence and intimidation.*

climax /ˈklaɪmæks/ **climaxes, climaxing, climaxed.** N-COUNT & VERB The **climax of** something is the most exciting or important moment in it, usually near the end. You can say something **climaxes with** a particular event. *Reaching an Olympics was the climax of her career... The poem climaxes with an outbreak of his jealousy.*

⭐ **climb** /klaɪm/ **climbs, climbing, climbed.** ① VERB & N-COUNT If you **climb** something such as a tree, mountain, or ladder, or if you **climb up** it, you move towards the top of it. Climbing something is called a **climb**. *Climb up the steps on to the bridge... Children love to climb. ...an hour's leisurely climb through olive groves.* ② VERB If you **climb** somewhere, you move there carefully and often awkwardly, for example because you are moving into a small space. *The girls climbed into the car.* ③ VERB When something like an aeroplane **climbs**, it moves upwards. *The plane climbed to 370 feet.* ④ VERB When something **climbs**, it increases in value or amount. *Prices have climbed by 21%.*

▶ **climb down.** ① PHR-VERB If you **climb down** something such as a tree, mountain, or ladder, you move towards the bottom of it. ② PHR-VERB If you **climb down** in an argument or dispute, you admit that you are wrong, or change your intentions or demands.

climber /ˈklaɪmə/ **climbers.** N-COUNT A **climber** is someone who climbs rocks or mountains as a sport.

climbing /ˈklaɪmɪŋ/. N-UNCOUNT **Climbing** is the activity of climbing rocks or mountains.

clinch /klɪntʃ/ **clinches, clinching, clinched.** VERB To **clinch** an agreement or argument means to settle it. [INFORMAL] *He is about to clinch a deal with an American engine manufacturer.*

cling /klɪŋ/ **clings, clinging, clung.** ① VERB If you **cling to** or **onto** something or someone, you hold onto them tightly. *She had to cling onto the door handle... They hugged each other, clinging together.* ② VERB Clothes that **cling to** you stay pressed against your body when you move. *Her sweat-stained clothing clung to her body.* ③ VERB If you **cling to** an idea or way of behaving, you continue to believe in its value or importance, even though it may no longer be valid or useful. *She clings to a romantic fantasy of wedded bliss.*

⭐ **clinic** /ˈklɪnɪk/ **clinics.** N-COUNT A **clinic** is a building where people receive medical advice or treatment.

clinical /ˈklɪnɪkəl/. ① ADJ BEFORE N **Clinical** means involving or relating to the medical treatment or testing of patients. *...a clinical psychologist.* ♦ **clinically** ADV *She was diagnosed as being clinically depressed.* ② ADJ **Clinical** thought or behaviour is very logical and does not involve any emotion; used showing disapproval. *All this questioning is so analytical and clinical.*

clink /klɪŋk/ **clinks, clinking, clinked.** N-COUNT & VERB When glass or metal objects **clink**, or when you **clink** them, they touch each other and make a short light sound, called a **clink**. *She clinked her glass against his. ...the clink of a spoon in a cup.*

clip /klɪp/ **clips, clipping, clipped.** ① N-COUNT A **clip** is a small metal or plastic device that is used for holding things together. *She took the clip out of her hair.* ② VERB If you **clip** one thing to another, you fasten it there with a clip. You can also say that one thing **clips to** another. *He clipped his cufflinks neatly in place. ...an electronic pen which clips to the casing.* ③ N-COUNT A **clip** from a film or a radio or television programme is a short piece of it that is broadcast separately. *...an historical film clip of Lenin speaking.* ④ VERB If you **clip** something, you cut small pieces from it. *I saw an old man out clipping his hedge.*

clipped /klɪpt/. ① ADJ **Clipped** means neatly trimmed. *...a quiet street of clipped hedges.* ② ADJ If you have a **clipped** way of speaking, you speak with quick short sounds. *'Come in', a clipped voice said.*

clipping /ˈklɪpɪŋ/ **clippings.** N-COUNT A **clipping** is an article, picture, or advertisement that has been cut from a newspaper or magazine. *...newspaper clippings.*

clique /kliːk/ **cliques.** N-COUNT If you describe a group of people as a **clique**, you mean that they spend a lot of time together and seem unfriendly towards people who are not in the group; used showing disapproval. *...a clique of privileged students.*

cloak /kləʊk/ **cloaks, cloaking, cloaked.** ① N-COUNT A **cloak** is a wide loose coat that fastens at the neck and does not have sleeves. ② VERB & N-SING To **cloak** something, or to put a **cloak** around it, means to hide the truth about it or cover it up. *The subject remains cloaked in mythology and mystery... Preparations for the wedding were made under a cloak of secrecy.*

cloakroom /ˈkləʊkruːm/ **cloakrooms.** N-COUNT A **cloakroom** is a small room in a public building where people can leave their coats.

clobber /ˈklɒbə/ **clobbers, clobbering, clobbered.** VERB If you **clobber** someone, you hit them. [BRITISH, INFORMAL]

⭐ **clock** /klɒk/ **clocks, clocking, clocked.** N-COUNT A **clock** is an instrument, for example in a room or on the outside of a building, that shows you what the time is. → See Reference Page on Telling the Time. ● See also **o'clock**.

a
b
c
d
e
f
g
h
i
j
k
l
m
n
o
p
q
r
s
t
u
v
w
x
y
z

A

B

C

D

E

F

G

H

I

J

K

L

M

N

O

P

Q

R

S

T

U

V

W

X

Y

Z

PHRASES ● If you work **round** or **around the clock**, you work all day and all night without stopping. *She will no longer be guarded round the clock. ...an around-the-clock service.* ● If you want to **turn the clock back** or **put the clock back**, you want to return to a situation that used to exist, for example because you would like to have avoided certain things that have happened.
▸**clock up.** PHR-VERB To **clock up** a large total means to reach that total. [BRITISH] *Rude taxi drivers clocked up a total of 239 offences in 1990.*

clockwise /'klɒkwaɪz/ ADV & ADJ BEFORE N When something is moving **clockwise** or when it is moving in a **clockwise** direction, it is moving in a circle, in the same direction as the hands on a clock.

clockwork /'klɒkwɜːk/ [1] ADJ BEFORE N A **clockwork** toy or device has machinery inside it which makes it move or operate when it is wound up with a key. [2] PHRASE If something happens **like clockwork**, it happens without problems or delays. *The Queen's holiday is arranged to go like clockwork.*

clog /klɒg/ **clogs, clogging, clogged.** [1] VERB & PHR-VERB When something **clogs** a hole or place, or when it **clogs up** a hole or place, it blocks it so that nothing can pass through. *The traffic clogged the Thames bridges... The lungs clog up with a thick mucus.* ◆ **clogged** ADJ *The streets were clogged with people.* [2] N-COUNT **Clogs** are heavy leather or wooden shoes with thick wooden soles.

clone /kləʊn/ **clones, cloning, cloned.** [1] N-COUNT A **clone** is an animal or plant that has been produced artificially from a cell of another animal or plant, and is exactly the same as it. [2] N-COUNT If you say that someone is a **clone** of someone else, you disapprove of them because they try to look and behave exactly like that person. *They believe we all want to be supermodel clones.* [3] VERB To **clone** an animal or plant means to produce it as a clone.

close 1 verb uses

★ **close** /kləʊz/ **closes, closing, closed.** [1] VERB When you **close** a door, window, or lid, or when it **closes**, it moves so that a hole, gap, or opening is covered. *If you are cold, close the window... Zacharias heard the door close.* [2] VERB When a place **closes**, or when it **is closed**, people cannot use it, or all work stops there. *Shops close only on Christmas Day. ...if they do close the local college.* [3] VERB To **close** a matter or event means to bring it to an end. *He needs another $30,000 to close the deal. ...the closing ceremony of the National Political Conference.* [4] N-SING **The close of** a period of time or an activity is the end of it. To **bring** something **to a close** or to **draw** something **to a close** means to end it. *Applications would still be received until the close of business tomorrow.* [5] VERB If you **are closing on** someone or something that you are following, you are getting nearer and nearer to them. *I was within 15 seconds of the guy in second*

place and closing on him.
[6] See also **closing.**
▸**close down.** PHR-VERB If a factory or a business **closes down**, or if it **is closed down**, all work or activity stops there, usually for ever. *The Government has already closed down two newspapers.*
▸**close in.** PHR-VERB If people **close in on** a person or place, they come nearer and gradually surround them. *Forces were closing in on Berlin.*

close 2 adjective uses

★ **close** /kləʊs/ **closer, closest.** [1] ADJ AFTER LINK-V Something that is **close to** something else is near to it. *Her lips were close to his head... The man moved closer... The tables were pushed close together.* ◆ **closely** ADV *They were closely followed by security men.* [2] ADJ People who are **close** know each other well and like each other a lot. *She and Linda became very close. ...a close friend from school.* ◆ **closeness** N-UNCOUNT *...her closeness to her mother.* [3] ADJ BEFORE N Your **close** relatives are the members of your family most directly related to you, for example your parents, brothers, or sisters. [4] ADJ BEFORE N **Close** contact or co-operation involves seeing or communicating with someone often. *He lived alone, keeping close contact with his three grown-up sons.* ◆ **closely** ADV *We work closely with the careers officers.* [5] ADJ If there is a **close** connection or resemblance between two things, they are strongly connected or are very similar. *There is a close connection between pain and tension. ...Clare's close resemblance to his elder sister.* ◆ **closely** ADV *...a pattern closely resembling a cross.* [6] ADJ When a competition or election is **close**, it is only won or lost by a small amount. *It is still a close contest between two leading opposition parties.* [7] ADJ BEFORE N **Close** inspection or observation of something is careful and thorough. *Let's have a closer look.* ◆ **closely** ADV *...if you look closely at many of the problems in society.* [8] ADJ AFTER LINK-V If you are **close to** something, or if it is **close**, it is likely to happen or come soon. *She sounded close to tears... A senior White House official said the agreement is close... He's close to signing a contract.* [9] ADJ If the atmosphere in a place is **close**, it is uncomfortably warm and does not have enough fresh air.

PHRASES ● Something that is **close by** or **close at hand** is near to you. ● If you describe an event as a **close shave** or a **close call**, you mean that an accident nearly happened. ● If something is **close to** or **close on** a particular amount or distance, it is slightly less than that amount or distance. *Sisulu spent close to 30 years in prison.* ● If you look at something **close up** or **close to**, you look at it when you are very near to it. *They always look smaller close up.* ● See also **close-up.**

closed /kləʊzd/. ADJ A **closed** group of people does not welcome new people or ideas from outside. *It is a closed society in the sense that they've not been exposed to many things.*

,closed-'circuit. ADJ **Closed-circuit** television is a television system used to film people, for example in shops so thieves can be identified. *...closed-circuit cameras.*

closet /'klɒzɪt/ **closets.** [1] N-COUNT In American English, a **closet** is a piece of furniture with doors at the front and shelves inside, which is used for storing things. The usual British word is **cupboard.** [2] ADJ BEFORE N **Closet** is used to describe a person who has beliefs, habits, or feelings which they keep secret. *He is a closet Fascist.*

close-up /'kləʊs ʌp/ **close-ups.** N-COUNT A **close-up** is a photograph or a picture in a film that shows a lot of detail because it is taken very near to the subject.

closing /'kləʊzɪŋ/. ADJ BEFORE N The **closing** part of an activity or period of time is its final part. *...in the closing stages of the war.* ● See also **close.**

closure /'kləʊʒə/ **closures.** [1] N-VAR The **closure** of a business or factory is the permanent shutting of it. *Almost three in four clinics say they face closure.* [2] N-COUNT The **closure** of a road or border is the blocking of it to prevent people from using it.

clot /klɒt/ **clots, clotting, clotted.** [1] N-COUNT A blood **clot** is a thick lump of blood inside the body. *...surgery to remove a blood clot from his brain.* [2] VERB When blood **clots**, it thickens and forms a clot.

cloth /klɒθ, AM klɔːθ/ **cloths.** [1] N-VAR **Cloth** is fabric which is made by weaving or knitting a substance such as cotton or wool. [2] N-COUNT A **cloth** is a piece of cloth used for a particular purpose, such as cleaning. *...a damp cloth.*

clothed /kləʊðd/. ADJ AFTER LINK-V If you are **clothed** in a certain way, you are dressed in that way. *He lay down on the bed fully clothed... She was clothed in a flowered dress.*

⭐ **clothes** /kləʊðz/. N-PLURAL **Clothes** are the things that people wear, such as shirts, coats, trousers, and dresses. → See pictures on page 819 and 820.

> **USAGE** There is no singular form of **clothes**. You cannot talk about 'a clothe'. In formal English, you can talk about a **garment**, a **piece of clothing**, an **article of clothing**, or an **item of clothing**, but in ordinary conversation, you usually name the piece of clothing you are talking about. For the different verbs associated with clothes, see the note at **wear**.

⭐ **clothing** /'kləʊðɪŋ/. N-UNCOUNT **Clothing** is the clothes people wear. *...protective clothing.*

⭐ **cloud** /klaʊd/ **clouds, clouding, clouded.** [1] N-VAR A **cloud** is a mass of water vapour that is seen as a white or grey mass in the sky. *The sky was almost entirely obscured by cloud.* [2] N-COUNT A **cloud** of smoke or dust is a mass of it floating in the air.

[3] VERB If you say that something **clouds** your view of a situation, you mean that it makes you unable to understand the situation or judge it properly. *Religious mania clouded his mind.* [4] VERB If something **clouds** an event or situation, it makes it less pleasant. *Poor job prospects have clouded the outlook for the economy.*
▸ **cloud over.** PHR-VERB If your face or eyes **cloud over**, you suddenly look sad or angry.

cloudy /'klaʊdi/ **cloudier, cloudiest.** [1] ADJ If it is **cloudy**, there are a lot of clouds in the sky. [2] ADJ A **cloudy** liquid is less clear than it should be.

clout /klaʊt/ **clouts, clouting, clouted.** [1] VERB & N-COUNT If you **clout** someone, or if you give them a **clout**, you hit them. [INFORMAL] *The officer clouted her on the head... I was half tempted to give one of them a clout.* [2] N-UNCOUNT A person or institution that has **clout** has influence and power. *The two firms wield enormous clout in financial markets.*

clove /kləʊv/ **cloves.** [1] N-VAR **Cloves** are small dried flower buds used as a spice. [2] N-COUNT A **clove** of garlic is one of the small sections of a garlic bulb.

clown /klaʊn/ **clowns, clowning, clowned.** [1] N-COUNT A **clown** is a performer who wears funny clothes and bright make-up, and does silly things to make people laugh. [2] VERB If you **clown**, you do silly things to make people laugh.

⭐ **club** /klʌb/ **clubs, clubbing, clubbed.** [1] N-COUNT A **club** is an organization of people who are all interested in a particular activity. *...a chess club.* [2] N-COUNT A **club** is a team which competes in professional or amateur sporting competitions. *...the Italian football club, AC Milan.* [3] N-COUNT A **club** is a place where the members of a particular club or organization meet. [4] N-COUNT A **club** is the same as a **nightclub**. *...an occasional night of dancing at a club.* [5] N-COUNT A **club** is a thick heavy stick that can be used as a weapon. [6] VERB To **club** a person or animal means to hit them hard with a thick heavy stick or a similar weapon. *Riot police clubbed a student to death.* [7] N-COUNT A golf **club** is a long thin metal stick with a piece of wood or metal at one end. [8] N-VAR **Clubs** is one of the four suits in a pack of playing cards. Each card in the suit is called a **club** and is marked with one or more black symbols: ♣.

clubhouse (or **club house**) /'klʌbhaʊs/ **clubhouses.** N-COUNT A **clubhouse** is the place where the members of a sports club meet.

clue /kluː/ **clues.** [1] N-COUNT A **clue to** a problem, mystery, or puzzle is something that helps you find the answer. *...a crossword puzzle clue. ...clues to the girls' killer.* [2] PHRASE If you **haven't a clue** about something, you know nothing about it. *I haven't a clue what I'll give Carl for his birthday.*

clump /klʌmp/ **clumps.** N-COUNT A **clump of** things is a small group of them growing together

a
b
c
d
e
f
g
h
i
j
k
l
m
n
o
p
q
r
s
t
u
v
w
x
y
z

or collected together in one place. ...*a clump of trees... Her hair fell out in clumps.*

clumsy /ˈklʌmzi/ **clumsier, clumsiest.** 1 ADJ A **clumsy** person moves or handles things in an awkward way. ♦ **clumsily** /ˈklʌmzɪli/ ADV *She rose clumsily.* ♦ **clumsiness** N-UNCOUNT *His clumsiness embarrassed him.* 2 ADJ A **clumsy** action or statement is not skilful or is without tact and likely to upset people. ...*the German bank's clumsy handling of German monetary policy.* ♦ **clumsily** ADV ...*the exciting but clumsily written account of a captured crew of an RAF Tornado.* ♦ **clumsiness** N-UNCOUNT ...*clumsiness of expression.* 3 ADJ A **clumsy** object is ugly and awkward to use. *The keyboard is a large and clumsy instrument.*

clung /klʌŋ/. **Clung** is the past tense and past participle of **cling**.

cluster /ˈklʌstə/ **clusters, clustering, clustered.** 1 N-COUNT A **cluster of** people or things is a small group of them close together. 2 VERB If people or things **cluster** together, they gather together or are found together in small groups. *The children clustered around me.* ...*small cottages that are clustered together.*

clutch /klʌtʃ/ **clutches, clutching, clutched.** 1 VERB If you **clutch** something, you hold it very tightly. *Michelle clutched my arm.* 2 N-PLURAL If you are in another person's **clutches**, that person has control over you. 3 N-COUNT In a car, the **clutch** is the pedal that you press before you change gear, and the mechanism that it operates.

clutter /ˈklʌtə/ **clutters, cluttering, cluttered.** 1 N-UNCOUNT **Clutter** is a lot of unnecessary or useless things in an untidy state. *Caroline prefers her worktops to be clear of clutter.* 2 VERB If things **clutter** a place, they fill it untidily. *The roads were cluttered with cars.* ♦ **cluttered** ADJ ...*a cluttered desk.*

cm. cm is the written abbreviation for **centimetre**. *His height had increased by 2.5 cm.*

co- /ˌkəʊ-/. **Co-** is used to form words that refer to people sharing things or doing things together. *He co-produced the album with Bowie... His co-workers hated him.*

⭐ **coach** /kəʊtʃ/ **coaches, coaching, coached.** 1 N-COUNT A **coach** is a large comfortable bus that carries passengers on long journeys. → See picture on page 835. *I hate travelling by coach.* 2 N-COUNT A **coach** is one of the separate sections of a train that carries passengers. [BRITISH] 3 N-COUNT A **coach** is an enclosed four-wheeled vehicle pulled by horses, in which people used to travel. 4 VERB If you **coach** someone, you help them to become better at a particular sport or subject. *He coached the North Carolina State University basketball team.* 5 N-COUNT A **coach** is someone who coaches a person or sports team. ...*a drama coach.* ...*a football coach.*

⭐ **coal** /kəʊl/ **coals.** 1 N-UNCOUNT **Coal** is a hard black substance taken from underground and

burned as fuel. 2 N-PLURAL **Coals** are burning pieces of coal.

⭐ **coalition** /ˌkəʊəˈlɪʃən/ **coalitions.** 1 N-COUNT A **coalition** is a government consisting of people from two or more political parties. ...*a coalition government.* 2 N-COUNT A **coalition** is a group consisting of people from different political or social groups. ...*a coalition of consumer and environmental groups.*

coarse /kɔːs/ **coarser, coarsest.** 1 ADJ **Coarse** things have a rough texture. ...*a beach of coarse sand.* ♦ **coarsely** ADV ...*coarsely ground black pepper.* 2 ADJ A **coarse** person talks and behaves in a rude and offensive way. ♦ **coarsely** ADV *The women laughed coarsely at some vulgar joke.*

⭐ **coast** /kəʊst/ **coasts, coasting, coasted.** 1 N-COUNT The **coast** is an area of land next to the sea. ♦ **coastal** /ˈkəʊstəl/ ADJ BEFORE N ...*coastal areas.* 2 VERB If a person or a team **is coasting**, they are doing something easily and without effort. *Charles was coasting at school... Ivan Lendl coasted to a 6-3, 6-2, 6-3 victory.*

coastguard /ˈkəʊstɡɑːd/ **coastguards.** N-COUNT A **coastguard** is an official who watches the sea near a coast, in order to get help when it is needed and to prevent smuggling.

coastline /ˈkəʊstlaɪn/ **coastlines.** N-VAR A country's **coastline** is the edge of its coast. ...*two patrol boats to watch five miles of coastline.*

⭐ **coat** /kəʊt/ **coats, coating, coated.** 1 N-COUNT A **coat** is a piece of clothing with long sleeves worn over your other clothes when you go outside. → See picture on page 819. 2 N-COUNT An animal's **coat** is its fur or hair. 3 VERB If you **coat** something **with** a substance, you cover it with a thin layer of the substance. ...*a dying bird coated with oil.* ♦ **-coated** ...*chocolate-coated sweets.* 4 N-COUNT A **coat of** paint or varnish is a thin layer of it.

coating /ˈkəʊtɪŋ/ **coatings.** N-COUNT A **coating** of a substance is a thin layer of it. ...*a coating of breadcrumbs.*

coax /kəʊks/ **coaxes, coaxing, coaxed.** VERB If you **coax** someone **to** do something, you gently try to persuade them to do it. *I had to coax him to tell me what was wrong.*

cobble /ˈkɒbəl/ **cobbles, cobbling, cobbled.**
▶ **cobble together.** PHR-VERB If you say that someone has **cobbled** something **together**, you mean that they have produced it roughly or quickly. *The group had cobbled together a few decent songs.*

cobra /ˈkəʊbrə/ **cobras.** N-COUNT A **cobra** is a kind of poisonous snake.

cobweb /ˈkɒbweb/ **cobwebs.** N-COUNT A **cobweb** is the fine net that a spider makes in order to catch insects.

cocaine /kəʊˈkeɪn/. N-UNCOUNT **Cocaine** is an addictive drug which people take for pleasure.

cock /kɒk/ **cocks, cocking, cocked.** 1 N-COUNT A **cock** is an adult male chicken. 2 VERB If you **cock** a part of your body towards a particular direction, you lift it or point it in that direction. *He paused and cocked his head.*

cockpit /'kɒkpɪt/ **cockpits.** N-COUNT The **cockpit** in a small plane or racing car is the part where the pilot or driver sits.

cockroach /'kɒkrəʊtʃ/ **cockroaches.** N-COUNT A **cockroach** is a large brown insect that is often found in dirty or damp places. → See picture on page 824.

cocktail /'kɒkteɪl/ **cocktails.** ① N-COUNT A **cocktail** is an alcoholic drink containing several ingredients. *...a champagne cocktail.* ② N-COUNT A mixture of a number of different things can be called a **cocktail**. *...a fruit cocktail... Children and guns are a potentially lethal cocktail.*

cocky /'kɒki/ **cockier, cockiest.** ADJ A **cocky** person is very self-confident and pleased with themselves. [INFORMAL] *He had a confident, even cocky, air.*

cocoa /'kəʊkəʊ/. ① N-UNCOUNT **Cocoa** is a brown powder used in making chocolate. ② N-UNCOUNT **Cocoa** is a hot drink made with cocoa powder and milk.

coconut /'kəʊkənʌt/ **coconuts.** N-VAR A **coconut** is a very large nut with a hairy shell, white flesh, and milky juice inside. **Coconut** is the white flesh of a coconut.

cocoon /kə'kuːn/ **cocoons.** ① N-COUNT A **cocoon** is a covering of silky threads made by the larvae of moths and other insects before they grow into adults. ② N-COUNT You can use **cocoon** to describe a safe and protective environment. *She is looking for a cocoon to retreat to or bring up children.*

cod /kɒd/.

⚠ **Cod** is both the singular and the plural form.

N-VAR A **cod** is a large sea fish with white flesh. **Cod** is the flesh of this fish eaten as food.

⭐ **code** /kəʊd/ **codes.** ① N-COUNT A **code** is a set of rules about how people should behave. *...a strict code of practice. ...the strict Islamic dress code.* ② N-VAR A **code** is a system of replacing the words in a message with other words or symbols, so that people who do not know the system cannot understand it. *If you can't remember your number, write it in code in a diary.* ③ N-COUNT A **code** is a group of numbers or letters used to identify something such as a postal address. *Callers dialing the wrong area code will not get through.* ④ N-COUNT A **code** is any system of signs or symbols that has a meaning. *...digital code.*

coded /'kəʊdɪd/. ADJ **Coded** messages have words or symbols which represent other words, so that the message is secret unless you know the system behind the code. *...coded instructions to waiting terrorists.*

coding /'kəʊdɪŋ/. N-UNCOUNT **Coding** is a method of making it easy to see the difference between several things, for example by marking them in different colours.

coerce /kəʊ'ɜːs/ **coerces, coercing, coerced.** VERB If you **coerce** someone **into** doing something, you make them do it against their will. [FORMAL] *Clark had somehow been able to coerce Jenny into doing whatever he told her to do.* ♦ **coercion** /kəʊ'ɜːʃən/ N-UNCOUNT *The growth in its membership was due to official coercion.*

⭐ **coffee** /'kɒfi, AM 'kɔːfi/ **coffees.** ① N-VAR **Coffee** is the roasted beans of the coffee plant. ② N-VAR **Coffee** is a drink made from boiling water and ground roasted coffee beans. *Would you like to come back for coffee?*

'**coffee shop, coffee shops.** N-COUNT A **coffee shop** is a restaurant that sells coffee, tea, cakes, and sometimes sandwiches and snacks.

coffers /'kɒfəz/. N-PLURAL The **coffers** of an organization consist of the money that it has to spend.

coffin /'kɒfɪn, AM 'kɔːfɪn/ **coffins.** N-COUNT A **coffin** is a box in which a dead body is buried or cremated.

cognac /'kɒnjæk, AM 'kəʊn-/ **cognacs.** N-VAR **Cognac** is a kind of brandy.

cognitive /'kɒgnɪtɪv/. ADJ BEFORE N **Cognitive** means relating to the mental process involved in knowing, learning, and understanding things. [TECHNICAL] *...physical, emotional and cognitive growth.*

coherent /kəʊ'hɪərənt/. ① ADJ If something is **coherent**, it is well planned, so that it is clear and sensible. *...a coherent campaign to change the laws.* ♦ **coherence** /kəʊ'hɪərəns/ N-UNCOUNT *...political coherence.* ② ADJ If someone is **coherent**, they express their thoughts in a clear and calm way. *He appeared hardly capable of conducting a coherent conversation.*

♦ **coherently** ADV *Many young people are unable to express themselves coherently.*

cohesion /kəʊ'hiːʒən/. N-UNCOUNT If there is **cohesion** within a society, organization, or group, the different members fit together well and form a united whole. *The cohesion of the armed forces was rapidly breaking down.*

cohesive /kəʊ'hiːsɪv/. ADJ Something that is **cohesive** consists of parts that fit together well and form a united whole. *...a reasonably cohesive and supportive family.*

coil /kɔɪl/ **coils, coiling, coiled.** ① N-COUNT A **coil of** rope or wire is a length of it that has been wound into a series of loops. *He slung the coil of rope over his shoulder.* ② VERB & PHR-VERB If something **coils**, or if you **coil** it **up**, it curves into a series of loops or into the shape of a ring. *A huge rattlesnake lay coiled on the blanket... Once we have the wire, we can coil it up.*

coin /kɔɪn/ **coins, coining, coined.** ① N-COUNT A **coin** is a small piece of metal used as money. ② VERB If you **coin** a word or a phrase, you are the first person to say it. *Jaron Lanier coined the term 'virtual reality'.*

coinage /'kɔɪnɪdʒ/. ① N-UNCOUNT **Coinage** consists of the coins used in a country.

a b c d e f g h i j k l m n o p q r s t u v w x y z

A
B
C
D
E
F
G
H
I
J
K
L
M
N
O
P
Q
R
S
T
U
V
W
X
Y
Z

2 N-UNCOUNT **Coinage** is the system of money used in a country.

coincide /ˌkəʊɪnˈsaɪd/ **coincides, coinciding, coincided.** **1** VERB If one event **coincides with** another, they happen at the same time. *The shop's opening coincided with the Christmas rush.* **2** VERB If the opinions or ideas of two or more people **coincide**, they are the same. *The beliefs of the patient and the doctor ideally should coincide.*

coincidence /kəʊˈɪnsɪdəns/ **coincidences.** N-VAR A **coincidence** happens when two or more things occur at the same time by chance. *It's been pure coincidence that he's followed my career. ...a string of amazing coincidences.*

coincidentally /ˌkəʊɪnsɪˈdentli/. ADV You say **coincidentally** when you want to draw attention to a coincidence. *Coincidentally, I had once found myself in a similar situation.*

coke /kəʊk/ **cokes.** **1** N-VAR **Coke** is a sweet, brown, non-alcoholic fizzy drink. **Coke** is a trademark. **2** N-UNCOUNT **Coke** is **cocaine**. [INFORMAL]

cola /ˈkəʊlə/. N-UNCOUNT **Cola** is a sweet, brown, non-alcoholic fizzy drink.

⭐ **cold** /kəʊld/ **colder, coldest, colds.** **1** ADJ & N-UNCOUNT If something or someone is **cold**, they have a very low temperature. **The cold** is cold weather or a low temperature. *...cold running water... It was windy and Jake felt cold... He must have come inside to get out of the cold.* ◆ **coldness** N-UNCOUNT *...the coldness of the night.*

> **USAGE** If you want to emphasize how cold the weather is, you can say that it is **freezing**, especially in winter when there is ice or frost. In summer, if the temperature is below average, you can say that it is **cool**. In general, **cold** suggests a lower temperature than **cool**, and **cool** things may be pleasant or refreshing. *A cool breeze swept off the sea; it was pleasant out there.*

2 ADJ **Cold** food, such as salad or meat that has been cooked and cooled, is not intended to be eaten hot. **3** ADJ A **cold** person does not show much emotion or affection and therefore seems unfriendly. *What a cold, unfeeling woman she was.* ◆ **coldly** ADV *'I'll see you in the morning,' Hugh said coldly.* ◆ **coldness** N-UNCOUNT *His coldness angered her.* **4** N-COUNT & PHRASE If you have a **cold**, you have a mild, very common illness which makes you sneeze a lot and gives you a sore throat or a cough. If you **catch cold**, or if you **catch a cold**, you become ill with a cold. **5** **in cold blood**: see **blood**.

ˌcold ˈcalling. N-UNCOUNT **Cold calling** is phoning or visiting someone without their agreement in order to try to sell them something.

collaborate /kəˈlæbəreɪt/ **collaborates, collaborating, collaborated.** **1** VERB When people **collaborate**, they work together on a particular

project. *Students collaborate in group exercises and projects... He collaborated with his son Michael on the English translation.* ◆ **collaboration, collaborations** N-VAR *Drummond was working on a book in collaboration with the band.*
◆ **collaborator** /kəˈlæbəreɪtə/ **collaborators** N-COUNT *He completed the book in two years, with Hugh Lynn his collaborator.* **2** VERB If someone **collaborates with** an enemy which has occupied their country, he or she helps them; used showing disapproval. ◆ **collaboration** N-UNCOUNT *...rumors of his collaboration with the occupying forces.* ◆ **collaborator** N-COUNT *...a collaborator with the secret police.*

collaborative /kəˈlæbərətɪv, AM -reɪt-/. ADJ BEFORE N A **collaborative** piece of work is done by two or more people working together. [FORMAL]

collage /ˈkɒlɑːʒ, AM kəˈlɑːʒ/ **collages.** N-VAR A **collage** is a picture made by sticking pieces of paper or cloth onto paper. **Collage** is the method of making these pictures.

⭐ **collapse** /kəˈlæps/ **collapses, collapsing, collapsed.** **1** VERB & N-UNCOUNT If something **collapses**, or if there is a **collapse** of it, it suddenly falls down or falls inwards. *The roof support structure had collapsed. ...an inquiry into the freeway's collapse.* **2** VERB & N-UNCOUNT If you **collapse**, or if you have a **collapse**, you suddenly fall down because you are ill or tired. *Jimmy collapsed on the floor... A few days after his collapse he was sitting up in bed.* **3** VERB & N-UNCOUNT If a system or institution **collapses**, or if there is a **collapse**, it fails completely and suddenly. *His business empire collapsed under a massive burden of debt... The medical system is facing collapse.*

collar /ˈkɒlə/ **collars, collaring, collared.** **1** N-COUNT The **collar** of a shirt or coat is the part which fits round the neck and is usually folded over. → See picture on page 820. **2** N-COUNT A **collar** is a leather band which is put round the neck of a dog or cat. **3** VERB If you **collar** someone who has done something wrong or who is running away, you catch them and hold them so that they cannot escape. [INFORMAL] *As Kerr fled towards the exit, Boycott collared him at the ticket barrier.*

collate /kəˈleɪt/ **collates, collating, collated.** VERB When you **collate** pieces of information, you gather them all together and examine them. *The 2001 figures have not yet been collated.*

collateral /kəˈlætərəl/. N-UNCOUNT **Collateral** is money or property which is used as a guarantee that someone will repay a loan. [FORMAL] *Many people use personal assets as collateral for small business loans.*

⭐ **colleague** /ˈkɒliːg/ **colleagues.** N-COUNT Your **colleagues** are the people you work with, especially in a professional job. *...a business colleague.*

⭐ **collect** /kəˈlekt/ **collects, collecting, collected.** **1** VERB If you **collect** a number of things, you bring them together from several places. *Two young girls were collecting firewood... 1.5 million* signatures have been collected. **2** VERB If you **collect** things as a hobby, you get a large number of them over a period of time because you are interested in them. *He collected antique furniture.* ♦ **collecting** N-UNCOUNT *...stamp collecting.* ♦ **collector, collectors** N-COUNT *...a respected collector of Indian art.* **3** VERB When you **collect** someone or something, you go and get them from a place where they are waiting for you or have been left for you. *David always collects Alistair from school... After collecting the cash, the kidnapper made his escape.* ♦ **collection** N-UNCOUNT *...services such as rubbish collection.* **4** VERB If a substance **collects** somewhere, or if something **collects** it, it keeps arriving over a period of time and is held in that place or thing. *Methane gas does collect in the mines. ...water tanks which collect rainwater.* **5** VERB If you **collect for** a charity or **for** a present, you ask people to give you money for it. *They collected donations for a fund to help military families.* ♦ **collection, collections** N-COUNT *There was a collection for a wreath.* **6** VERB If you **collect yourself** or **collect** your thoughts, you make an effort to calm or prepare yourself. *...a chance to relax and collect his thoughts.*

⭐ **collection** /kə'lekʃən/ **collections. 1** N-COUNT A **collection of** things is a group of similar or related things. *...the world's largest collection of sculptures by Henry Moore. ...a collection of essays from foreign affairs experts. ...Guy Laroche's autumn collection of day and evening wear.* **2** See also **collect.**

⭐ **collective** /kə'lektɪv/ **collectives. 1** ADJ BEFORE N **Collective** means shared by or involving every member of a group of people. *It was a collective decision... Scientists breathed a collective sigh of relief about the finding.* ♦ **collectively** ADV *The Cabinet is collectively responsible for policy.* **2** N-COUNT A **collective** is a business or farm whose employees share the decision-making and the profits.

collector /kə'lektə/ **collectors. 1** N-COUNT A **collector** is someone whose job is to take something such as money or tickets from people. *...rent collectors. ...Council rubbish collectors.* **2** See also **collect.**

⭐ **college** /'kɒlɪdʒ/ **colleges. 1** N-VAR A **college** is an institution where students study after they have left school. *Joanna is doing business studies at a local college... I'm going to college in September.* **2** N-COUNT A **college** in a university is one of the institutions which some British universities are divided into. *...Balliol College, Oxford.* **3** N-COUNT A **college** of a particular kind is an organized group of people who have special duties and powers. [FORMAL] *...the Royal College of Nursing.*

collide /kə'laɪd/ **collides, colliding, collided.** VERB If people or vehicles **collide**, they bump into each other. *Two trains collided head-on... Racing up the stairs, he almost collided with Daisy.*

colliery /'kɒljəri/ **collieries.** N-COUNT A **colliery** is a coal mine. [BRITISH]

collision /kə'lɪʒən/ **collisions.** N-VAR A **collision** occurs when a moving object hits something. *Their van was involved in a collision with a car. ...a head-on collision between two aeroplanes.*

collude /kə'luːd/ **colludes, colluding, colluded.** VERB If one person **colludes with** another, they co-operate secretly or illegally. *Several local officials are in jail on charges of colluding with the Mafia.* ♦ **collusion** /kə'luːʒən/ N-UNCOUNT *Critics have accused banks of being in collusion over the plans.*

colon /'kəʊlən/ **colons.** N-COUNT A **colon** is the punctuation mark (:). → See also Reference Page on Punctuation.

⭐ **colonel** /'kɜːnəl/ **colonels.** N-COUNT & N-TITLE A **colonel** is a senior military officer.

colonial /kə'ləʊniəl/. ADJ BEFORE N **Colonial** means relating to countries that are colonies, or to colonialism. *...independence from British colonial rule. ...the colonial civil service.*

colonialism /kə'ləʊniəlɪzəm/. N-UNCOUNT **Colonialism** is the practice by which a powerful country directly controls less powerful countries. *...the residual effects of colonialism.*

colonist /'kɒlənɪst/ **colonists.** N-COUNT **Colonists** are people who start a colony. *...the early American colonists.*

colonize (BRIT also **colonise**) /'kɒlənaɪz/ **colonizes, colonizing, colonized.** VERB When large numbers of people or animals **colonize** a place, they go to live there and make it their home. *The first British attempt to colonize Ireland was in the twelfth century... Toads are colonising the whole place.* ♦ **colonization** N-UNCOUNT *...the European colonization of America.*

colony /'kɒləni/ **colonies. 1** N-COUNT A **colony** is a country which is controlled by a more powerful country. **2** N-COUNT A **colony** is a group of people or animals of a particular sort living together. *...an artists' colony. ...a seal colony.*

color /'kʌlə/. See **colour.**

colorless /'kʌlələs/. See **colourless.**

colossal /kə'lɒsəl/. ADJ Something that is **colossal** is very large. *...a colossal waste of money.*

⭐ **colour** (AM **color**) /'kʌlə/ **colours, colouring, coloured. 1** N-COUNT The **colour** of something is the appearance that it has as a result of reflecting light. Red, blue, and green are colours. *'What colour is the car?' – 'Red.'... Her silk dress was sky-blue, the colour of her eyes.* **2** N-COUNT Someone's **colour** is the colour of their skin. People often use **colour** in this way to refer to a person's race. *...colour and ethnic origins were utterly irrelevant.* **3** ADJ A **colour** television, film, or photograph shows things in all their colours, and not just in black and white. *...colour illustrations.* **4** N-UNCOUNT **Colour** is a quality that makes something interesting or exciting. *Check shirts add colour to a sober work suit.* **5** VERB If something **colours** your opinion, it affects your opinion.

⭐ Bank of English® frequent word　　　For a full explanation of all grammatical labels, see pages vii-x

a
b
c
d
e
f
g
h
i
j
k
l
m
n
o
p
q
r
s
t
u
v
w
x
y
z

▶ **colour in.** PHR-VERB If you **colour in** a drawing, you give it different colours using crayons or paints.

★ **coloured** (AM **colored**) /'kʌləd/. **1** ADJ **Coloured** means having a particular colour or combination of colours. ...a cheap gold-coloured bracelet. ...brightly coloured silks. **2** ADJ A **coloured** person belongs to a race of people with dark skins; an offensive use.

colourful (AM **colorful**) /'kʌləfʊl/. **1** ADJ Something that is **colourful** has bright colours. ...colourful flowers. **2** ADJ **Colourful** means interesting and exciting. ...boxing's colourful history. ...the island's colourful past.

colouring (AM **coloring**) /'kʌlərɪŋ/ **colourings.** **1** N-UNCOUNT Someone's **colouring** is the colour of their hair, skin, and eyes. **2** N-UNCOUNT **Colouring** is a substance that is used to give colour to food.

colourless (AM **colorless**) /'kʌlələs/. **1** ADJ A **colourless** substance is clear or invisible. ...a colourless, almost odourless liquid. **2** ADJ **Colourless** people or places are dull and uninteresting. We hurried through the colourless little town.

colt /kəʊlt/ **colts.** N-COUNT A **colt** is a young male horse.

★ **column** /'kɒləm/ **columns.** **1** N-COUNT A **column** is a tall solid cylinder, especially one supporting part of a building. **2** N-COUNT A **column** is something that has a tall narrow shape. ...a column of smoke. **3** N-COUNT A **column** of people, animals, or vehicles is a group of them moving in a line. → See picture on page 826. ...a column of tanks. **4** N-COUNT In a newspaper or magazine, a **column** is a vertical section of writing, or a regular section written by the same person. He writes a column for The Wall Street Journal.

columnist /'kɒləmɪst/ **columnists.** N-COUNT A **columnist** is a journalist who writes a regular article in a newspaper or magazine.

coma /'kəʊmə/ **comas.** N-COUNT If someone is **in a coma**, they are deeply unconscious.

comb /kəʊm/ **combs, combing, combed.** **1** N-COUNT A **comb** is a flat piece of plastic or metal with long thin pointed parts, which you use to tidy your hair. **2** VERB When you **comb** your hair, you tidy it using a comb. **3** VERB If you **comb** a place **for** something, you search thoroughly for it. Officers combed the woods for the murder weapon.

★ **combat** /'kɒmbæt/ **combats, combating, combated.** **1** N-VAR **Combat** is fighting that takes place in a war. Over 16 million men had died in combat. **2** VERB /kəm'bæt/ If people in authority **combat** something, they try to stop it happening. ...new government measures to combat crime.

combatant /'kɒmbətənt, AM kəm'bæt-/ **combatants.** N-COUNT A **combatant** is someone who takes part in a fight or a war.

combative /'kɒmbətɪv, AM kəm'bætɪv/. ADJ A **combative** person is aggressive and eager to fight or argue.

★ **combination** /ˌkɒmbɪ'neɪʃən/ **combinations.** **1** N-COUNT A **combination** is a mixture of things. ...a fantastic combination of colours. **2** N-COUNT The **combination** of a lock is the series of letters or numbers used to open it. He's the only one who knows the combination to the safe.

★ **combine, combines, combining, combined.** **1** VERB /kəm'baɪn/ If you **combine** two or more things, or if they **combine**, they exist or join together. Combine the flour with 3 tablespoons water... Disease and starvation combine to kill thousands. ♦ **combined** ADJ BEFORE N Their combined assets total £20 billion. **2** VERB If someone or something **combines** two qualities or features, they have both of them. Their system seems to combine the two ideals... He combines legal expertise with social concern. **3** VERB If someone **combines** two activities, they do them both at the same time. It is possible to combine a career with being a mother... He will combine the two jobs. **4** N-COUNT /'kɒmbaɪn/ A **combine** is a group of people or organizations that are working together.

combustion /kəm'bʌstʃən/. N-UNCOUNT **Combustion** is the act of burning something or the process of burning. [TECHNICAL]

★ **come** /kʌm/ **comes, coming, came, come.** **1** VERB You use **come** to say that someone or something arrives somewhere, or moves towards you. Two police officers came into the hall... He came to a door... Beryl came round this morning to apologize. **2** VERB If something **comes** to a particular point, it reaches it. I wore a large shirt of Jamie's which came down over my hips. **3** VERB You use **come** in expressions which state what happens to someone or something. The door knobs came off... The Communists came to power in 1944... Their worst fears may be coming true. **4** VERB If someone **comes to** do something, they gradually start to do it. She said it so many times that she came to believe it. **5** VERB When a particular time or event **comes**, it arrives or happens. The announcement came after a meeting at the Home Office... The time has come for us to move on. **6** VERB If a thought or idea **comes to** you, you suddenly realize it. **7** VERB If something such as a sum **comes to** a particular amount, it adds up to it. Lunch came to $80. **8** VERB If someone or something **comes from** a particular place or thing, that place or thing is their origin or source. Nearly half the students come from abroad... Chocolate comes from the cacao tree. **9** VERB Something that **comes from** something else or **comes of** it is the result of it. ...a feeling of power that comes from driving fast. **10** VERB If someone or something **comes** first, next, or last, they are first, next, or last in a series, list, or competition. **11** VERB If a type of thing **comes in** a range of colours, styles, or sizes, it can have any of those colours, styles, or sizes. The wallpaper comes in black and white only. **12** See note at **bring.**
● See also **coming.**

►**come about.** PHR-VERB When you say how or when something **came about**, you say how or when it happened. *This situation came about when I encouraged him to give up his job.*

►**come across.** [1] PHR-VERB If you **come across** someone or something, or **come upon** them, you meet or find them by chance. *This is the worst place I've come across.* [2] PHR-VERB The way that someone **comes across** is the impression they make on other people. *He can come across as an extremely pleasant young man.*

►**come along.** [1] PHR-VERB If you ask someone to **come along** to a place or event where you are going to be, you are inviting them to come with you or go there. [2] PHR-VERB When something **comes along**, it arrives or happens, perhaps by chance. *It was lucky you came along.* [3] PHR-VERB If something **is coming along**, it is developing or making progress. *How's your husband's research coming along?*

►**come around** or **come round.** [1] PHR-VERB If you **come around to** an idea, you eventually change your mind and accept it. *It looks like they're coming around to our way of thinking.* [2] PHR-VERB When something **comes around**, it happens as a regular or predictable event. *...when the World Cup comes around next year.* [3] PHR-VERB When someone who is unconscious **comes around** or **comes to**, they recover consciousness.

►**come at.** PHR-VERB If a person or animal **comes at** you, they move towards you in a threatening way and try to attack you.

►**come back.** [1] PHR-VERB If something that you had forgotten **comes back to** you, you remember it. *I'll think of his name in a moment when it comes back to me.* [2] PHR-VERB When something **comes back**, it becomes fashionable again. *I'm glad hats are coming back.*
♦ **comeback, comebacks.** N-COUNT *Tight fitting T-shirts are making a comeback.*

►**come by.** PHR-VERB To **come by** something means to find or obtain it.

►**come down.** [1] PHR-VERB If the cost, level, or amount of something **comes down**, it becomes less than it was before. *The price of petrol is coming down.* [2] PHR-VERB If something **comes down**, it falls to the ground.

►**come down on.** [1] PHR-VERB If you **come down on** one side of an argument, you declare that you support that side. [2] PHR-VERB To **come down on** someone means to criticize them or treat them harshly.

►**come down to.** PHR-VERB If a problem or decision **comes down to** a particular thing, that thing is the most important factor involved. *The problem comes down to money.*

►**come down with.** PHR-VERB If you **come down with** an illness, you get it.

►**come for.** PHR-VERB If people such as soldiers **come for** you, they come to find you.

►**come forward.** PHR-VERB If someone **comes forward**, they offer to do something in response to a request for help. *A vital witness came forward to say that she saw Tanner wearing the boots.*

►**come in.** [1] PHR-VERB If information or a report **comes in**, you receive it. *Reports are now coming in of trouble at yet another jail.* [2] PHR-VERB If you have money **coming in**, you receive it regularly as your income. [3] PHR-VERB If someone or something **comes in**, or **comes into** a situation, they are involved in it. *Finally, he could do no more, which is where Jacques came in.* [4] PHR-VERB When a new idea, fashion, or product **comes in**, it becomes popular or available.

►**come in for.** PHR-VERB If someone or something **comes in for** criticism or blame, they receive it.

►**come into.** [1] PHR-VERB If someone **comes into** money or property, they inherit it. [2] See also **come in** 3.

►**come off.** PHR-VERB If something **comes off**, it is successful or effective. *It was a good try but it didn't quite come off.*

►**come on.** [1] PHR-VERB You say **'Come on'** to someone to encourage them to do something. *Come on Doreen, let's dance.* [2] PHR-VERB When a machine **comes on**, it starts working. [3] PHR-VERB If you have an illness or a headache **coming on**, you can feel it starting. [4] PHR-VERB If something **is coming on**, it is developing or making progress. *The knee's coming on fine, I'm walking comfortably already.*

►**come on to.** PHR-VERB When you **come on to** a particular topic, you start discussing it. *We're now looking at a smaller system but I'll come on to that later.*

►**come out.** [1] PHR-VERB When a new product **comes out**, it becomes available to the public. *Christian Slater has a new movie coming out.* [2] PHR-VERB If a fact **comes out**, it becomes known to people. *The truth is beginning to come out about what happened.* [3] PHR-VERB If you **come out for** or **against** something, you declare that you support it or that you do not support it. [4] PHR-VERB If a photograph does not **come out**, it is blank or unclear when it is developed and printed. [5] PHR-VERB When the sun, moon, or stars **come out**, they appear in the sky.

►**come over.** PHR-VERB If a feeling **comes over** you, it affects you. *An eerie feeling came over me.*

►**come round.** See **come around.**

►**come through.** [1] PHR-VERB To **come through** a dangerous or difficult situation means to survive it. *The city had faced racial crisis and come through it.* [2] PHR-VERB If something **comes through**, you receive it. *The news came through at about five o'clock.* [3] PHR-VERB If a quality or impression **comes through**, it is clearly shown in what is said or done. *I hope my love for the material came through.*

►**come to.** See **come around** 3.

►**come under.** [1] PHR-VERB If you **come under** attack or pressure, for example, people attack you or put pressure on you. [2] PHR-VERB If something **comes under** your authority, you control how it is managed.

►**come up.** [1] PHR-VERB If someone **comes up to** you, they walk over to you. [2] PHR-VERB If an event **is coming up**, it is about to take place. *We do have elections coming up.* [3] PHR-VERB If something **comes up**, it happens unexpectedly. *I was delayed – something came up at home.* [4] PHR-VERB If a topic **comes up** in a conversation, it is mentioned. [5] PHR-VERB If a job **comes up** or if something **comes up for sale**, it becomes available. [6] PHR-VERB When the sun or moon **comes up**, it rises.

►**come up against.** PHR-VERB If you **come up against** a problem or difficulty, you have to deal with it. *We came up against a great deal of resistance in dealing with the case.*

►**come upon.** See **come across** 1.

comeback /'kʌmbæk/ **comebacks.** See **come back** 2.

comedian /kə'miːdiən/ **comedians.** N-COUNT A **comedian** is an entertainer whose job is to make people laugh by telling jokes.

⭐ **comedy** /'kɒmədi/ **comedies.** [1] N-UNCOUNT **Comedy** consists of types of entertainment that are intended to make people laugh. *...his career in comedy. ...a TV comedy series.* [2] N-COUNT A **comedy** is a play, film, or television programme that is intended to make people laugh.

comet /'kɒmɪt/ **comets.** N-COUNT A **comet** is an object that travels around the sun leaving a bright trail behind it.

⭐ **comfort** /'kʌmfət/ **comforts, comforting, comforted.** [1] N-UNCOUNT **Comfort** is the state of being physically or mentally relaxed. *The shoe has padding around the collar, heel and tongue for added comfort.* [2] N-UNCOUNT If you are living **in comfort**, you have enough money to have everything you need. [3] N-COUNT **Comforts** are things that make your life easier and more pleasant. *She enjoys the material comforts married life has brought her.* [4] VERB & N-UNCOUNT If you **comfort** someone, or if you offer them **comfort**, you make them feel less worried or unhappy. *Ned put his arm around her, trying to comfort her... We have offered comfort to some new residents who felt lost and lonely.*

⭐ **comfortable** /'kʌmftəbəl/ [1] ADJ You describe things such as furniture as **comfortable** when they make you feel physically relaxed. When you are physically relaxed you can also say that you are **comfortable**. *...a comfortable fireside chair... Lie down on your bed and make yourself comfortable.* ♦ **comfortably** ADV *Are you sitting comfortably?* [2] ADJ If someone is **comfortable**, they have enough money to be able to live without financial problems. ♦ **comfortably** ADV *Cayton describes himself as comfortably well-off.* [3] ADJ AFTER LINK-V If you feel **comfortable with** a particular situation or person, you feel confident and relaxed with them. *I felt comfortable with him... I'll talk to them, but I won't feel comfortable about it.*

comforting /'kʌmfətɪŋ/ ADJ If something is **comforting**, it makes you feel less worried or unhappy. *It may be comforting to know that some things never change.*

comic /'kɒmɪk/ **comics.** [1] ADJ Something that is **comic** makes you want to laugh. *The novel is comic and tragic. ...a fine comic actor.* [2] N-COUNT A **comic** is an entertainer who tells jokes in order to make people laugh. [3] N-COUNT In British English, a **comic** is a magazine that contains stories told in pictures. The usual American term is **comic book**.

comical /'kɒmɪkəl/. ADJ If something is **comical**, it makes you want to laugh because it seems funny or silly. *Her expression is almost comical.*

comic book, comic books. N-COUNT A **comic book** is the same as a **comic**. [AMERICAN]

⭐ **coming** /'kʌmɪŋ/. ADJ BEFORE N A **coming** event or time will happen soon. *...the weather in the coming months.*

comma /'kɒmə/ **commas.** N-COUNT A **comma** is the punctuation mark (,). → See Reference Page on Punctuation.

⭐ **command** /kə'mɑːnd, -'mænd/ **commands, commanding, commanded.** [1] VERB & N-COUNT If you **command** someone **to** do something, or if you give them a **command to** do it, you order them to do it. *'Get in your car and follow me,' he commanded... The tanker failed to respond to a command to stop.* [2] VERB If you **command** something such as obedience or attention, you obtain it as a result of being popular or important. *...an excellent physician who commanded the respect of all his colleagues.* [3] VERB & N-COUNT An officer who **commands** part of an army, navy, or air force or has **command of** it, is in charge of it. *Who would command the troops in the event of war?... In 1942 he took command of 108 Squadron.* [4] N-UNCOUNT Your **command of** something is your knowledge of it and ability to use it. *...his excellent command of English.*

commandant /'kɒməndænt/ **commandants.** N-COUNT A **commandant** is an army officer in charge of a particular place or group of people.

⭐ **commander** /kə'mɑːndə/ **commanders.** [1] N-COUNT & N-TITLE A **commander** is an officer in charge of a military operation. [2] N-COUNT & N-TITLE A **commander** is an officer in the navy.

commanding /kə'mɑːndɪŋ/. [1] ADJ If you are in a **commanding** position, you are in a strong or powerful position. *The French vessel has a commanding lead.* [2] ADJ If you have a **commanding** voice or manner, you seem powerful and confident. *...his commanding presence.*

commando /kə'mɑːndəʊ/ **commandos** (or **commandoes**). N-COUNT **Commandos** are soldiers specially trained to carry out raids.

commemorate /kə'meməreɪt/ **commemorates, commemorating, commemorated.** VERB If you **commemorate** a person or event, you remember them by means of a special action or ceremony,

A B C D E F G H I J K L M N O P Q R S T U V W X Y Z

or a specially created object. ...*a plaque commemorating the 169 Australians who died.*
♦ **commemoration, commemorations** N-VAR ...*a service of commemoration.*

commemorative /kə'memərətɪv/. ADJ BEFORE N A **commemorative** object or event is intended to make people remember an event or person. ...*a commemorative plaque.*

commence /kə'mens/ **commences, commencing, commenced.** VERB When something **commences**, or when you **commence** it, it begins. [FORMAL] *He commenced laughing.* ♦ **commencement** N-UNCOUNT ...*the subsequent commencement of oil and gas production.*

commend /kə'mend/ **commends, commending, commended.** VERB If you **commend** someone or something, you praise them formally to other people. *I commended her for that action.*
♦ **commendation, commendations** N-VAR ...*a letter of commendation.*

commendable /kə'mendəbəl/. ADJ If you describe someone's behaviour as **commendable**, you approve of it. [FORMAL] *Mr Sparrow has acted with commendable speed.* ♦ **commendably** ADV *Her manner was commendably restrained.*

⭐ **comment** /'kɒment/ **comments, commenting, commented.** VERB & N-VAR If you **comment** on something, or if you make a **comment on** it, you give your opinion about it or make a statement about it. *Police have refused to comment on whether anyone has been arrested... Stuart commented that this was very true... He made his comments at a news conference.*

commentary /'kɒməntri, AM -teri/ **commentaries.** [1] N-VAR A **commentary** is a spoken description of an event that is broadcast on radio or television while it is taking place. *He turned on his car radio to listen to the commentary.* [2] N-COUNT A **commentary** is a book or article which explains or discusses something. ...*a lengthy commentary on the situation in India.*

commentate /'kɒmənteɪt/ **commentates, commentating, commentated.** VERB To **commentate** means to give a radio or television commentary on an event. *They are in Sweden to commentate on the European Championships.*

⭐ **commentator** /'kɒmənteɪtə/ **commentators.** [1] N-COUNT A **commentator** is a broadcaster who gives a commentary on an event. [2] N-COUNT A **commentator** is someone who often writes or broadcasts about a particular subject. ...*Hugo Young, the political commentator of the Guardian.*

⭐ **commerce** /'kɒmɜːs/. N-UNCOUNT **Commerce** is the activity of buying and selling things on a large scale. *They have made their fortunes from industry and commerce.*

⭐ **commercial** /kə'mɜːʃəl/ **commercials.** [1] ADJ **Commercial** means relating to the buying and selling of goods. ...*English commercial law.* [2] ADJ **Commercial** activities, organizations, and products are concerned with making a profit. ...*the commercial exploitation of the forests.*

♦ **commercially** ADV *About five more species are grown commercially.* [3] ADJ **Commercial** television and radio are paid for by advertising. [4] N-COUNT A **commercial** is an advertisement broadcast on television or radio.

⭐ **commission** /kə'mɪʃən/ **commissions, commissioning, commissioned.** [1] VERB & N-COUNT If you **commission** a piece of work, or if you give someone a **commission** to do it, you formally arrange to pay for someone to do it for you. *A Japanese publishing house commissioned a book from me.* [2] N-VAR **Commission** is a sum of money paid to a salesperson for every sale that they make. *The adviser gets commission on every new policy sold.* [3] N-COUNT A **commission** is a group of people appointed to find out about something or to control something. **Commission** can take the singular or plural form of the verb. ...*the Press Complaints Commission.* [4] VERB & N-COUNT If a member of the armed forces is **commissioned**, or if they receive a **commission**, they are made an officer.

⭐ **commissioner** /kə'mɪʃənə/ **commissioners.** N-COUNT A **commissioner** is an important official in a government department or other organization. ...*the European Commissioner for External Affairs.*

⭐ **commit** /kə'mɪt/ **commits, committing, committed.** [1] VERB If someone **commits** a crime or a sin, they do something illegal or bad. *They believe they know who committed the murder.* [2] VERB To **commit** money or resources **to** something means to use them for a particular purpose. ...*one of the first nations to commit forces to the Gulf.* [3] VERB If you **commit yourself** to a way of life or course of action, you accept it fully or definitely decide to do it. *Mary had committed herself to becoming a teacher.* ♦ **commitment, commitments** N-VAR ...*commitment to the ideals of Bolshevism... They made a commitment to peace.* [4] VERB If someone **is committed to** a hospital or prison, they are officially sent there.

⭐ **commitment** /kə'mɪtmənt/ **commitments.** N-COUNT A **commitment** is a regular task which takes up some of your time. *I've got a lot of work commitments.*

⭐ **committee** /kə'mɪti/ **committees.** N-COUNT A **committee** is a group of people who represent a larger group or organization and make decisions for them. **Committee** can take the singular or plural form of the verb. ...*the Committee for Safety in Medicine.*

commodity /kə'mɒdɪti/ **commodities.** N-COUNT A **commodity** is something that is sold for money. [TECHNICAL] ...*basic commodities like bread and meat.*

⭐ **common** /'kɒmən/ **commoner, commonest; commons.** [1] ADJ If something is **common**, it is found in large numbers or it happens often. ...*Hansen, a common name in Norway. ...a common mistake.* ♦ **commonly** ADV *Parsley is probably the most commonly used of all herbs.* [2] ADJ If something is **common to** two or more

⭐ Bank of English® frequent word   For a full explanation of all grammatical labels, see pages vii-x

a
b
c
d
e
f
g
h
i
j
k
l
m
n
o
p
q
r
s
t
u
v
w
x
y
z

A B C D E F G H I J K L M N O P Q R S T U V W X Y Z

people or groups, it is possessed, done, or used by them all. *Such behaviour is common to all young people... Moldavians and Romanians share a common language.* [3] PHRASE If two or more people or things have something **in common**, they have the same interests, experiences, characteristics or features. [4] ADJ BEFORE N **Common** is used to indicate that something is ordinary and not special. *The scientific name for common salt is sodium chloride.* [5] ADJ If you describe someone as **common**, you mean they behave in a way that shows lack of taste, education, and good manners. [6] N-COUNT A **common** is an area of grassy land where the public is allowed to go.

common 'law. [1] N-UNCOUNT **Common law** is the system of law which is based on judges' decisions and on custom rather than on written laws. [2] ADJ BEFORE N A **common law** relationship is regarded as a marriage because it has lasted a long time, although no official marriage contract has been signed. *...his common law wife.*

commonplace /ˈkɒmənpleɪs/ **commonplaces.** ADJ & N-COUNT If something is **commonplace** or a **commonplace**, it happens often or is often found. *...a commonplace event. ...the sort of comment that has become a commonplace among conservatives.*

common 'sense (or **commonsense**). N-UNCOUNT **Common sense** is the natural ability to make good judgments and behave sensibly.

Commonwealth /ˈkɒmənwelθ/. N-PROPER **The Commonwealth** is an association of countries that used to belong to the British Empire.

commotion /kəˈməʊʃən/ **commotions.** N-VAR A **commotion** is a lot of noise and confusion. *I heard yelling and a lot of commotion.*

communal /ˈkɒmjʊnəl, AM kəˈmjuːnəl/. [1] ADJ BEFORE N **Communal** means relating to particular groups in a country or society. *...the communal violence in Sri Lanka.* [2] ADJ Something that is **communal** is shared by a group of people. *...communal ownership.*

commune /ˈkɒmjuːn/ **communes.** N-COUNT A **commune** is a group of people who live together and share everything.

⭐ **communicate** /kəˈmjuːnɪkeɪt/ **communicates, communicating, communicated.** [1] VERB If you **communicate with** someone, you give them information, for example by speaking, writing, or sending radio signals. *My natural mother has never communicated with me... They communicated in sign language.* ♦ **communication** N-UNCOUNT *She has no means of communication.* [2] VERB If you **communicate** an idea or a feeling **to** someone, you make them aware of it. *I was having trouble communicating my feelings to others.* [3] VERB If you say that people are able to **communicate**, you mean they talk to each other openly, which allows them to understand each other's feelings or attitudes.

...the inability of husbands and wives to communicate.

⭐ **communication** /kəˌmjuːnɪˈkeɪʃən/ **communications.** [1] N-PLURAL **Communications** are the systems and processes that are used to communicate or broadcast information. *...a communications satellite.* [2] N-COUNT A **communication** is a message that is sent to someone by, for example, sending a letter. [FORMAL]

communion /kəˈmjuːnjən/. [1] N-UNCOUNT **Communion** is the Christian ceremony in which people eat bread and drink wine as a symbol of Christ's death and resurrection. [2] N-UNCOUNT **Communion with** nature or some other power or spirit, or **communion with** a person, is the feeling that you are sharing thoughts or feelings with them.

communiqué /kəˈmjuːnɪkeɪ, AM -ˈkeɪ/ **communiqués.** N-COUNT A **communiqué** is an official statement. *...the joint communiqué, issued by China and Saudi Arabia.*

⭐ **communist** /ˈkɒmjʊnɪst/ **communists.** N-COUNT & ADJ A **communist** is someone who supports a political system in which the state controls the means of production, and everyone is supposed to be equal. *...communist rebels.* ♦ **communism** N-UNCOUNT *...the ultimate triumph of communism in the world.*

⭐ **community** /kəˈmjuːnɪti/ **communities.** [1] N-SING & N-COUNT A **community** is a group of people who live in a particular area or are alike in some way. *The event was well supported by the local community. ...the business community.* [2] N-UNCOUNT **Community** is friendship between different people or groups, and a sense of having something in common. **Community** can take the singular or plural form of the verb. *...a neighbourhood which has no sense of community.*

com'munity centre (AM **community center**) **community centres.** N-COUNT A **community centre** is a place where the people, groups, and organizations in a particular area can go and meet one another and do things.

com,munity 'service. N-UNCOUNT **Community service** is unpaid work that criminals sometimes do as a punishment instead of being sent to prison. *He was sentenced to 140 hours community service.*

commute /kəˈmjuːt/ **commutes, commuting, commuted.** [1] VERB If you **commute**, you travel a long distance to work every day. ♦ **commuter,** **commuters** N-COUNT *The number of commuters to London has dropped by 100,000.* [2] VERB If a prisoner's sentence **is commuted**, it is changed to a less serious sentence.

compact /kəmˈpækt/ **compacts, compacting, compacted.** [1] ADJ Something that is **compact** is small or takes up very little space. *...a compact camera.* [2] VERB To **compact** something means to press it so that it becomes more dense.

[FORMAL] *The boy was compacting the trash. ...a pile of compacted earth.*

compact disc /ˌkɒmpækt ˈdɪsk/ **compact discs.** N-COUNT **Compact discs** are small discs on which sound, especially music, is recorded. The abbreviation **CD** is also used.

companion /kəmˈpænjən/ **companions.** N-COUNT A **companion** is someone who you spend time with or travel with. *He has been her constant companion for the last four months.*

companionship /kəmˈpænjənʃɪp/. N-UNCOUNT **Companionship** is having someone you know and like with you, rather than being on your own. *I was glad of her companionship.*

⭐ **company** /ˈkʌmpəni/ **companies.** [1] N-COUNT A **company** is a business organization that makes money by selling goods or services. *...an insurance company.* [2] N-COUNT A **company** is a group of opera singers, dancers, actors, or other performers who work together. [3] N-UNCOUNT **Company** is the state of having companionship. *'I won't stay long.'—'No, please. I need the company'.* [4] PHRASE If you **keep** someone **company**, you spend time with them and stop them feeling lonely or bored.

comparable /ˈkɒmpərəbəl/. [1] ADJ Something that is **comparable to** something is roughly similar, for example in amount or importance. *Farmers were meant to get an income comparable to that of townspeople.* ◆ **comparably** ADV *...comparably qualified students.* [2] ADJ If two or more things are **comparable**, they are similar and so can be reasonably compared. *In other comparable countries real wages increased much more rapidly.* ◆ **comparability** N-UNCOUNT *...comparability between the accounts of similar companies.*

comparative /kəmˈpærətɪv/ **comparatives.** [1] ADJ BEFORE N You use **comparative** to show that your description of something is accurate only when it is compared to something else, or to what is usual. *He met the higher demands with comparative ease.* ◆ **comparatively** ADV *...a comparatively small nation.* [2] ADJ BEFORE N A **comparative** study involves the comparison of two or more things of the same kind. *...the comparative study of English and Latin authors.* [3] N-COUNT & ADJ BEFORE N In grammar, the **comparative** or the **comparative** form of an adjective or adverb is used to indicate that something has more of a quality than it used to have or than something else has. For example, 'bigger' is the comparative form of 'big'. ● Compare **superlative**.

⭐ **compare** /kəmˈpeə/ **compares, comparing, compared.** [1] VERB If you **compare** things, you consider them and discover the differences or similarities between them. *Compare the two illustrations in Fig 60.* [2] VERB If you **compare** one person or thing **to** another, you say that they are like the other person or thing. *Some commentators compared his work to that of James Joyce.*

⭐ **compared** /kəmˈpeəd/. PREP You can use **compared with** and **compared to** when you want to contrast two things or situations. For example, if you say that one thing is large compared with another or compared to another, you mean that it is larger than the other thing.

⭐ **comparison** /kəmˈpærɪsən/ **comparisons.** [1] N-VAR When you make a **comparison** between two or more things, you consider them and discover the differences between them. *...a comparison of the British and German economies.* [2] N-VAR When you make a **comparison**, you say that one thing is like another in some way. *...the comparison of her life to a sea voyage.*

compartment /kəmˈpɑːtmənt/ **compartments.** [1] N-COUNT A **compartment** is one of the separate sections of a railway carriage. [2] N-COUNT A **compartment** is one of the separate parts of an object that is used for keeping things in. *I put a bottle of champagne in the freezer compartment.*

compass /ˈkʌmpəs/ **compasses.** [1] N-COUNT A **compass** is an instrument that you use for finding directions. It has a dial and a magnetic needle that always points to the north. [2] N-PLURAL **Compasses** are a hinged V-shaped instrument that you use for drawing circles accurately. *...a pair of compasses.*

compassion /kəmˈpæʃən/. N-UNCOUNT **Compassion** is a feeling of pity, sympathy, and understanding for people who are suffering. *...his compassion and concern for a helpless woman.*

compassionate /kəmˈpæʃənət/. ADJ A **compassionate** person feels pity, sympathy, and understanding for people who are suffering. *...a deeply compassionate man.* ◆ **compassionately** ADV *He smiled compassionately at her.*

compatible /kəmˈpætɪbəl/. [1] ADJ If things, systems, or ideas are **compatible**, they work well together or can exist together successfully. *His evidence is fully compatible with other data.* ◆ **compatibility** N-UNCOUNT *...compatibility with VHS video recorders.* [2] ADJ If you are **compatible with** someone, you have a good relationship with them because you have similar opinions and interests. ◆ **compatibility** N-UNCOUNT *The basis of friendship is compatibility.*

compatriot /kəmˈpætriət, AM -ˈpeɪt-/ **compatriots.** N-COUNT Your **compatriots** are people from your own country.

compel /kəmˈpel/ **compels, compelling, compelled.** VERB If a situation, a rule, or a person **compels** you **to** do something, they force you to do it. *...legislation to compel cyclists to wear a helmet.*

compelling /kəmˈpelɪŋ/. ADJ A **compelling** argument or reason for something conv... that something is true or that someth... be done. *...a compelling reason to s...*

compensate /ˈkɒmpənseɪt/ **c...** **compensating, compensated.** [1] V... **compensated for** somethi... has happened to them, th...

compensation for it. *Farmers could be compensated for their loss of subsidies... The allied nations want Iraq to compensate victims of the war.* 2 VERB To **compensate for** something, especially something harmful or unwanted, means to do something that balances it or makes it ineffective. *The built-in safety device compensates for a fall in water pressure.*

★ **compensation** /ˌkɒmpənˈseɪʃən/ **compensations.** 1 N-UNCOUNT **Compensation** is money that someone who has undergone loss or suffering claims from the person or organization responsible. *He received one year's salary as compensation.* 2 N-VAR If something is a **compensation**, it reduces the effects of something bad that has happened. *Helen gained some compensation for her earlier defeat by winning the final open class.*

★ **compete** /kəmˈpiːt/ **competes, competing, competed.** 1 VERB If one person or organization **competes with** another **for** something, they try to get that thing for themselves and stop the other getting it. *Local residents fear competing with foreigners for jobs.* 2 VERB If you **compete** in a contest or a game, you take part in it. *Eight entrants competed for prizes totalling $1000.*

competent /ˈkɒmpɪtənt/. ADJ Someone who is **competent** is efficient and effective. *He was a very competent civil servant.* ♦ **competently** ADV *The government performed competently.* ♦ **competence** N-UNCOUNT *They have a high level of competence.*

★ **competition** /ˌkɒmpɪˈtɪʃən/ **competitions.** 1 N-UNCOUNT **Competition** is a situation in which two or more people or groups are trying to get something which not everyone can have. *There's been some fierce competition for the title.* 2 N-VAR A **competition** is an event in which people take part in order to find out who is best at a particular activity. *...a surfing competition.*

★ **competitive** /kəmˈpetɪtɪv/. 1 ADJ **Competitive** situations or activities are ones in which people compete with each other. *We are working in a very competitive market.* ♦ **competitively** ADV *...skiing competitively.* 2 ADJ A **competitive** person is eager to be more successful than other people. *...ambitious and fiercely competitive.* ♦ **competitively** ADV *They worked hard together, competitively and under pressure.* ♦ **competitiveness** N-UNCOUNT *I can't stand the pace, I suppose, and the competitiveness.* 3 ADJ You can say goods or services are at a **competitive** price or rate when they are less expensive than other goods of the same kind. ♦ **competitively** ADV *...competitively priced vehicles.*

★ **competitor** /kəmˈpetɪtə/ **competitors.** 1 N-COUNT A company's **competitors** are other companies that sell similar kinds of goods or services. *The bank isn't performing as well as some of its competitors.* 2 N-COUNT A **competitor** is a person who takes part in a competition.

compilation /ˌkɒmpɪˈleɪʃən/ **compilations.** N-COUNT A **compilation** is a record containing music from many different artists or music from different periods of one artist's career. *...a compilation of his jazz works over the past decade.*

compile /kəmˈpaɪl/ **compiles, compiling, compiled.** VERB If you **compile** something such as a book, report, or TV programme, you produce it by putting together pieces of information. *Councils were required to compile a register of all adults living in their areas.* ♦ **compilation** /ˌkɒmpɪˈleɪʃən/ N-UNCOUNT *...the compilation of data.*

complacent /kəmˈpleɪsənt/. ADJ If someone is **complacent** about something like a threat or danger, they behave as if there is nothing to worry about. *We cannot afford to be complacent about our health.* ♦ **complacency** /kəmˈpleɪsənsi/ N-UNCOUNT *...complacency about the risks of infection from AIDS.* ♦ **complacently** ADV *...smiling complacently at his own cleverness.*

★ **complain** /kəmˈpleɪn/ **complains, complaining, complained.** 1 VERB If you **complain about** something, you say you are not satisfied with it. *The American couple complained about the high cost of visiting Europe... People always complain that the big banks are unfriendly and unhelpful... They are liable to face more mistreatment if they complain to the police.* 2 VERB If you **complain of** a pain or illness, you say you have it.

★ **complaint** /kəmˈpleɪnt/ **complaints.** 1 N-VAR A **complaint** is a statement of dissatisfaction about a situation or a reason for it. *...complaints about the standard of service on Britain's railways.* 2 N-COUNT A **complaint** is an illness. *Eczema is a common skin complaint.*

complement, **complements, complementing, complemented.** 1 VERB /ˈkɒmplɪment/ If people or things **complement** each other, they have different qualities which go well together. *Choose a superb wine to complement your meal. ...a written examination to complement the practical test.* 2 N-COUNT /ˈkɒmplɪmənt/ Something that is a **complement** to something else complements it. *The green wallpaper is the perfect complement to the old pine.* 3 N-COUNT In grammar, the **complement** of a link verb is an adjective group or noun group which comes after the verb and describes or identifies the subject. For example, in the sentence 'They felt very tired', 'very tired' is the complement.

complementary /ˌkɒmplɪˈmentri/. ADJ If two different things are **complementary**, they form a complete unit when they are brought together, or they combine well with each other. *The two groups had complementary skills.*

★ **complete** /kəmˈpliːt/ **completes, completing, completed.** 1 ADJ If something is **complete**, it contains all the parts that it should contain. *No garden is complete without a bed of rose bushes. ...a complete set of keys to the shop.* 2 ADJ You use **complete** to emphasize that something is as great in degree or amount as it possibly can be.

The resignation came as a complete surprise.
♦ **completely** ADV *Dozens of flats had been completely destroyed.* [3] VERB If you **complete** something, you finish doing or producing it. *Peter Mayle has just completed his first novel.*
♦ **completion** N-UNCOUNT *The project is nearing completion.* [4] ADJ AFTER V-LINK If a task is **complete**, it is finished. *The work of restoring the farmhouse is complete.* [5] VERB To **complete** a set or group means to provide the last item that is needed to make it a full set or group. *Put a word in each space to complete the sentence.* [6] VERB To **complete** a form means to write the necessary information on it. [7] PHRASE If one thing comes **complete with** another, it has that thing as an extra or additional part. *The diary comes complete with a gold-coloured ballpoint pen.*

★ **complex** /'kɒmpleks/ **complexes.** [1] ADJ **Complex** things have many different parts and are hard to understand. *...a complex system of voting. ...her complex personality. ...complex machines.* [2] N-COUNT A **complex** is a group of buildings used for a particular purpose. *...a new stadium and leisure complex.* [3] N-COUNT If someone has a **complex** about something, they have a mental or emotional problem relating to it, often because of an unpleasant experience in the past. *I have never had a complex about my height.*

complexion /kəm'plekʃən/ **complexions.** N-COUNT Your **complexion** is the natural colour or condition of the skin on your face. *He had a pale complexion.*

complexity /kəm'pleksɪti/ **complexities.** N-VAR **Complexity** is the state of having many different parts connected or related to each other in a complicated way. *...the increasing complexity of modern weapon systems. ...legal complexities.*

compliance /kəm'plaɪəns/. N-UNCOUNT **Compliance with** something, for example a law or agreement, means doing what you are required or expected to do. [FORMAL] *The company says it is in full compliance with US labor laws.*

complicate /'kɒmplɪkeɪt/ **complicates, complicating, complicated.** VERB To **complicate** something means to make it more difficult to deal with or understand. *You have enough worries without me complicating matters.*

★ **complicated** /'kɒmplɪkeɪtɪd/. ADJ Something that is **complicated** has many parts and is therefore difficult to understand. *...the complicated voting system.*

complication /,kɒmplɪ'keɪʃən/ **complications.** N-COUNT A **complication** is a problem or difficulty. *The age difference was a complication in the relationship.*

complicity /kəm'plɪsɪti/. N-UNCOUNT **Complicity** is involvement with other people in an illegal activity. [FORMAL] *Recently a number of policemen were sentenced to death for their complicity in the murder.*

compliment, compliments, complimenting, complimented; verb /'kɒmplɪment/, noun /'kɒmplɪmənt/. [1] VERB & N-COUNT If you **compliment** someone, or if you pay them a **compliment**, you say something nice about them. *They complimented me on the way I looked.* [2] N-PLURAL **Compliments** is used in expressing good wishes or respect. [FORMAL] *My compliments to the chef.*

complimentary /,kɒmplɪ'mentəri/. [1] ADJ If you are **complimentary** about something, you express admiration for it. *We often get complimentary remarks regarding the cleanliness of our patio.* [2] ADJ A **complimentary** seat, ticket, or book is given to you free.

comply /kəm'plaɪ/ **complies, complying, complied.** VERB If you **comply with** a demand or rule, you do what you are required to do. [FORMAL] *The commander said that the army would comply with the ceasefire... There are calls for his resignation, but there is no sign yet that he will comply.*

★ **component** /kəm'pəʊnənt/ **components.** N-COUNT The **components** of something are its parts. *The management plan has four main components.*

compose /kəm'pəʊz/ **composes, composing, composed.** [1] VERB The things that something **is composed of** are its parts or members. The separate things that **compose** something are the parts or members that form it. *The force would be composed of troops from NATO countries... Protein molecules compose all the complex working parts of living cells.* [2] VERB When someone **composes** music, a speech, or a letter, they write it. [3] VERB If you **compose yourself**, you become calm after being angry or excited. ♦ **composed** ADJ *Laura was standing beside him, very calm and composed.*

composer /kəm'pəʊzə/ **composers.** N-COUNT A **composer** is a person who writes music.

composite /'kɒmpəzɪt, AM kəm'pɑːzɪt/ **composites.** ADJ & N-COUNT A **composite** object or item is made up of several different things, parts, or substances. A **composite** is a composite object or item. *...composite pictures.*

composition /,kɒmpə'zɪʃən/ **compositions.** [1] N-UNCOUNT The **composition of** something is the things that it consists of and the way that they are arranged. *...the social composition of the audience... Forests vary greatly in composition.* [2] N-COUNT A **composition** is a piece of written work, especially one that children write at school. [3] N-COUNT A composer's **compositions** are the pieces of music he or she has written.

compost /'kɒmpɒst, AM -pəʊst/. N-UNCOUNT **Compost** is a mixture of decaying plants and manure which is used to improve soil. *...a small compost heap.*

composure /kəm'pəʊʒə/. N-UNCOUNT Someone's **composure** is their appearance or feeling of calm and their control of their feelings, often in a difficult situation. [FORMAL]

compound, compounds, compounding, compounded; noun and adjective /'kɒmpaʊnd/, verb

a
b
c
d
e
f
g
h
i
j
k
l
m
n
o
p
q
r
s
t
u
v
w
x
y
z

/kəm'paʊnd/. **1** N-COUNT A **compound** is an enclosed area of land used for a particular purpose. ...*a military compound.* **2** N-COUNT In chemistry, a **compound** is a substance consisting of two or more elements. **3** ADJ BEFORE N In grammar, a **compound** noun, adjective, or verb is made up of two or more words, for example 'fire engine'. **4** VERB To **compound** a problem means to make it worse by increasing it in some way. [FORMAL] *Additional bloodshed and loss of life will only compound the tragedy.*

comprehend /ˌkɒmprɪ'hend/ **comprehends, comprehending, comprehended.** VERB If you cannot **comprehend** something, you cannot understand it. [FORMAL] *Whenever she failed to comprehend she invariably laughed.*

comprehension /ˌkɒmprɪ'henʃən/ **comprehensions.** **1** N-UNCOUNT **Comprehension** is the ability to understand something or the process of understanding something. *This was utterly beyond her comprehension... They turned to one another with the same expression of dawning comprehension.* **2** N-VAR A **comprehension** is an exercise to find out how well you understand a piece of text.

⭐ **comprehensive** /ˌkɒmprɪ'hensɪv/ **comprehensives.** **1** ADJ Something that is **comprehensive** includes everything necessary or relevant. ...*a comprehensive guide to the region.* ◆ **comprehensively** ADV *The book is comprehensively illustrated.* ...**2** ADJ BEFORE N & N-COUNT In Britain, a **comprehensive school** or a **comprehensive** is a secondary school where children of all abilities are taught together.

compress /kəm'pres/ **compresses, compressing, compressed.** VERB If you **compress** something, or if it **compresses**, it is pressed or squeezed so that it takes up less space. *Compressing a gas heats it up... As air in the lungs compresses, the flexible ribs contract.* ◆ **compression** /kəm'preʃən/ N-UNCOUNT *The compression of the wood is easily achieved.*

comprise /kəm'praɪz/ **comprises, comprising, comprised.** VERB If something **comprises** or is **comprised of** a number of things or people, it has them as its parts or members. [FORMAL] *The exhibition comprises 50 oils and watercolours.*

⭐ **compromise** /'kɒmprəmaɪz/ **compromises, compromising, compromised.** **1** N-VAR & VERB If you reach a **compromise** with someone or if you **compromise with** them, you reach an agreement whereby you both give up something that you originally wanted. ...*the government's policy of compromise... He would be prepared to compromise on his original demands... Make an effort to compromise with colleagues.* **2** VERB If someone **compromises themselves** or their beliefs, they do something which causes people to doubt their honesty, loyalty, or moral principles. *He would rather shoot himself than compromise his principles.*

compromising /'kɒmprəmaɪzɪŋ/. ADJ If you describe information or a situation as

compromising, you mean that it reveals an embarrassing or guilty secret about someone. ...*compromising photographs.*

compulsion /kəm'pʌlʃən/ **compulsions.** **1** N-COUNT A **compulsion** is a strong desire to do something. *He felt a sudden compulsion to drop the bucket and run.* **2** N-UNCOUNT If someone uses **compulsion** to make you do something, they force you to do it. *They were in classes out of choice rather than compulsion.*

compulsive /kəm'pʌlsɪv/. **1** ADJ BEFORE N You use **compulsive** to describe people who cannot stop doing something. ...*a compulsive liar.* ◆ **compulsively** ADV *John is compulsively neat and clean.* **2** ADJ If you say a book is **compulsive** reading or a film is **compulsive** viewing, you find it so interesting that you do not want to stop reading the book or watching the film. [BRITISH]

compulsory /kəm'pʌlsəri/. ADJ If something is **compulsory**, you must do it because a law or someone in authority says you must. *In East Germany learning Russian was compulsory.*

⭐ **computer** /kəm'pjuːtə/ **computers.** N-COUNT A **computer** is an electronic machine which makes quick calculations and deals with large amounts of information.

computerize (BRIT also **computerise**) /kəm'pjuːtəraɪz/ **computerizes, computerizing, computerized.** VERB To **computerize** a system or type of work means to introduce computers into it. ◆ **computerized** ADJ *Organizations can access computerized data banks to search for information.*

computing /kəm'pjuːtɪŋ/. N-UNCOUNT **Computing** is the activity of using a computer and writing programs for it.

comrade /'kɒmreɪd, AM -ræd/ **comrades.** N-COUNT Someone's **comrades** are their friends or companions. [LITERARY]

con /kɒn/ **cons, conning, conned.** VERB & N-COUNT If someone **cons** you, or if what they do is a **con**, they trick you into doing or believing something by saying things that are not true. [INFORMAL] *The businessman had conned him of £10,000... It was all a con.* ● **pros and cons**: see **pro**.

conceal /kən'siːl/ **conceals, concealing, concealed.** VERB To **conceal** something means to hide it or keep it secret. *The hat concealed her hair... She knew at once that he was concealing something from her.* ◆ **concealment** N-UNCOUNT ...*the concealment of weapons.*

⭐ **concede** /kən'siːd/ **concedes, conceding, conceded.** VERB If you **concede** something, you admit it or accept that it is true, often unwillingly. *Bess finally conceded that Nancy was right... 'Well,' he conceded, 'I do sometimes mumble a bit'.*

conceivable /kən'siːvəbəl/. ADJ If something is **conceivable**, you can imagine it or believe it. *It is just conceivable that a single survivor might be found.* ◆ **conceivably** ADV *The mission could conceivably be accomplished within a week.*

conceive /kənˈsiːv/ **conceives, conceiving, conceived.**
[1] VERB If you cannot **conceive of** something, you cannot imagine it or believe it. *He couldn't conceive of anyone arguing with his results.*
[2] VERB If you **conceive** a plan or idea, you think of it and work out how it can be done. *He conceived the idea of making a photographic study of German society.* ♦ **conception** /kənˈsepʃən/ N-UNCOUNT *The symphony is admirable in conception.* [3] VERB When a woman **conceives**, she becomes pregnant. ♦ **conception, conceptions** N-VAR *Six weeks after conception your baby is the size of your little fingernail.* [4] See also **conception.**

★ **concentrate** /ˈkɒnsəntreɪt/ **concentrates, concentrating, concentrated.** [1] VERB If you **concentrate on** something, you give it all your attention. *He sat back and concentrated on his driving... At work you need to be able to concentrate.* [2] VERB When something **is concentrated** in one place, it is all there rather than being spread around. *The high-status jobs were increasingly concentrated in the big cities.*

concentrated /ˈkɒnsəntreɪtɪd/. [1] ADJ A **concentrated** liquid has been increased in strength by having water removed from it. [2] ADJ A **concentrated** activity is done with great intensity in one place. *...a more concentrated effort to reach out to troubled kids.*

★ **concentration** /ˌkɒnsənˈtreɪʃən/ **concentrations.** [1] N-UNCOUNT **Concentration** on something involves giving all your attention to it. *We lacked concentration and it cost us the goal.* [2] N-VAR A **concentration of** something is a large amount of it or large numbers of it in a small area. *...one of the world's greatest concentrations of wildlife.*

concenˈtration camp, concentration camps. N-COUNT A **concentration camp** is a prison where non-military prisoners are kept in very bad conditions, usually in wartime.

★ **concept** /ˈkɒnsept/ **concepts.** N-COUNT A **concept** is an idea or abstract principle. *...the concept of arranged marriages.* ♦ **conceptual** /kənˈseptʃuəl/ ADJ BEFORE N *...the conceptual framework for this evaluation.*

conception /kənˈsepʃən/ **conceptions.** [1] N-VAR A **conception** is an idea that you have in your mind. *...someone with not the slightest conception of teamwork.* [2] See also **conceive.**

★ **concern** /kənˈsɜːn/ **concerns, concerning, concerned.** [1] N-UNCOUNT **Concern** is worry about a situation. *There is no cause for concern.* [2] VERB If something **concerns** you, it worries you. *It concerns me that we're not being told about this.* ♦ **concerned** ADJ *I've been concerned about you lately.* [3] N-COUNT A **concern** is a fact or situation that worries you. *Unemployment was the electorate's main concern.* [4] VERB If you **concern yourself with** something, you give attention to it because you think that it is important. *I didn't concern myself with politics.* [5] N-UNCOUNT Your **concern for** someone is a feeling that you want them to be happy, safe, and well. *He had only*

gone along out of concern for his two grandsons. [6] VERB If a book, speech, or piece of information **concerns** a particular subject, it is about that subject. *Chapter 2 concerns itself with the methodological difficulties.* ♦ **concerned** ADJ AFTER LINK-V *Randolph's work was exclusively concerned with the effects of pollution.* [7] VERB If a situation, event, or activity **concerns** you, it affects you or involves you. *'That doesn't concern you,' Zlotin retorted sharply.* ♦ **concerned** ADJ *It's a very stressful situation for everyone concerned.* [8] N-SING If a situation or problem is your **concern**, it is your duty or responsibility. *The technical aspects were the concern of the Army.* [9] N-COUNT A **concern** is a company or business. *The Minos Beach Hotel is a family concern.*
PHRASES ● You say **as far as** something **is concerned** to indicate the subject that you are talking about. *As far as my career was concerned, the affair did me more good than harm.* ● You say **as far as I'm concerned** to indicate that you are giving your own opinion. *The only problem, as far as I'm concerned, is Iris.*

concerning /kənˈsɜːnɪŋ/. PREP You use **concerning** to indicate what a question or piece of information is about. *...various questions concerning pollution and the environment.*

★ **concert** /ˈkɒnsət/ **concerts.** N-COUNT A **concert** is a performance of music. *...live rock concerts.*

concerted /kənˈsɜːtɪd/. [1] ADJ A **concerted** action is done by several people or groups working together. *...a concerted attack on poverty.* [2] ADJ If you make a **concerted** effort to do something, you try very hard to do it. *I'm going to make a concerted effort to write more letters.*

concerto /kənˈtʃeətəʊ/ **concertos.** N-COUNT A **concerto** is a piece of music for a solo instrument and an orchestra.

★ **concession** /kənˈseʃən/ **concessions.** N-COUNT If you make a **concession to** someone, you agree to let them do or have something, especially in order to end an argument or conflict. *He has refused to make any concessions to the kidnappers.*

conciliation /kənˌsɪliˈeɪʃən/. N-UNCOUNT **Conciliation** is trying to end a disagreement. *...a mood of conciliation.*

conciliatory /kənˈsɪliətri, AM -tɔːri/. ADJ If you are **conciliatory** in your actions or behaviour, you show you are willing to end a disagreement with someone. *...a conciliatory gesture.*

concise /kənˈsaɪs/. ADJ Something that is **concise** gives all the necessary information in a very brief form. *Burton's text is concise and informative.* ♦ **concisely** ADV *He'd delivered his report clearly and concisely.*

★ **conclude** /kənˈkluːd/ **concludes, concluding, concluded.** [1] VERB If you **conclude** that something is true, you decide that it is true using the facts you know. *He concluded that Oswald was somewhat abnormal... So what can we conclude from this debate?* [2] VERB When you **conclude** something, or when it **concludes**, it finishes.

[FORMAL] *I would like to conclude by saying that I do enjoy your magazine... The evening concluded with dinner and speeches.* **3** VERB If people or groups **conclude** a treaty or business deal, they arrange it or agree it. [FORMAL]

⭐ **conclusion** /kən'kluːʒən/ **conclusions.** **1** N-COUNT When you come to a **conclusion**, you decide that something is true after you have thought about it carefully. *I've come to the conclusion that she's a very great musician... Other people will no doubt draw their own conclusions.* **2** N-SING The **conclusion** of something is its ending. **3** PHRASE You can describe something that seems certain to happen as a **foregone conclusion**. **4** PHRASE You say **'in conclusion'** to introduce the last thing that you want to say. *In conclusion, walking is a cheap, safe, enjoyable and readily available form of exercise.*

conclusive /kən'kluːsɪv/. ADJ **Conclusive** evidence shows that something is definitely true. *There is no conclusive proof that this is harmful.* ♦ **conclusively** ADV *A new study proved conclusively that smokers die younger than non-smokers.*

concoct /kən'kɒkt/ **concocts, concocting, concocted.** **1** VERB If you **concoct** an excuse, you invent one. *The prisoner concocted the story to get a lighter sentence.* **2** VERB If you **concoct** something, especially something unusual, you make it by mixing several things together. *Eugene was concocting Rossini Cocktails.*

concoction /kən'kɒkʃən/ **concoctions.** N-COUNT A **concoction** is something that has been made out of several things mixed together. *...a concoction of honey, yogurt, oats, and apples.*

⭐ **concrete** /'kɒŋkriːt/. **1** N-UNCOUNT **Concrete** is a substance used for building. It is made from cement, sand, small stones, and water. **2** ADJ Something that is **concrete** is definite and specific. *He had no concrete evidence.*

concur /kən'kɜː/ **concurs, concurring, concurred.** VERB If two or more people **concur**, they agree. [FORMAL] *Local feeling does not necessarily concur with the press.*

concurrent /kən'kʌrənt, AM -'kɜːr-/. ADJ If two things are **concurrent**, they happen at the same time. *He will actually be serving three concurrent five-year sentences.* ♦ **concurrently** ADV *There were three races running concurrently.*

concussion /kən'kʌʃən/. N-UNCOUNT If you suffer **concussion** after a blow to your head, you lose consciousness or feel sick or confused.

⭐ **condemn** /kən'dem/ **condemns, condemning, condemned.** **1** VERB If you **condemn** something, you say that it is bad and unacceptable. *Mr Davies condemned the fee increase.* ♦ **condemnation** /ˌkɒndem'neɪʃən/ **condemnations** N-VAR *There was widespread condemnation of Saturday's killings.* **2** VERB If someone **is condemned to** a punishment, they are given it. *He was condemned to life imprisonment.* **3** VERB If authorities **condemn** a

building, they officially decide that it is not safe and must be pulled down.

condemned /kən'demd/. ADJ A **condemned** prisoner is going to be executed. *...a condemned man's last request.*

condense /kən'dens/ **condenses, condensing, condensed.** **1** VERB If you **condense** a piece of writing or speech, you make it shorter. *...how to condense serious messages into short, self-contained sentences.* **2** VERB When a gas or vapour **condenses**, or when you **condense** it, it changes into a liquid.

condescend /ˌkɒndɪ'send/ **condescends, condescending, condescended.** **1** VERB If you say that someone **condescends to** do something, you disapprove of them because they agree to do it in a way which shows that they think they are superior to other people and should not have to do it. *He wouldn't condescend to talk to the nurse.* **2** VERB If you say that someone **condescends to** other people, you disapprove of them because they behave in a way which shows that they think they are superior to other people. *Don't condescend to me.* ♦ **condescending** ADJ *...his condescending attitude.* ♦ **condescension** /ˌkɒndɪ'senʃən/ N-UNCOUNT *...a smile of condescension.*

⭐ **condition** /kən'dɪʃən/ **conditions, conditioning, conditioned.** **1** N-SING The **condition** of someone or something is the state they are in. *He remains in a critical condition in a California hospital... The boat is in good condition.* **2** N-PLURAL The **conditions** in which people live or do things are the factors that affect their comfort, safety, or success. *People are living in appalling conditions. ...the adverse weather conditions.* **3** N-COUNT A **condition** is something which must happen in order for something else to be possible. *One of the conditions of our release was that we had to leave the country immediately.* **4** PHRASE When you agree to do something **on condition that** something else happens, you mean that you will only do it if this other thing happens or is agreed to first. *He spoke to reporters on condition that he was not identified.* **5** N-COUNT You can refer to an illness or medical problem as a particular **condition.** *...a heart condition.* **6** VERB If someone **is conditioned to** think or do something in a particular way, they do it as a result of their upbringing or training. *You have been conditioned to believe that it is weak to be scared.* ♦ **conditioning** N-UNCOUNT *...social conditioning.*

conditional /kən'dɪʃənəl/. ADJ If a situation or agreement is **conditional on** something, it will only happen if this thing happens. *Their support is conditional on his proposals meeting their approval. ...a conditional offer.*

condolence /kən'dəʊləns/ **condolences.** N-PLURAL & N-UNCOUNT When you offer your **condolences**, or when you send a message of **condolence**, you express sympathy for someone whose friend or relative has died recently.

condom /ˈkɒndɒm/ **condoms.** N-COUNT A **condom** is a rubber covering which a man wears on his penis as a contraceptive.

condone /kənˈdəʊn/ **condones, condoning, condoned.** VERB If someone **condones** behaviour that is wrong, they accept it and allow it to happen. *I cannot condone violence.*

conducive /kənˈdjuːsɪv, AM -ˈduːsɪv/. ADJ If one thing is **conducive to** another, it makes the other thing likely to happen. *Make your bedroom as conducive to sleep as possible.*

★ **conduct, conducts, conducting, conducted;** verb /kənˈdʌkt/, noun /ˈkɒndʌkt/. ☐ VERB & N-SING When you **conduct** an activity or task, you organize it and do it. You can also talk about the **conduct** of an activity or task. *I decided to conduct an experiment. ...the conduct of free and fair elections.* ☐ N-UNCOUNT & VERB Your **conduct**, or the way you **conduct yourself**, is the way you behave. *...basic principles of civilised conduct... The way he conducts himself reflects on the party.* ☐ VERB When someone **conducts** an orchestra or choir, they stand in front of it and direct its performance. *Solti will continue to conduct here and abroad.* ◆ **conductor, conductors** N-COUNT *Several hundred musicians and their conductor.* ☐ VERB If something **conducts** heat or electricity, it allows heat or electricity to pass through it.

cone /kəʊn/ **cones.** ☐ N-COUNT A **cone** is a shape with a circular base and smooth curved sides ending in a point at the top. → See picture on page 829. ☐ N-COUNT A **cone** is the fruit of a pine or fir tree. It consists of a cluster of scales containing seeds.

confederation /kənˌfedəˈreɪʃən/ **confederations.** N-COUNT A **confederation** is an organization of groups or states, especially one that exists for political or business purposes. *...a confederation of independent republics.*

confer /kənˈfɜː/ **confers, conferring, conferred.** ☐ VERB When you **confer with** someone, you discuss something with them in order to make a decision. *He conferred with Hill... His doctors conferred by telephone.* ☐ VERB If someone or something **confers** power or honour on you, they give it to you. *Never imagine that rank confers genuine authority.*

★ **conference** /ˈkɒnfrəns/ **conferences.** N-COUNT A **conference** is a meeting, often lasting a few days, which is organized on a particular subject. *...a conference on education. ...the Conservative Party conference.*

confess /kənˈfes/ **confesses, confessing, confessed.** VERB If you **confess to** doing something wrong or something that you are ashamed of, you admit that you did it. *He had confessed to seventeen murders... Ed later confessed that he was worried.*

confession /kənˈfeʃən/ **confessions.** ☐ N-COUNT A **confession** is a signed statement by someone in which they admit that they have committed a particular crime. *They forced him to sign a confession.* ☐ N-VAR **Confession** is the act of

admitting that you have done something that you are ashamed of or embarrassed about. *I have a confession to make.*

confide /kənˈfaɪd/ **confides, confiding, confided.** VERB If you **confide in** someone, you tell them a secret. *She confided in me earlier... He confided to me that he felt like he was being punished.*

★ **confidence** /ˈkɒnfɪdəns/ **confidences.** ☐ N-UNCOUNT If you have **confidence in** someone, you feel you can trust them. *I have every confidence in you.* ☐ N-UNCOUNT If you have **confidence**, you feel sure about your abilities, qualities, or ideas. *The team was full of confidence.* ☐ N-UNCOUNT If you tell someone something **in confidence**, you tell them a secret. *We told you all these things in confidence.*

★ **confident** /ˈkɒnfɪdənt/. ☐ ADJ If you are **confident** about something, you are certain that it will happen in the way you want it to. *I'm confident that we will succeed.* ◆ **confidently** ADV *I can confidently promise that this year is going to be very different.* ☐ ADJ People who are **confident** feel sure of their own abilities, qualities, or ideas. *In time he became more confident and relaxed.* ◆ **confidently** ADV *She walked confidently across the hall.*

confidential /ˌkɒnfɪˈdenʃəl/. ADJ Information that is **confidential** is meant to be kept secret. *...confidential information about her private life.* ◆ **confidentially** ADV *Any information they give will be treated confidentially.* ◆ **confidentiality** N-UNCOUNT *...the confidentiality of the client-solicitor relationship.*

configuration /kənˌfɪgʊˈreɪʃən, AM -ˌfɪgjə-/ **configurations.** N-COUNT A **configuration** is an arrangement of a group of things. [FORMAL] *...an ancient configuration of giant stones.*

configure /kənˈfɪgə, AM -ˈfɪgjər/ **configures, configuring, configured.** VERB If you **configure** a piece of computer equipment, you set it up so that it is ready for use. [COMPUTING] *How easy was it to configure the software?*

confine, confines, confining, confined. ☐ VERB /kənˈfaɪn/ To **confine** something or someone **to** a particular place or group means to prevent them from spreading beyond it or from leaving it. *The US will soon be taking steps to confine the conflict... The army and police had been confined to barracks.* ◆ **confinement** N-UNCOUNT *...his confinement to a wheelchair.* ☐ VERB If you **confine yourself** or your activities **to** something, you do only that thing. *Yoko had largely confined her activities to the world of big business.* ☐ N-PLURAL /ˈkɒnfaɪnz/ The **confines** of a building or area are its boundaries. [FORMAL]

confined /kənˈfaɪnd/. ☐ ADJ AFTER LINK-V If something is **confined to** a particular place or group, it exists only there. *The problem is not confined to Germany.* ☐ ADJ A **confined** space or area is small and enclosed by walls.

★ **confirm** /kənˈfɜːm/ **confirms, confirming, confirmed.** ☐ VERB If something **confirms** what you believe,

it shows that it is definitely true. *X-rays have confirmed that he has not broken any bones... These new statistics confirm our worst fears.*
♦ **confirmation** /ˌkɒnfəˈmeɪʃən/ N-UNCOUNT *Rejections are simply confirmation of what they thought all along.* [2] VERB If you **confirm** something that has been stated or suggested, you say that it is definitely true. *The spokesman confirmed that the area was now in rebel hands.*
♦ **confirmation** N-UNCOUNT *She glanced over at James for confirmation.* [3] VERB If you **confirm** an arrangement or appointment, you make it definite. *You make the reservation, and I'll confirm it in writing.* ♦ **confirmation** N-UNCOUNT *Travel arrangements are subject to confirmation.*

confiscate /ˈkɒnfɪskeɪt/ **confiscates, confiscating, confiscated.** VERB If you **confiscate** something from someone, you take it away from them, often as a punishment. *The court confiscated his passport.*

⭐ **conflict, conflicts, conflicting, conflicted.**
[1] N-UNCOUNT /ˈkɒnflɪkt/ **Conflict** is serious disagreement and argument. If two people or groups are **in conflict**, they have had a serious disagreement and have not yet reached agreement. *Try to keep any conflict between you and your ex-partner to a minimum.* [2] N-VAR **Conflict** is fighting between countries or groups of people. *...a military conflict.* [3] VERB /kənˈflɪkt/ If ideas, beliefs, or accounts **conflict**, they are very different from each other and it seems impossible for them to exist together. *...opinions which usually conflicted with my own.*
♦ **conflicting** ADJ *...conflicting reports about the identity of the hostage.*

conform /kənˈfɔːm/ **conforms, conforming, conformed.** [1] VERB If something **conforms to** a law or **to** someone's wishes, it is what is required or wanted. *The lamp conforms to new safety requirements... These activities do not conform with diplomatic rules.* [2] VERB If you **conform**, you behave in the way that you are expected to behave. *People feel a failure if they don't conform.*

conformity /kənˈfɔːmɪti/ N-UNCOUNT **Conformity** is behaviour, thought, or appearance that is the same as that of most other people.

confound /kənˈfaʊnd/ **confounds, confounding, confounded.** VERB If someone or something **confounds** you, they make you confused or surprised. *The choice of Governor may confound us all.*

⭐ **confront** /kənˈfrʌnt/ **confronts, confronting, confronted.** [1] VERB If you **are confronted with** a problem or task, you have to deal with it. *She was confronted with severe money problems. ...the magnitude of the task confronting them.* [2] VERB If you **confront** someone, you stand or sit in front of them, especially when you are going to fight or argue with them. *The candidates confronted each other during a televised debate.* [3] VERB If you **confront** someone **with** evidence, you present it to them in order to accuse them of something. *How do managers react when we confront them with this fact?*

⭐ **confrontation** /ˌkɒnfrʌnˈteɪʃən/ **confrontations.** N-VAR A **confrontation** is a dispute, fight, or battle. *...confrontation with the enemy.*
♦ **confrontational** /ˌkɒnfrʌnˈteɪʃənəl/ ADJ *...the committee's confrontational style of campaigning.*

confuse /kənˈfjuːz/ **confuses, confusing, confused.** [1] VERB If you **confuse** two things, you get them mixed up, so that you think one is the other. *I can't see how anyone could confuse you with another!* ♦ **confusion** N-UNCOUNT *Use different colours of felt pen on your sketch to avoid confusion.* [2] VERB To **confuse** someone means to make it difficult for them to know what is happening or what to do. *German politics surprised and confused him.* [3] VERB To **confuse** a situation means to make it complicated or difficult to understand. *In attempting to present two sides, you managed only to confuse the issue.*

confused /kənˈfjuːzd/. [1] ADJ If you are **confused**, you do not know what to do or you do not understand what is happening. *People are confused about what they should eat to stay healthy.* [2] ADJ Something that is **confused** does not have any order or pattern and is difficult to understand. *...a modern society in which values have become increasingly confused.*

confusing /kənˈfjuːzɪŋ/. ADJ Something that is **confusing** makes it difficult for people to know what to do or what is happening. *This situation must be confusing for you.*

confusion /kənˈfjuːʒən/ [1] N-UNCOUNT If there is **confusion** about something, it is not clear what the true situation is. *There's still confusion about the number of casualties.* [2] N-UNCOUNT **Confusion** is a situation in which everything is in disorder, especially because there are lots of things happening at the same time. *There was confusion when a man fired shots.* [3] N-UNCOUNT If your mind is in a state of **confusion**, you do not know what to believe or what you should do. [4] See also **confuse.**

congenial /kənˈdʒiːniəl/. ADJ A **congenial** person, place, or environment is pleasant. [FORMAL]

congested /kənˈdʒestɪd/. ADJ A **congested** road or area is extremely crowded and blocked with traffic or people.

congestion /kənˈdʒestʃən/. N-UNCOUNT If there is **congestion** in a place, the place is extremely congested. *...the problems of traffic congestion.*

conglomerate /kənˈglɒmərət/ **conglomerates.** N-COUNT A **conglomerate** is a large business consisting of several different companies. *Fiat is Italy's largest industrial conglomerate.*

congratulate /kənˈgrætʃʊleɪt/ **congratulates, congratulating, congratulated.** VERB If you **congratulate** someone, you express pleasure for something good that has happened to them, or you praise them for something they have achieved. *She congratulated him on the birth of his son.* ♦ **congratulation** N-UNCOUNT *...letters of congratulation.*

congratulations /kənˌgrætʃʊ'leɪʃənz/.
CONVENTION You say **'congratulations'** to
someone in order to congratulate them.
Congratulations, you have a healthy baby boy.

congregate /'kɒŋgrɪgeɪt/ **congregates,**
congregating, congregated. VERB When people
congregate, they gather together. *Youngsters
love to congregate here in the evenings.*

congregation /ˌkɒŋgrɪ'geɪʃən/ **congregations.**
N-COUNT The people who attend a church service
are the **congregation**. **Congregation** can take
the singular or plural form of the verb.

congress /'kɒŋgres/ **congresses.** N-COUNT A
congress is a large meeting held to discuss ideas
and policies. **Congress** can take the singular or
plural form of the verb.

★ **Congress** /'kɒŋgres/. N-PROPER **Congress** is the
elected group of politicians that is responsible for
making the law in the USA. ♦ **congressional**
/kən'greʃənəl/ ADJ BEFORE N ...*a congressional
report.* ● See note at **government**.

congressman /'kɒŋgrɪsmən/ **congressmen.**
N-COUNT & N-TITLE A **congressman** is a male
member of the US Congress. ● See note at
government.

congresswoman /'kɒŋgrɪswʊmən/
congresswomen, N-COUNT & N-TITLE A
congresswoman is a female member of the US
Congress. ● See note at **government**.

conjecture /kən'dʒektʃə/ **conjectures.** N-VAR
Conjecture is a guess based on incomplete or
doubtful information. [FORMAL] *The attitudes of
others were matters of conjecture.*

conjoined twin /kənˌdʒɔɪnd 'twɪn/ **conjoined**
twins. N-COUNT **Conjoined twins** are twins who
are born with their bodies joined.

conjunction /kən'dʒʌŋkʃən/ **conjunctions.**
[1] PHRASE If one thing is done or used **in**
conjunction with another, the two things are
done or used together. [FORMAL] *The army should
have operated in conjunction with the fleet.*
[2] N-COUNT In grammar, a **conjunction** is a word
that joins together words, groups, or clauses. For
example, 'and' and 'or' are conjunctions.

conjure /'kʌndʒə, AM 'kɑːn-/ **conjures, conjuring,**
conjured. VERB & PHR-VERB If you **conjure** something
out of nothing, or if you **conjure up** something,
you produce it as if by magic. *Every day a different
chef will be conjuring up delicious dishes.*
▶**conjure up.** PHR-VERB To **conjure up** a
memory, picture, or idea means to create it in
your mind. *He could conjure up in exact colour
almost every event of his life.*

connect /kə'nekt/ **connects, connecting, connected.**
[1] VERB To **connect** one thing **to** another means
to join them together. *Connect the wires... The
trailer was connected to the car.* [2] VERB If a piece
of equipment or a place **is connected to** a source
of power or water, it is joined to that source.
*Ischia was now connected to the mainland water
supply.* [3] VERB If a telephone operator **connects**
you, he or she enables you to speak to another

person by telephone. [4] VERB If one train or
plane **connects with** another, it arrives at a time
which allows passengers to change to the other
one in order to continue their journey. ...*a train
connecting with a ferry to Ireland.* [5] VERB If you
connect a person or thing **with** something, you
realize that there is a link between them. *I hoped
he would not connect me with the article.*

connected /kə'nektɪd/. ADJ If one thing is
connected with another, there is a link between
them. ...*skin problems connected with exposure to
the sun... The dispute is not directly connected to
the negotiations.*

★ **connection** /kə'nekʃən/ **connections.** [1] N-COUNT
A **connection** is a relationship between two
people, groups, or things. *He had no connection
with the security forces.* [2] N-COUNT A **connection**
is the joint where two wires or pipes are joined
together. [3] N-COUNT If you get a **connection** at a
station or airport, you continue your journey by
catching another train, bus, or plane. *My flight
was late and I missed the connection.* [4] PHRASE If
you talk to someone **in connection with**
something, you talk to them about that thing. *I
am writing in connection with Michael Shower's
letter.*

connoisseur /ˌkɒnə'sɜː/ **connoisseurs.** N-COUNT A
connoisseur is someone who knows a lot about
the arts, food, or drink. ...*connoisseurs of good
food.*

connotation /ˌkɒnə'teɪʃən/ **connotations.**
N-COUNT The **connotations** of a word are the
ideas or qualities that it makes you think of. ...*the
title's sexual connotations.*

conquer /'kɒŋkə/ **conquers, conquering, conquered.**
[1] VERB If one country or group of people
conquers another, they take complete control of
their land. *During 1936, Mussolini conquered
Abyssinia.* ♦ **conqueror, conquerors** N-COUNT ...*the
attitudes of European conquerors.* [2] VERB If you
conquer something such as a problem, you
succeed in ending it or dealing with it. *He has
never conquered his addiction.*

conquest /'kɒŋkwest/. N-UNCOUNT **Conquest** is
the act of conquering a country or group of
people. *He had led the conquest of southern
Poland.*

conscience /'kɒnʃəns/ **consciences.** [1] N-COUNT
Your **conscience** is the part of your mind that
tells you if what you are doing is wrong. If you
have a **guilty conscience**, or if you have
something **on** your **conscience**, you feel guilty
because you know you have done something
wrong. *I have battled with my conscience over
whether I should actually send this letter.*
[2] N-UNCOUNT **Conscience** is doing what you
believe is right even though it might be
unpopular or difficult. *He refused for reasons of
conscience to sign a new law legalising abortion.*

conscientious /ˌkɒnʃi'enʃəs/. ADJ Someone
who is **conscientious** is very careful to do their
work properly. ...*a conscientious and dedicated*

a
b
c
d
e
f
g
h
i
j
k
l
m
n
o
p
q
r
s
t
u
v
w
x
y
z

mother. ✦ **conscientiously** ADV *He studied conscientiously.*

⭐ **conscious** /'kɒnʃəs/. **1** ADJ AFTER LINK-V If you are **conscious of** something, you notice it or are aware of it. *He was conscious of the faint, musky aroma of aftershave.* **2** ADJ **Conscious** is used in expressions such as 'politically conscious' to describe someone who believes that a particular aspect of life is important. *She was very health-conscious.* **3** ADJ BEFORE N A **conscious** decision or effort is one that you are aware of making. *I don't think we ever made a conscious decision to have a big family.* ✦ **consciously** ADV *Sophie was not consciously seeking a replacement after her father died.* **4** ADJ Someone who is **conscious** is awake rather than asleep or unconscious. *She was fully conscious.*

⭐ **consciousness** /'kɒnʃəsnəs/. **1** N-UNCOUNT Your **consciousness** consists of your mind, thoughts, beliefs and attitudes. *She let her consciousness drift. ...a necessary change in the European consciousness.* **2** N-UNCOUNT If you **lose consciousness**, you become unconscious. When you **regain consciousness**, you become conscious again.

conscript, conscripts, conscripting, conscripted. **1** VERB /kən'skrɪpt/ If someone **is conscripted**, they are officially made to join the armed forces of a country. *He was conscripted into the army.* ✦ **conscription** N-UNCOUNT *All adult males will be liable for conscription.* **2** N-COUNT /'kɒnskrɪpt/ A **conscript** is a person who has been made to join the armed forces of a country.

consecrate /'kɒnsɪkreɪt/ **consecrates, consecrating, consecrated.** VERB When a building, place, or object **is consecrated**, it is officially declared to be holy. ✦ **consecration** N-UNCOUNT *...the consecration of the new Coventry Cathedral.*

consecutive /kən'sekjʊtɪv/. ADJ **Consecutive** events or periods of time happen one after the other without interruption. *...his second consecutive win.*

consensus /kən'sensəs/. N-SING A **consensus** is general agreement amongst a group of people. *There is a growing consensus in Europe that more vigorous action is needed.*

consent /kən'sent/ **consents, consenting, consented.** **1** N-UNCOUNT **Consent** is permission given to someone to do something. *Can my child be medically examined without my consent?* **2** N-UNCOUNT **Consent** is agreement about something between people. *By common consent it was the best game of these Championships.* **3** VERB If you **consent to** something, you agree to do it or agree to it being done.

⭐ **consequence** /'kɒnsɪkwens/ **consequences.** **1** N-COUNT The **consequences of** something are the results or effects of it. *One consequence of the reforms was a sharp tax increase.* **2** PHRASE If one thing happens and then another thing happens **in consequence**, the second thing happens as a

result of the first. *His death was totally unexpected and, in consequence, no plans had been made for his replacement.* **3** N-UNCOUNT Someone or something that is **of consequence** is important or valuable. Someone or something that is **of no consequence** is not important or valuable.

consequent /'kɒnsɪkwənt/. ADJ **Consequent** means happening as a direct result of something. [FORMAL] *...the warming of the Earth and the consequent climatic changes.* ✦ **consequently** ADV *Ellen's father teased her about her weight. Consequently, she sees herself as much heavier than she really is.*

conservation /,kɒnsə'veɪʃən/. N-UNCOUNT **Conservation** is the preservation and protection of the environment. *...wildlife conservation.* ● See also **conserve**.

conservationist /,kɒnsə'veɪʃənɪst/ **conservationists.** N-COUNT A **conservationist** is someone who works and campaigns for the conservation of the environment.

⭐ **conservative** /kən'sɜːvətɪv/ **conservatives.** **1** N-COUNT & ADJ A **Conservative** or a **Conservative** politician or voter is a member of or votes for the Conservative Party. *...Conservative MPs.* ✦ **conservatism** N-UNCOUNT *...one of the hallmarks of Conservatism under John Major.* **2** ADJ & N-COUNT Someone who is **conservative** or who is a **conservative** has right-wing views. **3** ADJ Someone who is **conservative** is unwilling to accept changes and new ideas. *Older people tend to be more conservative than younger ones.* ✦ **conservatism** N-UNCOUNT *Designers blame UK manufacturers' conservatism.* **4** ADJ A **conservative** estimate is very cautious. *Conservative estimates put her wealth at £5 million.* ✦ **conservatively** ADV *...a player conservatively valued at £500,000.*

conservatory /kən'sɜːvətri, AM -tɔːri/ **conservatories.** N-COUNT A **conservatory** is a glass room built onto a house.

conserve /kən'sɜːv/ **conserves, conserving, conserved.** **1** VERB If you **conserve** a supply of something, you use it carefully so that it lasts longer than it normally would. *Rationing has been introduced to conserve stocks.* ✦ **conservation** N-UNCOUNT *...energy conservation.* **2** VERB To **conserve** something means to protect it from harm, loss, or change. *...aid to help developing countries conserve their forests.*

⭐ **consider** /kən'sɪdə/ **considers, considering, considered.** **1** VERB If you **consider** a person or thing to be something, this is your opinion of them. *I consider him a coward... Others consider the move premature... He considers that this is the worst recession this century.* **2** VERB If you **consider** something, you think about it carefully. *You do have to consider the feelings of those around you.* ✦ **consideration** N-UNCOUNT *He said the draft* *treaty needed further consideration.* [3] See also **considering**.

⭐ **considerable** /kən'sɪdərəbəl/. ADJ **Considerable** means great in amount or degree. *...his considerable wealth... Vets' fees can be considerable.* ♦ **considerably** ADV *Children vary considerably in the rate at which they learn.*

considerate /kən'sɪdərət/. ADJ A **considerate** person pays attention to the needs, wishes, or feelings of other people.

⭐ **consideration** /kən,sɪdə'reɪʃən/ **considerations.** [1] N-UNCOUNT Someone who shows **consideration** pays attention to the needs, wishes, or feelings of other people. *Show consideration for other rail travellers.* [2] N-COUNT A **consideration** is something that should be thought about when you are planning or deciding something. *A further important consideration is the weather.* [3] See also **consider**. PHRASES ● If you **take** something **into consideration**, you think about it because it is relevant to what you are doing. *In sentencing, he took into consideration the defendants' ages.* ● If something is **under consideration**, it is being discussed. *Several proposals are under consideration.*

⭐ **considering** /kən'sɪdərɪŋ/. CONJ & PREP You use **considering** to indicate that you are taking a particular fact into account when giving an opinion. *Considering that you are no longer involved with this man, your response is a little extreme... The former hostage is in remarkably good shape considering his ordeal.*

consign /kən'saɪn/ **consigns, consigning, consigned.** VERB If you **consign** someone or something **to** a particular place or situation, you put or place them there. *For decades, many of Malevich's works were consigned to the basements of Soviet museums.*

consignment /kən'saɪnmənt/ **consignments.** N-COUNT A **consignment of** goods is a load that is being delivered to a place or person.

⭐ **consist** /kən'sɪst/ **consists, consisting, consisted.** VERB Something that **consists of** particular things is formed from them. *His diet consisted of bread, cheese and lager.*

consistency /kən'sɪstənsi/. N-UNCOUNT The **consistency** of a substance is the extent to which it is thick or smooth. *Dilute the paint with water.*

⭐ **consistent** /kən'sɪstənt/. [1] ADJ A **consistent** person always behaves or responds in the same way. *Becker has never been the most consistent of players.* ♦ **consistency** N-UNCOUNT *He has shown remarkable consistency throughout.* ♦ **consistently** ADV *...something I have consistently denied.* [2] ADJ If facts or ideas are **consistent**, there is no contradiction between or within them. *This result is consistent with the findings.*

consolation /,kɒnsə'leɪʃən/ **consolations.** N-VAR If something is a **consolation**, it makes you feel more cheerful when you are unhappy. *He knew then he was right, but it was no consolation.*

console, consoles, consoling, consoled. [1] VERB /kən'səʊl/ If you **console** someone who is unhappy, you try to make them more cheerful. *I could say nothing to console him.* [2] N-COUNT /'kɒnsəʊl/ A **console** is a panel with switches or knobs that is used to operate a machine.

consolidate /kən'sɒlɪdeɪt/ **consolidates, consolidating, consolidated.** VERB If you **consolidate** something such as your power or success, you strengthen it so that it becomes more effective or secure. *This album should further consolidate their success.* ♦ **consolidation** N-UNCOUNT *The report recommended some consolidation of police powers.*

consonant /'kɒnsənənt/ **consonants.** N-COUNT A **consonant** is a sound such as 'p' or 'f' which you pronounce by stopping the air flowing freely through your mouth.

consortium /kən'sɔːtiəm/ **consortiums** or **consortia** /kən'sɔːtiə/. N-COUNT A **consortium** is a group of people or firms who have agreed to work together. **Consortium** can take the singular or plural form of the verb.

conspicuous /kən'spɪkjuəs/. ADJ If someone or something is **conspicuous**, people can see or notice them very easily. *I felt very conspicuous.* ♦ **conspicuously** ADV *Johnston's name was conspicuously absent from the list.*

conspiracy /kən'spɪrəsi/ **conspiracies.** N-VAR **Conspiracy** is the secret planning by a group of people to do something wrong or illegal. *...a conspiracy to undermine public education.*

conspirator /kən'spɪrətə/ **conspirators.** N-COUNT A **conspirator** is a person who joins a conspiracy.

conspire /kən'spaɪə/ **conspires, conspiring, conspired.** [1] VERB If two or more people **conspire to** do something illegal or harmful, they make a secret agreement to do it. *...a defendant convicted of conspiring with his brother to commit robberies.* [2] VERB If events **conspire to** produce a particular result, they seem to cause this result. *The weather and the recession conspired to hit wine production and sales.*

constable /'kʌnstəbəl, 'kɒn-/ **constables.** N-COUNT & N-TITLE In Britain, a **constable** is a police officer of the lowest rank.

⭐ **constant** /'kɒnstənt/. [1] ADJ Something that is **constant** happens all the time or is always there.

...*constant interruptions.* ...*constant noise.*

♦ **constantly** ADV *The direction of the wind is constantly changing.* [2] ADJ An amount or level that is **constant** stays the same over a particular period of time. *The temperature remains more or less constant.*

constellation /ˌkɒnstəˈleɪʃən/ **constellations.** N-COUNT A **constellation** is a group of stars which form a fixed pattern.

consternation /ˌkɒnstəˈneɪʃən/ N-UNCOUNT **Consternation** is a feeling of anxiety or fear. [FORMAL] *The announcement has caused consternation.*

constipation /ˌkɒnstɪˈpeɪʃən/ N-UNCOUNT **Constipation** is a medical condition which causes people to have difficulty getting rid of waste matter from their bowels.

constituency /kənˈstɪtʃʊənsi/ **constituencies.** N-COUNT A **constituency** is an area for which someone is elected as the representative in parliament.

constituent /kənˈstɪtʃʊənt/ **constituents.** [1] N-COUNT A **constituent** is someone who lives in a particular constituency. [2] N-COUNT & ADJ BEFORE N A **constituent** or a **constituent** part of something is one of the things that it is made from. ...*caffeine, one of the major constituents of coffee.*

constitute /ˈkɒnstɪtjuːt, AM -tuːt/ **constitutes, constituting, constituted.** [1] LINK-VERB If something **constitutes** a particular thing, it can be regarded as being that thing. ...*the question of what constitutes normal behaviour.* [2] LINK-VERB If a number of things or people **constitute** something, they are the parts or members that form it. *Hindus constitute 83% of India's population.*

⭐ **constitution** /ˌkɒnstɪˈtjuːʃən, AM -ˈtuː-/ **constitutions.** [1] N-COUNT The **constitution** of a country or organization is the system of laws which formally states people's rights and duties. ...*the French constitution.* ♦ **constitutional** /ˌkɒnstɪˈtjuːʃənəl, AM -ˈtuː-/ ADJ ...*Italy's constitutional reforms.* [2] N-COUNT Your **constitution** is your health. *He must have an extremely strong constitution.*

constrain /kənˈstreɪn/ **constrains, constraining, constrained.** VERB To **constrain** someone or something means to limit their development or activities. [FORMAL] *Women are too often constrained by family commitments.*

♦ **constrained** ADJ ...*constrained budgets.*

constraint /kənˈstreɪnt/ **constraints.** [1] N-COUNT A **constraint** is something that limits or controls what you can do. ...*new legal constraints.* [2] N-UNCOUNT **Constraint** is control over the way you behave which prevents you from doing what you want to do. *The Republics wanted democracy after years of constraint.*

constrict /kənˈstrɪkt/ **constricts, constricting, constricted.** [1] VERB If a part of your body, especially your throat, **is constricted**, something causes it to become narrower. ...*a drug which*

constricts the blood vessels... *His throat began to feel swollen and constricted.* ♦ **constriction** N-UNCOUNT ...*constriction of the blood vessels.* [2] VERB If something **constricts** you, it limits your actions so that you cannot do what you want to do. *Men and women alike have been constricted by traditional sexual roles.* ♦ **constriction, constrictions** N-COUNT ...*the constrictions placed upon me as a child.*

construct, constructs, constructing, constructed. [1] VERB /kənˈstrʌkt/ If you **construct** something, you build, make, or create it. ...*the campaign to construct a temple on the site... Construct a spending plan.* [2] N-COUNT /ˈkɒnstrʌkt/ A **construct** is a complex idea. [FORMAL]

⭐ **construction** /kənˈstrʌkʃən/ **constructions.** [1] N-UNCOUNT **Construction** is the building or creating of something. ...*a new community centre is under construction... This is the finest wood for boat construction.* [2] N-COUNT A **construction** is an object that has been made or built. ...*an impressive steel and glass construction.*

constructive /kənˈstrʌktɪv/ ADJ A **constructive** discussion, comment, or approach is useful and helpful. ...*constructive criticism.* ♦ **constructively** ADV *Use the time constructively.*

construe /kənˈstruː/ **construes, construing, construed.** VERB If something **is construed** in a particular way, its nature or meaning is interpreted in that way. [FORMAL] *She construed my concern as nosiness.*

consul /ˈkɒnsəl/ **consuls.** N-COUNT A **consul** is a government official who lives in a foreign city and looks after all the people there who are from his or her own country. ♦ **consular** /ˈkɒnsjʊlə, AM -sə-/ ADJ BEFORE N ...*British Consular officials.*

consulate /ˈkɒnsjʊlət, AM -sə-/ **consulates.** N-COUNT A **consulate** is the place where a consul works. ...*the British consulate in Lyons.*

⭐ **consult** /kənˈsʌlt/ **consults, consulting, consulted.** [1] VERB If you **consult** someone or something, you refer to them for advice or information. *Consult your doctor about how much exercise you should attempt... He needed to consult with an attorney... Consult the chart on page 44 for the correct cooking times.* ♦ **consultation, consultations** N-VAR ...*a consultation with a nutritionist.* [2] See also **consultation**.

consultancy /kənˈsʌltənsi/ **consultancies.** [1] N-COUNT A **consultancy** is a company that gives expert advice on a particular subject. ...*a management consultancy.* [2] N-UNCOUNT **Consultancy** is expert advice which a person or group is paid to provide. *The project provides both consultancy and training.*

⭐ **consultant** /kənˈsʌltənt/ **consultants.** [1] N-COUNT A **consultant** is an experienced doctor specializing in one area of medicine. [BRITISH] ...*a consultant heart surgeon.* [2] N-COUNT A **consultant** is a person who gives expert advice on a particular subject. *He was a consultant to the Swedish government.*

consultation /ˌkɒnsəlˈteɪʃən/ **consultations.**
1 N-VAR **Consultations** are meetings which are held to discuss something. **Consultation** is discussion about something. *...consultations with President Mitterrand.* **2** See also **consult**.

consultative /kənˈsʌltətɪv/. ADJ A **consultative** committee or document is one which gives advice or makes proposals about a particular problem or subject.

consume /kənˈsjuːm, AM -ˈsuːm/ **consumes, consuming, consumed.** **1** VERB If you **consume** something, you eat or drink it. [FORMAL] *Martha would consume nearly a pound of cheese per day.* **2** VERB To **consume** an amount of fuel, energy, or time means to use it up. *A computer circuit consumes a tiny amount of electricity.* ♦ **-consuming** *...oil-consuming countries. ...a time-consuming job.*

consumed /kənˈsjuːmd, AM -ˈsuːmd/. ADJ AFTER LINK-V If you are **consumed with** a feeling or idea, it affects you very strongly. *He's consumed with ambition.*

★ **consumer** /kənˈsjuːmə, AM -ˈsuː-/ **consumers.** N-COUNT A **consumer** is a person who buys things or uses services. *...consumer rights.*

consuming /kənˈsjuːmɪŋ, AM -ˈsuː-/. ADJ A **consuming** passion or interest is more important to you than anything else. *He has developed a consuming passion for chess.*

consummate, consummates, consummating, consummated. **1** ADJ /ˈkɒnsjəmət/ You use **consummate** to describe someone who is extremely skilful. [FORMAL] *...a consummate politician... He acted the part with consummate skill.* **2** VERB /ˈkɒnsəmeɪt/ If two people **consummate** a marriage or relationship, they make it complete by having sex. ♦ **consummation** N-UNCOUNT *...the consummation of their marriage.* **3** VERB To **consummate** an agreement means to complete it. [FORMAL] *No one has been able to consummate a deal.*

consumption /kənˈsʌmpʃən/. **1** N-UNCOUNT The **consumption** of fuel or energy is the amount of it that is used, or the act of using it. *...a reduction in fuel consumption.* **2** N-UNCOUNT The **consumption** of food or drink is the act of eating or drinking something. [FORMAL] *The wine was unfit for human consumption.* **3** N-UNCOUNT **Consumption** is the act of buying and using things. [TECHNICAL] *...the production and consumption of goods and services.*

★ **contact** /ˈkɒntækt/ **contacts, contacting, contacted.** **1** N-VAR **Contact** involves meeting or communicating with someone. *I had very little contact with teenagers... I shall be in contact with my family by telephone... He started writing poetry, and making contact with other poets.* **2** VERB If you **contact** someone, you telephone them or write to them. *Could he be contacted?* **3** N-UNCOUNT If you come **into contact with** something, you have some experience of it in the

course of your work or other activities. *The college has brought me into contact with western ideas.* **4** N-COUNT A **contact** is someone you know in an organization who helps you or gives you information. *Their contact in the United States Embassy was called Phil.* **5** N-UNCOUNT If people or things are **in contact**, they are touching each other. *...where the foot and shoe are in contact... There was no physical contact.*

¹contact lens, contact lenses. N-COUNT **Contact lenses** are small lenses that you put on your eyes to help you to see better.

contagious /kənˈteɪdʒəs/. **1** ADJ A **contagious** disease can be caught by touching people or things that are infected with it. **2** ADJ A **contagious** feeling or attitude spreads quickly among a group of people. *Laughing is contagious.*

★ **contain** /kənˈteɪn/ **contains, containing, contained.** **1** VERB If something such as a box or a room **contains** things, those things are in it. *The bag contained a Christmas card... The 77,000-acre estate contains five of the highest peaks in Scotland.* **2** VERB If something **contains** a particular substance, that substance is part of it. *Alcohol contains sugar.* **3** VERB To **contain** something such as a feeling, problem, or activity means to control it and prevent it from increasing. *Evans could barely contain his delight... Firemen are still trying to contain the fire.*

container /kənˈteɪnə/ **containers.** **1** N-COUNT A **container** is something such as a box or bottle that is used to hold things. **2** N-COUNT A **container** is a very large metal or wooden box used for transporting goods so that they can be loaded easily onto ships and lorries. *...the country's busiest container port.*

contaminate /kənˈtæmɪneɪt/ **contaminates, contaminating, contaminated.** VERB If something **is contaminated** by dirt, chemicals, or radiation, it becomes impure or harmful. *...waste water contaminated by hazardous chemicals... He received a contaminated blood transfusion.* ♦ **contamination** N-UNCOUNT *...the contamination of the sea.*

contemplate /ˈkɒntəmpleɪt/ **contemplates, contemplating, contemplated.** **1** VERB If you **contemplate** something, you consider it as a possibility. *He contemplated a career as an army medical doctor... He will not contemplate discussion on the issue.* **2** VERB If you **contemplate** an idea or subject, you think about it for a long time. *He cried as he contemplated his future.* ♦ **contemplation** N-UNCOUNT *It is a place of quiet contemplation.* **3** VERB To **contemplate** something or someone means to look at them for a long time. *He contemplated his hands.*

★ **contemporary** /kənˈtempərəri, AM -pəreri/ **contemporaries.** **1** ADJ **Contemporary** means existing now or at the time you are talking about. *...contemporary music. ...the reports of contemporary witnesses.* **2** N-COUNT Someone's

contemporaries are people who are or were alive at the same time as them. ...*Shakespeare and his contemporaries.*

contempt /kən'tempt/. N-UNCOUNT If you have **contempt for** someone or something, you have no respect for them. *He has contempt for most politicians... They were regarded with contempt.*

contemptuous /kən'temptʃuəs/. ADJ If you are **contemptuous of** someone or something, you have no respect for them. *He's openly contemptuous of all the major political parties.* ♦ **contemptuously** ADV *'A deal!' she said contemptuously, 'I hate all deals.'*

contend /kən'tend/ **contends, contending, contended.** [1] VERB If you have to **contend with** a problem or difficulty, you have to deal with it or overcome it. *They had a severely disturbed child to contend with.* [2] VERB If you **contend for** something, you compete with them to try to get it. ...*the two main groups contending for power.* ♦ **contender** /kən'tendə/ **contenders** N-COUNT ...*a strong contender for an Olympic gold medal.* [3] VERB If you **contend** that something is true, you state or argue that it is true. [FORMAL] *Lawyers contend that smokers use the tobacco products voluntarily.*

content 1 noun uses

⭐ **content** /'kɒntent/ **contents.** [1] N-PLURAL The **contents of** a container such as a bottle, box, or room are the things inside it. *Empty the contents of the pan into the sieve. ...Sandon Hall and its contents.* [2] N-VAR The **content** of a piece of writing, speech, or television programme is its subject and the ideas expressed in it. *Stricter controls were placed on the content of video films. ...the letter's contents.* [3] N-PLURAL The **contents** of a book are its different chapters and sections. *There is no initial list of contents.* [4] N-SING You can use **content** to refer to the amount or proportion of something that a substance contains. **Content** is always used after a noun for this meaning. *Sunflower margarine has the same fat content as butter.*

content 2 adjective and verb uses

content /kən'tent/ **contents, contenting, contented.** [1] ADJ AFTER LINK-V If you are **content to** do something or **content with** something, you are willing to accept it, rather than wanting something more or better. *I am content to admire the mountains from below... Not content with rescuing one theatre, Sally Green has taken on another.* [2] VERB If you **content yourself with** something, you accept it and do not try to do or have other things. *He wisely contented himself with his family.* [3] ADJ AFTER LINK-V If you are **content**, you are happy and satisfied with your way of life. [4] See also **contentment**.

contented /kən'tentɪd/. ADJ If you are **contented**, you are satisfied with your life or the situation you are in. ♦ **contentedly** ADV *The landlady sighed contentedly.*

contention /kən'tenʃən/ **contentions.** [1] N-COUNT Someone's **contention** is the opinion that they are expressing. *My contention is not that men don't talk. We do.* [2] N-UNCOUNT **Contention** is disagreement or argument about something. *The major area of contention among the Democrats is abortion.* [3] PHRASE If you are **in contention** in a contest, you have a chance of winning it. *Four others are in contention for the prize.*

contentious /kən'tenʃəs/. ADJ A **contentious** issue causes disagreement and arguments. *The strategy was highly contentious.*

contentment /kən'tentmənt/. N-UNCOUNT **Contentment** is the feeling of being content.

⭐ **contest, contests, contesting, contested.** [1] N-COUNT /'kɒntest/ A **contest** is a competition or game. ...*a writing contest.* [2] N-COUNT A **contest** is a struggle to win power or control. ...*next year's presidential contest.* [3] VERB /kən'test/ If someone **contests** an election or competition, they take part in it in order to win. [4] VERB If you **contest** a statement or decision, you disagree with it formally. *He has to reply within 14 days in order to contest the case.*

contestant /kən'testənt/ **contestants.** N-COUNT A **contestant** in a competition or quiz is a person who takes part in it.

⭐ **context** /'kɒntekst/ **contexts.** [1] N-VAR The **context of** an idea or event is the general situation in which it occurs. *It is important that we put Jesus into the context of history... The drugs problem has to be seen in context.* [2] N-VAR The **context** of a word or sentence consists of the words or sentences before it and after it. *He said his remarks had been taken out of context.*

⭐ **continent** /'kɒntɪnənt/ **continents.** [1] N-COUNT A **continent** is a very large area of land, such as Africa or Asia, that consists of several countries. [2] N-PROPER In Britain, the mainland of Europe is sometimes referred to as **the Continent**. ♦ **continental** ADJ BEFORE N ...*the continental street-side cafe.*

contingency /kən'tɪndʒənsi/ **contingencies.** N-COUNT A **contingency** is something that might happen in the future. *I need to examine all possible contingencies. ...military contingency plans.*

contingent /kən'tɪndʒənt/ **contingents.** [1] N-COUNT A **contingent** is a group of people representing a country or organization. *A contingent of Belgian paratroops is also said to have arrived. ...European scientists, including a British contingent.* [2] ADJ If an event is **contingent on** something, it can only happen if that thing happens or exists. [FORMAL] ...*the premise that people's rights are contingent on their abilities.*

continual /kən'tɪnjuəl/. ADJ BEFORE N **Continual** means happening without stopping, or happening again and again. ...*continual pain... She suffered continual police harassment.*

♦ **continually** ADV *Malcolm was continually changing his mind.*

USAGE Both **continual** and **continuous** can be used to say that something continues without interruption, but only **continual** can correctly be used to say that something keeps happening repeatedly. *There have been continual demands to cut costs... Calder became conscious of a continuous background noise.*

---

continuation /kən,tɪnjʊ'eɪʃən/. [1] N-UNCOUNT The **continuation** of something is the fact that it continues to happen or exist. *...the continuation of the war.* [2] N-SING Something that is a **continuation of** something else is closely connected with it and develops it in some way. *This chapter is a continuation of Chapter 8.*

⭐ **continue** /kən'tɪnjuː/ **continues, continuing, continued.** [1] VERB If something **continues**, it does not stop. If you **continue to** do something, you do not stop doing it. *The conflict would continue until conditions were met for a ceasefire... Interest rates continue to fall... Diana and Roy are determined to continue working.* [2] VERB If something **continues**, or if you **continue** it, it starts again after stopping for a period of time. *The trial continues today... I went up to my room to continue with my packing.* [3] VERB To **continue** means to begin speaking again after a pause or interruption. *'Anyway, that was what gave us the idea,' she continued after a pause.* [4] VERB If you **continue** in a particular direction, you keep going in that direction. *He continued rapidly up the path.*

continuity /kɒntɪ'njuːɪti, AM -'nuː-/ **continuities.** N-VAR The **continuity** of something is the fact that it happens, exists, or develops without stopping or changing suddenly. *...political stability and continuity.*

continuous /kən'tɪnjʊəs/. [1] ADJ A **continuous** process or event continues for a period of time without stopping. *...a continuous stream of phone calls.* ♦ **continuously** ADV *The machinery should go on working continuously for twelve hours.* [2] ADJ A **continuous** line or surface has no gaps in it. [3] ADJ In English grammar, **continuous** tenses are formed using the auxiliary 'be' and the present participle of a verb, as in 'I'm feeling a bit tired'. Compare **simple**.

contort /kən'tɔːt/ **contorts, contorting, contorted.** VERB When something **contorts**, it changes into an unnatural and unattractive shape. *His face contorted with pain.* ♦ **contortion, contortions** N-VAR *...the contortions of the gymnasts.*

contour /'kɒntʊə/ **contours.** [1] N-COUNT The **contours of** something are its shape or outline. *...the contours of the body.* [2] N-COUNT On a map, a **contour** is a line joining points of equal height.

contraception /,kɒntrə'sepʃən/. N-UNCOUNT

Methods of preventing pregnancy are called **contraception**.

contraceptive /,kɒntrə'septɪv/ **contraceptives.** N-COUNT A **contraceptive** is a device or pill used to prevent pregnancy.

⭐ **contract, contracts, contracting, contracted.** [1] N-COUNT /'kɒntrækt/ A **contract** is a legal agreement, usually between two companies or between an employer and employee, which involves doing work for a stated sum of money. *...a prestigious contract for work on Europe's tallest building.* [2] VERB /kən'trækt/ If you **contract with** someone **to** do something, you legally agree to do it for them or for them to do it for you. [FORMAL] *You can contract with us to deliver your cargo.* [3] VERB When something **contracts**, it becomes smaller or shorter. *When you are anxious, your muscles contract.* ♦ **contraction, contractions.** N-VAR *...the contraction and expansion of blood vessels.* [4] VERB If you **contract** a serious illness, you become ill with it. [FORMAL]

contractor /'kɒntræktə, kən'træk-/ **contractors.** N-COUNT A **contractor** is a person or company that works for other people or companies.

contractual /kən'træktʃʊəl/. ADJ A **contractual** arrangement or relationship involves a legal agreement between people. [FORMAL] ♦ **contractually** ADV *Rank was contractually obliged to hand him a cheque for $30 million.*

contradict /,kɒntrə'dɪkt/ **contradicts, contradicting, contradicted.** [1] VERB If you **contradict** someone, you say or suggest that what they have just said is wrong. *She dared not contradict her.* [2] VERB If one statement or action **contradicts** another, the first one makes the second appear to be wrong. *Her version contradicted the Government's claim.*

contradiction /,kɒntrə'dɪkʃən/ **contradictions.** [1] N-VAR A **contradiction** is an aspect of a situation which appears to conflict with other aspects, so that they cannot all exist or be successful. *...the contradictions between her private life and the public persona.* [2] PHRASE If you say that something is **a contradiction in terms**, you mean that it is described as having a quality that it cannot have. *A public service run for profit – a contradiction in terms if there ever was one.*

contradictory /,kɒntrə'dɪktəri, AM -tɔːri/. ADJ If two or more facts, ideas, or statements are **contradictory**, they state or imply that opposite things are true. *...advice that sometimes is contradictory and confusing.*

contrary /'kɒntrəri, AM -treri/. [1] ADJ **Contrary** ideas or opinions are completely different from each other. *Clearly there's room for a contrary view to mine... Contrary to popular belief, moderate exercise actually decreases your appetite.* [2] PHRASE You use **on the contrary** when you are contradicting what has just been

a b c d e f g h i j k l m n o p q r s t u v w x y z

said. 'People just don't do things like that.'—'On the contrary, they do them all the time.'

> **USAGE** Do not confuse **on the contrary** with **on the other hand**. **On the contrary** is used to contradict someone or something, to say that they are wrong. **On the other hand** is used to state a different, often contrasting aspect of the situation you are considering. *Prices of other foods and consumer goods fell. Wages on the other hand increased.*

3 PHRASE Evidence or statements **to the contrary** contradict what you are saying or what someone else has said. *Despite the report's conclusions to the contrary, the city had an excellent emergency plan.*

⭐ **contrast, contrasts, contrasting, contrasted.** **1** N-VAR /'kɒntrɑːst, -træst/ A **contrast** is a great difference between two or more things. *...the contrast between town and country... His public statements have always been in marked contrast to those of his son.* **2** PHRASE You use **contrast** in expressions such as **by contrast** or **in contrast**, to show that you are mentioning a very different situation from the one you have just mentioned. *After the ecstatic hugs and kisses of the team-members, the award ceremony was, in contrast, cold and flat.* **3** VERB /kən'trɑːst, -'træst/ If one thing **contrasts with** another, it is very different from it. *The latest news contrasts markedly with earlier reports... Paint the wall in a contrasting colour.* **4** VERB If you **contrast** one thing **with** another, you show the differences between them. *She contrasted the situation then with the present crisis... In this section we contrast four possible broad approaches.*

contravene /ˌkɒntrə'viːn/ **contravenes, contravening, contravened.** VERB To **contravene** a law or rule means to do something that is forbidden by it. [FORMAL] ◆ **contravention** /ˌkɒntrə'venʃən/ **contraventions** N-VAR *Child labour is exploited in contravention of labour laws.*

⭐ **contribute** /kən'trɪbjuːt/ **contributes, contributing, contributed.** **1** VERB If you **contribute to** something, you say or do something to help make it successful. *Each of the girls is expected to contribute to community work.* **2** VERB If a person, organization, or country **contributes** money or resources **to** something, they help to pay for it or achieve it. *They would like to contribute more to charity.* ◆ **contributor** /kən'trɪbjʊtə/ **contributors** N-COUNT *...contributors to EU funds.* **3** VERB If something **contributes** to a situation, it is one of its causes. *The report says design faults contributed to the tragedy... Stress, both human and mechanical, may also be a contributing factor.* ◆ **contributor** N-COUNT *Old buses are major contributors to pollution.* **4** VERB If you **contribute to** a magazine or book, you write things that are published in it. *She contributes*

regularly to Vogue magazine. ◆ **contributor** N-COUNT *...a regular contributor to this magazine.*

⭐ **contribution** /ˌkɒntrɪ'bjuːʃən/ **contributions.** **1** N-COUNT If you make a **contribution to** something, you do something to help make it successful or to produce it. *He was awarded a prize for his contribution to world peace.* **2** N-COUNT A **contribution** is a sum of money that you give in order to help pay for something. *...companies that make charitable contributions.*

contrive /kən'traɪv/ **contrives, contriving, contrived.** **1** VERB If you **contrive to** do something difficult, you manage to do it. [FORMAL] *He contrived to see her most days and nights.* **2** VERB If you **contrive** an event or situation, you succeed in making it happen. [FORMAL] *The oil companies were accused of contriving a shortage of gasoline.*

contrived /kən'traɪvd/ ADJ If you say that something is **contrived**, you think it is false or unconvincing; used showing disapproval. *The plotting is contrived, the dialogue inane and the romance implausible.*

⭐ **control** /kən'trəʊl/ **controls, controlling, controlled.** **1** VERB & N-UNCOUNT If someone **controls** an organization, place, or system, or if they have **control** of it, they have the power to take all the important decisions about the way it is run. You can also say they are **in control** of it or it is **under** their **control**. *The restructuring involves Mr Ronson giving up control of the company... People feel more in control of their own lives. ...its controlling interest in both firms.* ◆ **-controlled** *AGA Gas is Swedish-controlled.* ◆ **controller, controllers** N-COUNT *...the job of controller of BBC 1.* **2** VERB & N-UNCOUNT If you **control** a person or machine, or if you have **control of** them, you are able to make them do what you want them to do. *I can't control what the judge says or what people think... He lost control of his car... Some teachers have more control over pupils than their parents have.* **3** VERB & N-UNCOUNT If you **control yourself** or your feelings, or show **control**, you make yourself behave calmly even though you are feeling angry, excited, or upset. *I couldn't control my temper... Sometimes he would completely lose control.* ◆ **controlled** ADJ *Her manner was quiet and very controlled.* **4** VERB & N-UNCOUNT To **control** prices, wages, or undesirable activities means to restrict them to an acceptable level. **Control** is the act of controlling something in this way. If something is **out of control**, it cannot be restricted by anyone. If it is **under control**, it is being dealt with successfully. *The priorities are to control prices. ...the need to control environmental pollution... Control of inflation remains the government's absolute priority... The fire is burning out of control.* **5** N-PLURAL **Controls** are the methods an organization uses to restrict something. *The price controls announced yesterday will lower electricity bills.* **6** N-UNCOUNT A **control** is a device such as a switch or lever which you use in order to operate a machine or other piece of equipment. *He was at the controls of the plane when it crashed.*

USAGE You do not use **control** as a verb to talk about inspecting documents. The word you use is **check**. *Police were searching cars and checking identity documents.* However, at an airport or port, the place where passports are checked is called **passport control**.

★ **controversial** /ˌkɒntrə'vɜːʃəl/. ADJ Someone or something that is **controversial** causes intense public argument, disagreement, or disapproval. *...the controversial new book.*

★ **controversy** /'kɒntrəvɜːsi, kən'trɒvəsi/ **controversies.** N-VAR **Controversy** is a lot of discussion and disagreement about something, often involving strong anger or disapproval. *...a fierce political controversy over human rights.*

convalesce /ˌkɒnvə'les/ **convalesces, convalescing, convalesced.** VERB If you **are convalescing**, you are resting and regaining your health after an illness or operation. *...those convalescing from illness or surgery.* ◆ **convalescent** ADJ *...his convalescent wife.* ◆ **convalescence** /ˌkɒnvə'lesəns/ ADJ *I visited him during his convalescence.*

convene /kən'viːn/ **convenes, convening, convened.** VERB If you **convene** a meeting, you arrange for it to take place. You can also say that people **convene** at a meeting. *Senior officials convened in October.*

convenience /kən'viːniəns/ **conveniences.** [1] N-UNCOUNT If something is done for your **convenience**, it is done in a way that is useful or suitable for you. *He was happy to make a detour for her convenience.* [2] N-COUNT If you describe something as a **convenience**, you mean it is useful. *Mail order is a convenience for buyers who are too busy to shop.* [3] N-COUNT **Conveniences** are pieces of equipment designed to make your life easier. *...an apartment with all the modern conveniences.*

convenient /kən'viːniənt/. [1] ADJ Something that is **convenient** is easy, useful, or suitable for a particular purpose. *...a flexible and convenient way of paying... It was more convenient to eat in the kitchen.* ◆ **conveniently** ADV *The body spray slips conveniently into your sports bag.* ◆ **convenience** /kən'viːniəns/ N-UNCOUNT *...the convenience of a fast non-stop flight.* [2] ADJ A place that is **convenient** is near to where you are, or near to another place where you want to go. *Martin drove along until he found a convenient parking place.* ◆ **conveniently** ADV *The resort is conveniently close to Phoenix International Airport.* [3] ADJ A **convenient** time to do something is a time when you are free to do it or would like to do it. *Would this evening be convenient for you?*

convent /'kɒnvənt/ **convents.** N-COUNT A **convent** is a building in which a community of nuns live.

★ **convention** /kən'venʃən/ **conventions.** [1] N-VAR A **convention** is an accepted way of behaving or of doing something. *It's just a social convention that men don't wear skirts.* [2] N-COUNT A **convention** is an official agreement between countries or organizations. *...the UN convention on climate change.* [3] N-COUNT A **convention** is a large meeting of an organization or group. *...the annual convention of the World Boxing Council.*

★ **conventional** /kən'venʃənəl/. [1] ADJ **Conventional** people behave in a way that is accepted as normal in their society. *...a respectable married woman with conventional opinions.* ◆ **conventionally** ADV *People still wore their hair short and dressed conventionally.* [2] ADJ A **conventional** method or product is the one that is usually used. *...a conventional computer floppy disk.* ◆ **conventionally** ADV *...conventionally grown crops.* [3] ADJ **Conventional** wars and weapons do not involve nuclear explosives.

converge /kən'vɜːdʒ/ **converges, converging, converged.** [1] VERB When roads or lines **converge**, they meet or join. *As they flow south, the five rivers converge.* [2] VERB When people or vehicles **converge on** a place, they move towards it from different directions. *Hundreds of coaches will converge on the capital.* [3] VERB If different ideas or societies **converge**, they gradually become similar to each other. *The views of the richest householders converged with those of the poorest.* ◆ **convergence** /kən'vɜːdʒens/ **convergences** N-VAR *...economic convergence between the European economies.*

★ **conversation** /ˌkɒnvə'seɪʃən/ **conversations.** [1] N-VAR If you have a **conversation** with someone, you talk to each other, usually in an informal situation. *I struck up a conversation with him.* ◆ **conversational** ADJ *...the author's easy, conversational style.* ◆ **conversationally** ADV *Lyrics are written almost conversationally, yet sung with passion.* [2] PHRASE When you **make conversation**, you talk to someone in order to be polite rather than because you want to.

converse, converses, conversing, conversed. [1] VERB /kən'vɜːs/ If you **converse with** someone, you talk to each other. [FORMAL] *Luke conversed with the pilot... They were conversing in German.* [2] N-SING /'kɒnvɜːs/ **The converse** of a statement or fact is its opposite or reverse. *If great events produce great men, the converse is also true.* ◆ **conversely** /'kɒnvɜːsli, kən'vɜːsli/ ADV *Some people mistake politeness for weakness, and conversely, they think that rudeness is a sign of strength.*

★ **convert, converts, converting, converted.** [1] VERB /kən'vɜːt/ To **convert** one thing **into** another means to change it into a different shape or form. *The signal will be converted into digital code. ...a table that converts into an ironing board. ...a converted farmhouse.* ◆ **conversion** /kən'vɜːʃən/ **conversions** N-VAR *...the conversion of military industries to civilian use.* [2] VERB If

a
b
c
d
e
f
g
h
i
j
k
l
m
n
o
p
q
r
s
t
u
v
w
x
y
z

★ Bank of English® frequent word   For a full explanation of all grammatical labels, see pages vii-x someone **converts** you, they persuade you to change your religious or political beliefs. *He converted to Catholicism in 1917.* ◆ **conversion** N-VAR *...his conversion to Christianity.* ⟨3⟩ N-COUNT /'kɒnvɜːt/ A **convert** is someone who has changed their religious or political beliefs. *...new converts to democracy.*

convertible /kən,vɜːtɪbəl/ **convertibles.**
⟨1⟩ N-COUNT A **convertible** is a car with a soft roof that can be folded down or removed. ⟨2⟩ ADJ **Convertible** money can be easily exchanged for other forms of money. [TECHNICAL]

convey /kən'veɪ/ **conveys, conveying, conveyed.**
⟨1⟩ VERB To **convey** facts or feelings means to cause them to be known or understood. *I tried to convey the wonder of this machine to my husband... Officials convey a sense of alarm.*
⟨2⟩ VERB To **convey** someone or something to a place means to transport them there. [FORMAL] *The minibus picked us up and conveyed us to the centre.*

conveyor belt /kən'veɪə belt/ **conveyor belts.**
N-COUNT A **conveyor belt** or a **conveyor** is a continuously moving strip which is used in factories for moving objects along.

⭐ **convict, convicts, convicting, convicted.** ⟨1⟩ VERB /kən'vɪkt/ If someone **is convicted of** a crime, they are found guilty of it in a law court. *He was convicted of murder... There was insufficient evidence to convict him.* ⟨2⟩ N-COUNT /'kɒnvɪkt/ A **convict** is someone who is in prison, convicted of committing a crime.

⭐ **conviction** /kən'vɪkʃən/ **convictions.** ⟨1⟩ N-COUNT A **conviction** is a strong belief or opinion. *...the conviction that Europe may be losing its competitive edge... We had an absolute conviction that we were on the side of good.* ⟨2⟩ N-COUNT If someone has a **conviction**, they have been found guilty of a crime. *He will appeal against his conviction.*

⭐ **convince** /kən'vɪns/ **convinces, convincing, convinced.** ⟨1⟩ VERB If someone or something **convinces** you **of** something, they make you believe that it is true or that it exists. *I soon convinced him of my innocence... The waste disposal industry is finding it difficult to convince the public that its operations are safe.*
◆ **convinced** ADJ *He became convinced that the marriage could soon end.* ⟨2⟩ VERB If someone or something **convinces** you **to** do something, they persuade you to do it. *He convinced her to go ahead and marry Bud.*

convincing /kən'vɪnsɪŋ/. ADJ If someone or something is **convincing**, you believe them. *He sounded very convincing.* ◆ **convincingly** ADV *He argued forcefully and convincingly.*

convoy /'kɒnvɔɪ/ **convoys.** N-COUNT A **convoy** is a group of vehicles or ships travelling together. *They travel in convoy.*

convulsion /kən'vʌlʃən/ **convulsions.** N-COUNT If someone has **convulsions**, they suffer uncontrollable movements of their muscles.

⭐ **cook** /kʊk/ **cooks, cooking, cooked.** ⟨1⟩ VERB When you **cook** a meal, you prepare and heat food so it can be eaten. *Let the vegetables cook gently for about 10 minutes... Chefs at the St James Court restaurant have cooked for the Queen... We'll cook them a nice Italian meal.* ◆ **cooking** N-UNCOUNT *You do a lot of cooking, don't you?*

> **USAGE** You often use a more specific verb instead of **cook** when you are talking about preparing food using heat. For example, you **roast** meat in an oven, but you **bake** bread and cakes. You can **boil** vegetables in hot water, or you can **steam** them over a pan of boiling water. You can **fry** meat and vegetables in oil or fat. You can also **grill** them directly under or over a flame. In American English, **broil** is used instead of **grill**. You do not normally talk about **grilling** bread. Instead, you **toast** it.

⟨2⟩ N-COUNT A **cook** is a person whose job is to prepare and cook food. ⟨3⟩ See also **cooking**.
▶ **cook up.** PHR-VERB If someone **cooks up** a dishonest scheme, they plan it. [INFORMAL] *He must have cooked up his scheme on the spur of the moment.*

cookbook /'kʊkbʊk/ **cookbooks.** N-COUNT A **cookbook** is a book that contains recipes for preparing food.

cooker /'kʊkə/ **cookers.** N-COUNT A **cooker** is a large metal device used for cooking food using gas or electricity.

cookery /'kʊkəri/. N-UNCOUNT **Cookery** is the activity of preparing and cooking food.

cookie /'kʊki/ **cookies.** N-COUNT In American English, a **cookie** is a small, sweet, flat cake. The usual British word is **biscuit**.

⭐ **cooking** /'kʊkɪŋ/. ⟨1⟩ N-UNCOUNT **Cooking** is cooked food. *I like your cooking.* ⟨2⟩ See also **cook**.

⭐ **cool** /kuːl/ **cooler, coolest, cools, cooling, cooled.** ⟨1⟩ ADJ Something that is **cool** has a low temperature but is not cold. *There was a cool breeze... The vaccines were kept cool in refrigerators.*
◆ **coolness** N-UNCOUNT *...the coolness of the tiled floor.* ● See note at **cold**. ⟨2⟩ VERB When something **cools** or when you **cool** it, it becomes lower in temperature. You can also say it **cools down** or you **cool** it **down**. *As the droplets evaporated they cooled the air... Avoid putting your car away until the engine has cooled down.* ⟨3⟩ ADJ If you stay **cool** in a difficult situation, you remain calm. ◆ **coolly** ADV *Everyone must think this situation through calmly and coolly.* ◆ **coolness** N-UNCOUNT *Detectives praised him for his coolness.* ⟨4⟩ ADJ If you say that a person or their behaviour is **cool**, you mean that they are unfriendly or lack enthusiasm. ◆ **coolly** ADV *'It's your choice, Nina,' David said coolly.* ◆ **coolness** N-UNCOUNT *...the sudden coolness of her friend's manner.* ⟨5⟩ ADJ If you say that someone is **cool**, you mean that they are fashionable and attractive. [INFORMAL]

corner

►**cool down.** 1 See **cool** 2. 2 PHR-VERB If someone **cools down** or if you **cool** them **down**, they become less angry. *He has had time to cool down.*

►**cool off.** PHR-VERB If someone or something **cools off** or if you **cool** them **off**, they become cooler after being hot. *Cool off in the pool.*

⭐ **co-operate** /kəʊ-ˈɒpəreɪt/ **co-operates, co-operating, co-operated.** 1 VERB If you **co-operate with** someone, you work with them or help them. *The UN had been co-operating with the State Department... The couple spoke about how they would co-operate in the raising of their child.* ♦ **co-operation** /kəʊ-ˌɒpəˈreɪʃən/ N-UNCOUNT ...*economic co-operation with East Asia.* 2 VERB If you **co-operate**, you do what someone asks you to do. *He agreed to co-operate with the police investigation.* ♦ **co-operation** N-UNCOUNT ...*the importance of the public's co-operation in the hunt for the bombers.*

co-operative /kəʊ-ˈɒpərətɪv/ **co-operatives.** 1 N-COUNT A **co-operative** is a business or organization run by the people who work for it, who share its benefits and profits. 2 ADJ A **co-operative** activity is done by people working together. ...*a smooth co-operative effort between Egyptian and US authorities.* ♦ **co-operatively** ADV *They agreed to work co-operatively.* 3 ADJ Someone who is **co-operative** does what you ask them to. *I made every effort to be co-operative.*

co-ordinate (or **coordinate**) **co-ordinates, co-ordinating, co-ordinated.** 1 VERB /kəʊˈɔːdɪneɪt/ If you **co-ordinate** an activity, you organize it. ...*an advisory committee to co-ordinate police work. ...a rapid and well co-ordinated international rescue operation.* ♦ **co-ordination** N-UNCOUNT ...*more effective co-ordination of disaster relief.* ♦ **co-ordinator, co-ordinators** N-COUNT ...*the party's campaign co-ordinator.* 2 VERB If you **co-ordinate** the parts of your body, you make them work together efficiently. ♦ **co-ordination** N-UNCOUNT ...*clumsiness and lack of co-ordination.* 3 N-COUNT /kəʊˈɔːdɪnət/ The **co-ordinates** of a point on a map or graph are the two sets of numbers or letters that you need in order to find that point.

cop /kɒp/ **cops.** N-COUNT A **cop** is a policeman or policewoman. [INFORMAL]

⭐ **cope** /kəʊp/ **copes, coping, coped.** VERB If you **cope with** a problem, task, or difficult situation, you deal with it successfully. *She has had to cope with losing all her money... Don't worry, Clarrie. I'll cope.*

copious /ˈkəʊpiəs/. ADJ A **copious** amount is a large amount. ...*copious amounts of red wine.* ♦ **copiously** ADV *He bled copiously.*

copper /ˈkɒpə/ **coppers.** 1 N-UNCOUNT **Copper** is a soft reddish-brown metal. 2 N-COUNT A **copper** is a policeman or policewoman. [BRITISH, INFORMAL] 3 N-COUNT **Coppers** are brown metal coins of low value. [BRITISH] *I gave him a few coppers.*

⭐ **copy** /ˈkɒpi/ **copies, copying, copied.** 1 N-COUNT If you make a **copy of** something, you produce something that looks like the original thing. ...*a copy of Steve's resignation letter.* 2 VERB & PHR-VERB If you **copy** something which has been written or **copy** it **out**, you write it again exactly. *He copied the data into a notebook... We're copying from textbooks... Concentrating hard, the pupils copied out the text.* 3 VERB If you **copy** a person or their ideas, you behave like them. *Children can be seen to copy the behaviour of others whom they admire.* 4 N-COUNT A **copy of** a book, newspaper, or record is one of many identical ones that have been printed or produced. ...*a copy of 'USA Today'.*

►**copy down.** PHR-VERB If you **copy down** what someone says or writes, you write it down yourself. *I copied it down the way my lawyer read it.*

►**copy out.** See **copy** 2.

copyright /ˈkɒpiraɪt/ **copyrights.** N-VAR If someone has the **copyright** on a piece of writing or music, it is illegal to reproduce or perform it without their permission.

coral /ˈkɒrəl, AM ˈkɔː-/. N-UNCOUNT **Coral** is a hard substance formed from the skeletons of very small sea animals.

cord /kɔːd/ **cords.** 1 N-VAR **Cord** is strong thick string. ...*a length of nylon cord.* 2 N-VAR **Cord** is electrical wire covered in rubber or plastic. ...*electrical cord.*

cordial /ˈkɔːdiəl, AM -dʒəl/. ADJ **Cordial** means warm and friendly. *They struck up a cordial relationship.* ♦ **cordiality** /ˌkɔːdiˈælɪti, AM -ˈdʒæl-/ N-UNCOUNT ...*an atmosphere of cordiality.* ♦ **cordially** ADV *They all greeted me very cordially.*

cordon /ˈkɔːdən/ **cordons, cordoning, cordoned.** N-UNCOUNT A **cordon** is a line of police, soldiers, or vehicles preventing people from entering or leaving an area.

►**cordon off.** PHR-VERB If police or soldiers **cordon off** an area, they prevent people from entering or leaving it.

⭐ **core** /kɔː/ **cores.** 1 N-COUNT The **core** of a fruit is the central part containing seeds or pips. ...*an apple core.* 2 N-COUNT The **core** of something is the central or most important part. ...*the core of the city... Get straight to the core of a problem.*

cork /kɔːk/ **corks.** 1 N-UNCOUNT **Cork** is a soft light substance which forms the bark of a Mediterranean tree. 2 N-COUNT A **cork** is a piece of cork or plastic that is pushed into the opening of a bottle to close it.

corkscrew /ˈkɔːkskruː/ **corkscrews.** N-COUNT A **corkscrew** is a device for pulling corks out of bottles. → See picture on page 825.

corn /kɔːn/. 1 N-UNCOUNT **Corn** refers to crops such as wheat and barley, or their seeds. [BRITISH] ...*fields of corn.* 2 N-UNCOUNT **Corn** is the same as **maize.** [AMERICAN] ...*fresh-baked corn bread.*

⭐ **corner** /ˈkɔːnə/ **corners, cornering, cornered.** 1 N-COUNT A **corner** is a place where two sides or edges of something meet, or where a road meets

a
b
c
d
e
f
g
h
i
j
k
l
m
n
o
p
q
r
s
t
u
v
w
x
y
z

another road. ...*a card table in the corner of the living room... He waited until the man had turned a corner.* **2** VERB If you **corner** a person or animal, you force them into a place they cannot escape from. *The gang was cornered by armed police. ...like a cornered animal.* **3** VERB If a company or place **corners** an area of trade, they gain control over it so that no one else can have any success in it. *This restaurant has cornered the Madrid market for specialist paellas.* **4** PHRASE If you say that something is **around the corner**, you mean that it will happen very soon. *...economic recovery is just around the corner.*

cornerstone /'kɔːnəstəʊn/ **cornerstones.** N-COUNT The **cornerstone of** something is the basis of its existence or success. [FORMAL] *Research is the cornerstone of the profession.*

corny /'kɔːni/. ADJ If you describe something as **corny**, you mean that it is obvious or sentimental and not at all original. *I know it sounds corny, but I'm really not motivated by money.*

coronary /'kɒrənri, AM 'kɔːrəneri/ **coronaries.**
1 ADJ BEFORE N **Coronary** means relating to the heart. [TECHNICAL] *...the coronary arteries.*
2 N-COUNT If someone has a **coronary**, blood cannot reach their heart because of a blood clot.

coronation /ˌkɒrə'neɪʃən, AM ˌkɔːr-/ **coronations.**
N-COUNT A **coronation** is the ceremony at which a king or queen is crowned.

coroner /'kɒrənə, AM 'kɔːr-/ **coroners.** N-COUNT A **coroner** is an official who is responsible for investigating sudden or unusual deaths.

corporal /'kɔːprəl/ **corporals.** N-COUNT & N-TITLE A **corporal** is a non-commissioned officer in the army.

corporal 'punishment. N-UNCOUNT **Corporal punishment** is the punishment of people by hitting them.

⭐ **corporate** /'kɔːprət/. ADJ BEFORE N **Corporate** means relating to business corporations. *...a corporate lawyer.*

⭐ **corporation** /ˌkɔːpə'reɪʃən/ **corporations.** N-COUNT A **corporation** is a large business or company.

corps /kɔː/.

✔ **Corps** is both the singular and the plural form.

1 N-COUNT A **corps** is a part of the army which has special duties. *...the Army Medical Corps.*
2 N-COUNT A **corps** is a small group of people who do a special job. *...the diplomatic corps.*

corpse /kɔːps/ **corpses.** N-COUNT A **corpse** is a dead body.

⭐ **correct** /kə'rekt/ **corrects, correcting, corrected.**
1 ADJ Something that is **correct** is accurate and has no mistakes. *Check the label is correct.*
♦ **correctly** ADV *Did I pronounce your name correctly?* **2** ADJ AFTER LINK-V If you are **correct**, what you have said or thought is true. *If Casey is correct, the total cost of the cleanup would come to $110 billion.* **3** ADJ BEFORE N The **correct** thing or method is the one that is most suitable in a

particular situation. *...the correct way to produce a crop of tomato plants.* ♦ **correctly** ADV *The exercises, correctly performed, will stretch and tone muscles.* **4** VERB If you **correct** a mistake, problem, or fault, you put it right. *Most companies willingly correct what went wrong.* **5** VERB When someone **corrects** a piece of writing, they mark the mistakes in it. **6** VERB If you **correct** someone, you say something which is more accurate or appropriate than what they have just said. *I must correct him on a minor point.* **7** ADJ **Correct** behaviour is considered socially acceptable. ♦ **correctly** ADV *The High Court of Parliament began very correctly.* ♦ **correctness** N-UNCOUNT *...political correctness.*

correction /kə'rekʃən/ **corrections.** **1** N-VAR A **correction** is something which puts right something that is wrong. *We will then make the necessary corrections.* **2** N-COUNT **Corrections** are marks or comments made on a piece of written work which indicate where there are mistakes and what are the right answers.

corrective /kə'rektɪv/. ADJ **Corrective** measures are intended to put right something that is wrong. *...corrective surgery.*

correlate /'kɒrəleɪt, AM 'kɔːr-/ **correlates, correlating, correlated.** VERB If one thing **correlates with** another, there is a close similarity or connection between them. *Obesity correlates with increased risk for hypertension and stroke... Earnings and performance aren't always correlated.*

correlation /ˌkɒrə'leɪʃən, AM ˌkɔːr-/ **correlations.**
N-COUNT A **correlation between** things is a link between them. [FORMAL] *...the correlation between smoking and disease.*

correspond /ˌkɒrɪ'spɒnd, AM ˌkɔːr-/ **corresponds, corresponding, corresponded.** **1** VERB If one thing **corresponds to** another, there is a close similarity or connection between them. *The numerals in brackets correspond to page numbers... The two maps of London correspond closely.* ♦ **corresponding** ADJ BEFORE N *March and April sales this year were up 8% on the corresponding period in 1992.*

♦ **correspondingly** ADV *Local loans are easier to monitor and are correspondingly less risky.* **2** VERB If you **correspond with** someone, you write letters to them. *She still corresponds with her American friends... We corresponded regularly.*

correspondence /ˌkɒrɪ'spɒndəns, AM ˌkɔːr-/ **correspondences.** **1** N-UNCOUNT **Correspondence** is the act of writing letters to someone. *...a long correspondence with a close college friend.*
2 N-UNCOUNT Someone's **correspondence** is the letters that they receive or send. **3** N-COUNT If there is a **correspondence between** two things, there is a similarity between them.
...correspondences between Eastern religions and Christianity.

⭐ **correspondent** /ˌkɒrɪ'spɒndənt, AM ˌkɔːr-/ **correspondents.** N-COUNT A **correspondent** is a television or newspaper reporter.

corridor /'kɒrɪdɔː, AM 'kɔːrɪdər/ **corridors.**
N-COUNT A **corridor** is a long passage in a building
or train, with rooms on one or both sides.

corroborate /kə'rɒbəreɪt/ **corroborates,
corroborating, corroborated.** VERB To **corroborate**
something that has been said means to provide
evidence that supports it. [FORMAL] ...*a wide range
of documents which corroborated the story.*
♦ **corroboration** N-UNCOUNT ...*independent
corroboration.*

corrode /kə'rəʊd/ **corrodes, corroding, corroded.**
VERB When metal or stone **corrodes**, it is
gradually destroyed by rust or by a chemical. *The
structure had been corroded by moisture.*
♦ **corroded** ADJ *The underground pipes were
badly corroded.* ♦ **corrosion** N-UNCOUNT *Zinc is
used to protect other metals from corrosion.*

corrugated /'kɒrəgeɪtɪd, AM 'kɔːr-/. ADJ
Corrugated metal or cardboard has been folded
into a series of small parallel folds to make it
stronger.

corrupt /kə'rʌpt/ **corrupts, corrupting, corrupted.**
[1] ADJ A **corrupt** person behaves in a way that is
morally wrong, especially by doing illegal things
for money. [2] VERB If someone **is corrupted** by
something, it causes them to become dishonest
and unable to be trusted. ...*a man so corrupted by
the desire for money.*

⭐ **corruption** /kə'rʌpʃən/. N-UNCOUNT **Corruption**
is dishonesty and illegal behaviour by people in
positions of power. *The President faces 54 charges
of corruption and tax evasion.*

cosmetic /kɒz'metɪk/ **cosmetics.** [1] N-COUNT
Cosmetics are substances such as lipstick or face
powder. [2] ADJ **Cosmetic** measures or changes
improve the appearance of something without
changing its basic character or without solving a
basic problem. *They believe the changes in South
Africa are still largely cosmetic.*

cosmic /'kɒzmɪk/. ADJ **Cosmic** means occurring
in, or coming from, the part of space that lies
outside Earth and its atmosphere. ...*cosmic
radiation.*

cosmopolitan /ˌkɒzməˈpɒlɪtən/. ADJ
Cosmopolitan means influenced by many
different countries and cultures. *London has
always been a cosmopolitan city.*

cosmos /'kɒzmɒs, AM -məs/. N-SING The
cosmos is the universe. [TECHNICAL]

⭐ **cost** /kɒst, AM kɔːst/ **costs, costing, cost.** [1] N-COUNT
The **cost** of something is the amount of money
needed to buy, do, or make it. *Badges are also
available at a cost of £2.50.* [2] VERB If something
costs a particular amount of money, you can buy,
do, or make it for that amount. *It's going to cost
me over $100,000 to buy new trucks.* [3] N-SING The
cost of achieving something is the loss, damage
or injury involved in achieving it. *Factories in the
West Country are to be closed at a cost of 150 jobs.*
[4] VERB If an event or mistake **costs** you
something, you lose that thing because of it. ...*an
operation that cost him his sight.* [5] PHRASE If you

say that something must be avoided **at all costs**,
you are emphasizing that it must not be allowed
to happen under any circumstances.

'**co-star**, co-stars, co-starring, co-starred. [1] N-COUNT
An actor or actress who is a **co-star** of a film has
one of the most important parts in it. [2] VERB If
an actor or actress **co-stars** with another actor or
actress, the two of them have the main parts in a
film. ...*a film in which she co-starred with her
father... They co-starred in the movie State Of
Grace.*

ˌ**cost-ef'fective.** ADJ Something that is **cost-
effective** saves or makes more money than it
costs to make or maintain.

costly /'kɒstli, AM 'kɔːst-/ **costlier, costliest.** [1] ADJ
Something that is **costly** is very expensive. [2] ADJ
If you describe someone's action or mistake as
costly, you mean that it results in a serious
disadvantage for them. *This sort of scandal in
international banking has been politically costly.*

ˌ**cost of 'living.** N-SING The **cost of living** is the
average amount of money that people need to
spend on food, housing, and clothing.

costume /'kɒstjuːm, AM -tuːm/ **costumes.**
N-UNCOUNT A **costume** is a set or style of clothes
worn by people at a particular time in history, or
in a particular country.

cosy (AM **cozy**) /'kəʊzi/ **cosier, cosiest.** [1] ADJ A
cosy house or room is comfortable and warm.
[2] ADJ You use **cosy** to describe activities that are
pleasant and friendly. ...*a cosy chat between
friends.*

cot /kɒt/ **cots.** N-COUNT In British English, a **cot** is a
bed for a baby, with bars or panels round it so
that the baby cannot fall out. The American word
is **crib**.

cottage

⭐ **cottage** /'kɒtɪdʒ/ **cottages.** N-COUNT A **cottage** is
a small house, usually in the country.

⭐ **cotton** /'kɒtən/ **cottons, cottoning, cottoned.**
[1] N-VAR **Cotton** is cloth made from the soft fibres
from the cotton plant. *Summer sheets are
generally made of cotton.* ...*a cotton shirt.*
[2] N-UNCOUNT **Cotton** is a plant which produces
the soft fibres used in making cotton cloth.
[3] N-VAR **Cotton** is sewing thread. [BRITISH] ...*a
needle and cotton.*
▸**cotton on.** PHR-VERB If you **cotton on to**
something, you understand it or realize it.

a b c d e f g h i j k l m n o p q r s t u v w x y z

⭐ Bank of English® frequent word   For a full explanation of all grammatical labels, see pages vii-x

A
B
C
D
E
F
G
H
I
J
K
L
M
N
O
P
Q
R
S
T
U
V
W
X
Y
Z

[INFORMAL] *She had cottoned on to the fact that he was not all he appeared.*

cotton 'wool. N-UNCOUNT **Cotton wool** is soft fluffy cotton, often used for applying creams to your skin. [BRITISH]

couch /kaʊtʃ/ **couches, couching, couched.** [1] N-COUNT A **couch** is a long piece of furniture for sitting or lying on. [2] VERB If a statement **is couched in** a particular style of language, it is expressed in that style of language. [WRITTEN] *The statement was couched in polite terms.*

★ **cough** /kɒf, AM kɔːf/ **coughs, coughing, coughed.** [1] VERB & N-COUNT When you **cough**, you force air out of your throat with a sudden harsh noise. A **cough** is an act of coughing. *Graham began to cough violently... She heard a muffled cough.* ♦ **coughing** N-UNCOUNT *...a terrible fit of coughing.* [2] N-COUNT A **cough** is an illness in which you cough. *Contact your doctor if the cough persists.* [3] VERB If you **cough** blood, it comes up out of your throat or mouth when you cough.
▸**cough up.** PHR-VERB If you **cough up** money, you give someone money, usually when you would prefer not to. [INFORMAL] *I'll have to cough up $10,000 a year for tuition.*

★ **could** /kəd, STRONG kʊd/ [1] MODAL If you **could** do something, you were able to do it. *I could see that something was terribly wrong... He could not resist telling her the truth... I couldn't read or write.* [2] MODAL You use **could** after 'if' when you are imagining what would happen if something was the case. *If I could afford it I'd have four television sets.* [3] MODAL You use **could** to indicate that something sometimes happened. *He could be very pleasant when he wanted to.* [4] MODAL You use **could have** to indicate that something was a possibility in the past, although it did not actually happen. *He could have made a fortune as a lawyer.* [5] MODAL You use **could** to indicate that something is possibly true, or that it may possibly happen. *The disease could have been caused by years of working in smokey clubs.* [6] MODAL You use **could** when making offers and suggestions. *I could call the local doctor... Couldn't you go for walks with your friends?* [7] MODAL You use **could** in questions to make polite requests. *Could I stay tonight?... He asked if he could have a coffee.*

couldn't /'kʊdənt/. **Couldn't** is the usual spoken form of 'could not'.

could've /'kʊdəv/. **Could've** is the usual spoken form of 'could have', when 'have' is an auxiliary verb.

★ **council** /'kaʊnsəl/ **councils.** [1] N-COUNT A **council** is a group of people elected to govern a town or other area. *...Cheshire County Council.* [2] ADJ BEFORE N **Council** houses or flats are owned by the local council and people pay rent to live in them. [BRITISH]

councillor (AM **councilor**) /'kaʊnsələ/ **councillors.** N-COUNT A **councillor** is a member of a local council.

★ **counsel** /'kaʊnsəl/ **counsels, counselling, counselled** (or AM **counseling, counseled**). [1] N-UNCOUNT **Counsel** is careful advice. [FORMAL] *It is wise to seek help and counsel.* [2] VERB If you **counsel** someone **to** do something, you advise them to do it. [FORMAL] *My advisers counselled me to do nothing.* [3] VERB If you **counsel** people, you give them advice about their problems. *...a psychologist who counsels people with eating disorders.* ♦ **counselling** N-UNCOUNT *...marriage counseling.* ♦ **counsellor, counsellors** N-COUNT *Take your problems to a trained counsellor.* [4] N-COUNT Someone's **counsel** is the lawyer who gives advice on a legal case and speaks for them in court.

★ **count** /kaʊnt/ **counts, counting, counted.** [1] VERB When you **count**, you say all the numbers in order up to a particular number. *He was counting slowly under his breath... Brian counted to twenty.* [2] VERB & PHR-VERB If you **count** all the things in a group, or if you **count** them **up**, you add them up to see how many there are. *I counted the money... They counted up all the hours the villagers work.* [3] N-COUNT A **count** is the action of counting, or the number that you get after counting. *Bill's mother had been five times divorced at the last count.* [4] VERB If something or someone **counts for** something, or if they **count**, they are important or valuable. *Experience counts for a lot in poker... It's as if your opinions, your likes and dislikes just don't count.* [5] VERB If something **counts as** a particular thing, it is regarded as being that thing. *A conservatory counts as an extension... It can be counted a success.* [6] N-COUNT & N-TITLE A **Count** is a male member of the nobility. [7] PHRASE If you **keep count of** a number of things, you keep a record of how many have occurred. If you **lose count of** a number of things, you cannot remember how many have occurred. *She'd lost count of the interviews she'd been called for.*
▸**count against.** PHR-VERB If something **counts against** you, it may cause you to be punished or rejected. *...his youth might count against him.*
▸**count on** or **count upon.** PHR-VERB If you **count on** someone or something, you rely on them to support you. *I can always count on you to cheer me up.*
▸**count out.** PHR-VERB If you **count out** a sum of money, you count it as you put the notes or coins in a pile.
▸**count up.** See **count** 2.
▸**count upon.** See **count on**.

countable noun /ˌkaʊntəbəl 'naʊn/ **countable nouns.** N-COUNT A **countable noun** is the same as a **count noun.**

countdown /'kaʊntdaʊn/ **countdowns.** N-COUNT A **countdown** is the counting aloud of numbers in reverse order before something happens.

countenance /'kaʊntɪnəns/ **countenances, countenancing, countenanced.** [1] VERB If someone will not **countenance** something, they do not agree with it and will not allow it to happen. [FORMAL]

Jake would not countenance Janis's marrying.
[2] N-COUNT Someone's **countenance** is their face. [LITERARY]

⭐ **counter** /'kaʊntə/ **counters, countering, countered.**
[1] N-COUNT In a shop, a **counter** is a long flat surface at which customers are served. ...*the cosmetics counter.* [2] VERB & N-SING If you **counter** something that is being done, or do something as **a counter to** it, you take action to make it less effective. ...*those who are working to counter the drug problem.* ...*a danger that Muslim terrorism will emerge as a counter to Hindu violence.*
[3] VERB If you **counter** something that has been said, you say something in reaction to it or in opposition to it. *They had to counter fierce criticism.* [4] PHRASE If one thing **runs counter to** another, or if one thing **is counter to** another, the first thing is the opposite of the second thing or conflicts with it. *The plan runs counter to European Community policy.* [5] N-COUNT A **counter** is a small, flat, round object used in a board game.

counteract /'kaʊntərækt/ **counteracts, counteracting, counteracted.** VERB To **counteract** something means to reduce its effect by doing something that has the opposite effect. ...*pills to counteract high blood pressure.*

'**counter-attack, counter-attacks, counter-attacking, counter-attacked.** VERB & N-VAR When an army **counter-attacks**, or when it makes a **counter-attack**, it attacks an enemy that has just attacked it.

counterclockwise /ˌkaʊntə'klɒkwaɪz/. ADV & ADJ **Counterclockwise** means the same as **anti-clockwise.** [AMERICAN]

counterfeit /'kaʊntəfɪt/ **counterfeits, counterfeiting, counterfeited.** [1] N-COUNT & ADJ **Counterfeits**, or **counterfeit** banknotes, goods, or documents, are not genuine, but have been made to look exactly like genuine ones in order to deceive people. *Counterfeits of the jeans are flooding Europe.* ...*counterfeit currency.* [2] VERB To **counterfeit** something means to make a counterfeit version of it. ♦ **counterfeiting** N-UNCOUNT ...*the business of counterfeiting.*

⭐ **counterpart** /'kaʊntəpɑːt/ **counterparts.** N-COUNT Someone's or something's **counterpart** is another person or thing that has a similar function in a different place. *The Foreign Secretary telephoned his German and Italian counterparts.*

'**counter-pro'ductive** (or **counterproductive**). ADJ Something that is **counter-productive** has the opposite effect from what you intend. *Exercising alone can be boring and often counter-productive.*

countess /'kaʊntɪs/ **countesses.** N-COUNT & N-TITLE A **Countess** is a female member of the nobility.

countless /'kaʊntləs/. ADJ BEFORE N **Countless** means very many. *She brought joy to countless people.*

'**count noun, count nouns.** N-COUNT A **count noun** is a noun such as 'bird', 'chair', or 'year'

which has a singular and a plural form and is always used after a determiner in the singular.

⭐ **country** /'kʌntri/ **countries.** [1] N-COUNT A **country** is one of the political areas which the world is divided into, covering a particular area of land. You can refer to the people who live in a particular country as **the country**. *Indonesia is the fifth most populous country in the world... The country was going through the throes of civil war.*

> **USAGE Country** is the most usual word to use when you are talking about the major political units that the world is divided into. **State** is used when you are talking about politics or government institutions. ...*the new German state created by the unification process.* ...*Italy's state-controlled telecommunications company.* **State** can also refer to a political unit within a particular country. ...*the American state of California.* **Nation** is often used when you are talking about a country's inhabitants, and their cultural or ethnic background. *Wales is a proud nation with its own traditions... A senior government spokesman will be coming to address the nation.* **Land** is a less precise and more literary word, which you can use, for example, to talk about the feelings you have for a particular country. *She was fascinated to learn about this strange land at the edge of Europe.*

[2] N-SING **The country** is land away from towns and cities. ...*a healthy life in the country.*
[3] N-UNCOUNT **Country** is used to refer to an area with particular characteristics or connections. ...*mountainous country east of Genoa.*
[4] N-UNCOUNT **Country** music is a style of popular music from the USA.

countryman /'kʌntrimən/ **countrymen.** N-COUNT Your **countrymen** are people from your own country.

⭐ **countryside** /'kʌntrisaɪd/. N-UNCOUNT The **countryside** is land away from towns and cities.

> **USAGE** Do not confuse **countryside**, **landscape**, **scenery**, and **nature**. **Countryside** is land which is away from towns and cities. ...*3,500 acres of mostly flat countryside.* With **landscape**, the emphasis is on the physical features of the land, while **scenery** includes everything you can see when you look out over an area of land, usually in the country. ...*the landscape of steep woods and distant mountains. ...unattractive urban scenery.* **Nature** includes the landscape, the weather, animals, and plants. *These creatures roamed the Earth as the finest and rarest wonders of nature.*

A B **C** D E F G H I J K L M N O P Q R S T U V W X Y Z

⭐ **county** /'kaʊnti/ **counties.** N-COUNT A **county** is a region of Britain, Ireland, or the USA with its own local government.

⭐ **coup** /kuː/ **coups.** [1] N-COUNT A **coup** is the same as a **coup d'état.** [2] N-COUNT A **coup** is an achievement thought to be especially brilliant because of its difficulty. *The sale is a big coup for the auction house.*

coup d'état /ˌkuː deɪ'tɑː/ **coups d'état.**

✅ The plural is pronounced the same as the singular.

N-COUNT When there is a **coup d'état**, a group of people seize power in a country.

⭐ **couple** /'kʌpəl/ **couples, coupling, coupled.** [1] QUANT If you refer to **a couple of** people or things, you mean two or approximately two of them. *I think the trouble will clear up in a couple of days.* [2] N-COUNT A **couple** is two people who are married, or having a sexual or romantic relationship. *The couple have no children.* [3] N-COUNT A **couple** is two people that you see together on a particular occasion or that are associated in some way. *The four couples began the opening dance.* [4] VERB If one thing produces a particular effect when it **is coupled with** another, the two things combine to produce that effect. *Over-use of those drugs, coupled with poor diet, leads to physical degeneration.*

coupon /'kuːpɒn/ **coupons.** [1] N-COUNT A **coupon** is a piece of printed paper which is issued by the maker or supplier of a product and which allows you to pay less than usual for something. [2] N-COUNT A **coupon** is a small form which you fill in and send off to ask for information, to order something, or to enter a competition.

⭐ **courage** /'kʌrɪdʒ, AM 'kɜːr-/. N-UNCOUNT **Courage** is the quality shown by someone who does something difficult or dangerous, even though they may be afraid. *The girls plucked up the courage to tell police he was a drugs dealer.*

courageous /kə'reɪdʒəs/. ADJ Someone who is **courageous** shows courage. *...his courageous defiance of the government.* ♦ **courageously** ADV *Smith fought courageously.*

courgette /kʊə'ʒet/ **courgettes.** N-VAR In British English, **courgettes** are long thin green vegetables. The American word is **zucchini**. → See picture on page 836.

courier /'kʊriə/ **couriers, couriering, couriered.** [1] N-COUNT A **courier** is a person who is paid to take letters and parcels direct from one place to another. [2] N-COUNT A **courier** is a person employed by a travel company to look after people who are on holiday. [3] VERB If you **courier** something somewhere, you send it there by courier. *I couriered the report to Darren in New York.*

⭐ **course** /kɔːs/ **courses, coursing, coursed.** [1] See **of course.** [2] N-UNCOUNT The **course** of a vehicle is the route along which it is travelling. *The captain altered course a few degrees to the right.*

[3] N-COUNT A **course** of action is an action or a series of actions that you can do in a particular situation. *Vietnam is trying to decide on its course for the future.* [4] N-SING You can refer to the way that events develop as **the course of** history, nature, or events. [5] N-COUNT A **course** is a series of lessons or lectures on a particular subject. *...a course in business administration.* [6] N-COUNT A **course of** medical treatment is a series of treatments that a doctor gives someone. *...a course of antibiotics.* [7] N-COUNT A **course** is one part of a meal. *...a three-course dinner.* [8] VERB If a liquid **courses** somewhere, it flows there quickly. [LITERARY] *The tears coursed down his cheeks.* [9] N-COUNT In sport, a **course** is an area of land where races are held or golf is played.

PHRASES ● If you are **on course for** something, you are likely to achieve it. ● If something **runs its course** or **takes its course**, it develops naturally and comes to a natural end. *20,000 cows would die before the epidemic had run its course.* ● **in due course**: see **due.**

⭐ **court** /kɔːt/ **courts, courting, courted.** [1] N-COUNT A **court** is a place where legal matters are decided by a judge and jury or by a magistrate. You can also refer to a judge, jury, or magistrates as a **court**. *Would she be willing to testify in court?... The court awarded the man one and a half million pounds.* [2] N-COUNT A **court** is an area for playing a game such as tennis or squash. [3] N-COUNT The **court** of a king or queen is the place where he or she lives and works. [4] PHRASE You can say someone **holds court** when they are surrounded by a lot of people who are paying them a lot of attention because they are interesting or famous; used showing disapproval. [5] VERB If you say that someone **is courting** disaster, you think they are acting in a way that makes it likely to happen. [6] VERB If you **court** something such as publicity or popularity, you try to obtain it for yourself.

courteous /'kɜːtiəs/. ADJ Someone who is **courteous** is polite, respectful, and considerate. *He is so courteous and so helpful.* ♦ **courteously** ADV *He nodded courteously to me.*

courtesy /'kɜːtɪsi/ **courtesies.** [1] N-UNCOUNT **Courtesy** is polite, respectful, and considerate behaviour. [2] N-COUNT **Courtesies** are polite and respectful things that you say or do. [FORMAL] *Hugh and John were exchanging courtesies.* [3] ADJ BEFORE N **Courtesy** is used to describe services that are provided free of charge by an organization to its customers. *A courtesy bus operates between the hotel and the town.*

courthouse /'kɔːthaʊs/ **courthouses.** N-COUNT In American English, a **courthouse** is a building in which a law court meets. The usual British word is **court**.

courtier /'kɔːtiə/ **courtiers.** N-COUNT **Courtiers** were members of the nobility at the court of a king or queen.

,court-'martial, court-martials, court- martialling, court-martialled. [1] N-VAR A **court-martial** is a trial in a military court of a member of the armed forces. [2] VERB If a member of the armed forces **is court-martialled**, he or she is tried in a military court.

courtroom /'kɔːtruːm/ courtrooms. N-COUNT A **courtroom** is a room in which a law court meets.

courtship /'kɔːtʃɪp/. N-UNCOUNT **Courtship** is the activity in which a man and a woman spend a lot of time together, because they are intending to get married. [FORMAL]

courtyard /'kɔːtjɑːd/ courtyards. N-COUNT A **courtyard** is a flat open area of ground surrounded by buildings or walls.

★ cousin /'kʌzən/ cousins. N-COUNT Your **cousin** is the child of your uncle or aunt.

cove /kəʊv/ coves. N-COUNT A **cove** is a small bay on the coast.

covenant /'kʌvənənt/ covenants. [1] N-COUNT A **covenant** is a formal written agreement between two or more people which is recognized in law. [2] N-COUNT A **covenant** is a formal written promise to pay a sum of money each year for a fixed period, especially to a charity.

★ cover /'kʌvə/ covers, covering, covered. [1] VERB & PHR-VERB If you **cover** one thing **with** another, or if you **cover** it **up**, you place the second thing over the first in order to protect it, hide it, or close it. *Cover the casserole with a tight-fitting lid. ...the black patch which covered his left eye.* [2] N-COUNT A **cover** is something which is put over an object, usually in order to protect it. The **cover** of a book or a magazine is the protective outside part of it. [3] N-PLURAL Bed **covers** are sheets, blankets, and quilts. [4] VERB If one thing **is covered with** or **in** another, the second forms a layer over its surface. *The desk was covered with papers... Black clouds covered the sky.* [5] VERB If you **cover** a particular distance, you travel that distance. [6] VERB & N-UNCOUNT When an insurance policy **covers** a person or thing, or provides **cover**, it guarantees that money will be paid in relation to that person or thing. *...travel insurance covering you and your family against theft. ...unlimited cover for Freezer Contents.* [7] VERB If you **cover** a particular topic, you discuss it in a lecture, course, or book. *Other subjects covered included nerves and how to overcome them.* [8] VERB If a journalist **covers** an event, he or she reports on it. [9] VERB If a sum of money **covers** something, it is enough to pay for it. *...£1.50 to cover postage and administration.* [10] N-UNCOUNT & PHRASE You can refer to trees, rocks, or other places where you shelter from the weather or hide from someone as **cover**. If you **take cover**, you shelter from the weather or from an attack. *They ran for cover.*

▶ cover up. [1] PHR-VERB If you **cover up** something that you do not want people to know about, you conceal the truth about it. *How do we know you're not just covering up for*

your friend? [2] See also **cover** 1. ● See also **cover-up**.

★ coverage /'kʌvərɪdʒ/. N-UNCOUNT The **coverage** of something in the news is the reporting of it. *...TV coverage of college football.*

covering /'kʌvərɪŋ/ coverings. N-VAR A **covering** is a layer of something over something else. *Sawdust was used as a hygienic floor covering.*

covert /'kʌvət, 'kəʊvɜːt/. ADJ **Covert** activities or situations are secret or hidden. [FORMAL] *They have been supplying covert military aid to the rebels.* ◆ **covertly** ADV *Joanna studied him covertly through her lashes.*

'cover-up, cover-ups. N-COUNT A **cover-up** is an attempt to hide a crime or mistake.

covet /'kʌvɪt/ covets, coveting, coveted. VERB If you **covet** something belonging to someone else, you want very much to have it for yourself. [FORMAL] *She coveted his job so openly that conversations between them were tense.*

coveted /'kʌvɪtɪd/. ADJ You use **coveted** to describe something that very many people would like to have. *...one of sport's most coveted trophies.*

★ cow /kaʊ/ cows, cowing, cowed. [1] N-COUNT A **cow** is a large female animal kept on farms for its milk. → See picture on page 815. [2] N-COUNT Some female animals, including elephants and whales, are called **cows**. [3] VERB If someone **is cowed**, they are frightened into behaving in a particular way. [FORMAL] *The government, far from being cowed by these threats, has vowed to continue its policy.* ◆ **cowed** ADJ *She was so cowed by the beatings that she meekly obeyed.*

coward /kaʊəd/ cowards. N-COUNT A **coward** is someone who is easily frightened and avoids dangerous or difficult situations.

cowardice /'kaʊədɪs/. N-UNCOUNT **Cowardice** is cowardly behaviour.

cowardly /kaʊədli/. ADJ Someone who is **cowardly** is easily frightened and so avoids doing dangerous or difficult things. *I know it would be cowardly not to respond to the invitation.*

cowboy /'kaʊbɔɪ/ cowboys. [1] N-COUNT A **cowboy** is a man employed to look after cattle in the United States of America. [2] N-COUNT You can refer to someone, especially a builder, as a **cowboy** if you think they are dishonest or do bad work. [BRITISH]

coy /kɔɪ/. [1] ADJ If you describe someone as **coy**, you disapprove of them pretending to be shy and modest. *Carol charmed all the men by turning coy.* ◆ **coyly** ADV *She smiled coyly at Algie as he took her hand.* ◆ **coyness** N-UNCOUNT *...her coyness and flirting.* [2] ADJ If someone is being **coy**, they are unwilling to talk about something that they feel guilty or embarrassed about. *The hotel are understandably coy about the incident.*

cozy /'kəʊzi/. See **cosy**.

crab /kræb/ crabs. N-COUNT A **crab** is a sea creature with a flat round body covered by a shell, and five pairs of legs with claws on the front pair. Crabs walk sideways.

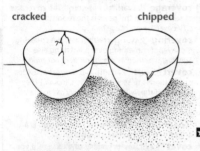

cracked   chipped

crack 1 verb uses

crack /kræk/ **cracks, cracking, cracked.** **1** VERB If something **cracks**, or if you **crack** it, it becomes slightly damaged, with lines appearing on its surface. *One of the stones cracked the glass panel in the front door. ...a cracked mirror.* **2** VERB If you **crack** something, you hit it and it breaks or is damaged. *Crack the eggs into a bowl... He cracked his head on the pavement.* **3** VERB If you **crack** a problem or a code, you solve it, especially after a lot of thought. *He has finally cracked the system.* **4** VERB If someone **cracks**, they lose control of their emotions or actions because they are under a lot of pressure. *She's calm and strong, and she is just not going to crack.* **5** VERB If you **crack** a joke, you tell it.

▸ **crack down.** PHR-VERB If people in authority **crack down on** a group of people, they become stricter in making them obey rules or laws. *The government is cracking down on drug users.* • See also **crackdown**.

▸ **crack up.** PHR-VERB If someone **cracks up**, they are under such emotional strain that they become mentally ill. [INFORMAL]

crack 2 noun and adjective uses

crack /kræk/ **cracks.** **1** N-COUNT A **crack** is a very narrow gap between two things. *Kathryn had seen him through a crack in the curtains.* **2** N-COUNT A **crack** is a line that appears on the surface of something when it is slightly damaged. *The plate had a crack in it.* **3** N-COUNT A **crack** is a sharp sound, like the sound of a piece of wood breaking. *There was a loud crack and glass flew into the car.* **4** N-COUNT If you have a **crack at** something, you make an attempt to do or achieve something. [INFORMAL] *I should love to have a crack at the Olympic title.* **5** N-COUNT A **crack** is a slightly rude or cruel joke. **6** ADJ BEFORE N A **crack** soldier or sportsman is highly trained and very skilful. *...a crack undercover police officer.*

crackdown /ˈkrækdaʊn/ **crackdowns.** N-COUNT A **crackdown** is strong official action taken to punish people who break laws.

cracker /ˈkrækə/ **crackers.** N-COUNT A **cracker** is a hollow cardboard tube covered with coloured paper. Crackers make a bang when they are pulled apart and usually contain a small toy, a joke, and a paper hat.

crackle /ˈkrækəl/ **crackles, crackling, crackled.** VERB & N-COUNT When something **crackles**, it makes a series of short harsh noises called **crackles**. *The radio crackled again. ...the crackle of gunfire.*

cradle /ˈkreɪdəl/ **cradles, cradling, cradled.** **1** N-COUNT A **cradle** is a baby's bed with high sides. **2** N-SING A place that is referred to as **the cradle of** something is the place where it began. *...New York, the cradle of capitalism.* **3** VERB If you **cradle** someone or something in your arms, you hold them carefully. *I stood cradling the phone.*

⭐ **craft** /krɑːft, kræft/ **crafts, crafting, crafted.**

✓ In meaning 1, **craft** is both the singular and the plural form.

1 N-COUNT You can refer to a boat, a spacecraft, or an aircraft as a **craft**. *Hundreds of small craft sounded their foghorns.* **2** N-COUNT A **craft** is an activity that involves doing something skilfully, especially an activity such as weaving, carving, or pottery that involves making things skilfully with your hands. *...the craft of writing. ...traditional arts and crafts.* **3** VERB If something **is crafted**, it is made skilfully. *Many delegates were willing to craft a compromise.*

craftsman /ˈkrɑːftsmən, ˈkræft-/ **craftsmen.** N-COUNT A **craftsman** is a man who makes things skilfully with his hands.

craftsmanship /ˈkrɑːftsmənʃɪp, ˈkræft-/. **1** N-UNCOUNT **Craftsmanship** is the skill that someone uses when they make beautiful things with their hands. *...the craftsmanship of Armani.* **2** N-UNCOUNT **Craftsmanship** is the quality that something has when it is beautiful and has been carefully made. *His canoes are known for their style, fine detail and craftsmanship.*

crafty /ˈkrɑːfti, ˈkræfti/ **craftier, craftiest.** ADJ If you describe someone as **crafty**, you mean that they get what they want in a clever way, often by deceiving people. *...a crafty, lying character.*

cram /kræm/ **crams, cramming, crammed.** VERB If you **cram** things or people **into** a place, or if they **cram** it, there are so many of them in it at one time that it is completely full. *She crammed her hat into a wastebasket... I crammed my bag full of T-shirts... Friends crammed the chapel.*

crammed /kræmd/. ADJ If a place is **crammed with** things or people, it is very full of them. *The house is crammed with priceless furniture.*

cramp /kræmp/ **cramps.** N-UNCOUNT & N-PLURAL **Cramp** is a sudden strong pain caused by a muscle suddenly contracting. *...stomach cramps.*

cramped /kræmpt/. ADJ A **cramped** room or building is not big enough for the people or things in it. *...a rather cramped little flat.*

crane /kreɪn/ **cranes, craning, craned.** **1** N-COUNT A **crane** is a large machine that moves heavy things by lifting them in the air. → See picture on page 155.

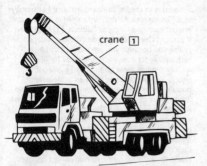

crane 1

2 N-COUNT A **crane** is a kind of large bird with a long neck and long legs. **3** VERB If you **crane** your neck, you stretch your neck in a particular direction in order to see or hear something better. *She craned forward to look at me.*

crank /kræŋk/ **cranks, cranking, cranked.** **1** N-COUNT If you call someone a **crank**, you think they have peculiar ideas or behaviour. [INFORMAL] **2** VERB If you **crank** a device or machine, you make it move by turning a handle. *The chauffeur got out to crank the motor.*

⭐ **crash** /kræʃ/ **crashes, crashing, crashed.** **1** VERB & N-COUNT If a moving vehicle **crashes**, or if it has a **crash**, it hits something and is damaged or destroyed. *His car crashed into the rear of a van... His mother crashed her car into a tree. ...a car crash.* **2** VERB & N-COUNT To **crash** means to move or fall violently, making a sudden loud noise, called a **crash**. *The walls above us crashed down... Two people in the flat recalled hearing a loud crash about 1.30 a.m.* **3** VERB & N-COUNT If a business or financial system **crashes**, it fails suddenly, often with serious effects. Its sudden failure is called a **crash**. *When the market crashed, they assumed the deal would be cancelled. ...a stock market crash.* **4** VERB If a computer or a computer program **crashes**, it fails suddenly. [COMPUTING]

crass /kræs/. ADJ **Crass** behaviour is stupid and insensitive.

crate /kreɪt/ **crates.** N-COUNT A **crate** is a large box used for transporting or storing things.

crater /'kreɪtə/ **craters.** N-COUNT A **crater** is a large hole in the ground, which has been caused by something hitting it or by an explosion.

crave /kreɪv/ **craves, craving, craved.** VERB If you **crave** something, you want to have it very much. *...a vulnerable, unhappy girl who craved affection... You may be craving for some fresh air.* ♦ **craving,** **cravings** N-COUNT *...a craving for sugar.*

crawl /krɔːl/ **crawls, crawling, crawled.** **1** VERB When you **crawl**, you move forward on your hands and knees. *I began to crawl towards the door.* **2** VERB & N-SING If someone or something **crawls** somewhere, or if they move there at **a crawl**, they move there slowly or with great difficulty. *I watched the moth crawl up the outside of the*

lampshade... The traffic on the approach road slowed to a crawl. **3** VERB If you say that a place **is crawling with** people or things, you mean that it is full of them. [INFORMAL] *This place is crawling with police.* **4** N-UNCOUNT The **crawl** is a kind of swimming stroke which you do lying on your front, swinging one arm over your head and then the other arm, and kicking your legs.

crayon /'kreɪɒn/ **crayons.** N-COUNT A **crayon** is a rod of coloured wax used for drawing.

craze /kreɪz/ **crazes.** N-COUNT If there is a **craze** for something, it is very popular for a short time. *Walking is the latest fitness craze.*

crazed /kreɪzd/. ADJ **Crazed** people are wild and uncontrolled, and perhaps insane. *A crazed gunman slaughtered five people last night.*

⭐ **crazy** /'kreɪzi/ **crazier, craziest.** **1** ADJ If you describe someone or something as **crazy**, you think they are very foolish or strange. [INFORMAL] *People thought they were all crazy to try to make money from manufacturing.* ♦ **crazily** ADV *Our policies are crazily extravagant.* **2** ADJ AFTER LINK-V If you are **crazy about** something, you are very enthusiastic about it. If you are **crazy about** someone, you are deeply in love with them. *He was crazy about gardening... We're crazy about each other.* **3** ADJ AFTER LINK-V If something makes or drives you **crazy**, it makes you extremely annoyed or upset. *This sitting around is driving me crazy.*

creak /kriːk/ **creaks, creaking, creaked.** VERB & N-COUNT If something **creaks**, it makes a short high-pitched sound, called a **creak**, when it moves. *The steps creaked beneath his feet... The door was pulled open with a creak.*

⭐ **cream** /kriːm/ **creams, creaming, creamed.** **1** N-UNCOUNT **Cream** is a thick liquid that is produced from milk. You can use it in cooking or put it on fruit or puddings. *...strawberries and cream.* **2** N-VAR A **cream** is a substance that you rub into your skin, for example to keep it soft or to heal or protect it. *...sun protection creams.* **3** ADJ Something that is **cream** in colour is yellowish-white. **4** N-SING The **cream** is used to refer to the best people or things of a particular kind. *...the cream of society.*
▸ **cream off.** PHR-VERB If you **cream off** part of a group of people, you separate them and treat them differently, because you think they are better than the rest. *The private schools cream off many of the best pupils.*

creamy /'kriːmi/. ADJ **Creamy** food or drink contains a lot of cream or milk or has a soft, smooth texture like cream. *...rich, creamy coffee. ...creamy mashed potato.*

crease /kriːs/ **creases, creasing, creased.** **1** VERB & N-COUNT If cloth or paper **creases**, or if you **crease** it, lines called **creases** form in it because it has been crushed or folded. *If you iron the collar last, you will crease the rest of the shirt... Papa flattened the creases of the map.* ♦ **creased** ADJ *His clothes were creased, as if he had slept in them.* **2** VERB &

a
b
c
d
e
f
g
h
i
j
k
l
m
n
o
p
q
r
s
t
u
v
w
x
y
z

N-COUNT If your face **creases**, lines called **creases** appear on it because you are frowning or smiling. *His face creased into an unwilling smile. ...the tiny creases at the corners of his eyes.* ♦ **creased** ADJ *...Jock's creased drunken face.*

⭐ **create** /kriˈeɪt/ **creates, creating, created.** VERB To **create** something means to cause it to happen or exist. *It is really great for a radio producer to create a show like this... She could create a fight out of anything.* ♦ **creator, creators** N-COUNT *...Ian Fleming, the creator of James Bond.*

creation /kriˈeɪʃən/ **creations.** [1] N-UNCOUNT The **creation of** something is the act of bringing it into existence. *These businesses stimulate the creation of local jobs.* [2] N-UNCOUNT In many religions, **creation** is the making of the universe, earth, and creatures by God. *...the biblical story of creation.* [3] N-COUNT You can refer to something that someone has made as a **creation**. *The bathroom is entirely my own creation.*

⭐ **creative** /kriˈeɪtɪv/. [1] ADJ A **creative** person has the ability to invent and develop original ideas, especially in art. **Creative** activities involve inventing and developing original ideas. *...creative writing.* ♦ **creativity** /ˌkriːeɪˈtɪvɪti/ N-UNCOUNT *American art reached a peak of creativity in the '50s and 60s.* [2] ADJ If you use something in a **creative** way, you use it in a new way that produces interesting and unusual results. *...his creative use of words.*

creature /ˈkriːtʃə/ **creatures.** N-COUNT You can refer to any living thing that is not a plant as a **creature**. *Like all living creatures, birds need a regular supply of water.*

crèche /krɛʃ/ **crèches.** N-COUNT A **crèche** is a place where small children are left and looked after while their parents are doing something else.

credence /ˈkriːdəns/. N-UNCOUNT If something gives or lends **credence** to a theory or story, it makes it easier to believe.

credentials /krɪˈdenʃəlz/. [1] N-PLURAL Your **credentials** are your previous achievements, training, and general background, which indicate that you are qualified to do something. *I can testify to the credentials of the clientele.* [2] N-PLURAL Someone's **credentials** are a letter or certificate that proves their identity or qualifications. *Britain's new ambassador to Lebanon has presented his credentials to the President.*

credible /ˈkredɪbəl/. [1] ADJ **Credible** means able to be trusted or believed. *We have two very credible witnesses.* ♦ **credibility** N-UNCOUNT *The police have lost their credibility.* [2] ADJ A **credible** candidate, policy, or system is one that appears to have a chance of being successful. *...a more credible opponent.*

⭐ **credit** /ˈkredɪt/ **credits, crediting, credited.** [1] N-UNCOUNT **Credit** is a system where you pay for goods or services several weeks or months after you have received them. *Pay cash or buy on credit.* [2] N-UNCOUNT If a person or their bank account is **in credit**, the bank account has money in it. *I made sure the account stayed in credit. ...the interest earned on a credit balance.* [3] N-UNCOUNT If you get **the credit for** something good, people praise you because you are thought to be responsible for it. *Some of the credit for her relaxed manner must go to Andy.* [4] VERB If people **credit** someone **with** an achievement, people say or believe that they were responsible for it. *The staff are crediting him with having saved Hythe's life.* [5] N-COUNT **The credits** refers to the list of people who helped to make a film, a record, or a television programme.

PHRASES ● If you say that, **to** someone's **credit**, they did something, you mean that they deserve praise for it. *To his credit, he had always opposed the use of violence.* ● If you have one or more achievements **to** your **credit**, you have achieved them. *I have countless magazine stories to my credit.*

creditable /ˈkredɪtəbəl/. ADJ A **creditable** performance or achievement is of a reasonably high standard.

'credit card, credit cards. N-COUNT A **credit card** is a plastic card that you use to buy goods on credit.

creditor /ˈkredɪtə/ **creditors.** N-COUNT Your **creditors** are the people who you owe money to.

creed /kriːd/ **creeds.** [1] N-COUNT A **creed** is a set of beliefs or principles that influence the way people live or work. *...their devotion to their creed of self-help.* [2] N-COUNT A **creed** is a religion. [FORMAL] *...young South Africans of every race and creed.*

creek /kriːk/ **creeks.** [1] N-COUNT A **creek** is a narrow inlet where the sea comes a long way into the land. [BRITISH] [2] N-COUNT A **creek** is a small stream or river. [AMERICAN]

creep /kriːp/ **creeps, creeping, crept.** [1] VERB To **creep** somewhere means to move there quietly and slowly. *He crept up the stairs... Mist had crept in again from the sea.* [2] VERB **Creep** can be used to indicate that something gradually reaches a particular level or that it is gradually introduced into a particular situation. *The inflation rate has been creeping up to 9.5 per cent. ...if you suspect a fault is creeping into your game.* [3] N-COUNT If you describe someone as a **creep**, you mean that you dislike them, because they flatter people but are not sincere. [INFORMAL]

creepy /ˈkriːpi/. ADJ If you say that something or someone is **creepy**, you mean they make you feel very uneasy. [INFORMAL] *...places that were really creepy at night.*

cremate /krɪˈmeɪt/, AM /ˈkriːmeɪt/ **cremates, cremating, cremated.** VERB When someone **is cremated**, their dead body is burned, usually as part of a funeral service. ♦ **cremation, cremations** N-VAR *We finalized the arrangements for her cremation.*

crept /krept/. **Crept** is the past tense and past participle of **creep**.

cricket 1

crescendo /krɪˈʃendəʊ/ **crescendos.** N-COUNT A **crescendo** is a noise that gets louder and louder. Some people use **crescendo** to refer to the point when a noise is at its loudest. *The applause quickly rose to a crescendo.*

crescent /ˈkresənt, ˈkrez-/ **crescents.** N-COUNT A **crescent** is a curved shape like the shape of the moon during its first and last quarters. → See picture on page 829.

crest /krest/ **crests.** 1 N-COUNT The **crest** of a hill or a wave is the highest part of it. 2 N-COUNT A **crest** is a design that is the symbol of a noble family, a town, or an organization.

crevice /ˈkrevɪs/ **crevices.** N-COUNT A **crevice** is a narrow crack in a rock.

⭐ **crew** /kruː/ **crews.** 1 N-COUNT The **crew** of a ship, an aircraft, or a spacecraft consists of the people who work on it and operate it. **Crew** can take the singular or plural form of the verb. 2 N-COUNT A **crew** is a group of people with special technical skills who work together on a task or project. **Crew** can take the singular or plural form of the verb. *...a two-man film crew.*

crib /krɪb/ **cribs.** N-COUNT In American English, a **crib** is a bed for a baby, with bars or panels round it so that the baby cannot fall out. The British word is **cot**.

⭐ **cricket** /ˈkrɪkɪt/ **crickets.** 1 N-UNCOUNT **Cricket** is an outdoor game played by two teams who try to score points, called runs, by hitting a ball with a wooden bat. 2 N-COUNT A **cricket** is a small jumping insect that produces sharp sounds by rubbing its wings together. → See picture on page 824.

cricketer /ˈkrɪkɪtə/ **cricketers.** N-COUNT A **cricketer** is a person who plays cricket.

⭐ **crime** /kraɪm/ **crimes.** N-VAR A **crime** is an illegal action or activity for which a person can be punished by law. *...the scene of the crime. ...the alarming rise in crime... It's not a crime to be stupid.*

⭐ **criminal** /ˈkrɪmɪnəl/ **criminals.** 1 N-COUNT A **criminal** is a person who has committed a crime. 2 ADJ **Criminal** means connected with crime. *He*

had a criminal record for petty theft. ...criminal assault.* ◆ **criminally** ADV *...a hospital for the criminally insane.*

crimson /ˈkrɪmzən/. ADJ Something that is **crimson** is deep red in colour.

cringe /krɪndʒ/ **cringes, cringing, cringed.** VERB If you **cringe at** something, you feel embarrassed or disgusted, and perhaps show this in your expression or by making a slight movement. *Chris had cringed at the thought of using her own family for publicity.*

cripple /ˈkrɪpəl/ **cripples, crippling, crippled.** 1 N-COUNT A person with a physical disability or a serious permanent injury is sometimes referred to as a **cripple**. Some people find this use offensive. 2 VERB If someone **is crippled** by an injury, they are so seriously affected by it that they can never move their body properly again. 3 VERB To **cripple** a machine, organization, or system means to damage it severely or prevent it from working properly. *A total cut-off of supplies would cripple Jordan's economy.*

crippling /ˈkrɪplɪŋ/. 1 ADJ BEFORE N A **crippling** illness or disability severely damages your health or body. *...crippling diseases such as arthritis.* 2 ADJ If you say that an action, policy, or situation has a **crippling** effect on something, you mean it has a very harmful effect.

⭐ **crisis** /ˈkraɪsɪs/ **crises** /ˈkraɪsiːz/. N-VAR A **crisis** is a situation in which something or someone is affected by one or more very serious problems. *...the continent's economic crisis. ...someone to turn to in moments of crisis.*

crisp /krɪsp/ **crisper, crispest; crisps.** 1 ADJ **Crisp** food is pleasantly hard and crunchy. *Grill under a medium grill until the bacon is crisp. ...crisp lettuce.* 2 N-COUNT In British English, **crisps** are very thin slices of potato that have been fried until they are hard and crunchy and that are eaten cold as a snack. The American word is **chips** or **potato chips**. 3 ADJ **Crisp** air is pleasantly fresh, cold, and dry. 4 ADJ A **crisp** remark or response is brief and perhaps unfriendly. *'Very well,' I said, adopting a crisp authoritative tone.*

criss-cross /'krɪs krɒs, ᴀᴍ - krɔːs/ **criss-crosses, criss-crossing, criss-crossed.** [1] VERB If a person or thing **criss-crosses** an area, they travel from one side to the other and back again many times. If a number of things **criss-cross** an area, they cross it, and cross over each other. *They criss-crossed the country by bus.* [2] ADJ BEFORE N A **criss-cross** pattern or design consists of lines crossing each other.

criterion /kraɪ'tɪəriən/ **criteria** /kraɪ'tɪəriə/. N-COUNT A **criterion** is a factor on which you judge or decide something. *The bank is reassessing its criteria for lending money.*

★ **critic** /'krɪtɪk/ **critics.** [1] N-COUNT A **critic** is a person who writes reviews and expresses opinions about books, films, music, and art. *Mather was film critic on the Daily Telegraph.* [2] N-COUNT Someone who is a **critic** of a person or system disapproves of them and criticizes them publicly. *Her critics accused her of caring only about success.*

★ **critical** /'krɪtɪkəl/. [1] ADJ A **critical** time or situation is extremely important. *The incident happened at a critical point in the campaign... How you finance a business is critical to the success of your venture.* ♦ **critically** ADV *Economic prosperity depends critically on an open world trading system.* [2] ADJ A **critical** situation is very serious and dangerous. *The German authorities are considering an airlift if the situation becomes critical.* ♦ **critically** ADV *Moscow is running critically low on food supplies.* [3] ADJ If you are **critical of** someone or something, you criticize them. *His report is highly critical of the judge... He has apologised for critical remarks he made about the referee.* ♦ **critically** ADV *She spoke critically of Laura.* [4] ADJ BEFORE N A **critical** approach to something involves examining and judging it carefully. *...the critical analysis of political ideas.* ♦ **critically** ADV *Wyman watched them critically.*

★ **criticism** /'krɪtɪsɪzəm/ **criticisms.** [1] N-VAR **Criticism** is the action of expressing disapproval of something or someone. A **criticism** is a statement that expresses disapproval. *...the criticism that the English do not truly care about their children.* [2] N-UNCOUNT **Criticism** is a serious examination and judgement of something such as a book or play. *...literary criticism.*

★ **criticize** (BRIT also **criticise**) /'krɪtɪsaɪz/ **criticizes, criticizing, criticized.** VERB If you **criticize** someone or something, you express your disapproval of them by saying what you think is wrong with them. *The regime has been harshly criticized for serious human rights violations.*

critique /krɪ'tiːk/ **critiques.** N-COUNT A **critique** is a written examination and judgement of a situation or of a person's work or ideas. [FORMAL] *...a feminist critique of Victorian lady novelists.*

croak /krəʊk/ **croaks, croaking, croaked.** [1] VERB When a frog or bird **croaks**, it makes a harsh low sound. [2] VERB When someone **croaks** something, they say it in a hoarse rough voice. *Tiller moaned and managed to croak, 'Help me'.*

crockery /'krɒkəri/. N-UNCOUNT **Crockery** consists of plates, cups, and saucers.

crocodile /'krɒkədaɪl/ **crocodiles.** N-COUNT A **crocodile** is a large reptile with a long body. Crocodiles live in rivers.

croissant /'kwæsɒn, ᴀᴍ kwɑː'sɑːn/ **croissants.** N-VAR **Croissants** are small crescent-shaped pieces of sweetened bread that are often eaten for breakfast.

crony /'krəʊni/ **cronies.** N-COUNT Your **cronies** are the friends who you spend a lot of time with. [INFORMAL] *...the governor and his cronies.*

crook /krʊk/ **crooks.** [1] N-COUNT A **crook** is a criminal or a dishonest person. [INFORMAL] *The man is a crook and a liar.* [2] N-COUNT The **crook of** your arm or leg is the soft inside part where you bend your elbow or knee.

crooked /'krʊkɪd/. [1] ADJ Something that is **crooked** is bent or twisted. *She has a crooked nose.* [2] ADJ If you describe a person or an activity as **crooked**, you mean that they are dishonest or criminal. *...crooked business deals.*

croon /kruːn/ **croons, crooning, crooned.** VERB If you **croon**, you sing or say something quietly and gently. *Lewis began to croon another Springsteen song.*

★ **crop** /krɒp/ **crops, cropping, cropped.** [1] N-COUNT **Crops** are plants such as wheat and potatoes that are grown in large quantities for food. *Farmers here still plant and harvest their crops by hand.* [2] N-COUNT The plants or fruits that are collected at harvest time are referred to as a **crop**. *...this year's corn crop.* [3] N-SING You can refer to a group of people or things that have appeared together as a **crop** of them. *...the current crop of young British designers.* [4] VERB To **crop** someone's hair means to cut it short.

▸ **crop up.** PHR-VERB If something **crops up**, it happens or appears unexpectedly. *Problems will crop up and hit you before you are ready.*

croquet /'krəʊkeɪ, ᴀᴍ krəʊ'keɪ/. N-UNCOUNT **Croquet** is a game in which the players use long-handled wooden mallets to hit balls through metal arches stuck in a lawn.

cross 1 verb and noun uses

★ **cross** /krɒs, ᴀᴍ krɔːs/ **crosses, crossing, crossed.** [1] VERB If you **cross** a room, road, or area of land, you move to the other side of it. If you **cross to** a place, you move over a room, road, or area in order to reach that place. *Nine Albanians have crossed the border into Greece... Egan crossed to the drinks cabinet and poured a Scotch.* [2] VERB A road, railway, or bridge that **crosses** an area of land or water passes over it. *The Defford to Eckington road crosses the river.* [3] VERB When lines or roads **cross**, they meet and go across each other. [4] VERB If you **cross** your arms, legs, or fingers, you put one of them on top of the other. *Pop crossed his arms over his chest.* [5] VERB If an expression **crosses** someone's face, it appears briefly on their face. [LITERARY] [6] VERB When a thought **crosses** your mind, you think of

crucify

something or remember something. **7** N-COUNT A **cross** is a shape that consists of a vertical line with a shorter horizontal line across it. → See picture on page 829. ...a cross on a silver chain **8** N-COUNT A **cross** is a written mark in the shape of an X. **9** N-COUNT Something that is a **cross between** two things is neither one thing nor the other, but a mixture of both. The snowmobile is a cross between a sledge and a motorcycle.
▸**cross out.** PHR-VERB If you **cross out** words, you draw a line through them.

cross 2 adjective use

cross /krɒs, AM krɔːs/ **crosser, crossest.** ADJ Someone who is **cross** is angry or irritated. I'm terribly cross with him. ♦ **crossly** ADV 'No, no, no,' Morris said crossly.

cross-'country. **1** N-UNCOUNT **Cross-country** is the sport of running, riding, or skiing across open countryside. **2** ADJ BEFORE N & ADV A **cross-country** journey involves less important roads or railway lines, or takes you from one side of a country to the other. ...cross-country rail services... I drove cross-country in his van.

cross-ex'amine, cross-examines, cross-examining, cross-examined. VERB When a lawyer **cross-examines** someone during a trial or hearing, he or she questions them about the evidence that they have given. ♦ **cross-examination, cross-examinations** N-VAR ...the cross-examination of a witness.

crossing /'krɒsɪŋ, AM 'krɔːs-/ **crossings.** **1** N-COUNT A **crossing** is a boat journey to the other side of a sea. **2** N-COUNT A **crossing** is a place where you can cross something such as a road or a border.

crossover /'krɒsəʊvə, AM 'krɔːs-/ **crossovers.** **1** N-VAR A **crossover** of one style and another is a combination of the two different styles. ...the contemporary crossover of pop, jazz and funk. **2** N-SING A **crossover** is a change from one type of activity to another. ...the crossover from actress to singer.

crossroads /'krɒsrəʊdz, AM 'krɔːs-/.

☑ **Crossroads** is both the singular and the plural form.

N-COUNT A **crossroads** is a place where two roads meet and cross.

'cross-section, cross-sections. **1** N-COUNT A **cross-section of** something such as a group of people is a typical or representative sample. I was surprised at the cross-section of people there. **2** N-COUNT A **cross-section of** an object is what you would see if you cut straight through the middle of it. ...a cross-section of an airplane.

crossword /'krɒsw3ːd, AM 'krɔːs-/ **crosswords.** N-COUNT A **crossword** or a **crossword puzzle** is a word game in which you work out answers to clues, and write the answers in the white squares of a pattern of black and white squares. ...doing the crossword puzzle in the daily paper.

crotch /krɒtʃ/ **crotches.** **1** N-COUNT Your **crotch** is the part of your body between the tops of your legs. **2** N-COUNT The **crotch** of a pair of trousers is the part that covers the area between the tops of your legs.

crouch /kraʊtʃ/ **crouches, crouching, crouched.** **1** VERB & N-SING If you **are crouching**, or if you **crouch down**, your legs are bent under you so that you are close to the ground and leaning forward slightly. If you are **in a crouch**, your body is in this position. → See picture on page 532. We were crouching in the bushes... He crouched down beside him... They walked in a crouch. **2** VERB If you **crouch over** something, you bend over it so that you are very near to it. He crouched over the steering wheel.

crow /krəʊ/ **crows, crowing, crowed.** **1** N-COUNT A **crow** is a large black bird which makes a loud harsh noise. **2** VERB When a cock **crows**, it utters a loud sound, early in the morning. **3** VERB If you say that someone **is crowing about** something they have achieved, they keep talking about it proudly in a way that annoys them. [INFORMAL] They outraged journalists by crowing about America's superiority to England.

★ **crowd** /kraʊd/ **crowds, crowding, crowded.** **1** N-COUNT A **crowd** is a large group of people who have gathered together. A huge crowd had gathered. **2** N-COUNT A particular **crowd** is a group of friends, or people with the same interests or occupation. [INFORMAL] All the old crowd have come out. **3** VERB When people **crowd around** someone or something, they gather closely together around them. The children crowded around him. **4** VERB If people **crowd into** a place or **are crowded into** it, large numbers of them enter it so that it becomes very full. One group of journalists were crowded into a minibus.

crowded /'kraʊdɪd/. ADJ A **crowded** place is full of people or things. The old town square was crowded with people. ...a crowded city.

★ **crown** /kraʊn/ **crowns, crowning, crowned.** **1** N-COUNT A **crown** is a circular ornament, usually made of gold and jewels, which a king or queen wears on their head at official ceremonies. **2** VERB When a king or queen **is crowned**, a crown is placed on their head as part of a ceremony in which they are officially made king or queen. **3** VERB If one thing **crowns** another, it is on top of it. [LITERARY] Another rugged castle crowns the cliffs. **4** N-COUNT Your **crown** is the top part of your head, at the back.

★ **crucial** /'kruːʃəl/. ADJ Something that is **crucial** is extremely important. An animal's sense of smell is still crucial to its survival. ...crucial decisions. ♦ **crucially** ADV Education is crucially important.

crucify /'kruːsɪfaɪ/ **crucifies, crucifying, crucified.** VERB In former times, if someone **was crucified**, they were killed by being tied or nailed to a cross and left to die. ♦ **crucifixion** /ˌkruːsɪ'fɪkʃən/ **crucifixions** N-VAR ...the crucifixion of Christians in Rome.

a
b
c
d
e
f
g
h
i
j
k
l
m
n
o
p
q
r
s
t
u
v
w
x
y
z

crude /kruːd/ **cruder, crudest.** [1] ADJ Something that is **crude** is simple and not sophisticated. *...an important but crude way of assessing the risk of heart disease. ...crude wooden boxes.* ♦ **crudely** ADV *...a crudely carved wooden form.* [2] ADJ If you describe someone as **crude**, you disapprove of them because they speak or behave in a rude or offensive way. *...crude sexual jokes.* ♦ **crudely** ADV *He hated it when she spoke so crudely.*

crude 'oil. N-UNCOUNT **Crude oil** is oil in its natural state before it has been processed.

cruel /ˈkruːəl/ **crueller, cruellest.** ADJ Someone who is **cruel** deliberately causes pain or distress. *Children can be so cruel. ...her cruel and abusive husband.* ♦ **cruelly** ADV *...the cruelly treated, faithful wife.* ♦ **cruelty** /ˈkruːəlti/ **cruelties** N-VAR *Britain has laws against cruelty to animals.*

⭐ **cruise** /kruːz/ **cruises, cruising, cruised.** [1] N-COUNT A **cruise** is a holiday spent on a ship or boat which visits a number of places. *He and his wife were planning to go on a world cruise.* [2] VERB If you **cruise** a sea, river, or canal, you travel around it or along it on a cruise. *You could cruise to Australia.* [3] VERB If a car or a ship **cruises**, it moves at a constant moderate speed. *A black and white police car cruised past.*

cruiser /ˈkruːzə/ **cruisers.** [1] N-COUNT A **cruiser** is a motor boat with a cabin for people to sleep in. [2] N-COUNT A **cruiser** is a large fast warship.

crumb /krʌm/ **crumbs.** N-COUNT **Crumbs** are tiny pieces that fall from bread, biscuits, or cake when you cut or eat them.

crumble /ˈkrʌmbəl/ **crumbles, crumbling, crumbled.** [1] VERB When something soft or brittle **crumbles**, or when you **crumble** it, it breaks into a lot of small pieces. *The flint crumbled into fragments.* [2] VERB If an old building or piece of land **is crumbling**, or if it **is crumbling away**, parts of it keep breaking off. *...a big gray mountain crumbling into the sea.* [3] VERB If something such as a system, relationship, or hope **crumbles**, it comes to an end. *The traditional marriage is crumbling fast.*

crumbly /ˈkrʌmbli/. ADJ Something that is **crumbly** is easily broken into a lot of little pieces. *...crumbly cheese.*

crumple /ˈkrʌmpəl/ **crumples, crumpling, crumpled.** [1] VERB & PHR-VERB If you **crumple** something such as paper or cloth, or if you **crumple** it **up**, you squash it and it becomes full of creases and folds. *She crumpled the paper in her hand... Nancy looked at the note angrily, then crumpled it up.* ♦ **crumpled** ADJ *His uniform was crumpled.* [2] VERB If someone's face **crumples**, they suddenly look very disappointed or as if they want to cry.
▶**crumple up.** See **crumple** 1.

crunch /krʌntʃ/ **crunches, crunching, crunched.** [1] VERB If you **crunch** something hard, you crush it noisily between your teeth. *Richard crunched into the apple.* [2] VERB & N-COUNT If something **crunches**, it makes a breaking or crushing noise,

called a **crunch**. *...wheels crunching over a stony surface. ...the crunch of tires on the gravel driveway.*

crunchy /ˈkrʌntʃi/. ADJ **Crunchy** food is pleasantly hard or crisp, and makes a noise when you eat it.

crusade /kruːˈseɪd/ **crusades.** N-COUNT A **crusade** is a long and determined attempt to achieve something. *He made it his crusade to teach children to love books.* ♦ **crusader, crusaders** N-COUNT *...a crusader for the rights of women.*

crush /krʌʃ/ **crushes, crushing, crushed.** [1] VERB To **crush** something means to press it very hard so that its shape is destroyed or so that it breaks into pieces. *Andrew crushed his empty can. ...crushed ice.* [2] VERB If you **are crushed against** someone or something, you are pushed or pressed against them. *We were at the front, crushed against the stage.* [3] N-COUNT A **crush** is a dense crowd of people. *He somehow got separated in the crush.* [4] VERB To **crush** a protest, army, or political organization means to defeat it completely. ♦ **crushing** N-UNCOUNT *...the violent crushing of anti-government demonstrations.* [5] N-COUNT If you have a **crush on** someone, you feel you are in love with them but you do not have a relationship with them. [INFORMAL]

crust /krʌst/ **crusts.** [1] N-COUNT The **crust** on a loaf of bread is the outside part. [2] N-COUNT The earth's **crust** is its outer layer.

crusty /ˈkrʌsti/. ADJ Something that is **crusty** has a hard, crisp, outer layer. *...crusty French loaves.*

crutch /krʌtʃ/ **crutches.** N-COUNT A **crutch** is a stick which someone with an injured foot or leg uses to support them when walking.

crux /krʌks/. N-SING The **crux of** a problem or argument is the most important or difficult part, which affects everything else. *The crux of their disagreement came down to two things: money and power.*

⭐ **cry** /kraɪ/ **cries, crying, cried.** [1] VERB & N-SING When you **cry**, or when you have a **cry**, tears come from your eyes, usually because you are unhappy or hurt. *I hung up the phone and started to cry... He cried with anger and frustration... I like a good cry.* ♦ **crying** N-UNCOUNT *...her 13-week-old son's crying.* [2] VERB & PHR-VERB To **cry** something, or to **cry** something **out**, means to shout or say something loudly. *'Nancy Drew,' she cried, 'you're under arrest!'... 'You're wrong, quite wrong!' Henry cried out.* [3] N-COUNT A **cry** is a loud high sound that you make when you feel a strong emotion such as fear, pain, or pleasure. *A cry of horror broke from me.* [4] PHRASE If you say that something is **a far cry from** something else, you mean it is very different from it. *Their lives are a far cry from his own poor childhood.*
▶**cry out.** [1] PHR-VERB If you **cry out**, you call out loudly because you are frightened, unhappy or in pain. *He was crying out in pain when the ambulance arrived.* [2] See **cry** 2.

▶**cry out for.** PHR-VERB If you say that something **cries out for** a particular thing, you mean that it needs that thing very much. *His body was crying out for some exercise.*

cryptic /ˈkrɪptɪk/. ADJ A **cryptic** remark or message contains a hidden meaning. *My father's notes are more cryptic here.* ♦ **cryptically** ADV *'Not necessarily,' she says cryptically.*

★ **crystal** /ˈkrɪstəl/ **crystals.** ① N-COUNT A **crystal** is a piece of a mineral that has formed naturally into a regular symmetrical shape. *...salt crystals.* ② N-UNCOUNT **Crystal** is a transparent rock used in jewellery and ornaments. ③ N-UNCOUNT **Crystal** is very high quality glass, usually with its surface cut into patterns. *...crystal glasses.*

ˌcrystal ˈclear. ADJ An explanation that is **crystal clear** is very easy to understand. *The message is crystal clear – if you lose weight, you will have a happier, healthier, better life.*

crystallize (BRIT also **crystallise**) /ˈkrɪstəlaɪz/ **crystallizes, crystallizing, crystallized.** ① VERB If you **crystallize** an opinion or idea, or if it **crystallizes**, it becomes fixed and definite in your mind. *I hope the above points have helped to crystallize your thoughts.* ② VERB When a substance **crystallizes**, it turns into crystals. *Don't stir or the sugar will crystallise.*

cub /kʌb/ **cubs.** N-COUNT A **cub** is a young wild animal such as a lion, wolf, or bear. *...three five-week-old lion cubs.*

cube /kjuːb/ **cubes.** N-COUNT A **cube** is a solid shape with six square surfaces which are all the same size. → See picture on page 829.

cubic /ˈkjuːbɪk/. ADJ BEFORE N **Cubic** is used to express units of volume. *...3 billion cubic metres of soil.*

cubicle /ˈkjuːbɪkəl/ **cubicles.** N-COUNT A **cubicle** is a small enclosed area, for example one where you can have a shower or change your clothes.

cuckoo /ˈkʊkuː/ **cuckoos.** N-COUNT A **cuckoo** is a grey bird which makes an easily recognizable sound consisting of two quick notes.

cucumber /ˈkjuːkʌmbə/ **cucumbers.** N-VAR A **cucumber** is a long dark green vegetable. → See picture on page 836.

cuddle /ˈkʌdəl/ **cuddles, cuddling, cuddled.** VERB & N-COUNT If you **cuddle** someone, or if you give them a **cuddle**, you put your arms round them and hold them close. *They used to kiss and cuddle in front of everyone... It would have been nice to give him a cuddle.*

cuddly /ˈkʌdəli/ **cuddlier, cuddliest.** ADJ If you describe people or animals as **cuddly**, you find them attractive because they are plump or soft and look nice to cuddle.

★ **cue** /kjuː/ **cues.** ① N-COUNT A **cue** is something said or done by a performer that is a signal for another performer to begin speaking or to begin doing something. *I had never known him miss a cue.* ② N-COUNT A **cue** is a long, thin wooden stick that is used to hit the ball in games such as snooker, billliards, and pool. ③ PHRASE If you

take your **cue from** someone, you use their behaviour as an indication of what you should do. *Taking his cue from his companion, he apologized.* ④ PHRASE If you say that something happened **on cue**, you mean that it happened just when it was expected to happen, or just at the right time. *Kevin arrived right on cue.*

cuff /kʌf/ **cuffs.** ① N-COUNT The **cuffs** of a piece of clothing are the end parts of the sleeves. ② PHRASE An **off-the-cuff** remark is made without being prepared or thought about in advance. *Mr Baker was speaking off the cuff when he made those suggestions.*

cuisine /kwɪˈziːn/ **cuisines.** N-VAR The **cuisine** of a region is its characteristic style of cooking. *...traditional French cuisine.*

culinary /ˈkʌlɪnəri, AM ˈkjuːləneri/. ADJ BEFORE N **Culinary** means related to cooking. *...culinary delights.*

cull /kʌl/ **culls, culling, culled.** ① VERB If items or ideas **are culled from** a particular source or number of sources, they are taken and gathered together. *All this, needless to say, had been culled second-hand from radio reports.* ② VERB & N-COUNT To **cull** animals means to kill some of them in order to reduce their numbers. You can also talk about a **cull**. *...a proposal to cull the Forest deer. ...the annual seal cull off the Namibian coast.* ♦ **culling** N-UNCOUNT *The culling of seal cubs has led to an outcry.*

culminate /ˈkʌlmɪneɪt/ **culminates, culminating, culminated.** VERB If you say that an activity, process, or series of events **culminates in** or **with** a particular event, you mean that event happens at the end of it. *They had an argument, which culminated in Tom getting drunk.* ♦ **culmination** N-SING *The protests were the culmination of a week of demonstrations.*

culprit /ˈkʌlprɪt/ **culprits.** ① N-COUNT The person who committed a crime or did something wrong can be referred to as the **culprit**. *The real culprits in the fight have not been identified.* ② N-COUNT The cause of a problem or bad situation can be referred to as the **culprit**. *...carbon dioxide – the main culprit in the greenhouse effect.*

cult /kʌlt/ **cults.** ① N-COUNT A **cult** is a fairly small religious group, especially one which is considered strange. *The teenager may have been abducted by a religious cult.* ② N-SING & ADJ When a person, object, or activity becomes a **cult**, they become very popular or fashionable. *The film is destined to become a cult classic.*

cultivate /ˈkʌltɪveɪt/ **cultivates, cultivating, cultivated.** ① VERB If you **cultivate** land, you prepare it and grow crops on it. *She also cultivated a small garden of her own. ...cultivated land.* ♦ **cultivation** N-UNCOUNT *...the cultivation of fruit and vegetables.* ② VERB If you **cultivate** an attitude, image, or skill, you develop it and make it stronger. *He has cultivated the image of an elder statesman.* ♦ **cultivation** N-UNCOUNT *...the cultivation of a positive approach to life.*

a
b
c
d
e
f
g
h
i
j
k
l
m
n
o
p
q
r
s
t
u
v
w
x
y
z

cultivated /ˈkʌltɪveɪtɪd/. **1** ADJ If you describe someone as **cultivated**, you mean that they are well-educated and have good manners. *...an elegant, cultivated woman.* **2** ADJ BEFORE N **Cultivated** plants have been developed for growing on farms or in gardens. *...a mixture of wild and cultivated varieties.*

⭐ **cultural** /ˈkʌltʃərəl/. ADJ **Cultural** means relating to the arts generally, or to the arts and customs of a particular society. *...sports and cultural events. ...cultural and educational exchanges between Britain and India.*
♦ **culturally** ADV *Culturally, they have much in common with their neighbours just across the border.*

⭐ **culture** /ˈkʌltʃə/ **cultures. 1** N-UNCOUNT **Culture** consists of activities such as the arts and philosophy, which are considered to be important for the development of civilization and of people's minds. *...France's Minister of Culture and Education.* **2** N-COUNT A **culture** is a particular society or civilization, especially considered in relation to its beliefs, way of life, or art. *...people from different cultures.* **3** N-COUNT In science, a **culture** is a group of bacteria or cells grown in a laboratory as part of an experiment.

cultured /ˈkʌltʃəd/. ADJ If you describe someone as **cultured**, you mean that they are well educated and know a lot about the arts. *He is a cultured man with a wide circle of friends.*

-cum- /-kʌm-/. You put **-cum-** between two words to form a compound noun referring to something or someone that is partly one thing and partly another. *...a dining-room-cum-study.*

cumbersome /ˈkʌmbəsəm/. **1** ADJ Something that is **cumbersome** is large and heavy and difficult to carry, wear, or handle. *Although the machine looks cumbersome, it is actually easy to use.* **2** ADJ A **cumbersome** system or process is complicated and inefficient. *The proposed regulations are ill-defined and cumbersome.*

cumulative /ˈkjuːmjʊlətɪv/. ADJ If a series of events have a **cumulative** effect, each event makes the effect greater. *The benefits from eating fish are cumulative.*

cunning /ˈkʌnɪŋ/. **1** ADJ A **cunning** person is clever and deceitful. ♦ **cunningly** ADV *They were cunningly disguised in golf clothes.* **2** N-UNCOUNT **Cunning** is the ability to plan things cleverly, often by deceiving people. *...one more example of the cunning of today's art thieves.*

⭐ **cup** /kʌp/ **cups, cupping, cupped. 1** N-COUNT A **cup** is a small round container with a handle, which you drink from. **2** N-COUNT A **cup** is something which is small, round, and hollow, like a cup. *...the brass cups of the small chandelier.* **3** N-COUNT A **cup** is a large metal cup on a stem given as a prize to the winner of a game or competition. **4** VERB If you **cup** your **hands**, you make them into a curved dish-like shape. *He cupped his hands around his mouth and called out for Diane.*

5 VERB If you **cup** something in your hands, you make your hands into a curved dish-like shape and support it or hold it gently. *He cupped her chin in the palm of his hand.*

cupboard /ˈkʌbəd/ **cupboards.** N-COUNT A **cupboard** is a piece of furniture with doors at the front and usually shelves inside.

curable /ˈkjʊərəbəl/. ADJ A **curable** disease or illness can be cured.

curate /ˈkjʊərət/ **curates.** N-COUNT A **curate** is a clergyman who helps a vicar or priest.

curator /kjʊˈreɪtə/ **curators.** N-COUNT The **curator** of a museum or art gallery is the person in charge of the exhibits or works of art.

curb /kɜːb/ **curbs, curbing, curbed. 1** VERB & N-COUNT If you **curb** something, you control it and keep it within limits. You can also talk about a **curb on** something. *...advertisements aimed at curbing the spread of Aids... He called for much stricter curbs on immigration.* **2** See also **kerb**.

⭐ **cure** /kjʊə/ **cures, curing, cured. 1** VERB If a doctor or a medical treatment **cures** someone, or **cures** their illness, they make the person well again. *Now doctors believe they have cured him of the disease.* **2** N-COUNT A **cure for** an illness is a medicine or other treatment that cures the illness. **3** VERB If someone or something **cures** a problem, they bring it to an end. *We need to cure our environmental problems.* **4** N-COUNT A **cure for** a problem is something which brings it to an end. *The magic cure for inflation does not exist.* **5** VERB When food, tobacco, or animal skin **is cured**, it is dried, smoked, or salted so that it will last for a long time. *...sliced cured ham.*

curfew /ˈkɜːfjuː/ **curfews.** N-COUNT A **curfew** is a law stating that people must stay inside their houses after a particular time at night. *The village was placed under curfew.*

curiosity /ˌkjʊəriˈɒsɪti/ **curiosities. 1** N-UNCOUNT **Curiosity** is a desire to know about things. *To satisfy our own curiosity we traveled to Baltimore.* **2** N-COUNT A **curiosity** is something which is interesting and fairly rare. *...castles, curiosities, and museums.*

⭐ **curious** /ˈkjʊəriəs/. **1** ADJ If you are **curious** about something, you are interested in it and want to learn more about it. *Steve was intensely curious about the world I came from. ...a group of curious villagers.* ♦ **curiously** ADV *The woman in the shop had looked at them curiously.* **2** ADJ Something that is **curious** is unusual or difficult to understand. *There is a curious thing about her writings.* ♦ **curiously** ADV *Harry was curiously silent through all this.*

curl /kɜːl/ **curls, curling, curled. 1** N-COUNT **Curls** are lengths of hair shaped in curves and circles. *...the little girl with blonde curls.* **2** VERB If your hair **curls**, or if you **curl** it, it is full of curls. *Maria had curled her hair for the event.* **3** N-COUNT A **curl of** something is a piece or quantity of it that is curved or spiral in shape. *...curls of lemon peel.* **4** VERB If something **curls** somewhere, it moves

there in circles or spirals. *Smoke was curling up the chimney... He curled the ball into the net.*
▸**curl up.** ☐ PHR-VERB When someone who is lying down **curls up**, they bring their arms, legs, and head in towards their stomach. *In colder weather, your cat will curl up into a tight, heat-conserving ball.* ② PHR-VERB When something such as a leaf or a piece of paper **curls up**, its edges bend up or towards its centre. *The corners of the lino were curling up.*

curly /'kɜːli/ **curlier, curliest.** ☐ ADJ **Curly** hair is full of curls. → See picture on page 312. ② ADJ **Curly** objects are curved or spiral-shaped. *...cauliflowers with extra long curly leaves.*

⭐ **currency** /'kʌrənsi, AM 'kɜːr-/ **currencies.** ☐ N-VAR The money used in a country is referred to as its **currency**. *...a single European currency. ...foreign currency.* ② N-UNCOUNT If ideas, expressions, or customs have **currency**, they are generally used and accepted by people at that time. [FORMAL] *'Loop' is one of those computer words that has gained currency.*

⭐ **current** /'kʌrənt, AM 'kɜːr-/ **currents.** ☐ N-COUNT A **current** is a steady, continuous, flowing movement of water or air. *The couple were swept away by the strong current.* ② N-COUNT An electric **current** is electricity flowing through a wire or circuit. ③ ADJ Something that is **current** is happening, being done, or being used at the present time. *The current situation is very different... He plans to repeal a number of current policies.* ♦ **currently** ADV *Twelve potential vaccines are currently being tested.*

,**current ac'count, current accounts.** N-COUNT A **current account** is a bank account which you can take money out of at any time. [BRITISH]

,**current af'fairs.** N-PLURAL **Current affairs** are political events and problems which are discussed in the media. *...the BBC's current affairs programme 'Panorama'.*

curriculum /kə'rɪkjʊləm/ **curriculums** (or **curricula** /kə'rɪkjʊlə/). ☐ N-COUNT A **curriculum** consists of all the different courses of study that are taught in a school, college, or university. *Not having Shakespeare in the school curriculum is madness.* ② N-COUNT A particular course of study can be referred to as a **curriculum**. *...the history curriculum.*

curry /'kʌri, AM 'kɜːri/ **curries.** N-VAR **Curry** is an Asian dish made with hot spices. *I went for a curry last night.*

curse /kɜːs/ **curses, cursing, cursed.** ☐ VERB & N-COUNT If you **curse**, or if you utter a **curse**, you swear or say rude words because you are angry about something. [WRITTEN] *I cursed and hobbled to my feet... Groans and curses filled the air.* ② VERB If you **curse** someone or something, you say insulting things to them or complain strongly about them because you are angry with them. *We set off again, cursing the delay... He cursed himself for not making a note of it.* ③ N-COUNT If you say that there is a **curse on** someone, you

mean that a supernatural power is causing unpleasant things to happen to them. ④ N-COUNT You can refer to something that causes a lot of trouble as a **curse**. *...the curse of high unemployment.*

cursor /'kɜːsə/ **cursors.** N-COUNT On a computer screen, the **cursor** is a small, movable shape which indicates where anything typed by the user will appear. [COMPUTING]

curt /kɜːt/. ADJ If someone is **curt**, they speak in a brief and rather rude way. *'The matter is closed,' was the curt reply.* ♦ **curtly** ADV *'I'm leaving,' she said curtly.*

curtail /kɜː'teɪl/ **curtails, curtailing, curtailed.** VERB If you **curtail** something, you reduce or restrict it. *Public spending is far too high, and must be curtailed.* ♦ **curtailment** N-UNCOUNT *...the curtailment of presidential power.*

⭐ **curtain** /'kɜːtən/ **curtains.** ☐ N-COUNT **Curtains** are hanging pieces of material which you can pull across a window to keep light out or prevent people from looking in. *Her bedroom curtains were drawn.* ② N-SING In a theatre, the **curtain** is a large piece of material that hangs in front of the stage until a performance begins.

curve /kɜːv/ **curves, curving, curved.** ☐ N-COUNT A **curve** is a smooth, gradually bending line, for example part of the edge of a circle. *...a curve in the road.* ② VERB If something **curves**, it is shaped like a curve, or moves in a curve. *A stone wall curves away to the left... The ball curved strangely in the air.* ♦ **curved** ADJ *...a curved blade.* ③ N-COUNT You can refer to a change in something as a particular **curve**, especially when it is represented on a graph. *...the rising curve of youth unemployment.*

cushion /'kʊʃən/ **cushions, cushioning, cushioned.** ☐ N-COUNT A **cushion** is a fabric case filled with soft material, which you put on a seat to make it more comfortable. ② VERB To **cushion** an impact means to reduce its effect. *...steps to cushion the impact of the economic slump.*

custard /'kʌstəd/. N-UNCOUNT **Custard** is a sweet yellow sauce made from milk and eggs or from milk and a powder. It is eaten with puddings.

custodial /kʌ'stəʊdiəl/. ADJ BEFORE N **Custodial** means relating to keeping people in prison. [FORMAL] *He will be given a custodial sentence.*

custodian /kʌ'stəʊdiən/ **custodians.** N-COUNT The **custodian** of an official building, a company's assets, or other valuable thing is the person in charge of it. *The Prime Minister is the ultimate custodian of the national interest.*

custody /'kʌstədi/. ☐ N-UNCOUNT **Custody** is the legal right to look after a child, especially the right given to a child's father or mother when they get divorced. *I'm going to go to court to get custody of the children.* ② PHRASE Someone who is **in custody** has been arrested and is being kept in prison until they can be tried.

a b c d e f g h i j k l m n o p q r s t u v w x y z

custom /'kʌstəm/ **customs.** ⚀ N-VAR A **custom** is an activity, a way of behaving, or an event which is usual or traditional in a particular society or in particular circumstances. *...an ancient Japanese custom... It was the custom to give presents at such occasions.* ⚁ See also **customs**.

customary /'kʌstəmri, AM -meri/. ADJ **Customary** means usual. *It is customary to offer a drink or a snack to guests... Yvonne took her customary seat.*

★ **customer** /'kʌstəmə/ **customers.** N-COUNT A **customer** is someone who buys goods or services, especially from a shop. *The shop was full of customers.*

> **USAGE** When you buy goods from a particular shop or company, you are one of its **customers**. If you use the professional services of someone such as a lawyer or an accountant, you are one of their **clients**. Doctors and hospitals have **patients**, while hotels have **guests**. People who travel on public transport are referred to as **passengers**.

,customer 'service. N-UNCOUNT **Customer service** refers to the way that companies behave towards their customers, for example how well they treat them. *...a mail-order business with a strong reputation for customer service.*

customize /'kʌstəmaɪz/ (BRIT also **customise**) **customizes, customizing, customized.** VERB If you **customize** something, you change its appearance or features to suit your tastes or needs. *Kids customised their bikes.*

customs /'kʌstəmz/. ⚀ N-PROPER **Customs** is the official organization responsible for collecting taxes on goods coming into a country and preventing illegal goods from being brought in. *Spanish customs seized 400lb of marijuana. ...customs officers.* ⚁ N-UNCOUNT **Customs** is the place where people arriving from a foreign country have to declare goods that they bring with them. *He walked through customs.*

★ **cut** /kʌt/ **cuts, cutting, cut.** ⚀ VERB & N-COUNT If you **cut** something, or if you make a **cut** in it, you push a knife or similar tool into it in order to remove a piece of it, or to mark or damage it. *Cut the tomatoes in half... The thieves cut a hole in the fence... You've had your hair cut, it looks great... The operation involves making several cuts in the cornea.* ⚁ VERB If you **cut yourself**, you accidentally injure yourself on a sharp object and you bleed. *Johnson cut himself shaving. ...blood from his cut lip.* ⚂ N-COUNT A **cut** is an injury caused by touching or being touched by something sharp. *...a cut on his left eyebrow.* ⚃ VERB If you **cut across** or **through** an area, you go through it because it is a short route to another place. *He decided to cut across the Heath.* ⚄ VERB & N-COUNT To **cut** something, or to make a **cut** in it, means to reduce it. *The first priority is to*

cut costs. ...a deal to cut 50 billion dollars from the federal deficit. ...an immediate 2 per cent cut in interest rates. ⚅ VERB & N-COUNT When a part of a piece of writing or performance **is cut**, or when **cuts** have been made to it, parts of it are not printed, broadcast, or performed. *We've cut some scenes... It has been found necessary to make some cuts in the text.* ⚆ VERB & N-COUNT To **cut** a supply of something means to stop providing it or stop it being provided. A **cut** in the supply of something is the action of stopping it. *...cutting food and water supplies. ...cuts in electricity supplies.* ⚇ PHRASE If something is **a cut above** other things of the same kind, it is better than them. ⚈ See also **cutting**.

▸ **cut across.** PHR-VERB If an issue or problem **cuts across** the division between two or more groups of people, it affects or matters to people in all the groups. *This health-care issue cuts across all the generations.*

▸ **cut back.** PHR-VERB If you **cut back** some money that you are spending, or if you **cut back on** it, you reduce it. *They will be concerned to cut back expenditure... The Government has cut back on defence spending.* ● See also **cutback**.

▸ **cut down.** ⚀ PHR-VERB If you **cut down on** something, you use or do less of it. *He cut down on coffee... Car owners were asked to cut down travel.* ⚁ PHR-VERB If you **cut down** a tree, you cut through its trunk so that it falls to the ground. ⚂ PHR-VERB If you **cut down** something, you reduce it. *We'd like politicians to agree ways to cut down atmospheric pollution.*

▸ **cut off.** ⚀ PHR-VERB If you **cut** something **off**, you remove it with a knife or a similar tool. *Mrs Kreutz cut off a generous piece of the meat... He threatened to cut my hair off.* ⚁ PHR-VERB To **cut off** a place or a person means to separate them from things they are normally connected with. *The storm has cut us off... Without a car we still felt very cut off.* ⚂ PHR-VERB To **cut off** a supply of something means to stop providing it or stop it being provided. *The rebels have cut off electricity from the capital.* ⚃ PHR-VERB If you get **cut off** when you are talking on the telephone, the line is suddenly disconnected.

▸ **cut out.** ⚀ PHR-VERB If you **cut** something **out**, you remove it from what surrounds it using scissors or a knife. *Cut out the coupon and send those cheques off today.* ⚁ PHR-VERB If you **cut out** a part of a text, you do not print, publish, or broadcast that part, in order to shorten the text or make it more acceptable. *They'd cut out all the interesting stuff.* ⚂ PHR-VERB To **cut out** something unnecessary means to remove it completely from a situation. *It would be wiser to cut out all alcohol during pregnancy.* ⚃ PHR-VERB If an object **cuts out** the light, it prevents light from reaching a place. *The curtains were half drawn to cut out the sunlight.* ⚄ PHR-VERB If an engine **cuts out**, it suddenly stops working.

▸ **cut up.** PHR-VERB If you **cut** something **up**, you cut it into several pieces. *Halve the tomatoes, then cut them up.*

cutback (or **cut-back**) /ˈkʌtbæk/ **cutbacks.**
N-COUNT A **cutback** is a reduction in something.
...cutbacks in defence spending.

cute /kjuːt/ **cuter, cutest.** ADJ **Cute** means pretty or
attractive. Oh, look at that dog! He's so cute. ...a
cute little house.

cutlery /ˈkʌtləri/. N-UNCOUNT The knives, forks,
and spoons that you eat with are referred to as
cutlery.

ˈcut-off (or **cutoff**) **cut-offs.** N-COUNT A **cut-off** or
a **cut-off** point is the level or limit at which you
decide that something should stop happening.
The cut-off date for registering is yet to be
announced.

cutter /ˈkʌtə/ **cutters.** N-VAR A **cutter** is a tool that
you use for cutting something. ...a pastry cutter.
...a pair of wire cutters.

⭐ **cutting** /ˈkʌtɪŋ/ **cuttings.** [1] N-COUNT A **cutting** is
a piece of writing cut from a newspaper or
magazine. [BRITISH] ...old newspaper cuttings.
[2] N-COUNT A **cutting** is a piece of stalk that you
cut from a plant and use to grow a new plant.
[3] ADJ A **cutting** remark is unkind and hurts
people's feelings.

ˌ**cutting** ˈ**edge.** N-SING If you are **at the cutting
edge** of a field of activity, you are involved in its
most important or exciting developments. This
shipyard is at the cutting edge of world
shipbuilding technology.

CV /ˌsiː ˈviː/ **CVs.** N-COUNT In British English, your
CV is a brief written account of your personal
details, your education, and jobs you have had,
which you send when you are applying for a job.
The American word is **resumé.**

cyanide /ˈsaɪənaɪd/. N-UNCOUNT **Cyanide** is a
highly poisonous substance.

cybercafé /ˈsaɪbəkæfeɪ/ **cybercafés.** N-COUNT A
cybercafé is a café where people can pay to use
the Internet.

cyberspace /ˈsaɪbəspeɪs/. N-UNCOUNT In
computer technology, **cyberspace** refers to data
banks and networks, considered as a space.
[COMPUTING]

⭐ **cycle** /ˈsaɪkəl/ **cycles, cycling, cycled.** [1] VERB If you
cycle, you ride a bicycle. I cycle to work at least
twice a week. ♦ **cycling** N-UNCOUNT Quiet country
roads are ideal for cycling. [2] N-COUNT A **cycle** is a
bicycle. [3] N-COUNT A **cycle** is a series of events or
processes that is continually repeated, always in
the same order. ...the cycles of nature... They must
break out of the cycle of violence.

cyclical /ˈsɪklɪkəl, ˈsaɪk-/ or **cyclic** /ˈsɪklɪk,
ˈsaɪk-/. ADJ A **cyclical** process happens again and
again in cycles. ...the cyclical downturns that the
stockmarket was bound to suffer.

cyclist /ˈsaɪklɪst/ **cyclists.** N-COUNT A **cyclist** is
someone who rides a bicycle.

cyclone /ˈsaɪkləʊn/ **cyclones.** N-COUNT A **cyclone**
is a violent tropical storm.

cylinder /ˈsɪlɪndə/ **cylinders.** N-COUNT A **cylinder** is
a shape or container with flat circular ends and
long straight sides. → See picture on page 829.
...a cylinder of foam. ...a gas cylinder.

cynic /ˈsɪnɪk/ **cynics.** N-COUNT A **cynic** is someone
who always thinks the worst of people or things.

cynical /ˈsɪnɪkəl/. ADJ If you describe someone
as **cynical**, you think that they always think the
worst of people or things. ...his cynical view of the
world... It has also made me more cynical about
relationships. ♦ **cynically** ADV He laughed
cynically, but without bitterness. ♦ **cynicism**
/ˈsɪnɪsɪzəm/ N-UNCOUNT ...growing public cynicism
about politicians.

cyst /sɪst/ **cysts.** N-COUNT A **cyst** is a growth
containing liquid that appears inside your body
or under your skin.

D d

dab /dæb/ **dabs, dabbing, dabbed.** [1] VERB If you
dab something, you touch it several times using
quick light movements. She dabbed iodine on the
cuts... He dabbed at his lips with the napkin.
[2] N-COUNT A **dab of** something is a small amount
of it that is put onto a surface. [INFORMAL] ...a dab of
glue.

dabble /ˈdæbəl/ **dabbles, dabbling, dabbled.** VERB If
you **dabble** in something, you take part in it but
not very seriously. He dabbled in politics.

⭐ **dad** /dæd/ **dads.** N-COUNT & N-VOC Your **dad** is your
father. [INFORMAL] Help me Dad!... He's living with his
mum and dad.

daddy /ˈdædi/ **daddies.** N-COUNT & N-VOC Children
often call their father **daddy.** [INFORMAL] Little
children like to watch their daddies shave... Look at
me, Daddy!

daffodil /ˈdæfədɪl/ **daffodils.** N-COUNT A **daffodil**
is a yellow flower that blooms in the spring.

daft /dɑːft, dæft/ **dafter, daftest.** ADJ **Daft** means
stupid and not sensible. [BRITISH, INFORMAL] That's a
daft question.

dagger /ˈdægə/ **daggers.** N-COUNT A **dagger** is a
weapon like a knife with two sharp edges.

⭐ **daily** /ˈdeɪli/ **dailies.** [1] ADV & ADJ BEFORE N If
something happens **daily**, it happens every day.
The exhibition is open daily from 11am... I set out
for my daily walk. [2] ADJ BEFORE N **Daily** means
relating to a single day or to one day at a time.
...the recommended daily intake of vitamins.
[3] N-COUNT & ADJ BEFORE N A **daily** or a **daily**
newspaper is a newspaper that is published
every day except Sunday.

dainty /ˈdeɪnti/. ADJ A **dainty** movement,
person, or object is small, delicate, or pretty.
...dainty feet. ♦ **daintily** ADV He noticed how
daintily they all ate.

a b c d e f g h i j k l m n o p q r s t u v w x y z

dairy /'deəri/ **dairies.** 1 N-COUNT A **dairy** is a shop or company that sells milk, butter, and cheese. 2 N-COUNT A **dairy** on a farm is a building where milk is kept or where cream, butter, and cheese are made. 3 ADJ BEFORE N **Dairy** is used to refer to foods such as butter and cheese that are made from milk. ...*dairy products.*

daisy /'deɪzi/ **daisies.** N-COUNT A **daisy** is a small wild flower with a yellow centre and white petals.

dam /dæm/ **dams, damming, dammed.** 1 N-COUNT A **dam** is a wall built across a river to stop the flow of the water and make a lake. 2 VERB To **dam** a river means to build a dam across it.

⭐ **damage** /'dæmɪdʒ/ **damages, damaging, damaged.** 1 VERB To **damage** something means to injure or harm it. *Halliday damaged his knee during training.* ...*the attempt to damage his reputation.* ♦ **damaging** ADJ ...*damaging allegations about his relationship with an actress.* 2 N-UNCOUNT **Damage** is injury or harm that is caused to something. *The bomb caused extensive damage to the restaurant.* ...*the damage done to our international image by the recent violence.* 3 N-PLURAL When a court of law awards **damages** to someone, it orders money to be paid to them by a person who has harmed them.

dame /deɪm/ **dames.** N-TITLE In Britain, **Dame** is a title given to a woman as a special honour. ...*Dame Joan Sutherland.*

damn /dæm/. 1 EXCLAM & ADJ BEFORE N & ADV **Damn** is a swear word which people use to express anger or frustration or for emphasis. *Damn! she muttered... The damn thing's burst... As it turned out, I was damn right.* 2 PHRASE If you say that someone **does not give a damn** about something, you mean that they do not care about it at all. [INFORMAL]

damned /dæmd/. ADJ BEFORE N & ADV **Damned** is a swear word which people use to express anger or frustration or for emphasis. ...*a damned nuisance... We are making a damned good profit.*

damning /'dæmɪŋ/. ADJ Something that is **damning** suggests strongly that someone is guilty of a crime or error. ...*damning evidence.*

damp /dæmp/ **damper, dampest; damps, damping, damped.** 1 ADJ **Damp** means slightly wet. ...*a damp towel.* ♦ **dampness** N-UNCOUNT ...*the dampness of the wall.* 2 N-UNCOUNT **Damp** is slight moisture in the air or on the walls of a house.

▸ **damp down.** PHR-VERB To **damp down** a difficult situation means to make it calmer or less intense. *Mr Brown tried to damp down the row yesterday.*

dampen /'dæmpən/ **dampens, dampening, dampened.** 1 VERB To **dampen** something means to make it less lively or intense. *It did nothing to dampen his enthusiasm for motor sport.* 2 VERB If you **dampen** something, you make it slightly wet. *Dampen a sponge.*

⭐ **dance** /dɑːns, dæns/ **dances, dancing, danced.** 1 VERB When you **dance**, you move around in time to music. ...*a couple dancing together... We all danced the Charleston.* ♦ **dancing** N-UNCOUNT *Let's go dancing tonight.* 2 N-COUNT A **dance** is a series of steps and rhythmic movements which you do to music. It is also a piece of music which people can dance to. *She describes the tango as a very sexy dance.* 3 N-COUNT A **dance** is a social event where people dance with each other. 4 N-UNCOUNT **Dance** is the activity of performing dances as a public entertainment or art form. ...*an evening of dance.*

'dance floor (or **dancefloor**) **dance floors.** N-COUNT In a restaurant or night club, the **dance floor** is the area where people can dance.

dancer /'dɑːnsə, 'dæns-/ **dancers.** N-COUNT A **dancer** is a person who earns money by dancing, or a person who is dancing.

dandelion /'dændɪlaɪən/ **dandelions.** N-COUNT A **dandelion** is a wild plant which has yellow flowers first, then fluffy balls of seeds.

⭐ **danger** /'deɪndʒə/ **dangers.** 1 N-UNCOUNT **Danger** is the possibility that someone may be harmed or killed. *My friends endured tremendous danger in order to help me... Your life is in danger.* 2 N-COUNT A **danger** is something or someone that can hurt or harm you. ...*the dangers of smoking.* 3 N-SING If there is a **danger of** something unpleasant happening, it is possible that it will happen. *There is a danger of infection developing.*

⭐ **dangerous** /'deɪndʒərəs/. ADJ If something is **dangerous**, it may hurt or harm you. ...*dangerous drugs.* ♦ **dangerously** ADV *He rushed downstairs dangerously fast.*

dangle /'dæŋgəl/ **dangles, dangling, dangled.** VERB If something **dangles** from somewhere, it hangs or swings loosely. *A gold bracelet dangled from his left wrist.*

⭐ **dare** /deə/ **dares, daring, dared.** 1 VERB & MODAL If you **dare to** do something, you have enough courage to do it. *He has also dared to take unpopular, but principled stands at times... I didn't dare look at Ellen... They daren't leave him.*

USAGE You can leave out the word **to** after **dare**. *Nobody dared complain.* The form **dares** is never used in a question or in a negative statement. You use **dare** instead. *Dare she tell?... He dare not enter.*

2 VERB & N-COUNT If you **dare** someone **to** do something, or challenge them to do it **for a dare**, you challenge them to prove that they are not frightened of doing it. *He glared at the German, daring him to disagree.* ...*two students accused of murdering a stranger for a dare.*

PHRASES ● You say **'how dare you'** when you are very shocked and angry about something that someone has done. *How dare you insult my singing!* ● You say **I dare say** or **I daresay** to show that you think something is probably true. [SPOKEN] *I dare say they're right.*

daren't /deənt/. 'Dare not' is usually written or said as **daren't**. [INFORMAL]

daring /'deərɪŋ/. **1** ADJ A **daring** person does things which might be dangerous or shocking. *...a daring escape by helicopter.* **2** N-UNCOUNT **Daring** is the courage to do things which might be dangerous or shocking. *His daring may have cost him his life.*

★ **dark** /dɑːk/ **darker, darkest. 1** ADJ When it is **dark**, there is not enough light to see properly. *People usually draw the curtains once it gets dark. ...a dark corridor... After dark, park in a well-lit, busy place.* ◆ **darkness** N-UNCOUNT *The whole city was plunged into darkness.* **2** N-SING **The dark** is the lack of light in a place. *I've always been afraid of the dark.* **3** ADJ Something that is **dark** or a **dark** colour is black or a shade close to black. *...a dark suit. ...a dark blue dress.* **4** ADJ Someone who is **dark** has brown or black hair, and often brown skin. **5** ADJ **Dark** looks or remarks suggest that something horrible is going to happen. *Dark rumours abound.* ◆ **darkly** ADV *They shake their heads and mutter darkly.* **6** PHRASE If you are **in the dark about** something, you do not know anything about it.

darken /'dɑːkən/ **darkens, darkening, darkened. 1** VERB If something **darkens**, it becomes darker. [WRITTEN] *The sky darkened abruptly... He may have darkened his hair.* **2** VERB If someone's face **darkens**, they suddenly look angry. [WRITTEN]

darkroom /'dɑːkruːm/ **darkrooms.** N-COUNT A **darkroom** is a room which is lit only by red light, so that photographs can be developed there.

darling /'dɑːlɪŋ/ **darlings. 1** N-VOC You call someone **darling** if you love them or like them very much. *Thank you, darling.* **2** ADJ BEFORE N & N-COUNT You can describe someone as **darling** or say that they are a **darling** when you love or like them very much. *...our darling child.*

darn /dɑːn/ **darns, darning, darned. 1** VERB When you **darn** something made of cloth, you mend a hole in it by sewing stitches across the hole and then weaving stitches in and out of them. **2** ADJ BEFORE N & ADV People sometimes use **darn** or **darned** to express anger or frustration or for emphasis. *...darned kids... You're darn right.*

dart /dɑːt/ **darts, darting, darted. 1** VERB If a person or animal **darts** somewhere, they move there suddenly and quickly. [WRITTEN] *Ingrid darted across the deserted street.* **2** VERB If you **dart** a glance at someone or something, or if your eyes **dart** to them, you look at them very quickly. [WRITTEN] *Her eyes darted from one face to another.* **3** N-COUNT A **dart** is a small, narrow object with a sharp point which you can throw or shoot. **4** N-UNCOUNT **Darts** is a game in which you throw darts at a round board with numbers on it.

dash /dæʃ/ **dashes, dashing, dashed. 1** VERB & N-SING If you **dash** somewhere, or if you make a **dash** there, you go there quickly and suddenly. *He*

dashed upstairs... Frank considered making a dash for the front door. **2** N-COUNT A **dash of** something is a small quantity or amount of it. *Add a dash of lemon juice.* **3** VERB If an event or person **dashes** someone's hopes, it destroys them by making it impossible that the thing that is hoped for will ever happen. *...the injury which dashed his hopes of Olympic gold.* **4** N-COUNT A **dash** is a short horizontal line (—) used in writing.

▸ **dash off. 1** PHR-VERB If you **dash off** to a place, you go there very quickly. **2** PHR-VERB If you **dash off** a letter, you write it quickly without thinking much about it.

dashboard /'dæʃbɔːd/ **dashboards.** N-COUNT The **dashboard** in a car is the panel facing the driver's seat where most of the instruments and switches are.

★ **data** /'deɪtə/. **1** N-UNCOUNT & N-PLURAL **Data** is information, usually in the form of facts or statistics, that you can analyse. *The study was based on data from 2,100 women.* **2** N-UNCOUNT & N-PLURAL **Data** is information that can be stored and used by a computer program. *...a disk that holds huge amounts of data.*

database (or **data base**) /'deɪtəbeɪs/ **databases.** N-COUNT A **database** is a collection of data stored in a computer in a way that makes it easy to obtain. [COMPUTING] *...a database of hotels that cater for businesswomen.*

★ **date** /deɪt/ **dates, dating, dated. 1** N-COUNT A **date** is a particular day or year, for example 7th June 2002, or 1066. → See Reference Page on Times and Dates. *What's the date today?... You will need to give the dates you wish to stay.* **2** VERB When you **date** something, you give the date when it began or was made. *Archaeologists have dated the fort to the reign of Emperor Antoninus Pius.* **3** VERB When you **date** a letter or a cheque, you write a particular day's date on it. **4** PHRASE **To date** means up until the present time. *'Dottie' is by far his best novel to date.* **5** VERB If something **dates**, it goes out of fashion. ◆ **dated** ADJ *...people in dated dinner-jackets.* **6** N-COUNT A **date** is an appointment to meet someone or go out with them, especially someone of the opposite sex. You can also refer to the person you go out with as your **date**. *I have a date with Bob... His date was one of the girls in the show.* **7** VERB If you **are dating** someone of the opposite sex, you go out regularly with them. *For a year I dated a woman who was a research assistant... They've been dating for three months.* **8** N-COUNT A **date** is a small, sticky, dark brown fruit with a stone inside. **9** See also **out of date**, **up-to-date**.

▸ **date back** or **date from.** PHR-VERB If something **dates back to** a particular time, or **dates from** that time, it started or was made at that time. *The treasure dates back to the sixth century BC.*

'**date rape.** N-UNCOUNT **Date rape** is when a man rapes a women whom he has met socially.

★ Bank of English® frequent word   For a full explanation of all grammatical labels, see pages vii–x

a
b
c
d
e
f
g
h
i
j
k
l
m
n
o
p
q
r
s
t
u
v
w
x
y
z

daub /dɔːb/ **daubs, daubing, daubed.** VERB When you **daub** a substance such as mud or paint on something, you spread it on that thing roughly or carelessly. *They daubed his home with slogans.*

⭐ **daughter** /'dɔːtə/ **daughters.** N-COUNT Your **daughter** is your female child.

'daughter-in-law, daughters-in-law. N-COUNT Your **daughter-in-law** is the wife of your son.

daunt /dɔːnt/ **daunts, daunting, daunted.** VERB If something **daunts** you, it makes you feel afraid or worried about dealing with it. *...a gruelling journey that would have daunted a woman half her age.* ♦ **daunted** ADJ AFTER LINK-V *I was quite daunted by the prospect of coping with teenagers.* ♦ **daunting** ADJ *...the daunting task of restoring the gardens to their former splendour.*

dawn /dɔːn/ **dawns, dawning, dawned.** [1] N-VAR **Dawn** is the time of day when light first appears in the sky, before the sun rises. *Nancy woke at dawn.* [2] VERB When you say that a particular day **dawned**, you mean it began. [WRITTEN] *The next day dawned sombre and gloomy.* [3] N-SING The **dawn of** a period of time or a situation is the beginning of it. [LITERARY] *...the dawn of the radio age.* [4] VERB If something **is dawning**, it is beginning to develop or come into existence. [LITERARY] *A new railway age has dawned.* ♦ **dawning** N-COUNT *...the dawning of the space age.*

▶**dawn on** or **dawn upon.** PHR-VERB If a fact or idea **dawns on** you, or if it **dawns upon** you, you realize it. *It gradually dawned on me that I still had talent.*

⭐ **day** /deɪ/ **days.** [1] N-COUNT A **day** is one of the seven twenty-four hour periods of time in a week. → See Reference Page on Times and Dates. [2] N-VAR **Day** is the part of a day when it is light or the time when you are awake and doing things. *He arranged for me to go down to London one day a week... The snack bar is open during the day.* [3] N-COUNT You can refer to a period in history as a particular **day** or as particular **days**. *He began to talk about the Ukraine of his uncle's day.*

PHRASES ● If you **call it a day**, you stop what you are doing and leave it to be finished later. *I'm tired, let's call it a day.* ● **One day**, **some day**, or **one of these days** means at some future time. *Maybe one day you'll find true love.* ● **day and night**: see **night**. ● **night and day**: see **night**.

'day care. N-UNCOUNT **Day care** is care that is provided during the day for people who cannot look after themselves, such as small children, old people, or people who are ill.

daydream /'deɪdriːm/ **daydreams, daydreaming, daydreamed.** VERB & N-COUNT When you **daydream**, or when you have a **daydream**, you think about pleasant things that you would like to happen. *He daydreams of being a famous journalist... Janis emerged from her daydream.*

daylight /'deɪlaɪt/ N-UNCOUNT **Daylight** is the light that there is during the day, or the time of

day when it is light. *It was still daylight... Quinn returned shortly after daylight.*

daytime /'deɪtaɪm/ N-UNCOUNT **Daytime** is the part of a day when it is light. *In the daytime he stayed up in his room.*

,day-to-'day. ADJ BEFORE N **Day-to-day** things or activities exist or happen every day as part of ordinary life. *...the day-to-day lives of students.*

dazed /deɪzd/ ADJ If someone is **dazed**, they are confused and unable to think clearly, often because of shock or a blow to the head.

dazzle /'dæzəl/ **dazzles, dazzling, dazzled.** [1] VERB If someone or something **dazzles** you, you are extremely impressed by their skill or beauty. *George dazzled her with his knowledge of the world.* [2] N-UNCOUNT The **dazzle** of a light is its brightness, which makes it impossible for you to see properly for a short time. [3] VERB If a bright light **dazzles** you, you cannot see properly for a short time.

dazzling /'dæzlɪŋ/ [1] ADJ Something that is **dazzling** is very impressive or beautiful. *...a dazzling smile.* ♦ **dazzlingly** ADV *The view was dazzlingly beautiful.* [2] ADJ A **dazzling** light is very bright and makes you unable to see properly for a short time. ♦ **dazzlingly** ADV *The bay seemed dazzlingly bright.*

⭐ **dead** /ded/ [1] ADJ & N-PLURAL **Dead** people or **the dead** are no longer living. *My husband's been dead a year now.*

> **USAGE** Do not confuse **dead** with **died**. **Died** is the past tense and past participle of the verb **die**, and thus indicates the action of dying. *She died in 1934... Two men have died since the rioting broke out.* You do not use **died** as an adjective. You use **dead** instead. *More than 2,200 dead birds have been found.*

[2] ADJ A telephone or piece of electrical equipment that is **dead** is not functioning. *Duke answered the phone and the line went dead.* [3] ADJ BEFORE N **Dead** is used to mean complete or absolute, especially with the words 'silence', 'centre', and 'stop'. *He adjusted each chesspiece so that it stood dead centre in its square.* [4] ADV **Dead** means precisely or exactly. *Mars was visible, dead in the centre of the telescope... A fishing boat came out of nowhere, dead ahead.* [5] ADV **Dead** is sometimes used to mean very. [INFORMAL] *His poems sound dead boring, actually.* [6] PHRASE To **stop dead** means to suddenly stop moving or doing something. *We all stopped dead and looked at it.*

,dead 'end, dead ends. [1] N-COUNT If a street is a **dead end**, there is no way out at one end of it. [2] N-COUNT A job or course of action that is a **dead end** does not lead to further developments or progression. *Waitressing was a dead-end job.*

⭐ **deadline** /'dedlaɪn/ **deadlines.** N-COUNT A **deadline** is a time or date before which a particular task must be finished or a particular thing must be done. *The deadline for submissions to the competition will be Easter.*

deadlock /'dedlɒk/. N-UNCOUNT If a dispute or series of negotiations reaches **deadlock**, neither side is willing to give in, and so no agreement can be reached. *Peace talks between the two sides ended in deadlock.*

deadly /'dedli/ **deadlier, deadliest.** 1 ADJ If something is **deadly**, it is likely or able to cause death. *...a deadly disease...* *Some have turned to more deadly weapons.* 2 ADJ If you describe a person or their behaviour as **deadly**, you mean they are unpleasant or dangerous. A **deadly** situation has unpleasant or dangerous consequences. *My aim was deadly accurate. ...the deadliest blizzard to hit the United States since January 1966.*

deaf /def/ **deafer, deafest.** 1 ADJ & N-PLURAL **Deaf** people or **the deaf** are unable to hear anything or unable to hear very well. *She is now profoundly deaf... Many regular TV programs are captioned for the deaf.* ♦ **deafness** N-UNCOUNT *...permanent deafness.* 2 ADJ AFTER LINK-V If you say that someone is **deaf to** people's pleas or criticisms, you disapprove of them because they refuse to pay attention to them. *She kept her eyes down, deaf to what was happening around her.*

deafen /'defən/ **deafens, deafening, deafened.** VERB If you **are deafened** by a noise, it is so loud that you cannot hear anything else. *The noise of the traffic deafened her.*

deafening /'defənɪŋ/. ADJ A **deafening** noise is a very loud noise.

⭐ **deal** /diːl/ **deals, dealing, dealt** /delt/. 1 QUANT A **good deal** or **a great deal of** something is a lot of it. *Lawrence Durrell wrote a great deal of poetry... She had certainly known a good deal more than she'd admitted.* 2 N-COUNT A **deal** is an agreement or arrangement, especially in business. *Japan will have to do a deal with America on rice imports.* 3 VERB If a person, company, or shop **deals in** a particular type of goods, their business involves buying or selling those goods. *They deal in antiques.* ♦ **dealer, dealers** N-COUNT *...an antique dealer.* 4 VERB & PHR-VERB When you **deal** cards, or when you **deal** them **out**, you give them out to the players in a game of cards. *The croupier dealt each player a card... Dalton dealt out five cards to each player.*
▸**deal out.** PHR-VERB If someone **deals out** a punishment or harmful action, they punish or harm someone. *It also deals out sharp criticism to the Department.* ● See also **deal** 4.
▸**deal with.** 1 PHR-VERB When you **deal with** a situation or problem, you do what is necessary to achieve the result you want. *...the way that building societies deal with complaints.*
2 PHR-VERB If a book, speech, or film **deals with** a subject, it is concerned with it. *...the parts of his book which deal with contemporary Paris.*
3 PHR-VERB If you **deal with** a particular person or organization, you have business relations with

them. *When I worked in Florida I dealt with British people all the time.*

dealings /'diːlɪŋz/. N-PLURAL Someone's **dealings with** a person or organization are the relations that they have with them or the business that they do with them. *He has learnt little in his dealings with the international community.*

dean /diːn/ **deans.** 1 N-COUNT A **dean** is an important administrator at a university or college. 2 N-COUNT A **dean** is a priest who is the main administrator of a large church.

⭐ **dear** /dɪə/ **dearer, dearest; dears.** 1 ADJ BEFORE N You use **dear** to describe someone or something that feel affection for. *Mrs Cavendish is a dear friend of mine.* 2 ADJ AFTER LINK-V If something is **dear to** you or **dear to** your heart, you care deeply about it. *His family life was very dear to him.* 3 N-VOC You can call someone **dear** as a sign of affection. *You're a lot like me, dear.* 4 ADJ BEFORE N **Dear** is written at the beginning of a letter, followed by the name or title of the person you are writing to. *'Dear sir,' she began.* 5 ADJ Something that is **dear** costs a lot of money. *They're too dear.*

dearest /'dɪərɪst/. 1 N-VOC You can call someone **dearest** when you are very fond of them. [DATED] *What's wrong, my dearest? You look tired.* 2 ADJ When you are writing to someone you are very fond of, you can use **dearest** at the beginning of the letter before the person's name. *Dearest Maria, Sorry I haven't written for so long.*

dearly /'dɪəli/. 1 ADV If you love someone **dearly**, you love them very much. 2 ADV If you would **dearly** like to do or have something, you would very much like to do it or have it. *I would dearly love to marry.* 3 PHRASE If you **pay dearly for** doing something or if it **costs** you **dearly**, you suffer a lot as a result. [FORMAL] *He drank too much and is paying dearly for the pleasure.*

⭐ **death** /deθ/ **deaths.** N-VAR **Death** is the end of the life of a person or animal. *1.5 million people are in immediate danger of death from starvation. ...the thirtieth anniversary of her death.*

PHRASES ● If you say that something is a matter of **life and death**, you are emphasizing that it is extremely important, often because someone may die if people do not act immediately. *We're dealing with a life-and-death situation here.* ● If someone **is put to death**, they are executed.
● You use **to death** to indicate that a particular action or process results in someone's death. *He was stabbed to death.* ● You use **to death** after an adjective or a verb to emphasize the action, state, or feeling mentioned. *He scares teams to death with his pace and power... I went out last night, but not for very long. I was bored to death.*

'death penalty. N-SING The **death penalty** is the punishment of death, used in some countries for people who have committed very serious crimes. *Both youngsters could face the death penalty.*

⭐ Bank of English® frequent word   For a full explanation of all grammatical labels, see pages vii–x

a
b
c
d
e
f
g
h
i
j
k
l
m
n
o
p
q
r
s
t
u
v
w
x
y
z

death row /ˌdeθ ˈrəʊ/. N-UNCOUNT If someone is **on death row**, they are in the part of a prison which contains the cells for criminals who have been sentenced to death.

'**death toll** (or **death-toll**) **death tolls.** N-COUNT The **death toll** of an accident, disaster, or war is the number of people who die in it.

debacle (or **débâcle**) /deɪˈbɑːkəl, AM ˈdɪbˈ-/ **debacles.** N-COUNT A **debacle** is an event or attempt that is a complete failure. *It will be hard for the republic to recover from this debacle.*

debatable /dɪˈbeɪtəbəl/. ADJ Something that is **debatable** is not definitely true or not certain. *Whether the Bank of England would do any better is highly debatable.*

⭐ **debate** /dɪˈbeɪt/ **debates, debating, debated.**
[1] N-VAR A **debate** is a discussion about a subject on which people have different views. *There has been a lot of debate among scholars about this.*
[2] VERB When people **debate** a topic, they discuss it fairly formally, putting forward different views. You can also say that one person **debates** a topic **with** another person. *The United Nations Security Council will debate the issue today.*
[3] N-COUNT A **debate** is a formal discussion, for example in a parliament, in which people express different opinions about a subject and then vote on it. *...a debate on defence spending.* [4] VERB If you **debate** what to do, you think about possible courses of action before deciding what to do. *At the moment we are debating what furniture to buy for the house... I debated going back inside.*

debit /ˈdebɪt/ **debits, debiting, debited.** [1] VERB When your bank **debits** your account, money is taken from it and paid to someone else.
[2] N-COUNT A **debit** is a record of the money taken from your bank account.

'**debit card, debit cards.** N-COUNT A **debit card** is a bank card that you can use to pay for things. When you use it the money is taken out of your bank account immediately.

debris /ˈdeɪbri, AM deɪˈbriː/. N-UNCOUNT **Debris** consists of pieces of things that have been destroyed, or rubbish that is lying around. *A number of people were killed by flying debris.*

⭐ **debt** /det/ **debts.** [1] N-VAR A **debt** is a sum of money that you owe someone. *He is still paying off his debts.* [2] N-UNCOUNT **Debt** is the state of owing money. *He was already deeply in debt through gambling losses.*

debtor /ˈdetə/ **debtors.** N-COUNT A **debtor** is a country, organization, or person who owes money.

⭐ **debut** /ˈdeɪbjuː, AM deɪˈbjuː/ **debuts.** N-COUNT The **debut** of a performer or sports player is his or her first public performance or recording. *...her debut album 'Sugar Time'.*

⭐ **decade** /ˈdekeɪd/ **decades.** N-COUNT A **decade** is a period of ten years, especially one that begins with a year ending in 0, for example 1980 to 1989. *...the last decade of the nineteenth century.*

decadent /ˈdekədənt/. ADJ If you say that a person or society is **decadent**, you mean that they have low standards, especially low moral standards. *...their decadent rock 'n' roll lifestyles.* ♦ **decadence** N-UNCOUNT *The empire had for years been falling into decadence.*

decay /dɪˈkeɪ/ **decays, decaying, decayed.** [1] VERB & N-UNCOUNT When something **decays**, it becomes rotten. This process is called **decay**. *The bodies buried in the fine ash slowly decayed. ...decaying leaves.* ♦ **decayed** ADJ *...decayed teeth.* [2] VERB & N-UNCOUNT If a society, system, or institution **decays**, it gradually becomes weaker or its condition gets worse. This process is called **decay**. *...decaying urban and rural areas. ...a film about inner city decay.*

deceased /dɪˈsiːst/.
☑ **Deceased** is both the singular and the plural form.
[1] N-COUNT The **deceased** is used to refer to a person or a group of people who have recently died. [FORMAL] *Do you know the last address of the deceased?* [2] ADJ A **deceased** person is one who has recently died. [FORMAL] *...his recently deceased mother.*

deceit /dɪˈsiːt/ **deceits.** N-VAR **Deceit** is behaviour that is intended to make people believe something which is not true. *...the deceit and lies of the past.*

deceitful /dɪˈsiːtfʊl/. ADJ If you say that someone is **deceitful**, you mean that they behave in a dishonest way by making other people believe something that is not true. *The ambassador called the report deceitful and misleading.*

deceive /dɪˈsiːv/ **deceives, deceiving, deceived.** VERB If you **deceive** someone, you make them believe something that is not true. *I was really hurt that he had deceived me... The alleged offences include deceiving the council into giving her son a house.*

⭐ **December** /dɪˈsembə/. N-UNCOUNT **December** is the twelfth and last month of the year in the Western calendar. → See Reference Page on Times and Dates.

decency /ˈdiːsənsi/. N-UNCOUNT **Decency** is behaviour which follows accepted moral standards. *His sense of decency forced him to resign... No-one had the decency to tell me to my face.*

decent /ˈdiːsənt/. [1] ADJ **Decent** means acceptable in standard or quality. *The lack of a decent education did not defeat Rey.* ♦ **decently** ADV *The allies say they will treat their prisoners decently.* [2] ADJ **Decent** is used to describe behaviour which is morally correct or acceptable. *After a decent interval, trade relations began to return to normal.* ♦ **decently** ADV *I don't want to go back to the regiment in Egypt, if I can decently avoid it.*

decentralized (BRIT also **decentralised**) /ˌdiːˈsentrəlaɪzd/. ADJ In a **decentralized** political system, decisions are made by departments in local areas. *This decentralized structure made it difficult to control developments within the various party branches.* ◆ **decentralization** /ˌdiːˌsentrəlaɪˈzeɪʃən/ N-UNCOUNT *He seems set against the idea of increased decentralisation.*

deception /dɪˈsepʃən/ **deceptions.** N-VAR **Deception** is the act of deceiving someone. *He admitted conspiring to obtain property by deception.*

deceptive /dɪˈseptɪv/. ADJ If something is **deceptive**, it encourages you to believe something which is not true. *First impressions proved deceptive.* ◆ **deceptively** ADV *The storyline is deceptively simple.*

decibel /ˈdesɪbel/ **decibels.** N-COUNT A **decibel** is a unit of measurement which is used to indicate how loud a sound is.

⭐ **decide** /dɪˈsaɪd/ **decides, deciding, decided.** 1 VERB If you **decide to** do something, you choose to do it. *She decided to do a secretarial course... He decided that he would drive back to town at once.* 2 VERB If a person or group of people **decides** something, they choose what something should be like or how a particular problem should be solved. *She was still young, he said, and that would be taken into account when deciding her sentence.* 3 VERB If you **decide** that something is the case, you form that opinion after considering the facts. *He decided Franklin must be suffering from a bad cold... For a long time I couldn't decide whether the original settlers were insane or just stupid.* 4 VERB If an event or fact **decides** something, it makes a particular result definite or unavoidable. *The results will decide if he will win a place at a good university... Luck is certainly not the only deciding factor.*
▸ **decide on.** PHR-VERB If you **decide on** something or **decide upon** something, you choose it from two or more possibilities. *Therese decided on a career in publishing.*

decided /dɪˈsaɪdɪd/. ADJ BEFORE N **Decided** means clear and definite. *He's a man of very decided opinions.*

decidedly /dɪˈsaɪdɪdli/. ADV **Decidedly** means to a great extent and in a way that is obvious. *He admits there will be moments when he's decidedly uncomfortable at what he sees.*

deciduous /dɪˈsɪdʒuəs/. ADJ A **deciduous** tree loses its leaves in autumn every year.

decimal /ˈdesɪməl/ **decimals.** 1 ADJ A **decimal** system involves counting in units of ten. *...the decimal system of metric weights and measures.* 2 N-COUNT A **decimal** is a fraction written in the form of a dot followed by one or more numbers representing tenths, hundredths, and so on, for example .5, .51, .517.

decimal point, decimal points. N-COUNT A **decimal point** is the dot in front of a decimal fraction.

decimate /ˈdesɪmeɪt/ **decimates, decimating, decimated.** VERB To **decimate** a group of people or animals means to destroy a very large number of

them. *The pollution could decimate the river's thriving population of kingfishers.*

decipher /dɪˈsaɪfə/ **deciphers, deciphering, deciphered.** VERB If you **decipher** a piece of writing or a message, you work out what it says, even though it is difficult to read or understand.

⭐ **decision** /dɪˈsɪʒən/ **decisions.** 1 N-COUNT When you make a **decision**, you choose what should be done or which is the best of various alternatives. *I think I made the right decision... The decision to discipline Marshall was taken by the party chairman.* 2 N-UNCOUNT **Decision** is the act of deciding something. *The moment of decision can't be too long delayed.*

decision-making. N-UNCOUNT **Decision-making** is the process of reaching decisions, especially in a large organization or in government. *She wants to see more women involved in decision-making.*

decisive /dɪˈsaɪsɪv/. 1 ADJ If a fact, action, or event is **decisive**, it makes it certain that there will be a particular result. *The election campaign has now entered its final, decisive phase.* ◆ **decisively** ADV *The plan was decisively rejected.* 2 ADJ If someone is **decisive**, they have the ability to make quick decisions. *He should give way to a younger, more decisive leader.* ◆ **decisively** ADV *'I'll call for you at half ten,' she said decisively.* ◆ **decisiveness** N-UNCOUNT *His supporters admire his decisiveness.*

⭐ **deck** /dek/ **decks, decking, decked.** 1 N-COUNT A **deck** on a bus or ship is a downstairs or upstairs area. *...the top deck of the number 13 bus.* 2 N-SING The **deck** of a ship is a floor in the open air which you can walk on. 3 N-COUNT A tape **deck** or a record **deck** is a piece of equipment on which you play tapes or records. 4 N-COUNT In American English, a **deck of** cards is a complete set of playing cards. The usual British word is **pack**.
▸ **deck out.** PHR-VERB If someone or something **is decked out with** or **in** something, they are decorated with it or wearing it. *She had decked him out from head to foot in expensive clothes.*

⭐ **declaration** /ˌdekləˈreɪʃən/ **declarations.** 1 N-COUNT A **declaration** is an official announcement or statement. *...the country's declaration of independence.* 2 N-COUNT A **declaration** is a firm statement which shows that you have no doubts about what you are saying. *...a declaration of undying love.*

⭐ **declare** /dɪˈkleə/ **declares, declaring, declared.** 1 VERB If you **declare** that something is the case, you say that it is true in a firm deliberate way. *He declared his intention to become the best golfer in the world.* 2 VERB If you **declare** something, you state it officially and formally. *The government is ready to declare a ceasefire... The judges will declare him innocent.* 3 VERB If you **declare** goods that you have bought abroad or money that you have earned, you say how much you have bought or earned so that you can pay tax on it.

a
b
c
d
e
f
g
h
i
j
k
l
m
n
o
p
q
r
s
t
u
v
w
x
y
z

A B C D E F G H I J K L M N O P Q R S T U V W X Y Z

⭐ **decline** /dɪ'klaɪn/ **declines, declining, declined.**
1 VERB & N-VAR If something **declines**, or if there is a **decline in** something, it becomes smaller, weaker, or worse. *The number of staff has declined from 217,000 to 114,000. ...declining standards of literacy. ...the rate of decline in tobacco consumption.* **2** PHRASE If something is **in decline**, falling **into decline**, or **on the decline**, it is gradually growing smaller, weaker, or worse. *U.S. oil production is in decline... Thankfully the smoking of cigarettes is on the decline.* **3** VERB If you **decline** something or **decline to** do something, you politely refuse to accept it or do it. [FORMAL] *I declined his offer of coffee and dessert... He declined to comment on the story.*

decode /diː'kəʊd/ **decodes, decoding, decoded.** VERB If you **decode** a message that has been written or spoken in a code, you change it into ordinary language. *The secret documents were decoded.*

decompose /,diːkəm'pəʊz/ **decomposes, decomposing, decomposed.** VERB When dead plants, humans, or animals **decompose**, they change chemically and begin to rot. *The debris slowly decomposes into compost... Her decomposed body was found in a remote wood.* ♦ **decomposition** /,diː,kɒmpə'zɪʃən/ N-UNCOUNT *The four mutilated bodies were all in advanced stages of decomposition.*

decor /'deɪkɔː/. N-UNCOUNT The **decor** of a house or of a room is the style in which it is furnished and decorated.

⭐ **decorate** /'dekəreɪt/ **decorates, decorating, decorated.** **1** VERB If you **decorate** something, you make it more attractive by adding things to it. *He decorated his room with pictures.* **2** VERB If you **decorate** a building or room, you paint it or wallpaper it. ♦ **decorating** N-UNCOUNT *I did a lot of the decorating myself.* ♦ **decorator, decorators** N-COUNT *...a firm of painters and decorators.* **3** VERB If someone **is decorated**, they are given a medal or other honour as an official reward for something that they have done.

decoration /,dekə'reɪʃən/ **decorations.** **1** N-VAR **Decorations** are features added to something to make it look more attractive. *...Christmas decorations... Whole currants look very pretty as decoration for cakes.* **2** N-UNCOUNT The **decoration** of a room or building is the furniture, wallpaper, and ornaments there. *Everybody has their own ideas on decoration.* **3** N-COUNT A **decoration** is a medal or a title given to someone as an official honour.

decorative /'dekərətɪv/. ADJ Something that is **decorative** is intended to look attractive. *...decorative accessories, designed to give your kitchen that personal touch.*

decoy /'diːkɔɪ/ **decoys.** N-COUNT A **decoy** is a person or object that you use to lead someone away from where they intended to go, especially so that you can catch them.

decrease, decreases, decreasing, decreased. **1** VERB /dɪ'kriːs/ When something **decreases**, or when you **decrease** it, it becomes less in quantity, size, or intensity. *Population growth is decreasing by 1.4% each year... Some groups have decreased their cigarette consumption. ...decreasing interest rates.* **2** N-COUNT /'diːkriːs/ A **decrease** is a reduction in the quantity or size of something. *...a decrease in the number of young people out of work.*

decree /dɪ'kriː/ **decrees, decreeing, decreed.** **1** VERB If someone in authority **decrees** that something must happen, they order this officially. *The government decreed that all who wanted to live and work in Kenya must hold Kenyan passports.* **2** N-COUNT A **decree** is an official order, especially one made by the ruler of a country. *...reform by presidential decree.*

dedicate /'dedɪkeɪt/ **dedicates, dedicating, dedicated.** **1** VERB If you say that someone **has dedicated themselves to** something, you approve of the fact that they have given a lot of time and effort to it because they think that it is important. *He dedicated himself to politics... Bessie has dedicated her life to caring for others.* ♦ **dedicated** ADJ *...a dedicated doctor.* ♦ **dedication** N-UNCOUNT *...his obvious dedication to the job.* **2** VERB If you **dedicate** something such as a book or a piece of music **to** someone, you say that the work is written for them, as a sign of affection or respect. ♦ **dedication, dedications** N-COUNT *Normally such dedications are reserved for special concert guests.*

deduce /dɪ'djuːs, AM -'duːs/ **deduces, deducing, deduced.** VERB If you **deduce** that something is true, you reach that conclusion because of what you know to be true. *Galileo deduced that the planets were closer to Earth than the stars were... The date of the document can be deduced from references to the Civil War.*

deduct /dɪ'dʌkt/ **deducts, deducting, deducted.** VERB When you **deduct** an amount **from** a total, you subtract it from the total. *The company deducted this payment from his compensation... He could deduct the fees he paid to the accountant.*

deduction /dɪ'dʌkʃən/ **deductions.** **1** N-VAR A **deduction** is a conclusion that you reach because of what you know to be true. *...her own shrewd deductions about what was going on.* **2** N-VAR A **deduction** is an amount subtracted from a total. *...tax deductions.*

deed /diːd/ **deeds.** **1** N-COUNT A **deed** is something that is done, especially something very good or very bad. [LITERARY] *...the warm feeling one gets from doing a good deed.* **2** N-COUNT A **deed** is a legal document containing the terms of an agreement, especially one concerning the ownership of land or a building.

deem /diːm/ **deems, deeming, deemed.** VERB If something **is deemed to** have a quality or **to** do something, it is considered to have that quality or do that thing. [FORMAL] *Many people have ideas that their society deems to be outrageous... She leads polls, but lacks the political machine deemed necessary to win.*

⭐ **deep** /diːp/ **deeper, deepest.** 1 ADJ & ADV If something is **deep**, it extends a long way down from the surface. *The water is very deep. ...the deep cut on his left hand... Gingerly, she put her hand in deeper.* 2 ADJ You use **deep** to talk or ask about how much something measures from the surface to the bottom, or from front to back. *I found myself in water only three feet deep.* 3 ADJ **Deep** in an area means a long way inside it. *Oil and gas were trapped deep inside the earth when it was formed. ...invasion armies advancing deep into Europe.* 4 ADJ You use **deep** to emphasize the seriousness, strength, importance, or degree of something. *...his deep love of Italy.* ♦ **deeply** ADV *Our conversations left me deeply depressed... She slept deeply.* 5 ADJ A **deep** breath uses the whole of your lungs. ♦ **deeply** ADV *She sighed deeply.* 6 ADJ A **deep** colour is strong and fairly dark. 7 ADJ A **deep** sound is a low one. *His voice was deep and mellow.* 8 ADJ You can describe someone as **deep** when you think that they have qualities such as intelligence or determination. 9 PHRASE If you say that something **goes deep** or **runs deep**, you mean that it is very serious or strong and is hard to change. *His anger and anguish clearly went deep.*

deepen /ˈdiːpən/ **deepens, deepening, deepened.** 1 VERB If a situation or emotion **deepens**, or if something **deepens** it, it becomes more intense. *As her feelings for Jay deepened, so did her desire for a permanent relationship.* 2 VERB When a sound **deepens** or **is deepened**, it becomes lower in tone. *Her voice has deepened.* 3 VERB To **deepen** something means to make it deeper.

ˌdeep-'seated. ADJ A **deep-seated** problem, feeling, or belief is difficult to change because its causes have been there for a long time. *...deep-seated economic problems.*

deer /dɪə/.

> ✓ **Deer** is both the singular and the plural form.

N-COUNT A **deer** is a large wild animal. Male deer usually have large, branching horns.

deface /dɪˈfeɪs/ **defaces, defacing, defaced.** VERB If someone **defaces** something such as a wall, they spoil it by writing or drawing things on it.

default /dɪˈfɔːlt/ **defaults, defaulting, defaulted.** 1 VERB & N-UNCOUNT If someone **defaults on** something that they have legally agreed to do, or if they are **in default on** it, they fail to do it. *More borrowers are defaulting on loans.* 2 N-UNCOUNT The **default** is a particular set of instructions which the computer always uses unless the person using the computer gives other instructions. [COMPUTING] *...default settings.* 3 PHRASE If something happens **by default**, it happens only because something else has not happened.

⭐ **defeat** /dɪˈfiːt/ **defeats, defeating, defeated.** 1 VERB If you **defeat** someone, you win a victory over them in a battle or contest. *His forces were defeated by government troops last October.* 2 VERB To **defeat** an action, plan, or proposal means to cause it to fail. *The socialist motion was defeated by 88 votes to 489.* 3 VERB If a task or a problem **defeats** you, it is so difficult that you cannot do it or solve it. *The structural challenges of constructing such a huge novel almost defeated her.* 4 N-VAR **Defeat** is the state of being beaten in a battle, game, or contest, or of failing to achieve what you wanted to. *The most important thing is not to admit defeat... The vote is seen as something of a defeat for the anti-abortion lobby.*

defect, defects, defecting, defected. 1 N-COUNT /ˈdiːfekt/ A **defect** is a fault or imperfection in a person or thing. *He was born with a hearing defect.* 2 VERB /dɪˈfekt/ If someone **defects**, they leave their own country, political party, or other group, and join an opposing one. *He tried to defect to the West last year.* ♦ **defection, defections** N-VAR *...the defection of at least sixteen Parliamentary deputies.* ♦ **defector, defectors** N-COUNT *...defectors from other parties.*

defective /dɪˈfektɪv/. ADJ If something is **defective**, there is something wrong with it. *...defective brakes.*

⭐ **defence** (AM **defense**) /dɪˈfens/ **defences.** 1 N-UNCOUNT **Defence** is action taken to protect someone or something from attack. *The land was flat, giving no scope for defence. ...chanting slogans in defence of freedom.* 2 N-UNCOUNT **Defence** is the organization of a country's armies and weapons to protect the country or its interests. *Twenty eight percent of the federal budget is spent on defense.* 3 N-PLURAL The **defences** of a country or region are its armed forces and weapons. 4 N-COUNT A **defence** is something that people or animals can use or do to protect themselves. *The immune system is our main defence against disease.* 5 N-COUNT A **defence** is something that you say or write in support of ideas or actions that have been criticized. *The defendant yesterday published a 10,000-word defence of his action.* 6 N-COUNT In a court of law, an accused person's **defence** is the process of presenting evidence in their favour. *He has insisted on conducting his own defence.* 7 N-SING **The defence** is the case presented by a lawyer in a trial for the person who has been accused of a crime. You can also refer to the lawyers for this person as **the defence**. 8 N-COUNT In a sports team, **the defence** is the group of players who try to stop the opposing team scoring. For this meaning, **defence** can take the singular or plural form of the verb.

defenceless (AM **defenseless**) /dɪˈfensləs/. ADJ If someone is **defenceless**, they are weak and cannot defend themselves. *...a savage attack on a defenceless young girl.*

⭐ **defend** /dɪˈfend/ **defends, defending, defended.** 1 VERB If you **defend** someone or something, you take action to protect them. *In 1991 he and his friends defended themselves against some racist thugs.* 2 VERB If you **defend** someone or something when they have been criticized, you

a b c d e f g h i j k l m n o p q r s t u v w x y z

argue in support of them. *Clarence's move was unpopular, but Matt had to defend it... He is defending himself against a charge of sexual harassment.* [3] VERB When a lawyer **defends** a person who has been accused of something, the lawyer argues on their behalf in a court of law that the charges are not true. [4] VERB If a sports champion **defends** his or her title, he or she is in a contest against someone who will become the new champion if they win.

defendant /dɪˈfendənt/ **defendants.** N-COUNT The **defendant** in a trial is the person accused of a crime.

defender /dɪˈfendə/ **defenders.** [1] ADJ If you are a **defender** of a particular thing or person that has been criticized or attacked, you support that thing or person in public. *...a strong defender of human rights or religious freedom.* [2] N-COUNT A **defender** in a game such as football is a player whose main task is to try and stop the other side scoring.

defense /dɪˈfens/. See **defence**.

defensive /dɪˈfensɪv/. [1] ADJ You use **defensive** to describe things that are intended to protect someone or something. *The union leaders were pushed into a more defensive position.* [2] ADJ & PHRASE If someone is **defensive**, or if they are **on the defensive**, they are behaving in a way that shows that they feel unsure or threatened. *She heard the blustering, defensive note in his voice.* ♦ **defensively** ADV *'It's nothing to be ashamed of', she replied somewhat defensively.*

defer /dɪˈfɜː/ **defers, deferring, deferred.** [1] VERB If you **defer** an event or action, you arrange that it will take place at a later date than was planned. *Customers often defer payment for as long as possible.* [2] VERB If you **defer to** someone, you accept their opinion or do what they want because you respect them. *She defers to her husband on everything.*

deference /ˈdefərəns/. N-UNCOUNT **Deference** is polite and respectful behaviour to someone in a superior social position.

defiance /dɪˈfaɪəns/. N-UNCOUNT **Defiance** is behaviour or an attitude which shows that you are not willing to obey someone. *...his courageous defiance of the government... People have taken to the streets in defiance of the curfew.*

defiant /dɪˈfaɪənt/. ADJ If you are **defiant**, you refuse to obey someone or you ignore their disapproval of you. *The newspaper remained defiant over its latest confrontation with the royals.* ♦ **defiantly** ADV *They defiantly rejected any talk of a compromise.*

deficiency /dɪˈfɪʃənsi/ **deficiencies.** [1] N-VAR **Deficiency** in something, especially something that your body needs, is a lack of it. [FORMAL] *...iron deficiency.* [2] N-VAR A **deficiency** is a weakness or imperfection in someone or something. [FORMAL] *...the deficiencies of the British transport system.*

deficient /dɪˈfɪʃənt/. [1] ADJ If someone or something is **deficient in** a particular thing, they

do not have as much of it as they need. [FORMAL] *...a diet deficient in vitamin B.* [2] ADJ Something that is **deficient** is not good enough. [FORMAL] *...deficient landing systems.*

⭐ **deficit** /ˈdefəsɪt/ **deficits.** N-COUNT A **deficit** is the amount by which the money received by a country or organization is less than the money it has spent. *...Britain's trade deficit.*

⭐ **define** /dɪˈfaɪn/ **defines, defining, defined.** VERB If you **define** something, you say exactly what it is or exactly what it means. *...a speech defining America's role in modern Europe... My dictionary defines morning as 'the first part of the day, ending at or about noon'.*

definite /ˈdefɪnɪt/. [1] ADJ If something is **definite**, it is firm and clear, and unlikely to be changed. *It's too soon to give a definite answer.* [2] ADJ **Definite** means true rather than being someone's opinion or guess. *The police had nothing definite against her.*

definite article, definite articles. N-COUNT In grammar, the word 'the' is sometimes called **the definite article**.

⭐ **definitely** /ˈdefɪnɪtli/. ADV You use **definitely** to emphasize that something is the case and will not change. *I definitely agree with you... They've definitely decided on the name Fiona.*

⭐ **definition** /ˌdefɪˈnɪʃən/ **definitions.** [1] N-COUNT A **definition** of a word or term is a statement giving its meaning, especially in a dictionary. [2] PHRASE If you say that something has a particular quality **by definition**, you mean that it has this quality simply because of what it is. *Fashion is by definition fickle.* [3] N-UNCOUNT **Definition** is the quality of being clear and distinct. *Their foreign policy lacks definition.*

definitive /dɪˈfɪnɪtɪv/. [1] ADJ Something that is **definitive** provides a firm, unquestionable conclusion. *No one has come up with a definitive answer as to why this should be so.* ♦ **definitively** ADV *The Constitution did not definitively rule out divorce.* [2] ADJ A **definitive** book or performance is thought to be the best of its kind ever.

deflate /dɪˈfleɪt/ **deflates, deflating, deflated.** [1] VERB If you **deflate** a person, you cause them to lose confidence. ♦ **deflated** ADJ *When she refused I felt deflated.* [2] VERB When a tyre or balloon **deflates**, all the air comes out of it.

deflect /dɪˈflekt/ **deflects, deflecting, deflected.** [1] VERB If you **deflect** something such as someone's attention, you cause them to turn their attention to something else or to do something different. *We won't let it deflect us from what we are doing.* [2] VERB If you **deflect** something that is moving, you make it go in a slightly different direction, for example by hitting it or pushing it. *He stuck out his boot and deflected the shot over the bar.* ♦ **deflection, deflections** N-VAR *...the gravitational deflection of light-rays by the Sun.*

deforestation /ˌdiːˈfɒrɪsˈteɪʃən, AM -ˈfɔːr-/. N-UNCOUNT **Deforestation** is the cutting down of trees over a large area. ...*the deforestation of the Amazon.*

deform /dɪˈfɔːm/ **deforms, deforming, deformed.** VERB If something **deforms** something such as a person's body, it causes it to have an unnatural shape. ...*people hideously deformed by acne.* ◆ **deformed** ADJ *He was born with a deformed right leg.*

deformity /dɪˈfɔːmɪti/ **deformities.** [1] N-COUNT A **deformity** is a part of someone's body which is not the normal shape because of injury or illness, or because they were born this way. [2] N-UNCOUNT **Deformity** is the condition of having a deformity. *The bones begin to grind against each other, leading to pain and deformity.*

defraud /dɪˈfrɔːd/ **defrauds, defrauding, defrauded.** VERB If someone **defrauds** you, they use tricks or lies to take something away from you or stop you from getting something that belongs to you. *He was convicted of defrauding investors out of millions of dollars.*

deft /deft/. ADJ A **deft** action is skilful and often quick. [WRITTEN] ◆ **deftly** ADV *One of the waiting servants deftly caught him as he fell.*

defunct /dɪˈfʌŋkt/. ADJ If something is **defunct**, it no longer exists or it is no longer functioning. ...*the now defunct Social Democratic Party.*

defuse /ˌdiːˈfjuːz/ **defuses, defusing, defused.** [1] VERB If you **defuse** a dangerous or tense situation, you calm it. ...*a series of measures to try to defuse the crisis.* [2] VERB If someone **defuses** a bomb, they remove the fuse from it so that it cannot explode.

defy /dɪˈfaɪ/ **defies, defying, defied.** [1] VERB If you **defy** people or laws, you refuse to obey them. *Nearly eleven thousand people have been arrested for defying the ban on street trading.* [2] VERB If you **defy** someone **to** do something which you think is impossible, you challenge them to do it. *I defy you not to want to know what happens next.* [3] VERB If something **defies** description or understanding, it is so strange or surprising that it is almost impossible to describe it or understand it. ...*a devastating and barbaric act that defies all comprehension.*

degenerate, degenerates, degenerating, degenerated. [1] VERB /dɪˈdʒenəreɪt/ To **degenerate** means to become worse. ...*fear that the present unrest could degenerate into violence.* ◆ **degeneration** N-UNCOUNT ...*the degeneration of our political system.* [2] ADJ & N-COUNT /dɪˈdʒenərət/ If you say that someone is **degenerate**, or if you say that they are a **degenerate**, you think they show very low standards of morality.

degrade /dɪˈɡreɪd/ **degrades, degrading, degraded.** [1] VERB Something that **degrades** someone humiliates them and makes them feel they are not respected. ...*the notion that pornography degrades women.* ◆ **degrading** ADJ ...*degrading*

treatment. ◆ **degradation** /ˌdeɡrəˈdeɪʃən/ **degradations** N-VAR *She described the degradations she had been forced to suffer.* [2] VERB To **degrade** something means to damage it so that it becomes worse or weaker. [FORMAL] *The very success of tourism has degraded the natural environment.* ◆ **degradation** N-UNCOUNT ...*the degradation of democracy.*

⭐ **degree** /dɪˈɡriː/ **degrees.** [1] N-COUNT You use **degree** to indicate the extent to which something happens or is the case. *These barriers will ensure a very high degree of protection.* [2] N-COUNT A **degree** is a unit of measurement for temperatures, angles, and longitude and latitude; often written as *°*, for example 23°. [3] N-COUNT A **degree** is a university qualification gained after completing a course of study there. *She has a degree in English.*

dehydrate /ˌdiːhaɪˈdreɪt, -ˈhaɪdreɪt/ **dehydrates, dehydrating, dehydrated.** [1] VERB When food **is dehydrated**, all the water is removed from it. ...*dehydrated soup.* [2] VERB If you **are dehydrated**, you feel ill because you have lost too much water from your body. ◆ **dehydration** N-UNCOUNT *I needed to drink three litres a day to prevent dehydration.*

deity /ˈdeɪɪti, AM ˈdiː-/ **deities.** N-COUNT A **deity** is a god or goddess. [FORMAL]

⭐ **delay** /dɪˈleɪ/ **delays, delaying, delayed.** [1] VERB If you **delay** doing something, you do not do it until a later time. *This morning's decision to delay the launch stems from unfavorable weather conditions.* [2] VERB To **delay** someone or something means to make them late or slow them down. *Various set-backs and problems delayed production.* [3] N-VAR If there is a **delay**, something does not happen until later than planned or expected. ...*a seven-hour stoppage that caused delays on most flights.*

⭐ **delegate, delegates, delegating, delegated.** [1] N-COUNT /ˈdelɪɡət/ A **delegate** is a person chosen to vote or make decisions on behalf of a group of people, especially at a conference or meeting. [2] VERB /ˈdelɪɡeɪt/ If you **delegate** duties, responsibilities, or power **to** someone, you give them those duties or responsibilities or that power, so that they can act on your behalf.

⭐ **delegation** /ˌdelɪˈɡeɪʃən/ **delegations.** N-COUNT A **delegation** is a group of people chosen to represent a larger group of people.

delete /dɪˈliːt/ **deletes, deleting, deleted.** VERB If you **delete** something that has been written down or stored in a computer, you cross it out or remove it.

deli /ˈdeli/ **delis.** N-COUNT A **deli** is a shop or part of a shop that sells unusual or foreign foods. **Deli** is an abbreviation for 'delicatessen'.

⭐ **deliberate, deliberates, deliberating, deliberated.** [1] ADJ /dɪˈlɪbərət/ If something that you do is **deliberate**, you intended to do it. ...*a deliberate act of sabotage.* ◆ **deliberately** ADV *It looks as if the blaze was started deliberately.* [2] ADJ A

A
B
C
D
E
F
G
H
I
J
K
L
M
N
O
P
Q
R
S
T
U
V
W
X
Y
Z

deliberate action or movement is slow and careful. ♦ **deliberately** ADV *He spoke slowly and deliberately.* [3] VERB/dɪ'lɪbəreɪt/ If you **deliberate**, you think about something carefully before making a decision. *The jury deliberated for five days before reaching a verdict.*

deliberation /dɪ,lɪbə'reɪʃən/ **deliberations.**
[1] N-UNCOUNT **Deliberation** is careful consideration of a subject. *After much deliberation, the winners have been chosen.* [2] N-PLURAL **Deliberations** are formal discussions.

delicacy /'delɪkəsi/ **delicacies.** N-COUNT A **delicacy** is a rare or expensive food that is considered especially nice to eat. *...delicacies such as smoked salmon.*

delicate /'delɪkət/. [1] ADJ Something that is **delicate** is narrow and graceful or attractive. *...her long, delicate nose.* ♦ **delicately** ADV *...a small and delicately formed chin.* ♦ **delicacy** N-UNCOUNT *...the delicacy of his features.* [2] ADJ A **delicate** colour, taste, or smell is pleasant and not intense. *Smoked trout has a delicate flavour.* ♦ **delicately** ADV *...a soup delicately flavoured with nutmeg.* [3] ADJ A **delicate** object is fragile and needs to be handled carefully. [4] ADJ Someone who is **delicate** is not healthy and strong, and becomes ill easily. *He was a delicate child.* [5] ADJ A **delicate** situation or problem needs very careful and tactful treatment. *...the delicate issue of adoption.* ♦ **delicately** ADV *...a delicately-worded memo.* ♦ **delicacy** N-UNCOUNT *...a matter of some delicacy.*

delicatessen /,delɪkə'tesən/ **delicatessens.** N-COUNT A **delicatessen** is a shop that sells unusual or foreign foods.

delicious /dɪ'lɪʃəs/. ADJ **Delicious** food or drink has an extremely pleasant taste. ♦ **deliciously** ADV *This new yoghurt has a deliciously creamy flavour.*

⭐ **delight** /dɪ'laɪt/ **delights, delighting, delighted.**
[1] N-UNCOUNT **Delight** is a feeling of very great pleasure. *Andrew roared with delight... To my great delight, it worked.* [2] N-COUNT You can refer to someone or something that gives you great pleasure as a **delight**. *The aircraft was a delight to fly.* [3] VERB If something **delights** you, it gives you a lot of pleasure. *...a style of music that has delighted audiences all over the world.* [4] VERB & PHRASE If you **delight in** something, especially doing something, or if you **take delight in** it, you get a lot of pleasure from it. *Ford delighted in showing visitors around... He took obvious delight in proving his critics wrong.*

⭐ **delighted** /dɪ'laɪtɪd/. ADJ If you are **delighted**, you are extremely pleased and excited about something. *He said that he was delighted with the public response.* ♦ **delightedly** ADV *She smiled delightedly up at him.*

delightful /dɪ'laɪtful/. ADJ Someone or something that is **delightful** is very pleasant. *...a most delightful woman.* ♦ **delightfully** ADV *...a delightfully mellow flavour.*

delinquent /dɪ'lɪŋkwənt/ **delinquents.** N-COUNT & ADJ A **delinquent** is a young person who repeatedly commits minor crimes. You can also describe their behaviour as **delinquent**. ♦ **delinquency** N-UNCOUNT *He had no history of delinquency.*

delirious /dɪ'lɪərɪəs/. [1] ADJ Someone who is **delirious** is unable to think or speak in a rational way, usually because they have a fever. [2] ADJ Someone who is **delirious** is extremely excited and happy. *I was delirious with joy.* ♦ **deliriously** ADV *Chelsea fans went home deliriously happy.*

⭐ **deliver** /dɪ'lɪvə/ **delivers, delivering, delivered.**
[1] VERB If you **deliver** something somewhere, you take it there. *The Canadians plan to deliver more food to southern Somalia... We were told the pizza would be delivered in 20 minutes.* [2] VERB If you **deliver** a lecture or speech, you give it. [3] VERB When someone **delivers** a baby, they help the woman who is giving birth. [4] VERB If someone **delivers** a blow to someone else, they hit them. *Those blows to the head could have been delivered by a woman.*

⭐ **delivery** /dɪ'lɪvəri/ **deliveries.** [1] N-UNCOUNT **Delivery** is the act of bringing letters, parcels, or goods to someone's house or office. *Please allow 28 days for delivery.* [2] N-COUNT A **delivery of** letters or goods is an occasion when they are delivered. *I got a delivery of fresh eggs this morning.* [3] N-UNCOUNT Someone's **delivery** of a speech is the way in which they give it. *His speeches were magnificently written but his delivery was hopeless.* [4] N-VAR **Delivery** is the process of giving birth to a baby. *In the end, it was an easy delivery: a fine baby boy.*

delta /'deltə/ **deltas.** N-COUNT A **delta** is a triangle-shaped area of flat land, where a river spreads out into several smaller rivers before entering the sea.

delude /dɪ'luːd/ **deludes, deluding, deluded.** VERB If you **delude** someone, you make them believe something that is not true. *We delude ourselves that we are in control.*

deluge /'deljuːdʒ/ **deluges, deluging, deluged.**
[1] VERB & N-COUNT If you **are deluged with** things, or if you receive a **deluge** of things, a very large number of them arrive or happen at the same time. *Papen's office was deluged with complaints... A deluge of manuscripts began to arrive in the post.* [2] N-COUNT & VERB A **deluge** is a sudden heavy fall of rain. You can say that rain **deluges** a place when it falls very heavily there.

delusion /dɪ'luːʒən/ **delusions.** N-VAR A **delusion** is a false belief. *I was under the delusion that intended to marry me.*

deluxe (or **de luxe**) /dɪ'lʌks/. ADJ BEFORE N **Deluxe** goods or services are better and more expensive than ordinary ones. *...a five-star deluxe hotel.*

delve /delv/ **delves, delving, delved.** [1] VERB If you **delve into** a subject, you try to discover more about it. *Jenny delved into her mother's past.*

☐2 VERB If you **delve** inside something such as a bag, you search inside it. *She delved into her rucksack and pulled out a folder.*

⭐ **demand** /dɪˈmɑːnd, -ˈmænd/ **demands, demanding, demanded.** ☐1 VERB & N-COUNT If you **demand** something, or if you make a **demand for** something, you ask for it forcefully. *The Labour Party has demanded an explanation from the government... They demanded that a police officer arrest the pair... They consistently rejected the demand to remove US troops. ...the demand for higher wages.* ☐2 PHRASE If something is available **on demand**, you can have it whenever you ask for it. ☐3 VERB If one thing **demands** another, the first needs the second in order to happen or be dealt with successfully. *The task of rebuilding would demand much patience.* ☐4 N-UNCOUNT & PHRASE If there is **demand for** something, a lot of people want it. You can also say that something or someone is **in demand**. *Demand for coal is down... He was much in demand as a lecturer.* ☐5 N-COUNT You talk about the **demands of** something or someone, or their **demands on** you when you mean the things they require or want from you, which will take a lot of effort on your part. *...the demands and challenges of a new job... I had no right to make demands on his time.*

demanding /dɪˈmɑːndɪŋ, -ˈmænd-/. ☐1 ADJ A **demanding** job requires a lot of time, energy, or attention. ☐2 ADJ Someone who is **demanding** always wants something and is not easily satisfied. *...a very demanding child.*

demean /dɪˈmiːn/ **demeans, demeaning, demeaned.** VERB To **demean** someone or something means to make people have less respect for them. *Pornography demeans women.* ◆ **demeaning** ADJ *Addressing women as 'girls' is demeaning.*

demeanour (AM **demeanor**) /dɪˈmiːnə/. N-UNCOUNT Your **demeanour** is the way you behave, which gives people an impression of your character and feelings. [FORMAL] *...a cheerful demeanour.*

demented /dɪˈmentɪd/. ☐1 ADJ Someone who is **demented** is mentally ill. ☐2 ADJ If you describe someone as **demented**, you think that their actions are strange, foolish, or uncontrolled.

dementia /dɪˈmenʃə/ **dementias.** N-VAR **Dementia** is a disease of the brain which leads to a progressive loss of intellectual power and memory. [TECHNICAL] *...senile dementia.*

demilitarize (BRIT also **demilitarise**) /ˌdiːˈmɪlɪtəraɪz/ **demilitarizes, demilitarizing, demilitarized.** VERB To **demilitarize** an area means to remove all military forces from it.

demise /dɪˈmaɪz/. N-SING The **demise** of something or someone is their end or death. [FORMAL] *...the demise of the reform movement.*

demo /ˈdeməʊ/ **demos.** N-COUNT A **demo** is a demonstration by a group of people to show their opposition to something or their support for something. [BRITISH] *...an anti-racist demo.*

demobilize (BRIT also **demobilise**) /ˌdiːˈməʊbɪlaɪz/ **demobilizes, demobilizing, demobilized.** VERB If a country **demobilizes** its troops, or if its troops **demobilize**, they are released from service and go home. ◆ **demobilization** N-UNCOUNT *...the demobilisation of its 100,000 strong army.*

⭐ **democracy** /dɪˈmɒkrəsi/ **democracies.** ☐1 N-UNCOUNT **Democracy** is a political system in which people choose their government by voting for them in elections. ☐2 N-COUNT A **democracy** is a country in which the people choose their government by voting for it.

⭐ **democrat** /ˈdeməkræt/ **democrats.** N-COUNT A **democrat** is a person who believes in the ideals of democracy, personal freedom, and equality.

⭐ **democratic** /ˌdeməˈkrætɪk/. ☐1 ADJ A **democratic** country, organization, or system is governed by representatives who are elected by the people. ◆ **democratically** ADV *...Russia's first democratically elected President.* ☐2 ADJ Something that is **democratic** is based on the idea that everyone should have equal rights and should be involved in making important decisions. *We work in a very democratic way.* ◆ **democratically** ADV *This committee will enable decisions to be made democratically.*

demolish /dɪˈmɒlɪʃ/ **demolishes, demolishing, demolished.** ☐1 VERB When a building is **demolished**, it is knocked down, often because it is old or dangerous. *A storm moved directly over the island, demolishing buildings.* ◆ **demolition** /ˌdeməˈlɪʃən/ **demolitions** N-VAR *The project required the total demolition of the old bridge.* ☐2 VERB If you **demolish** someone's idea, argument, or belief, you prove that it is completely wrong.

demon /ˈdiːmən/ **demons.** N-COUNT A **demon** is an evil spirit. ◆ **demonic** /dɪˈmɒnɪk/ ADJ *...a form of demonic possession.*

⭐ **demonstrate** /ˈdemənstreɪt/ **demonstrates, demonstrating, demonstrated.** ☐1 VERB To **demonstrate** a fact or theory means to make it clear to people. *Women's groups said the case demonstrated the law's bias against women... They are anxious to demonstrate to the voters that they have practical policies.* ◆ **demonstration, demonstrations** N-COUNT *We want a demonstration of commitment.* ☐2 VERB If you **demonstrate** a skill, quality, or feeling, you show that you have it. *He demonstrated his courage in the Korean war.* ☐3 VERB If you **demonstrate** something to someone, you show them how to do it or how it works. *The BBC has just successfully demonstrated a new digital radio transmission system.* ◆ **demonstration** N-COUNT *...a cookery demonstration.* ☐4 VERB When people **demonstrate**, they take part in a march or a meeting to show that they oppose or support something. *In Rostock, more than 10,000 people demonstrated against racism yesterday.* ◆ **demonstration** N-COUNT *Riot police used tear gas and truncheons this afternoon to break up a*

a b c d e f g h i j k l m n o p q r s t u v w x y z

A B C D E F G H I J K L M N O P Q R S T U V W X Y Z

demonstration. ◆ **demonstrator, demonstrators**
N-COUNT ...a crowd of demonstrators.

demoralize (BRIT also **demoralise**)
/dɪˈmɒrəlaɪz, AM -ˈmɔːr-/ **demoralizes, demoralizing,
demoralized.** VERB If something **demoralizes** you, it
makes you lose confidence and feel depressed.
◆ **demoralized** ADJ ...a demoralized police force.
◆ **demoralizing** ADJ It can be very demoralizing
to struggle with a painting which offers little
possibility of success. ◆ **demoralization**
N-UNCOUNT ...the lingering demoralization that
followed defeat.

demote /dɪˈməʊt/ **demotes, demoting, demoted.**
VERB If someone in authority **demotes** you, they
lower your rank, often as a punishment.
◆ **demotion, demotions** N-VAR He faces demotion
or even the sack.

den /den/ **dens.** [1] N-COUNT A **den** is the home of
certain types of wild animals such as foxes.
[2] N-COUNT A **den** is a secret place where people
meet, usually for a dishonest purpose. ...illegal
drinking dens.

denial /dɪˈnaɪəl/ **denials.** [1] N-VAR A **denial of**
something such as an accusation is a statement
that it is not true, does not exist, or did not
happen. ...denial of the Russian Mafia's existence.
[2] N-UNCOUNT If there is **denial of** something to
someone, they are not allowed to have it. ...the
denial of visas to international relief workers.

denigrate /ˈdenɪɡreɪt/ **denigrates, denigrating,
denigrated.** VERB If you **denigrate** someone or
something, you criticize or insult them, damaging
their reputation. [FORMAL] The article denigrated
Aboriginal ceremonies. ◆ **denigration** N-UNCOUNT
...men's denigration of women.

denim /ˈdenɪm/. N-UNCOUNT **Denim** is a thick
cotton cloth used to make clothes.

denomination /dɪˌnɒmɪˈneɪʃən/ **denominations.**
[1] N-COUNT A **denomination** is a religious group
which has slightly different beliefs from other
groups within the same faith. [2] N-COUNT The
denomination of a banknote or coin is its official
value. ...a pile of bank notes, mostly in small
denominations.

denote /dɪˈnəʊt/ **denotes, denoting, denoted.** VERB If
one thing **denotes** another, it is a sign or
indication of it. [FORMAL] Red eyes denote strain and
fatigue.

denounce /dɪˈnaʊns/ **denounces, denouncing,
denounced.** VERB If you **denounce** someone or
something, you criticize them severely and
publicly. Some 25,000 demonstrators denounced
him as a traitor. ● See also **denunciation**.

dense /dens/ **denser, densest.** [1] ADJ Something
that is **dense** contains a lot of things or people in
relation to its size. ...a dense forest. ◆ **densely**
ADV ...a densely populated island. [2] ADJ **Dense**
fog or smoke is thick and difficult to see through.

density /ˈdensɪti/ **densities.** [1] N-VAR The **density
of** something is the extent to which it fills a
place. ...the law which restricts the density of
housing. [2] N-VAR The **density** of a substance or

object is the relation of its mass or weight to its
volume.

dent /dent/ **dents, denting, dented.** [1] VERB If
something **dents** your ideas or your pride, it
makes you believe that you or your ideas are not
as good as you thought. [2] VERB & N-COUNT If you
dent something, you damage it by hitting or
pressing it, causing a hollow dip to form in it. The
hollow is called a **dent**. There was a dent in the
bonnet.

dental /ˈdentəl/. ADJ BEFORE N **Dental** is used to
describe things relating to teeth. ...free dental
treatment.

dentist /ˈdentɪst/ **dentists.** N-COUNT A **dentist** is a
person qualified to treat people's teeth.

dentures /ˈdentʃəz/.

✔ The form **denture** is used as a modifier.

N-PLURAL **Dentures** are artificial teeth.

denunciation /dɪˌnʌnsiˈeɪʃən/ **denunciations.**
N-VAR A **denunciation of** someone or something
is a severe public criticism of them.

★ **deny** /dɪˈnaɪ/ **denies, denying, denied.** [1] VERB If you
deny something, you say that it is not true. She
denied both accusations... The government has
denied that anybody died during the demolition.
[2] VERB If you **deny** someone something, you do
not let them have it. His ex-partner denies him
access to his children.

deodorant /diˈəʊdərənt/ **deodorants.** N-VAR
Deodorant is a substance that you put on your
body to reduce or hide the smell of perspiration.

depart /dɪˈpɑːt/ **departs, departing, departed.** VERB
To **depart from** a place means to leave it and
start a journey to another place. [FORMAL] Our tour
departs from Heathrow Airport.

★ **department** /dɪˈpɑːtmənt/ **departments.** N-COUNT
A **department** is one of the sections of a large
shop or organization such as a university.
...Bloomingdale's cosmetics department. ...the
geography department of Moscow University.
◆ **departmental** /ˌdiːpɑːtˈmentəl/ ADJ BEFORE N
...a bigger departmental budget.

de'partment store, department stores. N-COUNT
A **department store** is a large shop which sells
many different kinds of goods.

★ **departure** /dɪˈpɑːtʃə/ **departures.** [1] N-VAR
Departure is the act of leaving a place or a job.
...the President's departure for Helsinki. ...his
departure from the post of Prime Minister.
[2] N-VAR If an action is a **departure from** what
was planned or what is usually done, it is
different from it. That decision is a major
departure from previous American policy.

de'parture lounge, departure lounges. N-COUNT
In an airport, the **departure lounge** is the place
where passengers wait before they get onto their
plane.

★ **depend** /dɪˈpend/ **depends, depending, depended.**
[1] VERB If you say that one thing **depends on**
another, you mean that the first thing will be
affected or decided by the second. The cooking

time needed depends on the size of the potato. [2] VERB & PHRASE You use **depends** in expressions such as **it depends** or **depending on** to indicate that you cannot give a clear answer to a question because other factors will affect the answer. 'But how long can you stay in the house?'—'I don't know. It depends.' [3] VERB If you **depend on** someone or something, you need them in order to be able to survive. Their survival depends on him. [4] VERB If you can **depend on** someone or something, you know that they will help you or support you when you need them. You can depend on me.

dependable /dɪ'pendəbəl/. ADJ If someone or something is **dependable**, you know that they will always do what you need or expect them to do. ...a faithful and dependable companion.

dependant (or **dependent**) /dɪ'pendənt/ **dependants**. N-COUNT Your **dependants** are the people who you support financially, such as your children. ...a single man with no dependants.

dependent /dɪ'pendənt/. ADJ AFTER LINK-V To be **dependent on** someone or something means to need them in order to succeed or be able to survive. Britain became increasingly dependent on American technology. ♦ **dependence** N-UNCOUNT ...the effects of alcoholism and drug dependence. ♦ **dependency** N-UNCOUNT Ukraine is handicapped by its near-total dependency on Russian oil.

depict /dɪ'pɪkt/ **depicts, depicting, depicted.** VERB To **depict** someone or something means to represent them in drawing, painting, or writing. ...pictures depicting Nelson's most famous battles. ♦ **depiction, depictions** N-VAR ...their depiction in the book as thieves.

deplete /dɪ'pliːt/ **depletes, depleting, depleted.** VERB To **deplete** a stock or amount of something means to reduce it, usually to a very low level. ...substances that deplete the ozone layer. ♦ **depleted** ADJ ...Robert E. Lee's worn and depleted army. ♦ **depletion** N-UNCOUNT ...the depletion of underground water supplies.

deplorable /dɪ'plɔːrəbəl/. ADJ If you say that something is **deplorable**, you mean that it is extremely bad or unpleasant. [FORMAL] ...deplorable working and living conditions.

deplore /dɪ'plɔː/ **deplores, deploring, deplored.** VERB If you **deplore** something, you think it is very wrong or immoral. [FORMAL] He deplores violence.

deploy /dɪ'plɔɪ/ **deploys, deploying, deployed.** VERB To **deploy** troops or resources means to organize or position them so that they are ready to be used. ♦ **deployment** N-UNCOUNT ...the deployment of extra forces in the area.

deport /dɪ'pɔːt/ **deports, deporting, deported.** VERB If a government **deports** someone, it sends them out of the country. More than 240 England football fans are being deported from Italy. ♦ **deportation, deportations** N-VAR ...migrants facing deportation.

depose /dɪ'pəʊz/ **deposes, deposing, deposed.** VERB If a ruler or political leader **is deposed**, they are forced to give up their position. ♦ **deposition** /ˌdepə'zɪʃən/ N-UNCOUNT ...the deposition of the king.

⭐ **deposit** /dɪ'pɒzɪt/ **deposits, depositing, deposited.** [1] N-COUNT A **deposit** is a sum of money given as part payment for something, or as security when you rent something. A £50 deposit is required when ordering. ...the equivalent of a month's rent as a deposit. [2] VERB & N-COUNT If you **deposit** a sum of money into your bank account, or if you put a **deposit** in your account, you pay a sum of money into a bank account or other savings account. The customer has to deposit a minimum of £100 monthly. [3] N-COUNT & VERB A **deposit** is an amount of a substance that has been left somewhere as a result of a chemical or geological process. You say the substance has been **deposited** there. ...underground deposits of gold and diamonds.

depot /'depəʊ, AM 'diː-/ **depots.** [1] N-COUNT A **depot** is a place where large amounts of raw materials, equipment, or other supplies are kept. ...a government arms depot. [2] N-COUNT A **depot** is a large building or yard where buses or railway engines are kept when they are not being used. [3] N-COUNT A **depot** is a bus station or a railway station.

depreciate /dɪ'priːʃieɪt/ **depreciates, depreciating, depreciated.** VERB If something such as currency **depreciates**, or if something **depreciates** it, it loses some of its original value. The pound depreciated by a quarter. ♦ **depreciation, depreciations** N-VAR ...machinery depreciation and wages.

depress /dɪ'pres/ **depresses, depressing, depressed.** [1] VERB If someone or something **depresses** you, they make you feel sad and disappointed. The state of the country depresses me. [2] VERB If something **depresses** prices, wages, or figures, it causes them to become less. The stronger U.S. dollar depressed sales.

depressed /dɪ'prest/. [1] ADJ If you are **depressed**, you are sad and feel you cannot enjoy anything, because your situation is difficult and unpleasant. He seemed somewhat depressed. [2] ADJ A **depressed** place or industry does not have enough business or employment to be prosperous. The construction industry is no longer as depressed as it was.

depressing /dɪ'presɪŋ/. ADJ Something that is **depressing** makes you feel sad and disappointed. The hospital was a very depressing place to be. ♦ **depressingly** ADV It all sounded depressingly familiar.

⭐ **depression** /dɪ'preʃən/ **depressions.** [1] N-VAR **Depression** is a mental state in which someone feels unhappy and has no energy or enthusiasm. ...suffering from depression... I slid into a depression. [2] N-COUNT A **depression** is a time when there is very little economic activity, which results in a lot of unemployment and poverty.

a
b
c
d
e
f
g
h
i
j
k
l
m
n
o
p
q
r
s
t
u
v
w
x
y
z

A
B
C
D
E
F
G
H
I
J
K
L
M
N
O
P
Q
R
S
T
U
V
W
X
Y
Z

3 N-COUNT A **depression** in a surface is an area which is lower than the parts surrounding it.

deprive /dɪ'praɪv/ **deprives, depriving, deprived.** VERB If you **deprive** someone **of** something that they want or need, you take it away from them or prevent them from having it. *She was deprived of her passport.* ♦ **deprived** ADJ *...a deprived inner city area.* ♦ **deprivation** /ˌdeprɪ'veɪʃən/ **deprivations** N-VAR *Crime flourishes in conditions of deprivation.*

dept. Dept is a written abbreviation for 'department'.

⭐ **depth** /depθ/ **depths.** **1** N-VAR The **depth** of something such as a hole is the distance between its top and bottom surfaces. *The water was some 12 to 18 inches in depth.* **2** N-VAR The **depth** of a solid structure is the distance between its front surface and its back. **3** N-UNCOUNT If an emotion is very strongly felt, you can talk about its **depth**. *I am well aware of the depth of feeling that exists in Londonderry.* **4** N-PLURAL The **depths of** an area are the parts of it which are very remote. *...somewhere in the depths of the pine forest.* **5** N-PLURAL The **depths of** something difficult or unpleasant are the middle and most severe or intense parts of it. *...the depths of a recession. ...the depths of winter... I was in the depths of despair.* **6** PHRASE If you deal with a subject **in depth**, you consider all the aspects of it thoroughly. *...an in-depth investigation.* **7** PHRASE If you say that someone is **out of their depth**, you mean that they are in a situation that is much too difficult for them to be able to cope with it.

⭐ **deputy** /'depjʊti/ **deputies.** N-COUNT A **deputy** is the second most important person in an organization or department. Someone's deputy often acts on their behalf when they are absent. *...the academy's deputy director.*

derail /ˌdiː'reɪl/ **derails, derailing, derailed.** **1** VERB If someone or something **derails** a plan or a series of negotiations, they prevent it from continuing as planned. *...people trying to derail peace talks.* **2** VERB If a train **is derailed**, or it **derails**, it comes off the track on which it is running. ♦ **derailment** /ˌdiː'reɪlmənt/ **derailments** N-VAR *Rail services have been suspended because of a derailment.*

deranged /dɪ'reɪndʒd/. ADJ Someone who is **deranged** behaves in a wild or strange way, often as a result of mental illness. *A deranged man shot and killed 14 people.*

derelict /'derɪlɪkt/. ADJ A **derelict** place is empty and in a bad condition because it has not been used or lived in for a long time. *...a derelict warehouse.*

deride /dɪ'raɪd/ **derides, deriding, derided.** VERB If you **deride** someone or something, you say they are stupid or have no value. [FORMAL] *Other countries are derided for selling arms to the enemy.* ♦ **derision** /dɪ'rɪʒən/ N-UNCOUNT *He tried to calm the crowd, but was greeted with shouts of derision.*

derivative /dɪ'rɪvətɪv/ **derivatives.** **1** N-COUNT A **derivative** is something which has been developed or obtained from something else. *...a*

poppy-seed derivative similar to heroin.* **2** ADJ If you say that something is **derivative**, you are criticizing it because it is not new or original but has been developed from something else. *...their dull, derivative debut album.*

derive /dɪ'raɪv/ **derives, deriving, derived.** **1** VERB If you **derive** something such as pleasure or benefit **from** someone or something, you get it from them. *...one of those happy people who derive pleasure from helping others.* **2** VERB If something **derives** or **is derived from** something else, it comes from that thing. *The name Anastasia is derived from a Greek word meaning 'of the resurrection'.*

descend /dɪ'send/ **descends, descending, descended.** **1** VERB If you **descend**, or if you **descend** something, you move downwards. [FORMAL] *...as we descend to the cellar.* **2** VERB If a mood **descends** somewhere, it starts to affect the people there. *An uneasy calm descended on the area.* **3** VERB If people **descend on** a place, a lot of them arrive there suddenly. *Reporters from around the globe are descending on the peaceful villages.* **4** VERB If you say that someone **descends to** something which you consider unacceptable or unworthy of them, you are expressing your disapproval of the fact that they do it. *We're never going to descend to such methods.*

descendant /dɪ'sendənt/ **descendants.** N-COUNT Someone's **descendants** are the people in later generations who are related to them.

descended /dɪ'sendɪd/. ADJ AFTER LINK-V A person who is **descended from** someone who lived a long time ago is directly related to them. *She was descended from some Scottish Lord.*

descent /dɪ'sent/ **descents.** **1** N-VAR A **descent** is a movement from a higher to a lower level. *The airliner began its descent towards the airfield.* **2** N-COUNT A **descent** is a surface that slopes downwards, for example the side of a steep hill. **3** N-UNCOUNT You use **descent** to talk about a person's family background, for example their nationality or social status. *All the contributors were of African descent.*

⭐ **describe** /dɪ'skraɪb/ **describes, describing, described.** **1** VERB If you **describe** someone or something, you say what they are like. *We asked her to describe what kind of things she did in her spare time. ...a poem by Carver which describes their life together.* **2** VERB If you **describe** someone or something **as** a particular thing, you say that they are like that thing. *They described themselves as liberals.*

> **USAGE** When you use **describe** with an indirect object, you must put **to** in front of the indirect object. *He later described to me what he had found... Could you describe the man to the police?* You do not say, for example, 'He described me what he had found'.

⭐ **description** /dɪ'skrɪpʃən/ **descriptions.** **1** N-VAR A **description of** someone or something is an account which explains what they are or what they look like. *Police have issued a description of the man.* **2** N-SING If something is **of** a particular **description**, it belongs to the general class of items that are mentioned. *Events of this description occurred daily.*

descriptive /dɪ'skrɪptɪv/. ADJ **Descriptive** language indicates what something is like. *The poem is very descriptive.*

desecrate /'desɪkreɪt/ **desecrates, desecrating, desecrated.** VERB If someone **desecrates** something considered sacred or special, they deliberately damage or insult it. ◆ **desecration** N-UNCOUNT *...the desecration of the cemetery.*

⭐ **desert, deserts, deserting, deserted.** **1** N-VAR /'dezət/ A **desert** is a large area of land, usually in a hot region, which has almost no water, rain, trees, or plants. **2** VERB /dɪ'zɜːt/ If people **desert** a place, they leave it and it becomes empty. *Medical staff have deserted the city's main hospital.* ◆ **deserted** ADJ *...a new deserted side street.* **3** VERB If someone **deserts** you, they leave you and no longer help or support you. *Mrs Roding's husband deserted her years ago.* ◆ **desertion, desertions** N-VAR *...alone and vulnerable after her father's desertion.* **4** VERB If someone **deserts** from the armed forces, they leave without permission. ◆ **desertion** N-UNCOUNT *Two soldiers face charges of desertion.* ◆ **deserter, deserters** N-COUNT *...a young army deserter.*

⭐ **deserve** /dɪ'zɜːv/ **deserves, deserving, deserved.** VERB If you say that someone **deserves** something, you mean that they should have it or do it because of their qualities or actions. *It's your money. You deserve it... 'He deserved to die,' said Penelope viciously.*

deserving /dɪ'zɜːvɪŋ/. ADJ If you describe a person or organization as **deserving**, you think they should be helped. [FORMAL] *The money saved could be used for more deserving causes.*

⭐ **design** /dɪ'zaɪn/ **designs, designing, designed.** **1** VERB & N-UNCOUNT When you **design** something new, or when you are responsible for its **design**, you plan what it should be like. *He approached me to create and design the restaurant... The plan is designed to reduce some of the company's mountainous debt. ...a new mechanic with a flair for design.* **2** N-UNCOUNT The **design** of something is the way in which it has been planned and made. *...a new design of clock.* **3** N-COUNT A **design** is a drawing which someone produces to show how they would like something to be built or made. *...his design for a new office tower.* **4** N-COUNT A **design** is a decorative pattern of lines or shapes.

designate, designates, designating, designated. **1** VERB /'dezɪgneɪt/ When you **designate** something or someone **as** a particular thing, you formally give them a description or name. *The area has been designated a national park... Designate someone as the spokesperson.*

◆ **designation, designations** N-VAR *...the designation of Madrid as European City of Culture.* **2** VERB If something **is designated** for a particular purpose, it is set aside for that purpose. *Smoking is allowed in designated areas.* ADJ /'dezɪgnət/ You use **designate** after a job title to refer to someone who has been formally chosen to do that job, but has not yet started doing it.

⭐ **designer** /dɪ'zaɪnə/ **designers.** **1** N-COUNT A **designer** is a person whose job involves planning the form of a new object. *...a fashion designer.* **2** ADJ BEFORE N **Designer** clothes are expensive fashionable clothes created by a famous designer.

de,signer 'baby, designer babies. N-COUNT People use the term **designer baby** to refer to a baby that has developed from an embryo with certain desired characteristics.

desirable /dɪ'zaɪərəbəl/. **1** ADJ Something that is **desirable** is worth having or doing. *Prolonged negotiation was not desirable.* ◆ **desirability** N-UNCOUNT *...the debate on the desirability of banning the ivory trade.* **2** ADJ Someone who is **desirable** is sexually attractive.

⭐ **desire** /dɪ'zaɪə/ **desires, desiring, desired.** **1** VERB & N-COUNT If you **desire** something, or if you have a **desire** for it, you want it. [FORMAL] *Fred was bored and desired to go home... I had a strong desire to help and care for people... They seem to have lost their desire for life.* ◆ **desired** ADJ *His warnings have provoked the desired response.* **2** VERB & N-UNCOUNT If you **desire** someone, or if you feel **desire** for them, you want to have sex with them.

⭐ **desk** /desk/ **desks.** N-COUNT A **desk** is a table which you sit at in order to write or work.

desktop /'desktɒp/ **desktops.** **1** N-COUNT The **desktop** of a computer is the display of icons that you see on the screen when the computer is ready to use. [COMPUTING] **2** N-COUNT A **desktop** or a **desktop computer** is a computer that is small enough to fit onto a desk but too big to carry around with you.

desolate /'desələt/. **1** ADJ A **desolate** place is empty and lacking in comfort. **2** ADJ If someone is **desolate**, they feel very lonely and depressed.

desolation /ˌdesə'leɪʃən/. **1** N-UNCOUNT The **desolation** of a place is its depressing emptiness. *...a scene of desolation and ruin.* **2** N-UNCOUNT **Desolation** is a feeling of great unhappiness.

despair /dɪ'speə/ **despairs, despairing, despaired.** **1** VERB & N-UNCOUNT If you **despair**, you feel that everything is wrong and that nothing will improve. *I despair at the attitude with which their work is received... I looked at my wife in despair.* **2** VERB If you **despair of** something, you feel that there is no hope that it will happen or improve. *They despaired of ever having a family of their own.*

despatch /dɪ'spætʃ/. See **dispatch**.

⭐ **desperate** /'despərət/. **1** ADJ If you are **desperate**, you are in such a bad situation that you will try anything to change it. *...a desperate*

a
b
c
d
e
f
g
h
i
j
k
l
m
n
o
p
q
r
s
t
u
v
w
x
y
z

attempt to hijack a plane... Many refugees were in a desperate state. ♦ **desperately** ADV I tried desperately to bandage him. **2** ADJ AFTER LINK-V If you are **desperate for** something or **desperate to** do something, you want to have it or do it very much. People are desperate for him to do something. ♦ **desperately** ADV ...a boy who desperately needed affection.

desperation /ˌdespəˈreɪʃən/. N-UNCOUNT **Desperation** is the feeling that you have when you are in such a bad situation that you will try anything to change it. ...acts of sheer desperation.

despicable /dɪˈspɪkəbəl, AM ˈdespɪk-/. ADJ If you say that a person or action is **despicable**, you are emphasizing that they are extremely nasty or cruel. It was a despicable crime.

despise /dɪˈspaɪz/ **despises, despising, despised.** VERB If you **despise** someone or something, you hate them very much. How I despised myself for my cowardice!

⭐ **despite** /dɪˈspaɪt/. PREP You use **despite** to introduce a fact which makes the other part of the sentence surprising. Despite a thorough investigation, no trace of Dr Southwell has been found.

dessert /dɪˈzɜːt/ **desserts.** N-VAR **Dessert** is something sweet, such as fruit or a pudding, that you eat at the end of a meal. She had homemade ice cream for dessert.

destabilize (BRIT also **destabilise**) /diːˈsteɪbɪlaɪz/ **destabilizes, destabilizing, destabilized.** VERB To **destabilize** something such as a country or government means to create a situation which reduces its power or influence. Their sole aim is to destabilize the Indian government.

destination /ˌdestɪˈneɪʃən/ **destinations.** N-COUNT Your **destination** is the place you are going to. ...his preferred holiday destination, Hawaii.

destined /ˈdestɪnd/. ADJ AFTER LINK-V If something is **destined to** happen, or if someone is **destined to** do something, that thing will definitely happen. He feels that he was destined to become a musician... Muriel was destined for great things.

destiny /ˈdestɪni/ **destinies.** **1** N-COUNT A person's **destiny** is everything that happens to them during their life, including what will happen in the future. **2** N-UNCOUNT **Destiny** is the force which some people believe controls the things that happen to you. Is it destiny that brings people together?

destitute /ˈdestɪtjuːt, AM -tuːt/. ADJ Someone who is **destitute** has no money or possessions. [FORMAL] ...destitute people living on the streets.

⭐ **destroy** /dɪˈstrɔɪ/ **destroys, destroying, destroyed.** VERB To **destroy** something means to cause so much damage to it that it is completely ruined or does not exist any more. He destroyed my confidence... The building was completely destroyed. ♦ **destruction** /dɪˈstrʌkʃən/ N-UNCOUNT ...the destruction of the ozone layer.

destructive /dɪˈstrʌktɪv/. ADJ Something that is **destructive** causes or is capable of causing great damage, harm, or injury. ...the awesome destructive power of nuclear weapons... Guilt can be very destructive.

detach /dɪˈtætʃ/ **detaches, detaching, detached.** VERB If you **detach** one thing **from** another that it is fixed to, you remove it. If one thing **detaches from** another, it becomes separated from it. Detach the currants from the stems... Detach the white part of the application form.

detached /dɪˈtætʃt/ **1** ADJ Someone who is **detached** is not emotionally or personally involved in something. He tries to remain emotionally detached from the prisoners. **2** ADJ A **detached** house is not joined to any other house.

detachment /dɪˈtætʃmənt/. N-UNCOUNT **Detachment** is a feeling of not being emotionally or personally involved in something. ...a well-developed sense of professional detachment.

⭐ **detail** /ˈdiːteɪl/ **details, detailing, detailed.** **1** N-VAR The **details of** something are its small, individual features or elements. If you examine or discuss something **in detail**, you examine all these features. ...the details of a peace agreement... I recall every detail of the party. ...his scrupulous attention to detail. **2** N-PLURAL **Details** about something are items of information about it. See the bottom of this page for details of how to apply. **3** VERB If you **detail** things, you list them or give full information about them. [FORMAL] The report detailed the human rights abuses committed during the war.

⭐ **detailed** /ˈdiːteɪld, AM dɪˈteɪld/. ADJ A **detailed** report or plan contains a lot of details. ...a detailed account of the decisions.

detain /dɪˈteɪn/ **detains, detaining, detained.** **1** VERB When people such as the police **detain** someone, they keep them in a place under their control. The act allows police to detain a suspect for up to 48 hours. **2** VERB To **detain** someone means to delay them, for example by talking to them. [FORMAL] Thank you. We won't detain you any further.

detainee /ˌdiːteɪˈniː/ **detainees.** N-COUNT A **detainee** is someone who is being held prisoner by a government or being held by the police.

detect /dɪˈtekt/ **detects, detecting, detected.** VERB If you **detect** something, you find it or notice it. ...equipment used to detect radiation... Arnold could detect a certain sadness in the old man's face. ♦ **detection** N-UNCOUNT ...the early detection of breast cancer.

⭐ **detective** /dɪˈtektɪv/ **detectives.** N-COUNT A **detective** is someone whose job is to discover the facts about a crime or other situation.

detector /dɪˈtektə/ **detectors.** N-COUNT A **detector** is an instrument which is used to find or measure something. ...smoke detectors.

detente (or **détente**) /deɪˈtɒnt/. N-UNCOUNT **Detente** is a state of friendly relations between two countries when previously there had been problems between them. [FORMAL] ...*a policy of detente.*

detention /dɪ'tenʃən/ **detentions.** N-VAR
Detention is the arrest or imprisonment of someone, especially for political reasons. ...*the detention without trial of government critics.*

deter /dɪ't3ː/ **deters, deterring, deterred.** VERB To **deter** someone **from** doing something means to make them not want to do it. *It would deter criminals from carrying guns... Tougher sentences would do nothing to deter crime.*

detergent /dɪ't3ːdʒənt/ **detergents.** N-VAR
Detergent is a chemical substance used for washing things such as clothes or dishes.

deteriorate /dɪ'tɪəriəreɪt/ **deteriorates, deteriorating, deteriorated.** VERB If something **deteriorates**, it becomes worse. *Grant's health steadily deteriorated.* ♦ **deterioration** N-UNCOUNT ...*a sharp deterioration in Anglo-Irish relations.*

determination /dɪˌt3ːmɪ'neɪʃən/. N-UNCOUNT
Determination is the quality that you show when you have decided to do something and you will not let anything stop you. ...*the government's determination to beat inflation.*

⭐ **determine** /dɪ't3ːmɪn/ **determines, determining, determined.** [1] VERB If something **determines** what will happen, it controls it. *The size of the chicken pieces will determine the cooking time.*
♦ **determination** N-UNCOUNT *We must take into our own hands the determination of our future.* ...*the gene which is responsible for male sex determination.* [2] VERB To **determine** something means to discover it or discover the facts about it. *The investigation will determine what really happened... My aim was first of all to determine what to do next.* ♦ **determination** N-UNCOUNT ...*procedures for the determination of refugee status.*

⭐ **determined** /dɪ't3ːmɪnd/. ADJ If you are **determined to** do something, you have made a firm decision to do it and will not let anything stop you. *His enemies are determined to ruin him... England made several determined efforts to score.*
♦ **determinedly** ADV *She shook her head, determinedly.*

determiner /dɪ't3ːmɪnə/ **determiners.** N-COUNT In grammar, a **determiner** is a word such as 'the' or 'my' that is used before a noun to indicate which particular thing or person you are referring to.

deterrent /dɪ'terənt, AM -'t3ːr-/ **deterrents.** N-COUNT & ADJ BEFORE N A **deterrent**, or something that has a **deterrent** effect, is something that prevents people from doing something by making them afraid of what will happen to them if they do. *They seriously believe that capital punishment is a deterrent.* ♦ **deterrence** N-UNCOUNT ...*nuclear deterrence.*

detest /dɪ'test/ **detests, detesting, detested.** VERB If you **detest** someone or something, you dislike them very much. *Jean detested being photographed.*

detonate /'detəneɪt/ **detonates, detonating, detonated.** VERB If someone **detonates** a bomb, or if it **detonates**, it explodes. ♦ **detonation, detonations** N-VAR ...*accidental detonation of nuclear weapons.*

detour /'diːtʊə/ **detours.** N-COUNT If you make a **detour** on a journey, you go by a route which is not the shortest way.

detract /dɪ'trækt/ **detracts, detracting, detracted.** VERB If one thing **detracts from** another, it makes it seem less good or less impressive. *Even Sarah's sour comments could not detract from the excitement Meg felt.*

detriment /'detrɪmənt/. PHRASE If something happens **to the detriment of** something or someone, it causes them harm or damage. [FORMAL] *These tests will give too much importance to written exams to the detriment of other skills.*

detrimental /ˌdetrɪ'mentəl/. ADJ Something that is **detrimental to** something else has a harmful or damaging effect on it. *Many foods are suspected of being detrimental to health... The experts emphasized the detrimental effects of these drugs.*

devalue /ˌdiː'væljuː/ **devalues, devaluing, devalued.** [1] VERB To **devalue** something means to cause it to be thought less important or less worthy of respect. *They spread tales about her in an attempt to devalue her work.* [2] VERB To **devalue** the currency of a country means to reduce its value in relation to other currencies. ♦ **devaluation, devaluations** N-VAR ...*the devaluation of the dollar.*

devastate /'devəsteɪt/ **devastates, devastating, devastated.** VERB If something **devastates** a place, it damages it very badly or destroys it. *A fire had devastated large parts of Windsor Castle.*
♦ **devastation** N-UNCOUNT *A huge bomb blast brought chaos and devastation.*

devastated /'devəsteɪtɪd/. ADJ AFTER LINK-V If you are **devastated** by something, you are very shocked and upset by it.

devastating /'devəsteɪtɪŋ/. ADJ You describe something as **devastating** when it is very damaging or upsetting. *Affairs do have a devastating effect on marriages... The diagnosis was devastating. She had cancer.*

⭐ **develop** /dɪ'veləp/ **develops, developing, developed.** [1] VERB When someone or something **develops**, or when someone **develops** something, the person or thing grows or changes over a period of time and usually becomes more advanced or complete. *As children develop, some of the most important things they learn have to do with their sense of self... Most of these settlements developed from agricultural centres... These clashes could develop into open warfare... We must develop closer ties with Germany.* ♦ **development** N-UNCOUNT ...*the development of the embryo.* [2] VERB If someone **develops** something such as a habit or illness, they begin to have it. *She later developed a taste for expensive nightclubs... Smokers are most prone to develop lung cancer.*

a
b
c
d
e
f
g
h
i
j
k
l
m
n
o
p
q
r
s
t
u
v
w
x
y
z

A
B
C
D
E
F
G
H
I
J
K
L
M
N
O
P
Q
R
S
T
U
V
W
X
Y
Z

3 VERB If someone **develops** a new product, they design it and produce it. *He claims that several countries have developed nuclear weapons secretly.* ♦ **developer, developers** N-COUNT ...*a software developer.* ♦ **development, developments** N-VAR ...*investment in product development.* **4** VERB When a country **develops**, it changes from being a poor agricultural country to a rich industrial country. ♦ **developed** ADJ ...*the developed nations.* **5** VERB To **develop** an area of land means to build houses or factories on it to make it more useful or profitable. ...*the cost of acquiring or developing property.* ♦ **developer** N-COUNT ...*property developers.* ♦ **development** N-UNCOUNT ...*the fostering of development in the rural areas.* **6** VERB When a photographic film **is developed**, prints or negatives are made from it.

developing /dɪ'veləpɪŋ/. ADJ BEFORE N If you talk about **developing** countries or **the developing world**, you mean the countries or the parts of the world that are poor and have little industry.

⭐ **development** /dɪ'veləpmənt/ **developments**. **1** N-COUNT A **development** is an event which is likely to have an effect on a situation. ...*the latest developments in Moscow.* **2** N-COUNT A **development** is an area of houses or buildings which have been built by property developers.

deviant /'di:viənt/ **deviants**. N-COUNT & ADJ A **deviant** or someone who shows **deviant** behaviour behaves in a way that is different from what is normally considered to be acceptable. *Not all alcoholics and drug abusers produce deviant offspring.* ♦ **deviance** N-UNCOUNT ...*social deviance.*

deviate /'di:vieɪt/ **deviates, deviating, deviated**. VERB To **deviate from** a plan or **from** a usual way of behaving means not to behave in the planned or usual way. *He planned his schedule far in advance, and he didn't deviate from it.* ♦ **deviation, deviations** N-VAR *Deviation from the norm is not tolerated.*

⭐ **device** /dɪ'vaɪs/ **devices**. **1** N-COUNT A **device** is an object that has been made for a particular purpose. ...*a timer device for a bomb.* **2** N-COUNT A **device** is a method of achieving something. ...*a device to pressurise Mr Neill into negotiating.* **3** PHRASE If you **leave** someone **to** their **own devices**, you leave them alone to do as they wish.

devil /'devəl/ **devils**. **1** N-PROPER In Christianity, Judaism, and Islam, **the Devil** is the most powerful evil spirit. **2** N-COUNT A **devil** is an evil spirit. **3** N-COUNT You can use **devil** when showing how you feel about someone. For example, you can call someone 'a poor devil' to show that you feel sorry for them. [INFORMAL]

devious /'di:viəs/. ADJ A **devious** person does dishonest things in a clever complicated way. *You have a very devious mind.*

devise /dɪ'vaɪz/ **devises, devising, devised**. VERB If you **devise** something, you have the idea for it and design it. *We devised a plan.*

devoid /dɪ'vɔɪd/. ADJ AFTER LINK-V If you say that someone or something is **devoid of** a quality or thing, you are emphasizing that they have none of it. ...*a face that was devoid of feeling.*

devolve /dɪ'vɒlv/ **devolves, devolving, devolved**. VERB If you **devolve** power, authority, or responsibility **to** a less important or powerful person or group, or if it **devolves upon** them, it is transferred to them. *Companies have been learning to devolve authority.* ♦ **devolution** /ˌdi:və'lu:ʃən, ˌdev-/ N-UNCOUNT ...*the devolution of power to the regions.*

devote /dɪ'vəʊt/ **devotes, devoting, devoted**. VERB If you **devote yourself**, your time, or your energy **to** something, you spend all or most of your time or energy on it. *He abandoned his political life and devoted himself to business.*

devoted /dɪ'vəʊtɪd/. ADJ If you are **devoted to** someone or something, you care about them or love them very much. ...*a loving and devoted husband... Horace is so devoted to his garden.*

devotee /ˌdevə'ti:/ **devotees**. N-COUNT A **devotee of** a subject or activity is someone who is very enthusiastic about it.

devotion /dɪ'vəʊʃən/. N-UNCOUNT Your **devotion** to someone or something is your great love of them and commitment to them. *At first she was flattered by his devotion. ...his devotion to his job.*

devour /dɪ'vaʊə/ **devours, devouring, devoured**. VERB If a person or animal **devours** something, they eat it quickly and eagerly. *She devoured two bars of chocolate.*

devout /dɪ'vaʊt/. **1** ADJ A **devout** person has deep religious beliefs. *They were devout, serious girls.* **2** ADJ BEFORE N A **devout** believer in something supports it very strongly and enthusiastically. ...*devout Marxists.*

dew /dju:/. N-UNCOUNT **Dew** is small drops of water that form on the ground and other surfaces outdoors during the night.

diabetes /ˌdaɪə'bi:ti:z, AM -tɪs/. N-UNCOUNT **Diabetes** is a condition in which someone's body is unable to control the level of sugar in their blood.

diabetic /ˌdaɪə'betɪk/ **diabetics**. N-COUNT & ADJ A **diabetic** or a person who is **diabetic** suffers from diabetes.

diagnose /'daɪəgnəʊz, AM -nəʊs/ **diagnoses, diagnosing, diagnosed**. VERB If someone or something **is diagnosed as** having a particular illness or problem, their illness or problem is identified. *The soldiers were diagnosed as having flu... He could diagnose an engine problem simply by listening.*

diagnosis /ˌdaɪəg'nəʊsɪs/ **diagnoses**. N-VAR **Diagnosis** is identifying what is wrong with someone who is ill or with something that is not working properly. ...*a doctor making a diagnosis.*

diagnostic /ˌdaɪəgˈnɒstɪk/. ADJ BEFORE N **Diagnostic** devices or methods are used for discovering what is wrong with someone or something. ...*X-rays and other diagnostic tools.*

diagonal /daɪˈægənəl/. ADJ A **diagonal** line or movement goes in a slanting direction.
♦ **diagonally** ADV *He ran diagonally across the pitch.*

diagram /ˈdaɪəgræm/ **diagrams.** N-COUNT A **diagram** is a drawing which is used to explain something.

dial /daɪəl/ **dials, dialling, dialled** (AM **dialing, dialed**).
[1] N-COUNT The **dial** on a clock or meter is the part where the time or a measurement is indicated. [2] N-COUNT The **dial** on a radio is the control which you move in order to change the frequency. [3] N-COUNT The **dial** on some telephones is a circular disc that you rotate according to the number that you want to call. [4] VERB If you **dial**, or if you **dial** a number, you turn the dial or press the buttons on a telephone.

dialect /ˈdaɪəlekt/ **dialects.** N-VAR A **dialect** is a form of a language spoken in a particular area. *They began to speak rapidly in dialect.*

'dialog ˌbox, dialog boxes. N-COUNT A **dialog box** is a small area containing information or questions that appears on a computer screen when you are performing particular operations. [COMPUTING]

⭐ **dialogue** (AM **dialog**) /ˈdaɪəlɒg, AM -lɔːg/ **dialogues.** [1] N-VAR **Dialogue** is communication or discussion between people or groups. ...*a direct dialogue between the two nations.* [2] N-VAR The **dialogue** in a book, film, or play consists of the things the characters in it say to each other. *He writes great dialogue.*

diameter /daɪˈæmɪtə/ **diameters.** N-COUNT The **diameter** of a circle or sphere is the length of a straight line through the middle of it. ...*thin pancakes 6 inches in diameter.*

diamond /ˈdaɪəmənd/ **diamonds.** [1] N-COUNT A **diamond** is a hard bright precious stone. ...*diamond earrings.* [2] N-COUNT A **diamond** is a shape which has four straight sides of equal length which are not at right angles to each other. → See picture on page 829. [3] N-UNCOUNT **Diamonds** is one of the four suits in a pack of playing cards. Each card in the suit is called a **diamond** and is marked with one or more red symbols: ♦.

diaper /ˈdaɪəpə/ **diapers.** N-COUNT In American English, a **diaper** is something which you put round a baby's bottom in order to soak up its urine and faeces. The British word is **nappy**.

diaphragm /ˈdaɪəfræm/ **diaphragms.** N-COUNT Your **diaphragm** is a muscle between your lungs and your stomach.

diarrhoea (AM **diarrhea**) /ˌdaɪəˈriːə/. N-UNCOUNT When someone has **diarrhoea**, a lot of liquid faeces comes out of their body because they are ill.

⭐ **diary** /ˈdaɪəri/ **diaries.** N-COUNT A **diary** is a notebook with a separate space for each day of the year.

dice [1]

dice /daɪs/ **dices, dicing, diced.**

✔ **Dice** is both the singular and the plural form of the noun.

[1] N-COUNT A **dice** is a small cube with one to six spots on each face, used in games. *Roll the dice.* [2] VERB When you **dice** food, you cut it into small cubes.

dictate, dictates, dictating, dictated. [1] VERB /dɪkˈteɪt, AM ˈdɪkteɪt/ If you **dictate** something, you say it aloud for someone else to write down. *Mr Phillips dictated a memo to his secretary.* [2] VERB If you **dictate to** someone, you tell them what they must do. *What gives them the right to dictate to us what we should eat?... What right has one country to dictate the environmental standards of another?* [3] N-COUNT /ˈdɪkteɪt/ A **dictate** is an order which you have to obey. [FORMAL] ...*the dictates of the Party.*

dictation /dɪkˈteɪʃən/ **dictations.** N-VAR **Dictation** is the speaking or reading aloud of words for someone else to write down.

dictator /dɪkˈteɪtə, AM ˈdɪkteɪt-/ **dictators.** N-COUNT A **dictator** is a ruler who has complete power in a country; used showing disapproval.

dictatorial /ˌdɪktəˈtɔːriəl/. ADJ If you describe someone's behaviour as **dictatorial**, you mean that they tell people what to do in a forceful and unfair way; used showing disapproval. ...*his dictatorial management style.*

dictatorship /dɪkˈteɪtəʃɪp/ **dictatorships.** [1] N-VAR **Dictatorship** is system in which a country is governed by a dictator. [2] N-COUNT A **dictatorship** is a country ruled by a dictator.

dictionary /ˈdɪkʃənri, AM -neri/ **dictionaries.** N-COUNT A **dictionary** is a book in which the words and phrases of a language are listed, usually in alphabetical order, together with their meanings or their translations in another language.

did /dɪd/. **Did** is the past tense of **do**.

didn't /ˈdɪdənt/. **Didn't** is the usual spoken form of 'did not'.

⭐ **die** /daɪ/ **dies, dying, died.** [1] VERB When people, animals, or plants **die**, they stop living. *My mother*

a
b
c
d
e
f
g
h
i
j
k
l
m
n
o
p
q
r
s
t
u
v
w
x
y
z

died of cancer. ...*friends who died young.* ● See note at **dead.** [2] VERB When something **dies**, or when it **dies away** or **dies down**, it becomes less intense, until it disappears. *My love for you will never die. ...the echoes of the thunder dying away across the peaks... The wind had died down.* [3] PHRASE If you say that old habits or attitudes **die hard**, you mean that they take a very long time to change, and may never disappear completely. [4] See also **dying.**

▶ **die out.** PHR-VERB If something **dies out**, it becomes less and less common and eventually disappears. *How did the dinosaurs die out?*

diesel /'diːzəl/ **diesels.** [1] ADJ **Diesel** describes a type of engine in which oil is burnt by very hot air. It also describes a vehicle with this type of engine, or the heavy oil used as fuel in it. *Many people think diesel cars are smelly and dirty.* [2] N-VAR A **diesel** is a vehicle which has a diesel engine, or the heavy oil used as fuel in it.

⭐ **diet** /daɪət/ **diets, dieting, dieted.** [1] N-VAR Your **diet** is the type and range of food that you regularly eat. *...a healthy diet.* [2] N-COUNT & VERB If you are **on** a **diet**, or if you **are dieting**, you eat only certain foods because you are trying to lose weight. ◆ **dieter, dieters** N-COUNT *Most dieters are miserable.*

dietary /'daɪətri, AM -teri/ ADJ **Dietary** means relating to the kind of food you eat. *...dietary changes.*

differ /'dɪfə/ **differs, differing, differed.** [1] VERB If two or more things **differ**, they are not like each other. *Their attitudes to promotion also differ from ours.* [2] VERB If people **differ**, they disagree with each other about something. *They differ on lots of issues.*

⭐ **difference** /'dɪfrəns/ **differences.** [1] N-VAR The **difference** between things is the way in which they are different from each other. *...the vast difference in size... The difference is that I expect so much of her, but not of him.* [2] N-SING The **difference** between two amounts is the amount by which one is less than the other. [3] N-COUNT If people have their **differences**, they disagree about things. [4] PHRASE If something **makes a difference**, it changes a situation. If it **makes no difference**, it does not change a situation. *We had terrible rows over his homework, but it made no difference.*

⭐ **different** /'dɪfrənt/ [1] ADJ If one thing is **different from** another, it is not like the other thing. *London was different from most European capitals... We have totally different views.* ◆ **differently** ADV *Every individual learns differently.* [2] ADJ BEFORE N When you refer to two or more **different** things of a particular kind, you mean two or more separate things of that kind. *...different brands of drinks.* [3] ADJ AFTER LINK-V You can describe something as **different** when it is unusual and not like other things of the

same kind. *The result is interesting and different.*

> **USAGE** In British English, people sometimes say that one thing is **different to** another. *You're so different to what I imagined.* Some people consider this use to be incorrect, and insist that you should say **different from.** *We human beings are vastly different from all other species.* In American English, you can say that one thing is **different than** another. This use is often considered incorrect in British English, but it is sometimes the simplest possibility when the comparison involves a clause. *I am no different than I was 50 years ago.*

differential /ˌdɪfə'renʃəl/ **differentials.** N-COUNT A **differential** is a difference between two values in a scale, for example a difference between rates of pay within a company. [TECHNICAL] *...the differential between their two currencies. ...wage differentials.*

differentiate /ˌdɪfə'renʃieɪt/ **differentiates, differentiating, differentiated.** VERB To **differentiate between** things means to show or recognize the difference between them. *A child may not differentiate between his imagination and the real world... At this age your baby cannot differentiate one person from another. ...policies that differentiate them from the other parties.* ◆ **differentiation** N-UNCOUNT *...the differentiation between the sexes.*

⭐ **difficult** /'dɪfɪkəlt/ [1] ADJ Something that is **difficult** is not easy to do, understand, or cope with. *I find it difficult to speak up for myself.* [2] ADJ If you say that someone is **difficult**, you think they are behaving in an unreasonable and unhelpful way. *I could be difficult about it, but why bother?*

⭐ **difficulty** /'dɪfɪkəlti/ **difficulties.** [1] N-VAR A **difficulty** is a problem. If you are **in difficulty** or **in difficulties**, you are having a lot of problems. *Rumours spread about banks being in difficulty. ...economic difficulties.* [2] N-UNCOUNT If you have **difficulty** doing something, you are not able to do it easily. *Do you have difficulty getting up?*

diffident /'dɪfɪdənt/ ADJ Someone who is **diffident** is shy and lacks confidence. ◆ **diffidence** /'dɪfɪdəns/ N-UNCOUNT *...her diffidence towards the opposite sex.*

diffuse, diffuses, diffusing, diffused. [1] VERB /dɪ'fjuːz/ If something such as knowledge or information **is diffused**, or if it **diffuses**, it is made available over a wide area or to a lot of people. [FORMAL] *Interest in books is more widely diffused than ever.* ◆ **diffusion** /dɪ'fjuːʒən/ N-UNCOUNT *...the diffusion of political power.* [2] ADJ /dɪ'fjuːs/ Something that is **diffuse** is spread over a large area rather than concentrated in one place. [FORMAL] *...a cold, diffuse light.*

⭐ **dig** /dɪg/ **digs, digging, dug** /dʌg/. **1** VERB When people or animals **dig**, they make a hole in the ground or in a pile of stones or debris. *He dug a hole in the lawn... Rescue workers are digging through the rubble.* **2** VERB If you **dig** one thing **into** another, or if one thing **digs into** another, the first thing is pushed hard into the second, or presses hard into it. *He could feel the beads digging into his palm.* **3** N-COUNT A **dig** is a critical remark. *They have used the occasion to have a dig at the Press.*
▶**dig out** or **dig up**. PHR-VERB If you **dig** something **out** or **dig** it **up**, you discover it after it has been stored, hidden, or forgotten for a long time.

digest /daɪˈdʒest/ **digests, digesting, digested.** **1** VERB When you **digest** food, it passes through your body to your stomach, your stomach removes the substances that you need, and your body gets rid of the rest. *Fats are hard to digest.* ♦ **digestion** N-UNCOUNT *...a fruit which aids digestion.* **2** VERB If you **digest** information, you think about it carefully so that you understand it or are capable of dealing with it. *She read everything, digesting every fragment of news.*

digestive /daɪˈdʒestɪv/. ADJ BEFORE N **Digestive** refers to the digestion of food. *...digestive disorders.*

digit /ˈdɪdʒɪt/ **digits.** **1** N-COUNT A **digit** is a written symbol for any of the ten numbers from 0 to 9. **2** N-COUNT A **digit** is a finger, thumb, or toe. [FORMAL]

digital /ˈdɪdʒɪtəl/. **1** ADJ **Digital** systems record or transmit information in the form of thousands of very small signals. *...digital audio broadcasting.* **2** ADJ BEFORE N **Digital** watches or clocks show the time by displaying numbers.

ˌdigital ˈcamera, digital cameras. N-COUNT A **digital camera** is a camera that produces digital images that can be stored on a computer.

ˌdigital ˈradio. N-UNCOUNT **Digital radio** is radio in which the signals are transmitted in digital form and decoded by the radio receiver.

ˌdigital ˈtelevision. N-UNCOUNT **Digital television** is television in which the signals are transmitted in digital form and decoded by the television receiver.

dignified /ˈdɪgnɪfaɪd/. ADJ If you say that someone or something is **dignified**, you mean they are calmly impressive and worthy of respect.

dignitary /ˈdɪgnɪtri, AM -teri/ **dignitaries.** N-COUNT A **dignitary** is someone who has a high rank in government or in the Church.

dignity /ˈdɪgnɪti/. **1** N-UNCOUNT If someone behaves with **dignity**, they are serious, calm, and controlled. **2** N-UNCOUNT **Dignity** is the quality of being worthy of respect. *...respect for human dignity.*

dike /daɪk/. See **dyke**.

dilapidated /dɪˈlæpɪdeɪtɪd/. ADJ A **dilapidated** building is old and in bad condition.

dilate /daɪˈleɪt/ **dilates, dilating, dilated.** VERB When things such as blood vessels or the pupils of your eyes **dilate**, or when something **dilates** them, they become wider or bigger. *Exercise dilates blood vessels.* ♦ **dilated** ADJ *His eyes seemed slightly dilated.*

dilemma /daɪˈlemə, AM dɪl-/ **dilemmas.** N-COUNT A **dilemma** is a difficult situation in which you have to choose between two or more alternatives. *...the dilemma of whether or not to return to his country.*

diligent /ˈdɪlɪdʒənt/. ADJ **Diligent** people work hard and carefully. *...a diligent student.* ♦ **diligence** N-UNCOUNT *The police are pursuing their inquiries with great diligence.* ♦ **diligently** ADV *We worked diligently on our school assignments.*

dilute /daɪˈluːt/ **dilutes, diluting, diluted.** VERB If a liquid **is diluted**, or if it **dilutes**, it is added to or mixes with water or another liquid, and becomes weaker. *Dilute it well with cooled, boiled water.*

dim /dɪm/ **dimmer, dimmest; dims, dimming, dimmed.** **1** ADJ **Dim** light is not bright. You can also say that something is **dim** when the light is not bright enough to see very well. *Below decks, the lights were dim... He saw a dim outline of a small boat.* ♦ **dimly** ADV *...a dimly lit kitchen... The shoreline could be dimly seen.* **2** VERB If you **dim** a light, or if it **dims**, it becomes less bright.

dime /daɪm/ **dimes.** N-COUNT A **dime** is an American coin worth ten cents.

dimension /daɪˈmenʃən, dɪm-/ **dimensions.** **1** N-COUNT A particular **dimension** of something is a particular aspect of it. *Works of art have a spiritual dimension.* **2** N-PLURAL You can refer to the measurements of something as its **dimensions**. *...the dimensions of the new oilfield.*

diminish /dɪˈmɪnɪʃ/ **diminishes, diminishing, diminished.** VERB When something **diminishes**, or when it **is diminished**, its importance, size, or intensity is reduced. *The threat of nuclear war has diminished.*

diminutive /dɪˈmɪnjʊtɪv/. ADJ A **diminutive** person or object is very small. [FORMAL] *...the diminutive figure of Mr. Nerette.*

din /dɪn/. N-SING A **din** is a very loud and unpleasant noise that lasts for some time. *...the din of the crowd.*

dine /daɪn/ **dines, dining, dined.** VERB When you **dine**, you have dinner. [FORMAL] *The two men dined at Wilson's club.*

diner /ˈdaɪnə/ **diners.** **1** N-COUNT In the United States, a **diner** is a small cheap restaurant that is open all day. **2** N-COUNT The **diners** in a restaurant are the people who are eating there.

dinghy /ˈdɪŋgi/ **dinghies.** N-COUNT A **dinghy** is a small boat that you sail or row.

   For a full explanation of all grammatical labels, see pages vii-x

a b c d e f g h i j k l m n o p q r s t u v w x y z

dingy /'dɪndʒi/. ADJ A **dingy** place is dark and depressing. ...*his rather dingy office.*

'**dining room, dining rooms.** N-COUNT The **dining room** is the room in a house or hotel where people have their meals.

⭐ **dinner** /'dɪnə/ **dinners.** ① N-VAR **Dinner** is the main meal of the day, eaten in the evening. *She invited us to her house for dinner.* ② N-VAR Some people use **dinner** to refer to the meal you eat in the middle of the day. [BRITISH] ③ N-COUNT A **dinner** is a formal social event in the evening at which a meal is served. *The Foundation is holding a dinner.* ④ See note at **meal**.

'**dinner table, dinner tables.** N-COUNT You refer to a table as the **dinner table** when it is being used for dinner. [BRITISH] *Sam was left at the dinner table with Peg.*

dinosaur /'daɪnəsɔː/ **dinosaurs.** N-COUNT **Dinosaurs** were large reptiles which lived in prehistoric times.

dip /dɪp/ **dips, dipping, dipped.** ① VERB If you **dip** something **into** a liquid, you put it in and then quickly take it out again. *They dip the food into the sauce.* ② VERB If something **dips**, it makes a downward movement. *The sun dipped below the horizon.* ③ N-COUNT A **dip** in a surface is a place that is lower than the rest of the surface. *The pitch has a slight dip in the middle.*

diploma /dɪ'pləʊmə/ **diplomas.** N-COUNT A **diploma** is a university or college qualification.

diplomacy /dɪ'pləʊməsi/. ① N-UNCOUNT **Diplomacy** is the activity of managing relations between the governments of different countries. *Force will have to be used if diplomacy fails.* ② N-UNCOUNT **Diplomacy** is the skill of saying or doing things without offending people. *Mr Smith sometimes lacked diplomacy.*

⭐ **diplomat** /'dɪpləmæt/ **diplomats.** N-COUNT A **diplomat** is a senior official, usually based at an embassy, who negotiates with another country on behalf of his or her own country.

⭐ **diplomatic** /,dɪplə'mætɪk/. ① ADJ **Diplomatic** means relating to diplomacy and diplomats. *There was an attempt to resume diplomatic relations.* ♦ **diplomatically** ADV *The conflict can be resolved diplomatically.* ② ADJ Someone who is **diplomatic** is able to say or do things without offending people. ♦ **diplomatically** ADV *She could have put it more diplomatically.*

dire /daɪə/. ADJ **Dire** is used to emphasize how serious or terrible a situation or event is. *He was in dire need of hospital treatment.*

⭐ **direct** /daɪ'rekt, dɪ-/ **directs, directing, directed.** ① ADJ & ADV **Direct** means going or aimed straight towards a place or object. ...*a direct train service from Calais to Strasbourg... You can fly direct to Amsterdam from most British airports.* ♦ **directly** ADV *Roads and railways went directly to seaports.* ● See also **directly.** ② ADJ & ADV You use **direct** to describe something such as contact or a relationship between two things or people which only involves the things or people that are mentioned, with nothing or nobody in between them. *He seemed to be in direct contact with the Boss... 100 million have died this century as a direct result of war... Ensure that babies are kept out of direct sunlight... I can deal direct with your Inspector.* ♦ **directly** ADV *People lost money directly because of some kind of criminal action.* ③ ADJ If you describe a person or their behaviour as **direct**, you mean that they are honest and say exactly what they mean. *He avoided giving a direct answer.* ♦ **directness** N-UNCOUNT *I like the openness and directness of northerners.* ④ VERB Something that **is directed at** a particular person or thing is aimed at them or is intended to affect them. *The demonstrators directed their rage at symbols of wealth.* ⑤ VERB If you **direct** someone somewhere, you tell them how to get there. *Could you direct them to Dr Lamont's office, please?* ⑥ VERB If someone **directs** a project or a group of people, they organize it and are in charge of it. ♦ **director, directors** N-COUNT ...*the director of the intensive care unit.* ⑦ VERB If someone **directs** a film, play, or television programme, they decide how it should be made and performed. *Andrew acts and directs.* ♦ **director** N-COUNT ...*the film director Franco Zeffirelli.* ● See also **director.**

⭐ **direction** /daɪ'rekʃən, dɪr-/ **directions.** ① N-VAR A **direction** is the general line that someone or something is moving or pointing in. *St Andrews was ten miles in the opposite direction... Civilians were fleeing in all directions.* ② N-VAR **Directions** are instructions that tell you what to do or how to get to a place. *He proceeded to give Dan directions to the computer room... The house was built under the direction of John's partner.*

directive /daɪ'rektɪv, dɪr-/ **directives.** N-COUNT A **directive** is an official instruction that is given by someone in authority. ...*a new EU directive.*

directly /daɪ'rektli, dɪr-/. ① ADV If something is, for example, **directly** above something or in front of something, it is in exactly that position. *There, directly below me, was a guy.* ② ADV If you do one action **directly** after another, you do the second action as soon as the first one is finished. *Directly after lunch we were packed and ready to go.* ③ See also **direct.**

di,rect 'object, direct objects. N-COUNT The **direct object** of a transitive verb is the noun group which is used to refer to someone or something directly affected by or involved in the action performed by the subject. For example, in 'I saw him yesterday', 'him' is the direct object. Compare **indirect object.**

⭐ **director** /daɪ'rektə, dɪr-/ **directors.** N-COUNT The **directors** of a company are its most senior managers. ...*the board of directors.* ● See also **direct.**

directorate /daɪ'rektərət, dɪr-/ **directorates.** ① N-COUNT A **directorate** is a board of directors in a company. ② N-COUNT A **directorate** is a part of a government department which is responsible for one particular thing. ...*the Health and Safety Directorate of the EU.*

di,rector 'general, directors general. N-COUNT The **director general** of a large organization is the person who is in charge of it.

directory /daɪ'rektəri, dɪr-/ **directories.**
[1] N-COUNT A **directory** is a book which gives lists of information such as people's names, addresses, and telephone numbers. ...*a telephone directory.* [2] N-COUNT A **directory** is an area of a computer disk which contains one or more files or other directories. [COMPUTING]

dirt /dɜːt/. [1] N-UNCOUNT If there is **dirt** on something, there is dust, mud, or a stain on it. [2] N-UNCOUNT You can refer to the earth on the ground as **dirt**.

⭐ **dirty** /'dɜːti/ **dirtier, dirtiest; dirties, dirtying, dirtied.**
[1] ADJ & VERB If you get something **dirty**, or if you **dirty** it, it becomes marked or covered with stains, spots, or mud. *The kids have got their clothes dirty... The dog's hairs might dirty the seats.* [2] ADJ **Dirty** jokes, books, or language refer to sex in a way that many people find obscene or offensive.

disability /,dɪsə'bɪlɪti/ **disabilities.** N-COUNT A **disability** is a physical or mental condition that restricts the way someone can live their life. ...*facilities for people with disabilities.*

disable /dɪ'seɪbəl/ **disables, disabling, disabled.**
[1] VERB If an injury or illness **disables** someone, it restricts the way they can live their life. [2] VERB To **disable** a system or mechanism means to stop it working. ...*if you need to disable a car alarm.*

disabled /dɪ'seɪbəld/. ADJ & N-PLURAL **Disabled** people or **the disabled** have an illness, injury, or condition that restricts the way they can live their lives.

disadvantage /,dɪsəd'vɑːntɪdʒ, -'væn-/
disadvantages. [1] N-COUNT A **disadvantage** is a part of a situation which causes problems. ...*the advantages and disadvantages of allowing their soldiers to marry.* [2] PHRASE If you are **at a disadvantage**, you have a problem that other people do not have. *The children from poor families were at a distinct disadvantage.*

disadvantaged /,dɪsəd'vɑːntɪdʒd, -'væn-/.
ADJ & N-PLURAL **Disadvantaged** people or **the disadvantaged** live in bad economic or social conditions.

disaffected /,dɪsə'fektɪd/. ADJ **Disaffected** people no longer fully support something which they previously supported. ...*people disaffected with the government.*

disagree /,dɪsə'griː/ **disagrees, disagreeing, disagreed.** [1] VERB If you **disagree** with someone, you have a different opinion to them about something. *I respect him even though I often disagree with him... They can communicate even when they strongly disagree... Well, I disagree.* [2] VERB If you **disagree with** an action or suggestion, you disapprove of it. *I disagree with drug laws in general.*

disagreement /,dɪsə'griːmənt/ **disagreements.**
[1] N-UNCOUNT **Disagreement** means objecting to something. *Britain and France have expressed some disagreement with the proposal.* [2] N-VAR When there is a **disagreement** about something, people disagree or argue about what should be done. *My driving instructor and I had a brief disagreement.*

disallow /,dɪsə'laʊ/ **disallows, disallowing, disallowed.** VERB If something **is disallowed**, it is not allowed or accepted officially, because it has not been done correctly. *The goal was disallowed.*

⭐ **disappear** /,dɪsə'pɪə/ **disappears, disappearing, disappeared.** [1] VERB If someone or something **disappears**, they go where they cannot be seen or found. *The airliner disappeared off their radar.* ...*a Japanese woman who disappeared thirteen years ago.* ♦ **disappearance, disappearances** N-VAR *Her disappearance has baffled police.* [2] VERB To **disappear** means to stop existing or happening. *Year by year great swathes of this small nation's countryside disappear.* ♦ **disappearance** N-UNCOUNT ...*the virtual disappearance of common dolphins.*

disappoint /,dɪsə'pɔɪnt/ **disappoints, disappointing, disappointed.** VERB If things or people **disappoint** you, they are not as good as you had hoped, or do not do what you hoped they would do. *I'm sorry if this reply will disappoint you.* ♦ **disappointing** ADJ *The food was disappointing.* ♦ **disappointingly** ADV *Progress is disappointingly slow.*

⭐ **disappointed** /,dɪsə'pɔɪntɪd/. ADJ If you are **disappointed**, you are sad because something has not happened or because something is not as good as you hoped it would be. *I was disappointed that Kluge was not there... I'm surprised and disappointed in you.*

disappointment /,dɪsə'pɔɪntmənt/ **disappointments.** [1] N-UNCOUNT **Disappointment** is the state of feeling disappointed. *Book early to avoid disappointment.* [2] N-COUNT Someone or something that is a **disappointment** is not as good as you had hoped. *He was such a disappointment to his family.*

disapproval /,dɪsə'pruːvəl/. N-UNCOUNT If you express **disapproval** of something, you indicate that you do not like it or that you think it is wrong. ...*a society that registered its disapproval of alcohol by banning it... His action had been greeted with almost universal disapproval.*

disapprove /,dɪsə'pruːv/ **disapproves, disapproving, disapproved.** VERB If you **disapprove of** something, you do not like it or you think it is wrong. *Her mother disapproved of her working in a pub... No matter how much I disapprove, I still love her.* ♦ **disapproving** ADJ *Janet gave him a disapproving look.* ♦ **disapprovingly** ADV *Antonio looked at him disapprovingly.*

disarm /dɪs'ɑːm/ **disarms, disarming, disarmed.**
[1] VERB To **disarm** a person or group means to take away their weapons. *We will agree to*

a
b
c
d
e
f
g
h
i
j
k
l
m
n
o
p
q
r
s
t
u
v
w
x
y
z

disarming troops. **2** VERB If a country or group **disarms**, it gives up the use of its weapons. *We're not ready to disarm ourselves.* **3** VERB If a person or their behaviour **disarms** you, they cause you to feel less angry, hostile, or critical towards them. *She did her best to disarm her critics.*
♦ **disarming** ADJ *...a disarming smile.*
♦ **disarmingly** ADV *He is, as ever, business-like, and disarmingly honest.*

disarmament /,dɪs'ɑːməmənt/. N-UNCOUNT **Disarmament** is the act of reducing the number of weapons that a country has.

disarray /,dɪsə'reɪ/. N-UNCOUNT If people or things are **in disarray** they have become very confused and disorganized. *The nation is in disarray following rioting.*

⭐ **disaster** /dɪ'zɑːstə, -'zæs-/ **disasters.** **1** N-COUNT A **disaster** is a very bad accident such as an earthquake or a plane crash. *It was the second air disaster in the region.* **2** N-COUNT If you refer to something as a **disaster**, you are emphasizing that you think it is extremely bad. *It would be a disaster for them not to reach the semi-finals.* **3** N-UNCOUNT **Disaster** is something which has very bad consequences for you. *'The potential for disaster is enormous,' he says.*

disastrous /dɪ'zɑːstrəs, -'zæs-/. ADJ Something that is **disastrous** has extremely bad consequences and effects or is very unsuccessful. *...the recent, disastrous earthquake... England's cricketers have had another disastrous day.*
♦ **disastrously** ADV *Their scheme went disastrously wrong.*

disband /,dɪs'bænd/ **disbands, disbanding, disbanded.** VERB If someone **disbands** a group of people, it stops operating as a single unit. *All the armed groups will be disbanded... The rebels were to have fully disbanded by June.*

disbelief /,dɪsbɪ'liːf/. N-UNCOUNT **Disbelief** is not believing that something is true or real. *She looked at him in complete disbelief.*

disc (AM **disk**) /dɪsk/ **discs.** **1** N-COUNT A **disc** is a flat, circular shape or object. **2** N-COUNT A **disc** is a piece of cartilage between the bones in your spine. **3** N-COUNT A **disc** is a gramophone record or a compact disc. **4** See also **disk**.

discard /dɪs'kɑːd/ **discards, discarding, discarded.** VERB If you **discard** something, you get rid of it because it is not wanted. *Read the manufacturer's guidelines before discarding the box. ...discarded cigarette butts.*

discern /dɪ'sɜːn/ **discerns, discerning, discerned.** **1** VERB If you can **discern** something, you are aware of it and know what it is. [FORMAL] *It was hard to discern why this was happening.* **2** VERB If you can **discern** something, you can just see it, but not clearly. [FORMAL] *We could just discern a narrow, weedy ditch.*

discernible /dɪ'sɜːnəbəl/. ADJ If something is **discernible**, you can see it or recognize that it exists. *Far away the outline of the island is just discernible.*

discerning /dɪ'sɜːnɪŋ/. ADJ A **discerning** person is good at judging the quality of something. *...holidays to suit the more discerning traveller.*

discharge, discharges, discharging, discharged. verb /dɪs'tʃɑːdʒ/, noun /'dɪstʃɑːdʒ/. **1** VERB & N-UNCOUNT When someone **is discharged** from hospital, prison, or the armed forces, or when they are given a **discharge**, they are allowed to leave, or told that they must leave. *He has a broken nose but may be discharged today... He was given a conditional discharge.* **2** VERB If someone **discharges** their duties or responsibilities, they carry them out. [FORMAL] *...the quiet competence with which he discharged his many college duties.* **3** VERB If something **is discharged** from inside a place, it comes out. [FORMAL] *The resulting salty water will be discharged at sea.* **4** N-COUNT When there is a **discharge** of a substance, the substance comes out from inside somewhere. *...a watery discharge from their eyes.*

disciple /dɪ'saɪpəl/ **disciples.** N-COUNT If you are someone's **disciple**, you are influenced by their teachings and try to follow their example. *...a major intellectual figure with disciples throughout Europe.*

disciplinary /'dɪsɪplɪnəri, AM -neri/. ADJ BEFORE N **Disciplinary** matters are concerned with rules, making sure that people obey them, and punishing people who do not.

⭐ **discipline** /'dɪsɪplɪn/ **disciplines, disciplining, disciplined.** **1** N-UNCOUNT **Discipline** is the practice of making people obey rules or standards of behaviour, and punishing them when they do not. *...discipline problems in the classroom.* **2** VERB If someone **is disciplined** for something that they have done wrong, they are punished for it. *The workman was disciplined by his company but not dismissed.* **3** N-UNCOUNT **Discipline** is the quality of being able to behave or work in a controlled way. *...calm, control and discipline.* **4** N-COUNT A **discipline** is an area of study, especially a subject of study in a college or university. [FORMAL] *...people from a wide range of disciplines.*

¹**disc jockey, disc jockeys.** N-COUNT A **disc jockey** is the same as a **DJ**.

disclose /dɪs'kləʊz/ **discloses, disclosing, disclosed.** VERB If you **disclose** new or secret information, you tell it to someone. *He will not disclose the names of his patients... The company disclosed that its chairman will step down in May.*

disclosure /dɪs'kləʊʒə/ **disclosures.** N-VAR **Disclosure** is the act of revealing new or secret information. *...a series of unauthorised newspaper disclosures.*

disco /'dɪskəʊ/ **discos.** N-COUNT A **disco** is a place or event where people dance to pop music.

discomfort /dɪs'kʌmfət/ **discomforts.** **1** N-UNCOUNT **Discomfort** is an unpleasant or painful feeling in a part of your body. *Steve had some discomfort, but no real pain.* **2** N-UNCOUNT

Discomfort is a feeling of worry or embarrassment. *He sniffed, fidgeting in discomfort.* [3] N-COUNT **Discomforts** are conditions which cause you to feel physically uncomfortable. *...the discomforts of camping.*

disconcerting /ˌdɪskən'sɜːtɪŋ/. ADJ If you say that something is **disconcerting**, you mean that it makes you feel uneasy, confused, or embarrassed. *He had a disconcerting habit of looking down at the ground as he spoke.*
♦ **disconcertingly** ADV *She could be almost disconcertingly absent-minded.*

disconnect /ˌdɪskə'nekt/ **disconnects, disconnecting, disconnected.** VERB To **disconnect** a piece of equipment means to detach it from its source of power.

disconnected /ˌdɪskə'nektɪd/. ADJ **Disconnected** things are not linked in any way. *...sequences of utterly disconnected events.*

discontent /ˌdɪskən'tent/. N-UNCOUNT **Discontent** is the feeling of not being satisfied with your situation.

discontinue /ˌdɪskən'tɪnjuː/ **discontinues, discontinuing, discontinued.** [1] VERB If you **discontinue** something that you have been doing regularly, you stop doing it. [FORMAL] *Do not discontinue the treatment without consulting your doctor.* [2] VERB If a product **is discontinued**, the manufacturer stops making it.

discord /'dɪskɔːd/ **discords.** N-UNCOUNT **Discord** is disagreement. [LITERARY] *...arranging schedules so as to prevent discord.*

⭐ **discount, discounts, discounting, discounted.** [1] N-COUNT /'dɪskaʊnt/ A **discount** is a reduction in the price of something. *All full-time staff get a 20% discount.* [2] VERB /dɪs'kaʊnt/ If you **discount** something, you reject or ignore it. *Traders tended to discount the rumor.*

discourage /dɪs'kʌrɪdʒ, AM -'kɜːr-/ **discourages, discouraging, discouraged.** [1] VERB If someone or something **discourages** you, they cause you to lose your enthusiasm about doing something. *It may be difficult to do at first. Don't let this discourage you.* ♦ **discouraged** ADJ *She was determined not to be too discouraged.*
♦ **discouraging** ADJ *Today's report is more discouraging for the economy.* [2] VERB To **discourage** an action, or to **discourage** someone **from** doing it, means to try and persuade them not to do it. *...a campaign to discourage children from smoking.* ♦ **discouragement** N-UNCOUNT *...active discouragement from teachers.*

discourse /'dɪskɔːs/ N-UNCOUNT **Discourse** is spoken or written communication between people. *...a long tradition of political discourse.*

⭐ **discover** /dɪs'kʌvə/ **discovers, discovering, discovered.** [1] VERB If you **discover** something that you did not know about before, you become aware of it or learn of it. *She discovered that they'd escaped... It was difficult for the inspectors to discover which documents were important.* [2] VERB If someone or something **is discovered**,

someone finds them. *A few days later his badly beaten body was discovered.* [3] VERB When someone **discovers** something new, they are the first person to find it or become aware of it. *...the first European to discover America... People discovered how to cultivate cereals thousands of years ago.*

⭐ **discovery** /dɪs'kʌvəri/ **discoveries.** [1] N-VAR If someone makes a **discovery**, they become aware of something or learn of something that they did not know about before. *I felt I'd made an incredible discovery.* [2] N-COUNT If someone makes a **discovery**, they are the first person to find or become aware of something that no one knew about before. *...the discovery of the ozone hole over the South Pole.* [3] N-VAR When the **discovery** of people or objects happens, someone finds them.

discredit /dɪs'kredɪt/ **discredits, discrediting, discredited.** [1] VERB To **discredit** someone or something means to cause other people to stop trusting or respecting them. *...trying to discredit government foreign-aid policies.* ♦ **discredited** ADJ *...discredited police evidence.* [2] VERB To **discredit** evidence or an idea means to make it appear false or doubtful.

discreet /dɪs'kriːt/. ADJ If you are **discreet**, you are careful to avoid attracting attention or revealing private information. *He followed at a discreet distance. ...discreet jewellery. ...discreet inquiries.* ♦ **discreetly** ADV *He glanced discreetly around the room.*

discrepancy /dɪs'krepənsi/ **discrepancies.** N-COUNT If there is a **discrepancy** between two things that ought to be the same, there is a difference between them. *...discrepancies in their accounting systems.*

discretion /dɪs'kreʃən/. [1] N-UNCOUNT **Discretion** is the quality of behaving in a quiet and controlled way without attracting attention or giving away private information. *Larsson sometimes joined in the fun, but with more discretion.* [2] N-UNCOUNT If someone in a position of authority has **the discretion** to do something in a situation, they have the freedom and authority to decide what to do. [FORMAL] *School governors have the discretion to allow parents to withdraw pupils... The rules are often bent at the organiser's discretion.*

discretionary /dɪs'kreʃənri, AM -neri/. ADJ **Discretionary** matters are not fixed by rules but are decided by the people in authority. *You are entitled to a discretionary grant for your course.*

discriminate /dɪs'krɪmɪneɪt/ **discriminates, discriminating, discriminated.** [1] VERB If you can **discriminate between** two things, you can recognize the difference between them. *He is incapable of discriminating between a good idea and a terrible one.* [2] VERB To **discriminate against** a group of people or in favour of a group of people means to unfairly treat them worse or better than other groups. *They believe the law discriminates against women.*

a
b
c
d
e
f
g
h
i
j
k
l
m
n
o
p
q
r
s
t
u
v
w
x
y
z

discrimination /dɪsˌkrɪmɪ'neɪʃən/.
[1] N-UNCOUNT **Discrimination** is the practice of treating one person or group of people less fairly or less well than other people or groups. ...*sex discrimination laws. ...discrimination against immigrants.* [2] N-UNCOUNT **Discrimination** is awareness of what is good or of high quality. *They cooked without skill and ate without discrimination.*

discriminatory /dɪs'krɪmɪnətri, AM -tɔːri/. ADJ **Discriminatory** laws or practices are unfair because they treat one group of people worse than other groups. ...*racially discriminatory laws.*

⭐ **discuss** /dɪs'kʌs/ **discusses, discussing, discussed.** VERB If people **discuss** something, they talk about it, often in order to reach a decision. *I will be discussing the situation with colleagues tomorrow... The groups are also to discuss how to bring peace and unity to the country.*

> **USAGE** Note that **discuss** is never used as an intransitive verb. You cannot say, for example, 'They discussed', 'I discussed with him', or 'They discussed about politics'. Instead, you can say that you **have a discussion** with someone about something. *I had a long discussion about all this with Stephen.* You can also add an object and say that you **discuss** something **with** someone. If the discussion is less formal, you can simply use the verb **talk**. *They come here and sit for hours talking about politics... We talked all night long.*

⭐ **discussion** /dɪs'kʌʃən/ **discussions.** N-VAR If there is **discussion** about something, people talk about it, often in order to reach a decision. *Council members are due to have informal discussions later on today... The proposals are still under discussion.*

disdain /dɪs'deɪn/. N-UNCOUNT If you feel **disdain** for someone or something, you dislike them because you think they are inferior or unimportant. *Janet looked at him with disdain.*

⭐ **disease** /dɪ'ziːz/ **diseases.** N-VAR A **disease** is an illness which affects people, animals, or plants. ...*the rapid spread of disease in the area. ...heart disease.*

diseased /dɪ'ziːzd/. [1] ADJ Something that is **diseased** is affected by a disease. *Clear away dead or diseased plants.* [2] ADJ If you say that someone's mind is **diseased**, you are emphasizing that you think it is not normal or balanced. *Gardner describes the book as 'the product of a diseased and evil mind'.*

disenchanted /ˌdɪsɪn'tʃɑːntɪd, -'tʃænt-/. ADJ If you are **disenchanted with** something, you no longer think that it is good. *I'm disenchanted with the state of British theatre.* ♦ **disenchantment** /ˌdɪsɪn'tʃɑːntmənt, -'tʃænt-/ N-UNCOUNT *There's growing disenchantment with the Government.*

disengage /ˌdɪsɪn'geɪdʒ/ **disengages, disengaging, disengaged.** [1] VERB If you **disengage** something, you separate it from the thing which it has become attached to. *John gently disengaged himself from his sister's tearful embrace... His front brake cable disengaged.* [2] VERB If an army **disengages from** a conflict or an area, it withdraws from the fight or the area.
♦ **disengagement** N-UNCOUNT ...*the policy of disengagement from the European war.*

disengaged /ˌdɪsɪn'geɪdʒd/. ADJ If someone is **disengaged from** something, they are not as involved with it as you would expect. *Both of the parents are emotionally disengaged from the patient.*

disfigure /dɪs'fɪgə, AM -gjər/ **disfigures, disfiguring, disfigured.** [1] VERB If someone **is disfigured**, their appearance is spoiled. *Many of the wounded had been badly disfigured.* ♦ **disfigured** ADJ ...*the scarred, disfigured face.* [2] VERB To **disfigure** an object or a place means to spoil its appearance. *Wind turbines are noisy and they disfigure the landscape.*

disgrace /dɪs'greɪs/ **disgraces, disgracing, disgraced.** [1] N-UNCOUNT & N-SING If you say that someone is **in disgrace**, you are emphasizing that other people disapprove of them and do not respect them because of something they have done. *His vice president also had to resign in disgrace... What went on was a scandal. It was a disgrace to Britain.* [2] N-SING If you say that something is **a disgrace**, you are emphasizing that it is very bad or wrong. *To withhold any information is an absolute disgrace.* [3] VERB If you say that someone **disgraces** someone else, you are emphasizing that their behaviour causes the other person to feel ashamed. *I have disgraced my family's name.*

disgraced /dɪs'greɪst/. ADJ You use **disgraced** to describe someone whose bad behaviour has caused them to lose the approval and respect of the public or of people in authority. ...*the disgraced leader of the coup.*

disgraceful /dɪs'greɪsfʊl/. ADJ If you say that something is **disgraceful**, you disapprove of it strongly. ...*his most disgraceful behaviour.*
♦ **disgracefully** ADV *His brother had behaved disgracefully.*

disgruntled /dɪs'grʌntəld/. ADJ If you are **disgruntled**, you are cross and dissatisfied about something. *Disgruntled employees recently called for his resignation.*

disguise /dɪs'gaɪz/ **disguises, disguising, disguised.** [1] VERB & N-VAR If you **disguise yourself**, or if you are **in disguise**, you alter your appearance so that people will not recognize you. *She disguised herself as a man... He was wearing that ridiculous disguise.* ♦ **disguised** ADJ *The extremists entered the building disguised as medical workers.* [2] VERB To **disguise** something means to hide it or change its appearance, so that people do not know about it or will not recognize it. *He made no attempt to disguise his agitation.* ♦ **disguised** ADJ ...*a thinly disguised warning.*

a

disgust /dɪs'gʌst/ **disgusts, disgusting, disgusted.** [1] N-UNCOUNT **Disgust** is a strong feeling of dislike or disapproval. *He spoke of his disgust at the incident.* [2] VERB To **disgust** someone means to make them feel a strong sense of dislike and disapproval. *He disgusted many with his boorish behaviour.*

disgusted /dɪs'gʌstɪd/. ADJ If you are **disgusted**, you have a strong feeling of dislike or disapproval. *I'm disgusted with the way that he was treated.* ♦ **disgustedly** ADV *'It's a little late for that,' Ritter said disgustedly.*

disgusting /dɪs'gʌstɪŋ/. ADJ If you say that something is **disgusting**, you think it is extremely unpleasant or unacceptable. *...one of the most disgusting sights I have ever seen... i think it's disgusting that women of 60 are having babies.*

⭐ **dish** /dɪʃ/ **dishes, dishing, dished.** [1] N-COUNT A **dish** is a shallow container used for cooking or serving food. *...a dish of spaghetti.* [2] N-COUNT Food that is prepared in a particular style or combination can be referred to as a **dish**. *There are plenty of vegetarian dishes to choose from.* [3] N-COUNT You can use **dish** to refer to anything that is round and hollow in shape with a wide uncovered top. *...a satellite dish.*

▸**dish out** [1] PHR-VERB If you **dish out** something, you distribute it among a number of people. [INFORMAL] *Doctors, not pharmacists, are responsible for dishing out drugs.* [2] PHR-VERB If someone **dishes out** criticism or punishment, they give it to someone. [3] PHR-VERB If you **dish out** food, you serve it to people. *She dished him out a plate of stew.*

▸**dish up.** PHR-VERB If you **dish up** food, you serve it to people. *They dished up a superb meal... I'll dish up.*

dishonest /dɪs'ɒnɪst/. ADJ If you say someone is **dishonest**, you mean that they are not honest and you cannot trust them. *It would be dishonest to mislead people.* ♦ **dishonestly** ADV *They acted dishonestly.*

dishonesty /dɪs'ɒnɪsti/. N-UNCOUNT **Dishonesty** is dishonest behaviour.

disillusion /ˌdɪsɪ'luːʒən/ **disillusions, disillusioning, disillusioned.** [1] VERB If someone or something **disillusions** you, they make you realize that something is not as good as you thought. *He said he had been bitterly disillusioned by his country's failure to change.* ♦ **disillusioned** ADJ *I've become very disillusioned with local politics.* [2] N-UNCOUNT **Disillusion** is the same as **disillusionment**.

disillusionment /ˌdɪsɪ'luːʒənmənt/. N-UNCOUNT **Disillusionment** is the disappointment that you feel when you discover that someone or something is not as good as you had expected or thought. *...a general sense of disillusionment with the government.*

disinfect /ˌdɪsɪn'fekt/ **disinfects, disinfecting, disinfected.** VERB If you **disinfect** something, you

clean it using a substance that kills germs. *Your contact lenses should be disinfected daily.*

disinfectant /ˌdɪsɪn'fektənt/ **disinfectants.** N-VAR **Disinfectant** is a substance that kills germs.

disintegrate /dɪs'ɪntɪgreɪt/ **disintegrates, disintegrating, disintegrated.** [1] VERB If something **disintegrates**, it becomes seriously weakened and is divided or destroyed. *During October 1918 the Austro-Hungarian Empire began to disintegrate.* ♦ **disintegration** N-UNCOUNT *...the disintegration of an ordinary marriage.* [2] VERB If an object **disintegrates**, it breaks into many small pieces and is destroyed. *At 420 mph the windscreen disintegrated.*

disinterested /dɪs'ɪntrəstɪd/. [1] ADJ Someone who is **disinterested** is not involved in a situation or not likely to benefit from it and is therefore able to act in a fair and unselfish way. *Scientists, of course, can be expected to be impartial and disinterested.* [2] ADJ If you are **disinterested in** something, you are not interested in it. *Doran was disinterested in food.*

disk /dɪsk/. N-COUNT In a computer, the **disk** is the part where information is stored. [COMPUTING] *The program takes up 2.5 megabytes of disk space.*

'**disk drive, disk drives.** N-COUNT The **disk drive** on a computer is the part that contains the hard disk or into which a disk can be inserted. [COMPUTING]

dislike /dɪs'laɪk/ **dislikes, disliking, disliked.** [1] VERB & N-UNCOUNT If you **dislike** someone or something, or if you have a feeling of **dislike** towards them, you think they are unpleasant and you do not like them. *David began to dislike all his television heroes who smoked... She looked at him with dislike.* [2] N-PLURAL Your **dislikes** are the things that you do not like. *Consider what your likes and dislikes are about your job.*

dislocate /'dɪsləkeɪt/ **dislocates, dislocating, dislocated.** VERB If you **dislocate** a bone or a joint in your body, it moves out of its proper position. *Harrison dislocated a finger. ...a dislocated shoulder.*

dislodge /ˌdɪs'lɒdʒ/ **dislodges, dislodging, dislodged.** VERB To **dislodge** someone or something **from** a place or position means to make them move from that place or position. *Rainfall from a tropical storm dislodged the debris from the slopes of the volcano.*

dismal /'dɪzməl/. [1] ADJ Something that is **dismal** is depressingly bad. *My prospects of returning to a suitable job are dismal.* [2] ADJ Something that is **dismal** is bleak, sad, and depressing. *The main hospital is pretty dismal. ...a dark dismal day.*

dismantle /ˌdɪs'mæntəl/ **dismantles, dismantling, dismantled.** VERB If you **dismantle** a machine or structure, you take it apart carefully.

dismay /ˌdɪs'meɪ/ **dismays, dismaying, dismayed.** N-UNCOUNT & VERB If you have a feeling of **dismay**, or if something **dismays** you, it makes you feel afraid, worried, or disappointed. [FORMAL] *Mr*

b
c
d
e
f
g
h
i
j
k
l
m
n
o
p
q
r
s
t
u
v
w
x
y
z

Reynolds expressed dismay at this idea... McKee suddenly realized she was crying and the thought dismayed him. ♦ **dismayed** ADJ He was dismayed to find that his hands were shaking.

dismember /ˌdɪsˈmembə/ **dismembers, dismembering, dismembered.** VERB To **dismember** the body of a dead person means to cut or pull it to pieces. ♦ **dismemberment** N-UNCOUNT ...many bodies in various states of decay and dismemberment.

⭐ **dismiss** /ˌdɪsˈmɪs/ **dismisses, dismissing, dismissed.** ☐1 VERB If you **dismiss** something, you decide that it is not important enough for you to think about. Mr Wakeham dismissed the reports as speculation. ☐2 VERB When an employer **dismisses** an employee, they order the employee to leave his or her job. He was dismissed for incompetence. ☐3 VERB If you **are dismissed** by someone in authority, they tell you that you can go away from them. Two more witnesses were called, heard and dismissed.

dismissal /ˌdɪsˈmɪsəl/ **dismissals.** ☐1 N-VAR When an employee is dismissed from their job, you can refer to their **dismissal**. ...Mr Low's dismissal from his post at the head of the commission. ☐2 N-UNCOUNT **Dismissal of** something means deciding or saying that it is not important. ...high-handed dismissal of public opinion.

dismissive /ˌdɪsˈmɪsɪv/. ADJ If you are **dismissive of** someone or something, you say or show that you think they are not important or have no value. Mr Jones was dismissive of the report. ...the dismissive attitude scientists often take. ♦ **dismissively** ADV He describes Sally dismissively as 'that woman'.

disobedience /ˌdɪsəˈbiːdiəns/. N-UNCOUNT **Disobedience** is deliberately refusing to do what someone in authority tells you to do, or to follow rules. The penalty for disobedience was death.

disobey /ˌdɪsəˈbeɪ/ **disobeys, disobeying, disobeyed.** VERB When someone **disobeys** a person or an order, they deliberately do not do what they have been told to do. ...a naughty boy who often disobeyed his mother and father.

disorder /ˌdɪsˈɔːdə/ **disorders.** ☐1 N-VAR A **disorder** is a problem or illness which affects a person's mind or body. ...a rare nerve disorder that can cause paralysis of the arms. ☐2 N-UNCOUNT **Disorder** is a state of being untidy, badly prepared, or badly organized. The emergency room was in disorder. ☐3 N-UNCOUNT **Disorder** is violence or rioting in public. ...forms of civil disorder – most notably, football hooliganism.

disorderly /ˌdɪsˈɔːdəli/. ADJ If you describe something as **disorderly**, you mean that it is untidy, irregular, or disorganized. [FORMAL] ...the large and disorderly room.

disorganized (BRIT also **disorganised**) /ˌdɪsˈɔːgənaɪzd/. ADJ **Disorganized** means badly organized, planned, or managed, often leading to a state of confusion. The lectures are very disorganized... I'm completely disorganized.

disorientated /ˌdɪsˈɔːrienteɪtɪd/. ADJ **Disorientated** means the same as **disoriented**.

disoriented (BRIT also **disorientated**) /ˌdɪsˈɔːrientɪd/. ADJ If you feel **disoriented**, you lose your sense of direction, or you feel generally lost and uncertain. He is completely disoriented by what is going on.

disown /dɪsˈəʊn/ **disowns, disowning, disowned.** VERB If you **disown** someone or something, you no longer have any connection with them. His wealthy parents had disowned him.

disparage /ˌdɪsˈpærɪdʒ/ **disparages, disparaging, disparaged.** VERB If you **disparage** someone or something, you speak about them in a way which shows that you do not have a good opinion of them. ...Larkin's tendency to disparage literature. ♦ **disparagement** N-UNCOUNT ...their disparagement of this book. ♦ **disparaging** ADJ A lot of very disparaging things have been said about Seattle.

disparate /ˈdɪspərət/. ADJ **Disparate** things are clearly different from each other in quality or type. [FORMAL] Scientists are trying to pull together disparate ideas in astronomy.

disparity /ˌdɪsˈpærɪti/ **disparities.** N-VAR A **disparity between** two or more things is a noticeable difference between them. [FORMAL] ...disparities between poor and wealthy school districts.

dispatch (BRIT also **despatch**) /dɪsˈpætʃ/ **dispatches, dispatching, dispatched.** ☐1 VERB & N-UNCOUNT If you **dispatch** someone or something to a place, you send them there. You can also talk about the **dispatch** of people or things to a place. The Italian government was preparing to dispatch 4,000 soldiers to search the island. ☐2 N-COUNT A **dispatch** is an official report sent to a person or organization by their representative in another place.

dispel /dɪsˈpel/ **dispels, dispelling, dispelled.** VERB To **dispel** an idea or feeling means to stop people believing in it or feeling it. The President is attempting to dispel the notion that he has neglected the economy.

dispense /dɪsˈpens/ **dispenses, dispensing, dispensed.** ☐1 VERB To **dispense** something means to give it to people. [FORMAL] ...High Court circuit judges dispensing justice. ☐2 VERB When a chemist **dispenses** medicine, he or she prepares it and gives it to the patient.

▸**dispense with.** PHR-VERB If you **dispense with** something, you stop using it or get rid of it altogether. The princess dispensed with her official bodyguards at the beginning of the year.

dispenser /dɪsˈpensə/ **dispensers.** N-COUNT A **dispenser** is a machine or container from which you can get things. ...cash dispensers.

disperse /dɪsˈpɜːs/ **disperses, dispersing, dispersed.** ☐1 VERB When a group of people **disperses**, the group splits up and the people leave in different directions. The crowd dispersed peacefully... Police eventually dispersed them with tear gas. ☐2 VERB

When things **disperse**, or when you **disperse** them, they spread over a wide area. *The leaflets were dispersed throughout the country.*

displace /dɪs'pleɪs/ **displaces, displacing, displaced.**
1 VERB If one thing **displaces** another, it forces the other thing out and occupies its position. *It might even displace the war news from the front page.* 2 VERB If someone **is displaced**, they are forced to move away from the area where they live. *...resettling refugees and displaced persons.*
♦ **displacement** N-UNCOUNT *...the gradual displacement of the American Indian.*

⭐ **display** /dɪs'pleɪ/ **displays, displaying, displayed.**
1 VERB & N-UNCOUNT If you **display** something, or if you put it **on display**, you put it in a place where people can see it. *...war veterans proudly displaying their medals. ...the other artists whose work is on display.* 2 VERB & N-VAR If you **display** a quality or emotion, you behave in a way which shows that you have it. You can also talk about a **display of** a particular quality or emotion. *It was unlike Gordon to display his feelings. ...his determined display of courage.* 3 N-COUNT A **display** is something which is intended to attract people's attention, for example an event or attractive arrangement of different things. *...a permanent display of 300 of the artist's paintings. ...the firework display.*

displeasure /dɪs'pleʒə/. N-UNCOUNT
Displeasure with someone or something is a feeling of annoyance towards that person or about that thing. *He has been very vocal in his displeasure over the results.*

disposable /dɪs'pəʊzəbəl/. ADJ **Disposable** things are designed to be thrown away after use. *...disposable nappies.*

disposal /dɪs'pəʊzəl/. 1 PHRASE If you have something **at your disposal**, you are able to use it whenever you want. If you are **at** someone's **disposal**, you are willing to help them in any way you can. *Do you have this information at your disposal?* 2 N-UNCOUNT The **disposal of** something is the act of getting rid of it. *...the permanent disposal of radioactive wastes.*

dispose /dɪs'pəʊz/ **disposes, disposing, disposed.**
▶ **dispose of.** PHR-VERB If you **dispose of** something, you get rid of it, usually because you no longer want or need it. *Matthew told police he disposed of the murder weapon for Charles.*

disposed /dɪs'pəʊzd/. 1 ADJ AFTER LINK-V If you are **disposed to** do something, you are willing to do it. [FORMAL] *We passed one or two dwellings, but were not disposed to stop.* 2 ADJ You can use **disposed** when you are talking about someone's general attitude or opinion. *Every government is ill-disposed to the press.*

disposition /ˌdɪspə'zɪʃən/. **dispositions.** N-COUNT
Your **disposition** is the way that you tend to behave or feel. *...people of a nervous disposition.*

disprove /dɪs'pruːv/ **disproves, disproving, disproved.** VERB If you **disprove** an idea or belief, you show that it is not true.

⭐ **dispute** /dɪs'pjuːt/ **disputes, disputing, disputed.**
1 N-VAR A **dispute** is a disagreement or quarrel between people. *...pay disputes with the government.* 2 VERB & PHRASE If you **dispute** a fact or opinion, you say that it is incorrect or untrue. If an issue is **in dispute**, people cannot agree about whether it is correct or true. *Nobody disputed that Davey was clever.* 3 VERB When people **dispute** something, they fight for control of it. *Fishermen from Bristol disputed fishing rights with the Danes.*

disqualify /dɪs'kwɒlɪfaɪ/ **disqualifies, disqualifying, disqualified.** VERB When someone **is disqualified from** an event or an activity, they are officially stopped from taking part in it. *He was disqualified from driving for three years.* ♦ **disqualification** /ˌdɪs,kwɒlɪfɪ'keɪʃən/ **disqualifications** N-VAR *...a four-year disqualification from athletics.*

disquiet /ˌdɪs'kwaɪət/. N-UNCOUNT **Disquiet** is a feeling of worry or anxiety. [FORMAL] *There is growing disquiet about the cost of such policing.*

disregard /ˌdɪsrɪ'gɑːd/ **disregards, disregarding, disregarded.** VERB & N-UNCOUNT If you **disregard** something, or if you show **disregard for** it, you ignore it or do not take account of it. *He disregarded the advice of his executives. ...a total disregard for the safety of the public.*

disrepute /ˌdɪsrɪ'pjuːt/. PHRASE If something is brought **into disrepute** or falls **into disrepute**, it loses its good reputation, because it is connected with activities that people do not approve of.

disrupt /dɪs'rʌpt/ **disrupts, disrupting, disrupted.**
VERB If someone or something **disrupts** an event or process, they cause problems that prevent it from continuing normally. *Anti-war protesters disrupted the debate.* ♦ **disruption, disruptions** N-VAR *The strike is expected to cause delays and disruption to flights.*

disruptive /dɪs'rʌptɪv/. ADJ If you say that someone is **disruptive**, you think they are preventing an activity or system from continuing normally. *He was a disruptive influence.*

diss /dɪs/ **disses, dissing, dissed.** VERB If someone **disses** you, they criticize you unfairly or speak to you in a way that does not show respect. [INFORMAL] *He dissed me about my clothes.*

dissatisfaction /ˌdɪˌsætɪs'fækʃən/. N-UNCOUNT
If you feel **dissatisfaction with** something, you are not satisfied with it. *She has already expressed her dissatisfaction with the policy... Low pay is the main cause of job dissatisfaction among teachers.*

dissatisfied /ˌdɪ'sætɪsfaɪd/. ADJ If you are **dissatisfied with** something, you are not contented or pleased with it. *82% of voters are dissatisfied with the way their country is being governed.*

dissect /daɪ'sekt, dɪ-/ **dissects, dissecting, dissected.**
VERB To **dissect** a dead body means to cut it up in order to examine it. ♦ **dissection, dissections** N-VAR *Researchers need a growing supply of corpses for dissection.*

---

disseminate /dɪˈsemɪneɪt/ **disseminates, disseminating, disseminated.** VERB To **disseminate** information means to distribute it, so that it reaches many people. [FORMAL] *It took years to disseminate information about Aids.*
♦ **dissemination** N-UNCOUNT *...the dissemination of scientific ideas.*

dissent /dɪˈsent/ **dissents, dissenting, dissented.** VERB & N-UNCOUNT If you **dissent**, or if you express **dissent**, you express disagreement with a decision or established opinion. [FORMAL] *One member Martha Seger dissented from the final vote. ...voices of dissent.* ♦ **dissenting** ADJ *He suppressed dissenting views among his colleagues.*
♦ **dissenter, dissenters** N-COUNT *The Party does not tolerate dissenters in its ranks.*

dissertation /ˌdɪsəˈteɪʃən/ **dissertations.** N-COUNT A **dissertation** is a long formal piece of writing, especially for a university degree.

dissident /ˈdɪsɪdənt/ **dissidents.** N-COUNT **Dissidents** are people who criticize their repressive government. *...arrests of political dissidents.*

dissipate /ˈdɪsɪpeɪt/ **dissipates, dissipating, dissipated.** [1] VERB When something **dissipates**, or when you **dissipate** it, there is less of it or it becomes less strong, until it goes away completely. *The tension in the room had dissipated.* ♦ **dissipation** N-UNCOUNT *...the dissipation of my child-rearing energies.* [2] VERB If someone **dissipates** money, time, or effort, they waste it. *A wayward son dissipated the fortune.*
♦ **dissipation** N-UNCOUNT *...the dissipation of remaining pensions assets.*

dissociate /dɪˈsəʊʃieɪt/ **dissociates, dissociating, dissociated.** VERB If you **dissociate** yourself **from** someone or something, you say that you are not connected with them. *It seems harder and harder for the president to dissociate himself from the scandals.*

dissolve /dɪˈzɒlv/ **dissolves, dissolving, dissolved.** [1] VERB If a substance **dissolves** in liquid, or if you **dissolve** a substance, it mixes with the liquid, becoming weaker until it finally disappears. *Heat gently until the sugar dissolves.* [2] VERB When something **is dissolved**, it is officially ended. [FORMAL] *The marriage was dissolved in 1976.* ♦ **dissolution** /ˌdɪsəˈluːʃən/ N-UNCOUNT *...the dissolution of parliament.*

dissuade /dɪˈsweɪd/ **dissuades, dissuading, dissuaded.** VERB If you **dissuade** someone **from** doing something, you persuade them not to do it. [FORMAL] *Doctors had tried to dissuade patients from smoking... He considered emigrating, but his family managed to dissuade him.*

⭐ **distance** /ˈdɪstəns/ **distances, distancing, distanced.** [1] N-VAR The **distance between** two places is the amount of space between them. *...the distance between the island and the nearby shore. ...within walking distance.* [2] PHRASE If you are **at a distance from** something, or if you remember it **from a distance**, you are thinking about

something which happened a long time ago. *...now that I can look back on the whole tragedy from a distance of nearly forty years.* [3] N-UNCOUNT **Distance** is detachment and remoteness in the way that someone behaves, so that they do not seem friendly. *There were periods of sulking, and of pronounced distance.* [4] VERB If you **distance yourself from** someone or something, you become less involved with them. *The United States has distanced itself from the British plan.*
♦ **distanced** ADJ AFTER LINK-V *He'd become too distanced from his fans.*

distant /ˈdɪstənt/. [1] ADJ **Distant** means far away. [WRITTEN] *The mountains rolled away to a distant horizon.* ♦ **distantly** ADV *Rose heard a buzzer sound distantly.* [2] ADJ An event or time that is **distant** is far away in the past or future. *Things will improve in the not too distant future.* [3] ADJ A **distant** relative is one that you are not closely related to. ♦ **distantly** ADV *His father's distantly related to the Royal family.* [4] ADJ AFTER LINK-V If you describe someone as **distant**, you find them emotionally detached and unfriendly. [5] ADJ If you describe someone as **distant**, you mean that they are not paying attention because they are thinking about something else. *There was a distant look in her eyes.* ♦ **distantly** ADV *'He's in the interview room,' she said distantly.*

distaste /ˌdɪsˈteɪst/. N-UNCOUNT If you feel **distaste for** someone or something, you dislike or disapprove of them. *He professed a violent distaste for everything related to commerce... Roger looked at her with distaste.*

distasteful /ˌdɪsˈteɪstfʊl/. ADJ If something is **distasteful to** you, you dislike or disapprove of it. *Such ideas are distasteful to them... I find her gossip distasteful.*

distil (AM **distill**) /dɪˈstɪl/ **distils, distilling, distilled.** VERB If a liquid such as whisky **is distilled**, it is heated until it evaporates and then cooled until it becomes liquid again. *...a gallon of distilled water.*
♦ **distillation** N-UNCOUNT *The water is warm because of the distillation process.*

distinct /dɪˈstɪŋkt/. [1] ADJ If one thing is **distinct from** another, there is an important difference between them. *Engineering and technology are disciplines distinct from one another. ...oily fish, as distinct from fatty meat.*
♦ **distinctly** ADV *...a banking industry with two distinctly different sectors.* [2] ADJ If something is **distinct**, you hear or see it clearly. *...a distinct smell of burning coal.* ♦ **distinctly** ADV *I distinctly heard the loudspeaker.* [3] ADJ If an idea, thought, or intention is **distinct**, it is clear and definite. *There was a distinct change in her attitude.*
♦ **distinctly** ADV *I distinctly remember wishing I had not got involved.*

distinction /dɪˈstɪŋkʃən/ **distinctions.** [1] N-COUNT A **distinction** is a difference between similar things. If you **draw** or **make** a **distinction between** two things, you say that they are different. *...obvious distinctions between the two wine-making areas... He draws a distinction* between art and culture. **2** N-UNCOUNT **Distinction** is the quality of being excellent. ...furniture of distinction.

distinctive /dɪˈstɪŋktɪv/. ADJ Something that is **distinctive** has special qualities that make it easily recognizable. His voice was very distinctive. ♦ **distinctively** ADV ...the distinctively fragrant taste of elderflowers.

distinguish /dɪˈstɪŋgwɪʃ/ **distinguishes, distinguishing, distinguished.** **1** VERB If you can **distinguish** one thing **from** another, you can see or understand the difference between them. Could he distinguish right from wrong? ...distinguishing between areas of light and dark. **2** VERB A feature or quality that **distinguishes** one thing **from** another causes the two things to be regarded as different. There is something about music that distinguishes it from all other art forms. **3** VERB If you can **distinguish** something, you can see, hear, or taste it although it is very difficult to detect. [FORMAL] He could distinguish voices. **4** VERB If you **distinguish yourself**, you do something that makes you famous or important. He distinguished himself as a long distance runner.

distinguished /dɪˈstɪŋgwɪʃt/. ADJ A **distinguished** person is very successful, famous, or important. ...a distinguished academic family.

distinguishing /dɪˈstɪŋgwɪʃɪŋ/. ADJ The **distinguishing** features of something are the features which make it different from other things of the same type. One of the most distinguishing characteristics of the Algerians was religion.

distort /dɪˈstɔːt/ **distorts, distorting, distorted.** **1** VERB If you **distort** a statement, fact, or idea, you report or represent it in an untrue way. The media distorts reality. ♦ **distorted** ADJ These figures give a distorted view. ♦ **distortion, distortions** N-VAR He later accused reporters of wilful distortion and bias. **2** VERB If something you can see or hear **is distorted**, its appearance or sound is changed so that it seems strange. A painter may exaggerate or distort shapes. ♦ **distorted** ADJ ...the slightly distorted image caused by the projector. ♦ **distortion** N-VAR Audio signals could be transmitted along cables without distortion.

distract /dɪˈstrækt/ **distracts, distracting, distracted.** VERB If something **distracts** you, or if it **distracts** your **attention**, it stops you concentrating. Playing video games sometimes distracts him from his homework. ♦ **distracting** ADJ The barking of the little dog was very distracting.

distracted /dɪˈstræktɪd/. ADJ If you are **distracted**, you are very worried or are not concentrating. ♦ **distractedly** ADV He looked up distractedly. 'Be with you in a second'.

distraction /dɪˈstrækʃən/ **distractions.** **1** N-VAR A **distraction** is something that takes your attention away from what you are doing. This is getting to be a distraction from what I really want to do. **2** N-COUNT A **distraction** is an activity that

is intended to entertain people. Their national distraction is going to the disco.

distraught /dɪˈstrɔːt/. ADJ If someone is **distraught**, they are extremely upset or worried. Mr Barker's distraught parents were last night being comforted by relatives.

distress /dɪˈstres/ **distresses, distressing, distressed.** **1** N-UNCOUNT **Distress** is extreme sorrow, suffering, or pain. Jealousy causes distress and painful emotions. **2** N-UNCOUNT **Distress** is the state of being in extreme danger and needing urgent help. The ship might be in distress. **3** VERB If someone or something **distresses** you, they cause you to be upset or worried. The idea of Toni being in danger distresses him enormously. ♦ **distressed** ADJ She was too exhausted and distressed to talk. ♦ **distressing** ADJ ...distressing news. ♦ **distressingly** ADV Her face had grown distressingly old.

distribute /dɪˈstrɪbjuːt/ **distributes, distributing, distributed.** **1** VERB If you **distribute** things, you hand them or deliver them to a number of people. Soldiers are working to distribute food and blankets. ♦ **distribution** N-UNCOUNT ...the distribution of leaflets and posters. **2** VERB When a company **distributes** goods, it supplies them to the shops or businesses that sell them. ♦ **distribution** N-UNCOUNT ...the production and distribution of goods and services. ♦ **distributor, distributors** N-COUNT ...Spain's largest distributor of petroleum products. **3** VERB If you **distribute** things **among** the members of a group, you share them among those members. Distribute chores evenly among all family members.

⭐ **distribution** /ˌdɪstrɪˈbjuːʃən/ **distributions.** N-VAR The **distribution of** something is how much of it there is in each place or at each time. ...a more equitable distribution of wealth.

⭐ **district** /ˈdɪstrɪkt/ **districts.** **1** N-COUNT A **district** is an area of a town or country. I drove around the business district. **2** N-COUNT A **district** is an area of a town or country which has been given official boundaries for the purpose of administration. ...Glasgow District Council.

district at'torney, district attorneys. N-COUNT In the United States, a **District Attorney** is a lawyer who works as the State prosecutor in a district. The abbreviation **D.A.** is also used.

distrust /ˌdɪsˈtrʌst/ **distrusts, distrusting, distrusted.** VERB & N-UNCOUNT If you **distrust** someone or something, or if you feel **distrust** for them, you think that they are not honest, reliable, or safe. I don't have any particular reason to distrust them. ...a profound distrust of all political authority.

disturb /dɪˈstɜːb/ **disturbs, disturbing, disturbed.** **1** VERB If you **disturb** someone, you interrupt what they are doing and cause them inconvenience. She slept in a separate room in order not to disturb him. **2** VERB If something **disturbs** you, it makes you feel upset or worried. ...dreams so vivid that they disturb me for days.

A
B
C
D
E
F
G
H
I
J
K
L
M
N
O
P
Q
R
S
T
U
V
W
X
Y
Z

3 VERB If something **is disturbed**, its position or shape is changed. *He'd placed his notes in the brown envelope. They hadn't been disturbed.*

disturbance /dɪˈstɜːbəns/ **disturbances.**
1 N-COUNT A **disturbance** is an incident in which people behave violently in public. *During the disturbance which followed, three Englishmen were hurt.* **2** N-UNCOUNT **Disturbance** means upsetting or disrupting something which was previously in a calm and orderly state. *The old people's home would cause less disturbance to local residents than a school.*

disturbed /dɪˈstɜːbd/. ADJ Someone who is **disturbed** is extremely worried, unhappy, or mentally ill. *...severely emotionally disturbed children.*

disturbing /dɪˈstɜːbɪŋ/. ADJ Something that is **disturbing** makes you feel upset or worried. *There was something about him she found disturbing.* ♦ **disturbingly** ADV *...the disturbingly high frequency of racial attacks.*

disused /ˌdɪsˈjuːzd/. ADJ A **disused** place or building is no longer used. *...a disused airfield.*

ditch /dɪtʃ/ **ditches, ditching, ditched.** **1** N-COUNT A **ditch** is a long narrow channel cut into the ground at the side of a road or field. **2** VERB If you **ditch** something, you get rid of it. [INFORMAL] *I decided to ditch the sofa bed.*

dither /ˈdɪðə/ **dithers, dithering, dithered.** VERB If someone **dithers**, they hesitate because they are unable to make a quick decision about something. *We're still dithering over whether to marry.*

dive /daɪv/ **dives, diving, dived** (AM also **dove**).
1 VERB & N-COUNT If you **dive**, or if you do a **dive**, you jump head-first into water with your arms straight above your head. *She was standing by a pool, about to dive in. ...a dive of 80 feet from the Chasm Bridge.* **2** VERB & N-COUNT If you **dive**, or if you do a **dive**, you go under the surface of the sea or a lake, using special breathing equipment. ♦ **diver, divers** N-COUNT *Police divers have recovered the body of a sixteen year old boy.* ♦ **diving** N-UNCOUNT *...the most popular spots to go diving.* **3** VERB When birds and animals **dive**, they go quickly downwards, head-first, through the air or water. *The shark dived down and swam under the boat.* **4** VERB & N-COUNT If you **dive**, or if you make a **dive**, in a particular direction, you jump or rush in that direction. *They dived into a taxi... He made a sudden dive for Uncle Jim's legs.*

diverge /daɪˈvɜːdʒ/ **diverges, diverging, diverged.** **1** VERB When things **diverge**, they are different, or become different. *His interests increasingly diverged from those of his colleagues.* **2** VERB When roads or paths **diverge**, they begin leading in different directions. *At Orte, the railway lines for Florence and Ancona diverge.*

divergent /daɪˈvɜːdʒənt, AM dɪ-/. ADJ Things that are **divergent** are different from each other. *Similar customs were known in widely divergent cultures.* ♦ **divergence, divergences** N-VAR *There's*

a substantial divergence of opinion within the party.

diverse /daɪˈvɜːs, AM dɪ-/. ADJ If a group or range is **diverse**, it is made up of a wide variety of things. *...shops selling a diverse range of gifts.*

diversify /daɪˈvɜːsɪfaɪ, AM dɪ-/ **diversifies, diversifying, diversified.** VERB When an organization or person **diversifies into** other things, or when they **diversify** their activities, they increase the variety of things that they do or make. *The company's troubles started when it diversified into new products.* ♦ **diversification** /daɪˌvɜːsɪfɪˈkeɪʃən, AM dɪ-/ **diversifications** N-VAR *...diversification of agriculture.*

diversion /daɪˈvɜːʃən, AM dɪˈvɜːrʒən/ **diversions.** **1** N-COUNT A **diversion** is an action or event that attracts your attention away from what you are doing. *...armed robbers who escaped after throwing smoke bombs to create a diversion.* ♦ **diversionary** ADJ *...a diversionary tactic, taking attention away from what the case is all about.* **2** N-COUNT A **diversion** is a special route arranged for traffic when the normal route cannot be used. [BRITISH] ● See also **divert**.

diversity /daɪˈvɜːsɪti, AM dɪ-/ **diversities.** **1** N-VAR The **diversity** of something is the fact that it contains many very different elements. *...to introduce more choice and diversity into the education system.* **2** N-SING A **diversity of** things is a range of things which are very different from each other. *...how to grow a diversity of vegetables.*

divert /daɪˈvɜːt, AM dɪ-/ **diverts, diverting, diverted.** **1** VERB To **divert** people or vehicles means to change their course. *Police are diverting traffic away from the Square.* **2** VERB To **divert** money or resources means to cause them to be used for a different purpose. *The government is trying to divert more public funds from west to east.* ♦ **diversion** N-UNCOUNT *...the illegal diversion of profits from secret arms sales.* **3** VERB If someone **diverts** your attention **from** something important or serious, they stop you thinking about it by making you think about something else. *They want to divert the attention of the people from the real issues.*

★ **divide** /dɪˈvaɪd/ **divides, dividing, divided.** **1** VERB & PHR-VERB To **divide** something or to **divide** it **up**, means to split it up and separate it into two or more parts. *Divide the pastry in half... The idea is to divide up the country into four sectors... Paul divides most of his spare time between the study and his bedroom.* **2** VERB If you **divide** a larger number by a smaller number, you calculate how many times the smaller number can go exactly into the larger number. *Measure the floor area of the greenhouse and divide it by six.* **3** VERB If a border or line **divides** two areas, it keeps them separate from each other. *...the long frontier dividing Mexico from the United States.* **4** VERB If something **divides** people, it causes strong disagreement between them. *...the enormous differences that still divide the two sides.*

♦ **divided** ADJ *The democrats are divided over whether to admit him into their group.* [5] N-COUNT A **divide** is a significant difference between two groups. *...a Hindu-Muslim divide.*
▶**divide up.** See **divide** 1.

⭐ **dividend** /'dɪvɪdend/ **dividends.** [1] N-COUNT A **dividend** is the part of a company's profits which is paid to people who have shares in the company. [2] PHRASE If something **pays dividends**, it brings advantages at a later date. *Steps taken now to maximise your health will pay dividends later on.*

divine /dɪ'vaɪn/. ADJ You use **divine** to describe something that is provided by or relates to a god or goddess. *...a divine punishment.* ♦ **divinely** ADV *The law was divinely ordained.* ♦ **divinity** /dɪ'vɪnɪti/ N-UNCOUNT *...the divinity of Christ's word.*

diving /'daɪvɪŋ/. See **dive**.

⭐ **division** /dɪ'vɪʒən/ **divisions.** [1] N-UNCOUNT The **division of** something is the act of separating it into two or more different parts. *...the unification of Germany, after its division into two states. ...the current division of labor between workers and management.* [2] N-COUNT A **division** is a significant distinction or difference of opinion between two groups. *...the division between the prosperous west and the impoverished east.* [3] N-UNCOUNT **Division** is the mathematical process of dividing one number by another. [4] N-COUNT A **division** is a department in a large organization. *...the bank's Latin American division.* ♦ **divisional** ADJ BEFORE N *...the divisional headquarters.*

divisive /dɪ'vaɪsɪv/. ADJ Something that is **divisive** causes hostility between people. [FORMAL] *Abortion has always been a divisive issue.*

⭐ **divorce** /dɪ'vɔːs/ **divorces, divorcing, divorced.** [1] VERB & N-VAR When someone **divorces** their husband or wife, or obtains a **divorce** from them, their marriage is legally ended. *He and Lillian had got divorced... Numerous marriages now end in divorce.* ♦ **divorced** ADJ *Princess Margaret is divorced from Lord Snowdon.* [2] VERB If one thing **is divorced from** another, they become separate from each other. [FORMAL] *You can't divorce finance from manufacturing.*

divorcee /dɪvɔː'siː/ **divorcees.** N-COUNT A **divorcee** is someone who is divorced.

divulge /daɪ'vʌldʒ, AM dɪ-/ **divulges, divulging, divulged.** VERB If you **divulge** a piece of information, you tell someone about it. [FORMAL] *I do not want to divulge where the village is.*

DIY /,diː aɪ 'waɪ/. N-UNCOUNT **DIY** is the activity of making or repairing things in your home. **DIY** is an abbreviation for 'do-it-yourself'.

dizzy /'dɪzi/. ADJ If you feel **dizzy**, you feel that you are losing your balance and are about to fall. *He kept getting dizzy spells.* ♦ **dizziness** N-UNCOUNT *A wave of dizziness swept over her.*

DJ (or **dj**) /'diː ,dʒeɪ/ **DJs.** N-COUNT A **DJ** is someone who plays and introduces pop records on the radio or at a club.

DNA /,diː en 'eɪ/. N-UNCOUNT **DNA** is an acid that is contained in the cells of living things. It determines the particular structure and functions of every cell. **DNA** is an abbreviation for 'deoxyribonucleic acid'.

⭐ **do** /də, STRONG duː/: **does, doing, did, done.**

✔ Two of the major uses of **do** are in forming negatives and questions.

[1] VERB You use **do** to say that someone performs an action, activity, or task. [2] VERB To **do** something about a problem means to try to solve it. *Though he didn't like it there wasn't much he could do about it.* [3] VERB You use **do** to say that something has a particular result or effect. *A few bombs can do a lot of damage... The publicity did her career no harm.* [4] VERB If you ask someone what they **do**, you are asking what their job is. [5] VERB If someone **does** well or badly, they are successful or unsuccessful. *Connie did well at school.* [6] VERB If you **do** a subject, you study it at school or college. *I'd like to do maths at university.* [7] VERB You use **do** when referring to the speed that something achieves or can achieve. *They were doing 70 miles an hour.* [8] VERB If you say that something will **do**, you mean that it is satisfactory. *Give them a prize. Anything will do.* [9] N-COUNT A **do** is a party, dinner party, or other social event. [BRITISH, INFORMAL] *A friend of his is having a do in Stoke... They always have all-night dos there.* [10] See also **done.**

PHRASES ● If you say that you **could do with** something, you mean that you need it or would benefit from it. *I could do with a cup of tea.* ● If you ask **what** someone **is doing** in a particular place, you are expressing surprise that they are there. *What was he doing in Hyde Park at that time of the morning?* ● What something **has to do with** or **is to do with** is what it is connected or concerned with. *They were shouting at each other. It was something to do with money.*
▶**do away with.** PHR-VERB To **do away with** something means to get rid of it. *The long-range goal must be to do away with nuclear weapons.*
▶**do out of.** PHR-VERB If you **do** someone **out of** something, you unfairly cause them not to have it. [INFORMAL] *The others have done him out of his share.*
▶**do up.** [1] PHR-VERB If you **do** something **up**, you fasten it. *Mari did up the buttons... Do your coat up.* [2] PHR-VERB To **do up** an old building means to repair and decorate it. *Nicholas has bought a barn in Provence and is spending August doing it up.*
▶**do without.** PHR-VERB If you **do without** something, you manage or survive in spite of not having it. *We can't do without the help of your organisation.*

dock /dɒk/ **docks, docking, docked.** [1] N-COUNT A **dock** is an enclosed area of water where ships are loaded, unloaded, or repaired. [2] VERB When a ship **docks** or **is docked**, it is brought into a dock. *The vessel docked at Liverpool.* [3] VERB

a b c d e f g h i j k l m n o p q r s t u v w x y z

⭐ Bank of English® frequent word   For a full explanation of all grammatical labels, see pages vii-x

A
B
C
D ★
E
F
G
H
I
J
K
L
M ★
N
O
P
Q
R
S
T
U
V
W
X
Y
Z

When one spacecraft **docks** or **is docked with** another, they join together in space. [4] N-SING In a law court, **the dock** is the place where the person accused of a crime sits. [BRITISH] [5] VERB If you **dock** something such as someone's salary, you take some of it away as a punishment. *Soccer's governing body has recommended docking two points from the league champions.*

★ **doctor** /'dɒktə/ **doctors, doctoring, doctored.** [1] N-COUNT & N-TITLE & N-VOC A **doctor** is someone qualified in medicine who treats people who are ill. *Don't hesitate to call the doctor if you are at all uneasy... Doctor Paige will be here right after lunch.* [2] N-SING **The doctor's** is used to refer to the surgery or clinic where a doctor works. *I have an appointment at the doctor's.* [3] N-COUNT & N-TITLE **Doctor** is the title given to someone who has been awarded the highest academic degree by a university. ...*a doctor of philosophy.* [4] VERB To **doctor** something means to deliberately change it in order to deceive people. *They doctored the prints, deepening the lines to make her look as awful as possible.*

doctorate /'dɒktərət/ **doctorates.** N-COUNT A **doctorate** is the highest degree awarded by a university.

doctrine /'dɒktrɪn/ **doctrines.** N-VAR A **doctrine** is a set of principles or beliefs. ...*orthodox Christian doctrine.* ♦ **doctrinal** /dɒk'traɪnəl, AM 'dɑːktrɪnəl/ ADJ ...*the pursuit of doctrinal goals.*

★ **document, documents, documenting, documented.** [1] N-COUNT /'dɒkjəmənt/ A **document** is an official piece of paper with writing on it. ...*travel documents.* [2] VERB /'dɒkjəment/ If you **document** something, you make a detailed record of it on film, tape, or paper. ...*a book documenting his prison experiences.*

documentary /,dɒkjə'mentri/ **documentaries.** [1] N-COUNT A **documentary** is a radio or television programme or a film which provides factual information about a particular subject. ...*a TV documentary on homelessness.* [2] ADJ BEFORE N **Documentary** evidence consists of things that are written down.

documentation /,dɒkjəmen'teɪʃən/. N-UNCOUNT **Documentation** consists of documents which provide a record of something. *I had full documentation of our additional expenses.*

docusoap /'dɒkjəsəʊp/ **docusoaps.** N-COUNT A **docusoap** is a television programme that shows the daily lives of real ordinary people.

dodge /dɒdʒ/ **dodges, dodging, dodged.** [1] VERB If you **dodge** somewhere, you move there suddenly to avoid being hit, caught, or seen. *We dodged behind a pillar out of sight of the tourists.* [2] VERB If you **dodge** a moving object, you avoid it by quickly moving aside. *He desperately dodged a speeding car trying to run him down.* [3] VERB If you **dodge** something such as a problem, you avoid thinking about it or dealing with it. ...*dodging military service by feigning illness.*

dodgy /'dɒdʒi/ **dodgier, dodgiest.** [1] ADJ If you describe someone or something as **dodgy**, you disapprove of them because they seem rather dishonest and unreliable. [2] ADJ If you say that something is **dodgy**, you mean that it seems rather risky or unreliable. ...*some pretty dodgy airport food.*

does /dəz, STRONG dʌz/. **Does** is the third person singular of the present tense of **do**.

doesn't /'dʌzənt/. **Doesn't** is the usual spoken form of 'does not'.

★ **dog** /dɒg, AM 'dɔːg/ **dogs, dogging, dogged.** [1] N-COUNT A **dog** is an animal that is often kept as a pet or used to guard or hunt things. → See picture on page 815. [2] VERB If problems or injuries **dog** you, they keep affecting you. *His retirement was dogged by illnesses.*

dogged /'dɒgɪd, AM 'dɔː-/. ADJ BEFORE N If you describe someone's actions as **dogged**, you mean that they are determined to continue with something, however difficult it becomes. ...*one man's dogged determination to do something everyone else considered eccentric.* ♦ **doggedness** N-UNCOUNT *Most of my accomplishments came as the result of sheer doggedness.* ♦ **doggedly** ADV *She would fight doggedly for her rights.*

dogma /'dɒgmə, AM 'dɔːg-/ **dogmas.** N-VAR If you refer to a belief or a system of beliefs as a **dogma**, you are criticizing it for expecting people to accept that it is true without questioning it. *The unions accuse the government of political dogma.*

dogmatic /dɒg'mætɪk, AM dɔːg-/. ADJ If you say that someone is **dogmatic**, you are criticizing them for following rules or principles rigidly without paying any attention to other factors. ...*a dogmatic approach to solving political issues.* ♦ **dogmatically** ADV *He would not dogmatically oppose government intervention.* ♦ **dogmatism** /'dɒgmətɪzəm, AM 'dɔːg-/ N-UNCOUNT *We cannot allow dogmatism to stand in the way of progress.*

do-it-your'self. N-UNCOUNT **Do-it-yourself** is the activity of making or repairing things in your home yourself, rather than employing other people.

doldrums /'dɒldrəmz/. PHRASE If an area of activity is **in the doldrums**, nothing new or exciting is happening.

dole /dəʊl/ **doles, doling, doled.** [1] N-UNCOUNT In British English, **the dole** is money that is given regularly by the government to people who are unemployed. The usual American word is **welfare**. [2] PHRASES In British English, someone who is **on the dole** is registered as unemployed and receives money to live on from the government. The usual American expression is **on welfare**.

▶**dole out.** PHR-VERB If you **dole** something **out**, you give a certain amount of it to each member of a group.

doll /dɒl/ **dolls.** N-COUNT A **doll** is a child's toy which looks like a small person or baby.

⭐ **dollar** /'dɒlə/ **dollars.** N-COUNT The **dollar** is a unit of money in the USA, Canada, and some other countries. It is represented by the symbol $.

dolphin /'dɒlfɪn/ **dolphins.** N-COUNT A **dolphin** is a mammal with fins and a pointed nose which lives in the sea.

domain /dəʊ'meɪn/ **domains.** ☐1 N-COUNT A **domain** is a particular area of activity or interest. [FORMAL] ...the great experimenters in the domain of art. ☐2 N-COUNT Someone's **domain** is the area where they have control or influence. [FORMAL] The kitchen is by no means his wife's domain.

dome /dəʊm/ **domes.** N-COUNT A **dome** is a round roof. ...the dome of St Paul's cathedral.

⭐ **domestic** /də'mestɪk/. ☐1 ADJ **Domestic** political activities and situations happen or exist within one particular country. ...a mixture of domestic and foreign news. ...over 100 domestic flights a day to 15 UK destinations. ☐2 ADJ BEFORE N **Domestic** means relating to or concerned with the home and family. ...domestic violence between husband and wife. ...domestic appliances. ☐3 ADJ BEFORE N **Domestic** animals are not wild, and are kept as pets or on farms.

dominant /'dɒmɪnənt/. ADJ Someone or something that is **dominant** is more powerful or noticeable than other people or things. She was a dominant figure in the French film industry. ♦ **dominance** N-UNCOUNT ...the dominance of the scientific method in the modern world.

⭐ **dominate** /'dɒmɪneɪt/ **dominates, dominating, dominated.** ☐1 VERB To **dominate** a situation means to be the most powerful or important person or thing in it. The book is expected to dominate the best-seller lists. ...countries where life is dominated by war. ♦ **domination** N-UNCOUNT ...the domination of the market by a small number of organizations. ☐2 VERB If one person **dominates** another, they have power over them. Women are no longer dominated by the men in their relationships. ♦ **dominating** ADJ He had a very dominating personality. ♦ **domination** N-UNCOUNT ...five centuries of domination by the Romans.

dominion /də'mɪnjən/ **dominions.** ☐1 N-UNCOUNT **Dominion** is control or authority. [FORMAL] They truly believe they have dominion over us. ☐2 N-COUNT A **dominion** is an area of land that is controlled by a ruler. The Republic is a dominion of the Brazilian people.

domino /'dɒmɪnəʊ/ **dominoes.** N-VAR **Dominoes** is a game played using small rectangular blocks, called **dominoes**, which are marked with two groups of spots on one side.

donate /dəʊ'neɪt/ **donates, donating, donated.** ☐1 VERB If you **donate** something to a charity or other organization, you give it to them. Others donated second-hand clothes. ♦ **donation, donations** N-VAR ...the donation of his collection to the art gallery. ☐2 VERB If you **donate** your blood or a part of your body, you allow doctors to use it to help somebody who is ill. ♦ **donation** N-UNCOUNT ... kidney donation.

⭐ **done** /dʌn/. ☐1 **Done** is the past participle of **do.** ☐2 ADJ AFTER LINK-V A task that is **done** has been completed. The damage was done by the time Giggs came... As soon as the cake is done, remove it from the oven.

donkey /'dɒŋki/ **donkeys.** N-COUNT A **donkey** is an animal like a small horse with long ears. → See picture on page 815.

donor /'dəʊnə/ **donors.** ☐1 N-COUNT A **donor** is someone who gives a part of their body or some of their blood to be used by doctors to help a person who is ill. ☐2 N-COUNT A **donor** is someone who gives something such as money to a charity or other organization.

don't /dəʊnt/. **Don't** is the usual spoken form of **do not.**

donut /'dəʊnʌt/ **donuts.** See **doughnut.**

doom /duːm/. N-UNCOUNT **Doom** is a terrible state or event in the future which you cannot prevent. I awoke with a terrible sense of doom and fear.

doomed /duːmd/. ☐1 ADJ Someone or something that is **doomed** is certain to fail. ...a doomed attempt to rescue the children. ☐2 ADJ If someone is **doomed** to an unpleasant fate, they are certain to suffer it. If he lived, he would be doomed to spend the war as a prisoner.

⭐ **door** /dɔː/ **doors.** ☐1 N-COUNT A **door** is a swinging or sliding piece of wood, glass, or metal, which is used to open and close the entrance to a building, room, cupboard, or vehicle. I was knocking at the front door; there was no answer. ☐2 N-COUNT A **door** is the space in a wall when a door is open. She looked through the door. PHRASES ● When you **answer the door**, you go and open the door because a visitor has knocked on it or rung the bell. ● If someone goes **from door to door** or goes **door to door**, they go along a street calling at each house in turn, for example selling something. ● When you are **out of doors**, you are not inside a building, but in the open air. The weather was fine enough for working out of doors. ● See also **next door.**

doorstep /'dɔːstep/ **doorsteps.** ☐1 N-COUNT A **doorstep** is a step on the outside of a building, in front of a door. ☐2 PHRASE If a place is **on** your **doorstep**, it is very near to where you live. ...a giant oil refinery right on their doorstep.

doorway /'dɔːweɪ/ **doorways.** N-COUNT A **doorway** is the space in a wall where a door opens and closes. He stood in the doorway, smiling.

dope /dəʊp/ **dopes, doping, doped.** ☐1 N-UNCOUNT **Dope** is an illegal drug, especially cannabis. [INFORMAL] ☐2 VERB If someone **dopes** a person or animal, they force them or trick them into taking drugs.

dormant /'dɔːmənt/. ADJ Something that is **dormant** has not been active or used for a long

a b c d e f g h i j k l m n o p q r s t u v w x y z

A
B
C
D
E
F
G
H
I
J
K
L
M
N
O
P
Q
R
S
T
U
V
W
X
Y
Z

time, but is capable of becoming active. *...the long dormant volcano... The buds will remain dormant until spring.*

dormitory /ˈdɔːmɪtri, AM -tɔːri/ **dormitories.** N-COUNT A **dormitory** is a large bedroom where several people sleep, for example in a boarding school.

dosage /ˈdəʊsɪdʒ/ **dosages.** N-COUNT The **dosage** of a medicine or drug is the amount that should be taken. *...the correct dosage of insulin.*

dose /dəʊs/ **doses, dosing, dosed.** ☐1 N-COUNT A **dose** of a medicine or drug is a measured amount of it. *One dose of penicillin can wipe out the infection.* ☐2 VERB To **dose** someone means to give them a medicine or drug. *...the machine that was dosing her with painkillers.*

dosh /dɒʃ/. N-UNCOUNT **Dosh** is money. [BRITISH, INFORMAL]

dossier /ˈdɒsieɪ, -iə/ **dossiers.** N-COUNT A **dossier** is a collection of papers containing information on a particular subject. *The government kept dossiers on thousands of its citizens.*

dot /dɒt/ **dots.** N-COUNT A **dot** is a very small round mark. *...a black dot in the middle of the circle.*

ˌdot-ˈcom (or **dot com**), **dot-coms.** N-COUNT A **dot-com** is a company that does all or most of its business on the Internet.

dote /dəʊt/ **dotes, doting, doted.** VERB If you **dote on** someone, you love them very much and ignore their faults. *He dotes on his nine-year-old son.* ♦ **doting** ADJ *...his doting parents.*

dotted /ˈdɒtɪd/. ☐1 ADJ **Dotted** lines are made of a row of dots. *Cut along the dotted line.* ☐2 ADJ AFTER LINK-V If an area is **dotted with** things, it has many of those things scattered over its surface. *The maps were dotted with the names of small towns... Many pieces of sculpture are dotted around the house.*

⭐ **double** /ˈdʌbəl/ **doubles, doubling, doubled.** ☐1 ADJ BEFORE N You use **double** to describe a pair of similar things. *...a pair of double doors... Ring four two, double two, double two if you'd like to speak to our financial adviser. ...an extremely nasty double murder.* ☐2 ADJ You use **double** to describe something which is twice the normal size or twice the normal capacity. *...a large double garage... Allow the loaves to rise until just about double in size.* ☐3 ADJ & N-COUNT A **double** room, or a **double**, is a room that is intended to be used by two people. *The Great Western Hotel is ideal, costing around £60 a night for a double.* ☐4 VERB If something **doubles**, or if you **double** it, it becomes twice as large. *The program will double the amount of money available.* ☐5 VERB If a person or thing **doubles as** someone or something else, they have a second job or purpose as well as their main one. *...drug dealers who double as police informers.* ☐6 N-UNCOUNT **Doubles** is a game of tennis or badminton in which two people play against two other people. ☐7 PHRASE If you **bend double**, you bend right

over. If you **are bent double**, you are bending right over. ☐8 **in double figures**: see **figure**.
▶**double up** or **double over.** PHR-VERB If you **double up**, or if you **double over**, you bend your body quickly or violently. *She doubled up with laughter... I was doubled over in agony.*

double bass /ˌdʌbəl ˈbeɪs/ **double basses.** N-VAR A **double bass** is the largest instrument in the violin family. You play it standing up. → See picture on page 827.

ˌdouble-ˈglaze, double-glazes, double-glazing, double-glazed. VERB If someone **double-glazes** a house or its windows, they fit the windows with a second layer of glass which keeps the inside of the house warmer and quieter. ♦ **double-glazing** N-UNCOUNT *Doreen had double-glazing put into their bungalow.*

doubly /ˈdʌbli/. ☐1 ADV You use **doubly** to say that a situation has two aspects or features. *She now felt doubly guilty; she had embarrassed Franklin and she had cost her partner money.* ☐2 ADV You use **doubly** to say that something happens or is true to a greater degree than usual. *In pregnancy a high fibre diet is doubly important.*

⭐ **doubt** /daʊt/ **doubts, doubting, doubted.** ☐1 N-VAR If you feel **doubt** or **doubts** about something, you feel uncertain about it. *This raises doubts about the point of advertising... There can be little doubt that you can try too hard.* ☐2 VERB If you **doubt** something, or if you **doubt** whether something is true or possible, you believe that it is probably not true, genuine, or possible. *No one doubted his ability... He doubted if he would learn anything new.* ☐3 VERB If you **doubt** someone, or if you **doubt** their **word**, you think they might not be telling the truth. *Don't think I'm doubting you.*
PHRASES ● If you are **in doubt** about something, or if it is **in doubt**, you are uncertain about it. *He is in no doubt as to what is needed... The outcome was still in doubt.* ● If something is **beyond doubt**, or if it is **beyond reasonable doubt**, you are certain that it is true. *She knew now beyond doubt that her husband loved her.* ● You use **no doubt** to emphasize that something seems very likely to you. *No doubt we will meet again.* ● You use **without doubt** or **without a doubt** to emphasize that something is true. *He is, without doubt, the best player in the world.* ● to **give** someone the **benefit of the doubt**: see **benefit**.

doubtful /ˈdaʊtfʊl/. ☐1 ADJ Something that is **doubtful** seems unlikely or uncertain. *It is doubtful whether he will appear again.* ☐2 ADJ If you are **doubtful** about something, you are uncertain about it. *I was still very doubtful about the chances for success.* ♦ **doubtfully** ADV *Keeton shook his head doubtfully.*

doubtless /ˈdaʊtləs/. ADV If you say that something is **doubtless** the case, you mean that you think it is probably or almost certainly the case. *They will doubtless get their land back.*

dough /dəʊ/. N-UNCOUNT **Dough** is a mixture of flour and water, and sometimes also sugar and fat, which is cooked to make bread, pastry, and biscuits.

doughnut (or **donut**) /'dəʊnʌt/ **doughnuts.**
N-COUNT A **doughnut** is a lump or ring of sweet dough cooked in hot fat.

dour /dʊə, daʊə/. ADJ Someone who is **dour** has a severe and unfriendly manner.

douse (or **dowse**) /daʊs/ **douses, dousing, doused.**
[1] VERB If you **douse** a fire, you stop it burning by pouring a lot of water over it. [2] VERB If you **douse** someone or something **with** a liquid, you throw a lot of that liquid over them. *They doused their victim with petrol.*

dove, doves. [1] N-COUNT /dʌv/ A **dove** is a bird that looks like a pigeon. [2] /dəʊv/ **Dove** is a past tense of **dive.** [AMERICAN]

down 1 preposition and adverb uses

⭐ **down** /daʊn/. [1] PREP & ADV **Down** means towards the ground or a lower level, or in a lower place. *A man came down the stairs. ...a ledge 40ft down the rock face... She was still looking down at her papers.* [2] ADV If you put something **down,** you put it onto a surface. *Danny put down his glass.* [3] PREP If you go **down** a road or river, you go along it. *...a few miles down the road at Burnham.* [4] ADV **Down** is often used to mean in the south or towards the south. *I went down to L.A. all the way from Seattle.* [5] ADV If the amount or level of something goes **down,** it decreases. *My weight went down to seventy pounds.* [6] PREP If someone or something is **down for** something, it has been arranged that they will do it or it will happen to them. *Mark had told me that he was down for an interview.* [7] **up and down:** see **up.**
● **ups and downs:** see **up.**

down 2 adjective uses

down /daʊn/. [1] ADJ AFTER LINK-V If you are feeling **down,** you are feeling unhappy or depressed. [INFORMAL] [2] ADJ AFTER LINK-V If something is **down on** paper, it has been written on the paper. *That date wasn't down on our news sheet.* [3] ADJ AFTER LINK-V If a piece of equipment, especially a computer system, is **down,** it is temporarily not working because of a fault. [COMPUTING]

down 3 noun use

down /daʊn/. N-UNCOUNT **Down** consists of the small soft feathers on young birds.

downfall /'daʊnfɔːl/. [1] N-UNCOUNT The **downfall** of a successful or powerful person or institution is their failure. *His lack of experience had led to his downfall.* [2] N-UNCOUNT Something that is someone's **downfall** is the thing that causes them to fail. *His honesty had been his downfall.*

downgrade /daʊn'grɪd/ **downgrades, downgrading, downgraded.** VERB If someone or something **is downgraded,** their situation is changed to a lower level of importance or value. *The boy's condition has been downgraded from critical to serious... I was downgraded to a clerical job.*

downhill /daʊn'hɪl/. [1] ADV & ADJ BEFORE N If someone or something is moving **downhill,** they are moving down a slope. *He headed downhill towards the river. ...downhill ski runs.* [2] ADV You can say that something is going **downhill** when it is becoming worse.

Downing Street /'daʊnɪŋ striːt/. N-PROPER **Downing Street** is the street in London in which the Prime Minister and the Chancellor of the Exchequer live. You can also use **Downing Street** to refer to the Prime Minister and his or her officials.

download /ˌdaʊn'ləʊd/ **downloads, downloading, downloaded.** VERB To **download** data means to transfer it to or from a computer along a line such as a telephone line, a radio link, or a computer network. [COMPUTING] *Users can download their material to a desktop PC back in the office.*

'down payment, down payments. N-COUNT If you make a **down payment on** something, you pay a percentage of the total cost when you buy it. You pay the remaining amount later.

downpour /'daʊnpɔː/ **downpours.** N-COUNT A **downpour** is a heavy fall of rain.

downright /'daʊnraɪt/. ADV & ADJ BEFORE N You use **downright** to emphasize unpleasant or bad qualities or behaviour. *...ideas that would have been downright dangerous. ...suspicion and downright hostility.*

downside /'daʊnsaɪd/. N-SING The **downside** of a situation is the aspect of it which is less positive, pleasant, or useful than its other aspects. *The downside of this approach is a lack of clear leadership.*

downstairs /ˌdaʊn'steəz/. [1] ADV If you go **downstairs** in a building, you go down a staircase towards the ground floor. [2] ADV & ADJ BEFORE N If something or someone is **downstairs,** they are on the ground floor or on a lower floor than you. *...the flat downstairs. ...the downstairs rooms.*

downstream /ˌdaʊn'striːm/. ADV & ADJ BEFORE N **Downstream** means towards the mouth of a river. *We had drifted downstream... Breaking the dam could submerge downstream cities.*

,down-to-'earth. ADJ Someone who is **down-to-earth** is concerned with practical things, rather than with theories; used showing approval.

downtown /'daʊntaʊn/. ADV & ADJ BEFORE N **Downtown** means in or towards the centre of a city. *By day he worked downtown. ...downtown Chicago.*

downturn /'daʊntɜːn/ **downturns.** N-COUNT If there is a **downturn in** the economy, it becomes worse or less successful.

downwards /'daʊnwədz/.

☑ In usual British English, **downwards** is an adverb and **downward** is an adjective. In formal British English and in American English, **downward** is both an adjective and an adverb.

A B C D E F G H I J K L M N O P Q R S T U V W X Y Z

[1] ADV & ADJ If you move or look **downwards**, you move or look towards the ground or a lower level. *Benedict pointed downwards. ...a firm downward movement of the hands.* **[2]** ADV & ADJ If an amount or rate moves **downwards**, it decreases. *...the downward trend in home ownership.*

dowse /daʊs/. See **douse**.

doze /dəʊz/ **dozes, dozing, dozed.** VERB & N-SING When you **doze**, or when you have **a doze**, you sleep lightly or for a short period.
▸ **doze off.** PHR-VERB If you **doze off**, you fall into a light sleep. *Salter dozed off for a few moments.*

⭐ **dozen** /'dʌzən/ **dozens. [1]** NUM A **dozen** means twelve. *...two dozen eggs.* **[2]** QUANT If you refer to **dozens of** things or people, you are emphasizing that there are many of them. *...dozens of homes.*

⭐ **Dr, Drs. Dr** is a written abbreviation for **Doctor**.

drab /dræb/. ADJ Something that is **drab** is dull and not attractive or exciting. ♦ **drabness** N-UNCOUNT *...the dusty drabness of nearby villages.*

draconian /drə'kəʊniən/. ADJ **Draconian** laws or measures are extremely harsh. [FORMAL]

⭐ **draft** /drɑːft, dræft/ **drafts, drafting, drafted.** **[1]** VERB & N-COUNT When you **draft** a piece of writing, you write the first version of it, called a **draft**. *He drafted a standard letter to the editors.* **[2]** VERB If you **are drafted**, you are ordered to serve in the armed forces. **[3]** VERB If people **are drafted into** a place, they are moved there to do a particular job. *Extra police have been drafted into the town.* **[4]** See also **draught**.

⭐ **drag** /dræg/ **drags, dragging, dragged. [1]** VERB If you **drag** something or someone somewhere, you pull them there with difficulty. *He got up and dragged his chair towards the table... He drags his leg, and he can hardly lift his arm.* **[2]** VERB To **drag** a computer image means to use the mouse to move the position of the image on the screen, or to change its size or shape. *Use your mouse to drag the pictures to their new size.* **[3]** VERB If you **drag** someone somewhere, you make them go there, although they may be unwilling. *...when you can drag him away from his work... I find it really hard to drag myself out and exercise regularly.* **[4]** VERB If a period of time or an event **drags**, it is very boring and seems to last a long time. *The minutes dragged past.* **[5]** VERB If the police **drag** a river or lake, they pull nets or hooks across the bottom of it in order to look for something.

PHRASES ● If you **drag** your **feet**, or if you **drag** your **heels**, you delay doing something or do it very slowly because you do not want to do it. ● If a man is **in drag**, he is wearing women's clothes.
▸ **drag out. [1]** PHR-VERB If you **drag** something **out**, you make it last for longer than is necessary. *...a company that was willing to drag out the proceedings for years.* **[2]** PHR-VERB If you **drag** something **out of** someone, you persuade them to tell you something that they do not want to tell you.

dragon /'drægən/ **dragons.** N-COUNT In stories and legends, a **dragon** is an animal like a big lizard. It has wings and claws, and breathes out fire.

dragonfly /'drægənflaɪ/ **dragonflies.** N-COUNT A **dragonfly** is a brightly coloured insect with a long thin body and two sets of wings. → See picture on page 824.

⭐ **drain** /dreɪn/ **drains, draining, drained. [1]** VERB If you **drain** a liquid from a place or object, you remove the liquid by causing it to flow somewhere else. If a liquid **drains** somewhere, it flows there. *Miners built the tunnel to drain water out of the mines.* **[2]** N-COUNT A **drain** is a pipe that carries water or sewage away from a place, or an opening in a surface that leads to the pipe. **[3]** VERB If you **drain** a place or object, you remove the liquid that has been in it or surrounding it. *Drain the pasta well... The soil drains freely.* **[4]** VERB If something **drains** you, it exhausts you physically and emotionally. ♦ **drained** ADJ *She sighed and collapsed, completely drained.* ♦ **draining** ADJ *I've been through a very draining time.* **[5]** N-SING If something or someone is **a drain on** resources, they use them up. *...citizens who are a drain on public resources.* **[6]** PHRASE If you say that something is going **down the drain**, you mean that it is being destroyed or wasted. [INFORMAL]

drainage /'dreɪnɪdʒ/. N-UNCOUNT **Drainage** is the system or process by which water or other liquids are drained from a place.

⭐ **drama** /'drɑːmə/ **dramas. [1]** N-COUNT A **drama** is a serious play for the theatre, television, or radio. **[2]** N-UNCOUNT You refer to plays in general as **drama**. *He knew nothing of Greek drama.* **[3]** N-VAR You can refer to exciting or dangerous aspects of a real situation as its **drama**. *...all the ingredients of high political drama.*

⭐ **dramatic** /drə'mætɪk/ **dramatics. [1]** ADJ A **dramatic** change is sudden and noticeable. *Air safety has not improved since the dramatic advances of the 1970s.* ♦ **dramatically** ADV *The cost of living has increased dramatically.* **[2]** ADJ A **dramatic** action, event, or situation is exciting and impressive. *...a dramatic display of fireworks.*

dramatics /drə'mætɪks/.

☑ The form **dramatic** is used as a modifier.

N-UNCOUNT You use **dramatics** to refer to activities connected with the theatre and drama. *...an amateur dramatics class. ...a dramatic arts major in college.*

dramatist /'dræmətɪst/ **dramatists.** N-COUNT A **dramatist** is someone who writes plays.

dramatize (BRIT also **dramatise**) /'dræmətaɪz/ **dramatizes, dramatizing, dramatized.** **[1]** VERB If a book or story **is dramatized**, it is written or presented as a play, a film, or a television drama. ♦ **dramatization, dramatizations** N-COUNT *...a dramatisation of D H Lawrence's novel, 'Lady Chatterley's Lover'.* **[2]** VERB If someone **dramatizes** an event or situation, they try to make it seem more serious or exciting than it really is; used showing disapproval. *They* *have tried very hard to dramatize their own experience as victims.*

drank /dræŋk/. **Drank** is the past tense of **drink**.

drape /dreɪp/ **drapes, draping, draped.** ① VERB If you **drape** a piece of cloth somewhere, you place it there so that it hangs down. *Natasha took the coat and draped it over her shoulders... He draped himself in the Canadian flag.* ② N-PLURAL In American English, **drapes** are pieces of heavy fabric you hang across a window and close to keep the light out or stop people looking in. The British word is **curtains**.

drastic /ˈdræstɪk/. ① ADJ A **drastic** course of action is extreme and is usually taken urgently. *He's not going to do anything drastic about economic policy.* ② ADJ A **drastic** change is a very great change. ♦ **drastically** ADV *Services have been drastically reduced.*

draught (AM **draft**) /drɑːft, dræft/ **draughts.** N-COUNT A **draught** is an unwelcome current of air coming into a room or vehicle. *You need fresh air but obviously don't want to be in a draught.*

⭐ **draw** /drɔː/ **draws, drawing, drew, drawn.** ① VERB When you **draw**, or when you **draw** something, you use a pencil, pen, or crayon to produce a picture, pattern, or diagram. *He starts a painting by quickly drawing simplified shapes.* ♦ **drawing** N-UNCOUNT *I like dancing, singing and drawing.* ② VERB You can use **draw** to indicate that someone or something moves somewhere or is moved there. *Claire had seen the taxi drawing away... He drew her close to him... He drew his chair nearer the fire.* ③ VERB If you **draw** a curtain or blind, you pull it across a window to cover or uncover the window. ④ VERB If someone **draws** a gun, knife, or other weapon, they pull it out of its holder so that it is ready to use. ⑤ VERB If you **draw** a deep breath, you breathe in deeply once. ⑥ VERB If you **draw** something into or out of a particular place, you cause it to go into or come out of that place. *Villagers still have to draw their water from wells.* ⑦ VERB If you **draw** money out of a bank or building society, you take it out so that you can use it. ⑧ VERB If you **draw** a comparison, conclusion, or distinction, you decide that it exists or is true. *...literary critics drawing comparisons between George Sand and George Eliot.* ⑨ VERB If you **draw** someone's attention **to** something, you make them aware of it. *He wants to draw attention to the plight of the unemployed.* ⑩ VERB If someone or something **draws** a particular reaction, people react to it in that way. *Such a policy would inevitably draw fierce resistance from farmers.* ⑪ PHRASE When an event or period of time **draws to an end**, or when it **draws to a close**, it finishes. *The conflict was drawing to a close.* ⑫ See also **drawing, drawn**.

▸**draw in** or **draw into.** PHR-VERB If you **draw** someone **in**, or if you **draw** them **into** something you are involved with, you cause them to become involved in it. *She is said to be the*

perfect hostess, drawing everyone into the conversation.

▸**draw on.** ① PHR-VERB If you **draw on** or **draw upon** something such as your skills or experience, you use them. *He drew on his experience as a yachtsman to make a documentary programme.* ② PHR-VERB As a period of time **draws on**, it passes and the end of it gets closer. *...as the afternoon drew on.*

▸**draw up.** ① PHR-VERB When you **draw up** a document, list, or plan, you prepare it and write it out. *...a working party to draw up a formal agreement.* ② PHR-VERB If you **draw up** a chair, you move it nearer to a person or place.

▸**draw upon.** See **draw on** 1.

drawback /ˈdrɔːbæk/ **drawbacks.** N-COUNT A **drawback** is an aspect of something that makes it less acceptable. *The apartment's only drawback was that it was too small.*

drawer /ˈdrɔːə/ **drawers.** N-COUNT A **drawer** is a part of a desk or other piece of furniture that is shaped like a rectangular box. You pull it towards you to open it.

drawing /ˈdrɔːɪŋ/ **drawings.** N-COUNT A **drawing** is a picture made with a pencil, pen, or crayon. *She did a drawing of me.* ● See also **draw**.

'**drawing room, drawing rooms.** N-COUNT A **drawing room** is a room, especially a large room in a large house, where people sit and relax. [DATED]

drawl /drɔːl/ **drawls, drawling, drawled.** VERB & N-COUNT If someone **drawls**, or if they speak in a **drawl**, they speak slowly, with long vowel sounds. *'You guys don't mind if I smoke?' he drawled. ...Jack's southern drawl.*

drawn /drɔːn/. ① **Drawn** is the past participle of **draw**. ② ADJ If someone looks **drawn**, they look very tired or ill.

,**drawn-'out.** ADJ You describe something as **drawn-out** when it lasts longer than you think it should. *...a long drawn-out war.*

dread /dred/ **dreads, dreading, dreaded.** ① VERB If you **dread** something unpleasant which may happen, you feel anxious about it. *I dreaded coming back... I'd been dreading that the birth would take a long time.* ② N-UNCOUNT **Dread** is a feeling of great anxiety and fear about something that may happen.

dreaded /ˈdredɪd/. ADJ BEFORE N **Dreaded** means terrible and greatly feared. *...how to treat this dreaded disease.*

dreadful /ˈdredfʊl/. ADJ If you say that something is **dreadful**, you mean that it is very unpleasant or very poor in quality. *They told us the dreadful news... My financial situation is dreadful.* ♦ **dreadfully** ADV *I've behaved absolutely dreadfully.*

⭐ **dream** /driːm/ **dreams, dreaming, dreamed** or **dreamt** /dremt/. ① VERB & N-COUNT When you **dream**, or when you **have** a **dream**, you experience imaginary events in your mind while you are asleep. *Ivor dreamed that he was on a bus... He*

had a dream about Claire. **2** VERB If you often think about something that you would very much like to happen or have, you can say that you **dream of** it. *As a schoolgirl, she had dreamed of becoming an actress.* **3** N-COUNT You can describe something that you would very much like to happen or have as your **dream**. *...his dream of becoming a pilot.* **4** VERB If you say you **would not dream of** doing something, you are emphasizing that you would not do it. *I wouldn't dream of making fun of you.*
▸**dream up.** PHR-VERB If you **dream up** a plan or idea, you work it out or create it in your mind. *I dreamed up a plan to solve both problems.*

dreamer /ˈdriːmə/ **dreamers.** N-COUNT Someone who is a **dreamer** looks forward to pleasant things that may never happen, rather than being realistic and practical.

dreamy /ˈdriːmi/ **dreamier, dreamiest.** ADJ If someone has a **dreamy** expression, they are not paying attention to things around them and look as if they are thinking about something pleasant. *He smiled, an odd, dreamy smile.*

dreary /ˈdrɪəri/ **drearier, dreariest.** ADJ If something is **dreary**, it is so dull that it makes you feel bored or depressed. *...a dreary little town.*

dredge /dredʒ/ **dredges, dredging, dredged.** VERB To **dredge** a river means to clear a channel by removing mud from the bottom.
▸**dredge up.** PHR-VERB If someone **dredges up** a piece of information they learnt a long time ago, or if they **dredge up** a distant memory, they manage to remember it. *...an American trying to dredge up some French or German learned in high school.*

drench /drentʃ/ **drenches, drenching, drenched.** VERB To **drench** something or someone means to make them completely wet. *...getting drenched by icy water.* ◆ **drenched** ADJ *We were completely drenched and cold.*

★ **dress** /dres/ **dresses, dressing, dressed.** **1** N-COUNT A **dress** is a piece of clothing worn by a woman or girl which covers her body and extends down over her legs. → See picture on page 819. **2** N-UNCOUNT You can refer to clothes worn by men or women as **dress**. *He's usually smart in his dress. ...evening dress.* **3** VERB When you **dress**, or when you **dress yourself**, you put clothes on yourself. *He told Sarah to wait while he dressed.* ● See note at **wear**.
▸**dress up.** PHR-VERB If you **dress up**, you put on different clothes, in order to look smarter or to disguise yourself. *You do not need to dress up for dinner... He was dressed up as Father Christmas.*
▸**dress down.** PHR-VERB If you **dress down**, you wear clothes that are less smart than usual.

★ **dressed** /drest/ **1** ADJ AFTER LINK-V If you are **dressed**, you are wearing clothes rather than being naked. *He was fully dressed, including shoes.* ● See note at **wear**. **2** ADJ AFTER LINK-V If you are **dressed** in a particular way, you are wearing clothes of a particular kind or colour. *He was dressed in a black suit.*

dresser /ˈdresə/ **dressers.** **1** N-COUNT A **dresser** is a piece of furniture which is usually used for storing china. [BRITISH] **2** N-COUNT A **dresser** is a chest of drawers, usually with a mirror on the top. [AMERICAN] **3** N-COUNT You use **dresser** to refer to the kind of clothes that a person wears. *...smart dressers.*

dressing /ˈdresɪŋ/ **dressings.** **1** N-COUNT A **dressing** is a protective covering that is put on a wound. **2** N-VAR A salad **dressing** is a mixture of oil, vinegar, salt and pepper, which you pour over a salad.

'**dressing gown, dressing gowns.** N-COUNT A **dressing gown** is a loose-fitting coat worn over pyjamas or other night clothes.

'**dressing room, dressing rooms.** N-COUNT A **dressing room** is a room in a theatre or sports stadium where performers or players can change their clothes.

'**dressing table, dressing tables.** N-COUNT A **dressing table** is a small table in a bedroom with drawers and a mirror.

drew /druː/. **Drew** is the past tense of **draw**.

dribble /ˈdrɪbəl/ **dribbles, dribbling, dribbled.** **1** VERB If a liquid **dribbles** somewhere, or if you **dribble** it, it drips down slowly or flows in a thin stream. *Sweat dribbled down Hart's face.* **2** VERB When a person **dribbles**, saliva trickles from their mouth. **3** VERB When players **dribble** the ball in a game such as football, they give it several quick kicks or taps in order to keep it moving.

dried /draɪd/. **Dried** is the past tense and past participle of **dry**.

drier /ˈdraɪə/. See **dry, dryer**.

★ **drift** /drɪft/ **drifts, drifting, drifted.** **1** VERB When something **drifts** somewhere, it is carried there by the wind or by water. *Mist drifted silently across the water.* **2** VERB & N-COUNT To **drift** somewhere, or to move there in a **drift**, means to move there slowly or gradually. *Half the crowd drifted outside before the end. ...the drift towards the cities.* **3** VERB To **drift into** a situation means to get into it in a way that is not planned or controlled. *...young people drifting into crime.* **4** N-COUNT A **drift** of snow is a deep pile formed by the wind.
▸**drift off.** PHR-VERB If you **drift off** or **drift off to sleep**, you gradually fall asleep.

drill /drɪl/ **drills, drilling, drilled.** **1** N-COUNT A **drill** is a tool for making holes. → See picture on page 833. *...pneumatic drills.* **2** VERB When you **drill into** something or **drill** a hole in it, you make a hole using a drill. **3** N-VAR A **drill** is a procedure which a group of people, especially soldiers, practise so that they can do something quickly and efficiently. *...the military drill used by soldiers to load and fire the big guns.*

★ **drink** /drɪŋk/ **drinks, drinking, drank, drunk.** **1** VERB When you **drink** a liquid, you take it into your mouth and swallow it. *He drank some tea.* ◆ **drinker, drinkers** N-COUNT *...a coffee drinker.* **2** N-COUNT A **drink** is an amount of a liquid

which you drink. *I'll get you a drink of water.*
3 VERB To **drink** means to drink alcohol. *He was smoking and drinking too much.* ♦ **drinking** N-UNCOUNT *She left him because of his drinking.* ♦ **drinker** N-COUNT *He was a heavy drinker.* **4** N-VAR **Drink** is alcohol, such as beer, wine, or whisky. A **drink** is an alcoholic drink. *Too much drink is bad for your health.* **5** See also **drunk**.
▶ **drink to.** PHR-VERB If you **drink to** someone or something, you raise your glass before drinking, and say that you hope they will be happy or successful. *We drank to our success.*

,drink 'driver, **drink drivers.** N-COUNT In British English, a **drink driver** is someone who drives after drinking more than the amount of alcohol that is legally allowed. The American term is **drunk driver.** ♦ **drink driving** N-UNCOUNT *...a drink driving conviction.*

drip /drɪp/ **drips, dripping, dripped.** **1** VERB When liquid **drips** somewhere, it falls in small drops. *Rain dripped from the brim of his baseball cap.* **2** VERB When something **drips**, drops of liquid fall from it. *A tap in the kitchen was dripping.* **3** N-COUNT A **drip** is a small individual drop of a liquid. *...drips of water.* **4** N-COUNT A **drip** is a piece of medical equipment by which a liquid is slowly passed through a tube into a patient's bloodstream. *I had to be put on a drip.*

⭐ **drive** /draɪv/ **drives, driving, drove, driven** /'drɪvən/. **1** VERB To **drive** a vehicle means to control it so that it goes where you want it to go. *She never learned to drive... His daughter Carly drove him to the train station.* ♦ **driving** N-UNCOUNT *...dangerous driving.* ♦ **driver, drivers** N-COUNT *The driver got out of his van.* **2** N-COUNT A **drive** is a journey in a vehicle such as a car. *I thought we might go for a drive.* **3** N-COUNT A **drive** is a private road leading from a public road to a house. **4** VERB If something **drives** a machine, it supplies the power that makes it work. *...electric motors that drive the wheels.* **5** N-COUNT You use **drive** to refer to the mechanical part of a computer which reads the data on disks and tapes, or writes data onto them. [COMPUTING] **6** VERB If you **drive** one thing **into** another, you push it in or hammer it in using a lot of effort. *Drive the pegs into the side of the path.* **7** VERB If you **drive** people or animals somewhere, you make them go to or from that place. *The last offensive drove thousands of people into Thailand.* **8** VERB The desire or feeling that **drives** someone **to** do something, especially something extreme, is what causes them to do it. *Jealousy drives people to murder.* **9** N-UNCOUNT **Drive** is energy and determination. *John will be best remembered for his drive and enthusiasm.* **10** N-SING A **drive** is a special effort by a group of people to achieve something. *...a drive to end child poverty.* **11** See also **driving, drove**.
▶ **drive away.** PHR-VERB To **drive** people **away** means to make them want to go away or stay away. *Increased crime is driving away customers.*

'drive-by. ADJ BEFORE N A **drive-by** killing

involves shooting someone from a moving car. *...a drive-by shooting.*

driver /'draɪvə/ **drivers.** **1** N-COUNT The **driver** of a vehicle is the person who is driving it. *The driver got out of his van.* **2** N-COUNT A **driver** is a computer program that controls a device such as a printer. [COMPUTING]

'drive-through. ADJ BEFORE N A **drive-through** shop or restaurant is one where you can buy things without leaving your car.

driveway /'draɪvweɪ/ **driveways.** N-COUNT A **driveway** is a private road that leads from a public road to a house or garage.

driving /'draɪvɪŋ/. ADJ BEFORE N The **driving** force behind something is the person, group, or thing mainly responsible for it. *...the driving force behind the economic growth.*

'driving licence, **driving licences.** N-COUNT In British English, a **driving licence** is a card showing that you are qualified to drive. The usual American term is **driver's license.**

drizzle /'drɪzəl/ **drizzles, drizzling, drizzled.** **1** VERB If **it is drizzling**, light rain in falling in fine drops. **2** N-UNCOUNT **Drizzle** is light rain falling in fine drops.

drone /drəʊn/ **drones, droning, droned.** VERB & N-SING If something **drones**, it makes a low continuous humming noise called a **drone**. *The occasional plane droned overhead. ...the constant drone of the motorways.*
▶ **drone on.** PHR-VERB If someone **drones on about** something, they keep talking about it in a boring way.

drool /druːl/ **drools, drooling, drooled.** **1** VERB If someone **drools**, saliva falls from their mouth. **2** VERB If you **drool over** someone or something, you look at them with great pleasure; used showing disapproval. *She is drooled over by men.*

droop /druːp/ **droops, drooping, drooped.** VERB If something **droops**, it hangs or leans downwards with no strength or firmness. *Pale wilting roses drooped from a blue vase.*

⭐ **drop** /drɒp/ **drops, dropping, dropped.** **1** VERB & N-COUNT If a level or amount **drops**, or if there is a **drop in** it, it quickly becomes less. *Temperatures can drop to freezing at night... He had dropped the price of his London home by £1.25m... She was prepared to take a drop in wages.* **2** VERB If you **drop** something, or if it **drops**, it falls straight down. *I dropped my glasses and broke them... He dropped his plate into the sink.* ♦ **dropping** N-UNCOUNT *...the dropping of the first atomic bomb.* **3** N-COUNT You use **drop** to talk about vertical distances. *It's only a four-foot drop.* **4** VERB If a person or a part of their body **drops** to a lower position, or if they **drop** a part of their body to a lower position, they move to that position, often in a tired way. *Nancy dropped into a nearby chair... She let her head drop.* **5** VERB If your voice **drops**, or if you **drop** your voice, you speak more quietly. *He dropped his voice and glanced round at the door.* **6** VERB & PHR-VERB If the driver of a

A
B
C
D
E
F
G
H
I
J
K
L
M
N
O
P
Q
R
S
T
U
V
W
X
Y
Z

vehicle **drops** you somewhere, or if they **drop** you **off**, they stop the vehicle and you get out. *He dropped me outside the hotel... Just drop me off at the airport.* [7] VERB If you **drop** an idea, course of action, or habit, you decide not to continue with it. *He was told to drop the idea.* [8] PHRASE If you **drop a hint**, you give someone a hint in a casual way. [9] N-COUNT A **drop of** a liquid is a very small amount of it shaped like a little ball.

▶**drop by** or **drop in**. PHR-VERB If you **drop by**, or if you **drop in**, you visit someone informally. *He tried to drop by the office... Why not drop in for a chat?*

▶**drop off**. [1] See drop 6 [2] PHR-VERB If you **drop off** or **drop off to sleep**, you go to sleep.

▶**drop out**. PHR-VERB If someone **drops out of** college or a race, for example, they leave it without finishing what they started.

droplet /'drɒplət/ **droplets**. N-COUNT A **droplet** is a very small drop of liquid. *...droplets of water.*

drought /draʊt/ **droughts**. N-VAR A **drought** is a long period of time during which no rain falls. *...drought and famines have killed up to two million people.*

drove /drəʊv/ **droves**. [1] **Drove** is the past tense of **drive**. [2] N-COUNT **Droves of** people are very large numbers of them. *Droves of young men were strolling along the quays... They are leaving in droves.*

drown /draʊn/ **drowns, drowning, drowned**. [1] VERB When someone **drowns**, or when they **are drowned**, they die because they have gone under water and cannot breathe. *Forty-eight people have drowned after their boat capsized... She fell into the water and was drowned.* [2] VERB & PHR-VERB If something **drowns** a sound, or if it **drowns** it **out**, it is louder than the sound and makes it impossible to hear it. *His speech was drowned by loud cries... Her voice was drowned out by a loud crash.*

drowsy /'draʊzi/ **drowsier, drowsiest**. ADJ If you are **drowsy**, you feel sleepy and cannot think clearly. *He felt pleasantly drowsy.* ♦ **drowsiness** N-UNCOUNT *Big meals during the day cause drowsiness.*

⭐ **drug** /drʌɡ/ **drugs, drugging, drugged**. [1] N-COUNT A **drug** is a chemical substance given to people to treat or prevent an illness or disease. [2] N-COUNT **Drugs** are substances that some people smoke or inject into their blood because of their stimulating effects. *She was sure Leo was taking drugs.* [3] VERB If you **drug** a person or animal, you give them a chemical substance in order to make them sleepy or unconscious. *They drugged the guard dog.*

'drug ,addict, drug addicts. N-COUNT A **drug addict** is someone who is addicted to illegal drugs.

drugstore /'drʌɡstɔː/ **drugstores**. N-COUNT In America, a **drugstore** is a shop where medicines, cosmetics, and some other goods are sold. ● See note at **pharmacy**.

⭐ **drum** /drʌm/ **drums, drumming, drummed**. [1] N-COUNT A **drum** is a musical instrument consisting of a skin stretched tightly over a round frame. → See picture on page 828. ♦ **drummer, drummers** N-COUNT *...a pop-group drummer.* [2] N-COUNT A **drum** is a large container in the shape of a cylinder which is used for storing fuel or other substances. *...an oil drum.* [3] VERB If something **drums on** a surface, or if you **drum** something **on** a surface, it hits it regularly, making a continuous beating sound. *He drummed his fingers on the leather top of his desk.*

▶**drum into**. PHR-VERB If you **drum** something **into** someone, you keep saying it to make them understand or remember it. *We had it drummed into us that you need a degree to get a job.*

▶**drum up**. PHR-VERB If you **drum up** support or business, you try to get it. *The organisers failed to drum up much public support.*

drunk /drʌŋk/ **drunks**. [1] ADJ If someone is **drunk**, they have consumed too much alcohol. *I got drunk.* [2] N-COUNT A **drunk** is someone who is drunk or who often gets drunk. [3] **Drunk** is the past participle of **drink**.

,drunk 'driver, drunk drivers. N-COUNT In American English, a **drunk driver** is someone who drives after drinking more than the amount of alcohol that is legally allowed. The usual British term is **drink driver**. ♦ **drunk driving** N-UNCOUNT *...his sixth drunk driving offense.*

drunken /'drʌŋkən/. ADJ BEFORE N A **drunken** person is drunk or is frequently drunk; used showing disapproval. *...groups of drunken hooligans.* ♦ **drunkenly** ADV *Bob stormed drunkenly into her house.* ♦ **drunkenness** N-UNCOUNT *He was arrested for drunkenness.*

⭐ **dry** /draɪ/ **drier** (or **dryer**), **driest; dries, drying, dried**. [1] ADJ If something is **dry**, it has no water or other liquid on it or in it. *...a soft dry cloth... Pat it dry with a soft towel.* ♦ **dryness** N-UNCOUNT *...the parched dryness of the air.* [2] VERB When you **dry** something, or when it **dries**, it becomes dry. *Wash and dry the lettuce... Leave your hair to dry naturally.* [3] ADJ When the weather or a place is **dry**, there is no rain or much less rain than average. [4] ADJ If you say that your skin or hair is **dry**, you mean that it is less oily or soft than normal. *Dry hair is damaged by washing it too frequently.* ♦ **dryness** N-UNCOUNT *...dryness of the skin.* [5] ADJ **Dry** humour is amusing, mocking people in a subtle way. ♦ **dryly** ADV *'I've never done anything like this,' he said. – 'That's a comfort,' she replied dryly.* [6] ADJ If you describe something such as a book, play, or activity as **dry**, you mean that it is dull and uninteresting. *...the dry, academic phrases.* [7] ADJ **Dry** sherry or wine does not taste sweet. [8] See also **dried, dryer**.

▶**dry off**. PHR-VERB If something **dries off**, or if you **dry** it **off**, the moisture on its surface disappears or is removed. *I got out, dried myself off, and dressed.*

▶**dry out**. PHR-VERB If something **dries out**, it

becomes completely dry. *If the soil is allowed to dry out the tree could die.*

▶**dry up.** **1** PHR-VERB If something **dries up**, it loses all its water or moisture. *As the day goes on, the pollen dries up and becomes hard.* **2** PHR-VERB If a supply of something **dries up**, it stops. *Tourism is expected to dry up completely this summer.* **3** PHR-VERB If you **dry up** or **dry up the dishes**, you wipe the water off them with a cloth after they have been washed.

,dry-'clean, **dry-cleans, dry-cleaning, dry-cleaned.** VERB When clothes **are dry-cleaned**, they are cleaned with a liquid chemical rather than with water.

dryer (or **drier**) /ˈdraɪə/ **dryers.** N-COUNT A **dryer** is a machine for drying things, for example clothes or people's hair. *...hair dryers.* ● See also **dry**.

,dry 'run, **dry runs.** N-COUNT If you have a **dry run**, you practise something to make sure that you are ready to do it properly. *The competition is planned as a dry run for the World Cup finals.*

dual /ˈdjuːəl, AM ˈduːl-/. ADJ BEFORE N **Dual** means having two parts, functions, or aspects. *...his dual role as head of the party and head of state. ...dual nationality.*

dub /dʌb/ **dubs, dubbing, dubbed.** **1** VERB If someone or something **is dubbed** a particular thing, it is given that description or name. *Orson Welles dubbed her 'the most exciting woman in the world'.* **2** VERB If a film **is dubbed**, a different soundtrack is added with actors speaking in a different language. *It was dubbed into Spanish for Mexican audiences.*

dubious /ˈdjuːbiəs, AM ˈduː-/. **1** ADJ You describe something as **dubious** when you think it is not completely honest, safe, or reliable. *This claim seems to us to be rather dubious.* ♦ **dubiously** ADV *He was dubiously convicted of shooting three white men.* **2** ADJ AFTER LINK-V If you are **dubious about** something, you are unsure about it. *My parents were a bit dubious about it all at first.* ♦ **dubiously** ADV *He eyed Coyne dubiously.*

duchess /ˈdʌtʃɪs/ **duchesses.** N-COUNT A **duchess** is a woman who has the same rank as a duke, or is a duke's wife or widow.

duck /dʌk/ **ducks, ducking, ducked.** **1** N-COUNT A **duck** is a common water bird with short legs and a large flat beak. → See picture on page 815. **2** N-UNCOUNT **Duck** is the meat of a duck eaten as food. **3** VERB If you **duck**, you move your head or body quickly downwards to avoid being seen or hit. *He ducked in time to save his head from a blow... I wanted to duck down and slip past but they saw me... Hans deftly ducked their blows.* **4** VERB You say that someone **ducks** a duty or responsibility when you disapprove of the fact that they avoid it. *He is an indecisive leader who ducks crucial decisions.*

▶**duck out.** PHR-VERB If you **duck out of** something that you are supposed to do, you

avoid doing it. *George ducked out of his forced marriage to a cousin.*

duct /dʌkt/ **ducts.** N-COUNT A **duct** is a pipe or channel which carries a liquid or gas. *...a big air duct in the ceiling.*

dud /dʌd/ **duds.** ADJ & N-COUNT You say that something is **dud** or a **dud** when it does not work properly. [INFORMAL] *He replaced a dud valve.*

dude /djuːd, AM duːd/ **dudes.** N-COUNT A **dude** is a man. [INFORMAL] *My doctor is a real cool dude.*

⭐ **due** /djuː, AM duː/ **dues.** **1** PREP If an event or situation is **due to** something else, it happens or exists as a result of it. *A lot of this will be due to Mr Green's efforts.* **2** ADJ AFTER LINK-V If something is **due** at a particular time, it is expected to happen or to arrive at that time. *The results are due at the end of the month... Mr Carter is due in London on Monday.* **3** PHRASE If you say that something will happen **in due course**, you mean that it will happen eventually, when the time is right. *The arrangements will be published in due course.* **4** ADJ AFTER LINK-V If something is **due to** you, you have a right to it. *I've got some leave due to me... No further pension was due.* **5** ADJ AFTER LINK-V If someone is **due for** something, that thing is planned to happen or be given to them now, or very soon. *Miss Smith, you know you are due for a move?* **6** ADJ BEFORE N If you give something **due** consideration, you give it the consideration it deserves. *After due consideration it was decided to send him away.* **7** N-PLURAL **Dues** are sums of money that you pay regularly to an organization that you belong to. **8** PHRASE You can say **'with due respect'** when you are about to disagree politely with someone. *With all due respect I submit to you that you're asking the wrong question.*

duel /ˈdjuːəl, AM ˈduː-/ **duels.** **1** N-COUNT A **duel** is a fight between two people in which they use guns or swords in order to settle a quarrel. **2** N-COUNT You can refer to a conflict between two people or groups as a **duel**.

duet /djuˈet, AM duː-/ **duets.** N-COUNT A **duet** is a piece of music sung or played by two people.

dug /dʌg/. **Dug** is the past tense and past participle of **dig**.

duke /djuːk, AM duːk/ **dukes.** N-COUNT A **duke** is a noble of high rank.

dull /dʌl/ **duller, dullest; dulls, dulling, dulled.** **1** ADJ If you describe someone or something as **dull**, you mean that they are not interesting or exciting. *They are both nice people but can be rather dull.* ♦ **dullness** N-UNCOUNT *...the dullness of their routine life.* **2** ADJ A **dull** colour or light is not bright. *The stamp was a dark, dull blue colour.* ♦ **dully** ADV *The street lamps gleamed dully.* **3** ADJ A **dull** sound or feeling is weak and not intense. *...the dull boom of the explosion. ...a dull ache.* ♦ **dully** ADV *His arm throbbed dully.* **4** VERB If something **dulls**, or if it **is dulled**, it becomes less intense, bright, or lively. *He can dull your senses with facts.*

a
b
c
d
e
f
g
h
i
j
k
l
m
n
o
p
q
r
s
t
u
v
w
x
y
z

duly /ˈdjuːli, AM ˈduː-/. ADV **Duly** is used to say that something is done at the correct time or in the correct way. [FORMAL] *He is a duly elected president of the country.*

dumb /dʌm/ **dumber, dumbest; dumbs, dumbing, dumbed.** ☐1 ADJ Someone who is **dumb** is completely unable to speak. *...a young deaf and dumb man.* ☐2 ADJ AFTER LINK-V If someone is **dumb** on a particular occasion, they cannot speak because they are angry or shocked. *We were all struck dumb for a minute.* ☐3 ADJ If you call a person **dumb**, you mean that they are stupid or foolish. *I've met a lot of dumb people.* ☐4 ADJ If you say that something is **dumb**, you think that it is silly and annoying. [AMERICAN, INFORMAL] *I came up with this dumb idea.* ►**dumb down.** PHR-VERB If you **dumb down** something, you make it easier for people to understand, especially when this spoils it. *This sounded like a case for dumbing down the magazine, which no one favoured.* ♦ **dumbing down** N-UNCOUNT *He accused broadcasters of contributing to the dumbing down of America.*

dummy /ˈdʌmi/ **dummies.** ☐1 N-COUNT A **dummy** is a model of a person, often used to display clothes. *...a shop-window dummy.* ☐2 N-COUNT In British English, a **dummy** is a rubber or plastic object that you give to a baby to suck so that it feels comforted. The American word is **pacifier.** ☐3 ADJ You use **dummy** to describe objects that are not real, but have been made to look as if they are real. *...dummy weapons.*

⭐ **dump** /dʌmp/ **dumps, dumping, dumped.** ☐1 VERB If something **is dumped** somewhere, it is put there because it is no longer wanted or needed. *The getaway car was dumped near a motorway tunnel.* ♦ **dumping** N-UNCOUNT *...the dumping of hazardous waste.* ☐2 VERB If you **dump** something somewhere, you put it there quickly and carelessly. [INFORMAL] *We dumped our bags at the nearby Grand Hotel and hurried towards the market.* ☐3 N-COUNT A **dump** is a site provided for people to leave their rubbish. ☐4 N-COUNT If you refer to a place as a **dump**, you mean it is unattractive and unpleasant to live in or visit. [INFORMAL]

dune /djuːn, AM duːn/ **dunes.** N-COUNT A **dune** is a hill of sand near the sea or in a desert.

dung /dʌŋ/. N-UNCOUNT **Dung** is faeces from large animals. *...little piles of cow dung.*

dungeon /ˈdʌndʒən/ **dungeons.** N-COUNT A **dungeon** is a dark underground prison in a castle.

dunno /dəˈnəʊ/. **Dunno** is sometimes used to represent a way of saying 'don't know'. [WRITTEN, INFORMAL] *'How did she get it?'—'I dunno.'*

duo /ˈdjuːəʊ, AM ˈduː-/ **duos.** N-COUNT A **duo** consists of two people who do something together, especially perform together. *...a famous dancing and singing duo.*

dupe /djuːp, AM duːp/ **dupes, duping, duped.** VERB If someone **dupes** you, they trick you. *...a plot to dupe stamp collectors into buying fake rarities.*

duplicate, duplicates, duplicating, duplicated; verb /ˈdjuːplɪkeɪt, AM ˈduː-/, noun /ˈdjuːplɪkət, AM ˈduː-/. ☐1 VERB & N-COUNT If you **duplicate** something that has already been done, or if you perform a **duplicate of** it, you repeat or copy it. *His task will be to duplicate his success overseas here at home... It was an exact duplicate of what happened in Vegas.* ♦ **duplication** N-UNCOUNT *...unnecessary duplication of work.* ☐2 VERB If you **duplicate** something which has been written, drawn, or recorded onto tape, you make exact copies of it. *...a business which duplicates video and cinema tapes.* ☐3 N-COUNT A **duplicate** is an object which is a copy of something. *I've lost my card. I've got to get a duplicate. ...a duplicate key.*

durable /ˈdjʊərəbəl, AM ˈduː-/. ADJ **Durable** materials or products are strong and last a long time. *...hard, durable plastic.* ♦ **durability** N-UNCOUNT *Airlines recommend hard-sided cases for durability.*

duration /djʊˈreɪʃən, AM dʊr-/. N-UNCOUNT The **duration** of an event or state is the time that it lasts for. *Courses are of two years' duration.*

⭐ **during** /ˈdjʊərɪŋ, AM ˈdʊrɪŋ/. ☐1 PREP If something happens **during** a period of time or **during** an event, it happens continuously, or happens several times between the beginning and end of that period or event. *Sandstorms are common during the Saudi Arabian winter.* ☐2 PREP An event that happens **during** a period of time happens at some point or moment in that period. → See Reference Page on Times and Dates. *During the night a gust of wind had blown the pot over.*

> **USAGE** You do not use **during** to say how long something lasts. You use **for.** You do not say, for example, 'I went to Wales during two weeks'. You say **'I went to Wales for two weeks'.**

dusk /dʌsk/. N-UNCOUNT **Dusk** is the time just before night when it is not yet completely dark.

⭐ **dust** /dʌst/ **dusts, dusting, dusted.** ☐1 N-UNCOUNT **Dust** consists of very small dry particles of earth, sand, or dirt. *I could see a thick layer of dust on the stairs.* ☐2 VERB When you **dust** furniture or other objects, you remove dust from them using a dry cloth. ☐3 PHRASE If you say that **the dust has settled**, you mean that a situation has become calmer after a series of confusing or chaotic events.

dustbin /ˈdʌstbɪn/ **dustbins.** N-COUNT In British English, a **dustbin** is a large container for rubbish. The usual American term is **garbage can.**

dusty /ˈdʌsti/ **dustier, dustiest.** ADJ Something that is **dusty** is covered with dust.

dutiful /ˈdjuːtɪfʊl, AM ˈduː-/. ADJ If you are **dutiful**, you do everything that you are expected to do. ...*the dutiful wife, who sacrifices her career for her husband.* ♦ **dutifully** ADV *The inspector dutifully recorded the date.*

⭐ **duty** /'djuːti, AM 'duːti/ **duties.** ① N-VAR **Duty** is the work that you have to do as your job. *Staff must report for duty at their normal place of work... I carried out my duties conscientiously.* ② PHRASE If someone such as a policeman or a nurse is **off duty**, they are not working. If they are **on duty**, they are working. *Extra staff had been put on duty.* ③ N-SING If you say that something is your **duty**, you believe that you ought to do it because it is your responsibility. *I consider it my duty to write to you and thank you.* ④ N-VAR **Duties** are taxes which you pay to the government on goods that you buy. ...*import duties.*

⸴**duty-'free.** ADJ **Duty-free** goods are sold at airports or on planes or ships at a cheaper price than usual because they are not taxed.

duvet /'duːveɪ, AM duː'veɪ/ **duvets.** N-COUNT A **duvet** is a large cover filled with feathers or similar material, which you use to cover yourself in bed instead of a sheet and blankets. [BRITISH]

DVD /ˌdiː viː 'diː/ **DVDs.** N-COUNT A **DVD** is a disc similar to a compact disc on which a film or music is recorded. **DVD** is an abbreviation for 'digital video disc' or 'digital versatile disc'. ...*a DVD player.*

DVT /ˌdiː viː 'tiː/ N-VAR **DVT** is a serious medical condition caused by blood clots in the legs. **DVT** is an abbreviation for 'deep vein thrombosis'.

dwarf /dwɔːf/ **dwarfs, dwarfing, dwarfed.** VERB If one person or thing **is dwarfed** by another, the second is so much bigger than the first that it makes them look very small. *The US air travel market dwarfs that of Britain.*

dwell /dwel/ **dwells, dwelling, dwelled** or **dwelt.** ① VERB If you **dwell on** something, especially something unpleasant, you think, speak, or write about it a lot or for quite a long time. *I'd rather not dwell on the past.* ② VERB If you **dwell** somewhere, you live there. [FORMAL] ...*the fate of the forest and the Indians who dwell in it.*

dweller /'dwelə/ **dwellers.** N-COUNT A city **dweller** or slum **dweller**, for example, is a person who lives in the kind of place or house indicated. ...*to encourage town dwellers to grow vegetables.*

dwelling /'dwelɪŋ/ **dwellings.** N-COUNT A **dwelling** is a house or other place where someone lives. [FORMAL]

dwelt /dwelt/. **Dwelt** is the past tense and past participle of **dwell.**

dwindle /'dwɪndəl/ **dwindles, dwindling, dwindled.** VERB If something **dwindles**, it becomes smaller, weaker, or less in number. *The factory's workforce has dwindled from over 4,000 to a few hundred.* ...*his dwindling authority.*

dye /daɪ/ **dyes, dyeing, dyed.** ① VERB If you **dye** something, you change its colour by soaking it in a special liquid. *The women prepared, spun and dyed the wool.* ② N-VAR **Dye** is a substance which is used to dye something.

dying /'daɪɪŋ/. ① **Dying** is the present participle of **die.** ② ADJ BEFORE N & N-PLURAL **Dying** people or **the dying** are people who are very ill and likely to die soon. ...*a dying man... The dead and the dying were everywhere.* ③ ADJ BEFORE N A **dying** tradition or industry is becoming less important and is likely to end altogether. ④ ADJ AFTER LINK-V You say that you **are dying for** something or **are dying to** do something to emphasize that you very much want to have it or do it. [INFORMAL] *I was dying for a cigarette... She was dying to talk to Frank.*

dyke (or **dike**) /daɪk/ **dykes.** N-COUNT A **dyke** is a thick wall that prevents river or sea water flooding onto land.

dynamic /daɪ'næmɪk/ **dynamics.** ① ADJ A **dynamic** person is full of energy; used showing approval. ...*a dynamic and energetic leader.* ♦ **dynamically** ADV ...*one of the most dynamically imaginative jazz pianists.* ♦ **dynamism** /'daɪnəmɪzəm/ N-UNCOUNT ...*a situation that calls for dynamism and new thinking.* ② N-PLURAL The **dynamics** of a situation or group of people are the opposing forces within it that cause it to change. ...*an understanding of family dynamics.*

dynamite /'daɪnəmaɪt/. N-UNCOUNT **Dynamite** is a type of explosive.

dynamo /'daɪnəməʊ/ **dynamos.** N-COUNT A **dynamo** is a device that uses the movement of a machine to produce electricity.

dynasty /'dɪnəsti, AM 'daɪn-/ **dynasties.** N-COUNT A **dynasty** is a series of rulers of a country who all belong to the same family.

E e

⭐ **each** /iːtʃ/. ① QUANT If you refer to **each** thing or person in a group, or if you refer to **each one** of the members of a group, you are referring to every member, considered as individuals. *Each book is beautifully illustrated.* ...*two bedrooms, each with three beds.* ...*tickets at six pounds each... He handed each of them a page of photos... He picked up forty of these publications and read each one of them.* ② PRON You use **each other** when

you are saying that each member of a group does something to the others. *We stared at each other.*

⭐ **eager** /'iːgə/. ADJ If you are **eager to** do or have something, you very much want to do it or have it. *They're very eager to get money.* ...*the crowd of eager faces around him.* ♦ **eagerly** ADV *Scientists throughout Europe are eagerly awaiting the results.* ♦ **eagerness** N-UNCOUNT ...*an eagerness to learn.*

⭐ Bank of English® frequent word   For a full explanation of all grammatical labels, see pages vii–x

a
b
c
d
e
f
g
h
i
j
k
l
m
n
o
p
q
r
s
t
u
v
w
x
y
z

eagle /'iːɡəl/ **eagles.** N-COUNT An **eagle** is a large bird that hunts and kills small animals for food.

⭐ **ear** /ɪə/ **ears.** **1** N-COUNT Your **ears** are the two parts of your body with which you hear sounds. → See picture on page 823. **2** N-SING If you have **an ear for** music or language, you are able to hear its sounds accurately and to interpret them or reproduce them well. **3** N-COUNT The **ears** of a cereal plant such as wheat are the top parts containing the seeds.

⭐ **earlier** /'ɜːliə/. **1** **Earlier** is the comparative of **early**. **2** ADJ & ADV **Earlier** means occurring at a point in time before the present or before the one you are talking about. ...*earlier reports of gunshots.* ...*political reforms announced earlier this year.*

earliest /'ɜːliɪst/. **1** **Earliest** is the superlative of **early**. **2** PHRASE **At the earliest** means not before the date or time mentioned. *The tests won't be completed until next April at the earliest.*

earlobe /'ɪələʊb/ **earlobes.** N-COUNT Your **earlobes** are the soft parts at the bottom of your ears. → See picture on page 823.

⭐ **early** /'ɜːli/ **earlier, earliest.** **1** ADV & ADJ BEFORE N **Early** means before the usual time that something happens or before the time that was arranged or expected. *Why do we have to go to bed so early?.* ...*early retirement.* **2** ADV & ADJ BEFORE N **Early** means near the beginning of an activity, process, or period of time. ...*the early stages of pregnancy... It's too early to declare his efforts a success. ...an incident which occurred much earlier in the game. ...the early 1980s.*

earmark /'ɪəmɑːk/ **earmarks, earmarking, earmarked.** VERB If something **is earmarked for** a particular purpose, it is reserved for that purpose. *China has earmarked more than $20bn for oil exploration.*

⭐ **earn** /ɜːn/ **earns, earning, earned.** **1** VERB If you **earn** money, you receive it in return for work that you do. *She earns £17,000 a year.* **2** VERB If something **earns** money, it produces money as profit. ...*a current account which earns little or no interest.* ...*the money earned from oil imports.* **3** VERB If you **earn** something such as praise, you get it because you deserve it. *Companies must earn a reputation for honesty... I think that's earned him very high admiration.*

earner /'ɜːnə/ **earners.** N-COUNT An **earner** is someone or something that earns money or produces profit. ...*a typical wage earner... Sugar is Fiji's second biggest export earner.*

earnest /'ɜːnɪst/. **1** PHRASE If something is done **in earnest**, it is done to a much greater extent and more seriously than before. *Campaigning will begin in earnest tomorrow.* **2** ADJ **Earnest** people are very serious and sincere. ♦ **earnestly** ADV *I earnestly hope Mrs Smith will find it in her heart to forgive me.*

⭐ **earnings** /'ɜːnɪŋz/. N-PLURAL Your **earnings** are the money that you earn by working. *Average weekly earnings rose by 1.5% in July.*

earring /'ɪərɪŋ/ **earrings.** N-COUNT **Earrings** are pieces of jewellery which you attach to your ears.

⭐ **earth** /ɜːθ/ **earths.** **1** N-PROPER The **Earth** is the planet on which we live. **2** N-SING The **earth** is the surface of the Earth. *The earth shook.* **3** N-UNCOUNT **Earth** is the substance on the land surface of the earth in which plants grow. ...*a huge mound of earth.* **4** N-SING The **earth** in an electric plug or appliance is a wire through which electricity can pass into the ground, to make the equipment safe even if something goes wrong with it.

PHRASES ● You use **on earth** for emphasis in questions which begin with words such as 'how', 'why', 'what', or 'where'. *Why on earth would he want to go to such a place?* ● If you come **down to earth**, you have to face the reality of everyday life after a period of great excitement. *I was shocked, brought down to earth by this revelation.* ● See also **down-to-earth**.

earthly /'ɜːθli/. **1** ADJ BEFORE N **Earthly** means happening in the material world of our life on earth and not in any spiritual life or life after death. *The priest emphasized the need to confront evil during the earthly life.* **2** PHRASE If you say that there is no **earthly reason** for something, you are emphasizing that there is no possible reason for it. *What earthly reason would they have for lying?*

earthquake /'ɜːθkweɪk/ **earthquakes.** N-COUNT An **earthquake** is a shaking of the ground caused by movement of the earth's crust.

earthy /'ɜːθi/ **earthier, earthiest.** **1** ADJ If you describe someone as **earthy**, you mean they are open and direct about subjects which other people avoid or feel ashamed about. ...*his extremely earthy humour.* **2** ADJ Something that is **earthy** looks, smells, or feels like earth. ...*a strong, earthy smell.*

earwig /'ɪəwɪg/ **earwigs.** N-COUNT An **earwig** is a small, thin brown insect that has a pair of pincers at the back end of its body. → See picture on page 824.

⭐ **ease** /iːz/ **eases, easing, eased.** **1** PHRASE If you do something **with ease**, you do it without difficulty or effort. *Anne was intelligent and capable of passing her exams with ease.* **2** N-UNCOUNT If you talk about the **ease of** a particular activity, you mean that it is easy to do or has been made easier to do. *For ease of reference, only the relevant extracts are included. ...the camera's ease of use.* **3** PHRASE If you are **at ease**, you feel confident and comfortable. If you are **ill at ease**, you feel anxious or awkward. **4** VERB If something **eases**, or if it **eases off**, it is reduced in degree, speed, or intensity. *I gave him some brandy to ease the pain... These days, the pressure has eased off... The rain had eased up.* ♦ **easing** N-UNCOUNT ...*the easing of sanctions.* **5** VERB If you **ease** your way somewhere or **ease** somewhere, you move there slowly, carefully, and gently. If you **ease** something somewhere, you move it there slowly, carefully, and gently.

She eased back into the chair... He eased his foot off the accelerator.

▶**ease up.** PHR-VERB If you **ease up**, you start to make less effort. *He told supporters not to ease up even though he's leading in the presidential race.*

easel /'iːzəl/ **easels.** N-COUNT An **easel** is a wooden frame that supports a picture which an artist is painting.

⭐ **easily** /'iːzɪli/. **1** ADV You use **easily** to emphasize that something is very likely to happen, or is certainly true. *The cost could easily be three times that amount. ...an ancient barn that is easily the length of two tennis courts.* **2** ADV You use **easily** to say that something happens more quickly than normal. *He had always cried very easily.* **3** See also **easy.**

⭐ **east** /iːst/. **1** N-SING The **east** is the direction in which you look to see the sun rise. **2** N-SING & ADJ The **east** of a place, or the **east** part of a place, is the part which is towards the east. *...a village in the east of the country. ...the east coast.* **3** ADV **East** means towards the east, or positioned to the east of a place or thing. *Go east on Route 9. ...just east of the center of town.* **4** ADJ An **east** wind blows from the east. **5** N-SING The **East** is used to refer either to the countries in the southern and eastern part of Asia, including India, China, and Japan, or to the former USSR and other countries in eastern Europe. ● See also **Far East, Middle East.**

Easter /'iːstə/. N-UNCOUNT **Easter** is a Christian festival and holiday, when the resurrection of Jesus Christ is celebrated.

easterly /'iːstəli/. **1** ADJ An **easterly** point, area, or direction is to the east or towards the east. *...a more easterly direction.* **2** ADJ An **easterly** wind blows from the east.

⭐ **eastern** /'iːstən/. **1** ADJ **Eastern** means in or from the east of a region or country. **2** ADJ **Eastern** means coming either from the people or countries of the East, such as India, China, and Japan, or from the countries in the East of Europe and the former USSR.

easterner /'iːstənə/ **easterners.** N-COUNT An **easterner** is a person who was born in or who lives in the eastern part of a place or country.

eastward /'iːstwəd/ (or **eastwards**). ADV & ADJ **Eastward** or **eastwards** means towards the east. *A powerful snowstorm is moving eastwards. ...travel in an eastward direction.*

⭐ **easy** /'iːzi/ **easier, easiest.** **1** ADJ If a job or action is **easy**, you can do it without difficulty. *That kind of calculation is fairly easy to do. ...making easy conversation with people she has never met before.* ◆ **easily** ADV *These journeys are most easily made by plane.* **2** ADJ An **easy** life or time is comfortable and without any problems. *It ought to make life much easier.* **3** PHRASE If someone tells you to **take it easy**, they mean that you should relax and not do very much. [INFORMAL]

,**easy-'going.** ADJ If you describe someone as **easy-going**, you mean that they are not easily worried or upset; used showing approval.

⭐ **eat** /iːt/ **eats, eating, ate, eaten.** VERB When you **eat** something, you put it into your mouth, chew it, and swallow it. *I ate my chicken quickly.*

▶**eat away.** PHR-VERB If one thing **eats away** another or **eats away at** another, it gradually destroys it or uses it up. *The sea eats away at coastlines.*

▶**eat into.** PHR-VERB If something **eats into** your time or resources, it uses them, when they should be used for other things. *Responsibilities at home and work eat into his time.*

eater /'iːtə/ **eaters.** N-COUNT You use **eater** to refer to someone who eats in a particular way or eats particular kinds of food. *...a fussy eater. ...meat eaters.*

eavesdrop /'iːvzdrɒp/ **eavesdrops, eavesdropping, eavesdropped.** VERB If you **eavesdrop on** someone, you listen secretly to what they are saying. ◆ **eavesdropper, eavesdroppers** N-COUNT *...a telephone call recorded by an eavesdropper.*

ebb /eb/ **ebbs, ebbing, ebbed.** **1** VERB When the tide or the sea **ebbs**, its level falls. **2** N-COUNT The **ebb** or the **ebb tide** is one of the regular periods when the sea gradually falls to a lower level. **3** VERB If a feeling or a person's strength **ebbs** or **ebbs away**, it weakens and gradually disappears. [FORMAL] *Popular sympathy for the government could ebb.*

PHRASES ● If someone or something is **at a low ebb**, they are not being very successful or profitable. *The club's fortunes were at a low ebb.* ● You can use **ebb and flow** to describe the way that something repeatedly increases and decreases. *...the ebb and flow of the fighting.*

ebullient /ɪ'bʌliənt, -'bʊl-/. ADJ An **ebullient** person is lively and full of enthusiasm or excitement about something. [FORMAL] ◆ **ebullience** N-UNCOUNT *...his characteristic ebullience.*

eccentric /ɪk'sentrɪk/ **eccentrics.** ADJ & N-COUNT An **eccentric** person or an **eccentric** has habits or opinions that other people think strange. ◆ **eccentricity** /,eksen'trɪsɪti/ **eccentricities** N-VAR *...a performer noted for his eccentricity... We all have our eccentricities.*

ecclesiastical /ɪ,kliːzi'æstɪkəl/. ADJ **Ecclesiastical** means belonging to or connected with the Christian church.

echelon /'eʃəlɒn/ **echelons.** N-COUNT An **echelon** in an organization or society is a level or rank in it. [FORMAL] *...the lower echelons of society.*

⭐ **echo** /'ekəʊ/ **echoes, echoing, echoed.** **1** N-COUNT An **echo** is a sound caused by a noise being reflected off a surface such as a wall. *He heard the echo of his footsteps along the hallway.* **2** VERB If sounds **echo**, or a place **echoes with** sounds, the sounds are reflected off a surface there and can be heard again. *The corridor echoed with the*

a b c d e f g h i j k l m n o p q r s t u v w x y z

barking of a dozen dogs. ...the echoing hall.
3 VERB If you **echo** someone's words, you repeat them or express the same thing. *Other US military personnel echoed the sentiments of Captain Ryan.* **4** N-COUNT An **echo** is an expression of an attitude, opinion, or statement which has already been expressed. *Political attacks work only if they find an echo with voters.*

eclectic /ɪ'klektɪk/. ADJ If you describe a collection of objects, ideas, or beliefs as **eclectic**, you mean that they are wide-ranging and come from many different sources. [FORMAL] ...*the most eclectic mix of styles imaginable.*

eclipse /ɪ'klɪps/ **eclipses, eclipsing, eclipsed.**
1 N-COUNT When there is an **eclipse** of the sun or a **solar eclipse**, the moon is between the Earth and the sun, so that part or all of the sun is hidden. When there is an **eclipse** of the moon or a **lunar eclipse**, the Earth is between the sun and the moon, so that part or all of the moon is hidden. **2** VERB If one thing **eclipses** another, the first thing becomes more important so that the second thing is no longer noticed. *Nothing is going to eclipse winning the Olympic title.*

'eco-,friendly. ADJ **Eco-friendly** products or services are less harmful to the environment than other similar products or services. ...*eco-friendly washing powder.*

ecology /ɪ'kɒlədʒi/. **1** N-UNCOUNT When you talk about the **ecology** of a place, you are referring to the relationships between living things and their environment. *The region has a unique ecology.* ◆ **ecological** /,i:kə'lɒdʒɪkəl/ ADJ BEFORE N ...*Siberia's delicate ecological balance.* ◆ **ecologically** ADV *China is very ecologically conscious.* **2** N-UNCOUNT **Ecology** is the study of the relationship between living things and their environment. ◆ **ecologist, ecologists** N-COUNT ...*an ecologist who visited Sri Lanka to study endangered animals.*

⭐ **economic** /,i:kə'nɒmɪk, ,ek-/. **1** ADJ **Economic** means concerned with the organization of the money, industry, and trade of a country, region, or society. ...*Poland's radical economic reforms.* ◆ **economically** ADV ...*an economically depressed area.* **2** ADJ If something is **economic**, it produces a profit. *The new system may be more economic.*

economical /,i:kə'nɒmɪkəl, ,ek-/. **1** ADJ Something that is **economical** does not require a lot of money to operate. ...*economical cars.* ◆ **economically** ADV *Services could be operated more efficiently and economically.* **2** ADJ If someone is **economical**, they spend money carefully and sensibly. ◆ **economically** ADV *We must all live as economically as possible.*

⭐ **economics** /,i:kə'nɒmɪks, ,ek-/. **1** N-UNCOUNT **Economics** is the study of the way in which money, industry, and trade are organized in a society. **2** N-UNCOUNT The **economics** of a society

or industry is the system of organizing money and trade in it. ...*the economics of the newspaper business.*

⭐ **economist** /ɪ'kɒnəmɪst/ **economists.** N-COUNT An **economist** is a person who studies, teaches, or writes about economics.

⭐ **economy** /ɪ'kɒnəmi/ **economies.** **1** N-COUNT The **economy** of a country or region is the system by which money, industry, and trade are organized. ...*changes in the Indian economy.* **2** N-UNCOUNT **Economy** is careful spending or the careful use of things to save money or avoid waste. ...*improvements in the fuel economy of cars.*

ecosystem /'i:kəʊsɪstəm, AM 'ekə-/ **ecosystems.** N-COUNT An **ecosystem** is all the plants and animals that live in a particular area together with the relationship that exists between them and their environment. [TECHNICAL] ...*Antarctica's ecosystem.*

ecstasy /'ekstəsi/ **ecstasies.** **1** N-VAR **Ecstasy** is a feeling of great happiness. ...*a state of almost religious ecstasy... The dancing roused the audience to ecstasies.* **2** N-UNCOUNT **Ecstasy** is an illegal drug which acts as a stimulant and can cause hallucinations.

ecstatic /ek'stætɪk/. ADJ If you are **ecstatic**, you feel very enthusiastic and happy. *The audience reception was ecstatic... The Russian President was given an ecstatic welcome.* ◆ **ecstatically** ADV ...*ecstatically happy.*

eczema /'eksmə, AM ɪg'zi:mə/. N-UNCOUNT **Eczema** is a skin condition which makes your skin itch and become sore and broken.

⭐ **edge** /edʒ/ **edges, edging, edged.** **1** N-COUNT The **edge** of something is the place or line where it stops, or the part of it that is furthest from the middle. *We were on a hill, right on the edge of town... She was standing at the water's edge.* **2** N-COUNT The **edge** of something sharp such as a knife is its sharp or narrow side. ...*the sharp edge of the sword.* **3** VERB If you **edge** somewhere, you move there very slowly. *He edged closer to the telephone.* **4** N-SING If you have an **edge over** someone, you have an advantage over them. *The three days France have to prepare could give them the edge over England... Manufacturers will do almost anything to gain a competitive edge.* **5** PHRASE If you are **on edge**, you are nervous and unable to relax.

▶**edge out.** PHR-VERB If someone **edges out** someone else, they just manage to beat them or get in front of them in a contest. *McGregor's effort was enough to edge Johnson out of top spot.*

edgy /'edʒi/. ADJ If you feel **edgy**, you are nervous and anxious. [INFORMAL]

edible /'edɪbəl/. ADJ If something is **edible**, it is safe to eat. ...*edible mushrooms.*

edict /'i:dɪkt/ **edicts.** N-COUNT An **edict** is a command given by someone in authority. [FORMAL]

edifice /'edɪfɪs/ **edifices.** ⬛1 N-COUNT An **edifice** is a large impressive building. [FORMAL] ...*a large sandstone edifice built in the early part of the century.* ⬛2 N-COUNT You can describe a system of beliefs or a traditional institution as an **edifice**. ...*the ancient edifice of monarchy.*

★ **edit** /'edɪt/ **edits, editing, edited.** ⬛1 VERB If you **edit** a text, you correct it so that it is suitable for publication. *She had helped him by editing his manuscript.* ⬛2 VERB If you **edit** a book, you collect pieces of writing by different authors and prepare them for publication. ...*a collection of essays, edited by Toni Morrison.* ⬛3 VERB If you **edit** a film or a television or radio programme, you choose some of what has been filmed or recorded and arrange it in a particular order. *He taught me to edit and splice film... He is editing together excerpts of some of his films.* ⬛4 VERB Someone who **edits** a newspaper or magazine is in charge of it and makes decisions concerning the contents.
▸ **edit out.** PHR-VERB If you **edit** something **out** of a book or film, you remove it. *His voice will be edited out of the final film.*

★ **edition** /ɪ'dɪʃən/ **editions.** ⬛1 N-COUNT An **edition** is a particular version of a book, magazine, or newspaper that is printed at one time. *This is the second edition of a popular book. ...a paperback edition.* ⬛2 N-COUNT An **edition** is a single television or radio programme that is one of a series. ...*the Monday edition of 'Eastenders'.*

★ **editor** /'edɪtə/ **editors.** ⬛1 N-COUNT An **editor** is a person in charge of a newspaper or magazine, or a section of a newspaper or magazine, who makes decisions concerning the contents. ⬛2 N-COUNT An **editor** is a person who checks and corrects texts before they are published. ⬛3 N-COUNT An **editor** is a person who is collecting pieces of writing by different authors and preparing them for publication. *Michael Rosen is the editor of the anthology.* ⬛4 N-COUNT An **editor** is a person who selects recorded material for a film or for a radio or television programme.

★ **editorial** /,edɪ'tɔːriəl/ **editorials.** ⬛1 ADJ BEFORE N **Editorial** means involved in preparing a newspaper, magazine, or book for publication. ...*the editorial staff of 'Private Eye'.* ⬛2 ADJ BEFORE N **Editorial** means involving the attitudes, opinions, and contents of a newspaper, magazine, or television programme. *We are not about to change our editorial policy.* ⬛3 N-COUNT An **editorial** is an article in a newspaper which gives the opinion of the editor or publisher on a particular topic.

educate /'edʒʊkeɪt/ **educates, educating, educated.** ⬛1 VERB When someone **is educated**, they are taught at a school or college. *He was educated at Haslingden Grammar School.* ⬛2 VERB To **educate** people means to improve their understanding of a particular problem or issue.

...*a game designed to help educate teenagers about AIDS.*

> **USAGE** Note that you do not use **educate** or **education** to talk about the way parents look after their children and gradually teach them about good behaviour and life in general. Instead, you should use the verb **bring up** or the noun **upbringing**, but not the verb **grow up**, which is always used without an object. *His parents brought him up to be polite and courteous. ...the effect that this religious upbringing has had on me... I grew up in a very rural area.*

educated /'edʒʊkeɪtɪd/. ADJ **Educated** people have reached a high standard of learning.

★ **education** /,edʒʊ'keɪʃən/ **educations.** N-VAR **Education** means learning and teaching. *They're cutting funds for education... Parents are the most important factor in a child's education.*
◆ **educational** ADJ ...*declining educational standards.*

Edwardian /ed'wɔːdiən/ **Edwardians.** ⬛1 ADJ **Edwardian** means connected with or typical of Britain in the first decade of the 20th century, when Edward VII was King. ...*the Edwardian era.* ⬛2 N-COUNT People associated with the Edwardian period are sometimes called **Edwardians**.

eel /iːl/ **eels.** N-COUNT An **eel** is a fish with a long, thin body.

eerie /'ɪəri/. ADJ Something that is **eerie** is strange and frightening. ...*an eerie silence.*
◆ **eerily** ADV *The streets were eerily deserted.*

★ **effect** /ɪ'fekt/ **effects, effecting, effected.** ⬛1 N-VAR An **effect** is a change, reaction, or impression that is caused by something or is the result of something. ...*the effect of divorce on children... Head injuries can cause long-lasting psychological effects... She paused, obviously for effect.* ⬛2 VERB If you **effect** something, you succeed in causing it to happen. [FORMAL] ...*prospects for effecting real political change.* ⬛3 See also **side-effect**.
PHRASES ● You add **in effect** to a statement which you feel is a reasonable description or summary of something. *That deal would create, in effect, the world's biggest airline.* ● You use **to this effect**, **to that effect**, or **to the effect that** when you are summarizing what someone has said, rather than repeating their actual words. ...*statements to the effect that they're not prepared to negotiate with this regime.* ● When something **takes effect**, **comes into effect**, or **is put into effect**, it begins to apply or starts to have results. ● You use **effect** in expressions such as **to good effect** and **to no effect** in order to indicate how successful or impressive an action is. *Mr Charles complained, to no effect.*

★ **effective** /ɪ'fektɪv/. ⬛1 ADJ Something that is **effective** produces the intended results. ...*the most effective way of teaching writing... The*

a
b
c
d
e
f
g
h
i
j
k
l
m
n
o
p
q
r
s
t
u
v
w
x
y
z

vaccine is effective against most allergies.
♦ **effectively** ADV *I learned to exert my authority more effectively.* ♦ **effectiveness** N-UNCOUNT *...the effectiveness of computers as an educational tool.* [2] ADJ BEFORE N **Effective** means having a particular role or result in practice, though not officially. *The rebels have been in effective control of the island since March.* [3] ADJ AFTER LINK-V When a law or an agreement becomes **effective**, it begins officially to apply.

effectively /ɪˈfektɪvli/. ADV You use **effectively** with a statement which you feel is a reasonable description or summary of a particular situation. *The President has effectively lost power.*

efficacy /ˈefɪkəsi/. N-UNCOUNT The **efficacy** of something is its effectiveness in producing the intended results. *The World Health Organisation is to analyse the drug to test its safety and efficacy.*

⭐ **efficient** /ɪˈfɪʃənt/. ADJ Something or someone that is **efficient** does a job successfully, without wasting time or energy. *Cycling is the most efficient form of transport. ...energy-efficient lighting.* ♦ **efficiently** ADV *...a campaign to encourage consumers to use energy more efficiently.* ♦ **efficiency** /ɪˈfɪʃənsi/ N-UNCOUNT *They marvelled at her efficiency.*

⭐ **effort** /ˈefət/ **efforts.** [1] N-VAR If you make an **effort** to do something, you try hard to do it. *He made no effort to hide his disappointment... He died despite the frantic efforts of lifeguards.* [2] N-VAR If you do something **with effort**, or if it is an **effort**, you can do it but you find it physically or mentally demanding. *She took a deep breath and sat up slowly and with great effort... With an effort he rose to his feet... Even carrying the camcorder while hiking in the forest was an effort.*

effortless /ˈefətləs/. ADJ If an action is **effortless**, it is achieved easily. *...the sense of seemingly effortless movement.* ♦ **effortlessly** ADV *Peter adapted effortlessly to his new surroundings.*

EFL /ˌiː ef ˈel/. N-UNCOUNT **EFL** is used to describe things connected with the teaching of English to people whose first language is not English. **EFL** is an abbreviation for 'English as a Foreign Language'. *...an EFL teacher.*

e.g. /ˌiː ˈdʒiː/. **e.g.** is an abbreviation that means 'for example'. It is used before a noun, or to introduce another sentence. *...products made from cream, e.g. cheese, butter, etc.*

⭐ **egg** /eg/ **eggs, egging, egged.** [1] N-COUNT An **egg** is the rounded object produced by a female bird from which a baby bird later emerges. Reptiles, fish, and insects also produce eggs. *...a baby bird hatching from its egg.* [2] N-VAR An **egg** is a hen's egg considered as food. *Break the eggs into a shallow bowl. ...bacon and egg.* [3] N-COUNT An **egg** is a cell in a female person or animal which can develop into a baby.

▶**egg on.** PHR-VERB If you **egg** someone **on**, you encourage them to do something that is daring or foolish.

ego /ˈiːgəʊ, ˈegəʊ/ **egos.** N-VAR Someone's **ego** is their sense of their own self and their own worth. *It's a great blow to your ego... She's got a lot of ego invested in her career.*

eh /eɪ/. **Eh** is used to represent a noise that people make in conversation, for example to show agreement or to ask for something to be explained or repeated. *Let's talk all about it outside, eh?... 'He's um ill in bed.' — 'Eh?' — 'He's ill in bed.'*

⭐ **eight** /eɪt/ **eights.** NUM **Eight** is the number 8.

⭐ **eighteen** /ˌeɪˈtiːn/. NUM **Eighteen** is the number 18.

⭐ **eighteenth** /ˌeɪˈtiːnθ/. ORD The **eighteenth** item in a series is the one that you count as number eighteen.

⭐ **eighth** /eɪtθ/ **eighths.** [1] ORD The **eighth** item in a series is the one that you count as number eight. *...the eighth century.* [2] N-COUNT An **eighth** is one of eight equal parts of something. *...an eighth of an inch thick.*

⭐ **eightieth** /ˈeɪtiəθ/. ORD The **eightieth** item in a series is the one that you count as number eighty.

⭐ **eighty** /ˈeɪti/ **eighties.** [1] NUM **Eighty** is the number 80. [2] N-PLURAL When you talk about **the eighties**, you are talking about numbers between 80 and 89. For example, if you are **in your eighties**, you are aged between 80 and 89. If the temperature is **in the eighties**, the temperature is between 80 and 89 degrees. If something happened **in the eighties**, it happened between 1980 and 1989.

⭐ **either** /ˈaɪðə, ˈiːðə/. [1] CONJ You use **either** in front of the first of two or more alternatives, when you are stating the only possibilities or choices that there are. The other alternatives are introduced by 'or'. *Sightseeing is best done either by tour bus or by bicycles... He should be either put on trial or set free... Either she goes or I go.* [2] PRON & DET You can use **either** to refer to one of two things, people, or situations, when you want to say that they are both possible and it does not matter which one is chosen or considered. *There were glasses of iced champagne and cigars. Unfortunately not many of either were consumed. ...the authority to pursue suspects into either country... Do either of you smoke cigarettes?* [3] PRON & DET & CONJ You can use **either** in a negative statement to refer to each of two things, people, or situations to indicate that the negative statement includes both of them. *She warned me that I'd never marry or have children.—'I don't want either.'... He sometimes couldn't remember either man's name. ...music that fails to be either funny or funky.* [4] DET You use **either** to introduce a noun that refers to each of two things when you are talking about both of them. *The basketball nets hung down from the ceiling at* *either end of the gymnasium.* **5** ADV You use **either** by itself in negative statements to indicate that there is a similarity or connection with a person or thing that you have just mentioned. *He did not even say anything to her, and she did not speak to him either.*

eject /ɪ'dʒekt/ **ejects, ejecting, ejected.** **1** VERB If someone **ejects** you from a place, they force you to leave. *Officials used guard dogs to eject the protesters.* ♦ **ejection, ejections** N-VAR *...the ejection and manhandling of hecklers at the meeting.* **2** VERB To **eject** something means to remove it or push it out forcefully. *...the volcanic dust that is sometimes ejected into the stratosphere.*

elaborate, elaborates, elaborating, elaborated. **1** ADJ /ɪ'læbərət/ You use **elaborate** to describe something that consists of many different parts, making it very detailed or complex. *...an elaborate ceremony that lasts for eight days.* ♦ **elaborately** ADV *...elaborately costumed dolls.* **2** VERB /ɪ'læbəreɪt/ If you **elaborate on** a plan or a theory, or if you **elaborate** a plan or theory, you give more details about it. *Lieutenant Cerezzi refused to elaborate on possible motives for the killing.* ♦ **elaboration** N-UNCOUNT *...the elaboration of specific policies.*

elapse /ɪ'læps/ **elapses, elapsing, elapsed.** VERB When time **elapses**, it passes. [FORMAL] *Forty-eight hours have elapsed since his arrest.*

elastic /ɪ'læstɪk/ **1** N-UNCOUNT **Elastic** is a rubber material that stretches when you pull it and returns to its original size when you let it go. *...bouncing around on a piece of elastic.* **2** ADJ Something that is **elastic** stretches easily. *Like all arteries, it is elastic and muscular.*

elasticity /ˌiːlæ'stɪsɪti, ɪˌlæst-/. N-UNCOUNT The **elasticity** of a material or substance is its ability to return to its original shape, size, and condition after it has been stretched. *Daily facial exercises help her to retain the skin's elasticity.*

elated /ɪ'leɪtɪd/. ADJ If you are **elated**, you are extremely happy and excited because of something that has happened. *'That was one of the best races of my life,' said an elated Hakkinen.* ♦ **elation** /ɪ'leɪʃən/ N-UNCOUNT *His supporters have reacted to the news with elation.*

elbow /'elbəʊ/ **elbows, elbowing, elbowed.** **1** N-COUNT Your **elbow** is the joint where your arm bends in the middle. → See picture on page 822. **2** VERB If you **elbow** someone away, you push them aside with your elbow. If you **elbow** your way somewhere, you move there by pushing other people out of the way, using your elbows. *The security team elbowed aside a steward... Her burly boyfriend elbowed him into the gutter.* **3** VERB If someone **elbows** you, they intentionally hurt you by hitting you with their elbow. *He blatantly elbowed Harding right in the eye.*

elder /'eldə/ **elders.** **1** ADJ The **elder** of two

people is the one who was born first. *...his elder brother.*

USAGE In British English, the adjective **elder** is usually only used to describe brothers and sisters. *...her elder sister.* You use **older** to talk about the age of other people or things. **Elder** cannot be followed by **than** but **older** can be followed by **than**. *I've got a sister who is older than me.*

2 N-COUNT A person's **elder** is someone who is older than them. **3** N-COUNT In some societies, an **elder** is one of the respected older people who have influence and authority.

★ **elderly** /'eldəli/. ADJ & N-PLURAL You use **elderly** as a polite way of saying that someone is old. **The elderly** are people who are old. *...an elderly couple. ...programs that provide health care to the elderly.*

eldest /'eldɪst/. ADJ The **eldest** person in a group is the one who was born before all the others. *...her eldest daughter, Lisa.*

★ **elect** /ɪ'lekt/ **elects, electing, elected.** **1** VERB When people **elect** someone, they choose that person to represent them, by voting. *Manchester College elected him Principal in 1956. ...electing a woman as its new president. ...the country's democratically elected president.* **2** VERB If you **elect to** do something, you choose to do it. [FORMAL] *Those electing to smoke will be seated at the rear.*

★ **election** /ɪ'lekʃən/ **elections.** **1** N-VAR An **election** is a process in which people vote to choose a person or group of people to hold an official position. *...Poland's first fully free elections for more than fifty years. ...his election campaign.* **2** N-UNCOUNT The **election** of a person or a political party is their success in winning an election. *...the election of the Labour government in 1964. ...Vaclav Havel's election as president.* **3** See also **by-election, general election.**

elector /ɪ'lektə/ **electors.** N-COUNT An **elector** is a person who has the right to vote in an election.

★ **electoral** /ɪ'lektərəl/. ADJ BEFORE N **Electoral** means connected with an election. *...Italy's electoral system.* ♦ **electorally** ADV *A period of recession was electorally damaging.*

electorate /ɪ'lektərət/ **electorates.** N-COUNT The **electorate** of a country is the people there who have the right to vote in an election. **Electorate** can take the singular or plural form of the verb. *He has the backing of almost a quarter of the electorate.*

★ **electric** /ɪ'lektrɪk/. **1** ADJ BEFORE N An **electric** device works by means of electricity. **2** ADJ BEFORE N An **electric** current, voltage, or charge is one that is produced by electricity. **Electric** plugs, sockets, or power lines are designed to carry electricity. **3** ADJ If you describe the atmosphere of a place or event as **electric**, you mean that people are in a state of great excitement.

A
B
C
D
E
F
G
H
I
J
K
L
M
N
O
P
Q
R
S
T
U
V
W
X
Y
Z

electrical /ɪˈlektrɪkəl/. [1] ADJ BEFORE N
Electrical devices work by means of electricity.
...*electrical equipment.* ◆ **electrically** ADV
...*electrically-powered vehicles.* [2] ADJ BEFORE N
Electrical engineers and industries are involved
in the production or maintenance of electricity or
electrical goods.

electrician /ɪlekˈtrɪʃən, ˌiːlek-/ **electricians.**
N-COUNT An **electrician** is a person whose job is
to install and repair electrical equipment.

★ **electricity** /ɪlekˈtrɪsɪti, ˌiːlek-/. N-UNCOUNT
Electricity is a form of energy used for heating
and lighting, and to provide power for machines.

e,lectric 'shock, electric shocks. See **shock**
meaning 7.

electrify /ɪˈlektrɪfaɪ/ **electrifies, electrifying,
electrified.** [1] VERB If something **electrifies** you, it
excites and surprises you a lot. *The world was
electrified by his courage and resistance.*
◆ **electrifying** ADJ ...*an electrifying performance.*
[2] VERB When a railway system **is electrified**, it is
connected by overhead wires or by a special rail
to a supply of electricity. ◆ **electrification**
/ɪˌlektrɪfɪˈkeɪʃən/ N-UNCOUNT ...*the electrification of
the Oxted to Uckfield line.*

electrocute /ɪˈlektrəkjuːt/ **electrocutes,
electrocuting, electrocuted.** VERB If someone **is
electrocuted**, they are accidentally killed or
injured when they touch something connected
to a source of electricity. *He accidentally
electrocuted himself.* ◆ **electrocution** N-UNCOUNT
...*safety switches designed to switch off in a second
to prevent electrocution.*

electron /ɪˈlektrɒn/. N-COUNT An **electron** is a
tiny particle of matter that is smaller than an
atom and has a negative electrical charge.

★ **electronic** /ɪlekˈtrɒnɪk, ˌiː-/. [1] ADJ BEFORE N
An **electronic** device has transistors, silicon chips,
or valves which control and change the electric
current passing through it. [2] ADJ An **electronic**
process involves the use of electronic devices.
...*electronic surveillance.* ◆ **electronically** ADV
...*electronically operated gates.*

electronics /ɪlekˈtrɒnɪks/. [1] N-UNCOUNT
Electronics is the technology of using transistors
and silicon chips, especially in devices such as
radios, televisions, and computers. ...*Europe's
three main electronics companies.* [2] N-PLURAL
You can refer to electronic devices, or the part of
a piece of equipment that consists of electronic
devices, as **the electronics**. *It is hoped that all
the electronics could be contained in a microchip.*

★ **elegant** /ˈelɪɡənt/. [1] ADJ If you describe a
person or thing as **elegant**, you think they are
pleasing and graceful. ...*an elegant restaurant.*
◆ **elegance** N-UNCOUNT ...*Princess Grace's
understated elegance.* ◆ **elegantly** ADV ...*a tall,
elegantly dressed man.* [2] ADJ If you describe a
piece of writing, an idea, or a plan as **elegant**,
you mean that it is simple, clear, and clever.
◆ **elegance** N-UNCOUNT *The delight comes from*

the simple elegance of the writing. ◆ **elegantly**
ADV ...*her funny and elegantly written memoirs.*

★ **element** /ˈelɪmənt/ **elements.** [1] N-COUNT An
element of something is one of the parts which
make up the whole thing. ...*one of the key
elements of the UN's peace plan... Fitness has now
become an important element in our lives.*
[2] N-COUNT When you talk about the particular
elements within a society or organization, you
are referring to groups of people who have
similar aims, beliefs, or habits. ...*criminal elements.*
[3] N-COUNT If something has an **element of** a
particular quality, it has a certain amount of it.
*These reports clearly contain elements of
propaganda.* [4] N-COUNT The **element** in an
electrical appliance is the metal part which
changes the electric current into heat.
[5] N-PLURAL You can refer to the weather,
especially wind and rain, as **the elements**. *Our
open boat is exposed to the elements.* [6] PHRASE If
someone is **in** their **element**, they are doing
something that they enjoy and do well. *My
stepmother was in her element, organizing
everything.*

elemental /ˌelɪˈmentəl/. ADJ **Elemental**
feelings and behaviour are simple and forceful.
[LITERARY] *Jamie resorted to a more elemental tactic.*

elementary /ˌelɪˈmentri/. ADJ **Elementary**
things are very simple, straightforward, and basic.
...*elementary computer skills.*

elephant /ˈelɪfənt/ **elephants.** N-COUNT An
elephant is a very large animal with a long trunk.
→ See picture on page 816.

elevate /ˈelɪveɪt/ **elevates, elevating, elevated.**
[1] VERB When someone or something **is
elevated to** a more important rank or status,
they achieve it. [FORMAL] *He was elevated to the
post of prime minister.* ◆ **elevation** N-UNCOUNT
...*his elevation to the papacy.* [2] VERB To **elevate**
something means to increase it in amount or
intensity. [FORMAL] *Emotional stress can elevate
blood pressure.* [3] VERB If you **elevate** something,
you raise it above a horizontal level. [FORMAL]

elevation /ˌelɪˈveɪʃən/ **elevations.** N-COUNT The
elevation of a place is its height above sea level.

elevator /ˈelɪveɪtə/ **elevators.** N-COUNT In
American English, an **elevator** is a device that
carries people up and down inside buildings. The
usual British word is **lift**.

★ **eleven** /ɪˈlevən/. NUM **Eleven** is the number 11.

★ **eleventh** /ɪˈlevənθ/. ORD The **eleventh** item in
a series is the one that you count as number
eleven.

elicit /ɪˈlɪsɪt/ **elicits, eliciting, elicited.** [1] VERB If you
elicit a response or a reaction, you do or say
something which makes other people respond or
react. *He was hopeful that his request would elicit
a positive response.* [2] VERB If you **elicit** a piece of
information, you get it by asking the right
questions. *Several phone calls elicited no further
information.*

eligible /ˈelɪdʒɪbəl/. ADJ Someone who is **eligible for** something is entitled or able to have it. *You could be eligible for a grant... Almost half the population are eligible to vote.* ◆ **eligibility** N-UNCOUNT *...the rules covering eligibility for benefits.*

⭐ **eliminate** /ɪˈlɪmɪneɪt/ **eliminates, eliminating, eliminated.** [1] VERB To **eliminate** something means to remove it completely. [FORMAL] *If you think you may be allergic to a food or drink, eliminate it from your diet.* ◆ **elimination** N-UNCOUNT *...the complete elimination of nuclear weapons.* [2] VERB When a person or team **is eliminated from** a competition, they are defeated and so take no further part in it.

elite /ɪˈliːt, eɪ-/ **elites.** N-COUNT & ADJ BEFORE N You can refer to the most powerful, rich, or talented people within a particular group or society as the **elite**. You can also talk about an **elite** group of people. *...China's intellectual elite. ...elite troops.*

elitist /ɪˈliːtɪst, eɪ-/ **elitists.** [1] ADJ If you describe an activity, a profession, or a system as **elitist**, you mean that it is practised only by a small group of powerful, rich, or talented people, or that it favours only this group of people; used showing disapproval. *The legal profession is starting to be less elitist.* ◆ **elitism** N-UNCOUNT *...the arrogance and elitism of gallery owners. ...a conference against elitism.* [2] N-COUNT An **elitist** is someone who believes that they are part of an elite; used showing disapproval.

elm /elm/ **elms.** N-VAR An **elm** is a tree with broad leaves which it loses in winter.

eloquent /ˈeləkwənt/. ADJ A person who is **eloquent** is good at speaking and able to persuade people; used showing approval. *...one particularly eloquent German critic. ...a very eloquent speech.* ◆ **eloquence** N-UNCOUNT *...his eloquence and persuasiveness.* ◆ **eloquently** ADV *Jan speaks eloquently about her art.*

⭐ **else** /els/. [1] ADV You use **else** after words such as 'anywhere', 'someone', 'what', 'everyone' and 'everything' to refer vaguely to another place, person, or thing, or to refer to all the other people, places, or things except the one you are talking about. *What else have you had for your birthday?... I never wanted to live anywhere else... Cigarettes are in short supply, like everything else here... London seems so much dirtier than everywhere else.* [2] CONJ You use **or else** after stating a logical conclusion, to indicate that what you are about to say is evidence for that conclusion. *Evidently no lessons have been learnt or else the government would not have handled the problem so sloppily.* [3] CONJ You use **or else** to introduce a possibility or alternative. *Make sure you are strapped in very well, or else you will fall out... You are either a total genius or else you must be absolutely raving mad.* [4] PHRASE You can say **'if nothing else'** to indicate that what you are mentioning is, in your opinion, the only good thing in a particular situation. *If nothing else, you'll really enjoy meeting them.*

⭐ **elsewhere** /ˌelˈsweə/. ADV **Elsewhere** means in other places or to another place. *Almost 80 percent of the state's residents were born elsewhere... But if you are not satisfied then go elsewhere.*

ELT /ˌiː el ˈtiː/. **ELT** is the teaching of English to people whose first language is a language other than English. **ELT** is an abbreviation for 'English Language Teaching'.

elude /ɪˈluːd/ **eludes, eluding, eluded.** [1] VERB If something that you want **eludes** you, you fail to obtain it. *Sleep eluded her... The appropriate word eluded him.* [2] VERB If you **elude** someone or something, you avoid them or escape from them. *He eluded the police for 13 years.*

elusive /ɪˈluːsɪv/. ADJ Something or someone that is **elusive** is difficult to find, achieve, describe, or remember. *In London late-night taxis are always elusive.*

e-mail (or **E-mail**) /ˈiːmeɪl/ **e-mails, e-mailing, e-mailed.** [1] N-VAR **E-mail** is a system of sending written messages electronically from one computer to another. **E-mail** is an abbreviation for 'electronic mail'. [COMPUTING] *Do you want to send an E-mail?* [2] VERB If you **e-mail** someone, you send them an e-mail. *Jamie e-mailed me to say he couldn't come.*

emanate /ˈeməneɪt/ **emanates, emanating, emanated.** [1] VERB If a quality, idea, or feeling **emanates from** you, or if you **emanate** a quality or feeling, you give people a strong sense that you have that quality or feeling. [FORMAL] *He emanates sympathy.* [2] VERB If something **emanates from** somewhere, it comes from there. [FORMAL] *...reports emanating from America.*

emancipate /ɪˈmænsɪpeɪt/ **emancipates, emancipating, emancipated.** VERB If people **are emancipated**, they are freed from unpleasant or degrading social, political, or legal restrictions. [FORMAL] *That war preserved the Union and emancipated the slaves.* ◆ **emancipation** N-UNCOUNT *...women's emancipation.*

embankment /ɪmˈbæŋkmənt/ **embankments.** N-COUNT An **embankment** is a thick wall built of earth, often supporting a railway line or road.

embargo /ɪmˈbɑːgəʊ/ **embargoes.** N-COUNT An **embargo** is an order made by a government to stop trade with another country.

embark /ɪmˈbɑːk/ **embarks, embarking, embarked.** [1] VERB If you **embark on** something new, you start doing it. *He's embarking on a new career as a writer.* [2] VERB When you **embark** on a ship, you go on board before the start of a journey.

embarrass /ɪmˈbærəs/ **embarrasses, embarrassing, embarrassed.** [1] VERB If something or someone **embarrasses** you, it makes you feel shy or ashamed. *It embarrassed him that he had no idea of what was going on.* ◆ **embarrassing** ADJ *That was an embarrassing situation for me.* ◆ **embarrassingly** ADV *Stephens had beaten him embarrassingly easily.* [2] VERB If something **embarrasses** a politician, it causes political

a
b
c
d
e
f
g
h
i
j
k
l
m
n
o
p
q
r
s
t
u
v
w
x
y
z

problems for them. *The Government has been embarrassed by the affair.* ♦ **embarrassing** ADJ *He has put the Bonn government in an embarrassing position.*

embarrassed /ɪmˈbærəst/. ADJ A person who is **embarrassed** feels shy, ashamed, or guilty about something.

embarrassment /ɪmˈbærəsmənt/ **embarrassments.** [1] N-UNCOUNT **Embarrassment** is a feeling of shyness, shame, or guilt. *We apologise for any embarrassment this may have caused.* [2] N-SING If you refer to a person as **an embarrassment**, you mean that you disapprove of them but cannot avoid your connection with them. *His wife's family were something of an embarrassment to him.*

★ **embassy** /ˈembəsi/ **embassies.** N-COUNT An **embassy** is a group of officials, headed by an ambassador, who represent their government in a foreign country. The building in which they work is also called an **embassy**.

embedded /ɪmˈbedɪd/. [1] ADJ If an object is **embedded in** something, it is fixed there firmly and deeply. *There is glass embedded in the cut.* [2] ADJ If an attitude or feeling is **embedded in** a society or **in** someone's personality, it has become a permanent feature of it. *...the racism still so strongly embedded in our society.*

embellish /ɪmˈbelɪʃ/ **embellishes, embellishing, embellished.** [1] VERB If something **is embellished with** decorative features, they are added to make it more attractive. *The stern was embellished with carvings... Ivy leaves embellish the front of the dresser.* ♦ **embellishment** /ɪmˈbelɪʃmənt/ **embellishments** N-VAR *...buildings with little bits of decoration and embellishment.* [2] VERB If you **embellish** a story, you make it more interesting by adding details which may be untrue.

embezzle /ɪmˈbezəl/ **embezzles, embezzling, embezzled.** VERB If someone **embezzles** money that their organization or company has placed in their care, they take it and use it illegally for their own purposes. ♦ **embezzlement** N-UNCOUNT *...charges of forgery and embezzlement.*

emblem /ˈembləm/ **emblems.** [1] N-COUNT An **emblem** is a design representing a country or organization. [2] N-COUNT An **emblem** is something symbolizing a quality or idea. *The eagle was an emblem of strength and courage.*

embodiment /ɪmˈbɒdimənt/. N-SING If you describe someone or something as **the embodiment of** a quality or idea, you mean that it is their most noticeable characteristic, or the basis of all they do. [FORMAL] *A baby is the embodiment of vulnerability.*

embody /ɪmˈbɒdi/ **embodies, embodying, embodied.** [1] VERB If someone or something **embodies** an idea or quality, they are a symbol or expression of that idea or quality. *Jack Kennedy embodied all the hopes of the 1960s.* [2] VERB If something **is embodied in** a particular thing, the second thing

contains or consists of the first. *This strategy was embodied in two early pieces of legislation.*

embrace /ɪmˈbreɪs/ **embraces, embracing, embraced.** [1] VERB & N-COUNT When you **embrace** someone, you put your arms around them in order to show your affection for them. This action is called an **embrace**. *The couple in the corridor were embracing each other. ...a young couple locked in an embrace.* [2] VERB If you **embrace** a change, political system, or idea, you start supporting it or believing in it wholeheartedly. [FORMAL] *The new rules have been embraced by government watchdog organizations.* [3] VERB If something **embraces** a group of people, things, or ideas, it includes them. [FORMAL] *...a theory that would embrace the whole field of human endeavour.*

embroider /ɪmˈbrɔɪdə/ **embroiders, embroidering, embroidered.** VERB If cloth **is embroidered with** a design, the design is stitched into it. *The collar was embroidered with red strawberries... Matilda was embroidering an altar cloth.*

embroidery /ɪmˈbrɔɪdəri/ **embroideries.** [1] N-VAR **Embroidery** consists of designs sewn onto cloth. [2] N-UNCOUNT **Embroidery** is the activity of sewing designs onto cloth.

embroiled /ɪmˈbrɔɪld/. ADJ If you become **embroiled** in an argument or **with** a person, you become deeply involved in that argument or in a relationship with that person, often causing problems for yourself.

embryo /ˈembriəʊ/ **embryos.** N-COUNT An **embryo** is an animal or human in the very early stages of development in the womb.

embryonic /ˌembriˈɒnɪk/. ADJ **Embryonic** means in a very early stage of development. [FORMAL] *...an embryonic democracy.*

emerald /ˈemərəld/ **emeralds.** N-COUNT An **emerald** is a bright green precious stone.

★ **emerge** /ɪˈmɜːdʒ/ **emerges, emerging, emerged.** [1] VERB When you **emerge**, you come out from a place where you could not be seen. *The postman emerged from his van.* [2] VERB If you **emerge from** a difficult or bad experience, you come to the end of it. *The nation is emerging from the recession slowly.* [3] VERB When something such as a political movement **emerges**, it comes into existence. [JOURNALISM] ♦ **emergence** N-UNCOUNT *...the emergence of new political groups.*

★ **emergency** /ɪˈmɜːdʒənsi/ **emergencies.** [1] N-COUNT An **emergency** is an unexpected and serious situation such as an accident, which must be dealt with quickly. *The hospital will cater only for emergencies.* [2] ADJ BEFORE N An **emergency** action is one that is done or arranged quickly, in response to an emergency. *...an emergency meeting of parliament.* [3] ADJ BEFORE N **Emergency** equipment or supplies are those intended for use in an emergency. *...an emergency exit.*

emigrate /ˈemɪɡreɪt/ **emigrates, emigrating, emigrated.** VERB If you **emigrate**, you leave your own country to live in another. *He emigrated to*

Belgium. ✦ **emigration** N-UNCOUNT *...the huge emigration of workers to the West.*

eminent /'emɪnənt/. ADJ An **eminent** person is well-known and respected. *...an eminent scientist.* ✦ **eminence** /'emɪnəns/ N-UNCOUNT *Beveridge was a man of great eminence.*

eminently /'emɪnəntli/. ADV You use **eminently** in front of an adjective describing a positive quality in order to emphasize the quality expressed by that adjective. *His family was eminently respectable.*

emission /ɪ'mɪʃən/ **emissions.** N-VAR An **emission** of light, heat, radiation, or a harmful gas is the release of it into the atmosphere. [FORMAL]

emit /ɪ'mɪt/ **emits, emitting, emitted.** VERB To **emit** a sound, smell, or substance means to produce it or send it out. [FORMAL] *Polly blinked and emitted a long, low whistle.*

⭐ **emotion** /ɪ'məʊʃən/ **emotions.** N-VAR Emotion is strong feeling such as joy or love. An **emotion** is one of these feelings. *Her voice trembled with emotion... Jealousy is a destructive emotion, and one I avoid.*

⭐ **emotional** /ɪ'məʊʃənəl/. ☐ ADJ **Emotional** means relating to emotions and feelings. ✦ **emotionally** ADV *He'd learned never to become emotionally involved.* ☐ ADJ When someone is **emotional**, they show their feelings openly, especially because they are upset.

emotive /ɪ'məʊtɪv/. ADJ An **emotive** situation or issue is likely to make people feel strong emotions. *Embryo research is an emotive issue.*

empathy /'empəθi/. N-UNCOUNT **Empathy** is the ability to share another person's feelings as if they were your own feelings. *He had a natural empathy with children.*

emperor /'empərə/ **emperors.** N-COUNT An **emperor** is a man who rules an empire.

emphasis /'emfəsɪs/ **emphases** /'emfəsiːz/. ☐ N-VAR **Emphasis** is special importance that is given to one part or aspect of something. *...a family-run hotel and restaurant, with the emphasis firmly on comfort.* ☐ N-VAR **Emphasis** is extra force that you put on a syllable, word, or phrase when you are speaking. *The emphasis is on the first syllable of the last word.*

⭐ **emphasize** (BRIT also **emphasise**) /'emfəsaɪz/ **emphasizes, emphasizing, emphasized.** VERB To **emphasize** something means to indicate that it is particularly important or true, or to draw special attention to it. *Your letter should emphasize how your skills will benefit the employer.*

emphatic /ɪm'fætɪk/. ☐ ADJ An **emphatic** statement is made forcefully. ✦ **emphatically** ADV *The president emphatically denied that suggestion.* ☐ ADJ An **emphatic** victory is one where the winner wins easily.

⭐ **empire** /'empaɪə/ **empires.** ☐ N-COUNT An **empire** is a group of countries controlled by one powerful country. ☐ N-COUNT A business **empire** is a group of companies controlled by one powerful person. *...the Mondadori publishing empire.*

empirical /ɪm'pɪrɪkəl/. ADJ **Empirical** knowledge or evidence is based on observation, experiment, and experience rather than theories. ✦ **empirically** ADV *To some extent it can be demonstrated empirically.*

⭐ **employ** /ɪm'plɔɪ/ **employs, employing, employed.** ☐ VERB If a person or company **employs** you, they pay you to work for them. *3,000 local workers are employed in the tourism industry.* ☐ VERB If you **employ** methods, materials, or expressions, you make use of them. [FORMAL] *...the clever advertising employed by U.S. cigarette companies.*

⭐ **employee** /ɪm'plɔɪiː/ **employees.** N-COUNT An **employee** is a person who is paid to work for a company or organization. *He is an employee of Fuji Bank.*

⭐ **employer** /ɪm'plɔɪə/ **employers.** N-COUNT Your **employer** is the organization or person that you work for.

⭐ **employment** /ɪm'plɔɪmənt/. N-UNCOUNT If you are in **employment**, you have a paid job. *She was unable to find employment.*

empower /ɪm'paʊə/ **empowers, empowering, empowered.** VERB If someone or something **empowers** you, they give you the means to achieve something, for example to become more successful. *...to empower people, to give them ways to help them get well.* ✦ **empowerment** N-UNCOUNT *...the empowerment of women.*

empress /'emprɪs/ **empresses.** N-COUNT An **empress** is a woman who rules an empire, or the wife of an emperor.

⭐ **empty** /'empti/ **emptier, emptiest; empties, emptying, emptied.** ☐ ADJ An **empty** place, vehicle, or container has no people or things in it. *The room was bare and empty... The roads were nearly empty of traffic.* ✦ **emptiness** N-UNCOUNT *...the emptiness of the desert.* ☐ VERB If you **empty** a container, or if you **empty** something out of it, you remove its contents. *Empty the noodles and liquid into a serving bowl... He emptied the contents out into the palm of his hand.* ☐ VERB If someone **empties** a room or place, or if it **empties**, everyone in that place leaves. *The stadium emptied at the end of the first day of athletics.* ☐ ADJ If you describe something as **empty**, you mean that it has no real value or meaning. *Sometimes I even make empty threats that I have no intention of carrying out.* ✦ **emptiness** N-UNCOUNT *In my private life there was emptiness.*

empty-handed. ADJ If you come back from somewhere **empty-handed**, you have failed to get what you intended to get.

emulate /'emjʊleɪt/ **emulates, emulating, emulated.** VERB If you **emulate** someone or something, you imitate them because you admire them. [FORMAL] *Sons are traditionally expected to emulate their fathers.*

a
b
c
d
e
f
g
h
i
j
k
l
m
n
o
p
q
r
s
t
u
v
w
x
y
z

enable /ɪnˈeɪbəl/ **enables, enabling, enabled.** VERB If someone or something **enables** you **to** do something, they make it possible for you to do it. *The new test should enable doctors to detect the disease early.*

enact /ɪnˈækt/ **enacts, enacting, enacted.** [1] VERB When a government **enacts** a proposal, they make it into a law. [TECHNICAL] ♦ **enactment, enactments** N-VAR *...the enactment of a Bill of Rights.* [2] VERB If people **enact** a story or play, they act it. [FORMAL]

enamel /ɪˈnæməl/. N-UNCOUNT **Enamel** is a substance which can be heated and put onto metal in order to decorate or protect it.

encapsulate /ɪnˈkæpsjʊleɪt/ **encapsulates, encapsulating, encapsulated.** VERB If something **encapsulates** facts or ideas, it contains or represents them in a very small space or in a single object or event. *The editorial encapsulated the views of many conservatives.*

encase /ɪnˈkeɪs/ **encases, encasing, encased.** VERB If something **is encased in** a container or material, it is completely enclosed within it or covered by it. *When nuclear fuel is manufactured it is encased in metal cans.*

enchant /ɪnˈtʃɑːnt, -ˈtʃænt/ **enchants, enchanting, enchanted.** [1] VERB If you **are enchanted** by someone or something, you think they are very pleasing. ♦ **enchanting** ADJ *She's an absolutely enchanting child.* [2] VERB In fairy stories and legends, to **enchant** someone means to put a magic spell on them.

encircle /ɪnˈsɜːkəl/ **encircles, encircling, encircled.** VERB To **encircle** something or someone means to surround them completely. *A forty-foot-high concrete wall encircles the jail.*

enclave /ˈeŋkleɪv/ **enclaves.** N-COUNT An **enclave** is a place that is different from the areas surrounding it, for example because the people there are from a different culture.

enclose /ɪnˈkləʊz/ **encloses, enclosing, enclosed.** [1] VERB If a place or object **is enclosed** by something, the place or object is completely surrounded by that thing or is inside it. *The garden was enclosed by a privet hedge... Enclose the pot in a clear polythene bag.* [2] VERB If you **enclose** something with a letter, you put it in the same envelope. *Please remember to enclose a stamped addressed envelope when writing.*

enclosure /ɪnˈkləʊʒə/ **enclosures.** N-COUNT An **enclosure** is an area of land surrounded by a wall or fence and used for a special purpose. *...seats in the VIP enclosure.*

encode /ɪˈnkəʊd/ **encodes, encoding, encoded.** VERB When information **is encoded**, it is put into a code. *Throughout the 20th century spies used random noise to encode their messages.*

encompass /ɪnˈkʌmpəs/ **encompasses, encompassing, encompassed.** VERB If something **encompasses** certain things, it includes all of them. *The map shows the rest of the western region, encompassing nine states.*

encore /ˈɒŋkɔː, -ˈkɔː/ **encores.** N-COUNT & CONVENTION An **encore** is a short extra performance at the end of a longer one, which an entertainer gives because the audience asks for it, often by shouting **'encore'**.

encounter /ɪnˈkaʊntə/ **encounters, encountering, encountered.** [1] VERB If you **encounter** problems or difficulties, you experience them. *...the practical problems encountered by disabled people.* [2] VERB & N-COUNT If you **encounter** someone, or if you have an **encounter** with them, you meet them. [FORMAL] *...that first encounter with Daniel.*

encourage /ɪnˈkʌrɪdʒ, AM -ˈkɜːr-/ **encourages, encouraging, encouraged.** [1] VERB If you **encourage** someone, you give them confidence, for example by letting them know that what they are doing is good. *When things aren't going well, he encourages me, telling me not to give up.* [2] VERB If someone **is encouraged by** something, it gives them hope or confidence. *She has been encouraged by the unwavering support of her family.* ♦ **encouraged** ADJ *He was encouraged that there seemed to be some progress.* [3] VERB If you **encourage** someone **to** do something, you try to persuade them to do it, for example by trying to make it easier for them to do it. *We want to encourage people to go fishing... Their task is to help encourage private investment.* [4] VERB If something **encourages** a particular activity or state, it causes it to happen or increase. *...a natural substance that encourages cell growth.*

encouragement /ɪnˈkʌrɪdʒmənt, AM -ˈkɜːr-/ **encouragements.** N-VAR **Encouragement** is the activity of encouraging someone, or something that is said or done in order to encourage them. *Thanks for your advice and encouragement.*

encouraging /ɪnˈkʌrɪdʒɪŋ, AM -ˈkɜːr-/. ADJ Something that is **encouraging** gives you hope or confidence. *It was encouraging that he recognised the dangers.* ♦ **encouragingly** ADV *...encouragingly large audiences.*

encroach /ɪnˈkrəʊtʃ/ **encroaches, encroaching, encroached.** [1] VERB If one thing **encroaches on** or **upon** another, it spreads or becomes stronger, and slowly begins to restrict the power, range, or effectiveness of the second thing; used showing disapproval. *The Church is resisting government attempts to encroach upon its authority.* ♦ **encroachment, encroachments** N-VAR *...the encroachment of commercialism in medicine.* [2] VERB If something **encroaches on** a place, it spreads and takes over more and more of that place. [FORMAL] *Sand dunes began encroaching on agricultural land.*

encyclopedia (BRIT also **encyclopaedia**) /ɪn,saɪkləˈpiːdiə/ **encyclopedias.** N-COUNT An **encyclopedia** is a book, set of books, or CD-ROM in which many facts are arranged for reference.

end /end/ **ends, ending, ended.** [1] N-SING **The end of** something such as a period of time or an activity is the last part of it or the final point in it. *...at the end of the 18th century... You will have the chance to ask questions at the end.* [2] VERB & PHRASE

When a situation, process, or activity **ends**, or when something or someone **ends** it, it reaches its final point and stops. You can also say that something has **come to an end** or is **at an end**. *The Vietnam War was just about to end... She began to weep. That ended our discussion... The cold war came to an end.* ♦ **ending** N-SING *...the ending of a marriage.* [3] VERB A journey, road, or river that **ends** at a particular place stops there. *The road ended at a T-junction.* [4] N-COUNT The **end** of a long narrow object is the tip or smallest edge of it. *...the end of her cigarette.* [5] N-COUNT An **end** is the purpose for doing something. *The police force is being manipulated for political ends.* [6] See also **ending**, **dead end**.
PHRASES ● If you find it difficult to **make ends meet**, you do not have enough money. ● When something happens for days or weeks **on end**, it happens continuously during that time.
▶**end up.** PHR-VERB If you **end up** in a particular place or situation, you are in that place or situation after a series of events. *The painting ended up at the Tate Gallery... You might end up getting something you don't want.*

endanger /ɪnˈdeɪndʒə/ **endangers, endangering, endangered.** VERB To **endanger** something or someone means to put them in a situation where they might be harmed or destroyed. *Toxic waste could endanger lives. ...endangered species.*

endear /ɪnˈdɪə/ **endears, endearing, endeared.** VERB If something **endears** you **to** someone, or if you **endear yourself to** them, you become well liked by them. *He has endeared himself to the public.*
♦ **endearing** ADJ *...an endearing personality.*

endeavour (AM **endeavor**) /ɪnˈdevə/ **endeavours, endeavouring, endeavoured.** [1] VERB If you **endeavour to** do something, you try to do it. [FORMAL] *I will endeavour to arrange it.* [2] N-VAR An **endeavour** is an attempt to do something, especially if it is new and original. *...scientific endeavour.*

endemic /enˈdemɪk/. ADJ If a disease or illness is **endemic** in a place, it is frequently found among the people who live there. [FORMAL] *Polio was then endemic among children my age.*

ending /ˈendɪŋ/ **endings.** N-COUNT The **ending** of a book, play, or film is the last part of it. *The film has a Hollywood happy ending.* ● See also **end**.

endless /ˈendləs/ [1] ADJ If you describe something as **endless**, you mean that it lasts so long that it seems as if it will never end. *...endless meetings and tedious functions.* ♦ **endlessly** ADV *They talk about it endlessly.* [2] ADJ **Endless** means very large or long, with no variation.
♦ **endlessly** ADV *Rolling green pastures stretch endlessly to the horizon.*

endorse /ɪnˈdɔːs/ **endorses, endorsing, endorsed.** [1] VERB If you **endorse** someone or something, you say publicly that you support or approve of them. *I can endorse their opinion wholeheartedly.*
♦ **endorsement, endorsements** N-COUNT *...the committee's endorsement of the idea.* [2] VERB If you **endorse** a product or company, you appear in advertisements for it. *The twins endorsed a line of household cleaning products.* ♦ **endorsement** N-COUNT *Her income from endorsements is around $7 million a year.*

endow /ɪnˈdaʊ/ **endows, endowing, endowed.** [1] VERB If someone or something **is endowed with** a quality, they have it or are given it. [FORMAL] *Herbs endow food with subtle flavours.* [2] VERB If someone **endows** an institution, they provide it with a large amount of money which is invested to produce an annual income.

endowment /ɪnˈdaʊmənt/ **endowments.** [1] N-COUNT An **endowment** is a gift of money that is made to an institution such as a school. [2] N-COUNT Someone's **endowments** are their natural qualities and abilities. [FORMAL] *...their natural mental endowments.*

endurance /ɪnˈdjʊərəns, AM -ˈdʊr-/. N-UNCOUNT **Endurance** is the ability to continue with a difficult experience or activity over a long period of time. *...his powers of endurance.*

endure /ɪnˈdjʊə, AM -ˈdʊr/ **endures, enduring, endured.** [1] VERB If you **endure** a painful or difficult situation, you bear it calmly and patiently, usually because you have no other choice. *The company endured heavy financial losses. ...unbearable pain, which they had to endure in solitude.* [2] VERB If something **endures**, it continues to exist. *Somehow the language endures.* ♦ **enduring** ADJ *...the start of an enduring friendship.*

¹**end ˌuser, end users.** N-COUNT The **end user** of a product or service is the person that it has been designed for, not the person who installs or maintains it. *You have to be able to describe things in a form that the end user can understand.*

⭐ **enemy** /ˈenəmi/ **enemies.** [1] N-COUNT Your **enemy** is someone who intends to harm you. [2] N-SING In a war, the **enemy** is the army or country that you are fighting. **Enemy** can take the singular or plural form of the verb for this meaning. *The enemy are all around us.*

energetic /ˌenəˈdʒetɪk/. ADJ An **energetic** person has a lot of energy. **Energetic** activities require a lot of energy. *As young people we were very energetic. ...an energetic display.*
♦ **energetically** ADV *...dancing energetically around the fire.*

⭐ **energy** /ˈenədʒi/ **energies.** [1] N-UNCOUNT **Energy** is the ability and strength to do active physical things. *He was saving his energy for next week's race.* [2] N-VAR If you put all your **energy** or **energies** into something, you put all your time and effort into it. *He began to put more of his energies into bringing up his son.* [3] N-UNCOUNT **Energy** is power obtained from electricity, coal, or water, that makes machines work or provides heat. *...nuclear energy.*

ˌ**energy-efˈficient.** ADJ A device or building that is **energy-efficient** uses relatively little energy to provide the power it needs. *...energy-efficient light bulbs.*

a
b
c
d
e
f
g
h
i
j
k
l
m
n
o
p
q
r
s
t
u
v
w
x
y
z

A
B
C
D
E
F
G
H
I
J
K
L
M
N
O
P
Q
R
S
T
U
V
W
X
Y
Z

enforce /ɪnˈfɔːs/ **enforces, enforcing, enforced.**
[1] VERB If people in a position of authority **enforce** a law or rule, they make sure that it is obeyed. *The government was going to enforce a ban on any new refugees.* ♦ **enforcement** N-UNCOUNT *The doctors want stricter enforcement of existing laws.* [2] VERB If you **enforce** a particular condition, you force it to be done or to happen. ...*the enforced intimacy of life on a small, overcrowded island.*

★ **engage** /ɪnˈɡeɪdʒ/ **engages, engaging, engaged.**
[1] VERB If you **are engaged in** an activity, you are doing it. [FORMAL] *I have never engaged in the drug trade.* [2] VERB If something **engages** you, it keeps you interested in it and thinking about it. [FORMAL] *The subject has been engaging the attention of many researchers.* [3] VERB If you **engage** someone **in** conversation, you have a conversation with them. [FORMAL] *We want to engage recognized leaders in discussion.* [4] VERB If you **engage** someone to do a particular job, you hire them to do it. [FORMAL]

engaged /ɪnˈɡeɪdʒd/. [1] ADJ If two people are **engaged**, they have agreed to marry each other. [2] ADJ AFTER LINK-V Someone who is **engaged in** or **on** a particular activity is doing it or involved with it. *The police said they found the three engaged in target practice.* [3] ADJ AFTER LINK-V When a telephone line is **engaged**, it is already being used, so that you are unable to speak to the person you are phoning.

engagement /ɪnˈɡeɪdʒmənt/ **engagements.**
[1] N-COUNT An **engagement** is an arrangement that you have made to do something at a particular time. [FORMAL] *He had an engagement at a restaurant in Greek Street at eight.* [2] N-COUNT An **engagement** is an agreement that two people have made to get married. You can also refer to the period of time during which they have this agreement as their **engagement**. [3] N-COUNT A military **engagement** is a battle.

engaging /ɪnˈɡeɪdʒɪŋ/. ADJ An **engaging** person or thing is pleasant, interesting, or entertaining.

engender /ɪnˈdʒendə/ **engenders, engendering, engendered.** VERB If someone or something **engenders** a particular feeling or situation, they cause it. [FORMAL] *He has what it takes to engender loyalty.*

★ **engine** /ˈendʒɪn/ **engines.** [1] N-COUNT A vehicle's **engine** is the part that produces the power to make it move. [2] N-COUNT An **engine** is the large vehicle that pulls a railway train.

★ **engineer** /ˌendʒɪˈnɪə/ **engineers, engineering, engineered.** [1] N-COUNT An **engineer** is a skilled person who uses scientific knowledge to design, construct, and maintain engines and machines or structures such as roads and bridges. [2] VERB When a vehicle, bridge, or building **is engineered**, it is planned and constructed using scientific methods. [3] N-COUNT An **engineer** is a person who repairs mechanical or electrical devices. ...*a service engineer.* [4] VERB If you

engineer an event or situation, you cause it to happen, in a clever or indirect way. *The officers engineered a second coup on 19th June.*

★ **engineering** /ˌendʒɪˈnɪərɪŋ/. N-UNCOUNT **Engineering** is the work involved in designing and constructing machinery, electrical devices, or roads and bridges.

★ **English** /ˈɪŋɡlɪʃ/. [1] ADJ **English** means belonging or relating to England. ...*the English way of life.* [2] N-PLURAL **The English** are the people who come from England. [3] N-UNCOUNT **English** is the language spoken by people who live in Great Britain and Ireland, the United States, Canada, Australia, and many other countries.

engraved /ɪnˈɡreɪvd/. ADJ If an object is **engraved**, a design or some writing has been cut into its surface. ...*a headstone engraved with the Star of David.* ...*exquisite engraved glass.*

engrossed /ɪnˈɡrəʊst/. ADJ If you are **engrossed in** something, it holds your attention completely. *Tony didn't notice because he was too engrossed in his work.*

engulf /ɪnˈɡʌlf/ **engulfs, engulfing, engulfed.** [1] VERB If one thing **engulfs** another, it spreads quickly through it or over it, covering it completely. [LITERARY] *A landslide engulfed a block of flats.* [2] VERB If something such as a conflict or hatred **engulfs** a place or a group of people, it spreads uncontrollably through that place or group, effecting everybody strongly. [LITERARY] *A revolutionary wave now threatens to engulf the country.*

★ **enhance** /ɪnˈhɑːns, -ˈhæns/ **enhances, enhancing, enhanced.** VERB To **enhance** something means to improve its value, quality, or attractiveness. *They'll be keen to enhance their reputation abroad.* ♦ **enhancement, enhancements** N-VAR *He was concerned with the enhancement of the human condition.*

enigma /ɪˈnɪɡmə/ **enigmas.** N-COUNT If you describe something or someone as an **enigma**, you mean they are mysterious or difficult to understand.

enigmatic /ˌenɪɡˈmætɪk/. ADJ **Enigmatic** means mysterious and difficult to understand. ...*one of Orson Welles's most enigmatic films.* ♦ **enigmatically** ADV *His words hung enigmatically in the air.*

★ **enjoy** /ɪnˈdʒɔɪ/ **enjoys, enjoying, enjoyed.** [1] VERB If you **enjoy** something, it gives you pleasure and satisfaction. *I enjoyed playing cricket.* [2] VERB If you **enjoy yourself**, you do something you like doing. *Eleanor went to Baltimore with Franklin, but did not enjoy herself.* [3] VERB If you **enjoy** something such as a privilege, you have it. *The average German will enjoy 40 days' paid holiday this year.*

enjoyable /ɪnˈdʒɔɪəbəl/. ADJ Something that is **enjoyable** gives you pleasure. *Shopping for clothes should be an enjoyable experience.*

enjoyment /ɪnˈdʒɔɪmənt/. N-UNCOUNT Your **enjoyment of** something is the pleasure you get from having or experiencing it. *I apologise if your enjoyment of the movie was spoiled.*

enlarge /ɪnˈlɑːdʒ/ **enlarges, enlarging, enlarged.** ☐1 VERB If you **enlarge** something, or if it **enlarges**, it becomes bigger. *...the plan to enlarge Ewood Park into a 30,000 all-seater stadium... The glands in the neck may enlarge. ...an enlarged peacekeeping force.* ♦ **enlargement** N-UNCOUNT *...the enlargement of the European Union.* ☐2 VERB If you **enlarge on** or **upon** something that has been mentioned, you give more details about it.

enlighten /ɪnˈlaɪtən/ **enlightens, enlightening, enlightened.** VERB To **enlighten** someone means to give them more knowledge and greater understanding about something. [FORMAL] *This book will entertain and enlighten the reader.* ♦ **enlightening** ADJ *...an enlightening talk on the work done at the zoo.*

enlightened /ɪnˈlaɪtənd/. ADJ If you describe someone as **enlightened**, you admire them for having sensible modern attitudes. You can also talk about an **enlightened** place or period of history. *We now live in more enlightened times.*

enlist /ɪnˈlɪst/ **enlists, enlisting, enlisted.** ☐1 VERB If someone **enlists**, he or she joins the army, navy, or air force. *He enlisted as a private in the Mexican War... Many students sought to avoid being drafted and sent to Vietnam as enlisted men.* ☐2 VERB If you **enlist** someone's help or support, you persuade them to help you or support you.

enliven /ɪnˈlaɪvən/ **enlivens, enlivening, enlivened.** VERB If something **enlivens** an event or situation, it makes it more lively or cheerful. *Flirtation can enliven even the most mundane situation.*

en masse /ˌɒn ˈmæs/. ADV If a group of people do something **en masse**, they all do it together. *They were threatening to resign en masse.*

⭐ **enormous** /ɪˈnɔːməs/. ADJ **Enormous** means extremely large in size, amount, or degree. *The main bedroom is enormous... It was an enormous disappointment.* ♦ **enormously** ADV *I admired him enormously.*

⭐ **enough** /ɪˈnʌf/. ☐1 QUANT **Enough** means as much as you need or as much as is necessary. *They had enough cash for a one-way ticket... I was old enough to work and earn money... Although the UK says efforts are being made, they are not doing enough.* ☐2 QUANT If you say that something is **enough**, you mean that you do not want it to continue. *I think I have said enough... Ann had heard enough of this... Would you shut up, please! I'm having enough trouble with these children!* ☐3 ADV You use **enough** to say that something is the case to a moderate or fairly large degree. *Winter is a common enough German surname... The rest of the evening passed pleasantly enough.* ☐4 ADV You use **enough** in expressions such as **strangely enough** and **interestingly enough** to indicate that you think a fact is strange or interesting. *...an Italian who, interestingly enough, doesn't speak a word of his native language.* ● **sure enough**: see **sure**.

enquire /ɪnˈkwaɪə/. See **inquire**.
enquiry /ɪnˈkwaɪəri/. See **inquiry**.
enrage /ɪnˈreɪdʒ/ **enrages, enraging, enraged.** VERB If you **are enraged** by something, it makes you extremely angry. *He enraged the government by renouncing the agreement.* ♦ **enraged** ADJ *I began getting more and more enraged at my father.*

enrich /ɪnˈrɪtʃ/ **enriches, enriching, enriched.** VERB To **enrich** something means to improve its quality by adding something to it. *It is important to enrich the soil prior to planting.* ♦ **enrichment** N-UNCOUNT *...spiritual enrichment.*

enrol (AM **enroll**) /ɪnˈrəʊl/ **enrols, enrolling, enrolled.** VERB If you **enrol** for a course, or if you **are enrolled** in a college or university, you officially join it and pay a fee. *Cherny was enrolled at the University in 1945... I thought I'd enrol you with an art group at the school.* ♦ **enrolment** N-UNCOUNT *A fee is payable at enrolment.*

en route /ˌɒn ˈruːt/. ADV If you are **en route to** a place, you are travelling there.

enshrined /ɪnˈʃraɪnd/. ADJ If something such as an idea or a right is **enshrined in** a society, constitution, or a law, it is protected by it. *Freedom of speech is enshrined in the US constitution.*

ensue /ɪnˈsjuː, AM -ˈsuː/ **ensues, ensuing, ensued.** VERB If something **ensues**, it happens immediately after something else, usually as a result of else. *A brief but rather embarrassing silence ensued.*

ensuing /ɪnˈsjuːɪŋ/. ADJ BEFORE N **Ensuing** events happen immediately after other events. *The ensuing argument had been bitter.*

⭐ **ensure** /ɪnˈʃʊə/ **ensures, ensuring, ensured.** VERB To **ensure** that something happens means to make certain that it happens. [FORMAL] *Ensure that your name and address is correct.*

entail /ɪnˈteɪl/ **entails, entailing, entailed.** VERB If one thing **entails** another, it involves it or causes it. *The job entails dealing with members of the public.*

entangle /ɪnˈtæŋɡəl/ **entangles, entangling, entangled.** ☐1 VERB If something **is entangled** in something such as a rope or net, it is caught in it very firmly. *Drift nets entangle hundreds of thousands of animals annually.* ☐2 VERB If something **entangles** you **in** problems or difficulties, it involves you in problems or difficulties from which you find it hard to escape. *Military involvement could eventually entangle Britain in a war.* ♦ **entangled** ADJ *He became entangled in further controversy.* ♦ **entanglement, entanglements** N-VAR *...the US becoming involved in foreign entanglements.*

⭐ **enter** /ˈentə/ **enters, entering, entered.** ☐1 VERB When you **enter** a place, you come or go into it. [FORMAL] *He entered the room briskly and stood near the door... As soon as I entered, they stopped.* ☐2 VERB If you **enter** an organization or institution, you start to work there or become a member of it. *She entered Parliament in 1959.*

3 VERB When something **enters** a new period in its development or history, it begins this period. ...*as the war enters its second month.* **4** VERB If you **enter** a competition, race, or examination, you officially take part in it. *His wife Marie secretly entered him for the Championship.* **5** VERB When you **enter** something in a book or computer, you write or type it in. *Prue entered the passage in her notebook.*

▶**enter into.** **1** PHR-VERB If you **enter into** something such as an agreement, discussion, or relationship with someone, you become involved in it. [FORMAL] *She is prepared to enter into talks with the strike leaders.* **2** PHR-VERB Something that **enters into** something else is a factor in it. *Self-interest didn't enter into it.*

★ **enterprise** /'entəpraɪz/ **enterprises.** **1** N-COUNT An **enterprise** is a company or business. ...*state-owned enterprises.* **2** N-COUNT An **enterprise** is something new that you try to do, especially something difficult or involving a degree of risk. *Horse breeding is indeed a risky enterprise.* **3** N-UNCOUNT If you say that someone shows **enterprise**, you approve of their willingness to try out new ways of doing something. *Sadly, his enterprise was not rewarded.* ♦ **enterprising** ADJ ...*an enterprising young man.*

★ **entertain** /,entə'teɪn/ **entertains, entertaining, entertained.** **1** VERB If you **entertain** people, you do something that amuses or interests them. *Children's television not only entertains but also teaches.* ♦ **entertaining** ADJ ...*a highly entertaining movie.* **2** VERB If you **entertain** guests, you give them food and hospitality. ...*an enthusiastic cook who loves to entertain.* ♦ **entertaining** N-UNCOUNT *The magnificent hall is often used for entertaining.* **3** VERB If you **entertain** an idea or suggestion, you consider it. [FORMAL] *They flatly refuse to entertain any idea of reform.*

entertainer /,entə'teɪnə/ **entertainers.** N-COUNT An **entertainer** is a person whose job is to entertain audiences, for example by telling jokes, singing, or dancing.

★ **entertainment** /,entə'teɪnmənt/ **entertainments.** N-VAR **Entertainment** consists of performances or activities that give people pleasure. *We have to present athletics as entertainment.* ...*discos and other entertainments.*

enthral (AM **enthrall**) /ɪn'θrɔːl/ **enthrals, enthralling, enthralled.** VERB To **enthral** someone means to hold their attention and interest completely. *He enthralled audiences in Paris.* ♦ **enthralling** ADJ ...*an enthralling book.*

enthuse /ɪn'θjuːz/, AM -'θuːz/ **enthuses, enthusing, enthused.** **1** VERB If you **enthuse** about something, you talk about it in a way that shows how excited you are about it. *'I've found the most wonderful house to buy!' she enthused.* **2** VERB If you **are enthused** by something, it makes you feel enthusiastic. *Holst was enthused by William Morris's ideas on art.*

★ **enthusiasm** /ɪn'θjuːziæzəm, AM -'θuː-/ **enthusiasms.** **1** N-UNCOUNT **Enthusiasm** is great eagerness to do something or to be involved in something. *If her son showed enough enthusiasm, maybe Warren would take him into the business.* **2** N-COUNT An **enthusiasm** is an activity or subject that interests you a lot. *Racing was one of Pat Meaney's many enthusiasms.*

enthusiast /ɪn'θjuːziæst, AM -'θuː-/ **enthusiasts.** N-COUNT An **enthusiast** is a person who is very interested in a particular activity or subject. ...*keep-fit enthusiasts.*

enthusiastic /ɪn,θjuːzi'æstɪk, AM -,θuː-/. ADJ If you are **enthusiastic about** something, you show how much you like or enjoy it by the way that you behave and talk. *They are very enthusiastic about the proposal.* ♦ **enthusiastically** ADV *The announcement was greeted enthusiastically.*

entice /ɪn'taɪs/ **entices, enticing, enticed.** VERB To **entice** someone means to try to persuade them to go somewhere or to do something. *She resisted attempts to entice her into politics.* ♦ **enticement, enticements** N-VAR *There is a range of enticements to open an account.*

enticing /ɪn'taɪsɪŋ/. ADJ Something that is **enticing** is extremely attractive. *It was an enticing proposition.*

★ **entire** /ɪn'taɪə/. ADJ You use **entire** when you want to emphasize that you are referring to the whole of something. *He had spent his entire life in China as a doctor... The entire family was staring at him.*

★ **entirely** /ɪn'taɪəli/. ADV **Entirely** means completely. ...*an entirely new approach... Paul was not entirely happy with this suggestion... I agree with you entirely.*

entirety /ɪn'taɪərɪti/. PHRASE If you refer to something **in its entirety**, you mean all of it. ...*plans to publish the journal in its entirety.*

★ **entitle** /ɪn'taɪtəl/ **entitles, entitling, entitled.** **1** VERB If you **are entitled to** something, you have the right to have it or do it. *They are also entitled to free school meals.* ♦ **entitlement, entitlements** N-VAR *They lose their entitlement to benefit when they start work.* **2** VERB You say that a book, film, or painting **is entitled** a particular thing when you are mentioning its title. ...*a book entitled Decorative Designs.*

entity /'entɪti/ **entities.** N-COUNT An **entity** is something that exists separately from other things and has a clear identity. [FORMAL] *The domestic and international tourism markets are separate entities.*

entourage /,ɒntʊ'rɑːʒ/ **entourages.** N-COUNT The **entourage** of someone famous or important is the group of assistants or other people who travel with them. *Her entourage included her personal assistant, hairdresser, and bodyguard.*

★ **entrance**, **entrances, entranced.** **1** N-COUNT /'entrəns/ An **entrance** is a way into a place, for example a door or gate. *Beside the* *entrance to the church, turn right.* [2] N-COUNT Someone's **entrance** is their arrival in a room. *If she had noticed her father's entrance, she gave no indication.* [3] N-UNCOUNT If you gain **entrance** to a place, profession, or institution, you are able to go into it or are accepted as a member of it. *Entrance to universities and senior secondary schools was restricted.* [4] VERB /ɪn'trɑːns, -'træns/ If something **entrances** you, it makes you feel delight and wonder. *She entranced the audience with classical Indian singing.* ♦ **entranced** ADJ *For the next three hours we sat entranced.*

entrant /'entrənt/ **entrants.** N-COUNT An **entrant** is a person who officially enters a competition or institution. *...competition entrants. ...a young school entrant.*

entrench /ɪn'trentʃ/ **entrenches, entrenching, entrenched.** VERB If something such as power, a custom, or an idea is **entrenched**, it is firmly established and difficult to change. ♦ **entrenched** ADJ *Religious disputes are deeply entrenched and will not be easily overcome.*

entrepreneur /,ɒntrəprə'nɜː/ **entrepreneurs.** N-COUNT An **entrepreneur** is a person who sets up businesses and business deals. ♦ **entrepreneurial** ADJ *...his entrepreneurial skills.*

entrust /ɪn'trʌst/ **entrusts, entrusting, entrusted.** VERB If you **entrust** something important **to** someone, or if you **entrust** them **with** it, you make them responsible for it. *Miss Conway was entrusted with the children's education.*

⭐ **entry** /'entri/ **entries.** [1] N-COUNT An **entry** is something that you complete in order to take part in a competition, for example the answers to a set of questions. *The closing date for entries is 31st December.* [2] N-COUNT An **entry** in a diary, computer file, or reference book is a single short item in it. *The event is recorded in Waite's diary, in the entry for 23 March 1936.* [3] N-COUNT A person's **entry** is their arrival in a room. *They hardly noticed Sue's triumphant entry into the room.* [4] N-UNCOUNT If you gain **entry** to a particular place, you are able to go in. *He was refused entry to France... No entry after 11pm.* [5] N-UNCOUNT Someone's **entry** into a society or group is their joining of it. *His entry into the navy had to be delayed.* [6] N-COUNT The **entry** to a place is the way into it, for example a door or gate.

envelop /ɪn'veləp/ **envelops, enveloping, enveloped.** VERB If one thing **envelops** another, it covers or surrounds it completely. *A thick fog enveloped the airport.*

envelope /'envələʊp, 'ɒn-/ **envelopes.** N-COUNT An **envelope** is the rectangular paper cover in which you send a letter through the post.

enviable /'enviəbl/. ADJ An **enviable** quality is one that someone else has and that you wish you had too. *They have enviable reputations as athletes.*

envious /'enviəs/. ADJ If you are **envious of**

someone else, you **envy** them. ♦ **enviously** ADV *Ferguson could only look on enviously.*

⭐ **environment** /ɪn'vaɪərənmənt/ **environments.** [1] N-VAR Someone's **environment** is their surroundings, especially the conditions in which they grow up, live, or work. *The twins were separated at birth and brought up in entirely different environments.* [2] N-SING The **environment** is the natural world of land, sea, air, plants, and animals. *...persuading people to respect the environment.* ♦ **environmental** /ɪn,vaɪərən'mentəl/ ADJ BEFORE N *Ireland's strict environmental protection laws ensure that these industries operate safely and cleanly.*

environmentalist /ɪn,vaɪərən'mentəlɪst/ **environmentalists.** N-COUNT An **environmentalist** is a person who wants to protect and preserve the natural environment.

envisage /ɪn'vɪzɪdʒ/ **envisages, envisaging, envisaged.** VERB If you **envisage** a situation or event, you imagine it, or think that it is likely to happen. *He had never envisaged spending the whole of his working life in that particular job.*

envision /ɪn'vɪʒən/ **envisions, envisioning, envisioned.** VERB If you **envision** something, you envisage it. [AMERICAN]

envoy /'envɔɪ/ **envoys.** N-COUNT An **envoy** is a diplomat sent to a foreign country.

envy /'envi/ **envies, envying, envied.** VERB & N-UNCOUNT If you **envy** someone, you wish that you had the same things or qualities that they have. This feeling is called **envy**. *I envied her relationship with our mother... Her sisters watched with envy.*

enzyme /'enzaɪm/ **enzymes.** N-COUNT An **enzyme** is a chemical substance that is found in living creatures which produces changes in other substances without being changed itself. [TECHNICAL]

epic /'epɪk/ **epics.** [1] N-COUNT An **epic** is a long book, poem, or film whose story extends over a long period of time or tells of great events. *...Mel Gibson's historical epic, Braveheart.* [2] ADJ Something that is described as **epic** is considered very impressive or ambitious. *...Columbus's epic voyage of discovery.*

epidemic /,epɪ'demɪk/ **epidemics.** N-COUNT If there is an **epidemic** of a particular disease somewhere, it spreads quickly to a very large number of people there. *...a flu epidemic.*

epilepsy /'epɪlepsi/. N-UNCOUNT **Epilepsy** is a brain condition which causes a person to suddenly lose consciousness and sometimes to have fits.

epileptic /,epɪ'leptɪk/ **epileptics.** [1] N-COUNT An **epileptic** is a person who suffers from epilepsy. [2] ADJ **Epileptic** means suffering from or relating to epilepsy. *...an epileptic fit.*

episode /'epɪsəʊd/ **episodes.** [1] N-COUNT You can refer to an event or a short period of time as an **episode** if you want to suggest that it is important or unusual, or has some particular

a
b
c
d
e
f
g
h
i
j
k
l
m
n
o
p
q
r
s
t
u
v
w
x
y
z

quality. ...*an unhappy episode in our long (and previously friendly) relationship.* **2** N-COUNT An **episode** is one of the programmes in a serial on television or radio.

epitome /ɪˈpɪtəmi/. N-SING If you say that someone or something is **the epitome of** a particular thing, you mean that they are a perfect example of it. *Maureen was the epitome of sophistication.*

epitomize (BRIT also **epitomise**) /ɪˈpɪtəmaɪz/. **epitomizes, epitomizing, epitomized.** VERB If you say that someone or something **epitomizes** a particular thing, you mean that they are a perfect example of it. ...*the American heiress who is said to have epitomised Parisian chic in her day.*

epoch /ˈiːpɒk, AM ˈepək/ **epochs.** N-COUNT If you refer to a long period of time as an **epoch**, you mean that important events or great changes took place during it. *The birth of Christ was the beginning of a major epoch of world history.*

⭐ **equal** /ˈiːkwəl/ **equals, equalling, equalled** (AM **equaling, equaled**). **1** ADJ If two things are **equal**, or if one thing is **equal to** another, they are the same in size, number, or value. ...*equal numbers of men and women... Research and teaching are of equal importance. ...an amount equal to their monthly wages.* ◆ **equally** ADV *All these techniques are equally effective... The prize was divided equally between the six of us.* **2** ADJ If people are **equal**, they all have the same rights and are treated in the same way. ...*the commitment to equal opportunities... They have agreed to meet on reasonably equal terms.* ◆ **equally** ADV ...*a court system that is supposed to treat everyone equally.* **3** N-COUNT If someone is your **equal**, they have the same ability or status that you have. *You should have married somebody more your equal.* **4** VERB To **equal** something or someone means to be as good as or as great as them. *The victory equalled Southend's best in history.* **5** ADJ AFTER LINK-V If someone is **equal to** a job or situation, they have the necessary abilities, strength, or courage to deal successfully with it. *He was confident that the two people would be equal to the task ahead of them.*

equality /ɪˈkwɒlɪti/. N-UNCOUNT **Equality** is a situation or state where all the members of a society or group have the same status, rights, and opportunities. ...*equality of the sexes.*

equalize (BRIT also **equalise**) /ˈiːkwəlaɪz/ **equalizes, equalizing, equalized.** VERB To **equalize** a situation means to give everyone the same rights or opportunities. ...*modern divorce laws that equalize the rights of husbands and wives.* ◆ **equalization** N-UNCOUNT ...*the equalization of parenting responsibilities between men and women.*

⭐ **equally** /ˈiːkwəli/. ADV **Equally** is used to introduce a comment which balances or contrasts with another comment that has just been made. *In that situation, he would lie. Equally, in my situation, I would want to believe he was lying.* ● See also **equal**.

equate /ɪˈkweɪt/ **equates, equating, equated.** VERB If you **equate** one thing with another, or if one thing **equates with** another, you believe that they are strongly connected. *I'm always wary of men wearing suits, as I equate this with power and authority... The author doesn't equate liberalism and conservatism.*

equation /ɪˈkweɪʒən/ **equations.** N-COUNT An **equation** is a mathematical statement saying that two amounts or values are the same, for example $6 \times 4 = 12 \times 2$.

equator /ɪˈkweɪtə/. N-SING **The equator** is an imaginary line round the middle of the earth, halfway between the North and South poles.

equestrian /ɪˈkwestriən/. ADJ **Equestrian** means connected with the activity of riding horses. ...*equestrian skills.*

equilibrium /ˌiːkwɪˈlɪbriəm/. N-VAR **Equilibrium** is a state of balance or stability in a situation or in someone's mind. *For the economy to be in equilibrium, income must equal expenditure... He had recovered his equilibrium and even his good humour.*

equip /ɪˈkwɪp/ **equips, equipping, equipped.** **1** VERB If you **equip** a person or thing **with** something such as a tool or a machine, you provide them with it. *They equipped their vehicle with all sorts of gadgets. ...well-equipped research buildings.* **2** VERB If something **equips** you **for** a particular task or experience, it gives you the knowledge, skills, and personal qualities you need for it. *These skills will equip you for what lies ahead... A basic two-hour first aid course would equip you to deal with any of these incidents.*

⭐ **equipment** /ɪˈkwɪpmənt/. N-UNCOUNT **Equipment** consists of the things such as tools or machines which are used for a particular purpose.

equitable /ˈekwɪtəbəl/. ADJ Something that is **equitable** is fair and reasonable in a way that gives equal treatment to everyone. ...*a fair and equitable settlement.*

⭐ **equivalent** /ɪˈkwɪvələnt/ **equivalents.** **1** N-SING & ADJ If one amount or value is **the equivalent of** another, or if one is **equivalent to** the other, they are the same. *It is common to ask for the equivalent of one month's rent as a deposit... A unit is equivalent to a glass of wine.* **2** N-COUNT & ADJ The **equivalent** of someone or something is a person or thing that has the same function in a different place, time, or system. ...*the Red Cross and its equivalent in Muslim countries, the Red Crescent. ...a decrease of 10% in property investment compared with the equivalent period in 1991.*

ER /ˌiː ˈɑː/ **ERs.** N-COUNT In American English, the **ER** is the part of a hospital where people are taken for emergency treatment. **ER** is an abbreviation for 'emergency room'. The usual British words are **casualty** or **A&E**.

er /ɜː/. **Er** is used to represent the sound that people make when they hesitate, especially while they decide what to say next. *I would challenge the, er, suggestion that we're in third place.*

★ **era** /ˈɪərə/ **eras.** N-COUNT An **era** is a period of time that is considered as a single unit because it has a particular feature.

eradicate /ɪˈrædɪkeɪt/ **eradicates, eradicating, eradicated.** VERB To **eradicate** something means to get rid of it completely. [FORMAL] *They are already battling to eradicate illnesses such as malaria and tetanus.* ♦ **eradication** N-UNCOUNT *...the eradication of corruption.*

erase /ɪˈreɪz, AM ɪˈreɪs/ **erases, erasing, erased.** 1 VERB If you **erase** a thought or feeling, you destroy it completely so that you can no longer remember it or feel it. *They are desperate to erase the memory of that last defeat.* 2 VERB If you **erase** sound which has been recorded on a tape or information which has been stored in a computer, you completely remove or destroy it. *The names were accidentally erased from computer disks.* 3 VERB If you **erase** something such as writing or a mark, you remove it.

erect /ɪˈrekt/ **erects, erecting, erected.** 1 VERB If people **erect** something such as a building or bridge, they build it. [FORMAL] *The Eiffel Tower was erected for the World Exhibition in 1889.* ♦ **erection** N-UNCOUNT *...the erection of temporary fencing.* 2 ADJ People or things that are **erect** are straight and upright. *Her head was erect and her back was straight.*

erection /ɪˈrekʃən/ **erections.** N-COUNT If a man has an **erection**, his penis is stiff and sticking up because he is sexually aroused.

erode /ɪˈrəʊd/ **erodes, eroding, eroded.** 1 VERB If rock or soil **erodes**, or if it **is eroded** by the weather or sea, it cracks and breaks so that it is gradually destroyed. *Soil is quickly eroded by wind and rain.* ♦ **erosion** /ɪˈrəʊʒən/ N-UNCOUNT *...erosion of the river valleys.* 2 VERB If something strong or something with a high value **erodes** or **is eroded**, it gradually weakens or decreases. [FORMAL] *His fumbling of the issue of reform has eroded his authority.* ♦ **erosion** N-UNCOUNT *...the erosion of moral standards.*

erotic /ɪˈrɒtɪk/ ADJ If you describe something as **erotic**, you mean that it involves or arouses sexual desire. *It wasn't an erotic experience at all.*

err /ɜː/ **errs, erring, erred.** 1 VERB If you **err**, you do something wrong. [FORMAL] *If you make a threat be sure to carry it out if he errs again.* 2 PHRASE If you **err on the side of** a way of behaving, you tend to behave in that way. *They may be wise to err on the side of caution.*

errand /ˈerənd/ **errands.** N-COUNT If you go on an **errand** for someone, you go a short distance in order to do something for them, for example to buy something from a shop.

erratic /ɪˈrætɪk/ ADJ Something that is **erratic** happens at unexpected times or moves in an irregular way. *...Argentina's erratic inflation rate.* ♦ **erratically** ADV *Police stopped him for driving erratically.*

erroneous /ɪˈrəʊniəs/ ADJ **Erroneous** beliefs or opinions are incorrect. *...the erroneous notion that one can contract AIDS by giving blood.* ♦ **erroneously** ADV *It had been widely and erroneously reported that Armstrong had refused.*

★ **error** /ˈerə/ **errors.** 1 N-VAR An **error** is a mistake. *NASA discovered a mathematical error in its calculations... The plane was shot down in error.* 2 **trial and error:** see **trial**.

erupt /ɪˈrʌpt/ **erupts, erupting, erupted.** 1 VERB When a volcano **erupts**, it throws out a lot of hot lava, ash, and steam. ♦ **eruption, eruptions** N-VAR *...the volcanic eruption of Tambora in 1815.* 2 VERB **Erupt** is used to indicate that something suddenly begins or intensifies. *Heavy fighting erupted there today... The neighborhood known as Watts erupted into riots... Without warning she erupts into laughter.* ♦ **eruption** N-COUNT *...this sudden eruption of violence.*

escalate /ˈeskəleɪt/ **escalates, escalating, escalated.** VERB If an unpleasant situation **escalates**, or if someone or something **escalates** it, it becomes worse. [JOURNALISM] *Protests escalated into five days of rioting.* ♦ **escalation** N-SING *...a sudden escalation of violence.*

escalator /ˈeskəleɪtə/ **escalators.** N-COUNT An **escalator** is a moving staircase.

★ **escape** /ɪˈskeɪp/ **escapes, escaping, escaped.** 1 VERB & N-COUNT If you **escape from** a place, or if you make your **escape** from a place, you succeed in getting away from it. *A prisoner has escaped from a jail in northern England.* 2 VERB & N-COUNT You can say that you **escape** when you survive something such as an accident. You can also talk about a particular kind of **escape**. *The two officers were extremely lucky to escape serious injury... The man's girlfriend managed to escape unhurt... I hear you had a very narrow escape.* 3 N-COUNT If something is an **escape**, it makes people think about pleasant things instead of the tedious unpleasant aspects of their life. *For me television is an escape.* 4 VERB If something **escapes** you, or if it **escapes** your **attention**, you forget it or are unaware of it. *...an actor whose name escapes me for the moment.*

escapism /ɪˈskeɪpɪzəm/. N-UNCOUNT If you describe an activity or type of entertainment as **escapism**, you mean that it makes people think about pleasant things instead of the boring or unpleasant aspects of their life. ♦ **escapist** ADJ *...escapist movies.*

escort, escorts, escorting, escorted. 1 N-COUNT & PHRASE /ˈeskɔːt/ An **escort** is a person or group of people travelling with someone in order to protect or guard them. If someone is taken somewhere **under escort**, they are accompanied by guards, either because they have been arrested or because they need to be protected. *He arrived with a police escort.* 2 N-COUNT An **escort** is a person who accompanies someone of the opposite sex to a social event. [FORMAL] 3 VERB /ɪsˈkɔːt/ If you **escort** someone

a b c d e f g h i j k l m n o p q r s t u v w x y z

somewhere, you go there with them to make sure that they go. *I escorted him to the door.*

esoteric /ˌiːsəʊ'terɪk, AM ˌesə-/. ADJ Something that is **esoteric** is understood by only a small number of people with special knowledge. [FORMAL] *Where did you obtain this esoteric piece of information?*

⭐ **especially** /ɪ'speʃəli/. **1** ADV You use **especially** to emphasize that what you are saying applies more to one person or thing than to any others. *Re-apply sunscreen every two hours, especially if you have been swimming... He liked the American country singers, especially George Jones.* **2** ADV You use **especially** to emphasize a characteristic or quality. *She was especially fond of a little girl named Betsy.*

espionage /'espiənɑːʒ/. N-UNCOUNT **Espionage** is the activity of finding out the political, military, or industrial secrets of your enemies or rivals by using spies.

espouse /ɪ'spaʊz/ **espouses, espousing, espoused.** VERB If you **espouse** a policy or plan, you support it. [FORMAL]

essay /'eseɪ/ **essays.** N-COUNT An **essay** is a piece of writing on a particular subject. *...Thomas Malthus's essay on population.*

essence /'esəns/. N-UNCOUNT **The essence of** something is its basic and most important characteristic. *The essence of good managing is caring.*

PHRASES ● You use **in essence** to indicate that you are talking about the basic and most important characteristics of something. [FORMAL] *Local taxes are in essence simple.* ● If you say that something **is of the essence**, you mean that it is absolutely necessary in a particular situation. *Time is of the essence – a matter of life and death.*

⭐ **essential** /ɪ'senʃəl/ **essentials.** **1** ADJ Something that is **essential** is absolutely necessary. *It is essential that you take specialist legal advice... Play is an essential part of a child's development.* **2** N-COUNT **The essentials** are things that are absolutely necessary in a situation. *The flat contained the basic essentials.*

⭐ **essentially** /ɪ'senʃəli/. **1** ADV You use **essentially** to emphasize that you are talking about the most basic and important aspects of someone or something. *He was essentially a simple man.* **2** ADV You use **essentially** to indicate that what you are saying is basically or generally true, although it may not cover all the minor details. *He develops his opinions essentially by reading the newspapers.*

⭐ **establish** /ɪ'stæblɪʃ/ **establishes, establishing, established.** **1** VERB If someone **establishes** an organization or a system, they create it. *...the right to establish independent trade unions.* ● **establishment** N-SING *...the establishment of the regional government.* **2** VERB If you **establish** contact with a group of people, you start to have discussions with them. [FORMAL] ● **establishment** N-SING *...discussions to explore*

the establishment of diplomatic relations. **3** VERB If you **establish** that something is true, you discover facts that show that it is definitely true. [FORMAL] *Medical tests established that she was not their own child... An autopsy was being done to establish the cause of death. ...an established medical fact.*

established /ɪ'stæblɪʃt/. ADJ An **established** person or organization has a good reputation or a secure position, usually because they have existed for a long time. *...the established names of Paris fashion.*

⭐ **establishment** /ɪ'stæblɪʃmənt/ **establishments.** **1** N-COUNT An **establishment** is a shop, restaurant, or other business premises. [FORMAL] *...a scientific research establishment. ...commercial establishments.* **2** N-SING You refer to the people who have power and influence in the running of a country or organization as **the establishment**. *...the literary establishment.*

⭐ **estate** /ɪ'steɪt/ **estates.** **1** N-COUNT An **estate** is a large area of land in the country owned by one person or organization. **2** N-COUNT In Britain, people sometimes use **estate** to refer to a housing estate. **3** N-COUNT Someone's **estate** is the money and property they leave when they die. *His estate was valued at $150,000.* **4** See also **housing estate, real estate.**

es'tate agent, estate agents. N-COUNT In British English, an **estate agent** is someone who works for a company selling houses and land. The American word is **realtor**.

esteem /ɪ'stiːm/. N-UNCOUNT **Esteem** is admiration and respect. [FORMAL] *He is held in very high esteem by colleagues.*

esthetic /iːs'θetɪk, AM es'θ-/. See **aesthetic**.

⭐ **estimate, estimates, estimating, estimated;** verb /'estɪmeɪt/, noun /'estɪmət/. **1** VERB & N-COUNT If you **estimate** a quantity or value, or if you make an **estimate**, you make an approximate judgement or calculation of it. *It's difficult to estimate how much money is involved. ...the official estimate of the election result.* ♦ **estimated** ADJ *There are an estimated 90,000 gangsters in the country.* **2** N-COUNT An **estimate** is a judgement about a person or situation which you make based on the available evidence. *...my estimate of his grandson's capabilities.*

estranged /ɪ'streɪndʒd/. ADJ You refer to someone as **estranged from** their family or friends when they are living separately from them and not communicating with them because they have quarrelled. [FORMAL] *...his estranged wife... She spent most of her twenties virtually estranged from her father.* ♦ **estrangement** N-UNCOUNT *They are anxious to end the estrangement between them.*

estuary /'estʃʊri, AM 'estʃʊeri/ **estuaries.** N-COUNT An **estuary** is the wide part of a river where it joins the sea.

⭐ **etc. etc** is used at the end of a list to indicate that there are other items which you could mention if you had enough time or space. **etc** is a written abbreviation for **etcetera**. *She knew all about my schoolwork, my hospital work, etc.*

etcetera (or **et cetera**) /et'setrə/. See **etc**.

etch /etʃ/ **etches, etching, etched.** ⟦1⟧ VERB If a line or pattern **is etched** into a surface, it is cut into the surface using acid or a sharp tool. *Crosses were etched into the walls.* ⟦2⟧ VERB If something **is etched** on your memory, you remember it very clearly because it made a strong impression on you. [LITERARY] *The ugly scene in the study was still etched in her mind.*

etching /'etʃɪŋ/ **etchings.** N-COUNT An **etching** is a picture printed from a metal plate that has had a design cut into it.

eternal /ɪ'tɜːnəl/. ⟦1⟧ ADJ Something that is **eternal** lasts for ever. *...eternal life. ...the quest for eternal youth.* ◆ **eternally** ADV *She is eternally grateful to her family for their support.* ⟦2⟧ ADJ BEFORE N **Eternal** truths and values never change and are thought to be true in all situations. *...the eternal and immutable principles of right and wrong.*

eternity /ɪ'tɜːnɪti/. ⟦1⟧ N-UNCOUNT **Eternity** is time without an end, or a state of existence outside time, especially the state which some people believe they will pass into after they have died. *I have always found the thought of eternity terrifying.* ⟦2⟧ N-SING You can refer to a period of time as **an eternity** when it seems very long. [INFORMAL] *The war continued for an eternity.*

ethereal /ɪ'θɪəriəl/. ADJ If you describe someone or something as **ethereal**, you mean that they have a delicate beauty that seems almost supernatural. [FORMAL]

ethic /'eθɪk/ **ethics.** ⟦1⟧ N-PLURAL **Ethics** are moral beliefs and rules about right and wrong. *Its members are bound by a rigid code of ethics.* ⟦2⟧ N-SING An **ethic** of a particular kind is moral belief that influences the behaviour and attitudes of a group of people. *The work ethic is very strong in their household.*

ethical /'eθɪkəl/. ⟦1⟧ ADJ **Ethical** means influenced by a system of moral beliefs about right and wrong. *...the ethical aspects of animal experimentation.* ◆ **ethically** ADV *We can defend ethically and morally everything we stand for.* ⟦2⟧ ADJ If you describe something you do as **ethical**, you mean that it is morally right or acceptable. *My involvement has not been altogether, shall we say, ethical.* ◆ **ethically** ADV *Mayors want local companies to behave ethically.*

⭐ **ethnic** /'eθnɪk/. ADJ **Ethnic** means relating to different racial or cultural groups of people. *...Britain's ethnic minorities.* ◆ **ethnically** /'eθnɪkli/ ADV *...a predominantly young, ethnically mixed audience.*

ethos /'iːθɒs/. N-SING The **ethos** of a group of people is the set of ideas and attitudes associated with it. *The whole ethos of the hotel is effortless service.*

etiquette /'etɪket/. N-UNCOUNT **Etiquette** is a set of customs and rules for polite behaviour. *...the rules of diplomatic etiquette.*

⭐ **EU** /,iː 'juː/. N-PROPER **The EU** is an organization of European countries which have joint policies on matters such as trade, agriculture, and finance. **EU** is an abbreviation for 'European Union'.

euphemism /'juːfəmɪzəm/ **euphemisms.** N-COUNT A **euphemism** is a polite word or expression that people use to talk about something unpleasant or embarrassing, such as death or sex.

euphemistic /'juːfəmɪstɪk/. ADJ **Euphemistic** language consists of polite words or expressions for unpleasant or embarrassing things. ◆ **euphemistically** ADV *...political prisons, called euphemistically 're-education camps'.*

euphoria /juː'fɔːriə/. N-UNCOUNT **Euphoria** is a feeling of great happiness. ◆ **euphoric** /juː'fɒrɪk/ ADJ *It had received euphoric support from the public.*

euro /'jʊərəʊ/ **euros.** N-COUNT The **euro** is a unit of currency that is used by the member countries of the European Union which have joined the European Monetary union.

Euroland /'jʊərəʊlænd/. N-PROPER **Euroland** is the group of countries in the European Union which have the euro as a common currency. [JOURNALISM]

⭐ **European** /,jʊərə'piːən/ **Europeans.** ⟦1⟧ ADJ **European** means coming from or relating to Europe. *...European countries.* ⟦2⟧ N-COUNT A **European** is a person who comes from Europe.

⭐ **European 'Union.** N-PROPER **The European Union** is an organization of European countries which have joint policies on matters such as trade, agriculture, and finance.

euthanasia /,juːθə'neɪziə, AM -ʒə/. N-UNCOUNT **Euthanasia** is the practice of painlessly killing a dying person in order to stop their suffering.

evacuate /ɪ'vækjʊeɪt/ **evacuates, evacuating, evacuated.** VERB If people **are evacuated from** a place, or if they **evacuate** a place, they move out of it because it has become dangerous. *18,000 people have been evacuated from the area... Officials ordered the residents to evacuate.* ◆ **evacuation, evacuations** N-VAR *...the mass evacuation of the Bosnian town of Srebrenica.*

evacuee /ɪ,vækjʊ'iː/ **evacuees.** N-COUNT An **evacuee** is someone who has been sent away from a dangerous place to somewhere safer.

evade /ɪ'veɪd/ **evades, evading, evaded.** VERB If you **evade** something unpleasant or difficult, you avoid it. *By his own admission, he evaded taxes... He managed to evade capture.*

evaluate /ɪ'væljʊeɪt/ **evaluates, evaluating, evaluated.** VERB If you **evaluate** something or someone, you consider them in order to make a judgement about them, for example about how good or bad they are. *Evaluate what you are doing and work to get better.* ◆ **evaluation,**

a
b
c
d
e
f
g
h
i
j
k
l
m
n
o
p
q
r
s
t
u
v
w
x
y
z

evaluations N-VAR ...*the opinions and evaluations of college supervisors.*

evaporate /ɪ'væpəreɪt/ **evaporates, evaporating, evaporated.** VERB When a liquid **evaporates**, it changes into a gas, because its temperature has increased. ◆ **evaporation** N-UNCOUNT ...*the evaporation of the sweat on the skin.*

evasion /ɪ'veɪʒən/ **evasions.** N-VAR If you accuse someone of **evasion**, you mean that they are deliberately avoiding dealing with something that is unpleasant or difficult. ...*an evasion of responsibility.*

evasive /ɪ'veɪsɪv/. ADJ If you describe someone as **evasive**, you mean that they deliberately avoid answering questions. ◆ **evasively** ADV *'I can't come to any conclusion about that,' Millson said evasively.*

eve /iːv/ **eves.** N-COUNT The **eve** of an event is the day before it, or the period of time just before it. [JOURNALISM] ...*on the eve of his 27th birthday.*

⭐ **even** /'iːvən/. [1] ADV You use **even** to suggest that what comes just after or just before it in the sentence is surprising. *He kept calling me for years, even after he got married... Even dark-skinned women should use sunscreens.* [2] PHRASE You use **even so** to introduce a surprising fact that relates to what you have just said. *The bus was only half full. Even so, a young man asked Nina if the seat next to her was taken.* [3] ADV You use **even** with comparative adjectives and adverbs to emphasize a quality that someone or something has. *It was on television that he made an even stronger impact as an interviewer... Stan was speaking even more slowly than usual.* [4] CONJ You use **even if** or **even though** to indicate that a particular fact does not make the rest of your statement untrue. *Even if you are on a fairly strict diet you can still go out for a good meal.*

even /'iːvən/. [1] ADJ An **even** measurement or rate stays at about the same level. *How important is it to have an even temperature?* ◆ **evenly** ADV *He looked at Ellen, breathing evenly in her sleep.* [2] ADJ An **even** surface is smooth and flat. *The tables are fitted with a glass top to provide an even surface.* [3] ADJ If there is an **even** division of something, each person, group, or area involved has an equal amount. *Divide the dough into 12 even pieces.* ◆ **evenly** ADV *The money will be evenly distributed.* [4] ADJ If a contest or competition is **even**, the people taking part are all equally skilful. ◆ **evenly** ADV ...*two evenly matched candidates.* [5] ADJ AFTER LINK-V If you are **even with** someone, you do not owe them anything, such as money or a favour. [6] PHRASE When a company or a person running a business **breaks even**, they make neither a profit nor a loss. [7] PHRASE If you say you will **get even with** someone, you mean that you intend to harm them because they have harmed you. [INFORMAL]

[8] ADJ An **even** number can be divided exactly by the number two.

even /'iːvən/ **evens, evening, evened.**
►**even out.** PHR-VERB When an amount of something **evens out**, or when you **even** it **out**, it becomes more evenly distributed or steadier. *Rates of house price inflation have evened out.*

⭐ **evening** /'iːvnɪŋ/ **evenings.** N-VAR The **evening** is the part of each day between the end of the afternoon and the time when you go to bed. *All he did that evening was sit around. ...6.00 in the evening. ...a proper evening meal.*

⭐ **event** /ɪ'vent/ **events.** [1] N-COUNT An **event** is something that happens. ...*recent events in Europe... The event was an undoubted success.* [2] N-COUNT An **event** is an organized occasion. ...*major sporting events.* [3] PHRASE You use **in the event of**, **in the event that**, and **in that event** when you are talking about a possible future situation, especially when you are planning what to do if it occurs. ...*in the unlikely event of an error being made.*

eventual /ɪ'ventʃuəl/. ADJ BEFORE N The **eventual** result of something is what happens at the end of it. ...*events leading to his imprisonment and his eventual death.*

eventuality /ɪˌventʃu'ælɪti/ **eventualities.** N-COUNT An **eventuality** is a possible future event or result. [FORMAL] *Every eventuality is covered, from running out of petrol to needing water.*

⭐ **eventually** /ɪ'ventʃuəli/. [1] ADV **Eventually** means in the end, especially after a lot of delays, problems, or arguments. *The flight eventually got away six hours late.* [2] ADV **Eventually** means at the end of a situation or process or as the final result of it. *She eventually plans to run her own chain of country inns.*

⭐ **ever** /'evə/. [1] ADV **Ever** means at any time. It is used in questions and negative statements. *Neither of us had ever skied... Have you ever experienced failure?... You won't hear from Gaston ever again.* [2] ADV You use **ever** after comparatives and superlatives to emphasize the degree to which something is true. *She's got a great voice and is singing better than ever... This is the most awful evening I can ever remember.*
PHRASES ● You say **as ever** in order to indicate that something is not unusual. *He was by himself, alone as ever.* ● You use **ever since** to emphasize that something has been true since the time mentioned, and is still true now. *He's been there ever since you left!* ● You use **ever so** and **ever such** to emphasize that someone or something has a lot of a particular quality. [BRITISH, INFORMAL] *He was very lively and ever such a good dancer... I like him ever so much.*

ever- /'evə-/. You use **ever-** in adjectives such as **ever-increasing** and **ever-present**, to show that something exists or continues all the time. ...*an ever-changing world.*

evergreen /'evəgriːn/evergreens. N-COUNT An **evergreen** is a tree or bush which has green leaves all the year round.

⭐ **every** /'evri/. **1** DET & ADJ You use **every** to indicate that you are referring to all the members of a group or all the parts of something. ...*recipes for every occasion.* ...*parents who would fulfil his every need.* **2** DET You use **every** to say how often something happens or to indicate that something happens at regular intervals. *We were made to attend meetings every day... A burglary occurs every three minutes in London.* **3** DET You use **every** before some nouns in order to emphasize what you are saying. *There is every chance that you will succeed... I made every effort to be co-operative... He has every intention of staying.*

PHRASES ● You use the expressions **every now and then**, **every now and again**, **every once in a while**, and **every so often** to indicate that something happens occasionally. ● If something happens **every other** day or week, for example, or **every second** day or week, it happens on one day or week in each period of two days or weeks. *Their local committees are usually held every other month.*

⭐ **everybody** /'evrɪbɒdi/. See **everyone**.

everyday /'evrideɪ/. ADJ You use **everyday** to describe something which happens or is used every day, or forms a regular and basic part of your life. ...*your everyday routine.* ...*the joys and sorrows of everyday living.*

⭐ **everyone** /'evriwʌn/ (or **everybody**). PRON **Everyone** or **everybody** means all the people in a group or all people in general. *Everyone in the street was shocked... Everyone else goes home around 7 p.m... Everyone needs some free time for rest and relaxation.*

> **USAGE** Do not confuse **everyone** with **every one**. **Everyone** always refers to people. In the phrase **every one**, 'one' is a pronoun that can refer to any person or thing, depending on the context. It is often followed by the word **of**. *We've saved seeds from every one of our plants... Every one of them phoned me.* In these examples, **every one** is a more emphatic way of saying **all**.

⭐ **everything** /'evrɪθɪŋ/. **1** PRON You use **everything** to refer to all the objects, activities, or facts in a situation. *Everything else in his life had changed.* ...*everything that they will need for the day's hike.* **2** PRON You use **everything** to refer to a whole situation or to life in general. *Is everything all right?*

⭐ **everywhere** /'evriweə/. **1** ADV You use **everywhere** to refer to a whole area or to all the places in a particular area. *Working people everywhere object to paying taxes... We went everywhere together.* **2** ADV You use **everywhere**

to refer to all the places that someone goes to. *Everywhere he went he was introduced as the current United States Open Champion.* **3** PRON If you say that someone or something is **everywhere**, you mean that they are present in a place in very large numbers. *There were cartons of cigarettes everywhere.*

evict /ɪ'vɪkt/evicts, evicting, evicted. VERB When people **are evicted**, they are officially forced to leave the house where they are living. *The city police evicted ten families.* ◆ **eviction, evictions** N-VAR *He was facing eviction, along with his wife and family.*

⭐ **evidence** /'evɪdəns/. N-UNCOUNT **Evidence** is anything that makes you believe that something is true or exists. ...*evidence that stress is partly responsible for disease... There is no evidence to support this theory.*

PHRASES ● If you **give evidence** in a court of law, you give a statement saying what you know about something. ● If someone or something is **in evidence**, they are present and can be clearly seen. *Few soldiers were in evidence.*

evident /'evɪdənt/. ADJ If something is **evident**, you notice it easily and clearly. *His footprints were clearly evident in the heavy dust... It was evident that she had once been a beauty.*

evidently /'evɪdəntli/. ADV You use **evidently** to say that something is true, because you have seen evidence of it yourself or because someone has told you it is true. *The two Russians evidently knew each other.*

⭐ **evil** /'iːvəl/evils. **1** N-UNCOUNT **Evil** is used to refer to all the wicked and bad things that happen in the world. ...*a conflict between good and evil.* **2** N-COUNT An **evil** is a very unpleasant or harmful situation or activity. ...*the evils of alcohol.* **3** ADJ If you describe someone or something as **evil**, you mean that they are wicked and cause harm to people. ...*the country's most evil terrorists.* ...*condemning slavery as evil.*

evocative /ɪ'vɒkətɪv/. ADJ If something like a description is **evocative**, it strongly reminds you of something or gives you a powerful impression of what it is like. *Her story is sharply evocative of Italian provincial life.*

evoke /ɪ'vəʊk/evokes, evoking, evoked. VERB To **evoke** a particular memory, idea, emotion, or response means to cause it to happen or exist. ...*the scene evoking memories of those old movies.*

evolution /ˌiːvə'luːʃən, ˌev-/. **1** N-UNCOUNT **Evolution** is a process of gradual change during which animals and plants change some of their characteristics and sometimes develop into new species. **2** N-UNCOUNT You can use **evolution** to refer to any gradual process of change and development. ...*the evolution of modern physics.*

evolutionary /ˌiːvə'luːʃənri, AM -neri/. ADJ **Evolutionary** means relating to a process of gradual change and development. ...*a period of evolutionary change.*

a
b
c
d
e
f
g
h
i
j
k
l
m
n
o
p
q
r
s
t
u
v
w
x
y
z

A
B
C
D
E
F
G
H
I
J
K
L
M
N
O
P
Q
R
S
T
U
V
W
X
Y
Z

evolve /ɪ'vɒlv/ **evolves, evolving, evolved.** ☐1 VERB When animals and plants **evolve**, they gradually change and develop into different forms. *Maize evolved from a wild grass. ...when amphibians evolved into reptiles.* ☐2 VERB If something **evolves**, or if you **evolve** it, it gradually develops into something different and usually more advanced. *...a tiny airline which eventually evolved into Pakistan International Airlines.*

ewe /juː/ **ewes.** N-COUNT A **ewe** is an adult female sheep.

exacerbate /ɪg'zæsəbeɪt/ **exacerbates, exacerbating, exacerbated.** VERB If something **exacerbates** a bad situation, it makes it worse. [FORMAL] ♦ **exacerbation** N-UNCOUNT *...the exacerbation of global problems.*

⭐ **exact** /ɪg'zækt/ **exacts, exacting, exacted.** ☐1 ADJ Something that is **exact** is correct, accurate, and complete in every way. *I don't remember the exact words... The exact number of protest calls has not been revealed... A small number – five, to be exact – have been bad.* ♦ **exactly** ADV *Try to locate exactly where the smells are entering the room.* ☐2 ADJ BEFORE N You use **exact** before a noun to emphasize that you are referring to that particular thing and no other. *Do you really think I could get the exact thing I want?* ☐3 VERB When someone **exacts** something, they demand and obtain it from someone else. [FORMAL] *Already he has exacted a written apology from the chairman of the commission.* ☐4 See also **exactly**.

exacting /ɪg'zæktɪŋ/. ADJ An **exacting** person or task requires you to work very hard. *They seem to have the same exacting standards.*

⭐ **exactly** /ɪg'zæktli/. ☐1 ADV **Exactly** means precisely, and not just approximately. *Agnew's car pulled into the driveway at exactly five o'clock. ...exactly in the middle of the picture.* ☐2 ADV If you say **'Exactly'**, you are agreeing with someone or emphasizing the truth of what they say. If you say **'Not exactly'**, you are telling them politely that not everything they are saying is true or accurate. *'We don't know the answer to that.'—'Exactly, so shut up... 'And you refused?'—'Well, not exactly. I couldn't say yes.'* ☐3 ADV You use **not exactly** to indicate that a meaning or situation is slightly different from what people think or expect. *He's not exactly homeless, he just hangs out in this park.*

exaggerate /ɪg'zædʒəreɪt/ **exaggerates, exaggerating, exaggerated.** ☐1 VERB If you **exaggerate**, you make the thing that you are talking about seem bigger or more important than it actually is. *She did sometimes exaggerate the demands of her job.* ♦ **exaggeration, exaggerations** N-VAR *It would be an exaggeration to call the danger urgent.* ☐2 VERB If something **exaggerates** a situation, quality, or feature, it makes it appear greater, more obvious, or more important than it really is. *The dress exaggerates her slim waist.*

exaggerated /ɪg'zædʒəreɪtɪd/. ADJ Something that is **exaggerated** is or seems larger, better,

worse, or more important than it needs to be. *...exaggerated claims for what such courses can achieve.*

exalted /ɪg'zɔːltɪd/. ADJ An **exalted** person is very important. [LITERARY] *...the more exalted members of the British government.*

exam /ɪg'zæm/ **exams.** N-COUNT An **exam** is a formal test taken to show your knowledge of a subject. *Did you pass any exams?... I was due to sit exams at university.*

USAGE Note that to **pass** an exam always means to succeed in it. If you do not pass an exam, you **fail** it. If you simply do an exam or take part in it, you can say that you **take** the exam, or, in British English, that you **sit** the exam.

⭐ **examination** /ɪg,zæmɪ'neɪʃən/ **examinations.** N-COUNT An **examination** is an exam. [FORMAL]

⭐ **examine** /ɪg'zæmɪn/ **examines, examining, examined.** ☐1 VERB If you **examine** something, you look at it or consider it carefully. *He examined her passport... The plans will be examined by EU environment ministers.* ♦ **examination, examinations** N-VAR *Further examination is needed to exclude the chance of disease.* ☐2 VERB If you **are being examined**, you are being given a formal test in order to show your knowledge of a subject

examiner /ɪg'zæmɪnə/ **examiners.** N-COUNT An **examiner** is a person who sets or marks an exam.

⭐ **example** /ɪg'zɑːmpəl, -'zæmp-/ **examples.** ☐1 N-COUNT An **example** is something which represents or is typical of a particular group of things. *...an outstanding example of a small business that grew into a big one... Let me give another example.* ☐2 PHRASE You use **for example** to show that you are giving an example of a particular kind of thing. *...intelligent money management, for example paying big bills monthly.* ☐3 N-COUNT In a dictionary entry, an **example** is a phrase which shows how a word is used. ☐4 N-COUNT If you refer to a person as an **example** to other people, you mean that he or she behaves in a good way that other people should copy. *He had always been held up as an example to the younger ones.*
PHRASES If you **follow** someone's **example**, you copy their behaviour, especially because you admire them. If you **set an example**, you encourage people by your behaviour to behave in a similar way.

exasperate /ɪg'zɑːspəreɪt, -'zæs-/ **exasperates, exasperating, exasperated.** VERB If someone or something **exasperates** you, they annoy you, making you feel frustrated. *The sheer futility of it all exasperates her.* ♦ **exasperated** ADJ *Bertha was exasperated at the delay.* ♦ **exasperation** N-UNCOUNT *Mahoney clenched his fist in exasperation.*

---

excavate /'ekskəveɪt/ **excavates, excavating, excavated.** VERB To **excavate** a piece of land means to remove earth carefully from it and look for the remains of objects or buildings, in order to find out about the past. ♦ **excavation, excavations** N-VAR ...*the excavation of a bronze-age boat.*

exceed /ɪk'siːd/ **exceeds, exceeding, exceeded.** 1 VERB If something **exceeds** a particular amount, it is greater than that amount. *Its research budget exceeds $700 million a year.* 2 VERB If you **exceed** a limit, you go beyond it. *I would be exceeding my powers if I ordered the march to be halted.*

exceedingly /ɪk'siːdɪŋli/. ADV **Exceedingly** means very much indeed. [DATED] ...*an exceedingly good lunch.*

excel /ɪk'sel/ **excels, excelling, excelled.** VERB If someone **excels in** or **at** something, they are very good at it. *She excelled at outdoor sports... Academically he began to excel.*

Excellency /'eksələnsi/ **Excellencies.** N-VOC People use expressions such as **Your Excellency** or **His Excellency** when they are addressing or referring to officials of very high rank, for example ambassadors or governors. ...*His Excellency the President.*

★ **excellent** /'eksələnt/. ADJ Something that is **excellent** is very good indeed. *Sue is very efficient and does an excellent job as Fred's personal assistant.* ♦ **excellence** N-UNCOUNT ...*the top US award for excellence in journalism.* ♦ **excellently** ADV *They're both playing excellently.*

★ **except** /ɪk'sept/. PREP & CONJ You use **except** or **except for** to introduce the only thing or person that a statement does not apply to, or a fact that prevents a statement from being completely true. *I don't take any drugs whatsoever, except aspirin... Everyone was late, except for Richard... The log cabin stayed empty, except when we came.*

★ **exception** /ɪk'sepʃən/ **exceptions.** N-VAR An **exception** is a situation, thing, or person that is not included in a general statement. *Normally she wore little make-up, but this evening was clearly an exception. ...a day off for everybody, with the exception of Lawrence.*
  PHRASES • If you **make an exception**, you consider or allow something that you would normally not consider or allow. *It is not a good idea to eat in hotels, but I made an exception for the Chinese restaurant in the Mandarin Hotel.* • If you **take exception to** something, you feel offended or annoyed by it. *He took exception to having been spied on.*

exceptional /ɪk'sepʃənəl/. 1 ADJ You use **exceptional** to describe someone or something that has a particular quality to an unusually high degree. ...*children with exceptional ability.* ♦ **exceptionally** ADV ...*an exceptionally talented dancer.* 2 ADJ **Exceptional** situations are very unusual or rare. *The courts hold that this case is exceptional.*

★ **excerpt** /'eksɜːpt/ **excerpts.** N-COUNT An **excerpt** is a short piece of writing or music taken from a larger piece. ...*an excerpt from Tchaikovsky's Nutcracker.*

★ **excess, excesses;** noun /ɪk'ses/, adjective /'ekses/. 1 N-VAR & ADJ BEFORE N An **excess of** something or an **excess** amount of it is a larger amount than is needed or usual. ...*the problems created by an excess of wealth... The major reason for excess weight is excess eating.* 2 PHRASE **In excess of** means more than a particular amount. *Avoid deposits in excess of £20,000 in any one account.* 3 N-VAR **Excess** is behaviour that is unacceptable because it is too extreme or immoral. ...*the bloody excesses of warfare.* 4 PHRASE If you do something **to excess**, you do it too much. *Red meat, eaten to excess, is very high in fat.*

excessive /ɪk'sesɪv/. ADJ If something is **excessive**, it is too great in amount or degree. ...*use of excessive force by police.* ♦ **excessively** ADV ...*excessively high salaries.*

★ **exchange** /ɪks'tʃeɪndʒ/ **exchanges, exchanging, exchanged.** 1 VERB & N-COUNT If two or more people **exchange** things, or if there is an **exchange of** them, they give them to each other at the same time. *We exchanged addresses... He exchanged a quick smile with her. ...the exchange of prisoners of war.* 2 VERB If you **exchange** something, or if you **exchange** it **for** something else, you replace it with something. *We will gladly exchange your goods, or refund your money.* 3 PHRASE If you give someone one thing **in exchange for** another, you give it to them because they are giving the other thing to you. If you do something for someone **in exchange for** another, you do it for someone because they did something for you. *It is illegal for public officials to solicit gifts in exchange for favours.* 4 N-COUNT An **exchange** is a brief conversation. [FORMAL] ...*angry exchanges between opposition and government delegates.*

★ **ex'change rate, exchange rates.** N-COUNT The **exchange rate** of a country's unit of currency is the amount of another country's currency that you get in exchange for it.

excise /'eksaɪz/. N-UNCOUNT **Excise** is a tax that the government of a country puts on goods produced for sale in that country.

excitable /ɪk'saɪtəbəl/. ADJ An **excitable** person becomes excited very easily.

excite /ɪk'saɪt/ **excites, exciting, excited.** 1 VERB If something **excites** you, it makes you feel happy or enthusiastic. *I only take on work that excites me.* 2 VERB If something **excites** a reaction or feeling, it causes it. *These comings and goings excited some curiosity.*

excited /ɪk'saɪtɪd/. ADJ If you are **excited**, you are looking forward to something eagerly. *I'm very excited about the possibility of playing for England's first team.* ♦ **excitedly** ADV *A little boy came running up and tugged at his coat sleeve excitedly.*

a b c d e f g h i j k l m n o p q r s t u v w x y z

excitement /ɪk'saɪtmənt/ **excitements.** N-VAR You use **excitement** to refer to the state of being excited, or to something that excites you. ...*in a state of great excitement... This game had its challenges, excitements and rewards.*

⭐ **exciting** /ɪk'saɪtɪŋ/. ADJ Something that is **exciting** makes you feel very happy or enthusiastic. ...*the most exciting adventure of their lives.*

exclaim /ɪks'kleɪm/ **exclaims, exclaiming, exclaimed.** VERB Writers sometimes use **exclaim** to show that someone is speaking suddenly, loudly, or emphatically. *'There!' Jackson exclaimed delightedly... She exclaimed that she could not possibly do something like that.*

excla'mation mark, exclamation marks. N-COUNT In British English, an **exclamation mark** is the punctuation mark (!). The American term is **exclamation point.** → See Reference Page on Punctuation.

exclude /ɪks'klu:d/ **excludes, excluding, excluded.** ①VERB If you **exclude** someone **from** a place or activity, you prevent them from entering it or taking part in it. *The Academy excluded women from its classes... Many of the youngsters feel excluded.* ♦ **exclusion** /ɪk'sklu:ʒən/ **exclusions** N-VAR ...*his continued exclusion from the team.* ②VERB If you **exclude** something that has some connection with what you are doing, you deliberately do not use it or consider it. *Christmas carols are being modified to exclude any reference to Christ.* ♦ **exclusion** N-VAR ...*the exclusion of all commercial lending institutions from the college loan program.* ③VERB To **exclude** a possibility means to decide or prove that it is wrong and not worth considering.

excluding /ɪk'sklu:dɪŋ/. PREP You use **excluding** before mentioning a person or thing to show that you are not including them in your statement. *Excluding water, half of the body's weight is protein.*

exclusive /ɪk'sklu:sɪv/. ①ADJ Something that is **exclusive** is available only to people who are rich. ...*Britain's most exclusive club.* ②ADJ **Exclusive** means used or owned by only one person or group. *Our group will have exclusive use of a 60-foot boat.* ③ADJ If two things are **mutually exclusive**, they cannot exist together. *Ambition and successful fatherhood can be mutually exclusive.*

exclusively /ɪk'sklu:sɪvli/. ADV **Exclusively** is used to refer to situations or activities that involve only the thing or things mentioned, and nothing else. ...*an exclusively male domain.*

excrete /ɪk'skri:t/ **excretes, excreting, excreted.** VERB When you **excrete** waste matter from your body, you get rid of it. [FORMAL]

excruciating /ɪk'skru:ʃieɪtɪŋ/. ADJ **Excruciating** pain is extremely painful.

excursion /ɪk'skɜ:ʃən, AM -ʒən/ **excursions.** N-COUNT An **excursion** is a short journey or visit. ...*a coach excursion to Trondheim.*

⭐ **excuse, excuses, excusing, excused.** ①N-COUNT /ɪk'skju:s/ An **excuse** is a reason which you give in order to explain why something has been done or has not been done, or to avoid doing something. *I made some excuse and bolted for the exit... Once I had had a baby I had the perfect excuse to stay at home.* ②VERB /ɪk'skju:z/ To **excuse** someone or to **excuse** their behaviour means to provide reasons for their actions, especially when other people disapprove of these actions. *That doesn't excuse my mother's behaviour.* ③VERB If you **excuse** someone **for** something wrong that they have done, you forgive them. *Many people might have excused them for avoiding some of their responsibilities.* ④VERB If someone **is excused from** a duty or responsibility, they are told that they do not have to carry it out. ...*a medical certificate excusing him from court.* ⑤VERB If you **excuse yourself**, you use a phrase such as **'Excuse me'** as a polite way of saying that you are about to leave. *He excused himself and went up to his room.*

PHRASES ● You say **'Excuse me'** when you want to politely get someone's attention. *Excuse me, but are you Mr Honig?* ● You use **'Excuse me'** to apologize for interrupting someone. *Excuse me interrupting, but there's a thing I feel I've got to say.*

⭐ **execute** /'eksɪkju:t/ **executes, executing, executed.** ①VERB To **execute** someone means to kill them as a punishment. *This boy's father had been executed for conspiring against the throne.* ♦ **execution, executions** N-VAR ...*execution by lethal injection.* ♦ **executioner, executioners** N-COUNT ...*the executioner's axe.* ②VERB If you **execute** a plan, you carry it out. [FORMAL] ♦ **execution** N-UNCOUNT ...*the making and execution of monetary policy.* ③VERB If you **execute** a difficult action or movement, you perform it. *The landing was skilfully executed.*

⭐ **executive** /ɪg'zekjʊtɪv/ **executives.** ①N-COUNT An **executive** is someone employed by a company at a senior level. ②N-SING The **executive** of an organization is a committee which makes important decisions. *Some executive members have called for his resignation.*

exemplary /ɪg'zempləri/. ADJ If you describe someone or something as **exemplary**, you consider them to be extremely good. *He showed outstanding and exemplary courage.*

exemplify /ɪg'zemplɪfaɪ/ **exemplifies, exemplifying, exemplified.** VERB If something or someone **exemplifies** something, they are a typical example of it. *The room's style exemplifies Conran's ideal of 'beauty and practicality'.*

exempt /ɪg'zempt/ **exempts, exempting, exempted.** ①ADJ If you are **exempt from** a rule or duty, you do not have to obey it or perform it. *Men in college were exempt from military service.* ②VERB To **exempt** a person **from** a rule or duty means to state officially that they do not have to obey it or perform it. ♦ **exemption, exemptions** N-VAR ...*new exemptions for students and the low-paid.*

⭐ **exercise** /'eksəsaɪz/ **exercises, exercising, exercised.**
[1] VERB & N-SING If you **exercise** your authority,
your rights, or a good quality such as mercy, you
put it into use. **The exercise of** these things is
the act of using them. [FORMAL] *They are merely
exercising their right to free speech. ...the exercise
of political and economic power.* [2] VERB &
N-UNCOUNT When you **exercise**, you move your
body energetically in order to get fit and remain
healthy. The activity is referred to as **exercise**.
*Exercising the body does a great deal to improve
one's health... Lack of exercise can lead to feelings
of depression. ...stomach exercises.* [3] N-COUNT
Exercises are a series of movements you do in
order to get fit or remain healthy. [4] N-COUNT
Exercises are activities which you do to in order
to maintain a skill or to train for a particular skill.
...creative writing exercises. ...military exercises.

exert /ɪg'zɜːt/ **exerts, exerting, exerted.** [1] VERB If
someone or something **exerts** influence or
pressure **on** someone, they use their influence or
put pressure on that person to do something.
...exerting political influence on newspaper editors.
[2] VERB If you **exert yourself**, you make a
physical or mental effort to do something. *Do not
exert yourself unnecessarily.* ◆ **exertion, exertions**
N-VAR *He clearly found the physical exertion
exhilarating.*

exhale /eks'heɪl/ **exhales, exhaling, exhaled.** VERB
When you **exhale**, you breathe out. [FORMAL]

⭐ **exhaust** /ɪg'zɔːst/ **exhausts, exhausting, exhausted.**
[1] VERB If something **exhausts** you, it makes you
very tired. *Walking in deep snow had totally
exhausted him.* ◆ **exhausted** ADJ *She was too
exhausted and distressed to talk.* ◆ **exhausting**
ADJ *It's a pretty exhausting job.* ◆ **exhaustion**
N-UNCOUNT *He is suffering from exhaustion.* [2] VERB
If a supply of something such as money or food
is exhausted, it has all been spent or eaten.
*People are now living longer and exhausting
natural resources.* [3] VERB If you **have exhausted**
a subject, you have talked about it so much that
there is nothing more to say about it. [4] N-COUNT
The **exhaust** on a motor vehicle is the series of
pipes which carry waste gases from the engine.
[5] N-UNCOUNT **Exhaust** is the waste gases
produced by the engine of a motor vehicle.

exhaustive /ɪg'zɔːstɪv/. ADJ An **exhaustive**
study or search is thorough and complete.
...exhaustive inquiries. ◆ **exhaustively** ADV *You
covered everything pretty exhaustively.*

exhibit /ɪg'zɪbɪt/ **exhibits, exhibiting, exhibited.**
[1] VERB To **exhibit** a particular quality, feeling, or
type of behaviour means to show it. [FORMAL] *He
has exhibited symptoms of anxiety.* [2] VERB When
an object of interest **is exhibited**, it is put in a
public place for people to come and look at it. *...a
massive elephant exhibited by London Zoo.*
◆ **exhibition** N-UNCOUNT *Pieces of the wall are
currently on exhibition.* [3] N-COUNT An **exhibit** is
an object of interest that is displayed in a
museum or art gallery. [4] VERB When artists
exhibit, they show their work in public. *By 1936

she was exhibiting at the Royal Academy.
[5] N-COUNT An **exhibit** is an object that is shown
in court as evidence in a legal case.

⭐ **exhibition** /ˌeksɪ'bɪʃən/ **exhibitions.** [1] N-COUNT
An **exhibition** is an event at which objects of
interest are displayed in a public place. *...an
exhibition of expressionist art.* [2] N-SING If a player
or team plays particularly well in a game, you can
say that they give an **exhibition of** their skills.
*...treating the fans to an exhibition of power and
speed.* [3] See also **exhibit**.

exhibitor /ɪg'zɪbɪtə/ **exhibitors.** N-COUNT An
exhibitor is a person whose work is being shown
in an exhibition.

exhilarating /ɪg'zɪləreɪtɪŋ/. ADJ If you describe
an experience or feeling as **exhilarating**, you
mean that it makes you feel very happy and
excited. *The effect is exhilarating.*

exhort /ɪg'zɔːt/ **exhorts, exhorting, exhorted.** VERB If
you **exhort** someone **to** do something, you try
hard to persuade them to do it. [FORMAL] *Kennedy
exhorted his listeners to turn away from violence.*
◆ **exhortation, exhortations** N-VAR *...exhortations
to reform.*

⭐ **exile** /'eksaɪl, 'egz-/ **exiles, exiling, exiled.** [1] VERB &
N-UNCOUNT If someone **is exiled**, or if they are
living **in exile**, they are living in a foreign country
because they cannot live in their own country,
usually for political reasons. *Napoleon was exiled
to St Helena... He is now living in exile in Egypt.*
[2] N-COUNT An **exile** is someone who lives in exile.

⭐ **exist** /ɪg'zɪst/ **exists, existing, existed.** [1] VERB If
something **exists**, it is present in the world as a
real thing. *He thought that if he couldn't see
something, it didn't exist. ...if you hide away your
problems and pretend that they don't exist.* [2] See
also **existing**.

⭐ **existence** /ɪg'zɪstəns/ **existences.** [1] N-UNCOUNT
The **existence** of something is the fact that it is
present in the world as a real thing. *...the
existence of other galaxies.* [2] N-COUNT You can
refer to someone's way of life as a particular
existence. *She has led a fairly comfortable
existence.*

⭐ **existing** /ɪg'zɪstɪŋ/. ADJ BEFORE N **Existing** is
used to describe something which is now present
or available. *...the need to improve existing
products.*

exit /'egzɪt, 'eksɪt/ **exits, exiting, exited.** [1] N-COUNT
An **exit** is a doorway through which you can
leave a public building. *He picked up the case and
walked towards the exit.* [2] N-COUNT An **exit** on a
motorway is a place where traffic can leave it.
Take the A422 exit at Old Stratford. [3] N-COUNT If
you refer to someone's **exit**, you are referring to
the fact that they left it. *I made a hasty exit.*
[4] VERB If you **exit** a room or building, you leave
it. [FORMAL] [5] VERB If you **exit** a computer
program or system, you stop running it. *Do you
want to exit this program?*

exodus /'eksədəs/. N-SING When there is an
exodus of people from a place, a lot of people

a
b
c
d
e
f
g
h
i
j
k
l
m
n
o
p
q
r
s
t
u
v
w
x
y
z

leave it at the same time. ...*the exodus of refugees from a war zone.*

exotic /ɪg'zɒtɪk/. ADJ Something that is **exotic** is unusual and interesting, usually because it comes from a distant tropical country. ...*brilliantly coloured, exotic flowers.* ♦ **exotically** ADV ...*an exotically plumed bird.*

⭐ **expand** /ɪk'spænd/ **expands, expanding, expanded.** VERB If something **expands**, it becomes larger. *The money supply expanded by 14.6%... I owned a bookshop and desired to expand the business.* ♦ **expansion** /ɪk'spænʃən/ **expansions** N-VAR *The company has abandoned plans for further expansion.*

▸**expand on** or **expand upon**. PHR-VERB If you **expand on** something, you give more information about it. *The president used today's speech to expand on remarks he made last month.*

expanse /ɪk'spæns/ **expanses.** N-COUNT An **expanse of** sea, sky, or land is a very large area of it.

expansion /ɪk'spænʃən/. See **expand**.

expansive /ɪk'spænsɪv/. [1] ADJ BEFORE N **Expansive** means covering or including a large area or many things. ...*an expansive grassy play area.* [2] ADJ If you are **expansive**, you talk a lot, or are friendly or generous, because you are happy and relaxed. *Fritz was a large and expansive man who loved to entertain.*

expatriate /ek'spætriət, -'peɪt-/ **expatriates.** N-COUNT An **expatriate** is someone who is living in a country other than the one where they were born.

⭐ **expect** /ɪk'spekt/ **expects, expecting, expected.** [1] VERB If you **expect** something **to** happen, you believe that it will happen. *He expects to lose his job in the next few weeks... They no longer expect profits to improve.* [2] VERB If you **are expecting** something or someone, you believe that they will be delivered or arrive soon. *I am expecting several important letters... We were expecting him home.* [3] VERB If you **expect** something, or if you **expect** someone **to** do something, you believe that it is your right to have that thing, or it is that person's duty to do it for you. *I do expect to have some time to myself... I wasn't expecting you to help.* [4] VERB If a woman **is expecting** a baby, she is pregnant. *I hear Dawn's expecting again.*

expectant /ɪk'spektənt/. [1] ADJ If you are **expectant**, you are excited because you think something interesting is about to happen. ♦ **expectantly** ADV *The others waited, looking at him expectantly.* ♦ **expectancy** N-UNCOUNT ...*a tremendous air of expectancy.* ● See also **life expectancy.** [2] ADJ BEFORE N An **expectant** mother or father is someone whose baby is going to be born soon.

⭐ **expectation** /,ekspek'teɪʃən/ **expectations.** [1] N-VAR Your **expectations** are your beliefs that a particular thing will happen. *One broker said, 'My expectation is that the stock will go as high as $2.50'... Even the dark night air was tense with*

expectation. [2] N-COUNT A person's **expectations** are beliefs which they have about the way someone should behave or something should happen. ...*living up to other people's expectations.*

expedient /ɪk'spi:diənt/ **expedients.** N-COUNT & ADJ An **expedient** is an action that achieves a particular purpose, but may not be morally right. You can also say that **it is expedient** to do something. *I cut my purchases dramatically by the simple expedient of destroying my credit card... It was expedient to be nice to him if you wanted to get on.* ♦ **expediency** N-UNCOUNT *Their enthusiasm was partly motivated by political expediency.*

expedition /,ekspɪ'dɪʃən/ **expeditions.** N-COUNT An **expedition** is a journey made for a particular purpose such as exploration. ...*Byrd's 1928 expedition to Antarctica.*

expel /ɪk'spel/ **expels, expelling, expelled.** [1] VERB If someone **is expelled from** a school or organization, they are officially told to leave because they have behaved badly. ...*a 14-year-old boy expelled from school for refusing to take a shower.* ♦ **expulsion** /ɪk'spʌlʃən/ N-UNCOUNT ...*her expulsion from high school.* [2] VERB If people **are expelled from** a place, they are made to leave it, usually by force. ...*numerous examples of patients being expelled from hospital.* ♦ **expulsion** N-UNCOUNT ...*the expulsion of illegal immigrants.* [3] VERB To **expel** something such as a gas means to force it out. *He groaned, expelling the air from his lungs.*

expend /ɪk'spend/ **expends, expending, expended.** VERB To **expend** energy, time, or money means to spend it or use it.

expenditure /ɪk'spendɪtʃə/ **expenditures.** [1] N-VAR **Expenditure** is the spending of money on something, or the money that is spent on something. ...*reduced public expenditure... They should cut their expenditure on defence.* [2] N-UNCOUNT **Expenditure of** energy or time is using it for a particular purpose.

⭐ **expense** /ɪk'spens/ **expenses.** [1] N-VAR **Expense** is the money that something costs you or that you need to spend in order to do something. *The tunnel is an unnecessary expense. ...household expenses.* [2] N-PLURAL Your **expenses** are the money you spend while doing something in the course of your work, which will be paid back to you afterwards. ...*travelling expenses.*
PHRASES ● If you do something **at** your **own expense**, you pay for it. *She traveled at her own expense to Russia.* ● If someone makes a joke **at** your **expense**, they do it to make you seem foolish.

⭐ **expensive** /ɪk'spensɪv/. ADJ If something is **expensive**, it costs a lot of money. *Wine's so expensive in this country. ...a lot of expensive equipment.* ♦ **expensively** ADV *She was expensively dressed.*

⭐ **experience** /ɪk'spɪəriəns/ **experiences, experiencing, experienced.** [1] N-UNCOUNT **Experience** is knowledge or skill in a particular job or activity, which you have gained from doing that job or activity. *He has also had managerial experience on every level.* ♦ **experienced** ADJ *...very experienced nurses.* [2] N-UNCOUNT **Experience** is used to refer to the past events, knowledge, and feelings that make up someone's life or character. *Experience has taught me caution.* [3] N-COUNT An **experience** is something that happens to you or something that you do. *Unfair dismissal can be a traumatic experience for an employee.* [4] VERB If you **experience** a situation or feeling, it happens to you or you are affected by it. *Widows seem to experience more distress than do widowers.*

⭐ **experiment** /ɪkˈsperɪmənt/ **experiments, experimenting, experimented.** [1] N-VAR An **experiment** is a scientific test which is done to discover what happens to something in particular conditions. *...conducting experiments on behalf of NASA and the Japanese scientific community.* [2] VERB If you **experiment with** something, or if you **experiment on** it, you do scientific tests to discover what happens to that thing in particular conditions. *...a professor who had been experimenting on rabbits.* ♦ **experimentation** N-UNCOUNT *...animal experimentation.* [3] N-VAR An **experiment** is the trying out of a new idea or method in order to see what it is like and what effects it has. *...the country's five year experiment in democracy.* [4] VERB To **experiment** means to try out a new idea or method, in order to see what it is like and what kind of effects it has. *Students should be encouraged to experiment with bold ideas.* ♦ **experimentation** N-UNCOUNT *...sexual experimentation.*

experimental /ɪkˌsperɪˈmentəl/. [1] ADJ Something that is **experimental** is new or uses new ideas or methods. *...highly experimental pieces of music.* [2] ADJ BEFORE N **Experimental** means relating to scientific experiments. *Scientists know that all experimental results are variable.* ♦ **experimentally** ADV *A species can be studied experimentally.*

⭐ **expert** /ˈekspɜːt/ **experts.** [1] ADJ & N-COUNT If someone is **expert at** doing something, or if they are an **expert**, he or she is very skilled at doing something or knows a lot about a particular subject. *The Japanese are expert at lowering manufacturing costs. ...an expert gardener. ...experts on terrorism.* ♦ **expertly** ADV *Shopkeepers expertly rolled spices up in bay leaves.* [2] ADJ BEFORE N **Expert** advice or help is given by someone who has studied a subject thoroughly or who is very skilled at a particular job. *We'll need an expert opinion.*

expertise /ˌekspɜːˈtiːz/. N-UNCOUNT **Expertise** is special skill or knowledge. *...legal expertise.*

expire /ɪkˈspaɪə/ **expires, expiring, expired.** [1] VERB When something such as a contract or a visa **expires**, it comes to an end or is no longer valid. *My passport has expired.* [2] VERB When someone **expires**, they die. [LITERARY]

⭐ **explain** /ɪkˈspleɪn/ **explains, explaining, explained.** [1] VERB If you **explain** something, you give details about it or describe it so that it can be understood. *Don't sign anything until your solicitor has explained the contract to you... 'He and Mrs Stein have a plan,' she explained.* [2] VERB If you **explain** something that has happened, you give reasons for it. *The receptionist apologized for the delay, explaining that it had been a hectic day... Explain yourself to me.*
▸**explain away** PHR-VERB If someone **explains away** a mistake or a bad situation that they are responsible for, they try to indicate that it is unimportant or that it is not really their fault. *I had noticed blood on my husband's clothing but he explained it away.*

⭐ **explanation** /ˌekspləˈneɪʃən/ **explanations.** N-VAR If you give an **explanation**, you give reasons why something happened, or describe something in detail. *The authorities have given no explanation for his arrest. ...an in-depth explanation of the gas furnace and how it works.*

explanatory /ɪkˈsplænətəri, AM -tɔːri/. ADJ Something that is **explanatory** explains something by giving details about it. [FORMAL] *...explanatory notes.*

explicit /ɪkˈsplɪsɪt/. [1] ADJ Something that is **explicit** is shown or expressed clearly and openly, without hiding anything. *...sexually explicit scenes in films.* ♦ **explicitly** ADV *...explicitly political activities.* [2] ADJ AFTER LINK-V If you are **explicit about** something, you express yourself clearly and openly. *He has been so vocal and so explicit about his annoyance.* ♦ **explicitly** ADV *She has been talking very explicitly about AIDS.*

⭐ **explode** /ɪkˈspləʊd/ **explodes, exploding, exploded.** [1] VERB If something such as a bomb **explodes**, it bursts with great force. *The grenade exploded, killing both men. ...gunfire which exploded the fuel tank.* [2] VERB You can say that a person **explodes** when they express strong feelings suddenly and violently. *Simon exploded with anger.*

⭐ **exploit, exploits, exploiting, exploited.** [1] VERB /ɪkˈsplɔɪt/ If someone **exploits** you, they unfairly use your work or ideas and give you little in return. *Critics claim he exploited black musicians.* ♦ **exploitation** N-UNCOUNT *...to protect the interests of the staff and prevent exploitation.* [2] VERB To **exploit** something means to use it to gain an advantage for yourself. *...a talent for seeing, creating and exploiting opportunities.* ♦ **exploitation** N-UNCOUNT *...her exploitation of the social security system.* [3] VERB To **exploit** resources or raw materials means to develop them and use them for industry or commercial activities. ♦ **exploitation** N-UNCOUNT *...the planned exploitation of its potential oil and natural gas reserves.* [4] N-COUNT /ˈeksplɔɪt/ Someone's **exploits** are the brave or interesting things they have done. *...his wartime exploits.*

exploratory /ɪkˈsplɒrətri, AM -ˈplɔːrətɔːri/. ADJ

a
b
c
d
e
f
g
h
i
j
k
l
m
n
o
p
q
r
s
t
u
v
w
x
y
z

Exploratory actions are done to discover or learn something. ...*exploratory surgery*.

⭐ **explore** /ɪkˈsplɔː/ **explores, exploring, explored.**
[1] VERB If you **explore** a place, you travel around it to find out what it is like. *The best way to explore the area is in a boat.* ♦ **exploration** /ˌekspləˈreɪʃən/. ♦ **explorer, explorers** N-COUNT ...*Arctic explorers.* [2] VERB If you **explore** an idea, you think about it carefully to decide whether it is a good one. *The city is exploring the idea of converting the building into a youth hostel.* [3] VERB If people **explore for** a substance such as oil or minerals, they study an area and do tests on the land to see whether they can find it. ♦ **exploration** N-UNCOUNT ...*oil exploration.*

⭐ **explosion** /ɪkˈspləʊʒən/ **explosions.** [1] N-COUNT An **explosion** is a sudden violent burst of energy, for example one caused by a bomb. *Six soldiers were injured in the explosion.* [2] N-COUNT An **explosion** of something is a large and rapid increase of it. ...*the population explosion in North Africa.*

explosive /ɪkˈspləʊsɪv/ **explosives.** [1] N-VAR & ADJ An **explosive**, or an **explosive** substance or device, is a substance or device that can cause an explosion. [2] ADJ An **explosive** situation is likely to have serious or dangerous effects.

exponent /ɪkˈspəʊnənt/ **exponents.** [1] N-COUNT An **exponent** of an idea, theory, or plan is someone who speaks or writes in support of it. [FORMAL] ...*an exponent of free speech.* [2] N-COUNT An **exponent of** a particular skill or activity is a person who is good at it. ...*the great exponent of expressionist dance, Kurt Jooss.*

⭐ **export, exports, exporting, exported;** verb /ɪkˈspɔːt/, noun /ˈekspɔːt/. [1] VERB & N-UNCOUNT To **export** goods means to sell them to another country. Selling goods to another country is called **export**. *The lumber is exported worldwide.* ...*200,000 cars a year, mostly for export.* ♦ **exporter, exporters** N-COUNT ...*arms exporters.* [2] N-COUNT **Exports** are goods which are sold to another country and sent there. *Ghana's main export is cocoa.*

⭐ **expose** /ɪkˈspəʊz/ **exposes, exposing, exposed.**
[1] VERB To **expose** something means to uncover it and make it visible. *For an instant his whole back was exposed.* [2] VERB If you **are exposed to** something dangerous, you are put in a situation in which it might harm you. ...*workers exposed to chemicals that damage their health.* [3] VERB To **expose** a person or situation means to reveal the truth about them. ...*church officials exposed him as a fake.* [4] ADJ An **exposed** place has no natural protection against bad weather or enemies. ...*an exposed hillside.*

exposition /ˌekspəˈzɪʃən/ **expositions.** N-COUNT An **exposition of** an idea or theory is a detailed explanation of it. [FORMAL]

⭐ **exposure** /ɪkˈspəʊʒə/ **exposures.** [1] N-UNCOUNT **Exposure to** something dangerous means being in a situation where it might affect you. *Exposure*

to lead is known to damage the brains of young children. [2] N-UNCOUNT **Exposure** is the harmful effect on your body caused by very cold weather. *At least two people died of exposure.* [3] N-UNCOUNT **Exposure** is publicity. *His aim is to get the artists more exposure.* [4] N-UNCOUNT The **exposure** of a well-known person is the revealing of the fact that they are bad or immoral in some way. ...*the exposure of Anthony Blunt as a former Soviet spy.* [5] N-COUNT In photography, an **exposure** is a single photograph.

expound /ɪkˈspaʊnd/ **expounds, expounding, expounded.** VERB If you **expound** an idea or opinion, you give a clear and detailed explanation of it. [FORMAL] *Schmidt continued to expound his views on economics.*

⭐ **express** /ɪkˈspres/ **expresses, expressing, expressed.**
[1] VERB When you **express** an idea or feeling, you show what you think or feel. *He expressed grave concern... I didn't know how to express myself properly.* [2] VERB If an idea or feeling **expresses itself** in some way, it can be clearly seen in someone's actions. *The anxiety of the separation often expresses itself as anger.* [3] VERB If you **express** a quantity in a particular form, you write it down in that form. [TECHNICAL] *It is expressed as a percentage.* [4] ADJ BEFORE N An **express** command or order is stated clearly. [FORMAL] *The visit to the nightclub was against the express wishes of the coach.* ♦ **expressly** ADV *Suicide is expressly forbidden in Buddhism.* [5] ADJ BEFORE N An **express** intention or purpose is deliberate or specific. *I had obtained my first camera for the express purpose of taking railway photographs.* ♦ **expressly** ADV ...*projects expressly designed to support cattle farmers.* [6] ADJ BEFORE N An **express** service is one in which things are done faster than usual. ...*an express delivery service.* [7] N-COUNT An **express** is a fast train or coach which stops at very few places.

⭐ **expression** /ɪkˈspreʃən/ **expressions.** [1] N-COUNT An **expression** is a word or phrase. ...*an Irish expression for fun.* [2] N-VAR The **expression** of ideas or feelings is the showing of them through words, actions, or art. *The announcement led to some expressions of concern from ministers.* ...*freedom of artistic expression.* [3] N-VAR Your **expression** is the way that your face shows what you are thinking or feeling.

expressive /ɪkˈspresɪv/. ADJ Something that is **expressive** indicates clearly a person's feelings or intentions. ...*her wonderfully expressive face.* ...*love poems, expressive of love for someone.* ♦ **expressively** ADV *He moved his hands very expressively.*

expulsion /ɪkˈspʌlʃən/. See **expel**.

exquisite /ɪkˈskwɪzɪt, ˈekskwɪzɪt/. ADJ **Exquisite** means extremely beautiful. *His voice is exquisite.* ...*her exquisite manners.* ♦ **exquisitely** ADV ...*exquisitely crafted dolls' houses.*

⭐ **extend** /ɪkˈstend/ **extends, extending, extended.**
[1] VERB If something **extends for** a particular distance or time, it continues for that distance or

time. *The caves extend for 18 kilometres. ...a playing career in first-class cricket that extended from 1894 to 1920.* [2] VERB If an object **extends from** a surface, it sticks out from it. *...a brightly coloured awning extended from the wall.* [3] VERB If something **extends to** a group of people, things, or activities, it includes or affects them. *The service also extends to wrapping and delivering gifts... His influence extends beyond the TV viewing audience.* [4] VERB If you **extend** something, you make it bigger, or make it last longer or include more. *We thought about extending the house... They have extended the deadline by twenty-four hours.* [5] VERB If you **extend** a part of your body, you straighten it or stretch it out. *Marshall extended his hand to Kelly.* [6] VERB To **extend** an offer or invitation to someone means to make it. [FORMAL]

extension /ɪkˈstenʃən/ **extensions.** [1] N-COUNT An **extension** is a new room or building which is added to an existing building. *...the new extension to London's National Gallery.* [2] N-COUNT An **extension** is an extra period of time for which something continues to exist or be valid. *...an extension to their visas.* [3] N-COUNT Something that is an **extension** of something else is a development of it that includes or affects more people, things, or activities. *...the difficulties of an extension of unemployment benefits.* [4] N-COUNT An **extension** is a telephone line that is connected to the switchboard of a company or institution, and that has its own number. *...extension 308.*

⭐ **extensive** /ɪkˈstensɪv/. [1] ADJ Something that is **extensive** covers a large area. *The hospital stands in extensive grounds.* ♦ **extensively** ADV *She has travelled extensively.* [2] ADJ If something is **extensive**, it is very great. *The blast caused extensive damage.* ♦ **extensively** ADV *This edition has been extensively revised.* [3] ADJ **Extensive** means covering many details, ideas, or items. *The summit is given extensive coverage in today's newspapers.* ♦ **extensively** ADV *All these issues have been extensively researched.*

⭐ **extent** /ɪkˈstent/. [1] N-SING **The extent of** something is its length, area, or size. *Climatic alterations reduced the extent of the rain forest.* [2] N-SING **The extent of** a situation is how great, important, or serious it is. *There's no word on the extent of his injuries.* [3] N-UNCOUNT You use **extent** to say how true something is. *It was and, to a large extent, still is a good show... I was getting more nervous to the extent that I was almost physically sick.*

exterior /ɪkˈstɪəriə/ **exteriors.** [1] N-COUNT The **exterior** of something is its outside surface. *...the stone exterior of the building.* [2] N-COUNT You can refer to someone's outward appearance and behaviour as their **exterior**. *Pat's tough exterior hides a shy and sensitive soul.* [3] ADJ BEFORE N use **exterior** to refer to the outside parts of something, or to things that are outside something. *...exterior walls.*

exterminate /ɪkˈstɜːmɪneɪt/ **exterminates, exterminating, exterminated.** VERB To **exterminate** a group of people or animals means to kill all of them. *A huge effort was made to exterminate the rats.* ♦ **extermination** N-UNCOUNT *...the extermination of wild dogs.*

external /ɪkˈstɜːnəl/. [1] ADJ BEFORE N **External** means happening, coming from, or existing outside a place, person, or area of activity. *...external walls. ...the commissioner for external affairs.* ♦ **externally** ADV *Vitamins can be applied externally to the skin.* [2] ADJ BEFORE N **External** is used to describe people who come into an organization from outside to do a job there. *...external examiners.*

extinct /ɪkˈstɪŋkt/. [1] ADJ If a species of animals is **extinct**, it no longer has any living members. *It is 250 years since the wolf became extinct in Britain.* [2] ADJ An **extinct** volcano does not erupt or is unlikely to erupt.

extinction /ɪkˈstɪŋkʃən/. N-UNCOUNT The **extinction** of a species of animal is the death of all its remaining members. *Tigers could face extinction within 10 years.*

extinguish /ɪkˈstɪŋgwɪʃ/ **extinguishes, extinguishing, extinguished.** VERB If you **extinguish** a fire or a light, you stop it burning or shining. *It took about 50 minutes to extinguish the fire.*

extol /ɪkˈstəʊl/ **extols, extolling, extolled.** VERB If you **extol** something, you praise it enthusiastically. *You hear people extolling the virtues of higher education.*

⭐ **extra** /ˈekstrə/ **extras.** [1] ADJ BEFORE N & ADV An **extra** thing, person, or amount is another one that is added to others of the same kind. *...extra blankets. ...extra staff... They should get up to £13,500 extra a year to spend on staff.* [2] N-COUNT **Extras** are things that are not necessary but make something more comfortable, useful, or enjoyable. *Extras include an introduction to scuba diving.* [3] N-COUNT **Extras** are additional amounts of money added to the basic price of something. *There are no hidden extras.* [4] N-COUNT An **extra** is a person who plays an unimportant part in a film. [5] ADV You can use **extra** in front of adjectives and adverbs to emphasize the quality that they are describing. [INFORMAL] *I'd have to be extra careful.*

extract, extracts, extracting, extracted; verb /ɪkˈstrækt/, noun /ˈekstrækt/. [1] VERB & N-VAR To **extract** a substance means to obtain it from something else, for example by using industrial or chemical processes. An **extract** is a substance that has been obtained in this way. *Citric acid can be extracted from the juice of oranges. ...a plant extract which acts as a natural tonic.* ♦ **extraction** N-UNCOUNT *...the extraction of oil.* [2] VERB If you **extract** something **from** a place, you take it out or pull it out. [LITERARY] *He extracted a small notebook from his pocket... She reached into the wardrobe and extracted another tracksuit.* [3] VERB If you **extract** information or a response **from** someone, you get it from them with

a
b
c
d
e
f
g
h
i
j
k
l
m
n
o
p
q
r
s
t
u
v
w
x
y
z

difficulty. *He was unable to extract any information from the three men.* **4** VERB When a dentist **extracts** a tooth, he or she removes it from the patient's mouth. ♦ **extraction, extractions** N-VAR *Extractions were carried out without anaesthetic.* **5** N-COUNT An **extract from** a book or piece of writing is a small part of it that is printed or published separately.

extradite /ˈekstrədaɪt/ **extradites, extraditing, extradited.** VERB If someone **is extradited**, they are officially sent back to their own country to stand trial for a crime. [FORMAL] ♦ **extradition** /ˌekstrəˈdɪʃən/ **extraditions** N-VAR ...*the British government's request for his extradition.*

⭐ **extraordinary** /ɪkˈstrɔːdənri, AM -neri/. **1** ADJ An **extraordinary** person or thing has some extremely good or special quality. ...*an extraordinary musician... We've made extraordinary progress.* ♦ **extraordinarily** /ɪkˈstrɔːdənrɪli, AM -nerɪli/ ADV *She's extraordinarily disciplined.* **2** ADJ If you describe something as **extraordinary**, you mean that it is very unusual or surprising. *What an extraordinary thing to happen!* ♦ **extraordinarily** ADV *Rainfall was extraordinarily high.*

extravagance /ɪkˈstrævəgəns/ **extravagances.** N-COUNT An **extravagance** is something that you spend money on but cannot really afford. *Her only extravagance was horses.*

extravagant /ɪkˈstrævəgənt/. **1** ADJ Someone who is **extravagant** spends more money than they can afford or uses more of something than is reasonable. *We are not extravagant; restaurant meals are a luxury.* ♦ **extravagantly** ADV *Jeff had shopped extravagantly for presents.* ♦ **extravagance** N-UNCOUNT ...*gross mismanagement and financial extravagance.* **2** ADJ Something that is **extravagant** costs more money than you can afford or uses more of something than is reasonable. *Her Aunt Sallie gave her an uncharacteristically extravagant gift.* ♦ **extravagantly** ADV ...*an extravagantly expensive piece of equipment.* **3** ADJ **Extravagant** behaviour is extreme behaviour that is often done for a particular effect. ...*extravagant shows of generosity.* ♦ **extravagantly** ADV *She had on occasion praised him extravagantly.* **4** ADJ **Extravagant** claims or ideas are unrealistic or impractical; used showing disapproval. ...*extravagant claims for success.*

extravaganza /ɪkˌstrævəˈgænzə/ **extravaganzas.** N-COUNT An **extravaganza** is a very elaborate and expensive show or performance. ...*a magnificent firework extravaganza.*

⭐ **extreme** /ɪkˈstriːm/ **extremes.** **1** ADJ **Extreme** means very great in degree or intensity. ...*people living in extreme poverty. ...Japan, with its extreme housing shortage.* ♦ **extremely** ADV *My mobile phone is extremely useful.* **2** ADJ You use **extreme** to describe situations and behaviour which are much more severe or unusual than you would

expect. *'I would rather die than do anything so extreme,' she said.* **3** ADJ The **extreme** point or edge of something is its farthest point or edge. ...*the extreme north.* **4** N-COUNT You can use **extremes** to refer to situations or types of behaviour that have completely opposite qualities to each other. ...*the extremes of success and failure.* **5** PHRASE You use **in the extreme** after an adjective to emphasize how bad or undesirable something is. *He had been foolish in the extreme.*

extremist /ɪkˈstriːmɪst/ **extremists.** N-COUNT If you describe someone as an **extremist**, you disapprove of them because they try to bring about political change by using violent or extreme methods. ...*a previously unknown extremist group.* ♦ **extremism** N-UNCOUNT ...*right-wing extremism.*

extrovert /ˈekstrəvɜːt/ **extroverts.** N-COUNT & ADJ An **extrovert**, or someone who is **extrovert**, is very active, lively, and sociable. *His extrovert personality won the hearts of the public.*

exuberant /ɪgˈzjuːbərənt, AM -ˈzuːb-/. **1** ADJ Someone who is **exuberant** is full of energy, excitement, and cheerfulness. *She was a bubbly, exuberant personality.* ♦ **exuberance** N-UNCOUNT ...*her burst of exuberance.* ♦ **exuberantly** ADV *They both laughed exuberantly.* **2** ADJ If you describe something as **exuberant**, you like it because it is lively, exciting, and full of energy and life. *His clothes had a kind of exuberant style.* ♦ **exuberance** N-UNCOUNT ...*the sheer exuberance of the sculpture.* ♦ **exuberantly** ADV ...*exuberantly decorated.*

exude /ɪgˈzjuːd, AM -ˈzuːd/ **exudes, exuding, exuded.** **1** VERB If someone **exudes** a quality or feeling, or if it **exudes**, they show that they have it to a great extent. [FORMAL] *Men dressed like this exude an air of quiet confidence.* **2** VERB If something **exudes** a liquid or smell, or if a liquid or smell **exudes from** it, the liquid or smell comes out of it. [FORMAL] ...*a factory which exuded a pungent smell.*

⭐ **eye** /aɪ/ **eyes, eyeing** (or **eying**), **eyed.** **1** N-COUNT Your **eyes** are the parts of your body with which you see. → See picture on page 823. ♦ **-eyed** ...*a blonde-haired, blue-eyed little girl... She watched open-eyed.* **2** N-COUNT You use **eye** when you are talking about a person's ability to judge things or about the way in which they are considering or dealing with things. ...*a man of discernment, with an eye for quality... He turned his critical eye on the United States... The practice of religion in America sometimes seems strange to European eyes.* **3** VERB If you **eye** someone or something in a particular way, you look at them carefully in that way. *Sally eyed Claire with interest... Martin eyed the bottle.* **4** N-COUNT An **eye** is a small metal loop which a hook fits into. → See picture on page 249.

PHRASES ● If you say that something happens **before** your **eyes**, **in front of** your **eyes**, or **under** your **eyes**, you are emphasizing that it happens where you can see it clearly or while you are watching it. *The man was bleeding to death before his eyes.* ● If something **catches** your **eye**, you suddenly notice it. *A quick movement across the aisle caught his eye.* ● If you **catch** someone's **eye**, you do something to attract their attention, so that you can speak to them. *He tried to catch her eye, but she was sunk in deep thought.* ● To **clap eyes on** someone or something, or to **set** or **lay eyes on** them, means to see them. [INFORMAL] *It was the most cruel, evil human face I ever set eyes on.* ● If you **have** your **eye on** something, you want to have it. [INFORMAL] *...a new outfit you've had your eye on.* ● If you **keep an eye on** something or someone, you watch them carefully, for example to make sure that they are safe, or are not causing trouble. *He had been sent here to keep an eye on Benedict.* ● If you **keep** your **eyes open** or **keep an eye out for** someone or something, you watch for them carefully. [INFORMAL] *As we walked along, we kept our eyes open for mushrooms... Keep an eye out for the police.* ● If you **look** someone **in the eye** or **meet** their **eyes**, you look directly at them in a bold open way, for example in order to make them realize that you are not afraid of them or that you are telling the truth. *She felt so foolish she could barely look Robert in the eye... She met*

my eyes steadily, but offered no explanations. ● If someone sees something **through** your **eyes**, they see it from your point of view.

eyeball /ˈaɪbɔːl/ **eyeballs.** N-COUNT Your **eyeballs** are the parts of your eyes that are like white balls.

eyebrow /ˈaɪbraʊ/ **eyebrows.** [1] N-COUNT Your **eyebrows** are the lines of hair which grow above your eyes. → See picture on page 823. [2] PHRASE If something causes you to **raise an eyebrow** or to **raise** your **eyebrows**, it causes you to feel surprised or disapproving. *He raised his eyebrows over some of the suggestions.*

'**eye-catching.** ADJ Something that is **eye-catching** is very noticeable. *...an eye-catching headline on the front page of the Sunday Times.*

eyelash /ˈaɪlæʃ/ **eyelashes.** N-COUNT Your **eyelashes** are the hairs which grow on the edges of your eyelids. → See picture on page 823.

eyelid /ˈaɪlɪd/ **eyelids.** N-COUNT Your **eyelids** are the two flaps of skin which cover your eyes when they are closed. → See picture on page 823.

eyesight /ˈaɪsaɪt/. N-UNCOUNT Your **eyesight** is your ability to see. *He suffered from poor eyesight.*

eyewitness /ˈaɪwɪtnəs/ **eyewitnesses.** N-COUNT An **eyewitness** is a person who has seen an event and can therefore describe it, for example in a law court.

F f

fable /ˈfeɪbəl/ **fables.** N-VAR A **fable** is a traditional story which teaches a moral lesson.

★ **fabric** /ˈfæbrɪk/ **fabrics.** [1] N-VAR **Fabric** is cloth. *...red cotton fabric. ...silk and other delicate fabrics.* [2] N-SING The **fabric** of a society is its structure and customs. [FORMAL] *Years of civil war have wrecked the country's social fabric.* [3] N-SING The **fabric** of a building is its walls, roof, and other parts. [FORMAL]

fabricate /ˈfæbrɪkeɪt/ **fabricates, fabricating, fabricated.** VERB If someone **fabricates** information, they invent it in order to deceive people. [FORMAL] *Officers fabricated evidence against them.*
♦ **fabrication, fabrications** N-VAR *China calls the report pure fabrication.*

fabulous /ˈfæbjʊləs/. ADJ You use **fabulous** to emphasize how wonderful or impressive you think something is. ♦ **fabulously** ADV *...their fabulously rich parents.*

facade or **façade** /fəˈsɑːd/ **facades.** [1] N-COUNT The **facade** of a large building is the outside of its front wall. *...the refurbishing of the cathedral's facade.* [2] N-SING You say that something is a **facade** when its outward appearance deliberately gives a wrong impression. *They hid behind a facade of family togetherness.*

face 1 noun uses

★ **face** /feɪs/ **faces.** [1] N-COUNT Your **face** is the front of your head from your chin to your forehead. → See picture on page 822. *She had a beautiful*

face... His face was covered with wrinkles. [2] N-COUNT The **face** of a cliff, mountain, or building is a vertical surface or side of it. [3] N-COUNT The **face** of a clock is the surface which shows the time. [4] N-SING If you refer to a particular **face of** something, you mean one particular aspect of it. *...the unacceptable face of capitalism.* [5] N-UNCOUNT If you **lose face**, something that you do or something that happens makes people lose respect for you. If you are able to **save face**, you do something which restores your reputation. *England doesn't want a war but it doesn't want to lose face.* [6] See also **face value**.

PHRASES ● If you take a particular action or attitude **in the face of** a problem or difficulty, you respond to that problem or difficulty in that way. *He persevered in the face of active discouragement from those around him.* ● If an action or belief **flies in the face of** accepted ideas or rules, it seems to completely contradict them. *...scientific principles that seem to fly in the face of common sense.* ● If you **make** or **pull a face**, you show your dislike for something by, for example, sticking out your tongue. ● If you manage to keep **a straight face**, you manage to look serious, although you want to laugh.

face 2 verb uses

★ **face** /feɪs/ **faces, facing, faced.** [1] VERB To **face** a particular direction means to look in that

a b c d e f g h i j k l m n o p q r s t u v w x y z

A B C D E **F** G H I J K L M N O P Q R S T U V W X Y Z

direction from a position directly opposite it. *They stood facing each other... The garden faces south.* [2] VERB If you **are faced with** something difficult or unpleasant, you have to deal with it. *We are faced with a serious problem.* [3] VERB If you cannot **face** something, you do not feel able to deal with it because it seems so difficult or unpleasant. *My children want me with them for Christmas Day, but I can't face it... I couldn't face seeing anyone.*
▶**face up to.** PHR-VERB If you **face up to** something difficult or unpleasant, you accept it and try to deal with it. *You can help an alcoholic parent by facing up to the problem.*

faceless /'feɪsləs/. ADJ If you describe someone or something as **faceless**, you dislike them because they have no character or individuality. *...faceless bureaucrats.*

facet /'fæsɪt, -set/**facets.** N-COUNT A **facet** of something is a single part or aspect of it. *The government is involved in every facet of people's lives.*

,face 'value. [1] N-SING The **face value** of things such as banknotes or tickets is the price stated on it. *Tickets were selling at twice their face value.* [2] PHRASE If you take something **at face value**, you accept it without thinking about it very much.

facial /'feɪʃəl/. ADJ BEFORE N **Facial** is used to describe things that relate to your face. *...his facial expression.*

facilitate /fə'sɪlɪteɪt/**facilitates, facilitating, facilitated.** VERB To **facilitate** a process means to make it easier. [FORMAL] *...facilitating the release of hostages.*

⭐ **facility** /fə'sɪlɪti/**facilities.** [1] N-COUNT **Facilities** are buildings, equipment, or services that are provided for a particular purpose. *...nursery facilities.* [2] N-COUNT A **facility** is a useful service or feature provided by an organization or a machine. *...an overdraft facility... This system has an electronic mail facility.*

⭐ **fact** /fækt/**facts.** [1] N-COUNT **Facts** are pieces of information which can be proved to be true. *...the facts about the murder.* [2] N-UNCOUNT When you refer to something as **fact**, you mean that it is true or correct. *...a statement of verifiable historical fact.*
PHRASES ● You use **the fact that** after some verbs and prepositions, for example in expressions such as **despite the fact that** and **apart from the fact that**, to link the verb or preposition with a clause. *Despite the fact that the disease is so prevalent, treatment is still far from satisfactory... My family now accepts the fact that I don't eat sugar or bread.* ● You use **in fact**, **in actual fact**, **as a matter of fact**, or **in point of fact** to indicate that you are giving more detailed information about what you have just said. *We've had a pretty bad time while you were away. In fact, we very nearly split up.*

⭐ **faction** /'fækʃən/**factions.** N-COUNT A **faction** is an organized group of people within a larger group who oppose some of the ideas of the larger group. *...the leaders of the country's warring factions.* ◆ **factional** ADJ *The factional fighting has killed more than 4,000 people.*

⭐ **factor** /'fæktə/**factors.** N-COUNT A **factor** is one of the things that affects an event or situation. *...environmental factors, such as air pollution.*

⭐ **factory** /'fæktri/**factories.** N-COUNT A **factory** is a large building where machines are used to make goods in large quantities.

factual /'fæktʃʊəl/. ADJ Something that is **factual** contains or refers to facts rather than theories or opinions. *The editorial contained several factual errors.*

faculty /'fækəlti/**faculties.** [1] N-COUNT Your **faculties** are your physical and mental abilities. *...losing our faculties of memory and reason.* [2] N-COUNT In some universities, a **faculty** is a group of related departments. *...the Faculty of Social and Political Sciences.*

fad /fæd/**fads.** N-COUNT You can refer to an activity or topic of interest that is very popular for a short time as a **fad**.

⭐ **fade** /feɪd/**fades, fading, faded.** [1] VERB When something **fades**, or when something **fades** it, it slowly becomes less intense in brightness, colour, or sound. *They observed the comet for 70 days before it faded from sight... Ultraviolet light will fade the colours in organic materials... His voice faded away.* ◆ **faded** ADJ *...faded blue jeans.* [2] VERB If memories, feelings, or possibilities **fade**, they slowly become less strong. *Prospects for peace had already started to fade.*
▶**fade away** or **fade out.** PHR-VERB When something **fades away** or **fades out**, it slowly becomes less noticeable or less important until it ends completely. *With time, they said, criticism will fade away.*

faeces (AM **feces**) /'fiːsiːz/. N-UNCOUNT **Faeces** is the solid waste substance that people and animals get rid of from their body through the anus. [FORMAL]

Fahrenheit /'færənhaɪt/. ADJ & N-UNCOUNT **Fahrenheit** is a scale for measuring temperature, in which water freezes at 32 degrees and boils at 212 degrees. It is represented by the symbol °F. ● See note at **temperature**.

⭐ **fail** /feɪl/**fails, failing, failed.** [1] VERB If you **fail to** do something that you were trying to do, you do not succeed in doing it. *He failed to win sufficient votes... We tried to develop plans for them to get along, which all failed miserably.* [2] VERB If someone or something **fails to** do something that they should have done, they do not do it. *He failed to file tax returns for 1982... The bomb failed to explode.* [3] VERB If someone **fails** you, they do not do what you expected or trusted them to do. *...communities who feel that the political system has failed them.* [4] VERB If someone **fails** an examination, they do not reach the standard that is required. ● See note at **exam**. [5] VERB If something **fails**, it stops working properly. *The lights mysteriously failed.*

failing /'feɪlɪŋ/ **failings.** [1] N-COUNT The **failings** of someone or something are their faults or unsatisfactory features. *The new law's failings could soon make many companies bankrupt.* [2] PHRASE You say **failing that** to introduce an alternative, in case what you have just said is not possible. *Talk things through, or failing that, write down your thoughts.*

⭐ **failure** /'feɪljə/ **failures.** [1] N-VAR **Failure** is a lack of success in doing or achieving something. *This policy is doomed to failure... The marriage was a failure.* [2] N-UNCOUNT Your **failure to** do something you were expected to do is the fact that you do not do it. *...their disgraceful failure to support British citizens.* [3] N-VAR When there is a **failure** of something, it stops working properly. *...engine failures... Anthony was being treated for kidney failure.*

faint /feɪnt/ **fainter, faintest; faints, fainting, fainted.** [1] ADJ Something that is **faint** is not strong or intense. *...the soft, faint sounds of water dripping... Their voices grew fainter.* ♦ **faintly** ADV *She smiled faintly.* [2] VERB & N-COUNT If you **faint**, or if you fall into a **faint**, you lose consciousness for a short time. [3] ADJ AFTER LINK-V Someone who feels **faint** feels dizzy and unsteady.

⭐ **fair** /feə/ **fairer, fairest; fairs.** [1] ADJ Something or someone that is **fair** is reasonable, right, and just. *It didn't seem fair to leave out her father. ...a very fair and broadminded man... He has been critical of me but, to be fair, he's always very encouraging and wants me to perform at my best.* ♦ **fairly** ADV *...solving their problems quickly and fairly.* ♦ **fairness** N-UNCOUNT *...concern about the fairness of the election campaign.* [2] ADJ BEFORE N A **fair** amount, degree, size, or distance is quite large. *I spent a fair bit of time finding directions.* [3] ADJ **Fair** hair or skin is light or pale in colour. [4] ADJ When the weather is **fair**, it is not cloudy or rainy. [FORMAL] [5] N-COUNT A **fair** is an event held in a field on which people pay to ride on machines for amusement or try to win prizes in games. [BRITISH] [6] N-COUNT A **fair** is an event at which people display or sell goods. *...an antiques fair.* [7] See also **fairly**.
PHRASES ● You use **fair enough** when you want to say that a statement, decision, or action seems reasonable to a certain extent, but that perhaps someone has gone beyond what is reasonable. *If you don't like it, fair enough, but that's hardly a justification to attack the whole thing.* ● You say **fair enough** to acknowledge what someone has just said and to indicate that you think it is reasonable. 'The message was addressed to me and I don't see why I should show it to you.'—'Fair enough'.

fairground /'feəgraʊnd/ **fairgrounds.** N-COUNT A **fairground** is a part of a park or field where people pay to ride on various machines for amusement or try to win prizes in games.

⭐ **fairly** /'feəli/. ADV **Fairly** means to quite a large degree. *We did fairly well... Were you always fairly bright at school?* ● See note at **rather**. ● See also **fair**.

fairy /'feəri/ **fairies.** N-COUNT A **fairy** is an imaginary creature with magical powers.

'fairy tale, fairy tales. N-COUNT A **fairy tale** is a story for children involving magical events and imaginary creatures.

⭐ **faith** /feɪθ/ **faiths.** [1] N-UNCOUNT If you have **faith in** someone or something, you feel confident about their ability or goodness. *She had placed a great deal of faith in Mr Penleigh... People have lost faith in the British Parliament.* [2] N-COUNT A **faith** is a particular religion, such as Christianity or Buddhism. *The College welcomes students of all races, faiths, and nationalities.* [3] N-UNCOUNT **Faith** is strong religious belief. *I don't think his faith should be ridiculed.* [4] PHRASE If you do something **in good faith**, you sincerely believe that it is the right thing to do in the circumstances.

faithful /'feɪθfʊl/. [1] ADJ & N-PLURAL If you are **faithful to** a person, organization, or idea, you remain firm in your support for them. People like this can be referred to as **the faithful**. *The government remained faithful to its peace initiative. ...gatherings of the Party faithful.* ♦ **faithfully** ADV *She had served the police force faithfully for so many years.* [2] ADJ Someone who is **faithful to** their husband, wife, or lover does not have a sexual relationship with anyone else. *She insisted that she had remained faithful to her husband.* [3] ADJ A **faithful** account, version, or copy of something represents or reproduces the original accurately. *Colin Welland's screenplay is faithful to the novel.* ♦ **faithfully** ADV *I translate from one meaning to another as faithfully as I can.*

faithfully /'feɪθfʊli/. CONVENTION In British English, when you start a formal or business letter with 'Dear Sir' or 'Dear Madam', you write **Yours faithfully** before your signature at the end. The usual American expression is **Sincerely yours**.

fake /feɪk/ **fakes, faking, faked.** [1] ADJ & N-COUNT **Fake** things or **fakes** have been made to look valuable or genuine, although they are not. *The bank manager is said to have issued fake certificates... It is filled with famous works of art, and every one of them is a fake.* [2] VERB If someone **fakes** something, they try to make it look genuine, although it is not. *He faked his own death... I leant against the glass partition and faked a yawn.*

⭐ **fall** /fɔːl/ **falls, falling, fell, fallen.** [1] VERB If someone or something **falls**, they move quickly downwards. *Her father fell into the sea... He held the bag so that everything fell out... Bombs fell in the town.* [2] VERB & N-COUNT If a person or structure **falls**, **falls down**, or **falls over**, they move from an upright position, so that they are lying on the ground. You can also say that a

a b c d e f g h i j k l m n o p q r s t u v w x y z

A
B
C
D
E
F
G
H
I
J
K
L
M
N
O
P
Q
R
S
T
U
V
W
X
Y
Z

person has a **fall**. *The woman gripped the shoulders of her man to stop herself from falling... We watched buildings fall on top of people... I hit him so hard he fell down... Roads have been blocked by fallen trees.*

USAGE You can use **fall down** to talk about people and objects, but not about things like **prices**. Instead you should use the verb **fall** by itself. *Jolil tripped and fell down as we were coming back... Share prices fell sharply during the day in New York.*

3 VERB & N-COUNT When rain or snow **falls**, or when there is a **fall of** it, it comes down from the sky. **4** VERB & N-COUNT If something **falls**, or if there is a **fall in** it, it decreases in amount, value, or strength. *Her weight fell to under seven stones... Oil product prices fell 0.2 per cent. ...a sharp fall in the value of the pound.* **5** VERB & N-SING If a powerful or successful person **falls**, they suddenly lose their power or position. You can also talk about that person's **fall**. *Mrs Thatcher fell from power. ...the fall of the military dictator.* **6** VERB You can use **fall** to show that someone or something passes into another state. For example, if someone **falls** ill, they become ill. *These women fall victim to exploitation.* **7** VERB If you say that something or someone **falls into** a particular category, you mean that they belong in that category. *Both women fall into the highest-risk group.* **8** VERB If silence or a feeling of sadness or tiredness **falls on** a group of people, they become silent, sad, or tired. [WRITTEN] *Silence fell on the passengers as the police checked identity cards.* **9** VERB When light or shadow **falls** on something, it covers it. *...the shadow that suddenly fell across the doorway.* **10** VERB When night or darkness **falls**, night begins and it becomes dark. **11** N-PLURAL You can refer to a waterfall as the **falls**. *...Niagara Falls.* **12** N-VAR In American English, **fall** is the season between summer and winter. The British word is **autumn**. *...in the fall of 1991... The Supreme Court will not hear the case until next fall.* **13** to **fall flat**: see **flat**.

▶**fall apart.** **1** PHR-VERB If something **falls apart**, it breaks into pieces because it is old or badly made. *Bit by bit the building fell apart.* **2** PHR-VERB If an organization or system **falls apart**, it becomes disorganized and inefficient. *Europe's monetary system is falling apart... I've tried everything to stop our marriage falling apart.*

▶**fall back on.** PHR-VERB If you **fall back on** something, you do it or use it after other things have failed. *Unable to defeat him by logical discussion, she fell back on her old habit of criticizing his speech.*

▶**fall behind.** PHR-VERB If you **fall behind**, you do not make progress or move forward as fast as

other people. *He missed school and fell behind... Boris is falling behind all the top players.*

▶**fall for.** **1** PHR-VERB If you **fall for** someone, you are strongly attracted to them and start loving them. *I just fell for him right away.* **2** PHR-VERB If you **fall for** a lie or trick, you believe it or are deceived by it. [INFORMAL] *It was just a line to get you out here, and you fell for it!*

▶**fall off.** PHR-VERB If something **falls off**, it separates from the thing to which it was attached. *When your exhaust falls off, you have to replace it.*

▶**fall out.** **1** PHR-VERB If a person's hair or a tooth **falls out**, it becomes loose and separates from their body. **2** PHR-VERB If you **fall out with** someone, you have an argument with them and stop being friendly. *She fell out with her husband... Mum and I used to fall out a lot.* ● See also **fallout**.

▶**fall through.** PHR-VERB If an arrangement **falls through**, it fails to happen. *My house sale is just on the verge of falling through.*

▶**fall to.** PHR-VERB If a responsibility or duty **falls to** someone, it becomes their responsibility or duty. *It fell to me to get rid of them.*

fallacy /ˈfæləsi/ **fallacies.** N-COUNT A **fallacy** is an idea which many people believe to be true, but which is false. *It is a fallacy that mass tourism has spoiled Mallorca.*

fallen /ˈfɔːlən/. **Fallen** is the past participle of **fall**.

fallout /ˈfɔːlaʊt/. N-UNCOUNT **Fallout** is the radiation that affects an area after a nuclear explosion.

⭐ **false** /fɔːls/. **1** ADJ If something is **false**, it is incorrect, untrue, or mistaken. *The President was being given false information... He had deliberately given the hospital a false name.* ♦ **falsely** ADV *...a man who is falsely accused of a crime.* **2** ADJ You use **false** to describe objects which are artificial but which are intended to look like the real thing or to be used instead of the real thing. *...the false bottom of her suitcase. ...a set of false teeth.* **3** ADJ If you describe a person or their behaviour as **false**, you are criticizing them for not being sincere or for hiding their real feelings. *She bowed her head and smiled in false modesty.* ♦ **falsely** ADV *He was falsely jovial.*

false alarm, false alarms. N-COUNT When you think something dangerous was about to happen, but then discover that you were mistaken, you can say that it was a **false alarm**. *...a bomb threat that turned out to be a false alarm.*

false start, false starts. N-COUNT A **false start** is an attempt to start something, such as a speech, project, or plan, which fails because you were not properly prepared or ready to begin.

falsify /ˈfɔːlsɪfaɪ/ **falsifies, falsifying, falsified.** VERB If someone **falsifies** a written record, they change it in a misleading way or add untrue details to it in order to deceive people. *Wise allegedly falsified bank records.*

falter /ˈfɔːltə/ **falters, faltering, faltered.** **1** VERB If something **falters**, it weakens and seems likely to collapse or to stop. *The economy is faltering. ...the faltering peace process.* **2** VERB If you **falter**, you hesitate and become unsure or unsteady. *Her voice faltered and she had to stop a moment to control it.*

fame /feɪm/. N-UNCOUNT If you achieve **fame**, you become very well-known. *The film earned him international fame.*

famed /feɪmd/. ADJ If you are **famed for** something, you are very well-known because of it. *The city is famed for its outdoor restaurants.*

⭐ **familiar** /fəˈmɪliə/. **1** ADJ If someone or something is **familiar to** you, you recognize them or know them well. *...a culture that was quite familiar to him... They are already familiar faces on our TV screens.* ♦ **familiarity** /fəmɪliˈærɪti/ N-UNCOUNT *...the uncanny familiarity of her face.* **2** ADJ AFTER LINK-V If you are **familiar with** something, you know it or understand it well. *He was not very familiar with the area.* ♦ **familiarity** N-UNCOUNT *The enemy would always have the advantage of familiarity with the rugged terrain.* **3** ADJ If you behave in a **familiar** way towards someone, you treat them very informally, so that you may offend them if you are not close friends. *John's 'crime' was being too familiar with the manager.* ♦ **familiarly** ADV *'Gerald, isn't it?' I began familiarly.* ♦ **familiarity** N-UNCOUNT *...the easy familiarity with which her host greeted the head waiter.*

⭐ **family** /ˈfæmɪli/ families.

✓ **Family** can take the singular or plural form of the verb.

1 N-COUNT A **family** is a group of people who are related to each other, especially parents and their children. *...a family of five... His family are completely behind him... They decided to start a family.* **2** N-COUNT When people talk about their **family**, they sometimes mean their ancestors. *Her family came to Los Angeles at the turn of the century.*

ˌfamily ˈplanning. N-UNCOUNT **Family planning** is the practice of using contraception to control the number of children you have.

famine /ˈfæmɪn/ famines. N-VAR A **famine** is a serious shortage of food in a country, which may cause many deaths.

⭐ **famous** /ˈfeɪməs/. ADJ Someone or something that is **famous** is very well known. *...England's most famous landscape artist... New Orleans is famous for its cuisine.*

USAGE A **famous** person or thing is known to more people than a **well-known** one. A **notorious** person or thing is famous because they are connected with something bad or undesirable. **Infamous** is not the opposite of famous. It has a similar meaning to notorious, but is a stronger word. Someone or something that is **notable** is important or remarkable.

famously /ˈfeɪməsli/. ADV You use **famously** to refer to a fact that is well known, usually because it is remarkable. *Authors are famously ignorant about the realities of publishing.*

⭐ **fan** /fæn/ fans, fanning, fanned. **1** N-COUNT If you are a **fan** of someone or something, you admire them and are very interested in them. *If you're a Billy Crystal fan, you'll love this movie.* **2** N-COUNT A **fan** is a flat object that a person waves to keep cool or a device that keeps a room or machine cool. **3** VERB If you **fan yourself**, you wave a fan or other flat object in order to make yourself cooler. **4** VERB If you **fan** a fire, you wave something flat next to it in order to make it burn more strongly.

▸**fan out.** PHR-VERB If a group of people or things **fan out**, they move forwards away from a particular point in different directions. *The main body of British, American, and French troops had fanned out to the west.*

fanatic /fəˈnætɪk/ fanatics. **1** N-COUNT If you describe someone as a **fanatic**, you disapprove of them because you consider their behaviour or opinions to be very extreme. *I am not a religious fanatic but I am a Christian.* ♦ **fanatical** ADJ *...a fanatical group of fundamentalists.* **2** N-COUNT If you say that someone is a **fanatic**, you mean that they are very enthusiastic about a particular activity, sport, or way of life. [INFORMAL] *Both Rod and Phil are football fanatics.*

fanciful /ˈfænsɪful/. ADJ If you describe an idea as **fanciful**, you disapprove of it because you think it comes from someone's imagination, and is therefore unrealistic or unlikely to be true. *...fanciful ideas about Martian life.*

fancy 1 wanting, liking, or thinking

⭐ **fancy** /ˈfænsi/ fancies, fancying, fancied. **1** VERB If you **fancy** something, you want to have it or do it. [BRITISH, INFORMAL] *Do you fancy going to see a movie sometime?... I just fancied a drink.* **2** VERB If you **fancy** someone, you feel attracted to them, especially in a sexual way. [INFORMAL] *I didn't really fancy him anyway.* **3** N-VAR A **fancy** is an idea that is unlikely, untrue, or imaginary. [LITERARY] *...a childhood fancy.* **4** EXCLAM You say **'fancy'** or **'fancy that'** when you want to express surprise or disapproval. *Fancy coming to a funeral in brown boots!*

PHRASE If something **takes** your **fancy** when you see or hear it, you like it. [INFORMAL] *...copying any fashion which takes her fancy.*

fancy 2 elaborate or expensive

fancy /ˈfænsi/ fancier, fanciest. **1** ADJ If you describe something as **fancy**, you mean that it is special, unusual, or elaborate. *...fancy jewellery.* **2** ADJ If you describe something as **fancy**, you mean that it is very expensive or of very high quality, and you often dislike it because of this. *They sent me to a fancy private school.*

fanfare /ˈfænfeə/ fanfares. N-COUNT A **fanfare** is a short loud tune played on trumpets to announce a special event.

a
b
c
d
e
f
g
h
i
j
k
l
m
n
o
p
q
r
s
t
u
v
w
x
y
z

fang /fæŋ/ **fangs.** N-COUNT **Fangs** are the two long, sharp, upper teeth that some animals have.

fantasize (BRIT also **fantasise**) /ˈfæntəsaɪz/ **fantasizes, fantasizing, fantasized.** VERB If you **fantasize about** something that you would like to happen, you think imaginatively about it. *I fantasised about writing music... She fantasised that he was still alive.*

fantastic /fænˈtæstɪk/. [1] ADJ If you say that something is **fantastic**, you are emphasizing that you think it is very good. [INFORMAL] *I have a fantastic social life.* [2] ADJ BEFORE N You use **fantastic** to emphasize the size, amount, or degree of something. [INFORMAL] *...fantastic amounts of money.* ♦ **fantastically** ADV *...a fantastically expensive restaurant.* [3] ADJ You describe something as **fantastic** when it seems strange and wonderful or unlikely. *Unlikely and fantastic legends grew up around a great many figures.*

⭐ **fantasy** /ˈfæntəzi/ **fantasies.** [1] N-COUNT A **fantasy** is a situation or event that you think about and that you want to happen, especially one that is unlikely to happen. *...fantasies of romance and true love.* [2] N-VAR You can refer to a story or situation that someone creates from their imagination and that is not based on reality as **fantasy**. *...the words from a Disney fantasy.*

FAQ /fæk/ **FAQs. FAQ** is used especially on websites to refer to questions about computers and the Internet. **FAQ** is an abbreviation for 'frequently asked questions'. [COMPUTING]

⭐ **far** /fɑː/ **farther** (or **further**) **farthest** (or **furthest**).

✓ **Far** has two comparatives, **farther** and **further**, and two superlatives, **farthest** and **furthest**. **Farther** and **farthest** are used mainly in sense 1, and are dealt with here. **Further** and **furthest** are dealt with in separate entries.

[1] ADV If one place, thing, or person is **far** away **from** another, there is a great distance between them. *...a nice little Italian restaurant not far from here... Both of my sisters moved even farther away from home... He had wandered to the far end of the room.* [2] ADV You use **far** in questions and statements about distances. *How far is it to Malcy?... How far can you throw?... She followed the tracks as far as the road.*

USAGE Far is used in negative sentences and questions about distance, but not usually in affirmative sentences. If you want to state the distance of a particular place from where you are, you can say that it is that distance **away**. *...Durban, which is over 300 kilometres away.* If a place is very distant, you can say that it is **a long way away**, or that it is **a long way from** another place. *It is a long way from London... Anna was still a long way away.*

[3] ADJ BEFORE N You use **far** to refer to the part of an area or object that is the greatest distance from the centre in a particular direction. *...at the far left of the blackboard.* [4] ADV A time or event that is **far** away in the future or the past is a long time from the present. *...conflicts whose roots lie far back in time... I can't see any farther than the next six months... The first day of term seemed so far away.* [5] ADV You use **far** to indicate the extent to which something happens. *How far did the film tell the truth about Barnes Wallis?* [6] ADV You can use **far** when talking about the progress that someone or something makes. *Discussions never progressed very far.* [7] ADV You can use **far** when talking about the degree to which someone's behaviour or actions are extreme. *This time he's gone too far.* [8] ADV You can use **far** to mean 'very much' when you are comparing two things and emphasizing the difference between them. *Women who eat plenty of fresh vegetables are far less likely to suffer anxiety... These trials are simply taking far too long.*

PHRASES ● You can use **by far** or **far and away** in comparisons to emphasize that something is better or greater than anything else. *By far the most important issue for them is unemployment... Rangers are far and away the best team.* ● If you say that something is **far from** a particular thing or **far from** being the case, you are emphasizing that it is not that particular thing or not at all the case. *Much of what they recorded was far from the truth.* ● If an answer or idea is **not far wrong**, **not far out**, or **not far off**, it is almost correct. *I hadn't been far wrong in my estimate.* ● **So far** means up until the present point in time or in a situation. *So far, they have met with no success.* ● If people come **from far and wide**, they come from a large number of places, some of them far away. If things spread **far and wide**, they spread over a very large area or distance. ● **as far as** I am **concerned**: see **concern.** ● **a far cry from**: see **cry.**

faraway /ˌfɑːrəˈweɪ/. [1] ADJ BEFORE N **Faraway** means a long distance from you or from a particular place. *...photographs of a faraway country.* [2] ADJ BEFORE N If you describe someone or their thoughts as **faraway**, you mean that they are thinking about something that is very different from the situation around them. *She smiled with a faraway look in her eyes.*

farce /fɑːs/ **farces.** [1] N-COUNT A **farce** is a humorous play in which the characters become involved in unlikely and complicated situations. [2] N-COUNT If you describe a situation or event as a **farce**, you mean that it is so disorganized or ridiculous that you cannot take it seriously. *The increasing traffic on our roads is going to make cycling a complete farce.* ♦ **farcical** ADJ *The whole scheme is farcical.*

⭐ **fare** /feə/ **fares, faring, fared.** [1] N-COUNT The **fare** is the money that you pay for a journey by bus, taxi, train, boat, or aeroplane. *He could barely afford the railway fare.* [2] VERB If you say that someone or something **fares** well or badly, you are referring to the degree of success they achieve in a particular situation or activity. *It is unlikely that the marine industry will fare any better in September.*

,**Far 'East.** N-PROPER **The Far East** consists of all the countries of Eastern Asia, including China and Japan.

farewell /,feə'wel/ **farewells.** CONVENTION & N-COUNT **Farewell** means goodbye. [LITERARY] *'Farewell', my friend... They said their farewells.*

,**far-'fetched.** ADJ If you describe a story or idea as **far-fetched**, you are criticizing it because you think it is unlikely to be true or practical. *The storyline was too far-fetched.*

★ **farm** /fɑːm/ **farms, farming, farmed.** ☐ N-COUNT A **farm** is an area of land consisting of fields and buildings, where crops are grown or animals are raised. *Both boys liked to work on the farm.* ☐ VERB If you **farm** an area of land, you grow crops or raise animals on it. *He has lived and farmed in the area for 46 years.*

★ **farmer** /'fɑːmə/ **farmers.** N-COUNT A **farmer** is a person who owns or manages a farm.

farmhouse /'fɑːmhaʊs/ **farmhouses.** N-COUNT A **farmhouse** is the main house on a farm, usually where the farmer lives.

farming /'fɑːmɪŋ/. N-UNCOUNT **Farming** is the activity of growing crops or keeping animals on a farm.

farmland /'fɑːmlænd/ **farmlands.** N-VAR **Farmland** is land which is farmed or which is suitable for farming.

farmyard /'fɑːmjɑːd/ **farmyards.** N-COUNT On a farm, the **farmyard** is an area near the farmhouse which is enclosed by walls or buildings.

,**far 'off, further off, furthest off.** ☐ ADJ A **far off** time is a long time away in the future or past. *The day this would happen was not far off.* ☐ ADJ & ADV A **far off** place is a long distance away. *...stars in far-off galaxies... The children who lived far off didn't go home.*

,**far-'reaching.** ADJ **Far-reaching** actions, events, or changes have a very great influence and affect a great number of things. *...technology with far-reaching effects on human society.*

farther /'fɑːðə/. **Farther** is a comparative of **far**.

farthest /'fɑːðɪst/. **Farthest** is a superlative of **far**.

fascinate /'fæsɪneɪt/ **fascinates, fascinating, fascinated.** VERB If something or someone **fascinates** you, you find them extremely interesting. *Politics fascinated Franklin's father.*

Fastenings

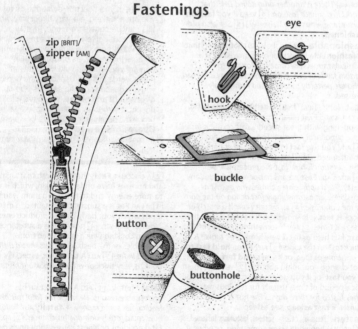

zip [BRIT]/
zipper [AM]

eye

hook

buckle

button

buttonhole

fascinated /'fæsɪneɪtɪd/. ADJ If you are **fascinated**, you are extremely interested by something. *I sat on the stairs and watched, fascinated.*

fascinating /'fæsɪneɪtɪŋ/. ADJ If you find something **fascinating**, you find it extremely interesting. *Madagascar is the most fascinating place I have ever been to.*

fascination /,fæsɪ'neɪʃən/. N-UNCOUNT **Fascination** is the state of being extremely interested in something. *I've had a lifelong fascination with the sea.*

fascist /'fæʃɪst/ **fascists.** [1] N-COUNT & ADJ A **fascist** or a person with **fascist** views has a set of right-wing political beliefs that includes strong control by the state and a powerful role for the armed forces. ♦ **fascism** N-UNCOUNT *...the menace of fascism.* [2] N-COUNT If you refer to someone as a **fascist**, you disapprove of the fact that they have extreme views on something, and do not tolerate alternative views.

★ **fashion** /'fæʃən/ **fashions, fashioning, fashioned.** [1] N-UNCOUNT **Fashion** is the area of activity that involves styles of clothing and appearance. [2] N-COUNT & PHRASE A **fashion** is a style of clothing or a way of behaving that is popular at a particular time. If something is **in fashion**, it is a fashion at a particular time, and if it is **out of fashion** it is not. [3] N-SING If you do something **in** a particular **fashion**, you do it in that way. [FORMAL] *There is another drug called DHE that works in a similar fashion.* [4] VERB If you **fashion** something, you make it. [FORMAL] [5] See also **old-fashioned**.

fashionable /'fæʃənəbəl/. ADJ Something that is **fashionable** is popular or approved of at a particular time. *It became fashionable to eat certain kinds of fish.* ♦ **fashionably** ADV *...women who are perfectly made up and fashionably dressed.*

★ **fast** /fɑːst, fæst/ **faster, fastest; fasts, fasting, fasted.** [1] ADJ & ADV **Fast** means moving, acting, or happening with great speed. *...fast cars. ...a faster pace of political reform... They work terrifically fast.* [2] ADV You use **fast** in questions or statements about speed. *How fast were you driving?... The only question is how fast the process will be.* [3] ADV & ADJ **Fast** means happening without any delay. *We'd appreciate your leaving as fast as possible. ...an astonishingly fast action on the part of the Congress.* [4] ADJ AFTER V-LINK If a watch or clock is **fast**, it is showing a time that is later than the real time. [5] ADV If something is held or fixed **fast**, it is held or fixed very firmly. *The tanker is stuck fast on the rocks.* [6] ADV If you **hold fast to** a principle or idea, or if you **stand fast**, you do not change your mind about it. [7] VERB & N-COUNT If you **fast**, or if you go on a **fast**, you eat no food for a period of time, usually for religious reasons. *They fasted for three days... The fast is broken at sunset.* ● **fast asleep**: see **asleep**.

fasten /'fɑːsən, 'fæs-/ **fastens, fastening, fastened.** [1] VERB When you **fasten** something, or when it fastens, you do it up or close it by means of buttons or a strap, buckle, or other device. *Fasten your seat belt. ...the dress, which fastens with a long back zip.* [2] VERB If you **fasten** one thing **to** another, you attach the first thing to the second.

fastening /'fɑːsənɪŋ, 'fæs-/ **fastenings.** N-COUNT A **fastening** is something that you use to fasten something. → See picture on page 249.

,**fast 'food.** N-UNCOUNT **Fast food** is hot food such as hamburgers which is served quickly after you order it.

fastidious /fæ'stɪdiəs/. ADJ If you say that someone is **fastidious**, you mean that they pay great attention to detail because they like everything to be accurate and very orderly. *He was fastidious about his appearance.* ♦ **fastidiously** ADV *He fastidiously copied every word of his notes.*

'**fast lane, fast lanes.** [1] N-COUNT On a motorway, the **fast lane** is the part of the road where the vehicles that are travelling fastest go. [BRITISH] [2] N-SING If someone is living in the **fast lane**, they have a very busy, exciting life, although they sometimes seem to take a lot of risks.

★ **fat** /fæt/ **fatter, fattest; fats.** [1] ADJ A **fat** person has a lot of flesh on their body and weighs too much. *I could eat what I liked without getting fat.* ♦ **fatness** N-UNCOUNT *...a child's tendency towards fatness.*

> **USAGE** If you describe someone as **fat**, you are speaking in a very direct way, and this may be considered rude. If you want to say more politely that someone is rather fat, it is better to describe them as **plump**, or more informally, as **chubby**, but in general you should avoid using any of these words in the presence of the person you are describing. The same is true of **overweight** and **obese**, which are used to describe someone who may have health problems because of their size or weight. **Obese** is also a medical term used to describe someone who is extremely fat or overweight.

[2] N-UNCOUNT **Fat** is the extra flesh that animals and humans have under their skin, which is used to store energy and to help keep them warm. [3] N-VAR **Fat** is a substance contained in many foods which your body uses to produce energy. *...low-fat yogurts.* [4] N-VAR **Fat** is a substance used in cooking which is obtained from vegetables or the flesh of animals. *Avoid dishes cooked in fat.* [5] ADJ A **fat** object, especially a book, is very thick or wide. *He took out his fat wallet.*

fatal /'feɪtəl/. [1] ADJ A **fatal** action has undesirable results. *He made the fatal mistake of lending her some money.* ♦ **fatally** ADV *Failure now could fatally damage his chances.* [2] ADJ A **fatal** accident or illness causes someone's death.

...*the fatal stabbing of a police sergeant.*
♦ **fatally** ADV *He was shot and fatally injured.*

fatality /fə'tælɪti/ **fatalities.** N-COUNT A **fatality** is a person's death, caused by an accident or violence. [FORMAL]

★ **fate** /feɪt/ **fates.** **1** N-UNCOUNT **Fate** is a power that some people believe controls everything that happens. *Could these facts be attributed to fate?* **2** N-COUNT Someone's **fate** is what happens to them. *His fate is now in the hands of his bankers.*

fateful /'feɪtfʊl/. ADJ If you describe an action or event as **fateful**, you mean that it had important, and often bad, effects on later events. *It was a fateful decision, one which was to break the Government.*

★ **father** /'fɑːðə/ **fathers, fathering, fathered.** **1** N-COUNT Your **father** is your male parent. **2** VERB When a man **fathers** a child, he makes a woman pregnant and their child is born. **3** N-COUNT The **father of** something is the man who invented or started it. ...*Max Dupain, regarded as the father of modern photography.* **4** N-VOC & N-TITLE In some Christian churches, priests are addressed or referred to as **Father**.

fatherhood /'fɑːðəhʊd/. N-UNCOUNT **Fatherhood** is the state of being a father. ...*the joys of fatherhood.*

'father-in-law, fathers-in-law. N-COUNT Your **father-in-law** is the father of your husband or wife.

fathom /'fæðəm/ **fathoms, fathoming, fathomed.** **1** N-COUNT A **fathom** is a unit of length used for describing the depth of the sea. One fathom is equal to 6 feet or approximately 1.8 metres. **2** VERB & PHR-VERB If you cannot **fathom** something, or you cannot **fathom** it **out**, you cannot understand it, although you think carefully about it. *I really couldn't fathom what Steiner was talking about.*

fatigue /fə'tiːg/. N-UNCOUNT **Fatigue** is a feeling of extreme physical or mental tiredness.

fatigues /fə'tiːgz/. N-PLURAL **Fatigues** are clothes that soldiers wear when they are on the battlefield or when they are doing routine jobs.

fattening /'fætənɪŋ/. ADJ **Fattening** food is thought to make people fat.

fatty /'fæti/. **1** ADJ **Fatty** food contains a lot of fat. ...*fatty meat such as sausages.* **2** ADJ BEFORE N **Fatty** acids or **fatty** tissue contain or consist of fat.

★ **fault** /fɔːlt/ **faults, faulting, faulted.** **1** N-SING & PHRASE If a bad situation is your **fault**, or if you are **at fault**, you caused it or are responsible for it. *It was all his fault... Individuals had suffered hardship through no fault of their own... He could never accept that he had been at fault.* **2** N-COUNT A **fault** is a weakness or imperfection in a person or a piece of equipment. *His biggest fault was his desire to do too much... There is a fault in the computer program.* **3** VERB If you say that you cannot **fault** someone, you approve of the hard

work they put into doing something or the efficient way that they do it. *It is hard to fault the way he runs his own operation.* **4** N-COUNT A **fault** is a large crack in the earth's surface. ...*the San Andreas Fault.* **5** PHRASE If you **find fault with** something, you complain about it.

faultless /'fɔːltləs/. ADJ Something that is **faultless** contains no mistakes. *Hans's English was faultless.*

faulty /'fɔːlti/. ADJ A **faulty** machine or piece of equipment is not working properly. *His car has faulty brakes.*

fauna /'fɔːnə/. N-PLURAL Animals, especially those in a particular area, can be referred to as **fauna**. [TECHNICAL] ...*the Lake's remarkable flora and fauna.*

★ **favour** (AM **favor**) /'feɪvə/ **favours, favouring, favoured.** **1** N-UNCOUNT If you regard something or someone with **favour**, you like or support them. *The changes favour our most competitors.* **2** N-COUNT If you ask someone to do a **favour** for you, you ask them to do something which will help you. *Can you do me a favour?* **3** VERB If you **favour** something, you prefer it to the other choices available. *They favour a transition to democracy.* **4** VERB If you **favour** someone, you treat them better than you treat other people. *My brother felt that my mum favoured me.*

PHRASES ● If you are **in favour of** something, you think that it is a good thing. *I wouldn't be in favour of income tax cuts.* ● If one thing is rejected **in favour of** another, the second thing is done or chosen instead of the first. ...*when ordinary machine tools are scrapped in favour of new computerized ones.* ● If someone makes a judgement **in** your **favour**, they say that you are right. *A federal judge ruled in their favour.* ● If something is **in** your **favour**, it helps you or gives you an advantage. ...*the allegation that the media were biased in favour of Mr Blair.* ● If someone or something is **in favour**, people like or support them. If they are **out of favour**, people no longer like or support them.

favourable (AM **favorable**) /'feɪvərəbəl/. **1** ADJ If you are **favourable to** something, you agree with it or approve of it. *Many banks are favourable to the idea... We've already had a lot of favourable comment from customers.*
♦ **favourably** ADV *He listened intently, and responded favourably to both my suggestions.* **2** ADJ If something makes a **favourable** impression on you, or if it is **favourable to** you, you like it and approve of it. *He was desperate to make a favourable impression on General Macarthur... These terms were favourable to India.* **3** ADJ If you make a **favourable** comparison between two things, you say that the first is better than or as good as the second.
♦ **favourably** ADV *These figures compare favourably with more established methods.* **4** ADJ **Favourable** conditions make something more likely to succeed. ...*attempts to influence the government to choose policies favourable to*

a
b
c
d
e
f
g
h
i
j
k
l
m
n
o
p
q
r
s
t
u
v
w
x
y
z

industry. ...*favourable weather conditions.*
♦ **favourably** ADV *Japan is thus favourably placed to maintain its economic lead.*

⭐ **favourite** (AM **favorite**)/'feɪvərɪt/**favourites.**
1 N-COUNT & ADJ BEFORE N Your **favourite**, or your **favourite** thing or person, is the one that you like most. *I love all sports but soccer is my favourite... Her favourite writer is Hans Christian Andersen.*
2 N-COUNT The **favourite** in a race or contest is the person or animal expected to win. *The Belgian Cup has been won by the favourites F.C. Liège.*

fawn /fɔːn/ **fawns, fawning, fawned.** 1 ADJ & N-UNCOUNT Something that is **fawn** is pale yellowish-brown. 2 N-COUNT A **fawn** is a very young deer. 3 VERB If you say that someone **fawns over** a powerful or rich person, you disapprove of them because they flatter that person in order to get something for themselves. *People fawn over you when you're famous. ...200 pages of fawning praise.*

fax /fæks/ **faxes, faxing, faxed.** 1 N-COUNT A **fax** or a **fax machine** is a piece of equipment used to send and receive documents electronically along a telephone line. 2 VERB & N-COUNT If you **fax** a document, you send a document from one fax machine to another. *Did you fax him a reply?... Pop it in the post, or get your secretary to fax it.* 3 N-COUNT You can refer to a copy of a document that is transmitted by a fax machine as a **fax**. *I sent him a fax... Did she get my fax yesterday?*

⭐ **fear** /fɪə/ **fears, fearing, feared.** 1 N-VAR **Fear** is the unpleasant feeling of worry that you get when you think that you are in danger or that something horrible is going to happen. *I stood there crying and shaking with fear. ...his fears about the forthcoming operation.* 2 PHRASE If you do not do something **for fear of** another thing happening, you do not do it because you do not wish that other thing to happen. *He did not dare move his feet for fear of disturbing anything.* 3 VERB If you **fear** something unpleasant, you are worried that it might happen, or might have happened. *She had feared she was going down with pneumonia... More than two million refugees have fled the area, fearing attack.* 4 VERB & N-VAR If you **fear** for someone or something, or if you have **fears for** them, you are worried that they might be in danger. *Carla fears for her son... There are fears for the safety of a 15-year-old girl.*

fearful /'fɪəfʊl/. 1 ADJ If you are **fearful of** something, you are afraid of it. *Bankers were fearful of a world banking crisis.* ♦ **fearfully** ADV *'What are you going to do to me?' Alex asked fearfully.* 2 ADJ BEFORE N You use **fearful** to emphasize how serious or bad something is. *The region is in a fearful recession.* ♦ **fearfully** ADV *It's fearfully expensive!*

fearless /'fɪələs/. ADJ If you describe someone as **fearless**, you admire their courage. *They were*

young and strong and fearless. ♦ **fearlessly** ADV ...*a fearlessly outspoken politician.*

fearsome /'fɪəsəm/. ADJ If you describe something as **fearsome**, you are emphasizing the fact that it is terrible or frightening. ...*a fearsome array of weapons.*

feasible /'fiːzəbəl/. ADJ If something is **feasible**, it can be done, made, or achieved. *Are these experiments technically feasible?* ♦ **feasibility** N-UNCOUNT *Two companies are studying the feasibility of building a mill in the region.*

feast /fiːst/ **feasts, feasting, feasted.** 1 N-COUNT A **feast** is a large and special meal. ...*wedding feasts.* 2 VERB If you **feast**, you take part in a feast. [LITERARY] ♦ **feasting** N-UNCOUNT *The marriage is celebrated with much dancing and feasting.* 3 VERB If you **feast on** a particular food, you eat a large amount of it with great enjoyment. *We feasted on nuts and candies and cake.* 4 N-SING You can refer to a large number of good, interesting, or enjoyable things as a **feast of** them. ...*a feast of special effects.*

feat /fiːt/ **feats.** N-COUNT A **feat** is an impressive and difficult act or achievement. *A racing car is an extraordinary feat of engineering.*

feather /'feðə/ **feathers.** N-COUNT A bird's **feathers** are the light soft things covering its body.

feathered /'feðəd/. ADJ **Feathered** is used to describe something covered in feathers or made from feathers. ...*extravagant feathered hats.*

⭐ **feature** /'fiːtʃə/ **features, featuring, featured.** 1 N-COUNT A particular **feature of** something is an interesting or important part or characteristic of it. *The spacious gardens are a special feature of this property... The making of pilgrimages is an essential feature of Hindu life.* 2 N-PLURAL Your **features** are your eyes, nose, mouth, and other parts of your face. 3 VERB When a film or exhibition **features** someone or something, they are an important part of it. *The series featured top stars from snooker, cricket and rugby.* 4 VERB If someone or something **features in** something such as an exhibition or magazine, they are an important part of it. *Most projects featured in the book are small scale.* 5 N-COUNT A **feature** is a special article in a newspaper or magazine, or a special programme on radio or television. ...*our special feature on breast cancer.* 6 N-COUNT A **feature** or a **feature film** is a full-length film about a fictional subject.

⭐ **February** /'febjʊəri, AM -jʊeri/. N-UNCOUNT **February** is the second month of the year. → See Reference Page on Times and Dates.

feces /'fiːsiːz/. See **faeces.**

fed /fed/. **Fed** is the past tense and past participle of **feed.** ● See also **fed up.**

⭐ **federal** /'fedərəl/. 1 ADJ BEFORE N In a **federal** country or system, a group of states is controlled by a central government. 2 ADJ BEFORE N **Federal** means belonging or relating to the national government of a federal country rather than to

fell

one of the states within it. *...a federal judge.*
♦ **federally** ADV *...federally subsidized apartments.*

⭐ **federation** /ˌfedəˈreɪʃən/ **federations.** N-COUNT A **federation** is a group of organizations or states that have joined together for a common purpose. *...the British Athletic Federation.*

ˌfed ˈup. ADJ AFTER LINK-V Someone who is **fed up** is bored or annoyed. [INFORMAL] *I am fed up with reading how women should dress to please men.*

⭐ **fee** /fiː/ **fees.** ☐1 N-COUNT A **fee** is a sum of money that you pay to be allowed to do something. *...the television licence fee.* ☐2 N-COUNT A **fee** is the money that someone is paid for a particular job or service. *...solicitors' fees.*

feeble /ˈfiːbəl/ **feebler, feeblest.** ☐1 ADJ If you describe someone or something as **feeble**, you mean that they are physically weak. *He was old and feeble.* ♦ **feebly** ADV *His left hand moved feebly at his side.* ☐2 ADJ If you say that someone or something is **feeble**, you mean that they are not very good, convincing, or effective. *This is a particularly feeble argument.* ♦ **feebly** ADV *I said 'Sorry', very feebly, feeling rather embarrassed.*

⭐ **feed** /fiːd/ **feeds, feeding, fed.** ☐1 VERB If you **feed** a person or animal, you give them food. *She fed him a cookie... He spooned the ice cream into a cup and fed it to her.* ♦ **feeding, feedings** N-VAR *...the feeding of dairy cows.* ☐2 VERB To **feed** a family or a community means to supply food for them. *Feeding a hungry family can be expensive.* ☐3 VERB When an animal **feeds**, it eats something. *...insects that feed on wood.* ☐4 VERB & N-COUNT When a baby **feeds**, or when it has a **feed**, it drinks breast milk or milk from its bottle. ☐5 VERB If you **feed** something somewhere, you put it in there at a steady rate. *She was feeding documents into a paper shredder. ...blood vessels that feed blood to the brain.*

feedback /ˈfiːdbæk/. N-UNCOUNT When you get **feedback** on your work or progress, someone tells you how well or badly you are doing.

⭐ **feel** /fiːl/ **feels, feeling, felt.** ☐1 LINK-VERB If you **feel** an emotion or a physical sensation, you experience it. *I am feeling very depressed... I felt a sharp pain in my shoulder.* ☐2 LINK-VERB If you talk about how an experience or event **feels**, you are describing the emotions and sensations connected with it. *It feels good to have finished a piece of work... It felt like I'd had two babies instead of one.* ☐3 N-SING & LINK-VERB The **feel** of an object, or the way it **feels**, is the physical quality that you notice when you touch it. *He remembered the feel of her skin... The metal felt smooth and cold.* ☐4 VERB If you **feel** an object, you touch it so that you can learn what it is like. *The doctor felt his head... Feel how soft the skin is.* ☐5 VERB If you **feel** something, you are aware that it is touching or happening to your body. *He felt her leg against his... I felt myself blush.* ☐6 VERB If you **feel** something, you become aware of it, even though you cannot see or hear it. *I could feel that a man was watching me.* ☐7 VERB If you **feel** that something is the case, you have a strong idea in your mind that it is the case. *I feel certain that it will all turn out well... She felt him to be responsible.* ☐8 VERB If you **feel** that you should do something, you think that you should do it. *You need not feel obliged to contribute.* ☐9 VERB If you talk about how you **feel about** something, you talk about your opinion, attitude, or reaction to it. *She feels guilty about spending less time lately with her two kids.* ☐10 VERB If you **feel like** doing or having something, you want to do or have it. *Neither of them felt like going back to sleep.* ☐11 N-SING The **feel** of something is the general impression that it gives you. *The room has a warm, cosy feel.* ☐12 See also **feeling, felt**.
▸ **feel for.** ☐1 PHR-VERB If you **feel for** something, you try to find it using your hands rather than your eyes. *I felt for my wallet.* ☐2 PHR-VERB If you **feel for** someone, you have sympathy for them.

feelgood /ˈfiːlɡʊd/. ☐1 ADJ BEFORE NOUN A **feelgood** film presents people and life in a way which makes the people who watch it feel happy and optimistic. ☐2 PHRASE The **feelgood factor** is the fact that people are feeling hopeful and optimistic about the future. [JOURNALISM]

⭐ **feeling** /ˈfiːlɪŋ/ **feelings.** ☐1 N-VAR A **feeling** is an emotion. *It gave me a feeling of satisfaction.* ☐2 PHRASE **Bad feeling** or **ill feeling** is resentment or anger which exists between people, for example after an argument. *There's been some bad feeling between the two families.* ☐3 N-COUNT If you have a **feeling** that something is the case, you think that it is probably the case. *I have a feeling that everything will come right for us.* ☐4 N-SING If you have a **feeling of** being in a particular situation, you feel that you are in that situation. *I had the terrible feeling of being left behind.* ☐5 N-PLURAL Your **feelings about** something are the things that you think and feel about it, or your attitude towards it. *I had mixed feelings about meeting him.* ☐6 N-PLURAL When you refer to someone's **feelings**, you are talking about the things that might embarrass or upset them. If you hurt someone's **feelings**, you say or do something that upsets them. ☐7 N-UNCOUNT **Feeling** for someone is affection or sympathy for them. *It's incredible that Peter can behave with such stupid lack of feeling.* ☐8 N-COUNT A **feeling** is a physical sensation. *I also had a strange feeling in my neck.* ☐9 N-UNCOUNT **Feeling** in part of your body is the ability to experience the sense of touch in this part of the body. *After the accident he had no feeling in his legs.*

feet /fiːt/. **Feet** is the plural of **foot**.

feign /feɪn/ **feigns, feigning, feigned.** VERB If someone **feigns** a feeling or attitude, they pretend to have it. [FORMAL] *I didn't want to go to school, and decided to feign illness.*

fell /fel/ **fells, felling, felled.** ☐1 **Fell** is the past tense of **fall**. ☐2 VERB If trees are **felled**, they are cut down.

⭐ Bank of English® frequent word   For a full explanation of all grammatical labels, see pages vii-x

a b c d e f g h i j k l m n o p q r s t u v w x y z

fella (or **feller**) /'felə/**fellas.** N-COUNT You can refer to a man as a **fella**. [INFORMAL] *He's an intelligent man and a nice fella.*

⭐ **fellow** /'feləʊ/**fellows.** [1] ADJ BEFORE N You use **fellow** to describe people who are in the same situation as you, or people you feel you have something in common with. *He knew his fellow teachers in Cincinnati shared his frustrations.* [2] N-COUNT A **fellow** is a man or boy. [DATED, INFORMAL] *...the fellow who came to collect our drinks.* [3] N-COUNT A **fellow** of a society or academic institution is a member of it.

fellowship /'feləʊʃɪp/**fellowships.** [1] N-COUNT A **fellowship** is a group of people that join together for a common purpose. *...the Fellowship of World Christians.* [2] N-UNCOUNT **Fellowship** is a feeling of friendship that people have when they are talking or doing something together. *...a sense of community and fellowship.* [3] N-COUNT A **fellowship** at a university is a post which involves research work.

felony /'feləni/**felonies.** N-COUNT A **felony** is a very serious crime such as armed robbery. [TECHNICAL]

felt /felt/. [1] **Felt** is the past tense and past participle of **feel**. [2] N-UNCOUNT **Felt** is a type of thick cloth made from wool or other fibres packed tightly together.

⭐ **female** /'fiːmeɪl/**females.** [1] ADJ Someone who is **female** is a woman or a girl. *...a female singer.* [2] N-COUNT Women and girls are sometimes referred to as **females** when they are being considered as a type. *Hay fever affects males more than females.* [3] ADJ BEFORE N **Female** is used to describe things that relate to or affect women rather than men. *...female infertility.* [4] N-COUNT & ADJ You can refer to any creature that can lay eggs or produce babies from its body as a **female**, or as a **female** creature. *Each female will lay just one egg. ...the female blue whale.*

feminine /'femɪnɪn/. ADJ **Feminine** means relating to women or considered typical of or suitable for them. *...traditional feminine roles.* ♦ **femininity** /,femɪ'nɪnɪti/ N-UNCOUNT *...the ideology of motherhood and femininity.*

feminism /'femɪnɪzəm/. N-UNCOUNT **Feminism** is the belief that women should have the same rights and opportunities as men. ♦ **feminist, feminists** N-COUNT *...the feminist movement.*

⭐ **fence** /fens/**fences, fencing, fenced.** [1] N-COUNT A **fence** is a barrier made of wood or wire supported by posts. [2] VERB & PHR-VERB If you **fence** an area of land, if you **fence** it **off**, or if you **fence** it **in**, you surround it with a fence. *We could fence off the cliff top... He plans to fence in about 100 acres of his ranch.* [3] PHRASE You say that someone **is sitting on the fence** to express their disapproval of them because they refuse to state a definite opinion or to say who they support in a conflict. *The Republicans criticised the president for sitting on the fence.*

fencing /'fensɪŋ/. [1] N-UNCOUNT **Fencing** is a sport in which two competitors fight using very thin swords. [2] N-UNCOUNT **Fencing** consists of materials that are used to make fences.

fend /fend/**fends, fending, fended.** VERB If you have to **fend for yourself**, you have to look after yourself without relying on other people. ▶**fend off.** PHR-VERB If you **fend off** someone or something, you defend yourself against them, using either words or physical strength. *Earlier, Marianne had fended off questions about her marriage... I fended him off with my elbow.*

ferment, ferments, fermenting, fermented. [1] N-UNCOUNT /'fɜːment/ **Ferment** is excitement and trouble caused by change or uncertainty. *The whole country has been in a state of political ferment.* [2] VERB /fə'ment/ If a food or drink **ferments**, or if it **is fermented**, a chemical change takes place in it so that alcohol is produced. ♦ **fermentation** N-UNCOUNT *...the fermentation that produces alcohol.*

fern /fɜːn/**ferns.** N-COUNT A **fern** is a plant with long stems, thin leaves, and no flowers.

ferocious /fə'rəʊʃəs/. ADJ A **ferocious** animal, person, or action is fierce and violent. *...a pack of ferocious dogs.* ♦ **ferociously** ADV *She kicked out ferociously.*

ferocity /fə'rɒsɪti/. N-UNCOUNT When something is done with **ferocity**, it is done in a fierce and violent way.

ferry /'feri/**ferries, ferrying, ferried.** [1] N-COUNT A **ferry** is a boat that carries passengers or vehicles across a river or a narrow stretch of sea. [2] VERB To **ferry** people or goods means to transport them, usually by means of regular journeys between the same two places. *A plane arrives to ferry guests to and from Bird Island Lodge.*

fertile /'fɜːtaɪl, AM -təl/. [1] ADJ Land or soil that is **fertile** is able to support a large number of strong healthy plants. ♦ **fertility** /fɜː'tɪlɪti/ N-UNCOUNT *...the fertility of the soil.* [2] ADJ BEFORE N You describe a place or situation as **fertile** ground when you think that something is likely to succeed or develop there. *...a fertile breeding ground for this kind of violent racism.* [3] ADJ Someone who is **fertile** is able to reproduce and have babies. ♦ **fertility** N-UNCOUNT *Pregnancy is the only sure test for fertility.*

fertilize (BRIT also **fertilise**) /'fɜːtɪlaɪz/**fertilizes, fertilizing, fertilized.** [1] VERB When an egg or plant **is fertilized**, the process of reproduction begins by sperm joining with the egg, or by pollen coming into contact with the reproductive part of a plant. ♦ **fertilization** N-UNCOUNT *...the average length of time from fertilization until birth.* [2] VERB To **fertilize** land means to spread manure or chemicals on it to make plants grow well.

fertilizer (BRIT also **fertiliser**) /'fɜːtɪlaɪzə/**fertilizers.** N-VAR **Fertilizer** is a substance that you spread on the ground to make plants grow more successfully.

fibre

fervent /'fɜːvənt/. ADJ Someone who is **fervent** about something has strong and enthusiastic feelings about it. ...*a fervent admirer of Morisot's work.* ♦ **fervently** ADV *Their claims will be fervently denied.*

fervour (AM **fervor**) /'fɜːvə/. N-UNCOUNT **Fervour** is a very strong enthusiasm for something or belief in something. [FORMAL] ...*religious fervour.*

fester /'festə/ **festers, festering, festered.** 1 VERB If a situation or problem **is festering**, it is growing worse, because it is not being properly recognized or dealt with. *Resentments are starting to fester.* 2 VERB If a wound **festers**, it becomes infected. [LITERARY]

⭐ **festival** /'festɪvəl/ **festivals.** 1 N-COUNT A **festival** is an organized series of events and performances. ...*summer festivals of music, theatre, and dance.* 2 N-COUNT A **festival** is a day or period when people have a holiday and celebrate some special event, often a religious one.

festive /'festɪv/. 1 ADJ Something that is **festive** is special, colourful, or exciting, especially because of a holiday or celebration. *The town has a festive holiday atmosphere.* 2 ADJ BEFORE N **Festive** means relating to a holiday or celebration, especially Christmas. ...*the festive period.*

festivity /fes'tɪvɪti/ **festivities.** 1 N-UNCOUNT **Festivity** is the celebration of something in a happy way. *There was a general air of festivity and abandon.* 2 N-PLURAL **Festivities** are events organized to celebrate something.

fetch /fetʃ/ **fetches, fetching, fetched.** 1 VERB If you **fetch** something or someone, you go and get them from where they are. *Sylvia fetched a towel from the bathroom... Fetch me a glass of water.* 2 VERB If something **fetches** a particular sum of money, it is sold for that amount. *The house is expected to fetch around £400,000.* 3 See also **far-fetched**.

fete /feɪt/ **fetes, feting, feted.** 1 N-COUNT A **fete** is an event held out of doors that includes competitions and the selling of home-made goods. 2 VERB If someone **is feted**, they are celebrated, welcomed, or admired by the public.

fetus /'fiːtəs/. See **foetus**.

feud /fjuːd/ **feuds, feuding, feuded.** 1 N-COUNT A **feud** is a long-lasting and bitter dispute between two people or groups. 2 VERB If two people or groups **feud**, there is a feud between them. *He feuded with his ex-wife.*

feudal /'fjuːdəl/. ADJ BEFORE N **Feudal** means relating to the system in which people were given land and protection by people of higher rank, and worked and fought for them in return.

fever /'fiːvə/ **fevers.** 1 N-VAR If you have a **fever**, your temperature is higher than usual because you are ill. ♦ See also **hay fever**. 2 N-COUNT A **fever** is extreme excitement or agitation. *Angie waited in a fever of excitement.*

feverish /'fiːvərɪʃ/. 1 ADJ **Feverish** emotion or activity shows great excitement or agitation. ...*feverish last minute negotiations.* ♦ **feverishly** ADV *Volunteers are working feverishly to remove the heavy snow.* 2 ADJ If you are **feverish**, you are suffering from a fever.

⭐ **few** /fjuː/ **fewer, fewest.** 1 QUANT **Few** is used to indicate a small number of things or people. *I gave a dinner party for a few close friends... A strict diet is appropriate for only a few. ...a little tea-party I'm giving for a few of the teachers.* 2 QUANT **Few** is used to indicate that a number of things or people is smaller than is desirable or than was expected. *She had few friends... The trouble is that few want to buy... Few of the beach houses still have lights on.*

> **USAGE** **Few** and **a few** are both used in front of the plural of count nouns, but they do not have the same meaning. For example, if you say '**I have a few friends**', this is a positive statement and you are saying that you have some friends. However, if you say '**I have few friends**', this is a kind of negative statement and you are saying that you have almost no friends or that you do not have enough friends.
> You use **fewer** to talk about things that can be counted, for example *fewer than five visits*. When you are talking about amounts that cannot be counted, you should use **less**, for example *less money.*

PHRASES ● You use **a good few** when you are referring to quite a lot of things or people. *He was a good few years older than me.* ● You use **as few as** before a number to suggest that it is surprisingly small. *The factory may make as few as 1,500 cars this year.* ● Things that are **few and far between** are very rare or uncommon. *Successful women politicians are few and far between.* ● You use **no fewer than** to suggest that a number is surprisingly large. *He had invited no fewer than 4,000 young people.*

fiancé /fi'ɒnseɪ, AM ˌfiːɑːn'seɪ/ **fiancés.** N-COUNT A woman's **fiancé** is the man to whom she is engaged to be married.

fiancée /fi'ɒnseɪ, AM ˌfiːɑː'nseɪ/ **fiancées.** N-COUNT A man's **fiancée** is the woman to whom he is engaged to be married.

fiasco /fi'æskəʊ/ **fiascos.** N-COUNT When something fails completely, you can describe it as a **fiasco**, especially if it seems ridiculous or disorganized. *The race had been a complete fiasco.*

fibre (AM **fiber**) /'faɪbə/ **fibres.** 1 N-COUNT A **fibre** is a thin thread of a natural or artificial substance, especially one used to make cloth or rope. 2 N-COUNT A **fibre** is a thin piece of flesh like a thread which connects nerve cells in your body or which muscles are made of. ...*the nerve fibres.* 3 N-UNCOUNT **Fibre** consists of the parts of

a b c d e f g h i j k l m n o p q r s t u v w x y z

plants or seeds that your body cannot digest, but which help food pass quickly through your digestive system.

fickle /'fɪkəl/. **1** ADJ A **fickle** person keeps changing their mind about what they like or want; used showing disapproval. ...*a handsome but fickle young actor.* **2** ADJ If you say that something is **fickle**, you mean that it often changes and is unreliable. *Orta's weather can be fickle.*

fiction /'fɪkʃən/ **fictions. 1** N-UNCOUNT **Fiction** is stories about imaginary people and events.
♦ **fictional** ADJ *Ulverton is a fictional village on the Wessex Downs.* **2** N-VAR A statement or report that is **fiction** is not true. *The truth or fiction of this story has never been truly determined.*

fictitious /fɪk'tɪʃəs/. ADJ Something that is **fictitious** is false or does not exist. *We're interested in the source of these fictitious rumours.*

fiddle /'fɪdəl/ **fiddles, fiddling, fiddled. 1** VERB If you **fiddle with** an object, you keep moving it or touching it with your fingers. *She fiddled nervously with the buttons of her cardigan.* **2** VERB If someone **fiddles** financial documents, they alter them dishonestly to get money for themselves. [INFORMAL] ♦ **fiddling** N-UNCOUNT ...*evidence of fiddling in the firm's Treasury-bond department.* **3** N-COUNT A **fiddle** is a dishonest action or scheme to get money. [BRITISH, INFORMAL] ...*a £10 million car insurance fiddle.* **4** N-COUNT Some people call violins **fiddles**.

fiddly /'fɪdəli/. ADJ Something that is **fiddly** is difficult to do or use, because it involves small or complicated objects. [INFORMAL] *Fish can be fiddly to cook.*

fidelity /fɪ'delɪti/. **1** N-UNCOUNT **Fidelity** is loyalty to a person, organization, or set of beliefs. [FORMAL] *I had to promise fidelity to the Queen.* **2** N-UNCOUNT The **fidelity** of something such as a report or translation is its degree of accuracy. [FORMAL]

fidget /'fɪdʒɪt/ **fidgets, fidgeting, fidgeted.** VERB If you **fidget**, you keep moving your hands or feet or changing position slightly, because you are nervous or bored. *Brenda fidgeted in her seat... He fidgeted with his tie.*

⭐ **field** /fiːld/ **fields, fielding, fielded. 1** N-COUNT A **field** is an enclosed area of land where crops are grown or animals are kept. ...*a field of wheat.* **2** N-COUNT A sports **field** is a grassy area where sports are played. **3** N-COUNT A **field** is an area of land or sea bed under which large amounts of a mineral are found. ...*an extensive natural gas field.* ● See also **minefield**, **playing field**. **4** PHRASE Your **field of vision** is the area that you can see without turning your head. *A big red rubber ball bounced suddenly across his field of vision.* **5** N-COUNT A particular **field** is a subject or area of interest. *Each of the authors of the tapes is an expert in his field.* **6** ADJ **Field** work involves research that is done in a real, natural environment rather than in a theoretical way or

in controlled conditions. ...*field trips to observe plants and animals.* **7** VERB The team that is **fielding** in a game of cricket or baseball is the team trying to catch the ball. ♦ **fielder, fielders** N-COUNT *The right fielder threw the ball back.* ♦ **fielding** N-UNCOUNT *Their bowling performance was very good, their fielding very sharp.* **8** PHRASE If someone **is having a field day**, they are very busy doing something that they enjoy, even though it may hurt other people. *In our absence the office gossips are probably having a field day.*

⭐ **fierce** /fɪəs/ **fiercer, fiercest. 1** ADJ A **fierce** animal or person is very aggressive or angry. ♦ **fiercely** ADV *'I don't know,' she said fiercely.* **2** ADJ **Fierce** feelings, actions, or conditions are very intense and strong. ...*a fierce storm which went on for five days.* ♦ **fiercely** ADV *He has always been ambitious and fiercely competitive.*

fiery /'faɪəri/. **1** ADJ Something that is **fiery** is burning strongly or contains fire. [LITERARY] *A helicopter crashed in a fiery explosion in Vallejo.* **2** ADJ You can use **fiery** for emphasis when you are referring to bright colours such as red or orange. [LITERARY] *Overhead the sky is a fiery red.* **3** ADJ If you describe someone as **fiery**, you mean that they express very strong emotions, especially anger. *She had a fiery temper.*

⭐ **fifteen** /ˌfɪf'tiːn/. NUM **Fifteen** is the number 15.

⭐ **fifteenth** /ˌfɪf'tiːnθ/. ORD The **fifteenth** item in a series is the one that you count as number fifteen.

⭐ **fifth** /fɪfθ/ **fifths. 1** ORD The **fifth** item in a series is the one that you count as number five. **2** N-COUNT A **fifth** is one of five equal parts of something.

⭐ **fiftieth** /'fɪftiəθ/. ORD The **fiftieth** item in a series is the one that you count as number fifty.

⭐ **fifty** /'fɪfti/ **fifties.** NUM **Fifty** is the number 50. For examples of how numbers such as fifty and eighty are used see **eighty**.

fig /fɪg/ **figs.** N-COUNT A **fig** is a soft sweet fruit full of tiny seeds. Figs grow on trees in hot countries.

⭐ **fight** /faɪt/ **fights, fighting, fought** /fɔːt/. **1** VERB & N-COUNT If you **fight** something, you try in a determined way to prevent it or stop it happening. A **fight against** something is an attempt to stop it. *More units to fight forest fires are planned... I've spent a lifetime fighting against racism. ...the fight against drug addiction.* **2** VERB & N-COUNT If you **fight for** something, you try in a determined way to get it or achieve it. A **fight for** something is an attempt to get it. *We had fought to hold on to the company. ...the fight for justice.* **3** VERB If a person or army **fights**, they oppose each other with weapons. *I would sooner go to prison than fight for this country... The rival militias have been fighting for more than two years.*
♦ **fighting** N-UNCOUNT *More than nine hundred people have died in the fighting.* **4** VERB & N-COUNT If one person **fights with** another, or if they have a **fight**, they hit or kick each other because they want to hurt each other. *I did fight him, I punched*

him but it was like hitting a wall... He had had a fight with Smith. [5] VERB & N-COUNT When people **fight about** something, or when they have a **fight**, they quarrel. *Mostly, they fight about paying bills... He had a big fight with his dad.* [6] VERB When politicians **fight** an election, they try to win it. [7] VERB If you **fight** your **way** to a place, you move towards it with great difficulty, usually because there are a lot of people in your way. *Female fans fought their way past bodyguards and tore at his clothes.* [8] VERB When you **fight** an emotion or desire, you try very hard not to feel it, show it, or act on it. *He fought with the urge to smoke.*

▸**fight back.** [1] PHR-VERB If you **fight back** against someone who has attacked you or made difficulties for you, you defend yourself by taking action against them. *The teenage attackers fled when the two men fought back.* [2] PHR-VERB When you **fight back** an emotion, you try very hard not to feel it, show it, or act on it. *She fought back the tears.*

▸**fight off.** [1] PHR-VERB If you **fight off** something such as an illness, a desire, or unpleasant feeling, you succeed in getting rid of it. *All day she had fought off the impulse to telephone Harry.* [2] PHR-VERB If you **fight off** someone who has attacked you, you succeed in driving them away by fighting them. *The woman fought off her attacker.*

⭐ **fighter** /ˈfaɪtə/ **fighters.** [1] N-COUNT A **fighter** or a **fighter plane** is a fast military aircraft used for destroying other aircraft. [2] N-COUNT A **fighter** is someone who physically fights another person, especially a boxer.

figurative /ˈfɪɡərətɪv, AM -ɡjər-/. ADJ If you use a word or expression in a **figurative** sense, you use it with a more abstract or imaginative meaning than its ordinary literal one. ♦ **figuratively** ADV *A lot more children are abandoned today both literally and figuratively.*

⭐ **figure** /ˈfɪɡə, AM -ɡjər/ **figures, figuring, figured.** [1] N-COUNT A **figure** is a particular amount expressed as a number, especially a statistic. *Government figures predict that one in two marriages will end in divorce.* [2] N-COUNT A **figure** is any of the ten written symbols from 0 to 9 that are used to represent a number. [3] N-PLURAL An amount or number that is **in single figures** is between nought and nine. An amount or number that is **in double figures** is between ten and ninety-nine. [4] N-COUNT A **figure** is the shape of a person you cannot see clearly. *A figure in a blue dress appeared in the doorway.* [5] N-COUNT In art, a **figure** is a person in a drawing or a painting, or a statue of a person. [6] N-COUNT Your **figure** is the shape of your body. *Janet was a natural blonde with a good figure.* [7] N-COUNT Someone who is referred to as a particular type of **figure** is well-known and important in some way. *...key figures in the three main political parties.* [8] N-COUNT If you say that someone is, for example, a mother **figure** or a hero **figure**, you mean that they have

the qualities typical of mothers or heroes. *...authority figures such as parents and teachers.* [9] VERB If you **figure** that something is the case, you think or guess that it is the case. [INFORMAL] *I figured that's what she wanted.* [10] VERB A thing or person that **figures in** something appears in it or is included in it. *Human rights violations figured prominently in the report.*

▸**figure out.** PHR-VERB If you **figure out** a solution to a problem or the reason for something, you succeed in solving it or understanding it. [INFORMAL] *It took them about one month to figure out how to start the equipment.*

figurehead /ˈfɪɡəhed, AM -ɡjə-/ **figureheads.** N-COUNT If you refer to someone as the **figurehead** of an organization or political movement, you mean that they are recognized as its leader, although they have no real power.

⭐ **file** /faɪl/ **files, filing, filed.** [1] N-COUNT A **file** is a box or folder in which documents are kept. [2] N-COUNT A **file** is a set of related data that has its own name. [COMPUTING] [3] N-COUNT & PHRASE To keep a **file on** someone or something means to collect information about them. Information that is **on file** is recorded as part of a collection of information. *We already have files on people's tax details... We'll keep your details on file.* [4] VERB & PHR-VERB If you **file** a document, or if you **file** it **away**, you put it in the correct file. *I'd completed all the case notes and filed them away.* [5] VERB When you **file** an accusation, complaint, or request, you make it officially. *I filed for divorce on the grounds of adultery.* [6] VERB & PHRASE When a group of people **files** somewhere, or when they walk somewhere **in single file**, they walk one behind the other in a line. *The children filed out of the house.* [7] N-COUNT A **file** is a tool with rough surfaces, used for smoothing and shaping hard materials. [8] VERB If you **file** an object, you smooth or shape it with a file.

⭐ **fill** /fɪl/ **fills, filling, filled.** [1] VERB & PHR-VERB If you **fill** a container, or if you **fill** it **up**, you keep putting or pouring something into it until it is full. You can also say a container or something shaped like a container **fills with** something. *Fill a saucepan with water... The victims' lungs fill quickly with fluid... Pass me your cup, Amy, and I'll fill it up for you.* [2] VERB & PHR-VERB If something **fills** a space, or if it **fills up** a space, it is so large, or there are such large quantities of it, that there is very little room left. *The text fills 231 pages. ...the complicated machines that fill up today's laboratories.* ♦ **filled** ADJ *...four museum buildings filled with historical objects. ...a flower-filled garden.* [3] VERB & PHR-VERB If you **fill** a crack or hole, or if you **fill** it **in**, you put a substance into it in order to make the surface smooth again. [4] VERB If something **fills** you **with** an emotion, you experience this emotion strongly. *He was filled with pride at his creation.* [5] VERB & PHR-VERB If you **fill** a period of time with a particular activity, or if you **fill** it **up** with that activity, you spend the time in this way. *She went to her yoga*

a
b
c
d
e
f
g
h
i
j
k
l
m
n
o
p
q
r
s
t
u
v
w
x
y
z

class, glad to have something to fill up the evening. **6** VERB If something **fills** a need or gap, it means that the need or gap no longer exists. *...a sense of fun, of gaiety that filled a gap in his life.* **7** VERB If something **fills** a role or position, that is their role or position. *I was asked to fill the role of escort.* **8** PHRASE If you **have had** your **fill** of something, you do not want to experience it or do it any more.

▶**fill in.** **1** PHR-VERB When you **fill in** a form, you write information in the spaces on it. **2** PHR-VERB If you **fill** someone **in**, you give them detailed information about something. [INFORMAL] *He filled her in on Wilbur Kantor's visit.* **3** PHR-VERB If you **fill in for** someone else, you do their job for them in their absence. **4** See also **fill** 3.

▶**fill out.** PHR-VERB To **fill out** a form means the same as to **fill in** a form. *Fill out the application carefully, and keep copies of it.*

▶**fill up.** **1** PHR-VERB A type of food that **fills you up** makes you feel that you have eaten a lot, even though you have only eaten a small amount. **2** See also **fill** 1, 2, 5.

fillet /ˈfɪlɪt, AM fɪˈleɪ/ **fillets, filleting, filleted.** **1** N-VAR A **fillet** of fish or meat is a piece that has no bones in it. *...chicken fillets.* **2** VERB When you **fillet** fish or meat, you prepare it by taking the bones out.

filling /ˈfɪlɪŋ/ **fillings.** **1** N-COUNT A **filling** is a small amount of metal or plastic that a dentist puts in a hole in a tooth. **2** N-VAR The **filling** in a pie, chocolate, sandwich or cake is the mixture inside it. **3** ADJ Food that is **filling** makes you feel full when you have eaten it. *...a filling meal.*

⭐ **film** /fɪlm/ **films, filming, filmed.** **1** N-VAR A **film** consists of moving pictures that have been recorded so that they can be shown in a cinema or on television. *In the evening we saw a film starring William Holden... The programme showed film of the four children laughing.* **2** VERB If you **film** someone or something, you use a camera to take moving pictures which can be shown in a cinema or on television. *...a camera crew filming her for French television.* ◆ **filming** N-UNCOUNT *Filming begins early next year.* **3** N-VAR A **film** is the roll of thin plastic that you use in a camera to take photographs. *...a roll of film.* **4** N-COUNT A **film of** powder, liquid, or grease is a very thin layer of it. *A film of dust covered every surface.*

filter /ˈfɪltə/ **filters, filtering, filtered.** **1** VERB To **filter** a substance, or to **filter** particles out of a substance, means to pass it through a device which removes the particles from it. *The best prevention for cholera is to boil or filter water.* **2** N-COUNT A **filter** is a device through which a substance is passed when it is being filtered. *...an oil filter.* **3** VERB When light or sound **filters into** a place, it comes in faintly. **4** N-COUNT A **filter** is a device through which sound or light is passed and which blocks or reduces particular frequencies. *...a pale blue filter gives the correct colour balance.* **5** VERB When news or information **filters through to** people, it

gradually reaches them. *It took months before the findings began to filter through to the politicians.*

filth /fɪlθ/ **1** N-UNCOUNT **Filth** is a disgusting amount of dirt. *The floor and furniture are covered in filth.* **2** N-UNCOUNT People refer to words or pictures as **filth** when they think that they describe or represent something such as sex or nudity in a disgusting way.

filthy /ˈfɪlθi/ **filthier, filthiest.** **1** ADJ Something that is **filthy** is very dirty indeed. *...a pair of filthy jeans.* **2** ADJ People describe things as **filthy** when they think that they are disgusting. *...a filthy habit.*

fin /fɪn/ **fins.** **1** N-COUNT A fish's **fins** are the flat objects which stick out of its body and help it to swim. **2** N-COUNT A **fin** on something such as an aeroplane is a flat part which sticks out and helps to control its movement.

⭐ **final** /ˈfaɪnəl/ **finals.** **1** ADJ BEFORE N In a series of events, things, or people, the **final** one is the last one, or the one that happens at the end. *This is my final offer... The final effect was eerily realistic.* **2** ADJ If a decision is **final**, it cannot be changed or questioned. *I'm not going, and that's final.* **3** N-COUNT A **final** is the last game or contest in a series, which decides the overall winner. *...the Scottish Cup Final.* ● See also **quarter-final**, **semi-final**. **4** N-PLURAL **Finals** are the last and most important examinations in a university course. *Anna sat her finals in the summer.*

finale /fɪˈnɑːli, -ˈnæli/ **finales.** **1** N-COUNT The **finale** is the last section of a show or a piece of music. *... the finale of Shostakovich's Fifth Symphony.* **2** N-COUNT If you say that an event provides a particular kind of **finale to** something, you mean that it provides it with that kind of ending. *...a sad finale to an otherwise spectacular career.*

finalist /ˈfaɪnəlɪst/ **finalists.** N-COUNT A **finalist** is a person or team that takes part in the final of a competition. *...World Cup finalists.*

finalize (BRIT also **finalise**) /ˈfaɪnəlaɪz/ **finalizes, finalizing, finalized.** VERB If you **finalize** something that you are arranging, you complete the arrangements for it. *They have until today to finalise their orders.*

⭐ **finally** /ˈfaɪnəli/ **1** ADV If something **finally** happens, it happens after a long delay. *Finally, he answered the phone himself.* **2** ADV You use **finally** to indicate that something is the last in a series. *She moves from Germany to Russia and finally America.* **3** ADV You use **finally** to introduce a final point or topic. *And finally, a word about the winner.*

⭐ **finance** /ˈfaɪnæns, fɪˈnæns/ **finances, financing, financed.** **1** VERB & N-UNCOUNT To **finance** a project or purchase, or to provide **finance** for it, means to provide money to pay for it. *These funds are then used to finance the purchase of equipment. ...an American whom he hoped would provide finance for the magazine.* **2** N-UNCOUNT **Finance** is the management of money, especially on a

national level. ...*the world of high finance.*
3 N-PLURAL Your **finances** are the amount of money that you have.

⭐ **financial** /faɪˈnænʃəl, fɪ-/. ADJ **Financial** means relating to or involving money. ...*financial difficulties.* ◆ **financially** ADV *She would like to be more financially independent.*

fi,nancial adˈviser, financial advisers. N-COUNT A **financial adviser** is someone whose job it is to advise people about financial products and services.

fi,nancial ˈservices. N-PLURAL A company or organization that provides **financial services** is able to help you do things such as make investments or buy a pension or mortgage.

fi,nancial ˈyear, financial years. N-COUNT A **financial year** is a twelve month period beginning and ending in April, which governments and businesses use to plan their finances. [BRITISH]

financier /faɪˈnænsɪə, fɪ-/ **financiers.** N-COUNT A **financier** is a person who provides money for projects or enterprises.

⭐ **find** /faɪnd/ **finds, finding, found.** **1** VERB If you **find** someone or something, you see them or learn where they are. *The police also found a pistol... I can't find the boys' shampoo.* **2** VERB If you **find** something that you need or want, you succeed in getting it. *We have to find him a job... My sister helped me find the money for a private operation.* **3** PASSIVE-VERB If you say that something **is found** in a particular place, you mean that it is in that place. *Fibre is found in cereal foods, beans, fruit and vegetables.* **4** VERB If you **find yourself** doing something, you are doing it without intending to. *It's not the first time that you've found yourself in this situation.* **5** VERB If you **find** that something is the case, you become aware of it or realize it. *At my age I would find it hard to get another job... I've never found my diet a problem... She returned to her east London home to find her back door forced open.* **6** VERB When a court or jury finds a person guilty or not guilty, they decide if that person is guilty or innocent. *She was found guilty of manslaughter.* **7** VERB You can use **find** to express your reaction to someone or something. *We're sure you'll find it exciting!... But you'd find him a good worker if you showed him what to do.* **8** N-COUNT If you describe something that has been discovered as a **find**, you mean that it is good or useful. ...*the botanical find of the century.* **9** PHRASE If you **find your way** somewhere, you get there by choosing the right way to go. *He was an expert at finding his way, even in strange surroundings.* **10** See also **finding, found.** ● to **find fault with**: see **fault.**

▶**find out.** **1** PHR-VERB If you **find** something **out**, you learn it, often by making a deliberate effort. ...*their campaign to find out the truth.* **2** PHR-VERB If you **find** someone **out**, you discover they have been doing something dishonest.

finding /ˈfaɪndɪŋ/ **findings.** N-COUNT Someone's **findings** are the information they get as the result of an investigation. *The committee has just reported its findings.*

fine 1 adjective uses

⭐ **fine** /faɪn/ **finer, finest.** **1** ADJ You use **fine** to describe someone or something that is very good. ...*an excellent journalist and a very fine man.* ...*London's finest art deco cinema.* ◆ **finely** ADV *They are finely engineered boats.* **2** ADJ AFTER LINK-V If you say that you are **fine**, you mean that you are feeling well and reasonably happy. **3** ADJ & ADV If you say that something is **fine**, you mean that it is satisfactory or acceptable. *All the instruments are working fine.* **4** ADJ When the weather is **fine**, it is sunny and not raining. **5** ADJ Something that is **fine** is very delicate, narrow, or small. ...*the fine hairs on her arms.* ◆ **finely** ADV *Chop the ingredients finely.* **6** ADJ A **fine** adjustment, detail, or distinction is very delicate, small, or exact.

fine 2 punishment

⭐ **fine** /faɪn/ **fines, fining, fined.** N-COUNT & VERB If you get a **fine**, or if you **are fined**, you are punished by being ordered to pay a sum of money. *They fined him $10,000.*

ˌfine ˈart, fine arts. N-VAR Painting and sculpture can be referred to as **fine art** or as **the fine arts**.

finesse /fɪˈnes/. N-UNCOUNT If you do something with **finesse**, you do it with great skill and elegance. *His boxing style lacks finesse.*

ˌfine-ˈtune, fine-tunes, fine-tuning, fine-tuned. VERB If you **fine-tune** something, you make very small and precise changes to it to make it work better.

⭐ **finger** /ˈfɪŋɡə/ **fingers, fingering, fingered.** **1** N-COUNT Your **fingers** are the four long moveable parts at the end of your hands. → See picture on page 823. *There was a ring on each of his fingers.* **2** VERB If you **finger** something, you touch or feel it with your fingers. *He fingered the few coins in his pocket.*

PHRASES ● If you **cross** your **fingers**, you put one finger on top of another and hope for good luck. If someone **is keeping** their **fingers crossed**, they are hoping for good luck. ● If you **point the finger at** someone, you blame them or accuse them of something. *He said he wasn't pointing an accusing finger at anyone in the government.* ● If you **put** your **finger on** something such as a problem or an idea, you see and identify exactly what it is. *He could never quite put his finger on who or what was responsible for all this.*

fingernail /ˈfɪŋɡəneɪl/ **fingernails.** N-COUNT Your **fingernails** are the hard areas on the ends of your fingers. → See picture on page 823.

fingerprint /ˈfɪŋɡəprɪnt/ **fingerprints.** N-COUNT & PHRASE Your **fingerprints** are the unique marks made by the tip of your fingers when you touch something. If the police **take** someone's **fingerprints**, they make a record of that person's fingerprints.

a
b
c
d
e
f
g
h
i
j
k
l
m
n
o
p
q
r
s
t
u
v
w
x
y
z

fingertip /ˈfɪŋɡətɪp/ **fingertips.** [1] N-COUNT Your **fingertips** are the ends of your fingers. [2] PHRASE If something is **at** your **fingertips**, you can reach or get it easily. *I had the information at my fingertips.*

⭐ **finish** /ˈfɪnɪʃ/ **finishes, finishing, finished.** [1] VERB & PHR-VERB When you **finish** doing something, or when you **finish** it **off**, you do the last part of it, so that there is no more for you to do. In American English, you can also say **finish up**. *I've practically finished the ironing... The consultants had been working to finish a report... She is busy finishing off a biography.* [2] PHRASE If you **put the finishing touches to** something, you do the last things that are necessary to complete it. [3] VERB When something **finishes**, it ends. *The teaching day finishes at around 4pm.* [4] N-SING The **finish** of something is the last part of it. *I intend to continue it and see the job through to the finish.* [5] N-COUNT An object's **finish** is the appearance or texture of its surface. *...the finish and workmanship of the woodwork.* [6] See also **finished**.
▸**finish off.** PHR-VERB When you **finish off** something that you have been eating or drinking, you eat or drink the last part of it. • See also **finish** 2.
▸**finish up.** PHR-VERB If you **finish up** in a particular place or situation, you are in that place or situation after doing something. *He's probably going to finish up in jail.* • See also **finish** 2.
▸**finish with.** PHR-VERB When you **finish with** someone or something, you stop being involved with them. *My boyfriend was threatening to finish with me.*

finished /ˈfɪnɪʃt/. [1] ADJ AFTER LINK-V If you are **finished with** something, you are no longer doing it or interested in it. *One suspects he will be finished with boxing.* [2] ADJ AFTER LINK-V Someone or something that is **finished** is no longer important or effective. *Her power over me is finished... I thought I was finished.*

finite /ˈfaɪnaɪt/. ADJ Something that is **finite** has a limited size or extent. [FORMAL] *Coal and oil are finite resources.*

fir /fɜː/ **firs.** N-COUNT A **fir** or a **fir tree** is a tall pointed evergreen tree.

fire 1 burning, heat

⭐ **fire** /faɪə/ **fires.** [1] N-UNCOUNT **Fire** consists of the flames produced by things that are burning. *...a great orange ball of fire.* [2] N-VAR A **fire** is an occurrence of uncontrolled burning which destroys things. *Much of historic Rennes was destroyed by fire. ...a forest fire.* [3] N-COUNT A **fire** is a burning pile of coal, wood, or other fuel that you make. *I started to clear the grate to light a fire.* [4] N-COUNT A **fire** is a device that uses electricity or gas to heat a room.
PHRASES • If something **catches fire**, it starts burning. • If something is **on fire**, it is burning fiercely. • If you **set fire** to something, or if you set it **on fire**, you start it burning.

fire 2 shooting or attacking

⭐ **fire** /faɪə/ **fires, firing, fired.** [1] VERB & N-UNCOUNT If someone **fires** a gun or a bullet, a bullet is sent from a gun that they are using. You can refer to the shots fired as **fire**. *...an exchange of fire during a police raid.* ♦ **firing** N-UNCOUNT *The firing continued.* [2] VERB If you **fire** questions **at** someone, you ask them a lot of questions very quickly, one after another.

fire 3 dismiss

fire /faɪə/ **fires, firing, fired.** VERB If your employer **fires** you, he or she dismisses you from your job. *You're fired!*

firearm /ˈfaɪərɑːm/ **firearms.** N-COUNT **Firearms** are guns. *...illegal possession of firearms.*

ˈfire brigade, fire brigades. N-COUNT The **fire brigade** is an organization which has the job of putting out fires.

ˈfire engine, fire engines. N-COUNT In British English, a **fire engine** is a large vehicle that carries firemen and equipment for putting out fires. The usual American term is **fire truck**.

fireman /ˈfaɪəmən/ **firemen.** N-COUNT A **fireman** is a person whose job is to put out fires.

fireplace /ˈfaɪəpleɪs/ **fireplaces.** N-COUNT In a room, the **fireplace** is the place where a fire can be lit.

firepower /ˈfaɪəpaʊə/. N-UNCOUNT The **firepower** of an army or military vehicle is the amount of ammunition it can fire.

firewood /ˈfaɪəwʊd/. N-UNCOUNT **Firewood** is wood that has been cut up for burning on a fire.

firework /ˈfaɪəwɜːk/ **fireworks.** N-COUNT **Fireworks** are small objects that are lit to entertain people on special occasions. They burn in a bright, attractive, and often noisy way.

⭐ **firm** /fɜːm/ **firms; firmer, firmest.** [1] N-COUNT A **firm** is a business selling or producing something. *...a firm of heating engineers.* [2] ADJ Something that is **firm** is fairly hard and does not change much in shape when it is pressed. *Choose a soft, medium or firm mattress.* ♦ **firmness** N-UNCOUNT *Vegetables should retain some firmness.* [3] ADJ A **firm** grasp or push is one which is strong and controlled. *The quick handshake was firm and cool.* ♦ **firmly** ADV *She held me firmly by the elbow.* [4] ADJ A **firm** person behaves in a fairly strict way, and will not change their mind. *She had to be firm with him. 'I don't want to see you again'.* ♦ **firmly** ADV *'A good night's sleep is what you want,' he said firmly.* ♦ **firmness** N-UNCOUNT *...a manner that combines friendliness with compassion and firmness.* [5] PHRASE If someone **stands firm**, they refuse to surrender or change their mind about something. *The council is standing firm against the barrage of protest.* [6] ADJ A **firm** decision or piece of information is definite and unlikely to change. *We have no firm evidence.* ♦ **firmly** ADV *He is firmly convinced that it is vital to do this.*

⭐ **first** /fɜːst/. **1** ORD & PRON & ADV The **first** thing or person is the one that happens or comes before all the others of the same kind. ...*the first month of her diet... Johnson came first in the one hundred metres... The second paragraph startled me even more than the first. ...two years after they had first started going out.* **2** ADV If you do something **first**, you do it before anyone else does, or before you do anything else. *I do not remember who spoke first... First, tell me what you think of my products.* **3** N-SING An event that is described as **a first** has never happened before. *The meeting between financial analysts was a first for the company.* **4** PRON **The first** you hear of something or **the first** you know about it is the time when you first become aware of it. *That was the first we heard of it.* **5** ADV & ORD You use **first** when you are talking about what happens in the early part of an event or process, in contrast to what happens later. *At first, he seemed surprised by my questions... Her first reaction was disgust.* **6** ADV & PHRASE You use **first** or **first of all** to introduce the first of a number of things that you want to say. *First of all, we can encourage people to buy their homes.* **7** ADJ **First** refers to the best or most important thing or person of a particular kind. *The first duty of any government must be to protect the interests of the taxpayers.* **8** PHRASE If you **put** someone or something **first**, you treat them as more important than anything else.

first 'aid. N-UNCOUNT **First aid** is medical treatment given as soon as possible to a sick or injured person. *Onlookers thought she was giving first aid.*

first 'class. **1** ADJ Something or someone that is **first class**, is of the highest quality or standard. *The food was first class.* **2** N-UNCOUNT & ADJ & ADV **First class**, or **first class** accommodation, is the best and most expensive accommodation on an aeroplane, ship, or train. ...*a cabin in first class. ...two first class tickets to Dublin... She had never flown first class before.*

first-'hand (or firsthand). ADJ **First-hand** information or experience is gained directly, rather than from other people. *She has little first-hand knowledge of Quebec... We've been through Germany and seen first-hand what's happening there.*

firstly /ˈfɜːstli/. ADV You use **firstly** when you are about to mention the first in a series of items. *Noise affects us in two ways. Firstly, it can damage hearing.*

first 'name, first names. N-COUNT Your **first name** is the first of the names that you were given when you were born, as opposed to your surname. *Her first name is Mary.*

first 'rate. ADJ If someone or something is **first rate**, they are of the highest quality. ...*a first-rate scientist.*

⭐ **fiscal** /ˈfɪskəl/. ADJ BEFORE N **Fiscal** means related to government money or public money, especially taxes. ...*fiscal policy.*

⭐ **fish** /fɪʃ/ **fishes, fishing, fished.**

✅ The plural is **fish** or **fishes**.

1 N-VAR A **fish** is a creature with a tail and fins that lives in water. **Fish** is the flesh of a fish eaten as food. **2** VERB If you **fish**, you try to catch fish. **3** VERB If you **fish** a particular area of water, you try to catch fish there. *On Saturday we fished the River Arno.*
▶ **fish out.** PHR-VERB If you **fish** something **out** from somewhere, you take or pull it out. *He fished out three files from the cabinet.*

fisherman /ˈfɪʃəmən/ **fishermen.** N-COUNT A **fisherman** is a person who catches fish as a job or for sport.

⭐ **fishing** /ˈfɪʃɪŋ/. N-UNCOUNT **Fishing** is the sport or business of catching fish.

fist /fɪst/ **fists.** N-COUNT You refer to someone's hand as their **fist** when they have bent their fingers towards their palm. *He swore and shook his fist at me.*

fit 1 being right or going in the right place

⭐ **fit** /fɪt/ **fits, fitting, fitted** (AM **fit**). **1** VERB & N-SING If something **fits**, or if it is a good **fit**, it is the right size and shape to go onto a person's body or into a particular position. *The garments were made to fit a child. ...a pocket computer which is small enough to fit into your pocket... The sills and doors were a reasonably good fit.* **2** VERB If you **fit** something into a particular space or place, you put it there. ...*she fitted her key in the lock.* **3** VERB If you **fit** something somewhere, you attach it there securely. *Fit hinge bolts to give extra support to the door lock... Peter had built the overhead ladders, and the next day he fitted them to the wall.* **4** ADJ If someone or something is **fit for** a particular purpose, they are suitable or appropriate for it. *Only two of the bicycles were fit for the road... You're not fit to be a mother!... The meat is fit to eat.* ♦ **fitness** N-UNCOUNT *You should consult your doctor about your fitness to travel.* **5** PHRASE If someone **sees fit to** do something, they decide that it is the right thing to do; used showing disapproval. *He's not a friend, you say, yet you saw fit to lend him money.*
▶ **fit in.** **1** PHR-VERB If you manage to **fit** a person or task **in**, you manage to find time to deal with them. *I find that I just can't fit in regular domestic work. You're not fit to be a mother!...* **2** PHR-VERB If you **fit into** a group, or if you **fit in**, you seem to belong in the group because you are similar to other people in it. *It's hard to see how he would fit into the team.*
▶ **fit out** or **fit up.** PHR-VERB If you **fit** someone or something **out**, or if you **fit** them **up**, you provide them with equipment and other things that they need. *We helped to fit him out for a trip to the Baltic.*

fit 2 healthy

⭐ **fit** /fɪt/ **fitter, fittest.** ADJ Someone who is **fit** is healthy and physically strong. ♦ **fitness**

a
b
c
d
e
f
g
h
i
j
k
l
m
n
o
p
q
r
s
t
u
v
w
x
y
z

N-UNCOUNT ...*women who regularly engage in sports and fitness activities.*

fit 3 uncontrollable movements or emotions

fit /fɪt/ **fits.** **1** N-COUNT If someone has a **fit**, they suddenly lose consciousness and their body makes uncontrollable movements. ...*epileptic fits.* **2** N-COUNT A **fit of** coughing, laughter, anger, or panic is a sudden uncontrolled outburst of it. *Pattie shot Tom in a fit of jealous rage.*

fitted /'fɪtɪd/. **1** ADJ **Fitted** clothes or furnishings are designed to be exactly the right size for their purpose. ...*a fitted jacket.* ...*a fitted carpet.* **2** ADJ **Fitted** furniture is designed to fill a particular space and is fixed in place. ...*fitted wardrobes.* **3** ADJ If a room is **fitted with** objects, those objects are in the room and are normally fixed in place. ...*an exercise room fitted with an electronic bicycle.*

fitting /'fɪtɪŋ/ **fittings.** **1** ADJ If something is **fitting**, it is right or suitable. ...*a fitting end to a bitter campaign.* ♦ **fittingly** ADV *Fittingly, the hearing is being conducted by a former Supreme Court judge.* **2** N-COUNT A **fitting** is a small part on the outside of a piece of equipment or furniture, such as a handle or a tap. ...*brass light fittings.* **3** N-PLURAL **Fittings** are things such as cookers or electric fires that are fixed inside a building but can be removed if necessary.

⭐ **five** /faɪv/ **fives.** NUM **Five** is the number 5.

fiver /'faɪvə/ **fivers.** N-COUNT A **fiver** is a British five pound note. [INFORMAL]

⭐ **fix** /fɪks/ **fixes, fixing, fixed.** **1** VERB If something **is fixed** somewhere, it is attached there securely. *It is fixed on the wall... He fixed a bayonet to the end of his rifle.* **2** VERB If you **fix** something, for example a date, price, or policy, you decide what it will be or you arrange it. *He's going to fix a time when I can see him... He vanished after you fixed him with a job.* **3** VERB To **fix** something means to repair it or to make it satisfactory. *If something is broken, we get it fixed... It's not too late to fix the problem.* **4** VERB If you **fix** your eyes or attention **on** something, you look at it or think about it with concentration. *Her soft brown eyes fixed on Kelly... Fix your attention on the practicalities of financing your schemes.* **5** VERB & N-COUNT If someone **fixes** a race, election, contest, or other event, they make unfair or illegal arrangements to affect the result. A **fix** is a situation where this happens. *They offered opposing players bribes to fix a decisive league match... It's all a fix, a deal they've made.* **6** N-COUNT An injection of an addictive drug such as heroin can be referred to as a **fix**. [INFORMAL] **7** See also **fixed**.

▸ **fix up.** **1** PHR-VERB If you **fix** someone **up with** something they need, you provide it. *He was fixed up with a job.* **2** PHR-VERB If you **fix** something **up**, you arrange it. *I fixed up an appointment to see her.*

⭐ **fixed** /fɪkst/. ADJ You use **fixed** to describe something which stays the same and does not

vary. ...*fixed interest rates.* ...*people who have fixed ideas about things.* ...*a fixed grin.*

fixture /'fɪkstʃə/ **fixtures.** **1** N-COUNT **Fixtures** are pieces of furniture or equipment, for example baths, which are permanently fixed inside a building. **2** N-COUNT If something or someone is a **fixture** in a particular place, they are always there. *She was a fixture in New York's nightclubs.* **3** N-COUNT In sport, a **fixture** is a competition arranged for a particular date. [BRITISH] *City won this fixture 3-0.*

fizz /fɪz/ **fizzes, fizzing, fizzed.** VERB & N-UNCOUNT If a drink **fizzes**, or if it has **fizz**, it produces lots of little bubbles of gas and makes a hissing sound. ...*what is it that makes cola fizz... The champagne began to lose its fizz.*

fizzy /'fɪzi/. ADJ **Fizzy** drinks are full of little bubbles of gas.

⭐ **flag** /flæg/ **flags, flagging, flagged.** **1** N-COUNT A **flag** is a piece of coloured cloth used as a sign for something or as a signal. ...*the American flag.* **2** PHRASE If you **fly the flag**, you show that you are proud of your country, or that you support a particular cause. *Don't expect him to be flying the flag for his home country.* **3** VERB If you **flag**, or if your spirits **flag**, you begin to lose enthusiasm or energy. *By 4,000m he was beginning to flag.*

flagrant /'fleɪgrənt/. ADJ BEFORE N You can use **flagrant** to describe an action or situation that is bad or shocking in an obvious or deliberate way. ...*a flagrant violation of international law.*

flagship /'flægʃɪp/ **flagships.** **1** N-COUNT A **flagship** is the most important ship in a fleet. **2** N-COUNT The **flagship** of a group of things that are owned or produced by a particular organization is the most important one. *The hospital has been the government's flagship.*

flail /fleɪl/ **flails, flailing, flailed.** VERB If your arms or legs **flail**, **flail around**, or **flail about**, they wave about in an energetic but uncontrolled way. *His arms were flailing in all directions.*

flair /fleə/. **1** N-SING If you have a **flair for** a particular thing, you have a natural ability to do it well. ...*a friend who has a flair for languages.* **2** N-UNCOUNT If you have **flair**, you do things in an interesting, and stylish way. *Their work has all the usual punch, panache and flair you'd expect.*

flak /flæk/. N-UNCOUNT If you get a lot of **flak** from someone, they criticize you severely. If you take **the flak**, you get the blame for something. [INFORMAL]

flake /fleɪk/ **flakes, flaking, flaked.** **1** N-COUNT A **flake** is a small thin piece of something that has broken off a larger piece. *A flake of plaster from the ceiling fell into his eye.* **2** VERB If paint **flakes**, or if it **flakes off**, small pieces of it come off.

flamboyant /flæm'bɔɪənt/. ADJ If you say that someone or something is **flamboyant**, you mean that they are very noticeable and stylish. *Freddie Mercury was a flamboyant star.* ♦ **flamboyance** N-UNCOUNT ...*his usual mixture of flamboyance and* *flair.* ◆ **flamboyantly** ADV *She dressed flamboyantly.*

flame /fleɪm/ **flames.** N-VAR A **flame** is a hot bright stream of burning gas that comes from something that is burning. *The heat from the flames was so intense that roads melted.* PHRASES ● If something is **in flames**, it is on fire. ● If something **bursts into flames**, it suddenly starts burning fiercely.

flaming /ˈfleɪmɪŋ/. 1 ADJ **Flaming** is used to describe something that is burning and producing a lot of flames. *...the crash, which sent flaming debris hurtling through the city centre.* 2 ADJ BEFORE N Something that is **flaming** red or **flaming** orange is bright red or orange in colour.

flank /flæŋk/ **flanks, flanking, flanked.** 1 N-COUNT An animal's **flanks** are the sides of its body. 2 N-COUNT A **flank** of an army or naval force is one side of it when it is organized for battle. 3 VERB If something **is flanked** by things, it has them at its side. *Bookcases flank the bed.*

flannel /ˈflænəl/ **flannels.** N-UNCOUNT **Flannel** is a lightweight cloth for making clothes. *...a faded red flannel shirt.*

flap /flæp/ **flaps, flapping, flapped.** 1 VERB If something that is attached at one end **flaps**, or if you **flap** it, it moves quickly up and down or from side to side. *The bird flapped its wings furiously.* 2 N-COUNT A **flap of** cloth or skin is a flat piece of it that moves freely because it is attached by only one edge. *...a loose flap of skin... He drew back the tent flap.*

flare /fleə/ **flares, flaring, flared.** 1 N-COUNT A **flare** is a small device that produces a bright flame. Flares are used as signals, for example on ships. 2 VERB If a fire **flares**, or if it **flares up**, the flames suddenly become larger. *Don't spill too much fat on the barbecue as it could flare up.* 3 VERB If something such as violence or anger **flares**, or if it **flares up**, it becomes worse. *Trouble flared in several American cities... Dozens of people were injured as fighting flared up.*

'flare-up, flare-ups. N-COUNT If there is a **flare-up** of violence or of an illness, it suddenly starts or gets worse. *...a flare-up in her arthritis.*

★ **flash** /flæʃ/ **flashes, flashing, flashed.** 1 N-COUNT A **flash of** light is a sudden, short burst of it. *A sudden flash of lightning lit everything up.* 2 VERB If a light **flashes**, or if you **flash** a light, it shines brightly and suddenly. *Lightning flashed among the distant dark clouds... A driver flashed her headlights.* 3 VERB Something that **flashes** past moves or happens very quickly. *Cars flashed by every few minutes... A ludicrous thought flashed through Harry's mind.* 4 PHRASE If you say that something happens **in a flash**, you mean that it happens very quickly. *The answer had come to him in a flash.*

flashback /ˈflæʃbæk/ **flashbacks.** 1 N-COUNT In a film, novel, or play, a **flashback** is a scene that returns to events in the past. 2 N-COUNT If you have a **flashback to** a past experience, you have a sudden and vivid memory of it. *He has recurring flashbacks to the night his friends died.*

flashlight /ˈflæʃlaɪt/ **flashlights.** N-COUNT A **flashlight** is a small portable electric light which gets its power from batteries.

flashy /ˈflæʃi/ **flashier, flashiest.** ADJ If you describe a person or thing as **flashy**, you mean they are smart and noticeable, but in a rather vulgar way. [INFORMAL] *...a flashy sports car.*

flask /flɑːsk, flæsk/ **flasks.** N-COUNT A **flask** is a bottle used for carrying alcoholic or hot drinks around with you. *...a flask of coffee.*

★ **flat** /flæt/ **flats; flatter, flattest.** 1 N-COUNT In British English, a **flat** is a set of rooms for living in, that is part of a larger building. The usual American word is **apartment**. *...a block of flats.* 2 ADJ Something that is **flat** is level and smooth, rather than sloping, curved, or bumpy. *His right hand moved across the cloth, smoothing it flat... The sea was calm, perfectly flat.* 3 ADJ A **flat** object is not very tall or deep in relation to its length and width. *...a square flat box.* 4 ADJ A **flat** tyre or ball does not have enough air in it. 5 ADJ A **flat** battery has lost some or all of its electrical power. 6 ADJ BEFORE N A **flat** refusal or rejection is definite and firm. *The Foreign Ministry has issued a flat denial of any involvement.* ◆ **flatly** ADV *He flatly refused to discuss it.* 7 ADV If something is done in a particular amount of time **flat**, it is done in exactly that amount of time. *I had it all explained to me in two minutes flat.* 8 ADJ You use **flat** to describe someone's voice when they are saying something without expressing any emotion. *'Whatever you say,' he said in a deadly flat voice.* ◆ **flatly** ADV *I know you,' he said flatly.* 9 ADJ BEFORE N A **flat** rate, price, or percentage is one that is fixed and which applies in every situation. *Sometimes there's a flat fee for carrying out a particular task.* 10 ADJ **Flat** is used after a letter representing a musical note to show that the note should be played or sung half a tone lower than the note which otherwise corresponds to that letter. **Flat** is often represented by the symbol ♭ after the letter. 11 ADV & ADJ If a musical note is played or sung **flat**, it is slightly lower in pitch than it should be. PHRASES ● If an event or attempt to do something **falls flat**, it fails. *Liz meant it as a joke but it fell flat.* ● If you do something **flat out**, you do it as fast or as hard as you can. [BRITISH] *He is working flat out to trap those responsible.*

flatten /ˈflætən/ **flattens, flattening, flattened.** 1 VERB & PHR-VERB If you **flatten** something, or if you **flatten** it **out**, you make it flat or flatter. You can also say that something **flattens** or **flattens out**. *Flatten the dough out and cut it into six pieces.* 2 VERB If you **flatten yourself against** something, you press yourself flat against it. *He flattened himself against a brick wall as I passed.*

flatter /ˈflætə/ **flatters, flattering, flattered.** 1 VERB If someone **flatters** you, they praise you in an exaggerated way that is not sincere. *I knew she was just flattering me.* 2 VERB If you **flatter**

yourself that something is the case, you believe, perhaps wrongly, something good about yourself. *He flatters himself that his work will be found useful.*

flattered /'flætəd/. ADJ AFTER LINK-V If you are **flattered** by something that has happened, you are pleased about it because it makes you feel important. *I am flattered that they should be so supportive.*

flattering /'flætərɪŋ/. 1 ADJ If something is **flattering**, it makes you appear more attractive. *Her hair has been cut in a shorter, more flattering style.* 2 ADJ If someone's remarks or behaviour are **flattering**, they are pleasing because they show that the person has a high opinion of you. *It is always flattering to be asked to judge.*

flaunt /flɔːnt/ **flaunts, flaunting, flaunted.** VERB If you say that someone **flaunts** their possessions or qualities, you mean that they display them in a very obvious way. *They drove around in Rolls-Royces, openly flaunting their wealth.*

⭐ **flavour** (AM **flavor**) /'fleɪvə/ **flavours, flavouring, flavoured.** 1 N-VAR The **flavour** of a food or drink is its taste. *This cheese has a crumbly texture with a strong flavour.* ♦ **-flavoured** ...*fruit-flavoured sparkling water.* 2 VERB If you **flavour** food or drink, you add something to give it a particular taste. *Flavour your favourite dishes with exotic herbs and spices.* 3 N-UNCOUNT The **flavour** of something is its distinctive characteristic or quality. *Claude's landscapes have a strong Italian flavour.*

flavouring (AM **flavoring**) /'fleɪvərɪŋ/ **flavourings.** N-VAR **Flavourings** are substances that are added to food or drink to give it a particular taste.

flaw /flɔː/ **flaws.** 1 N-COUNT A **flaw in** something such as a theory is a mistake in it. *There were a number of flaws in his theory... Almost all of these studies have serious flaws.* 2 N-COUNT A **flaw in** someone's character is an undesirable quality which they have. *The only flaw in his character seems to be a short temper.*

flawed /flɔːd/. ADJ Something that is **flawed** has a mark or fault in it. *The research was seriously flawed. ...a flawed genius.*

flawless /'flɔːləs/. ADJ If you say that something or someone is **flawless**, you mean that they have no faults or imperfections. *...her flawless complexion.* ♦ **flawlessly** ADV *I wanted to do my job flawlessly.*

flea /fliː/ **fleas.** N-COUNT A **flea** is a small jumping insect that sucks human or animal blood. → See picture on page 824.

fleck /flek/ **flecks.** N-COUNT **Flecks** are small marks on a surface, or objects that look like small marks. *Flecks of dark blue paint.*

fled /fled/. **Fled** is the past tense and past participle of **flee**.

fledgling /'fledʒlɪŋ/ **fledglings.** 1 N-COUNT A **fledgling** is a young bird. 2 ADJ BEFORE N You

use **fledgling** to describe an inexperienced person or a new organization. *...fledgling writers.*

⭐ **flee** /fliː/ **flees, fleeing, fled.** VERB If you **flee** from something or someone, or if you **flee** them, you escape from them by running away. *In 1984 he fled to Costa Rica to avoid military service. ...refugees fleeing persecution.*

fleece /fliːs/ **fleeces, fleecing, fleeced.** 1 N-COUNT A sheep's **fleece** is its coat of wool. 2 N-COUNT A **fleece** is the wool, in a single piece, that is cut off one sheep during shearing. 3 VERB If someone **fleeces** you, they get a lot of money from you by tricking you. [INFORMAL] *He fleeced her out of thousands of pounds.*

⭐ **fleet** /fliːt/ **fleets.** 1 N-COUNT A **fleet** is an organized group of ships. *...local fishing fleets.* 2 N-COUNT You can refer to a group of vehicles as a **fleet**, especially when they all belong to a particular organization or when they are all going somewhere together. *With its own fleet of trucks, the company delivers most orders overnight.*

fleeting /'fliːtɪŋ/. ADJ **Fleeting** is used to describe something which lasts only for a very short time. *The girls caught only a fleeting glimpse of the driver.* ♦ **fleetingly** ADV *He smiled fleetingly.*

flesh /fleʃ/ **fleshes, fleshing, fleshed.** 1 N-UNCOUNT **Flesh** is the soft part of a person's or animal's body between the bones and the skin. *...the pale pink flesh of trout.* 2 N-UNCOUNT You can use **flesh** to refer to human skin and the human body, especially when you are considering it in a sexual way. *...the sins of the flesh.* 3 N-UNCOUNT The **flesh** of a fruit or vegetable is the soft inner part. 4 PHRASE If you meet or see someone **in the flesh**, you meet or see them in person. 5 PHRASE If you say that someone is your **own flesh and blood**, you are emphasizing that they are a member of your family.
▶ **flesh out.** PHR-VERB If you **flesh out** something such as a story, you add more details to it. *He talked with him for an hour and a half, fleshing out the details of his original five-minute account.*

flew /fluː/. **Flew** is the past tense of **fly**.

flex /fleks/ **flexes, flexing, flexed.** 1 N-VAR A **flex** is an electric cable containing wires that is connected to an electrical appliance. 2 VERB If you **flex** your muscles or parts of your body, you bend, move, or stretch them to exercise them.

⭐ **flexible** /'fleksɪbəl/. 1 ADJ A **flexible** object or material can be bent easily without breaking. *...brushes with long, flexible bristles.* ♦ **flexibility** N-UNCOUNT *The plastic's flexibility makes it possible to create a much larger range of shapes.* 2 ADJ Something or someone that is **flexible** is able to change and adapt easily to new conditions and circumstances. *Look for software that's flexible enough for a range of abilities.* ♦ **flexibility** N-UNCOUNT *Manville has the financial flexibility to buy other companies at the best moment.*

flick /flɪk/ **flicks, flicking, flicked.** 1 VERB & N-COUNT If something **flicks** in a particular direction, or if someone **flicks** it, it moves with a short, sudden movement. This action is called a **flick**. *His tongue flicked across his lips... She sighed and flicked a dishcloth at the counter. ...a flick of the whip.* [2] VERB If you **flick** a switch, you press it quickly. *He flicked a light-switch... Pearle flicked off the TV.* [3] VERB If you **flick through** a book or magazine, you turn the pages quickly.

flicker /ˈflɪkə/ **flickers, flickering, flickered.** [1] VERB & N-COUNT If a light or flame **flickers**, it shines unsteadily. You can also talk about a **flicker of** light. *A television flickered in the corner... I saw the flicker of flames.* [2] N-COUNT A **flicker of** feeling is one that is experienced or visible only faintly and briefly. *He felt a flicker of regret.* [3] VERB If an expression **flickers** across your face, it appears briefly. *A smile flickered across Vincent's grey features.*

⭐ **flight** /flaɪt/ **flights.** [1] N-COUNT A **flight** is a journey made by flying, usually in an aeroplane. *The flight will take four hours.* [2] N-COUNT You can refer to an aeroplane carrying passengers on a particular journey as a particular **flight**. *I'll try to get on the flight down to Karachi tonight... BA flight 286 was two hours late.* [3] N-UNCOUNT **Flight** is the action of flying, or the ability to fly. *...supersonic flight... These hawks are magnificent in flight.* [4] N-UNCOUNT **Flight** is the act of running away from something. *Frank was in full flight when he reached them. ...others who came to this country in desperate flight from wars or famines.* [5] PHRASE If someone **takes flight**, they run away. [6] N-COUNT A **flight of** steps or stairs is a row of them leading from one level to another.

flimsy /ˈflɪmzi/ **flimsier, flimsiest.** [1] ADJ Something that is **flimsy** is easily damaged because it is badly made or made of a weak material. *...a flimsy wooden door.* [2] ADJ **Flimsy** cloth or clothing is thin and does not give much protection. [3] ADJ If you describe something such as evidence or an excuse as **flimsy**, you mean that it is not very convincing.

flinch /flɪntʃ/ **flinches, flinching, flinched.** [1] VERB If you **flinch**, you make a small, sudden movement without meaning to, usually because you are startled or frightened. *She flinched as though he'd slapped her.* [2] VERB If you do not **flinch from** something unpleasant, you do not attempt to avoid it. *He has never flinched from harsh financial decisions.*

fling /flɪŋ/ **flings, flinging, flung** /flʌŋ/. [1] VERB If you **fling** something or someone somewhere, you throw them there suddenly, using a lot of force. *Peter flung his shoes into the corner... He flung himself to the floor.* [2] N-COUNT If two people have a **fling**, they have a brief sexual relationship. [INFORMAL] [3] N-SING You can refer to a short period of enjoyment as a **fling**, especially when it might be the last one that you will have. *...that last fling before you finally give up and take up a job.*

flip /flɪp/ **flips, flipping, flipped.** [1] VERB If you **flip through** a book, you turn the pages quickly. [2] VERB If something **flips over**, or if you **flip** it

over, it suddenly turns over. *The plane then flipped over and burst into flames... He flipped it neatly on to the plate.*

flirt /flɜːt/ **flirts, flirting, flirted.** [1] VERB If you **flirt with** someone, you behave as if you are sexually attracted to them, in a playful or not very serious way. *Dad's flirting with all the ladies... He flirts outrageously.* ♦ **flirtation, flirtations** N-VAR *...a professor who has a flirtation with a student.* [2] N-COUNT A **flirt** is someone who flirts a lot. [3] VERB If you **flirt with** an idea or belief, you consider it or adopt it briefly, but do not become completely committed to it. *My mother used to flirt with Anarchism.*

flit /flɪt/ **flits, flitting, flitted.** [1] VERB If someone **flits from** one place, thing or situation **to** another, they move or turn their attention from one to the other very quickly. *She is restless, flitting between London and Glasgow... Nick flits from job to job.* [2] VERB If something such as a bird or a bat **flits** about, it flies quickly from one place to another. *A butterfly flits from flower to flower.*

⭐ **float** /fləʊt/ **floats, floating, floated.** [1] VERB If something **is floating** in or on a liquid, it is lying or moving slowly on or just below the surface. *A tree branch was floating down the river.* [2] VERB Something that **floats** in the air hangs in it or moves slowly through it. *The white cloud of smoke floated away.* [3] N-COUNT A **float** is a light object that is used to help someone or something float in water. [4] VERB To **float** a new company means to make shares in it available for the public to buy. To **float** new shares means to make them available for the public to buy.

flock /flɒk/ **flocks, flocking, flocked.** [1] N-COUNT A **flock of** birds, sheep, or goats is a group of them. **Flock** can take the singular or plural form of the verb. [2] N-COUNT You can refer to a group of people or things as a **flock of** them to emphasize that there are a lot of them. *These cases all attracted flocks of famous writers.* [3] VERB If people **flock** to a place or event, a lot of them go there. *The criticisms will not stop people flocking to see the film.*

flog /flɒg/ **flogs, flogging, flogged.** [1] VERB If someone tries to **flog** something, they try to sell it. [BRITISH, INFORMAL] [2] VERB If something **is flogged**, they are hit very hard with a whip or stick as a punishment. ♦ **flogging, floggings** N-VAR *He urged the restoration of hanging and flogging.*

⭐ **flood** /flʌd/ **floods, flooding, flooded.** [1] N-VAR If there is a **flood**, a large amount of water, for example from an overflowing river, covers an area which is usually dry. *More than 70 people were killed in the floods.* [2] VERB If something such as a river or a burst pipe **floods** an area that is usually dry, or if the area **floods**, it becomes covered with water. *The Chicago River flooded the city's underground tunnel system... That February the river flooded.* ♦ **flooding** N-UNCOUNT *The flooding is thought to be the worst this century.* [3] VERB & N-COUNT If you say that people or things **flood into** a place, or that there is a **flood of**

a
b
c
d
e
f
g
h
i
j
k
l
m
n
o
p
q
r
s
t
u
v
w
x
y
z

them arriving somewhere, you are emphasizing that they arrive there in large numbers. *Large numbers of immigrants flooded into the area... He received a flood of letters.*

floodlight /'flʌdlaɪt/ **floodlights, floodlighting, floodlit.** ⓵ N-COUNT **Floodlights** are powerful lamps which are used to light sports grounds and the outsides of public buildings. ⓶ VERB If a building or place **is floodlit**, it is lit by floodlights. *A police helicopter hovered above, floodlighting the area. ...a floodlit forecourt.*

★ **floor** /flɔː/ **floors, flooring, floored.** ⓵ N-COUNT The **floor** of a room is the part that you walk on. *Jack's sitting on the floor watching TV.* ⓶ N-COUNT A **floor** of a building is all the rooms on a particular level. *It is on the fifth floor of the hospital.*

> **USAGE** In British English, the **ground floor** of a building is the floor which is level with the ground. The floor on the next level is called the **first floor**. In American English, the **first floor** is the floor which is level with the ground and the next floor up is the **second floor**.

⓷ N-COUNT The ocean **floor** is the ground at the bottom of an ocean. The valley **floor** is the ground at the bottom of a valley. ⓸ VERB If you **are floored** by something, you are unable to respond to it because you are so surprised by it. *He was floored by the announcement.* ⓹ VERB If someone **is floored**, they are knocked to the ground. *Police Sergeant John Shepherd floored him with a rugby tackle.* ⓺ See also **shop floor**.

floorboard /'flɔːbɔːd/ **floorboards.** N-COUNT **Floorboards** are the long pieces of wood that some floors are made of.

flop /flɒp/ **flops, flopping, flopped.** ⓵ VERB If someone or something **flops** somewhere, they fall there heavily or untidily. *His hair flopped over his left eye.* ⓶ VERB & N-COUNT If something **flops**, or if it is a **flop**, it is a total failure. *The film flopped badly at the box office... The policy is destined to be another embarrassing flop.*

floppy /'flɒpi/. ADJ **Floppy** things are loose and tend to hang downwards. *...a floppy hat.*

floppy 'disk (BRIT also **floppy disc**) **floppy disks.** N-COUNT A **floppy disk** is a small magnetic disk that is used for storing computer data and programs. [COMPUTING]

flora /'flɔːrə/. N-UNCOUNT You can refer to plants as **flora**, especially the plants growing in a particular area. **Flora** can take the singular or plural form of the verb. [TECHNICAL] *The soil is rich in lime and affects the flora.*

floral /'flɔːrəl/. ⓵ ADJ A **floral** fabric or design has a pattern of flowers on it. ⓶ ADJ BEFORE N You use **floral** to describe something that contains flowers or is made of flowers. *...eye-catching floral arrangements.*

florist /'flɒrɪst, AM 'flɔːr-/ **florists.** ⓵ N-COUNT A **florist** is a shopkeeper who sells flowers and indoor plants. ⓶ N-COUNT A **florist** or a **florist's** is a shop where flowers and indoor plants are sold.

flounder /'flaʊndə/ **flounders, floundering, floundered.** ⓵ VERB If something **is floundering**, it has many problems and may soon fail completely. *What a pity that his career was left to flounder.* ⓶ VERB If someone **is floundering**, they do not know what to do or say. *I was floundering. I worked in a number of jobs. I had no direction in my life.*

flour /flaʊə/ **flours.** N-VAR **Flour** is a white or brown powder that is made by grinding grain. It is used to make bread, cakes, and pastry.

flourish /'flʌrɪʃ, AM 'flɜːr-/ **flourishes, flourishing, flourished.** ⓵ VERB If something **flourishes**, it is successful or widespread, and developing quickly and strongly. *Business flourished and within six months they were earning 18,000 roubles a day.* ♦ **flourishing** ADJ *London quickly became a flourishing port.* ⓶ VERB If a plant or animal **flourishes**, it grows well or is healthy. ♦ **flourishing** ADJ *...the largest and most flourishing fox population in Europe.* ⓷ N-COUNT If you do something with a **flourish**, you do it with a bold sweeping movement, intended to make people notice it. *She tended to finish dancing with a flourish.*

flout /flaʊt/ **flouts, flouting, flouted.** VERB If you **flout** a law, order, or rule of behaviour, you deliberately and openly disobey it.

★ **flow** /fləʊ/ **flows, flowing, flowed.** ⓵ VERB & N-VAR If a liquid, gas, or electrical current **flows** somewhere, it moves there steadily and continuously. This movement is called a **flow**. *A stream flowed gently down into the valley. ...increases in blood flow.* ⓶ VERB & N-COUNT If a number of people or things **flow** from one place to another, they move there steadily in large groups. This movement is called a **flow**. *Refugees continue to flow from the region. ...the frantic river of cars and buses along the street.* ⓷ VERB & N-COUNT If information or money **flows** somewhere, it moves freely between people or organizations. This movement is called a **flow**. *A lot of this information flowed through other police departments. ...the opportunity to control the flow of information.* ⓸ VERB If someone's hair or clothing **flows**, it hangs freely and loosely. [LITERARY]

★ **flower** /flaʊə/ **flowers, flowering, flowered.** ⓵ N-COUNT A **flower** is the brightly coloured part of a plant which grows at the end of a stem. *...a bunch of flowers.* ⓶ VERB & PHRASE When a plant **flowers**, or when it is **in flower**, its flowers have appeared and opened. ⓷ VERB When something **flowers**, it gets stronger and more successful. *Their relationship flowered.* ♦ **flowering** N-UNCOUNT *...the flowering of new thinking.*

'flower ,bed, flower beds. N-COUNT A **flower bed** is an area of earth in which you grow plants.

flown /fləʊn/. **Flown** is the past participle of **fly**.

flu /fluː/. N-UNCOUNT **Flu** is an illness caused by a virus. The symptoms are like those of a bad cold but more serious. *He had come down with the flu.*

fluctuate /ˈflʌktʃueɪt/ **fluctuates, fluctuating, fluctuated.** VERB If something **fluctuates**, it changes a lot in an irregular way. *Body temperature can fluctuate if you are ill.* ♦ **fluctuation, fluctuations** N-VAR *Don't worry about tiny fluctuations in your weight.*

fluent /ˈfluːənt/. [1] ADJ Someone who is **fluent in** a particular language can speak it easily and correctly. You can also say that someone speaks **fluent** French, Chinese, or other language. ♦ **fluently** ADV *He spoke three languages fluently.* ♦ **fluency** N-UNCOUNT *To work as a translator, you need fluency in at least one foreign language.* [2] ADJ If your speech, reading, or writing is **fluent**, you speak, read, or write easily, with no hesitation or mistakes. ♦ **fluently** ADV *Alex didn't read fluently till he was nearly seven.*

fluff /flʌf/ **fluffs, fluffing, fluffed.** [1] N-UNCOUNT **Fluff** is the small masses of soft light thread that you find on clothes or in dusty corners of a room. *...some bits of fluff on the sleeve of her sweater.* [2] VERB & PHR-VERB If you **fluff** something, or if you **fluff** it **up**, you get a lot of air into it, for example by shaking or brushing it, in order to make it seem larger and lighter. *She stood up and fluffed her hair.*

fluffy /ˈflʌfi/. ADJ Something such as a towel or a toy animal that is **fluffy** is very soft and woolly.

fluid /ˈfluːɪd/ **fluids.** [1] N-VAR A **fluid** is a liquid. [FORMAL] *Make sure that you drink plenty of fluids.* [2] ADJ **Fluid** movements, lines, or designs are smooth and graceful. ♦ **fluidity** /fluːˈɪdɪti/ N-UNCOUNT *...an exquisite fluidity of movement.* [3] ADJ A situation that is **fluid** is likely to change often.

fluke /fluːk/ **flukes.** N-COUNT If you say that something good is a **fluke**, you mean that it happened accidentally rather than by being planned or arranged. [INFORMAL] *The discovery was something of a fluke.*

flung /flʌŋ/. **Flung** is the past tense and past participle of **fling**.

fluorescent /fluəˈresənt/. [1] ADJ A **fluorescent** surface or colour has a very bright appearance when light is directed onto it. *...a piece of fluorescent tape.* [2] ADJ A **fluorescent** light shines with a very hard bright light and is usually in the form of a long strip.

flurry /ˈflʌri/, AM /ˈflɜːri/ **flurries.** [1] N-COUNT A **flurry of** activity or speech is a short, energetic amount of it. *...a flurry of diplomatic activity aimed at ending the war.* [2] N-COUNT A **flurry of** snow or wind is a small amount of it that moves suddenly.

flush /flʌʃ/ **flushes, flushing, flushed.** [1] VERB & N-COUNT If you **flush**, or if there is a **flush** on your cheeks, your face goes red because you are embarrassed or hot. *There was a slight flush on his cheeks.* ♦ **flushed** ADJ *Her face was flushed with anger.* [2] VERB & N-COUNT When you **flush** a toilet, or when it **flushes**, you press a handle and water flows into the toilet bowl, cleaning it. This action is called a **flush**. [3] VERB If you **flush** people or animals out of a place, you force them to come out. *...operations to flush out anti-government rebels.* [4] ADJ AFTER LINK-V If something is **flush with** a surface, it is level with it and does not stick up. *Make sure the tile is flush with the surrounding tiles.*

fluster /ˈflʌstə/ **flusters, flustering, flustered.** VERB If you **fluster** someone, you make them feel nervous and confused by hurrying or interrupting them. *She was a very calm person. Nothing could fluster her.* ♦ **flustered** ADJ *She was so flustered that she forgot her reply.*

flute /fluːt/ **flutes.** N-COUNT A **flute** is a musical wind instrument consisting of a long tube with holes in it. You play it by blowing over a hole at one end while holding it sideways. → See picture on page 828.

flutter /ˈflʌtə/ **flutters, fluttering, fluttered.** [1] VERB If something light **flutters**, or if you **flutter** it, it moves through the air with small quick movements. *Her chiffon skirt was fluttering in the night breeze.* [2] VERB If your heart or stomach **flutters**, you experience a strong feeling of excitement or anxiety.

flux /flʌks/. N-UNCOUNT If something is in a state of **flux**, it is changing constantly. *...a period of economic flux.*

★ **fly** /flaɪ/ **flies, flying, flew, flown.** [1] N-COUNT A **fly** is a small insect with two wings. → See picture on page 824. [2] VERB When something such as a bird, insect, or aircraft **flies**, it moves through the air. *The planes flew through the clouds... The bird flew away.* ♦ **flying** ADJ BEFORE N *...species of flying insects.* [3] VERB If you **fly** somewhere, you travel there in an aircraft. If you **fly** something or someone somewhere, you send them there in an aircraft. *It may be possible to fly the women and children out on Thursday.* [4] VERB When a pilot **flies** an aircraft, he or she controls its movement. *He flew a small plane to Cuba. ...his inspiration to fly.* ♦ **flyer, flyers** N-COUNT *...a highly experienced flyer.* [5] VERB If something **flies** or is **flying**, it moves about freely and loosely. *His long, uncovered hair flew back in the wind... A red and black flag was flying from the balcony.* [6] VERB If you say that someone or something **flies** in a particular direction, you are emphasizing that they move there with a lot of speed or force. *She flew to their bedsides when they were ill... The blow sent the young man flying.* [7] N-COUNT The front opening on a pair of trousers is referred to as the **fly** or the **flies**. [8] PHRASE If you **get off to a flying start**, you start something very well, for example a race or a new job.

▶ **fly into.** PHR-VERB If you **fly into** a rage or a panic, you suddenly become very angry or anxious and show this in your behaviour. *Losing a game would cause him to fly into a rage.*

flyer /ˈflaɪə/ **flyers.** N-COUNT A **flyer** is a small printed notice which is used to advertise a particular company or event. ● See also **fly**.

foal /fəʊl/ **foals.** N-COUNT A **foal** is a very young horse.

foam /fəʊm/ **foams, foaming, foamed.** [1] N-UNCOUNT **Foam** consists of a mass of small bubbles that are formed when air and a liquid are mixed together. *The water curved round the rocks in great bursts of foam.* [2] N-COUNT If a liquid **foams**, it is full of small bubbles and keeps moving slightly. [3] N-UNCOUNT **Foam** or **foam rubber** is soft rubber full of small holes which is used, for example, to make mattresses and cushions.

focal point /ˈfəʊkəl pɔɪnt/ **focal points.** N-COUNT The **focal point** of something is the thing that people concentrate on or pay most attention to.

⭐ **focus** /ˈfəʊkəs/ **focuses, focusing, focused (or focusses, focussing, focussed).** [1] VERB If you **focus on** a particular topic, or if your attention **is focused on** it, you concentrate on it and deal with it. *Today he was able to focus his message exclusively on the economy.* [2] N-COUNT The **focus of** something is the main topic or main thing that it is concerned with. *The new system is the focus of controversy.* [3] N-COUNT Your **focus on** something is the special attention that you pay it. *...his sudden focus on foreign policy... IBM has also shifted its focus from mainframes to personal computers.* [4] VERB If you **focus** your eyes, or if your eyes **focus**, your eyes adjust so that you can clearly see the thing that you want to look at. If you **focus** a camera, telescope, or other instrument, you adjust it so that you can see clearly through it. *His eyes slowly began to focus on what looked like a small black ball.* [5] PHRASE If an image or a camera, telescope, or other instrument is **in focus**, the edges of what you see are clear and sharp. If it is **out of focus**, the edges of what you see are blurred. [6] VERB If you **focus** rays of light on a particular point, you pass them through a lens or reflect them from a mirror so that they meet at that point.

'**focus group, focus groups.** N-COUNT A **focus group** is a group of people who are intended to represent the general public. Focus groups have discussions in which their opinions are recorded as a form of market research.

fodder /ˈfɒdə/. N-UNCOUNT **Fodder** is food that is given to animals such as cows or horses.

foe /fəʊ/ **foes.** N-COUNT Someone's **foe** is their enemy. [LITERARY]

foetus (or **fetus**) /ˈfiːtəs/ **foetuses.** N-COUNT A **foetus** is an unborn animal or human being in its later stages of development.

fog /fɒg/ **fogs.** N-VAR When there is **fog**, there are tiny drops of water in the air which form a thick cloud and make it difficult to see things. *The crash happened in thick fog... Halfway down the river we ran into a bank of fog.*

foggy /ˈfɒgi/ **foggier, foggiest.** ADJ When it is **foggy**, there is fog.

foil /fɔɪl/ **foils, foiling, foiled.** [1] N-UNCOUNT **Foil** is metal that is as thin as paper. It is used to wrap food in. [2] VERB If you **foil** someone's plan or attempt at something, you prevent it from being successful. [JOURNALISM] *He foiled an armed robbery.* [3] N-COUNT If you say that one thing or person is a **foil for** another, you think that they contrast with each other and go well together. *A cold beer is the perfect foil for a curry.*

⭐ **fold** /fəʊld/ **folds, folding, folded.** [1] VERB & PHR-VERB If you **fold** a piece of paper or cloth, or if you **fold** it **up**, you bend it so that one part covers another part. *He folded the paper carefully... Fold the omelette in half.* [2] N-COUNT A **fold** in a piece of paper or cloth is a bend that you make in it when you put one part of it over another part and press the edge. [3] N-COUNT The **folds** in a piece of cloth are the curved shapes which are formed when it is not hanging or lying flat. [4] VERB & PHR-VERB If a piece of furniture or equipment **folds**, or if you **fold** it **up**, you make it smaller or flatter by bending or closing parts of it. *This portable seat folds flat for easy storage... Fold the ironing board up so that it is flat. ...a folding beach chair.* [5] VERB If you **fold** your arms or hands, you bring them together and cross them or link them. [6] VERB If a business or organization **folds**, it is unsuccessful and has to close.

folder /ˈfəʊldə/ **folders.** N-COUNT A **folder** is a thin piece of cardboard in which you can keep loose papers.

foliage /ˈfəʊliɪdʒ/. N-UNCOUNT The **foliage** of a plant consists of its leaves.

⭐ **folk** /fəʊk/ **folks.** [1] N-PLURAL & N-VOC You can refer to people as **folk** or **folks.** *...country folk... It's a question of money, folks.* [2] N-PLURAL You can refer to your close family, especially your mother and father, as your **folks.** [INFORMAL] *I've been avoiding my folks lately.* [3] ADJ BEFORE N **Folk** art and customs are traditional or typical of a particular community or nation. *...Irish folk music.*

folklore /ˈfəʊklɔː/. N-UNCOUNT **Folklore** consists of the traditional stories, customs, and habits of a particular community or nation. *In Chinese folklore the bat is an emblem of good fortune.*

⭐ **follow** /ˈfɒləʊ/ **follows, following, followed.** [1] VERB If you **follow** someone who is going somewhere, you move along behind them. *We followed him up the steps... They took him into a small room and I followed.* [2] VERB If you **follow** someone to a place, you go to join them there at a later time. *He followed Janice to New York.* [3] VERB To **follow** an event, activity, or period of time means to happen or come after it, at a later time. *...the days following Daddy's death... He was arrested in the confusion which followed.* [4] VERB & PHR-VERB If you **follow** one thing with another, or if you **follow** it **up with** another, you do or say the second thing after you have done or said the first thing. *Warm up first, then follow this with a series of stretching exercises.* [5] PHRASE You use **followed by** to say what comes after something else in a list or ordered set of things. *Potatoes are* *still the most popular food, followed by white bread.* **6** VERB If it **follows** that a particular thing is the case, that thing is a logical result of something else being true or being the case. *Just because a bird does not breed one year, it does not follow that it will fail the next.* **7** PHRASE You use **as follows** to introduce something such as a list, description, or explanation. *The winners are as follows: E. Walker; R. Foster; R. Gates.* **8** VERB If you **follow** a path or route, you go somewhere using the path or route to direct you. **9** VERB If you **follow** advice or instructions, you act or do something in the way that it indicates. **10** VERB If you **follow** something, you understand it. *Do you follow the plot so far?* **11** VERB If you **follow** something, you take an interest in it. *Do you follow the football at all?*

▶**follow through.** PHR-VERB If you **follow through** an action or plan, you continue doing or thinking about it until it is completed.

follower /'fɒləʊə/**followers.** N-COUNT The **followers** of a person or belief are the people who support the person or accept the belief.

★ **following** /'fɒləʊɪŋ/. **1** PREP **Following** a particular event means after that event. *...the centuries following Christ's death.* **2** ADJ The **following** day, week, or year is the day, week, or year after the one you have just mentioned. → See Reference Page on Times and Dates. *We went to dinner the following Monday evening.* **3** ADJ & PRON You use **the following** to refer to something that you are about to mention. *The method of helping such patients is explained in the following chapters... Add small pinches of any of the following: paprika, nutmeg, dried herbs.* **4** N-SING If you have a **following**, a group of people support or admire your beliefs or actions. *Australian rugby league enjoys a huge following in New Zealand.*

'follow-up, follow-ups. N-VAR A **follow-up** is something that is done as a continuation or second part of something done previously. *Patients are asked to return for a one-day follow-up workshop.*

folly /'fɒli/**follies.** N-VAR If you say that an action or way of behaving is **folly** or is a **folly**, you mean that it is foolish. *...the follies of war.*

fond /fɒnd/**fonder, fondest.** **1** ADJ AFTER LINK-V If you are **fond of** someone or something, you like that person or thing. *I am very fond of Michael.* ♦ **fondness** N-UNCOUNT *I've always had a fondness for jewels.* **2** ADJ BEFORE N You use **fond** to describe people or their behaviour when they show affection. *He gave me a fond smile.* ♦ **fondly** ADV *Their eyes meet fondly across the table.* **3** ADJ BEFORE N If you have **fond** memories of someone or something, you remember them with pleasure. ♦ **fondly** ADV *I remembered it fondly.*

★ **food** /fuːd/**foods.** **1** N-VAR **Food** is what people and animals eat. *Enjoy your food. ...frozen foods.* **2** PHRASE If you give someone **food for thought**, you make them think carefully about

something. *Lord Fraser's speech offers much food for thought.*

foodstuff /'fuːdstʌf/**foodstuffs.** N-COUNT **Foodstuffs** are substances which people eat. *...basic foodstuffs such as sugar, cooking oil and cheese.*

★ **fool** /fuːl/**fools, fooling, fooled.** **1** N-COUNT If you call someone a **fool**, you are indicating that you think they are not sensible and show a lack of good judgement. *'You fool!' she shouted... He'd been a fool to get involved with her!* **2** PHRASE If you **make a fool of** someone, you make people think they are silly. *He was drinking and making a fool of himself.* **3** VERB If someone **fools** you, they deceive or trick you. *They tried to fool you into coming after us.*

▶**fool about** or **fool around.** PHR-VERB If you **fool about**, or if you **fool around**, you behave in a playful and silly way.

foolish /'fuːlɪʃ/. ADJ If you say that someone's behaviour is **foolish**, you mean that it is not sensible and shows a lack of good judgement. *It would be foolish to raise hopes unnecessarily.* ♦ **foolishly** ADV *He admitted that he had acted foolishly.* ♦ **foolishness** N-UNCOUNT *They don't accept any foolishness.*

★ **foot** /fʊt/**feet.**

✓ In meaning 3, the plural can be either **foot** or **feet**.

1 N-COUNT & PHRASE Your **feet** are the parts of your body that are at the ends of your legs and that you stand on. If you are **on** your **feet**, you are standing up. If you rise **to** your **feet**, you stand up. → See picture on page 822. *Everyone was on their feet applauding.* **2** N-SING The **foot of** something is the part that is farthest from its top. *David called to the children from the foot of the stairs.* **3** N-COUNT A **foot** is a unit of length, equal to 12 inches or 30.48 centimetres. *...a cell 6 foot wide and 10 foot high.*

PHRASES ● If you say that someone or something is **on** their **feet** again after a difficult period, you mean that they have recovered and are back to normal. ● If you go somewhere **on foot**, you walk, rather than use any form of transport. ● If someone **puts** their **foot down**, they use their authority in order to stop something happening. *He had planned to go skiing on his own in March but his wife had decided to put her foot down.* ● If you **put** your **feet up**, you relax or have a rest, especially by sitting or lying with your feet supported off the ground. ● To **set foot** in a place means to go there. *I left that place and never set foot in Texas again.* ● If someone has to **stand on** their **own two feet**, they have to manage without help from other people.

footage /'fʊtɪdʒ/. N-UNCOUNT **Footage** of a particular event is a film, or the part of a film, showing this event. *...exclusive footage from this summer's festivals.*

a
b
c
d
e
f
g
h
i
j
k
l
m
n
o
p
q
r
s
t
u
v
w
x
y
z

⭐ **football** /'fʊtbɔːl/ **footballs.** **1** N-UNCOUNT In British English, **football** is a game played by two

football [BRIT]/**soccer** [AM]

teams of eleven players who try to score by kicking or heading a ball into their opponent's goal. The American word is **soccer**. *Several boys were still playing football.*

American football [BRIT]/**football** [AM]

2 N-UNCOUNT In American English, **football** is a game played by two teams of eleven players who try to score by taking the ball into their opponent's end. The British term is **American football**. **3** N-COUNT A **football** is a ball that is used for playing football.

footballer /'fʊtbɔːlə/ **footballers.** N-COUNT In British English, a **footballer** is a person who plays football. The American term is **soccer player**.

footer /'fʊtə/ **footers.** N-COUNT A **footer** is text such as a name or page number that can be automatically displayed at the bottom of each page of a printed document.

foothills /'fʊthɪlz/. N-PLURAL The **foothills of** a mountain or a range of mountains are the lower hills or mountains around its base. *Pasadena lies in the foothills of the San Gabriel mountains.*

foothold /'fʊthəʊld/ **footholds.** **1** N-COUNT A **foothold** is a strong position from which further advances or progress may be made. *Companies must establish a firm foothold in Europe.* **2** N-COUNT A **foothold** is a ledge or hollow where you can safely put your foot when climbing.

footing /'fʊtɪŋ/. **1** N-UNCOUNT You use **footing** to describe the basis on which something is done or exists. *...research that is aimed at placing training on a more scientific footing.* **2** N-UNCOUNT You use **footing** to refer to your position and

how securely your feet are placed on the ground. *He lost his footing and slid into the water.*

footnote /'fʊtnəʊt/ **footnotes.** N-COUNT A **footnote** is a note at the bottom of a page which gives more information about something on the page.

footpath /'fʊtpɑːθ, -pæθ/ **footpaths.** N-COUNT A **footpath** is a path for people to walk on.

footprint /'fʊtprɪnt/ **footprints.** N-COUNT A **footprint** is the mark of a person's or animal's foot left on a surface.

footstep /'fʊtstep/ **footsteps.** **1** N-COUNT A **footstep** is the sound made by someone's feet touching the ground when they are walking or running. *They heard footsteps in the main room.* **2** PHRASE If you **follow in** someone's **footsteps**, you do the same things as they did earlier. *He followed in the footsteps of his father, a former professional boxer.*

footwear /'fʊtweə/. N-UNCOUNT **Footwear** refers to things that people wear on their feet, for example shoes, boots, and sandals.

⭐ **for** /fə, STRONG fɔː/. **1** PREP If something is **for** someone, they are intended to have it or benefit from it. *I have some free advice for you. ...a table for two.* **2** PREP If you work **for** someone, you are employed by them. *...a buyer for one of the largest chain stores.* **3** PREP & ADV If you are **for** something, you are in favour of it. *Are you for or against public transport?.* **4** PHRASE If you are **all for** something, you are very much in favour of it. *I was all for it, but Wolfe said no.* **5** PREP If you are **for** something, or if something is **for** you, you like it or intend to do it or have it. *Right, who's for a toasted sandwich then?... I'm afraid German beer isn't for me.* **6** PREP You use **for** after words such as 'time', 'space', 'money', or 'energy' when you say how much there is or whether there is enough of it in order to be able to do or use a particular thing. *Many new trains have space for wheelchair users... It would take three to six hours for a round trip.* **7** PREP You use **for** when you are describing the purpose of something, the reason for something, or the cause of something. *...a room for rent. ...a comfortable chair, suitable for use in the living room. ...a speech in parliament explaining his reasons for going.* **8** PREP A word or term **for** something is a way of referring to it. *The technical term for sunburn is erythema.* **9** PREP You use **for** to say how long something lasts or continues. *For a few minutes she sat on her bed... They talked for a bit.* **10** PHRASE You use an expression such as **for the first time** when you are talking about how often something has happened. *He was married for the second time, this time to a Belgian.* **11** PREP You use **for** to say how far something extends. *We drove on for a few miles.* **12** PREP You use **for** with 'every' when you state the second part of a ratio. *There had been one divorce for every 100 marriages before the war.* **13** PREP You use **for** when you are talking about the cost of something. *The Martins sold their house for about 1.4 million pounds.*

14 PREP You use **for** when you are mentioning a person or thing that you have feelings about. *He began to feel sympathy for this slightly mysterious man.* **15** PREP You use **for** when you are saying how something affects someone. *It would be excellent experience for him to travel a little.*
16 PREP You use **for** when you say that an aspect of something or someone is surprising in relation to other aspects of them. *He was tall for an eight-year-old.* **17** PREP If something is planned **for** a particular time or occasion, it is planned to happen then. *The party was scheduled for 7:00... I'll be home for Christmas.* **18** PREP If you leave **for** a place, or if you take a train, plane, or boat **for** a place, you are going there. **19** **as for**: see **as**. ● **but for**: see **but**. ● **for all**: see **all**.

forage /'fɒrɪdʒ, AM 'fɔːr-/ **forages, foraging, foraged.** **1** VERB To **forage** for something such as food means to search for it. *They were forced to forage for clothing and fuel.* **2** N-UNCOUNT **Forage** is crops that are grown as food for cattle and horses.

foray /'fɒreɪ, AM 'fɔːreɪ/ **forays.** **1** N-COUNT If you make a **foray into** a new or unfamiliar type of activity, you start to become involved in it. *...her first forays into politics.* **2** N-COUNT If a group of soldiers make a **foray into** an area, they make a quick attack there, usually in order to steal supplies.

forbid /fə'bɪd/ **forbids, forbidding, forbade** /fə'bæd, -'beɪd/, **forbidden.** **1** VERB If you **forbid** someone **to** do something, or if you **forbid** an activity, you order that it must not be done. *They'll forbid you to marry... Brazil's constitution forbids the military use of nuclear energy.* **2** VERB If something **forbids** an event or course of action, it makes it impossible. *His own pride forbids him to ask Arthur's help.*

forbidden /fə'bɪdən/. ADJ If something is **forbidden**, you are not allowed to do it or have it. *Smoking was forbidden... It is forbidden to drive faster than 20mph.*

⭐ **force** /fɔːs/ **forces, forcing, forced.** **1** VERB If something or someone **forces** you **to** do something, they make you do it, even though you do not want to. *A back injury forced her to withdraw from the competition... I cannot force you in this. You must decide... He tried to force her into a car... To force this agreement on the nation is wrong.* **2** VERB If you **force** something, you use a lot of strength to move it. *He forced the key clumsily into the ignition... Police forced the door of the flat and arrested Mr Roberts.* **3** N-UNCOUNT **Force** is power or strength. *...the guerrillas' efforts to seize power by force... The force of the explosion shattered the windows.* **4** N-COUNT Someone or something that is a **force** in a situation has a strong influence on it. *The FLN is still a big political force in the country.* **5** VERB If you **force** a smile or a laugh, you manage to smile or laugh even though you do not want to. ♦ **forced** ADJ *He pushed her away with a forced smile.*
6 N-COUNT A **force** in physics is the pulling or

pushing effect that one thing has on another. *...the earth's gravitational force.* **7** N-COUNT **Forces** are groups of soldiers or military vehicles that are organized for a particular purpose. *...the deployment of American forces in the region.*
PHRASES ● A law or system that is **in force** exists or is being used. *Martial law is in force.* ● If you **join forces with** someone, you work together to achieve a common aim or purpose. *He joined forces with his brother to launch the company.* ● to **force** someone's **hand**: see **hand**.

forceful /'fɔːsful/. **1** ADJ Someone who is **forceful** expresses their opinions in a strong and confident way. *She was a forceful intellectual, unafraid to speak her mind.* ♦ **forcefully** ADV *He argued forcefully and convincingly.* **2** ADJ Something that is **forceful** causes you to think or feel something very strongly. *The recent bomb attack is a forceful reminder that we must continue to strive for peace.*

forcible /'fɔːsɪbəl/. ADJ **Forcible** actions involve physical force or violence. *...the forcible resettlement of villagers.* ♦ **forcibly** ADV *Student leaders were forcibly removed from the university.*

ford /fɔːd/ **fords.** A **ford** is a shallow place in a river where it is possible to cross safely without using a boat.

fore /fɔː/. **1** PHRASE When something or someone comes **to the fore**, they suddenly become important or popular. *A number of low-budget independent films brought new directors and actors to the fore.* **2** ADJ BEFORE N & ADV **Fore** is used to refer to parts at the front of a ship or aircraft. *Our yacht was well equipped with two double cabins fore and aft.*

forearm /'fɔːrɑːm/ **forearms.** N-COUNT Your **forearms** are the parts of your arms between your elbows and your wrists.

⭐ **forecast** /'fɔːkɑːst, -kæst/ **forecasts, forecasting, forecasted** or **forecast.** VERB & N-COUNT If you **forecast** future events, you say what you think is going to happen. A **forecast** is a prediction of future events. *He forecasts that average salary increases will remain around 4 per cent... The forecast is for changeable weather.* ♦ **forecaster, forecasters** N-COUNT *...our senior weather forecaster.*

forefinger /'fɔːfɪŋgə/ **forefingers.** N-COUNT Your **forefinger** is the finger next to your thumb.
→ See picture on page 823.

forefront /'fɔːfrʌnt/. N-SING If you are **at the forefront of** a campaign or other activity, you have a leading and influential position in it. *They have been at the forefront of the campaign for political change.*

forego (or **forgo**) /fɔː'gəʊ/ **foregoes, foregoing, forewent, foregone.** VERB If you **forego** something, you decide not to have it or do it, although you would like to. [FORMAL] *Keen skiers are happy to forego a summer holiday to go skiing.*

foreground /'fɔːgraʊnd/. **1** N-SING The **foreground** of a picture is the part that seems nearest to you. *...the bowler-hatted figure in the*

a
b
c
d
e
f
g
h
i
j
k
l
m
n
o
p
q
r
s
t
u
v
w
x
y
z

A
B
C
D
E
F
G
H
I
J
K
L
M
N
O
P
Q
R
S
T
U
V
W
X
Y
Z

foreground. **2** N-SING If something or someone is **in the foreground**, they receive a lot of attention. *...issues that were placed in the foreground.*

forehead /'fɒrɪd, 'fɔːhed/**foreheads.** N-COUNT Your **forehead** is the flat area at the front of your head above your eyebrows and below where your hair grows. → See picture on page 823.

☆ **foreign** /'fɒrɪn, AM 'fɔːr-/. **1** ADJ Something that is **foreign** comes from or relates to a country that is not your own. *She was on her first foreign holiday without her parents. ...a foreign language.* **2** ADJ BEFORE N In politics and journalism, **foreign** is used to describe people and activities relating to countries that are not the country of the person or government concerned. *...the German foreign minister. ...the effects of US foreign policy.* **3** ADJ A **foreign body** is an object that has got into something, usually by accident, and should not be there. [FORMAL] *...a foreign body in the eye.* **4** ADJ Something that is **foreign to** a particular person or thing is not typical of them or is unknown to them. *The whole concept of being gentle with anyone is foreign to most men.*

☆ **foreigner** /'fɒrɪnə, AM 'fɔːr-/**foreigners.** N-COUNT A **foreigner** is someone who belongs to a country that is not your own. ● See note at **stranger**.

,**foreign ex'change, foreign exchanges.** **1** N-PLURAL **Foreign exchanges** are the institutions or systems involved with changing one currency into another. *On the foreign exchanges, the US dollar is up point forty-five.* **2** N-UNCOUNT **Foreign exchange** is foreign currency that is obtained through the foreign exchange system.

'**Foreign ,Office, Foreign Offices.** N-COUNT The **Foreign Office** is the government department, especially in Britain, which is responsible for the government's relations with foreign governments.

foreman /'fɔːmən/**foremen.** N-COUNT A **foreman** is a person who is in charge of a group of workers.

foremost /'fɔːməʊst/. **1** ADJ The **foremost** thing or person in a group is the most important or best. *...one of the world's foremost scholars of ancient Indian culture.* **2** PHRASE You use **first and foremost** to emphasize the most important quality of something or someone. *This book aims first and foremost to improve your painting skills.*

forename /'fɔːneɪm/**forenames.** N-COUNT Your **forenames** are your first names, as opposed to your surname. [FORMAL]

forensic /fə'rensɪk/. **1** ADJ BEFORE N When a **forensic** analysis is done, objects are examined scientifically in order to discover information about a crime. *Forensic experts searched the area for clues.* **2** ADJ BEFORE N **Forensic** means relating to the legal profession. *...a senior forensic psychiatrist.*

forerunner /'fɔːrʌnə/**forerunners.** N-COUNT The **forerunner of** something is a similar thing that existed before it and influenced its development. *...a machine which, in some respects, was the forerunner of the modern helicopter.*

foresee /fɔː'siː/**foresees, foreseeing, foresaw, foreseen.** VERB If you **foresee** something, you expect and believe that it will happen. *He did not foresee any problems. ...a dangerous situation which could have been foreseen.*

foreseeable /fɔː'siːəbəl/. PHRASE When you talk about **the foreseeable future**, you are referring to the period of time in the future during which it is possible to say what will happen. *She will not be seeking a divorce in the foreseeable future.*

foresight /'fɔːsaɪt/. N-UNCOUNT **Foresight** is the ability to see what might happen in the future and to take appropriate action; used showing approval. *Thankfully they had the foresight to invest in new technology.*

☆ **forest** /'fɒrɪst, AM 'fɔːr-/**forests.** N-VAR A **forest** is a large area where trees grow close together. *...25 million hectares of forest.*

forestall /fɔː'stɔːl/**forestalls, forestalling, forestalled.** VERB If you **forestall** someone, you realize what they are likely to do and prevent them from doing it. *O'Leary made to open the door, but Bunbury forestalled him.*

forestry /'fɒrɪstri, AM 'fɔːr-/. N-UNCOUNT **Forestry** is the science or skill of growing trees in forests.

forever /fə'revə/.

☑ **Forever** is also spelled **for ever** for meanings 1 and 2.

1 ADV Something that will happen or continue **forever** will always happen or continue. *It was great fun but we knew it wouldn't go on for ever... I am forever grateful to the friend who helped us.* **2** ADV If something has gone or changed **forever**, it has gone and will never reappear. *The old social order was gone forever.* **3** ADV If you say that someone is **forever** doing something, you are emphasizing that they do it very often. *He was forever attempting to arrange deals.*

forewent /fɔː'went/. **Forewent** is the past tense of **forego**.

forfeit /'fɔːfɪt/**forfeits, forfeiting, forfeited.** **1** VERB If you **forfeit** a right, privilege, or possession, you have to give it up because you have done something wrong. *He argues that murderers forfeit their own right to life.* **2** N-COUNT A **forfeit** is something that you have to give up because you have done something wrong. *That is the forfeit he must pay.*

forgave /fə'geɪv/. **Forgave** is the past tense of **forgive**.

forge /fɔːdʒ/**forges, forging, forged.** **1** VERB If someone **forges** banknotes, documents, or paintings, they make false copies of them in order to deceive people. *Taylor had forged her signature.* ◆ **forger, forgers** N-COUNT *...the most* *prolific art forger in the country.* 2 VERB If you **forge** an alliance or relationship, you succeed in creating it. *The programme aims to forge links between higher education and small businesses.* 3 N-COUNT A **forge** is a place where a blacksmith makes metal things such as horseshoes.

▸**forge ahead.** PHR-VERB If you **forge ahead** with something, you make a lot of progress with it. *George began to forge ahead with his studies.*

forgery /ˈfɔːdʒəri/ **forgeries.** 1 N-UNCOUNT **Forgery** is the crime of forging banknotes, documents, or paintings. 2 N-COUNT You can refer to a forged banknote, document, or painting as a **forgery.**

⭐ **forget** /fəˈget/ **forgets, forgetting, forgot, forgotten.** 1 VERB If you **forget** something, or if you **forget how to** do something, you cannot think of it or think of how to do it, although you knew in the past. *I forgot how to speak English, I could only speak Spanish... She forgot where she left the car.* 2 VERB If you **forget to** do something, you do not remember to do it. *She forgot to lock her door one day and two men got in... Don't forget that all dogs need a supply of fresh water.* 3 VERB If you **forget** something that you had intended to bring with you, you do not remember to bring it. *Once when we were going to Paris, I forgot my passport.*

> **USAGE** Note that you cannot use the verb **forget** to say that you have put something somewhere and left it there. Instead you use the verb **leave**. *I left my bag on the bus.*

4 VERB If you **forget** something or someone, you deliberately do not think about them any more. *I can't forget what happened... I found it very easy to forget about Sam.* 5 VERB If someone **forgets himself** or **herself**, he or she behaves in an uncontrolled or unacceptable way.

forgetful /fəˈgetfʊl/. ADJ Someone who is **forgetful** often forgets things. ♦ **forgetfulness** N-UNCOUNT *Her forgetfulness is due to advancing age.*

forgive /fəˈgɪv/ **forgives, forgiving, forgave, forgiven.** VERB If you **forgive** someone who has done something wrong, you stop being angry with them. *She'd find a way to forgive him for the theft of the money.* ♦ **forgiving** ADJ *I don't think people are in a very forgiving mood.*
♦ **forgiveness** N-UNCOUNT *He would fall to his knees sobbing and begging for forgiveness.*

forgo /fɔːˈgəʊ/. See **forego.**

forgot /fəˈgɒt/. **Forgot** is the past tense of **forget.**

forgotten /fəˈgɒtən/. **Forgotten** is the past participle of **forget.**

fork /fɔːk/ **forks, forking, forked.** 1 N-COUNT A **fork** is an implement that you use when you are eating food. It consists of three or four long thin points on the end of a handle. → See picture on page 825. 2 N-COUNT A garden **fork** is a tool that

you use to dig your garden. It consists of three or four long thin points attached to a long handle. → See picture on page 832. 3 N-COUNT & VERB If there is a **fork** in something such as a road or a river, or if it **forks**, it divides into two parts in the shape of a 'Y'. *You should take the right fork... The path dipped down to a sort of cove, and then it forked in two directions.*

▸**fork out.** PHR-VERB If you **fork out for** something, you pay for it. [INFORMAL] *He will have to fork out for private school fees... Britons fork out more than a billion pounds a year on toys.*

forlorn /fəˈlɔːn/. 1 ADJ If you are **forlorn**, you are lonely and unhappy. ♦ **forlornly** ADV *...waiting forlornly in the rain.* 2 ADJ A **forlorn** hope or attempt has no chance of success. *...the forlorn hope of finding a better life in cities.*

form 1 type and shape

⭐ **form** /fɔːm/ **forms.** 1 N-COUNT A **form of** something is a type or kind of it. *He contracted a rare form of cancer... I am against hunting in any form.* 2 PHRASE If someone's behaviour is **true to form**, it is typical of them. *True to form, she kept her guests waiting for more than 90 minutes.* 3 N-COUNT The **form** of something is its shape. *...the form of the body.* 4 N-COUNT You can refer to something that you can see as a **form**, especially if you cannot see it clearly. *She thought she'd never been so glad to see his bulky form.*

form 2 making things

⭐ **form** /fɔːm/ **forms, forming, formed.** 1 VERB When a particular shape **forms** or **is formed**, people or things move or are arranged so that this shape is made. *They formed a circle and sang... The General gave orders for the cadets to form into lines.* 2 VERB If something is arranged so that it has a particular shape or function, you can say that it **forms** something with that shape or function. *All the buildings have names and form a half circle.* 3 VERB If something consists of particular things or people, you can say that they **form** that thing. *Cereals form the staple diet.* 4 VERB If you **form** an organization, group, or company, you start it. ♦ **formation** N-UNCOUNT *...the formation of a new government.* 5 VERB When something **forms**, it begins to exist. *Huge ice sheets were formed.*

form 3 document

⭐ **form** /fɔːm/ **forms.** N-COUNT A **form** is a piece of paper with questions on it. You write the answers on the same piece of paper. *You will be asked to fill in a form.*

form 4 someone's physical condition

form /fɔːm/. N-UNCOUNT & PHRASE In sport, an athlete's **form** refers to their ability or success over a period of time. If they are **off form**, they are performing badly; if they are **on form**, they are performing well. *His form this season has been brilliant.*

⭐ **formal** /ˈfɔːməl/. 1 ADJ **Formal** speech or behaviour is correct and serious, rather than relaxed and friendly, and is used especially in official situations. *...a formal letter of apology.*

a
b
c
d
e
f
g
h
i
j
k
l
m
n
o
p
q
r
s
t
u
v
w
x
y
z

◆ **formally** ADV *'Good afternoon, Mr Benjamin,'* *Schumacher said formally.* ◆ **formality** /fɔːˈmælɪti/ N-UNCOUNT *...the stifled formality of the office.* [2] ADJ BEFORE N A **formal** statement, action, or event is an official one. *No formal announcement had been made. ...a formal dinner.* ◆ **formally** ADV *They are now formally separated.* [3] ADJ BEFORE N **Formal** education or training is given in a school or college. *Although his formal education stopped after primary school, he was an avid reader.*

formality /fɔːˈmælɪti/ **formalities.** [1] N-COUNT **Formalities** are formal actions that are carried out on particular occasions. *...immigration and customs formalities.* [2] See also **formal**.

formalize (BRIT also **formalise**) /ˈfɔːməlaɪz/ **formalizes, formalizing, formalized.** VERB If you **formalize** a plan or arrangement, you make it official. *The arrangement, he added, need not be formalized in court.*

format /ˈfɔːmæt/ **formats, formatting, formatted.** [1] N-COUNT The **format** of something is the way it is arranged and presented. *I had met with him to explain the format of the programme.* [2] VERB To **format** a computer disk means to run a program so that the disk can be written on. [COMPUTING]

formation /fɔːˈmeɪʃən/ **formations.** [1] N-UNCOUNT The **formation** of something is its start or creation. *The name was changed two years after the club's formation. ...the formation of an interim government.* [2] N-COUNT A rock or cloud **formation** is rock or clouds of a particular shape. [3] N-UNCOUNT If things are **in formation**, they are arranged in a particular pattern. *He was flying in formation with seven other jets.*

formative /ˈfɔːmətɪv/. ADJ A **formative** period in your life or experience is one that has an important influence on your character and attitudes. *She spent her formative years growing up in east London.*

⭐ **former** /ˈfɔːmə/. [1] ADJ BEFORE N **Former** is used to indicate what someone or something used to be, but no longer is. *...former President Bill Clinton. ...the former home of Sir Christopher Wren.* [2] ADJ BEFORE N **Former** is used to describe a situation or period of time which came before the present one. *He would want you to remember him as he was in former years.* [3] PRON When two people, things, or groups have just been mentioned, you can refer to the first of them as **the former**. *If the family home and joint pension rights are of equal value, the wife may choose the former and the husband the latter.*

formerly /ˈfɔːməli/. ADV If something happened or was **formerly** true, it happened or was true in the past. *He had formerly been in the Navy.*

formidable /ˈfɔːmɪdəbəl, fəˈmɪd-/. ADJ If you describe something or someone as **formidable**, you mean that you feel frightened by them because they are very impressive or considerable. *We have a formidable task ahead of us.*

⭐ **formula** /ˈfɔːmjʊlə/ **formulas** (or **formulae** /ˈfɔːmjʊliː/). [1] N-COUNT A **formula** is a plan that is made as a way of dealing with a problem. *...this simple formula for a long and happy life.* [2] N-COUNT A **formula** is a group of letters, numbers, or other symbols which represents a scientific or mathematical rule. *...a mathematical formula.* [3] N-COUNT In science, the **formula** for a substance tells you what amounts of other substances are needed in order to make that substance. [4] N-UNCOUNT **Formula** is a powder which you mix with water to make artificial milk for babies.

formulate /ˈfɔːmjʊleɪt/ **formulates, formulating, formulated.** [1] VERB If you **formulate** a plan or proposal, you develop it, thinking about the details carefully. ◆ **formulation** N-UNCOUNT *...the process of policy formulation.* [2] VERB If someone **formulate** a thought or opinion, you express it in words.

forsake /fəˈseɪk/ **forsakes, forsaking, forsook** /fəˈsʊk/, **forsaken.** [1] VERB If someone **forsakes** you, they leave you when they should have stayed, or stop helping you or looking after you. *...children who've been forsaken by individual teachers.* [2] VERB If you **forsake** something, you stop doing or having it. [LITERARY] *She forsook her notebook for new technology.*

fort /fɔːt/ **forts.** N-COUNT A **fort** is a strong building that is used as a military base.

⭐ **forth** /fɔːθ/. [1] ADV To go **forth** from a place means to leave it. [LITERARY] *Go forth into the desert.* [2] ADV To bring something **forth** means to produce it or make it visible. [LITERARY] *...ways to bring forth new ideas.* [3] **and so forth**: see **so**. ● **back and forth**: see **back**.

forthcoming /ˌfɔːθˈkʌmɪŋ/. [1] ADJ BEFORE N A **forthcoming** event is going to happen soon. *...the forthcoming election.* [2] ADJ AFTER LINK-V When something such as help or information is **forthcoming**, it is provided or made available. *They promised that the money would be forthcoming.* [3] ADJ If someone is **forthcoming**, they willingly give you information when you ask.

forthright /ˈfɔːθraɪt/. ADJ If you describe someone as **forthright**, you admire them because they say clearly and forcefully what they think and feel. *...forthright language.*

⭐ **fortieth** /ˈfɔːtiəθ/. ORD The **fortieth** item in a series is the one that you count as number forty.

fortify /ˈfɔːtɪfaɪ/ **fortifies, fortifying, fortified.** [1] VERB To **fortify** a place means to make it stronger and less easy to attack, often by building a wall or ditch round it. *...British soldiers working to fortify an airbase.* [2] VERB If food or drink **is fortified**, another substance is added to it to make it healthier or stronger. *...wine fortified with brandy.*

fortnight /ˈfɔːtnaɪt/ **fortnights.** N-COUNT A **fortnight** is a period of two weeks. *I hope to be back in a fortnight.*

fortress /ˈfɔːtrɪs/ **fortresses.** N-COUNT A **fortress** is a castle or other strong, well protected building, which is difficult for enemies to enter.

fortunate /'fɔːtʃunɪt/. ADJ If someone or something is **fortunate**, they are lucky. *He was extremely fortunate to survive.* ♦ **fortunately** ADV *Fortunately, the weather that winter was reasonably mild.*

★ **fortune** /'fɔːtʃuːn/**fortunes.** 1 N-UNCOUNT **Fortune** or **good fortune** is good luck. **Ill fortune** is bad luck. 2 N-PLURAL The **fortunes** of someone or something are the extent to which they are doing well or being successful. *The film follows the fortunes of two women.* 3 N-COUNT A **fortune** is a very large amount of money.

★ **forty** /'fɔːti/**forties.** NUM **Forty** is the number 40. For examples of how numbers such as forty and eighty are used see **eighty**.

forum /'fɔːrəm/**forums.** N-COUNT A **forum** is a place, situation, or event in which people exchange ideas and discuss issues that are important to them. *The organisation would provide a forum where problems could be discussed.*

★ **forward** /'fɔːwəd/**forwards, forwarding, forwarded.**

☑ **Forwards** is often used as an adverb instead of **forward** in senses 1 and 4.

1 ADV If you move or look **forward** or **forwards**, you move or look in a direction that is in front of you. *She fell forwards on to her face... He continued to walk, didn't look at the car, kept his face forward.* 2 ADV & ADJ BEFORE N **Forward** means in a position near the front of something such as a building or vehicle. *The best seats are in the aisle and as far forward as possible. ...to allow more troops to move to forward positions.* 3 ADV If something or someone is put **forward**, they are suggested or offered as suitable for a particular purpose. If someone **comes forward**, they present themselves as suitable for a particular purpose. *Next month the Commission is to bring forward its first proposals... No witnesses have come forward.* 4 ADV **Forward** and **forwards** are used to indicate that someone is making progress. *They just couldn't see any way forward.* 5 VERB If a letter or message **is forwarded to** someone, it is sent to the place where they are, after having been sent to a different place earlier. 6 ADJ If you describe someone as **forward**, you mean they speak very confidently and openly, sometimes offending people or not showing them enough respect. ♦ **forwardness** N-UNCOUNT *He shocked me with his forwardness.* 7 **backwards and forwards**: see **backwards**.

fossil /'fɒsəl/**fossils.** N-COUNT A **fossil** is the hardened remains or impression of a prehistoric animal or plant inside a rock.

fossil 'fuel, fossil fuels. N-VAR **Fossil fuels** are fuels such as coal, oil, and natural gas.

foster /'fɒstə, AM 'fɔːst-/**fosters, fostering, fostered.** 1 ADJ BEFORE N **Foster** parents are people who officially take a child into their family for a period of time, without becoming the child's legal

parents. The child is referred to as their **foster** child. 2 VERB If you **foster** a child, you take him or her into your family as a foster child. 3 VERB If you **foster** a feeling, activity, or idea, you help it to develop. *...a responsibility to foster global economic growth.*

fought /fɔːt/. **Fought** is the past tense and past participle of **fight**.

foul /faʊl/**fouler, foulest; fouls, fouling, fouled.** 1 ADJ If you describe something as **foul**, you mean it is dirty and smells or tastes unpleasant. 2 VERB If a place **is fouled** by someone or something, they make it dirty. *Two oil-related accidents near Los Angeles have fouled the ocean.* 3 ADJ **Foul** language is offensive and contains swear words or rude words. 4 ADJ If someone is in a **foul** temper or mood, they are very angry. 5 PHRASE If you **fall foul of** someone, you do something which gets you into trouble with them. 6 N-COUNT In sports such as football, a **foul** is an action that is against the rules.

★ **found** /faʊnd/**founds, founding, founded.** 1 **Found** is the past tense and past participle of **find**. 2 VERB When an organization, company, or city **is founded** by someone, they start it or create it. *He founded the Centre for Journalism Studies at University College Cardiff.* ♦ **foundation** N-SING *...the foundation of Kew Gardens.* ♦ **founder, founders** N-COUNT *He was one of the founders of the university's medical faculty.*

★ **foundation** /faʊn'deɪʃən/**foundations.** 1 N-COUNT The **foundation of** something such as a belief or way of life is the idea or experience on which it is based. *The issue strikes at the very foundation of our community... This laid the foundations for later modern economic growth.* 2 N-PLURAL The **foundations** of a building or other structure are the layer of bricks or concrete below the ground that it is built on. 3 N-COUNT A **foundation** is an organization which provides money for a special purpose. *...the National Foundation for Educational Research.* 4 N-UNCOUNT If a story, idea, or argument has no **foundation**, there are no facts to prove that it is true. *The allegations were without foundation.*

founded /'faʊndɪd/. ADJ AFTER LINK-V If something is **founded on** a particular thing, it is based on it. *The criticisms are founded on facts.*

★ **founder** /'faʊndə/**founders, foundering, foundered.** 1 VERB If something such as a plan or a project **founders**, it fails. 2 VERB If a ship **founders**, it fills with water and sinks.

founding /'faʊndɪŋ/. N-SING & ADJ The **founding** of an organization, tradition, or club is the creation of it. You can also use **founding** to describe a person or thing relating to the founding of something. *I have been a member of The Wine Club since its founding in 1973. ...a founding member of the Communist Party.*

foundry /'faʊndri/**foundries.** N-COUNT A **foundry** is a place where metal or glass is melted and made into particular objects.

a b c d e f g h i j k l m n o p q r s t u v w x y z

fountain /ˈfaʊntɪn/ **fountains.** [1] N-COUNT A **fountain** is an ornamental feature in a pool which consists of a jet of water that is forced up into the air by a pump. [2] N-COUNT A **fountain of** a liquid is an amount of it which is sent up into the air and falls back.

★ **four** /fɔː/ **fours.** [1] NUM **Four** is the number 4. [2] PHRASE If you are **on all fours**, your knees, feet, and hands are on the ground. → See picture on page 532. *She crawled on all fours over to the window.*

foursome /ˈfɔːsəm/ **foursomes.** N-COUNT A **foursome** is a group of four people or things.

★ **fourteen** /ˌfɔːˈtiːn/. NUM **Fourteen** is the number 14.

★ **fourteenth** /ˌfɔːˈtiːnθ/. ORD The **fourteenth** item in a series is the one that you count as number fourteen.

★ **fourth** /fɔːθ/ **fourths.** [1] ORD The **fourth** item in a series is the one that you count as number four. [2] N-COUNT In American English, a **fourth** is one of four equal parts of something. The British word is **quarter**.

four-wheel ˈdrive, four-wheel drives. N-COUNT A **four-wheel drive** is a vehicle in which all four wheels receive power from the engine.

fowl /faʊl/.

✓ The plural is **fowl** or **fowls**.

N-COUNT A **fowl** is a bird, especially a duck, goose, or chicken.

fox /fɒks/ **foxes, foxing, foxed.** [1] N-COUNT A **fox** is a wild animal which looks like a dog and has reddish-brown fur and a thick tail. [2] VERB If you **are foxed** by something, you cannot understand it or solve it. [BRITISH] *...a question which foxed one of these formidable experts.*

foyer /ˈfɔɪə, ˈfwaɪeɪ/ **foyers.** N-COUNT The **foyer** is the large area where people meet or wait just inside the doors of a theatre, cinema, or hotel.

fraction /ˈfrækʃən/ **fractions.** [1] N-COUNT A **fraction** is a tiny amount or proportion of something. *I opened my eyes just a fraction.* [2] N-COUNT In arithmetic, a **fraction** is a part of a whole number. For example, $\frac{1}{2}$ and $\frac{1}{3}$ are fractions of 1.

fracture /ˈfræktʃə/ **fractures, fracturing, fractured.** [1] VERB If something such as a bone **fractures**, or if it **is fractured**, it cracks or breaks. *He suffered a fractured skull.* [2] N-COUNT A **fracture** is a crack or break in something. *...a hip fracture.*

fragile /ˈfrædʒaɪl, AM -dʒəl/. [1] ADJ If you describe a situation as **fragile**, you mean that it is weak or uncertain, and unlikely to be able to resist strong pressure or attack. *...the fragile peace agreed this month.* ♦ **fragility** /frəˈdʒɪlɪti/ N-UNCOUNT *...the fragility of the environment.* [2] ADJ Something that is **fragile** is easily broken or damaged. *He leaned back in his fragile chair.* ♦ **fragility** N-UNCOUNT *...the fragility of their bones.* [3] ADJ Something that is **fragile** is very delicate in appearance. *...her fragile beauty.*

fragment, fragments, fragmenting, fragmented. [1] N-COUNT /ˈfrægmənt/ A **fragment of** something is a small piece or part of it. *...glass fragments... She read everything, digesting every fragment of news.* [2] VERB /fræɡˈment/ If something **fragments**, or if another thing **fragments** it, it breaks or separates into small pieces. *By the first century BC, Buddhism was in danger of fragmenting into small sects.* ♦ **fragmentation** N-UNCOUNT *...the fragmentation of the Soviet Union.* ♦ **fragmented** ADJ *Europe had become infinitely more unstable and fragmented.*

fragrance /ˈfreɪgrəns/ **fragrances.** N-VAR A **fragrance** is a pleasant or sweet smell.

fragrant /ˈfreɪgrənt/. ADJ Something that is **fragrant** has a sweet or pleasant smell. *The air was fragrant with the smell of orange blossoms.*

frail /freɪl/ **frailer, frailest.** [1] ADJ Someone who is **frail** is not very strong or healthy. [2] ADJ Something that is **frail** is easily broken or damaged.

★ **frame** /freɪm/ **frames, framing, framed.** [1] N-COUNT The **frame** of a picture or mirror is the part around its edges. *...a photograph of her mother in a silver frame.* [2] VERB If a picture or photograph **is framed**, it is put in a frame. [3] N-COUNT A **frame** is a structure, for example of bars or posts, which gives an object its shape and strength. *We painted our table to match the window frame.* [4] N-COUNT A **frame** of cinema film is one of the many separate photographs that it consists of. [5] N-COUNT You can refer to someone's body as their **frame**, especially when you are describing its general shape. *...their bony frames.* [6] VERB If you **frame** something in a particular kind of language, you express it in that way. *Let me frame the question a little differently.* [7] VERB If someone **frames** an innocent person, they make other people think that person is guilty of a crime, by lying or inventing evidence. [INFORMAL] *He had been framed by the police.*

ˌframe of ˈmind. N-SING Your **frame of mind** is your mood or attitude at a particular time. *Clearly, Lewis was not in the right frame of mind to continue.*

framework /ˈfreɪmwɜːk/ **frameworks.** [1] N-COUNT A **framework** is a set of rules, ideas, or beliefs which you use in order to decide what to do. *...topical issues within a Christian framework.* [2] N-COUNT A **framework** is a structure that forms a support or frame for something. *...wooden shelves on a steel framework.*

franchise /ˈfræntʃaɪz/ **franchises.** [1] N-COUNT If a large company or organization grants a **franchise** to a smaller company, the smaller company is allowed to sell the products of the larger company or participate in an activity controlled by the larger company. *...the franchise to build and operate the tunnel.* [2] N-SING In politics, **the franchise** is the right to vote in an election, especially one to elect a parliament.

frank /fræŋk/ **franker, frankest.** ADJ If someone is **frank**, they state things openly and honestly. ...*a frank discussion.* ◆ **frankly** ADV *You can talk frankly to me.* ◆ **frankness** N-UNCOUNT *The reaction to his frankness was hostile.*

frankly /fræŋkli/. ADV You use **frankly** when you are expressing an opinion or feeling to emphasize that you mean what you are saying. *Frankly, Thomas, this question of your loan is beginning to worry me.*

frantic /fræntɪk/. ADJ If someone is **frantic**, they are behaving in a desperate, wild, and disorganized way, because they are frightened, worried, or in a hurry. *A bird had been locked in and was by now quite frantic.* ◆ **frantically** ADV *We have been frantically trying to save her life.*

fraternity /frəˈtɜːnɪti/ **fraternities.** [1] N-UNCOUNT **Fraternity** is friendship between people who feel they are closely linked to each other. *Bob needs the fraternity of others who share his mission.* [2] N-COUNT You can refer to a group of people with the same profession or interests as a particular **fraternity**. ...*the sailing fraternity.* [3] N-COUNT In the United States, a **fraternity** is a society of male students at a university or college.

⭐ **fraud** /frɔːd/ **frauds.** [1] N-VAR **Fraud** is the crime of gaining money by deceit. *He was jailed for two years for fraud.* ...*tax frauds.* [2] N-COUNT If you call someone or something a **fraud**, you are criticizing them because you think they are not genuine, or are less good than they claim or appear to be. *You're a fraud and a spy, Simons.*

fraudulent /ˈfrɔːdʒʊlənt/. ADJ **fraudulent** activity is deceitful or dishonest. ...*fraudulent claims about being a nurse.* ◆ **fraudulently** ADV *All 5,000 of the homes were fraudulently obtained.*

fraught /frɔːt/. [1] ADJ AFTER LINK-V If a situation or action is **fraught with** problems or difficulties, it is full of them. *Operations employing this technique were fraught with dangers.* [2] ADJ If you say that a situation or action is **fraught**, you mean that it is worrying or stressful. ...*a somewhat fraught day.*

fray /freɪ/ **frays, fraying, frayed.** [1] VERB If something such as cloth or rope **frays**, its threads or fibres become worn and it is likely to tear or break. *The stitching had begun to fray at the edges.* [2] N-SING If you say that someone joins **the fray**, you mean that they become involved in an exciting or challenging activity or situation. ...*a second round of voting when new candidates can enter the fray.*

freak /friːk/ **freaks.** [1] ADJ BEFORE N A **freak** event or action is very unusual or extreme. ...*a freak accident.* [2] N-COUNT People are sometimes referred to as **freaks** when their behaviour or appearance is very different from that of most people; used showing disapproval. ...*a place where minorities are treated like freaks.*

freckle /ˈfrekəl/ **freckles.** N-COUNT If someone has **freckles**, they have small light brown spots on their skin.

⭐ **free** /friː/ **freer, freest; frees, freeing, freed.** [1] ADJ If something is **free**, you can have it or use it without paying. ...*a free brochure... The company won the contract by essentially saying it would do the job for free.* ● **free of charge:** see **charge.** [2] ADJ Someone or something that is **free** is not controlled or limited by rules or custom or by other people. *Women should be free to dress and act as they please.* ...*organising free and fair elections.* [3] PHRASE You say **'feel free'** to someone who has asked you if they can do something as a way of giving them permission. *Go right ahead. Feel free... If you have any questions at all, please feel free to ask me.* [4] VERB If you **free** someone **of** something unpleasant or restricting, you remove it from them. *It will free us of a whole lot of debt.* [5] ADJ A person or thing that is **free of** something unpleasant does not have it or is not affected by it. ...*a future far more free of fear... The carnival got off to a virtually trouble-free start.* [6] ADJ Someone who is **free** is no longer a prisoner or a slave. *He walked from the court house a free man... More than ninety prisoners have been set free.* [7] VERB To **free** a prisoner or slave means to release them. [8] VERB If you **free** someone or something, you make them available for a task or purpose. *His deal with Disney will run out shortly, freeing him to pursue his own project.* [9] ADJ If you have a **free** period of time, or if you are **free** at a particular time, you are not working or occupied then. *She spent her free time shopping.* [10] ADJ If something such as a table or seat is **free**, it is not being used or occupied, or is not reserved for someone to use. *They took the only free table.* [11] ADJ AFTER LINK-V If something gets **free**, it is no longer trapped by something or attached to something. *He pulled his arm free.* [12] VERB If you **free** someone or something, you remove or loosen them from the place where they have been trapped or become fixed. *Firemen tried to free the injured and put out the blaze.*

⭐ **freedom** /ˈfriːdəm/ **freedoms.** [1] N-VAR **Freedom** is the state of being allowed to do what you want. ...*freedom of speech.* ...*the need for individual freedoms and human rights.* [2] N-UNCOUNT When prisoners or slaves gain their **freedom**, they are set free or they escape. *What he wanted was release from prison and freedom.* [3] N-UNCOUNT **Freedom from** something you do not want means not being affected by it. ...*all the freedom from pain that medicine could provide.*

free 'enterprise. N-UNCOUNT **Free enterprise** is an economic system in which businesses compete for profit without much government control.

freelance /ˈfriːlɑːns, -læns/. ADJ & ADV Someone who works **freelance** or who is, for example, a **freelance** journalist or photographer, organizes their own work, income, and taxes,

a
b
c
d
e
f
g
h
i
j
k
l
m
n
o
p
q
r
s
t
u
v
w
x
y
z

rather than being employed by someone who pays them regularly. *She decided to go freelance.*

freely /ˈfriːli/. **1** ADV You use **freely** to indicate that something happens or is done many times or in large quantities, often without restraint. *We have referred freely to his ideas... Consumer goods are freely available.* **2** ADV If you can talk **freely**, you do not need to be careful about what you say. **3** ADV If someone gives or does something **freely**, they give or do it without being forced to do it. *Danny shared his knowledge freely.* **4** ADV If something or someone moves **freely**, they move easily and smoothly, without any obstacles or resistance. *...to ensure that traffic flows freely throughout the country.*

freer /ˈfriːə/. **Freer** is the comparative of **free**.

freest /ˈfriːɪst/. **Freest** is the superlative of **free**.

freeway /ˈfriːweɪ/ **freeways.** N-COUNT In American English, a **freeway** is a major road that has been specially built for fast travel over long distances. The usual British word is **motorway**.

free 'will. PHRASE If you do something **of** your **own free will**, you do it because you want to and not because you are forced to. *If he does not leave of his own free will then we will have to force him out.*

⭐ **freeze** /friːz/ **freezes, freezing, froze, frozen. 1** VERB If a liquid **freezes**, or if something **freezes** it, it becomes solid because of low temperatures. *If the temperature drops below 0°C, water freezes.* **2** VERB If you **freeze** something such as food, you preserve it by storing it at a temperature below 0° Celsius. You can also talk about how well food **freezes**. **3** VERB If you **freeze**, you feel very cold. *Your hands will freeze doing this.* **4** VERB If someone who is moving **freezes**, they suddenly stop and become completely still. *She froze when the beam of the flashlight struck her.* **5** VERB & N-COUNT If the government or a company **freeze** an activity, prices, or wages, or if it puts a **freeze** on them, it states officially that it will not allow them to increase for a fixed period of time. *OPEC has agreed to freeze its global oil production. ...a wage freeze.* **6** VERB If someone in authority **freezes** your bank accounts or other financial concerns, they obtain a legal order which stops you having access to them or using them. **7** See also **freezing, frozen.**
▸**freeze out.** PHR-VERB If you **freeze** someone **out** of an activity or situation, you prevent them from being involved in it by creating difficulties or by being unfriendly.

freezer /ˈfriːzə/ **freezers.** N-COUNT A **freezer** is a fridge in which the temperature is kept below freezing point so that you can store food inside it for long periods.

freezing /ˈfriːzɪŋ/. ADJ If you say that something or someone is **freezing** or **freezing cold**, you are emphasizing that they are very cold. *...a freezing January afternoon... You must be freezing.* ● See note at **cold.**

freight /freɪt/. **1** N-UNCOUNT **Freight** is the movement of goods by lorries, trains, ships, or aeroplanes. *The whole thing will have to go by air freight.* **2** N-UNCOUNT **Freight** consists of the goods that are transported by lorries, trains, ships, or aeroplanes. *...26 tons of freight.*

freighter /ˈfreɪtə/ **freighters.** N-COUNT A **freighter** is a ship or aeroplane designed to carry goods.

frenetic /frɪˈnetɪk/. ADJ **Frenetic** activity is fast and energetic, but rather uncontrolled. *...the frenetic pace of life in New York.*

frenzied /ˈfrenzid/. ADJ **Frenzied** actions are carried out by someone who has lost control of their mind, senses, or feelings and is acting in a wild and violent way. *...a frenzied attack.*

frenzy /ˈfrenzi/ **frenzies.** N-VAR **Frenzy** is great excitement or wild behaviour that often results from losing control of your feelings. *'Get out!' she ordered in a frenzy.*

frequency /ˈfriːkwənsi/ **frequencies. 1** N-UNCOUNT The **frequency** of an event is the number of times it happens. *The frequency of Kara's phone calls increased.* **2** N-VAR The **frequency** of a sound wave or radio wave is the rate at which it vibrates. [TECHNICAL]

⭐ **frequent, frequents, frequenting, frequented. 1** ADJ /ˈfriːkwənt/ If something is **frequent**, it happens often. *She gives frequent performances of her work... He is a frequent visitor to the house.*
♦ **frequently** ADV *He was frequently depressed.* **2** VERB /frɪˈkwent/ If someone **frequents** a particular place, they regularly go there. [FORMAL] *I hear he frequents Kenny's, the Cajun restaurant.*

fresco /ˈfreskəʊ/ **frescoes.** N-COUNT A **fresco** is a picture that is painted on a plastered wall when the plaster is still wet.

⭐ **fresh** /freʃ/ **fresher, freshest. 1** ADJ BEFORE N A **fresh** thing or amount replaces or is added to a previous one. *Make fresh inquiries... I need a new challenge and a fresh start.* **2** ADJ Something that is **fresh** has been done, made, or experienced recently. *There were no fresh car tracks. ...with the memory of the bombing fresh in her mind.*
♦ **freshly** ADV *...a freshly painted porch.* **3** ADJ **Fresh** food has been produced or picked recently, and has not been preserved. *...locally caught fresh fish.* ♦ **freshly** ADV *...freshly baked bread.* ♦ **freshness** N-UNCOUNT *Pay attention to the freshness of your food.* **4** ADJ If you describe something as **fresh**, you mean you like it because it is new and exciting. *These designers are full of fresh ideas.* ♦ **freshness** N-UNCOUNT *There was a freshness and enthusiasm about the new students.* **5** ADJ If something smells, tastes, or feels **fresh**, it is clean, cool, or refreshing. *The air was fresh.* **6** ADJ **Fresh** water is water that is not salty, for example the water in streams and lakes. ● See also **freshwater.** **7** ADJ AFTER LINK-V If you **are fresh from** or **are fresh out of** a particular place or experience, you have just come from that place or you have just had that experience. *I returned to the office, fresh from Heathrow.*

,**fresh 'air.** N-UNCOUNT You can describe the air outside as **fresh air**, especially when you mean that it is good for you. *Take exercise, preferably in the fresh air.*

freshman /'freʃmən/ **freshmen.** N-COUNT **Freshmen** are students who are in their first year at an American university or college.

freshwater /'freʃwɔːtə/. ADJ BEFORE N A **freshwater** lake or pool contains water that is not salty.

fret /fret/ **frets, fretting, fretted.** VERB If you **fret about** something, you worry about it. *Vera is fretting about her sick children.*

friction /'frɪkʃən/ **frictions.** [1] N-VAR **Friction** between people is disagreement and quarrels between them. *The friction between us was becoming evident.* [2] N-UNCOUNT **Friction** is the force that makes it difficult for things to move freely when they are touching each other. [3] N-UNCOUNT **Friction** is the rubbing of one thing against another. *...the friction of his leg against hers.*

⭐ **Friday** /'fraɪdeɪ, -di/ **Fridays.** N-VAR **Friday** is the day after Thursday and before Saturday. → See Reference Page on Times and Dates.

fridge /frɪdʒ/ **fridges.** N-COUNT In British English, a **fridge** is a large metal container for storing food at low temperatures to keep it fresh. The usual American word is **refrigerator**.

⭐ **friend** /frend/ **friends.** [1] N-COUNT A **friend** is someone who you know well and like, but who is not related to you. *Joanie's my best friend.* [2] N-PLURAL If you are **friends with** someone, you are their friend and they are yours. *I still wanted to be friends with her... Sarah and Ella have been friends for seven years.* [3] PHRASE If you **make friends with** someone, you begin a friendship with them. *He has made friends with the kids on the street... I've never found it hard to make friends.* [4] N-PLURAL The **friends of** an organization, a country, or a cause are the people and organizations who help and support them. *...The Friends of Birmingham Royal Ballet.*

⭐ **friendly** /'frendli/ **friendlier, friendliest; friendlies.** [1] ADJ A **friendly** person is kind and pleasant. *...a man with a pleasant, friendly face.* ♦ **friendliness** N-UNCOUNT *She also loves the friendliness of the people.* [2] ADJ AFTER LINK-V If you are **friendly with** someone, you like each other and enjoy spending time together. *I'm friendly with his mother.* [3] N-COUNT In sport, a **friendly** is a game which is not part of a competition, and is played for entertainment or practice.

-friendly /-'frendli/. **-friendly** combines with nouns to form adjectives which describe things that do not harm or that help the thing or person mentioned. *Palm oil is environment-friendly. ...ozone-friendly fridges. ...customer-friendly banking facilities.*

⭐ **friendship** /'frendʃɪp/ **friendships.** N-VAR A **friendship** is a relationship or state of friendliness between two people who like each other. *...the quickest way to end a good friendship... The two countries signed treaties of friendship and co-operation.*

frigate /'frɪgət/ **frigates.** N-COUNT A **frigate** is a small naval ship that can move at fast speeds.

fright /fraɪt/ **frights.** [1] N-UNCOUNT **Fright** is a sudden feeling of fear. *Franklin uttered a shriek and jumped with fright.* [2] N-COUNT A **fright** is an experience which makes you suddenly afraid. *The last time you had a real fright, you nearly crashed the car.* [3] PHRASE If someone **takes fright**, they experience a sudden feeling of fear.

frighten /'fraɪtən/ **frightens, frightening, frightened.** VERB If something or someone **frightens** you, they cause you to suddenly feel afraid or anxious. *He knew that Soli was trying to frighten him.*
▶ **frighten away** or **frighten off.** [1] PHR-VERB If you **frighten away** a person or animal, or if you **frighten** them **off**, you make them afraid so that they run away or stay some distance away from you. *The fishermen said the company's seismic survey was frightening away fish.* [2] PHR-VERB To **frighten** someone **away** or **frighten** them **off** means to make them nervous so that they decide not to do something. *Let's not frighten visitors off by making them feel they're not welcome.*
▶ **frighten into.** PHR-VERB If you **frighten** someone **into** doing something, you force them to do it by making them afraid.
▶ **frighten off.** See **frighten away**.

frightened /'fraɪtənd/. ADJ If you are **frightened**, you feel anxious or afraid. *She was frightened of flying.*

frightening /'fraɪtənɪŋ/. ADJ If something is **frightening**, it makes you feel afraid or anxious. *It was a very frightening experience.* ♦ **frighteningly** ADV *She was frighteningly ill.*

frightful /'fraɪtfʊl/. [1] ADJ Something that is **frightful** is very bad or unpleasant. [DATED] *My father was unable to talk about the war, it was so frightful.* [2] ADJ BEFORE N **Frightful** is used to emphasize the extent or degree of something. [DATED] *He got himself into a frightful muddle.* ♦ **frightfully** ADV *I'm most frightfully sorry.*

frill /frɪl/ **frills.** [1] N-COUNT A **frill** is a long, narrow, folded strip of cloth which is attached to something as a decoration. [2] N-PLURAL If something has no **frills**, it is simple and has no unnecessary or additional features. *...Volkswagen's no-frills cars.*

fringe /frɪndʒ/ **fringes.** [1] N-COUNT In British English, a **fringe** is hair which is cut so that it hangs over your forehead. The usual American word is **bangs**. → See picture on page 312. [2] N-COUNT A **fringe** is a decoration attached to clothes and other objects, consisting of a row of hanging threads. *...curtains of white silk with a fringe edging.* [3] N-COUNT To be **on the fringe** or **on the fringes of** a place means to be on the outside edge of it. *...black townships located on the fringes of the city.* [4] N-COUNT The **fringe** or **fringes of** an activity or organization are its least typical or most extreme parts. *The party remained on the fringe of the political scene. ...fringe theatre style.* **5** N-COUNT **Fringe benefits** are extra things that some people get from their job in addition to their salary, for example a car.

fringed /frɪndʒd/. **1** ADJ BEFORE N **Fringed** clothes, curtains, or furnishings are decorated with fringes. **2** ADJ AFTER LINK-V If a place or object is **fringed with** things, they are situated along its edges. *...tiny islands fringed with golden sand.*

frivolous /ˈfrɪvələs/. **1** ADJ If you describe someone as **frivolous**, you mean they behave in a silly or light-hearted way, rather than being serious and sensible. *Isabelle was a frivolous little fool.* **2** ADJ If you describe an activity as **frivolous**, you disapprove of it because it is not useful and wastes time or money. *...a business as fickle and frivolous as fashion.*

fro /frəʊ/. **to and fro**: see **to**.

frock /frɒk/. **frocks.** N-COUNT A **frock** is a woman's or girl's dress. [DATED]

frog /frɒg, AM frɔːg/. **frogs.** N-COUNT A **frog** is a small creature with smooth skin, big eyes, and long back legs which it uses for jumping.

frolic /ˈfrɒlɪk/. **frolics, frolicking, frolicked.** VERB & N-VAR When people or animals **frolic**, they run around and play in a lively way. **Frolic** is this behaviour. *Tourists sunbathe and frolic in the ocean. ...fun and frolic.*

★ **from** /frəm, STRONG frɒm, AM frʌm/. **1** PREP You use **from** to say what the source, origin, or starting point of something is. *...an anniversary present from his wife... The results were taken from six surveys. ...wines from France.* **2** PREP If someone or something moves or is taken **from** a place, they leave it or are removed from it. *The guests watched as she fled from the room... Remove the bowl from the ice.* **3** PREP If you take something **from** an amount, you reduce the amount by that much. *The £103 is deducted from Mrs Adams' salary every month.* **4** PREP If you are away **from** a place, you are not there. *Her husband worked away from home a lot.* **5** PREP If you return **from** a place or activity, you return after being there or doing it. *My son Colin has just returned from Amsterdam.* **6** PREP If you see or hear something **from** a particular place, you are in that place when you see it or hear it. *They see the painting from behind a plate glass window.* **7** PREP Something that sticks out or hangs **from** an object is attached to it or touches it. *Hanging from his right wrist is a heavy gold bracelet. ...large fans hanging from ceilings.* **8** PREP You can use **from** when giving distances. For example, if one place is fifty miles **from** another, the distance between them is fifty miles. *How far is it from here?* **9** PREP If a road goes **from** one place to another, you can travel along it between the two places. *...the road from St Petersburg to Tallinn.* **10** PREP **From** is used, especially in the expression **made from**, to say what substance has been used to make something. *...bread made*

from white flour. **11** PREP If something happens **from** a particular time, it begins to happen then. *She studied painting from 1926.* **12** PREP You say **from** one thing **to** another when you are stating the range of things that are possible. *There are 94 countries represented in Barcelona, from Algeria to Zimbabwe.* **13** PREP If something changes **from** one thing **to** another, it stops being the first thing and becomes the second thing. *The expression on his face changed from sympathy to surprise.* **14** PREP You use **from** when mentioning the cause of something. *The problem simply resulted from a difference of opinion... He is suffering from eye ulcers.* **15** PREP You use **from** to give the reason for an opinion. *I guessed from his name that Jose must have been Spanish.*

★ **front** /frʌnt/. **fronts.** **1** N-COUNT & ADJ BEFORE N The **front** of something, or the **front** part of it, is the part of it that faces you or faces forward. *Stand at the front of the line... Her cotton dress had ripped down the front... She was only six and still missing her front teeth.* **2** N-COUNT In a war, **the front** is the place where two armies are fighting. *Her husband is fighting at the front.* **3** N-COUNT If something happens on a particular **front**, it happens with regard to a particular situation or activity. *...research across a wide academic front.* **4** N-SING If someone puts on a **front**, they pretend to have feelings which they do not have. *Michael kept up a brave front.* **5** N-COUNT An organization or activity that is a **front for** another one that is illegal or secret is used to hide it. *...a firm later identified by the police as a front for crime syndicates in the city.*

PHRASES ● If a person or thing is **in front**, they are ahead of others in a moving group. *...motorists who speed or drive too close to the car in front.* ● If you are **in front** in a competition or contest, you are winning. ● If someone or something is **in front of** a particular thing, they are facing it, ahead of it, or close to the front part of it. *She sat down in front of her dressing-table mirror... Something darted out in front of my car.* ● If you do something **in front of** someone, you do it in their presence. *They never argued in front of their children.*

frontal /ˈfrʌntəl/. **1** ADJ A **frontal** attack or challenge criticizes or threatens something in a very strong direct way. *...a frontal attack on conventional marriage.* **2** ADJ **Frontal** means relating to or involving the front of something. *...the frontal region of the brain.*

frontier /ˈfrʌntɪə, -ˈtɪə/. **frontiers.** **1** N-COUNT A **frontier** is a border between two countries. **2** N-COUNT The **frontiers of** a subject are the limits to which it can be known or done. *...pushing back the frontiers of science.*

front 'line, front lines. N-COUNT The **front line** is the place where two armies are fighting each other.

front-'page. ADJ A **front-page** article or picture appears on the front page of a newspaper because it is very important or interesting.

,front-'runner, front-runners. N-COUNT In a competition or contest, the **front-runner** is the person who seems most likely to win it.

frost /frɒst/, AM frɔːst/ **frosts.** N-VAR When there is a **frost**, the outside temperature drops below freezing and the ground is covered with ice crystals.

frosty /'frɒsti, AM 'frɔːsti/. [1] ADJ If the weather is **frosty**, the temperature is below freezing. ...*sharp, frosty nights.* [2] ADJ You describe the ground or an object as **frosty** when it is covered with frost. ...*the frosty stones.* [3] ADJ If you describe someone's behaviour as **frosty**, you think it is unfriendly. ...*Ros's frosty glance.*

froth /frɒθ, AM frɔːθ/ **froths, frothing, frothed.** [1] VERB If a liquid **froths**, small bubbles appear on the surface. *The sea froths over my feet.* [2] N-UNCOUNT **Froth** is a mass of small bubbles on the surface of a liquid. ...*the froth of bubbles on the top of a glass of beer.*

frown /fraʊn/ **frowns, frowning, frowned.** VERB & N-COUNT If you **frown**, or if you have a **frown** on your face, you move your eyebrows close together because you are annoyed, worried, or thinking hard. *He frowned at her anxiously... There was a deep frown on the boy's face.*

▶ **frown on** or **frown upon.** PHR-VERB If something **is frowned on**, or if it **is frowned upon**, people disapprove of it. *This practice is frowned upon as being wasteful.*

froze /frəʊz/. **Froze** is the past tense of **freeze**.

frozen /'frəʊzən/. [1] **Frozen** is the past participle of **freeze**. [2] ADJ If the ground is **frozen**, it has become very hard because the weather is very cold. *It was bitterly cold now and the ground was frozen hard.* [3] ADJ **Frozen** food has been preserved by being kept at a very low temperature. *Frozen fish is a very healthy convenience food.* [4] ADJ If you say that you are **frozen**, you mean that you are very cold. *He put one hand up to his frozen face.*

frugal /'fruːɡəl/. [1] ADJ Someone who is **frugal** spends very little money on themselves. *She lives a frugal life.* ♦ **frugality** /fruː'ɡælɪti/ N-UNCOUNT *We must practise the strictest frugality and economy.* [2] ADJ A **frugal** meal is small and inexpensive. *The diet was frugal.*

■ **fruit** /fruːt/.

✓ The plural is **fruit** or **fruits**.

[1] N-VAR **Fruit** is something which grows on a tree or bush and which contains seeds or a stone covered by edible flesh. Apples, oranges, and bananas are all fruit. *Fresh fruit and vegetables provide fibre and vitamins.* → See picture on page 821. [2] N-COUNT **The fruit** or **fruits of** someone's work or activity are the good things that result from it. *The findings are the fruit of more than three years research.* [3] PHRASE If an action **bears fruit**, it produces good results.

fruitful /'fruːtfʊl/. ADJ Something that is **fruitful** produces good and useful results. ...*a long, happy, fruitful relationship.*

fruition /fruː'ɪʃən/. N-UNCOUNT When something comes to **fruition**, it starts to produce the intended results. *These plans take time to come to fruition.*

fruitless /'fruːtləs/. ADJ **Fruitless** actions, events, or efforts do not achieve anything at all. *It was a fruitless search... Talks have so far have been fruitless.*

fruity /'fruːti/ **fruitier, fruitiest.** [1] ADJ Something that is **fruity** smells or tastes of fruit. *This shampoo smells fruity. ...a lovely rich fruity wine.* [2] ADJ A **fruity** laugh or voice is rich and deep.

⭐ **frustrate** /frʌ'streɪt, AM 'frʌstreɪt/ **frustrates, frustrating, frustrated.** [1] VERB If something **frustrates** you, it upsets or angers you because you are unable to do anything about the problems it creates. *These questions frustrated me... Do you get very frustrated by slow-moving traffic?* ♦ **frustrated** ADJ *Roberta felt frustrated and angry.* ♦ **frustrating** ADJ *I found it very frustrating to teach Ted.* ♦ **frustration, frustrations** N-VAR *...frustration among hospital doctors.* [2] VERB To **frustrate** something such as a plan means to prevent it. *The government has deliberately frustrated his efforts to gain work permits.*

⭐ **fry** /fraɪ/ **fries, frying, fried.** [1] VERB When you **fry** food, you cook it in a pan containing hot fat. *Fry the breadcrumbs until golden brown.* ♦ **fried** ADJ *...fried fish.* ● See note at **cook.** [2] N-PLURAL **Fry** are very small young fish. [3] N-PLURAL **Fries** are the same as **chips**.

'frying pan, frying pans. N-COUNT A **frying pan** is a flat metal pan with a long handle, in which you fry food. → See picture on page 825.

ft. N-COUNT **ft** is a written abbreviation for **foot** or **feet**. ...*flying at 1,000 ft.*

fudge /fʌdʒ/ **fudges, fudging, fudged.** [1] N-UNCOUNT **Fudge** is a soft brown sweet made from butter, milk, and sugar. [2] VERB If you **fudge** something, you avoid making clear or definite decisions about it. *Both have fudged their calculations.*

⭐ **fuel** /'fjuːəl/ **fuels, fuelling, fuelled** (AM **fueling, fueled**). [1] N-VAR **Fuel** is a substance such as coal, oil, or petrol that is burned to provide heat or power. ...*the fuel necessary to heat their homes.* ● See also **fossil fuel.** [2] VERB A machine or vehicle that **is fuelled** by a particular substance works by burning that substance. ...*power stations fuelled by oil.*

fugitive /'fjuːdʒɪtɪv/ **fugitives.** N-COUNT A **fugitive** is someone who is running away or hiding, usually in order to avoid being caught by the police.

⭐ **fulfil** (or **fulfill**) /fʊl'fɪl/, **fulfils, fulfilling, fulfilled.** [1] VERB If you **fulfil** a promise, dream, or ambition, you do what you said or hoped you would do. ...*to fulfil her ambitions and become an actress.* [2] VERB To **fulfil** a task, role, or function means to do what is required by it. [3] VERB If something **fulfils** you, you feel happy and satisfied with what you are doing. ...*a hobby that*

fulfilled her. ♦ **fulfilling** ADJ ...a fulfilling career. ♦ **fulfilled** ADJ I feel more fulfilled doing this than I've ever done. ♦ **fulfilment** N-UNCOUNT ...a great sense of fulfilment.

⭐ **full** /fʊl/ **fuller, fullest.** ☐1 ADJ Something that is **full** contains as much of a substance or as many objects as it can. ...a full tank of petrol... The main car park was full. ☐2 ADJ AFTER LINK-V If a place is **full of** things or people, it contains a large number of them. His mouth was full of peas. ...a useful recipe leaflet full of ideas. ☐3 ADJ AFTER LINK-V If someone or something is **full of** a feeling or quality, they have a lot of it. I feel full of confidence. ☐4 ADJ AFTER LINK-V If you feel **full**, you have eaten so much that you do not want anything else. ♦ **fullness** N-UNCOUNT High fibre diets give the feeling of fullness. ☐5 ADJ BEFORE N & ADV You can use **full** to indicate the greatest possible amount of something. ...the sound of Mahler, playing at full volume. ...in full daylight. ...a two-seater Lotus, parked with its headlamps full on. ☐6 ADJ BEFORE N You can use **full** to indicate that you are referring to the whole of something, or to emphasize the amount of a quality that it has. Full details will be sent to you... May I have your full name?... The farm was in full view of the house. ☐7 ADJ If someone has a **full** life, they are always busy. ☐8 ADJ When there is a **full** moon, the moon appears as a bright, complete circle. ☐9 ADJ A **full** flavour is strong and rich. ...a dry, grapey wine with a full flavour.
PHRASES ● Something that has been done **in full** has been done or finished completely. The medical experts have yet to report in full.
● Something that is done or experienced **to the full** is done to as great an extent as is possible. ...a good mind which should be used to the full.

,full-'blown. ADJ BEFORE N **Full-blown** means having all the characteristics of a particular type of thing or person. Before becoming a full-blown director, he worked as a film editor.

,full-'length. ☐1 ADJ BEFORE N A **full-length** book, record, or film is the normal length, rather than being shorter than normal. ☐2 ADJ BEFORE N A **full-length** coat or skirt is long enough to reach the lower part of a person's leg. ☐3 ADJ BEFORE N A **full-length** mirror or portrait shows the whole of a person. ☐4 ADV Someone who is lying **full-length** is lying down flat and stretched out. She stretched herself out full-length.

,full-'scale. ☐1 ADJ BEFORE N **Full-scale** means as complete, intense, or great in extent as possible. ...a full-scale nuclear war. ☐2 ADJ BEFORE N A **full-scale** drawing or model is the same size as the thing that it represents.

,full-'size (or **full-sized**). ADJ BEFORE N A **full-size** or **full-sized** model or picture is the same size as the thing or person that it represents.

,full 'stop, full stops. N-COUNT In British English, a **full stop** is the punctuation mark (.) which you use at the end of a sentence when it is not a question or exclamation. The American word is **period**. → See Reference Page on Punctuation.

,full-'time (or **full time**). ADJ & ADV **Full-time** work or study takes up the whole of each normal working week. ...a full-time job... Deirdre works full-time.

⭐ **fully** /'fʊli/. ☐1 ADV **Fully** means to the greatest degree or extent possible. She was fully aware of my thoughts... I don't fully agree. ☐2 ADV If you describe, answer, or deal with something **fully**, you leave out nothing that should be mentioned or dealt with. These debates are discussed more fully later in this book.

fumble /'fʌmbəl/ **fumbles, fumbling, fumbled.** VERB If you **fumble for** something, or if you **fumble with** it, you clumsily try and reach for it or hold it. She crept from the bed and fumbled for her dressing gown.

fume /fjuːm/ **fumes, fuming, fumed.** ☐1 N-PLURAL **Fumes** are unpleasantly strong or harmful gases or smells. ...car exhaust fumes. ☐2 VERB If you **are fuming** over something, you are very angry about it. 'It's monstrous!' Jackie fumed... Mrs. Vine was still fuming.

⭐ **fun** /fʌn/. ☐1 N-UNCOUNT **Fun** is pleasant, enjoyable, and light-hearted activity or amusement. We had so much fun doing it... You still have time to join in the fun. ☐2 ADJ If someone is **fun**, you enjoy their company. If something is **fun**, you enjoy doing it. Liz was wonderful fun to be with... It was a fun evening.
PHRASES ● If you do something **in fun**, you do it as a joke or for amusement, without intending to cause any harm. Don't say such things, even in fun.
● If you **make fun of** someone or something, or if you **poke fun at** them, you tease them or make jokes about them. They all made fun of my plan.

⭐ **function** /'fʌŋkʃən/ **functions, functioning, functioned.** ☐1 N-COUNT The **function** of something or someone is the useful thing that they do or are intended to do. The main function of the merchant banks is to raise capital for industry. ☐2 VERB If a machine or system **is functioning**, it is working or operating. Conservation programs cannot function without local support. ☐3 VERB If someone or something **functions as** a particular thing, they do the work or fulfil the purpose of that thing. One third of the room functions as workspace. ☐4 N-COUNT A **function** is a large formal dinner or party.

functional /'fʌŋkʃənəl/. ☐1 ADJ **Functional** things are useful rather than decorative. ...modern, functional furniture. ☐2 ADJ **Functional** equipment works or operates in the way that it is supposed to. We have fully functional smoke alarms. ☐3 ADJ BEFORE N **Functional** means relating to the way something works or operates. ...decreased functional ability in the knees.

⭐ **fund** /fʌnd/ **funds, funding, funded.** ☐1 N-PLURAL **Funds** are amounts of money that are available to be spent. The concert will raise funds for research into Aids. ...government funds. ☐2 N-COUNT A **fund** is an amount of money that is collected for a particular purpose. ...a scholarship fund for undergraduate engineering students.

3 VERB To **fund** something means to provide money for it. *They will use the grant to fund the appointment of a Welfare Visitor. ...government-funded institutions.* ♦ **funding** N-UNCOUNT *They hope for government funding for the scheme.*
4 N-COUNT If you have a **fund of** something, you have a lot of it. *...an extraordinary fund of energy.*

fundamental /ˌfʌndəˈmentəl/. ADJ If something is **fundamental**, it is very important or basic. *Technical skill is a fundamental basis for most, if not all, great art... Better relations with its neighbours are fundamental to the well-being of the area.* ♦ **fundamentally** ADV *He can be very charming but he is fundamentally a bully.*

fundamentalism /ˌfʌndəˈmentəlɪzəm/. N-UNCOUNT **Fundamentalism** is belief in the original form of a religion or theory, without accepting any later ideas. ♦ **fundamentalist** /ˌfʌndəˈmentəlɪst/ **fundamentalists** N-COUNT *...fundamentalist Christians.*

fundamentals /fʌndəˈmentəlz/. N-PLURAL The **fundamentals of** something are its simplest, most important elements, ideas, or principles. *...the fundamentals of road safety.*

fundraiser /ˈfʌndreɪzə/ **fundraisers.** **1** N-COUNT A **fundraiser** is an event which is intended to raise money for a particular purpose. *Organize a fundraiser for your church.* **2** N-COUNT A **fundraiser** is someone who works to raise money for a particular purpose.

'fund-raising. N-UNCOUNT **Fund-raising** is the activity of collecting money for a particular purpose.

funeral /ˈfjuːnərəl/ **funerals.** N-COUNT A **funeral** is a ceremony for the burial or cremation of someone who has died. *His funeral will be on Thursday at Blackburn Cathedral.*

fungus /ˈfʌŋgəs/ **fungi** /ˈfʌŋgiː, ˈfʌndʒaɪ/. N-VAR A **fungus** is a plant that has no flowers, leaves, or green colouring, such as a mushroom or mould. ♦ **fungal** /ˈfʌŋgəl/ ADJ *...fungal growth.*

funnel /ˈfʌnəl/ **funnels, funnelling, funnelled** (AM **funneling, funneled**). **1** N-COUNT A **funnel** is an object with a wide top and a tube at the bottom, which is used to pour substances into a container. → See picture on page 825. **2** N-COUNT A **funnel** is a chimney on a ship. **3** VERB If something **funnels** somewhere, or if it **is funnelled**, it is directed through a narrow space. *The winds came from the north, across the plains, funnelling down the valley.* **4** VERB If you **funnel** money or resources somewhere, you send them there from several sources. *...a plan to funnel environmental aid through the World Bank.*

funny /ˈfʌni/ **funnier, funniest.** **1** ADJ **Funny** things are amusing and make you smile or laugh. *...a funny story... What's so funny?* **2** ADJ You say that something is **funny** when it is strange, surprising, or puzzling. *It's funny how fast things change.* **3** ADJ If you feel **funny**, you feel slightly ill. [INFORMAL]

fur /fɜː/ **furs.** **1** N-UNCOUNT **Fur** is the thick hair that grows on the bodies of many animals, and is sometimes used to make clothes or rugs. You can also refer to an artificial material that resembles this hair as **fur.** *...a black coat with a fur collar.* **2** N-COUNT A **fur** is a coat made from fur. *...women in furs.*

furious /ˈfjʊəriəs/. **1** ADJ If someone is **furious**, they are extremely angry. *He is furious at the way his wife has been treated.* ♦ **furiously** ADV *'You clumsy idiot,' he said furiously.* ● See note at **angry**. **2** ADJ You can use **furious** to indicate that something involves great energy, speed, or violence. *...months of furious debate.* ♦ **furiously** ADV *I started writing furiously.*

furlong /ˈfɜːlɒŋ, AM -lɔːŋ/ **furlongs.** N-COUNT A **furlong** is an imperial unit of length that is equal to 220 yards or 201.2 metres.

furnace /ˈfɜːnɪs/ **furnaces.** N-COUNT A **furnace** is a container or enclosed space in which a very hot fire is made, for example to melt metal, burn rubbish, or produce steam.

furnish /ˈfɜːnɪʃ/ **furnishes, furnishing, furnished.** **1** VERB When you **furnish** a room, you put furniture in it. ♦ **furnished** ADJ *...a furnished flat... The room was tastefully furnished.* **2** VERB To **furnish** something means to provide it or supply it. [FORMAL] *They'll be able to furnish you with the rest of the details.*

furnishings /ˈfɜːnɪʃɪŋz/. N-PLURAL The **furnishings** of a room or house are the furniture, curtains, carpets, and decorations such as pictures.

★ **furniture** /ˈfɜːnɪtʃə/. N-UNCOUNT **Furniture** consists of large movable objects such as tables, chairs, or beds that are used in a room for sitting or lying on, or for putting things on or in. *...bedroom furniture.*

> **USAGE** Note that **furniture** is only ever used as an uncount noun. You cannot say 'a furniture' or 'furnitures'. If you want to refer in general terms to something such as a table, a chair, or a bed, you can say a **piece of furniture** or an **item of furniture**.

furore (AM **furor**) /fjʊˈrɔːri, ˈfjʊərɔː/. N-SING A **furore** is a very angry or excited reaction by people to something. *...the furore over his remarks about Northern Ireland.*

furrow /ˈfʌrəʊ, AM ˈfɜːr-/ **furrows, furrowing, furrowed.** **1** N-COUNT A **furrow** is a long line in the earth made for planting seeds. **2** N-COUNT The **furrows** in someone's skin are deep folds or lines. *...the deep furrows that marked the corners of his mouth.* **3** VERB If someone **furrows** their brow or forehead, deep folds appear in it because they are frowning. [WRITTEN] *Her father furrowed his forehead... Occasionally her brow furrowed.*

furry /ˈfɜːri/ **furrier, furriest.** **1** ADJ A **furry** animal is covered with thick soft hair. *...a long furry tail.*

a b c d e f g h i j k l m n o p q r s t u v w x y z

A

2 ADJ Something that is **furry** resembles fur. ...*a furry hat.*

★ **further** /'fɜːðə/, **furthers, furthering, furthered. 1** ADV **Further** means to a greater degree or extent. *Inflation is below 5% and set to fall further.* **2** ADV If someone or something goes **further** or takes something **further**, they progress to a more advanced or detailed stage. *He did not develop that idea any further.* **3** ADJ BEFORE N A **further** thing or amount is an additional one. *Doctors are carrying out further tests.* **4** ADV **Further** means a greater distance than before or than something else. *Now we live further away from the city centre.* ...*a crossroads fifty yards further on.* **5** ADV **Further** is used in expressions such as **'further back'** and **'further ahead'** to refer to a point in time that is earlier or later than the time you are talking about. *Ministers have been looking further ahead, beyond the current conflicts in the region.* **6** VERB If you **further** something, you help it to progress or to be successful. *Education needn't only be about furthering your career.*

,**further edu'cation.** N-UNCOUNT In Britain, **further education** is education after leaving school, at a college rather than at a university. The usual American term is **continuing education.**

furthermore /,fɜːðə'mɔː/. ADV **Furthermore** is used to introduce a statement adding to or supporting the previous one. *It is nearly dark, and furthermore it's going to rain.*

furthest /'fɜːðɪst/. **1** ADV **Furthest** means to a greater extent or degree than ever before or than anything or anyone else. ...*the south of England, where prices have fallen furthest.* **2** ADJ & ADV The **furthest** one of a number of things is the one that is the greatest distance away. ...*the furthest point from earth.* ...*areas furthest from the coast.*

furtive /'fɜːtɪv/. ADJ If you describe someone's behaviour as **furtive**, you disapprove of them behaving as if they want to keep something secret or hidden. ...*furtive meetings.* ♦ **furtively** ADV *He glanced around furtively.*

fury /'fjʊəri/. N-UNCOUNT **Fury** is very strong anger. *His face was contorted with fury.*

fuse /fjuːz/ **fuses, fusing, fused. 1** N-COUNT In an electrical appliance, a **fuse** is a wire safety device which melts and stops the electric current if there is a fault. **2** VERB When an electric device **fuses**, or when you **fuse** it, it stops working because of a fault. *The light fused.* **3** N-COUNT A **fuse** is part of a bomb or firework which delays the explosion and gives people time to move away. **4** VERB When one thing **fuses with** another, they join together, usually to become one thing. *Conception occurs when a sperm fuses with an egg... Manufactured glass is made by fusing various types of sand.* **5** VERB To **fuse** ideas, qualities, or things means to combine them. ...*Latin American music fused with jazz.*

fuselage /'fjuːzɪlɑːʒ/ **fuselages.** N-COUNT The

fuselage of an aeroplane or rocket is its main part.

fusion /'fjuːʒən/ **fusions. 1** N-VAR When two ideas, qualities, or things are combined, you can say that there is a **fusion** of them. ...*a fusion of Eastern and Western cooking.* **2** N-UNCOUNT **Fusion** is the process in which atomic particles combine and produce a large amount of nuclear energy. [TECHNICAL] ...*research into nuclear fusion.*

fuss /fʌs/ **fusses, fussing, fussed. 1** N-SING & N-UNCOUNT **Fuss** is unnecessarily anxious or excited behaviour. *I don't know what all the fuss is about.* **2** VERB When people **fuss**, they behave in an unnecessarily anxious or excited way. *My mother is fussing about the journey.* **3** VERB If you **fuss over** someone or something, you pay them too much attention or worry about them too much. *All the Sisters fussed over her.* **4** PHRASE If you **make a fuss of** someone, you pay a lot of attention to them.

fussy /'fʌsi/ **fussier, fussiest. 1** ADJ Someone who is **fussy** is very concerned with unimportant details and is difficult to please. *He was very fussy about cleanliness.* **2** ADJ If you describe things as **fussy**, you are criticizing them because they are too elaborate or detailed. ...*fussy curtains.*

futile /'fjuːtaɪl, AM -təl/. ADJ If you say that something is **futile**, you mean there is no point in doing it, usually because it has no chance of succeeding. ...*their futile attempts to avoid publicity.* ♦ **futility** /fjuː'tɪləti/ N-UNCOUNT ...*the futility of arguing with him.*

★ **future** /'fjuːtʃə/ **futures. 1** N-SING **The future** is the period of time after the present. *No decision on the proposal was likely in the immediate future.* **2** ADJ BEFORE N **Future** things will happen or exist after the present time. ...*the UK's future role in Europe.* **3** N-COUNT The **future** of someone or something is what will happen to them after the present time. ...*his future as prime minister.* **4** N-COUNT Something that has a **future** is likely to be successful or to survive. *There's no future in this relationship.*

PHRASES ● You use **in future** when you are telling someone what you want or expect to happen from now on. *Be more careful in future.* ● If you say something will happen **in the near future**, you mean it will happen quite soon.

,**future 'tense.** N-SING In grammar, the **future tense** is used to refer to things that will come after the present.

futuristic /,fjuːtʃə'rɪstɪk/. ADJ Something that is **futuristic** looks like something from the future. ...*a futuristic building.*

fuzzy /'fʌzi/ **fuzzier, fuzziest. 1** ADJ **Fuzzy** hair sticks up in a soft curly mass. **2** ADJ A **fuzzy** picture or image is blurred and unclear. ...*fuzzy photographs.* **3** ADJ BEFORE N **Fuzzy** logic is a type of computer logic that is supposed to imitate the way that humans think. [COMPUTING]

G g

gadget /'gædʒɪt/ **gadgets.** N-COUNT A **gadget** is a small machine or device which does a useful task. *...consumer gadgets such as CD players.*

gag /gæg/ **gags, gagging, gagged.** ▢1 N-COUNT A **gag** is a piece of cloth that is tied round or put inside someone's mouth to stop them from speaking. ▢2 VERB If someone **gags** you, they tie a piece of cloth around your mouth in order to stop you from speaking. *The raiders bound and gagged her.* ▢3 VERB If a person **is gagged** by someone in authority, they are prevented from expressing their opinion or from publishing certain information; used showing disapproval. ▢4 N-COUNT A **gag** is a joke. [INFORMAL]

gain /geɪn/ **gains, gaining, gained.** ▢1 VERB If you **gain** something, you acquire it gradually. *Students can gain valuable experience by working on the campus radio... The helicopter gained speed as it headed toward the mainland.* ▢2 VERB If you **gain from** something, you get some advantage from it. *Many areas of the world would actually gain from global warming.* ▢3 N-COUNT A **gain** is an improvement or increase. *News on new home sales is brighter, showing a gain of nearly 8% in June.* ▢4 PHRASE If you do something **for gain**, you do it in order to get some profit for yourself. [FORMAL] *...buying art solely for financial gain.* ▢5 VERB If you **gain** something, you obtain it, usually after a lot of effort. *Passing exams is no longer enough to gain a place at university.*

gait /geɪt/ **gaits.** N-COUNT Someone's **gait** is their particular way of walking. [WRITTEN] *...a rolling gait.*

gala /'gɑːlə, AM 'geɪlə/ **galas.** N-COUNT A **gala** is a special public celebration, performance, or festival. *...a gala evening at the Royal Opera House.*

galaxy /'gæləksi/ **galaxies.** N-COUNT A **galaxy** is a huge group of stars and planets extending over millions of miles.

gale /geɪl/ **gales.** N-COUNT A **gale** is a very strong wind. *...fierce winter gales.*

gall /gɔːl/ **galls, galling, galled.** ▢1 N-SING If someone has the **gall to** do something dangerous or dishonest, they have the daring to do it; used showing disapproval. *She had the gall to suggest that I might supply her with information.* ▢2 VERB If someone's action **galls** you, it makes you angry because you cannot do anything about it. *What really galled Dana was that Caroline knew where she would be staying.*

gallant /'gælənt/.

☑ The pronunciation /gə'lænt/ is also used for meaning 2.

▢1 ADJ A **gallant** person behaves very bravely and honourably in a dangerous or difficult situation. *...gallant soldiers.* ◆ **gallantly** ADV *The town responded gallantly to the War.* ▢2 ADJ If you say that a man is **gallant**, you think he is polite and considerate towards other people, especially women. [DATED]

★ **gallery** /'gæləri/ **galleries.** ▢1 N-COUNT A **gallery** is a place that has permanent exhibitions of works of art in it. *...an art gallery.* ▢2 N-COUNT The **gallery** in a theatre or concert hall is a raised area at the back like a large balcony.

galley /'gæli/ **galleys.** N-COUNT On a ship or aircraft, the **galley** is the kitchen.

gallon /'gælən/ **gallons.** N-COUNT A **gallon** is a unit of measurement for liquids that is equal to eight pints. In Britain, it is equal to 4.564 litres. In America, it is equal to 3.785 litres.

gallop /'gæləp/ **gallops, galloping, galloped.** ▢1 VERB & N-SING When a horse **gallops**, or when it runs at **a gallop**, it runs very fast, so that during each stride all four legs are off the ground at the same time. *The horses galloped away... He whipped his horse into a gallop.* ▢2 VERB & N-COUNT If you **gallop**, you ride a horse that is galloping. A **gallop** is a ride on a galloping horse. *Major Winston galloped into the distance. ...early morning gallops at his Lambourne stables.*

galore /gə'lɔː/. ADJ You use **galore** to emphasize that something you like exists in very large quantities. *There were bargains galore.*

galvanize (BRIT also **galvanise**) /'gælvənaɪz/ **galvanizes, galvanizing, galvanized.** VERB If you **are galvanized into** doing something, you are motivated by excitement, fear, or anger into doing it straight away. *These murders may galvanise the country into throwing the weight of the state against racial violence.*

gamble /'gæmbəl/ **gambles, gambling, gambled.** ▢1 VERB & N-SING If you **gamble on** something, or if you take a **gamble**, you take a risky action or decision in the hope of gaining money, success, or an advantage. *Few firms will be willing to gamble on new products... They are not prepared to gamble their careers on this matter. ...the French president's risky gamble in calling a referendum.* ▢2 VERB If you **gamble**, you bet money on the result of a game, a race, or competition. *John gambled heavily on the horses... He gambled away his family estates.*
◆ **gambler, gamblers** N-COUNT *I used to be a very heavy gambler.* ◆ **gambling** N-UNCOUNT *The laws regulating gambling are quite tough.*

★ **game** /geɪm/ **games.** ▢1 N-COUNT A **game** is an activity or sport usually involving skill, knowledge, or chance, in which you follow fixed rules and try to win against an opponent or to solve a puzzle. *...the wonderful game of football.* ▢2 N-COUNT In sport, a **game** is a match, or part of a match. *We won three games against Australia. ...the last three points of the second game.* ▢3 N-PLURAL **Games** are organized events involving several different sports. *...the 1996*

a
b
c
d
e
f
g
h
i
j
k
l
m
n
o
p
q
r
s
t
u
v
w
x
y
z

Olympic Games. **4** N-COUNT You can describe a way of behaving as a **game** when it is used to try to gain advantage. *The Americans have been playing a very delicate political game.* **5** N-UNCOUNT **Game** is wild animals or birds that are hunted for sport or food. **6** ADJ AFTER LINK-V If you say that someone is **game** or **game for** something, you mean that they are willing to do something new, unusual, or risky. *He still had new ideas and was game to try them... He said he's game for a similar challenge next year.*

PHRASES ● If someone or something **gives the game away**, they reveal a secret or reveal their feelings. *The faces of the two conspirators gave the game away!* ● If you beat someone **at their own game**, you use the same methods that they have used, but more successfully, so that you gain an advantage over them. ● If you say that something is **the name of the game**, you mean that it is the most important aspect of the activity you are talking about. *In the current economic climate, survival is the name of the game.*

gaming /'geɪmɪŋ/. N-UNCOUNT **Gaming** means the same as **gambling**, especially at cards, roulette, and other games of chance.

⭐ **gang** /gæŋ/ **gangs, ganging, ganged.** **1** N-COUNT A **gang** is a group of people who join together for some purpose, often criminal. *...members of a rival gang. ...a gang of masked robbers.* **2** N-COUNT A **gang** is a group of manual workers who work together. *...a gang of labourers.*

▶ **gang up.** PHR-VERB If people **gang up on** someone, they unite against them. [INFORMAL] *All the girls in my class seemed to gang up on me.*

gangster /'gæŋstə/ **gangsters.** N-COUNT A **gangster** is a member of a group of violent criminals.

gaol /dʒeɪl/. See **jail**.

⭐ **gap** /gæp/ **gaps.** **1** N-COUNT A **gap** is a space between two things or a hole in something solid. *...the wind tearing through gaps in the window frames.* **2** N-COUNT A **gap** is a period of time when you are not doing what you normally do. *There followed a gap of four years, during which William joined the Army.* **3** N-COUNT If there is something missing from a situation which prevents it from being complete, you can also say that there is a **gap**. *Tony recognised a gap in the market for a true specialist in cheese.* **4** N-COUNT A **gap** is a great difference between two things, people, or ideas. *...the gap between rich and poor... America's trade gap widened.*

gape /geɪp/ **gapes, gaping, gaped.** **1** VERB If you **gape**, you look at someone or something in surprise, with your mouth open. *His secretary stopped taking notes to gape at me.* **2** VERB If you say that something such as a hole or a wound **gapes**, you are emphasizing that it is deep or wide. *A hole gaped in the roof.* ♦ **gaping** ADJ *...a gaping wound in her back.*

'**gap year.** N-SING A **gap year** is a period of time during which a student takes a break from studying after they have finished school and before they start college or university. [BRITISH]

garage /'gæraːʒ, -rɪdʒ, AM gə'raːʒ/ **garages.** **1** N-COUNT A **garage** is a building in which you keep a car. **2** N-COUNT A **garage** is a place where you can get your car repaired, buy a car, or buy petrol.

garbage /'gaːbɪdʒ/. N-UNCOUNT In American English, **garbage** is rubbish, especially waste from a kitchen. The usual British word is **rubbish**. *...garbage collection.*

> **USAGE** In American English, the words **garbage** and **trash** are most commonly used to refer to waste material that is thrown away. *...the smell of rotting garbage... She threw the bottle into the trash.* In British English, **rubbish** is the usual word. **Garbage** and **trash** are sometimes used in British English, but only informally and metaphorically. *I don't have to listen to this garbage... The book was trash* .

⭐ **garden** /'gaːdən/ **gardens, gardening, gardened.** **1** N-COUNT In British English, a **garden** is an area of land next to a house, with plants, trees, and grass. The usual American word is **yard**. **2** VERB If you **are gardening**, you are doing work in your garden such as weeding or planting. ♦ **gardener, gardeners** N-COUNT *...a keen gardener.* ♦ **gardening** N-UNCOUNT *I have taken up gardening again.* **3** N-COUNT **Gardens** are a park with plants, trees, and grass. *...the botanical gardens.*

garish /'geərɪʃ/. ADJ If you describe something as **garish**, you dislike it because it is very bright in an unattractive, showy way. *...garish, illuminated signs.*

garland /'gaːlənd/ **garlands.** N-COUNT A **garland** is a circular decoration made from flowers and leaves, worn round the neck or head.

garlic /'gaːlɪk/. N-UNCOUNT **Garlic** is the small, white, round bulb of a plant related to the onion plant, which is used as a flavouring. *...a clove of garlic.*

garment /'gaːmənt/ **garments.** N-COUNT A **garment** is a piece of clothing. [FORMAL] ● See note at **clothes**.

garner /'gaːnə/ **garners, garnering, garnered.** VERB If you say that someone has **garnered** something useful or valuable, you mean that they have collected or gained it. [FORMAL]

garnish /'gaːnɪʃ/ **garnishes, garnishing, garnished.** **1** N-VAR A **garnish** is a small amount of herbs, salad, or other food that is used to decorate prepared food. **2** VERB To **garnish** food means to decorate it with a garnish.

garrison /'gærɪsən/ **garrisons.** N-COUNT A **garrison** is a group of soldiers whose job is to guard the town or building where they live. You can also refer to the buildings which the soldiers live in as a **garrison**.

⭐ **gas** /gæs/ **gases, gasses, gassing, gassed.**

> ✔ The form **gases** is the plural of the noun. The form **gasses** is the third person singular of the verb.

☐1☐ N-VAR A **gas** is any substance that is neither liquid nor solid, such as oxygen or hydrogen. Some gases burn easily and are used as a fuel for heating and cooking. ...*gas and dust from the volcanic eruption.* ● See also **tear gas.** ☐2☐ N-VAR **Gas** is a poisonous gas that can be used as a weapon. ...*mustard gas.* ☐3☐ VERB To **gas** a person or animal means to kill them by making them breathe poisonous gas. ☐4☐ N-UNCOUNT In American English, **gas** is the liquid used as a fuel for motor vehicles. The British word is **petrol.**

gash /gæʃ/ **gashes, gashing, gashed.** ☐1☐ N-COUNT A **gash** is a long deep cut. ☐2☐ VERB If you **gash** something, you accidentally make a long deep cut in it. *He gashed his leg while felling trees.*

'**gas mask, gas masks.** N-COUNT A **gas mask** is a device worn over someone's face in order to protect them from poisonous gases.

gasoline /'gæsəli:n/. N-UNCOUNT In American English, **gasoline** is the liquid used as a fuel for motor vehicles. The British word is **petrol.**

gasp /gɑːsp, gæsp/ **gasps, gasping, gasped.** VERB & N-COUNT If you **gasp,** or if you give a **gasp,** you take a short, quick breath through your mouth, especially when you are surprised or in pain. *She gasped for air... An audible gasp went round the court.*

gastric /'gæstrɪk/. ADJ BEFORE N **Gastric** is used to describe things which occur in the stomach. [TECHNICAL] ...*gastric ulcers.*

▪ **gate** /geɪt/ **gates.** ☐1☐ N-COUNT A **gate** is a structure like a door which is used at the entrance to a field, a garden, or the grounds of a building. ☐2☐ N-COUNT In an airport, a **gate** is an exit through which passengers reach their aeroplane. ...*the departure gate.*

gateway /'geɪtweɪ/ **gateways.** ☐1☐ N-COUNT A **gateway** is an entrance where there is a gate. *The ruined castle has an attractive gateway.* ☐2☐ N-COUNT A **gateway to** something is a way of reaching, achieving, or discovering it. *New York is the great gateway to America.*

▪ **gather** /'gæðə/ **gathers, gathering, gathered.** ☐1☐ VERB When people **gather** somewhere, or if someone **gathers** them there, they come together in a group. *We gathered around the fireplace... The man signalled for me to gather the children together.* ☐2☐ VERB & PHR-VERB If you **gather** things, or if you **gather** them **up,** you collect them together. *I suggest we gather enough firewood to last the night. ...a private detective using a hidden tape recorder to gather information... I needed a few minutes to gather my thoughts... When Sutcliffe had gathered up his papers, he went out.* ☐3☐ VERB If something **gathers** speed, momentum, or force, it gradually becomes faster or more powerful. *Demands for his dismissal have gathered momentum in recent weeks.* ☐4☐ VERB You use **gather** in expressions such as '**I gather**' and '**as far as I can gather**' when you are introducing information that you have found out, especially when you have found it out in an indirect way. *I gather his report is highly critical of the trial judge...*

'He speaks English,' she said to Graham.— 'I gathered that.'
▸ **gather up.** See **gather** 2.

gathering /'gæðərɪŋ/ **gatherings.** N-COUNT A **gathering** is a group of people meeting together. ...*polite social gatherings.*

gaudy /'gɔːdi/ **gaudier, gaudiest.** ADJ If you describe something as **gaudy,** you mean it is very bright-coloured and obvious, and often you are suggesting that it is vulgar. ...*gaudy fake jewellery.*

gauge /geɪdʒ/ **gauges, gauging, gauged.** ☐1☐ VERB If you **gauge** something, you measure it or judge it. *He gauged the wind at over thirty knots... To gauge consumer reaction, we canvassed shoppers in London's West End.* ☐2☐ N-COUNT A **gauge** is a device that measures the amount or quantity of something and shows the amount measured. ...*temperature gauges.* ☐3☐ N-SING A **gauge of** a situation is a fact or event that can be used to judge it. *They run businesses and see money as a gauge of efficiency.*

gaunt /gɔːnt/. ADJ If someone looks **gaunt,** they look very thin, usually because of illness.

gauntlet /'gɔːntlɪt/ **gauntlets.** N-COUNT **Gauntlets** are long, thick, protective gloves.
PHRASES ● If you **run the gauntlet,** you are attacked or criticized by a lot of hostile people, especially because you are obliged to pass through a group of them. *She was forced to run a gauntlet of some 300 jeering demonstrators.* ● If you **throw down the gauntlet** to someone, you say or do something that challenges them to argue or compete with you. If someone **takes up the gauntlet,** they accept a challenge that has been offered.

gave /geɪv/. **Gave** is the past tense of **give.**

★ **gay** /geɪ/ **gays; gayer, gayest.** ☐1☐ ADJ & N-PLURAL **Gay** people or **gays** are homosexuals. ☐2☐ ADJ **Gay** means lively and cheerful. [DATED] *I felt almost gay as I waited for Hank.*

gaze /geɪz/ **gazes, gazing, gazed.** ☐1☐ VERB If you **gaze at** someone or something, you look steadily at them for a long time. *He gazed reflectively at the fire... The girls stood still, gazing around the building.* ☐2☐ N-COUNT You can talk about someone's **gaze** as a way of describing how they are looking at something, especially when they are looking steadily at it. *She felt increasingly uncomfortable under the woman's steady gaze.*

USAGE The verbs **gaze** and **stare** are both used to talk about looking at something for a long time. If you **gaze at** something, it is often because you think it is marvellous or impressive. *A fresh-faced little girl gazes in wonder at the bright fairground lights.* If you **stare at** something or someone, it is often because you think they are strange or shocking. *Various families came out and stared at us.*

gazette /gə'zet/ **gazettes.** N-COUNT A **gazette** is a newspaper or journal. ...*the Arkansas Gazette.*

GCE /ˌdʒiː siː 'iː/ **GCEs.** N-VAR A **GCE** is an examination taken by British school students at Advanced level, during their last year at school. **GCE** is an abbreviation for 'General Certificate of Education'. ● See also **A level.**

GCSE /ˌdʒiː siː es 'iː/ **GCSEs.** N-VAR A **GCSE** is an examination taken by British school students when they are fifteen or sixteen years old. **GCSE** is an abbreviation for 'General Certificate of Secondary Education'.

⭐ **gear** /gɪə/ **gears, gearing, geared.** [1] N-COUNT A **gear** is a piece of machinery, for example in a car or on a bicycle, which controls the rate at which energy is converted into motion. When a vehicle's engine is operating at a particular rate, you can say it is **in** a particular **gear**. *The car was in fourth gear... He put the truck in gear and drove on.* [2] N-UNCOUNT The **gear** for a particular activity is the equipment and special clothes that you use. ...*fishing gear.* [3] ADJ If someone or something is **geared to** or **geared towards** a particular purpose, they are organized or designed in order to achieve that purpose. *My training was geared towards winning gold in Munich.*

▸**gear up.** PHR-VERB If someone **is gearing up** for a particular activity, they are preparing to do it. If they **are geared up for** it, they are prepared and able to do it. *All the parties will be gearing up for a general election... The factory was geared up to make 1,100 cars a day.*

gearbox /'gɪəbɒks/ **gearboxes.** N-COUNT A **gearbox** is the system of gears in an engine or vehicle.

gee /dʒiː/. EXCLAM People sometimes say **gee** in order to express a strong reaction to something or to introduce a remark or response. [AMERICAN, INFORMAL] *Gee, it's hot.*

geese /giːs/. **Geese** is the plural of **goose.**

gel (or **jell**) /dʒel/ **gels, gelling, gelled.** [1] VERB If people, things, or ideas **gel**, they or their different parts begin to work well together to form a successful whole. *They have gelled very well with the rest of the team. ...episodes that never quite manage to gel into a plot.* [2] N-VAR **Gel** is a smooth, soft, jelly-like substance, especially one used to keep your hair in a particular style.

gem /dʒem/ **gems.** [1] N-COUNT A **gem** is a jewel. ...*precious gems.* [2] N-COUNT If you describe something or someone as a **gem**, you mean that they are especially good or helpful. ...*a gem of a hotel.*

gender /'dʒendə/ **genders.** [1] N-VAR A person's **gender** is the fact that they are male or female. *Women are sometimes denied opportunities solely because of their gender.* [2] N-COUNT You can refer to all male people or all female people as a particular **gender**. ...*the different abilities and skills of the two genders.*

⭐ **gene** /dʒiːn/ **genes.** N-COUNT A **gene** is the part of

a cell in a living thing which controls its physical characteristics, growth, and development.

genealogy /ˌdʒiːni'ælədʒi/ **genealogies.** [1] N-UNCOUNT **Genealogy** is the study of the history of families. ◆ **genealogical** /ˌdʒiːniə'lɒdʒɪkəl/ ADJ BEFORE N ...*genealogical research on his family.* [2] N-COUNT A **genealogy** is the history of a family over several generations.

genera /'dʒenərə/. **Genera** is the plural of **genus.**

⭐ **general** /'dʒenrəl/ **generals.** [1] N-COUNT & N-TITLE A **general** is an officer of a high rank in the armed forces. [2] ADJ BEFORE N If you talk about the **general** situation somewhere or if you talk about something in **general** terms, you are describing the situation as a whole rather than considering its details or exceptions. *The figures represent a general decline in employment... She recounted in very general terms some of the events of recent months.* [3] ADJ BEFORE N You use **general** to describe something that involves or affects most people, or most people in a group. ...*general awareness about bullying.* [4] ADJ BEFORE N **General** is used to describe something that is not restricted to any one thing or area. ...*a general store. ...a general ache radiating from the back of the neck. ...a general sense of well-being.* [5] ADJ BEFORE N **General** is used to describe a person who has an average amount of knowledge or interest in a particular subject. *This book is intended for the general reader.* [6] ADJ BEFORE N **General** is used to describe someone's job, to indicate that they have responsibility for the whole of an organization. *He is the general manager of the museum.* [7] See also **generally.**
PHRASES ● You say **in general** when you are talking about the whole of a situation without going into details, or when you are referring to most people or things in a group. *We need to improve our educational system in general... People in general will support us.* ● **In general** is used to indicate that a statement is true in most cases. *In general, it was the better-educated voters who voted Yes.*

⭐ **general e'lection, general elections.** N-COUNT A **general election** is an election for a new government, in which all the citizens of a country may vote.

generalize (BRIT also **generalise**) /'dʒenrəlaɪz/ **generalizes, generalizing, generalized.** VERB If you **generalize**, you say something that is true in most cases. *It is virtually impossible to generalize about the state of the country's health.* ◆ **generalization, generalizations** N-VAR *You cannot make sweeping generalizations out of the isolated cases.*

generalized (BRIT also **generalised**) /'dʒenrəlaɪzd/. ADJ **Generalized** means involving many different things, rather than one or two specific things. *The symptoms may have become more generalized and less easily detected.*

⭐ **generally** /'dʒenrəli/. [1] ADV You use **generally** to summarize a situation, activity, or idea without referring to the particular details of it. *University teachers generally have admitted a lack of enthusiasm.* [2] ADV You use **generally** to say that something happens or is used on most occasions but not on every occasion. *As women we generally say and feel too much.*

,general prac'titioner, general practitioners.
N-COUNT A **general practitioner** is a doctor who treats all types of illnesses instead of specializing in one area of medicine. The abbreviation **GP** is also used.

,general 'public. N-SING The **general public** is all the people in a society. *You get to know what the general public is really thinking.*

★ generate /'dʒenəreɪt/ generates, generating, generated. [1] VERB To **generate** something means to cause it to begin and develop. *The reforms would generate new jobs.* [2] VERB To **generate** electricity or other forms of energy means to produce it. *...solar panels for generating power.* ◆ **generation** N-UNCOUNT *...the fuels used for electricity generation.*

★ generation /,dʒenə'reɪʃən/ generations. [1] N-COUNT A **generation** consists of all the people in a group or country who are of a similar age. *He's of a younger generation. ...the leading American playwright of his generation.* [2] N-COUNT A **generation** is the period of time that it takes for children to grow up and become adults and have children of their own. *Its centuries-old culture will be wiped out within a few generations.* [3] N-COUNT You can use **generation** to refer to a stage of development in the design and manufacture of machines or equipment. *...the next generation of computers.*

generator /'dʒenəreɪtə/ generators. N-COUNT A **generator** is a machine which produces electricity.

generic /dʒɪ'nerɪk/ generics. [1] ADJ BEFORE N **Generic** means applying to a whole group of similar things. [FORMAL] *Parmesan is a generic term used to describe a family of hard Italian cheeses.* [2] N-COUNT & ADJ A **generic** or a **generic** drug is a drug that does not have a trademark and is known by a general name. [TECHNICAL]

★ generous /'dʒenərəs/. [1] ADJ A **generous** person gives more of something, especially money, than is usual or expected. *German banks are more generous in their lending... The gift is generous by any standards.* ◆ **generosity** /,dʒenə'rɒsɪti/ N-UNCOUNT *She is well known for her generosity.* ◆ **generously** ADV *...the judges who gave so generously of their time.* [2] ADJ **Generous** means friendly, helpful, and willing to see the good qualities in people or things. *That's a very generous interpretation of what he said.* ◆ **generously** ADV *He said, very generously, that the campaign had been a huge success.* [3] ADJ Something that is **generous** is much larger than is usual or necessary. *...a generous portion of spaghetti.* ◆ **generously** ADV *Sprinkle generously with sugar.*

,genetically 'modified. ADJ **Genetically modified** plants and animals have had one or more genes changed. The abbreviation **GM** is often used. *... genetically modified foods.*

genetics /dʒɪ'netɪks/.

☑ The form **genetic** is used as a modifier.

[1] N-UNCOUNT **Genetics** is the study of how characteristics are passed from one generation to another by means of genes. [2] ADJ **Genetic** means concerned with genetics or genes. *...genetic scientists.* ◆ **genetically** ADV *...genetically altered tomatoes.*

genial /'dʒiːniəl/. ADJ A **genial** person is kind and friendly. ◆ **genially** ADV *Liz laughed genially.* ◆ **geniality** N-UNCOUNT *...his habitual geniality.*

genitals /'dʒenɪtəls/. N-PLURAL Your **genitals** are your external sexual organs.

genius /'dʒiːniəs/ geniuses. [1] N-UNCOUNT **Genius** is very great ability or skill in something. *...his genius for chess.* [2] N-COUNT A **genius** is a highly intelligent, creative, or talented person.

genocide /'dʒenəsaɪd/. N-UNCOUNT **Genocide** is the murder of a whole community or race. [FORMAL]

genre /'ʒɒnrə/ genres. N-COUNT A **genre** is a particular style of literature, art, or music. [FORMAL] *...novels in the horror genre.*

gent /dʒent/ gents. [1] N-COUNT A **gent** is a gentleman. [DATED] [2] N-SING People sometimes refer to a men's public toilet as **the gents**. [BRITISH, INFORMAL]

genteel /dʒen'tiːl/. ADJ A **genteel** person is polite, respectable, and refined. *...a genteel middle-class family.*

★ gentle /'dʒentəl/ gentler, gentlest. [1] ADJ A **gentle** person is kind, mild, and calm. *...a quiet and gentle man. ...her gentle nature.* ◆ **gently** ADV *She smiled gently.* ◆ **gentleness** N-UNCOUNT *...his gentleness towards the children.* [2] ADJ If an action is **gentle**, it has little force. *...light, gentle strokes. ...a gentle breeze.* ◆ **gently** ADV *Patrick took her gently by the arm.* [3] ADJ A **gentle** slope or curve is not steep or severe. *...gentle, rolling meadows.* ◆ **gently** ADV *...a gently sloping hill.* [4] ADJ A **gentle** heat is a fairly low heat.

★ gentleman /'dʒentəlmən/ gentlemen. [1] N-COUNT A **gentleman** is a man from a family of high social standing. *...the traditional country gentleman.* [2] N-COUNT A **gentleman** is a man who is polite and well-educated. *He was always such a gentleman.* [3] N-COUNT You can refer politely to men as **gentlemen**. *This way, please, gentlemen.*

gentry /'dʒentri/. N-PLURAL The **gentry** are people of high social status. [BRITISH, DATED]

★ genuine /'dʒenjuɪn/. [1] ADJ Something that is **genuine** is real and exactly what it appears to be. *...genuine leather... They're convinced the picture is genuine.* ◆ **genuinely** ADV *I was genuinely surprised.* [2] ADJ Someone who is **genuine** is

a b c d e f g h i j k l m n o p q r s t u v w x y z

honest and sincere. *She was a very genuine woman.*

genus /ˈdʒɛnəs, AM ˈdʒiː-/ **genera**. N-COUNT A **genus** is a class or group of similar animals or plants. [TECHNICAL]

geographical /ˌdʒiːəˈɡræfɪkəl/ (or **geographic** /ˌdʒiːəˈɡræfɪk/). ADJ **Geographical** means relating to geography. *...a vast geographical area.* ♦ **geographically** ADV *Geographically, it's the highest point in London.*

geography /dʒiˈɒɡrəfi/ **1** N-UNCOUNT **Geography** is the study of the countries of the world and of such things as land formations, seas, and climate. **2** N-UNCOUNT The **geography** of a place is the way that features such as rivers, mountains, and towns are arranged. *...policemen who knew the local geography.*

geology /dʒiˈɒlədʒi/. **1** N-UNCOUNT **Geology** is the study of the earth's structure, surface, and origins. ♦ **geological** /ˌdʒiːəˈlɒdʒɪkəl/ ADJ *...a lengthy geological survey.* ♦ **geologist**, **geologists** N-COUNT *...the latest discovery by geologists in Australia.* **2** N-UNCOUNT The **geology** of an area is the structure of its land.

geometric /ˌdʒiːəˈmetrɪk/. **1** ADJ **Geometric** means relating to geometry. *...geometric laws.* **2** ADJ **Geometric** patterns or shapes consist of regular shapes or lines. *...geometric designs.*

geometry /dʒiˈɒmɪtri/. **1** N-UNCOUNT **Geometry** is a mathematical science concerned with the measurement of lines, angles, curves, and shapes. **2** N-UNCOUNT The **geometry** of an object is its shape or the relationship of its parts to each other. [FORMAL] *...the geometry of the car's nose.*

geriatric /ˌdʒeriˈætrɪk/. ADJ BEFORE N **Geriatric** is used to describe things relating to the illnesses and medical care of old people. [TECHNICAL] *...the future of geriatric care.*

germ /dʒɜːm/ **germs**. **1** N-COUNT A **germ** is a very small organism that causes disease. *...cholera germs.* **2** N-COUNT The **germ of** something such as an idea is the beginning of it.

germinate /ˈdʒɜːmɪneɪt/ **germinates, germinating, germinated**. VERB If a seed **germinates** or **is germinated**, it starts to grow. [TECHNICAL] *Heat will encourage seeds to germinate.* ♦ **germination** N-UNCOUNT *To speed up germination, it is worth soaking the seed in water.*

⭐ **gesture** /ˈdʒestʃə/ **gestures, gesturing, gestured**. **1** VERB & N-COUNT If you **gesture**, you use movements of your hands or head called **gestures** to convey a message or feeling. *She gestured towards the front door... With a gesture of the head, she beckoned him back.* **2** N-COUNT A **gesture** is something that you say or do in order to express your attitude or intentions. *Iraq said it made the offer as a gesture of goodwill.*

get 1 changing, causing, moving, or reaching

⭐ **get** /ɡet/ **gets, getting, got** (AM also **gotten**).

✓ In most of its uses **get** is a fairly informal word.

1 LINK-VERB **Get** often has the same meaning as 'become'. For example, if something **gets** cold, it becomes cold. *The boys were getting bored... From here on, it can only get better... It's getting late.* **2** **Get** is often used in place of 'be' as an auxiliary verb to form the passive. *Does she ever get asked for her autograph?... A pane of glass got broken.* **3** VERB If someone or something **gets** into a particular state or situation, or if someone or something **gets** them into it, they start being in that state or situation. *Perhaps I shouldn't say that – I might get into trouble... How did we get into this recession... I don't know if I can get it clean... Brian will get them out of trouble.* **4** VERB To **get** somewhere means to move or arrive there. *I got off the bed and opened the door... Generally I get to work at 9.30am... It was dark by the time she got home.* **5** VERB If you **get** something or someone into a particular place or position, you move them there by means of a particular action or effort. *Mack got his wallet out... Go and get your coat on... The UN was supposed to be getting aid to where it was most needed.* **6** VERB If you **get** someone to do something, they do it because you asked, persuaded, or told them to do it. *Tom's on the phone. Can I get him to call you back?* **7** VERB If you **get** something done, you arrange for it to be done. *I have to get my car repaired.* **8** VERB If you **get to** do something, you manage to do it or have the opportunity to do it. *Do you get to see him often?... They get to stay in nice hotels.* **9** VERB You can use **get** in expressions like **get moving**, **get going**, and **get working** when you want to tell people to begin moving, going, or working quickly. **10** VERB If you **get** to a particular stage in an activity, you reach that stage. *Patrick had got as far as finding some clients.* **11** VERB If something **gets** you, it annoys you. [INFORMAL] *What gets me is the attitude of so many of the people.*

get 2 obtaining, receiving, or catching

⭐ **get** /ɡet/ **gets, getting, got** (or AM **gotten**). **1** VERB If you **get** something that you want or need, you obtain it or receive it. *The problem was how to get enough food to sustain life... I asked him to get me some information... They get a salary of $11,000 a year... Whenever I get the chance I go to Maxim's for dinner.* **2** VERB If you **get** someone or something, you go and bring them to a particular place. *Go and get your daddy for me... Get me a large brandy.* **3** VERB You can use **you get** instead of 'there is' or 'there are' to say that something exists, happens, or can be experienced. [SPOKEN] *You get a lot of youngsters hanging around the Common.* **4** VERB If you **get** an illness or disease, you become ill with it. *When I was five I got measles.* **5** VERB If you **get** an idea, impression, or feeling, you have it or experience it. *Charles got a shock when he saw him... I get the feeling that you're an honest man.* **6** VERB If you **get** a joke or **get** the point of something, you understand it. **7** VERB When you **get** a train, bus, plane, or boat, you travel by that means of transport. $\boxed{8}$ See also **got**. ● to **give as good as you get**: see **give**.

⭐ **get** /get/ **gets, getting, got** (or AM **gotten**).

▶ **get about.** $\boxed{1}$ PHR-VERB If you **get about**, you move or travel from place to place. *Rail travel through France is the perfect way to get about.* $\boxed{2}$ See **get around**.

▶ **get across.** PHR-VERB If you **get** an idea or argument **across**, you succeed in making people understand it. *Officers felt their point of view was not getting across to ministers... Wally got his message across very well.*

▶ **get along.** PHR-VERB If you **get along with** someone, you have a friendly relationship with them. *It's impossible to get along with him.*

▶ **get around.** $\boxed{1}$ PHR-VERB If you **get around**, you go to a lot of different places as part of your way of life. $\boxed{2}$ PHR-VERB If news **gets around**, **gets about**, or **gets round**, it is told to lots of people. *Word got around that he was taking drugs.* $\boxed{3}$ PHR-VERB If you **get around** or **get round** a difficulty or restriction, you manage to avoid it or deal with it. *Although tobacco ads are prohibited, companies get around the ban by sponsoring music shows.*

▶ **get around to** or **get round to.** PHR-VERB When you **get around to** doing something that you have delayed or have been too busy to do, you finally do it. *I haven't got round to talking to him yet.*

▶ **get at.** $\boxed{1}$ PHR-VERB To **get at** something means to succeed in reaching it. *A goat was standing up against a tree on its hind legs, trying to get at the leaves.* $\boxed{2}$ PHR-VERB If you **get at** someone, you keep criticizing or teasing them in an unkind way. [INFORMAL] *I'm just tired of you getting at me all the time.* $\boxed{3}$ PHR-VERB If you ask someone what they **are getting at**, you ask them to explain what they mean. *What are you getting at now?*

▶ **get away.** $\boxed{1}$ PHR-VERB If you **get away**, you succeed in leaving a place or situation that you do not want to be in. *Dr Dunn was apparently trying to get away when he was shot.* $\boxed{2}$ PHR-VERB If you **get away**, you go away for a period of time in order to have a holiday.

▶ **get away with.** PHR-VERB If you **get away with** doing something wrong or risky, you do not suffer any punishment or other bad consequences because of it. *The criminals know how to play the system and get away with it.*

▶ **get back.** PHR-VERB If you **get** something **back** after you have lost it or after it has been taken from you, you have it again. *You can cancel the contract and get your money back.*

▶ **get back to.** $\boxed{1}$ PHR-VERB If you **get back to** a previous activity or subject, you start doing the activity or talking about the subject again. *I couldn't get back to sleep... We got back to the subject of Tom Halliday.* $\boxed{2}$ PHR-VERB To **get back**

to a previous state or level means to return to it. *Life started to get back to normal.*

▶ **get by.** PHR-VERB If you can **get by** with the few resources you have, you can manage to live or do things satisfactorily. *Melville managed to get by on a small amount of money.*

▶ **get down to.** PHR-VERB When you **get down to** something, you start doing it. *With the election out of the way, the government can get down to business.*

▶ **get in.** $\boxed{1}$ PHR-VERB When a train, bus, or plane **gets in**, it arrives. *Her train gets in at about ten to two.* $\boxed{2}$ PHR-VERB When a political party or a politician **gets in**, they are elected. $\boxed{3}$ PHR-VERB If you **get** something you want to say **in**, you eventually manage to say it, usually in a situation where other people are talking a lot. *It was hard to get a word in.*

▶ **get in on.** PHR-VERB If you **get in on** an activity, you start taking part in it, perhaps without being invited. [INFORMAL] *Now baseball is trying to get in on the European market.*

▶ **get into.** $\boxed{1}$ PHR-VERB If you **get into** an activity, you start doing it or being involved in it. *He was eager to get into politics.* $\boxed{2}$ PHR-VERB If you **get into** a school, college, or university, you are accepted there as a student. $\boxed{3}$ PHR-VERB If you ask what has **got into** someone, you mean that they are behaving in an unexpected way. [INFORMAL] *He didn't know what could have got into him, to steal a watch.*

▶ **get off.** $\boxed{1}$ PHR-VERB If someone who has broken a law or rule **gets off**, they are not punished, or only slightly punished. *He is likely to get off with a small fine.* $\boxed{2}$ PHR-VERB You can tell someone to **get off** when they are touching you and you do not want them to. *I kept telling him to get off... 'Get off me!' I screamed.*

▶ **get off with.** PHR-VERB If you **get off with** someone, you have a romantic or sexual encounter with them. [INFORMAL]

▶ **get on.** $\boxed{1}$ PHR-VERB If you **get on with** someone, you have a friendly relationship with them. *I get on very well with his wife.* $\boxed{2}$ PHR-VERB If you **get on with** an activity, you continue doing it or start doing it. *Jane got on with her work.* $\boxed{3}$ PHR-VERB If someone **is getting on** well or badly, they are making good or bad progress. *Livy's getting on very well in Russian.* $\boxed{4}$ PHR-VERB If you try to **get on**, you try to be successful in your career. *She's keen. She's ambitious. She wants to get on.* $\boxed{5}$ PHR-VERB If someone **is getting on**, they are getting old. [INFORMAL]

▶ **get on to.** $\boxed{1}$ PHR-VERB If you **get on to** a particular topic, you start talking about it. *We got on to the subject of relationships.* $\boxed{2}$ PHR-VERB If you **get on to** someone, you contact them. *I got on to him and explained some of the things.*

▶ **get out.** $\boxed{1}$ PHR-VERB If you **get out of** a place or situation, you leave it. *I told him to leave and get out... Getting out of the contract would be no problem.* $\boxed{2}$ PHR-VERB If you **get out**, you go to places and meet people. *Get out and enjoy*

a b c d e f **g** h i j k l m n o p q r s t u v w x y z

yourself, make new friends. **3** PHR-VERB If news or information **gets out**, it becomes known. *If word got out now, a scandal could be disastrous.*

▸**get out of.** PHR-VERB If you **get out of** doing something that you do not want to do, you avoid doing it. *It's amazing what people will do to get out of paying taxes.*

▸**get over.** **1** PHR-VERB If you **get over** an unpleasant experience or an illness, you recover from it. *It took me a very long time to get over the shock of her death.* **2** PHR-VERB If you **get over** a problem, you manage to deal with it.

▸**get over with.** PHR-VERB If you **get** something unpleasant **over with**, you do it or experience it quickly, since you cannot avoid it. *The sooner we start, the sooner we'll get it over with.*

▸**get round.** **1** See **get around**. **2** PHR-VERB If you **get round** someone, you persuade them to like you or do what you want, by pleasing or flattering them. *Max could always get round her.*

▸**get round to.** See **get around to**.

▸**get through.** **1** PHR-VERB If you **get through** a task, you complete it. *I think you can get through the first two chapters.* **2** PHR-VERB If you **get through** an unpleasant experience or time, you manage to live through it. *It is hard to see how people will get through the winter.* **3** PHR-VERB If you **get through** a large amount of something, you use it up. *You'll get through at least ten nappies a day.* **4** PHR-VERB If you **get through** to someone, you succeed in making them understand what you are trying to say. *An old friend might well be able to get through to her and help her.* **5** PHR-VERB If you **get through to** someone, you succeed in contacting them on the telephone. *I can't get through to this number... I've been trying to ring up all day and I couldn't get through.*

▸**get together.** **1** PHR-VERB When people **get together**, they meet in order to discuss something or to spend time together. **2** PHR-VERB If you collect or assemble things or people for a particular purpose, you can say that you **get** them **together**. *We'll give you three days to get the money together.*

▸**get up.** **1** PHR-VERB If you are sitting or lying and then **get up**, you rise to a standing position. **2** PHR-VERB When you **get up**, you get out of bed. *They have to get up early in the morning.*

▸**get up to.** PHR-VERB If you say that someone **gets up to** something, you mean that they do it and you do not approve of it. [BRITISH] *They get up to all sorts behind your back.*

getaway /ˈgetəweɪ/ **getaways.** N-COUNT When someone makes a **getaway**, they leave a place in a hurry, especially after committing a crime. *They made their getaway on a stolen motorcycle.*

ghastly /ˈgɑːstli, ˈgæstli/ **ghastlier, ghastliest.** ADJ If you describe someone or something as **ghastly**, you mean that they are very unpleasant. *...a mother accompanied by her ghastly unruly child.*

ghetto /ˈgetəʊ/ **ghettos** or **ghettoes.** N-COUNT A **ghetto** is a part of a town in which many poor people or many people of a particular race, religion, or nationality live. *...the black ghettos of New York.*

ghost /gəʊst/ **ghosts.** N-COUNT A **ghost** is the spirit of a dead person that someone believes they can see or feel. *...the ghost of the drowned girl.*

ghostly /ˈgəʊstli/. ADJ Something that is **ghostly** seems unreal or supernatural and may be frightening because of this. *The moon shone, shedding a ghostly light on the fields.*

GI /ˌdʒiː ˈaɪ/ **GIs.** N-COUNT A **GI** is a soldier in the United States army.

⭐ **giant** /ˈdʒaɪənt/ **giants.** **1** ADJ BEFORE N You use **giant** to describe something that is much larger or more important than most other things of its kind. *...Italy's giant car maker, Fiat. ...a giant oak table.* **2** N-COUNT A large successful organization or country can be referred to as a **giant**. [JOURNALISM] *...Japanese electronics giant Sony.* **3** N-COUNT In children's stories, a **giant** is a person who is very big and strong.

gibe /dʒaɪb/. See **jibe**.

giddy /ˈgɪdi/. ADJ If you feel **giddy**, you feel that you are about to fall over, usually because you are not well.

⭐ **gift** /gɪft/ **gifts.** **1** N-COUNT A **gift** is something that you give someone as a present. *...suggestions for Christmas gifts.* **2** N-COUNT If someone has a **gift for** doing something, they have a natural ability for doing it. *He discovered a gift for teaching.*

gifted /ˈgɪftɪd/. ADJ A **gifted** person has a natural ability for doing most things or for doing a particular activity. *...a school for gifted children.*

gig /gɪg/ **gigs.** N-COUNT A **gig** is a live performance by a pop or jazz musician, comedian, or disc jockey. [INFORMAL] *The Stones only do outdoor gigs.*

gigabyte /ˈgɪgəbaɪt/ **gigabytes.** N-COUNT In computing, a **gigabyte** is one thousand and twenty-four megabytes.

gigantic /dʒaɪˈgæntɪk/. ADJ If you describe something as **gigantic**, you are emphasizing that it is extremely large in size, amount, or degree. *...a gigantic oak tree... It's come as a gigantic surprise.*

giggle /ˈgɪgəl/ **giggles, giggling, giggled.** VERB & N-COUNT If you **giggle**, or if you let out a **giggle**, you laugh in a childlike, helpless way. *'I beg your pardon?' she giggled... She gave a little giggle.*

gilded /ˈgɪldɪd/. ADJ If something is **gilded**, it has been covered with a thin layer of gold or gold paint. *...gilded statues.*

gilt /gɪlt/. ADJ A **gilt** object is covered with a thin layer of gold or gold paint.

gimmick /ˈgɪmɪk/ **gimmicks.** N-COUNT A **gimmick** is an unusual and unnecessary feature or action whose purpose is to attract attention or publicity; used showing disapproval. *It is just a public relations gimmick.*

For a full explanation of all grammatical labels, see pages vii-x　　⭐ Bank of English® frequent word

gin /dʒɪn/ **gins. N-VAR** **Gin** is a colourless alcoholic drink.

ginger /'dʒɪndʒə/. **1** N-UNCOUNT **Ginger** is the root of a plant that is used to flavour food. It has a sweet spicy flavour. **2** ADJ & N-UNCOUNT **Ginger** is used to describe something, usually a person's hair, that is orange-brown.

gingerly /'dʒɪndʒəli/. ADV If you do something **gingerly**, you do it in a careful, hesitant manner. [WRITTEN] I drove gingerly past the security check points.

gipsy /'dʒɪpsi/ **gipsies**. See **gypsy**.

giraffe /dʒɪ'rɑːf, -'ræf/ **giraffes**. N-COUNT A **giraffe** is a large African animal with a very long neck, long legs, and dark patches on its body.
→ See picture on page 816.

⭐ **girl** /ɡɜːl/ **girls**. **1** N-COUNT A **girl** is a female child. **2** N-COUNT Young women are often referred to as **girls**. Some people find this use offensive. ...a pretty twenty-year old girl.

'girl band, girl bands. N-COUNT A **girl band** is a band consisting of young women who sing popular music and dance.

girlfriend /'ɡɜːlfrend/ **girlfriends**. **1** N-COUNT Someone's **girlfriend** is a girl or woman with whom they are having a romantic or sexual relationship. He had been going out with his girlfriend for seven months. **2** N-COUNT A **girlfriend** is a female friend. I met a girlfriend for lunch.

girth /ɡɜːθ/ **girths**. N-VAR The **girth** of an object is its width or thickness. [FORMAL] ...a 43 inch long fish with a 9 inch girth.

gist /dʒɪst/. N-SING The **gist of** a speech, conversation, or piece of writing is its general meaning. I could not get the gist of their conversation.

give 1 used with nouns describing actions

⭐ **give** /ɡɪv/ **gives, giving, gave, given**. **1** VERB You can use **give** with nouns that refer to physical actions. The whole expression refers to the performing of the action. For example, 'She gave a smile' means almost the same as 'She smiled'. George gave a tremendous yawn... She gave my hand a quick squeeze. **2** VERB You use **give** to say that a person does a particular thing for someone else. For example, if you **give** someone a lift, you take them somewhere in your car. She began to give piano lessons to some of the local children... He was given mouth-to-mouth resuscitation. **3** VERB You use **give** with nouns that refer to information, opinions, or greetings to indicate that something is communicated. For example, if you **give** someone some news, you tell it to them. He gave no details... He asked me to give his regards to all of you. **4** VERB If someone or something **gives** you a particular idea, impression, or feeling, they cause you to have it. They gave me the impression that they were doing exactly what they wanted... It will give great pleasure to many thousands of children. **5** VERB If you **give** something thought or attention, you

think about it or deal with it. I've been giving it some thought... Priority will be given to those who apply early. **6** VERB If you **give** a speech or a performance, you speak or perform in public. ...Mrs Butler who gave us such an interesting talk last year. **7** VERB If you **give** a party or other social event, you organize it.

give 2 transferring

⭐ **give** /ɡɪv/ **gives, giving, gave, given**. **1** VERB If you **give** someone something that you own or have bought, you provide them with it, so that they have it or can use it. Many leading industrialists gave money to the Conservative Party... She gave me a doll for my birthday. **2** VERB If you **give** someone something that you are holding or that is near you, you pass it to them, so that they are then holding it. He pulled a handkerchief from his pocket and gave it to him. **3** VERB To **give** someone or something a particular right or power means to allow them to have it. ...a citizen's charter giving rights to gays.

give 3 other uses, phrases, and phrasal verbs

⭐ **give** /ɡɪv/ **gives, giving, gave, given**. **1** VERB If something **gives**, it collapses or breaks under pressure. My knees gave under me. **2** VERB You use **give** in phrases such as **I'd give anything**, **I'd give my right arm**, and **what wouldn't I give** to emphasize that you are very keen to do or have something. I'd give anything to be like you.
PHRASES ● If someone **gives as good as** they get, they fight or argue as well or intensely as the person they are fighting or arguing with. ● If you say something requires **give and take**, you mean that people must compromise for it to be successful. ● **Give or take** is used to indicate that an amount is approximate. They grow to a height of 12 inches – give or take a couple of inches. ● to **give way**: see **way**.

▶**give away. 1** PHR-VERB If you **give away** something that you own, you give it to someone because you no longer want it. He was giving his collection away for nothing. **2** PHR-VERB If you **give away** information that should be kept secret, you reveal it to other people. Her voice gave nothing away.

▶**give back.** PHR-VERB If you **give** something **back**, you return it to the person who gave it to you. I gave the textbook back to him.

▶**give in. 1** PHR-VERB If you **give in**, you admit that you are defeated or that you cannot do something. All right. I give in. What did you do with the ship? **2** PHR-VERB If you **give in**, you agree to do something that you do not want to do. They won't give in to the workers' demands.

▶**give off** or **give out.** PHR-VERB If something **gives off** or **gives out** a gas, heat, or a smell, it produces it and sends it out into the air. ...natural gas, which gives off less carbon dioxide than coal.

▶**give out.** PHR-VERB If you **give out** a number of things, you distribute them among a group of people. They were giving out leaflets. ● See also **give off**.

A
B
C
D
E
F
G
H
I
J
K
L
M
N
O
P
Q
R
S
T
U
V
W
X
Y
Z

▶**give up.** 1 PHR-VERB If you **give up** something, you stop doing it or having it. *I was trying to give up drugs... The doctors gave up hope as her condition worsened.* 2 PHR-VERB If you **give up**, you decide that you cannot do something and stop trying to do it. *After a fruitless morning sitting at his desk he had given up.* 3 PHR-VERB If you **give up** your job, you resign from it.
▶**give up to.** See **give over to**.

⭐ **given** /'gɪvən/. 1 **Given** is the past participle of **give**. 2 ADJ AFTER LINK-V If you are **given to** doing something, you often do it. [FORMAL] *I am not very given to emotional displays.* 3 ADJ If something happens in a **given** situation, it happens in that particular situation. If something happens at a **given** time, it happens at that particular time. *Do you regularly work for more than 10 hours on any given day?* 4 PREP **Given** is used when indicating a possible situation in which someone has the opportunity or ability to do something. For example, **given the chance** means 'if I had the chance'. *Given patience, successful breeding of this species can be achieved.* 5 CONJ If you say **given that** something is the case, you mean 'taking that fact into account'. *This may seem an odd view to take, given that I am strongly in favour of the Maastricht treaty.* 6 PREP If you say **given** a particular thing, you mean 'taking that thing into account'. *Given the uncertainty over Leigh's future I was left with little other choice.*

glacial /'gleɪʃəl/. ADJ **Glacial** means relating to or produced by glaciers or ice. [TECHNICAL] *...a true glacial landscape with U-shaped valleys.*

glacier /'glæsɪə, AM 'gleɪʃə/glaciers. N-COUNT A **glacier** is a huge mass of ice which moves very slowly, often down a mountain.

⭐ **glad** /glæd/. 1 ADJ AFTER LINK-V If you are **glad about** something, you are happy and pleased about it. *I'm glad I relented in the end... The people seem genuinely glad to see you... I ought to be glad about what happened.* ♦ **gladly** ADV *If this offer is genuine I will gladly accept it.* 2 ADJ If you say that you will be **glad to** do something, you mean that you are willing and eager to do it. *I'll be glad to show you everything.* ♦ **gladly** ADV *If you'd prefer something else I'll gladly have it changed for you.*

glamorous /'glæmərəs/. ADJ If you describe someone or something as **glamorous**, you mean that they are more attractive, exciting, or interesting than ordinary people or things. *...the glamorous lifestyle of the rich and famous.*

glamour (AM **glamor**) /'glæmə/. N-UNCOUNT **Glamour** is the quality of being more attractive, exciting, or interesting than ordinary people or things. *He loved the glamour of show business.*

⭐ **glance** /glɑːns, glæns/glances, glancing, glanced. 1 VERB & N-COUNT If you **glance at** someone or something, or if you give them a **glance**, you look at them very quickly and then look away. *He glanced at his watch... The boys exchanged glances.* 2 VERB If you **glance through** or **at** a newspaper or book, you spend a short time looking at it without reading it carefully. *She*

glanced at her diary. 3 PHRASE If you say that something seems to be true **at first glance**, you mean that it seems to be true when you first see it, but that your first impression may be wrong. *At first glance, everything appeared normal.*

gland /glænd/glands. N-COUNT **Glands** are organs in your body that produce chemical substances which your body needs in order to function. *...sweat glands.*

glare /gleə/glares, glaring, glared. 1 VERB & N-COUNT If you **glare at** someone, or if you give them a **glare**, you look at them angrily. *Joe glared at his brother... The waiter lowered his eyes to avoid Harold's furious glare.* 2 VERB & N-SING If the sun or a light **glares**, it shines with a very bright light which is difficult to look at, called a **glare**. *The sun glared down on the station platform. ...the glare of the headlights.* 3 N-SING If you are in the **glare of** publicity or public attention, you are constantly being watched and talked about by the public.

glaring /'gleərɪŋ/. ADJ If you describe something bad as **glaring**, you mean that it is very obvious. *...glaring errors.* ♦ **glaringly** ADV *It was glaringly obvious.*

⭐ **glass** /glɑːs, glæs/glasses. 1 N-UNCOUNT **Glass** is the hard transparent substance that windows and bottles are made from. *...a pane of glass. ...a sliding glass door.* 2 N-COUNT A **glass** is a container made of glass which you can drink from. *Jack held his glass out and Carl poured it full... I drank a glass of water.* 3 N-UNCOUNT Objects made of glass can be referred to as **glass**. *...a glittering array of glass.* 4 N-PLURAL **Glasses** are two lenses in a frame that some people wear in front of their eyes in order to see better. *He took off his glasses.*

glaze /gleɪz/glazes. N-COUNT A **glaze** is a thin layer of a hard shiny substance on a piece of pottery.

glazed /gleɪzd/. 1 ADJ If someone's eyes are **glazed**, their expression is dull or dreamy, because they are tired or are having difficulty concentrating. *There was a glazed look in her eyes.* 2 ADJ **Glazed** pottery is covered with a thin layer of a hard shiny substance. 3 ADJ A **glazed** window or door has glass in it.

gleam /gliːm/gleams, gleaming, gleamed. 1 VERB & N-SING If an object or the surface of something **gleams**, it shines because it is reflecting light. The light reflecting off something is called a **gleam**. *The cutlery gleamed... I could see the gleam of brass.* 2 N-COUNT A **gleam of** light is a faint light. [WRITTEN] *...the first gleam of dawn.* 3 VERB & N-SING If your eyes **gleam**, or if there is a **gleam** in your eyes, your eyes look bright and show that you are excited or happy. [WRITTEN]

glean /gliːn/gleans, gleaning, gleaned. VERB If you **glean** information, you obtain it slowly and with difficulty. *At present we're gleaning information from all sources.*

glee /gliː/. N-UNCOUNT **Glee** is a feeling of happiness and excitement, often caused by someone else's misfortune. *Investors have reacted with glee.*

gleeful /'gli:fəl/. ADJ Someone who is **gleeful** is happy or excited, often because of someone else's misfortune. ♦ **gleefully** ADV *The media gleefully reports the bitterness between the two groups.*

glib /glɪb/. ADJ If you describe what someone says as **glib**, you disapprove of it because it suggests that something is simple or easy, when this is not the case. ♦ **glibly** ADV *We talk glibly of equality of opportunity.*

glide /glaɪd/**glides, gliding, glided.** [1] VERB If you **glide** somewhere, you move there smoothly and silently. *Waiters glide between tightly packed tables bearing trays.* [2] VERB When birds or aeroplanes **glide**, they float on air currents. *Pelicans glide over the waves.*

glider /'glaɪdə/**gliders.** N-COUNT A **glider** is an aircraft without an engine which flies by floating on air currents.

glimmer /'glɪmə/**glimmers, glimmering, glimmered.** [1] VERB & N-COUNT If something **glimmers**, it produces a faint, often unsteady light called a **glimmer**. *...a few stars still glimmered. ...the glimmer of daylight.* [2] N-COUNT A **glimmer of** something is a faint sign of it. *...the first glimmer of hope.*

glimpse /glɪmps/**glimpses, glimpsing, glimpsed.** [1] VERB & N-COUNT If you **glimpse** someone or something, or if you get a **glimpse** of them, you see them very briefly and not very well. *...a window through which you could glimpse a few of the soldiers inside... I had a glimpse of a swimming pool through the trees.* [2] N-COUNT A **glimpse of** something is a brief experience of it or an idea about it that helps you understand it better. *The trip will give them a glimpse of a world they have barely encountered.*

glint /glɪnt/**glints, glinting, glinted.** [1] VERB & N-COUNT If something **glints**, or if there is a **glint of** light from it, it produces or reflects a quick flash of light. [WRITTEN] *The sea glinted in the sun. ...the glint of gold.* [2] VERB & N-SING If someone's eyes **glint**, they shine and express a particular emotion. You can talk about a **glint** in someone's eyes. [WRITTEN] *...her eyes glinting with pride... Was there a glint of mockery in his eyes?*

glisten /'glɪsən/**glistens, glistening, glistened.** VERB If something **glistens**, it shines, because it is smooth, wet, or oily. *Her eyes glistened with tears. ... a man with glistening black hair.*

glitter /'glɪtə/**glitters, glittering, glittered.** [1] VERB If something **glitters**, it shines and sparkles. *The sunlight made the water glitter.* [2] N-UNCOUNT You can use **glitter** to refer to the superficial attractiveness or excitement connected with something. *...the glitter of the pop world.*

gloat /gləʊt/**gloats, gloating, gloated.** VERB When someone **gloats**, they show great pleasure at their own success or at other people's failure. *No doubt you're gloating over the result.*

★ **global** /'gləʊbəl/. ADJ **Global** means concerning or including the whole world. *...a global ban on nuclear testing.* ♦ **globally** ADV *...products sold globally.*

,**global 'village.** N-SING People sometimes use **global village** to refer to the world as a single community linked together by electronic communications.

,**global 'warming.** N-UNCOUNT The problem of the gradual rise in the earth's temperature is referred to as **global warming**.

globe /gləʊb/**globes.** [1] N-SING You can refer to the Earth as **the globe**. *...performers from around the globe.* [2] N-COUNT A **globe** is a ball-shaped object with a map of the world on it.

gloom /glu:m/. [1] N-SING **Gloom** is a state of partial darkness. *My eyes were becoming accustomed to the gloom.* [2] N-UNCOUNT **Gloom** is a feeling of unhappiness or despair. *...the deepening gloom over the economy.*

gloomy /'glu:mi/**gloomier, gloomiest.** [1] ADJ Something that is **gloomy** is dark and rather depressing. *...the gloomy days of winter.* [2] ADJ If someone is **gloomy**, they are unhappy and have no hope. *They are gloomy about their chances of success.* ♦ **gloomily** ADV *Mark shook his head gloomily.* [3] ADJ If a situation is **gloomy**, it does not give you much hope of success or happiness. *The economic outlook remains gloomy.*

glorify /'glɔ:rɪfaɪ/**glorifies, glorifying, glorified.** VERB If you say that someone **glorifies** something, you mean that they praise it or make it seem good or special, usually when it is not. *...music which glorifies drugs.* ♦ **glorification** /,glɔ:rɪfɪ'keɪʃən/ N-UNCOUNT *...the increasing glorification of violence.*

glorious /'glɔ:riəs/. [1] ADJ If you describe something as **glorious**, you are emphasizing that it is very beautiful and wonderful. *...a glorious rainbow.* ♦ **gloriously** ADV *...a gloriously sunny morning.* [2] ADJ A **glorious** career, victory, or occasion involves great fame or success.

glory /'glɔ:ri/**glories, glorying, gloried.** [1] N-UNCOUNT **Glory** is fame and admiration that you get for an achievement. *It was her moment of glory.* [2] N-UNCOUNT The **glory** of something is its great beauty or quality of being impressive. *Spring arrived in all its glory.*

▸**glory in.** PHR-VERB If you **glory in** a situation or activity, you enjoy it very much. *The workers were glorying in their new-found freedom.*

gloss /glɒs, AM glɔ:s/**glosses, glossing, glossed.** [1] N-SING A **gloss** is a bright shine on a surface. *It gives hair a rich gloss.* [2] N-VAR **Gloss** or **gloss paint** is paint that forms a shiny surface when it dries.

▸**gloss over.** PHR-VERB If you **gloss over** a problem or mistake, you try to make it seem unimportant by ignoring it or by dealing with it very quickly.

glossy /'glɒsi, AM 'glɔ:si/**glossier, glossiest.** [1] ADJ Something that is **glossy** is smooth and shiny. *...glossy black hair.* [2] ADJ BEFORE N **Glossy**

a
b
c
d
e
f
g
h
i
j
k
l
m
n
o
p
q
r
s
t
u
v
w
x
y
z

magazines, brochures, or photographs are produced on expensive shiny paper.

glove /glʌv/ **gloves.** N-COUNT **Gloves** are pieces of clothing which cover your hand and wrist and have individual sections for each finger.

glow /gləʊ/ **glows, glowing, glowed.** [1] VERB & N-COUNT If something **glows**, it produces a dull, steady light called a **glow**. *He blew on the charcoal until it glowed orange. ...the glow of the fire.* [2] VERB If something **glows**, it looks bright because it is reflecting light. *The ship's sails glowed in the morning sun.* [3] VERB & N-SING If someone's skin **glows**, or if there is a **glow** to their skin, it looks healthy and pink, for example because they are excited or have been exercising. *Alison's skin seemed to glow with health.* [4] VERB & N-SING If someone **glows with** an emotion such as pride or pleasure, the expression in their face shows they feel it. A **glow** of something like pride or pleasure is a strong feeling of it. *I felt a glow of achievement.*

glowing /ˈgləʊɪŋ/. ADJ A **glowing** description of someone or something praises them highly. *...glowing school reports.*

glucose /ˈgluːkəʊz, -əʊs/. N-UNCOUNT **Glucose** is a type of sugar.

glue /gluː/ **glues, glueing** (or **gluing**)**, glued.** [1] N-VAR **Glue** is a sticky substance used for joining things together. [2] VERB If you **glue** one object to another, you stick them together, using glue. *Glue the two halves together.* [3] PASSIVE-VERB If you say that someone **is glued to** something, you mean that they are giving it all their attention. *She was glued to the television.*

glum /glʌm/ **glummer, glummest.** ADJ Someone who is **glum** is sad and quiet, because they are disappointed or unhappy. ♦ **glumly** ADV *Charles was sitting glumly in the front seat.*

glut /glʌt/ **gluts.** N-COUNT If there is a **glut** of something such as goods or raw materials, there is so much of it that it cannot all be sold or used.

GM /ˌdʒiː ˈem/. [1] ADJ **GM** crops have had one or more genes changed, for example in order to make them resist pests better. **GM** is an abbreviation for 'genetically modified'. *...food containing GM ingredients.* [2] ADJ In Britain, **GM** schools receive money directly from the government rather than from a local authority. **GM** is an abbreviation for 'grant-maintained'. *...GM schools.*

gm. gm is a written abbreviation for **gram.**

ˈGM-free. ADJ **GM-free** products or crops are products or crops that do not contain any genetically modified material. *...GM-free soya.*

GMO /ˌdʒiː em ˈəʊ/ **GMOs.** N-COUNT A **GMO** is an animal, plant, or other organism whose genetic structure has been changed by genetic engineering. **GMO** is an abbreviation for 'genetically modified organism'.

GMT /ˌdʒiː em ˈtiː/. **GMT** is an abbreviation for 'Greenwich Mean Time', the standard time in Great Britain which is used to calculate the time

in the rest of the world.

gnaw /nɔː/ **gnaws, gnawing, gnawed.** [1] VERB If animals or people **gnaw** something, they bite it repeatedly. *Woodlice attack living plants and gnaw at the stems.* [2] VERB If a feeling or thought **gnaws at** you, it causes you to keep worrying. [LITERARY] *...a question gnawed at him. ...gnawing doubts about the whole affair.*

gnome /nəʊm/ **gnomes.** N-COUNT In children's stories, a **gnome** is a tiny old man with a beard and pointed hat.

go 1 moving or leaving

⭐ **go** /gəʊ/ **goes, going, went, gone.**

> ✔ In most cases the past participle of **go** is **gone**, but occasionally you use 'been': see **been.**

[1] VERB When you **go** somewhere, you move or travel there. *We went to Rome... I went home at the weekend... It took us an hour to go three miles.* [2] VERB You use **go** to say that someone leaves the place where they are and does an activity, often a leisure activity. *We went swimming very early... He went for a walk.* [3] VERB When someone **goes to** do something, they move somewhere in order to do it, and they do it. In British English, someone can also **go and** do something. In American English, someone can also **go do** something, but you say that someone **went and** did something. *Paddy had gone to live in Canada... I must go and see this film.* [4] VERB When you **go**, you leave the place where you are. *Let's go.* [5] VERB If you **go to** school, work, or church, you attend it regularly as part of your normal life. *His son went to a top university.* [6] VERB When you say where a road or path **goes**, you are saying where it begins or ends, or what places it is in. *...a mountain road that goes from Blairstown to Millbrook Village.* [7] VERB If you say where money **goes**, you are saying what it is spent on. *Most of my money goes on bills.* [8] VERB If you say that something **goes to** someone, you mean that it is given to them. *A lot of credit must go to the chairman... The job went to Yuri Skokov.* [9] VERB If something **goes**, someone gets rid of it. *100,000 jobs will go.* [10] VERB If something **goes** into something else, it fits into it or it is put into it. *He was trying to push it through the hole and it wouldn't go... This knob goes here... The shoes go on the shoe shelf.* [11] VERB If something such as a piece of machinery **is going**, it is no longer working properly and may soon stop working altogether. You can also talk, for example, about someone's hearing or mental powers **going**. *The battery was going... His eyes are going.* [12] See note at **bring.**

go 2 link verb uses

⭐ **go** /gəʊ/ **goes, going, went, gone.** [1] LINK-VERB You can use **go** to say that someone or something changes to another state or condition. For example, if someone **goes crazy**, they become crazy. *50,000 companies have gone out of business.* [2] LINK-VERB You can use **go** when indicating whether or not someone wears or has something. For example, if someone **goes barefoot**, they do not wear any shoes.

go 3 other verb uses, noun uses, and phrases

go /ɡəʊ/ **goes, going, went, gone.** [1] VERB You use **go** to talk about how successful an event or situation is. For example, if you say that an event **went well**, you mean that it was successful, and if you ask how something **is going**, you are asking how much success people are having with it. [2] VERB If something **goes with** something else, they look or taste nice together. *I was searching for a pair of grey gloves to go with my new gown... Some colours go together and some don't.* [3] N-COUNT A **go** is an attempt at doing something. *I always wanted to have a go at football.* [4] N-COUNT If it is your **go** in a game, it is your turn to do something. [5] See also **going**, **gone**.

> **PHRASES** ● If you **go all out to** do something or **go all out for** something, you make the greatest possible effort to do it or get it. [INFORMAL] ● If someone **has a go at** you, they criticize you, often unfairly. [INFORMAL] ● If someone is **making a go of** something such as a business or relationship, they are beginning to make it successful. ● If you **have** something **on the go**, you have started it and are busy doing it. *Do you like to have many projects on the go at any one time?* ● If someone is always **on the go**, they are busy and active. [INFORMAL] ● If you say that there is a certain amount of time **to go**, you mean that there is that amount of time left before something happens or ends. *There is a week to go until the first German elections.* ● **to go without saying**: see **say**. ● **there you go**: see **there**.

go 4 phrasal verbs

go /ɡəʊ/ **goes, going, went, gone.**
▸**go about.** [1] PHR-VERB The way you **go about** a task or problem is the way you deal with it. [2] PHR-VERB When you **are going about** your normal activities, you are doing them. [3] PHR-VERB If you **go about** in a particular way, you behave or dress in that way. *He went about looking ill and unhappy.*
▸**go after.** PHR-VERB If you **go after** something, you try to get it, catch it, or hit it. *We're not going after civilian targets.*
▸**go against.** PHR-VERB If someone **goes against** your wishes, beliefs, or expectations, their behaviour is the opposite of what you want, believe in, or expect.
▸**go ahead.** [1] PHR-VERB If someone **goes ahead with** something, they begin to do it or make it. [2] PHR-VERB If a process or an organized event **goes ahead**, it takes place or is carried out.
▸**go along with.** [1] PHR-VERB If you **go along with** someone or something such as a rule or an idea, you agree with that person or you accept that idea. [2] PHR-VERB If you **go along with** a person or an idea, you agree with them.
▸**go around** or **go round.** [1] PHR-VERB If you **go around to** or **go round to** someone's house, you visit them at their house. [INFORMAL] [2] PHR-VERB If there is enough of something **to**

go around or **to go round**, there is enough of it for people's needs.
▸**go around with** or **go round with.** PHR-VERB If you **go around with** or **go round with** a person or group of people, you are friends with them and go to places together. [BRITISH]
▸**go back on.** PHR-VERB If you **go back on** a promise or agreement, you do not do what you promised or agreed to do.
▸**go back to.** PHR-VERB If you **go back to** a task or activity, you start doing it again after you have stopped for a period of time.
▸**go before.** PHR-VERB When someone or their case **goes before** a judge, they appear in court as part of a legal process.
▸**go down.** [1] PHR-VERB If a price, level, or amount **goes down**, it becomes lower than it was. *Crime has gone down 70%.* [2] PHR-VERB If you **go down on** your knees or **on** all fours, you lower your body until it is supported by your knees, or by your hands and knees. [3] PHR-VERB When the sun **goes down**, it drops below the horizon. [4] PHR-VERB If a ship **goes down**, it sinks. If a plane **goes down**, it crashes. [5] PHR-VERB If you say that a remark, idea, or type of behaviour **goes down** in a particular way, you mean that it gets that reaction. *Solicitors advised their clients that a tidy look went down well with the magistrates.*
▸**go down with.** PHR-VERB If you **go down with** an illness or a disease, you catch it.
▸**go for.** [1] PHR-VERB If you **go for** a particular thing or way of doing something, you choose it. *People tried to persuade him to go for a more gradual reform programme.* [2] PHR-VERB If you **go for** someone or something, you like them very much. [INFORMAL] *I tend to go for large dark men.* [3] PHR-VERB If someone **goes for** you, they attack you. *Pantieri went for him, gripping him by the throat.*
▸**go in.** PHR-VERB If the sun **goes in**, it becomes covered by a cloud.
▸**go in for.** PHR-VERB If you **go in for** a particular activity, you start doing it.
▸**go into.** [1] PHR-VERB If you **go into** something, you describe it in detail. *I don't want to go into details about what was said.* [2] PHR-VERB If you **go into** a particular occupation, you start doing that job. *Mr Pok has now gone into the tourism business.*
▸**go off.** [1] PHR-VERB If you **go off** something or someone, you stop liking them. [INFORMAL] [2] PHR-VERB If an explosive device or a gun **goes off**, it explodes or fires. [3] PHR-VERB If an alarm bell **goes off**, it makes a sudden loud noise. [4] PHR-VERB If an electrical device **goes off**, it stops operating. *All the lights went off.* [5] PHR-VERB Food or drink that has **gone off** is unfit to eat or drink. [BRITISH]
▸**go on.** [1] PHR-VERB If you **go on** doing something, or **go on with** an activity, you continue to do it. *I'm all right here. Go on with your work.* [2] PHR-VERB If a process or institution **goes on**, it continues to happen or exist. *The*

a
b
c
d
e
f
g
h
i
j
k
l
m
n
o
p
q
r
s
t
u
v
w
x
y
z

A

population failed to understand the necessity for the war to go on. **3** PHR-VERB If something **is going on**, it is happening. *While this conversation was going on, I was listening.* **4** PHR-VERB If you **go on**, you continue saying something or talking about something. *Meer cleared his throat several times before he went on.* **5** PHR-VERB The information you have **to go on** is the information you have available to base an opinion or judgement on. **6** PHR-VERB If an electrical device **goes on**, it begins operating.

▸**go out.** **1** PHR-VERB When you **go out**, you do something enjoyable away from your home, for example you go to a bar or the cinema. **2** PHR-VERB If you **go out with** someone, you have a romantic or sexual relationship with them. **3** PHR-VERB If a light **goes out**, it stops shining. **4** PHR-VERB If flames **go out**, they stop burning. **5** PHR-VERB When the tide **goes out**, the level of sea in a particular place gets lower.

▸**go over.** PHR-VERB If you **go over** a document, incident, or problem, you examine it very carefully and systematically. *An accountant has gone over the books.*

▸**go over to.** **1** PHR-VERB If someone or something **goes over to** a different way of doing things, they change to it. **2** PHR-VERB If you **go over to** a group or political party, you join them after previously belonging to an opposing group or party. *Only a small number of tanks and paratroops have gone over to his side.*

▸**go round.** PHR-VERB **Go round** means the same as **go around**.

▸**go through.** **1** PHR-VERB If you **go through** a difficult experience or period of time, you experience it. **2** PHR-VERB If you **go through** a lot of things such as papers or clothes, you look at them, usually in order to search for a particular item. *Someone had gone through my possessions.* **3** PHR-VERB When someone **goes through** a particular routine, they perform a task in a particular way. **4** PHR-VERB If a law, agreement, or official decision **goes through**, it is approved by a parliament or committee.

▸**go through with.** PHR-VERB If you **go through with** an action you have decided on, you do it, even though it may be very difficult for you.

▸**go towards.** PHR-VERB If an amount of money **goes towards** something, it is used to pay part of the cost of it.

▸**go under.** **1** PHR-VERB If a business **goes under**, it becomes bankrupt. **2** PHR-VERB If a boat or a person **goes under**, they sink below the surface of some water.

▸**go up.** **1** PHR-VERB If a price, amount, or level **goes up**, it becomes higher or greater than it was. **2** PHR-VERB If something **goes up**, it explodes or suddenly starts to burn. *The hotel went up in flames.*

▸**go with.** **1** PHR-VERB If one thing **goes with** another thing, the two things officially belong together, so that if you get one, you also get the other. *...the lucrative £150,000 salary that goes with the job.* **2** PHR-VERB If one thing **goes with**

another thing, they are usually found or experienced together. *...the shame that goes with being on the dole.*

▸**go without.** PHR-VERB If you **go without** something that you need, you do not get it. *I have known what it is like to go without food for days.*

goad /gəʊd/ **goads, goading, goaded.** VERB If you **goad** someone, you deliberately make them angry in order to get them to react in some way. *The psychiatrist was trying to goad him into some unguarded response.*

'go-ahead. **1** N-SING If you give someone **the go-ahead**, you give them permission to do something. *The Greek government today gave the go-ahead for five major road schemes.* **2** ADJ BEFORE N A **go-ahead** person or organization tries hard to succeed, often by using new methods.

⭐ **goal** /gəʊl/ **goals.** **1** N-COUNT In games such as football or hockey, the **goal** is the space into which the players try to get the ball in order to score. **2** N-COUNT In games such as football or hockey, if a player scores a **goal**, they get the ball into the goal. **3** N-COUNT Your **goal** is something that you hope to achieve. *The goal is to raise as much money as possible.*

goalie /'gəʊli/ **goalies.** N-COUNT A **goalie** is a **goalkeeper.** [INFORMAL]

goalkeeper /'gəʊlkiːpə/ **goalkeepers.** N-COUNT A **goalkeeper** is the player in a sports team whose job is to guard the goal.

goalless /'gəʊllɪs/. ADJ In football, a **goalless** game is one which ends with neither team having scored a goal. *The fixture ended in a goalless draw.*

goalpost (or **goal post**) /'gəʊlpəʊst/ **goalposts.** N-COUNT A **goalpost** is one of the two upright posts that are connected by a crossbar and form the goal in games such as football and hockey.

goat /gəʊt/ **goats.** N-COUNT A **goat** is an animal which is a bit bigger than a sheep and has horns. → See picture on page 815.

gobble /'gɒbəl/ **gobbles, gobbling, gobbled.** VERB If you **gobble** food, you eat it quickly and greedily.

'go-between. N-COUNT **go-betweens.** If someone acts as a **go-between**, they take messages between people who are unable or unwilling to meet each other.

⭐ **god** /gɒd/ **gods.** **1** N-PROPER The name **God** is given to the spirit or being who is worshipped as the creator and ruler of the world, especially by Christians, Jews, and Muslims. **2** CONVENTION People sometimes use **God** in exclamations for emphasis, or to express surprise, fear, or excitement. Some people find this use offensive. *Oh my God he's shot somebody.* **3** N-COUNT A **god** is one of the spirits or beings believed in many religions to have power over an aspect of the world. *...Pan, the God of nature.*

goddess /'gɒdes/ **goddesses.** N-COUNT In many religions, a **goddess** is a female spirit or being that is believed to have power over a particular aspect of the world. ...*Diana, the goddess of war.*

goggles /'gɒgəlz/. N-PLURAL **Goggles** are large glasses that fit closely to your face around your eyes to protect them.

going /'gəʊɪŋ/. **1** VERB If you say that something **is going to** happen, you mean that it will happen in the future. *I think it's going to be successful... You're going to enjoy this... He's going to resign.* **2** N-UNCOUNT **The going** is the conditions that affect your ability to do something. *He has her support to fall back on when the going gets tough.* **3** ADJ BEFORE N The **going** rate for something is the usual amount of money that you expect to pay or receive for it. **4** See also **go**.

PHRASES • When you **get going**, you start doing something or start a journey, especially after a delay. • If you **keep going**, you continue doing something difficult or tiring. • If someone or something **has** a lot **going for** them, they have a lot of advantages.

goings-'on. N-PLURAL **Goings-on** are strange, amusing, or improper activities.

gold /gəʊld/ **golds.** **1** N-UNCOUNT **Gold** is a valuable yellow-coloured metal used for making jewellery, and as an international currency. *The price of gold was going up. ...gold coins.* **2** N-UNCOUNT **Gold** is jewellery and other things that are made of gold. *We handed over all our gold and money.* **3** ADJ & N-COUNT Something that is **gold** in colour is bright yellow. ...*Michel's black and gold shirt.*

golden /'gəʊldən/. **1** ADJ Something that is **golden** is bright yellow. ...*an endless golden beach.* **2** ADJ **Golden** things are made of gold. **3** ADJ BEFORE N If you describe something as **golden**, you mean it is wonderful because it is likely to be successful, or because it is the best of its kind. *There's a golden opportunity for peace.*

goldfish /'gəʊldfɪʃ/.

☑ **Goldfish** is both the singular and the plural form.

N-COUNT A **goldfish** is a small orange-coloured fish which is often kept as a pet in a bowl or a garden pond.

gold 'medal, gold medals. N-COUNT A **gold medal** is a medal made of gold which is awarded as first prize in a contest or competition.

golf /gɒlf/. N-UNCOUNT **Golf** is a game in which you use long sticks called clubs to hit a ball into holes that are spread out over a large area of grassy land. ♦ **golfer, golfers** N-COUNT *About 150 golfers had arrived for a match.* ♦ **golfing** N-UNCOUNT ...*a golfing holiday in Spain.*

golf club, golf clubs. **1** N-COUNT A **golf club** is a long, thin, metal stick with a piece of wood or metal at one end that you use to hit the ball in golf. **2** N-COUNT A **golf club** is a social organization which provides a golf course and a clubhouse for its members.

'golf course, golf courses. N-COUNT A **golf course** is an area of land where people play golf.

⭐ **gone** /gɒn, AM gɑːn/. **1 Gone** is the past participle of **go**. **2** ADJ AFTER LINK-V Someone or something that is **gone** is no longer present or no longer exists. *While he was gone she had tea with the Colonel... By morning the smoke will be all gone.* **3** PREP If it is **gone** a particular time, it is later than that time. [BRITISH, INFORMAL] *It was just gone 7 o'clock this evening when I finished.*

gong /gɒŋ, AM gɔːŋ/ **gongs.** N-COUNT A **gong** is a flat, circular piece of metal that you hit with a hammer to make a loud sound.

gonna /'gɒnə, AM 'gɔːnə/. **Gonna** is used to represent the words 'going to' when they are pronounced informally. [WRITTEN] *What am I gonna do?*

⭐ **good** /gʊd/ **better, best.** **1** ADJ **Good** means pleasant or enjoyable. *We had a really good time together... There's nothing better than a cup of hot coffee... It's so good to hear your voice after all this time.* **2** ADJ **Good** means of a high quality, standard, or level. *Exercise is just as important to health as good food... He was very good at his work.* **3** ADJ A **good** idea, reason, method, or decision is a sensible or valid one. *It was a good idea to make some offenders do community service... Could you give me some advice on the best way to do this?* **4** ADJ Someone who is in a **good** mood is cheerful and pleasant to be with. **5** ADJ A **good** person is kind and thoughtful. *You are good to me.* **6** ADJ A child or animal that is **good** is well-behaved. **7** N-UNCOUNT **Good** is what is considered to be right according to moral standards or religious beliefs. ...*good and evil.* **8** N-SING If something is done for the **good** of a person or organization, it is done in order to benefit them. *I'm only telling you this for your own good!* **9** N-UNCOUNT If you say that doing something is **no good** or does **not** do **any good**, you mean that doing it is not of any use or will not bring any success. *It's no good worrying about it now... We gave them water and kept them warm, but it didn't do any good.* **10** ADJ BEFORE N You use **good** to emphasize the great extent or degree of something. *We waited a good fifteen minutes.*

PHRASES • **As good as** can be used to mean 'almost'. *His career is as good as over.* • If something changes or disappears **for good**, it never changes back or reappears as it was before. *This drug cleared up the disease for good.* • If someone **is good for** something, you can rely on them to provide that thing. *He was good for a few laughs.* • If you **make good** some damage or a loss, you repair the damage or replace what has been lost. • If someone **makes good**, they become successful. *Both men are poor boys made good.* • See also **better, best, goods.**

good after'noon. CONVENTION You say **'Good afternoon'** when you are greeting someone in the afternoon. [FORMAL] → See Reference Page on Greetings and Goodbyes.

⬛ Bank of English® frequent word   For a full explanation of all grammatical labels, see pages vii-x

a b c d e f g h i j k l m n o p q r s t u v w x y z

goodbye (or **good-bye**) /ˌɡʊdˈbaɪ/ **goodbyes.**
[1] CONVENTION You say **'Goodbye'** to someone when you or they are leaving, or at the end of a telephone conversation. → See Reference Page on Greetings and Goodbyes. [2] N-VAR When you say **goodbye** to someone or say your **goodbyes**, you say something such as 'goodbye' or 'bye' when you leave. *They came to the front door to wave goodbye.*

good 'evening. CONVENTION You say **'Good evening'** when you are greeting someone in the evening. [FORMAL] → See Reference Page on Greetings and Goodbyes.

goodie /ˈɡʊdi/. See **goody**.

good-'looking, better-looking, best-looking. ADJ A **good-looking** person has an attractive face.
● See note at **beautiful**.

good 'morning. CONVENTION You say **'Good morning'** when you are greeting someone in the morning. [FORMAL] → See Reference Page on Greetings and Goodbyes.

good-'natured. ADJ A **good-natured** person or animal is naturally friendly and does not get angry easily.

goodness /ˈɡʊdnəs/. [1] CONVENTION People say **'goodness'** or **'my goodness'** to express surprise or for emphasis. *Goodness, I wonder if he knows... My goodness, he's earned millions in his career.*
● **thank goodness**: see **thank**. [2] N-UNCOUNT **Goodness** is the quality of being kind and honest. *He retains a faith in human goodness.*

goodnight (or **good night**) /ˌɡʊdˈnaɪt/. CONVENTION You say **'Goodnight'** to someone late in the evening, before one of you goes home or goes to sleep. → See Reference Page on Greetings and Goodbyes.

⭐ **goods** /ɡʊdz/. N-PLURAL **Goods** are things that are made to be sold. *...consumer goods.*

goodwill /ˌɡʊdˈwɪl/. N-UNCOUNT **Goodwill** is a friendly or helpful attitude towards other people, countries, or organizations. *...a gesture of goodwill.*

goody (or **goodie**) /ˈɡʊdi/ **goodies.** [1] N-COUNT You can refer to pleasant, exciting, or attractive things as **goodies**. [INFORMAL] *...a little bag of goodies.* [2] N-COUNT You can refer to the heroes or the morally good characters in a story or situation as the **goodies**. [INFORMAL] *There are few goodies and baddies in this industrial dispute.*

goose /ɡuːs/ **geese.** N-VAR A **goose** is a large bird similar to a duck, with a long neck. The meat of this bird is also referred to as **goose**. → See picture on page 815.

gore /ɡɔː/ **gores, goring, gored.** [1] VERB If someone **is gored** by an animal, they are badly wounded by its horns or tusks. *Carruthers had been gored by a rhinoceros.* [2] N-UNCOUNT **Gore** is blood from a wound that has become thick. [LITERARY]

gorge /ɡɔːdʒ/ **gorges, gorging, gorged.** [1] N-COUNT A **gorge** is a narrow steep-sided valley, usually where a river passes through mountains or an area of hard rock. [2] VERB If you **gorge on** something, you eat lots of it in a very greedy way. *We gorged ourselves on delicious bread.*

gorgeous /ˈɡɔːdʒəs/. ADJ Someone or something that is **gorgeous** is extremely pleasant or attractive. [INFORMAL] *It's a gorgeous day... All the girls in my house are mad about Ryan, they think he's gorgeous.*

gorilla /ɡəˈrɪlə/ **gorillas.** N-COUNT A **gorilla** is a very large ape. → See picture on page 816.

gosh /ɡɒʃ/. CONVENTION Some people say **'Gosh'** to indicate surprise or shock. [INFORMAL] *Gosh, that was a heavy bag!*

gospel /ˈɡɒspəl/ **gospels.** [1] N-COUNT The **Gospels** are the four books of the Bible describing the life and teachings of Jesus Christ. [2] N-COUNT You can use **gospel** to refer humorously to a particular way of thinking that a person or group urges others to accept. *...the gospel according to my mom.* [3] ADJ If you take something **as gospel**, or **as the gospel truth**, you believe that it is completely true. [4] N-UNCOUNT **Gospel** or **gospel music** is a style of religious music that uses strong rhythms and vocal harmony.

gossip /ˈɡɒsɪp/ **gossips, gossiping, gossiped.** [1] N-UNCOUNT **Gossip** is informal conversation, often about other people's private affairs. *There has been much gossip about the possible reasons for his absence.* [2] VERB If you **gossip with** someone, you talk informally with them, especially about other people or local events. *Eva gossiped with Sarah... We spoke, debated, gossiped into the night.* [3] N-COUNT If you describe someone as a **gossip**, you disapprove of them because they often talk about other people's private affairs.

⭐ **got** /ɡɒt/. [1] **Got** is the past tense and past participle of **get**. [2] VERB You use **have got** in spoken English when you are saying that someone owns, possesses, or is holding a particular thing, or when you are mentioning a quality or characteristic that someone or something has. In American English, the 'have' is sometimes omitted. *I've got a coat just like this... Have you got any ideas?... After a pause he asked, 'You got any identification?'* [3] VERB You use **have got to** in spoken English when you are saying that something is necessary or must happen in the way stated. In American English, the 'have' is sometimes omitted. *I'm not happy with the situation, but I've just got to accept it... See, you got to work very hard.* [4] VERB People sometimes use **have got to** in spoken English in order to emphasize that they are certain that something is true. In American English, the 'have' is sometimes omitted. *He's got to be very happy with these results.*

Gothic /ˈɡɒθɪk/. [1] ADJ **Gothic** is used to describe a style of architecture or church art, dating from the Middle Ages, that is distinguished by tall pillars, high curved ceilings, and pointed arches. [2] ADJ **Gothic** is used to describe stories in which strange, mysterious adventures happen in dark and lonely places such as the ruins of a castle.

gotta /ˈɡɒtə/. **Gotta** is used to represent the words 'got to' when they are pronounced informally, as a way of saying 'have to' or 'must'. [WRITTEN] *Prices are high and our kid's gotta eat.*

gotten /'gɒtən/. **Gotten** is the past participle of **get** in American English.

gouge /gaʊdʒ/ **gouges, gouging, gouged.** VERB If you **gouge** something, you make a hole or a long cut in it, usually with a sharp object. *...quarries which have gouged great holes in the hills.*
▶ **gouge out.** PHR-VERB To **gouge out** a piece or part of something means to cut, dig, or force it from the surrounding surface. *...threatening to gouge his eyes out.*

gourmet /'gʊəmeɪ/ **gourmets.** [1] ADJ BEFORE N **Gourmet** food is more unusual or sophisticated than ordinary food. [2] N-COUNT A **gourmet** is someone who enjoys good food, and who knows a lot about food and wine.

⭐ **govern** /'gʌvən/ **governs, governing, governed.** [1] VERB To **govern** a country means to officially control and organize its economic, social, and legal systems. [2] VERB If a situation or activity **is governed** by a particular factor or rule, it is controlled by or depends on that factor or rule. *Marine insurance is governed by a strict series of rules and regulations.*

⭐ **government** /'gʌvənmənt/ **governments.** [1] N-COUNT The **government** of a country is the group of people who are responsible for governing it. When it is singular, **government** can take the singular or plural form of the verb. *The Government are to carry out a review of the Shops Act. ...fighting between government forces and left-wing rebels.* [2] N-UNCOUNT **Government** consists of the activities, methods, and principles involved in governing a country or other political unit. *...our system of government.*
♦ **governmental** /,gʌvən'mentəl/ ADJ BEFORE N *...participation in the governmental process.*

USAGE In Britain, the head of the government is the **Prime Minister**. The Prime Minister appoints the other **ministers**, who are responsible for particular areas of policy. The Prime Minister and other senior ministers together form the **Cabinet**. The policies of the government are debated and approved by **Parliament**, which consists of the **House of Commons** and the **House of Lords**. There are about 650 elected **Members of Parliament** (or **MPs**) in the House of Commons.
In the United States, the head of the government is the **President**, who appoints the members of his **administration**. Policies are debated and approved by **Congress**, which consists of the **House of Representatives** and the **Senate**. Members of the House of Representatives are known as **congressmen** and **congresswomen**, and members of the Senate are called **senators**.

⭐ **governor** /'gʌvənə/ **governors.** N-COUNT A **governor** is a person who is responsible for the political administration of a region, or for the administration of an institution. *Governor Deukmejian called for an inquiry. ...the BBC board of governors. ...the prison governor.*

gown /gaʊn/ **gowns.** [1] N-COUNT A **gown** is a long dress which women wear on formal occasions. [2] N-COUNT A **gown** is a loose black cloak worn on formal occasions by lawyers and academics.

GP /,dʒi: 'pi:/ **GPs.** N-COUNT A **GP** is a doctor who treats all types of illness, instead of specializing in one area of medicine. **GP** is an abbreviation for 'general practitioner'.

⭐ **grab** /græb/ **grabs, grabbing, grabbed.** [1] VERB If you **grab** something, you take it or pick it up roughly. *I grabbed him by the neck.* [2] VERB & N-COUNT If you **grab at** something, or if you make a **grab for** it, you try to get hold of it. *I made a grab for the knife.* [3] VERB If you **grab** an opportunity, you take advantage of it eagerly. *She grabbed the chance of a job interview.* [4] PHRASE If something is **up for grabs**, it is available to anyone who is interested. [INFORMAL]

grace /greɪs/ **graces, gracing, graced.** [1] N-UNCOUNT If someone moves with **grace**, they move smoothly and elegantly. [2] N-UNCOUNT If someone behaves with **grace**, they behave in a polite and dignified way, even when they are upset. *He accepted defeat with grace.* [3] VERB If you say that something or someone **graces** a place, you mean that they make the place more pleasant or attractive. [FORMAL] *The Tartar cities were graced with many gates and temples... Her face graced the cover of more than 500 magazines.* [4] N-UNCOUNT A period of **grace** is an extra period of time that you have been given to do something. *Businesses were given a year's grace and payments will begin from March 1, 2003.* [5] PHRASE If you refer to someone's **fall from grace**, you are talking about the fact that they are suddenly no longer approved of or popular, often because they have done something unacceptable. You can also say that someone **has fallen from grace**.

graceful /'greɪsfʊl/. [1] ADJ Someone or something that is **graceful** moves in a smooth and elegant way that is attractive to watch.
♦ **gracefully** ADV *She stepped gracefully onto the stage.* [2] ADJ Something that is **graceful** is attractive because it has a pleasing shape or style. *...a graceful medieval cathedral.* [3] ADJ **Graceful** behaviour is polite and pleasant.
♦ **gracefully** ADV *We managed to decline gracefully.*

gracious /'greɪʃəs/. [1] ADJ If someone is **gracious**, they are considerate and pleasant. *...a gracious speech of thanks.* ♦ **graciously** ADV *Hospitality at the Presidential guest house was graciously declined.* [2] ADJ You use **gracious** to describe the comfortable way of life of wealthy people. *...gracious suburbs with swimming pools and tennis courts.*

a
b
c
d
e
f
g
h
i
j
k
l
m
n
o
p
q
r
s
t
u
v
w
x
y
z

A
B
C
D
E
F
G
H
I
J
K
L
M
N
O
P
Q
R
S
T
U
V
W
X
Y
Z

★ **grade** /greɪd/ **grades, grading, graded.** **1** VERB If something **is graded**, its quality is judged or classified. *The oil is tasted and graded according to quality... South Point College does not grade the students' work.* **2** N-COUNT The **grade** of a product is its quality. *...a good grade of plywood.* **3** N-COUNT Your **grade** in an examination is the mark that you get. *...GCSE O level, grade B.* **4** N-COUNT Your **grade** in a company or organization is your level of importance or your rank. *...senior management grades.* **5** N-COUNT In schools in the United States, a **grade** is a group of classes in which all the children are of a similar age. **6** PHRASE If someone **makes the grade**, they succeed, especially by reaching the required standard. [INFORMAL]

gradient /'greɪdiənt/ **gradients.** N-COUNT A **gradient** is a slope or the degree to which the ground slopes.

gradual /'grædʒʊəl/. ADJ A **gradual** change or process happens in small stages over a long period of time, rather than suddenly. *You can expect her progress at school to be gradual rather than brilliant.* ♦ **gradually** ADV *Gradually we learned to cope.*

★ **graduate, graduates, graduating, graduated;** verb /'grædʒʊeɪt/, noun /'grædʒʊət/. **1** VERB & N-COUNT In Britain, when a student **graduates** from university, they have successfully completed a first degree course. A **graduate** is someone who has graduated from university. *She graduated in English and Drama from Manchester University. ...graduates in engineering.* **2** VERB In the United States, when a student **graduates**, they have successfully completed their university, college, or school studies. **3** N-COUNT In the United States, a **graduate** is a student who has successfully completed high school. **4** VERB If you **graduate from** one thing **to** another, you go from a less important job or position to a more important one. *From commercials she quickly graduated to television shows.*

graduation /,grædʒʊ'eɪʃən/ **graduations.** **1** N-UNCOUNT **Graduation** is the successful completion of a course of study at a university, college, or school, for which you receive a degree or diploma. *Upon graduation he joined a small law firm.* **2** N-COUNT A **graduation** is a special ceremony at which degrees or diplomas are given to students who have successfully completed their studies.

graffiti /grə'fiːti/. N-UNCOUNT **Graffiti** is words or pictures that are scribbled or drawn in public places, for example on walls or trains.

graft /grɑːft, græft/ **grafts, grafting, grafted.** **1** VERB If a piece of healthy skin or bone **is grafted on to** a damaged part of your body, it is attached to that part of your body by a medical operation. **2** N-COUNT A **graft** is skin or bone which is grafted onto your body. *I am having a skin graft on my arm soon.* **3** VERB If a part of one plant **is grafted onto** another plant, they are joined together so that they will become one

plant. **4** N-UNCOUNT **Graft** means hard work. [BRITISH] *His career has been one of hard graft.* **5** N-UNCOUNT **Graft** refers to the activity of using power to obtain money dishonestly. [AMERICAN] *Her wealth was obtained by graft and corruption.*

Grail /greɪl/. **1** N-PROPER **The Grail** or **the Holy Grail** is the cup that was used by Jesus Christ at the Last Supper. **2** N-SING If you describe something as a **grail** or a **holy grail**, you mean that someone is trying very hard to obtain or achieve it.

★ **grain** /greɪn/ **grains.** **1** N-COUNT A **grain** of wheat, rice, or other cereal crop is a seed from it. **2** N-VAR **Grain** is a cereal crop, especially wheat or corn, that has been harvested for food. *...a bag of grain.* **3** N-COUNT A **grain** of something such as sand or salt is a tiny piece of it. **4** N-SING A **grain of** a quality is a very small amount of it. *There's more than a grain of truth in that.* **5** N-COUNT The **grain** of a piece of wood is the direction of its fibres. You can also refer to the pattern of lines on the surface of the wood as **the grain**. *Brush the paint generously over the wood in the direction of the grain.* **6** PHRASE If you say that an idea or action **goes against the grain**, you mean it is very difficult to accept it or do it, because it conflicts with your beliefs.

gram (BRIT also **gramme**) /græm/ **grams.** N-COUNT A **gram** is a unit of weight equal to one thousandth of a kilogram.

grammar /'græmə/ **grammars.** **1** N-UNCOUNT **Grammar** is the ways that words can be put together in order to make sentences. *He studied hard at his Latin grammar.* **2** N-UNCOUNT Someone's **grammar** is the way in which they obey or do not obey the rules of a language. *...a deterioration in spelling and grammar among teenagers.* **3** N-COUNT A **grammar** is a book that describes the rules of a language.

'grammar school, grammar schools. N-COUNT A **grammar school** is a school in Britain for children aged between eleven and eighteen with a high academic ability.

grammatical /grə'mætɪkəl/. ADJ BEFORE N **Grammatical** is used to describe something relating to grammar.

gramme /græm/. See **gram**.

gran /græn/ **grans.** N-COUNT & N-VOC Your **gran** is your grandmother. [INFORMAL]

★ **grand** /grænd/ **grander, grandest.** **1** ADJ If you describe a building or landscape as **grand**, you mean that it is splendid or impressive. *...their rather grand house.* **2** ADJ **Grand** plans or actions are ambitious and intended to achieve important results. *The grand design of Europe's monetary union is already agreed.* **3** ADJ If you describe people as **grand**, you mean they seem or act important or socially superior. **4** ADJ If you describe an activity or experience as **grand**, you think that it is pleasant and enjoyable. *He was having a grand time meeting new sorts of people.* **5** ADJ BEFORE N A **grand** total is a total obtained by adding a series of things together. **6** N-SING A **grand** is a thousand pounds or a thousand dollars. [INFORMAL]

grandad (or **granddad**) /'grændæd/ **grandads.** N-COUNT & N-VOC Your **grandad** is your grandfather. [INFORMAL]

grandchild /'græntʃaɪld/ **grandchildren.** N-COUNT Someone's **grandchild** is the child of their son or daughter.

granddaughter /'grændɔːtə/ **granddaughters.** N-COUNT Someone's **granddaughter** is the daughter of their son or daughter.

grandeur /'grændʒə/. **1** N-UNCOUNT **Grandeur** is the quality in something which makes it seem impressive and elegant. ...the grandeur of the country mansion. **2** N-UNCOUNT Someone's **grandeur** is the great importance and social status that they have, or think that they have. ...mansions built by nineteenth-century men with delusions of grandeur.

grandfather /'grændfɑːðə/ **grandfathers.** N-COUNT & N-VOC Your **grandfather** is the father of your father or mother.

grandiose /'grændiəʊs/. ADJ If you describe something as **grandiose**, you mean it is bigger or more elaborate than necessary; used showing disapproval. Not one of Kim's grandiose plans has even begun.

grand 'jury, grand juries. N-COUNT A **grand jury** is a jury, usually in the United States, which considers a criminal case in order to decide if someone should be tried in a court of law.

grandma /'grænmɑː/ **grandmas.** N-COUNT & N-VOC Your **grandma** is your grandmother. [INFORMAL]

grandmother /'grænmʌðə/ **grandmothers.** N-COUNT & N-VOC Your **grandmother** is the mother of your father or mother.

grandpa /'grænpɑː/ **grandpas.** N-COUNT & N-VOC Your **grandpa** is your grandfather. [INFORMAL]

grandparent /'grænpeərənt/ **grandparents.** N-COUNT Your **grandparents** are the parents of your father or mother.

grandson /'grænsʌn/ **grandsons.** N-COUNT Someone's **grandson** is the son of their son or daughter.

grandstand /'grændstænd/ **grandstands.** N-COUNT A **grandstand** is a covered stand for spectators at sporting events.

granite /'grænɪt/. N-UNCOUNT **Granite** is a very hard rock used in building.

granny (or **grannie**) /'græni/ **grannies.** N-COUNT & N-VOC Your **granny** is your grandmother. [INFORMAL]

⭐ **grant** /grɑːnt, grænt/ **grants, granting, granted.** **1** N-COUNT A **grant** is an amount of money that the government or other institution gives to a person or an organization for a particular purpose. They'd got a special grant to encourage research. **2** VERB If someone in authority **grants** you something, they give it to you. Permission was granted a few weeks ago. **3** VERB If you

grant that something is true, you admit that it is true. [FORMAL] The magistrates granted that the RSPCA was justified in bringing the action.

PHRASES ● If you say that someone **takes** you **for granted**, you are complaining that they benefit from your help, efforts, or presence without showing that they are grateful. ● If you **take it for granted** that something is the case, or if you **take** something **for granted**, you believe that it is true or you accept it as normal without thinking about it. He seemed to take it for granted that he should speak as a representative... All the things I took for granted up north just didn't happen in London.

grant-main'tained. ADJ A **grant-maintained** school is one which receives money directly from the national government rather than from a local authority. [BRITISH]

grape /greɪp/ **grapes.** **1** N-COUNT **Grapes** are small green or purple fruit that can be eaten raw or used for making wine. → See picture on page 821. **2** PHRASE If you describe someone's attitude as **sour grapes**, you mean that they say something is worthless or undesirable because they want it but cannot have it themselves.

grapefruit /'greɪpfruːt/.

☑ The plural is **grapefruit** or **grapefruits**.

N-VAR A **grapefruit** is a large, round, yellow fruit that has a sharp taste.

grapevine /'greɪpvaɪn/ **grapevines.** **1** PHRASE If you hear something **on the grapevine**, you hear it in casual conversation with other people. **2** N-COUNT A **grapevine** is a climbing plant on which grapes grow.

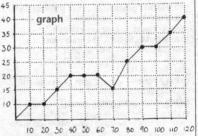

graph /grɑːf, græf/ **graphs.** N-COUNT A **graph** is a mathematical diagram which shows the relationship between two or more sets of numbers or measurements.

graphic /'græfɪk/ **graphics.** **1** ADJ A **graphic** description or account of something unpleasant is very clear and detailed. ...graphic scenes of drug taking. ◆ **graphically** ADV Here, graphically displayed, was confirmation of the entire story. **2** N-UNCOUNT **Graphics** is the activity of drawing or making pictures, especially in publishing, industry, or computing. **3** N-COUNT **Graphics** are drawings and pictures that are made using simple lines. *The Agriculture Department today released a new graphic to replace the old symbol.*

graphite /'græfaɪt/. N-UNCOUNT **Graphite** is a hard black substance that is a form of carbon.

grapple /'græpəl/ **grapples, grappling, grappled.** [1] VERB If you **grapple with** someone, you take hold of them and struggle with them. *He was grappling with an alligator... They grappled desperately for control of the weapon.* [2] VERB If you **grapple with** a problem, you try hard to solve it.

grasp /grɑːsp, græsp/ **grasps, grasping, grasped.** [1] VERB & N-SING If you **grasp** something, you hold it firmly. A **grasp** is a firm hold or grip. *She was trying to grasp at something... His hand was taken in a warm, firm grasp.* [2] N-SING If something is **in** your **grasp**, you possess or control it. If something slips **from** your **grasp**, you lose it or lose control of it. *She allowed victory to slip from her grasp.* [3] VERB & N-SING If you **grasp** something that is complicated or difficult to understand, you understand it. A **grasp** of something is an understanding of it. *He instantly grasped that Stephen was talking about his wife... They have a good grasp of foreign languages.* [4] N-SING If you say that something is **within** someone's **grasp**, you mean that it is very likely that they will achieve it.

★ **grass** /grɑːs, græs/ **grasses.** N-VAR **Grass** is a very common green plant with narrow leaves that forms a layer covering an area of ground.

grasshopper /'grɑːshɒpə, 'græs-/ **grasshoppers.** N-COUNT A **grasshopper** is an insect with long back legs that jumps high into the air and makes a high, vibrating sound. → See picture on page 824.

grassland /'grɑːslænd, 'græs-/ **grasslands.** N-VAR **Grassland** is land covered with wild grass.

grass 'roots (also **grass-roots** or **grassroots**). N-PLURAL The **grass roots** of an organization are the ordinary people in it, rather than its leaders. *You have to join the party at grass-roots level.*

grassy /'grɑːsi, 'græs-/. ADJ A **grassy** area of land is covered in grass.

grate /greɪt/ **grates, grating, grated.** [1] N-COUNT A **grate** is a framework of bars in a fireplace, which holds the coal or wood. [2] VERB When you **grate** food, you shred it into very small pieces using a tool called a grater. → See picture on page 825. [3] VERB When something **grates**, it rubs against something else, making a harsh unpleasant sound. *The gun barrel grated against the floor.* [4] VERB If something such as someone's behaviour **grates on** you, it irritates you. *His manner always grated on me. ...a loud, grating Brooklyn accent.*

grateful /'greɪtfʊl/. ADJ If you are **grateful for** something that someone has given you or done for you, you are pleased and wish to thank them. *I am grateful to you for your help.* ♦ **gratefully** ADV *I gratefully accepted the offer.*

gratify /'grætɪfaɪ/ **gratifies, gratifying, gratified.** [1] VERB If you **are gratified** by something, it gives you pleasure or satisfaction. [FORMAL] *Sarah was gratified by the figures.* ♦ **gratifying** ADJ *It is very gratifying to watch our business grow.* ♦ **gratification** /,grætɪfɪ'keɪʃən/ N-UNCOUNT *Israelis reacted with gratification.* [2] VERB If you **gratify** a desire, you satisfy it. [FORMAL] *We gratified our friend's curiosity.* ♦ **gratification** N-UNCOUNT *...sexual gratification.*

gratitude /'grætɪtjuːd, AM -tuːd/. N-UNCOUNT **Gratitude** is the state of feeling grateful. *I wish to express my gratitude to Kathy Davis for her help.*

gratuitous /grə'tjuːɪtəs, AM -'tuː-/. ADJ If you describe something as **gratuitous**, you mean that it is unnecessary, and often harmful or upsetting. *...gratuitous violence.* ♦ **gratuitously** ADV *...something less gratuitously offensive.*

★ **grave** /greɪv/ **graves; graver, gravest.** [1] N-COUNT A **grave** is a place where a dead person is buried. [2] ADJ A **grave** situation is very serious. *...the grave crisis facing the country.* ♦ **gravely** ADV *...his gravely ill wife.* [3] ADJ A **grave** person is quiet and serious. *Mrs Williams was looking very grave.* ♦ **gravely** ADV *'I think you should see this', she said gravely.*

gravel /'grævəl/. N-UNCOUNT **Gravel** consists of very small stones. *...a gravel path.*

graveyard /'greɪvjɑːd/ **graveyards.** N-COUNT A **graveyard** is an area of land where dead people are buried.

gravitational /,grævɪ'teɪʃənəl/. ADJ BEFORE N **Gravitational** means relating to the force of gravity. *...the earth's gravitational pull.*

gravity /'grævɪti/. [1] N-UNCOUNT **Gravity** is the force which makes things fall when you drop them. [2] N-UNCOUNT **The gravity of** a situation is its importance and seriousness. *No one questioned the gravity of the crime itself.*

gravy /'greɪvi/. N-UNCOUNT **Gravy** is a sauce made from the juices that come from meat when it cooks.

gray /greɪ/. See **grey**.

graze /greɪz/ **grazes, grazing, grazed.** [1] VERB When animals **graze**, or when they **are grazed**, they eat the grass or other plants that are growing in a particular place. *He used to graze some sheep up on the high slopes.* [2] VERB If you **graze** a part of your body, you injure the skin by scraping against something. [3] N-COUNT A **graze** is a small wound caused by scraping against something. *...minor cuts and grazes.* [4] VERB If one thing **grazes** another thing, it touches that thing lightly as it passes by. *A bullet grazed my cheek.*

grease /griːs/ **greases, greasing, greased.** [1] N-UNCOUNT **Grease** is a thick substance used to oil the moving parts of machines. [2] N-UNCOUNT **Grease** is an oily substance produced by your skin. [3] N-UNCOUNT **Grease** is animal fat produced by cooking meat. *...bacon grease.* [4] VERB If you **grease** something, you put grease or fat on it. *Lightly grease a baking tray.*

greasy /'gri:si, -zi/ **greasier, greasiest.** ADJ
Something that is **greasy** is covered with grease
or contains a lot of grease. ...*greasy hair.*

⭐ **great** /greɪt/ **greats; greater, greatest.** 1 ADJ BEFORE
N You use **great** to describe something that is
very large. ...*great columns of ice.* 2 ADJ **Great** is
used to emphasize the large amount or degree of
something. *She had great difficulty in keeping her
eyes open.* ♦ **greatly** ADV *He will be greatly
missed.* 3 ADJ You use **great** to describe
someone or something that is important, famous,
or exciting. ...*the great novels of the 19th century.*
...*the greatest scientist since Einstein.*
♦ **greatness** N-UNCOUNT ...*her conviction of her
husband's greatness.* 4 ADJ If something is **great**,
it is very good. [INFORMAL] *I thought it was a great
idea... It would make a great film... Oh great! That'll
be good for Fergus.*

USAGE Great, **big**, and **large** are all
used to talk about size. In general, **large** is
more formal than **big**, and **great** is more
formal than **large**.
Big and **large** are normally used to
describe objects. If you use **great** to
describe an object, you are suggesting
that it is impressive because of its size.
*The great bird of prey was a dark smudge
against the sun.*
You can use **large** or **great**, but not **big**, to
describe amounts. *He noticed a large
amount of blood on the laundry floor... The
coming of tourists in great numbers
changes things.*
Great is often used with nouns referring to
things such as feelings or ideas. It is the
only one of the three words that can be
used in front of an uncount noun. *It gives
me very great pleasure to welcome you to
Kings Norton.*
Remember that **great** has several other
meanings, when it does not refer to size,
but to something that is remarkable, very
good, or enjoyable.

---

greed /gri:d/. N-UNCOUNT **Greed** is a desire for
more of something than is necessary or fair.

greedy /'gri:di/. **greedier, greediest.** ADJ Someone
who is **greedy** wants more of something than is
necessary or fair. ...*greedy bosses who award
themselves huge pay rises.* ♦ **greedily** ADV *Livy
ate the pasties greedily.*

⭐ **green** /gri:n/ **greener, greenest; greens.** 1 ADJ &
N-VAR Something that is **green** is the colour of
grass or leaves. ...*green olives.* ...*a paler and softer
shade of green.* 2 ADJ A place that is **green** is
covered with grass, plants, and trees.
♦ **greenness** N-UNCOUNT ...*the lush greenness of
the river valleys.* 3 ADJ BEFORE N **Green** issues
relate to the protection of the environment. ...*the
power of the Green movement in Germany.*
4 N-COUNT A **green** is a smooth, flat area of grass,

for example the area around a hole on a golf
course.

greenery /'gri:nəri/. N-UNCOUNT Plants that
make a place look attractive are referred to as
greenery.

greenhouse /'gri:nhaʊs/ **greenhouses.** N-COUNT A
greenhouse is a glass building in which you
grow plants that need to be protected from bad
weather.

'greenhouse effect. N-SING The **greenhouse
effect** is the rise in the earth's temperature
caused by a build-up of gases around the earth.

greet /gri:t/ **greets, greeting, greeted.** 1 VERB When
you **greet** someone, you say something friendly
such as 'hello' when you meet them. → See
Reference Page on Greetings and Goodbyes.
2 VERB If something **is greeted** in a particular
way, people react to it in that way. *The move was
greeted with dismay by union leaders.* 3 VERB If
you **are greeted** by something, it is the first
thing you notice in a place. [LITERARY] *Customers
are greeted by a wonderful waft of smells from the
kitchen.*

greeting /'gri:tɪŋ/ **greetings.** N-VAR A **greeting** is
something friendly that you say or do when you
meet someone. *He raised a hand in greeting.*

grenade /grɪ'neɪd/ **grenades.** N-COUNT A **grenade**
is a small bomb that can be thrown by hand.

grew /gru:/. **Grew** is the past tense of **grow**.

⭐ **grey** (AM **gray**) /greɪ/ **greyer, greyest; greys.** ADJ &
N-VAR **Grey** is the colour of ashes or of clouds on
a rainy day. ...*grey trousers... His hair is a dark
shade of grey.*

greyhound /'greɪhaʊnd/ **greyhounds.** N-COUNT A
greyhound is a thin dog that can run very fast.

grid /grɪd/ **grids.** 1 N-COUNT A **grid** is a pattern of
straight lines that cross over each other to form
squares. ...*a grid of narrow streets.* 2 N-COUNT A
grid is a network of wires and cables by which
sources of power, such as electricity, are
distributed throughout an area. ...*the national
electricity grid.*

gridlock /'grɪdlɒk/. 1 N-UNCOUNT **Gridlock** is
the situation that exists when all the roads in a
particular place are so full of vehicles that none
of them can move. 2 N-UNCOUNT You can use
gridlock to refer to a situation in an argument or
dispute when neither side is prepared to give in,
so no agreement can be reached. ...*political
gridlock.*

grief /gri:f/. 1 N-UNCOUNT **Grief** is extreme
sadness. ...*her grief at her husband's suicide.*
2 PHRASE If someone or something **comes to
grief**, they fail or are harmed. *So many marriages
have come to grief over lack of money.*

grievance /'gri:vəns/ **grievances.** N-VAR A
grievance is a reason for complaining. ...*an
opportunity for them to air their grievances.*

grieve /gri:v/ **grieves, grieving, grieved.** 1 VERB If
you **grieve** over something, especially someone's
death, you feel very sad about it. *He still grieves
for his wife, who died of cancer three years ago.*

a b c d e f **g** h i j k l m n o p q r s t u v w x y z

⭐ Bank of English® frequent word   For a full explanation of all grammatical labels, see pages vii-x

2 VERB If something **grieves** you, it makes you feel unhappy or upset. *It grieved Elaine to be separated from her son.*

grievous /ˈgriːvəs/. ADJ Something that is **grievous** is extremely serious or worrying in its effects. [FORMAL] *...a very grievous mistake.*
♦ **grievously** ADV *Michael was grievously injured.*

grill /grɪl/ **grills, grilling, grilled.** **1** VERB In British English, if you **grill** food, you cook it using strong heat directly above or below it. The American word is **broil**. ● See note at **cook**. **2** N-COUNT A **grill** is a part of a cooker where food is grilled. **3** VERB If you **grill** someone, you ask them a lot of questions for a long period of time. [INFORMAL] *The police grilled him for hours.* ♦ **grilling, grillings** N-COUNT *Bank chiefs face a grilling over the plan.*

grille /grɪl/ **grilles.** N-COUNT A **grille** is a protective framework of bars or wire placed in front of a window or a piece of machinery.

grim /grɪm/ **grimmer, grimmest.** **1** ADJ A situation or news that is **grim** is unpleasant. *There was further grim economic news yesterday.* **2** ADJ A **grim** place is unattractive and depressing. **3** ADJ If someone is **grim**, they are very serious or stern. [LITERARY] *Her face was grim.* ♦ **grimly** ADV *'That was no accident,' Frank said grimly.*

grimace /grɪˈmeɪs, ˈgrɪməs/ **grimaces, grimacing, grimaced.** VERB & N-COUNT If you **grimace**, or if you make a **grimace**, you twist your face in an ugly way because you are unhappy, disgusted, or in pain. *He grimaced at his reflection. ...a little grimace of pain.*

grin /grɪn/ **grins, grinning, grinned.** VERB & N-COUNT If you **grin**, or if you give a **grin**, you smile broadly. *Nancy grinned at him.*

grind /graɪnd/ **grinds, grinding, ground.** **1** VERB When something such as corn or coffee **is ground**, it is crushed until it becomes a fine powder. *...freshly ground coffee.* **2** VERB If you **grind** something into a surface, you press it hard into the surface. *He ground his cigar stub into the ashtray.* **3** PHRASE If something **grinds to a halt**, it gradually slows down until it stops completely. *The industry would grind to a halt.* **4** N-SING You can refer to tiring, boring, and routine work as a **grind**. [INFORMAL] *...the daily grind of shaving.* **5** See also **ground**.

▸**grind down.** PHR-VERB If you **grind** someone **down**, you treat them very harshly, so that they do not have the will to resist you.

grinder /graɪndə/ **grinders.** N-COUNT A **grinder** is a machine or device which crushes something into small pieces. *...coffee grinders.*

★ **grip** /grɪp/ **grips, gripping, gripped.** **1** VERB & N-SING If you **grip** something, or if you take a **grip** on it, you hold it firmly. *She gripped the rope... His strong hand eased the bag from her grip.* **2** N-UNCOUNT If things such as shoes or car tyres have **grip**, they do not slip. **3** N-SING Someone's **grip** on a person or situation is the control they have over them. If you **get a grip on** something,

you make an effort to control it. *The president maintains an iron grip on his country... He wondered if he was getting old and losing his grip.* **4** VERB If something **grips** you, it affects you strongly and your attention is concentrated on it. *The entire community has been gripped by fear.* ♦ **gripping** ADJ *The film turned out to be a gripping thriller.*
PHRASES If you **get to grips with** a problem, or if you **come to grips with** it, you consider it seriously, and start taking action to deal with it. *The government's first task is to get to grips with the economy.*

gripe /graɪp/ **gripes, griping, griped.** VERB & N-COUNT If you say that someone **is griping about** something, you mean they are complaining about something in an annoying way. A **gripe** is a complaint. [INFORMAL] *I am sick of hearing motorists griping about the state of the roads.*
♦ **griping** N-UNCOUNT *Still, the griping went on.*

grisly /ˈgrɪzli/ **grislier, grisliest.** ADJ Something that is **grisly** is horrible and shocking. *...grisly murders.*

grit /grɪt/ **grits, gritting, gritted.** **1** N-UNCOUNT **Grit** consists of tiny pieces of stone, often put on roads in winter to make them less slippery. **2** N-UNCOUNT If you say that someone has **grit**, you mean that they have determination and courage. *...the inner grit to hang on when things go wrong.* **3** VERB If you **grit** your **teeth**, you decide to say nothing or to carry on, even though you are very angry or the situation is very difficult. *Ms Warner said she coped with such abuse 'through gritted teeth'.*

gritty /ˈgrɪti/ **grittier, grittiest.** **1** ADJ Something that is **gritty** is covered with grit or has a texture like grit. *...coarse, gritty ash.* **2** ADJ Someone who is **gritty** is determined and courageous. *...gritty determination.*

groan /grəʊn/ **groans, groaning, groaned.** VERB & N-COUNT If you **groan**, you make a long low sound of pain, unhappiness, or disapproval, called a **groan**. *He began to groan with pain... A groan of disappointment went up from the crew.*

grocer /ˈgrəʊsə/ **grocers.** N-COUNT A **grocer** is a shopkeeper who sells foods such as flour, sugar, and tinned foods. You can refer to a shop where these goods are sold as a **grocer** or a **grocer's**.

grocery /ˈgrəʊsəri/ **groceries.** **1** N-COUNT A **grocery** or a **grocery store** is a grocer's shop. [AMERICAN] **2** N-PLURAL **Groceries** are foods you buy at a grocer's or at a supermarket. *...two bags of groceries.*

groin /grɔɪn/ **groins.** N-COUNT Your **groin** is the part of your body where your legs meet your abdomen.

groom /gruːm/ **grooms, grooming, groomed.**
1 N-COUNT A **groom** is the same as a **bridegroom**. **2** N-COUNT A **groom** is someone whose job is to look after horses in a stable. **3** VERB If you **groom** an animal, you brush its fur. **4** VERB If you **are groomed for** a special job,

someone prepares you for it. *George was being groomed for the top job.*

groomed /gruːmd/. ADJ You use **groomed** in expressions such as **well groomed** and **badly groomed** to say how neat, clean, and smart a person is. *...a well-groomed appearance.*

grooming /ˈgruːmɪŋ/. N-UNCOUNT **Grooming** refers to the things that people do to keep themselves clean and make their face, hair, and skin look nice. *...a growing concern for personal grooming.*

groove /gruːv/ **grooves.** N-COUNT A **groove** is a deep line cut into a surface.

grope /grəʊp/ **gropes, groping, groped.** [1] VERB If you **grope for** something that you cannot see, you search for it with your hands. *Bunbury groped in his breast pocket for his wallet... I didn't turn on the light, but groped my way across the room.* [2] VERB If you **grope for** something such as the solution to a problem, you try to think of it, when you have no real idea what it could be. *She groped for a simple word to express a simple idea.*

★ **gross** /grəʊs/ **grosser, grossest.** [1] ADJ BEFORE N You use **gross** to emphasize the degree to which something is unacceptable or unpleasant. *He was dismissed from his job for gross misconduct.*
♦ **grossly** ADV *...grossly overpaid corporate lawyers.* [2] ADJ If you describe something or someone as **gross**, you think that they are very ugly, tasteless, or repulsive. [INFORMAL] *He wears really gross holiday outfits... Don't be so gross!* [3] ADJ BEFORE N & ADV A **gross** amount is the total amount after all the relevant amounts have been added together, and before any deductions are made. *Gross sales in June totalled £709 million. ...a father earning £20,000 gross a year.* [4] ADJ BEFORE N The **gross** weight of something is its total weight, including its container or wrapping.

grotesque /grəʊˈtesk/. [1] ADJ You say that something is **grotesque** when it is so unnatural, unpleasant, or exaggerated that it upsets or shocks you. *...a country where grotesque abuses are taking place.* ♦ **grotesquely** ADV *He says the law is grotesquely unfair.* [2] ADJ If something is **grotesque**, it is very ugly. *...a grotesque face with its gaping mouth.* ♦ **grotesquely** ADV *...grotesquely deformed beggars.*

★ **ground** /graʊnd/ **grounds, grounding, grounded.** [1] N-SING The **ground** is the surface of the earth or the floor of a room. *We slid down the roof and dropped to the ground. ...the marshy ground of the river delta... They sat on the ground.* [2] N-SING If you say that something takes place **on the ground**, you mean that it takes place on the surface of the earth and not in the air. *The war was largely fought on the ground. ...American naval, air and ground forces.* [3] N-UNCOUNT A **ground** is an area which is used for a particular purpose. *...Indian hunting grounds. ...the city's football ground.* [4] N-PLURAL The **grounds** of a large or important building are the garden or area of land which surrounds it. *...the palace grounds. ...the grounds of the University.* [5] VERB If aircraft or

pilots **are grounded**, they are not allowed to fly. [6] N-VAR You can use **ground** to refer to a place or situation in which particular methods or ideas can develop and be successful. *The company has maintained its reputation as the developing ground for new techniques.* [7] N-UNCOUNT **Ground** is used in expressions such as **gain ground** and **lose ground** in order to talk about the progress which someone or something makes in a situation or in a particular field. [JOURNALISM] *The election campaign gained ground during the last week... These novels are breaking new ground.* [8] N-VAR The **ground** or **grounds** for a particular feeling or course of action are the reason or justification for it. *Owen was against it, on the grounds of expense.* [9] VERB If an argument or opinion **is grounded in** or **on** something, it is based on that thing. *Her argument was grounded in fact.* [10] **Ground** is the past tense and past participle of **grind**.

PHRASES ● If something such as a project **gets off the ground**, it begins or starts functioning. *We help small companies to get off the ground.* ● If you **stand your ground** or **hold your ground**, you do not run away from a danger or threat, but face it bravely. ● If people or things of a particular kind are **thin on the ground**, there are very few of them. [BRITISH] *Good managers are thin on the ground.*

grounding /ˈgraʊndɪŋ/. N-SING If you have a **grounding in** a subject, you know the basic facts or principles of that subject. *The degree provides a grounding in law.*

'ground rule, ground rules. N-COUNT The **ground rules for** something are the basic principles on which future action will be based. *Rudy set ground rules for our meeting.*

groundwork /ˈgraʊndwɜːk/. N-SING The **groundwork for** something is the early work on it which forms the basis for the rest. *Yesterday's meeting was to lay the groundwork for the task ahead.*

★ **group** /gruːp/ **groups, grouping, grouped.**
[1] N-COUNT A **group of** people or things is a number of them together in one place at one time. **Group** can take the singular or plural form of the verb. *The trouble involved a small group of football supporters... The students work in groups.* [2] N-COUNT A **group** is a set of people who have the same interests or objectives, and who organize themselves to work or act together. *...the Minority Rights Group. ...members of an environmental group.* [3] N-COUNT A **group** is a set of people or things which have something in common. *...the most promising players in her age group.* ● See also **focus group, pressure group**. [4] N-COUNT A **group** is a number of musicians who perform pop music together. [5] VERB If a number of things or people **are grouped together**, they are together in one place or within one organization or system. *The fact sheets are grouped into seven sections. ...the Arab*

a
b
c
d
e
f
g
h
i
j
k
l
m
n
o
p
q
r
s
t
u
v
w
x
y
z

A
B
C
D
E
F
G
H
I
J
K
L
M
N
O
P
Q
R
S
T
U
V
W
X
Y
Z

Maghreb Union, which groups together the five North African states.

grouping /ˈgruːpɪŋ/ **groupings.** N-COUNT A **grouping** is a set of people or things that have something in common. *There were two main political groupings.*

grouse /graʊs/ **grouses, grousing, groused.**

✓ In meaning 1, **grouse** is both the singular and the plural form.

1 N-COUNT **Grouse** are small fat birds which are often shot for sport and can be eaten. **2** VERB & N-COUNT If you **grouse**, you complain. A **grouse** is a complaint. *They groused about the parking regulations.*

grove /grəʊv/ **groves.** N-COUNT A **grove** is a group of trees that are close together. *...an olive grove.*

grovel /ˈgrɒvəl/ **grovels, grovelling, grovelled** (AM **groveling, groveled**). **1** VERB If someone **grovels**, they behave very humbly towards another person, for example because they are frightened or because they want something; used showing disapproval. *I don't grovel to anybody.*
♦ **grovelling** ADJ *The Senator has been accused of grovelling.* **2** VERB If you **grovel**, you crawl on the ground, for example in order to find something. *We grovelled around the club on our knees.*

⭐ **grow** /grəʊ/ **grows, growing, grew, grown.** **1** VERB When something or someone **grows**, they develop and increase in size or intensity. *All children grow at different rates... The economy continues to grow... This political row threatens to grow into a full blown crisis.* **2** VERB If a plant or tree **grows** in a particular place, it is alive there. *Trees and bushes grew down to the water's edge.* **3** VERB When you **grow** something, you cause it to develop or increase in size or length. *I always grow a few red onions... I'm growing my hair.*
♦ **grower, growers** N-COUNT *...England's apple growers.* **4** LINK-VERB You use **grow** to say that someone or something gradually changes until they have a new quality, feeling, or attitude. *I grew a little afraid of the guy next door... He's growing old... He grew to love his work.* **5** See also **grown.**

▸ **grow apart.** PHR-VERB If people who have a close relationship **grow apart**, they gradually start to have different interests and opinions, and their relationship starts to fail. *It sounds as if you have grown apart from Tom.*

▸ **grow into.** PHR-VERB When a child **grows into** a piece of clothing that is too big for them, they get bigger so that it fits them properly.

▸ **grow on.** PHR-VERB If someone or something **grows on** you, you start to like them more and more. *The place began to grow on me.*

▸ **grow out of.** **1** PHR-VERB If you **grow out of** a type of behaviour, you stop behaving in that way as you develop or change. *Most children who stammer grow out of it.* **2** PHR-VERB When a child **grows out of** a piece of clothing, they become so big that it no longer fits them.

▸ **grow up.** **1** PHR-VERB When someone **grows up**, they gradually change from being a child into being an adult. **2** PHR-VERB If something **grows up**, it starts to exist and becomes larger or more important. *A variety of heavy industries grew up alongside the port.* **3** See also **grown-up.**

growl /graʊl/ **growls, growling, growled.** **1** VERB & N-COUNT When an animal **growls**, it makes a low rumbling noise, called a **growl**, usually because it is angry. *The dog growled at him.* **2** VERB & N-COUNT If someone **growls** something, they say it in a low rough voice, called a **growl**. [WRITTEN] *'I should have killed him,' Sharpe growled.*

grown /grəʊn/. **1 Grown** is the past participle of **grow.** **2** ADJ A **grown** man or woman is one who is fully developed and mature. *Dad, I'm a grown woman. I know what I'm doing.*

grown-ˈup, grown-ups. **1** N-COUNT Children, or people talking to children, often refer to adults as **grown-ups**. *Tell children to tell a grown-up if they're being bullied.* **2** ADJ Someone who is **grown-up** is mature and no longer dependent on their parents or another adult. *She was a widow with grown-up children.*

⭐ **growth** /grəʊθ/ **growths.** **1** N-UNCOUNT The **growth of** something such as an industry, organization, or idea is its development in size, wealth, or importance. *...the growth of nationalism. ...Japan's enormous economic growth.* **2** N-UNCOUNT **Growth** in a person, animal, or plant is the process of increasing in size and development. *...hormones which control fertility and body growth.* **3** N-COUNT A **growth** is an abnormal lump that grows inside or on a person, animal, or plant.

grub /grʌb/ **grubs.** **1** N-COUNT A **grub** is an insect which has just hatched from its egg. **2** N-UNCOUNT **Grub** is food. [INFORMAL]

grubby /ˈgrʌbi/ **grubbier, grubbiest.** ADJ **Grubby** people or things are rather dirty. [INFORMAL] *...kids with grubby faces.*

grudge /grʌdʒ/ **grudges.** N-COUNT If you have a **grudge against** someone, you have unfriendly feelings towards them because they have harmed you in the past.

grudging /ˈgrʌdʒɪŋ/. ADJ A **grudging** feeling or action is one that you feel or do unwillingly. *He even earned his opponents' grudging respect.*
♦ **grudgingly** ADV *The studio grudgingly agreed to allow him to continue working.*

gruelling (AM **grueling**) /ˈgruːəlɪŋ/. ADJ A **gruelling** activity is extremely difficult and tiring.

gruesome /ˈgruːsəm/. ADJ Something that is **gruesome** is horrible and shocking. *...gruesome murders.*

grumble /ˈgrʌmbəl/ **grumbles, grumbling, grumbled.** VERB & N-COUNT If you **grumble about** something, you complain about it. You can refer to complaints like this as **grumbles**. *I shouldn't grumble about Mum... A tourist grumbled that the waiter spoke too much Spanish... Its high price has brought grumbles from some customers.*

grumpy /ˈɡrʌmpi/ **grumpier, grumpiest.** ADJ If you say that someone is **grumpy**, you think they are bad-tempered and miserable. [INFORMAL]
♦ **grumpily** ADV I rolled grumpily out of bed.

grunt /ɡrʌnt/ **grunts, grunting, grunted.** 1 VERB & N-COUNT If someone **grunts**, they make a low rough noise called a **grunt**, often because they do not want to talk. 'Rubbish,' I grunted... He grunted his thanks. ...grunts of acknowledgement. 2 VERB When an animal, usually a pig, **grunts**, it makes a low rough noise.

⭐ **guarantee** /ˌɡærənˈtiː/ **guarantees, guaranteeing, guaranteed.** 1 VERB & N-COUNT If one thing **guarantees** another, or if one thing is a **guarantee** of another, the first is certain to cause the second thing to happen. ...a man whose fame guarantees that his calls will nearly always be returned... Reports of this kind are guaranteed to cause anxiety... A famous old name on a firm is not necessarily a guarantee of quality. 2 VERB & N-COUNT If you **guarantee** something, you promise that it is definitely true, or that you will do or provide it for someone. You refer to a promise like this as your **guarantee**. We guarantee to refund your money if you are not delighted. ...a guaranteed income... The Editor can give no guarantee that they will fulfil their obligations. 3 VERB & N-COUNT If a company **guarantees** its product or work it has carried out, it provides a written promise called a **guarantee** which states that if the product or work has any faults within a specified time, it will be repaired or replaced free of charge.

⭐ **guard** /ɡɑːd/ **guards, guarding, guarded.** 1 VERB If you **guard** a place, person, or object, you watch them carefully, either to protect them or to stop them from escaping. A few men were left outside to guard her. ...the heavily guarded border. 2 N-COUNT & PHRASE A **guard** is someone such as a soldier or prison officer who is guarding a particular place or person. When a soldier or prison officer is guarding someone or something, you say that they are **on guard** or **standing guard**. 3 N-SING A **guard** is a specially organized group of people, such as soldiers or policemen, who protect or watch someone or something. We have a security guard around the whole area. 4 N-COUNT A **guard** is a person whose job is to check tickets on a train and ensure that the train travels safely and punctually. 5 VERB If you **guard** something important or secret, you protect or hide it. He closely guarded her identity.
♦ **guarded** ADJ He was hoping to keep the visit a closely guarded secret. 6 N-COUNT A **guard** is a protective device which covers a part of someone's body or a dangerous part of a piece of equipment. ...safety guards.
PHRASES ● If someone **catches** you **off guard**, they surprise you by doing something when you are not expecting it. ● If you are **on** your **guard**, or if you are **on guard**, you are being very careful because you think a situation might become

difficult or dangerous. He is constantly on guard against any threat of humiliation.
▸ **guard against.** PHR-VERB If you **guard against** something, you are careful to prevent it from happening, or you take action to avoid being affected by it. We always have to guard against complacency.

guardian /ˈɡɑːdiən/ **guardians.** 1 N-COUNT A **guardian** is someone who has been legally appointed to look after another person's affairs, for example those of a child or someone who is mentally ill. 2 N-COUNT If you consider someone a defender or protector of something, you can call them its **guardian**. ...guardians of public morality.

⭐ **guerrilla** (or **guerilla**) /ɡəˈrɪlə/ **guerrillas.** N-COUNT A **guerrilla** is a person who fights as part of an unofficial army, usually an army which is fighting against the existing government of a country.

⭐ **guess** /ɡes/ **guesses, guessing, guessed.** 1 VERB & N-COUNT If you **guess** something, or if you make a **guess** about something, you form an idea or opinion about it, knowing that it may not be true or accurate because you do not have all the relevant facts. Wood guessed that he was a very successful publisher or a banker... You can only guess at what mental suffering they endure... My guess is that the answer will be negative. 2 VERB If you **guess** that something is the case, you correctly form the opinion that it is the case, although you do not have definite knowledge about it. He should have guessed what would happen... Someone might have guessed our secret. 3 PHRASE You say **I guess** to indicate slight uncertainty or reluctance about what you are saying. I guess he's right.

⭐ **guest** /ɡest/ **guests, guesting, guested.** 1 N-COUNT A **guest** is someone who has been invited to stay in your home, attend an event, or appear on a radio or television show. She was a guest at the wedding. ...a frequent chat show guest. 2 VERB If someone **guests** on something such as a television show, they appear or perform on it as a guest. Last month she guested with New York City Ballet. 3 N-COUNT A **guest** is someone who is staying in a hotel.

guidance /ˈɡaɪdəns/. N-UNCOUNT **Guidance** is help and advice. ...the reports which were produced under his guidance.

⭐ **guide** /ɡaɪd/ **guides, guiding, guided.** 1 N-COUNT A **guide** is a person who shows tourists round places such as museums or cities, or shows people the way through difficult country. 2 VERB If you **guide** someone somewhere, you go there with them in order to show them the way, and perhaps to explain points of interest to them. He took the bewildered Elliott by the arm and guided him out. ...a guided tour of the eight-bedroom mansion. 3 N-COUNT A **guide** or **guide book** is a book which gives information about a town, area, or country, or information to help you understand something. ...the Pocket Guide to Butterflies. 4 N-COUNT A **guide** is something that

a b c d e f g h i j k l m n o p q r s t u v w x y z

can be used to help you plan your actions or to form an opinion about something. *As a rough guide, a horse needs 2.5 per cent of his body weight in food every day.* **5** VERB If you **guide** someone, you influence their actions or decisions. *He should have let his instinct guide him.*

guideline /ˈgaɪdlaɪn/ **guidelines.** N-COUNT A **guideline** is a rule or piece of advice about how to do something. *Are there strict guidelines for animal experimentation?*

guild /gɪld/ **guilds.** N-COUNT A **guild** is an organization of people who do the same job or who share an interest. *...the Guild of Food Writers.*

guilt /gɪlt/. **1** N-UNCOUNT **Guilt** is an unhappy feeling that you have because you have done something bad. *...his feeling of guilt towards his son.* **2** N-UNCOUNT **Guilt** is the fact that you have done something bad or illegal. *...the determination of guilt according to criminal law.*

⭐ **guilty** /ˈgɪlti/ **guiltier, guiltiest.** **1** ADJ If you feel **guilty**, you feel unhappy because you have done something bad or have failed to do something which you should have done. ♦ **guiltily** ADV *He glanced guiltily over his shoulder.* **2** ADJ BEFORE N You use **guilty** to describe an action or fact that you feel guilty about. *...a guilty secret.* **3** ADJ If someone is **guilty** of doing something bad or committing a crime, they have done a bad thing or committed a crime. *Mr Brooke had been guilty of a 'gross error of judgment'... He has agreed to plead guilty to six felonies.*

'guinea pig, guinea pigs. **1** N-COUNT If someone is used as a **guinea pig** in an experiment, a drug or other treatment is tested for the first time on them. *The Doctor used himself as a human guinea pig to perfect a treatment.* **2** N-COUNT A **guinea pig** is a small furry animal without a tail.

guise /gaɪz/ **guises.** N-COUNT If something is done or appears **under the guise** of something else, the first thing looks like the second thing or is made to look like it, in order to hide its true appearance or nature. *...the men who committed this murder under the guise of a political act... The new leaders are merely the old guard in a different guise.*

⭐ **guitar** /gɪˈtɑː/ **guitars.** N-COUNT A **guitar** is a wooden musical instrument with six strings which are plucked or strummed. → See picture on page 827. ♦ **guitarist** /gɪˈtɑːrɪst/ **guitarists** N-COUNT *...the world's best jazz guitarists.*

gulf /gʌlf/ **gulfs.** **1** N-COUNT A **gulf** is an important or significant difference between two people, things, or groups. *There is a growing gulf between rich and poor.* **2** N-COUNT A **gulf** is a large area of sea which extends a long way into the surrounding land. *...the Gulf of Mexico.*

gullible /ˈgʌlɪbəl/. ADJ If you say that someone is **gullible**, you think they are easily tricked. ♦ **gullibility** N-UNCOUNT *...the unending gullibility of his poor customers.*

gully /ˈgʌli/ **gullies.** N-COUNT A **gully** is a long narrow valley with steep sides.

gulp /gʌlp/ **gulps, gulping, gulped.** **1** VERB & N-COUNT If you **gulp** food or drink, or if you take **gulps** of food or drink, you swallow large quantities of it. *She quickly gulped her tea... He'd gulped it down in one bite. ...a large gulp of whisky... He took the burger carefully from my fingers and swallowed it in two gulps.* **2** VERB & N-COUNT If you **gulp**, you swallow air, making a noise in your throat called a **gulp** as you do so, usually because you are nervous. *I gulped, and then proceeded to tell her the whole story... He slumped back, gulping for air.*

gum /gʌm/ **gums.** **1** N-UNCOUNT **Gum** is a substance, often mint-flavoured, which you chew for a long time but do not swallow. **2** N-UNCOUNT **Gum** is a type of glue that you use to stick paper together. **3** N-COUNT Your **gums** are the areas of firm pink flesh inside your mouth, which your teeth grow out of. → See picture on page 823.

⭐ **gun** /gʌn/ **guns, gunning, gunned.** **1** N-COUNT A **gun** is a weapon from which bullets or pellets are fired. **2** PHRASE If you **stick to** your **guns**, you continue to have your own opinion about something, even though other people disagree or try to make you change your mind. [INFORMAL] ▶ **gun down.** PHR-VERB If someone **is gunned down**, they are shot and severely injured or killed.

gunfire /ˈgʌnfaɪə/. N-UNCOUNT **Gunfire** is the repeated shooting of guns. *He died during an exchange of gunfire.*

gunman /ˈgʌnmən/ **gunmen.** N-COUNT A **gunman** is someone who uses a gun to commit a crime. [JOURNALISM]

gunpoint /ˈgʌnpɔɪnt/. PHRASE If someone holds you **at gunpoint**, they threaten to shoot you if you do not obey them.

gunshot /ˈgʌnʃɒt/ **gunshots.** **1** N-COUNT A **gunshot** is the firing of a gun or the sound of a gun being fired. *He heard gunshots.* **2** N-UNCOUNT **Gunshot** is used to refer to bullets that are fired from a gun. *A policeman suffered gunshot wounds.*

gurgle /ˈgɜːgəl/ **gurgles, gurgling, gurgled.** **1** VERB When water **gurgles**, it makes a bubbling sound. *...the sound of hot water gurgling through the van's engine.* **2** VERB When a baby **gurgles**, it makes bubbling sounds in its throat, usually because it is happy.

guru /ˈguːruː/ **gurus.** **1** N-COUNT A **guru** is a spiritual leader and teacher, especially in Hinduism. **2** N-COUNT A **guru** is someone that many people regard as an expert or leader. *...fashion gurus.*

gush /gʌʃ/ **gushes, gushing, gushed.** **1** VERB & N-SING When liquid **gushes** out of something, or if there is a **gush of** liquid from something, a large quantity of liquid flows out very quickly. *Piping-hot water gushed out... A supertanker continues to gush oil off the coast of Spain... I heard a gush of water.* **2** VERB If you say that someone **gushes about** something, you mean that they express their admiration or pleasure in a way that seems exaggerated and false. *He gushes about his new-found happiness with a girl almost half his age.* ♦ **gushing** ADJ *She was very gushing and very effusive.*

gust /gʌst/ **gusts, gusting, gusted.** 1 N-COUNT A **gust** is a short, strong, sudden rush of wind. 2 VERB When the wind **gusts**, it blows with short, strong, sudden rushes. *The wind gusted up to 164 miles an hour.*

gut /gʌt/ **guts, gutting, gutted.** 1 N-PLURAL A person's or animal's **guts** are all their internal organs. 2 VERB If someone **guts** a fish or a dead animal, they remove its internal organs. 3 N-SING **The gut** is the tube inside your body through which food passes while it is being digested. 4 N-UNCOUNT **Guts** is courage. [INFORMAL] *The new Chancellor has the guts to push through unpopular tax increases.* 5 ADJ A **gut** feeling or response is based on instinct or emotion rather than on reason. *My gut reaction was very positive.* 6 VERB If a building **is gutted**, the inside is destroyed, leaving only the outside walls. *A firebomb gutted a building where 60 people lived.*

gutter /'gʌtə/ **gutters.** 1 N-COUNT The **gutter** is the edge of a road next to the pavement, where rain collects and flows away. 2 N-COUNT A **gutter** is a channel fixed to the edge of a roof, which rain water drains into. 3 N-SING You can use **the gutter** to refer to a condition of life in which

someone is poor and has no self-respect. *Instead of ending up in jail or in the gutter he was remarkably successful.*

⭐ **guy** /gaɪ/ **guys.** 1 N-COUNT A **guy** is a man. [INFORMAL] *I was working with a guy from Manchester.* 2 N-VOC & N-PLURAL Americans sometimes address a group of people, whether they are male or female, as **guys** or **you guys**.

gym /dʒɪm/ **gyms.** 1 N-COUNT A **gym** is the same as a **gymnasium**. 2 N-UNCOUNT **Gym** means **gymnastics**.

gymnasium /dʒɪm'neɪziəm/ **gymnasiums.** N-COUNT A **gymnasium** is a club or room, usually containing special equipment, where people can exercise.

gymnastic /dʒɪm'næstɪk/ **gymnastics.**

☑ The form **gymnastic** is used as a modifier.

N-PLURAL **Gymnastics** consists of physical exercises that develop your strength, co-ordination, and agility. *...gymnastic exercises.*

gynaecology (AM **gynecology**) /,gaɪnɪ'kɒlədʒi/. N-UNCOUNT **Gynaecology** is the branch of medical science which deals with women's diseases and medical conditions.

gypsy (or **gipsy**) /'dʒɪpsi/ **gypsies.** N-COUNT A **gypsy** is a member of a race of people who travel from place to place in caravans, rather than living in one place.

H h

⭐ **habit** /'hæbɪt/ **habits.** 1 N-VAR A **habit** is something that you do often or regularly. *He had the endearing habit of smiling at everyone he saw... After twenty years as a chain smoker Mr Nathe has given up the habit. ...a survey on eating habits in the UK.* 2 PHRASE If you **are in the habit of** doing something or **make a habit of** doing it, you do it regularly or often. If you **get into the habit of** doing something, you begin to do it regularly or often. *You can phone me at work as long as you don't make a habit of it.* 3 N-COUNT A drug **habit** is an addiction to a drug such as heroin.

habitat /'hæbɪtæt/ **habitats.** N-COUNT The **habitat** of an animal or plant is its natural environment in which it normally lives or grows.

habitual /hə'bɪtʃuəl/. ADJ A **habitual** state or way of behaving is one that someone usually has or does, especially one that is considered to be typical or characteristic of them. *He soon recovered his habitual geniality.* ♦ **habitually** ADV *They habitually used foul language.*

hack /hæk/ **hacks, hacking, hacked.** 1 VERB PHR-VERB If you **hack** something, or if you **hack away at** it, you cut it with strong, rough strokes using a sharp tool such as an axe or knife. *Some were hacked to death with machetes... He started to hack away at the tree bark.* 2 N-COUNT If you refer to a professional writer such as a journalist as a

hack, you disapprove of them because they write for money without worrying very much about the quality of their writing. 3 VERB When someone **hacks into** a computer system, they break into the system, especially in order to get secret information that is stored there. [COMPUTING] ♦ **hacker** /'hækə/ **hackers** N-COUNT *Once inside their systems, the hackers could steal information.* ♦ **hacking** N-UNCOUNT *...the common and often illegal art of computer hacking.*
▸**hack away.** See **hack** 1.
▸**hack off.** PHR-VERB If you **hack** something **off**, you cut it off with strong, rough strokes using a sharp tool such as an axe or knife. *Kim even hacked off her long hair.*

had /hæd/. **Had** is the past tense and past participle of **have**.

haddock /'hædək/.

☑ The form **haddock** is also used as the plural.

N-VAR A **haddock** is a type of sea fish. **Haddock** is the flesh of this fish eaten as food.

hadn't /'hædənt/. **Hadn't** is the usual spoken form of 'had not'.

haemorrhage (AM **hemorrhage**) /'hemərɪdʒ/ **haemorrhages, haemorrhaging, haemorrhaged.** VERB & N-VAR If someone **is haemorrhaging**, or if they have a **haemorrhage**, they are bleeding heavily because of broken

A B C D E F G H I J K L M N O P Q R S T U V W X Y Z

Hair

curly hair

fringe

bun

straight hair

wavy hair

ponytail

blood vessels inside their body. *If this is left untreated, one can actually haemorrhage to death.* ♦ **haemorrhaging** N-UNCOUNT *A post mortem showed he died from shock and haemorrhaging.*

haggle /ˈhægəl/ **haggles, haggling, haggled.** VERB If you **haggle**, you argue about something before reaching an agreement, especially about the cost of something. *Of course he'll still haggle over the price.* ♦ **haggling** N-UNCOUNT *After months of haggling, they recovered only three-quarters of what they had lent.*

hail /heɪl/ **hails, hailing, hailed.** [1] VERB If a person or event **is hailed as** important or successful, they are praised publicly. *US magazines hailed her as the greatest rock'n'roll singer in the world.* [2] N-UNCOUNT **Hail** consists of tiny balls of ice that fall like rain from the sky. [3] N-SING A **hail of** things, usually small objects, is a large number of them that hit you at the same time and with great force. *The riot police were met with a hail of stones.* [4] VERB If someone or something **hails from** a particular place or background, they come from it. *I hail from Brighton.* [5] VERB If you **hail** a taxi, you wave at it in order to stop it and ask the driver to take you somewhere.

⭐ **hair** /heə/ **hairs.** [1] N-VAR Your **hair** is the mass of fine thread-like strands that grow on your head. [2] N-VAR **Hair** is all the short, fine, thread-like

material that grows on different parts of your body. *The majority of men have hair on their chest.* [3] N-VAR **Hair** is the rough, thread-like material that covers the body of an animal such as a dog, or makes up a horse's mane and tail. [4] N-COUNT **Hairs** are very fine thread-like strands that grow on some insects and plants.

haircut /ˈheəkʌt/ **haircuts.** [1] N-COUNT If you have a **haircut**, someone cuts your hair for you. [2] N-COUNT A **haircut** is the style in which your hair has been cut. *Who's that guy with the funny haircut?*

hairdresser /ˈheədresə/ **hairdressers.** N-COUNT A **hairdresser** is a person who cuts, washes, and styles people's hair. You can refer to the shop where a hairdresser works as a **hairdresser** or a **hairdresser's**. ♦ **hairdressing** N-UNCOUNT *...personal services such as hairdressing.*

hairstyle /ˈheəstaɪl/ **hairstyles.** N-COUNT Your **hairstyle** is the style in which your hair has been cut or arranged. *I think her new short hairstyle looks simply great.*

hairy /ˈheəri/ **hairier, hairiest.** [1] ADJ Someone or something that is **hairy** is covered with a lot of hair. [2] ADJ If you describe a situation as **hairy**, you mean that it is exciting but rather frightening. [INFORMAL] *His driving was a bit hairy.*

halal /həˈlɑːl/. N-UNCOUNT **Halal** is meat from animals that have been killed according to Muslim law. ...*halal meat*.

⭐ **half** /hɑːf, AM hæf/ **halves.** [1] N-COUNT & PREDET & ADJ **Half** of an amount or object is one of two equal parts that together make up the whole amount or object. *Cut the tomatoes in half vertically... The bridge was re-built in two halves... She's half his age. ...the first half hour.* [2] N-COUNT In games such as football and rugby, matches are divided into two equal periods of time which are called **halves**. ...*early in the second half*. [3] ADV You use **half** to say that something is only partly the case or happens to only a limited extent. *His refrigerator frequently looked half empty... She'd half expected him to withdraw from the course.* [4] ADV You can use **half** to say that someone has parents of different nationalities. For example, if you are **half** German, one of your parents is German. [5] PREP You use **half past** to refer to a time that is thirty minutes after a particular hour. → See Reference Page on Telling the Time. ...*half past twelve.* [6] PHRASE If you increase something **by half**, half of the original amount is added to it. If you decrease it **by half**, half of the original amount is taken away from it. *The number of 7 year olds who read poorly has increased by half over the past 5 years.*

'**half-brother, half-brothers.** N-COUNT Someone's **half-brother** is a boy or man who has either the same mother or the same father as they have. *Peter, my half-brother, considers himself Canadian.*

,**half-'hearted.** ADJ If someone does something in a **half-hearted** way, they do it without any real interest or effort. ...*a half-hearted apology... Her application was a bit half-hearted.* ♦ **half-heartedly** ADV *I can't do anything half-heartedly. I have to do everything 100 per cent.*

'**half-sister, half-sisters.** N-COUNT Someone's **half-sister** is a girl or woman who has either the same mother or the same father as they have.

,**half-'time.** N-UNCOUNT In sport, **half-time** is the short rest period between the two parts of a game.

halfway (or **half-way**) /,hɑːfˈweɪ, AM ,hæf-/. [1] ADV **Halfway** means in the middle of a place or in between two points, at an equal distance from each of them. *He was halfway up the ladder.* [2] ADV & ADJ BEFORE N **Halfway** means in the middle of a period of time or an event. *We were more than halfway through our tour. ...the halfway point of the tournament.*

⭐ **hall** /hɔːl/ **halls.** [1] N-COUNT In a house or flat, the **hall** is the area just inside the front door. [2] N-COUNT A **hall** is a large room or building which is used for public events such as concerts, exhibitions, and meetings. ...*a dance in the village hall. ...the Royal Albert Hall.*

hallmark /ˈhɔːlmɑːk/ **hallmarks.** [1] N-COUNT The **hallmark** of something or someone is their most typical quality or feature. *It's a technique that has become the hallmark of Amber Films.* [2] N-COUNT A **hallmark** is an official mark that is put on objects

made of gold, silver, or platinum that indicates the quality of the metal.

hallo /hæˈləʊ/. See **hello**.

hallowed /ˈhæləʊd/. [1] ADJ **Hallowed** is used to describe something that is respected and admired, usually because it is old or important. ...*the hallowed turf of Lord's Cricket Ground.* [2] ADJ **Hallowed** is used to describe something that is considered to be holy. ...*hallowed ground.*

Halloween (or **Hallowe'en**) /,hæləʊˈiːn/. N-UNCOUNT **Halloween** is the night of the 31st of October and it is traditionally said to be the time when ghosts and witches can be seen.

hallucination /hə,luːsɪˈneɪʃən/ **hallucinations.** N-COUNT A **hallucination** is something that is not real that someone sees because they are ill or have taken a drug. *The drug induces hallucinations at high doses.*

hallway /ˈhɔːlweɪ/ **hallways.** N-COUNT A **hallway** is the entrance hall of a house or other building.

halo /ˈheɪləʊ/ **haloes** or **halos.** N-COUNT A **halo** is a circle of light that is drawn in pictures round the head of a holy figure such as a saint.

⭐ **halt** /hɔːlt/ **halts, halting, halted.** [1] VERB & PHRASE When a vehicle or person **halts** or when something **halts** them, they stop moving along and stand still. You can also say that they come **to a halt**. *She held her hand out flat, to halt him... The elevator creaked to a halt.* [2] VERB & PHRASE When something such as development or activity **halts**, or when you **halt** it, it stops completely. You can also say that these things come **to a halt**. *He criticised the government for failing to halt economic decline... In the ensuing chaos, agricultural production was brought to a halt.*

halve /hɑːv, AM hæv/ **halves, halving, halved.** [1] VERB When you **halve** something, or when it **halves**, it is reduced to half its previous size or amount. *Sales of vinyl records halved in 1992 to just 6.7m.* [2] VERB If you **halve** something, you divide it into two equal parts. *Halve the pineapple and scoop out the inside.* [3] **Halves** is the plural of **half**.

ham /hæm/ **hams.** N-VAR **Ham** is meat from the top of the back leg of a pig, usually eaten cold. ...*a huge baked ham. ...ham sandwiches.*

hamburger /ˈhæmbɜːgə/ **hamburgers.** N-COUNT A **hamburger** is a flat round mass of minced beef, fried and eaten in a bread roll.

hammer /ˈhæmə/ **hammers, hammering, hammered.** [1] N-COUNT A **hammer** is a tool used for hitting things. It consists of a heavy piece of metal at the end of a handle. → See picture on page 833. [2] VERB & PHR-VERB If you **hammer** something such as a nail, you hit it with a hammer. If you **hammer** it **in**, you hit it into a surface, using a hammer. *Hammer a wooden peg into the hole.* [3] VERB If you **hammer** a surface or **hammer on** it, you hit it several times. *He hammered his two clenched fists on the table.* [4] VERB If a person or organization **is being hammered**, they are being severely attacked, defeated, or harmed. [BRITISH,

INFORMAL] *The company has been hammered by the downturn in the construction and motor industries.*

▸**hammer in.** See **hammer** 2.

▸**hammer out.** PHR-VERB If you **hammer out** something such as a plan, you reach an agreement about it after a long or difficult discussion. *Diplomats met to hammer out a draft resolution.*

hamper /'hæmpə/ **hampers, hampering, hampered.**
[1] VERB If someone or something **hampers** you, they make it difficult for you to do what you are trying to do. *I was hampered by a lack of information.* [2] N-COUNT A picnic **hamper** is a large basket with a lid, used for carrying food. → See picture on page 48.

hamstring /'hæmstrɪŋ/ **hamstrings, hamstringing, hamstrung.** [1] N-COUNT A **hamstring** is a tendon behind your knee joining the muscles of your thigh to the bones of your lower leg. [2] VERB If you **are hamstrung** by something, it makes it very difficult for you to take any action. [JOURNALISM] *These countries are often hamstrung by lack of money and facilities.*

hand 1 noun and phrase uses

⭐ **hand** /hænd/ **hands.** [1] N-COUNT Your **hands** are the parts of your body at the end of your arms, below the wrist. → See picture on page 822. [2] N-COUNT The **hands** of a clock or watch are the thin pieces of metal or plastic that indicate what time it is. [3] N-SING If you ask someone for **a hand** with something, you are asking them to help you. *Come and give me a hand in the garden... I'd be glad to lend a hand.* [4] N-COUNT In a game of cards, your **hand** is the cards which are dealt to you.

PHRASES • If something is **at hand**, **near at hand**, or **close at hand**, it is very near in place or time. *His retirement was near at hand.* • If you do something **by hand**, you do it using your hands rather than a machine. *...quilts stitched entirely by hand.* • When something **changes hands**, its ownership changes, usually because it is sold to someone else. • If you **force** someone's **hand**, you force them to do something before they are ready to do it, or to do something they do not want to do. • If someone gives you **a free hand**, they allow you to do what you want in a particular situation. • If two things **go hand in hand**, they are closely connected and cannot be considered separately from each other. *Yvette's rise to fame went hand in hand with the growth of the club.* • If you **have a hand in** something, you are one of the people involved in doing it or creating it. • If a situation is **in hand**, it is under control. *The Olympic organisers say that matters are well in hand.* • If someone **lives from hand to mouth**, they have hardly enough food or money to live on. • If someone or something is **on hand**, they are near and able to be used if they are needed. *The Bridal Department will have experts on hand to give you all the help and advice you need.* • You use **on the other hand** to introduce the second of two contrasting points,

facts, or ways of looking at something. You can use **on the one hand** in an earlier sentence to introduce the first part of the contrast. *On the one hand, if the body doesn't have enough cholesterol, we would not be able to survive. On the other hand, if the body has too much cholesterol, the excess begins to line the arteries.*

> **USAGE** Do not confuse **on the contrary** with **on the other hand**. **On the contrary** is used to contradict someone or something, to say that they are wrong. **On the other hand** is used to state a different, often contrasting aspect of the situation you are considering. *Prices of other foods and consumer goods fell. Wages on the other hand increased... He had no wish to hurt her. On the contrary, he thought of her with warmth and affection.*

• If you reject an idea **out of hand**, you reject it without hesitating and without discussing it or considering it first. *I initially dismissed the idea out of hand.* • If you have something **to hand** or **near to hand**, you have it with you or near you, ready to be used when needed. *You may want to keep this brochure safe, so you have it to hand whenever you may need it.* • If you **try** your **hand** at an activity, you attempt to do it, usually for the first time. • If you **wash** your **hands of** someone or something, you refuse to be involved with them any more or to take responsibility for them.

hand 2 verb uses

⭐ **hand** /hænd/ **hands, handing, handed.** VERB If you **hand** something to someone, you pass it to them. *He handed me a little bit of white paper.*

▸**hand down** or **hand on.** PHR-VERB If you **hand** something such as your knowledge or possessions **down**, or **hand** it **on**, you pass it on to other people, often people of a younger generation. *...a Ukrainian folk heritage handed down from their parents.*

▸**hand in.** PHR-VERB If you **hand** something **in**, you give it to someone in authority, so that they can deal with it. *My advice to anyone who finds anything on a bus is to hand it in to the police... All eighty opposition members of parliament have handed in their resignation.*

▸**hand on.** See **hand down**.

▸**hand out.** [1] PHR-VERB If you **hand** something **out**, you give it to people. *One of my jobs was to hand out the prizes.* [2] See also **handout**.

▸**hand over.** PHR-VERB If you **hand** something **over** to someone, you give it to them. *He handed over a letter of apology from the Minister.*

▸**hand over to.** PHR-VERB If you **hand over to** someone, you give them the responsibility for dealing with a particular situation which was previously your responsibility. *The present leaders have to decide whether to stand down and hand over to a younger generation.*

handbag /'hændbæg/ **handbags.** N-COUNT In British English, a **handbag** is a small bag used by women to carry things such as money and keys. The usual American word is **purse.** → See picture on page 48.

handbook /'hændbʊk/ **handbooks.** N-COUNT A **handbook** is a book giving advice or instructions on how to do a practical task.

handcuffs

handcuff /'hændkʌf/ **handcuffs, handcuffing, handcuffed.** [1] N-PLURAL **Handcuffs** are two metal rings linked by a short chain which are locked round a prisoner's wrists. *He was led away to jail in handcuffs.* [2] VERB If the police **handcuff** someone, they put handcuffs around their wrists. *She was handcuffed to a woman police officer during the court hearing.*

handful /'hændfʊl/ **handfuls.** [1] N-SING If there is only a **handful of** people or things, there are not very many of them. *...the handful of customers at the bar.* [2] N-COUNT A **handful of** something is the amount of it that you can hold in your hand. *She scooped up a handful of sand.* [3] N-COUNT If you describe someone, especially a child, as a **handful**, you mean that he or she is difficult to control. [INFORMAL]

handicap /'hændikæp/ **handicaps, handicapping, handicapped.** [1] N-COUNT A **handicap** is a physical or mental disability. [DATED] *He lost his leg when he was ten, but learnt to overcome his handicap.* [2] VERB & N-COUNT If an event or a situation **handicaps** someone or something, or if it is a **handicap to** them, it places them at a disadvantage. *Greater levels of stress may seriously handicap some students... The tax issue was undoubtedly a handicap to Labour.*

handicapped /'hændikæpt/. ADJ & N-PLURAL A **handicapped** person has a physical or mental disability. You can refer to people who are handicapped as **the handicapped.** [DATED] *Alex was mentally handicapped.*

handkerchief /'hæŋkətʃɪf/ **handkerchiefs.** N-COUNT A **handkerchief** is a small square of fabric which you use for blowing your nose.

⭐ **handle** /'hændəl/ **handles, handling, handled.** [1] N-COUNT A **handle** is the part of an object such as a tool, bag, or cup that you hold in order to be able to pick up and use the object. [2] N-COUNT A **handle** is a small round object or a lever that is attached to a door and is used for opening and closing it. *I turned the handle and went in.* [3] VERB

When you **handle** something such as a weapon or car, you use or control it effectively. You can also say that a vehicle **handles** well or badly, depending on how easy it is to steer. *I wanted someone who could handle a gun, just in case... His ship had handled like a dream!* [4] VERB If you **handle** a problem or a particular area of work, you deal with it. *You must learn how to handle your feelings... She handled travel arrangements for the press.* ♦ **handling** N-UNCOUNT *The family has criticized the military's handling of Robert's death.* [5] VERB When you **handle** an object or a person, you hold them or touch them with your hands. *When it sunk in that I might be handling a new born baby my heart skipped a beat.*

handler /'hændlə/ **handlers.** N-COUNT A **handler** is someone whose job is to be in charge of a particular type of thing. *...baggage handlers at Gatwick airport. ...dog handlers.*

handmade /,hænd'meɪd/. ADJ If something is **handmade**, it is made without using machines. *...a pair of handmade shoes.*

handout /'hændaʊt/ **handouts.** [1] N-COUNT A **handout** is money, clothing, or food which is given to people who are badly in need of it. *Soldiers oversee the food handouts.* [2] N-COUNT A **handout** is a document which gives information about something.

'**hands-free.** ADJ BEFORE N A **hands-free** phone or other device can be used without being held in your hand.

handshake /'hændʃeɪk/ **handshakes.** N-COUNT If you give someone a **handshake**, you grasp their right hand with your right hand and move it up and down as a greeting, or to show that you have agreed about something.

handsome /'hænsəm/. [1] ADJ A **handsome** man has an attractive face. [2] ADJ A **handsome** woman has an attractive appearance with large regular features rather than small delicate ones. [3] ADJ BEFORE N A **handsome** sum of money is a large or generous amount of it. [FORMAL] *They will make a handsome profit.* [4] See note at **beautiful**.

,**hands-'on.** ADJ **Hands-on** experience or work involves actually doing a particular thing, rather than just talking about it or getting someone else to do it. *...hands-on experience of computers.*

handwriting /'hændraɪtɪŋ/. N-UNCOUNT Your **handwriting** is your style of writing with a pen or pencil.

handwritten /,hænd'rɪtən/. ADJ A **handwritten** piece of writing was written with a pen or pencil, rather than being typed.

handy /'hændi/ **handier, handiest.** [1] ADJ Something that is **handy** is useful. *...handy hints on looking after indoor plants.* [2] ADJ A thing or place that is **handy** is nearby and convenient. [INFORMAL] *Keep a pen and pad handy by the phone.* [3] ADJ AFTER LINK-V Someone who is **handy with** a particular tool or weapon is skilful at using it. [INFORMAL]

a b c d e f g h i j k l m n o p q r s t u v w x y z

A B C D E F G **H** I J K L M N O P Q R S T U V W X Y Z

★ **hang** /hæŋ/ **hangs, hanging, hung.**

> ✓ The form **hanged** is used as the past tense and past participle in meaning 3.

1 VERB & PHR-VERB If something **hangs** in a high place or position, or if you **hang** it there, it is attached there so it does not touch the ground. **Hang up** means the same as **hang**. *A young woman came out of the house to hang clothes on a line... Some of the prisoners climbed onto the roof and hung up a banner... The walls are hung with old cinema posters.* **2** VERB If a piece of clothing or fabric **hangs** in a particular way or position, that is how it is worn or arranged. *...the shawl hanging loose from her shoulders.* **3** VERB If someone **is hanged**, they are killed by having a rope tied around their neck and the support taken away from under their feet. *He was hanged last month after being found guilty of spying.* **4** VERB If a future event or a possibility **hangs over** you, it worries you. *Threat of unemployment hangs over thousands of university researchers.* **5** PHRASE If you **get the hang of** something, you begin to understand how to do it. [INFORMAL]

▶ **hang about** or **hang around** or **hang round.** PHR-VERB If you **hang about, hang around**, or **hang round** somewhere, you stay or wait there. [INFORMAL] *He got sick of hanging around waiting for me.*

▶ **hang back.** PHR-VERB If you **hang back**, you move or stay slightly behind a person or group, usually because you are nervous about something. *He hung back shyly.*

▶ **hang on.** **1** PHR-VERB If you ask someone to **hang on**, you mean you want them to wait for a moment. [INFORMAL] *Hang on a second. I'll come with you.* **2** PHR-VERB If you **hang on**, you manage to survive until a situation improves. *Manchester United hung on to take the Cup.* **3** PHR-VERB If you **hang on to** or **hang onto** something that gives you an advantage, you succeed in keeping it for yourself. *The President has been trying hard to hang onto power.* **4** PHR-VERB If you **hang on to** or **hang onto** something, you hold it very tightly. **5** PHR-VERB If one thing **hangs on** another, it depends on it. *The survival of the sport hangs on this race.*

▶ **hang out.** **1** PHR-VERB When you **hang out** washing, you hang it on a clothes line to dry. **2** PHR-VERB If you **hang out** in a particular place or area, you go and stay there for no particular reason, or spend a lot of time there. [INFORMAL] *We can just hang out and have a good time.*

▶ **hang round.** See **hang around.**

▶ **hang up.** **1** See **hang 1. 2** PHR-VERB If you **hang up** when you are on the phone, or if you **hang up** on someone, you end the phone call suddenly and unexpectedly by putting back the receiver. *Don't hang up!... He said he'd call again, and hung up on me.*

hangar /'hæŋə/ **hangars.** N-COUNT A **hangar** is a large building in which aircraft are kept.

hanger /'hæŋə/ **hangers.** N-COUNT A **hanger** is a curved piece of metal or wood used for hanging clothes on.

hangover /'hæŋəʊvə/ **hangovers.** **1** N-COUNT A **hangover** is a headache and feeling of sickness that you have after drinking too much alcohol. **2** N-COUNT Something that is a **hangover from** the past is an idea or way of behaving which people used to have in the past but which people no longer generally have. *...the official trade union, a hangover from the past.*

haphazard /hæp'hæzəd/. ADJ If you describe something as **haphazard**, you are critical of it because it is not at all organized or is not arranged according to a plan. *Students find the transition from school to college haphazard and confusing.* ♦ **haphazardly** ADV *...books jammed haphazardly in the shelves.*

hapless /'hæpləs/. ADJ BEFORE N A **hapless** person is unlucky. [FORMAL] *...his hapless victim.*

★ **happen** /'hæpən/ **happens, happening, happened.** **1** VERB When something **happens**, it occurs or is done without being planned. *Tell me what happened... The accident was similar to one that happened in 1973.* **2** VERB When something **happens to** you, it takes place and affects you. *It's the best thing that ever happened to me.* **3** VERB If you **happen** to do something, you do it by chance. If **it happens that** something is the case, it occurs by chance. *I looked in the nearest paper, which happened to be the Daily Mail.* **4** PHRASE You use **as it happens** in order to introduce a statement, especially one that is rather surprising. *As it happened, the demonstration was smaller than expected.*

happening /'hæpənɪŋ/ **happenings.** N-COUNT **Happenings** are things that happen, often in a way that is unexpected or hard to explain. *They plan to hire freelance reporters to cover the latest happenings in the towns.*

★ **happy** /'hæpi/ **happier, happiest.** **1** ADJ Someone who is **happy** has feelings of joy or contentment. *Marina was a confident, happy child.* ♦ **happily** ADV *Joe and Irene were still happily married.* ♦ **happiness** N-UNCOUNT *Money can't buy happiness.* **2** ADJ A time or place that is **happy** is full of pleasant feelings, or has an atmosphere in which people feel happy. *She had had a particularly happy childhood.* **3** ADJ AFTER LINK-V If you are **happy with** a situation or arrangement, you are satisfied with it. *I wasn't too happy with what I'd written so far.* **4** ADJ AFTER LINK-V If you are **happy to** do something, you are willing to do it. *That's a risk I'm happy to take.* **5** ADJ BEFORE N You use **happy** in greetings to say that you hope someone will enjoy a special occasion. *Happy Birthday!* ● **many happy returns**: see **return.** **6** ADJ You use **happy** to describe something that is fortunate or lucky. *By happy coincidence, Robert met Richard and Julia.* ♦ **happily** ADV *Happily, his neck injuries were not serious.*

harass /'hærəs, hə'ræs/ **harasses, harassing, harassed.** VERB If you **harass** someone, you continually trouble them. *We are almost routinely*

harassed by the police. ♦ **harassment** N-UNCOUNT
...sexual harassment.

harassed /'hærəst, hə'ræst/. ADJ If you are
harassed, you are anxious and tense because
you have too much to do or too many problems
to cope with. I grew more and more harassed over
lack of funds and too much to do.

⭐ **harbour** (AM **harbor**) /'hɑːbə/ **harbours,
harbouring, harboured.** [1] N-COUNT A **harbour** is an
area of deep water which is protected from the
sea by land or walls, so that boats can be left
there safely. [2] VERB If you **harbour** an emotion,
you have it for a long period of time. He had
always harboured political ambitions. [3] VERB If a
person or country **harbours** someone who is
wanted by the police, they let them stay in their
house or country and offer them protection.

⭐ **hard** /hɑːd/ **harder, hardest.** [1] ADJ Something that
is **hard** is very firm to touch and is not easily
bent, cut, or broken. ...the hard wooden floor.
♦ **hardness** N-UNCOUNT ...the hardness of the iron
railing. [2] ADJ Something that is **hard** is very
difficult. At my age I would find it hard to get
another job... I have had a hard life... It was a very
hard problem. [3] ADV & ADJ If you try **hard** or work
hard, you make a great effort to achieve
something. Am I trying too hard?... I admired him
as a true scientist and hard worker... Their work is
hard and unglamorous. [4] ADV & ADJ **Hard** means
with a lot of force. I kicked a dustbin very hard...
He gave her a hard push. [5] ADJ & ADV Someone
who is **hard** shows no kindness or pity. His father
was a hard man... Don't be so hard on him... The
security forces would continue to crack down hard
on the protesters. [6] ADJ A **hard** winter or a **hard**
frost is very cold. [7] ADJ BEFORE N **Hard** evidence
or facts are definitely true. He wanted more hard
evidence. [8] ADJ **Hard** drugs are strong illegal
drugs such as heroin.
PHRASES ● If you say that something is **hard
going**, you mean it is difficult and requires a lot
of effort. The talks had been hard going at the
start. ● If someone is **hard put to** or **hard
pushed to** do something, they have difficulty
doing it. I'd be hard pushed to teach him anything.

hardback /'hɑːdbæk/ **hardbacks.** N-VAR A
hardback is a book which has a stiff cover. 'The
Secret History' was published in hardback.

'**hard core.** N-SING You can refer to the
members of a group who are most involved with
its activities as the **hard core.** ...a hard-core group
of right-wing senators.

'**hard 'currency, hard currencies.** N-VAR A **hard
currency** is one which is unlikely to lose its value
and so is considered to be a good one to have or
to invest in.

'**hard disk, hard disks.** N-COUNT A **hard disk** is a
hard plastic disk inside a computer on which data
and programs are stored. [COMPUTING]

harden /'hɑːdən/ **hardens, hardening, hardened.**
[1] VERB When something **hardens**, it becomes
stiff or firm. Give the cardboard two or three coats

of varnish to harden it. [2] VERB When you **harden**
your ideas or attitudes, they become fixed and
you become determined that you will not change
them. ♦ **hardening** N-UNCOUNT ...a hardening of
the government's attitude. [3] VERB When people
harden, or when events **harden** them, they
become less sympathetic and gentle. Witnessing
the horrors of the Bosnian war hardened her.

hardline (or **hard-line**) /,hɑːd'laɪn/. ADJ If you
describe someone's policy or attitude as
hardline, you mean that it is strict or extreme,
and they refuse to change it. He will continue with
the same hardline policies towards drugs.

⭐ **hardly** /'hɑːdli/. [1] ADV You use **hardly** to say
that something is only just true. I hardly know
you... Hardly anyone slept that night. [2] ADV If you
say **hardly** had one thing happened when
something else happened, you mean that the
first event was followed immediately by the
second. He had hardly collected the papers on his
desk when the door burst open. [3] ADV You use
hardly to mean 'not' when you want to suggest
that you are expecting your listener or reader to
agree with your comment. It's hardly surprising his
ideas didn't catch on.

,**hard-'pressed.** [1] ADJ If someone is **hard-
pressed**, they are under a lot of strain and worry.
...hard-pressed, poorly paid professionals. [2] ADJ If
you will be **hard-pressed to** do something, you
will have great difficulty doing it. The airline will
be hard-pressed to make a profit.

hardship /'hɑːdʃɪp/ **hardships.** N-VAR **Hardship** is
a situation in which your life is difficult or
unpleasant. Many people are suffering economic
hardship.

hardware /'hɑːdweə/. [1] N-UNCOUNT Computer
hardware is computer equipment as opposed to
the programs that are written for it. [COMPUTING]
[2] N-UNCOUNT Military **hardware** is the equipment
that is used by the armed forces, such as tanks
and missiles. [3] N-UNCOUNT **Hardware** is
equipment such as hammers and screws for use
in the home and garden.

hardy /'hɑːdi/ **hardier, hardiest.** ADJ People,
animals, and plants that are **hardy** are strong and
able to endure difficult conditions. ...the ten hardy
football supporters who had made the trek to
Dublin.

hare /heə/ **hares.** N-COUNT A **hare** is an animal like
a large rabbit, but with longer ears and legs.

hark /hɑːk/ **harks, harking, harked.**
▸**hark back to.** [1] PHR-VERB If you say that one
thing **harks back to** another thing in the past,
you mean that it is similar to it or takes it as a
model. ...pitched roofs, which hark back to the
Victorian era. [2] PHR-VERB When people **hark
back to** something in the past, they remember it
or tell someone about it. ...whether Puttnam
should be harking back to a conflict that happened
nearly fifty years ago.

⭐ **harm** /hɑːm/ **harms, harming, harmed.** [1] VERB &
N-UNCOUNT To **harm** someone or something, or to

a
b
c
d
e
f
g
h
i
j
k
l
m
n
o
p
q
r
s
t
u
v
w
x
y
z

⭐ Bank of English® frequent word   For a full explanation of all grammatical labels, see pages vii-x

cause them **harm**, means to injure or damage them. *The hijackers seemed anxious not to harm anyone... To cut taxes would probably do the economy more harm than good.* **2** PHRASE If you say that **there is no harm in** doing something, you mean that it might be worth doing, and you will not be blamed for doing it. *They are not always willing to take on untrained workers, but there's no harm in asking.*

harmful /'hɑːmfʊl/. ADJ Something that is **harmful** has a bad effect on someone or something else. ...*the harmful effects of smoking.*

harmless /'hɑːmləs/. **1** ADJ Something that is **harmless** does not have any bad effects. *This experiment was harmless to the animals.* **2** ADJ If you describe someone or something as **harmless**, you mean that they are not important and therefore unlikely to annoy other people or cause trouble. *He seemed harmless enough.*

harmonic /hɑː'mɒnɪk/. ADJ **Harmonic** means composed, played, or sung using two or more notes which sound right and pleasing together. ...*harmonic and rhythmic structures.*

harmonious /hɑː'məʊnɪəs/. **1** ADJ A **harmonious** relationship, agreement, or discussion is friendly and peaceful.
♦ **harmoniously** ADV *It is unfortunate when neighbours cannot live harmoniously.* **2** ADJ Something that is **harmonious** has parts which go well together. ...*a harmonious balance of mind, body, and spirit.*

harmonize (BRIT also **harmonise**) /'hɑːmənaɪz/ **harmonizes, harmonizing, harmonized.** VERB If two or more things **harmonize with** each other, they fit in well with each other. ...*slabs of pink and beige stone that harmonize with the carpet... Their tastes don't harmonize.*

harmony /'hɑːməni/ **harmonies.** **1** N-UNCOUNT If people are living **in harmony with** each other, they are in a state of peaceful agreement and co-operation. ...*racial harmony. ...the notion that man should dominate nature rather than live in harmony with it.* **2** N-VAR **Harmony** is the pleasant combination of different notes of music played at the same time. ...*complex vocal harmonies. ...singing in harmony.* **3** N-UNCOUNT The **harmony** of something is the way in which its parts are combined into a pleasant arrangement. ...*the ordered harmony of the universe.*

harness /'hɑːnɪs/ **harnesses, harnessing, harnessed.** **1** VERB To **harness** something means to control it and use it. ...*the movement's ability to harness the anger of all Ukrainians... Turkey plans to harness the waters of the Tigris and Euphrates rivers.* **2** N-COUNT A **harness** is a set of straps which fits around a person or animal, for example to attach a piece of equipment to them. **3** VERB If a horse or other animal **is harnessed**, a harness is put on it. *The horses were harnessed to a heavy wagon.*

harp /hɑːp/ **harps, harping, harped.** N-COUNT A **harp** is a large musical instrument consisting of a triangular frame with vertical strings which you pluck with your fingers. → See picture on page 827.

▸**harp on.** PHR-VERB If someone **harps on about** something, they keep talking about it; used showing disapproval. *She concentrated on the good parts of her trip instead of harping on about the bad.*

harrowing /'hærəʊɪŋ/. ADJ A **harrowing** sight or experience is very upsetting or disturbing. ...*harrowing pictures of the children who had been murdered.*

harsh /hɑːʃ/ **harsher, harshest.** **1** ADJ **Harsh** climates or living conditions are very difficult for people, animals, and plants to exist in. *The weather grew harsh, chilly and unpredictable.*
♦ **harshness** N-UNCOUNT ...*the harshness of their living conditions.* **2** ADJ **Harsh** actions or remarks are unkind and show no understanding or sympathy. ...*the cold, harsh cruelty of her husband.*
♦ **harshly** ADV *Her husband is being harshly treated in prison.* ♦ **harshness** N-UNCOUNT *She apologizes for the harshness of her words.* **3** ADJ Something that is **harsh** is so hard, bright, or rough that it seems unpleasant or harmful. ...*harsher detergents that can leave hair brittle.*

harvest /'hɑːvɪst/ **harvests, harvesting, harvested.** **1** VERB & N-SING When farmers **harvest** a crop, they gather it in. You can refer to this activity as **the harvest.** ...*there was about 300 million tons of grain in the fields at the start of the harvest.* **2** N-COUNT A crop is called a **harvest** when it has been gathered. ...*a bumper potato harvest.*

has

☑ The auxiliary verb is pronounced /həz, STRONG hæz/. The main verb is usually pronounced /hæz/.

Has is the third person singular of the present tense of **have**.

hash /hæʃ/. PHRASE If you **make a hash of** a job, you do it very badly. [INFORMAL] *Watson had made a thorough hash of it.*

hasn't /'hæzənt/. **Hasn't** is the usual spoken form of 'has not'.

hassle /'hæsəl/ **hassles, hassling, hassled.** **1** N-VAR A **hassle** is a situation that is difficult and involves problems, effort, or arguments with people. ...*all the usual hassles at airport check-in.* **2** VERB If someone **hassles** you, they irritate you by repeatedly telling you or asking you to do something that you do not want to do. [INFORMAL] ...*if you are tired of being hassled by unreasonable parents.*

haste /heɪst/. N-UNCOUNT **Haste** is the quality of doing something too quickly, so that you are careless and make mistakes. *The translations bear the signs of inaccuracy and haste... Loneliness can lead to people remarrying in haste.*

hasten /'heɪsən/ **hastens, hastening, hastened.** **1** VERB If you **hasten** an event or process, you make it happen faster or sooner. [WRITTEN] *He may hasten the collapse of his own country.* [2] VERB If you **hasten to** do something, you are quick to do it. *'There's no threat in this, Freddie,' Arnold hastened to say.*

hasty /ˈheɪsti/ **hastier, hastiest.** [1] ADJ **Hasty** means done or arranged in a hurry, without planning or preparation. *The signs of their hasty departure could be seen everywhere.* ◆ **hastily** ADV *'No, I'm sure it's not,' said Virginia hastily.* [2] ADJ If you describe what someone does or says as **hasty**, you mean that they are acting too quickly, without thinking carefully; used showing disapproval. *The Government should not be pressured into making hasty decisions.*

⭐ **hat** /hæt/ **hats.** N-COUNT A **hat** is a covering that you wear on your head. → See picture on page 819.

hatch /hætʃ/ **hatches, hatching, hatched.** [1] VERB When an egg **hatches**, or when it **is hatched**, a baby bird or animal comes out by breaking the shell. *The young disappeared soon after they were hatched.* [2] VERB If someone **hatches** a plot or a scheme, they think of it and work it out; used showing disapproval. *He has accused opposition parties of hatching a plot to assassinate the Pope.* [3] N-COUNT A **hatch** is a small covered opening in a floor, wall, or ceiling.

hatchet /ˈhætʃɪt/ **hatchets.** N-COUNT A **hatchet** is a small axe.

⭐ **hate** /heɪt/ **hates, hating, hated.** [1] VERB & N-UNCOUNT If you **hate** someone or something, or if you have feelings of **hate** towards them, you have an extremely strong dislike for them. *Most people hate him, but they don't dare to say so. ...a violent bully, destructive and full of hate.* [2] VERB You can use **hate** in expressions such as '**I hate to say it**' and '**I hate to tell you**' when you want to express regret about what you are about to say. *I hate to tell you this, but tomorrow's your last day.*

hatred /ˈheɪtrɪd/. N-UNCOUNT **Hatred** is an extremely strong feeling of dislike for someone or something. *Her hatred of authority led to her expulsion from high school.*

'**hat-trick, hat-tricks.** N-COUNT A **hat-trick** is a series of three achievements, for example three goals scored by the same person in a football match.

haul /hɔːl/ **hauls, hauling, hauled.** [1] VERB If you **haul** a heavy object somewhere, you pull it there with a great effort. *A crane had to be used to haul the car out of the stream.* [2] PHRASE If you say that a task or a journey is **a long haul**, you mean that it takes a long time and a lot of effort. *Revitalising the economy will be a long haul.*

haunt /hɔːnt/ **haunts, haunting, haunted.** [1] VERB If something unpleasant **haunts** you, you keep thinking or worrying about it over a long period of time. *The decision to leave her children now haunts her.* [2] N-COUNT A place that is the **haunt** of a particular person is one which they often visit because they enjoy going there. *Morris came up to*

New York to revisit his old haunts. [3] VERB If people say that a ghost or spirit **haunts** a place or a person, they mean that a ghost or spirit regularly appears in that place or is seen by that person.

haunted /ˈhɔːntɪd/. [1] ADJ A **haunted** building or other place is one where a ghost regularly appears. [2] ADJ Someone who has a **haunted** expression looks very worried or troubled. *She looked so haunted, I almost didn't recognize her.*

haunting /ˈhɔːntɪŋ/. ADJ **Haunting** sounds, images, or words remain in your thoughts because they are very beautiful or sad. *...the haunting calls of wild birds.* ◆ **hauntingly** ADV *Each one of these ancient towns is hauntingly beautiful.*

⭐ **have,** STRONG hæv, **has, having, had.** [1] MODAL You use **have to** when you are saying that something is necessary, obligatory, or must happen. If you do not **have to** do something, it is not necessary or obligatory for you to do it. *He had to go to Germany... We'll have to find a taxi... They didn't have to pay tax.* [2] VERB You use **have** when you are saying that someone or something owns, possesses, or holds a particular thing, or when you are mentioning one of their qualities or characteristics. *Oscar had a new bicycle... You have beautiful eyes... Do you have any brothers and sisters?... I have no doubt at all in my own mind about this... I have my microphone with me.* [3] VERB If a woman **has** a baby, she gives birth to it. If she **is having** a baby, she is pregnant. [4] VERB If you **have** something **to** do, you are responsible for doing it or must do it. *He had plenty of work to do... I have some important calls to make.* [5] VERB If you **have** something such a part of your body in a particular position or state, it is in that position or state. *Mary had her eyes closed... They had the curtains open.* [6] VERB If someone **has** you **by** a part of your body, they are holding you there and they are trying to hurt you or force you to go somewhere. *Larry had him by the ear and was beating his head against the pavement.* [7] VERB If you **have** something done, someone does it for you or you arrange for it to be done. *I had your rooms cleaned and aired... You've had your hair cut.* [8] VERB If someone or something **has** something happen to them, usually something unpleasant, it happens to them. *We had our money stolen.* [9] PHRASE You can use **has it** in expressions like '**rumour has it that**' and '**as legend has it**' when you are quoting something that you have heard, but you do not necessarily think it is true. *Rumour has it that tickets were being sold for £300.*

haven /ˈheɪvən/ **havens.** N-COUNT A **haven** is a place where people or animals are safe from trouble or danger. *...Lake Baringo, a freshwater haven for a mixed variety of birds.*

haven't /ˈhævənt/. **Haven't** is the usual spoken form of 'have not'.

havoc /ˈhævək/. [1] N-UNCOUNT **Havoc** is a state of chaos, confusion, and disorder. *Rioters caused havoc in the centre of the town.* [2] PHRASE If one thing **plays havoc with** another or **wreaks**

havoc on it, it prevents it from continuing or functioning as normal, or damages it. *The weather played havoc with airline schedules.*

hawk /hɔːk/ **hawks.** N-COUNT A **hawk** is a large bird that hunts other animals.

hay /heɪ/. N-UNCOUNT **Hay** is grass which has been cut and dried so that it can be used to feed animals. *...bales of hay.*

'**hay fever.** N-UNCOUNT If someone suffers from **hay fever**, they have an allergy to pollen which makes their nose, throat, and eyes become red and swollen.

hazard /'hæzəd/ **hazards, hazarding, hazarded.** **1** N-COUNT A **hazard** is something which could be dangerous to you. *The deer are a hazard to motorists.* **2** VERB If you **hazard** a guess that something is the case, you make a guess about it which you know might be wrong.

hazardous /'hæzədəs/. ADJ **Hazardous** things are dangerous, especially to people's health or safety. *Lead is hazardous to unborn babies.*

haze /heɪz/ **hazes.** **1** N-VAR **Haze** is a light mist caused by heat or dust in the air. *...the shimmering heat haze.* **2** N-SING If there is a **haze** of something such as smoke or steam, you cannot see clearly through it. [LITERARY] *...a haze of cigarette smoke.*

hazel /'heɪzəl/ **hazels.** **1** N-VAR A **hazel** is a small tree which produces edible nuts. **2** ADJ **Hazel** eyes are greenish-brown.

hazy /'heɪzi/ **hazier, haziest.** **1** ADJ When the sky or a view is **hazy**, you cannot see it clearly because there is a haze. *...a warm, hazy summer afternoon.* **2** ADJ If you are **hazy about** things, or if your thoughts are **hazy**, you are confused. *I'm a bit hazy about that... I have only a hazy memory of what he was really like.*

★ **he** /hɪ, STRONG hiː/. PRON You use **he** to refer to a man, boy, or male animal. **He** is used as the subject of a verb. *He lives in Rapid City.*

head 1 noun uses

★ **head** /hed/ **heads.** **1** N-COUNT Your **head** is the part of your body which has your eyes, mouth, nose, and brain in it. → See picture on page 822. *She turned her head away from him.* **2** N-COUNT You can use **head** to refer to your mind and your mental abilities. *I can't get that song out of my head. ...an exceptional analyst who could do complex maths in his head.* **3** N-COUNT The **head** of an organization, school, or department is the person in charge of it. *...heads of government from more than 100 countries... She became head of a girls' school.* **4** N-SING The **head** of something is the top, start, or most important end of it. *...the head of the stairs*

head 2 verb uses

★ **head** /hed/ **heads, heading, headed.** **1** VERB If someone or something **heads** a line or procession, they are at the front of it. **2** VERB If something **heads** a list or group, it is at the top of it. *Running a business heads the list of ambitions.* **3** VERB If a piece of writing **is headed**

a particular title, it has that title written at the beginning of it. *One chapter is headed, 'Beating the Test'.* **4** VERB If you **are heading for** a particular place or in a particular direction, you are going towards that place or in that direction. You can also say that you **are headed for** a particular place. *He headed for the bus stop... It is not clear how many of them will be heading back to Saudi Arabia.* **5** VERB If something or someone **is heading for** a particular result, the situation they are in is developing in a way that makes that result very likely. You can also say that something or someone **is headed** towards a particular result. *The centuries-old ritual seems headed for extinction.* **6** VERB When you **head** a ball, you hit it with your head. *He headed the ball across the face of the goal.* **7** See also **heading.**

head 3 phrases

★ **head** /hed/ **heads.**

PHRASES ● The cost or amount **per head** or a **head** is the cost or amount for one person. *This simple chicken dish costs less than £1 a head.* ● If a problem or disagreement **comes to a head** or if you **bring** it **to a head**, it reaches a state where you have to do something about it urgently. *These problems came to a head in September when five of the station's journalists were sacked.* ● If you **get** something **into** your **head**, you suddenly decide that it is true and you will not change your mind about it. ● If you say that something such as praise or success **goes to** someone's **head**, you mean that they become arrogant as a result of it. ● If you **keep** your **head**, you remain calm in a difficult situation. If you **lose** your **head**, you panic or do not remain calm.

headache /'hedeɪk/ **headaches.** **1** N-COUNT If you have a **headache**, you have a pain in your head. **2** N-COUNT If you say that something is a **headache**, you mean that it causes you difficulty or worry. *The biggest headache for mothers hoping to return to study is childcare.*

header /'hedə/ **headers.** N-COUNT A **header** is text such as a name or a page number that can be automatically displayed at the top of each page of a printed document.

heading /'hedɪŋ/ **headings.** N-COUNT A **heading** is the title of a piece of writing, written or printed at the top of the page. *...chapter headings.*

headlight /'hedlaɪt/ **headlights.** N-COUNT A vehicle's **headlights** are the large bright lights at the front.

★ **headline** /'hedlaɪn/ **headlines.** **1** N-COUNT A **headline** is the title of a newspaper story, printed in large letters at the top of it. *The headline says 'Pentagon plans major cuts'.* **2** N-PLURAL The **headlines** are the main points of a radio or television news broadcast. **3** PHRASE Someone or something that **hits the headlines** gets a lot of publicity from the media.

headlined /'hedlaɪnd/. ADJ AFTER LINK-V If a newspaper story is **headlined** something, that is its title. *...an article headlined 'Don't Panic'.*

headlong /'hedlɒŋ, ᴀᴍ -lɔːŋ/. **1** ADV If you move **headlong** in a particular direction, you move there very quickly. *He ran headlong for the open door.* **2** ADV & ADJ BEFORE N If you rush **headlong** into something, you do it quickly, without thinking carefully about it. *Do not leap headlong into decisions. ...the headlong rush to independence will create further problems.*

headmaster /,hed'mɑːstə, -'mæst-/ **headmasters.** N-COUNT A **headmaster** is a man who is the head teacher of a school. [BRITISH]

headmistress /,hed'mɪstrɪs/ **headmistresses.** N-COUNT A **headmistress** is a woman who is the head teacher of a school. [BRITISH]

,head of 'state, heads of state. N-COUNT A **head of state** is the leader of a country, for example a president or queen.

,head-'on. **1** ADV & ADJ BEFORE N If two vehicles hit each other **head-on**, they hit each other with their front parts pointing towards each other. *The car collided head-on with a van. ...a head-on collision.* **2** ADJ BEFORE N & ADV A **head-on** disagreement is firm and direct and has no compromises. *...a head-on clash between the president and the assembly... I chose to confront the issue head-on.*

headphones /'hedfəʊnz/. N-PLURAL **Headphones** are small speakers which you wear over your ears in order to listen to music or other sounds without other people hearing.

⭐ **headquarters** /'hedkwɔːtəz/. N-COUNT The **headquarters** of an organization are its main offices. **Headquarters** can take the singular or plural form of the verb. *...the army's headquarters in Buenos Aires.*

,head 'start. N-SING If you have a **head start** on other people, you have an advantage over them in a competition or race. *A good education gives your child a head start in life.*

,head 'teacher (or **headteacher**) **head teachers.** N-COUNT A **head teacher** is a teacher who is in charge of a school. [BRITISH]

headway /'hedweɪ/. PHRASE If you **make headway**, you make progress towards achieving something. *Police were making little headway in the investigation.*

heady /'hedi/ **headier, headiest.** ADJ A **heady** atmosphere or experience strongly affects your senses, for example by making you feel drunk or excited. *...the heady days just after their marriage.*

⭐ **heal** /hiːl/ **heals, healing, healed.** **1** VERB When an injury such as a broken bone **heals**, it becomes healthy and normal again. *It will take three to four weeks before the fracture fully heals.* **2** VERB If you **heal** something such as a disagreement between people, you restore the situation to its former state. *...the man most likely to heal the wounds in the party.*

healer /'hiːlə/ **healers.** N-COUNT A **healer** is a person who treats sick people, especially one who believes that they are able to heal people through prayer or a supernatural power.

⭐ **health** /helθ/. **1** N-UNCOUNT Your **health** is the condition of your body. *Smoking is bad for your health.* **2** N-UNCOUNT **Health** is a state in which you are fit and well. *They nursed me back to health.* **3** N-UNCOUNT The **health** of an organization or system is the success that it has and the fact that it is working well. *...the longer-term improvement in the health of the economy.*

⭐ **healthy** /'helθi/ **healthier, healthiest.** **1** ADJ Someone who is **healthy** is well and is not suffering from any illness. Something that is **healthy** shows that a person is well. *She was a very healthy child. ...the glow of healthy skin.* ♦ **healthily** ADV *What I really want is to live healthily for as long as possible.* **2** ADJ Something that is **healthy** is good for you. *...a healthy diet.* **3** ADJ A **healthy** organization or system is successful. *...recent collapses of apparently healthy companies.* **4** ADJ A **healthy** amount of something is a large amount that shows success. *...healthy profits.*

heap /hiːp/ **heaps, heaping, heaped.** **1** N-COUNT A **heap of** things is an untidy pile of them. *...a heap of clothes.*

> **USAGE** A **heap** of things is usually untidy, and often has the shape of a hill or mound. *Now, the house is a heap of rubble.* A **stack** is usually tidy, and often consists of flat objects placed directly on top of each other. *...a neat stack of dishes.* A **pile** of things can be tidy or untidy. *...a neat pile of clothes.*

2 VERB & PHR-VERB If you **heap** things, or if you **heap** them **up**, you arrange them in a pile. *Mrs. Madrigal heaped more carrots onto Michael's plate... The militia was heaping up wood for a bonfire.* **3** VERB If you **heap** praise or criticism **on** someone or something, you give them a lot of praise or criticism. **4** QUANT **Heaps of** something or a **heap of** it is a large quantity of it. [INFORMAL] *You have heaps of time... I got in a heap of trouble.*

⭐ **hear** /hɪə/ **hears, hearing, heard** /hɜːd/. **1** VERB When you **hear** sounds, you are aware of them because they reach your ears. *I heard the sound of gunfire.*

> **USAGE** Do not confuse **hear** and **listen**. You use **hear** to talk about sounds that you are aware of because they reach your ears. You often use **can** with **hear**. *I can hear him yelling and swearing.* If you want to say that someone is paying attention to something they can hear, you say that they **are listening to** it. *He turned on the radio and listened to the news.* Note that **listen** is not followed directly by an object. You must always say that you listen **to** something. However, **listen** can also be used on its own without an object. *I was laughing too much to listen.*

a
b
c
d
e
f
g
h
i
j
k
l
m
n
o
p
q
r
s
t
u
v
w
x
y
z

A B C D E F G H I J K L M N O P Q R S T U V W X Y Z

2 VERB When a judge or a court **hears** a case or **hears** evidence, they listen to it officially in order to make a decision about it. [FORMAL] *The case will be heard next week.* **3** VERB If you **hear from** someone, you receive a letter or a telephone call from them. *The police are anxious to hear from anyone who may know her.* **4** VERB If you **hear** some news or information, you learn it because someone tells it to you or it is mentioned on the radio or television. *My mother heard of this school through Leslie... I heard that he was forced to resign... You mean you still haven't heard anything of Ian?*

PHRASES ● If you **have** never **heard of** someone or something, you know nothing about them. ● If you **won't hear of** someone doing something, you refuse to let them do it.

★ **hearing** /'hɪərɪŋ/ **hearings.** **1** N-UNCOUNT **Hearing** is the sense which makes it possible for you to be aware of sounds. *My hearing has grown sharper.* **2** N-COUNT A **hearing** is an official meeting held to collect facts about an incident or problem. **3** N-COUNT If someone gives you a **hearing** or a **fair hearing**, they listen to you when you give your opinion about something.

★ **heart** /hɑːt/ **hearts.** **1** N-COUNT Your **heart** is the organ in your chest that pumps the blood around your body. *...the beating of his heart.* **2** N-COUNT You can refer to someone's **heart** when you are talking about their deep feelings and beliefs. [LITERARY] *Alik's words filled her heart with pride.* **3** N-VAR You use **heart** when you are talking about someone's character and attitude towards other people. *She's got a good heart.* **4** N-SING If you refer to things **of the heart**, you mean love and romance. **5** N-SING The **heart of** something is the most important part of it. *The heart of the problem is supply and demand.* **6** N-SING The **heart of** a place is its centre. *...the heart of London's West End.* **7** N-COUNT A **heart** is a shape that is sometimes used as a symbol of love. → See picture on page 829. **8** N-VAR **Hearts** is one of the four suits in a pack of playing cards. Each card in the suit is called a **heart** and is marked with one or more symbols: ♥.

PHRASES ● If you feel or believe something **with all** your **heart**, you feel or believe it very strongly. *My own family I loved with all my heart.* ● If someone is a particular kind of person **at heart**, this is what they are really like. ● If someone or something **breaks** your **heart**, or if they give you a **broken heart**, they make you very unhappy. ● If you know something such as a poem **by heart**, you have learnt all the words and can remember them. ● If you have a **change of heart**, your feelings about something change. ● If something is **close to** your **heart**, or if it is **dear to** your **heart**, you care deeply about it. ● If you say something **from the heart**, you sincerely mean what you say. *I don't want to go away without thanking you from the bottom of my heart.* ● If your **heart sinks**, you suddenly feel very disappointed or unhappy. *Our hearts sank*

when we saw this awful hotel. ● If you **take heart from** something, you are made to feel encouraged and optimistic by it. ● If you **take** something **to heart**, you are deeply affected and upset by it.

heartache /'hɑːteɪk/ **heartaches.** N-VAR **Heartache** is very great sadness and emotional suffering. [JOURNALISM] *...the heartache of her divorce.*

'**heart attack, heart attacks.** N-COUNT If someone has a **heart attack**, their heart begins to beat irregularly or stops completely.

heartbeat /'hɑːtbiːt/ **heartbeats.** **1** N-SING Your **heartbeat** is the regular movement of your heart as it pumps blood around your body. *Your baby's heartbeat will be monitored continuously.* **2** N-COUNT A **heartbeat** is one of the movements of your heart. *Smoking could lead to irregular heartbeats.*

heartbreak /'hɑːtbreɪk/ **heartbreaks.** N-VAR **Heartbreak** is very great sadness or unhappiness. *...suffering and heartbreak for those close to the victims.*

heartbreaking /'hɑːtbreɪkɪŋ/. ADJ Something that is **heartbreaking** makes you feel extremely sad and upset. *They have taken the heartbreaking decision to have no more children.*

heartbroken /'hɑːtbrəʊkən/. ADJ Someone who is **heartbroken** is extremely sad and upset.

hearten /'hɑːtən/ **heartens, heartening, heartened.** VERB If you **are heartened** by something, it encourages you and makes you cheerful. *The news heartened everybody.* ◆ **heartened** ADJ AFTER LINK-V *I feel heartened by her progress.* ◆ **heartening** ADJ *It has been very heartening to see new writing emerging.*

'**heart failure.** N-UNCOUNT **Heart failure** is a serious medical condition in which someone's heart stops working properly or stops completely.

heartfelt /'hɑːtfelt/. ADJ **Heartfelt** is used to describe a deep or sincere feeling or wish. *My heartfelt sympathy goes out to all the relatives.*

hearth /hɑːθ/ **hearths.** N-COUNT The **hearth** is the floor of a fireplace, which sometimes extends into the room.

heartland /'hɑːtlænd/ **heartlands.** N-COUNT **Heartland** or **heartlands** is used to refer to the area or region where a particular set of activities or beliefs is most significant. *...the industrial heartland of America.*

hearty /'hɑːti/ **heartier, heartiest.** **1** ADJ **Hearty** people or actions are loud, cheerful, and energetic. ◆ **heartily** ADV *He laughed heartily.* **2** ADJ **Hearty** feelings or opinions are strongly felt. *Arnold was in hearty agreement.* ◆ **heartily** ADV *I heartily agree with her favourable comments.* **3** ADJ A **hearty** meal is large and very satisfying. *The boys ate a hearty breakfast.*

★ **heat** /hiːt/ **heats, heating, heated.** **1** VERB & PHR-VERB When you **heat** something, or when you **heat** it **up**, you raise its temperature. *Heat the tomatoes and oil in a pan... Freda heated up a pie for me.*

2 N-UNCOUNT **Heat** is warmth or the quality of being hot. ...*the fierce heat of the sun.*
3 N-UNCOUNT The **heat** of something is its temperature. *Adjust the heat of the barbecue.*
4 N-SING The **heat of** a particular activity is the point when there is the greatest activity or excitement. ...*in the heat of the election campaign.*
5 N-COUNT A **heat** is one of a series of races or competitions. The winners of a heat take part in another race or competition, against the winners of other heats.
▸**heat up.** **1** PHR-VERB When something **heats up**, it gradually becomes hotter. ...*when her mobile home heats up like an oven.* **2** See also **heat** 1.

heated /ˈhiːtɪd/. ADJ If someone is **heated** about something, they get angry and excited about it. A **heated** discussion or quarrel is one where the people involved are angry and excited.
♦ **heatedly** ADV *The crowd continued to argue heatedly about the best way to tackle the problem.*

heater /ˈhiːtə/ **heaters.** N-COUNT A **heater** is a piece of equipment which is used to warm a place or to heat water.

heather /ˈhɛðə/. N-UNCOUNT **Heather** is a low spreading plant with small purple, pink, or white flowers that grows wild on hills or moorland.

heating /ˈhiːtɪŋ/. N-UNCOUNT **Heating** is the process or equipment involved in keeping a building warm. ...*cottages for £150 a week, including heating.* ● See also **central heating.**

heave /hiːv/ **heaves, heaving, heaved.** **1** VERB & N-COUNT If you **heave** an object that is heavy or difficult to move, or if you move it with a **heave**, you push, pull, or lift it using a lot of effort. *It took five strong men to heave it up a ramp... It took only one heave to hurl him into the river.* **2** VERB If something **heaves**, it moves up and down with large regular movements. *His chest heaved, and he took a deep breath.*

⭐ **heaven** /ˈhɛvən/ **heavens.** **1** N-PROPER In some religions, **heaven** is said to be the place where God lives and where good people go when they die. **2** N-PLURAL The **heavens** are the sky. [DATED] *The stars glittered in the heavens.*
PHRASES ● You say **'good heavens'** to express surprise. *Good Heavens! That explains a lot!* ● You can say **'Heaven knows'** to emphasize that you do not know something, or that you find something very surprising. [BRITISH, INFORMAL] *Heaven knows what they put in it.* ● You can say **'Heaven knows'** to emphasize something that you feel or believe very strongly. [BRITISH, INFORMAL] *Heaven knows they have enough money.* ● **thank heavens:** see **thank.**

heavenly /ˈhɛvənli/. **1** ADJ **Heavenly** describes things relating to heaven. ...*heavenly beings whose function it is to serve God.* **2** ADJ If you describe something as **heavenly**, you mean that it is very pleasant and enjoyable. [INFORMAL] *The idea of spending two weeks with him may seem heavenly.*

heavily /ˈhɛvɪli/. ADV You can use **heavily** to indicate that something is great in amount, degree, or intensity. ...*heavily armed soldiers... The agency was heavily criticised.*

⭐ **heavy** /ˈhɛvi/ **heavier, heaviest.** **1** ADJ Something that is **heavy** weighs a lot. *He opened the heavy Bible.* ♦ **heaviness** N-UNCOUNT ...*a sensation of warmth and heaviness in the muscles.* **2** ADJ You use **heavy** to ask or talk about how much someone or something weighs. *How heavy are you?... Protons are nearly 2000 times as heavy as electrons.* **3** ADJ Someone or something that is **heavy** is solid in appearance or structure. ...*heavy old brown furniture... He was short and heavy.*
♦ **heavily** ADV ...*a big man of about forty, wide-shouldered and heavily built.* **4** ADJ **Heavy** means great in amount, degree, or intensity. *Heavy fighting has been going on. ...the heavy responsibility that parents take on.* ♦ **heaviness** N-UNCOUNT ...*the heaviness of the blood loss.* **5** ADJ If a person's breathing is **heavy**, it is very loud and deep. ♦ **heavily** ADV *She sank back on the pillow and closed her eyes, breathing heavily.*
6 ADJ BEFORE N A **heavy** movement or action is done with a lot of force or pressure. *You sustained a heavy blow on the back of the skull.* ♦ **heavily** ADV *I sat down heavily on the ground.* **7** ADJ If you describe a period of time or a schedule as **heavy**, you mean it involves a lot of work. *It's been a heavy day and I'm tired.* **8** ADJ **Heavy** work requires a lot of physical strength. **9** ADJ **Heavy** air or weather is unpleasantly still, hot, and damp. **10** ADJ A situation that is **heavy** is serious and difficult to cope with. [INFORMAL] ...*when you can't handle your best friends' heavy conversation.*

heavy-'duty. ADJ A **heavy-duty** machine is strong and can be used a lot. ...*a heavy-duty polythene bag.*

heavy-'handed. ADJ If you say that someone is **heavy-handed**, you mean they are unnecessarily forceful and thoughtless. ...*heavy-handed police tactics.*

heavyweight /ˈhɛviweɪt/ **heavyweights.**
1 N-COUNT A **heavyweight** is a boxer or wrestler in the heaviest class. **2** N-COUNT If you refer to a person or organization as a **heavyweight**, you mean that they have a lot of influence, experience, and importance in a particular field. ...*a political heavyweight.*

Hebrew /ˈhiːbruː/. N-UNCOUNT **Hebrew** is a language spoken by Jews.

heck /hɛk/. **1** EXCLAM You say **'heck!'** to express slight irritation or surprise. [INFORMAL] *Oh, heck. What can I write about?... What the heck's that?* **2** PHRASE People use **a heck of** to emphasize how big something is or how much of it there is. [INFORMAL] *They're spending a heck of a lot of money.*

heckle /ˈhɛkəl/ **heckles, heckling, heckled.** VERB & N-COUNT If people in an audience **heckle** public speakers, they interrupt them by making rude remarks, called **heckles.** *A small group of youths stayed behind to heckle. ...a heckle from an*

Height

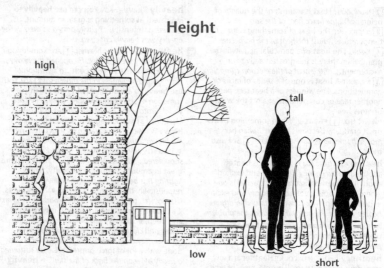

high

tall

low

short

audience member. ♦ **heckling** N-UNCOUNT ...*the heckling and jeers of his audience.* ♦ **heckler, hecklers** N-COUNT *He was interrupted by hecklers.*

hectare /'hekteə/ **hectares.** N-COUNT A **hectare** is a unit of area equal to 10,000 square metres.

hectic /'hektɪk/. ADJ A **hectic** situation involves a lot of rushed activity. ...*his hectic work schedule.*

he'd /hɪd, hiːd/. **He'd** is the usual spoken form of 'he had', especially when 'had' is an auxiliary verb. **He'd** is also a spoken form of 'he would'.

hedge /hedʒ/ **hedges, hedging, hedged.** ① N-COUNT A **hedge** is a row of bushes along the edge of a garden, field, or road. ② VERB If you **hedge**, you avoid answering a question or committing yourself to a particular action. *'I can't give you an answer now,' he hedged.* ③ PHRASE If you **hedge** your **bets**, you reduce the risk of losing a lot by supporting more than one person or thing.

hedgehog /'hedʒhɒg, AM -hɔːg/ **hedgehogs.** N-COUNT A **hedgehog** is a small brown animal with sharp spikes covering its back. → See picture on page 815.

hedgerow /'hedʒrəʊ/ **hedgerows.** N-COUNT A **hedgerow** is a row of bushes, trees, and plants, usually growing along a country lane or between fields.

hedonist /'hiːdənɪst/ **hedonists.** N-COUNT A **hedonist** is someone who believes that having pleasure is the most important thing in life. [FORMAL] ♦ **hedonistic** ADJ ...*the hedonistic pleasures of partying.* ♦ **hedonism** N-UNCOUNT ...*a life of hedonism and glamour.*

heed /hiːd/ **heeds, heeding, heeded.** ① VERB If you **heed** someone's advice or warning, you pay attention to it and do what they suggest. [FORMAL] *Few at the conference in London last week heeded*

his warning. ② PHRASE If you **take heed of** what someone says, or if you **pay heed to** them, you pay attention to them and consider carefully what they say.

heel /hiːl/ **heels.** ① N-COUNT Your **heel** is the back part of your foot, just below your ankle. See picture at **human.** ② N-COUNT The **heel** of a shoe is the raised part on the bottom at the back.

hefty /'hefti/ **heftier, heftiest.** ADJ **Hefty** means very large in size, weight, or amount. [INFORMAL] *He faces a hefty fine.*

⭐ **height** /haɪt/ **heights.** ① N-VAR The **height** of a person or thing is their measurement from bottom to top. *Her weight is about normal for her height.* ② N-UNCOUNT **Height** is the quality of being tall. *Her height is intimidating for some men.* ③ N-VAR A particular **height** is the distance that something is above the ground. ...*a 6.3 kilogram weight was dropped on it from a height of 1 metre.* ④ N-COUNT A **height** is a high position or place above the ground. *From a height, it looks like a desert.* ⑤ N-SING When an activity, situation, or organization is **at** its **height**, it is at its most successful, powerful, or intense. *Emigration from Britain to Brittany was at its height.* ⑥ N-SING If you say that something is **the height of** a quality, you are emphasizing that it has that quality to the greatest degree possible. *I think it's the height of bad manners to be dressed badly.*

heighten /'haɪtən/ **heightens, heightening, heightened.** VERB If something **heightens** a feeling, the feeling increases in degree or intensity. *The move has heightened tension in the state... Cross's interest heightened.*

heir /eə/ **heirs.** N-COUNT Someone's **heir** is the person who will inherit their money, property, or title when they die. *Her son was the sole heir to his grandparents' fortune.*

heiress /'eərɪs/ **heiresses.** N-COUNT An **heiress** is a woman who will inherit property, money, or a title.

held /held/. **Held** is the past tense and past participle of **hold**.

★ **helicopter** /'helɪkɒptə/ **helicopters.** N-COUNT A **helicopter** is an aircraft with no wings. It hovers or moves vertically and horizontally by means of large overhead blades which rotate.

★ **hell** /hel/ **hells.** [1] N-PROPER According to some religions, **Hell** is the place where the Devil lives, and where wicked people are sent to be punished when they die. [2] N-VAR If you say that a particular situation or place is **hell**, you are emphasizing that it is extremely unpleasant. [INFORMAL] *June says her life has been hell since her marriage ended nine months ago.* [3] PHRASE You can use **from hell** after a noun when you are emphasizing that something or someone is extremely unpleasant or evil. *...the holiday from hell.*

he'll /hɪl, hiːl/. **He'll** is the usual spoken form of 'he will'.

★ **hello** (also **hallo** or **hullo**) /he'ləʊ/ **hellos.** CONVENTION & N-COUNT You say '**Hello**' when you are greeting someone or starting a telephone conversation. → See Reference Page on Greetings and Goodbyes. *Hello, Trish. I won't shake hands, because I'm filthy... The salesperson greeted me with a warm hello.*

helmet /'helmɪt/ **helmets.** N-COUNT A **helmet** is a hard hat which you wear to protect your head.

★ **help** /help/ **helps, helping, helped.** [1] VERB If you **help** someone, you make something easier for them to do, for example by doing part of their work or by giving them advice or money. *He has helped to raise a lot of money... America's priority is to help nations defend themselves... You can of course help by giving them a donation directly... He began to help with the chores.* [2] VERB & N-SING If something **helps**, or if someone or something is a **help**, they make something easier to do or get, or they improve a situation. *The right style of swimsuit can help to hide a lot... It will do very little indeed to help our environment... The books were not much help.* [3] VERB If you **help yourself to** something, you serve yourself or you take it for yourself. *'Help yourself to a Pepsi.'... There's bread on the table. Help yourself.* [4] N-UNCOUNT & EXCLAM **Help** is the assistance that someone gives when they go to rescue a person who is in danger. You shout '**help!**' when you are in danger in order to attract someone's attention so that they can come and rescue you. *He was screaming for help.* **PHRASES** ● If you **can't help** the way you feel or behave, you cannot control it or stop it happening. You can also say that you **can't help yourself.** *'Please don't cry.'--'I can't help it.'* ● See note at **avoid.** ● If something or someone **is of**

help, they make things easier or better. *Can I be of help to you?*
▶**help out.** PHR-VERB If you **help** someone **out**, you help them by doing some work for them or by lending them some money.

helper /'helpə/ **helpers.** N-COUNT A **helper** is a person who helps another person or group with a job they are doing, usually an organized activity.

helpful /'helpful/. [1] ADJ If someone is **helpful**, they help you by doing work for you or by giving you advice or information. *The staff in the London office are helpful.* ♦ **helpfully** ADV *They had helpfully provided us with instructions.* [2] ADJ Something that is **helpful** makes a situation more pleasant or easier to tolerate. *Having the right equipment at hand will be enormously helpful.*

helpless /'helpləs/. ADJ If you are **helpless**, you do not have the strength or power to do anything useful or to protect yourself. *...seeing your child develop from a helpless baby to an independent toddler.* ♦ **helplessly** ADV *Their son watched helplessly as they vanished beneath the waves.* ♦ **helplessness** N-UNCOUNT *...his overwhelming sense of helplessness.*

hem /hem/ **hems, hemming, hemmed.** [1] N-COUNT The **hem** of a piece of cloth is an edge which is folded over and sewn. The **hem** of a skirt or dress is the hem along its lower edge. [2] VERB If you **hem** a piece of cloth, you fold the edge over and sew it to make it neat.
▶**hem in.** PHR-VERB If you are **hemmed in** by something, you are completely surrounded by it so that you cannot move. You can also say that a place is **hemmed in** when it is surrounded by something tall such as mountains or tall buildings. *You feel hemmed in. Find open spaces, get in touch with nature. ...a small valley hemmed in by rocks.*

hemisphere /'hemɪsfɪə/ **hemispheres.** N-COUNT A **hemisphere** is one half of the earth. *...the northern hemisphere.*

hemorrhage /'hemərɪdʒ/. See **haemorrhage**.

hen /hen/ **hens.** [1] N-COUNT A **hen** is a female chicken. → See picture on page 815. [2] N-COUNT The female of any bird can be referred to as a **hen**. *...ostrich hens.*

hence /hens/. [1] ADV **Hence** means for the reason just mentioned. *The Socialist Party was profoundly divided and hence very weak.* [2] ADV If something will happen a particular length of time **hence**, it will happen that length of time from now. *The election two years hence may seem a long way off.*

henceforth /ˌhens'fɔːθ/. ADV **Henceforth** means from this time onwards. [FORMAL] *Henceforth, all churches and religious societies will be legally recognised.*

hepatitis /ˌhepə'taɪtɪs/. N-UNCOUNT **Hepatitis** is a serious disease which affects the liver.

a
b
c
d
e
f
g
h
i
j
k
l
m
n
o
p
q
r
s
t
u
v
w
x
y
z

★ **her** /hə, STRONG hɜː/. **1** PRON & DET You use **her** to refer to a woman, girl, or female animal. *I really thought I'd lost her... Liz travelled round the world for a year with her boyfriend James.* **2** PRON & DET **Her** is sometimes used to refer to a country or nation. *...Britain's apparently deep-rooted distrust of her EU partner.* **3** PRON & DET People sometimes use **her** to refer informally to a car, ship, or machine. *Kemp got out of his car. 'Just fill her up, thanks.'*

herald /'herəld/ **heralds, heralding, heralded.** **1** VERB & N-COUNT Something that **heralds** a future event or situation, or is a **herald of** it, is a sign that it is going to appear or happen. *Their discovery could herald a cure for some forms of impotence.* **2** VERB If an important event or action **is heralded** by people, announcements are made about it so that it is publicly known and expected. *Tonight's clash between Real Madrid and Arsenal is being heralded as the match of the season.*

herb /hɜːb, AM ɜːb/ **herbs.** N-COUNT A **herb** is a plant whose leaves are used in cookery to add flavour to food, or as a medicine. ♦ **herbal** /'hɜːbəl, AM 'ɜːb-/ ADJ *...herbal remedies for colds.*

herd /hɜːd/ **herds, herding, herded.** **1** N-COUNT A **herd** is a large group of animals of one kind that live together. *...dairy herds.* **2** VERB If you **herd** people or animals somewhere, you make them move there in a group. *The group was herded into a bus.*

★ **here** /hɪə/. **1** ADV You use **here** when you are referring to the place where you are. *I'm here all by myself... Well, I can't stand here chatting all day... Sheila was in here a minute ago.* **2** ADV You use **here** when you are pointing towards a place that is near you, in order to draw someone else's attention to it. *...if you will just sign here... Come and sit here, Lauren.* **3** ADV You use **here** at the beginning of a sentence in order to draw attention to something or someone who has just arrived in the place where you are, or to draw attention to the place you have just arrived at. *'Here's the taxi,' she said politely... Here comes your husband.* **4** ADV You use **here** to refer to a particular point or stage of a situation or subject that you have come to or that you are dealing with. *The book goes into recent work in greater detail than I have attempted here.* **5** ADV You use **here** when you are offering or giving something to someone. *Here's my mother's number... Here's some letters I want you to sign.*

hereditary /hɪ'redɪtri/. **1** ADJ A **hereditary** characteristic or illness is passed on to a child from its parents before it is born. *Cystic fibrosis is the commonest fatal hereditary disease.* **2** ADJ A **hereditary** title or position in society is passed on as a right from parent to child.

heresy /'herɪsi/ **heresies.** N-VAR **Heresy** is a belief or way of behaving that disagrees with generally accepted beliefs, especially religious ones. *Galileo's heresy lay in declaring the Sun to be the fixed point and not the Earth.*

heritage /'herɪtɪdʒ/. N-SING A country's **heritage** consists of all the qualities and traditions that have continued over many years, especially when they are considered to be of historical importance. *Bullfighting is part of Spain's heritage.*

hermit /'hɜːmɪt/ **hermits.** N-COUNT A **hermit** is a person who deliberately lives alone, away from people and society.

hernia /'hɜːniə/ **hernias.** N-COUNT A **hernia** is a medical condition in which one of your internal organs sticks through a weak point in the surrounding tissue.

★ **hero** /'hɪərəʊ/ **heroes.** **1** N-COUNT The **hero** of a book, play, or film is the main male character, who usually has good qualities. **2** N-COUNT A **hero** is someone who has done something brave or good and is admired by a lot of people. *He called Mr Mandela a hero who had inspired millions.*

heroic /hɪ'rəʊɪk/ **heroics.** **1** ADJ **Heroic** people or actions are brave and determined. *A heroic six-year-old saved his playmate from being burned to death. ...his heroic effort to negotiate the release of hostages.* ♦ **heroically** ADV *He had acted heroically.* **2** N-PLURAL You can describe actions involving bravery or determination as **heroics**. *...his wartime heroics as a fighter pilot.* **3** N-PLURAL If you describe someone's actions as **heroics**, you mean that they are foolish or dangerous because they are too difficult for the situation in which they occur. [SPOKEN] *His advice was: 'No heroics, stay within the law'.*

heroin /'herəʊɪn/. N-UNCOUNT **Heroin** is a powerful addictive drug used to prevent pain. Some people take it for pleasure.

heroine /'herəʊɪn/ **heroines.** **1** N-COUNT The **heroine** of a book, play, or film is its main female character, who usually has good qualities. **2** N-COUNT A **heroine** is a woman who has done something brave or good and is admired by a lot of people. *...our national heroines.*

heroism /'herəʊɪzəm/. N-UNCOUNT **Heroism** is great courage and bravery. *...acts of heroism.*

herpes /'hɜːpiːz/. N-UNCOUNT **Herpes** is the name used for several viruses which cause painful red spots to appear on the skin. [TECHNICAL]

herring /'herɪŋ/.

☑ The plural is **herring** or **herrings**.

N-VAR A **herring** is a long silver-coloured fish. **Herring** is the flesh of this fish eaten as food.

hers /hɜːz/. PRON You use **hers** to indicate that something belongs or relates to a woman, girl, or female animal that has already been mentioned, or whose identity is known. *His hand as it shook hers was warm and firm. ...a great friend of hers.*

★ **herself** /hə'self/. **1** PRON You use **herself** to refer to the same woman, girl, or female animal that is mentioned as the subject of the clause, or as a previous object in the clause. *She let herself out of the room... Robin didn't feel good about herself.* **2** PRON You use **herself** to emphasize the female subject or object of a clause, and to make it clear who you are referring to. *Has anyone thought of consulting Bethan herself?* **3** PRON If a girl or woman does something **herself**, she does it without any help or interference from anyone else. *The jam was marvellous. She had made it herself.*

he's /hɪz, hiːz/. **He's** is the usual spoken form of 'he is' or 'he has', especially when 'has' is an auxiliary verb.

hesitant /'hezɪtənt/. ADJ If you are **hesitant about** doing something, you do not do it quickly or immediately, usually because you are uncertain, embarrassed, or worried. *She was hesitant about coming forward with her story... At first he was hesitant to accept the role.*
♦ **hesitancy** /'hezɪtənsi/ N-UNCOUNT *...Ukraine's hesitancy over abandoning the weapons.*
♦ **hesitantly** ADV *'Would you do me a favour?' she asked hesitantly.*

hesitate /'hezɪteɪt/ **hesitates, hesitating, hesitated.** **1** VERB If you **hesitate**, you pause slightly while you are doing something or just before you do it, usually because you are uncertain, embarrassed, or worried. *She hesitated before replying.*
♦ **hesitation, hesitations** N-VAR *After a moment's hesitation, the others followed him.* **2** VERB If you **hesitate to** do something, you are unwilling to do it because you are not certain whether it is the right thing to do. *Many women hesitate to discuss money... Don't hesitate to say no if you'd rather not.* ♦ **hesitation** N-VAR *He promised there would be no more hesitations in pursuing reforms.*

heterosexual /,hetərəʊ'sekʃʊəl/ **heterosexuals.** ADJ & N-COUNT Someone who is **heterosexual** or a **heterosexual**, is sexually attracted to people of the opposite sex. ♦ **heterosexuality** N-UNCOUNT *...the assumption that heterosexuality was 'normal'.*

hey /heɪ/. CONVENTION You say or shout **'hey'** to attract someone's attention or show surprise, interest, or annoyance. [INFORMAL] *Hey! You!*

heyday /'heɪdeɪ/. N-SING The **heyday** of someone or something is the time when they are most powerful, successful, or popular. *...the heyday of the railways.*

hi /haɪ/. CONVENTION You say **'hi'** when you are greeting someone. [INFORMAL] *'Hi, Darren.'*

hiccup (or **hiccough**) /'hɪkʌp/ **hiccups, hiccuping, hiccuped** (or **hiccupping, hiccupped**). **1** VERB & N-UNCOUNT When you **hiccup**, or when you have **hiccups**, you make repeated sharp sounds in your throat, often because you have been eating or drinking too quickly. **2** N-COUNT You can refer to a minor problem as a **hiccup**. *Preparations have been hit by only one slight hiccup.*

hid /hɪd/. **Hid** is the past tense of **hide**.

hidden /'hɪdən/. **1** **Hidden** is the past participle of **hide**. **2** ADJ Something that is **hidden** is not easily noticed. *...hidden dangers.* **3** ADJ A place that is **hidden** is difficult to find. *...a hidden valley.*

⭐ **hide** /haɪd/ **hides, hiding, hid, hidden.** **1** VERB To **hide** something means to cover it or put it somewhere so that it cannot be seen. *She hid her face in her hands. ...a bomb hidden in a briefcase.* **2** VERB If you **hide**, or if you **hide yourself**, you go somewhere where you cannot easily be seen or found. *They hid themselves behind a tree.* **3** VERB If you **hide** what you feel or know, you keep it a secret. *Lee tried to hide his excitement.* **4** N-COUNT A **hide** is a place which is built to look like its surroundings, so that people can watch or photograph animals and birds without being seen by them. [BRITISH] **5** N-VAR A **hide** is the skin of a large animal, used for making leather. *...cow hides.*

hideous /'hɪdiəs/. ADJ If you say that someone or something is **hideous**, you mean that they are extremely unpleasant or ugly. *...a hideous crime. ...his hideous face.* ♦ **hideously** ADV *He has been left hideously disfigured.*

hiding /'haɪdɪŋ/. N-UNCOUNT If someone is **in hiding**, they have secretly gone somewhere where they cannot be found. *He is thought to be in hiding... He went into hiding 18 months ago.*

hierarchy /'haɪərɑːki/ **hierarchies.** **1** N-VAR A **hierarchy** is a system in which people have different ranks or positions depending on how important they are. *...a society which is ordered by hierarchy.* ♦ **hierarchical** /haɪə'rɑːkɪkəl/ ADJ *...a hierarchical society.* **2** N-COUNT The **hierarchy** of an organization such as the Church is the group of people who manage and control it.

hi-fi /'haɪ faɪ/ **hi-fis.** N-COUNT A **hi-fi** is a set of stereo equipment which you use to play records, tapes, and compact discs.

⭐ **high** /haɪ/ **higher, highest; highs.** **1** ADJ & ADV A **high** structure or mountain covers a great amount from the bottom to the top. → See picture on page 324. *...a house, with a high wall all around it. ...the highest mountain in the Adirondacks. ...high-heeled shoes. ...a sofa piled high with cushions.*

> **USAGE** You do not use **high** to describe people. The word you should use is **tall**. *She was rather tall for a woman.* **Tall** is also used to describe buildings such as skyscrapers and other things whose height is much greater than their width. *...tall pine trees. ...a tall glass vase.*

2 ADJ You use **high** to talk or ask about how much something upright measures from the bottom to the top. *...an elegant bronze horse only nine inches high... How high is the door?* **3** ADJ & ADV If something is **high**, it is a long way above the ground, above sea level, or above a person or thing. *I looked down from the high window... The sun was high in the sky. ...being able to run faster or jump higher than other people.* **4** ADJ & ADV **High** means great in amount, degree, or intensity. *Official reports said casualties were* high... *High winds have knocked down trees and power lines.* **5** ADJ If a number or level is in the **high** eighties, it is more than eighty-five, but not as much as ninety. **6** ADJ AFTER LINK-V If a food or other substance is **high in** a particular ingredient, it contains a large amount of that ingredient. *...a superb compost, high in calcium.* **7** N-COUNT If something reaches a **high** of a particular amount or degree, that is the greatest it has ever been. *Sales of Russian vodka have reached an all-time high.* **8** ADJ If you say that something is a **high** priority or is **high** on your list, you mean that you consider it to be one of the most important things you have to do. **9** ADJ **High** means advanced or complex. *...the rise of Japan's high technology industries.* **10** ADJ Someone who is **high** in a particular profession or society, or who has a **high** position, has an important position and has great authority and influence. **11** ADJ If people have a **high** opinion of you, they respect you very much. **12** ADJ If the quality or standard of something is **high**, it is very good indeed. **13** ADJ If someone has **high** principles or standards, they are morally good. **14** ADJ If your spirits are **high**, you feel happy and excited. **15** to **be high time**: see **time**.

ˌhigh-'class. ADJ **High-class** is used to describe people and things which are the very best of their type. *...a high-class hotel. ...a high-class international jockey.*

higher /haɪə/. **Higher** is the comparative form of **high**.

ˌhigher edu'cation. N-UNCOUNT **Higher education** is education at universities and colleges.

ˌhigh-'flying. ADJ A **high-flying** person is very ambitious and is likely to be successful in their career. *...a high-flying executive.*

ˌhigh-'impact. ADJ **High-impact** exercise puts a lot of stress on your body. *...high-impact aerobics.*

highlands /'haɪləndz/. N-PLURAL **Highlands** are mountainous areas. *...the highlands of Scotland.*

⭐ **highlight** /'haɪlaɪt/ **highlights, highlighting, highlighted.** **1** VERB If you **highlight** a point or problem, you draw attention to it. *The report highlights the need to set aside areas for the development of airports.* **2** N-COUNT The **highlights** of an event, activity, or period of time are the most interesting or exciting parts of it.

⭐ **highly** /'haɪli/. **1** ADV You use **highly** to emphasize that a particular quality exists to a great degree. *...highly confidential information. ...highly skilled craftsmen.* **2** ADV You use **highly** to indicate that someone has an important position in an organization or set of people. *...a highly placed government source.* **3** ADV If you think **highly** of something or someone, you think they are very good indeed.

Highness /'haɪnɪs/ **Highnesses.** N-VOC You use expressions such as **Your Highness** and **His Highness** to address a member of a royal family.

ˌhigh-'pitched. ADJ A **high-pitched** sound is high and shrill. *...a high-pitched scream.*

ˌhigh-'powered. ADJ **High-powered** professional people are in a job which carries a lot of responsibility or status.

ˌhigh-'profile. ADJ A **high-profile** person or event attracts a lot of attention or publicity.

'high-rise. N-COUNT & ADJ BEFORE N A **high-rise**, or a **high-rise** building, is a very tall modern building. *...high-rise flats.*

'high school, high schools. **1** N-VAR In Britain, a **high school** is a school for children aged between eleven and eighteen. **2** N-VAR In the United States, a **high school** is a school for children aged between fourteen and eighteen.

'high street, high streets. N-COUNT The **high street** of a town is the main street where most of the shops and banks are. [BRITISH]

ˌhigh 'tech (or hi tech). ADJ **High tech** activities or equipment involve or result from the use of high technology. *...such high-tech industries as computers.*

ˌhigh tech'nology. N-UNCOUNT **High technology** is the development and use of advanced electronics and computers.

highway /'haɪweɪ/ **highways.** N-COUNT A **highway** is a main road, especially one that connects towns or cities. [AMERICAN]

hijack /'haɪdʒæk/ **hijacks, hijacking, hijacked.** VERB & N-COUNT If someone **hijacks** a plane or other vehicle, they illegally take control of it by force while it is travelling from one place to another. An illegal action like this is called a **hijack**.
♦ **hijacker, hijackers** N-COUNT *There was a scuffle between the hijackers and the pilots.*
♦ **hijacking, hijackings** N-COUNT *Car hijackings are running at a rate of nearly 50 a day.*

hike /haɪk/ **hikes, hiking, hiked.** **1** VERB & N-COUNT If you **hike**, or if you go on a **hike**, you go for a long walk in the country. *You could hike through the Fish River Canyon.* ♦ **hiker, hikers** N-COUNT *...hikers with rucksacks and maps.* ♦ **hiking** N-UNCOUNT *...strenuous hiking on cliff pathways.*
2 VERB & PHR-VERB To **hike** prices, rates, or taxes, or to **hike** them **up**, means to increase them suddenly or by a large amount. [JOURNALISM] *The federal government hiked the tax on hard liquor.*

hilarious /hɪ'leərɪəs/. ADJ If something is **hilarious**, it is extremely funny. ♦ **hilariously** ADV *She found it hilariously funny.*

⭐ **hill** /hɪl/ **hills.** N-COUNT A **hill** is an area of land that is higher than the land that surrounds it, but not as high as a mountain.

hilly /'hɪli/ **hillier, hilliest.** ADJ A **hilly** area has a lot of hills.

⭐ **him** /hɪm/. **1** PRON You use **him** to refer to a man, boy, or male animal. *Elaine met him at the bus station.* **2** PRON **Him** can be used to refer to someone whose sex is not known or stated. [WRITTEN]

⭐ **himself** /hɪm'self/. **1** PRON You use **himself** to refer to the same man, boy, or male animal that is mentioned as the subject of the clause. *A driver blew up his car and himself... He poured himself a whisky... William went away muttering to himself.* ☐2 PRON You use **himself** to emphasize the male subject or object of a clause, and to make it clear who you are referring to. *...the judgment pronounced by Pope John Paul II himself.* ☐3 PRON If a man or boy does something **himself**, he does it without any help. *Goldrims had written it himself.*

hind /haɪnd/ **hinds.** ☐1 ADJ BEFORE N An animal's **hind** legs are at the back of its body. ☐2 N-COUNT A **hind** is a female deer.

hinder /'hɪndə/ **hinders, hindering, hindered.** VERB If something **hinders** you, it makes it more difficult for you to do something. *A thigh injury increasingly hindered her mobility.*

hindrance /'hɪndrəns/ **hindrances.** ☐1 N-COUNT A **hindrance** is someone or something that hinders you. ☐2 N-UNCOUNT **Hindrance** is the act of hindering someone or something. *They boarded their flight to Paris without hindrance.*

hindsight /'haɪndsaɪt/. N-UNCOUNT **Hindsight** is the ability to understand something about an event after it has happened, although you did not understand or realize it at the time. *With hindsight, we'd all do things differently.*

Hindu /'hɪnduː, hɪn'duː/ **Hindus.** ☐1 N-COUNT A **Hindu** is a person who believes in Hinduism. ☐2 ADJ **Hindu** is used to describe things that belong or relate to Hinduism. *...a Hindu temple.*

Hinduism /'hɪnduːɪzəm/. N-UNCOUNT **Hinduism** is an Indian religion, which has many gods and teaches that people have another life after they die.

hinge /hɪndʒ/ **hinges, hinging, hinged.** ☐1 N-COUNT A **hinge** is a moveable joint made of metal, wood, or plastic that joins two things so that one of them can swing freely. ☐2 ADJ Something that is **hinged** is joined to another thing by means of a hinge. *The hinged seat lifts up to reveal a useful storage space.*
▸**hinge on.** PHR-VERB Something that **hinges on** one thing or event depends entirely on it. *The plan hinges on a deal being struck.*

☆ **hint** /hɪnt/ **hints, hinting, hinted.** ☐1 VERB & N-COUNT If you **hint at** something, or if you **drop** a **hint** about it, you suggest it in an indirect way. *She suggested a trip to the shops and hinted at the possibility of a treat... The President hinted he might make some changes.* ☐2 N-COUNT A **hint** is a helpful piece of advice. *The book gives handy hints on looking after indoor plants.* ☐3 N-SING A **hint of** something is a very small amount of it. *She added only a hint of vermouth to the gin.*

☆ **hip** /hɪp/ **hips.** ☐1 N-COUNT Your **hips** are the two areas or bones at the sides of your body between the tops of your legs and your waist. → See picture on page 822. ☐2 ADJ If you say that someone is **hip**, you mean that they are fashionable. [INFORMAL] *...a hip young character with tight-cropped blond hair.*

hippie (or **hippy**) /'hɪpi/ **hippies.** N-COUNT In the 1960s and 1970s, **hippies** were people who rejected conventional society and tried to live a life based on peace and love.

☆ **hire** /haɪə/ **hires, hiring, hired.** ☐1 VERB & N-UNCOUNT If you **hire** something, or if you have it **on hire**, you pay money to use it for a period of time. [BRITISH] *The bikes are on hire... Hire of skis, boots and clothing, are all available.* ☐2 PHRASE If something is **for hire**, it is available for you to hire. [BRITISH] ☐3 VERB If you **hire** someone, you pay them to work for you. *He will be in charge of all hiring and firing at PHA.*
▸**hire out.** PHR-VERB If you **hire out** something such as a car or a person's services, you allow them to be used in return for payment. *His agency hires out security guards and bodyguards.*

☆ **his** /hɪz/. ☐1 DET & PRON You use **his** to indicate that something belongs or relates to a man, boy, or male animal. *He spent a large part of his career in Hollywood... My dinner jacket is every bit as good as his.* ☐2 DET **His** can be used to refer to someone whose sex is not known or stated. *...the relations between a teacher and his pupils.*

Hispanic /hɪ'spænɪk/ **Hispanics.** ADJ & N-COUNT If you describe someone from the United States as **Hispanic**, or if you refer to them as a **Hispanic**, you mean that they or their family originally came from Latin America.

hiss /hɪs/ **hisses, hissing, hissed.** ☐1 VERB & N-COUNT To **hiss** means to make a sound like a long 's', called a **hiss**. *The tires of Lenny's bike hissed over the wet pavement.* ♦ **hissing** N-UNCOUNT *...a silence broken only by a steady hissing from above my head.* ☐2 VERB If you **hiss** something, you say it in a strong angry whisper. *'Now, quiet,' my mother hissed.*

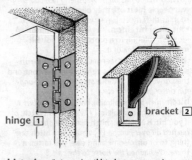

hinge ☐1   bracket ☐2

historian /hɪ'stɔːriən/ **historians.** N-COUNT A **historian** is a person who specializes in the study of history and who writes about it.

☆ **historic** /hɪ'stɒrɪk, AM -'tɔːr-/. ADJ A **historic** event is important in history, or likely to be considered important at some time in the future. *...the historic changes in Eastern Europe.*

☆ **historical** /hɪ'stɒrɪkəl, AM -tɔːr-/. ☐1 ADJ BEFORE N **Historical** people, situations, or things existed in the past and are considered to be a part of history. ♦ **historically** ADV *Historically, royal marriages have been cold, calculating affairs.* 2 ADJ BEFORE N **Historical** books, works of art, or studies are concerned with people, situations, or things that existed in the past.

⭐ **history** /ˈhɪstəri/ **histories.** 1 N-UNCOUNT You can refer to the events of the past as **history**. You can also refer to the past events which concern a particular topic or place as its **history**. *He later studied history and folklore at Indiana University. ...great moments in baseball history.* 2 N-COUNT **history** is an account of events that have happened in the past in a particular subject. *...his magnificent history of broadcasting.* 3 N-COUNT Someone's **history** is the set of facts that are known about their past. *...the boy's medical history.* 4 N-COUNT If someone has a **history of** something bad, they keep doing that thing or it keeps happening to them. *He had a long history of drink problems.*

⭐ **hit** /hɪt/ **hits, hitting, hit.** 1 VERB If you **hit** someone or something, you deliberately strike or touch them forcefully, with your hand or with an object held in your hand. *Both men had been hit in the stomach with baseball bats.* 2 VERB & N-COUNT When a moving object **hits** another object, it strikes or touches it with a lot of force. This impact is called a **hit**. *The car had apparently hit a traffic sign... A house took a direct hit and then the rocket exploded.* 3 VERB If something **hits** a person, place, or thing, it affects them badly. *...the earthquake which hit northern Peru.* 4 VERB When a feeling or an idea **hits** you, it suddenly comes into your mind. *Then the answer hit me.* 5 N-COUNT If a record, play, or film is a **hit**, it is very popular and successful. 6 N-COUNT A **hit** is a single visit to a website. [COMPUTING] *Our company has had 78,000 hits on its website.* 7 PHRASE If two people **hit it off**, they become friendly as soon as they meet. [INFORMAL]

▶**hit on** or **hit upon**. PHR-VERB If you **hit on** an idea or a solution to a problem, or if you **hit upon** it, you think of it.

,**hit-and-'run.** ADJ BEFORE N In a **hit-and-run** accident, the driver of a vehicle hits someone and then drives away without stopping. *...a hit-and-run driver in a stolen car.*

hitch /hɪtʃ/ **hitches, hitching, hitched.** 1 N-COUNT A **hitch** is a slight problem. 2 VERB If you **hitch**, or if you **hitch** a lift, you hitch-hike. *Philippe had hitched all over Europe.* 3 VERB If you **hitch** one thing **to** or **onto** something else, you fasten it there. *We hitched the horse to the cart.*

hitchhike (or **hitch-hike**) /ˈhɪtʃhaɪk/ **hitchhikes, hitchhiking, hitchhiked.** VERB If you **hitchhike**, you travel by getting free lifts from passing vehicles. *Neff hitchhiked to New York.* ♦ **hitchhiker, hitchhikers** N-COUNT *On my way to Vancouver I picked up a hitchhiker.*

,**hi 'tech.** See **high tech**.

hitherto /ˌhɪðəˈtuː/. ADV You use **hitherto** to indicate that something was true up until the

time you are talking about, although it may no longer be the case. [FORMAL] *Hitherto, emphasis has been on the need to resist aggression.*

'**hit list, hit lists.** N-COUNT A terrorist's or gangster's **hit list** are the people they intend to kill.

⭐ **HIV** /ˌeɪtʃ aɪ ˈviː/. 1 N-UNCOUNT **HIV** is a virus which reduces people's resistance to illness and can cause AIDS. **HIV** is an abbreviation for 'human immunodeficiency virus'. 2 PHRASE If someone is **HIV positive**, they are infected with the HIV virus, and may develop AIDS.

hive /haɪv/ **hives.** 1 N-COUNT A **hive** is a structure in which bees are kept. 2 N-COUNT If you describe a place as a **hive of** activity, you approve of the fact that there is a lot of activity there or that people are busy working there.

hoard /hɔːd/ **hoards, hoarding, hoarded.** 1 VERB If you **hoard** things such as food or money, you save or store them, often in secret, because they are valuable or important to you. *They've begun to hoard food and gasoline and save their money.* 2 N-SING A **hoard** is a store of things you have hoarded or secretly hidden.

hoarding /ˈhɔːdɪŋ/ **hoardings.** N-COUNT In British English, a **hoarding** is a large board used for advertising which stands at the side of a road. The usual American word is **billboard**.

hoarse /hɔːs/ **hoarser, hoarsest.** ADJ If you are **hoarse**, your voice sounds rough and unclear, for example because your throat is sore. ♦ **hoarsely** ADV *'Thank you,' Maria said hoarsely.*

hoax /həʊks/ **hoaxes.** N-COUNT A **hoax** is a trick in which someone tells people something that is not true, for example that there is a bomb somewhere.

hob /hɒb/ **hobs.** N-COUNT A **hob** is a surface on top of a cooker which can be heated in order to cook things.

hobble /ˈhɒbəl/ **hobbles, hobbling, hobbled.** 1 VERB If you **hobble**, you walk with difficulty because you are in pain. *He got up slowly and hobbled over to the coffee table.* 2 VERB To **hobble** something or someone means to make it more difficult for them to be successful or to achieve what they want. *...the poor transport system that has hobbled the area.*

hobby /ˈhɒbi/ **hobbies.** N-COUNT A **hobby** is something that you enjoy doing in your spare time.

hockey

hockey /'hɒki/. [1] N-UNCOUNT **Hockey** is a sport played between two teams of 11 players who use long curved sticks to hit a small ball and try to score goals. [2] See also **ice hockey**.

hoe /həʊ/ **hoes**. N-COUNT A **hoe** is a gardening tool with a long handle and a small square blade, which you use to remove small weeds and break up the surface of the soil.

hog /hɒg, AM hɔːg/ **hogs, hogging, hogged.** [1] N-COUNT A **hog** is a pig. [2] VERB If you **hog** something, you take all of it in a selfish or rude way. [INFORMAL] *Have you done hogging the bathroom?*

hoist /hɔɪst/ **hoists, hoisting, hoisted.** [1] VERB If you **hoist** a heavy object somewhere, you lift it or pull it up there, often using equipment or machinery of some kind. *Hoisting my suitcase on to my shoulder, I turned and headed toward my hotel... A twenty-foot steel pyramid is to be hoisted into position.* [2] N-COUNT A **hoist** is a machine for lifting heavy things. [3] VERB If you **hoist** a flag or a sail, you pull it up to its correct position using ropes.

hold 1 physically touching, supporting, or containing

⭐ **hold** /həʊld/ **holds, holding, held.** [1] VERB & N-COUNT When you **hold** something, you carry or support it, using your hands or your arms. Your **hold on** something is the fact that you are holding it. *Hold the knife at an angle... Hold the baby while I load the car... He released his hold on the camera.* [2] N-UNCOUNT **Hold** is used in expressions such as **grab hold of**, **catch hold of**, and **get hold of**, to indicate that you close your hand tightly around something. *Mother took hold of the barking dogs by their collars.* [3] VERB If you **hold** your body or part of your body in a particular position, you keep it in that position. *Hold your hands in front of your face.* [4] VERB If one thing **holds** another in a particular position, it keeps it in that position. *...the wooden wedge which held the heavy door open.* [5] VERB If one thing is used to **hold** another, it is used to store it. *Two knife racks hold her favourite knives.* [6] VERB If something **holds** a particular amount of something, it can contain that amount. *The small bottles don't seem to hold much.* [7] N-COUNT The **hold** of a ship or aeroplane is the place where cargo is stored. [8] See also **holding**.

hold 2 having or doing

⭐ **hold** /həʊld/ **holds, holding, held.** [1] VERB If you **hold** a particular opinion or belief, that is your opinion or belief. *He held firm opinions which usually conflicted with my own.* [2] VERB You can use **hold** to say that something has a particular quality or characteristic. *Death doesn't hold any fear for me.* [3] VERB **Hold** is used with nouns such as 'office', 'power', and 'responsibility' to indicate that someone has a particular position of power or authority. *She has never held ministerial office.* [4] VERB **Hold** is used with nouns such as 'permit', 'degree', or 'ticket' to indicate that someone has a particular document that allows them to do something. *He did not hold a firearm*

certificate. ♦ **holder, holders** N-COUNT *...season-ticket holders.* [5] VERB If you **hold** an event, you organize it and it takes place. *The German sports federation said it would hold an investigation.* [6] VERB If you **hold** a conversation with someone, you talk with them. *The Prime Minister is holding consultations with his colleagues.* [7] VERB If you **hold** someone's interest or attention, you keep them interested. *It's done in a way that will hold children's attention.* [8] See also **holding**.

hold 3 controlling or remaining

⭐ **hold** /həʊld/ **holds, holding, held.** [1] VERB If someone **holds** you in a place, they keep you there as a prisoner. *Somebody is holding your wife hostage.* [2] N-SING If you have a **hold over** or **on** someone, you have power or control over them. *Because he once loved her, she still has a hold on him.* [3] VERB You ask someone to **hold** when you are answering a telephone if you are asking them to wait for a short time. *Could you hold the line and I'll just get my pen.* [4] VERB If something **holds**, it remains the same. *Cattle prices held at yesterday's sales... Would the weather hold?* [5] CONVENTION If you say **'Hold it'**, you are telling someone to stop what they are doing and to wait. [6] CONVENTION If you say **'Hold on'**, you are telling someone to wait a short time. [7] See also **holding**.

hold 4 phrases

⭐ **hold** /həʊld/ **holds, holding, held.** PHRASES ● If you **get hold of** something or someone, you manage to get them or find them. *It is hard to get hold of guns in this country.* ● If you **put** something **on hold**, you decide not to do it now, but to leave it till later. *He put his retirement on hold to work 16 hours a day.* ● If you **hold your own**, you are not defeated by someone. *She can hold her own against almost any player.* ● If something **takes hold**, it finally gains complete control or influence over something or someone. *She felt a strange excitement taking hold of her.*

hold 5 phrasal verbs

⭐ **hold** /həʊld/ **holds, holding, held.**
▸**hold against.** PHR-VERB If you **hold** something **against** someone, you resent or dislike them because of something which they did in the past.
▸**hold back.** [1] PHR-VERB If you **hold back**, you hesitate before doing something. *My fear of failure always held me back.* [2] PHR-VERB If you **hold** someone or something **back**, you prevent them from advancing or increasing. *Stagnation in home sales is holding back economic recovery.* [3] PHR-VERB If you **hold** something **back**, you do not tell someone the full details about it. *You seem to be holding something back.*
▸**hold down.** PHR-VERB If you **hold down** a job, you manage to keep it.
▸**hold off.** PHR-VERB If you **hold off** doing something, you delay doing it or delay making a

a b c d e f g h i j k l m n o p q r s t u v w x y z

decision about it. *They have threatened military action but held off until now.*

▶**hold on** or **hold onto.** [1] PHR-VERB If you **hold on** or **hold onto** something, you keep your hand firmly round something. [2] PHR-VERB If you **hold onto** something that gives you an advantage, you succeed in keeping it for yourself, and prevent other people getting it. *...a politician who knew how to hold onto power.* [3] PHR-VERB If you **hold onto** something, you keep it for a longer time than would normally be expected. *People hold onto letters for years and years.*

▶**hold out.** [1] PHR-VERB If you **hold out** your hand or something that is in your hand, you move it towards someone. *'I'm Nancy Drew,' she said, holding out her hand.* [2] PHR-VERB If you **hold out** for something, you refuse to accept something inferior or you refuse to surrender. *He can only hold out a few more weeks.*

▶**hold up.** [1] PHR-VERB If someone or something **holds** you **up**, they delay you. [2] PHR-VERB If someone **holds up** a place such as a bank, they rob it using a weapon. ● See also **hold-up**.

▶**hold with.** PHR-VERB If you do not **hold with** something, you do not approve of it.

⭐ **holder** /'həʊldə/ **holders.** N-COUNT A **holder** is a device for storing a particular thing. *...a Victorian cigar holder. ...a toothbrush holder.*

holding /'həʊldɪŋ/ **holdings.** [1] N-COUNT If you have a **holding** in a company, you own shares in it. *...holdings in commercial and merchant banks.* [2] N-COUNT A **holding** is an area of farm land rented or owned by the person who cultivates it. [3] N-PLURAL The **holdings** of a place such as a library or art gallery consists of the collection of items which are kept there.

'**hold-up, hold-ups.** [1] N-COUNT A **hold-up** is a situation in which someone is threatened with a weapon in order to make them hand over money or valuables. [2] N-COUNT A **hold-up** is something which causes a delay, for example traffic delays.

⭐ **hole** /həʊl/ **holes, holing, holed.** N-COUNT A **hole** is an opening or hollow space in something. *The builders had cut holes into the soft stone.*

▶**hole up.** PHR-VERB If you **hole up** somewhere, you hide or shut yourself away there. [INFORMAL] *She spent her free time holed up in her apartment with a book.*

⭐ **holiday** /'hɒlɪdeɪ/ **holidays, holidaying, holidayed.** [1] N-COUNT & PHRASE In British English, a **holiday** is a period of time when you are not working and are away from home for relaxation. You can also say that you are **on holiday** during this time. The American word is **vacation**. *We're going to Scotland for our holidays... I went on holiday with friends to Ibiza.* [2] VERB If you **are holidaying** in a place, you are on holiday there. [BRITISH] [3] N-COUNT A **holiday** is a day when people do not go to work or school because of a religious or national festival. *...dozens of flight cancellations over the holiday weekend.* ● See also **bank holiday**. [4] N-PLURAL In British English, the

holidays are the time when children do not have to go to school. The American word is **vacation**. *...the first day of the school holidays.*

holidaymaker (or **holiday-maker**) /'hɒlɪdeɪmeɪkə/ **holidaymakers.** N-COUNT In British English, a **holidaymaker** is a person who is away from home on holiday. The American word is **vacationer**.

holiness /'həʊlɪnəs/. [1] N-UNCOUNT **Holiness** is the state or quality of being holy. [2] N-VOC People say **Your Holiness** or **His Holiness** when they address or refer respectfully to the Pope or to leaders of some other religions.

holistic /həʊ'lɪstɪk/. ADJ A **holistic** approach to something treats it as a whole, rather than as a number of different parts. [FORMAL]

holler /'hɒlə/ **hollers, hollering, hollered.** VERB If you **holler**, you shout loudly. [AMERICAN, INFORMAL] *He'll be hollering at me for coming in late.*

hollow /'hɒləʊ/ **hollows, hollowing, hollowed.** [1] ADJ Something that is **hollow** has a hole or space inside it. *...a hollow tree.* [2] ADJ A surface that is **hollow** curves inwards. *...sharp-featured, with hollow cheeks.* [3] N-COUNT A **hollow** is an area that is lower than the surrounding surface. *Water gathers in a hollow and forms a pond.* [4] ADJ If you describe a statement, situation, or person as **hollow**, you mean they have no real value, worth, or effectiveness. ◆ **hollowness** N-UNCOUNT *...the hollowness of these promises.* [5] ADJ BEFORE N A **hollow** sound is dull and echoing. *...the hollow sound of a gunshot.*

▶**hollow out.** PHR-VERB If you **hollow** something **out**, you remove the inside part of it. *Someone had hollowed out a large block of stone.*

holly /'hɒli/ **hollies.** N-VAR **Hollies** are a group of evergreen trees and shrubs which have hard, shiny, prickly leaves, and also have bright red berries in winter.

holocaust /'hɒləkɔːst/ **holocausts.** [1] N-VAR A **holocaust** is an event in which there is large-scale destruction and loss of life, especially in war. *...nuclear holocaust.* [2] N-SING **The holocaust** was the killing by the Nazis of millions of Jews during the Second World War.

⭐ **holy** /'həʊli/ **holier, holiest.** [1] ADJ Something that is **holy** is considered to be special because it relates to God or to a particular religion. *This is a holy place.* [2] ADJ Someone who is **holy** leads a pure and good life which is dedicated to God or to a particular religion.

homage /'hɒmɪdʒ/. N-UNCOUNT **Homage** is respect shown towards someone or something you admire, or to someone who is in authority. *...films that pay homage to our literary heritage.*

⭐ **home** /həʊm/ **homes, homing, homed.** [1] N-COUNT & ADV Someone's **home** is the house or flat where they live. *They stayed at home and watched TV... She wanted to go home... Hi, Mom, I'm home!* [2] N-COUNT Your **home** is the place or country where you live or feel that you belong. *Ms*

Highsmith has made Switzerland her home.
3 N-COUNT A **home** is a building where people who cannot care for themselves are looked after. *...a home for handicapped children.* **4** N-SING The **home** of something is the place where it began or where it is most typically found. *This southwest region of France is the home of claret.* **5** ADV If you **press**, **drive**, or **hammer** a message or an opinion **home**, you emphasize it strongly. *It is now up to all of us to debate this issue and press home the argument.* **6** N-UNCOUNT & ADJ BEFORE N When a team plays **at home**, or when they play a **home** game, they play a game on their own ground, rather than on the opposing team's ground. **7** PHRASE If you feel **at home**, you feel comfortable and at ease in the place or situation that you are in.
▸**home in.** PHR-VERB If you **home in on** one particular aspect of something, you concentrate all your attention on it. *You must home in on what is important to your topic.*

homecoming /ˈhəʊmkʌmɪŋ/ **homecomings.** N-COUNT Your **homecoming** is your return to your home or country after you have been away for a long time.

home-'grown. **1** ADJ **Home-grown** fruit and vegetables have been grown in your garden, rather than bought in a shop. **2** ADJ If you describe something as **home-grown**, you mean it develops in your own country or area rather than another country or area.

homeland /ˈhəʊmlænd/ **homelands.** N-COUNT Your **homeland** is your native country.

⭐ **homeless** /ˈhəʊmləs/. ADJ & N-PLURAL You describe people who have nowhere to live as **homeless**. You can also refer to them as **the homeless**. ♦ **homelessness** N-UNCOUNT *...the only way to solve homelessness.*

homely /ˈhəʊmli/. ADJ If you describe a room or house as **homely**, you like it because it makes you feel comfortable and at ease. *...a very homely atmosphere.*

home-'made (also **homemade**). ADJ **Home-made** things are made in someone's home, rather than in a shop or factory. *...a home-made bomb.*

'Home ,Office. N-PROPER **The Home Office** Is the department of the British government which is responsible for domestic affairs, including the police, immigration, and broadcasting.

homeopathy (BRIT also **homoeopathy**) /ˌhəʊmiˈɒpəθi/. N-UNCOUNT **Homeopathy** is a way of treating illness in which the patient is given very small amounts of a drug which would produce symptoms of the illness if taken in large quantities. ♦ **homeopathic** /ˌhəʊmiəʊˈpæθɪk/ ADJ *...homeopathic medicine.*

homepage /ˈhəʊmpeɪdʒ/ **homepages.** N-COUNT On the Internet, a person's or organization's **homepage** is the main page of information about them. [COMPUTING]

,Home 'Secretary, Home Secretaries. N-COUNT The **Home Secretary** is the member of the British government who is in charge of the Home Office.

homesick /ˈhəʊmsɪk/. ADJ If you are **homesick**, you feel unhappy because you are away from home and are missing your family and friends. ♦ **homesickness** N-UNCOUNT *There were inevitable bouts of homesickness.*

homestead /ˈhəʊmsted/ **homesteads.** N-COUNT A **homestead** is a farmhouse, together with the land around it.

,home 'town (also **hometown**) **home towns.** N-COUNT Someone's **home town** is the town where they live or the town that they come from.

homework /ˈhəʊmwɜːk/. **1** N-UNCOUNT **Homework** is school work given to pupils to do at home. *Have you done your homework?* **2** N-UNCOUNT If you **do** your **homework**, you find out what you need to know in preparation for something. *Serious bargain hunters will do their homework before taking a tour.*

homicidal /ˌhɒmɪˈsaɪdəl/. ADJ **Homicidal** is used to describe someone who is dangerous because they are likely to kill someone.

homicide /ˈhɒmɪsaɪd/ **homicides.** N-VAR **Homicide** is the deliberate and unlawful killing of a person.

homogeneous (also **homogenous**) /ˌhɒməˈdʒiːniəs, ˈhəʊ-/. ADJ **Homogeneous** is used to describe a group or thing which has members or parts that are all the same. *The unemployed are not a homogeneous group.*

homophobia /ˌhɒməˈfəʊbiə/. N-UNCOUNT **Homophobia** is a strong and unreasonable dislike of homosexual people. ♦ **homophobic** ADJ *...homophobic violence.*

⭐ **homosexual** /ˈhɒməʊˌsekʃʊəl, ˈhəʊ-/ **homosexuals.** ADJ & N-COUNT Someone who is **homosexual**, or who is a **homosexual**, is sexually attracted to people of the same sex. *...a homosexual relationship.* ♦ **homosexuality** N-UNCOUNT *...a place where gays could openly discuss homosexuality.*

hone /həʊn/ **hones, honing, honed.** VERB If you **hone** something, for example a skill or idea, you carefully develop it for a special purpose. *His body is honed and kept in trim with constant exercise.*

⭐ **honest** /ˈɒnɪst/. **1** ADJ If you describe someone as **honest**, you mean that they always tell the truth, and do not try to deceive people or break the law. *He is a very honest, decent man.* ♦ **honestly** ADV *She fought honestly for a just cause and for freedom.* **2** ADJ If you are being **honest** in a particular situation, you are telling the complete truth or giving your sincere opinion, even if this is not very pleasant. *What do you think of the school, in your honest opinion?* ♦ **honestly** ADV *It came as a shock to hear an old friend speak so honestly about Ted.* **3** ADV You say **'honest'** before or after a statement to emphasize that you are telling the truth. [INFORMAL]

a b c d e f g **h** i j k l m n o p q r s t u v w x y z

I'm not sure, honest. ◆ **honestly** ADV *Honestly, I don't know anything about it.*

honestly /'ɒnɪstli/. ADV You use **honestly** to emphasize that you are annoyed or impatient. [SPOKEN] *Oh, honestly, I don't know what they will think of next.*

honesty /'ɒnɪsti/. N-UNCOUNT **Honesty** is the quality of being honest. *I can answer you with complete honesty.*

honey /'hʌni/. N-UNCOUNT **Honey** is a sweet, sticky, edible substance made by bees.

honeymoon /'hʌnimuːn/ **honeymoons, honeymooning, honeymooned.** [1] N-COUNT A **honeymoon** is a holiday taken by a couple who have just married. [2] VERB When a couple who have just married **honeymoon** somewhere, they go there on their honeymoon. *They honeymooned in Venice.* [3] N-COUNT You can use **honeymoon** to refer to a period of time when someone has just started in a new job or role and everyone is pleased with them and does not criticize them. *The new Prime Minister will enjoy a honeymoon period.*

honor /'ɒnə/. See **honour**.

honorable /'ɒnərəbəl/. See **honourable**.

honorary /'ɒnərəri, AM -reri/. [1] ADJ BEFORE N An **honorary** title or membership is given as a mark of respect to someone who does not qualify for it in the normal way. *...an honorary member of the Golf Club.* [2] ADJ BEFORE N **Honorary** is used to describe an official job that is done without payment. *...the honorary secretary of the Cheshire Beekeepers' Association.*

⭐ **honour** (AM **honor**) /'ɒnə/ **honours, honouring, honoured.** [1] N-UNCOUNT **Honour** means doing what you believe to be right and being confident that you have done what is right. *I do not believe I can any longer serve with honour as a member of your government.* [2] N-COUNT An **honour** is a special award or job that is given to someone for something they have done. *He was showered with honours – among them an Oscar.* [3] VERB If someone **is honoured**, they are given public praise or an award for something they have done. *Two American surgeons were honoured with the 1990 Nobel Prize for Medicine and Physiology.* [4] PHRASE If something is arranged **in honour of** a particular event, it is arranged in order to celebrate that event. [5] N-SING If you describe something that has happened to you as **an honour**, you mean that you are pleased and proud about it. *It's an honour to finally work with her.* [6] VERB If you say that you would **be honoured to** do something, you are saying very politely and formally that you would be pleased to do it. *I'd be honoured to accept.* [7] VERB If you **honour** an arrangement or promise, you keep to it. *The two sides agreed to honour a new ceasefire.* [8] N-VOC Judges are sometimes called **Your Honour** or referred to as **His Honour** or **Her Honour**.

honourable (AM **honorable**) /'ɒnrəbəl/. ADJ If you describe people or actions as **honourable**, you mean that they are worthy of being respected or admired. ◆ **honourably** ADV *She had not behaved honorably in the election.*

hood /hʊd/ **hoods.** [1] N-COUNT A **hood** is a part of some coats which covers your head. [2] N-COUNT A **hood** is a bag made of cloth, which is put over someone's head and face so that they cannot be recognized or so that they cannot see. [3] N-COUNT In American English the **hood** of a car is the cover over the engine at the front. The British word is **bonnet**.

hooded /'hʊdɪd/. [1] ADJ A **hooded** piece of clothing has a hood. *...a hooded sweatshirt.* [2] ADJ A **hooded** person is wearing a hood or a piece of clothing pulled down over their face, so they are difficult to recognize. *...a hooded gunman.*

hoof /huːf/ **hoofs** or **hooves.** N-COUNT The **hooves** of an animal such as a horse are the hard parts of its feet.

⭐ **hook** /hʊk/ **hooks, hooking, hooked.** [1] N-COUNT A **hook** is a bent piece of metal or plastic that is used for catching or holding things, or for hanging things up. → See picture on page 249. *He felt a fish pull at his hook. ...curtain hooks.* [2] VERB If you **hook** one thing onto another, you attach it there using a hook. If something **hooks** somewhere, it can be hooked there. *...one of those can openers that hooked onto the wall.* [3] N-COUNT A **hook** is a short sharp punch that you make with your elbow bent.
PHRASES ● If someone **gets off the hook**, they manage to get out of the awkward or unpleasant situation that they are in. *Government officials accused of bribery and corruption often get off the hook.* ● If you take a phone **off the hook**, you take the receiver off the part that it normally rests on, so that the phone will not ring.
▸**hook up.** PHR-VERB When someone **hooks up** a computer or other electronic machine, they connect it to other similar machines or to a central power supply. *...technicians who hook up computer systems and networks.*

hooked /hʊkt/. [1] ADJ **Hooked** objects are shaped like a hook. *...hooked claws.* [2] ADJ AFTER LINK-V If you are **hooked on** something, you enjoy it so much that it takes up a lot of your interest and attention. *Many of the leaders have become hooked on power... Open this book and read a few pages and you will be hooked.* [3] ADJ AFTER LINK-V If someone is **hooked on** a drug, they are addicted to it.

hooker /'hʊkə/ **hookers.** N-COUNT A **hooker** is a prostitute. [INFORMAL]

hooligan /'huːlɪgən/ **hooligans.** N-COUNT If you describe young people as **hooligans**, you are critical of them because they behave in a noisy and violent way in a public place.

hooliganism /'huːlɪgənɪzəm/. N-UNCOUNT

Hooliganism is the behaviour and action of hooligans. ...*football hooliganism*.

hoop /huːp/ **hoops**. N-COUNT A **hoop** is a large ring made of wood, metal, or plastic.

hoot /huːt/ **hoots, hooting, hooted.** 1 VERB & N-COUNT If you **hoot** the horn on a vehicle, it makes a loud noise called a **hoot**. *I never hoot my horn when I pick a girl up for a date.* 2 VERB & N-COUNT If you **hoot**, you make a loud high-pitched noise, called a **hoot**, when you are laughing. *Bev hooted with laughter. ...derisive hoots.* 3 VERB & N-COUNT When an owl **hoots**, it makes a sound like a long 'oo'. The sound is called a **hoot**.

hoover /ˈhuːvə/ **hoovers, hoovering, hoovered.** 1 N-COUNT A **hoover** is an electric machine which sucks up dust and dirt from carpets. **Hoover** is a trademark. [BRITISH] 2 VERB If you **hoover** a carpet, you clean it using a vacuum cleaner. [BRITISH] ♦ **hoovering** N-UNCOUNT *I finished off the hoovering.*

hooves /huːvz/. **Hooves** is a plural of **hoof**.

hop /hɒp/ **hops, hopping, hopped.** 1 VERB & N-COUNT When you **hop**, you move along by jumping on one foot. A movement like this is called a **hop**. 2 VERB & N-COUNT When birds and some small animals **hop**, they move in small jumps, called **hops**, with two feet together. ...*toads hopping across the road.* 3 VERB If you **hop** somewhere, you move there quickly or suddenly. [INFORMAL] *I hopped out of bed quickly.* 4 N-COUNT A **hop** is a short quick journey, usually by plane. ...*a 20-minute hop in a private helicopter.*

⭐ **hope** /həʊp/ **hopes, hoping, hoped.** 1 VERB If you **hope** that something is true, or if you **hope for** something, you want it to be true or to happen, and you usually believe that it is possible and likely. *He hesitates before leaving, almost as though he had been hoping for conversation... I hope to get a job within the next two weeks... 'Will it happen again?'—'I hope not, but you never know.'* 2 N-VAR **Hope** is a feeling of desire and expectation that things will go well in the future. *Kevin hasn't given up hope of being fit.* 3 N-COUNT If someone wants something to happen, and considers it likely or possible, you can refer to their **hopes** of doing that thing, or to their **hope that** it will happen. *My hope is that, in the future, I will go over there and marry her.*

PHRASES ● If you **hope for the best**, you hope that everything will happen in the way you want, although you know that it may not. *Some companies are cutting costs and hoping for the best.* ● If you do one thing **in the hope of** another thing happening, you do it because you think it might cause or help the other thing to happen, which is what you want. *He was studying in the hope of being admitted to an engineering college.*

hopeful /ˈhəʊpfʊl/ **hopefuls.** 1 ADJ If you are **hopeful**, you are fairly confident that something that you want to happen will happen. *Surgeons were hopeful of saving the sight in Sara's left eye.* 2 ADJ If something such as a sign or event is **hopeful**, it makes you feel that what you want to happen will happen. ...*hopeful forecasts that the economy will improve.* 3 N-COUNT If you refer to someone as a **hopeful**, you mean that they have a particular ambition and it is possible that they will achieve it. ...*his job as football coach to young hopefuls.*

hopefully /ˈhəʊpfʊli/. ADV **Hopefully** is often used when mentioning something that you hope and are fairly confident will happen. *Hopefully, you won't have any problems after reading this.*

hopeless /ˈhəʊpləs/. 1 ADJ If you feel **hopeless**, you feel desperate because there seems to be no possibility of success. *Even able pupils feel hopeless about job prospects.* ♦ **hopelessly** ADV ...*a young woman hopelessly in love with a handsome hero.* ♦ **hopelessness** N-UNCOUNT *She had a feeling of hopelessness about the future.* 2 ADJ Someone or something that is **hopeless** is certain to be unsuccessful. *I don't believe your situation is as hopeless as you think.* 3 ADJ You use **hopeless** to emphasize how bad an event or situation is. ♦ **hopelessly** ADV *He was hopelessly in debt.*

horde /hɔːd/ **hordes.** N-COUNT If you describe a large crowd of people as a **horde**, you mean that they are excited and, often, rather frightening or unpleasant. ...*a horde of people was screaming for tickets.*

horizon /həˈraɪzən/ **horizons.** 1 N-SING The **horizon** is the distant line where the sky seems to touch the land or the sea. 2 N-COUNT Your **horizons** are the limits of what you want to do or of what you are interested or involved in. *As your horizons expand, these new ideas can give a whole new meaning to life.* 3 PHRASE If something is **on the horizon**, it is going to happen or be done quite soon.

horizontal /ˈhɒrɪˌzɒntəl, AM ˈhɔːr-/ **horizontals.** 1 ADJ Something that is **horizontal** is flat and parallel with the ground. *The board consists of vertical and horizontal lines.* ♦ **horizontally** ADV ...*a horizontally striped tie.* 2 N-COUNT The **horizontal** is a line or structure that is horizontal. *Do not raise your left arm above the horizontal.*

hormone /ˈhɔːməʊn/ **hormones.** N-COUNT A **hormone** is a chemical, usually occurring naturally in your body, that stimulates certain organs of your body. ♦ **hormonal** /hɔːˈməʊnəl/ ADJ ...*our individual hormonal balance.*

horn /hɔːn/ **horns.** 1 N-COUNT On a vehicle such as a car, the **horn** is the device that makes a loud noise as a signal or warning. 2 N-COUNT The **horns** of an animal such as a cow or deer are the hard pointed things that grow from its head. 3 N-UNCOUNT **Horn** is the hard substance that the horns of animals are made of. 4 N-COUNT A **horn** is a brass musical instrument, consisting of a pipe that is narrow at one end and wide at the other.

a
b
c
d
e
f
g
h
i
j
k
l
m
n
o
p
q
r
s
t
u
v
w
x
y
z

horoscope /ˈhɒrəskəʊp, AM ˈhɔːr-/ **horoscopes.** N-COUNT Your **horoscope** is a forecast of events which some people believe will happen to you in the future, based on the position of the stars when you were born.

horrendous /həˈrendəs, AM hɔːˈr-/. ADJ Something that is **horrendous** is very bad or unpleasant. *The violence used was horrendous.* ◆ **horrendously** ADV *The restaurant is horrendously expensive.*

horrible /ˈhɒrɪbəl, AM ˈhɔːr-/. ADJ If you say that something is **horrible**, you mean that it is very unpleasant. *...a horrible small boy... Unless you respect other people's religions, horrible mistakes and conflict will occur.* ◆ **horribly** /ˈhɒrɪbli, AM ˈhɔːr-/ ADV *Everything's gone horribly wrong.*

horrid /ˈhɒrɪd, AM ˈhɔːr-/. ADJ If you describe someone or something as **horrid**, you mean they are very unpleasant. [INFORMAL] *What a horrid smell!... I love both my parents, but they're horrid to each other.*

horrific /həˈrɪfɪk, AM hɔːˈr-/. ADJ If you describe something as **horrific**, you mean that it is so bad that people are horrified and shocked by it. *I have never seen such horrific injuries.* ◆ **horrifically** ADV *He had been horrifically assaulted.*

horrify /ˈhɒrɪfaɪ, AM ˈhɔːr-/ **horrifies, horrifying, horrified.** VERB If someone **is horrified**, they feel shocked, disappointed, or disgusted. *...a crime trend that will horrify all parents.* ◆ **horrifying** ADJ *These were such horrifying experiences.*

⭐ **horror** /ˈhɒrə, AM ˈhɔːr-/ **horrors.** [1] N-UNCOUNT **Horror** is a strong feeling of alarm caused by something extremely unpleasant. *I felt numb with horror.* [2] N-SING If you have a **horror of** something, you are afraid of it or dislike it strongly. *...his horror of death.* [3] N-COUNT You can refer to extremely unpleasant or frightening experiences as **horrors**. *...the horrors of war.* [4] ADJ A **horror** film or story is intended to be very frightening.

⭐ **horse** /hɔːs/ **horses.** N-COUNT A **horse** is a large animal which people can ride. → See picture on page 815.

horseback /ˈhɔːsbæk/. [1] N-UNCOUNT If you do something **on horseback**, you do it while riding a horse. [2] ADJ BEFORE N & ADV **Horseback** riding is the activity of riding a horse. *Many people in this area ride horseback.*

horseman /ˈhɔːsmən/ **horsemen.** N-COUNT A **horseman** is a man who is riding a horse, or who rides horses well.

horsepower /ˈhɔːspaʊə/. N-UNCOUNT **Horsepower** is a unit of power used for measuring how powerful an engine is.

horseshoe /ˈhɔːsʃuː/ **horseshoes.** N-COUNT A **horseshoe** is a piece of metal shaped like a U which is fixed to a horse's hoof.

horticulture /ˈhɔːtɪkʌltʃə/. N-UNCOUNT **Horticulture** is the study and practice of growing plants. ◆ **horticultural** /ˌhɔːtɪˈkʌltʃərəl/ ADJ *...the horticultural show.*

hose /həʊz/ **hoses, hosing, hosed.** [1] N-COUNT A **hose** is a long, flexible pipe through which water is carried in order to do things such as put out fires or water gardens. [2] VERB & PHR-VERB If you **hose** something, or if you **hose** it **down**, you wash it using a hose. *The beaches were hosed with hot water... Crewmen hosed down the decks.*

hospice /ˈhɒspɪs/ **hospices.** N-COUNT A **hospice** is a hospital for people who are dying.

hospitable /hɒˈspɪtəbəl, ˈhɒspɪt-/. ADJ A **hospitable** person is friendly, generous, and welcoming to guests or strangers. *He was very hospitable to me when I came to New York.*

⭐ **hospital** /ˈhɒspɪtəl/ **hospitals.** N-VAR A **hospital** is a place where people who are ill are looked after by doctors and nurses. *My mother went into hospital.*

hospitality /ˌhɒspɪˈtælɪti/. N-UNCOUNT **Hospitality** is friendly, welcoming behaviour towards guests or strangers.

hospitalize (BRIT also **hospitalise**) /ˈhɒspɪtəlaɪz/ **hospitalizes, hospitalizing, hospitalized.** VERB If someone **is hospitalized**, they are sent or admitted to hospital. ◆ **hospitalization** N-UNCOUNT *Occasionally hospitalization is required.*

⭐ **host** /həʊst/ **hosts, hosting, hosted.** [1] N-COUNT & VERB The **host** at a party is the person who has invited the guests and who provides the food, drink, or entertainment. You can say they **host** the party. *He attended a private lunch hosted by the Prime Minister.* [2] N-COUNT & VERB A country, city, or organization that is the **host** of an event provides the facilities for that event to take place. You can say they **host** the event. *In March Luxembourg hosted a meeting of justice-ministry officials.* [3] N-COUNT & VERB The **host** of a radio or television show is the person who introduces it and talks to the people taking part. You can say they **host** the show. [4] QUANT A **host of** things is a lot of them. *...a whole host of gadgets powered by electricity.*

⭐ **hostage** /ˈhɒstɪdʒ/ **hostages.** N-COUNT & PHRASE A **hostage** is a person who is illegally held prisoner and threatened with injury or death unless certain demands are met by other people. If someone **is taken hostage** or **is held hostage**, they are captured and kept in this way.

hostel /ˈhɒstəl/ **hostels.** N-COUNT A **hostel** is a large house where people can stay cheaply for a short time.

hostess /ˈhəʊstɪs/ **hostesses.** N-COUNT The **hostess** at a party is the woman who has invited the guests and provides the food, drink, or entertainment.

hostile /ˈhɒstaɪl, AM -təl/. [1] ADJ If someone is **hostile** to another person or to an idea or suggestion, they show their dislike for them in an aggressive way. *The Governor faced hostile*

Houses

bungalow

cottage

semi-detached house

terraced house

crowds. ♦ **hostility** /hɒˈstɪlɪti/ N-UNCOUNT
...*hostility to Black and ethnic groups.* [2] ADJ A
hostile environment is one in which humans and
animals find it difficult to live. ...*some of the most
hostile climatic conditions in the world.* [3] ADJ A
hostile takeover bid is one that is opposed by
the company that is being bid for.

hostilities /hɒˈstɪlɪtiz/. N-PLURAL You can refer
to fighting between two countries or groups who
are at war as **hostilities**.

★ **hot** /hɒt/ **hotter, hottest, hots, hotting, hotted.** [1] ADJ If
something is **hot**, it has a high temperature. ...*hot
water.* ...*a hot meal.*

> **USAGE** In informal English, if you want to
> emphasize how hot the weather is, you can
> say that it is **boiling** or **scorching**. In winter,
> if the temperature is above average, you can
> say that it is **mild**. In general, **hot** suggests a
> higher temperature than **warm**, and **warm**
> things are usually pleasant. *I would imagine
> that I was back home in England, sitting in
> the garden on a warm evening.*

[2] ADJ If you are **hot**, you feel uncomfortable
because of the high temperature of your body or
your surroundings. [3] ADJ You can say food is **hot**
when it has a burning taste caused by spices. ...*hot*

curries. [4] ADJ You can use **hot** to describe an issue
or event that is very important, exciting, or popular
at the present time. [INFORMAL] ...*the hottest movie of
the summer... Atlantic City is the hot favourite to stage
the fight.*

▸ **hot up.** PHR-VERB When something **hots up**, it
becomes more active or exciting. [BRITISH] *Poland's
presidential campaign is hotting up.*

,**hot 'air balloon.** See **balloon.**

'**hot dog, hot dogs.** N-COUNT A **hot dog** is a long
bread roll with a sausage in it.

★ **hotel** /həʊˈtel/ **hotels.** N-COUNT A **hotel** is a
building where people stay, paying for their
rooms and meals.

hotelier /ˌhəʊˈtelɪə, AM ˌəʊtelˈljeɪ/ **hoteliers.**
N-COUNT A **hotelier** is a person who owns or
manages a hotel or several hotels.

hotline /ˈhɒtlaɪn/ **hotlines.** [1] N-COUNT A **hotline**
is a telephone line that the public can use to
contact an organization about a particular
subject. [2] N-COUNT A **hotline** is a direct
telephone line between heads of government for
use in an emergency.

hotly /ˈhɒtli/. [1] ADV If you say something
hotly, you say it angrily. *'That's not true,' Robyn
said hotly... The bank hotly denies any wrongdoing.*
[2] ADV If something is being **hotly** pursued or
hotly contested, the people involved are very

★ Bank of English® frequent word   For a full explanation of all grammatical labels, see pages vii–x

A
B
C
D
★ E
F
G
H
I
J
K
L
M
N
O
P
Q
R
S
T
U
V
W
X
Y
Z

determined to catch it or to win it. *This year's final will be as hotly contested as ever.*

hound /haʊnd/ **hounds, hounding, hounded.**
[1] N-COUNT A **hound** is a type of dog, often used for hunting or racing. *...a pack of hounds.* [2] VERB If someone **hounds** you, they constantly disturb you or pester you. *I was constantly hounded by classmates.*

★ **hour** /aʊə/ **hours.** [1] N-COUNT An **hour** is a period of sixty minutes. → See Reference Page on Telling the Time. *The journey took three hours... They returned half an hour later.* [2] N-PLURAL You can refer to the period of time during which something happens or operates each day as the **hours** during which it happens or operates. *...the hours of darkness... Phone us during office hours... Peter came home in the early hours of the morning.* [3] N-SING **The hour** is used in expressions like **on the hour** to refer to times when it is exactly one o'clock, two o'clock, and so on. → See Reference Page on Telling the Time. *Trains will leave Reading at 36 minutes past the hour.* [4] See also **rush hour**.

hourly /aʊəli/. [1] ADJ BEFORE N & ADV An **hourly** event happens once every hour. *...hourly news bulletins... The hospital issued press releases hourly.* [2] ADJ BEFORE N Your **hourly** earnings are the amount of money that you earn each hour. *...the decision to cut their hourly pay.*

★ **house, houses** /haʊzɪz/, **housing, housed.**
[1] N-COUNT /haʊs/ A **house** is a building in which people live. You can also refer to all the people who live together in a house as the **house**. *It would wake the whole house.* → See picture on page 337. [2] PHRASE If someone **puts** their **house in order**, they arrange their affairs and solve their problems. [3] N-COUNT **House** is used in the names of some types of companies and establishments. *...a steak house. ...a publishing house.* [4] N-COUNT You can refer to the two main bodies of Britain's and the United States of America's parliament as **the House** or a **House**. *Some members of the House and Senate worked all day yesterday.* [5] N-COUNT In a theatre or cinema, the **house** is the part where the audience sits. *The show played to packed houses.* [6] VERB /haʊz/ To **house** someone means to provide a house or flat for them to live in. [7] VERB If a building **houses** something, that thing is kept or located in the building. *The gallery will house the university's art collection.*

house ar'rest. N-UNCOUNT If someone is **under house arrest**, they are officially ordered not to leave their home, because they are suspected of being involved in an illegal activity.

★ **household** /haʊshəʊld/ **households.** [1] N-COUNT A **household** is all the people in a family or group who live together in a house. *...women-only households.* [2] N-SING The **household** is your home and everything connected with looking after it. *My husband gave me cash to manage the household. ...household chores.* [3] ADJ BEFORE N Someone or something that is a **household** name is very well known.

householder /haʊshəʊldə/ **householders.**
N-COUNT A **householder** is the owner or tenant of a house.

housekeeper /haʊskiːpə/ **housekeepers.**
N-COUNT A **housekeeper** is a person employed to do the cleaning and cooking in a house.

housekeeping /haʊskiːpɪŋ/. N-UNCOUNT **Housekeeping** is the work, organization, and financial planning involved in running a home.

,**House of 'Commons.** N-PROPER **The House of Commons** is the more powerful of the two parts of parliament in Britain and Canada. The building where the members meet is also called **the House of Commons.**

,**House of 'Lords.** N-PROPER **The House of Lords** is the less powerful of the two parts of parliament in Britain and Canada. The building where the members meet is also called **the House of Lords.**

housewife /haʊswaɪf/ **housewives.** N-COUNT A **housewife** is a married woman who does not have a paid job, but instead looks after her home and children.

housework /haʊswɜːk/. N-UNCOUNT **Housework** is the work such as cleaning and cooking that you do in your home.

★ **housing** /haʊzɪŋ/. N-COUNT **Housing** is the buildings that people live in. *...affordable housing.*

'**housing estate, housing estates.** N-COUNT A **housing estate** is a large number of houses or flats built close together. [BRITISH]

hover /hɒvə, AM hʌv-/ **hovers, hovering, hovered.**
[1] VERB To **hover** means to stay in the same position in the air without moving forwards or backwards. *Butterflies hovered above the wild flowers... A police helicopter hovered overhead.* [2] VERB If someone **is hovering**, they are hesitating because they cannot decide what to do. *Judith was hovering in the doorway.*

★ **how** /haʊ/.

> ✓ **How** is mainly used in questions.

[1] ADV & CONJ You use **how** to ask about the way in which something happens or is done. *I don't want to know how he died... How do you manage to keep the place so tidy?* [2] ADV & CONJ You use **how** when you are asking for news about someone's health or life, or whether something was successful or enjoyable. *Hi! How are you doing?... How's the job?... How was your trip down to Orlando?... She asked how he had been feeling.* [3] ADV You use **how** in expressions such as '**how about...**' or '**how would you like...**' when you are making an offer or a suggestion. *How about a cup of coffee?* [4] ADV You use **how** to emphasize the degree to which something is true. *I didn't realize how heavy that shopping was going to be.* [5] ADV You use **how** to ask questions about the quantity or degree of something. *How long will you be staying?... How old is your son now?* [6] CONVENTION You can say '**How about you?'**

when you are asking someone their opinion. *Well, I enjoyed that. How about you two?*

> **USAGE** You do not use **how** to ask questions about the appearance or character of someone or something. You use an expression with **what** and **like**. For example, if you ask '**How is Susan?**', you are asking about her health. If you want to know about her appearance, you ask '**What does Susan look like?**' If you want to know about her personality, you ask '**What is Susan like?**'

★ **however** /haʊ'evə/. ⓵ ADV You use **however** when you are adding a comment which contrasts with what has just been said. *Some of the food crops failed. However, the cotton did quite well.* ⓶ CONJ & ADV You use **however** to say that it makes no difference how something is done or to what degree or extent something is done. *Wear your hair however you want... However hard she tried, nothing seemed to work.* ⓷ ADV & CONJ You can use **however** in questions to express surprise at something. *However did you find this place?*

howl /haʊl/ **howls, howling, howled.** ⓵ VERB & N-COUNT If a wolf or a dog **howls** or lets out a **howl**, it utters a long, loud, crying sound. ⓶ VERB & N-COUNT If a person **howls** or lets out a **howl**, they make a long, loud cry expressing pain, anger, or unhappiness. *Vincent let out a howl of anguish.* ⓷ VERB & N-COUNT If people **are howling with** laughter, or if there are **howls of** laughter, people are laughing very loudly. ⓸ VERB When the wind **howls**, it blows hard, making a loud noise.

HQ /,eɪtʃ 'kjuː/ **HQs.** N-VAR **HQ** is an abbreviation for 'headquarters'.

hr, hrs. hr is a written abbreviation for 'hour'. *...1 hr 15 mins.*

HTML /,eɪtʃ tiː em 'el/. N-UNCOUNT **HTML** is a system of codes for producing documents for the Internet. **HTML** is an abbreviation for 'hypertext markup language'. [COMPUTING]

hub /hʌb/ **hubs.** ⓵ N-COUNT The **hub** of a wheel is the part at the centre. ⓶ N-COUNT If you describe a place as a **hub of** an activity, you mean that it is a very important centre for that activity. *The area was the hub of Moscow's business life.*

huddle /'hʌdəl/ **huddles, huddling, huddled.** ⓵ VERB If you **huddle** somewhere, you sit, stand, or lie there holding your arms and legs close to your body, usually because you are cold or frightened. *She huddled inside the porch.* ⓶ VERB If people **huddle together** or **huddle round** something, they stand, sit, or lie close to each other, usually because they all feel cold or frightened. *We huddled round a small coal fire.* ⓷ N-COUNT A **huddle of** people or things is a small group standing or sitting close together. *...a huddle of stone buildings.*

hue /hjuː/ **hues.** N-COUNT A **hue** is a colour. [LITERARY] *...an intricately woven cloth of many hues.*

huff /hʌf/ **huffs, huffing, huffed.** ⓵ VERB If you **huff**, you indicate that you are annoyed or offended about something, usually by the way that you say something. *'I don't like ultimatums,' Michelle huffed.* ⓶ PHRASE If someone is **in a huff**, they are behaving in a bad-tempered way because they are annoyed or offended.

hug /hʌg/ **hugs, hugging, hugged.** ⓵ VERB & N-COUNT If you **hug** someone, or if you give them a **hug**, you put your arms around them and hold them tightly, as a sign of affection. *Lynn and I hugged each other... There were lots of hugs and kisses.* ⓶ VERB If you **hug** something, you hold it close to your body with your arms tightly round it. *She hugged her legs tight to her chest.* ⓷ VERB Something that **hugs** the ground or a stretch of land or water stays very close to it. [WRITTEN] *The road hugs the coast for hundreds of miles.*

★ **huge** /hjuːdʒ/. ADJ Something that is **huge** is extremely large in size, amount, or degree. *...a huge window... They have made huge profits.* ♦ **hugely** ADV *...a hugely successful career.*

hull /hʌl/ **hulls.** N-COUNT The **hull** of a boat is the main part of its body.

hullo /hʌ'ləʊ/. See **hello**.

hum /hʌm/ **hums, humming, hummed.** ⓵ VERB & N-SING If something **hums**, or if it makes a **hum**, it makes a low continuous noise. *The air conditioner hummed. ...the hum of traffic.* ⓶ VERB When you **hum** a tune, you sing it with your lips closed. *She was humming to herself.*

★ **human** /'hjuːmən/ **humans.** ⓵ ADJ BEFORE N **Human** means relating to or concerning people. *...the human body. ...human history... The crash was the result of human error.* ⓶ N-COUNT You can refer to people as **humans** when you are comparing them with animals or machines. *In humans, the same process takes about three months.*

human 'being, human beings. N-COUNT A **human being** is a man, woman, or child.

humane /,hjuː'meɪn/. ADJ Someone who is **humane** is kind and compassionate. *...the desire for a more humane society.* ♦ **humanely** ADV *All detainees are being humanely treated.*

humanism /'hjuːmənɪzəm/. N-UNCOUNT **Humanism** is the belief that people can achieve happiness and fulfilment without the need for religion. ♦ **humanist, humanists** N-COUNT *...the country's leading humanists.*

humanitarian /hjuː,mænɪ'teəriən/ **humanitarians.** N-COUNT & ADJ If someone is a **humanitarian**, or if they hold **humanitarian** views, they try to avoid making people suffer or to help people who are suffering. *He says he acted on humanitarian grounds.*

humanity /hjuː'mænɪti/ **humanities.** ⓵ N-UNCOUNT All the people in the world can be referred to as **humanity**. *He has rendered a great service to humanity.* ⓶ N-UNCOUNT A person's **humanity** is their state of being a human being, rather than an animal or an object. [FORMAL] *He*

a
b
c
d
e
f
g
h
i
j
k
l
m
n
o
p
q
r
s
t
u
v
w
x
y
z

was under discussion and it made him feel deprived of his humanity. **3** N-UNCOUNT **Humanity** is the quality of being kind, thoughtful, and sympathetic. *Her speech showed great maturity and humanity.* **4** N-PLURAL **The humanities** are subjects such as literature, philosophy, and history which are concerned with human ideas and behaviour.

,human 'nature. N-UNCOUNT **Human nature** is the natural qualities and behaviour that most people show. *It seems to be human nature to worry.*

,human 'race. N-SING You can refer to all the people in the world as **the human race**.

★ ,human 'rights. N-PLURAL **Human rights** are basic rights which many societies believe that all people should have.

humble /'hʌmbəl/ **humbler, humblest; humbles, humbling, humbled.** **1** ADJ A **humble** person is not proud and does not believe that they are better than other people. ♦ **humbly** ADV *'I'm a lucky man, undeservedly lucky,' he said humbly.* **2** ADJ People and things that are considered very ordinary and unimportant can be described as **humble**. *...a humble fisherman. ...the humble potato.* **3** VERB If something or someone **humbles** you, they make you realize that you are not as important or clever as you thought you were. *I felt humbled by the power of the sea.* ♦ **humbling** ADJ *...a very humbling experience.*

humid /'hju:mɪd/. ADJ You use **humid** to describe an atmosphere or climate that is very damp, and usually very hot. *Visitors can expect hot and humid conditions.*

humidity /hju:'mɪdɪti/. N-UNCOUNT **Humidity** is dampness in the air. *The humidity is relatively low.*

humiliate /hju:'mɪlieɪt/ **humiliates, humiliating, humiliated.** VERB To **humiliate** someone means to say or do something which makes them feel ashamed or stupid. *He enjoyed humiliating me.* ♦ **humiliated** ADJ *I have never felt so humiliated in my life.* ♦ **humiliating** ADJ *...a humiliating defeat.*

humiliation /hju:,mɪli'eɪʃən/ **humiliations.** N-VAR **Humiliation** is the embarrassment and shame you feel when someone makes you appear stupid, or when you make a mistake in public. A **humiliation** is an occasion or situation in which you feel this. *The result is a humiliation for the prime minister.*

humility /hju:'mɪlɪti/. N-UNCOUNT Someone who has **humility** is not proud and does not believe that they are better than other people. *He should learn a little humility.*

humor /'hju:mə/. See **humour**.

humorous /'hju:mərəs/. ADJ If someone or something is **humorous**, they are amusing and witty. *...humorous stories.* ♦ **humorously** ADV *He regarded the whole thing humorously.*

★ **humour** (AM **humor**) /'hju:mə/ **humours, humouring, humoured.** **1** N-UNCOUNT You can refer to the amusing things that people say as their

humour. *She is a fan of his outrageous humour.* **2** N-UNCOUNT If something has **humour**, it is funny and makes you want to laugh. *He tries to find the humour in most situations.* **3** N-UNCOUNT If you are in good **humour**, you feel happy. [WRITTEN] **4** VERB If you **humour** someone, you try to please them, so that they will not become upset. *I nodded, partly to humour him.*

hump /hʌmp/ **humps, humping, humped.** **1** N-COUNT A **hump** is a small hill or raised piece of ground. *The path goes over a large hump.* **2** N-COUNT A camel's **hump** is the large lump on its back. **3** VERB If you **hump** a heavy object somewhere, you carry it there with difficulty. [BRITISH, INFORMAL] *Charlie humped his rucksack up the stairs.*

hunch /hʌntʃ/ **hunches, hunching, hunched.** **1** N-COUNT If you **have** a **hunch** that something is true, you think that it is likely to be true. [INFORMAL] *I had a hunch it was lead poisoning.* **2** VERB If you **hunch** your shoulders or **hunch** forward, you raise your shoulders, lower your head, and lean forward. *Pupils sat hunched over their books.*

★ **hundred** /'hʌndrəd/ **hundreds.** **1** NUM A **hundred** or **one hundred** is the number 100. **2** N-PLURAL & PRON You can use **hundreds** to mean an extremely large number. *He received hundreds of letters... Hundreds died in the fighting.* **3** PHRASE You can use **a hundred per cent** or **one hundred per cent** to emphasize that something is definitely the case. [INFORMAL] *I'm a hundred per cent certain that's what I saw.*

★ **hundredth** /'hʌndrədθ/ **hundredths.** **1** ORD The **hundredth** item in a series is the one that you count as number one hundred. *...the hundredth anniversary of his birth.* **2** N-COUNT A **hundredth** is one of a hundred equal parts of something. *...one hundredth of a second.*

hung /hʌŋ/. **1** **Hung** is the past tense and past participle of most senses of **hang**. **2** ADJ A **hung** parliament, council, or jury consists of different groups of people who have different opinions, but no group forms a majority.

hunger /'hʌŋgə/ **hungers, hungering, hungered.** **1** N-UNCOUNT **Hunger** is the feeling of weakness or discomfort that you get when you need something to eat. *...pangs of hunger.* **2** N-UNCOUNT **Hunger** is a serious lack of food which causes suffering or death. *...thousands could easily die of hunger.* **3** VERB & N-SING If you **hunger for** something, or if you have a **hunger for** it, you want it very much. [FORMAL] *Jules hungered for adventure.*

'hunger strike, hunger strikes. N-VAR If someone goes **on hunger strike**, they refuse to eat as a way of protesting about something. *The protesters have been on hunger strike for 17 days.*

hungry /'hʌŋgri/ **hungrier, hungriest.** **1** ADJ When you are **hungry**, you want food. ♦ **hungrily** ADV *James ate hungrily.* **2** PHRASE If people **go hungry**, they suffer from hunger, either for a long period because they are poor or for a short period because they miss a meal. **3** ADJ If you are **hungry for** something, you want it very much. [LITERARY] ...*an ambitious club who are hungry for success.*

hunk /hʌŋk/ **hunks.** N-COUNT A **hunk of** something is a large piece of it. ...*a hunk of cheese.*

⭐ **hunt** /hʌnt/ **hunts, hunting, hunted.** 1 VERB & N-COUNT When people or animals **hunt**, or when they go on a **hunt**, they chase and kill wild animals for food or as a sport. *He liked to hunt rabbits.* ...*a bear hunt.* ♦ **hunting** N-UNCOUNT ...*a ban on fox hunting.* 2 VERB & N-COUNT If you **hunt for** someone or something, or if you have a **hunt for** them, you search for them. *He hunted for an apartment... More than 70 police officers are involved in the hunt for her killer.* ♦ **hunting** N-UNCOUNT ...*job hunting.*
▶ **hunt down.** PHR-VERB If you **hunt** someone or something **down**, you succeed in finding them after searching for them. *It took her four months to hunt him down.*

⭐ **hunter** /ˈhʌntə/ **hunters.** 1 N-COUNT A **hunter** is a person who hunts wild animals for food or as a sport. ...*deer hunters.* 2 N-COUNT People who are searching for things of a particular kind can be referred to as **hunters**. ...*bargain hunters.*

hurdle /ˈhɜːdəl/ **hurdles.** 1 N-COUNT A **hurdle** is a difficulty that you must overcome in order to achieve something. ...*preparing a CV, the first hurdle in a job search.* 2 N-COUNT **Hurdles** is a race in which people run and jump over a number of obstacles that are also called hurdles.

hurdler /ˈhɜːdlə/ **hurdlers.** N-COUNT A **hurdler** is an athlete whose special event is the hurdles.

hurl /hɜːl/ **hurls, hurling, hurled.** 1 VERB If you **hurl** an object, you throw it with a lot of force. *Groups of angry youths hurled stones at police.* 2 VERB If you **hurl** abuse or insults at someone, you shout at them aggressively.

hurricane /ˈhʌrɪkən, AM ˈhɜːrɪkeɪn/ **hurricanes.** N-COUNT A **hurricane** is a very violent storm with strong winds.

hurried /ˈhʌrid, AM ˈhɜːr-/. ADJ A **hurried** action is done quickly. ...*a hurried breakfast.*
♦ **hurriedly** ADV *She blushed and hurriedly left the room.*

hurry /ˈhʌri, AM ˈhɜːri/ **hurries, hurrying, hurried.** 1 VERB If you **hurry** somewhere, you go there quickly. *Claire hurried along the road... She had to hurry home and look after her son.* 2 VERB If you **hurry to** do something, you start doing it as soon as you can, or you try to get it done quickly. *Traders hurried to buy up supplies before the long weekend.* 3 VERB & PHR-VERB If you **hurry** someone or something, **hurry** them **up**, or **hurry** them **along**, you try to make something happen more quickly. *Sorry to hurry you, John... Can you advise me how I can hurry up the process?... Petter saw no reason to hurry the divorce along.* 4 PHRASE If you are **in a hurry to** do something, you need or want to do something quickly. If you

do something **in a hurry**, you do it quickly. *My colleague was in a hurry to get back to work.*
▶ **hurry up.** 1 PHR-VERB If you tell someone to **hurry up**, you are telling them to do something more quickly. *Hurry up with that coffee, will you.* 2 See **hurry** 3.

⭐ **hurt** /hɜːt/ **hurts, hurting, hurt.** 1 VERB & ADJ If you **hurt yourself**, or **hurt** a part of your body, or if you are **hurt**, you are injured. *He fell and hurt his back... His comrades asked him if he was hurt.* 2 VERB If you **hurt** someone, you cause them to feel pain. *I didn't mean to hurt her... Ouch. That hurt.* 3 VERB If a part of your body **hurts**, you feel pain there. *His collar bone only hurt when he lifted his arm.* 4 VERB & ADJ If someone **hurts** you, or if you are **hurt**, you are upset because someone has said or done something rude or inconsiderate. *He is afraid of hurting Bessy's feelings... He gave me a slightly hurt look.* 5 VERB You can say that something **hurts** someone or something when it damages them. *They may fear hurting their husbands' careers.*

hurtle /ˈhɜːtəl/ **hurtles, hurtling, hurtled.** VERB If someone or something **hurtles** somewhere, they move there very quickly, often in a rough or violent way. *I hurtled down the stairs.*

⭐ **husband** /ˈhʌzbənd/ **husbands.** N-COUNT A woman's **husband** is the man she is married to.

hush /hʌʃ/ **hushes, hushing, hushed.** 1 CONVENTION You say **'Hush!'** to someone when you are asking or telling them to be quiet. 2 N-SING You say that there is a **hush** in a place when it is quiet and peaceful, or when it suddenly becomes quiet. *A hush fell over the crowd.*
▶ **hush up.** PHR-VERB If someone in authority **hushes up** something bad or wrong, they prevent other people from finding out about it. *They had to hush it up.*

hushed /hʌʃt/. ADJ **Hushed** means quiet and calm. ...*a hushed and dignified atmosphere.*

hustle /ˈhʌsəl/ **hustles, hustling, hustled.** 1 VERB If you **hustle** someone, you make them move quickly, usually by pulling or pushing them. *The guards hustled Harry out of the car.* 2 VERB If you **hustle**, you go somewhere or do something hurriedly. *He hustled straight up the aircraft steps.*

hut /hʌt/ **huts.** N-COUNT A **hut** is a small, simple building, often made of wood, mud, or grass.

hybrid /ˈhaɪbrɪd/ **hybrids.** 1 N-COUNT A **hybrid** is an animal or plant that has been bred from two different types of animal or plant. [TECHNICAL] 2 N-COUNT You can use **hybrid** to refer to something that is a mixture of other things. ...*a hybrid of solid and liquid fuel.*

hydraulic /haɪˈdrɒlɪk, AM -ˈdrɔːl-/. ADJ BEFORE N **Hydraulic** means involving a fluid that is under pressure, such as water or oil. ...*hydraulic pumps.*

hydrogen /ˈhaɪdrədʒən/. N-UNCOUNT **Hydrogen** is a colourless gas that is the lightest and most common element in the universe.

hygiene /ˈhaɪdʒiːn/. N-UNCOUNT **Hygiene** is the practice of keeping yourself and your surroundings clean, especially in order to prevent the spread of disease. ◆ **hygienic** /haɪ'dʒiːnɪk, AM ,haɪ'dʒienɪk/ ADJ ...*extremely hygienic conditions.*

hymn /hɪm/ **hymns.** N-COUNT A **hymn** is a song sung by Christians to praise God.

hype /haɪp/. N-UNCOUNT If you describe the publicity for something such as a new film as **hype**, you disapprove of it because it is very intensive and exaggerated. *My products aren't based on advertising hype, they sell by word of mouth.*

hyperlink /'haɪpəlɪŋk/ **hyperlinks.** N-COUNT In an HTML document, a **hyperlink** is a link to another part of the document or to another document. Hyperlinks are shown as words with a line under them. [COMPUTING]

hyphen /'haɪfən/ **hyphens.** N-COUNT A **hyphen** is the punctuation sign (-) used to join words together to make a compound. → See Reference Page on Punctuation.

hypnosis /hɪp'nəʊsɪs/. [1] N-UNCOUNT **Hypnosis** is a state of unconsciousness produced when someone has been hypnotized. [2] N-UNCOUNT **Hypnosis** is the art or practice of hypnotizing someone.

hypnotic /hɪp'nɒtɪk/. [1] ADJ Something that is **hypnotic** makes you feel as if you have been hypnotized. ...*the TV screen's hypnotic power.* [2] ADJ If someone is in a **hypnotic** state, they have been hypnotized.

hypnotize (BRIT also **hypnotise**) /'hɪpnətaɪz/ **hypnotizes, hypnotizing, hypnotized.** [1] VERB If someone **hypnotizes** you, they put you into a state of unconsciousness in which you seem to be asleep but can respond to certain things you see or hear. ◆ **hypnotism** /'hɪpnətɪzəm/ N-UNCOUNT ...*the use of acupuncture and hypnotism.* ◆ **hypnotist, hypnotists** N-COUNT ...*regular visits to a hypnotist.* [2] VERB If you **are hypnotized** by someone or something, you are so fascinated by them that you cannot think of anything else. *He's hypnotized by that black hair and that white face.*

hypocrisy /hɪ'pɒkrɪsi/ **hypocrisies.** N-VAR If you accuse someone of **hypocrisy**, you disapprove of them because they act in a way which goes against the beliefs or qualities they say they have. *He accused newspapers of hypocrisy in their*

treatment of the story.

hypocrite /'hɪpəkrɪt/ **hypocrites.** N-COUNT If you accuse someone of being a **hypocrite**, you disapprove of them because they act in a way which goes against the beliefs or qualities they say they have.

hypocritical /,hɪpə'krɪtɪkəl/. ADJ If you accuse someone of being **hypocritical**, you disapprove of them because they act in a way which goes against the beliefs or qualities they say they have. *If someone is being hypocritical then it is fair to expose that.*

hypothesis /haɪ'pɒθɪsɪs/ **hypotheses.** N-COUNT A **hypothesis** is an explanation or theory which has not yet been proved to be correct. [FORMAL]

hypothetical /,haɪpə'θetɪkəl/. ADJ If something is **hypothetical**, it is based on possible situations, not actual ones. ...*a purely hypothetical question.* ◆ **hypothetically** /,haɪpə'θetɪkli/ ADV *We're talking hypothetically.*

hysterectomy /,hɪstə'rektəmi/ **hysterectomies.** N-COUNT A **hysterectomy** is a surgical operation to remove a woman's womb.

hysteria /hɪ'stɪəriə, AM -'ster-/. [1] N-UNCOUNT **Hysteria** among a group of people is a state of uncontrolled excitement or panic. *No one could help getting carried away by the hysteria.* [2] N-UNCOUNT A person who is suffering from **hysteria** is mentally disturbed, often as a result of shock. [TECHNICAL]

hysterical /hɪ'sterɪkəl/. [1] ADJ Someone who is **hysterical** is in a state of uncontrolled excitement or panic. *Calm down. Don't get hysterical.* ◆ **hysterically** ADV *Everyone was laughing hysterically.* [2] ADJ If you describe someone or something as **hysterical**, you mean that you think they are very funny. [INFORMAL] ◆ **hysterically** ADV *It wasn't supposed to be a comedy but I found it hysterically funny.* [3] ADJ A **hysterical** illness is caused by mental disturbance that is often the result of shock. [TECHNICAL] *Her hysterical symptoms included paralysis.*

hysterics /hɪ'sterɪks/. [1] N-PLURAL If someone is **in hysterics** or **is having hysterics**, they are in a state of uncontrolled excitement or panic. [2] N-PLURAL You can say that someone is **in hysterics** or **is having hysterics** when they are laughing uncontrollably. [INFORMAL] *She collapsed in hysterics when I told her about the horse.*

I i

⭐ **I** /aɪ/. PRON **I** is used as the subject of a verb. A speaker or writer uses **I** to refer to himself or herself. *She liked me, I think... Jim and I are getting married.*

⭐ **ice** /aɪs/ **ices, icing, iced.** [1] N-UNCOUNT **Ice** is frozen water. *Hans ground his skate blade against the ice. ...a bitter lemon with ice.* [2] VERB To **ice** cakes means to cover them with icing. *We were all*

given little iced cakes. [3] N-COUNT An **ice** is an ice cream.

PHRASES ● If you **break the ice** at a party or meeting, or in a new situation, you do something to make people feel relaxed. *Break the ice with tea or coffee and get to know your client a little better.* ● If you say that something **cuts no ice** with you, you mean that you are not impressed or influenced by it. *That sort of romantic attitude cuts no ice with money-men.* ● If someone puts a plan or project **on ice**, they delay doing it. ● See also **iced**, **icing**.

iceberg /'aɪsbɜːg/ **icebergs.** N-COUNT An **iceberg** is a large, tall mass of ice floating in the sea. ● **tip of the iceberg**: see **tip**.

,**ice 'cream, ice creams.** ① N-UNCOUNT **Ice cream** is a very cold sweet food made from frozen milk, fats, and sugar. ② N-COUNT An **ice cream** is a portion of ice cream.

iced /aɪst/. ADJ BEFORE N An **iced** drink has been made very cold, often by putting ice in it. *...iced tea.* ● See also **ice**.

'**ice hockey.** N-UNCOUNT **Ice hockey** is a game like hockey played on ice.

ice-skating

'**ice-skate, ice-skates.** N-COUNT **Ice-skates** are boots with a thin metal bar underneath that people wear to move about on ice.

'**ice-skater, ice-skaters.** N-COUNT An **ice-skater** is someone who moves about on ice wearing ice-skates.

'**ice-skating.** N-UNCOUNT **Ice-skating** is a sport or leisure activity which involves people moving about on ice wearing ice-skates.

icicle /'aɪsɪkəl/ **icicles.** N-COUNT An **icicle** is a long pointed piece of ice hanging from a surface.

icing /'aɪsɪŋ/. N-UNCOUNT **Icing** is a sweet substance made from powdered sugar that is used to cover and decorate cakes.

icon (or **ikon**) /'aɪkɒn/ **icons.** ① N-COUNT If you describe something or someone as an **icon**, you mean that they are important as a symbol of something. *...Britain's favourite fashion icon, the Princess of Wales. ...Picasso and the other icons of modernism.* ② N-COUNT An **icon** is a picture of Christ or of a saint painted on a wooden panel. Icons are regarded as holy by some Christians. ③ N-COUNT An **icon** is a picture on a computer screen representing a particular computer function. If you want to use it, you move the cursor onto the icon using a mouse. [COMPUTING]

icy /'aɪsi/ **icier, iciest.** ① ADJ **Icy** air or water is extremely cold. *...an icy wind... His shoes and clothing were wet through and icy cold.* ② ADJ An **icy** road has ice on it.

ID /ˌaɪ 'diː/ **IDs.** N-VAR If you have **ID**, you are carrying a document such as an identity card or driving licence which proves that you are a particular person. *I had no ID on me so the police couldn't establish I was the owner of the car.*

I'd /aɪd/. **I'd** is the usual spoken form of 'I had', especially when 'had' is an auxiliary verb. **I'd** is also a spoken form of 'I would'. *I'd seen her before... There are some questions I'd like to ask.*

★ **idea** /aɪ'dɪə/ **ideas.** ① N-COUNT An **idea** is a plan or possible course of action. *It's a good idea to avoid refined food... I really like the idea of helping people... She told me she'd had a brilliant idea.* ② N-COUNT Your **idea of** something is your belief about what it is like or what it should be like. *My idea of physical perfection is to be very slender... Everyone has their own ideas about how to bring up children. ...a theory which supports the idea that there are many other solar systems.* ③ N-SING If you have an **idea of** something, you have some general understanding or knowledge of it, although you may not know many details about it. *Could you give us an idea of the range of complaints you've been receiving?... I had an idea that he joined the army later, after university... We haven't the faintest idea where he is.* ④ N-SING The **idea** of an action or activity is its aim or purpose. *The idea is to give children the freedom to explore.* ⑤ PHRASE If someone **gets the idea**, they understand how to do something or understand what you are telling them. *It isn't too difficult once you get the idea.*

★ **ideal** /aɪ'diːəl/ **ideals.** ① N-COUNT An **ideal** is a principle, idea, or standard that you believe is right and worth trying to achieve. *...pursuing his ideals of democracy, justice and human rights.* ② N-SING Your **ideal** of something is the person or thing that seems to you to be the best possible example of it. *Throughout her career she remained his feminine ideal.* ③ ADJ The **ideal** person or thing for a particular purpose is the best one for it. *I was the ideal person to take over the job... The conditions were ideal for racing.* ◆ **ideally** ADV *The hotel is ideally situated for country walks.* ④ ADJ BEFORE N An **ideal** society or world is the best possible one that you can imagine. ● See also **ideally**.

idealise /aɪ'diːəlaɪz/. See **idealize**.

idealism /aɪ'diːəlɪzəm/. N-UNCOUNT **Idealism** is the behaviour and beliefs of someone who has ideals and tries to follow them, even though this may be impractical or naive. ◆ **idealist, idealists** N-COUNT *He is not such an idealist that he cannot see the problems.*

idealistic /ˌaɪdɪə'lɪstɪk/. ADJ **Idealistic** people base their behaviour on ideals, even though this may be impractical or naive.

idealize (BRIT also **idealise**) /aɪ'diːəlaɪz/ **idealizes, idealizing, idealized.** VERB If you **idealize** someone or something, you think of them as perfect or much better than they really are. *People idealize the past.*

a b c d e f g h i j k l m n o p q r s t u v w x y z

A
B
C
D
E
F
G
H ★
I
J
K
L
M
N
O
P
Q
R
S
T
U
V
W
X
Y
Z

ideally /aɪˈdiːəli/. ADV If you say that **ideally** something should happen, you mean that you would like it to happen, although it may not be possible. *Ideally, she would love to become pregnant again.* ● See also **ideal**.

identical /aɪˈdentɪkəl/. ADJ Things that are **identical** are exactly the same. *Nearly all the houses were identical.* ◆ **identically** ADV *...nine identically dressed female dancers.*

identifiable /aɪˌdentɪˈfaɪəbəl/. ADJ Something or someone that is **identifiable** can be recognized. *It is instantly identifiable as a Catholic church.*

identification /aɪˌdentɪfɪˈkeɪʃən/. N-UNCOUNT When someone asks you for **identification**, they are asking to see something such as a driving licence which proves who you are.

★ **identify** /aɪˈdentɪfaɪ/ **identifies, identifying, identified.** [1] VERB If you can **identify** someone or something, you can recognize them and say who or what they are. *Police have already identified around 10 murder suspects... Having identified the problem, the question arises of how to overcome it.* ◆ **identification** /aɪˌdentɪfɪˈkeɪʃən/ **identifications** N-VAR *He's made a formal identification of the body.* [2] VERB If something **identifies** you, it makes it possible for people to recognize you. *She wore a little nurse's hat on her head to identify her.* [3] VERB If you **identify with** someone or something, you feel that you understand them. *She would only play a role if she could identify with the character.* ◆ **identification** N-VAR *Marilyn had an intense identification with animals.* [4] VERB If you **identify** one thing with another, you consider them to be closely associated. *Candidates want to identify themselves with reform.* ◆ **identification** N-VAR *...the identification of Spain with Catholicism.*

★ **identity** /aɪˈdentɪti/ **identities.** [1] N-COUNT Your **identity** is who you are. *The police soon established his true identity.* [2] N-VAR The **identity** of a person or place is the characteristics that they have that distinguish them from others. *Palestinians see Jerusalem as a symbol of national identity.*

i'dentity card, identity cards. N-COUNT An **identity card** is a card with a person's name, photograph, date of birth, and other information about them on it.

ideology /ˌaɪdiˈɒlədʒi/ **ideologies.** N-VAR An **ideology** is a set of beliefs, especially the political beliefs on which people, parties, or countries base their actions. *...capitalist ideology.* ◆ **ideological** /ˌaɪdiəˈlɒdʒɪkəl/ ADJ *...the ideological divisions between the parties.* ◆ **ideologically** ADV *The army was ideologically opposed to the kind of economic solution proposed.*

idiom /ˈɪdiəm/ **idioms.** [1] N-COUNT A particular **idiom** is a particular style of something such as music or architecture. [FORMAL] *McCartney was also keen to write in a classical idiom, rather than a pop*

onc. [2] N-COUNT An **idiom** is a group of words which have a different meaning when used together from the one they would have if you took the meaning of each word individually. For example, 'to give someone the cold shoulder' is an idiom meaning to ignore someone.

idiot /ˈɪdiət/ **idiots.** N-COUNT If you call someone an **idiot**, you mean that they are very stupid. *I knew I'd been an idiot to stay there.*

idle /ˈaɪdəl/ **idles, idling, idled.** [1] ADJ If you describe someone as **idle** you disapprove of them not doing anything when they should be doing something. *...idle bureaucrats who spent the day reading newspapers.* ◆ **idly** ADV *We were not idly sitting around.* [2] ADJ AFTER LINK-V Workers that are **idle** have no jobs or work. Machines or factories that are **idle** are not being used. *The machine is lying idle.* [3] ADJ BEFORE N **Idle** is used to describe something that is done for no particular reason, or does not achieve anything useful. *...idle chatter.* ◆ **idly** ADV *We talked idly about magazines.*

idol /ˈaɪdəl/ **idols.** N-COUNT An **idol** is someone such as a film star or pop star, who is greatly admired or loved by their fans. *...a teen idol.*

idolize (BRIT also **idolise**) /ˈaɪdəlaɪz/ **idolizes, idolizing, idolized.** VERB If you **idolize** someone, you admire them very much. *Naomi idolised her father.*

idyllic /ɪˈdɪlɪk, AM aɪd-/. ADJ Something that is **idyllic** is extremely pleasant and peaceful without any difficulties. *...an idyllic setting for a summer romance... Married life was not as idyllic as he had imagined.*

i.e. /ˌaɪ ˈiː/. **i.e.** is used to introduce a word or sentence expressing what you have just said in a different and clearer way. *The Uzbeks speak a Turkic language (i.e. one related to Turkish).*

★ **if** /ɪf/. [1] CONJ You use **if** in conditional sentences to introduce the circumstances in which an event or situation might happen or might have happened. *She gets very upset if I exclude her from anything... Are you a student with a knack for coming up with great ideas? If so, we would love to hear from you.* [2] CONJ You use **if** in indirect questions when the answer is either 'yes' or 'no'. *I wonder if you'd be kind enough to give us some information, please?* [3] CONJ You use **if** to suggest that something might be slightly different from what you are stating in the main part of the sentence, for example that there might be slightly more or less of a particular quality. *That standard is quite difficult, if not impossible, to achieve... What one quality, if any, do you like the most about your partner?*

PHRASES ● You use **'if anything'** when you are saying something which confirms a negative statement that you have just made. *There has yet to be an improvement. If anything, the situation has deteriorated.* ● You use **as if** to describe something or someone by comparing them with another thing or person. *He points two fingers at his head, as if he were holding a gun.* ● You use **if**

only when you are mentioning a reason for doing something. *She always writes me once a month, if only to scold me because I haven't answered her last letter yet.* ● You use **if only** to express a wish or desire, especially one that cannot be fulfilled. *If only you had told me that some time ago... If only it were that simple!*

ignite /ɪg'naɪt/ **ignites, igniting, ignited.** VERB When you **ignite** something, or when it **ignites**, it starts burning. *The bombs ignited a fire which destroyed some 60 houses.*

ignition /ɪg'nɪʃən/. N-SING In a car, the **ignition** is the mechanism which ignites the fuel and starts the engine, usually operated by turning a key. *Uncle Jim put the key in the ignition.*

ignorant /'ɪgnərənt/. [1] ADJ If you refer to someone as **ignorant**, you mean that they are not very knowledgeable or well educated. If someone is **ignorant** of a fact, they do not know it. *People don't like to ask questions for fear of appearing ignorant... Many people are worryingly ignorant of the facts about global warming.*
♦ **ignorance** N-UNCOUNT *I am embarrassed by my complete ignorance of non-European history.* [2] ADJ People are sometimes described as **ignorant** when they behave in a rude or inconsiderate way. Some people think this use is not correct.

ignore /ɪg'nɔː/ **ignores, ignoring, ignored.** VERB If you **ignore** someone or something, you deliberately take no notice of them. *Her husband ignored her... She ignored legal advice to drop the case.*

ikon /'aɪkɒn/. See **icon**.

ill /ɪl/ **ills.** [1] ADJ & N-PLURAL Someone who is **ill** is suffering from a disease or health problem. People who are ill in some way can be referred to as, for example, **the** mentally **ill**. *I was feeling ill.*

USAGE The words **ill** and **sick** are very similar in meaning but are used in slightly different ways. **Ill** is generally not used before a noun, and can be used in verbal expressions such as **fall ill** and **be taken ill**. *He fell ill shortly before Christmas... The trial was delayed after one of the jury members was taken ill.* **Sick** is often used before a noun. *...sick children.*
In British English, **ill** is a slightly more polite, less direct word than **sick**. **Sick** often suggests the actual physical feeling of being ill, for example nausea or vomiting. *I spent the next 24 hours in bed, groaning and being sick.*
In American English, **sick** is often used where British people would say **ill**. *Some people get hurt in accidents or get sick.*

[2] N-PLURAL Difficulties or problems can be referred to as **ills**. [FORMAL] *His critics maintain that he's responsible for many of Algeria's ills.* [3] ADJ BEFORE N **Ill** can be used in front of some nouns

to mean 'bad'. [FORMAL] *She had brought ill luck into her family.* [4] N-UNCOUNT **Ill** is evil or harm. [LITERARY] *They say they mean you no ill.* [5] **ill at ease:** see **ease**.

I'll /aɪl/. **I'll** is the usual spoken form of 'I will' or 'I shall'. *I'll drive you back to your hotel later, if you like.*

★ **illegal** /ɪ'liːgəl/. ADJ If something is **illegal**, the law says that it is not allowed. *It is illegal to intercept radio messages. ...illegal drugs.*
♦ **illegally** ADV *The previous government had acted illegally... Illegally parked cars will be towed away.*

illegitimate /ˌɪlɪ'dʒɪtɪmət/. [1] ADJ A person who is **illegitimate** was born of parents who were not legally married to each other. [2] ADJ Something that is **illegitimate** is not right, according to the law or to accepted standards. *The election would have been dismissed as illegitimate by the international community.*

,ill-'fated. ADJ If you describe something as **ill-fated**, you mean that it ended or will end in an unsuccessful or unfortunate way. *...Scott's ill-fated expedition to the South Pole.*

,ill 'health. N-UNCOUNT Someone who suffers from **ill health** has an illness or is often ill.

illicit /ɪ'lɪsɪt/. ADJ An **illicit** activity or substance is not allowed according to the law or to social customs. *...the use of illicit drugs.*

illiterate /ɪ'lɪtərət/. ADJ Someone who is **illiterate** cannot read or write.

★ **illness** /'ɪlnəs/ **illnesses.** [1] N-UNCOUNT **Illness** is the fact or experience of being ill. *Mental illness is still a taboo subject... He has not taken a day off work due to illness in 25 years.* [2] N-COUNT An **illness** is a particular disease such as a cold, measles, or pneumonia.

illogical /ɪ'lɒdʒɪkəl/. ADJ An **illogical** feeling or action is not rational and does not result from ordered thinking. *It is illogical to have two houses of parliament with the same powers. ...his completely illogical arguments.*

illuminate /ɪ'luːmɪneɪt/ **illuminates, illuminating, illuminated.** [1] VERB To **illuminate** something means to shine light on it and make it brighter. [WRITTEN] *The sandstone walls were illuminated by moonlight.* ♦ **illumination** N-UNCOUNT *...the days before illumination by electricity.* [2] VERB If you **illuminate** something that is difficult to understand, you make it clearer by explaining it or giving examples. [FORMAL] *The instructors use games and drawings to illuminate their subject.*
♦ **illuminating** ADJ *This is a most illuminating book.* ♦ **illumination** N-UNCOUNT *...a growing sense of illumination.*

illusion /ɪ'luːʒən/ **illusions.** [1] N-VAR An **illusion** is a false idea or belief. *No one really has any illusions about winning the war.* [2] N-COUNT An **illusion** is something that appears to exist or to be a particular thing but in reality does not exist or is something else. *Her upswept hair gave the illusion of above average height.*

a b c d e f g h i j k l m n o p q r s t u v w x y z

★ **illustrate** /'ɪləstreɪt/ **illustrates, illustrating, illustrated.** [1] VERB If something **illustrates** a situation, it shows that the situation exists. *The incident illustrates how tricky it is to design a safe system... The case also illustrates that some women are now trying to fight back.* ♦ **illustration, illustrations** N-VAR *An illustration of China's dynamism is that a new company is formed in Shanghai every 11 seconds.* [2] VERB If you use an example, story, or diagram to **illustrate** a point, you use it show that what you are saying is true or to make your meaning clearer. *Throughout, she illustrates her analysis with excerpts from discussions.* ♦ **illustration** N-VAR *Here, by way of illustration, are some extracts from our new catalogue.* [3] VERB To **illustrate** a book means to put pictures or diagrams into it. ♦ **illustration** N-VAR *The text is embellished with medical illustrations.*

illustrious /ɪ'lʌstriəs/. ADJ An **illustrious** person is famous and distinguished.

I'm /aɪm/. **I'm** is the usual spoken form of 'I am'. *I'm having a bath and going to bed.*

★ **image** /'ɪmɪdʒ/ **images.** [1] N-COUNT If you have an **image** of someone or something, you have a picture or idea of them in your mind. *The words 'Cote d'Azur' conjure up images of sunny days in Mediterranean cafés.* [2] N-COUNT The **image** of a person or organization is the way that they appear to other people. *He has cultivated the image of an elder statesman... The tobacco industry has been trying to improve its image.* [3] N-COUNT An **image** is a picture or reflection of someone or something. *...glamorous images of women on record sleeves.* [4] N-COUNT An **image** is a description or symbolic representation of something in a poem or other work of art. *...the image of 'star-laden seas' in the first stanza.*

imagery /'ɪmɪdʒri/. N-UNCOUNT You can talk about, for example, a poem's or film's **imagery** when you are referring to the symbols or descriptions in it which create a strong picture in your mind. *...the nature imagery of the ballad.*

imaginable /ɪ'mædʒɪnəbəl/. ADJ You use **imaginable** in expressions like 'the worst thing imaginable' or 'every imaginable thing' to emphasize that it is the most extreme example of something, or all the possible examples of something. *...their imprisonment under some of the most horrible circumstances imaginable... He had had the worst imaginable day.*

imaginary /ɪ'mædʒɪnəri, AM -neri/. ADJ An **imaginary** person, place, or thing exists only in your mind or in a story, and not in real life. *Lots of children have imaginary friends.*

★ **imagination** /ɪˌmædʒɪ'neɪʃən/ **imaginations.** N-VAR Your **imagination** is your ability to form pictures or ideas in your mind of new, exciting, or imaginary things. *Antonia is a woman with a vivid imagination... Long before I ever went there, Africa was alive in my imagination... The Government approach displays a lack of imagination.*

imaginative /ɪ'mædʒɪnətɪv/. ADJ Someone who is **imaginative** or who has **imaginative** ideas is easily able to think of or create new or exciting things. *...hundreds of cooking ideas and imaginative recipes.* ♦ **imaginatively** ADV *The hotel is decorated imaginatively and attractively.*

★ **imagine** /ɪ'mædʒɪn/ **imagines, imagining, imagined.** [1] VERB If you **imagine** a situation, your mind forms a picture or idea of it. *He could not imagine a more peaceful scene... Can you imagine how she must have felt?... Imagine you're lying on a beach.* [2] VERB If you **imagine** that something is true, you think that it is true. *We tend to imagine that the Victorians were very prim and proper... 'Was he meeting someone?'—'I imagine so.'* [3] VERB If you **imagine** something, you think that you have seen, heard, or experienced something, although actually you have not. *I realised that I must have imagined the whole thing.*

imbalance /ɪm'bæləns/ **imbalances.** N-VAR If there is an **imbalance** in a situation, the things involved are not the same size, or are not the right size in proportion to each other. *...the imbalance between the two sides in this war.*

imbue /ɪm'bjuː/ **imbues, imbuing, imbued.** VERB If you **imbue** something **with** a quality, you fill it with the quality. [FORMAL] *His presence imbued her with a feeling of security.*

imitate /'ɪmɪteɪt/ **imitates, imitating, imitated.** [1] VERB If you **imitate** someone, you copy what they do or produce. *...a genuine German musical which does not try to imitate the American model.* ♦ **imitator, imitators** N-COUNT *...that slickness which sets Bruce Willis's movies apart from their imitators.* [2] VERB If you **imitate** someone or something, you copy the way they speak or behave, often as a joke.

imitation /ˌɪmɪ'teɪʃən/ **imitations.** [1] N-COUNT An **imitation** of something is a copy of it. *...the most accurate imitation of Chinese architecture in Europe.* [2] N-UNCOUNT **Imitation** means copying someone else's actions. *Molly learned her golf by imitation.* [3] ADJ BEFORE N **Imitation** things are not genuine but are made to look as if they are. *...imitation leather.* [4] N-COUNT If someone **does** an **imitation** of another person, they copy the way they speak or behave, often as a joke.

immaculate /ɪ'mækjʊlət/. [1] ADJ If something is **immaculate**, it is extremely clean, tidy, or neat. *Her front room was kept immaculate.* ♦ **immaculately** ADV *As always he was immaculately dressed.* [2] ADJ If something is **immaculate**, it is perfect, without any mistakes or flaws at all. *Moreno produced an immaculate performance.*

immaterial /ˌɪmə'tɪəriəl/. ADJ AFTER LINK-V If something is **immaterial**, it is not important or not relevant. *Whether we like him or not is immaterial.*

immature /ˌɪmə'tjʊə, AM -'tʊr/. [1] ADJ Something that is **immature** is not yet fully developed. *...babies with particularly immature*

impact

respiratory systems. [2] ADJ If you describe someone as **immature**, you mean that they do not behave in a sensible and adult way. ...*grossly immature drivers who flout the rules of the road... She's just being childish and immature.*

immediate /ɪˈmiːdiət/. [1] ADJ An **immediate** result, action, or reaction happens or is done without any delay. *These tragic incidents have had an immediate effect... My immediate reaction was just disgust.* ◆ **immediately** ADV *He immediately flung himself to the floor... Ingrid answered Peter's letter immediately.* [2] ADJ **Immediate** needs and concerns must be dealt with quickly. *The immediate problem is not a lack of food, but transportation.* [3] ADJ BEFORE N **Immediate** means very close to something or someone else in time or space, or in a sequence. ...*the immediate aftermath of the riots. ...his immediate superior, General Geichenko.* ◆ **immediately** ADV *She always sits immediately behind the driver.* [4] ADJ BEFORE N Your **immediate** family are your parents, brothers, and sisters.

immediately /ɪˈmiːdiətli/. [1] ADV If something is **immediately** apparent, it can be seen or understood without any delay. *The reasons for this may not be immediately obvious.* [2] CONJ If one thing happens **immediately** something else happens, it happens after that event, without any delay. *Immediately he had said it, Leonidas cursed himself.* [3] See also **immediate**.

immense /ɪˈmens/. ADJ **Immense** means extremely large or great. *With immense relief I stopped running... The job ahead is immense and will take time.*

immensely /ɪˈmensli/. ADV **Immensely** means to a very great extent or degree. *Chess is immensely popular in Russia... I enjoyed this movie immensely.*

immerse /ɪˈmɜːs/ **immerses, immersing, immersed.** [1] VERB If you **immerse yourself in** something that you are doing, you become completely involved in it. *I had to immerse myself in the new job.* ◆ **immersed** ADJ AFTER LINK-V *He's really becoming immersed in his work.* [2] VERB If you **immerse** something **in** a liquid, you put it into the liquid so that it is completely covered.

immigrant /ˈɪmɪɡrənt/ **immigrants.** N-COUNT An **immigrant** is a person who has come to live in a country from another country.

immigration /ˌɪmɪˈɡreɪʃən/. [1] N-UNCOUNT **Immigration** is the fact or process of people coming into a country in order to live and work there. *The government has decided to tighten its immigration policy.* [2] N-UNCOUNT **Immigration** or **immigration control** is the place at a port, airport, or international border where officials check the passports of people who wish to come into the country.

imminent /ˈɪmɪnənt/. ADJ Something that is **imminent** will happen very soon. *There appeared no imminent danger.*

immoral /ɪˈmɒrəl, AM -ˈmɔːr-/. ADJ If you describe someone or their behaviour as **immoral**, you mean that their behaviour is morally wrong. ...*those who think that birth control and abortion are immoral.*

immortal /ɪˈmɔːtəl/ **immortals.** [1] ADJ & N-COUNT Someone or something that is **immortal** or an **immortal** is famous and likely to be remembered for a long time. ...*Wuthering Heights, Emily Bronte's immortal love story... He called Moore 'one of the immortals of soccer'.* ◆ **immortality** /ˌɪmɔːˈtælɪti/ N-UNCOUNT *Some people want to achieve immortality through their works.* [2] ADJ & N-COUNT In stories, someone who is **immortal** or an **immortal** lives for ever. ◆ **immortality** N-UNCOUNT *The Greeks accepted belief in the immortality of the soul.*

immortalize (BRIT also **immortalise**) /ɪˈmɔːtəlaɪz/ **immortalizes, immortalizing, immortalized.** VERB If someone or something **is immortalized** in something such as a film or a book, they are made famous and will be remembered for a very long time because of it.

immune /ɪˈmjuːn/. [1] ADJ AFTER LINK-V If you are **immune to** a disease, you cannot be affected by it. *Most adults are immune to Rubella.* ◆ **immunity** /ɪˈmjuːnɪti/ N-UNCOUNT *Birds in outside cages develop immunity to airborne bacteria.* [2] ADJ AFTER LINK-V If you are **immune to** something that happens or is done, you are not affected by it. *He did not become immune to the sight of death.* [3] ADJ AFTER LINK-V Someone or something that is **immune from** a particular process or situation is able to escape it. *No one is immune from scandal.* ◆ **immunity** N-UNCOUNT *The police are offering immunity to witnesses who help identify the murderers.*

im'mune system, immune systems. N-COUNT Your **immune system** consists of all the cells and processes in your body which protect you from illness and infection.

immunize (BRIT also **immunise**) /ˈɪmjʊnaɪz/ **immunizes, immunizing, immunized.** VERB If you **are immunized against** a disease, you are given with a drug which prevents you from being affected by it. *Every student is immunized against hepatitis B.. He proposed a national program to immunize children.* ◆ **immunization, immunizations** N-VAR ...*universal immunization against childhood diseases.*

impact, impacts, impacting, impacted; noun /ˈɪmpækt/, verb /ɪmˈpækt/. [1] N-COUNT & VERB If something makes an **impact on** a situation or person, or if something **impacts on** a situation or person, it has a strong effect on them. *They expect the meeting to have a marked impact on the future of the country... Such schemes mean little unless they impact on people.* [2] N-UNCOUNT The **impact** of one object on another is the force with which it hits it. *A running track should be capable of absorbing the impact of a runner's foot landing on it.*

impair /ɪm'peə/ **impairs, impairing, impaired.** VERB
To **impair** something such as an ability or the way that something functions means to damage it, preventing it from working properly. [FORMAL] *Consumption of alcohol impairs your ability to drive a car.* ♦ **impaired** ADJ *...permanently impaired hearing.*

impairment /ɪm'peəmənt/ **impairments.** N-COUNT
If someone has an **impairment**, they have a medical condition which prevents their eyes, ears, or brain from working properly.

impart /ɪm'pɑːt/ **imparts, imparting, imparted.**
1 VERB If you **impart** information **to** someone, you tell it to them. [FORMAL] 2 VERB If something **imparts** a particular quality to something, it gives it that quality. [FORMAL] *She managed to impart great elegance to the unpretentious dress she was wearing.*

impartial /ɪm'pɑːʃəl/. ADJ Someone who is **impartial** is able to act fairly because they are not personally involved in a situation. *...impartial advice on investments.* ♦ **impartially** ADV *He has vowed to oversee the elections impartially.*
♦ **impartiality** /ˌɪmpɑːʃiˈælɪti/ N-UNCOUNT *...a justice system lacking impartiality.*

impasse /'æmpæs, 'ɪm-/. N-SING An **impasse** is a situation in which it is impossible to make any progress. *The company says it has reached an impasse in negotiations with the union.*

impassioned /ɪm'pæʃənd/. ADJ If someone makes an **impassioned** speech or plea, they express strong personal feelings about an issue in a forceful way. [WRITTEN]

impassive /ɪm'pæsɪv/. ADJ An **impassive** person does not show any emotion.
♦ **impassively** ADV *Mr Miyazawa had sat impassively through a barrage of insults from the opposition.*

impatient /ɪm'peɪʃənt/. 1 ADJ If you are **impatient**, you are annoyed because you have had to wait too long for something. *Some countries are growing impatient with the slow pace of reform.* ♦ **impatiently** ADV *Frank hit the elevator button and waited impatiently for the elevator to arrive.* ♦ **impatience** /ɪm'peɪʃəns/ N-UNCOUNT *There is considerable impatience with the slow pace of political change.* 2 ADJ AFTER LINK-V If you are **impatient to** do something or **impatient for** something to happen, you are eager to do it or eager for it to happen and do not want to wait. *He was impatient to get home.*

impeccable /ɪm'pekəbəl/. ADJ If you describe something such as someone's behaviour or appearance as **impeccable**, you are emphasizing that it is excellent and has no faults. *She had impeccable taste in clothes.* ♦ **impeccably** ADV *...the impeccably manicured garden.*

impede /ɪm'piːd/ **impedes, impeding, impeded.** VERB
To **impede** someone or something means to make their movement, development, or progress difficult. [FORMAL] *Fallen rocks are impeding the progress of the rescue workers.*

impediment /ɪm'pedɪmənt/ **impediments.**
1 N-COUNT An **impediment to** something prevents it from happening, or from progressing or developing easily. [FORMAL] *The current level of rates was not an impediment to economic recovery.* 2 N-COUNT A speech **impediment** is a disability such as a stammer which makes speaking difficult.

impending /ɪm'pendɪŋ/. ADJ BEFORE N An **impending** event is one that is going to happen very soon. [FORMAL] *...a feeling of impending disaster.*

impenetrable /ɪm'penɪtrəbəl/. 1 ADJ An **impenetrable** wall or barrier is impossible to get through. 2 ADJ If you describe something such as a book as **impenetrable**, you are emphasizing that it is impossible to understand.

imperative /ɪm'perətɪv/ **imperatives.** 1 ADJ & N-COUNT You can say that it is **imperative** that something is done, or that there is an **imperative to** do it when you want to emphasize that it must be done. *The killings made it all the more imperative that that cycle of violence be ended... Many see it as a moral imperative to reduce animal experiments.* 2 N-SING In grammar, a clause that is in the **imperative** contains the base form of a verb and usually has no subject. Imperative clauses are used to tell someone to do something. Examples are 'Go away' and 'Please be careful'.

imperfect /ɪm'pɜːfɪkt/. 1 ADJ Something that is **imperfect** has faults. *...an imperfect world.* 2 N-SING In grammar, **the imperfect** or **the imperfect tense** of a verb is used in describing continuous situations or repeated actions in the past.

imperfection /ˌɪmpə'fekʃən/ **imperfections.** N-VAR
An **imperfection** is a fault or weakness.

imperial /ɪm'pɪəriəl/. 1 ADJ BEFORE N **Imperial** means belonging or relating to an empire, emperor, or empress. *...the Imperial Palace in Tokyo.* 2 ADJ BEFORE N The **imperial** system of measurement uses miles, yards, feet, and inches to measure length, ounces and pounds to measure weight, and pints and gallons to measure volume.

imperialism /ɪm'pɪəriəlɪzəm/. N-UNCOUNT
Imperialism is a system in which a rich and powerful country controls other countries.
♦ **imperialist, imperialists** N-COUNT *...an imperialist power that insists on meddling in the affairs of weaker countries.*

impersonal /ɪm'pɜːsənəl/. 1 ADJ If you describe a place, organization, or activity as **impersonal**, you think that the people there are acting in an unfriendly way towards you, making you feel unimportant or unwanted. *...impersonal cold rooms in large, cheap, white hotels.* 2 ADJ **Impersonal** means not concerned with any particular person. *Redundancy selection will probably be carried out on a fairly impersonal basis.*

impersonate /ɪmˈpɜːsəneɪt/ **impersonates, impersonating, impersonated.** VERB If you **impersonate** someone, you pretend to be that person, either to deceive people or to entertain them. *He was once jailed for impersonating a doctor.* ♦ **impersonation, impersonations** N-COUNT *He was doing an impersonation of Elvis.*

impetus /ˈɪmpɪtəs/. N-UNCOUNT Something that gives a process **impetus** or gives it an **impetus** makes it happen or progress more quickly. *The article gave new impetus to the debate over mercy killing.*

implacable /ɪmˈplækəbəl/. ADJ If you describe someone as **implacable**, you mean that their attitude or feelings about something are firm and will not be changed by other people's opinions. *...a ruthless and implacable enemy.* ♦ **implacably** ADV *His union was implacably opposed to the privatization of the company.*

implant, implants, implanting, implanted. 1 VERB /ɪmˈplɑːnt, -ˈplænt/ If something such as a heart **is implanted** into a person's body, it is put there by means of a medical operation. *For diabetes the capsule is implanted under the skin.* 2 N-COUNT /ˈɪmplɑːnt, -plænt/ An **implant** is something implanted into a person's body. *...silicone breast implants.*

⭐ **implement, implements, implementing, implemented.** 1 VERB /ˈɪmplɪment/ If you **implement** a plan, system, or law, you carry it out. ♦ **implementation** N-UNCOUNT *...the implementation of the peace agreement.* 2 N-COUNT /ˈɪmplɪmənt/ An **implement** is a tool or other piece of equipment.

implicate /ˈɪmplɪkeɪt/ **implicates, implicating, implicated.** VERB If you **implicate** someone **in** a crime or something bad, you show that they were involved in it. *Allegations had appeared in the press implicating the army and police in some of the killings.*

⭐ **implication** /ˌɪmplɪˈkeɪʃən/ **implications.** N-COUNT The **implications** of something are the things that are likely to happen as a result of it. *...the political implications of his decision.*

implicit /ɪmˈplɪsɪt/. 1 ADJ Something that is **implicit** is expressed in an indirect way. ♦ **implicitly** ADV *Mr Jones's role was implicitly criticised in the report.* 2 ADJ If you have an **implicit** belief or faith in something, you believe it completely and have no doubts about it. *He had implicit faith in the noble intentions of the Emperor.* ♦ **implicitly** ADV *I trust him implicitly.*

implore /ɪmˈplɔː/ **implores, imploring, implored.** VERB If you **implore** someone **to** do something, you beg them to do it. [FORMAL] *Opposition leaders implored the president to break the deadlock... Michael, I implore you. Don't say anything.*

⭐ **imply** /ɪmˈplaɪ/ **implies, implying, implied.** VERB To **imply** that something is the case means to say or do something to make it appear that it is the case. *The tone of the report implied that his death*

was inevitable... *The meeting in no way implies a resumption of contacts with the terrorists.*

⭐ **import, imports, importing, imported.** 1 VERB /ɪmˈpɔːt/ When a country or organization **imports** a product, they buy it from another country for use in their own country. *To import from Russia, a Ukrainian firm needs Russian roubles. ...the price of imported oil.* ♦ **importation** N-UNCOUNT *...restrictions concerning the importation of birds.* ♦ **importer, importers** N-COUNT *...oil importers.* 2 N-COUNT /ˈɪmpɔːt/ **Imports** are products or raw materials bought from another country for use in your own country.

⭐ **important** /ɪmˈpɔːtənt/. 1 ADJ Something that is **important** is very significant, valuable, or necessary. *Her sons are the most important thing in her life.* ♦ **importantly** ADV *I was hungry, and, more importantly, my children were hungry.* ♦ **importance** N-UNCOUNT *Safety is of paramount importance.* 2 ADJ An **important** person has influence or power. *...a very important criminal lawyer.* ♦ **importance** N-UNCOUNT *Penn photographed just about everyone of importance in the arts.*

> **USAGE** You do not use **important** to say that an amount or quantity is very large. You do not talk, for example, about 'an important sum of money'. Instead, you use words such as **large**, **considerable**, or **substantial**. *...a large sum of money. ...a man with considerable influence... Britain's armed forces face substantial cuts.*

⭐ **impose** /ɪmˈpəʊz/ **imposes, imposing, imposed.** 1 VERB If you **impose** something **on** people, you force them to accept it. *Parents should beware of imposing their own tastes on their children.* ♦ **imposition** /ˌɪmpəˈzɪʃən/ N-UNCOUNT *...the imposition of a day-time ban on cycling in the city centre.* 2 VERB If someone **imposes on** you, they expect you to do something for them which you do not want to do. *I was afraid you'd simply feel we were imposing on you... I didn't want to impose myself on my married friends.* ♦ **imposition, impositions** N-COUNT *I know this is an imposition. But please hear me out.*

imposing /ɪmˈpəʊzɪŋ/. ADJ If you describe someone or something as **imposing**, you think their appearance or manner is very impressive. *...the imposing gates at the entrance to the estate.*

⭐ **impossible** /ɪmˈpɒsɪbəl/. 1 ADJ Something that is **impossible** cannot be done or cannot happen. *The tax is impossible to administer.* ♦ **impossibly** ADV *Mathematical physics is an almost impossibly difficult subject.* ♦ **impossibility, impossibilities** N-VAR *...the impossibility of knowing absolute truth.* 2 ADJ You can say that a situation or person is **impossible** when they are very difficult to deal with. *The Government was now in an almost impossible position... You are an impossible man!*

impotent /ˈɪmpətənt/. [1] ADJ If someone feels **impotent**, they feel that they have no power to influence people or events. *The aggression of a bully leaves people feeling hurt, angry and impotent.* ♦ **impotence** N-UNCOUNT *...a sense of impotence in the face of deplorable events.* [2] ADJ If a man is **impotent**, he is unable to have sex normally. ♦ **impotence** N-UNCOUNT *...the many men who suffer from impotence.*

impound /ɪmˈpaʊnd/ **impounds, impounding, impounded.** VERB If policemen or other officials **impound** something that you own, they legally confiscate it. [FORMAL] *The police moved in, arrested him and impounded the cocaine.*

impoverish /ɪmˈpɒvərɪʃ/ **impoverishes, impoverishing, impoverished.** VERB To **impoverish** someone or something means to make them poor. *We need to reduce the burden of taxes that impoverish the economy.* ♦ **impoverished** ADJ *...one of the most impoverished and crime-infested suburbs of Rio de Janeiro.*

impractical /ɪmˈpræktɪkəl/. ADJ If an idea or course of action is **impractical**, it is not sensible or practical. *Narrow fields several kilometres in length are highly impractical for farmers.*

⭐ **impress** /ɪmˈpres/ **impresses, impressing, impressed.** [1] VERB If someone or something **impresses** you, you feel great admiration for them. *...a group of students who were trying to impress their girlfriends.* ♦ **impressed** ADJ AFTER LINK-V *I'm very impressed with the new airport.* [2] VERB If you **impress** something **on** or **upon** someone, you make them understand its importance. *I had always impressed upon the children that if they worked hard they would succeed.*

⭐ **impression** /ɪmˈpreʃən/ **impressions.** [1] N-COUNT Your **impression** of someone or something is what you think they are like. Your **impression** of a situation is what you think is going on. *What were your first impressions of college?... My impression is that they are totally out of control.* [2] N-SING If someone or something gives a particular **impression**, they cause you to believe that something is the case, often when it is not actually the case. *They certainly gave the impression of a carefree couple who delighted in each other's company.* [3] N-COUNT If you **do** an **impression** of someone, you imitate their voice or manner in an amusing way. [4] N-COUNT An **impression** of an object is the mark that it has left after being pressed hard onto a surface.
PHRASES ● If you are **under the impression** that something is the case, you believe it to be the case. *His family was under the impression that he died while en route to the hospital.* ● If someone or something **makes an impression**, they have a strong effect on people or a situation. *He has told me his plans and he's made a good impression on me.*

⭐ **impressive** /ɪmˈpresɪv/. ADJ **Impressive** is used to describe people or things which impress you.

The film's special effects are particularly impressive. ♦ **impressively** ADV *...an impressively bright and energetic American woman.*

imprint, **imprints, imprinting, imprinted;** noun /ˈɪmprɪnt/ verb /ɪmˈprɪnt/. [1] N-COUNT & VERB If something leaves an **imprint on** your mind, or if it **is imprinted on** your mind, you cannot forget it because it has had a strong effect on you. *The problem of unemployment left a deep imprint on his attitude towards such social issues... He could not dislodge the images imprinted on his brain.* [2] N-COUNT An **imprint** is a mark made by the pressure of an object on a surface. [3] VERB If a surface **is imprinted with** a mark or design, that mark or design is printed on the surface or pressed into it.

imprison /ɪmˈprɪzən/ **imprisons, imprisoning, imprisoned.** VERB If someone **is imprisoned**, they are locked up or kept somewhere. ♦ **imprisonment** N-UNCOUNT *She was sentenced to seven years' imprisonment.*

improbable /ɪmˈprɒbəbəl/. [1] ADJ Something that is **improbable** is unlikely to be true or to happen. *It is improbable that the Prime Minister will be forced to resign.* ♦ **improbability, improbabilities** N-VAR *...the improbability of such an outcome.* [2] ADJ If you describe something as **improbable**, you mean it is strange or ridiculous. *Their marriage seems an improbable alliance.* ♦ **improbably** ADV *...an improbably glamorous female cop.*

impromptu /ɪmˈprɒmptjuː, AM -tuː/. ADJ An **impromptu** action is one that you do without planning it in advance. *The children put on an impromptu concert for the visitors.*

improper /ˌɪmˈprɒpə/. [1] ADJ **Improper** activities are illegal or dishonest. [FORMAL] *Mr Matthews maintained that he had done nothing improper.* ♦ **improperly** ADV *I acted neither fraudulently nor improperly.* [2] ADJ BEFORE N **Improper** conditions or methods of treatment are not suitable or adequate for a particular purpose. *The improper use of medicine could lead to severe adverse reactions.* ♦ **improperly** ADV *Doctors were improperly trained.* [3] ADJ If you describe someone's behaviour as **improper**, you mean that it is rude or shocking. [DATED] *It would be improper to speculate on Dr Holt's suicide.* ♦ **improperly** ADV *...improperly dressed.*

⭐ **improve** /ɪmˈpruːv/ **improves, improving, improved.** [1] VERB If something **improves**, or if you **improve** it, it gets better. *The weather is beginning to improve... He improved their house.* ♦ **improvement** /ɪmˈpruːvmənt/ **improvements** N-VAR *There is considerable room for improvement in state facilities for treating the mentally handicapped.* [2] VERB If you **improve on** a previous achievement, you achieve a better standard or result. *...whether annual profits can improve on last year's £65.8 million.* ♦ **improvement** N-COUNT *The system we introduced in 1990 has been a great improvement.*

improvise /'ɪmprəvaɪz/ **improvises, improvising, improvised.** ☐1 VERB If you **improvise**, you make or do something using whatever you have or without having planned it in advance. ...*tents improvised from sheets of heavy plastic... His improvised bomb must have started a fire.* ☐2 VERB When actors or musicians **improvise**, they make up the words or music while they are performing. *He'd had to improvise a dramatic suicide scene.*

impulse /'ɪmpʌls/ **impulses.** ☐1 N-COUNT An **impulse** is a sudden desire to do something. *All day she had fought off the impulse to telephone Harry.* ☐2 PHRASE If you do something **on impulse**, you suddenly decide to do it, without planning it. *After lunch she decided on impulse to take a bath.* ☐3 N-COUNT An **impulse** is a short electrical signal sent along a wire or nerve, or through the air.

impulsive /ɪm'pʌlsɪv/. ADJ Someone who is **impulsive** does things suddenly without thinking about them carefully first. *Avoid making an impulsive decision.* ♦ **impulsively** ADV *Impulsively she patted him on the arm.*

impure /ɪm'pjʊə/. ADJ An **impure** substance is not of good quality because it has other substances mixed with it.

impurity /ɪm'pjʊərɪti/ **impurities.** N-COUNT **Impurities** are substances that are present in small quantities in another substance and make it dirty or of an unacceptable quality.

in 1 position or movement

☆ **in** /ɪn/. ☐1 PREP Something that is **in** something else is enclosed by it or surrounded by it. *He was in his car... Put the knives in the kitchen drawer... Mix the sugar and the water in a cup.* ☐2 PREP If something happens **in** a place, it happens there. *Those rockets landed in the desert.* ☐3 ADV If you are **in**, you are present at your home or place of work. *My flatmate was in at the time.* ☐4 ADV When someone comes **in**, they enter a room or building. *They shook hands and went in.* ☐5 ADV If a train, boat, or plane is **in** or has come **in**, it has arrived. *Look. The train's in.* ☐6 ADV When the sea or tide comes **in**, the sea moves towards the shore rather than away from it. ☐7 PREP Something that is **in** a window, especially a shop window, is just behind the window so that you can see it from outside. *There was a camera for sale in the window.* ☐8 PREP When you see something **in** a mirror, you see its reflection. ☐9 PREP If you are dressed **in** a piece of clothing, you are wearing it. *They were still in their pyjamas. ...three women in black.*

in 2 inclusion or movement

☆ **in** /ɪn/. ☐1 PREP If something is **in** a book, film, play, or picture, you can read it or see it there. *...one of the funniest scenes in the film.* ☐2 PREP If you are **in** something such as a play or a race, you are one of the people taking part. *Alf offered her a part in the play he was directing.* ☐3 PREP Something that is **in** a group or collection is a member of it or part of it. *There were about 12 students in my class.* ☐4 PREP You use **in** to specify a general subject or field of activity. *...future developments in medicine and surgery.*

in 3 time and numbers

☆ **in** /ɪn/. ☐1 PREP If something happens **in** a particular year, month, or other period of time, it happens during that time. *In the evening, the people assemble in the mosques... He believes food prices will go up in the future.* ☐2 PREP If you do something **in** a particular period of time, that is how long it takes you to do it. *He completed the book in two years.* ☐3 PREP If something will happen **in** a particular length of time, it will happen after that length of time. *They'll be back in a few months.* ☐4 PREP You use **in** to indicate roughly how old someone is. For example, if someone is **in** their fifties, they are between 50 and 59 years old. ☐5 PREP You use **in** to indicate roughly how many people or things do something. *The jugs were produced in their millions.* ☐6 PREP You use **in** to express a ratio, proportion, or probability. *He had a one in 500 chance of survival.*

in 4 states and qualities

☆ **in** /ɪn/. ☐1 PREP If something or someone is **in** a particular state or situation, that is their present state or situation. *Their equipment was in poor condition... Dave was in a hurry.* ☐2 PREP You use **in** to indicate the feeling or desire which someone has when they do something, or which causes them to do it. *Simpson looked at them in surprise... Carl pushed ahead in his eagerness to reach the wall.* ☐3 PREP You use **in** to indicate how someone is expressing something. *'Good evening,' Frank said in Russian... All requests must be made in writing.* ☐4 PREP You use **in** to describe the arrangement or shape of something. *He was curled up in a ball.* ☐5 PREP You use **in** to specify which feature or aspect of something you are talking about. *The movie is nearly two hours in length. ...a real increase in the standard of living.*

in 5 other uses and phrases

☆ **in** /ɪn/. ADJ Something that is **in** is fashionable or popular. [INFORMAL] *A few years ago jogging was the in thing.*

PHRASES ● If you say that someone **is in for** a shock or a surprise, you mean they are going to experience it. ● If someone **has it in for** you, they dislike you and try to cause problems for you. [INFORMAL] ● If you are **in on** something, you are involved in it or know about it. *I'm going to let you in on a little secret.* ● You use **in that** to explain a statement you have just made. *I'm lucky in that I've got four sisters.*

in.

☑ The plural can be **in.** or **ins.**

In. is a written abbreviation for **inch**.

inability /ˌɪnə'bɪlɪti/. N-UNCOUNT Someone's **inability to** do something is the fact that they are unable to do it. *...her inability to concentrate.*

inaccessible /ˌɪnək'sesɪbəl/. ☐1 ADJ An **inaccessible** place is impossible or very difficult

a b c d e f g h i j k l m n o p q r s t u v w x y z

A

to reach. *It is far away in a wild, inaccessible part of the island.* **2** ADJ Someone or something that is **inaccessible** is difficult or impossible to understand or appreciate. *...language that is inaccessible to working people.*

inaccurate /ɪnˈækjʊrət/. ADJ If a statement or measurement is **inaccurate**, it is not accurate or correct. ♦ **inaccuracy, inaccuracies** N-VAR *There are many inaccuracies in her article.*

inaction /ɪnˈækʃən/. N-UNCOUNT If you refer to someone's **inaction**, you disapprove of the fact that they are doing nothing. *He is bitter about the inaction of the other political parties.*

inactive /ɪnˈæktɪv/. ADJ Someone or something that is **inactive** is not doing anything or is not working. *Most volcanoes are inactive most of the time.* ♦ **inactivity** /ˌɪnækˈtɪvɪti/ N-UNCOUNT *After years of inactivity I started running.*

inadequate /ɪnˈædɪkwət/. **1** ADJ If something is **inadequate**, there is not enough of it or it is not good enough. *The problem lies with inadequate staffing.* ♦ **inadequacy, inadequacies** N-VAR *...the inadequacy of the water supply.* ♦ **inadequately** ADV *The projects were inadequately funded.* **2** ADJ If someone feels **inadequate**, they feel that they do not have the qualities necessary to do something or to cope with life. ♦ **inadequacy** N-UNCOUNT *...her chronic sense of inadequacy.*

inadvertent /ˌɪnədˈvɜːtənt/. ADJ An **inadvertent** action is one that you do without realizing what you are doing. *She giggled at the inadvertent pun.* ♦ **inadvertently** ADV *You may have inadvertently pressed the wrong button.*

inappropriate /ˌɪnəˈprəʊprɪət/. ADJ Something that is **inappropriate** is not suitable for a particular situation or purpose. *His behavior was inappropriate and insensitive.*

inasmuch as (or **in as much as**) /ˌɪnəzˈmʌtʃ æz/. CONJ You use **inasmuch as** to introduce a statement which explains something you have just said, and adds to it. [FORMAL] *I am extremely lucky in as much as I have a very strong and loving wife.*

inaugural /ɪnˈɔːgjʊrəl/. ADJ BEFORE N An **inaugural** meeting or speech is the first one of a new organization or leader.

inaugurate /ɪnˈɔːgjʊreɪt/ **inaugurates, inaugurating, inaugurated.** **1** VERB When a new leader **is inaugurated**, they are formally given their new position at an official ceremony. ♦ **inauguration, inaugurations** N-VAR *...the inauguration of the new Governor.* **2** VERB If you **inaugurate** a new system or organization, you start it. [FORMAL]

incapable /ɪnˈkeɪpəbəl/. ADJ Someone who is **incapable of** doing something is unable to do it. *He was a man incapable of violence.*

incarcerate /ɪnˈkɑːsəreɪt/ **incarcerates, incarcerating, incarcerated.** VERB If someone **is incarcerated**, they are imprisoned. [FORMAL]

♦ **incarceration** N-UNCOUNT *...her mother's incarceration in a psychiatric hospital.*

incarnation /ˌɪnkɑːˈneɪʃən/ **incarnations.** **1** N-COUNT If you say that someone is the **incarnation of** a particular quality, you mean that they represent that quality or are typical of it in an extreme form. *She is the incarnation of courage.* **2** N-COUNT An **incarnation** is one of the lives that a person has, according to some religions.

incendiary /ɪnˈsendiəri, AM -eri/. ADJ BEFORE N **Incendiary** attacks or weapons are ones which cause large fires. *More than 10,000 incendiary bombs were dropped.*

incense, incenses, incensing, incensed. **1** N-UNCOUNT /ˈɪnsens/ **Incense** is a substance that is burned for its sweet smell, often during a religious ceremony. **2** VERB /ɪnˈsens/ Something that **incenses** you makes you extremely angry. ♦ **incensed** ADJ *Mum was incensed at his lack of compassion.*

incentive /ɪnˈsentɪv/ **incentives.** N-VAR An **incentive** is something that encourages you to do something. *...tax incentives for companies that create jobs.*

incessant /ɪnˈsesənt/. ADJ An **incessant** process or activity never stops. *...incessant rain.* ♦ **incessantly** ADV *Dee talked incessantly.*

incest /ˈɪnsest/. N-UNCOUNT **Incest** is the crime of two members of the same family having sexual intercourse.

⭐ **inch** /ɪntʃ/ **inches, inching, inched.** **1** N-COUNT An **inch** is a unit of length, equal to 2.54 centimetres. **2** VERB To **inch** somewhere means to move there very slowly and carefully. To **inch** something somewhere means to move it there in this way. *...a climber inching up a vertical wall of rock... He inched the van forward.*

incidence /ˈɪnsɪdəns/ **incidences.** N-VAR The **incidence** of something bad is the frequency with which it occurs, or the occasions when it occurs. *...the high incidence of child mortality.*

⭐ **incident** /ˈɪnsɪdənt/ **incidents.** N-COUNT An **incident** is an event, especially one involving something unpleasant. [FORMAL] *Police were still investigating the incident yesterday.*

incidental /ˌɪnsɪˈdentəl/. ADJ If one thing is **incidental to** another, it is less important than the other thing or is not a major part of it. *The playing of music proved to be incidental to the main business of the evening... At the bottom of the bill, you will notice various incidental expenses.*

incidentally /ˌɪnsɪˈdentli/. ADV You use **incidentally** to introduce a point which is not directly relevant to what you are saying. *The tower, incidentally, dates from the twelfth century.*

incinerate /ɪnˈsɪnəreɪt/ **incinerates, incinerating, incinerated.** VERB When authorities **incinerate** rubbish or waste material, they burn it in a furnace. ♦ **incineration** N-UNCOUNT *...an incineration plant.*

incinerator /ɪnˈsɪnəreɪtə/ **incinerators.** N-COUNT An **incinerator** is a furnace for burning rubbish.

incisive /ɪnˈsaɪsɪv/. ADJ **Incisive** speech or writing is clear and forceful.

incite /ɪnˈsaɪt/ **incites, inciting, incited.** VERB If someone **incites** people **to** behave in a violent or unlawful way, they encourage them to behave in that way. *The party agreed not to incite its supporters to violence. ...material likely to incite racial hatred.* ◆ **incitement, incitements** N-VAR *British law forbids incitement to murder.*

inclination /ˌɪnklɪˈneɪʃən/ **inclinations.** N-VAR An **inclination** is a feeling that makes you want to act in a particular way. *She showed no inclination to go. ...his artistic inclinations.*

incline, inclines, inclining, inclined. [1] VERB /ɪnˈklaɪn/ If you **incline to** a particular view or action, you want to take that view or perform that action, or often take or perform it. [FORMAL] *I incline to the view that he is right.* ◆ **inclined** ADJ AFTER LINK-V *Nobody felt inclined to argue with Smith.* [2] N-COUNT /ˈɪnklaɪn/ An **incline** is a slope. [FORMAL]

inclined /ɪnˈklaɪnd/. [1] ADJ AFTER LINK-V If you say that you are **inclined** to have a particular opinion, you mean that you hold this opinion but you are not expressing it strongly. *I am inclined to agree with Alan.* [2] ADJ Someone who is, for example, mathematically or artistically **inclined** has a natural talent for mathematics or art.

⭐ **include** /ɪnˈkluːd/ **includes, including, included.** VERB If something **includes** something else, it has it as one of its parts. If you **include** one thing **in** another, you make it part of it. *The program includes swimming, fishing and canoeing... Food is included in the price... Most people, myself included, aren't very happy about it.*

⭐ **including** /ɪnˈkluːdɪŋ/. PREP You use **including** to introduce examples of people or things that are part of the group of people or things that you are talking about. *Twelve people, including six police officers, were taken to hospital.*

inclusion /ɪnˈkluːʒən/ **inclusions.** N-VAR The **inclusion** of one thing in another is the act of making it a part of the second thing. *...his inclusion in the team.*

inclusive /ɪnˈkluːsɪv/. [1] ADJ & ADV If a price is **inclusive**, it includes all the charges connected with the goods or services offered. *The price of the trip was £824 (inclusive of flights). ...a special introductory offer of £5,995 fully inclusive.* [2] ADJ You use **inclusive** to indicate that the first and last things mentioned are included in a series. *Only children aged 6 to 15 inclusive are eligible.*

incoherent /ˌɪnkəʊˈhɪərənt/. ADJ If someone is **incoherent**, they are talking in a confused and unclear way. *The man was almost incoherent with fear.*

⭐ **income** /ˈɪnkʌm/ **incomes.** N-COUNT The **income** of a person or organization is the money that they earn or receive. *...families on low incomes.* ● See note at **pay.**

income tax, income taxes. N-VAR **Income tax** is a part of your income that you have to pay regularly to the government.

incoming /ˈɪnkʌmɪŋ/. [1] ADJ BEFORE N An **incoming** message or phone call is one that you receive. *We keep a tape of incoming calls.* [2] ADJ BEFORE N An **incoming** plane or passenger is one that is arriving at a place. *...a passenger off the incoming flight.*

incompatible /ˌɪnkəmˈpætɪbəl/. ADJ If one thing or person is **incompatible with** another, they are very different from each other and therefore cannot exist or work together. *His behavior has been incompatible with his role as head of state... Their interests were mutually incompatible.* ◆ **incompatibility** N-UNCOUNT *He sees no incompatibility between poetry and science.*

incompetent /ɪnˈkɒmpɪtənt/. ADJ If you describe someone as **incompetent**, you are criticizing them because they cannot do their job or a task properly. *...lazy and incompetent colleagues.* ◆ **incompetence** N-UNCOUNT *Our manager was sacked for incompetence.*

incomplete /ˌɪnkəmˈpliːt/. ADJ Something that is **incomplete** is not yet finished, or does not have all the parts or details that it needs. *The clearing of rubbish and drains is still incomplete.*

incomprehensible /ˌɪnkɒmprɪˈhensɪbəl/. ADJ Something that is **incomprehensible** is impossible to understand.

inconceivable /ˌɪnkənˈsiːvəbəl/. ADJ If something is **inconceivable**, it is very unlikely to happen or be true. *It was inconceivable that he was a criminal.*

inconclusive /ˌɪnkənˈkluːsɪv/. ADJ If something is **inconclusive**, it does not provide any clear answer or result. *Our research has so far proved inconclusive.*

incongruous /ɪnˈkɒŋgruəs/. ADJ Something that is **incongruous** seems strange because it does not fit in with the rest of a situation. [FORMAL] *She was small and fragile and looked incongruous in an army uniform.* ◆ **incongruously** ADV *...Western-style buildings perched incongruously in a high green valley.*

inconsiderate /ˌɪnkənˈsɪdərət/. ADJ If you describe someone as **inconsiderate**, you are criticizing them for not taking enough care over how their behaviour affects other people.

inconsistent /ˌɪnkənˈsɪstənt/. [1] ADJ If you describe someone as **inconsistent**, you are criticizing them for not behaving in the same way every time a similar situation occurs. *...the leadership's hesitant and inconsistent behaviour.* ◆ **inconsistency, inconsistencies** N-VAR *His worst fault was his inconsistency.* [2] ADJ AFTER LINK-V Something that is **inconsistent with** a particular set of ideas or values is not in accordance with them. *His theory is inconsistent with modern observations.*

a
b
c
d
e
f
g
h
i
j
k
l
m
n
o
p
q
r
s
t
u
v
w
x
y
z

incontinent /ɪnˈkɒntɪnənt/. ADJ Someone who is **incontinent** is unable to control their bladder or bowels. ♦ **incontinence** N-UNCOUNT *Incontinence is not just a condition of old age.*

inconvenience /ˌɪnkənˈviːniəns/ **inconveniences, inconveniencing, inconvenienced.** [1] N-VAR If someone or something causes **inconvenience**, they cause problems or difficulties. *We apologize for any inconvenience caused during the repairs.* [2] VERB If someone **inconveniences** you, they cause problems or difficulties for you. *He promised to be very quick so as not to inconvenience them any further.*

inconvenient /ˌɪnkənˈviːniənt/. ADJ Something that is **inconvenient** causes problems or difficulties for someone. *She arrived at an extremely inconvenient moment.*

incorporate /ɪnˈkɔːpəreɪt/ **incorporates, incorporating, incorporated.** VERB If something such as a group or device **incorporates** a particular thing, the group or device has that thing in it as one of its parts. [FORMAL] *The new cars will incorporate a number of major improvements.*

incorrect /ˌɪnkəˈrekt/. ADJ Something that is **incorrect** is wrong or untrue. *The findings were based on incorrect data.* ♦ **incorrectly** ADV *The doors had been fitted incorrectly.*

⭐ **increase, increases, increasing, increased;** verb /ɪnˈkriːs/, noun /ˈɪnkriːs/. [1] VERB & N-COUNT If something **increases**, or if there is an **increase in** it, it becomes larger in number, level, or amount. *Japan's industrial output increased by 2%... We are experiencing an increasing number of problems. ...a sharp increase in productivity.* [2] PHRASE If something is **on the increase**, it is becoming more frequent. *Divorce rates and births outside marriage are on the increase.*

⭐ **increasingly** /ɪnˈkriːsɪŋli/. ADV You use **increasingly** to indicate that a situation or quality is becoming greater in intensity or more common. *He was finding it increasingly difficult to make decisions... Increasingly, their goals have become more radical.*

⭐ **incredible** /ɪnˈkredɪbəl/. [1] ADJ If you describe someone or something as **incredible**, you like them very much or are impressed by them, because they are extremely or unusually good. *The wildflowers will be incredible after this rain.* [2] ADJ Something that is **incredible** is amazing or very difficult to believe. ...*the incredible stories that children may tell us.* ♦ **incredibly** ADV *Incredibly, some people don't like the name.* [3] ADJ You use **incredible** to emphasize the amount or intensity of something. *We import an incredible amount of cheese from the Continent.* ♦ **incredibly** ADV *It was incredibly hard work.*

incredulous /ɪnˈkredʒʊləs/. ADJ If someone is **incredulous**, they cannot believe something because it is very surprising or shocking. *There was a brief, incredulous silence.* ♦ **incredulously** ADV *'You told Pete?' Rachel said incredulously.*

incriminate /ɪnˈkrɪmɪneɪt/ **incriminates, incriminating, incriminated.** VERB If something **incriminates** you, it suggests that you are the person responsible for something bad, especially a crime. *They are afraid of incriminating themselves and say no more than is necessary.* ♦ **incriminating** ADJ ...*incriminating evidence.*

incumbent /ɪnˈkʌmbənt/ **incumbents.** N-COUNT An **incumbent** is the person who is holding an official post at a particular time. [FORMAL] *In general, incumbents have a 94% chance of being re-elected.*

incur /ɪnˈkɜː/ **incurs, incurring, incurred.** VERB If you **incur** something unpleasant, it happens to you because of something you have done. [FORMAL] *The government had also incurred huge debts.*

incurable /ɪnˈkjʊərəbəl/. [1] ADJ An **incurable** disease cannot be cured. ♦ **incurably** ADV ...*youngsters who are disabled, or incurably ill.* [2] ADJ You can use **incurable** to indicate that someone has a particular quality or attitude and will not change. *Poor old William is an incurable romantic.* ♦ **incurably** ADV *I know you think I'm incurably nosey.*

indebted /ɪnˈdetɪd/. ADJ AFTER LINK-V If you say that you are **indebted to** someone, you mean that you are very grateful to them for something. *I am deeply indebted to him for his help.*

indecent /ɪnˈdiːsənt/. ADJ Something that is **indecent** is shocking, usually because it relates to sex or nakedness. *He accused Mrs Moore of making an indecent suggestion.* ♦ **indecency** N-UNCOUNT ...*the indecency of their language.* ♦ **indecently** ADV ...*an indecently short skirt.*

indecision /ˌɪndɪˈsɪʒən/. N-UNCOUNT **Indecision** is uncertainty about what you should do. *After months of indecision, the government finally gave the plan the go-ahead.*

indecisive /ˌɪndɪˈsaɪsɪv/. ADJ If someone is **indecisive**, they find it difficult to make decisions.

⭐ **indeed** /ɪnˈdiːd/. [1] ADV You use **indeed** to confirm or agree in an emphatic way with something that has just been said. *The payments had indeed been made... 'Did you know him?'—'I did indeed.'... 'Know what I mean?'—'Indeed I do.'* [2] ADV You use **indeed** to introduce a further comment or statement which strengthens the point you have already made. *We have nothing against diversity; indeed, we want more of it.* [3] ADV You use **indeed** at the end of a clause to give extra force to the word 'very', or to emphasize a particular word. *The wine was very good indeed... Of course, these occasions are rare indeed.*

indefinite /ɪnˈdefɪnɪt/. [1] ADJ If something is **indefinite**, people have not decided when it will end. *The trial was adjourned for an indefinite period.* ♦ **indefinitely** ADV *The visit has now been postponed indefinitely.* [2] ADJ If something such as a plan is **indefinite**, it is not exact or clear. ...*at some indefinite time in the future.*

in,definite 'article, indefinite articles. N-COUNT In grammar, the words 'a' and 'an' are sometimes called **indefinite articles**.

in,definite 'pronoun, indefinite pronouns. N-COUNT An **indefinite pronoun** is a pronoun such as 'someone', 'anything', or 'nobody', which you use to refer in a general way to a person or thing without saying who or what they are, or what kind of person or thing you mean.

⭐ **independent** /ˌɪndɪˈpendənt/. [1] ADJ If one thing or person is **independent of** another, they are separate and not connected, so the first one is not affected or influenced by the second. *Your questions should be independent of each other.* ♦ **independently** ADV *...several people working independently in different areas of the world.* [2] ADJ Someone who is **independent** does not rely on other people. *She would like to be financially independent.* ♦ **independently** ADV *...helping disabled students to live and study as independently as possible. ...the independently-minded females of the Nineties.* ♦ **independence** N-UNCOUNT *He was afraid of losing his independence.* [3] ADJ **Independent** countries and states are not ruled by other countries but have their own government. ♦ **independence** N-UNCOUNT *In 1816, Argentina declared its independence from Spain.*

⭐ **index** /ˈɪndeks/ **indices, indexes, indexing, indexed.**

> ✓ **Indexes** is the usual plural, but the form **indices** /ˈɪndɪsiːz/ can be used for meaning 1.

[1] N-COUNT An **index** is a system by which changes in the value of something can be compared or measured. *...the UK retail price index.* [2] VERB If a quantity or value **is indexed to** another, a system is arranged so that it increases or decreases whenever the other one increases or decreases. *Minimum pensions and wages are to be indexed to inflation.* [3] N-COUNT An **index** is an alphabetical list at the back of a book saying where particular things are referred to in the book. [4] VERB If a book or collection of books **has been indexed**, someone has made an alphabetical list of the items in it. *A quarter of this vast archive has been indexed.*

⭐ **indicate** /ˈɪndɪkeɪt/ **indicates, indicating, indicated.** [1] VERB If one thing **indicates** another, the first thing shows that the second is true or exists. *A survey of retired people has indicated that most are independent and enjoying life.* [2] VERB If you **indicate** an opinion, an intention, or a fact, you mention it in a rather indirect way. *Mr Rivers has indicated that he may resign.* [3] VERB If you **indicate** something to someone, you point to it. *He indicated a chair.* [4] VERB When the driver of a car **indicates**, they operate flashing lights on one side of their vehicle which show the direction they are going to turn.

⭐ **indication** /ˌɪndɪˈkeɪʃən/ **indications.** N-VAR An **indication** is a sign which gives you an idea of what someone feels, what is happening, or what

is likely to happen. *I cannot come to a decision about it now or even give any indication of my own views... He gave no indication that he was ready to compromise.*

indicative /ɪnˈdɪkətɪv/. [1] ADJ If something is **indicative of** the existence or nature of something, it is a sign of it. *Often physical appearance is indicative of how a person feels.* [2] N-SING In grammar, a clause that is in **the indicative**, or in **the indicative mood**, has a subject followed by a verb group. Examples are 'I'm hungry' and 'She was followed'.

indicator /ˈɪndɪkeɪtə/ **indicators.** [1] N-COUNT An **indicator** is a measurement or value which gives you an idea of what something is like. *...vital economic indicators, such as inflation, growth and the trade gap.* [2] N-COUNT A car's **indicators** are the flashing lights that tell you that it is going to turn left or right.

indices /ˈɪndɪsiːz/. **Indices** is one of the plurals of **index**.

indict /ɪnˈdaɪt/ **indicts, indicting, indicted.** VERB When someone **is indicted for** a crime, they are officially charged with it. *She has been indicted for possessing cocaine... Jones was later indicted on criminal charges.* ♦ **indictment, indictments** N-VAR *He is currently under indictment in Switzerland.*

indictment /ɪnˈdaɪtmənt/ **indictments.** N-COUNT If you say that a fact or situation is an **indictment of** something, you mean that it shows how bad that thing is. *It's a sad indictment of society that policeman are regarded as easy targets by thugs.*

indifferent /ɪnˈdɪfərənt/. [1] ADJ If you are **indifferent to** something, you have no interest in it. *People have become indifferent to the suffering of others.* ♦ **indifferently** ADV *'Not that it matters,' said Tench indifferently.* ♦ **indifference** N-UNCOUNT *...the prejudice and indifference which surround the Aids epidemic.* [2] ADJ If you describe something or someone as **indifferent**, you mean that it is of a rather low standard. *She had starred in several very indifferent movies.*

indigenous /ɪnˈdɪdʒɪnəs/. ADJ **Indigenous** people or things belong to the country in which they are found, rather than coming there or being brought there from another country. *The Chumash were a tribe indigenous to California.*

indigestion /ˌɪndɪˈdʒestʃən/. N-UNCOUNT If you have **indigestion**, you have pains in your stomach that are caused by difficulties in digesting food.

indignant /ɪnˈdɪgnənt/. ADJ If you are **indignant**, you are shocked and angry, because you think that something is unjust or unfair. ♦ **indignantly** ADV *'That is not true,' Erica said indignantly.*

indignation /ˌɪndɪgˈneɪʃən/. N-UNCOUNT **Indignation** is a feeling of shock and anger which you have when you think that something is unjust or unfair. *He could hardly contain his indignation.*

a
b
c
d
e
f
g
h
i
j
k
l
m
n
o
p
q
r
s
t
u
v
w
x
y
z

indignity /ɪnˈdɪgnɪti/ **indignities.** N-VAR If you talk about the **indignity of** doing something, you mean that doing it is humiliating or embarrassing. *He suffered the indignity of having to flee angry protesters.*

indirect /ˌɪndaɪˈrekt, -dɪr-/. **1** ADJ An **indirect** result or effect is not caused immediately and obviously by a thing or person, but happens because of something else that they have done. *Millions could die of hunger as an indirect result of the war.* ♦ **indirectly** ADV *Drugs are directly or indirectly responsible for much of the violence.* **2** ADJ An **indirect** route or journey does not use the shortest way between two places. **3** ADJ An **indirect** answer or reference does not directly mention the thing that is actually being talked about.

indirect 'object, indirect objects. N-COUNT An **indirect object** is an object which is used with a transitive verb to indicate who benefits from an action or gets something as a result. For example, in 'She gave him her address', 'him' is the indirect object. Compare **direct object**.

indirect 'speech. Indirect speech is the same as **reported speech**.

indiscriminate /ˌɪndɪˈskrɪmɪnət/. ADJ If you describe an action as **indiscriminate**, you are critical of it because it does not involve any careful thought or choice. *...the indiscriminate killing of refugees.* ♦ **indiscriminately** ADV *It is worth being patient rather than buying indiscriminately.*

indispensable /ˌɪndɪˈspensəbəl/. ADJ If someone or something is **indispensable**, they are absolutely essential and other people or things cannot function without them. *She was becoming indispensable to him.*

indisputable /ˌɪndɪˈspjuːtəbəl/. ADJ If a fact is **indisputable**, it is obviously and definitely true. *It is indisputable that birds in the UK are harbouring this illness.* ♦ **indisputably** ADV *She has an indisputably lovely voice.*

indistinguishable /ˌɪndɪˈstɪŋgwɪʃəbəl/. ADJ If one thing is **indistinguishable from** another, the two things are so similar that it is difficult to know which is which. *In most cases the copies were indistinguishable from the originals.*

⭐ **individual** /ˌɪndɪˈvɪdʒʊəl/ **individuals.** **1** ADJ BEFORE N **Individual** means relating to one person or thing, rather than to a large group. *Homeopathic treatment is always geared towards each individual person.* ♦ **individually** ADV *...cheeses which come in individually wrapped segments.* **2** N-COUNT An **individual** is a person.

individuality /ˌɪndɪvɪdʒʊˈælɪti/. N-UNCOUNT The **individuality** of a person or thing consists of the qualities that make them different from other people or things. *People should be free to express their individuality.*

indoor /ˈɪndɔː/. ADJ BEFORE N **Indoor** activities or things are ones that happen or are used inside a building, rather than outside. *...a weekly indoor market.*

indoors /ˌɪnˈdɔːz/. ADV If something happens **indoors**, it happens inside a building. *Perhaps we should go indoors.*

induce /ɪnˈdjuːs, AM -ˈduːs/ **induces, inducing, induced.** **1** VERB To **induce** a particular state or condition means to cause it. *Surgery could induce a heart attack.* **2** VERB If you **induce** someone **to** do something, you persuade or influence them to do it. *I would do anything to induce them to stay.*

inducement /ɪnˈdjuːsmənt, AM -ˈduːs-/ **inducements.** N-COUNT An **inducement** is something which might persuade someone to do a particular thing. *My friends were offered financial inducements to give the press information.*

induction /ɪnˈdʌkʃən/ **inductions.** N-VAR **Induction** is a procedure or ceremony for introducing someone to a new job or way of life. *...the induction of the girls into the sport. ...Elvis' induction into the army.*

indulge /ɪnˈdʌldʒ/ **indulges, indulging, indulged.** **1** VERB If you **indulge** in something, you allow yourself to have or do something that you know you will enjoy. *Only rarely will she indulge in a glass of wine... You can indulge yourself without spending a fortune.* **2** VERB If you **indulge** someone, you let them have or do whatever they want. *He did not really agree with indulging children.*

indulgent /ɪnˈdʌldʒənt/. ADJ If you are **indulgent**, you treat a person with special kindness. *His indulgent mother was willing to let him do anything he wanted.* ♦ **indulgently** ADV *Ned smiled at him indulgently.* ♦ **indulgence,** **indulgences** N-VAR *...the king's indulgence towards his sons.*

⭐ **industrial** /ɪnˈdʌstriəl/. **1** ADJ **Industrial** means relating to industry. *...industrial machinery and equipment.* **2** ADJ An **industrial** city or country is one in which industry is important or highly developed.

in,dustrial 'action. N-UNCOUNT If a group of workers **take industrial action**, they stop working or take other action to protest about their pay or working conditions.

in'dustrial estate, industrial estates. N-COUNT An **industrial estate** is an area which has been specially planned for a lot of factories. [BRITISH]

industrialist /ɪnˈdʌstriəlɪst/ **industrialists.** N-COUNT An **industrialist** is a person who owns or controls large industrial companies or factories.

industrialize (BRIT also **industrialise**) /ɪnˈdʌstriəlaɪz/ **industrializes, industrializing, industrialized.** VERB When a country **industrializes**, or when it **is industrialized**, it develops a lot of industries. *Energy consumption rises as countries industrialise... these methods had industrialized the Russian economy.* ♦ **industrialization** N-UNCOUNT *Industrialization began early in Spain.*

in,dustrial re'lations. N-PLURAL **Industrial**

relations refers to the relationship between employers and workers.

⭐ **industry** /'ɪndəstri/**industries.** [1] N-UNCOUNT **Industry** is the work and processes involved in making things in factories. [2] N-COUNT A particular **industry** consists of all the people and activities involved in making a particular product or providing a particular service. ...*the motor vehicle and textile industries.*

inedible /ɪn'edɪbəl/. ADJ Something that is **inedible** is poisonous or tastes too bad to eat.

ineffective /ˌɪnɪ'fektɪv/. ADJ If you say that something is **ineffective**, you mean that it has no effect on a process or situation. ...*an ineffective method of controlling your dog.*

ineffectual /ˌɪnɪ'fektʃʊəl/. ADJ If someone or something is **ineffectual**, they fail to do what they are expected to do or are trying to do. *The government appears to be both ineffectual and indecisive.* ♦ **ineffectually** ADV *I tried, ineffectually, to comfort her.*

inefficient /ˌɪnɪ'fɪʃənt/. ADJ A person, organization, system, or machine that is **inefficient** does not work in the most economical way. ...*the closure of outdated and inefficient factories.* ♦ **inefficiency** N-UNCOUNT ...*the inefficiency of the system.* ♦ **inefficiently** ADV *We still use power very inefficiently.*

inept /ɪn'ept/. ADJ Someone who is **inept** does something with a complete lack of skill. *You are completely inept at writing.*

inequality /ˌɪnɪ'kwɒlɪti/**inequalities.** N-VAR **Inequality** is a difference in social status, wealth, or opportunity between people or groups. *People are concerned about social inequality.*

inert /ɪn'ɜːt/. ADJ Someone or something that is **inert** does not move at all and appears to be lifeless. *The body was cold and inert.*

inertia /ɪn'ɜːʃə/. N-UNCOUNT If you have a feeling of **inertia**, you feel very lazy and unwilling to do anything. *He resented her inertia, her lack of energy.*

inescapable /ˌɪnɪ'skeɪpəbəl/. ADJ If something is **inescapable**, it is impossible not to notice it or be affected by it. *That is the inescapable conclusion of the reports.*

⭐ **inevitable** /ɪn'evɪtəbəl/. ADJ & N-SING If something is **inevitable**, it is certain to happen and cannot be prevented or avoided. You can refer to something inevitable as **the inevitable**. *If the case succeeds, it is inevitable that other trials will follow... There's no point in putting off the inevitable.* ♦ **inevitability** N-UNCOUNT *We are all bound by the inevitability of death.* ♦ **inevitably** /ɪn'evɪtəbli/ ADV *Technological changes will inevitably lead to unemployment.*

inexorable /ɪn'eksərəbəl/. ADJ Something that is **inexorable** cannot be prevented from continuing. [FORMAL] ...*the seemingly inexorable rise in unemployment.* ♦ **inexorably** ADV *The crisis is moving inexorably towards war.*

inexpensive /ˌɪnɪk'spensɪv/. ADJ Something

that is **inexpensive** does not cost much. ...*a large variety of good inexpensive restaurants.*

inexperience /ˌɪnɪk'spɪəriəns/. N-UNCOUNT If you refer to someone's **inexperience**, you mean that they have little knowledge or experience of a particular situation or activity. *Critics attacked the youth and inexperience of his staff.*

inexperienced /ˌɪnɪk'spɪəriənst/. ADJ If you are **inexperienced**, you have little or no experience of a particular activity. *They are inexperienced when it comes to decorating.*

inexplicable /ˌɪnɪk'splɪkəbəl/. ADJ If something is **inexplicable**, you cannot explain it. ♦ **inexplicably** ADV *She suddenly and inexplicably announced her retirement.*

inextricably /ˌɪnek'strɪkəbəli/. ADV If two or more things are **inextricably** linked, they cannot be separated. *Our survival is inextricably linked to the survival of the rainforest.*

infamous /'ɪnfəməs/. ADJ **Infamous** people or things are well-known because of something bad. ● See note at **famous**.

infancy /'ɪnfənsi/. [1] N-UNCOUNT **Infancy** is the period in your life when you are a very young child. *Fewer children die at birth or in infancy than ever before.* [2] N-UNCOUNT If something is in its **infancy**, it is new and has not developed very much. *Computing science was still in its infancy.*

infant /'ɪnfənt/**infants.** N-COUNT An **infant** is a very young child or baby. [FORMAL]

infantry /'ɪnfəntri/. N-UNCOUNT The **infantry** are the soldiers in an army who fight on foot.

⭐ **infect** /ɪn'fekt/**infects, infecting, infected.** [1] VERB To **infect** people, animals, plants, or food means to cause them to suffer from germs or to carry germs. ...*people infected with HIV... Europeans infected Indians with smallpox.* ♦ **infection** N-UNCOUNT ...*plants that are resistant to infection.* [2] VERB If a virus **infects** a computer, it affects the computer by damaging or destroying programs. [COMPUTING] *This virus infected thousands of computers.*

⭐ **infection** /ɪn'fekʃən/**infections.** N-COUNT An **infection** is a disease caused by germs. *I had an ear infection.*

infectious /ɪn'fekʃəs/. [1] ADJ If you have an **infectious** disease, people near you can catch it from you. [2] ADJ If a feeling is **infectious**, it spreads to other people. ...*the infectious enthusiasm of the workforce.*

infer /ɪn'fɜː/**infers, inferring, inferred.** VERB If you **infer** that something is true, you decide that it is true on the basis of information you have. ...*information from which he can infer the future course of events.*

inference /'ɪnfərəns/**inferences.** N-COUNT An **inference** is a conclusion that you draw about something. *There were two inferences to be drawn from her letter.*

inferior /ɪn'fɪəriə/**inferiors.** [1] ADJ Something that is **inferior** is not as good as something else. *The cassettes were of inferior quality...*

⭐ Bank of English® frequent word   For a full explanation of all grammatical labels, see pages vii-x

Comprehensive schools were perceived as inferior to grammar schools. [2] ADJ & N-COUNT If one person is regarded as **inferior to** another or as that person's **inferior**, they are considered to have less ability, status, or importance. *He preferred the company of those who were intellectually inferior to himself... Most career women make me feel inferior... It was a gentleman's duty always to be civil, even to his inferiors.* ♦ **inferiority** /ɪnfɪəri'ɒrɪti, AM -'ɔːr-/ N-UNCOUNT *...feelings of inferiority that come from childhood.*

infertile /ɪn'fɜːtaɪl, AM -təl/. [1] ADJ Someone who is **infertile** is unable to produce babies. ♦ **infertility** /,ɪnfɜː'tɪlɪti/ N-UNCOUNT *Male infertility is becoming commonplace.* [2] ADJ **Infertile** land has poor quality soil, so plants cannot grow well there.

infested /ɪn'festɪd/. ADJ If a place is **infested with** something undesirable such as insects or other pests, there are lots of them in it. *The prison is infested with rats. ...shark-infested waters.*

infidelity /,ɪnfɪ'delɪti/ **infidelities.** N-VAR **Infidelity** occurs when a person who is married or in a steady relationship has sex with another person. *Andrews learned of his wife's infidelity.*

infiltrate /'ɪnfɪltreɪt/ **infiltrates, infiltrating, infiltrated.** VERB If people **infiltrate** an organization, they join it secretly in order to spy on it or influence it. *The movement has been infiltrated by anarchists.* ♦ **infiltration, infiltrations** N-VAR *...the problem of Communist infiltration of the armed forces.*

infinite /'ɪnfɪnɪt/. ADJ Something that is **infinite** is extremely large in amount or degree, or has no limit. *No company has infinite resources.* ♦ **infinitely** ADV *His design was infinitely better than anything I could have done.*

infinitive /ɪn'fɪnɪtɪv/ **infinitives.** N-COUNT The **infinitive** of a verb is its base form or simplest form, such as 'do', 'take', and 'eat'. The infinitive is often used with 'to' in front of it.

infinity /ɪn'fɪnɪti/. [1] N-UNCOUNT **Infinity** is a number that is larger than any other number and so can never be given an exact value. [2] N-UNCOUNT **Infinity** is a point that is further away than any other point and so can never be reached. *...the darkness of a starless night stretching to infinity.*

infirmary /ɪn'fɜːməri/ **infirmaries.** N-COUNT Some hospitals are called **infirmaries**. *...the Radcliffe Infirmary in Oxford.*

inflame /ɪn'fleɪm/ **inflames, inflaming, inflamed.** VERB If something **inflames** a situation, or if it **inflames** people's feelings, it makes people more angry or feel more strongly. [JOURNALISM] *Political passions have been inflamed by the scandal.*

inflamed /ɪn'fleɪmd/. ADJ If part of your body is **inflamed**, it is red or swollen because of an infection or injury. [FORMAL]

inflammation /,ɪnflə'meɪʃən/ **inflammations.** N-VAR An **inflammation** is a swelling in your body

that results from an infection or injury. [FORMAL] *...inflammation of the liver.*

inflammatory /ɪn'flæmətəri, AM -tɔːri/. ADJ An **inflammatory** action or remark is likely to make people react very angrily. *Someone made an inflammatory racist remark.*

inflatable /ɪn'fleɪtəbəl/. ADJ An **inflatable** object is one that you fill with air when you want to use it. *...an inflatable boat.*

inflate /ɪn'fleɪt/ **inflates, inflating, inflated.** VERB If you **inflate** something such as a balloon or tyre, or if it **inflates**, it becomes bigger as it is filled with air or another gas. *Don's lifejacket had failed to inflate.*

inflated /ɪn'fleɪtɪd/. [1] ADJ If you say that someone has an **inflated** opinion of themselves, you mean that they think that they are better or more important than they really are. [2] ADJ If you describe a price or salary as **inflated**, you mean that it is higher than is reasonable.

★ **inflation** /ɪn'fleɪʃən/. N-UNCOUNT **Inflation** is a general increase in the prices of goods and services in a country. *...an inflation rate of only 2.2%.*

inflationary /ɪn'fleɪʃənri, AM -neri/. ADJ **Inflationary** means connected with inflation or causing inflation. *...inflationary wage claims.*

inflect /ɪn'flekt/ **inflects, inflecting, inflected.** VERB If a word **inflects**, its ending or form changes in order to show its grammatical function or number. If a language **inflects**, it has words in it that inflect. ♦ **inflection, inflections** N-VAR *...the rules of inflection.*

inflexible /ɪn'fleksɪbəl/. ADJ Something or someone that is **inflexible** cannot or will not change or be altered, even if the situation changes. *Workers insisted the new system was too inflexible.* ♦ **inflexibility** N-UNCOUNT *Joyce was irritated by the inflexibility of her colleagues.*

inflict /ɪn'flɪkt/ **inflicts, inflicting, inflicted.** VERB To **inflict** something unpleasant **on** someone or something means to make them suffer it. *...sports that inflicted cruelty on animals.*

★ **influence** /'ɪnflʊəns/ **influences, influencing, influenced.** [1] N-UNCOUNT **Influence** is the power to make other people agree with your opinions or make them do what you want. *Did Eva Braun have any influence on Hitler?... The government should continue to use its influence for the release of all hostages.* [2] VERB If you **influence** someone, you use your power to make them agree with you or do what you want. *My dad influenced me to do electronics.* [3] N-COUNT & VERB If someone or something has an **influence** on people or events, or if they **influence** people or events, they affect the way people think or act, or what happens. *The Shropshire landscape was an influence on Owen. ...driving under the influence of alcohol... What you eat may influence your risk of getting cancer.* [4] N-COUNT Someone or something that is a good or bad **influence** has a good or bad effect on someone. *TV is a bad influence on people.*

influential /ˌɪnfluˈenʃəl/. ADJ Someone who is **influential** has a lot of influence over people or events. *It helps to have influential friends... He had been influential in shaping economic policy.*

influx /ˈɪnflʌks/. N-SING An **influx of** people or things into a place is their steady arrival there in large numbers. *...an influx of refugees.*

info /ˈɪnfəʊ/. N-UNCOUNT **Info** is information. [INFORMAL] *For more info phone 414-3935.*

◨ **inform** /ɪnˈfɔːm/**informs, informing, informed.** VERB If you **inform** someone **of** something, you tell them about it. *They would inform him of any progress they had made. ...efforts to inform people about the dangers of AIDS... My daughter informed me that she was pregnant.* ● See also **informed.**

informal /ɪnˈfɔːməl/. ADJ You use **informal** to describe behaviour, speech, or situations that are relaxed and casual rather than correct and serious. *She is refreshingly informal.*
◆ **informally** ADV *They frequently chat informally over coffee.*

informant /ɪnˈfɔːmənt/**informants.** N-COUNT An **informant** is someone who gives another person information, especially someone who gives information to the police.

◨ **information** /ˌɪnfəˈmeɪʃən/. N-UNCOUNT If you have **information** about a particular thing, you know something about it. *We will be looking at every piece of information we receive... For further information contact the number below.*

> **USAGE** Note that **information** is only ever used as an uncount noun. You cannot say 'an information' or 'informations'. However, you can say a **piece of information** or an **item of information** when you are referring to a particular fact that someone has informed you of.

infor,mation tech'nology. N-UNCOUNT **Information technology** is the theory and practice of using computers to store and analyse information. [COMPUTING]

informative /ɪnˈfɔːmətɪv/. ADJ Something that is **informative** gives you useful information. *It is an informative and readable book.*

informed /ɪnˈfɔːmd/. ADJ Someone who is **informed** knows about a subject. An **informed** guess or decision is based on knowledge about a subject. *Consumers can now make a more informed choice about what they buy.*

informer /ɪnˈfɔːmə/**informers.** N-COUNT An **informer** is someone who tells the police that another person has done something wrong.

infra-red /ˌɪnfrə ˈred/. ADJ BEFORE N **Infra-red** radiation is similar to light but has a longer wavelength, so you cannot see it without special equipment, referred to as **infra-red** equipment.

infrastructure /ˈɪnfrəstrʌktʃə/**infrastructures.** N-VAR The **infrastructure** of a country or society consists of the basic facilities such as transport, communications, power supplies, and buildings, which enable the country or society to function properly.

infringe /ɪnˈfrɪndʒ/**infringes, infringing, infringed.** ▢1 VERB If someone **infringes** a law or an agreement, they break it. *The film exploited his image and infringed his copyright.*
◆ **infringement** /ɪnˈfrɪndʒmənt/**infringements** N-VAR *Infringement of the regulation is punishable by a fine.* ▢2 VERB If something **infringes** people's rights or freedoms, or if it **infringes on** them, it prevents them from having the rights or freedoms they are entitled to. ◆ **infringement** N-VAR *The wide-ranging police powers are an infringement of civil liberties.*

infuriate /ɪnˈfjʊərieɪt/**infuriates, infuriating, infuriated.** VERB If something or someone **infuriates** you, they make you extremely angry. *...a teenage craze guaranteed to infuriate your parents.* ◆ **infuriating** ADJ *Lizzie is messy to an infuriating degree.*

infuse /ɪnˈfjuːz/**infuses, infusing, infused.** VERB To **infuse** a quality **into** someone or something, or to **infuse** them **with** a quality, means to fill them with it. [FORMAL] *The girls seemed to be infused with excitement on seeing the snow.*

ingenious /ɪnˈdʒiːniəs/. ADJ Something that is **ingenious** is very clever and involves new ideas or equipment. *...a truly ingenious invention.*

ingenuity /ˌɪndʒəˈnjuːɪti, AM -ˈnuː-/. N-UNCOUNT **Ingenuity** is skill at inventing things or at working out how to achieve things.

ingrained /ˌɪnˈɡreɪnd/. ADJ **Ingrained** habits and beliefs are difficult to change or remove. *...deeply ingrained family loyalty.*

★ **ingredient** /ɪnˈɡriːdiənt/**ingredients.** ▢1 N-COUNT **Ingredients** are the things that are used to make something, especially all the different foods you use when you are cooking a particular dish. ▢2 N-COUNT An **ingredient** of a situation is one of the essential parts of it.

inhabit /ɪnˈhæbɪt/**inhabits, inhabiting, inhabited.** VERB If a place or region **is inhabited** by a group of people or a species of animal, those people or animals live there. *...the people who inhabit these beautiful islands.*

inhabitant /ɪnˈhæbɪtənt/**inhabitants.** N-COUNT The **inhabitants** of a place are the people who live there.

inhale /ɪnˈheɪl/**inhales, inhaling, inhaled.** VERB When you **inhale**, you breathe in. When you **inhale** something such as smoke, you take it into your lungs when you breathe in. *He was treated for the effects of inhaling smoke.*

inherent /ɪnˈherənt, -ˈhɪər-/. ADJ The **inherent** qualities of something are the necessary and natural parts of it. *...the dangers inherent in an outbreak of war.* ◆ **inherently** ADV *Aeroplanes are not inherently dangerous.*

inherit /ɪnˈherɪt/**inherits, inheriting, inherited.** ▢1 VERB If you **inherit** money or property, you

a
b
c
d
e
f
g
h
i
j
k
l
m
n
o
p
q
r
s
t
u
v
w
x
y
z

receive it from someone who has died. ...*paintings that he inherited from his father.* ② VERB If you **inherit** something such as a situation or attitude, you take it over from people who came before you. *The government inherited an impossibly difficult situation from its predecessors.* ③ VERB If you **inherit** a characteristic, you are born with it, because your parents or ancestors had it. *Her children have inherited her love of sport.*

inheritance /ɪnˈherɪtəns/ **inheritances.** ① N-VAR An **inheritance** is money or property which you receive from someone who is dead. ...*families fighting over their inheritance.* ② N-COUNT If you get something such as a problem or attitude from someone who used to have it, you can refer to this as an **inheritance.** ...*starvation and disease over much of Europe and Asia, which was Truman's inheritance as President.*

inhibit /ɪnˈhɪbɪt/ **inhibits, inhibiting, inhibited.** VERB If something **inhibits** an event or process, it prevents it or slows it down. *Wine or sugary drinks inhibit digestion.*

inhibited /ɪnˈhɪbɪtɪd/. ADJ If you say that someone is **inhibited**, you mean they find it difficult to behave naturally and show their feelings, and that you think this is a bad thing. *The English are very inhibited.*

inhibition /ˌɪnɪˈbɪʃən/ **inhibitions.** N-VAR **Inhibitions** are feelings of fear or embarrassment that make it difficult for you to behave naturally. *They behave with a total lack of inhibition.*

inhuman /ˌɪnˈhjuːmən/. ① ADJ If you describe something as **inhuman**, you mean that it is extremely cruel. *The barbaric slaughter of whales is unnecessary and inhuman.* ② ADJ Something that is **inhuman** is not human or does not seem human, and is strange or frightening. ...*inhuman shrieks.*

☆ **initial** /ɪˈnɪʃəl/ **initials, initialling, initialled** (AM **initialing, initialed**). ① ADJ BEFORE N You use **initial** to describe something that happens at the beginning of a process. *The initial reaction has been excellent.* ② N-COUNT **Initials** are the capital letters which begin each word of a name. ③ VERB When you **initial** a document, you write your initials on it to show that you have seen it or have officially approved it.

☆ **initially** /ɪˈnɪʃəli/. ADV **Initially** means in the early stages of a process or situation. *Initially, they were wary of Simon.*

initiate /ɪˈnɪʃieɪt/ **initiates, initiating, initiated.** ① VERB If you **initiate** something, you start it or cause it to happen. *They wanted to initiate a discussion on economics.* ✦ **initiation** N-UNCOUNT *There was a year between initiation and completion.* ② VERB If someone **is initiated into** a particular group or society, they become a member of it by taking part in ceremonies at which they learn its special knowledge or customs. *She was initiated into the London Temple*

of the Alpha and Omega in 1919. ✦ **initiation, initiations** N-VAR ...*initiation rites.*

☆ **initiative** /ɪˈnɪʃətɪv/ **initiatives.** ① N-COUNT An **initiative** is an important act intended to solve a problem. *There's talk of a new peace initiative.* ② N-SING In a fight or contest, if you have **the initiative**, you are in a stronger position than your opponents. ③ N-UNCOUNT If you have **initiative**, you are able to take action without needing other people to tell you what to do. *She was disappointed by his lack of initiative.* ④ PHRASE If you **take the initiative** in a situation, you are the first person to act, and are therefore able to control the situation.

inject /ɪnˈdʒekt/ **injects, injecting, injected.** ① VERB To **inject** someone **with** a substance such as a medicine, or to **inject** it **into** them, means to use a needle and a syringe to put it into their body. *His son was injected with strong drugs... The technique consists of injecting healthy cells into the weakened muscles.* ② VERB If you **inject** a new, exciting, or interesting quality **into** a situation, you add it. *She kept trying to inject a little fun into their relationship.* ③ VERB If you **inject** money or resources **into** a business or organization, you provide more money or resources for it.

injection /ɪnˈdʒekʃən/ **injections.** ① N-COUNT If you have an **injection**, a doctor or nurse puts a medicine into your body using a needle and a syringe. *It has to be given by injection, usually twice daily.* ② N-COUNT An **injection of** money or resources into a business or organization is the act of providing more money or resources for it.

injunction /ɪnˈdʒʌŋkʃən/ **injunctions.** N-COUNT An **injunction** is a court order, usually one telling someone not to do something. [LEGAL] ...*an injunction banning her from his home.*

injure /ˈɪndʒə/ **injures, injuring, injured.** VERB If you **injure** a person or animal, you damage some part of their body. ...*motorists who kill, maim, and injure.* ● See note at **wound**.

☆ **injured** /ˈɪndʒəd/. ① ADJ & N-PLURAL An **injured** person has physical damage to part of their body, usually as a result of an accident or fighting. **The injured** are people who are injured. *Many of them will have died because they were so badly injured.* ● See note at **wound**. ② ADJ If you feel **injured**, or if your feelings are **injured**, you feel upset because you believe something unfair has been done to you. ...*a look of injured pride.*

☆ **injury** /ˈɪndʒəri/ **injuries.** N-VAR An **injury** is damage done to a person's body. *The two other passengers escaped serious injury.* ● See note at **wound**.

injustice /ɪnˈdʒʌstɪs/ **injustices.** N-VAR **Injustice** is a lack of fairness in a situation. ...*the injustice and futility of terrorism.*

ink /ɪŋk/ **inks, inking, inked.** ① N-VAR **Ink** is the coloured liquid used for writing or printing. *The letter was handwritten in black ink.* ② VERB If you **ink** something, you put ink on it.

inland. 1 ADV /ɪnˈlænd/ If something is situated **inland**, it is away from the coast, towards or near the middle of a country. *The vast majority live further inland.* 2 ADJ BEFORE N /ˈɪnlænd/ **Inland** lakes and places are not on the coast, but in or near the middle of a country.

'in-laws. N-PLURAL Your **in-laws** are the parents and close relatives of your husband or wife.

inlet /ˈɪnlet/ **inlets.** N-COUNT An **inlet** is a narrow strip of water which goes from a sea or lake into the land.

inmate /ˈɪnmeɪt/ **inmates.** N-COUNT The **inmates** of a prison or a psychiatric hospital are the prisoners or patients who are living there.

inn /ɪn/ **inns.** N-COUNT An **inn** is a small hotel or a pub, usually an old one. [DATED]

innate /ɪˈneɪt/. ADJ An **innate** quality or ability is one which a person is born with. *Americans have an innate sense of fairness.* ♦ **innately** ADV *...her innately feminine qualities.*

⭐ **inner** /ˈɪnə/. 1 ADJ BEFORE N The **inner** parts of something are the parts which are contained or enclosed inside the other parts, and which are closest to the centre. *She got up and went into an inner office.* 2 ADJ BEFORE N Your **inner** feelings are feelings which you have but do not show to other people.

,inner 'circle, inner circles. N-COUNT An **inner circle** is a group of people who have a lot of power or control in a group or organization, and who work together in secretive ways. *...the inner circle of scientists who produced the atomic bomb.*

,inner 'city, inner cities. N-COUNT You use **inner city** to refer to areas near the centre of a city where people live and where there are often social and economic problems. *...the fear of living in the inner city. ...inner-city areas.*

innings /ˈɪnɪŋz/.

✅ **Innings** is both the singular and the plural form.

N-COUNT An **innings** is a period in a game of cricket during which a particular player or team is batting.

innocence /ˈɪnəsəns/. 1 ADJ **Innocence** is the quality of having no experience or knowledge of the more complex or unpleasant aspects of life. *...childhood innocence.* 2 N-UNCOUNT If someone proves their **innocence**, they prove that they are not guilty of a crime.

⭐ **innocent** /ˈɪnəsənt/ **innocents.** 1 ADJ If someone is **innocent**, they did not commit a crime which they have been accused of. *He was sure that the man was innocent of any crime.* 2 ADJ & N-COUNT If someone is **innocent** or is an **innocent**, they have no experience or knowledge of the more complex or unpleasant aspects of life. *They seemed so young and innocent. ...a hopeless innocent where women were concerned.* ♦ **innocently** ADV *The baby gurgled innocently on the bed.* 3 ADJ **Innocent** people are those who are not involved in a crime, conflict, or other situation, but who nevertheless get injured or

killed. *All those wounded were innocent victims.* 4 ADJ An **innocent** remark or action is not meant to offend people, although it may do so. *It was probably an innocent question.*

innocuous /ɪˈnɒkjuəs/. ADJ Something that is **innocuous** is not at all harmful. [FORMAL] *Both mushrooms look innocuous but are in fact deadly.*

innovation /ˌɪnəˈveɪʃən/ **innovations.** 1 N-COUNT An **innovation** is a new thing or new method of doing something. 2 N-UNCOUNT **Innovation** is the introduction of new things or new methods. *We must promote originality, inspire creativity and encourage innovation.*

innovative /ˈɪnəveɪtɪv/. 1 ADJ Something that is **innovative** is new and original. 2 ADJ An **innovative** person introduces changes and new ideas.

innovator /ˈɪnəveɪtə/ **innovators.** N-COUNT An **innovator** is someone who introduces changes and new ideas.

innuendo /ˌɪnjuˈendəʊ/ **innuendoes** or **innuendos.** N-VAR **Innuendo** is indirect reference to something rude or unpleasant. *...magazines which are full of sexual innuendo.*

innumerable /ɪˈnjuːmərəbəl, AM -ˈnuː-/. ADJ **Innumerable** means very many, or too many to be counted. *He has invented innumerable excuses, told endless lies.*

inordinate /ɪnˈɔːdɪnɪt/. ADJ If you describe something as **inordinate**, you are emphasizing that it is unusually or excessively great in amount or degree. [FORMAL] *...their inordinate number of pets.* ♦ **inordinately** ADV *He is inordinately proud of his wife.*

input /ˈɪnpʊt/ **inputs, inputting, input.** 1 N-VAR **Input** consists of information or resources that a group or project receives. *...inputs and advice on how to improve the management of their farms.* 2 VERB If you **input** information into a computer, you feed it in, for example by typing it on a keyboard. [COMPUTING] 3 N-UNCOUNT **Input** is information fed into a computer. [COMPUTING]

inquest /ˈɪnkwest/ **inquests.** N-COUNT An **inquest** is an official inquiry into the cause of someone's death.

inquire (or **enquire**) /ɪnˈkwaɪə/ **inquires, inquiring, inquired.** 1 VERB If you **inquire** about something, you ask for information about it. [FORMAL] *'Is something wrong?' he enquired... He asked for his key and inquired whether there had been any messages for him.* 2 VERB If you **inquire into** something, you investigate it carefully. *Inspectors were appointed to inquire into the affairs of the company.*
▶**inquire after.** PHR-VERB If you **inquire after** someone, you ask how they are or what they are doing. *Elsie called to inquire after my health.*

inquiring (or **enquiring**) /ɪnˈkwaɪərɪŋ/. 1 ADJ BEFORE N If you have an **inquiring** mind, you have a great interest in learning new things. *...an inquiring attitude to learning.* 2 ADJ BEFORE N If someone has an **inquiring** expression on their face, they are showing that they want to know something. [WRITTEN]

⭐ **inquiry** (or **enquiry**) /ɪnˈkwaɪəri/ **inquiries.**
1 N-COUNT An **inquiry** is a question which you ask in order to get information. *He made some inquiries and discovered she had gone to the Continent.* **2** N-COUNT An **inquiry** is an official investigation. **3** N-UNCOUNT **Inquiry** is the process of investigating something to get information about it. *...a new line of inquiry.*

inquisitive /ɪnˈkwɪzɪtɪv/. ADJ An **inquisitive** person likes finding out about things, especially secret things. *Barrow had an inquisitive nature.*

inroads /ˈɪnrəʊdz/. PHRASE If one thing **makes inroads into** another, the first thing starts affecting or destroying the second. *...television has made deep inroads into cinema.*

insane /ɪnˈseɪn/. **1** ADJ & N-PLURAL Someone who is **insane** has a mind that does not work in a normal way, with the result that their behaviour is very strange. **The insane** are people who are insane. *His first wife went insane.* ♦ **insanity** /ɪnˈsænɪti/ N-UNCOUNT *...a woman's descent into insanity.* **2** ADJ If you describe a decision or action as **insane**, you think it is very foolish or excessive. ♦ **insanely** ADV *I would be insanely jealous if Bill left me for another woman.*
♦ **insanity** N-UNCOUNT *...the final financial insanity of the 1980s.*

insatiable /ɪnˈseɪʃəbəl/. ADJ If someone has an **insatiable** desire for something, they want as much of it as they can possibly get. *He had an insatiable appetite for publicity.*

inscribe /ɪnˈskraɪb/ **inscribes, inscribing, inscribed.**
VERB If you **inscribe** words on an object, you write or carve the words on it. *...stone slabs inscribed with Buddhist texts.*

inscription /ɪnˈskrɪpʃən/ **inscriptions.** N-COUNT An **inscription** is a piece of writing carved into a surface, or written on a book or photograph.

insect /ˈɪnsekt/ **insects.** N-COUNT An **insect** is a small creature with six legs. Most insects have wings. → See pictures on page 824.

insecticide /ɪnˈsektɪsaɪd/ **insecticides.** N-VAR **Insecticide** is a chemical used to kill insects.

insecure /ˌɪnsɪˈkjʊə/. **1** ADJ If you feel **insecure**, you feel that you are not good enough or are not loved. *Most mothers are insecure about their performance as mothers.* ♦ **insecurity** /ˌɪnsɪˈkjʊərɪti/ N-VAR *It was his shyness and insecurity which let him down.* **2** ADJ Something that is **insecure** is not safe or protected. *...low-paid, insecure jobs.*
♦ **insecurity** N-UNCOUNT *...the insecurity of agricultural life.*

insensitive /ɪnˈsensɪtɪv/. ADJ If you describe someone as **insensitive**, you mean that they are not aware of or sympathetic to other people's feelings or problems. *My husband is very insensitive about my problem.* ♦ **insensitivity** /ɪnˌsensɪˈtɪvɪti/ N-UNCOUNT *...my clumsiness and insensitivity towards her.*

inseparable /ɪnˈseprəbəl/. **1** ADJ If two things are **inseparable**, they cannot be considered separately. *Liberty is inseparable from social justice.* **2** ADJ Friends who are **inseparable** spend a lot of time together.

insert /ɪnˈsɜːt/ **inserts, inserting, inserted.** **1** VERB If you **insert** an object **into** something, you put the object inside it. *He took a small key from his pocket and slowly inserted it into the lock.*
♦ **insertion, insertions** N-VAR *...the insertion of needles at precise points on the body.* **2** VERB If you **insert** a comment or detail in a piece of writing or a speech, you include it.

⭐ **inside** /ˌɪnˈsaɪd/ **insides.** **1** PREP & ADV Something or someone that is **inside** a place, container, or object is in it or surrounded by it. *Inside the box were a dozen or so papers... There is a telephone inside the entrance hall... He ripped open the envelope and read what was inside.* **2** N-COUNT The **inside** of something is the part or area that its sides surround or contain. *I painted the inside of the house. ...an inside lavatory.* **3** ADJ BEFORE N On a wide road, the **inside** lanes are the ones closest to the edge of the road. **4** N-PLURAL Your **insides** are your internal organs, especially your stomach. [INFORMAL] **5** ADJ BEFORE N **Inside** knowledge is obtained from someone who is involved in a situation and therefore knows a lot about it. *The attackers had inside information about the targets.* **6** PHRASE If something such as a piece of clothing is **inside out**, the inside part has been turned so that it faces outwards.

insider /ˌɪnˈsaɪdə/ **insiders.** N-COUNT An **insider** is someone who is involved in a situation and who knows more about it than other people. *Insiders say there are simply too many chiefs. ...insider knowledge.*

insidious /ɪnˈsɪdiəs/. ADJ Something that is **insidious** is unpleasant and develops gradually without being noticed. *The changes are insidious, and will not produce a noticeable effect for 15 to 20 years.*

insight /ˈɪnsaɪt/ **insights.** N-VAR If you gain **insight into** a complex situation or problem, you learn something useful or valuable about it. *...an insight into the practical problems encountered by disabled people.*

insignificant /ˌɪnsɪgˈnɪfɪkənt/. ADJ Something that is **insignificant** is unimportant, especially because it is very small. *In 1949 Bonn was a small, insignificant city.* ♦ **insignificance** N-UNCOUNT *...the sense of insignificance that everybody has felt.*

⭐ **insist** /ɪnˈsɪst/ **insists, insisting, insisted.** **1** VERB If you **insist** that something should be done, you say very firmly that it must be done. *She insisted on being present... I didn't want to join in, but Kenneth insisted.* ♦ **insistence** N-UNCOUNT *She had attended an interview at her boyfriend's insistence.* **2** VERB If you **insist** that something is true, you say it very firmly and refuse to change your mind. *The president insisted that he was acting out of compassion.*

insistent /ɪnˈsɪstənt/. [1] ADJ Someone who is **insistent** keeps insisting that a particular thing should be done or is the case. *Abramov had been insistent that the matter be resolved quickly.* ◆ **insistently** ADV *'What is it?' his wife asked again, gently but insistently.* [2] ADJ An **insistent** noise or rhythm continues for a long time and holds your attention.

insofar as /ˌɪnsəˈfɑːr æz/. CONJ You use **insofar as** to introduce a statement which explains and adds to something you have just said. [FORMAL] *She was not ashamed of her addiction, except insofar as it troubled her husband.*

insomnia /ɪnˈsɒmniə/. N-UNCOUNT Someone who suffers from **insomnia** finds it difficult to sleep.

⭐ **inspect** /ɪnˈspekt/ **inspects, inspecting, inspected.** VERB If you **inspect** something, you examine it or check it carefully. *His wife tilted his head to the side and inspected the wound.* ◆ **inspection, inspections** N-VAR *Officials will have to make an inspection of the dam.*

⭐ **inspector** /ɪnˈspektə/ **inspectors.** [1] N-COUNT An **inspector** is someone whose job is to inspect things. *The mill was finally shut down by state safety inspectors.* [2] N-COUNT & N-TITLE In Britain, an **inspector** is a police officer who is higher in rank than a sergeant and lower in rank than a superintendent. *...Inspector Joplin.*

inspiration /ˌɪnspɪˈreɪʃən/. [1] N-UNCOUNT **Inspiration** is a feeling of excitement and enthusiasm gained from new ideas. *Daphne played extremely well and it will give a lot of inspiration to other women.* [2] N-SING The **inspiration for** something such as a piece of work or a theory is the person or thing that provides the basic idea or example for it. *India's myths and songs are the inspiration for her book... My inspiration comes from poets like Baudelaire.*

inspire /ɪnˈspaɪə/ **inspires, inspiring, inspired.** [1] VERB If a work of art or an action **is inspired** by something, that thing is the source of the idea or the motivation for it. *The book was inspired by a real person... What inspired you to change your name?* ◆ **-inspired** *...Mediterranean-inspired ceramics.* [2] VERB If someone or something **inspires** you, they give you new ideas and a strong feeling of enthusiasm. *...the personal charisma to inspire people.* ◆ **inspiring** ADJ *...a brilliant and inspiring young teacher.* [3] VERB Someone or something that **inspires** a particular emotion or reaction in people makes them feel it. *He inspires fierce loyalty in his friends.*

instability /ˌɪnstəˈbɪlɪti/ **instabilities.** N-VAR **Instability** is a lack of stability in a place, situation, or person. *...political instability.*

⭐ **install** /ɪnˈstɔːl/ **installs, installing, installed.** [1] VERB If you **install** a piece of equipment, you fit it or put it somewhere so that it is ready to be used. *They had installed a new phone line.* ◆ **installation** /ˌɪnstəˈleɪʃən/ N-UNCOUNT *...the installation of alarms.* [2] VERB If someone **is installed** in a new job or important position, they are officially given the job or position. *The army has promised to install a new government within a week.*

instalment (AM **installment**) /ɪnˈstɔːlmənt/ **instalments.** [1] N-COUNT If you pay for something in **instalments**, you pay small sums of money at regular intervals over a period of time. *...his next instalment on the mortgage.* [2] N-COUNT An **instalment** of a story is one of its separate parts that are published or broadcast one after the other. *...the latest instalment in Douglas Adams's 'Hitchhiker' trilogy.*

⭐ **instance** /ˈɪnstəns/ **instances.** [1] PHRASE You use **for instance** when you are mentioning something or someone that is an example of what you are talking about. *They will be concerned to do the right thing – to dress properly, for instance.* [2] N-COUNT An **instance** is a particular example or occurrence of something. *...another instance of robbery.* [3] PHRASE You say **in the first instance** to mention the first of a series of actions or possibilities. [FORMAL] *Try to resolve the problem with the Tax Office in the first instance.*

⭐ **instant** /ˈɪnstənt/ **instants.** [1] N-COUNT An **instant** is an extremely short period of time or a point in time. *The pain disappeared in an instant... At that instant the museum was plunged into total darkness.* [2] CONJ If you say that someone does something **the instant** something else happens, you are emphasizing that they do the first thing immediately after the second thing happens. *She would know the instant he walked in whether it was true.* [3] ADJ You use **instant** to describe something that happens immediately. *He had taken an instant dislike to Mortlake.* ◆ **instantly** ADV *The man was killed instantly.* [4] ADJ BEFORE N **Instant** food can be prepared very quickly, for example by just adding water. *...instant coffee.*

instantaneous /ˌɪnstənˈteɪniəs/. ADJ Something that is **instantaneous** happens immediately and very quickly. *The coroner said that death was instantaneous.* ◆ **instantaneously** ADV *Airbags inflate instantaneously on impact.*

⭐ **instead** /ɪnˈsted/. PREP & ADV If you do one thing **instead of** another, you do the first thing and not the second thing, especially as the result of a choice or a change of behaviour. *She had to spend nearly four months away from him that summer, instead of the usual two... When we feel anger, we bury the emotion and feel guilty instead.*

instigate /ˈɪnstɪgeɪt/ **instigates, instigating, instigated.** VERB To **instigate** an event or situation means to cause it to happen. *...those who are instigating violence.* ◆ **instigation** N-UNCOUNT *The talks are taking place at the instigation of Germany.* ◆ **instigator, instigators** N-COUNT *He was accused of being the main instigator of the coup.*

instil (AM **instill**) /ɪnˈstɪl/ **instils, instilling, instilled.** VERB If you **instil** an idea or feeling **in** or **into**

someone, you make them think it or feel it. *Their work will instil a sense of responsibility in children.*

instinct /'ɪnstɪŋkt/**instincts.** **1** N-VAR An **instinct** is the natural tendency that a person has to behave or react in a particular way. *I didn't have a strong maternal instinct. ...the dog's natural instinct to hunt.* **2** N-COUNT An **instinct** is a feeling that you have about a particular situation, rather than an opinion based on facts. *I should've gone with my first instinct, which was not to do the interview.*

instinctive /ɪn'stɪŋktɪv/. ADJ An **instinctive** feeling, idea, or action is one that you have or do without thinking. *It's an absolutely instinctive reaction – if a child falls down, you pick it up.* ♦ **instinctively** ADV *He knew instinctively that here was more bad news.*

★ **institute** /'ɪnstɪtjuːt, AM -tuːt/**institutes, instituting, instituted.** **1** N-COUNT An **institute** is an organization or building where a particular type of work is done, especially research or teaching. *...the National Cancer Institute.* **2** VERB If you **institute** a system, rule, or plan, you start it. [FORMAL] *We will institute a number of measures to better safeguard the public.*

★ **institution** /ˌɪnstɪ'tjuːʃən, AM -'tuː-/**institutions.** **1** N-COUNT An **institution** is an official organization which is important in society. Parliament, the Church, and large banks are all institutions. ♦ **institutional** ADJ BEFORE N *...the power of the institutional church.* **2** N-COUNT An **institution** is a place such as a mental hospital, children's home, or prison, where people are kept and looked after. *Larry has been in an institution since he was four.* **3** N-COUNT An **institution** is a custom that is considered an important or typical feature of society, because it has existed for a long time. *...the institution of marriage.*

institutionalized (BRIT also **institutionalised**) /ˌɪnstɪ'tjuːʃənəlaɪzd, AM -'tuː-/. ADJ If you say that something bad has become **institutionalized**, you are critical of the fact that it has become part of a culture, social system, or organization.

in-'store. ADJ & ADV **In-store** facilities are facilities that are available within a department store, supermarket or other large shop. *...an in-store bakery... Ask in-store for details.*

instruct /ɪn'strʌkt/**instructs, instructing, instructed.** **1** VERB If you **instruct** someone **to** do something, you formally tell them to do it. *The family has instructed solicitors to sue the company.* **2** VERB Someone who **instructs** people **in** a subject or skill teaches it to them. *He instructed family members in nursing techniques.*

★ **instruction** /ɪn'strʌkʃən/**instructions.** **1** N-PLURAL **Instructions** are clear and detailed information on how to do something. *...some basic instructions on how to cook a turkey.* **2** N-COUNT An **instruction** is something that someone tells you to do. *He had instructions to keep this guest satisfied.* **3** N-UNCOUNT **Instruction** in a subject or

skill is teaching that someone gives you about it. *...religious instruction.*

instructive /ɪn'strʌktɪv/. ADJ Something that is **instructive** gives useful information. *...an entertaining and instructive documentary.*

instructor /ɪn'strʌktə/**instructors.** N-COUNT An **instructor** is a teacher, especially of driving, skiing, or swimming. *...his karate instructor.*

★ **instrument** /'ɪnstrəmənt/**instruments.** **1** N-COUNT An **instrument** is a tool or device that is used to do a particular task. *...navigation instruments. ...instruments for cleaning and polishing teeth.* **2** N-COUNT A musical **instrument** is an object such as a piano, guitar, or flute which you play in order to produce music. **3** N-COUNT Something that is an **instrument** for achieving a particular aim is used by people to achieve that aim. *...the use of the law as an instrument of political repression.*

instrumental /ˌɪnstrə'mentəl/**instrumentals.** **1** ADJ Someone or something that is **instrumental** in a process or event helps to make it happen. *He was instrumental in getting the legislation passed.* **2** ADJ & N-COUNT **Instrumental** music is performed using musical instruments and not voices. An **instrumental** is a piece of instrumental music.

insufficient /ˌɪnsə'fɪʃənt/. ADJ Something that is **insufficient** is not enough for a particular purpose. [FORMAL] *There are insufficient funds to pay the debt.* ♦ **insufficiently** ADV *The general workforce is insufficiently educated.*

insular /'ɪnsjʊlə, AM -sə-/. ADJ **Insular** people are unwilling to meet new people or to consider new ideas. ♦ **insularity** /ˌɪnsjʊ'lærɪti, AM -sə-/ N-UNCOUNT *...the growing insularity of Russian politics.*

insulate /'ɪnsjʊleɪt, AM -sə-/**insulates, insulating, insulated.** **1** VERB To **insulate** something means to cover it or surround it in a thick layer, in order to prevent heat or sound from passing through it. *Is there any way we can insulate our home from the noise?* **2** VERB If a person or group **is insulated from** harmful things, they are protected from them. *The country was insulated from the worst effects of the recession.* **3** VERB If a piece of equipment **is insulated**, it is covered with rubber or plastic to prevent electricity passing through it and giving the person using it an electric shock.

insulation /ˌɪnsjʊ'leɪʃən, AM -sə-/. N-UNCOUNT **Insulation** is a thick layer of material used to insulate something.

insulin /'ɪnsjʊlɪn, AM -sə-/. N-UNCOUNT **Insulin** is a substance that most people produce naturally in their body and which controls the level of sugar in their blood.

insult, insults, insulting, insulted. **1** VERB/ɪn'sʌlt/ If you **insult** someone, you offend them by being rude to them. *I did not mean to insult you.* ♦ **insulted** ADJ *I was deeply insulted.* ♦ **insulting** ADJ *...an insulting remark.* **2** N-COUNT/'ɪnsʌlt/ An **insult** is a rude remark or action which offends someone. *They shouted insults at each other.* **3** PHRASE If an action or event **adds insult to injury**, it makes an unfair or unacceptable situation even worse.

⭐ **insurance** /ɪnˈʃʊərəns/. **1** N-UNCOUNT **Insurance** is an arrangement in which you pay money regularly to a company, and they pay money to you if something unpleasant happens to you, for example if your property is stolen. *...health insurance.* **2** N-SING If you do something as an **insurance against** something unpleasant, you do it in order to protect yourself in case the unpleasant thing happens. *Farmers grow a mixture of crops as an insurance against crop failure.*

insure /ɪnˈʃʊə/ **insures, insuring, insured.** VERB If you **insure yourself** or your property, you pay money to an insurance company so that if you become ill or if your property is stolen, the company will pay you a sum of money. *Women can now insure themselves against contracting breast cancer.* ● See also **ensure**.

insurer /ɪnˈʃʊərə/ **insurers.** N-COUNT An **insurer** is a company that sells insurance.

insurgency /ɪnˈsɜːdʒənsi/ **insurgencies.** N-VAR An **insurgency** is an attempt by a group of people to remove the government of their country by force.

insurrection /ˌɪnsəˈrekʃən/ **insurrections.** N-VAR An **insurrection** is violent action taken by a group of people against the rulers of their country. *...an armed insurrection.*

intact /ɪnˈtækt/. ADJ Something that is **intact** is complete and has not been damaged or spoilt. *The roof was still intact... His reputation remained intact.*

intake /ˈɪnteɪk/ **intakes.** **1** N-COUNT Your **intake** of food, drink, or air is the amount that you eat, drink, or breathe in, or the process of taking it into your body. *Cut down your alcohol intake.* **2** N-COUNT The people who are accepted into an institution or organization at a particular time are referred to as a particular **intake**. *...one of this year's intake of students.*

intangible /ɪnˈtændʒɪbəl/ **intangibles.** ADJ & N-PLURAL A quality or idea that is **intangible** is hard to define or explain. You can refer to qualities or ideas like this as **intangibles**. *The culture is shaped by many factors, some of them intangible.*

integral /ˈɪntɪgrəl/. ADJ If something is an **integral** part of another thing, it is an essential part of it. *The nude scenes were integral to the story.*

⭐ **integrate** /ˈɪntɪgreɪt/ **integrates, integrating, integrated.** **1** VERB If people **integrate into** a social group, or if they **are integrated into** it, they join it and become a part of it. *...attempts to integrate immigrants more firmly into French society.* ♦ **integrated** ADJ *...integrated schooling.* ♦ **integration** N-UNCOUNT *...the integration of disabled people into mainstream society.* **2** VERB

If you **integrate** things, you combine them so that they are closely linked or so that they form one thing. *The two airlines will integrate their services.* ♦ **integrated** ADJ *...integrated computer systems.*

integrity /ɪnˈtegrɪti/. N-UNCOUNT **Integrity** is the quality of being honest and firm in your moral principles. *...a man of integrity.*

intellect /ˈɪntɪlekt/ **intellects.** **1** N-VAR **Intellect** is the ability to think and to understand ideas and information. *...good health and a lively intellect.* **2** N-VAR **Intellect** is the quality of being very intelligent or clever. *I was intrigued by him, stirred by his intellect.*

⭐ **intellectual** /ˌɪntɪˈlektʃuəl/ **intellectuals.** **1** ADJ BEFORE N **Intellectual** means involving a person's ability to think and to understand ideas and information. *...the intellectual development of children.* ♦ **intellectually** ADV *...intellectually demanding work.* **2** N-COUNT & ADJ An **intellectual** is someone who spends a lot of time studying and thinking about complicated ideas. You can say that someone like this is **intellectual**. *They were very intellectual and she found it difficult, I think, to fit in.*

⭐ **intelligence** /ɪnˈtelɪdʒəns/. **1** N-UNCOUNT Someone's **intelligence** is their ability to understand and learn things. *...a woman of exceptional intelligence.* **2** N-UNCOUNT **Intelligence** is the ability to think and understand instead of doing things by instinct. *Whales have intelligence and are capable of exercising choice.* **3** N-UNCOUNT **Intelligence** is information gathered by the government about their country's enemies. *...the intelligence services.*

⭐ **intelligent** /ɪnˈtelɪdʒənt/. **1** ADJ An **intelligent** person has the ability to think, understand, and learn things quickly and well. *...the most intelligent man I have ever met.* ♦ **intelligently** ADV *They are incapable of thinking intelligently about politics.* **2** ADJ Something that is **intelligent** has the ability to think and understand instead of doing things by instinct. *...the biggest-ever search for intelligent life elsewhere in the universe.*

intelligible /ɪnˈtelɪdʒəbəl/. ADJ Something that is **intelligible** can be understood. *The women made no intelligible response.*

⭐ **intend** /ɪnˈtend/ **intends, intending, intended.** **1** VERB If you **intend to** do something, you have decided or planned to do it. *I intend to go to university. ...the hotel in which they intended staying.* **2** VERB Something that is **intended for** a particular person or purpose, or **is intended to** have a particular effect, has been planned for that person or purpose, or planned to have that effect. *The money is intended for food and medical supplies... Her behaviour was intended to drive him away... Today's announcement was intended as a warning.*

⭐ **intense** /ɪnˈtens/. **1** ADJ Something that is **intense** is very great in strength or degree. *The*

a
b
c
d
e
f
g
h
i
j
k
l
m
n
o
p
q
r
s
t
u
v
w
x
y
z

pain was intense. ...intense heat. ♦ **intensely** ADV She is intensely irritating. ♦ **intensity** /ɪnˈtensɪti/ N-UNCOUNT ...the intensity of the work. [2] ADJ An **intense** person is very serious. ...an intense young man.

intensify /ɪnˈtensɪfaɪ/ **intensifies, intensifying, intensified.** VERB If you **intensify** something, or if it **intensifies**, it becomes greater in strength or degree. His lawyers have intensified their efforts to halt his execution.

intensive /ɪnˈtensɪv/. [1] ADJ An **intensive** activity involves the concentration of energy or people on one particular task. ...four weeks of intensive study. ♦ **intensively** ADV Wilson has worked intensively on his speed and strength. [2] ADJ **Intensive** farming involves producing as many crops or animals as possible from your land, usually with the aid of chemicals.

in,tensive 'care. N-UNCOUNT If someone is in **intensive care**, they are in hospital being cared for very thoroughly and watched very closely because they are seriously ill.

intent /ɪnˈtent/ **intents.** [1] N-UNCOUNT A person's **intent** is their intention to do something. [FORMAL] ...his intent to appeal against the decision. ...this strong statement of intent on arms control. [2] ADJ If someone is **intent**, they appear to be concentrating very seriously on what they are doing or feeling. [WRITTEN] Amy watched the child's intent face. ♦ **intently** ADV She stared intently at the TV screen. [3] ADJ AFTER LINK-V If you are **intent on** doing something, you are determined to do it. He is intent on repeating his victory. [4] PHRASE You say **to all intents and purposes** to suggest that a situation is not exactly as you describe it but the effect is the same as if it were. To all intents and purposes he was my father.

⭐ **intention** /ɪnˈtenʃən/ **intentions.** N-VAR An **intention** is an idea or plan of what you are going to do. ...his intention to return to Berlin... I have no intention of resigning.

intentional /ɪnˈtenʃənəl/. ADJ Something that is **intentional** is deliberate. The kick was intentional. ♦ **intentionally** ADV I've never intentionally hurt anyone.

interact /ˌɪntəˈrækt/ **interacts, interacting, interacted.** VERB The way that two people or things **interact** is the way that they communicate or work in relation to each other. Addictive substances interact with the chemicals in the brain. ♦ **interaction, interactions** N-VAR ...studies on parent-child interaction.

interactive /ˌɪntəˈræktɪv/. ADJ An **interactive** computer program or television system is one which allows direct communication between the user and the machine.

intercept /ˌɪntəˈsept/ **intercepts, intercepting, intercepted.** VERB If you **intercept** someone or something that is travelling from one place to another, you stop them. He asked why the bombers had not been intercepted by Army patrols. ♦ **interception, interceptions** N-VAR ...the

interception of a ship off the west coast of Scotland.

interchange, interchanges; verb /ˌɪntəˈtʃeɪndʒ/, noun /ˈɪntətʃeɪndʒ/. VERB & N-VAR If you **interchange** things, or if there is an **interchange of** things, you exchange one thing for the other. Your task is to interchange words so that the sentence makes sense.

interchangeable /ˌɪntəˈtʃeɪndʒəbəl/. ADJ Things that are **interchangeable** can be exchanged with each other without making any difference. ♦ **interchangeably** ADV ...two different words used interchangeably to describe one action.

interconnect /ˌɪntəkəˈnekt/ **interconnects, interconnecting, interconnected.** VERB Things that **interconnect** or that **are interconnected** are connected to or with each other. Virtually all urban problems are really interconnected with each other. ...interconnecting rooms. ♦ **interconnection, interconnections** N-VAR ...the variety of interconnections between music and other arts.

intercontinental /ˌɪntəkɒntɪˈnentəl/. ADJ BEFORE N **Intercontinental** is used to describe something that exists or happens between continents. ...intercontinental flights.

intercourse /ˈɪntəkɔːs/. N-UNCOUNT If people have **intercourse**, they have sex. [FORMAL]

interdependent /ˌɪntədɪˈpendənt/. ADJ People or things that are **interdependent** all depend on each other. Most economies today are highly interdependent. ♦ **interdependence** N-UNCOUNT ...the interdependence of the world's economies.

⭐ **interest** /ˈɪntrəst, -tərest/ **interests, interesting, interested.** [1] N-SING & N-UNCOUNT If you have an **interest** in something, you like it and want to learn or hear more about it. He showed a great interest in animals... She'd liked him at first, but soon lost interest. [2] N-COUNT Your **interests** are the things that you enjoy doing. His interests include cooking and photography. [3] VERB If something **interests** you, you want to learn more about it or to continue doing it. These are the stories that interest me. [4] N-COUNT If you have an **interest** in something being done, you want it to be done because you will benefit from it. The US clearly has an interest in promoting free trade. [5] N-COUNT A person or organization that has **interests** in a company owns shares in this company. Her other business interests include a theme park in Scandinavia. [6] N-UNCOUNT **Interest** is extra money that you receive if you have invested a sum of money, or extra money that you pay if you have borrowed money. Does your current account pay interest? [7] See also **self-interest, vested interest**.

PHRASES • Something that is **in the interests of** a person or group will benefit them in some way. ...a compromise that would be in the interests of the British fishing industry. • If you do something **in the interests of** a particular result or situation, you do it in order to achieve that result or maintain that situation. ...*a call for all businessmen to work together in the interests of national stability.*

⭐ **interested** /'ɪntrestɪd/. **1** ADJ AFTER LINK-V If you are **interested in** something, you think it is important and you are keen to learn more about it or spend time doing it. *I wasn't particularly interested in physics... I'd be interested to know what people's views were.* **2** ADJ BEFORE N An **interested** party or group of people is affected by or involved in a particular event or situation.

⭐ **interesting** /'ɪntrestɪŋ/. ADJ If you find something **interesting**, it attracts you or holds your attention. *It was interesting to be in a different environment. ...a very interesting book.* ♦ **interestingly** ADV *Interestingly enough, a few weeks later, Benjamin remarried.*

interface /'ɪntəfeɪs/ **interfaces.** N-COUNT The **interface** of a piece of computer software is the way it appears on screen and how easy it is to operate. [COMPUTING] ...*the development of better user interfaces.*

interfere /ˌɪntə'fɪə/ **interferes, interfering, interfered.** **1** VERB If someone **interferes** in a situation, they get involved in it although it does not concern them and their involvement is not wanted. *I wish everyone would stop interfering. ...interfering neighbours.* **2** VERB If something **interferes with** a situation, process, or activity, it has a damaging effect on it. *Drug problems frequently interfered with his work.*

interference /ˌɪntə'fɪərəns/. **1** N-UNCOUNT **Interference** is the act of interfering in something. ...*interference in the republic's internal affairs.* **2** N-UNCOUNT When there is **interference**, a radio signal is affected by other radio waves so that it cannot be received properly.

⭐ **interim** /'ɪntərɪm/. **1** ADJ BEFORE N **Interim** describes things that are intended to be used until something permanent is arranged or established. ...*an interim government. ...an interim report.* **2** PHRASE **In the interim** means until a particular thing happens.

⭐ **interior** /ɪn'tɪəriə/ **interiors.** **1** N-COUNT The **interior** of something is the inside or central part of it. ...*the boat's interior. ...the interior walls.* **2** N-SING **The interior** of a country or continent is the central area of it. ...*a 5-day hike into the interior.*

interlude /'ɪntəluːd/ **interludes.** N-COUNT An **interlude** is a short period of time during which an activity or event stops. ...*a happy interlude in the Kents' life.*

intermediary /ˌɪntə'miːdiəri/ **intermediaries.** N-COUNT An **intermediary** is a person who passes messages between two people or groups.

intermediate /ˌɪntə'miːdiət/. **1** ADJ An **intermediate** stage or level is one that occurs between two other stages or levels. **2** ADJ **Intermediate** students are no longer beginners, but are not yet advanced.

interminable /ɪn'tɜːmɪnəbəl/. ADJ If you describe something as **interminable**, you think it lasts too long and wish it would stop. ...*an interminable wait of six hours.* ♦ **interminably** ADV *The programme droned interminably on.*

intermittent /ˌɪntə'mɪtənt/. ADJ Something that is **intermittent** happens occasionally rather than continuously. ...*three hours of intermittent rain.* ♦ **intermittently** ADV *The talks went on intermittently for years.*

intern /ɪn'tɜːn/ **interns, interning, interned.** VERB If someone **is interned**, they are put in prison for political reasons. *He was interned as an enemy alien.*

⭐ **internal** /ɪn'tɜːnəl/. **1** ADJ BEFORE N You use **internal** to describe things that exist or happen inside a place or organization. *The country stepped up internal security. ...the internal mail box.* **2** ADJ BEFORE N **Internal** is used to describe things that exist or happen inside a particular person, object, or place. *The internal bleeding had been massive.* ♦ **internally** ADV *The herb has gentle calming effects when taken internally.*

⭐ **international** /ˌɪntə'næʃənəl/. ADJ **International** means between or involving different countries. ...*an international embargo on arms supplies to Iraq.* ♦ **internationally** ADV ...*internationally recognised certificates.*

Internet /'ɪntənet/. N-PROPER **The Internet** is the worldwide network of computer links which allows computer users to connect with computers all over the world. [COMPUTING]

'**Internet** ˌcafé, **Internet cafés.** N-COUNT An **Internet café** is a café with computers where people can pay to use the Internet. [COMPUTING]

interpersonal /ˌɪntə'pɜːsənəl/. ADJ BEFORE N **Interpersonal** means relating to relationships between people. ...*interpersonal relationships.*

interpret /ɪn'tɜːprɪt/ **interprets, interpreting, interpreted.** **1** VERB If you **interpret** something in a particular way, you decide that this is its meaning or significance. *The judge has to interpret the law as it's been passed.* **2** VERB If you **interpret** what someone is saying, you translate it immediately into another language. *The chambermaid spoke little English, so her husband came with her to interpret.* ♦ **interpreter, interpreters** N-COUNT *Interpreters and translators are employed by local authorities.*

interpretation /ɪnˌtɜːprɪ'teɪʃən/ **interpretations.** **1** N-VAR An **interpretation** of something is an opinion of what it means. *The opposition party put a different interpretation on the figures.* **2** N-VAR A performer's **interpretation** of a piece of music or a dance is the particular way in which they choose to perform it.

interrogate /ɪn'terəgeɪt/ **interrogates, interrogating, interrogated.** VERB If someone, especially a police officer, **interrogates** someone, they question him or her for a long time, in order to get information from them. ♦ **interrogation,**

⭐ Bank of English® frequent word   For a full explanation of all grammatical labels, see pages vii-x

a b c d e f g h i j k l m n o p q r s t u v w x y z

A
B
C
D
E
F
G
H
I
J
K
L
M
N
O
P
Q
R
S
T
U
V
W
X
Y
Z

interrogations N-VAR *Two men have died under interrogation.*

interrogative /ˌɪntəˈrɒɡətɪv/. N-SING A clause that is in **the interrogative** is in the form of a question.

interrupt /ˌɪntəˈrʌpt/ **interrupts, interrupting, interrupted.** [1] VERB If you **interrupt** someone who is speaking, you say or do something that causes them to stop. *They interrupted me every time I tried to say something... Turkin tapped him on the shoulder. 'Sorry to interrupt, Colonel.'* ♦ **interruption, interruptions** N-VAR *The sudden interruption stopped Beryl in mid-flow. ...the constant interruptions of delivery men.* [2] VERB If someone or something **interrupts** a process or activity, they stop it for a period of time. *He has rightly interrupted his holiday in Spain.* ♦ **interruption** N-VAR *...interruptions in the supply of food.*

intersection /ˌɪntəˈsekʃən/ **intersections.** N-COUNT An **intersection** is a place where roads cross each other. *...a busy highway intersection.*

interspersed /ˌɪntəˈspɜːst/. ADJ If one group of things are **interspersed with** or **among** another, the second things occur between or among the first things. *...a series of bursts of gunfire, interspersed with single shots.*

interstate /ˈɪntəsteɪt/ **interstates.** [1] ADJ BEFORE N **Interstate** means between states, especially the states of the United States. *The action prohibits interstate movement of certain fruits.* [2] N-COUNT In the US, an **interstate** is a major road linking states.

interval /ˈɪntəvəl/ **intervals.** [1] N-COUNT The **interval** between two events or dates is the period of time between them. *There was a long interval of silence.* [2] N-COUNT An **interval** during a play, concert, or game is a short break between two of the parts.

PHRASES ● If something happens **at intervals**, it happens several times with gaps or pauses in between. ● If things are placed **at** particular **intervals**, there are spaces of a particular size between them. *Several barriers marked the road at intervals of about a mile.*

intervene /ˌɪntəˈviːn/ **intervenes, intervening, intervened.** VERB If you **intervene in** a situation, you become involved in it and try to change it. *The Government is doing nothing to intervene in the crisis... The situation calmed down when police intervened.* ♦ **intervention** /ˌɪntəˈvenʃən/ **interventions** N-VAR *...its intervention in the internal affairs of many countries.*

intervening /ˌɪntəˈviːnɪŋ/. [1] ADJ BEFORE N An **intervening** period of time is one which separates two events or points in time. *I had spent the intervening time in London.* [2] ADJ BEFORE N An **intervening** object or area comes between two other objects or areas.

⭐ **interview** /ˈɪntəvjuː/ **interviews, interviewing, interviewed.** [1] VERB & N-COUNT When an employer **interviews** you, or when you go for an

interview, he or she asks you questions in order to find out whether you are suitable for a job. *He was interviewed for a management job. ...an interview for a job as a TV researcher.* [2] VERB & N-COUNT When a journalist **interviews** someone such as a famous person, they ask them a series of questions. This type of discussion is also called an **interview**. *...an interview with American Vogue fashion editor Carlyn Cerf.* ♦ **interviewer, interviewers** N-COUNT *...a wealthy figure much sought after by TV interviewers.*

interviewee /ˌɪntəvjuːˈiː/ **interviewees.** N-COUNT An **interviewee** is a person who is being interviewed.

intestine /ɪnˈtestɪn/ **intestines.** N-COUNT Your **intestines** are the tubes in your body through which food from your stomach passes. ♦ **intestinal** /ɪnˈtestɪnəl/ ADJ BEFORE N *...the intestinal wall.*

intimacy /ˈɪntɪməsi/. N-UNCOUNT When there is **intimacy** between people, they have a close relationship. *...a few precious moments of intimacy with a lover.*

intimate, intimates, intimating, intimated; adjective and noun /ˈɪntɪmət/, verb /ˈɪntɪmeɪt/. [1] ADJ If two people have an **intimate** friendship, they are very good friends. ♦ **intimately** ADV *He did not feel he had got to know them intimately.* [2] ADJ You use **intimate** to describe an occasion or the atmosphere of a place that you like because it is quiet and pleasant, and seems suitable for close conversations between friends. *...an intimate candlelit dinner for two.* [3] ADJ To be **intimate with** someone means to have a sexual relationship with them. *...their intimate moments with their boyfriends.* ♦ **intimately** ADV *Get to know yourself and your partner intimately.* [4] ADJ If you have an **intimate** knowledge of something, you know it in great detail. *...their intimate knowledge of the motor industry.* ♦ **intimately** ADV *...musicians whose work she knew intimately.* [5] VERB If you **intimate** that something is the case, you say it in an indirect way. [FORMAL] *He went on to intimate that he was indeed contemplating a shake-up of the company.*

intimidate /ɪnˈtɪmɪdeɪt/ **intimidates, intimidating, intimidated.** VERB To **intimidate** someone means to frighten them, sometimes as a deliberate way of making them do something. *...attempts to intimidate people into voting for the governing party.* ♦ **intimidated** ADJ *Women can come in here and not feel intimidated.* ♦ **intimidating** ADJ *...the intimidating atmosphere that greeted them as they took to the pitch.* ♦ **intimidation** N-UNCOUNT *...an aggressive campaign of intimidation against supporters of the prime minister.*

⭐ **into** /ˈɪntuː/.

✓ In addition to the uses shown below, **into** is used with verbs of movement, such as 'walk into', and in phrasal verbs such as 'enter into'.

1 PREP To go **into** a place or object means to go inside it. *I have no idea how he got into Iraq... He got into bed... Put them into a dish... All olives were packed into jars by hand.* **2** PREP If you bump or crash **into** something, you hit it accidentally. *The Belgian hit the kerb and smashed into the barriers.* **3** PREP If you get **into** a piece of clothing, you put it on. *She could change into a different outfit.* **4** PREP To get **into** a particular state means to start being in that state. *That caused him to get into trouble... I slid into a depression.* **5** PREP If something changes **into** something else, it then has a new form, shape, or nature. *...to turn a nasty episode into a little bit of a joke.* **6** PREP An investigation **into** a subject or event is concerned with that subject or event. *...research into Aids.* **7** PREP You use **into** with many verbs to do with persuading someone to do something. *Gerome tried to talk her into taking an apartment in Paris.* **8** PREP If something is cut or split **into** a number of pieces or sections, it is divided so that it becomes several smaller pieces or sections. *Sixteen teams are taking part, divided into four groups.*

intolerable /ɪnˈtɒlərəbəl/. ADJ If something is **intolerable**, it is so bad that no one can accept it. *This would put intolerable pressure on them.* ♦ **intolerably** ADV *...intolerably cramped conditions for the actors.*

intolerant /ɪnˈtɒlərənt/. ADJ If you describe someone as **intolerant**, you mean that they do not accept behaviour and opinions that are different from their own; used showing disapproval. *He was intolerant of both suggestions and criticisms.* ♦ **intolerance** N-UNCOUNT *...his intolerance of any opinion other than his own.*

intoxicated /ɪnˈtɒksɪkeɪtɪd/. **1** ADJ Someone who is **intoxicated** is drunk. [FORMAL] **2** ADJ If you are **intoxicated by** something, you are so excited that you find it hard to think clearly and sensibly. *They seem to have become intoxicated by their success.*

intractable /ɪnˈtræktəbəl/. **1** ADJ **Intractable** people are very difficult to influence or control. [FORMAL] *He protested, but Wright was intractable.* **2** ADJ **Intractable** problems are very difficult to deal with. [FORMAL] *A final settlement of the intractable Afghan conflict is still far off.*

intranet /ˈɪntrənet/**intranets.** N-COUNT An **intranet** is a network of computers, similar to the Internet, within a company or organization. [COMPUTING]

intransigent /ɪnˈtrænsɪdʒənt/. ADJ If you describe someone as **intransigent**, you mean that they refuse to change their behaviour or opinions; used showing disapproval. [FORMAL] *They put pressure on the Government to change its intransigent stance.* ♦ **intransigence** N-UNCOUNT *He often appeared angry and frustrated by the intransigence of both sides.*

intransitive /ɪnˈtrænsɪtɪv/. ADJ An **intransitive** verb does not have an object.

intravenous /ˌɪntrəˈviːnəs/. ADJ **Intravenous** foods or drugs are given to sick people through their veins, rather than their mouths. *...an intravenous drip.* ♦ **intravenously** ADV *Premature babies have to be fed intravenously.*

intrepid /ɪnˈtrepɪd/. ADJ An **intrepid** person acts bravely, ignoring difficulties and danger. *...an intrepid space traveller.*

intricate /ˈɪntrɪkət/. ADJ Something that is **intricate** has many small parts or details. *...intricate patterns and motifs.* ♦ **intricately** ADV *...intricately carved sculptures.* ♦ **intricacy** N-UNCOUNT *...the rich intricacy of traditional Japanese porcelain.*

intrigue, intrigues, intriguing, intrigued. **1** N-VAR /ˈɪntriːg/ **Intrigue** is the making of secret plans that are intended to harm or deceive other people. *...the plots and intrigues in the novel.* **2** VERB /ɪnˈtriːg/ If something **intrigues** you, you are fascinated by it and curious about it. *She had hesitated, even though the job intrigued her.* ♦ **intrigued** ADJ *I would be intrigued to hear others' views.*

intriguing /ɪnˈtriːgɪŋ/. ADJ If you describe someone or something as **intriguing**, you mean that they interest you and you are curious about them. *This intriguing book is both thoughtful and informative.* ♦ **intriguingly** ADV *The results are intriguingly different each time.*

intrinsic /ɪnˈtrɪnsɪk/. ADJ If something has **intrinsic** value or **intrinsic** interest, it is valuable or interesting because of its basic nature or character, and not because of its connection with other things. [FORMAL] *Diamonds have little intrinsic value.* ♦ **intrinsically** ADV *Sometimes I wonder if people are intrinsically evil.*

⭐ **introduce** /ˌɪntrəˈdjuːs, AM -ˈduːs/**introduces, introducing, introduced.** **1** VERB To **introduce** something means to cause it to enter a place or exist in a system for the first time. *The word 'Pagoda' was introduced to Europe by the 17th century Portuguese.* **2** VERB If you **introduce** someone **to** something, you cause them to learn about it or to have their first experience of it. *He introduced her to both literature and drugs.* **3** VERB If you **introduce** one person **to** another, or if you **introduce** two people, you tell them each other's names, so that they can get to know each other. *Tim, may I introduce you to my uncle's secretary?... Let me introduce myself.* **4** VERB The person who **introduces** a television or radio programme speaks at the beginning of it, and often between the different items in it, in order to explain what the programme or the items are about. *'Health Matters' is introduced by Dick Oliver.*

introduction /ˌɪntrəˈdʌkʃən/**introductions.** **1** N-UNCOUNT The **introduction** of something into a place or system is the occasion when it enters the place or exists in the system for the first time. *...the introduction of student loans.* **2** N-SING Someone's **introduction to** something is the occasion when they experience it for the first time. *His introduction to public life came as an*

a
b
c
d
e
f
g
h
i
j
k
l
m
n
o
p
q
r
s
t
u
v
w
x
y
z

office-holder in a trade union. **3** N-VAR When you make an **introduction**, you tell two people each other's names so that they can get to know each other. **4** N-COUNT The **introduction** to a book or talk comes at the beginning and tells you what the rest of the book or talk is about. **5** N-COUNT If you refer to a book as an **introduction to** a particular subject, you mean that it explains the basic facts about it.

introductory /ˌɪntrə'dʌktəri/. **1** ADJ An **introductory** remark, book, or course is intended to give you a general idea of a particular subject, often before more detailed information is given. **2** ADJ An **introductory** offer or price on a new product is something such as a free gift or a low price that is meant to attract new customers.

intrude /ɪn'truːd/ **intrudes, intruding, intruded.** VERB If you say that someone or something **is intruding into** a particular place or situation, you mean that they are not wanted or welcome there. The press has been blamed for intruding into people's personal lives... I hope I'm not intruding... Personal feelings cannot be allowed to intrude.

intruder /ɪn'truːdə/ **intruders.** N-COUNT An **intruder** is a person who enters a place without permission.

intrusion /ɪn'truːʒən/ **intrusions.** N-VAR If you describe something as an **intrusion**, you mean that it disturbs you when you are in a private place or in a private situation. I hope you don't mind this intrusion. ...intrusion into private grief.

intrusive /ɪn'truːsɪv/. ADJ Something that is **intrusive** disturbs your mood or your life in an unwelcome way. Staff are courteous but never intrusive.

intuition /ˌɪntjʊ'ɪʃən, AM -tʊ-/ **intuitions.** N-VAR Your **intuitions** are feelings you have that something is true even when you have no evidence or proof of it. Her intuition was telling her that something was wrong.

intuitive /ɪn'tjuːɪtɪv, AM -'tuː-/. ADJ If you have an **intuitive** idea or feeling about something, you feel that it is true although you have no evidence or proof of it. ◆ **intuitively** ADV He seemed to know intuitively that I must be missing my mother.

inundate /'ɪnʌndeɪt/ **inundates, inundating, inundated.** VERB If you **are inundated with** letters or demands, you receive so many that you cannot deal with them all. They have inundated me with fan letters.

invade /ɪn'veɪd/ **invades, invading, invaded.** **1** VERB To **invade** a country means to enter it by force with an army. ◆ **invader, invaders** N-COUNT ...action against a foreign invader. **2** VERB If you say that people or animals **invade** a place, you mean that they enter it in large numbers, often in a way that is unpleasant or difficult to deal with. Every so often the kitchen would be invaded by ants.

invalid, invalids. **1** N-COUNT /'ɪnvəlɪd/ An **invalid** is someone who is very ill or disabled and needs to be cared for by someone else. **2** ADJ /ɪn'vælɪd/

If an action, procedure, or document is **invalid**, it cannot be accepted, because it breaks the law or some official rule. The trial was stopped and the results declared invalid. **3** ADJ An **invalid** argument or conclusion is wrong because it is based on a mistake.

invaluable /ɪn'væljəbəl/. ADJ If you describe something as **invaluable**, you mean that it is extremely useful. I was able to gain invaluable experience over that year.

invariably /ɪn'veəriəbli/. ADV If something **invariably** happens or is **invariably** true, it always happens or is always true. They almost invariably get it wrong.

★ **invasion** /ɪn'veɪʒən/ **invasions.** **1** N-VAR If there is an **invasion** of a country, a foreign army enters it by force. ...the Roman invasion of Britain. **2** N-UNCOUNT If you refer to the arrival of a large number of people or things as an **invasion**, you are emphasizing that they are unpleasant or difficult to deal with. ...this year's annual invasion of flies. **3** N-VAR If you describe an action as an **invasion**, you disapprove of it because it affects someone or something in a way that is not desirable. Is reading a child's diary always a gross invasion of privacy?

invasive /ɪn'veɪsɪv/. ADJ You use **invasive** to describe something undesirable which spreads very quickly and which is very difficult to stop from spreading. They found invasive cancer during a routine examination.

invent /ɪn'vent/ **invents, inventing, invented.** **1** VERB If you **invent** something, you are the first person to think of it or make it. He invented the first electric clock. ◆ **inventor, inventors** N-COUNT ...Alexander Graham Bell, the inventor of the telephone. **2** VERB If you **invent** a story or excuse, you try to persuade people that it is true when it is not. I must invent something I can tell my mother.

invention /ɪn'venʃən/ **inventions.** **1** N-COUNT An **invention** is a machine or system that has been invented by someone. The spinning wheel was a Chinese invention. **2** N-VAR If you refer to someone's account of something as an **invention**, you mean that it is not true and that they have made it up. The story was certainly a favourite one, but it was undoubtedly pure invention. **3** N-UNCOUNT **Invention** is the act of inventing something that has never been made or used before. ...the invention of the wheel.

inventive /ɪn'ventɪv/. ADJ An **inventive** person is good at inventing things or has clever and original ideas. She inspired me to be more inventive with my own cooking.
◆ **inventiveness** N-UNCOUNT He has surprised us before with his inventiveness.

inventory /'ɪnvəntri, AM -tɔːri/ **inventories.** **1** N-COUNT An **inventory** is a written list of all the objects in a place. **2** N-COUNT An **inventory** is a supply or stock of something. [AMERICAN]

invert /ɪnˈvɜːt/ **inverts, inverting, inverted.** [1] VERB If you **invert** something, you turn it upside down or back to front. [FORMAL] *Invert the cake onto a cooling rack. ...a black inverted triangle.* [2] VERB If you **invert** something, you change it to its opposite. [FORMAL] *...inverted moral values.*

inˌverted ˈcommas. N-PLURAL In British English, **inverted commas** are the punctuation marks (' ') or (" ") which are used in writing to show where speech or a quotation begins and ends. The usual American term is **quotation marks.** → See Reference Page on Punctuation.

⭐ **invest** /ɪnˈvest/ **invests, investing, invested.** [1] VERB If you **invest in** something, or if you **invest** a sum of money, you use your money in a way that you hope will increase its value, for example by buying shares or property. *They intend to invest directly in shares... He wants advice on how to invest the money.* ♦ **investor, investors** N-COUNT *It is likely that investors will face losses.* [2] VERB If you **invest in** something useful, you buy it because it will help you to do something more efficiently or more cheaply. *The company has invested a six-figure sum in an electronic order-control system.* [3] VERB If you **invest** time or energy in something, you spend a lot of time or energy on something that you consider to be useful or likely to be successful. *I would rather invest time in Rebecca than in the kitchen.* [4] VERB To **invest** someone **with** rights or responsibilities means to give them those rights or responsibilities legally or officially. [FORMAL] *The constitution had invested him with certain powers.*

⭐ **investigate** /ɪnˈvestɪɡeɪt/ **investigates, investigating, investigated.** VERB If someone, especially an official, **investigates** an event or allegation, they try to find out what happened or what is the truth. *Police are still investigating how the accident happened.* ♦ **investigation, investigations** N-VAR *He is currently under investigation for corruption.*

investigative /ɪnˈvestɪɡətɪv, AM -ɡeɪt-/. ADJ **Investigative** work, especially journalism, involves investigating things. *...an investigative reporter.*

investigator /ɪnˈvestɪɡeɪtə/ **investigators.** N-COUNT An **investigator** is someone who investigates things, especially as part of their job.

⭐ **investment** /ɪnˈvesmənt/ **investments.** [1] N-UNCOUNT **Investment** is the activity of investing money. *The government must introduce tax incentives to encourage investment.* [2] N-COUNT An **investment** is an amount of money that you invest, or the thing that you invest in it. *...an average rate of return of 8% on your investments. ...people's desire to buy a house as an investment.* [3] N-COUNT If you describe something you buy as an **investment**, you mean that it will be useful, especially because it will help you to do a task more cheaply or efficiently. *A small-screen portable TV can be a good investment.*

invigorating /ɪnˈvɪɡəreɪtɪŋ/. ADJ Something that is **invigorating** makes you feel refreshed and more energetic. *...the invigorating northern air.*

invincible /ɪnˈvɪnsɪbəl/. ADJ If you describe an army or a sports team as **invincible**, you believe that they cannot be defeated. *He knocked out the seemingly invincible Mike Tyson.*

invisible /ɪnˈvɪzɪbəl/. [1] ADJ If something is **invisible**, you cannot see it, because it is hidden or because it is very small or faint. *The belt is invisible even under the thinnest garments.* ♦ **invisibly** ADV *A thin coil of smoke rose almost invisibly.* [2] ADJ If you say that a particular problem or situation is **invisible**, you are complaining that it is being ignored. *The problems of the poor are largely invisible.* ♦ **invisibility** N-UNCOUNT *...the invisibility of women and women's concerns in society.*

⭐ **invitation** /ˌɪnvɪˈteɪʃən/ **invitations.** [1] N-COUNT An **invitation** is a written or spoken request to come to an event such as a party or a meeting. *The Syrians have not yet accepted an invitation to attend.* [2] N-COUNT An **invitation** is the card or paper on which an invitation is written or printed. [3] N-SING If you believe that someone's action is likely to have a particular result, especially a bad one, you can refer to the action as an **invitation** to that result. *Don't leave your shopping on the back seat of your car – it's an open invitation to a thief.*

⭐ **invite, invites, inviting, invited.** [1] VERB /ɪnˈvaɪt/ If you **invite** someone to something such as a party or a meal, you ask them to come to it. *She invited him to her 26th birthday party... I invited her in for a coffee... Barron invited her to accompany him to the races.* [2] VERB If you **are invited to** do something, you are formally asked to do it. *Managers will be invited to apply for a management buy-out.* [3] VERB If something you say or do **invites** trouble or criticism, it makes trouble or criticism more likely. *Their refusal to compromise will inevitably invite more criticism from the UN.* [4] N-COUNT /ˈɪnvaɪt/ An **invite** is an invitation to something such as a party or a meal. [INFORMAL]

inviting /ɪnˈvaɪtɪŋ/. ADJ If you say that something is **inviting**, you mean it has qualities that attract you. *The February air was soft, cool, and inviting.* ♦ **invitingly** ADV *The waters of the tropics are invitingly clear.*

invoice /ˈɪnvɔɪs/ **invoices, invoicing, invoiced.** [1] N-COUNT An **invoice** is an official document that lists goods or services that you have received and says how much money you owe for them. [2] VERB If you **invoice** someone, you send them an invoice.

invoke /ɪnˈvəʊk/ **invokes, invoking, invoked.** [1] VERB If you **invoke** a law, you state that you are taking a particular action because that law allows or obliges you to. *The judge invoked an international law that protects refugees.* [2] VERB If you **invoke** something such as a saying or a famous person, you refer to them in order to support what you

a
b
c
d
e
f
g
h
i
j
k
l
m
n
o
p
q
r
s
t
u
v
w
x
y
z

⭐ Bank of English® frequent word — For a full explanation of all grammatical labels, see pages vii-x are saying. *Adam Smith's name is frequently invoked by the promoters of such policies.*

involuntary /ɪnˈvɒləntri/. ADJ If you make an **involuntary** movement or sound, you make it suddenly and without intending to. *Pain in my ankle caused me to give an involuntary shudder.* ♦ **involuntarily** /ˈɪnvɒləntrəli/ ADV *His left eyelid twitched involuntarily.*

⭐ **involve** /ɪnˈvɒlv/ **involves, involving, involved.** **1** VERB If an activity **involves** something, that thing is a necessary part of it. *Nicky's job as a public relations director involves spending quite a lot of time with other people.* **2** VERB If a situation or activity **involves** someone, they are taking part in it. *...a riot involving a hundred inmates.* **3** VERB If you **involve** someone **in** something, you get them to take part in it. *Before too long he started involving me in the more confidential aspects of the job.*

⭐ **involved** /ɪnˈvɒlvd/. **1** ADJ AFTER LINK-V If you are **involved in** a situation or activity, you are taking part in it or have a strong connection with it. *...an organisation for people involved in agriculture.* **2** ADJ AFTER LINK-V The things **involved** in something such as a job or system are the necessary parts of it. *Let's take a look at some of the figures involved.* **3** ADJ If a situation or activity is **involved**, it is very complicated. **4** ADJ AFTER LINK-V If one person is **involved with** another, especially someone they are not married to, they are having a close relationship. *He became romantically involved with a married woman.*

⭐ **involvement** /ɪnˈvɒlvmənt/. N-UNCOUNT Your **involvement in** something is the fact that you are taking part in it. *You have no proof of my involvement in anything... She disliked his involvement with the group.*

inward /ˈɪnwəd/. **1** ADJ BEFORE N Your **inward** thoughts or feelings are the ones that you do not express or show to other people. *I sighed with inward relief.* ♦ **inwardly** ADV *He pretended to be mildly affronted, but inwardly he was pleased.* **2** ADJ BEFORE N An **inward** movement is one towards the inside or centre of something. *...a sharp, inward breath like a gasp.*

inwards /ˈɪnwədz/.

> ✅ The form **inward** is also used. In American English, **inward** is more usual.

ADV If something moves or faces **inwards**, it moves or faces towards the inside or centre of something. *She pressed back against the door until it swung inwards.*

iodine /ˈaɪədiːn, AM -daɪn/. N-UNCOUNT **Iodine** is a dark-coloured substance often used in medicine and photography.

IP address /aɪ ˈpiː əˌdres, AM ˌædres/ **IP addresses.** N-COUNT An **IP address** is a series of numbers that identifies which particular computer or network is connected to the Internet. **IP** is an abbreviation for 'Internet Protocol'. [COMPUTING]

IQ /ˌaɪ ˈkjuː/ **IQs.** N-VAR Your **IQ** is your level of intelligence, as indicated by a special test. *His IQ is above average.*

irate /aɪˈreɪt/. ADJ If someone is **irate**, they are very angry about something. *Bob was very irate, shouting and swearing about the flight delay.*

iris /ˈaɪərɪs/ **irises. 1** N-COUNT The **iris** is the round coloured part of a person's eye. **2** N-COUNT An **iris** is a tall plant with long leaves and large purple, yellow, or white flowers.

⭐ **iron** /aɪən/ **irons, ironing, ironed. 1** N-UNCOUNT **Iron** is an element which usually takes the form of a hard, dark-grey metal. *...the huge, iron gate.* **2** ADJ BEFORE N You can use **iron** to describe the character or behaviour of someone who is very firm in their decisions and actions, or who can control their feelings well. *...a man of icy nerve and iron will.* **3** N-COUNT An **iron** is an electrical device with a flat metal base. You heat it until the base is hot, then rub it over clothes to remove creases. **4** VERB If you **iron** clothes, you remove the creases from them using an iron. *...a freshly ironed shirt.* ♦ **ironing** N-UNCOUNT *I managed to get all the ironing done.* **5** See also **cast-iron.**
▸ **iron out.** PHR-VERB If you **iron out** difficulties, you resolve them and bring them to an end.

ironic /aɪˈrɒnɪk/. **1** ADJ When you make an **ironic** remark, you say something that you do not mean, as a joke. *People used to call me Mr Popularity at high school, but they were being ironic.* ♦ **ironically** ADV *'A very good year for women!' she said ironically.* **2** ADJ An **ironic** situation is strange or amusing because it is the opposite of what you expect. *It seems ironic that it takes a recession to improve choice.*
♦ **ironically** ADV *Ironically, for a man who hated war, he would have made a superb war cameraman.*

irony /ˈaɪrəni/ **ironies. 1** N-UNCOUNT **Irony** is a form of humour which involves saying things that you do not mean. *There seemed to be no hint of irony in his voice.* **2** N-VAR The **irony** of a situation is an aspect of it which is strange or amusing, because it is just the opposite of what you expect. *The irony is this document may become more available in the US than in Britain where it was commissioned.*

irrational /ɪˈræʃənəl/. ADJ **Irrational** feelings or behaviour are not based on logical reasons or thinking. *...an irrational fear of science.*
♦ **irrationally** ADV *He is in a disturbed state of mind and could act irrationally.* ♦ **irrationality** N-UNCOUNT *His cruelty increased, as did his irrationality.*

irreconcilable /ɪˌrekənˈsaɪləbəl/. **1** ADJ If two things such as opinions or proposals are **irreconcilable**, they are so different from each other that it is not possible to have them both. [FORMAL] *These old concepts are irreconcilable with modern life.* **2** ADJ An **irreconcilable** disagreement is so serious that it cannot be settled. [FORMAL] *...an irreconcilable clash of personalities.*

irregular /ɪˈreɡjʊlə/. [1] ADJ If events or actions occur at **irregular** intervals, the periods of time between them are of different lengths. *She was taken to hospital suffering from an irregular heartbeat... He worked irregular hours.*
♦ **irregularly** ADV *Epileptic fits occur irregularly and without warning.* ♦ **irregularity** /ɪˌreɡjʊˈlærɪti/ **irregularities** N-VAR *...a dangerous irregularity in her heartbeat.* [2] ADJ Something that is **irregular** is not smooth or straight, or does not form a regular pattern. *The paint was drying in irregular patches.* ♦ **irregularly** ADV *...the irregularly shaped lake.* [3] ADJ **Irregular** behaviour is dishonest or not in accordance with the normal rules. *...the minister accused of irregular business practices.* ♦ **irregularity** N-VAR *...alleged financial irregularities.*

irrelevant /ɪˈrelɪvənt/. ADJ If you say that something is **irrelevant**, you mean that it is not important to or not connected with the present situation or discussion. *He either ignored questions or gave irrelevant answers... He said politics has become increasingly irrelevant to most Americans.*
♦ **irrelevance** N-SING *Whether the book shocks or not is an irrelevance.*

irresistible /ˌɪrɪˈzɪstɪbəl/. [1] ADJ If your wish to do something is **irresistible**, it is so powerful that you cannot prevent yourself doing it. *He experienced an irresistible urge to yawn.*
♦ **irresistibly** ADV *He found himself being irresistibly drawn to Gail's home.* [2] ADJ If you describe something or someone as **irresistible**, you mean that they are so good or attractive that you cannot stop yourself from liking them or wanting them. *What is it about Tim that you find so irresistible?* ♦ **irresistibly** ADV *She had a charm which men found irresistibly attractive.*

irrespective /ˌɪrɪˈspektɪv/. PREP If something is true or happens **irrespective of** other things, those things do not affect it. [FORMAL] *This service should be available to everybody, irrespective of whether they can afford it.*

irresponsible /ˌɪrɪˈspɒnsɪbəl/. ADJ If you describe someone as **irresponsible**, you are criticizing them because they do things without properly considering their possible consequences. *Many people have an irresponsible attitude towards marriage.* ♦ **irresponsibly** ADV *They have behaved irresponsibly.*
♦ **irresponsibility** N-UNCOUNT *She was greatly embarrassed by her son's irresponsibility.*

irreverent /ɪˈrevərənt/. ADJ If you describe someone as **irreverent**, you mean that they do not show respect for people or things that are generally respected. ♦ **irreverence** N-UNCOUNT *...his irreverence for authority.*

irreversible /ˌɪrɪˈvɜːsɪbəl/. ADJ If a change is **irreversible**, things cannot be changed back to the way they were before. *She could suffer irreversible brain damage.*

irrevocable /ɪˈrevəkəbəl/. ADJ Actions or decisions that are **irrevocable** cannot be stopped or changed. [FORMAL] *His mother's death was an irrevocable loss.* ♦ **irrevocably** ADV *My relationships with friends have been irrevocably altered.*

irrigate /ˈɪrɪɡeɪt/ **irrigates, irrigating, irrigated.** VERB To **irrigate** land means to supply it with water in order to help crops to grow. *None of the water from Lake Powell is used to irrigate the area.*
♦ **irrigation** N-UNCOUNT *...a sophisticated irrigation system.*

irritable /ˈɪrɪtəbəl/. ADJ If you are **irritable**, you are easily annoyed. *He had missed his dinner, and grew irritable.* ♦ **irritably** ADV *'Why are you whispering?' he asked irritably.* ♦ **irritability** N-UNCOUNT *She showed no sign of irritability.*

irritant /ˈɪrɪtənt/ **irritants.** [1] N-COUNT If you describe something as an **irritant**, you mean that it keeps annoying you. [FORMAL] *He said the issue was not a major irritant.* [2] N-COUNT An **irritant** is a substance which causes a part of your body to become tender, sore, or itchy. [FORMAL]

irritate /ˈɪrɪteɪt/ **irritates, irritating, irritated.** [1] VERB If something **irritates** you, it keeps annoying you. *Her high voice really irritated Maria.* ♦ **irritated** ADJ *Her teacher is getting irritated with her.* ● See note at **angry.** ♦ **irritating** ADJ *...the irritating habit of interrupting.* ♦ **irritatingly** ADV *They can be irritatingly indecisive at times.* [2] VERB If something **irritates** a part of your body, it causes it to itch or be sore. *Skin is easily irritated.*

irritation /ˌɪrɪˈteɪʃən/ **irritations.** [1] N-UNCOUNT **Irritation** is a feeling of annoyance. *He tried not to let his irritation show.* [2] N-COUNT An **irritation** is something that keeps annoying you. *He describes the tourists as an irritation.* [3] N-UNCOUNT **Irritation** in your skin or eyes is a feeling of soreness or itching there.

is /ɪz/. **Is** is the third person singular of the present tense of **be.**

★ **Islam** /ˈɪzlɑːm, AM ɪsˈlɑːm/. N-UNCOUNT **Islam** is the religion of the Muslims, which teaches that there is only one God and that Mohammed is His prophet. ♦ **Islamic** /ɪzˈlæmɪk/ ADJ *...Islamic law.*

★ **island** /ˈaɪlənd/ **islands.** N-COUNT An **island** is a piece of land that is completely surrounded by water. *...the picturesque island of Gozo... We spent a day on Caldey Island.*

islander /ˈaɪləndə/ **islanders.** N-COUNT **Islanders** are people who live on an island.

isle /aɪl/ **isles.** N-COUNT **Isle** is used in the names of some islands. *...the Isle of Man.*

isn't /ˈɪzənt/. **Isn't** is the usual spoken form of 'is not'.

isolate /ˈaɪsəleɪt/ **isolates, isolating, isolated.** VERB To **isolate** someone or something means to make them become separate from other people or things of the same kind, either physically or socially. *We can use genetic engineering techniques to isolate the gene.* ♦ **isolated** ADJ *They are finding themselves increasingly isolated within the teaching profession.* ♦ **isolation** N-UNCOUNT *...the public isolation of the Prime Minister.*

a
b
c
d
e
f
g
h
i
j
k
l
m
n
o
p
q
r
s
t
u
v
w
x
y
z

isolated /'aɪsəleɪtɪd/. [1] ADJ An **isolated** place is a long way away from large towns and is difficult to reach. *Aubrey's family's farm is very isolated.* [2] ADJ BEFORE N An **isolated** example is an example of something that is not very common. *...an isolated case of cheating.*

isolation /,aɪsə'leɪʃən/. [1] PHRASE If someone does something **in isolation**, they do it without other people being present or without their help. [2] See also **isolate**.

ISP /,aɪ es 'piː/ **ISPs**. N-COUNT An **ISP** is a company that provides Internet and e-mail services. **ISP** is an abbreviation for 'Internet service provider'. [COMPUTING]

⭐ **issue** /'ɪsjuː, 'ɪʃuː/ **issues, issuing, issued.** [1] N-COUNT An **issue** is an important subject that people are arguing about or discussing. *...the issue of human rights... Is it right for the Church to express a view on political issues?* [2] N-SING If something is **the issue**, it is the thing you consider to be the most important part of a situation or discussion. *I was earning a lot of money, but that was not the issue... She avoided the issue.* [3] N-COUNT An **issue** of a magazine or newspaper is a particular edition of it. *...the latest issue of the Lancet.* [4] VERB If someone makes a statement, they make it formally or publicly. *His kidnappers issued a second threat to kill him.* [5] VERB If you **are issued with** something, it is officially given to you. *Staff will be issued with new grey-and-yellow designer uniforms.* [6] VERB When something such as a liquid, sound, or smell **issues from** something, it comes out of that thing. [FORMAL] [7] PHRASE The question or point **at issue** is the question or point that is being argued about or discussed. *The point at issue is who controls the company.*

⭐ **it** /ɪt/

✔ **It** is used as the subject of a verb or as the object of a verb or preposition.

[1] PRON You use **it** to refer to an object, animal, or other thing that you have already been mentioning, or to a situation that you have just described. *He saw the grey Land-Rover down the by-pass. It was more than a hundred yards from him... Antonia will not be jealous, or if she is, she will not show it.* [2] PRON You use **it** before certain nouns, adjectives, and verbs to introduce your feelings or point of view about a situation. *It was nice to see Steve again... It's a pity you never got married, Sarah.* [3] PRON You use **it** in passive clauses which report a situation or event. *It has been said that stress causes cancer.* [4] PRON You use **it** to say what the time, day, or date is. → See Reference Pages on Times and Dates and Telling the Time. *It's three o'clock in the morning... It was a Monday, so she was at home.* [5] PREP You use **it** to describe the weather, the light, or the temperature. *It was very wet and windy... It's getting dark. Let's go inside.* [6] PRON You use **it** when you are telling someone who you are, or asking them who they are. *'Who is it?' he called... Hello Freddy, it's only me, Maxine.* [7] PREP When you are emphasizing or drawing attention to

something, you can put that thing immediately after **it** and a form of the verb 'be'. *It's my father they're accusing.*

italic /ɪ'tælɪk/ **italics.** N-PLURAL & ADJ **Italics** or **italic** letters are letters which slope to the right. They can be used to emphasize particular words. The examples in this dictionary are printed in italics.

itch /ɪtʃ/ **itches, itching, itched.** [1] VERB & N-COUNT If you **itch**, or if a part of your body **itches**, you have an unpleasant feeling on your skin, called an **itch**, that makes you want to scratch. *His body regularly itched from head to toe... Scratch my back – I've got an itch.* ♦ **itching** N-UNCOUNT *The itching is caused by contact with irritant material.* ♦ **itchy** ADJ *...itchy, sore eyes.* [2] VERB & N-SING If you **are itching** to do something, or if you have an **itch to** do something, you are very eager or impatient to do it. [INFORMAL] *I was itching to get involved. ...those with an itch to be rich.*

it'd /ɪtəd/. **It'd** is a spoken form of 'it had', especially when 'had' is an auxiliary. **It'd** is also a spoken form of 'it would'. *It'd just started... It'd be fun.*

⭐ **item** /'aɪtəm/ **items.** [1] N-COUNT An **item** is one of a collection or list of objects. *The most valuable item on show will be a Picasso drawing.* [2] N-COUNT An **item** is one of a list of things for someone to do, deal with, or talk about. *The other item on the agenda is the tour.*

itinerary /aɪ'tɪnərəri, AM -eri/ **itineraries.** N-COUNT An **itinerary** is a plan of a journey, including the route and the places that will be visited. *The next place on our itinerary was Silistra.*

it'll /ɪtəl/. **It'll** is a spoken form of 'it will'. *It'll be nice to meet her.*

⭐ **its** /ɪts/. DET You use **its** to indicate that something belongs or relates to a thing, place, or animal that has just been mentioned or whose identity is known. *The British Labor Party concludes its annual conference today.*

USAGE Do not confuse **its** and **it's**. **Its** means 'belonging to it'. **It's** is short for 'it is' or 'it has'. *The horse raised its head... It's hot in here... It's stopped raining.*

it's /ɪts/. **It's** is a spoken form of 'it is' or 'it has', especially when 'has' is an auxiliary verb.

⭐ **itself** /ɪt'self/. [1] PRON **Itself** is used as the object of a verb or preposition when it refers to something that is the same thing as the subject of the verb. *The body rebuilds itself while we sleep... The back part of the chair bends double and folds into itself.* [2] PRON You use **itself** to emphasize the thing you are referring to. *I think life itself is a learning process.* [3] PRON If you say that someone is, for example, politeness **itself** or kindness **itself**, you are emphasizing they are extremely polite or extremely kind.

I've /aɪv/. **I've** is the usual spoken form of 'I have', especially when 'have' is an auxiliary verb. *I think I've got a stomach ulcer.*

IVF /ˌaɪ viː 'ef/. N-UNCOUNT **IVF** is a method of helping a woman to have a baby by fertilizing an egg outside her body. **IVF** is an abbreviation for 'in vitro fertilization'.

ivory /'aɪvəri/. N-UNCOUNT **Ivory** is a valuable type of bone, which forms the tusks of an elephant. ...*intricate ivory carvings.*

ivy /'aɪvi/. N-UNCOUNT **Ivy** is an evergreen plant that grows up walls or along the ground.

J j

jab /dʒæb/ **jabs, jabbing, jabbed.** ☐ VERB If you **jab** something, you push it with a quick sudden movement. *A needle was jabbed into the baby's arm... He jabbed at me with his forefinger.* ☐ N-COUNT A **jab** is an injection to prevent illness. [INFORMAL, BRITISH]

jack /dʒæk/ **jacks, jacking, jacked.** ☐ N-COUNT A **jack** is a device for lifting a heavy object such as a car off the ground. ☐ N-COUNT A **jack** is a playing card whose value is between a ten and a queen. ▸**jack up.** PHR-VERB If you say that someone or something **jacks up** a price or amount, you mean the price or amount rises to an unreasonable level. [INFORMAL] *Inflation has jacked up the rate of unemployment.*

⭐ **jacket** /'dʒækɪt/ **jackets.** ☐ N-COUNT A **jacket** is a short coat. → See picture on page 820. ● See also **lifejacket.** ☐ N-COUNT The **jacket** of a book is the paper cover that protects it. ☐ N-COUNT In American English, the **jacket** of a record is the cover in which it is kept. The usual British word is **sleeve.**

jackpot /'dʒækpɒt/ **jackpots.** N-COUNT A **jackpot** is a large sum of money which is the most valuable prize in a game or lottery.

Jacuzzi /dʒə'kuːzi/ **Jacuzzis.** N-COUNT A **Jacuzzi** is a large round bath which is fitted with a special device that makes the water bubble. **Jacuzzi** is a trademark.

jade /dʒeɪd/. N-UNCOUNT **Jade** is a hard green type of stone used for making jewellery and ornaments.

jaded /'dʒeɪdɪd/. ADJ If you are **jaded**, you have no enthusiasm because you are tired and bored.

jagged /'dʒægɪd/. ADJ Something that is **jagged** has a rough uneven shape or edge with lots of sharp points. → See picture on page 526. ...*a piece of iron with jagged edges.*

⭐ **jail** /dʒeɪl/ **jails, jailing, jailed.** ☐ N-VAR A **jail** is a place where criminals are kept in order to punish them. *He served six months in jail for theft.* ☐ VERB If someone **is jailed**, they are put in jail.

jam /dʒæm/ **jams, jamming, jammed.** ☐ N-VAR **Jam** is a food that you spread on bread, made by cooking fruit with a large amount of sugar. The usual American word is **jelly.** ☐ VERB If you **jam** something somewhere, you push it there roughly. *Pete jammed his hands into his pockets.* ☐ VERB If something **jams**, or if you **jam** it, it becomes fixed in one position and cannot move freely or work properly. *The second time he fired, his gun jammed... A rope jammed the boat's*

propeller. ☐ VERB To **jam** a radio or electronic signal means to interfere with it and prevent it from being received or heard clearly.
♦ **jamming** N-UNCOUNT *The plane is used for electronic jamming and radar detection.* ☐ VERB If a lot of people **jam** a place, or if they **jam into** it, they are packed tightly together and can hardly move. *Thousands of people jammed the streets... They jammed into buses provided by the Red Cross.*
♦ **jammed** ADJ *The stadium was jammed.* ☐ N-COUNT If there is a **jam** on a road, there are so many vehicles there that they cannot move. ☐ N-SING If you are **in a jam**, you are in a very difficult situation. [INFORMAL]

jangle /'dʒæŋgəl/ **jangles, jangling, jangled.** VERB & N-COUNT If metal objects **jangle**, or if they **are jangled**, they strike against each other and make an unpleasant ringing noise, called a **jangle.** ...*her jangling bracelets.*

janitor /'dʒænɪtə/ **janitors.** N-COUNT A **janitor** is a person whose job is to look after a building. [AMERICAN]

⭐ **January** /'dʒænjəri, AM -jueri/. N-UNCOUNT **January** is the first month of the year in the Western calendar. → See Reference Page on Times and Dates.

jar /dʒɑː/ **jars, jarring, jarred.** ☐ N-COUNT A **jar** is a glass container with a lid, used for storing food. ...*two jars of filter coffee.* ☐ VERB If something **jars on** you, you find it unpleasant or shocking. *Sometimes a light remark jarred on her father.*
♦ **jarring** ADJ *Dore's comments strike a jarring note.* ☐ VERB If an object **jars**, or if something **jars** it, the object moves with a fairly hard shaking movement. *The impact jarred his arm.*

jargon /'dʒɑːgən/. N-UNCOUNT **Jargon** consists of words and expressions that are used in special or technical ways by particular groups of people, often making the language difficult to understand. ...*600,000 C2 males (marketing jargon for skilled manual workers).*

jaunty /'dʒɔːnti/ **jauntier, jauntiest.** ADJ If you describe someone or something as **jaunty**, you mean that they are full of confidence and energy. *Tremain's novel is altogether jauntier.* ♦ **jauntily** ADV *He walked jauntily into the cafe.*

javelin /'dʒævlɪn/ **javelins.** ☐ N-COUNT A **javelin** is a long spear that is thrown in sports competitions. ☐ N-SING You can refer to the competition in which the javelin is thrown as **the javelin.**

jaw /dʒɔː/ **jaws.** ☐ N-COUNT Your **jaw** is the part of your face below your mouth. → See picture on page 823. **2** N-COUNT A person's or animal's **jaws** or **jawbones** are the two bones in their head which their teeth are attached to.

★ **jazz** /dʒæz/. N-UNCOUNT **Jazz** is a style of music invented by black American musicians in the early part of the twentieth century. It has very strong rhythms and the musicians often improvise.

jealous /'dʒeləs/. **1** ADJ If someone is **jealous**, they feel angry or bitter because they think that another person is trying to take a lover, friend, or possession away from them. *She got insanely jealous and there was a terrible fight.* ♦ **jealously** ADV *The formula is jealously guarded.* **2** ADJ If you are **jealous of** another person's possessions or qualities, you feel angry or bitter because you do not have them. *You're jealous because the record company rejected your idea... She was jealous of his wealth.* ♦ **jealously** ADV *Gloria eyed them jealously.*

jealousy /'dʒeləsi/ **jealousies.** N-VAR **Jealousy** is the feeling of anger or bitterness which someone has when they think that another person is trying to take a lover, friend, or possession away from them, or when they wish that they could have the qualities or possessions that another person has. *We all know the sharp stab of jealousy as an old girlfriend comes back into view... Her beauty causes envy and jealousy.*

jeans /dʒiːnz/. N-PLURAL **Jeans** are casual trousers that are usually made of strong blue denim. You can also say **a pair of jeans**. → See picture on page 819.

Jeep /dʒiːp/ **Jeeps.** N-COUNT A **Jeep** is a small four-wheeled vehicle that can travel over rough ground. **Jeep** is a trademark. → See picture on page 834.

jeer /dʒɪə/ **jeers, jeering, jeered. 1** VERB If people **jeer at** someone, they show that they do not respect them by saying rude and insulting things to them. *His motorcade was jeered by angry residents... Marchers jeered at white passers-by.* ♦ **jeering** N-UNCOUNT *There was constant jeering and interruption from the floor.* **2** N-COUNT **Jeers** are the rude and insulting things which people shout in order to show that they do not respect someone.

jell /dʒel/. See **gel**.

jelly /'dʒeli/ **jellies. 1** N-VAR **Jelly** is a transparent food made from gelatine, fruit juice, and sugar, which is eaten as a dessert. [BRITISH] **2** N-VAR **Jelly** is a food that you spread on bread, made by cooking fruit with a large amount of sugar. The British word is **jam**.

jeopardize (BRIT also **jeopardise**) /'dʒepədaɪz/ **jeopardizes, jeopardizing, jeopardized.** VERB If someone or something **jeopardizes** a situation or activity, they do something that may destroy it or cause it to fail. *The talks may still be jeopardized by disputes.*

jeopardy /'dʒepədi/. PHRASE If someone or something is **in jeopardy**, they are in a

dangerous situation. *A series of setbacks have put the whole project in jeopardy.*

jerk /dʒɜːk/ **jerks, jerking, jerked.** VERB & N-COUNT If you **jerk** something or someone, or if they **jerk** in a particular direction, they move a short distance very suddenly and quickly. A **jerk** is a short sudden movement. *...jerking his head in my direction... The car jerked to a halt... He indicated the bedroom with a jerk of his head.*

jerky /'dʒɜːki/ **jerkier, jerkiest.** ADJ **Jerky** movements are very sudden and abrupt and do not flow smoothly. *Mr Griffin made a jerky gesture.* ♦ **jerkily** ADV *... he moved jerkily towards the car.*

★ **jersey** /'dʒɜːzi/ **jerseys. 1** N-COUNT A **jersey** is a knitted piece of clothing that covers the upper part of your body and your arms. [DATED] **2** N-UNCOUNT **Jersey** is a knitted fabric used especially to make women's clothing. *... a black jersey top.*

Jesus /'dʒiːzəs/. N-PROPER **Jesus** or **Jesus Christ** is the name of the man who Christians believe was the son of God, and whose teachings are the basis of Christianity.

★ **jet** /dʒet/ **jets, jetting, jetted. 1** N-COUNT A **jet** is an aeroplane that is powered by jet engines. **2** VERB If you **jet** somewhere, you travel there in a fast aeroplane. *Val will be jetting off on a two-week holiday.* **3** N-COUNT A **jet** of liquid or gas is a strong, fast, thin stream of it. *...a jet of water.*

,**jet 'engine, jet engines.** N-COUNT A **jet engine** works by pushing hot air and gases out at the back.

'**jet lag** (also **jetlag**). N-UNCOUNT If you are suffering from **jet lag**, you feel tired and slightly confused after a long journey by aeroplane.

'**jet ski** (also **jet-ski**), **jet skis.** N-COUNT A **jet ski** is a small machine like a motorcycle that is powered by a jet engine and can travel on the surface of water. **Jet ski** is a trademark.

jettison /'dʒetɪsən/ **jettisons, jettisoning, jettisoned.** VERB If someone **jettisons** something that is not needed, they throw it away or get rid of it. *The crew jettisoned excess fuel... The Government seems to have jettisoned the plan.*

jetty /'dʒeti/ **jetties.** N-COUNT A **jetty** is a wide stone wall or wooden platform where boats stop to let people get on and off, or to load or unload goods.

★ **Jew** /dʒuː/ **Jews.** N-COUNT A **Jew** is a person who believes in and practises the religion of Judaism.

jewel /'dʒuːəl/ **jewels.** N-COUNT A **jewel** is a precious stone used to decorate valuable things such as rings or necklaces. *...precious jewels.*

jeweller (AM **jeweler**) /'dʒuːələ/ **jewellers. 1** N-COUNT A **jeweller** is a person who makes, sells, and repairs jewellery and watches. **2** N-COUNT A **jeweller** or a **jeweller's** is a shop where jewellery and watches are made, sold, and repaired.

jewellery (AM **jewelry**) /'dʒuːəlri/. N-UNCOUNT **Jewellery** consists of ornaments that people wear such as rings and bracelets.

a

Jewish /ˈdʒuːɪʃ/. ADJ **Jewish** means belonging or relating to the religion of Judaism or to Jews. ...the Jewish festival of the Passover.

jibe (also **gibe**) /dʒaɪb/ **jibes, jibing, jibed.** VERB & N-COUNT If someone **jibes**, they say something rude and insulting, called a **jibe**, which is intended to make another person look foolish. [WRITTEN] 'No doubt he'll give me the chance to fight him again,' he jibed. ...a cheap jibe about his loss of hair.

jig /dʒɪg/ **jigs, jigging, jigged.** [1] N-COUNT A **jig** is a lively folk dance. [2] VERB To **jig** means to dance or move energetically.

jigsaw /ˈdʒɪgsɔː/ **jigsaws.** N-COUNT A **jigsaw** or **jigsaw puzzle** is a picture on cardboard or wood that has been cut up into odd shapes and which has to be put back together again.

jingle /ˈdʒɪŋgəl/ **jingles, jingling, jingled.** [1] VERB When something **jingles**, or when you **jingle** it, it makes a gentle ringing noise, like small bells. Brian put his hands in his pockets and jingled some change. [2] N-COUNT A **jingle** is a short and simple tune, often with words, used to advertise a product on radio or television.

jitters /ˈdʒɪtəz/. N-PLURAL If someone has **the jitters**, they are very nervous or uncertain about something. [INFORMAL] He cut interest rates in December to calm the jitters of investors.

jittery /ˈdʒɪtəri/. ADJ If someone is **jittery**, they are very nervous or uncertain about something. [INFORMAL] International investors have become jittery about the country's economy.

job /dʒɒb/ **jobs.** [1] N-COUNT A **job** is the work that someone does to earn money. Once I'm in America I can get a job... Thousands have lost their jobs. [2] N-COUNT A **job** is a particular task. He was given the job of tending the fire... Save major painting jobs for the spring or summer. [3] N-COUNT The **job** of a particular person or thing is their duty or function. Their main job is to preserve health rather than treat illness. [4] N-SING If you say, for example, that someone has done a good **job** or an excellent **job** of something, you mean that they have done it well. You could make a better job of running a restaurant.

jobless /ˈdʒɒbləs/. ADJ Someone who is **jobless** does not have a job, but would like one.

'job ,satisfaction. N-UNCOUNT **Job satisfaction** is the pleasure that you get from doing your job.

'job share, job shares, job sharing, job shared. VERB & N-COUNT If two people **job share**, or if they do a **job share**, they share the same job by working part-time, for example one person in the mornings and the other in the afternoons. They both want to job share... She works in a bank job share.

jockey /ˈdʒɒki/ **jockeys.** N-COUNT A **jockey** is someone who rides a horse in a race.

jog /dʒɒg/ **jogs, jogging, jogged.** [1] VERB & N-COUNT If you **jog**, or if you go for a **jog**, you run slowly, often as a form of exercise. I got up early to jog. ◆ **jogger, joggers** N-COUNT The park was full of joggers. ◆ **jogging** N-UNCOUNT Many students are keeping fit through jogging. [2] VERB If you **jog**

something, you push or bump it slightly so that it or moves. Avoid jogging the camera.

join /dʒɔɪn/ **joins, joining, joined.** [1] VERB If one person or vehicle **joins** another, they move or go to the same place. His wife and children moved to join him in their new home. [2] VERB If you **join** an organization, you become a member of it. He joined the Army five years ago. [3] VERB & PHR-VERB If you **join** an activity, or if you **join in** an activity, you become involved in it. The Egyptian Prime Minister has now joined the debate... Tens of thousands of people are expected to join in the celebrations. [4] VERB If you **join** a queue, you go and stand at the end of it. [5] VERB If two roads or rivers **join**, or if one **joins** the other, they meet or come together at a particular point. Do you know the highway to Tulsa? The airport road joins it. [6] VERB & N-COUNT To **join** two things means to fasten, fix, or connect them together. A **join** is a place where two things are fastened or fixed together. 'And' is frequently used to join two sentences. ...the conjunctiva, the skin which joins the eye to the lid... Don't worry – you can't see the join. [7] to **join forces**: see **force**. ● to **join the ranks**: see **rank**.
▶**join in.** See **join** 3.
▶**join up.** PHR-VERB If someone **joins up**, they become a member of the armed forces. [BRITISH]

joint /dʒɔɪnt/ **joints.** [1] ADJ BEFORE N **Joint** means shared by or belonging to two or more people. ...a joint bank account. ◆ **jointly** ADV The Port Authority is an agency jointly run by New York and New Jersey. [2] N-COUNT A **joint** is a part of your body such as your elbow or knee where two bones meet and are able to move together. Her joints ache if she exercises. [3] N-COUNT A **joint** is a place where two things meet or are fixed together.

,joint 'venture, joint ventures. N-COUNT A **joint venture** is a business or project in which two or more companies or individuals have invested, with the intention of working together.

joke /dʒəʊk/ **jokes, joking, joked.** [1] VERB & N-COUNT If you **joke**, or if you **make** a **joke**, you say something amusing or tell a funny story to make people laugh. She would joke about her appearance... Don't get defensive, Charlie. I was only joking... He made a joke about poisoning his wife. ◆ **joker, jokers** N-COUNT He is, by nature, a joker. [2] N-SING If you say that someone or something is **a joke**, you mean that they are ridiculous and not worthy of respect. [INFORMAL] The decision was a joke.
PHRASES ● You say **you're joking** or **you must be joking** to someone when they have just told you something very surprising or difficult to believe. [SPOKEN] One hundred and forty quid for a pair of headphones, you've got to be joking! ● If you describe a situation as **no joke**, you are emphasizing that it is very difficult or unpleasant. [INFORMAL] Two hours on a bus is no joke.

joker /ˈdʒəʊkə/ **jokers.** N-COUNT The **joker** in a

b
c
d
e
f
g
h
i
j
k
l
m
n
o
p
q
r
s
t
u
v
w
x
y
z

pack of cards is the card which does not belong to any of the four suits.

jolly /'dʒɒli/ **jollier, jolliest.** [1] ADJ A **jolly** person is happy and cheerful. [2] ADJ A **jolly** event is lively and enjoyable. *I was looking forward to a jolly party.* [3] ADV You can use **jolly** to emphasize something. [BRITISH, DATED] *It was jolly hard work.*

jolt /dʒəʊlt/ **jolts, jolting, jolted.** [1] VERB & N-COUNT If something **jolts**, or if something else **jolts** it, it moves suddenly and violently. A **jolt** is a sudden violent movement. *The train jolted into motion... Three people fell overboard when their raft was jolted... One tiny jolt could worsen her injuries.* [2] VERB & N-COUNT If you **are jolted** by something, it gives you an unpleasant surprise or shock. A **jolt** is a surprise or shock like this. *...scandals that have jolted the Catholic church... An uproar from the hallway jolted her awake... The campaign came at a time when America needed such a jolt.*

jostle /'dʒɒsəl/ **jostles, jostling, jostled.** [1] VERB If people **jostle** you, they bump against you or push you in a crowd. *I was jostled by a group of fans... Journalists and photographers jostled for space... Chee jostled his way through the crowd.* [2] VERB If people or things **are jostling for** something such as attention or a reward, they are competing with each other for it. *...the contenders who have been jostling for the top job.*

jot /dʒɒt/ **jots, jotting, jotted.**
▸**jot down.** PHR-VERB If you **jot** something **down**, you write it down in the form of a short informal note. *Keep a pad handy to jot down your queries.*

⭐ **journal** /'dʒɜːnəl/ **journals.** [1] N-COUNT A **journal** is a magazine or newspaper, especially one that deals with a specialized subject. *...scientific journals.* [2] N-COUNT A **journal** is an account which you write of your daily activities. *On the plane he wrote in his journal.*

⭐ **journalist** /'dʒɜːnəlɪst/ **journalists.** N-COUNT A **journalist** is a person whose job is to collect news, and write about it in newspapers and magazines or talk about it on television or radio. *...a journalist with the Financial Times.*
♦ **journalism** N-UNCOUNT *He began a career in journalism.*

⭐ **journey** /'dʒɜːni/ **journeys, journeying, journeyed.** VERB & N-COUNT If you **journey** somewhere, or if you make a **journey** there, you travel there. *Naomi journeyed to the United States for the first time... During the journey to the airport he was pursued by photographers.*

⭐ **joy** /dʒɔɪ/ **joys.** [1] N-UNCOUNT **Joy** is a feeling of great happiness. *Salter shouted with joy. ...tears of joy.* [2] N-COUNT Something that is a **joy** makes you feel happy or gives you great pleasure. *That is one of the joys of being a chef.*

joyful /'dʒɔɪfʊl/. [1] ADJ Something that is **joyful** causes happiness and pleasure. *A wedding is a joyful celebration of love.* [2] ADJ A **joyful** person is extremely happy. *...crowds of joyful students.*
♦ **joyfully** ADV *They greeted him joyfully.*

joyous /'dʒɔɪəs/. ADJ **Joyous** means extremely happy. [LITERARY] *...a joyous celebration of life.*
♦ **joyously** ADV *Sarah accepted joyously.*

joyrider /'dʒɔɪraɪdə/ **joyriders.** N-COUNT A **joyrider** is someone who steals a car and drives it around at high speed for fun.

jubilant /'dʒuːbɪlənt/. ADJ If you are **jubilant**, you feel extremely happy because of a success. *I was jubilant at how things had gone.*

jubilee /'dʒuːbɪliː/ **jubilees.** N-COUNT A **jubilee** is a special anniversary of an event, especially the 25th or 50th anniversary. *...Queen Victoria's jubilee.*

Judaism /'dʒuːdeɪɪzəm/. N-UNCOUNT **Judaism** is the religion of the Jewish people, which is based on the Old Testament of the Bible and the laws written in the Talmud.

⭐ **judge** /dʒʌdʒ/ **judges, judging, judged.** [1] N-COUNT A **judge** is the person in a court of law who decides how the law should be applied, for example how criminals should be punished. *Tomorrow they will be brought before a judge... Judge Mr Justice Schiemann jailed him for life.* [2] VERB If you **judge** someone or something, you form an opinion about them based on the evidence or information that you have. *It will take a few more years to judge the impact of these ideas... He judged that this was the moment to say what had to be said... Judging by the opinion polls, he seems to be succeeding.* [3] N-COUNT If someone is a good **judge** of something, they can understand it and make decisions about it. *I think I am a reasonable judge of character.* [4] N-COUNT A **judge** is a person who chooses the winner of a competition. *A panel of judges is now selecting the finalists.* [5] VERB If you **judge** a competition, you decide who the winner is. *Entrants will be judged in two age categories.*

⭐ **judgment** (BRIT also **judgement**)
/'dʒʌdʒmənt/ **judgments.** [1] N-COUNT A **judgment** is an opinion that you have or express after thinking carefully about something. *In your judgment, what has changed over the past few years?... I don't really want to make any judgments on the decisions they made.* [2] N-UNCOUNT **Judgment** is the ability to make sensible guesses about a situation or sensible decisions about what to do. *I think you have made a bad error of judgement... I have never had anyone question my judgement.* [3] N-VAR A **judgment** is a decision made by a judge or by a court of law. *The industry was awaiting a judgment from the European Court... The Appeal Court reserved judgment on Mrs Thornton's second appeal.*

judicial /dʒuː'dɪʃəl/. ADJ BEFORE N **Judicial** means relating to the legal system and to judgements made in a court of law. *...an independent judicial inquiry.*

judiciary /dʒuː'dɪʃəri, AM -ʃieri/. N-SING The **judiciary** is the branch of authority in a country which is concerned with justice and the legal system. [FORMAL]

judicious /dʒuːˈdɪʃəs/. ADJ An action or decision that is **judicious** shows very good judgment and sense. [FORMAL] *The President authorizes the judicious use of military force to protect our citizens.* ◆ **judiciously** ADV *Fertilisers should be used judiciously.*

judo /ˈdʒuːdəʊ/. N-UNCOUNT **Judo** is a sport or martial art in which two people wrestle and try to throw each other to the ground.

jug /dʒʌg/ **jugs.** N-COUNT A **jug** is a container which is used for holding and pouring liquids.

juggle 2

juggle /ˈdʒʌgəl/ **juggles, juggling, juggled.** 1 VERB If you have to **juggle** lots of different things, you have difficulty fitting them all in so that you have enough time for all of them. *Mike juggled the demands of a family of 11 with a career as a TV reporter.* 2 VERB If you **juggle**, you entertain people by throwing things into the air, catching each one and throwing it up again so that there are several of them in the air at the same time. *Soon she was juggling five eggs.* ◆ **juggling** N-UNCOUNT *...mime and juggling.* ◆ **juggler, jugglers** N-COUNT *...a professional juggler.*

juice /dʒuːs/ **juices.** 1 N-VAR **Juice** is the liquid that can be obtained from a fruit. *...a glass of fresh orange juice.* 2 N-PLURAL The **juices** of a joint of meat are the liquid that comes out of it when you cook it. 3 N-PLURAL The **juices** in your stomach are the fluids that help you to digest food.

juicy /ˈdʒuːsi/ **juicier, juiciest.** 1 ADJ If food is **juicy**, it has a lot of juice in it and is very enjoyable to eat. *...a thick, juicy steak.* 2 ADJ You can describe information as **juicy** if it is exciting or scandalous. [INFORMAL]

July /dʒuˈlaɪ/. N-UNCOUNT **July** is the seventh month of the year. → See Reference Page on Times and Dates.

jumble /ˈdʒʌmbəl/ **jumbles, jumbling, jumbled.** 1 N-COUNT A **jumble of** things is a lot of different things that are all mixed together in a disorganized or confused way. *...a jumble of huge boulders. ...a meaningless jumble of words.* 2 VERB & PHR-VERB If you **jumble** things, or if they **jumble**, they become mixed together so that they are untidy or not in the correct order. To **jumble up** means the same as to **jumble**. *They jumble together shampoos, toys, chocolate,*

clothes, electronic goods and hair slides. *...wires jumbled up, tied together, all painted black.* 3 N-UNCOUNT **Jumble** is old or unwanted things that people give away to charity. [BRITISH]

jumbo /ˈdʒʌmbəʊ/ **jumbos.** 1 ADJ BEFORE N **Jumbo** is used to describe things which are very large. *...a jumbo box of tissues.* 2 N-COUNT A **jumbo** or a **jumbo jet** is a very large jet aeroplane.

⭐ **jump** /dʒʌmp/ **jumps, jumping, jumped.** 1 VERB & N-COUNT When you **jump**, you bend your knees, push against the ground with your feet, and move quickly upwards into the air. This action is called a **jump**. *He jumped 25 feet from his third floor flat to avoid the man. ...the longest jumps by a man.* 2 VERB If you **jump** something such as a fence, you move quickly up and through the air over or across it. 3 VERB If you **jump** somewhere, you move there quickly and suddenly. *She jumped to her feet and ran downstairs.* 4 VERB If something makes you **jump**, it makes you make a sudden movement because you are frightened or surprised. 5 VERB & N-COUNT If an amount or level **jumps**, or if there is a **jump** in an amount or level, it suddenly increases by a large amount in a short time. *Sales jumped from $94 million to over $101 million. ...a big jump in energy conservation.* 6 VERB If you **jump at** an offer or opportunity, you accept it quickly and eagerly. *Members of the public would jump at the chance to become part owners.*

jumper /ˈdʒʌmpə/ **jumpers.** N-COUNT In British English, a **jumper** is a knitted piece of clothing which covers the upper part of your body and your arms. The American word is **sweater**.

junction /ˈdʒʌŋkʃən/ **junctions.** N-COUNT A **junction** is a place where roads or railway lines join. The usual American word is **intersection**. *Follow the road to a junction and turn left.*

⭐ **June** /dʒuːn/. N-UNCOUNT **June** is the sixth month of the year. → See Reference Page on Times and Dates.

jungle /ˈdʒʌŋgəl/ **jungles.** 1 N-VAR A **jungle** is a forest in a tropical country where tall trees and other plants grow very closely together. 2 N-SING If you describe a situation as a **jungle**, you dislike it because it is complicated and difficult to get what you want from it. *...a jungle of complex rules.*

⭐ **junior** /ˈdʒuːniə/ **juniors.** 1 N-COUNT & ADJ A **junior**, or a **junior** official or employee, holds a lower-ranking position in an organization or profession. *...a junior minister attached to the prime minister's office.* 2 N-SING If you are someone's **junior**, you are younger than they are. *...a woman 12 years his junior.*

junior 'high, junior highs. N-VAR In the United States, **junior high** is the school that young people attend between the ages of 11 or 12 and 14 or 15.

junk /dʒʌŋk/. 1 N-UNCOUNT **Junk** is an amount of old or useless things. [INFORMAL] *What are you going to do with all that junk, Larry?* 2 N-UNCOUNT

a b c d e f g h i j k l m n o p q r s t u v w x y z

You can use **junk** to refer to old and second-hand goods that people buy and collect.

junkie /'dʒʌŋki/**junkies.** N-COUNT A **junkie** is a drug addict. [INFORMAL]

junta /'dʒʌntə, 'hʊntə/**juntas.** N-COUNT If you refer to a government as a **junta**, you mean that it is a military dictatorship that has taken power by force.

jurisdiction /,dʒʊərɪs'dɪkʃən/. N-UNCOUNT **Jurisdiction** is the power that a court of law or an official has to carry out legal judgements or enforce laws. *The British police have no jurisdiction over foreign bank accounts.*

juror /'dʒʊərə/**jurors.** N-COUNT A **juror** is a member of a jury.

⭐ **jury** /'dʒʊəri/**juries.**

> ✔ When it is in the singular, **jury** can take the singular or plural form of the verb.

1 N-COUNT In a court of law, the **jury** is the group of people who have been chosen from the general public to listen to the facts about a crime and to decide whether the person accused is guilty or not. *The jury found him guilty of murder.* **2** N-COUNT A **jury** is a group of people who choose the winner of a competition.

just 1 adverb uses and phrases

⭐ **just** /dʒʌst/. **1** ADV If you say that something has **just** happened, you mean that it happened a very short time ago. *I've just bought a new house.* **2** ADV If you say that you are **just** doing something, you mean that you will finish doing it very soon. If you say that you are **just** going to do something, you mean that you will do it very soon. *I'm just making the sauce for the cauliflower... I'm just going to walk down the lane now and post some letters.* **3** ADV You use **just** to indicate that something is no more important, interesting, or difficult, for example, than you say it is. *It's just a suggestion... I am sure you can tell just by looking at me that I am all right.* **4** ADV You use **just** to indicate that what you are saying is the case, but only by a very small degree or amount. *Her hand was just visible.* **5** ADV You use **just** to emphasize the word or phrase following it, in order to express feelings such as annoyance, admiration, or certainty. *She just won't relax... I don't see the point in it really. It's just stupid.* **6** ADV You use **just** with instructions, polite requests, or statements of intention, to make your request or statement seem less difficult than someone might think. *I'm just going to ask you a bit more about your father's business.* **7** ADV You use **just** to mean exactly, when you are specifying something precisely or asking for precise information. *There are no statistics about just how many people won't vote... My arm hurts too, just here.*

> PHRASES ● You use **just about** to indicate that what you are talking about is so close to being the case that it can be regarded as being the case. *What does she read? Just about everything.*
> ● You use **it's just that** when you are making a

complaint, suggestion, or excuse, so that the person you are talking to will not get annoyed with you. *Your hair is all right; it's just that you need a haircut.* ● **just now:** see **now.** ● **only just:** see **only.**

just 2 adjective use

just /dʒʌst/. ADJ If you describe a situation, action, or idea as **just**, you mean that it is right or acceptable according to particular moral principles. [FORMAL] *...a just cause.* ♦ **justly** ADV *They were not treated justly in the past.*

⭐ **justice** /'dʒʌstɪs/**justices.** **1** N-UNCOUNT **Justice** is fairness in the way that people are treated. *He only wants freedom, justice and equality.* **2** N-UNCOUNT The **justice of** a claim, argument, or cause is its quality of being reasonable and right. *We must win people round to the justice of our cause.* **3** N-UNCOUNT **Justice** is the system that a country uses in order to deal with people who break the law. *A lawyer is part of the machinery of justice.* **4** N-COUNT In American English, a **justice** is a judge. **5** N-TITLE **Justice** is used before the names of judges. *...Mr Justice Hutchison.*

> PHRASES ● If a criminal **is brought to justice,** he or she is tried in a court of law and punished. *They demanded that those responsible be brought to justice.* ● If you **do justice** to someone or something, you deal with them properly and completely. *No one article can ever do justice to the topic of fraud.*

justifiable /,dʒʌstɪ'faɪəbəl/. ADJ An opinion, action, or fact that is **justifiable** is acceptable or correct because there is a good reason for it. *When, if ever, is it morally justifiable to allow a patient to die?* ♦ **justifiably** ADV *He was justifiably proud of his achievements.*

justification /,dʒʌstɪfɪ'keɪʃən/**justifications.** N-VAR A **justification for** something is an acceptable reason or explanation for it. *To me the only justification for a zoo is educational.*

justified /'dʒʌstɪfaɪd/. ADJ AFTER LINK-V An action that is **justified** is reasonable and acceptable. *In my opinion, the decision was wholly justified... He's absolutely justified in resigning.*

⭐ **justify** /'dʒʌstɪfaɪ/**justifies, justifying, justified.** VERB If someone or something **justifies** a particular decision, action, or idea, they show or prove that it is reasonable or necessary. *No argument can justify a war.*

jut /dʒʌt/**juts, jutting, jutted.** VERB If something **juts out**, it sticks out above or beyond a surface. *The northern end of the island juts out like a long, thin finger into the sea.*

juvenile /'dʒuːvənaɪl/**juveniles.** **1** N-COUNT A **juvenile** is a child or young person who is not yet old enough to be regarded as an adult. [FORMAL] **2** ADJ If you describe someone's behaviour as **juvenile**, you are critical of it because you think that it is silly or immature.

juxtapose /,dʒʌkstə'pəʊz/**juxtaposes, juxtaposing, juxtaposed.** VERB If you **juxtapose** two contrasting objects, images, or ideas, you put them together, so that the differences between them are strongly emphasized. [FORMAL] *Interviews with politicians were juxtaposed with news items of quite astonishing triviality.* ♦ **juxtaposition** /ˌdʒʌkstəpəˈzɪʃən/ **juxtapositions** N-VAR *...the juxtaposition of sound and picture.*

K k

k /keɪ/. **K** or **k** is used to represent the number 1000, especially when referring to sums of money. For example, £10k means £10,000.

kangaroo /ˌkæŋgəˈruː/ **kangaroos.** N-COUNT A **kangaroo** is a large Australian animal. Female kangaroos carry their babies in a pouch on their stomachs.

karate /kəˈrɑːti/. N-UNCOUNT **Karate** is a martial art in which people fight using their hands, elbows, feet, and legs.

keel /kiːl/ **keels, keeling, keeled.** PHRASE If something is **on an even keel**, it is working or progressing smoothly and steadily, without any sudden changes. *There is enough income to keep the family on an even keel.*
▸ **keel over.** PHR-VERB If something or someone **keels over**, they fall over sideways. *She must have had a heart attack and keeled over.*

⭐ **keen** /kiːn/ **keener, keenest.** ① ADJ AFTER LINK-V If you are **keen on** doing something, you very much want to do it. If you are **keen** that something should happen, you very much want it to happen. *He's keen on a return match... She's still keen to keep in touch.* ♦ **keenness** N-UNCOUNT *...the country's keenness for better economic ties with its neighbours.* ② ADJ AFTER LINK-V If you are **keen on** something or someone, you like them a lot. ♦ **keenness** N-UNCOUNT *...his keenness for the arts.* ③ ADJ If someone is **keen**, they have a lot of enthusiasm for a particular activity or for things in general. *I've interviewed him and he seems very keen... She was a keen amateur photographer.* ♦ **keenness** N-UNCOUNT *...the keenness of the students.* ④ ADJ A **keen** sense or emotion is very strong and intense. *...his keen sense of loyalty.* ♦ **keenly** ADV *Charles listened keenly... The 1994 contest was very keenly fought.*

⭐ **keep** /kiːp/ **keeps, keeping, kept.** ① LINK-VERB If someone **is kept** in a particular state, they remain in it. *The noise kept him awake... To keep warm they burnt wood... Their main aim is to help keep youngsters out of trouble.* ② VERB If you **keep** in a particular position or place, or if someone **keeps** you in it, you remain in it. *Keep away from the doors while the train is moving... He kept his head down... Doctors will keep her in hospital for at least another week.* ③ VERB & PHR-VERB If you **keep** doing something, or if you **keep on** doing it, you do it repeatedly or continue to do it. You can also say that someone or something **keeps** you doing something. *I keep forgetting it's December... Did he give up or keep on trying?* ④ VERB **Keep** is used with some nouns to indicate that someone does something for a period of time or continues to do it. For example,

if you **keep a grip on** something, you continue to hold or control it. *One of them would keep a look-out on the road.* ⑤ VERB If you **keep** something that you possess, you continue to have it. If you **keep** it somewhere, you store it there. *The city of Leningrad was deciding whether to keep its name... To make it easier to contact us, keep this card handy... She kept her money under the mattress.* ⑥ VERB When you **keep** something such as a promise or an appointment, you do what you said you would do. ⑦ VERB If you **keep** a record of a series of events, you make a written record of it. *Eleanor began to keep a diary.* ⑧ VERB If someone or something **keeps** you **from** doing something, they prevent you from doing it. *What can you do to keep it from happening again?* ⑨ VERB If someone or something **keeps** you, they delay you and make you arrive somewhere later than expected. *'What kept you?'—'I went in the wrong direction'.* ⑩ VERB If you **keep** something **from** someone, you do not tell them about it. *He had to keep the truth from his children.* ⑪ N-SING Your **keep** is the cost of food and other things that you need every day. *Ray will earn his keep on local farms while studying.*
PHRASES ● If you **keep yourself to yourself**, or if you **keep to yourself**, you stay on your own most of the time and do not mix with other people. ● If something is **in keeping with** something else, it is appropriate or suitable according to that thing. *In keeping with tradition, the Emperor and Empress did not attend the ceremony.* ● to **keep** your **head**: see **head**.
▸ **keep down.** PHR-VERB If you **keep** the amount of something **down**, you do not let it increase. *Administration costs were kept down to just £460.*
▸ **keep on** ① See **keep** 3. ② PHR-VERB If you **keep** someone **on**, you continue to employ them, for example after other employees have lost their jobs. *A skeleton staff of 20 is being kept on.*
▸ **keep to.** ① PHR-VERB If you **keep to** a rule, plan, or agreement, you do exactly what you are expected or supposed to do. *You've got to keep to the speed limit.* ② PHR-VERB If you **keep** something **to** a particular number or quantity, you limit it to that number or quantity. *Keep costs to a minimum.*
▸ **keep up.** ① PHR-VERB If someone or something **keeps up with** another person or thing, the first one moves or progresses as fast as the second. *She shook her head and started to walk on. He kept up with her... Things are changing so fast, it's hard to keep up.* ② PHR-VERB If you **keep** something **up**, you continue to do it or provide it. *They can no longer keep up the repayments.*

a
b
c
d
e
f
g
h
i
j
k
l
m
n
o
p
q
r
s
t
u
v
w
x
y
z

keeper /'kiːpə/ **keepers.** [1] N-COUNT In football, the **keeper** is the same as the **goalkeeper**. [BRITISH, INFORMAL] [2] N-COUNT A **keeper** at a zoo is a person who takes care of the animals.

kennel /'kenəl/ **kennels.** [1] N-COUNT A **kennel** is a small hut made for a dog to sleep in. [2] N-COUNT **Kennels** or **a kennels** or **a kennel** is a place where dogs are bred and trained, or looked after when their owners are away.

kept /kept/. **Kept** is the past tense and past participle of **keep**.

kerb (AM **curb**) /kɜːb/ **kerbs.** N-COUNT The **kerb** is the raised edge of a pavement which separates it from the road.

kerosene /'kerəsiːn/. N-UNCOUNT In American English, **kerosene** is a strong-smelling liquid which is used as a fuel in heaters, lamps, and engines. The usual British word is **paraffin**.

kettle /'ketəl/ **kettles.** N-COUNT A **kettle** is a covered container that you use for boiling water.

⭐ **key** /kiː/ **keys.** [1] N-COUNT A **key** is a specially shaped piece of metal which fits in a lock and is turned in order to open it. [2] N-COUNT The **keys** of a typewriter or computer keyboard are the buttons that you press in order to operate it. [3] N-COUNT The **keys** of a piano or organ are the black and white bars that you press in order to play it. [4] N-COUNT In music, a **key** is a scale of musical notes that starts at one particular note. ...*the key of A minor.* [5] ADJ BEFORE N The **key** person or thing in a group is the most important one. *Education is likely to be a key issue in the next election.* [6] N-COUNT The **key to** a desirable situation or result is the way in which it can be achieved. *Diet and relaxation are two important keys to good health.*

keyboard /'kiːbɔːd/ **keyboards.** [1] N-COUNT The **keyboard** of a typewriter or computer is the set of keys that you press in order to operate it. [2] N-COUNT The **keyboard** of a piano or organ is the set of black and white keys that you press in order to play it.

'**key card, key cards.** N-COUNT A **key card** is a small plastic card which you can use instead of a key to open a door or barrier, for example in some hotels and car parks.

kg. kg is the written abbreviation for **kilogram**.

khaki /'kɑːki, AM 'kæki/. ADJ Something that is **khaki** is greenish brown.

⭐ **kick** /kɪk/ **kicks, kicking, kicked.** [1] VERB & N-COUNT If you **kick** someone or something, or if you give them a **kick**, you hit them with your foot. *She kicked him in the leg... He escaped by kicking open the window... He suffered a kick to the knee.* [2] VERB If you **kick**, you move your legs with very quick, small, and forceful movements, once or repeatedly. *They were dragged away struggling and kicking... The baby beamed and kicked her legs.* [3] PHRASE If someone **gets a kick from** something, they get pleasure or excitement from it. [INFORMAL] [4] VERB If you **kick** a bad habit, you stop having that habit. [INFORMAL] *I've kicked cigarettes.*

▶**kick off.** PHR-VERB If an event, game, series, or discussion **kicks off**, or if someone **kicks** it **off**, it begins. [INFORMAL] *The Mayor kicked off the party.*

▶**kick out.** PHR-VERB To **kick** someone **out** of a place means to force them to leave it. [INFORMAL] *Her family kicked her out.*

'**kick-off, kick-offs.** N-VAR In football, **kick-off** is the time at which a particular match starts.

'**kick-start, kick-starts, kick-starting, kick-started.** VERB To **kick-start** a process that has stopped working or progressing is to take a course of action that will quickly start it going again. *The President has chosen to kick-start the economy by slashing interest rates.*

⭐ **kid** /kɪd/ **kids, kidding, kidded.** [1] N-COUNT You can refer to a child as a **kid**. [INFORMAL] *They've got three kids.* [2] N-COUNT Young people who are no longer children are sometimes referred to as **kids**. [INFORMAL] ...*gangs of kids on motorbikes.* [3] VERB If you **are kidding**, you are saying something that is not really true, as a joke. [INFORMAL] *Oh come on, I was just kidding... I'm not kidding, Frank. There's a cow out there.* [4] VERB If people **kid themselves**, they allow themselves to believe something that is not true. [INFORMAL] *Anyone who thinks he'll resign is kidding himself.* [5] N-COUNT A **kid** is a young goat.

kidnap /'kɪdnæp/ **kidnaps, kidnapping, kidnapped** (AM **kidnaping, kidnaped**). [1] VERB To **kidnap** someone is to take them away illegally and by force, and usually to hold them prisoner in order to demand something from their family, employer, or government. *Police in Brazil uncovered a plot to kidnap him.* ♦ **kidnapper, kidnappers** N-COUNT *He has been set free by his kidnappers.* ♦ **kidnapping, kidnappings** N-VAR *He was shot during the kidnapping.* [2] N-VAR **Kidnap** or a **kidnap** is the crime of kidnapping someone. *He was charged with the kidnap of a 25 year-old woman.*

kidney /'kɪdni/ **kidneys.** N-COUNT Your **kidneys** are the two organs in your body that filter waste matter from your blood and send it out of your body in your urine. ...*kidney disease.*

⭐ **kill** /kɪl/ **kills, killing, killed.** [1] VERB If a person, animal, or other living thing **is killed**, something or someone causes them to die. *Six people have been killed in a road crash... The earthquake killed 62 people... Heroin can kill.* ♦ **killing, killings** N-VAR ...*a brutal killing.*

USAGE There are several words which mean similar things to kill. To **murder** someone means to kill them deliberately. **Assassinate** is used to talk about the murder of an important person, often for political reasons. If a large number of people are murdered, the words **slaughter** or **massacre** are sometimes used. **Slaughter** can also be used to talk about killing animals for their meat.

---

2 VERB & PHR-VERB If something **kills** an activity, process, or feeling or **kills** it **off**, it prevents it from continuing. *His objective was to kill the space station project altogether... An election like that kills off your interest in politics for ever.* **3** VERB If you **are killing** time, you are doing something because you have some time available, not because you really want to do it. *To kill the hours while she waited, Anna worked in the garden.*
▶ **kill off.** **1** See kill 2. **2** PHR-VERB If you **kill** things **off**, you destroy or kill all of them. *Their natural predators have all been killed off... All blood products are now heat treated to kill off any infection.*

★ **killer** /'kɪlə/ **killers.** **1** N-COUNT A **killer** is a person who has killed someone. *The police are searching for his killers.* **2** N-COUNT You can refer to anything that causes death as a **killer**. *Heart disease is the biggest killer of men in most developed countries.*

kilo /'kiːləʊ/ **kilos.** N-COUNT A **kilo** is the same as a **kilogram.**

kilogram (or **kilogramme**) /'kɪləɡræm/ **kilograms.** N-COUNT A **kilogram** is a metric unit of weight. One kilogram is a thousand grams, and is equal to 2.2 pounds.

★ **kilometre** (AM **kilometer**) /'kɪləmiːtə, kɪ'lɒmɪtə/ **kilometres.** N-COUNT A **kilometre** is a metric unit of distance or length. One kilometre is a thousand metres, and is equal to 0.62 miles.

kin /kɪn/. N-PLURAL Your **kin** are your relatives. [DATED]

★ **kind** /kaɪnd/ **kinds; kinder, kindest.** **1** N-VAR If you talk about a particular **kind of** thing, you are talking about one of the classes or sorts of that thing. *Had Jamie ever been in any kind of trouble?... I'm not the kind of person to get married... This book prize is the biggest of its kind in the world... Donations came from all kinds of people.* **2** ADJ Someone who is **kind** behaves in a gentle, caring, and helpful way towards other people. *She is warm-hearted and kind to everyone... It was very kind of you to come.*
♦ **kindly** ADV *He had very kindly asked me to the cocktail party.* ♦ **kindness** N-UNCOUNT *We have been treated with such kindness by everybody.*
3 ADJ AFTER LINK-V You can use **kind** in expressions such as **please be so kind as to** in order to ask someone to do something in a firm but polite way. *I wonder if you'd be kind enough to call him.*
PHRASES ● You use **kind of** when you want to say that something or someone can be roughly described in a particular way. [SPOKEN] *She wasn't beautiful. But she was kind of cute... It kind of gives us an idea of what's happening.* ● Payment **in kind** is payment in the form of goods or services, rather than money. *...the child's dream of working in a chocolate factory and being paid in kind.*
● See also **kindly.**

kindergarten /'kɪndəɡɑːtən/ **kindergartens.** N-VAR A **kindergarten** is a school for young children who are not old enough to go to a primary school. *She's in kindergarten now.*

kindly /'kaɪndli/ **kindlier, kindliest.** **1** ADJ A **kindly** person is kind, caring, and sympathetic. **2** ADV If someone asks you to **kindly** do something, they are asking you in a way which shows that they have authority over you, or that they are angry with you. *Will you kindly obey the instructions?* **3** PHRASE If someone **does not take kindly to** something, they do not like it. *She did not take kindly to being offered advice.* ● See also **kind.**

★ **king** /kɪŋ/ **kings.** **1** N-COUNT A **king** is a man who is a member of the royal family of his country, and who is the head of state of that country. *...the king and queen of Spain.* **2** N-COUNT In chess, the **king** is the piece which each player must try to capture. **3** N-COUNT A **king** is a playing card with a picture of a king on it.

kingdom /'kɪŋdəm/ **kingdoms.** **1** N-COUNT A **kingdom** is a country or region that is ruled by a king or queen. **2** N-SING All the animals, birds, and insects in the world can be referred to together as the animal **kingdom**. All the plants can be referred to as the plant **kingdom**.

kiosk /'kiːɒsk/ **kiosks.** N-COUNT A **kiosk** is a small shop in a public place such as a street or station. It sells things such as snacks or newspapers which you buy through a window.

★ **kiss** /kɪs/ **kisses, kissing, kissed.** VERB & N-COUNT If you **kiss** someone, or if you give them a **kiss**, you touch them with your lips to show affection or to greet them. *She leaned up and kissed him on the cheek... They kissed for almost half-a-minute.*

kit /kɪt/ **kits, kitting, kitted.** **1** N-COUNT A **kit** is a group of items that are kept together because they are used for similar purposes. *...a first aid kit.* **2** N-UNCOUNT Your **kit** is the special clothing you use for a particular activity or sport. [BRITISH] *I forgot my gym kit.* **3** N-COUNT A **kit** is a set of parts that can be put together in order to make something. *...model aeroplane kits.*
▶ **kit out.** PHR-VERB If someone or something **is kitted out**, they have all the clothing or equipment they need at a particular time. [BRITISH, INFORMAL] *Kit yourself out in crash helmet and goggles.*

★ **kitchen** /'kɪtʃɪn/ **kitchens.** N-COUNT A **kitchen** is a room used for cooking and related jobs such as washing dishes.

kite /kaɪt/ **kites.** N-COUNT A **kite** is an object consisting of a light frame covered with paper or cloth, which you fly in the air at the end of a long string.

kitsch /kɪtʃ/. N-UNCOUNT & ADJ You can refer to a work of art or an object as **kitsch** if it is showy and in bad taste, for example because it is designed to appeal to people's sentimentality. *...collectors of Fifties kitsch... Green eye shadow has long been considered kitsch.*

kitten /'kɪtən/ **kittens.** N-COUNT A **kitten** is a very young cat.

kitty /'kɪti/ **kitties.** N-COUNT A **kitty** is an amount of money collected from several people, which is used to buy things that they will share or use together. *You haven't put any money in the kitty.*

'kiwi fruit, kiwi fruits.

☑ Kiwi fruit can also be used as the plural form.

N-VAR A **kiwi fruit** is a fruit with a brown hairy skin and green flesh. → See picture on page 821.

km, km is a written abbreviation for **kilometre.**

knack /næk/ N-SING If you have the **knack of** doing something difficult or skilful, you are able to do it easily. *He's got the knack of getting people to listen.*

knead /niːd/ **kneads, kneading, kneaded.** VERB When you **knead** dough, you press and squeeze it with your hands to make it smooth.

☆ **knee** /niː/ **knees.** [1] N-COUNT Your **knee** is the place where your leg bends. → See picture on page 822. *The snow was up to his knees. ...a knee injury.* [2] N-COUNT If something or someone is **on** your **knee**, they are resting or sitting on the upper part of your legs when you are sitting down. *I sat in the back of the taxi with my son on my knee.* [3] N-PLURAL If you are **on** your **knees**, you are kneeling. *She fell to the ground on her knees and prayed.* [4] PHRASE If a country or organization **is brought to its knees**, it is almost completely destroyed by someone or something.

kneel /niːl/ **kneels, kneeling, knelt** /nelt/ (or **kneeled**). VERB & PHR-VERB When you **kneel** or **kneel down**, you move your body into a position with your knees on the ground and your lower legs stretched out behind them. If you **are kneeling**, you are in this position. → See picture on page 532. *She kneeled down beside him... She was kneeling in prayer.*

knew /njuː, AM nuː/. **Knew** is the past tense of **know.**

knickers /'nɪkəz/ N-PLURAL **Knickers** are a piece of underwear worn by women and girls which have holes for the legs and elastic around the top. [BRITISH] *...six pairs of knickers.*

☆ **knife** /naɪf/ **knives, knifes, knifing, knifed.**

☑ **Knives** is the plural form of the noun and **knifes** is the third person singular of the present tense of the verb.

[1] N-COUNT A **knife** is a tool consisting of a sharp flat piece of metal attached to a handle, used to cut things or as a weapon. → See picture on page 825. *...a knife and fork. ...a surgeon's knife.* [2] VERB To **knife** someone means to attack and injure them with a knife. *She was knifed in the back.*

knight /naɪt/ **knights, knighting, knighted.** [1] N-COUNT In medieval times, a **knight** was a man of noble birth, who served his king or lord in battle. [2] VERB If someone **is knighted**, they are given a knighthood. [3] N-COUNT In chess, a **knight** is a piece shaped like a horse's head.

knighthood /'naɪthʊd/ **knighthoods.** N-COUNT A **knighthood** is a title given to a man in Britain for outstanding achievements or for service to his country. A man with a knighthood puts 'Sir' in front of his name.

knit /nɪt/ **knits, knitting, knitted.** VERB When someone **knits** something, they make it from wool or a similar thread using knitting needles or a machine. *She knitted him 10 pairs of socks. ...her grey knitted cardigan.* ♦ **knitting** N-UNCOUNT *...a relaxing hobby, such as knitting.*

knitting /'nɪtɪŋ/. N-UNCOUNT **Knitting** is something, such as a piece of clothing, that is being knitted. *Miss Marple sits in the corner with her knitting.*

knives /naɪvz/. **Knives** is the plural of **knife.**

knob /nɒb/ **knobs.** [1] N-COUNT A **knob** is a round handle or switch. *She reached for the door knob... He twiddled a knob on the dashboard.* [2] N-COUNT A **knob of** butter is a small amount of it. [BRITISH]

☆ **knock** /nɒk/ **knocks, knocking, knocked.** [1] VERB & N-COUNT If you **knock on** something such as a door or window, you hit it, usually several times, to attract someone's attention. A **knock** is the action or sound of knocking. *She went directly to Simon's apartment and knocked on the door... They heard a knock.* ♦ **knocking** N-SING *...a loud knocking at the door.* [2] VERB & N-COUNT If you **knock** something, or if you give it a **knock**, you touch it or hit it roughly and it moves or falls over. *She accidentally knocked the tea tin off the shelf. ...materials to protect against knocks.* [3] VERB To **knock** someone into a particular place or condition means to hit them very hard so that they fall over or become unconscious. *Someone had knocked him unconscious.* [4] VERB If something **knocks**, it makes a repeated banging noise. *The walls squeaked and the pipes knocked.* [5] VERB If you **knock** something or someone, you criticize them. [INFORMAL]

▶**knock about** or **knock around.** [1] PHR-VERB If someone **knocks** you **around** or **knocks** you **about**, they hit or kick you several times. [BRITISH, INFORMAL] *He started knocking her about.* [2] PHR-VERB If someone **knocks around** or **knocks about** somewhere, they spend time there. [BRITISH, INFORMAL] *Do you have a big group of friends that you knock around with?*

▶**knock down.** [1] PHR-VERB If someone **is knocked down**, they are hit by a vehicle and are injured or killed. [2] PHR-VERB To **knock down** a building means to demolish it.

▶**knock off.** PHR-VERB To **knock off** an amount from a price, time, or level means to reduce it by that amount. *He has knocked 10 seconds off the world record.*

▶**knock out.** [1] PHR-VERB To **knock** someone **out** means to cause them to become unconscious. *I nearly knocked him out.* [2] PHR-VERB If a person or team **is knocked out of** a competition, they are defeated in a game, so that they take no more part in the competition. ● See also **knockout.**

Koran

'knock-on. ADJ BEFORE N If something has a **knock-on** effect, it causes a series of events to happen, one after another. [BRITISH] *Their problems could have a knock-on effect on the banking sector.*

knockout (or **knock-out**) /'nɒkaʊt/ **knockouts.** [1] N-COUNT If a boxer wins a fight by a **knockout**, his opponent falls to the ground and is unable to stand up before the referee has counted to ten. [2] ADJ BEFORE N A **knockout** blow is an action or event that completely destroys an opponent. [3] ADJ BEFORE N In a **knockout** competition, the loser of each game leaves the competition, until one competitor is left as the winner. [BRITISH]

knot /nɒt/ **knots, knotting, knotted.** [1] VERB & N-COUNT If you **knot** something such as a piece of string, or if you tie a **knot** in it, you pass one end of it through a loop and pull it tight. [2] PHRASE If you say that two people **tie the knot**, you mean that they get married. [INFORMAL] [3] N-SING A **knot** of people is a group of them standing very close together. *...a little knot of children.* [4] VERB & N-COUNT If your stomach **knots**, or if there is a **knot** in your stomach, it feels tight because you are afraid or excited. *I felt my stomach knot with apprehension.* [5] N-COUNT A **knot** is a unit used for measuring the speed of ships and aircraft, equal to approximately 1.85 kilometres per hour. *...speeds of up to 30 knots.*

⭐ **know** /nəʊ/ **knows, knowing, knew, known.** [1] VERB If you **know** something, you have it correctly in your mind. *Everyone knows his name... We know what happened there... 'How did he meet your mother?'—'I don't know.'* [2] VERB If you **know about** something or **know how to** do something, you understand part or all of it, or have the necessary skills and understanding to do it. *She didn't know anything about music... Do you know any English?... The health authorities now know how to deal with the disease.* [3] VERB If you **know of** something, you have heard about it but you do not necessarily have a lot of information about it. *We know of the incident but have no further details.* [4] VERB If you **know** a person, place, or thing, you are familiar with them. *I'd known him for nine years... I know Birmingham quite well.* [5] VERB If someone or something **is known as** a particular name, they are called by that name. *The disease is more commonly known as Mad Cow Disease... Everyone knew him as Dizzy.* [6] See also **known**.
PHRASES ● If you **get to know** someone, you find out what they are like by spending time with them. ● You say **'I know'** to indicate that you agree with what has just been said, or to indicate that you realize something is true. *'This country is so awful.'—'I know, I know.'* ● Someone who is **in the know** has information about something that only a few people have any knowledge of. ● You say **'you know'** to emphasize something or to make your statement clearer. *The conditions in there are awful, you know.* ● You say **'You never know'** or **'One never knows'** to indicate that something is possible, although it is unlikely. *There might be an even bigger one – I doubt it, but you never know.*

'know-how (also **knowhow**). N-UNCOUNT **Know-how** is knowledge of the methods or techniques of doing something. [INFORMAL] *...technical know-how.*

knowingly /'nəʊɪŋli/. [1] ADV If you **knowingly** do something wrong, you are aware that it is wrong when you do it. *He had never knowingly taken illegal drugs.* [2] ADV If you look or gesture **knowingly**, you show that you understand something, even though it has not been mentioned directly. *The officers nodded knowingly to each other.*

⭐ **knowledge** /'nɒlɪdʒ/. N-UNCOUNT **Knowledge** is information and understanding about a subject, which someone has in their mind. *He denies any knowledge of the payments. ...the latest advances in scientific knowledge.*
PHRASES ● If you say that something is true **to the best of** your knowledge, you mean that you think that it is true, although you are not completely sure. ● If you do something **safe in the knowledge** that something else is the case, you do the first thing confidently because you are sure of the second thing. [WRITTEN] *I arrived late, safe in the knowledge that no demonstration leaves on time.*

knowledgeable /'nɒlɪdʒəbəl/. ADJ A **knowledgeable** person knows a lot about many different things or a lot about a particular subject. *Youngsters seem very knowledgeable about drugs.*

known /nəʊn/. [1] **Known** is the past participle of **know**. [2] ADJ You use **known** to describe someone or something that is clearly recognized by or familiar to all people, or to a particular group of people. *...a known criminal.* [3] PHRASE If you **let it be known** that something is the case, you make sure that people know it, without telling them directly. *The Prime Minister has let it be known that he is against it.* [4] See also **well-known**.

knuckle /'nʌkəl/ **knuckles.** N-COUNT Your **knuckles** are the rounded pieces of bone where your fingers join your hands, and where your fingers bend. → See picture on page 823.

Koran /kɔː'rɑːn/. N-PROPER **The Koran** is the sacred book on which the religion of Islam is based.

a b c d e f g h i j k l m n o p q r s t u v w x y z

L l

l. l is a written abbreviation for 'litre'.

lab /læb/ **labs.** N-COUNT A **lab** is the same as a **laboratory**. [INFORMAL]

★ **label** /ˈleɪbəl/ **labels, labelling, labelled, (AM labeling, labeled).** [1] N-COUNT A **label** is a piece of paper or plastic that is attached to an object, giving information about it. [2] VERB If something **is labelled**, a label is attached to it, giving information about it. *All the products are labelled with comprehensive instructions.* [3] N-COUNT If you say that someone gets a particular **label**, you mean that people describe them with a particular critical word or phrase. *Her treatment of her husband earned her the label of the most hated woman in America.* [4] VERB If you say that someone or something **is labelled** as a particular thing, you mean that people generally describe them that way and you think that this is unfair. *They are afraid to contact the social services in case they are labelled a problem family.*

labor /ˈleɪbə/. See **labour.**

★ **laboratory** /ləˈbɒrətri, AM ˈlæbrətɔːri/ **laboratories.** N-COUNT A **laboratory** is a building or room where scientific experiments and research are carried out.

laborer. See **labourer.**

laborious /ləˈbɔːriəs/. ADJ A **laborious** task or process takes a lot of effort. ♦ **laboriously** ADV *He sat behind a desk laboriously writing.*

★ **labour** (AM **labor**) /ˈleɪbə/ **labours, labouring, laboured.** [1] ADJ A **Labour** politician or voter is a member of the Labour Party or votes for the Labour Party. [2] N-VAR **Labour** is very hard work. *...the labour of seeding, planting and harvesting... The chef at the barbecue looked up from his labours.* [3] VERB If you **labour to** do something, you do it with difficulty. *For 25 years now he has laboured to build a religious community.* [4] N-UNCOUNT **Labour** is used to refer to the people who work in a country or industry. *...skilled labour.* [5] VERB If you **labour under** an illusion that something is the case, you continue to believe it to be true when it is not. *Both authors labour under the strange delusion that the world is run by feminists.* [6] VERB If you **labour** a point or an argument, you keep making the same point or saying the same thing, although it is unnecessary. [7] N-UNCOUNT **Labour** is the last stage of pregnancy, in which a woman gives birth to a baby. *She was in labour.*

labourer /ˈleɪbərə/ **labourers.** N-COUNT A **labourer** is a person who does a job which involves a lot of hard physical work. *...a farm labourer.*

'Labour ,Party. N-PROPER In Britain, **the Labour Party** is one of the main political parties. It believes that wealth and power should be shared fairly and public services should be free for everyone.

labyrinth /ˈlæbɪrɪnθ/ **labyrinths.** [1] N-COUNT A **labyrinth** is a complicated series of paths or passages, through which it is difficult to find your way. [2] N-COUNT If you describe a situation, process, or area of knowledge as a **labyrinth**, you mean that it is very complicated. *...the labyrinth of human nature.*

lace /leɪs/ **laces, lacing, laced.** [1] N-UNCOUNT **Lace** is very delicate cloth which is made by twisting together fine threads, leaving holes in between. [2] N-COUNT **Laces** are thin pieces of material that are used to fasten some types of clothing, especially shoes. *He'd put on his shoes and tied the laces.* [3] VERB & PHR-VERB If you **lace** something such as a pair of shoes, or if you **lace** them **up**, you tighten them by pulling the laces through the holes, and tying them together. [4] VERB To **lace** food or drink **with** a substance such as alcohol or a drug means to put a small amount of the substance into the food or drink. *She laced his food with sleeping pills.*

★ **lack** /læk/ **lacks, lacking, lacked.** [1] N-UNCOUNT If there is a **lack of** something, there is not enough of it, or there is none at all. *Despite his lack of experience, he got the job... The charges were dropped for lack of evidence.* [2] VERB If you say that someone or something **lacks** something, or that something **is lacking** in them, you mean they do not have any or enough of that thing. *It lacked the power of the Italian cars... Certain vital information is lacking in the report.* ♦ **lacking** ADJ AFTER LINK-V *She felt nervous, increasingly lacking in confidence.*

lacklustre (AM **lackluster**) /ˈlæklʌstə/. ADJ If you describe something or someone as **lacklustre**, you mean that they are not very impressive or lively. *...his party's lacklustre performance during the election campaign.*

lacquer /ˈlækə/ **lacquers.** N-VAR **Lacquer** is a special type of liquid which is put on wood or metal to protect it and make it shiny.

lacy /ˈleɪsi/. ADJ **Lacy** things are made from lace or have pieces of lace attached to them. *...lacy nightgowns.*

★ **lad** /læd/ **lads.** N-COUNT A **lad** is a boy or young man. [BRITISH, INFORMAL] *He's always been a big lad for his age.*

ladder /ˈlædə/ **ladders.** N-COUNT A **ladder** is a piece of equipment used for climbing up something such as a wall. It consists of two long

★ Bank of English® frequent word

pieces of wood or metal with steps fixed between them.

laddish /'lædɪʃ/. ADJ A **laddish** person behaves in a way that seems typical of young men, for example by being noisy, drinking a lot of alcohol, and having a bad attitude towards women; used showing disapproval. [BRITISH] ...the laddish culture of English football. ◆ **laddishness** N-UNCOUNT They revel in lager and laddishness.

laden /'leɪdən/. [1] ADJ If someone or something is **laden** with a lot of heavy things, they are holding or carrying them. [LITERARY] ...buffet tables laden with exotic fruit. ...a car heavily laden with skis. [2] VERB If you describe a person or thing as **laden with** something, particularly something bad, you mean that they have a lot of it or are full of it. We're so laden with guilt.

⭐ **lady** /'leɪdi/ **ladies.** [1] N-COUNT & N-VOC You can use the word **lady** when you are referring to a woman, especially when you are showing politeness or respect. Shall we rejoin the ladies?... Your table is ready, ladies. [2] N-TITLE **Lady** is a title used in front of the names of some women from the upper classes. ...Lady Diana Spencer. [3] N-SING People sometimes refer to a public toilet for women as **the ladies**.

lag /læg/ **lags, lagging, lagged.** [1] VERB To **lag behind** someone or something means to make slower progress than them. He now lags 10 points behind the champion. [2] N-COUNT A time **lag** is a period of time between two related events. There's a time lag between infection with HIV and developing AIDS.

lager /'lɑːɡə/ **lagers.** N-VAR **Lager** is a kind of pale beer.

lagoon /lə'ɡuːn/ **lagoons.** N-COUNT A **lagoon** is an area of calm sea water that is separated from the ocean by sand or rock.

laid /leɪd/. **Laid** is the past tense and past participle of **lay**.

laid-'back. ADJ If you describe someone as **laid-back**, you mean that they behave in a calm relaxed way as if nothing ever worries them.

lain /leɪn/. **Lain** is the past participle of some meanings of **lie**.

⭐ **lake** /leɪk/ **lakes.** N-COUNT A **lake** is a large area of fresh water, surrounded by land.

lamb /læm/ **lambs.** [1] N-COUNT A **lamb** is a young sheep. [2] N-UNCOUNT **Lamb** is the flesh of a lamb eaten as food. ...leg of lamb.

lame /leɪm/. [1] ADJ A **lame** person cannot walk properly because an injury or illness has damaged one or both of their legs. She was lame in one leg... His horse went lame. [2] ADJ If you describe an excuse or effort as **lame**, you mean that it is weak. He mumbled some lame excuse about having gone to sleep. ◆ **lamely** ADV 'Lovely house,' I said lamely.

lament /lə'ment/ **laments, lamenting, lamented.** [1] VERB If you **lament** something, you express

your regret about it. [LITERARY] He laments that people in Villa El Salvador are suspicious of the police... 'Prices are down 40 per cent since Christmas,' he lamented. [2] N-COUNT Someone's **lament** is something that they say that expresses their regret or disappointment about something. ...the professional woman's lament that a woman's judgment is questioned more than a man's.

lamp /læmp/ **lamps.** N-COUNT A **lamp** is a light that works by using electricity or by burning oil or gas. She switched on the bedside lamp.

⭐ **land** /lænd/ **lands, landing, landed.** [1] N-UNCOUNT **Land** is an area of ground. ...agricultural land... It isn't clear whether the plane went down over land or sea. [2] N-COUNT A particular **land** is a particular country. [LITERARY] ...2,000 miles away in a strange land. ● See note at **country**. [3] VERB When someone or something **lands**, they come down to the ground after moving through the air or falling. He was sent flying into the air and landed 20ft away. [4] VERB When a plane or spacecraft **lands**, or when someone **lands** it, it arrives somewhere after a journey. The jet landed after a flight of just under three hours. ◆ **landing, landings** N-COUNT I had to make a controlled landing into the sea. [5] VERB To **land** goods somewhere means to successfully unload them there at the end of a journey, especially by ship. The vessels will have to land their catch at designated ports. [6] VERB If something **lands** you **in** an unpleasant situation, or it if **lands** you **with** it, it causes you to have to deal with it. [BRITISH, INFORMAL] This is not the first time his exploits have landed him in trouble... The other options simply complicate the situation and could land him with more expense.

landfill /'lændfɪl/ **landfills.** N-VAR **Landfill** is a method of disposing of very large amounts of rubbish by burying it in a large deep hole. A **landfill** is a large deep hole that rubbish is buried in. ...the environmental costs of landfill.

landing /'lændɪŋ/ **landings.** N-COUNT In a building, a **landing** is a flat area at the top of a staircase.

landlady /'lændleɪdi/ **landladies.** N-COUNT Someone's **landlady** is the woman who allows them to live or work in a building which she owns, in return for rent.

landlord /'lændlɔːd/ **landlords.** N-COUNT Someone's **landlord** is the man who allows them to live or work in a building which he owns, in return for rent.

landmark /'lændmɑːk/ **landmarks.** [1] N-COUNT A **landmark** is a building or feature which is easily noticed and can be used to judge your position or the position of other buildings or features. The Ambassador Hotel is a Los Angeles landmark. [2] N-COUNT You can refer to an important stage in the development of something as a **landmark**. The baby was one of the big landmarks in our relationship.

a
b
c
d
e
f
g
h
i
j
k
l
m
n
o
p
q
r
s
t
u
v
w
x
y
z

A

★ **landscape** /'lændskeɪp/ **landscapes, landscaping, landscaped.** [1] N-VAR The **landscape** is everything that you can see when you look across an area of land, including hills, rivers, buildings, and trees. *...Arizona's harsh desert landscape.*

USAGE Do not confuse **landscape**, **scenery**, **countryside**, and **nature**. With **landscape**, the emphasis is on the physical features of the land, while **scenery** includes everything you can see when you look out over an area of land usually in the country. *...the landscape of steep woods and distant mountains. ...unattractive urban scenery.* **Countryside** is land which is away from towns and cities. *...3,500 acres of mostly flat countryside.* **Nature** includes the landscape, the weather, animals, and plants. *These creatures roamed the Earth as the finest and rarest wonders of nature.*

---

[2] N-COUNT A **landscape** is a painting of the countryside. [3] VERB If an area of land **is landscaped**, it is altered to create a pleasing artistic effect. ♦ **landscaping** N-UNCOUNT *The landowner insisted on a high standard of landscaping.*

landslide /'lændslaɪd/ **landslides.** [1] N-COUNT If an election is won by a **landslide**, it is won by a large number of votes. [2] N-COUNT A **landslide** is a large amount of earth and rocks falling down a cliff or the side of a mountain.

★ **lane** /leɪn/ **lanes.** [1] N-COUNT A **lane** is a type of road, especially in the country. [2] N-COUNT Roads, race courses, and swimming pools are sometimes divided into parallel strips called **lanes.** *...the slow lane.* [3] N-COUNT A **lane** is a route that is frequently used by aircraft or ships. *...the busiest shipping lanes in the world.*

★ **language** /'læŋgwɪdʒ/ **languages.** [1] N-COUNT A **language** is a system of sounds and written symbols used by the people of a particular country, area, or tribe to communicate with each other. *...the English language... Students are expected to master a second language.* [2] N-UNCOUNT **Language** is the ability to use words in order to communicate. *...how children acquire language.* [3] N-UNCOUNT You can refer to the words used in connection with a particular subject as the **language** of that subject. *...the language of business.* [4] N-UNCOUNT The **language** of a piece of writing or a speech is the style in which it is written or spoken. *...a booklet summarising it in plain language.*

languid /'læŋgwɪd/. ADJ If someone is **languid**, they show little energy or interest and are very slow and casual in their movements. [LITERARY] ♦ **languidly** ADV *We sat about languidly.*

languish /'læŋgwɪʃ/ **languishes, languishing, languished.** VERB If someone **languishes** somewhere, they are forced to remain and suffer in an unpleasant situation. *Pollard continues to languish in prison.*

lantern /'læntən/ **lanterns.** N-COUNT A **lantern** is a lamp in a metal frame with glass sides.

★ **lap** /læp/ **laps, lapping, lapped.** [1] N-COUNT Your **lap** is the flat area formed by your thighs when you are sitting down. *She waited quietly with her hands in her lap.* [2] N-COUNT In a race, you say that a competitor has completed a **lap** when he or she has gone round the course once. [3] VERB If you **lap** another competitor in a race, you pass them while they are still on the previous lap. [4] VERB When water **laps** against something such as the shore or the side of a boat, it touches it gently and makes a soft sound. [WRITTEN] *Water lapped the walls.* ♦ **lapping** N-UNCOUNT *The only sound was the lapping of the waves.* [5] VERB & PHR-VERB When an animal **laps** a drink, or when it **laps** it **up**, it uses its tongue to flick the liquid into its mouth.

▶ **lap up.** PHR-VERB If someone **laps up** information or attention, they accept it eagerly. *They just haven't been to school before. They're so eager to learn, they lap it up.* ● See **lap** 5.

lapel /lə'pel/ **lapels.** N-COUNT The **lapels** of a jacket or coat are the two flaps at the front that are folded back on each side. → See picture on page 820.

lapse /læps/ **lapses, lapsing, lapsed.** [1] N-COUNT A **lapse of** something such as concentration or judgement is a temporary lack of it, which can cause you to make a mistake. [2] VERB & N-COUNT If you **lapse into** a particular kind of behaviour, or have a **lapse into** that behaviour, you start behaving that way. *He lapsed into long silences... Her lapse into German didn't seem peculiar.* [3] N-SING A **lapse of** time is a period that is long enough for a situation to change. *Traditional management is being restored after a lapse of nearly 50 years.* [4] VERB If a period of time **lapses**, it passes. *...in the days that had lapsed since Grace's death.* [5] VERB If a situation, relationship, or legal contract **lapses**, it is allowed to end or to become invalid.

laptop /'læptɒp/ **laptops.** N-COUNT A **laptop** or a **laptop computer** is a small computer that you can carry around with you. [COMPUTING]

★ **large** /lɑːdʒ/ **larger, largest.** [1] ADJ A **large** thing or person is greater in size than usual or average. *The pike swims mainly in large rivers and lakes... He was a large man with a thick square head.* [2] ADJ A **large** amount or number of people or things is more than the average amount or number. *There are a large number of centres where you can take full-time courses.* [3] ADJ **Large** is used to indicate that a problem or issue which is being discussed is very important or serious. *...the already large problem of under-age drinking.*

USAGE Large, big, and great are all used to talk about size. In general, **large** is more formal than **big**, and **great** is more formal than **large**.
Big and **large** are normally used to describe objects. If you use **great** to describe an object, you are suggesting that it is impressive because of its size. *The great bird of prey was a dark smudge against the sun.*
You can use **large** or **great**, but not **big**, to describe amounts. *He noticed a large amount of blood on the laundry floor... The coming of tourists in great numbers changes things.*
Great is often used with nouns referring to things such as feelings or ideas. It is the only one of the three words that can be used in front of an uncount noun. *It gives me very great pleasure to welcome you to Kings Norton.*

PHRASES ● You use **at large** to indicate that you are talking about most of the people mentioned. *...the chances of getting reforms accepted by the community at large.* ● You use **by and large** to indicate that a statement is mostly but not completely true. *By and large, he does not watch many movies.*

⭐ **largely** /ˈlɑːdʒli/. [1] ADV You use **largely** to say that a statement is mostly but not completely true. *The early studies were done on men, largely by male researchers.* [2] ADV You use **largely** to introduce the main reason for an event or situation. *Today, largely because of their diets, over 50% of Americans are at risk for heart disease.*

large-ˈscale (or **large scale**). [1] ADJ BEFORE N A **large-scale** action or event happens over a wide area or involves a lot of people or things. *...a large-scale military operation.* [2] ADJ BEFORE N A **large-scale** map or diagram represents a small area of land or a building or machine in a way that shows small details of it.

lark /lɑːk/ **larks**. N-COUNT A **lark** is a small brown bird that has a pleasant song.

larva /ˈlɑːvə/ **larvae** /ˈlɑːviː/. N-COUNT A **larva** is an insect at the stage before it becomes an adult.

laser /ˈleɪzə/ **lasers**. [1] N-COUNT A **laser** is a narrow beam of concentrated light produced by a special machine. [2] N-COUNT A **laser** is a machine that produces a laser beam.

lash /læʃ/ **lashes, lashing, lashed**. [1] N-COUNT Your **lashes** are the hairs that grow on the edge of your eyelids. [2] VERB If you **lash** something somewhere, you tie it firmly to something. *Secure the anchor by lashing it to the rail... All the equipment is very securely lashed down.* [3] VERB If wind, rain, or water **lashes** someone or something, it hits them violently. [WRITTEN] *Suddenly rain lashed against the windows.* [4] VERB & N-COUNT If someone **lashes** another person, they

hit that person with a whip. This action is called a **lash**. *The villagers sentenced him to five lashes.*
▶**lash out.** [1] PHR-VERB If you **lash out**, you try to hit someone with your hands or feet or with a weapon. [2] PHR-VERB If you **lash out at** someone or something, you speak to them very angrily or cruelly, criticizing or scolding them.

lass /læs/ **lasses**. N-COUNT A **lass** is a young woman or girl. [INFORMAL, BRITISH]

⭐ **last** /lɑːst, læst/ **lasts, lasting, lasted**. [1] ADJ & PRON You use **last** to describe the most recent period of time, event, or thing. *I got married last July... Much has changed since my last visit... The next tide would be even higher than the last.* [2] ORD & PRON The **last** thing, person, event, or period of time is the one that happens or comes after all the others of the same kind. *...the last three pages of the chapter... The trickiest bits are the last on the list.* [3] DET & N-SING **Last** is used to refer to the only thing, person, or part of something that remains. *...the last piece of pizza... He finished off the last of the wine.* [4] ADJ & PRON You can use **last** to emphasize that you do not want to do something or that something is unlikely to happen. *The last thing I wanted to do was teach... I would be the last to say that science has explained everything.* [5] ADV If something **last** happened on a particular occasion, it has not happened since then. *When were you there last?... The house is a little more dilapidated than when I last saw it.* [6] ADV If something happens **last**, it happens after everything else. *I was always picked last for the football team.* [7] PRON If you are **the last to** do or know something, everyone else does or knows it before you. [8] VERB If something **lasts**, it continues to exist or happen. *The games lasted only half the normal time... Enjoy it because it won't last.* [9] VERB If something **lasts** for a particular length of time, it continues to be able to be used for that time, for example because there is some of it left. *This battery lasts twice as long as batteries made by other battery makers.* [10] See also **lasting**.
PHRASES ● If something has happened **at last** or **at long last**, it has happened after you have been hoping for it for a long time. *I'm so glad that we've found you at last!* ● You use expressions such as **the night before last**, **the election before last**, and **the leader before last**, to refer to the period of time, event, or person that happened or came immediately before the most recent one in a series. ● You can use expressions such as **the last I heard** and **the last she heard** to introduce a piece of information that is most recent that you have on a particular subject. *The last I heard, Joe and Irene were still happily married.* ● You use expressions such as **to the last detail** and **to the last man** to indicate that a plan, situation, or activity includes every single person, thing, or part involved. ● to **have the last laugh**: see **laugh**. ● **the last straw**: see **straw**.

last-ˈditch. ADJ BEFORE N A **last-ditch** action is done only because there are no other ways left to try to achieve something or to prevent something happening. ...*a last-ditch attempt to prevent civil war.*

lasting /'lɑːstɪŋ, 'læst-/. ADJ Something that is **lasting** continues to exist or to be effective for a very long time. *She left a lasting impression on him.*

lastly /'lɑːstli, 'læst-/. [1] ADV You use **lastly** when you want to make a final point that is connected with the ones you have already mentioned. *Lastly, I would like to ask about your future plans.* [2] ADV You use **lastly** when you are saying what happens after everything else in a series of actions or events. *Spot all the differences between the two pictures opposite, then circle them in red. Lastly, complete the tie-breaker.*

last-'minute. See **minute.**

latch /lætʃ/ **latches, latching, latched.** [1] N-COUNT A **latch** is a fastening on a door or gate. It consists of a metal bar which you lower to lock the door and raise to open it. [2] N-COUNT A **latch** is a lock on a door which locks automatically when you shut the door.
▸**latch onto** or **latch on.** [1] PHR-VERB If someone **latches onto** a person or an idea, or if someone **latches on**, they become very interested in the person or idea, often because they find them useful. *Other trades have been quick to latch on.* [2] PHR-VERB If one thing **latches onto** another, or if it **latches on**, it attaches itself to it. *Antibodies in their blood latch onto the virus.*

⭐ **late** /leɪt/ **later, latest.** [1] ADV & ADJ BEFORE N **Late** means near the end of a period of time. *It was late in the afternoon... ...the late 1960s.* [2] ADV & ADJ **Late** means after the time that was arranged or expected. *Steve arrived late... His campaign got off to a late start.* [3] ADJ AFTER LINK-V If it is **late**, it is near the end of the day or it is past the time that you feel something should have been done. *We've got to go now. It's getting late.* ♦ **lateness** N-UNCOUNT *A large crowd had gathered despite the lateness of the hour.* [4] ADV & ADJ BEFORE N **Late** means after the usual time that a particular event or activity happens. *We went to bed very late... They had a late lunch.* ♦ **lateness** N-UNCOUNT *He apologised for his lateness.* [5] ADJ BEFORE N You use **late** when you are talking about someone who is dead. *...the late Mr Parkin.* [6] See also **later, latest.**
PHRASES ● If you say that someone is doing something **late in the day**, you mean that it may fail because they have waited too long before doing it. *I'd left it all too late in the day to get anywhere with these strategies.* ● You use **of late** to refer to an event or state of affairs that happened or began to exist a short time ago. [FORMAL] *Neither player has been well of late.*

lately /'leɪtli/. ADV **Lately** means recently. *Dad's health hasn't been too good lately.*

latent /'leɪtənt/. ADJ **Latent** is used to describe something which is hidden and not obvious at the moment, but which may develop further in the future. *It may also appeal to the latent chauvinism of many ordinary people.*

⭐ **later** /'leɪtə/. [1] **Later** is the comparative of **late.** [2] ADV You use **later** or **later on** to refer to a time or situation that is after the one that you have been talking about or after the present one. *Later on I'll be speaking to Patty... The competition should have been re-scheduled for a later date.* [3] ADJ You use **later** to refer to the last part of someone's life or career or of a period in history. *He found happiness in later life.*

lateral /'lætərəl/. ADJ **Lateral** means relating to the sides of something, or moving in a sideways direction. *...the lateral movement of the bridge.*

⭐ **latest** /'leɪtɪst/. [1] **Latest** is the superlative of **late.** [2] ADJ You use **latest** to describe something that is the most recent thing of its kind. *...her latest book.* [3] ADJ You can use **latest** to describe something that is extremely modern and up-to-date, and is therefore better than the other things of its type. *Computers have always represented the latest in technology.* [4] PHRASE You use **at the latest** to emphasize that something must happen at or before a particular time. *She should be back by ten at the latest.*

lathe /leɪð/ **lathes.** N-COUNT A **lathe** is a machine for shaping wood or metal.

Latin A'merican, Latin Americans. ADJ & N-COUNT **Latin American** means belonging or relating to the countries of South America, Central America, and Mexico. A **Latin American** is someone who lives in or comes from Latin America. *...Latin American art.*

latitude /'lætɪtjuːd, AM -tuːd/ **latitudes.** [1] N-VAR The **latitude** of a place is its distance from the Equator. Compare **longitude**. *The army must cease military operations above 36 degrees latitude north.* [2] N-UNCOUNT **Latitude** is the freedom to choose how to do something. [FORMAL] *He was given every latitude in forming a new government.*

⭐ **latter** /'lætə/. [1] PRON & ADJ BEFORE N When two people, things, or groups have just been mentioned, you can refer to the second one as **the latter** or describe them as **the latter** person, thing, or group. *He tracked down his cousin and uncle. The latter was sick.*

USAGE The latter should only be used to refer to the second of two items which have already been mentioned: *Given the choice between working for someone else and being on call day and night for the family business, she'd prefer the latter.* The last of three or more items can be referred to as **the last-named.** Compare this with **the former** which is used to talk about the first of two things already mentioned.

---

[2] ADJ BEFORE N You use **latter** to describe the later part of a period of time or an event. *The latter part of the debate concentrated on abortion.*

'**latter-day.** ADJ BEFORE N **Latter-day** is used to describe a person or thing that is a modern equivalent of someone or something in the past. *He holds the sincere belief that he is a latter-day prophet.*

lattice /'lætɪs/ **lattices.** N-COUNT A **lattice** is a pattern or structure made of strips which cross over each other diagonally leaving holes in between. *...the narrow steel lattice of the bridge.*

◪ **laugh** /lɑːf, læf/ **laughs, laughing, laughed.** ☐ VERB & N-COUNT When you **laugh**, or when you give a **laugh**, you make a sound with your throat while smiling. *The British don't laugh at the same jokes as the French... He gave a deep rumbling laugh.* ☐ VERB If people **laugh at** someone or something, they mock them or make jokes about them. *I thought they were laughing at me because I was ugly.* ☐ PHRASE If you say that you **have the last laugh**, you mean that you make your critics or opponents look foolish or wrong, by being successful when you were not expected to be.
▶ **laugh off.** PHR-VERB If you **laugh off** a difficult or serious situation, you try to suggest that it is amusing and unimportant. *Whilst I used to laugh it off, I'm now getting irritated by it.*

◪ **laughter** /'lɑːftə, 'læf-/. N-UNCOUNT **Laughter** consists of people laughing. *Everybody in the room roared with laughter.*

◪ **launch** /lɔːntʃ/ **launches, launching, launched.** ☐ VERB & N-COUNT To **launch** a ship or a lifeboat means to put it into water, often for the first time. The occasion when this happens is called its **launch.** *Coastguards launched three lifeboats... The launch of a ship was a big occasion.* ☐ VERB & N-VAR To **launch** a rocket, missile, or satellite means to send it into the air or into space. You can also refer to its **launch.** *A Delta II rocket was launched from Cape Canaveral... This morning's launch of the space shuttle Columbia has been delayed.* ☐ VERB & N-COUNT To **launch** a large and important activity, for example a military attack, means to start it. The start of something like this is its **launch.** *The President was on holiday when the coup was launched. ...the launch of a campaign to restore law and order.* ☐ VERB & N-COUNT If a company **launches** a new product, it starts to make it available to the public. You say this is the **launch** of the product. *Crabtree & Evelyn has just launched a new jam... The company's spending has risen following the launch of a new Sunday magazine.*
▶ **launch into.** PHR-VERB If you **launch into** something such as a speech, task, or fight, you start it enthusiastically. *Geoff has launched himself into fatherhood with great enthusiasm.*

launder /'lɔːndə/ **launders, laundering, laundered.** ☐ VERB When you **launder** clothes, bed linen, or towels, you wash and iron them. *...a freshly laundered and starched white shirt.* ☐ VERB To **launder** money that has been obtained illegally means to process it through a legitimate business or to send it abroad to a foreign bank, so that nobody knows that it was illegally obtained.

...banks that launder drug money. ◆ **launderer, launderers** N-COUNT *...a businessman and self-described money launderer and arms dealer.*

laundry /'lɔːndri/ **laundries.** ☐ N-UNCOUNT **Laundry** is used to refer to clothes, sheets, and towels that are about to be washed, are being washed, or have just been washed. *I'll do your laundry. ...dirty laundry.* ☐ N-COUNT A **laundry** is a place where clothes, sheets, and towels are washed and dried.

laurel /'lɒrəl, AM 'lɔːr-/ **laurels.** N-VAR A **laurel** or a **laurel tree** is a small evergreen tree with shiny leaves.

lava /'lɑːvə/. N-UNCOUNT **Lava** is the very hot liquid rock that comes out of a volcano.

lavatory /'lævətri, AM -tɔːri/ **lavatories.** N-COUNT A **lavatory** is a toilet. [BRITISH]

lavender /'lævɪndə/. N-UNCOUNT **Lavender** is a garden plant with sweet-smelling purple flowers.

lavish /'lævɪʃ/ **lavishes, lavishing, lavished.** ☐ ADJ If you describe something as **lavish**, you mean that a lot of time, effort, or money has been spent on it to make it as impressive as possible. *...a lavish party.* ◆ **lavishly** ADV *IBM spent lavishly on their workers' education.* ☐ ADJ If you say that something is **lavish**, you mean it is extravagant and wasteful. *...stealing antique jewellery and paintings to finance a lavish lifestyle.* ☐ VERB If you **lavish** something such as money, affection, or time **on** someone or something, you spend a lot of money on them or give them a lot of affection or attention. *Prince Sadruddin lavished praise on Britain's contribution to world diplomacy... The emperor promoted the general and lavished him with gifts.*

⭐ **law** /lɔː/ **laws.** ☐ N-SING The **law** is a system of rules that a society or government develops in order to deal with crime, business agreements, and social relationships. *Obscene and threatening phone calls are against the law.* ☐ N-PLURAL The **laws** of an organization or activity are its rules, which are used to organize and control it. ☐ N-COUNT A **law** is a rule or set of rules for good behaviour which is considered right and important by the majority of people for moral, religious, or emotional reasons. *...inflexible moral laws.* ☐ N-COUNT A **law** is a natural process in which a particular event or thing always leads to a particular result, or a scientific rule that someone has invented to explain such a process. *...the law of gravity.* ☐ N-UNCOUNT **Law** or the **law** is all the professions which deal with advising people about the law, representing people in court, or giving decisions and punishments. **Law** is also the study of systems of law and how laws work. *...a career in law. ...a law degree.* ☐ PHRASE If someone **takes the law into** their **own hands**, they punish someone according to their own ideas of justice, often when this involves breaking the law.

'**law-abiding.** ADJ A **law-abiding** person

a
b
c
d
e
f
g
h
i
j
k
l
m
n
o
p
q
r
s
t
u
v
w
x
y
z

always obeys the law. *Gun ownership by law-abiding people was not a problem.*

,law and 'order. N-UNCOUNT When there is **law and order** in a country, the laws are generally accepted and obeyed there. *If there were a breakdown of law and order, the army might be tempted to intervene.*

lawful /'lɔːfʊl/. ADJ If an activity, organization, or product is **lawful**, it is allowed by law. [FORMAL]
♦ **lawfully** ADV *...whether the police acted lawfully in shooting him.*

lawless /'lɔːləs/. ADJ **Lawless** actions break the law, especially in a wild and violent way. *...the lawless gangs who have been terrorizing the city.*
♦ **lawlessness** N-UNCOUNT *...acts of lawlessness.*

lawn /lɔːn/ **lawns.** N-VAR A **lawn** is an area of grass that is kept cut short and is usually part of a garden or park.

lawnmower (also **lawn mower**) /'lɔːnməʊə/ **lawnmowers.** N-COUNT A **lawnmower** is a machine for cutting grass on lawns. → See picture on page 832.

lawsuit /'lɔːsuːt/ **lawsuits.** N-COUNT A **lawsuit** is a case in a court of law which concerns a dispute between two people or organizations. [FORMAL]

⭐ **lawyer** /'lɔɪə/ **lawyers.** N-COUNT A **lawyer** is a person who is qualified to advise people about the law and represent them in court.

lax /læks/. ADJ If you say that a person's behaviour or a system is **lax**, you mean they are not careful or strict in making or obeying rules or maintaining high standards. *One of the problem areas is lax security.* ♦ **laxity** N-UNCOUNT *The laxity of export control authorities has made a significant contribution to the problem.*

laxative /'læksətɪv/ **laxatives.** N-VAR & ADJ A **laxative**, or a **laxative** substance, is something which you eat or drink which helps you to pass faeces through your body.

lay 1 placing and putting

⭐ **lay** /leɪ/ **lays, laying, laid.** [1] **Lay** is the past tense of some meanings of **lie**. [2] VERB If you **lay** something somewhere, you put it there in a careful or neat way. *Mothers routinely lay babies on their backs to sleep.* [3] VERB If you **lay** something such as carpets, cables, or foundations, you put them into their permanent position. *Public utilities dig up roads to lay pipes.* [4] VERB When someone **lays** a trap, they prepare it to catch someone or something. *They were laying a trap for the kidnapper.* [5] VERB When a female bird **lays** an egg, an egg comes out of its body. [6] VERB **Lay** is used with some nouns to talk about making preparations for something. For example, if you **lay the basis for** something or **lay plans for** it, you prepare it carefully so that you can continue with it, develop it, or benefit from it later. *His work laid the foundations of modern psychology.* [7] VERB **Lay** is used with some nouns in expressions about accusing or blaming someone. For example, if you **lay the**

blame for a mistake on someone, you say it is their fault. *Police have decided not to lay charges.*

USAGE Do not confuse the verb **lay** with the verb **lie**. The past tense and past participle of **lay** are **laid** and it is usually a transitive verb. *They laid him on the floor.* However, **lie** is an intransitive verb with the past tense **lay** and the past participle **lain**. *I lay on the floor with my legs in the air... He had lain in great pain in a darkened room.* Because **lay** is used to talk about putting something in a particular place or position, it is related to the verb **lie**. If someone **lays** something somewhere, it **lies** there. Because of their related meaning, people sometimes confuse the two verbs.

▶ **lay aside.** PHR-VERB If you **lay aside** a feeling or belief, you reject it or give it up in order to progress with something. *To make a success of any future talks, both sides will have to lay aside their long-term differences.*

▶ **lay down.** PHR-VERB If rules or people in authority **lay down** what people must do, they tell people what they must do. *The Companies Act lays down a set of minimum requirements.*

▶ **lay into.** PHR-VERB If you **lay into** someone, you start attacking them physically or criticizing them severely. [INFORMAL] *A mob of women laid into him with handbags.*

▶ **lay off.** [1] PHR-VERB If workers **are laid off** by their employers, they are told to leave their jobs, usually because there is no more work for them to do. *They did not sell a single car for a month and had to lay off workers.* [2] PHR-VERB If you tell someone to **lay off**, you mean that they should leave you or someone else alone. [INFORMAL]

▶ **lay on.** PHR-VERB If you **lay on** food, entertainment, or a service, you provide it or supply it, especially in a generous or grand way. *They laid on a superb evening.*

▶ **lay out.** [1] PHR-VERB To **lay out** ideas or plans means to explain or present them clearly, for example in a document or a meeting. *Maxwell listened closely as Johnson laid out his plan.* [2] PHR-VERB To **lay out** an area of land or a building means to plan and design how its different parts should be arranged. [3] See also **layout.**

lay 2 non-professional

lay /leɪ/. [1] ADJ BEFORE N You use **lay** to describe people who are involved with a Christian church but are not monks, nuns, or members of the clergy. *...a Methodist lay preacher.* [2] ADJ BEFORE N You use **lay** to describe someone who is not an expert or professional in a particular subject or activity. *It is difficult for a lay person to gain access to medical libraries.*

⭐ **layer** /'leɪə/ **layers, layering, layered.** [1] N-COUNT A **layer** of a material or substance is a quantity or flat piece of it that covers a surface or that is between two other things. *A fresh layer of snow covered the street... Dress warmly, in layers.* **2** N-COUNT If something such as a system or an idea has many **layers**, it has many different levels or parts. *He is not concerned with deeper layers of meaning.* **3** VERB If you **layer** something, you arrange it in layers. *Continue layering the pastry sheets. ...a layered white dress.*

layman /'leɪmən/ **laymen.** N-COUNT A **layman** is a person who is not an expert or a professional in a particular subject or activity. *...explaining scientific breakthroughs in layman's terms.*

layout /'leɪaʊt/ **layouts.** N-COUNT The **layout** of a garden, building, or piece of writing is the way in which the parts of it are arranged.

lazy /'leɪzi/ **lazier, laziest.** **1** ADJ If someone is **lazy**, they do not want to work or make an effort. *I was too lazy to learn how to read music.* ♦ **laziness** N-UNCOUNT *I dislike laziness.* **2** ADJ BEFORE N **Lazy** actions or activities are done in a slow and relaxed way, without making much effort. *We would have a lazy lunch and then lie on the beach.* ♦ **lazily** ADV *She smiled lazily.*

lb.

> ☑ The plural is **lbs** or **lb.**

lb is a written abbreviation for **pound**, when 'pound' refers to weight.

lead 1 being ahead or taking someone somewhere

⭐ **lead** /li:d/ **leads, leading, led.** **1** VERB If you **lead** a group of moving people, you walk or ride in front of them. *They threatened to lead a mass walkout... Tom was leading, a rifle slung over his back.* **2** VERB If you **lead** someone to a particular place or thing, you take them there. *The nurse led me to a large room.* **3** VERB If something such as a road or door **leads** to a place, you can get to that place by following the road or going through the door. *...a main highway leading north.* **4** VERB If you **are leading** in a race or competition, you are winning. *So far Fischer leads by five wins to two.* **5** N-SING If you have **the lead** or are **in the lead** in a race or competition, you are winning. The amount by which someone is winning can also be referred to as their **lead**. *England took the lead after 31 minutes... Sainz now has a lead of 28 points.* **6** VERB If you **lead** a group, an organization, or an activity, you are in charge of it. *He led the country between 1949 and 1984.* **7** N-COUNT If you give a **lead**, you do something which is considered a good example to follow. *...the need for the president to give a moral lead... Many others followed his lead.* **8** VERB You can use **lead** when you are saying what kind of life someone has. For example, if you **lead** a busy life, your life is busy. *If you lead a busy life...* **9** VERB If something **leads to** a situation or event, it causes that situation or event to happen. *Ethnic tensions among the republics could lead to civil war... What led you to do this work?* **10** VERB If someone or something **leads** you **to** think or expect something, they cause you to think or expect it, although it is not true or does not happen. *It was not as*

straightforward as we were led to believe.* **11** VERB To **lead** a discussion or person onto a particular subject means to cause the discussion to develop in such a way that the subject is introduced. *After a while I led the conversation around to her job.* **12** N-COUNT A **lead** is a piece of information or an idea which may help people to discover the facts in a situation. *Police say they have no leads so far on the murder.* **13** N-SING The **lead** in a play, film, or show is the most important role in it. The person who plays this part can also be called **the lead**. *She has recently played the lead in Pearl Harbor.* **14** N-COUNT A dog's **lead** is a long chain or piece of leather attached to the dog's collar so that you can control the dog. **15** N-COUNT A **lead** in a piece of electrical equipment is a piece of wire which supplies electricity to the equipment. **16** See also **leading.** ● to **lead** someone **astray**: see **astray**.

▶**lead on to.** PHR-VERB If one event or action **leads on to** another, it causes it or makes it possible. [BRITISH] *This discovery led on to studies of the immune system.*

▶**lead up to.** **1** PHR-VERB Events that **lead up to** a situation happen one after the other until that situation is reached. *...the events that led up to the deaths.* **2** PHR-VERB The period of time **leading up to** an event is the period of time immediately before it happens. *...the weeks leading up to Christmas.*

lead 2 substances

lead /led/ **leads.** **1** N-UNCOUNT **Lead** is a soft, grey, heavy metal. **2** N-COUNT The **lead** in a pencil is the central part of it which makes a mark on paper.

⭐ **leader** /'li:də/ **leaders.** **1** N-COUNT The **leader** of an organization or a group of people is the person who is in charge of it. *...the Liberal Party leader.* **2** N-COUNT The **leader** in a race or competition is the person who is winning at a particular time.

⭐ **leadership** /'li:dəʃɪp/. **1** N-SING You can refer to the people who are in charge of a group or organization as **the leadership**. *...the Labour leadership of Haringey council.* **2** N-UNCOUNT Someone's **leadership** is their position or state of being in control of a group of people. *The agency quadrupled in size under her leadership.* **3** N-UNCOUNT **Leadership** refers to the qualities or methods that make someone a good leader. *There will be times when firm leadership is required.*

⭐ **leading** /'li:dɪŋ/. **1** ADJ BEFORE N The **leading** people or things in a group are the most important or successful. *...a leading industrial nation.* **2** ADJ BEFORE N The **leading** role in a play or film is the main one. A **leading** lady or man is an actor who plays this role.

⭐ **leaf** /li:f/ **leaves; leafs, leafing, leafed.**

> ☑ The plural of the noun is **leaves**; the third person singular, present tense of the phrasal verb is **leafs**.

a b c d e f g h i j k l m n o p q r s t u v w x y z

N-COUNT A **leaf** is one of the parts of a tree or plant that is flat, thin, and usually green.
▸**leaf through.** PHR-VERB If you **leaf through** a book or magazine, you turn the pages quickly without looking at them carefully.

leaflet /'liːflət/ **leaflets.** N-COUNT A **leaflet** is a little book or a piece of paper containing information about a particular subject. *...a leaflet called 'Sexual Harassment at Work'.*

leafy /'liːfi/. ① ADJ **Leafy** trees and plants have a lot of leaves. *...green leafy vegetables.* ② ADJ You say that a place is **leafy** when there are a lot of trees and plants there. *...London's leafy suburbs.*

★ **league** /liːg/ **leagues.** ① N-COUNT A **league** is a group of people, clubs, or countries that have joined together for a particular purpose or because they share a common interest. *...the League of Nations.* ② N-COUNT You use **league** to make comparisons between different people or things, especially in terms of their quality. *Their record sales would put them in the same league as The Rolling Stones.* ③ PHRASE If you say that someone is **in league with** someone else to do something bad, they are working together to do that thing. *Secretly, he was in league with the nation's top mobsters.*

★ **leak** /liːk/ **leaks, leaking, leaked.** ① VERB & N-COUNT If a container or other object **leaks**, or if it has a **leak**, there is a hole or crack in it which lets liquid or gas escape. You can also say the liquid or gas **leaks** from its container. *The roof leaked... The tanker is still leaking oil. ...a gas leak.* ② VERB & N-COUNT If a secret document or piece of information **is leaked** or if there is a **leak** involving it, someone lets the public know about it. *A civil servant was imprisoned for leaking a document to the press. ...serious leaks, possibly involving national security.*

leakage /'liːkɪdʒ/ **leakages.** N-VAR **Leakage** is the escape of liquid or gas from a container through a crack or hole.

★ **lean** /liːn/ **leans, leaning, leaned** (BRIT also **leant** /lɛnt/); **leaner leanest.** ① VERB When you **lean** in a particular direction, you bend your body in that direction. *They stopped to lean over a gate.* ② VERB If you **lean on** something, you rest against it so that it partly supports you. If you **lean** an object somewhere, you place the object so that its weight is partly supported. *A man was leaning on the railing... Lean the plants against a wall.* ③ VERB If you **lean** towards an idea or a way of behaving, you tend to think or act in that way. *Voters have been leaning in the direction of the Democrats.* ④ ADJ A **lean** person is thin but looks strong and fit. ⑤ ADJ **Lean** meat has very little fat. ⑥ ADJ A **lean** period of time is one in which people have little money or success. *It is a lean time for the oil business.*
▸**lean on.** PHR-VERB If you **lean on** someone, you depend on them for support and help. *You can lean on me.*

★ **leap** /liːp/ **leaps, leaping, leaped, leapt** /lɛpt/.

✓ In British English, the form **leapt** is usually used in the past tense and past participle. American English usually uses **leaped.**

① VERB & N-COUNT If you **leap**, or if you take a **leap**, you jump high in the air or jump a long distance. *He had leapt from a window in the building and escaped.* ② VERB To **leap** somewhere means to move there suddenly and quickly. *The two men leaped into the jeep... The car leapt forward.* ③ VERB & N-COUNT You can say that things **leap** or take a **leap** when they suddenly advance or increase by a large amount. *Their share will leap to about 15 per cent. ...a giant leap in productivity.* ④ VERB If you **leap at** a chance or opportunity, you accept it quickly and eagerly.

★ **learn** /lɜːn/ **learns, learning, learned** (BRIT also **learnt** /lɜːnt/). ① VERB When you **learn**, you obtain knowledge or a skill through studying or training. *Their children were going to learn English... He is learning to play the piano... You need to learn how to use the office computer.* ♦ **learner, learners** N-COUNT *...a new aid for younger children or slow learners.* ♦ **learning** N-UNCOUNT *...a bilingual approach to the learning of English.* ② VERB If you **learn** something such as a poem or the script of a play, you study or repeat the words so that you can remember them. ③ VERB If people **learn to** behave or react in a particular way, their attitudes gradually change and they start behaving in that way. *He learned to conceal his views... We are learning how to confront death.* ④ VERB If you **learn from** an experience, you change the way you behave so that it does not happen again, or so that you can deal with it if it happens again. *He has learned from his mistakes.* ⑤ VERB If you **learn of** something, you find out about it. *She learned of his affair with Betty... She wasn't surprised to learn that he was involved.*

learned /'lɜːnɪd/. ADJ A **learned** person has gained a lot of knowledge by studying. **Learned** books have been written by a learned person. *...a genuinely learned man.*

★ **lease** /liːs/ **leases, leasing, leased.** ① N-COUNT A **lease** is a legal agreement under which someone pays money to another person in exchange for the use of a building or piece of land for a specified period of time. *He took up a 10 year lease on the house.* ② VERB If you **lease** property or something such as a car, or if someone **leases** it **to** you, they allow you to use it in return for regular payments of money. *He leased an apartment... She hopes to lease the building to students.* ③ PHRASE If you say that someone or something has been given **a new lease of life**, you are emphasizing that they are much more lively or successful than they have been in the past.

★ **least** /liːst/.

✓ **Least** is often considered to be the superlative form of **little**.

① ADJ & ADV & PRON You use **the least** to mean a smaller amount or extent than anyone or anything else, or the smallest amount or extent possible. *If you like cheese, go for the ones with the least fat... I'm the least experienced guy... We might get caught when we least expect it. ...the gap between those earning the most and those earning the least.* [2] ADJ You use **least** in structures where you are emphasizing that a particular situation or event is much less important or serious than other possible or actual ones. *Feeling sick is the least of her worries.*

PHRASES • You use **at least** to say that a number, amount, or action is the minimum possible or likely, and that more may be possible. The forms **at least** and **at the very least** are also used. *...a dinner menu featuring at least 15 different sorts of fish... She could take a nice holiday at least.* • You use **at least** when you are mentioning an advantage that still exists in a bad situation. *At least we know he is still alive.* • You can use **in the least** and **the least bit** to emphasize a negative. *I'm not like that at all. Not in the least... Alice wasn't the least bit frightened.* • You can use **not least** to emphasize an important example or reason. *Dieting itself can be bad for you, not least because it is a cause of chronic stress.* • You can use **to say the least** to suggest that a situation is actually much more extreme or serious than you say it is. *Accommodation was basic to say the least.*

leather /'leðə/ **leathers.** [1] N-VAR **Leather** is treated animal skin which is used for making shoes, clothes, bags, and furniture. *...a leather jacket.* [2] N-PLURAL **Leathers** are leather clothes, especially those worn by motorcyclists.

leave /li:v/ **leaves, leaving, left** /left/. [1] VERB If you **leave** a place or person, you go away from that place or person. *I simply couldn't bear to leave my little girl... My flight leaves in less than an hour... The last of the older children had left for school.* [2] VERB If you **leave** an institution, group, or job, you stop attending that institution, being a member of that group, or doing that job. *He left school with no qualifications. ...a leaving present.* [3] VERB If someone **leaves** their husband, wife, or partner, they end the relationship and stop living with him or her. *Bill left me for another woman.* [4] VERB If you **leave** something somewhere, you put it there and it remains there when you go away. *I left my bags in the car... Leave your key with a neighbour... He left me a nice little welcoming note.* [5] VERB If someone or something **leaves** an amount of something, that amount remains available after the rest has been used or has gone. *He always left a little food for the next day... It doesn't leave me much time.* [6] VERB If something **leaves** a mark, effect, or sign, it causes that mark, effect, or sign to remain as a result. *A muscle tear will leave a scar after healing... She left a lasting impression on him.* [7] VERB If an event **leaves** people or things in a particular state, they are in that state when the event has finished. *...violent disturbances which have left at least ten people dead.* [8] VERB If you

leave someone **to** do something, you go away from them so that they do it on their own, or you give them the responsibility for dealing with it. *I'd better leave you to get on with it... Left to myself, I don't go to church much.* [9] PHRASE If you **leave** someone or something **alone**, you do not bother them or try to do anything with them. *He just would not leave me alone, he followed me everywhere... Cigarettes and alcohol are best left alone.* [10] VERB If you **leave** something until a particular time, you delay dealing with it. *Don't leave it all until the last minute.* [11] VERB If you **leave** property or money **to** someone, you arrange for it to be given to them after you have died.* [12] VERB If you say that someone **leaves** a wife, husband, or a particular number of children, you mean that the wife, husband, or children remain alive after that person has died. [13] N-UNCOUNT & PHRASE **Leave** is a period of time when you are not working at your job. If you are **on leave**, you are not at your job. *Why don't you take a few days' leave?*

▶**leave behind.** [1] PHR-VERB If you **leave** someone or something **behind**, you go away permanently from them. *When he fled Liberia, he left behind a wife and two young children.* [2] PHR-VERB If someone or something **leaves behind** an object or a situation, that object or situation remains after they have gone. *The tenant has already left, leaving behind a mess of broken furniture.* [3] PHR-VERB If a person, country, or organization **is left behind**, they do not achieve as much as others or they do not progress as quickly, so they are at a disadvantage.

▶**leave off.** PHR-VERB If someone or something **is left off** a list, they are not included on that list.

▶**leave out.** PHR-VERB If you **leave** someone or something **out of** something such as an activity or a collection, you do not include them in it. *I never left him out of my team.*

leaves /li:vz/. **Leaves** is the plural form of **leaf**.

lecture /'lektʃə/ **lectures, lecturing, lectured.** [1] N-COUNT A **lecture** is a talk that someone gives in order to teach people about a particular subject, usually at a university. [2] VERB If you **lecture** on a particular subject, you give a lecture or a series of lectures about it. *She then invited him to Atlanta to lecture on the history of art.* [3] VERB & N-COUNT If someone **lectures** you about something, or if they give you a **lecture**, they criticize you or tell you how they think you should behave. *Chuck would lecture me, telling me to get a haircut... Our captain gave us a stern lecture on safety.*

lecturer /'lektʃərə/ **lecturers.** N-COUNT A **lecturer** is a teacher at university or college.

led /led/. **Led** is the past tense and past participle of **lead**.

ledge /ledʒ/ **ledges.** [1] N-COUNT A **ledge** is a narrow shelf along the bottom edge of a window. [2] N-COUNT A **ledge** is a piece of rock

a
b
c
d
e
f
g
h
i
j
k
l
m
n
o
p
q
r
s
t
u
v
w
x
y
z

shaped like a narrow shelf on the side of a cliff or mountain.

ledger /ˈledʒə/ **ledgers.** N-COUNT A **ledger** is a book in which a company or other organization writes down the amounts of money it spends and receives.

leek /liːk/ **leeks.** N-VAR **Leeks** are long green and white vegetables. → See picture on page 836.

leer /lɪə/ **leers, leering, leered.** VERB & N-COUNT If someone **leers at** you, or if they look at you with a **leer**, they smile unpleasantly, usually in a sexually suggestive way; used showing disapproval. *The soldier leered at Thomasina... He gave it to me with a leer.*

⭐ **left** /left/. **1** **Left** is the past tense and past participle of **leave**. **2** ADJ & PHRASE If there is a certain amount of something **left**, or if you have a certain amount of it **left over**, it remains when the rest has gone or been used. *Is there any gin left?... They still have six games left to play.* **3** N-SING & ADV & ADJ BEFORE N The **left** is one of two opposite directions, sides, or positions. In the word 'to', the 't' is to the left of the 'o'. If you are facing north and you turn **left**, you will be facing west. **Left** is used to describe the one of two things that someone has, for example their arm or leg, that is on the left. *In Britain cars drive on the left... To my left, I noticed a light... Go left at the traffic lights... Drummond had the baton in his left hand.* **4** N-SING You can refer to political ideas which are closer to socialism than to capitalism or conservatism, or to people who support these ideas, as **the left**. *The change has been bitterly opposed by the left.*

'left-click, left-clicks, left-clicking, left-clicked. VERB To **left-click** or to **left-click on** something means to press the left-hand button on a computer mouse. [COMPUTING] *Left-click on one of the choices to make it operate.*

'left-hand. ADJ BEFORE N **Left-hand** describes the position of something when it is on the left side. *...the back left-hand corner of the drawer.*

,left-'handed. ADJ Someone who is **left-handed** finds it easier to use their left hand rather than their right hand for activities such as writing and throwing a ball.

leftist /ˈleftɪst/ **leftists.** N-COUNT & ADJ BEFORE N Socialists and communists are sometimes referred to as **leftists.** *...an alliance of leftist parties.*

leftover /ˈleftəʊvə/ **leftovers.** ADJ BEFORE N & N-PLURAL **Leftover** things or **leftovers** are things which remain after the other similar things have been used, especially food which remains after a meal.

,left-'wing (or **left wing**). **1** ADJ **Left-wing** people have political ideas that are based on socialism. *They would not be voting for him because he was too left-wing.* **2** N-SING The **left wing** of a political group consists of the members of it whose beliefs are closer to socialism than are those of its other members.

⭐ **leg** /leg/ **legs.** **1** N-COUNT A person's or animal's **legs** are the long parts of their body that they use to stand on and walk with. → See picture on page 822. **2** N-COUNT The **legs** of a pair of trousers are the parts that cover your legs. **3** N-COUNT A **leg** of lamb or pork is a piece of meat from the thigh of a sheep, lamb, or pig. **4** N-COUNT The **legs** of a table, chair, or other piece of furniture are the parts that rest on the floor, supporting the furniture's weight. **5** N-COUNT A **leg** of a long journey is one part of it. *The first leg of the journey was by boat.*

legacy /ˈlegəsi/ **legacies.** **1** N-COUNT A **legacy** is money or property which someone leaves to you in their will when they die. **2** N-COUNT The **legacy** of an event or period of history is something which is a direct result of it and which continues to exist after it is over. *...the legacy of inequality and injustice created by apartheid.*

⭐ **legal** /ˈliːgəl/. **1** ADJ BEFORE N **Legal** is used to describe things that relate to the law. *He vowed to take legal action. ...the British legal system.* ♦ **legally** ADV *It could be a bit problematic, legally speaking.* **2** ADJ An action or situation that is **legal** is allowed by law. *...drivers who drink more than the legal limit of alcohol.* ♦ **legally** ADV *...a legally binding contract.* ♦ **legality** /liːˈgæləti/ N-UNCOUNT *The auditor questioned the legality of the deal.*

legalize (BRIT also **legalise**) /ˈliːgəlaɪz/ **legalizes, legalizing, legalized.** VERB If something **is legalized**, the law is changed so that it is allowed. *...a 1973 ruling which legalized abortion.*

legend /ˈledʒənd/ **legends.** **1** N-VAR A **legend** is a very old and popular story that may be based on real events. *...the legends of ancient Greece.* **2** N-COUNT If you refer to someone as a **legend**, you mean that they are very famous and admired. *...Hollywood legend Audrey Hepburn.*

legendary /ˈledʒəndri, AM -deri/. **1** ADJ If you describe someone or something as **legendary**, you mean that they are very famous and that many stories are told about them. *...the legendary jazz singer Adelaide Hall.* **2** ADJ A **legendary** person, place, or event is described in a legend.

leggings /ˈlegɪŋz/. N-PLURAL **Leggings** are tight trousers that are made out of a fabric which stretches easily.

legion /ˈliːdʒən/ **legions.** **1** N-COUNT A **legion** is a large group of soldiers who form one section of an army. **2** N-COUNT A **legion of** people or things is a large number of them.

legislate /ˈledʒɪsleɪt/ **legislates, legislating, legislated.** VERB When a government **legislates**, it passes a new law. *You can't legislate against prejudice.*

⭐ **legislation** /ˌledʒɪˈsleɪʃən/. N-UNCOUNT **Legislation** consists of a law or laws passed by a government. *...legislation to protect women's rights.*

legislative /ˈledʒɪslətɪv, AM -leɪ-/. ADJ BEFORE N **Legislative** means involving or relating to the process of making and passing laws.

legislator /'ledʒɪsleɪtə/ **legislators.** N-COUNT A **legislator** is someone involved in making or passing laws.

legislature /'ledʒɪslətʃə, AM -leɪ-/ **legislatures.** N-COUNT The **legislature** of a state or country is the group of people within it who have the power to make and pass laws.

legitimate /lɪ'dʒɪtɪmət/. ① ADJ Something that is **legitimate** is acceptable according to the law. ...the restoration of the legitimate government. ◆ **legitimacy** /lɪ'dʒɪtɪmɪsi/ N-UNCOUNT ...the legitimacy of the board's activities. ◆ **legitimately** ADV He still claims to be the legitimately elected president. ② ADJ If you say that something such as a feeling or opinion is **legitimate**, you think that it is reasonable and acceptable. That's a perfectly legitimate fear. ◆ **legitimacy** N-UNCOUNT The comment is not without legitimacy. ◆ **legitimately** ADV You can legitimately claim to feel angry and disappointed.

leisure /'leʒə, AM 'liːʒ-/. ① N-UNCOUNT **Leisure** is the time when you do not have to work and can do things that you enjoy. ...a relaxing way to fill my leisure time. ② PHRASE If someone does something **at leisure** or **at their leisure,** they do it when they want to, without hurrying. Stroll at leisure through the gardens.

leisurely /'leʒəli, AM 'liːʒ-/. ADJ & ADV A **leisurely** action is done in a relaxed and unhurried way. Tweed walked at a leisurely pace.

lemon /'lemən/ **lemons.** N-VAR A **lemon** is a sour yellow citrus fruit. → See picture on page 821. ...a slice of lemon.

lemonade /,lemə'neɪd/. N-UNCOUNT **Lemonade** is a clear, sweet, fizzy drink, or a drink that is made from lemons, sugar, and water.

⭐ **lend** /lend/ **lends, lending, lent.** ① VERB When people or organizations such as banks **lend** you money, they give it to you and you agree to pay it back at a future date, often with an extra amount as interest. I had to lend him ten pounds to take his children to the pictures... The White House said that America would lend another $1.5 billion. ◆ **lender, lenders** N-COUNT ...the six leading mortgage lenders. ◆ **lending** N-UNCOUNT ...a slump in bank lending. ② VERB If you **lend** something that you own, you allow someone to have or to use it for a period of time. Will you lend me your jacket? ③ VERB To **lend** something such as a particular quality **to** something means to give it that quality. Enthusiastic applause lent a sense of occasion to the proceedings... He lent his support to the abolition of existing divorce laws. ④ VERB If something **lends itself to** a particular activity, it is very suitable for it. The room lends itself well to summer eating.

⭐ **length** /leŋθ/ **lengths.** ① N-VAR The **length** of something is the amount that it measures from one end to the other. It is about a metre in length. ...the length of the fish. ② N-UNCOUNT The **length** of something is its quality of being long. I noticed, too, the length of her fingers. ③ N-VAR The **length**
of something such as a piece of writing is the amount of writing that is contained in it. ④ N-VAR The **length** of an event, activity, or situation is the time it lasts. The film is over two hours in length. ⑤ N-COUNT A **length of** wood, string, cloth, or other material is a piece of it. Hang lengths of fabric behind the glass. ⑥ N-COUNT If you swim a **length** in a swimming pool, you swim from one end to the other. ⑦ N-SING If something happens or exists along **the length of** something, it happens or exists for the whole way along it. I looked along the length of the building.

PHRASES ● If someone does something **at length**, they do it for a long time and in great detail. They spoke at length. ● If someone **goes to great lengths to** achieve something, they try very hard and may do extreme things in order to achieve it. Garbo went to great lengths to hide from reporters.

lengthen /'leŋθən/ **lengthens, lengthening, lengthened.** VERB When something **lengthens**, or when you **lengthen** it, it becomes longer. Vacations have lengthened.

lengthy /'leŋθi/. ① ADJ Something that is **lengthy** lasts for a long time. ...the lengthy process of filling out passport application forms. ② ADJ A **lengthy** report, book, or document contains a lot of speech or writing.

lenient /'liːniənt/. ADJ When someone in authority is **lenient**, they are not as strict or as severe as expected. He received an unexpectedly lenient sentence. ◆ **leniently** ADV Reckless drivers are treated too leniently.

⭐ **lens** /lenz/ **lenses.** N-COUNT A **lens** is a thin, curved piece of glass or plastic in something such as a camera or pair of glasses which makes things appear larger or clearer.

lent /lent/. **Lent** is the past tense and past participle of **lend**.

lentil /'lentɪl/ **lentils.** N-COUNT **Lentils** are a type of dried seed used in cooking.

leopard /'lepəd/ **leopards.** N-COUNT A **leopard** is a type of large wild cat from Africa or Asia. Leopards have yellow fur and black spots. → See picture on page 816.

⭐ **lesbian** /'lezbiən/ **lesbians.** N-COUNT & ADJ A **lesbian** or a **lesbian** woman is a woman who is sexually attracted to women.

⭐ **less** /les/. ① QUANT & ADV You use **less** to indicate that there is a smaller number of things or a smaller amount of something than before or than average, or than something else. People should eat less fat... Over here, things have been a bit less dramatic... He still eats cheese, but far less often. ...spending less and saving more... Last year less of the money went into high-technology companies. ② PREP You use **less than** before a number or amount to say that the actual number or amount is smaller than this. Motorways actually cover less than 0.1 percent of the countryside. ③ PREP When you are referring to

a b c d e f g h i j k **l** m n o p q r s t u v w x y z

amounts, you use **less** in front of a number or quantity to indicate that it is to be subtracted from another number or quantity already mentioned. ...Fees: £750, less £400.

> **USAGE** You use **less** to talk about amounts that cannot be counted, except in the phrase **no less than**. ...less money. ...no less than nine goals. When you are talking about things that can be counted, you should use **fewer**, for example fewer than five visits.

PHRASES ● You use **less and less** to say that something is becoming smaller all the time in degree or amount. The couple seem to spend less and less time together. ● You can use **no less** as an emphatic way of expressing surprise or admiration at the amount or importance of someone or something. He had returned to England in an aircraft carrier no less. ● You use **no less than** before an amount to indicate that you think the amount is larger than you expected. He is lined up for no less than four US television interviews. ● You use **less than** to say that something does not have a particular quality. For example, something that is **less than** perfect is not perfect. ● **more or less**: see **more**.

lessen /'lesən/ **lessens, lessening, lessened.** VERB If something **lessens**, or if you **lessen** it, it becomes smaller in amount, degree, or importance. ...changes to their diet that would lessen the risk of premature death. ◆ **lessening** N-UNCOUNT ...a lessening of tension.

lesser /'lesə/. ADJ & ADV You use **lesser** in order to indicate that something is smaller in extent or amount than another thing that has been mentioned. The responsibility lies with Harris and, to a lesser extent, Clarke. ...lesser known works by famous artists.

⭐ **lesson** /'lesən/ **lessons.** 1 N-COUNT A **lesson** is a fixed period of time during which people are taught something. Johanna took piano lessons. 2 N-COUNT If an experience teaches you a **lesson**, it makes you realize the truth or realize what should be done. There's still one lesson to be learned from the crisis. 3 PHRASE If you say that you are going to **teach** someone **a lesson**, you mean that you are going to punish them for something that they have done so that they do not do it again.

lest /lest/. CONJ If you do something **lest** something unpleasant should happen, you do it to try to prevent the unpleasant thing from happening. [FORMAL] I was afraid to open the door lest he should follow me.

⭐ **let** /let/ **lets, letting, let.** 1 VERB If you **let** something happen, you allow it to happen. Thorne let him talk... I love sweets but Mum doesn't let me have them... I can't let myself be distracted. 2 VERB If you **let** someone into, out of, or through a place, you allow them to enter, leave,

or go through it. I let myself into the flat... I'd better go and let the dog out. 3 VERB You use **let me** when you are introducing something you want to do, or something you are offering to do. Let me explain... Let me get you something to drink. 4 VERB You use **let's** or **let us** when you are making a suggestion. I'm bored. Let's go home... 'Shall we go in and have some supper?'— 'Yes, let's.' 5 VERB & PHR-VERB If you **let** your house or land to someone, or if you **let** it **out**, you allow them to use it in exchange for regular payments.

PHRASES ● **Let alone** is used after a statement, usually a negative one, to indicate that the statement is even more true of the person or situation that you are going to mention next. It is incredible that the 12-year-old managed to even reach the pedals, let alone drive the car. ● If you **let go of** someone or something, you stop holding them. She let go of Mona's hand. ● If you **let** someone **know** something, you make sure that they know about it. If you do want to go, please let me know.

▶**let down.** 1 PHR-VERB If you **let** someone **down**, you disappoint them, usually by not doing something that you said you would do. Don't worry, Xiao, I won't let you down. 2 PHR-VERB If you **let down** something filled with air, such as a tyre, you allow air to escape from it.

▶**let in.** PHR-VERB If an object **lets in** something such as air or water, it allows air or water to get into it or pass through it. There is no glass in the front door to let in light.

▶**let in on.** PHR-VERB If you **let** someone **in on** something that is a secret from most people, you allow them to know about it.

▶**let off.** 1 PHR-VERB If someone in authority **lets** you **off** a task or duty, they give you permission not to do it. [BRITISH] Having a new baby lets you off going to boring dinner-parties. 2 PHR-VERB If you **let** someone **off**, you give them a lighter punishment than they expect or no punishment at all. 3 PHR-VERB If you **let off** an explosive or a gun, you explode or fire it. His neighbourhood had let off fireworks to celebrate the Revolution.

▶**let on.** PHR-VERB If you do not **let on** that something is true, you do not tell anyone that it is true. [BRITISH] I'd be in trouble if I let on.

▶**let out.** 1 PHR-VERB If something or someone **lets** water, air, or breath **out**, they allow it to flow out or escape. It lets sunlight in but doesn't let heat out. 2 See also **let** 5.

▶**let up.** PHR-VERB If an unpleasant, continuous process **lets up**, it stops or reduces. The rain had let up.

lethal /'li:θəl/. ADJ Something that is **lethal** can kill you. ...a lethal dose of sleeping pills.

lethargic /lɪ'θɑːdʒɪk/. ADJ If you are **lethargic**, you have no energy or enthusiasm. He felt too miserable and lethargic to get dressed.

lethargy /'leθədʒi/. N-UNCOUNT **Lethargy** is a

condition in which you have no energy or enthusiasm.

⭐ **let's** /lets/. **Let's** is the usual spoken and written form of **let us**.

⭐ **letter** /'letə/letters. **1** N-COUNT When you write a **letter**, you write a message on paper and send it to someone. *I had received a letter from a very close friend. ...a letter of resignation.* **2** N-COUNT **Letters** are written symbols which represent the sounds of a language. *...the letter E.*

letterbox (or **letter box**) /'letəbɒks/letterboxes. N-COUNT A **letterbox** is a rectangular hole in a door through which letters are delivered.

lettering /'letərɪŋ/. N-UNCOUNT You can use **lettering** to refer to writing, especially when you are describing the type of letters used. *...a small blue sign with white lettering.*

lettuce /'letɪs/lettuces. N-VAR A **lettuce** is a plant with large green leaves that you eat in salads. → See picture on page 836.

leukaemia (AM **leukemia**) /luː'kiːmiə/. N-UNCOUNT **Leukaemia** is a serious disease of the blood.

⭐ **level** /'levəl/levels, levelling, levelled (AM leveling, leveled). **1** N-COUNT A **level** is a point on a scale, for example a scale of amount, importance, or difficulty. *...the lowest level of inflation for some years... Michael's roommate had been pleasant on a superficial level.* **2** N-SING The **level** of something is its height or the height of its surface. *He had the gun held at waist level... The water level of the Mississippi River is already 6.5 feet below normal.* **3** ADJ AFTER LINK-V If one thing is **level with** another thing, it is at the same height. *He leaned over the counter so his face was almost level with the boy's.* **4** ADJ Something that is **level** is completely flat. *...a plateau of fairly level ground.* **5** VERB If someone or something such as a violent storm **levels** a building or area of land, they flatten or demolish it completely. *Further tremors could level more buildings.* **6** ADV & ADJ AFTER LINK-V If you **draw level with** someone or something, you get closer to them until you are by their side. *Everyone waited till she drew level with them on the platform... He waited until they were level with the door.* **7** VERB If an accusation or criticism is **levelled** at someone, they are criticized for something they have done or are accused of doing something wrong. *Allegations of corruption were levelled at him.*
● **a level playing field**: see **playing field**.
▶**level off** or **level out.** PHR-VERB If an amount or something that is changing **levels off** or **levels out**, it stops changing so quickly. *Inflation is finally levelling out at around 11% a month.*

lever /'liːvə, AM 'lev-/levers. **1** N-COUNT A **lever** is a handle or bar that you pull or push to operate a piece of machinery. *Pull the gear lever.* **2** N-COUNT A **lever** is a long bar, one end of which is placed under a heavy object so that when you press down on the other end you can move the object. **3** N-COUNT A **lever** is an idea or action that you can use to make people do what you want them to do. *...using the hostages as a lever to gain concessions.*

leverage /'liːvərɪdʒ, AM 'lev-/. **1** N-UNCOUNT **Leverage** is the ability to influence and control situations or people. *His function as a Mayor affords him the leverage to get things done.* **2** N-UNCOUNT **Leverage** is the force that is applied to an object when something such as a lever is used.

levy /'levi/levies, levying, levied. **1** N-COUNT A **levy** is a sum of money that you have to pay, for example as a tax to the government. **2** VERB If a government or organization **levies** a tax or other sum of money, it demands it.

liability /ˌlaɪə'bɪlɪti/liabilities. **1** N-COUNT If you say that someone or something is a **liability**, you mean that they cause a lot of problems or embarrassment. *She had become a liability to her party.* **2** N-COUNT An organization's **liabilities** are the sums of money which it owes.

liable /'laɪəbəl/. **1** ADJ AFTER LINK-V If people or things are **liable to** do something or **liable to** something, they have a tendency to do it or to experience it. [FORMAL] *...equipment that is liable to break. ...a woman particularly liable to depression.* **2** ADJ AFTER LINK-V If you are **liable for** something, you are legally responsible for it. *The airline's insurer is liable for damages.* ◆ **liability** /ˌlaɪə'bɪlɪti/N-UNCOUNT *The Government will not admit liability for his injuries.*

liaise /li'eɪz/liaises, liaising, liaised. VERB When organizations or people **liaise**, or when one organization **liaises** with another, they co-operate and inform each other about their work. [BRITISH] *Social services and health workers liaise closely.*

liaison /li'eɪzɒn, AM 'liːeɪz-/liaisons. **1** N-UNCOUNT **Liaison** is co-operation and the exchange of information between different organizations or people. *We work in close liaison with the Doping Control Unit.* **2** N-COUNT You can refer to a romantic relationship between two people as a **liaison**.

liar /'laɪə/liars. N-COUNT A **liar** is someone who tells lies.

libel /'laɪbəl/libels, libelling, libelled. **1** N-VAR **Libel** is something in writing which wrongly accuses someone of something, and which is therefore against the law. [LEGAL] *Warren sued him for libel over the remarks.* **2** VERB If someone **libels** you, they write something in a newspaper or book which wrongly damages your reputation and is therefore against the law.

⭐ **liberal** /'lɪbərəl/liberals. **1** ADJ & N-COUNT If someone has **liberal** views, or if they are a **liberal**, they are tolerant and believe in people's right to behave differently or hold their own opinions. *She is known to have liberal views on divorce.* **2** ADJ BEFORE N & N-COUNT A **Liberal** politician or voter or a **Liberal** is a member of a

Liberal Party or votes for a Liberal Party. [3] ADJ **Liberal** means giving, using, or taking a lot of something. ...*the country's liberal use of the death penalty.* ♦ **liberally** ADV ...*coffee liberally laced with whiskey.*

,**Liberal 'Democrat Party.** N-PROPER **The Liberal Democrat Party** is the third largest political party in Britain and the main centre party.

liberalize (BRIT also **liberalise**) /'lɪbrəlaɪz/ **liberalizes, liberalizing, liberalized.** VERB When a country or government **liberalizes**, or **liberalizes** its laws or its attitudes, it allows people more freedom in their actions. ...*the decision to liberalize travel restrictions.* ♦ **liberalization** N-UNCOUNT ...*the liberalization of divorce laws.*

★ **liberate** /'lɪbəreɪt/ **liberates, liberating, liberated.** [1] VERB To **liberate** a place or the people in it means to free them from the political or military control of another country, area, or group of people. *They planned to march on and liberate the city.* ♦ **liberation** N-UNCOUNT ...*a mass liberation movement.* [2] VERB To **liberate** someone **from** something means to help them escape from it or overcome it, and lead a better way of life. *He asked how committed the leadership was to liberating its people from poverty.* ♦ **liberating** ADJ *It can be a very liberating experience.* ♦ **liberation** N-UNCOUNT ...*the women's liberation movement.*

liberated /'lɪbəreɪtɪd/. ADJ If you describe someone as **liberated**, you mean that they do not accept their society's traditional values or restrictive way of behaving.

★ **liberty** /'lɪbəti/ **liberties.** [1] N-VAR **Liberty** is the freedom to live your life in the way that you want and go where you want to go. ...*the rights and liberties of the English people.* [2] PHRASE If someone is **at liberty to** do something, they have been given permission to do it. *We are not at liberty to disclose that information.*

librarian /laɪ'breərɪən/ **librarians.** N-COUNT A **librarian** is a person who works in, or is in charge of a library.

★ **library** /'laɪbrəri/ AM -breri/ **libraries.** N-COUNT A public **library** is a building where things such as books, newspapers, videos, and music are kept for people to read, use, or borrow.

lice /laɪs/. **Lice** is the plural of **louse.**

★ **licence** (AM **license**) /'laɪsəns/ **licences.** [1] N-COUNT A **licence** is an official document which gives you permission to do, use, or own something. ...*his pilot's licence.* [2] PHRASE If someone does something **under licence**, they do it by special permission from a government or some other authority.

license /'laɪsəns/ **licenses, licensing, licensed.** VERB If a government or other authority **licenses** a person, organization, or activity, they officially give permission for the person or organization to do something, or for the activity to take place.

The council can license a U.S. company to produce the drug.

licensed /'laɪsənst/. [1] ADJ If you are **licensed to** do something, you are given the official authority to do it. *The club was licensed to hold parties.* [2] ADJ If something that you own or use is **licensed**, you have official permission to own it or use it. ...*a licensed rifle.*

'**license plate, license plates.** N-COUNT In American English, a **license plate** is a sign on the front and back of a vehicle that shows its registration number. The British term is **number plate.**

lick /lɪk/ **licks, licking, licked.** VERB & N-COUNT When you **lick** something, or when you give it a **lick**, you move your tongue across its surface. *She folded up her letter, licking the envelope flap.* ...*taking tiny licks at a pistachio ice-cream.*

lid /lɪd/ **lids.** [1] N-COUNT A **lid** of a container is the top which you open to reach inside. [2] N-COUNT Your **lids** are the pieces of skin which cover your eyes when you close them.

lie 1 position or situation

★ **lie** /laɪ/ **lies, lying, lay, lain.** [1] VERB If you **are lying** somewhere, you are in a horizontal position and are not standing or sitting. *There was a child lying on the ground... He lay awake watching her.* [2] VERB If an object **lies** in a particular place, it is in a flat position in that place. *Broken glass lay scattered on the carpet.* [3] VERB If a place **lies** in a particular position, it is situated there. *The islands lie at the southern end of the Kurile chain.* [4] LINK-VERB You can use **lie** to say that something is or remains in a particular state or condition. *His country's economy lies in ruins.* [5] VERB You can use **lie** to say what position someone is in during a competition. [BRITISH] *Blyth Tait is lying in second place.* [6] VERB You can talk about where something such as a problem, solution, or fault **lies** to say what you think it involves or is caused by. *The problem lay in the large amounts spent on defence.* [7] VERB If something **lies** ahead, it is going to happen in the future.

USAGE Do not confuse the verb **lie** with the verb **lay**. The past tense of **lie** is **lay** and the past participle is **lain**. It is an intransitive verb. *I lay on the floor with my legs in the air... He had lain in great pain in a darkened room.* However, **lay**, whose past tense and past participle are **laid**, is usually a transitive verb. *They laid him on the floor.* Because **lay** is used to talk about putting something in a particular place or position, it is related to the verb **lie**. If someone **lays** something somewhere, it **lies** there. Because of their related meanings, people sometimes confuse the two verbs.

▶**lie around.** PHR-VERB If things are left **lying around** or **lying about**, they are not tidied away. *My dad had a couple of Bob Dylan and Beatles song-books lying around the house.*

▶**lie behind.** PHR-VERB If you refer to what **lies behind** a situation or event, you are referring to the reason the situation exists or the event happened. *What lay behind the clashes was disagreement over the list of candidates.*

lie 2 things that are not true

⭐ **lie** /laɪ/ **lies, lying, lied.** ☐1 VERB & N-COUNT If someone **is lying**, or if they are telling a **lie**, they are saying something which they know is untrue. *He lies about his age... She lied to her husband so she could meet her lover... All the boys told lies about their adventures.* ♦ **lying** N-UNCOUNT *Lying is something that I will not tolerate.* ☐2 PHRASE If you say that someone **is living a lie**, you mean that in every part of their life they are hiding the truth about themselves from other people.

lieutenant /lef'tenənt, AM lu:-/ **lieutenants.** A **lieutenant** is a junior officer in the army, navy, or air force.

lifeboat

⭐ **life** /laɪf/ **lives.** ☐1 N-UNCOUNT **Life** is the quality which people, animals, and plants have when they are not dead. *...a baby's first minutes of life.* ☐2 N-UNCOUNT You can use **life** to refer to things or groups of things which are alive. *...some useful facts about animal and plant life.* ☐3 N-COUNT Someone's **life** is their state of being alive, or the period of time during which they are alive. *Your life is in danger... He spent the last fourteen years of his life in retirement.* ☐4 N-UNCOUNT **Life** is the events and experiences that happen to people. *...the sort of life we can only fantasise about living.* ☐5 N-COUNT You can use **life** to refer to particular activities which people regularly do during their lives. *My personal life has had to take second place to my career.* ☐6 N-UNCOUNT A person or place that is full of **life** is full of activity and excitement. *The town itself was full of life and character.* ☐7 N-SING The **life** of something such as a machine or organization is the period of time that it lasts for. *The repairs did not increase the value or the life of the equipment.* ☐8 N-UNCOUNT If someone is sentenced to **life**, they are sent to prison for the rest of their life, or for a very long time. ☐9 PHRASE If someone **is fighting for** their **life**, they are very

seriously ill or injured and may die. [JOURNALISM] ● a new lease of life: see lease.

lifeboat /'laɪfbəʊt/ **lifeboats.** N-COUNT A **lifeboat** is a boat used to rescue people who are in danger at sea.

'**life-cycle, life-cycles.** N-COUNT The **life-cycle** of an animal or plant is the series of changes it passes through from the beginning of its life until its death.

,**life ex'pectancy, life expectancies.** N-VAR The **life expectancy** of a person, animal, or plant is the length of time that they are normally likely to live. *Smoking reduces life expectancy.*

lifeguard /'laɪfɡɑːd/ **lifeguards.** N-COUNT A **lifeguard** is a person who works at a beach or swimming pool and rescues people when they are in danger of drowning.

lifejacket (or **life jacket**) /'laɪfdʒækɪt/ **lifejackets.** N-COUNT A **lifejacket** is a sleeveless jacket which keeps you afloat in water. [BRITISH]

lifeless /'laɪfləs/ ☐1 ADJ A person or animal that is **lifeless** is dead, or so still that they appear to be dead. ☐2 ADJ A **lifeless** place or area does not have anything living or growing there at all. *...the Antarctic, mile for mile one of the planet's most lifeless areas.* ☐3 ADJ If you describe a person, or something such as an artistic performance or a town as **lifeless**, you mean they lack any lively or exciting qualities. *With one exception his novels are shallow and lifeless things.*

lifeline /'laɪflaɪn/ **lifelines.** N-COUNT A **lifeline** is something that enables an organization or group to survive or to continue with an activity. *The orders will throw a lifeline to Britain's shipyards.*

lifelong /'laɪflɒŋ, AM -lɔːŋ/. ADJ BEFORE N **Lifelong** means existing or happening for the whole of a person's life. *...her lifelong friendship with Naomi.*

lifespan /'laɪfspæn/ **lifespans.** N-COUNT The **lifespan** of a person, animal, or plant is the period of time for which they live or are normally expected to live. *A 15-year lifespan is not uncommon for a dog.*

lifestyle (or **life-style**) /'laɪfstaɪl/ **lifestyles.** ☐1 N-COUNT Your **lifestyle** is the way you live, for example the things you normally do. *They enjoyed an income and lifestyle that many people would envy.* ☐2 ADJ **Lifestyle** magazines, television programmes and products are aimed at people who wish to be associated with glamorous and successful lifestyles.

'**life-threatening.** ADJ A **life-threatening** situation or illness is one in which there is a strong possibility that someone will die.

lifetime /'laɪftaɪm/ **lifetimes.** ☐1 N-COUNT A **lifetime** is the length of time that someone is alive. *During my lifetime I haven't got around to much travelling.* ☐2 N-SING The **lifetime** of something is the period of time that it lasts. *...the lifetime of a parliament.* ☐3 PHRASE If you describe something, for example an opportunity, as the opportunity **of a lifetime**, you are emphasizing

⭐ Bank of English® frequent word　　For a full explanation of all grammatical labels, see pages vii-x

a
b
c
d
e
f
g
h
i
j
k
l
m
n
o
p
q
r
s
t
u
v
w
x
y
z

that it is the most memorable or important opportunity that you are ever likely to have.

⭐ **lift** /lɪft/ **lifts, lifting, lifted.** 1 VERB & PHR-VERB If you **lift** something, or if you **lift** it **up**, you move it to a higher position. *She lifted the last of her drink to her lips... Amy lifted her arm to wave... She put her arms around him and lifted him up.* 2 VERB If fog, cloud, or mist **lifts**, it reduces, making the weather brighter or less misty. 3 N-COUNT In British English, a **lift** is a device that carries people or goods up and down inside tall buildings. The American word is **elevator.** 4 N-COUNT If you give someone a **lift**, you drive them from one place to another. 5 VERB If people in authority **lift** a law or rule, they end it. *The European Commission has urged France to lift its ban on imports of British beef.* 6 VERB To **lift** something means to increase it. *The bank has lifted its basic home loans rate.*

ligament /ˈlɪɡəmənt/ **ligaments.** N-COUNT A **ligament** is a band of strong tissue in your body, which connects bones.

light 1 brightness or illumination

⭐ **light** /laɪt/ **lights, lighting, lit, lighted; lighter, lightest.**

✓ The form **lit** is the usual past tense and past participle, but the form **lighted** is also used.

1 N-UNCOUNT **Light** is the brightness that lets you see things. Light comes from the sun, moon, lamps, and fire. *It was difficult to see in the dim light. ...ultraviolet light.* 2 N-COUNT A **light** is anything that produces light, especially an electric bulb. *The janitor comes round to turn the lights out. ...street lights.* 3 VERB A place or object that **is lit** by something has light shining in it or on it. *The room was lit by only the one light.* 4 ADJ If it is **light**, there is enough natural daylight to see by. *It was still light when we arrived.* 5 ADJ If a building or room is **light**, it has a lot of natural light in it. 6 VERB If you **light** something, you make it start burning. *She lit the fire as soon as I arrived.* 7 N-SING If someone asks you for a **light**, they want a match or a cigarette lighter so they can start smoking. [INFORMAL] 8 N-COUNT If something is presented **in** a particular **light**, it is presented so that you think about it in a particular way or so that it appears to be of a particular nature. *He has worked hard in recent months to portray New York in a better light.*

PHRASES ● If you **set light to** something, you make it start burning. ● If someone or something **sheds light on**, **throws light on**, or **casts light on** something, they add to the information people have about it, helping them to understand it more. *A new approach offers an answer, and may shed light on an even bigger question.* ● If something **comes to light** or is **brought to light**, it becomes known. *The truth is unlikely to be brought to light by the promised enquiry.* ● If something is possible **in the light of** particular information or knowledge, it becomes possible because you have this information or knowledge. *In the light of this information it is*

now possible to identify a number of key issues.
● See also **lighter, lighting.**

►**light up.** 1 PHR-VERB If you **light** something **up**, or if it **lights up**, it becomes bright. *...a keypad that lights up when you pick up the handset.* 2 PHR-VERB If your face or eyes **light up**, you suddenly look very surprised or happy.

light 2 not great in weight, amount, or intensity

⭐ **light** /laɪt/ **lighter, lightest.** 1 ADJ Something that is **light** does not weigh very much. *Try to wear light, loose clothes.* ◆ **lightness** N-UNCOUNT *It is fashioned completely of steel for lightness and strength.* 2 ADJ Something that is **light** is not very great in amount, degree, or intensity. *...the usual light traffic in the city... There was a light knock at the door.* ◆ **lightly** ADV *Put the onions in the pan and cook until lightly browned... He kissed her lightly on the mouth.* 3 ADJ Something that is **light** is very pale in colour. *He is light haired with gray eyes... We know he has a light green van.* 4 ADJ **Light** work does not involve much physical effort.

light 3 unimportant or not serious

⭐ **light** /laɪt/ **lighter, lightest.** 1 ADJ You can describe things such as books or music as **light** when they are entertaining without making you think very deeply. 2 ADJ If you say something in a **light** way, you sound as if you think it is not important or serious. *Talk to him in a friendly, light way about the relationship. ...to finish on a lighter note.* ◆ **lightly** ADV *'Once a detective, always a detective,' he said lightly.*

'light bulb, light bulbs. N-COUNT A **light bulb** is the round glass part of an electric light or lamp which light shines from.

lighten /ˈlaɪtən/ **lightens, lightening, lightened.** 1 VERB When something **lightens**, or when you **lighten** it, it becomes less dark. *She was asked to lighten her hair for a TV series.* 2 VERB If your attitude or mood **lightens**, you feel more cheerful, happy, and relaxed. *The sun was streaming in through the window, yet it did nothing to lighten his mood.* 3 VERB If you **lighten** something, you make it less heavy.

lighter /ˈlaɪtə/ **lighters.** N-COUNT A **lighter** is a small device that produces a flame that you can use to light cigarettes.

,light-'hearted. 1 ADJ **Light-hearted** things are intended to be entertaining or amusing, and not at all serious. *The opera is viewed as light-hearted fantasy.* 2 ADJ Someone who is **light-hearted** is cheerful and happy. *They were light-hearted and prepared to enjoy life.*

lighthouse /ˈlaɪthaʊs/ **lighthouses.** N-COUNT A **lighthouse** is a tower near the sea which contains a powerful flashing lamp to guide ships or to warn them of danger.

lighting /ˈlaɪtɪŋ/ N-UNCOUNT The **lighting** in a place is the way that it is lit, or the quality of the light in it. *The whole room is bathed in soft lighting. ...street lighting.*

lightning /'laɪtnɪŋ/. **1** N-UNCOUNT **Lightning** is the bright flashes of light in the sky that you see during a thunderstorm. **2** ADJ BEFORE N **Lightning** describes things that happen very quickly or last for only a short time. *Driving today demands lightning reflexes.*

lightweight /'laɪtweɪt/. **1** ADJ Something that is **lightweight** weighs less than most other things of the same type. *The company manufactures a range of lightweight cycles.* **2** N-COUNT A **lightweight** is a boxer or wrestler in one of the lightest classes. **3** ADJ & N-COUNT If you describe someone as **lightweight**, or as a **lightweight**, you are criticizing them for not being important or skilful in a particular area of activity. *Some of the discussion in the book is lightweight and unconvincing.*

'light year, light years. 1 N-COUNT A **light year** is the distance that light travels in a year. **2** N-COUNT You can say that two things are **light years** apart to emphasize a very great difference or a very long distance or period of time between them. [INFORMAL] *She says the French education system is light years ahead of the English one.*

likable /'laɪkəbəl/. See **likeable**.

like 1 expressing similarity

★ **like** /laɪk/ **likes. 1** PREP If one person or thing is **like** another, they have similar characteristics or behave in similar ways. *Kathy is a great mate, we are like sisters... It's a bit like going to the dentist; it's never as bad as you fear.* ♦ **-like** ...*flu-like illnesses.* **2** PREP If you ask or talk about what someone or something is **like**, you are asking or talking about their qualities, features, or characteristics. *What was Bulgaria like?* **3** PREP You use **like** to introduce an example of the thing that you have just mentioned. *The neglect that large cities like New York have received over the past 12 years is tremendous.* **4** PREP If you say that someone is behaving **like** something or someone else, you mean that they are behaving in a way that is typical of that kind of thing or person. *Greenfield was behaving like an irresponsible idiot.* **5** PREP **Like** is sometimes used in order to say that something appears to be the case when it is not. Some people consider this use to be incorrect and prefer to use 'as if'. *I felt like I was going on an adventure.* **6** PREP You can use **like** in expressions such as **nothing like** to make an emphatic negative statement. *Three hundred million dollars will be nothing like enough.* **PHRASES** ● You say **'and the like'** to indicate that there are other similar things or people that can be included in what you are saying. ...*keeping fit through jogging, aerobics, weight training, and the like.* ● You say **'like this'**, **'like that'**, or **'like so'** when you are showing someone how something is done. *It opens and closes, like this.* ● You use the expression **something like** with an amount, number, or description to indicate that it is approximately accurate. *They can get something like £3,000 a year.*

like 2 expressing preferences and wishes

★ **like** /laɪk/ **likes, liking, liked. 1** VERB If you **like** something or someone, you think they are interesting, enjoyable, or attractive. *I can't think why Grace doesn't like me... Do you like to go swimming?... That's one of the things I like about you.* **2** N-PLURAL Someone's **likes** are the things that they enjoy or find pleasant. *I knew everything about Jemma: her likes and dislikes.* **3** VERB If you **like** something such as a particular course of action or way of behaving, you approve of it. *Opal, his wife, didn't really like him drinking so much.* **4** VERB If you say that you **would like** something or **would like to** do something, you are expressing a wish or desire. *I'd like a huge bubble bath... Would you like to come back for coffee?* **5** PHRASE You say **if you like** when you are expressing something in a different way, or in a way that you think some people might disagree with or find strange. *This is more like a down payment, or a deposit, if you like.* **6** See also **liking**.

likeable (or **likable**) /'laɪkəbəl/. ADJ Someone or something that is **likeable** is pleasant and easy to like. *He was an immensely likeable chap.*

likelihood /'laɪklihʊd/. N-UNCOUNT The **likelihood of** something happening is how likely it is to happen. *The likelihood of infection is minimal... There is every likelihood that sanctions will work.*

★ **likely** /'laɪkli/ **likelier, likeliest. 1** ADJ If something is **likely to** happen, it probably will happen. *Once people have seen that something actually works, they are much more likely to accept change.* **2** ADJ If something is **likely**, it is probably true. *It appeared most likely that a new engine would be required.* **3** ADJ BEFORE N A **likely** person, place, or thing is one that will probably be suitable for a particular purpose. *He had always seemed a likely candidate to become Prime Minister.*

'like-minded. ADJ **Like-minded** people have similar opinions, ideas, or interests.

liken /'laɪkən/ **likens, likening, likened.** VERB If you **liken** one thing or person **to** another, you say that they are similar. *She likens marriage to slavery.*

likeness /'laɪknəs/ **likenesses. 1** N-SING If one thing has a **likeness to** another, it is similar to it. *These myths have a startling likeness to one another... There might be a likeness between their features, but their eyes were totally dissimilar.* **2** N-COUNT If a picture is a good **likeness of** someone, it looks very much like them.

likewise /'laɪkwaɪz/. **1** ADV You use **likewise** when you are comparing two things and saying that they are similar. *The V2 was not an ordinary weapon: it could only be used against cities. Likewise the atom bomb.* **2** ADV If you do one thing, and someone else does **likewise**, they do the same thing. *He lent money, made donations and encouraged others to do likewise.*

a b c d e f g h i j k l m n o p q r s t u v w x y z

liking /'laɪkɪŋ/. N-SING If you have a **liking for** something or someone, you like them. *She had a liking for good clothes.*

PHRASES ● If something is, for example, too fast for your **liking**, you would prefer it to be slower. *He had become too powerful for their liking.* ● If something is **to** your **liking**, it suits your interests, tastes, or wishes. *London was more to his liking than Rome.*

lilac /'laɪlək/.

✔ The plural is **lilac** or **lilacs**.

[1] N-VAR A **lilac** is a small tree with pleasant-smelling purple, pink, or white flowers. [2] ADJ & N-COUNT Something that is **lilac** is pale pinkish-purple in colour.

lily /'lɪli/ **lilies.** N-COUNT A **lily** is a plant with large sweet-smelling flowers.

limb /lɪm/ **limbs.** N-COUNT [1] Your **limbs** are your arms and legs. *She would be able to stretch out her cramped limbs.* [2] PHRASE If someone **has gone out on a limb**, they have done or said something that is risky or extreme.

limbo /'lɪmbəʊ/. N-UNCOUNT If you are **in limbo**, you are in a situation where you seem to be caught between two stages and it is unclear what will happen next. *I've made no firm decisions yet—I'm in limbo.*

lime /laɪm/ **limes.** [1] N-COUNT A **lime** is a small, round citrus fruit with green skin. [2] N-UNCOUNT **Lime** is a drink that tastes of limes. [3] N-COUNT A **lime** is a large tree with pale green leaves. [4] N-UNCOUNT **Lime** is a substance containing calcium. It is found in soil and water.

limelight /'laɪmlaɪt/. N-UNCOUNT If someone is **in the limelight**, they are getting a lot of attention, because they are famous or because they have done something unusual or exciting.

limestone /'laɪmstəʊn/ **limestones.** N-VAR **Limestone** is a white rock which is used for building and making cement.

⭐ **limit** /'lɪmɪt/ **limits, limiting, limited.** [1] N-COUNT A **limit** is the greatest amount, extent, or degree of something that is possible. *Her love for him was being tested to its limits... There is no limit to how much fresh fruit you can eat in a day.* [2] N-COUNT A **limit** is the largest or smallest amount of something such as time or money that is allowed because of a rule, law, or decision. *The three month time limit will be up in mid-June.* [3] VERB If you **limit** something, you prevent it from becoming greater than a particular amount or degree. *This would limit unemployment to around 2.5 million.* ◆ **limitation** N-UNCOUNT *...the limitation of nuclear weapons.* [4] VERB If you **limit yourself to** something, or if someone or something **limits** you, the number of things that you have or do is reduced. *Men should limit themselves to 20 units of alcohol a week.* ◆ **limiting** ADJ *The conditions laid down to me were not too limiting.* [5] VERB If something **is limited to** a particular place or group of people, it exists only in that place, or is had or done only

by that group. *Entry to this prize draw is limited to UK residents only.*

PHRASES ● If a place is **off limits**, you are not allowed to go there. *These establishments are off limits to ordinary citizens.* ● If someone **is over the limit**, they have drunk more alcohol than they are legally allowed to when driving a vehicle. [BRITISH]

limitation /ˌlɪmɪ'teɪʃən/ **limitations.** [1] N-VAR A **limitation on** something is a rule or decision which prevents that thing from growing or extending beyond certain limits. *...a limitation on the tax deductions for top earners.* [2] N-PLURAL The **limitations** of someone or something are the things that they cannot do, or the things that they do badly. *Parents are too likely to blame schools for the educational limitations of their children.* [3] N-VAR A **limitation** is a fact or situation that allows only some actions and makes others impossible. *...an acute disc collapse in the spine, causing limitation of movement.* [4] See also **limit**.

⭐ **limited** /'lɪmɪtɪd/. [1] ADJ Something that is **limited** is not very great in amount, range, or degree. *They may only have a limited amount of time.* [2] ADJ BEFORE N A **limited** company is one in which the shareholders are legally responsible for only a part of any money that it may owe if it goes bankrupt. [BRITISH]

ˌlimited e'dition, **limited editions.** N-COUNT A **limited edition** is something such as a book or a set of coins which has been produced in very small numbers, so that each one will be valuable in the future.

limitless /'lɪmɪtləs/. ADJ If you describe something as **limitless**, you mean that there is or appears to be so much of it that it will never be used up. *...a limitless supply of energy.*

limousine /ˌlɪmə'ziːn/ **limousines.** N-COUNT A **limousine** is a large and very comfortable car. Limousines are usually driven by a chauffeur and are used by very rich or important people.

limp /lɪmp/ **limps, limping, limped.** [1] VERB & N-COUNT If you **limp**, or if you walk with a **limp**, you walk in an uneven way because one of your legs or feet is hurt. *He had to limp off with a leg injury... A stiff knee following surgery forced her to walk with a limp.* [2] ADJ If something is **limp**, it is soft or weak when it should be firm or strong. *...adding volume and lift to limp hair.* ◆ **limply** ADV *He let the newspaper hang limply from his fingers.*

line 1 noun uses

⭐ **line** /laɪn/ **lines.** [1] N-COUNT A **line** is a long thin mark on a surface. *Draw a line down that page's center.* [2] N-COUNT The **lines** on someone's face are the wrinkles that appear there as they grow older. [3] N-COUNT A **line** of people or things is a number of them that are arranged in a row. *...a line of women queueing for bread.* → See pictures on page 826. [4] N-COUNT You can refer to a long piece of string or wire as a **line** when it is being used for a particular purpose. *She put her washing*

on the line. ...a piece of fishing-line. **5** N-COUNT
Line is used to refer to a route along which
people or things move or are sent. The telephone
lines went dead... They've got to ride all the way to
the end of the line. **6** N-COUNT You can use **line** to
refer to the edge, outline, or shape of something.
7 N-COUNT **Line** refers to the boundary between
certain areas, things, or types of people. ...just
over the California state line in Nevada... Thirteen
per cent of the population live below the poverty
line. **8** N-COUNT An actor's **lines** are the words
they speak in a play or film. **9** N-COUNT The **line**
that someone takes on a problem or topic is their
attitude or policy towards it. ...countries which
take a hard line on terrorism. **10** N-COUNT Your
line of work is the kind of work that you do.
11 N-COUNT A **line** is a type of product that a
company makes or sells. His best selling line is the
cheapest lager. **12** See also **lining**, **bottom line**,
front line, **production line**.

line 2 verb uses

★ **line** /laɪn/ **lines, lining, lined.** **1** VERB If people or
things **line** a place such as a road, large numbers
of them are present along its edges or sides.
Thousands of local people lined the streets. ...a long
tree-lined drive. **2** VERB If you **line** something
such as a container, you put a layer of something
on the inside surface of it. Bears tend to line their
dens with leaves or grass. **3** VERB If something
lines a container or area, it forms a layer on the
inside surface. ...the muscles that line the
intestines.
▶ **line up.** **1** PHR-VERB If people or things **are
lined up**, they move so that they stand in a row
or form a queue. I would line up my toys on this
windowsill and play... The senior leaders lined up
behind him in orderly rows. **2** PHR-VERB If you **line
up** an event or activity, you arrange for it to
happen. If you **line** someone **up** for an event or
activity, you arrange for them to be available for
that event or activity. Bob Dylan was lining up a
two-week UK tour.

line 3 phrases

★ **line** /laɪn/ **lines.**
PHRASES ● If something happens somewhere
along the line or somewhere **down the line**, it
happens during the course of a situation or
activity. Somewhere along the line he picked up an
engineering degree. ● If you **draw the line at** a
particular activity, you refuse to do it, usually
because you disapprove of it. They would draw
the line at hitting an old lady. ● If you are **in line
for** something, you are likely to get it. He must be
in line for a place in the Guinness Book of Records.
● If one thing is **in line with** another, or is
brought **into line with** it, the first thing is, or
becomes, similar to the second, especially in a
way that has been agreed, planned, or expected.
The structure of our schools is now broadly in line
with the major countries of the world. ● If you do
something **on line**, you do it using a computer or
a computer network. [COMPUTING] ● If something
such as your job, career, or reputation is **on the**

line, you may lose or harm it as a result of the
situation you are in. He wouldn't put his career on
the line to help a friend. ● If someone steps **out of
line**, they disobey someone or behave in an
unacceptable way. ● If you **read between the
lines**, you understand what someone really
means, or what is really happening in a situation,
even though it is not said openly. ● to **toe the
line**: see **toe**.

linear /ˈlɪnɪə/. **1** ADJ A **linear** process is one in
which something progresses straight from one
stage to another. ...life as a series of events,
progressing in a linear way from beginning to end.
2 ADJ A **linear** shape consists of straight lines.

linen /ˈlɪnɪn/. N-UNCOUNT **Linen** is a kind of cloth
that is made from a plant called flax.

liner /ˈlaɪnə/ **liners.** N-COUNT A **liner** is a large
passenger ship.

liner

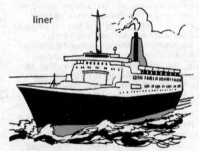

linesman /ˈlaɪnzmən/ **linesmen.** N-COUNT A
linesman is an official in games such as football
and tennis who indicates when the ball goes
outside the boundary lines.

'line-up, line-ups. N-COUNT A **line-up** is a group of
people or a series of things that are assembled to
take part in a particular activity or event. ...a new
series with a great line-up of musicians.

linger /ˈlɪŋgə/ **lingers, lingering, lingered.** **1** VERB If
something **lingers**, it continues to exist for a long
time. The scent of her perfume lingered on in the
room. ...the lingering effects of radiation. **2** VERB
If you **linger** somewhere, you stay there for a
longer time than is necessary. Customers are
welcome to linger over coffee until around
midnight.

lingerie /ˈlænʒəri, AM -ˈreɪ/. N-UNCOUNT You can
refer to women's underwear and night clothes as
lingerie.

linguist /ˈlɪŋgwɪst/ **linguists.** **1** N-COUNT A
linguist is someone who is good at speaking or
learning foreign languages. **2** N-COUNT A **linguist**
is someone who studies or teaches linguistics.

linguistics /lɪŋˈgwɪstɪks/.

☑ The form **linguistic** is used as a modifier.

1 N-UNCOUNT **Linguistics** is the study of the way
in which language works. **2** ADJ **Linguistic**

abilities or ideas relate to language or linguistics. ...*linguistic theory.*

lining /'laɪnɪŋ/ **linings.** ☐1 N-COUNT The **lining** of a piece of clothing or a curtain is a material attached to the inside of it in order to make it thicker or warmer, or to make it hang better. ...*a padded satin jacket with quilted lining.* ☐2 N-COUNT The **lining** of your stomach or other organ is a layer of tissue on the inside of it. ...*the uterine lining.*

⭐ **link** /lɪŋk/ **links, linking, linked.** ☐1 VERB & N-COUNT If something **links** two things, or if there is a **link between** them, there is a logical relationship between them. *Liver cancer is linked to the hepatitis B virus.* ...*the link between alcohol and violence.* ☐2 VERB & N-COUNT If something **links** two places or objects, or if there is a **link between** them, there is a physical connection between them. ...*the Rama Road, which links the capital, Managua, with the Caribbean coast.* ...*the high-speed rail link between London and the Channel Tunnel.* ☐3 VERB If you **link** one person or thing **to** another, you claim that there is a relationship or connection between them. *Jones has linked the crime to social circumstances.* ☐4 VERB If you **link** one thing with another, you join them by putting one thing through the other. *She linked her arm through his.* ☐5 N-COUNT A **link** of a chain is one of the rings in it.

▶**link up.** ☐1 PHR-VERB If you **link up with** someone, you join them for a particular purpose. *They linked up with a series of local anti-nuclear groups... The Russian and American armies linked up for the first time.* ☐2 PHR-VERB If one thing **is linked up to** another, the two things are connected to each other. ...*CD-ROM discs, which can be linked up to a hi-fi and personal computer.*

'link-up, link-ups. N-COUNT A **link-up** is a relationship or partnership between two organizations. *The US airline has just announced a formal link-up with British Airways.*

lion /'laɪən/ **lions.** N-COUNT A **lion** is a large wild member of the cat family that is found in Africa. Lions have yellowish fur, and male lions have long hair on their head and neck. → See picture on page 816.

'lion's share. N-SING If a person, group, or project gets the **lion's share of** something, they get the largest part of it. *The lion's share of the work will go to American companies.*

⭐ **lip** /lɪp/ **lips.** ☐1 N-COUNT Your **lips** are the two outer parts of the edge of your mouth. → See picture on page 823. ☐2 PHRASE If you say that someone keeps a **stiff upper lip**, you mean that they do not show any emotion even though it is difficult for them not to. ☐3 to **bite** your **lip**: see bite.

'lip-service. N-UNCOUNT If you say that someone **pays lip-service** to an idea, you are criticizing them because they say they are in favour of it, but do nothing to support it. *He had done no more than pay lip service to their views.*

lipstick /'lɪpstɪk/ **lipsticks.** N-VAR **Lipstick** is a coloured substance which women put on their lips.

liqueur /lɪ'kjʊə, AM -'kɜːr/ **liqueurs.** N-VAR A **liqueur** is a strong sweet alcoholic drink.

liquid /'lɪkwɪd/ **liquids.** N-VAR A **liquid** is a substance such as water which is not solid and which can be poured. *Solids turn to liquids at certain temperatures.* ...*liquid nitrogen.*

liquidate /'lɪkwɪdeɪt/ **liquidates, liquidating, liquidated.** VERB To **liquidate** a company means to close it down and sell all its assets, usually because it is in debt. ♦ **liquidation, liquidations** N-VAR *The company went into liquidation.* ♦ **liquidator, liquidators** N-COUNT *The firm has been passed into the hands of liquidators.*

liquor /'lɪkə/ **liquors.** N-VAR In American English, alcoholic drink such as whisky and vodka is sometimes referred to as **liquor**. The British word is **spirits**.

⭐ **list** /lɪst/ **lists, listing, listed.** ☐1 N-COUNT A **list** is a set of things which all belong to a particular category, written down one below the other. ...*the hotel's exhaustive wine list.* ☐2 VERB To **list** a set of things means to write them or say them one after another, usually in a particular order. *Ingredients are listed in order of the amount used.*

⭐ **listen** /'lɪsən/ **listens, listening, listened.** ☐1 VERB If you **listen to** someone who is talking or **to** a sound, you give your attention to them. *Sonia was not listening... He spent his time listening to the radio.* ☐2 VERB If you **listen for** a sound, you keep alert, ready to hear it if it occurs. *They spend the flight listening for any little noise that may seem odd.* ☐3 VERB If you **listen to** someone, you do what they advise you to do, or you believe them. *When I asked him to stop, he would not listen... Anne, you need to listen to me this time.* ☐4 CONVENTION You say **listen** when you want someone to pay attention to you because you are going to say something. *Listen, I finish at one.*

USAGE Do not confuse **listen** and **hear**. If you want to say that someone is paying attention to something they can hear, you say that they **are listening** to it. *He turned on the radio and listened to the news.* Note that **listen** is not followed directly by an object. You must always say that you listen **to** something. However, **listen** can also be used on its own without an object. *I was laughing too much to listen.* You use **hear** to talk about sounds that you are aware of because they reach your ears. You often use **can** with **hear**. *I can hear him yelling and swearing.*

▶**listen in.** PHR-VERB If you **listen in to** or **on** a private conversation, you secretly listen to it. *He assigned federal agents to listen in on Martin Luther King's phone calls.*

listener /ˈlɪsnə/ **listeners.** N-COUNT People who listen to the radio are often referred to as **listeners**. *I'm a regular listener to her show.*

listless /ˈlɪstləs/. ADJ Someone who is **listless**, has no energy or enthusiasm. ♦ **listlessly** ADV *Usually, you would just sit listlessly, too hot to do anything.*

lit /lɪt/. **Lit** is a past tense and past participle of **light**.

liter /ˈliːtə/. See **litre**.

literacy /ˈlɪtərəsi/. N-UNCOUNT **Literacy** is the ability to read and write. *Many adults have some problems with literacy and numeracy.*

literal /ˈlɪtərəl/. [1] ADJ The **literal** meaning of a word is its most basic meaning. *People there are fighting, in a literal sense, for their homes.* [2] ADJ A **literal** translation is one in which you translate each word separately, rather than expressing the meaning in a more natural way. *A literal translation of the name Tapies is 'walls'.* ♦ **literally** ADV *The word 'volk' translates literally as 'folk'.*

literally /ˈlɪtərəli/. ADV You can use **literally** to emphasize a word or expression which is being used in a creative way to exaggerate a situation. Some careful speakers of English think that this use is incorrect. *The views are literally breath-taking.*

⭐ **literary** /ˈlɪtərəri, AM -reri/. [1] ADJ **Literary** means connected with literature. *...a literary masterpiece.* [2] ADJ **Literary** words are often unusual in some way and are used to create a special effect in a poem, speech, or novel.

literate /ˈlɪtərət/. [1] ADJ Someone who is **literate** is able to read and write. *Over one-quarter of the adult population are not fully literate.* [2] ADJ If you describe someone as **literate**, you mean that they are intelligent and well-educated, especially about literature and the arts. *Scientists should be literate and articulate as well as able to handle figures.*

⭐ **literature** /ˈlɪtrətʃə, AM -tərətʃʊr/. [1] N-UNCOUNT Novels, plays, and poetry are referred to as **literature**. *...teaching literature to large groups of young people.* [2] N-UNCOUNT **Literature** is printed information about something. *...the literature on immigration policy.*

litigation /ˌlɪtɪˈgeɪʃən/. N-UNCOUNT **Litigation** is the process of taking legal action. [TECHNICAL] *The settlement ends more than four years of litigation on behalf of the residents.*

litre (AM **liter**) /ˈliːtə/ **litres.** N-COUNT A **litre** is a metric unit of volume. It is equal to approximately 1.76 British pints or 2.11 American pints. *...15 litres of water.*

litter /ˈlɪtə/ **litters, littering, littered.** [1] N-UNCOUNT **Litter** is rubbish which is left lying around outside. [2] VERB If a number of things **litter** a place, they are scattered around in it. *Glass from broken bottles litters the pavement.* ♦ **littered** ADJ *Debris was littered over the race track.* [3] ADJ AFTER

LINK-V If you say that something such as history or someone's speech is **littered with** something, you mean that there are many examples of the second thing in the first. *Charles' speech is littered with lots of marketing buzzwords like 'package' and 'product'.*

⭐ **little** /ˈlɪtəl/. [1] QUANT You use **little** to emphasize that there is only a small amount of something. *I need very little sleep these days... Little is known about his childhood.* [2] QUANT A **little of** something is a small amount of it. *A little food would do us all some good... Pour a little of the sauce over the chicken.* [3] ADV **Little** means not very often or to only a small extent. *On their way back to Marseille they spoke very little.* [4] ADJ **Little** things are small in size. **Little** is slightly more informal than **small**. *We sat around a little table. ...the little group of art students.* [5] ADJ BEFORE N A **little** distance, period of time, or event is short in length. *Just go down the road a little way.* [6] ADJ BEFORE N You use **little** to indicate that something is not serious or important. *Harry found himself getting angry over little things.*

> **USAGE** You can use the adjective **little** to talk about things that are small, for example *a little house* and *little children*, but it is not normally used to emphasize or draw attention to the fact that something is small. For instance, you cannot say 'The town is little' or 'I have a very little car', but you can say '**The town is small**' or '**I have a very small car**'. **Little** is a less precise word than **small**, and may be used to suggest the speaker's feelings or attitude towards the person or thing being described. For that reason, **little** is often used after another adjective. *What a nice little house you've got here!... Shut up, you horrible little boy!*
> **Little** and **a little** are both used as determiners in front of uncount nouns, but they do not have the same meaning. For example, if you say '**I have a little money**', this is a positive statement and you are saying that you have some money. However, if you say '**I have little money**', this is a kind of negative statement and you are saying that you have almost no money or that you do not have enough money.

PHRASES ● **A little** or **a little bit** means to a small extent or degree or for a short period. *He was a little bit afraid of his father's reaction... He walked a little by himself.* ● If something happens **little by little**, it happens very gradually. *Little by little he was becoming weaker.*

live 1 verb uses

⭐ **live** /lɪv/ **lives, living, lived.** [1] VERB If someone **lives** in a particular place, their home is there. *She has*

a b c d e f g h i j k l m n o p q r s t u v w x y z

lived here for 10 years... We used to live in the same road... He still lives with his parents.

USAGE When you are talking about someone's home, the verb **live** has a different meaning in the continuous tenses than it does in the simple tenses. For example, if you say '**I'm living in London**', this suggests that the situation is temporary and you may soon move to a different place. If you say '**I live in London**', this suggests that London is your permanent home.
The verb **work** behaves in a similar way. You use the continuous tenses, with the '-ing' form, to talk about a temporary job, but the simple tenses to talk about a permanent job.

2 VERB The way someone **lives** is the kind of life they have or the circumstances they are in. *We lived quite grandly... We can start living a normal life again.* **3** VERB To **live** means to be alive. If you say that someone **lived** to a particular age, you mean that they stayed alive until that age. *He's got a terrible disease and will not live long... He lived to be 103... Ian was her only living relative.* **4** VERB If people **live by** doing a particular activity, they get the money, food, or clothing they need by doing that activity. *...the last people to live by hunting.* **5** VERB If you say that someone **lives for** a particular thing, you are emphasizing that it is the most important thing in their life. *She lived for those kids.* **6** PHRASE If you **live it up**, you have a very enjoyable and exciting time. [INFORMAL] **7** to **live from hand to mouth**: see **hand**. ● to **live a lie**: see **lie**.
▸**live down.** PHR-VERB If you are unable to **live down** a mistake, failure, or bad reputation, you are unable to make people forget about it. *I thought I'd never live it down.*
▸**live off.** **1** PHR-VERB If you **live off** another person, you rely on them to provide you with money. *...a man who all his life had lived off his father.* **2** See **live on** 1.
▸**live on.** **1** PHR-VERB If you **live on** a particular amount of money, or if you **live off** it, you have that amount of money to buy things. *Most students are unable to live on £4000 per year.* **2** PHR-VERB If someone **lives on** a particular kind of food, it is, or seems to be, the only thing that they eat. *The children live on chips.* **3** PHR-VERB If a person or occasion **lives on** in someone's mind or in history, they are remembered because they are significant or important.
▸**live up to.** PHR-VERB If someone or something **lives up to** what they were expected to be or do, they achieve what they expected.

live 2 adjective and adverb uses

★ **live** /laɪv/ **1** ADJ BEFORE N **Live** animals or plants are alive, rather than being dead or artificial. **2** ADJ & ADV A **live** television or radio programme is one in which an event is broadcast

at the time that it happens. *...live pictures of the current weather... It was broadcast live in 50 countries.* **3** ADJ & ADV A **live** performance is given in front of an audience, rather than being recorded. *She's much happier performing live.* **4** ADJ A **live** wire or piece of electrical equipment is directly connected to a source of electricity.

livelihood /ˈlaɪvlihʊd/ **livelihoods.** N-VAR Your **livelihood** is your job or the source of your income. *...fishermen who depend on the seas for their livelihood.*

lively /ˈlaɪvli/ **livelier, liveliest.** **1** ADJ You can describe someone as **lively** when they behave in an enthusiastic and cheerful way. ◆ **liveliness** N-UNCOUNT *Amy could sense his liveliness.* **2** ADJ A **lively** event or a **lively** discussion, for example, has lots of interesting and exciting things happening or being said in it. *...a lively debate.* **3** ADJ BEFORE N You use **lively** to describe a feeling which is strong and enthusiastic. *He had a lively interest in Buddhism.*

liven /ˈlaɪvən/ **livens, livening, livened.**
▸**liven up.** **1** PHR-VERB If a place or event **livens up**, or if you **liven it up**, it becomes more interesting and exciting. *How could we decorate the room to liven it up?* **2** PHR-VERB If people **liven up**, or if something **livens** them **up**, they become more cheerful and energetic. *Talking about her daughters livens her up.*

liver /ˈlɪvə/ **livers.** **1** N-COUNT Your **liver** is a large organ in your body which cleans your blood. **2** N-UNCOUNT **Liver** is the liver of some animals, which is cooked and eaten.

lives. **1** /laɪvz/ **Lives** is the plural of **life**. **2** /lɪvz/ **Lives** is the third person singular form of **live**.

livestock /ˈlaɪvstɒk/. N-UNCOUNT Animals such as cattle and sheep which are kept on a farm are referred to as **livestock**.

livid /ˈlɪvɪd/. ADJ Someone who is **livid** is extremely angry. [INFORMAL] *I am absolutely livid about it.*

★ **living** /ˈlɪvɪŋ/ **1** N-SING The work that you do for a **living** is the work that you do to earn the money that you need. *He earns his living doing all kinds of things.* **2** N-UNCOUNT You use **living** when talking about the quality of people's daily lives. *...the stresses of urban living.* **3** N-PLURAL **The living** are people who are alive, rather than people who have died.

'living-room, living-rooms. N-COUNT The **living-room** in a house is the room where people sit and relax.

lizard /ˈlɪzəd/ **lizards.** N-COUNT A **lizard** is a reptile with short legs and a long tail.

★ **load** /ləʊd/ **loads, loading, loaded.** **1** VERB & PHR-VERB If you **load** a vehicle or container, or if you **load** it **up**, you put a large quantity of things or heavy things into it. *The three men seemed to have finished loading the truck... Mr. Dambar had loaded his plate with lasagne.* **2** N-COUNT A **load** is something large or heavy which is being carried. *...a big load of hay.* **3** VERB To **load** a gun, camera, or other piece of equipment means to put something such as a bullet or film in it so that it is ready to use. *He carried a loaded gun.* 4 QUANT **A load of** something or **loads of** it is a large amount of it. **A load of** people or things or **loads of** them is a large number of them. *I've got loads of money.*

loaded /ˈləʊdɪd/ 1 ADJ A **loaded** remark or question has more meaning or purpose than it appears to have, because the person who uses it hopes it will cause people to respond in a particular way. 2 ADJ If something is **loaded with** things, it has a large number of them in it or on it. *...a fully loaded jet airliner. ...a truck loaded with fruit.* 3 ADJ If you say that something is **loaded in favour of** someone or something, you mean that it works unfairly to their advantage. If you say it is **loaded against** them, you mean that it works unfairly to their disadvantage.

loaf /ləʊf/ **loaves** /ləʊvz/. N-COUNT A **loaf** of bread is bread in a shape that can be cut into slices.

⭐ **loan** /ləʊn/ **loans, loaning, loaned.** 1 N-COUNT A **loan** is a sum of money that you borrow. 2 VERB & N-SING If someone **loans** something to you, or if they give you a **loan** of it, they lend it to you. 3 PHRASE If something or someone is **on loan to** a person or organization, that person or organization is borrowing them.

loath or **loth** /ləʊθ/. ADJ AFTER LINK-V If you are **loath to** do something, you do not want to do it.

loathe /ləʊð/ **loathes, loathing, loathed.** VERB If you **loathe** something or someone, you dislike them very much. *...a play universally loathed by the critics.* ◆ **loathing** N-UNCOUNT *She looked at him with loathing.*

loaves /ləʊvz/. **Loaves** is the plural of **loaf**.

lob /lɒb/ **lobs, lobbing, lobbed.** VERB & N-COUNT If you **lob** something such as a ball, you throw or hit it high in the air. A **lob** is a throw or hit like this. *Thugs lobbed a grenade into the crowd.*

⭐ **lobby** /ˈlɒbi/ **lobbies, lobbying, lobbied.** 1 N-COUNT The **lobby** of a building is the main entrance area with corridors and staircases leading off it. 2 VERB To **lobby** a member of a government means to try to persuade them that a particular thing should be done. *Gun control advocates are lobbying hard for new laws.* 3 N-COUNT A **lobby** is a group of people who represent a particular organization or campaign, and who try to persuade the government to do something. *...a fierce anti-nuclear lobby.*

lobe /ləʊb/ **lobes.** N-COUNT The **lobe** of your ear is the soft part at the bottom.

lobster /ˈlɒbstə/ **lobsters.** N-COUNT A **lobster** is a sea creature with a hard shell, two large claws, and eight legs.

⭐ **local** /ˈləʊkəl/ **locals.** 1 ADJ **Local** means existing in or belonging to the area where you live, or to the area that you are talking about. *...the local newspaper... Some local residents joined the students' protest.* ◆ **locally** ADV *Her clothes were bought locally.* 2 N-COUNT You can refer to the

people who live in a particular district as **the locals.** [INFORMAL]

locality /ləʊˈkælɪti/ **localities.** N-COUNT A **locality** is a small area of a country or city. *...details of the drinking water quality in your locality.*

locate /ləʊˈkeɪt, AM ˈləʊkeɪt/ **locates, locating, located.** 1 VERB If you **locate** something or someone, you find them. [FORMAL] 2 VERB If you **locate** something in a particular place, you put, build, or set it there. [FORMAL] ◆ **located** ADJ *The restaurant is located near the cathedral.*

⭐ **location** /ləʊˈkeɪʃən/ **locations.** 1 N-COUNT A **location** is a place, especially the place where something happens or is situated. *Macau's newest small luxury hotel has a beautiful location.* 2 PHRASE If a film is made **on location**, it is made away from a studio.

loch /lɒx, lɒk/ **lochs.** N-COUNT A **loch** is a large Scottish lake.

⭐ **lock** /lɒk/ **locks, locking, locked.** 1 VERB When you **lock** something, you fasten it by means of a key. *...the locked door.* 2 N-COUNT The **lock** on something such as a door is the device which fastens it when you turn a key in it. *He heard a key turning in the lock.* 3 VERB If you **lock** something or someone in a place, room, or container, you put them there and fasten the lock. *They beat them up and locked them in a cell.* 4 VERB When you **lock** something in a particular position or place, or when it **locks** there, it is held or fitted firmly in that position or place. *He locked his fingers behind his head... The undercarriage locked into position.* 5 N-COUNT A **lock** is a place on a canal or river which can be closed at each end by gates, so boats can move to a higher or lower section by changing the water level inside the gates. 6 N-COUNT A **lock** of hair is a small bunch of hairs on your head that grow together in the same direction.

▶**lock away.** 1 PHR-VERB If you **lock** something **away** in a place or container, you put or hide it there and fasten the lock. *He had even locked away all the videos.* 2 PHR-VERB To **lock** someone **away** or to **lock** them **up** means to put them in prison or in a secure psychiatric hospital. *Locking them away is not sufficient, you have to give them treatment.*

▶**lock up.** 1 PHR-VERB When you **lock up** a building or car, or when you **lock up**, you make sure that all the doors and windows are locked so that nobody can get in. 2 See **lock away** 2.

locker /ˈlɒkə/ **lockers.** N-COUNT A **locker** is a small cupboard for someone's personal belongings, for example in a changing room.

locomotive /ˌləʊkəˈməʊtɪv/ **locomotives.** N-COUNT A **locomotive** is a railway engine. [FORMAL]

locust /ˈləʊkəst/ **locusts.** N-COUNT **Locusts** are insects that live in hot countries. They fly in large groups and eat crops. → See picture on page 824.

lodge /lɒdʒ/ **lodges, lodging, lodged.** 1 N-COUNT A **lodge** is a house or hut in the country or the mountains where people stay on holiday. *...a*

a
b
c
d
e
f
g
h
i
j
k
l
m
n
o
p
q
r
s
t
u
v
w
x
y
z

Victorian hunting lodge. **2** VERB If you **lodge** in someone else's house, you live there paying rent. ◆ **lodger, lodgers** N-COUNT *Jennie took in a lodger to help with the mortgage.* **3** VERB If something **lodges** somewhere, it becomes stuck there. *The bullet lodged in the sergeant's leg... His car has a bullet lodged in the passenger door.* **4** VERB If you **lodge** a complaint, you formally make it.

lodging /ˈlɒdʒɪŋ/**lodgings.** N-VAR You can refer to a room that is rented in someone's house as a person's **lodging** or **lodgings**. *He was given free lodging.*

loft /lɒft, AM lɔːft/**lofts.** N-COUNT A **loft** is the space inside the sloping roof of a building.

lofty /ˈlɒfti, AM ˈlɔːf-/. **1** ADJ A **lofty** idea or aim is noble, important, and admirable. *...the gap between lofty ideals and grubby reality.* **2** ADJ A **lofty** building or room is very high. [FORMAL] *...a light, lofty apartment.* **3** ADJ If you say that someone behaves in a **lofty** way, you are criticizing them for behaving in a proud way, as if they think they are very important. *...the lofty disdain he often expresses for his profession.*

log /lɒg, AM lɔːg/**logs, logging, logged.** **1** N-COUNT A **log** is a thick piece of wood cut from a branch or trunk of a tree. **2** N-COUNT A **log** is an official written account of what happens each day, for example on a ship. *He wrote about what he had seen in his ship's log.* **3** VERB If you **log** an event or fact, you record it officially in writing. *Details of the crime are then logged in the computer.*
▶**log in** or **log on.** PHR-VERB When someone **logs in** or **logs on**, or when they **log into** a computer system, they gain access to the system, usually by typing their name and a password. [COMPUTING]
▶**log out** or **log off.** PHR-VERB When someone who is using a computer system **logs out** or **logs off**, they finish using it by typing a particular command. [COMPUTING]

logic /ˈlɒdʒɪk/. N-UNCOUNT **Logic** is a way of reasoning that involves a series of statements, each of which must be true if the statement before it is true.

logical /ˈlɒdʒɪkəl/. **1** ADJ In a **logical** argument or analysis, each step or point must be true if the step before it is true. *Each logical step has been checked by other mathematicians.* ◆ **logically** ADV *My professional training has taught me to look at things logically.* **2** ADJ A **logical** conclusion or result is the only reasonable one. *If the climate gets drier, then the logical conclusion is that even more drought will occur.* ◆ **logically** ADV *Logically, the Universe cannot be younger than any of the stars it contains.* **3** ADJ A **logical** course of action seems reasonable or sensible in the circumstances. *It is logical to take precautions.*

logistics /ləˈdʒɪstɪks/.

☑ The form **logistic** is used as a modifier.

1 N-PLURAL If you refer to **the logistics of** doing a complicated task, you are referring to the skilful

organization of people and equipment, so that it can be done. *...the logistics of getting such a big show on the road.* **2** ADJ **Logistic** or **logistical** means relating to the organization of something complicated. *Producing a musical so far from home posed a variety of logistical problems.*

logo /ˈləʊgəʊ/**logos.** N-COUNT The **logo** of an organization is the special design that it puts on all its products.

loiter /ˈlɔɪtə/**loiters, loitering, loitered.** VERB If you **loiter** somewhere, you stay there or walk about there without any real purpose. *Men loiter at the entrance of the factory.*

lone /ləʊn/. ADJ BEFORE N A **lone** person or thing is alone or is the only one in a particular place. *He was shot by a lone gunman.*

lonely /ˈləʊnli/**lonelier, loneliest.** **1** ADJ A **lonely** person is unhappy because they are alone, or because they do not have any friends. You can also use **lonely** to describe a situation or period of time in which someone feels lonely. *...those long, lonely nights.* ◆ **loneliness** N-UNCOUNT *He felt a sudden inexpressible loneliness.* **2** ADJ A **lonely** place is one where very few people come. *...dark, lonely streets.*

loner /ˈləʊnə/**loners.** N-COUNT A **loner** is a person who likes being alone.

long 1 time

☆ **long** /lɒŋ, AM lɔːŋ/**longer, longest.** **1** ADV & ADJ **Long** means a great amount of time or for a great amount of time. *Repairs to the cable did not take too long... I learned long ago to avoid these invitations... The railway had obviously been built long after the house... I went for a long walk around Odessa.* **2** ADV & ADJ You use **long** to ask or talk about amounts of time. *How long can you stay?... The average commuter journey there is five hours long.*

PHRASES ● If you say that something is true **as long as** or **so long as** something else is true, you mean that it is true only if the second thing is true. *Tiles can be fixed to any surface as long as it's flat.* ● The expression **for long** is used to mean 'for a great amount of time'. *'Did you live there?'—'Not for long'.* ● Something that is **no longer** true, or that is not true **any longer**, used to be true but is not true now. *Food shortages are no longer a problem... He wasn't sitting by the door any longer.* ● If you say that someone **won't be long**, you think that they will arrive or return soon.

long 2 distance and size

☆ **long** /lɒŋ, AM lɔːŋ/**longer, longest.** **1** ADJ Something that is **long** measures a great distance from one end to the other. *...a long table. ...places quite a long way from here.* **2** ADJ You use **long** to talk or ask about the distance something measures from one end to the other. *An eight-week-old embryo is only an inch long... How long is the tunnel? ...centipedes as long as a pencil.* **3** ADJ A **long** book or other piece of writing contains a lot of words.

⭐ **long** /lɒŋ, AM lɔːŋ/ **longs, longing, longed.** VERB If you **long for** something, you want it very much. *He longed for the winter to be over... I'm longing to meet her.* ◆ **longing, longings** N-VAR *...her longing to return home.*

,long-'distance. ADJ BEFORE N & ADV **Long-distance** travel or communication involves places that are far apart. *...long-distance journeys... I phoned Nicola long-distance.*

longevity /lɒn'dʒevɪti/. N-UNCOUNT **Longevity** is living for a long time or lasting for a long time. [FORMAL] *He attributed his longevity to a happy family life.*

longitude /'lɒndʒɪtjuːd, AM -tuːd/ **longitudes.** N-VAR The **longitude** of a place is its distance to the west or east of a line passing through Greenwich in England. Compare **latitude**.

,long-'lost. ADJ BEFORE N You use **long-lost** to describe someone or something that you have not seen for a long time. *...the arrival of their long-lost cousins.*

,long-'range. ADJ A **long-range** plan or prediction relates to a period extending a long time into the future. *...a long-range strategy for improving US education.*

,long-'standing. ADJ A **long-standing** situation has existed for a long time. *...their long-standing dispute over money.*

,long-'suffering. ADJ Someone who is **long-suffering** patiently bears continual trouble or bad treatment. *...his loyal, long-suffering wife.*

,long 'term. ① ADJ Something that is **long term** has continued for a long time or will continue for a long time in the future. *...the long-term unemployed. ...a long-term solution to credit card fraud.* ② N-SING When you talk about what happens **in the long term**, you are talking about what happens over a long period of time. *In the long term the company hopes to open a shop in Moscow.*

⭐ 'long-time. ADJ You use **long-time** to describe something that has existed or been a particular thing for a long time. *...her long-time boyfriend.*

loo /luː/ **loos.** N-COUNT A **loo** is a toilet. [BRITISH, INFORMAL]

⭐ **look** /lʊk/ **looks, looking, looked.** ① VERB & N-SING If you **look**, or if you have a **look**, in a particular direction, you direct your eyes there in order to see what is there. *I looked down the hallway... Ducks! Look, right there!... Lucille took a last look in the mirror... Assisi has a couple of churches that are worth a look.* ● See note at **see.** ② N-COUNT A **look** is an expression on someone's face, showing what they are feeling or thinking. *He gave her a blank look, as if he had no idea who she was... A look of disgust came over his face.* ③ VERB & N-COUNT If you **look for** something or someone, or if you have a **look for** them, you try to find them. *I'm looking for my friend... Have you looked on the piano?... Go and have another look.* ④ VERB

& N-COUNT To **look at** a subject or situation, or to have a **look at** it, means to examine it, consider it, or judge it. *Can you look at my back? I think something's wrong... Next term we'll be looking at the Second World War period. ...a quick look at the morning newspapers... Brian had learned to look at her with new respect.* ⑤ VERB You can use **look** to draw attention to something or someone, for example because you find them very significant or annoying. *Look what a mess you've made of your life.* ⑥ CONVENTION You say **look** when you want someone to pay attention to what you are going to say. *Look, I'm sorry. I didn't mean it.* ⑦ VERB If a building or part of a building **looks out** onto something, it has a view of it. *We sit on the terrace, which looks out on the sea.* ⑧ to **look** someone **in the eye**: see **eye.**

▶**look after.** ① PHR-VERB If you **look after** someone or something, you keep them healthy, safe, or in good condition. *I love looking after the children.* ② PHR-VERB If you **look after** something, it is your responsibility to deal with it. *We'll help you look after your finances.*

▶**look around.** See **look round.**

▶**look back.** PHR-VERB If you **look back**, you think about things that happened in the past. *Looking back, I see that I did the best I could.*

▶**look down on.** PHR-VERB If you say that someone **looks down on** someone or something, you mean that they consider that person or thing to be inferior, usually when this is not the case. *I wasn't successful, so they looked down on me.*

▶**look forward to.** PHR-VERB If you **are looking forward to** something, you want it to happen because you think you will enjoy it. *I'm really looking forward to meeting him.*

▶**look into.** PHR-VERB If you **look into** something, you find out about it. *He had once looked into buying his own island.*

▶**look on.** ① PHR-VERB If you **look on** while something happens, you watch it happening without taking part yourself. *Local people looked on in silence as the two coffins were taken into the church.* ② PHR-VERB If you **look on** someone or something in a particular way, you think of them in that way. *Employers look favourably on applicants who have work experience.*

▶**look out.** PHR-VERB You say '**look out**' to warn someone of danger. ● See also **lookout.**

▶**look out for.** PHR-VERB If you **look out for** something, you stay alert so that you will notice it if or when it happens. *Look out for special deals.*

▶**look round.** PHR-VERB If you **look round** a place, or if you **look around** it, you walk round it and look at the different parts of it. *We went to look round the show homes... I'm going to look around and see what I can find.*

▶**look through.** PHR-VERB If you **look through** a book, a magazine, or a group of things, you get an idea of what is in it by examining a lot of the items in it. *Peter starts looking through the mail as soon as the door shuts.*

a
b
c
d
e
f
g
h
i
j
k
l
m
n
o
p
q
r
s
t
u
v
w
x
y
z

look 412

▶**look to.** PHR-VERB If you **look to** someone or something for a particular thing, you expect or hope that they will provide it. *The nation looks to them for guidance.*

▶**look up.** **1** PHR-VERB If you **look up** a piece of information, you find it out by looking in a book or list. *I looked your address up in the personnel file.* **2** PHR-VERB If you **look** someone **up**, you visit them after you have not seen them for a long time. **3** PHR-VERB If a situation **is looking up**, it is improving. [INFORMAL]

▶**look up to.** PHR-VERB If you **look up to** someone, you respect and admire them.

look 2 appearance

★ **look** /lʊk/ **looks, looking, looked.** **1** LINK-VERB & N-SING You use **look** when describing the appearance of a person or thing or the impression that they give. *I shall use the money to make my home look lovely... They look like stars to the naked eye... He looked as if he was going to smile... She had the look of someone deserted and betrayed.*

> **USAGE** If you want to say that someone is paying attention to something they can see, you say that they **are looking at** it or **watching it**. In general, you **look at** something that is not moving, while you **watch** something that is moving or changing. *I asked him to look at the picture above his bed... He watched Blake run down the stairs.* **Look** is never followed by an object. You must always use **at** or some other preposition. *I looked towards the plane.* You use **see** to talk about things that you are aware of because a visual impression reaches your eyes. You often use **can** in this case. *I can see the fax here on the desk.*

2 N-PLURAL When you refer to someone's **looks**, you are referring to how physically attractive they are. *...a young woman with wholesome good looks.* **3** LINK-VERB You use **look** when indicating what you think will happen in the future or how a situation seems to you. *He had lots of time to think about the future, and it didn't look good... It looks like Warner Brothers' gamble is paying off.* **PHRASES** ● You use expressions such as **by the look of him** or **by the looks of it** when you want to give an opinion based on the appearance of someone or something. *He was not a well man by the look of him.* ● If you **don't like the look of** something or someone, their appearance suggests that they might be the cause of something unpleasant. *I don't like the look of those clouds... I didn't like the look of him one bit.*

lookout /'lʊkaʊt/ **lookouts.** **1** N-COUNT A **lookout** is a place from which you can see clearly in all directions. *Troops tried to set up a lookout post.* **2** N-COUNT A **lookout** is someone who is watching for danger. **3** PHRASE If you are **on the**

lookout for something, you are watching out for it. *He was always on the lookout for good new music.*

loom /luːm/ **looms, looming, loomed.** **1** VERB If something **looms** over you, or if it **looms up**, it appears as a large or unclear shape, often in a frightening way. *...the bleak mountains that loomed out of the blackness.* **2** VERB If a worrying or threatening event or situation **is looming**, it seems likely to happen soon. *The threat of renewed civil war looms ahead.* **3** PHRASE If a problem or event **looms large**, it occupies a lot of your thoughts and seems to be a frightening prospect that you cannot avoid. *...the terrible problem of armed crime now looming large in our society.* **4** N-COUNT A **loom** is a device that is used for weaving thread into cloth.

loony /'luːni/ **loonies.** ADJ & N-COUNT If you describe someone's behaviour as **loony**, or if you refer to someone as a **loony**, you mean that they behave in a way that seems mad or strange. [INFORMAL] *...loony feminist nonsense... They all thought I was a loony.*

loop /luːp/ **loops, looping, looped.** **1** N-COUNT A **loop** is a curved or circular shape in something long, such as a piece of string. **2** VERB If you **loop** something such as a piece of rope around an object, you tie a length of it in a loop around the object. *He looped the rope over the wood.* **3** VERB If something **loops** somewhere, it goes there in a circular direction. *...the road which looped through the hills.*

loophole /'luːphəʊl/ **loopholes.** N-COUNT A **loophole** in the law is a small mistake or omission which some people use to avoid doing something that the law intends them to do. *...exploiting some loophole in the law to avoid prosecution.*

★ **loose** /luːs/ **looser, loosest.** **1** ADJ Something that is **loose** is not firmly held or fixed in place. *Two wooden beams had come loose from the ceiling. ...a loose thread.* ◆ **loosely** ADV *...a shirt tied loosely at the waist.* **2** ADJ If people or animals break **loose** or are set **loose**, they are freed after they have been restrained. *She broke loose from his embrace.* **3** PHRASE If a person or animal is **on the loose**, they are free because they have escaped from a person or place. **4** ADJ **Loose** clothes do not fit closely. ◆ **loosely** ADV *His shirt hung loosely over his thin shoulders.* **5** ADJ A **loose** grouping or arrangement is flexible rather than strictly controlled or organized. *...a loose coalition of leftwing forces.* ◆ **loosely** ADV *...a loosely organised studio band.*

,**loose 'end, loose ends.** N-COUNT A **loose end** is part of a story or situation that has not yet been explained. *There are some annoying loose ends in the plot.*

loosen /'luːsən/ **loosens, loosening, loosened.** **1** VERB If someone in authority **loosens** restrictions or rules, they make them less severe. ◆ **loosening** N-SING *...a loosening of state control over economic matters.* **2** VERB If you **loosen**

something that is tied or fastened, you move it or undo it slightly so that it is less tight or less firmly held in place.

▸**loosen up.** [1] PHR-VERB If a person or situation **loosens up**, they become more relaxed. [2] PHR-VERB If you **loosen up**, you do simple exercises to get your muscles ready for a physical activity.

loot /luːt/ **loots, looting, looted.** [1] VERB If people **loot** a building, or if they **loot** things from it, they steal things from it during a battle or a riot. ...*thugs who have looted food supplies.* ◆ **looting** N-UNCOUNT *There has been rioting and looting.* ◆ **looter, looters** N-COUNT *He saw looters carrying off items from evacuated apartments.* [2] N-UNCOUNT **Loot** is stolen money and goods. [INFORMAL]

lopsided (or **lop-sided**) /ˌlɒpˈsaɪdɪd/. ADJ Something that is **lopsided** is uneven because one side is, for example, higher or much greater than the other. ...*a friendly, lopsided grin.* ...*lopsided economic relations.*

⭐ **lord** /lɔːd/ **lords.** [1] N-COUNT In Britain, a **lord** is a man who has a high rank in the nobility. *She married a lord.* [2] N-TITLE **Lord** is a title used in front of the names of some male members of the nobility, and of judges, bishops, and some high ranking officials. [BRITISH] *He was Lord Chancellor from 1970 until 1974.* [3] N-PROPER In the Christian church, people refer to God and to Jesus Christ as **the Lord**.

lore /lɔː/. N-UNCOUNT The **lore** of a particular country or culture is its traditional stories and history. ...*ancient Catalan lore.* ● See also **folklore**.

lorry /ˈlɒri/, AM /ˈlɔːri/ **lorries.** N-COUNT In British English, a **lorry** is a large vehicle used to transport goods by road. The American word is **truck.** → See picture on page 834.

⭐ **lose** /luːz/ **loses, losing, lost.** [1] VERB If you **lose** a fight or an argument, someone else defeats you. *A C Milan lost the Italian Cup Final... No one likes to be on the losing side.* [2] VERB If you **lose** something, you cannot find it, or you no longer have it because it has been taken away from you. *I lost my keys... He lost his place in the team.* [3] VERB If someone **loses** a quality or belief, they no longer have it. *He lost all sense of reason.* [4] VERB You say you **lose** something when you have less of it. *She lost a lot of blood... The best way to lose weight is to exercise... The company was losing money.* [5] VERB If you **lose** a relative or friend, they die. [6] VERB If you **lose** an opportunity or **lose** time, you waste it. *They did not lose the opportunity to say what they thought of events.* [7] **Lose** is used in a large number of expressions which are explained under other words in this dictionary. For example, the expression **lose** your **balance** is explained at **balance.** ● See also **lost.**

▸**lose out.** PHR-VERB If you **lose out**, you suffer a loss or disadvantage. *Women have lost out in this new pay flexibility.*

loser /ˈluːzə/ **losers.** N-COUNT The **losers** of a contest or struggle are the people who are defeated. If you say someone is a **good loser** you mean that they accept that they have lost a contest without complaining. If you say that someone is a **bad loser**, you mean that they hate losing and complain a lot about it.

⭐ **loss** /lɒs, AM lɔːs/ **losses.** [1] N-UNCOUNT **Loss** is the fact of no longer having something or of having less of it than before. ...*loss of sight... The loss of income for the government is about $250 million a month.* [2] N-COUNT A **loss** is the disadvantage you suffer when a valuable and useful person or thing leaves or is taken away. *His death was a great loss to herself. ...a terrible loss of human life... Military sources put the army's losses at about twenty.* [3] N-UNCOUNT **Loss** is the feeling of sadness you experience when someone you like is taken away from you. ...*your feelings of loss and grief.* [4] N-VAR If a business makes a **loss**, it earns less than it spends.

PHRASES ● If you are **at a loss**, you do not know what to do in a particular situation. ● If you **cut** your **losses**, you stop what you are doing because it is making a bad situation become worse.

⭐ **lost** /lɒst, AM lɔːst/. [1] **Lost** is the past tense and past participle of **lose.** [2] ADJ If you are **lost**, you do not know where you are or you are unable to find your way. *I realised I was lost.* [3] ADJ If something gets **lost**, you cannot find it. [4] ADJ If you feel **lost**, you feel uncomfortable or vulnerable because you are in an unfamiliar situation. [5] PHRASE If advice or a comment **is lost on** someone, they do not understand it, or they pay no attention to it.

⭐ **lot** /lɒt/ **lots.** [1] QUANT A **lot of** something or **lots of** it is a large amount of it. *A lot of our land is used to grow crops... He drank lots of milk... I learned a lot from him.* [2] ADV A **lot** means to a great extent or degree. *They went out a lot.* [3] N-COUNT You can use **lot** to refer to a set or group of things or people. *We've just sacked one lot of builders.* [4] N-SING You can refer to a specific group of people as a particular **lot.** [INFORMAL] *They're a boring lot.* [5] N-COUNT A **lot** in an auction is one of the objects or groups of objects that is being sold. *Lot 432 is described as a Baroque Pearl and Diamond Pin.* [6] PHRASE If people **draw lots** to decide who will do something, they each take a piece of paper from a container. One or more pieces of paper is marked, and the people who take marked pieces are chosen. [7] See also **parking lot.**

loth /ləʊθ/. See **loath.**

lotion /ˈləʊʃən/ **lotions.** N-VAR A **lotion** is a liquid that you use to clean, improve, or protect your skin or hair. ...*suntan lotion.*

lottery /ˈlɒtəri/ **lotteries.** [1] N-COUNT A **lottery** is a type of gambling in which people bet on a number or a series of numbers being chosen as the winner. Lotteries usually offer large cash prizes and are often organized so that a

a b c d e f g h i j k l m n o p q r s t u v w x y z

⭐ Bank of English® frequent word   For a full explanation of all grammatical labels, see pages vii-x

percentage of the profits is donated to good causes. [2] N-SING If you describe something as a **lottery**, you mean that what happens depends entirely on luck or chance. *Which judges are assigned to a case is always a bit of a lottery.*

⭐ **loud** /laʊd/ **louder, loudest.** [1] ADJ & ADV If a noise is **loud**, the level of sound is very high and it can easily be heard. Someone or something that is **loud** produces a lot of noise. *There was a loud bang... He turns the television up very loud.*
♦ **loudly** ADV *His footsteps echoed loudly in the tiled hall.* [2] PHRASE If you say something **out loud**, you say it so that it can be heard, rather than just thinking it. *I laughed out loud.* [3] ADJ If someone is **loud in** their support or condemnation of something, they express their opinion very often and in a very strong way.
♦ **loudly** ADV *Mac talked loudly in favour of the good works done by the Church.* [4] ADJ If you describe a piece of clothing as **loud**, you dislike it because it is too bright and tasteless.

loudspeaker /ˌlaʊdˈspiːkə/ **loudspeakers.** N-COUNT A **loudspeaker** is a piece of equipment, for example part of a radio, through which sound comes out.

lounge /laʊndʒ/ **lounges, lounging, lounged.** [1] N-COUNT A **lounge** is a room in a house, or in a hotel, where people sit and relax. [2] N-COUNT At an airport, the departure **lounge** is a large room where passengers go before boarding their plane. [3] VERB If you **lounge** somewhere, you lean against something or lie somewhere in a relaxed way. *They ate and drank and lounged in the shade.*
▸ **lounge about** or **lounge around.** PHR-VERB If you **lounge about** or **lounge around**, you spend your time in a relaxed and lazy way. *He remembered mowing the lawn, lounging around the swimming pool.*

louse /laʊs/ **lice.** N-COUNT **Lice** are small insects that live on the bodies of people or animals.

lousy /ˈlaʊzi/ [1] ADJ If you describe something as **lousy**, you mean that it is of very bad quality. [INFORMAL] *The food was lousy.* [2] ADJ If you feel **lousy**, you feel very ill. [INFORMAL] *I felt lousy.*

lout /laʊt/ **louts.** N-COUNT If you describe a young man as a **lout**, you are critical of him because he behaves in a rude or aggressive way. *...a drunken lout.*

lovable /ˈlʌvəbəl/. ADJ If you describe someone as **lovable**, you mean they have attractive qualities and are easy to like.

⭐ **love** /lʌv/ **loves, loving, loved.** [1] VERB & N-UNCOUNT If you **love** someone, or if you feel **love for** them, you feel romantically or sexually attracted to them, and they are very important to you. *Oh, Amy, I love you... Our love for each other has increased by what we've been through together.* [2] VERB & N-UNCOUNT If you **love** someone, or if you have **love for** them, you care for them very much. *You'll never love anyone the way you love your baby... My love for all my children is*

unconditional. [3] VERB & N-UNCOUNT If you **love** something, or if you have a **love of** it, you like it very much. *I love taking photographs. ...one of these people that loves to be in the outdoors. ...a love of literature.* [4] VERB You can say that you **love** something when you consider that it is important and want to protect or support it. *I love my country as you love yours.* [5] VERB If you **would love to** have or do something, you very much want to have or do it. *I would love a hot bath and clean clothes... His wife would love him to give up his job.* [6] CONVENTION You can write **love** or **love from**, followed by your name, when you end an informal letter. *...with love from Grandma.* [7] N-VOC Some people use **love** as an affectionate way of addressing someone. [INFORMAL] *Well, I'll take your word for it then, love.* [8] NUM In tennis, **love** is a score of zero.
PHRASES ● If you **fall in love with** someone, you start to feel romantically or sexually attracted to them, and they are very important to you. *I fell in love with him... We fell madly in love.* ● When two people **make love**, they have sex. ● See also **loving**.

'**love affair, love affairs.** N-COUNT A **love affair** is a romantic and usually sexual relationship between two people.

'**love life, love lives.** N-COUNT Someone's **love life** is the part of their life that consists of their romantic and sexual relationships.

⭐ **lovely** /ˈlʌvli/ **lovelier, loveliest.** ADJ If you describe someone or something as **lovely**, you mean that they are very beautiful or that you like them very much. *You look lovely, Marcia... He had a lovely voice.* ♦ **loveliness** N-UNCOUNT *You are a vision of loveliness.*

'**love-making.** N-UNCOUNT **Love-making** refers to sexual activities that take place between two people who love each other.

⭐ **lover** /ˈlʌvə/ **lovers.** [1] N-COUNT Someone's **lover** is someone who they are having a sexual relationship with but are not married to. [2] N-COUNT If you are a **lover of** something such as animals or the arts, you enjoy them very much and take great pleasure in them. *She is a great lover of horses. ...art lovers.*

loving /ˈlʌvɪŋ/ [1] ADJ Someone who is **loving** feels or shows love to other people. *...a most loving husband.* ♦ **lovingly** ADV *Brian gazed lovingly at Mary Ann.* [2] ADJ **Loving** actions are done with great enjoyment and care. *The house has been restored with loving care.* ♦ **lovingly** ADV *...lovingly prepared food.*

⭐ **low** /laʊ/ **lower, lowest; lows.** [1] ADJ Something that is **low** measures a short distance from the bottom to the top. → See picture on page 324. *She put it down on the low table. ...low, rolling hills.* [2] ADJ If something is **low**, it is close to the ground, to sea level, or to the bottom of something. *He bumped his head on the low beams... It was late afternoon and the sun was low in the sky.* [3] ADJ **Low** means small in amount or degree, or at the bottom of a particular scale or system. ...*low incomes.* ...*temperatures in the low 80s...* *World stocks of wheat were getting very low.* ...*the low rank of 'legal adviser'.* **4** N-COUNT A **low** is a level or amount that is less than it was before. *The shares plunged to a new low.* **5** ADJ If the quality or standard of something is **low**, it is poor. ...*work of very low quality.* **6** ADJ If someone is **low**, or if their spirits are **low**, they are feeling depressed. *We are all very tired and morale is low.* **7** ADJ If you have a **low** opinion of someone, you disapprove of them or dislike them. **8** ADJ A **low** sound is deep and quiet. *Father whistled a few low notes...* *'The police are here,' she said in a low voice.* **9** ADJ If something such as a radio or a light is **low**, it is only producing a small amount of sound, heat, or light. *I've got the heater on low.* **10** PHRASE If you **are lying low**, you are avoiding being seen or drawing attention to yourself. [INFORMAL] *It would be safer to lie low till the men were gone.* ● **at a low ebb**: see **ebb**. ● **a low profile**: see **profile**.

⭐ **lower** /ˈləʊə/ **lowers, lowering, lowered.** **1** **Lower** is the comparative of **low**. **2** ADJ You can use **lower** to refer to the bottom one of a pair of things. *She bit her lower lip.* **3** VERB If you **lower** something, you move it slowly downwards. *She lowered herself into a chair.* **4** VERB To **lower** an amount, value, or quality means to make it less. *The bank has lowered interest rates.* ◆ **lowering** N-SING ...*the lowering of the voting age to 18.*

lower 'class (or **lower-class**) **lower classes.** N-COUNT & ADJ Some people use **the lower class** or **the lower classes** to refer to the division of society that they consider to have the lowest social status. **The lower class** can take the singular or plural form of the verb. *Most of the victims come from the lower classes.* ...*students from lower-class families.*

low-'impact. ADJ **Low-impact** exercise does not put a lot of stress on your body.

low-'key. ADJ Something that is **low-key** is restrained rather than noticeable or intense. *The wedding will be a very low-key affair.*

lowly /ˈləʊli/ **lowlier, lowliest.** ADJ Something that is **lowly** is low in position or status. ...*the team's lowly position in the First Division.*

loyal /ˈlɔɪəl/. ADJ If you describe someone as **loyal**, you mean they remain firm in their friendship or support for someone or something. *They had remained loyal to the president.* ◆ **loyally** ADV *They have loyally supported their party.*

loyalty /ˈlɔɪəlti/ **loyalties.** **1** N-UNCOUNT **Loyalty** is behaviour in which you stay firm in your friendship or support for someone or something. *I have sworn an oath of loyalty to the monarchy.* **2** N-COUNT **Loyalties** are feelings of friendship, support, or duty. *Mr Armstrong has divided loyalties when England play Scotland at rugby.*

LP /ˌel ˈpiː/ **LPs.** N-COUNT An **LP** is a record which usually has about 25 minutes of music or speech on each side.

⭐ **Ltd.** In Britain, **Ltd** is a written abbreviation for **limited**, used after the name of a company.

lubricate /ˈluːbrɪkeɪt/ **lubricates, lubricating, lubricated.** VERB If you **lubricate** something such as a part of a machine, you put oil onto it to make it move smoothly. *Lubricate the hinges and springs.* ◆ **lubrication** N-UNCOUNT *Use a touch of linseed oil for lubrication.*

lucid /ˈluːsɪd/. **1** ADJ **Lucid** writing or speech is clear and easy to understand. ...*his lucid explanation of the work.* ◆ **lucidly** ADV ...*the ability to present complex matters lucidly.* ◆ **lucidity** /luːˈsɪdɪti/ N-UNCOUNT ...*the force and lucidity of his arguments.* **2** ADJ When someone is **lucid**, they are able to think clearly again after a period of illness or confusion. ◆ **lucidity** N-UNCOUNT *Gordie had occasional months of lucidity.*

⭐ **luck** /lʌk/. N-UNCOUNT **Luck** is success or good things that happen to you, which do not come from your own abilities or efforts. *He does deserve some good luck...* *We have had no luck finding accommodation.*
　PHRASES ● You can say **'Bad luck'**, **'Hard luck'**, or **'Tough luck'** to someone when you want to express your sympathy to them. ● You say **'Good luck'** or **'Best of luck'** to someone when you are wishing them success in something they are trying to do. ● When someone **tries** their **luck at** something, they try to succeed at it. *She went back to Japan last June to try her luck at modelling.* ● You can add **with luck** or **with any luck** to a statement to indicate that you hope that a particular thing will happen. *With any luck, she thought, the money would turn up somewhere.*

luckily /ˈlʌkɪli/. ADV You add **luckily** to your statement to indicate that you are glad that something happened or is the case. *Luckily, we both love football.*

⭐ **lucky** /ˈlʌki/ **luckier, luckiest.** **1** ADJ If someone is **lucky**, they are in a very desirable situation. *I am luckier than most. I have a job.* **2** ADJ A **lucky** person always has good luck. *He had always been lucky at cards.* **3** ADJ If an event or situation is **lucky**, it has good effects or consequences, which happen by chance. *Five of the kids were taken to hospital, it's just lucky that no lives were lost.* **4** ADJ A **lucky** object is something that someone believes helps them to be successful. *Seven is my lucky number.* **5** PHRASE If you say that someone **will be lucky to** do or get something, you mean that they are very unlikely to be able to do or get it. *You'll be lucky to have change out of £750.*

lucrative /ˈluːkrətɪv/. ADJ A **lucrative** business or activity earns you a lot of money.

ludicrous /ˈluːdɪkrəs/. ADJ If you describe something as **ludicrous**, you mean that it is very foolish or unreasonable. *It was ludicrous to suggest that the visit could be kept secret.* ◆ **ludicrously** ADV *The prices are ludicrously low.*

lug /lʌɡ/ **lugs, lugging, lugged.** VERB If you **lug** a heavy object somewhere, you carry it there with

a
b
c
d
e
f
g
h
i
j
k
l
m
n
o
p
q
r
s
t
u
v
w
x
y
z

difficulty. [INFORMAL] *Nobody wants to lug around huge suitcases.*

luggage /ˈlʌgɪdʒ/. N-UNCOUNT **Luggage** consists of the suitcases and bags that take when you travel.

> **USAGE Luggage** is an uncount noun. You can have **a piece of luggage** or **some luggage** but you cannot have 'a luggage' or 'some luggages'.

lukewarm /ˌluːkˈwɔːm/. [1] ADJ **Lukewarm** water is only slightly warm. [2] ADJ If you describe a person or their attitude as **lukewarm** towards someone or something, you mean they do not show much enthusiasm or interest towards them. *The new design received the same lukewarm response as his first proposal.*

lull /lʌl/ **lulls, lulling, lulled.** [1] N-COUNT A **lull** is a period of quiet or of little activity. *...a lull in the conversation.* [2] VERB If you **are lulled into** feeling safe, someone or something causes you to feel safe at a time when you are not safe. *It is easy to be lulled into a false sense of security.*

lumber /ˈlʌmbə/ **lumbers, lumbering, lumbered.** [1] N-UNCOUNT In American English, **lumber** consists of wood that has been roughly cut up. The British word is **timber**. [2] VERB If someone **lumbers** around, they move slowly and clumsily. *He turned and lumbered back to his chair.*
▸**lumber with.** PHR-VERB If you **are lumbered with** someone or something, you have to take responsibility for them, although you do not want to. [BRITISH, INFORMAL] *I was lumbered with the job of taking charge of all the money.*

luminous /ˈluːmɪnəs/. ADJ Something that is **luminous** shines or glows in the dark. *...the luminous dial on the clock.*

lump /lʌmp/ **lumps, lumping, lumped.** [1] N-COUNT A **lump** is a solid piece of something. *...a lump of clay.* [2] N-COUNT A **lump** on someone's body is a small, hard piece of flesh caused by an injury or an illness.
▸**lump together.** PHR-VERB If a number of different people or things **are lumped together**, they are considered as a group rather than separately. [INFORMAL] *People tend to lump them all together.*

'lump sum, lump sums. N-COUNT A **lump sum** is a large amount of money that is given or received all at once. *...a tax-free lump sum of £50,000.*

lumpy /ˈlʌmpi/ **lumpier, lumpiest.** ADJ Something that is **lumpy** contains lumps or is covered in lumps. *She stretched out on the lumpy mattress.*

lunar /ˈluːnə/. ADJ BEFORE N **Lunar** means relating to the moon. *...man's first lunar landing.*

lunatic /ˈluːnətɪk/ **lunatics.** N-COUNT & ADJ If you describe someone as a **lunatic**, or if you say that

their behaviour is **lunatic**, you mean that they behave in a stupid and possibly dangerous way.

⭐ **lunch** /lʌntʃ/ **lunches, lunching, lunched.** [1] N-VAR **Lunch** is a meal that you have in the middle of the day. *We all went out for lunch.* ● See note at **meal.** [2] VERB When you **lunch** somewhere, you eat lunch there. [FORMAL]

luncheon /ˈlʌntʃən/ **luncheons.** N-VAR **Luncheon** is a formal meal in the middle of the day.

lunchtime (also **lunch time**) /ˈlʌntʃtaɪm/ **lunchtimes.** N-VAR **Lunchtime** is the period of the day when people have their lunch. *Could we meet at lunchtime?*

lung /lʌŋ/ **lungs.** N-COUNT Your **lungs** are the two organs inside your chest which you use for breathing.

lunge /lʌndʒ/ **lunges, lunging, lunged.** VERB & N-COUNT If you **lunge**, or if you make a **lunge**, in a particular direction, you move there suddenly and clumsily. *He lunged at me, grabbing me violently.*

lurch /lɜːtʃ/ **lurches, lurching, lurched.** VERB & N-COUNT To **lurch**, or to give a **lurch**, means to make a sudden, jerky movement, especially forwards. *Henry looked, stared, and lurched to his feet... The car took a lurch forward.*

lure /ljʊə, AM lʊr/ **lures, luring, lured.** [1] VERB To **lure** someone means to trick them into a particular place or to trick them into doing something that they should not do. *They were being lured into a trap.* [2] N-COUNT A **lure** is an attractive quality that something has. *The lure of rural life is proving as strong as ever.*

lurid /ˈljʊərɪd, AM ˈlʊrɪd/. [1] ADJ If you say that something is **lurid**, you disapprove of it because it involves a lot of violence, sex, or shocking detail. *...lurid accounts of Claire's sexual exploits.* [2] ADJ If you describe something as **lurid**, you do not like it because it is very brightly coloured. *...a lurid red.*

lurk /lɜːk/ **lurks, lurking, lurked.** [1] VERB If someone **lurks** somewhere, they hide there, usually because they intend to do something bad. *...the trees where Harper lurked with his seven-barrelled gun.* [2] VERB If something such as a memory, suspicion, or danger **lurks**, it exists, but you are only slightly aware of it. *Around every corner lurked doubt and uncertainty.*

luscious /ˈlʌʃəs/. ADJ **Luscious** food is juicy and delicious.

lush /lʌʃ/ **lusher, lushest.** ADJ **Lush** fields or gardens have a lot of very healthy grass or plants.

lust /lʌst/ **lusts, lusting, lusted.** [1] VERB & N-UNCOUNT If you **lust after** someone or **lust for** them, you feel a very strong sexual desire for them. **Lust** is this feeling. *He is obsessed by his lust for her.* [2] VERB & N-UNCOUNT If you **lust for** something or **lust after** it, you have a very strong and eager desire to have it. A **lust for** something is this desire. *Sheard lusted after the Directorship.*

luxurious /lʌgˈʒʊəriəs/. [1] ADJ Something that is **luxurious** is very comfortable and expensive.

...*Roberto's luxurious life-style.* ♦ **luxuriously** ADV *The dining-room is luxuriously furnished.* **2** ADJ **Luxurious** actions express great pleasure and comfort. ♦ **luxuriously** ADV *Liz laughed, stretching luxuriously.*

⭐ **luxury** /'lʌkʃəri/ **luxuries. 1** N-UNCOUNT **Luxury** is very great comfort, especially among beautiful and expensive surroundings. *He leads a life of considerable luxury.* **2** N-COUNT & ADJ BEFORE N A **luxury** is something expensive which you do not really need but which you enjoy. *I do like the luxuries of life – good wine, clothes, holidays. ...luxury food.* **3** N-SING A **luxury** is a pleasure which you do not often experience. *Hot baths are my favourite luxury.*

lying /'laɪɪŋ/. **Lying** is the present participle of **lie**.

lynch /lɪntʃ/ **lynchs, lynching, lynched.** VERB If an angry crowd of people **lynch** someone they believe is guilty of committing a crime, they kill that person by hanging them, without letting them have a trial.

lyric /'lɪrɪk/ **lyrics. 1** ADJ BEFORE N **Lyric** poetry is written in a simple and direct style. **2** N-PLURAL The **lyrics** of a song are its words.

lyrical /'lɪrɪkəl/. ADJ Something that is **lyrical** is poetic and romantic. *His paintings became more lyrical.*

M m

m. m is a written abbreviation for **metres** or **metre**. *...a ditch 1m wide.*

ma'am /mæm, mɑːm/. N-VOC People sometimes say **ma'am** as a formal and polite way of addressing a woman whose name they do not know, or a woman of superior rank.

macabre /mə'kɑːbrə/. ADJ You describe something such as an event or story as **macabre** when it is strange and horrible, usually because it involves death or injury.

machete /mə'ʃeti/ **machetes.** N-COUNT A **machete** is a large knife with a broad blade.

⭐ **machine** /mə'ʃiːn/ **machines. 1** N-COUNT A **machine** is a piece of equipment which uses electricity or an engine in order to do a particular kind of work. *...a machine to pump water out of mines.* **2** N-COUNT You use **machine** to refer to a large, well-controlled organization. *...the party's publicity machine.*

ma'chine gun, machine guns. N-COUNT A **machine gun** is a gun which fires a lot of bullets very quickly one after the other. *...a burst of machine-gun fire.*

machinery /mə'ʃiːnəri/. **1** N-UNCOUNT **Machinery** is machines in general, or machines that are used in a factory. **2** N-UNCOUNT The **machinery** of a government or organization is the system that it uses to deal with things. *...strengthening the machinery of the United Nations.*

machinist /mə'ʃiːnɪst/ **machinists.** N-COUNT A **machinist** is a person whose job is to operate a machine, especially in a factory.

macho /'mætʃəʊ, AM 'mɑː-/. ADJ You use **macho** to describe men who behave in an aggressively masculine way. [INFORMAL] *He likes to project a macho image.*

mackerel /'mækərəl/.

✅ **Mackerel** is both the singular and the plural form.

N-VAR A **mackerel** is a greenish-blue edible sea fish. **Mackerel** is the flesh of this fish eaten as food.

⭐ **mad** /mæd/ **madder, maddest. 1** ADJ Someone who is **mad** has a mental illness which makes them behave in strange ways. *She was afraid of going mad.* ♦ **madness** N-UNCOUNT *...the classic symptoms of madness.* **2** ADJ You describe someone as **mad** when they do or say things that you think are very foolish. *He'd be mad to refuse.* ♦ **madness** N-UNCOUNT *It would be madness to lose the jury system.* **3** ADJ You use **mad** to describe wild uncontrolled behaviour. *There would be a mad rush for our bicycles... The audience went mad.* **4** ADJ You can say that someone is **mad** when they are very angry. [INFORMAL] *They both got mad at me for interfering.* **5** ADJ AFTER LINK-V If you are **mad about** something or someone, you like them very much indeed. [INFORMAL] *He was mad about golf.* PHRASES ● If you say that someone or something **drives** you **mad**, you mean that you find them extremely annoying. [INFORMAL] *This itching is driving me mad.* ● If you do something **like mad**, you do it very energetically or enthusiastically. [INFORMAL] *We trained like mad.*

madam /'mædəm/. N-VOC **Madam** is a formal and polite way of addressing a woman. *This way, madam.*

madden /'mædən/ **maddens, maddening, maddened.** VERB If something **maddens** you, it makes you feel very angry or annoyed. ♦ **maddening** ADJ *...her maddening vagueness.* ♦ **maddeningly** ADV *The service is maddeningly slow.*

made /meɪd/. **1** **Made** is the past tense and past participle of **make**. **2** ADJ AFTER LINK-V If something is **made of** or **made out of** a particular substance or material, that substance or material was used to build or construct it. *...a cross made of silver.*

madly /'mædli/. **1** ADV If you do something **madly**, you do it in a fast, excited, or eager way. *...waving madly to catch the attention of those on*

a
b
c
d
e
f
g
h
i
j
k
l
m
n
o
p
q
r
s
t
u
v
w
x
y
z

board. **2** ADV If you are **madly** in love with someone, you love them very much.

mag /mæg/ **mags.** N-COUNT A **mag** is the same as a **magazine.** [INFORMAL] ...*sports mags.*

⭐ **magazine** /ˌmægəˈziːn, AM -ziːn/ **magazines.** N-COUNT A **magazine** is a weekly or monthly publication which contains articles, stories, photographs and advertisements. ...*a women's magazine.*

maggot /ˈmægət/ **maggots.** N-COUNT **Maggots** are tiny creatures that look like very small worms and turn into flies.

⭐ **magic** /ˈmædʒɪk/. **1** N-UNCOUNT & ADJ **Magic** is a special power that occurs in stories and that some people believe in, that can make apparently impossible things happen. ...*a magic charm.* **2** N-UNCOUNT **Magic** is the art of performing tricks to entertain people, for example by seeming to make things appear and disappear. **3** N-UNCOUNT & ADJ The **magic of** something is a special quality that makes it seem wonderful and exciting. ...*part of the magic of Christmas.* ...*those magic moments.*

magical /ˈmædʒɪkəl/. **1** ADJ Something that is **magical** seems to use magic or to be able to produce magic. ...*a little boy who has magical powers.* ♦ **magically** ADV *Rub gently with a pencil and the picture will magically appear.* **2** ADJ You can say that something is **magical** when it has a special mysterious quality that makes it seem wonderful and exciting. *Paris is a magical city.*

magician /məˈdʒɪʃən/ **magicians.** **1** N-COUNT A **magician** is a person who entertains people by doing magic tricks. **2** N-COUNT In fairy stories, a **magician** is a man who has magic powers.

magistrate /ˈmædʒɪstreɪt/ **magistrates.** N-COUNT A **magistrate** is a person who is appointed to act as a judge in law courts which deal with minor crimes or disputes.

magnate /ˈmægneɪt/ **magnates.** N-COUNT A **magnate** is someone who has earned a lot of money from a particular business or industry. ...*a shipping magnate.*

magnet /ˈmægnɪt/ **magnets.** N-COUNT A **magnet** is a piece of iron which attracts iron or steel towards it.

magnetic /mægˈnetɪk/. **1** ADJ If something is **magnetic**, it has the power of a magnet or functions like a magnet. ...*magnetic particles.* **2** ADJ **Magnetic** tapes or objects are coated in a magnetic substance which contains coded information that can be read or written on by computers. ...*a magnetic strip.* [COMPUTING] **3** ADJ If you describe something or someone as **magnetic**, you mean that they have qualities which people find very attractive. ...*her magnetic personality.*

magnetism /ˈmægnɪtɪzəm/. **1** N-UNCOUNT **Magnetism** is a power that attracts some substances towards others. **2** N-UNCOUNT Someone with **magnetism** has unusual and exciting qualities which people find very attractive. ...*his animal magnetism.*

magnificent /mægˈnɪfɪsənt/. ADJ Something or someone that is **magnificent** is extremely good, beautiful, or impressive. ...*a magnificent achievement.* ♦ **magnificence** N-UNCOUNT ...*the magnificence of the sunset.* ♦ **magnificently** ADV *The team played magnificently.*

magnify /ˈmægnɪfaɪ/ **magnifies, magnifying, magnified.** **1** VERB To **magnify** an object means to make it appear larger than it really is, by means of a special lens or mirror. ...*classifying lenses by how much they magnify the image.* ♦ **magnification** /ˌmægnɪfɪˈkeɪʃən/ N-UNCOUNT *Pores are visible without magnification.* **2** VERB To **magnify** something means to increase its effect, size, or intensity. *Advances in shipping have magnified the problem.*

magnitude /ˈmægnɪtjuːd, AM -tuːd/. N-UNCOUNT The **magnitude** of something is its great size or importance. *They underestimated the magnitude of the task.*

magpie /ˈmægpaɪ/ **magpies.** N-COUNT A **magpie** is a black and white bird with a long tail.

mahogany /məˈhɒɡəni/. N-UNCOUNT **Mahogany** is a dark reddish-brown wood that is used to make furniture.

maid /meɪd/ **maids.** N-COUNT A **maid** is a female servant.

maiden /ˈmeɪdən/ **maidens.** **1** N-COUNT A **maiden** is a young girl or woman. [LITERARY] **2** ADJ BEFORE N **Maiden** is used to describe some activities and events when they are the first of that kind that a particular person or thing has done. ...*the ship's maiden voyage.*

⭐ **mail** /meɪl/ **mails, mailing, mailed.** **1** N-UNCOUNT **Mail** is the letters and parcels that are delivered to you. *Nora looked through the mail.* **2** N-SING **The mail** is the system used for collecting and delivering letters and parcels. *It's illegal to use the mail for those purposes... Ford will contact owners by mail.* **3** VERB If you **mail** something, you post it. *I just mailed a letter to you yesterday... Mail me the current issue immediately.* **4** See also **e-mail.**

mailbox /ˈmeɪlbɒks/ **mailboxes.** **1** N-COUNT In the United States, a **mailbox** is a box outside your house where letters are delivered. **2** N-COUNT In American English, a **mailbox** is a metal box with a hole in it where you put letters that you want to send. The British term is **post box**.

ˌmail ˈorder. N-UNCOUNT If you buy things by **mail order**, you chose them from a catalogue and they are sent to you by post.

mailshot /ˈmeɪlʃɒt/ **mailshots.** N-COUNT A **mailshot** is a letter advertising something or asking for money for charity that is sent to a large number of people at the same time. [BRITISH]

maim /meɪm/ **maims, maiming, maimed.** VERB To **maim** someone means to injure them so badly that part of their body is permanently damaged. *She saw children horrifically maimed by landmines.*

★ **main** /meɪn/ **mains.** ☐ ADJ The **main** thing is the most important one. ...*one of the main tourist areas of Amsterdam*... *My main concern now is to protect the children.* ② PHRASE If something is true **in the main**, it is generally true, although there may be exceptions. *In the main, her old friends are happy for her.* ③ N-COUNT The **mains** are the pipes which supply gas or water to buildings, or which take sewage away from them. ...*a new gas main.* ④ N-PLURAL The **mains** are the wires which supply electricity to buildings, or the place where the wires end inside the building. [BRITISH] ...*amplifiers which plug into the mains.*

,main 'clause, main clauses. N-COUNT In grammar, a **main clause** is a clause that can stand alone as a complete sentence.

mainframe /meɪnfreɪm/ **mainframes.** N-COUNT A **mainframe** or a **mainframe computer** is a large computer which can be used by many people at the same time. [COMPUTING]

mainland /meɪnlænd/. N-SING The **mainland** is the large main part of a country, in contrast to the islands around it. ...*the coast of mainland Britain.* ...*the ferry to the mainland.*

★ **mainly** /meɪnli/. ADV You use **mainly** to say that a statement is true in most cases or to a large extent. *The staff were mainly Russian.*

,main 'road, main roads. N-COUNT A **main road** is an important road that leads from one town or city to another.

mainstay /meɪnsteɪ/ **mainstays.** N-COUNT The **mainstay** of something is the most important part of it. *Fish and rice were the mainstays of the country's diet.*

mainstream /meɪnstriːm/. N-SING People or ideas that are part of **the mainstream** are regarded as normal and conventional. ...*those outside the mainstream of society.* ...*mainstream opinion.*

★ **maintain** /meɪnteɪn/ **maintains, maintaining, maintained.** ☐ VERB If you **maintain** something, you continue to have it, and do not let it stop or grow weaker. *I've tried to maintain contact with the children.* ② VERB If you **maintain** something **at** a particular rate or level, you keep it at that rate or level. *The government was right to maintain interest rates at a high level.* ③ VERB To **maintain** someone means to provide them with money and the things that they need. ...*the basic costs of maintaining a child.* ④ VERB If you **maintain** a building, vehicle, road, or machine, you keep it in good condition. ⑤ VERB If you **maintain** that something is true, you state your opinion very strongly. *He had always maintained his innocence.*

maintenance /meɪntɪnəns/. ☐ N-UNCOUNT The **maintenance** of a building, road, vehicle, or machine is the process of keeping it in good condition. ② N-UNCOUNT **Maintenance** is money that someone gives regularly to another person to pay for the things that they need.

maize /meɪz/. N-UNCOUNT **Maize** is a tall plant which produces sweetcorn.

majestic /mədʒestɪk/. ADJ If you describe something or someone as **majestic**, you think they are very beautiful, dignified, and impressive. ...*a majestic country home.* ♦ **majestically** ADV *She rose majestically to her feet.*

majesty /mædʒɪsti/ **majesties.** ☐ N-VOC & N-COUNT **Your Majesty, His Majesty, Her Majesty,** or **Their Majesties** are used to address or refer to Kings or Queens. ② N-UNCOUNT The **majesty** of a place or thing is its quality of being beautiful, dignified, and impressive. ...*the breathtaking majesty of the view.*

★ **major** /meɪdʒə/ **majors.** ☐ ADJ BEFORE N You use **major** to describe something that is more important, serious, or significant than other things. *Drug abuse has long been a major problem.* ② N-COUNT & N-TITLE A **major** is an army officer of medium rank.

★ **majority** /mədʒɒrɪti, AM -dʒɔːr-/ **majorities.** ☐ N-SING & PHRASE The **majority of** people or things in a group is more than half of them. When there is more of one group than another, you can say that they are **in a majority** or **in the majority**. *The vast majority of our cheeses are made with pasteurised milk*... *Supporters of the treaty are still in the majority.* ② N-COUNT In an election or vote, a **majority** is the difference between the number of votes gained by the winner and the number gained by the person or party that comes second. *The decision was passed by a majority of eight to two.*

★ **make** /meɪk/ **makes, making, made.**

> ✓ **Make** is used with many nouns to talk about performing actions, and creating, constructing, or preparing something.

☐ VERB If someone or something **makes** you do something, they cause or force you to do it. *Mama made him clean up the plate*... *Grit from the highway made him cough*... *I was made to feel guilty.* ② VERB You use **make** to talk about causing someone or something to be a particular thing or to have a particular quality. ...*James Bond, the role that made him a star*... *She made life very difficult for me.* ③ VERB If you **make yourself** understood, heard, or known, you succeed in getting people to understand you, hear you, or know that you are there. *He almost had to shout to make himself heard above the music.* ④ VERB If you **make** something **into** something else, you change it in some way so that it becomes that other thing. *The middle valley was made into public gardens for recreation.* ⑤ VERB If you **make** money, you get it by working, by selling something, or by winning it. *What interested Dyer was making money.* ⑥ VERB If you **make** friends or enemies, someone becomes your friend or enemy, often because of a particular thing you have done. ⑦ VERB If something **makes** something else, it is responsible for the success of that thing. *What*

a b c d e f g h i j k l **m** n o p q r s t u v w x y z

really makes the book are the beautiful designs. [8] VERB You can use **make** to say that someone or something has the right qualities for a particular task or role. *She'll make a good actress, if she gets the right training.* [9] VERB If someone **makes** a particular team or **makes** a particular high position, they do so well that they are put in that team or get that position. *The athletes are just happy to make the British team.* [10] VERB You can use **make** to say what two numbers add up to. *Four twos make eight.* [11] N-COUNT The **make of** a product such as a car or radio is the name of the company that made it. *...a certain make of wristwatch.*

PHRASES ● If you **make do with** something, you use or have it instead of something else that you do not have, although it is not as good. *Why make do with a copy if you can afford the genuine article?* ● If you **make it** somewhere, you succeed in getting there, especially in time to do something. *So you did make it to America, after all.* ● If you **make it**, you are successful in achieving something difficult, or in surviving through a very difficult period. *You're brave and courageous. You can make it.*

▶**make for.** PHR-VERB If you **make for** a place, you move towards it. *He rose from his seat and made for the door.*

▶**make of.** PHR-VERB If you ask someone what they **make of** something, you want to know what their impression or opinion of it is. *Nancy wasn't sure what to make of Mick's apology.*

▶**make off.** PHR-VERB If you **make off**, you leave somewhere as quickly as possible. *They broke free and made off in a stolen car.*

▶**make out.** [1] PHR-VERB If you can **make** something **out**, you can see, hear, or understand it. *I could just make out a tall, pale, shadowy figure... For a moment he couldn't make out what she was saying.* [2] PHR-VERB If you **make out** that something is the case, you try to get people to believe it. *They were trying to make out that I'd actually done it.* [3] PHR-VERB When you **make out** a cheque or receipt, you write all the necessary information on it.

▶**make up.** [1] PHR-VERB The people or things that **make up** something are the members or parts that form that thing. *Women officers make up 13 per cent of the police force.* [2] PHR-VERB If you **make up** a story or excuse, you invent it. [3] PHR-VERB If two people **make up** after a quarrel or disagreement, or if they **make it up**, they become friends again. [4] PHR-VERB To **make up for** something that is lost or missing means to replace it or compensate for it. *...an extra compensation payment to make up for the stress you have been caused.* [5] PHR-VERB If you **make it up to** someone for disappointing them, you do something for them to show how sorry you are. *I must make it up to him for the awful intrusion of last night.*

⭐ **maker** /'meɪkə/ **makers.** N-COUNT The **maker** of

something is the person or company that makes it. *...Japan's two largest car makers.*

makeshift /'meɪkʃɪft/. ADJ **Makeshift** things are temporary and of poor quality, and are used because there is nothing better available. *20,000 Liberians were living in makeshift shelters.*

⭐ '**make-up.** [1] N-UNCOUNT **Make-up** consists of things such as lipstick and eye shadow which you can put on your face to make yourself look more attractive. [2] N-UNCOUNT The **make-up** of something is the different parts that it consists of, and the way these parts are arranged. *...the chemical make-up of the oceans and atmosphere.*

making /'meɪkɪŋ/ **makings.** N-UNCOUNT The **making** of something is the act of producing, constructing, or creating it. *...the making of this movie.*

PHRASES ● If you describe a person or thing as something **in the making**, you mean that they are going to become known or recognized as that thing. *Her drama teacher is confident Julie is a star in the making.* ● If something **is the making of** a person or thing, it is the reason that they become successful or become very much better than they used to be. ● If someone or something has **the makings of** something, it seems possible or likely that they will become that thing, as they have the necessary qualities. *Godfrey had the makings of a successful journalist.* ● If something such as a problem you have is **of your own making**, you have caused or created it yourself. *The university's financial troubles are of its own making.*

malaria /mə'leəriə/. N-UNCOUNT **Malaria** is a serious disease caught from mosquitoes.

⭐ **male** /meɪl/ **males.** [1] N-COUNT & ADJ A **male** is a person or animal that belongs to the sex that cannot have babies or lay eggs. *...a deep male voice.* [2] ADJ A **male** flower or plant fertilizes the part that will become the fruit.

malfunction /ˌmæl'fʌŋkʃən/ **malfunctions, malfunctioning, malfunctioned.** VERB & N-COUNT If a machine or computer **malfunctions**, it fails to work properly. If this happens, you say there is a **malfunction**. *...a malfunctioning satellite. ...a technical malfunction.*

malice /'mælɪs/. N-UNCOUNT **Malice** is a deliberate desire to harm people. *There was no malice on his part.*

malicious /mə'lɪʃəs/. ADJ **Malicious** talk or behaviour is intended to harm people or their reputation, or to embarrass or upset them. *...malicious gossip.* ◆ **maliciously** ADV *Sue grinned maliciously in the darkness.*

malignant /mə'lɪgnənt/. ADJ A **malignant** tumour or disease is serious, spreads rapidly to other parts of the body, and may cause death.

maligned /mə'laɪnd/. ADJ If you describe someone or something as **maligned**, you mean that people often criticize them and say unpleasant things about them, and that this is unfair. *Potatoes are a much-maligned vegetable.*

mall /mɔːl, mæl/ **malls**. N-COUNT A **mall** is a large enclosed shopping area.

mallet /'mælɪt/ **mallets**. N-COUNT A **mallet** is a wooden hammer with a square head. → See picture on page 833.

malnutrition /ˌmælnjuːˈtrɪʃən, AM -nuːt-/. N-UNCOUNT If someone is suffering from **malnutrition**, they are physically weak and extremely thin because they have not eaten enough food.

malpractice /ˌmælˈpræktɪs/ **malpractices**. N-VAR If you accuse someone of **malpractice**, you are accusing them of breaking the law or the rules of their profession in order to gain some advantage for themselves. [FORMAL]

malt /mɔːlt/. N-UNCOUNT **Malt** is a substance made from grain that is used to make some alcoholic drinks.

mammal /'mæməl/ **mammals**. N-COUNT **Mammals** are animals that give birth to babies rather than laying eggs, and feed their young with milk.

mammoth /'mæməθ/ **mammoths**. [1] ADJ You can use **mammoth** to emphasize that a task is very great and needs a lot of effort to achieve. ...*the mammoth task of relocating the library*. [2] N-COUNT A **mammoth** was a prehistoric animal like a large elephant with long curling tusks.

★ **man** /mæn/ **men; mans, manning, manned**. [1] N-COUNT A **man** is an adult male human. [2] N-VAR **Man** and **men** are sometimes used to refer to all humans. Some people dislike this use. *Anxiety is modern man's natural state.* [3] N-PLURAL In the armed forces, the **men** are the ordinary soldiers, sailors, or airmen, but not the officers. [4] VERB. If you **man** something such as a place, vehicle or machine, you operate it or are in charge of it. *The station is seldom manned in the evening.* [5] **the man in the street**: see **street**.

★ **manage** /'mænɪdʒ/ **manages, managing, managed**. [1] VERB If someone **manages** an organization, business, or system, they are responsible for controlling it. *Within two years he was managing the store.* [2] VERB If you **manage** time, money, or other resources, you deal with them carefully and do not waste them. *In a busy world, managing your time is increasingly important.* [3] VERB If you **manage to** do something, especially something difficult, you succeed in doing it. *I managed to pull myself up onto a wet, sloping ledge.* [4] VERB If you **manage**, you succeed in coping with a difficult situation. *How did your mother manage when your father left?*

manageable /'mænɪdʒəbəl/. ADJ Something that is **manageable** is of a size, quantity, or level of difficulty that people are able to deal with. *Cut down the task to a manageable size.*

★ **management** /'mænɪdʒmənt/ **managements**. [1] N-UNCOUNT **Management** is the control and organizing of something. *The zoo needed better management.* ...*time management.* [2] N-VAR You can refer to the people who control and organize a business or other organization as the

management. Management can take the singular or plural form of the verb. *The management is doing its best.*

★ **manager** /'mænɪdʒə/ **managers**. N-COUNT A **manager** is the person responsible for running part of or the whole of a business organization.

manageress /ˌmænɪdʒəˈres/ **manageresses**. N-COUNT The **manageress** of a shop, restaurant, or other small business is the woman who is responsible for running it.

managerial /ˌmænɪˈdʒɪəriəl/. ADJ **Managerial** means relating to the work of a manager. ...*managerial skills.*

managing di'rector, managing directors. N-COUNT The **managing director** of a company is the most important working director, and is in charge of the way the company is managed.

mandate /'mændeɪt/ **mandates, mandating, mandated**. [1] N-COUNT A government's **mandate** is the authority it has to carry out particular policies or tasks as a result of winning an election or vote. ...*a mandate for continued economic reform.* [2] VERB & N-COUNT When someone **is mandated to** do something, or when they are given a **mandate** to do it, they are given the authority to do it, or are instructed to do it. *He'd now been mandated by the West African Economic Community to go in and to enforce a ceasefire.*

mandatory /'mændətri, AM -tɔːri/. ADJ If an action or procedure is **mandatory**, people have to do it, because it is a rule or it is fixed by law. [FORMAL] ...*the mandatory life sentence for murder.*

mane /meɪn/ **manes**. N-COUNT The **mane** on a horse or lion is the long thick hair that grows from its neck.

maneuver /məˈnuːvə/. See **manoeuvre**.

mangle /'mæŋgəl/ **mangles, mangling, mangled**. VERB If something **is mangled**, it is very forcefully crushed and twisted out of shape. ...*the mangled wreckage.*

mango /'mæŋgəʊ/ **mangoes** or **mangos**. N-COUNT A **mango** is a large, sweet yellowish fruit which grows in hot countries.

manhood /'mænhʊd/. N-UNCOUNT **Manhood** is the state of being a man rather than a boy, or the period of a man's adult life. *They were failing to help their sons grow from boyhood to manhood.*

mania /'meɪniə/ **manias**. N-COUNT If you say that a person or group has a **mania** for something, you mean that they enjoy it very much or devote a lot of time to it. *It seemed to some observers that the English had a mania for travelling.*

maniac /'meɪniæk/ **maniacs**. N-COUNT A **maniac** is a mad person who is violent and dangerous.

manic /'mænɪk/. ADJ If you describe someone as **manic**, you mean that they do things extremely quickly or energetically, often because they are very excited or anxious. ♦ **manically** ADV *We cleaned the house manically.*

manicure /'mænɪkjʊə/ **manicures, manicuring, manicured**. VERB & N-COUNT If you **manicure** your hands or nails, or if you have a **manicure**, you

a
b
c
d
e
f
g
h
i
j
k
l
m
n
o
p
q
r
s
t
u
v
w
x
y
z

A B C D E F G H I J K L M N O P Q R S T U V W X Y Z

care for them by softening your skin and cutting and painting your nails.

manifest /ˈmænɪfest/ **manifests, manifesting, manifested.** [1] ADJ If you say that something is **manifest**, you mean it is clearly true and that nobody would disagree with it if they saw it or considered it. [FORMAL] ...*the manifest failure of the policies.* ♦ **manifestly** ADV *She manifestly failed to last the mile and a half of the race.* [2] VERB & ADJ If you **manifest** a particular quality, feeling, or illness, or if it becomes **manifest**, it becomes visible or obvious. [FORMAL] *The virus needs two weeks to manifest itself... The same alarm is manifest everywhere.*

manifestation /ˌmænɪfeˈsteɪʃən/ **manifestations.** N-COUNT A **manifestation** of something is one of the different ways in which it can appear. [FORMAL] ... *different manifestations of the disease.*

manifesto /ˌmænɪˈfestəʊ/ **manifestos** or **manifestoes.** N-COUNT A **manifesto** is a statement published by a person or group of people, especially a political party, in which they say what their aims and policies are. ...*the Labour Party's election manifesto.*

manipulate /məˈnɪpjʊleɪt/ **manipulates, manipulating, manipulated.** [1] VERB If you say that someone **manipulates** people or events, you disapprove of them because they control or influence them to produce a particular result. *They felt he had been cowardly in manipulating the system.* ♦ **manipulation, manipulations** N-VAR ...*accusations of political manipulation.* [2] VERB If you **manipulate** something that requires skill, such as a complicated piece of equipment or a difficult idea, you operate it or process it. *The technology uses a pen to manipulate a computer.* ♦ **manipulation** N-VAR *Making circuits requires controlled manipulation.*

manipulative /məˈnɪpjʊlətɪv/ ADJ If you describe someone as **manipulative**, you disapprove of them because they manipulate people. ...*aggressive and manipulative behaviour.*

mankind /ˌmænˈkaɪnd/ N-UNCOUNT You can refer to all human beings as **mankind** when you are considering them as a group. ...*the evolution of mankind.*

manly /ˈmænli/ ADJ If you describe a man's behaviour as **manly**, you approve of it because it shows qualities that are considered ideal in a man. ♦ **manliness** N-UNCOUNT *He has no doubts about his manliness.*

man-ˈmade ADJ **Man-made** things are created or caused by people, rather than occurring naturally. ...*man-made lakes.*

manned /mænd/. See **man.**

⭐ **manner** /ˈmænə/ **manners.** [1] N-SING The **manner** in which you do something is the way that you do it. *She smiled again in a friendly manner.* [2] N-SING Someone's **manner** is the way in which they behave and talk when they are with other people. *His manner was self-assured.* ♦ **-mannered** *He was a quiet, mild-mannered* man. [3] N-PLURAL If someone has **good manners**, they are polite and observe social customs. If someone has **bad manners**, they are not polite and do not observe these customs. [4] PHRASE If you refer to **all manner of** objects or people, you are talking about objects or people of many different kinds. ...*all manner of wildlife.*

manoeuvre (AM **maneuver**) /məˈnuːvə/ **manoeuvres, manoeuvring, manoeuvred.** [1] VERB & N-VAR If you **manoeuvre** something into or out of an awkward position, you skilfully move it there. A **manoeuvre** is a movement like this. *I manoeuvred my way among the tables.* ...*a ship capable of high speed and rapid manoeuvre.* [2] N-COUNT A **manoeuvre** is something clever which you do to change a situation to your advantage. ...*manoeuvres to block the electoral process.* [3] PHRASE If you have **room for manoeuvre**, you have the opportunity to change your plans if it becomes necessary or desirable. *With an election looming, he has little room for manoeuvre.* [4] N-PLURAL Military **manoeuvres** are training exercises which involve the movement of soldiers and equipment over a large area.

manor /ˈmænə/ **manors.** N-COUNT A **manor** is a large country house with land.

manpower /ˈmænpaʊə/. N-UNCOUNT Workers are sometimes referred to as **manpower** when they are being considered as a part of the process of producing goods or providing services.

mansion /ˈmænʃən/ **mansions.** N-COUNT A **mansion** is a very large house.

manslaughter /ˈmænslɔːtə/. N-UNCOUNT **Manslaughter** is the unlawful killing of a person by someone who did not intend to kill them. [TECHNICAL] ...*she was guilty of manslaughter, not murder.*

mantelpiece (or **mantlepiece**) /ˈmæntəlpiːs/ **mantelpieces.** N-COUNT A **mantelpiece** is a shelf over a fireplace.

mantra /ˈmæntrə/ **mantras.** N-COUNT A **mantra** is a chant used by Buddhists and Hindus when they meditate.

manual /ˈmænjʊəl/ **manuals.** [1] ADJ **Manual** work is unskilled work using your hands or your physical strength. ...*skilled manual workers.* [2] ADJ BEFORE N **Manual** equipment is operated by hand, rather than by electricity or by a motor. ♦ **manually** ADV *The device is manually operated.* [3] N-COUNT A **manual** is a book which tells you how to do something or how a piece of machinery works. ...*the instruction manual.*

⭐ **manufacture** /ˌmænjʊˈfæktʃə/ **manufactures, manufacturing, manufactured.** [1] VERB & N-UNCOUNT To **manufacture** things means to make them in a factory. The **manufacture** of things is the process of making them in a factory. *They manufacture the class of plastics known as thermoplastic materials.* ♦ **manufacturing** N-UNCOUNT ...*management headquarters for manufacturing in China.* [2] VERB If you say that someone

manufactures information, you are criticizing them because the information is not true. *The officers manufactured an elaborate story.*

manufacturer/ˌmænjʊˈfæktʃərə/ **manufacturers.** N-COUNT A **manufacturer** is a business that makes goods in large quantities.

manure/məˈnjʊə, AM -ˈnʊr/. N-UNCOUNT **Manure** is animal faeces that is spread on the ground in order to improve the growth of plants.

manuscript/ˈmænjʊskrɪpt/ **manuscripts.** [1] N-COUNT A **manuscript** is a handwritten or typed document, especially a writer's first version of a book before it is published. [2] N-COUNT A **manuscript** is an old document that was written by hand before printing was invented. *...early printed books and rare manuscripts.*

many/ˈmeni/. [1] QUANT **Many** is used to indicate a large number of people or things. *I don't think many people would argue with that... In many of these neighborhoods a lot of people don't have telephones.* [2] QUANT **Many** is used to talk and ask questions about numbers or quantities. *No-one knows how many people have been killed... How many do you smoke a day?*

> **USAGE** You only use **many** to talk about things that can be counted. You use **much** if you want to talk about a large amount of something. *...too much money... There are many books on the subject.*

PHRASES ● You use **as many as** before a number to suggest that it is surprisingly large. *As many as four and a half million people watched today's parade.* ● You use **a good many** or **a great many** to emphasize that you are referring to a large number of things or people. *We've both had a good many beers.* ● **in so many words**: see **word**.

map/mæp/ **maps, mapping, mapped.** N-COUNT A **map** is a drawing of a particular area, showing its main features as they would appear if you looked at them from above. *Have you got a map of the city centre?*

▶ **map out.** PHR-VERB If you **map out** a plan or task, you work out how you will do it. *We had mapped out our future.*

maple/ˈmeɪpəl/ **maples.** N-VAR A **maple** is a tree with large leaves with five points. **Maple** is the wood of this tree.

mar/mɑː/ **mars, marring, marred.** VERB To **mar** something means to spoil or damage it. [WRITTEN] *That election was marred by massive cheating.*

marathon/ˈmærəθən, AM -θɒn/ **marathons.** [1] N-COUNT A **marathon** is a race in which people run a distance of 26 miles (about 42 km). [2] ADJ BEFORE N A **marathon** task takes a long time to do and is very tiring. *...a marathon session of talks.*

marble/ˈmɑːbəl/ **marbles.** [1] N-UNCOUNT **Marble** is a very hard rock used, for example, to make statues and fireplaces. *...classical marble busts of Caesar.* [2] N-VAR **Marbles** are small coloured

glass balls used by children to play a game called **marbles**.

★ **march**/mɑːtʃ/ **marches, marching, marched.** [1] VERB & N-COUNT When soldiers **march** somewhere, or when a commanding officer **marches** them somewhere, they walk there with very regular steps, as a group. You can also say they go on a **march**. *We marched fifteen miles to Yadkin River.* [2] VERB & N-COUNT When a large group of people **march**, or when they hold a **march**, they walk somewhere together in order to protest about something. *The demonstrators then marched through the capital. ...a march for peace.*
♦ **marcher, marchers** N-COUNT *Police stopped the marchers.* [3] VERB If you **march** somewhere, you walk there quickly, for example because you are angry. *He marched into the kitchen without knocking.* [4] VERB If you **march** someone somewhere, you force them to walk there with you by holding their arm. *I marched him across the room and out on to the doorstep.* [5] N-SING **The march of** something is its steady progress. *...the relentless march of technology.* [6] PHRASE If you give someone their **marching orders**, you tell them that you no longer want or need them. [BRITISH] *Seven board members either resigned or were given their marching orders.*

★ **March**/mɑːtʃ/. N-UNCOUNT **March** is the third month of the year. → See Reference Page on Times and Dates.

mare/meə/ **mares.** N-COUNT A **mare** is an adult female horse.

margarine/ˌmɑːdʒəˈriːn, AM -rɪn/. N-UNCOUNT **Margarine** is a substance similar to butter, made from vegetable oil and sometimes animal fats.

★ **margin**/ˈmɑːdʒɪn/ **margins.** [1] N-COUNT A **margin** is the difference between two amounts, especially the difference in the number of votes or points between the winner and the loser in a contest. *They could end up with a 50-point winning margin.* [2] N-COUNT If there is a **margin for** something in a situation, there is some freedom to choose what to do or decide how to do it. *He knew he had to be very fast; there was no margin for error.* [3] N-COUNT The **margins** on a page are the blank spaces at each side.

marginal/ˈmɑːdʒɪnəl/. ADJ Something that is **marginal** is small and not very important. *...a marginal improvement in output.* ♦ **marginally** ADV *Sales last year were marginally higher than in 1991.*

marijuana/ˌmærɪˈwɑːnə/. N-UNCOUNT **Marijuana** is an illegal drug which is usually smoked.

marina/məˈriːnə/ **marinas.** N-COUNT A **marina** is a small harbour for pleasure boats.

marinade/ˌmærɪˈneɪd/ **marinades, marinading, marinaded.** [1] N-COUNT A **marinade** is a sauce of oil, vinegar, and spices, which you soak meat or fish in before cooking it, in order to flavour it. [2] VERB To **marinade** means the same as to **marinate**.

marinate /'mærɪneɪt/ **marinates, marinating, marinated.** VERB If you **marinate** meat or fish or if it **marinates**, you soak it in oil, vinegar, and spices before cooking it, in order to flavour it.

★ **marine** /mə'riːn/ **marines.** ① N-COUNT A **marine** is a soldier who is trained for duties at sea and on land. ② ADJ BEFORE N **Marine** is used to describe things relating to the sea. ...marine life. ...a solicitor specialising in marine law.

marital /'mærɪtəl/. ADJ BEFORE N **Marital** means relating to marriage. ...their marital problems.

maritime /'mærɪtaɪm/. ADJ BEFORE N **Maritime** means relating to the sea and to ships. ...the National Maritime Museum.

★ **mark** /mɑːk/ **marks, marking, marked.** ① VERB & N-COUNT If something **marks** a surface, or if it makes a **mark** on it, a small area of the surface is stained or damaged. Wood marks easily... The dogs are always rubbing against the wall and making dirty marks. ② VERB & N-COUNT If you **mark** something with a particular word or symbol, you write that word or symbol on it. This word or symbol is called a **mark**. The bank marks the check 'certified'... He made marks with a pencil. ③ VERB & N-COUNT When a teacher **marks** a student's work, he or she decides how good it is and writes comments or a score on it. This score is called a **mark**. He was marking essays in his small study... He did well to get such a good mark. ④ N-COUNT When something reaches a particular **mark**, it reaches that particular number, point, or stage. Unemployment is rapidly approaching the one million mark. ⑤ N-COUNT The **mark of** a particular thing, feeling, or quality is something which enables you to recognize it or which shows that it exists. The mark of a civilized society is that it looks after its weakest members. ⑥ VERB If something **marks** a place or position, it shows where a particular thing is or was. ...the river which marks the border with Thailand.
 ♦ **marker, markers** N-COUNT ...a boundary marker. ⑦ VERB An event that **marks** a particular stage or point is a sign that something different is about to happen. The announcement marks the end of an extraordinary period in European history. ⑧ See also **marked, marking.**
 PHRASES ● If something or someone **leaves** their **mark** or **leaves a mark**, they have a lasting effect. His experiences in Spain have left their mark on him. ● If you **make** your **mark** or **make a mark**, you become noticed or famous by doing something impressive or unusual. She made her mark in the film industry in the 1960s. ● If something is **off the mark** or **wide of the mark**, it is inaccurate or incorrect. If it is **on the mark**, it is accurate or correct. That comparison isn't as wide of the mark as it seems.

▶ **mark down.** ① PHR-VERB If you **mark** something **down**, you write it down. I had the date marked down in my diary. ② PHR-VERB To **mark** an item **down** or **mark** its price **down** means to reduce its price. Clothes are the best bargain, with many items marked down.

▶ **mark off.** PHR-VERB If you **mark off** an item on a list, you put a mark on it, for example to indicate that it has been dealt with. Read the text through and mark off the sections you find particularly applicable.

★ **marked** /mɑːkt/. ADJ Something that is **marked** is very obvious and easily noticed. ...a marked increase in crimes against property. ♦ **markedly** /'mɑːkɪdli/ ADV The film is markedly different from the play.

★ **market** /'mɑːkɪt/ **markets, marketing, marketed.** ① N-COUNT A **market** is a place where goods are bought and sold, usually in the open air. He sold boots on a market stall. ② N-COUNT The **market** for a commodity or product is the total number of people who want to buy it. The housing market was in a state of serious decline. ③ VERB To **market** a product means to organize its sale, by deciding on its price, where it should be sold, and how it should be advertised. Touch-tone telephones have been marketed in America since 1963. ♦ **marketing** N-UNCOUNT ...Renault's marketing department. ④ PHRASE If something is **on the market** or comes **onto the market**, it is available for people to buy.

marketplace (or **market place**) /'mɑːkɪtpleɪs/, **marketplaces.** ① N-COUNT In business, **the marketplace** refers to the activity of buying and selling products. Alternative fuels can't compete in the marketplace alongside gasoline. ② N-COUNT A **marketplace** is a small area in a town where goods are bought and sold, often in the open air.

marking /'mɑːkɪŋ/ **markings.** N-COUNT **Markings** are lines or patterns on an animal or object which help to identify it. ...the distinctive markings on their tails.

marmalade /'mɑːməleɪd/ **marmalades.** N-VAR **Marmalade** is a food like jam made from oranges or lemons.

maroon /mə'ruːn/ **maroons, marooning, marooned.** ① ADJ & N-UNCOUNT Something that is **maroon** is a dark reddish-purple. ...maroon velvet curtains. ② VERB If someone **is marooned** somewhere, they are left in a place that is difficult for them to escape from. He spent twenty-four hours marooned in the cab of his vehicle.

marquis (or **marquess**) /'mɑːkwɪs/ **marquises.** N-COUNT A **marquis** is a male member of the nobility.

★ **marriage** /'mærɪdʒ/ **marriages.** ① N-VAR A **marriage** is the relationship between a husband and wife, or the state of being married. ...a good marriage. ...six years of marriage. ② N-VAR A **marriage** is the act of marrying someone, or the ceremony at which this is done. I opposed her marriage to Darryl.

★ **married** /'mærɪd/. ① ADJ If you are **married**, you have a husband or wife. She is married to an Englishman. ...a married man. ② ADJ BEFORE N **Married** means relating to marriage. ...the first ten years of our married life.

⭐ **marry** /ˈmæri/ **marries, marrying, married.** 1 VERB When two people **get married** or **marry**, they become each other's husband and wife during a special ceremony. *Laura just got married to Jake... They married a month after they met... He wants to marry her.* 2 VERB When a clergyman or registrar **marries** two people, he or she is in charge of their marriage ceremony.

marsh /mɑːʃ/ **marshes.** N-VAR A **marsh** is a wet muddy area of land.

marshal /ˈmɑːʃəl/ **marshals, marshalling, marshalled** (AM **marshaling marshaled**). 1 VERB If you **marshal** people or things, you gather them together and organize them. *Richard was marshalling the doctors and nurses.* 2 N-COUNT A **marshal** is an official who helps to organize a public event. *The grand prix is controlled by well-trained marshals.* 3 N-COUNT In the United States and some other countries, a **marshal** is a police officer, often one who is responsible for a particular area.

martial /ˈmɑːʃəl/. ADJ **Martial** is used to describe things that relate to soldiers or war. [FORMAL] *He declared martial law and immediately started arresting political opponents.* ● See also **court-martial**.

martial ˈart, martial arts. N-COUNT A **martial art** is one of the techniques of self-defence that come from the Far East, for example karate and judo.

martyr /ˈmɑːtə/ **martyrs, martyred.** 1 N-COUNT A **martyr** is someone who is killed or made to suffer greatly because of their religious or political beliefs. *...a Christian martyr.* 2 VERB If someone **is martyred**, they are killed or made to suffer greatly because of their religious or political beliefs.

marvel /ˈmɑːvəl/ **marvels, marvelling, marvelled** (AM **marveling, marveled**). 1 VERB If you **marvel at** something, you express your great surprise or admiration. *Her fellow members marveled at her seemingly infinite energy.* 2 N-COUNT A **marvel** is something that makes you feel great surprise or admiration. *...the marvels of creation.*

marvellous (AM **marvelous**) /ˈmɑːvələs/. ADJ If you describe someone or something as **marvellous**, you are emphasizing that they are very good indeed. *...a marvellous actor... He looked marvellous.* ● **marvellously** ADV *He always painted marvellously.*

Marxism /ˈmɑːksɪzəm/. N-UNCOUNT **Marxism** is a political philosophy based on the writings of Karl Marx which stresses the importance of the struggle between different social classes.

Marxist /ˈmɑːksɪst/ **Marxists.** ADJ & N-COUNT Marxist means based on Marxism or relating to Marxism. A **Marxist** is a person who believes in Marxism or who is a member of a Marxist party. *...Marxist ideology.*

mascara /mæˈskɑːrə, AM -ˈkær-/. N-UNCOUNT **Mascara** is a substance used to colour eyelashes.

mascot /ˈmæskɒt/ **mascots.** N-COUNT A **mascot** is an animal, toy, or symbol which is associated with a particular organization or event, and which is thought to bring good luck. *...the official mascot of the Barcelona Games.*

masculine /ˈmæskjʊlɪn/. ADJ **Masculine** characteristics or things relate to or are considered typical of men, rather than women. *...masculine characteristics like a husky voice and facial hair.* ● **masculinity** /ˌmæskjʊˈlɪnɪti/ N-UNCOUNT *Why do men seem to need to prove their masculinity?*

mash /mæʃ/ **mashes, mashing, mashed.** VERB If you **mash** food that is solid but soft, you crush it so that it forms a soft mass. *Mash the bananas with a fork.*

⭐ **mask** /mɑːsk, mæsk/ **masks, masking, masked.** 1 N-COUNT A **mask** is something which you wear over your face for protection or to disguise yourself. *...actors wearing masks.* 2 VERB & N-COUNT If you **mask** your feelings, you deliberately do not show them. This type of behaviour can be referred to as a **mask**. *His mask of detachment cracked.* 3 VERB If one thing **masks** another, the first thing prevents people from noticing or recognizing the second thing. *A thick grey cloud masked the sun.*

masked /mɑːskt/. ADJ Someone who is **masked** is wearing a mask.

masochism /ˈmæsəkɪzəm/. N-UNCOUNT **Masochism** is behaviour in which someone gets sexual pleasure from their own pain or their own suffering. ● **masochist, masochists** N-COUNT *...sexual masochists.* ● **masochistic** /ˌmæsəˈkɪstɪk/ ADJ *...masochistic tendencies.*

mason /ˈmeɪsən/ **masons.** N-COUNT A **mason** is a person who makes things out of stone.

masonry /ˈmeɪsənri/. N-UNCOUNT **Masonry** consists of the parts of a building which are built from brick or stone.

masquerade /ˌmæskəˈreɪd/ **masquerades, masquerading, masqueraded.** VERB To **masquerade as** someone or something means to pretend to be that person or thing. *He masqueraded as a doctor and fooled everyone.*

⭐ **mass** /mæs/ **masses, massing, massed.** 1 N-SING A **mass of** something is a large amount of it. *She had a mass of auburn hair.* 2 QUANT **Masses of** something means a large amount of it. [INFORMAL] *There's masses of work for her to do.* 3 ADJ BEFORE N **Mass** is used to describe something which involves or affects a very large number of people. *...weapons of mass destruction.* 4 N-PLURAL **The masses** are the ordinary people in society. *His music is commercial. It is aimed at the masses.* 5 VERB When people or things **mass** somewhere, large numbers of them gather there. *The General was massing his troops for a counterattack.* ● **massed** ADJ BEFORE N *...the massed ranks of newsmen.* 6 N-VAR The **mass** of an object is the amount of physical matter that it has. [TECHNICAL] 7 N-VAR **Mass** is a Christian church ceremony during which people eat bread and drink wine in order to remember the last meal of Jesus Christ.

massacre/'mæsəkə/**massacres, massacring, massacred.** ☐1 N-VAR A **massacre** is the killing of many people in a violent and cruel way. ☐2 VERB If people **are massacred**, a large number of them are killed in a violent and cruel way. *300 civilians are believed to have been massacred by the rebels.* ☐3 See note at **kill**.

massage/'mæsɑːʒ, AM məˈsɑːʒ/**massages, massaging, massaged.** VERB & N-VAR If you **massage** someone, or if you give them a **massage**, you rub their body to make them relax or to stop their muscles from hurting. *She continued massaging her right foot... Massage isn't a long-term cure for stress.*

masse. See **en masse**.

⭐ **massive**/'mæsɪv/. ADJ Something that is **massive** is very large in size. *There was evidence of massive fraud.* ♦ **massively**ADV *Interest rates will rise massively.*

,mass 'media.N-SING The **mass media** are television, radio, and newspapers.

,mass-pro'duce.**mass-produces, mass-producing, mass-produced.** VERB To **mass-produce** something means to manufacture it in large quantities, using machinery. *...machinery to mass-produce footwear.* ♦ **mass-produced**ADJ BEFORE N *...the first mass-produced mountain bike.*

mast/mɑːst, mæst/**masts.** ☐1 N-COUNT The **masts** of a boat are the tall upright poles that support its sails. ☐2 N-COUNT A radio or television **mast** is a very tall pole that is used as an aerial.

⭐ **master**/'mɑːstə, 'mæs-/**masters, mastering, mastered.** ☐1 N-COUNT A servant's **master** is the man that he or she works for. [DATED] ☐2 ADJ BEFORE N You use **master** to describe someone's job when they are very skilled at it. *...a master craftsman.* ☐3 N-UNCOUNT If you are **master of** a situation, you have control over it. *Jackson remained calm and always master of his passions.* ☐4 VERB If you **master** something, you manage to learn how to do it properly or understand it completely. *Students are expected to master a second language.* ☐5 N-COUNT A **master** is a male schoolteacher. [BRITISH] ● See also **headmaster**.

mastermind/'mɑːstəmaɪnd, 'mæs-/**masterminds, masterminding, masterminded.** ☐1 VERB If you **mastermind** a complicated activity, you plan and organize it. *The finance minister will continue to mastermind Poland's economic reform.* ☐2 N-COUNT The **mastermind** behind a complicated plan, often a criminal one, is the person who plans and organizes it.

masterpiece/'mɑːstəpiːs, 'mæs-/**masterpieces.** N-COUNT A **masterpiece** is an extremely good painting, novel, film, or other work of art.

mastery/'mɑːstəri, 'mæs-/. ☐1 N-UNCOUNT If you show **mastery of** a particular skill or language, you show you have learnt or understood it completely and have no difficulty using it. *He doesn't have mastery of the basic rules*

of grammar. ☐2 N-UNCOUNT **Mastery** is power or control over something. *...his mastery over early, painful emotions.*

mat/mæt/**mats.** ☐1 N-COUNT A **mat** is a small piece of material which you put on a table to protect it from a hot plate or cup. ☐2 N-COUNT A **mat** is a small piece of carpet or other thick material that you put on the floor.

⭐ **match**/mætʃ/**matches, matching, matched.** ☐1 N-COUNT A **match** is an organized game of football, cricket, or other sport. ☐2 N-COUNT A **match** is a small wooden stick with a substance on one end that produces a flame when you strike it against a rough surface. ☐3 VERB If one thing **matches** another, or if the two things **match**, they look good together, usually because they have similar colours or designs. *You don't have to match your lipstick exactly to your outfit.* ♦ **matching**ADJ BEFORE N *...a matching handbag.* ☐4 VERB If something such as an amount or a quality **matches with** another, or if the two things **match**, they are both the same or equal. *Our value system does not match with their value system... Their strengths in memory and spatial skills matched.* ☐5 VERB To **match** something means to be equal to it in speed, size, or quality. *They played some fine attacking football, but I think we matched them in every department.* ☐6 PHRASE If one person or thing is **no match for** another, they are unable to compete successfully with the other person or thing. *Hand-held guns proved no match for heavy armor.*

matched/mætʃt/. ☐1 ADJ If two people are well **matched**, they are suited to one another and are likely to have a successful relationship. *My parents were not very well matched.* ☐2 ADJ In competitive situations, if opponents are well **matched**, they are both of the same standard in strength or ability.

⭐ **mate**/meɪt/**mates, mating, mated.** ☐1 N-COUNT You can refer to someone's friends as their **mates**. [BRITISH, INFORMAL]. ☐2 N-COUNT An animal's **mate** is its sexual partner. ☐3 VERB When animals **mate**, they have sex in order to produce young. *They want the males to mate with wild females.*

⭐ **material**/məˈtɪəriəl/**materials.** ☐1 N-VAR A **material** is a solid substance. *...a conducting material such as a metal.* ☐2 N-VAR **Material** is cloth. *...the thick material of her skirt.* ☐3 N-PLURAL **Materials** are the things that you need for a particular activity. *...sewing materials.* ☐4 ADJ **Material** things are possessions or money, rather than abstract things. *She enjoys the material comforts married life has brought her.* ♦ **materially**ADV *He has tried to help this child materially and spiritually.*

materialism/məˈtɪəriəlɪzəm/. N-UNCOUNT **Materialism** is the attitude of someone who attaches a lot of importance to money and possessions.

materialize(BRIT also **materialise**)/məˈtɪəriəlaɪz/**materializes, materializing, materialized.** VERB If an event does not **materialize**, it does not happen. *A rebellion by radicals failed to materialize.*

maternal /mə'tɜ:nəl/. ADJ **Maternal** feelings or actions are typical of those of a mother towards her child. *She had little maternal instinct.*

maternity /mə'tɜ:nɪti/. ADJ BEFORE N **Maternity** is used to describe things relating to pregnancy and birth. *...the city's maternity hospital.*

math /mæθ/. See **maths**.

mathematical /,mæθə'mætɪkəl/. ADJ BEFORE N Something that is **mathematical** involves numbers and calculations. ♦ **mathematically** ADV *...a mathematically complicated formula.*

mathematician /,mæθəmə'tɪʃən/ **mathematicians.** N-COUNT A **mathematician** is a person who is trained in the study of numbers and in the study of calculations.

mathematics /,mæθə'mætɪks/. N-UNCOUNT **Mathematics** is the study of numbers, quantities, or shapes.

maths /mæθs/. N-UNCOUNT In British English, mathematics is usually referred to as **maths**. The American word is **math**.

matinee (or **matinée**) /'mætɪneɪ, AM -'neɪ/ **matinees.** N-COUNT A **matinee** is a performance of a play or a showing of a film in the afternoon.

matrix /'meɪtrɪks/ **matrices** /'meɪtrɪsi:z/. N-COUNT A **matrix** is the environment in which something such as a society develops and grows. [FORMAL] *...the matrix of their culture.*

matt /mæt/. ADJ A **matt** colour, paint, or surface is dull rather than shiny.

⭐ **matter** /'mætə/ **matters, mattering, mattered.** ① N-COUNT A **matter** is a task, situation, or event which you have to deal with or think about. *...business matters.* ② N-PLURAL You use **matters** to refer to the situation you are talking about. *It is hard to see how this would improve matters.* ③ N-UNCOUNT You can refer to books, newspapers, and other texts as printed **matter** or reading **matter**. ④ N-UNCOUNT **Matter** is the physical part of the universe consisting of solids, liquids, and gases. ⑤ N-SING You use **matter** in expressions such as **'What's the matter?'** or **'Is anything the matter?'** when you think that someone has a problem and you want to know what it is. ⑥ N-SING You can use matter in expressions such as **'a matter of weeks'** when you are emphasizing that it is a short period of time. ⑦ VERB If something **matters**, it is important because it has an effect on a situation. *It does not matter how long their hair is.*

PHRASES ● If you say that something is **another matter** or **a different matter**, you mean that it is very different from the situation that you have just discussed or is an exception to a rule or general statement that you have just made. *Being responsible for one's own health is one thing, but being responsible for another person's health is quite a different matter.* ● You say **'it doesn't matter'** to tell someone who is apologizing to you that you are not angry or upset, and that

they should not worry. ● You use **no matter** in expressions such as **no matter how** and **no matter what** to indicate that something is true or happens in all circumstances. *Any dog bite, no matter how small, needs immediate medical attention.* ● If you are going to do something **as a matter of** urgency or priority, you are going to do it as soon as possible, because it is important. ● If you say that something is just **a matter of time**, you mean that it is certain to happen at some time in the future. *It would be only a matter of time before he went through with it.* ● **as a matter of fact**: see **fact**.

matter-of-'fact. ADJ If you say someone is being **matter-of-fact**, you mean that they are being unemotional in a tense or difficult situation. *John was doing his best to give Francis the news in a matter-of-fact way.* ♦ **matter-of-factly** ADV *'She thinks you're a spy,' Scott said matter-of-factly.*

mattress /'mætrəs/ **mattresses.** N-COUNT A **mattress** is a large flat pad which is put on a bed to make it comfortable to sleep on.

mature /mə'tjʊə/ **matures, maturing, matured.** ① VERB When a child or young animal **matures**, it becomes an adult. ② ADJ A **mature** person or animal is fully grown. ♦ **maturity** /mə'tjʊərɪti/ N-UNCOUNT *We stop growing at maturity.* ③ ADJ If you describe someone as **mature**, you think that their behaviour is responsible and sensible. ♦ **maturity** N-UNCOUNT *Her speech showed great maturity.* ④ VERB When something **matures**, it reaches a state of complete development. *When the trees matured they were cut.*

maul /mɔ:l/ **mauls, mauling, mauled.** VERB If someone **is mauled** by an animal, they are attacked and badly injured by it. *The dog went berserk and mauled one of the girls.*

maverick /'mævərɪk/ **mavericks.** N-COUNT If you describe someone as a **maverick**, you mean that they do not think or behave in the same way as other people.

maxim /'mæksɪm/ **maxims.** N-COUNT A **maxim** is a rule for good or sensible behaviour, especially one in the form of a saying. *I believe in the maxim 'if it ain't broke, don't fix it'.*

maximize (BRIT also **maximise**) /'mæksɪmaɪz/ **maximizes, maximizing, maximized.** VERB To **maximize** something means to make it as large or important as you can. *In order to maximize profit the firm would obviously seek to maximize output.*

⭐ **maximum** /'mæksɪməm/. ① ADJ BEFORE N & N-SING The **maximum** amount or the **maximum** is the amount which is the largest that is possible, allowed, or required. *The maximum height for a fence or hedge is 2 metres. ...a maximum of two years in prison.* ② ADJ BEFORE N You use **maximum** to emphasize how great an amount is. *...the maximum amount of information... It was achieved with minimum fuss and maximum efficiency.* ③ ADV If you say that

a
b
c
d
e
f
g
h
i
j
k
l
m
n
o
p
q
r
s
t
u
v
w
x
y
z

something is a particular amount **maximum**, you mean that this is the greatest amount it should be or could possibly be, although a smaller amount is acceptable or very possible. *We need an extra 6g a day maximum.*

⭐ **may** /meɪ/. **1** MODAL If you say that something **may** happen or be true, you mean that it is possible. *We may have some rain today... I don't know if they'll publish it or not. They may... Cancer may not show up for many years.* **2** MODAL If someone **may** do something, they are allowed to do it. *May we come in?... You may leave... Adolescents under the age of 18 may not work in jobs that require them to drive.* **3** MODAL You use **may** in statements where you are accepting the truth of a situation, but contrasting it with something that is more important. *I may be almost 50, but there's not a lot of things I've forgotten.*

⭐ **May** /meɪ/. N-UNCOUNT **May** is the fifth month of the year. → See Reference Page on Times and Dates.

⭐ **maybe** /'meɪbi/. **1** ADV You use **maybe** to express uncertainty, for example when you do not know that something is definitely true. *Maybe she is in love... I do think about having children, maybe when I'm 40... 'Is she coming back?'— 'Maybe'.* **2** ADV You use **maybe** when you are making a rough guess at a number, quantity, or value, rather than stating it exactly. *The men were maybe a hundred feet away.*

mayhem /'meɪhem/. N-UNCOUNT **Mayhem** is a situation that is not controlled or ordered, when people are behaving in a disorganized, confused, and often violent way. *Their arrival caused mayhem as crowds of refugees rushed towards them.*

mayonnaise /ˌmeɪə'neɪz/. N-UNCOUNT **Mayonnaise** is a sauce made from egg yolks, oil, and vinegar, eaten cold.

⭐ **mayor** /meə, 'meɪə/ **mayors**. N-COUNT The **mayor** of a town or city is the person who has been elected to represent it for a fixed period of time.

maze /meɪz/ **mazes**. N-COUNT A **maze** is a complex system of passages or paths separated by walls or hedges.

⭐ **me** /mi, STRONG miː/. PRON A speaker or writer uses **me** to refer to himself or herself. **Me** is a first person singular pronoun. **Me** is used as the object of a verb or a preposition. *...decisions that would affect me for the rest of my life... She looked up at me.*

meadow /'medəʊ/ **meadows**. N-COUNT A **meadow** is a field with grass and flowers growing in it.

meagre (AM **meager**) /'miːgə/. ADJ Something that is **meagre** is very small in amount. *...a meagre 3.1% pay rise... Their food supply is meager and they are frequently without water.*

⭐ **meal** /miːl/ **meals**. N-COUNT A **meal** is an occasion when people eat. You can refer to the food that they eat at that time as a **meal**. *The waiter offered him red wine or white wine with his meal.*

USAGE The first meal of the day is called **breakfast**. The most common word for the midday meal is **lunch**, but in some parts of Britain, and in some contexts, **dinner** is used as well. *...school dinners. ...Christmas dinner.* However, **dinner** is used mainly to refer to a meal in the evening. In British English, it may also suggest a formal or special meal. **Supper** and **tea** are sometimes also used to refer to this meal, though for some people, **supper** is a snack in the late evening and **tea** is a light meal in the afternoon.

---

mean 1 signify

⭐ **mean** /miːn/ **means, meaning, meant**. **1** VERB If you want to know what something or someone **means**, you want to know what they are referring to, or what message they are conveying. *What does 'evidence' mean?... What do you think he means by that?... In modern Welsh, 'glas' means 'blue'... The red signal means you can shoot.* **2** VERB If something **means** a lot to you, it is important to you. *It would mean a lot to them to win.* **3** VERB If one thing **means** another, it shows that the second thing is true or makes it certain to happen. *Becoming a millionaire didn't mean an end to money worries.* **4** VERB If you **mean** what you say, you are serious and not joking, exaggerating, or just being polite. *He could see I meant what I said... Does he really mean it when he says he is sorry?* **5** VERB If you **mean to** do something, you intend to do it. *I have been meaning to write this letter for some time now... I didn't mean to hurt you.*

PHRASES ● You say **'I mean'** when you are explaining, justifying, or correcting what you have just said. *It was his idea. Gordon's, I mean... I'm sure he wouldn't mind. I mean, I was the one who asked him... It was law or classics – I mean English or classics.* ● to **mean business**: see **business**.

mean 2 unkind

mean /miːn/ **meaner, meanest**. **1** ADJ If you say that someone is **mean**, you disapprove of them because they are unwilling to spend much money or to use much of a particular thing. *He's basically mean with money. ...a rather mean portion of apple tart.* ♦ **meanness** N-UNCOUNT *...the meanness of some employers.* **2** ADJ If you are **mean** to someone, you are unkind to them. ♦ **meanness** N-UNCOUNT *You provoked him out of meanness.* **3** PHRASE You use **no mean** to emphasize that someone or something is good or remarkable. *She was no mean performer.*

mean 3 average

mean /miːn/. N-SING The **mean** is a number that is the average of a set of numbers. *...the mean score for 26-year-olds.* ● See also **means**.

meander /miˈændə/ **meanders, meandering, meandered.** [1] VERB If a river or road **meanders**, it has a lot of bends in it. *A rural single railway track meanders through the valley.* [2] VERB If you **meander** through a place, you move slowly through it for pleasure. *It's so restful to meander along Irish country roads.*

★ **meaning** /ˈmiːnɪŋ/ **meanings.** [1] N-VAR The **meaning** of something such as a word, symbol, or gesture is the thing that it refers to or the message that it conveys. *...two words with similar meanings... I have been trying hard to interpret the meaning of this dream.* [2] N-UNCOUNT If an activity or action has **meaning**, it has a purpose and is worthwhile. *...a challenge that gives meaning to life.*

meaningful /ˈmiːnɪŋfʊl/. [1] ADJ If you describe something as **meaningful**, you mean that it is serious, important, or useful in some way. *...satisfying, meaningful work.*
♦ **meaningfully** ADV *By joining voluntary organisations they can participate actively and meaningfully.* [2] ADJ BEFORE N A **meaningful** look, gesture, or remark is intended to express something which is not obvious, but which is understood. ♦ **meaningfully** ADV *She rolled her eyes meaningfully.*

meaningless /ˈmiːnɪŋləs/. ADJ Something that is **meaningless** has no meaning or purpose. *The sentence 'kicked the ball the man' is meaningless. ...the conviction that life is meaningless.*

★ **means** /miːnz/.

☑ In meaning 1, **means** is both the singular and the plural form.

[1] N-COUNT A **means of** doing something is a method or instrument which can be used to do it. *They didn't provide me with any means of transport... The move is a means to fight crime.* [2] N-PLURAL You can refer to the money that someone has as their **means**. [FORMAL] *...a health service that's available to all, regardless of means... As a student you're always living beyond your means.*

PHRASES ● You can say **'by all means'** to tell someone that you are willing to allow them to do something. *'Can I come and have a look at your house?'—'Yes, by all means'.* ● If you do something **by means of** a particular method or instrument, you do it using that method or instrument. *This is a two year course taught by means of lectures and seminars.* ● You use expressions such as **'by no means'** and **'not by any means'** to emphasize that something is not true. *This is by no means out of the ordinary.*

meant /ment/. [1] **Meant** is the past tense and past participle of **mean**. [2] ADJ AFTER LINK-V If something or someone is **meant to** do a particular thing or is **meant for** a particular purpose, that is what was intended or planned. *The tales were never meant for publication... I'm meant to be on holiday.* [3] ADJ AFTER LINK-V If you say that something is **meant to** have a particular

quality or characteristic, you mean it has a reputation for being like that. *Spurs are meant to be one of the top teams in the world.*

meantime /ˈmiːntaɪm/. N-UNCOUNT **In the meantime** means in the period of time between two events, or while an event is happening. *Reduce the heat and simmer for 30 minutes. In the meantime, fry the spicy sausage.*

★ **meanwhile** /ˈmiːnwaɪl/. ADV **Meanwhile** means in the period of time between two events, or while an event is happening. *I'll be ready to greet them. Meanwhile I'm off to discuss the Fowler's party with Felix.*

measles /ˈmiːzəlz/. N-UNCOUNT **Measles** is an infectious illness that gives you a high temperature and red spots.

measurable /ˈmeʒərəbəl/. ADJ If something is **measurable**, it is large enough to be noticed or to be significant. [FORMAL] *Both leaders seemed to expect measurable progress.*

★ **measure** /ˈmeʒə/ **measures, measuring, measured.** [1] VERB If you **measure** the quality, quantity, or value of something, you decide how great it is, by using particular procedures or instruments. *I continued to measure his progress against the charts in the doctor's office... The swelling is measured with a ruler.* [2] VERB If something **measures** a particular length, width, or amount, that is its size or intensity, expressed in numbers. *This hand-decorated plate measures 30cm across.* [3] N-SING A **measure of** a particular quality, feeling, or activity is a fairly large amount of it. [FORMAL] *Each attained a measure of success.* [4] N-SING If something is a **measure of** a particular situation, it shows that the situation is very serious or has developed to a very great extent. *That is a measure of how bad things have become.* [5] N-COUNT When someone takes **measures** to do something, they carry out particular actions in order to achieve a particular result. *...new government measures to combat crime.* [6] PHRASE If something is done **for good measure**, it is done in addition to a number of other things. *I repeated my question for good measure.*

▶**measure up.** PHR-VERB If you do not **measure up to** a standard or **to** someone's expectations, you are not good enough to achieve the standard or fulfil the person's expectations. *It was fatiguing sometimes to try to measure up to her standard of perfection.*

measurement /ˈmeʒəmənt/ **measurements.** [1] N-COUNT A **measurement** is a result that you obtain by measuring something. *We took lots of measurements.* [2] N-VAR **Measurement** of something is the process or activity of measuring it. [3] N-PLURAL Your **measurements** are the size of your chest, waist, hips, and other parts of your body.

★ **meat** /miːt/ **meats.** N-VAR **Meat** is the flesh of a dead animal that people cook and eat. *...cold meats and salads.*

a
b
c
d
e
f
g
h
i
j
k
l
m
n
o
p
q
r
s
t
u
v
w
x
y
z

mechanic/mɪˈkænɪk/ **mechanics.** 1 N-COUNT A **mechanic** is someone whose job is to repair and maintain machines and engines, especially car engines. 2 N-PLURAL **The mechanics of** a system or activity are the way in which it works or the way in which it is done. *What are the mechanics of this new process?*

mechanical/mɪˈkænɪkəl/. 1 ADJ A **mechanical** device has moving parts and uses power in order to do a particular task. ♦ **mechanically** ADV *The locks are mechanically operated.* 2 ADJ A **mechanical** action is done automatically, without thinking about it. ♦ **mechanically** ADV *He nodded mechanically.*

★ **mechanism**/ˈmekənɪzəm/ **mechanisms.** 1 N-COUNT A **mechanism** is a part of a machine that does a particular task. *...the locking mechanism.* 2 N-COUNT A **mechanism** is a way of getting something done within a particular system. *...a mechanism for protecting rights.*

mechanize(BRIT also **mechanise**) /ˈmekənaɪz/ **mechanizes, mechanizing, mechanized.** VERB If a type of work **is mechanized**, it is done by machines. ♦ **mechanization** N-UNCOUNT *...the mechanisation of agriculture.*

★ **medal**/ˈmedəl/ **medals.** N-COUNT A **medal** is a small metal disc, given as an award for bravery or as a prize in a sporting event.

medallist/ˈmedəlɪst/ **medallists.** N-COUNT A **medallist** is a person who has won a medal in sport.

meddle/ˈmedəl/ **meddles, meddling, meddled.** VERB If you say that someone **meddles in** something, you are criticizing the fact that they try to influence or change it without being asked. *She told me not to meddle in things that don't concern me.*

★ **media**/ˈmiːdiə/. 1 N-SING You can refer to television, radio, and newspapers as **the media**. Media can take the singular or plural form of the verb. *The media has brought more unwelcome attention to the Royal Family.* 2 Media is a plural of **medium**.

,media ˈcircus,media circuses. N-COUNT If an event is described as a **media circus**, a large group of people from the media is there to report on it and take photographs. *The couple married in the Caribbean to avoid a media circus.*

mediaeval. See **medieval**.

mediate/ˈmiːdieɪt/ **mediates, mediating, mediated.** VERB If someone **mediates between** two groups, or **mediates** an agreement **between** them, they try to settle a dispute between them. *The Vatican successfully mediated in a territorial dispute between Argentina and Chile.* ♦ **mediation** N-UNCOUNT *...United Nations mediation between the two sides.* ♦ **mediator,mediators** N-COUNT *An archbishop has been acting as mediator between the rebels and the authorities.*

★ **medical**/ˈmedɪkəl/ **medicals.** 1 ADJ BEFORE N **Medical** means relating to illness and injuries and to their treatment or prevention. *Four of our men needed medical treatment.* ♦ **medically** ADV

I am not medically qualified. 2 N-COUNT A **medical** is a thorough examination of your body by a doctor.

medication/,medɪˈkeɪʃən/ **medications.** N-VAR **Medication** is medicine that is used to cure an illness. *She is not on any medication.*

medicinal/meˈdɪsənəl/. ADJ **Medicinal** substances are used to treat and cure illness.

★ **medicine**/ˈmedsən, AM ˈmedɪsɪn/ **medicines.** 1 N-UNCOUNT **Medicine** is the treatment of illness and injuries by doctors and nurses. *He pursued a career in medicine.* 2 N-VAR A **medicine** is a substance that you swallow in order to cure an illness.

medieval(or **mediaeval** /,medɪˈiːvəl, AM ,miːd-/. ADJ **Medieval** things relate to or date from the period in European history between about 500 AD and about 1500 AD. *...a medieval castle.*

mediocre/,miːdiˈəʊkə/. ADJ If you describe someone or something as **mediocre**, you mean that it is of rather poor quality. *His school record was mediocre.* ♦ **mediocrity** /,miːdiˈɒkrɪti, ,med-/ N-UNCOUNT *...the mediocrity of most contemporary literature.*

meditate/ˈmedɪteɪt/ **meditates, meditating, meditated.** 1 VERB If you **meditate on** something, you think about it carefully and deeply for a long time. 2 VERB If you **meditate**, you remain in a calm, silent state for a period of time, often as part of a religious training. ♦ **meditation** N-UNCOUNT *Many busy executives have begun to practice meditation.*

★ **medium**/ˈmiːdiəm/.

> ✓ The plural of the noun is **mediums** or **media**.

1 ADJ You use **medium** to describe something which is average in size, degree or amount, or approximately half way along a scale between two extremes. *He was of medium height... Only a low or medium heat is necessary. ...medium brown hair.* 2 N-COUNT A **medium** is the means that you use to communicate or express something. *In Sierra Leone, English is used as the medium of instruction.* ● See also **media**.

meek/miːk/. ADJ & N-PLURAL A **meek** person is quiet and timid and does what other people say. **The meek** are people who are meek. ♦ **meekly** ADV *'Thank you, Peter', Amy said meekly.*

★ **meet**/miːt/ **meets, meeting, met.** 1 VERB If you **meet** someone, or if you **meet up with** them, you happen to be in the same place as them and have a conversation with them. *He's the kindest and sincerest person I've ever met... Hey, Terry, come and meet my Dad... We met by chance... When he was parking my automobile, he met up with a buddy he had at Oxford.* 2 VERB If two or more people **meet**, or if they **meet up**, they go to the same place, which they have earlier arranged to do, so that they can talk or do something together. *Meet me down at the beach tomorrow... Mr Levy will meet with President Bush on*

Thursday... We tend to meet up for lunch once a week... The committee met twice last week to discuss the company's problems. **3** VERB If you **meet** someone who is travelling, or if you **meet** their train, plane, or bus, you go to the station, airport, or bus stop in order to be there when they arrive. *Lili and my father met me off the boat.* **4** VERB If something **meets** a need, requirement, or condition, it is satisfactory or sufficiently large to fulfil it. *Employees must meet certain eligibility requirements.* **5** VERB If you **meet** something such as a problem or challenge, you deal satisfactorily with it. *They had worked heroically to meet the deadline.* **6** VERB If you **meet** the cost of something, you provide the money for it. *The government said it will help meet some of the cost of the damage.* **7** VERB If someone or something **meets** an attitude or reaction, or if they **meet with** it, they experience that attitude or get that reaction from people. *Never had she met such spite and pettiness... The idea met with a cool response.* **8** VERB The place where two areas or lines **meet** is the place where they are next to one another or join. *The track widened as it met the road.* **9** to **make ends meet**: see end. ● to **meet** someone's **eyes**: see eye.
▸**meet up.** See meet 1, 2.

⭐ **meeting** /'miːtɪŋ/ **meetings.** **1** N-COUNT A **meeting** is an event at which a group of people come together to discuss things or make decisions. You can also refer to the people at a meeting as **the meeting**. *He still travels to London regularly for business meetings... The meeting decided that further efforts were needed.* **2** N-COUNT A **meeting** is an occasion when you meet someone. *...a chance meeting.*

megabyte /'meɡəbaɪt/ **megabytes.** N-COUNT In computing, a **megabyte** is one million bytes of data.

melancholy /'melənkɒli/. ADJ & N-UNCOUNT Someone who is **melancholy** or who has **melancholy** feelings has an intense feeling of sadness. This feeling can be called **melancholy**. [LITERARY]

mellow /'meləʊ/ **mellower, mellowest; mellows, mellowing, mellowed.** **1** ADJ **Mellow** is used to describe things that have a pleasant, soft, rich colour, usually red, yellow, or brown. *...the softer, mellower light of evening.* **2** ADJ A **mellow** flavour or sound is pleasant, smooth, and rich. **3** VERB & ADJ If someone **mellows**, or if they become more **mellow**, they become kinder or less extreme in their behaviour. *Marriage had not mellowed him... Is she more mellow and tolerant?*

melodrama /'melədrɑːmə/ **melodramas.** N-VAR A **melodrama** is a story or play in which there are a lot of exciting or sad events and in which people's emotions are very exaggerated.

melodramatic /ˌmelədrə'mætɪk/. ADJ If you are being **melodramatic**, you treat a situation as much more serious than it really is.

melody /'melədi/ **melodies.** N-COUNT A **melody** is a tune. [LITERARY]

melon /'melən/ **melons.** N-VAR A **melon** is a large, sweet, juicy fruit with a thick green or yellow skin.
➔ See picture on page 821.

melt /melt/ **melts, melting, melted.** **1** VERB When a solid substance **melts**, or when it **is melted**, it changes to a liquid because of being heated. *The snow had melted... Break up the chocolate and melt it.* **2** VERB & PHR-VERB If something **melts**, or if it **melts away**, it gradually disappears. *The youths dispersed and melted into the darkness... His anger melted away.*
▸**melt down.** PHR-VERB If an object **is melted down**, it is heated until it melts. *Their equipment would be melted down as scrap metal.*

⭐ **member** /'membə/ **members.** N-COUNT A **member of** a group or organization is one of the people, animals, or things belonging to it. *Their lack of training could put members of the public at risk. ...a sunflower or a similar member of the daisy family... Britain is a full member of NATO.*

Member of 'Parliament, Members of Parliament. N-COUNT A **Member of Parliament** is a person who has been elected to represent people in a country's parliament. It is usually abbreviated to **MP**. ● See note at **government**.

⭐ **membership** /'membəʃɪp/ **memberships.** **1** N-UNCOUNT **Membership** is the fact or state of being a member of an organization. *...his membership of the Communist Party.* **2** N-VAR The **membership** of an organization is the people who belong to it. *The party membership reached 97,000.*

membrane /'membreɪn/ **membranes.** N-COUNT A **membrane** is a thin skin which connects or covers parts of a person's or animal's body.

memo /'meməʊ/ **memos.** N-COUNT A **memo** is an official note from one person to another within the same organization.

memoirs /'memwɑːz/. N-PLURAL If someone writes their **memoirs**, they write a book about their life.

memorabilia /ˌmemərə'bɪliə/. N-PLURAL **Memorabilia** consists of things that you collect because they are connected with a person or an organization in which you are interested. *...rock and pop memorabilia.*

memorable /'memərəbəl/. ADJ Something that is **memorable** is likely to be remembered, because it is special or unique. *It had been a memorable day.*

memorandum /ˌmemə'rændəm/.

✅ The plural is **memoranda** or **memorandums**.

N-COUNT A **memorandum** is a **memo**. [FORMAL]

memorial /mɪ'mɔːriəl/ **memorials.** **1** N-COUNT A **memorial** is a structure built in order to remind people of a famous person or event. *...a memorial to Columbus... Every village had its war memorial.* **2** ADJ BEFORE N A **memorial** event or prize is in honour of someone who has died, so that they will be remembered. *A memorial service is being held for her at St Paul's Church.*

a
b
c
d
e
f
g
h
i
j
k
l
m
n
o
p
q
r
s
t
u
v
w
x
y
z

memorize (BRIT also **memorise**) /'meməraɪz/ memorizes, memorizing, memorized. VERB If you **memorize** something, you learn it so that you can remember it exactly.

⭐ **memory** /'meməri/ **memories.** ⚊1⚊ N-COUNT Your **memory** is your ability to remember things. *All the details of the meeting are fresh in my memory... He had a good memory for faces... He claims to have lost his memory.* ⚊2⚊ N-COUNT A **memory** is something that you remember about the past. *He had happy memories of his father.* ⚊3⚊ N-SING If you talk about the **memory** of someone who has died, especially someone who was loved or respected, you are referring to the ways in which they are remembered. *The congress opened with a minute's silence in memory of those who died in the struggle.* ⚊4⚊ N-COUNT A computer's **memory** is the capacity of the computer to store information. ⚊5⚊ PHRASE If you do something **from memory**, you do it without looking at anything written or printed. *Many members of the church sang from memory.*

men /men/. **Men** is the plural of **man**.

menace /'menɪs/ **menaces, menacing, menaced.** ⚊1⚊ N-COUNT Something or someone that is a **menace** is likely to cause serious harm. *In my view you are a menace to the public. ...the menace of fascism.* ⚊2⚊ N-UNCOUNT **Menace** is a quality or atmosphere of danger or threat. *...a vague feeling of menace.* ⚊3⚊ VERB If someone or something **menaces** you, they threaten to harm you or are likely to do so. *...a Franco-Spanish fleet which menaced the English coast.* ◆ **menacing** ADJ *Mary Ann gave her a menacing look.*
◆ **menacingly** ADV *James moved menacingly towards him.*

mend /mend/ **mends, mending, mended.** ⚊1⚊ VERB If you **mend** something that is damaged or broken, you do something to it so that it works properly or can be used. *My father always mended shoes... I should have had the catch mended.* ⚊2⚊ PHRASE If you are **on the mend**, you are recovering after an illness or injury.

meningitis /ˌmenɪn'dʒaɪtɪs/. N-UNCOUNT **Meningitis** is a serious infectious illness which affects your brain and spinal cord.

menopause /'menəpɔːz/. N-SING The **menopause** is the time during which a woman stops menstruating, usually when she is about fifty. ◆ **menopausal** ADJ *...a menopausal woman.*

menstrual /'menstruəl/. ADJ BEFORE N **Menstrual** means relating to menstruation. *...the menstrual cycle.*

menstruate /'menstrueɪt/ **menstruates, menstruating, menstruated.** VERB When a woman **menstruates**, a flow of blood comes from her womb. [FORMAL] ◆ **menstruation** N-UNCOUNT *...the cycles of menstruation and fertility.*

menswear /'menzweə/. N-UNCOUNT **Menswear** is clothing for men.

⭐ **mental** /'mentəl/. ⚊1⚊ ADJ BEFORE N **Mental** means relating to the mind and the process of thinking. *...the mental development of children.*
◆ **mentally** ADV *He became mentally ill.* ⚊2⚊ ADJ BEFORE N A **mental** act is one that involves only thinking and not physical action. *...mental arithmetic.* ◆ **mentally** ADV *I mentally rehearsed what I would do.*

mentality /men'tælɪti/ **mentalities.** N-COUNT Your **mentality** is your attitudes or ways of thinking. *...the criminal mentality.*

⭐ **mention** /'menʃən/ **mentions, mentioning, mentioned.** ⚊1⚊ VERB & N-VAR If you **mention** something, or if you give a **mention** to it, you say something about it, usually briefly. *I may not have mentioned it to her... She had mentioned that it was her husband's birthday... There was no mention of elections.* ⚊2⚊ PHRASE You use **not to mention** when you want to add extra information which emphasizes the point that you are making. *The audience, not to mention the bewildered cast, were not amused.*

mentor /'mentɔː/ **mentors.** N-COUNT Someone's **mentor** is a person who teaches them and gives them a lot of advice over a period of time. [FORMAL] *...his political mentor.*

menu /'menjuː/ **menus.** ⚊1⚊ N-COUNT In a restaurant or café, the **menu** is a list of the available meals and drinks. *They ordered everything on the menu.* ⚊2⚊ N-COUNT On a computer, a **menu** is a list of choices of things that you can do using the computer. [COMPUTING]

MEP /ˌem iː 'piː/ **MEPs.** N-COUNT An **MEP** is a person who has been elected to the European Parliament. **MEP** is an abbreviation for 'Member of the European Parliament'.

mercenary /'mɜːsənri, AM -neri/ **mercenaries.** ⚊1⚊ N-COUNT A **mercenary** is a soldier who is paid to fight for a country or group that he or she does not belong to. ⚊2⚊ ADJ If you describe someone as **mercenary**, you mean that they are only interested in the money that they can get from a particular person or situation.

merchandise /'mɜːtʃəndaɪz, -daɪs/. N-UNCOUNT **Merchandise** is goods that are bought or sold. [FORMAL] *The merchandise is reasonably priced.*

merchandising /'mɜːtʃəndaɪzɪŋ/. N-UNCOUNT **Merchandising** is used to refer to the way shops and businesses organize the sale of their products, for example the way they are displayed and the prices that are chosen.

⭐ **merchant** /'mɜːtʃənt/ **merchants.** ⚊1⚊ N-COUNT A **merchant** is a person whose business is buying or selling goods in large quantities. *...a wine merchant.* ⚊2⚊ ADJ BEFORE N **Merchant** seamen or ships are involved in carrying goods for trade.

mercifully /'mɜːsɪfʊli/. ADV You can use **mercifully** to show that you are glad about something, because it avoids a dangerous or unpleasant situation. *Mercifully, a friend came to the rescue... Crime is mercifully rare here.*

merciless /'mɜːsɪləs/. ADJ If you describe someone as **merciless**, you mean that they are very cruel or determined and do not show any concern for the effect that their actions have on other people. ♦ **mercilessly** ADV *We teased him mercilessly.*

mercury /'mɜːkjʊri/. N-UNCOUNT **Mercury** is a silver-coloured liquid metal, used in thermometers.

mercy /'mɜːsi/. [1] N-UNCOUNT If someone in authority shows **mercy**, they choose not to harm or punish someone they have power over. *They cried for mercy.* [2] PHRASE If you are **at the mercy of** something or someone, you cannot prevent yourself being affected or harmed by them. *Ordinary people are at the mercy of faceless bureaucrats.*

⭐ **mere** /mɪə/ **merest.** ADJ BEFORE N You use **mere** to emphasize how unimportant, insufficient, or small something is. **Mere** does not have a comparative form. The superlative form **merest** is used for emphasis, rather than in comparisons. *Tickets are a mere £7.50... She'd never received the merest hint of any communication from him.* ♦ **merely** ADV *The brain accounts for merely three per cent of body weight.*

⭐ **merely** /'mɪəli/. [1] ADV You use **merely** to emphasize that something is only what you say and not better, more important, or more exciting. *Michael is now merely a good friend.* [2] ADV You use **not merely** before the less important of two statements, as a way of emphasizing the more important statement. *His were not merely crimes of theft but of violence.*

merge /mɜːdʒ/ **merges, merging, merged.** VERB If one thing **merges with** another, or if one thing **is merged with** another, they combine or come together to make one whole thing. *The two countries merged into one. ...how to merge the graphic with text on the same screen.*

⭐ **merger** /'mɜːdʒə/ **mergers.** N-COUNT A **merger** is the joining together of two separate companies or organizations so that they become one. *...the proposed merger of two Japanese banks.*

merit /'merɪt/ **merits, meriting, merited.** [1] N-VAR If you refer to the **merit** or **merits** of something, you mean that it has good or useful qualities. *Box-office success mattered more than artistic merit... Whatever its merits, their work would never be used.* [2] VERB If someone or something **merits** a particular action or treatment, they are good, important, or serious enough for someone to treat them in this way. [FORMAL] *Such ideas merit careful consideration.* [3] PHRASE If you judge something or someone **on merit** or **on** their **merits**, your judgement is based on their actual qualities, rather than on particular rules, traditions, or prejudices. *Everybody is selected on merit... Each case is judged on its merits.*

mermaid /'mɜːmeɪd/ **mermaids.** N-COUNT In fairy stories and legends, a **mermaid** is a woman with a fish's tail instead of legs, who lives in the sea.

merry /'meri/. ADJ **Merry** means happy and cheerful. *...a merry little tune... We wished them a*

Merry Christmas. ♦ **merrily** ADV *Chris threw back his head and laughed merrily.*

mesh /meʃ/ **meshes, meshing, meshed.** [1] N-VAR **Mesh** is material like a net made from wire, thread, or plastic. *...wire mesh.* [2] VERB If two things or ideas **mesh**, or if they **are meshed**, they go together well. *This story never quite meshed with the facts.*

mesmerize (BRIT also **mesmerise**) /'mezməraɪz/ **mesmerizes, mesmerizing, mesmerized.** VERB If you **are mesmerized** by something, you are so fascinated by it that you cannot think about anything else. *Jack walked around the hotel and was mesmerized by its sheer size.*

⭐ **mess** /mes/ **messes, messing, messed.** [1] N-SING If something is a **mess** or **in a mess**, it is dirty or untidy. *I'll clear up the mess later... The wrong shampoo can leave curly hair in a tangled mess.* [2] N-COUNT If you say that a situation is a **mess**, you mean that it is full of trouble or problems. You can also say that something is **in a mess**. *I've made such a mess of my life. ...the many reasons why the economy is in such a mess.*
▸**mess around** or **mess about.** [1] PHR-VERB If you **mess around**, you spend time doing silly or casual things without any particular purpose or result. *Boys and girls will enjoy messing about with any kind of machine.* [2] PHR-VERB If you say that someone **is messing around** with something, you mean that they are interfering with it in a harmful way. *I'd like to know who's been messing about with the pram.*
▸**mess up.** [1] PHR-VERB If someone **messes** something **up**, or if they **mess up**, they cause something to fail or be spoiled. [INFORMAL] *He had messed up one career... If I messed up, I would probably be fired.* [2] PHR-VERB If you **mess up** a place or a thing, you make it untidy or dirty. *I hope they haven't messed up your video tapes.*

⭐ **message** /'mesɪdʒ/ **messages.** [1] N-COUNT A **message** is a piece of information or a request that you send to someone or leave for them when you cannot speak to them directly. *I got a message you were trying to reach me.* [2] N-COUNT The **message** that someone is trying to communicate is the idea, argument, or opinion that they are trying to communicate. *I think they got the message that this is wrong.*

messenger /'mesɪndʒə/ **messengers.** N-COUNT A **messenger** takes a message to someone, or takes messages regularly as their job. *...instruction for the document to be sent by messenger.*

Messiah /mɪ'saɪə/. N-PROPER For Jews, **the Messiah** is a king or leader who will be sent to them by God. For Christians, **the Messiah** is Jesus Christ.

Messrs /'mesəz/. **Messrs** is used as the plural of **Mr** in front of the names of two or more men. [FORMAL] *...Messrs Clegg & Sons of Balham.*

messy /'mesi/. [1] ADJ A **messy** person or activity makes things dirty or untidy. *She was a good, if messy, cook... The work tends to be a bit*

a
b
c
d
e
f
g
h
i
j
k
l
m
n
o
p
q
r
s
t
u
v
w
x
y
z

messy. [2] ADJ Something that is **messy** is dirty or untidy. *This first coat of paint looks messy.* [3] ADJ If you describe a situation as **messy**, you dislike it because it is confused or complicated. *Negotiations would be messy and time-consuming.*

met /met/. **Met** is the past tense and past participle of **meet**.

metabolic /,metə'bɒlɪk/. ADJ BEFORE N **Metabolic** means relating to a person's or animal's metabolism. [TECHNICAL] *People who have inherited a low metabolic rate will gain weight.*

metabolism /mɪ'tæbəlɪzəm/ **metabolisms**. N-VAR Your **metabolism** is the way that chemical processes in your body cause food to be used in an efficient way, for example to give you energy. [TECHNICAL]

⭐ **metal** /'metəl/ **metals**. N-VAR **Metal** is a hard substance such as iron, steel, copper, or lead. *...furniture in wood, metal and glass. ...a metal bar.*

metallic /mə'tælɪk/. ADJ **Metallic** things consist of metal or sound or look like they consist of metal. *...a nonstick metallic dish... It gave a metallic clang, like a cracked bell.*

metamorphosis /,metə'mɔːfəsɪs/ **metamorphoses**. N-VAR When a **metamorphosis** occurs, a person or thing develops and changes into something completely different. [FORMAL] *...his metamorphosis from a Republican to a Democrat.*

metaphor /'metəfɔːr/ **metaphors**. N-VAR A **metaphor** is an imaginative way of describing something by referring to something else which has the qualities that you want to express. *...using a dinner party as a metaphor for life.*

metaphorical /,metə'fɒrɪkəl, AM -'fɔːr-/. ADJ You use **metaphorical** to indicate that you are not using words with their ordinary meaning, but are describing something by means of an image or symbol. *The ride is the literal and metaphorical high point of the park.* ♦ **metaphorically** ADV *You're speaking metaphorically, I hope.*

mete /miːt/ **metes, meting, meted.**
▸**mete out.** PHR-VERB To **mete out** a punishment means to punish someone. [FORMAL] *...the two year sentence meted out to a convicted child molester.*

meteor /'miːtiə/ **meteors**. N-COUNT A **meteor** is a piece of rock flying through space, especially one that is shining or burning brightly.

meteorite /'miːtiəraɪt/ **meteorites**. N-COUNT A **meteorite** is a large piece of rock or metal from space that has landed on the earth.

meteorological /,miːtiərə'lɒdʒɪkəl/. ADJ BEFORE N **Meteorological** means relating to the weather or to weather forecasting. [TECHNICAL] *...adverse meteorological conditions.*

meter /'miːtə/ **meters**. [1] N-COUNT A **meter** is a device that measures and records something such as the amount of gas or electricity that you have used. *...the electricity meter.* [2] See also **metre**.

methane /'miːθeɪn, AM 'meθ-/. N-UNCOUNT **Methane** is a colourless gas that has no smell.

⭐ **method** /'meθəd/ **methods**. N-VAR A **method** is a particular way of doing something. *The pill is the most efficient method of birth control. ...new teaching methods.*

methodical /mə'θɒdɪkəl/. ADJ If you describe someone as **methodical**, you mean that they do things carefully, thoroughly, and in order. *Da Vinci was methodical in his research.*
♦ **methodically** ADV *She methodically put the things into her suitcase.*

methodology /,meθə'dɒlədʒi/ **methodologies**. N-VAR A **methodology** is a system of methods and principles for doing something. [FORMAL] *Teaching methodologies vary according to the topic.* ♦ **methodological** ADJ *...methodological issues raised by the study of literary texts.*

meticulous /mə'tɪkjʊləs/. ADJ If someone is **meticulous**, they do things very carefully and with great attention to detail. ♦ **meticulously** ADV *The flat had been meticulously cleaned.*

⭐ **metre** (AM **meter**) /'miːtə/ **metres**. N-COUNT A **metre** is a unit of length equal to 100 centimetres. *The scarves are 2.3 metres long.*

metric /'metrɪk/. ADJ The **metric** system of measurement uses metres, grammes, and litres.

metro /'metrəʊ/ **metros**. N-COUNT The **metro** is the underground railway system in some cities, for example in Paris.

metropolis /mə'trɒpəlɪs/ **metropolises**. N-COUNT You can refer to a large, important, busy city as a **metropolis**. *Ho Chi Minh City will be a thriving metropolis in the future.*

metropolitan /,metrə'pɒlɪtən/. ADJ BEFORE N **Metropolitan** means belonging to or typical of a large busy city. *...major metropolitan hospitals.*

mg. **mg** is a written abbreviation for **milligram** or **milligrams**. *...300 mg of calcium.*

mice /maɪs/. **Mice** is the plural of **mouse**.

microbe /'maɪkrəʊb/ **microbes**. N-COUNT A **microbe** is a very small living thing, which you can only see with a microscope.

microchip /'maɪkrəʊtʃɪp/ **microchips**. N-COUNT A **microchip** is a small piece of silicon inside a computer, on which electronic circuits are printed. [COMPUTING]

microcosm /'maɪkrəʊkɒzəm/ **microcosms**. N-COUNT A place or event that is a **microcosm** of a larger one has all the main features of the larger one and seems like a smaller version of it. [FORMAL] *In many ways, Pennsylvania is a microcosm of the United States.*

micro-'organism, **micro-organisms**. N-COUNT A **micro-organism** is a very small living thing which you can only see with a powerful microscope. [TECHNICAL]

microphone /'maɪkrəfəʊn/ **microphones**. N-COUNT A **microphone** is a device used to record sounds or make them louder.

microprocessor /,maɪkrəʊ'prəʊsesə/ **microprocessors**. N-COUNT A **microprocessor** is a microchip which can be programmed to do a large number of tasks or calculations.

microscope/'maɪkrəskəʊp/ **microscopes.** N-COUNT A **microscope** is an instrument which magnifies very small objects so that you can study them.

microscopic/,maɪkrə'skɒpɪk/. ADJ **Microscopic** objects are extremely small, and usually can be seen only through a microscope. ...*microscopic particles.*

microwave/'maɪkrəʊweɪv/ **microwaves, microwaving, microwaved.** ① N-COUNT A **microwave** or a **microwave oven** is an oven which cooks food very quickly by a kind of radiation rather than by heat. ② VERB To **microwave** food or drink means to cook or heat it in a microwave oven.

mid-'air(or **midair**). N-UNCOUNT If something happens **in mid-air**, it happens in the air rather than on the ground. *The aircraft exploded in mid-air.* ...*a mid-air collision.*

midday/,mɪd'deɪ/. N-UNCOUNT **Midday** is twelve o'clock in the middle of the day. → See Reference Page on Telling the Time.

⭐ **middle**/'mɪdəl/ **middles.** ① N-COUNT The **middle** of something is the part that is farthest from its edges, ends, or outside surface. *Howard stood in the middle of the room... Father told her to make sure the roast potatoes weren't raw in the middle.* ② ADJ BEFORE N The **middle** thing or person in a row or series is the one with an equal number of things or people on each side, or before it and after it. *The middle drawer contained stockings.* ...*the middle child in a family of seven children.* ③ N-SING & ADJ BEFORE N The **middle** of an event or period of time, or the **middle** part of it, is the part that comes after the first part and before the last part. *I woke up in the middle of the night.* ...*the middle month of each quarter.* ④ ADJ BEFORE N The **middle** course or way is a moderate course of action that lies between two opposite and extreme courses. ...*an attempt to find a middle way between doing nothing and doing everything.* PHRASES ● If you are **in the middle of** doing something, you are busy doing it. *I'm in the middle of writing a book.* ● **the middle of nowhere**: see **nowhere.**

middle 'age. N-UNCOUNT **Middle age** is the period in your life when you are between about 40 and 60 years old.

middle-'aged. ADJ **Middle-aged** people are between the ages of about 40 and 60.

⭐ **middle 'class, middle classes.** N-COUNT & ADJ The **middle class** or **middle classes** are the people in a society who are not working class or upper class, for example managers, doctors, and lawyers. You can say people like this are **middle class.** ...*middle-class voters.*

⭐ **Middle 'East.** N-PROPER **The Middle East** is the area around the eastern Mediterranean that includes Iran and all the countries in Asia that are to the west and south-west of Iran. ...*the two great rivers of the Middle East.*

middleman/'mɪdəlmæn/ **middlemen.** ① N-COUNT A **middleman** is a person or company that buys things from the people who produce them and sells them to other people at a profit. ② N-COUNT A **middleman** is a person who helps in negotiations between people who are unwilling to meet each other directly. *The two sides would only meet indirectly, through middlemen.*

Midlands/'mɪdləndz/. N-PROPER **The Midlands** is the region in the central part of a country, in particular the central part of England.

⭐ **midnight**/'mɪdnaɪt/. N-UNCOUNT **Midnight** is twelve o'clock in the middle of the night. → See Reference Page on Telling the Time.

midst/mɪdst/.
PHRASES ● If you are **in the midst of** doing something, you are doing it at present. *Susan's students are in the midst of their first research project.* ● If something happens **in the midst of** a situation or an event, it happens during that situation or event. *Eleanor arrived in the midst of a blizzard.* ● If someone or something is **in the midst of** a group of people or things, they are among them or surrounded by them. ...*a house in the midst of huge trees.*

midway/,mɪd'weɪ/. ① ADV & ADJ BEFORE N If something is **midway between** two places, it is between them and the same distance from each of them. ...*a cottage midway between London and Oxford.* ...*the midway point between Gloucester, Hereford and Worcester.* ② ADV & ADJ BEFORE N If something happens **midway through** a period of time, it happens during the middle part of it. *He returned midway through the afternoon.* ...*the midway point in the season.*

midweek/,mɪd'wiːk/. ADJ BEFORE N & ADV **Midweek** describes something that happens in the middle of the week. ...*midweek flights from Gatwick... They'll be able to go up to London midweek.*

midwife/'mɪdwaɪf/ **midwives.** N-COUNT A **midwife** is a nurse who advises pregnant women and helps them to give birth.

⭐ **might**/maɪt/. ① MODAL You use **might** to indicate that something will possibly happen or be true in the future. *Smoking might be banned totally in most buildings... I might well regret it later... He might not be back until tonight.* ② MODAL You use **might** to indicate that there is a possibility that something is true. *You might be right... He might not be interested in her any more... I heard what might have been an explosion.* ③ MODAL You use **might** to make a suggestion or to give advice in a very polite way. *You might try the gas station down the street... I thought we might go for a drive on Sunday.* ④ MODAL You use **might** as a polite way of interrupting someone, asking a question, making a request, or introducing what you are going to say next. [FORMAL, SPOKEN] *Might I make a suggestion?... Might*

a b c d e f g h i j k l m n o p q r s t u v w x y z

I trouble you for a drop more tea? **5** N-UNCOUNT **Might** is power or strength. [FORMAL] *The might of the army could prove a decisive factor.*

mightily /'maɪtɪli/. ADV **Mightily** means to a great extent or to a great degree. [DATED] *I was mightily impressed.*

mightn't /'maɪtənt/. **Mightn't** is a spoken form of 'might not'.

might've /'maɪtəv/. **Might've** is the usual spoken form of 'might have', especially when 'have' is an auxiliary verb.

mighty /'maɪti/ **mightier, mightiest.** **1** ADJ **Mighty** means very large or powerful. [LITERARY] *...a mighty explosion. ...one of the mightiest armies in history.* **2** ADV **Mighty** means very. [AMERICAN, INFORMAL] *You look mighty pretty tonight.*

migraine /'mi:greɪn, AM 'maɪ-/ **migraines.** N-VAR A **migraine** is a very severe headache.

migrant /'maɪgrənt/ **migrants.** N-COUNT A **migrant** is a person who moves from one place to another, especially in order to find work. *...migrant workers.*

migrate /maɪ'greɪt, AM 'maɪgreɪt/ **migrates, migrating, migrated.** **1** VERB If people **migrate**, they move from one place to another, especially in order to find work. *Lacking opportunities in the countryside, peasants have migrated to the cities.* ♦ **migration, migrations** N-VAR *...the migration of Soviet Jews to Israel.* **2** VERB When birds, fish, or animals **migrate**, they go and live in a different area for part of the year, in order to breed or to find food. ♦ **migration** N-VAR *...the migration of swallows.*

mike /maɪk/ **mikes.** N-COUNT A **mike** is a microphone. [INFORMAL]

⭐ **mild** /maɪld/ **milder, mildest.** **1** ADJ Something that is **mild** is not very strong or severe. *...a mild onion flavour. ...a mild headache.* ♦ **mildly** ADV *...mildly spiced rice... I felt mildly alarmed.* **2** ADJ **Mild** weather is less cold than usual. ● See note at **hot.**

⭐ **mile** /maɪl/ **miles.** **1** N-COUNT A **mile** is a unit of distance equal to approximately 1.6 kilometres. *The hurricane is moving to the west at about 18 miles per hour.* **2** N-PLURAL **Miles** is used to refer to a long distance. *The nearest doctor is miles away... 'Shall I come to see you?'—'Are you kidding? It's miles.'*

mileage /'maɪlɪdʒ/ **mileages.** **1** N-VAR **Mileage** refers to a distance that is travelled, measured in miles. *They had to keep track of their mileage.* **2** N-UNCOUNT The **mileage** in a particular course of action is its usefulness in getting you what you want. *It's obviously important to get as much mileage out of the convention as possible.*

milestone /'maɪlstəʊn/ **milestones.** N-COUNT A **milestone** is an important event in the history or development of something. *The decision is being seen as a milestone in relations between the two countries.*

milieu /'mi:ljɜː, AM mɪ'lju:/ **milieux** or **milieus.** N-COUNT The **milieu** in which you live or work is

the group of people that you live or work among. [FORMAL] *...a very different cultural milieu.*

⭐ **militant** /'mɪlɪtənt/ **militants.** ADJ & N-COUNT Someone who is **militant**, or who is a **militant**, is active in trying to bring about political change. *...one of the most militant unions. ...an attack by militants.* ♦ **militancy** N-UNCOUNT *...the growing militancy of French university students.*

⭐ **military** /'mɪlɪtri, AM -teri-/. **1** ADJ **Military** means relating to a country's armed forces. *Military action may become necessary.* ♦ **militarily** /ˌmɪlɪ'teərɪli/ ADV *...suggestions that the United States should intervene militarily.* **2** N-SING **The military** are the armed forces of a country, especially the officers of high rank. **Military** can take the singular or plural form of the verb. *Did you serve in the military?*

militia /mɪ'lɪʃə/ **militias.** N-COUNT A **militia** is an organization that operates like an army but whose members are not professional soldiers.

⭐ **milk** /mɪlk/ **milks, milking, milked.** **1** N-UNCOUNT **Milk** is the white liquid produced by cows and goats, which people drink and make into butter, cheese, and yoghurt. **2** VERB When someone **milks** a cow or goat, they get milk from it from an organ called the udder, which hangs beneath its body. ♦ **milking** N-UNCOUNT *...helping to bring in the cows for milking.* **3** N-UNCOUNT **Milk** is the white liquid produced by women to feed their babies. **4** VERB If you say that someone **milks** something, you mean that they get as much benefit or profit as they can from it, without caring about other people; used showing disapproval. *The callous couple milked money from a hospital charity to fund a lavish lifestyle.*

milky /'mɪlki/. **1** ADJ Something that is **milky** in colour is pale white. *A milky mist filled the valley.* **2** ADJ **Milky** food or drink contains a lot of milk. *...milky coffee.*

⭐ **mill** /mɪl/ **mills, milling, milled.** **1** N-COUNT A **mill** is a building where grain is crushed to make flour. **2** N-COUNT A **mill** is a small device used for grinding something such as coffee or pepper. *...a pepper mill.* **3** N-COUNT A **mill** is a factory used for making and processing materials such as steel, wool, or cotton.
▸ **mill around** or **mill about.** PHR-VERB When a crowd of people **are milling around**, they are moving around in a disorganized way.

millennium /mɪ'leniəm/ **millennia** or **millenniums.** N-COUNT A **millennium** is a thousand years.

milligram (or **milligramme**) /'mɪlɪgræm/ **milligrams.** N-COUNT A **milligram** is a metric unit of weight equal to one thousandth of a gram. *...0.5 milligrams of mercury.*

millilitre (AM **milliliter**) /'mɪlɪliːtə/ **millilitres.** N-COUNT A **millilitre** is a metric unit of volume for liquids and gases that is equal to a thousandth of a litre. *...100 millilitres of blood.*

millimetre (AM **millimeter**) /'mɪlɪmiːtə/ **millimetres.** N-COUNT A **millimetre** is a metric unit of length equal to one tenth of a centimetre. *The* *dots can be as small as a quarter of a millimetre across.*

⭐ **million** /ˈmɪliən/ **millions.** ☐1 NUM **A million** or **one million** is the number 1,000,000. ☐2 QUANT People say that there are **millions of** people or things when they are emphasizing that there is a very large number of them. *The programme was viewed on television in millions of homes... This long and wretched war has brought misery to millions.*

millionaire /ˌmɪliəˈneə/ **millionaires.** N-COUNT A **millionaire** is someone who has money or property worth at least a million pounds or dollars.

⭐ **millionth** /ˈmɪliənθ/. ORD The **millionth** item in a series is the one you count as number one million.

mime /maɪm/ **mimes, miming, mimed.** ☐1 N-VAR **Mime** is the use of movements and gestures to express something or tell a story without using speech. *...a mime artist.* ☐2 VERB If you **mime** something, you describe or express it using mime rather than speech. *I remember asking her to mime getting up in the morning.*

mimic /ˈmɪmɪk/ **mimics, mimicking, mimicked.** ☐1 VERB If you **mimic** someone's actions or voice, you imitate them in an amusing or entertaining way. *He could mimic anybody.* ☐2 N-COUNT A **mimic** is a person who is able to mimic people.

min. Min. is a written abbreviation for **minimum**, or for **minutes** or **minute**.

mince /mɪns/ **minces, mincing, minced.** ☐1 N-UNCOUNT In British English, **mince** is meat cut into very small pieces. The usual American word is **hamburger meat.** ☐2 VERB If you **mince** food such as meat, you cut it into very small pieces. ☐3 PHRASE If you say someone does not **mince** their **words** or does not **mince words**, you mean they speak in a forceful direct way, especially when saying something unpleasant to someone.

mind 1 thinking

⭐ **mind** /maɪnd/ **minds.** N-COUNT Your **mind** is your ability to think and reason. You also talk about someone having a particular type of **mind** when it is part of their character, or a result of their education or professional training. *She moved to London, meeting some of the best minds of her time... Andrew, you have a very suspicious mind.* PHRASES ● If you say that an idea or possibility never **crossed** your **mind**, you mean that you did not think of it. ● If you see something **in** your **mind's eye**, you are able to imagine it clearly in your mind. *In his mind's eye, he could see the headlines in the newspapers.* ● If you tell someone to **bear** something **in mind** or to **keep** something **in mind**, you are reminding or warning them about something important which they should think about and remember. ● If you **make up** your **mind** or **make** your **mind up**, you decide which of a number of possible things you will have or do. ● If something is **on** your **mind**, you are worried or concerned about it and think

about it a lot. *This game has been on my mind all week.* ● If your **mind is on** something or you **have** your **mind on** something, you are thinking about that thing rather than something else. *He tried the first page but his mind was on other things.* ● If you have or keep **an open mind**, you avoid forming an opinion or making a decision until you know all the facts. *Police said they were keeping an open mind about the mystery death.* ● If you say that someone is **out of** their **mind**, you mean that they are mad or very foolish. ● Your **state of mind** is your mental state at a particular time. *Over time the patient's state of mind gradually improved.* ● If something **takes** your **mind off** a problem or unpleasant situation, it helps you to forget about it for a while.

mind 2 expressing opinion

⭐ **mind** /maɪnd/ **minds, minding, minded.** ☐1 VERB If you do not **mind** something, you are not annoyed or bothered by it. *Do you mind being alone?... I hope you don't mind me calling in like this, without an appointment... It involved a little extra work, but nobody seemed to mind.* ☐2 VERB If someone does not **mind** what happens or what something is like, they do not have a strong preference for any particular thing. *I don't mind what we play, really.*

PHRASES ● If you **change** your **mind**, or if someone or something **changes** your **mind**, you change a decision you have made or an opinion that you had. ● You use **never mind** to tell someone that you do not think that they need to do something or to worry about something. *'I'll go up in one second, I promise.'—'Never mind,' I said with a sigh. 'I'll do it.'... 'Was his name David?'—'No I don't think it was, but never mind, go on.'* ● You use **to my mind** to indicate that the statement you are making is your own opinion. *There are scenes in this play which to my mind are incredibly violent.* ● If you say that you **wouldn't mind** something, you mean that you would quite like it. *I wouldn't mind a coffee... Anne said she wouldn't mind going to Italy to live.*

mind 3 care

mind /maɪnd/ **minds, minding, minded.** ☐1 VERB If you tell someone to **mind** something or to **mind** that they do something, you are warning them to be careful so that they do not hurt themselves or other people, or damage something. *Mind that bike!... Mind you don't burn those sausages.* ☐2 VERB If you **mind** a child or something such as a shop or luggage, you look after it, usually while the person who owns it or is usually responsible for it is elsewhere. *Jim Coulters will mind the store while I'm away.*

minder /ˈmaɪndə/ **minders.** N-COUNT A **minder** is a person whose job is to protect someone such as a celebrity or businessman.

mindful /ˈmaɪndfʊl/. ADJ AFTER LINK-V If you are **mindful of** something, you think about it and consider it when taking action. [FORMAL] *Always be mindful of safety.*

a
b
c
d
e
f
g
h
i
j
k
l
m
n
o
p
q
r
s
t
u
v
w
x
y
z

A
B
C
D
E
F
G
H
I
J
K
L
M
N
O
P
Q
R
S
T
U
V
W
X
Y
Z

mindless/'maɪndləs/. ⓵ ADJ If you describe a destructive action as **mindless**, you mean that it is not at all sensible and is done for no good reason. ...*mindless violence*. ⓶ ADJ If you describe an activity as **mindless**, you mean that it is so dull that people do it without thinking. ...*the mindless repetitiveness of some tasks*. ♦ **mindlessly**ADV ...*mindlessly banging a tennis ball against the wall*.

★ **mine**/maɪn/ **mines, mining, mined.** ⓵ PRON **Mine** is the first person singular possessive pronoun. A speaker or writer uses **mine** to indicate that something belongs or relates to himself or herself. *Her right hand is inches from mine... That wasn't his fault, it was mine*. ⓶ N-COUNT A **mine** is a place where deep holes or tunnels are dug under the ground in order to extract minerals. ...*a coal mine*. ⓷ VERB When a mineral **is mined**, it is obtained from the ground by digging deep holes and tunnels. *The pit no longer has enough coal that can be mined economically*. ♦ **miner,miners** N-COUNT *My father was a miner*. ♦ **mining** N-UNCOUNT ...*traditional industries such as coal mining*. ⓸ N-COUNT A **mine** is a bomb hidden in the ground or in water which explodes when something touches it.

minefield/'maɪnfiːld/ **minefields**. N-COUNT A **minefield** is an area of land or water where explosive mines have been hidden.

mineral/'mɪnərəl/ **minerals**. N-COUNT A **mineral** is a substance such as tin, salt, or coal that is formed naturally in rocks and in the earth.

'**mineral water,mineral waters**. N-VAR **Mineral water** is water that comes out of the ground naturally and is considered healthy to drink.

mingle/'mɪŋgəl/ **mingles, mingling, mingled.** ⓵ VERB If things such as sounds, smells, or feelings **mingle**, they become mixed together but are usually still recognizable. *Foreboding mingled with his excitement. ...the mingled scents of flowers, cigar smoke and Chanel*. ⓶ VERB If you **mingle**, you move among a group of people, chatting to different people. *Guests ate and mingled. ...reporters who mingled with the crowd*.

miniature/'mɪnɪtʃə, AM 'mɪniətʃʊr/ **miniatures.** ⓵ ADJ BEFORE N **Miniature** things are much smaller than other things of the same kind. ...*miniature roses*. ⓶ PHRASE If you describe one thing as another thing **in miniature**, you mean that it is much smaller than the other thing, but is otherwise exactly the same. *Ecuador provides a perfect introduction to South America; it's a continent in miniature*.

minibus/'mɪnɪbʌs/ **minibuses**. N-COUNT A **minibus** is a large van which has seats in the back and windows along its sides. → See picture on page 835. *He was then taken there by minibus*.

minidisc/'mɪnɪdɪsk/ **minidiscs**. N-COUNT A **minidisc** is a small compact disc on which you can record music or data. **Minidisc** is a trademark.

minimal/'mɪnɪməl/. ADJ Something that is **minimal** is very small in quantity or degree. *The*

co-operation between the two is minimal. ♦ **minimally**ADV *He was paid, but only minimally*.

minimalist/'mɪnɪməlɪst/ **minimalists**. ADJ & N-COUNT **Minimalist** ideas, artists, or designers are influenced by a style in which a small number of very simple things are used to create a particular effect. Artists and designers like this are called **minimalists**. *The two designers settled upon a minimalist approach*. ♦ **minimalism**N-UNCOUNT ...*austere minimalism*.

minimize(BRIT also **minimise**/'mɪnɪmaɪz/ **minimizes, minimizing, minimized.** ⓵ VERB If you **minimize** a risk or problem, you reduce it to the lowest possible level. *Concerned people want to minimize the risk of developing cancer*. ⓶ VERB If you **minimize** something, you make it seem smaller or less important than it really is. *At his trial, he had tried to minimize his behavior*.

★ **minimum**/'mɪnɪməm/. ⓵ ADJ BEFORE N & N-SING A **minimum** amount of something, or a **minimum**, is the smallest amount that is possible, allowed, or required. ...*five feet nine, the minimum height for a policeman... This will take a minimum of one hour*. ⓶ ADJ BEFORE N & N-SING You use **minimum**, or a **minimum**, to state how small an amount is. *He goes about his job with a minimum of fuss*.

mining/'maɪnɪŋ/. See **mine**.

★ **minister**/'mɪnɪstə/ **ministers, ministering, ministered.** ⓵ N-COUNT A **minister** is a person who is in charge of a government department. ...*the new Defence Minister*. ● See note at **government**. ⓶ N-COUNT A **minister** is a member of the clergy, especially in a Protestant church. ⓷ VERB If you **minister to** people or **to** their needs, you serve them or help them, for example by making sure that they have everything they need or want. *For 44 years he had ministered to the poor*.

ministerial/,mɪnɪ'stɪəriəl/. ADJ BEFORE N **Ministerial** means relating to government ministers. *A ministerial meeting was being held*.

★ **ministry**/'mɪnɪstri/ **ministries.** ⓵ N-COUNT A **ministry** is a government department. ...*the Ministry of Justice*. ⓶ N-COUNT The **ministry** of a religious person is the work that they do that is inspired by their religious beliefs. *His ministry is among the poor*. ⓷ N-SING Members of the clergy belonging to some branches of the Christian church are referred to as **the ministry**. *So what prompted him to enter the ministry?*

mink/mɪŋk/.

☑ The plural is **mink** or **minks**.

⓵ N-COUNT A **mink** is a small furry animal with highly valued fur. ⓶ N-UNCOUNT **Mink** is the fur of a mink. ⓷ N-COUNT A **mink** is a coat or other garment made from the fur of a mink.

★ **minor**/'maɪnə/ **minors.** ⓵ ADJ You use **minor** to describe something that is less important, serious, or significant than other things in a group or situation. ...*a number of minor roles in* *films... The problem is minor, and should be quickly overcome.* [2] N-COUNT A **minor** is a person who is still legally a child. In Britain, people are minors until they reach the age of eighteen.

⭐ **minority** /maɪˈnɒrɪti, AM -ˈnɔːr-/ **minorities.**
[1] N-SING If you talk about a **minority of** people or things in a larger group, you are referring to a number of them that forms less than half of the larger group. *In a tiny minority of cases mistakes have been made. ...minority shareholders.*
[2] PHRASE If people are **in a minority** or **in the minority**, they belong to a group of people or things that form less than half of a larger group.
[3] N-COUNT A **minority** is a group of people of the same race, culture, or religion who live in a place where most of the people around them are of a different race, culture, or religion. *...the region's ethnic minorities.*

mint /mɪnt/ **mints, minting, minted.** [1] N-UNCOUNT **Mint** is a fresh-tasting herb. [2] N-COUNT A **mint** is a sweet with a peppermint flavour. [3] N-SING The **mint** is the place where the official coins of a country are made. [4] VERB To **mint** coins or medals means to make them in a mint.
♦ **minting** N-UNCOUNT *...the minting of new gold coins.*

minus /ˈmaɪnəs/ **minuses.** [1] CONJ You use **minus** to show that one number or quantity is being subtracted from another. *One minus one is zero. ...their full July salary minus the hardship payment.* [2] ADJ **Minus** before a number or quantity means that the number or quantity is less than zero. *...temperatures of minus 65 degrees.* [3] PREP If someone or something is **minus** something, they do not have that thing. *The film company collapsed, leaving Chris jobless and minus his life savings.* [4] N-COUNT A **minus** is a disadvantage. *The minuses far outweigh that possible gain.*

minuscule /ˈmɪnɪskjuːl/. ADJ If you describe something as **minuscule**, you mean it is very small.

⭐ **minute, minutes.** [1] N-COUNT /ˈmɪnɪt/ A **minute** is one of the sixty equal parts of an hour. People often say **'a minute'** or **'minutes'** when they mean a short length of time. → See Reference Page on Telling the Time. *The pizza will then take about twenty minutes to cook... See you in a minute.* [2] CONVENTION People often use expressions such as **'wait a minute'** or **'just a minute'** when they want to stop you doing or saying something. *Wait a minute, folks, something is wrong here.* [3] N-PLURAL The **minutes** of a meeting are the written records of the things that are discussed or decided at it. [4] ADJ /maɪˈnjuːt, AM -ˈnuːt/. If you say that something is **minute**, you mean that it is very small. *Only a minute amount is needed.* ♦ **minutely** ADV *The benefit of an x-ray far outweighs the minutely increased risk of cancer.*

PHRASES ● If you say that something will or may happen **at any minute** or **any minute now**, you are emphasizing that it is likely to happen very soon. ● A **last-minute** action is done at the latest

time possible. *He will probably wait until the last minute.* ● You use **the next minute** or expressions such as **'one minute** he was there, **the next** he was gone'** to emphasize that something happens suddenly. *The next minute my father came in.* ● If you say that something happens **the minute** something else happens, you are emphasizing that it happens immediately after the other thing. *The minute you do this, you'll lose control.* ● If you say that something must be done **this minute**, you mean that it must be done immediately. *Sit down this minute.*

miracle /ˈmɪrəkəl/ **miracles.** [1] N-COUNT If you say that an event or invention is a **miracle**, you mean that it is very surprising and fortunate. *It is a miracle no one was killed.* [2] N-COUNT A **miracle** is a wonderful and surprising event that is believed to be caused by God.

miraculous /mɪˈrækjʊləs/. [1] ADJ If you describe something as **miraculous**, you mean that it is very surprising and fortunate. *The horse made a miraculous recovery.* ♦ **miraculously** ADV *Miraculously, the guards escaped death.* [2] ADJ If someone describes a wonderful event as **miraculous**, they believe the event has been caused by God. ♦ **miraculously** ADV *He was miraculously healed of a severe fever.*

⭐ **mirror** /ˈmɪrə/ **mirrors, mirroring, mirrored.**
[1] N-COUNT A **mirror** is an object made of glass in which you can see your reflection. [2] VERB If you see something reflected in water, you can say that the water **mirrors** it. [LITERARY] [3] VERB If something **mirrors** something else, it has similar features to it, and therefore seems like a copy or representation of it. *The book inevitably mirrors my own interests and experiences.*

miscalculate /ˌmɪsˈkælkjʊleɪt/ **miscalculates, miscalculating, miscalculated.** VERB If you **miscalculate**, you make a mistake in judging a situation or in making a calculation. *He has badly miscalculated the mood of the people.*
♦ **miscalculation, miscalculations** N-VAR *The coup failed because of miscalculations by the plotters.*

miscarriage /ˌmɪsˈkærɪdʒ/ **miscarriages.** N-COUNT If a woman has a **miscarriage**, she gives birth to a foetus before it is properly formed and it dies.

miscellaneous /ˌmɪsəˈleɪniəs/. ADJ BEFORE N A **miscellaneous** group consists of many different kinds of things or people that are difficult to put into a particular category. *...a hoard of miscellaneous junk.*

mischief /ˈmɪstʃɪf/. [1] N-UNCOUNT **Mischief** is eagerness to have fun, especially by embarrassing people or by playing harmless tricks. *He was always up to mischief.* [2] N-UNCOUNT **Mischief** is trouble or harm that is caused by something. *...the mischief that young people get up to when they're not employed. ...old attitudes and prejudices which have done so much mischief.*

mischievous /ˈmɪstʃɪvəs/. [1] ADJ A **mischievous** person is eager to have fun by embarrassing people or by playing harmless

A
B
C
D
E
F
G
H
I
J
K
L
M
N
O
P
Q
R
S
T
U
V
W
X
Y
Z

tricks. ◆ **mischievously** ADV *Kathryn winked mischievously.* [2] ADJ A **mischievous** act or suggestion is intended to cause trouble. *The Foreign Office dismissed the story as mischievous and false.*

misconception /ˌmɪskən'sepʃən/ **misconceptions.** N-COUNT A **misconception** is an idea that is not correct or which has been misunderstood. *There are many fears and misconceptions about cancer.*

misconduct /ˌmɪs'kɒndʌkt/. N-UNCOUNT **Misconduct** is bad or unacceptable behaviour, especially by a professional person or someone who is normally respected by people. *She was found guilty of professional misconduct.*

misdemeanour (AM **misdemeanor**) /ˌmɪsdɪ'miːnə/ **misdemeanours.** N-COUNT A **misdemeanour** is an act that some people consider to be wrong or unacceptable. [FORMAL] *Emily knew nothing about her husband's misdemeanours.*

miserable /'mɪzərəbəl/. [1] ADJ If you are **miserable**, you are very unhappy. ◆ **miserably** ADV *He looked miserably down at his plate.* [2] ADJ A **miserable** place or **miserable** weather makes you feel depressed, for example because it is very dull. *...a grey, wet, miserable day.*

misery /'mɪzəri/ **miseries.** [1] N-VAR **Misery** is great unhappiness. *All that money brought nothing but sadness and misery.* [2] N-UNCOUNT **Misery** is the way of life and unpleasant living conditions of people who are very poor. *A tiny, educated elite profited from the misery of their two million fellow countrymen.*

misfit /'mɪsfɪt/ **misfits.** N-COUNT A **misfit** is a person who is not easily accepted by other people, often because their behaviour is very different from that of everyone else.

misfortune /ˌmɪs'fɔːtʃuːn/ **misfortunes.** N-VAR A **misfortune** is something unpleasant or unlucky that happens to someone. *She seemed to enjoy the misfortunes of others.*

misgiving /ˌmɪs'gɪvɪŋ/ **misgivings.** N-VAR If you have **misgivings** about something that is being proposed or done, you feel that it is not quite right, and are worried that it may have undesirable consequences. *I have misgivings about going anywhere away from home.*

misguided /ˌmɪs'gaɪdɪd/. ADJ If you describe an opinion or plan as **misguided**, you are critical of it because you think it is based on a mistake or misunderstanding. *He is misguided in expecting honesty from her.*

mishap /'mɪshæp/ **mishaps.** N-VAR A **mishap** is an unfortunate but not very serious event that happens to you. *After a number of mishaps she did manage to get back to Germany.*

misinterpret /ˌmɪsɪn'tɜːprɪt/ **misinterprets, misinterpreting, misinterpreted.** VERB If you **misinterpret** something, you understand it wrongly. *He was totally amazed that he'd misinterpreted the situation so completely.*

◆ **misinterpretation** N-UNCOUNT *The message left no room for misinterpretation.*

misjudge /ˌmɪs'dʒʌdʒ/ **misjudges, misjudging, misjudged.** VERB If you say that someone **has misjudged** a person or situation, you mean that they have formed an incorrect idea or opinion about them, and often that they have made a wrong decision as a result of this. *Perhaps I had misjudged him, and he was not so predictable after all.*

mislead /ˌmɪs'liːd/ **misleads, misleading, misled.** VERB If you say that someone **has misled** you, you mean that they have made you believe something which is not true, either by telling you a lie or by giving you a wrong idea or impression.

misleading /ˌmɪs'liːdɪŋ/. ADJ If you describe something as **misleading**, you mean that it gives you a wrong idea or impression. *It would be misleading to say that we were friends.* ◆ **misleadingly** ADV *The data had unfortunately been presented misleadingly.*

misled /ˌmɪs'led/. **Misled** is the past tense and past participle of **mislead**.

mismanage /ˌmɪs'mænɪdʒ/ **mismanages, mismanaging, mismanaged.** VERB To **mismanage** something means to manage it badly. *75% of voters think the President has mismanaged the economy.* ◆ **mismanagement** N-UNCOUNT *His gross mismanagement left the company desperately in need of restructuring.*

misplaced /ˌmɪs'pleɪst/. ADJ If you describe a feeling or action as **misplaced**, you are critical of it because you think it is inappropriate, or directed towards the wrong thing or person. *Your concern is misplaced. Ackroyd is no threat to anyone.*

misread, misreads, misreading, misread; present tense /ˌmɪs'riːd/, past tense and past participle /ˌmɪs'red/. [1] VERB If you **misread** a situation or someone's behaviour, you do not understand it properly. *The government largely misread the mood of the electorate.* ◆ **misreading, misreadings** N-COUNT *...a misreading of opinion in France.* [2] VERB If you **misread** something that has been written or printed, you look at it and think that it says something that it does not say. *I misread the map.*

misrepresent /ˌmɪsreprɪ'zent/ **misrepresents, misrepresenting, misrepresented.** VERB If someone **misrepresents** a person or situation, they give a wrong or inaccurate account of what the person or situation is like. *The press had misrepresented him as arrogant and bullying.*

◆ **misrepresentation** N-UNCOUNT *The programme's researchers are most certainly guilty of bias and misrepresentation.*

⭐ **miss** /mɪs/ **misses, missing, missed.** [1] N-TITLE You use **Miss** in front of the name of a girl or unmarried woman. *The club was run by Miss Ivy Streeter.* [2] VERB & N-COUNT If you **miss** when you are trying to hit something, you fail to hit it. A **miss** is an occasion when you miss something.

She hurled the ashtray across the room, narrowly missing my head... Striker Alan Smith was guilty of two glaring misses. [3] VERB If you **miss** something, you fail to notice it. *It's the first thing you see as you come round the corner. You can't miss it.* [4] VERB If you **miss** the point or **miss** the joke, you fail to understand or appreciate a particular point or joke that someone is making. [5] VERB If you **miss** someone or something, you feel sad because the person is no longer with you, or because you no longer have the thing. *Your mama and I are gonna miss you at Christmas... He missed having good friends.* [6] VERB If you **miss** something such as a plane or train, you arrive too late to catch it. *He missed the last bus home.* [7] VERB If you **miss** an event or activity, you do not go to it or take part in it, because you are unable to or have forgotten to. *Makku and I had to miss our lesson... 'Are you coming to the show?'—'I wouldn't miss it for the world.'* [8] See also **missing**.
▸ **miss out.** [1] PHR-VERB If you **miss out on** something that would be beneficial or interesting to you, you are not involved in it or do not take part in it. *We're missing out on a tremendous opportunity.* [2] PHR-VERB If you **miss out** something or someone, you do not include them. [BRITISH] *What about Sally? You've missed her out.*

⭐ **missile** /'mɪsaɪl, AM -səl/ **missiles.** [1] N-COUNT A **missile** is a tube-shaped weapon that moves long distances through the air and explodes when it reaches its target. [2] N-COUNT Anything that is thrown as a weapon can be called a **missile**. [FORMAL] *Supporters hurled missiles at rival fans.*

⭐ **missing** /'mɪsɪŋ/. [1] ADJ If someone or something is **missing** or has **gone missing**, they are not where you expect them to be, and you cannot find them. *His wallet was missing... She reported him to the police as a missing person.* [2] ADJ If a part of something is **missing**, it has been removed or has come off and has not been replaced. *Three buttons were missing from his shirt.*

⭐ **mission** /'mɪʃən/ **missions.** [1] N-COUNT A **mission** is an important task that you are given to do, especially one that involves travelling to another country. *In 1987, he disappeared on a mission to Beirut.* [2] N-COUNT A **mission** is a group of people who have been sent to a foreign country to carry out an official task. *...the head of South Africa's trade mission to Zimbabwe.* [3] N-COUNT A **mission** is a special journey made by a military aeroplane or space rocket. *The plane was on a bombing mission.* [4] N-COUNT If you have a **mission**, there is something that you believe it is your duty to try to achieve. *Her mission in life is to show that being disabled doesn't mean being helpless.*

missionary /'mɪʃənri, -neri/ **missionaries.** N-COUNT A **missionary** is a Christian who has been sent to a foreign country to teach people about Christianity.

mist /mɪst/ **mists, misting, misted.** N-VAR **Mist** consists of many tiny drops of water in the air, which make it difficult to see very far. *I couldn't see anything through the mist.*
▸ **mist over** or **mist up.** PHR-VERB When a piece of glass **mists over** or **mists up**, it becomes covered with tiny drops of water, so that you cannot see through it easily. *The windscreen was misting up.*

⭐ **mistake** /mɪ'steɪk/ **mistakes, mistaking, mistook, mistaken.** [1] N-COUNT & PHRASE If you **make** a **mistake**, or if you do something **by mistake**, you do something wrong, for example because you do not know what is right or because you are not thinking clearly. *...spelling mistakes... The official who ignored the warning might have made a mistake... Someone must have sold it by mistake.* [2] VERB If you **mistake** one person or thing **for** another, you wrongly think that they are the other person or thing. *I mistook you for Carlos.* [3] PHRASE You can say **there is no mistaking** something when you are emphasizing that you cannot fail to recognize or understand it. *There's no mistaking his voice.*

mistaken /mɪ'steɪkən/. ADJ If you are **mistaken**, or if you have a **mistaken** belief, you are wrong about something. *You couldn't be more mistaken, Alex. ...a victim of mistaken identity.*
♦ **mistakenly** ADV *Some of the crew mistakenly believed the ship was under attack.*

mister /'mɪstə/. See **Mr**.

mistook /mɪ'stʊk/. **Mistook** is the past tense and past participle of **mistake**.

mistress /'mɪstrəs/ **mistresses.** [1] N-COUNT A married man's **mistress** is a woman he is having a sexual relationship with, but who is not his wife. [2] N-COUNT A **mistress** is a female teacher. [BRITISH, DATED] *...Miss Moore, the geography mistress.*

mistrust /,mɪs'trʌst/ **mistrusts, mistrusting, mistrusted.** VERB & N-UNCOUNT If you **mistrust** someone or something, you do not trust them. **Mistrust** is the feeling that you have towards someone who you do not trust. *There was mutual mistrust between the two men.*

misty /'mɪsti/. ADJ If it is **misty**, there is a lot of mist in the air.

misunderstand /,mɪsʌndə'stænd/ **misunderstands, misunderstanding, misunderstood.** VERB If you **misunderstand** someone or something, you do not understand them properly. *He had misunderstood the rules.*

misunderstanding /,mɪsʌndə'stændɪŋ/ **misunderstandings.** [1] N-VAR A **misunderstanding** is a failure to understand something such as a situation or a person's remarks. *It is a simple misunderstanding.* [2] N-COUNT You can refer to a disagreement or slight quarrel as a **misunderstanding**. *We had a misunderstanding.*

misunderstood /,mɪsʌndə'stʊd/. [1] **Misunderstood** is the past tense and past participle of **misunderstand**. [2] ADJ If you describe someone as **misunderstood**, you mean

a
b
c
d
e
f
g
h
i
j
k
l
m
n
o
p
q
r
s
t
u
v
w
x
y
z

that people have wrong ideas about them, and do not recognize their qualities or achievements. ...*a misunderstood genius.*

misuse, misuses, misusing, misused. [1] VERB /ˌmɪsˈjuːz/ If you **misuse** something, you use it incorrectly, carelessly, or dishonestly. *Mr Chung was accused of misusing company funds.* [2] N-VAR /ˌmɪsˈjuːs/ The **misuse** of something is incorrect, careless, or dishonest use of it. ...*the misuse of language.*

mite /maɪt/ **mites.** [1] PHRASE A **mite** means to a small extent or degree. *I can't help feeling just a mite uneasy about it.* [2] N-COUNT **Mites** are very tiny creatures that live, for example, on plants or in animals' fur.

mitigate /ˈmɪtɪɡeɪt/ **mitigates, mitigating, mitigated.** VERB To **mitigate** something means to make it less unpleasant, less serious, or less painful. [FORMAL] ...*ways of mitigating the effects of an explosion.*

mitigating /ˈmɪtɪɡeɪtɪŋ/. ADJ BEFORE N **Mitigating** circumstances are facts which make a crime less serious or more justifiable. [FORMAL]

⭐ **mix** /mɪks/ **mixes, mixing, mixed.** [1] VERB If two substances **mix**, or if you **mix** one substance **with** another, they combine to form a single substance. *Oil and water don't mix.., Mix the cinnamon with the rest of the sugar.* [2] VERB If you **mix** something, you prepare it by mixing two or more things together. *He mixed himself a drink.* [3] N-VAR A **mix** is a powder containing all the substances that you need in order to make something, to which you add liquid. ...*cake mix.* [4] N-COUNT A **mix** is two or more things combined together. *The story is a magical mix of fantasy and reality.* [5] VERB If you **mix with** other people, you meet them and talk to them. *The secret of staying young was to mix with older people. ...giving both younger and older students the opportunity to mix.* [6] See also **mixed up.**
▸**mix up.** PHR-VERB If you **mix up** two things or people, you confuse them, so that you think that one of them is the other one. *I had mixed her up with someone else.*

⭐ **mixed** /mɪkst/. [1] ADJ You use **mixed** to describe something which consists of different people or things of the same general kind. *His clubs attract a mixed crowd... I had mixed feelings about this news.* [2] ADJ **Mixed** means involving people from two or more different races. ...*a woman of mixed race. ...mixed marriages.* [3] ADJ **Mixed** education or accommodation is intended for both males and females. ...*a mixed secondary school.*

ˌ**mixed 'up.** [1] ADJ If you are **mixed up**, you are confused. *I get mixed up about times and places... Elena is a very mixed up child.* [2] ADJ AFTER LINK-V If you say that someone is **mixed up with** a person or **in** an activity that you disapprove of, you mean they are involved with that person or activity. *She got herself mixed up in terrorism.*

mixer /ˈmɪksə/ **mixers.** N-COUNT A **mixer** is a machine used for mixing things together. ...*a food mixer.*

⭐ **mixture** /ˈmɪkstʃə/ **mixtures.** [1] N-SING A **mixture of** things consists of several different things together. ...*trembling in a mixture of fear and excitement.* [2] N-COUNT A **mixture** is a substance that consists of other substances which have been stirred or shaken together. ...*a sticky mixture of flour and water.*

ml. ml is a written abbreviation for **millilitre** or **millilitres**. ...*300 ml water.*

⭐ **mm. mm** is a written abbreviation for **millimetre** or **millimetres**. *45 mm of rain fell.*

moan /məʊn/ **moans, moaning, moaned.** [1] VERB & N-COUNT If you **moan**, you make a low, miserable cry called a **moan**, because you are unhappy or in pain. *Lauren moaned in her sleep... She let out a faint moan.* [2] VERB To **moan** means to speak in a way which shows that you are very unhappy. *'Look what he did,' she moaned... Carol is always moaning about how she detests her bottom.*

mob /mɒb/ **mobs, mobbing, mobbed.** [1] N-COUNT A **mob** is a large disorganized crowd of people. *The mob then set fire to the police station.* [2] VERB If someone **is mobbed**, a disorderly crowd of people gathers very closely around them. *They are mobbed by fans wherever they go.*

⭐ **mobile** /ˈməʊbaɪl, AM -bəl/. [1] ADJ Something or someone that is **mobile** is able to move or be moved easily. *He is now mobile thanks to a powered wheelchair. ...a mobile library.*
♦ **mobility** /məʊˈbɪlɪti/ N-UNCOUNT *It's intended to give patients greater mobility.* [2] ADJ If you are socially **mobile**, you are able to move to a different social class. ♦ **mobility** N-UNCOUNT ...*class barriers which prevented social mobility.*

ˌ**mobile 'phone, mobile phones.** N-COUNT In British English, a **mobile phone** is a telephone that you can carry with you and use to make or receive calls wherever you are. The usual American word is **cellphone**.

mobilize (BRIT also **mobilise**) /ˈməʊbɪlaɪz/ **mobilizes, mobilizing, mobilized.** [1] VERB If you **mobilize** a group of people, or if you **mobilize** support, you get people to support something in an active way. *The king had wanted to mobilise popular support.* ♦ **mobilization** N-UNCOUNT ...*the rapid mobilization of international opinion in support of the revolution.* [2] VERB If a country **mobilizes** its armed forces, or if it **mobilizes**, it prepares for war. [FORMAL] *The French mobilized 160,000 troops.* ♦ **mobilization** N-UNCOUNT ...*a demand for full-scale mobilisation to defend the republic.*

mock /mɒk/ **mocks, mocking, mocked.** [1] VERB If you **mock** someone, you laugh at them, tease them, or try to make them look foolish. ♦ **mocking** ADJ ...*his deliberately mocking tone.* [2] ADJ BEFORE N You use **mock** to describe something which is not genuine, but which is intended to be very similar to the real thing. *Tex's voice was raised in mock horror. ...mock exams.*

mockery/'mɒkəri/. [1] N-UNCOUNT **Mockery** is words, behaviour, or opinions that are unkind and scornful. *There was a hint of mockery in his voice.* [2] N-SING If something **makes a mockery of** something, it makes it appear worthless and foolish. *Allowing her to avoid prison would make a mockery of the law.*

modal/'məʊdəl/**modals.** N-COUNT In grammar, a **modal** or a **modal verb** is a word such as 'can' or 'would' which is used in a verbal group and which expresses ideas such as possibility, intention, and necessity.

mode/məʊd/**modes.** N-COUNT A **mode of** something is one of the different forms it can take. [FORMAL] *...road, rail and other modes of transport.*

model/'mɒdəl/**models, modelling, modelled** (AM **modeling, modeled**). [1] N-COUNT A **model** of an object is a smaller copy of it that shows what it looks like or how it works. *...an architect's model of a wooden house. ...model aeroplane.* [2] N-COUNT A **model** is a system that is being used and that people might want to copy in order to achieve similar results. *...the Chinese model of economic reform.* [3] N-COUNT If you say that someone or something is a **model of** a particular quality, you approve of them because they have that quality to a large degree. *His marriage is a model of propriety.* [4] ADJ BEFORE N A **model** wife or a **model** teacher, for example, is an excellent wife or an excellent teacher. *She had been a model pupil.* [5] VERB If one thing **is modelled on** another, the first thing is made so that it is like the second thing in some way. *She asked the author if she had modelled her hero on anybody in particular.* [6] N-COUNT A particular **model** of a machine is a version of it. *To keep the cost down, opt for a basic model.* [7] N-COUNT An artist's **model** is a person who is painted, drawn, or sculpted by them. [8] N-COUNT A fashion **model** is a person whose job is to display clothes by wearing them. [9] VERB If someone **models** clothes, they display them by wearing them. ♦ **modelling**N-UNCOUNT *She was being offered a modelling contract.*

moderate/**moderates, moderating, moderated.** [1] ADJ & N-COUNT /'mɒdərət/ **Moderate** political opinions or policies are not extreme. A person who has these opinions can be referred to as a **moderate.** *...an easy-going man of very moderate views.* [2] ADJ A **moderate** amount is neither large nor small. *...moderate exercise.* ♦ **moderately**ADV *...a moderately attractive woman.* [3] VERB /'mɒdəreɪt/ If you **moderate** something, or if it **moderates**, it becomes less extreme or violent. *The immediate sense of crisis has moderated somewhat.*

moderation/,mɒdə'reɪʃən/. [1] N-UNCOUNT If someone's behaviour shows **moderation**, they act in a way that is reasonable and not extreme. *He urged the party to show moderation.* [2] PHRASE

If you do something **in moderation**, you do not do it too much. *Many adults are able to drink in moderation.*

modern/'mɒdən/. [1] ADJ BEFORE N **Modern** means relating to the present time. *...the risks facing every modern marriage.* [2] ADJ Something that is **modern** is new and involves the latest ideas or equipment. *...modern technology.*

modernize(BRIT also **modernise**) /'mɒdənaɪz/**modernizes, modernizing, modernized.** VERB To **modernize** a system means to replace old equipment or methods with new ones. *...plans to modernize the refinery.* ♦ **modernization**N-UNCOUNT *...a five-year modernization programme.*

modest/'mɒdɪst/. [1] ADJ A **modest** house or other building is not large or expensive. *She lives in a modest apartment in Santa Monica.* [2] ADJ Something that is **modest** is quite small in amount. *...a modest improvement.* ♦ **modestly** ADV *Sales are expected to drop only modestly this year.* [3] ADJ If you say that someone is **modest**, you approve of them because they do not talk much about their abilities, achievements, or possessions. ♦ **modestly**ADV *Hubbard modestly described himself as an average runner.*

modesty/'mɒdɪsti/. N-UNCOUNT Someone who shows **modesty** does not talk much about their abilities, achievements, or possessions; used showing approval.

modifier/'mɒdɪfaɪə/**modifiers.** N-COUNT A **modifier** is a word which comes in front of a noun in a noun group.

modify/'mɒdɪfaɪ/**modifies, modifying, modified.** VERB If you **modify** something, you change it slightly in order to improve it. *He planned to modify existing legislation.* ♦ **modification** /,mɒdɪfɪ'keɪʃən/**modifications.** N-COUNT *Relatively minor modifications were required.*

module/'mɒdʒuːl/**modules.** [1] N-COUNT A **module** is one of the units that some university or college courses are divided into. [BRITISH] [2] N-COUNT A **module** is part of a spacecraft which can operate independently of the main part, often at a distance from it.

moist/mɔɪst/**moister, moistest.** ADJ Something that is **moist** is slightly wet.

moisture/'mɔɪstʃə/. N-UNCOUNT **Moisture** is tiny drops of water in the air or on a surface.

mold/məʊld/. See **mould**.

mole/məʊl/**moles.** [1] N-COUNT A **mole** is a natural dark spot on someone's skin. [2] N-COUNT A **mole** is a small animal with black fur that lives underground. [3] N-COUNT A **mole** is a member of a government or organization who secretly reveals confidential information to the press or to a rival organization.

molecular/mə'lekjʊlə/. ADJ BEFORE N **Molecular** means relating to molecules. *...recent advances in molecular genetics.*

molecule/'mɒlɪkjuːl/**molecules.** N-COUNT A

a
b
c
d
e
f
g
h
i
j
k
l
m
n
o
p
q
r
s
t
u
v
w
x
y
z

molecule is the smallest amount of a chemical substance which can exist. ...*water molecules.*

molest /mə'lest/ **molests, molesting, molested.** VERB A person who **molests** someone touches them sexually against their will.

molten /'məʊltən/. ADJ **Molten** rock, metal, or glass has been heated to a very high temperature and has become a hot thick liquid.

mom /mɒm/ **moms.** N-COUNT & N-VOC Your **mom** is your mother. [AMERICAN, INFORMAL]

⭐ **moment** /'məʊmənt/ **moments.** [1] N-COUNT A **moment** is a very short period of time. *She stared at him a moment, then turned away... In moments, I was asleep.* [2] N-COUNT A particular **moment** is the point in time at which something happens. *Many people remember the moment they heard that President Kennedy had been assassinated.*
PHRASES ● You use **at the moment** to indicate that a particular situation exists at the time when you are speaking. *At the moment, no one is talking to me.* ● If someone does something **at the last moment**, they do it at the latest possible time. *They changed their minds at the last moment and refused to go.* ● You use **for the moment** to indicate that something is true now, even if it will not be true later or in the future. *For the moment, however, the government is happy to live with it.* ● If you say that something happens **the moment** something else happens, you are emphasizing that it happens immediately after the other thing. *The moment I closed my eyes, I fell asleep.*

momentary /'məʊməntəri, AM -teri/. ADJ Something that is **momentary** lasts for only a very short time. ♦ **momentarily** /,məʊmən'teərɪli/ ADV *She paused momentarily.*

momentous /məʊ'mentəs/. ADJ A **momentous** event is very important.

momentum /məʊ'mentəm/. [1] N-UNCOUNT If a process or movement gains **momentum**, it develops or progresses increasingly quickly, and becomes increasingly less likely to stop. *The campaign against him was gathering momentum.* [2] N-UNCOUNT **Momentum** is the force that causes an object to continue moving, because of its mass and speed. [TECHNICAL]

monarch /'mɒnək/ **monarchs.** N-COUNT A **monarch** is a king or queen.

monarchist /'mɒnəkɪst/ **monarchists.** ADJ & N-COUNT If someone has **monarchist** opinions or if they are a **monarchist**, they believe that their country should have a monarch.

monarchy /'mɒnəki/ **monarchies.** N-COUNT A **monarchy** is a system in which a monarch rules over a country. ...*the future of the monarchy.*

monastery /'mɒnəstri, AM -teri/ **monasteries.** N-COUNT A **monastery** is a building in which monks live.

⭐ **Monday** /'mʌndeɪ, -di/ **Mondays.** N-VAR **Monday** is the day after Sunday and before Tuesday. → See Reference Page on Times and Dates.

⭐ **monetary** /'mʌnɪtri, AM 'mɑːnɪteri/. ADJ BEFORE N **Monetary** means relating to money, or to the money supply. [FORMAL] ...*monetary policy.*

⭐ **money** /'mʌni/. [1] N-UNCOUNT **Money** consists of the coins or banknotes that you can spend, or a sum that can be represented by these. *They spent all their money on that building... I needed to earn some money.* [2] PHRASE If you **get** your **money's worth,** you are satisfied with it because you think it is worth the amount of money you have spent on it. *The fans get their money's worth.*

'**money laundering.** N-UNCOUNT **Money laundering** is the crime of processing stolen money through a legitimate business or sending it abroad to a foreign bank, to hide the fact that the money was obtained illegally.

⭐ **monitor** /'mɒnɪtə/ **monitors, monitoring, monitored.** [1] VERB If you **monitor** something, you regularly check its development or progress. *Officials had not been allowed to monitor the voting.* [2] N-COUNT A **monitor** is a machine used to check or record things. ...*a heart monitor.* [3] N-COUNT A **monitor** is a machine similar to a television that shows information on a screen.

monk /mʌŋk/ **monks.** N-COUNT A **monk** is a member of a male religious community.

monkey /'mʌŋki/ **monkeys.** N-COUNT A **monkey** is an animal that lives in hot countries, has a long tail and climbs trees. → See picture on page 816.

monogamy /mə'nɒgəmi/. N-UNCOUNT **Monogamy** is the state or custom of having a sexual relationship with only one partner or of being married to only one person.
♦ **monogamous** ADJ ...*a monogamous relationship.*

monolithic /,mɒnə'lɪθɪk/. ADJ If you describe an organization or system as **monolithic**, you are critical of it because it is very large and very slow to change. ...*a monolithic bureaucracy.*

monologue /'mɒnəlɒg, AM -lɔːg/ **monologues.** N-COUNT If you refer to a long speech by one person during a conversation as a **monologue**, you mean it prevents other people from talking or expressing their opinions.

monopolize (BRIT also **monopolise**) /mə'nɒpəlaɪz/ **monopolizes, monopolizing, monopolized.** VERB If someone **monopolizes** something, they have a very large share of it and prevent other people from having a share. *Johnson, as usual, monopolized the conversation.*

monopoly /mə'nɒpəli/ **monopolies.** [1] N-VAR If a company, person, or state has a **monopoly on** something such as an industry, they have complete control over it. ...*a state monopoly on land ownership.* [2] N-COUNT A **monopoly** is a company which is the only one that makes a particular product or offers a particular service and which completely controls an industry.

monotonous /mə'nɒtənəs/. ADJ Something that is **monotonous** is very boring because it has a regular repeated pattern which never changes. *It's monotonous work, like most factory jobs.*

monsoon /mɒn'suːn/ **monsoons.** N-COUNT The **monsoon** is the season of very heavy rain in Southern Asia.

monster /'mɒnstə/ **monsters.** 1 N-COUNT A **monster** is a large imaginary creature that is very frightening. 2 ADJ BEFORE N **Monster** means extremely large. [INFORMAL] *The film will be a monster hit.*

monstrous /'mɒnstrəs/. 1 ADJ If you describe a situation or someone's actions as **monstrous**, you mean that it is very shocking or unfair. ♦ **monstrously** ADV *Your husband's family has behaved monstrously.* 2 ADJ If you describe something, especially an unpleasant thing, as **monstrous**, you mean that it is extremely large. *...monstrous waves and severe winds.*

⭐ **month** /mʌnθ/ **months.** N-COUNT A **month** is one of the twelve periods of time that a year is divided into, for example January or February. → See Reference Page on Times and Dates.

⭐ **monthly** /'mʌnθli/. ADJ BEFORE N & ADV A **monthly** publication or event appears or happens every month. *...a monthly newsletter... I get paid monthly.*

monument /'mɒnjʊmənt/ **monuments.** N-COUNT A **monument** is a large structure, usually made of stone, which is built to remind people of an event in history or of a famous person.

monumental /ˌmɒnjʊ'mentəl/. ADJ You can use **monumental** to emphasize the size or extent of something. *It had been a monumental blunder. ...his monumental work on Chinese astronomy.*

⭐ **mood** /muːd/ **moods.** 1 N-COUNT Your **mood** is the way you are feeling at a particular time. *Lily was in one of her aggressive moods.* 2 N-SING The **mood** of a group of people is the way that they think and feel about an idea, event, or question at a particular time. *They largely misread the mood of the electorate.* 3 N-COUNT If someone is **in a mood**, their behaviour shows that they are feeling angry and impatient.

moody /'muːdi/. ADJ A **moody** person often becomes depressed or angry without any warning. ♦ **moodily** ADV *He sat and stared moodily out of the window.* ♦ **moodiness** N-UNCOUNT *His moodiness may have been caused by his poor health.*

⭐ **moon** /muːn/ **moons.** 1 N-SING The **moon** is the object in the sky that goes round the Earth once every four weeks and that you can often see at night as a circle or part of a circle. *...the light of a full moon.* 2 N-COUNT A **moon** is an object like a small planet that travels around a planet. *...Neptune's large moon.* 3 PHRASE If you say that you are **over the moon**, you mean that you are very pleased about something. [BRITISH, INFORMAL]

moonlight /'muːnlaɪt/ **moonlights, moonlighting, moonlighted.** 1 N-UNCOUNT **Moonlight** is the light that comes from the moon at night. *They walked along the road in the moonlight.* 2 VERB If someone **moonlights**, they have a second job in addition to their main job, often without

informing their main employers or the tax office. *...an engineer who was moonlighting as a taxi driver.*

moor /mʊə/ **moors, mooring, moored.** 1 N-VAR A **moor** is an area of high open ground covered mainly with rough grass and heather. [BRITISH] 2 VERB If you **moor** a boat, you attach it to the land with a rope or cable so that it cannot drift away. *I decided to moor near some tourist boats.*

mooring /'mʊərɪŋ/ **moorings.** N-COUNT A **mooring** is a place or object on land to which a boat is tied so that it cannot drift away.

moorland /'mʊələnd/ **moorlands.** N-VAR **Moorland** is land which consists of moors.

moose /muːs/.

✅ **Moose** is both the singular and the plural form.

N-COUNT A **moose** is a large North American deer.

mop /mɒp/ **mops, mopping, mopped.** 1 N-COUNT A **mop** consists of a sponge or many pieces of string attached to a long handle and is used for washing floors. 2 VERB If you **mop** a floor, you clean it with a mop. 3 VERB If you **mop** sweat from your forehead, you wipe the sweat away with a handkerchief. *The Inspector took out a handkerchief and mopped his brow.*
▶ **mop up.** PHR-VERB If you **mop up** a liquid, you clean it with a cloth so that the liquid is absorbed. *A waiter mopped up the mess.*

mope /məʊp/ **mopes, moping, moped.** VERB If you **mope**, or if you **mope around** or **mope about**, you feel miserable and are not interested in anything. *Get on with life and don't sit back and mope... He moped around the office for a while, feeling bored.*

moped /'məʊped/ **mopeds.** N-COUNT A **moped** is a kind of motorcycle with a very small engine. → See picture on page 817.

⭐ **moral** /'mɒrəl, AM 'mɔːr-/ **morals.** 1 N-PLURAL **Morals** are principles and beliefs concerning right and wrong behaviour. *They have no morals.* 2 ADJ BEFORE N **Moral** means relating to beliefs about what is right or wrong. ♦ **morally** ADV *When, if ever, is it morally justifiable to allow a patient to die?* 3 ADJ A **moral** person behaves in a way that is believed by most people to be good and right. ♦ **morally** ADV *Art is not there to improve you morally.* 4 ADJ BEFORE N If you give someone **moral** support, you encourage them in what they are doing by expressing approval. 5 N-SING The **moral** of a story or event is what you learn from it about how you should or should not behave.

morale /mə'rɑːl, -'ræl/. N-UNCOUNT **Morale** is the amount of confidence and optimism that people have. *Many pilots are suffering from low morale.*

morality /mə'rælɪti/ **moralities.** 1 N-UNCOUNT **Morality** is the belief that some behaviour is right and acceptable and that other behaviour is wrong. *...standards of morality and justice.* 2 N-UNCOUNT The **morality** of something is how

a
b
c
d
e
f
g
h
i
j
k
l
m
n
o
p
q
r
s
t
u
v
w
x
y
z

right or acceptable it is. ...*debates over the morality of the death penalty.*

moratorium /ˌmɒrəˈtɔːriəm, AM ˌmɔːr-/ **moratoriums** or **moratoria**. N-COUNT If there is a **moratorium on** a particular activity, it is officially stopped for a period of time. [FORMAL] *Spain imposed a moratorium on the building of nuclear power stations.*

morbid /ˈmɔːbɪd/. ADJ If someone has a **morbid** interest in a particular subject, especially a strange or unpleasant subject, they are fascinated by it. ...*a morbid fear of cancer.* ◆ **morbidly** ADV *I slid into a depression and became morbidly fascinated with death.*

⭐ **more** /mɔː/.

✔ **More** is often considered to be the comparative form of **much** and **many**.

1 QUANT You use **more** to indicate that there is a greater number of things or a greater amount of something than before or than average, or than something else. ...*teaching more children foreign languages... Prison conditions have become more brutal... We can satisfy our basic wants more easily than in the past... He had four hundred dollars in his pocket. Billy had more... As the afternoon drew on we were joined by more of the regulars.* **2** PREP You use **more than** before a number or amount to say that the actual number or amount is even greater. ...*a survey of more than 1,500 schools.* **3** ADV You can use **more** or **some more** to indicate that something continues to happen for a further period of time. *We can talk more about Leo on Thursday... Would you mind if I just stayed in my room and read some more?* **4** ADV You use **more** to indicate that something is repeated. *Aubrey sighed once more... The breathing exercises should be repeated several times more.* **5** DET & PRON You use **more** to refer to an additional thing or amount. *Are you sure you wouldn't like some more wine?... They should do more to help themselves.*

PHRASES ● You can use **more and more** to indicate that something is becoming greater in amount, extent, or degree all the time. *Bob became more and more furious... More and more women are wearing men's fragrances.* ● You use **more than** to say that something is true to a greater degree than is necessary or than average. *Lithuania produces more than enough food to feed itself.* ● You use **no more than** or **not more than** when you want to emphasize how small a number or amount is. *Each box requires no more than a few hours of labor to build.* ● If something is **more or less** true, it is true in a general way, but it is not completely true. *The Conference is more or less over.* ● You can use **what is more** or **what's more** to introduce an extra piece of information which supports or emphasizes the point you are making. *You should remember it, and what's more, you should get it right.* ● **all the more:** see **all.** ● **any more:** see **any.**

⭐ **moreover** /mɔːˈrəʊvə/. ADV You use **moreover** to introduce a piece of information that adds to

or supports the previous statement. [FORMAL] *There was indeed a man immediately behind her. Moreover, he was observing her strangely.*

morgue /mɔːg/ **morgues**. N-COUNT A **morgue** is a building or room where dead bodies are kept before being cremated or buried.

⭐ **morning** /ˈmɔːnɪŋ/ **mornings.** **1** N-VAR The **morning** is the part of a day between the time that people wake up and noon. *On Sunday morning Bill was woken by the telephone.* **2** N-COUNT If you refer to a particular time **in the morning**, you mean a time during the part of a day between midnight and noon. *I often stayed up until two or three in the morning.* **3** PHRASE If you say that something will happen **in the morning**, you mean that it will happen during the morning of the following day.

morose /məˈrəʊs/. ADJ Someone who is **morose** is miserable, bad-tempered, and not willing to talk very much to other people.. ◆ **morosely** ADV *One elderly man sat morosely at the bar.*

morphine /ˈmɔːfiːn/. N-UNCOUNT **Morphine** is a drug used to relieve pain.

morsel /ˈmɔːsəl/ **morsels.** N-COUNT A **morsel** is a very small amount of something, especially a very small piece of food. ...*a delicious little morsel of meat.*

mortal /ˈmɔːtəl/ **mortals.** **1** ADJ If you refer to the fact that people are **mortal**, you mean that they have to die and cannot live forever. ◆ **mortality** N-UNCOUNT *She has suddenly come face to face with her own mortality.* **2** N-COUNT You can describe someone as a **mortal** when you want to say that they are an ordinary person, rather than someone who has power or has achieved something. *Musicians, like the rest of us, are mere mortals.* **3** ADJ BEFORE N You can use **mortal** to show that something is very serious or may cause death. *Our citizens' lives were in mortal danger.* ◆ **mortally** ADV ...*a mortally wounded soldier.*

mortality /mɔːˈtælɪti/. N-UNCOUNT The **mortality** in a particular place or situation is the number of people who die. ...*the infant mortality rate in Britain is higher.*

mortar /ˈmɔːtə/ **mortars.** **1** N-COUNT A **mortar** is a short cannon which fires shells high into the air for a short distance. **2** N-UNCOUNT **Mortar** is a mixture of sand, water, and cement, which is put between bricks to make them stay firmly together.

⭐ **mortgage** /ˈmɔːgɪdʒ/ **mortgages, mortgaging, mortgaged.** **1** N-COUNT A **mortgage** is a loan of money which you get from a bank or building society in order to buy a house. **2** VERB If you **mortgage** your house or land, you use it as a guarantee to a company in order to borrow money from them.

mortician /mɔːˈtɪʃən/ **morticians.** N-COUNT In American English, a **mortician** is a person whose job is to deal with the bodies of people who have died and to arrange funerals. The British word is **undertaker**.

mortuary/'mɔːtʃʊəri, ᴀᴍ -eri/**mortuaries.**
ɴ-ᴄᴏᴜɴᴛ A **mortuary** is building or a room in a hospital where dead bodies are kept before they are buried or cremated.

mosaic/məʊ'zeɪɪk/**mosaics.** ɴ-ᴠᴀʀ A **mosaic** is a design made of small pieces of coloured stone or glass set in concrete or plaster.

Moslem/'mʊzlɪm/. See **Muslim**.

mosque/mɒsk/**mosques.** ɴ-ᴄᴏᴜɴᴛ A **mosque** is a building where Muslims go to worship.

mosquito/mɒ'skiːtəʊ/**mosquitoes or mosquitos.**
ɴ-ᴄᴏᴜɴᴛ **Mosquitoes** are small flying insects which bite people in order to suck their blood.
→ See picture on page 824.

moss/mɒs, ᴀᴍ mɔːs/**mosses.** ɴ-ᴠᴀʀ **Moss** is a very small soft green plant which grows on damp soil, or on wood or stone.

◪ **most**/məʊst/.

☑ **Most** is often considered to be the superlative form of **much** and **many**.

☐**1** ǫᴜᴀɴᴛ You use **most** to refer to the majority of a group of people or things or the largest part of something. *Most people think the Queen has done a good job... Most of the book is completely true... All of the rooms have private baths, and most have radios and TV.*

USAGE Note that you can say '**Most children love sweets**', but you cannot say 'Most of children love sweets'. However, when a pronoun is used, you can say '**Most of them love sweets**'.

☐**2** ᴀᴅᴊ & ᴘʀᴏɴ You use **the most** to mean a larger amount than anyone or anything else, or the largest amount possible. *The President himself won the most votes... The most they earn in a day is ten roubles.* ☐**3** ᴀᴅᴠ & ᴘʜʀᴀsᴇ You use **most** or **most of all** to indicate that something is true or happens to a greater degree or extent than anything else. *What she feared most was becoming like her mother. ...Professor Morris, the person he most hated... She said she wanted most of all to be fair.* ☐**4** ᴀᴅᴠ You use **most** to indicate that someone or something has a greater amount of a particular quality than other things of its kind. *He was one of the most influential performers of modern jazz.* ☐**5** ᴀᴅᴠ If you do something **the most**, you do it to the greatest extent possible or with the greatest frequency. *What question are you asked the most?* ☐**6** ᴀᴅᴠ You use **most** to emphasize an adjective or adverb. [ғᴏʀᴍᴀʟ] *I believe he is most painfully anxious about Diana.*
PHRASES ● You use **at most** or **at the most** to say that a number or amount is the maximum that is possible or likely. *I was probably only about twelve or thirteen years old at most.* ● If you **make the most of** something, you get the maximum

use or advantage from it. *Make the most of every opportunity.*

★ **mostly**/'məʊstli/. ᴀᴅᴠ You use **mostly** to indicate that a statement is true about the majority of a group of things or people, true most of the time, or true in most respects. *I am working with mostly highly motivated people... Cars are mostly metal.*

motel/məʊ'tel/**motels.** ɴ-ᴄᴏᴜɴᴛ A **motel** is a hotel intended for people who are travelling by car.

moth/mɒθ, ᴀᴍ mɔːθ/**moths.** ɴ-ᴄᴏᴜɴᴛ A **moth** is an insect like a butterfly, which usually flies about at night. → See picture on page 824.

★ **mother**/'mʌðə/**mothers, mothering, mothered.**
☐**1** ɴ-ᴄᴏᴜɴᴛ & ɴ-ᴠᴏᴄ Your **mother** is the woman who gave birth to you. *She's an English teacher and a mother of two children.* ☐**2** ᴠᴇʀʙ If you **mother** someone, you treat them with great care and affection, as if they were a small child.

motherhood/'mʌðəhʊd/. ɴ-ᴜɴᴄᴏᴜɴᴛ **Motherhood** is the state of being a mother.

'mother-in-law,mothers-in-law. ɴ-ᴄᴏᴜɴᴛ Someone's **mother-in-law** is the mother of their husband or wife.

motherland/'mʌðəlænd/. ɴ-sɪɴɢ The **motherland** is the country in which you were born and to which you still feel emotionally linked.

motherly/'mʌðəli/. ᴀᴅᴊ **Motherly** feelings or actions are like those of a mother. *It was an incredible display of motherly love and forgiveness.*

motif/məʊ'tiːf/**motifs.** ɴ-ᴄᴏᴜɴᴛ A **motif** is a design used as a decoration or as part of an artistic pattern. *...a rose motif.*

★ **motion**/'məʊʃən/**motions, motioning, motioned.**
☐**1** ɴ-ᴜɴᴄᴏᴜɴᴛ **Motion** is continual movement. *The wind from the car's motion whipped her hair around her head.* ☐**2** ɴ-ᴄᴏᴜɴᴛ A **motion** is an action, gesture, or movement. *He made a neat chopping motion with his hand.* ☐**3** ᴠᴇʀʙ If you **motion** to someone, you move your hand or head as a way of telling them to do something or where to go. *She motioned for the locked front doors to be opened... I motioned him to join us.* ☐**4** ɴ-ᴄᴏᴜɴᴛ A **motion** in a meeting or debate is a proposal which is discussed and voted on. ☐**5** See also **slow motion**.
PHRASES ● If you say that someone **is going through the motions**, you think they are only saying or doing something because it is expected of them and not because they are interested in it, enthusiastic about it, or sympathetic to it. ● If a process or event is **set in motion**, something causes it to begin or begin to happen. *Our desires in food are largely set in motion by our sense of smell.*

motionless/'məʊʃənləs/. ᴀᴅᴊ Someone or something that is **motionless** is not moving at all. *He remained quite motionless behind his desk.*

'motion picture,motion pictures. ɴ-ᴄᴏᴜɴᴛ A

a b c d e f g h i j k l m n o p q r s t u v w x y z

A

motion picture is a film made for cinema. [AMERICAN]

B

★ **motivate** /'məʊtɪveɪt/ **motivates, motivating, motivated.** [1] VERB If you **are motivated** by something, especially an emotion, it causes you to behave in a particular way. *The crime was not politically motivated... What motivates athletes to takes drugs?* [2] VERB If someone **motivates** you **to** do something, they make you feel determined to do it. *Better schools are able to motivate students to do their best.* ♦ **motivated** ADJ *...highly motivated employees.*

C

D

E

motivation /,məʊtɪ'veɪʃən/ **motivations.** [1] N-COUNT Your **motivation** for doing something is what causes you to want to do it. *The prime motivation is usually money.* [2] N-UNCOUNT If you have the **motivation** to do something, you feel determined to do it. *The players were tired and they lacked motivation.*

F

G

H

motive /'məʊtɪv/ **motives.** N-COUNT Your **motive** for doing something is your reason for doing it. *He ruled out robbery as a motive for the killing.*

I

J

★ **motor** /'məʊtə/ **motors, motoring, motored.** [1] N-COUNT A **motor** in a machine, vehicle, or boat is the part that uses electricity or fuel to produce movement, so that the machine, vehicle, or boat can work. [2] ADJ BEFORE N **Motor** vehicles and boats have a petrol or diesel engine. [3] ADJ BEFORE N **Motor** is used to describe activities relating to motor vehicles. *...the future of the British motor industry.* [4] See also **motoring.**

K

L

M

motorbike /'məʊtəbaɪk/ **motorbikes.** N-COUNT A **motorbike** is the same as a **motorcycle.** → See picture on page 817.

N

'**motor car, motor cars.** N-COUNT A **motor car** is the same as a **car.** [DATED]

O

motorcycle /'məʊtəsaɪkəl/ **motorcycles.** N-COUNT A **motorcycle** is a two-wheeled vehicle with an engine. → See picture on page 817.

P

motorcyclist /'məʊtəsaɪklɪst/ **motorcyclists.** N-COUNT A **motorcyclist** is someone who rides a motorcycle.

Q

R

motoring /'məʊtərɪŋ/. ADJ BEFORE N **Motoring** means relating to cars and to driving. *...one of Britain's largest motoring organisations.*

S

motorist /'məʊtərɪst/ **motorists.** N-COUNT A **motorist** is someone who drives a car.

T

motorized (BRIT also **motorised**) /'məʊtəraɪzd/. ADJ A **motorized** vehicle has an engine. *...the first time motorized vehicles were used in a war.*

U

V

motorway /'məʊtəweɪ/ **motorways.** N-VAR In British English, a **motorway** is a wide road specially built for fast travel over long distances. The usual American word is **freeway.**

W

X

motto /'mɒtəʊ/ **mottoes** or **mottos.** N-COUNT A **motto** is a short sentence or phrase that expresses the attitude to life of a particular person or group. *The motto of the club is: THINK QUICK!*

Y

Z

mould (AM **mold**) /məʊld/ **moulds, moulding, moulded.** [1] N-COUNT A **mould** is a container used

to make something into a particular shape. [2] VERB If you **mould** plastic or clay, you make it into a particular shape. *Mould the cheese mixture into small balls.* [3] VERB To **mould** someone or something means to change or influence them over a period of time so that they develop in a particular way. *We try to mold our children into something they do not wish to be.* [4] N-VAR **Mould** is a soft grey, green, or blue substance that sometimes forms on old food or on damp walls or clothes.

mound /maʊnd/ **mounds.** N-COUNT A **mound of** things is a large heap or pile of them. *The bulldozers piled up huge mounds of dirt.*

★ **mount** /maʊnt/ **mounts, mounting, mounted.** [1] VERB To **mount** a campaign or event means to organize it and make it take place. *The group announced it was mounting a major campaign of mass political protests.* [2] VERB If something **mounts**, or if it **mounts up**, it increases. *For several hours, tension mounted... Her medical bills mounted up.* [3] VERB If you **mount** the stairs or a platform, you go up the stairs or go up onto the platform. [FORMAL] *The vehicle mounted the pavement.* [4] VERB If you **mount** a horse or cycle, you climb on to it so that you can ride it. *They all mounted and rode off.* [5] VERB If you **mount** an object **on** something, you fix it there firmly. *Her husband mounts the work on velour paper.* ♦ **-mounted** *...a wall-mounted electric fan.* [6] **Mount** is used as part of the name of some mountains. *...Mount Everest.* [7] See also **mounted.**

★ **mountain** /'maʊntɪn, AM -tən/ **mountains.** [1] N-COUNT A **mountain** is a very high area of land with steep sides. *...the north side of the mountain. ...a lovely little mountain village.* [2] N-COUNT A **mountain** of something is a very large amount of it. [INFORMAL] *They have mountains of coffee to sell.*

'**mountain bike, mountain bikes.** N-COUNT A **mountain bike** is a type of bicycle with a strong frame and thick tyres.

mountaineer /,maʊntɪ'ɪə/ **mountaineers.** N-COUNT A **mountaineer** is someone who climbs mountains as a hobby or sport.

mountainous /'maʊntɪnəs/. ADJ A **mountainous** place has a lot of mountains. *...the mountainous region of Campania.*

mountainside /'maʊntɪnsaɪd/ **mountainsides.** N-COUNT A **mountainside** is one of the steep sides of a mountain.

mounted /'maʊntɪd/. ADJ BEFORE N **Mounted** police or soldiers ride horses when they are on duty. ● See also **mount.**

mourn /mɔːn/ **mourns, mourning, mourned.** [1] VERB If you **mourn** someone who has died, you are very sad that they have died and show your sorrow in the way that you behave. *The whole nation had mourned the death of their great leader.* [2] VERB If you **mourn** something, you regret that you no longer have it and show your regret in the way that you behave. *We mourned the loss of our cities.*

mourner /ˈmɔːnə/ **mourners.** N-COUNT You can refer to the people at a funeral as the **mourners.**

mournful /ˈmɔːnfʊl/. ADJ If you are **mournful,** you are very sad. *He looked mournful, even near to tears.* ♦ **mournfully** ADV *He stood mournfully at the gate waving bye bye.*

mouse /maʊs/ **mice** /maɪs/. [1] N-COUNT A **mouse** is a small furry animal with a long tail. [2] N-COUNT A **mouse** is a device that you use to perform operations on a computer without using the keyboard. [COMPUTING]

mousse /muːs/ **mousses.** N-VAR **Mousse** is a sweet light food made from eggs and cream.

moustache (AM **mustache**) /məˈstɑːʃ, AM ˈmʊstæʃ/ **moustaches.** N-COUNT A man's **moustache** is the hair that grows on his upper lip.

⭐ **mouth, mouths, mouthing, mouthed;** noun /maʊθ/ in the singular, /maʊðz/ in the plural. [1] N-COUNT Your **mouth** is your lips, or the space behind your lips where your teeth and tongue are. → See picture on page 823. *She clamped her hand against her mouth... His mouth was full of peas.* ♦ **-mouthed** *...a tough, wide-mouthed, gray-haired policeman.* [2] N-COUNT The **mouth** of a cave, hole, or bottle is its entrance or opening. [3] N-COUNT The **mouth** of a river is the place where it flows into the sea. [4] VERB /maʊð/ If you **mouth** something, you form words with your lips without making any sound. *I mouthed a goodbye and hurried in... 'It's for you,' he mouthed.* [5] to **live from hand to mouth:** see **hand.**

mouthful /ˈmaʊθfʊl/ **mouthfuls.** N-COUNT A **mouthful** of food or drink is an amount that you put or have in your mouth. *She gulped down a mouthful of coffee.*

mouthpiece /ˈmaʊθpiːs/ **mouthpieces.** [1] N-COUNT The **mouthpiece** of a telephone is the part that you speak into. [2] N-COUNT The **mouthpiece** of a musical instrument is the part that you blow into. [3] N-COUNT The **mouthpiece** of an official person or organization is someone who informs other people of the opinions and policies of that organization or person. *Their mouthpiece is the vice-president.*

movable (or **moveable**) /ˈmuːvəbəl/. ADJ Something that is **movable** can be moved from one place or position to another. *It's a vinyl doll with movable arms and legs.*

⭐ **move** /muːv/ **moves, moving, moved.** [1] VERB When you **move** something, or when it **moves,** its position changes. *She moved the sheaf of papers into position... The train began to move.* [2] VERB & N-COUNT When you **move,** or when you make a **move,** you change your position or go to a different place. *She moved away from the window... Daniel's eyes followed her every move.* [3] VERB & N-COUNT If a person or company **moves,** they leave the building where they have been living or working, and go to live or work in a different place. A **move** is an act of moving. *She*

had often considered moving to London... The move to Prague was a daunting prospect. [4] VERB & N-COUNT If you **move** from one job or interest to another, you change to it. A **move** is an act of moving. *Christina moved jobs to get experience. ...his move to the chairmanship.* [5] VERB & N-COUNT If you **move** towards a particular state, activity, or opinion, you start to be in that state, do that activity, or have that opinion. A **move** is an act of moving in this way. *...the need to move towards greater economic convergence... Fifteen Japanese banks made a move to pull out.* [6] VERB If a situation **is moving,** it is developing or progressing. *Events are moving fast.* [7] VERB If something **moves** you **to** do something, it causes you to do it. *It was punk that first moved him to join a band.* [8] VERB If something **moves** you, it causes you to feel a deep emotion, usually sadness or sympathy. *His prayer moved me to tears.* ♦ **moved** ADJ AFTER LINK-V *Those who listened to him were deeply moved.* [9] N-COUNT A **move** is an action that you take in order to achieve something. *It may also be a good move to suggest she talks things over.* [10] PHRASE If you are **on the move,** you are going from one place to another. [11] See also **moving.**

▶ **move about** or **move around.** PHR-VERB If you **move about** or **move around,** you keep changing your job or keep changing the place where you live. *He moved around the country working in orange groves.*

▶ **move in.** [1] PHR-VERB If you **move in** somewhere, or if you **move into** a new house or place, you begin to live in a different house or place. *Her husband had moved in with a younger woman... I want you to move into my apartment.* [2] PHR-VERB If soldiers or police **move in,** they go towards a place or person in order to attack them or deal with them. *Forces were moving in on the town of Knin.*

▶ **move off.** PHR-VERB When vehicles or people **move off,** they start moving away from a place. *Gil waved his hand and the car moved off.*

▶ **move on.** PHR-VERB When you **move on** somewhere, you leave the place where you have been staying or waiting and go or travel somewhere else. *What's wrong with his wanting to sell his land and move on?... Mr Brooke moved on from Paris to Belgrade.*

▶ **move out.** PHR-VERB If you **move out,** you leave the house or place where you have been living, and go and live somewhere else.

▶ **move up.** PHR-VERB If you **move up,** you change your position, especially in order to be nearer someone or to make room for someone else. *Move up, John, and let the lady sit down.*

moveable /ˈmuːvəbəl/. See **movable.**

⭐ **movement** /ˈmuːvmənt/ **movements.** [1] N-VAR **Movement** involves changing position or going from one place to another. *They actually monitor the movement of the fish going up river... Her hand movements are becoming more animated.* [2] N-VAR **Movement** is a gradual development or

a b c d e f g h i j k l **m** n o p q r s t u v w x y z

change of an attitude, opinion, or policy. ...*the movement towards democracy in Latin America.* **3** N-PLURAL Your **movements** are everything which you do or plan to do during a period of time. *I want a full account of your movements the night Mr Gower was killed.* **4** N-COUNT A **movement** is a group of people who share the same beliefs, ideas, or aims. ...*the women's movement.*

★ **movie** /'muːvi/ **movies.** **1** N-COUNT In American English, a **movie** is a motion picture. The British word is **film**. ...*a horror movie.* **2** N-PLURAL In American English, when people go to **the movies**, they see a movie in a movie theater. The British term is **the cinema**.

moving /'muːvɪŋ/. **1** ADJ If something is **moving**, it makes you feel a strong emotion such as pity. *It was a moving moment.* ♦ **movingly** ADV *You write very movingly of your sister Amy's suicide.* **2** ADJ BEFORE N A **moving** model or part of a machine moves or is able to move. **3** See also **move**.

mow /məʊ/ **mows, mowing, mowed, mown** (or **mowed**). VERB If you **mow** an area of grass, you cut it using a lawnmower or a mower.
▸ **mow down.** PHR-VERB If a large number of people **are mown down**, they are killed violently by a vehicle or gunfire.

mower /'məʊə/ **mowers.** N-COUNT A **mower** is a machine for cutting grass, corn, or wheat.

★ **MP** /,em 'piː/ **MPs.** N-COUNT In Britain, an **MP** is a person who has been elected to represent the people from a particular area in the House of Commons. **MP** is an abbreviation for 'Member of Parliament'.

MP3 /'em piː θriː/. N-COUNT **MP3** is a kind of technology that enables you to record and play music from the Internet. [COMPUTING] ...*MP3 files.*

mph. mph is written after a number to indicate the speed of something such as a vehicle. **mph** is an abbreviation for 'miles per hour'.

★ **Mr** /'mɪstə/. N-TITLE **Mr** is used before a man's name when you are speaking or referring to him. *Hello, Mr Simpson. ...Mr Bob Price.*

★ **Mrs** /'mɪsɪz/. N-TITLE **Mrs** is used before the name of a married woman when you are speaking or referring to her. *Hello, Mrs Miles. ...Mrs Anne Pritchard.*

★ **Ms** /məz, mɪz/. N-TITLE **Ms** is used before a woman's name when you are speaking to her or referring to her. If you use **Ms**, you are not specifying if the woman is married or not. ...*Ms Elizabeth Harman.*

MSP /'em es piː/ **MSPs.** N-COUNT An **MSP** is someone who has been elected as a member of the Scottish Parliament. **MSP** is an abbreviation for 'Member of the Scottish Parliament'.

★ **much** /mʌtʃ/. **1** ADV You use **much** to indicate the great intensity, extent, or degree of something such as an action, feeling, or change. **Much** is usually used with 'so', 'too', and 'very',

and in negative clauses for this meaning. *She laughs too much... Thank you very much... My hairstyle hasn't changed much since I was five.* **2** ADV You use **much** in order to emphasize that there is a large amount of a particular quality. *The skin is much too delicate... You'd be so much happier if you could see yourself the way I see you.* **3** ADV If one thing is **much** the same as another thing, it is very similar to it. *Sheep's milk is produced in much the same way as goat's milk... It looks pretty much like Michael's signature.* **4** QUANT You use **much** to indicate that you are referring to a large amount of something. *They are grown on the hillsides in full sun, without much water... There was so much to talk about... She does much of her work abroad.*

5 QUANT You use **much** to ask questions or make statements about the amount or degree of something. *How much do you earn?... She knows how much this upsets me.* **6** ADV If something does not happen **much**, it does not happen very often. *His father never talked much about the war.* PHRASES ● If you describe something as **not much of** a particular type of thing, you mean that it is small or of poor quality. *It hasn't been much of a holiday.* ● If something is **not so much** one thing as another, it is more like the second thing than the first. *I don't really think of her as a daughter so much as a very good friend.* ● You say **nothing much** to refer to something that is not very interesting or important. *'What was stolen?'—'Oh, nothing much.'* ● You use **much less** after a statement to indicate that the statement is even more true of the person, thing, or situation that you are going to mention next. *They are always short of water to drink, much less to bathe in.* ● If you say **so much for** a particular thing, you mean that it has not been successful or helpful. [INFORMAL] *So much for all his damn theories!* ● If a situation or action is **too much for** you, you cannot cope with it. *His inability to stay at one job for long had finally proved too much for her.* ● **a bit much**: see **bit**.

muck /mʌk/ **mucks, mucking, mucked.** N-UNCOUNT **Muck** is dirt or some other unpleasant substance. [INFORMAL]
▸ **muck about** or **muck around.** PHR-VERB If you **muck about** or **muck around**, you behave in a stupid way and waste time. [BRITISH, INFORMAL] *He'd spent his boyhood summers mucking about in boats.*

mucus /'mjuːkəs/. N-UNCOUNT **Mucus** is a liquid that is produced in some parts of your body, for example the inside of your nose. [FORMAL]

mud /mʌd/. N-UNCOUNT **Mud** is a sticky mixture of earth and water.

muddle /'mʌdəl/ **muddles, muddling, muddled.**
[1] N-VAR A **muddle** is a confused state or situation. *My thoughts are all in a muddle.* [2] VERB & PHR-VERB If you **muddle** things or people, or if you **muddle** them **up**, you get them mixed up, so that you do not know which is which. *One or two critics have begun to muddle the two names... He sometimes muddles me up with other patients.* ♦ **muddled up** ADJ *I am getting my words muddled up.*
▸**muddle through.** PHR-VERB If you **muddle through**, you manage to do something even though you do not really know how to do it properly.
▸**muddle up.** See **muddle** 2.

muddled /'mʌdəld/. ADJ If someone is **muddled**, they are confused about something.

muddy /'mʌdi/ **muddier, muddiest; muddies, muddying, muddied.** [1] ADJ Something that is **muddy** contains or is covered in mud. *...his muddy boots.* [2] ADJ BEFORE N A **muddy** colour is dull and brownish. *...a muddy green-brown.* [3] VERB If you **muddy** something, you cause it to be muddy. *They muddied their shoes.* [4] VERB If someone or something **muddies** a situation or issue, they cause it to seem less clear and less easy to understand. *Their relationship has sometimes been muddied by politics and personal rivalry.*

muffle /'mʌfəl/ **muffles, muffling, muffled.** VERB If something **muffles** a sound, it makes it quieter and more difficult to hear. *Blake held his handkerchief over the mouthpiece to muffle his voice.*

mug /mʌg/ **mugs, mugging, mugged.** [1] N-COUNT A **mug** is a large deep cup with straight sides. *She sipped from her coffee mug. ...a mug of sweet tea.* [2] VERB If someone **mugs** you, they attack you in order to steal your money. ♦ **mugging, muggings** N-VAR *...a victim of mugging.* ♦ **mugger, muggers** N-COUNT *If you come face to face with a mugger, what do you do?*

mule /mju:l/ **mules.** N-COUNT A **mule** is an animal whose parents are a horse and a donkey.

mull /mʌl/ **mulls, mulling, mulled.**
▸**mull over.** PHR-VERB If you **mull** something **over**, you think about it for a long time before deciding what to do.

multilateral /,mʌlti'lætərəl/. ADJ **Multilateral** means involving at least three different groups of people or nations. *...multilateral trade talks in Geneva.*

multimedia /,mʌlti'mi:diə/. [1] N-UNCOUNT In computing, you use **multimedia** to refer to programs and products which involve the use of sound, pictures, and film, as well as ordinary text. [2] N-UNCOUNT In education, **multimedia** is the use of television and other different media in a lesson, instead of only textbooks.

multinational (or**multi-national**) /,mʌlti'næʃənəl/ **multinationals.** [1] ADJ & N-COUNT A **multinational** company or a **multinational** has branches in many different countries. *...multinationals such as Ford and IBM.* [2] ADJ **Multinational** is used to describe something that involves several different countries. *The US troops would be part of a multinational force.*

multiple /'mʌltɪpəl/ **multiples.** [1] ADJ You use **multiple** to describe things that consist of many parts, involve many people, or have many uses. *He died of multiple injuries... The most common multiple births are twins.* [2] N-COUNT If one number is a **multiple** of a smaller number, it can be exactly divided by that smaller number. *We count the seconds, minutes and hours in multiples of six and ten.*

multiple sclerosis /,mʌltɪpəl sklə'rəʊsɪs/. N-UNCOUNT **Multiple sclerosis** is a serious disease of the nervous system. The abbreviation **MS** is also used.

multiplicity /,mʌltɪ'plɪsɪti/. QUANT A **multiplicity of** things is a large number or large variety of them. [FORMAL] *...a writer who uses a multiplicity of styles.*

multiply /'mʌltɪplaɪ/ **multiplies, multiplying, multiplied.** [1] VERB When something **multiplies**, or when you **multiply** it, it increases greatly in number or amount. *Her husband multiplied his demands on her time.* ♦ **multiplication** /,mʌltɪplɪ'keɪʃən/ N-UNCOUNT *...the multiplication of bacteria.* [2] VERB If you **multiply** one number **by** another, you calculate the total which you get when you add the number to itself as many times as is indicated by the second number. *Twenty-five multiplied by one point one two is twenty eight. ...the remarkable ability to multiply huge numbers.* ♦ **multiplication** N-UNCOUNT *...subtraction, multiplication and division.*

multitude /'mʌltɪtju:d, AM -tu:d/ **multitudes.** QUANT A **multitude of** things or people is a very large number of them. *There are a multitude of small quiet roads to cycle along.*

⭐ **mum** /mʌm/ **mums.** N-COUNT & N-VOC Your **mum** is your mother. [BRITISH, INFORMAL] *He misses his mum.*

mumble /'mʌmbəl/ **mumbles, mumbling, mumbled.** VERB & N-COUNT If you **mumble** something, or if you speak in a **mumble**, you speak very quietly and not clearly so that the words are difficult to understand. *He mumbled a few words.*

mummy /'mʌmi/ **mummies.** [1] N-COUNT & N-VOC Some people, especially children, call their mother **mummy**. [BRITISH, INFORMAL] [2] N-COUNT A **mummy** is a dead body which was preserved long ago by being rubbed with oils and wrapped in cloth.

munch /mʌntʃ/ **munches, munching, munched.** VERB To **munch** food means to chew it steadily and thoroughly. *Sheep were munching their way through a yellow carpet of leaves.*

mundane /,mʌn'deɪn/. ADJ Something that is

a
b
c
d
e
f
g
h
i
j
k
l
m
n
o
p
q
r
s
t
u
v
w
x
y
z

mundane is ordinary and not interesting. ...*the mundane realities of life.*

municipal /mjuː'nɪsɪpəl/. ADJ BEFORE N **Municipal** means associated with the local government of a city or town.

municipality /mjuː,nɪsɪ'pælɪti/ **municipalities.** N-COUNT A **municipality** is a city or town with its own local council and officials. You can also refer to that city or town's local government as **the municipality.** ...*public woodlands, belonging to the municipality.*

munitions /mjuː'nɪʃənz/. N-PLURAL **Munitions** are bombs, guns, and other military supplies.

mural /'mjʊərəl/ **murals.** N-COUNT A **mural** is a picture which is painted on a wall.

★ **murder** /'mɜːdə/ **murders, murdering, murdered.** **1** N-VAR **Murder** is the crime of deliberately killing a person. *He was jailed for life after being found guilty of murder... She was convicted of three murders.* **2** VERB To **murder** someone means to commit the crime of killing them deliberately. ◆ **murderer, murderers** N-COUNT ...*a notorious murderer.* **3** See note at **kill.**

murderous /'mɜːdərəs/. ADJ If you describe a person or their actions as **murderous**, you mean that they intend to kill someone or are likely to kill someone. *This murderous lunatic could kill them both.*

murky /'mɜːki/ **murkier, murkiest.** **1** ADJ A **murky** place or time of day is dark and rather unpleasant. ...*one murky November afternoon.* **2** ADJ **Murky** water is dark and dirty. **3** ADJ If you describe an activity or situation as **murky**, you suspect that it is dishonest. [BRITISH] ...*a murky conspiracy to keep them out of power.* **4** ADJ If you describe something as **murky**, you mean that it is difficult to understand. *The law here is a little bit murky.*

murmur /'mɜːmə/ **murmurs, murmuring, murmured.** **1** VERB & N-COUNT If you **murmur** something, or if you speak in a **murmur**, you speak very quietly, so that not many people can hear what you are saying. *He turned and murmured something to the professor... They spoke in low murmurs.* **2** N-SING A **murmur** is a continuous low sound, like the noise of a river or of distant voices. *I could hear the murmur of the sea.*

★ **muscle** /'mʌsəl/ **muscles, muscling, muscled.** **1** N-VAR Your **muscles** are the internal pieces of body tissue which connect your bones together, and which you expand and contract when you make a movement. *Exercise will tone up your stomach muscles.* **2** N-UNCOUNT If you say that someone has **muscle**, you mean that they have power and influence. *Eisenhower used his muscle to persuade Congress to change the law.* **3** PHRASE If a group, organization, or country **flexes** its **muscles**, it behaves in a way designed to show people that it has power and is considering using it.

▶ **muscle in.** PHR-VERB If someone **muscles in on** something, they force their way into a situation

where they have no right to be and where they are not welcome; used showing disapproval. *Cohen complained that Kravis was muscling in on his deal.*

muscular /'mʌskjʊlə/. **1** ADJ BEFORE N **Muscular** means involving or affecting your muscles. ...*muscular effort.* **2** ADJ A **muscular** person has strong, firm muscles. ...*his tanned muscular legs.*

muse /mjuːz/ **muses, musing, mused.** VERB If you **muse on** something, you think about it, usually saying or writing what you are thinking at the same time. [WRITTEN] *Many of the papers muse on the fate of the President... General George Patton once mused that Americans love a winner.* ◆ **musing, musings** N-COUNT *His musings were interrupted by Montagu.*

★ **museum** /mjuː'ziːəm/ **museums.** N-COUNT A **museum** is a public building where interesting and valuable objects are kept and displayed.

mushroom /'mʌʃruːm/ **mushrooms, mushrooming, mushroomed.** **1** N-VAR **Mushrooms** are fungi with short stems and round tops. You can eat some kinds of mushrooms. → See picture on page 836. ...*mushroom omelette.* **2** VERB If something **mushrooms**, it grows or appears very quickly. *A sleepy capital of a few hundred thousand people has mushroomed to a crowded city of 2 million.*

★ **music** /'mjuːzɪk/. **1** N-UNCOUNT **Music** is the pattern of sounds produced by people singing or playing instruments. ...*classical music.* **2** N-UNCOUNT **Music** is the symbols written on paper that represent musical sounds. *He's never been able to read music.*

★ **musical** /'mjuːzɪkəl/ **musicals.** **1** ADJ BEFORE N **Musical** describes things that are concerned with playing or studying music. ...*Stan Getz's musical career.* ◆ **musically** ADV *Musically there is a lot to enjoy.* **2** N-COUNT A **musical** is a play or film that uses singing and dancing in the story. **3** ADJ Someone who is **musical** has a natural ability in music. *My father was very musical.*

musical instrument, musical instruments. N-COUNT A **musical instrument** is an object such as a piano, guitar, or violin which you play in order to produce music. → See pictures on pages 827 and 828.

★ **musician** /mjuː'zɪʃən/ **musicians.** N-COUNT A **musician** is a person who plays a musical instrument as their job or hobby.

★ **Muslim** (or **Moslem**) /'mʊzlɪm/ **Muslims.** N-COUNT & ADJ A **Muslim** or a person who is **Muslim** is someone who believes in Islam and lives according to its rules.

muslin /'mʌzlɪn/. N-UNCOUNT **Muslin** is a very thin cotton cloth.

mussel /'mʌsəl/ **mussels.** N-COUNT A **mussel** is a kind of shellfish.

★ **must** /məst, STRONG mʌst/. **1** MODAL You use **must** to indicate that you think it is very important or necessary for something to happen. *What you wear should be stylish and clean, and* *must definitely fit well... The doctor must not allow the patient to be put at risk.* [2] MODAL You use **must** to express your firm intention to do something. *I must be getting back.* [3] MODAL You use **must** to make forceful suggestions or invitations. *You must see a doctor, Frederick... You must see the painting Paul has given me.* [4] MODAL You use **must** in questions to express your anger or irritation about something that someone has done. *Why must you do everything as if you have to win?* [5] PHRASE You say **'if you must'** when you know that you cannot stop someone doing something that you think is wrong, stupid, or annoying. *'Could I have a word?'—'Oh dear, if you must.'* [6] N-COUNT If something is a **must**, it is absolutely necessary. [INFORMAL] *A trip to this important religious monument is a must for all visitors.* [7] MODAL You use **must** to indicate that you are fairly sure that something is the case, often because of the available evidence. *At 29 Russell must be one of the youngest ever Wembley referees... He must have brought them home in order to continue his work.*

mustache /məˈstɑːʃ, AM ˈmʊstæʃ/. See **moustache**.

mustard /ˈmʌstəd/. N-UNCOUNT **Mustard** is a yellow or brown paste made from seeds which tastes spicy.

muster /ˈmʌstə/ **musters, mustering, mustered.** [1] VERB If you **muster** support, strength, or energy, you gather as much as you can in order to do something. *He travelled around West Africa trying to muster support for his movement.* [2] VERB When soldiers **muster** or **are mustered**, they gather in one place in order to take part in military action.

mustn't /ˈmʌsənt/. **Mustn't** is the usual spoken form of 'must not'.

must've /ˈmʌstəv/. **Must've** is a spoken form of 'must have', especially when 'have' is an auxiliary verb.

mutant /ˈmjuːtənt/ **mutants.** N-COUNT A **mutant** is an animal or plant that is physically different from others of the same species as the result of a change in its genetic structure.

mutate /mjuːˈteɪt, AM ˈmjuːteɪt/ **mutates, mutating, mutated.** VERB If an animal or plant **mutates**, or if something **mutates** it, it develops different characteristics as a result of a change in its genes. *HIV may have mutated into a new, as yet undetected virus.* ♦ **mutation, mutations** N-VAR *...accidental mutations of the genes.*

mute /mjuːt/ **mutes, muting, muted.** [1] ADJ Someone who is **mute** does not speak. *He was mute, distant, and indifferent.* [2] VERB If you **mute** a noise or sound, you make it quieter. ♦ **muted** ADJ *'Yes,' he muttered, his voice so muted I hardly heard his reply.* [3] VERB If someone **mutes** something such as their feelings or their activities, they reduce the strength or intensity of them. *The threat contrasted sharply with his*

previous muted criticism. ♦ **muted** ADJ *Reaction to the news was muted.*

mutilate /ˈmjuːtɪleɪt/ **mutilates, mutilating, mutilated.** VERB If a person or animal **is mutilated**, their body is damaged very severely, usually by someone who physically attacks them. ♦ **mutilation, mutilations** N-VAR *...cases of torture and mutilation.*

mutiny /ˈmjuːtɪni/ **mutinies.** N-VAR A **mutiny** is a rebellion by a group of people, usually soldiers or sailors, against a person in authority.

mutter /ˈmʌtə/ **mutters, muttering, muttered.** VERB & N-COUNT If you **mutter**, or if you speak in a **mutter**, you speak very quietly so that you cannot easily be heard, often because you are complaining about something. *She can hear the old woman muttering about consideration. ...a mutter of protest.* ♦ **muttering, mutterings** N-VAR *He heard muttering from the front of the crowd.*

mutton /ˈmʌtən/. N-UNCOUNT **Mutton** is meat from an adult sheep.

⭐ **mutual** /ˈmjuːtʃʊəl/. ADJ You use **mutual** to describe a situation, feeling, or action that is experienced, felt, or done by both of two people mentioned. *The East and the West can work together for their mutual benefit... It's plain that he adores his daughter, and the feeling is mutual.* ♦ **mutually** ADV *...a mutually convenient time.*

muzzle /ˈmʌzəl/ **muzzles, muzzling, muzzled.** [1] N-COUNT The **muzzle** of a gun is the end where the bullets come out when it is fired. [2] N-COUNT A **muzzle** is a device that is put over a dog's nose and mouth so that it cannot bite people or bark. [3] VERB If you **muzzle** a dog, you put a muzzle over its nose and mouth.

⭐ **my** /maɪ/. DET A speaker or writer uses **my** to indicate that something belongs or relates to himself or herself. *I invited him back to my flat... John's my best friend.*

myriad /ˈmɪriəd/ **myriads.** QUANT You can use **myriad** to refer to a very large number or great variety of people or things. *They face a myriad of problems bringing up children. ...the myriad other tasks we are trying to perform in the world. ...these myriads of fish.*

⭐ **myself** /maɪˈself/. [1] PRON A speaker or writer uses **myself** to refer to himself or herself. **Myself** is used as the object of a verb or preposition when the subject refers to the same person. *I asked myself what I would have done... I looked at myself in the mirror.* [2] PRON You use **myself** to emphasize a first person singular subject. Some speakers use **myself** instead of 'me' as the object of a verb or preposition. *I myself enjoy cinema. ...a complete beginner like myself.* [3] PRON If you say something such as 'I did it **myself**', you are emphasizing that you did it, rather than anyone else.

mysterious /mɪˈstɪəriəs/. [1] ADJ Someone or something that is **mysterious** is strange, not known about, or not understood. *He died in mysterious circumstances. ...a mysterious illness.*

a
b
c
d
e
f
g
h
i
j
k
l
m
n
o
p
q
r
s
t
u
v
w
x
y
z

A

♦ **mysteriously** ADV *A couple of messages had mysteriously disappeared.* [2] ADJ AFTER LINK-V If someone is **mysterious about** something, they deliberately do not talk about it, often because they want people to be curious about it. *As for his job—well, he was very mysterious about it.* ♦ **mysteriously** ADV *Asked what she meant, she said mysteriously: 'Work it out for yourself'.*

⭐ **mystery** /ˈmɪstəri/ **mysteries.** [1] N-COUNT A **mystery** is something that is not understood or known about. *The source of the gunshots still remains a mystery.* [2] N-UNCOUNT If you talk about the **mystery** of someone or something, you are talking about how difficult they are to understand or to know about. *She's a lady of mystery... It is an elaborate ceremony, shrouded in mystery.* [3] ADJ BEFORE N A **mystery** person or thing is one whose identity or nature is not known. *A mystery buyer purchased 1.5 million MGN shares.* [4] N-COUNT A **mystery** is a story in which strange things happen that are not explained until the end.

mystic /ˈmɪstɪk/ **mystics.** [1] N-COUNT A **mystic** is a person who believes in religious practices in which people search for truth, knowledge, and unity with God through meditation and prayer. ♦ **mysticism** /ˈmɪstɪsɪzəm/ N-UNCOUNT *...a mixture of mysticism and Roman Catholicism.* [2] ADJ BEFORE N **Mystic** means the same as **mystical.** *...mystic union with God.*

mystical /ˈmɪstɪkəl/. ADJ Something that is **mystical** involves spiritual powers and influences that most people do not understand. *That was clearly a deep mystical experience.*

mystify /ˈmɪstɪfaɪ/ **mystifies, mystifying, mystified.** VERB If you **are mystified** by something, you find it impossible to explain or understand. *There was something strange in her attitude which mystified me.* ♦ **mystifying** ADJ *I find your attitude a little mystifying.*

mystique /mɪˈstiːk/. N-UNCOUNT **Mystique** is an atmosphere of mystery and secrecy which is associated with a particular person or thing. *...the mystique that surrounds fine art.*

⭐ **myth** /mɪθ/ **myths.** [1] N-VAR A **myth** is a well-known story which was made up in the past to explain natural events or to justify religious beliefs or social customs. *...a famous Greek myth.* ♦ **mythical** ADJ *...the Hydra, the mythical beast that had seven or more heads.* [2] N-VAR If you describe a belief or explanation as a **myth**, you mean that many people believe it but it is actually untrue. *Contrary to the popular myth, women are not reckless spendthrifts.*

mythical /ˈmɪθɪkəl/. ADJ If you describe something as **mythical**, you think it is untrue or does not exist. *...the mythical, romanticized West of cowboys.*

mythology /mɪˈθɒlədʒi/. N-UNCOUNT **Mythology** is a group of myths, especially those from a particular country, religion, or culture. *...Greek mythology.* ♦ **mythological** ADJ *...the mythological beast that was part lion and part goat.*

N n

nag /næg/ **nags, nagging, nagged.** [1] VERB If you say that someone **is nagging** you, you are annoyed with them because they are continuously asking you to do something. *My girlfriend nagged me to cut my hair.* ♦ **nagging** N-UNCOUNT *Her endless nagging drove him away from home.* [2] VERB If something such as a doubt or worry **nags at** you, or **nags** you, it keeps worrying you. *...the anxiety that had nagged Amy all through lunch.*

nail /neɪl/ **nails, nailing, nailed.** [1] N-COUNT A **nail** is a thin piece of metal with one pointed end and one flat end. You hit the flat end with a hammer in order to push the nail into something such as a wall. → See picture on page 833. [2] VERB If you **nail** something somewhere, you fix it there using one or more nails. *The windows were all nailed shut.* [3] N-COUNT Your **nails** are the thin hard parts that grow at the ends of your fingers and toes. → See picture on page 823.

nail down. [1] PHR-VERB If you **nail down** something unknown or uncertain, you find out exactly what it is. *It would be useful if you could nail down the source of this tension.* [2] PHR-VERB If you **nail down** an agreement, you manage to reach a firm agreement with a definite result.

naive (or **naïve**) /naɪˈiːv, AM nɑːˈ-/. ADJ If you describe someone as **naive**, you think they lack experience, causing them to expect things to be uncomplicated or easy, or people to be honest or kind when they are not. *I must have been naive to think we would get my parents' blessing.* ♦ **naively** ADV *...naively applying Western solutions to Eastern problems.* ♦ **naivety** /naɪˈiːvɪti/ N-UNCOUNT *I was alarmed by his naivety and ignorance of international affairs.*

naked /ˈneɪkɪd/. [1] ADJ Someone who is **naked** is not wearing any clothes. *Her naked body was found wrapped in a sheet.* ♦ **nakedness** N-UNCOUNT *He had pulled the blanket over his body to hide his nakedness.* [2] ADJ You can describe an object as **naked** when it does not have its normal covering. *...a naked light bulb.* [3] ADJ BEFORE N **Naked** emotions are easily recognized because they are very strongly felt. [WRITTEN] *...the naked hatred in the woman's face.* ♦ **nakedly** ADV *...showing her fear so nakedly.* [4] PHRASE If you say that something cannot be seen by **the naked eye**, you mean that it cannot be seen without the help of equipment such as a telescope or microscope.

name/neɪm/**names, naming, named.** [1] N-COUNT The **name** of a person, thing, or place is the word or words that you use to identify them. *His name is Michael... They changed the name of the street.* [2] VERB When you **name** someone or something, you give them a name. If you **name** someone or something **after** a person or thing, you give them the same name as that person or thing. *My mother insisted on naming me Horace... Why have you not named any of your sons after yourself?* [3] VERB If you **name** someone, you identify them by stating their name. *One of the victims of the weekend's snowstorm has been named as twenty-year-old John Barr.* [4] N-COUNT You can refer to the reputation of a person or thing as their **name**. *He had a name for good judgement... She's never done anything to give jazz a bad name.* [5] See also **brand name, Christian name.**

PHRASES ● You can use **by name**, or **by the name of**, when you are saying what someone is called. *This guy, Jack Smith, does he go by the name of Jackal?* ● If someone **calls** you **names**, they insult you by saying unpleasant things to you or about you. *They had called her rude names.* ● If something is **in** your **name**, it officially belongs to you or has been reserved for you. *A double room had been reserved for him in the name of Muller.* ● If you do something **in the name of** an ideal or a person, you do it because you believe in or represent that ideal or person. *...the things people did in the name of business.* ● If you **make a name for** yourself or **make** your **name** as something, you become well-known for that thing. *She was beginning to make a name for herself as a portrait photographer.* ● If you say that something is **the name of the game**, you mean that it is the most important aspect of a situation. [INFORMAL] *Family values are suddenly the name of the game.* ● If something such as a newspaper or an official body **names and shames** people who have performed badly or who have done something wrong, it identifies those people by name. *The government will also name and shame the worst performing airlines.*

namely/ˈneɪmli/. ADV You use **namely** to introduce more detailed information about what you have just said. *One group of people seems to be forgotten, namely pensioners.*

nanny/ˈnæni/**nannies.** N-COUNT A **nanny** is a woman who is paid by parents to look after their children.

nap/næp/**naps, napping, napped.** VERB & N-COUNT If you **nap**, or if you have a **nap**, you sleep for a short period of time, usually during the day.

napkin/ˈnæpkɪn/**napkins.** N-COUNT A **napkin** is a small piece of cloth or paper used to protect your clothes when you are eating.

nappy/ˈnæpi/**nappies.** N-COUNT In British English, a **nappy** is a piece of thick cloth or paper which is fastened round a baby's bottom in order to soak up its urine and faeces. The usual American word is **diaper.**

narcotic/nɑːˈkɒtɪk/**narcotics.** N-COUNT & ADJ **Narcotics**, or **narcotic** drugs, are drugs such as

opium or heroin which make you sleepy and stop you feeling pain, but are also addictive.

narrate/nəˈreɪt, AM ˈnæreɪt/**narrates, narrating, narrated.** VERB If you **narrate** a story, you tell it. [FORMAL] *The book is narrated by Richard Papen.* ◆ **narration** N-UNCOUNT *...its story-within-a-story method of narration.* ◆ **narrator, narrators** N-COUNT *The story's narrator is an actress in her late thirties.*

narrative/ˈnærətɪv/**narratives.** N-COUNT A **narrative** is a story or an account of events.

★ **narrow**/ˈnærəʊ/**narrower, narrowest; narrows, narrowing, narrowed.** [1] ADJ Something that is **narrow** measures a very small distance from one side to the other, especially compared to its length or height. *...the town's narrow streets... She had long, narrow feet.* ◆ **narrowness** N-UNCOUNT *...the narrowness of the river mouth.* [2] VERB If something **narrows**, it becomes less wide. *The wide track narrows before crossing another stream.* [3] ADJ If you describe someone's ideas, attitudes, or beliefs as **narrow**, you disapprove of them because they are not imaginative but are old-fashioned or very strict, and often ignore the more important aspects of a situation. *...a narrow and outdated view of family life.* ◆ **narrowness** N-UNCOUNT *...the narrowness of their mental and spiritual outlook.* [4] VERB If something **narrows**, or if you **narrow** it, its extent, range, or scope becomes smaller. *The European Union and America had narrowed their differences over farm subsidies.* ◆ **narrowing** N-UNCOUNT *...a narrowing of the gap between rich members and poor.* [5] ADJ If you have a **narrow** victory, you succeed in winning but only by a small amount. *Delegates have voted by a narrow majority in favour of considering electoral reform.* ◆ **narrowly** ADV *She narrowly failed to win enough votes.* [6] ADJ BEFORE N If you have a **narrow** escape, something unpleasant nearly happens to you. ◆ **narrowly** ADV *Five firemen narrowly escaped death.*

▶ **narrow down.** PHR-VERB If you **narrow down** a range of things, you reduce the number of things included in it. *I've managed to narrow the list down to twenty-three.*

nasal/ˈneɪzəl/. [1] ADJ If someone's voice is **nasal**, it sounds as if air is passing through their nose as well as their mouth while they are speaking. *She talked in a deep nasal monotone.* [2] ADJ BEFORE N **Nasal** is used to describe things relating to the nose. *...inflamed nasal passages.*

nasty/ˈnɑːsti, ˈnæsti/**nastier, nastiest.** [1] ADJ Something that is **nasty** is very unpleasant or unattractive. *This divorce could turn nasty.* ◆ **nastiness** N-UNCOUNT *...the nastiness of war.* [2] ADJ A **nasty** problem or question is a difficult one. *This firm action had defused a very nasty situation.* [3] ADJ If you describe a disease or injury as **nasty**, you mean that it is serious or looks very unpleasant. *Lili had a nasty chest infection.* [4] ADJ If you describe a person or their behaviour as **nasty**, you mean that they behave in an unkind and unpleasant way. *The guards looked really*

a
b
c
d
e
f
g
h
i
j
k
l
m
n
o
p
q
r
s
t
u
v
w
x
y
z

nasty... *She is so nasty to me.* ✦ **nastily** ADV *She took the money and eyed me nastily.*

⭐ **nation** /'neɪʃən/ **nations.** N-COUNT A **nation** is an individual country, especially when it is considered from the point of view of its cultural or ethnic identity. *...the Arab nations of the Gulf.* ● See note at **country**.

⭐ **national** /'næʃənəl/ **nationals.** 1 ADJ **National** means relating to the whole of a country, rather than to part of it or to other nations. *...national and local elections. ...major national and international issues.* ✦ **nationally** ADV *...a nationally televised speech.* 2 ADJ BEFORE N **National** means typical of the people or customs of a particular country or nation. *Baseball is the national pastime.* 3 N-COUNT A **national** of a country is a citizen of that country who is staying in a different country. *...a Sri Lankan-born British national.*

,**national 'anthem, national anthems.** N-COUNT A **national anthem** is a nation's official song.

nationalise /'næʃənəlaɪz/. See **nationalize**.

⭐ **nationalist** /'næʃənəlɪst/ **nationalists.** 1 ADJ BEFORE N & N-COUNT **Nationalist** ideas or movements are connected with attempts to obtain political independence for a particular group of people. A **nationalist** is a person with nationalist beliefs. *The crisis has set off a wave of nationalist feelings in Quebec.* ✦ **nationalism** N-UNCOUNT *...the rising tide of nationalism.* 2 ADJ BEFORE N & N-COUNT **Nationalist** is used when describing people's great love for their nation, or their belief that their nation is better than others. A **nationalist** is someone with nationalist views. *Political life has been infected by growing nationalist sentiment.* ✦ **nationalistic** ADJ *There is still a lot of nationalistic pride in being the best in the country.* ✦ **nationalism** N-UNCOUNT *...this kind of fierce nationalism.*

nationality /,næʃə'næliti/ **nationalities.** N-VAR If you have the **nationality** of a particular country, you have the legal right to be a citizen of it. *Asked his nationality, he said British.*

nationalize (BRIT also **nationalise**) /'næʃənəlaɪz/ **nationalizes, nationalizing, nationalized.** VERB If a government **nationalizes** a private industry, that industry becomes owned by the state and controlled by the government. *The coffee industry was nationalised at the time of independence.* ✦ **nationalization, nationalizations** N-VAR *...the nationalization of the coal mines.*

,**national 'park, national parks.** N-COUNT A **national park** is a large area of natural land protected by the government because of its natural beauty, plants, or animals.

nationwide /,neɪʃən'waɪd/. ADJ & ADV **Nationwide** activities or situations happen or exist in all parts of a country. You can say they happen or exist **nationwide**. *The rising number of car crimes is a nationwide problem. ...available from department stores nationwide.*

⭐ **native** /'neɪtɪv/ **natives.** 1 ADJ BEFORE N Your **native** country or area is the country or area where you were born and brought up. *Mother Teresa visited her native Albania.* 2 N-COUNT & ADJ A **native** of a particular country or region, or a person who is **native to** that country or region, is a person who was born there. *Dr Aubin is a native of St Blaise. ...men and women native to countries such as Japan.* 3 ADJ BEFORE N Your **native** language or tongue is the first language that you learned to speak when you were a child. 4 N-COUNT & ADJ Animals or plants that are **natives** of a region, or are **native to** it, grow there naturally and have not been introduced there. *The coconut palm is a native of Malaysia... Many of the plants are native to Brazil.*

⭐ **natural** /'nætʃərəl/ **naturals.** 1 ADJ If you say that it is **natural** for someone to act in a particular way, you mean that it is reasonable in the circumstances. *It is only natural for youngsters to crave excitement... Grief is a perfectly natural response.* 2 ADJ If someone's behaviour is **natural**, they are relaxed and do not appear to be hiding anything or pretending to be something they are not. ✦ **naturally** ADV *You can talk quite naturally to her.* ✦ **naturalness** N-UNCOUNT *...the naturalness of the acting.* 3 ADJ **Natural** behaviour or ability is instinctive and has not been learned. *...the insect's natural instinct to feed... Martin was a natural communicator.* ✦ **naturally** ADV *Some children are naturally more timid than others.* 4 N-COUNT If you describe someone as a **natural**, you mean that they do something very well and very easily. *He's a natural with any kind of engine.* 5 ADJ BEFORE N **Natural** things exist in nature and were not created by people. *...a natural disaster like an earthquake. ...the gigantic natural harbour of Poole.* ✦ **naturally** ADV *Nitrates are chemicals that occur naturally in water.*

naturalist /'nætʃərəlɪst/ **naturalists.** N-COUNT A **naturalist** is a person who studies plants, animals, and other living things.

⭐ **naturally** /'nætʃərəli/. 1 ADV You use **naturally** to indicate that something is obvious and not surprising. *He will never play again. Naturally he is devastated.* 2 ADV If one thing develops **naturally** from another, it develops as a normal result of it. *A study of yoga leads naturally to meditation.* 3 PHRASE If a skill or quality **comes naturally to** you, you have it instinctively, without having to work very hard to get it. *Ambition and self-confidence came naturally to Sergei.*

,**natural re'sources.** N-PLURAL The **natural resources** of a place are all its land, forests, energy sources, and minerals which exist naturally there and can be used by people. *...a country rich in natural resources.*

⭐ **nature** /'neɪtʃə/ **natures.** 1 N-UNCOUNT **Nature** refers to all the animals, plants, and other things in the world that are not made by people, and all the events and processes that are not caused by people. ...*grasses that grow wild in nature.* ...*the ecological balance of nature.*

> **USAGE** Do not confuse **nature**, **landscape**, **scenery**, and **countryside**. **Nature** includes the landscape, the weather, animals, and plants. *These creatures roamed the Earth as the finest and rarest wonders of nature.* With **landscape**, the emphasis is on the physical features of the land, while **scenery** includes everything you can see when you look out over an area of land, usually in the country. ...*the landscape of steep woods and distant mountains.* ...*unattractive urban scenery.* **Countryside** is land which is away from towns and cities. ...*3,500 acres of mostly flat countryside.*

[2] N-UNCOUNT The **nature** of something is its basic quality or character. ...*the ambitious nature of the programme... The protests had been non-political by nature.* [3] N-COUNT Someone's **nature** is their character, which they show by their behaviour. *Her ambitious nature made him unsuitable for an arranged marriage... He was by nature affectionate.*
PHRASES ● If you say that something has a particular characteristic **by** its **nature** or **by** its **very nature**, you mean that things of that type always have that characteristic. *Youth is by its very nature rebellious.* ● If a way of behaving is **second nature to** you, you do it almost without thinking because it is easy or obvious to you. *Secrecy is second nature to these people.*

naughty /'nɔːti/. [1] ADJ You say that small children are **naughty** when they behave badly. *Girls, you're being very naughty.* [2] ADJ **Naughty** books, pictures, or words are slightly rude or relate to sex. ...*naughty magazines.*

nausea /'nɔːziə/. N-UNCOUNT **Nausea** is a feeling of sickness and dizziness. *I was overcome with a feeling of nausea.*

nautical /'nɔːtɪkəl/. ADJ **Nautical** things and people are involved with ships. ...*a nautical chart of the region.*

⭐ **naval** /'neɪvəl/. ADJ BEFORE N **Naval** people and things belong to a country's navy. ...*the US naval base at Guantanamo Bay.*

navel /'neɪvəl/ **navels.** N-COUNT Your **navel** is the small hollow just below your waist at the front of your body.

navigate /'nævɪgeɪt/ **navigates, navigating, navigated.** [1] VERB When someone **navigates** an area, or when they **navigate**, they steer a ship or plane through the area towards a particular destination. *Every year they navigate the Greek and Turkish islands in a sailing boat.*
♦ **navigation** N-UNCOUNT *The expedition was wrecked by bad planning and poor navigation.*
♦ **navigator, navigators** N-COUNT *He became an*

RAF navigator during the war.* [2] VERB If a passenger in a car **navigates**, he or she tells the driver, often using a road map, what roads the car should be driven along in order to get somewhere. *You drive. I'll navigate.* [3] VERB If you **navigate** your way somewhere, you go there with difficulty, because the route is complicated or there are obstacles. *He attempted to navigate his way through the crowds.*

⭐ **navy** /'neɪvi/ **navies.** [1] N-COUNT A country's **navy** is the part of its armed forces that fights at sea. *Her own son was also in the Navy.* [2] ADJ & N-UNCOUNT **Navy** or **navy blue** is very dark blue.

NB /ˌen 'biː/. You write **NB** to draw someone's attention to what you are going to write next. *NB: A small charge will be made.*

⭐ **near** /nɪə/ **nearer, nearest; nears, nearing, neared.** [1] PREP & ADV If something is **near** a place or thing or **near to** it, it is a short distance from it. ...*a farmhouse near the cottage... He crouched as near to the door as he could... He collapsed into the nearest chair.* [2] ADV & PREP & ADJ If you are **near to** a particular state or **near** it, you have almost reached it. *The repairs to the Hafner machine were near to completion... He was near tears... She was believed to have died in near poverty.* [3] ADV & PREP If two things are similar, you can say that they are **near to** each other or **near** each other. ...*a sickening sensation that was near to nausea... The legal profession is the nearest thing to a recession-proof industry... Her feelings were nearer hatred than love.* [4] PREP & ADV If something happens **near** a particular time or **near to** it, it happens just before or just after that time. *I'll tell you nearer the day... The announcement, so near to Christmas, had come as a shock.* [5] ADV If a time or event is **near**, it will happen very soon. *The time for my departure from Japan was drawing nearer.* [6] VERB If someone or something **is nearing** a particular place, stage, or point in time, they will soon reach it. *As he neared the stable, he slowed the horse... His age was hard to guess – he must have been nearing fifty.* [7] PREP & ADV You use **near** to say that something is a little more or less than an amount or number stated. ...*the pound, which ended last year near its annual low.* ...*the near 5 per cent fall in the exchange rate.*
PHRASES ● If something is **near enough** a quantity or **near enough** true, it is almost that quantity or almost true. *I've been working at it now for near enough an hour.* ● You use **nowhere near** and **not anywhere near** to emphasize that something is not the case. *They are nowhere near good enough.* ● **in the near future:** see **future.**

⭐ **nearby** /ˌnɪə'baɪ/. ADV & ADJ If something is **nearby**, it is only a short distance away. ...*someone who lived nearby.* ...*a nearby table.*

⭐ **nearly** /'nɪəli/. [1] ADV If something is **nearly** a quantity, it is very close to that quantity but slightly less than it. If something is **nearly** a certain state, it is very close to that state but has not quite reached it. *Goldsworth stared at me in silence for nearly twenty seconds... It was already* nearly eight o'clock... I've nearly finished. [2] PHRASE You use **not nearly** to emphasize that something is not the case. For example, if something is **not nearly** big enough, it is much too small. Father's flat in Paris wasn't nearly as grand as this.

⭐ **neat**/niːt/ **neater, neatest.** [1] ADJ A **neat** place, thing, or person is tidy, smart, and orderly. She undressed and put her wet clothes in a neat pile.
♦ **neatly**ADV He folded his paper neatly.
♦ **neatness**N-UNCOUNT ...the crisp neatness of her appearance. [2] ADJ A **neat** explanation or method is clever and convenient. It had been such a neat, clever plan. ♦ **neatly**ADV Real people do not fit neatly into these categories. ♦ **neatness** N-UNCOUNT ...the extreme neatness of his conclusions. [3] ADJ If you drink an alcoholic drink **neat**, you drink it without anything added. ...neat whisky.

⭐ **necessarily**/ˌnesɪˈserɪli, -srɪli/. [1] ADV If you say that something is **not necessarily** true, you mean that it may not be true or is not always true. Women do not necessarily have to imitate men to be successful... 'He was lying, of course.'—'Not necessarily.' [2] ADV If you say that something **necessarily** happens, you mean that it has to happen and cannot be any different. Business relationships are necessarily a bit more formal.

⭐ **necessary**/ˈnesɪsəri/. [1] ADJ Something that is **necessary** is needed to get a particular result or effect. It might be necessary to leave fast... We will do whatever is necessary... The army needs men who are willing to fight, when necessary. [2] ADJ BEFORE N A **necessary** consequence or connection must happen or exist, because of the nature of the things or events involved. Wastage was no doubt a necessary consequence of war.

necessitate/nɪˈsesɪteɪt/ **necessitates, necessitating, necessitated.** VERB If something **necessitates** a particular course of action, it makes it necessary. [FORMAL] ...a letter to the Pope, which necessitates careful phrasing.

necessity/nɪˈsesɪti/ **necessities.** [1] N-UNCOUNT **Necessity** is the need to do something. He'd learned the necessity of hiding his feelings... Most women, like men, work from economic necessity. [2] PHRASE If something is **of necessity** true, it is true because nothing else is possible or imaginable in the circumstances. [3] N-COUNT **Necessities** are things that you must have to live. Water is a basic necessity of life.

⭐ **neck**/nek/ **necks.** [1] N-COUNT Your **neck** is the part of your body which joins your head to the rest of your body. → See picture on page 822. She threw her arms round his neck and hugged him. [2] N-COUNT The **neck** of a dress or shirt is the part which is round your neck or just below it. [3] N-COUNT The **neck** of something such as a bottle or a guitar is the long narrow part at one end of it. [4] PHRASE If two or more competitors are **neck and neck**, they are level with each other and have an equal chance of winning. [5] a **pain in the neck**: see **pain**.

necklace/ˈneklɪs/ **necklaces.** N-COUNT A **necklace**

is a piece of jewellery such as a chain or string of beads, which someone wears round their neck.

nectarine/ˈnektəriːn, -rɪn/ **nectarines.** N-COUNT A **nectarine** is a fruit similar to a peach with a smooth skin. → See picture on page 821.

née/neɪ/. **née** is used before a name to indicate that it was a woman's surname before she got married. [FORMAL] ...Nicola Lewis (née May).

⭐ **need**/niːd/ **needs, needing, needed.** [1] VERB If you **need** something, or **need to** do something, you cannot successfully achieve what you want or live properly without it. He desperately needed money... I need to make a phone call... I need you to do something for me... I need you here, Wally. [2] N-COUNT If you have a **need to** do or have something, you cannot successfully achieve what you want without it. Charles has never felt the need to compete. ...his need for attention. [3] VERB If an object or place **needs** something doing to it, that action must or should be done to improve the object or place, or to improve a situation. If a task **needs** doing, it must or should be done to improve a situation. The building needs quite a few repairs... The flavour sometimes needs to be disguised. [4] N-SING If there is a **need for** something, that thing would improve a situation. There is a need for other similar schools. [5] MODAL & VERB If you say that someone **needn't** do something, or that they **don't need to** do it, you are telling them not to do it, or advising or suggesting that they should not do it. Look, you needn't shout... She need not know I'm here... Come along, Mother, we don't need to take up any more of Mr Kemp's time. [6] MODAL & VERB If you **needn't** have done something, or if they **didn't need to** do it, it was not necessary or useful for them to do it, although they did it. I was a little nervous when I announced my engagement to Grace, but I needn't have worried... You didn't need to give me any more money you know.

PHRASES ● If you say that you will do something, especially an extreme action, **if need be**, or **if needs be**, you mean that you will do it if it is necessary. We can survive down here for three months, if need be. ● People **in need** do not have enough of essential things such as money, food, or good health. When both of you were in need, I was the one who loaned you money. ● If someone or something is **in need of** something, they need it or ought to have it. I was all right but in need of rest.

needle/ˈniːdəl/ **needles, needling, needled.** [1] N-COUNT A **needle** is a small very thin piece of metal with a hole at one end and a sharp point at the other, which is used for sewing. [2] N-COUNT Knitting **needles** are thin metal or plastic sticks that are used for knitting. [3] N-COUNT The **needle** on a record player is the small pointed instrument that touches the record and picks up the sound signals. [4] N-COUNT A **needle** is a thin hollow metal rod with a sharp point, which forms part of a syringe. It is used to give injections. [5] N-COUNT On an instrument measuring speed, weight, or electricity, the **needle** is the thin piece of metal or plastic which moves backwards and forwards and shows the measurement. **6** N-COUNT The **needles** of a fir or pine tree are its thin pointed leaves. **7** VERB If someone **needles** you, they annoy you by criticizing you repeatedly. He had needled Jerrold, which might be unwise.

needless /'niːdləs/. **1** ADJ Something that is **needless** is completely unnecessary. His death was so needless. ◆ **needlessly** ADV A lot of women suffer needlessly. **2** PHRASE You say **needless to say** to emphasize that what you are saying is obvious. Needless to say, I am thrilled.

needn't /'niːdənt/. **Needn't** is the usual spoken form of 'need not'.

needy /'niːdi/**needier, neediest.** ADJ & N-PLURAL **Needy** people do not have enough food, medicine, or clothing or an adequate house to live in. The **needy** are people who are needy....housing for needy families. ...raising funds for the needy.

negate /nɪ'geɪt/**negates, negating, negated.** VERB If one thing **negates** another, it causes that other thing to lose the effect or value that it had. [FORMAL] An incorrect diet may negate the effects of training.

⭐ **negative** /'negətɪv/**negatives.** **1** ADJ A fact, situation, or experience that is **negative** is unpleasant, depressing, or harmful. The news is not all negative. ...the negative effect of persistent job insecurity. **2** ADJ A **negative** reply or decision indicates the answer 'no'. The question invites a negative response. ◆ **negatively** ADV 60 percent of the sample answered negatively. **3** ADJ If someone is **negative**, they consider only the bad aspects of a situation, rather than the good ones. ...the public's overall negative view of the Government's economic policies. ◆ **negatively** ADV Why do so many people think negatively? ◆ **negativity** N-UNCOUNT She has been accused of negativity. **4** N-COUNT A **negative** is a word, expression, or gesture that means 'no' or 'not'. He uses five negatives in fifty-three words. **5** ADJ If a medical test or scientific test is **negative**, it shows that something has not happened or is not present. The results were negative. **6** N-COUNT A **negative** is the image that is first produced when you take a photograph. **7** ADJ A **negative** number is less than zero.

neglect /nɪ'glekt/**neglects, neglecting, neglected.** **1** VERB & N-UNCOUNT If you **neglect** someone or something, you do not look after them properly. **Neglect** is failure to look after someone or something properly. Don't neglect your health... The house had suffered years of neglect. ◆ **neglected** ADJ ...neglected children. **2** VERB If you **neglect to** do something, you fail to do it. He had neglected to give her his telephone number... They never neglect their duties.

negligent /'neglɪdʒənt/. ADJ When someone is **negligent**, they fail to do something that they should do. The doctors have denied they were negligent. ◆ **negligently** ADV ...a claim that they have acted negligently. ◆ **negligence** N-UNCOUNT They accuse the airline of negligence.

negligible /'neglɪdʒɪbəl/. ADJ Something that is **negligible** is so small or unimportant that it is not worth considering. The risks are negligible.

negotiable /nɪ'gəʊʃəbəl/. ADJ Something that is **negotiable** can be changed or agreed by means of discussion. The fee is negotiable.

⭐ **negotiate** /nɪ'gəʊʃieɪt/**negotiates, negotiating, negotiated.** **1** VERB If one person or group **negotiates with** another, they talk about a problem or a situation such as a business arrangement in order to solve the problem or complete the arrangement. You can also say that two people or groups **negotiate**. It is not clear whether the president is willing to negotiate with the Democrats... The local government and the army negotiated a truce... His publishing house had just begun negotiating for her next books. ◆ **negotiator**, **negotiators** N-COUNT ...Japanese trade negotiators. **2** VERB If you **negotiate** a place or an obstacle, you successfully travel across it or around it. I negotiated my way out of the airport.

ne'gotiating table. N-SING If you say that people are **at the negotiating table**, you mean that they are having discussions in order to settle a dispute or reach an agreement.

⭐ **negotiation** /nɪ,gəʊʃi'eɪʃən/**negotiations.** N-VAR **Negotiations** are discussions that take place between people with different interests, in which they try to reach an agreement. Four years of negotiation ended fruitlessly.

Negro /'niːgrəʊ/**Negroes.** N-COUNT A **Negro** is someone with dark skin who comes from Africa or whose ancestors came from Africa. Many people find this word offensive.

⭐ **neighbour** (AM**neighbor**) /'neɪbə/**neighbours.** **1** N-COUNT Your **neighbours** are the people who live near you, especially the people who live in the house or flat which is next to yours. **2** N-COUNT Your **neighbour** is the person who is standing or sitting next to you. The woman prodded her neighbour. **3** N-COUNT You can refer to something which is near or next to something else of the same kind as its **neighbour**. Consider the shape and colour of each plant in relation to its neighbours.

neighbourhood (AM**neighborhood**) /'neɪbəhʊd/**neighbourhoods.** N-COUNT A **neighbourhood** is one of the parts of a town where people live. Margaret no longer takes evening strolls around her neighbourhood.

neighbouring (AM**neighboring**) /'neɪbərɪŋ/. ADJ BEFORE N **Neighbouring** describes the places and things that are near to the place or thing that you are talking about. ...Thailand and its neighbouring countries.

⭐ **neither** /'naɪðə, 'niːðə/. **1** CONJ You use **neither** in front of the first of two or more words or expressions when you are linking two or more things which are not true or do not happen. The other thing, or the last of the other things, is introduced by 'nor'. Professor Hisamatsu spoke neither English nor German... The play is neither as

a
b
c
d
e
f
g
h
i
j
k
l
m
n
o
p
q
r
s
t
u
v
w
x
y
z

A

funny nor as disturbing as Tabori thinks it is.
2 DET & PRON You use **neither** to refer to each of
two things or people, when you are making a
negative statement that includes both of *At first,
neither man could speak... Neither of us felt like
going out... Neither seemed likely to be aware of
my absence for long.* **3** CONJ If you say that one
person or thing does not do something and
neither does another, what you say is true of all
the people or things that you are mentioning. *I
never learned to swim and neither did they.*

neon /ˈniːɒn/. **1** N-UNCOUNT **Neon** is a gas
which exists in very small amounts in the
atmosphere. **2** ADJ **Neon** lights or signs are
made from glass tubes filled with neon gas which
produce a bright electric light.

nephew /ˈnefjuː, ˈnev-/ **nephews**. N-COUNT Your
nephew is the son of your sister or brother.

★ **nerve** /nɜːv/ **nerves. 1** N-COUNT **Nerves** are long
thin fibres that transmit messages between your
brain and other parts of your body. **2** N-PLURAL If
you talk about someone's **nerves**, you mean their
ability to remain calm and not become worried in
a stressful situation. *Jill's nerves are stretched to
breaking point.* **3** N-PLURAL You can refer to
someone's feelings of anxiety or tension as
nerves. *I don't suffer from nerves.* **4** N-UNCOUNT
Nerve is the courage you need to do something
difficult or dangerous. *He never got up enough
nerve to meet me.*
PHRASES ● If someone or something **gets on**
your **nerves**, they annoy or irritate you. [INFORMAL]
● If you say that someone **had a nerve** or **had
the nerve** to do something, you mean that they
made you angry by doing something rude or
lacking in respect. [INFORMAL] *He had the nerve to
ask me to prove who I was.*

★ **nervous** /ˈnɜːvəs/. **1** ADJ If you are **nervous**,
you are worried and frightened, and show this in
your behaviour. *It has made me very nervous
about going out.* ♦ **nervously** ADV *Joe giggled
nervously.* ♦ **nervousness** N-UNCOUNT *I smiled
warmly so he wouldn't see my nervousness.* **2** ADJ
A **nervous** person is very tense and easily upset.
3 ADJ BEFORE N A **nervous** illness or condition is
one that affects your mental state.

nervous 'breakdown, nervous breakdowns.
N-COUNT If someone has a **nervous breakdown**,
they become extremely depressed and anxious,
and have to be treated by a psychiatrist.

'nervous system, nervous systems. N-COUNT Your
nervous system is all the nerves in your body
together with your brain and spinal cord, which
control your movements and feelings.

nest /nest/ **nests, nesting, nested. 1** N-COUNT A **nest**
is a place that birds, insects and other animals
make to lay eggs in or give birth to their young
in. *...a wasps' nest.* **2** VERB When a bird **nests**
somewhere, it builds a nest and settles there to
lay its eggs. *Owls nested in the trees.*

nestle /ˈnesəl/ **nestles, nestling, nestled. 1** VERB If
you **nestle** somewhere, you move into a

comfortable position, often by pressing against
someone or something soft. *The two little girls
nestled against their mother.* **2** VERB If a building,
place, or thing **nestles** somewhere, it is in that
place or position and seems safe or sheltered. *The
house nestles in 40 acres of parkland.*

★ **net** /net/ **nets, netting, netted.**

✔ Net is also spelled **nett** in British English for
meanings 5 and 6.

1 N-UNCOUNT **Net** is a kind of material made of
threads, strings, or wires woven together so that
there are small equal spaces between them. *...net
curtains.* **2** N-COUNT A **net** is a piece of net which
you use, for example, to protect something or to
catch fish. *...a fisherman who sat mending his nets.*
3 N-COUNT The **net** is the piece of netting used to
divide the two halves of a tennis court, or to form
the back of a goal in football. *Both girls were
eager to come to the net to volley.* **4** VERB If you
net something, you manage to get it, often by
using skill. *He stands to net a fortune.* **5** ADJ
BEFORE N & ADV A **net** amount or result is the final
amount or result, when everything necessary has
been considered or included. *...a rise in sales and
net profit. ...a net gain of nearly 50 seats... The
London Share Account now pays 7.75% gross
5.81% net.* **6** ADJ BEFORE N The **net** weight of
something is its weight without its container or
wrapping.

netball

netball /ˈnetbɔːl/. N-UNCOUNT **Netball** is a game
played by two teams of seven players, usually
women. Each team tries to score goals by
throwing a ball through a net at the top of a pole
at each end of the court.

nett. See **net**.

nettle /ˈnetəl/ **nettles.** N-COUNT A **nettle** is a wild
plant with leaves that sting when you touch them.

★ **network** /ˈnetwɜːk/ **networks. 1** N-COUNT A
network of lines, roads, veins, or other long thin
things is a large number of them which cross
each other or meet at many points. *...the network
of streets surrounding the park... Butterfly wings
are covered with a network of veins.* **2** N-COUNT A
network of people or organizations is a large
number of them that have a connection with
each other and work together as a system. *...their
widespread network of offices.* **3** N-COUNT A radio

or television **network** is a company or group of companies that broadcasts the same radio or television programmes throughout an area.

'**network card, network cards.** N-COUNT A **network card** is a card that connects a computer to a network. [COMPUTING].

networking /'netwɜːkɪŋ/. N-UNCOUNT **Networking** is the process of establishing business contacts, often through social activities. *Quite a bit of networking goes on.*

neurosis /njʊəˈrəʊsɪs, AM nʊr-/ **neuroses.** N-VAR **Neurosis** is a mental condition which causes people to have unreasonable fears and worries. *She got a neurosis about chemicals.*

neurotic /njʊəˈrɒtɪk, AM nʊr-/ **neurotics.** ADJ & N-COUNT If someone is **neurotic**, or if they are a **neurotic**, they continually show a lot of unreasonable fears and worry. *They were neurotic about their health.*

neutral /'njuːtrəl, AM 'nuːt-/. [1] ADJ A **neutral** person or country does not support anyone in a disagreement, war, or contest. *It is morally impossible to remain neutral in this conflict.*
♦ **neutrality** /njuːˈtrælɪti, AM 'nuːt-/ N-UNCOUNT *...a reputation for political neutrality.* [2] ADJ If someone's facial expression or language is **neutral**, they do not show what they are thinking or feeling. *After a pause I said in my most neutral voice: 'Really'.* [3] N-UNCOUNT **Neutral** is the position between the gears of a vehicle, in which the gears are not connected to the engine. *Graham put the van in neutral and jumped out.* [4] ADJ In an electrical device or system, the **neutral** wire is one of the three wires needed to complete the circuit so that the current can flow.

neutralize (BRIT also **neutralise**) /'njuːtrəlaɪz, AM 'nuːt-/ **neutralizes, neutralizing, neutralized.** VERB To **neutralize** something means to prevent it from having any effect or from working properly. *Does alcohol neutralise the effects of contraceptive measures?*

⭐ **never** /'nevə/. [1] ADV **Never** means at no time in the past or future. *I have never lost the weight I put on in my teens... Never say that... This is never to happen again.* [2] ADV **Never** means not in any circumstances. *Divorce is never easy for children.* [3] PHRASE **Never ever** is an emphatic expression for 'never'. [SPOKEN] *He's vowed never ever to talk about it.* [4] ADV **Never** is used to refer to the past and to say that something did not happen. *He never achieved anything... I was to meet Nick in London, but he never appeared.* [5] **never mind**: see **mind**.

,**never-'ending.** ADJ If you describe something bad or unpleasant as **never-ending**, you are emphasizing that it seems to last a very long time. *...a never-ending series of scandals.*

⭐ **nevertheless** /ˌnevəðəˈles/. ADV You use **nevertheless** when saying something that contrasts with what has just been said. [FORMAL] *All of this is perfectly true, but the episode is incredible nevertheless.*

⭐ **new** /njuː, AM nuː/ **newer, newest.** [1] ADJ Something that is **new** has been recently created or invented. *They've just opened a new hotel... These ideas are nothing new in America.* [2] ADJ Something that is **new** has not been used or owned by anyone. *There are many boats, new and used, for sale.* [3] ADJ You use **new** to describe something which has replaced another thing because someone no longer has it, or because it is no longer useful. *I had to find somewhere new to live... They told me I needed a new battery.* [4] ADJ **New** is used to describe something that has only recently been discovered or noticed. *The new planet is about ten times the size of the earth.* [5] ADJ BEFORE N **New** is used to describe someone or something that has recently acquired a particular status. *...a new mother.* [6] ADJ AFTER LINK-V If you are **new to** a situation or place, or if the situation or place is **new to** you, you have not previously seen it or had any experience of it. *She wasn't new to the company... His name was new to me then.*

newborn (or **new-born**)/'njuːbɔːn, AM 'nuː-/ **newborns.** ADJ & N-COUNT A **newborn** baby or animal or a **newborn** is a baby or animal that has just been born. *...a cradle for his newborn child.*

newcomer /'njuːkʌmə, AM 'nuː-/ **newcomers.** N-COUNT A **newcomer** is a person who has recently started a new activity, arrived in a place, or joined an organization. *The candidates are both relative newcomers to politics.*

,**new-'found** (or **newfound**). ADJ BEFORE N A **new-found** quality or ability is one that you have discovered recently. *...his new-found sense of confidence.*

⭐ **newly** /'njuːli, AM 'nuːli/. ADV **Newly** is used before past participles or adjectives to indicate that an action or a situation is very recent. *...a newly married man. ...the newly independent countries of Africa and Asia.*

⭐ **news** /njuːz, AM nuːz/. [1] N-UNCOUNT **News** is information about a recently changed situation or a recent event. *We waited and waited for news of him... I wish I had better news for you... Mr Forsberg welcomed the news.* [2] N-UNCOUNT **News** is information that is published in newspapers and broadcast on radio and television. *...some of the top stories in the news.* [3] N-SING **The news** is a television or radio broadcast which consists of information about recent events. *...the six o'clock news.*

> **USAGE** Note that, although **news** looks like a plural, it is in fact an uncount noun in meanings 1 and 2. *Good news is always worth waiting for.* You cannot say 'a news', but you can say a **piece of news** when you are referring to a particular fact or message. *One of my Dutch colleagues told me a very exciting piece of news.* When you are talking about television and radio news, or newspapers, you can refer to an individual story or report as a **news item**.

⭐ Bank of English® frequent word   For a full explanation of all grammatical labels, see pages vii–x

a
b
c
d
e
f
g
h
i
j
k
l
m
n
o
p
q
r
s
t
u
v
w
x
y
z

'news agency, news agencies. N-COUNT A **news agency** is an organization which collects news stories from all over the world and sells them to journalists.

newsagent /'njuːzeɪdʒənt, AM 'nuːz-/ **newsagents.** N-COUNT In Britain, a **newsagent** or a **newsagent's** is a shop where newspapers, sweets, cigarettes, and stationery are sold. You can also refer to the shopkeeper as a **newsagent**.

newscaster /'njuːzkɑːstə, AM 'nuːzkæstə/ **newscasters.** N-COUNT A **newscaster** is a person who reads the news on television or radio.

'news conference, news conferences. N-COUNT A **news conference** is a meeting held by a famous or important person in which they answer journalists' questions.

newsgroup /'njuːzɡruːp, AM 'nuːz-/ **newsgroups.** N-COUNT A **newsgroup** is an Internet site where people can put information and opinions about a particular subject for other people to read. [COMPUTING]

newsletter /'njuːzletə, AM 'nuːz-/ **newsletters.** N-COUNT A **newsletter** is one or more printed sheets of paper containing information about an organization that is sent regularly to its members.

⭐ **newspaper** /'njuːspeɪpə, AM 'nuːz-/ **newspapers.** **1** N-VAR A **newspaper** is a publication consisting of a number of large sheets of folded paper, on which news is printed. *They read their daughter's allegations in the newspaper... two pots, each wrapped in newspaper.* **2** N-COUNT A **newspaper** is an organization that produces a newspaper. *He worked for a small newspaper in Queensland.*

newsprint /'njuːzprɪnt, AM 'nuːz-/. N-UNCOUNT **Newsprint** is the cheap paper on which newspapers are printed.

, new 'wave, new waves. N-COUNT In the arts or in politics, a **new wave** is a group or movement that deliberately introduces new or unconventional ideas. *...the new wave of satirical comedy.*

, New 'Year. 1 N-UNCOUNT **New Year** or the **New Year** is the time when people celebrate the start of a year. *Happy New Year, everyone... The restaurant was closed over the New Year.* **2** N-SING **The New Year** is the first few weeks of a year. *Isabel was expecting their baby in the New Year.*

⭐ **next** /nekst/. **1** ORD The **next** period of time, event, person, or thing is the one that comes immediately after the present one or after the previous one. *I got up early the next morning. ...the next available flight... Who will be the next prime minister?... I don't want to be the next to die.* **2** DET & PRON You use **next** in expressions such as **next Friday** and **next year** to refer, for example, to the Friday or year which follows immediately after the present one or after the previous one. *Let's plan a big night next week... John would be coming the weekend after next.* **3** ADJ The **next** place or person is the one nearest to you or the first one that you come to. *Trish could hear it in the next room... Stop at the next corner.* **4** ADV The

thing that happens **next** is the thing that happens immediately after something else. *Allow the sauce to cool. Next, add the parsley... The news is next.* **5** ADV When you **next** do something, you do it for the first time since you last did it. *I next saw him at his house.* **6** ADV You use **next** to say that something has more of a quality than all other things except one. *He didn't have a son. I think he felt that a grandson is the next best thing.* **7** PHRASE You can say **the next thing I knew** to suggest that a new situation which you are describing was surprising because it happened very suddenly. [INFORMAL, SPOKEN] *The next thing I knew, the bungalow was on fire.* **8** PREP If one thing is **next to** another, it is at the side of it. *She sat down next to him on the sofa.* **9** PHRASE You use **next to** before a negative, or a word that suggests something negative, to mean almost. *Most pre-prepared weight loss products are next to useless.*

, next 'door. 1 ADV & ADJ BEFORE N If a room or building is **next door**, it is the next one to the right or left. *He lived in the house next door to me. ...the old lady who lived next door... Juan came out of the next-door room.* **2** ADV & ADJ The people **next door** are the people who live in the house to the right or left of yours. *...our next door neighbour.*

nibble /'nɪbəl/ **nibbles, nibbling, nibbled. 1** VERB & N-COUNT If you **nibble** food, or if you eat it in **nibbles**, you eat it by biting very small pieces off it. *She nibbled at the corner of a piece of dry toast.* **2** VERB When animals **nibble** at something, or when they **nibble away at** it, they take small bites of it quickly and repeatedly.

⭐ **nice** /naɪs/ **nicer, nicest. 1** ADJ If you say that something is **nice**, you mean that it is pleasant, enjoyable, or attractive. → See Reference Page on Greetings and Goodbyes. *It's nice to be here together again... We had a nice meal.* ♦ **nicely** ADV *He's just written a book, nicely illustrated and not too technical.* **2** ADJ If you say that it is **nice of** someone to say or do something, you are saying that they are being kind and thoughtful. This is often used as a way of thanking someone. *'How are your boys?' — 'How nice of you to ask.'* **3** ADJ If someone is **nice**, they are friendly and pleasant. *He was a nice fellow, very quiet and courteous... They were extremely nice to me.* ♦ **nicely** ADV *He treated you very nicely.*

nicely /'naɪsli/. ADV Something that is happening or working **nicely** is happening or working in a satisfactory way. *She has a bit of private money, so they manage quite nicely.*

niche /niːʃ, AM nɪtʃ/ **niches. 1** N-COUNT A **niche** is a hollow area in a wall or a natural hollow part in a cliff. *...a niche in the rock where the path ended.* **2** N-COUNT Your **niche** is the job or activity which is exactly suitable for you. *Simon Lane quickly found his niche as a busy freelance model maker.*

nick /nɪk/ **nicks, nicking, nicked. 1** VERB If someone **nicks** something, they steal or take it. [INFORMAL, BRITISH] *He's nicked all your ideas... Michelle had her* *purse nicked.* [2] VERB If you **nick** something, you accidentally make a small cut or scratch into the surface of it. *He'd also nicked himself on the chin with his razor.* [3] N-COUNT A **nick** is a small cut or scratch in the surface of something. *There was a bad nick at the nape of his neck.* [4] PHRASE If something is achieved **in the nick of time**, it is achieved successfully, at the last possible moment. [INFORMAL] *Seems we got here just in the nick of time.*

nickel /ˈnɪkəl/ **nickels.** [1] N-UNCOUNT **Nickel** is a silver-coloured metal that is used in making steel. [2] N-COUNT In the United States and Canada, a **nickel** is a coin worth five cents.

nickname /ˈnɪkneɪm/ **nicknames, nicknaming, nicknamed.** [1] N-COUNT A **nickname** is an informal name for someone or something. *Red got his nickname for his red hair.* [2] VERB If someone or something **is nicknamed** a particular name, they are given that name as a nickname. *Which newspaper was once nicknamed The Thunderer?*

nicotine /ˈnɪkɪtiːn/. N-UNCOUNT **Nicotine** is an addictive substance in tobacco.

niece /niːs/ **nieces.** N-COUNT Your **niece** is the daughter of your sister or brother.

niggle /ˈnɪɡəl/ **niggles, niggling, niggled.** VERB & N-COUNT If something **niggles** you, it makes you worry slightly over a long time. You can call a worry like this a **niggle**. *The truth might niggle him for ever... Why is there a little niggle at the back of my mind?*

⭐**night** /naɪt/ **nights.** [1] N-VAR The **night** is the part of each period of twenty-four hours when it is dark outside, especially the time when most people are sleeping. *He didn't leave the house all night... Finally night fell.* [2] N-COUNT The **night** is the period of time between the end of the afternoon and the time that you go to bed. *So whose party was it last night?... I really enjoy going out on Friday night.* [3] N-UNCOUNT If you refer to a particular time **at night**, you mean a time during the part of a day when it gets dark and before midnight. *We got back about eleven o'clock at night.*

PHRASES ● If something happens **day and night** or **night and day**, it happens all the time without stopping. *His team is working day and night to finish.* ● If you have **an early night**, you go to bed early. If you have **a late night**, you go to bed late.

nightclub /ˈnaɪtklʌb/ **nightclubs.** N-COUNT A **nightclub** is a place where people go late in the evening to drink and dance.

nightlife /ˈnaɪtlaɪf/. N-UNCOUNT The **nightlife** in a place is the entertainment and social activities that are available at night, such as nightclubs and bars. *It's a university town, with lots of nightlife.*

nightly /ˈnaɪtli/. ADJ BEFORE N & ADV A **nightly** event happens every night. *Air raids were a nightly occurrence... Dinner is served nightly.*

⭐**nightmare** /ˈnaɪtmeə/ **nightmares.** [1] N-COUNT A **nightmare** is a very frightening dream. *All the*

victims still suffered nightmares. [2] N-COUNT If you say that an experience is a **nightmare**, you mean that it is very unpleasant. [INFORMAL] *The bus journey up there was a nightmare.*

'**night time.** N-UNCOUNT **Night time** is the period of time between when it gets dark and when the sun rises. *He likes to have his bath at night time.*

nil /nɪl/. [1] NUM **Nil** means the same as zero. It is often used in scores of sports games. *They lost two nil to Italy.* [2] N-UNCOUNT If you say that something is **nil**, you mean that it does not exist at all. *Their legal rights are virtually nil.*

nimble /ˈnɪmbəl/ **nimbler, nimblest.** [1] ADJ Someone who is **nimble** is able to move their fingers, hands, or legs quickly and easily. *...jobs which demand nimble fingers.* [2] ADJ Someone who has a **nimble** mind is clever and can think quickly.

⭐**nine** /naɪn/ **nines.** NUM **Nine** is the number 9.

⭐**nineteen** /ˌnaɪnˈtiːn/ **nineteens.** NUM **Nineteen** is the number 19.

⭐**nineteenth** /ˌnaɪnˈtiːnθ/. ORD The **nineteenth** item in a series is the one that you count as number nineteen.

⭐**ninetieth** /ˈnaɪntiəθ/. ORD The **ninetieth** item in a series is the one that you count as number ninety.

⭐**ninety** /ˈnaɪnti/ **nineties.** NUM **Ninety** is the number 90. For examples of how numbers such as ninety and eighty are used see **eighty**.

⭐**ninth** /naɪnθ/. ORD The **ninth** item in a series is the one that you count as number nine.

nip /nɪp/ **nips, nipping, nipped.** [1] VERB If you **nip** somewhere, usually somewhere nearby, you go there quickly or for a short time. [INFORMAL, BRITISH] *Should I nip out and get some groceries?* [2] VERB If a person or an animal **nips** you, they pinch or bite you lightly. *He was nipped by a rat.* ● to **nip** something **in the bud**: see **bud**.

nipple /ˈnɪpəl/ **nipples.** N-COUNT The **nipples** on someone's body are the two small pieces of slightly hard flesh on their chest. Babies suck milk through their mothers' nipples.

nitrate /ˈnaɪtreɪt/ **nitrates.** N-VAR A **nitrate** is a chemical compound that includes nitrogen and oxygen. Nitrates are used as fertilizers.

nitrogen /ˈnaɪtrədʒən/. N-UNCOUNT **Nitrogen** is a colourless element that has no smell and is usually found as a gas.

⭐**no** /nəʊ/.

☑ The plural of the noun can be **noes** or **no's**.

[1] CONVENTION You use **no** to give a negative answer to a question, to say that something is not true, to refuse an offer, or to refuse permission. *'Any problems?'—'No, I'm O.K.'... 'You're getting worse than me.'—'No I'm not.'... 'Here, have mine.'—'No, this is fine.'... No. I forbid it.* [2] CONVENTION You use **no** to say that you agree with or understand a negative statement that someone else has made. *'I don't know him, do*

I?'—'*No, you don't.*' ③ CONVENTION You use **no** to express shock or disappointment at something. *Oh no, not another day of this.* ④ CONVENTION You use **no** as a way of introducing a correction to what you have just said. *It means the whole group, no, more than that, it means the entire species.* ⑤ DET You use **no** to mean not any or not one person or thing. *He had no intention of paying the cash... No letters survive from this early period.* ⑥ DET You use **no** to emphasize that someone or something is not a particular thing or does not have a particular quality. *He is no singer... Today's elections are of no great importance.* ⑦ ADV You use **no** when emphasizing that something does not exceed a particular amount or number, or does not have more of a particular quality than something else. *...no later than the end of 1994... No fewer than thirty climbers reached the summit... He will be no more effective than his predecessors.* ⑧ DET **No** is used in notices or instructions to say that a particular thing is forbidden. *...'no smoking' signs... No talking after lights out.* ⑨ N-COUNT A **no** is the answer 'no' or a vote against something. *Is that a yes or a no?* ⑩ PHRASE If you say **there is no** doing a particular thing, you mean that it is impossible to do that thing. *There is no going back to the life she had.*

No., Nos. No. is a written abbreviation for **number**. *...No. 10 Downing Street.*

nobility /nəʊ'bɪlɪti/. ① N-UNCOUNT **Nobility** is the quality of being noble. [FORMAL] *...instincts of nobility and generosity.* ② N-SING **The nobility** of a society are all the people who have titles and high social rank. *They married into the nobility.*

noble /'nəʊbəl/ **nobler, noblest; nobles.** ① ADJ If you say that someone is a **noble** person or their behaviour is **noble**, you admire and respect them because they are honest, brave, and not selfish. *He was an upright and noble man who was always willing to help.* ♦ **nobly** ADV *They have supported us nobly in this war.* ② ADJ Something that is **noble** is very impressive in quality or appearance. *...the great parks with their noble trees.* ③ ADJ & N-COUNT If someone is **noble** or a **noble**, they belong to a high social class and have a title. *...rich and noble families.*

★ **nobody** /'nəʊbɒdi/ **nobodies.** ① PRON **Nobody** means not a single person. *Nobody realizes how bad things are... For a long time, nobody spoke.* ② N-COUNT If someone says that a person is a **nobody**, they are saying in an unkind way that the person is not at all important. *A man in my position has nothing to fear from a nobody like you.*

> **USAGE** You do not use **nobody** or **no one** in front of **of** to talk about a particular group of people. The word you need is **none**. *None of the men have been injured... None of the victims has been identified.*

nocturnal /nɒk'tɜːnəl/. ① ADJ **Nocturnal** means occurring at night. *...teenagers' nocturnal activities.* ② ADJ **Nocturnal** creatures are active mostly at night.

★ **nod** /nɒd/ **nods, nodding, nodded.** ① VERB & N-COUNT If you **nod**, or if you give a **nod**, you move your head down and up to show that you are answering 'yes' to a question, or to show agreement, understanding, or approval. *'Are you okay?' I asked. She nodded... Todd agreed with a nod of his head.* ② VERB & N-COUNT If you **nod** in a particular direction, or if you give a **nod** in a particular direction, you bend your head once in a that direction in order to indicate something. *'Does it work?' he asked, nodding at the piano... 'It was on the news earlier,' said Leo, with a nod towards the television.* ③ VERB & N-COUNT If you **nod**, or if you give a **nod**, you bend your head once, as a way of saying hello or goodbye. *All the girls nodded and said 'Hi'... He gave Sabrina a quick nod of acknowledgement.*

▶ **nod off.** PHR-VERB If you **nod off**, you fall asleep, especially when you had not intended to. [INFORMAL] *I almost nodded off listening to it.*

★ **noise** /nɔɪz/ **noises.** ① N-UNCOUNT **Noise** is a loud or unpleasant sound. *There was too much noise in the room.* ② N-COUNT A **noise** is a sound that someone or something makes. *...animal noises... He heard a noise somewhere under his window.*

noisy /'nɔɪzi/ **noisier, noisiest.** ① ADJ Someone or something that is **noisy** makes a lot of loud or unpleasant noise. *...my noisy old typewriter.* ♦ **noisily** ADV *He slammed the car door noisily.* ② ADJ A place that is **noisy** is full of loud or unpleasant noise. *...the crowded and noisy terrace of the café.*

nomadic /nəʊ'mædɪk/. ADJ **Nomadic** people travel from place to place rather than living in one place all the time. *...gypsies who have given up their nomadic way of life.*

'no-man's land. N-UNCOUNT **No-man's land** is an area of land that is not owned or controlled by anyone, for example the area of land between two opposing armies. *...the no-man's land between the two countries.*

nominal /'nɒmɪnəl/. ① ADJ You use **nominal** to indicate that someone or something is supposed to have a particular identity or status, but in reality does not have it. *As he was still not allowed to run a company, his wife became its nominal head.* ♦ **nominally** ADV *Nominally she is the king's prisoner.* ② ADJ A **nominal** price or sum of money is very small in comparison with the real cost or value of the thing that is being bought or sold. *All the ferries carry bicycles free or for a nominal charge.*

nominate /'nɒmɪneɪt/ **nominates, nominating, nominated.** VERB If someone **is nominated for** a job, position, or prize, their name is formally suggested as a candidate for it. *...a presidential decree nominating him as sports ambassador... The public will be able to nominate candidates for awards such as the MBE.*

nomination /ˌnɒmɪˈneɪʃən/ **nominations.** N-COUNT A **nomination** is an official suggestion of someone for a job, position, or prize. ...*a list of nominations for senior lectureships.*

nominee /ˌnɒmɪˈniː/ **nominees.** N-COUNT A **nominee** is someone who is nominated for something. ...*nominees for the Nobel Peace Prize.*

nonchalant /ˈnɒnʃələnt, AM -ˈlɑːnt/. ADJ Someone who is **nonchalant** seems very calm and appears not to worry or care about things. *Denis tried to look nonchalant and uninterested.* ♦ **nonchalance** /ˈnɒnʃələns/ N-UNCOUNT *Despite everyone's apparent nonchalance the air crackled with nervous energy.* ♦ **nonchalantly** ADV *'Does Will intend to return with us?' Joanna asked as nonchalantly as she could.*

⭐ **none** /nʌn/. QUANT **None of** something means not even a small amount of it. **None of** a group of people or things means not even one of them. *She did none of the maintenance on the vehicle... None of us knew how to treat her... They asked me for fresh ideas, but I had none.* **PHRASES** ● You use **none the** to say that someone or something does not have any more of a particular quality than they did before. *He became convinced that his illness was purely imaginary: that made it none the better.* ● You use **none too** in front of an adjective or adverb in order to emphasize that the quality mentioned is not present. *He was none too thrilled to hear from me at that hour.*

nonetheless /ˌnʌnðəˈles/. ADV You use **nonetheless** when saying something that contrasts with what has just been said. [FORMAL] *His face is serious but nonetheless very friendly.*

non-ex'istent. ADJ If you say that something is **non-existent**, you mean that it does not exist when you feel that it should. *Hygiene was non-existent: no running water, no bathroom.*

no-'nonsense. ADJ If you describe someone as a **no-nonsense** person or something as a **no-nonsense** thing, you approve of the fact that they are efficient and concentrate on important matters rather than trivial things. *The decor is straightforward and no-nonsense.*

nonsense /ˈnɒnsəns/. **1** N-UNCOUNT If you say that something spoken or written is **nonsense**, you mean that you consider it to be untrue or silly. ...*all that poetic nonsense about love... 'I'm putting on weight.'—'Nonsense my dear.'* **2** N-UNCOUNT You can use **nonsense** to refer to something that you think is foolish or that you disapprove of. *I think there is a limit to how much of this nonsense people are going to put up with.* **3** PHRASE To **make a nonsense of** something or to **make nonsense of** it means to make it seem ridiculous or pointless. *The fighting made a nonsense of peace pledges made in London last week.*

non-'smoker, non-smokers. N-COUNT A **non-smoker** is someone who does not smoke.

non-'stick. ADJ **Non-stick** cooking equipment such as pans or baking tins has a special coating, which prevents food from sticking to it.

non-'stop (or **nonstop**). ADJ Something that is **non-stop** continues without any pauses or breaks. ...*80 minutes of non-stop music.*

non-'violent. **1** ADJ **Non-violent** methods of bringing about change do not involve hurting people or causing damage. ♦ **non-violence** N-UNCOUNT ...*a firm public commitment to non-violence.* **2** ADJ You can refer to someone or to something such as a crime as **non-violent** when that person or thing does not hurt or injure people. ...*non-violent offenders.*

noodle /ˈnuːdəl/ **noodles.** N-COUNT **Noodles** are long, thin pieces of pasta.

noon /nuːn/. N-UNCOUNT **Noon** is twelve o'clock in the middle of the day. → See Reference Page on Telling the Time. *The long day of meetings started at noon.*

⭐ **'no one** (or **no-one**). PRON **No one** means not a single person, or not a single member of a particular group or set. *No one can open mail except the person to whom it has been addressed.* ● See note at **nobody**.

noose /nuːs/ **nooses.** N-COUNT A **noose** is a loop at the end of a piece of rope or wire that is used to trap animals or hang people.

nope /nəʊp/. CONVENTION **Nope** is sometimes used instead of 'no' as a response; INFORMAL, SPOKEN. *'Has the prisoner next door talked to you'—'Nope,' the man answered.*

⭐ **nor** /nɔː/. **1** CONJ You use **nor** after 'neither' to introduce the second thing that a negative statement applies to. *Neither Mr Rose nor Mr Woodhead was available for comment... I can give you neither an opinion nor any advice.* **2** CONJ You use **nor** after a negative statement in order to indicate that the negative statement also applies to you or to someone or something else. *'If my husband has no future,' she said, 'then nor do my children.'*

norm /nɔːm/ **norms.** **1** N-COUNT **Norms** are ways of behaving that are considered normal in a particular society. ...*the commonly accepted norms of democracy.* ...*a social norm that says drunkenness is inappropriate behaviour.* **2** N-SING If you say that a situation is **the norm**, you mean that it is usual and expected. *Families of six or seven are the norm in Borough Park.*

⭐ **normal** /ˈnɔːməl/. ADJ Something that is **normal** is usual and ordinary, and in accordance with what people expect. *There's no reason why you can't have a perfectly normal child... The two countries resumed normal diplomatic relations.*

normality /nɔːˈmælɪti/. N-UNCOUNT **Normality** is a situation in which everything is normal. *A semblance of normality has returned.*

normalize (BRIT also **normalise**) /ˈnɔːməlaɪz/ **normalizes, normalizing, normalized.** VERB When you **normalize** a situation, or when it **normalizes**, it becomes normal or returns to normal. *The two*

governments were close to normalizing relations.
...some deep-seated emotional reason which has to
be dealt with before your eating habits normalize.
♦ **normalization** N-UNCOUNT ...the normalisation
of diplomatic relations between them.

⭐ **normally** /'nɔːməli/. **1** ADV If you say that
something **normally** happens or that you
normally do a particular thing, you mean that it
is what usually happens or what you usually do.
All airports in the country are working normally
today... Normally, the transportation system in
Paris carries 950,000 passengers a day. **2** ADV If
you do something **normally**, you do it in the
usual or conventional way. She would apparently
eat normally and then make herself sick.

⭐ **north** /nɔːθ/. **1** N-SING The **north** is the
direction on your left when you are looking
towards the direction where the sun rises. Birds
usually migrate from north to south. **2** N-SING & ADJ
The **north** of a place or the **north** part of it is the
part which is towards the north. ...people in the
North and Midlands. ...the north coast of Crete.
3 ADV **North** means towards the north, or
positioned to the north of a place. Anita drove
north up Pacific Highway. ...a little village a few
miles north of Portsmouth. **4** ADJ A **north** wind
blows from the north.

⭐ **north-'east.** **1** N-SING The **north-east** is the
direction halfway between north and east. The
land to the north-east fell away into meadows.
2 N-SING & ADJ The **north-east** of a place or the
north-east part of it is the part which is towards
the north-east. ...in the north-east of England.
...the north-east outskirts of London. **3** ADV
North-east means towards the north-east, or
positioned to the north-east of a place or thing.
...army convoys moving north-east. ...Careysburg,
twenty miles north-east of the capital, Monrovia.
4 ADJ A **north-east** wind blows from the north-
east.

,**north-'eastern** (or**north eastern**). ADJ
North-eastern means in or from the north-east
of a region or country. ...the north-eastern coast of
the United States.

northerly /'nɔːðəli/. **1** ADJ **Northerly** means
towards the north. ...the most northerly island in
the British Isles... I wanted to go a more northerly
route across Montana. **2** ADJ A **northerly** wind
blows from the north.

⭐ **northern** /'nɔːðən/. ADJ **Northern** means in or
from the north of a region or country. ...Northern
Ireland... Prices at three-star hotels fell furthest in
several northern cities.

northward /'nɔːθwəd/ (or**northwards**
/'nɔːθwədz/). ADV & ADJ **Northward** or
northwards means towards the north. ...the flow
of immigrants northward... The northward journey
from Jalalabad was no more than 120 miles.

⭐ ,**north-'west.** **1** N-SING The **north-west** is the
direction halfway between north and west.
...Ushant, five miles out to the north-west.
2 N-SING & ADJ The **north-west** of a place or the

north-west part of it is the part which is towards
the north-west. ...the extreme north-west of South
America. ...the North-West Regional Health
Authority. **3** ADV **North-west** means towards the
north-west, or positioned to the north-west of a
place or thing. Take the narrow lane going north-
west parallel with the railway line. **4** ADJ A
north-west wind blows from the north-west.

,**north-'western.** ADJ **North-western** means in
or from the north-west of a region or country. He
was from north-western Russia.

⭐ **nose** /nəʊz/ **noses.** **1** N-COUNT Your **nose** is the
part of your face which sticks out above your
mouth. You use it for smelling and breathing.
→ See picture on page 823. **2** N-COUNT The **nose**
of a car or plane is its front part. **3** PHRASE If you
do something **under** someone's **nose**, you do it in
front of them, so that they could easily see you
doing it. She stole items from right under the noses
of other shoppers.

nostalgia /nɒ'stældʒə/. N-UNCOUNT **Nostalgia** is
an affectionate feeling for things you have
experienced in the past.

nostalgic /nɒs'tældʒɪk/. ADJ If you feel
nostalgic, you think affectionately about
experiences you have had in the past. Many
people were nostalgic for the good old days.
♦ **nostalgically** ADV People look back
nostalgically on the period.

nostril /'nɒstrɪl/ **nostrils.** N-COUNT Your **nostrils**
are the two openings at the end of your nose.
→ See picture on page 823.

⭐ **not** /nɒt/. **1** You use **not**, usually in the form
n't, to form questions to which you expect the
answer 'yes'. Haven't they got enough problems
there already? **2** You use **not**, usually in the form
n't, in questions which imply that someone
should have done something or should do
something, or to express surprise that something
is not the case. Why didn't you do it months ago?...
Hasn't anyone ever kissed you before? **3** You use
not, usually in the form **n't**, in question tags after
a positive statement. You will take me tomorrow,
won't you? **4** You use **not**, usually in the form
n't, in polite suggestions. Why don't you fill out
our application? **5** You use **not** to represent the
negative of a word, group, or clause that has just
been used. 'Have you found Paula?'—'I'm afraid
not.'... I really didn't care whether he came or not.
6 You use **not** before 'all', 'every', or 'always' to
say that there are exceptions to something that is
generally true. You also use **not** before words like
'only' and 'just' to say that something is true, but
it is not the whole truth. Not every applicant had
a degree... Brendel is not only a great pianist, but a
great musician. **7** You can use **not** or **not even**
in front of 'a' or 'one' to emphasize that there is
none at all of what is being mentioned. I sent
report after report. But not one word was
published. **8** You use **not** when you are
contrasting something that is true with
something that people might wrongly believe to
be true. Training is an investment not a cost.

9 CONJ You use **not that** to introduce a negative clause that contradicts or modifies what the previous statement implies. *His death took me a year to get over; not that you're ever really over it.* **10** CONVENTION **Not at all** is an emphatic way of saying 'No' or of agreeing that the answer to a question is 'No'. *'Sorry. I sound like Abby, don't I?'—'No. Not at all.'* **11** **not least**: see **least**. ● **not to mention**: see **mention**. ● **nothing if not**: see **nothing**. ● **more often than not**: see **often**.

notable/ˈnəʊtəbəl/. ADJ Something or someone that is **notable** is important or interesting. *...a sleepy fishing town notable for its church.* ● See note at **famous**.

notably/ˈnəʊtəbli/. ADV You use **notably** before mentioning the most important example of the thing you are talking about. *...more important problems, notably the fate of the children.*

notch/nɒtʃ/ **notches, notching, notched.** **1** N-COUNT A **notch** is a small V-shaped or circular cut in the surface or edge of something. **2** N-COUNT You can refer to a step on a scale of measurement or achievement as a **notch**. [JOURNALISM] *Average earnings in the economy moved up another notch in August.* ▸ **notch up.** PHR-VERB If you **notch up** something such as a score or total, you achieve it. [JOURNALISM] *Selfridges notched up sales worth £1 million before lunch.*

★ **note**/nəʊt/ **notes, noting, noted.** **1** N-COUNT A **note** is a short letter. *I'll have to leave a note for Karen... Remember to write a note to say where you are.* **2** N-COUNT A **note** is something that you write down to remind you about something. *Take notes during the consultation.* **3** VERB & PHR-VERB When you **note** something, or when you **note down**, you write it down so that you have a record of it. You can also say that a piece of writing **notes** something when it is recorded there. *She was, she noted in her diary, 'very indignant with him.'... He noted down the address... The report notes that a dramatic drop in military violence took place.* **4** VERB If you **note** a fact, you become aware of it. *Those who met her noted the facial resemblance to the famous actress... Please note that there are a limited number of tickets.* **5** N-COUNT In a book or article, a **note** is a short piece of additional information. *See Note 16 on page p. 223.* **6** N-COUNT In music, a **note** is a sound of a particular pitch, or a written symbol representing this sound. **7** N-COUNT In British English, a **note** is a piece of paper money. The usual American word is **bill**. *...a five pound note.* **8** N-SING You can use **note** to refer to a quality or feeling that something has, or the impression that it gives you. You can say that someone or something strikes or sounds a particular **note**. *He could discern the note of urgency in their voices... The film ends on a positive note... He welcomed the campaign but sounded a note of caution.* PHRASES ● If you **compare notes with** someone

or if the two of you **compare notes**, you talk to them and find out whether they have the same opinion, information, or experiences as yourself. *...the chance to compare notes with other suffering mothers.* ● Someone or something that is **of note** is important, worth mentioning, or well-known. *He has published nothing of note in the last ten years.* ● If you **take note of** something, you pay attention to it because you think that it is important. *He advises you to take note of where the exits are.* ● See also **noted**. ▸ **note down.** See **note** 3.

notebook/ˈnəʊtbʊk/ **notebooks.** N-COUNT A **notebook** is a small book for writing notes in.

★ **noted**/ˈnəʊtɪd/. ADJ Someone who is **noted for** something they do or have is well-known and admired for it. *...a television programme noted for its attacks on organised crime.*

★ **nothing**/ˈnʌθɪŋ/. **1** PRON **Nothing** means not a single thing, or not a single part of something. *He said nothing to reporters... There is nothing wrong with the car.* **2** PRON You use **nothing** to indicate that something or someone is not important or significant. *Because he had always had money it meant nothing to him... She kept bursting into tears over nothing.* PHRASES ● **Nothing but** a particular thing means only that thing. *All that money brought nothing but sadness... She did nothing but complain about him.* ● You use **nothing if not** to indicate that someone or something clearly has a lot of a particular quality. *Professor Fish has been nothing if not professional.* ● You can use **nothing less than** to emphasize your next words, often indicating that something seems very surprising or important. *You're nothing less than a murderer!* ● You say **nothing of the sort** to emphasize a refusal or a negative statement. *It was supposed to have been a triumph. It was nothing of the sort.* ● to **say nothing of**: see **say**. ● to **think nothing of**: see **think**.

★ **notice**/ˈnəʊtɪs/ **notices, noticing, noticed.** **1** VERB If you **notice** something, you become aware of it. *You didn't notice anything special about him?... Mrs Shedden noticed a bird sitting on the garage... She noticed he was acting strangely.* **2** PHRASE If something **comes to** your **notice** or is **brought to** your **notice**, you become aware of it. If it **escapes** your **notice**, you are not aware of it. *He was later thanked for bringing the matter to their notice.* **3** PHRASE If you **take notice of** something, you pay attention to it. *Noel was someone people took notice of... I always knew something was wrong, but no one would take any notice.* **4** N-COUNT A **notice** is a written announcement in a place where everyone can read it. *A few guest houses had 'No Vacancies' notices in their windows.* **5** N-UNCOUNT **Notice** is advance warning about something. *I was given four days' notice to prepare for the wedding... She was transferred without notice... Thank you all for coming along at such short notice.* PHRASES ● If a situation will exist **until further**

a b c d e f g h i j k l m n o p q r s t u v w x y z

notice, it will continue until someone changes it.
● If your employer **gives** you **notice**, he or she tells you that you must leave within a set period of time. If you **give notice** or **hand in** your **notice**, you tell your employer that you intend to leave within a set period of time.

noticeable /'nəʊtɪsəbəl/. ADJ Something that is **noticeable** is very obvious, so that it is easy to see or recognize. *It was noticeable that his face and arms were red.* ♦ **noticeably** ADV *The baby became noticeably more agitated.*

notify /'nəʊtɪfaɪ/ **notifies, notifying, notified.** VERB If you **notify** someone **of** something, you officially inform them of it. *The skipper notified the coastguard of the tragedy... We have notified the police.* ♦ **notification** /,nəʊtɪfɪ'keɪʃən/ **notifications** N-VAR *All clubs should have received notification by now.*

★ **notion** /'nəʊʃən/ **notions.** N-COUNT A **notion** is a belief or idea. *...the notion that pornography degrades women.*

notoriety /,nəʊtə'raɪɪti/. N-UNCOUNT If someone or something achieves **notoriety**, they become well-known for something bad.

notorious /nəʊ'tɔːriəs/. ADJ Someone or something that is **notorious** is well known for something bad. *The area is notorious for drug dealing.* ♦ **notoriously** ADV *Doctors notoriously neglect their own health.* ● See note at **famous**.

notwithstanding /,nɒtwɪð'stændɪŋ/. PREP & ADV If something is true **notwithstanding** something else, it is true in spite of that other thing. [FORMAL] *He despised William Pitt, notwithstanding the similar views they both held... Such realism notwithstanding, the film was a disaster.*

nought /nɔːt/ **noughts. Nought** is the number 0.

USAGE In spoken British English, **nought** is much more common than **zero**. *The acceleration is so extreme, from nought to 60 in a fraction of one second.* As a number, **zero** is used mainly in scientific contexts, or when you want to be precise. However, when you are stating a telephone number, you say O (/əʊ/). In some sports contexts, especially football scores, **nil** is used. *England beat Poland two-nil at Wembley.* In tennis, **love** is the usual word. *He won the first set and took a two-games-to-love lead in the second.*

---

noun /naʊn/ **nouns.** N-COUNT A **noun** is a word such as 'woman', 'guilt', or 'John' which is used to refer to a person or thing.

nourish /'nʌrɪʃ, AM 'nɜːrɪʃ/ **nourishes, nourishing, nourished.** VERB To **nourish** a person, animal, or plant means to provide them with the food that is necessary for growth and health. *...microbes in the soil which nourish the plant.* ♦ **nourishing** ADJ *...sensible, nourishing food.* ♦ **nourishment**

N-UNCOUNT *Breast milk is your baby's best source of nourishment.*

★ **novel** /'nɒvəl/ **novels.** 1 N-COUNT A **novel** is a book containing a long story about imaginary people and events. 2 ADJ **Novel** things are unlike anything that has been done, experienced, or created before. *...taking scraps of past music and making them into something novel.*

novelist /'nɒvəlɪst/ **novelists.** N-COUNT A **novelist** is a person who writes novels.

novelty /'nɒvəlti/ **novelties.** 1 N-UNCOUNT **Novelty** is the quality of being different, new, and unusual. *The novelty of the situation intrigued him.* 2 N-COUNT A **novelty** is something that is new and therefore interesting. *...the days when a motor car was a novelty.* 3 N-COUNT **Novelties** are cheap unusual objects sold as gifts or souvenirs.

★ **November** /nəʊ'vembə/. N-UNCOUNT **November** is the eleventh month of the year.
→ See Reference Page on Times and Dates.

novice /'nɒvɪs/ **novices.** N-COUNT A **novice** is someone who has been doing a job or other activity for only a short time and so is not experienced at it. *Most of us are novices on the computer. ...a novice writer.*

★ **now** /naʊ/. 1 ADV & PRON You use **now** to refer to the present time, often in contrast to the past or the future. *Beef steak now costs well over £3 a pound... I must go now... She should know that by now... Now is your chance to talk to him.* 2 CONJ You use **now** or **now that** to indicate that an event has occurred and as a result something else may or will happen. *Now you're settled, why don't you take up some serious study?* 3 ADV You use **now** in statements which specify the length of time up to the present that something has lasted. *They've been married now for 30 years.* 4 ADV You can say **'Now'** to introduce new information into a story or account. *Now, I hadn't told him these details, so he must have done some research on his own.*
PHRASES ● If you say that something will happen **any day now, any moment now,** or **any time now**, you mean that it will happen very soon. *We were expecting him home again any day now.* ● **Just now** means a very short time ago. *You looked pretty upset just now.* ● If you say that something happens **now and then** or **every now and again**, you mean that it happens sometimes but not very often or regularly. *Now and then they heard the roar of a heavy truck.*

nowadays /'naʊədeɪz/. ADV **Nowadays** means at the present time, in contrast with the past. *I don't see much of Tony nowadays.*

★ **nowhere** /'nəʊweə/. 1 ADV You use **nowhere** to emphasize that a place has more of a particular quality than any other places, or that it is the only place where something happens or exists. *Nowhere is language a more serious issue than in Hawaii... This kind of forest exists nowhere else in the world.* 2 ADV You use **nowhere** when making negative statements to say that a suitable place of the specified kind does not exist. *There was nowhere to hide and nowhere to run... I have nowhere else to go.*

PHRASES • If you say that something or someone appears **from nowhere** or **out of nowhere**, you mean that they appear suddenly and unexpectedly. *A car came from nowhere, and I had to jump back.* • If you say that you **are getting nowhere** or that something **is getting** you **nowhere**, you mean that you are not achieving anything or having any success. *Oh, stop it! This is getting us nowhere.* • If you say that a place is **in the middle of nowhere**, you mean it is a long way from other places. • **nowhere near:** see **near**.

nuance /'njuːɑːns, AM 'nuː-/ **nuances.** N-VAR A **nuance** is a small and subtle difference in sound, feeling, appearance, or meaning. *...every subtle nuance of emotion.*

⭐ **nuclear** /'njuːkliə, AM 'nuːk-/. ADJ BEFORE N **Nuclear** means relating to the nuclei of atoms, or to the energy produced when these nuclei are split or combined. *...a nuclear power station. ...nuclear weapons.*

nuclear reˈactor, nuclear reactors. N-COUNT A **nuclear reactor** is a machine which produces nuclear energy.

nucleus /'njuːkliəs, AM 'nuː-/ **nuclei.** ① N-COUNT The **nucleus** of an atom or cell is the central part of it. ② N-COUNT The **nucleus** of a group of people is the small number of members which form the most important part of the group. *...the nucleus of people who started Private Eye magazine.*

nude /njuːd, AM nuːd/ **nudes.** ① ADJ & PHRASE Someone who is **nude** or who is **in the nude** is not wearing any clothes. • **nudity** /'njuːdɪti, AM 'nuː-/ N-UNCOUNT *...nudity and bad language on TV.* ② N-COUNT A **nude** is a picture or statue of a nude person.

nudge /nʌdʒ/ **nudges, nudging, nudged.** VERB & N-COUNT If you **nudge** someone, or if you give them a **nudge**, you push them gently with your elbow.

nuisance /'njuːsəns, AM 'nuː-/ **nuisances.** N-COUNT If you say that someone or something is a **nuisance**, you mean that they annoy you or cause you problems. If you say that someone **makes a nuisance of** themselves, you mean that they are a nuisance. *He could be a bit of a nuisance when he was drunk.*

numb /nʌm/ **numbs, numbing, numbed.** ① ADJ If a part of your body is **numb**, you cannot feel anything there. *He could feel his fingers growing numb.* • **numbness** N-UNCOUNT *Nerve injury can cause numbness in the thigh.* ② VERB If a blow or cold weather **numbs** a part of your body, you can no longer feel anything in it. *The cold numbed my fingers.* ③ ADJ If you are **numb with** shock or fear, you are so shocked or frightened that you cannot think clearly or feel any emotion. ④ VERB

If an event or experience **numbs** you, you can no longer think clearly or feel any emotion. • **numbed** ADJ *I'm so numbed with shock that I can hardly think.*

⭐ **number** /'nʌmbə/ **numbers, numbering, numbered.** ① N-COUNT A **number** is a word such as 'two', 'nine', or 'twelve', or a symbol such as 1, 3, or 47, which is used in counting something. *I don't know the room number. ...number 3, Argyll Street.* ② N-COUNT Someone's **number** is the series of digits that you dial when you telephone them. *Sarah sat down and dialled a number... 'You must have a wrong number,' she said. 'There's no one of that name here.'* ③ VERB If you **number** something, you give it a number in a series and write the number on it. *He cut his paper up into tiny squares, and he numbered each one.* ④ N-COUNT You use **number** with words such as 'large' or 'small' to say approximately how many things or people there are. *I have had an enormous number of letters.* ⑤ N-SING If there are **a number of** things or people, there are several of them. If there are **any number of** things or people, there is a large quantity of them. *Sam told a number of lies... There must be any number of people in my position.* ⑥ VERB If a group of people or things **numbers** a particular total, that is how many there are. *...a paramilitary force which numbered 100,000 men.*

ˌnumber ˈone. ADJ **Number one** means better, more important, or more popular than anything else of its kind. *The economy is the number one issue by far.*

ˈnumber plate, number plates. N-COUNT In British English, a **number plate** is a sign on the front and back of a vehicle that shows its registration number. The American term is **license plate**.

numerical /njuː'merɪkəl, AM 'nuː-/. ADJ **Numerical** means expressed in numbers or relating to numbers. *Put them in numerical order.* • **numerically** ADV *...a numerically small nation.*

⭐ **numerous** /'njuːmərəs, AM 'nuːm-/. ADJ If people or things are **numerous**, they exist or are present in large numbers. *Sex crimes were just as numerous as they are today.*

nun /nʌn/ **nuns.** N-COUNT A **nun** is a member of a female religious community.

⭐ **nurse** /nɜːs/ **nurses, nursing, nursed.** ① N-COUNT A **nurse** is a person whose job is to care for people who are ill. ② VERB If you **nurse** someone, you care for them while they are ill. *In hospital they nursed me back to health.* • **nursing** N-UNCOUNT *I wanted to go into something like nursing or dentistry.*

nursery /'nɜːsəri/ **nurseries.** ① N-COUNT A **nursery** is a place where children who are not old enough to go to school are looked after. *Her company ran its own workplace nursery.* ② N-COUNT A **nursery** is a place where plants are grown in order to be sold to the public.

ˈnursery rhyme, nursery rhymes. N-COUNT A

a
b
c
d
e
f
g
h
i
j
k
l
m
n
o
p
q
r
s
t
u
v
w
x
y
z

A
B
C
D
E
F
G
H
I
J
K
L
M
N
O
P
Q
R
S
T
U
V
W
X
Y
Z

nursery rhyme is a traditional poem or song for young children.

'nursing home, nursing homes. N-COUNT A **nursing home** is a private hospital for old people.

nurture/'nɜːtʃə/ **nurtures, nurturing, nurtured.** 1 VERB If you **nurture** a young child or a young plant, you care for it while it is growing and developing. [FORMAL] *Parents want to know the best way to nurture and raise their child.* 2 VERB If you **nurture** plans, ideas, or people, you encourage their development and success. [FORMAL] *She has always interrupted her own work to nurture the talent of others.*

nut/nʌt/ **nuts.** 1 N-COUNT The firm shelled fruit of some trees and bushes are called **nuts**. 2 N-COUNT A **nut** is a small piece of metal with a hole through which you put a bolt. Nuts and bolts are used to hold things together such as pieces of machinery. → See picture on page 833.

nutrient/'njuːtriənt, AM 'nuː-/ **nutrients.** N-COUNT **Nutrients** are chemical substances that people and animals need from food and plants need from soil. *...minerals and other essential nutrients.*

nutrition/njuːˈtrɪʃən, AM 'nuː-/. N-UNCOUNT **Nutrition** is the process of taking and absorbing nutrients from food. *There are alternative sources of nutrition to animal meat.*

nutritional/njuːˈtrɪʃənəl, AM 'nuː-/. ADJ The **nutritional** content of food is all the proteins, vitamins, and minerals that are in it which help you to remain healthy. ♦ **nutritionally**ADV *...a nutritionally balanced diet.*

nutritious/njuːˈtrɪʃəs, AM nuː-/. ADJ **Nutritious** food contains the proteins, vitamins, and minerals which help your body to be healthy. *...a hot, nutritious meal.*

nylon/'naɪlɒn/. N-UNCOUNT **Nylon** is a strong, flexible, artificial material. *Green nylon nets were piled up.*

O o

oak/əʊk/ **oaks.** N-VAR An **oak** or an **oak tree** is a type of large tree. **Oak** is the wood of this tree. *...a stout oak door.*

oar/ɔː/ **oars.** N-COUNT **Oars** are long poles with flat ends which are used for rowing a boat.

oasis/əʊˈeɪsɪs/ **oases**/əʊˈeɪsiːz/. 1 N-COUNT An **oasis** is a small area in a desert where water and plants are found. 2 N-COUNT You can refer to any pleasant place or situation as an **oasis** when it is surrounded by unpleasant ones. *The gardens are an oasis in the midst of Cairo's urban sprawl.*

oath/əʊθ/ **oaths.** 1 N-COUNT An **oath** is a formal promise. *He took an oath of loyalty to the government.* 2 N-SING In a court of law, if someone **takes the oath**, they formally promise to tell the truth . You can say that someone is **on oath** or **under oath** when they have made this promise.

oats/əʊts/. N-COUNT **Oats** are a cereal crop or its grains, used for making porridge or for feeding animals.

obedient/əʊˈbiːdiənt/. ADJ An **obedient** person or animal does what they are told to do. *He was always very obedient to his parents.* ♦ **obedience**N-UNCOUNT *...unquestioning obedience to the law.* ♦ **obediently**ADV *He was looking obediently at Keith.*

obese/əʊˈbiːs/. ADJ Someone who is **obese** is extremely fat. *Three-fifths of English women are overweight or obese.* ♦ **obesity**N-UNCOUNT *There is a link between diet, obesity, and disease.* ● See note at **fat**.

obey/əʊˈbeɪ/ **obeys, obeying, obeyed.** VERB If you **obey** a rule, instruction, or person, you do what you are told to do. *Most people obey the law... It was Baker's duty to obey.*

obituary/əʊˈbɪtʃʊəri, AM -ʃʊeri/ **obituaries.** N-COUNT Someone's **obituary** is an account of their character and achievements which is published shortly after they have died. *I read your brother's obituary in the Times.*

★ **object, objects, objecting, objected.** 1 N-COUNT /'ɒbdʒɪkt/ An **object** is anything that has a fixed shape or form and that is not alive. *...an object the shape of a coconut. ...everyday objects such as wooden spoons.* 2 N-COUNT The **object** of what someone is doing is their aim or purpose. *The object of the exercise is to raise money.* 3 N-COUNT The **object of** a particular feeling or reaction is the person or thing it is directed towards, or the person or thing that causes it. *The object of her hatred was 24-year-old Ros French.* 4 N-COUNT In grammar, the **object** of a clause is a noun group which refers to a person or thing that is affected by the action of the verb. In the sentence 'She married a young engineer', 'a young engineer' is the object. ● See also **direct object**, **indirect object** . 5 PHRASE If you say, for example, that **money is no object**, you are emphasizing that you are willing or able to spend as much money as necessary. *For him price is no object.* 6 VERB /əbˈdʒekt/ If you **object** to something, you express your dislike or disapproval of it. *Working people everywhere object to paying taxes... The Labour Party objects that the government's scheme is elitist.*

objection/əbˈdʒekʃən/ **objections.** N-VAR If you make an **objection to** something, you say that you do not like it or agree with it. *Two main objections to the proposal have been raised... I have no objection to banks making money.*

★ **objective**/əbˈdʒektɪv/ **objectives.** 1 N-COUNT Your **objective** is what you are trying to achieve. *His objective was to win.* 2 ADJ BEFORE N

Objective means based on facts and not influenced by personal feelings. *He had no objective evidence that anything extraordinary was happening... A journalist should be completely objective.* ♦ **objectively** ADV *We simply want to inform people objectively about events.* ♦ **objectivity** /ˌɒbdʒekˈtɪvɪti/ N-UNCOUNT *...the objectivity of science.*

obligation /ˌɒblɪˈgeɪʃən/ **obligations.** N-VAR If you have an **obligation to** do something, it is your duty to do it. If you have an **obligation to** a person, it is your duty to look after them. *He had not felt an obligation to help save his friend... We have an obligation to the children.*

obligatory /əˈblɪgətri, AM -tɔːri/. 1 ADJ If something is **obligatory**, you must do it, because there is a rule or law about it. *Sixteenth-century dress was obligatory for guests. ...an obligatory AIDS test.* 2 ADJ BEFORE N If you describe something as **obligatory**, you mean that it is done from habit or custom rather than out of enthusiasm. *His lips curved up in the obligatory smile.*

oblige /əˈblaɪdʒ/ **obliges, obliging, obliged.** 1 VERB If you **oblige** someone, you help them by doing what they have asked you to do. *If you ever need help with the babysitting, I'd be glad to oblige... They obliged with very straightforward answers.* 2 VERB If a situation or law **obliges** you **to** do something, it makes it necessary for you to do it. [FORMAL] *This decree obliges unions to delay strikes.*

obliged /əˈblaɪdʒd/. ADJ If you feel **obliged to** do something, you feel that you should do it, or a rule insists that you do it.

obliging /əˈblaɪdʒɪŋ/. ADJ If you describe someone as **obliging**, you think that they are willing and eager to be helpful. *...an extremely pleasant and obliging man.* ♦ **obligingly** ADV *Benedict obligingly held the door open.*

oblique /əʊˈbliːk/. ADJ An **oblique** statement is not expressed directly or openly, making it difficult to understand. *Mr Golding delivered an oblique warning.* ♦ **obliquely** ADV *He obliquely referred to the US.*

obliterate /əˈblɪtəreɪt/ **obliterates, obliterating, obliterated.** 1 VERB If something **obliterates** an object or place, it destroys it completely. *Whole villages were obliterated by fire.* ♦ **obliteration** N-UNCOUNT *...the obliteration of three rainforests.* 2 VERB If you **obliterate** something such as a memory or emotion, you remove it completely from your mind. [LITERARY] *There was time enough to obliterate memories of how things once were.*

oblivion /əˈblɪviən/. 1 N-UNCOUNT **Oblivion** is the state of not being aware of what is happening around you, for example because you are asleep or unconscious. *He had slipped once again into deep and dreamless oblivion.* 2 N-UNCOUNT **Oblivion** is the state of having been forgotten. *His football career seemed to be heading for oblivion.*

oblivious /əˈblɪviəs/. ADJ If you are **oblivious to** something, you are not aware of it. *She lay motionless where she was, oblivious to pain.*

obnoxious /ɒbˈnɒkʃəs/. ADJ If you describe someone as **obnoxious**, you think that they are very unpleasant. *He was a most obnoxious character. No-one liked him.*

obscene /ɒbˈsiːn/. ADJ If you describe something as **obscene**, you mean it offends you because it relates to sex or violence in an unpleasant and shocking way. *I think all these photographs are obscene.*

obscenity /ɒbˈsenɪti/ **obscenities.** 1 N-UNCOUNT **Obscenity** is behaviour that offends people because it relates to sex in an unpleasant or indecent way. *The photographs were not art but obscenity.* 2 N-COUNT An **obscenity** is a very rude word or expression. *They shouted obscenities at us.*

obscure /ɒbˈskjʊə/ **obscurer, obscurest; obscures, obscuring, obscured.** 1 ADJ If something or someone is **obscure**, they are unknown, or are known by only a few people. *The origin of the custom is obscure. ...an obscure Greek composer.* ♦ **obscurity** N-UNCOUNT *The latter half of his life was spent in obscurity.* 2 VERB If one thing **obscures** another, it prevents it from being seen or heard properly. *Trees obscured his vision; he couldn't see much of the square.* 3 ADJ If you describe something as **obscure**, you find it is difficult to understand or deal with, usually because it involves so many parts or details. *The contracts are written in obscure language.* ♦ **obscurity** N-UNCOUNT *Hunt was irritated by the obscurity of Henry's reply.*

observation /ˌɒbzəˈveɪʃən/ **observations.** 1 N-UNCOUNT **Observation** is the action or process of carefully watching someone or something. *...careful observation of the movement of the planets... In hospital she'll be under observation all the time.* ♦ **observational** ADJ *...observational studies of the early emotional relationships of young children.* 2 N-COUNT An **observation** is something that you have learned by seeing or watching something and thinking about it. *This book contains observations about the causes of addictions.* 3 N-COUNT If a person makes an **observation**, they make a comment about something or someone, usually as a result of watching how they behave. *He makes the observation that writing can be a kind of salvation for certain people.* 4 N-UNCOUNT **Observation** is the ability to notice things that are not usually noticed. *My powers of observation and memory had improved.*

observatory /əbˈzɜːvətri, AM -tɔːri/ **observatories.** N-COUNT An **observatory** is a building with a large telescope from which scientists study the stars and planets.

⭐ **observe** /əbˈzɜːv/ **observes, observing, observed.** 1 VERB If you **observe** someone or something, you watch them carefully. *Professor Stern studies and observes the behaviour of babies.* 2 VERB If

a b c d e f g h i j k l m n **o** p q r s t u v w x y z

you **observe** someone or something, you see or notice them. [FORMAL] *Hooke observed a reddish spot on the surface of the planet.* **3** VERB If you **observe** something such as a law or custom, you obey it or follow it. *...forcing motorists to observe speed restrictions.* ♦ **observance** N-UNCOUNT *...the observance of religious rituals.*

⭐ **observer** /əb'zɜːvə/ **observers.** **1** N-COUNT An **observer** is someone who sees or notices something. *Observers say the woman pulled a knife out and stabbed him.* **2** N-COUNT An **observer** is someone who studies current events and situations. *...an independent political observer.*

obsess /əb'ses/ **obsesses, obsessing, obsessed.** VERB If something **obsesses** you, you keep thinking about it and find it difficult to think about anything else. *The idea of hunting big game had obsessed me since I was about six... She stopped drinking but began obsessing about her weight.* ♦ **obsessed** ADJ *He was obsessed with American gangster movies.*

obsession /əb'seʃən/ **obsessions.** N-VAR If you say that someone has an **obsession with** someone or something, you feel they are spending too much of their time thinking about that person or thing. *She would try to forget her obsession with Christopher.*

obsessive /əb'sesɪv/. ADJ If someone's behaviour is **obsessive**, they cannot stop doing something or thinking about something. *Williams is obsessive about motor racing.* ♦ **obsessively** ADV *He couldn't help worrying obsessively about what would happen.*

obsolete /ˌɒbsə'liːt/. ADJ Something that is **obsolete** is no longer needed because a better thing now exists. *So much equipment becomes obsolete almost as soon as it's made.*

obstacle /'ɒbstəkəl/ **obstacles.** N-COUNT An **obstacle** is something which makes it difficult for you to go forward or do something. *A rabbit can jump obstacles up to three feet high... Overcrowding remains a large obstacle to improving housing conditions.*

obstetrician /ˌɒbstə'trɪʃən/ **obstetricians.** N-COUNT An **obstetrician** is a doctor who is trained to deal with childbirth and the care of pregnant women.

obstinate /'ɒbstɪnət/. ADJ If you describe someone as **obstinate**, you are critical of them because they are very determined to do what they want, and refuse to be persuaded to do something else. *He is obstinate and determined and will not give up.* ♦ **obstinately** ADV *Smith obstinately refused to carry out the order.* ♦ **obstinacy** N-UNCOUNT *She was capable of great obstinacy.*

obstruct /əb'strʌkt/ **obstructs, obstructing, obstructed.** **1** VERB To **obstruct** someone or something means to block their path, making it difficult for them to move forward. *Lorries have completely obstructed the road.* **2** VERB To **obstruct** something such as justice or progress means to prevent it from happening properly or from developing. *The authorities are obstructing a United Nations investigation.*

obstruction /əb'strʌkʃən/ **obstructions.** **1** N-VAR An **obstruction** is something that blocks a road or path. *...drivers parking near his house and causing an obstruction.* **2** N-UNCOUNT **Obstruction** is the act of deliberately preventing something from happening. *Obstruction of justice is a federal offence.*

⭐ **obtain** /əb'teɪn/ **obtains, obtaining, obtained.** VERB To **obtain** something means to get it or achieve it. [FORMAL] *Evans was trying to obtain a false passport.*

⭐ **obvious** /'ɒbviəs/. ADJ If something is **obvious**, it is easy to see or understand. *It's obvious he's worried about us. ...her obvious creative talents.*

⭐ **obviously** /'ɒbviəsli/. **1** ADV You use **obviously** when you are stating something that you expect your listener to know already. *Obviously I'd be disappointed if we don't make it, but it wouldn't be the end of the world.* **2** ADV You use **obviously** to indicate that something is easily noticed, seen, or recognized. *They obviously appreciate you very much.*

⭐ **occasion** /ə'keɪʒən/ **occasions.** **1** N-COUNT An **occasion** is a time when something happens. *On one occasion, his father threw a radio at his mother.* **2** N-COUNT An **occasion** is an important event, ceremony, or celebration. *The launch of a ship was a big occasion.* **3** N-COUNT An **occasion for** doing something is an opportunity for doing it. [FORMAL] *It is an occasion for all the family to celebrate.* **4** PHRASE If something happens **on occasion** or **on occasions**, it happens sometimes, but not very often. *Some of the players may, on occasion, break the rules.*

⭐ **occasional** /ə'keɪʒənəl/. ADJ **Occasional** means happening sometimes, but not regularly or often. *I've had occasional mild headaches.* ♦ **occasionally** ADV *He still misbehaves occasionally.*

occult /ɒ'kʌlt, 'ɒkʌlt/. N-SING **The occult** is the knowledge and study of supernatural or magical forces.

occupancy /'ɒkjʊpənsi/. N-UNCOUNT **Occupancy** is the act of using a room, building, or area of land for a fixed period of time. *Hotel occupancy has been as low as 40%.*

occupant /'ɒkjʊpənt/ **occupants.** N-COUNT The **occupants** of a building or room are the people who live or work there. *Most of the occupants had left before the fire broke out.*

⭐ **occupation** /ˌɒkjʊ'peɪʃən/ **occupations.** **1** N-COUNT Your **occupation** is your job or your profession. ♦ **occupational** ADJ *...the occupational hazards of mining.* **2** N-COUNT An **occupation** is something that you do for pleasure or as part of your daily life. *Parachuting is a dangerous occupation.* **3** N-UNCOUNT The **occupation** of a country is its invasion and control by a foreign army. ...*the deportation of Jews from Paris during the German occupation.*

⭐ **occupy** /'ɒkjʊpaɪ/ **occupies, occupying, occupied.** **1** VERB The people who **occupy** a building or place are the people who live or work there. *Land is, in most instances, purchased by those who occupy it.* ♦ **occupier, occupiers** N-COUNT ...*junk mail addressed to 'the occupier'.* **2** PASSIVE-VERB If something such as a seat **is occupied**, someone is using it, so that it is not available for anyone else. *I saw three camp beds, two of which were occupied.* **3** VERB If something **occupies** you, or if you **occupy yourself with** it, you are busy doing it or thinking about it. *Her parliamentary career has occupied all of her time... He occupied himself with packing the car.* ♦ **occupied** ADJ *I had been so occupied with other things.* **4** VERB If soldiers **occupy** a place or country, they move into it, using force in order to gain control of it. *U.S. forces now occupy a part of the country.* **5** VERB If someone or something **occupies** a particular place in a system, process, or plan, they have that place. *Many men still occupy more positions of power than women.*

⭐ **occur** /ə'kɜː/ **occurs, occurring, occurred.** **1** VERB When an event **occurs**, it happens. *The crash occurred on a sharp bend... Events of this description occurred daily.* **2** VERB When something **occurs** in a particular place, it exists or is present there. *Nitrates are chemicals that occur naturally in water.* **3** VERB If a thought or idea **occurs to** you, you suddenly think of it or realize it. *It did not occur to me to check my insurance policy... It occurred to me that I could have the book sent to me.*

occurrence /ə'kʌrəns, AM -'kɜːr-/ **occurrences.** N-COUNT An **occurrence** is something that happens. [FORMAL] *Complaints seemed to be an everyday occurrence.*

⭐ **ocean** /'əʊʃən/ **oceans.** N-COUNT **The ocean** is the sea. *There were few sights as beautiful as the calm ocean. ...the Indian Ocean.*

⭐ **o'clock** /ə'klɒk/. ADV You use **o'clock** after numbers from one to twelve to say what time it is. *It's almost eight o'clock. ...ten o'clock last night.*

⭐ **October** /ɒk'təʊbə/. N-UNCOUNT **October** is the tenth month of the year. → See Reference Page on Times and Dates.

octopus /'ɒktəpəs/ **octopuses.** N-VAR An **octopus** is a sea creature with eight tentacles.

⭐ **odd** /ɒd/ **odder, oddest.** **1** ADJ If you say that someone or something is **odd**, you mean that they are strange or unusual. *He'd always been odd... What an odd coincidence.* ♦ **oddly** ADV ...*an oddly shaped hill... He was behaving extremely oddly.* **2** ADJ You use **odd** before a noun to indicate that the type or size of something is not important. ...*moving from place to place where she could find the odd bit of work... He likes the odd drink.* **3** ADJ You say that two things are **odd** when they do not belong to the same set or pair. ...*odd socks.* **4** ADJ **Odd** numbers cannot be

divided exactly by the number two. **5** ADV You use **odd** after a number to indicate that it is approximate. [INFORMAL] *I've lived here for forty odd years.* **6** PHRASE In a group of people or things, **the odd one out** is the one that is different from all the others.

oddity /'ɒdɪti/ **oddities.** **1** N-COUNT An **oddity** is someone or something that is strange or unusual. *Tourists are still something of an oddity.* **2** N-COUNT The **oddity** of something is the fact that it is strange. ...*one of the oddities of human intelligence.*

odds /ɒdz/. N-PLURAL You refer to the probability of something happening as **the odds** that it will happen. *What are the odds of winning a prize?* PHRASES ● If something happens **against all odds**, it happens or succeeds although it seemed impossible or very unlikely. *Some women do manage to achieve business success against all odds.* ● If you are **at odds with** someone, you are disagreeing or quarrelling with them.

odour (AM **odor**) /'əʊdə/ **odours.** N-COUNT An **odour** is a smell. ...*the odour of tobacco.*

odyssey /'ɒdɪsi/ **odysseys.** N-COUNT An **odyssey** is a long exciting journey on which a lot of things happen. [LITERARY]

⭐ **of** /əv, STRONG ɒv, AM ʌv/. **1** PREP You use **of** to say who or what someone or something belongs to, or is connected with. ...*the immaculately maintained homes of the rich. ...the new mayor of Los Angeles. ...the superb temples of India.* **2** PREP You use **of** to say what something relates to or concerns. ...*her feelings of jealousy. ...cancer of the breast.* **3** PREP You use **of** to say who or what a feeling or quality relates to. *I have grown very fond of Alec... She would be guilty of betraying her mother.* **4** PREP You use **of** to talk about someone or something else who is also involved in an action. *He'd been dreaming of her... The Americans cannot accuse him of ignoring the problem.* **5** PREP You use **of** to show that someone or something is part of a larger group. *Gita Saghal is the youngest child of three. ...a blade of grass.* **6** PREP You use **of** to talk about amounts. ...*a rise of 13.8%. ...a glass of beer. ...eight years of war.* **7** PREP You use **of** to say how old someone or something is. *She is a young woman of twenty-six... I feel like a girl of 18.* **8** PREP You use **of** to say the date when talking about what day of the month it is. ...*the 4th of July.* **9** PREP You use **of** to say when something happened. *Some of the economic errors of the past are at last being put right... Rene announced his retirement at the end of the month.* **10** PREP You use **of** to say what substance or materials something is formed from. ...*a mixture of paint-thinner and petrol... The traditional thermometer is made of brass.* **11** PREP You use **of** to say what caused or is causing a person's or animal's death. *One of her ex-husbands is dying of cancer.* **12** PREP You use **of** to talk about someone's qualities or characteristics. *Andrew is a man of honour... She's a woman of few words, but the few*

⭐ Bank of English® frequent word   For a full explanation of all grammatical labels, see pages vii-x

a b c d e f g h i j k l m n o p q r s t u v w x y z

words are potent. [13] PREP You use **of** to describe someone's behaviour. *That's very kind of you.*

⭐ **of 'course.** [1] ADV You say **of course** to say that something is not surprising because it is normal, obvious, or well-known. *Of course there were lots of other interesting things at the exhibition.* [2] ADV You use **of course** in order to emphasize a statement that you are making. *Of course I'm not afraid!* [3] CONVENTION You say **of course** as a polite way of giving permission. [SPOKEN] *'Could I see these documents?'—'Of course.'* [4] CONVENTION **Of course not** is an emphatic way of saying no. [SPOKEN] *'You won't tell him, will you?'—'Of course not.'*

⭐ **off** /ɒf, AM ɔ:f/. [1] PREP & ADV When something is taken **off** something else or moves **off** it, it is no longer touching that thing. *He took his feet off the desk... Hugh wiped the blood off his face... Lee broke off a small piece of orange.* [2] PREP & ADV When you get **off** a bus, train, or plane, you get out of it. *As he stepped off the aeroplane, he was shot dead... At the next stop the man got off too and introduced himself.* [3] ADV When you go **off**, you leave the place where you were. *He was just about to drive off.* [4] PREP & ADV If you keep **off** a street or piece of land, you do not go onto it. *The police had warned visitors to keep off the beach. ...a sign saying 'Keep Off'.* [5] PREP & ADV If something is situated **off** a place such as a room or road, it is near to it, but not exactly in it. *The boat was anchored off the northern coast. ...a penthouse just off Park Avenue.* [6] ADV If you fight something **off** or keep it **off**, you make it go away or prevent it. *...the body's effort to fight off the common cold.* [7] ADV & PREP If you have time **off**, you do not go to work for a period of time. *The rest of the men had the day off... He could not get time off work.* [8] ADJ & ADV If something such as a machine or an electric light is **off**, it is not in use. *He saw her bedroom light was off... The microphones have been switched off.* [9] ADJ If an agreement or an arranged event is **off**, it has been cancelled. *The deal's off... Greenpeace refused to call off the event.* [10] ADJ AFTER LINK-V If food has gone **off**, it tastes and smells unpleasant because it is going bad. [11] PREP If you are **off** something, you have stopped using it or liking it. [INFORMAL] *I'm off coffee at the moment... The psychiatrist took her off drug therapy.* [12] ADV If something is a long time **off**, it will not happen for a long time. *The required technology is probably still two years off.* [13] PHRASE If something happens **on and off** or **off and on**, it happens occasionally, or only for part of a period of time, not in a regular or continuous way. *I was still working on and off as a waitress.*

offal /'ɒfəl, AM 'ɔ:fəl/. N-UNCOUNT **Offal** is the liver, kidneys, and other internal organs of an animal, when they are used for food.

,**off-'balance** (or**off balance**). ADJ AFTER LINK-V If someone or something is **off-balance**, they can easily fall or be knocked over because

they are not standing firmly. *She was thrown off-balance.*

,**off 'duty** (or**off-duty**). ADJ When someone such as a soldier or policeman is **off duty**, they are not working. *...an off-duty policeman.*

⭐ **offence** (AM**offense**) /ə'fens/ **offences.** [1] N-COUNT An **offence** is a crime. [FORMAL] *He has committed hundreds of offences.* [2] N-UNCOUNT If you give **offence**, you upset or embarrass someone. *We did not mean to cause any offence.* [3] PHRASE If you **take offence**, you are upset by something that someone says or does. *She never takes offence at anything.*

offend /ə'fend/ **offends, offending, offended.** [1] VERB If you **offend** someone, you upset or embarrass them. ♦ **offended** ADJ *She is terribly offended and hurt by this.* [2] VERB To **offend against** a law, rule, or principle means to break it. *This bill offends against good sense.* [3] VERB If someone **offends**, they commit a crime. *Girls are far less likely to offend than boys.* ♦ **offender, offenders** N-COUNT *...a prison for young offenders.*

offense /ə'fens, 'ɒfens/. See **offence**.

⭐ **offensive** /ə'fensɪv/ **offensives.** [1] ADJ Something that is **offensive** upsets or embarrasses people because it is rude or insulting. *...an offensive remark.* [2] N-COUNT An **offensive** is a strong attack. *...a military offensive on the guerrilla base.* [3] PHRASE If you **go on the offensive, go over to the offensive**, or **take the offensive**, you begin to take strong action against people who have been attacking you.

⭐ **offer** /'ɒfə, AM 'ɔ:fər/ **offers, offering, offered.** [1] VERB If you **offer** something **to** someone, you ask them if they would like to have it or to use it. *I was brought up to offer my seat to a lady on the tube... She offered him a cup of tea. ...a new magazine offering advice on finance.* [2] VERB If you **offer to** do something, you say that you are willing to do it. *Greg offered to teach him to ski... 'Can I get you a drink,' she offered.* [3] VERB If you **offer** a particular amount of money **for** something, you say that you will pay that much for it. *The UN has offered $25,000 reward for information leading to his arrest.* [4] N-COUNT An **offer** is something that someone says they will give you or do for you. *He was made a film offer he could not refuse... Ingrid would not accept Steele's offer to drive her to her car.* [5] N-COUNT An **offer** in a shop is a specially low price for a product, or something extra that you get by buying the product. *...special offers on alcohol.* [6] PHRASE If something is **on offer**, it is available to be used or bought. *...some of the excellent books on offer.*

offering /'ɒfərɪŋ, AM 'ɔ:f-/ **offerings.** N-COUNT An **offering** is something that is specially produced to be sold.

⭐ **office** /'ɒfɪs, AM 'ɔ:f-/ **offices.** [1] N-COUNT An **office** is a room or a part of a building where people work sitting at desks. *I arrived at the office early.* [2] N-COUNT An **office** is a department of an organization, especially the government, where people deal with a particular kind of administrative work. *Contact your local tax office.* ③ N-COUNT An **office** is a small building or room where people can go for information, tickets, or a service of some kind. *...the tourist office.* ④ N-UNCOUNT Someone who holds **office** has an important job or a position of authority in government or in an organization. *...events to mark the President's first ten years in office.*

★ **officer**/'ɒfɪsə, AM 'ɔːf-/• **officers.** ① N-COUNT In the armed forces, an **officer** is a person in a position of authority. *...army officers.* ② N-COUNT An **officer** is a person who has a responsible position in an organization, especially a government organization. *...a local authority education officer.* ③ N-COUNT & N-VOC Members of the police force can be referred to as **officers**. *...senior police officers... Thank you, Officer.*

★ **official**/ə'fɪʃəl/• **officials.** ① ADJ Something that is **official** is approved by the government or by someone else in authority. *...the official unemployment figures.* ♦ **officially** ADV *The election results have still not been officially announced.* ② ADJ BEFORE N **Official** is used to describe things which are done or used by people in authority as part of their job or position. *Mr Ridley is currently on an official visit to Hungary. ...the Irish President's official residence.* ③ N-COUNT An **official** is a person who holds a position of authority in an organization. *...a senior UN official.*

'**off-licence**, **off-licences.** N-COUNT In Britain, an **off-licence** is a shop which sells alcoholic drinks. The usual American expression is **liquor store**.

offline(also **off-line**)/,ɒf'laɪn, AM ,ɔːf-/. ADJ & ADV If a computer is **offline**, it is not connected to the Internet. [COMPUTING] *Most software programs allow you to compose emails offline.*

,**off-'peak** ADJ BEFORE N & ADV **Off-peak** things are available at a time when there is little demand for them, so that they are cheaper than usual. *...off-peak electricity... Calls cost 39p a minute off-peak.*

offset/,ɒf'set, AM ,ɔːf-/• **offsets, offsetting, offset.** VERB If one thing **is offset** by another, the effect of the first thing is reduced by the second, so that any advantage or disadvantage is cancelled out. *The slump in sales was offset by a surge in exports.*

offshoot/'ɒfʃuːt, AM 'ɔːf-/• **offshoots.** N-COUNT If one thing is an **offshoot** of another thing, it has developed from the other thing. *The technology we use is an offshoot of the motor industry.*

offshore(or **off-shore**)/,ɒf'ʃɔː, AM ,ɔːf-/. ADJ & ADV **Offshore** means situated or happening in the sea, near to the coast. *...an offshore island... One day a larger ship anchored offshore.*

offside(or **off-side**)/,ɒf'saɪd, AM ,ɔːf-/. ① ADJ & ADV If a player in a game of football or hockey is **offside**, they have broken the rules by moving too far forward. *Rush was clearly offside... Wise*

was standing at least ten yards offside. ② N-SING The **offside** of a vehicle is the side farthest from the pavement when you are driving. [BRITISH]

offspring/'ɒfsprɪŋ, AM 'ɔːf-/.

✓ **Offspring** is both the singular and the plural form.

N-COUNT You can refer to a person's children or to an animal's young as their **offspring**. [FORMAL]

★ **often**/'ɒfən, AM 'ɔːf-/. ① ADV If something happens **often**, it happens many times or much of the time. *They often spent Christmas at Prescott Hill... They used these words freely, often in front of their parents too... That doesn't happen very often.* ② ADV You use **often** after 'how' to ask questions about frequency. You also use **often** in statements to give information about the frequency of something. *How often do you brush your teeth?... They jog twice as often as the general population.*

> **USAGE** You do not use **often** to talk about something that happens several times within a short period of time. You do not say, for example, 'I often phoned her yesterday'. You say **'I phoned her several times yesterday'** or **'I kept phoning her yesterday'**.

PHRASES ● If something happens **every so often**, it happens regularly, but with fairly long intervals between each occasion. *Every so often he would turn and look at her.* ● If you say that something happens **more often than not** or **as often as not**, you mean that it happens fairly frequently, and that this can be considered as typical of the kind of situation you are talking about. *Behind many successful men there is, more often than not, a woman who makes this success possible.*

★ **oh**/əʊ/. ① CONVENTION You use **oh** to introduce a response or a comment on something that has just been said. [SPOKEN] *'Would you like me to phone and explain the situation?'—'Oh, would you?'.* ② EXCLAM You use **oh** to express a feeling such as surprise, pain, annoyance, or joy. [SPOKEN] *'Oh!' Kenny blinked. 'Has everyone gone?'... 'Oh, my God,' Korontzis moaned.* ③ CONVENTION You use **oh** when you are hesitating while speaking, for example because you are trying to estimate something, or because you are searching for the right word. *I've been here, oh, since the end of June.*

★ **oil**/ɔɪl/• **oils, oiling, oiled.** ① N-VAR **Oil** is a smooth thick liquid used as a fuel and for lubricating machines. Oil is found underground. *The company buys and sells about 600,000 barrels of oil a day. ...a small oil-lamp.* ② VERB If you **oil** something, you put oil onto it or into it in order to make it work smoothly or to protect it. *A crew of assistants oiled and adjusted the release mechanism.* ③ N-VAR **Oil** is a smooth thick liquid

a b c d e f g h i j k l m n o p q r s t u v w x y z

made from plants or fish and used in cookery. *...olive oil.*

'oil paint, oil paints. N-VAR **Oil paint** is a thick paint used by artists.

'oil painting, oil paintings. N-COUNT An **oil painting** is a picture which has been painted using oil paints.

'oil slick, oil slicks. N-COUNT An **oil slick** is a layer of oil that floats on the sea or on a lake. It is formed when oil accidentally spills out of a ship or container.

oily /ˈɔɪli/ **oilier, oiliest.** ADJ Something that is **oily** is covered with oil, contains oil, or looks, feels, or tastes like oil. *...an oily rag... Paul found the tomato sauce too oily. ...a skin tonic for oily, blemished complexions.*

ointment /ˈɔɪntmənt/ **ointments.** N-VAR An **ointment** is a smooth thick substance that is put on sore skin or a wound to help it heal. *A range of ointments and creams is available for the treatment of eczema.*

⭐ **okay** (or **OK**) /ˌəʊˈkeɪ/. **1** ADJ & ADV If you say that something is **okay**, you mean that it is acceptable. [INFORMAL] *Is it okay if I come by myself?... We seemed to manage okay for the first year.* **2** ADJ AFTER LINK-V If you say that someone is **okay**, you mean that they are safe and well. *Check that the baby's okay.* **3** CONVENTION You can say **okay** to show that you agree to something. *'Shall I give you a ring on Friday?'—'Yeah okay.'* **4** CONVENTION You can say **'Okay?'** to check whether the person you are talking to understands what you have said and accepts it. *We'll get together next week, OK?*

⭐ **old** /əʊld/ **older, oldest.** **1** ADJ & N-PLURAL Someone who is **old** has lived for many years and is no longer young. You can refer to old people as **the old**. *...a white-haired old man.* **2** ADJ Something that is **old** has existed for a long time. *These books must be very old. ...an old Arab proverb.* **3** ADJ Something that is **old** is no longer in good condition because of its age or because it has been used a lot. *...an old toothbrush.* **4** ADJ You use **old** to talk or ask about the age of someone or something. ● See note at **elder**. *The paintings in the chapel were perhaps a thousand years old... How old are you now?* **5** ADJ BEFORE N You use **old** to refer to something that is no longer used, that no longer exists, or that has been replaced by something else. *The old road had disappeared under grass.* **6** ADJ BEFORE N You use **old** to refer to something that used to belong to you, or to a person or thing that used to have a particular role in your life. *I'll make up the bed in your old room. ...when Jane returned to her old boyfriend.* **7** ADJ BEFORE N An **old** friend or enemy is someone who has been your friend or enemy for a long time. **8** PHRASE You use **any old** to emphasize that the quality or type of something is not important. If you say that a particular thing is not **any old** thing, you are emphasizing how special or famous it is. *Any old paper will do... This is not just any old front room.*

,old 'age. **1** N-UNCOUNT Your **old age** is the period of years towards the end of your life. *They worry about how they will support themselves in their old age.* **2** N-UNCOUNT **Old age** is the quality or state of being old and near the end of one's life. *We tend to consider old age as a social problem.*

,old-'fashioned. ADJ Something that is **old-fashioned** is no longer used, done, or believed by most people, because it has been replaced by something that is more modern. *The house was dull, old-fashioned and in bad condition... They still make cheese the old-fashioned way.*

olive /ˈɒlɪv/ **olives.** **1** N-VAR **Olives** are small green or black fruit with a bitter taste. The tree on which olives grow is called an **olive tree** or an **olive.** **2** ADJ & N-VAR Something that is **olive** is yellowish-green in colour.

'olive oil. N-UNCOUNT **Olive oil** is edible oil obtained by pressing olives.

⭐ **Olympic** /əˈlɪmpɪk/ **Olympics.** **1** ADJ BEFORE N **Olympic** means relating to the Olympic Games. *...Gao, the reigning Olympic champion.* **2** N-PROPER **The Olympics** are the **Olympic Games.**

O,lympic 'Games. N-PROPER **The Olympic Games** are a set of international sports competitions which take place every four years, each time in a different country. **Olympic Games** can take the singular or plural form of the verb.

omelette (AM **omelet**) /ˈɒmlət/ **omelettes.** N-COUNT An **omelette** is a food made by beating eggs and cooking them in a flat pan.

omen /ˈəʊmen/ **omens.** N-COUNT If you say that something is an **omen**, you think it indicates what is likely to happen in the future and whether it will be good or bad. *Her appearance at this moment is an omen of disaster.*

ominous /ˈɒmɪnəs/. ADJ If you describe something as **ominous**, you mean that it worries you because it makes you think that something unpleasant is going to happen. *The rolls of distant thunder were growing more ominous.*
◆ **ominously** ADV *The bar seemed ominously quiet.*

omission /əʊˈmɪʃən/ **omissions.** N-VAR An **omission** is the act of not including something or not doing something. *We overcame the prosecution's seemingly malicious omission of recorded evidence.*

omit /əʊˈmɪt/ **omits, omitting, omitted.** **1** VERB If you **omit** something, you do not include it in an activity or piece of work. *Omit the salt in this recipe... Our apologies to David Pannick for omitting his name from last week's article.* **2** VERB If you **omit to** do something, you do not do it. [FORMAL] *His new girlfriend had omitted to tell him she was married.*

⭐ **on** /ɒn/. **1** PREP If someone or something is **on** a surface or object, the surface or object is underneath them and is supporting their weight. *He is sitting beside her on the sofa... On top of the* cupboards are vast straw baskets. ...the Chinese rug on the floor. **2** PREP If something is **on** a surface or object, it is stuck to it or attached to it. ...the peeling paint on the ceiling... There was a smear of gravy on his chin. **3** PREP If you get **on** a bus, train, or plane, you go in it in order to travel somewhere. You say you are **on** the bus, train, or plane when you are travelling in it. I never go on the bus into the town. **4** PREP If there is something **on** a piece of paper, it has been written or printed there. ...the writing on the back of the card. ...the numbers she put on the chart. **5** ADV When you put a piece of clothing **on**, you place it over a part of your body in order to wear it. If you have it **on**, you are wearing it. He put his coat on... I had a hat on. **6** PREP You can say that you have something **on** you if you are carrying it in your pocket or in a bag. I didn't have any money on me. **7** PREP If something happens **on** a particular day or date, that is when it happens. → See Reference Page on Times and Dates. This year's event will take place on June 19th... She travels to Korea on Monday. **8** PREP You use **on** when mentioning an event that was followed by another one. She waited in her hotel to welcome her children on their arrival from London... On reaching Dubai the evacuees were taken straight to Dubai international airport. **9** PREP If something is done **on** an instrument, machine, or system, it is done using that instrument, machine, or system. I could do all my work on the computer. **10** ADJ & ADV If something such as a machine or an electric light is **on**, it is functioning or in use. The light was on and the door was open... I've turned the central heating on again. **11** PREP Books, discussions, or ideas **on** a particular subject are concerned with that subject. ...any book on baby care. ...a free counselling service which can offer help and advice on legal matters. **12** PREP If something affects you, you can say that it has an effect **on** you. **13** PREP When you buy something or pay for something, you spend money **on** it. I resolved not to waste money on a hotel. **14** PREP When you spend time or energy **on** a particular activity, you spend time or energy doing it. Children spend so much time on computer games. **15** ADV You use **on** to say that someone is continuing to do something. They walked on in silence... Read on for further hints. **16** PREP If you are **on** a council or committee, you are a member of it. Claire and Beryl were on the organizing committee. **17** PREP If someone is **on** a medicine or drug, they are taking it regularly. If someone lives **on** a particular kind of food, they eat it. She was on antibiotics for an eye infection... The caterpillars feed on a wide range of trees, shrubs and plants. **18** PREP If you are **on** a particular kind of income, that is the kind of income you have. ...young people who are unemployed or on low wages. **19** ADV When an activity is taking place, you can say that it is **on**. It tells you what here what's on at the cinema. **20** PREP If something is being broadcast, you can say that it is **on** the radio or television.

...every sporting event on television and satellite. **21** ADV If you say that someone goes **on at** you, you mean that they continually criticize you, complain to you, or ask you to do something. She's been on at me for weeks to show her round the stables... He used to keep on at me about the need to win. **22** PHRASE If you **have a lot on**, you are very busy. If you **do not have much on**, you are not busy. [SPOKEN] **23** **and so on**: see **so**.

⭐ **once** /wʌns, wɒns/. **1** ADV If something happens **once**, it happens one time only, or one time within a particular period of time. I met Wilma once, briefly... Since then I haven't once slept through the night... Mary had only been to Manchester once before. **2** ADV If something was **once** true, it was true at some time in the past, but is no longer true. The house where she lives was once the village post office. **3** CONJ If something happens **once** another thing has happened, it happens immediately afterwards. Once customers come to rely on these systems they almost never take their business elsewhere.
　PHRASES ● If something happens **once and for all**, it happens completely or finally. We have to resolve this matter once and for all. ● If you do something **at once**, you do it immediately. I have to go, I really must, at once. ● If several things happen **at once** or **all at once**, they all happen at the same time. You can't be doing two things at once. ● **For once** is used to emphasize that something happens on this particular occasion, especially if it has never happened before, and may never happen again. For once, dad is not complaining. ● **once upon a time**: see **time**. ● **once in a while**: see **while**.

⭐ **one** /wʌn, wɒn /ones. **1** NUM **One** is the number 1. They had three sons and one daughter. ...one thousand years ago. ...one of the children killed in the crash. **2** DET & PRON You can use **one** to refer to the first of two or more things that you are comparing. Prices vary from one shop to another... The twins were dressed differently and one was thinner than the other. **3** PRON You can use **one** or **ones** when it is clear what type of thing or person you are referring to and you are describing them or giving more information about them. They are selling their house to move to a smaller one. **4** DET You can use **one** when referring to a time in the past or in the future. For example, if you say that you did something **one day**, you mean that you did it on a day in the past. How would you like to have dinner one night? **5** PRON Speakers and writers sometimes use **one** to make statements about people in general which also apply to themselves. **One** can be used as the subject or object of a sentence. [FORMAL] Where does one go from there?... Shares and bonds can bring one quite a considerable additional income.
　PHRASES ● If you say that someone is **at one with** the world, their feelings, or other people, you mean that they feel happy and relaxed in

the situation they are in. *Take a stroll through the countryside and be at one with nature.* ● You use **one or other** to refer to one or more things or people in a group, when it does not matter which one is thought of or chosen. *...discrimination against one or other of the sexes.* ● **One or two** means a few. *We may make one or two changes.* ● **one another**: see **another**.

,one-'off, one-offs. [1] N-COUNT A **one-off** is something that is made or happens only once. [MAINLY BRITISH] [2] ADJ BEFORE N A **one-off** thing is made or happens only once. [MAINLY BRITISH] *...one-off cash benefits.*

onerous /'əʊnərəs, AM 'ɑːn-/. ADJ If you describe a task as **onerous**, you dislike having to do it because you find it difficult or unpleasant. [FORMAL] *...the onerous task of bringing up a very difficult child.*

⭐ **one's** /wʌnz/. [1] DET Speakers and writers use **one's** to indicate that something belongs or relates to people in general, or to themselves in particular. [FORMAL] *It is natural to care for one's family and one's children.* [2] **One's** can be used as a spoken form of 'one is' or 'one has', especially when 'has' is an auxiliary verb. *No one's going to hurt you... 'No-one's got respect for him any more.'*

oneself /wʌn'self/. [1] PRON A speaker or writer uses **oneself** to refer to themselves or to any person in general. *...a way of making oneself feel sophisticated... To work one must have time to oneself.* [2] PRON To do something **oneself** means to do it without any help or interference from anyone else. [FORMAL] *Some things one must do oneself.* [3] PRON You use **oneself** to emphasize that something happens to you rather than to people in general. *It is better to die oneself than to kill.*

,one-'sided. [1] ADJ In a **one-sided** activity or relationship, one of the people or groups involved does much more than the other or is much stronger than the other. *The negotiating was completely one-sided. ...a very one-sided match.* [2] ADJ If you describe someone as **one-sided**, you are critical of them because they have considered only one side of an issue or event. *Historians should be less one-sided, pay more attention to the contributions of women.*

'one-time (or **onetime**). ADJ BEFORE N **One-time** can be used to describe something such as a job or role which someone used to have, or something which happened or existed in the past. *...a one-time body builder.*

,one-to-'one. ADJ BEFORE N & ADV In a **one-to-one** relationship, you deal with only one other person. *...one-to-one counselling is the answer... She would like to talk to people one to one.*

,one-'way. [1] ADJ In **one-way** streets or traffic systems, vehicles can only travel in one direction.

[2] ADJ A **one-way** ticket enables you to travel to a place, but not to come back again. *The fare is £85 one-way.*

ongoing /,ɒn'gəʊɪŋ/. ADJ An **ongoing** situation is continuing to happen. *There is an ongoing debate on the issue.*

onion /'ʌnjən/ **onions.** N-VAR An **onion** is a small round vegetable. It is white with a brown skin, and has a strong smell and taste. → See picture on page 836.

⭐ **online** (or **on-line**) /,ɒn'laɪn/. ADJ & ADV **Online** means available on or connected to the Internet. [COMPUTING] *...an online catalogue... You can chat to other people online.*

onlooker /'ɒnlʊkə/ **onlookers.** N-COUNT An **onlooker** is someone who is watching an event. *A small crowd of onlookers were there to watch Mrs Thatcher.*

⭐ **only** /'əʊnli/. [1] ADV You use **only** to indicate the one thing that is true, appropriate, or necessary in a particular situation. *Only the President could authorize the use of the atomic bomb... A business can only be built on a sound financial base.* [2] ADV You use **only** to introduce the thing which must happen before the thing mentioned in the main part of the sentence can happen. *The lawyer is paid only if he wins.* [3] ADJ BEFORE N If you talk about the **only** person or thing involved in a particular situation, you mean there are no others involved in it. *She was the only woman in the legal department.* [4] ADJ BEFORE N An **only** child is a child who has no brothers or sisters. [5] ADV You use **only** to emphasize that something is unimportant or small. *I was only joking... Child car seats only cost about £10 a week to hire... Teenagers typically earn only half the adult wage.* [6] ADV You use **only** to emphasize a wish or hope. *We can only hope that she can recover.* [7] CONJ **Only** can be used to add a comment which slightly changes or corrects what you have just said. [INFORMAL] *It's a bit like my house, only nicer... It's just as dramatic as a film, only it's real.* [8] CONJ **Only** can be used after a clause with 'would' to indicate why something is not done. [SPOKEN] *I'd invite you to come with me, only it's such a long way.* [9] ADV You can use **only** before an infinitive to introduce an event which happens immediately after one you have just mentioned, and which is rather surprising or unfortunate. *I tried ringing them dozens of times only to find the number engaged.* [10] ADV You can use **only** to emphasize how appropriate a certain course of action or type of behaviour is. *It's only fair to let her know that you intend to apply... She appeared to have changed considerably, which was only to be expected.*

PHRASES ● You can say that something has **only just** happened when you want to emphasize that it happened a very short time ago. *I've only just arrived.* ● You use **only just** to emphasize that something is true, but by such a small degree that it is almost not true at all. *For centuries*

farmers there have only just managed to survive.
● **if only**: see **if**.

USAGE When **only** is used as an adverb, its position in the sentence depends on the word or phrase it applies to. If **only** applies to the subject of a clause, you put it in front of the subject. *Only strong characters can make such decisions.* Otherwise, you normally put it in front of the verb, or after the first auxiliary, or after the verb **be**. *I only want my son back, that is all... He had only agreed to see me because we had met before... I was only able to wash four times in 66 days.* However, some people think it is more correct to put **only** directly in front of the word or phrase it applies to. This is the best position if you want to be quite clear or emphatic. *It applies only to passengers carrying British passports... She'd done it only because it was necessary.* For extra emphasis, you can put **only** after the word or phrase it applies to. *The event will be for women only... I'll say this once and once only.*

on-'screen(or **onscreen**). **1** ADJ BEFORE N **On-screen** means appearing on the screen of a television, cinema, or computer. *...a clear and easy-to-follow menu-driven on-screen display.* **2** ADJ BEFORE N & ADV **On-screen** means relating to the roles being played by film or television actors. *...her on-screen romance with Pierce Lawton... He was immensely attractive to women, onscreen and offscreen.*

onset/'ɒnset/. N-SING The **onset** of something unpleasant is the beginning of it. *...the onset of the disease.*

onslaught/'ɒnslɔːt/ **onslaughts**. **1** N-COUNT An **onslaught on** someone or something is a very violent attack against them. *The attackers launched another vicious onslaught on their victim.* **2** N-COUNT If you refer to an **onslaught of** something, you mean that there is a large amount of it, often so that it is very difficult to deal with. *The onslaught of orders should keep aircraft manufacturers busy.*

onto(or **on to**) /'ɒntuː/. **1** PREP If someone or something moves **onto** an object, or if they are put **onto** it, they are then on that object or surface. *I lowered myself onto the bed and switched on the TV... Smear cream on to your baby's skin.* **2** PREP When you get **onto** a bus, train, or plane, you enter it. **3** PREP **Onto** is used after verbs such as 'hold', 'hang', and 'cling' to indicate what someone is holding firmly or where something is being held firmly. *She had to cling onto the door handle until the pain passed.* **4** PREP If people who are talking get **onto** a different subject, they begin talking about it. *Let's get on to more important matters.* **5** PREP If someone is **onto** something, they are about to

make a discovery. [INFORMAL] *Archaeologists knew they were onto something big when they started digging.* **6** PREP If someone is **onto** you, they have discovered that you are doing something illegal or wrong. [INFORMAL] *I had told people what he had been doing, so the police were onto him.*

onus/'əʊnəs/. N-SING If you say that the **onus** is **on** someone **to** do something, you mean it is their duty or responsibility to do it. *The onus is on the shopkeeper to provide quality goods.*

onward/'ɒnwəd/ (or **onwards**/'ɒnwədz/). **1** ADJ & ADV **Onward** means moving forward or continuing a journey. *British Airways have two flights a day to Bangkok, and there are onward flights to Phnom Penh... He led us onwards through the forest... The bus continued onward.* **2** ADJ & ADV **Onward** means developing, progressing, or becoming more important over a period of time. *...the onward march of progress in the British aircraft industry... The White House feels no compulsion to rush onwards to a new agreement.* **3** ADV If something happens from a particular time **onwards** or **onward**, it begins to happen at that time and continues to happen afterwards. *...from the turn of the century onward.*

ooze/uːz/ **oozes, oozing, oozed**. **1** VERB When a thick or sticky liquid **oozes** from something, the liquid flows slowly and in small quantities. *The wounds were still oozing blood... He could see the cut now, still oozing slightly.* **2** VERB If you say that someone or something **oozes** a quality or characteristic, you mean that they show it very strongly. *The Elizabethan house oozes charm.*

opaque/əʊ'peɪk/. **1** ADJ If an object or substance is **opaque**, you cannot see through it. *...opaque glass windows.* **2** ADJ If you say that something is **opaque**, you mean that it is difficult to understand. *...the opaque language of the inspector's reports.*

open 1 *uncovering*

★ **open**/'əʊpən/ **opens, opening, opened**. **1** VERB When you **open** something such as a door or the lid of a box, or when it **opens**, you move it so that it no longer covers a hole or gap. *He opened the window... The church doors would open and the crowd would surge out.* **2** VERB If you **open** something such as a container or a letter, you move, remove, or cut part of it so that you can take out what is inside. *The Inspector opened the packet of cigarettes.* **3** VERB If you **open** something such as a book, an umbrella, or your hand, or if it **opens**, the different parts of it move away from each other so that the inside of it can be seen. *He opened the heavy Bible... The officer's mouth opened.* **4** VERB When you **open** your eyes, or when they **open**, you move your eyelids upwards so that you can see. **5** VERB If people **open** something such as a blocked road or a border, or if it **opens**, people can then pass along it or through it. *The rebels have opened the road from Monrovia to the Ivory Coast.* **6** ADJ You use **open** to describe something which has been opened. *...an open window... I tore the letter* open... *Her eyes were open.* **7** ADJ If an item of clothing is **open**, it is not fastened. *His open shirt revealed a fat gold chain.* **8** VERB When flowers **open**, their petals spread out.

> **USAGE** You do not use **open** as a verb or adjective to talk about electrical devices. If someone causes an electrical device to work by pressing a switch or turning a knob, you say that they **put it on**, **switch it on**, or **turn it on**. If the device is already working, you say that it is **on**. *The answering machine is on... He cannot sleep with the light on.*

open 2 buildings, places, and events

☆ **open** /'əʊpən/ **opens, opening, opened.** **1** VERB When a shop, office, or public building **opens**, or when it **is opened**, its doors are unlocked and the people in it start working. *Banks closed on Friday afternoon and did not open again until Monday morning.* **2** ADJ AFTER LINK-V When a shop, office, or public building is **open**, its doors are unlocked and the people in it are working. *His shop is open Monday through Friday.* **3** VERB When a public building, factory, or company **opens** or when someone **opens** it, it starts operating for the first time. *The original station opened in 1754.* ♦ **opening, openings** N-COUNT *He was there for the official opening.* **4** VERB When an event such as a conference or a play **opens**, it begins to take place or to be performed. *...an emergency session of Parliament due to open later this morning.* ♦ **opening** N-SING *...the opening of the talks.* **5** VERB If a place **opens into** another, larger place, you can move from one directly into the other. *The corridor opened into a low smoky room.* **6** ADJ An **open** area is a large area that does not have many structures or obstructions in it. *Officers will continue their search of nearby open ground.* **7** ADJ BEFORE N An **open** structure or object is not covered or enclosed. *...a room with an open fire.*

open 3 other meanings

☆ **open** /'əʊpən/ **opens, opening, opened.** **1** ADJ If you describe a person or their character as **open**, you mean they are honest and do not want or try to hide anything or to deceive anyone. *He had always been open with her.* ♦ **openness** N-UNCOUNT *I was impressed by his openness.* **2** ADJ AFTER LINK-V If you are **open to** suggestions or ideas, you are ready and willing to consider or accept them. *They are open to suggestions on how working conditions might be improved.* **3** ADJ AFTER LINK-V If you say that a system, person, or idea is **open to** something such as abuse or criticism, you mean they might receive abuse or criticism because of the qualities they possess or the effects they have had. *They left themselves wide open to accusations of double standards.* **4** VERB If you **open** an account with a bank or a commercial organization, you begin to use their services. **5** See also **opening, openly.**

open 4 phrases and phrasal verbs

☆ **open** /'əʊpən/ **opens, opening, opened.**
   PHRASES ● If you do something **in the open**, you do it out of doors. ● If a situation is brought out **into the open**, people are told about it and it is no longer a secret.
▶**open up.** **1** PHR-VERB If something **opens up** opportunities or possibilities, or if opportunities or possibilities **open up**, they are able to arise or develop. *New opportunities are opening up for investors.* **2** PHR-VERB If a place, economy, or area of interest **opens up**, or if someone **opens** it **up**, it becomes accessible to more people. *As the market opens up, I think people are going to be able to spend more money on consumer goods.* **3** PHR-VERB When you **open up** a building, you unlock and open the door so that people can get in. *The postmaster and his wife arrived to open up the shop.*

,open-'air (or **open air**). **1** ADJ An **open-air** place or event is outside rather than in a building. *...the Open Air Theatre in Regents Park.* **2** N-SING If you are **in the open air**, you are outside rather than in a building.

,open-'ended. ADJ When people begin an **open-ended** discussion or activity, they do not start with any intention of achieving a particular decision or result. *...open-ended questions about what passengers expect of an airline.*

opener /'əʊpənə/ **openers.** N-COUNT An **opener** is a tool which is used to open containers. → See picture on page 825.

☆ **opening** /'əʊpənɪŋ/ **openings.** **1** ADJ BEFORE N The **opening** event, item, day, or week in a series is the first one. *...the season's opening game.* **2** N-SING The **opening** of something such as a book or concert is the first part of it. *...the opening of the film.* **3** N-COUNT An **opening** is a hole or empty space through which things can pass. *...a narrow opening in the fence.* **4** N-COUNT An **opening** is a good opportunity to do something. *All she needed was an opening to show her capabilities.* **5** N-COUNT An **opening** is a job that is available. *We don't have any openings now.* **6** See also **open.**

openly /'əʊpənli/. ADV If you do something **openly**, you do it without trying to hide anything. *We can now talk openly about AIDS... They were openly gay.*

,open-'minded. ADJ If you describe someone as **open-minded**, you approve of them because they are willing to listen to and consider other people's ideas. ♦ **open-mindedness** N-UNCOUNT *...honesty, open-mindedness and willingness to learn.*

☆ **opera** /'ɒpərə/ **operas.** N-VAR An **opera** is a musical entertainment. It is like a play, but most of the words are sung. ♦ **operatic** /ˌɒpə'rætɪk/ ADJ *...the local amateur operatic society.*

☆ **operate** /'ɒpəreɪt/ **operates, operating, operated.** **1** VERB If you **operate** a business or organization, you work to keep it running properly. If a business or organization **operates**, it carries out its work. *Greenwood owned and operated an enormous pear orchard. ...allowing commercial banks to operate in the country.* ♦ **operation** N-UNCOUNT *...funds for the everyday operation of the business.* **2** VERB The way that something **operates** is the way that it works or has an effect. *Ceiling and wall lights can operate independently.* ♦ **operation** N-UNCOUNT *The operation of the new tax is being studied.* **3** VERB When you **operate** a machine or device, you make it work. ♦ **operation** N-UNCOUNT *...the operation of the aeroplane.* **4** VERB When surgeons **operate on** a patient, they cut open the patient's body in order to remove, replace, or repair a diseased or damaged part.

'**operating theatre, operating theatres.** N-COUNT In British English, an **operating theatre** is a room in a hospital where surgeons carry out operations. The usual American term is **operating room**.

⭐ **operation** /ˌɒpəˈreɪʃən/ **operations.** **1** N-COUNT An **operation** is a highly organized activity that involves many people doing different things. *The rescue operation began on Friday afternoon. ...a military operation.* **2** N-COUNT A business or company can be referred to as an **operation**. *...Thorn's electronics operation.* **3** N-COUNT If a patient has an **operation**, a surgeon cuts open their body in order to remove, replace, or repair a diseased or damaged part. **4** N-UNCOUNT If a system is **in operation**, it is being used. *Until the rail links are in operation, passengers can only travel through the tunnel by coach.* **5** N-UNCOUNT If a machine or device is **in operation**, it is working. *There are three ski lifts in operation.* **6** See also **operate**.

operational /ˌɒpəˈreɪʃənəl/. **1** ADJ A machine or piece of equipment that is **operational** is in use or is ready to be used. *The whole system will be fully operational by December 1995.* **2** ADJ **Operational** factors or problems relate to the working of a system, device, or plan. *Every operational aspect had been fully researched.* ♦ **operationally** ADV *An all-female political section would have been operationally ineffective.*

operative /ˈɒpərətɪv/ **operatives.** **1** ADJ Something that is **operative** is working or having an effect. *The Youth Training Scheme was operative by the end of 1983.* **2** N-COUNT An **operative** is a worker, especially one with a manual skill. [FORMAL] **3** N-COUNT An **operative** is someone who works for a government agency such as the intelligence service. [AMERICAN]

⭐ **operator** /ˈɒpəreɪtə/ **operators.** **1** N-COUNT An **operator** is a person who works at a telephone exchange or on the switchboard of an office or hotel. *He dialled the operator.* **2** N-COUNT An **operator** is someone who is employed to operate or control a machine. **3** N-COUNT An **operator** is a person or a company that runs a business. *...the nation's largest cable TV operator.*

⭐ **opinion** /əˈpɪnjən/ **opinions.** **1** N-COUNT Your **opinion** about something is what you think or believe about it. *I wasn't asking for your opinion.* **2** N-SING Your **opinion of** someone is your judgment of their character or ability. *That improved Mrs Goole's already favourable opinion of him.* **3** N-UNCOUNT You can refer to the beliefs or views that people have as **opinion**. *Scientific opinion is divided over the health risks.*

o'**pinion poll, opinion polls.** N-COUNT An **opinion poll** involves asking people for their opinion on a particular subject, especially one concerning politics.

opium /ˈəʊpiəm/. N-UNCOUNT **Opium** is a powerful drug made from the seeds of a type of poppy.

⭐ **opponent** /əˈpəʊnənt/ **opponents.** **1** N-COUNT A politician's **opponents** are other politicians who belong to a different party or have different aims or policies. **2** N-COUNT In a sporting contest, your **opponent** is the person who is playing against you. **3** N-COUNT The **opponents** of an idea or policy do not agree with it. *...opponents of the spread of nuclear weapons.*

opportunist /ˌɒpəˈtjuːnɪst, AM -ˈtuːn-/ **opportunists.** **1** ADJ & N-COUNT If you describe someone as **opportunist**, or if you call them an **opportunist**, you are critical of them because they take advantage of situations in order to gain money or power. *...corrupt and opportunist politicians.* ♦ **opportunism** N-UNCOUNT *...political opportunism.* **2** ADJ **Opportunist** actions are not planned, but take advantage of the immediate situation. *...a brilliant opportunist goal.*

opportunistic /ˌɒpətjuːˈnɪstɪk, AM -tuːn-/. ADJ If you describe someone's behaviour as **opportunistic**, you are critical of them because they take advantage of situations in order to gain money or power. *Many of the party's members joined only for opportunistic reasons.*

⭐ **opportunity** /ˌɒpəˈtjuːnɪti, AM -ˈtuːn-/ **opportunities.** N-VAR An **opportunity** is a situation in which it is possible for you to do something that you want to do. *I had an opportunity to go to New York... The best reason for a trip to London is the super opportunity for shopping.*

⭐ **oppose** /əˈpəʊz/ **opposes, opposing, opposed.** VERB If you **oppose** someone or their plans or ideas, you disagree with what they want to do and try to prevent them from doing it. *...protesters opposing planned nuclear tests by France.*

⭐ **opposed** /əˈpəʊzd/. **1** ADJ AFTER LINK-V If you are **opposed to** something, you disagree with it or disapprove of it. *I am utterly opposed to any form of terrorism.* **2** ADJ You say that two ideas or systems are **opposed** when they are opposite to each other or very different from each other. *...two opposed ideologies.* **3** PHRASE You use **as opposed to** when you want to make it clear that you are talking about a particular thing and not something else. *We ate in the restaurant, as opposed to the bistro.*

a b c d e f g h i j k l m n o p q r s t u v w x y z

⭐ Bank of English® frequent word   For a full explanation of all grammatical labels, see pages vii-x

opposing/ə'pəʊzɪŋ/. [1] ADJ BEFORE N **Opposing** ideas or tendencies are totally different from each other. *I have a friend who has the opposing view.* [2] ADJ BEFORE N **Opposing** groups of people disagree about something or are in competition with one another.

☆ **opposite**/'ɒpəzɪt/**opposites.** [1] PREP & ADV If one thing is **opposite** another, it is facing it. *Two young people sat opposite me... I glanced up at the building opposite.* [2] ADJ BEFORE N The **opposite** side or part of something is the one that is farthest away from you. *...the opposite corner of the room.* [3] ADJ **Opposite** is used to describe things of the same kind which are as different as possible in a particular way. *...a word with the opposite meaning. ...a car going in the opposite direction.* [4] N-COUNT The **opposite of** someone or something is the person or thing that is most different from them. *He was the complete opposite of Raymond.*

,**opposite** '**sex.**N-SING If you are talking about men and refer to **the opposite sex**, you mean women. If you are talking about women and refer to **the opposite sex**, you mean men.

☆ **opposition**/,ɒpə'zɪʃən/. [1] N-UNCOUNT **Opposition** is strong, angry, or violent disagreement and disapproval. *The government is facing a new wave of opposition.* [2] N-SING The **opposition** refers to the politicians or political parties that form part of a country's parliament but are not in the government.

oppress/ə'pres/**oppresses, oppressing, oppressed.** [1] VERB To **oppress** someone means to treat them cruelly and unfairly. *These people often are oppressed by their governments.* ◆ **oppressed** ADJ *...oppressed minorities.* ◆ **oppression** /ə'preʃən/N-UNCOUNT *...the oppression of black people throughout history.* ◆ **oppressor, oppressors** N-COUNT *They sought to drive out their oppressors.* [2] VERB If something **oppresses** you, it makes you feel depressed and uncomfortable. [LITERARY] *It was not just the weather which oppressed her.*

oppressive/ə'presɪv/. [1] ADJ **Oppressive** laws, societies, and customs treat people cruelly and unfairly. *The new laws will be just as oppressive as those they replace.* [2] ADJ You say that the weather is **oppressive** when it is hot and humid. *...the oppressive afternoon heat.* [3] ADJ An **oppressive** situation makes you feel depressed or uncomfortable. *...the oppressive sadness that weighed upon him.*

☆ **opt**/ɒpt/**opts, opting, opted.** VERB If you **opt** for something, you choose it or decide to do it in preference to anything else. *Depending on your circumstances you may wish to opt for one method or the other... She opted to spend Christmas with her younger brother.*

▸ **opt out.** PHR-VERB If you **opt out of** something, you choose not to be involved in it. *...powers for hospitals to opt out of health authority control... The Vietnamese can opt out at any time.*

optic/'ɒptɪk/. ADJ BEFORE N **Optic** means relating to the eyes or to sight. *...the optic nerve.*

optical/'ɒptɪkəl/. [1] ADJ **Optical** instruments, devices, or processes involve or relate to vision or light. *...optical telescopes.* [2] ADJ BEFORE N **Optical** means relating to the way that things appear to people. *...an optical illusion.*

optician/ɒp'tɪʃən/**opticians.** N-COUNT An **optician** is someone whose job involves testing people's eyesight and making and selling glasses and contact lenses.

optimism/'ɒptɪmɪzəm/. N-UNCOUNT **Optimism** is the feeling of being hopeful about the future or about the success of something. *The president expressed optimism about reaching a peaceful settlement.* ◆ **optimist, optimists** N-COUNT *Susan remains an optimist.*

☆ **optimistic**/,ɒptɪ'mɪstɪk/. ADJ Someone who is **optimistic** is hopeful about the future or about the success of something. *She is optimistic that an agreement can be worked out soon.*
◆ **optimistically** ADV *He talked optimistically about the future.*

optimum/'ɒptɪməm/. ADJ The **optimum** level or state of something is the best level or state that it could achieve. [FORMAL] *...the basic requirements for optimum health.*

☆ **option**/'ɒpʃən/**options.** [1] N-COUNT An **option** is a choice between one or more things. *...frustrated artists who became lawyers at an early age because it seemed a safe option... What other options do you have?* [2] N-SING If you have **the option of** doing something, you can choose whether to do it or not. *Women should be given the option of having the treatment.* [3] PHRASE If you **keep** your **options open** or **leave** your **options open**, you avoid making an immediate decision about something.

optional/'ɒpʃənəl/. ADJ If something is **optional**, you can choose whether or not you do it or have it. *Optional extras include cooking tuition.*

optometrist/ɒp'tɒmətrɪst/**optometrists.** N-COUNT An **optometrist** is the same as an **optician**.

opulent/'ɒpjʊlənt/. ADJ **Opulent** things look grand and expensive. [FORMAL] *...his opulent new office.* ◆ **opulence** N-UNCOUNT *...the opulence of Napoleon III's court.*

opus/'əʊpəs, 'ɒpəs/**opuses** or **opera.** N-COUNT An **opus** is a musical composition.

☆ **or**/ə, STRONG ɔː/. [1] CONJ You use **or** to link alternatives. *Would you like tea or coffee?... He said he would try to write or call... Everyone thought she was either lying or mad... I don't know whether people will buy it or not.* [2] CONJ **Or** is used between two numbers to indicate that you are giving an approximate amount. *Drink two or three glasses of water after exercising.* [3] CONJ You use **or** to introduce a comment which corrects or modifies what you have just said. *The man was a fool, or at least incompetent... There was nothing* more he wanted, or so he thought. **4** CONJ You can use **or** to introduce an explanation or justification for what you have just said. *She had to have the operation, or she would die... He must have thought Jane was worth it or he wouldn't have wasted time on her.* **5** **or else**: see **else**. ● **or so**: see **so**.

> **USAGE** You do not use **or** after **neither**. You use **nor** instead. *He speaks neither English nor German.*

oral /'ɔːrəl/ **orals. 1** ADJ **Oral** is used to describe things that involve speaking rather than writing. *...an oral exam in the form of an interview.* ♦ **orally** ADV *...the tradition that is passed down orally.* **2** N-COUNT An **oral** is an examination, especially in a foreign language, that is spoken rather than written. **3** ADJ BEFORE N **Oral** medicines are ones that you swallow. *...an oral typhoid vaccine.* ♦ **orally** ADV *...tablets taken orally.*

⭐ **orange** /'ɒrɪndʒ, AM 'ɔːr-/ **oranges. 1** ADJ & N-VAR Something that is **orange** is of a colour between red and yellow. **2** N-COUNT An **orange** is a round orange fruit that is juicy and sweet. → See picture on page 821. **3** N-UNCOUNT **Orange** is a drink that is made from or tastes of oranges.

oratory /'ɒrətəri, AM 'ɔːrətɔːri/. N-UNCOUNT **Oratory** is the art of making formal speeches. [FORMAL] *...American political oratory.*

orbit /'ɔːbɪt/ **orbits, orbiting, orbited. 1** N-VAR An **orbit** is the curved path followed by an object going round a planet, a moon, or the sun. *Mars and Earth have orbits which change with time.* **2** VERB If something such as a satellite **orbits** a planet, a moon, or the sun, it goes round and round it.

orbital /'ɔːbɪtəl/. **1** ADJ BEFORE N An **orbital** road goes all the way round a large city. **2** ADJ BEFORE N **Orbital** describes things relating to the orbit of an object in space. *...the Earth's orbital path.*

orchard /'ɔːtʃəd/ **orchards.** N-COUNT An **orchard** is an area of land on which fruit trees are grown.

orchestra /'ɔːkɪstrə/ **orchestras.** N-COUNT An **orchestra** is a large group of musicians who play a variety of different instruments together. ♦ **orchestral** /ɔːˈkestrəl/ ADJ BEFORE N *...orchestral music.*

orchestrate /'ɔːkɪstreɪt/ **orchestrates, orchestrating, orchestrated. 1** VERB If you **orchestrate** something, you organize it very carefully in order to produce a particular result or situation. *The colonel was able to orchestrate a rebellion from inside an army jail.* ♦ **orchestration** N-UNCOUNT *...the orchestration of criminal justice policy.* **2** VERB When someone **orchestrates** a piece of music, they rewrite it so that it can be played by an orchestra. ♦ **orchestration** N-UNCOUNT *...Ravel's orchestration of Mussorgsky's piano work.*

orchid /'ɔːkɪd/ **orchids.** N-COUNT An **orchid** is a plant which has brightly coloured, unusually shaped flowers.

ordain /ɔːˈdeɪn/ **ordains, ordaining, ordained.** VERB When someone **is ordained**, they are made a member of the clergy in a religious ceremony.

ordeal /ɔːˈdiːl/ **ordeals.** N-COUNT An **ordeal** is an extremely unpleasant and difficult experience. *She described her agonising ordeal.*

order 1 conjunction uses

⭐ **order** /'ɔːdə/. **1** CONJ If you do something **in order to** achieve a particular thing, you do it because you want to achieve that thing. *Schools are extremely unwilling to cut down on staff in order to cut costs... No agenda was drawn up, in order that all matters could be raised.* **2** CONJ If something must happen **in order for** something else to happen, the second thing cannot happen if the first thing does not happen. *In order for him to win, he has to get at least nine Democratic votes.*

order 2 commands and requests

⭐ **order** /'ɔːdə/ **orders, ordering, ordered. 1** VERB & N-COUNT If someone in authority **orders** something, **orders** you to do something, or gives you an **order**, they tell you to do something. *The President has ordered a full investigation... He ordered his men to cease firing... She was fined £1,200 for disobeying orders.* **2** N-COUNT An **order** is something that you ask to be brought or sent to you, and that you are going to pay for. *The waiter returned with their order.* **3** VERB When you **order** something that you are going to pay for, you ask for it to be brought or sent to you. *Iris ordered coffees for herself and Tania.* **4** PHRASE If you are **under orders to** do something, you have been told not to do it by someone in authority. *I am under orders not to discuss his mission.* **5** See also **mail order.** ● **a tall order**: see **tall**.

▸**order around** or**order about.** PHR-VERB If someone **is ordering** you **around**, they are telling you what to do as if they have authority over you.

order 3 arrangements, situations, and groupings

⭐ **order** /'ɔːdə/ **orders. 1** N-UNCOUNT If a set of things are arranged or done **in** a particular **order**, one thing is put first or done first, another thing second, another thing third, and so on. *Arrange the entries in numerical order.* **2** N-UNCOUNT **Order** is the situation that exists when everything is in the correct place or is done at the correct time. *She ached for some order in her life.* **3** N-UNCOUNT **Order** is the situation that exists when people live together peacefully rather than fighting or causing trouble. *Troops were sent to the islands to restore order.* **4** N-SING When people talk about a particular **order**, they mean the way society is organized at a particular time. *...questioning the existing social order.* **5** N-COUNT A religious **order** is a group of monks or nuns who live according to certain rules. **6** N-COUNT If you refer to something **of** a particular **order**, you mean

a
b
c
d
e
f
g
h
i
j
k
l
m
n
o
p
q
r
s
t
u
v
w
x
y
z

something of a particular quality, amount, or degree. [FORMAL] ...*a poet of the highest order.*

7 PREP You use **in the order of** or **of the order of** when giving an approximate figure. *They borrowed something in the order of £10 million.*

8 See also **law and order.**

PHRASES • A machine or device that is **in working order** is functioning properly and is not broken. ...*a ten-year-old car that is in perfect working order.* • A machine or device that is **out of order** is broken and does not work.

orderly /ˈɔːdəli/ **orderlies.** **1** ADJ Something that is **orderly** is well organized or well arranged. ...*a beautiful, clean and orderly city.* ◆ **orderliness** N-UNCOUNT ...*parents' concerns with neatness and orderliness.* **2** N-COUNT An **orderly** is an untrained hospital attendant.

ordinal /ˈɔːdɪnəl/ **ordinals.** N-COUNT An **ordinal** or an **ordinal number** is a number such as 'first', 'third', or 'tenth', which tells you what position something has in an ordered group of things.

ordinance /ˈɔːdɪnəns/ **ordinances.** N-COUNT An **ordinance** is an official rule or order. [FORMAL]

ordinarily /ˈɔːdɪnərəli, AM -ˈnerɪli/. ADV If something is **ordinarily** the case, it is usually the case. *The streets would ordinarily have been full of people.*

⭐ **ordinary** /ˈɔːdɪnri, AM -neri/. **1** ADJ **Ordinary** people or things are not special or different in any way. *Most ordinary people would agree with me... It was just an ordinary weekend.* **2** PHRASE Something that is **out of the ordinary** is unusual or different. *The boy's knowledge was out of the ordinary.*

ordination /ˌɔːdɪˈneɪʃən/ **ordinations.** N-VAR When someone's **ordination** takes place, they are made a member of the Christian clergy in a special ceremony.

ore /ɔː/ **ores.** N-VAR **Ore** is rock or earth from which metal can be obtained.

organ /ˈɔːgən/ **organs.** **1** N-COUNT An **organ** is a part of your body that has a particular purpose or function, for example your heart or your lungs. ...*the liver and other organs.* **2** N-COUNT An **organ** is a large musical instrument with pipes of different lengths through which air is forced. It has keys and pedals rather like a piano. ◆ **organist, organists** N-COUNT ...*the acclaimed organist Christopher Wrench.*

organic /ɔːˈgænɪk/. **1** ADJ **Organic** gardening or farming uses only natural animal and plant products and does not use artificial fertilizers or pesticides. ◆ **organically** ADV ...*organically grown vegetables.* **2** ADJ Something that is **organic** is produced by or found in living things. ...*decaying organic matter.*

organisation /ˌɔːgənaɪˈzeɪʃən/. See **organization.**

organisational /ˌɔːgənaɪˈzeɪʃənəl/. See **organizational.**

organise /ˈɔːgənaɪz/. See **organize.**

organism /ˈɔːgənɪzəm/ **organisms.** N-COUNT An **organism** is an animal or plant, especially one that is so small that you cannot see it without using a microscope.

⭐ **organization** (BRIT also **organisation**) /ˌɔːgənaɪˈzeɪʃən/ **organizations.** **1** N-COUNT An **organization** is an official group of people, for example a political party, a business, a charity, or a club. ...*charitable organizations.* ...*the International Labour Organisation.*

◆ **organizational** ADJ BEFORE N *This problem needs to be dealt with at an organizational level.* **2** N-UNCOUNT The **organization** of something is the way in which its different parts are arranged or relate to each other. ...*the proposed changes in the organization of the Health Service.*

◆ **organizational** ADJ BEFORE N *Big organisational changes are needed.* **3** N-UNCOUNT The **organization** of an activity or public event involves making all the arrangements for it. *He was involved in the organization of conferences and seminars.* ◆ **organizational** ADJ BEFORE N ...*Evelyn's excellent organisational skills.*

⭐ **organize** (BRIT also **organise**) /ˈɔːgənaɪz/ **organizes, organizing, organized.** **1** VERB If you **organize** an activity or event, you make all the arrangements for it. *Maggie was the one that organized the trip to the railway museum.*

◆ **organizer, organizers** N-COUNT ...*the complete lack of planning by festival organizers.* **2** VERB If you **organize** something that someone wants or needs, you make sure that it is provided. *He asked her to organize coffee and sandwiches.* **3** VERB If you **organize** things, you put them into order. *He began to organize his materials.*

⭐ **organized** (BRIT also **organised**) /ˈɔːgənaɪzd/. **1** ADJ BEFORE N An **organized** activity or group involves a number of people doing something together in a structured way, rather than doing it by themselves. ...*organised groups of art thieves.* ...*organised religion.* **2** ADJ People who are **organized** work in an efficient and effective way.

orgasm /ˈɔːgæzəm/ **orgasms.** N-COUNT An **orgasm** is the moment of greatest pleasure and excitement during sexual activity.

orgy /ˈɔːdʒi/ **orgies.** **1** N-COUNT An **orgy** is a party in which people behave in a very uncontrolled way, especially one involving sexual activity. **2** N-COUNT You can refer to an activity as an **orgy** to emphasize that it is done to an excessive extent. ...*an orgy of destruction.*

orient /ˈɔːriənt/ **orients, orienting, oriented.**

☑ The form **orientate** is also used.

1 VERB When your **orient yourself to** a new situation or course of action, you learn about it and prepare to deal with it. [FORMAL] *You will need the time to orient yourself to your new way of eating.* **2** VERB When you **orient yourself**, you find out exactly where you are and which direction you are facing. *She lay still for a few seconds, trying to orient herself.*

oriental /ˌɔːriˈentəl/. ADJ **Oriental** means coming from or associated with eastern Asia, especially China and Japan. ...*oriental carpets*.

orientated /ˈɔːriənteɪtɪd/. ADJ **Orientated** means the same as **oriented**. ...*a lesbian and gay orientated radio programme*.

orientation /ˌɔːriənˈteɪʃən/. [1] N-UNCOUNT You can refer to the aims and interests of an organization as its **orientation**. ...*a marketing orientation*. [2] N-UNCOUNT Someone's **orientation** is their basic beliefs or preferences. ...*sexual orientation*.

oriented /ˈɔːrientɪd/. ADJ AFTER LINK-V You use **oriented** to indicate what someone or something is interested in or concerned with. For example, if someone is politically **oriented**, they are interested in politics. *Most students here are oriented to computers*.

⭐ **origin** /ˈɒrɪdʒɪn, AM ˈɔːr-/ **origins**. [1] N-VAR You can refer to the beginning, cause, or source of something as its **origin** or its **origins**. ...*theories about the origin of life*. ...*many drugs which have their origins in herbs*. [2] N-VAR Your **origin** or **origins** is the country, race, or social class of your parents or ancestors. ...*people of Asian origin*. ...*their country of origin*.

⭐ **original** /əˈrɪdʒɪnəl/ **originals**. [1] ADJ You use **original** to refer to something that existed at the beginning of a process or activity, or the characteristics that something had when it first existed. ...*Strathclyde police, which carried out the original investigation*. ◆ **originally** ADV *France originally refused to sign the treaty*. [2] N-COUNT If something such as a document or work of art is an **original**, it is not a copy or a later version. *Copy the questionnaire and send the original to your employer*. [3] ADJ An **original** piece of writing or music was written recently and has not been published or performed before. ...*its policy of commissioning original work*. [4] ADJ If you describe someone or their work as **original**, you mean that they are very imaginative and have new ideas. ...*a wholly original form of humour*. ◆ **originality** /əˌrɪdʒɪˈnælɪti/ N-UNCOUNT *He was capable of writing things of startling originality*.

originate /əˈrɪdʒɪneɪt/ **originates, originating, originated**. VERB If something **originated** at a particular time or in a particular place, it began to happen or exist at that time or in that place. *All carbohydrates originate from plants*.

ornament /ˈɔːnəmənt/ **ornaments**. [1] N-COUNT An **ornament** is an attractive object that you display in your home or garden. [2] N-UNCOUNT **Ornament** refers to decorations and patterns on a building or piece of furniture.

ornamental /ˌɔːnəˈmentəl/. ADJ Something that is **ornamental** is intended to be attractive rather than useful. ...*an ornamental pond*.

ornate /ɔːˈneɪt/. ADJ Something that is **ornate** has a lot of decoration on it. ...*an ornate iron staircase*.

orphan /ˈɔːfən/ **orphans, orphaned**. [1] N-COUNT An **orphan** is a child whose parents are dead. [2] PASSIVE-VERB If a child **is orphaned**, his or her parents die. *Jones was orphaned at the age of ten*.

orphanage /ˈɔːfənɪdʒ/ **orphanages**. N-COUNT An **orphanage** is a place where orphans are looked after.

orthodox /ˈɔːθədɒks/. [1] ADJ **Orthodox** beliefs, methods, or systems are the ones that are accepted or used by most people. ...*orthodox medicine*. [2] ADJ If you describe someone as **orthodox**, you mean that they hold the older and more traditional ideas of their religion or party. ...*Orthodox Jews*.

orthodoxy /ˈɔːθədɒksi/ **orthodoxies**. [1] N-COUNT An **orthodoxy** is an accepted view about something. *These ideas rapidly became the new orthodoxy in linguistics*. [2] N-VAR The old traditional beliefs of a religion, political party, or philosophy can be referred to as **orthodoxy**. ...*a return to political orthodoxy*.

ostensibly /ɒˈstensɪbli/. ADV If something is **ostensibly** true, it seems or is officially stated to be true, but you or other people have doubts about whether it is. ...*ostensibly independent organisations*.

ostentatious /ˌɒstenˈteɪʃəs/. [1] ADJ If you describe something or someone as **ostentatious**, you disapprove of them because their content, appearance, or behaviour is intended to impress people with its wealth and importance. ...*an ostentatious wedding reception*. ◆ **ostentatiously** ADV *They lived comfortably, but not ostentatiously*. [2] ADJ An **ostentatious** action is done in an exaggerated way in order to attract people's attention. ◆ **ostentatiously** ADV *He yawned ostentatiously*.

ostrich /ˈɒstrɪtʃ, AM ˈɔːst-/ **ostriches**. N-COUNT An **ostrich** is a very large African bird that cannot fly.

⭐ **other** /ˈʌðə/ **others**.

✅ When **other** follows the determiner 'an', it is written as one word: see **another**.

[1] ADJ BEFORE N & PRON You use **other** to refer to an additional thing or person of the same type as one that has been mentioned or is known about. *They were just like any other young couple... Four crewmen were killed, one other was injured*. [2] ADJ BEFORE N & PRON You use **other** to indicate that something is not the thing already mentioned, but something else. *Calls cost 36p per minute cheap rate and 48p per minute at all other times... Some of these methods will work. Others will not*. [3] ADJ BEFORE N & PRON You use **other** to refer to the second of two things or people when the identity of the first is already known or understood, or has already been mentioned. *The Captain was at the other end of the room. ...a cigarette in one hand and a martini in the other*. [4] ADJ BEFORE N & PRON You use **other** to refer to the rest of the people or things in a group, or to people or things like the ones just mentioned. *When the other pupils were taken to an exhibition,*

he was left behind. ...the new physics and astronomy of Copernicus, Galileo, and others. **5** ADJ BEFORE N & PRON **Other** people are people in general, excluding yourself or the particular person you have mentioned. *She likes to be with other people. ...a brave man who died helping others.* **6** ADJ BEFORE N You use **other** in expressions of time such as **the other day** or **the other week** to refer to a day or week in the recent past. [INFORMAL] *The other evening we had a party.*

PHRASES ● You use **none other than** and **no other than** to emphasize the name of a person or thing when something about that person or thing is surprising. *The manager was none other than his son.* ● You use **other than** after a negative in order to introduce an exception to what you have said. *Geoffrey was left no choice other than to resign.* ● **each other**: see **each**. ● **every other**: see **every**. ● **one or other**: see **one**. ● **in other words**: see **word**.

⭐ **otherwise** /'ʌðəwaɪz/. **1** ADV You use **otherwise** after stating a situation or fact, to say what the result or consequence would be if this situation or fact was not the case. *I'm lucky that I'm interested in school work, otherwise I'd go mad.* **2** ADV You use **otherwise** when stating the general condition or quality of something, when you are also mentioning an exception to this. *He woke at about 7 am, very hungry but otherwise happy.* **3** ADV You use **otherwise** to refer to actions or ways of doing something that are different from the one mentioned in your main statement. *Take approximately 60mg up to four times a day, unless advised otherwise by a doctor.*

⭐ **ought** /ɔːt/. **1** MODAL If you say that someone **ought to** do something, you mean that it is the right or sensible thing to do. If you say that someone **ought to have** done something, you mean that it would have been the right or sensible thing to do, but they did not do it. *You've got a good wife. You ought to take care of her... You ought to ask a lawyer's advice... Perhaps I ought not to interfere... I realize I ought to have told you about it.* **2** MODAL If you say that something **ought to** be true, you mean that you expect it to be true. If you say that something **ought to have** happened, you mean that you expect it to have happened. *'This ought to be fun,' he told Alex, eyes gleaming... The meal ought to have reached the house some time ago.*

oughtn't /'ɔːtənt/. **Oughtn't** is a spoken form of 'ought not'.

ounce /aʊns/ **ounces. 1** N-COUNT An **ounce** is a unit of weight used in Britain and the USA. There are sixteen ounces in a pound and one ounce is equal to 28.35 grams. **2** N-SING You can refer to a very small amount of something, such as a quality or characteristic, as an **ounce of** that thing. *I spent every ounce of energy trying to hide.*

⭐ **our** /aʊə/. **1** DET A speaker or writer uses **our** to indicate that something belongs or relates both to himself or herself and to one or more other

people. *We're expecting our first baby... I locked myself out of our apartment.* **2** DET A speaker or writer sometimes uses **our** to indicate that something belongs or relates to people in general. *The quality of our life depends on keeping well.*

ours /aʊəz/. PRON A speaker or writer uses **ours** to refer to something that belongs or relates to a group of people which includes himself or herself. *There are few strangers in a town like ours.*

⭐ **ourselves** /aʊə'selvz/. **1** PRON A speaker or writer uses **ourselves** to refer to himself or herself and one or more other people as a group. *We sat round the fire to keep ourselves warm... We admitted to ourselves that we were tired.* **2** PRON A speaker or writer sometimes uses **ourselves** to refer to people in general. *When we exert ourselves our heart rate increases.* **3** PRON You use **ourselves** to emphasize the first person plural subject, or to emphasize that you are referring to a particular group of people and nobody else. *Others are feeling just the way we ourselves would feel in the same situation... We did it ourselves.*

oust /aʊst/ **ousts, ousting, ousted.** VERB If someone **is ousted from** a position of power or **from** a job or place, they are forced to leave it. *The leaders have been ousted from power by nationalists... They tried to oust him in a parliamentary vote of no confidence.* ◆ **ousting** N-UNCOUNT ...*the ousting of the radicals.*

⭐ **out** /aʊt/. **1** ADV When you go **out of** a place or get **out of** something such as a vehicle, you leave it, so that you are no longer inside it. You keep **out of** a place, you do not go into it. *The waitress came out of the kitchen... She got out of bed and put on her robe... Nurses and doctors rushed out... Electric fences are erected to keep out animals.* **2** ADV If you are **out**, you are not at home or not at your usual place of work. *She almost certainly left the house while you were out... I went out looking for the kids.* **3** ADV If you take something **out of** a place or container, you remove it from there. *Carefully pull out the centre pages... He took out his notebook... I always took my key out of my bag and put it in my pocket.* **4** ADV If you look or shout **out of** a window, you look or shout through it at someone or something that is outside. *He went to the window and stared out at the dark sky... Her mother waved at her out of the train window.* **5** PREP If you get **out of** a situation or **out of** something such as the rain or wind, you are no longer in it. *Children may lie to get out of trouble... Stay out of politics... Keep your child out of the sun.* **6** ADJ AFTER LINK-V & ADV If a light or fire is **out**, it is no longer shining or burning. If it goes **out**, it stops burning or shining. *The candle went out.* **7** ADJ AFTER LINK-V & ADV If flowers are **out**, their petals have opened. If they come **out**, their petals open. **8** ADJ AFTER LINK-V & ADV If something such as a book or record is **out** or comes **out**, it is available for people to buy. *Our new spring '93 catalogue is out now.* **9** ADJ AFTER LINK-V In a game or sport, if someone is **out**, they can no longer take part either because the rules say so or because they are unable to. **10** ADJ AFTER LINK-V If you say that a proposal or suggestion is **out**, you mean that it is unacceptable or impossible. **11** ADJ AFTER LINK-V If you say that a calculation or measurement is **out**, you mean that it is incorrect. *They were only a few inches out.* **12** ADJ AFTER LINK-V If you say that someone is **out to** do something, usually something that you disapprove of, you mean they intend to do it. [INFORMAL] *Most companies these days are just out to make a quick profit.* **13** PREP You use **out of** to say what causes someone to do something. For example, if you do something **out of** pity, you do it because you pity someone. *He took up office out of a sense of duty.* **14** PREP If you get something such as pleasure, an advantage, or information **out of** something or someone, they give it to you or cause you to have it. *To get the most out of your money, you have to invest... Employers are looking to get more work out of fewer people.* **15** PREP If you are **out of** something, you no longer have any of it. *We're out of milk.* **16** PREP If something is made **out of** a particular material, it is formed or constructed using it. **17** PREP You use **out of** to indicate what proportion of a group of things something is true of. For example, if something is true of one **out of** five things, it is true of one fifth of all things of that kind. *One out of every two households owns a microwave.*

outback /'aʊtbæk/. N-SING The parts of Australia where very few people live are referred to as **the outback**.

outbreak /'aʊtbreɪk/ **outbreaks**. N-COUNT An **outbreak** of something unpleasant is a sudden occurrence of it. *...the outbreak of war.*

outburst /'aʊtbɜːst/ **outbursts**. **1** N-COUNT An **outburst of** an emotion, especially anger, is a sudden strong expression of that emotion. *...a spontaneous outburst of cheers and applause.* **2** N-COUNT An **outburst of** violent activity is a sudden period of this activity. *Five people were reported killed today in a fresh outburst of violence.*

outcast /'aʊtkɑːst, -kæst/ **outcasts**. N-COUNT An **outcast** is someone who is rejected by a group of people. *All of us felt like social outcasts.*

★ **outcome** /'aʊtkʌm/ **outcomes**. N-COUNT The **outcome** of an action or process is the result of it. *It's too early to know the outcome of her illness.*

outcry /'aʊtkraɪ/ **outcries**. N-COUNT An **outcry** is a reaction of strong disapproval and anger shown by the public or media about a recent event. *The killing caused an international outcry.*

outdated /,aʊt'deɪtɪd/. ADJ Something that is **outdated** is old-fashioned and no longer useful. *...outdated and inefficient factories.*

outdo /,aʊt'duː/ **outdoes, outdoing, outdid, outdone**. VERB If you **outdo** someone, you are more successful than they are at a particular activity. *...each man trying to outdo the other in boasts of his wartime exploits.*

outdoor /,aʊt'dɔː/. ADJ BEFORE N **Outdoor** activities or things take place or are used outside, rather than in a building. *She excelled at outdoor sports. ...outdoor furniture.*

outdoors /,aʊt'dɔːz/. ADV & N-SING If something happens **outdoors**, or if it happens **in the outdoors**, it happens outside in the fresh air rather than in a building. *It was warm enough to be outdoors all afternoon.*

outer /'aʊtə/. ADJ BEFORE N The **outer** parts of something are the parts which enclose the other parts, and which are farthest from the centre. *...burns that damage only the outer layer of skin. ...the outer suburbs of the city.*

outer 'space. N-UNCOUNT **Outer space** refers to the area outside the Earth's atmosphere where planets and stars are.

outfit /'aʊtfɪt/ **outfits, outfitting, outfitted**. **1** N-COUNT An **outfit** is a set of clothes. *...smart new outfits for work. ...a maid's outfit.* **2** N-COUNT You can refer to a group of people or an organization as an **outfit**. [INFORMAL] *We are a professional outfit.* **3** VERB To **outfit** someone or something means to provide them with equipment for a particular purpose. [AMERICAN] *I outfitted an attic bedroom as a studio.*

outflow /'aʊtfləʊ/ **outflows**. N-COUNT When there is an **outflow of** money or people, a large amount of money or people move from one place to another.

outgoing /,aʊt'gəʊɪŋ/. **1** ADJ BEFORE N An **outgoing** president, chairman, or minister is one who is going to leave. **2** ADJ An **outgoing** person is very friendly and likes meeting people. **3** ADJ BEFORE N **Outgoing** things such as planes, mail, and passengers are leaving somewhere or being sent somewhere.

outgoings /'aʊtgəʊɪŋz/. N-PLURAL Your **outgoings** are the regular amounts of money which you have to spend every week or every month, for example in order to pay your rent or bills. [BRITISH]

outgrow /,aʊt'grəʊ/ **outgrows, outgrowing, outgrew, outgrown**. VERB If you **outgrow** a piece of clothing, you get bigger and can no longer wear it.

outing /'aʊtɪŋ/ **outings**. N-COUNT An **outing** is a short enjoyable trip, usually with a group of people, away from your home, school, or place of work. *...a family outing to London.*

outlaw /'aʊtlɔː/ **outlaws, outlawing, outlawed**. **1** VERB When something **is outlawed**, it is made illegal. *In 1975, gambling was outlawed.* **2** N-COUNT An **outlaw** is a criminal who is hiding from the authorities. [DATED]

outlay /'aʊtleɪ/ **outlays**. N-COUNT An **outlay** is an amount of money that is invested in a piece of equipment, project, or business. [FORMAL]

outlet /'aʊtlet/ **outlets**. **1** N-COUNT If someone has an **outlet for** their feelings or ideas, they have a means of expressing and releasing them. *Boxing now became one of the main outlets for his*

a
b
c
d
e
f
g
h
i
j
k
l
m
n
o
p
q
r
s
t
u
v
w
x
y
z

incredible energy. **2** N-COUNT An **outlet** is a shop or organization which sells the goods made by a particular manufacturer. *...the largest retail outlet in the city.* **3** N-COUNT An **outlet** is a hole or pipe through which water or air can flow away. *...the sewage outlet.* **4** N-COUNT In American English, an **outlet** is a device in a wall where you can connect electrical equipment to the electricity supply. The British word is **socket**.

⭐ **outline** /'aʊtlaɪn/ **outlines, outlining, outlined.** **1** VERB & N-COUNT If you **outline** an idea or plan, or if you present an **outline of** it, you explain it in a general way. *The mayor outlined his plan to clean up the town's image. ...an outline of the survey findings.* **2** N-COUNT The **outline of** an object is the general shape of it that you can see, for example when there is a light behind it. *...the hazy outline of the goalposts.* **3** VERB When an object **is outlined**, you can see its general shape because there is a light behind it. *The hotel was outlined against the lights.*

outlive /,aʊt'lɪv/ **outlives, outliving, outlived.** VERB If one person **outlives** another, they are still alive after the other person has died. If one thing **outlives** another thing, the first thing continues to exist after the second has disappeared or been replaced. *I'm sure Rose will outlive many of us... Khrushchev predicted that Communism would outlive Capitalism.*

outlook /'aʊtlʊk/ **outlooks.** **1** N-COUNT Your **outlook** is your general attitude towards life. *The experience improved my outlook on life.* **2** N-SING The **outlook** for something is whether or not it is going to be prosperous, successful, or safe. *He said the inflation outlook remained good.*

outlying /'aʊtlaɪɪŋ/. ADJ BEFORE N **Outlying** places are far away from the main cities of a country. *Tourists can visit outlying areas like the Napa Valley.*

outnumber /,aʊt'nʌmbə/ **outnumbers, outnumbering, outnumbered.** VERB If one group of people or things **outnumbers** another, the first group has more people or things in it than the second group. *...a town where men outnumber women four to one.*

out of 'date. ADJ Something that is **out of date** is old-fashioned and no longer useful. *Think how rapidly medical knowledge has gone out of date. ...out-of-date computers.*

out of 'work. ADJ Someone who is **out of work** does not have a job.

outpost /'aʊtpəʊst/ **outposts.** N-COUNT An **outpost** is a small settlement in a foreign country or in a distant area. *...a remote mountain outpost.*

⭐ **output** /'aʊtpʊt/ **outputs.** **1** N-VAR You use **output** to refer to the amount of something that a person or thing produces. *...the largest drop in industrial output for ten years.* **2** N-VAR The **output** from a computer is the information that it displays on a screen or prints on paper as a result of a particular program. [COMPUTING]

outrage, outrages, outraging, outraged; verb /,aʊt'reɪdʒ/, noun /'aʊtreɪdʒ/. **1** VERB If something **outrages** you, it makes you extremely shocked and angry. *The Civil Liberties Union is outraged by the court's decision.* ♦ **outraged** ADJ *Outraged readers said the story was extremely offensive.* **2** N-UNCOUNT **Outrage** is a feeling of shock and anger about something. *The decision provoked outrage from women.* **3** N-COUNT You can refer to an act or event which you find very shocking as an **outrage**. *It is an outrage that women are denied the same financial assistance as men.*

outrageous /aʊt'reɪdʒəs/. ADJ If you describe something as **outrageous**, you are emphasizing that it is unacceptable or very shocking. *...his outrageous drunken behaviour.* ♦ **outrageously** ADV *...outrageously expensive clothes.*

outright; adjective /'aʊtraɪt/, adverb /,aʊt'raɪt/. **1** ADJ BEFORE N & ADV You use **outright** to describe actions and behaviour that are open and direct, rather than indirect. *...an outright lie... Why don't you tell me outright?* **2** ADJ BEFORE N & ADV **Outright** means complete and total. *She had failed to win an outright victory... The peace plan wasn't rejected outright.* **3** PHRASE If someone **is killed outright**, they die immediately, for example in an accident.

outset /'aʊtset/. PHRASE If something happens **at the outset** of an event, process, or period of time, it happens at the beginning of it. If something happens **from the outset**, it happens from the beginning and continues to happen. *Decide at the outset what kind of learning programme you want... It's clear from the outset that their love is doomed.*

⭐ **outside** /,aʊt'saɪd/ **outsides.** **1** N-COUNT & ADJ BEFORE N The **outside** of something such as a building or a container is the part which surrounds or encloses the rest of it. *The moth was on the outside of the glass. ...the outside wall.* **2** ADV & PREP & ADJ BEFORE N If you are **outside** a building, place, or country, you are not in it. *They heard voices coming from outside... The victim was outside a shop when he was attacked. ...an outside lavatory.* **3** ADJ BEFORE N When you talk about the **outside** world, you are referring to things that happen or exist in places other than your own home or community. *...a side of her character she hid carefully from the outside world.* **4** ADJ BEFORE N On a road with two or more lanes, the **outside** lane is the one for overtaking or for travelling at high speed. **5** ADJ BEFORE N & PREP **Outside** people or organizations are not part of a particular organization or group. *...outside consultants... He is hoping to recruit a chairman from outside the company.* **6** PREP You use **outside** to refer to a particular thing or range of things which are not part of something or not included within it. *She is a beautiful boat, but way, way outside my price range.* **7** PREP Something that happens **outside** a particular period of time does not happen during that time. *They are open outside normal daily banking hours.*

outsider /ˌaʊtˈsaɪdə/ **outsiders.** [1] N-COUNT An **outsider** is someone who does not belong to a particular group or organization, or is not accepted by them. *Malone, a cop, felt as much an outsider as any of them.* [2] N-COUNT In a competition, an **outsider** is a competitor who is unlikely to win.

outskirts /ˈaʊtskɜːts/. N-PLURAL The **outskirts** of a city or town are the parts that are farthest from its centre. ...*the outskirts of New York.*

outspoken /ˌaʊtˈspəʊkən/. ADJ If you are **outspoken**, you give your opinions about things openly, even if they shock people. ...*his outspoken criticism of the prime minister.*

♦ **outspokenness** N-UNCOUNT *Her outspokenness had alienated many voters.*

⭐ **outstanding** /ˌaʊtˈstændɪŋ/. [1] ADJ If you describe a person or their work as **outstanding**, you think that they are remarkable and impressive. ...*an outstanding athlete.*

♦ **outstandingly** ADV ...*outstandingly successful schools.* [2] ADJ **Outstanding** means very obvious or important. ...*an outstanding example of a small business that grew into a big one.* [3] ADJ Money that is **outstanding** has not yet been paid and is still owed to someone. *The total debt outstanding is $70 billion.* [4] ADJ **Outstanding** issues or problems have not yet been resolved.

outstretched /ˌaʊtˈstretʃt/. ADJ If your arms, fingers, legs, or feet are **outstretched**, they are stretched as far as they can go. *He was wrapped in a blanket and held his arms outstretched.*

outstrip /ˌaʊtˈstrɪp/ **outstrips, outstripping, outstripped.** VERB If one thing **outstrips** another, the first thing becomes larger in amount, or more successful or important, than the second thing. ...*wage rises that far outstripped productivity.*

outward /ˈaʊtwəd/. [1] ADJ BEFORE N An **outward** journey is a journey that you make away from a place that you are intending to return to later. *Tickets must be bought in advance, with outward and return dates specified.* [2] ADJ BEFORE N The **outward** feelings, qualities, or attitudes of someone or something are the ones they appear to have rather than the ones that they actually have. *What the military rulers have done is to restore the outward appearance of order.* ♦ **outwardly** ADV *People were outwardly hostile.* [3] ADJ BEFORE N The **outward** features of something are the ones that you can see from the outside. *Mark was lying unconscious but with no outward sign of injury.*

outwards /ˈaʊtwədz/.

✓ The form **outward** is also used. In American English, **outward** is more usual.

ADV If something moves or faces **outwards**, it moves or faces away from the place you are in or the place you are talking about. *The top door opened outwards.*

outweigh /ˌaʊtˈweɪ/ **outweighs, outweighing, outweighed.** VERB If, for example, the benefits of something **outweigh** the disadvantages, it has some disadvantages but is more beneficial than harmful. [FORMAL] *The medical benefits of x-rays far outweigh the risk of having them.*

outwit /ˌaʊtˈwɪt/ **outwits, outwitting, outwitted.** VERB If you **outwit** someone, you use your intelligence or a clever trick to defeat them or to gain an advantage over them. *To win the presidency he had first to outwit his rivals.*

oval /ˈəʊvəl/ **ovals.** N-COUNT & ADJ An **oval** or an **oval** shape is a round shape which is similar to a circle, but is wider in one direction than the other. → See picture on page 829. ...*a pale oval face.*

ovary /ˈəʊvəri/ **ovaries.** N-COUNT A woman's **ovaries** are the two organs in her body that produce eggs.

ovation /əʊˈveɪʃən/ **ovations.** N-COUNT An **ovation** is a long burst of applause from an audience for a particular performer.

oven /ˈʌvən/ **ovens.** N-COUNT An **oven** is a cooker or part of a cooker that is like a box with a door. You cook food inside an oven.

over 1 position and movement

⭐ **over** /ˈəʊvə/. [1] PREP & ADV If one thing is **over** another thing or is moving **over** it, the first thing is directly above the second, either resting on it, or with a space between them. *He looked at himself in the mirror over the table.* ...*the small iron bridge over the stream.* ...*planes flying over every 10 or 15 minutes.* [2] PREP & ADV If one thing is **over** another thing, it covers part or all of it. *He was wearing a light-grey suit over a shirt... The workers decided it would be too difficult to recover it so they covered it over.* [3] PREP & ADV If you lean **over** an object, you bend your body so that the top part of it is above the object. *She bent over the table, frowning... Sam leant over to open the door of the car.* [4] PREP If you look **over** an object, you look or talk across the top of it. *I went and stood beside him, looking over his shoulder.* [5] PREP If a window has a view **over** an area of land or water, you can see the land or water through the window. [6] PREP & ADV If someone or something goes **over** a barrier or boundary, they get to the other side of it by going across it, or across the top of it. *Policemen jumped over the wall in pursuit... I climbed over into the back seat.* [7] PREP If something is on the opposite side of a road or river, you can say that it is **over** the road or **over** the river. ...*Richard Garrick, who lived in the house over the road.* [8] ADV You use **over** to indicate a particular position or place away from you. *He noticed Rolfe standing silently over by the window.* [9] PHRASE **Over here** means near you, or in the country you are in. **Over there** means in a place a short distance away from you, or in another country. *Why don't you come over here tomorrow evening... She'd married some American and settled down over there.* [10] ADV If something rolls **over** or is turned **over**, its position changes so that the part that was facing upwards is now facing downwards. *His car rolled over after a tyre was punctured.*

over 2 amounts and time

⭐ **over** /ˈəʊvə/. **1** PREP & ADV If something is **over** a particular amount, measurement, or age, it is more than that amount, measurement, or age. *Cigarettes kill over a hundred thousand Britains every year. ...people aged 65 and over.* **2** PHRASE **Over and above** an amount, especially a normal amount, means more than that amount or in addition to it. *Expenditure on education has gone up by seven point eight per cent over and above inflation.* **3** ADJ AFTER LINK-V If an activity is **over** or **all over**, it is completely finished. *The bad times were over... I am glad it's all over.* **4** PREP If something happens **over** a period of time, it happens during that time. → See Reference Page on Times and Dates. *Many strikes over the last few years have not ended successfully.* **5** PREP If you are **over** an illness or an experience, it has finished and you have recovered from its effects. *I'm glad that you're over the flu.*

over 3 cause and influence

⭐ **over** /ˈəʊvə/. **1** PREP You use **over** to indicate what a disagreement or feeling relates to or is caused by. *...concern over recent events in Burma.* **2** PREP If you have control or influence **over** someone or something, you are able to control them or influence them. *The oil companies have lost their power over oil prices.*

⭐ **overall, overalls**; adjective and adverb /ˌəʊvərˈɔːl/, noun /ˈəʊvərɔːl/. **1** ADJ BEFORE N & ADV You use **overall** to indicate that you are talking about a situation in general or about the whole of something. *Cut down your overall amount of physical activity. ...the quality of education overall.* **2** N-PLURAL **Overalls** are a piece of clothing that combine trousers and a shirt which you wear over your clothes to protect them while you are working. **3** N-COUNT An **overall** is a type of coat that you wear over your clothes to protect them while you are working.

overboard /ˈəʊvəbɔːd/. ADV If you fall **overboard**, you fall over the side of a ship into the water.

overcame /ˌəʊvəˈkeɪm/. **Overcame** is the past tense of **overcome**.

overcharge /ˌəʊvəˈtʃɑːdʒ/ **overcharges, overcharging, overcharged.** VERB If someone **overcharges** you, they charge you too much for their goods or services.

overcoat /ˈəʊvəkəʊt/ **overcoats.** N-COUNT An **overcoat** is a thick warm coat.

⭐ **overcome** /ˌəʊvəˈkʌm/ **overcomes, overcoming, overcame, overcome.** **1** VERB If you **overcome** a problem or a feeling, you successfully deal with it and control it. *Molly had fought and overcome her fear of flying.* **2** VERB If you **are overcome** by a feeling, you feel it very strongly. *The night before the test I was overcome by fear and despair.*

3 VERB If you **are overcome** by smoke or a poisonous gas, you become very ill or die from breathing it in.

overcrowded /ˌəʊvəˈkraʊdɪd/. ADJ An **overcrowded** place has too many things or people in it. *...one of the most overcrowded prisons in the country.*

overcrowding /ˌəʊvəˈkraʊdɪŋ/. N-UNCOUNT If there is **overcrowding** in a place, there are more people living there than it was designed for. *...overcrowding and lack of facilities for patients.*

overdo /ˌəʊvəˈduː/ **overdoes, overdoing, overdid, overdone.** **1** VERB If someone **overdoes** something, they behave in an exaggerated or extreme way. *He thought Dan was overdoing the charity bit.* **2** VERB If you **overdo** an activity, you try to do more than you can physically manage. *Satisfy your urge to take exercise but don't overdo it.*

overdose /ˈəʊvədəʊs/ **overdoses, overdosing, overdosed.** N-COUNT & VERB If someone takes an **overdose** of a drug, or if they **overdose on** it, they take more of it than is safe. *Guitarist Jimi Hendrix died of a drug overdose... He'd overdosed on heroin.*

overdraft /ˈəʊvədrɑːft, -dræft/ **overdrafts.** N-COUNT If you have an **overdraft**, you have spent more money than you have in your bank account, and so you are in debt to the bank.

overdue /ˌəʊvəˈdjuː, AM -ˈduː/. **1** ADJ If you say that a change or an event is **overdue**, you mean that it should have happened before now. *This debate is long overdue.* **2** ADJ **Overdue** sums of money have not been paid, even though it is later than the date on which they should have been paid.

overeat /ˌəʊvəˈiːt/ **overeats, overeating, overate, overeaten.** VERB If you **overeat**, you eat more than you should.

overestimate /ˌəʊvərˈestɪmeɪt/ **overestimates, overestimating, overestimated.** VERB If you **overestimate** someone or something, you think that they are better, bigger, or more important than they really are. *I think you overestimate me, Fred.*

overflow, overflows, overflowing, overflowed. **1** VERB /ˌəʊvəˈfləʊ/ If a liquid or a river **overflows**, it flows over the edges of the container or the place it is in. *The sewers were overflowing and the river was bursting its banks.* **2** VERB If a place or container **is overflowing with** people or things, there are too many of them in it. *The great hall was overflowing with people.* **3** VERB If someone **is overflowing with** a feeling, or if the feeling **overflows**, the person is experiencing it very strongly and shows this in their behaviour. *Kenneth overflowed with friendliness and hospitality.* **4** N-COUNT /ˈəʊvəfləʊ/ An **overflow** is a hole or pipe through which liquid can flow out of a container when it gets too full.

overgrown /ˌəʊvəˈɡrəʊn/. ADJ If a place is **overgrown**, it is thickly covered with plants because it has not been looked after. ...*a courtyard overgrown with weeds.*

overhang /ˌəʊvəˈhæŋ/ **overhangs, overhanging, overhung.** VERB If one thing **overhangs** another, it sticks out over and above it. *Part of the rock wall overhung the path.*

overhaul, overhauls, overhauling, overhauled; verb /ˌəʊvəˈhɔːl/, noun /ˈəʊvəhɔːl/. [1] VERB & N-COUNT If a piece of equipment **is overhauled**, or if you give it an **overhaul**, it is cleaned, checked thoroughly, and repaired if necessary. *He had had his little Fiat car overhauled three times.* [2] VERB & N-COUNT If you **overhaul** a system or method, or if you give it an **overhaul**, you examine it carefully and change it in order to improve it. ...*a complete overhaul of air traffic control systems.*

overhead; adjective /ˈəʊvəhed/, adverb /ˌəʊvəˈhed/. ADJ BEFORE N & ADV You use **overhead** to indicate that something is above you or above the place you are talking about. ...*the overhead light... Helicopters have been flying overhead.*

overheads /ˈəʊvəhedz/. N-PLURAL The **overheads** of a business are its regular and essential expenses.

overhear /ˌəʊvəˈhɪə/ **overhears, overhearing, overheard.** VERB If you **overhear** someone, you hear what they are saying when they are not talking to you and do not know that you are listening. *I overheard two doctors discussing my case.*

overheat /ˌəʊvəˈhiːt/ **overheats, overheating, overheated.** VERB If a machine **overheats**, or if you **overheat** it, it becomes hotter than is necessary or desirable. *The engine was overheating and the car was not handling well.* ◆ **overheated** ADJ ...*that stuffy, overheated apartment.*

overhung /ˌəʊvəˈhʌŋ/. **Overhung** is the past tense and past participle of **overhang**.

overjoyed /ˌoʊvərˈdʒɔɪd/. ADJ If you are **overjoyed**, you are extremely pleased about something. *Shelley was overjoyed to see me.*

overland /ˈəʊvəlænd/. ADJ BEFORE N & ADV An **overland** journey is made across land rather than by ship or aeroplane. ...*the overland route... They're travelling to Baghdad overland.*

overlap, overlaps, overlapping, overlapped; verb /ˌəʊvəˈlæp/, noun /ˈəʊvəlæp/. [1] VERB If one thing **overlaps** another, one part of the first thing covers a part of the other. You can also say that two things **overlap**. *Overlap the slices carefully so there are no gaps... The edges must overlap each other.* [2] VERB & N-COUNT If one idea or activity **overlaps** another, they involve some of the same subjects, people, or periods of time. You can also say that two ideas or activities **overlap**, or that there is an **overlap** between them. ...*the overlap between civil and military technology.*

overleaf /ˌəʊvəˈliːf/. ADV **Overleaf** is used in books and magazines to say that something is on the other side of the page you are reading. *Answer the questionnaire overleaf.*

overload /ˌəʊvəˈləʊd/ **overloads, overloading, overloaded.** [1] VERB If you **overload** a vehicle, you put more things or people in it than it was designed to carry. *Don't overload the boat or it will sink.* ◆ **overloaded** ADJ *Some trains were so overloaded that their suspension collapsed.* [2] VERB & N-COUNT To **overload** someone **with** work or problems means to give them more work or problems than they can manage. This can also be called an **overload**. ...*an effective method that will not overload staff with yet more paperwork... 57 per cent complained of work overload.* ◆ **overloaded** ADJ *The bar waiter was already overloaded with orders.*

overlook /ˌəʊvəˈlʊk/ **overlooks, overlooking, overlooked.** [1] VERB If a building or window **overlooks** a place, you can see the place from the building or window. *Pretty and comfortable rooms overlook a flower-filled garden.* [2] VERB If you **overlook** a fact or problem, you do not notice it, or do not realize how important it is. *We overlook all sorts of warning signals about our own health.* [3] VERB If you **overlook** someone's faults or bad behaviour, you forgive them and take no action. ...*satisfying relationships that enable them to overlook each other's faults.*

overly /ˈəʊvəli/. ADV **Overly** means more than is normal, necessary, or reasonable. *Employers may become overly cautious about taking on new staff.*

★ **overnight** /ˌəʊvəˈnaɪt/. [1] ADV & ADJ BEFORE N **Overnight** means throughout the night or at some point during the night. *The weather remained calm overnight.* ...*overnight accommodation.* [2] ADV & ADJ BEFORE N You can say that something happens **overnight** when it happens quickly and unexpectedly. *The rules are not going to change overnight... He became an overnight success.*

overpower /ˌəʊvəˈpaʊə/ **overpowers, overpowering, overpowered.** [1] VERB If you **overpower** someone, you seize them despite their struggles because you are stronger than they are. *It took ten guardsmen to overpower him.* [2] VERB If a feeling **overpowers** you, it suddenly affects you very strongly. *A sudden dizziness overpowered him.* ◆ **overpowering** ADJ *The desire for revenge can be overpowering.*

overpowering /ˌəʊvəˈpaʊərɪŋ/. ADJ An **overpowering** person makes other people feel uncomfortable because they have such a strong personality.

overran (or **over-ran**) /ˌəʊvəˈræn/. **Overran** is the past tense of **overrun**.

overrate (or **over-rate**) /ˌəʊvəˈreɪt/ **overrates, overrating, overrated.** VERB If you say that something or someone **is overrated**, you mean that people have a higher opinion of them than they deserve. *More men are finding out that the joys of work*

a
b
c
d
e
f
g
h
i
j
k
l
m
n
o
p
q
r
s
t
u
v
w
x
y
z

A
B
C
D
E
F
G
H
I
J
K
L ⭐
M
N
O
P
Q
R
S
T
U
V
W
X
Y
Z

have been overrated. ♦ **overrated** ADJ *Life in the wild is vastly overrated.*

override (or **over-ride**) /ˌəʊvəˈraɪd/ **overrides, overriding, overrode, overridden.** ☐ VERB If one thing in a situation **overrides** other things, it is more important than them. *The welfare of a child should always override the wishes of its parents.* ♦ **overriding** ADJ *...the overriding need to cut the budget.* ☐ VERB If someone in authority **overrides** a person or their decisions, they cancel their decisions. *...the authority to override him.*

overrule (or **over-rule**) /ˌəʊvəˈruːl/ **overrules, overruling, overruled.** VERB If someone in authority **overrules** a person or their decision, they officially decide that the decision is incorrect or not valid. *In 1991, the Court of Appeal overruled this decision.*

overrun (or **over-run**) /ˌəʊvəˈrʌn/ **overruns, overrunning, overran.** ☐ VERB If an army **overruns** a country, it succeeds in occupying it quickly. ☐ VERB If you say that a place **is overrun with** things that you consider undesirable, you mean that there are a large number of them there. *The flower beds were overrun with grasses.* ☐ VERB If an event or meeting **overruns**, it continues for a longer time than it should have. *Tuesday's lunch overran by three-quarters of an hour.*

⭐ **overseas** /ˌəʊvəˈsiːz/ ☐ ADJ BEFORE N & ADV You use **overseas** to describe things that happen or exist abroad. *...his long overseas trip. ...if you're staying for more than three months or working overseas.* ☐ ADJ BEFORE N An **overseas** student or visitor comes from abroad.

oversee /ˌəʊvəˈsiː/ **oversees, overseeing, oversaw, overseen.** VERB If someone in authority **oversees** a job or an activity, they make sure that it is done properly. *...an architect or surveyor to oversee the work.*

overshadow /ˌəʊvəˈʃædəʊ/ **overshadows, overshadowing, overshadowed.** ☐ VERB If an unpleasant event or feeling **overshadows** something, it makes it less happy or enjoyable. *Fears for the President's safety could overshadow his peace-making mission.* ☐ VERB If someone or something **is overshadowed** by another person or thing, they are less successful, important, or impressive than the other person or thing. *Hester is overshadowed by her younger and more attractive sister.*

oversight /ˈəʊvəsaɪt/ **oversights.** N-COUNT If there has been an **oversight**, someone has forgotten to do something which they should have done. *By an unfortunate oversight, full instructions do not come with the product.*

oversized /ˈəʊvəsaɪzd/. ADJ **Oversized** things are bigger than usual. *...an oversized bed.*

overstate /ˌəʊvəˈsteɪt/ **overstates, overstating, overstated.** VERB If you say that someone is **overstating** something, you mean they are describing it in a way that makes it seem more important or serious than it really is. *Many scientists think this method overstates the dangers.*

overt /ˌəʊˈvɜːt/. ADJ An **overt** action or attitude is done or shown in an open and obvious way. *Although there is no overt hostility, black and white students do not mix much.* ♦ **overtly** ADV *...overtly political issues.*

overtake /ˌəʊvəˈteɪk/ **overtakes, overtaking, overtook, overtaken.** ☐ VERB If you **overtake** a moving vehicle or person, you pass them because you are moving faster than they are. ☐ VERB If an event **overtakes** you, it happens unexpectedly or suddenly. *Something like panic overtook me in a flood.*

overthrow, overthrows, overthrowing, overthrew, overthrown; verb /ˌəʊvəˈθrəʊ/, noun /ˈəʊvəθrəʊ/. VERB & N-SING When a government or a leader **is overthrown**, they are removed from power by force. You can also talk about the **overthrow** of a government or leader. *That government was overthrown in a military coup. ...the overthrow of the government.*

overtime /ˈəʊvətaɪm/. N-UNCOUNT **Overtime** is time that you spend doing your job in addition to your normal working hours. *He would work overtime, without pay, to finish a job.*

overtone /ˈəʊvətəʊn/ **overtones.** N-COUNT If something has **overtones** of a particular thing or quality, it has a small amount of that thing or quality but does not openly express it. *...a speech that had overtones of a sermon.*

overtook /ˌəʊvəˈtʊk/. **Overtook** is the past tense of **overtake.**

overture /ˈəʊvətʃʊə/ **overtures.** N-COUNT An **overture** is a piece of music, often one that is used as the introduction to an opera or play.

overturn /ˌəʊvəˈtɜːn/ **overturns, overturning, overturned.** ☐ VERB If something **overturns**, or if you **overturn** it, it turns upside down or on its side. *Alex jumped up so violently that he overturned his glass of sherry.* ☐ VERB If someone in authority **overturns** a legal decision, they officially decide that that decision is incorrect or not valid. ☐ VERB To **overturn** a government or system means to remove it or destroy it.

overview /ˈəʊvəvjuː/ **overviews.** N-COUNT An **overview of** a situation is a general understanding or description of it as a whole. *...a historical overview of drug use.*

overweight /ˌəʊvəˈweɪt/. ADJ Someone who is **overweight** weighs more than is considered healthy or attractive. ● See note at **fat.**

overwhelm /ˌəʊvəˈwelm/ **overwhelms, overwhelming, overwhelmed.** ☐ VERB If you **are overwhelmed** by a feeling or event, it affects you very strongly and you do not know how to deal with it. *Her brightness overwhelmed me.* ♦ **overwhelmed** ADJ *...overwhelmed by the crowds and noise.* ☐ VERB If a group of people **overwhelm** a place or another group, they gain control over them. *One massive Allied offensive would overwhelm the weakened enemy.*

⭐ **overwhelming** /ˌəʊvəˈwelmɪŋ/. ☐ ADJ If something is **overwhelming**, it affects you very strongly, and you do not know how to deal with it. ...*an overwhelming desire to have another child.* ♦ **overwhelmingly** ADV *Women found him overwhelmingly attractive.* [2] ADJ You can use **overwhelming** to emphasize that an amount or quantity is much greater than other amounts or quantities. *The overwhelming majority of small businesses go broke within the first twenty-four months.* ♦ **overwhelmingly** ADJ *The House of Commons has overwhelmingly rejected calls to bring back the death penalty.*

overwork /ˌəʊvəˈwɜːk/ **overworks, overworking, overworked.** VERB & N-UNCOUNT If you **overwork**, or if you suffer from **overwork**, you work too hard, and are likely to become very tired or ill. *He overworks and underpays the poor clerk.* ...*a heart attack brought on by overwork.* ♦ **overworked** ADJ ...*an overworked doctor.*

ovulate /ˈɒvjʊleɪt/ **ovulates, ovulating, ovulated.** VERB When a woman **ovulates**, she produces eggs from her ovary [FORMAL]. ♦ **ovulation** N-UNCOUNT *The woman can tell when ovulation is about to occur.*

⭐ **owe** /əʊ/ **owes, owing, owed.** [1] VERB If you **owe** money to someone, they have lent it to you and you have not yet paid it back. *The company owes money to more than 60 banks... Blake already owed him nearly £50.* [2] VERB If someone or something **owes** a particular quality, their success, or their existence to a person or thing, they only have it because of that person or thing. *I owe him my life.* [3] VERB If you say that you **owe** someone gratitude, respect, or loyalty, you mean that they deserve it from you. [FORMAL] *I owe you an apology... I owe a big debt of gratitude to her.* [4] VERB If you say that you **owe it to** someone **to** do something, you mean that you should do that thing because they deserve it. *I can't go. I owe it to him to stay.* [5] PREP You use **owing to** to introduce the reason for something. *He was out of work owing to a physical injury.*

owl /aʊl/ **owls.** N-COUNT An **owl** is a bird with large eyes which hunts small animals at night.

⭐ **own** /əʊn/ **owns, owning, owned.** [1] ADJ & PRON You use **own** to indicate that something belongs to

or is typical of a particular person or thing. *My wife decided I should have my own shop... I let her tell me about it in her own way. ...a sense of style that is very much her own.* [2] ADJ & PRON You use **own** to emphasize that someone does something without any help from other people. *He'll have to make his own arrangements... There's no career structure, you have to create your own.* [3] VERB If you **own** something, it is your property. *His father owns a local pub.*
PHRASES ● When you are **on** your **own**, you are alone. ● If you do something **on** your **own,** you do it without any help from other people. *I work best on my own.* ● If someone or something **comes into** their **own**, they become very successful or start to perform very well because the circumstances are right. *The goalkeeper came into his own with a series of brilliant saves.*
►**own up.** PHR-VERB If you **own up to** something wrong that you have done, you admit that you did it. *Last year my husband owned up to an affair.*

⭐ **owner** /ˈəʊnə/ **owners.** N-COUNT The **owner** of something is the person to whom it belongs. ...*the owner of the store... Every pet owner knows their animal has its own personality.*

⭐ **ownership** /ˈəʊnəʃɪp/. N-UNCOUNT **Ownership** of something is the state of owning it. ...*the growth of home ownership in Britain.*

ox /ɒks/ **oxen.** N-COUNT An **ox** is a castrated bull.

oxygen /ˈɒksɪdʒən/. N-UNCOUNT **Oxygen** is a colourless gas in the air which is needed by all plants and animals.

oyster /ˈɔɪstə/ **oysters.** N-COUNT An **oyster** is a large flat shellfish.

oz. oz is a written abbreviation for **ounce**.

ozone /ˈəʊzəʊn/. N-UNCOUNT **Ozone** is a form of oxygen. There is a layer of ozone high above the earth's surface.

ozone-ˈfriendly. ADJ **Ozone-friendly** chemicals, products, or technology do not cause harm to the ozone layer.

ˈozone layer. N-SING The **ozone layer** is the part of the Earth's atmosphere that has the highest number of ozone molecules.

P p

p /piː/. **p** is an abbreviation for **pence** or **page**. *They cost 5p each... See Note 16 on p. 223.*

⭐ **pace** /peɪs/ **paces, pacing, paced.** [1] N-UNCOUNT The **pace** of something is the speed at which it happens or is done. *Many people were not satisfied with the pace of change.* [2] N-SING Your **pace** is the speed at which you walk. *He moved at a brisk pace.* [3] N-COUNT A **pace** is the distance you move when you take one step. *I took a pace backwards.* [4] VERB If you **pace** a small area, you keep walking up and down it, because you are anxious or impatient. *Kravis paced the room nervously... He found John pacing around the flat.*

PHRASES ● To **keep pace with** something that is changing means to change quickly in response to it. ...*the rise fails to keep pace with inflation.* ● If you do something **at** your **own pace**, you do it at a speed that is comfortable for you.

pacifier /ˈpæsɪfaɪər/ **pacifiers.** N-COUNT In American English, a **pacifier** is a rubber or plastic object that you give to a baby to suck so that it feels comforted. The British word is **dummy**.

pacifist /ˈpæsɪfɪst/ **pacifists.** N-COUNT & ADJ A **pacifist** or someone with **pacifist** views believes that war and violence are always wrong. ♦ **pacifism** N-UNCOUNT *He didn't hide his pacifism.*

a
b
c
d
e
f
g
h
i
j
k
l
m
n
o
p
q
r
s
t
u
v
w
x
y
z

⭐ Bank of English® frequent word   For a full explanation of all grammatical labels, see pages vii–x

pack /pæk/ **packs, packing, packed.** ☐1 VERB & PHR-VERB When you **pack**, or when you **pack up**, you put your belongings into a bag, because you are leaving. *I packed my bags and left home... He began packing up his things.* ◆ **packing** N-UNCOUNT *She left Frances to finish her packing.* ☐2 VERB To **pack** things, for example in a factory, means to put them into containers or parcels so that they can be transported and sold. *Machines now exist to pack olives in jars.* ☐3 VERB If people or things **pack into** a place, or if they **pack** a place, there are so many of them that the place is full. *A thousand supporters packed into the stadium... Thousands of people packed the square.* ◆ **packed** ADJ *The stores were packed with shoppers.* ☐4 N-COUNT A **pack of** things is a collection of them in one packet. *...a free information pack. ...a pack of cigarettes.* ☐5 N-COUNT A **pack** is a bag containing your belongings that you carry on your back when you are travelling. *I hid the money in my pack.* ☐6 N-COUNT A **pack of** wolves or dogs is a group of them hunting together. ☐7 N-COUNT In British English, a **pack of** cards is a complete set of playing cards. The usual American word is **deck**. ▸**pack off.** PHR-VERB If you **pack** someone **off** somewhere, you send them there. [INFORMAL] *At the age of nine she was packed off to boarding school in England.*

⭐ **package** /'pækɪdʒ/ **packages, packaging, packaged.** ☐1 N-COUNT A **package** is a small parcel. *The package was addressed to Yusuf.* ☐2 N-COUNT A **package** is a set of proposals that are made by a government or organization. *...a Western economic aid package.* ☐3 VERB When something **is packaged**, it is put into packets to be sold.

packaging /'pækɪdʒɪŋ/. N-UNCOUNT **Packaging** is the container or wrappings that something is sold in. *...layers of expensive, wasteful packaging.*

packet /'pækɪt/ **packets.** N-COUNT A **packet** is a small box, bag, or envelope in which a quantity of something is sold. *The packet says the product contains cream... She was eating a packet of peanuts.*

⭐ **pact** /pækt/ **pacts.** N-COUNT A **pact** is a formal agreement between two or more people, organizations, or governments. *He signed a new non-aggression pact with Germany.*

pad /pæd/ **pads.** ☐1 N-COUNT A **pad** is a thick flat piece of a material such as cloth or foam rubber. Pads are used, for example, to clean things or for protection. *...a pad of cotton-wool.* ☐2 N-COUNT A **pad** of paper is a number of pieces of paper which are fixed together along the top or the side, so that each piece can be torn off when it has been used. *Keep a pad handy to jot down queries as they occur.*

padded /'pædɪd/. ADJ Something that is **padded** has soft material on it or inside it which makes it less hard, protects it, or gives it a different shape. *...a man in a padded jacket.*

padding /'pædɪŋ/. N-UNCOUNT **Padding** is soft material on the outside or inside of something

which makes it less hard, protects it, or gives it a different shape. *Players must wear padding to protect them from injury.*

paddle /'pædəl/ **paddles, paddling, paddled.** ☐1 N-COUNT A **paddle** is a short pole with a wide flat part at one end or at both ends, used to move a small boat through water. ☐2 VERB & N-COUNT If you **paddle**, or if you go for a **paddle**, you walk or stand in shallow water, for example at the edge of the sea, for pleasure. *...a lovely little stream that you can paddle in.*

paddock /'pædək/ **paddocks.** ☐1 N-COUNT A **paddock** is a small field where horses are kept. ☐2 N-COUNT In horse racing, the **paddock** is the place where the horses walk about before a race.

paddy /'pædi/ **paddies.** N-COUNT A **paddy** or a **paddy field** is a flooded field that is used for growing rice.

padlock

padlock /'pædlɒk/ **padlocks, padlocking, padlocked.** N-COUNT & VERB A **padlock** is a lock used for fastening two things or two parts of something together. When you **padlock** something, you lock it or fasten it using a padlock. *Eddie parked his cycle against a lamp post and padlocked it.*

paediatrician (AM **pediatrician**) /ˌpiːdiə'trɪʃən/ **paediatricians.** N-COUNT A **paediatrician** is a doctor who specializes in treating sick children.

paediatrics (AM **pediatrics**) /ˌpiːdi'ætrɪks/ **paediatric.**

✅ The form **paediatric** is used as a modifier.

N-UNCOUNT **Paediatrics** is the area of medicine that is concerned with the treatment of children's illnesses. *...a paediatric surgeon.*

pagan /'peɪgən/. ADJ **Pagan** beliefs and activities do not belong to any of the main religions of the world and take nature and a belief in many gods as a basis. They are older than other religions.

⭐ **page** /peɪdʒ/ **pages, paging, paged.** ☐1 N-COUNT A **page** is a side of one of the pieces of paper in a book, magazine, or newspaper. *Turn to page 4.* ☐2 N-COUNT The **pages** of a book, magazine, or newspaper are the pieces of paper it consists of. *He turned the pages of his notebook.*

pageant /'pædʒənt/ **pageants.** N-COUNT A **pageant** is a colourful public parade, show, or ceremony, often organized to celebrate a historic event.

paid /peɪd/. [1] **Paid** is the past tense and past participle of **pay**. [2] ADJ **Paid** means to do with the money a worker receives from his or her employer. You can say, for example, that someone is **well paid** when they receive a lot of money for the work that they do. ...a legal right to paid holiday leave.

⭐ **pain** /peɪn/ **pains, paining, pained.** [1] N-VAR If you feel **pain**, or if you are **in pain**, you feel great discomfort in a part of your body, because of illness or an injury. ...a bone disease that caused excruciating pain... I felt a sharp pain in my lower back. [2] N-UNCOUNT **Pain** is the unhappiness that you feel when something very upsetting happens. ...grey eyes that seemed filled with pain. [3] VERB If something **pains** you, it makes you feel upset or unhappy. It pains me to think of you struggling all alone. ◆ **pained** ADJ A pained expression came over her face.
PHRASES ● If you say that something or someone is **a pain** or **a pain in the neck**, you mean they are very annoying or irritating. [INFORMAL] You can be a real pain in the neck sometimes. ● If you **take pains to** do something, you try hard to do it successfully. He took great pains to entertain me.

⭐ **painful** /'peɪnfʊl/. [1] ADJ If a part of your body is **painful**, it hurts. Her glands were swollen and painful. ◆ **painfully** ADV His tooth had started to throb painfully. [2] ADJ If something such as an illness, injury, or operation is **painful**, it causes you a lot of physical pain. ...a painful back injury. ◆ **painfully** ADV ...cracking his head painfully against the cupboard. [3] ADJ Situations, memories, or experiences that are **painful** are difficult and unpleasant to deal with, and often make you feel sad and upset. She finds it too painful to return there without him.

painfully /'peɪnfʊli/. ADV You use **painfully** to emphasize a quality or situation that is undesirable. Things are moving painfully slowly... He was painfully aware of the gaps in his education.

painkiller /'peɪnkɪlə/ **painkillers.** N-COUNT A **painkiller** is a drug which reduces or stops physical pain.

painless /'peɪnləs/. [1] ADJ Something such as a treatment that is **painless** causes no physical pain. The operation itself is a brief, painless procedure. ◆ **painlessly** ADV She died peacefully and painlessly. [2] ADJ If a process or activity is **painless**, you do not have to make a great effort or suffer in any way. There are no easy or painless solutions to the nation's economic ills.
◆ **painlessly** ADV ...a game for children which painlessly teaches essential pre-reading skills.

painstaking /'peɪnsteɪkɪŋ/. ADJ A **painstaking** search, examination, or investigation is done extremely carefully and thoroughly.

◆ **painstakingly** ADV Broken bones were painstakingly pieced together.

⭐ **paint** /peɪnt/ **paints, painting, painted.** [1] N-VAR **Paint** is a coloured liquid that you put on a wall or other surface with a brush in order to protect the surface or to make it look nice, or that you use to produce a picture. They saw some large letters in white paint... The paint was peeling on the window frames. [2] VERB If you **paint** a wall or an object, you cover it with paint. I painted the walls white. [3] VERB If you **paint** something, or if you **paint** a picture of it, you produce a picture of it using paint. He is painting a huge volcano.

paintbrush /'peɪntbrʌʃ/ **paintbrushes.** N-COUNT A **paintbrush** is a brush which you use for painting. → See picture on page 833.

painter /'peɪntə/ **painters.** [1] N-COUNT A **painter** is an artist who paints pictures. ...England's greatest modern painter. [2] N-COUNT A **painter** is someone who paints walls, doors, and some other parts of buildings as their job.

⭐ **painting** /'peɪntɪŋ/ **paintings.** [1] N-COUNT A **painting** is a picture which someone has painted. [2] N-UNCOUNT **Painting** is the activity of painting pictures. She really enjoyed painting and gardening.

⭐ **pair** /peə/ **pairs.** [1] N-COUNT A **pair of** things are two things of the same size and shape that are intended to be used together. ...a pair of socks. ...a pair of earrings. [2] N-COUNT Some objects that have two main parts of the same size and shape are referred to as a **pair**. ...a pair of faded jeans. ...a pair of binoculars. [3] N-SING You can refer to two people as a **pair** when they are standing or walking together. A pair of teenage boys were smoking cigarettes. [4] See also **au pair**.

USAGE The noun **pair** can take either a singular verb or a plural verb, depending on whether it refers to one thing seen as a unit or a collection of two things or people. A good, supportive and protective pair of trainers is essential... The pair are still friends and attend functions together.

pajamas /pə'dʒɑːməz/. See **pyjamas**.

pal /pæl/ **pals.** N-COUNT Your **pals** are your friends. [INFORMAL] The two women became close pals.

⭐ **palace** /'pælɪs/ **palaces.** N-COUNT A **palace** is a very large splendid house, especially the home of a king, queen, or president.

palatable /'pælətəbəl/. [1] ADJ If you describe food or drink as **palatable**, you mean that it tastes pleasant. [FORMAL] ...some very palatable red wines. [2] ADJ If you describe an idea or proposal as **palatable**, you mean that it is easy to accept. ...direct payments to make the cuts more palatable to farmers.

palate /'pælɪt/ **palates.** [1] N-COUNT Your **palate** is the top part of the inside of your mouth. [2] N-COUNT You can refer to someone's ability to judge good food and wine as their **palate**.

a
b
c
d
e
f
g
h
i
j
k
l
m
n
o
p
q
r
s
t
u
v
w
x
y
z

...fresh pasta sauces to tempt more demanding palates.

★ **pale** /peɪl/ **paler, palest.** 1 ADJ Something that is **pale** is not strong or bright in colour. ...pale blue. 2 ADJ If someone looks **pale**, their face is a lighter colour than usual, because they are ill, frightened, or shocked.

palette /'pælɪt/ **palettes.** N-COUNT A **palette** is a flat piece of wood or plastic on which an artist mixes paints.

pall /pɔːl/ **palls, palling, palled.** 1 VERB If something **palls**, it becomes less interesting or less enjoyable. The job was beginning to pall. 2 N-COUNT A **pall of** smoke is a thick cloud of it. [LITERARY]

palm /pɑːm/ **palms.** 1 N-COUNT A **palm** or **palm tree** is a tree that grows in hot countries. It has long leaves at the top and no branches. 2 N-COUNT The **palm of** your hand is the flat surface which your fingers can bend towards. → See picture on page 823.

palpable /'pælpəbəl/. ADJ Something that is **palpable** is very obvious. The tension was palpable. ♦ **palpably** /'pælpəbli/ ADV The policeman was palpably nervous.

paltry /'pɔːltri/. ADJ A **paltry** amount of money or something else is very small. ...a paltry 0.2% rise in manufacturing.

pamper /'pæmpə/ **pampers, pampering, pampered.** VERB If you **pamper** someone, you do everything for them, and give them everything they want. ♦ **pampered** ADJ I was a very pampered child.

pamphlet /'pæmflət/ **pamphlets.** N-COUNT A **pamphlet** is a very thin book with a paper cover, which gives information about something.

★ **pan** /pæn/ **pans.** N-COUNT A **pan** is a round metal container with a long handle, which is used for cooking things, usually on top of a cooker. → See picture on page 825.

panacea /,pænə'siːə/ **panaceas.** N-COUNT If you say that something is not a **panacea** for a particular set of problems, you mean that it will not solve all those problems. [JOURNALISM] Western aid may help but will not be a panacea.

panache /pə'næʃ/. N-UNCOUNT If you do something **with panache**, you do it in a confident and stylish way. The whole orchestra performed with great panache.

pancake /'pænkeɪk/ **pancakes.** N-COUNT A **pancake** is a thin, flat, circular piece of cooked batter that is usually eaten hot, often with a sweet or savoury filling.

panda /'pændə/ **pandas.** N-COUNT A **panda** is a large animal with black and white fur which lives in China. → See picture on page 816.

pander /'pændə/ **panders, pandering, pandered.** VERB If you **pander to** someone, you do everything they want, often to get some advantage for yourself; used showing disapproval. ...politicians who pander to millionaires.

pane /peɪn/ **panes.** N-COUNT A **pane of** glass is a flat sheet of glass in a window or door.

★ **panel** /'pænəl/ **panels.** 1 N-COUNT A **panel** is a small group of people who are chosen to do something, for example to discuss something in public or to make a decision. The case will now go before a panel of judges. 2 N-COUNT A **panel** is a flat rectangular piece of wood or other material that forms part of a larger object such as a door. 3 N-COUNT A control **panel** or instrument **panel** is a board containing switches and controls.

panelled (AM **paneled**) /'pænəld/. ADJ If something such as a room or door is **panelled**, its walls or surface are covered in decorative wooden panels. ...panelled walls.

pang /pæŋ/ **pangs.** N-COUNT A **pang** is a sudden strong feeling, for example of sadness or pain. Ruth felt a pang of guilt.

★ **panic** /'pænɪk/ **panics, panicking, panicked.** 1 N-VAR **Panic** is a strong feeling of anxiety or fear that makes you act without thinking carefully. He felt a sudden rush of panic at the thought... In a panic, I rushed to the kitchen. 2 VERB If you **panic**, or if someone or something **panics** you, you become anxious or afraid, and act without thinking carefully. Jason panicked when the spider fell onto his knee.

panorama /,pænə'rɑːmə, -'ræmə/ **panoramas.** N-COUNT A **panorama** is a view in which you can see a long way over a wide area of land. You look out onto a breathtaking panorama of London. ♦ **panoramic** /,pænə'ræmɪk/ ADJ We had a panoramic view of the beach.

pant /pænt/ **pants, panting, panted.** VERB If you **pant**, you breathe quickly and loudly, because you have been doing something energetic. She was panting for air.

pantomime /'pæntəmaɪm/ **pantomimes.** N-VAR A **pantomime** is a funny musical play for children, usually performed at Christmas. She regularly appeared in pantomime.

pants /pænts/. 1 N-PLURAL In British English, **pants** are a piece of underwear with two holes to put your legs through and elastic around the top. The usual American word is **underpants**. 2 N-PLURAL In American English, **pants** are a piece of clothing that you wear over your body from the waist downwards, and that cover each leg separately. The usual British word is **trousers**.

papa /pə'pɑː, AM 'pɑːpə/ **papas.** N-COUNT & N-VOC Some people refer to or address their father as **papa**. [DATED]

papal /'peɪpəl/. ADJ BEFORE N **Papal** is used to describe things relating to the Pope. ...a papal visit to Japan.

★ **paper** /'peɪpə/ **papers, papering, papered.** 1 N-UNCOUNT **Paper** is a material that you write on or wrap things with. ...a piece of paper. ...a paper bag. 2 PHRASE If you put your thoughts down **on paper**, you write them down. 3 N-COUNT A **paper** is a newspaper. ...the daily papers. 4 N-PLURAL **Papers** are sheets of paper with information on them. ...a briefcase carrying personal papers. 5 N-PLURAL Your **papers** are your official documents, for example your passport or identity card. *To his surprise the officer asked him in English for his papers.* ⑥ N-COUNT A **paper** is a long essay on an academic subject. ⑦ N-COUNT A **paper** prepared by a government or a committee is a report on a question they have been considering or a set of proposals for changes in the law. *...a new government paper on European policy.* ⑧ VERB If you **paper** a wall, you put wallpaper on it. *We papered all four bedrooms.*

paperback /ˈpeɪpəbæk/ **paperbacks.** N-VAR A **paperback** is a book with a paper cover. *...a cheap paperback... The book is now out in paperback.*

paperwork /ˈpeɪpəwɜːk/. N-UNCOUNT **Paperwork** consists of the letters, reports, and records which have to be dealt with as the routine part of a job. *He does his paperwork here.*

par /pɑː/.
PHRASES ● If you say that someone or something is **below par**, you mean that they are below the standard you expected. *Duffy's guitar playing is well below par.* ● If one thing is **on a par** with another, the two things are equally good or bad. *This match was on a par with the German Cup Final.*

parable /ˈpærəbəl/ **parables.** N-COUNT A **parable** is a short story which makes a moral or religious point.

parachute /ˈpærəʃuːt/ **parachutes, parachuting, parachuted.** ① N-COUNT A **parachute** is a device which enables a person to jump from an aircraft and float safely to the ground. It consists of a large piece of thin cloth attached to your body by strings. ② VERB If a person **parachutes**, or if someone **parachutes** them somewhere, they jump from an aircraft using a parachute. *They had been parachuted into the country at night.*

parade /pəˈreɪd/ **parades, parading, paraded.** ① N-COUNT A **parade** is a line of people or vehicles moving together through a public place in order to celebrate an important day or event. → See picture on page 826. ② VERB When people **parade**, they walk together in a formal group or in a line, usually in front of spectators. *Soldiers paraded down the Champs Elysées.* ③ VERB If someone **parades** something, they show it in public in order to impress people or to gain some advantage for themselves. *I paraded all the paintings in front of them... Five US fighter pilots have been captured and paraded before the media.*

paradise /ˈpærədaɪs/ **paradises.** ① N-PROPER According to some religions, **paradise** is a wonderful place where people go after they die, if they have led good lives. ② N-VAR You can refer to a place or situation that seems perfect as **paradise** or a **paradise**.

paradox /ˈpærədɒks/ **paradoxes.** ① N-COUNT You describe a situation as a **paradox** when it involves two or more facts or qualities which seem to contradict each other. ♦ **paradoxical** ADJ *Some sedatives produce the paradoxical effect of making the person more anxious.* ♦ **paradoxically** ADV *Paradoxically, the less you have to do the more you may resent the work that does come your way.* ② N-VAR A **paradox** is a statement in which it seems that if one part of it is true, the other part of it cannot be true.

paraffin /ˈpærəfɪn/. N-UNCOUNT **Paraffin** is a strong-smelling liquid which is used as a fuel in heaters, lamps, and engines. The usual American word is **kerosene**.

paragon /ˈpærəgɒn/ **paragons.** N-COUNT If you say that someone is a **paragon** of virtue, or some other good quality, you mean that they have a lot of that quality. *...a paragon of neatness, efficiency and reliability.*

paragraph /ˈpærəgrɑːf, -græf/ **paragraphs.** N-COUNT A **paragraph** is a section of a piece of writing. A paragraph always begins on a new line and contains at least one sentence.

parallel /ˈpærəlel/ **parallels, parallelling, parallelled** (AM **paralleling, paralleled**). ① N-COUNT If something has a **parallel**, or if there are **parallels** between two or more things, they are similar to each other in some way. *It's an ecological disaster with no parallel anywhere else in the world... Detailed study of folk music from a variety of countries reveals many close parallels.* ② VERB & ADJ If one thing **parallels** another, or if two things are **parallel**, they happen at the same time or are similar, and often seem to be connected. *His remarks paralleled those of the president. ...parallel talks between the two countries' Foreign Ministers.* ③ ADJ If two lines or two objects are **parallel**, they are the same distance apart along their whole length.

paralyse (AM **paralyze**) /ˈpærəlaɪz/ **paralyses, paralysing, paralysed.** ① VERB If someone **is paralysed** by an accident or illness, they have no feeling in their body, or in part of their body, and are unable to move. ♦ **paralysed** ADJ *...a paralysed right arm.* ② VERB If a person, place, or organization **is paralysed** by something, they are unable to act or function properly. *The government has been paralysed by indecision.*

paralysis /pəˈræləsɪs/. N-UNCOUNT **Paralysis** is the loss of feeling in all or part of your body and the inability to move. *...paralysis of the leg.*

parameter /pəˈræmɪtə/ **parameters.** N-COUNT **Parameters** are factors or limits which affect the way that something can be done or made. *...the parameters of our loan agreement.*

paramilitary /ˌpærəˈmɪlɪtri, AM -teri/ **paramilitaries.** ADJ BEFORE N & N-COUNT **Paramilitary** organizations are groups who are organized like an army but do not belong to any official army. **Paramilitaries** are members of a paramilitary organization.

paramount /ˈpærəmaʊnt/. ADJ Something that is **paramount** or of **paramount** importance is

a
b
c
d
e
f
g
h
i
j
k
l
m
n
o
p
q
r
s
t
u
v
w
x
y
z

more important than anything else. *The child's welfare must be seen as paramount.*

paranoia /ˌpærəˈnɔɪə/. **1** N-UNCOUNT If you say that someone suffers from **paranoia**, you think that they are too suspicious and afraid of other people. *...the mounting paranoia with which he viewed the world.* **2** N-UNCOUNT If someone suffers from **paranoia**, they are suffering from a mental illness which makes them wrongly believe that other people are trying to harm them. [TECHNICAL]

paranoid /ˈpærənɔɪd/. **1** ADJ If you say that someone is **paranoid**, you mean that they are extremely suspicious and afraid of other people. *I'm not going to get paranoid about it.* **2** ADJ Someone who is **paranoid** suffers from the mental illness of paranoia. [TECHNICAL] *...a paranoid schizophrenic.*

paraphernalia /ˌpærəfəˈneɪliə/. N-UNCOUNT You can refer to a large number of objects that someone has with them or that are connected with a particular activity as **paraphernalia**. *...cigarettes and ashtrays and other paraphernalia associated with smoking.*

paraphrase /ˈpærəfreɪz/ **paraphrases, paraphrasing, paraphrased.** VERB & N-COUNT If you **paraphrase** someone, or if you **paraphrase** something that they have said or written, you express what they have said or written in a different way. A **paraphrase** is something that has been paraphrased. *I'm paraphrasing but this is honestly what he said... The writer here has attempted a paraphrase of Mabry's words.*

parasite /ˈpærəsaɪt/ **parasites.** **1** N-COUNT A **parasite** is a small animal or plant that lives on or inside a larger animal or plant. ♦ **parasitic** /ˌpærəˈsɪtɪk/ ADJ *...parasitic worms.* **2** N-COUNT If you call someone a **parasite**, you disapprove of them because you think that they get money or other things from people without doing anything in return.

paratrooper /ˈpærətruːpə/ **paratroopers.** N-COUNT **Paratroopers** are soldiers who are trained to be dropped by parachute into battle or into enemy territory.

parcel /ˈpɑːsəl/ **parcels.** N-COUNT A **parcel** is something wrapped in paper, usually so that it can be sent to someone by post. The more usual American word is **package**. ● **part and parcel**: see **part**.

parched /pɑːtʃt/. **1** ADJ If the ground is **parched**, it is very dry, because there has been no rain. *...a hill of parched brown grass.* **2** ADJ If your mouth, throat, or lips are **parched**, they are unpleasantly dry. **3** ADJ AFTER LINK-V If you say you are **parched**, you mean that you are very thirsty.

pardon /ˈpɑːdən/ **pardons, pardoning, pardoned.** **1** CONVENTION You say **'Pardon?'**, or **'I beg your pardon?'** or, in American English, **'Pardon me?'** when you want someone to repeat what they

have just said, either because you have not heard or understood it or because you are surprised by it. *'Will you let me open it?'—'Pardon?'—'Can I open it?'* **2** CONVENTION You say **'I beg your pardon'** or **'I do beg your pardon'** as a way of apologizing for accidentally doing something wrong, such as disturbing someone or making a mistake. *I was impolite and I do beg your pardon.* **3** VERB & N-COUNT If someone who has been found guilty of a crime **is pardoned** or is given a **pardon**, they are officially allowed to go free and are not punished.

pare /peə/ **pares, paring, pared.** **1** VERB When you **pare** something, or **pare** part of it **off** or **away**, you cut off its skin or its outer layer. *He took out a slab of cheese and pared off a slice.* **2** VERB & PHR-VERB If you **pare** something **down** or **back**, or if you **pare** it, you reduce it. *The number of Ministries has been pared down by a third.*

⭐ **parent** /ˈpeərənt/ **parents.** N-COUNT Your **parents** are your father and mother. ♦ **parental** /pəˈrentəl/ ADJ *Parental attitudes vary widely.*

parenthood /ˈpeərənthʊd/. N-UNCOUNT **Parenthood** is the state of being a parent.

parenting /ˈpeərəntɪŋ/. N-UNCOUNT **Parenting** is the activity of bringing up and looking after your child.

parish /ˈpærɪʃ/ **parishes.** **1** N-COUNT A **parish** is a village or part of a town which has its own church and clergyman. **2** N-COUNT A **parish** is a small country area in England with its own elected council.

parishioner /pəˈrɪʃənə/ **parishioners.** N-COUNT A clergyman's **parishioners** are the people in his parish.

parity /ˈpærɪti/. N-UNCOUNT If there is **parity** between two things, they are equal. [FORMAL] *Women have yet to achieve wage or occupational parity.*

⭐ **park** /pɑːk/ **parks, parking, parked.** **1** N-COUNT A **park** is a public area of land with grass and trees, usually in a town, where people go to relax and enjoy themselves. **2** N-VAR In Britain, a private area of grass and trees around a large country house is referred to as a **park**. **3** VERB When you **park** a vehicle, or when you **park** somewhere, you drive the vehicle into a position where it can stay for a period of time and leave it. *Could you park over there?* ♦ **parked** ADJ *...rows of parked cars.* ♦ **parking** N-UNCOUNT *...parking is allowed only on one side of the street.* ● See also **car park**, **national park**.

USAGE Note that you do not use the word **parking** to refer to a place where cars are parked. Instead, you refer to a **car park** in British English, and a **parking lot** in American English. **Parking** is used only to refer to the action of parking your car, or the state of being parked. *...a 'No Parking' sign.*

'parking lot, parking lots. N-COUNT In American English, a **parking lot** is an area of ground where people can leave their cars. The British term is **car park**.

⭐ **parliament** /'pɑːləmənt/ **parliaments.** N-VAR The **parliament** of a country is the group of people who make or change its laws. ● See note at **government**. ● See also **Member of Parliament**.

⭐ **parliamentary** /ˌpɑːlə'mentəri/. ADJ BEFORE N **Parliamentary** is used to describe things that are connected with a parliament. ...a parliamentary candidate.

parlour (AM **parlor**) /'pɑːlə/ **parlours.** N-COUNT **Parlour** is used in the names of some types of shops which provide a service. ...a pizza parlour.

parochial /pə'rəʊkiəl/. ADJ If you describe someone as **parochial**, you are critical of them because they are too concerned with their own local affairs and interests.

parody /'pærədi/ **parodies, parodying, parodied.** VERB & N-VAR When someone **parodies** a particular work, thing, or person, they imitate them in an amusing or exaggerated way. You call an imitation like this a **parody**. ...parodying a number of television and film genres. ...a parody of his favourite comic book.

parole /pə'rəʊl/ **paroles, paroling, paroled.** [1] N-UNCOUNT & PASSIVE-VERB When prisoners are given **parole**, or when they **are paroled**, they are released before their sentence is due to end, on condition that they behave well. [2] PHRASE If someone is **on parole**, they will stay out of prison if they behave well.

parrot /'pærət/ **parrots, parroting, parroted.** [1] N-COUNT A **parrot** is a tropical bird with a curved beak and brightly-coloured or grey feathers. Parrots can be kept as pets. [2] VERB If you **parrot** what someone else has said, you repeat it without really understanding what it means. Students all over the world have learnt to parrot the standard explanations.

parsley /'pɑːsli, AM -zli/. N-UNCOUNT **Parsley** is a small plant with curly leaves used for flavouring or decorating savoury food.

parsnip /'pɑːsnɪp/ **parsnips.** N-COUNT A **parsnip** is a root vegetable similar in shape to a carrot. → See picture on page 836.

part 1 piece, section

⭐ **part** /pɑːt/ **parts.** [1] N-VAR If one thing is a **part of** another thing or **part of** it, the first thing is one of the pieces, sections, or elements that the second thing consists of. I like that part of Cape Town... Respect is a very important part of any relationship... Switzerland is not part of the EC. [2] N-COUNT A **part** for a machine or vehicle is one of the smaller pieces that is used to make it. ...spare parts for military equipment.

PHRASES ● **The best part of** or **the better part of** a period of time or an amount means most of that time or that amount. We spent the better part of an hour searching for her. ● You use **in part** to indicate that something exists or happens to

some extent but not completely. The levels of blood glucose depend in part on what you eat. ● **For the most part** means mostly or usually. For the most part, the travellers lived as the locals did. ● If you say that something is **part and parcel of** something else, you mean that it is involved or included in it. Violence is part and parcel of everyday life round here.

part 2 role

⭐ **part** /pɑːt/ **parts.** [1] N-COUNT A **part** in a play or film is one of the roles in it. I'd love a part in a romantic comedy. [2] N-SING Your **part in** something that happens is your involvement in it. If only he could conceal his part in the accident.

PHRASES ● You can say, for example, that **for your part** you thought or did something, to introduce what you feel or do. The soldiers, for their part, agreed not to disrupt the election campaign. ● If someone **looks the part**, they dress or behave in the way that is characteristic of a particular kind of person. If you go to an interview looking the part you can command a much higher salary. ● If you talk about a feeling or action **on** someone's **part**, you are referring to something that they feel or do. That was actually an error on my part. ● You can say that someone or something **plays a part in** something to talk about the fact that they are involved in it and the effect they have on it. Work plays an important part in a single woman's life. ● If you **take part in** an activity, you are involved in it with other people. He did not take part in the meeting.

part 3 separate

⭐ **part** /pɑːt/ **parts, parting, parted.** [1] VERB If things which are touching **part**, or if they **are parted**, they move away from each other. Her lips parted and she smiled... Livy parted the curtains. [2] VERB If your hair is **parted**, it is combed in two different directions so that there is a straight line from the front of your head to the back. [3] VERB When two people **part**, they leave each other or separate. [FORMAL] He is parting from his Swedish-born wife Eva. ◆ **parting, partings** N-VAR After her parting with Jackson she lived in Provence.
▶**part with.** PHR-VERB If you **part with** something that you would prefer to keep, you give it or sell it to someone else. Think carefully before parting with money.

partial /'pɑːʃəl/. [1] ADJ You use **partial** to refer to something that is true or exists to some extent, but is not complete or total. The event was only a partial success. ◆ **partially** ADV I am partially deaf. [2] ADJ AFTER LINK-V If you are **partial to** something, you like it. Wasn't his uncle rather partial to asparagus?

participant /pɑː'tɪsɪpənt/ **participants.** N-COUNT The **participants** in an activity are the people who take part in it.

⭐ **participate** /pɑː'tɪsɪpeɪt/ **participates, participating, participated.** VERB If you **participate in** an activity, you are involved in it with other people. All the warring parties agreed to

a b c d e f g h i j k l m n o p q r s t u v w x y z

participate in talks. ◆ **participation** N-UNCOUNT
...participation in religious activities.

participle /'pɑːtɪsɪpəl/ **participles.** N-COUNT In
grammar, a **participle** is a form of a verb that can
be used in compound tenses of the verb. English
verbs have a past participle, which usually ends
in '-ed', and a present participle, which ends in
'-ing'.

particle /'pɑːtɪkəl/ **particles.** N-COUNT A **particle
of** something is a very small piece or amount of
it. ...food particles. ...a particle of hot metal.

⭐ **particular** /pə'tɪkjʊlə/ **particulars.** [1] ADJ BEFORE
N You use **particular** to emphasize that you are
talking about one thing or one kind of thing
rather than other similar ones. One particular
memory still haunts me. [2] PHRASE You use **in
particular** to indicate that what you are saying
applies especially to one thing or person. Why
should he notice her car in particular? [3] ADJ
BEFORE N If a person or thing has a **particular**
quality or possession, it belongs only to them. I
have a particular responsibility to ensure that I
make the right decision. [4] ADJ BEFORE N You can
use **particular** to emphasize that something is
greater or more intense than usual. Particular
emphasis will be placed on oral language training.
[5] ADJ Someone who is **particular** chooses or
does things very carefully and is not easily
satisfied. Ted was very particular about the colors
he used.

⭐ **particularly** /pə'tɪkjʊləli/. ADV You use
particularly to indicate that what you are saying
applies especially to one thing or situation. Keep
your office space looking good, particularly your
desk... I particularly liked the wooden chests and
chairs.

particulars /pə'tɪkjʊləz/. N-PLURAL The
particulars of something or someone are facts or
details about them which are kept as a record.
The nurses at the admission desk asked for her
particulars.

partisan /ˌpɑːtɪ'zæn, AM -zən/ **partisans.** [1] ADJ &
N-COUNT Someone who is **partisan** or a **partisan**
strongly supports a particular person or cause,
often without thinking carefully about what they
represent. [2] N-COUNT **Partisans** are people who
get together to fight enemy soldiers who are
occupying their country.

partition /pɑː'tɪʃən/ **partitions, partitioning,
partitioned.** [1] N-COUNT A **partition** is a wall or
screen separating one part of a room or vehicle
from another. [2] VERB If you **partition** a room,
you separate one part of it from another by
means of a partition. [3] VERB & N-UNCOUNT To
partition a country means to divide it into two or
more independent countries. The **partition** of a
country is the act of dividing it like this.

⭐ **partly** /'pɑːtli/. ADV You use **partly** to indicate
that something is true or exists to some extent,
but not completely. It's partly my fault... Margaret
was always several steps behind her sister, partly
because of her age.

⭐ **partner** /'pɑːtnə/ **partners, partnering partnered.**
[1] N-COUNT Your **partner** is the person you are
married to or are having a long-term sexual
relationship with. [2] N-COUNT Your **partner** in an
activity such as a game or dance is the person
you are playing or dancing with. [3] VERB If you
partner someone, you are their partner in a
game or in a dance. [4] N-COUNT The **partners** in a
firm or business are the people who share the
ownership of it. He's a partner in a Chicago law
firm. [5] N-COUNT The **partner** of a country or
organization is another country or organization
with which they have an alliance or agreement.
...Britain's major trading partners in Europe.

⭐ **partnership** /'pɑːtnəʃɪp/ **partnerships.** N-VAR A
partnership is a relationship in which two or
more people or organizations work together as
partners. Management must work in partnership
with their employees and unions.

ˌ**part-'time.** ADJ & ADV If someone is a **part-time**
worker or has a **part-time** job, they work for only
part of each day or week. You can also say that
they work **part-time**.

⭐ **party** /'pɑːti/ **parties, partying, partied.** [1] N-COUNT A
party is a social event at which people enjoy
themselves doing things such as eating, drinking,
or dancing. We threw a huge birthday party.
[2] N-COUNT A political **party** is an organization
whose members have similar aims and beliefs,
and that tries to get its members elected to
government. ...the Labour party. [3] N-COUNT A
party of people is a group of them doing
something together, for example travelling. ...a
party of sightseers. [4] VERB If you **party**, you
enjoy yourself doing things such as going
drinking and dancing. They drank and partied all
night. [5] N-COUNT One of the people involved in a
legal agreement or dispute can be referred to as
a particular **party**. [TECHNICAL] It has to be proved
that they are the guilty party. [6] PHRASE If you **are
party to** an action or agreement, or **are a party
to** it, you are involved in it, and are therefore
partly responsible for it. Crook had resigned his
post rather than be party to such treachery.

⭐ **pass** /pɑːs, pæs/ **passes, passing, passed.** [1] VERB To
pass someone or something means to go past
them. We passed the mountains of Torres Vedras...
Jane stood aside to let her pass. [2] VERB To **pass**
in a particular direction means to move or go in
that direction. He passed through the doorway
into Ward B... The route passes through St-Paul-
sur-Ubaye. [3] VERB If you **pass** something
through, over, or **round** something else, you
move or push it through, over, or round that
thing. She passed the needle through the rough
cloth... He passed a hand wearily over his eyes.
[4] VERB If you **pass** an object to someone, you
pick it up and give it to them. If you **pass** a ball to
someone, you hit, kick, or throw it to them. Pass
the salt, please. [5] VERB & PHR-VERB If something
passes from one person to another, or if it **is
passed to** them or **is passed on to** them, the
second person is given it. His mother's small

estate had passed to him after her death... He has written a note asking me to pass on his thanks. **6** VERB When a period of time **passes**, it happens and ends. *Several minutes passed before the girls were noticed.* ♦ **passing** N-SING ...*the passing of time.* **7** VERB If you **pass** time in a particular way, you spend it in that way. *The children passed the time playing in the streets.* **8** VERB If an amount **passes** a particular total or level, it becomes greater than that total or level. *Today the population of the globe has passed five billion.* **9** VERB & N-COUNT If someone or something **passes** a test or **is passed**, they are considered to be of an acceptable standard. To get a **pass** in a test means to pass it. *Kevin has just passed his driving test... The medical board would not pass him fit for General Service... It could mean the difference between a pass and a fail.* ● See note at **exam**. **10** N-COUNT A **pass** is a document that allows you to do something. *Don't let any cars onto the land unless they've got a pass.* **11** VERB When people in authority **pass** a new law or a proposal, they formally agree to it or approve it. *Congress passed a law that regulates the disposal of waste.* **12** VERB If something **passes** without comment or **passes** unnoticed, nobody comments on it or notices it. *I cannot allow this nonsense to pass unchallenged.* **13** VERB To **pass for** or to **pass as** a particular thing means to be accepted as that thing, in spite of not having all the right qualities. *...a woman passing as a man.* **14** N-COUNT A **pass** is a narrow way between two mountains. **15** See also **passing**. ● to **pass the buck**: see **buck**. ● to **pass sentence**: see **sentence**.

▸ **pass around** or **pass round.** PHR-VERB If a group of people **pass** something **around**, or **pass** it **round**, they each take it and then give it to the next person. *A bottle of whisky was passed around.*

▸ **pass away.** PHR-VERB You can say that someone **passed away** to mean that they died, if you want to avoid using the word 'die'.

▸ **pass off.** PHR-VERB If an event **passes off** without any trouble, it ends without any trouble. [BRITISH] *The main demonstration passed off peacefully.*

▸ **pass off as.** PHR-VERB If someone **passes** something **off** as another thing, they dishonestly convince people that it is that other thing. *She'd decided to pass herself off as a Canadian.*

▸ **pass on.** See **pass** 5.

▸ **pass out.** PHR-VERB If you **pass out**, you faint or collapse.

▸ **pass over.** PHR-VERB If someone **is passed over** for a job, they do not get the job and someone younger or less experienced is chosen instead. *She was repeatedly passed over for promotion.*

▸ **pass round.** See **pas around**.

▸ **pass up.** PHR-VERB If you **pass up** an opportunity, you do not take advantage of it. *We can't pass up a chance like this.*

★ **passage** /ˈpæsɪdʒ/ **passages.** **1** N-COUNT A **passage** is a long, narrow space between walls or fences, connecting one room or place with another. **2** N-COUNT A **passage** in a book, speech, or piece of music is a section of it. *He reads a passage from Milton.* **3** N-COUNT The **passage** of someone or something is their movement or progress from one place or stage to another. *...the passage of food through the digestive tract... Relief convoys were to be guaranteed safe passage through rebel-held areas.* **4** N-SING The **passage of** time is the fact of it passing.

passageway /ˈpæsɪdʒweɪ/ **passageways.** N-COUNT A **passageway** is a long, narrow space between walls or fences, connecting one room or place with another.

★ **passenger** /ˈpæsɪndʒə/ **passengers.** N-COUNT A **passenger** in a bus, boat, or plane is a person who is travelling in it, but who is not driving it or working on it.

passing /ˈpɑːsɪŋ, ˈpæs-/. **1** ADJ BEFORE N A **passing** feeling or action is brief and not very serious or important. *He had never taken more than a passing interest in the girl... It was just a passing comment.* **2** PHRASE If you mention something **in passing**, you mention it briefly while you are talking or writing about something else. **3** N-SING You can talk about **the passing of** a person or thing to mean the fact of their dying or coming to an end, especially when you are sad about this. *The business world is a duller place for his passing... We have mourned the passing of the old ways.* **4** See also **pass**.

★ **passion** /ˈpæʃən/ **passions.** **1** N-UNCOUNT **Passion** is a very strong feeling of sexual attraction for someone. *...my passion for a dark-haired, slender boy named James.* **2** N-UNCOUNT **Passion** is a very strong belief in something, to the point where you become excited or emotional about it. *He spoke with great passion.* **3** N-COUNT If you have a **passion for** something, you like it very much. *...her childhood passion for collecting.*

passionate /ˈpæʃənət/. **1** ADJ A **passionate** person has very strong feelings about something. *I'm a passionate believer in public art. ...his passionate commitment to peace.* ♦ **passionately** ADV *I am passionately opposed to the death penalty.* **2** ADJ A **passionate** person has strong romantic or sexual feelings and expresses them in their behaviour. ♦ **passionately** ADV *He was passionately in love with her.*

passive /ˈpæsɪv/. **1** ADJ If you describe someone as **passive**, you mean they do not take action but instead let things happen to them; used showing disapproval. ♦ **passively** ADV *...sitting passively in front of the TV.* **2** N-SING In grammar, **the passive** is formed using 'be' and the past participle of a verb. The subject of a passive clause does not perform the action expressed by the verb but is affected by it. For example, in 'He's been murdered', the verb is in the passive.

a
b
c
d
e
f
g
h
i
j
k
l
m
n
o
p
q
r
s
t
u
v
w
x
y
z

Passover /ˈpɑːsəʊvə, ˈpæs-/. N-UNCOUNT
Passover is a Jewish festival beginning in March or April and lasting for seven or eight days.

passport /ˈpɑːspɔːt, ˈpæs-/ **passports.** [1] N-COUNT
Your **passport** is an official document which you need to show when you enter or leave a country. [2] N-COUNT If you say that something is a **passport to** something such as success, you mean that it makes that thing possible. *It could be your passport to riches.*

password /ˈpɑːswɜːd, ˈpæs-/ **passwords.** N-COUNT
A **password** is a secret word or phrase that enables you to enter a place or use a computer system.

⭐ **past** /pɑːst, pæst/ **pasts.** [1] N-SING The **past** is the period of time before the present, and the things that happened in that period. *In the past they have been the target of racist abuse.* [2] ADJ BEFORE N **Past** events and things happened or existed before the present time. *...details of his past activities.* [3] N-COUNT Your **past** consists of all the things that you have done or that have happened to you. *...revelations about his past. ...Germany's recent past.* [4] ADJ BEFORE N You use **past** to talk about a period of time that has just finished. *...the momentous events of the past few days... I have been homeless for the past year.* [5] ADJ BEFORE N The **past tense** of a verb is used to refer to things that happened or existed before the time when you are speaking or writing. For regular verbs, the past tense is the '-ed' form, for example 'They walked back to the car'. [6] PREP & ADV You use **past** when you are stating the time, when it is thirty minutes or less after a particular hour. → See Reference Pages on Telling the Time, and Times and Dates. *It's ten past eleven... At a quarter past seven, we left the hotel... I have my lunch at half past.* [7] PREP & ADV If you go **past** someone or something, you go near them and keep moving, so that they are then behind you. *I dashed past him... An ambulance drove past.* [8] PREP If something is **past** a place, it is on the other side of it. *The farm was just past the next village.*

pasta /ˈpæstə, AM ˈpɑːstə/. N-UNCOUNT **Pasta** is a type of food made from a mixture of flour, eggs, and water that is formed into different shapes. Spaghetti and macaroni are types of pasta.

paste /peɪst/ **pastes, pasting, pasted.** [1] N-VAR **Paste** is a soft, wet, sticky mixture of a substance, which can be spread easily. *...wallpaper paste. ...tomato paste.* [2] VERB If you **paste** something on a surface, you stick it to the surface with glue or adhesive paste. *The children were busy pasting gold stars on a chart.*

pastel /ˈpæstəl, AM pæˈstel/ **pastels.** ADJ & N-COUNT
Pastel colours are pale rather than dark or bright. *...delicate pastel shades... The lobby is decorated in pastels.*

pastime /ˈpɑːstaɪm, ˈpæs-/ **pastimes.** N-COUNT A **pastime** is something that you enjoy doing in your spare time. *His favourite pastime is golf.*

pastoral /ˈpɑːstərəl, ˈpæst-/. [1] ADJ BEFORE N
The **pastoral** activities of a religious leader relate to the general needs of people, rather than just their religious needs. *...the pastoral care of the sick.* [2] ADJ BEFORE N **Pastoral** means characteristic of peaceful country life. *...the pastoral beauty of a park.*

pastry /ˈpeɪstri/ **pastries.** [1] N-UNCOUNT **Pastry** is a food made of flour, fat, and water that is used for making pies and flans. [2] N-COUNT A **pastry** is a small cake made with pastry.

pasture /ˈpɑːstʃə, ˈpæs-/ **pastures.** N-VAR **Pasture** is land that has grass growing on it and that is used for farm animals to graze on.

pat /pæt/ **pats, patting, patted.** VERB & N-COUNT If you **pat** something or someone, or if you give them a **pat**, you tap them lightly with your hand held flat, usually as a sign of encouragement, affection, or friendship. *'Don't you worry about any of this,' she said patting me on the knee... He gave her an encouraging pat on the shoulder.*

patch /pætʃ/ **patches, patching, patched.** [1] N-COUNT
A **patch** on a surface is a part of it which is different in appearance from the area around it. *...the bald patch on the top of his head. ...two big damp patches on the carpet.* [2] N-COUNT A **patch of** land is a small area of land, often one used for growing a particular crop. *...a patch of wild cornflowers. ...a vegetable patch.* [3] N-COUNT A **patch** is a piece of material used to cover a hole in something. [4] VERB If you **patch** something that has a hole in it, you mend it by fixing something over the hole. *He and Walker patched the barn roof.* [5] PHRASE If you go through **a bad patch** or **a rough patch**, you have a lot of problems for a time.
▸ **patch up.** [1] PHR-VERB If you **patch up** a quarrel or relationship, you try to be friendly again and not to quarrel any more. *She has gone on holiday with her husband to try to patch up their marriage.* [2] PHR-VERB If you **patch up** something which is damaged, you mend it.

patchwork /ˈpætʃwɜːk/. ADJ BEFORE N A **patchwork** quilt or dress has been made by sewing small pieces of material together.

patchy /ˈpætʃi/ **patchier, patchiest.** [1] ADJ A **patchy** substance or colour is not spread evenly, but is scattered around in small quantities. *...thick patchy fog.* [2] ADJ If something is **patchy**, it is not completely reliable or satisfactory because it is not always good. *The evidence is patchy.*

pâté /ˈpæteɪ, AM pɑːˈteɪ/ **pâtés.** N-VAR **Pâté** is a mixture of meat, fish, or vegetables with various flavourings, which is blended into a paste and eaten cold.

patent /ˈpeɪtənt, AM ˈpæt-/ **patents, patenting, patented.**

✔ The pronunciation /ˈpætənt/ is also used for meanings 1 and 2 in British English.

[1] N-COUNT A **patent** is an official right to be the only person or company to make and sell a new

product. *P&G applied for a patent on its cookies.*
2 VERB If you **patent** something, you obtain a patent for it. *The invention has been patented by the university.* **3** ADJ You use **patent** to emphasize that the nature or existence of something, especially something bad, is obvious. *This was patent nonsense.* ♦ **patently** ADV *He made his displeasure patently obvious.*

paternal /pə'tɜːnəl/. ADJ BEFORE N **Paternal** is used to describe feelings or actions which are typical of those of a father towards his child. *...paternal love for his children.*

⭐ **path** /pɑːθ, pæθ/ **paths.** **1** N-COUNT A **path** is a strip of ground that people walk along. *...the garden path.* **2** N-COUNT Your **path** is the space ahead of you as you move along. *A group of reporters blocked his path.* **3** N-COUNT The **path of** something is the line which it moves along in a particular direction. *He stepped without looking into the path of a reversing car.* **4** N-COUNT A **path** that you take is a particular course of action or way of doing something. *...a crucial step on the path of peace.*

pathetic /pə'θetɪk/. **1** ADJ If you describe a person or animal as **pathetic**, you mean that they are sad and weak or helpless, and they make you feel very sorry for them. *...a pathetic little dog with a curly tail.* ♦ **pathetically** ADV *She was pathetically thin.* **2** ADJ If you describe someone or something as **pathetic**, you mean that they make you feel impatient or angry, often because they are very bad or weak. *What pathetic excuses.* ♦ **pathetically** ADV *Five women in a group of 18 people is a pathetically small number.*

pathological /ˌpæθə'lɒdʒɪkəl/. **1** ADJ You describe a person as **pathological** when they behave in an extreme and unacceptable way, and have very powerful feelings which they cannot control. *He experiences chronic, almost pathological jealousy.* **2** ADJ **Pathological** means relating to pathology. *Students are trained in the use of pathological tests.* [TECHNICAL]

pathology /pə'θɒlədʒi/. N-UNCOUNT **Pathology** is the study of the way diseases and illnesses develop, and examining dead bodies in order to find out the cause of death. [TECHNICAL] ♦ **pathologist, pathologists** N-COUNT *...the pathologist who conducted the autopsy.*

pathos /'peɪθɒs/. N-UNCOUNT **Pathos** is a quality in a situation that makes people feel sadness and pity. *...the pathos of man's isolation.*

pathway /'pɑːθweɪ, 'pæθ-/ **pathways.** N-COUNT A **pathway** is the same as a **path**.

patience /'peɪʃəns/. N-UNCOUNT If you have **patience**, you are able to stay calm and not get annoyed, for example when something takes a long time. *He doesn't have the patience to wait.*

⭐ **patient** /'peɪʃənt/ **patients.** **1** N-COUNT A **patient** is a person who is receiving treatment from a doctor or who is registered with a doctor. *The earlier the treatment is given, the better the patient's chances.* **2** ADJ If you are **patient**, you

stay calm and do not get annoyed, for example when something takes a long time. *I've got to be patient and wait.* ♦ **patiently** ADV *She waited patiently for Frances to finish talking.*

patio /'pætiəʊ/ **patios.** N-COUNT A **patio** is a paved area in a garden, where people can sit to eat or relax. *We had lunch on the patio.*

patriot /'pætriət, 'peɪt-/ **patriots.** N-COUNT A **patriot** is someone who loves their country.

patriotic /ˌpætri'ɒtɪk, ˌpeɪt-/. ADJ Someone who is **patriotic** loves their country and feels very loyal towards it. ♦ **patriotism** /'pætriətɪzəm, 'peɪt-/ N-UNCOUNT *...a boy who had joined the army out of a sense of patriotism.*

patrol /pə'trəʊl/ **patrols, patrolling, patrolled.** **1** VERB & N-VAR When soldiers, police, or guards **patrol** an area or building, or when they do a **patrol** of it, they move around it in order to make sure that there is no trouble. *100 police were on patrol.* **2** N-COUNT A **patrol** is a group of soldiers or vehicles that are patrolling an area. *A hand grenade was thrown at an army patrol.*

patron /'peɪtrən/ **patrons.** **1** N-COUNT A **patron** is a person who supports and gives money to artists, writers, or musicians. *...a patron of modern art.* **2** N-COUNT The **patron** of a charity, group, or campaign is an important person who allows his or her name to be connected with it for publicity. *The duchess is a patron of the charity.* **3** N-COUNT The **patrons** of a place such as a pub or a hotel are its customers. *Many of the bar's patrons are military.*

patronage /'pætrənɪdʒ, 'peɪt-/. N-UNCOUNT **Patronage** is the support and money given by someone to a person or a group such as a charity. *...government patronage of the arts.*

patronize (BRIT also **patronise**) /'pætrənaɪz, AM 'peɪt-/ **patronizes, patronizing, patronized.** VERB If someone **patronizes** you, they speak or behave towards you in a way which seems friendly, but which shows that they think that they are superior to you. *Don't you patronize me!* ♦ **patronizing** ADJ *...his patronising attitude to the homeless.*

patter /'pætə/ **patters, pattering, pattered.** VERB & N-SING If something **patters** on a surface, it hits it quickly several times, making quiet tapping sounds. You can refer to these sounds as a **patter**. *Rain pattered gently outside. ...the patter of lots of little hands being clapped together.*

⭐ **pattern** /'pætən/ **patterns.** **1** N-COUNT A **pattern** is a particular way in which something is usually or repeatedly done. *His sleeping pattern was bad.* **2** N-COUNT A **pattern** is a design of lines or shapes repeated at regular intervals. *...a three-dimensional pattern of colored dots.* → See pictures on page 829. **3** N-COUNT A **pattern** is a diagram or shape that you can use as a guide when you are making something such as a model or a piece of clothing.

patterned /'pætənd/. ADJ Something that is

a
b
c
d
e
f
g
h
i
j
k
l
m
n
o
p
q
r
s
t
u
v
w
x
y
z

patterned is covered with a pattern or design. *...a patterned sweater.*

☆ **pause** /pɔːz/ **pauses, pausing, paused.** [1] VERB If you **pause** while you are speaking or doing something, you stop for a short time and then continue. *The crowd paused for a minute, wondering what to do next.* [2] N-COUNT A **pause** is a short period when something stops before it continues again. *There was a pause while the barmaid set down two plates.*

pave /peɪv/ **paves, paving, paved.** [1] VERB When an area of ground **has been paved**, it has been covered with blocks of stone or concrete. [2] PHRASE If one thing **paves the way for** another, it creates a situation in which the other thing is able to happen. *The invention of the first dynamo paved the way for the large scale generation of electric power.*

pavement /ˈpeɪvmənt/ **pavements.** [1] N-COUNT In British English, a **pavement** is a path with a hard surface by the side of a road. The usual American word is **sidewalk**. [2] N-COUNT The **pavement** is the hard surface of a road. [AMERICAN] *The car spun on the slippery pavement.*

pavilion /pəˈvɪliən/ **pavilions.** [1] N-COUNT A **pavilion** is a building on the edge of a sports field where players can change their clothes and wash. [BRITISH] [2] N-COUNT A **pavilion** is a large temporary structure such as a tent, which is used at outdoor public events.

paw /pɔː/ **paws, pawing, pawed.** [1] N-COUNT The **paws** of an animal such as a cat, dog, or bear are its feet. [2] VERB If an animal **paws** something, it draws its paw or hoof over it.

pawn /pɔːn/ **pawns, pawning, pawned.** [1] VERB If you **pawn** something that you own, you leave it with a pawnbroker, who gives you money for it and who can sell it if you do not pay back the money before a certain time. [2] N-COUNT In chess, a **pawn** is the smallest and least valuable playing piece. [3] N-COUNT If you say that someone is using you as a **pawn**, you mean that they are using you for their own advantage. *They are the pawns in the power game played by their unseen captors.*

pawnbroker /ˈpɔːnbrəʊkə/ **pawnbrokers.** N-COUNT A **pawnbroker** is a person who will lend you money if you give them something that you own. The pawnbroker can sell that thing if you do not pay back the money before a certain time.

☆ **pay** /peɪ/ **pays, paying, paid.** [1] VERB When you **pay** an amount of money to someone, you give it to them because you are buying something from them or because you owe it to them. When you **pay** something such as a bill or a debt, you pay the amount that you owe. *The wealthier may have to pay a little more in taxes... All you pay for is breakfast and dinner... We paid £35 for each ticket... You can pay by credit card.* [2] VERB & N-UNCOUNT When you are **paid**, or when you receive your **pay**, you get your wages or salary

from your employer. *I get paid monthly... They have not had a pay rise for two years.*

> **USAGE** When used as a noun, **pay** is a general word which you can use to refer to the money you get from your employer for doing your job. Professional people and office workers receive a **salary**, which is paid monthly. However, when talking about someone's salary, you usually give the annual figure. *I'm paid a salary of £15,000 a year.* Manual workers are paid **wages**, or **a wage**. The plural is more common than the singular, especially when you are talking about the actual cash that someone receives. *Every week he handed all his wages in cash to his wife.* Wages are usually paid, and quoted, as an hourly or a weekly sum. *...a starting wage of five dollars an hour.* Your **income** consists of all the money you receive from all sources, including your pay.

[3] VERB If a course of action **pays**, it results in some advantage or benefit for you. *It pays to invest in protective clothing.* [4] VERB If you **pay for** something that you do or have, you suffer as a result. *Britain was to pay dearly for its lack of resolve... She committed a terrible crime and will pay the penalty.* [5] VERB You use **pay** with some nouns, for example in the expressions **pay a visit** and **pay attention**, to indicate that something is given or done. *He felt a heavy bump, but paid no attention to it.* [6] PHRASE If you **pay your way**, you have or earn enough money to pay for what you need, without needing other people to give or lend you money. *I went to college anyway, as a part-time student, paying my own way.* [7] See also **paid**.

▸**pay back.** PHR-VERB If you **pay back** money that you have borrowed from someone, you give them an equal amount at a later time.

▸**pay off.** [1] PHR-VERB If you **pay off** a debt, you give someone all the money that you owe them. [2] PHR-VERB If an action **pays off**, it is successful. *Sandra was determined to become a doctor and her persistence paid off.* [3] See also **payoff**.

▸**pay out.** PHR-VERB If you **pay out** money, usually a large amount, you spend it on something. *...football clubs who pay out millions of pounds for players.*

▸**pay up.** PHR-VERB If you **pay up**, you give someone the money that you owe them.

payable /ˈpeɪəbəl/. [1] ADJ If an amount of money is **payable**, it has to be paid or it can be paid. *Tax was not payable on goods for export.* [2] ADJ If a cheque is made **payable to** you, it has your name written on it to indicate that you are the person who will receive the money.

payer /ˈpeɪə/ **payers.** N-COUNT You can refer to someone as a **payer** if they pay a particular kind of bill or fee. For example, a tax **payer** is someone who pays taxes.

⭐ **payment** /'peɪmənt/ **payments.** 1 N-UNCOUNT **Payment** is the act of paying money to someone or of being paid. *Players now expect payment for interviews.* 2 N-COUNT A **payment** is an amount of money that is paid to someone. *...mortgage payments.*

payoff /'peɪɒf/ **payoffs.** 1 N-COUNT A **payoff** is a payment which is made to someone, often secretly or illegally, so that they will not cause trouble. 2 N-COUNT A **payoff** is an advantage or benefit that results from an action.

payroll /'peɪrəʊl/ **payrolls.** N-COUNT The people on the **payroll** of a company or an organization are the people who work for it and are paid by it.

PC /,piː 'siː/ **PCs.** 1 N-COUNT & N-TITLE In Britain, a **PC** is a male police officer of the lowest rank. **PC** is an abbreviation for 'police constable'. 2 N-COUNT A **PC** is a computer that is used by one person in a small business, at school, or at home. **PC** is an abbreviation for 'personal computer'. [COMPUTING]

PDA /,piː diː 'eɪ/ **PDAs.** N-COUNT A **PDA** is a hand-held computer, used mainly for storing and accessing personal information such as addresses, telephone numbers, and memos. **PDA** is an abbreviation for 'personal digital assistant'.

pea /piː/ **peas.** N-COUNT **Peas** are small, round, green seeds eaten as a vegetable. → See picture on page 836.

⭐ **peace** /piːs/. 1 N-UNCOUNT **Peace** is a state of undisturbed quiet and calm. *One more question and I'll leave you in peace.* 2 N-UNCOUNT When there is **peace** in a country, it is not involved in a war. *...a shared commitment to world peace.* 3 N-UNCOUNT & PHRASE If there is **peace** among a group of people, or if they live or work **in peace** with each other, they live or work together without fighting or quarrelling. *...a period of relative peace in the country's industrial relations.*

⭐ **peaceful** /'piːsfʊl/. 1 ADJ A **peaceful** place or time is quiet, calm, and undisturbed. ♦ **peacefully** ADV *Except for traffic noise the night passed peacefully.* 2 ADJ Someone who feels or looks **peaceful** feels or looks calm and free from worry. ♦ **peacefully** ADV *Would she wake to find Gaston sleeping peacefully at her side?* 3 ADJ **Peaceful** means not involving violence or conflict. *...a peaceful demonstration.* ♦ **peacefully** ADV *Thousands have taken part in the protest which passed off peacefully.*

peach /piːtʃ/ **peaches.** 1 N-COUNT A **peach** is a soft, round, juicy fruit with sweet yellow flesh and pinky-yellow skin. → See picture on page 821. 2 ADJ & N-VAR Something that is **peach** is pale pinky-orange in colour. *...a peach silk blouse. ...a bedroom in peach and fern green.*

⭐ **peak** /piːk/ **peaks, peaking, peaked.** 1 N-COUNT The **peak** of a process or activity is the point at which it is at its strongest, most successful, or most fully developed. *...the peak of the morning rush hour.* 2 ADJ BEFORE N The **peak** level or value of something is its highest level or value. *...a 10 per*

cent reduction in traffic at peak times. 3 VERB When someone or something **peaks**, they reach their highest value or highest level of success. *Temperatures have peaked at over thirty degrees Celsius.* 4 N-COUNT A **peak** is a mountain, or the top of a mountain. *...snow-covered peaks.* 5 N-COUNT The **peak** of a cap is the part at the front that sticks out above your eyes.

peal /piːl/ **peals, pealing, pealed.** 1 VERB & N-COUNT When bells **peal**, or when there is a **peal of** bells, they ring one after the other, making a musical sound. *Church bells pealed at the stroke of midnight.* 2 N-COUNT A **peal of** laughter or thunder consists of a long loud series of sounds. [LITERARY]

peanut /'piːnʌt/ **peanuts.** N-COUNT **Peanuts** are small nuts often eaten as a snack.

pear /peə/ **pears.** N-COUNT A **pear** is a juicy fruit which is narrow at the top and wider at the bottom. It has white flesh and green or yellow skin. → See picture on page 821.

pearl /pɜːl/ **pearls.** N-COUNT A **pearl** is a hard, shiny, white ball-shaped object which grows inside the shell of an oyster. Pearls are used for making jewellery. *...a string of pearls. ...pearl earrings.*

peasant /'pezənt/ **peasants.** N-COUNT People refer to the small farmers or farm labourers in a poor country as **peasants**.

peat /piːt/. N-UNCOUNT **Peat** is dark decaying plant material which is found in some cool wet regions.

pebble /'pebəl/ **pebbles.** N-COUNT A **pebble** is a small stone.

peck /pek/ **pecks, pecking, pecked.** 1 VERB If a bird **pecks** something, it moves its beak forward quickly and bites at it. *A jay was pecking at a piece of bread someone had dropped... Chickens pecked in the dust.* 2 VERB & N-COUNT If you **peck** someone **on** the cheek, or if you give them a **peck on** the cheek, you give them a quick light kiss.

peculiar /pɪ'kjuːliə/. 1 ADJ If you describe someone or something as **peculiar**, you think that they are strange or unusual, often in an unpleasant way. *Rachel thought it tasted peculiar.* ♦ **peculiarly** ADV *His face had become peculiarly expressionless.* 2 ADJ AFTER LINK-V If something is **peculiar to** a particular thing, person, or situation, it belongs or relates only to that thing, person, or situation. *Hippies and Sumo wrestlers all have distinct hair styles, peculiar to their group.*

peculiarity /pɪ,kjuːli'ærɪti/ **peculiarities.** 1 N-COUNT A **peculiarity** is a characteristic or quality which belongs or relates only to one person or thing. *I usually get out of my car very quickly – it's a peculiarity of mine. ...a peculiarity of the Soviet system.* 2 N-COUNT A **peculiarity** that someone or something has is a strange or unusual characteristic or habit. *Joe's peculiarity was that he was constantly munching hard candy.*

pedal /'pedəl/ **pedals, pedalling, pedalled** (AM **pedaling, pedaled**). 1 N-COUNT The **pedals** on a bicycle are the two parts that you push with your feet in order to make the bicycle move. 2 VERB

a
b
c
d
e
f
g
h
i
j
k
l
m
n
o
p
q
r
s
t
u
v
w
x
y
z

When you **pedal** a bicycle, you push the pedals around with your feet to make it move. *I pedalled to school.* [3] N-COUNT A **pedal** in a car or on a machine is a lever that you press with your foot in order to control the car or machine. *...the brake pedal.*

peddle /'pedəl/ **peddles, peddling, peddled.** [1] VERB Someone who **peddles** things goes from place to place trying to sell them. [DATED] [2] VERB Someone who **peddles** drugs sells them illegally. ♦ **peddling** N-UNCOUNT *...the war against drug peddling.* [3] VERB If someone **peddles** an idea or piece of information, they try to get people to accept it; used showing disapproval. *Talk shows like these are a great place to peddle ideas to a large audience.*

pedestal /'pedɪstəl/ **pedestals.** N-COUNT A **pedestal** is the base on which a statue or a column stands.

pedestrian /pɪ'destriən/ **pedestrians.** [1] N-COUNT A **pedestrian** is a person who is walking, especially in a town. *...streets crowded with pedestrians.* [2] ADJ If you describe something as **pedestrian**, you mean that it is ordinary and not at all interesting. *This book is depressingly pedestrian.*

pediatrician. See **paediatrician**.

pediatrics. See **paediatrics**.

pedigree /'pedɪgriː/ **pedigrees.** [1] N-COUNT If a dog, cat, or other animal has a **pedigree**, its ancestors are known and recorded. [2] ADJ A **pedigree** animal is descended from animals which have all been of a particular breed, and is therefore considered to be of good quality. [3] N-COUNT Someone's **pedigree** is their background or ancestry. *Jones has an impeccable pedigree.*

peek /piːk/ **peeks, peeking, peeked.** VERB & N-COUNT If you **peek at** something or someone, or if you have a **peek** at them, you have a quick look at them, often secretly. [INFORMAL] *On two occasions she had peeked at him through a crack in the wall.*

peel /piːl/ **peels, peeling, peeled.** [1] N-UNCOUNT & N-COUNT The **peel** of a fruit such as a lemon or apple is its skin. In American English, you can also refer to a **peel**. *...grated lemon peel. ...a banana peel.* [2] VERB When you **peel** fruit or vegetables, you remove their skins. [3] VERB & PHR-VERB If you **peel** something **off** a surface, or if it **peels** or **peels off**, it comes away from the surface. *It took me two days to peel off the labels... Paint was peeling off the walls... The acid makes skin peel slightly, revealing new skin beneath.*

peep /piːp/ **peeps, peeping, peeped.** [1] VERB & N-SING If you **peep at** something, or if you take a **peep at** it, you have a quick look at it, often secretly. *Now and then she peeped to see if he was noticing her... 'Fourteen minutes,' Chris said, taking a peep at his watch.* [2] VERB If something **peeps out** from somewhere, a small part of it is visible. *Here and there a face peeped out from the shop doorway.*

★ **peer** /pɪə/ **peers, peering, peered.** [1] VERB If you **peer at** something, you look at it very hard, usually because it is difficult to see clearly. *I had been peering at a computer print-out... He watched the Customs official peer into the driver's window.* [2] N-COUNT A **peer** is a member of the group of people in society who have titles and high social rank. [3] N-PLURAL Your **peers** are people of the same age or status as you. *...children who are much cleverer than their peers.*

peerage /'pɪərɪdʒ/ **peerages.** [1] N-COUNT If someone has a **peerage**, they have the rank of a peer. [2] N-SING The peers of a country are referred to as **the peerage**.

★ **peg** /peg/ **pegs, pegging, pegged.** [1] N-COUNT A **peg** is a small hook or knob on a wall or door which is used for hanging things on. [2] N-COUNT A **peg** is a small device which you use to fasten clothes to a washing line. [BRITISH] [3] N-COUNT A tent **peg** is a small piece of wood or metal that is hammered into the ground, keeping a section of the tent in place. [4] VERB If the price of something **is pegged at** a particular level, it is fixed at that level. You can also say that one country's currency **is pegged to** another country's when the value of the first currency is fixed in relation to the second. [JOURNALISM] *A system was introduced, under which the peso is strictly pegged to the dollar.*

pellet /'pelɪt/ **pellets.** N-COUNT A **pellet** is a small ball of paper, mud, lead, or other material.

pelt /pelt/ **pelts, pelting, pelted.** [1] N-COUNT The **pelt** of an animal is its skin which can be used to make clothing or rugs. [2] VERB If you **pelt** someone **with** things, you throw things at them. *Crowds started to pelt police cars with stones.* [3] VERB If the rain **is pelting down**, it is raining very hard. [INFORMAL] *The rain now was pelting down... We drove through pelting rain.*

pelvic /'pelvɪk/. ADJ BEFORE N **Pelvic** means near or relating to your pelvis.

pelvis /'pelvɪs/ **pelvises.** N-COUNT Your **pelvis** is the wide curved group of bones at the level of your hips.

★ **pen** /pen/ **pens, penning, penned.** [1] N-COUNT A **pen** is a writing instrument, which you use to write in ink. [2] VERB If someone **pens** a letter, article, or book, they write it. *She penned a short memo to his private secretary.* [3] N-COUNT A **pen** is a small fenced area in which farm animals are kept for a short time. [4] VERB If people or animals **are penned** somewhere, they have to remain in a very small area. *I don't have to stay in my room penned up like a prisoner.*

penal /'piːnəl/. ADJ BEFORE N **Penal** means relating to the punishment of criminals. *...a penal colony.*

penalize (BRIT also **penalise**) /'piːnəlaɪz/ **penalizes, penalizing, penalized.** VERB If someone **is penalized** for something, they are made to suffer some disadvantage because of it. *Some of the* *players may, on occasion, break the rules and be penalized.*

⭐ **penalty** /'penəlti/ **penalties.** [1] N-COUNT A **penalty** is a punishment for doing something which is against a law or rule. *The death penalty for murder was abolished in Britain in 1969.* [2] N-COUNT In sports such as football and hockey, a **penalty** is a free kick or hit at a goal, which is given to the attacking team if the defending team commit a foul near their own goal.

pence /pens/. See **penny**.

penchant /'pɒnʃɒn, 'pentʃənt/. N-SING If someone has a **penchant for** something, they have a special liking for it or a tendency to do it. [FORMAL] *...a stylish woman with a penchant for dark glasses.*

pencil /'pensəl/ **pencils, pencilling, pencilled.** [1] N-COUNT A **pencil** is a thin wooden rod with graphite down the centre which is used for writing or drawing. [2] VERB If you **pencil** a letter or a note, you write it using a pencil. *He pencilled a note to Joseph Daniels.*

pendant /'pendənt/ **pendants.** N-COUNT A **pendant** is an ornament on a chain worn round your neck.

pending /'pendɪŋ/. [1] ADJ If something such as a legal procedure is **pending**, it is waiting to be dealt with or settled. [FORMAL] *As the court cases are pending we cannot say any more.* [2] PREP If something is done **pending** a future event, it is done until that event happens. *A judge has suspended a ban on the magazine pending a full inquiry.*

pendulum /'pendʒʊləm/ **pendulums.** [1] N-COUNT The **pendulum** of a clock is a rod with a weight at the end which swings from side to side in order to make the clock keep regular time. [2] N-SING People use the word **pendulum** as a way of talking about regular changes in a situation or in people's opinions. *The pendulum has swung back and the American car companies have made dramatic advances in safety.*

penetrate /'penɪtreɪt/ **penetrates, penetrating, penetrated.** [1] VERB If someone or something **penetrates** a physical object or an area, they succeed in getting into it or passing through it. *His men had been ordered to shoot on sight anyone trying to penetrate the area.*
♦ **penetration** N-UNCOUNT *The water has become clearer, permitting deeper penetration by the heat of the sun.* [2] VERB If someone **penetrates** an organization or a profession, they succeed in entering it although it is difficult to do so. *...the continuing failure of women to penetrate the higher levels of engineering.* [3] VERB If someone **penetrates** an enemy group, they succeed in joining it in order to get information or cause trouble. ♦ **penetration** N-UNCOUNT *...the successful penetration by the KGB of the French intelligence service.*

penetrating /'penɪtreɪtɪŋ/. [1] ADJ A **penetrating** sound is loud and clear. [2] ADJ If

someone gives you a **penetrating** look, you feel that they know what you are thinking. [3] ADJ Someone who has a **penetrating** mind understands and recognizes things quickly and thoroughly. *He never stopped asking penetrating questions.*

penguin /'peŋgwɪn/ **penguins.** N-COUNT A **penguin** is a black and white sea bird found mainly in the South Pole. Penguins cannot fly.

peninsula /pə'nɪnsjʊlə/ **peninsulas.** N-COUNT A **peninsula** is a long narrow piece of land that is joined at one part to the mainland and is almost completely surrounded by water.

penis /'piːnɪs/ **penises.** N-COUNT A man's **penis** is the part of his body that he uses when urinating and when having sex.

penniless /'penɪləs/. ADJ Someone who is **penniless** has not got any money.

⭐ **penny** /'peni/ **pennies, pence.**

✔ The form **pence** is used for the plural of meaning 1.

[1] N-COUNT In Britain, a **penny** is a coin or an amount which is worth one hundredth of a pound.

> **USAGE Pennies** usually refers to a number of individual coins. *He took two pennies out of his pocket.* You use **pence** or **p** when you are talking about a sum of money. *It only cost fifty pence... Admission for children is 50p.*

[2] N-COUNT In America, a **penny** is a coin or amount that is worth one cent.

⭐ **pension** /'penʃən/ **pensions.** N-COUNT A **pension** is a sum of money which a retired, widowed, or disabled person regularly receives from the state or from a former employer.

pensioner /'penʃənə/ **pensioners.** N-COUNT A **pensioner** is a person who receives a pension.

Pentagon /'pentəgən, AM -gɑːn/. N-PROPER The **Pentagon** is the main building of the US Defense Department in Washington.

penthouse /'penthaʊs/ **penthouses.** N-COUNT A **penthouse** is a luxurious flat or set of rooms at the top of a tall building.

pent-up /,pent 'ʌp/. ADJ **Pent-up** emotions have been held back and not expressed. *He still had a lot of pent-up anger to release.*

penultimate /pe'nʌltɪmət/. ADJ The **penultimate** thing in a series is the one before the last.

⭐ **people** /'piːpəl/ **peoples; peopled.**

✔ In meaning 1, **people** is normally used as the plural of **person**, instead of 'persons'.

[1] N-PLURAL **People** are men, women, and children. *Millions of people have lost their homes. ...the people of Angola.* [2] N-PLURAL **The people** is sometimes used to refer to ordinary men and women, in contrast to the upper classes or the

---

⭐ Bank of English® frequent word   For a full explanation of all grammatical labels, see pages vii-x

a
b
c
d
e
f
g
h
i
j
k
l
m
n
o
p
q
r
s
t
u
v
w
x
y
z

government. ...*a tremendous rift between the people and their leadership.* [3] N-COUNT A **people** consists of all the men, women, and children of a particular country or race. ...*the native peoples of Central and South America.* [4] PASSIVE-VERB If a place **is peopled by** a particular group of people, those people live there.

★ **pepper** /ˈpepə/ **peppers, peppering, peppered.**
[1] N-UNCOUNT **Pepper** is a hot-tasting spice which is used to flavour food. ...*freshly ground black pepper.* [2] N-COUNT A **pepper** is a hollow green, red or yellow vegetable. → See picture on page 836. [3] VERB If something **is peppered with** things, they hit it or are scattered over it. *The missile peppered the studio with jagged bits of metal.* ...*a retired bank manager who, like his son, peppers his conversation with jokes.*

peppermint /ˈpepəmɪnt/ **peppermints.**
[1] N-UNCOUNT **Peppermint** is a strong fresh-tasting flavouring that is obtained from the peppermint plant or made artificially. [2] N-COUNT A **peppermint** is a peppermint-flavoured sweet.

★ **per** /pɜː/. PREP You use **per** to express rates and ratios. For example, if a vehicle is travelling at 40 miles per hour, it will travel 40 miles in an hour.

per annum /pər ˈænəm/. ADV A particular amount **per annum** means that amount each year. ...*a fee of £35 per annum.*

per capita /pə ˈkæpɪtə/. ADJ BEFORE N & ADV The **per capita** amount of something is the average amount of it for each person in a particular area or country. [TECHNICAL] *They have the world's largest per capita income.* ...*the lowest oil consumption per capita in the world.*

perceive /pəˈsiːv/ **perceives, perceiving, perceived.**
[1] VERB If you **perceive** something, especially something that is not obvious, you see, notice, or realize it. ...*to get pupils to perceive for themselves the relationship between success and effort.*
[2] VERB If you **perceive** someone or something **as** doing or being a particular thing, it is your opinion that they do this thing or that they are that thing. *A woman cannot succeed if she is perceived as being too feminine.*

★ **per cent** (or **percent**) /pə ˈsent/.

☑ **Per cent** is both the singular and the plural form.

N-COUNT & ADJ BEFORE N You use **per cent** to talk about amounts. For example, if an amount is 10 per cent (10%) of a larger amount, it is equal to 10 hundredths of the larger amount.

★ **percentage** /pəˈsentɪdʒ/ **percentages.** N-COUNT A **percentage** is a fraction of an amount expressed as a particular number of hundredths.

perception /pəˈsepʃən/ **perceptions.** [1] N-COUNT Your **perception** of something is the way that you think about it or the impression you have of it. *Our perceptions of death affect the way we live.*
[2] N-UNCOUNT Someone who has **perception** realizes or notices things that are not obvious.
[3] N-UNCOUNT **Perception** is the recognition of

things by using your senses, especially the sense of sight.

perceptive /pəˈseptɪv/. ADJ A **perceptive** person realizes or notices things that are not obvious.

perch /pɜːtʃ/ **perches, perching, perched.** [1] VERB If you **perch on** something, you sit down lightly on the very edge of it. *I walked across the bridge, and perched on the narrow railing there.* [2] VERB If something **perches on** something, it is on the top or edge of something. ...*the vast slums that perch precariously on top of the hills.* [3] VERB If you **perch** one thing **on** another, you put it on the top or edge, so that it looks as if it might fall off. *He picked up one of the baseball caps and perched it on his head.* [4] VERB When a bird **perches on** a branch or a wall, it lands on it and stays there.

percussion /pəˈkʌʃən/. N-UNCOUNT **Percussion** instruments are musical instruments that you hit, such as drums.

perennial /pəˈreniəl/. ADJ You use **perennial** to describe problems or situations that keep occurring or which seem to exist all the time. ...*the perennial urban problems of drugs and homelessness.*

★ **perfect, perfects, perfecting, perfected.** [1] ADJ /ˈpɜːfɪkt/ Something that is **perfect** is as good as it can possibly be. *He spoke perfect English... Hiring a nanny has turned out to be the perfect solution.* ♦ **perfectly** ADV *The system worked perfectly.* [2] ADJ If you say that something is **perfect for** a particular person, thing, or activity, you are emphasizing that it is very suitable for them or for that activity. *Carpet tiles are perfect for kitchens because they're easy to take up and wash.*
[3] ADJ BEFORE N You can use **perfect** to add emphasis. *What he had said to her made perfect sense.* ♦ **perfectly** ADV *They made it perfectly clear that it was pointless to go on.* [4] ADJ BEFORE N The **perfect** tenses of a verb are the ones used to talk about things that happened or began before a particular time, as in 'He's already left' (present perfect) and 'They had always liked her' (past perfect). The present perfect tense is sometimes called the **perfect tense**. [5] VERB /pəˈfekt/ If you **perfect** something, you improve it so that it becomes as good as it can possibly be. *We perfected a hand-signal system.*

perfection /pəˈfekʃən/. N-UNCOUNT **Perfection** is the quality of being perfect. ...*fresh fish, cooked to perfection.*

perfectionist /pəˈfekʃənɪst/ **perfectionists.** N-COUNT Someone who is a **perfectionist** refuses to do or accept anything that is not perfect.

★ **perform** /pəˈfɔːm/ **performs, performing, performed.** [1] VERB When you **perform** a task or action, you do it. ...*people of all ages who have performed outstanding acts of bravery.* [2] VERB The way that someone or something **performs** is how well they work or achieve good results. *The point of the tables is to get a picture of how schools are*

performing. ◆ **performer, performers** N-COUNT
*Until 1987, Canada's industry had been the star
performer.* **3** VERB To **perform** a play, a piece of
music, or a dance means to do it in front of an
audience. *He began performing regularly in the
early fifties.* ◆ **performer** N-COUNT *...a solo
performer.*

★ **performance** /pə'fɔːməns/ **performances.**
1 N-COUNT A **performance** involves entertaining
an audience by singing, dancing, or acting. *...a
performance of Bizet's Carmen.* **2** N-VAR
Someone's or something's **performance** is how
well they do something. *That study looked at the
performance of 18 surgeons.*

perfume /'pɜːfjuːm, pə'fjuːm/ **perfumes.**
1 N-VAR **Perfume** is a pleasant-smelling liquid
which women put on their necks and wrists to
make themselves smell nice. **2** N-COUNT A
perfume is a pleasant smell. [LITERARY] *...the
perfume of roses.*

★ **perhaps** /pə'hæps, præps/. ADV You use
perhaps to indicate that you are not sure
whether something is true, possible, or likely. *In
the end they lose millions, perhaps billions... It was
bulky, perhaps three feet long and almost as high...
Perhaps, in time, the message will get through.*

peril /'perɪl/ **perils.** **1** N-VAR & PHRASE **Perils** are
great dangers. If someone or something is **in
peril**, they are in great danger. [FORMAL] *...the perils
of the sea.* **2** N-PLURAL The **perils of** a particular
activity or course of action are the dangers or
problems that can arise from doing it. *...the perils
of starring in a television commercial.*

perilous /'perɪləs/. ADJ Something that is
perilous is very dangerous. *...a perilous journey
across the war-zone.* ◆ **perilously** ADV *The track
snaked perilously upwards.*

perimeter /pə'rɪmɪtə/ **perimeters.** N-COUNT The
perimeter of an area of land is the whole of its
outer edge or boundary.

★ **period** /'pɪəriəd/ **periods.** **1** N-COUNT A particular
period is a particular length of time. *...a period of
a few months. ...a period of economic good health
and expansion. ...the Roman period.* **2** ADJ
Period costumes, furniture and instruments were
made at an earlier time in history, or look as if
they were made then. **3** N-COUNT When a woman
has a **period**, she bleeds from her womb. This
usually happens once a month, unless she is
pregnant. **4** N-COUNT In American English, a
period is the punctuation mark (.) which you use
at the end of a sentence when it is not a question
or an exclamation. The British term is **full stop**.

periodic /,pɪəri'ɒdɪk/. ADJ A **periodic** event or
situation happens occasionally, at fairly regular
intervals. *...periodic bouts of illness.*

periodical /,pɪəri'ɒdɪkəl/ **periodicals.** **1** N-COUNT
A **periodical** is a magazine. **2** ADJ **Periodical**
means the same as **periodic**. ◆ **periodically**
ADV *Meetings are held periodically to monitor the
project's progress.*

peripheral /pə'rɪfərəl/. **1** ADJ A **peripheral**
activity or issue is not very important compared
with other activities or issues. **2** ADJ **Peripheral**
areas of land are ones which are on the edge of
larger ones. *...peripheral regions beyond the reach
of powerful rulers.*

periphery /pə'rɪfəri/ **peripheries.** **1** N-COUNT If
something is on the **periphery** of an area, place,
or thing, it is on the edge of it. [FORMAL] **2** N-COUNT
The **periphery** of a subject is the part of it that is
not considered to be as central and important as
the main part. *He brought the centre and the
periphery of American politics together.*

perish /'perɪʃ/ **perishes, perishing, perished.** **1** VERB
To **perish** means to die or be destroyed. [WRITTEN]
*...the ferry disaster in which 193 passengers
perished.* **2** VERB If a substance or material
perishes, it starts to fall to pieces. *Their tyres are
slowly perishing.*

perjury /'pɜːdʒəri/. N-UNCOUNT If someone who
is giving evidence in a court of law commits
perjury, they lie. [TECHNICAL]

perk /pɜːk/ **perks perking perked.** N-COUNT **Perks** are
benefits that are given to people who have a
particular job or belong to a particular group.
One of the perks of being a student is cheap travel.
▸ **perk up.** PHR-VERB If something **perks** you **up**,
or if you **perk up**, you become cheerful, after
feeling tired, bored, or depressed. *...suggestions to
make you smile and perk you up.*

perm /pɜːm/ **perms, perming, permed.** VERB &
N-COUNT When a hair stylist **perms** someone's
hair, or when they give someone a **perm**, they
curl their hair it and treat it with chemicals so
that it stays curly for several months. [BRITISH] *She
had her hair permed.*

★ **permanent** /'pɜːmənənt/. ADJ **Permanent**
means lasting for ever or occurring all the time.
*...permanent damage to the brain... The ban is
intended to be permanent. ...a permanent state of
tension.* ◆ **permanently** ADV *She lived
permanently in Australia with her family. ...the only
way to lose weight permanently.* ◆ **permanence**
N-UNCOUNT *Anything which threatens the
permanence of the treaty is a threat to peace.*

permeate /'pɜːmieɪt/ **permeates, permeating,
permeated.** **1** VERB If an idea, feeling, or attitude
permeates society or a system, it affects every
part of it. *An obvious change of attitude at the top
will permeate through the system.* **2** VERB If a
liquid, smell, or flavour **permeates** something, it
spreads through it. *Eventually, the water will
permeate through the surrounding concrete.*

permissible /pə'mɪsəbəl/. ADJ Something that
is **permissible** is allowed because it does not
break any laws or rules. *Religious practices are
permissible under the Constitution.*

★ **permission** /pə'mɪʃən/. N-UNCOUNT If you give
someone **permission** to do something, you tell
them that they can do it. *He asked permission to
leave the room... They cannot leave the country*

a
b
c
d
e
f
g
h
i
j
k
l
m
n
o
p
q
r
s
t
u
v
w
x
y
z

A
B
C ☆
D
E
F
G
H
I
J
K
L
M
N
O
P
Q
R
S
T
U
V
W
X
Y
Z

without permission... He got permission from his commanding officer to join me.

permissive /pə'mɪsɪv/. ADJ A **permissive** person allows or tolerates things which other people disapprove of. ♦ **permissiveness** N-UNCOUNT ...*sexual permissiveness.*

☆ **permit, permits, permitting, permitted.** [1] VERB /pə'mɪt/ If someone **permits** you to do something, they allow you to do it. [FORMAL] *The guards permitted me to bring my camera.* [2] VERB If a situation **permits** something, it makes it possible for that thing to exist, happen, or be done. [FORMAL] *This method of cooking also permits heat to penetrate evenly.* [3] N-COUNT /'pɜːmɪt/ A **permit** is an official document allowing you to do something. ...*a work permit.*

pernicious /pə'nɪʃəs/. ADJ If you describe something as **pernicious**, you mean that it is very harmful. [FORMAL] ...*the pernicious influence of secret societies.*

perpetrate /'pɜːpɪtreɪt/ **perpetrates, perpetrating, perpetrated.** VERB If someone **perpetrates** an immoral or harmful act, they commit it. [FORMAL] *A high proportion of crime in any country is perpetrated by young males.* ♦ **perpetrator, perpetrators** N-COUNT ...*perpetrators of terrorist acts.*

perpetual /pə'petʃʊəl/. ADJ A **perpetual** feeling, state, or quality never ends or changes. [FORMAL] ...*his perpetual enthusiasm.*
♦ **perpetually** ADV *They were all perpetually starving.*

perpetuate /pə'petʃʊeɪt/ **perpetuates, perpetuating, perpetuated.** VERB To **perpetuate** a situation, system, or belief, especially one that is bad or wrong, means to cause it to continue. ...*adverts that perpetuate the worst stereotypes about the Irish.*

perplexed /pə'plekst/. ADJ If you are **perplexed**, you are puzzled or do not know what to do. *She is perplexed about what to do for her daughter.*

persecute /'pɜːsɪkjuːt/ **persecutes, persecuting, persecuted.** VERB If someone is **persecuted**, they are treated cruelly and unfairly, often because of their race or beliefs. *During the Middle Ages, the Church persecuted scientists like Copernicus.*
♦ **persecution** N-UNCOUNT ...*victims of political persecution.* ♦ **persecutor, persecutors** N-COUNT *How could he forgive his persecutors?*

persevere /ˌpɜːsɪ'vɪə/ **perseveres, persevering, persevered.** VERB If you **persevere with** something difficult, you continue doing it and do not give up. ...*a school with a reputation for persevering with difficult and disruptive children.*
♦ **perseverance** N-UNCOUNT *Adam's perseverance proved worthwhile.*

persist /pə'sɪst/ **persists, persisting, persisted.** [1] VERB If something undesirable **persists**, it continues to exist. *Contact your doctor if the cough persists.* [2] VERB If you **persist in** doing something, you continue to do it, even though other people oppose you or it is difficult. *She*

knows how much this upsets me but she persists in doing it... Their coach persisted with his own ideas.

persistent /pə'sɪstənt/. [1] ADJ If something undesirable is **persistent**, it continues to exist or happen for a long time. *His cough grew more persistent.* ♦ **persistently** ADV *The allegations have been persistently denied.* ♦ **persistence** N-UNCOUNT ...*concern at the persistence of inflation.* [2] ADJ **Persistent** people continue trying to do something, even though other people oppose them or it is difficult. *He phoned again this morning. He's very persistent.* ♦ **persistently** ADV *Rachel gently but persistently imposed her will upon Douglas.* ♦ **persistence** N-UNCOUNT *Chandra was determined to become a doctor and her persistence paid off.*

☆ **person** /'pɜːsən/ **persons.**

✓ The usual plural of person is **people**. The form **persons** is used as the plural in formal language.

[1] N-COUNT A **person** is a man, woman, or child. *The amount of sleep we need varies from person to person... At least fifty four people have been killed.* [2] PHRASE If you do something **in person**, you do it yourself rather than letting someone else do it for you. *You must collect the mail in person.* [3] PHRASE If you meet, hear, or see someone **in person**, you are in the same place as them, rather than speaking to them on the telephone or writing to them. [4] N-COUNT In grammar, the term **first person** is used when referring to 'I' and 'we', **second person** when referring to 'you', and **third person** when referring to 'he', 'she', 'it', 'they', and all other noun groups. **Person** is also used like this when referring to the verb forms that go with these pronouns and noun groups.

persona /pə'səʊnə/ **personas** or **personae.** N-COUNT Someone's **persona** is the aspect of their character or nature that they present to other people. [FORMAL] ...*the contradictions between her private life and the public persona.*

☆ **personal** /'pɜːsənəl/. [1] ADJ BEFORE N A **personal** opinion, quality, or thing belongs or relates to a particular person. *That's my personal opinion. ...books, furniture, and other personal belongings.* [2] ADJ BEFORE N If you give something your **personal** attention, you deal with it yourself rather than letting someone else deal with it. ...*a personal letter from the President's secretary.* [3] ADJ **Personal** matters relate to your feelings, relationships, and health. *He had resigned for personal reasons.* [4] ADJ **Personal** comments are critical of someone's appearance or character in an offensive way. *Newspapers resorted to personal abuse... It does concern me when it gets personal and people attack my family.*

ˌ**personal com'puter, personal computers.** N-COUNT A **personal computer** is a computer which is used by one person, normally independently. The abbreviation **PC** is also used. [COMPUTING]

⭐ **personality** /ˌpɜːsəˈnælɪti/ **personalities.** ①N-VAR
Your **personality** is your whole character and nature. *...a friendly personality... Nobody in politics doubts his force of personality.* ②N-COUNT You can refer to a famous person, especially in entertainment, broadcasting, or sport, as a **personality**. *...television personalities.*

personalized (BRIT also **personalised**) /ˈpɜːsənəlaɪzd/. ADJ **Personalized** objects are marked with the name or initials of their owner. *...personalised stationery.*

⭐ **personally** /ˈpɜːsənəli/. ①ADV You use **personally** to emphasize that you are giving your own opinion. *Personally I think it's a waste of time.* ②ADV If you do something **personally**, you do it yourself rather than letting someone else do it. *The minister is returning to Paris to answer the allegations personally.* ③ADV If you meet or know someone **personally**, you have met them or you know them, rather than knowing about them or knowing their work. *He did not know them personally, but he was familiar with their reputation.*

ˌpersonal ˈpronoun, personal pronouns. N-COUNT
A **personal pronoun** is a pronoun such as 'I', 'you', 'she', or 'they' which is used to refer to the speaker or the person listening to them, or to a person or thing whose identity is clear.

personify /pəˈsɒnɪfaɪ/ **personifies, personifying, personified.** VERB If you say that someone **personifies** a particular thing or quality, you mean that they are a perfect example of that thing, or they have a lot of that quality. *She seemed to personify goodness.*
♦ **personification** /pəˌsɒnɪfɪˈkeɪʃən/ N-SING *Joplin was the personification of the '60s female rock singer.*

⭐ **personnel** /ˌpɜːsəˈnel/. N-PLURAL The **personnel** of an organization are the people who work for it.

⭐ **perspective** /pəˈspektɪv/ **perspectives.** ①N-COUNT A **perspective** is a particular way of thinking about something. *The death of his father 18 months ago has given him a new perspective on life.* ②PHRASE If you get something **in perspective** or **into perspective**, you judge its real importance by considering it in relation to everything else. If you get something **out of perspective**, you fail to do this.

perspiration /ˌpɜːspɪˈreɪʃən/. N-UNCOUNT
Perspiration is the moisture that appears on your skin when you are hot or frightened. [FORMAL]

⭐ **persuade** /pəˈsweɪd/ **persuades, persuading, persuaded.** ①VERB If you **persuade** someone **to** do a particular thing, you get them to do it, usually by convincing them that it is a good idea. *My husband persuaded me to come.* ②VERB If you **persuade** someone that something is true, you say things that eventually make them believe that it is true. *I've managed to persuade Steve that it's for his own good.*

persuasion /pəˈsweɪʒən/ **persuasions.** ①N-UNCOUNT **Persuasion** is the act of persuading someone to do something or to believe that something is true. *Britain had achieved a great deal by persuasion.* ②N-COUNT If you are **of** a particular political or religious **persuasion**, you have that political or religious belief. [FORMAL]

persuasive /pəˈsweɪsɪv/. ADJ Someone or something that is **persuasive** is likely to persuade you to do or believe a particular thing. *This is hardly persuasive evidence.*
♦ **persuasively** ADV *...a trained lawyer who can be relied on to present arguments persuasively.*

pertain /pəˈteɪn/ **pertains, pertaining, pertained.** VERB Something that **pertains to** something else belongs or relates to it. [FORMAL] *...information pertaining to terrorist activities.*

pertinent /ˈpɜːtɪnənt/. ADJ Something that is **pertinent** is relevant to a particular subject. [FORMAL] *She had asked some pertinent questions.*

pervade /pəˈveɪd/ **pervades, pervading, pervaded.** VERB Something that **pervades** a place or thing is present or noticed throughout it. [FORMAL] *The smell of sawdust and glue pervaded the factory.*

pervasive /pəˈveɪsɪv/. ADJ Something that is **pervasive** is present or felt throughout a place or thing. [FORMAL] *...the pervasive influence of the army in national life.*

perverse /pəˈvɜːs/. ADJ Someone who is **perverse** deliberately does things that are unreasonable. ♦ **perversely** ADV *She was perversely pleased to be causing trouble.*
♦ **perversity** N-UNCOUNT *It would be wrong to continue out of perversity.*

perversion /pəˈvɜːʃən, -ʒən/ **perversions.** ①N-VAR A **perversion** is a sexual desire or action that is considered abnormal and unacceptable. ②N-VAR The **perversion** of something is the changing of it so that it is no longer what it should be. *...cases involving the perversion of justice.*

pervert, perverts, perverting, perverted. ①VERB /pəˈvɜːt/ If you **pervert** something, you interfere with it so that it is not what it used to be or should be. [FORMAL] *Any reform will destroy and pervert our constitution.* ②N-COUNT /ˈpɜːvɜːt/ People with abnormal or unacceptable sexual desires are called **perverts**.

perverted /pəˈvɜːtɪd/. ADJ Someone who is **perverted** has abnormal behaviour or ideas, especially sexual ones.

pessimism /ˈpesɪmɪzəm/. N-UNCOUNT
Pessimism is the belief that bad things are going to happen. ♦ **pessimist, pessimists** N-COUNT *I don't consider myself a pessimist.* ♦ **pessimistic** /ˌpesɪˈmɪstɪk/ ADJ *People are becoming much more pessimistic about the future.*

pest /pest/ **pests.** ①N-COUNT A **pest** is an insect or small animal which damages crops or food supplies. ②N-COUNT You can describe someone, especially a child, as a **pest** if they keep bothering you. [INFORMAL]

a
b
c
d
e
f
g
h
i
j
k
l
m
n
o
p
q
r
s
t
u
v
w
x
y
z

⭐ Bank of English® frequent word   For a full explanation of all grammatical labels, see pages vii-x

pester /'pestə/ **pesters, pestering, pestered.** VERB If you say that someone **is pestering** you, you mean that they keep asking you to do something, or keep talking to you, and you find this annoying. *He gets fed up with people pestering him for money.*

pesticide /'pestɪsaɪd/ **pesticides.** N-VAR **Pesticides** are chemicals which farmers put on their crops to kill harmful insects.

⭐ **pet** /pet/ **pets, petting, petted.** [1] N-COUNT A **pet** is an animal that you keep in your home to give you company and pleasure. *...dogs and other pets.* [2] ADJ BEFORE N Someone's **pet** subject is one that they particularly like. Someone's **pet** hate is something that they particularly dislike. [3] VERB If you **pet** an animal, you pat or stroke it affectionately.

petal /'petəl/ **petals.** N-COUNT The **petals** of a flower are the thin coloured outer parts which together form the flower.

peter /'piːtə/ **peters, petering, petered.**
▸**peter out.** PHR-VERB If something **peters out**, it gradually comes to an end. *The six-month strike seemed to be petering out.*

petite /pə'tiːt/ ADJ A **petite** woman is small and slim.

petition /pə'tɪʃən/ **petitions, petitioning, petitioned.** [1] N-COUNT A **petition** is a document signed by a lot of people which asks for some official action to be taken. *...a petition calling for a halt to nuclear tests.* [2] VERB If you **petition** someone in authority, you make a formal request to them. *Her followers petitioned the Vatican to make her a saint.*

petrified /'petrɪfaɪd/ ADJ If you are **petrified**, you are extremely frightened. *I've always been petrified of being alone.*

petrol /'petrəl/ N-UNCOUNT In British English, **petrol** is a liquid used as a fuel for motor vehicles. The usual American word is **gas** or **gasoline.**

petroleum /pə'trəʊliəm/ N-UNCOUNT **Petroleum** is oil which is found underground or under the sea bed. Petrol and other fuels are obtained from petroleum.

petty /'peti/ [1] ADJ You can use **petty** to describe things such as rules, problems, or arguments which you think are trivial or unimportant. *...endless rules and petty regulations.* [2] ADJ If you describe someone's behaviour as **petty**, you disapprove of it because you think it shows that they care too much about small, unimportant things. ♦ **pettiness** N-UNCOUNT *Never had she met such spite and pettiness.* [3] ADJ BEFORE N **Petty** is used to describe minor crimes or criminals. *...petty crime, such as handbag-snatching.*

petulant /'petʊlənt/ ADJ You can describe someone's behaviour as **petulant** when he or she is angry for no good reason and upset in a childish way. ♦ **petulance** N-UNCOUNT *His petulance made her impatient.*

pew /pjuː/ **pews.** N-COUNT A **pew** is a long wooden seat for people in church.

pewter /'pjuːtə/ N-UNCOUNT **Pewter** is a grey metal made by mixing tin and lead.

phantom /'fæntəm/ **phantoms.** [1] N-COUNT A **phantom** is a ghost. [2] ADJ BEFORE N You use **phantom** to describe something which does not really exist, but which someone believes or pretends does exist. *...a phantom pregnancy. ...phantom companies run by her relations.*

pharmaceutical /,fɑːmə'suːtɪkəl/ **pharmaceuticals.** [1] ADJ BEFORE N **Pharmaceutical** means connected with the industrial production of medicine. *...pharmaceutical companies.* [2] N-PLURAL **Pharmaceuticals** are medicines.

pharmacist /'fɑːməsɪst/ **pharmacists.** N-COUNT A **pharmacist** is a person who is qualified to prepare and sell medicines.

pharmacy /'fɑːməsi/ **pharmacies.** [1] N-COUNT A **pharmacy** is a place where medicines are sold or given out. [2] N-UNCOUNT **Pharmacy** is the job or the science of preparing medicines.

> **USAGE** In British English, **pharmacy** is not the usual way of referring to a shop where medicines are sold or given out. The usual term is **chemist** or **chemist's**. *She went into a chemist's and bought some aspirin.* In American English, the word **drugstore** is used, but this usually refers to a shop where you can buy drinks, snacks, and other small items, as well as medicines. *At the drugstore I bought a can of Coke and the local papers.*

⭐ **phase** /feɪz/ **phases, phasing, phased.** [1] N-COUNT A **phase** is a particular stage in a process or in the development of something. *This first phase of economic reform was very popular.* [2] VERB If an action or change **is phased** over a period of time, it is done in stages. *The redundancies will be phased over two years.*
▸**phase in.** PHR-VERB If a new way of doing something **is phased in**, it is introduced gradually. *...the government's policy of phasing in Arabic as the official academic language.*
▸**phase out.** PHR-VERB If something **is phased out**, people gradually stop using it or doing it. *16,000 jobs are being phased out.*

PhD /,piː eɪtʃ 'diː/ **PhDs.** N-COUNT A **PhD** is a degree awarded to people who have done advanced research. **PhD** is an abbreviation for 'Doctor of Philosophy'.

pheasant /'fezənt/.

> ☑ The plural is **pheasant** or **pheasants**.

N-COUNT A **pheasant** is a bird with a long tail, sometimes shot for sport and then eaten.

phenomenal /fɪ'nɒmɪnəl/ ADJ Something that is **phenomenal** is extraordinarily great or good. ♦ **phenomenally** ADV *...her phenomenally successful singing career.*

phenomenon /fɪ'nɒmɪnən, ᴀᴍ -nɑːn/
phenomena /fɪ'nɒmɪnə/. N-COUNT A **phenomenon**
is something that is observed to happen or exist.
[ғᴏʀᴍᴀʟ] ...*natural phenomena such as lightning.*

philosopher /fɪ'lɒsəfə/ **philosophers.** N-COUNT A
philosopher is a person who studies or writes
about philosophy.

philosophic /ˌfɪlə'sɒfɪk/. ADJ **Philosophic**
means the same as **philosophical**.

philosophical /ˌfɪlə'sɒfɪkəl/. 1 ADJ
Philosophical means concerned with or relating
to philosophy. ...*philosophical discussions.* 2 ADJ
Someone who is **philosophical** does not get
upset when disappointing or disturbing things
happen. *He was philosophical about his defeat.*
♦ **philosophically** ADV *She says philosophically:
'It could have been far worse'.*

⭐ **philosophy** /fɪ'lɒsəfi/ **philosophies.** 1 N-UNCOUNT
Philosophy is the study or creation of theories
about basic things such as the nature of
existence or how people should live. ...*traditional
Chinese philosophy.* 2 N-COUNT A **philosophy** is a
particular set of theories or beliefs. *Republicans
and Democrats have different philosophies.*

phobia /'fəʊbiə/ **phobias.** N-COUNT A **phobia** is an
irrational fear or hatred of something. *He had a
phobia about flying.*

⭐ **phone** /fəʊn/ **phones, phoning, phoned.**
1 N-UNCOUNT The **phone** is an electrical system
used to talk to someone in another place by
dialling a number on a piece of equipment and
speaking into it. *We never discuss any matters over
the phone... Do you have an address and phone
number for him?* 2 N-COUNT A **phone** is the piece
of equipment that is used to talk to someone by
phone. *Jamie answered the phone.* 3 VERB &
PHR-VERB When you **phone** someone, or when
you **phone** them **up**, you dial their phone
number and speak to them by phone. *He phoned
me to say he was visiting Manchester... I waited for
her to phone... I'll phone up and ask them.*
  PHRASES ● If you are **on the phone**, you are
speaking to someone by telephone. *He's
constantly on the phone to his girlfriend.* ● If
someone is **on the phone**, they have a telephone
in their house or office which is connected to the
rest of the telephone system.

'**phone booth, phone booths.** N-COUNT In
American English, a **phone booth** is a small
shelter in the street in which there is a public
telephone. The British term is **phone box**.

'**phone box, phone boxes.** N-COUNT In British
English, a **phone box** is a small shelter in the
street in which there is a public telephone. The
usual American term is **phone booth**.

⭐ '**phone call, phone calls.** N-COUNT If you make a
phone call, you speak to someone by phone.

phonecard /'fəʊnkɑːd/ **phonecards.** N-COUNT A
phonecard is a plastic card that you can use
instead of money in some public telephones.

'**phone-in, phone-ins.** N-COUNT A **phone-in** is a
radio or television programme in which people

telephone with questions or opinions and their
calls are broadcast.

phoney (or **phony**) /'fəʊni/ **phonier, phoniest;
phoneys.** 1 ADJ If you describe something as
phoney, you disapprove of it because it is not
genuine. [ɪɴғᴏʀᴍᴀʟ] *He'd telephoned with some
phoney excuse.* 2 ADJ & N-COUNT If you say that
someone is **phoney**, or if you say they are a
phoney, you disapprove of them because they
are pretending to be someone that they are not.

phosphate /'fɒsfeɪt/ **phosphates.** N-VAR A
phosphate is a chemical compound that is used
in fertilizers.

⭐ **photo** /'fəʊtəʊ/ **photos.** N-COUNT A **photo** is the
same as a **photograph**. [ɪɴғᴏʀᴍᴀʟ]

photocopier /'fəʊtəʊkɒpiə/ **photocopiers.**
N-COUNT A **photocopier** is a machine which
quickly copies documents by photographing
them.

photocopy /'fəʊtəʊkɒpi/ **photocopies,
photocopying, photocopied.** 1 VERB If you
photocopy a document, you make a copy of it
with a photocopier. 2 N-COUNT A **photocopy** is a
document made by a photocopier.

⭐ **photograph** /'fəʊtəgrɑːf, -græf/ **photographs,
photographing, photographed.** 1 N-COUNT A
photograph is a picture that is made using a
camera. *Her photograph appeared on the front
page of The New York Times.* 2 VERB When you
photograph someone or something, you use a
camera to obtain a picture of them. *They were
photographed kissing.*

⭐ **photographer** /fə'tɒgrəfə/ **photographers.**
N-COUNT A **photographer** is someone who takes
photographs, especially as their job.

photographic /ˌfəʊtə'græfɪk/. ADJ
Photographic means connected with
photographs or photography. ...*photographic
equipment.*

photography /fə'tɒgrəfi/. N-UNCOUNT
Photography is the skill, job, or process of
producing photographs. ...*fashion photography.*

'**photo shoot, photo shoots.** N-COUNT A **photo
shoot** is an occasion when a photographer takes
pictures, especially of models or famous people,
to be used in a newspaper or magazine.

phrasal verb /ˌfreɪzəl 'vɜːb/ **phrasal verbs.**
N-COUNT A **phrasal verb** is a combination of a
verb and an adverb or preposition, for example
'shut up' or 'look after', which together have a
particular meaning.

⭐ **phrase** /freɪz/ **phrases, phrasing, phrased.**
1 N-COUNT A **phrase** is a short group of words
that are used as a unit and whose meaning is not
always obvious from the words contained in it.
2 VERB If you **phrase** something in a particular
way, you say or write it in that way. *I would have
phrased it quite differently.* 3 PHRASE If someone
has a particular **turn of phrase**, they have a
particular way of saying or writing something.
*Rose's stories weren't bad; she had a nice turn of
phrase.*

a
b
c
d
e
f
g
h
i
j
k
l
m
n
o
p
q
r
s
t
u
v
w
x
y
z

A
B
C
D
E
F
G
H
I
J
K
L
M
N
O
P
Q
R
S
T
U
V
W
X
Y
Z

★ **physical** /'fɪzɪkəl/. [1] ADJ **Physical** means connected with a person's body, rather than with their mind. *Physical activity promotes good health... The attraction between them is physical.* ♦ **physically** ADV *...those who are physically disabled.* [2] ADJ BEFORE N **Physical** things are real things that can be touched or seen. *Physical and ideological barriers had come down in Eastern Europe.* [3] ADJ BEFORE N **Physical** means connected with physics. *...physical laws.*

physician /fɪ'zɪʃən/ **physicians.** N-COUNT A **physician** is a doctor. [AMERICAN]

physicist /'fɪzɪsɪst/ **physicists.** N-COUNT A **physicist** is a person who studies physics.

physics /'fɪzɪks/. N-UNCOUNT **Physics** is the scientific study of forces such as heat, light, sound, pressure, gravity, and electricity.

physiology /,fɪzi'ɒlədʒi/. [1] N-UNCOUNT **Physiology** is the scientific study of how people, animals, and plants grow and function. [2] N-SING The **physiology** of an animal or plant is the way that it functions. *...the reproductive physiology of rodents.* ♦ **physiological** /,fɪziə'lɒdʒɪkəl/ ADJ *...the physiological effects of stress.*

physiotherapist /,fɪziəʊ'θerəpɪst/ **physiotherapists.** N-COUNT A **physiotherapist** is a person whose job is using physiotherapy to treat people.

physiotherapy /,fɪziəʊ'θerəpi/. N-UNCOUNT **Physiotherapy** is medical treatment given to people who cannot move a part of their body and involves exercise, massage, or heat treatment.

physique /fɪ'ziːk/ **physiques.** N-VAR Your **physique** is the shape and size of your body. *He was strikingly handsome with a powerful physique.*

piano /pi'ænəʊ/ **pianos.** N-COUNT A **piano** is a large musical instrument with a row of black and white keys, which you strike with your fingers. → See picture on page 828. ♦ **pianist** /'piːənɪst, AM pi'æn-/ **pianists** N-COUNT *Howard is a talented pianist.*

★ **pick** /pɪk/ **picks, picking, picked.** [1] VERB If you **pick** a particular person or thing, you choose that one. *I had deliberately picked a city with a tropical climate.* [2] N-SING You can refer to the best things or people in a particular group as **the pick of** that group. *The corporation gets the pick of Japan's best graduates.* [3] VERB When you **pick** flowers, fruit, or leaves, you break them off the plant and collect them. [4] VERB If you **pick** something from a place, you take it from that place, using your fingers. *He picked the telephone off the wall bracket.* [5] VERB If you **pick** an argument or a fight with someone, you deliberately cause one. [6] VERB If someone **picks** a lock, they open it without using a key, for example by using a piece of wire. [7] PHRASE If you **pick** your **way** across an area, you walk across it very carefully in order to avoid obstacles or dangerous objects. *Rescue workers were still picking their way through tons of rubble.*

▸**pick at.** PHR-VERB If you **pick at** the food you are eating, you eat only very small amounts of it.
▸**pick on.** PHR-VERB If someone **picks on** you, they repeatedly criticize or attack you unfairly. *Bullies pick on younger children.*
▸**pick out.** PHR-VERB If you can **pick out** something or someone, you recognize them when it is difficult to see them. *Through my binoculars I pick out a group of figures a mile or so away.*
▸**pick up.** [1] PHR-VERB If you **pick** something **up**, you lift it upwards from a surface using your fingers. *Ridley picked up a pencil and fiddled with it.* [2] PHR-VERB When you **pick up** something or someone, you collect them from somewhere, usually in a car. *We drove to the airport the next morning to pick up Susan.* [3] PHR-VERB If you **pick up** a skill or an idea, you acquire it without effort. [INFORMAL] *Where did you pick up your English?* [4] PHR-VERB If a piece of equipment **picks up** a signal or sound, it receives it or detects it. *We can pick up Italian television.* [5] PHR-VERB If trade or the economy of a country **picks up**, it improves. [6] PHR-VERB If you **pick up** an illness, you get it from somewhere or something. *Passengers had picked up a food poisoning bug abroad.*

pickaxe (AM **pickax**) /'pɪkæks/ **pickaxes.** N-COUNT A **pickaxe** is a large tool consisting of a curved, pointed piece of metal with a long handle joined to the middle. Pickaxes are used for breaking up rocks or the ground. → See picture on page 833.

picket /'pɪkɪt/ **pickets, picketing, picketed.** [1] VERB If people who are demonstrating or on strike **picket** a place, they stand outside it in order to make a protest or to prevent people from going in. *More than 150 protesters picketed the Australian Embassy.* [2] N-COUNT A **picket** is a group of people who are picketing a place. *...a twenty-four hour picket.*

pickle /'pɪkəl/ **pickles.** [1] N-PLURAL **Pickles** are vegetables or fruit which have been kept in vinegar or salt water for a long time to give them a strong sharp taste. [2] N-VAR **Pickle** is a cold, spicy sauce that is made by boiling chopped vegetables and fruit with spices.

pickled /'pɪkəld/. ADJ **Pickled** food has been kept in vinegar and salt water so that it develops a strong sharp taste and does not go bad. *...pickled cabbage served with peppers.*

picnic /'pɪknɪk/ **picnics, picnicking, picnicked.** N-COUNT & VERB When people have a **picnic**, or when they **picnic** somewhere, they eat a meal in the open air. *I took the kids for a picnic... We picnicked on the riverbank.*

pictorial /pɪk'tɔːriəl/. ADJ **Pictorial** means relating to or using pictures. *...a pictorial history of the Special Air Service.*

★ **picture** /'pɪktʃə/ **pictures, picturing, pictured.** [1] N-COUNT A **picture** consists of lines and shapes which are drawn, painted, or printed on a surface and show a person, thing, or scene. [2] N-COUNT A **picture** is a photograph. *The Observer carries a*

a
b
c
d
e
f
g
h
i
j
k
l
m
n
o
p
q
r
s
t
u
v
w
x
y
z

big front-page picture of rioters. [3] VERB If someone or something **is pictured** in a newspaper or magazine, they appear in a photograph in it. *The proud owners are pictured with one of their winning entries.* [4] N-COUNT You can refer to the image you see on a television screen as a **picture**. [5] N-COUNT You can refer to a film as a **picture**. *...a director of epic action pictures.* [6] N-PLURAL In British English, if you go to **the pictures**, you go to a cinema to see a film. The American word is **movies**. [7] VERB & N-COUNT If you **picture** something, or if you have a **picture of** something in your mind, you have a clear idea or memory of it in your mind. *He pictured her with long black braided hair... We do have a picture of how we'd like things to be.* [8] N-COUNT If you give a **picture of** what something is like, you describe it. *Her book paints a bleak picture of the problems women now face.* [9] N-SING When you refer to the **picture** in a particular place, you are referring to the situation there. *It's a similar picture across the border in Ethiopia.*

PHRASES ● If you **get the picture**, you understand a particular situation, especially one which someone is describing to you. [INFORMAL] ● If you **put** someone **in the picture**, you tell them about a situation which they need to know about.

picturesque /ˌpɪktʃəˈresk/. ADJ A **picturesque** place is attractive, interesting, and unspoiled. *...a picturesque village in the Cotswolds.*

pie /paɪ/ **pies.** N-VAR A **pie** consists of meat, vegetables, or fruit, baked in pastry. *...a slice of apple pie.*

⭐ **piece** /piːs/ **pieces, piecing, pieced.** [1] N-COUNT A **piece** of something is a portion, part, or section of it that has been removed, broken off, or cut off. *...a piece of paper... Cut the ham into pieces... The vehicle was blown to pieces by the explosion.* [2] N-COUNT A **piece of** something of a particular kind is an individual thing of that kind. For example, you can refer to a particular thing that someone is advised to do as a **piece of advice**. *...a highly complex piece of legislation. ...a sturdy piece of furniture.* [3] N-COUNT A **piece** is something that is written or created, such as an article, work of art, or musical composition. *There was a piece about him on television... He replaced the stolen carvings with less valuable pieces.*

PHRASES ● If someone or something is still **in one piece** after a dangerous journey or experience, they are safe and not damaged or hurt. ● If you have to **pick up the pieces** after a disaster, you have to try to get the situation back to normal again. ● If you **go to pieces**, you are so upset or nervous that you lose control of yourself and cannot do what you should do. [INFORMAL]

▸**piece together.** [1] PHR-VERB If you **piece together** the truth about something, you gradually discover it. *Francis was able to piece together what had happened.* [2] PHR-VERB If you **piece** something **together,** you gradually make it

complete by joining its parts together. *Doctors painstakingly pieced together the broken bones.*

piecemeal /ˈpiːsmiːl/. ADJ & ADV A **piecemeal** process happens gradually and in irregular or unconnected stages. *The report is rightly critical of this piecemeal approach to welfare... It was built piecemeal over some 130 years.*

pier /pɪə/ **piers.** N-COUNT A **pier** is a large platform which sticks out into the sea and which people can walk along.

pierce /pɪəs/ **pierces, piercing, pierced.** VERB If a sharp object **pierces** something, or if you **pierce** something **with** a sharp object, the object goes into it and makes a hole in it. *Pierce the skin of the potato with a fork... I'm having my ears pierced.*

piercing /ˈpɪəsɪŋ/. [1] ADJ A **piercing** sound is high-pitched and sharp in an unpleasant way. *Suddenly there was a piercing scream.* [2] ADJ Someone with **piercing** eyes has bright eyes which seem to look at you very intensely.

piety /ˈpaɪəti/. N-UNCOUNT **Piety** is strong religious belief or behaviour.

pig /pɪg/ **pigs.** [1] N-COUNT A **pig** is a farm animal with a pink, white, or black skin. Pigs are kept for their meat, which is called pork, ham, or bacon. → See picture on page 815. [2] N-COUNT If you call someone a **pig**, you are insulting them, usually because you think that they are greedy or unkind.

pigeon /ˈpɪdʒɪn/ **pigeons.** N-COUNT A **pigeon** is a grey bird which is often seen in towns.

pigment /ˈpɪgmənt/ **pigments.** N-VAR A **pigment** is a substance that gives something a particular colour. [FORMAL] *Melanin is the dark pigment in our skin.*

pike /paɪk/.

☑ The plural is **pike** or **pikes**.

N-VAR **Pike** are a type of large river fish that eat other fish.

⭐ **pile** /paɪl/ **piles, piling, piled.** [1] N-COUNT A **pile** of things is a quantity of them lying on top of one another. *The leaves had been swept into huge piles. ...a pile of boxes.*

> **USAGE** A **pile** of things can be tidy or untidy. *...a neat pile of clothes.* A **heap** is usually untidy, and often has the shape of a hill or mound. *Now, the house is a heap of rubble.* A **stack** is usually tidy, and often consists of flat objects placed directly on top of each other. *...a neat stack of dishes.*

[2] VERB If you **pile** a quantity of things somewhere, you put them there so that they form a pile. You can also say a surface **is piled with** things. *He was piling clothes into the suitcase.* [3] QUANT A **pile of** something or **piles of** it is a large amount of it. [INFORMAL] *He had piles of money.* [4] VERB If people **pile into** or **out of** a place, they all get into it or out of it in a disorganized way. *A fleet of police cars suddenly*

arrived. *Dozens of officers piled out.* **5** N-UNCOUNT The **pile** of a carpet is its soft surface, which consists of lots of little threads standing on end.

▸**pile up.** **1** PHR-VERB If you **pile up** a quantity of things, or if they **pile up**, they gradually form a pile. *Mail was still piling up at the office.* **2** PHR-VERB If problems or losses **pile up**, or if you **pile** them **up**, you get more and more of them. *Problems were piling up at work... He piled up huge debts.*

pilgrim /ˈpɪlgrɪm/ **pilgrims.** N-COUNT A **pilgrim** is a person who makes a journey to a holy place.

pilgrimage /ˈpɪlgrɪmɪdʒ/ **pilgrimages.** N-VAR If someone makes a **pilgrimage** to a place, they make a journey there because the place is holy according to their religion, or very important to them personally. *...a private pilgrimage to family graves.*

⭐ **pill** /pɪl/ **pills.** **1** N-COUNT **Pills** are small solid round masses of medicine or vitamins that you swallow. **2** N-SING If a woman is **on the pill**, she takes a special pill that prevents her from becoming pregnant. *She had been on the pill for three years. ...the contraceptive pill.*

pillar /ˈpɪlə/ **pillars.** **1** N-COUNT A **pillar** is a tall solid structure which is usually used to support part of a building. **2** N-COUNT If you describe someone as a **pillar of** the community, you approve of them because they play an important and active part in the community.

pillow /ˈpɪləʊ/ **pillows.** N-COUNT A **pillow** is a rectangular cushion which you rest your head on when you are in bed.

⭐ **pilot** /ˈpaɪlət/ **pilots, piloting, piloted.** **1** N-COUNT A **pilot** is a person who is trained to fly an aircraft. **2** VERB When someone **pilots** an aircraft, they act as its pilot. **3** ADJ A **pilot** scheme or project is one which is used to test an idea before deciding whether to introduce it on a larger scale. **4** VERB If an organization or government **pilots** a new scheme, they test it before deciding whether to introduce it on a larger scale. *The Government piloted a scheme under which noisy neighbours faced instant fines.*

pimp /pɪmp/ **pimps.** N-COUNT A **pimp** is a man who finds clients for a prostitute and takes a large part of the prostitute's earnings.

⭐ **pin** /pɪn/ **pins, pinning, pinned.** **1** N-COUNT **Pins** are very small thin pieces of metal with points at one end, which are used to fasten things together. **2** VERB If you **pin** something somewhere, you fasten it there with a pin. *They pinned a notice to the door... General Carl Vuono pinned on the medals.* **3** N-COUNT You can refer to any long narrow piece of metal or wood with a blunt end, especially one that is used to fasten two things together, as a **pin**. *Surgeons will insert a 12-inch pin in his leg.* **4** VERB If someone **pins** you in a particular position, they press you firmly against something so that you cannot move. *I pinned him against the wall.* **5** VERB If someone tries to **pin** something bad **on** you, they say that you were

responsible for it. *They couldn't pin the killing on anyone.* **6** VERB If you **pin** your hopes **on** something or someone, your future success or happiness depends on them. *Are we right to pin our hopes on our young people?*

▸**pin down.** **1** PHR-VERB If you try to **pin** something **down**, you try to discover exactly what, where, or when it is. *It has taken until now to pin down its exact location.* **2** PHR-VERB If you **pin** someone **down**, you force them to make a definite statement. *She couldn't pin him down to a date.*

pincer /ˈpɪnsə/ **pincers.** **1** N-PLURAL **Pincers** consist of two pieces of metal that are hinged in the middle. They are used as a tool for gripping things or for pulling things out. → See picture on page 833. **2** N-COUNT The **pincers** of an animal such as a crab or a lobster are its front claws.

pinch /pɪntʃ/ **pinches, pinching, pinched.** **1** VERB & N-COUNT If you **pinch** someone, or if you give them a **pinch**, you squeeze a part of their body between your thumb and first finger. *She pinched his cheek.* **2** N-SING A **pinch of** an ingredient such as salt is the amount of it that you can hold between your thumb and your first finger. *...a pinch of cinnamon.* **3** VERB If someone **pinches** something, especially something of little value, they steal it. [INFORMAL] **4** PHRASE If a person or company **is feeling the pinch**, they do not have as much money as they used to, and cannot buy the things that they want.

pine /paɪn/ **pines, pining, pined.** **1** N-VAR A **pine** or a **pine tree** is a tall tree with long thin leaves which it keeps all year round. **Pine** is the wood of this tree. **2** VERB If you **are pining for** something or someone, you feel sad because you cannot have them or cannot be with them. *I pine for the countryside... Make sure your pet won't pine while you're away.*

pineapple /ˈpaɪnæpəl/ **pineapples.** N-VAR A **pineapple** is a large oval fruit with sweet, juicy, yellow flesh and thick, brown, skin. → See picture on page 821.

⭐ **pink** /pɪŋk/ **pinker, pinkest; pinks.** ADJ & N-VAR **Pink** is the colour between red and white. *...a soft pink.*

pinnacle /ˈpɪnəkəl/ **pinnacles.** **1** N-COUNT A **pinnacle** is a tall pointed piece of a building or a rock. **2** N-COUNT The **pinnacle of** something is the best or highest level of it. *Do you regard your selection as Captain as the pinnacle of your career?*

pinpoint /ˈpɪnpɔɪnt/ **pinpoints, pinpointing, pinpointed.** VERB If you **pinpoint** something, you discover or describe exactly what or where it is. *There is no possibility of pinpointing the exact time of death... The control room can always pinpoint the location of the car.*

pint /paɪnt/ **pints.** N-COUNT A **pint** is a unit of measurement for liquids. In Britain, it is equal to 568 cubic centimetres or one eighth of an imperial gallon. In America, it is equal to 473 cubic centimetres or one eighth of an American

Pipes

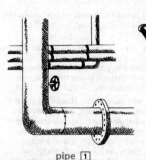

pipe $\boxed{1}$ pipe $\boxed{3}$ pipe $\boxed{4}$

gallon. *...a pint of milk. ...glasses which can hold a full pint.*

'pin-up, pin-ups. N-COUNT A **pin-up** is a picture of an attractive woman or man who appears on posters, often wearing very few clothes. *She was already a famous model and pin-up.*

pioneer /ˌpaɪə'nɪə/ **pioneers, pioneering, pioneered.** $\boxed{1}$ VERB & N-COUNT Someone who **pioneers** a new activity, invention, or process is one of the first people to do it. You can also refer to them as a **pioneer of** it. *...Professor Alec Jeffreys, who invented and pioneered DNA tests. ...one of the leading pioneers of British photo journalism.* ♦ **pioneering** ADJ *The school has won awards for its pioneering work with the community.* $\boxed{2}$ N-COUNT **Pioneers** are people who leave their own country to go and settle in a part of another country that has not been settled in before.

pious /paɪəs/. ADJ Someone who is **pious** is very religious and moral. *He was brought up by pious female relatives.* ♦ **piously** ADV *Conti kneeled and crossed himself piously.*

pip /pɪp/ **pips, pipping, pipped.** $\boxed{1}$ N-COUNT **Pips** are the small hard seeds in a fruit such as an apple or orange. $\boxed{2}$ VERB In British English, if someone **is pipped to** something, such as a prize or an award, they are narrowly defeated. *She pipped actress Meryl Streep to the part... Lewis was pipped for the gold medal by world record-holder Evans.*

★ **pipe** /paɪp/ **pipes, piping, piped.** $\boxed{1}$ N-COUNT A **pipe** is a long, round, hollow object through which a liquid or gas can flow. *...water pipes.* $\boxed{2}$ VERB If liquid or gas **is piped** somewhere, it is transferred from one place to another through a pipe. *Clean water is piped into our own homes.* $\boxed{3}$ N-COUNT A **pipe** is an object which is used for smoking tobacco. $\boxed{4}$ N-COUNT Organ **pipes** are the long hollow tubes which produce musical notes from an organ.

pipeline /'paɪplaɪn/ **pipelines.** $\boxed{1}$ N-COUNT A **pipeline** is a large pipe used for carrying oil or gas over a long distance. $\boxed{2}$ PHRASE If something is **in the pipeline**, it has already been planned or begun. *There are still four movies in the pipeline.*

piping /'paɪpɪŋ/. $\boxed{1}$ N-UNCOUNT **Piping** is lengths of pipe or tube made from metal or plastic. *...rolls of bright yellow plastic piping.* $\boxed{2}$ N-UNCOUNT **Piping** is cloth made into a narrow tube, used to decorate the edges of clothing.

piracy /'paɪrəsi/. $\boxed{1}$ N-UNCOUNT **Piracy** was robbery at sea carried out by pirates. $\boxed{2}$ N-UNCOUNT You can refer to the illegal copying of things such as video tapes and computer programs as **piracy**.

pirate /'paɪrət/ **pirates, pirating, pirated.** $\boxed{1}$ N-COUNT **Pirates** were sailors who attacked other ships and stole property from them. $\boxed{2}$ VERB Someone who **pirates** tapes, books, or computer programs copies and sells them when they have no right to do so. *...a pirated edition of the book.*

piste /piːst/ **pistes.** N-COUNT A **piste** is a track of firm snow to ski on.

pistol /'pɪstəl/ **pistols.** N-COUNT A **pistol** is a small handgun.

piston /'pɪstən/ **pistons.** N-COUNT A **piston** is a cylinder or metal disc that is part of an engine.

★ **pit** /pɪt/ **pits, pitting, pitted.** $\boxed{1}$ N-COUNT A **pit** is a coal mine. $\boxed{2}$ N-COUNT A **pit** is a large hole that is dug in the ground. $\boxed{3}$ N-COUNT In motor racing, the **pits** are the areas where drivers stop for fuel and repairs during races. $\boxed{4}$ VERB If two opposing things or people **are pitted against** one another, they are in conflict. *These were two strong men who pitted their skills against each other.* $\boxed{5}$ See also **pitted**.

★ **pitch** /pɪtʃ/ **pitches, pitching, pitched.** $\boxed{1}$ N-COUNT In British English, a **pitch** is an area of ground that is marked out and used for playing a game such as football, cricket, or hockey. The more usual American word is **field**. *...cricket pitches.* $\boxed{2}$ VERB If you **pitch** something somewhere, you throw it forcefully while aiming carefully. *Simon pitched the empty bottle into the lake.* $\boxed{3}$ VERB If someone or something **pitches** somewhere, or if they **are pitched** somewhere, they fall forwards suddenly and with a lot of force. *I was pitched into the water and swam ashore.* $\boxed{4}$ N-UNCOUNT The **pitch** of a sound is how high or low it is. *He raised his voice to an even higher pitch.* $\boxed{5}$ VERB If

★ Bank of English® frequent word   For a full explanation of all grammatical labels, see pages vii-x

a b c d e f g h i j k l m n o p q r s t u v w x y z

pitcher

something **is pitched at** a particular level, it is set at that level. *Prices at the budget hotel would be pitched at just over £40 a night.* 6 N-SING If something such as a feeling or a situation rises to a high **pitch**, it rises to a high level. ...*the competitors who have all worked themselves up to a very high pitch.* 7 VERB To **pitch** a tent means to put it up in a place where you are going to stay.
▸ **pitch in.** PHR-VERB If you **pitch in**, you join in and help with an activity. [INFORMAL] *The entire company pitched in to help.*

pitcher /'pɪtʃə/ **pitchers.** 1 N-COUNT A **pitcher** is a jug. 2 N-COUNT In baseball, the **pitcher** is the person who throws the ball to the person who is batting.

pitfall /'pɪtfɔːl/ **pitfalls.** N-COUNT The **pitfalls** involved in a particular activity or situation are the things that may go wrong or may cause problems. *The pitfalls of working abroad are numerous.*

pitiful /'pɪtɪfʊl/. 1 ADJ Someone or something that is **pitiful** is so sad, weak, or small that you feel pity for them. *It was the most pitiful sight I had ever seen.* ♦ **pitifully** ADV *His legs were pitifully thin.* 2 ADJ If you describe something as **pitiful**, you mean that it does not deserve respect or consideration. *This argument seems to show a pitiful lack of confidence in the capabilities of our juries.*

pitted /'pɪtɪd/. ADJ If the surface of something is **pitted**, it is covered with a lot of small shallow holes. ...*the pitted surface of the moon.*

pity /'pɪti/ **pities, pitying, pitied.** 1 N-UNCOUNT & VERB If you feel **pity for** someone, or if you **pity** them, you feel very sorry for them. *He felt a sudden tender pity for her... I don't know whether to hate or pity him.* 2 PHRASE If you **take pity on** someone, you feel sorry for them and help them. *No woman had ever felt the need to take pity on him.* 3 N-SING If you say that it is **a pity** that something is the case, you mean that you feel disappointment or regret about it. *It is a great pity that all pupils in the city cannot have the same chances.*

pivot /'pɪvət/ **pivots, pivoting, pivoted.** 1 N-COUNT The **pivot** in a situation is the most important thing which everything else is based on or arranged around. *It was Johnny, however, who was the pivot of her life.* 2 VERB If something or someone **pivots**, they balance or turn on a central point. *He pivoted around sharply and punched Graham.* 3 N-COUNT A **pivot** is the pin or central point on which something balances or turns.

pivotal /'pɪvətəl/. ADJ A **pivotal** role, point, or figure in something is one that is very important and affects the success of that thing. *The Court of Appeal has a pivotal role in the English legal system.*

pizza /'piːtsə/ **pizzas.** N-VAR A **pizza** is a flat piece of dough covered with tomatoes, cheese, and other savoury food, which is baked in an oven.

placard /'plækɑːd/ **placards.** N-COUNT A **placard** is a large notice that is carried in a march or demonstration.

placate /plə'keɪt, AM 'pleɪkeɪt/ **placates, placating, placated.** VERB If you **placate** someone, you stop them feeling angry or resentful by doing or saying things that will please them. ...*a gesture intended to placate me.*

⭐ **place** /pleɪs/ **places, placing, placed.** 1 N-COUNT A **place** is any point, building, area, town, or country. ...*Temple Mount, the place where the Temple actually stood... The snow along the roadside was five or six feet deep in places.* 2 N-SING **Place** can be used after 'any', 'no', 'some', or 'every' to mean 'anywhere', 'nowhere', 'somewhere', or 'everywhere'. [AMERICAN, INFORMAL] *The poor guy obviously didn't have any place to go... Why not go out and see if there's some place we can dance?* 3 N-COUNT Your **place** is the house or flat where you live. [INFORMAL] *Let's all go back to my place!* 4 N-COUNT & PHRASE You can refer to the position where something belongs, or where it is supposed to be, as its **place**. If something is **in place**, it is in its correct or usual position. If it is **out of place**, it is not in its correct or usual position. *He returned the album to its place on the shelf.* 5 N-COUNT A **place** is a position that is available for someone to occupy. *I found a place to park.* 6 N-COUNT The **place** of someone or something in a society, system, or situation is their position or role in relation to it. *They want to see more women take their place higher up the corporate or professional ladder.* 7 N-COUNT & VERB Your **place** in a race or competition is your position in relation to the other competitors. If, for example, a competitor **is placed** first, second, or last, that is their position at the end of a race or competition. 8 N-COUNT If you get a **place** in a team, on a committee, or on a course, you are allowed to join the team, committee, or course. *I eventually got a place at York University.* 9 VERB If you **place** something somewhere, you put it in a particular position. *Brand folded it in his handkerchief and placed it in the inside pocket of his jacket.* 10 VERB You can use **place** instead of 'put' or 'lay' in certain expressions where the meaning is carried by the associated noun. *His government is placing its faith in international diplomacy.* 11 VERB If you **place** someone or something in a particular class or group, you classify them in that way. *The authorities have placed the drug in Class A.* 12 VERB If you **place** an order for some goods or for a meal, you ask a company to send you the goods or a waiter to bring you the meal. 13 VERB If you **place** an advertisement in a newspaper, you arrange for the advertisement to appear in the newspaper. *They placed an advertisement in the local paper for a secretary.* 14 VERB If you say that you cannot **place** someone, you mean that you recognize them but cannot remember exactly who they are or where you have met them before. *He felt he should know him, but could not quite place him.*

> **USAGE** You do not normally use **place** on its own to refer to somewhere where someone can sit. The word you need is **seat**. *There was only one seat free on the train.* More generally, you can refer to a **space** which someone or something can occupy. *He was clearing a space for her to lie down.*
>
> You do not use **place** as an uncount noun to refer to an open or empty area. You should use **room** or **space** instead. **Room** is more likely to be used when you are talking about space inside an enclosed area. *There's not enough room in the bathroom for both of us... Leave plenty of space between you and the car in front.*

PHRASES • If you have been trying to understand something puzzling and then everything **falls into place**, you suddenly understand how different pieces of information are connected and everything becomes clearer. • If things **fall into place**, events happen naturally to produce a situation you want. *Once the decision was finally made, things fell into place rapidly.* • If something such as a law, a policy, or an administrative structure is **in place**, it is working or able to be used. *Similar legislation is already in place in Wales.* • If one thing or person is used or appears **in place of** another or **in** another's **place**, they replace the other thing or person. *Cooked kidney beans can be used in place of French beans.* • You say **in the first place** when you are talking about the beginning of a situation or about the situation as it was before a series of events. *What brought you to Washington in the first place?* • If you **put** someone **in** their **place**, you show them that they are less important or clever than they think they are. • When something **takes place**, it happens, especially in a controlled or organized way. *The discussion took place in a famous villa.*

placement /ˈpleɪsmənt/**placements.**
[1] N-UNCOUNT The **placement of** something is the act of putting it in a particular place. *...the placement of the gun just beyond the victim's right hand.* [2] N-COUNT If someone who is training gets a **placement**, they get a job for a period of time which is intended to give them experience in the work they are training for. [3] N-UNCOUNT The **placement** of someone in a job, home, or school is the act or process of finding them a job, home, or school. *...placement in a foster care home.*

placid /ˈplæsɪd/. ADJ If you describe a person or animal as **placid**, you mean they are calm and do not become excited, angry, or upset very easily.

plague /pleɪg/ **plagues, plaguing, plagued.**
[1] N-COUNT A **plague** is an infectious disease that spreads quickly and kills large numbers of

people. *A cholera plague had been killing many prisoners of war.* [2] N-COUNT A **plague of** unpleasant things is a large number of them that arrive or happen at the same time. *...a plague of rats.* [3] VERB If you **are plagued** by unpleasant things, they continually cause you a lot of trouble or suffering. *Fears about job security plague nearly half the workforce.* [4] VERB If someone **plagues** you, they keep bothering you or asking you for something. *I'm not going to plague you with a lot more questions.*

plaice /pleɪs/.

> ☑ **Plaice** is both the singular and the plural form.

N-VAR A **plaice** is a flat sea fish. **Plaice** is the flesh of this fish eaten as food.

★ **plain** /pleɪn/ **plains; plainer, plainest.** [1] ADJ A **plain** object, surface, or fabric is entirely in one colour and has no pattern, design, or writing on it. *A plain carpet makes a room look bigger.* [2] ADJ **Plain** things are very simple in style. *...plain food, freshly made from good quality ingredients.*
♦ **plainly** ADV *...plainly dressed.* [3] ADJ If a fact, situation, or statement is **plain**, it is easy to recognize or understand. *It was plain to him that I was having a nervous breakdown.* [4] ADJ If you describe someone, especially a woman or girl, as **plain**, you think they look ordinary and are not at all beautiful. [5] N-COUNT A **plain** is a large, flat area of land with very few trees on it.

plainly /ˈpleɪnli/. [1] ADV If something is **plainly** the case, it is obviously the case. *The judge's conclusion was plainly wrong.* [2] ADV You use **plainly** to indicate that something is easily seen, noticed, or recognized. *I could plainly see him turning his head.* [3] ADV If you say something **plainly**, it is easy to understand and cannot be mistaken. *'You're a coward,' Mark said very plainly.*

plaintiff /ˈpleɪntɪf/ **plaintiffs.** N-COUNT A **plaintiff** is a person who brings a legal case against someone in a court of law.

plaintive /ˈpleɪntɪv/. ADJ A **plaintive** sound or voice is sad and high-pitched. [LITERARY] *...the plaintive cry of the seagulls.*

plait /plæt, AM pleɪt/ **plaits, plaiting, plaited.** [1] VERB If you **plait** three or more lengths of hair or rope together, you twist them over and under each other to make one thick length. [2] N-COUNT In British English, a **plait** is a length of hair that has been plaited. The American word is **braid**.

★ **plan** /plæn/ **plans; planning, planned.** [1] N-COUNT & PHRASE A **plan** is a method of achieving something that you have worked out carefully in advance. When things are going **according to plan**, they are working out in the way that you had planned. *...a peace plan... It seemed a trouble-free race, everything going to plan, until lap nineteen.* [2] VERB If you **plan** what you are going to do, you decide in detail what you are going to do. *He planned to leave Baghdad on Monday... Plan for the future. ...when we plan road construction.* [3] N-PLURAL If you have **plans**, you are intending to do a particular thing. *'I'm sorry,'* she said. *'I have plans for tonight.'* [4] N-COUNT A **plan of** something that is going to be built or made is a detailed diagram or drawing of it. [5] See also **planning**.

▶ **plan on.** PHR-VERB If you **plan on** doing something, you intend to do it. *They were planning on getting married.*

★ **plane** /pleɪn/ **planes, planing, planed.** [1] N-COUNT A **plane** is a vehicle with wings and engines which can fly. *He had plenty of time to catch his plane.* [2] N-COUNT A **plane** is a flat level surface which may be sloping at a particular angle. *...a building with angled planes.* [3] N-COUNT If you say that something is **on a higher plane**, you mean that it is more spiritual or less concerned with worldly things. *...a mind nostalgic for a higher plane.* [4] N-COUNT A **plane** is a tool that has a flat bottom with a sharp blade in it, used for shaping wood. → See picture on page 833. [5] VERB If you **plane** a piece of wood, you make it smaller or smoother by using a plane.

★ **planet** /'plænɪt/ **planets.** N-COUNT A **planet** is a large, round object in space that moves around a star. The Earth is a planet. *...the nine planets in the solar system.*

planetary /'plænɪtri, AM -teri/. ADJ BEFORE N **Planetary** means relating to or belonging to planets. *...planetary systems.*

plank /plæŋk/ **planks.** N-COUNT A **plank** is a long rectangular piece of wood.

planner /'plænə/ **planners.** N-COUNT **Planners** are people whose job is to make decisions about what is going to be done in the future. *...James, a 29-year-old town planner.*

★ **planning** /'plænɪŋ/. [1] N-UNCOUNT **Planning** is the process of deciding in detail how to do something before you actually start to do it. *The trip needs careful planning.* [2] N-UNCOUNT **Planning** is control by the local government of the way that land is used and of what new buildings are built.

★ **plant** /plɑːnt, plænt/ **plants, planting, planted.** [1] N-COUNT A **plant** is a living thing that grows in earth and has a stem, leaves, and roots. *Water each plant as often as required.* [2] VERB When you **plant** a seed, plant, or young tree, you put it into earth so that it will grow. ◆ **planting** N-UNCOUNT *Flooding in the country has delayed planting.* [3] VERB When someone **plants** land, they put plants or seeds into the land to grow. *Much of their energy has gone into planting a large vegetable garden.* [4] N-COUNT A **plant** is a factory, or a place where power is generated. *...car assembly plants.* [5] N-UNCOUNT **Plant** is large machinery used in industrial processes. [TECHNICAL] [6] VERB If you **plant** something somewhere, you put it there firmly. *She planted her feet wide.* [7] VERB If someone **plants** a bomb somewhere, they hide it in the place where they want it to explode. [8] VERB If something such as a weapon or drug **is planted** on someone, it is put amongst

their belongings or in their house so that they will be wrongly accused of a crime.

plantation /plɑːn'teɪʃən, plæn-/ **plantations.** [1] N-COUNT A **plantation** is a large piece of land, where crops such as cotton, tea, or sugar are grown. [2] N-COUNT A **plantation** is a large number of trees planted together.

plaque /plæk, plɑːk/ **plaques.** [1] N-COUNT A **plaque** is a flat piece of metal or wood, which is fixed to a wall or monument in memory of a person or event. [2] N-UNCOUNT **Plaque** is a harmful substance that forms on the surface of your teeth.

plasma /'plæzmə/. N-UNCOUNT **Plasma** is the clear fluid part of blood which contains the red and white cells.

plaster /'plɑːstə, 'plæs-/ **plasters, plastering, plastered.** [1] N-UNCOUNT **Plaster** is a smooth paste made of sand, lime, and water which dries and forms a hard layer. Plaster is used to cover walls and ceilings. [2] VERB If you **plaster** a wall or ceiling, you cover it with a layer of plaster. [3] N-COUNT A **plaster** is a strip of sticky material with a small pad, used for covering small cuts or sores on your body. [BRITISH] [4] PHRASE If a broken leg or arm is **in plaster**, it is covered in a hard case made from a special type of plaster to protect the broken bones.

plastered /'plɑːstəd, 'plæs-/. [1] ADJ AFTER LINK-V If something is **plastered** to a surface, it is sticking to the surface. *His hair was plastered down to his scalp.* [2] ADJ AFTER LINK-V If a surface is **plastered** with something, it is covered with it. *My hands, boots and trousers were plastered with mud.*

★ **plastic** /'plæstɪk/ **plastics.** N-VAR **Plastic** is a light but strong material produced by a chemical process. *...a black plastic bag.*

,plastic 'surgery. N-UNCOUNT **Plastic surgery** is the practice of performing operations to repair or replace skin which has been damaged, or to improve people's appearance.

★ **plate** /pleɪt/ **plates.** [1] N-COUNT A **plate** is a round or oval flat dish used to hold food. A **plate of** food is the amount of food on the plate. *...a huge plate of bacon and eggs.* [2] N-COUNT A **plate** is a flat piece of metal, for example on part of a machine. [3] N-UNCOUNT **Plate** is dishes, bowls, and cups that are made of precious metal. [4] N-COUNT A **plate** in a book is a picture or photograph which takes up a whole page. [5] N-COUNT A dental **plate** is a piece of shaped plastic which a set of false teeth is attached to. [6] See also **number plate**.

plateau /'plætəʊ, AM plæ'təʊ/ **plateaus** or **plateaux.** [1] N-COUNT A **plateau** is a large area of high fairly flat land. [2] N-COUNT If an activity or process has reached a **plateau**, it is going through a stage where there is no change or development.

plated /'pleɪtɪd/. ADJ AFTER LINK-V If something made of metal is **plated with** a thin layer of another type of metal, it is covered with it. *...solid brass, plated with 24-carat gold.*

platform /'plætfɔːm/ **platforms.** **1** N-COUNT A **platform** is a flat raised structure or area on which someone or something can stand. *He walked towards a platform to begin his speech. ...a rocky platform where they could pitch their tents.* **2** N-COUNT A **platform** in a railway station is the area beside the rails where you wait for or get off a train. **3** N-COUNT The **platform** of a political party is what they say they will do if they are elected. *...a landslide victory on a nationalist platform.*

platinum /'plætɪnəm/. N-UNCOUNT **Platinum** is a very valuable silvery-grey metal.

platitude /'plætɪtjuːd, AM -tuːd/ **platitudes.** N-COUNT A **platitude** is a statement considered to be meaningless because it has been made many times before in similar situations. *I had told her the truth, while everyone else had been mouthing platitudes.*

platonic /plə'tɒnɪk/. ADJ A **platonic** relationship is one of friendship and does not involve sexual attraction.

platter /'plætə/ **platters.** N-COUNT A **platter** is a large flat plate used for serving food.

plausible /'plɔːzɪbəl/. ADJ A **plausible** explanation or statement seems likely to be true or valid. *Is it plausible that the President did not know what was going on?* ♦ **plausibly** /'plɔːzɪbli/ ADV *He could plausibly have been in contact with all these people.* ♦ **plausibility** N-UNCOUNT *...the plausibility of the theory.*

⭐ **play** /pleɪ/ **plays, playing, played.** **1** VERB & N-UNCOUNT When children or animals **play**, or when they spend time in **play**, they spend time doing enjoyable things, such as using toys and taking part in games. *Polly was playing with her teddy bear. ...a few hours of play until the baby-sitter takes them off to bed.* **2** VERB & N-UNCOUNT When you **play** a sport, game, or match, you take part in it. **Play** is the activity of playing sport or the time during which a game or match is played. *Alain was playing cards with his friends... I want to play for my country. ...the Continental style of play.* **3** VERB When one person or team **plays** another, or **plays against** them, they compete against them in a sport or game. *Northern Ireland will play Latvia.* **4** N-COUNT A **play** is a piece of writing performed in a theatre, on the radio, or on television. *It's my favourite Shakespeare play.* **5** VERB If an actor **plays** a character in a play or film, he or she performs as that character. *His ambition is to play the part of Dracula.* **6** VERB If you **play** a musical instrument, or if you **play** a tune on it, you produce music from it. **7** VERB If you **play** a record, CD, or tape, you put it onto a record player or into a CD-player or tape recorder and sound is produced. *There is classical music playing in the background.* **8** VERB If you **play** a joke or a trick **on** someone, you deceive them or give them a surprise in a way that you think is funny, but may cause them problems or annoy

them. *Someone had played a trick on her, stretched a piece of string at the top of those steps.* PHRASES ● If you ask **what** someone **is playing at**, you are angry because you think they are doing something stupid or wrong. [INFORMAL] ● If something or someone **plays a part** or **plays a role** in a situation, they are involved in it and have an effect on it. *The UN would play a major role in monitoring a ceasefire.*

▶**play along.** PHR-VERB If you **play along with** a person, you appear to agree with them and do what they want, even though you are not sure whether they are right. *I had to play along with her and pretend that we really had a relationship.*

▶**play around.** **1** PHR-VERB If you **play around**, you behave in a silly way to amuse yourself or other people. [INFORMAL] *Stop playing around and eat!* **2** PHR-VERB If you **play around with** a problem or an arrangement of objects, you try different ways of organizing it in order to find the best solution or arrangement. [INFORMAL]

▶**play at.** PHR-VERB If you say that someone is **playing at** an activity, you disapprove of the fact that they are doing it casually and not very seriously. *He had the afternoon off and spent it at her stall, playing at being a market trader.*

▶**play back.** PHR-VERB When you **play back** a tape or film, you listen to the sounds or watch the pictures after recording them.

▶**play down.** PHR-VERB If you **play down** something, you try to make people think that it is less important than it really is. *The team coach played down the rivalry between the sides.*

▶**play off against.** PHR-VERB If you **play** people **off against** each other, you make them compete or argue, so that you gain some advantage. *Gregory would interview them, and would play one off against the other.*

▶**play on.** PHR-VERB If you **play on** someone's fears, you deliberately use them in order to achieve what you want. *...an election campaign which plays on the population's fear of change.*

▶**play up.** PHR-VERB If something such as a machine or a part of your body **is playing up**, or if it **is playing** you **up**, it is not working properly. [INFORMAL, BRITISH] *The engine had been playing up... It was his back playing him up.*

⭐ **player** /'pleɪə/ **players.** **1** N-COUNT A **player** in a sport or game is a person who takes part. **2** N-COUNT You can use **player** to refer to a musician. *...a professional trumpet player.* **3** N-COUNT A **player** is an actor. *Oscar nominations went to all five leading players.* **4** See also **record player.**

playful /'pleɪfʊl/. ADJ A **playful** gesture is friendly and cheerful. *...a playful kiss.* ♦ **playfully** ADV *She pushed him away playfully.* ♦ **playfulness** N-UNCOUNT *...the child's natural playfulness.*

playground /'pleɪgraʊnd/ **playgrounds.** N-COUNT A **playground** is a piece of land where children can play.

⭐ Bank of English® frequent word   For a full explanation of all grammatical labels, see pages vii-x

playgroup /'pleɪgruːp/ **playgroups.** N-VAR A **playgroup** is an informal kind of school for very young children where they learn by playing.

playing cards (pl)

'**playing card, playing cards.** N-COUNT **Playing cards** are thin pieces of card with numbers and pictures on them, which are used to play games.

'**playing field, playing fields.** ① N-COUNT A **playing field** is a large area of grass where people play sports. ② PHRASE You talk about a **level playing field** to mean a situation that is fair, because no competitor or opponent has an advantage over another.

'**play-off** (or **playoff**) **playoffs.** N-COUNT A **playoff** is an extra game played to decide the winner of a sports competition when two or more people have got the same score.

playwright /'pleɪraɪt/ **playwrights.** N-COUNT A **playwright** is a person who writes plays.

plaza /'plɑːzə, AM 'plæzə/ **plazas.** N-COUNT A **plaza** is an open square in a city.

plc (or **PLC**) /,piː el 'siː/ **plcs.** In Britain, **plc** is an abbreviation for 'public limited company'. It is used after the name of a company whose shares can be bought by the public. ...*British Telecommunications plc.*

plea /pliː/ **pleas.** ① N-COUNT A **plea** is a request for something made in an intense or emotional way. [JOURNALISM] ...*his emotional plea for help in solving the killing.* ② N-COUNT In a court of law, a person's **plea** is the answer that they give when they have been charged with a crime. ...*a plea of not guilty.*

plead /pliːd/ **pleads, pleading, pleaded.** ① VERB If you **plead with** someone **to** do something, you ask them in an intense, emotional way to do it. *He was kneeling on the floor pleading for mercy... The lady pleaded with her daughter to come back home.* ② VERB When someone charged with a crime **pleads guilty** or **not guilty** in a court of law, they officially state that they are guilty or not guilty of the crime. ③ VERB If someone **pleads the case** or **cause** of someone or something, they speak out in their support or defence. *He would plead the cause of Russian unity.* ④ VERB If you **plead** a particular thing as a reason for doing

or not doing something, you give it as your excuse. *Mr Giles pleads ignorance as his excuse.*

pleading /'pliːdɪŋ/ **pleadings.** ① ADJ A **pleading** expression or gesture shows that you want something very much. ...*his pleading eyes.* ② N-VAR **Pleading** is asking someone for something you want very much, in an intense and emotional way. *His mother simply ignored Sid's pleading.*

★ **pleasant** /'plezənt/ **pleasanter, pleasantest.** ① ADJ Something that is **pleasant** is enjoyable or attractive. *It's always pleasant to do what you're good at doing.* ◆ **pleasantly** ADV *The room was pleasantly warm.* ② ADJ Someone who is **pleasant** is friendly and likeable.

★ **please** /pliːz/ **pleases, pleasing, pleased.**
① CONVENTION You say **please** when you are politely asking or inviting someone to do something, or when you are asking someone for something. *Can you help us please?... Please come in.* ② CONVENTION You say **please** when you are accepting something politely. *'Tea?'—'Yes, please.'* ③ VERB If someone or something **pleases** you, they make you feel happy and satisfied. *I was tidying my bedroom to please mum... Nothing pleased him.* ④ PHRASE You use **please** in expressions such as **as she pleases, whatever you please,** and **anything he pleases** to indicate that someone can do or have whatever they want. *Women should be free to dress and act as they please.* ⑤ CONVENTION You say **'please yourself'** to indicate in a rather rude way that you do not mind or care whether the person you are talking to does a particular thing or not. [INFORMAL]

★ **pleased** /pliːzd/ ① ADJ AFTER LINK-V If you are **pleased,** you are happy about something or satisfied with it. *I think he's going to be pleased that we identified the real problems... I'm pleased with the way things have been going... They're pleased to be going home.* ② CONVENTION You say **'Pleased to meet you'** as a polite way of greeting someone you are meeting for the first time.

pleasing /'pliːzɪŋ/. ADJ Something that is **pleasing** gives you pleasure and satisfaction. ...*a pleasing climate.* ◆ **pleasingly** ADV *The interior design is pleasingly simple.*

pleasurable /'pleʒərəbəl/. ADJ **Pleasurable** experiences or sensations are pleasant and enjoyable. *He found sailing more pleasurable than skiing.*

★ **pleasure** /'pleʒə/ **pleasures.** ① N-UNCOUNT If something gives you **pleasure,** you get a feeling of happiness, satisfaction, or enjoyment from it. *Everybody takes pleasure in eating.* ② N-UNCOUNT **Pleasure** is the activity of enjoying yourself rather than working. *He mixed business and pleasure.* ③ N-COUNT A **pleasure** is an activity or experience that you find very enjoyable and satisfying. *Watching TV is our only pleasure.* ④ CONVENTION You can say **'It's a pleasure'** or **'My pleasure'** as a polite way of replying to someone who has just thanked you for doing something. *'Thanks very much anyhow.'—'It's a pleasure.'*

pleat /pliːt/ **pleats.** N-COUNT A **pleat** in a piece of clothing is a permanent fold made in the cloth.

pleated /'pliːtɪd/. ADJ A **pleated** piece of clothing has pleats in it.

★ **pledge** /pledʒ/ **pledges, pledging, pledged.** [1] VERB & N-COUNT When someone **pledges to** do something, or when they make a **pledge to** do it, they promise solemnly that they will do it or provide it. *Britain pledged $36 million to the refugees... Both sides pledged that a nuclear war must never be fought. ...a pledge to step up cooperation.* [2] VERB If you **pledge yourself to** something, you promise to follow a particular course of action. *The treaties pledge the two countries to co-operation.*

plentiful /'plentɪfʊl/. ADJ Things that are **plentiful** exist in such large amounts or numbers that there is enough for people's wants or needs. *...a plentiful supply of vegetables.*

★ **plenty** /'plenti/. QUANT If there is **plenty of** something, there is a large amount of it, often more than is needed. *There was still plenty of time to take Jill out for pizza... I don't believe in long interviews. Fifteen minutes is plenty.*

pliers /'plaɪəz/. N-PLURAL **Pliers** are a tool with two handles at one end and two hard, flat, metal parts at the other. **Pliers** are used to hold or pull out things such as nails, or to bend or cut wire.
→ See picture on page 833.

plight /plaɪt/. N-SING If you talk about someone's **plight**, you mean the difficult or dangerous situation they are in. [FORMAL] *...the worsening plight of Third World countries.*

plod /plɒd/ **plods, plodding, plodded.** [1] VERB If someone **plods** somewhere, they walk there slowly and heavily. *He plodded down the road at an unhurried pace.* [2] VERB If you **plod on with** a job, you keep on doing it, without worrying about how fast you are progressing. *He is plodding on with negotiations... Aircraft production continued to plod along at an agonizingly slow pace.*

★ **plot** /plɒt/ **plots, plotting, plotted.** [1] N-COUNT & VERB If there is a **plot to** do something illegal or wrong, or if people **plot to** do something like this, they plan secretly to do it. *...a plot to overthrow the government... By the time they were married, she was already plotting against him.*
♦ **plotter, plotters** N-COUNT *Plotters tried to seize power in Moscow.* [2] N-VAR The **plot** of a film, novel, or play is the story and the way in which it develops. [3] N-COUNT A **plot** is a small piece of land, especially one that is intended for a purpose such as building houses or growing vegetables. [4] VERB When people **plot** a strategy or a course of action, they carefully plan each step of it. [5] VERB When someone **plots** something on a graph, they mark certain points on it and then join the points up. [6] VERB To **plot**

the position or progress of something means to follow its position or progress and show it on a map or diagram.

plough (AM **plow**) /plaʊ/ **ploughs, ploughing, ploughed.** [1] N-COUNT A **plough** is a large farming tool with sharp blades, which is attached to a tractor or an animal and used to turn over the soil before planting. [2] VERB When a farmer **ploughs** an area of land, they turn the soil using a plough.
▸ **plough into.** [1] PHR-VERB If something, for example a car, **ploughs into** something else, it crashes violently into it. [2] PHR-VERB If you say that money **is ploughed into** something such as a business, you are emphasizing that a large amount of money is being invested in it. *...the need to plough even more money into education and training.*
▸ **plough on.** PHR-VERB If you **plough on**, you continue moving or trying to complete something, even though it takes a lot of effort. *This will not deter the Government from ploughing on with the sale.*
▸ **plough through.** [1] PHR-VERB If you **plough through** something such as a large meal or a long piece of work, you finally finish it, although it takes a lot of effort. [2] PHR-VERB If a person or vehicle **ploughs through** a place or substance, they move through it with great force or effort. *...the satisfying noise made by the boat as it ploughs through the water.*

plow /plaʊ/. See **plough**.

ploy /plɔɪ/ **ploys.** N-COUNT If you describe something someone does as a **ploy**, you mean that they have planned it carefully and are doing it in order to gain an advantage for themselves. *That's only a ploy to get me to take Chris's place.*

pluck /plʌk/ **plucks, plucking, plucked.** [1] VERB If you **pluck** a fruit, flower, or leaf, you take it between your fingers and pull it from its stalk. [WRITTEN] *I plucked a lemon from the tree.* [2] VERB If you **pluck** something from somewhere, you take it in your fingers or hands and pull it sharply from where it is. *He plucked the cigarette from his mouth and tossed it out into the street.* [3] VERB If you **pluck** the strings of a musical instrument such as a guitar, you pull them with your fingers and let them go, so that they make a sound. [4] VERB If you **pluck** a bird that has been killed to be eaten, you pull its feathers out to prepare it for cooking. [5] VERB If you **pluck** your eyebrows, you shape them by pulling out some of the hairs, using a device called a tweezers. [6] VERB If someone is rescued from a dangerous or bad situation, you can say that they **are plucked from** it or **are plucked to safety.** [JOURNALISM] *They were plucked from the icy river when residents heard cries for help.* [7] PHRASE If you **pluck up the courage to** do something frightening, you make an effort to be brave enough to do it. *I slept in my car for two more days until I plucked up the courage to go home.*

▸**pluck at.** PHR-VERB If you **pluck at** something, you take it between your fingertips and pull it sharply but gently. *The boy plucked at Adam's sleeve.*

plug /plʌg/ **plugs, plugging, plugged.** [1] N-COUNT A **plug** on a piece of electrical equipment is a small plastic object with two or three metal pins which fit into the holes of an electric socket. [2] N-COUNT A **plug** is a thick circular piece of rubber or plastic that you use to block the hole in a bath or sink. when it is filled with water. [3] VERB If you **plug** a hole, a gap, or a leak, you block it with something. *Chet tore off his shirt and used it to plug the hole in the canoe.* [4] VERB & N-COUNT If someone **plugs** something such as a book or a film, or if they give it a **plug**, they talk about it in order to encourage people to buy it or see it. [INFORMAL] *...another actor plugging his latest book.* [5] PHRASE If someone in a position of power **pulls the plug on** a project or on someone's activities, they use their power to stop them continuing.

▸**plug in** or **plug into.** PHR-VERB If you **plug** a piece of electrical equipment **into** an electricity supply, or if you **plug** it **in**, you push its plug into an electric socket so that it can work. *I filled the kettle while she was talking and plugged it in.*

plum /plʌm/ **plums.** [1] N-COUNT A **plum** is a small sweet fruit with a smooth red or yellow skin and a stone in the middle. → See picture on page 821. [2] ADJ BEFORE N A **plum** job is a very good job that a lot of people would like.

plumber /ˈplʌmə/ **plumbers.** N-COUNT A **plumber** is a person whose job is to connect and repair things such as water and drainage pipes, baths, and toilets.

plumbing /ˈplʌmɪŋ/. [1] N-UNCOUNT The **plumbing** in a building consists of the water and drainage pipes, baths, and toilets in it. [2] N-UNCOUNT **Plumbing** is the work of connecting and repairing water and drainage pipes, baths, and toilets.

plume /pluːm/ **plumes.** N-COUNT A **plume of** smoke, dust, fire, or water is a large quantity of it that rises into the air in a column.

plummet /ˈplʌmɪt/ **plummets, plummeting, plummeted.** VERB If an amount, rate, or price **plummets**, it decreases quickly by a large amount. [JOURNALISM] *In Tokyo share prices have plummeted.*

plump /plʌmp/ **plumper, plumpest; plumps, plumping, plumped.** ADJ A **plump** person is rather fat. ● See note at **fat**.

▸**plump for.** PHR-VERB If you **plump for** someone or something, you choose them after hesitating and thinking. *They may well plump for a candidate with a higher qualification.*

plunder /ˈplʌndə/ **plunders, plundering, plundered.** VERB & N-UNCOUNT If someone **plunders** a place, or if they are involved in the **plunder** of a place, they steal things from it. [WRITTEN] *This has been done by plundering £4 billion from the Government*

reserves. *...a guerrilla group infamous for torture and plunder.*

⭐ **plunge** /plʌndʒ/ **plunges, plunging, plunged.** [1] VERB If something or someone **plunges** in a particular direction, especially into water, they fall, rush, or throw themselves in that direction. *At least 50 people died when a bus plunged into a river.* [2] VERB If you **plunge** an object **into** something, you push it quickly or violently into it. *She plunged the knife into his chest.* [3] VERB If something **plunges** someone or something **into** a particular state or situation, or if they **plunge into** it, they are suddenly in that state or situation. *8,000 homes were plunged into darkness as electricity cables crashed down... The economy is plunging into recession.* [4] VERB If you **plunge into** an activity or **are plunged into** it, you become very involved in it. *He plunged himself into work.* [5] VERB & N-COUNT If an amount or rate **plunges**, or if there is a **plunge** in an amount or rate, it decreases quickly and suddenly. *His weight began to plunge.* [6] PHRASE If you **take the plunge**, you decide to do something that you consider difficult or risky. *Lesley took the plunge and invited him back.*

plural /ˈplʊərəl/ **plurals.** N-COUNT & ADJ BEFORE N The **plural** of a word or its **plural** form is the form that is used when referring to more than one person or thing. *What is the plural of 'person'? ...the plural pronoun 'we'.*

pluralism /ˈplʊərəlɪzəm/. N-UNCOUNT If there is **pluralism** within a society, it has many different groups and political parties. [FORMAL]

⭐ **plus** /plʌs/ **pluses** or **plusses.** [1] CONJ You use **plus** to show that one number or quantity is being added to another. *Two plus two equals four... Send a cheque for £18.99 plus £2 for postage and packing.* [2] ADJ **Plus** before a number or quantity means that the number or quantity is greater than zero. *The aircraft was subjected to temperatures of minus 65 degrees and plus 120 degrees.* [3] CONJ You can use **plus** when mentioning an additional item or fact. *There's easily enough room for two adults and three children, plus a dog in the boot.* [4] ADJ You use **plus** after a number or quantity to indicate that the actual number or quantity is greater than the one mentioned. *There are only 35 staff to serve 30,000-plus customers.* [5] N-COUNT A **plus** is an advantage or benefit. [INFORMAL] *Experience of any career in sales is a big plus.*

plush /plʌʃ/ **plusher, plushest.** ADJ If you describe something as **plush**, you mean that it is very smart, comfortable, or expensive. *...a plush, four-storey, Georgian house in Mayfair.*

plutonium /pluːˈtəʊniəm/. N-UNCOUNT **Plutonium** is a radioactive element used especially in nuclear weapons and as a fuel in nuclear power stations.

ply /plaɪ/ **plies, plying, plied.** [1] VERB If someone **plies** you **with** food or drink, they keep giving it to you in an insistent way. *There they ply you with drink until you are throwing your money at them in* handfuls. **2** VERB If a ship, aircraft, or vehicle **plies** a route, it makes regular journeys along that route.

plywood /'plaɪwʊd/. N-UNCOUNT **Plywood** is wood that consists of thin layers of wood stuck together.

p.m. /ˌpiː 'em/. ADV **p.m.** is used after a number to show that you are referring to a particular time between noon and midnight. → See Reference Page on Telling the Time. *The spa is open from 7:00 a.m. to 9:00 p.m. every day.*

⭐ **PM** /ˌpiː 'em/ **PMs**. N-COUNT The **PM** is an abbreviation for the **Prime Minister.** [INFORMAL]

pneumonia /njuː'məʊniə/. N-UNCOUNT **Pneumonia** is a serious disease which affects your lungs and makes breathing difficult.

poach /pəʊtʃ/ **poaches, poaching, poached. 1** VERB If someone **poaches** animals, fish, or birds, they illegally catch them on someone else's property. ♦ **poacher, poachers** N-COUNT *Security cameras have been installed to guard against poachers.* ♦ **poaching** N-UNCOUNT *...a man accused of salmon poaching.* **2** VERB If an organization **poaches** members or customers **from** another organization, they secretly or dishonestly persuade them to join them or become their customers. *...allegations that it had poached members from other unions.* ♦ **poaching** N-UNCOUNT *Measures were introduced to conserve labour and prevent poaching.* **3** VERB If you **poach** food such as fish or eggs, you cook it gently in boiling water or milk. *...a poached egg.*

⭐ **pocket** /'pɒkɪt/ **pockets, pocketing, pocketed. 1** N-COUNT A **pocket** is a small bag or pouch that forms part of a piece of clothing. *...his jacket pocket.* **2** N-COUNT You can use **pocket** in expressions that refer to money that people have, get, or spend. *Tax cuts will put money in taxpayers' pockets.* **3** ADJ BEFORE N You use **pocket** to describe something that is small enough to fit into a pocket. *...a pocket calculator.* **4** VERB If someone **pockets** something, usually something that does not belong to them, they keep it or steal it. [INFORMAL] *O'Connor pocketed the money to reduce his bank overdraft.* **5** PHRASE If you are **out of pocket**, you have less money than you should have or than you intended. *You're going to be out of pocket because the interest is more than the income.*

'**pocket money.** N-UNCOUNT In British English, **pocket money** is a small amount of money given regularly to children by their parents. The usual American word is **allowance.**

pod /pɒd/ **pods**. N-COUNT A **pod** is a seed container that grows on some plants such as peas.

podium /'pəʊdiəm/ **podiums**. N-COUNT A **podium** is a small platform on which someone stands in order to give a lecture or conduct an orchestra.

⭐ **poem** /'pəʊɪm/ **poems**. N-COUNT A **poem** is a piece of writing in which the words are chosen for their beauty and sound and are carefully arranged, often in short lines.

⭐ **poet** /'pəʊɪt/ **poets**. N-COUNT A **poet** is a person who writes poems.

poetic /pəʊ'etɪk/. **1** ADJ Something that is **poetic** is very beautiful, expressive, and sensitive. *...a witty and eloquent portrait of contemporary Dublin.* **2** ADJ **Poetic** means relating to poetry. *There's a very rich poetic tradition in Gaelic.*

⭐ **poetry** /'pəʊɪtri/. N-UNCOUNT Poems, considered as a form of literature, are referred to as **poetry.** *Lawrence Durrell wrote a great deal of poetry. ...a poetry book.*

poignant /'pɔɪnjənt/. ADJ Something that is **poignant** makes you feel very sad or full of pity. *A poignant moment in the movie is the untimely death of one of the characters.*

⭐ **point** /pɔɪnt/ **points, pointing, pointed. 1** N-COUNT A **point** is an opinion or fact expressed by someone. *The research made some valid points... He illustrates his point with an anecdote.* **2** N-COUNT If you say that someone has a **point**, or if you take their **point** or see their **point**, you mean that you accept that what they have said is worth considering. *'If he'd already killed once, surely he'd have killed Sarah?' She had a point there.* **3** N-SING The **point of** what you are saying or discussing is the most important part. If you say that something is **beside the point**, you mean it is not relevant to what you are saying or discussing. *My point is that I'm not going to change... He has completely missed the point of recent student protests... He came straight to the point. 'It's bad news,' he said.* **4** N-SING If you ask what **the point of** something is, or say that there is **no point in** it, you are indicating that a particular action has no purpose or would not be useful. *Many do not even turn up to classes. They cannot see the point... There was no point in staying any longer.* **5** N-COUNT A **point** is an aspect or quality of something or someone. *Science was never my strong point at school.* **6** N-COUNT A **point** is a particular position or time. *The pain originated from a point in his right thigh... At this point Diana arrived.* **7** N-COUNT The **point** of something such as a needle or knife is the thin, sharp end of it. **8** N-COUNT In some sports and games, a **point** is one of the single marks that are added together to give the total score. *New Zealand have beaten Scotland by 21 points to 18.* **9** N-COUNT You use **point** to refer to the dot or mark in a decimal number that separates the whole numbers from the fractions. [SPOKEN] *...seven point eight per cent.* **10** N-COUNT The **points** of a compass are the marks on it that show the directions, especially north, south, east, and west. **11** VERB If you **point at** or **to** a thing or person, you hold out your finger or an object such as a stick to show someone where the thing or person is. *He pointed to a chair, signalling for her to sit.* **12** VERB If you **point** something **at** someone, you aim the tip or end of it towards them. *A man pointed a gun at them.* **13** VERB If

a b c d e f g h i j k l m n o p q r s t u v w x y z

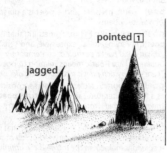

jagged

pointed [1]

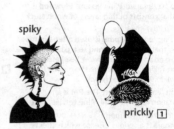

spiky

prickly [1]

something **points to** a place or **points** in a particular direction, it shows where that place is or faces in that direction. *An arrow pointed to the toilets.* [14] VERB If something **points to** a particular situation, it suggests that the situation exists or is likely to occur. *Private polls and embassy reports pointed to a no vote.*

PHRASES ● If you **make a point of** doing something, you do it in a deliberate or obvious way. *He had made a point of never talking about the episode.* ● If you are **on the point of** doing something, you are about to do it. *He was on the point of saying something when the phone rang.* ● If you say that something is true **up to a point**, you mean that it is partly but not completely true. *It worked up to a point.* ● See also **pointed**. ● **in point of fact**: see **fact**. ● **to point the finger at** someone: see **finger**.

▸**point out.** [1] PHR-VERB If you **point out** an object or place to someone, you direct their attention to it. *They kept standing up to take pictures and point things out to each other.* [2] PHR-VERB If you **point out** a fact or mistake, you tell someone about it. *Critics point out that the prince, on his income, should be paying tax.*

,**point-'blank.** [1] ADV & ADJ BEFORE N If you say something **point-blank**, you say it very directly, without explaining or apologizing. *I asked him point-blank why he was doing it. ...their point-blank refusal.* [2] ADV & ADJ BEFORE N If someone or something is shot **point-blank** or **at point-blank range**, they are shot by a gun which is held extremely close to them.

pointed /'pɔɪntɪd/. [1] ADJ An object that is **pointed** has a narrow end or tip. *...pointed shoes. ...pointed roofs.* [2] ADJ **Pointed** comments or behaviour express criticism in a clear and direct way. *The senators asked Klein some rather pointed questions.* ◆ **pointedly** ADV *They were pointedly absent from the news conference.*

pointer /'pɔɪntə/ **pointers.** N-COUNT A **pointer** is a piece of advice or information which helps you to understand a situation or solve a problem. *Here are a few pointers to help you make a choice.*

pointless /'pɔɪntləs/. ADJ Something that is **pointless** has no purpose. *Violence is always*

pointless. ◆ **pointlessly** ADV *More than four years of my life had been ruined, quite pointlessly.*

★ ,**point of 'view, points of view.** [1] N-COUNT You can refer to the opinions that you have about something as your **point of view**. [2] PHRASE If you consider something **from** a particular **point of view**, you are using one aspect of a situation to judge it. *Do you think that, from the point of view of results, this exercise was worth the cost?*

poise /pɔɪz/. N-UNCOUNT If someone has **poise**, they are calm, dignified, and self-controlled. *It took a moment for Mark to recover his poise.*

poised /pɔɪzd/. [1] ADJ If a part of your body is **poised**, it is completely still but ready to move at any moment. *He studied the keyboard carefully, one finger poised.* [2] ADJ AFTER LINK-V If someone is **poised to** do something, they are ready to take action at any moment. *Britain was poised to fly medical staff to the country... US forces are poised for a massive air, land and sea assault.* [3] ADJ If you are **poised**, you are calm, dignified, and in control of your emotions.

poison /'pɔɪzən/ **poisons, poisoning, poisoned.** [1] N-VAR **Poison** is a substance that harms or kills people or animals if they swallow or absorb it. *Mercury is a known poison.* [2] VERB To **poison** someone or something means to give poison to them or to add poison to them, causing them harm. *...the rumours that she had poisoned him... The land has been completely poisoned by chemicals.* ◆ **poisoning, poisonings** N-VAR *She was sentenced to twenty years' imprisonment for poisoning.* [3] VERB Something that **poisons** a good situation or relationship spoils it or destroys it. *The letter poisoned her relationship with her family for ever.*

poisonous /'pɔɪzənəs/. [1] ADJ Something that is **poisonous** will kill you or harm you if you swallow or absorb it. *Ten workmen breathed in poisonous gas.* [2] ADJ A **poisonous** animal produces a poison that will kill you or make you ill if the animal bites you.

poke /pəʊk/ **pokes, poking, poked.** [1] VERB & N-COUNT If you **poke** someone or something, or if

you give them a **poke**, you quickly push them with your finger or a sharp object. You can also say that you **poke** your finger or an object **into** someone or something. *Her mother opened the oven door and poked a fork into the turkey skin... John smiled at them and gave Richard a playful poke.* [2] VERB If something **pokes from** behind or under something, or if someone **pokes** it there, you can see part of it appearing from behind or under that thing. *His tiny head poked from the covers... Julie tapped on my door and poked her head in.* [3] to **poke fun at**: see **fun**.
▸ **poke around.** PHR-VERB If you **poke around** for something, you search for it, usually by moving lots of objects around. [INFORMAL] *We opened up the car bonnet and he started poking around in my engine.*
▸ **poke at.** PHR-VERB If you **poke at** something, you make lots of little pushing movements at it with a sharp object.

poker /ˈpəʊkə/. N-UNCOUNT **Poker** is a card game that people usually play in order to win money.

polar /ˈpəʊlə/. ADJ BEFORE N **Polar** refers to the area around the North and South Poles. *...the rigours of life in the polar regions.*

polarize (BRIT also **polarise**) /ˈpəʊləraɪz/ **polarizes, polarizing, polarized.** VERB If something **polarizes** people, it causes them to become two separate groups with opposite opinions or positions. *The issue of free trade was polarizing the country.* ♦ **polarization** N-UNCOUNT *...polarization between the blacks and whites in the US.*

⭐ **pole** /pəʊl/ **poles.** [1] N-COUNT A **pole** is a long, thin piece of wood or metal, used especially for supporting things. *...a telegraph pole.* [2] N-COUNT The earth's **poles** are the two opposite ends of its axis.

polemic /pəˈlemɪk/ **polemics.** N-VAR A **polemic** is a fierce written or spoken attack on, or defence of, a particular belief or opinion. *...Edmund Burke's polemic against the French Revolution.*

⭐ **police** /pəˈliːs/ **polices, policing, policed.** [1] N-SING & N-PLURAL The **police** are the official organization that is responsible for making sure that people obey the law. The **police** can take the singular or plural form of the verb. The men and women who belong to this organization are referred to as **police**. *Police say they have arrested twenty people... More than one hundred police have ringed the area.* [2] VERB To **police** a place, an event, or an activity means to preserve law and order within it or to ensure that what is done is fair and legal. *It is extremely difficult to police the border effectively. ...the Securities and Exchange Commission, which polices the stockmarkets.*

po'lice force, police forces. N-COUNT A **police force** is the police organization in a particular country or area.

⭐ **policeman** /pəˈliːsmən/ **policemen.** N-COUNT A **policeman** is a man who is a member of the police force.

⭐ **po'lice officer, police officers.** N-COUNT A **police officer** is a member of the police force.

po'lice station, police stations. N-COUNT A **police station** is the local office of a police force in a particular area.

policewoman /pəˈliːswʊmən/ **policewomen.** N-COUNT A **policewoman** is a woman who is a member of the police force.

⭐ **policy** /ˈpɒlɪsi/ **policies.** [1] N-VAR A **policy** is a set of plans or principles that is used as a basis for making decisions, especially in politics, economics, or business. *What is their policy on nuclear testing?* [2] N-COUNT An insurance **policy** is a document which shows the agreement that you have made with an insurance company.

polio /ˈpəʊliəʊ/. N-UNCOUNT **Polio** is a serious infectious disease which can cause paralysis.

polish /ˈpɒlɪʃ/ **polishes, polishing, polished.** [1] N-UNCOUNT **Polish** is a substance that you put on the surface of an object in order to clean it, protect it, and make it shine. *...furniture polish.* [2] VERB If you **polish** something, you put polish on it or rub it with a cloth to make it shine. ♦ **polished** ADJ *...a highly polished floor.* [3] N-UNCOUNT If you say that a person, performance, or piece of work has **polish**, you mean that they show confidence and sophistication. ♦ **polished** ADJ *He is polished, charming, articulate.* [4] VERB & PHR-VERB If you **polish** your technique, performance, or skill at doing something, or if you **polish** it **up**, you work on improving it. *Polish up your writing skills.*
▸ **polish off.** PHR-VERB If you **polish off** food or drink, you finish it. [INFORMAL]

polite /pəˈlaɪt/ **politer, politest.** ADJ A **polite** person has good manners and is not rude to other people. *...polite conversation.* ♦ **politely** ADV *'Your home is beautiful,' I said politely.* ♦ **politeness** N-UNCOUNT *She listened to him, but only out of politeness.*

⭐ **political** /pəˈlɪtɪkəl/. [1] ADJ **Political** means relating to the way power is achieved and used in a country or society. *All other political parties there have been completely banned.* ♦ **politically** ADV *The killings were politically motivated.* [2] ADJ If you are **political**, you are interested in politics and hold strong beliefs about it.

⭐ **politician** /ˌpɒlɪˈtɪʃən/ **politicians.** N-COUNT A **politician** is a person whose job is in politics, especially a member of parliament.

⭐ **politics** /ˈpɒlɪtɪks/. [1] N-UNCOUNT **Politics** is the actions or activities which people use to achieve power in a country or organization. **Politics** can take the singular or plural form of the verb. *Politics is by no means the only arena in which women are excelling.* [2] N-PLURAL Your **politics** are your beliefs about how a country ought to be governed. *His politics began in the Communist Party.*

⭐ **poll** /pəʊl/ **polls.** [1] N-COUNT A **poll** is a survey in which people are asked their opinions about something. ● See also **opinion poll.** [2] N-PLURAL

a
b
c
d
e
f
g
h
i
j
k
l
m
n
o
p
q
r
s
t
u
v
w
x
y
z

The polls means an election for a country's government, or the place where people go to vote in an election. *Voters are due to go to the polls on Sunday.*

pollen /'pɒlən/. N-UNCOUNT **Pollen** is a powder produced by flowers in order to fertilize other flowers.

polling /'pəʊlɪŋ/. N-UNCOUNT **Polling** is the act of voting in an election.

pollutant /pə'luːtənt/ **pollutants.** N-VAR **Pollutants** are substances that pollute the environment, especially poisonous chemicals that are produced as waste by vehicles and by industry.

pollute /pə'luːt/ **pollutes, polluting, polluted.** VERB To **pollute** water, air, or land means to make it dirty and dangerous to live in or to use, especially with poisonous chemicals or sewage. ♦ **polluted** ADJ ...*foul polluted water.*

⭐ **pollution** /pə'luːʃən/. [1] N-UNCOUNT **Pollution** is poisonous substances that are polluting water, air, or land. *The level of pollution in the river was falling.* [2] N-UNCOUNT **Pollution** is the process of polluting the water, air, or land.

polo

polo /'pəʊləʊ/. N-UNCOUNT **Polo** is a ball game played between two teams of players riding on horses.

polyester /,pɒli'estə, AM 'pɒliestə/ **polyesters.** N-VAR **Polyester** is a type of synthetic cloth used especially to make clothes.

polythene /'pɒlɪθiːn/. N-UNCOUNT **Polythene** is a type of plastic made into thin sheets or bags.

pomp /pɒmp/. N-UNCOUNT **Pomp** is the use of a lot of fine clothes, and decorations, and formal words or actions. ...*the pomp and ceremony of the Pope's visit.*

pompous /'pɒmpəs/. ADJ If you describe someone as **pompous**, you mean that they behave or speak in a very serious way because they think they are more important than they really are; used showing disapproval. ♦ **pomposity** /pɒm'pɒsɪti/ N-UNCOUNT ...*a scientist who hated pomposity.* ♦ **pompously** ADV '*This is clearly a very important project,*' I said pompously.

pond /pɒnd/ **ponds.** N-COUNT A **pond** is a small, usually man-made, area of water. ...*a garden pond.*

ponder /'pɒndə/ **ponders, pondering, pondered.** VERB If you **ponder** a question, you think about it carefully. *I'm continually pondering how to improve the team.*

ponderous /'pɒndərəs/. [1] ADJ **Ponderous** speech or writing is dull and serious. ♦ **ponderously** ADV ...*the ponderously named Association of Residential Letting Agents.* [2] ADJ A movement or action that is **ponderous** is very slow or clumsy. [WRITTEN] ♦ **ponderously** ADV *Wilson shifted ponderously in his chair.*

pony /'pəʊni/ **ponies.** N-COUNT A **pony** is a type of small horse.

ponytail /'pəʊniteɪl/ **ponytails.** N-COUNT If someone has their hair in a **ponytail**, it is tied up at the back so that it hangs down like a tail. → See picture on page 312.

poodle /'puːdəl/ **poodles.** N-COUNT A **poodle** is a type of dog with thick curly hair.

⭐ **pool** /puːl/ **pools, pooling, pooled.** [1] N-COUNT A **pool** is the same as a **swimming pool**. [2] N-COUNT A **pool** is a small area of still water. ...*beautiful gardens filled with pools.* [3] N-COUNT A **pool of** liquid or light is a small area of it. *She was found lying in a pool of blood.* [4] N-COUNT A **pool of** people, money, or things is a number or quantity of them that is available for use. ...*a reserve pool of cash.* [5] VERB If people **pool** their money, knowledge, or equipment, they share it or put it together so that it can be used for a particular purpose. *Philip and I pooled our savings to start up my business.* [6] N-UNCOUNT **Pool** is a game played on a special table. Players use a long stick called a cue to hit a white ball so that it knocks coloured balls into six holes around the edge of the table. [7] N-PLURAL If you do **the pools**, you take part in a gambling competition in which people try to guess the results of football matches. [BRITISH]

⭐ **poor** /pʊə, pɔː/ **poorer, poorest.** [1] ADJ & N-PLURAL Someone who is **poor** has very little money and few possessions. **The poor** are people who are poor. *He was one of thirteen children from a poor family... Even the poor have their pride.* [2] ADJ A **poor** country or area is inhabited by people who are poor. ...*children in a poor neighborhood.* [3] ADJ BEFORE N You use **poor** to express sympathy for someone. *Poor Gordon!* [4] ADJ If you describe something as **poor**, you mean that it is of a low quality or standard. *The flat was in a poor state of repair.* ♦ **poorly** ADV ...*poorly built dormitories.* [5] ADJ If you describe an amount, rate, or number as **poor**, you mean that it is less than expected or less than is considered reasonable. ...*poor wages and working conditions.* ♦ **poorly** ADV *The evening meetings were poorly attended.* [6] ADJ You use **poor** to describe someone who is not very skilful in a particular activity. *He was a poor actor.* ♦ **poorly** ADV *Today I played as poorly as I ever have.* [7] ADJ AFTER

LINK-V If something is **poor in** a particular quality or substance, it contains very little of the quality or substance. *Some foods are very rich in energy but poor in vitamins.*

poorly /'puəli, 'pɔː-/. ADJ If someone is **poorly**, they are ill. [INFORMAL, BRITISH] *Miss Cartwright looks very poorly.*

⭐ **pop** /pɒp/ **pops, popping, popped.** ☐ N-UNCOUNT Pop is modern music that usually has a strong rhythm and uses electronic equipment. *...a life-size poster of a pop star.* ☐ VERB & N-COUNT If something **pops**, it makes a short sharp sound, called a **pop**. *The cork popped and shot to the ceiling... His back tyre just went pop on a motorway.* ☐ VERB & PHR-VERB If your eyes **pop**, or if they **pop out**, you look very surprised or excited. [INFORMAL] *My eyes popped at the sight of the rich variety of food on show.* ☐ VERB If you **pop** something somewhere, you put it there. [BRITISH, INFORMAL] *He popped some chewing-gum into his mouth.* ☐ VERB If someone **pops** somewhere, they go there for a short time. [BRITISH, INFORMAL] *He's just popped out to the shops. He won't be a minute.*

▸**pop up.** PHR-VERB If someone or something **pops up**, they appear in a place or situation unexpectedly. *You solved one problem and another would immediately pop up.*

popcorn /'pɒpkɔːn/. N-UNCOUNT **Popcorn** is a snack which consists of grains of maize that have been heated until they have burst and become large and light.

Pope /pəup/ **Popes.** N-COUNT & N-TITLE The **Pope** is the head of the Roman Catholic Church. *...Pope John Paul II.*

poppy /'pɒpi/ **poppies.** N-COUNT A **poppy** is a plant with large, delicate, red flowers.

populace /'pɒpjuləs/. N-SING The **populace** of a country is its people. [FORMAL] *...a large section of Pakistan's populace.*

⭐ **popular** /'pɒpjulə/. ☐ ADJ Someone or something that is **popular** is liked by a lot of people. *...the most popular politician in France... These delicious pastries will be very popular.* ◆ **popularity** /,pɒpju'læriti/ N-UNCOUNT *...his popularity with ordinary people... Golf increased in popularity during the 1980s.* ☐ ADJ **Popular** ideas or attitudes are approved of or held by most people. *The military government has been unable to win popular support.* ◆ **popularity** N-UNCOUNT *Watson's views gained in popularity.* ☐ ADJ BEFORE N **Popular** newspapers, television programmes, or forms of art are aimed at ordinary people and not at experts or intellectuals. *...one of the classics of modern popular music.* ☐ ADJ BEFORE N **Popular** is used to describe political activities which involve the ordinary people of a country. *President Ferdinand Marcos was overthrown by a popular uprising.*

popularize (BRIT also **popularise**) /'pɒpjuləraɪz/ **popularizes, popularizing, popularized.** VERB To **popularize** something means to make a lot of people interested in it and able to enjoy or understand it. ◆ **popularization** N-UNCOUNT *...the popularisation of sport through television.*

popularly /'pɒpjuləli/. ☐ ADV If something or someone is **popularly** known as something, most people call them that, although it is not their official name or title. *...an infection popularly called mad cow disease.* ☐ ADV If something is **popularly** believed or supposed to be the case, most people believe or suppose it to be the case, although it may not be true. *Schizophrenia is not a 'split mind' as is popularly believed.*

populate /'pɒpjuleɪt/ **populates, populating, populated.** VERB If an area **is populated** by people or animals, those people or animals live there. *Before all this the island was populated by native American Arawaks.* ◆ **populated** ADJ *The southeast is the most densely populated area.*

⭐ **population** /,pɒpju'leɪʃən/ **populations.** ☐ N-VAR The **population** of a place is the people who live there, or the number of people living there. *Bangladesh now has a population of about 110 million. ...a massive increase in population.* ☐ N-COUNT If you refer to a particular type of **population** in a place, you are referring to all the people or animals of that type there. [FORMAL] *...75.6 per cent of the male population over sixteen.*

porcelain /'pɔːsəlɪn/. N-UNCOUNT **Porcelain** is a hard, shiny substance made by heating clay. It is used to make cups, plates, and ornaments.

porch /pɔːtʃ/ **porches.** ☐ N-COUNT A **porch** is a sheltered area at the entrance to a building. It has a roof and sometimes walls. ☐ N-COUNT In American English, a **porch** is a raised platform built along the outside wall of a house and often covered with a roof. The British word is **veranda**.

pore /pɔː/ **pores, poring, pored.** ☐ N-COUNT Your **pores** are the tiny holes in your skin. ☐ N-COUNT The **pores** of a plant are the tiny holes on its surface.

▸**pore over.** PHR-VERB If you **pore over** or **through** information, you look at it, studying it very carefully. *We spent hours poring over travel brochures.*

pork /pɔːk/. N-UNCOUNT **Pork** is meat from a pig, usually fresh and not smoked or salted.

porn /pɔːn/. N-UNCOUNT **Porn** is the same as **pornography**. [INFORMAL]

pornography /pɔː'nɒgrəfi/. N-UNCOUNT **Pornography** refers to books, magazines, and films that are designed to cause sexual excitement; used showing disapproval. ◆ **pornographic** /,pɔːnə'græfɪk/ ADJ *...pornographic videos.*

porous /'pɔːrəs/. ADJ Something that is **porous** has many small holes in it, allowing water and air to pass through. *...a porous material like sand or charcoal.*

porridge /'pɒrɪdʒ, AM 'pɔːr-/. N-UNCOUNT **Porridge** is a thick sticky food made from oats that are cooked in water or milk and eaten hot, especially for breakfast.

★ **port** /pɔːt/ **ports. 1** N-COUNT A **port** is a town or a harbour area with docks and warehouses, where ships load or unload goods or passengers. ...*the Mediterranean port of Marseilles.* **2** ADJ & N-UNCOUNT The **port** side of a ship is the left side when you are on it and facing towards the front. ...*turn to port.* **3** N-VAR **Port** is a type of strong, sweet red wine.

portable /'pɔːtəbəl/ **portables.** ADJ & N-COUNT A **portable** machine or device is designed to be easily carried or moved. The machine or device can be called a **portable.** ...*portable computer... We bought a colour portable for the bedroom.*

porter /'pɔːtə/ **porters. 1** N-COUNT A **porter** is a person whose job is to be in charge of the entrance of a building such as a hotel. [BRITISH] **2** N-COUNT A **porter** is a person whose job is to carry things, for example people's luggage at a railway station.

portfolio /pɔːt'fəuliəu/ **portfolios.** N-COUNT A **portfolio** is a set of pictures or photographs of someone's work, which they show to potential employers. *Edith showed them a portfolio of her own political cartoons.*

portion /'pɔːʃən/ **portions. 1** N-COUNT A **portion of** something is a part of it. *Damage was confined to a small portion of the castle... I have spent a fairly considerable portion of my life here.* **2** N-COUNT A **portion** is the amount of food that is given to one person at a meal. *Desserts can be substituted by a portion of fresh fruit.*

★ **portrait** /'pɔːtreɪt/ **portraits.** N-COUNT A **portrait** is a painting, drawing, or photograph of a person. ...*a portrait of the Queen.*

portray /pɔː'treɪ/ **portrays, portraying, portrayed. 1** VERB When an actor or actress **portrays** someone, he or she plays that person in a play or film. *He portrayed the king in a Los Angeles revival of 'Camelot'.* **2** VERB To **portray** someone or something in a particular way means to represent them in that way, for example in a book or film. ...*this northern novelist, who accurately portrays provincial domestic life.*

portrayal /pɔː'treɪəl/ **portrayals.** N-COUNT A **portrayal of** someone or something is a representation of them in a book, film, or play. ...*a sensitive and often funny portrayal of a friendship between two 11-year-old boys.*

★ **pose** /pəʊz/ **poses, posing, posed. 1** VERB If something **poses** a problem or danger, it is the cause of that problem or danger. *His ill health poses serious problems for the future.* **2** VERB If you **pose** a question, you ask it. [FORMAL] **3** VERB If you **pose as** someone, you pretend to be that person in order to deceive people. *The team posed as drug dealers to trap the ringleaders.* **4** VERB & N-COUNT If you **pose for** a photograph or painting, you stay in a particular position so that someone can photograph or paint you. This position is called a **pose.** *How did you get him to pose for this picture?*

posh /pɒʃ/. **1** ADJ If you describe something as **posh**, you mean that it is smart, fashionable, and expensive. [INFORMAL] ...*a posh hotel.* **2** ADJ If you describe a person as **posh**, you mean that they belong to or behave as if they belong to a high social class. *He sounded so posh on the phone.*

★ **position** /pə'zɪʃən/ **positions, positioning, positioned. 1** N-COUNT The **position** of someone or something is the place where they are. *The ship's name and position were reported to the coastguard.* **2** N-COUNT When someone or something is in a particular **position**, they are sitting, lying, or arranged in that way. *The upper back and neck are held in an erect position.* **3** VERB & PHRASE If you **position** someone or something somewhere, or if you place them **in position**, you put them exactly where you want them to be. *Position trailing plants near the edges... Some 28,000 US troops are moving into position.* **4** N-COUNT Your **position** in society is the role and the importance that you have in it. ...*adjustment to their changing role and position in society.* **5** N-COUNT A **position** in a company or organization is a job. [FORMAL] *He left a career in teaching to take up a position with the Council.* **6** N-COUNT Your **position** in a race or competition is how well you did in relation to the other competitors or how well you are doing. *The car was running in eighth position.* **7** N-COUNT You can describe your situation at a particular time by saying that you are in a particular **position**. *He's going to be in a very difficult position.* **8** PHRASE If you are **in a position to** do something, you are able to do it. *I am not in a position to comment.* **9** N-COUNT Your **position on** a particular matter is your attitude towards it. [FORMAL] *What's your position on abortion?*

★ **positive** /'pɒzɪtɪv/. **1** ADJ If you are **positive**, you are hopeful and confident, and think of the good aspects of a situation rather than the bad ones. *Be positive about your future.* ♦ **positively** ADV *Try thinking positively about yourself.* **2** ADJ A **positive** situation or experience is pleasant and helpful to you in some way. *Working abroad should be an exciting and positive experience.* **3** ADJ If you make a **positive** decision or take **positive** action, you do something definite in order to deal with a task or problem. *He was expected to make a very positive contribution to the 1996 Games organisation.* **4** ADJ A **positive** response shows agreement, approval, or encouragement. ♦ **positively** ADV *Voters would respond positively to a good campaign argument.* **5** ADJ AFTER LINK-V If you are **positive about** something, you are completely sure about it. *I'm as positive as I can be about it.* **6** ADJ BEFORE N **Positive** evidence gives definite proof of something. *We have positive proof that he was a blackmailer.* ♦ **positively** ADV *He has positively identified the body.* **7** ADJ AFTER LINK-V If a medical or scientific test is **positive**, it shows that something has happened or is present. *If the test* *is positive, a course of antibiotics may be prescribed.*

positively /'pɒzɪtɪvli/. ADV You use **positively** to emphasize that something is the case. *This is positively the worst thing that I can imagine.*

possess /pə'zes/ **possesses, possessing, possessed.** [1] VERB If you **possess** something, you have it or own it. *He is said to possess a fortune.* [2] VERB To **possess** a quality, ability, or feature means to have it. *...the practical skills that some people possess.*

possession /pə'zeʃən/ **possessions.** [1] N-UNCOUNT If you are **in possession of** something, you have it, because you have obtained it or because it belongs to you. [FORMAL] *Those documents are now in the possession of the Guardian. ...illegal possession of firearms.* [2] N-COUNT Your **possessions** are the things that you own or have with you at a particular time. *People had lost their homes and all their possessions.*

possessive /pə'zesɪv/ **possessives.** [1] ADJ If someone is **possessive**, they want all their partner's love and attention. *She became increasingly possessive and jealous.*
♦ **possessiveness** N-UNCOUNT *I've ruined every relationship with my possessiveness.* [2] N-COUNT In grammar, **the possessive** is the form of a noun or pronoun used to indicate possession, for example 'George's' and 'his'.

possibility /ˌpɒsɪ'bɪlɪti/ **possibilities.** [1] N-COUNT If you say there is a **possibility** that something is the case or that something will happen, you mean that it might be the case or it might happen. *Tax on food has become a very real possibility.* [2] N-COUNT A **possibility** is one of several things that could be done. *There were several possibilities open to each manufacturer.*

> **USAGE** Note that you do not use **possibility** in sentences like 'I had the possibility to do it'. The words you need are **opportunity** or **chance**. *Later Donald had the opportunity of driving the car... The people of Northern Ireland would have the chance to shape their own future.*

⭐ **possible** /'pɒsɪbəl/. [1] ADJ If it is **possible to** do something, it can be done. *If it is possible to find out where your brother is, we shall... I need to see you, right away if possible.* [2] ADJ If you do something **as** soon **as possible**, you do it as soon as you can. If you get **as** much **as possible** of something, you get as much of it as you can. *Mrs. Pollard decided to learn as much as possible about the People's Republic of China.* [3] ADJ A **possible** event is one that might happen. *Her family is discussing a possible move to America.* [4] ADJ If you say that it is **possible** that something is true or correct, you mean that you do not know whether it is true or correct, but you accept that it might be. *It is possible that there's an*

explanation for all this. [5] ADJ You use **possible** with superlative adjectives to emphasize that something has more of a quality than anything else of its kind. *They have joined the job market at the worst possible time... He is doing the best job possible.* [6] N-SING **The possible** is everything that can be done in a situation. *He is a democrat with the skill, nerve, and ingenuity to push the limits of the possible.*

⭐ **possibly** /'pɒsɪbli/. [1] ADV You use **possibly** to indicate that you are not sure whether something is true or will happen. *This camera was rare and possibly a collector's item.* [2] ADV You use **possibly** to emphasize that you are surprised or puzzled. *How could they possibly eat that stuff?... What could this possibly mean?* [3] ADV You use **possibly** with a negative modal to emphasize that something cannot happen or cannot be done. *No I really can't possibly answer that!... There's nothing more they can possibly do.*

post 1 letters, parcels, and information

⭐ **post** /pəʊst/ **posts, posting, posted.** [1] N-SING In British English, **the post** is the public service by which letters and parcels are collected and delivered. The American word is **mail**. *The winner will be notified by post... The cheque is in the post.*
♦ **postal** ADJ BEFORE N *...the American postal service.* [2] N-UNCOUNT In British English, you can use **post** to refer to letters and parcels that are delivered to you. The American word is **mail**. *He flipped through the post without opening any of it.* [3] VERB In British English, if you **post** a letter or parcel, you send it to someone by putting it in a letterbox or taking it to a post office. The American word is **mail**. *I'm posting you a cheque tonight.*

post 2 jobs and places

⭐ **post** /pəʊst/ **posts, posting, posted.** [1] N-COUNT A **post** in a company or organization is a job or official position in it. [FORMAL] *She had earlier resigned her post as President Menem's assistant.* [2] VERB If you **are posted** somewhere, you are sent there by your employers to work. *Eric was posted to the South Seas for a year.* [3] See also **posting**.

post 3 poles

post /pəʊst/ **posts.** N-COUNT A **post** is an upright pole fixed into the ground. *The device is fixed to a post.*

postage /'pəʊstɪdʒ/. N-UNCOUNT **Postage** is the money that you pay for sending letters and parcels by post. *Send a cheque for £18.99 plus £2 for postage and packing.*

'post box, post boxes. N-COUNT In British English, a **post box** is a metal box with a hole in it where you put letters that you want to send. The American word is **mailbox**.

postcard /'pəʊstkɑːd/ **postcards.** N-COUNT A **postcard** is a piece of card, often with a picture on one side, which you can write on and post to someone without using an envelope.

postcode /'pəʊstkəʊd/ **postcodes.** N-COUNT In British English, your **postcode** is a short

a
b
c
d
e
f
g
h
i
j
k
l
m
n
o
p
q
r
s
t
u
v
w
x
y
z

Postures

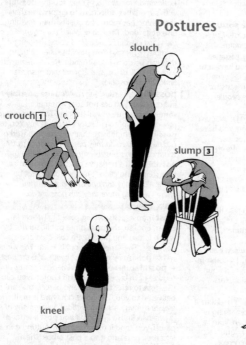

slouch

crouch [1]

slump [3]

squat [1]

kneel

on all fours

sequence of numbers and letters at the end of your address. The American term is **zip code**.

poster /'pəʊstə/ **posters.** N-COUNT A **poster** is a large notice, advertisement, or picture that you stick on a wall.

posterity /pɒ'steriti/. N-UNCOUNT You can refer to everyone who will be alive in the future as **posterity.** [FORMAL] *A photographer recorded the scene on video for posterity.*

postgraduate /,pəʊst'grædʒʊət/ **postgraduates.** N-COUNT A **postgraduate** is a student with a first degree from a university who is studying or doing research at a more advanced level. [BRITISH]

posting /'pəʊstɪŋ/ **postings.** 1 N-COUNT A **posting** is a job which involves going to a different town or country. *Relevant work experience is required for overseas postings.*
2 N-COUNT A **posting** is a message that is placed on the Internet, for example on a bulletin board or website, for everyone to read. [COMPUTING] ● See also **post**.

postman /'pəʊstmən/ **postmen.** N-COUNT In British English, a **postman** is a man whose job is to collect and deliver letters and parcels that are sent by post. The usual American word is **mailman**.

post-mortem /,pəʊst 'mɔːtəm/ **post-mortems.** 1 N-COUNT A **post-mortem** is a medical

examination of a dead person's body to find out how they died. 2 N-COUNT A **post-mortem** is an examination of something that has recently happened, especially something that has failed or gone wrong. *...the election post-mortem.*

'**post office, post offices.** N-COUNT A **post office** is a building where you can buy stamps, post letters and parcels, and use other services provided by the national postal service.

postpone /pəʊs'pəʊn/ **postpones, postponing, postponed.** VERB If you **postpone** an event, you arrange for it to take place at a later time than was originally planned. *The visit has now been postponed indefinitely.* ♦ **postponement, postponements** N-VAR *There were several postponements of the flight.*

postulate /'pɒstʃʊleɪt/ **postulates, postulating, postulated.** VERB If you **postulate** something, you suggest it as the basis for a theory, argument, or calculation. [FORMAL] *Freud postulated that we all have a death instinct.*

posture /'pɒstʃə/ **postures.** 1 N-VAR Your **posture** is the position or manner in which you stand or sit. *You can make your stomach look flatter instantly by improving your posture.*
2 N-COUNT A **posture** is an attitude that you have towards something. [FORMAL]

,**post-'war** (or **postwar**). ADJ **Post-war** is used

to describe things that happened, existed, or were made in the period immediately after a war, especially the Second World War (1939-45). *...postwar architecture.*

⭐ **pot** /pɒt/ **pots, potting, potted.** ☐1 N-COUNT A **pot** is a deep round container for cooking food. *...metal cooking pots.* ☐2 N-COUNT A **pot** is a teapot or coffee pot. *There's tea in the pot.* ☐3 VERB If you **pot** a plant, you put it into a flowerpot filled with soil.

⭐ **potato** /pə'teɪtəʊ/ **potatoes.** N-VAR **Potatoes** are vegetables with brown or red skins and white insides. → See picture on page 836.

potent /'pəʊtənt/. ADJ Something that is **potent** is effective and powerful. *The drug is extremely potent, but causes unpleasant side effects.* ♦ **potency** /'pəʊtənsi/ N-UNCOUNT *Sunscreen can lose its potency if left over winter in the bathroom cabinet.*

⭐ **potential** /pə'tenʃəl/. ☐1 ADJ BEFORE N You use **potential** to say that someone or something is capable of developing into a particular kind of person or thing. *The firm has identified 60 potential customers.* ♦ **potentially** ADV *This is a potentially dangerous situation.* ☐2 N-UNCOUNT If something has **potential**, it is capable of being useful or successful in the future. *The boy has great potential.* ☐3 N-UNCOUNT If you say that someone or something has **potential for** doing something, you mean that it is possible that they may do it. If there is **the potential for** something, it may happen. *John seemed as horrified as I about his potential for violence.*

potion /'pəʊʃən/ **potions.** N-COUNT A **potion** is a drink that contains medicine, poison, or something that is supposed to have magic powers. *...a magic potion to get him better.*

potter /'pɒtə/ **potters, pottering, pottered.** N-COUNT A **potter** is someone who makes pottery.
▸ **potter about** or **potter around.** PHR-VERB If you **potter about** or **potter around**, you spend your time slowly doing a few pleasant or unimportant tasks. [BRITISH]

pottery /'pɒtəri/. ☐1 N-UNCOUNT **Pottery** is objects made from clay. ☐2 N-UNCOUNT **Pottery** is the craft or activity of making objects out of clay. *...pottery classes.*

potty /'pɒti/ **potties.** ☐1 N-COUNT A **potty** is a deep bowl which a small child uses as a toilet. ☐2 ADJ If you say that someone is **potty**, you think that they are crazy or foolish. [BRITISH, INFORMAL] *I have to get out of here. I'll go potty if I stay.*

pouch /paʊtʃ/ **pouches.** ☐1 N-COUNT A **pouch** is a flexible container like a small bag. *On my belt in its little leather pouch was my Swiss penknife.* ☐2 N-COUNT The **pouch** of an animal such as a kangaroo is the pocket of skin on its stomach in which its baby grows.

poultry /'pəʊltri/. N-UNCOUNT You can refer to chickens, ducks, and other birds that are kept for their eggs and meat as **poultry**. Meat from these birds is also referred to as **poultry**. *...intensive*

methods of rearing poultry... *The menu features roast meats and poultry.*

pounce /paʊns/ **pounces, pouncing, pounced.** ☐1 VERB If a person or animal **pounces on** another person or animal, they leap towards them and try to take hold of them or attack them. *He pounced on the photographer, beat him up and smashed his camera... Before I could get the pigeon the cat pounced.* ☐2 VERB If someone **pounces on** something such as a mistake, they draw attention to it, usually in order to gain some sort of advantage for themselves. *The Democrats were ready to pounce on any Republican failings.*

⭐ **pound** /paʊnd/ **pounds, pounding, pounded.** ☐1 N-COUNT The **pound** is the unit of money which is used in Britain. It is represented by the symbol £. Some other countries, for example Egypt, also have a unit of money called a **pound**. *Beer cost three pounds a bottle.* ☐2 N-COUNT A **pound** is a unit of weight used mainly in Britain, America, and other countries where English is spoken. One pound is equal to 0.454 kilograms. *Her weight was under ninety pounds. ...a pound of cheese.* ● See note at **weight**. ☐3 VERB If you **pound** something, or if you **pound on** it, you hit it loudly and repeatedly with your fists. *He pounded the table with his fist... Somebody began pounding on the front door.* ☐4 VERB If your heart **is pounding**, it is beating with a strong fast rhythm, usually because you are afraid or excited. *I'm sweating, my heart is pounding. I can't breathe.* ♦ **pounding** N-UNCOUNT *...the fast pounding of her heart.*

⭐ **pour** /pɔː/ **pours, pouring, poured.** ☐1 VERB If you **pour** a liquid, you make it flow steadily out of a container by holding the container at an angle. *She poured some water into a plastic bowl.* ☐2 VERB If you **pour** someone a drink, you fill a cup or glass with it so that they can drink it. *He poured himself a Scotch.* ☐3 VERB When a liquid or other substance **pours** somewhere, it flows there quickly and in large quantities. *There was dense smoke pouring from all four engines... Tears poured down both our faces.* ☐4 VERB When it rains very heavily, you can say that **it is pouring**. *The rain was pouring down.* ♦ **pouring** ADJ *They left the school in pouring rain.* ☐5 VERB If people **pour into** or **out of** a place, they go there quickly and in large numbers. *At six p.m. large groups poured out of the numerous offices.* ☐6 VERB If something **pours** into a place, a lot of it is obtained or given. *Letters and cards of support have been pouring in.*
▸ **pour out.** PHR-VERB If you **pour out** a drink, you fill a cup or glass with it. *Carefully and slowly he poured the beer out.*

pout /paʊt/ **pouts, pouting, pouted.** VERB If you **pout**, you stick out your lips, usually as a way of showing that you are annoyed. *He whined and pouted when he did not get what he wanted.*

⭐ **poverty** /'pɒvəti/. N-UNCOUNT **Poverty** is the state of being very poor. *...people living in poverty.*

powder /'paʊdə/ **powders.** N-VAR **Powder** consists

a
b
c
d
e
f
g
h
i
j
k
l
m
n
o
p
q
r
s
t
u
v
w
x
y
z

of many tiny particles of a solid substance. *Her face was covered with white powder.*

powdered /'paʊdəd/. ADJ A **powdered** substance is one which is in the form of a powder. *...powdered milk.*

⭐ **power** /paʊə/ **powers, powering, powered.**
[1] N-UNCOUNT If someone has **power**, they have a lot of control over people and activities. *...women who have reached positions of great power and influence.* [2] N-UNCOUNT Your **power to** do something is your ability to do it. *Fathers have the power to dominate children... He was so drunk that he had lost the power of speech.* [3] N-UNCOUNT If it is **in** your **power** to do something, you are able to do it or you have the resources to deal with it. *We must do everything in our power to ensure the success of the conference.* [4] N-VAR If someone in authority has the **power to** do something, they have the legal right to do it. *The Prime Minister has the power to appoint senior ministers. ...the legal powers of British Customs officers.* [5] N-UNCOUNT If people take **power** or come to **power**, they take charge of a country's affairs. People who are **in power** are in charge of a country's affairs. [6] N-UNCOUNT The **power** of something is its physical strength or other capability. *The Roadrunner had better power, better tyres, and better brakes. ...massive computing power.* [7] N-UNCOUNT **Power** is energy, especially electricity, that is obtained in large quantities from a fuel source. *Power has been restored to most parts that were hit last night by high winds.* [8] VERB The device or fuel that **powers** a machine provides the energy that makes the machine work.

⭐ **powerful** /'paʊəfʊl/. [1] ADJ A **powerful** person or organization is able to control or influence people and events. *...Russia and India, two large, powerful countries.* [2] ADJ You say that someone's body is **powerful** when it is physically strong. *...his powerful muscles.* ♦ **powerfully** ADV *...a strong, powerfully-built man.* [3] ADJ A **powerful** machine or substance is effective because it is very strong. *...powerful computer systems.* ♦ **powerfully** ADV *...this powerfully alcoholic wine.* [4] ADJ A **powerful** smell is very strong. [5] ADJ A **powerful** voice is loud and can be heard from a long way away. [6] ADJ You describe a piece of writing, speech, or work of art as **powerful** when it has a strong effect on people's feelings or beliefs. ♦ **powerfully** ADV *...a powerfully acted play.*

powerless /'paʊələs/. [1] ADJ Someone who is **powerless** is unable to control or influence events. ♦ **powerlessness** N-UNCOUNT *...childhood feelings of powerlessness.* [2] ADJ AFTER LINK-V If you are **powerless to** do something, you are unable to do it. *He was sympathetic, but powerless to help.*

'**power line, power lines.** N-COUNT A **power line** is a cable, especially above ground, along which electricity passes to an area or building.

'**power plant, power plants.** N-COUNT A **power plant** is a place where electricity is generated.

'**power station, power stations.** N-COUNT A **power station** is a place where electricity is generated.

⭐ **pp. pp.** is the plural of 'p' and means 'pages'. *See chapter 6, pp. 137-41.*

practicable /'præktɪkəbəl/. ADJ If a task or plan is **practicable**, people are able to do it or carry it out. *Teachers can only be expected to do what is reasonable and practicable.*

⭐ **practical** /'præktɪkəl/ **practicals.** [1] ADJ **Practical** means involving real situations, rather than ideas and theories. *They offer practical suggestions for healthy eating.* [2] ADJ You describe people as **practical** when they make sensible decisions and deal effectively with problems. *We are practical people who judge ideas and policies by results.* [3] ADJ **Practical** ideas and methods are likely to be effective or successful in a real situation. *Our system is the most practical way of preventing crime.* [4] ADJ You can describe clothes and things in your house as **practical** when they are useful rather than just being fashionable or attractive. *Our clothes are lightweight, fashionable, practical for holidays.* [5] N-COUNT A **practical** is an examination or lesson in which you make things or do experiments rather than simply write answers to questions.

practicality /ˌpræktɪ'kælɪti/ **practicalities.** N-COUNT The **practicalities of** a situation are the aspects of it which are concerned with real events rather than with ideas or theories. *...the practicalities of financing your schemes.*

practically /'præktɪkəli/. [1] ADV **Practically** means almost. *He'd known the old man practically all his life.* [2] ADV You use **practically** to describe something which involves real actions or events rather than ideas or theories. *The course is essentially more practically based than the Masters degree.*

⭐ **practice** /'præktɪs/ **practices.** [1] N-COUNT You can refer to something that people do regularly as a **practice**. *...the modern practice of using chemicals to colour the hair.* [2] N-VAR **Practice** means doing something regularly in order to do it better. A **practice** is a session of this. *...basketball practice... He recorded the fastest time in a final practice today.* [3] N-UNCOUNT The work done by doctors and lawyers is referred to as the **practice** of medicine and law. People's religious activities are referred to as the **practice** of a religion. *I had to change my attitude toward medical practice. ...freedom of conscience and religious practice.* [4] N-COUNT A doctor's or lawyer's **practice** is his or her business, often shared with other doctors or lawyers. [5] See also **practise**.
PHRASES ● What happens **in practice** is what actually happens, in contrast to what is supposed to happen. *This theoretical freedom of choice is not in practice available to the majority of the population.* ● If you are **out of practice** at doing something, you have not had much experience

of it recently, although you used to do it a lot or be quite good at it. ● If you **put** an idea or method **into practice,** you make use of it. *The prime minister has another chance to put his new ideas into practice.*

practise (AM **practice**) /'præktɪs/**practises, practising, practised.** [1] VERB If you **practise** something, you keep doing it regularly in order to do it better. *Lauren practises the piano every day.* [2] VERB When people **practise** something such as a custom, craft, or religion, they take part in the activities associated with it. *...a family which practised traditional Judaism... Acupuncture was practised in China as long ago as the third millennium BC.* ◆ **practising** ADJ BEFORE N *All employees must be practising Christians.* [3] VERB Someone who **practises** medicine or law works as a doctor or lawyer. *He practised as a lawyer until his retirement last year. ...a practising architect.*

practised (AM **practiced**) /'præktɪst/. ADJ Someone who is **practised** at something is good at it because they have had a lot of experience of it. *...once you are practised at this sort of relaxation. ...a practised and experienced surgeon.*

practitioner /præk'tɪʃənə/ **practitioners.** N-COUNT Doctors are sometimes referred to as **practitioners.** [FORMAL]

pragmatic /præg'mætɪk/. ADJ A **pragmatic** way of dealing with something is based on practical considerations, rather than theoretical ones. A **pragmatic** person deals with things in a practical way. ◆ **pragmatically** ADV *These firms respond pragmatically to local conditions.*

pragmatism /'prægmətɪzəm/. N-UNCOUNT **Pragmatism** means thinking or dealing with problems in a practical way, rather than by using theory or abstract principles. [FORMAL] ◆ **pragmatist, pragmatists** N-UNCOUNT *He is a political pragmatist, not an idealist.*

prairie /'preəri/ **prairies.** N-VAR A **prairie** is a large area of flat grassy land in North America.

⭐ **praise** /preɪz/ **praises, praising, praised.** [1] VERB & N-UNCOUNT If you **praise** someone or something, or if you express your **praise for** them, you express approval for their achievements or qualities. *He praised the fans for their continued support... She is full of praise for the range of excellent services available.* [2] VERB & N-UNCOUNT If you **praise** God, or if you offer him your **praise,** you express your respect, honour, and thanks to God. *Hindus were singing hymns in praise of the god Rama.* [3] PHRASE If you **sing** someone's **praises,** you praise them in an enthusiastic way.

pram /præm/ **prams.** N-COUNT A **pram** is like a baby's cot on wheels, which you can push along when you want to take the baby somewhere.

prank /præŋk/ **pranks.** N-COUNT A **prank** is a childish trick. [DATED]

prawn /prɔːn/ **prawns.** N-COUNT In British English, a **prawn** is a small edible shellfish, similar to a shrimp. The usual American word is **shrimp.**

pray /preɪ/ **prays, praying, prayed.** VERB When people **pray,** they speak to God in order to give thanks or to ask for help. *Kelly prayed that God would judge her with mercy.*

prayer /preə/ **prayers.** [1] N-UNCOUNT **Prayer** is the activity of speaking to God. *The night was spent in prayer.* [2] N-COUNT A **prayer** is the words that someone says when they speak to God. [3] N-COUNT You can refer to a strong hope that you have as your **prayer.** *This drug could be the answer to our prayers.* [4] N-PLURAL A short religious service at which people gather to pray can be referred to as **prayers.** *...Muslims attending prayers.*

preach /priːtʃ/ **preaches, preaching, preached.** [1] VERB When someone, especially a member of the clergy, **preaches,** he or she gives a talk on a religious or moral subject as part of a church service. *The bishop preached to a crowd of several hundred local people.* ◆ **preacher, preachers** N-COUNT *...acceptance of women preachers.* [2] VERB When people **preach** a belief or a course of action, they try to persuade other people to accept the belief or take the course of action. *For many years I have preached against war.*

precarious /prɪ'keəriəs/. [1] ADJ If your situation is **precarious,** you are not in complete control of events and might fail in what you are doing at any moment. ◆ **precariously** ADV *This left him clinging precariously to his job.* [2] ADJ Something that is **precarious,** is not securely held in place and is likely to fall at any moment. *...a very precarious ladder.* ◆ **precariously** ADV *One of my grocery bags was still precariously perched on the car bumper.*

precaution /prɪ'kɔːʃən/ **precautions.** N-COUNT A **precaution** is an action that is intended to prevent something dangerous or unpleasant from happening. *They took the precaution of seeking legal advice. ...safety precautions.*

precede /prɪ'siːd/ **precedes, preceding, preceded.** VERB If one event or period of time **precedes** another, it happens before it. [FORMAL] *The earthquake was preceded by several smaller tremors. ...friends I had already met during the preceding months.*

precedence /'presɪdəns/. PHRASE If one thing **takes precedence over** another, the first thing is regarded as more important than the second one. *He took precedence over everyone else.*

precedent /'presɪdənt/ **precedents.** N-VAR If there is a **precedent for** an action or event, it has happened before, and this can be regarded as an argument for doing it again. [FORMAL] *There are plenty of precedents in Hollywood for letting people out of contracts.*

precept /'priːsept/ **precepts.** N-COUNT A **precept** is a general rule that helps you to decide how you should behave in particular circumstances. [FORMAL] *...the moral precepts that govern civilised society.*

a
b
c
d
e
f
g
h
i
j
k
l
m
n
o
p
q
r
s
t
u
v
w
x
y
z

precinct /'priːsɪŋkt/ **precincts.** [1] N-COUNT A shopping **precinct** is an area in the centre of a town in which cars are not allowed. [BRITISH] [2] N-COUNT In the United States, a **precinct** is a part of a city which has its own police force and fire service. [3] N-PLURAL The **precincts** of an institution are its buildings and land. [FORMAL]

precious /'preʃəs/. [1] ADJ If you say that something such as a resource is **precious**, you mean that it is valuable and should not be wasted or used badly. *A family break allows you to spend precious time together.* [2] ADJ **Precious** objects and materials are worth a lot of money because they are rare. [3] ADJ If something is **precious** to you, you regard it as important and do not want to lose it. *Her family's support is particularly precious to Josie.* [4] PHRASE If you say that there is **precious little** of something, you are emphasizing that there is very little of it, and that it would be better if there were more. *They have had precious little to celebrate... Precious few home-buyers will notice any reduction in their monthly repayments.*

precipitate, precipitates, precipitating, precipitated. [1] VERB /prɪ'sɪpəteɪt/ If something **precipitates** an event or situation, usually a bad one, it causes it to happen suddenly or sooner than normal. [FORMAL] *A slight mistake could precipitate a disaster.* [2] ADJ /prɪ'sɪpɪtət/ A **precipitate** action or decision happens or is made more quickly or suddenly than most people think is sensible. [FORMAL] ♦ **precipitately** ADV *I fled precipitately in the opposite direction.*

precise /prɪ'saɪs/. [1] ADJ You use **precise** to emphasize that you are referring to an exact thing, rather than something vague. *...the precise location of the wreck.* [2] ADJ Something that is **precise** is exact and accurate in all its details. *They speak very precise English.*

⭐ **precisely** /prɪ'saɪsli/. [1] ADV **Precisely** means accurately and exactly. *The meeting began at precisely 4.00 p.m.* [2] ADV You use **precisely** to emphasize that a reason or fact is the only important one there is, or that it is obvious. *That is precisely the result the system is designed to produce.*

precision /prɪ'sɪʒən/. N-UNCOUNT If you do something with **precision**, you do it exactly as it should be done. *The choir sang with precision.*

preclude /prɪ'kluːd/ **precludes, precluding, precluded.** VERB If something **precludes** you **from** doing something or going somewhere, it prevents you from doing it or going there. *Poor English precluded them from ever finding a job.*

precocious /prɪ'kəʊʃəs/. ADJ **Precocious** children do or say things that seem very advanced for their age.

preconception /ˌpriːkən'sepʃən/ **preconceptions.** N-COUNT Your **preconceptions** about something are the beliefs you form about it before you have enough information or experience.

...preconceptions about the sort of people who did computing.

precondition /ˌpriːkən'dɪʃən/ **preconditions.** N-COUNT If one thing is a **precondition for** another, it must happen or be done before the second thing can happen or exist. [FORMAL] *Some basic preconditions are necessary for unions to work well.*

precursor /priː'kɜːsə/ **precursors.** N-COUNT A **precursor of** something is a similar thing that happened or existed before it. *...the European Monetary Institute, the precursor of a European central bank.*

predator /'predətə/ **predators.** N-COUNT A **predator** is an animal that kills and eats other animals.

predatory /'predətri, AM -tɔːri/. ADJ **Predatory** animals or birds kill and eat other animals. *...predatory birds like the eagle.*

predecessor /'priːdɪsesə, AM 'pred-/ **predecessors.** [1] N-COUNT Your **predecessor** is the person who had your job before you. *He learned everything he knew from his predecessor.* [2] N-COUNT The **predecessor** of an object or machine is the object or machine that came before it in a sequence or process of development. *The car is some 40mm shorter than its predecessor.*

predicament /prɪ'dɪkəmənt/ **predicaments.** N-COUNT If you are **in a predicament**, you are in a difficult situation. *The decision will leave her in a peculiar predicament.*

⭐ **predict** /prɪ'dɪkt/ **predicts, predicting, predicted.** VERB If you **predict** an event, you say that it will happen. *He predicted that my hair would grow back 'in no time'.*

predictable /prɪ'dɪktəbəl/. ADJ Something that is **predictable** is obvious in advance and will happen. *The result was entirely predictable.* ♦ **predictably** ADV *His article is, predictably, a scathing attack on capitalism.* ♦ **predictability** N-UNCOUNT *...the predictability of climate in the North Atlantic.*

prediction /prɪ'dɪkʃən/ **predictions.** N-VAR If you make a **prediction**, you say what you think will happen. *...their prediction that he would change her life drastically.*

predispose /ˌpriːdɪ'spəʊz/ **predisposes, predisposing, predisposed.** [1] VERB If something **predisposes** you **to** think or behave in a particular way, it makes it likely that you will think or behave in that way. [FORMAL] *His wife's suicide predisposed him to pessimism.* ♦ **predisposed** ADJ AFTER LINK-V *Franklin was predisposed to believe him.* [2] VERB If something **predisposes** you **to** a disease or condition, it makes it likely that you will suffer from that disease or condition. ♦ **predisposed** ADJ AFTER LINK-V *Some people are genetically predisposed to diabetes.*

predisposition /ˌpriːdɪspə'zɪʃən/ **predispositions.** N-COUNT If you have a **predisposition to** a particular disease, condition, or way of behaving, something in your nature makes it likely that you will suffer from that disease or condition, or that you will behave in that way. ...*a predisposition to alcoholism.* ...*a woman's predisposition to use the right side of her brain.*

predominant /prɪˈdɒmɪnənt/. ADJ If something is **predominant**, it is more important or noticeable than anything else in a set of people or things. *Amanda's predominant emotion was that of confusion.* ◆ **predominantly** ADV *Business is conducted predominantly by phone.* ◆ **predominance** N-UNCOUNT ...*the predominance of men in entertainment TV.*

predominate /prɪˈdɒmɪneɪt/ **predominates, predominating, predominated.** VERB When one type of person or thing **predominates** in a group, there are more of that type than any other. [FORMAL] *In older age groups women predominate because men tend to die younger.*

pre-ˈeminent. ADJ The **pre-eminent** person in a group is the most important or powerful one. [FORMAL] ...*the pre-eminent political figure in the country.* ◆ **pre-eminence** N-UNCOUNT ...*the pre-eminence of post-war US literature.*

pre-empt /priːˈempt/ **pre-empts, pre-empting, pre-empted.** VERB If you **pre-empt** an action, you prevent it from happening by doing something before it can happen. *You can pre-empt pain by taking a painkiller at the first warning sign.*

pre-emptive /priːˈemptɪv/. ADJ A **pre-emptive** attack or strike is intended to weaken or damage an enemy or opponent, for example by destroying their weapons before they can do any harm.

preface /ˈprefɪs/ **prefaces, prefacing, prefaced.** [1] N-COUNT A **preface** is an introduction at the beginning of a book. [2] VERB If you **preface** an action or speech **with** something else, you do or say this other thing first. *She prefaced everything with, 'The trouble with doing that is...'*

⭐ **prefer** /prɪˈfɜː/ **prefers, preferring, preferred.** VERB If you **prefer** someone or something, you like that person or thing better than another. *Does he prefer a particular sort of music?... I preferred books and people to politics.*

> **USAGE** Note that **prefer** can often sound rather formal in ordinary conversation. Verbal expressions such as **like...better** and **would rather** are used more frequently. For example, instead of saying '**I prefer football to tennis**', you can say '**I like football better than tennis**', instead of '**I'd prefer an apple**', you can say '**I'd rather have an apple**', and instead of '**I'd prefer to walk**', you can say '**I'd rather walk**'.

preferable /ˈprefrəbəl/. ADJ If one thing is **preferable to** another, it is more desirable or suitable. *A big earthquake a long way off is*

preferable to a smaller one nearby... It is preferable to use only vegetable oil for cooking.
◆ **preferably** ADV *Take exercise, preferably in the fresh air.*

preference /ˈprefərəns/ **preferences.** [1] N-VAR If you have a **preference for** something, you would like to have or do that thing rather than something else. *His designs show a preference for using natural materials.* [2] N-UNCOUNT If you **give preference to** someone, you choose them rather than someone else. *The company gave preference to local workers.*

preferential /ˌprefəˈrenʃəl/. ADJ If you get **preferential** treatment, you are treated better than other people.

prefix /ˈpriːfɪks/ **prefixes.** N-COUNT A **prefix** is a letter or group of letters which is added to the beginning of a word in order to form a different word. For example, the prefix 'un-' is added to 'happy' to form 'unhappy'.

⭐ **pregnant** /ˈpregnənt/. ADJ If a woman or female animal is **pregnant**, she has a baby or babies developing in her body. *Lena got pregnant... Tina was pregnant with their first daughter.* ◆ **pregnancy** /ˈpregnənsi/ N-UNCOUNT *It would be wiser to cut out all alcohol during pregnancy.*

preheat /ˌpriːˈhiːt/ **preheats, preheating, preheated.** VERB If you **preheat** an oven, you switch it on and allow it to reach a certain temperature before you put food inside it.

prehistoric /ˌpriːhɪˈstɒrɪk, AM -ˈtɔːr-/. ADJ **Prehistoric** people and things existed at a time before information was written down. ...*the famous prehistoric cave paintings of Lascaux.*

prejudice /ˈpredʒʊdɪs/ **prejudices, prejudicing, prejudiced.** [1] N-VAR **Prejudice** is an unreasonable dislike of someone or something, or an unreasonable preference for one group over another. ...*a deep-rooted racial prejudice... There is widespread prejudice against workers over 45.* [2] VERB To **prejudice** someone or something means to influence them in such a way that they are no longer fair and objective. *I think your South American youth has prejudiced you.* [3] VERB If someone **prejudices** another person's situation, they do something which makes it worse than it should be. *The council has prejudiced their health by failing to deal with the asbestos.*

prejudiced /ˈpredʒʊdɪsd/. ADJ If someone is **prejudiced** against a particular group, they have an unreasonable dislike of them. *Some landlords and landladies are racially prejudiced.*

preliminary /prɪˈlɪmɪnri, AM -neri/ **preliminaries.** N-COUNT & ADJ **Preliminaries,** or **preliminary** activities or discussions, take place in preparation for an event before it starts. ...*alternative treatment as a preliminary to surgery.* ...*preliminary tests.*

prelude /ˈpreljuːd, AM ˈpreɪluːd/ **preludes.** N-COUNT You describe an event as a **prelude to** a more important event when it happens before it

a
b
c
d
e
f
g
h
i
j
k
l
m
n
o
p
q
r
s
t
u
v
w
x
y
z

and acts as an introduction to it. *For some, retirement can be a boring prelude to senility and death.*

premature /ˌpreməˈtʃʊə, AM ˌpriː-/. **1** ADJ Something that is **premature** happens too early or earlier than expected. *His career was brought to a premature end.* ♦ **prematurely** ADV *The years in the harsh mountains had prematurely aged him.* **2** ADJ A **premature** baby is born before the date when it was due to be born.

★ **premier** /ˈpremiə, AM prɪˈmɪr/ **premiers.** **1** N-COUNT The leader of a government can be referred to as the **premier.** *...Australian premier Paul Keating.* **2** ADJ BEFORE N **Premier** is used to describe something that is considered to be the best or most important thing of its kind. *...the country's premier opera company.*

premiere /ˈpremiə, AM prɪˈmjer/ **premieres.** N-COUNT The **premiere** of a new play or film is the first public performance of it.

premiership /ˈpremiəʃɪp, AM prɪˈmɪr-/. N-SING **Premiership** is the position of being the leader of a government. *...the final years of Margaret Thatcher's premiership.*

premise /ˈpremɪs/ **premises.**

☑ **Premiss** is also used in British English for sense 2.

1 N-PLURAL The **premises** of a business are all the buildings and land that it occupies. *There is a kitchen on the premises... The business moved to premises in Brompton Road.* **2** N-COUNT A **premise** is something that you suppose is true and that you use as a basis for developing an idea. [FORMAL] *...the premise that men and women are on equal terms.*

★ **premium** /ˈpriːmiəm/ **premiums.** **1** N-COUNT A **premium** is money that you pay regularly to an insurance company for an insurance policy. **2** N-COUNT A **premium** is a sum of money that you have to pay for something in addition to the normal cost. *Callers are charged a premium rate of 48p a minute.* **3** PHRASE If something is **at a premium**, it is wanted or needed, but is difficult to get or achieve. *If space is at a premium, choose adaptable furniture.*

premonition /ˌpreməˈnɪʃən, AM ˌpriː-/ **premonitions.** N-COUNT If you have a **premonition**, you have a feeling that something is going to happen, often something unpleasant. *She had a premonition of disaster before the flight.*

prenatal /ˌpriːˈneɪtəl/. ADJ **Prenatal** things relate to the medical care of pregnant women.

preoccupy /prɪˈɒkjʊpaɪ/ **preoccupies, preoccupying, preoccupied.** VERB If something **is preoccupying** you, you are thinking about it a lot. *...matters which were also increasingly preoccupying me.* ♦ **preoccupied** ADJ *He's become preoccupied with insurance policies.* ♦ **preoccupation, preoccupations** N-VAR *In his preoccupation with Robyn, Crook had neglected everything.*

★ **preparation** /ˌprepəˈreɪʃən/ **preparations.** **1** N-UNCOUNT **Preparation** is the process of getting something ready for use or for a particular purpose. *Behind any successful event lay months of preparation. ...food preparation.* **2** N-PLURAL **Preparations** are the arrangements that are made for a future event. *...preparations for the wedding.*

preparatory /prɪˈpærətrɪ, AM -tɔːri/. ADJ **Preparatory** actions are done as a preparation for something else. [FORMAL] *At least a year's preparatory work will be necessary before building can start.*

★ **prepare** /prɪˈpeə/ **prepares, preparing, prepared.** **1** VERB If you **prepare** something, you make it ready for something that is going to happen. *Two technicians were preparing a videotape recording of last week's programme.* **2** VERB If you **prepare for** an event or action that will happen soon, you get yourself ready for it or make the necessary arrangements. *The Party is using management consultants to help prepare for the next election... He had to go back to his hotel and prepare to catch a train.* **3** VERB When you **prepare** food, you get it ready to be eaten.

★ **prepared** /prɪˈpeəd/. **1** ADJ AFTER LINK-V If you are **prepared** to do something, you are willing to do it. *I'm prepared to take any advice.* **2** ADJ AFTER LINK-V If you are **prepared for** something that you think is going to happen, you are ready for it. *Be prepared for both warm and cool weather.* ♦ **preparedness** N-UNCOUNT *...the city's preparedness for war.* **3** ADJ Something that is **prepared** has been done or made beforehand, so that it is ready when it is needed. *He ended his prepared statement by thanking the police.*

preposition /ˌprepəˈzɪʃən/ **prepositions.** N-COUNT A **preposition** is a word such as 'by', 'for', 'into', or 'with', which usually has a noun group as its object. → See Reference Page on Times and Dates.

preposterous /prɪˈpɒstərəs/. ADJ If you describe something as **preposterous**, you mean that it is extremely unreasonable and foolish. ♦ **preposterously** ADV *Some prices are preposterously high.*

prerequisite /ˌpriːˈrekwɪzɪt/ **prerequisites.** N-COUNT If one thing is a **prerequisite for** another, it must happen or exist before the second thing is possible. *Good self-esteem is a prerequisite for a happy life.*

prerogative /prɪˈrɒgətɪv/ **prerogatives.** N-COUNT Something that is the **prerogative** of a particular person or group is a privilege or a power that only they have. [FORMAL] *Constitutional changes are exclusively the prerogative of the parliament.*

prescribe /prɪˈskraɪb/ **prescribes, prescribing, prescribed.** **1** VERB If a doctor **prescribes** treatment, he or she states what medicine or treatment a patient should have. **2** VERB If a person or set of laws or rules **prescribes** an action or duty, they state that it must be carried out. [FORMAL] ...*article II of the constitution, which prescribes the method of electing a president.*

prescription /prɪˈskrɪpʃən/ **prescriptions.**
1 N-COUNT A **prescription** is a medicine which a doctor has told you to take, or the form on which the doctor has written the details of that medicine. **2** PHRASE If a medicine is available **on prescription**, you can get it from a chemist if a doctor gives you a prescription for it.

⭐ **presence** /ˈprezəns/. **1** N-SING Someone's **presence** in a place is the fact that they are there. *His presence in the village could only stir up trouble.* **2** N-UNCOUNT If you say that someone has **presence**, you mean that they impress people by their appearance and manner. *They do not seem to have the vast, authoritative presence of those great men.*
PHRASES ● If someone or something **makes** their **presence felt**, they do something which forces people to pay attention to them. ● If you are **in** someone's **presence**, you are in the same place as they are, and are close enough to them to be seen or heard.

present 1 existing or happening now

⭐ **present** /ˈprezənt/. **1** ADJ BEFORE N You use **present** to describe people and things that exist now, rather than in the past or the future. *...the government's present economic difficulties... No statement can be made at the present time.* **2** N-SING The **present** is the period of time that we are in now and the things that are happening now. *...his struggle to reconcile the past with the present.* **3** ADJ BEFORE N The **present** tenses of a verb are the ones used to talk about things that happen regularly or situations that exist at this time.
PHRASES ● A situation that exists **at present** exists now, although it may change. ● The **present day** is the period of history that we are in now. *...Western European art from the period of Giotto to the present day.*

present 2 being somewhere

⭐ **present** /ˈprezənt/. **1** ADJ If someone is **present** at an event, they are there. *The whole family was present.* **2** ADJ If something, especially a substance or disease, is **present in** something else, it exists within that thing. *This special form of vitamin D is naturally present in breast milk.*

present 3 gift

⭐ **present** /ˈprezənt/ **presents.** N-COUNT A **present** is something that you give to someone, for example for their birthday or for Christmas. *This book would make a great Christmas present.*

present 4 verb uses

⭐ **present** /prɪˈzent/ **presents, presenting, presented.**
1 VERB If you **present** someone **with** a prize or **with** information, or if you **present** it **to** them, you formally give it to them. *Prince Michael of Kent presented the prizes... We presented three options to the unions for discussion.*
● **presentation** /ˌprezənˈteɪʃən, AM ˌpriːzen-/ **presentations** N-VAR *Then came the presentation of*

the awards. **2** VERB Something that **presents** a difficulty or a challenge causes or provides it. *Public policy on the family presents liberals with a dilemma.* **3** VERB If you **present** someone or something in a particular way, you describe them in that way. *The British like to present themselves as a nation of dog-lovers.* **4** VERB If someone **presents** a programme on television or radio, they introduce each item in it. ● **presenter, presenters** N-COUNT *...the presenter of the BBC radio programme Law in Action.*

presentation /ˌprezənˈteɪʃən, AM ˌpriːzen-/ **presentations.** **1** N-UNCOUNT **Presentation** is the appearance of something, which someone has worked to create. *...traditional French food cooked in a lighter way, keeping the presentation simple.* **2** N-COUNT A **presentation** is a formal event at which someone is given a prize or award. **3** N-COUNT When someone gives a **presentation**, they give a formal talk. *...a slide and video presentation.* **4** N-COUNT A **presentation** is something that is performed before an audience. *...Blackpool Opera House's presentation of Buddy, the musical.*

ˌ**present-ˈday** (or **present day**). ADJ BEFORE N **Present-day** things, situations, and people exist at the time in history we are now in. *Even by present-day standards these were large aircraft.*

presently /ˈprezəntli/. **1** ADV If you say that something is **presently** happening, you mean that it is happening now. *She is presently developing a number of projects... The island is presently uninhabited.* **2** ADV You use **presently** to indicate that something happened quite a short time after something you have just mentioned. [WRITTEN] *He was shown to a small office. Presently, a young woman in a white coat came in.* **3** ADV If you say that something will happen **presently**, you mean that it will happen quite soon. *'Who's Agnes?'—'You'll be meeting her presently.'*

preservative /prɪˈzɜːvətɪv/ **preservatives.** N-VAR A **preservative** is a chemical that is added to substances to prevent them from decaying. *Nitrates are commonly used as preservatives in food manufacture.*

⭐ **preserve** /prɪˈzɜːv/ **preserves, preserving, preserved.**
1 VERB If you **preserve** a situation or condition, you make sure that it stays as it is, and does not change or end. *We will do everything to preserve peace.* ● **preservation** /ˌprezəˈveɪʃən/ N-UNCOUNT *...the preservation of the status quo.* **2** VERB If you **preserve** something, you take action to save it or protect it. *We need to preserve the forest.* ● **preservation** N-UNCOUNT *...the preservation of historic houses.* **3** VERB If you **preserve** food, you treat it in order to prevent it from decaying.

preside /prɪˈzaɪd/ **presides, presiding, presided.** VERB If you **preside over** a meeting or event, you are in charge or act as the chairperson.

⭐ **presidency** /ˈprezɪdənsi/. **presidencies.** N-COUNT The **presidency** of a country or organization is the position of being the president or the period of time during which someone is president. *Poverty had declined during his presidency.*

⭐ **president** /ˈprezɪdənt/ **presidents.** ☐ N-COUNT & N-TITLE The **president** of a country that has no king or queen is the person who has the highest political position and is the leader of the country. *...President Mubarak.* ● See note at **government**. ☐ N-COUNT The **president** of an organization is the person with the highest position in it. *...the president of the medical commission.*

⭐ **presidential** /ˌprezɪˈdenʃəl/. ADJ BEFORE N **Presidential** activities or things relate or belong to a president. *...campaigning for Peru's presidential election.*

⭐ **press** /pres/ **presses, pressing, pressed.** ☐ VERB If you **press** something somewhere, you push it firmly against something else. *He pressed his back against the door... They pressed the silver knife into the cake.* ☐ VERB & N-COUNT If you **press** a button or switch, or if you give it a **press**, you push it with your finger in order to make a machine or device work. *Drago pressed a button and the door closed. ...a TV which rises from a table at the press of a button.* ☐ VERB If you **press** something, or if you **press down on** it, you push against it with your hand or foot. *The engine stalled. He pressed the accelerator hard... She leaned forward with her hands pressing down on the desk.* ☐ VERB If you **press** clothes, you iron them. ☐ VERB If you **press for** something, you try hard to persuade someone to give it to you or agree to it. *Police might now press for changes in the law.* ☐ VERB If you **press** someone, you try hard to persuade them to do or say something. *Trade unions are pressing him to stand firm... Mr King seems certain to be pressed for further details.* ☐ VERB If you **press charges** against someone, you make an official accusation which has to be decided in a court of law. *Police have announced they will not be pressing charges.* ☐ N-SING The **press** refers to newspapers and the journalists who write them. **The press** can take the singular or plural form of the verb. *A meeting was promised, but the Press was not admitted.* ☐ N-COUNT A **press** or a **printing press** is a machine used for printing books, newspapers, and leaflets. ☐ See also **pressing**.

▸**press on** or **press ahead.** PHR-VERB If you **press on** or **press ahead**, you continue doing something in a determined way, and do not allow difficulties to delay you. *Poland pressed on with economic reform.*

'**press conference, press conferences.** N-COUNT A **press conference** is a meeting held by a famous or important person in which they answer journalists' questions.

pressing /ˈpresɪŋ/. ADJ A **pressing** problem, need, or issue has to be dealt with immediately.

'**press release, press releases.** N-COUNT A **press release** is a written statement about a matter of public interest which is given to the press by an organization involved in the matter. *The*

government had put out a press release naming the men.

'**press-up, press-ups.** N-COUNT In British English, **press-ups** are exercises that you do by lying with your face towards the floor and pushing with your hands to raise your body until your arms are straight. The usual American term is **push-up**. *He made me do 50 press-ups.*

⭐ **pressure** /ˈpreʃə/ **pressures, pressuring, pressured.** ☐ N-UNCOUNT **Pressure** is the force produced when you press hard on something. *The best way to treat such bleeding is to apply firm pressure.* ☐ N-UNCOUNT The **pressure** in a place or container is the force produced by the quantity of gas or liquid in that place or container. *...another high pressure area over the North Sea.* ● See also **blood pressure**. ☐ N-UNCOUNT If there is **pressure on** someone to do something, someone is trying to persuade or force them to do it. *He may have put pressure on her to agree... Its government is under pressure from the European Commission.* ☐ N-VAR If you feel **pressure**, you feel that you have too much to do and not enough time to do it, or that people expect a lot from you. *Can you work under pressure?... The pressures of modern life are great.* ☐ VERB If you **pressure** someone **to** do something, you try forcefully to persuade them to do it. *He will never pressure you to get married... Don't pressure me.* ◆ **pressured** ADJ *You're likely to feel anxious and pressured.*

'**pressure group, pressure groups.** N-COUNT A **pressure group** is an organization that campaigns to try to persuade a government to do something. *...the environmental pressure group Greenpeace.*

pressurize (BRIT also **pressurise**) /ˈpreʃəraɪz/ **pressurizes, pressurizing, pressurized.** VERB If you are **pressurized into** doing something, you are forcefully persuaded to do it. *Do not be pressurized into making your decision immediately.*

pressurized (BRIT also **pressurised**) /ˈpreʃəraɪzd/. ADJ In a **pressurized** container or area, the pressure inside is different from the pressure outside. *Supplementary oxygen is rarely needed in pressurized aircraft.*

prestige /preˈstiːʒ/. N-UNCOUNT If a person, a country, or an organization has **prestige**, they are admired and respected because they are important or successful. *...efforts to build up the prestige of the United Nations. ...high prestige jobs.*

prestigious /preˈstɪdʒəs/. ADJ A **prestigious** institution or activity is respected and admired by people. *...the largest and most prestigious businesses in America.*

⭐ **presumably** /prɪˈzjuːməbli, AM -ˈzuːm-/. ADV If you say that something is **presumably** the case, you mean that you think it is the case, although you are not certain. *Presumably the front door was locked?... He had gone to the reception desk, presumably to check out.*

presume /prɪ'zjuːm, AM -'zuːm/ **presumes, presuming, presumed.** [1] VERB If you **presume** that something is the case, you think that it is the case, although you are not certain. *I presume you're here on business... The missing person is presumed dead.* [2] VERB If you say that someone **presumes to** do something, you mean that they do it even though they have no right to do it. [FORMAL] *I wouldn't presume to question your judgement.*

presumption /prɪ'zʌmpʃən/ **presumptions.** N-COUNT A **presumption** is something that is accepted as true but is not certain to be true. *...the presumption that a defendant is innocent until proved guilty.*

presumptuous /prɪ'zʌmptʃʊəs/. ADJ If you describe someone as **presumptuous**, you disapprove of them because they do things that they have no right to do. *It would be presumptuous to judge what the outcome will be.*

pretence (AM **pretense**) /prɪ'tens, AM 'priːtens/ **pretences.** [1] N-VAR A **pretence** is a way of behaving that is intended to make people believe something that is not true. *Welland made a pretence of writing a note in his pad.* [2] PHRASE If you do something **under false pretences**, you do it when people do not know the truth about you and your intentions. *...a man who had married me under false pretences.*

pretend /prɪ'tend/ **pretends, pretending, pretended.** [1] VERB If you **pretend** that something is the case, you try to make people believe that it is the case, although it is not. *Sometimes the boy pretended to be asleep.* [2] VERB If you **pretend** that you are doing something, you imagine that you are doing it, for example as part of a game. *She can sunbathe and pretend she's in Spain.*

pretense. See **pretence.**

pretension /prɪ'tenʃən/ **pretensions.** N-VAR Someone with **pretensions** pretends that they are more important than they really are. *We like him for his honesty, his lack of pretension.*

pretentious /prɪ'tenʃəs/. ADJ Someone or something that is **pretentious** tries to appear more important or significant than they really are. *The film was too boring and pretentious for me.*

pretext /'priːtekst/ **pretexts.** N-COUNT A **pretext** is a reason which you pretend has caused you to do something. *I darted into the bedroom on the pretext of looking for a book.*

⭐ **pretty** /'prɪti/ **prettier, prettiest.** [1] ADJ If you describe someone, especially a girl, as **pretty**, you mean that they look nice and are attractive in a delicate way. *...a shy, delicately pretty girl with enormous blue eyes.* [2] ADJ A place or a thing that is **pretty** is attractive and pleasant. *...a pretty flowered cotton dress.* ♦ **prettily** ADV *The living-room was prettily decorated.* [3] ADV You can use **pretty** before an adjective or adverb to mean 'quite' or 'rather'. [INFORMAL] *I'm a pretty good judge of character.* [4] PHRASE **Pretty much** or **pretty**

well means 'almost'. [INFORMAL] *I travel pretty well every week.*

prevail /prɪ'veɪl/ **prevails, prevailing, prevailed.** [1] VERB If a proposal, principle, or opinion **prevails**, it gains influence or is accepted. *Political and personal ambitions are starting to prevail over economic interests.* [2] VERB If a situation or attitude **prevails** in a particular place at a particular time, it is normal or most common at that place and time. *...the confusion which had prevailed at the time of the revolution.* [3] VERB If you **prevail upon** someone **to** do something, you succeed in persuading them to do it. *He was prevailed upon to sign copies of his book.*

prevalent /'prevələnt/. ADJ A condition or belief that is **prevalent** is very common. *Smoking is becoming increasingly prevalent among younger women.* ♦ **prevalence** N-UNCOUNT *...the prevalence of behaviour problems in 3-year-old children.*

⭐ **prevent** /prɪ'vent/ **prevents, preventing, prevented.** VERB If you **prevent** something, you stop it happening or being done. *...measures to prevent the wastage of water. ...to prevent wild animals in Britain from suffering terrible cruelty.* ♦ **prevention** N-UNCOUNT *...crime prevention.*

preventative /prɪ'ventətɪv/. ADJ BEFORE N **Preventative** means the same as **preventive.**

preventive /prɪ'ventɪv/. ADJ BEFORE N **Preventive** actions are intended to help prevent things such as disease or crime. *...preventive medicine.*

preview /'priːvjuː/ **previews.** N-COUNT A **preview** is an opportunity to see something such as a film or invention before it is open or available to the public.

⭐ **previous** /'priːviəs/. ADJ BEFORE N A **previous** event or thing is one that occurred before the one you are talking about. *She has a teenage daughter from a previous marriage.*

⭐ **previously** /'priːviəsli/. [1] ADV **Previously** means at some time before the period that you are talking about. *Previously she had very little*

a
b
c
d
e
f
g
h
i
j
k
l
m
n
o
p
q
r
s
t
u
v
w
x
y
z

A
B
C
D
E
F
G
H
I
J
K
L
M
N
O
P
Q
R
S
T
U
V
W
X
Y
Z

time to work. [2] ADV You can use **previously** to say how much earlier one event was than another. *She had rented the flat from the council some fourteen months previously.*

pre-'war. ADJ **Pre-war** is used to describe things that happened, existed, or were made in the period immediately before a war, especially the Second World War (1939-45). *It was 1950 before he returned to his pre-war job at the British Museum.*

prey /preɪ/ **preys, preying, preyed.** [1] N-UNCOUNT A creature's **prey** are the creatures that it hunts and eats in order to live. [2] VERB A creature that **preys on** other creatures lives by catching and eating them. *...mountain lions and bears that prey on sheep.* [3] N-UNCOUNT If someone or something is **prey to** something bad, they have a tendency to let themselves be affected by it. *He was prey to a growing despair.* [4] PHRASE To **fall prey to** something bad means to be affected by it. *Children in evacuation centres are falling prey to disease.*

price /praɪs/ **prices, pricing, priced.** [1] N-VAR The **price** of something is the amount of money that you must pay to buy it. *They expected house prices to rise... They haven't come down in price.*

> **USAGE** The **price** of goods is the amount of money that the seller is asking people to pay in order to buy them. *The price marked on the box was five pounds.* When you are referring to services, or to things that you pay to use, you usually talk about a **charge** or a **fee**, rather than a **price**. *There is a 50p handling charge for postal bookings. ...£400 in unpaid parking fees.* The **cost** of something is the amount of money that you actually pay, or would pay, for it. *The total cost of modernising the room came to just £800.* The **cost** of goods is usually the same as their **price**.

[2] VERB If something **is priced at** a particular amount, the price is set at that amount. *The book is priced at £8.99.* ◆ **pricing** N-UNCOUNT *It's hard to maintain competitive pricing.* [3] N-SING The **price** that you pay **for** something is an unpleasant thing you have to do in order to get it. *Slovenia will have to pay a high price for independence.* [4] PHRASE If you want something **at any price**, you are determined to get it, even if unpleasant things happen as a result.

priceless /ˈpraɪsləs/. [1] ADJ Something that is **priceless** is worth a very large amount of money. *...his priceless collection of Chinese art.* [2] ADJ If you say that something is **priceless**, you mean that it is extremely useful. *Gillian is passing on some of her priceless skill and experience.*

pricey /ˈpraɪsi/ **pricier, priciest.** ADJ If something is **pricey**, it is expensive. [INFORMAL]

prick /prɪk/ **pricks, pricking, pricked.** [1] VERB If you **prick** something, you make small holes in it with

a sharp object such as a pin. *Prick the potatoes and rub the skins with salt.* [2] VERB & N-COUNT If something sharp **pricks** you, or if you feel a **prick**, something sticks into you and causes you pain. *She had just pricked her finger with the needle... She felt a prick on her neck.*

prickly /ˈprɪkli/ **pricklier, prickliest.** [1] ADJ Something that is **prickly** feels rough and uncomfortable, as if it has a lot of sharp points. → See picture on page 526. [2] ADJ Someone who is **prickly** loses their temper or gets upset very easily. *You know how prickly she can be sometimes.*

★ **pride** /praɪd/ **prides, priding, prided.** [1] N-UNCOUNT **Pride** is a feeling of satisfaction which you have because you or people close to you have done something good or possess something good. *...the sense of pride in a job well done... Take pride in your health and your figure.* [2] VERB If you **pride yourself on** a quality or skill that you have, you are very proud of it. *Smith prides himself on being able to organise his own life.* [3] N-UNCOUNT **Pride** is a sense of dignity and self-respect. *His own pride forbids him to ask Arthur's help.* [4] N-UNCOUNT Someone's **pride** is the feeling that they have that they are better or more important than other people; used showing disapproval. *His pride may still be his downfall.*
PHRASES ● Someone or something that is your **pride and joy** is very important to you and makes you feel very happy. *The bike soon became his pride and joy.* ● If something takes **pride of place**, it is treated as the most important thing in a group of things.

★ **priest** /priːst/ **priests.** [1] N-COUNT A **priest** is a member of the Christian clergy in the Catholic, Anglican, or Orthodox church. [2] N-COUNT In many non-Christian religions a **priest** is a man who has particular duties and responsibilities in a place where people worship.

priestess /ˈpriːstes/ **priestesses.** N-COUNT A **priestess** is a woman in a non-Christian religion who has particular duties and responsibilities in a place where people worship.

priesthood /ˈpriːsthʊd/. [1] N-UNCOUNT **Priesthood** is the position of being a priest or the period of time during which someone is a priest. *He spent the first twenty-five years of his priesthood as an academic.* [2] N-SING The **priesthood** consists of all the members of the Christian clergy.

prim /prɪm/ **primmer, primmest.** ADJ If you describe someone as **prim**, you mean that they behave too correctly and are too easily shocked by anything rude or improper. ◆ **primly** ADV *We sat primly at either end of a long settee.*

primal /ˈpraɪml/. ADJ **Primal** is used to describe something that relates to the origins of things or that is very basic. [FORMAL] *Jealousy is a primal emotion.*

primarily /ˈpraɪmərɪli, AM praɪˈmeərɪli/. ADV You use **primarily** to say what is mainly true in a

primary /ˈpraɪməri, AM -meri/. **1** ADJ BEFORE N You use **primary** to describe something that is extremely important or most important for someone or something. [FORMAL] *The primary source of water in the region is the river.* **2** ADJ BEFORE N In Britain, **primary** education is given to pupils between the ages of 5 and 11. The American equivalent is **elementary** education.

primate /ˈpraɪmət/ **primates.** N-COUNT A **primate** is a member of the group of mammals which includes humans, monkeys, and apes.

prime /praɪm/ **primes, priming, primed.** **1** ADJ BEFORE N You use **prime** to describe something that is most important in a situation. *The police will see me as the prime suspect... Its prime audience lies in the 17 to 24 age group.* **2** ADJ BEFORE N You use **prime** to describe something that is of the best possible quality. *...keeping a car in prime condition.* **3** ADJ BEFORE N A **prime** example of something is a very typical example of it. *New York is a prime example of a city where crime strangles small-business development.* **4** N-SING Your **prime** is the stage in your life when you are most active or most successful. *She was in her intellectual prime.* **5** VERB If you **prime** someone **to** do something, you prepare them to do it, for example by giving them information about it beforehand. *I'm pretty much primed to believe anything bad about her.*

Prime 'Minister, Prime Ministers. N-COUNT The leader of the government in some countries is called the **Prime Minister**.

primitive /ˈprɪmɪtɪv/. **1** ADJ **Primitive** means belonging to a society in which people live in a very simple way, usually without industries or a writing system. *...primitive tribes.* **2** ADJ **Primitive** means belonging to a very early period in the development of an animal or plant. *It is a primitive instinct to flee a place of danger.* **3** ADJ If you describe something as **primitive**, you mean that it is very simple in style or that it is very old-fashioned. *It's using some rather primitive technology.*

primrose /ˈprɪmrəʊz/ **primroses.** N-COUNT A **primrose** is a wild plant with pale yellow flowers.

prince /prɪns/ **princes.** N-COUNT & N-TITLE A **prince** is a male member of a royal family, especially the son of a king or queen.

princess /ˌprɪnˈses, AM -ˈsəs/ **princesses.** N-COUNT & N-TITLE A **princess** is a female member of a royal family, especially the daughter of a king or queen or the wife of a prince.

principal /ˈprɪnsɪpəl/ **principals.** **1** ADJ BEFORE N **Principal** means first in order of importance. *Salt is the principal source of sodium in our diets.* **2** N-COUNT The **principal** of a school or college is the person in charge of it.

principally /ˈprɪnsɪpəli/. ADV **Principally** means more than anything else. *A sport such as cycling is principally about athletic achievement.*

principle /ˈprɪnsɪpəl/ **principles.** **1** N-VAR A **principle** is a belief that you have about the way you should behave. *...moral principles. ...a man of principle.* **2** N-COUNT The **principles** of a particular theory or philosophy are its basic rules or laws. *...the principles of Buddhism.*
  PHRASES ● If you refuse to do something **on principle**, you refuse to do it because of your beliefs. *He would vote against it on principle.* ● If you agree with something **in principle**, you agree in general terms to the idea of it, although you do not know the details or know if it will be possible. *The conference approved in principle a new policy-making process.*

principled /ˈprɪnsɪpəld/. ADJ If you describe someone as **principled**, you approve of them because they have strong moral principles.

print /prɪnt/ **prints, printing, printed.** **1** VERB If someone **prints** a book, newspaper, or leaflet, they produce it in large quantities by a mechanical process. ♦ **printing** N-UNCOUNT *...a printing and publishing company.* **2** VERB If a newspaper or magazine **prints** a piece of writing, it includes it or publishes it. **3** VERB If numbers or letters **are printed** on an object, they appear on it. *The company has for some time printed its phone number on its products.* **4** VERB If a text or a picture **is printed**, a copy of it is produced by means of a computer printer or some other type of equipment. *...machines that can print on both sides of a page.* **5** VERB If you **print**, you write in letters that are not joined together. **6** N-UNCOUNT **Print** is used to refer to letters and numbers as they appear on the pages of a printed document. *...columns of tiny print.*
  PHRASES ● If you or your words appear **in print**, or get **into print**, what you say or write is published in a book or newspaper. ● If a book is **in print**, it is available from a publisher. If it is **out of print**, it is no longer available.
  ▶**print out.** PHR-VERB If you **print out** a document or some information, you produce a copy of it on paper using a computer. You can also say that a computer **prints** something **out**. *Print it out and compare it to the old version of your file.* ● See also **printout**.

printer /ˈprɪntə/ **printers.** **1** N-COUNT A **printer** is a machine that can be connected to a computer in order to make copies on paper of information held by the computer. [COMPUTING] **2** N-COUNT A **printer** is a person or firm whose job is printing books, leaflets, or similar material.

printout (or **print-out**) /ˈprɪntaʊt/ **printouts.** N-VAR A **printout** is a piece of paper on which information from a computer has been printed. [COMPUTING]

prior /ˈpraɪə/. **1** ADJ BEFORE N You use **prior** to indicate that something has already happened, or must happen, before another event takes place. [FORMAL] → See Reference Page on Times and Dates. *These courses require prior knowledge of computing.* **2** PREP If something happens **prior to** a particular time or event, it happens before it. [FORMAL] ...*a man seen hanging around the area prior to the shooting.*

⭐ **priority** /praɪˈɒrɪti, AM -ˈɔːr-/ **priorities.** N-COUNT If something is a **priority**, it is the most important thing you have to achieve or deal with before everything else. *Quality is our number one priority... Her first priority was to knock down the wall between the kitchen and dining area.*

PHRASES ● If you **give priority to** something or someone, you treat them as more important than anything or anyone else. *The school will give priority to science and maths.* ● If something **takes priority over** other things or **has priority over** them, it is regarded as being more important than them and is dealt with first. *Academic work takes priority over politics or social life for most students.*

priory /ˈpraɪəri/ **priories.** N-COUNT A **priory** is a place where a small number of monks live and work together.

prise (AM **prize**) /praɪz/ **prises, prising, prised.** [1] VERB If you **prise** something open, or if you **prise** it away from a surface, you force it to open or force it to come away from the surface. *She prised open the window... We were unable to prise the lids off.* [2] VERB If you **prise** information **out of** someone, you persuade them to tell you although they may be very unwilling to.

⭐ **prison** /ˈprɪzən/ **prisons.** N-COUNT A **prison** is a building where criminals are kept.

⭐ **prisoner** /ˈprɪzənə/ **prisoners.** [1] N-COUNT A **prisoner** is a person who is kept in a prison as a punishment or because they have been captured by an enemy. [2] PHRASE If someone **is taken prisoner**, they are captured. If someone **is held prisoner**, they are guarded so that they cannot escape.

pristine /ˈprɪstiːn/ ADJ **Pristine** things are extremely clean or new. *The house is in pristine condition.*

privacy /ˈprɪvəsi, AM ˈpraɪ-/ N-UNCOUNT **Privacy** is the fact of being alone so that you can do things without being seen or disturbed. *...exercises you can do in the privacy of your own home... I've always enjoyed my privacy.*

⭐ **private** /ˈpraɪvɪt/ **privates.** [1] ADJ **Private** industries and services are owned and controlled by an individual person or group, rather than by the state. *...private education.* ♦ **privately** ADV *...privately owned businesses.* [2] ADJ If something is **private**, it is for the use of one person or group, rather than for the general public. *...his father's private plane. ... a private golf club.* [3] ADJ **Private** activities involve only a small number of people, and very little information about them is given to other people. ♦ **privately** ADV *I had not talked to Winnette privately for weeks.* [4] PHRASE If you do something **in private**, you do it without other people being present, often because it is something that you want to keep secret. [5] ADJ Your **private** life is that part of your life that is concerned with your personal relationships and

activities, rather than with your work or business. [6] ADJ Your **private** thoughts or feelings are ones that you do not talk about to other people. *We felt as if we were intruding on his private grief.* ♦ **privately** ADV *Privately, she worries about whether she's really good enough.* [7] ADJ If you describe a place as **private**, you mean that it is a quiet place and you can be alone there without being disturbed. *Can't we go somewhere private to discuss this?* [8] N-COUNT & N-TITLE A **private** is a soldier of the lowest rank.

,**private 'school, private schools.** N-COUNT A **private school** is a school which is not supported financially by the government and which parents have to pay for their children to go to.

⭐ **privatize** (BRIT also **privatise**) /ˈpraɪvətaɪz/ **privatizes, privatizing, privatized.** VERB If an organization owned by the state **is privatized**, the government sells it to one or more private companies. ♦ **privatization, privatizations** N-VAR *...the privatisation of British Rail.*

privilege /ˈprɪvɪlɪdʒ/ **privileges.** [1] N-COUNT A **privilege** is a special right or advantage that only one person or group has. *...special privileges for government officials.* [2] N-UNCOUNT **Privilege** is the power and advantages that belong to a small group of people, usually because of their wealth or their high social class. *...a life of privilege.*

privileged /ˈprɪvɪlɪdʒd/ ADJ Someone who is **privileged** has an advantage or opportunity that most other people do not have, often because of their wealth or high social class. *...a very wealthy, privileged elite.*

⭐ **prize** /praɪz/ **prizes, prizing, prized.** [1] N-COUNT A **prize** is something valuable, such as money or a trophy, that is given to the winner of a game or competition. *He won first prize... The winner won about £300 in prize money.* [2] ADJ BEFORE N You use **prize** to describe things that are of such good quality that they win prizes or deserve to win prizes. *...a prize bull.* [3] VERB Something that **is prized** is wanted and admired because it is considered to be very valuable or very good quality. *These shells were highly prized by the Indians.* [4] See also **prise**.

pro /prəʊ/ **pros.** [1] N-COUNT A **pro** is a professional, especially a professional sportsman or sportswoman. [2] PHRASE The **pros and cons** of something are its advantages and disadvantages.

probability /ˌprɒbəˈbɪlɪti/ **probabilities.** [1] N-VAR The **probability of** something happening is how likely it is to happen, sometimes expressed as a fraction or a percentage. *Without a transfusion, the victim's probability of dying was 100%.* [2] N-VAR You say that there is a **probability that** something will happen when it is likely to happen. *The probability is that he will return to Gloucestershire.* [3] PHRASE You use **in all probability** when you are confident that something is true or correct, or is likely to happen. *In all probability, we shall never know.*

probable /'prɒbəbəl/. ADJ Something that is **probable** is likely to be true or likely to happen. *It is probable that the volcano will erupt again.*

⭐ **probably** /'prɒbəbli/. ADV If you say that something is **probably** the case, you think that it is likely to be the case, although you are not sure. *You probably won't understand this word... Van Gogh is probably the best-known painter in the world.*

probation /prə'beɪʃən, AM 'prəʊ-/. N-UNCOUNT **Probation** is a period of time during which a person who has committed a crime is supervised to ensure that they do not break the law again, rather than being put in prison. *The young woman admitted three theft charges and was put on probation for two years.*

pro'bation officer, probation officers. N-COUNT A **probation officer** is a person whose job is to supervise and help people who have been put on probation.

probe /prəʊb/ **probes, probing, probed.** 1 VERB & N-COUNT If you **probe into** something, you ask questions or make enquiries in order to discover facts about it. This questioning or enquiring is called a **probe**. *The more they probed into his background, the more suspicious they became. ...a new probe into burglary in Queensland.* 2 VERB If you **probe** a place, you search in it in order to find someone or something that you looking for. *I probed around for some time in the bushes.*

⭐ **problem** /'prɒbləm/ **problems.** 1 N-COUNT A **problem** is an unsatisfactory situation that causes difficulties for people. *He left home at the age of 16 because of family problems... The main problem was that I had very little experience.* 2 N-COUNT A **problem** is a puzzle that requires logical thought or mathematics to solve it.

problematic /ˌprɒblə'mætɪk/. ADJ Something that is **problematic** involves problems and difficulties. *Some places are more problematic than others for women traveling alone.*

procedural /prə'siːdʒərəl/. ADJ **Procedural** means involving a formal procedure. [FORMAL] *The discussions will probably focus on procedural matters.*

⭐ **procedure** /prə'siːdʒə/ **procedures.** N-VAR A **procedure** is a way of doing something, especially the usual or correct way. *The procedure is lengthy, complicated and quite secretive. ...safety procedures.*

⭐ **proceed, proceeds, proceeding, proceeded.** 1 VERB /prə'siːd/ If you **proceed to** do something, you do it after doing something else. *He then proceeded to tell us everything.* 2 VERB To **proceed** means to continue as planned. [FORMAL] *I do not believe that would be a sensible way to proceed.* 3 VERB If you **proceed** in a particular direction, you go in that direction. [FORMAL] *He proceeded down the spiral stairway.* 4 N-PLURAL /'prəʊsiːdz/ The **proceeds** of an event or activity are the money that has been obtained from it.

The proceeds from the concert will go towards famine relief.

proceedings /prə'siːdɪŋz/. 1 N-PLURAL Legal **proceedings** are legal action taken against someone. [FORMAL] *...a man facing criminal proceedings for kidnapping his daughter.* 2 N-PLURAL You can refer to an organized series of events that happen in a place as **the proceedings**. [FORMAL] *...the proceedings of the enquiry.*

⭐ **process** /'prəʊses, AM 'prɑːses/ **processes, processing, processed.** 1 N-COUNT A **process** is a series of actions or events which have a particular result. *...the 12-week training process. ...factors that accelerate the ageing process.* 2 VERB When raw materials or foods **are processed**, they are treated by a chemical or industrial process before they are used or sold. *...diets high in refined and processed foods.* ♦ **processing** N-UNCOUNT *...nuclear fuel processing plant.* 3 VERB When a person or computer **processes** information, they deal with the information by putting it through a system or into a computer. ♦ **processing** N-UNCOUNT *...data processing.* 4 See also **word processing**.

PHRASES ● If you **are in the process of** doing something, you have started to do it and are still doing it. ● If you are doing something and you do something else **in the process**, you do the second thing as a result of doing the first thing. *You have to let us struggle for ourselves, even if we must die in the process.*

procession /prə'seʃən/ **processions.** N-COUNT A **procession** is a group of people who are walking, riding, or driving in a line as part of a public event. → See picture on page 826. *A funeral procession was coming up the hill.*

processor /'prəʊsesə, AM 'prɑːs-/ **processors.** N-COUNT A **processor** is the part of a computer that interprets commands and performs the processes the user has requested. [COMPUTING]

proclaim /prəʊ'kleɪm/ **proclaims, proclaiming, proclaimed.** VERB If people **proclaim** something, they formally announce it or make it known. *He still proclaims himself a believer in the Revolution.*

proclamation /ˌprɒklə'meɪʃən/ **proclamations.** N-COUNT A **proclamation** is a public announcement about something important.

procure /prə'kjʊə/ **procures, procuring, procured.** VERB If you **procure** something, especially something that is difficult to get, you obtain it. [FORMAL] *It remained very difficult to procure food.* ♦ **procurement** N-UNCOUNT *...procurement of new weapons.*

prod /prɒd/ **prods, prodding, prodded.** 1 VERB & N-COUNT If you **prod** someone or something, or if you give them a **prod**, you give them a quick push with your finger or with a pointed object. *He prodded Murray with the shotgun.* 2 VERB If you **prod** someone **into** doing something, you remind them or persuade them to do it. *This question is designed to prod students into*

⭐ Bank of English® frequent word   For a full explanation of all grammatical labels, see pages vii-x

a
b
c
d
e
f
g
h
i
j
k
l
m
n
o
p
q
r
s
t
u
v
w
x
y
z

examining the idea. ♦ **prodding** N-UNCOUNT *She did her chores without prodding.*

prodigious /prə'dɪdʒəs/. ADJ Something that is **prodigious** is very large or impressive. [LITERARY] *...prodigious amounts of work.* ♦ **prodigiously** ADV *She ate prodigiously.*

prodigy /'prɒdɪdʒi/ **prodigies.** N-COUNT A **prodigy** is someone who has a great natural talent for something which shows itself at an early age.

⭐ **produce, produces, producing, produced.** [1] VERB /prə'djuːs, AM -'duːs/ To **produce** something means to cause it to happen. *The drug is known to produce side-effects.* [2] VERB If you **produce** something, you make or create it. *We try to produce items that are the basics of a stylish wardrobe.* ♦ **producer, producers** N-COUNT *...the world's leading oil producer.* [3] VERB If you **produce** evidence or an argument, you show it or explain it to people. *They challenged him to produce evidence to support his allegations.* [4] VERB If you **produce** an object from somewhere, you bring it out so that it can be seen. *To hire a car you must produce a passport.* [5] VERB If someone **produces** a play, film, programme, or record, they organize it and decide how it should be made. ♦ **producer** N-COUNT *...a freelance film producer.* [6] N-UNCOUNT /'prɒdjuːs, AM -duːs/ **Produce** is food such as fruit and vegetables that are grown in large quantities to be sold.

⭐ **product** /'prɒdʌkt/ **products.** [1] N-COUNT A **product** is something that is produced and sold in large quantities. [2] N-COUNT If you say that someone or something is a **product of** a particular situation or process, you mean that the situation or process made that person or thing what they are. *The bank is the product of a 1971 merger of two Japanese banks.*

⭐ **production** /prə'dʌkʃən/ **productions.** [1] N-UNCOUNT **Production** is the process of manufacturing or growing something in large quantities, or the amount of goods manufactured or grown. *That model won't go into production before 2005... We needed to increase the volume of production.* [2] N-UNCOUNT The **production of** something is its creation as the result of a natural process. *These proteins stimulate the production of blood cells.* [3] N-UNCOUNT **Production** is the process of organizing and preparing a play, film, programme, or record. [4] N-COUNT A **production** is a play, opera, or other show that is performed in a theatre. *...a new production of The Rocky Horror Show.*

pro'duction line, production lines. N-COUNT A **production line** is an arrangement of machines in a factory where the products pass from one machine to another until they are finished.

productive /prə'dʌktɪv/. [1] ADJ Something or someone that is **productive** is very efficient at producing something. *Training makes workers highly productive.* [2] ADJ If you say that a relationship is **productive**, you mean that good

or useful things happen as a result of it. *Our discussions were amicable and productive.*

productivity /,prɒdʌk'tɪvɪti/. N-UNCOUNT **Productivity** is the rate at which goods are produced. *...continued improvements in productivity.*

Prof. /prɒf/. N-TITLE **Prof.** is a written abbreviation for **professor**. *...Prof. Richard Joyner.*

profess /prə'fes/ **professes, professing, professed.** [1] VERB If you **profess to** do or have something, you claim that you do it or have it, often when you do not. [FORMAL] *She professed to hate her nickname... Why do organisations profess that they care?* [2] VERB If you **profess** a feeling, opinion, or belief, you express it. [FORMAL] *He professed to be content... Bacher professed himself pleased with the Indian tour.*

⭐ **profession** /prə'feʃən/ **professions.** [1] N-COUNT A **profession** is a type of job that requires advanced education or training. [2] N-COUNT You use **profession** to refer to all the people who have the same profession. *...the medical profession.*

⭐ **professional** /prə'feʃənəl/ **professionals.** [1] ADJ BEFORE N **Professional** means relating to a person's work, especially work that requires special training. *His professional career started at Liverpool University.* ♦ **professionally** ADV *...a professionally-qualified architect.* [2] N-COUNT & ADJ BEFORE N A **professional**, or a **professional** person, has a job that requires advanced education or training. *My father wanted me to become a professional and have more stability.* [3] ADJ BEFORE N & N-COUNT You use **professional** to describe people who do a particular thing to earn money rather than as a hobby. You call these people **professionals**. *...a professional footballer... He had been a professional since March 1985.* ♦ **professionally** ADV *By age 16 he was playing professionally with bands.* [4] ADJ If you say that something that someone does or produces is **professional**, you approve of it because you think it shows skill and high standards. *...a truly professional but personal touch.* ♦ **professionalism** N-UNCOUNT *American companies pride themselves on their professionalism.* ♦ **professionally** ADV *These tickets have been produced very professionally.*

⭐ **professor** /prə'fesə/ **professors.** [1] N-COUNT & N-TITLE A **professor** in a British university is the most senior teacher in a department. *In 1979, only 2% of British professors were female.* [2] N-COUNT & N-TITLE A **professor** in an American or Canadian university or college is a teacher there.

proffer /'prɒfə/ **proffers, proffering, proffered.** VERB If you **proffer** something to someone, you offer it to them. [FORMAL] *The army has not yet proffered an explanation.*

proficient /prə'fɪʃənt/. ADJ If you are **proficient in** something, you can do it well. *A great number of Egyptians are proficient in foreign languages.*

♦ **proficiency** N-UNCOUNT ...*basic proficiency in English.*

⭐ **profile** /'prəʊfaɪl/ **profiles, profiling, profiled.** N-COUNT Your **profile** is the outline of your face seen from the side.
PHRASES ● If someone has a **high profile**, people notice them and what they do. *Football is a high profile business.* ● If you **keep a low profile**, you avoid doing things that will make people notice you.

⭐ **profit** /'prɒfɪt/ **profits, profiting, profited.** [1] N-VAR A **profit** is an amount of money that you gain when you are paid more for something than it cost you. *The bank made pre-tax profits of £3.5 million.* [2] VERB If you **profit from** something, you earn a profit from it or gain some advantage or benefit from it. *Jennifer wasn't convinced that she'd profit from a more relaxed lifestyle... The dealers profited shamefully at the expense of my family.*

profitable /'prɒfɪtəbəl/ [1] ADJ A **profitable** activity or organization makes a profit. *It was profitable for them to produce large amounts of food.* ♦ **profitably** ADV *The 28 French stores are trading profitably.* ♦ **profitability** N-UNCOUNT ...*an effort to increase profitability.* [2] ADJ Something that is **profitable** results in some benefit for you. ...*a profitable exchange of personnel and ideas.*
♦ **profitably** ADV *He could scarcely have spent his time more profitably.*

profound /prə'faʊnd/ [1] ADJ You use **profound** to emphasize that something is very great or intense. ...*discoveries which had a profound effect on many areas of medicine.*
♦ **profoundly** ADV *This has profoundly affected my life.* [2] ADJ A **profound** idea or work shows great intellectual depth and understanding. ...*one of the country's most profound minds.*

profuse /prə'fjuːs/. ADJ **Profuse** means doing something or happening a lot. *He gave profuse thanks to Jimmy.* ♦ **profusely** ADV *He was bleeding profusely.*

profusion /prə'fjuːʒən/. N-SING & N-UNCOUNT If there is a **profusion of** something or if it occurs **in profusion**, there is a very large quantity or variety of it. [FORMAL] *Wild flowers grew in profusion.*

prognosis /prɒg'nəʊsɪs/ **prognoses** /prɒg'nəʊsiːz/. N-COUNT A **prognosis** is an estimate about the future of someone or something. [FORMAL] *His wife had a brain tumour and the prognosis was poor.*

⭐ **program** /'prəʊgræm/ **programs, programming, programmed.** VERB & N-COUNT When you **program** a computer, you give it a set of instructions called a **program**, to make it able to perform a particular task. [COMPUTING] ♦ **programming** N-UNCOUNT ...*programming skills.* ♦ **programmer, programmers** N-COUNT ...*a computer programmer.*

⭐ **programme** (AM **program**) /'prəʊgræm/ **programmes, programming, programmed.** [1] N-COUNT A **programme** of actions or events is a series of actions or events that are planned to be done. *The nuclear programme should still continue.* [2] N-COUNT A television or radio **programme** is something that is broadcast on television or radio. ...*local news programmes.* [3] N-COUNT A theatre or concert **programme** is a booklet giving information about the play or concert. [4] VERB When you **programme** a machine or system, you set its controls so that it will work in a particular way. *Parents can programme the machine not to turn on at certain times.*

⭐ **progress, progresses, progressing, progressed.** [1] N-UNCOUNT /'prəʊgres, AM 'prɑː-/ **Progress** is the process of gradually improving or getting nearer to achieving or completing something. *His teacher sees signs of progress in his reading.* [2] N-SING **The progress of** a situation or action is the way in which it develops. *He had retained a keen interest in the progress of the work.* [3] PHRASE If something is **in progress**, it has started and is still continuing. [4] VERB /prə'gres/ To **progress** means to improve or to become more advanced or higher in rank. *He started only five years ago, sketching first and then progressing to painting.* [5] VERB If events **progress**, they continue to happen gradually over a period of time. *As her career progressed she made three other short films.*

progression /prə'greʃən/ **progressions.** N-COUNT A **progression** is a gradual development from one state to another. *Both drugs slow the progression of AIDS.*

progressive /prə'gresɪv/ **progressives.** [1] ADJ & N-COUNT Someone who is **progressive** has modern ideas about how things should be done, rather than traditional ones. You can call someone like this a **progressive**. ...*one of the country's most progressive young theatre companies... The Republicans were deeply split between progressives and conservatives.* [2] ADJ A **progressive** change happens gradually over a period of time. ...*progressive loss of memory.*
♦ **progressively** ADV *Her symptoms became progressively worse.*

prohibit /prə'hɪbɪt, AM prəʊ-/ **prohibits, prohibiting, prohibited.** VERB If someone **prohibits** something, they forbid it or make it illegal. [FORMAL] ...*a law that prohibits tobacco advertising.*
♦ **prohibition** N-UNCOUNT *The review recommended prohibition of cannabis.*

prohibitive /prə'hɪbɪtɪv, AM prəʊ-/. ADJ If something's cost is **prohibitive**, it is so high that many people cannot afford it. ...*the prohibitive prices charged for seats at the opera.*
♦ **prohibitively** ADV *Meat and butter were prohibitively expensive.*

⭐ **project, projects, projecting, projected.** [1] N-COUNT /'prɒdʒekt/ A **project** is a carefully planned task that requires a lot of time and effort. ...*local development projects such as hospitals and schools.* [2] N-COUNT A **project** is a detailed study of a subject by a pupil or student. [3] VERB /prə'dʒekt/ If something **is projected**, it is planned or expected. *The industry is projecting a* small increase in exports. [4] VERB If you **project** a film or picture onto a screen or wall, you make it appear there. ...a high-tech production projected onto a giant Cinemascope screen. [5] VERB If you **project** a particular feeling or quality, you show it in your behaviour. If you **project** someone or something in a particular way, you try to make people see them in that way. He just hasn't been able to project himself as the strong leader... His first job will be to project Glasgow as a friendly city. [6] VERB If something **projects**, it sticks out beyond a particular surface or edge. [FORMAL] ...brown-coloured boulders projecting above the oily surface.

projection /prə'dʒekʃən/ **projections.** [1] N-COUNT A **projection** is an estimate of a future amount. ...sales projections. [2] N-UNCOUNT The **projection** of a film or picture is the act of projecting it onto a screen or wall. ...the most up to date projection facilities in the world.

projector /prə'dʒektə/ **projectors.** N-COUNT A **projector** is a machine that projects films or slides onto a screen or wall.

proliferate /prə'lɪfəreɪt/ **proliferates, proliferating, proliferated.** VERB If things **proliferate**, they increase in number very quickly. [FORMAL] Computerized data bases are proliferating fast. ♦ **proliferation** N-UNCOUNT ...the proliferation of nuclear weapons.

prolific /prə'lɪfɪk/. ADJ A **prolific** writer, artist, or composer produces a large number of works.

prologue /'prəʊlɒg, AM -lɔːg/ **prologues.** N-COUNT A **prologue** is a speech or section of text that introduces a play or book.

prolong /prə'lɒŋ, AM -lɔːŋ/ **prolongs, prolonging, prolonged.** VERB To **prolong** something means to make it last longer. Foreign military aid was prolonging the war.

prolonged /prə'lɒŋd, AM -lɔːŋd/. ADJ A **prolonged** event or situation continues for a long time. ...a prolonged period of low interest rates.

⭐ **prominent** /'prɒmɪnənt/. [1] ADJ Someone or something that is **prominent** is well-known and important or respected. ...the children of very prominent or successful parents. ...Romania's most prominent independent newspaper. ♦ **prominence** N-UNCOUNT Crime prevention had to be given more prominence. [2] ADJ Something that is **prominent** is very noticeable. ...his prominent nose. ♦ **prominently** ADV Entries will be prominently displayed in the exhibition hall.

promiscuous /prə'mɪskjʊəs/. ADJ Someone who is **promiscuous** has sex with many different people; used showing disapproval. ♦ **promiscuity** /ˌprɒmɪ'skjuːɪti/ N-UNCOUNT ...an attempt to limit promiscuity.

⭐ **promise** /'prɒmɪs/ **promises, promising, promised.** [1] VERB & N-COUNT If you **promise** that you will do something, or if you make a **promise** that you will do it, you say that you will definitely do it. He promised to wait... Promise me you will not waste

your time. [2] VERB & N-COUNT If you **promise** someone something, or if you make them a **promise** about it, you tell them that you will definitely give it to them or make sure that they have it. We promise you an exciting and exhilarating trip. [3] VERB If a situation or event **promises to** have a particular quality, it shows signs that it will have that quality. The seminar also promises to be most instructive. [4] N-UNCOUNT If someone or something shows **promise**, they seem likely to be very good or successful.

promising /'prɒmɪsɪŋ/. ADJ Someone or something that is **promising** seems likely to be very good or successful. ...one of the most promising poets of his generation.

⭐ **promote** /prə'məʊt/ **promotes, promoting, promoted.** [1] VERB If people **promote** something, they help to make it happen, increase, or become more popular. In many ways, our society actively promotes alcoholism... The island could be promoted as a tourist destination. ♦ **promotion, promotions** N-VAR ...TV commercials and other promotions. [2] VERB If someone **is promoted**, they are given a more important job in the organization they work for. I was promoted to editor. ♦ **promotion** N-VAR Consider changing jobs or trying for promotion.

promoter /prə'məʊtə/ **promoters.** [1] N-COUNT A **promoter** is a person who helps organize and finance an event, especially a sports event. [2] N-COUNT The **promoter of** a cause or idea tries to make it become popular. ...the most energetic promoter of American music.

promotional /prə'məʊʃənəl/. ADJ **Promotional** material, events, or ideas are designed to advertise a product or service and increase its sales.

⭐ **prompt** /prɒmpt/ **prompts, prompting, prompted.** [1] VERB If something **prompts** someone **to** do something, it makes them decide to do it. Japan's recession has prompted consumers to cut back on buying cars. [2] VERB If you **prompt** someone, you encourage or remind them to do something or to continue doing something. 'Well, Daniels?' Wilson prompted. ♦ **prompting, promptings** N-VAR She telephoned Wychwood House at your prompting. [3] ADJ A **prompt** action is done without any delay. It is not too late, but prompt action is needed.

promptly /'prɒmptli/. [1] ADV If you do something **promptly**, you do it immediately. I set my watch alarm for seven-thirty and promptly fell asleep. [2] ADV If you do something **promptly at** a particular time, you do it at exactly that time. Promptly at a quarter past seven, we left the hotel and made our way to the car.

prone /prəʊn/. ADJ AFTER LINK-V If someone or something is **prone to** something, usually something bad, they have a tendency to be affected by it or to do it. We know males are more prone to violence. ♦ **-prone** ...the most injury-prone rider on the circuit.

pronoun /ˈprəʊnaʊn/ **pronouns.** N-COUNT A **pronoun** is a word which is used instead of a noun group to refer to someone or something. 'He', 'she', 'them', and 'something' are pronouns.

pronounce /prəˈnaʊns/ **pronounces, pronouncing, pronounced.** [1] VERB To **pronounce** a word means to say it. *He pronounced it Per-sha, the way the English do.* [2] VERB If you **pronounce** something, you state it formally or publicly. [FORMAL] *The authorities took time to pronounce their verdicts.*

pronounced /prəˈnaʊnst/. ADJ Something that is **pronounced** is very noticeable. *Most of the art exhibitions have a pronounced Scottish theme.*

pronouncement /prəˈnaʊnsmənt/ **pronouncements.** N-COUNT **Pronouncements** are public or official statements on an important subject. ...*the President's pronouncements.*

pronunciation /prəˌnʌnsiˈeɪʃən/ **pronunciations.** N-VAR The **pronunciation** of words is the way they are pronounced. *You're going to have to forgive my pronunciation.*

★ **proof** /pruːf/ **proofs.** N-VAR **Proof** is a fact or a piece of evidence which shows that something is true or exists. *This is not necessarily proof that he is wrong.*

-proof /-pruːf/ **-proofs, -proofing, -proofed.** [1] **-proof** combines with nouns and verbs to form adjectives which indicate that something cannot be damaged or badly affected by a particular thing or person. ...*a large microwave-proof dish.* [2] **-proof** combines with nouns to form verbs which refer to protecting something against being damaged or badly affected by the thing mentioned. ...*the cost of draught-proofing your home.*

prop /prɒp/ **props, propping, propped.** [1] VERB & PHR-VERB If you **prop** an object **on** or **against** something, or if you **prop** it **up**, you support it by putting something underneath it or by resting it against something. *He propped his feet on the desk... Prop up your back against a wall.* [2] N-COUNT A **prop** is a stick or other object used to support something. [3] N-COUNT The **props** in a play or film are the objects and furniture used in it.

▸**prop up.** [1] PHR-VERB To **prop up** something means to support it or help it to survive. *Investments in the U.S. money market have propped up the American dollar.* [2] See **prop** 1.

propaganda /ˌprɒpəˈɡændə/. N-UNCOUNT **Propaganda** is information, often inaccurate information, which an organization publishes or broadcasts in order to influence people; used showing disapproval. ...*anti-European propaganda.*

propagate /ˈprɒpəɡeɪt/ **propagates, propagating, propagated.** VERB If people **propagate** an idea or a piece of information, they spread it and try to make people believe it or support it. [FORMAL] ♦ **propagation** N-UNCOUNT ...*the propagation of true Buddhism.*

propel /prəˈpel/ **propels, propelling, propelled.** [1] VERB To **propel** something in a certain direction means to cause it to move in that direction. *Rebecca took Steve's elbow and propelled him towards the staircase.* [2] VERB If something **propels** you into a particular activity, it causes you to be involved in it. *University fees was the issue which propelled her into politics.*

propeller /prəˈpelə/ **propellers.** N-COUNT A **propeller** on a boat or aircraft is a device with blades which is turned by the engine, causing the boat or aircraft to move.

propensity /prəˈpensɪti/ **propensities.** N-COUNT If someone has a **propensity to** do something or a **propensity for** something, they tend to behave in a particular way. [FORMAL] *Mr Bint has a propensity to put off decisions.*

★ **proper** /ˈprɒpə/. [1] ADJ BEFORE N You use **proper** to describe things that you consider to be real or satisfactory. *Two out of five people lack a proper job.* ♦ **properly** ADV *You're too thin. You're not eating properly.* [2] ADJ BEFORE N The **proper** thing is the one that is correct or most suitable. *The proper procedures have been followed.* [3] ADJ If you say that a way of behaving is **proper**, you mean that it is considered socially acceptable and right. *It was not thought entirely proper for a woman to be on the stage.* ♦ **properly** ADV *It's about time he learnt to behave properly.*

ˈproper ˌnoun, proper nouns. N-COUNT In grammar, a **proper noun** is a noun which refers to a particular person, place, or institution. Proper nouns begin with a capital letter.

★ **property** /ˈprɒpəti/ **properties.** [1] N-UNCOUNT Someone's **property** consists of all the things that belong to them, or something that belongs to them. [FORMAL] ...*stolen property.* [2] N-COUNT A **property** is a building and the land belonging to it. [FORMAL] [3] N-COUNT The **properties** of a substance or object are the ways in which it behaves in particular conditions. [TECHNICAL] *A radio signal has both electrical and magnetic properties.*

prophecy /ˈprɒfɪsi/ **prophecies.** N-VAR A **prophecy** is a statement in which someone says they strongly believe that something will happen.

prophesy /ˈprɒfɪsaɪ/ **prophesies, prophesying, prophesied.** VERB If you **prophesy** something, you say that you strongly believe that it will happen. *She prophesied a bad ending for the expedition.*

prophet /ˈprɒfɪt/ **prophets.** N-COUNT A **prophet** is a person believed to be chosen by God to say the things that God wants to tell people.

prophetic /prəˈfetɪk/. ADJ If something was **prophetic**, it described or suggested something that did actually happen later. *This ominous warning soon proved prophetic.*

proponent /prəˈpəʊnənt/ **proponents.** N-COUNT A **proponent of** a particular idea or course of action actively supports it. [FORMAL] *He's a hard-line proponent of law and order.*

a
b
c
d
e
f
g
h
i
j
k
l
m
n
o
p
q
r
s
t
u
v
w
x
y
z

proportion /prə'pɔːʃən/ **proportions. 1** N-COUNT
A **proportion of** an amount or group is a part of
it. [FORMAL] *A large proportion of the dolphins in
that area will eventually die.* **2** N-COUNT The
proportion of one kind of person or thing in a
group is the number of people or things of that
kind compared to the total number in the group.
*The proportion of women in the profession had
risen to 17.3%.* **3** N-PLURAL If you refer to the
proportions of something, you are referring to
its size, usually when this is extremely large.
[WRITTEN] *In the tropics plants grow to huge
proportions.*
PHRASES ● If one thing increases or decreases **in
proportion to** another thing, it increases or
decreases to the same degree as that thing. *The
pressure in the cylinders would go up in proportion
to the boiler pressure.* ● If something is small or
large **in proportion to** something else, it is small
or large when you compare it with that thing.
*Children tend to have relatively larger heads than
adults in proportion to the rest of their body.* ● If
you get something **out of proportion**, you think
it is more important or worrying than it really is. If
you keep something **in proportion**, you have a
realistic view of how important it is.

proportional /prə'pɔːʃənəl/. ADJ If one
amount is **proportional** to another, the two
amounts increase and decrease at the same rate
so there is always the same relationship between
them. *Loss of weight is directly proportional to the
rate at which the disease is progressing.*

proportionate /prə'pɔːʃənət/. ADJ
Proportionate means the same as **proportional**.
♦ **proportionately** ADV *Proportionately more
Americans get married nowadays than before.*

proposal /prə'pəuzəl/ **proposals. 1** N-COUNT A
proposal is a suggestion or plan, often a formal
or written one. *...the government's proposals to
abolish free health care.* **2** N-COUNT A **proposal** is
the act of asking someone to marry you.

propose /prə'pəuz/ **proposes, proposing, proposed.**
1 VERB If you **propose** a plan or idea, you
suggest it. *Britain is about to propose changes to
European Community institutions.* **2** VERB If you
propose to do something, you intend to do it.
*It's still far from clear what action the government
proposes to take... And where do you propose
building such a huge thing?* **3** VERB If you
propose to someone, you ask them to marry
you.

proposition /ˌprɒpə'zɪʃən/ **propositions.**
1 N-COUNT If you describe something such as a
task or an activity as, for example, a difficult
proposition or an attractive **proposition**, you
mean that it is difficult or pleasant to do. *Making
easy money has always been an attractive
proposition.* **2** N-COUNT A **proposition** is a
statement or an idea which people can consider
or discuss to decide whether it is true. [FORMAL]
3 N-COUNT A **proposition** is an offer or
suggestion. *You came to see me at my office the
other day with a business proposition.*

proprietary /prə'praɪətri, AM -teri/. ADJ BEFORE
N **Proprietary** substances are ones sold under a
trade name. [FORMAL] *...some proprietary brands of
dog food.*

proprietor /prə'praɪətə/ **proprietors.** N-COUNT The
proprietor of a hotel, shop, newspaper, or other
business is the person who owns it.

prosaic /prəu'zeɪɪk/. ADJ Something that is
prosaic is dull and lacks interest. *The truth is more
prosaic.*

prose /prəuz/. N-UNCOUNT **Prose** is ordinary
written language, in contrast to poetry. *He writes
in prose.*

prosecute /'prɒsɪkjuːt/ **prosecutes, prosecuting,
prosecuted.** VERB If someone **is prosecuted**, they
are charged with a crime and put on trial. *The
police have decided not to prosecute.*
♦ **prosecution, prosecutions** N-VAR *The head of
government called for the prosecution of those
responsible.*

prosecution /ˌprɒsɪ'kjuːʃən/. N-SING The
lawyers who try to prove that a person on trial is
guilty are called **the prosecution**. *Colonel Pugh,
for the prosecution, said that the offences occurred
over a six-year period.*

prosecutor /'prɒsɪkjuːtə/ **prosecutors.** N-COUNT In
some countries, a **prosecutor** is a lawyer or
official who brings charges against alleged
criminals or tries to prove in a trial that they are
guilty.

prospect, prospects, prospecting, prospected.
1 N-VAR /'prɒspekt/ A **prospect** is a possibility or
a possible event. *There is little prospect of seeing
these big questions answered... They now face the
prospect of having to wear a cycling helmet by law.*
2 N-PLURAL Someone's **prospects** are their
chances of being successful. *I chose to work
abroad to improve my career prospects.* **3** VERB
/prə'spekt, AM 'prɑːspekt/ To **prospect for** a
substance such as oil or gold means to look for it
in the ground or under the sea. *He had
prospected for minerals everywhere.*

prospective /prə'spektɪv, AM prɑː-/. ADJ
BEFORE N You use **prospective** to describe a
person who wants to be the thing mentioned or
is likely to be the thing mentioned. *The story
should act as a warning to other prospective
buyers.*

prospectus /prə'spektəs, AM prɑː-/ **prospectuses.**
N-COUNT A **prospectus** is a document produced
by a college, school, or company which gives
details about it.

prosper /'prɒspə/ **prospers, prospering, prospered.**
VERB If people or businesses **prosper**, they are
financially successful.

prosperity /prɒ'sperɪti/. N-UNCOUNT **Prosperity**
is a condition in which a person or community is
being financially successful. *...a new era of peace
and prosperity.*

prosperous /'prɒspərəs/. ADJ **Prosperous**
people or places are rich and successful.

prostitute /'prɒstɪtjuːt, AM -tuːt/ **prostitutes.**
N-COUNT A **prostitute** is a person, usually a woman, who has sex with men in exchange for money.

prostitution /ˌprɒstɪ'tjuːʃən, AM -'tuː-/.
N-UNCOUNT **Prostitution** involves having sex in exchange for money.

protagonist /prə'tægənɪst, AM prəʊ-/
protagonists. [1] N-COUNT A **protagonist** in a play, novel, or real event is one of the main people in it. [FORMAL] ...*the main protagonists in the row are Visa and Mastercard.* [2] N-COUNT A **protagonist of** an idea or movement is a supporter of it.

⭐ **protect** /prə'tekt/ **protects, protecting, protected.**
VERB To **protect** someone or something means to prevent them from being harmed or damaged. *What can women do to protect themselves from heart disease?... The government is committed to protecting the interests of tenants.* ♦ **protector, protectors** N-COUNT *The best protector of women in childbirth is a trained midwife.*

⭐ **protection** /prə'tekʃən/. N-UNCOUNT If something gives **protection against** something unpleasant, it prevents people or things from being harmed or damaged by it. *Such a diet is widely believed to offer protection against a number of cancers.*

protective /prə'tektɪv/. [1] ADJ **Protective** means designed or intended to protect something or someone from harm. *She had to wear protective gloves.* [2] ADJ If someone is **protective** towards you, they show a strong desire to keep you safe. *Glynis was beside her, putting a protective arm around her shoulders.*

protégé /'prɒtɪʒeɪ, AM 'prəʊt-/ **protégés.**

✔ The spelling **protégée** is also used when referring to a woman.

N-COUNT The **protégé** of an older and more experienced person is a young person who is helped and guided by them over a period of time.

⭐ **protein** /'prəʊtiːn/ **proteins.** N-VAR **Protein** is a substance which the body needs and which is found in meat, eggs, and milk. ...*a high protein diet.*

⭐ **protest, protests, protesting, protested.** [1] VERB /prə'test/ To **protest** means to say or show publicly that you object to something. In British English, you **protest about** something or **against** something. In American English, you **protest** something. *Groups of women took to the streets to protest against the arrests... They were protesting soaring prices.* ♦ **protester, protesters** N-COUNT ...*anti-abortion protesters.* [2] VERB If you **protest** that something is the case, you insist that it is the case, when other people think that it may not be. *She protested that she was a patriot, not a collaborator... 'I never said any of that to her,' he protested... He has always protested his innocence.* [3] N-VAR /'prəʊtest/ A **protest** is the act of saying or showing publicly that you do not approve of something. ...*a protest against the company's tests*

on live animals... Councillors walked out of the meeting in protest.

Protestant /'prɒtɪstənt/ **Protestants.** N-COUNT A **Protestant** is someone who belongs to the branch of the Christian church which separated from the Catholic church in the sixteenth century.

protocol /'prəʊtəkɒl, AM -kɔːl/ **protocols.** N-VAR **Protocol** is a system of rules or agreements about the correct way to act in formal situations. ...*minor breaches of protocol.*

prototype /'prəʊtətaɪp/ **prototypes.** N-COUNT A **prototype** is the first model or example of a new type of thing. *Dave set about obtaining a patent for his invention and building a prototype.*

protracted /prə'træktɪd, AM prəʊ-/. ADJ Something that is **protracted** lasts longer than usual or longer than you had hoped. *After protracted negotiations Ogden got the deal he wanted.*

protrude /prə'truːd, AM prəʊ-/ **protrudes, protruding, protruded.** VERB If something **protrudes from** somewhere, it sticks out. [FORMAL] ...*a huge round mass of smooth rock protruding from the water.*

⭐ **proud** /praʊd/ **prouder, proudest.** [1] ADJ If you feel **proud**, you feel pleasure and satisfaction at something that you own, have done, or are connected with. *I felt proud of his efforts... They are proud that she is doing well at school. ...the proud father of a 5-month-old baby son.* ♦ **proudly** ADV *'That's the first part finished,' he said proudly.* [2] ADJ Someone who is **proud** has a lot of dignity and self-respect. *He was too proud to ask his family for help.* [3] ADJ Someone who is **proud** feels that they are better or more important than other people.

⭐ **prove** /pruːv/ **proves, proving, proved** or **proven.** [1] LINK-VERB If something **proves to** be true or to have a particular quality, it becomes clear after a period of time that it is true or has that quality. *Our reports proved to be true... This process of transition has often proven difficult. ...an experiment which was to prove a source of inspiration.* [2] VERB If you **prove** that something is true, you show by means of argument or evidence that it is definitely true. *Professor Cantor set out to prove his theory. ...trying to prove how groups of animals have evolved... That made me determined to prove him wrong.* [3] VERB If you **prove yourself**, you show by your actions that you have a certain good quality. *I have to prove myself as a respectable, balanced person.*

proverb /'prɒvɜːb/ **proverbs.** N-COUNT A **proverb** is a short sentence that people often quote, which gives advice or tells you something about life.

proverbial /prə'vɜːbiəl/. ADJ BEFORE N You use **proverbial** to show that you know the way you are describing something is one that is often used or is part of a popular saying. *My audience certainly isn't the proverbial man in the street.*

provide /prə'vaɪd/ **provides, providing, provided.** ① VERB If you **provide** something that someone needs or wants, you give it to them or make it available to them. *They would not provide any details... The government was not in a position to provide them with food.* ② VERB If a law or agreement **provides** that something will happen, it states that it will happen. [FORMAL] *The treaty provides that, by the end of the century, the United States must have removed its bases.*

▸**provide for.** ① PHR-VERB If you **provide for** someone, you support them financially and make sure that they have the things that they need. *Elaine wouldn't let him provide for her... Her father always ensured she was well provided for.* ② PHR-VERB If you **provide for** something that might happen or that might need to be done, you make arrangements to deal with it. [FORMAL] *James had provided for just such an emergency.*

provided /prə'vaɪdɪd/. CONJ If something will happen **provided** or **providing** that something else happens, the first thing will happen only if the second thing also happens. *Provided they are fit I see no reason why they shouldn't go on playing.*

providence /'prɒvɪdəns/. N-UNCOUNT **Providence** is God, or a force which is believed to arrange the things that happen to us. [LITERARY]

providing /prə'vaɪdɪŋ/. See **provided.**

⭐ **province** /'prɒvɪns/ **provinces.** ① N-COUNT A **province** is a large section of a country which has its own administration. ② N-PLURAL The **provinces** are all the parts of a country except the part where the capital is situated. *The government plans to transfer some 30,000 government jobs from Paris to the provinces.*

provincial /prə'vɪnʃəl/. ① ADJ BEFORE N **Provincial** means connected with the parts of a country outside the capital. *...provincial towns.* ② ADJ If you describe someone or something as **provincial**, you disapprove of them because you think that they are not sophisticated. *The audience was dull and very provincial.*

⭐ **provision** /prə'vɪʒən/ **provisions.** ① N-UNCOUNT The **provision** of something is the act of giving it or making it available to people who need or want it. *The department is responsible for the provision of residential care services.* ② N-UNCOUNT If you make **provision for** a future need, you make arrangements to ensure that it is dealt with. *Mr King asked if it had ever occurred to her to make provision for her own pension.* ③ N-COUNT A **provision** in an agreement or law is an arrangement included in it. ④ N-PLURAL **Provisions** are supplies of food.

provisional /prə'vɪʒənəl/. ADJ You use **provisional** to describe something that has been arranged or appointed for the present, but may be changed soon. *...a provisional coalition government.* ♦ **provisionally** ADV *The European Community has provisionally agreed.*

provocation /,prɒvə'keɪʃən/ **provocations.** N-VAR **Provocation** is a deliberate attempt to make someone react angrily. *The soldiers fired without provocation.*

provocative /prə'vɒkətɪv/. ① ADJ Something that is **provocative** is intended to make people react angrily. *...outspoken and sometimes provocative speeches.* ② ADJ **Provocative** behaviour or dress is intended to make someone feel sexual desire.

⭐ **provoke** /prə'vəʊk/ **provokes, provoking, provoked.** ① VERB If you **provoke** someone, you deliberately annoy them and try to make them behave aggressively. *I provoked him into doing something really stupid.* ② VERB If something **provokes** a violent or unpleasant reaction, it causes it. *The destruction of the mosque has provoked anger throughout the Muslim world.*

prowess /'praʊɪs/. N-UNCOUNT Someone's **prowess** is their great ability at doing a particular thing. [FORMAL] *...his prowess as a cricketer.*

prowl /praʊl/ **prowls, prowling, prowled.** VERB When animals or people **prowl around**, they move around quietly, for example when they are hunting. *He prowled around the room, not sure what he was looking for.*

proximity /prɒk'sɪmɪti/. N-UNCOUNT **Proximity to** a place or person is the fact of being near to them. [FORMAL] *Families are no longer in close proximity to each other.*

proxy /'prɒksi/ **proxies.** N-VAR A **proxy** is a person or thing that is acting or being used in the place of someone or something else. If you do something **by proxy**, you arrange for someone else to do it for you. *Those not attending the meeting may vote by proxy.*

prude /pru:d/ **prudes.** N-COUNT If you call someone a **prude**, you disapprove of them because you think that they are too easily shocked and embarrassed by nudity or sex.

prudent /'pru:dənt/. ADJ Someone who is **prudent** is sensible and careful. *It is always prudent to start any exercise programme gradually.* ♦ **prudently** ADV *Prudently, Joanna spoke none of this aloud.* ♦ **prudence** N-UNCOUNT *A lack of prudence may lead to financial problems.*

prune /pru:n/ **prunes, pruning, pruned.** ① N-COUNT A **prune** is a dried plum. ② VERB When you **prune** a tree or bush, you cut off some of the branches so that it will grow better the next year.

pry /praɪ/ **pries, prying, pried.** ① VERB If you say that someone is **prying**, you disapprove of them because they are trying to find out about someone else's private affairs. *We do not want people prying into our affairs.* ② VERB If you **pry** something **open** or **pry** it away from a surface, you force it open or away from a surface. *She pried open his jaws... I pried the top off a can of chilli.*

PS /,pi: 'es/. You write **PS** before a comment you add at the end of a letter, after you have signed it. *PS. Please show your friends this letter.*

pseudonym /'sjuːdənɪm, AM 'suː-/ **pseudonyms.**
N-COUNT A **pseudonym** is a name which
someone, usually a writer, uses instead of his or
her real name.

psyche /'saɪki/ **psyches.** N-COUNT Your **psyche** is
your mind and your deepest feelings and
attitudes. ...*disturbing elements of the human
psyche.*

psychedelic /,saɪkə'delɪk/. ADJ **Psychedelic** art
has bright colours and strange patterns.

psychiatry /saɪ'kaɪətri, AM sɪ-/. N-UNCOUNT
Psychiatry is the branch of medicine concerned
with the treatment of mental illness.
♦ **psychiatric** /,saɪki'ætrɪk/ ADJ ...*chronic
psychiatric illnesses.* ♦ **psychiatrist**
/saɪ'kaɪətrɪst, AM sɪ-/ **psychiatrists** N-COUNT A
colleague urged him to see a psychiatrist.

psychic /'saɪkɪk/. [1] N-COUNT & ADJ If you
believe that someone is a **psychic**, or is **psychic**,
you believe that they have strange mental
powers, such as being able to read the minds of
other people or to see into the future. [2] ADJ
Psychic means relating to the mind rather than
the body. [FORMAL] ...*psychic powers.*

psychoanalysis /,saɪkəʊə'nælɪsɪs/. N-UNCOUNT
Psychoanalysis is the treatment of someone
who has mental problems by asking them about
their feelings and their past in order to discover
what may be causing their condition.
♦ **psychoanalyst** /,saɪkəʊ'ænəlɪst/
psychoanalysts N-COUNT *Jane is seeing a
psychoanalyst.*

⭐ **psychological** /,saɪkə'lɒdʒɪkəl/. ADJ
Psychological means concerned with a person's
mind and thoughts. *Robyn's loss of memory is a
psychological problem.* ♦ **psychologically** ADV *It
was very important psychologically for us to
succeed.*

psychology /saɪ'kɒlədʒi/. [1] N-UNCOUNT
Psychology is the scientific study of the human
mind and the reasons for people's behaviour.
♦ **psychological** /,saɪkə'lɒdʒɪkəl/. ADJ
...*psychological testing.* ♦ **psychologist,
psychologists** N-COUNT *She was referred to a
psychologist.* [2] N-UNCOUNT The **psychology of** a
person is the kind of mind that they have, which
makes them think or behave in the way that they
do. ...*the psychology of murderers.*

psychopath /'saɪkəʊpæθ/ **psychopaths.** N-COUNT
A **psychopath** is someone who has serious
mental problems and who may act in a violent
way without feeling sorry for what they have
done.

psychosis /saɪ'kəʊsɪs/ **psychoses.** N-VAR
Psychosis is severe mental illness which can
make people lose contact with reality. [MEDICAL]

psychotherapy /,saɪkəʊ'θerəpi/. N-UNCOUNT
Psychotherapy is the use of psychological
methods to treat people who are mentally ill.
♦ **psychotherapist, psychotherapists** N-COUNT *He
arranged for him to see a psychotherapist.*

psychotic /saɪ'kɒtɪk/. N-COUNT & ADJ A
psychotic or someone who is **psychotic** has a
severe mental illness which has made them lose
contact with reality. [MEDICAL]

⭐ **pub** /pʌb/ **pubs.** N-COUNT In Britain, a **pub** is a
building where people can buy and drink
alcoholic drinks. ● See note at **café**.

puberty /'pjuːbəti/. N-UNCOUNT **Puberty** is the
stage in someone's life when their body starts to
become physically mature.

⭐ **public** /'pʌblɪk/.

> ✅ In meaning 1, **public** can take the singular
> or plural form of the verb.

[1] N-SING You can refer to people in general as
the public. *The public is certainly getting tired of
hearing about it... The public have flocked to the
show.* [2] ADJ BEFORE N **Public** means relating to all
the people in a country or community. *The
Turkish government is under pressure from public
opinion.* [3] ADJ BEFORE N **Public** statements,
actions, and events are made or done in such a
way that everyone can see them or be aware of
them. ...*the ministry's first detailed public
statement on the subject... Marilyn made her last
public appearance at Madison Square Garden.*
♦ **publicly** ADV *He never spoke publicly about the
affair.* [4] ADJ BEFORE N A **public** figure or a person
in **public** life is known about by many people
because they serve the public in their job. *Mr
Mandela is by far the most popular public figure in
South Africa.* [5] ADJ AFTER LINK-V If a fact is **made
public** or **becomes public**, it becomes known to
everyone rather than being kept secret. [6] ADJ
BEFORE N **Public** means relating to the
government or state, or things that are done by
the state for the people. *The social services
account for a substantial part of public spending.*
[7] ADJ BEFORE N **Public** things and places are
provided for everyone to use, or are open to
anyone. ...*the New York Public Library.* ...*public
transport.* ...*public areas of international airports.*
PHRASES ● If someone is in **the public eye**,
many people know who they are, because they
are famous or because they are often mentioned
on television or in the newspapers. *He has kept
his wife and daughter out of the public eye.* ● If
you say or do something **in public**, you say or do
it when a group of other people are present. *By-
laws are to make it illegal to smoke in public.*

⭐ **publication** /,pʌblɪ'keɪʃən/ **publications.**
[1] N-UNCOUNT The **publication** of a book or
magazine is the act of printing it and making it
available. *The final volume is due for publication in
October.* [2] N-COUNT A **publication** is a book,
magazine, or article that has been published.

publicist /'pʌblɪsɪst/ **publicists.** N-COUNT A
publicist is a person who publicizes things,
especially as part of a job in advertising or
journalism.

⭐ **publicity** /pʌ'blɪsɪti/. [1] N-UNCOUNT **Publicity** is
advertising, information, or actions intended to
attract the public's attention to someone or

something. *The publicity blitz uses stickers with bright red lettering.* [2] N-UNCOUNT When newspapers and television pay a lot of attention to something, you can say that it is receiving **publicity**. *Football now seems to be getting massive publicity.*

publicize (BRIT also **publicise**) /'pʌblɪsaɪz/ **publicizes, publicizing, publicized.** VERB If you **publicize** a fact or event, you make it widely known to the public. *The author appeared on television to publicize her latest book.*

ˌpublic reˈlations. [1] N-UNCOUNT **Public relations** is the part of an organization's work that is concerned with obtaining the public's approval for what it does. The abbreviation **PR** is also used. *The chairman's statement is merely a public relations exercise.* [2] N-PLURAL **Public relations** are the state of the relationship between an organization and the public. *His behaviour was not good for public relations.*

ˌpublic ˈschool, public schools. [1] N-VAR In Britain, a **public school** is a private school that provides secondary education which parents have to pay for. [2] N-VAR In the USA, Australia, and some other countries, a **public school** is a school that is supported financially by the government and usually provides free education.

ˌpublic ˈsector. N-SING The **public sector** is the part of a country's economy which is controlled or supported financially by the government.

⭐ **publish** /'pʌblɪʃ/ **publishes, publishing, published.** [1] VERB When a company **publishes** a book or magazine, it prints copies of it, which are sent to shops and sold. [2] VERB When the people in charge of a newspaper or magazine **publish** a piece of writing or a photograph, they print it in their newspaper or magazine. *The magazine published an article satirising the government.* [3] VERB If someone **publishes** a book or an article that they have written, they arrange to have it published. *He has published two collections of poetry.*

⭐ **publisher** /'pʌblɪʃə/ **publishers.** N-COUNT A **publisher** is a person or company that publishes books, newspapers, or magazines.

⭐ **publishing** /'pʌblɪʃɪŋ/. N-UNCOUNT **Publishing** is the business of publishing books.

ˈpublishing house, publishing houses. N-COUNT A **publishing house** is a company which publishes books.

pudding /'pʊdɪŋ/ **puddings.** [1] N-VAR A **pudding** is a cooked sweet food made with flour, fat, and eggs, and usually served hot. [2] N-UNCOUNT Some people refer to the sweet course of a meal as the **pudding**. [BRITISH] *What's for pudding?*

puddle /'pʌdəl/ **puddles.** N-COUNT A **puddle** is a small shallow pool of rain or other liquid on the ground.

puff /pʌf/ **puffs, puffing, puffed.** [1] VERB & N-COUNT If someone **puffs on** or **at** a cigarette, cigar, or pipe, or if they take a **puff** of it, they smoke it. *He nodded and puffed on a stubby pipe as he*

listened... *She was taking quick puffs at her cigarette.* [2] VERB If you **are puffing**, you are breathing loudly and quickly with your mouth open because you are out of breath after a lot of physical effort. [3] N-COUNT A **puff of** air or smoke is a small amount of it that is blown out from somewhere.

⭐ **pull** /pʊl/ **pulls, pulling, pulled.** [1] VERB & N-COUNT When you **pull** something, you hold it firmly and move it towards you or away from its previous position. A **pull** is an instance of pulling. *I helped pull him out of the water... Pull as hard as you can... The feather must be removed with a straight, firm pull.* [2] VERB When a vehicle, animal, or person **pulls** a cart or piece of machinery, they are attached to it or hold it, so that it moves along behind them when they move forward. ...*a freight train pulling wagons.* [3] VERB If you **pull** a part of your body in a particular direction, you move it with effort or force in that direction. *He pulled his arms out of the sleeves... She tried to pull her hand free.* [4] VERB If you **pull** a muscle, you injure it by straining it. [5] N-COUNT A **pull** is a strong physical force which causes things to move in a particular direction. ...*the pull of gravity.*

▸ **pull away.** [1] PHR-VERB When a vehicle or driver **pulls away**, the vehicle starts moving forward. [2] PHR-VERB If you **pull away from** someone that you have had close links with, you deliberately become less close to them. *The Soviet Union began pulling away from Cuba.*

▸ **pull back.** PHR-VERB If someone **pulls back from** an action, they decide not to continue or persist with it, because it could have bad consequences. *They will plead with him to pull back from confrontation.*

▸ **pull down.** PHR-VERB To **pull down** a building or statue means to deliberately destroy it.

▸ **pull in.** PHR-VERB When a vehicle or driver **pulls in** somewhere, the vehicle stops there. *He pulled in at the side of the road.*

▸ **pull into.** PHR-VERB When a vehicle or driver **pulls into** a road or driveway, the vehicle makes a turn into the road or driveway and stops there.

▸ **pull off.** PHR-VERB If you **pull off** something very difficult, you manage to achieve it successfully. *It will be a very, very fine piece of mountaineering if they pull it off.*

▸ **pull out.** [1] PHR-VERB When a vehicle or driver **pulls out**, the vehicle moves out into the road or nearer the centre of the road. *She pulled out into the street.* [2] PHR-VERB If you **pull out of** an agreement, a contest, or an organization, you withdraw from it. [3] PHR-VERB If troops **pull out** of a place, they leave it.

▸ **pull over.** PHR-VERB When a vehicle or driver **pulls over**, the vehicle moves closer to the side of the road and stops there.

▸ **pull through.** PHR-VERB If someone with a serious illness or in a very difficult situation **pulls through**, they recover.

▸ **pull together.** [1] PHR-VERB If people **pull together**, they co-operate with each other. *The* *nation was urged to pull together to avoid a slide into complete chaos.* **2** PHR-VERB If you are upset or depressed and someone tells you to **pull yourself together**, they are telling you in a rather unsympathetic way to control your feelings and behave calmly.

▶**pull up.** PHR-VERB When a vehicle or driver **pulls up**, the vehicle slows down and stops.

pullover /ˈpʊləʊvə/ **pullovers.** N-COUNT A **pullover** is a woollen piece of clothing that covers the upper part of your body and your arms. [BRITISH] → See picture on page 819.

pulp /pʌlp/. **1** N-SING If an object is pressed into a **pulp**, it is crushed or beaten until it is soft, smooth, and wet. **2** N-SING In fruit and vegetables, **the pulp** is the soft inner part.

pulpit /ˈpʊlpɪt/ **pulpits.** N-COUNT A **pulpit** is a small raised platform in a church with a rail around it, where a member of the clergy stands to preach.

pulsate /pʌlˈseɪt, AM ˈpʌlseɪt/ **pulsates, pulsating, pulsated.** VERB If something **pulsates**, it moves in and out or shakes with strong regular movements. *...a pulsating blood vessel.*

pulse /pʌls/ **pulses.** **1** N-COUNT Your **pulse** is the regular beating of blood through your body, which you can feel, for example, at your wrist or neck. *Mahoney's pulse was racing, and he felt confused.* **2** PHRASE When someone **takes** your **pulse** or **feels** your **pulse**, they find out the speed of your heartbeat by feeling the pulse in your wrist. **3** N-COUNT A **pulse** of electrical current, light, or sound is a sharp temporary increase in its level. **4** N-PLURAL Some large dried seeds which can be cooked and eaten are called **pulses**, for example the seeds of peas, beans, and lentils.

⭐ **pump** /pʌmp/ **pumps, pumping, pumped.** **1** N-COUNT A **pump** is a machine that is used to force a liquid or gas to flow in strong regular movements in a particular direction. *...a petrol pump.* **2** VERB To **pump** a liquid or gas in a certain direction means to force it to flow in that direction, using a pump. *Pumping out the air is a laborious process.* **3** N-COUNT A **pump** is a device for bringing water to the surface from below the ground. **4** VERB To **pump** water, oil, or gas means to get a supply of it from below the surface of the ground, using a pump. *The Russians have pumped huge amounts of oil... The water will be pumped up from chalk pits.* **5** N-COUNT A **pump** is a device that you use to force air into something, for example a tyre. *...a bicycle pump.* **6** VERB If someone has their stomach **pumped**, doctors remove the contents of their stomach. **7** VERB If you **pump** money **into** a project or an industry, you invest a lot of money in it. [INFORMAL] **8** N-COUNT **Pumps** are canvas shoes with flat rubber soles which people wear for sports and leisure. *There was a pair of pumps by the bed.*

▶**pump out.** PHR-VERB To **pump out** something means to produce or supply it continually and in

large amounts. *Japanese companies have been pumping out plenty of innovative products.*

▶**pump up.** PHR-VERB If you **pump up** something such as a tyre, you fill it with air, using a pump.

pumpkin /ˈpʌmpkɪn/ **pumpkins.** N-VAR A **pumpkin** is a large, round, orange-coloured vegetable with a thick skin.

pun /pʌn/ **puns.** N-COUNT A **pun** is a clever and amusing use of a word with more than one meaning, or a word that sounds like another word, so that what you say has two different meanings.

⭐ **punch** /pʌntʃ/ **punches, punching, punched.** **1** VERB & N-COUNT If you **punch** someone or something, or if you throw a **punch** at them, you hit them hard with your fist. *If anyone tried to stop me I'd punch him on the nose.* **2** VERB If you **punch** something such as the buttons on a keyboard, you touch them in order to store information on a machine such as a computer or to give the machine a command to do something. **3** VERB If you **punch holes** in something, you make holes in it by pushing or pressing it with something sharp. **4** N-COUNT A **punch** is a tool used for making holes in something. **5** PHRASE If you say that someone does not **pull** their **punches** when they are criticizing someone or something, you mean that they say exactly what they think and do not moderate their criticism. **6** N-VAR **Punch** is a drink usually made from wine or spirits mixed with sugar, fruit, and spices.

▶**punch in.** PHR-VERB If you **punch in** a number on a machine or **punch** numbers **into** it, you push the machine's numerical keys in order to give it a command to do something. *All you need to do is punch in a short code.*

punctual /ˈpʌŋktʃʊəl/. ADJ Someone who is **punctual** arrives somewhere or does something at the right time and is not late. *He's always very punctual.* ♦ **punctually** ADV *My guest arrived punctually.*

punctuate /ˈpʌŋktʃʊeɪt/ **punctuates, punctuating, punctuated.** VERB If an activity or situation **is punctuated** by particular things, it is interrupted by them at intervals. [FORMAL] *The silence of the night was punctuated by the distant rumble of traffic.*

punctuation /ˌpʌŋktʃʊˈeɪʃən/. N-UNCOUNT **Punctuation** is the system of signs such as full stops, commas, and question marks that you use in writing to divide words into sentences and clauses. → See Reference Page on Punctuation.

punctu'ation mark, punctuation marks. N-COUNT A **punctuation mark** is a sign such as a full stop, comma, or question mark.

puncture /ˈpʌŋktʃə/ **punctures, puncturing, punctured.** **1** N-COUNT A **puncture** is a small hole in a car or bicycle tyre that has been made by a sharp object. **2** VERB If a sharp object **punctures** something, it makes a hole in it. *A bullet punctured one of the front tyres.*

a
b
c
d
e
f
g
h
i
j
k
l
m
n
o
p
q
r
s
t
u
v
w
x
y
z

pundit /ˈpʌndɪt/ **pundits.** N-COUNT A **pundit** is a person who knows a lot about a subject and is often asked to give information or their opinion about it to the public.

pungent /ˈpʌndʒənt/. ADJ Something that is **pungent** has a strong bitter smell or taste. ...the pungent smell of smoked fish.

punish /ˈpʌnɪʃ/ **punishes, punishing, punished.** ☐ VERB To **punish** someone means to make them suffer in some way because they have done something wrong. I don't believe that George ever had to punish the children. ☐ VERB To **punish** a crime means to punish anyone who commits that crime. Such behaviour is unacceptable and will be punished.

punishing /ˈpʌnɪʃɪŋ/. ADJ A **punishing** schedule, activity, or experience requires a lot of physical effort and makes you very tired or weak.

punishment /ˈpʌnɪʃmənt/ **punishments.** ☐ N-UNCOUNT **Punishment** is the act of punishing someone or being punished. The man is guilty and he deserves punishment. ☐ N-VAR A **punishment** is a particular way of punishing someone. The usual punishment is a fine. ☐ See also **capital punishment, corporal punishment.**

punitive /ˈpjuːnɪtɪv/. ADJ **Punitive** actions are intended to punish people. [FORMAL] ...punitive measures such as curfews and fines.

punk /pʌŋk/ **punks.** ☐ N-UNCOUNT **Punk** or **punk rock** is rock music that is played in a fast, loud, and aggressive way. Punk rock was particularly popular in the late 1970s. ☐ N-COUNT A **punk** or a **punk rocker** is a person who likes punk music and dresses in a very noticeable and unconventional way. ☐ N-COUNT A **punk** is a young person who behaves in an unruly, aggressive, or anti-social manner. [AMERICAN, INFORMAL]

punter /ˈpʌntə/ **punters.** ☐ N-COUNT A **punter** is a person who bets money. [BRITISH, INFORMAL] ☐ N-COUNT People sometimes refer to their customers or clients as **punters.** [BRITISH, INFORMAL]

pup /pʌp/ **pups.** N-COUNT A **pup** is a young dog. The young of some other animals, for example seals, are called **pups.**

☆ **pupil** /ˈpjuːpɪl/ **pupils.** ☐ N-COUNT The **pupils** of a school are the children who go to it. ☐ N-COUNT A **pupil** of a painter, musician, or other expert is someone who studies with that expert, learning his or her skills. ☐ N-COUNT The **pupils** of your eyes are the small, round, black holes in the centre of them. → See picture on page 823.

puppet /ˈpʌpɪt/ **puppets.** ☐ N-COUNT A **puppet** is a doll that you can move, either by pulling strings which are attached to it, or by putting your hand inside its body and moving your fingers. ☐ N-COUNT You can refer to a person or country as a **puppet** when you mean their actions are controlled by a more powerful person or government, even though they may appear to be independent. ...a puppet government.

puppy /ˈpʌpi/ **puppies.** N-COUNT A **puppy** is a young dog.

☆ **purchase** /ˈpɜːtʃɪs/ **purchases, purchasing, purchased.** ☐ VERB When you **purchase** something, you buy it. [FORMAL] ♦ **purchaser, purchasers** N-COUNT The group is the second largest purchaser of fresh fruit in the US. ☐ N-UNCOUNT The **purchase of** something is the act of buying it. [FORMAL] This week he is to visit China to discuss the purchase of military supplies. ☐ N-COUNT A **purchase** is something that you buy. [FORMAL] She opened the box and looked at her purchase.

☆ **pure** /pjʊə/ **purer, purest.** ☐ ADJ **Pure** means not mixed with anything else. This dress is pure silk... His hair was pure white. ♦ **purity** /ˈpjʊərɪti/ N-UNCOUNT ...their obsession with ideological purity. ☐ ADJ Something that is **pure** is clean and does not contain any harmful substances. ...demands for purer and cleaner river water. ♦ **purity** N-UNCOUNT They worried about the purity of tap water. ☐ ADJ If you describe someone as **pure,** you mean that they are free from things that are considered to be sinful or bad, especially sex. [LITERARY] ♦ **purity** N-UNCOUNT ...sexual purity. ☐ ADJ BEFORE N **Pure** science or **pure** research is concerned only with theory and not with how this theory can be used in practical ways. ...pure maths. ☐ ADJ BEFORE N **Pure** means complete and total. This was pure coincidence. ...a look of pure surprise.

puree /ˈpjʊəreɪ, AM pjʊˈreɪ/ **purees.** N-VAR **Puree** is food which has been mashed, sieved, or blended so that it forms a thick, smooth sauce. ...a can of tomato puree.

purely /ˈpjʊəli/. ADV You use **purely** to emphasize that the thing you are mentioning is the most important feature or that it is the only thing which should be considered. It is a racing machine, designed purely for speed.

purge /pɜːdʒ/ **purges, purging, purged.** ☐ VERB & N-COUNT To **purge** an organization of its unacceptable members, or to make a **purge of** an organization, means to remove its unacceptable members from it. You can also talk about **purging** people **from** an organization. The leadership voted to purge the party of 'hostile elements'... Purges began soon after the election. ☐ VERB If you **purge** something of undesirable things, you get rid of them. He closed his eyes and lay still, trying to purge his mind of anxiety.

purify /ˈpjʊərɪfaɪ/ **purifies, purifying, purified.** VERB To **purify** a substance means to make it pure by removing any harmful, dirty, or inferior substances from it. ♦ **purification** N-UNCOUNT ...a water purification plant.

purist /ˈpjʊərɪst/ **purists.** N-COUNT A **purist** is someone who believes in absolute correctness, especially concerning a particular subject which they know a lot about.

puritan /ˈpjʊərɪtən/ **puritans.** N-COUNT & ADJ You describe someone as a **puritan,** or you describe their behaviour as **puritan,** when they live according to very strict moral or religious principles, especially by avoiding physical pleasures; used showing disapproval.

puritanical /ˌpjʊərɪ'tænɪkəl/. ADJ If you describe someone as **puritanical**, you mean that they disapprove of pleasure, for example because they are strictly religious; used showing disapproval. ...*a puritanical attitude towards sex.*

purity. See **pure.**

⭐ **purple** /'pɜːpəl/. ADJ Something that is **purple** is reddish-blue in colour.

purport /pə'pɔːt/ **purports, purporting, purported.** VERB If someone or something **purports to** do or be a particular thing, they claim to do or be that thing. [FORMAL] ...*a book that purports to tell the whole truth.*

⭐ **purpose** /'pɜːpəs/ **purposes.** 1 N-COUNT The **purpose** of something is the reason for which it is made or done. *What is the purpose of your visit?* ...*the use of nuclear energy for military purposes.* 2 N-COUNT Your **purpose** is the thing that you want to achieve. *I don't know exactly what their purpose is.* 3 N-UNCOUNT **Purpose** is the feeling of having a definite aim and of being determined to achieve it. *The teachers have a sense of purpose.* PHRASES ● You use **for all practical purposes** or **to all intents and purposes** to suggest that a situation is not exactly as you describe it, but the effect is the same as if it were. *To all intents and purposes he was my father.* ● If you do something **on purpose**, you do it deliberately. *Was it an accident or did David really do it on purpose?*

purpose-'built. ADJ A **purpose-built** building has been specially designed and built for a particular use.

purposeful /'pɜːpəsfʊl/. ADJ If someone is **purposeful**, they show that they have a definite aim and a strong desire to achieve it. *She had a purposeful air.* ◆ **purposefully** ADV *He strode purposefully towards the barn.*

purr /pɜː/ **purrs, purring, purred.** 1 VERB When a cat **purrs**, it makes a low vibrating sound with its throat. 2 VERB & N-COUNT When an engine or machine **purrs**, it makes a quiet, continuous, vibrating sound, called a **purr**. *Both boats purred out of the cave mouth and into open water.*

purse /pɜːs/ **purses, pursing, pursed.** 1 N-COUNT In British English, a **purse** is a very small bag that people, especially women, keep their money in. The usual American term is **change purse.** 2 N-COUNT In American English, a **purse** is a small bag that women carry. The usual British word is **handbag.** → See picture on page 48. 3 VERB If you **purse** your **lips**, you move them into a small rounded shape.

⭐ **pursue** /pə'sjuː, -'suː/ **pursues, pursuing, pursued.** 1 VERB If you **pursue** a particular aim or result, you make efforts to achieve it or to progress in it. [FORMAL] *She had come to England to pursue an acting career.* 2 VERB If you **pursue** a particular topic, you try to find out more about it by asking questions. [FORMAL] *If your original request is*

denied, don't be afraid to pursue the matter.* 3 VERB If you **pursue** a person, vehicle, or animal, you follow them, usually in order to catch them. [FORMAL] ◆ **pursuer, pursuers** N-COUNT *He could hear the pursuers getting closer.*

pursuit /pə'sjuːt, AM -'suːt/ **pursuits.** 1 N-UNCOUNT Your **pursuit of** something that you want consists of your attempts at achieving it. ...*the pursuit of happiness... They frequently move around the country in pursuit of a medical career.* 2 N-UNCOUNT If you are **in pursuit of** a person, vehicle, or animal, you are chasing them. [FORMAL] 3 N-COUNT Your **pursuits** are your activities, usually activities that you enjoy when you are not working. *They both love outdoor pursuits.*

purveyor /pə'veɪə/ **purveyors.** N-COUNT The **purveyors of** information, goods, or services are the people who provide them. [FORMAL] ...*the leading purveyors of traditional Irish music.*

⭐ **push** /pʊʃ/ **pushes, pushing, pushed.** 1 VERB When you **push** something, you use force to make it move away from you or away from its previous position. You can also say that you give it a **push.** *The woman pushed back her chair and stood up... He pushed the door open... He gave me a sharp push.* 2 VERB If you **push through** things that are blocking your way or **push** your **way** through them, you use force in order to move past them. *Dix pushed forward carrying a glass... He pushed his way towards him, laughing.* 3 VERB To **push** a value or amount **up** or **down** means to cause it to increase or decrease. *Interest had pushed the loan up to $27,000.* 4 VERB If you **push** someone to do something or **push** them **into** doing it, you urge, encourage, or force them to do it. A **push** is the action of pushing someone to do something. *James did not push her into stealing the money... We need a push to take the first step.* 5 VERB & N-COUNT If you **push for** something, or if you make a **push for** it, you try very hard to achieve it. *Keep pushing for everything that you want. ...a final push to arrive at an agreement.* 6 VERB If someone **pushes** an idea, a point, or a product, they try in a forceful way to convince people to accept it or buy it. ...*taking bribes from big business in return for pushing new projects.* 7 VERB When someone **pushes** drugs, they sell them illegally. [INFORMAL] ◆ **pusher, pushers** N-COUNT ...*drug pushers.*
▸**push ahead** or **push forward.** PHR-VERB If you **push ahead with** something or **push forward with** it, you make progress with it. *The governor has vowed to push ahead with the airport.*
▸**push around.** PHR-VERB If someone **pushes** you **around**, they give you orders in a rude and insulting way.
▸**push aside.** PHR-VERB If you **push** something **aside**, you ignore it or refuse to think about it. ...*pushing aside unpleasant thoughts.*
▸**push forward.** See **push ahead.**
▸**push in.** PHR-VERB When someone **pushes in**,

a b c d e f g h i j k l m n o p q r s t u v w x y z

they come into a queue in front of other people; used showing disapproval.

▶ **push on.** PHR-VERB When you **push on**, you continue with a journey or task. *Although the journey was a long and lonely one, Tumalo pushed on.*

▶ **push over.** PHR-VERB If you **push** someone or something **over**, you push them so that they fall onto the ground. *...people damaging hedges, uprooting trees and pushing over walls.*

▶ **push through.** PHR-VERB If someone **pushes through** a law, reform, or policy, they succeed in getting it accepted, often despite opposition. *Lord Wyatt tried to push the amendment through Parliament.*

pushchair /'pʊʃtʃeə/ **pushchairs.** N-COUNT In British English, a **pushchair** is a small chair on wheels, in which a small child can sit and be wheeled around. The usual American word is **stroller**.

⭐ **put** /pʊt/ **puts, putting, put.** **1** VERB When you **put** something in a particular place or position, you move it into that place or position. *Leaphorn put the photograph on the desk... Mishka put down a heavy shopping bag.* **2** VERB If you **put** someone somewhere, you cause them to go there and to stay there. *I'd put the children to bed.* **3** VERB To **put** someone or something in a particular state or situation means to cause them to be in that state or situation. *This is going to put them out of business... He was putting himself at risk.* **4** VERB If you **put** your trust, faith, or confidence **in** someone or something, you trust them or have faith in them. *Are we right to put our confidence in computers?* **5** VERB If you **put** time, strength, or energy **into** an activity, you use it in doing that activity. *Eleanor did not put much energy into the discussion.* **6** VERB When you **put** an idea or remark in a particular way, you express it in that way. *The security forces might have made some mistakes, as he put it... You can't put that sort of fear into words.* **7** VERB When you **put** a question to someone, you ask them the question. *Some workers may be afraid to put questions publicly.* **8** VERB If you **put** something **at** a particular value or **in** a particular category, or **put** a particular value **on** it, you estimate it to have that value or to be in that category. *I would put her age at about 50... All the more technically advanced countries put a high value on science.* **9** VERB If you **put** written information somewhere, you write, type, or print it there. *They put an announcement in the local paper.*

▶ **put across** or **put over.** PHR-VERB When you **put** something **across** or **put** it **over**, you succeed in describing or explaining it to someone. *Andrew really enjoys putting across a technical argument.*

▶ **put aside.** PHR-VERB If you **put** something **aside**, you keep it to be dealt with or used at a later time. *She took up a slice of bread, broke it nervously, then put it aside.*

▶ **put away.** **1** PHR-VERB If you **put** something **away**, you put it into the place where it is normally kept when it is not being used. *She finished putting the milk away.* **2** PHR-VERB If someone **is put away**, they are sent to prison or to a mental hospital for a long time. [INFORMAL]

▶ **put back.** PHR-VERB To **put** something **back** means to delay it or postpone it. *The trip has been put back to Easter.*

▶ **put by.** PHR-VERB If you **put** money **by**, you save it so that you can use it at a later time. *There was enough put by for her fare.*

▶ **put down.** **1** PHR-VERB If you **put** something **down** somewhere, you write or type it there. *I had prepared for the meeting by putting down what I wanted from them.* **2** PHR-VERB If you **put down** some money, you pay part of the price of something as a deposit. *He bought an investment property for $100,000 and put down $20,000.* **3** PHR-VERB When soldiers, police, or the government **put down** a riot or rebellion, they stop it by using force. **4** PHR-VERB If someone **puts** you **down**, they treat you in an unpleasant way by criticizing you in front of other people or making you appear foolish. [INFORMAL] **5** PHR-VERB When an animal **is put down**, it is killed because it is dangerous or very ill.

▶ **put down to.** PHR-VERB If you **put** something **down to** a particular thing, you believe that it is caused by that thing. *Sales remain constantly high. I put it down to having good staff.*

▶ **put forward.** PHR-VERB If you **put forward** a plan, proposal, or name, you suggest that it should be considered for a particular purpose or job. *I rang the Colonel and asked him to put my name forward for the vacancy in Zurich.*

▶ **put in.** **1** PHR-VERB If you **put in** an amount of time or effort doing something, you spend that time or effort doing it. *We had to put in three hours work a night.* **2** PHR-VERB If you **put in** a request or **put in for** something, you make a formal request or application. *I decided to put in for a job as deputy secretary.*

▶ **put off.** **1** PHR-VERB If you **put** something **off**, you delay doing it. *...women who put off having a baby.* **2** PHR-VERB If you **put** someone **off**, you make them wait for something that they want. *I got the impression she'd like a word or two with you, sir, and I didn't put her off.* **3** PHR-VERB To **put** someone **off** something means to cause them to dislike it. *His personal habits put them off.* **4** PHR-VERB If someone or something **puts** you **off**, they distract you from what you are trying to do and make it more difficult for you to do it. [BRITISH] *It put her off revising for her exams.*

▶ **put on.** **1** PHR-VERB When you **put on** clothing or make-up, you place it on your body in order to wear it. *I haven't even put any lipstick on.* ● See note at **wear.** **2** PHR-VERB If you **put on** a way of behaving, you behave in a way that is not natural to you or that does not express your real feelings. *It was hard to believe she was ill, she was putting it on.* **3** PHR-VERB When people **put on** a show, exhibition, or service, they perform it or organize it. *We put it on and everybody said 'Oh it's a brilliant production'.* **4** PHR-VERB If someone **puts on** weight, they become heavier. *Luther's put on three stone.* **5** PHR-VERB If you **put on** a piece of equipment or a device, you make it start working. *I put the radio on.* **6** PHR-VERB If you **put on** a record, tape, or CD, you place it on a record, tape, or CD player and listen to it. **7** PHR-VERB If you **put** something **on**, you begin to cook or heat it. *Put on a large pan of water to simmer.*

▸**put out.** **1** PHR-VERB If you **put out** an announcement or story, you make it known to a lot of people. *The French news agency put out a statement from the Trade Minister.* **2** PHR-VERB If you **put out** a fire, candle, or cigarette, you make it stop burning. *He lit a half-cigarette and almost immediately put it out again.* **3** PHR-VERB If you **put out** an electric light, you make it stop shining by pressing a switch. **4** PHR-VERB If you **put out** things that will be needed, you place them somewhere ready to be used. *I slowly unpacked the teapot and put it out on the table.* **5** PHR-VERB If you **put out** your **hand**, you move it forward, away from your body. *She put her hand out and tried to touch her mother's arm.* **6** PHR-VERB If you **put** someone **out**, you cause them trouble or inconvenience because they have to do something for you. *I've always put myself out for others.*

▸**put over.** See **put across**.

▸**put through.** **1** PHR-VERB When someone **puts through** a telephone call or a caller, they make the connection that allows the caller to speak to the person they are phoning. *The operator will put you through.* **2** PHR-VERB If someone **puts** you **through** an unpleasant experience, they make you experience it. *She wouldn't want to put them through the ordeal of a huge ceremony.*

▸**put together.** **1** PHR-VERB If you **put** something **together**, you join its different parts to each other so that it can be used. *He took it all to pieces, cleaned it inside and out and put it together again.* **2** PHR-VERB If you **put together** a group of people or things, you form them into a team or collection. *He is trying to put a team together for next season.* **3** PHR-VERB If you **put together** an agreement, plan, or product, you design and create it. *We got to work on putting the book together.*

▸**put up.** **1** PHR-VERB If people **put up** a wall,

building, tent, or other structure, they construct it. *They put up their tents and settled down for the night.* **2** PHR-VERB If you **put up** a poster or notice, you fix it to a wall or board. *They're putting new street signs up.* **3** PHR-VERB To **put up** resistance to something means to resist it. *He was old and very frail. He couldn't have put up a fight.* **4** PHR-VERB If you **put up** money for something, you provide the money that is needed to pay for it. *The merchant banks raise capital for industry. They don't actually put it up themselves.* **5** PHR-VERB To **put up** the price of something means to cause it to increase. *They know they would put their taxes up.* **6** PHR-VERB If a person or hotel **puts** you **up**, you stay at the person's home or at the hotel for one or more nights. *They put him up when he was homeless.*

▸**put up with.** PHR-VERB If you **put up with** something, you tolerate or accept it, even though you find it unpleasant or unsatisfactory. *You're late, Shelly; and I'll tell you, I won't put up with it.*

putt /pʌt/ **putts, putting, putted.** VERB In golf, when you **putt** the ball, you hit it a short distance on the green.

puzzle /'pʌzəl/ **puzzles, puzzling, puzzled.** **1** VERB If something or someone **puzzles** you, you do not understand them and find them confusing. *...a question which has puzzled me for years... My sister puzzles me.* ♦ **puzzled** ADJ *A puzzled look came across his face.* ♦ **puzzling** ADJ *Some of this book is rather puzzling.* **2** VERB If you **puzzle over** something, you try hard to think of the answer or the explanation for it. *She puzzled over his behavior for a moment.* **3** N-COUNT A **puzzle** is a question, game, or toy which you have to think about carefully in order to answer it correctly or put it together properly. **4** N-SING You can describe a person or thing that is hard to understand as **a puzzle**. *'Women are a puzzle,' he said.*

pyjamas (AM **pajamas**) /pɪ'dʒɑːməz/. N-PLURAL A pair of **pyjamas** consists of loose trousers and a loose jacket that are worn in bed.

pyramid /'pɪrəmɪd/ **pyramids.** N-COUNT A **pyramid** is a three-dimensional shape with a flat base and flat triangular sides which slope upwards to a point. → See picture on page 829.

python /'paɪθən/ **pythons.** N-COUNT A **python** is a type of large snake.

Q q

quadruple /ˌkwɒ'druːpəl/ **quadruples, quadrupling, quadrupled.** **1** VERB If someone **quadruples** an amount, or if it **quadruples**, it becomes four times bigger. *The price has quadrupled in the last few years.* **2** PREDET If one amount is **quadruple** another amount, it is four times bigger. **3** ADJ You use **quadruple** to indicate that something happens four times

or has four parts. *...a quadruple gold medalist.*

quail /kweɪl/.

✅ The plural is **quails** or **quail**.

N-COUNT A **quail** is a small bird which is often shot and eaten.

a
b
c
d
e
f
g
h
i
j
k
l
m
n
o
p
q
r
s
t
u
v
w
x
y
z

quaint /kweɪnt/ **quainter, quaintest.** ADJ Something that is **quaint** is attractive because it is unusual and rather old-fashioned. ...*a quaint little cottage.*

quake /kweɪk/ **quakes, quaking, quaked.** [1] N-COUNT A **quake** is the same as an **earthquake.** [INFORMAL] [2] VERB If you **quake**, you tremble or shake, usually because you are afraid. *I just stood there quaking with fear.*

qualification /ˌkwɒlɪfɪˈkeɪʃən/ **qualifications.** [1] N-COUNT Your **qualifications** are the examinations that you have passed. ...*people with good academic qualifications.* [2] N-COUNT The **qualifications** needed for a particular activity or task are the qualities and skills that you need in order to do it. *Responsibility and reliability are necessary qualifications.* [3] N-VAR A **qualification** is something that you add to a statement to make it less strong or less generalized. *This statement requires qualification and clarification.* [4] See also **qualify.**

⭐ **qualified** /ˈkwɒlɪfaɪd/. ADJ BEFORE N If you give someone or something **qualified** support or approval, you give support or approval that is not total and suggests that you have some doubts. *Wade answers both questions with a qualified yes.*

qualifier /ˈkwɒlɪfaɪə/ **qualifiers.** N-COUNT A **qualifier** is an early game or round in a competition. *Wales lost 5-1 to Romania in a World Cup qualifier last night.*

⭐ **qualify** /ˈkwɒlɪfaɪ/ **qualifies, qualifying, qualified.** [1] VERB When someone **qualifies**, they pass the examinations that they need to pass in order to work in a particular profession. *I qualified as a doctor. ...qualified teachers.* ♦ **qualification** /ˌkwɒlɪfɪˈkeɪʃən/ N-UNCOUNT *Following qualification, he worked as a social worker.* [2] VERB If someone **qualifies for** something, or if something **qualifies** them **for** it, they have the right to do it or to have it. *A few useful skills – English-teaching, for example – qualified foreigners for work visas.* [3] VERB If you **qualify** in a competition, you are successful in one part of it and go on to the next stage. *Nottingham Forest qualified for the final by beating Tranmere.* ♦ **qualifier, qualifiers** N-COUNT *Kenya's Robert Kibe was the fastest qualifier for the 800 metres final.* [4] VERB If you **qualify** a statement, you add a detail or explanation to it to make it less strong or less generalized. *I would qualify that by putting it into context.* [5] See also **qualification.**

qualitative /ˈkwɒlɪtətɪv, AM -teɪt-/. ADJ **Qualitative** means relating to the quality of something. [FORMAL] ...*qualitative research in psychology.*

⭐ **quality** /ˈkwɒlɪti/ **qualities.** [1] N-UNCOUNT The **quality** of something is how good or bad it is. ...*high quality paper.* [2] N-UNCOUNT Something **of quality** is of a high standard. ...*a college of quality... We are offering a quality service.* [3] N-COUNT Someone's **qualities** are their good characteristics. ...*mature people with leadership qualities.* [4] N-COUNT You can describe a particular characteristic of a person or thing as a

quality. *Thyme tea can be used by adults for its antiseptic qualities.*

qualm /kwɑːm/ **qualms.** N-COUNT If you **have no qualms about** what you are doing, you are not worried that it may be wrong. *I have no qualms about recommending the same approach to other doctors.*

quantifier /ˈkwɒntɪfaɪə/ **quantifiers.** N-COUNT In grammar, a **quantifier** is a word or phrase like 'plenty' or 'a lot', which allows you to refer to the quantity of something without being absolutely precise. It is often followed by 'of', as in 'a lot of money'.

quantitative /ˈkwɒntɪtətɪv, AM -teɪt-/. ADJ **Quantitative** means relating to the different sizes or amounts of things. ...*the quantitative analysis of migration.*

⭐ **quantity** /ˈkwɒntɪti/ **quantities.** [1] N-VAR A **quantity** is an amount that you can measure or count. ...*a small quantity of water... Cheap goods are available, but not in sufficient quantities.* [2] N-UNCOUNT Things that are produced or available **in quantity** are produced or available in large amounts. *They can afford to import basic food stuffs and raw materials in quantity.* [3] PHRASE If you say that someone or something is **an unknown quantity**, you mean that not much is known about what they are like or how they will behave.

quantum /ˈkwɒntəm/. [1] ADJ BEFORE N In physics, **quantum theory** and **quantum mechanics** are concerned with the behaviour of atomic particles. [2] ADJ BEFORE N You can use **quantum** in the expressions **quantum leap** and **quantum jump**, which mean a very great and sudden increase in size, amount, or quality. *A vaccine which can halt this suffering represents a quantum leap in healthcare.*

quarantine /ˈkwɒrəntiːn, AM ˈkwɔːr-/. N-UNCOUNT If a person or animal is **in quarantine**, they are kept separate from other people or animals in case they have an infectious disease.

quarrel /ˈkwɒrəl, AM ˈkwɔːr-/ **quarrels, quarrelling, quarrelled (AM quarreling, quarreled).** [1] N-COUNT & VERB If you have a **quarrel with** a friend or family member, or if you **quarrel with** them, you have an angry argument with them. *I had a terrible quarrel with my other brothers... My brother quarrelled with my father.* [2] N-SING If you say that you have **no quarrel with** someone, you mean that you do not disagree with them.

quarry /ˈkwɒri, AM ˈkwɔːri/ **quarries, quarrying, quarried.** [1] N-COUNT A **quarry** is an area that is dug out from a piece of land or mountainside in order to extract stone, slate, or minerals. [2] VERB When stone or minerals **are quarried**, or when an area **is quarried** for them, they are removed from the area by digging, drilling, or using explosives.

quart /kwɔːt/ **quarts.** N-COUNT A **quart** is a unit of volume that is equal to two pints.

★ **quarter** /'kwɔːtə/ **quarters.** 1 N-COUNT & PREDET & ADJ BEFORE N A **quarter** is one of four equal parts of something. *Cut the peppers into quarters. ...an asteroid about a quarter the size of the moon. ...the past quarter century.* 2 N-COUNT A **quarter** is a fixed period of three months. *We update that once a quarter.* 3 N-UNCOUNT When you are telling the time, you use **quarter** to talk about the fifteen minutes before or after the hour. For example, 8.15 is **quarter past** eight, and 8.45 is **quarter to** nine. In American English you can also say that 8.15 is a **quarter after** eight and 8.45 is a **quarter of** nine. → See Reference Page on Telling the Time. 4 N-COUNT You can refer to the area in a town where a particular group of people live or work as a particular **quarter**. *...the Chinese quarter.* 5 N-COUNT If you talk about feelings or reactions from a certain **quarter**, you mean the feelings or reactions of a group of people, but you do not want to mention the names of the people. *The threat of violence from this quarter has increased sharply.* 6 N-PLURAL You can refer to the room or rooms provided for a person such as a soldier to live in as that person's **quarters**. *...the officers' quarters.* 7 PHRASE If you do something **at close quarters**, you do it from a place that is very near to someone or something. *You can watch aircraft take off or land at close quarters.*

quarterback /'kwɔːtəbæk/ **quarterbacks.** N-COUNT In American football, a **quarterback** is the player on the attacking team who begins each play and decides which play to use.

ˌquarter-ˈfinal (or **quarterfinal**) **quarter-finals.** N-COUNT A **quarter-final** is one of the four matches in a competition which decides which four players or four teams will compete in the semi-final.

quarterly /'kwɔːtəli/. ADJ & ADV A **quarterly** event happens four times a year, at intervals of three months. *...the latest Bank of Japan quarterly survey... Dividends are paid quarterly or annually.*

ˌquarter ˈpounder, **quarter pounders.** N-COUNT A **quarter pounder** is a hamburger that weighs four ounces before it is cooked. Four ounces is a quarter of a pound.

quartet /kwɔːˈtet/ **quartets.** 1 N-COUNT A **quartet** is a group of four people who play musical instruments or sing together. 2 N-COUNT A **quartet** is a piece of music for four instruments or four singers.

quartz /kwɔːts/. N-UNCOUNT **Quartz** is a kind of hard shiny crystal, used in making electronic equipment and very accurate watches and clocks.

quash /kwɒʃ/ **quashes, quashing, quashed.** VERB If someone in authority **quashes** a decision or judgment, they officially reject it and it becomes no longer legally valid. *The Appeal Court has quashed the convictions of all eleven people.*

quay /kiː/ **quays.** N-COUNT A **quay** is a long platform beside the sea or a river where boats can be tied.

★ **queen** /kwiːn/ **queens.** 1 N-COUNT & N-TITLE A **queen** is a woman who rules a country as its monarch, or a woman who is married to a king. *...Queen Victoria... The king and queen had fled.* 2 N-COUNT In chess, the **queen** is the most powerful piece, which can be moved in any direction. 3 N-COUNT A **queen** is a playing card with a picture of a queen on it. *...the queen of spades.*

queer /kwɪə/ **queerer, queerest.** ADJ **Queer** means strange. [DATED] *There's something a bit queer going on.*

quell /kwel/ **quells, quelling, quelled.** 1 VERB To **quell** opposition or violence means to stop it by using persuasion or force. *Troops eventually quelled the unrest.* 2 VERB If you **quell** unpleasant feelings, you stop yourself or other people from having these feelings. *The Information Minister is trying to quell fears of a looming oil crisis.*

quench /kwentʃ/ **quenches, quenching, quenched.** VERB When you are thirsty, you can **quench your thirst** by having a drink. *He stopped to quench his thirst at a stream.*

query /'kwɪəri/ **queries, querying, queried.** 1 N-VAR A **query** is a question about a particular point. *He is unable to answer queries personally.* 2 VERB If you **query** something, you check it by asking about it because you are not sure if it is correct. *No one queried my decision.* 3 VERB To **query** means to ask a question. *People queried whether any harm had been done.*

quest /kwest/ **quests.** N-COUNT A **quest** is a long and difficult search for something. *My quest for a better bank continues.*

★ **question** /'kwestʃən/ **questions, questioning, questioned.** 1 N-COUNT A **question** is something which you say or write in order to ask about a particular matter. *He refused to answer further questions.* 2 VERB If you **question** someone, you ask them questions about something. *I had questioned him on his Western adventures.* ◆ **questioner, questioners** N-COUNT *He told the questioner: 'I don't know about their activities.'* ◆ **questioning** N-UNCOUNT *The police have detained thirty-two people for questioning.* 3 VERB If you **question** something, you express doubts about it. *It never occurs to them to question the doctor's decisions.* 4 N-UNCOUNT If there is some **question** about something, there is doubt about it. If something is **in question** or has been called **into question**, doubt has been expressed about it. *Why Marlowe was killed may be open to question.* 5 N-COUNT A **question** is a problem or point which needs to be discussed. *The whole question of aid is a tricky political one.* 6 N-COUNT The **questions** in an examination are the problems or topics which are set in order to test your knowledge or ability.

PHRASES ● The time, place, person, or thing **in question** is the one you have just been talking about. *The player in question is Mark Williams.* ● If something is **out of the question**, it is

a
b
c
d
e
f
g
h
i
j
k
l
m
n
o
p
q
r
s
t
u
v
w
x
y
z

impossible. *For the homeless, private medical care is simply out of the question.* ● If you say **there is no question of** something happening, you are emphasizing that it is not going to happen. *There was no question of betraying his own comrades.* ● If you do something **without question**, you do it without arguing or asking why it is necessary.

questionable /ˈkwestʃənəbəl/. ADJ If you say that something is **questionable**, you do not consider it to be completely honest or reasonable. *...questionable business practices.*

'question mark, question marks. N-COUNT A **question mark** is the punctuation mark (?) which is used in writing at the end of a question. → See Reference Page on Punctuation.

questionnaire /ˌkwestʃəˈneə, ˌkes-/ **questionnaires.** N-COUNT A **questionnaire** is a written list of questions which are answered by a number of people in order to provide information for a report or survey. *Please fill in the questionnaire.*

queue /kjuː/ **queues, queueing** (or **queuing**), **queued.** [1] N-COUNT In British English, a **queue** is a line of people or vehicles that are waiting for something. The American word is **line**. → See picture on page 826. *He got a tray and joined the queue.* [2] VERB & PHR-VB In British English, when people **queue**, or when they **queue up**, they stand in a line waiting for something. The American term is **line up**.

quibble /ˈkwɪbəl/ **quibbles, quibbling, quibbled.** [1] VERB When people **quibble**, they argue about a small matter which is not important. *It seems silly to quibble over such trivial details.* [2] N-COUNT A **quibble** is a minor objection to something.

⭐ **quick** /kwɪk/ **quicker, quickest.** [1] ADJ Someone or something that is **quick** moves or does things with great speed. *You'll have to be quick... He was a very quick learner.* ♦ **quickly** ADV *Stop me if I'm speaking too quickly.* ♦ **quickness** N-UNCOUNT *...the natural quickness of his mind.* [2] ADJ Something that is **quick** takes or lasts only a short time. *He took one last quick look about the room.* ♦ **quickly** ADV *You can become fitter than you are quite quickly.* [3] ADJ **Quick** means happening with very little delay. *They were quick to dismiss rumours of an off-screen romance. ...a quick end to the war.* ♦ **quickly** ADV *We need to get it back as quickly as possible.*

quicken /ˈkwɪkən/ **quickens, quickening, quickened.** VERB If something **quickens**, or if you **quicken** it, it becomes faster or moves at a greater speed. *He quickened his pace a little.*

quid /kwɪd/.

✓ **Quid** is both the singular and the plural form.

N-COUNT A **quid** is a pound in money. [BRITISH, INFORMAL] *It cost him five hundred quid.*

⭐ **quiet** /ˈkwaɪət/ **quieter, quietest.** [1] ADJ Something or someone that is **quiet** makes only a small amount of noise. *Tania kept the children reasonably quiet and content... The street was*

unnaturally quiet. ♦ **quietly** ADV *Two students whisper quietly to each other.* ♦ **quietness** N-UNCOUNT *I was impressed by the smoothness and quietness of the flight.* [2] ADJ If a place, situation, or time is **quiet**, there is no excitement, activity, or trouble. *She wanted a quiet life.* ♦ **quietly** ADV *He lives quietly in the country.* ♦ **quietness** N-UNCOUNT *I do very much appreciate the quietness and privacy here.* [3] ADJ AFTER LINK-V & N-UNCOUNT If you are **quiet**, you are not saying anything. You say there is **quiet** when no one is talking. *I told them to be quiet and go to sleep... He called for quiet.* ♦ **quietly** ADV *Amy stood quietly in the doorway watching him.* [4] PHRASE If you **keep quiet about** something, or if you **keep** something **quiet**, you do not say anything about it. *He denied the department had tried to keep the plan quiet.*

quieten /ˈkwaɪətən/ **quietens, quietening, quietened.** VERB If you **quieten** someone or something, or if they **quieten**, they become less noisy or less active. *A man shouted and the dogs suddenly quietened.*

quilt /kwɪlt/ **quilts.** [1] N-COUNT A **quilt** is a bed-cover filled with warm soft material, which is often decorated with lines of stitching. [2] N-COUNT A **quilt** is the same as a **duvet**. [BRITISH]

quip /kwɪp/ **quips, quipping, quipped.** VERB & N-COUNT To **quip** or to make a **quip** means to say something that is intended to be amusing or clever. [WRITTEN] *'He'll have to go on a diet,' Ballard quipped.*

quirk /kwɜːk/ **quirks.** [1] N-COUNT A **quirk** is a habit or aspect of a person's character which is odd or unusual. [2] N-COUNT A **quirk** is a strange occurrence that is difficult to explain.

quirky /ˈkwɜːki/ **quirkier, quirkiest.** ADJ Someone or something that is **quirky** is rather odd or unpredictable in their appearance, character, or behaviour. *...her quirky and original style.* ♦ **quirkiness** N-UNCOUNT *You will probably notice an element of quirkiness in his behaviour.*

quit /kwɪt/ **quits, quitting, quit.** [1] VERB If you **quit** something, you leave it or you stop doing it. *He refused to quit the building... Nicotine patches are now widely used to help smokers quit the habit.* [2] PHRASE If you say that you are going to **call it quits**, you mean that you have decided to stop doing something or being involved in something.

⭐ **quite** /kwaɪt/. [1] ADV You use **quite** to indicate that something is the case to a fairly great extent. **Quite** is less emphatic than 'very' and 'extremely'. *I felt quite bitter about it at the time... I was quite a long way away... I quite enjoy living here.* [2] ADV You use **quite** to indicate certainty or to emphasize that something is definitely the case. *It is quite clear that we were firing in self defence... I quite agree with you.* [3] ADV You use **quite** after a negative to weaken the force of your statement. *Something here is not quite right... I didn't quite understand what all this was about.* [4] PREDET You use **quite** in front of a noun group to emphasize that a person or thing is very

---

impressive or unusual. *He's quite a character.*
5 ADV You can say **'quite'** to express your
agreement with someone. [SPOKEN] *'And if you buy
the record it's your choice isn't it?' — 'Quite.'*

USAGE You can use **quite** in front of **a** or
an when it is followed by an adjective plus
noun. For example, you can say **'It's quite
an old car'** as well as **'The car is quite
old'**, and **'It was quite a warm day'** as
well as **'The day was quite warm'**. Note
that, in sentences like these, **quite** comes
in front of the indefinite article. You cannot
say, for example, **'It's a quite old car'**.
Quite can be used to modify adjectives
and adverbs, and is slightly stronger than
fairly but less strong than **very**. **Quite**
may suggest that something has more of
a quality than expected. *Nobody here's
ever heard of it but it is actually quite
common.*

quiver /'kwɪvə/ **quivers, quivering, quivered.** **1** VERB
If something **quivers**, it shakes with very small
movements. *Her bottom lip quivered.* **2** VERB &
N-COUNT If you say that someone **is quivering
with** an emotion such as rage or happiness, or if
they feel a **quiver of** emotion, you mean that
their appearance or voice clearly shows this
emotion. *I recognized it instantly and felt a quiver
of panic.*

quiz /kwɪz/ **quizzes, quizzing, quizzed.** **1** N-COUNT A
quiz is a game or competition in which someone
tests your knowledge by asking you questions.
2 VERB If you **are quizzed** by someone about
something, they ask you questions because they

want to get information from you. *Four men were
being quizzed by police.*

quota /'kwəʊtə/ **quotas.** **1** N-COUNT A **quota** is
the limited number or quantity which is officially
allowed. *...the quota of four tickets per person.*
2 N-COUNT Someone's **quota of** something is
their expected or deserved share of it. *They have
the usual quota of human weaknesses.*

quotation /kwəʊ'teɪʃən/ **quotations.** **1** N-COUNT
A **quotation** is a sentence or phrase taken from a
book, poem, or play. **2** N-COUNT When someone
gives you a **quotation**, they tell you how much
they will charge you to do a particular piece of
work. [BRITISH]

quo'tation mark, quotation marks. N-COUNT
Quotation marks are punctuation marks used in
writing to show where speech or a quotation
begins and ends. They are usually written or
printed as (' ') and (" "). → See Reference Page on
Punctuation.

★ **quote** /kwəʊt/ **quotes, quoting, quoted.** **1** VERB If
you **quote** someone as saying something, you
repeat what they have written or said. *She quoted
a great line from a book by Romain Gary.* **2** VERB
If you **quote** something such as a law or a fact,
you state it because it supports what you are
saying. *She quoted statistics to show how well
Britain is doing.* **3** N-COUNT A **quote** from a book,
poem, or play is a sentence or phrase from it.
4 VERB & N-COUNT If someone **quotes** you a price
for something, or if they give you a **quote
for** doing it, they say how much money they
would charge you to do it. *He quoted a price for
the repairs.* **5** N-PLURAL **Quotes** are the same as
quotation marks.

R r

rabbi /'ræbaɪ/ **rabbis.** N-COUNT & N-TITLE A **rabbi** is
a Jewish religious leader.

rabbit /'ræbɪt/ **rabbits.** **1** N-COUNT A **rabbit** is a
small furry animal with long ears. Rabbits live in
holes in the ground. **2** N-UNCOUNT **Rabbit** is the
flesh of this animal eaten as food.

rabble /'ræbəl/. N-SING A **rabble** is a crowd of
noisy disorganized people; used showing
disapproval.

rabies /'reɪbiːz/. N-UNCOUNT **Rabies** is a serious
infectious disease which humans can get from
the bite of an animal such as a dog which has the
disease.

★ **race** /reɪs/ **races, racing, raced.** **1** N-COUNT A **race** is
a competition to see who is the fastest, for
example in running or driving. **2** VERB If you
race, you take part in a race. *Morris is the only
other horse in the land who could race him... I
haven't raced against a lot of my rivals this year.*
3 N-COUNT A **race** is a situation in which people
or organizations compete with each other for

power or control. *The race for the White House
begins in earnest today.* **4** VERB If you **race**
somewhere, you go there as quickly as possible.
He raced across town to the State House building.
5 VERB If something **races**, it moves at a very
fast rate. *Her heart raced... Already her mind was
racing ahead to the hundred and one things she
had to do.* **6** N-VAR A **race** is one of the major
groups which human beings can be divided into
according to their physical features, such as their
skin colour. *Discrimination by employers on the
grounds of race and nationality was illegal.*
7 PHRASE You describe a situation as a **race
against time** when you have to work very fast in
order to do something before a particular time.
● See also **human race**.

racecourse (or **race course**) /'reɪskɔːs/
racecourses. N-COUNT In British English, a
racecourse is a track on which horses race. The
American word is **racetrack**.

racehorse (or **race horse**) /'reɪshɔːs/

★ Bank of English® frequent word   For a full explanation of all grammatical labels, see pages vii–x

A
B
C
D
E
F
G ★
H ★
I
J
K
L
M
N
O
P
Q
R
S
T
U
V
W
X
Y
Z

racehorses. N-COUNT A **racehorse** is a horse that is trained to run in races.

racer /'reɪsə/ **racers.** [1] N-COUNT A **racer** is a person or animal that takes part in races. ...*a former champion powerboat racer.* [2] N-COUNT A **racer** is a vehicle such as a car or bicycle that is designed to be used in races and therefore travels fast.

race re'lations. N-PLURAL **Race relations** are the ways in which people of different races living together in the same community behave towards each other.

racetrack (or **race track**) /'reɪstræk/ **racetracks.** N-COUNT A **racetrack** is a track for races.

racial /'reɪʃəl/ ADJ **Racial** describes things relating to people's race. ...*racial discrimination.*
♦ **racially** ADV ...*racially mixed marriages.*

racing /'reɪsɪŋ/ N-UNCOUNT **Racing** refers to races between animals, especially horses, or between vehicles.

racist /'reɪsɪst/ **racists.** N-COUNT & ADJ A **racist**, or a person with **racist** views, believes that people of some races are inferior to others. ...*a gang of white racists.* ...*dealing with a racist society.*
♦ **racism** /'reɪsɪzəm/ N-UNCOUNT ...*the fight against racism.*

rack /ræk/ **racks, racking, racked.**

☑ The verb is also spelled **wrack** in American English.

[1] N-COUNT A **rack** is a piece of equipment used for holding things or for hanging things on. ...*a luggage rack.* ...*racks of clothes.* [2] VERB If someone **is racked by** or **with** something, it causes them great suffering or pain. ...*a teenager racked with guilt.*

racket /'rækɪt/ **rackets.**

☑ The spelling **racquet** is also used in meaning 3.

[1] N-SING A **racket** is a loud unpleasant noise. *He makes such a racket.* [2] N-COUNT You can refer to an illegal activity used to make money as a **racket.** [INFORMAL] ...*a drugs racket.* [3] N-COUNT A **racket** is an oval-shaped bat with strings across it which is used in games such as tennis.

racy /'reɪsi/ **racier, raciest.** ADJ **Racy** writing or behaviour is lively and slightly shocking.

radar /'reɪdɑː/ N-UNCOUNT **Radar** is a way of discovering the position or speed of objects such as aircraft or ships by using radio signals.

radiant /'reɪdiənt/ [1] ADJ Someone who is **radiant** is so happy that their joy shows in their face. *The bride looked truly radiant.* ♦ **radiance** N-UNCOUNT *A sort of radiance envelops her.* [2] ADJ Something that is **radiant** glows brightly. *Out on the bay the morning is radiant.* ♦ **radiance** N-UNCOUNT ...*the radiance of early morning.*

radiate /'reɪdieɪt/ **radiates, radiating, radiated.** [1] VERB If things **radiate from** a place, they form a pattern that spreads out like lines drawn from the centre of a circle to its edge. ...*paths radiating from a central circular paved area.* [2] VERB If you

radiate an emotion or quality or if it **radiates from** you, people can see it very clearly in your face and in your behaviour. *She radiates happiness.*

radiation /,reɪdi'eɪʃən/. [1] N-UNCOUNT **Radiation** is very small particles of a radioactive substance. Large amounts of radiation can cause illness and death. [2] N-UNCOUNT **Radiation** is energy, often in waves of heat or light, that comes from a particular source.

radiator /'reɪdieɪtə/ **radiators.** [1] N-COUNT A **radiator** is a hollow metal device which is connected to a central heating system and used to heat a room. [2] N-COUNT A car **radiator** is the part of the engine which is used to cool the engine.

radical /'rædɪkəl/ **radicals.** [1] ADJ **Radical** changes and differences are very important and great in degree. ...*radical economic reforms.*
♦ **radically** ADV ...*radically different beliefs.*
[2] N-COUNT & ADJ A **radical** or a person who has **radical** views believes that there should be great changes in society and tries to bring about these changes. ...*tension between radical and conservative politicians.*

radii /'reɪdiaɪ/. **Radii** is the plural of **radius.**

radio /'reɪdiəʊ/ **radios, radioing, radioed.** [1] N-UNCOUNT **Radio** is the broadcasting of programmes for the public to listen to. You can refer to the programmes broadcast in this way as **the radio.** *The last 12 months have been difficult ones for local radio... He's been on the radio a lot recently.* [2] N-COUNT A **radio** is the piece of equipment used to listen to radio programmes. [3] N-UNCOUNT **Radio** is a system of sending sound over a distance using electrical signals. *They are in twice daily radio contact with the rebel leader.* [4] N-COUNT A **radio** is a piece of equipment that is used for sending and receiving messages. [5] VERB If you **radio** someone, you send a message to them by radio. *The officer radioed for advice.*

radioactive /,reɪdiəʊ'æktɪv/. ADJ Something that is **radioactive** contains a substance that produces energy in the form of powerful rays which are harmful in large doses. ...*radioactive waste.* ♦ **radioactivity** /,reɪdiəʊæk'tɪvɪti/ N-UNCOUNT ...*waste which is contaminated with low levels of radioactivity.*

radius /'reɪdiəs/ **radii** /'reɪdiaɪ/. [1] N-SING The **radius** around a point is the distance from it in any direction. *Nigel has searched for work in a ten-mile radius around his home.* [2] N-COUNT The **radius** of a circle is the distance from its centre to its outside edge.

RAF /,ɑːr eɪ 'ef, ræf/. N-PROPER **The RAF** is the air force of the United Kingdom. **RAF** is an abbreviation for 'Royal Air Force'.

raffle /'ræfəl/ **raffles.** N-COUNT A **raffle** is a competition in which you buy numbered tickets. If your ticket is chosen, you win a prize.

raft /rɑːft, ræft/ **rafts.** [1] N-COUNT A **raft** is a floating platform made from large pieces of wood tied together. [2] N-COUNT A **raft** is a small inflatable rubber or plastic boat. [3] N-COUNT A **raft of** people or things is a lot of them. *He has surrounded himself with a raft of advisers.*

rafter /ˈrɑːftə, ˈræf-/ **rafters.** N-COUNT **Rafters** are the sloping pieces of wood that support a roof.

rag /ræg/ **rags.** [1] N-VAR A **rag** is a piece of old cloth which you can use to clean or wipe things. *...dry it on some rag.* [2] N-PLURAL **Rags** are old torn clothes. *...small children, some dressed in rags.* [3] N-COUNT People refer to a newspaper as a **rag** when they have a low opinion of it. [INFORMAL] *I've read all about it in the local rag.*

⭐ **rage** /reɪdʒ/ **rages, raging, raged.** [1] N-VAR **Rage** is strong, uncontrollable anger. *I flew into a rage. ...a fit of rage.* [2] VERB You say that something powerful or unpleasant **rages** when it continues with great force or violence. *The fire raged for more than four hours.* ◆ **raging** ADJ BEFORE N *...kayaking on a raging river.* [3] VERB If you **rage** about something, you speak or think very angrily about it. *He began to rage against his bad luck.* [4] N-SING When something is popular and fashionable, you can say that it is **the rage.** [INFORMAL] *Chinese cooking is all the rage.*

ragged /ˈrægɪd/. [1] ADJ **Ragged** clothes are old and torn. If someone is **ragged**, they are wearing old torn clothing. *...ragged children played among the pot-holed streets.* [2] ADJ You can say that something is **ragged** when it is uneven or untidy. *O'Brien formed the men into a ragged line.*

⭐ **raid** /reɪd/ **raids, raiding, raided.** [1] VERB & N-COUNT When soldiers or the police **raid** a place, they enter it by force to attack it, or to look for someone or something. This action is called a **raid.** *...a raid on a house by thirty armed police.* ◆ **raider, raiders** N-COUNT *The raiders continued on their mission – to seek out and destroy American air and sea forces.* [2] VERB & N-COUNT If someone **raids** a building or place, they enter it by force in order to steal something. This action is called a **raid.** [BRITISH] *A 19-year-old man has been found guilty of raiding a bank.* ◆ **raider** N-COUNT *The raiders escaped with cash and jewellery.*

⭐ **rail** /reɪl/ **rails.** [1] N-COUNT A **rail** is a horizontal bar which is fixed to something and used as a fence or a support, or to hang things on. *She gripped the hand rail in the lift... This pair of curtains will fit a rail up to 7ft 6in wide.* [2] N-COUNT **Rails** are the steel bars which trains run on. [3] N-UNCOUNT If you travel or send something **by rail**, you travel or send it on a train. *The president traveled by rail to his home town. ...the electric rail link between Manchester and Sheffield.*

railing /ˈreɪlɪŋ/ **railings.** N-COUNT A fence made from metal bars is called a **railing** or **railings.**

railroad /ˈreɪlrəʊd/ **railroads.** N-COUNT In American English, a **railroad** is the same as a **railway.**

⭐ **railway** /ˈreɪlweɪ/ **railways.** [1] N-COUNT A **railway** is a route between two places along which trains travel on steel rails. [BRITISH] [2] N-COUNT A **railway** is a company or organization that operates railway routes. [BRITISH] *...the state-owned French railway. ...the privatisation of the railways.*

⭐ **rain** /reɪn/ **rains, raining, rained.** [1] N-UNCOUNT **Rain** is water that falls from the clouds in small drops. *I hope you didn't get soaked standing out in the rain. It is raining. It rained the whole weekend.* [3] VERB & PHR-VERB If things **rain on** a person or place, or if they **rain down**, they fall on that person or place in large quantities. *The masked attacker rained blows on him... Guerrillas rained down mortar machine-gun fire.* ▸ **rain off.** PHR-VERB If a sports match **is rained off**, it cannot take place because of the rain.

rainbow /ˈreɪnbəʊ/ **rainbows.** N-COUNT A **rainbow** is the arch of different colours that you sometimes see in the sky when it is raining.

raincoat /ˈreɪnkəʊt/ **raincoats.** N-COUNT A **raincoat** is a waterproof coat. → See picture on page 819.

raindrop /ˈreɪndrɒp/ **raindrops.** N-COUNT A **raindrop** is a single drop of rain.

rainfall /ˈreɪnfɔːl/ **rainfalls.** N-VAR **Rainfall** is the amount of rain that falls in a place during a particular period of time. *...below average rainfall.*

rainforest /ˈreɪnfɒrɪst, AM -fɔːr-/ **rainforests.** N-VAR A **rainforest** is a thick forest of tall trees found in tropical areas where there is a lot of rain.

rainy /ˈreɪni/ **rainier, rainiest.** ADJ If it is **rainy**, it is raining a lot. *...one rainy night in Seattle.*

⭐ **raise** /reɪz/ **raises, raising, raised.** [1] VERB If you **raise** something, you move it to a higher position. *She went to the window and raised the blinds... He raised his hand. ...a small raised platform.* [2] VERB If you **raise** the rate or level of something, you increase it. *The Republic of Ireland is expected to raise interest rates.* [3] VERB To **raise** the standard of something means to improve it. *...courses to raise the standard of coaching.* [4] VERB If you **raise** your voice, you speak more loudly. [5] VERB If an event **raises** a particular emotion or question, it makes people feel the emotion or consider the question. *The agreement has raised hopes that the war may end soon.* [6] VERB If you **raise** a subject, objection, or question, you mention it or bring it to someone's attention. *At no time did he raise the matter with me.* [7] N-COUNT In American English, a **raise** is an increase in your wages or salary. The British word is **rise.** [8] VERB To **raise** money for a particular cause means to get people to donate money towards it. [9] VERB To **raise** a child means to look after it until it is grown up. [10] VERB To **raise** a particular type of animal or crop means to breed

a
b
c
d
e
f
g
h
i
j
k
l
m
n
o
p
q
r
s
t
u
v
w
x
y
z

the animal or grow the crop. *They raise sheep for meat, skins, and wool.*

USAGE You should be careful not to confuse the verbs **raise** and **rise**. **Raise** is a transitive verb and is usually followed by an object, whereas **rise** is an intransitive verb and is not followed by an object. **Rise** can also not be used in the passive. *...the government's decision to raise prices... The number of dead is likely to rise.*

---

raisin /'reɪzən/ **raisins.** N-COUNT **Raisins** are dried grapes.

rake /reɪk/ **rakes, raking, raked.** [1] N-COUNT A **rake** is a garden tool consisting of a row of metal teeth attached to a long handle. → See picture on page 832. [2] VERB To **rake** leaves or soil means to use a rake to gather the leaves or to make the soil smooth.
▸**rake in.** PHR-VERB If someone **is raking in** money, they are earning a lot of it fairly easily. [INFORMAL] *He raked in £33,000 from his shares.*

★ **rally** /'ræli/ **rallies, rallying, rallied.** [1] N-COUNT A **rally** is a large public meeting held in support of something such as a political party. *...a pre-election rally.* [2] N-COUNT A **rally** is a competition in which vehicles are driven over public roads. *...an accomplished rally driver.* [3] VERB When people **rally to** something or when someone **rallies** them, they unite to support it. *He attempted to rally his supporters.* [4] VERB When someone or something **rallies**, they begin to recover or improve after having been weak. *Stock markets began to rally worldwide.*
▸**rally around** or **rally round.** PHR-VERB When people **rally around** or **rally round**, they work as a group in order to support someone at a difficult time. *Connie's friends rallied round her.*

ram /ræm/ **rams, ramming, rammed.** [1] VERB If one vehicle **rams** another, it crashes into it with a lot of force. [2] VERB If you **ram** something somewhere, you push it there with great force. *He rammed the key into the lock.* [3] N-COUNT A **ram** is an adult male sheep.

ramble /'ræmbəl/ **rambles, rambling, rambled.** [1] VERB & N-COUNT If you **ramble**, or if you go on a **ramble**, you go on a long walk in the countryside. *...an hour's ramble through the woods.* ♦ **rambler, ramblers** N-COUNT *...a popular route for ramblers.* [2] VERB & PHR-VB If someone **rambles**, or if they **ramble on**, they talk for a long time in a confused way. *She began rambling on about her childhood.*

ramification /,ræmɪfɪ'keɪʃən/ **ramifications.** N-COUNT The **ramifications** of a decision or event are all its consequences and effects, especially ones which were not obvious at first. *...the political ramifications of the riots.*

ramp /ræmp/ **ramps.** N-COUNT A **ramp** is a sloping surface between two places that are at different levels. *I pushed her wheelchair up the ramp.*

rampage, rampages, rampaging, rampaged; verb /ræm'peɪdʒ/; phrase /'ræmpeɪdʒ/. VERB & PHRASE If people or animals **rampage** through a place, or if they **go on the rampage** through a place, they rush about in a wild or violent way, causing damage or destruction. *Hundreds of fans went on the rampage after the match.*

rampant /'ræmpənt/. ADJ If something such as crime or a disease is **rampant**, it is growing or spreading in an uncontrolled way. *...rampant corruption.*

ramshackle /'ræmʃækəl/. ADJ A **ramshackle** building is badly made or in a very bad condition.

ran /ræn/. **Ran** is the past tense of **run.**

ranch /rɑːntʃ, ræntʃ/ **ranches.** N-COUNT A **ranch** is a large farm used for raising animals.

random /'rændəm/. ADJ & PHRASE Something that is done or chosen in a **random** way, or **at random**, is done or chosen without a definite plan or pattern. *...a random sample of 930 women... Names were selected at random by computer.* ♦ **randomly** ADV *...magazines left scattered randomly around.*

R & R. N-UNCOUNT **R&R** refers to time that you spend relaxing, when you are not working. **R&R** is an abbreviation for 'rest and recreation'. *Winter spas are the place for serious R&R.*

rang /ræŋ/. **Rang** is the past tense of some meanings of **ring.**

★ **range** /reɪndʒ/ **ranges, ranging, ranged.** [1] N-COUNT A **range of** things is a number of different things of the same general kind. *...a wide range of furniture. ...a range of environmental issues.* [2] N-COUNT A **range** is the complete group that is included between two points on a scale of measurement or quality. *The age range is from eighteen to forty. ...properties available in the price range they are looking for.* [3] N-COUNT The **range of** something is the maximum area within which it can reach things or detect things. *...a missile with a range of 2,000 kilometres... A newborn baby's range of vision is about a foot or so.* [4] VERB If things **range between** two points or **range from** one point **to** another, they vary within these points on a scale of measurement or quality. *They range in price from $3 to $15.* [5] VERB If people or things **are ranged** somewhere, they are arranged in a row or in lines. [FORMAL] *Wooden chairs were ranged against one wall.* [6] N-COUNT A **range** of mountains or hills is a line of them. [7] N-COUNT A rifle **range** or a firing **range** is a place where people can shoot at targets.
PHRASES ● If something is **in range** or **within range**, it is near enough to be reached or detected. If it is **out of range**, it is too far away to be reached or detected. *...within range of their aircraft... The fish stayed 50 yards offshore, well out of range.* ● If you see or hit something at **close range**, or **from close range**, you are very close to it when you see it or hit it. *...photographing wild animals from close range.*

---

ranger /'reɪndʒə/ **rangers.** N-COUNT A **ranger** is a person whose job is to look after a forest or park.

⭐ **rank** /ræŋk/ **ranks, ranking, ranked.** [1] N-VAR Someone's **rank** is their position in an organization, or in society. ...the rank of captain. ...a person of high rank. [2] VERB When someone or something **is ranked** a particular position, they are at that position on a scale. The British player, Michael Adams, already ranks 20th in the world. ...a remarkable scientist whose work ranked with that of Einstein. [3] N-PLURAL The **ranks** are the ordinary members of an organization, especially of the armed forces. ...a former Lieutenant-Colonel who had risen from the ranks. [4] N-PLURAL When you become a member of a large group of people, you can say that you are joining its **ranks**. He soon joined the ranks of the unemployed. [5] ADJ You can describe something as **rank** when it has a strong and unpleasant smell. [LITERARY] ...the rank smell of unwashed skin. [6] N-COUNT A taxi **rank** is a place where taxis park and wait to be hired.
PHRASES ● If a member of a group or organization **breaks ranks**, they disobey the instructions of their group or organization. ● If the members of a group **close ranks**, they support each other in a united way to oppose any attack or criticism.

rank and file. N-SING The **rank and file** of an organization are the ordinary members of an organization, rather than the leaders. The rank and file of the party hadn't been consulted.

ransack /'rænsæk/ **ransacks, ransacking, ransacked.** VERB If people **ransack** a building or a room, they disturb everything in it and leave it in a mess, often because they are looking for something. The thieves ransacked the house.

ransom /'rænsəm/ **ransoms.** [1] N-VAR A **ransom** is money that is demanded as payment for the return of someone who has been kidnapped. The kidnappers are demanding a ransom of five million dollars. [2] PHRASE If a kidnapper **holds** someone **to ransom**, they keep that person prisoner until they are given what they want.

rant /rænt/ **rants, ranting, ranted.** VERB & N-COUNT If someone **rants**, or if they have a **rant**, they talk in a loud, excited, and angry way. ...a rant against the meat industry. ◆ **ranting, rantings** N-VAR He had been listening to Goldstone's rantings all night.

rap /ræp/ **raps, rapping, rapped.** [1] N-VAR & VERB **Rap** is a type of music in which the words are not sung but are spoken in a rapid, rhythmic way. Someone who **raps** performs rap. ◆ **rapper, rappers** N-COUNT ...the French rapper MC Solaar. [2] VERB & N-COUNT If you **rap on** something or **rap** it, you hit it with a series of quick blows. A **rap** is a quick hit or knock on something. Mike rapped the table... There was a rap on the door.

⭐ **rape** /reɪp/ **rapes, raping, raped.** VERB & N-VAR If someone **is raped**, they are forced to have sex against their will. **Rape** is the crime of forcing someone to have sex. She despised the men who had raped her. ◆ **rapist, rapists** N-COUNT The judge sentenced the two rapists to five years in prison.

⭐ **rapid** /'ræpɪd/. ADJ If something is **rapid**, it happens or moves very quickly. His heart rate seemed abnormally rapid to him. ◆ **rapidly** ADV ...Queensland's rapidly increasing population. ◆ **rapidity** /rə'pɪdɪti/ N-UNCOUNT ...the rapidity with which the weather can change.

rapids /'ræpɪdz/. N-PLURAL **Rapids** are parts of a river where the water moves very fast.

rapport /ræ'pɔː/. N-UNCOUNT **Rapport** is a feeling of understanding and sympathy between two or more people. ...the extraordinary rapport between the two leaders.

rapture /'ræptʃə/ **raptures.** N-VAR **Rapture** is a feeling of extreme joy or pleasure. [LITERARY] They will be in raptures over the French countryside.

rapturous /'ræptʃərəs/. ADJ A **rapturous** feeling or reaction is one of great happiness or enthusiasm. ◆ **rapturously** ADV The performance was greeted rapturously by the audience.

⭐ **rare** /reə/ **rarer, rarest.** [1] ADJ If something is **rare**, it is not common, and is therefore interesting, valuable, or unusual. ...rare breeds of cattle. ...those rare occasions when he did eat alone. [2] ADJ Meat that is **rare** is cooked very lightly so that the inside is still red.

⭐ **rarely** /'reəli/. ADV **Rarely** means not very often. I very rarely wear a raincoat.

rarity /'reərɪti/ **rarities.** [1] N-COUNT If someone or something is a **rarity**, they are interesting or valuable because they are so unusual. Signatures on 18th century Irish furniture are a rarity. [2] N-UNCOUNT The **rarity** of something is the fact that it is very uncommon. It was a real prize due to its rarity and good condition.

rash /ræʃ/ **rasher, rashest; rashes.** [1] ADJ If someone is **rash** or does **rash** things, they act without thinking carefully first. I don't want to make any rash promises. ◆ **rashly** ADV I made quite a lot of money, but I rashly gave most of it away. [2] N-COUNT A **rash** is an area of red spots on your skin which appear when you are ill or have an allergy. [3] N-SING A **rash** of events or things is a large number of them that all happen or appear within a short period of time. ...a rash of scandals.

rasp /rɑːsp, ræsp/ **rasps, rasping, rasped.** [1] VERB & N-SING If someone **rasps**, their voice or breathing is harsh and unpleasant to listen to. A **rasp** is this sound. ...the rasp of Rennie's voice. [2] VERB & N-SING If something **rasps**, it makes a harsh, unpleasant sound as it rubs against something hard or rough. A **rasp** is this sound. ...the rasp of something being drawn across the sand.

raspberry /'rɑːzbri, AM 'ræzberi/ **raspberries.** N-COUNT **Raspberries** are small, soft, red fruit that grow on bushes. → See picture on page 821.

rat /ræt/ **rats.** N-COUNT A **rat** is an animal which has a long tail and looks like a large mouse.

⭐ **rate** /reɪt/ **rates, rating, rated.** [1] N-COUNT The **rate** at which something happens is the speed or frequency with which it happens. ...the rate at

a
b
c
d
e
f
g
h
i
j
k
l
m
n
o
p
q
r
s
t
u
v
w
x
y
z

which hair grows... New diet books appear at a rate of nearly one a week. **2** N-COUNT A **rate** is the amount of money that is charged for goods or services. ...specially reduced rates for travellers using Gatwick Airport. **3** N-COUNT The **rate** of taxation or interest is its level, expressed as a percentage. The richest Americans pay taxes at a rate of 28%. **4** VERB If you **rate** someone or something as good or bad, you consider them to be good or bad. The film was rated excellent. **5** See also **rating**.

PHRASES ● You use **at any rate** to indicate that the important thing is what you are going to say now, and not what was said before. Well, at any rate, let me thank you for all you did. ● If you say that **at this rate** something bad or extreme will happen, you mean that it will happen if things continue to develop as they have been doing. At this rate they'd be lucky to get home before eight.

⭐ **rather** /'rɑːðə, 'ræð-/. **1** PREP & CONJ You use **rather than** when you are contrasting two things or situations. **Rather than** introduces the thing or situation that is not the case or that you do not want or approve of. I use the bike if I can rather than the car... She made students think for themselves, rather than telling them what to think. **2** ADV You use **rather** to introduce a correction or contrast to what you have just said. Twenty million years ago, Idaho was not the arid place it is now. Rather, it was warm and damp. **3** PHRASE If you **would rather** do something, you would prefer to do it. Kids would rather play than study. ● See note at **prefer**. **4** ADV You use **rather** to indicate that something is true to a fairly great extent. ...rather unusual circumstances.

> **USAGE** Rather, pretty, quite, and fairly can all be used to modify adjectives and adverbs, but are all less strong than **very**. **Rather** and **pretty** are the strongest of these words and are the closest to **very**. **Pretty**, in this sense, is informal. Therefore, if you said to someone, '**Your work is rather good**' or '**Your work is pretty good**', they would be more likely to be pleased than if you said '**Your work is quite good**' or '**Your work is fairly good**'. However, **rather** is commonly used with words indicating negative qualities. I was feeling rather sad. It is the only one of these words that can be used with comparatives, and with **too**. Global warming could be rather worse than we think it will be... He was becoming rather too friendly with my ex-boyfriend. **Quite** is slightly stronger than **fairly**, and may suggest that something has more of a quality than expected. Nobody here's ever heard of it but it is actually quite common.

5 ADV You use **rather** before verbs that introduce your thoughts and feelings, in order to express your opinion politely, especially when a different opinion has been expressed. [BRITISH] I rather think he was telling the truth.

ratify /'rætɪfaɪ/ **ratifies, ratifying, ratified.** VERB When national leaders or organizations **ratify** a treaty or written agreement, they make it official by giving their formal approval to it, usually by signing it or voting for it. ♦ **ratification** /,rætɪfɪ'keɪʃən/ **ratifications** N-COUNT ...the ratification of the treaty.

⭐ **rating** /'reɪtɪŋ/ **ratings.** N-COUNT A **rating** of something is a score or assessment of how good or popular it is. A student with 95 percent in a final examination scored a rating of five.

ratio /'reɪʃiəʊ, AM -ʃəʊ/ **ratios.** N-COUNT The **ratio** of something is the relationship between two things expressed in numbers or amounts, to show how much greater one is than the other. The adult to child ratio is 1 to 6.

ration /'ræʃən/ **rations, rationing, rationed.** **1** N-COUNT When there is a shortage of something, your **ration** of it is the amount that you are allowed to have. Families get a ration of tea, oil, sugar and rice. **2** VERB When something **is rationed**, you are only allowed to have a limited amount of it. Motorists will be rationed to thirty litres of petrol a month. ♦ **rationing** N-UNCOUNT Tea rationing ended in Britain in 1952. **3** N-PLURAL **Rations** are the food which is given to people with food shortages.

rational /'ræʃənəl/. **1** ADJ **Rational** decisions and thoughts are based on reason rather than on emotion. Look at both sides of the case and come to a rational decision. ♦ **rationally** ADV We discussed it rationally. ♦ **rationality** /ræʃə'nælɪti/ N-UNCOUNT We live in an era of rationality. **2** ADJ A **rational** person is someone who thinks clearly and is not emotionally or mentally unbalanced. Rachel looked calmer and more rational now.

rationale /,ræʃə'nɑːl, -'næl/ **rationales.** N-COUNT The **rationale** for a course of action or a belief is the set of reasons on which it is based. The rationale behind the project was that 'where learning is fun, it is done better'.

rationalist /'ræʃənəlɪst/ **rationalists.** N-COUNT & ADJ A **rationalist**, or a person with **rationalist** views, believes that their life should be based on reason and logic, rather than emotions or religious beliefs. ♦ **rationalism** /'ræʃənəlɪzəm/ N-UNCOUNT ...the rationalism of Western culture.

rationalize (BRIT also **rationalise**) /'ræʃənəlaɪz/ **rationalizes, rationalizing, rationalized.** **1** VERB If you try to **rationalize** attitudes or actions that are difficult to accept, you think of reasons to justify or explain them. ...an attempt to rationalize my feelings. ♦ **rationalization** /,ræʃənəlaɪ'zeɪʃən/ N-VAR ...the rationalization of middle-class values. **2** VERB When a company, system, or industry **is rationalized**, it is made more efficient, usually by getting rid of staff and equipment. ♦ **rationalization** N-UNCOUNT ...the recent rationalization of the textile industry.

rationing /'ræʃənɪŋ/. See **ration**.

rattle /'rætəl/ **rattles, rattling, rattled.** [1] VERB &
N-COUNT When something **rattles**, or when you
rattle it, it makes short sharp knocking sounds
because it is being shaken or it keeps hitting
against something hard. A **rattle** is this noise. *...a
train rattled by... There was a rattle of rifle-fire.*
[2] N-COUNT A **rattle** is a baby's toy with loose bits
inside which make a noise when the baby shakes
it. [3] VERB If something or someone **rattles** you,
they make you nervous. *The question didn't rattle
her.* ◆ **rattled** ADJ *His supporters seem a bit
rattled.*
▸ **rattle off.** PHR-VERB If you **rattle off** something,
you say it or do it very quickly and without much
effort. *He rattled off the names.*

raucous /'rɔːkəs/. ADJ A **raucous** sound is loud,
harsh, and rather unpleasant. *...the raucous cries
of the sea-birds.* ◆ **raucously** ADV *They laughed
together raucously.*

ravage /'rævɪdʒ/ **ravages, ravaging, ravaged.** VERB A
town, country, or economy that **has been
ravaged** has been damaged so much that it is
almost completely destroyed. *The country has
been ravaged by civil war.*

ravages /'rævɪdʒɪz/. N-PLURAL The **ravages of**
time, war, or the weather are the damaging
effects that they have. *...the ravages of winter.*

rave /reɪv/ **raves, raving, raved.** [1] VERB If someone
raves, they talk in an excited and uncontrolled
way. *'What is wrong with you, acting like that,' she
raved.* [2] VERB If you **rave about** something, you
speak or write about it with great enthusiasm.
Rachel raved about the new foods she ate.
[3] N-COUNT A **rave** or a **rave review** is a very
enthusiastic review. *'Only the Truth is Funny', has
drawn raves from the critics.* [4] N-COUNT A **rave** is
a large musical event in a club or in the open air
which attracts people who like dancing to
modern, electronic, dance music. [5] See also
raving.

raven /'reɪvən/ **ravens.** [1] N-COUNT A **raven** is a
large bird with shiny black feathers and a deep
harsh call. [2] ADJ **Raven** hair is shiny, black, and
smooth. [WRITTEN]

ravine /rə'viːn/ **ravines.** N-COUNT A **ravine** is a
very deep narrow valley with steep sides.

raving /'reɪvɪŋ/. ADJ & ADV You use **raving** to
describe someone who you think is completely
mad. [INFORMAL] *Malcolm looked at her as if she
were a raving lunatic... Jean-Paul has gone raving
mad.*

★ **raw** /rɔː/. [1] ADJ A **raw** substance is in its
natural state before being processed. *...two ships
carrying raw sugar from Cuba.* [2] ADJ **Raw** food
has not been cooked, or has not been cooked
enough. *...a popular dish made of raw fish.* [3] ADJ
If a part of your body is **raw**, it is red and painful
because the skin has been damaged. [4] ADJ If
you describe someone in a new job as **raw**, or as
a **raw** recruit, you mean that they lack experience
in that job. *Davies is still raw but his potential*

shows. [5] PHRASE If you say that you are getting **a
raw deal**, you mean that you are being treated
unfairly. [INFORMAL]

★ **ray** /reɪ/ **rays.** [1] N-COUNT **Rays** of light are narrow
beams of light. [2] N-SING A **ray of** hope, comfort,
or other positive quality is a small amount that
makes a bad situation seem less bad. *The drug is
a ray of hope for the 500,000 victims of Alzheimer's
in Britain today.*

razor /'reɪzə/ **razors.** N-COUNT A **razor** is a tool
that people use for shaving.

Rd. Rd is a written abbreviation for 'road'. *...St
Pancras Library, 100 Euston Rd, London, NW1.*

-'re. -'re is a shortened form of 'are' that is used
in spoken English and in informal written English.
*We're not, are we?... What're you going to do?...
People're working on that now.*

★ **reach** /riːtʃ/ **reaches, reaching, reached.** [1] VERB
When someone or something **reaches** a place,
they arrive there. *He did not stop until he reached
the door.* [2] VERB If you **reach** somewhere, you
move your arm and hand to take or touch
something. *Judy reached into her handbag.*
[3] VERB If you can **reach** something, you are able
to touch it by stretching out your arm or leg. *Can
you reach your toes with your fingertips?* [4] VERB If
you try to **reach** someone, you try to contact
them, usually by telephone. *Has the doctor told
you how to reach him or her in emergencies?*
[5] VERB If someone or something **has reached** a
certain stage or amount, they are at that stage or
amount. *We're told the figure could reach 100,000
next year.* [6] VERB If something **reaches** a place
or level, it extends as far as that place or level. *...a
nightshirt which reached to his knees.* [7] VERB
When people **reach** an agreement or
compromise, they succeed in achieving it. *They
are meeting in Lusaka in an attempt to reach a
compromise.*

★ **react** /ri'ækt/ **reacts, reacting, reacted.** [1] VERB
When you **react to** something that has
happened to you, you behave in a particular way
because of it. *They reacted violently to the news...
It's natural to react with disbelief if your child is
accused of bullying.* [2] VERB If you **react against**
someone's way of behaving, you deliberately
behave in a different way. *My father never saved
and perhaps I reacted against that.* [3] VERB If you
react to a treatment or substance, you are
affected unpleasantly or made ill by it. *He reacted
very badly to the radiation therapy.* [4] VERB When
one chemical substance **reacts with** another,
they combine chemically to form another
substance. *Calcium reacts with water... These two
gases react readily to produce carbon dioxide and
water.*

★ **reaction** /ri'ækʃən/ **reactions.** [1] N-VAR Your
reaction to something that has happened or
something that you have experienced is what
you feel, say, or do because of it. *Reaction to the
visit is mixed... He was surprised that his answer
should have caused such a strong reaction.*
[2] N-COUNT A **reaction against** something is a

a
b
c
d
e
f
g
h
i
j
k
l
m
n
o
p
q
r
s
t
u
v
w
x
y
z

way of behaving or doing something that is deliberately different from what has been done before. *All new fashion starts out as a reaction against existing convention. ...a strong reaction against the reform.* **3** N-COUNT If you have a **reaction to** a treatment or substance, you are affected unpleasantly or made ill by it. *...life-threatening reactions to anaesthetics.* **4** N-PLURAL Your **reactions** are your ability to move quickly in response to something. *The sport requires very fast reactions.* **5** N-COUNT The **reaction between** two chemical substances is what happens when they combine to form another substance. *Ozone is produced by the reaction between oxygen and ultra-violet light. ...chemical reactions.*

reactionary /ri'ækʃənri, AM -neri/ **reactionaries.** N-COUNT & ADJ A **reactionary** or a **reactionary** person or group tries to prevent changes in the political or social system of their country; used showing disapproval. *...reactionary forces trying to spread fear, confusion and discontent.*

reactor /ri'æktə/ **reactors.** N-COUNT A **reactor** is a device which produces nuclear energy.

⭐ **read, reads, reading, read.**

✓ When it is the present tense, **read** is pronounced /riːd/; **read** is also the past tense and past participle, when it is pronounced /red/.

1 VERB & N-COUNT When you **read** something such as a book or article, you look at and understand or say aloud the words that are written there. You can also say you have a **read**. *He read through the pages slowly... I read them a story before tucking them in... I settled down to have a good read.* **2** VERB If you can **read** music, you have the ability to look at and understand the written symbols that are used to represent musical sounds. **3** VERB You can use **read** when saying what is written somewhere. For example, if a notice **reads** 'Exit', the word 'Exit' is written on it. **4** VERB If you refer to how a piece of writing **reads**, you are referring to its style. *It reads very awkwardly.* **5** N-COUNT If you say that a book is a good **read**, you mean that it is very enjoyable to read. **6** VERB If you **read** someone's mind or their mood, you know what they are thinking or feeling without them telling you. **7** VERB When you **read** a measuring device, you look at it to see what the measurement on it is. *It is essential that you are able to read a thermometer.* **8** See also **reading**. ● **to read between the lines**: see **line**.

▸**read into.** PHR-VERB If you **read** a meaning **into** something, you think it is there although it may not be. *It would be wrong to try to read too much into such a light-hearted production.*

▸**read out.** PHR-VERB If you **read** something **out**, you say the words aloud, especially in a loud, clear voice. *The evidence was read out to the court.*

▸**read up on.** PHR-VERB If you **read up on** a subject, you read a lot about it so that you become informed on it.

readable /'riːdəbəl/. ADJ If a book or article is **readable**, it is enjoyable and easy to read.

⭐ **reader** /'riːdə/ **readers.** N-COUNT The **readers** of a book, newspaper, or magazine are the people who read it.

readership /'riːdəʃɪp/. N-SING The **readership** of a book, newspaper, or magazine is the number or type of people who read it. *...a college-age readership.*

readily /'redɪli/. **1** ADV If you do something **readily**, you do it willingly. *When I was invited to the party, I readily accepted.* **2** ADV You use **readily** to say that something can be done or obtained quickly and easily. *I don't readily make friends.*

⭐ **reading** /'riːdɪŋ/ **readings.** **1** N-UNCOUNT **Reading** is the activity of reading books. *I have always loved reading.* **2** N-COUNT A **reading** is an event at which extracts from books are read to an audience. **3** N-COUNT The **reading** on a measuring device is the measurement that it shows.

readjust /ˌriːə'dʒʌst/ **readjusts, readjusting, readjusted.** **1** VERB When you **readjust to** a new situation, you adapt to it. *I can understand why astronauts find it difficult to readjust to life on earth.* ♦ **readjustment, readjustments** N-VAR *...a period of readjustment.* **2** VERB If you **readjust** something, you change it so that it is more effective or appropriate. *The rebel army has readjusted its strategy.* ♦ **readjustment** N-VAR *...readjustment of state borders.*

⭐ **ready** /'redi/ **readies, readying, readied.** **1** ADJ AFTER LINK-V If someone or something is **ready**, they have reached the required stage for something or they are properly prepared for action or use. *It took her a long time to get ready for church... Your breakfast's ready.* ♦ **readiness** N-UNCOUNT *The newsletter was printed towards the end of June in readiness for mailing.* **2** ADJ AFTER LINK-V If you are **ready to** do something, you are willing to do it. *She was always ready to give interviews.* ♦ **readiness** N-UNCOUNT *...his readiness to accept criticism.* **3** ADJ AFTER LINK-V If someone or something is **ready to** do something, they are about to do it or likely to do it. *It's like a volcano ready to erupt.* **4** ADJ AFTER LINK-V If you are **ready for** something, you need it or want it. *After five days in the heat of Bangkok, we were ready for the beach.* **5** ADJ BEFORE N You use **ready** to describe things that are able to be used quickly and easily. *...a ready supply of well-trained workers.* **6** VERB When you **ready** something, you prepare it for a particular purpose. [FORMAL] *Soldiers were readying themselves for the final assault.* **7** **Ready** combines with past participles to indicate that something has already been done, and that therefore you do not have to do it yourself. *...ready-printed forms.* **8** PHRASE If you have something **at the ready**, you have it in a position where it can be quickly and easily used. *...soldiers with guns at the ready.*

,ready-'made. [1] ADJ If something that you buy is **ready-made**, you can use it immediately. [2] ADJ **Ready-made** means extremely convenient or useful for a particular purpose. ....*a ready-made topic of conversation.*

reaffirm /ˌriːəˈfɜːm/ **reaffirms, reaffirming, reaffirmed.** VERB If you **reaffirm** something, you state it again clearly and firmly. [FORMAL] *Police reaffirmed that he was a top suspect.*

⭐ **real** /riːl/. [1] ADJ Something that is **real** actually exists and is not imagined or theoretical. *No, it wasn't a dream. It was real.* [2] ADJ A material or object that is **real** is genuine and not artificial or an imitation. ...*real leather... Who's to know if they're real guns or not?* [3] ADJ BEFORE N You can use **real** to say that someone or something has all the characteristics or qualities that such a person or thing typically has. ...*his first real girlfriend.* [4] ADJ BEFORE N You can use **real** to describe something that is the true or original thing of its kind. *Her real name had been Miriam Pinckus.* [5] ADV You can use **real** to emphasize an adjective or adverb. [INFORMAL, AMERICAN]
PHRASES ● If someone does something **for real**, they actually do it and do not just pretend to do it. *He thought it was all a big joke, he had no idea it was for real.* ● You use **in real terms** to refer to the actual value or cost of something. For example, if your pocket money rises by 5% but prices rise by 10%, in real terms you get less pocket money. ● If you say that a thing or event is **the real thing**, you mean that it is the actual thing or event, and not an imitation or rehearsal. *The counterfeits sell for $20 less than the real thing.*

'real estate. N-UNCOUNT **Real estate** is property in the form of buildings and land. [AMERICAN]

realise /ˈriːəlaɪz/. See **realize**.

realism /ˈriːəlɪzəm/. [1] N-UNCOUNT When people show **realism** in their behaviour, they recognize and accept the true nature of a situation and try to deal with it in a practical way. ◆ **realist, realists** N-COUNT *I see myself as a realist.* [2] N-UNCOUNT If things and people are presented with **realism** in painting, novels, or films, they are presented in a way that is like real life; used showing approval. ◆ **realist** ADJ BEFORE N ...*the foremost realist painter of our times.*

realistic /ˌriːəˈlɪstɪk/. [1] ADJ If you are **realistic** about a situation, you recognize and accept its true nature and try to deal with it practically. *It's only realistic to acknowledge that something, some time, will go wrong.* ◆ **realistically** ADV *As an adult, you can assess the situation realistically.* [2] ADJ You say that a painting, story, or film is **realistic** when the people and things in it are like people and things in real life. ◆ **realistically** ADV *The film starts off realistically and then develops into a ridiculous fantasy.*

⭐ **reality** /riːˈælɪti/ **realities.** [1] N-UNCOUNT You use **reality** to refer to real things or the real nature of things rather than imagined, invented, or theoretical ideas. *Fiction and reality were increasingly blurred.* [2] N-COUNT The **reality of** a

situation is the truth about it, especially when it is unpleasant. ...*the harsh reality of top international competition.* [3] N-VAR If something becomes a **reality**, it actually exists or is actually happening. *The reality is that they are poor.* [4] PHRASE You can use **in reality** to introduce a statement about the real nature of something, when it contrasts with something incorrect that has just been described. *He came across as streetwise, but in reality he was not.*

re'ality TV. N-UNCOUNT **Reality TV** is a type of television which aims to show how ordinary people behave in everyday life, or in situations, often created by the programme makers, which are intended to represent everyday life.

⭐ **realize** (BRIT also **realise**) /ˈriːəlaɪz/ **realizes, realizing, realized.** [1] VERB If you **realize** that something is true, you become aware of that fact or understand it. *People don't realize how serious this recession has actually been.* ◆ **realization, realizations** N-COUNT *There is now a growing realisation that things cannot go on like this.* [2] VERB When someone **realizes** a design or an idea, they make or organize something based on that design or idea. [FORMAL] *The characters in 'Terminator II' have been cleverly realised.* [3] VERB If your hopes, desires, or fears **are realized**, the things that you hope for, desire, or fear actually happen. [FORMAL] ◆ **realization** N-UNCOUNT ...*the realization of his worst fears.*

⭐ **really** /ˈriːəli/. [1] ADV You can use **really** to emphasize a statement. [SPOKEN] *I'm very sorry. I really am... I really do feel that some people are being unfair.* [2] ADV You use **really** when you are discussing the real facts about something, in contrast to the ones someone wants you to believe. *My father didn't really love her... What was really going on?* [3] ADV People sometimes use **really** to slightly reduce the force of a negative statement. *I'm not really surprised... 'Did they hurt you?'—'Not really'.* [4] CONVENTION You can say **'Really?'** to express surprise or disbelief. *'We saw a very bright shooting star.'—'Did you really?'*

> **USAGE** When **really** is used in a negative sentence, its position in relation to the verb affects the meaning. For instance, if you say **'I really don't like Richard'**, with **really** in front of the verb, you are emphasizing how much you dislike Richard. However, if you say **'I don't really like Richard'**, with **really** coming after the negative, you are still saying that you dislike Richard, but the feeling is not particularly strong.

realm /relm/ **realms.** N-COUNT You can use **realm** to refer to any area of activity, interest, or thought. [FORMAL] ...*the realm of politics.*

,real 'world. N-SING If you talk about **the real world**, you are referring to the world and life in general, in contrast to a particular person's own

a
b
c
d
e
f
g
h
i
j
k
l
m
n
o
p
q
r
s
t
u
v
w
x
y
z

life, experience, and ideas. *When they eventually leave the school they will be totally ill-equipped to deal with the real world.*

reap /riːp/ **reaps, reaping, reaped.** VERB If you **reap** the benefits or the rewards of something, you enjoy the good things that happen as a result of it.

reappear /ˌriːəˈpɪə/ **reappears, reappearing, reappeared.** VERB When people or things **reappear**, they return after they have been away or out of sight for some time. ♦ **reappearance, reappearances** N-COUNT ...*the reappearance of Cossack culture in Russia.*

⭐ **rear** /rɪə/. **rears, rearing, reared.** ❶ N-SING The **rear** of something is the back part of it. ...*the rear of the building... Manufacturers have been obliged to fit rear seat belts in all new cars.* ❷ VERB If you **rear** children or young animals, you look after them until they are old enough to look after themselves. *I was reared in east Texas.* ❸ VERB & PHR-VB If a horse **rears** or **rears up**, it moves the front part of its body upwards, so that its front legs are high in the air and it is standing on its back legs.

rearrange /ˌriːəˈreɪndʒ/ **rearranges, rearranging, rearranged.** VERB If you **rearrange** things, you change the way they are organized or ordered. *She rearranged the furniture.* ♦ **rearrangement, rearrangements** N-VAR ...*a rearrangement of our parliamentary institutions.*

⭐ **reason** /ˈriːzən/ **reasons, reasoning, reasoned.** ❶ N-COUNT The **reason for** something is a fact or situation which explains why it happens. *There is a reason for everything that happens... Who would have a reason to want to kill her? ...the reason why Italian tomatoes have so much flavour... For some reason Herman decided not to play the piece.* ❷ N-UNCOUNT If you say that you have **reason to** believe something or **to** have a particular emotion, you mean that you have evidence for your belief or there is a definite cause of your feeling. *He had every reason to be upset.* ❸ N-UNCOUNT The ability that people have to think and to make sensible judgments can be referred to as **reason**. ...*a conflict between emotion and reason.* ❹ VERB If you **reason** that something is true, you decide that it is true after thinking carefully about all the facts. *I reasoned that if he could do it, so could I... 'Motherhood would be a full-time job,' she reasoned.* ❺ PHRASE If one thing happens **by reason of** another, it happens because of it. [FORMAL] ❻ See also **reasoned, reasoning.**
▸**reason with.** PHR-VERB If you try to **reason with** someone, you try to persuade them to do something or to accept something by using sensible arguments.

⭐ **reasonable** /ˈriːzənəbəl/. ❶ ADJ If you think that someone is fair and sensible you can say they are **reasonable**. ...*this moderate and reasonable man. ...a perfectly reasonable decision.* ♦ **reasonably** ADV *'I'm sorry, Andrew,' she said reasonably.* ♦ **reasonableness** N-UNCOUNT *Bertha spoke with calm reasonableness.* ❷ ADJ If

you say that an expectation or explanation is **reasonable**, you mean that there are good reasons why it may be correct. *It seems reasonable to expect rapid urban growth.* ♦ **reasonably** ADV *Today's young adults can reasonably expect to live well into their 70s.* ❸ ADJ If you say that the price of something is **reasonable**, you mean that it is fair and not too high. ♦ **reasonably** ADV ...*reasonably priced accommodation.* ❹ ADJ You can use **reasonable** to describe something that is fairly good, but not very good. ♦ **reasonably** ADV *I can dance reasonably well.* ❺ ADJ A **reasonable** amount of something is a fairly large amount of it. *There are a reasonable number of people here.* ♦ **reasonably** ADV *The repairs were made reasonably quickly.*

reasoned /ˈriːzənd/. ADJ A **reasoned** discussion or argument is based on sensible reasons, rather than on feelings.

reasoning /ˈriːzənɪŋ/. N-UNCOUNT **Reasoning** is the process by which you reach a conclusion after considering all the facts. ...*the reasoning behind the decision.*

reassert /ˌriːəˈsɜːt/ **reasserts, reasserting, reasserted.** ❶ VERB If you **reassert** your control or authority, you make it clear that you are still in a position of power, or you strengthen the power that you had. ❷ VERB If something such as an idea or habit **reasserts itself**, it becomes noticeable again.

reassess /ˌriːəˈses/ **reassesses, reassessing, reassessed.** VERB If you **reassess** a situation, you think about it and decide whether you need to change your opinion about it. ♦ **reassessment, reassessments** N-VAR *We need an urgent reassessment of the entire programme.*

reassure /ˌriːəˈʃʊə/ **reassures, reassuring, reassured.** VERB If you **reassure** someone, you say or do things to make them stop worrying about something. ♦ **reassurance, reassurances** N-VAR *She needed reassurance that she belonged somewhere.*

reassured /ˌriːəˈʃʊəd/. ADJ If you feel **reassured**, you feel less worried about something. *We both felt reassured after a talk with the surgeon.*

reassuring /ˌriːəˈʃʊərɪŋ/. ADJ If you find someone's words or actions **reassuring**, they make you feel less worried. ♦ **reassuringly** ADV *'It's okay now,' he said reassuringly.*

rebate /ˈriːbeɪt/ **rebates.** N-COUNT A **rebate** is an amount of money which is paid to you when you have paid more tax, rent, or rates than you needed to.

⭐ **rebel, rebels, rebelling, rebelled;** verb /rɪˈbel/, noun /ˈrebəl/. ❶ N-COUNT **Rebels** are people who are fighting against their own country's army in order to change the political system there. ❷ VERB If politicians **rebel against** one of their own party's policies, they show that they oppose it. ❸ N-COUNT Politicians who show that they oppose their own party's policies are sometimes referred to as **rebels**. ☐4 VERB When someone **rebels**, they start to behave differently from other people and reject the values of society or of their parents. ☐5 N-COUNT If you say that someone is a **rebel**, you mean that they behave differently from other people and reject the values of society or of their parents.

rebellion /rɪ'beliən/ **rebellions**. ☐1 N-VAR A **rebellion** is a violent organized action by a large group of people who are trying to change their country's political system. ☐2 N-VAR A **rebellion** is a situation in which politicians show their opposition to their own party's policies.

rebellious /rɪ'beliəs/. ADJ A **rebellious** person behaves in an unacceptable way and does not do what they are told. ♦ **rebelliousness** N-UNCOUNT *With adolescence his rebelliousness only increased.*

rebirth /ˌriː'bɜːθ/. N-SING You can refer to a change that leads to a new period of growth and improvement in something as its **rebirth**. *...the rebirth of democracy in Latin America.*

rebound /rɪ'baʊnd/ **rebounds, rebounding, rebounded**. ☐1 VERB If something **rebounds** from a solid surface, it bounces or springs back from it. *The ball rebounded off the wall.* ☐2 VERB If an action or situation **rebounds on** you, it has an unpleasant effect on you, especially when this effect was intended for someone else. *Mia realised her trick had rebounded on her.*

rebuff /rɪ'bʌf/ **rebuffs, rebuffing, rebuffed**. VERB & N-VAR If someone **rebuffs** your suggestion or advice, or if they treat it with a **rebuff**, they respond in an unfriendly way and refuse to accept it.

rebuild /ˌriː'bɪld/ **rebuilds, rebuilding, rebuilt**. ☐1 VERB When people **rebuild** something such as a building, they build it again after it has been damaged or destroyed. ☐2 VERB When people **rebuild** something such as an institution, a system, or an aspect of their lives, they take action to restore it to its previous state.

rebuke /rɪ'bjuːk/ **rebukes, rebuking, rebuked**. VERB & N-VAR If you **rebuke** someone, or if you give them a **rebuke**, you speak severely to them because they have said or done something that you do not approve of. [FORMAL]

⭐ **recall** /rɪ'kɔːl/ **recalls, recalling, recalled**. ☐1 VERB When you **recall** something, you remember it. *I recalled all that Ray had told me... She could not recall ever seeing him drunk.* ☐2 VERB When you **recall** something, you remember it and tell others about it. *Henderson recalled that he first met Pollard during a business trip... 'That evening,' I felt he was friendly,' she recalled.* ☐3 VERB If you **are recalled** to your home, country, or the place where you work, you are ordered to return there. *Spain has recalled its Ambassador after a row over refugees.*

recapture /ˌriː'kæptʃə/ **recaptures, recapturing, recaptured**. ☐1 VERB & N-SING When soldiers **recapture** a place, they win control of it again

from an opposing army who had taken it from them. You can also refer to the **recapture** of a place. ☐2 VERB & N-SING To **recapture** a person or animal which has escaped from somewhere means to catch them again. You can also refer to the **recapture** of a person or animal. ☐3 VERB When you **recapture** something such as an experience, emotion, or a quality you had in the past, or when something **recaptures** it for you, you experience it again. *This macho behaviour is the way they try and recapture their youth.*

recede /rɪ'siːd/ **recedes, receding, receded**. ☐1 VERB If something **recedes** from you, it moves away into the distance. *Luke's footsteps receded into the night.* ☐2 VERB When something such as a quality, problem, or illness **recedes**, it becomes weaker, smaller, or less intense. ☐3 VERB If a man's hair starts to **recede**, it no longer grows on the front of his head.

receipt /rɪ'siːt/ **receipts**. ☐1 N-COUNT A **receipt** is a piece of paper that you get from someone as confirmation that they have received money or goods from you. *I wrote her a receipt for the money.* ☐2 N-PLURAL **Receipts** are the amount of money received during a particular period, for example by a shop or theatre. *On Saturdays Amos takes the week's receipts to the bank.* ☐3 N-UNCOUNT The **receipt of** something is the act of receiving it. [FORMAL] *We cannot acknowledge receipt of letters.*

⭐ **receive** /rɪ'siːv/ **receives, receiving, received**. ☐1 VERB When you **receive** something, you get it after someone gives it to you or sends it to you. *They will receive their awards at a ceremony in Stockholm.* ☐2 VERB You can use **receive** to say that certain kinds of thing happen to someone. For example if they are injured, you can say that they received an injury. *He received more of the blame than anyone.* ☐3 VERB If you say that something **is received** in a particular way, you mean that people react to it in that way. *The book's been well received.*

receiver /rɪ'siːvə/ **receivers**. ☐1 N-COUNT A telephone **receiver** is the part that you hold near to your ear and speak into. ☐2 N-COUNT A **receiver** is the part of a radio or television that picks up incoming signals and converts them into sound or pictures. ☐3 N-COUNT A **receiver** is someone who is officially appointed to manage the affairs of a business, usually when it has gone into bankruptcy.

⭐ **recent** /'riːsənt/. ADJ A **recent** event or period of time happened only a short while ago. *...her recent trip to Argentina... The situation has improved in recent years.*

⭐ **recently** /'riːsəntli/. ADV If you have done something **recently** or if something happened **recently**, it happened only a short time ago. *Mr Stevens recently celebrated his eightieth birthday... Until recently she was renting a house.*

reception /rɪ'sepʃən/ **receptions**. ☐1 N-UNCOUNT In a hotel, office, or hospital, **reception** is the place where people are received and their reservations,

a b c d e f g h i j k l m n o p q r s t u v w x y z

appointments, and inquiries are dealt with. *'For you,' the young lady at reception said. ...the hotel reception desk.* **2** N-COUNT A **reception** is a formal party which is given to celebrate a special event or to welcome someone. *The wedding and the reception will be held on Saturday.* **3** N-COUNT If something or someone has a particular kind of **reception**, that is the way people react to them. *He received a cool reception to his speech.* **4** N-UNCOUNT If you get good **reception** from your radio or television, the sound or picture is clear because the signal is strong.

receptionist /rɪ'sepʃənɪst/ **receptionists.** N-COUNT In a hotel, office, or hospital, the **receptionist** is the person whose job is to answer the telephone, arrange reservations or appointments, and deal with people when they first arrive.

receptive /rɪ'septɪv/. ADJ Someone who is **receptive to** new ideas or suggestions is prepared to consider them or accept them.

recess /rɪ'ses, 'riːses/ **recesses, recessing, recessed.** **1** N-VAR A **recess** is a break between the sessions of work of an official body such as a committee, a court of law, or a government. *The conference broke for a recess.* **2** VERB When formal proceedings **recess**, they stop temporarily. *The hearings have now recessed for dinner.* **3** N-COUNT In a room, a **recess** is part of a wall which is built further back than the rest of the wall. **4** N-COUNT The **recesses of** something are its deep or hidden parts. *He emerged from the dark recesses of the garage.*

☆ **recession** /rɪ'seʃən/ **recessions.** N-VAR A **recession** is a period when the economy of a country is not very successful. *The oil price increases sent Europe into deep recession.*

recipe /'resɪpi/ **recipes.** **1** N-COUNT A **recipe** is a list of ingredients and a set of instructions that tell you how to cook something. **2** N-SING If you say that something is **a recipe for** a particular situation, you mean that it is likely to result in that situation. *When two ladies are involved in the same kitchen, it is often a recipe for disaster.*

recipient /rɪ'sɪpiənt/ **recipients.** N-COUNT The **recipient of** something is the person who receives it. [FORMAL] *...recipients of government grants.*

reciprocal /rɪ'sɪprəkəl/. ADJ A **reciprocal** action or agreement involves two people or groups who do the same thing to each other or agree to help each other in a similar way. [FORMAL] *...the old reciprocal relationship that exists between workers and employers.*

reciprocate /rɪ'sɪprəkeɪt/ **reciprocates, reciprocating, reciprocated.** VERB If you reciprocate your feelings or actions towards someone **are reciprocated**, the other person feels or behaves in the same way towards you as you have felt or behaved towards them. *I hope they reciprocate by coming to support us.*

recital /rɪ'saɪtəl/ **recitals.** N-COUNT A **recital** is a performance of music or poetry, usually given by one person.

recite /rɪ'saɪt/ **recites, reciting, recited.** **1** VERB When someone **recites** a poem or other piece of writing, they say it aloud after they have learned it. **2** VERB If you **recite** something such as a list, you say it aloud. *All he could do was recite a list of Government failings.*

reckless /'rekləs/. ADJ A **reckless** person shows a lack of care about danger or about the results of their actions. *She was reckless and utterly without fear. ...reckless driving.* ♦ **recklessly** ADV *She spent money recklessly.* ♦ **recklessness** N-UNCOUNT *...the headstrong recklessness of youth.*

☆ **reckon** /'rekən/ **reckons, reckoning, reckoned.** **1** VERB If you **reckon** that something is true, you think that it is true. [INFORMAL] *Toni reckoned that it must be about three o'clock.* **2** VERB If something **is reckoned to** be a particular figure, it is calculated to be roughly that amount. *The market's revised threshold is now reckoned to be 22,000–22,500.*

▸ **reckon with.** **1** PHR-VERB If you had not **reckoned with** something, you had not expected it and so were not ready for it. *Giles had not reckoned with the strength of Sally's feelings for him.* **2** PHRASE If you refer to a person or force as someone or something **to be reckoned with**, you mean that they will be difficult to deal with because they are quite powerful or skilful. *Women have become a force to be reckoned with.*

reckoning /'rekənɪŋ/ **reckonings.** N-VAR Someone's **reckoning** is a calculation they make about something. *By my reckoning 50% of the people in our team will be available.*

reclaim /rɪ'kleɪm/ **reclaims, reclaiming, reclaimed.** **1** VERB If you **reclaim** something that you have lost or had taken away from you, you succeed in getting it back. *We can reclaim the income tax which you have already paid on this money.* **2** VERB When people **reclaim** land, they make it suitable for use by draining or irrigating it. *...1,100 acres of reclaimed land in Tokyo Bay.*

recline /rɪ'klaɪn/ **reclines, reclining, reclined.** **1** VERB If you **recline** on something, you sit or lie on it with the upper part of your body supported at an angle. *Some guests recline in lounge chairs.* **2** VERB If a seat **reclines**, you can lower the back so that it is more comfortable to sit in. *First-class seats recline almost like beds.*

recluse /rɪ'kluːs, AM 'rekluːs/ **recluses.** N-COUNT A **recluse** is a person who lives alone and deliberately avoids other people.

reclusive /rɪ'kluːsɪv/. ADJ If someone is **reclusive**, they prefer to live on their own and deliberately avoid other people.

☆ **recognition** /,rekəg'nɪʃən/. **1** N-UNCOUNT **Recognition** is the act of recognizing someone or identifying something when you see it. *He searched for a sign of recognition on her face.* **2** N-UNCOUNT **Recognition** of something is an understanding and acceptance of it. *...their*

recognition of the workers' right to strike.
3 N-UNCOUNT When a person receives **recognition** for the things that they have done, people acknowledge the value or skill of their work. *Her father's work has received popular recognition.* **4** PHRASE If something is done **in recognition** of someone's achievements, it is done as a way of showing official appreciation of them. *He was presented with a bottle of champagne in recognition of his services to Australian soccer.*

recognizable (BRIT also **recognisable**) /ˌrekəgˈnaɪzəbəl/. ADJ Something that is **recognizable** is easy to recognize or identify. *This tree is always recognizable by its extremely beautiful silvery bark.*

⭐ **recognize** (BRIT also **recognise**) /ˈrekəgnaɪz/ **recognizes, recognizing, recognized.** **1** VERB If you **recognize** someone or something, you know who or what they are, because you have seen or heard them before or because they have been described to you. *The receptionist recognized him at once. ...a man I easily recognized as Luke's father.* **2** VERB You say that you **recognize** something when you realize or accept that it exists or that it is true. *Of course I recognize that evil exists... They have been slow to recognize AIDS as a problem.* **3** VERB If people or organizations **recognize** something as valid, they officially accept it or approve of it. *Russia has recognized Ukraine independence.* **4** VERB When people **recognize** the work someone has done, they show their appreciation of it, often by giving that person an award.

recoil /rɪˈkɔɪl/ **recoils, recoiling, recoiled.** **1** VERB If something makes you **recoil**, you move your body quickly away from it because it frightens, offends, or hurts you. *I thought he was going to kiss me. I recoiled in horror.* **2** VERB If you say that someone **recoils from** doing something or **recoils at** the idea of something, you mean that they are reluctant to do it because they dislike it so much. *People used to recoil from the idea of getting into debt.*

recollection /ˌrekəˈlekʃən/ **recollections.** N-VAR If you have a **recollection of** something, you remember it. *Pat has vivid recollections of the trip... He had no recollection of the crash.*

⭐ **recommend** /ˌrekəˈmend/ **recommends, recommending, recommended.** **1** VERB If someone **recommends** something or someone **to** you, they suggest that you would find them good or useful. *I have just spent a holiday there and would recommend it to anyone... I'll recommend you for a promotion.* ♦ **recommended** ADJ *This book is highly recommended.* ♦ **recommendation, recommendations** N-COUNT *Most people choose a product often on the recommendation of others.* **2** VERB If you **recommend** that something is done, you advise that it should be done. *It is recommended that you should consult your doctor.* ♦ **recommendation** N-COUNT *The committee's recommendations are unlikely to be made public.*

3 VERB If something has a particular quality **to recommend** it, that quality makes it attractive or gives it an advantage over similar things. *La Noblesse restaurant has much to recommend it to diners.*

reconcile /ˈrekənsaɪl/ **reconciles, reconciling, reconciled.** **1** VERB If you **reconcile** two beliefs, facts, or demands that seem to be opposed or completely different, you find a way in which they can both be true or both be fulfilled. *It's difficult to reconcile the demands of my job and the desire to be a good father.* ♦ **reconciliation** /ˌrekənsɪliˈeɪʃən/ N-SING *...a reconciliation of the values of equality and liberty.* **2** VERB If you **are reconciled with** someone, you become friendly with them again after a disagreement. *He never believed he and Susan would be reconciled. ...my attempt to reconcile him with Toby.* ♦ **reconciliation, reconciliations** N-VAR *The couple have separated but he wants a reconciliation.* **3** VERB If you **reconcile yourself to** an unpleasant situation, you accept it. *She had reconciled herself to never seeing him again.* ♦ **reconciled** ADJ AFTER LINK-V *He seemed reconciled to defeat.*

reconnaissance /rɪˈkɒnɪsəns/. N-UNCOUNT **Reconnaissance** is the process of obtaining military information about a place using soldiers, planes, or satellites.

reconsider /ˌriːkənˈsɪdə/ **reconsiders, reconsidering, reconsidered.** VERB If you **reconsider** a decision or method, you think about it and try to decide whether it should be changed. *This has forced the United States to seriously reconsider its position.*

reconstruct /ˌriːkənˈstrʌkt/ **reconstructs, reconstructing, reconstructed.** **1** VERB If you **reconstruct** something that has been destroyed or badly damaged, you build it and make it work again. *He had plastic surgery to help reconstruct his badly damaged face.* ♦ **reconstruction** N-UNCOUNT *...the post-war reconstruction of Germany.* **2** VERB To **reconstruct** something such as a system means to change its construction so that it works in a different way. *She actually wanted to reconstruct the state and transform society.* **3** VERB If you **reconstruct** a past event, you obtain a complete description of it by combining a lot of small pieces of information. ♦ **reconstruction, reconstructions** N-COUNT *Mrs Kerr was too upset to take part in a reconstruction of her ordeal.*

⭐ **record, records, recording, recorded;** noun /ˈrekɔːd, AM -kərd/, verb /rɪˈkɔːd/. **1** N-COUNT If you keep a **record** of something, or if you keep something **on record**, you keep an account of it in writing, photographs, or on a computer so that it can be referred to later. *The result will go on your medical records... A photograph of each customer will be kept on record.* **2** N-COUNT Someone's **record** is the facts that are known about their achievements or character. *Professor Blainey has a distinguished record as a historical researcher.*

3 VERB If you **record** a piece of information or an event, you write it down, photograph it, or put it into a computer so that in the future people can refer to it. *Her letters record the domestic and social details of diplomatic life.* **4** VERB When music or speech **is recorded**, it is put onto a tape or a record, so that it can be heard again later. **5** N-COUNT A **record** is a round flat piece of black plastic on which music is stored. You listen to the sound by playing the record on a record player. **6** N-COUNT A **record** is the best result that has ever been achieved in a particular sport or activity, for example the fastest time or the furthest distance. *...the 800 metres, where she is the world record holder.* **7** See also **recording**, **track record**.

PHRASES ● If you say something **off the record**, you do not intend what you say to be taken as official, or published with your name attached to it. ● If you **set the record straight** or **put the record straight**, you show that something which has been regarded as true is in fact not true.

recorder /rɪˈkɔːdə/ **recorders**. N-COUNT A **recorder** is a hollow musical instrument that you play by blowing down one end and covering a series of holes with your fingers. → See picture on page 828.

★ **recording** /rɪˈkɔːdɪŋ/ **recordings**. **1** N-COUNT A **recording** of something is a record, tape, CD, or video of it. **2** N-UNCOUNT **Recording** is the process of making records, tapes, or videos. *...the recording industry.*

'record player, record players. N-COUNT A **record player** is a machine on which you play records.

recount, recounts, recounting, recounted. 1 VERB /rɪˈkaʊnt/ If you **recount** a story or event, you tell or describe it to people. [FORMAL] *He recounted how Williams had visited him.* **2** N-COUNT /ˈriːkaʊnt/ A **recount** is a second count of votes in an election when the result is very close.

recoup /rɪˈkuːp/ **recoups, recouping, recouped.** VERB If you **recoup** a sum of money that you have spent or lost, you get it back. *Insurance companies are trying to recoup their losses.*

recourse /rɪˈkɔːs/. N-UNCOUNT If you have **recourse to** something, you use it to help you in a difficult situation. *It enabled its members to settle their differences without recourse to war.*

★ **recover** /rɪˈkʌvə/ **recovers, recovering, recovered. 1** VERB When you **recover from** an illness or an injury, you become well again. *He is recovering from a knee injury... A policeman was recovering in hospital last night after being stabbed.* **2** VERB If you **recover from** an unhappy or unpleasant experience, you stop being upset by it. *...a tragedy from which he never fully recovered.* **3** VERB If you **recover** something that has been lost or stolen, you find it or get it back. *Police raided five houses in south-east London and recovered stolen goods.* **4** VERB If you **recover** your former mental or physical state, it comes back again. *She never recovered consciousness.*

★ **recovery** /rɪˈkʌvəri/ **recoveries. 1** N-VAR If a sick person makes a **recovery**, he or she becomes well again. *He had been given less than a one in 500 chance of recovery.* **2** N-VAR When there is a **recovery** in a country's economy, it improves. **3** N-UNCOUNT You talk about the **recovery of** something when you get it back after it has been lost or stolen. *A substantial reward is being offered for the recovery of a painting by Turner.* **4** N-UNCOUNT You talk about the **recovery of** someone's physical or mental state when they return to this state. *...the abrupt loss and recovery of consciousness.*

recreate /ˌriːkriˈeɪt/ **recreates, recreating, recreated.** VERB If you **recreate** something, you succeed in making it happen or exist again. *I am trying to recreate family life far from home.* ◆ **recreation, recreations** N-COUNT *...a faithful recreation of the original Elizabethan theatre.*

recreation /ˌrekriˈeɪʃən/ **recreations**. N-VAR **Recreation** consists of things that you do in your spare time to relax. *All the family members need to have their own interests and recreations.* ◆ **recreational** ADJ *...parks and other recreational facilities.*

recrimination /rɪˌkrɪmɪˈneɪʃən/ **recriminations**. N-VAR **Recriminations** are accusations that two people or groups make about each other. *The war sweeps up everyone in hatred and recrimination.*

★ **recruit** /rɪˈkruːt/ **recruits, recruiting, recruited. 1** VERB If you **recruit** people for an organization, you get them to join it or work for it. *The police are trying to recruit more black and Asian officers.* ◆ **recruiting** N-UNCOUNT *...an army recruiting office.* ◆ **recruitment** N-UNCOUNT *...a crisis in teacher recruitment.* **2** N-COUNT A **recruit** is a person who has recently joined an organization or army.

re,cruitment con'sultant, recruitment consultants. N-COUNT A **recruitment consultant** is a person who helps professional people to find work by introducing them to potential employers.

rectangle /ˈrektæŋɡəl/ **rectangles**. N-COUNT A **rectangle** is a shape with four sides whose angles are all right angles. Each side of a rectangle is the same length as the one opposite to it. → See picture on page 829.

rectangular /rekˈtæŋɡjʊlə/. ADJ Something that is **rectangular** is shaped like a rectangle. *...a rectangular table.*

rectify /ˈrektɪfaɪ/ **rectifies, rectifying, rectified.** VERB If you **rectify** something that is wrong, you change it so that it becomes correct or satisfactory. *Only an act of Congress could rectify the situation.*

recuperate /rɪˈkuːpəreɪt/ **recuperates, recuperating, recuperated.** VERB When you **recuperate**, you recover your health or strength after you have been ill or injured. *He is recuperating from a serious back injury.*

♦ **recuperation** N-UNCOUNT *Sleep is necessary for recuperation.*

recur /rɪ'kɜː/ **recurs, recurring, recurred.** VERB If something **recurs**, it happens more than once. *...a recurring nightmare she has had since childhood.* ♦ **recurrence** /rɪ'kʌrəns, AM -'kɜːr-/ **recurrences** N-VAR *Police are out in force to prevent a recurrence of the violence.*

recurrent /rɪ'kʌrənt, AM -'kɜːr-/. ADJ A **recurrent** event or feeling happens or is experienced more than once. *...buildings in which staff suffer recurrent illness.*

recycle /ˌriː'saɪkəl/ **recycles, recycling, recycled.** VERB If you **recycle** things that have already been used, such as bottles or sheets of paper, you process them so that they can be used again.

⭐ **red** /red/ **redder, reddest; reds.** [1] ADJ & N-VAR Something that is **red** is the colour of blood or of a ripe tomato. [2] ADJ You describe someone's hair as **red** when it is between red and brown in colour.

> **PHRASES** ● If a person or company is **in the red** or if their bank account is **in the red**, they have spent more money than they have in their account and therefore they owe money to the bank. ● If you **see red**, you become very angry.

ˌred 'card, red cards. N-COUNT In football or rugby, the **red card** is a card that the referee shows to a player who has to leave the pitch for breaking the rules.

reddish /'redɪʃ/. ADJ **Reddish** means slightly red in colour.

redeem /rɪ'diːm/ **redeems, redeeming, redeemed.** [1] VERB If you **redeem yourself**, you do something that gives people a good opinion of you again after you have behaved or performed badly. *He had realized the mistake he had made and wanted to redeem himself.* [2] VERB When something **redeems** an unpleasant thing or situation, it prevents it from being completely bad. *Work is the way that people seek to redeem their lives from futility.* [3] VERB If you **redeem** a debt or an obligation, you pay money that you owe or that you promised to pay.

redemption /rɪ'dempʃən/. N-UNCOUNT **Redemption** is the act of redeeming something or of being redeemed by something. *He craves redemption for his sins. ...redemption of the loan.*

redevelopment /ˌriːdɪ'veləpmənt/. N-UNCOUNT When **redevelopment** takes place, old buildings in a part of a town are knocked down and new ones are built in their place.

ˌred-'hot. ADJ Something that is **red-hot** is extremely hot.

redirect /ˌriːdɪ'rekt, -daɪ-/ **redirects, redirecting, redirected.** [1] VERB If you **redirect** your energy, resources, or ability, you begin doing something different or trying to achieve something different. *...the ability to redirect attention quickly.* [2] VERB If you **redirect** someone or something, you change their course. *She redirected them to the men's department.*

redistribute /ˌriːdɪ'strɪbjuːt/ **redistributes, redistributing, redistributed.** VERB If money or goods **are redistributed**, they are shared among people or organizations in a different way from the way that they were previously shared. *Taxes could be used to redistribute income.*

♦ **redistribution** N-UNCOUNT *...a redistribution of wealth.*

redress, /rɪ'dres/ **redresses, redressing, redressed.** [1] VERB If you **redress** something such as a wrong or a grievance, you do something to correct it or to improve things for the person who has been badly treated. [FORMAL] *...laws designed to redress racial inequality.* [2] VERB If you **redress** the balance or the imbalance between two things that have become unequal, you make them equal again. *...to redress the economic imbalance between the developed countries and the developing countries.* [3] N-UNCOUNT **Redress** is compensation for something wrong that has been done. [FORMAL] *...their legal battle to seek some kind of a redress from the government.*

ˌred 'tape. N-UNCOUNT You refer to official rules and procedures as **red tape** when they seem unnecessary and cause delay.

⭐ **reduce** /rɪ'djuːs, AM -'duːs/ **reduces, reducing, reduced.** [1] VERB If you **reduce** something, you make it smaller. *It reduces the risks of heart disease.* [2] VERB If someone **is reduced to** a weaker or inferior state, they become weaker or inferior as a result of something that happens to them. *They were reduced to extreme poverty.* [3] VERB If something is changed to a different or less complicated form, you can say that it **is reduced to** that form. *All the buildings in the town have been reduced to rubble.* [4] VERB If you say that someone **is reduced to** doing something, you mean that they have to do it, although it is unpleasant or humiliating. *He was reduced to begging for a living.*

⭐ **reduction** /rɪ'dʌkʃən/ **reductions.** N-VAR When there is a **reduction in** something, it is made smaller. *Many companies have announced dramatic reductions in staff.*

redundancy /rɪ'dʌndənsi/ **redundancies.** N-VAR If there are **redundancies** within an organization, some of its employees are dismissed because their jobs are no longer necessary or because the organization can no longer afford to pay them. [BRITISH] *Thousands of bank employees are facing redundancy.*

redundant /rɪ'dʌndənt/. [1] ADJ If you are made **redundant**, you lose your job because it is no longer necessary or because your employer cannot afford to keep paying you. [BRITISH] *...a redundant miner.* [2] ADJ Something that is **redundant** is no longer needed because it has been replaced by something else. *Changes in technology may mean that once-valued skills are now redundant.*

reed /riːd/ **reeds.** N-VAR **Reeds** are tall plants that grow in shallow water or wet ground.

a
b
c
d
e
f
g
h
i
j
k
l
m
n
o
p
q
r
s
t
u
v
w
x
y
z

⭐ Bank of English® frequent word　　　For a full explanation of all grammatical labels, see pages vii-x

reef /riːf/ **reefs.** N-COUNT A **reef** is a long line of rocks or sand, the top of which is just above or just below the surface of the sea.

reek /riːk/ **reeks, reeking, reeked.** [1] VERB & N-SING If something **reeks of** something else, usually something unpleasant, it smells very strongly of it. You can also talk about the **reek of** something. *Your breath reeks of stale cigar smoke... The entire house reeked... He smelt the reek of whisky.* [2] VERB If you say that something **reeks of** unpleasant ideas, feelings, or practices, you disapprove of it because it gives a firm impression that it involves those ideas, feelings, or practices. *The whole thing reeks of hypocrisy.*

⭐ **reel** /riːl/ **reels, reeling, reeled.** [1] N-COUNT A **reel** is a cylinder-shaped object around which you wrap something such as thread or cinema film. [2] VERB When someone **reels**, they move about unsteadily as if they were going to fall. *He lost his balance and reeled back.* [3] VERB If you are **reeling from** a shock, you are feeling extremely surprised or upset because of it. *I'm still reeling from the shock of hearing it... It left us reeling with disbelief.* [4] VERB If you say that your brain or your mind **is reeling**, you mean that you are very confused because you have too much to think about.

▸ **reel off.** PHR-VERB If you **reel off** information, you repeat it from memory quickly and easily. *She reeled off the titles of a dozen or so of the novels.*

re-e'lect, re-elects, re-electing, re-elected. VERB When someone such as a politician **is re-elected**, they win a new election and are therefore able to continue in their position as, for example, a member of parliament. *The president will pursue lower taxes if he is re-elected.* ♦ **re-election** N-UNCOUNT *I would like to see him stand for re-election.*

re-ex'amine, re-examines, re-examining, re-examined. VERB If a person or group of people **re-examine** their ideas or beliefs, they think about them carefully because they are no longer sure if they are correct. *The end of the cold war caused both France and Germany to re-examine their foreign policies.* ♦ **re-examination, re-examinations** N-VAR *It was time for a re-examination of the situation.*

⭐ **refer** /rɪˈfɜː/ **refers, referring, referred.** [1] VERB If you **refer to** a particular subject or person, you mention them. *In his speech, he referred to a recent trip to Canada.* ♦ **reference** /ˈrefərəns/ **references** N-VAR *He made no reference to any agreement.* [2] VERB If you **refer to** someone or something by a particular name, you call them this name. *He always referred to his friend as Mr Lowry.* [3] VERB If a word or expression **refers to** something, it is used as a name for it. *The word 'banquet' refers to a feast.* [4] VERB If you **refer to** a book or other source of information, you look at it in order to find something out. *He had to keep referring to the manual.* ♦ **reference** N-UNCOUNT *Keep this sheet for future reference.* [5] VERB If a

person or problem **is referred to** another person or to an organization, that person or organization is asked to deal with them. *I was referred to an ear specialist... He referred the matter to the Police Complaints Authority.*

referee /ˌrefəˈriː/ **referees, refereeing, refereed.** [1] N-COUNT The **referee** is the official who controls a sports match. [2] VERB If you **referee** a sports match, you act as referee.

⭐ **reference** /ˈrefərəns/ **references.** [1] N-COUNT A **reference** is something such as a number or a name that tells you where you can obtain information. *...a map reference.* [2] ADJ BEFORE N **Reference** books are ones you look at when you need specific information about a subject. [3] PHRASE You use **with reference to** or **in reference to** to indicate who or what you are referring to. *I am writing with reference to your article on salaries.* [4] N-COUNT A **reference** is a letter written by someone who knows you which describes your character and abilities. [5] See also **refer**.

⭐ **referendum** /ˌrefəˈrendəm/ **referendums** (or **referenda** /ˌrefəˈrendə/). N-COUNT A **referendum** is a vote in which all the people in a country are asked whether they agree or disagree with a particular policy. *The government might hold a referendum on the matter.*

referral /rɪˈfɜːrəl/ **referrals.** N-VAR **Referral** is the act of officially sending someone to a person or authority that is authorized or better qualified to deal with them. A **referral** is an instance of this. *...a 300% increase in referrals to his psychiatry practice.*

refill, refills, refilling, refilled; verb /ˌriːˈfɪl/, noun /ˈriːfɪl/. VERB & N-COUNT If you **refill** something, or if you give it a **refill**, you fill it again after it has been emptied. *Max held out his cup for a refill.*

refine /rɪˈfaɪn/ **refines, refining, refined.** [1] VERB When a substance **is refined**, it is made pure by the removal of other substances from it. *...refined sugar.* ♦ **refining** N-UNCOUNT *...oil refining.* [2] VERB If something such as a process, a theory, or a machine **is refined**, it is improved by being changed in small ways. *Surgical techniques are constantly being refined.* ♦ **refinement, refinements** N-VAR *Further refinements are needed.*

refined /rɪˈfaɪnd/. ADJ **Refined** people are polite and well-mannered.

refinery /rɪˈfaɪnəri/ **refineries.** N-COUNT A **refinery** is a factory which refines a substance such as oil or sugar.

refit, refits, refitting, refitted; verb /ˌriːˈfɪt/, noun /ˈriːfɪt/. VERB & N-COUNT When a ship **is refitted**, or when it is given a **refit**, it is repaired or is given new parts, equipment, or furniture.

⭐ **reflect** /rɪˈflekt/ **reflects, reflecting, reflected.** [1] VERB If something **reflects** an attitude or situation, it shows that the attitude or situation exists. *Concern at the economic situation was reflected in the government's budget.* [2] VERB When light or heat **is reflected** off a surface, it is sent back from the surface rather than passing through it. *The light reflects off the window. ...a layer of aluminium to reflect heat.* **3** VERB When something **is reflected** in a mirror or in water, you can see its image there. **4** VERB When you **reflect on** something, you think deeply about it. *I reflected on the child's future.* **5** VERB If an action or situation **reflects** in a particular way **on** someone or something, it gives people a good or bad impression of them. *The affair hardly reflected well on the British.*

reflection /rɪˈflekʃən/ **reflections.** **1** N-COUNT A **reflection** is an image that you can see in a mirror or in water. **2** N-COUNT A **reflection of** a person's attitude or a situation indicates that the attitude or situation exists. *Crumb's drawings turn out to be a reflection of his own self-loathing.* **3** N-SING If you say that something is a **reflection on** someone or a **sad reflection on** someone, you mean that it gives a bad impression of them. *It's no reflection on your ability as a mother.* **4** N-UNCOUNT **Reflection** is careful thought about a particular topic. *A moment's reflection reveals the weakness of such a defence... On reflection, he says, he very much regrets the comments.* **5** N-PLURAL Your **reflections** are your thoughts about a particular topic. *...his reflections on the church.*

reflective /rɪˈflektɪv/ **1** ADJ If you are **reflective**, you think deeply about things. [WRITTEN] ♦ **reflectively** ADV *He sipped his brandy reflectively.* **2** ADJ AFTER LINK-V If something is **reflective of** a particular situation or attitude, it shows that situation or attitude exists. *...a superb achievement reflective of rugby's booming popularity.* **3** ADJ A **reflective** surface or material sends back light or heat. [FORMAL] *...new reflective coatings.*

reflex /ˈriːfleks/ **reflexes.** **1** N-COUNT A **reflex** or a **reflex action** is a normal uncontrollable reaction of your body to something that you feel, see, or experience. *Blushing is a reflex action linked to the nervous system.* **2** N-PLURAL Your **reflexes** refer to your body's ability to react quickly when something unexpected happens. *...the reflexes of an athlete.*

reflexive pronoun /rɪˈfleksɪv ˈprəʊnaʊn/ **reflexive pronouns.** N-COUNT A **reflexive pronoun** is a pronoun such as 'myself' which refers back to the subject of a sentence or clause.

reflexive verb /rɪˈfleksɪv vɜːb/ **reflexive verbs.** N-COUNT A **reflexive verb** is a transitive verb whose subject and object always refer to the same person or thing, so the object is always a reflexive pronoun. An example is 'to enjoy yourself'.

⭐ **reform** /rɪˈfɔːm/ **reforms, reforming, reformed.** **1** N-VAR **Reform** consists of changes and improvements to a law, social system, or institution. These changes can be called **reforms**. *He has urged reform of the welfare system.* **2** VERB To **reform** something such as a law, a social system, or an institution means to improve it by

making changes. *...his proposals for reforming the legal system.* ♦ **reformer, reformers** N-COUNT *...prison reformers.* **3** VERB When someone **reforms**, they stop doing something that society does not approve of. ♦ **reformed** ADJ *...a reformed alcoholic.*

refrain /rɪˈfreɪn/ **refrains, refraining, refrained.** **1** VERB If you **refrain from** doing something, you deliberately do not do it. *He appealed to all factions to refrain from violence.* **2** N-COUNT A **refrain** is a short simple part of a song which you repeat several times.

refresh /rɪˈfreʃ/ **refreshes, refreshing, refreshed.** **1** VERB If something **refreshes** you when you are hot, tired, or thirsty, it makes you feel cooler or more energetic. ♦ **refreshed** ADJ *He awoke feeling completely refreshed.* ♦ **refreshing** ADJ *...refreshing drinks.* **2** PHRASE If someone **refreshes** your **memory**, they tell you something you have forgotten.

refreshing /rɪˈfreʃɪŋ/ ADJ If something is **refreshing**, it is pleasantly different from what you are used to. *It's refreshing to hear somebody speaking common sense.* ♦ **refreshingly** ADV *He was refreshingly honest.*

refreshment /rɪˈfreʃmənt/ **refreshments.** **1** N-PLURAL **Refreshments** are drinks and small amounts of food that are provided, for example, during a meeting or journey. **2** N-UNCOUNT You can refer to food and drink as **refreshment**. [FORMAL] *May I offer you some refreshment?*

refrigerate /rɪˈfrɪdʒəreɪt/ **refrigerates, refrigerating, refrigerated.** VERB If you **refrigerate** food, you make it cold, for example by putting it in a refrigerator. ♦ **refrigeration** N-UNCOUNT *Refrigeration slows down the growth of bacteria.*

refrigerator /rɪˈfrɪdʒəreɪtə/ **refrigerators.** N-COUNT A **refrigerator** is a large container which is kept cool inside, usually by electricity, so that the food and drink in it stays fresh.

refuel /ˌriːˈfjuːəl/ **refuels, refuelling, refuelled (AM refueling, refueled).** VERB When an aircraft or other vehicle **refuels**, or when someone **refuels** it, it is filled with more fuel so that it can continue its journey. ♦ **refuelling** N-UNCOUNT *It will make two refuelling stops.*

refuge /ˈrefjuːdʒ/ **refuges.** **1** N-UNCOUNT If you take **refuge** somewhere, you try to protect yourself from physical harm by going there. *Many Cubans took refuge in the United States.* **2** N-COUNT A **refuge** is a place where you go for safety and protection. *...a refuge for battered women.*

⭐ **refugee** /ˌrefjuˈdʒiː/ **refugees.** N-COUNT **Refugees** are people who have been forced to leave their country because there is a war there or because of their political or religious beliefs.

refund, refunds, refunding, refunded. **1** N-COUNT /ˈriːfʌnd/ A **refund** is a sum of money which is returned to you, for example because a shop returned goods to a shop. *Dissatisfied customers can return the product for a full refund.* **2** VERB

a
b
c
d
e
f
g
h
i
j
k
l
m
n
o
p
q
r
s
t
u
v
w
x
y
z

/rɪ'fʌnd/ If someone **refunds** your money, they return it to you.

refurbish /riː'fɜːbɪʃ/ **refurbishes, refurbishing, refurbished.** VERB To **refurbish** a building or room means to clean and decorate it, and make it more attractive or better equipped.
♦ **refurbishment, refurbishments** N-VAR *The gallery is now closed for refurbishment.*

refusal /rɪ'fjuːzəl/ **refusals.** N-VAR A **refusal** is the fact of firmly saying or showing that you will not do, allow, or accept something. *...the Prince's repeated refusals to attend peace negotiations.*

⭐ **refuse, refuses, refusing, refused.** [1] VERB /rɪ'fjuːz/ If you **refuse** to do something, you deliberately do not do it, or say firmly that you will not do it. *He refused to comment after the trial... He expects me to stay on here and I can hardly refuse.* [2] VERB If someone **refuses** you something, they do not allow you to have it. *The town council had refused permission for the march.* [3] VERB If you **refuse** something that is offered to you, you do not accept it. *The patient has the right to refuse treatment.* [4] N-UNCOUNT /'refjuːs/ **Refuse** consists of the rubbish and unwanted things in a house, shop, or factory that are regularly thrown away. [FORMAL]

refute /rɪ'fjuːt/ **refutes, refuting, refuted.** [1] VERB If you **refute** something such as a theory or argument, you prove that it is wrong. [FORMAL] *It was the kind of rumour that it is impossible to refute.* [2] VERB If you **refute** an allegation or accusation, you deny that it is true. [FORMAL] *He angrily refutes the charge.*

regain /rɪ'geɪn/ **regains, regaining, regained.** VERB If you **regain** something that you have lost, you get it back again. *Troops have regained control of the city.*

regal /'riːgəl/. ADJ If you describe something as **regal**, you mean that it is suitable for a king or queen, because it is very splendid or dignified. *...his regal manner.*

⭐ **regard** /rɪ'gɑːd/ **regards, regarding, regarded.** [1] VERB If you **regard** someone or something in a particular way, you think of them in that way, or have that opinion of them. *He regarded drug dealers with loathing... He was regarded as the most successful Chancellor of modern times.* [2] N-UNCOUNT If you have a high **regard** for someone, you have a lot of respect for them. *She was pleased by Hugh's regard for her parents.* [3] N-PLURAL **Regards** is used in expressions like **'best regards'** and **'with warm regards'** as a way of expressing friendly feelings towards someone. *Give my regards to your husband.* PHRASES ● You can use **as regards**, **with regard to**, or **in regard to** to indicate what you are referring to. *As regards the war, Haig believed in victory at any price.* ● You can use **in this regard** or **in that regard** to refer back to something you have just said. *In this regard nothing has changed.*

regarding /rɪ'gɑːdɪŋ/. PREP You can use **regarding** to indicate what you are referring to.

He refused to divulge any information regarding the man's whereabouts.

regardless /rɪ'gɑːdləs/. [1] PHRASE If something happens **regardless of** something else, it is not affected or influenced at all by that other thing. *Regardless of whether he is right or wrong, we have to abide by his decisions.* [2] ADV If you say someone did something **regardless**, you mean they did it even though there were problems that could have stopped them. *Britain's partners are pressing on regardless.*

regatta /rɪ'gætə/ **regattas.** N-COUNT A **regatta** is a sports event consisting of races between yachts or rowing boats.

regenerate /rɪ'dʒenəreɪt/ **regenerates, regenerating, regenerated.** VERB To **regenerate** something that has been declining means to develop and improve it to make it more active or successful. *The government will continue to try to regenerate inner city areas.* ♦ **regeneration** N-UNCOUNT *...plans for the regeneration of the area.*

reggae /'regeɪ/. N-UNCOUNT **Reggae** is a kind of West Indian popular music with a very strong beat.

⭐ **regime** /reɪ'ʒiːm/ **regimes.** N-COUNT If you refer to a government as a **regime**, you are critical of it because you think it is not democratic and uses unacceptable methods. *...a military regime.*

regiment /'redʒɪmənt/ **regiments.** N-COUNT A **regiment** is a large group of soldiers commanded by a colonel. ♦ **regimental** /ˌredʒɪ'mentəl/ ADJ BEFORE N *...the regimental headquarters.*

⭐ **region** /'riːdʒən/ **regions.** [1] N-COUNT A **region** is an area of a country or of the world. *...a remote mountainous region of Afghanistan.* ♦ **regional** ADJ *...regional conflicts.* [2] PHRASE You say **in the region of** to indicate that you are mentioning an approximate amount. *The scheme will cost in the region of six million pounds.*

⭐ **register** /'redʒɪstə/ **registers, registering, registered.** [1] N-COUNT A **register** is an official list or record. *...the register of voters.* [2] VERB If you **register for** something, you put your name on an official list. *He registered for a class in design.* [3] VERB If you **register** something, you have it recorded on an official list. *The boy's mother never registered his birth.* [4] VERB When something **registers** on a scale or measuring instrument, it shows a particular value. *The earthquake registered 5.3 points on the Richter scale.* [5] VERB If you **register** a feeling or opinion that you have, you make it clear to other people. *Her face registered her dismay... Workers stopped work to register their protest.*

registrar /ˌredʒɪ'strɑː, AM -'strɑːr/ **registrars.** [1] N-COUNT A **registrar** is a person whose job is to keep official records, especially of births, marriages, and deaths. [2] N-COUNT A **registrar** is a senior administrative official in a college or university.

registration /ˌredʒɪˈstreɪʃən/. N-UNCOUNT The **registration** of something is the recording of it in an official list.

registry /ˈredʒɪstri/ **registries.** N-COUNT A **registry** is a place where official records are kept.

regress /rɪˈgres/ **regresses, regressing, regressed.** VERB When people or things **regress**, they return to an earlier and less advanced stage of development. [FORMAL] ...if your child regresses to babyish behaviour. ♦ **regression** /rɪˈgreʃən/ N-UNCOUNT ...regression in a pupil's learning process.

⭐ **regret** /rɪˈgret/ **regrets, regretting, regretted.** ☐ VERB If you **regret** something that you have done, you wish that you had not done it. I simply gave in to him, and I've regretted it ever since. ☐ N-VAR **Regret** is a feeling of sadness or disappointment. He feels deep regret about his friend's death. ☐ N-UNCOUNT & VERB If someone expresses **regret** about something, or if they **regret** something, they are saying in a polite way that they are sorry about it. [FORMAL] She has accepted his resignation with regret... I regret to say that Mr Brand has been taken ill.

regrettable /rɪˈgretəbəl/. ADJ You describe something as **regrettable** when you think that it is bad and that it should not happen or have happened. Obviously, it is regrettable that we made the mistake. ♦ **regrettably** ADV Regrettably we could find no sign of the man.

regroup /ˌriːˈgruːp/ **regroups, regrouping, regrouped.** VERB If a group of people who work as a team **regroup**, they reorganize themselves because their previous attempt to do something has failed.

⭐ **regular** /ˈregjʊlə/ **regulars.** ☐ ADJ **Regular** things happen at equal intervals, or involve things happening at equal intervals. Keep your eyes closed and let your breathing become regular. ...a regular pattern of sleeping and waking. ♦ **regularly** ADV He also writes regularly for 'International Management' magazine. ♦ **regularity** /ˌregjʊˈlærɪti/ N-UNCOUNT ...the regularity of the beat. ☐ ADJ **Regular** events happen often. They'd agreed to meet on a regular basis. ♦ **regularly** ADV ...if you regularly take snacks instead of eating properly. ♦ **regularity** N-UNCOUNT Job losses are again being announced with monotonous regularity. ☐ N-COUNT & ADJ BEFORE N If you are a **regular** at a place, or a **regular** visitor there, you go there often. ...regulars at his local pub. ...regular churchgoers. ☐ ADJ BEFORE N **Regular** means 'normal'. The product looks and burns like a regular cigarette. ☐ ADJ If something has a **regular** shape, both halves are the same and it has straight edges or a smooth outline. ...a man of moderate height with regular features. ☐ ADJ A **regular** verb, noun, or adjective inflects in the same way as most other verbs, nouns, or adjectives in the same language.

regulate /ˈregjʊleɪt/ **regulates, regulating, regulated.** VERB To **regulate** an activity or process means to control it, especially by means of rules.

...proposals to regulate and limit animal testing. ♦ **regulation** N-UNCOUNT ...the regulation of nurseries.

⭐ **regulation** /ˌregjʊˈleɪʃən/ **regulations.** N-COUNT **Regulations** are rules made by a government or other authority in order to control the way something is done or the way people behave. ...the new safety regulations.

⭐ **regulator** /ˈregjʊleɪtə/ **regulators.** N-COUNT A **regulator** is a person or organization appointed by a government to regulate the activities of private companies who provide a service to the public. ♦ **regulatory** /ˌregjʊˈleɪtəri/ ADJ BEFORE N ...the UK's financial regulatory system.

rehabilitate /ˌriːhəˈbɪlɪteɪt/ **rehabilitates, rehabilitating, rehabilitated.** VERB To **rehabilitate** someone who has been ill or in prison means to help them to live a normal life again. ♦ **rehabilitation** N-UNCOUNT ...an alcohol and drug rehabilitation centre.

rehearsal /rɪˈhɜːsəl/ **rehearsals.** N-VAR A **rehearsal** of a play, dance, or piece of music is the time when those taking part practise it. ...rehearsals for a concert tour.

rehearse /rɪˈhɜːs/ **rehearses, rehearsing, rehearsed.** VERB When people **rehearse** a play, dance, or piece of music, they practise it. Tens of thousands of people have been rehearsing for the opening ceremony.

reign /reɪn/ **reigns, reigning, reigned.** ☐ VERB If you say, for example, that silence **reigns** in a place, you mean that the place is silent. A relative calm reigned over the city. ☐ VERB & N-COUNT When a king or queen **reigns**, he or she is the leader of the country. The **reign** of a king or queen is the period when they reign.

PHRASES ● Someone or something that **reigns supreme** is the most important or powerful element in a situation or period of time. The bicycle reigned supreme in Britain's most popular mode of transport. ● A **reign of terror** is a period during which there is a lot of violence and killing, especially by people who are in a position of power.

reimburse /ˌriːɪmˈbɜːs/ **reimburses, reimbursing, reimbursed.** VERB If you **reimburse** someone **for** something, you pay them back the money that they have spent or lost because of it. [FORMAL] I'll be happy to reimburse you for any expenses you might have incurred. ♦ **reimbursement, reimbursements** N-VAR She is demanding reimbursement for medical and other expenses.

rein /reɪn/ **reins, reining, reined.** ☐ N-PLURAL **Reins** are the leather straps attached to a horse's bridle which are used to control the horse. ☐ PHRASE If you **give free rein to** someone, you give them a lot of freedom to do what they want.
▶**rein in.** PHR-VERB To **rein in** something means to control it. He has had to rein in his enthusiasm.

reincarnation /ˌriːɪnkɑːˈneɪʃən/ **reincarnations.** ☐ N-UNCOUNT If you believe in **reincarnation**, you believe that people are born again as other

a
b
c
d
e
f
g
h
i
j
k
l
m
n
o
p
q
r
s
t
u
v
w
x
y
z

people or animals after they die. **2** N-COUNT A **reincarnation** is a person or animal who is believed to contain the spirit of a dead person.

reindeer /ˈreɪndɪə/.

☑ **Reindeer** is both the singular and the plural form.

N-COUNT A **reindeer** is a type of deer that lives in northern areas of Europe, Asia, and America.

reinforce /ˌriːɪnˈfɔːs/ **reinforces, reinforcing, reinforced.** **1** VERB If something **reinforces** something such as a feeling, process, or belief, it makes it stronger. *They are determined to reinforce the message that they will not tolerate drug abuse.* ♦ **reinforcement, reinforcements** N-VAR *...the role of science in the reinforcement of cruel but popular myths about race.* **2** VERB To **reinforce** an object means to make it stronger or harder. *They had to reinforce the walls with exterior beams. ...reinforced glass.*

reinforcements /ˌriːɪnˈfɔːsmənts/. N-PLURAL **Reinforcements** are soldiers who are sent to join an army in order to make it stronger.

reinstate /ˌriːɪnˈsteɪt/ **reinstates, reinstating, reinstated.** VERB If you **reinstate** someone, you give them back a job which had been taken from them. *They had not reinstated him as manager.* ♦ **reinstatement** N-UNCOUNT *Parents campaigned in vain for her reinstatement.*

reiterate /riːˈɪtəreɪt/ **reiterates, reiterating, reiterated.** VERB If you **reiterate** something, you say it again or emphasize it. [FORMAL] *Let me reiterate that I knew this about him.*

⭐ **reject, rejects, rejecting, rejected.** **1** VERB /rɪˈdʒekt/ If you **reject** something such as a proposal or request, you do not accept it or agree to it. *I think the president was correct to reject the offer.* ♦ **rejection** N-VAR *...his rejection of our values.* **2** VERB If someone **is rejected** for a job or course of study, it is not offered to them. ♦ **rejection** N-COUNT *Be prepared for lots of rejections before you land a job.* **3** VERB If you **reject** someone who feels affection for you, you show them that you do not feel affection for them. ♦ **rejection** N-COUNT *...feelings of rejection and hurt.* **4** N-COUNT /ˈriːdʒekt/ A **reject** is a product that has not been accepted for use or sale, because there is something wrong with it.

rejoice /rɪˈdʒɔɪs/ **rejoices, rejoicing, rejoiced.** VERB If you **rejoice**, you are very pleased about something and you show it in your behaviour. [LITERARY] ♦ **rejoicing** N-UNCOUNT *There was general rejoicing at the news.*

rejuvenate /rɪˈdʒuːvəneɪt/ **rejuvenates, rejuvenating, rejuvenated.** VERB If something **rejuvenates** you, it makes you feel or look young again. *The Italian climate would rejuvenate him.* ♦ **rejuvenating** ADJ *...rejuvenating face-cream.*

rekindle /ˌriːˈkɪndəl/ **rekindles, rekindling, rekindled.** VERB If something **rekindles** an interest, feeling, or thought that you used to have, it makes you think about it or feel it again. *The tragedy rekindled memories.*

relapse, relapses, relapsing, relapsed; verb /rɪˈlæps/, noun /ˈriːlæps/ or /ˈriːlæps/. **1** VERB & N-COUNT If someone **relapses into** a way of behaving, or if they have a **relapse**, they start to behave in that way again. *With this the Superintendent relapsed into silence. ...relapses into old habits.* **2** VERB & N-COUNT If a sick person **relapses**, or if they have a **relapse**, their health suddenly gets worse after it had been improving.

⭐ **relate** /rɪˈleɪt/ **relates, relating, related.** **1** VERB If something **relates to** a particular subject, it concerns that subject. *The word crafts relates to the production of the work.* ♦ **-related** *...smoking-related diseases.* **2** VERB The way that two things **relate** is the connection between them. *...a shift in thinking about how the two sciences relate.* ♦ **related** ADJ *Crime and poverty are closely related. ...diving and related activities.* **3** VERB The way that people **relate** is the way that they communicate with each other and behave towards each other. *They didn't know how to relate to my sister.* **4** VERB If you **relate** a story, you tell it. [FORMAL]

⭐ **related** /rɪˈleɪtɪd/. **1** ADJ AFTER LINK-V People who are **related** belong to the same family. *There are two families of Elwoods in Galway, and we're not related.* **2** See also **relate**.

⭐ **relation** /rɪˈleɪʃən/ **relations.** **1** N-PLURAL **Relations** between people, groups, or countries are contacts between them and the way they behave towards each other. *Greece has established full diplomatic relations with Israel.* **2** N-UNCOUNT The **relation of** one thing **to** another is the connection between them. *...the relation of artists to politics.* **3** PHRASE You can talk about something **in relation to** something else when you want to compare the size, condition, or position of the two things. *The money he'd been ordered to pay was minimal in relation to his salary.* **4** N-COUNT Your **relations** are the members of your family.

⭐ **relationship** /rɪˈleɪʃənʃɪp/ **relationships.** **1** N-COUNT The **relationship** between two people or groups is the way they feel and behave towards each other. *...close family relationships.* **2** N-COUNT A **relationship** is a close friendship between two people, especially one involving romantic or sexual feelings. *Both of us felt the relationship wasn't really going anywhere.* **3** N-COUNT The **relationship** between two things is the way in which they are connected. *...a relationship between diet and cancer.*

⭐ **relative** /ˈrelətɪv/ **relatives.** **1** N-COUNT Your **relatives** are the members of your family. *Get a relative to look after the children.* **2** ADJ You use **relative** when you are comparing two or more things, particularly their size or quality. *The fighting resumed after a period of relative calm. ...the relative merits of London and Paris as places to live... If you do 50mph on a motorway, it's very slow. It's all relative.* ♦ **relatively** ADV *The sums needed are relatively small.* **3** PHRASE **Relative to** something means with reference to it or in comparison with it. *Japanese interest rates rose relative to America's.*

,relative 'clause, relative clauses. N-COUNT A **relative clause** is a subordinate clause which specifies or gives information about a person or thing. Relative clauses come after a noun or pronoun and, in English, often begin with a relative pronoun such as 'who', 'which', or 'that'.

,relative 'pronoun, relative pronouns. N-COUNT A **relative pronoun** is a word such as 'who', 'that', or 'which' that is used to introduce a relative clause.

⭐ **relax** /rɪˈlæks/ **relaxes, relaxing, relaxed.** 1 VERB If you **relax**, or if something **relaxes** you, you feel calmer and less worried or tense. *I ought to relax and stop worrying about it... Do something that you know relaxes you.* ♦ **relaxation** N-UNCOUNT *...relaxation techniques.* ♦ **relaxed** ADJ *The atmosphere at lunch was relaxed.* ♦ **relaxing** ADJ *...a quiet, relaxing holiday.* 2 VERB When your body or a part of it **relaxes**, it becomes less stiff, firm, or tense. *Massage is used to relax muscles.* 3 VERB If you **relax** your grip on something, you hold it less tightly than before. 4 VERB If you **relax** a rule, you make it less strict. *Rules governing student conduct have relaxed somewhat in recent years.*

relay, relays, relaying, relayed. 1 N-COUNT /ˈriːleɪ/ A **relay** or a **relay race** is a race between two or more teams in which each member of the team runs or swims one section of the race. 2 VERB /rɪˈleɪ/ To **relay** television or radio signals means to send them on or broadcast them.

⭐ **release** /rɪˈliːs/ **releases, releasing, released.** 1 VERB & N-COUNT If a prisoner or animal **is released**, they are set free. You can also talk about someone's **release**. *He called for the release of all political prisoners.* 2 VERB & N-UNCOUNT To **release** someone **from** an obligation, task, or feeling, or to give them **release from** it means to free them from it. [FORMAL] *Many look on life at college as a release from the obligation to work.* 3 VERB & N-UNCOUNT If someone in authority **releases** information, they make it available. You can also talk about the **release** of information. 4 VERB If you **release** someone or something, you stop holding them. [FORMAL] *He stopped and faced her, releasing her wrist.* 5 VERB & N-COUNT When a form of energy or a substance such as a gas **is released** from something, it escapes from it. You can also talk about the **release** of energy or a substance. *...the release of radioactive materials into the environment.* 6 VERB & N-COUNT When a new record, video, or film **is released**, it becomes available so that people can buy it or see it. You refer to this new record, video or film as a new **release**. 7 See also **press release**.

relegate /ˈrelɪɡeɪt/ **relegates, relegating, relegated.** 1 VERB If a team that competes in a league **is relegated**, it is moved to a lower division because it finished at or near the bottom of its division at the end of a season. ♦ **relegation** N-UNCOUNT *Relegation to the Third Division would*

prove catastrophic. 2 VERB If someone or something **is relegated to** a less important position or role, they are moved to that position or role.

relent /rɪˈlent/ **relents, relenting, relented.** VERB If you **relent**, you allow someone to do something that you had previously refused to allow them to do. *Finally his mother relented and gave permission for her son to marry.*

relentless /rɪˈlentləs/. ADJ If something is **relentless**, it never stops or becomes less intense. *The pressure now was relentless... She moves with relentless energy from one project to another.* ♦ **relentlessly** ADV *The sun is beating down relentlessly.*

relevant /ˈreləvənt/. ADJ If something is **relevant to** a situation or person, it is important or significant in that situation or to that person. *I can think of nothing less relevant to Australians than a celebration of Queen Victoria's birthday... Dr Venter said the relevant authorities would be consulted.* ♦ **relevance** /ˈreləvəns/ N-UNCOUNT *Many of the experiments performed on animals had little relevance to humans.*

⭐ **reliable** /rɪˈlaɪəbəl/. 1 ADJ **Reliable** people or things can be trusted to work well or to behave in the way that you want them to. ♦ **reliably** ADV *It's been working reliably for years.* ♦ **reliability** N-UNCOUNT *He's worried about his car's reliability.* 2 ADJ **Reliable** information is very likely to be correct, because it comes from a trustworthy or accurate source. ♦ **reliably** ADV *Sonia, we are reliably informed, loves her family very much.* ♦ **reliability** N-UNCOUNT *Both questioned the reliability of recent opinion polls.*

reliant /rɪˈlaɪənt/. ADJ AFTER LINK-V A person or thing that is **reliant on** something needs it and often cannot live or work without it. ♦ **reliance** N-UNCOUNT *...the country's increasing reliance on foreign aid.*

relic /ˈrelɪk/ **relics.** 1 N-COUNT If you describe something or someone as a **relic of** or **from** an earlier period, you dislike them and think that they should not have survived into the present. *Their radio communication system is a relic from the 1950s which keeps on breaking down.* 2 N-COUNT A **relic** is something which was made or used a long time ago and which is kept for its historical significance. *...a museum of war relics.*

⭐ **relief** /rɪˈliːf/. 1 N-UNCOUNT If you feel a sense of **relief**, you feel glad because something unpleasant has not happened or is no longer happening. *I breathed a sigh of relief... It's a great relief to be back.* 2 N-UNCOUNT If something provides **relief from** pain or distress, it stops the pain or distress, or it makes it less intense. 3 N-UNCOUNT **Relief** is money, food, or clothing that is provided for people who are very poor or hungry, or who have been affected by war or a natural disaster.

relieve /rɪˈliːv/ **relieves, relieving, relieved.** 1 VERB To **relieve** an unpleasant feeling or situation

a
b
c
d
e
f
g
h
i
j
k
l
m
n
o
p
q
r
s
t
u
v
w
x
y
z

⭐ Bank of English® frequent word   For a full explanation of all grammatical labels, see pages vii–x

means to make it less unpleasant or cause it to disappear completely. *Drugs can relieve much of the pain.* [2] VERB If someone **relieves** you **of** something, they take it away from you. *A porter relieved her of the three large cases she had been pushing on a trolley.* [3] VERB If you **relieve** someone, you take their place and do the job or task being done previously by that person.

relieved /rɪˈliːvd/. ADJ If you are **relieved**, you feel glad because something unpleasant has not happened or is no longer happening.

★ **religion** /rɪˈlɪdʒən/ **religions.** [1] N-UNCOUNT **Religion** is belief in a god or gods. *...Indian philosophy and religion.* [2] N-COUNT A **religion** is a particular set of beliefs in a god or gods and the activities connected with these beliefs. *...the Christian religion.*

★ **religious** /rɪˈlɪdʒəs/. [1] ADJ BEFORE N **Religious** means connected with religion or with one particular religion. *...different religious beliefs.* [2] ADJ A **religious** person has a strong belief in a god or gods.

relinquish /rɪˈlɪŋkwɪʃ/ **relinquishes, relinquishing, relinquished.** VERB If you **relinquish** something such as power or control, you give it up. [FORMAL]

relish /ˈrelɪʃ/ **relishes, relishing, relished.** VERB & N-UNCOUNT If you **relish** something, or if you do something with **relish**, you get a lot of enjoyment from it. *I relish the challenge of doing jobs that others turn down.*

relive /ˌriːˈlɪv/ **relives, reliving, relived.** VERB If you **relive** something that has happened to you in the past, you remember it and imagine that you are experiencing it again.

relocate /ˌriːləʊˈkeɪt, AM -ˈləʊkeɪt/ **relocates, relocating, relocated.** VERB If people or businesses **relocate**, or if they **are relocated**, they move to a different place. *The firm plans to relocate its headquarters from Saint Louis to San Antonio.* ♦ **relocation** N-UNCOUNT *...the railroad station's relocation out of the center of town.*

★ **reluctant** /rɪˈlʌktənt/. ADJ If you are **reluctant to** do something, you do not really want to do it. ♦ **reluctantly** ADV *We have reluctantly agreed to let him go.* ♦ **reluctance** N-UNCOUNT *Frank boarded his train with great reluctance.*

★ **rely** /rɪˈlaɪ/ **relies, relying, relied.** [1] VERB If you **rely on** someone or something, you need them in order to live or work properly. *The Association relies on member subscriptions for most of its income.* [2] VERB If you can **rely on** someone to work well or behave as you want them to, you can trust them to do this.

★ **remain** /rɪˈmeɪn/ **remains, remaining, remained.** [1] LINK-VERB To **remain** in a particular state means to stay in that state and not change. *The three men remained silent... He remained a formidable opponent.* [2] VERB If you **remain** in a place, you do not move away from it. *She remained at home, waiting for the phone to ring.* [3] VERB You can say that something **remains** when it still exists. *Other dangers still remain.*

[4] LINK-VERB If something **remains to** be done, it still needs to be done. [5] N-PLURAL **The remains of** something are the parts of it that are left after most of it has been taken away or destroyed. *...the charred remains of a tank.* [6] N-PLURAL The **remains** of a person or animal are the parts of their body that are left after they have died. *...human remains.* [7] N-PLURAL **Remains** are objects and parts of buildings from an earlier period of history. *...valuable Roman remains.* [8] See also **remaining**.

remainder /rɪˈmeɪndə/. N-SING **The remainder of** something is the part of it that remains after the other parts have gone or been dealt with. *He gulped down the remainder of his coffee.*

★ **remaining** /rɪˈmeɪnɪŋ/. [1] ADJ BEFORE N The **remaining** things or people out of a group are the things or people that still exist, are still present, or have not yet been dealt with. *Stir in the remaining ingredients.* [2] See also **remain**.

remake, remakes, remaking, remade; verb /ˌriːˈmeɪk/, noun /ˈriːmeɪk/. VERB & N-COUNT If a film **is remade**, or if there is a **remake of** it, a new film is made that has the same story, and often the same title, as the original film.

remand /rɪˈmɑːnd, -ˈmænd/ **remands, remanding, remanded.** VERB & N-COUNT If a person who is accused of a crime **is remanded** in custody, or if they are **on remand**, they are kept in prison until their trial. If they **are remanded** on bail, they are released and told to return to the court at a later date, when their trial will take place. *She has already served a year on remand.*

★ **remark** /rɪˈmɑːk/ **remarks, remarking, remarked.** [1] VERB If you **remark** that something is the case, you say that it is the case. *'Some people have more money than sense,' Winston had remarked... On several occasions she had remarked on the boy's improvement.* [2] N-COUNT If you make a **remark** about something, you say something about it.

★ **remarkable** /rɪˈmɑːkəbəl/. ADJ Someone or something that is **remarkable** is very impressive or unusual. ♦ **remarkably** ADV *The book is remarkably accurate.*

remedial /rɪˈmiːdiəl/. ADJ **Remedial** activities are intended to improve something. [FORMAL] *How bad does all this have to get before remedial action is taken?*

remedy /ˈremədi/ **remedies, remedying, remedied.** [1] VERB & N-COUNT If you **remedy** something that is wrong or harmful, or if you find a **remedy for** it, you correct or improve it. *They took drastic action to remedy the situation. ... a remedy for unemployment.* [2] N-COUNT A **remedy** is something that is intended to stop illness or pain. *...Chinese herbal remedies.*

★ **remember** /rɪˈmembə/ **remembers, remembering, remembered.** [1] VERB If you **remember** people or events from the past, you still have an idea of them in your mind and you are able to think about them. *I remember her perfectly... I don't* remember talking to you at all... I remember that it used to snow quite a lot. [2] VERB If you **remember** that something is the case, you suddenly become aware of it again after a time when you did not think about it. *She remembered that she was going to the social club that evening... Then I remembered the cheque, which cheered me up.* [3] VERB If you **remember to** do something, you do it when you intend to. *Please remember to enclose a stamped addressed envelope when writing.*

remembrance /rɪ'membrəns/. N-UNCOUNT If you do something **in remembrance of** a dead person, you do it as a way of showing that you remember them and respect them. [FORMAL]

★ **remind** /rɪ'maɪnd/ **reminds, reminding, reminded.** [1] VERB If someone **reminds** you **of** a fact or event that you already know about, they say something which makes you think about it. *His father has constantly reminded him of the virtues of patience.* [2] VERB If someone **reminds** you **to** do something, they say something which makes you remember to do it. *Tutors always have to remind them to bring in their notes.* [3] VERB If someone or something **reminds** you **of** another person or thing, they are similar to the other person or thing and they make you think about them. *The president reminds me of some managers I've known in business.*

reminder /rɪ'maɪndə/ **reminders.** [1] N-COUNT If one thing is a **reminder of** another, the first thing makes you think about the second. *The British are about to be given a sharp reminder of what fighting abroad really means.* [2] N-COUNT A **reminder** is a letter that is sent to tell you that you have not done something such as pay a bill.

reminisce /,remɪ'nɪs/ **reminisces, reminiscing, reminisced.** VERB If you **reminisce** about something from your past, you write or talk about it with pleasure. [FORMAL]

reminiscence /,remɪ'nɪsəns/ **reminiscences.** N-COUNT Someone's **reminiscences** are things which they remember from the past, and which they talk or write about. [FORMAL]

reminiscent /,remɪ'nɪsənt/. ADJ AFTER LINK-V If one thing is **reminiscent of** another, the first thing reminds you of the second. [FORMAL] *...flat-roofed houses reminiscent of those found in the Atlas Mountains.*

remission /rɪ'mɪʃən/ **remissions.** [1] N-VAR If someone who has had a serious disease is **in remission** or if the disease is **in remission**, the disease has been controlled so that they are not as ill as they were. [2] N-UNCOUNT If someone in prison gets **remission**, their prison sentence is reduced, usually because they have behaved well. [BRITISH]

remit /'riːmɪt/ **remits.** N-COUNT Someone's **remit** is the area of activity which they are expected to deal with, or which they have authority to deal with. *The centre has a remit to advise Asian businesses.*

remnant /'remnənt/ **remnants.** N-COUNT A **remnant of** something is a small part of it that is left when the main part has disappeared or been destroyed. *Remnants of an older building are incorporated into its walls.*

remorse /rɪ'mɔːs/. N-UNCOUNT **Remorse** is a strong feeling of guilt and regret about something wrong that you have done. [FORMAL]

★ **remote** /rɪ'məʊt/ **remoter, remotest.** [1] ADJ **Remote** areas are far away from places where most people live. ♦ **remoteness** N-UNCOUNT *...the remoteness of the island.* [2] ADJ If something is **remote from** what people want or need, it is not relevant to it because it is so different from it or has no connection with it. *...teenagers forced to study subjects that seem remote from their daily lives.* [3] ADJ If you describe someone as **remote**, you mean that they are not friendly and do not get closely involved with other people. [4] ADJ If there is a **remote** possibility that something will happen, there is only a very small possibility that it will happen.

re,mote con'trol, **remote controls.** [1] N-UNCOUNT **Remote control** is a system of controlling a machine or vehicle from a distance by using radio or electronic signals. [2] N-COUNT The **remote control** for a television, video recorder, or music system is the device that you use to control it from a distance.

remotely /rɪ'məʊtli/. ADV You use **remotely** to emphasize a negative statement. *Nobody was remotely interested.*

removal /rɪ'muːvəl/ **removals.** [1] N-UNCOUNT The **removal** of something is the act of removing it. *...surgical removal of a tumor.* [2] N-VAR **Removal** is the process of transporting furniture from one building to another. [BRITISH] *He has bought 30 lorries to move into house removals. ...a removal van.*

★ **remove** /rɪ'muːv/ **removes, removing, removed.** [1] VERB If you **remove** something **from** a place, you take it away. *At least three bullets were removed from his wounds... He went to the refrigerator and removed a bottle of wine.* [2] VERB When you **remove** clothing, you take it off. [3] VERB If you **remove** an obstacle or a problem, you get rid of it. *Most of her fears had been removed.*

removed /rɪ'muːvd/. ADJ If an idea or situation is **far removed from** something, it is very different from it. *Her teen fantasy may not be all that far removed from reality.*

renaissance /rɪ'neɪsɒns, AM ,renɪ'sɑːns/. N-SING If something experiences a **renaissance**, it becomes popular or successful again after a time when people were not interested in it.

render /'rendə/ **renders, rendering, rendered.** [1] VERB You can use **render** to say that something is changed into a different state. *It contained so many errors as to render it worthless.* [2] VERB If you **render** someone help or assistance, you help them. [FORMAL] *He had a*

a
b
c
d
e
f
g
h
i
j
k
l
m
n
o
p
q
r
s
t
u
v
w
x
y
z

A B C D E F G H I J K L M N O P Q R S T U V W X Y Z

chance to render some service to his country.
3 VERB To **render** something in a particular language or in a particular way means to express it in that language or in that way. *All the signs and announcements were rendered in English and Spanish.* ♦ **rendering, renderings** N-COUNT *...a rendering of Verdi's Requiem by the LSO.*

rendezvous /'rɒndeɪvuː/ **rendezvous, rendezvousing** /'rɒndeɪvuːɪŋ/, **rendezvoused** /'rɒndeɪvuːd/.

✓ The form **rendezvous** is pronounced /'rɒndeɪvuːz/ when it is the plural of the noun or the third person singular of the verb.

VERB & N-COUNT If you **rendezvous with** someone or if the two of you **rendezvous**, you meet at a particular time and place, often secretly. Your meeting is called a **rendezvous**. *I rendezvoused with him at 1400 hours.*

renegade /'renɪgeɪd/ **renegades.** N-COUNT & ADJ BEFORE N A **renegade** is a person who abandons their former group and joins an opposing or different group. You use **renegade** to describe a person who does this. *Three men were shot dead by a renegade policeman.*

⭐ **renew** /rɪ'njuː, AM -'nuː/ **renews, renewing, renewed.** **1** VERB If you **renew** an activity or a relationship, you begin it again. *When the two men met again after the war they renewed their friendship. ...renewed fighting.* **2** VERB When you **renew** something such as a licence or a contract, you extend the period of time for which it is valid. *Larry's landlord threatened not to renew his lease.* **3** VERB You can say that something **is renewed** when it grows or succeeds again after a time when it was destroyed, lost, or failing. *...a renewed interest in public transport systems.*

renewable /rɪ'njuːəbəl, AM -'nuː-/. **1** ADJ **Renewable** resources are ones such as wind, water, and sunlight, which are constantly replacing themselves and therefore do not become used up. **2** ADJ If a contract or agreement is **renewable**, it can be extended when it reaches the end of a fixed period of time.

renewal /rɪ'njuːəl, -'nuː-/ **renewals. 1** N-SING If there is a **renewal of** an activity or situation, it starts again. **2** N-VAR The **renewal** of a document such as a licence or a contract is an official extension of the time for which it remains valid. *His contract came up for renewal.*

renounce /rɪ'naʊns/ **renounces, renouncing, renounced.** VERB If you **renounce** something, you reject it or give it up. *After a period of imprisonment she renounced terrorism... He renounced his claim to the French throne.*

renovate /'renəveɪt/ **renovates, renovating, renovated.** VERB If someone **renovates** an old building or machine, they repair it and get it back into good condition. ♦ **renovation, renovations** N-VAR *...a property which will need extensive renovation.*

renown /rɪ'naʊn/. N-UNCOUNT A person **of renown** is well-known, usually because they do or have done something good. *...a celebrity of world renown.*

renowned /rɪ'naʊnd/. ADJ A person or place that is **renowned for** something, usually something good, is well known because of it. *The hotel is renowned for its friendliness to all visitors.*

⭐ **rent** /rent/ **rents, renting, rented. 1** VERB If you **rent** something, you regularly pay its owner in order to have it and use it yourself. *...a rented car.* **2** VERB & PHR-VERB If you **rent** something **to** someone, or if you **rent** it **out** to them, you let them have it and use it in exchange for a sum of money which they pay you regularly. *She rented rooms to university students.* **3** N-VAR **Rent** is the amount of money that you pay regularly for the use of a house, flat, or piece of land. *They recently put my rent up.*

rental /'rentəl/ **rentals. 1** N-VAR The **rental** of something such as a car or television is the fact of paying an amount of money in order to have and use it. *...Scotland's largest video rental company.* **2** N-COUNT The **rental** is the amount of money that you have to pay to use something such as a television, telephone, car, or property. [BRITISH] **3** ADJ BEFORE N You use **rental** to describe things that are connected with the renting out of goods, properties, and services. *She picked up a rental car.*

reorganize (BRIT also **reorganise**) /ri'ɔːgənaɪz/ **reorganizes, reorganizing, reorganized.** VERB To **reorganize** something means to change the way in which it is organized or done. ♦ **reorganization, reorganizations** N-VAR *...the reorganization of the legal system.*

rep /rep/ **reps. 1** N-COUNT A **rep** is a person who travels round selling their company's products or services to other companies. **2** N-COUNT A **rep** is a person who acts as a representative for a group of people. *...the health and safety rep at your union.* **3** N-UNCOUNT In the theatre, **rep** is the same as **repertory**.

repaid /rɪ'peɪd/. **Repaid** is the past tense and past participle of **repay**.

⭐ **repair** /rɪ'peə/ **repairs, repairing, repaired. 1** VERB If you **repair** something that has been damaged or is not working properly, you mend it. *A woman drove her car to the garage to have it repaired.* ♦ **repairer, repairers** N-COUNT *...builders, plumbers and TV repairers.* **2** N-VAR A **repair** is something that you do to mend something that has been damaged. *Many women know how to carry out repairs on their cars... Her marriage is beyond repair.* **3** PHRASE If something such as a building is **in good repair**, it is in good condition. If it is **in bad repair**, it is in bad condition.

repatriate /ˌriː'pætrieɪt, AM -'peɪt-/ **repatriates, repatriating, repatriated.** VERB If a country **repatriates** someone, it sends them back to their home country. ♦ **repatriation, repatriations** N-VAR

...the forced repatriation of Vietnamese boat people.

repay /rɪ'peɪ/ **repays, repaying, repaid.** ☐1 VERB If you **repay** a debt, you pay back the money you owe to somebody. ☐2 VERB If you **repay** a favour that someone did for you, you do something or give them something in return. *It was very kind. I don't know how I can ever repay you.*

repayment /rɪ'peɪmənt/ **repayments.** ☐1 N-COUNT A **repayment** is an amount of money paid at regular intervals in order to repay a debt. ☐2 N-UNCOUNT The **repayment** of money is the act or process of paying it back to the person you borrowed it from.

repeal /rɪ'piːl/ **repeals, repealing, repealed.** VERB & N-COUNT If the government **repeals** a law, it officially ends it so that it is no longer valid. You call this the **repeal** of a law.

☆ **repeat** /rɪ'piːt/ **repeats, repeating, repeated.** ☐1 VERB If you **repeat** something, you say or write it again. *He repeated that he had been misquoted.* ☐2 VERB If you **repeat** something that someone else has said or written, you say or write the same thing. *She had an irritating habit of repeating everything I said to her.* ☐3 VERB If you **repeat** an action, you do it again. ☐4 VERB & N-COUNT If an event or series of events **repeats itself**, or if there is a **repeat of** an event, it happens again. *The UN will have to work hard to stop history repeating itself.* ☐5 N-COUNT A **repeat** is a television or radio programme that has been broadcast before.

repeated /rɪ'piːtɪd/ ADJ BEFORE N **Repeated** actions or events are ones which happen many times. ♦ **repeatedly** ADV *Both men have repeatedly denied the allegations.*

repel /rɪ'pel/ **repels, repelling, repelled.** ☐1 VERB When an army **repels** an attack or an invasion, they successfully fight and drive back soldiers from another army. [FORMAL] ☐2 VERB If something **repels** you, you find it horrible and disgusting. ♦ **repelled** ADJ *She was very striking but in some way I felt repelled.*

repellent /rɪ'pelənt/ **repellents.**

☑ The spelling **repellant** is also used for meaning 2.

☐1 ADJ If you think that something is horrible and disgusting, you can say it is **repellent**. [FORMAL] *...a very large, very repellent toad.* ☐2 N-VAR Insect **repellents** are chemical substances that you use to keep insects away.

repent /rɪ'pent/ **repents, repenting, repented.** VERB If you **repent**, you say or show you feel sorry for something wrong you have done. ♦ **repentance** /rɪ'pentəns/ N-UNCOUNT *They showed no repentance during their trial.* ♦ **repentant** ADJ *...a repentant criminal.*

repercussions /ˌriːpə'kʌʃənz/ N-PLURAL If an action or event has **repercussions**, it causes unpleasant things to happen some time after the original action or event. *...the political repercussions of voting for a big tax increase.*

repertoire /'repətwɑː/ N-SING A performer's **repertoire** is all the pieces of music or parts in plays that he or she has learned and can perform. *...a wide repertoire of songs.*

repertory /'repətri, AM -tɔːri/ ☐1 N-UNCOUNT A **repertory** company is a group of actors and actresses who perform plays for just a few weeks at a time. ☐2 N-SING **Repertory** means the same as **repertoire**.

repetition /ˌrepɪ'tɪʃən/ **repetitions.** N-VAR If there is a **repetition** of an event, it happens again. *...a repetition of last month's violence.*

repetitive /rɪ'petɪtɪv/ ADJ **Repetitive** actions are repeated many times and are therefore boring. *...factory workers who do repetitive jobs.*

☆ **replace** /rɪ'pleɪs/ **replaces, replacing, replaced.** ☐1 VERB To **replace** a person or thing means to put another person or thing in their place. *...the city lawyer who replaced Bob as chairman... I clean out all the grease and replace it with oil.* ♦ **replacement** N-UNCOUNT *...a gradual replacement of staff with less experienced contractors.* ☐2 VERB If you **replace** something that is damaged or lost, you get a new one. ♦ **replacement** N-UNCOUNT *...the replacement of damaged or lost books.* ☐3 VERB If you **replace** something, you put it back where it was before. *Replace the caps on all the bottles.*

☆ **replacement** /rɪ'pleɪsmənt/ **replacements.** N-COUNT One thing or person that replaces another can be referred to as their **replacement**. *Taylor has nominated Adams as his replacement.*

replay, replays, replaying, replayed; verb /ˌriː'pleɪ/, noun /'riːpleɪ/. ☐1 VERB & N-COUNT In sport, if a match **is replayed**, it is played again, usually because there is no winner from the first match. The second match is called a **replay**. ☐2 N-COUNT A **replay** of something which has been recorded on a video tape is another showing of it. *...a slow-motion videotape replay.*

replenish /rɪ'plenɪʃ/ **replenishes, replenishing, replenished.** VERB If you **replenish** something, you make it full or complete again. [FORMAL] *Three hundred thousand tons of cereals are needed to replenish stocks.* ♦ **replenishment** N-UNCOUNT *...the replenishment of its fuel supplies.*

replica /'replɪkə/ **replicas.** N-COUNT A **replica of** something such as a statue, machine, or weapon is an accurate copy of it.

☆ **reply** /rɪ'plaɪ/ **replies, replying, replied.** ☐1 VERB & N-COUNT When you **reply to** something that someone has said or written to you, you say or write something, called a **reply**, as an answer. *I've not replied to Lee's letter yet... David has had 12 replies to his ad.* ☐2 VERB If you **reply to** something such as an attack **with** a particular action, you do something in response. *Farmers threw eggs and empty bottles at police, who replied with tear gas.*

☆ **report** /rɪ'pɔːt/ **reports, reporting, reported.** ☐1 VERB If you **report** something that has happened, you tell people about it. *I reported the theft to the*

a b c d e f g h i j k l m n o p q r s t u v w x y z

police... Estate agents report that business is reasonable... The foreign secretary is reported as saying that force will have to be used... She reported him missing the next day. [2] VERB & N-COUNT If you **report on** an event or subject, or if you give someone a **report on** it, you tell people about it, because it is your job or duty to do so. *From now on I'll report back to you every night. ...a progress report on how the project is going.* [3] N-COUNT A **report** is a news article or broadcast which gives information about something that has just happened. [4] N-COUNT A school **report** is a written account of a pupil's work and behaviour for the previous term or year. [5] VERB If someone **reports** you **to** a person in authority, they tell the person about something wrong that you have done. *His ex-wife reported him to the police... The Princess was reported for speeding.* [6] VERB If you **report to** a person or place, you go to them and say that you are ready to start work. *Who do you report to?... None of the men had reported for duty.*

reportedly /rɪˈpɔːtɪdli/ ADV If you say that something is **reportedly** the case, you mean that someone has said that it is the case, but you have no evidence of it. [FORMAL] *More than two hundred people have reportedly been killed.*

re,ported 'speech. N-UNCOUNT **Reported speech** gives an account of something that someone has said, but without quoting their actual words. Reported speech is usually introduced by a verb such as 'say' or 'tell' followed by 'that', as in 'He said that he was tired'.

⭐ **reporter** /rɪˈpɔːtə/ **reporters.** N-COUNT A **reporter** is someone who writes news articles or broadcasts news reports. *...a TV reporter.*

⭐ **reporting** /rɪˈpɔːtɪŋ/. N-UNCOUNT **Reporting** is the presenting of news in newspapers, on radio, and on television. *...impartial political reporting.*

repository /rɪˈpɒzɪtri, AM -tɔːri/ **repositories.** [1] N-COUNT A **repository** is a place where something is kept safely. [FORMAL] *A church in Moscow became a repository for police files.* [2] N-COUNT A **repository** of information is someone who knows a lot of information about a particular subject. [LITERARY] *The repository of all important knowledge in a small town was the chief barman of the local pub.*

repossess /ˌriːpəˈzes/ **repossesses, repossessing, repossessed.** VERB If a person's house or car **is repossessed**, it is taken from them because the loan payments have not been paid.

repossession /ˌriːpəˈzeʃən/ **repossessions.** [1] N-VAR The **repossession** of someone's house is the act of repossessing it. [2] N-COUNT You can refer to a house or car that has been repossessed as a **repossession**. *Many of the cars you will see at auction are repossessions.*

⭐ **represent** /ˌreprɪˈzent/ **represents, representing, represented.** [1] VERB If someone **represents** you, they act on your behalf. *...the politicians we elect to represent us.* [2] VERB If you say that something

represents a change, achievement, or victory, you mean that it is a change, achievement, or victory. *These developments represented a major change in the established order.* [3] VERB If a sign or symbol **represents** something, it is accepted as meaning that thing. *...a black dot in the middle of the circle is supposed to represent the source of the radiation.* [4] VERB If you **represent** a person or thing **as** a particular thing, you describe them as being that thing. *She represented him as the best husband a woman could have.*

representation /ˌreprɪzenˈteɪʃən/ **representations.** [1] N-UNCOUNT If a group or person has **representation** in a parliament or on a committee, someone in parliament or on the committee will vote or make decisions on their behalf. *Puerto Ricans are U.S. citizens but they have no representation in Congress.* [2] N-COUNT You can describe a picture or statue of someone as a **representation** of them. [FORMAL] *...a lifelike representation of Christ.*

⭐ **representative** /ˌreprɪˈzentətɪv/ **representatives.** [1] N-COUNT A **representative** is a person who acts on behalf of another person or group of people. *...trade union representatives.* [2] ADJ BEFORE N A **representative** group acts on behalf of a larger group. [3] ADJ If something is **representative of** a group, it is typical of that group. *He was in no way representative of dog-trainers in general.*

repress /rɪˈpres/ **represses, repressing, repressed.** [1] VERB If you **repress** a feeling, you make a deliberate effort not to show or have this feeling; used showing disapproval. *People who repress their emotions risk having nightmares.*
♦ **repression** N-UNCOUNT *...the repression of his feelings about men.* [2] VERB If a section of society **is repressed**, their freedom is restricted by the people who have authority over them; used showing disapproval. *...a UN resolution banning him from repressing his people.* ♦ **repression, repressions** N-VAR *...a society conditioned by violence and repression.*

repressed /rɪˈprest/. ADJ **Repressed** people try to stop themselves having natural feelings and desires, especially sexual ones; used showing disapproval.

repressive /rɪˈpresɪv/. ADJ A **repressive** government is one which uses force to control people and to restrict their freedom.

reprieve /rɪˈpriːv/ **reprieves, reprieving, reprieved.** [1] VERB If someone who has been sentenced in court **is reprieved**, their punishment is officially postponed or cancelled. [2] N-COUNT A **reprieve** is a delay before a very unpleasant or difficult situation which may or may not take place. *Homebuyers may have won a reprieve from higher interest rates.*

reprimand /ˈreprɪmɑːnd, -ˈmænd/ **reprimands, reprimanding, reprimanded.** VERB & N-COUNT If someone in authority **reprimands** you, or if they give you a **reprimand**, they speak to you angrily or seriously for doing something wrong. *He was* *reprimanded by a teacher for talking in the corridor... He has been fined five thousand pounds and given a severe reprimand.*

reprint, reprints, reprinting, reprinted. [1] VERB /ˌriːˈprɪnt/ When a book **is reprinted**, further copies of it are printed after all the other ones have been sold. [2] N-COUNT /ˈriːprɪnt/ A **reprint** is a new copy of a book or article, printed because all the other ones have been sold or because minor changes have been made to the original.

reprisal /rɪˈpraɪzəl/ **reprisals.** N-VAR If you do something to someone in **reprisal**, you do something violent or unpleasant to them because they have done something similar to you. *Witnesses are unwilling to testify through fear of reprisals.*

reproach /rɪˈprəʊtʃ/ **reproaches, reproaching, reproached.** [1] VERB If you **reproach** someone, you say or show that you are disappointed, upset, or angry because they have done something wrong. *She had not even reproached him for breaking his promise.* [2] N-VAR If you look at or speak to someone with **reproach**, you indicate to them that you are sad and disappointed or angry because they have done something wrong. *Women in public life must be beyond reproach.*

reproduce /ˌriːprəˈdjuːs, AM -ˈduːs/ **reproduces, reproducing, reproduced.** [1] VERB If you **reproduce** something, you copy it. *I shall not try to reproduce the policemen's English.* [2] VERB When people, animals, or plants **reproduce**, they produce more of their own species. *...the mechanism by which human cells reproduce themselves.*

reproduction /ˌriːprəˈdʌkʃən/ **reproductions.** [1] N-COUNT A **reproduction** is a copy of something such as an antique or a painting. [2] N-UNCOUNT **Reproduction** is the process by which living things produce more of their own species.

reproductive /ˌriːprəˈdʌktɪv/. ADJ **Reproductive** processes and organs are concerned with the reproduction of living things.

reptile /ˈreptaɪl, AM -tɪl/ **reptiles.** N-COUNT **Reptiles** are a group of animals which have scales on their skin and lay eggs. Snakes and crocodiles are reptiles.

⭐ **republic** /rɪˈpʌblɪk/ **republics.** N-COUNT A **republic** is a country that has a president or whose system of government is based on the idea that every citizen has equal status. *In 1918 Austria became a republic. ...the Republic of Ireland.*

⭐ **republican** /rɪˈpʌblɪkən/ **republicans.** [1] ADJ & N-COUNT A **republican** government has a president or is based on the idea that every citizen has equal status. You can also talk about someone who has **republican** views, or who is a **republican**. *Some families have been republican for generations.* [2] N-COUNT & ADJ In Northern Ireland, if someone is a **Republican** or if they have **republican** views, they believe that Northern Ireland should not be ruled by Britain but should become part of the Republic of Ireland.

repudiate /rɪˈpjuːdieɪt/ **repudiates, repudiating, repudiated.** VERB If you **repudiate** something or someone, you show that you strongly disagree with them and do not want to be connected with them. *Leaders urged people to turn out in large numbers to repudiate the violence.*
♦ **repudiation** N-UNCOUNT *...his public repudiation of the conference decision.*

repulsive /rɪˈpʌlsɪv/. ADJ **Repulsive** means horrible and disgusting. *...repulsive fat white slugs.*

reputable /ˈrepjʊtəbəl/. ADJ A **reputable** company or person is reliable and trustworthy.

⭐ **reputation** /ˌrepjʊˈteɪʃən/ **reputations.** [1] N-COUNT To have a **reputation for** something means to be known or remembered for it. *...his reputation for honesty.* [2] N-COUNT Your **reputation** is the opinion that people have of you. *The stories ruined his reputation.*

reputed /rɪˈpjuːtɪd/. ADJ If something is **reputed to** be true or **to** exist, some people say that it is true or that it exists. *He is reputed to earn ten million pounds a year.* ♦ **reputedly** ADV *The beaches of the east coast are reputedly beautiful.*

⭐ **request** /rɪˈkwest/ **requests, requesting, requested.** [1] VERB If you **request** something, you ask for it politely or formally. *She had requested that the door to her room be left open.* [2] N-COUNT If you make a **request**, you politely ask for something or ask someone to do something. *Vietnam made an official request that the meeting be postponed.*
PHRASES ● If something is done **on request**, it is given or done when you ask for it. *Leaflets giving details are available on request.* ● If you do something **at** someone's **request**, you do it because they ask you to.

⭐ **require** /rɪˈkwaɪə/ **requires, requiring, required.** [1] VERB To **require** something means to need it. *...the kind of crisis that requires us to drop everything else.* [2] VERB If a law or rule **requires** you **to** do something, you have to do it. [FORMAL] *The rules require employers to provide safety training... Then he'll know exactly what's required of him.*

⭐ **requirement** /rɪˈkwaɪəmənt/ **requirements.** [1] N-COUNT A **requirement** is a quality or qualification that you must have in order to be allowed to do something or to be suitable for something. *Its products met all legal requirements.* [2] N-COUNT Your **requirements** are the things that you need. *Variations of this programme can be arranged to suit your requirements.*

requisite /ˈrekwɪzɪt/. ADJ **Requisite** means necessary for a particular purpose. [FORMAL] *She filled in the requisite paperwork.*

⭐ **rescue** /ˈreskjuː/ **rescues, rescuing, rescued.** [1] VERB & N-VAR If you **rescue** someone, you get them out of a dangerous or unpleasant situation. A **rescue** is an attempt to save someone from a situation like this. *He had rescued her from a horrible life. ...a major air-sea rescue... Lights clipped onto life*

a
b
c
d
e
f
g
h
i
j
k
l
m
n
o
p
q
r
s
t
u
v
w
x
y
z

A B C D E F G H I J K L M N O P Q R S T U V W X Y Z

jackets improve the chances of rescue. ♦ **rescuer, rescuers** N-COUNT *It took rescuers 90 minutes to reach the trapped men.* [2] PHRASE If you **go to** someone's **rescue** or **come to** their **rescue**, you help them when they are in danger or difficulty.

★ **research** /rɪ'sɜːtʃ/ **researches, researching, researched.** VERB & N-VAR If you **research** something or if you do **research into** it, you try to discover facts about it. *She spent two years in South Florida researching and filming her documentary. ...cancer research.* ♦ **researcher, researchers** N-COUNT *...a market researcher.*

resemblance /rɪ'zembləns/ **resemblances.** N-VAR If there is a **resemblance between** two people or things, they are similar to each other. *There was a remarkable resemblance between him and Pete.*

resemble /rɪ'zembəl/ **resembles, resembling, resembled.** VERB If one thing or person **resembles** another, they are similar to each other. *She so resembles her mother.*

resent /rɪ'zent/ **resents, resenting, resented.** VERB If you **resent** someone or something, you feel bitter and angry about them. *She resents her mother for being so tough on her.*

resentful /rɪ'zentfʊl/. ADJ If you are **resentful**, you feel resentment. *I felt very resentful and angry about losing my job.*

resentment /rɪ'zentmənt/ **resentments.** N-VAR **Resentment** is a feeling of bitterness and anger. *Inflation and unemployment still cause a lot of resentment.*

reservation /,rezə'veɪʃən/ **reservations.** [1] N-VAR If you have **reservations about** something, you are not sure that it is entirely good or right. [2] N-COUNT If you make a **reservation**, you arrange for something such as a table in a restaurant to be kept for you. *Can I use your telephone to make a reservation?*

★ **reserve** /rɪ'zɜːv/ **reserves, reserving, reserved.** [1] VERB If something **is reserved for** a particular person or purpose, it is kept specially for that person or purpose. *A double room had been reserved for him... They reserved two seats on a Malaysian Airlines flight.* [2] N-COUNT A **reserve** is a supply of something that is available for use when needed. *...the world's oil reserves.* [3] PHRASE If you have something **in reserve**, you have it available for use when it is needed. *...the bottle of whisky that he kept in reserve.* [4] N-COUNT In sport, a **reserve** is someone who is available to play in a team if one of the members cannot play. [BRITISH] [5] N-COUNT A nature **reserve** is an area of land where animals, birds, and plants are officially protected. [6] N-UNCOUNT If someone shows **reserve**, they keep their feelings hidden. *I do hope that you'll overcome your reserve and let me know.*

reserved /rɪ'zɜːvd/. ADJ Someone who is **reserved** keeps their feelings hidden. *Even though I'm quite a reserved person, I like meeting people.*

reservoir /'rezəvwɑː/ **reservoirs.** [1] N-COUNT A **reservoir** is a lake used for storing water before it is supplied to people. [2] N-COUNT A **reservoir of** something is a large quantity of it that is available for use when needed. *...the body's short-term reservoir of energy.*

reside /rɪ'zaɪd/ **resides, residing, resided.** VERB If someone **resides** somewhere, they live there or are staying there. [FORMAL] *Margaret resides with her invalid mother.*

residence /'rezɪdəns/ **residences.** [1] N-COUNT A **residence** is a house where people live. [FORMAL] *The hotel could easily convert back into a private residence.* [2] N-UNCOUNT Your place **of residence** is the place where you live. [FORMAL]
PHRASES ● If someone is **in residence** in a place, they are living there. ● If you **take up residence** somewhere, you start living there.

★ **resident** /'rezɪdənt/ **residents.** [1] N-COUNT The **residents** of a house or area are the people who live there. [2] ADJ AFTER LINK-V Someone who is **resident** in a country or town lives there. *He had been resident in Brussels since 1967.*

residential /,rezɪ'denʃəl/. [1] ADJ A **residential** area contains houses rather than offices or factories. [2] ADJ A **residential** institution is one where you can live while you are studying there or being cared for there. *...a residential home for children with disabilities.*

residual /rɪ'zɪdʒʊəl/. ADJ **Residual** is used to describe what remains of something when most of it has gone. *Allow the residual heat to keep the mixture simmering.*

residue /'rezɪdjuː, AM -duː/ **residues.** N-COUNT A **residue** of something is a small amount that remains after most of it has gone. *Always using the same shampoo means that a residue can build up on the hair.*

★ **resign** /rɪ'zaɪn/ **resigns, resigning, resigned.** [1] VERB If you **resign** from a job or position, you formally announce that you are leaving it. *He resigned as chairman of the Electricity Council.* [2] VERB If you **resign yourself to** an unpleasant situation or fact, you accept it because you cannot change it. *He seemed to resign himself to leaving me.* [3] See also **resigned**.

★ **resignation** /,rezɪg'neɪʃən/ **resignations.** [1] N-VAR Your **resignation** is a formal statement of your intention to leave a job or position. *I'm not prepared to carry on and here's my resignation.* [2] N-UNCOUNT **Resignation** is the acceptance of an unpleasant situation or fact because you cannot change it. *He sighed with profound resignation.*

resigned /rɪ'zaɪnd/. ADJ If you are **resigned to** an unpleasant situation or fact, you accept it because you cannot change it. *He is resigned to the noise, the mess, the constant upheaval.*

resilient /rɪ'zɪliənt/. ADJ **Resilient** people are able to recover easily and quickly from unpleasant or damaging events. ♦ **resilience**

N-UNCOUNT *His friend's resilience had helped them through the difficult times.*

resin /'rezɪn/ **resins.** [1] N-VAR **Resin** is a sticky substance produced by some trees. [2] N-VAR **Resin** is a chemically produced substance used to make plastics.

⭐ **resist** /rɪ'zɪst/ **resists, resisting, resisted.** [1] VERB If you **resist** a change, you refuse to accept it and try to prevent it. *Both governments continue to resist the introduction of political freedom.* [2] VERB To **resist** someone or to **resist** an attack by them means to fight back. *The man was shot outside his house as he tried to resist arrest.* [3] VERB If you **resist** the temptation to do something, you stop yourself from doing it although you would like to do it. *She cannot resist giving him advice.* [4] VERB If someone or something **resists** damage of some kind, they are not harmed or damaged by it. *...bodies trained and toughened to resist the cold.*

⭐ **resistance** /rɪ'zɪstəns/. [1] N-UNCOUNT **Resistance to** a change or a new idea is a refusal to accept it. *...his stubborn resistance to anything new.* [2] N-UNCOUNT When there is **resistance** to an attack, people fight back. *...the troops are encountering stiff resistance.* [3] N-UNCOUNT The **resistance** of your body **to** germs or diseases is its power to remain unharmed or unaffected by them.

resistant /rɪ'zɪstənt/. [1] ADJ People who are **resistant to** something are opposed to it and want to prevent it. *Some people are very resistant to the idea of exercise.* [2] ADJ If something is **resistant to** something else, it is not harmed by it. *...how to improve plants to make them more resistant to disease.*

resolute /'rezəluːt/. ADJ Someone who is **resolute** refuses to change their mind or to give up a course of action. [FORMAL] ♦ **resolutely** ADV *He resolutely refused to speak English.*

⭐ **resolution** /,rezə'luːʃən/ **resolutions.** [1] N-COUNT A **resolution** is a formal decision taken at a meeting by means of a vote. *...a resolution declaring the republic fully independent.* [2] N-COUNT If you make a **resolution**, you decide to try very hard to do something. *She made a resolution to get fit.* [3] N-UNCOUNT **Resolution** is determination to do something. *She acted with resolution, courage, and intelligence.* [4] N-UNCOUNT The **resolution of** a problem or difficulty is the solving of it. [FORMAL] *...the successful resolution of the dispute. ...a peaceful resolution to the crisis.*

⭐ **resolve** /rɪ'zɒlv/ **resolves, resolving, resolved.** [1] VERB To **resolve** a problem or argument, means to find a solution to it. [FORMAL] *We must find a way to resolve these problems.* [2] VERB If you **resolve to** do something, you make a firm decision to do it. [FORMAL] *She resolved to report the matter... She resolved that, if Mimi forgot this promise, she would remind her.* [3] N-UNCOUNT **Resolve** is determination to do something. [FORMAL] *...the American public's resolve to go to war if necessary.*

resolved /rɪ'zɒlvd/. ADJ If you are **resolved to** do something, you are determined to do it. [FORMAL] *He was resolved to marry Mrs Simpson.*

resonant /'rezənənt/ ADJ If a sound is **resonant**, it is deep, clear, and echoing. ♦ **resonance** N-UNCOUNT *His voice had lost its resonance; it was tense and strained.*

resonate /'rezəneɪt/ **resonates, resonating, resonated.** VERB If something **resonates**, it vibrates and produces a deep strong sound. *The bass guitar began to thump so loudly that it resonated in my head.*

⭐ **resort** /rɪ'zɔːt/ **resorts, resorting, resorted.** [1] VERB If you **resort to** a course of action that you disapprove of, you adopt it because you cannot see any other way of achieving what you want. *His punishing work schedule had made him resort to drugs.* [2] PHRASE If you do something **as a last resort**, you do it because you can find no other way of getting out of a difficult situation or of solving a problem. *Nuclear weapons should be used only as a last resort.* [3] N-COUNT A holiday **resort** is a place where people can spend their holidays.

resounding /rɪ'zaʊndɪŋ/. [1] ADJ **Resounding** means very successful. *The FIS won a resounding victory in local elections.* [2] ADJ A **resounding** sound is loud and echoing. *...a resounding slap on the face.*

⭐ **resource** /rɪ'zɔːs, AM 'riːsɔːrs/ **resources.** N-COUNT The **resources** of a country, organization, or person are the materials, money, and other things they have and can use. *...scarce water resources... Some families don't have the resources to feed themselves properly.*

resourceful /rɪ'zɔːsfʊl/. ADJ Someone who is **resourceful** is good at finding ways of dealing with problems. ♦ **resourcefulness** N-UNCOUNT *I envy Theo his stamina and resourcefulness.*

⭐ **respect** /rɪ'spekt/ **respects, respecting, respected.** [1] VERB & N-UNCOUNT If you **respect** someone, or if you have **respect for** them, you have a good opinion of their character or ideas. *I want him to respect me as a career woman.* [2] VERB & N-UNCOUNT If you **respect** someone's wishes, rights, or customs, or if you show **respect for** them, you avoid doing things that they would dislike or regard as wrong. *Finally, trying to respect her wishes, I said I'd leave.* [3] See also **respected.**
PHRASES ● You use expressions like **in this respect** and **in many respects** to indicate that what you are saying applies to the feature you have just mentioned or to many features of something. *In many respects Asian women see themselves as equal to their men.* ● You use **with respect to**, or in British English **in respect of**, to say what something relates to. [FORMAL] *Parents often have little choice with respect to the way their child is medically treated.* ● If you **pay** your **respects to** someone, you go to see them or speak to them in order to be polite. [FORMAL] *Carl*

a
b
c
d
e
f
g
h
i
j
k
l
m
n
o
p
q
r
s
t
u
v
w
x
y
z

had asked him to visit the hospital and to pay his respects to Francis.

respectable /rɪ'spektəbəl/. [1] ADJ Someone or something that is **respectable** is approved of by society and considered to be morally correct. ...*a teacher and a respectable member of the community.* ♦ **respectability** N-UNCOUNT *If she divorced Tony, she would lose all respectability.* [2] ADJ **Respectable** means adequate or acceptable. *At last I have something respectable to wear!*

respected /rɪ'spektɪd/. ADJ Someone or something that is **respected** is admired and considered important by many people. *She is a well respected member of the community.*

respectful /rɪ'spektfʊl/. ADJ If you are **respectful**, you show respect for someone. *The children in our family are always respectful.* ♦ **respectfully** ADV *'You are an artist,' she said respectfully.*

respective /rɪ'spektɪv/. ADJ BEFORE N **Respective** means relating separately to the people you have just mentioned. *They went into their respective bedrooms to pack.*

respectively /rɪ'spektɪvli/. ADV **Respectively** means in the same order as the items you have just mentioned. *Their sons, Ben and Jonathan, were three and six respectively.*

respiratory /'respərətri, AM -tɔːri/. ADJ **Respiratory** means relating to breathing. [MEDICAL] ...*respiratory disease.*

respite /'respaɪt, -pɪt/. N-SING A **respite** is a short period of rest from something unpleasant. [FORMAL] *The heat can be unbearable, the only respite comes with cooler evenings.*

'respite care. N-UNCOUNT **Respite care** is short-term care that is provided for very old or very sick people so that the person who usually cares for them can have a break.

⭐ **respond** /rɪ'spɒnd/ **responds, responding, responded.** VERB When you **respond to** something that is done or said, you react by doing or saying something. *They are likely to respond positively to the President's request for aid... The army responded with gunfire and tear gas.*

⭐ **response** /rɪ'spɒns/ **responses.** N-COUNT Your **response to** an event or **to** something that is said is your reply or reaction to it. *In response to my question he thought for a moment.*

⭐ **responsibility** /rɪ,spɒnsɪ'bɪlɪti/ **responsibilities.** [1] N-UNCOUNT If you have **responsibility for** something or someone, it is your job or duty to deal with them. *He has responsibility for five employees.* [2] N-PLURAL Your **responsibilities** are the duties that you have because of your job or position. ...*work and family responsibilities.* [3] N-SING If you think that you have a **responsibility to** do something, you feel that you ought to do it because it is morally right or your duty to do it. *The court feels it has a responsibility to ensure that customers are not misled.* [4] N-UNCOUNT If you accept **responsibility for** something that has happened, you agree that

you were to blame for it. *British Rail has now admitted responsibility for the accident.*

⭐ **responsible** /rɪ'spɒnsɪbəl/. [1] ADJ AFTER LINK-V If you are **responsible for** something bad that has happened, it is your fault. *He still felt responsible for her death.* [2] ADJ AFTER LINK-V If you are **responsible for** something, it is your job or duty to deal with it. ...*the minister responsible for the environment.* [3] ADJ AFTER LINK-V If you are **responsible to** a person or group, you are controlled by them and have to report to them about what you have done. *I'm responsible to my board of directors.* [4] ADJ **Responsible** people behave properly, without needing to be supervised. ♦ **responsibly** ADV *He urged everyone to act responsibly.*

responsive /rɪ'spɒnsɪv/. ADJ A **responsive** person is quick to react to people or events and to show emotions such as pleasure and affection. *Harriet was an easy, responsive little girl.* ♦ **responsiveness** N-UNCOUNT *Its success is based on its responsiveness to consumer demand.*

rest 1 quantifier uses

⭐ **rest** /rest/. [1] QUANT The **rest of** something is all that remains of it. *He was unable to travel to Barcelona with the rest of the team... Only 55 per cent of the raw material is canned. The rest is thrown away.*

> **USAGE** If you are talking about something that cannot be counted, the verb following **rest** is singular. *The rest of the food was delicious.* If you are talking about several people or things, the verb is plural. *The rest of the boys were delighted.*

[2] PHRASE You can add **and the rest** or **all the rest of it** to the end of a statement or list when you want to refer vaguely to other things associated with the ones you have already mentioned. *And what about racism and all the rest of it?*

rest 2 verb and noun uses

⭐ **rest** /rest/ **rests, resting, rested.** [1] VERB & N-VAR If you **rest**, or if you have a **rest**, you do not do anything active for a period of time. *Rest the injured limb as much as possible... I've worked for 47 years so I think I'm due for a rest by now.* ♦ **rested** ADJ AFTER LINK-V *He looked tanned and well rested after his vacation.* [2] VERB If something such as an idea **rests on** a particular thing, it depends on that thing. [FORMAL] *Such a view rests on a number of incorrect assumptions.* [3] VERB If something **rests** somewhere, or if you **rest** it there, its weight is supported there. *His head was resting on her shoulder... He rested his arms on the back of the chair... He rested on his pickaxe for a while.* [4] PHRASE When an object that has been moving **comes to rest**, it stops.

restate /,riː'steɪt/ **restates, restating, restated.** VERB If you **restate** something, you say or write it again, expressing the same message in a slightly different way. [FORMAL]

⭐ **restaurant** /'restərɒnt, AM -rənt/ **restaurants.**
N-COUNT A **restaurant** is a place where you can buy and eat a meal. ● See note at **café**.

restless /'restləs/. [1] ADJ If you are **restless**, you are bored or dissatisfied, and want to do something else. ◆ **restlessness** N-UNCOUNT Many fears and anxieties cause a feeling of restlessness. [2] ADJ You say that someone is **restless** when they keep moving around, because they find it difficult to stay still. ◆ **restlessly** ADV He paced up and down restlessly.

⭐ **restore** /rɪ'stɔː/ **restores, restoring, restored.** [1] VERB To **restore** something means to cause it to exist again. The army has recently been brought in to restore order. ◆ **restoration** /,restə'reɪʃən/ N-UNCOUNT ...the restoration of diplomatic relations. [2] VERB To **restore** someone or something **to** a previous state or condition means to cause them to be in that state or condition again. We will restore her to health... His country desperately needs Western aid to restore its ailing economy. [3] VERB To **restore** an old building, painting, or piece of furniture means to repair and clean it, so that it looks like it did when it was new. ◆ **restoration** N-UNCOUNT ...the restoration of fire-damaged Windsor Castle.

restrain /rɪ'streɪn/ **restrains, restraining, restrained.** [1] VERB If someone **restrains** you, they stop you from doing what you intended or wanted to do, usually by using physical strength. [2] VERB If you **restrain** an emotion or **restrain yourself from** doing something, you prevent yourself from showing that emotion or performing that action. Nancy restrained herself from bringing up the subject. ◆ **restrained** ADJ In the circumstances he felt he'd been very restrained. [3] VERB To **restrain** something that is growing or increasing means to prevent it from getting too large. ...efforts to restrain inflation.

restraint /rɪ'streɪnt/ **restraints.** [1] N-VAR **Restraints** are rules or conditions that limit or restrict someone or something. The Prime Minister is calling for new restraints on trade unions. [2] N-UNCOUNT **Restraint** is calm, controlled, and unemotional behaviour. They behaved with more restraint than I'd expected.

restrict /rɪ'strɪkt/ **restricts, restricting, restricted.** [1] VERB If you **restrict** something, you put a limit on it to stop it becoming too large. ...passing laws to restrict foreign imports. ◆ **restricted** ADJ Plants, like animals, often have restricted habitats. ◆ **restriction, restrictions** N-VAR ...restrictions on official spending. [2] VERB To **restrict** the movement or actions of someone or something means to prevent them from moving or acting freely. These dams have restricted the flow of the river downstream. ◆ **restricted** ADJ They warned that he was in restricted airspace. ◆ **restriction** N-VAR ...the relaxation of travel restrictions. [3] VERB If you **restrict** someone's activities **to** one thing, they can only do or deal with that thing. He was,

however, allowed to stay on at the temple as long as he restricted himself to his studies. [4] VERB If something **is restricted to** a particular group, only that group can have it or do it. Camping is restricted to designated campgrounds.

restrictive /rɪ'strɪktɪv/. ADJ **Restrictive** things make it difficult for you to do what you want to. ...increasingly restrictive immigration laws.

restructure /,riː'strʌktʃə/ **restructures, restructuring, restructured.** VERB To **restructure** an organization or system means to change the way it is organized, usually in order to make it work more effectively. ...his plans to restructure Russia's local government. ◆ **restructuring, restructurings** N-VAR The company's property losses will mean more financial restructuring.

⭐ **result** /rɪ'zʌlt/ **results, resulting, resulted.** [1] N-COUNT A **result** is something that happens or exists because of something else that has happened. ...people who have developed asthma as a direct result of their work... It's worth spending more to get better results. [2] VERB If something **results in** a particular situation or event, it causes that situation or event to happen. Fifty per cent of road accidents result in head injuries. [3] VERB If something **results from** a particular event or action, it is caused by that event or action. Many hair problems result from what you eat... Ignore the early warnings and illness could result. [4] N-COUNT A **result** is the situation that exists at the end of a contest. ...election results. [5] N-COUNT A **result** is the number that you get when you do a calculation. The laboratory, which calculated the results, had made an error. [6] N-COUNT Your **results** are the marks or grades that you get for examinations. Kate's exam results were excellent.

resultant /rɪ'zʌltənt/. ADJ BEFORE N **Resultant** means caused by the event just mentioned. [FORMAL] At least a quarter of a million people have died in the fighting and the resultant famines.

⭐ **resume** /rɪ'zjuːm, AM -'zuːm/ **resumes, resuming, resumed.** VERB If you **resume** an activity, or if it **resumes**, it begins again. [FORMAL] The search is expected to resume early today.

résumé (or **resumé**) /'rezjʊmeɪ, AM -zʊm-/ **résumés.** [1] N-COUNT A **résumé** is a short account of something that has happened or that someone has said or written. I will leave with you a resumé of his most recent speech. [2] N-COUNT In American English, your **résumé** is a brief account of your personal details, your education, and the jobs you have had. The usual British word is **CV**.

resumption /rɪ'zʌmpʃən/. N-UNCOUNT When there is a **resumption** in an activity, it begins again. ...the dispute over the resumption of nuclear testing.

resurgence /rɪ'sɜːdʒəns/. N-UNCOUNT If there is a **resurgence of** an attitude or activity, it reappears and grows. [FORMAL] ...the resurgence of nationalism in Europe.

resurrect /,rezə'rekt/ **resurrects, resurrecting, resurrected.** VERB When you **resurrect** something

a
b
c
d
e
f
g
h
i
j
k
l
m
n
o
p
q
r
s
t
u
v
w
x
y
z

that has ended, you cause it to exist again. *Attempts to resurrect the ceasefire have already failed once.*

resurrection /ˌrezəˈrekʃən/. N-UNCOUNT The **resurrection of** something that had ended is the act of making it exist again. *...a resourceful resurrection of wartime spirit.*

resuscitate /rɪˈsʌsɪteɪt/ **resuscitates, resuscitating, resuscitated.** VERB If you **resuscitate** someone who has stopped breathing, you cause them to start breathing again. [FORMAL] ♦ **resuscitation** N-UNCOUNT *Despite attempts at resuscitation, Mr Hunt died.*

⭐ **retail** /ˈriːteɪl/ **retails, retailing, retailed.** [1] N-UNCOUNT **Retail** is the activity of selling goods direct to the public. *Retail sales grew just 3.8 percent last year.* [2] VERB If an item in a shop **retails at** or **for** a particular price, it is for sale at that price.

retailer /ˈriːteɪlə/ **retailers.** N-COUNT A **retailer** is a person or business that sells goods to the public.

retailing /ˈriːteɪlɪŋ/. N-UNCOUNT **Retailing** is the activity of selling goods direct to the public.

'**retail park, retail parks.** N-COUNT A **retail park** is a large, specially built area usually at the edge of a town or city where there are a lot of large shops.

⭐ **retain** /rɪˈteɪn/ **retains, retaining, retained.** VERB To **retain** something means to continue to have that thing. [FORMAL] *This rice will retain its heat for a good hour.*

retaliate /rɪˈtælieɪt/ **retaliates, retaliating, retaliated.** VERB If you **retaliate** when someone harms you, you harm them in return. *The militia responded by saying it would retaliate against any attacks.* ♦ **retaliation** N-UNCOUNT *The attack was in retaliation for the death of the drug trafficker.*

retarded /rɪˈtɑːdɪd/. ADJ **Retarded** people are less advanced mentally than most people of their age. [DATED] *Doctors said he would probably be mentally retarded.*

retention /rɪˈtenʃən/. N-UNCOUNT The **retention of** something is the keeping of it. [FORMAL] *...the retention of sanctions.*

rethink /ˌriːˈθɪŋk/ **rethinks, rethinking, rethought.** VERB & N-SING If you **rethink** something such as a plan, or if you have a **rethink** about it, you think about it again and change it. *I think all of us need to rethink our attitudes toward health and sickness. ...calls for a rethink of Britain's military aid policy to Bogota.*

reticent /ˈretɪsənt/. ADJ If you are **reticent about** something, you do not talk about it. *She is so reticent about her achievements.* ♦ **reticence** N-UNCOUNT *Pearl didn't mind his reticence; in fact she liked it.*

retina /ˈretɪnə/ **retinas.** N-COUNT Your **retina** is the part of your eye at the back of your eyeball.

⭐ **retire** /rɪˈtaɪə/ **retires, retiring, retired.** [1] VERB When older people **retire**, they leave their job and stop working. *Why aren't MPs made to retire at 65? ...his decision to retire from grand prix racing at the end*

of the season. ♦ **retired** ADJ *...a retired policeman.* [2] VERB If you **retire to** another room or place, you go there. [FORMAL]

⭐ **retirement** /rɪˈtaɪəmənt/. [1] N-UNCOUNT **Retirement** is the time when a worker retires. *The Governor is going to take early retirement.* [2] N-UNCOUNT A person's **retirement** is the period in their life after they have retired. *...financial support during retirement.*

retort /rɪˈtɔːt/ **retorts, retorting, retorted.** VERB & N-COUNT To **retort**, or to answer with a **retort**, means to reply angrily. *Was he afraid, he was asked. 'Afraid of what?' he retorted... Others retort that strong central power is a dangerous thing.*

retrace /rɪˈtreɪs/ **retraces, retracing, retraced.** VERB If you **retrace** your steps, you return to where you started from, using the same route. *He retraced his steps to the spot where he'd left the case.*

retract /rɪˈtrækt/ **retracts, retracting, retracted.** VERB If you **retract** something that you have said or written, you say publicly that you did not mean it. [FORMAL] *He later retracted the statement, claiming he made it when drunk.* ♦ **retraction, retractions** N-COUNT *Miss Pearce said she expected an unqualified retraction of his comments.*

⭐ **retreat** /rɪˈtriːt/ **retreats, retreating, retreated.** [1] VERB If you **retreat** from someone or something, you move away from them. *He retreated to the kitchen to consider their quarrel.* [2] VERB & N-VAR If an army **retreats**, or if it is in **retreat**, it moves away from an enemy in order to avoid fighting. *The French, suddenly outnumbered, were forced to retreat. ...Napoleon's retreat from Moscow.* [3] N-COUNT A **retreat** is a quiet secluded place where you go to rest or to do something in private.

retribution /ˌretrɪˈbjuːʃən/. N-UNCOUNT **Retribution** is punishment for a crime. [FORMAL] *They did not want their names used for fear of retribution.*

retrieval /rɪˈtriːvəl/. N-UNCOUNT The **retrieval** of something is the process of getting it back. *Data is now usually stored in a computer as the sorting and retrieval can be done very easily.*

retrieve /rɪˈtriːv/ **retrieves, retrieving, retrieved.** VERB If you **retrieve** something, you get it back from the place where you left it. *He reached over and retrieved his jacket from the back seat.*

retro /ˈretrəʊ/. ADJ **Retro** clothes, music, and objects are based on the styles of the past. *...50s retro ballgowns.*

retrospect /ˈretrəspekt/. PHRASE The way that things seem **in retrospect** is the way they seem after an event, when you are able to consider them from a more experienced point of view. *In retrospect, I wish I hadn't done it.*

retrospective /ˌretrəˈspektɪv/ **retrospectives.** [1] N-COUNT A **retrospective** is an exhibition or showing of work done by an artist over many years, rather than his or her most recent work. [2] ADJ **Retrospective** laws or legal actions take effect from a date before the date when they are

officially approved. ♦ **retrospectively** ADV
...*governments that impose taxes retrospectively.*

⭐ **return** /rɪ'tɜːn/ **returns, returning, returned.** ☐1 VERB
& N-SING When you **return to** a place, you go back
there. Your **return** is your arrival back at a place.
*Three days after returning to Britain he was
arrested... She returned home to Birmingham...
Asthma had hardly bothered him since his return
from Berlin.* ☐2 VERB & N-SING If you **return**
something that you have borrowed or taken, you
give it back or put it back. The **return of**
something is the act of giving or putting it back.
*He returned her passport. ...Japan's demand for the
return of the islands.* ☐3 VERB If you **return**
someone's action, you do the same thing to
them as they have just done to you. If you **return**
someone's feeling, you feel the same way
towards them as they feel towards you. *I returned
his smile... Why couldn't she return his affection
and like him just a little?* ☐4 VERB & N-SING If you
return to a subject or an activity, you start
talking about that subject or doing that activity
again. A **return to** an activity is the starting of it
again. *He called for an end to strikes and a return
to work.* ☐5 VERB & N-SING If you **return to** a state
you were in before, you go back to that state
again. You can refer to a change back to a former
state as a **return to** that state. *Life has not yet
returned to normal. ...the conditions that would
allow a lasting peace and a return to normality.*
☐6 VERB When a judge or jury **returns** a verdict,
they announce whether a person is guilty or not.
☐7 N-COUNT A **return** or a **return ticket** is a ticket
that allows you to travel to a place and then back
again. ☐8 N-VAR The **return on** an investment is
the profit you get from it. *Investors require higher
returns on riskier investments.*
PHRASES ● If you do something **in return** for
what someone has done for you, you do it
because of what they did. *There's little I can do for
him in return.* ● You say **'many happy returns'** to
wish someone a happy birthday.

reunification /ˌriːjuːnɪfɪ'keɪʃən/. N-UNCOUNT
The **reunification** of a country or city that has
been divided into two or more parts for some
time is the joining of it together again.

reunion /riː'juːniən/ **reunions.** N-VAR A **reunion** is
a party or occasion when people who have not
seen each other for a long time meet again. *...a
family reunion... It was a very emotional reunion.*

reunite /ˌriːjuː'naɪt/ **reunites, reuniting, reunited.**
☐1 VERB If you **are reunited with** your family or
friends, you meet them again after being
separated from them. *For Mary it would mean the
chance to be reunited with her sister.* ☐2 VERB To
reunite a divided organization or country means
to cause it to be united again. *His first job will be
to reunite the army.*

rev /rev/ **revs, revving, revved.** ☐1 VERB & PHR-VERB To
rev the engine of a vehicle, or **rev up** the engine
of a vehicle, means to increase the engine speed
by pressing the accelerator. *The old bus was
revving its engine... The friend revved up his*

motorbike. ☐2 N-PLURAL An engine's **revs** are its
speed, which is measured in revolutions per
minute.

revamp /riː'væmp/ **revamps, revamping, revamped.**
VERB & N-COUNT If someone **revamps** something,
they change things about it in order to try and
improve it. **Revamps** are changes to something.
*It is time to revamp the system. ...major
organizational revamps.*

⭐ **reveal** /rɪ'viːl/ **reveals, revealing, revealed.** ☐1 VERB
To **reveal** something means to make people
aware of it. *Research revealed that neither the sex
nor the age of the student makes a difference.*
☐2 VERB If you **reveal** something that has been
out of sight, you uncover it so that people can
see it. *A grey carpet was removed to reveal the
original pine floor.*

revealing /rɪ'viːlɪŋ/. ☐1 ADJ A **revealing** action
or statement tells you something that you were
not aware of. *...a revealing comment.* ☐2 ADJ
Revealing clothes show a lot of your body.

revel /'revəl/ **revels, revelling, revelled** (AM **reveling
reveled**). VERB If you **revel in** a situation or
experience, you enjoy it very much. *He revelled in
his triumph.*

revelation /ˌrevə'leɪʃən/ **revelations.** ☐1 N-VAR The
revelation of something is the act of making it
known. A **revelation** is an interesting fact that is
made known to people. *...the revelation of his
affair with a former secretary. ...revelations about
his private life.* ☐2 N-SING If something is a
revelation to you, it makes you aware of
something that you did not know before. *The
expression on his father's face was a revelation to
him.*

revenge /rɪ'vendʒ/. N-UNCOUNT **Revenge**
involves hurting someone who has hurt you.
*...acts of revenge. The attackers were said to be
taking revenge on the 14-year-old, claiming he was
a school bully... The killings were said to have been
in revenge for the murder of her lover.*

⭐ **revenue** /'revənjuː/ **revenues.** N-UNCOUNT &
N-PLURAL **Revenue** or **revenues** is used to refer to
the money that a government or organization
receives from people. *...a boom year at the
cinema, with record advertising revenue. ...a 40%
increase in revenues.*

reverberate /rɪ'vɜːbəreɪt/ **reverberates,
reverberating, reverberated.** VERB When a loud sound
reverberates, it echoes through a place. *The
noise reverberated through the house.*

revere /rɪ'vɪə/ **reveres, revering, revered.** VERB If you
revere someone, you respect and admire them
greatly. [FORMAL] *He revered his father.* ♦ **revered**
ADJ *...some of the country's most revered
institutions.* ♦ **reverence** /'revərəns/ N-UNCOUNT
They shared a reverence for women.

Reverend /'revərənd/. N-TITLE **Reverend** is a
title used before the name of a member of the
clergy. *...the Reverend Jim Simons.*

reversal /rɪ'vɜːsəl/ **reversals.** N-COUNT When there
is a **reversal of** a process or policy, it is changed

a
b
c
d
e
f
g
h
i
j
k
l
m
n
o
p
q
r
s
t
u
v
w
x
y
z

to the opposite process or policy. *The move represents a complete reversal of previous US policy.*

⭐ **reverse** /rɪ'vɜːs/ **reverses, reversing, reversed.**
1 VERB To **reverse** a process, decision, or policy means to change it to its opposite. *Complaints are already rising, reversing the trend of recent years.* **2** VERB If you **reverse** the order of a set of things, you arrange them in the opposite order, so that the first thing comes last. **3** VERB & N-UNCOUNT When a car **is being reversed**, or when it is being driven **in reverse**, it is being driven backwards. **4** ADJ & N-SING **Reverse** or **the reverse** means opposite to what has just been described or mentioned. *Instead of bringing about peace the meeting may well have the reverse effect... It's not difficult, quite the reverse.* **5** PHRASE If something happens **in reverse** or goes **into reverse**, it happens in the opposite way to usual or to what has been happening. *The process also works in reverse.*

revert /rɪ'vɜːt/ **reverts, reverting, reverted.** VERB When people or things **revert to** a former state, system, or type of behaviour, they go back to it. *She reverted to her old ways.*

⭐ **review** /rɪ'vjuː/ **reviews, reviewing, reviewed.**
1 VERB & N-COUNT When someone **reviews** something such as a new book or play, they write a report or give a talk on television or radio in which they express their opinion of it. This report is called a **review**. ♦ **reviewer, reviewers** N-COUNT *...a film reviewer.* **2** VERB & N-VAR If you **review** a situation or system, you examine it in order to decide whether changes are needed. This process is called a **review**. *He said the Government would review the situation in June... That policy was due for review this year.* **3** PHRASE If something is **under review**, it is being examined in order to decide whether changes are needed.

revise /rɪ'vaɪz/ **revises, revising, revised.** **1** VERB If you **revise** something, you alter it in order to make it better or more accurate. *I found myself revising my opinion of him... Experts are starting to revise their estimates of how big the oil spill may be.* ♦ **revision** /rɪ'vɪʒən/ N-VAR *It is badly in need of revision.* **2** VERB When you **revise** for an examination, you read things again in order to learn them thoroughly. [BRITISH] *She got up early to revise.* ♦ **revision** N-UNCOUNT *...exam revision.*

revisit /ˌriː'vɪzɪt/ **revisits, revisiting, revisited.** VERB If you **revisit** a place, you return there for a visit after you have been away for a long time.

revitalize (BRIT also **revitalise**) /ˌriː'vaɪtəlaɪz/ **revitalizes, revitalizing, revitalized.** VERB To **revitalize** something means to make it more active or lively. *...Government plans for revitalising the economy of South Wales .*

revival /rɪ'vaɪvəl/ **revivals.** **1** N-VAR When there is a **revival of** something, it becomes active or popular again. *...recent signs of economic revival. ...a revival of interest in his work.* **2** N-COUNT A **revival** is a new production of a play, an opera,

or a ballet. *...John Clement's revival of Chekhov's 'The Seagull'.*

revive /rɪ'vaɪv/ **revives, reviving, revived.** **1** VERB When something such as a feeling or a practice **revives** or **is revived**, it becomes active or successful again. *...an attempt to revive the British economy.* **2** VERB When someone **revives** a play, opera, or ballet, they present a new production of it. **3** VERB If you **revive** someone who has fainted, or if they **revive**, they become conscious again. *She could not be revived.*

revoke /rɪ'vəʊk/ **revokes, revoking, revoked.** VERB When someone in authority **revokes** something such as an order, they cancel it. [FORMAL] *The council revoked its decision and the library remained open.*

revolt /rɪ'vəʊlt/ **revolts, revolting, revolted.** **1** N-VAR A **revolt** is a violent attempt by a group of people to change their country's political system. **2** VERB When people **revolt**, they use violence to try to change a country's political system. *In 1848 the Hungarians revolted against Austrian rule.* **3** N-VAR A **revolt** by a person or group against someone or something is a rejection of the authority of that person or thing. *The Prime Minister is facing a revolt by some of his MPs.* **4** VERB When people **revolt**, they reject the authority of someone or something. *Caroline revolted against her ballet training at sixteen.*

revolting /rɪ'vəʊltɪŋ/. ADJ **Revolting** means horrible and disgusting. *The smell was revolting.*

⭐ **revolution** /ˌrevə'luːʃən/ **revolutions.** **1** N-VAR A **revolution** is a successful attempt by a large group of people to change their country's political system, using force. *The period since the revolution has been one of political turmoil... There was talk of revolution.* **2** N-COUNT A **revolution** is an important change in a particular area of human activity. *...the industrial revolution.*

⭐ **revolutionary** /ˌrevə'luːʃənri, AM -neri/ **revolutionaries.** **1** ADJ **Revolutionary** activities, organizations, or people have the aim of causing a political revolution. *...the Cuban revolutionary leader, Jose Marti.* **2** N-COUNT A **revolutionary** is a person who tries to cause a revolution or who takes part in one. **3** ADJ **Revolutionary** ideas and developments involve great changes in the way something is done or made. *...a revolutionary concept in aviation.*

revolutionize (BRIT also **revolutionise**) /ˌrevə'luːʃənaɪz/ **revolutionizes, revolutionizing, revolutionized.** VERB When something **revolutionizes** an activity, it causes great changes in the way it is done. *...ideas that will revolutionize the way people use computers.*

revolve /rɪ'vɒlv/ **revolves, revolving, revolved.** **1** VERB If one thing **revolves around** another thing, the second thing is the main feature or focus of the first thing. *Since childhood, her life has revolved around tennis... The conversation revolved around the terrible condition of the road.* **2** VERB When something **revolves**, it moves or turns in a circle around a central point or line. *The satellite revolves around the Earth once every hundred minutes.*

revolver /rɪ'vɒlvə/ **revolvers.** N-COUNT A **revolver** is a kind of hand gun.

revue /rɪ'vjuː/ **revues.** N-COUNT A **revue** is a light theatrical entertainment consisting of songs, dances, and jokes about recent events.

revulsion /rɪ'vʌlʃən/. N-UNCOUNT **Revulsion** is a strong feeling of disgust or disapproval. *They expressed their revulsion at his violent death.*

⭐ **reward** /rɪ'wɔːd/ **rewards, rewarding, rewarded.** **1** N-COUNT A **reward** is something that you are given because you have behaved well, worked hard, or provided a service to the community. *As a reward for good behaviour, treat your child to a new toy.* **2** N-COUNT A **reward** is a sum of money offered to anyone who can give information about lost or stolen property or about someone who is wanted by the police. **3** VERB If you do something and **are rewarded with** a particular benefit, you receive that benefit as a result of doing it. *Impress the buyer and you will be rewarded with a quicker sale.*

rewarding /rɪ'wɔːdɪŋ/. ADJ Something that is **rewarding** gives you satisfaction or brings you benefits. *...a rewarding and full career.*

rewritable /ˌriː'raɪtəbəl/. ADJ A **rewritable** CD or DVD is a CD or DVD that you can record onto more than once. *...rewritable discs.*

rewrite /ˌriː'raɪt/ **rewrites, rewriting, rewritten.** VERB If someone **rewrites** a piece of writing such as a book, a script, or a law, they write it in a different way in order to improve it. *Students rewrite their papers and submit them for final evaluation.*

rhetoric /'retərɪk/. N-UNCOUNT **Rhetoric** is speech or writing that is meant to convince and impress people but may lack sincerity or honesty. *My speech contained facts, not empty rhetoric.*

rhetorical /rɪ'tɒrɪkəl, AM -'tɔːr-/. **1** ADJ A **rhetorical** question is used in order to make a statement rather than to get an answer. ◆ **rhetorically** ADV *'Do these kids know how lucky they are?' Jackson asked rhetorically.* **2** ADJ **Rhetorical** language is intended to be grand and impressive. [FORMAL]

rhino /'raɪnəʊ/ **rhinos.** N-COUNT A **rhino** is the same as a **rhinoceros**.

rhinoceros /raɪ'nɒsərəs/ **rhinoceroses.** N-COUNT A **rhinoceros** is a large African or Asian animal with thick grey skin and one or two horns on its nose. → See picture on page 816.

rhyme /raɪm/ **rhymes, rhyming, rhymed.** **1** VERB If one word **rhymes with** another, they have a very similar sound. *York rhymes with pork. ...names that rhyme: Donnie, Ronnie, Connie.* **2** N-COUNT A **rhyme** is a short poem with rhyming words at the ends of its lines. ● See also **nursery rhyme**. **3** N-UNCOUNT **Rhyme** is the use of rhyming words as a technique in poetry.

⭐ **rhythm** /'rɪðəm/ **rhythms.** N-VAR A **rhythm** is a regular series of sounds, movements, or actions. *His body twists and sways to the rhythm.*

rhythmic /'rɪðmɪk/ (or **rhythmical** /'rɪðmɪkəl/). ADJ A **rhythmic** movement or sound is repeated at regular intervals. *...the rhythmic beat of the surf.* ◆ **rhythmically** ADV *She stood, swaying her hips, moving rhythmically.*

rib /rɪb/ **ribs.** N-COUNT Your **ribs** are the curved bones that go from your backbone around your chest.

ribbon /'rɪbən/ **ribbons.** N-VAR A **ribbon** is a long narrow piece of cloth used as a fastening or decoration.

⭐ **rice** /raɪs/. N-UNCOUNT **Rice** consists of white or brown grains taken from a cereal plant.

⭐ **rich** /rɪtʃ/ **richer, richest; riches.** **1** ADJ & N-PLURAL A **rich** person has a lot of money or valuable possessions. **The rich** are rich people. *Their one aim in life is to get rich. ...the rich and famous.* **2** N-PLURAL **Riches** are valuable possessions or large amounts of money. *Some people want fame or riches.* **3** ADJ If something is **rich in** a useful or valuable substance, it has a lot of that substance. *Bananas are rich in vitamin A. ...Angola's northern oil-rich coastline.* **4** ADJ A **rich** life is one that is interesting because it is full of different events and activities. *...the rich history of the island.* ◆ **richness** N-UNCOUNT *...the richness of human life.* **5** ADJ **Rich** food contains a lot of fat or oil.

richly /'rɪtʃli/. **1** ADV If something is **richly** coloured, flavoured, or patterned, it has a pleasantly strong colour, flavour, or scent. *...richly coloured fabrics.* **2** ADV You use **richly** to say that a place or thing has a large amount of elaborate or valuable things. *...the richly decorated silver pot.* **3** ADV If you say that someone **richly** deserves an award, success, or victory, you feel very strongly that they deserve it. *He achieved the success he so richly deserved.*

rickety /'rɪkɪti/. ADJ A **rickety** building or piece of furniture seems likely to collapse or break.

⭐ **rid** /rɪd/ **rids, ridding, rid.** **1** PHRASE When you **get rid of** something that you do not want or like, you take action so that you no longer have it. *The owner needs to get rid of the car for financial reasons.* **2** PHRASE If you **get rid of** someone who is causing problems for you, you make them leave. *...a senior manager who wanted to get rid of him.* **3** VERB If you **rid** a place or person **of** something undesirable or unwanted, you succeed in removing it completely. *Why couldn't he ever rid himself of those thoughts?* **4** ADJ AFTER LINK-V If you **are rid of** someone or something unpleasant or annoying, they are no longer with you or causing problems for you. *The family had sought a way to be rid of her.*

ridden /'rɪdən/. **Ridden** is the past participle of **ride**.

riddle /'rɪdəl/ **riddles.** **1** N-COUNT A **riddle** is a puzzle in which you ask a question that seems to be nonsense but which has a clever or amusing answer. **2** N-COUNT You can describe something

a
b
c
d
e
f
g
h
i
j
k
l
m
n
o
p
q
r
s
t
u
v
w
x
y
z

that is puzzling as a **riddle**. *Do they know the answer to the riddle of why it was never finished?*

riddled /'rɪdəld/. **1** ADJ AFTER LINK-V If something is **riddled with** bullets or bullet holes, it is full of them. **2** ADJ If something is **riddled with** undesirable qualities or features, it is full of them. *The report was riddled with errors. ...a dangerous, crime-riddled, filthy city.*

⭐ **ride** /raɪd/ **rides, riding, rode, ridden. 1** VERB If you **ride** a horse, you sit on it and control its movements. *Can you ride?... He mounted his horse and rode away.* **2** VERB If you **ride** a bicycle or a motorcycle you sit on it, control it, and travel along on it. *He goes to work on a bicycle.* **3** VERB When you **ride** in a vehicle such as a car, you travel in it. **4** N-COUNT A **ride** is a journey on a horse or bicycle, or in a vehicle.

> **USAGE** When you want to mention that someone is controlling a horse, bicycle, or motorbike, you can use **ride** as a transitive verb, with the object coming immediately after it. *Whether you ride a motorbike, scooter or moped, get yourself properly trained.* However, if you want to mention that someone is a passenger in a vehicle, **ride** must be followed by a preposition. *I was riding on the back of a friend's bicycle... We are still letting our children ride in the front seat of our cars.* If **ride** is used without an object, a preposition, or any other phrase that specifies the context, it usually refers to the activity of riding a horse. *'Do you ride?'—'No, I've never been on a horse.'*

PHRASES ● If you say that someone or something **is riding high**, you mean that they are popular or successful at the present time. ● If you say that someone faces **a rough ride**, you think that things are going to be difficult for them. [INFORMAL] ● See also **riding**.

⭐ **rider** /'raɪdə/ **riders.** N-COUNT A **rider** is someone who rides a horse, bicycle, or motorcycle.

ridge /rɪdʒ/ **ridges. 1** N-COUNT A **ridge** is a long narrow piece of raised land. *...a narrow mountain ridge.* **2** N-COUNT A **ridge** is a raised line on a flat surface. *...the bony ridge of the eye socket.*

ridicule /'rɪdɪkjuːl/ **ridicules, ridiculing, ridiculed.** VERB & N-UNCOUNT If you **ridicule** someone or something, or if you consider them with **ridicule**, you make fun of them in an unkind way. *Mr Goss ridiculed that suggestion... The press has held the royals up to ridicule.*

ridiculous /rɪ'dɪkjʊləs/. ADJ If you say that something or someone is **ridiculous**, you mean that they are very foolish. *It is ridiculous to suggest we are having a romance.*

ridiculously /rɪ'dɪkjʊləsli/. ADV You use **ridiculously** to emphasize the fact that you think something is unreasonable or very surprising. *She looked ridiculously young to be a mother.*

riding /'raɪdɪŋ/. N-UNCOUNT **Riding** is the activity or sport of riding horses. *I went riding.*

rife /raɪf/. ADJ AFTER LINK-V If something bad or unpleasant is **rife**, it is very common. *Bribery and corruption were rife in the industry.*

rifle /'raɪfəl/ **rifles, rifling, rifled. 1** N-COUNT A **rifle** is a gun with a long barrel. **2** VERB If you **rifle through** things, or if you **rifle** them, you make a quick search among them in order to find something or steal something. *The thief rifled through her handbag.*

rift /rɪft/ **rifts. 1** N-COUNT A **rift** between people is a serious quarrel that stops them having a co-operative relationship. *The serious rifts within the country could lead to civil war.* **2** N-COUNT A **rift** is a large split that appears in the ground.

rig /rɪg/ **rigs, rigging, rigged. 1** VERB If someone **rigs** a contest, they dishonestly arrange it to get the result they want or to give someone an unfair advantage. *She accused her opponents of rigging the vote.* ◆ **rigging** N-UNCOUNT *There were reports of election rigging.* **2** N-COUNT A **rig** is a large structure that is used for extracting oil or gas from the ground or the sea bed. *...gas rigs in the North Sea.*

▸ **rig up.** PHR-VERB If you **rig up** a device or structure, you make it or fix it in place using any materials that are available. *I'll rig up a curtain.*

right 1 correctness and morality

⭐ **right** /raɪt/ **rights, righting, righted. 1** ADJ & ADV If something is **right**, it is correct according to the facts or plans. If someone is **right** about something, they are correct about it. *Clocks never told the right time. ...delivery of the right pizza to the right place... Am I right in thinking you've got something arranged?... He guessed right about some things.* **2** ADJ & N-UNCOUNT **Right** is used to refer to activities or actions that are considered to be morally or legally good and acceptable. If someone has behaved in a way which is **right**, you can say that they are **in the right**. *It was right and proper not to show the film... I was right to issue that order... At least he knew right from wrong... Legally, the local tax office is in the right.* ◆ **rightness** N-UNCOUNT *Many people have very strong opinions about the rightness or wrongness of abortion.* **3** N-COUNT If you have a **right to** do or **to** have something, you are morally or legally entitled to do it or to have it. Your **rights** are the things you are entitled to do or have. *People have the right to read any kind of material they wish. ...voting rights.* **4** ADJ If something such as an action or decision is the **right** one, it is the best or most suitable one. *They decided the time was right for their escape... She's the right person for the job.* **5** ADJ AFTER LINK-V If a situation or thing is **right**, it is satisfactory and as you would like it to be. If something is not **right** about a situation or thing, there is something unsatisfactory or odd about it. *I was pleased with my performance on Saturday – everything went right... The name Sue Anne never seemed quite right.* **6** ADJ If you say that someone is seen in all the **right** places or knows all the **right** people, you mean that they go to places which are socially acceptable or know people who are socially acceptable.

[7] VERB If you **right** a wrong, you do something to make up for a mistake or something bad you did in the past. [8] VERB If you **right** something that has fallen or rolled over, it returns to its normal upright position. *The boat righted itself.* [9] ADJ BEFORE N The **right** side of a material is the side that is intended to be seen.

PHRASES ● If something is not the case but you think that it should be, you can say that **by rights** it should be the case. *She did work which by rights should be done by someone else.* ● If someone is a successful or respected person **in** their **own right**, they are successful or respected because of their own efforts and talents rather than those of the people they are connected with. ● **it serves you right**: see **serve**. ● **on the right side of** someone: see **side**.

right 2 direction and political groups

★ **right** /raɪt/.

☑ The spelling **Right** is also used for meaning 2.

[1] N-SING & ADV & ADJ BEFORE N The **right** is one of two opposite directions, sides, or positions. If you are facing north and you turn to the right, you will be facing east. **Right** is used to describe things which are on the right side of your body. *Parking is on the right... To her left was an orange grove... Turn right into the street... Her right arm was broken.* [2] N-SING You can refer to political ideas based on capitalist or conservative ideas, or to the people who support these ideas, as **the right**. *The Tory Right despise him.*

right 3 used for emphasis or in speech

★ **right** /raɪt/. [1] ADV You can use **right** to emphasize the exact position or time of something. *The back of a car appeared right in front of him... I had to decide right then.* [2] ADJ You can use **right** to emphasize a noun, usually referring to something bad. [INFORMAL, BRITISH] *He made a right mess.* [3] PHRASE If you do something **right away** or **right off**, you do it immediately. [SPOKEN] *Right off I want to confess that I was wrong.* [4] ADV You use **right** in order to attract someone's attention or to indicate that you have dealt with one thing so you can go on to another. *Right, let's go to our next caller.* [5] See also **all right**.

'right angle, right angles. [1] N-COUNT A **right angle** is an angle of 90°. [2] PHRASE If two things are **at right angles**, they form an angle of 90° where they touch each other. You can also say that one thing is **at right angles to** another.

'right-click, right-clicks, right-clicking, right-clicked. VERB To **right-click** or to **right-click on** something means to press the right-hand button on a computer mouse. [COMPUTING] *Right-click on the desktop and select New Folder.*

righteous /ˈraɪtʃəs/. ADJ Someone who is **righteous** is morally good, especially according

to the rules of a religion. *He was full of righteous indignation.* ● See also **self-righteous**.

rightful /ˈraɪtfʊl/. ADJ BEFORE N If you say that someone or something has returned to their **rightful** place or position, you mean they have returned to the place or position that you think they should have. *The car must be returned to its rightful owner.* ◆ **rightfully** ADV *She's inherited the money which is rightfully hers.*

'right-hand. ADJ BEFORE N If something is on the **right-hand** side of something, it is positioned on the right of it. *...the upper right-hand corner of the picture.*

,right-'handed. ADJ & ADV Someone who is **right-handed**, or who does things **right-handed**, uses their right hand rather than their left hand for activities such as writing or picking things up.

,right-'wing.

☑ The spelling **right wing** is used for meaning 2.

[1] ADJ A **right-wing** person or group has conservative or capitalist views. ◆ **right-winger, right-wingers** N-COUNT *Right-wingers demanded tax cuts.* [2] N-SING **The right wing** of a political party consists of the members of it who have the most conservative or capitalist views.

rigid /ˈrɪdʒɪd/. [1] ADJ If you describe laws, systems, or attitudes as **rigid**, you disapprove of them because they cannot be changed or because someone refuses to change them. *Hospital routines for nurses are very rigid.* ◆ **rigidity** /rɪˈdʒɪdɪti/ N-UNCOUNT *...the rigidity of government policy.* ◆ **rigidly** ADV *Our rule is rigidly enforced.* [2] ADJ A **rigid** substance or object is stiff and does not bend or stretch easily. ◆ **rigidity** N-UNCOUNT *...the rigidity of glass.*

rigor. See **rigour**.

rigorous /ˈrɪgərəs/. ADJ If you describe something as **rigorous**, you approve of the fact that it is done thoroughly and strictly. *...rigorous military training.* ◆ **rigorously** ADV *...rigorously conducted research.*

rigour (AM **rigor**) /ˈrɪgə/ **rigours.** [1] N-PLURAL If you refer to **the rigours of** an activity or job, you mean the difficult or unpleasant things that are associated with it. *...the rigours of childbirth.* [2] N-UNCOUNT If something is done with **rigour**, it is done in a strict, thorough way.

rim /rɪm/ **rims.** N-COUNT The **rim** of a container or a circular object is the edge which goes all the way round the top or round the outside. *...a round mirror with a white metal rim.*

rind /raɪnd/ **rinds.** [1] N-VAR The **rind** of a fruit such as a lemon is its thick outer skin. [2] N-VAR The **rind** of cheese or bacon is the hard outer edge which you do not usually eat.

ring 1 telephoning or making a sound

★ **ring** /rɪŋ/ **rings, ringing, rang, rung.** [1] VERB & PHR-VERB & N-COUNT In British English, if you **ring** someone, or if you **ring** them **up**, or if you give them a **ring**, you phone them. The usual American

a b c d e f g h i j k l m n o p q r s t u v w x y z

word is **call**. *She has rung home just once... Could someone ring for a taxi?* [2] VERB & N-COUNT When a telephone **rings**, it makes a sound called a **ring**, to let you know that someone is phoning you. [3] VERB & N-COUNT When you **ring** a bell or when a bell **rings**, it makes a metallic sound called a **ring**. *He heard the school bell ring.* ♦ **ringing** N-UNCOUNT *...the ringing of church bells.* [4] N-SING You can use **ring** to describe a quality that something seems to have as a statement or argument seems to have. For example, if an argument has **a plausible ring**, it seems to be plausible. [5] PHRASE If a statement **rings true**, it seems to be true or genuine. If it **rings hollow**, it does not seem to be true or genuine.

▸**ring back.** PHR-VERB In British English, if you **ring** someone **back**, you phone them, either because they phoned you earlier and you were out or because you did not finish an earlier conversation. The American term is **call back**.

▸**ring off.** PHR-VERB In British English, when you **ring off** you put down the receiver at the end of a telephone call. The American term is **hang up**.

ring 2 shapes and groups

⭐ **ring** /rɪŋ/ **rings, ringing, ringed.** [1] N-COUNT A **ring** is a small circle of metal that you wear on your finger. [2] N-COUNT An object or substance that is in the shape of a circle can be described as a **ring**. *...a ring of blue smoke.* [3] N-COUNT At a boxing match or circus, the **ring** is the place where the contest or performance takes place. [4] PASSIVE-VERB If a place **is ringed with** or **by** something, it is surrounded by that thing. *The city is ringed by mountains.* [5] N-COUNT You can refer to an organized group of people who are involved in an illegal activity as a **ring**. *...an international spy ring.*

'**ring tone, ring tones.** N-COUNT The **ring tone** is the sound made by a telephone, especially a mobile phone, when it rings.

rink /rɪŋk/ **rinks.** N-COUNT A **rink** is a large area where people go to skate.

rinse /rɪns/ **rinses, rinsing, rinsed.** [1] VERB & N-COUNT When you **rinse** something, or when you give it a **rinse**, you wash it in clean water in order to remove dirt or soap from it. *Shampoo and rinse your hair.* [2] N-COUNT A hair **rinse** is a hair dye which is not permanent but gradually fades over time.

⭐ **riot** /raɪət/ **riots, rioting, rioted.** [1] VERB & N-COUNT When people **riot**, or when there is a **riot**, a crowd of people behave violently in a public place. *They rioted in protest against the Government.* ♦ **rioter, rioters** N-COUNT *The militia dispersed the rioters.* ♦ **rioting** N-UNCOUNT *...three days of rioting.* [2] PHRASE If people **run riot**, they behave in a wild and uncontrolled manner. *Parents use discipline to stop their child running riot.*

rip /rɪp/ **rips, ripping, ripped.** [1] VERB If you **rip** something, you tear it forcefully with your hands or with a tool such as a knife. If something **rips**, it is torn forcefully. *I tried not to rip the paper as I unwrapped it.* [2] N-COUNT A **rip** is a long cut or split in something made of cloth or paper. [3] VERB If you **rip** something away, you remove it

quickly and forcefully. *Her earring had been ripped off.*

▸**rip off.** PHR-VERB If someone **rips** you **off**, they cheat you by charging too much for goods or services. [INFORMAL] *People are buying them and getting ripped off.*

▸**rip up.** PHR-VERB If you **rip** something **up**, you tear it into small pieces.

ripe /raɪp/ **riper, ripest.** [1] ADJ **Ripe** fruit or grain is fully grown and ready to be harvested or eaten. [2] ADJ AFTER LINK-V If something is **ripe for** a change, that change is likely to happen soon. *The nation was ripe for revolution.* [3] PHRASE If you say **the time is ripe** for something, you mean that a suitable time has arrived for doing it. *The time is ripe to send our first female ambassador to the region.*

ripen /'raɪpən/ **ripens, ripening, ripened.** VERB When crops **ripen**, or when something **ripens** them, they become ripe. *You can ripen the tomatoes on a sunny windowsill.*

ripple /'rɪpəl/ **ripples, rippling, rippled.** [1] N-COUNT & VERB **Ripples** are little waves on the surface of water caused by the wind or by something moving. When water **ripples**, a number of little waves appear on its surface. [2] VERB If something such as a feeling **ripples** through a person or group, it gradually spreads across them. *A faint smile rippled across the landlady's face.*

⭐ **rise** /raɪz/ **rises, rising, rose, risen** /'rɪzən/. [1] VERB If something **rises** or **rises up**, it moves upwards. *Wilson watched the smoke rise from his cigarette.* [2] VERB When you **rise**, you stand up. [FORMAL] *Luther rose slowly from the chair.* [3] VERB When you **rise**, you get out of bed. [WRITTEN] *Tony had risen early.* [4] VERB When the sun or moon **rises**, it appears from below the horizon. [5] VERB If land **rises**, it slopes upwards. *He looked up the slope of land that rose from the house.* [6] VERB & N-COUNT If an amount **rises**, or if there is a **rise** in an amount, the amount increases. *Profits rose from £842,000 to £1.82m... He will get a pay rise of nearly £4,000.* [7] VERB & N-SING If someone **rises** to a higher position or status, they become more powerful or successful. You can also talk about someone's **rise**. *He has risen rapidly through the ranks of government... The rise of the Nazis forced the family to move to London.* [8] VERB If a sound **rises**, it becomes louder or higher. *His voice rose almost to a scream.* [9] PHRASE If something **gives rise to** an event or situation, it causes that event or situation to happen. [10] to **rise to the challenge**: see **challenge**.

USAGE You should be careful not to confuse the verbs **rise** and **raise**. **Rise** is an intransitive verb and cannot be followed by an object, whereas **raise** is a transitive verb and is usually followed by an object. **Rise** can also not be used in the passive. *The number of dead is likely to rise. ...the government's decision to raise prices.*

▶ **rise above.** PHR-VERB If you **rise above** a problem, you do not allow it to affect you. *We have to resolve to rise above our circumstances.*

▶ **rise up.** PHR-VERB When the people in a country **rise up**, they rebel against the people in authority and start fighting them. *People have risen up against their rulers.*

⭐ **risk** /rɪsk/ **risks, risking, risked.** 1 N-VAR If there is a **risk of** something unpleasant, there is a possibility that it will happen. *There is a small risk that his party might lose... There's no risk of them being sued.* 2 N-COUNT If you say that something or someone is a **risk**, you mean they are likely to cause harm. *Salmon cannot be regarded as a health risk... He is a risk to national security.* 3 N-COUNT If something that you do is a **risk**, it might have unpleasant or undesirable results. *You're taking a big risk showing this to Kravis.* 4 VERB If you **risk** something unpleasant, you do something knowing that the unpleasant thing might happen as a result. *He's willing to risk making a fool of himself.* 5 VERB If you **risk** doing something, you do it, even though you know that it might have undesirable consequences. *I risked a glance back.* 6 VERB If you **risk** your life or something that is worth having, you do something which might result in it being lost or harmed. *You shouldn't have risked your job for me.* PHRASES ● If someone or something is **at risk**, they are in a situation where something unpleasant might happen to them. *People are at risk of starvation.* ● If you tell someone that they are doing something **at** their **own risk**, you are warning them that, if they are harmed, it will be their own responsibility. ● If you **run the risk of** doing or experiencing something undesirable, you do something knowing that the undesirable thing might happen as a result. *The officers had run the risk of being dismissed.*

risky /'rɪski/ **riskier, riskiest.** ADJ If an activity or action is **risky**, it is dangerous or could fail. *Investing is risky.*

rite /raɪt/ **rites.** N-COUNT A **rite** is a traditional ceremony is carried out in a particular group or society. *...a fertility rite.*

ritual /'rɪtʃʊəl/ **rituals.** 1 N-VAR & ADJ BEFORE N A **ritual** is a religious service or other ceremony which involves a series of actions performed in a fixed order. **Ritual** activities happen as part of a ritual. *...ritual dances.* 2 N-COUNT A **ritual** is a way of behaving or a series of actions which people regularly carry out in a particular situation. *Cocktails at the Plaza was a nightly ritual of their sophisticated world.*

⭐ **rival** /'raɪvəl/ **rivals, rivalling, rivalled** (AM **rivaling, rivaled**). 1 N-COUNT & ADJ If people or groups are **rivals**, they are competing against each other. You can also talk about **rival** groups. *He is well ahead of his nearest rival. ...a dispute between rival teenage gangs.* 2 VERB If you say that one thing **rivals** another, you mean that they are both of the same standard or quality. *In my opinion,*

French cooking is rivalled only by the cuisine of China.

rivalry /'raɪvəlri/ **rivalries.** N-VAR **Rivalry** is competition or conflict between people or groups. *What causes rivalry between brothers?*

⭐ **river** /'rɪvə/ **rivers.** N-COUNT A **river** is a large amount of fresh water flowing continuously in a long line across land.

riverside /'rɪvəsaɪd/. N-SING The **riverside** is the area of land by the banks of a river. *...a riverside path.*

rivet /'rɪvɪt/ **rivets, riveting, riveted.** 1 VERB If you **are riveted** by something, it fascinates you and holds your interest completely. ♦ **riveting** ADJ *...the most riveting TV interview of the year.* 2 N-COUNT A **rivet** is a type of bolt used for fastening pieces of metal together.

roach /rəʊtʃ/ **roaches.** N-COUNT A **roach** is the same as a **cockroach.** [AMERICAN]

⭐ **road** /rəʊd/ **roads.** N-COUNT A **road** is a long piece of hard ground built between two places so that people can drive or ride easily from one to the other. *There was very little traffic on the roads... They will travel by road to Jordan.*

'**road rage.** N-UNCOUNT **Road rage** is an angry or violent reaction by a driver towards another road user. *He was clearly a victim of road rage.*

roadside /'rəʊdsaɪd/ **roadsides.** N-COUNT The **roadside** is the area at the edge of a road. *...roadside restaurants.*

roadworks /'rəʊdwɜːks/. N-PLURAL **Roadworks** are repairs or other work being done on a road.

roam /rəʊm/ **roams, roaming, roamed.** VERB If you **roam** an area or **roam** around it, you wander around without having a particular purpose. *Barefoot children roamed the streets.*

roar /rɔː/ **roars, roaring, roared.** 1 VERB & N-COUNT If something **roars**, it makes a very loud noise. This noise is called a **roar**. *Her heart was pounding and the blood roared in her ears... A police car roared past. ...the roar of traffic.* 2 VERB If someone **roars**, they shout very loudly. If they **roar with** laughter, they laugh very loudly. *'Tell us your name!' he roared.* 3 VERB & N-COUNT When a lion **roars**, or when it gives a **roar**, it makes the loud sound typical of a lion.

roaring /'rɔːrɪŋ/. 1 ADJ BEFORE N A **roaring** fire has large flames and is sending out a lot of heat. 2 ADJ BEFORE N If something is a **roaring** success, it is very successful indeed.

roast /rəʊst/ **roasts, roasting, roasted.** 1 VERB When you **roast** meat or other food, you cook it by dry heat in an oven or over a fire. ● See note at **cook.** 2 ADJ BEFORE N **Roast** meat has been roasted. *I love roast chicken.*

rob /rɒb/ **robs, robbing, robbed.** 1 VERB If a person or place **is robbed**, money or property is stolen from them, often using force. *He attempted to rob a bank.* ♦ **robber, robbers** N-COUNT *Armed robbers broke into a jeweller's.* 2 VERB If someone is **robbed of** something that they should have, it is

a
b
c
d
e
f
g
h
i
j
k
l
m
n
o
p
q
r
s
t
u
v
w
x
y
z

taken away from them. *Bad luck robbed him of victory.*

robbery /'rɒbəri/ **robberies.** N-VAR **Robbery** is the crime of stealing money or property, often using force. *The gang members committed dozens of armed robberies.*

robe /rəʊb/ **robes.** **1** N-COUNT A **robe** is a long, loose piece of clothing, usually worn in religious or official ceremonies. **2** N-COUNT A bath **robe** is a piece of clothing, similar to a coat, which people wear at home when they are not dressed.

robin /'rɒbɪn/ **robins.** N-COUNT A **robin** is a small brown bird with a red breast.

robot /'rəʊbɒt, AM -bət/ **robots.** N-COUNT A **robot** is a machine which moves and performs certain tasks automatically. *...a robot arm.*

robust /rəʊ'bʌst, 'rəʊbʌst/. ADJ Someone or something that is **robust** is very strong or healthy.

⭐ **rock** /rɒk/ **rocks, rocking, rocked.** **1** N-UNCOUNT **Rock** is the hard substance which the Earth is made of. *The hills above the valley are bare rock.* **2** N-COUNT A **rock** is a large piece of rock that sticks up out of the ground or the sea, or that has broken away from a mountain or a cliff. **3** N-COUNT A **rock** is a piece of rock that is small enough for you to pick up. **4** VERB When something **rocks**, or when you **rock** it, it moves slowly and regularly backwards and forwards or from side to side. *His body rocked from side to side with the train... She sat on the porch and rocked the baby.* **5** VERB If an event or a piece of news **rocks** people, it shocks and horrifies them. [JOURNALISM] *...the scandals that have rocked the country.* **6** N-UNCOUNT **Rock** or **rock music** is loud music with a strong beat that is played using instruments including electric guitars and drums.

PHRASES ● If you say that something such as a marriage or a business is **on the rocks**, you mean that it is having severe difficulties and looks likely to end soon. ● If you say that something has reached or hit **rock bottom**, you mean that it is at such a low level that it cannot go any lower. *Morale in the armed forces was at rock bottom.*
● to **rock the boat**: see **boat**.

,**rock and 'roll.** N-UNCOUNT **Rock and roll** is a kind of pop music developed in the 1950s which has a strong beat for dancing.

⭐ **rocket** /'rɒkɪt/ **rockets, rocketing, rocketed.**
1 N-COUNT A **rocket** is a space vehicle shaped like a long tube. **2** N-COUNT A **rocket** is a missile containing explosive and powered by gas. *...an anti-tank rocket.* **3** VERB If prices or profits **rocket**, they suddenly increase very quickly. [JOURNALISM] *The crisis has sent oil prices rocketing.*

rocky /'rɒki/ **rockier, rockiest.** ADJ A **rocky** place is covered with rocks or consists of large areas of bare rock. *We made our way down the rocky path.*

rod /rɒd/ **rods.** N-COUNT A **rod** is a long thin bar made of metal or wood.

rode /rəʊd/. **Rode** is the past tense of **ride**.

rodent /'rəʊdənt/ **rodents.** N-COUNT **Rodents** are small mammals, for example rats and squirrels, with sharp front teeth.

rodeo /'rəʊdiəʊ, rəʊ'deɪəʊ/ **rodeos.** N-COUNT In the United States, a **rodeo** is a public entertainment in which cowboys show skills such as riding wild horses.

rogue /rəʊg/ **rogues.** N-COUNT A **rogue** is a man who behaves in a dishonest way. [DATED]

⭐ **role** /rəʊl/ **roles.** **1** N-COUNT The **role** of someone or something in a situation is their function or position in it. *Parents need to be clear about their role in raising their children... Films have long played a major role in his life.* **2** N-COUNT A **role** is one of the characters that an actor or singer plays in a film, play, or opera. *He gave her a leading role in his film.*

'**role model, role models.** N-COUNT A **role model** is someone you admire and try to imitate.

⭐ **roll** /rəʊl/ **rolls, rolling, rolled.** **1** VERB If something **rolls** or if you **roll** it, it moves along a surface, turning over many times. *The ball rolled into the net... Roll the meat in coarsely ground black pepper.* **2** VERB When vehicles **roll** somewhere, they move there slowly. *Tanks rolled into eastern Croatia.* **3** VERB If drops of liquid **roll down** a surface, they move quickly down it. *Tears rolled down her cheeks.* **4** VERB & PHR-VERB If you **roll** something flexible **into** a cylinder or a ball, or if you **roll** it **up**, you form it into a cylinder or a ball by wrapping it around itself or by shaping it between your hands. *Stein rolled up the paper bag with the money inside.* **5** N-COUNT A **roll** of paper, cloth, or plastic is a cylinder of it that has been wrapped around itself or around a tube. *...a dozen rolls of film.* **6** N-COUNT A **roll** is a very small circular loaf of bread. **7** N-COUNT A **roll** is an official list of people's names. *A new electoral roll should be drawn up.* **8** See also **rolling**.
PHRASES ● If someone is **on a roll**, they are having great success which seems likely to continue. [INFORMAL] ● If something is several things **rolled into one**, it combines the main features or qualities of those things. *This is our kitchen, sitting and dining room all rolled into one.*
● to **start the ball rolling**: see **ball**.
▶**roll in.** PHR-VERB If money or profits **are rolling in**, they are being received in large quantities. [INFORMAL]
▶**roll up.** **1** PHR-VERB If you **roll up** your sleeves or trouser legs, you fold the ends back several times, making them shorter. **2** See also **roll 4**.

roller /'rəʊlə/ **rollers.** N-COUNT A **roller** is a cylinder that turns round in a machine or device.

Rollerblade /'rəʊləbleɪd/ **Rollerblades.** N-COUNT **Rollerblades** are a type of roller skates with a single line of wheels along the bottom. **Rollerblade** is a trademark. ◆ **rollerblader, rollerbladers** N-COUNT *...a collision between a rollerblader and a cyclist.* ◆ **rollerblading** N-UNCOUNT *At the weekend I like to go rollerblading.*

'roller-coaster (or **roller coaster**) roller-coasters. **1** N-COUNT A **roller-coaster** is a ride at a fairground consisting of a small railway that goes up and down steep slopes fast. **2** N-COUNT If you say that someone or something is **on a roller-coaster**, you mean that they go through many dramatic changes in a short time. [JOURNALISM] I've been on an emotional roller coaster since then.

roller-skate /'rəʊləskeɪt/ **roller-skates**. N-COUNT **Roller-skates** are shoes with four small wheels on the bottom.

rolling /'rəʊlɪŋ/. ADJ BEFORE N **Rolling** hills have gentle slopes that extend into the distance.

'roll-neck, roll-necks. ADJ & N-COUNT A **roll-neck** sweater or a **roll-neck** is a sweater with a high neck that can be rolled over. [BRITISH]

ROM /rɒm/. N-UNCOUNT **ROM** is the permanent part of a computer's memory. The information stored there can be used but not changed. **ROM** is an abbreviation for 'read-only memory'. [COMPUTING] ● See also **CD ROM**.

Roman /'rəʊmən/ **Romans**. **1** ADJ & N-COUNT **Roman** means related to or connected with ancient Rome and its empire. A **Roman** was a citizen of ancient Rome or its empire. **2** ADJ & N-COUNT Roman means related to or connected with modern Rome. A **Roman** is someone who lives in or comes from Rome.

,Roman 'Catholic, Roman Catholics. N-COUNT & ADJ **Roman Catholic** means the same as **Catholic**.

romance /rə'mæns, 'rəʊmæns/ **romances**. **1** N-COUNT A **romance** is a relationship between two people who are in love with each other. ...a whirlwind romance. **2** N-UNCOUNT **Romance** refers to the actions and feelings of people who are in love. He still finds time for romance by cooking candlelit dinners for his girlfriend. **3** N-UNCOUNT You can refer to the pleasure and excitement of doing something as **romance**. ...the romance of travel. **4** N-COUNT A **romance** is a novel about a love affair.

⭐ **romantic** /rəʊ'mæntɪk/ **romantics**. **1** ADJ Someone who is **romantic** or does **romantic** things says and does things that make their partner feel special and loved. ...a romantic dinner for two. **2** ADJ BEFORE N **Romantic** means connected with love. ...a romantic relationship. ● **romantically** ADV We are not romantically involved. **3** ADJ BEFORE N A **romantic** play, film, or story describes or represents a love affair. **4** ADJ & N-COUNT If you say that someone has a **romantic** view or idea of things, or that they are a **romantic**, you are criticizing them because their view of things is unrealistic. He has a romantic view of rural society.

romp /rɒmp/ **romps, romping, romped**. VERB When children **romp**, they play and move around in a noisy happy way.

⭐ **roof** /ruːf/ **roofs**.

✓ The plural can be pronounced /ruːfs/ or /ruːvz/.

1 N-COUNT The **roof** of a building or car is the covering on top of it. ...a white cottage with a red slate roof. **2** N-COUNT **The roof of** your mouth is the top part of the inside of it. **3** N-COUNT The **roof** of an underground space such as a cave or mine is the highest part of it.

PHRASES ● If the level or price of something **goes through the roof**, it increases very suddenly and rapidly. [INFORMAL] Prices for Korean art have gone through the roof. ● If someone **hits the roof** or **goes through the roof**, they are very angry indeed. [INFORMAL]

rooftop (or **roof-top**) /'ruːftɒp/ **rooftops**. N-COUNT A **rooftop** is the outside part of the roof of a building. ...views over the rooftops.

rookie /'rʊki/ **rookies**. N-COUNT A **rookie** is a person who does not have much experience because they are new to a job. [AMERICAN, INFORMAL]

⭐ **room** /ruːm, rʊm/ **rooms**. **1** N-COUNT & N-SING A **room** is one of the separate sections in a building. You can refer to all the people in a room as **the room**. The largest conference room could seat 5,000 people... The whole room roared with laughter. **2** N-COUNT If you talk about your **room**, you are referring to a room that you have some use, especially your bedroom or your office. Go to my room and bring down my sweater, please. **3** N-UNCOUNT If there is **room for** something, there is enough space for it. The shoe should have enough room for the toes to move.

> **USAGE** You should use **room** or **space** to refer to an open or empty area. You do not use **place** as an uncount noun in this sense. **Room** is more likely to be used when you are talking about space inside an enclosed area. There's not enough room in the bathroom for both of us... Leave plenty of space between you and the car in front.

4 N-UNCOUNT If there is **room for** a particular kind of behaviour, people are able to behave in that way. Mr Hedge left no room for doubt that he was in charge.

roommate (or **room-mate**) /'ruːmmeɪt, 'rʊm-/ **roommates**. **1** N-COUNT Your **roommate** is the person you share an apartment or house with. [AMERICAN] **2** N-COUNT Your **roommate** is the person you share a rented room with. [BRITISH]

roomy /'ruːmi/ **roomier, roomiest**. ADJ Something that is **roomy** has plenty of space. ...a roomy kitchen.

roost /ruːst/ **roosts, roosting, roosted**. **1** N-COUNT A **roost** is a place where birds or bats rest. **2** VERB When birds or bats **roost** somewhere, they rest there.

⭐ **root** /ruːt/ **roots, rooting, rooted**. **1** N-COUNT The **roots** of a plant are the parts that grow underground. **2** N-COUNT The **root** of a hair or tooth is the part beneath the skin. **3** N-PLURAL

⭐ Bank of English® frequent word   For a full explanation of all grammatical labels, see pages vii-x

a b c d e f g h i j k l m n o p q **r** s t u v w x y z

You can refer to the place or culture that a person or their family comes from as their **roots**. *I am proud of my Brazilian roots.* 4 N-COUNT You can refer to the cause of a problem or of an unpleasant situation as the **root of** it or the **roots of** it. *We got to the root of the problem... They were treating symptoms and not the root cause.* 5 VERB If you **root** through things, you search through them thoroughly. *Dogs root in the debris at the roadside.* 6 PHRASE If an idea, belief, or custom **takes root**, it becomes established among a group of people. *Time would be needed for democracy to take root.* 7 See also **grass roots**.

▸**root out.** 1 PHR-VERB If you **root out** a person, you find them and force them from the place they are in, usually in order to punish them. *It shouldn't take too long to root him out.* 2 PHR-VERB If you **root out** a problem or an unpleasant situation, you find out the cause of it and put an end to it. *...a major drive to root out corruption.*

rooted /'ru:tɪd/. 1 ADJ AFTER LINK-V If one thing is **rooted in** another, it is strongly influenced by it or has developed from it. *The crisis is rooted in deep rivalries between the two groups.* 2 ADJ A deeply **rooted** opinion is a firm one that is unlikely to change. *Racism is a deeply rooted prejudice.*

rope /rəʊp/ **ropes, roping, roped.** 1 N-VAR A **rope** is a very thick cord, made by twisting together several thinner cords. *He tied the rope around his waist.* 2 VERB If you **rope** one thing to another, you tie them together with a rope. *I roped myself to the chimney.*

▸**rope in.** PHR-VERB If you say that you **were roped in** to do a particular task, you mean that someone persuaded you to help them do that task. [INFORMAL]

⭐ **rose** /rəʊz/ **roses.** 1 N-COUNT A **rose** is a flower which has a pleasant smell and grows on a bush with thorns. 2 **Rose** is the past tense of **rise**.

rosé /'rəʊzeɪ, AM rəʊ'zeɪ/. N-UNCOUNT **Rosé** is wine which is pink in colour.

rosette /rəʊ'zet/ **rosettes.** N-COUNT A **rosette** is a large circular badge made from coloured ribbons which is worn as a prize or to show support for a sports team or political party.

roster /'rɒstə/ **rosters.** N-COUNT A **roster** is a list of people, especially one giving details about who is employed to do a particular job or the order in which people do their job.

rosy /'rəʊzi/ **rosier, rosiest.** 1 ADJ **Rosy** means pink in colour. *She had bright, rosy cheeks.* 2 ADJ If you say that a situation looks **rosy**, you mean that it is likely to be good or successful.

rot /rɒt/ **rots, rotting, rotted.** 1 VERB When food, wood, or other substances **rot**, or when something **rots** them, they decay and fall apart. *...rotting vegetation... Sugary canned drinks rot your teeth.* 2 N-UNCOUNT If there is **rot** in something made of wood, parts of it have

decayed and fallen apart. *...extensive rot in the main beams.* 3 N-SING You can use **the rot** to refer to a gradual worsening of something. *He made mistakes during the campaign but the rot had set in well before that.*

▸**rot away.** PHR-VERB When something **rots away**, it decays. *The pillars rotted away and were replaced.*

rota /'rəʊtə/ **rotas.** N-COUNT A **rota** is a list which gives details of the order in which different people have to do a particular job. [BRITISH] *...a careful rota which will make it clear who tidies the room on which day.*

rotary /'rəʊtəri/. ADJ BEFORE N **Rotary** means turning or able to turn in a circular movement round a fixed point.

rotate /rəʊ'teɪt, AM 'rəʊteɪt/ **rotates, rotating, rotated.** 1 VERB When something **rotates**, or when you **rotate** it, it turns with a circular movement. *Gently rotate your hips.* ◆ **rotation, rotations** N-VAR *...the daily rotation of the earth.* 2 VERB If people or things **rotate**, or if someone **rotates** them, they take it in turns to do something. ◆ **rotation** N-VAR *...crop rotation.*

rotten /'rɒtən/. 1 ADJ If food, wood, or another substance is **rotten**, it has decayed and can no longer be used. *The front bay window is rotten.* 2 ADJ If you say that something is **rotten**, you think it is bad, unpleasant, or unfair. [INFORMAL] *It's a rotten idea.*

rouble /'ru:bəl/ **roubles.** N-COUNT The **rouble** is the unit of currency used in Russia.

⭐ **rough** /rʌf/ **rougher, roughest; roughs, roughing, roughed.** 1 ADJ If a surface is **rough**, it is uneven and not smooth. *His hands were rough and calloused.* ◆ **roughness** N-UNCOUNT *...the roughness of his jacket.* 2 ADJ You say that people are **rough** when they use too much force. ◆ **roughly** ADV *A hand roughly pushed him aside.* 3 ADJ A **rough** place is unpleasant and dangerous because there is a lot of violence or crime there. *...a rough part of our town.* 4 ADJ A **rough** calculation or guess is approximate rather than exact or detailed. ◆ **roughly** ADV *Gambling and tourism pay roughly half the entire state budget.* 5 ADJ If someone is having a **rough** time, they are experiencing something difficult or unpleasant. *Tomorrow, he knew, would be a rough day.* 6 ADV You say that someone is **sleeping rough** or **living rough** when they have nowhere to live.

roulette /ru:'let/. N-UNCOUNT **Roulette** is a gambling game in which a ball is dropped onto a revolving wheel with numbered holes in it. The players bet on which hole the ball will end up in.

round 1 preposition and adverb uses

⭐ **round** /raʊnd/. 1 PREP & ADV To be positioned **round** a place or object means to surround it or be on all sides of it. *They were sitting round the kitchen table... Visibility was good all round.* 2 PREP If you move **round** a corner or obstacle, you move to the other side of it. If you look **round** a corner or obstacle, you look to see what is on the other side. *Suddenly a car came round a corner... One of his men tapped and looked round the door.* [3] PREP & ADV You use **round** to say that something happens in or is near different parts of a place or area. *He happens to own half the land round here... Shirley found someone to show them round.* [4] ADV If you move things **round**, you move them so they are in different places. *He will be glad to refurnish where possible, change things round.* [5] ADV & PREP If you go **round** to someone's house, you visit them. *He came round with a bottle of champagne... I went round to my wife's house.* [6] PREP If you get **round** a problem or difficulty, you find a way of dealing with it. ● **round the corner**: see **corner**. ● **all year round**: see **year**.

USAGE Round and around are used in various ways as prepositions and adverbs, often as part of phrasal verbs. In most cases, you can use either word without any difference of meaning. In American English, around is much more common than round.
When you are talking about movement in no particular direction, you can use about as well as around and round. *It's so romantic up there, flying around in a small plane... I spent a couple of hours driving round Richmond... Police constables walk about with guns on their hips.*
When you are talking about something being generally present or available, you can use around or about, but not round, as adverbs *There is a lot of talent around at the moment... There are not that many jobs about.*

---

round 2 noun uses

⭐ **round** /raʊnd/ **rounds.** [1] N-COUNT A **round of** events is a series of related events, especially one which comes after or before a similar series of events. *Another round of preliminary talks would be held.* [2] N-COUNT In a sporting competition, a **round** is a series of games in which the winner goes on to play in the next round. [3] N-COUNT In a boxing or wrestling match, a **round** is one of the periods during which the participants fight. [4] N-COUNT A **round of** golf is one game, usually including 18 holes. [5] N-COUNT A doctor's **rounds** are a series of visits they make as part of their job. [6] N-COUNT If you buy a **round of** drinks, you buy a drink for each member of the group of people that you are with. [7] N-COUNT A **round of** ammunition is a bullet.

round 3 adjective use

round /raʊnd/ **rounder, roundest.** ADJ If something has a **round** shape, it has a curved shape, like a circle or ball. *She had small feet and hands and a flat, round face.*

round 4 verb uses

round /raʊnd/ **rounds, rounding, rounded.** [1] VERB If you **round** a place or obstacle, you move in a curve past the edge or corner of it. *The house disappeared from sight as we rounded a corner.* [2] VERB If you **round** an amount **up** or **down**, or if you **round** it **off**, you change it to the nearest whole number or nearest multiple of a number. [3] See also **rounded**.
▶ **round on.** PHR-VERB In British English, if someone **rounds on** you, they criticize you fiercely. The usual American expression is **turn on**. *Brown rounded angrily on his press officer.*
▶ **round up.** PHR-VERB If people or animals **are rounded up**, someone gathers them together.

roundabout /ˈraʊndəbaʊt/ **roundabouts.** [1] N-COUNT In British English, a **roundabout** is a circle at a place where several roads meet. The American term is **traffic circle**. [2] N-COUNT In a fair or playground, a **roundabout** is a large circular platform with seats which goes round and round. [BRITISH] [3] ADJ If you do something in a **roundabout** way, you deliberately avoid doing or saying it in a simple, clear, and direct way.

rounded /ˈraʊndɪd/. ADJ Something that is **rounded** is curved rather than pointed or sharp.

‚round ˈtrip, **round trips.** N-COUNT If you make a **round trip**, you travel to a place and then back again.

rouse /raʊz/ **rouses, rousing, roused.** [1] VERB If someone **rouses** you when you are sleeping, or if you **rouse**, you wake up. [FORMAL] *When I put my hand on his, he stirs but doesn't quite rouse.* [2] VERB If you **rouse yourself** to do something, you make yourself get up and do it. *He roused himself to work only when he felt like earning some money.* [3] VERB If something **rouses** you, it makes you very emotional or excited. *...a man not quickly roused to anger.* ◆ **rousing** ADJ *...a rousing speech.*

rout /raʊt/ **routs, routing, routed.** VERB & N-COUNT If an army or a sports team **routs** its opponents, it defeats them completely and easily. You can refer to a defeat like this as a **rout**. *The retreat turned into a rout.*

⭐ **route** /ruːt, AM raʊt/ **routes, routing, routed.** [1] N-COUNT A **route** is a way from one place to another. *...the most direct route to the town centre.* [2] VERB If vehicles, goods, or passengers **are routed** in a particular direction, they are made to travel in that direction. [3] PHRASE **En route to** a place means on the way to it. *The ship in question is en route from Spain to the Molucca Islands. ...holiday makers en route for the US.* [4] N-COUNT You can refer to a way of achieving something as a **route**. *Researchers are trying to get at the same information through an indirect route.*

⭐ **routine** /ruːˈtiːn/ **routines.** [1] ADJ **Routine** activities are done regularly as a normal part of a job or process. *...a series of routine medical tests.* ◆ **routinely** ADV *Banks routinely send new debit cards through the post.* [2] N-VAR A **routine** is the

---

a
b
c
d
e
f
g
h
i
j
k
l
m
n
o
p
q
r
s
t
u
v
w
x
y
z

A
B
C
D
E
F
G
H
I
J
K
L
M
N
O
P
Q
R
S
T
U
V
W
X
Y
Z

usual series of things that you do at a particular time in a particular order. ...*their daily routine*... *He checked up on you as a matter of routine.*

roving /ˈrəʊvɪŋ/. ADJ BEFORE N You use **roving** to describe a person who travels around, rather than staying in a fixed place. ...*a roving reporter.*

⭐ **row, rows, rowing, rowed.** ☐ N-COUNT /rəʊ/ A **row of** things or people is a number of them arranged in a line. → See picture on page 826. ...*a row of pretty little cottages.* ☐ PHRASE If something happens several times **in a row**, it happens that number of times without a break. *They have won five championships in a row.* ☐ VERB When you **row** a boat, you make it move through the water by using oars. *The boatman refused to row him back.* ♦ **rowing** N-UNCOUNT ...*competitions in rowing, swimming and water skiing.* ☐ N-COUNT /raʊ/ A **row** is a serious disagreement between people or organizations, often one involving a noisy argument. *They risked what could be a major diplomatic row with France... Maxine and I had a terrible row about how I spent my money.* ☐ VERB If two people **row**, or if one person **rows with** another, they have a noisy argument. *They rowed all the time... He had earlier rowed with his girlfriend.* ☐ N-COUNT If you say that someone is making a **row**, you mean that they are making a loud unpleasant noise. [BRITISH, INFORMAL] *Our little van made an unholy row.* ☐ See also **death row.**

rowdy /ˈraʊdi/ **rowdier, rowdiest.** ADJ If people are **rowdy**, they are noisy, rough, and likely to cause trouble. *He has complained to the police about rowdy neighbours.*

⭐ **royal** /ˈrɔɪəl/. ADJ **Royal** means related or belonging to a king, queen, or emperor, or to a member of their family. ...*the Japanese royal couple.*

royalist /ˈrɔɪəlɪst/ **royalists.** N-COUNT A **royalist** is someone who thinks it is right that their country should have a royal family.

royalty /ˈrɔɪəlti/ **royalties.** ☐ N-UNCOUNT The members of a royal family can be referred to as **royalty.** ...*a ceremony attended by royalty.* ☐ N-PLURAL **Royalties** are payments made to authors and musicians when their work is sold or performed.

rub /rʌb/ **rubs, rubbing, rubbed.** ☐ VERB If you **rub** something, you move your hand or a cloth backwards and forwards over it while pressing firmly. *She took off her glasses and rubbed them hard.* ☐ VERB If you **rub** a part of your body against a surface, you move it backwards and forwards while pressing it against the surface. *A cat was rubbing against my leg... She rubbed her finger up and down the shiny bonnet.* ☐ VERB If you **rub** a substance onto a surface, you spread it over the surface using your hand. *He rubbed oil into my back.* ☐ VERB If two things **rub together**, or if you **rub** them **together**, they move backwards and forwards, pressing against each other. *He rubbed his hands together.* ☐ to **rub shoulders**: see **shoulder.**

▶**rub off on.** PHR-VERB If someone's habits or characteristics **rub off on** you, you start developing the same habits or characteristics after spending time with them. [INFORMAL] *He was a tremendously enthusiastic teacher and that rubbed off on all the children he taught.*

▶**rub out.** PHR-VERB If you **rub out** something written on paper or on a blackboard, you remove it by rubbing it with a rubber or a cloth.

rubber /ˈrʌbə/. ☐ N-UNCOUNT **Rubber** is a strong, waterproof, elastic substance used for making tyres, boots, and other products. ☐ N-COUNT A **rubber** is a small piece of rubber used to rub out mistakes that you have made while writing or drawing. [BRITISH]

,**rubber 'stamp** (or **rubber-stamp**) **rubber stamps, rubber stamping, rubber stamped.** VERB When someone in authority **rubber stamps** a decision, plan, or law, they agree to it. *A meeting of union leaders rubber stamped the deal.*

rubbish /ˈrʌbɪʃ/ **rubbishes, rubbishing, rubbished.** ☐ N-UNCOUNT **Rubbish** consists of unwanted things or waste material such as old food. ☐ N-UNCOUNT If you think that something is foolish or of very poor quality you can say that it is **rubbish.** [INFORMAL] *These reports are total and utter rubbish... He described her book as absolute rubbish.*

> **USAGE** In British English, **rubbish** is the word most commonly used to refer to waste material that is thrown away. In American English, the words **garbage** and **trash** are more usual. ...*the smell of rotting garbage... She threw the bottle into the trash.* **Garbage** and **trash** are sometimes used in British English, but only informally and metaphorically. *I don't have to listen to this garbage... The book was trash.*

☐ VERB If you **rubbish** a person, their ideas, or their work, you say they are of little value. *Five whole pages of script were devoted to rubbishing her political opponents.*

rubble /ˈrʌbəl/. N-UNCOUNT **Rubble** consists of the pieces of brick, stone, or other materials that remain when a building is destroyed.

ruby /ˈruːbi/ **rubies.** N-COUNT A **ruby** is a dark red precious stone.

rucksack /ˈrʌksæk/ **rucksacks.** N-COUNT A **rucksack** is a bag, often on a frame, used for carrying things on your back. → See picture on page 48.

rudder /ˈrʌdə/ **rudders.** N-COUNT A **rudder** is a device for steering a boat or aeroplane.

ruddy /ˈrʌdi/ **ruddier, ruddiest.** ADJ If someone has a **ruddy** complexion, their face is a reddish colour. *He had a ruddy face and sticking-out ears.*

rude /ruːd/ **ruder, rudest.** ☐ ADJ If someone is **rude**, they behave in a way that is not polite. *He's rude to her friends.* ♦ **rudely** ADV ...*why she felt*

compelled to behave so rudely to a friend.
♦ **rudeness** N-UNCOUNT Midge ignored Mary's rudeness. **2** ADJ **Rude** words and behaviour are likely to embarrass or offend people, because they relate to sex or other bodily functions. ...a rude joke. **3** ADJ BEFORE N **Rude** is used to describe events that are unexpected and unpleasant. It will come as a rude shock when their salary cannot be cashed. ♦ **rudely** ADV People were awakened rudely by a siren.

rudimentary /ˌruːdɪˈmentri/. ADJ **Rudimentary** means very basic or not developed to a satisfactory degree. He had nothing more than a rudimentary knowledge of banking. ...the country's rudimentary legal system.

rueful /ˈruːfʊl/. ADJ If someone is **rueful**, they feel or express regret or sorrow in a quiet and gentle way. [LITERARY] He shook his head and gave me a rueful smile. ♦ **ruefully** ADV He was left to reflect ruefully on how his side have failed to win a single game.

ruffle /ˈrʌfəl/ **ruffles, ruffling, ruffled.** **1** VERB If you **ruffle** someone's hair, you move your hand backwards and forwards through it as a way of showing your affection towards them. **2** VERB If a bird **ruffles** its feathers, or if its feathers **ruffle**, they stand out on its body, for example when it is cleaning itself. **3** N-COUNT **Ruffles** are folds of cloth at the neck or cuffs of a piece of clothing.

ruffled /ˈrʌfəld/. **1** ADJ Something that is **ruffled** is no longer smooth or neat. Her short hair was oddly ruffled. **2** ADJ BEFORE N **Ruffled** clothes are decorated with small folds of material.

rug /rʌg/ **rugs.** **1** N-COUNT A **rug** is a piece of thick material that you put on the floor and use like a carpet. ...a Persian rug. **2** N-COUNT A **rug** is a small blanket which you use to cover your shoulders or your knees.

rugby

⭐ **rugby** /ˈrʌgbi/. N-UNCOUNT **Rugby** is a game played by two teams, who try to get an oval ball past a line at their opponents' end of the pitch.

rugged /ˈrʌgɪd/. **1** ADJ A **rugged** area of land is rocky and uneven. [LITERARY] ...a rugged mountainous terrain. **2** ADJ If you describe a man as **rugged**, you mean that he has strong masculine features; used showing approval.

3 ADJ A **rugged** piece of equipment is made of strong long-lasting material. Due to the rugged construction of the 600 Series, no maintenance should be required.

⭐ **ruin** /ˈruːɪn/ **ruins, ruining, ruined.** **1** VERB To **ruin** something means to severely harm, damage, or spoil it. My wife was ruining her health through worry. **2** PHRASE If something is **in ruins**, it has gone completely wrong, and there is no chance of putting it right. His travel plans lay in ruins. **3** N-COUNT & PHRASE A **ruin** is a building that has been partly destroyed. You can say that a building like this is **in ruins**. It looked as though part of the roof had fallen in. Commonwood was a ruin... The ancient medieval town was in ruins. **4** N-PLURAL The **ruins of** something are the parts of it that remain after it has been severely damaged or weakened. The new Turkish republic he helped to build emerged from the ruins of a great empire. **5** VERB & N-UNCOUNT If someone or something **ruins** you, or if you face financial **ruin**, someone or something causes you to no longer have any money.

ruined /ˈruːɪnd/. ADJ BEFORE N A **ruined** building has been badly damaged or has fallen apart. ...a ruined church.

⭐ **rule** /ruːl/ **rules, ruling, ruled.** **1** N-COUNT **Rules** are specific, often written, instructions telling you what you can and cannot do. ...a thirty-two-page pamphlet explaining the rules of basketball... This was against the rules. **2** N-COUNT The **rules of** something such as a language or a science are statements that describe the way that things usually happen in a particular situation. ...the rules of quantum theory. **3** N-SING If something is **the rule**, it is the normal state of affairs. For most people, seven hours sleep a night is the rule. **4** VERB The person or group that **rules** a country controls its affairs. For four centuries, he says, foreigners have ruled Angola. **5** VERB When someone in authority **rules on** a particular matter, they give an official decision about it. [FORMAL] The Israeli court has not yet ruled on the case. **6** See also **ruling; ground rule.**

PHRASES ● If you say that something happens **as a rule**, you mean that it usually happens. As a rule she eats dinner with us. ● If someone in authority **bends the rules**, they allow you to do something, even though it is against the rules.

▶ **rule out.** **1** PHR-VERB If you **rule out** an idea or course of action, you reject it because it is impossible or unsuitable. **2** PHR-VERB If something **rules out** a situation, it prevents it from happening or from being possible. Agassi's chest injury ruled him out of the Davis Cup final.

ruler /ˈruːlə/ **rulers.** **1** N-COUNT A **ruler** is a person who rules a country. He was a weak-willed and indecisive ruler. **2** N-COUNT A **ruler** is a long flat object with straight edges used for measuring things or drawing straight lines.

⭐ **ruling** /ˈruːlɪŋ/ **rulings.** **1** ADJ BEFORE N The **ruling** group of people in an organization or country is the group that controls its affairs. ...voters'

growing dissatisfaction with the ruling party.
2 N-COUNT A **ruling** is an official decision made by a judge or court. *Goodwin tried to have the court ruling overturned.*

rum /rʌm/. N-UNCOUNT **Rum** is an alcoholic drink made from sugar cane juice.

rumble /ˈrʌmbəl/ **rumbles, rumbling, rumbled.** VERB & N-COUNT If something **rumbles**, or if it makes a **rumble**, it makes a low continuous noise, often while moving slowly. *...the distant rumble of traffic.*

rumbling /ˈrʌmblɪŋ/ **rumblings.** **1** N-COUNT A **rumbling** is a low continuous noise. *...the rumbling of an empty stomach.* **2** N-COUNT **Rumblings** are signs that a bad situation is developing or that people are becoming dissatisfied. *There were rumblings of discontent within the ranks.*

rummage /ˈrʌmɪdʒ/ **rummages, rummaging, rummaged.** VERB & N-COUNT If you **rummage** through something, or if you have a **rummage** through it, you search for something you want by moving things around in a careless or hurried way. *I like going down to the markets and rummaging around... Your sons have had a good rummage in the cupboard.*

⭐ **rumour** (AM **rumor**) /ˈruːmə/ **rumours.** N-COUNT A **rumour** is a piece of information that may or may not be true, but that people are talking about.

rumoured (AM **rumored**) /ˈruːməd/. PASSIVE-VERB If something **is rumoured to** be the case, people are suggesting that it is the case, but they do not know for certain. *Her parents are rumoured to be on the verge of splitting up.*

rump /rʌmp/ **rumps.** N-COUNT An animal's **rump** is its rear end.

⭐ **run** /rʌn/ **runs, running, ran, run.** **1** VERB & N-COUNT When you **run**, or when you have a **run**, you move quickly, leaving the ground during each stride. *I excused myself and ran back to the telephone... Antonia ran to meet them... After a six-mile run, Jackie returns home.* ♦ **running** N-UNCOUNT *...cross-country running. ...running shoes.* **2** VERB You say that something long, such as a road, **runs** in a particular direction when you are describing its course or position. *...the sun-dappled trail which ran through the beech woods... The hallway ran the length of the villa.* **3** VERB If you **run** an object or your hand **over** or **through** something, you move the object or your hand over it or through it. *He ran his hand over his ribs... Fumbling, he ran her card through the machine.* **4** VERB In American English, if someone **runs** in an election, they take part as a candidate. The usual British word is **stand**. *He announced he would run for president.* **5** VERB If you **run** an organization or an activity, you are in charge of it or you organize it. *Is this any way to run a country? ...a well-run, profitable organisation.* ♦ **running** N-SING *...the day-to-day running of the clinic.* **6** VERB If you talk about

how a system, an organization, or someone's life **is running**, you are saying how well it is operating or progressing. *...the staff who have kept the bank running.* **7** VERB If you **run** an experiment, computer program, or other process, you start it and let it continue. *He ran a lot of tests... The program runs on a standard personal computer.* **8** VERB When a machine **is running**, or when you **are running** it, it is switched on and operating. *She ran the tape and found a message from Charles.* **9** VERB A machine that **runs on** or **off** a particular source of energy functions using that source of energy. *Black cabs run on diesel.* **10** VERB If a train or bus **runs** somewhere, it travels on a regular route at set times. *A shuttle bus runs frequently between the Inn and the Country Club.* **11** VERB If you **run** somewhere in a car, you drive there. [INFORMAL] *Could you run me up to Baltimore?* **12** VERB If a liquid **runs** in a particular direction, it flows in that direction. *Tears were running down her cheeks.* **13** VERB If you **run** water, you cause it to flow from a tap. *They heard him running the kitchen tap... I ran a warm bath.* ♦ **running** ADJ BEFORE N *...cold running water.* **14** VERB If the dye in some cloth or the ink on some paper **runs**, it comes off or spreads when the cloth or paper gets wet. **15** VERB If a play, event, or legal contract **runs** for a particular period of time, it lasts for that period of time. *It pleased critics but ran for only three years in the West End... The contract was to run from 1992 to 2020.* **16** N-COUNT In the theatre, a **run** is the period of time during which performances of a play are given. **17** VERB **Run** is used in combination with other words and phrases, where the meaning of the combination depends mostly on the other word or phrase. *Time is running short... I'm running late again... Today's RPI figure shows inflation running at 10.9 per cent.* **18** See also **running**.

PHRASES ● If you talk about what will happen **in the long run**, you are saying that you think what will happen over a long period of time in the future. If you talk about what will happen **in the short run**, you are saying what you think will happen in the near future. ● If someone is **on the run**, they are trying to escape or hide from someone such as the police or an enemy.

▸**run across.** PHR-VERB If you **run across** someone or something, you meet them or find them unexpectedly. *We ran across some old friends.*

▸**run away.** PHR-VERB If you **run away from** a place, you secretly leave it. *I ran away from home when I was sixteen.*

▸**run away with.** PHR-VERB If you let your emotions **run away with** you, you fail to control them.

▸**run down.** **1** PHR-VERB If you **run down** people or things, you criticize them strongly. *...the British 'genius for running ourselves down'.* **2** PHR-VERB If a vehicle or its driver **runs** someone **down**, the vehicle hits them and injures them. **3** See also **run-down**.

▶ **run into.** 1 PHR-VERB If you **run into** problems or difficulties, you unexpectedly begin to experience them. *...companies that have run into trouble.* 2 PHR-VERB If you **run into** someone, you meet them unexpectedly. *He ran into Krettner in the corridor.* 3 PHR-VERB If a vehicle **runs into** something, it accidentally hits it. 4 PHR-VERB You use **run into** when indicating that the cost or amount of something is very great. *...tuition fees which could run into thousands of pounds.*

▶ **run off.** 1 PHR-VERB If you **run off with** someone, you secretly go away with them in order to live with them or marry them. *The last thing I'm going to do is run off with somebody's husband.* 2 PHR-VERB If you **run off** copies of a piece of writing, you produce them using a machine.

▶ **run out.** 1 PHR-VERB If you **run out of** something, or if it **runs out**, you have no more of it left. *They have run out of ideas... Time is running out.* 2 PHR-VERB When a legal document **runs out**, it stops being valid. 3 To **run out of steam**: see **steam**.

▶ **run over.** PHR-VERB If a vehicle **runs over** someone or something, it knocks them down. *He ran over a six-year-old child as he was driving back from a party.*

▶ **run through.** 1 PHR-VERB If you **run through** a performance or a series of actions, you rehearse it or practise it. 2 PHR-VERB If you **run through** a list of items, you read or mention all the items quickly. *I ran through the options with him.*

▶ **run up.** 1 PHR-VERB If someone **runs up** bills or debts, they acquire them by buying a lot of things or borrowing money. *He ran up a £1,400 bill at the Britannia Adelphi Hotel.* 2 See also **run-up.**

▶ **run up against.** PHR-VERB If you **run up against** problems, you suddenly begin to experience them.

runaway /ˈrʌnəweɪ/ **runaways.** 1 ADJ You use **runaway** to describe a situation in which something increases or develops very quickly and cannot be controlled. *Our Grand Sale in June was a runaway success.* 2 N-COUNT A **runaway** is someone, especially a child, who leaves home without telling anyone or without permission. 3 ADJ A **runaway** vehicle is moving and its driver has lost control of it. *The runaway car careered into a bench.*

run-down. 1 ADJ /ˌrʌn ˈdaʊn/ If someone is **run-down**, they are tired or slightly ill. [INFORMAL] 2 ADJ A **run-down** building or organization is in very poor condition. *...a run-down block of flats.* 3 N-SING /ˈrʌn daʊn/ If you give someone a **run-down of** a group of things or a **run-down on** something, you give them details of it. [INFORMAL] *Here's a run-down of the options.*

rung /rʌŋ/ **rungs.** 1 **Rung** is the past participle of **ring.** 2 N-COUNT The **rungs** of a ladder are the wooden or metal bars that form the steps. 3 N-COUNT If you reach a particular **rung** in an organization or in a process, you reach that level in it. *...the first rung of the property ladder.*

'run-in, run-ins. N-COUNT If you have a **run-in** with someone, you have an argument or quarrel with them. [INFORMAL]

★ **runner** /ˈrʌnə/ **runners.** 1 N-COUNT A **runner** is a person who runs, especially for sport or pleasure. *...a marathon runner... I am a very keen runner.* 2 N-COUNT A drugs **runner** or gun **runner** is someone who illegally takes drugs or guns into a country. 3 N-COUNT **Runners** are thin strips of wood or metal underneath something which help it to move smoothly. *...plastic drawer runners.*

'runner bean, runner beans. N-COUNT **Runner beans** are long green beans that are eaten as a vegetable. → See picture on page 836.

,runner-'up, runners-up. N-COUNT A **runner-up** is someone who finishes in second place in a race or competition.

★ **running** /ˈrʌnɪŋ/. 1 ADJ BEFORE N You use **running** to describe things that continue or keep occurring over a period of time. *The song turned into a running joke.* 2 ADJ BEFORE N You use **running** to describe something that keeps being changed or added to as something progresses. *John gave the police control room a running commentary on the driver's antics.* 3 ADJ You can use **running** when indicating that something keeps happening. *She'll wear the same thing two days running... Spain won the Cup for the third year running.* 4 See also **run.**

PHRASES ● If someone is **in the running for** something, they have a good chance of winning or obtaining it. If they are **out of the running**, they have no chance of winning or obtaining it.

'running mate, running mates. N-COUNT In an American election campaign, a candidate's **running mate** is the person that they have chosen to be their deputy if they win.

runny /ˈrʌni/ **runnier, runniest.** 1 ADJ Something that is **runny** is more liquid than usual or than was intended. *Warm the honey until it becomes runny.* 2 ADJ If someone's nose or eyes are **runny**, liquid is flowing from them.

'run-up. N-SING The **run-up to** an event is the period of time just before it. *...the run-up to the elections.*

runway /ˈrʌnweɪ/ **runways.** N-COUNT At an airport, the **runway** is the long strip of ground with a hard surface which an aeroplane takes off from or lands on.

rupture /ˈrʌptʃə/ **ruptures, rupturing, ruptured.** 1 VERB & N-COUNT If you **rupture** a part of your body, or if you have a **rupture**, a part of your body tears or bursts open. *His stomach might rupture from all the acid. ...a ruptured appendix.* 2 N-COUNT & VERB If someone or something **ruptures** relations between people, or if there is a **rupture** in relations, they damage them, causing them to become worse or to end. *...a rupture of the family unit.*

a
b
c
d
e
f
g
h
i
j
k
l
m
n
o
p
q
r
s
t
u
v
w
x
y
z

A

★ **rural** /'rʊərəl/. ADJ **Rural** means relating to country areas as opposed to large towns. ...*the closure of rural schools... He spoke with a heavy rural accent.*

B

ruse /ruːz, AM ruːs/ **ruses.** N-COUNT A **ruse** is an action or plan which is intended to deceive someone. [FORMAL] *The whole thing may be a ruse to up the price.*

C

D

★ **rush** /rʌʃ/ **rushes, rushing, rushed.** [1] VERB If you **rush** somewhere, you go there quickly. *I've got to rush. Got a meeting in a few minutes... Shop staff rushed to get help.* [2] VERB If people **rush to** do something, they do it as soon as they can, because they are very eager to do it. *Russian banks rushed to buy as many dollars as they could.* [3] N-SING A **rush** is a situation in which you need to go somewhere or do something very quickly. *The men left in a rush. ...the mad rush not to be late for school.* [4] N-SING If there is a **rush for** something, many people suddenly try to get it or do it. *...the rush for tickets.* [5] VERB If you **rush** something, you do it in a hurry. *Chew your food well and do not rush meals.* ♦ **rushed** ADJ *...a rushed job.* [6] VERB If you **rush** someone or something to a place, you take them there quickly. *We got an ambulance and rushed her to hospital.* [7] VERB If you **rush into** something, or if you **are rushed into** it, you do it without thinking about it for long enough. *He will not rush into any decisions... Don't be rushed into committing yourself.* ♦ **rushed** ADJ *At no time did I feel rushed or under pressure.* [8] VERB If you experience a **rush of** a feeling, you suddenly experience it very strongly. *A rush of pure affection swept over him.* [9] N-COUNT **Rushes** are plants with long thin stems that grow near water.

E

F

G

H

I

J

K

L

M

N

O

'**rush hour, rush hours.** N-COUNT The **rush hour** is one of the periods of the day when most people are travelling to or from work. *Try to avoid rush-hour traffic.*

P

rust /rʌst/ **rusts, rusting, rusted.** [1] N-UNCOUNT **Rust**

Q

is a brown substance that forms on iron or steel when it comes into contact with water. [2] VERB When a metal object **rusts**, it becomes covered in rust.

rustic /'rʌstɪk/. ADJ You can use **rustic** to describe things or people that are simple or unsophisticated in a way that is typical of the countryside; used showing approval. *...the rustic charm of a country lifestyle.*

rustle /'rʌsəl/ **rustles, rustling, rustled.** VERB & N-COUNT When something thin and dry **rustles**, it makes soft sounds as it moves, called **rustles.** *The leaves rustled in the wind... She rustled her papers impatiently. ...a rustle of her frilled petticoats.* ♦ **rustling, rustlings** N-VAR *There was a rustling of paper.*

rusty /'rʌsti/ **rustier, rustiest.** [1] ADJ A **rusty** metal object has a lot of rust on it. *...a rusty old van.* [2] ADJ If a skill that you have or your knowledge of something is **rusty**, it is not as good as it used to be, because you have not used it for a long time. *Ginny tried to sharpen up some rusty typing skills.*

rut /rʌt/ **ruts.** [1] N-COUNT If someone is **in a rut**, they have become fixed in their way of thinking and doing things, and find it difficult to change. *I don't like being in a rut - I like to keep moving on.* [2] N-COUNT A **rut** is a deep narrow mark made in the ground by the wheels of a vehicle.

ruthless /'ruːθləs/. ADJ Someone who is **ruthless** is very harsh or determined, and will do anything that is necessary to achieve their aim. *...his ruthless treatment of employees.* ♦ **ruthlessly** ADV *...the ruthlessly efficient woman her father wanted her to be.* ♦ **ruthlessness** N-UNCOUNT *...a mixture of ambition and ruthlessness.*

rye /raɪ/. N-UNCOUNT **Rye** is a cereal grown in cold countries. Its grains can be used to make flour, bread, or other foods.

S s

R

S

Sabbath /'sæbəθ/. N-PROPER The **Sabbath** is the day of worship and rest for the members of some religious groups, especially Jews and Christians. For Jews, it is Saturday; for Christians, it is Sunday.

T

U

sabotage /'sæbətɑːʒ/ **sabotages, sabotaging, sabotaged.** [1] VERB & N-UNCOUNT If a machine, railway line, or bridge **is sabotaged**, it is deliberately damaged or destroyed, for example in a war. **Sabotage** is the act of sabotaging something. *The bombing was a spectacular act of sabotage.* [2] VERB If someone **sabotages** a plan or a meeting, they deliberately prevent it from being successful. *...her attempt to sabotage his relationship with Sarah.*

V

W

X

Y

Z

★ **sack** /sæk/ **sacks, sacking, sacked.** [1] N-COUNT A **sack** is a large bag made of rough woven material.

[2] VERB & N-SING If your employers **sack** you from your job, or if they give you **the sack**, they tell you that you can no longer work for them. *One girl got the sack for telling lies.* ♦ **sacking, sackings** N-COUNT *...the sacking of twenty-three thousand miners.*

sacred /'seɪkrɪd/. [1] ADJ Something that is **sacred** is believed to be holy. ♦ **sacredness** N-UNCOUNT *...the sacredness of the site.* [2] ADJ BEFORE N Something connected with religion or used in religious ceremonies is described as **sacred**. *...sacred songs or music.* [3] ADJ You can describe something as **sacred** when you regard it as too important to be changed or interfered with. ♦ **sacredness** N-UNCOUNT *...the sacredness of life.*

★ **sacrifice** /'sækrɪfaɪs/ **sacrifices, sacrificing, sacrificed.** **1** VERB & N-COUNT To **sacrifice** an animal, or to offer it as a **sacrifice**, means to kill it in a special religious ceremony. ♦ **sacrificial** /ˌsækrɪ'fɪʃəl/ ADJ BEFORE N ...*the sacrificial altar.* **2** VERB & N-VAR If you **sacrifice** something valuable or important, you give it up, usually to obtain something else. You call the thing you give up a **sacrifice**. *He was willing to make any sacrifice for peace.*

★ **sad** /sæd/ **sadder, saddest.** **1** ADJ If you are **sad**, you feel unhappy. **Sad** stories, situations, or events make you feel unhappy. *I'm sad that Julie's marriage is on the verge of splitting up. ...a sad story of how a naive girl was seduced by money and glamour.* ♦ **sadly** ADV *He will be sadly missed by all who knew him.* ♦ **sadness** N-UNCOUNT *It is with great sadness we have to face this difficult decision.* **2** ADJ **Sad** means unfortunate or undesirable. ♦ **sadly** ADV *Sadly, bamboo plants die after flowering.*

sadden /'sædən/ **saddens, saddening, saddened.** VERB If something **saddens** you, it makes you feel sad. ♦ **saddened** ADJ AFTER LINK-V *He is saddened that they did not win anything.*

saddle /'sædəl/ **saddles, saddling, saddled.** **1** N-COUNT A **saddle** is a leather seat that you put on the back of an animal so that you can ride the animal. **2** N-COUNT A **saddle** is a seat on a bicycle or motorcycle. **3** VERB & PHR-VERB If you **saddle** an animal, or if you **saddle** it **up**, you put a saddle on it. **4** VERB If you **saddle** someone **with** a problem or **with** a responsibility, you put them in a position where they have to deal with it. *An extravagant lifestyle left him saddled with debts of almost 5 million dollars.*

▸**saddle up.** See **saddle** 3.

sadism /'seɪdɪzəm/. N-UNCOUNT **Sadism** is behaviour in which people get pleasure from hurting other people. ♦ **sadist** /'seɪdɪst/ **sadists** N-COUNT ...*a sadist who tortured animals and people.* ♦ **sadistic** ADJ ...*sadistic guards who would punch the hostages.*

sae (also **SAE** or **s.a.e.**) /ˌes eɪ 'iː/, **saes.** N-COUNT An **sae** is an envelope on which you put your name and address, and a stamp. You send it to someone in order to save them the cost of posting you something. **sae** is an abbreviation for **stamped addressed envelope.** [BRITISH]

safari /sə'fɑːri/ **safaris.** N-COUNT A **safari** is an expedition for hunting or observing wild animals, especially in East Africa.

★ **safe** /seɪf/ **safer, safest; safes.** **1** ADJ Something that is **safe** does not cause physical harm or danger. *The only place it is truly safe to swim in is on a patrolled beach... The doll is safe for children.* ♦ **safely** ADV *The dog was safely locked up... Learn to drive safely.* **2** ADJ AFTER LINK-V If someone or something is **safe**, they are not in danger of being harmed or damaged. *Crime Prevention Officers can visit your home and suggest ways to make it safer... Where is Sophy? Is she safe?* ♦ **safely** ADV *Guests were brought out of the building safely by firemen.* **3** ADJ BEFORE N If

people or things have a **safe** journey, they reach their destination without being harmed. ...*the safe delivery of food and other supplies.* ♦ **safely** ADV *Once Mrs Armsby was safely home, she called the police.* **4** ADJ A **safe** place is one where it is unlikely that any harm will happen to the people or things that are there. ♦ **safely** ADV *Guns cannot be safely stored in homes.* **5** ADJ If it is **safe to** say or assume something, you can say it with little risk of being wrong. ♦ **safely** ADV *If I go to a grocer I know and trust, I can safely assume the eggs will be fresh.* **6** N-COUNT A **safe** is a strong metal cupboard with special locks, in which you keep money, jewellery, or other valuable things.

PHRASES ● If you say that someone or something is **in safe hands**, you mean that they are being looked after by a reliable person and will not be harmed or damaged. ● If you say you are doing something **to be on the safe side**, you mean that you are doing it as a precaution, in case something unexpected or unpleasant happens.

safeguard /'seɪfɡɑːd/ **safeguards, safeguarding, safeguarded.** **1** VERB To **safeguard** something or someone means to protect them from being harmed or lost. [FORMAL] ...*precautionary measures to safeguard their forces from the effects of chemical weapons.* **2** N-COUNT A **safeguard** is a law or rule that is intended to prevent someone or something from being harmed. ...*civil rights legislation that offers safeguards against discrimination in the workplace.*

ˌsafe 'sex (or **safer sex**). N-UNCOUNT **Safe sex** is sexual activity in which people protect themselves against the risk of AIDS and other sexually transmitted diseases, usually by using condoms.

★ **safety** /'seɪfti/. **1** N-UNCOUNT **Safety** is the state of being safe from harm or danger. ...*a number of recommendations to improve safety on aircraft. ...the safety of one's own home.* **2** N-SING If you are concerned about the **safety** of something, you are concerned that it might be harmful or dangerous. If you are concerned for someone's **safety**, you are concerned that they might be in danger. ...*public fears about the safety of nuclear power... There is grave concern for the safety of witnesses.* **3** ADJ BEFORE N **Safety** features or measures are intended to make something less dangerous. *Inbuilt safety devices halted the train... It's wise to wear safety goggles.*

ˈsafety belt, **safety belts.** N-COUNT A **safety belt** is a strap that you fasten across your body for safety when travelling in a car or aeroplane.

ˈsafety net, **safety nets.** N-COUNT A **safety net** is something that you can rely on to help you if you get into a difficult situation. *Welfare is the only real safety net for low-income workers.*

sag /sæg/ **sags, sagging, sagged.** **1** VERB When something **sags**, it hangs down loosely or sinks downwards in the middle. ...*the sagging armchair.*

a b c d e f g h i j k l m n o p q r s t u v w x y z

A B C D E F G H I J K L M N O P Q R S T U V W X Y Z

2 VERB To **sag** means to become weaker. *Her energy seemed to sag. ...their sagging popularity.*

saga /ˈsɑːgə/ **sagas.** N-COUNT A **saga** is a long story, account, or sequence of events.

sage /seɪdʒ/ **sages.** **1** ADJ & N-COUNT **Sage** means wise and knowledgeable. A **sage** is a person who is regarded as being very wise. ♦ **sagely** ADV *We all nodded sagely and pretended we understood.* **2** N-UNCOUNT **Sage** is a herb.

said /sed/. **Said** is the past tense and past participle of **say**.

⭐ **sail** /seɪl/ **sails, sailing, sailed.** **1** N-COUNT **Sails** are large pieces of material attached to the mast of a boat. **2** VERB If you **sail** a boat, or if a boat **sails**, it moves across water using its sails. *I shall get myself a little boat and sail her around the world.* **3** VERB You say a ship **sails** when it moves over the sea. *The trawler had sailed from the port of Zeebrugge.* **4** PHRASE When a ship **sets sail**, it leaves a port. **5** VERB If someone or something **sails** somewhere, they move there steadily and fairly quickly. *We got into the lift and sailed to the top floor.*
▸**sail through.** PHR-VERB If someone or something **sails through** a difficult situation or experience, they deal with it easily and successfully. *She sailed through her maths exams.*

sailing /ˈseɪlɪŋ/ **sailings.** **1** N-COUNT A **sailing** is a voyage made by a ship carrying passengers. *We'll get the next sailing.* **2** N-UNCOUNT **Sailing** is the activity or sport of sailing boats. **3** PHRASE In British English, if you say that a task was not all **plain sailing**, you mean that it was not very easy. The American term is **clear sailing**. *Pregnancy wasn't all plain sailing and once again there were problems.*

sailor /ˈseɪlə/ **sailors.** N-COUNT A **sailor** is a person who works on a ship as a member of its crew.

⭐ **saint** /seɪnt/ **saints.** **1** N-COUNT & N-TITLE A **saint** is a dead person who is officially recognized and honoured by the Christian church because his or her life was a perfect example of the way Christians should live. **2** N-COUNT If you refer to a living person as a **saint**, you mean they are extremely kind and patient. ♦ **saintly** ADJ *...his saintly wife.*

⭐ **sake** /seɪk/ **sakes.**
PHRASES ● If you do something **for the sake of** a particular thing, you do it for that purpose or in order to achieve that result. *For the sake of argument, let's assume that you're right.* ● If you do something **for its own sake**, you do it because you enjoy it, and not for any other reason. *...the pursuit of power for its own sake.* ● When you do something **for** someone's **sake**, you do it in order to help them or make them happy. *Linda knew that for both their sakes she must take drastic action.*

salad /ˈsæləd/ **salads.** N-VAR A **salad** is a mixture of uncooked vegetables, eaten as part of a meal.

⭐ **salary** /ˈsæləri/ **salaries.** N-VAR Your **salary** is the money that you are paid each month by your employer.

⭐ **sale** /seɪl/ **sales.** **1** N-SING The **sale** of goods is the selling of them for money. *Efforts were made to limit the sale of alcohol.* **2** N-PLURAL The **sales** of a product are the quantity that is sold. *The newspaper has sales of 1.72 million.* **3** N-PLURAL You refer to the part of a company that deals with selling as **sales**. *Sonia and Sue also work in sales. ...the sales department.* **4** N-COUNT A **sale** is an occasion when a shop sells things at less than their normal price. *...a pair of jeans bought half-price in a sale.*
PHRASES ● If something is **for sale** or **up for sale**, it is available to buy. *The company is up for sale.* ● Products that are **on sale** can be bought in shops. [BRITISH] *Tickets go on sale this Friday.*

'sales clerk, sales clerks. N-COUNT In American English, a **sales clerk** is a person who works in a shop, selling things to customers. The British word is **shop assistant**.

salesman /ˈseɪlzmən/ **salesmen.** N-COUNT A **salesman** is a man whose job is selling things to people.

salesperson /ˈseɪlzpɜːsən/ **salespeople** or **salespersons.** N-COUNT A **salesperson** is a person whose job is selling things to people.

saliva /səˈlaɪvə/. N-UNCOUNT **Saliva** is the watery liquid that forms in your mouth.

salmon /ˈsæmən/.
✓ **Salmon** is both the singular and the plural form.
N-VAR A **salmon** is a large edible silver-coloured fish with pink flesh. **Salmon** is the flesh of this fish eaten as food.

salon /ˈsælɒn, AM səˈlɑːn/ **salons.** N-COUNT A **salon** is a place where people such as hairdressers work. *...a new hair salon.*

saloon /səˈluːn/ **saloons.** **1** N-COUNT In British English, a **saloon** or a **saloon car** is a car with seats for four or more people, a fixed roof, and a

boot that is separated from the rear seats.
[2] N-COUNT A **saloon** is a place where alcoholic drinks are sold and drunk. [AMERICAN]

★ **salt** /sɔːlt/ **salts, salting, salted.** [1] N-UNCOUNT **Salt** is a substance in the form of white powder or crystals, used to improve the flavour of food or to preserve it. [2] VERB When you **salt** food, you add salt to it. ♦ **salted** ADJ ...*lightly salted butter.*

salty /'sɔːlti/ **saltier, saltiest.** ADJ **Salty** things contain salt or taste of salt. ...*salty water.*

salute /sə'luːt/ **salutes, saluting, saluted.** [1] VERB & N-COUNT If you **salute** someone, you greet them or show your respect with a formal sign. Soldiers salute officers by raising their right hand so that their fingers touch their forehead. A **salute** is a formal sign of greeting or respect. *I stood to attention and saluted... The soldier gave the clenched-fist salute... He raised his arm in salute.* [2] VERB & N-COUNT To **salute** a person or an achievement means to publicly show or state your admiration for them. A public show of admiration for someone or something is called a **salute**. *The students' performance is a salute to Australian music.*

salvage /'sælvɪdʒ/ **salvages, salvaging, salvaged.** [1] VERB & N-UNCOUNT If something **is salvaged**, someone manages to save it, for example from a ship that has sunk or a building that has been destroyed. **Salvage** is the act of salvaging things from somewhere. ...*components salvaged from a crashed aircraft. ...a huge salvage operation.* [2] N-UNCOUNT The **salvage** from wrecked ships or destroyed buildings consists of the things that are saved from them. ...*the value of the salvage.* [3] VERB If you **salvage** something **from** a difficult situation, you manage to get something useful from it so that it is not a complete failure. *Diplomats are still hoping to salvage something from the meeting.*

salvation /sæl'veɪʃən/ [1] N-UNCOUNT In Christianity, **salvation** is being saved from sin. [2] N-UNCOUNT The **salvation** of someone or something is the act of saving them from harm. ...*those whose marriages are beyond salvation.*

★ **same** /seɪm/ [1] ADJ If two or more things, actions, or qualities are **the same**, or if one is **the same as** another, the two are very similar or exactly like each other in some way. *The houses were all the same... Driving a boat is not the same as driving a car... Try to find potatoes that are all the same size.* [2] ADJ You use **same** to indicate that you are referring to only one place, time, or thing, and not to different ones. *Your birthday is on the same day as mine.* [3] ADJ Something that is still **the same** has not changed in any way. *Only 17% said the economy would improve, but 25% believed it would stay the same.* [4] ADJ & PRON You use **same** to refer to something that has already been mentioned. *I had the same experience when I became a teacher myself... We made the decision which was right for us. Other parents must do the same.* [5] **at the same time**: see **time**.

PHRASES ● You say **all the same** or **just the same** to indicate that a situation or your opinion has not changed, in spite of what has happened or been said. *I had a lot of support along the way today, but it was hard all the same.* ● If you say that two or more people or things which are thought to be different are **one and the same**, you mean that they are in fact the same person or thing, or they are very similar and should be considered as one thing. *Luckily, Nancy's father and her attorney were one and the same person.*

★ **sample** /'sɑːmpəl, 'sæm-/ **samples, sampling, sampled.** [1] N-COUNT A **sample of** a substance or product is a small quantity of it, showing you what it is like. *You'll receive samples of paint... We're giving away 2000 free samples.* [2] N-COUNT A **sample of** a substance is a small amount of it that is examined and analyzed scientifically. *They took samples of my blood.* [3] N-COUNT A **sample of** people or things is a number of them chosen from a larger group and then used in tests or used to provide information about the whole group. ...*a random sample of more than 200 males.* [4] VERB If you **sample** food or drink, you taste a small amount of it in order to find out if you like it. [5] VERB If you **sample** a place or situation, you experience it for a short time in order to find out about it. ...*the chance to sample a different way of life.*

★ **sanction** /'sæŋkʃən/ **sanctions, sanctioning, sanctioned.** [1] VERB & N-UNCOUNT If someone in authority **sanctions** an action or practice, they officially approve of it and allow it to be done. The **sanction** of someone in authority is their official approval. *He may now be ready to sanction the use of force... The king could not enact plans without the sanction of Parliament.* [2] N-PLURAL **Sanctions** are measures taken by countries to restrict trade and official contact with a country that has broken international law. *He expressed his opposition to the lifting of sanctions.* [3] N-COUNT A **sanction** is a severe course of action which is intended to make people obey the law. *The ultimate sanction is expulsion from the League.*

sanctity /'sæŋktɪti/ N-UNCOUNT If you talk about the **sanctity** of something, you mean that it is very important and should be treated with respect. ...*the sanctity of marriage.*

sanctuary /'sæŋktʃʊəri, AM -tʃʊeri/ **sanctuaries.** [1] N-VAR A **sanctuary** is a place of safety for people who are being persecuted. *His church became a sanctuary for thousands of people... They sought sanctuary in the French embassy.* [2] N-COUNT A wildlife **sanctuary** is a place where birds or animals are protected and allowed to live freely.

★ **sand** /sænd/ **sands, sanding, sanded.** [1] N-UNCOUNT **Sand** is a powder that consists of extremely small pieces of stone. *They walked barefoot across the damp sand to the water's edge. ...grains of sand.* [2] N-PLURAL **Sands** are a large area of sand, for example a beach. ...*miles of golden sands.* [3] VERB

a
b
c
d
e
f
g
h
i
j
k
l
m
n
o
p
q
r
s
t
u
v
w
x
y
z

If you **sand** an object, you rub it with an abrasive paper called sandpaper in order to make it smooth or to get rid of paint or rust. *Sand the surface softly and carefully.*

sandal /'sændəl/ **sandals.** N-COUNT **Sandals** are light shoes that have straps instead of a solid part over the top of your foot. → See picture on page 820.

sandstone /'sændstəʊn/ N-UNCOUNT **Sandstone** is a type of rock which contains a lot of sand.

sandwich /'sænwɪdʒ, -wɪtʃ/ **sandwiches, sandwiched.** [1] N-COUNT A **sandwich** consists of two slices of bread with a layer of food between them. *...a ham sandwich.* [2] PASSIVE-VERB When something **is sandwiched between** two other things, it is in a narrow space between them. *...a small shop sandwiched between a bar and a laundrette.*

sandy /'sændi/ **sandier, sandiest.** ADJ A **sandy** area is covered with sand. *...sandy beaches.*

sane /seɪn/ **saner, sanest.** [1] ADJ Someone who is **sane** is able to think and behave normally and reasonably, and is not mentally ill. *He appears to be quite sane.* [2] ADJ If you describe an action or idea as **sane**, you mean that it is reasonable and sensible. *...extremely sane advice.*

sang /sæŋ/. **Sang** is the past tense of **sing**.

sanitary /'sænɪtri, AM -teri/. ADJ **Sanitary** means concerned with keeping things clean and hygienic. *Sanitary conditions are appalling.*

sanitation /,sænɪ'teɪʃən/. N-UNCOUNT **Sanitation** is the process of keeping places clean and hygienic, especially by providing a sewage system and a clean water supply. *...the hazards of contaminated water and poor sanitation.*

sanity /'sænɪti/. [1] N-UNCOUNT A person's **sanity** is their ability to think and behave normally and reasonably. *It was enough to make us question our sanity.* [2] N-UNCOUNT If there is **sanity** in a situation or activity, there is a purpose and a regular pattern, rather than confusion and worry. *She should do what she can to restore sanity to the situation.*

sank /sæŋk/. **Sank** is the past tense of **sink**.

sap /sæp/ **saps, sapping, sapped.** [1] VERB If something **saps** your strength or confidence, it gradually weakens or destroys it. *The illness sapped his strength.* [2] N-UNCOUNT **Sap** is the watery liquid in plants and trees.

sarcasm /'sɑːkæzəm/. N-UNCOUNT **Sarcasm** refers to speech or writing which actually means the opposite of what it seems to say. Sarcasm is usually intended to mock or insult someone. *'Congratulations. I'm pleased.' Alan spoke with a bitter sarcasm.*

sarcastic /sɑː'kæstɪk/. ADJ Someone who is **sarcastic** says the opposite of what they really mean in order to mock or insult someone. *...sarcastic remarks.* ♦ **sarcastically** ADV *'What a surprise!' Caroline murmured sarcastically.*

sardine /sɑː'diːn/ **sardines.** N-COUNT **Sardines** are a kind of small sea fish, often eaten as food.

sardonic /sɑː'dɒnɪk/. ADJ If you describe someone as **sardonic**, you mean that they are mocking or scornful, often in a rather calm, quiet way. *...a sardonic sense of humour.* ♦ **sardonically** ADV *He grinned sardonically.*

sat /sæt/. **Sat** is the past tense and past participle of **sit**.

Satan /'seɪtən/. N-PROPER **Satan** is a name sometimes given to the Devil. ♦ **satanic** ADJ *...satanic rituals.*

⭐ **satellite** /'sætəlaɪt/ **satellites.** [1] N-COUNT A **satellite** is an object which has been sent into space in order to collect information or to be part of a communications system. *The signals are sent by satellite link.* [2] N-COUNT A **satellite** is a natural object in space that moves round a planet or star.

'satellite dish, satellite dishes. N-COUNT A **satellite dish** is a piece of equipment which receives satellite television signals.

satin /'sætɪn, AM -tən/. N-UNCOUNT **Satin** is a smooth and shiny type of cloth.

satire /'sætaɪə/ **satires.** [1] N-UNCOUNT **Satire** is the use of humour to mock or criticize political ideas or the way that people behave. *The commercial side of the Christmas season is an easy target for satire.* [2] N-COUNT A **satire** is a play or piece of writing that uses satire. *...a sharp satire on the American political process.*

satirical /sə'tɪrɪkəl/. ADJ A **satirical** drawing, piece of writing, or comedy show uses satire to criticize something. *...a satirical novel about London life.*

satisfaction /,sætɪs'fækʃən/. [1] N-UNCOUNT **Satisfaction** is the pleasure you feel when you do something you wanted or needed to do. *Both sides expressed satisfaction with the progress so far. ...job satisfaction.* [2] N-UNCOUNT If you get **satisfaction** from someone, you get money or an apology from them because of some harm or injustice which has been done to you. *If you can't get any satisfaction, complain to the park owner.*

satisfactory /,sætɪs'fæktəri/. ADJ If something is **satisfactory**, it is acceptable to you or fulfils a particular need or purpose. *I never got a satisfactory answer.* ♦ **satisfactorily** /,sætɪs'fæktərɪli/ ADV *Their motives have never been satisfactorily explained.*

⭐ **satisfied** /'sætɪsfaɪd/. ADJ If you are **satisfied with** something, you are pleased because you have got what you wanted. *We are not satisfied with these results. ...satisfied customers.*

satisfy /'sætɪsfaɪ/ **satisfies, satisfying, satisfied.** [1] VERB If someone or something **satisfies** you, they give you enough of what you want to make you pleased or contented. *The pace of change has not been quick enough to satisfy everyone.* [2] VERB If someone **satisfies** you **that** something is true or has been done properly, they convince you by giving you more information or by showing you what has been done. *Satisfy yourself that it's safe.*

3 VERB If you **satisfy** the requirements for something, you are good enough or suitable to fulfil these conditions. *Candidates must satisfy the general conditions for admission.*

satisfying /'sætɪsfaɪɪŋ/. ADJ Something that is **satisfying** gives you a feeling of pleasure and fulfilment. *...intellectually satisfying work.*

saturate /'sætʃʊreɪt/ **saturates, saturating, saturated.**
1 VERB If people or things **saturate** a place or object, they fill it completely so that no more can be added. *No one wants to saturate the city with car parking.* ♦ **saturation** N-UNCOUNT *...the saturation of the market with various kinds of goods.* **2** VERB If someone or something **is saturated**, they become extremely wet. *His work clothes, having become saturated with oil, had to be cleaned.*

★ **Saturday** /'sætədeɪ, -di/ **Saturdays.** N-VAR **Saturday** is the day after Friday and before Sunday. → See Reference Page on Times and Dates.

★ **sauce** /sɔːs/ **sauces.** N-VAR A **sauce** is a thick liquid which is served with other food. *...a sauce of garlic, tomatoes, and cheese.*

saucepan /'sɔːspən, AM -pæn/ **saucepans.**
N-COUNT A **saucepan** is a deep metal cooking pot, usually with a long handle and a lid. → See picture on page 825.

saucer /'sɔːsə/ **saucers.** N-COUNT A **saucer** is a small curved plate on which you stand a cup.

saucy /'sɔːsi/ **saucier, sauciest.** ADJ Someone or something that is **saucy** refers to sex in a light-hearted, amusing way. *...a saucy joke.*

sauna /'sɔːnə/ **saunas.** **1** N-COUNT A **sauna** is a hot steam bath. **2** N-COUNT A **sauna** is a room or building where you can have a sauna.

saunter /'sɔːntə/ **saunters, sauntering, sauntered.**
VERB If you **saunter** somewhere, you walk there in a slow casual way. *He sauntered along the river.*

sausage /'sɒsɪdʒ, AM 'sɔː-/ **sausages.** N-VAR A **sausage** consists of minced meat, mixed with other ingredients, inside a long thin skin.

sauté /'sɔːteɪ, AM sɔː'teɪ/ **sautés, sautéing, sautéed.**
VERB When you **sauté** food, you fry it quickly in hot oil or butter.

savage /'sævɪdʒ/ **savages, savaging, savaged.** **1** ADJ If someone or something is **savage**, they are extremely cruel, violent, and uncontrolled. *...a savage attack on a defenceless young girl.*
♦ **savagely** ADV *He was savagely beaten.*
2 N-COUNT If you refer to people as **savages**, you dislike them because you think that they are cruel, violent, or uncivilized. **3** VERB If someone **is savaged** by a dog or other animal, the animal attacks them violently. **4** VERB If someone or something that they have done **is savaged** by another person, that person criticizes them severely. *The show had been savaged by critics.*

savagery /'sævɪdʒri/. N-UNCOUNT **Savagery** is extremely cruel and violent behaviour.

★ **save** /seɪv/ **saves, saving, saved.** **1** VERB If you **save** someone or something, you help them to avoid

harm or to escape from a dangerous or unpleasant situation. *To save his life, doctors amputated his legs. ...a final attempt to save 40,000 jobs.* **2** VERB & N-COUNT If a goalkeeper **saves** a shot, or if they make a **save**, they prevent the ball from going into the goal. **3** VERB If you **save** something, you keep it because it will be needed later. *Drain the beans thoroughly and save the stock for soup.* **4** VERB & PHR-VERB If you **save**, or if you **save up**, you gradually collect money by spending less than you get, usually in order to buy something that you want. *Tim and Barbara are now saving for a house... Put money aside in order to save up enough to make one major expenditure.* ♦ **saver, savers** N-COUNT *Low interest rates are bad news for savers.* **5** VERB If you **save** data in a computer, you give the computer an instruction to store the data on a tape or disk. [COMPUTING] *Try to get into the habit of saving your work regularly.* **6** VERB If you **save** something such as time or money, you prevent the loss or waste of it. *It saves time in the kitchen to have things you use a lot within reach. ...money-saving special offers.* **7** VERB If you **save** someone an unpleasant task or experience, you do something which helps or enables them to avoid it. *He arranges to collect the payment from the customer, thus saving the client the paperwork.* **8** PREP You can use **save** or **save for** to introduce the only things, people, or ideas that your main statement does not apply to. [FORMAL] *The parking lot was virtually empty save for a few cars.*

▸**save up.** See **save** 4.

savings /'seɪvɪŋz/. N-PLURAL Your **savings** are the money that you have saved, especially in a bank or a building society. *Her savings were in the Post Office Savings Bank.*

saviour (AM **savior**) /'seɪvjə/ **saviours.**
1 N-COUNT A **saviour** is a person who saves someone or something from danger, ruin, or defeat. *...the saviour of English football... She regarded him as her saviour.* **2** N-PROPER In the Christian religion, **the Saviour** is Jesus Christ.

savour (AM **savor**) /'seɪvə/ **savours, savouring, savoured.** VERB If you **savour** something pleasant, you enjoy it as much as you can or for as long as possible. *Savour the flavour of each mouthful... It makes you want to savour every moment.*

savoury (AM **savory**) /'seɪvəri/ **savouries.** **1** ADJ **Savoury** food has a salty or spicy flavour rather than a sweet one. *...savoury dishes.* **2** N-COUNT **Savouries** are small portions of savoury food, usually eaten as a snack. [BRITISH]

saw /sɔː/ **saws, sawing, sawed, sawn.** **1** **Saw** is the past tense of **see**. **2** N-COUNT A **saw** is a tool for cutting wood, which has a blade with sharp teeth along one edge. → See picture on page 833. **3** VERB If you **saw** something, you cut it with a saw.

sawdust /'sɔːdʌst/. N-UNCOUNT **Sawdust** is the very fine fragments of wood which are produced when you saw wood.

sawn /sɔːn/. **Sawn** is the past participle of **saw**.

A B C D E F G H I J K L M N O P Q R S T U V W X Y Z

sax /sæks/ **saxes.** N-COUNT A **sax** is the same as a **saxophone.** [INFORMAL]

saxophone /'sæksəfəʊn/ **saxophones.** N-COUNT A **saxophone** is a musical wind instrument in the shape of a curved metal tube with keys and a curved mouthpiece. → See picture on page 828.
♦ **saxophonist** /sæk'sɒfənɪst, AM 'sæksəfəʊn-/ **saxophonists** N-COUNT ...the great jazz saxophonist Sonny Rollins.

⭐ **say** /seɪ/ **says** /sez/ **saying, said.** ☐ VERB When you **say** something, you speak words. You can also use **say** to signal that you are stating a fact or your opinion. 'I'm sorry,' he said... I packed and said goodbye to Charlie... Did he say where he was going?... I would say that Susan will learn a lot from what she did. ② VERB You can mention the contents of a piece of writing by mentioning what it **says** or what someone **says** in it. Auntie Winnie wrote back saying Mam wasn't well. ③ VERB If you **say** something **to** yourself, you think it. Perhaps I'm still dreaming, I said to myself. ④ VERB You indicate the information given by something such as a clock, dial, or map by mentioning what it **says**. The clock said four minutes past eleven. ⑤ VERB If something **says** something **about** a person, situation, or thing, it reveals something about them. The building says something about the importance of the project. ⑥ CONVENTION You can use **say** when you mention something as an example or when you mention an approximate amount or time. Someone with, say, between 300 and 500 acres could be losing thousands of pounds a year. ⑦ N-SING If you **have a say in** something, you have the right to give your opinion and influence decisions. When you **have** your **say**, you use this right or give your opinion. It's time the people of Glasgow had a say in the future of Europe.

USAGE Note that, with the verb **say**, if you want to mention the person who is being addressed, you should use the preposition **to**. 'What did she say you?' is wrong. '**What did she say to you?**' is correct. The verb **tell**, however, is usually followed by a direct object indicating the person who is being addressed. He told Alison he was suffering from leukaemia... What did she tell you? 'What did she tell to you?' is wrong.
Say is the most general verb for reporting the words that someone speaks. **Tell** is used to report information that is given to someone. The manufacturer told me that the product did not contain corn. **Tell** can also be used with a 'to' infinitive to report an order or instruction. My mother told me to shut up and eat my dinner.

PHRASES ● You can use '**You can say that again**' to express strong agreement with what someone has just said. [INFORMAL] 'Must have been a fiddly job.'—'You can say that again.' ● If

something **goes without saying**, it is obvious or definitely true. It goes without saying that if someone has lung problems they should not smoke. ● If you say that something **says it all**, you mean that it shows you very clearly the truth about a situation or someone's feelings. This is my third visit in a week, which says it all. ● You use **to say nothing of** when you add something which gives even more strength to the point you are making. Unemployment leads to a sense of uselessness, to say nothing of financial problems. ● You use **that is to say** to indicate that you are about to express the same idea more clearly. [FORMAL] Good writers are those who keep the language efficient. That is to say, keep it accurate, keep it clear. ● If you say there is a lot **to be said for** something, you think it has a lot of good qualities or aspects. There's a lot to be said for being based in the country.

saying /'seɪɪŋ/ **sayings.** N-COUNT A **saying** is a traditional sentence that people often say and that gives advice or information about life. We also realize the truth of that old saying: Charity begins at home.

scaffolding /'skæfəldɪŋ/. N-UNCOUNT **Scaffolding** is a temporary framework of poles and boards that is used by workmen to stand on while they are working on the outside structure of a building.

scald /skɔːld/ **scalds, scalding, scalded.** ☐ VERB If you **scald yourself**, you burn yourself with very hot liquid or steam. A patient jumped into a bath being prepared by a member of staff and scalded herself. ...scalding hot water. ② N-COUNT A **scald** is a burn caused by very hot liquid or steam.

⭐ **scale** /skeɪl/ **scales, scaling, scaled.** ☐ N-SING If you refer to the **scale** of something, you are referring to its size or extent, especially when it is very big. ...killing on a massive scale... The British aid programme is small in scale. ② N-COUNT A **scale** is a set of levels or numbers which are used in a particular system of measuring things or comparing things. ...an earthquake measuring five-point-five on the Richter scale. ...those on the high end of the pay scale. ③ N-COUNT In music, a **scale** is a fixed sequence of musical notes, each one higher than the next, which begins at a particular note. ...the scale of C major. ④ N-VAR The **scale** of a map, plan, or model is the relationship between the size of something in the map, plan, or model and its size in the real world. ...the map, on a scale of 1:10,000. ⑤ ADJ A **scale model** of something is smaller than the original, but the sizes of all the parts are in the same, exact relation to each other. ...an intricately detailed scale model of the house. ⑥ PHRASE If the different parts of a map, drawing, or model are **to scale**, they are the right size in relation to each other. ⑦ N-PLURAL **Scales** are a piece of equipment for weighing things or people. ...kitchen scales... I step on the scales practically every morning. ⑧ N-COUNT The **scales** of a fish or reptile are the small flat pieces of hard skin that

cover its body. 9 VERB If you **scale** something such as a mountain or a wall, you climb up it or over it. ...*the first British woman to scale Everest.*
▸**scale down.** PHR-VERB If you **scale down** something, you make it smaller in size, amount, or extent than it used to be. *One Peking factory has had to scale down its workforce from six hundred to only six.*

scalp /skælp/ **scalps.** N-COUNT Your **scalp** is the skin under the hair on your head.

scamper /ˈskæmpə/ **scampers, scampering, scampered.** VERB When people or small animals **scamper** somewhere, they move there quickly with small light steps. *The child scampered off without waiting for his friend.*

scan /skæn/ **scans, scanning, scanned.** 1 VERB When you **scan** an area, a group of things, or a piece of writing, you look at it carefully, usually because you are looking for something in particular. *Joss scanned the crowd for the child's mother... She scanned the advertisement pages of the newspapers.* 2 VERB If a machine **scans** luggage or other items, it examines it quickly, for example by moving a beam of light or X-rays over it. 3 N-COUNT A **scan** is a medical test in which a machine sends a beam of X-rays over a part of your body in order to check whether your organs are healthy. ...*a brain scan.* 4 N-COUNT If a pregnant woman has a **scan**, a machine using sound waves produces an image of her womb on a screen so that a doctor can see if her baby is developing normally.

⭐ **scandal** /ˈskændəl/ **scandals.** 1 N-COUNT A **scandal** is a situation, event, or someone's behaviour that shocks a lot of people because they think it is immoral. ...*a financial scandal.* 2 N-SING If you say that something is a **scandal**, you are angry about it and think that the people responsible for it should be ashamed. *It is a scandal that a person can be stopped for no reason by the police.*

scandalous /ˈskændələs/. 1 ADJ You can describe something as **scandalous** if it makes you very angry and you think the people responsible for it should be ashamed. ...*a scandalous waste of money.* ♦ **scandalously** ADV *Many workers were being paid scandalously low wages.* 2 ADJ **Scandalous** behaviour or activity is considered immoral and shocking.

scanner /ˈskænə/ **scanners.** N-COUNT A **scanner** is a machine which is used to examine, identify, or record things, for example by moving a beam of light, sound, or X-rays over them.

scant /skænt/. ADJ You use **scant** to indicate that there is very little of something or not as much of something as there should be. *She began to criticise the police for paying scant attention to the theft.*

scapegoat /ˈskeɪpɡəʊt/ **scapegoats.** N-COUNT If someone is made a **scapegoat for** something bad that has happened, people blame them or punish them for it, although it may not be their fault. *I don't think I deserve to be messed about and made the scapegoat for a couple of bad results.*

scar /skɑː/ **scars, scarring, scarred.** 1 N-COUNT A **scar** is a mark on the skin which is left after a wound has healed. 2 VERB If your skin **is scarred**, it is badly marked as a result of a wound. *He was scarred for life during a pub fight.* 3 VERB If a surface **is scarred**, it is damaged and there are ugly marks on it. *The arena was scarred by deep muddy ruts.* 4 N-COUNT & VERB If an unpleasant physical or emotional experience leaves a **scar** on someone, or if it **scars** them, it has a permanent effect on their mind. *The emotional scars that he bears will never disappear.*

scarce /skeəs/ **scarcer, scarcest.** ADJ If something is **scarce**, there is not enough of it. *Jobs are becoming increasingly scarce.*

scarcely /ˈskeəsli/. 1 ADV You use **scarcely** to emphasize that something is only just true or only just the case. *He could scarcely breathe... Scarcely a week goes by without the news providing fresh examples of racism.* 2 ADV You can use **scarcely** to say that something is certainly not true or is certainly not the case. *It was scarcely in their interest to let too many people know.* 3 ADV If you say **scarcely** had one thing happened when something else happened, you mean that the first event was followed immediately by the second. *Bruce had scarcely shaken our hands when the phone rang.*

scarcity /ˈskeəsɪti/ **scarcities.** N-VAR If there is a **scarcity** of something, there is not enough of it. [FORMAL] *Successive bad harvests have created a severe food scarcity.*

scare /skeə/ **scares, scaring, scared.** 1 VERB & N-COUNT If someone or something **scares** you, or if they give you a **scare**, they frighten you. *I didn't mean to scare you... It scared him to realise how close he had come to losing everything... Don't you realize what a scare you've given us all?* 2 N-COUNT A **scare** is a situation in which many people are afraid or worried because they think something dangerous is happening which will affect them all. ...*an Aids scare.* 3 N-COUNT A **bomb scare** or a **security scare** is a situation in which there is believed to be a bomb in a place.
▸**scare off** or **scare away.** PHR-VERB If you **scare off** a person or animal, or if you **scare** them **away**, you frighten them so that they go away. ...*an alarm to scare off an attacker.*

scared /skeəd/. 1 ADJ If you are **scared of** someone or something, you are frightened of them. *I'm certainly not scared of him... I was too scared to move.* 2 ADJ If you are **scared** that something unpleasant might happen, you are nervous and worried because you think that it might happen. *I was scared that I might be sick... He was scared of letting us down.*

scarf /skɑːf/ **scarfs** or **scarves** /skɑːvz/. N-COUNT A **scarf** is a piece of cloth that you wear round your neck or head, usually to keep yourself warm.
→ See picture on page 819.

→ See picture on page 819.

a b c d e f g h i j k l m n o p q r s t u v w x y z

scarlet /'skɑːlət/. ADJ & N-UNCOUNT Something that is **scarlet** is bright red.

scary /'skeəri/ **scarier, scariest.** ADJ Something that is **scary** is rather frightening. [INFORMAL] *There's something very scary about him. ...scary movies.*

scathing /'skeɪðɪŋ/. ADJ If you say that someone is being **scathing** about something, you mean that they are being very critical and scornful of it. *He made some particularly scathing comments about the design.* ♦ **scathingly** ADV *'Oh, they want to be excused,' the other girl said scathingly.*

scatter /'skætə/ **scatters, scattering, scattered.**
[1] VERB If you **scatter** things over an area, you throw or drop them so that they spread all over the area. *She scattered the petals over the grave.*
[2] VERB If a group of people **scatter**, they suddenly separate and move in different directions. *They stared for a second, then scattered in panic.*

scattered /'skætəd/. [1] ADJ **Scattered** things are spread over an area in an untidy or irregular way. *He picked up the scattered toys... Food was scattered across the floor.* [2] ADJ AFTER LINK-V If something is **scattered with** a lot of small things, they are spread all over it. *Every surface is scattered with photographs.*

scattering /'skætərɪŋ/. N-SING A **scattering of** things is a small number of them spread over an area. *...a road with an inn, a few shops and a scattering of houses.*

scavenge /'skævɪndʒ/ **scavenges, scavenging, scavenged.** VERB If people or animals **scavenge for** food or other things, they collect them by searching among waste or unwanted objects. *Children had to scavenge for food to survive.*
♦ **scavenger, scavengers** N-COUNT *...scavengers such as rats.*

scenario /sɪ'nɑːriəʊ, AM -'ner-/ **scenarios.** N-COUNT If you talk about a likely or possible **scenario**, you are talking about the way in which a situation may develop. *In the worst-case scenario, you could become a homeless person.*

⭐ **scene** /siːn/ **scenes.** [1] N-COUNT A **scene** in a play, film, or book is part of it in which a series of events happen in the same place. *...the opening scene of 'A Christmas Carol'.* [2] N-COUNT You refer to a place as a **scene** when you are describing its appearance and indicating what impression it makes on you. *It's a scene of complete devastation.* [3] N-COUNT **The scene of** an event is the place where it happened. *The area has been the scene of fierce fighting.* [4] N-SING You can refer to an area of activity as a particular type of **scene**. *...the alternative music scene.* [5] N-COUNT If you **make a scene**, you embarrass people by publicly showing your anger about something.
PHRASES ● If something is done **behind the scenes**, it is done secretly rather than in public. *But behind the scenes Mr Cain will be working quietly to try to get a deal done.* ● Something that **sets the scene for** a particular event creates the

conditions in which the event is likely to happen. *Community leaders have set the scene for a substantial policy change.*

scenery /'siːnəri/. [1] N-UNCOUNT The **scenery** in a country area is the land, water, or plants that you can see around you. *...the island's spectacular scenery.*

> **USAGE** Do not confuse **scenery**, **landscape**, **countryside**, and **nature**. With **landscape**, the emphasis is on the physical features of the land, while **scenery** includes everything you can see when you look out over an area of land, usually in the country. *...the landscape of steep woods and distant mountains. ...unattractive urban scenery.* **Countryside** is land which is away from towns and cities. *...3,500 acres of mostly flat countryside.* **Nature** includes the landscape, the weather, animals, and plants. *These creatures roamed the Earth as the finest and rarest wonders of nature.*

[2] N-UNCOUNT In a theatre, the **scenery** is the painted cloth and boards at the back of the stage which represent where the action is taking place.

scenic /'siːnɪk/. ADJ **Scenic** places have attractive scenery. *...a well-known scenic spot.*

scent /sent/ **scents, scenting, scented.** [1] N-COUNT The **scent** of something is the pleasant smell that it has. *...shiny-leaved bushes with white flowers and a wonderful scent.* [2] N-VAR **Scent** is a pleasant-smelling liquid which women put on their necks and wrists to make themselves smell nice. [3] N-VAR The **scent** of a person or animal is the smell that they give off. *It wouldn't take long for the dogs to pick up our scent.* [4] VERB When an animal **scents** something, it becomes aware of it by smelling it. *The horse acted as if she had scented a wild cat.*

scented /'sentɪd/. ADJ **Scented** things have a pleasant smell, either naturally or because perfume has been added to them. *...scented soap.*

sceptic (AM **skeptic**) /'skeptɪk/ **sceptics.** N-COUNT A **sceptic** is a person who has doubts and asks questions about things that other people believe. *He now has to convince sceptics that he has a serious plan.*

sceptical (AM **skeptical**) /'skeptɪkəl/. ADJ If you are **sceptical** about something, you have doubts about it. *...his sceptical view of all ideologies.*

scepticism (AM **skepticism**) /'skeptɪsɪzəm/. N-UNCOUNT **Scepticism** is great doubt about whether something is true or useful. *The report has inevitably been greeted with scepticism.*

⭐ **schedule** /'ʃedjuːl, AM 'skedʒuːl/ **schedules, scheduling, scheduled.** [1] N-COUNT A **schedule** is a plan that gives a list of events or tasks and the times at which each one should happen or be done. *He has been forced to adjust his schedule.*

2 N-UNCOUNT You can use **schedule** to refer to the time or way something is planned to be done. For example, if something is completed **on schedule**, it is completed at the time planned. *The jet arrived in Johannesburg two minutes ahead of schedule.* **3** VERB If something **is scheduled to** happen at a particular time, arrangements are made for it to happen at that time. *The space shuttle had been scheduled to blast off at 04:38... The meeting with Mr Bush is scheduled for tomorrow morning.* **4** N-COUNT A **schedule** is a written list of things, for example a list of prices, details, or conditions.

⭐ **scheme** /skiːm/ **schemes, scheming, schemed.**
1 N-COUNT A **scheme** is a plan or arrangement, especially one produced by a government or other organization. *...schemes to help combat unemployment. ...a private pension scheme.*
2 VERB If you say that people **are scheming**, you mean that they are making secret plans in order to gain something for themselves; used showing disapproval. *The bride's family were scheming to prevent a wedding. ...a scheming career woman.*
3 PHRASE **The scheme of things** is the way that everything in the world or in a particular situation seems to be organized. *He spends rather too much time examining his own role in the scheme of things.*

schizophrenia /ˌskɪtsə'friːniə/. N-UNCOUNT
Schizophrenia is a serious mental illness that prevents people from relating their thoughts and feelings to what is happening around them.

schizophrenic /ˌskɪtsə'frenɪk/ **schizophrenics.**
ADJ & N-COUNT Someone who is **schizophrenic** or who is a **schizophrenic** is suffering from schizophrenia. *...a psychopath with schizophrenic tendencies.*

scholar /'skɒlə/ **scholars.** N-COUNT A **scholar** is a person who studies an academic subject and knows a lot about it. *...a leading biblical scholar.*

scholarly /'skɒləli/. **1** ADJ A **scholarly** person spends a lot of time studying and knows a lot about academic subjects. **2** ADJ A **scholarly** book or article contains a lot of academic information and is intended for academic readers.

scholarship /'skɒləʃɪp/ **scholarships.** **1** N-COUNT If you get a **scholarship** to a school or university, your studies are paid for by the school or university, or by some other organization.
2 N-UNCOUNT **Scholarship** is serious academic study and the knowledge that is obtained from it. *A new era of scholarship is now beginning.*

⭐ **school** /skuːl/ **schools.** **1** N-VAR A **school** is a place where children are educated. You usually refer to this place as **school** when you are talking about the time that children spend there. *...a school built in the Sixties. ...two boys wearing school uniform. ...a boy who was in my class at school.* **2** N-COUNT A **school** is the pupils or staff at a school. **School** can take the singular or plural form of the verb. *The whole school's going to hate you.* **3** N-COUNT A place where a particular skill or

subject is taught can be referred to as a **school**. *...a riding school.* **4** N-VAR A university, college, or university department specializing in a particular type of subject can be referred to as a **school**. *...the school of veterinary medicine at the University of Pennsylvania.* **5** N-VAR **School** is used to refer to university or college. [AMERICAN, INFORMAL] *Moving rapidly through school, he graduated from the University of Kentucky at age 18.* **6** PHRASE A **school of thought** is a theory or opinion shared by a group of people. *There are three main schools of thought on how the money would best be spent.* **7** N-COUNT A **school of** fish or dolphins is a large group of them.

schoolboy /'skuːlbɔɪ/ **schoolboys.** N-COUNT A **schoolboy** is a boy who goes to school.

schoolchild /'skuːltʃaɪld/ **schoolchildren.** N-COUNT **Schoolchildren** are children who go to school.

schooldays (or **school days**) /'skuːldeɪz/. N-PLURAL Your **schooldays** are the period of your life when you are at school. *...a girl he had known since his schooldays.*

schoolgirl /'skuːlgɜːl/ **schoolgirls.** N-COUNT A **schoolgirl** is a girl who goes to school.

schooling /'skuːlɪŋ/. N-UNCOUNT **Schooling** is education that children receive at school. *...children whose schooling has been disrupted by illness.*

schoolteacher /'skuːltiːtʃə/ **schoolteachers.** N-COUNT A **schoolteacher** is a teacher in a school.

⭐ **science** /saɪəns/ **sciences.** **1** N-UNCOUNT **Science** is the study of the nature and behaviour of natural things and the knowledge that we obtain about them. *Technically advanced countries put a high value on science.* **2** N-COUNT A **science** is a particular branch of science, for example physics or biology. **3** N-COUNT A **science** is the study of some aspect of human behaviour, for example sociology or anthropology. **4** See also **social science**.

science fiction. N-UNCOUNT **Science fiction** consists of stories and films about events that take place in the future or in other parts of the universe.

⭐ **scientific** /ˌsaɪən'tɪfɪk/. **1** ADJ **Scientific** is used to describe things that relate to science or to a particular science. *...scientific research.*
♦ **scientifically** ADV *...scientifically advanced countries.* **2** ADJ If you do something in a **scientific** way, you do it carefully and thoroughly, using experiments or tests. *It's not a scientific way to test their opinions.* ♦ **scientifically** ADV *Efforts are being made to research it scientifically.*

⭐ **scientist** /'saɪəntɪst/ **scientists.** N-COUNT A **scientist** is someone who has studied science and whose job is to teach or do research in science.

sci-fi /'saɪ faɪ/. N-UNCOUNT **Sci-fi** is **science fiction**. *...low-budget sci-fi films.*

scissors /'sɪzəz/. N-PLURAL **Scissors** are a small tool with two sharp blades which are screwed together. You use scissors for cutting things such as paper and cloth. → See picture on page 825. *She picked up a pair of scissors.*

scoff /skɒf/ **scoffs, scoffing, scoffed.** VERB If you **scoff**, you speak in a scornful, mocking way about something. *Some people may scoff at the idea that animals communicate.*

scold /skəʊld/ **scolds, scolding, scolded.** VERB If you **scold** someone, you speak angrily to them because they have done something wrong. [FORMAL] *'You should be at school,' he scolded.*

scoop /skuːp/ **scoops, scooping, scooped.** [1] VERB If you **scoop** someone or something somewhere, you put your hands or arms under or round them and quickly move them there. *Michael knelt next to her and scooped her into his arms.* [2] VERB To **scoop** something from a container means to remove it with something such as a spoon. *She scooped the chicken bones back into the stewpot.* [3] N-COUNT A **scoop** is an object like a spoon which is used for picking up a quantity of a food such as ice cream or flour. *She gave him an extra scoop of clotted cream.* [4] N-COUNT A **scoop** is an exciting news story which is reported in one newspaper before it appears anywhere else.
▶**scoop out.** PHR-VERB If you **scoop out** part of something, you remove it using a spoon or other tool. *Cut a marrow in half and scoop out the seeds.*
▶**scoop up.** PHR-VERB If you **scoop** something **up**, you put your hands or arms under it and lift it in a quick movement. *Use both hands to scoop up the leaves.*

scooter /'skuːtə/ **scooters.** [1] N-COUNT A **scooter** is a small lightweight motorcycle. → See picture on page 817. [2] N-COUNT A **scooter** is a child's toy which has two wheels joined by a board and a handle on a long pole attached to the front wheel. → See picture on page 817.

scope /skəʊp/. [1] N-UNCOUNT If there is **scope for** a particular kind of behaviour, you have the opportunity to act in this way. *He believed in giving his staff scope for initiative... Banks had increased scope to develop new financial products.* [2] N-UNCOUNT The **scope of** an activity, topic, or piece of work is the area which it deals with or includes. *...the huge scope of his novel. ...a job she is confident will grow in scope.*

scorch /skɔːtʃ/ **scorches, scorching, scorched.** VERB To **scorch** something means to burn it slightly or damage it with heat. *The bomb scorched the side of the building.* ♦ **scorched** ADJ *...scorched black earth.*

scorching /'skɔːtʃɪŋ/. ADJ **Scorching** or **scorching hot** weather or temperatures are very hot indeed. *It was a scorching hot day.* ● See note at **hot.**

⭐ **score** /skɔː/ **scores, scoring, scored.** [1] VERB In a sport or game, if a player **scores** a goal or a point, they gain a goal or point. *Gascoigne almost scored in the opening minute.* ♦ **scorer, scorers** N-COUNT *Who was the club's leading scorer?* [2] N-COUNT The **score** in a game is the number of goals, runs, or points obtained by the teams or players. *4-1 was*

the final score. [3] VERB If you **score** a success, a victory, or a hit, you are successful in what you are doing. *A multiple rocket launcher scored a direct hit on the steeple of a church.* [4] N-COUNT The **score** of a piece of music is the written version of it. [5] QUANT **Scores of** things or people means a large number of them. *Campaigners lit scores of bonfires... Two people were killed and scores were injured.* [6] VERB If you **score** a surface with something sharp, you cut or scratch a line in it.

PHRASES ● You can use **on that score** or **on this score** to refer to something that has just been mentioned, especially an area of difficulty or concern. *I became pregnant easily. At least I've had no problems on that score.* ● If you **settle a score** or **settle an old score** with someone, you take revenge on them for something they have done in the past.

scorn /skɔːn/ **scorns, scorning, scorned.** [1] N-UNCOUNT If you treat someone or something with **scorn**, you show contempt for them. *He became the object of ridicule and scorn.* [2] VERB If you **scorn** someone or something, you feel or show contempt for them. *People scorn me as a single parent.* [3] VERB If you **scorn** something, you refuse to accept it because you think it is not good enough or suitable for you. *...people who scorned traditional methods.*

scornful /'skɔːnfəl/. ADJ If you are **scornful of** someone or something, you show contempt for them. *He is deeply scornful of politicians.*
♦ **scornfully** ADV *They laughed scornfully.*

Scotch /skɒtʃ/ **Scotches.** N-VAR **Scotch** or **Scotch whisky** is whisky made in Scotland. *...a bottle of Scotch... She expected him to ask for a scotch.*

scour /skaʊə/ **scours, scouring, scoured.** [1] VERB If you **scour** a place **for** someone or something, you make a thorough search there for them. *They scoured antiques shops for honey-coloured furniture.* [2] VERB If you **scour** something such as a sink, floor, or pan, you clean its surface by rubbing it hard with something rough.

scourge /skɜːdʒ/ **scourges.** N-COUNT A **scourge** is something that causes a lot of trouble to a group of people. *...the scourge of terrorism.*

scout /skaʊt/ **scouts, scouting, scouted.** [1] N-COUNT A **scout** is someone who is sent to an area of countryside to find out the position of an enemy army. [2] VERB If you **scout** somewhere **for** something, you go through that area searching for it. *They scouted around for more fuel.*

scowl /skaʊl/ **scowls, scowling, scowled.** VERB & N-COUNT When someone **scowls**, they frown to show that they are angry. A **scowl** is the expression on someone's face when they scowl. *She scowled at the two men... Chris met the remark with a scowl.*

scramble /'skræmbəl/ **scrambles, scrambling, scrambled.** [1] VERB If you **scramble** over rough or difficult ground, you move quickly over it using your hands to help you. *She scrambled down* *rocks to reach him.* **2** VERB To **scramble** means to move somewhere in a hurried and awkward way. *She managed to scramble out of the vehicle as it burst into flames.* **3** VERB & N-COUNT If a number of people **scramble for** something, or if there is a **scramble for** it, they compete with each other for it, in a rough way. *Business is booming and foreigners are scrambling to invest. ...the scramble for jobs.* **4** VERB If you **scramble** eggs, you mix the whites and yolks of the eggs, then cook the mixture by stirring and heating it in a pan. ♦ **scrambled** ADJ *...scrambled eggs and bacon.*

scrap /skræp/ **scraps, scrapping, scrapped.** **1** N-COUNT A **scrap of** something is a very small piece or amount of it. *...a fire fueled by scraps of wood... They need every scrap of information they can get.* **2** VERB If you **scrap** something, you get rid of it or cancel it. *...the decision to scrap smoking compartments on Kent trains.* **3** N-UNCOUNT **Scrap** is metal from old or damaged machinery or cars. *...a lorry piled with scrap metal.* **4** N-COUNT You can refer to a fight or a quarrel as a **scrap**. [INFORMAL]

scrape /skreɪp/ **scrapes, scraping, scraped.** **1** VERB If you **scrape** something from a surface, you remove it, especially by pulling a sharp object over the surface. *She went round the car scraping the frost off the windows.* **2** VERB & N-SING If something **scrapes** against something else, it rubs against it, making a noise, called a **scrape**. *The cab driver struggled with her luggage, scraping a bag against the door. ...the scrape of a guard's boot.* ♦ **scraping** N-SING *...the scraping of a chair across the floor.* **3** VERB If you **scrape** a part of your body, you accidentally rub it against something hard and rough, and damage it slightly.
▸**scrape through.** PHR-VERB If you **scrape through** an examination, you succeed in passing it but with a score that is so low that you almost failed. *...the minimum amount of work necessary to scrape through.*
▸**scrape together.** PHR-VERB If you **scrape together** an amount of money or a number of things, you succeed in obtaining it with difficulty. *They only just managed to scrape the money together.*

scratch /skrætʃ/ **scratches, scratching, scratched.** **1** VERB If you **scratch yourself**, you rub your fingernails against your skin because it is itching. *He scratched himself under his arm... The old man lifted his cardigan to scratch his side.* **2** VERB If a sharp object **scratches** something or someone, it makes small shallow cuts on their surface or skin. *Knives will scratch the worktop.* **3** N-COUNT **Scratches** on someone or something are small shallow cuts.
PHRASES ● If you do something **from scratch**, you do it without making use of anything that has been done before. *...building a home from scratch.* ● If something is not **up to scratch**, it is

not good enough. *...keeping his health up to scratch.*

¹scratch card, scratch cards. N-COUNT A **scratch card** is a card with hidden words or symbols on it. You scratch the surface off to see the words or symbols and find out if you have won a prize.

scrawl /skrɔːl/ **scrawls, scrawling, scrawled.** **1** VERB If you **scrawl** something, you write it in a careless and untidy way. *He scrawled a hasty note to his wife.* **2** N-VAR You can refer to writing that looks careless and untidy as **scrawl**.

⭐ **scream** /skriːm/ **screams, screaming, screamed.** **1** VERB & N-COUNT When someone **screams**, they make a loud high-pitched cry, called a **scream**, usually because they are in pain or frightened. *He staggered around the playground, screaming in agony. ...screams of terror.* **2** VERB If you **scream** something, you shout it in a loud high-pitched voice. *I was screaming at them to get out of my house.*

screech /skriːtʃ/ **screeches, screeching, screeched.** **1** VERB & N-COUNT If a vehicle **screeches**, its tyres make an unpleasant high-pitched noise, called a **screech**, on the road. *A black Mercedes screeched to a halt beside the helicopter... He slowed the car with a screech of tyres.* **2** VERB & N-COUNT If you **screech** something, or if you give a **screech**, you shout something in a loud, unpleasant, high-pitched voice. *'Get me some water, Jeremy!' I screeched. ...her voice rising to a screech.*

⭐ **screen** /skriːn/ **screens, screening, screened.** **1** N-COUNT A **screen** is the flat vertical surface on which pictures or words are shown on a television, on a computer, or in a cinema. **2** VERB When a film or a television programme **is screened**, it is shown in the cinema or broadcast on television. *Channel Nine has again refused to screen the West Indies cricket tour.* ♦ **screening, screenings** N-VAR *The film-makers will be present at the screenings.* **3** N-COUNT A **screen** is a vertical panel that is used to separate different parts of a room. *They put a screen in front of me so I couldn't see what was going on.* **4** VERB If something **is screened** by another thing, it is behind it and hidden by it. *Most of the road behind the hotel was screened by a block of flats.* **5** VERB To **screen** people **for** a disease means to examine them to make sure that they do not have it. *...a quick saliva test that would screen for people at risk of tooth decay.* ♦ **screening** N-VAR *...breast screening for cancer.*

screenplay /'skriːnpleɪ/ **screenplays.** N-COUNT A **screenplay** is a script for a film including instructions for the cameras.

¸screen saver, screen savers. N-COUNT A **screen saver** is a moving picture which appears on a computer screen when the computer is not being used. [COMPUTING]

screenwriter /'skriːnraɪtə/ **screenwriters.** N-COUNT A **screenwriter** is a person who writes screenplays.

a
b
c
d
e
f
g
h
i
j
k
l
m
n
o
p
q
r
s
t
u
v
w
x
y
z

screw /skruː/ **screws, screwing, screwed.** **1** N-COUNT A **screw** is a small metal device for fixing things together. It has a wide top, a pointed end, and a raised spiral groove along its length. → See picture on page 833. **2** VERB If you **screw** something somewhere, you fix it there by means of a screw or screws. *I had screwed the shelf on the wall... Screw down any loose floorboards.* **3** VERB To **screw** something somewhere means to fasten or fix it in place by twisting it round and round. *He screwed the cap back on and laid the bottle on the table.* **4** VERB If you **screw** your face or your eyes **into** an expression of pain or discomfort, you tighten the muscles of your face showing that you are in pain or uncomfortable. *He screwed his face into a horrible grimace.* **5** VERB If someone **screws** something, especially money, **out of** you, they get it from you by putting strong pressure on you. [INFORMAL] *He's now screwing cheaper prices out of his own raw material suppliers.*
▶**screw up.** PHR-VERB If someone **screws** something **up**, or if they **screw up**, they cause something to fail or be spoiled. [INFORMAL] *You can't open the window because it screws up the air conditioning.*

screwdriver /ˈskruːdraɪvə/ **screwdrivers.** N-COUNT A **screwdriver** is a tool for fixing screws into place. → See picture on page 833.

scribble /ˈskrɪbəl/ **scribbles, scribbling, scribbled.** **1** VERB If you **scribble** something, you write it quickly and untidily. *Boxhall scribbled his calculation on a scrap of paper... As I scribbled in my diary, the light went out.* **2** VERB To **scribble** means to make meaningless marks or rough drawings using a pencil or pen. *When Caroline was five she scribbled on a wall.* **3** N-VAR **Scribble** is something that has been written or drawn quickly and roughly.

⭐ **script** /skrɪpt/ **scripts.** **1** N-COUNT The **script** of a play, film, or television programme is the written version of it. **2** N-VAR A **script** is a particular system of writing. *...written in Arabic script.*

scripture /ˈskrɪptʃə/ **scriptures.** N-VAR **Scripture** or **the scriptures** refers to writings that are regarded as sacred in a particular religion, for example the Bible in Christianity.

scroll /skrəʊl/ **scrolls, scrolling, scrolled.** **1** N-COUNT A **scroll** is a long roll of paper or other material with writing on it. *...ancient scrolls.* **2** VERB If you **scroll** through text on a computer screen, you move the text up or down to find the information that you need. [COMPUTING] *I scrolled down to find 'United States of America'.*

'scroll bar, scroll bars. N-COUNT On a computer screen, a **scroll bar** is a long thin box along one edge of a window, which you click on with the mouse to move the text up, down, or across the window. [COMPUTING]

scrub /skrʌb/ **scrubs, scrubbing, scrubbed.** **1** VERB & N-SING If you **scrub** something, or if you give it a **scrub**, you rub it hard in order to clean it, using a stiff brush and water. *The corridors are scrubbed*

clean... *I started to scrub off the dirt... That floor needs a jolly good scrub.* **2** N-UNCOUNT **Scrub** is land consisting of low trees and bushes in an area which gets very little rain.

scruffy /ˈskrʌfi/ **scruffier, scruffiest.** ADJ **Scruffy** things or people are dirty and untidy. *...a scruffy basement flat.*

scrupulous /ˈskruːpjʊləs/ **1** ADJ A **scrupulous** person or organization takes great care to do what is fair, honest, or morally right. *The case is pursued with scrupulous fairness according to the rules.* ♦ **scrupulously** ADV *He is scrupulously fair.* **2** ADJ **Scrupulous** means thorough, exact, and careful about details. *Observe scrupulous hygiene when preparing and cooking food.* ♦ **scrupulously** ADV *The streets and parks were scrupulously clean.*

scrutinize (BRIT also **scrutinise**) /ˈskruːtɪnaɪz/ **scrutinizes, scrutinizing, scrutinized.** VERB If you **scrutinize** something, you examine it very carefully. *The insurance industry will continue to be closely scrutinized by Congress.*

scrutiny /ˈskruːtɪni/ N-UNCOUNT If something is **under scrutiny**, it is being studied or observed very carefully. *His private life came under scrutiny... The holders of public office must always be subject to public scrutiny.*

scuffle /ˈskʌfəl/ **scuffles, scuffling, scuffled.** VERB & N-COUNT If people **are scuffling**, or if they are involved in a **scuffle**, they are fighting for a short time in a disorganized way. *Police scuffled with some of the protesters... Violent scuffles broke out between rival groups.*

sculpt /skʌlpt/ **sculpts, sculpting, sculpted.** VERB When an artist **sculpts** something, they carve it or shape it out of a hard material such as stone. *...figures sculpted in stone.* ♦ **sculptor, sculptors** N-COUNT *...a sculptor who takes inspiration from all kinds of natural things.*

sculpture /ˈskʌlptʃə/ **sculptures.** **1** N-VAR A **sculpture** is a work of art that is produced by carving or shaping materials such as stone or clay. **2** N-UNCOUNT **Sculpture** is the art and craft of making sculptures.

scum /skʌm/ N-UNCOUNT **Scum** is a layer of a substance on the surface of a liquid which looks unpleasant. *...areas where the water is especially hard and prone to form scum.*

scupper /ˈskʌpə/ **scuppers, scuppering, scuppered.** VERB To **scupper** a plan or attempt means to spoil it completely. [BRITISH] *...a deliberate attempt to scupper the peace talks.*

scurry /ˈskʌri, AM ˈskɜːri/ **scurries, scurrying, scurried.** **1** VERB When people or small animals **scurry** somewhere, they move quickly and hurriedly, especially because they are frightened. *The attack began, sending residents scurrying for cover.* **2** VERB If people **scurry to** do something, they do it as quickly as they can. *Reporters scurried to find telephones.*

scuttle /ˈskʌtəl/ **scuttles, scuttling, scuttled.** VERB When people or small animals **scuttle**

somewhere, they run there with short quick steps. *Two very small children scuttled away in front of them.*

⭐ **sea** /siː/ **seas.** ① N-SING **The sea** is the salty water that covers much of the earth's surface. *Most of the kids have never seen the sea.* ② N-COUNT A **sea** is a large area of salty water that is part of an ocean or is surrounded by land. You use **seas** when you are describing the sea at a particular time or in a particular area. *...the North Sea... The seas are warm further south.* ③ N-SING A **sea of** people or things is a very large number of them. *...the sea of bottles and glasses on the table.*

PHRASES ● **At sea** means on or under the sea, far away from land. *The boats remain at sea for an average of ten days.* ● If someone is **all at sea**, they are in a state of confusion.

seafood /ˈsiːfuːd/. N-UNCOUNT **Seafood** refers to shellfish and other sea creatures that you can eat.

seagull /ˈsiːɡʌl/ **seagulls.** N-COUNT A **seagull** is a type of bird that lives near the sea.

⭐ **seal** /siːl/ **seals, sealing, sealed.** ① N-COUNT A **seal** is an animal which eats fish and lives partly on land and partly in the sea. It has short fur and uses short limbs, called flippers, to enable it to swim. ② VERB When you **seal** an envelope, you close it by sticking down the flap. *Write your letter and seal it in a blank envelope.* ③ VERB & N-COUNT If you **seal** a container or an opening, or if you form a **seal**, you cover it with something in order to prevent air, liquid, or other material getting in or out. *...a lid to seal in heat and keep food moist... Wet the edges where the two crusts join, to form a seal.* ④ N-COUNT A **seal** is a device, used for example in a machine, which closes an opening tightly so that air, liquid, or other substances cannot get in or out. *Checks seals on fridges and freezers regularly.* ⑤ N-COUNT A **seal** is an official mark on a document which shows that it is genuine. ⑥ VERB & PHR-VERB If someone in authority **seals** an area, or if they **seal** it **off**, they stop people entering or passing through it, for example by placing barriers in the way. *The army has stepped up patrols in an effort to seal the border... Police and troops sealed off the area.*

'sea level. N-UNCOUNT If you are at **sea level**, you are at the same level as the surface of the sea. *The stadium was 2275 metres above sea level.*

seam /siːm/ **seams.** ① N-COUNT A **seam** is a line of stitches joining two pieces of cloth together. ② N-COUNT A **seam** of coal is a long narrow layer of it beneath the ground. ③ PHRASE If a place is very full, you can say that it is **bursting at the seams**.

seaman /ˈsiːmən/ **seamen.** N-COUNT A **seaman** is a sailor.

seamless /ˈsiːmləs/. ADJ You use **seamless** to describe something that has no breaks or gaps in it or which continues smoothly, without stopping. *It was a seamless procession of wonderful electronic music.* ◆ **seamlessly** ADV *...allowing new and old to blend seamlessly.*

⭐ **search** /sɜːtʃ/ **searches, searching, searched.** ① VERB If you **search for** something or someone, you look carefully for them. If you **search** a place, you look carefully for something there. *The Turkish security forces have started searching for the missing men... She searched her desk for the necessary information.* ② N-COUNT A **search** is an attempt to find something by looking for it carefully. *Following an hour-long search, police seized several items.* ③ VERB If the police **search** you, they examine your clothing for hidden objects. ④ PHRASE If you go **in search of** something, you try to find them. *...people in search of better economic opportunities.*

'search ˌengine, **search engines.** N-COUNT A **search engine** is a computer program that searches for documents on the Internet. [COMPUTING]

searching /ˈsɜːtʃɪŋ/. ADJ A **searching** question is intended to discover the truth about something.

searing /ˈsɪərɪŋ/. ① ADJ BEFORE N **Searing** is used to indicate that something such as pain or heat is very intense. *...the searing heat of the Saudi Arabian desert.* ② ADJ BEFORE N A **searing** speech or piece of writing is very critical. *...a searing indictment of corruption at the top.*

seaside /ˈsiːsaɪd/. N-SING You can refer to an area that is close to the sea, especially where people go for their holidays, as **the seaside**. [BRITISH]

⭐ **season** /ˈsiːzən/ **seasons, seasoning, seasoned.** ① N-COUNT The **seasons** are the periods into which a year is divided and which each have their own typical weather conditions. → See Reference Page on Times and Dates. *Autumn's my favourite season. ...the rainy season.* ② N-COUNT A **season** is the period during each year when something usually happens. *...the start of the football season.* ③ VERB If you **season** food, you add salt, pepper, or spices to it. *Season the meat with salt and pepper.*

PHRASES ● If fruit or vegetables are **in season**, it is the time of year when they are ready for eating and are widely available. ● If a female animal is **in season**, she is in a state where she is ready for mating.

seasonal /ˈsiːzənəl/. ADJ **Seasonal** means happening during one particular time of the year. *...seasonal variations in temperature.* ◆ **seasonally** ADV *...the seasonally adjusted unemployment figures.*

seasoned /ˈsiːzənd/. ADJ **Seasoned** is used to describe people who have a lot of experience of something. *...seasoned travellers.*

seasoning /ˈsiːzənɪŋ/. N-UNCOUNT **Seasoning** is salt, pepper, or spices that are added to food to improve its flavour.

'season ˌticket, **season tickets.** N-COUNT A **season ticket** is a ticket that you can use repeatedly over a certain period without having to pay each time.

a
b
c
d
e
f
g
h
i
j
k
l
m
n
o
p
q
r
s
t
u
v
w
x
y
z

⭐ **seat** /siːt/ **seats, seating, seated.** **1** N-COUNT A **seat** is an object that you can sit on, for example a chair. *...the back seat of their car... All seats for the Variety performance will be priced at £12.00.* ● See note at **place**. **2** N-COUNT The **seat** of a chair is the part that you sit on. **3** VERB If you **seat yourself** somewhere, you sit down. *I seated myself at the bar... The room was empty apart from one man seated beside the fire.* **4** VERB A building or vehicle that **seats** a particular number of people has enough seats for that number. *The theatre seats 570.* **5** N-COUNT When someone is elected to parliament, you can say that they or their party have won a **seat**. **6** N-COUNT If someone has a **seat** on the board of a company or on a committee, they are a member of it. PHRASES ● If you **take a back seat**, you allow other people to have all the power and to make all the decisions. ● If you say that someone is **in the driving seat** or **in the driver's seat**, you mean that they are in control in a situation. *...a more accountable system that would put voters back in the driving seat.* ● If you **take a seat**, you sit down. *Take a seat. What can I do for you?*

'**seat-belt** (or **seatbelt**) **seat-belts.** N-COUNT A **seat-belt** is a strap that you fasten across your body for safety when travelling in a car or aeroplane.

seating /'siːtɪŋ/. N-UNCOUNT The **seating** in a place consists of the seats there. *...the pleasant cafeteria, with seating for up to 200.*

seaweed /'siːwiːd/ **seaweeds.** N-VAR **Seaweed** is a plant that grows in the sea.

secluded /sɪ'kluːdɪd/. ADJ A **secluded** place is quiet, private, and undisturbed.

seclusion /sɪ'kluːʒən/. N-UNCOUNT If you are **in seclusion**, you are in a quiet place away from other people. *They lived in seclusion on their farm... They love the seclusion of their garden.*

second 1 part of a minute

⭐ **second** /'sekənd/ **seconds.** N-COUNT A **second** is one of the sixty parts that a minute is divided into. People often say **'a second'** or **'seconds'** when they simply mean a very short length of time. *It only takes forty seconds... Seconds later, firemen reached his door.*

second 2 coming after something else

⭐ **second** /'sekənd/ **seconds, seconding, seconded.** **1** ORD The **second** item in a series is the one that you count as number two. *It is the second time I have heard the name. ...Cambodia's second biggest city... First, interest rates may take longer to fall than is hoped. Second, in real terms, lending may fall.* **2** PHRASE If you say that something is **second to none**, you are emphasizing that it is very good indeed or very large indeed. **3** PHRASE If you say that something is **second only to** something else, you mean that it is the best or biggest that exists, except for that thing. *As a major health risk hepatitis is second only to tobacco.* **4** N-COUNT **Seconds** are goods that are sold cheaply because they are slightly faulty.

5 VERB If you **second** a proposal in a meeting or debate, you formally agree with it so that it can then be discussed or voted on. *...the members who proposed and seconded his nomination.* **6** VERB If you **second** what someone has said, you say that you agree with them or say the same thing yourself. *His concern was seconded by spokesmen from the National Association of Homebuilders.* **7** **second nature**: see **nature**.

second 3 sending someone to do a job

second /sɪ'kɒnd/ **seconds, seconding, seconded.** VERB If you **are seconded** somewhere, you are moved there temporarily by the organization you work for in order to do special duties. *Several hundred soldiers have been seconded to help farmers.*

secondary /'sekəndri, AM -deri/. **1** ADJ If you describe something as **secondary**, you mean that it is less important than something else. *Money is considered to be of secondary importance in this scheme of things.* **2** ADJ In Britain, **secondary** education is for pupils between the ages of 11 and 18.

,**second 'best.** ADJ & N-SING Something that is **second best** or **a second best** is not as good as the best thing of its kind but is better than all the other things. *...his second best suit... He refused to settle for anything that was second best.*

,**second-'class.** ADJ BEFORE N **Second-class** things are regarded as less valuable or less important than others of the same kind. *He was not prepared to see Uzbekistan become a second-class republic.*

,**second-'hand.** **1** ADJ & ADV **Second-hand** things are not new and have been owned by someone else. *Far more boats are bought second-hand than are bought brand new.* **2** ADJ BEFORE N A **second-hand** shop sells second-hand goods. **3** ADJ & ADV **Second-hand** information or opinions are those you learn about from other people rather than directly or from your own experience. *I heard stories second-hand that they were having a fantastic time.*

secondly /'sekəndli/. ADV You say **secondly** when you want to make a second point or give a second reason for something. *Firstly, I didn't know exactly when I was going to America; secondly, who was going to look after Doran?*

,**second-'rate.** ADJ If you describe something as **second-rate**, you mean that it is of poor quality.

,**second 'thoughts.** **1** N-PLURAL If you have **second thoughts about** a decision, you have doubts and begin to wonder if it was wise. **2** PHRASE In British English, you can say **on second thoughts** when you suddenly change your mind about something that you are saying or something that you have decided to do. In American English, you say **on second thought**. *'On second thoughts,' he said, 'I guess I'll come with you.'*

secrecy /'siːkrəsi/. N-UNCOUNT **Secrecy** is the act of keeping something secret, or the state of being kept secret. *He had signed a pledge of secrecy.*

★ **secret** /'si:krɪt/ **secrets.** **1** ADJ If something is **secret**, it is known about by only a small number of people, and is not told or shown to anyone else. *The police have been trying to keep the documents secret.* ◆ **secretly** ADV *The meeting had been secretly recorded.* **2** N-COUNT A **secret** is a fact that is known by only a small number of people, and is not told to anyone else. *He enjoyed keeping our love a secret.* **3** N-SING If a way of behaving is **the secret of** achieving something, it is the best way or the only way to achieve it. *The secret of success is honesty.* **4** PHRASE If you do something **in secret**, you do it without anyone else knowing. *The plans were drawn up in secret.*

secretarial /ˌsekrə'teəriəl/. ADJ **Secretarial** work or training involves the work of a secretary.

secretariat /ˌsekrə'teəriæt/ **secretariats.** N-COUNT A **secretariat** is a department responsible for the administration of an international political organization.

★ **secretary** /'sekrətri, AM -teri/ **secretaries.** **1** N-COUNT A **secretary** is a person who is employed to do office work, such as typing letters or answering phone calls. **2** N-COUNT The **secretary** of an organization such as a trade union or a club is its official manager. **3** N-COUNT The **secretary** of a company is the person who has the legal duty of keeping the company's records. **4** N-COUNT **Secretary** is used in the titles of ministers and officials who are in charge of main government departments. *...the British Foreign Secretary.*

★ **Secretary of 'State, Secretaries of State.** **1** N-COUNT In the United States, **the Secretary of State** is the head of the government department which deals with foreign affairs. **2** N-COUNT In Britain, **the Secretary of State** for a particular government department is the head of that department.

secrete /sɪ'kri:t/ **secretes, secreting, secreted.** VERB If part of a plant or animal **secretes** a liquid, it produces it. [FORMAL] ◆ **secretion** N-UNCOUNT *...insulin secretion.*

secretion /sɪ'kri:ʃən/ **secretions.** N-COUNT A **secretion** is a liquid that is produced by a plant or animal. [FORMAL]

secretive /'si:krətɪv, sɪ'kri:t-/. ADJ If you are **secretive**, you like to keep your knowledge, feelings, or intentions hidden.

secret po'lice. N-UNCOUNT The **secret police** is a police force, especially in a non-democratic country, that works secretly and is concerned with political crimes.

secret 'service, secret services. N-COUNT A country's **secret service** is a government department whose job is to find out enemy secrets and to prevent its own government's secrets from being discovered.

sect /sekt/ **sects.** N-COUNT A **sect** is a group of people that has separated from a larger group

and has a particular set of religious or political beliefs.

sectarian /sek'teəriən/. ADJ **Sectarian** means resulting from the differences between different religious sects. *The murder was sectarian.*

★ **section** /'sekʃən/ **sections.** N-COUNT A **section of** something is one of the parts that it is divided into. *A section of the Bay Bridge had collapsed... This paragraph is the longest section of the will.* ● See also **cross-section**.

★ **sector** /'sektə/ **sectors.** N-COUNT A **sector of** something, especially a country's economy, is a particular part of it. *...the nation's manufacturing sector. ...the poorest sectors of Pakistani society.*

secular /'sekjʊlə/. ADJ You use **secular** to describe things that have no connection with religion. *...a secular state.*

★ **secure** /sɪ'kjʊə/ **secures, securing, secured.** **1** ADJ If something such as a job or institution is **secure**, it is safe and reliable, and unlikely to be lost or fail. *The industry has a strong and secure future.* **2** ADJ A **secure** place is tightly locked or well protected, so that people cannot enter it or leave it. ◆ **securely** ADV *Drugs were always securely locked away.* **3** VERB If you **secure** a place, you make it safe from harm or attack. [FORMAL] *Troops had secured the airport.* **4** ADJ If an object is **secure**, it is fixed firmly in position. ◆ **securely** ADV *They tied the ends of the bags securely.* **5** VERB If you **secure** an object, you fasten it firmly to another object. *Rugs are secured to the floor with tacks.* **6** ADJ If you feel **secure**, you feel safe and happy and are not worried about your life. **7** VERB If you **secure** something, you get it after a lot of effort. [FORMAL] *He failed to secure enough votes for outright victory.*

★ **security** /sɪ'kjʊərɪti/ **securities.** **1** N-UNCOUNT **Security** refers to all the precautions that are taken to protect a place. *Airport security was tightened... ...security guards.* **2** N-UNCOUNT A feeling of **security** is a feeling of being safe and free from worry. *He loves the security of a happy home life.* **3** N-UNCOUNT The **security** of something such as a job is the fact that it is safe or reliable, and unlikely to be lost or to fail. *Fears about job security plague nearly half the workforce.* **4** N-UNCOUNT If you pledge something as **security** for a loan, you promise to give it to the person who lends you money, if you fail to pay all the money back. **5** See also **social security**.

se'curity ˌcamera, security cameras. N-COUNT A **security camera** is a video camera that records people's activities in order to detect and prevent crime.

sedate /sɪ'deɪt/ **sedates, sedating, sedated.** **1** ADJ If you describe someone as **sedate**, you mean that they are quiet and calm, though perhaps rather dull. **2** VERB If someone **is sedated**, they are given a drug to calm them or to make them sleep.

sedation /sɪ'deɪʃən/. N-UNCOUNT If someone is **under sedation**, they have been given medicine

a b c d e f g h i j k l m n o p q r s t u v w x y z

or drugs in order to calm them or make them sleep.

sedative/'sedətɪv/ **sedatives.** N-COUNT A **sedative** is a drug that calms you or makes you sleep. *Her doctor prescribed a sedative.*

sedentary/'sedəntəri, AM -teri/. ADJ Someone who has a **sedentary** lifestyle or job sits down a lot of the time and does not take much exercise.

sediment/'sedɪmənt/ **sediments.** N-VAR **Sediment** is solid material that settles at the bottom of a liquid.

seduce/sɪ'djuːs, AM -'duːs/ **seduces, seducing, seduced.** [1] VERB If something **seduces** you, it is so attractive that it tempts you to do something that you would not normally approve of. *We are seduced into buying all these brilliantly packaged items.* ◆ **seduction**/sɪ'dʌkʃən/ **seductions** N-VAR *The country had resisted the seductions of mass tourism.* [2] VERB If someone **seduces** another person, they use their charm to persuade that person to have sex with them. ◆ **seduction** N-VAR *Her methods of seduction are subtle.*

seductive/sɪ'dʌktɪv/. [1] ADJ Something that is **seductive** is very attractive or tempting. *It's a seductive argument.* [2] ADJ A **seductive** person is sexually attractive. ◆ **seductively** ADV *Her mouth is seductively large and full.*

⭐ **see**/siː/ **sees, seeing, saw, seen.** [1] VERB When you **see** someone or something, you notice them using your eyes. *Did you see that policeman?... I saw a man making his way towards me... I saw her get out of the car... It's dark and I can't see.*

> **USAGE** You use **see** to talk about things that you are aware of because a visual impression reaches your eyes. You often use **can** in this case. *I can see the fax here on the desk.* If you want to say that someone is paying attention to something they can see, you say that they **are looking at** it or **watching** it. In general, you **look at** something that is not moving, while you **watch** something that is moving or changing. *I asked him to look at the picture above his bed... He watched Blake run down the stairs.*

[2] VERB If you go to **see** someone, you visit them or meet them. *You need to see a doctor.* [3] VERB If you go to **see** an entertainment such as a film or sports game, you go to watch it. *It was one of the most amazing films I've ever seen.* [4] VERB If you **see** what something is or what it means, you realize or understand what it is or what it means. *Amy saw that he was challenging her... I really don't see any reason for changing it... 'He came home in my car.'—'I see.'* [5] VERB If you **see** someone or something **as** a certain thing or **see** a particular quality in them, you have the opinion that they are that thing or have that quality. *He saw her as a rival... I don't see it as my duty to take sides.* [6] VERB If you **see** something happening in

the future, you imagine it, or predict that it will happen. *I can see them doing really well.* [7] VERB If you say that a period of time or a person **sees** a particular change or event, you mean that the change or event takes place during that period of time or while that person is alive. *Yesterday saw the resignation of the acting Interior Minister... He had worked with the General for three years and was sorry to see him go.* [8] VERB If you say that you will **see** what is happening, you mean that you will try to find out what is happening. If you say that you will **see** if you can do something, you mean that you will try to do it. *Let me just see what the next song is... We'll see what we can do, miss.* [9] VERB & PHRASE If you **see** that something is done, or if you **see to it** that it is done, you make sure that it is done. *See that you take care of him... Catherine saw to it that the information went directly to Walter.* [10] VERB If you **see** someone to a particular place, you accompany them to make sure that they get there safely, or to show politeness. *'Goodnight.'—'I'll see you out.'* [11] VERB **See** is used in books to indicate to readers where they should look for more information. *See Chapter 7 below for further comments on the textile industry.*

PHRASES ● People say '**let me see**' or '**let's see**' when they are trying to remember or calculate something, or are trying to find something. *Let's see, they're six – no, make that five hours ahead of us.* ● People say '**I'll see**' or '**We'll see**' to indicate that they do not intend to make a decision immediately, and will decide later. ● You can use **seeing that** or **seeing as** to introduce a reason for what you are saying or a reason why you think something is the case. *Seeing as I pay half the rent, I should be allowed to smoke.* ● '**See you**', '**be seeing you**', and '**see you later**' are ways of saying goodbye to someone when you expect to meet them again soon. → See Reference Page on Greetings and Goodbyes.

▶ **see about.** PHR-VERB When you **see about** something, you arrange for it to be done or provided. *I must see about selling the house.*
▶ **see off.** [1] PHR-VERB If you **see off** an opponent, you defeat them. *He saw off a strong challenge from two other candidates.* [2] PHR-VERB When you **see** someone **off**, you go with them to the place that they are leaving from, and say goodbye to them there.
▶ **see through.** PHR-VERB If you **see through** someone or their behaviour, you realize what their intentions are, even though they are trying to hide them. *I saw through your little ruse from the start.* ● See also **see-through**.
▶ **see to.** PHR-VERB If you **see to** something that needs attention, you deal with it. *Franklin saw to the luggage.* ● See also **see 9**.

⭐ **seed**/siːd/ **seeds.** [1] N-VAR A **seed** is one of the small hard parts of a plant from which a new plant grows. [2] N-PLURAL You can refer to the beginning of a feeling or process that gradually develops as the **seeds of** that feeling or process.

...questions meant to plant seeds of doubts in the minds of jurors.

seedling /'si:dlɪŋ/ **seedlings.** N-COUNT A **seedling** is a young plant grown from a seed.

seedy /'si:di/ **seedier, seediest.** ADJ If you describe a person or place as **seedy**, you disapprove of them because they look dirty and not respectable. ...a seedy hotel.

⭐ **seek** /si:k/ **seeks, seeking, sought.** [1] VERB If you **seek** something, you try to find or obtain it. [FORMAL] Pat decided she would seek work. ♦ **seeker, seekers** N-COUNT The beaches draw sun-seekers from all over Europe. [2] VERB If you **seek** to do something, you try to do it. We have never sought to impose our views.
▸**seek out.** PHR-VERB If you **seek out** someone or something, you keep looking for them until you find them. The press began to seek him out.

⭐ **seem** /si:m/ **seems, seeming, seemed.** [1] LINK-VERB You use **seem** to say that someone or something gives the impression of having a particular quality, or that something gives the impression of happening in the way you describe. Everyone seems busy... They seemed an ideal couple... Audiences seem to love it... It seemed as if she'd been gone forever. [2] VERB You use **seem** when you are describing your own feelings or thoughts, in order to make your statement less forceful. I seem to have lost all my self-confidence... I seem to remember giving you very precise instructions. [3] VERB If you say that you **cannot seem to** or **could not seem to** do something, you mean that you have tried to do it and were unable to. Kim's mother couldn't seem to stop crying.

seeming /'si:mɪŋ/. ADJ BEFORE N **Seeming** means appearing to be the case, but not necessarily the case. [FORMAL] ...the company's seeming inability to control costs. ♦ **seemingly** ADV He has moved to Spain, seemingly to enjoy a slower style of life.

seen /si:n/. **Seen** is the past participle of **see**.

seep /si:p/ **seeps, seeping, seeped.** VERB If liquid or gas **seeps** into a place, it slowly leaks into it. The gas is seeping out of the rocks.

seethe /si:ð/ **seethes, seething, seethed.** [1] VERB If you **are seething**, you are very angry about something but do not openly reveal your feelings about it. I seethed with rage. [2] VERB If you say that a place **is seething**, you are emphasizing that it is very full of people or things and that they are all moving about. The bars and restaurants were seething with customers. ♦ **seething** ADJ ...a seething mass of soldiers.

'see-through. ADJ **See-through** clothes are made of thin cloth, so that you can see a person's body or underwear through them. ...a see-through dress.

⭐ **segment** /'segmənt/ **segments.** N-COUNT A **segment** of something is one part of it. → See picture on page 821. ...the poorer segments of society.

segregate /'segrɪgeɪt/ **segregates, segregating, segregated.** VERB To **segregate** two groups or types of people or things means to keep them apart. They segregate you from the rest of the community. ♦ **segregated** ADJ ...racially segregated schools. ♦ **segregation** N-UNCOUNT ...the sex segregation of work.

⭐ **seize** /si:z/ **seizes, seizing, seized.** [1] VERB If you **seize** something, you take hold of it quickly and firmly. He seized my arm. [2] VERB When a group of people **seize** a place or **seize** control of it, they take control of it quickly and suddenly, using force. Troops have seized the airport. [3] VERB When someone **is seized**, they are arrested or captured. Men carrying sub-machine guns seized the five soldiers. [4] VERB If you **seize** an opportunity, you take advantage of it and do something that you want to do. I seized the chance to interview Chris.
▸**seize on.** PHR-VERB If you **seize on** something, or if you **seize upon** it, you show great interest in it, often because it is useful to you. Opposition parties were quick to seize on the jobs figures.
▸**seize up.** PHR-VERB If an engine or part of your body **seizes up**, it stops working.
▸**seize upon.** See **seize on**.

seizure /'si:ʒə/ **seizures.** [1] N-COUNT If someone has a **seizure**, they have a heart attack or an epileptic fit. ...a mild cardiac seizure. [2] N-COUNT If there is a **seizure of** power in a place, a group of people suddenly take control of it, using force. ...the seizure of territory through force.

seldom /'seldəm/. ADV If something **seldom** happens, it does not happen often. They seldom speak... We were seldom at home.

⭐ **select** /sɪ'lekt/ **selects, selecting, selected.** [1] VERB If you **select** something, you choose it from a number of things of the same kind. A panel of judges is now selecting the finalists. ♦ **selection** N-UNCOUNT The selection of jurors had to be at random. [2] ADJ You use **select** to describe things that are considered to be among the best of their kind. ...a meeting of a very select club.

⭐ **selection** /sɪ'lekʃən/ **selections.** [1] N-COUNT A **selection of** people or things is a set of them chosen from a larger group. ...this selection of popular songs. [2] N-SING The **selection** of goods in a shop is the range of goods available. There is also a wide selection of silk ties at £10. [3] See also **select**.

selective /sɪ'lektɪv/. [1] ADJ BEFORE N A **selective** process applies only to a few things or people. ...selective education. ♦ **selectively** ADV They apply the rules selectively and in their own favour. [2] ADJ When someone is **selective**, they choose things carefully, for example the things that they buy or do. Sales still happen, but buyers are more selective. ♦ **selectively** ADV ...people on small incomes who wanted to shop selectively.

⭐ **self** /self/ **selves.** N-COUNT Your **self** is your basic personality or nature. You're looking more like your usual self.

A
B
C
D
E
F
G
H
I
J
K
L
M
N
O
P
Q
R
S
T
U
V
W
X
Y
Z

‚self-'confident. ADJ Someone who is **self-confident** behaves confidently because they feel sure of their abilities or value. *...a self-confident young woman.* ♦ **self-confidence** N-UNCOUNT *I've developed a lot of self-confidence.*

‚self-'conscious. ADJ Someone who is **self-conscious** is easily embarrassed and nervous about the way they look or appear. *I felt a bit self-conscious in my swimming costume.*

‚self-con'tained. 1 ADJ You can describe someone as **self-contained** when they do not need help or resources from other people. *She's very self-contained.* 2 ADJ A **self-contained** flat has all its own facilities including a kitchen and bathroom.

‚self-con'trol. N-UNCOUNT Your **self-control** is your ability to control your feelings and appear calm. *I began to wish I'd shown more self-control.*

‚self-de'fence (AM **self-defense**). N-UNCOUNT **Self-defence** is the use of force to protect yourself against someone who is attacking you. *He acted in self-defence.*

‚self-determi'nation. N-UNCOUNT **Self-determination** is the right of a country to be independent, instead of being controlled by a foreign country, and to choose its own form of government.

‚self-em'ployed. ADJ & N-PLURAL **Self-employed** people or **the self-employed** are people who organize their own work and taxes and are paid by people for a service they provide, rather than being paid a regular salary by a company. *...a self-employed builder.*

‚self-es'teem. N-UNCOUNT Your **self-esteem** is how you feel about yourself and whether you have a good opinion of yourself. *It was so humiliating, a terrible blow to my self-esteem.*

‚self-'evident. ADJ A fact or situation that is **self-evident** is so obvious that there is no need for proof or explanation. *It's self-evident that this man's not worth marrying.*

‚self-'help. N-UNCOUNT **Self-help** consists of people providing support and help for each other in an informal way, rather than relying on official organizations. *...a self-help group.*

‚self-'image. N-COUNT Your **self-image** is your opinion of yourself. *You must strive constantly to improve your self-image.*

‚self-im'posed. ADJ A **self-imposed** situation, restriction, or task is one that you have created or accepted for yourself. *All my problems were self-imposed. ...eleven years of self-imposed exile.*

‚self-in'dulgent. ADJ If you are **self-indulgent**, you allow yourself to have things that you enjoy but do not need. *To buy flowers for myself seems wildly self-indulgent.* ♦ **self-indulgence**, **self-indulgences** N-VAR *Those days of carefree self-indulgence are over.*

‚self-'interest. N-UNCOUNT If you accuse someone of **self-interest**, you disapprove of them because they always want to do what is best for themselves rather than for anyone else.

Their protests are motivated purely by self-interest.

selfish /'selfɪʃ/. ADJ If you say that someone is **selfish**, you disapprove of them because they care only about themselves, and not about other people. *...the selfish interests of a few people.* ♦ **selfishly** ADV *39% of women complain that their partners act selfishly.* ♦ **selfishness** N-UNCOUNT *They lead lives of utter selfishness.*

selfless /'selfləs/. ADJ If you say that someone is **selfless**, you approve of them because they care about other people more than themselves. *Her generosity to me was entirely selfless.*

‚self-'pity. N-UNCOUNT **Self-pity** is a feeling of unhappiness and depression that you have about your problems, especially when this is unnecessary or greatly exaggerated. *I was unable to shake off my self-pity.*

‚self-re'spect. N-UNCOUNT **Self-respect** is a feeling of confidence and pride in your own ability and worth. *I'd lost all my self-respect.*

‚self-'righteous. ADJ If you describe someone as **self-righteous**, you disapprove of them because they are convinced that they are morally right and that other people are wrong. *...self-righteous reformers.* ♦ **self-righteousness** N-UNCOUNT *...Heather's voice, resonant with self-righteousness.*

‚self-'study. N-UNCOUNT **Self-study** is study that you do on your own, without a teacher. *...self-study courses.*

‚self-'styled. ADJ BEFORE N If you describe someone as a **self-styled** leader or expert, you disapprove of them because they claim to be a leader or expert but they do not have the right to call themselves this. *Two of those arrested are said to be self-styled area commanders.*

‚self-suf'ficient. ADJ If a country or group is **self-sufficient**, it is able to produce or make everything that it needs. *Rural areas tend to be more self-sufficient.* ♦ **self-sufficiency** N-UNCOUNT *...Japan's self-sufficiency in rice.*

⭐ **sell** /sel/ **sells, selling, sold.** 1 VERB If you **sell** something that you own, you let someone have it in return for money. *The directors sold the business for £14.8 million.* 2 VERB If a shop **sells** a product, people can buy it from that shop. *We sell cosmetics.* 3 VERB If something **sells for** a particular price, or if it **sells at** that price, that is what it costs. 4 VERB If something **sells**, it is bought in fairly large quantities. *The products will sell well in the run-up to Christmas.*
▶ **sell out.** 1 PHR-VERB If a shop **sells out of** something, it sells all its stocks of it. 2 PHR-VERB If a performance of a play, film, or other entertainment **is sold out**, all the tickets have been sold. 3 PHR-VERB If you accuse someone of **selling out**, you disapprove of the fact that they do something which used to be against their principles. [INFORMAL] *They felt I had sold out to the liberals.*

seller /'selə/ **sellers.** 1 N-COUNT A **seller** is a person or business that sells something. *...Kraft,* the largest seller of cheese in the United States. [2] N-COUNT If you describe a product as, for example, a big **seller**, you mean that large numbers of it are being sold. ● See also **best-seller**.

'**sell-off, sell-offs.** N-COUNT The **sell-off** of something, for example an industry that is owned by the state, is the act of selling it.

'**sell-out, sell-outs.** [1] N-COUNT If a play, sports event, or other entertainment is a **sell-out**, all the tickets for it are sold. [2] N-COUNT If you describe someone's behaviour as a **sell-out**, you disapprove of them doing something which used to be against their principles. *He denounced the summit agreement as a sell-out.*

selves /selvz/. **Selves** is the plural of **self**.

semblance /'sembləns/. N-SING If there is a **semblance of** a particular condition or quality, it appears to exist, though in fact it may not. [FORMAL] *A semblance of normality has been restored.*

semen /'siːmen/. N-UNCOUNT **Semen** is the liquid containing sperm that is produced by the male sex organs.

semester /sə'mestə/ **semesters.** N-COUNT In colleges and universities in the United States and some other countries, a **semester** is one of two periods into which the year is divided.

,**semi-'colon, semi-colons.** N-COUNT A **semi-colon** is the punctuation mark (;). → See Reference Page on Punctuation.

semiconductor /,semɪkən'dʌktə/ **semiconductors.** N-COUNT A **semiconductor** is a substance used in electronics whose ability to conduct electricity increases with greater heat.

semi-detached house

,**semi-de'tached.** ADJ A **semi-detached** house is a house that is joined to another house on one side by a shared wall.

'**semi-final, semi-finals.** N-COUNT A **semi-final** is one of the two matches or races in a competition that are held to decide who will compete in the final.

seminal /'semɪnəl/. ADJ **Seminal** is used to describe things such as books or events that have a great influence in a particular field. [FORMAL] *He wrote a seminal book on the subject.*

seminar /'semɪnɑː/ **seminars.** N-COUNT A **seminar** is a class at a university in which the teacher and a small group of students discuss a topic.

semitic /sɪ'mɪtɪk/. [1] ADJ **Semitic** is sometimes used to mean Jewish. [2] ADJ **Semitic** is used to describe a group of languages that includes Arabic and Hebrew, or the people who speak these languages.

★ **Senate** /'senɪt/.

✓ **Senate** can take the singular or plural form of the verb.

N-PROPER **The Senate** is the smaller and more important of the two councils in the government of some countries, such as the United States of America. ● See note at **government**.

★ **senator** /'senɪtə/ **senators.** N-COUNT A **senator** is a member of a law-making Senate. ● See note at **government**.

★ **send** /send/ **sends, sending, sent.** [1] VERB When you **send** someone something, you arrange for them to receive it, for example by post. *Myra sent me a note thanking me for dinner... I sent a copy to the minister for transport... He could work and send money back to his mother.* ♦ **sender, senders** N-COUNT *£200 will go to the sender of the first correct answer.* [2] VERB If you **send** someone somewhere, you arrange for them to go there or stay there. *Tom came up to see her, but she sent him away... The government sent troops to the region... I was sent for blood tests.* [3] VERB If you **send** a signal or message, you cause it to go to a place by means of radio waves. *The space probe Voyager sent back pictures of Neptune.* [4] VERB If something **sends** things or people in a particular direction, it causes them to move in that direction. *The explosion sent shrapnel flying through the sides of cars.* [5] VERB If something **sends** someone or something into a particular state, it causes them to be in that state. *Famine sent the country plunging into anarchy.*

▸ **send for.** [1] PHR-VERB If you **send for** someone, you send them a message asking them to come and see you. *I've sent for the doctor.* [2] PHR-VERB If you **send for** something, or if you **send off for** it, you write and ask for it to be sent to you.

▸ **send off.** [1] PHR-VERB If you **send off** a letter or parcel, you send it somewhere by post. [2] PHR-VERB If a footballer **is sent off**, the referee makes him or her leave the field during a game, as a punishment for seriously breaking the rules.

▸ **send off for.** See **send for** 2.

▸ **send out.** [1] PHR-VERB If you **send out** things such as leaflets or bills, you send them to a large number of people at the same time. *She had sent out well over four hundred invitations.* [2] PHR-VERB To **send out** a signal, sound, light, or heat means to produce it.

▸ **send out for.** PHR-VERB If you **send out for** food, you phone and ask for it to be delivered to you. *Let's send out for a pizza.*

senile /'siːnaɪl/. ADJ If old people become **senile**, they become confused and are unable to look after themselves. ♦ **senility** /sɪ'nɪlɪti/ N-UNCOUNT *Alzheimer's disease causes premature senility.*

a
b
c
d
e
f
g
h
i
j
k
l
m
n
o
p
q
r
s
t
u
v
w
x
y
z

★ **senior** /ˈsiːnjə/ **seniors.** ① ADJ BEFORE N The **senior** people in an organization have the highest and most important jobs in it. ...*senior officials in the Israeli government.* ② ADJ & N-COUNT If someone is **senior to** you, or if they are your **senior**, they have a more important job or position than you. ③ N-SING **Senior** is used when indicating how much older one person is than another. *She became involved with a married man many years her senior.*

,senior 'citizen, senior citizens. N-COUNT A **senior citizen** is a person who is old enough to receive an old-age pension.

sensation /senˈseɪʃən/ **sensations.** ① N-VAR **Sensation** is the ability to feel things physically. A **sensation** is a particular physical feeling. *She had lost all sensation in her left leg.* ...*a tingling sensation.* ② N-COUNT A **sensation** is the general feeling caused by a particular experience. *It's a funny sensation to know someone's talking about you.* ③ N-COUNT If a person or event is a **sensation**, they cause great excitement and interest. ...*the film that turned her into an overnight sensation.*

sensational /senˈseɪʃənəl/. ① ADJ A **sensational** event or situation is so remarkable that it causes great excitement and interest. *The world champions suffered a sensational defeat.* ◆ **sensationally** ADV *He sensationally announced that he is to quit.* ② ADJ You can describe something as **sensational** when you think that it is extremely good. ◆ **sensationally** ADV ...*sensationally good food.*

★ **sense** /sens/ **senses, sensing, sensed.** ① N-COUNT Your **senses** are the physical abilities of sight, smell, hearing, touch, and taste. ...*a keen sense of smell.* ② VERB If you **sense** something, you become aware of it, although it is not very obvious. *She probably sensed that I wasn't telling her the whole story.* ③ N-SING If you have a **sense of** guilt or shame, for example, you feel guilty or ashamed. ...*the crushing sense of failure that redundancy often brings.* ④ N-UNCOUNT **Sense** is the ability to make good judgements and to behave sensibly. *They sometimes have the sense to seek help.* ⑤ N-COUNT A **sense** of a word or expression is one of its possible meanings. ⑥ See also **common sense, sense of humour.**

PHRASES ● If something **makes sense**, or if you **make sense of** it, you understand it or find it sensible. *From an early age we try to make sense of the world... It makes sense to look after yourself.* ● If you say that someone **has come to** their **senses** or **has been brought to** their **senses**, you mean that they have stopped being foolish and are being sensible again.

senseless /ˈsensləs/. ① ADJ A **senseless** action seems to have no meaning or purpose. ...*senseless violence.* ② ADJ AFTER LINK-V If someone is **senseless**, they are unconscious. *I was beaten senseless.*

,sense of 'humour. N-UNCOUNT Someone's **sense of humour** is the fact that they find certain

things amusing. *We share the same sense of humour... He's got no sense of humour.*

sensibility /ˌsensɪˈbɪlɪti/ **sensibilities.** N-VAR Someone's **sensibility** is their ability to experience deep feelings. [FORMAL]

★ **sensible** /ˈsensɪbəl/. ADJ A **sensible** person is able to make good decisions and judgements based on reason. *It might be sensible to get a solicitor.* ◆ **sensibly** ADV *They have very sensibly adjusted their diet.*

> **USAGE** You do not use **sensible** to describe someone whose feelings or emotions are strongly affected by their experiences. The word you need is **sensitive.** ...*a highly sensitive artist.*

★ **sensitive** /ˈsensɪtɪv/. ① ADJ If you are **sensitive to** other people's problems and feelings, you understand and are aware of them. *The teacher must be sensitive to the child's needs... He was always so sensitive and caring.* ◆ **sensitively** ADV *The abuse of women needs to be treated seriously and sensitively.* ◆ **sensitivity** /ˌsensɪˈtɪvɪti/ N-UNCOUNT ...*sensitivity for each other's feelings.* ② ADJ If you are **sensitive about** something, it worries or upsets you. *Young people are very sensitive about their appearance.* ◆ **sensitivity, sensitivities** N-VAR *Do not offend the sensitivities of religious groups.* ③ ADJ A **sensitive** subject or issue needs to be dealt with carefully because it is likely to cause disagreement or make people upset. *Employment is a very sensitive issue.* ④ ADJ Something that is **sensitive to** a physical force or substance can be affected by it. ...*a chemical which is sensitive to light.* ◆ **sensitivity** N-UNCOUNT ...*skin lacking all sensitivity to touch.* ⑤ ADJ A **sensitive** piece of scientific equipment is capable of measuring or recording very small changes. ...*an extremely sensitive microscope.*

sensor /ˈsensə/ **sensors.** N-COUNT A **sensor** is an instrument which reacts to certain physical conditions such as heat or light.

sensory /ˈsensəri/. ADJ BEFORE N **Sensory** means relating to the physical senses. ...*sensory awareness.*

sensual /ˈsenʃuəl/. ① ADJ A **sensual** person has a great liking for physical pleasures, especially sexual pleasures. ◆ **sensuality** /ˌsenʃuˈælɪti/ N-UNCOUNT *Her blonde curls gave her sensuality and youth.* ② ADJ Something that is **sensual** gives pleasure to your physical senses rather than to your mind. ...*sensual dance rhythms.* ◆ **sensuality** N-UNCOUNT *These perfumes have warmth and sensuality.*

sensuous /ˈsenʃuəs/. ① ADJ **Sensuous** things give pleasure to the mind or body through the senses. ...*sensuous, atmospheric camerawork.* ◆ **sensuously** ADV ...*sensuously shaped opaque glass vases.* ② ADJ **Sensuous** means showing or suggesting a great liking for sexual pleasure.

◆ **sensuously**ADV ...*a woman with a sensuously curved torso.*

sent/sent/. **Sent** is the past tense and past participle of **send**.

⭐ **sentence**/'sentəns/ **sentences, sentencing, sentenced.** [1] N-COUNT A **sentence** is a group of words which, when they are written down, begin with a capital letter and end with a full stop, question mark, or exclamation mark. Most sentences contain a subject and a verb. [2] N-VAR In a law court, a **sentence** is the punishment that a person receives after they have been found guilty of a crime. *He had served a prison sentence for bank robbery.* [3] VERB & PHRASE When judges **sentence** someone, or when they **pass sentence on** someone, they state in court what the person's punishment will be. *A military court sentenced him to death.*

sentiment/'sentɪmənt/ **sentiments.** [1] N-VAR A **sentiment** is an attitude, feeling, or opinion. *...nationalist sentiments.* [2] N-UNCOUNT **Sentiment** is an emotion such as tenderness, affection, or sadness, which influences a person's behaviour. *Laura kept the letter out of sentiment.*

sentimental/ˌsentɪ'mentəl/. [1] ADJ A **sentimental** person or thing feels or makes you feel emotions such as tenderness, affection, or sadness, sometimes in a way that is exaggerated or foolish. *...sentimental love songs... I'm trying not to be sentimental about the past.* ◆ **sentimentality**N-UNCOUNT *In this book there is no sentimentality.* ◆ **sentimentally**ADV *We look back sentimentally to a 'golden era'.* [2] ADJ **Sentimental** means relating to a person's emotions. *...objects of sentimental value.*

sentry/'sentri/ **sentries.** N-COUNT A **sentry** is a soldier who guards a camp or a building.

⭐ **separate, separates, separating, separated.** [1] ADJ /'sepərət/ If one thing is **separate from** another, the two things are apart and are not connected. *Business bank accounts were kept separate from personal ones... I've always kept my private and professional life separate... The word 'quarter' has two completely separate meanings.* ◆ **separately** ADV *Each case is dealt with separately.* [2] PHRASE When two or more people who have been together for some time **go** their **separate ways**, they go to different places or end their relationship. [3] VERB /'sepəreɪt/ If you **separate** people or things that are together, or if they **separate**, they move apart. *Fluff the rice with a fork to separate the grains... They separated. Stephen returned to the square.* ◆ **separation, separations** N-VAR *Mrs Holland is trying to cope with separation from her family.* [4] VERB & PHR-VERB If you **separate** one idea or fact **from** another, or if you **separate** it **out**, you consider individually and see or show that they are distinct and different things. *It is difficult to separate the two aims... It is virtually impossible to separate out biological from early social influences.* ◆ **separation**N-VAR *...the separation of church and state.* [5] VERB A quality or factor that

separates one thing **from** another is the reason why the two things are different from each other. *What separates man from machine is the ability to think.* [6] VERB If an object, distance, or period of time **separates** two people or things, it exists between them. *...the white-railed fence that separated the yard from the paddock... Just four miles separate the two communities.* [7] VERB & PHR-VERB If you **separate** a group of people or things, or if you **separate** them **up**, you divide them into smaller groups or elements. *The police had separated the men into three groups... If prepared many hours ahead, the mixture may separate out.* ◆ **separation**N-VAR *...the Northern League, which advocates the separation of Italy into three republics.* [8] VERB If a couple who are married or living together **separate**, they decide to live apart. ◆ **separated**ADJ AFTER LINK-V *Her parents are separated.* ◆ **separation**N-VAR *They agreed to a trial separation.* [9] N-PLURAL /'sepərəts/ **Separates** are clothes such as skirts, trousers, and shirts which cover just the top or bottom half of your body.
▸ **separate out.** See **separate** 4, 7.

separatist/'sepərətɪst/ **separatists.** N-COUNT **Separatists** are people of an ethnic or cultural group within a country who want to establish their own separate government. ◆ **separatism** N-UNCOUNT *...the issue of Sikh separatism.*

⭐ **September**/sep'tembə/. N-UNCOUNT **September** is the ninth month of the year. → See Reference Page on Times and Dates.

sequel/'si:kwəl/ **sequels.** [1] N-COUNT The **sequel to** a book or film is another book or film which continues the story. [2] N-COUNT The **sequel to** an event is something that happened after it or because of it. *The clash was a sequel to yesterday's nationwide strike.*

sequence/'si:kwəns/ **sequences.** [1] N-COUNT A **sequence** of things is a number of them that come one after another in a particular order. *...the sequence of events which led to the murder.* [2] N-COUNT A particular **sequence** is a particular order in which things happen or are arranged. *...the colour sequence yellow, orange, purple, blue, green.* [3] N-COUNT A film **sequence** is a short part of a film. *...the film's opening sequence.*

sequin/'si:kwɪn/ **sequins.** N-COUNT **Sequins** are small, shiny discs that are sewn on clothes to decorate them.

serene/sɪ'ri:n/. ADJ **Serene** means calm and quiet. ◆ **serenely**ADV *She carried on serenely sipping her gin and tonic.* ◆ **serenity**/sɪ'renɪti/ N-UNCOUNT *...the serenity of the mountains.*

sergeant/'sɑːdʒənt/ **sergeants.** [1] N-VOC & N-TITLE A **sergeant** is an officer of middle rank in the army or air force. [2] N-VOC & N-TITLE A **sergeant** is an officer in the police force.

'**sergeant major, sergeant majors.** N-VOC & N-TITLE A **sergeant major** is an army officer of high rank.

serial/'sɪəriəl/ **serials.** [1] N-COUNT A **serial** is a story which is broadcast or published in a

a
b
c
d
e
f
g
h
i
j
k
l
m
n
o
p
q
r
s
t
u
v
w
x
y
z

number of parts over a period of time. ...*a popular radio serial.* [2] ADJ BEFORE N **Serial** killings or attacks are a series of killings or attacks committed by the same person. This person is known as a **serial** killer or attacker. ...*a serial rapist.*

⭐ **series** /'sɪəriz/.

✓ **Series** is both the singular and the plural form.

[1] N-COUNT A **series of** things or events is a number of them that come one after the other. ...*a series of explosions.* [2] N-COUNT A radio or television **series** is a set of related programmes with the same title. ...*a new drama series called Under The Hammer.*

⭐ **serious** /'sɪəriəs/. [1] ADJ **Serious** problems or situations are very bad and cause people to be worried or afraid. *Crime is an increasingly serious problem in Russian society. ...a serious accident.* ♦ **seriously** ADV *His wife was seriously injured in the attack.* ♦ **seriousness** N-UNCOUNT ...*the seriousness of the crisis.* [2] ADJ **Serious** matters are important and deserve careful thought. *This latest incident has raised serious questions about the security precautions taken for such events... It was a question which deserved serious consideration.* ♦ **seriously** ADV *The management will have to think seriously about their positions.* [3] ADJ If you are **serious about** something, you are sincere about it, and not joking. *You really are serious about this, aren't you?* ♦ **seriously** ADV *I seriously hope it will never come to that.* ♦ **seriousness** N-UNCOUNT *In all seriousness, there is nothing else I can do.* [4] ADJ **Serious** people are thoughtful, quiet, and do not laugh very often. ♦ **seriously** ADV *They spoke to me very seriously but politely.*

⭐ **seriously** /'sɪəriəsli/. [1] ADV You say **seriously** to indicate that you really mean what you say, or to ask someone else if they really mean what they have said. *Seriously, I shall miss you... 'OK, eat it.'—'Seriously?'* [2] PHRASE If you **take** someone or something **seriously**, you believe that they are important and deserve attention. *The phrase was not meant to be taken seriously.*

sermon /'sɜːmən/ **sermons.** N-COUNT A **sermon** is a talk on a religious or moral subject given during a church service.

serpent /'sɜːpənt/ **serpents.** N-COUNT A **serpent** is a snake. [LITERARY]

serum /'sɪərəm/ **serums.** N-VAR A **serum** is a liquid that is injected into someone's blood to protect them against a poison or disease.

⭐ **servant** /'sɜːvənt/ **servants.** N-COUNT A **servant** is someone who is employed to work in another person's house, for example to cook or clean. ● See also **civil servant**.

⭐ **serve** /sɜːv/ **serves, serving, served.** [1] VERB If you **serve** your country, an organization, or a person, you do useful work for them. *They served the US government loyally for 30 years.* [2] VERB If something **serves as** a particular thing or **serves**

a particular purpose, that is its use or function. *The small building served as a school... This serves to make attackers think twice before attacking... I really do not think that an inquiry would serve any useful purpose.* [3] VERB If something **serves** people or an area, it provides them with something that they need. *A typical NHS hospital serves about 250,000 people. ...small businesses which serve the community.* [4] VERB If you **serve** people or if you **serve** food and drink, you give people food and drink. *Our waiter served us quickly... We used to serve dinner to the airmen.* [5] VERB Someone who **serves** customers in a shop or a bar helps them and provides them with what they want to buy. *They wouldn't serve me in any pubs because I looked too young.* [6] VERB If you **serve** a prison sentence, you spend a period of time in jail. *He is serving a five-year sentence for robbery.* [7] VERB & N-COUNT When you **serve** in a game like tennis, you start play by hitting the ball. A **serve** is the act of doing this. *He threw the ball up to serve... His second serve clipped the net.* [8] PHRASE If you say it **serves** someone **right** when something unpleasant happens to them, you mean that it is their own fault and you have no sympathy for them. *Serves her right for being so stubborn.* [9] See also **serving**.

▸**serve up.** PHR-VERB If you **serve up** food, you give it to people. *When the dish was finally finished, he served it up on delicate white plates.*

server /'sɜːvə/ **servers.** N-COUNT A **server** is part of a computer network which does a particular task, for example storing or processing information, for all or part of the network. [COMPUTING]

⭐ **service** /'sɜːvɪs/ **services, servicing, serviced.**

✓ In meaning 10, **services** is both the singular and the plural form.

[1] N-COUNT A **service** is an organization or system that provides something for the public. ...*the social services. ...the postal service. ...service industries, such as banks and airlines.* [2] N-COUNT A **service** is a job that an organization or business can do for you. ...*a one hour dry-cleaning service.* [3] N-COUNT **The services** are the army, navy, and air force. [4] N-UNCOUNT **Service** is the state or activity of working for a particular person or organization. *Pat is leaving the company after 12 years service.* [5] N-UNCOUNT The level or standard of **service** provided by an organization or company is the amount or quality of the work it can do for you. *How do you think we could improve customer service?* [6] N-UNCOUNT When you receive **service** in a restaurant, hotel, or shop, an employee asks you what you want or gives you what you have ordered. *Restaurants usually charge between 10 and 12.5 per cent for service.* [7] PHRASE If a machine or vehicle is **in service**, it is being used or is able to be used. If it is **out of service**, it cannot be used. [8] VERB & N-COUNT If you **service** a machine or vehicle, or if it has a **service**, it is examined, adjusted, and cleaned so that it will keep working efficiently and safely. *Make sure that all gas fires are serviced*

annually... *The car is due for a service.* [9] N-COUNT
A **service** is a religious ceremony. *...the chapel
where the wedding service was to have been held.*
[10] N-COUNT A **services** is a place on a motorway
where there is a petrol station, restaurant, shop,
and toilets. [BRITISH] *...a motorway services.* [11] See
also **Civil Service**.

serviceman /'sɜːvɪsmən/ **servicemen.** N-COUNT A
serviceman is a man who is in the army, navy, or
air force.

'**service pro,vider** **service providers.** N-COUNT A
service provider is a company that provides a
service, especially an Internet service.

serving /'sɜːvɪŋ/ **servings.** N-COUNT A **serving** is
an amount of food given to one person at a meal.
Each serving contains 240 calories.

⭐ **session** /'seʃən/ **sessions.** [1] N-COUNT A **session** is
a meeting or series of meetings of a court,
parliament, or other official group. *...an
emergency session of the UN Security Council.
...the start of the next parliamentary session in
November.* [2] N-COUNT A **session** of a particular
activity is a period of that activity. *...a photo
session.*

set 1 noun uses

⭐ **set** /set/ **sets.** [1] N-COUNT A **set** of things is a
number of things that are thought of as a group.
They had the spare set of keys. ...a chess set.
[2] N-COUNT In tennis, a **set** is one of the groups of
six or more games that form part of a match.
[3] N-COUNT The **set** for a play or film scene is the
scenery and furniture that is used on the stage or
in the studio. *...stars who behave badly on set.*
[4] N-COUNT A television **set** is a television.

set 2 verb and adjective uses

⭐ **set** /set/ **sets, setting, set.** [1] VERB If you **set**
something somewhere, you put it there,
especially in a careful or deliberate way. *He set
the glass on the counter.* [2] ADJ AFTER LINK-V If
something is **set** in a particular place or position,
it is in that place or position. *The castle is set in 25
acres of beautiful grounds.* [3] ADJ AFTER LINK-V If
something is **set** into a surface, it is fixed there
and does not stick out. *...a gate set in a high wall.*
[4] VERB You can use **set** to say that a person or
thing causes something to be in a particular
condition or situation. For example, if something
sets someone free, it causes them to be free. *A
phrase from the conference floor set my mind
wandering... Dozens of people have been injured
and many vehicles set on fire.* [5] VERB When you
set a clock or control, you adjust it to a particular
point or level. *Set the volume as high as possible.*
[6] VERB If you **set** a date, price, goal, or level, you
decide what it will be. *He has not yet set a date for
the wedding.* [7] VERB To **set** an examination or a
question paper means to decide what questions
will be asked in it. [8] VERB If you **set** something
such as a record, an example, or a precedent, you
create it for people to copy or to try to achieve. *If
you are smoking in front of the children then you
are setting them a bad example.* [9] VERB If

someone **sets** you a task or a target, you have to
do that task or achieve that target. *The secret to
happiness is to keep setting yourself new
challenges.* [10] ADJ AFTER LINK-V If a play, film, or
story is **set** in a particular place or period of time,
the events in it happen in that place or period.
[11] PHRASE Something that **sets the scene for** a
particular event, or **sets the stage for** a particular
event, creates the conditions in which the event
is likely to happen. *That assassination set the
stage for the 1986 revolution.* [12] ADJ You use **set**
to describe something which is fixed and cannot
be changed. *...a set price. ...a set menu.* [13] ADJ
AFTER LINK-V If you are **set to** do something, you
are ready to do it or are likely to do it. If
something is **set to** happen, it is about to happen
or likely to happen. *...a book which is set to
become a classic.* [14] ADJ AFTER LINK-V If you are
set on something, you are strongly determined
to do or have it. *She was set on going to an all-
girls school.* [15] VERB When something such as
jelly, glue, or cement **sets**, it becomes firm or
hard. [16] VERB When the sun **sets**, it goes below
the horizon. [17] See also **setting**. • to **set eyes
on** something: see **eye**. • to **set fire to**
something: see **fire**. • to **set foot** somewhere:
see **foot**. • to **set sail**: see **sail**.

▶ **set apart.** PHR-VERB If a characteristic **sets** you
apart from other people, it makes you different
from them in a noticeable way. *Even at that stage
his natural ability set him apart.*

▶ **set aside.** [1] PHR-VERB If you **set** something
aside for a special use or purpose, you keep it
available for that use or purpose. *Try to set aside
time each day to relax.* [2] PHR-VERB If you **set**
aside a belief, principle, or feeling, you decide
that you will not be influenced by it. *He urged the
participants to set aside minor differences.*

▶ **set back.** [1] PHR-VERB If something **sets** you
back or **sets back** a project or scheme, it causes
a delay. [2] PHR-VERB If something **sets** you **back** a
certain amount of money, it costs you that much
money. [INFORMAL] [3] See also **setback**.

▶ **set down.** PHR-VERB If a committee or
organization **sets down** rules or guidelines for
doing something, they decide what they should
be and officially record them. *...rules set down by
the Personal Investment Authority.*

▶ **set in.** PHR-VERB If something unpleasant **sets
in**, it begins and seems likely to continue or
develop. *Panic was setting in.*

▶ **set off.** [1] PHR-VERB When you **set off**, you
start a journey. *He set off for the station.*
[2] PHR-VERB If something **sets off** something
such as an alarm or a bomb, it activates it so that
the alarm rings or the bomb explodes.

▶ **set out.** [1] PHR-VERB When you **set out**, you
start a journey. *I set out for the cottage.*
[2] PHR-VERB If you **set out to** do something, you
start trying to do it. *We set out to find the truth
behind the mystery.* [3] PHR-VERB If you **set** things
out, you arrange or display them. *She set out the
cups and saucers.* [4] PHR-VERB If you **set out** facts
or opinions, you explain them in writing or

speech in a clear, organized way. *The agreement sets out how the two countries will co-operate.*

▶ **set up.** [1] PHR-VERB If you **set** something **up**, you make the preparations that are necessary for it to start. *She wants to set up children's ski schools.* ◆ **setting up** N-UNCOUNT *The government announced the setting up of a special fund.* [2] PHR-VERB If you **set up** a temporary structure, you place it or build it somewhere. *Brian set up a large, white tent on the lawn.* [3] PHR-VERB If you **set up** somewhere or **set yourself up** somewhere, you establish yourself in a new business or area. *The scheme offers incentives to firms setting up in lower Manhattan.* [4] See also **set-up**.

setback /'setbæk/ **setbacks.** N-COUNT A **setback** is an event that delays your progress or reverses some of the progress that you have made. *He has suffered a serious setback in his political career.*

settee /se'tiː/ **settees.** N-COUNT A **settee** is a long comfortable seat with a back and arms, for two or three people.

setting /'setɪŋ/ **settings.** [1] N-COUNT The **setting** for something is the particular place or the type of surroundings in which it is located or where it happens. *The house is in a lovely setting in the Malvern hills.* [2] N-COUNT A **setting** is one of the positions to which the controls of a device such as a cooker or heater can be adjusted. *You can boil the fish fillets on a high setting.*

★ **settle** /'setəl/ **settles, settling, settled.** [1] VERB If two people **settle** an argument or problem, or if someone or something **settles** it, they solve it by making a decision about who is right or about what to do. *Both sides are looking for ways to settle their differences.* [2] VERB If you **settle** a bill or debt, you pay the amount that you owe. [3] VERB If something **is settled**, it has all been decided and arranged. *That's settled then. We'll exchange addresses tonight.* [4] VERB When people **settle** in a place, they start living there permanently. *He visited Paris and eventually settled there.* [5] VERB If you **settle yourself** somewhere or **settle** somewhere, you sit down or make yourself comfortable. *He settled into a chair.* [6] VERB If something **settles**, it sinks slowly and becomes still. *A black dust settled on the walls.* [7] **when the dust settles**: see **dust**. ● **to settle a score**: see **score**.

▶ **settle down.** [1] PHR-VERB When someone **settles down**, they start living a quiet life in one place, especially when they get married or buy a house. [2] PHR-VERB If a situation or a person that has been going through a lot of problems or changes **settles down**, they become calm. *We saw the therapist four times, and the children have now settled down.* [3] PHR-VERB If you **settle down to** do something, or if you **settle down to** something, you prepare to do it and concentrate on it. *Daniel settled down to work.*

▶ **settle for.** PHR-VERB If you **settle for** something, you choose or accept it, especially when it is not what you really want but there is

nothing else available. *England will have to settle for third or fourth place.*

▶ **settle into.** PHR-VERB If you **settle into** a new place, job, or routine, or **settle in**, you become used to it. *I'm sure they will settle in very well.*

▶ **settle on.** PHR-VERB If you **settle on** a particular thing, you choose it after considering other possible choices.

▶ **settle up.** PHR-VERB When you **settle up**, you pay a bill or a debt.

settled /'setəld/. [1] ADJ A **settled** situation or system stays the same all the time. *...a period of settled weather.* [2] ADJ AFTER LINK-V If you feel **settled**, you have been living or working in a place long enough to feel comfortable.

★ **settlement** /'setəlmənt/ **settlements.** [1] N-COUNT A **settlement** is an official agreement between two sides who were involved in a conflict. *...a peace settlement. ...pay settlements.* [2] N-COUNT A **settlement** is a place where people have come to live and have built homes. *...the oldest settlement in New Brunswick.*

settler /'setələ/ **settlers.** N-COUNT **Settlers** are people who go to live in a new country. *...the early settlers in North America.*

,**set-top 'box,** set-top boxes. N-COUNT A **set-top box** is a piece of equipment that rests on top of your television and receives digital television signals.

★ '**set-up,** set-ups. N-COUNT A particular **set-up** is a particular system or way of organizing something. [INFORMAL] *It was a bit of a weird family set-up.*

★ **seven** /'sevən/ **sevens.** NUM **Seven** is the number 7.

★ **seventeen** /,sevən'tiːn/. NUM **Seventeen** is the number 17.

★ **seventeenth** /,sevən'tiːnθ/. ORD The **seventeenth** item in a series is the one that you count as number seventeen.

★ **seventh** /'sevənθ/ **sevenths.** [1] ORD The **seventh** item in a series is the one that you count as number seven. [2] N-COUNT A **seventh** is one of seven equal parts of something.

★ **seventieth** /'sevəntiəθ/. ORD The **seventieth** item in a series is the one that you count as number seventy.

★ **seventy** /'sevənti/ **seventies.** NUM **Seventy** is the number 70. For examples of how numbers such as seventy and eighty are used see **eighty**.

sever /'sevə/ **severs, severing, severed.** [1] VERB To **sever** something means to cut right through it or cut it off. *He was hit by a train and his left arm was almost severed. ...a severed fuel line.* [2] VERB If you **sever** a relationship or connection with someone, you end it suddenly and completely. *She severed her ties with England.*

★ **several** /'sevrəl/. QUANT **Several** is used to refer to a number of people or things that is not large but is greater than two. *Several hundred students gathered on campus... Several of my friends are doctors.*

⭐ **severe** /sɪˈvɪə/ **severer, severest.** [1] ADJ You use **severe** to emphasize how bad or serious something is. *This bomb would have caused severe damage. ...a severe shortage of drinking water.*
♦ **severely** ADV *He was severely injured in a fire.*
♦ **severity** /sɪˈverɪti/ N-UNCOUNT *Several drugs are used to lessen the severity of the symptoms.* [2] ADJ **Severe** punishments or actions are very extreme. *My mother launched into a severe reprimand.*
♦ **severely** ADV *...a campaign to try to change the law to punish dangerous drivers more severely.*
♦ **severity** N-UNCOUNT *The Bishop said he was sickened by the severity of the sentence.*

sew /səʊ/ **sews, sewing, sewed, sewn.** VERB When you **sew**, you use a needle and thread to make or mend something such as clothes. *Anyone can sew on a button... She taught her daughter to sew.*
♦ **sewing** N-UNCOUNT *I was very good at sewing.*

sewage /ˈsuːɪdʒ/. N-UNCOUNT **Sewage** is waste matter such as faeces or dirty water from homes and factories, which flows away through sewers.

sewer /ˈsuːə/ **sewers.** N-COUNT A **sewer** is a large underground channel that carries waste matter and rain water away.

sewing /ˈsəʊɪŋ/. N-UNCOUNT **Sewing** is clothes or other things that are being sewn. *She took out her sewing.* ● See also **sew.**

sewn /səʊn/. **Sewn** is the past participle of **sew.**

⭐ **sex** /seks/ **sexes, sexing, sexed.** [1] N-COUNT The **sexes** are the two groups, male and female, into which people and animals are divided. [2] N-COUNT The **sex** of a person or animal is their characteristic of being either male or female. *We don't plan to find out the sex of the child before its birth. ...victims of sex discrimination.* [3] N-UNCOUNT **Sex** is the physical activity by which people can produce children. If two people **have sex**, they perform the physical act of sex.
►**sex up.** PHR-VERB To **sex** something **up** means to make it more interesting and exciting. [INFORMAL] *They wanted to modernise the programme, sex it up.*

sexist /ˈseksɪst/ **sexists.** ADJ & N-COUNT If you describe someone as **sexist** or as a **sexist**, you mean that they show prejudice and discrimination against the members of one sex, usually women. *Old-fashioned sexist attitudes are still common.* ♦ **sexism** N-UNCOUNT *...their battle against sexism.*

⭐ **sexual** /ˈsekʃʊəl/. [1] ADJ **Sexual** feelings or activities are connected with the act of sex or with desire for sex. *This was the first sexual relationship I had.* ♦ **sexually** ADV *...sexually transmitted diseases.* [2] ADJ **Sexual** means relating to the differences between men and women. *...sexual discrimination.* [3] ADJ **Sexual** means relating to the biological process by which people and animals produce young. *...sexual maturity.* ♦ **sexually** ADV *...organisms which reproduce sexually.*

sexual ˈintercourse. N-UNCOUNT **Sexual intercourse** is the physical act of sex between two people. [FORMAL]

sexuality /ˌsekʃʊˈælɪti/. [1] N-UNCOUNT A person's **sexuality** is their sexual feelings. *...the growing discussion of women's sexuality.* [2] N-UNCOUNT You can refer to a person's **sexuality** when you are talking about whether they are heterosexual, homosexual, or bisexual.

sexy /ˈseksi/ **sexier, sexiest.** ADJ You can describe people and things as **sexy** if you think they are sexually exciting or sexually attractive.

sh /ʃ/. CONVENTION You can say **'Sh!'** to tell someone to be quiet. *Sh! I have only a moment to talk, and you must listen closely!*

shabby /ˈʃæbi/ **shabbier, shabbiest.** [1] ADJ **Shabby** things or places look old and in bad condition. [2] ADJ A **shabby** person is wearing old, worn clothes.

shack /ʃæk/ **shacks.** N-COUNT A **shack** is a small hut built from bits of wood or metal.

⭐ **shade** /ʃeɪd/ **shades, shading, shaded.** [1] N-UNCOUNT **Shade** is a cool area of darkness where the sun does not reach. *These plants need some shade, humidity and fresh air.* [2] VERB If a place **is shaded** by something, that thing prevents light from falling on it. *Most plants prefer to be lightly shaded from direct sunlight. ...a shaded spot.* [3] N-UNCOUNT **Shade** is darkness or shadows as they are shown in a picture. *...Rembrandt's skilful use of light and shade.* [4] N-COUNT The **shades of** a particular colour are its different forms. *The flowers were a lovely shade of pink.* [5] N-COUNT The **shades of** something abstract are its many, slightly different forms. *...newspapers of every shade of opinion.* [6] N-COUNT A **shade** is a decorative covering that is fitted round or over an electric light bulb.

⭐ **shadow** /ˈʃædəʊ/ **shadows, shadowing shadowed.** [1] N-COUNT A **shadow** is a dark shape on a surface that is made when something stands between a light and the surface. *An oak tree cast its shadow over a tiny round pool.* [2] N-UNCOUNT **Shadow** is darkness caused by light not reaching a place. *Most of the lake was in shadow.* [3] VERB If someone **shadows** you, they follow you very closely wherever you go. *I noticed a police car shadowing us.* [4] ADJ BEFORE N In Britain, **the Shadow Cabinet** consists of the leaders of the main opposition party.

shadowy /ˈʃædəʊi/. [1] ADJ A **shadowy** place is dark and full of shadows. [2] ADJ **Shadowy** activities or people are mysterious and secretive. *...the shadowy world of spies.*

shady /ˈʃeɪdi/ **shadier, shadiest.** [1] ADJ A **shady** place is pleasant because it is sheltered from bright sunlight. [2] ADJ **Shady** activities or people seem to be dishonest or illegal. *John was a bit of a shady character.*

shaft /ʃɑːft, ʃæft/ **shafts.** [1] N-COUNT A **shaft** is a long narrow passage made so that people or things can travel up and down it. *...a disused mine shaft.* [2] N-COUNT A **shaft** in a machine is a rod that turns round and round to transfer

a
b
c
d
e
f
g
h
i
j
k
l
m
n
o
p
q
r
s
t
u
v
w
x
y
z

movement in the machine. ...*the drive shaft.*
3 N-COUNT A **shaft** of light is a beam of light.

shaggy /'ʃægi/ **shaggier, shaggiest.** ADJ **Shaggy** hair or fur is long and untidy. ...*a dark shaggy beard.*

⭐ **shake** /ʃeɪk/ **shakes, shaking, shook, shaken** /'ʃeɪkən/.
1 VERB & N-COUNT If you **shake** someone or something, or if you give them a **shake**, you move them quickly backwards and forwards or up and down. *Shake the rugs well... As soon as he got inside, the dog shook himself... She gave me a little shake.* **2** VERB If something **shakes**, or if a force **shakes** it, it moves from side to side or up and down with quick small movements. ...*an explosion that shook buildings several kilometers away.* **3** VERB If an event or a piece of news **shakes** you, it makes you feel shocked or upset. *Well it shook me quite a bit, but I was feeling emotional.*
PHRASES ● If you **shake** someone**'s hand**, you hold their right hand in your own when you are meeting them, saying goodbye, congratulating them, or showing friendship. ● If you **shake** your **head**, you move it from side to side in order to say 'no'.
▸**shake off.** PHR-VERB If you **shake off** someone or something that you do not want, you manage to get away from them or get rid of them.

'shake-up (or **shakeup**) **shake-ups.** N-COUNT A **shake-up** is a major set of changes in an organization or system. ...*a radical shake-up of the welfare state.*

shaky /'ʃeɪki/ **shakier, shakiest.** **1** ADJ If your body or your voice is **shaky**, you cannot control it properly and it trembles, for example because you are ill or nervous. *Even small operations can leave you feeling a bit shaky.* ◆ **shakily** ADV *'I'm okay,' she said shakily.* **2** ADJ If you describe a situation as **shaky**, you mean that it is weak and unstable, and seems likely to end soon. *The Prime Minister's political position is becoming increasingly shaky.*

⭐ **shall** /ʃəl, STRONG ʃæl/.
☑ **Shall** is a modal verb. It is used with the base form of a verb.

1 MODAL You use **shall** with 'I' and 'we' in questions in order to make offers or suggestions, or to ask for advice. *Shall I get the keys?... Let's have a nice little stroll, shall we?... What shall I do?* **2** MODAL You use **shall**, usually with 'I' and 'we', when you are referring to something that you intend to do, or when you are referring to something that you are sure will happen to you in the future. *We shall be landing in Paris in sixteen minutes... I shall miss him terribly.* **3** MODAL If you say that something **shall** happen, you are saying that it must happen, usually because of a rule or law. [FORMAL] *The president shall hold office for five years.*

shallow /'ʃæləʊ/ **shallower, shallowest,.** **1** ADJ A **shallow** hole, container, or layer of water measures only a short distance from the top to

the bottom. *The water is quite shallow.* **2** ADJ If you describe a person, piece of work, or idea as **shallow**, you disapprove of them because they lack any serious or careful thought. **3** ADJ If your breathing is **shallow**, you take only a small amount of air into your lungs at each breath.

shallows /'ʃæləʊz/ N-PLURAL The **shallows** are the shallow part of an area of water.

sham /ʃæm/ **shams.** N-COUNT If you describe something as a **sham**, you disapprove of it because it is not what it seems to be. *The party's promises were exposed as a hollow sham.*

shambles /'ʃæmbəlz/. N-SING If a place, event, or situation is **a shambles**, everything is in disorder. *The ship's interior was an utter shambles.*

⭐ **shame** /ʃeɪm/ **shames, shaming, shamed.**
1 N-UNCOUNT **Shame** is an uncomfortable feeling that you have when you know that you have done something wrong or embarrassing, or when someone close to you has. *She felt a deep sense of shame... I was, to my shame, a coward.* **2** N-UNCOUNT If someone brings **shame** on you, they make other people lose their respect for you. *I don't want to bring shame on the family name.* **3** VERB If something **shames** you, it causes you to feel shame. *Her son's affair had humiliated and shamed her.* **4** VERB If you **shame** someone **into** doing something, you force them to do it by making them feel ashamed not to. **5** N-SING If you say that something is **a shame**, you are expressing your regret about it and indicating that you wish it had happened differently. *What a shame the weather was so poor... It would seem a shame to waste this opportunity.*

shameful /'ʃeɪmfʊl/. ADJ You can describe someone's actions or attitude as **shameful** when they act or think in a way that you find unacceptable, and for which you think they should feel ashamed. ...*the most shameful episode in US naval history.* ◆ **shamefully** ADV *They have been shamefully neglected.*

shameless /'ʃeɪmləs/. ADJ If you describe someone or their behaviour as **shameless**, you mean that their behaviour is extremely bad and they ought to be ashamed of it. ...*a shameless attempt to get votes under false pretenses.* ◆ **shamelessly** ADV *He admitted to lying to women and manipulating them shamelessly.*

shampoo /ʃæm'puː/ **shampoos, shampooing, shampooed.** **1** N-VAR **Shampoo** is a liquid that you use for washing your hair. **2** VERB When you **shampoo** your hair, you wash it using shampoo.

shan't /ʃɑːnt, ʃænt/. **Shan't** is the usual spoken form of 'shall not'.

⭐ **shape** /ʃeɪp/ **shapes, shaping, shaped.** **1** N-VAR The **shape of** an object, a person, or an area is the form or pattern of its outline. ...*a keyring in the shape of a fish... The room was square in shape.* **2** N-COUNT A **shape** is something which has a definite form, for example a circle or triangle. → See pictures on page 829. ...*a kidney shape.*

3 VERB If you **shape** an object, you cause it to have a particular shape. *Cut the dough in half and shape each half into a loaf.* **4** N-SING The **shape of** something such as a plan or organization is its structure and size. *...the future shape of Western Europe.* **5** VERB To **shape** a situation or an activity means to strongly influence the way it develops. *Like it or not, our families shape our lives and make us what we are.* **6** PHRASE If someone or something is **in** good **shape**, they are healthy and fit. If they are **out of shape**, they are unhealthy and unfit.

▸ **shape up.** PHR-VERB The way that someone or something **is shaping up** is the way that they are developing. *This is shaping up to be the closest governor's race in recent memory.*

⭐ **shaped** /ʃeɪpt/. ADJ AFTER LINK-V Something that is **shaped** in a particular way has the shape indicated. *...a helmet shaped like a wedge of cheese. ...large, heart-shaped leaves.*

⭐ **share** /ʃeə/ **shares, sharing, shared.** **1** VERB If you **share** something **with** another person, you both have it, use it, do it, or experience it. *The village tribe is friendly and they share their water supply with you... We share similar opinions about music. ...the huge house that he shared with his sisters... Two Americans will share this year's Nobel Prize for Medicine... Yes, I want to share my life with you.* **2** N-COUNT If you have or do your **share** of something, you have or do the amount that is reasonable or fair. *Women must receive their fair share of training.* **3** N-COUNT The **shares** of a company are the equal parts into which its ownership is divided. People can buy shares in a company as an investment.

▸ **share out.** PHR-VERB If you **share** something **out**, you give each person in a group an equal or fair part of it. *...a formula for sharing out power among the various clans.*

⭐ **shareholder** /ʃeəhəʊldə/ **shareholders.** N-COUNT In British English, a **shareholder** is a person who owns shares in a company. The usual American word is **stockholder**.

shark /ʃɑːk/ **sharks.** N-COUNT **Sharks** are very large fish with sharp teeth.

⭐ **sharp** /ʃɑːp/ **sharper, sharpest.** **1** ADJ A **sharp** point or edge is very small or thin and can cut through things very easily. *The other end of the twig is sharpened into a sharp point.* **2** ADJ & ADV A **sharp** bend or turn is one that changes direction suddenly. *...a fairly sharp bend that swept downhill to the left... Do not cross the bridge but turn sharp left.* ♦ **sharply** ADV *Downstream the canyon bent sharply to the north.* **3** ADJ If you describe someone as **sharp**, you are praising them because they are quick to notice or understand things or to react to them. *He is very sharp, a quick thinker.* ♦ **sharpness** N-UNCOUNT *I liked their enthusiasm and sharpness of mind.* **4** ADJ If someone says something in a **sharp** way, they say it suddenly and rather firmly or angrily. *His sharp reply clearly made an impact.* ♦ **sharply** ADV *Environmentalists were sharply critical of the*

policy. ♦ **sharpness** N-UNCOUNT *Malone was surprised at the sharpness in his voice.* **5** ADJ A **sharp** change, movement, or feeling occurs suddenly, and is great in amount, force, or degree. *There's been a sharp rise in the rate of inflation. ...a sharp pain.* ♦ **sharply** ADV *Theft from farms has risen sharply this year.* **6** ADJ A **sharp** difference, image, or sound is very easy to see, hear, or distinguish. *All the footmarks are quite sharp and clear.* ♦ **sharply** ADV *Opinions on this are sharply divided.* ♦ **sharpness** N-UNCOUNT *They were amazed at the sharpness of the first picture.* **7** ADJ A **sharp** taste or smell is rather strong or bitter, but is often also clear and fresh. ♦ **sharpness** N-UNCOUNT *The pesto vinaigrette added a stimulating sharpness.* **8** ADV **Sharp** is used after stating a particular time to show that something happens at exactly that time. *She planned to unlock the store at 8.00 sharp.* **9** ADJ **Sharp** is used after a letter representing a musical note to show that the note should be played or sung half a tone higher than the note which otherwise corresponds to that letter. **Sharp** is often represented by the symbol ♯.

sharpen /ʃɑːpən/ **sharpens, sharpening, sharpened.** **1** VERB If you **sharpen** an object, you make its edge very thin or you make its end pointed. **2** VERB If something **sharpens** your skills, senses, or understanding, it makes you better at noticing things, thinking, or doing something. *You can sharpen your skills with rehearsal.*

▸ **sharpen up.** PHR-VERB If you **sharpen** something **up**, or if it **sharpens up**, it becomes smarter or better than it was. [INFORMAL] *The fashion designers have sharpened up their act in the last few years.*

shatter /ʃætə/ **shatters, shattering, shattered.** **1** VERB If something **shatters**, or if someone or something **shatters** it, it breaks into a lot of small pieces. *The force of the explosion shattered the windows.* ♦ **shattering** N-UNCOUNT *...the shattering of glass.* **2** VERB If something **shatters** your beliefs or hopes, it destroys them. **3** VERB If someone **is shattered** by an event, it shocks and upsets them. *...the tragedy which had shattered his life.* ♦ **shattering** ADJ *Yesterday's decision was another shattering blow.*

shattered /ʃætəd/. **1** ADJ If you are **shattered**, you are shocked and upset. *His death was so sudden. I am shattered.* **2** ADJ If you say that you are **shattered**, you mean you are extremely tired and have no energy left. [BRITISH] *He was shattered and too tired to concentrate on schoolwork.*

shave /ʃeɪv/ **shaves, shaving, shaved.** **1** VERB & N-COUNT To **shave**, or to have a **shave**, means to cut hair from your face or body using a razor or shaver. *Many women shave their legs.* ♦ **shaving** N-UNCOUNT *...a range of shaving products.* **2** VERB If you **shave off** part of a piece of wood or other material, you cut very thin pieces from it. *She was shaving thin slices off a courgette.*

a
b
c
d
e
f
g
h
i
j
k
l
m
n
o
p
q
r
s
t
u
v
w
x
y
z

shaver /'ʃeɪvə/ **shavers.** N-COUNT A **shaver** is an electric device used for shaving hair from the face and body.

shaving /'ʃeɪvɪŋ/ **shavings.** N-COUNT **Shavings** are small, very thin pieces or wood or other material which have been cut from a larger piece. ...*metal shavings.*

shawl /ʃɔ:l/ **shawls.** N-COUNT A **shawl** is a large piece of woollen cloth worn over a woman's shoulders or head, or wrapped around a baby to keep it warm.

⭐ **she** /ʃi, STRONG ʃi:/. PRON You use **she** to refer to a woman, girl, or female animal. **She** is used as the subject of a verb. *She was seventeen.*

shear /ʃɪə/ **shears, shearing, sheared, shorn.**

✅ The past participle can be **sheared** or **shorn.**

1 VERB To **shear** a sheep means to clip all its wool off. ♦ **shearing** N-UNCOUNT ...*a display of sheep shearing.* **2** N-PLURAL A pair of **shears** is a garden tool like a large pair of scissors. → See picture on page 832.

sheath /ʃi:θ/ **sheaths.** N-COUNT A **sheath** is a covering for the blade of a knife.

⭐ **shed** /ʃed/ **sheds, shedding, shed.** **1** N-COUNT A **shed** is a small building used for storing things such as garden tools. **2** VERB When a tree **sheds** its leaves, its leaves fall off, usually in the autumn. When an animal **sheds** hair or skin, some of its hair or skin drops off. **3** VERB To **shed** something means to get rid of it. [JOURNALISM] *The firm is to shed 700 jobs.* **4** VERB If you **shed** tears, you cry. *They will shed a few tears at their daughter's wedding.* **5** VERB To **shed** blood means to kill people in a violent way. *Gunmen in Ulster shed the first blood of the new year.* **6** to **shed light on** something: see **light.**

she'd /ʃi:d, ʃɪd/. **She'd** is the usual spoken form of 'she had', especially when 'had' is an auxiliary verb. **She'd** is also a spoken form of 'she would'. *She'd found a job... She'd do anything for a bit of money.*

sheen /ʃi:n/. N-SING If something has a **sheen**, it has a smooth and gentle brightness.

sheep /ʃi:p/.

✅ **Sheep** is both the singular and the plural form.

N-COUNT A **sheep** is a farm animal with a thick woolly coat. → See picture on page 815.

sheepish /'ʃi:pɪʃ/. ADJ If you look **sheepish**, you look slightly embarrassed because you feel foolish. ♦ **sheepishly** ADV *He grinned sheepishly.*

sheer /ʃɪə/. **1** ADJ BEFORE N You can use **sheer** to emphasize that a state or situation is complete and does not involve anything else. ...*acts of sheer desperation.* **2** ADJ BEFORE N A **sheer** cliff or drop is extremely steep or completely vertical. **3** ADJ BEFORE N **Sheer** material is very thin, light, and delicate. ...*sheer black tights.*

⭐ **sheet** /ʃi:t/ **sheets.** **1** N-COUNT A **sheet** is a large rectangular piece of cloth that you sleep on or cover yourself with in a bed. **2** N-COUNT A **sheet**

of paper is a rectangular piece of paper. **3** N-COUNT A **sheet of** glass, metal, or wood is a large, flat, thin piece of it.

sheikh (or **sheik**) /ʃeɪk, AM ʃi:k/ **sheikhs.** N-COUNT A **sheikh** is a male Arab chief or ruler.

shelf /ʃelf/ **shelves.** N-COUNT A **shelf** is a flat piece of wood, metal, or glass which is attached to a wall or to the sides of a cupboard. *He took a book from the shelf.*

⭐ **shell** /ʃel/ **shells, shelling, shelled.** **1** N-VAR The **shell** of an egg or nut is the hard covering which surrounds it. The substance that a shell is made of is called **shell**. ...*beads made from ostrich egg shell.* **2** N-COUNT The **shell** of a tortoise, snail, or crab is the hard protective covering on its back. **3** N-COUNT **Shells** are the coverings which surround, or used to surround, small sea creatures. *The sand was pure white, scattered with sea shells.* **4** VERB If you **shell** nuts, peas, prawns, or other food, you remove their natural outer covering. **5** N-COUNT A **shell** is a weapon consisting of a metal container filled with explosives that can be fired from a large gun over long distances. **6** VERB To **shell** a place means to fire explosive shells at it. ♦ **shelling, shellings** N-VAR *Out on the streets, the shelling continued.*

▸ **shell out.** PHR-VERB If you **shell out for** something, you spend a lot of money on it. [INFORMAL] ...*an insurance premium which saves you from having to shell out for repairs.*

she'll /ʃi:l, ʃɪl/. **She'll** is the usual spoken form of 'she will'.

shellfish /'ʃelfɪʃ/.

✅ **Shellfish** is both the singular and the plural form.

N-COUNT A **shellfish** is a small creature with a shell that lives in the sea.

⭐ **shelter** /'ʃeltə/ **shelters, sheltering, sheltered.** **1** N-COUNT A **shelter** is a small building or covered place which is made to protect people from bad weather or danger. **2** N-UNCOUNT If a place provides **shelter**, it provides protection from bad weather or danger. *The number of families seeking shelter rose by 17 percent.* **3** VERB If you **shelter** in a place, you stay there and are protected from bad weather or danger. ...*a man sheltering in a doorway.* **4** VERB If a place or thing **is sheltered** by something, it is protected by it from wind and rain. **5** VERB If a person **shelters** someone, usually someone who is being hunted by police or other people, they provide them with a place to stay or live. *A neighbor sheltered the boy for seven days.*

sheltered /'ʃeltəd/. **1** ADJ A **sheltered** place is protected from wind and rain. ...*a shallow-sloping beach next to a sheltered bay.* **2** ADJ If you say someone has had a **sheltered** life, you mean that they have not experienced things that most people of their age have experienced, and that as a result they are rather naive.

shelve /ʃelv/ **shelves, shelving, shelved.** **1** VERB If someone **shelves** a plan, they decide not to

⭐ Bank of English® frequent word

continue with it at that time. *The project has now been shelved.* [2] **Shelves** is the plural of **shelf**.

shepherd /'ʃepəd/ **shepherds, shepherding, shepherded.** [1] N-COUNT A **shepherd** is a person whose job is to look after sheep. [2] VERB If you **are shepherded** somewhere, someone takes you there to make sure you arrive at the right place safely. *Supporters will then be shepherded on to a special fleet of buses.*

sheriff /'ʃerɪf/ **sheriffs.** N-COUNT & N-TITLE In the United States, a **sheriff** is a person who is elected to make sure that the law is obeyed in a particular county.

sherry /'ʃeri/ **sherries.** N-VAR **Sherry** is a type of strong wine that is made in south-western Spain.

she's /ʃiːz, ʃɪz/ **She's** is the usual spoken form of 'she is' or 'she has', especially when 'has' is an auxiliary verb. *She's having a baby... She's been married for seven years.*

shield /ʃiːld/ **shields, shielding, shielded.** [1] VERB If something or someone **shields** you **from** a danger or risk, they protect you from it. *He shielded his head from the sun with an old sack.* [2] N-COUNT A **shield** is a large piece of metal or leather which soldiers used to carry to protect their bodies while they were fighting.

⭐ **shift** /ʃɪft/ **shifts, shifting, shifted.** [1] VERB If you **shift** something, or if it **shifts**, it moves slightly. *He shifted from foot to foot.* [2] VERB & N-COUNT If someone's opinion, a situation, or a policy **shifts**, or if it **is shifted**, it changes slightly. You call a change like this a **shift**. *The emphasis should be shifted more towards Parliament.* [3] N-COUNT A **shift** is a set period of work in a place like a factory or hospital. *His father worked shifts in a steel mill. ...the afternoon shift.*

shimmer /'ʃɪmə/ **shimmers, shimmering, shimmered.** VERB & N-COUNT If something **shimmers**, it shines with a faint unsteady light called a **shimmer**. *The lights shimmered on the water.*

shin /ʃɪn/ **shins.** N-COUNT Your **shin** is the front part of your leg between your knee and ankle. → See picture on page 822.

shine /ʃaɪn/ **shines, shining, shined, shone.**

✔️ The past tense and past participle of the verb is **shone**, except for meaning 4 when it is **shined**.

[1] VERB When the sun or a light **shines**, it gives out bright light. [2] VERB If you **shine** a torch or lamp somewhere, you point its light there. *One of the men shone a torch in his face.* [3] VERB & N-SING Something that **shines**, or that has a **shine**, is very bright because it is reflecting light. *This gel gives a beautiful shine to the hair.* [4] VERB Someone who **shines** at a skill or activity does it very well. *He failed to shine academically.*

shingle /'ʃɪŋgəl/ N-UNCOUNT **Shingle** is a mass of small stones on the shore of a sea or river.

shining /'ʃaɪnɪŋ/ ADJ A **shining** achievement or quality is a very good one which should be admired. *She is a shining example to us all.*

shiny /'ʃaɪni/ **shinier, shiniest.** ADJ **Shiny** things are bright and reflect light. *...a shiny new sports car.*

⭐ **ship** /ʃɪp/ **ships, shipping, shipped.** [1] N-COUNT A **ship** is a large boat which carries passengers or cargo. *He will then go by ship to England.* [2] VERB If people or things **are shipped** somewhere, they are sent there by ship. ◆ **shipment** N-UNCOUNT *The furniture was ready for shipment.*

shipment /'ʃɪpmənt/ **shipments.** N-COUNT A **shipment** is an amount of a particular kind of cargo that is sent to another country on a ship.

shipping /'ʃɪpɪŋ/ N-UNCOUNT **Shipping** is the transport of cargo as a business, especially on ships.

shipwreck /'ʃɪprek/ **shipwrecks, shipwrecked.** [1] N-VAR When there is a **shipwreck**, a ship is destroyed in an accident at sea. *...the perils of storm and shipwreck.* [2] N-COUNT A **shipwreck** is a ship which has been destroyed in an accident at sea. [3] PASSIVE-VERB If someone **is shipwrecked**, their ship is destroyed in an accident at sea but they survive and reach land.

shipyard /'ʃɪpjɑːd/ **shipyards.** N-COUNT A **shipyard** is a place where ships are built and repaired.

⭐ **shirt** /ʃɜːt/ **shirts.** N-COUNT A **shirt** is a piece of clothing worn on the upper part of your body with a collar, sleeves, and buttons down the front. → See picture on page 820.

shiver /'ʃɪvə/ **shivers, shivering, shivered.** VERB & N-COUNT When you **shiver**, or when you feel a **shiver**, your body shakes slightly because you are cold or frightened. *The emptiness here sent shivers down my spine.*

shoal /ʃəʊl/ **shoals.** N-COUNT A **shoal of** fish is a large group of them swimming together.

⭐ **shock** /ʃɒk/ **shocks, shocking, shocked.** [1] N-COUNT If you have a **shock**, you suddenly have an unpleasant or surprising experience. *It took me a very long time to get over the shock of her death.* [2] N-UNCOUNT **Shock** is a person's emotional and physical condition when something frightening or upsetting has happened to them. *She's still in a state of shock.* [3] N-UNCOUNT If someone is **in shock**, they are suffering from a serious physical condition in which their blood cannot circulate properly, for example because they have had a bad injury. [4] VERB If something **shocks** you, it makes you feel very upset. *Her behaviour at her husband's funeral shocked her friends.* ◆ **shocked** ADJ *This was a nasty attack and the woman is still very shocked.* [5] VERB If someone or something **shocks** you, it upsets or offends you because you think it is rude or morally wrong. *Pictures of emaciated prisoners shocked the world.* ◆ **shocked** ADJ *I am very sad and very shocked by this terrible crime.* [6] N-VAR A **shock** is a slight movement in something when it is hit by something else. *Steel barriers can bend and absorb the shock.* [7] N-COUNT If you get a **shock** or an **electric shock**, you get a sudden painful feeling when you touch something which is connected to a supply of electricity.

shocking /'ʃɒkɪŋ/. ADJ You can say that something is **shocking** if you think that it is very bad. [INFORMAL] ♦ **shockingly** ADV *His memory was becoming shockingly bad.*

'**shock wave, shock waves.** [1] N-COUNT A **shock wave** is an area of intense pressure moving through the air caused by an explosion or an earthquake, or by an object travelling faster than the speed of sound. [2] N-COUNT If the effect of something unpleasant or surprising sends **shock waves** through a place, more and more people are offended, shocked, or surprised as they find out about it. *The crime sent shock waves throughout the country.*

shod /ʃɒd/. [1] ADJ You can use **shod** when you are describing the kind of shoes that a person is wearing. [FORMAL] *...her stoutly shod feet.* [2] **Shod** is the past tense and past participle of **shoe**.

shoddy /'ʃɒdi/. ADJ If you describe a product or someone's work as **shoddy**, you think that it has been made or done carelessly or badly.
♦ **shoddily** ADV *...shoddily-built cars.*

⭐ **shoe** /ʃuː/ **shoes, shoeing, shod.** [1] N-COUNT **Shoes** are objects worn on your feet. Shoes cover most of your foot but not your ankle. → See pictures on page 820. *I'll need a new pair of shoes.*
[2] PHRASE If you talk about being **in** someone's **shoes**, you talk about what you would do or how you would feel if you were in their situation. *I wouldn't want to be in his shoes.* [3] VERB To **shoe** a horse means to fix horseshoes onto its hooves.

shone /ʃɒn, AM ʃəʊn/. **Shone** is the past tense and past participle of **shine**.

shook /ʃʊk/. **Shook** is the past tense of **shake**.

⭐ **shoot** /ʃuːt/ **shoots, shooting, shot.** [1] VERB To **shoot** a person or animal means to kill or injure them by firing a gun at them. *Her father shot himself in the head.* ♦ **shooting, shootings** N-COUNT *Two more bodies were found nearby after the shooting.* [2] VERB To **shoot** means to fire a bullet from a weapon such as a gun. *They started shooting at us.* [3] VERB If someone or something **shoots** in a particular direction, they move in that direction quickly and suddenly. *Another car shot out of a junction and smashed into the back of them.* [4] VERB & N-COUNT When people **shoot** a film or **shoot** photographs, they make a film or take photographs using a camera. A **shoot** is an instance of shooting a film or photograph. *...a barn presently being used for a video shoot.*
[5] VERB In sports such as football or basketball, when someone **shoots**, they try to score by kicking, throwing, or hitting the ball towards the goal. [6] N-COUNT **Shoots** are plants that are beginning to grow, or new parts growing from a plant or tree. [7] See also **shot**.

▶**shoot down.** [1] PHR-VERB If someone **shoots down** an aeroplane or helicopter, they make it fall to the ground by hitting it with a bullet or missile. [2] PHR-VERB If you **shoot** someone **down** or **shoot down** their ideas, you ridicule that person or their ideas.

▶**shoot up.** PHR-VERB If something **shoots up**, it grows or increases very quickly. *Sales shot up by 9%.*

⭐ **shop** /ʃɒp/ **shops, shopping, shopped.** [1] N-COUNT In British English, a **shop** is a building or part of a building where things are sold. The usual American word is **store**. *She had run her own antiques shop.* [2] VERB When you **shop**, you go to shops and buy things. *He always shopped at the Co-op.* ♦ **shopper, shoppers** N-COUNT *...crowds of Christmas shoppers.* [3] See also **shopping, coffee shop.**

USAGE When you want to refer to a particular type of shop, you can often simply use the word for the person who owns or manages the shop. *Down the road there is another greengrocer... Bring me back a paper from the newsagent.* Alternatively, you can use the possessive form with **'s**, without a following noun. *...items which can be purchased at the greengrocer's... She also cleans offices and serves in a local newsagent's.* You can also use the same pattern with other words that refer to a person or business that provides a service, such as **hairdresser** or **dentist**. *Three or four times a week they'll go to the hairdresser... It's worse than being at the dentist's.*

▶**shop around.** PHR-VERB If you **shop around**, you go to different shops or companies and compare prices and quality before buying something.

'**shop assistant, shop assistants.** N-COUNT In British English, a **shop assistant** is a person who works in a shop selling things to customers. The usual American word is **sales clerk**.

,**shop 'floor.** N-SING The **shop floor** refers to all the workers in a factory or the area where they work, especially in contrast to the management. *Cost must be controlled, not just on the shop floor.*

shopkeeper /'ʃɒpkiːpə/ **shopkeepers.** N-COUNT A **shopkeeper** is a person who owns a small shop. [BRITISH]

shoplift /'ʃɒplɪft/ **shoplifts, shoplifting, shoplifted.** VERB If someone **shoplifts**, they steal goods from a shop during the time that the shop is open.
♦ **shoplifter, shoplifters** N-COUNT *...when staff confronted shoplifters.* ♦ **shoplifting** N-UNCOUNT *The grocer accused her of shoplifting.*

⭐ **shopping** /'ʃɒpɪŋ/. [1] N-UNCOUNT When you **do the shopping**, you go to shops and buy things.
[2] N-UNCOUNT Your **shopping** consists of things that you have just bought from shops, especially food.

'shopping centre (AM **shopping center**) shopping centres. N-COUNT A **shopping centre** is an area in a town where a lot of shops have been built close together.

'shopping mall, shopping malls. N-COUNT A **shopping mall** is a covered area where many shops have been built and where cars are not allowed.

⭐ **shore** /ʃɔː/ **shores, shoring, shored.** N-COUNT & PHRASE The **shore** of a sea, lake, or wide river is the land along the edge of it. Someone who is **on shore** is on the land rather than on a ship.

▸ **shore up.** PHR-VERB If you **shore up** something which is becoming weak, you do something in order to strengthen it. *The Secretary of State for Education must act to shore up the system.*

shoreline /'ʃɔːlaɪn/ **shorelines.** N-COUNT The **shoreline** is the edge of a sea, lake, or wide river.

shorn /ʃɔːn/. **1** ADJ If hair is **shorn**, it has been cut very short. [LITERARY] **2** **Shorn** is the past participle of **shear**.

short 1 adjective and adverb uses

⭐ **short** /ʃɔːt/ **shorter, shortest. 1** ADJ If something is **short** or lasts for a **short** time, it is not very long or does not last very long. *The announcement was made a short time ago... Mr Mandela took a short break before resuming his schedule.* **2** ADV If something is cut **short** or stops **short**, it is stopped before people expect it to or before it has finished. *Jackson cut short his trip to Africa.* **3** ADJ Someone who is **short** is not as tall as most people are. → See picture on page 324. **4** ADJ Something that is **short** measures only a small amount from one end to the other. *The city centre and shops are only a short distance away.* **5** ADJ AFTER LINK-V If a name or abbreviation is **short for** another name, it is the short version of that name. *...her friend Kes (short for Kesewa).* **6** ADJ AFTER LINK-V If you are **short of** something or if it is **short**, you do not have enough of it. *Her father's illness left the family short of money.* **7** ADJ If you have a **short** temper, you get angry easily.

PHRASES ● If something is **short of** a place or amount, it has not quite reached it. *They were still 91 short of their target.* ● If someone **stops short of** doing something, they nearly do it but do not actually do it. *He stopped short of explicitly criticizing the government.* ● You use the expression **in short** when you have been giving a lot of details and you want to give a conclusion or summary. *Try tennis, badminton or windsurfing. In short, anything challenging.*

short 2 noun uses

short /ʃɔːt/ **shorts. 1** N-PLURAL **Shorts** are trousers with short legs. *I decided to put on a pair of shorts.* **2** N-PLURAL **Shorts** are men's underpants with short legs. **3** N-COUNT A **short** is a small, strong alcoholic drink of a spirit such as whisky or gin. [BRITISH]

⭐ **shortage** /'ʃɔːtɪdʒ/ **shortages.** N-VAR If there is a **shortage of** something, there is not enough of it.

...a shortage of funds... Vietnam is suffering from food shortages.

shortcoming /'ʃɔːtkʌmɪŋ/ **shortcomings.** N-COUNT The **shortcomings** of a person or thing are their faults or weaknesses. *I recognize all of my own shortcomings.*

short 'cut, short cuts. 1 N-COUNT A **short cut** is a quicker route than the one that you usually take. *I tried to take a short cut and got lost.* **2** N-COUNT A **short cut** is a method of achieving something more quickly or more easily than if you use the usual methods. *Fame can be a shortcut to love and money.*

shorten /'ʃɔːtən/ **shortens, shortening, shortened. 1** VERB If you **shorten** an event or the length of time that something lasts, or if it **shortens**, it does not last as long as it would otherwise do or as it used to do. *Smoking can shorten your life. ...when the days shorten in winter.* **2** VERB If you **shorten** an object, or if it **shortens**, it becomes smaller in length. *...an operation to shorten her nose.*

shortfall /'ʃɔːtfɔːl/ **shortfalls.** N-COUNT If there is a **shortfall** in something, there is not enough of it. *The government has refused to make up a £30,000 shortfall in funding.*

shorthand /'ʃɔːthænd/. N-UNCOUNT **Shorthand** is a quick way of writing which uses signs to represent words or syllables.

shortlist /'ʃɔːtlɪst/ **shortlists, shortlisting, shortlisted. 1** N-COUNT A **shortlist** is a list of people or things which have been chosen from a larger group, for example for a job or a prize. The successful person or thing is then chosen from the small group. [BRITISH] *...the six books on the shortlist for the Booker prize.* **2** VERB If someone or something **is shortlisted**, they are put on a shortlist. [BRITISH]

short-'lived. ADJ Something that is **short-lived** does not last very long. *Her sense of triumph was short-lived.*

⭐ **shortly** /'ʃɔːtli/. **1** ADV If something happens **shortly** after or before something else, it happens a short amount of time after or before it. *The telephone call came shortly before dinnertime.* **2** ADV If something is going to happen **shortly**, it is going to happen soon. *Their trial will shortly begin.*

short-'sighted. 1 ADJ In British English, if you are **short-sighted**, you cannot see things properly when they are far away, because there is something wrong with your eyes. The American term is **near-sighted**. **2** ADJ If you say that someone's actions or decisions are **short-sighted**, you mean they fail to take account of things that will probably happen in the future. *This is a short-sighted approach to the problem of global warming.*

⭐ **'short-term.** ADJ **Short-term** is used to describe things that will last for a short time, or things that will have an effect soon rather than in the distant future. *They had a short-term vacancy*

A
B
C
D
E
F
G
H
I
J
K
L
M
N
O
P
Q
R
S
T
U
V
W
X
Y
Z

for a person on the foreign desk... *The short-term outlook for employment remains gloomy.*

⭐ **shot** /ʃɒt/ **shots.** **1** **Shot** is the past tense and past participle of **shoot.** **2** N-COUNT If you fire a **shot,** you fire a gun once. *My first two shots missed the target.* **3** N-COUNT Someone who is a **good shot** can shoot well. Someone who is a **bad shot** cannot shoot well. **4** N-COUNT In sport, a **shot** is the act of kicking or hitting a ball, especially in an attempt to score. *He had only one shot at goal.* **5** N-COUNT A **shot** is a photograph or a particular sequence of pictures in a film. *A video crew was taking shots of the lane.* **6** PHRASES If you **have a shot** at something, or if you **give it a shot,** you attempt to do it. [INFORMAL] **7** N-COUNT A **shot of** a drug is an injection of it. *The doctor administered a shot of Nembutal.* **PHRASES** ● If you **give** something your **best shot,** you do it as well as you possibly can. [INFORMAL] ● The person who **calls the shots** is in a position to tell others what to do. *There is no mistaking who calls the shots.* ● If you describe something as a **long shot,** you mean that it is unlikely to succeed, but is worth trying. *The deal was a long shot, but Bagley had little to lose.* ● a **shot in the arm:** see **arm.**

shotgun /ˈʃɒtɡʌn/ **shotguns.** N-COUNT A **shotgun** is a gun which fires a lot of small metal balls at one time.

⭐ **should** /ʃəd, STRONG ʃʊd/.

✓ **Should** is a modal verb. It is used with the base form of a verb.

1 MODAL You use **should** when you are giving advice or recommendations or when you are mentioning things that are not the case but that you think ought to be. *I should exercise more... Should our children be taught to swim at school?* **2** MODAL You use **should** to tell someone what to do or to report a rule or law which tells someone what to do. *A High Court judge has ruled that the two men should stand trial.* **3** MODAL You use **should** in questions when you are asking someone for advice, permission, or information. *Should I or shouldn't I go to university?* **4** MODAL If you say that something **should have** happened, you mean that it did not happen, but that you wish it had happened or that you expected it to happen. *I should have gone this morning but I was feeling a bit ill... I shouldn't have said what I did.* **5** MODAL You use **should** when you are saying that something is probably the case or will probably happen in the way you are describing. If you say that something **should have** happened by a particular time, you mean that it will probably have happened by that time. *You should have no problem with reading this language... We should have finished by a quarter past two.* **6** MODAL You use **should** in 'that' clauses after some verbs and adjectives when you are talking about a future event or situation. *He raised his glass and indicated that I should do the same.* **7** MODAL You use **should** in expressions such as **I should imagine** to indicate

that you think something is true but you are not sure. *I should think it's going to rain soon.*

⭐ **shoulder** /ˈʃəʊldə/ **shoulders, shouldering, shouldered.** **1** N-COUNT Your **shoulders** are the parts of your body between your neck and the tops of your arms. → See picture on page 822. *He glanced over his shoulder.* **2** VERB If you **shoulder** something heavy, you put it across one of your shoulders so that you can carry it more easily. *He shouldered his bike and walked across the finish line.* **3** N-PLURAL When you talk about someone's problems or responsibilities, you can say that they carry them **on** their **shoulders.** *He recognizes and understands the burden that's on his shoulders.* **4** VERB If you **shoulder** the responsibility or blame for something, you accept it. *He has had to shoulder the responsibility of his father's mistakes.* **5** PHRASE If you **rub shoulders with** famous people, you meet them and talk to them. ● **a chip on** someone's **shoulder:** see **chip.**

shouldn't /ˈʃʊdənt/. **Shouldn't** is the usual spoken form of 'should not'.

should've /ˈʃʊdəv/. **Should've** is the usual spoken form of 'should have', especially when 'have' is an auxiliary verb.

⭐ **shout** /ʃaʊt/ **shouts, shouting, shouted.** **1** VERB & PHR-VERB If you **shout,** or **shout** something **out,** you say it very loudly. *'She's alive!' he shouted triumphantly... Andrew rushed out of the house, shouting for help... You will have to shout out your name to the auctioneer.* ♦ **shouting** N-UNCOUNT *My grandchildren heard the shouting first.* **2** N-COUNT A **shout** is the noise made when someone speaks very loudly. *I heard a distant shout.*

▸**shout down.** PHR-VERB If people **shout down** someone who is trying to speak, they prevent them from being heard by shouting at them. *Hecklers began to shout down the speakers.*

▸**shout out.** See **shout** 1.

shove /ʃʌv/ **shoves, shoving, shoved.** VERB & N-COUNT If you **shove** someone or something, or if you give them a **shove,** you give them a hard push. *He shoved her out of the way... She gave Gracie a shove towards the house.*

shovel /ˈʃʌvəl/ **shovels, shovelling, shovelled** (AM **shoveling, shoveled**). **1** N-COUNT A **shovel** is a tool like a spade, used for lifting and moving earth, coal, or snow. → See picture on page 832. **2** VERB If you **shovel** earth, coal, or snow, you lift and move it with a shovel. **3** VERB If you **shovel** something somewhere, you push a lot of it there quickly. *...Randall, who was obliviously shoveling food into his mouth.*

⭐ **show** /ʃəʊ/ **shows, showing, showed, shown.** **1** VERB If something **shows** that a state of affairs exists, it gives information that proves it or makes it clear to people. *New research shows that an excess of meat and salt can contract muscles... These figures show an increase of over one million in unemployment. ...blood tests to show whether you* have been infected. **2** VERB If a picture, chart, film, or piece of writing **shows** something, it represents it or gives information about it. *Figure 4.1 shows the respiratory system.* **3** VERB If you **show** someone something, you give it to them, take them to it, or point to it, so that they can see it or know what you are referring to. *Cut out this article and show it to your bank manager... I showed them where the gun was.* **4** VERB If you **show** someone to a room or seat, you lead them to it. *Your office is ready for you. I'll show you the way.* **5** VERB If you **show** someone how to do something, you do it yourself so that they can watch and learn how to do it. *Claire showed us how to make a chocolate roulade... Dr. Reichert has shown us a new way to look at those behavior problems.* **6** VERB If something **shows**, or if you **show** it, it is visible or noticeable. *Faint glimmers of daylight were showing through the treetops... Ferguson was unhappy and it showed... He showed his teeth.* **7** VERB If something **shows** a quality or characteristic, or if that quality or characteristic **shows itself**, the quality or characteristic can be noticed or observed. *Peace talks in Washington showed signs of progress.* **8** N-COUNT A **show of** a feeling or quality is an attempt by someone to make it clear that they have that feeling or quality. *Miners gathered in the centre of Bucharest in a show of support for the government.* **9** PHRASE If you **have** something **to show for** your efforts, you have achieved something as a result of what you have done. *It's about time I had something to show for my time in my job.* **10** N-COUNT A television or radio **show** is a programme on television or radio. **11** N-COUNT A **show** in a theatre is an entertainment or concert, especially one that includes different items such as music, dancing, and comedy. **12** VERB When a film or television programme **is shown**, it appears in a cinema or is broadcast on television. *American films are showing at Moscow's cinemas.* **13** N-COUNT A **show** is a public exhibition. *...the Chelsea Flower Show.* PHRASES • If you say that something is **for show**, you mean that it has no real purpose and is done just to give a good impression. *Animals are not put on this earth just for show.* • If something is **on show**, it has been put in a place where it can be seen by the public. *...the most valuable item on show.*

▸ **show around.** PHR-VERB If you **show** someone **around** a place, you go round it with them, pointing out its interesting features.

▸ **show off.** **1** PHR-VERB If you say that someone **is showing off**, you are criticizing them for trying to impress people by showing in a very obvious way what they can do or what they own. *All right, there's no need to show off.* **2** PHR-VERB If you **show off** something that you have or own, you show it to a lot of people because you are proud of it. *Body builders shave their chests to show off their muscles.* • See also **show-off**.

'**show business.** N-UNCOUNT **Show business** is

the entertainment industry. *He started his career in show business by playing the saxophone.*

showdown /ˈʃəʊdaʊn/ **showdowns.** N-COUNT A **showdown** is a big argument or conflict which is intended to settle a dispute. *They may be pushing the Prime Minister towards a final showdown with his party.*

shower /ˈʃaʊə/ **showers, showering, showered.** **1** N-COUNT A **shower** is a device which sprays you with water so that you can wash yourself. *She heard him turn on the shower.* **2** N-COUNT & VERB If you have a **shower**, or if you **shower**, you wash yourself by standing under a shower. *She took two showers a day... There wasn't time to shower.* **3** N-COUNT A **shower** is a short period of light rain. *The weather forecast was for scattered showers.* **4** N-COUNT You can refer to a lot of things that are falling as a **shower of** them. *Showers of sparks flew in all directions.* **5** VERB If you **are showered with** a lot of small objects or pieces, they are scattered over you. *They were showered with rice in the traditional manner.* **6** VERB If you **shower** someone **with** presents or kisses, you give them a lot of them.

'**shower gel,** shower gels. N-VAR **Shower gel** is liquid soap you use in the shower.

shown /ʃəʊn/. **Shown** is the past participle of **show**.

'**show-off,** show-offs. N-COUNT If you say that someone is a **show-off**, you are criticizing them for trying to impress people by showing in a very obvious way what they can do or what they own. [INFORMAL] *I was an awful show-off as a child.*

showpiece /ˈʃəʊpiːs/ **showpieces.** N-COUNT A **showpiece** is something that is admired as a fine example of its type, especially something which is intended to make people admire its owner or creator. *The factory was to be a showpiece of Western investment in the East.*

showroom /ˈʃəʊruːm/ **showrooms.** N-COUNT A **showroom** is a shop in which goods such as cars, furniture, or electrical appliances are displayed for sale.

shrank /ʃræŋk/. **Shrank** is the past tense of **shrink**.

shrapnel /ˈʃræpnəl/. N-UNCOUNT **Shrapnel** consists of small pieces of metal scattered from exploding bombs and shells.

shred /ʃred/ **shreds, shredding, shredded.** VERB & N-COUNT If you **shred** something such as food or paper, or if you cut it into **shreds**, you cut or tear it into very small pieces. *Finely shred the carrots.*

shrewd /ʃruːd/ **shrewder, shrewdest.** ADJ A **shrewd** person is able to understand and judge situations quickly and to use this understanding to their own advantage. ♦ **shrewdly** ADV *She looked at him shrewdly.* ♦ **shrewdness** N-UNCOUNT *His natural shrewdness tells him what is needed to succeed.*

shriek /ʃriːk/ **shrieks, shrieking, shrieked.** VERB & N-COUNT If you **shriek**, you give a sudden loud scream, called a **shriek**. *She shrieked and leapt*

a
b
c
d
e
f
g
h
i
j
k
l
m
n
o
p
q
r
s
t
u
v
w
x
y
z

from the bed... *'Stop it! Stop it!'* shrieked Jane... Sue let out a terrific shriek.

shrill /ʃrɪl/ **shriller, shrillest.** ADJ A **shrill** sound is high-pitched, piercing, and unpleasant to listen to. ...*the shrill whistle of the engine.*

shrimp /ʃrɪmp/.

☑ The plural is **shrimps** or **shrimp.**

N-COUNT **Shrimps** are small shellfish with long tails and many legs.

shrine /ʃraɪn/ **shrines.** N-COUNT A **shrine** is a holy place associated with a sacred person or object. ...*the holy shrine of Mecca.*

shrink /ʃrɪŋk/ **shrinks, shrinking, shrank, shrunk.**
1 VERB If something **shrinks**, it becomes smaller. *The vast forests of West Africa have shrunk.* 2 VERB If you **shrink** away from someone or something, you move away because you are frightened or horrified by them. *He reached for Benjy, who shrank back in fear... They didn't shrink from danger.* 3 N-COUNT A **shrink** is a psychiatrist. [INFORMAL]

shrivel /ʃrɪvəl/ **shrivels, shrivelling, shrivelled** (AM **shriveling, shriveled**). VERB & PHR-VERB When something **shrivels** or **shrivels up**, it becomes dry and wrinkled. ...*dry weather that shrivelled this summer's crops... The leaves started to shrivel up.* ◆ **shrivelled** ADJ *It looked old and shrivelled.*

shroud /ʃraʊd/ **shrouds, shrouding, shrouded.**
1 N-COUNT A **shroud** is a cloth used for wrapping a dead body. 2 PHRASE If something is **shrouded in mystery** or **shrouded in secrecy**, very little information about it has been made available. *The origin of AIDS, like that of most diseases is shrouded in mystery.* 3 VERB If darkness, fog, or smoke **shrouds** an area, it covers it so that it is difficult to see. *The area is shrouded in smoke.*

shrub /ʃrʌb/ **shrubs.** N-COUNT **Shrubs** are low plants like small trees with several stems instead of a trunk.

shrug /ʃrʌg/ **shrugs, shrugging, shrugged.** VERB & N-COUNT If you **shrug**, you raise your shoulders to show that you are not interested in something or that you do not know or care about something. This movement is called a **shrug.** *Anne shrugged, as if she didn't know... 'I suppose so,' said Anna with a shrug.*
▸**shrug off.** PHR-VERB If you **shrug** something **off**, you treat it as not important or serious. *He shrugged off the criticism.*

shrunk /ʃrʌŋk/. **Shrunk** is the past participle of **shrink.**

shudder /ʃʌdə/ **shudders, shuddering, shuddered.**
1 VERB & N-COUNT If you **shudder**, you tremble with fear or disgust. This movement is called a **shudder.** *She had shuddered at the thought... She gave a violent shudder.* 2 VERB If something such as a machine **shudders**, it shakes suddenly and violently. *The whole ship shuddered and trembled.*

shuffle /ʃʌfəl/ **shuffles, shuffling, shuffled.** 1 VERB & N-SING If you **shuffle**, or if you walk with a **shuffle**, you walk without lifting your feet properly. *An old*

man shuffled out of a doorway... She is quite frail and can only walk with a shuffle.* 2 VERB If you **shuffle** when you are sitting or standing, you move your bottom or your feet about, because you feel uncomfortable or embarrassed. *He grinned and shuffled his feet.* 3 VERB If you **shuffle** things such as pieces of paper, you move them around so that they are in a different order.

shun /ʃʌn/ **shuns, shunning, shunned.** VERB If you **shun** someone or something, you deliberately avoid them. *Everybody shunned him.*

shunt /ʃʌnt/ **shunts, shunting, shunted.** VERB If someone or something **is shunted** somewhere, they are moved or sent there, usually because someone finds them inconvenient. *He spent eight years being shunted between prisons.*

⭐ **shut** /ʃʌt/ **shuts, shutting, shut.** 1 VERB & ADJ AFTER LINK-V If you **shut** something such as a door, you move it so that it covers a hole or a space. If it is **shut**, it covers a hole or space. *The screen door shut gently... The windows were fastened tight shut.* 2 VERB & ADJ AFTER LINK-V If you **shut** your eyes or your mouth, or if they are **shut**, your eyelids are closed or your lips are placed together. 3 VERB & ADJ AFTER LINK-V When a shop or pub **shuts**, or if it is **shut**, it is closed and you cannot go into it until it opens again. *What time do the pubs shut?... The local shop may be shut.*
▸**shut away.** PHR-VERB If you **shut yourself away**, you avoid going out and seeing other people. *She was desperately upset and shut herself away for the whole day.*
▸**shut down.** PHR-VERB If a factory or business is **shut down**, it is closed permanently. *Smaller contractors had been forced to shut down.* ● See also **shutdown.**
▸**shut in.** PHR-VERB If you **shut** someone or something **in** a room, you close the door so that they cannot leave it.
▸**shut off.** PHR-VERB If you **shut off** something such as an engine or a power supply, you turn it off to stop it working. *The water was shut off.*
▸**shut out.** 1 PHR-VERB If you **shut** someone or something **out**, you prevent them from getting into a place. *'I shut him out of the bedroom,' says Maureen.* 2 PHR-VERB If you **shut out** a thought or a feeling, you stop yourself thinking about it or feeling it. *I shut out the memory.*
▸**shut up.** PHR-VERB If you **shut up**, you stop talking. If you say **'shut up'** to someone, you are rudely telling them to stop talking. ...*the only way he knew of shutting her up.*

shutdown /ʃʌtdaʊn/ **shutdowns.** N-COUNT A **shutdown** is the closing of a factory or other business.

shutter /ʃʌtə/ **shutters.** 1 N-COUNT The **shutter** in a camera is the part which opens to allow light through the lens when a photograph is taken. 2 N-COUNT **Shutters** are wooden or metal covers fitted to a window.

shuttle /ʃʌtəl/ **shuttles, shuttling, shuttled.** 1 N-COUNT A **shuttle** is the same as a **space shuttle.** 2 ADJ A **shuttle** is a plane, bus, or train which makes frequent journeys between two places. [3] VERB If someone or something **is shuttled** from one place to another, they are frequently sent from one place to the other. *Refugees can be shuttled from one country to another.*

shuttlecock /'ʃʌtəlkɒk/ **shuttlecocks.** N-COUNT A **shuttlecock** is the small object that you hit over the net in a game of badminton.

shy /ʃaɪ/ **shyer, shyest; shies, shying, shied.** [1] ADJ A **shy** person is nervous and uncomfortable in the company of other people. *He is painfully shy of women.* ♦ **shyly** ADV *The children smiled shyly.* ♦ **shyness** N-UNCOUNT *He overcame his shyness.* [2] ADJ & VERB If you are **shy of** doing something, or if you **shy away from** doing it, you are unwilling to do it, often because you are afraid or not confident enough. *You should not be shy of having your say in the running of the school... We frequently shy away from making decisions.* [3] VERB When a horse **shies**, it moves away suddenly because something has frightened it.

sibling /'sɪblɪŋ/ **siblings.** N-COUNT Your **siblings** are your brothers and sisters. [FORMAL] ● See note at **brother**.

⭐ **sick** /sɪk/ **sicker, sickest.** [1] ADJ & N-PLURAL If you are **sick**, you are ill. **The sick** are people who are sick. *He's very sick. He needs medication... There were no doctors to treat the sick.* [2] ADJ AFTER LINK-V If you are being **sick**, the food that you have eaten comes up from your stomach and out of your mouth. If you feel **sick**, you feel as if you are going to be sick. *She got up and was sick in the handbasin.* [3] N-UNCOUNT **Sick** is vomit. [BRITISH] [4] ADJ If you are **sick of** something, you are annoyed or bored by it and want it to stop. *I am sick and tired of hearing all these people moaning.* [5] ADJ If you describe something such as a joke or story as **sick**, you mean that it deals with death or suffering in an unpleasantly frivolous way. [6] PHRASE If someone or something **makes** you **sick**, they make you feel angry or disgusted. *The pictures made me sick.*

USAGE The words **sick** and **ill** are very similar in meaning but are used in slightly different ways. **Ill** is generally not used before a noun, and can be used in verbal expressions such as **fall ill** and **be taken ill**. *He fell ill shortly before Christmas... The trial was delayed after one of the jurors was taken ill.* **Sick** is often used before a noun. *...sick children.*
In British English, **ill** is a slightly more polite, less direct word than **sick**. **Sick** often suggests the actual physical feeling of being ill, for example nausea or vomiting. *I spent the next 24 hours in bed, groaning and being sick.*
In American English, **sick** is often used where British people would say **ill**. *Some people get hurt in accidents or get sick.*

sicken /'sɪkən/ **sickens, sickening, sickened.** VERB If something **sickens** you, it makes you feel disgusted. ♦ **sickening** ADJ *...a sickening attack on a pregnant and defenceless woman.*

sickly /'sɪkli/ **sicklier, sickliest.** [1] ADJ A **sickly** person is weak and unhealthy. *He had been a sickly child.* [2] ADJ A **sickly** smell or taste is unpleasant and makes you feel slightly sick. *...the sickly smell of burnt human flesh.*

sickness /'sɪknəs/ **sicknesses.** [1] N-UNCOUNT **Sickness** is the state of being ill or unhealthy. *In fifty-two years of working he had one week of sickness.* [2] N-UNCOUNT **Sickness** is the uncomfortable feeling that you are going to vomit. [3] N-COUNT A **sickness** is a particular illness. *...radiation sickness.*

⭐ **side** /saɪd/ **sides, siding, sided.** [1] N-COUNT The **side** of something is a position to the left or right of it, rather than in front of it, behind it, or on it. *...the nations on either side of the Pacific. ...both sides of the border... Park on the side of the road.* [2] N-COUNT The **sides** of an object are the outside surfaces that are not the top or the bottom. *We put a notice on the side of the box... A carton of milk lay on its side.* [3] N-COUNT The **sides** of a hollow or a container are its inside vertical surfaces. *...narrow valleys with steep sides.* [4] N-COUNT The two **sides** of an area, surface, or object are its two halves or surfaces. *...the right side of your face... The new copiers only copy onto one side of the paper.* [5] N-COUNT Your **sides** are the parts of your body from your armpits down to your hips. [6] ADJ BEFORE N **Side** is used to describe things that are not the main or least important ones of their kind. *...a side door.* [7] N-COUNT You can call the two groups of people involved in an argument, war, or game the two **sides** of that argument, war, or game. [8] N-COUNT The two **sides** of an argument are the opposing points of view. *...sharp reactions from people on both sides of the issue.* [9] VERB If you **side with** someone, you support them in an argument. [10] N-COUNT A particular **side** of something is one aspect of it. *Anxiety has a mental and a physical side.*

PHRASES ● If someone stays **at** your **side** or **by** your **side**, they stay near you and support or comfort you. *He was constantly at his wife's side.* ● If two people or things are **side by side**, they are next to each other. *We sat side by side.* ● If something moves **from side to side**, it moves repeatedly to the left and to the right. *She was shaking her head from side to side.* ● If you are **on** someone's **side**, you are supporting them in an argument or a war. ● If you do something **on the side**, you do it in addition to your main work. *...ways of making a little bit of money on the side.* ● If you **put** something **to one side**, you temporarily ignore it in order to concentrate on something else. *Health and safety regulations are often put to one side.* ● If you get **on the wrong side of** someone, you do something to annoy them and make them dislike you. If you stay **on**

a b c d e f g h i j k l m n o p q r s t u v w x y z

the right side of someone, you try to please them and avoid annoying them. • to **err on the side of** something: see **err**. • to **be on the safe side**: see **safe**.

'side-effect, side-effects. N-COUNT The **side-effects** of a drug are the effects it has on you in addition to its function of curing illness or pain. ...*unpleasant side-effects, such as nausea, vomiting and sweating.*

sideline /'saɪdlaɪn/ **sidelines.** ① N-COUNT A **sideline** is something that you do in addition to your main job in order to earn extra money. *Mr. Means sold computer disks as a sideline.* ② N-COUNT The **sidelines** of a playing area such as a tennis court or football pitch are the lines marking the long sides. ③ N-PLURAL If you are **on the sidelines** in a situation, you are not involved in it. *France no longer wants to be left on the sidelines when critical decisions are taken.*

'side road, side roads. N-COUNT A **side road** is a road which leads off a busier, more important road.

'side salad, side salads. N-COUNT A **side salad** is a bowl of salad which is served with a main meal.

'side street, side streets. N-COUNT A **side street** is a quiet, often narrow street which leads off a busier street.

sidestep (or **side-step**) /'saɪdstɛp/ **sidesteps, sidestepping, sidestepped.** VERB If you **sidestep** a problem, you avoid dealing with it. *Rarely, if ever, does he sidestep a question.*

sidewalk /'saɪdwɔːk/ **sidewalks.** N-COUNT In American English, a **sidewalk** is a path with a hard surface by the side of a road. The British word is **pavement**.

sideways /'saɪdweɪz/. ADV & ADJ BEFORE N **Sideways** means from or to the side of something or someone. *I took a step sideways. ...a sideways glance.*

siege /siːdʒ/ **sieges.** N-VAR A **siege** is a military operation in which an army or police force surrounds a place in order to force the people to surrender and come out. *We must do everything possible to lift the siege. ...sending supplies to the city which has been under siege.*

sieve /sɪv/ **sieves, sieving, sieved.** ① N-COUNT A **sieve** is a tool consisting of a metal or plastic ring with a fine wire net attached. It is used for separating liquids from solids or larger pieces of something from smaller pieces. → See picture on page 825. ② VERB When you **sieve** a liquid or a powder, you put it through a sieve. *Sieve the flour into a mixing bowl.*

sift /sɪft/ **sifts, sifting, sifted.** ① VERB If you **sift** a substance such as flour or sand, you put it through a sieve to remove large lumps. ② VERB If you **sift through** something such as evidence, you examine it thoroughly. *Experts spent all day sifting through the wreckage.*

★ **sigh** /saɪ/ **sighs, sighing, sighed.** VERB & N-COUNT When you **sigh**, or when you let out a **sigh**, you let out a deep breath. *She sighed deeply... She kicked off her shoes with a sigh.*

★ **sight** /saɪt/ **sights, sighting, sighted.** ① N-UNCOUNT Your **sight** is your ability to see. *My sight is failing, and I can't see to read any more.* ② VERB If someone **is sighted** somewhere, they are seen there briefly or suddenly. *A woman looking like her was sighted near Enmore.* ③ N-SING **The sight of** something is the act of seeing it or an occasion on which you see it. *I faint at the sight of blood.* ④ N-PLURAL **The sights** are interesting places often visited by tourists. *We'd toured the sights of Paris.* ⑤ N-PLURAL The **sights** of a weapon such as a rifle are the part which help you aim it.

PHRASES • If one thing is **a sight** better or **a sight** worse than a similar thing, it is very much better or very much worse; informal. *She's looking a damn sight better than I am.* • If you **know** someone **by sight**, you can recognize them when you see them, but you have never spoken to them. • If you **catch sight of** someone, you see them suddenly or briefly. *Then he caught sight of her small black velvet hat in the crowd.* • If something is **in sight**, you can see it. If it is **out of sight**, you cannot see it. • If a result or a decision is **in sight** or **within sight**, it is likely to happen within a short time. *An agreement on many aspects of trade policy was in sight.* • If you **lose sight of** an important feature or detail, you no longer pay attention to it because you are worrying about less important things. • If members of a police force or an army have been ordered to arrest or shoot someone **on sight**, they have been told to arrest or shoot someone as soon as they see them. *Troops shot anyone suspicious on sight.* • If you **set** your **sights on** something, you are determined to have it. *They have set their sights on the world record.*

sighting /'saɪtɪŋ/ **sightings.** N-COUNT A **sighting of** something is an occasion on which it is seen. *...the sighting of a rare sea bird at Lundy island.*

sightseeing /'saɪtsiːɪŋ/. N-UNCOUNT **Sightseeing** is the activity of visiting the interesting places that tourists usually visit.

sign 1 indicators

★ **sign** /saɪn/ **signs.** ① N-COUNT A **sign** is a mark or shape with a particular meaning, for example in mathematics or music. *...an equals sign.* ② N-COUNT A **sign** is a movement of your arms, hands, or head which is intended to have a particular meaning. *Lech Walesa is pictured giving the V-for-victory sign.* ③ N-COUNT A **sign** is a piece of wood, metal, or plastic with words or pictures on it, giving information or instructions. *Follow the road signs on to the D111.* ④ N-COUNT If there is a **sign of** something, there is evidence that it exists. *They are prepared to hand back a hundred prisoners of war a day as a sign of good will... The sky is clear and there's no sign of rain or snow.* ⑤ N-COUNT In astrology, a zodiac **sign** is one of the twelve areas into which the heavens are divided.

★ **sign** /saɪn/ **signs, signing, signed.** ☐1 VERB When you **sign** a document, you put your signature on it. *Before an operation the patient will be asked to sign a consent form.* ♦ **signing** N-UNCOUNT *Spain's top priority is the signing of the treaty.* ☐2 VERB If an organization **signs** someone, or if someone **signs** for an organization, they sign a contract agreeing to work for that organization for a specified period of time. *He has signed to play rugby league with the London Broncos.*

▸ **sign away.** PHR-VERB If you **sign** something **away**, you sign official documents to say that you no longer have a right to it. *The Duke signed away his inheritance.*

▸ **sign for.** PHR-VERB If you **sign for** something, you officially state that you have received it, by signing a form or book.

▸ **sign in.** PHR-VERB If you **sign in**, you officially indicate that you have arrived at a hotel or club by signing a book or form.

▸ **sign on.** ☐1 PHR-VERB When an unemployed person **signs on**, they officially inform the authorities that they are unemployed, so that they can receive money from the government in order to live. [BRITISH] ☐2 PHR-VERB If you **sign on for** something, or if you **sign up for** it, you officially agree to work for an organization or do a course of study by signing a contract or form. *He had signed on for a driving course.*

▸ **sign out.** PHR-VERB If you **sign out**, you indicate that you have left a hotel or club by signing a book or form.

▸ **sign up.** See **sign on 2**.

★ **signal** /'sɪɡnəl/ **signals, signalling, signalled.** (AM **signaling, signaled**). ☐1 N-COUNT A **signal** is a sound or action which is intended to send a particular message. *They fired three distress signals... You mustn't fire without my signal.* ☐2 VERB If you **signal** something, or if you **signal** to someone, you make a gesture or sound in order to give someone a particular message. *She signalled a passing taxi.* ☐3 VERB & N-COUNT If something **signals** a situation, or if it is a **signal of** it, it suggests that the situation is happening or likely to happen. *The lifting of American sanctions signalled the end of an era... Rebel leaders saw the visit as an important signal of support.* ☐4 N-COUNT A **signal** is a piece of equipment beside a railway, which tells train drivers when to stop. ☐5 N-COUNT A **signal** is a series of sound or light waves which carry information. *...high-frequency radio signals.*

signatory /'sɪɡnətri, AM -tɔːri/ **signatories.** N-COUNT The **signatories** to an official document are the people who sign it. *Australia was a signatory to the International Convention on Civil and Political Rights.*

signature /'sɪɡnətʃə/ **signatures.** N-COUNT Your **signature** is your name, written in your own characteristic way.

significance /sɪɡ'nɪfɪkəns/. N-UNCOUNT The **significance** of something is its importance. *The President's visit to this country is loaded with symbolic significance.*

★ **significant** /sɪɡ'nɪfɪkənt/. ☐1 ADJ A **significant** amount of something is large enough to be important or noticeable. ♦ **significantly** ADV *Cars can be made significantly more fuel-efficient.* ☐2 ADJ A **significant** action or gesture is intended to have a special meaning. *Mrs Bycraft gave Rose a significant glance.*

signify /'sɪɡnɪfaɪ/ **signifies, signifying, signified.** VERB An event or a sign or gesture that **signifies** something has a particular meaning. *Becoming a father signified that he was now an adult.*

Sikh /siːk/ **Sikhs.** N-COUNT A **Sikh** is a member of an Indian religion which separated from Hinduism in the sixteenth century and which teaches that there is only one God.

★ **silence** /'saɪləns/ **silences, silencing, silenced.** ☐1 N-VAR If there is **silence**, it is completely quiet. *They stood in silence.* ☐2 N-UNCOUNT Someone's **silence** about something is their refusal to tell people anything about it. *He broke his silence for the first time yesterday about his lovechild.* ☐3 VERB To **silence** someone or something means to stop them speaking or making a noise. *A ringing phone silenced her.* ☐4 VERB If someone **silences** you, they stop you expressing opinions that they do not agree with. *He tried to silence anyone who spoke out against him.*

★ **silent** /'saɪlənt/. ☐1 ADJ AFTER LINK-V Someone or something that is **silent** is making no sound. *The heavy guns have again fallen silent.* ♦ **silently** ADV *She and Ned sat silently for a moment.* ☐2 ADJ BEFORE N If you describe someone as a **silent** person, you mean that they do not talk to people very much, sometimes giving the impression of being unfriendly. *He was the silent type who sat in a corner, painfully shy.* ☐3 ADJ AFTER LINK-V If you are **silent about** something, you do not tell people about it. *The government have told the scientists to remain silent about their work.*

silhouette /ˌsɪluˈet/ **silhouettes.** N-COUNT A **silhouette** is the outline of a dark shape against a bright light or pale background. *The dark silhouette of the castle ruins stood out boldly against the fading light.*

silicon /'sɪlɪkən/. N-UNCOUNT **Silicon** is a non-metallic element that is found combined with oxygen in sand and in minerals such as quartz and granite. Silicon is used to make parts of computers and other electronic equipment.

silicone /'sɪlɪkəʊn/. N-UNCOUNT **Silicone** is a substance made from silicon, which is used to make things such as oils and polishes.

silk /sɪlk/ **silks.** N-VAR **Silk** is a very smooth, fine cloth made from a substance produced by a kind of moth.

silky /'sɪlki/ **silkier, silkiest.** ADJ Something that is **silky** is smooth and soft. *...silky fabrics.*

sill /sɪl/ **sills.** N-COUNT A **sill** is a ledge at the bottom of a window.

a
b
c
d
e
f
g
h
i
j
k
l
m
n
o
p
q
r
s
t
u
v
w
x
y
z

silly /'sɪli/ **sillier, silliest.** ADJ Someone who is being **silly** is behaving in a foolish or childish way. ♦ **silliness** N-UNCOUNT *Let's not have any more of this silliness.*

silt /sɪlt/. N-UNCOUNT **Silt** is fine sand, soil, or mud which is carried along by a river.

⭐ **silver** /'sɪlvə/. **1** N-UNCOUNT **Silver** is a valuable greyish-white metal used for making jewellery and ornaments. *...a hand-crafted brooch made from silver.* **2** N-UNCOUNT **Silver** consists of coins that look like silver. *...£150,000 in silver.* **3** N-UNCOUNT You can use **silver** to refer to all the things in a house that are made of silver, especially the cutlery and dishes. *He beat the rugs and polished the silver.* **4** ADJ & N-COUNT **Silver** is used to describe things that are shiny greyish-white in colour. *He had thick silver hair.*

,**silver** '**medal, silver medals.** N-COUNT A **silver medal** is a medal made of silver which is awarded as second prize in a contest.

silvery /'sɪlvəri/. ADJ **Silvery** things look like silver or are the colour of silver. *...silvery hair.*

'**SIM card, SIM cards.** N-COUNT A **SIM card** is a microchip in a mobile phone that identifies the user and allows them to use the phone network. **SIM** is an abbreviation for 'Subscriber Identity Module'.

⭐ **similar** /'sɪmɪlə/. ADJ If one thing is **similar** to another, or if a number of things are **similar**, they have features that are the same. *...the accident was similar to one that happened in 1973. ...a group of similar pictures.*

similarity /,sɪmɪ'lærɪti/ **similarities.** N-VAR If there is a **similarity between** two or more things, they share some features that are the same. *...the astonishing similarity between my brother and my son... She is also 25 and a native of Birmingham, but the similarity ends there.*

similarly /'sɪmɪləli/. **1** ADV You use **similarly** to say that something is similar to something else. *...a self-help network for themselves and other similarly affected families.* **2** ADV You use **similarly** to say that there is a correspondence or similarity between the way two things happen or are done. *He learned his English mainly from comic books. Similarly, I owe most of my oral French to Tintin and Asterix.*

simmer /'sɪmə/ **simmers, simmering, simmered.** VERB When you **simmer** food, or when it **simmers**, you cook it gently at just below boiling point. *Turn the heat down so the sauce simmers gently.*

⭐ **simple** /'sɪmpəl/ **simpler, simplest.** **1** ADJ If something is **simple**, it is not complicated, and is therefore easy to understand or do. *...simple pictures and diagrams. ...simple maths.* ♦ **simply** ADV *State simply and clearly the reasons why you need an extension.* **2** ADJ **Simple** means containing just the basic or necessary things, but nothing extra. *...a simple dinner of rice and beans.* ♦ **simply** ADV *He dressed simply and led a quiet family life.* **3** ADJ BEFORE N You use **simple** to emphasize that the thing you are referring to is

the only important or relevant reason for something. *His refusal to talk was simple stubbornness.* **4** ADJ In English grammar, **simple** tenses are ones which are not formed using the auxiliary verb 'be', as in 'I dressed and went for a walk' and 'These wines taste awful'. Compare **continuous.** ● See also **simply.**

simplicity /sɪm'plɪsɪti/. **1** N-UNCOUNT The **simplicity** of something is the fact that it is uncomplicated and can be understood or done easily. *Because of its simplicity, this test could be carried out easily by a family doctor.* **2** N-UNCOUNT When you talk about something's **simplicity**, you approve of it because it is natural and simple rather than elaborate or ornate. *...the classical simplicity of the design.*

simplify /'sɪmplɪfaɪ/ **simplifies, simplifying, simplified.** VERB If you **simplify** something, you make it easier to understand. *The aim of the scheme is to simplify the complex social security system.* ♦ **simplified** ADJ *...a shorter, simplified version of his speech.* ♦ **simplification** /,sɪmplɪfɪ'keɪʃən/ **simplifications** N-VAR *...the simplification of court procedures.*

simplistic /sɪm'plɪstɪk/. ADJ A **simplistic** view or interpretation of something makes it seem much simpler than it really is. *He has a simplistic view of the treatment of eczema.*

⭐ **simply** /'sɪmpli/. **1** ADV You use **simply** to emphasize that something consists of only one thing, happens for only one reason, or is done in only one way. *Most of the damage that's occurred was simply because of fallen trees.* **2** ADV You use **simply** to emphasize what you are saying. *...nine out of ten thought it was simply marvellous.* ● See also **simple** .

simulate /'sɪmjʊleɪt/ **simulates, simulating, simulated.** VERB To **simulate** something means to pretend to do it or to produce something like it. *We used this trick in the Army to simulate illness... The wood had been painted to simulate stone.* ♦ **simulation, simulations** N-VAR *Training includes realistic simulation of typical casualty procedures.*

simultaneous /,sɪməl'teɪniəs, AM ,saɪm-/. ADJ Things which are **simultaneous** happen or exist at the same time. *...the simultaneous release of the book and the album.* ♦ **simultaneously** ADV *The two guns fired almost simultaneously.*

sin /sɪn/ **sins, sinning, sinned.** N-VAR & VERB If someone commits a **sin**, or if they **sin**, they do something which is believed to break the laws of God. *The Spanish Inquisition charged him with sinning against God and man.* ♦ **sinner, sinners** N-COUNT *I do not mean to imply that you are sinners.*

⭐ **since** /sɪns/. **1** PREP & ADV & CONJ You use **since** when you are mentioning a time or event in the past and indicating that a situation has continued from then until now. *This research has been in progress since 1961... I simply gave in to him, and I've regretted it ever since... I've been bored to death since I left the army.* **2** ADV & CONJ You use

since to mention a time or event in the past when you are describing an event or situation that has happened after that time. *I haven't seen powdered eggs since the war... So much has changed in the sport since I was a teenager.* **3** ADV When you are talking about an event or situation in the past, you use **since** to indicate that another event happened at some point later in time. *Six thousand people were arrested, several hundred of whom have since been released.* **4** PHRASE If you say that something has **long since** happened, you mean that it happened a long time ago. *Her parents have long since died.* **5** CONJ You use **since** to introduce a reason. *I'm forever on a diet, since I put on weight easily.*

sincere /sɪnˈsɪə/. ADJ If you say that someone is **sincere**, you approve of them because they really mean the things they say. ♦ **sincerity** /sɪnˈserɪti/ N-UNCOUNT *I was greatly impressed with his deep sincerity.*

sincerely /sɪnˈsɪəli/. **1** ADV If you say or feel something **sincerely**, you really mean it or feel it. *...sincerely held religious beliefs.* **2** CONVENTION In British English, people write **Yours sincerely** before their signature at the end of a formal letter when they have addressed it to someone by name. The usual American term is **Sincerely yours**.

sinful /ˈsɪnfʊl/. ADJ If you describe something or someone as **sinful**, you think that they are wicked or immoral. *...sinful thoughts about women.*

⭐ **sing** /sɪŋ/ **sings, singing, sang, sung.** **1** VERB If you **sing**, you make musical sounds with your voice, usually producing words that fit a tune. *Ms Turner sang the theme tune from Goldeneye... Sing us a song!* ♦ **singing** N-UNCOUNT *The dancing and singing ended at midnight.* **2** VERB When birds or insects **sing**, they make pleasant high-pitched sounds. *The bird was singing a beautiful song.* ♦ **singing** N-UNCOUNT *The singing of birds is drowned out by motorway traffic.* **3** to **sing** someone's **praises**: see **praise**.
▸ **sing along.** PHR-VERB If you **sing along** with a piece of music, you sing it while you are listening to someone else perform it. *...fifteen hundred people all singing along.*

⭐ **singer** /ˈsɪŋə/ **singers.** N-COUNT A **singer** is a person who sings, especially as a job.

⭐ **single** /ˈsɪŋɡəl/ **singles, singling, singled.** **1** ADJ BEFORE N You use **single** to emphasize that you are referring to one thing, and no more than one thing. *She hadn't uttered a single word.* **2** ADJ BEFORE N You use **single** to indicate that you are considering something on its own and separately from other things like it. *Every single house in town had been damaged. ...the world's single most important source of oil.* **3** ADJ Someone who is **single** is not married. *When I was single I never worried about money.* **4** ADJ A **single** bed or room is intended for one person. **5** ADJ & N-COUNT In British English, a **single ticket** or a **single** is a ticket for a journey from one place to another but

not back again. The usual American term is **one-way** ticket. **6** N-COUNT A **single** is a CD which has one main song on it. *...the band's British and American hit singles.* **7** N-UNCOUNT **Singles** is a game of tennis or badminton in which one player plays another.
▸ **single out.** PHR-VERB If you **single** someone **out**, you choose them and give them special attention or treatment. *His immediate superior has singled him out for a special mention.*

single-. **Single-** is used to form words which describe something that has one part or feature, rather than having two or more of them. *...a single-sex school. ...a single-track road.*

ˌsingle-ˈhanded. ADV If you do something **single-handed**, you do it without help from anyone else. *I brought up my seven children single-handed.* ♦ **single-handedly** ADV *Olga Korbut single-handedly turned gymnastics into a major event.*

ˌsingle-ˈminded. ADJ A **single-minded** person has only one aim and is determined to achieve it. *...a single-minded determination to win.*
♦ **single-mindedness** N-UNCOUNT *...the single-mindedness of the athletes as they train.*

ˌsingle ˈparent, single parents. N-COUNT A **single parent** is someone who is bringing up a child on their own, because the other parent is not living with them.

singular /ˈsɪŋɡjʊlə/. **1** ADJ BEFORE N & N-SING The **singular** form of a word or **the singular** is the form that is used when referring to one person or thing. *The word 'you' can be singular or plural... The inhabitants of the Arctic are known as the Inuit. The singular is Inuk.* **2** ADJ **Singular** means very great and remarkable. [FORMAL]
♦ **singularly** ADV *...a former sales executive singularly unsuited for the job.*

sinister /ˈsɪnɪstə/. ADJ Someone or something that is **sinister** seems evil or harmful. *There was something sinister about him that Elizabeth found disturbing.*

⭐ **sink** /sɪŋk/ **sinks, sinking, sank, sunk.** **1** N-COUNT A **sink** is a basin with taps that supply water. *There were dirty dishes in the sink.* **2** VERB If a boat **sinks**, or if something **sinks** it, it disappears below the surface of a mass of water. *In a naval battle your aim is to sink the enemy's ship.* **3** VERB If something **sinks**, it disappears below the surface of a mass of water. *A fresh egg will sink and an old egg will float.* **4** VERB If you **sink**, you move into a lower position, for example by sitting down in a chair or kneeling. *She sank into an armchair and crossed her legs.* **5** VERB If something **sinks** to a lower level or standard, it falls to that level or standard. *Pay increases have sunk to around seven per cent.* **6** VERB If your voice **sinks**, it becomes quieter. [WRITTEN] *She heard their voices sink into a confidential whisper.* **7** VERB To **sink into** an unpleasant or undesirable situation or state means to pass gradually into it. *Bulgaria's economy has sunk into chaos.* **8** PHRASE If your

a
b
c
d
e
f
g
h
i
j
k
l
m
n
o
p
q
r
s
t
u
v
w
x
y
z

A
B
C
D
E
F
G
H
I
J
K
L
M
N
O
P
Q
R
S
T
U
V
W
X
Y
Z

heart sinks, you become depressed. *My heart sank because I thought he was going to dump me for another girl.* **9** VERB If something sharp **sinks** or **is sunk into** something solid, it goes deeply into it. *He sinks the needle into my arm.* ● See also **sunken**.

▸ **sink in.** PHR-VERB When a statement or fact **sinks in**, you finally understand or realize it fully. *The implication took a while to sink in.*

sip /sɪp/ **sips, sipping, sipped.** VERB & N-COUNT If you **sip** a drink, or if you drink it in **sips**, you drink a small amount at a time. *She sipped from her coffee mug.*

siphon (or **syphon**) /ˈsaɪfən/ **siphons, siphoning, siphoned.** **1** VERB If you **siphon** a liquid, you draw it from somewhere through a tube by using atmospheric pressure. *The town wasn't able to siphon any water out of the river.* **2** N-COUNT A **siphon** is a tube which is used for siphoning liquid.

☆ **sir** /sɜː/. **1** N-VOC People sometimes say **sir** as a polite way of addressing a man whose name they do not know or a man of superior rank. 'Dear Sir' is used at the beginning of official letters addressed to men. *Good afternoon, sir, and welcome to The New World Diner.* **2** N-TITLE **Sir** is the title used in front of the name of a knight or baronet. *...Sir Geoffrey Howe.*

siren /ˈsaɪərən/ **sirens.** N-COUNT A **siren** is a warning device which makes a long, loud, wailing noise. Most fire engines, ambulances, and police cars have sirens.

☆ **sister** /ˈsɪstə/ **sisters.** **1** N-COUNT Your **sister** is a girl or woman who has the same parents as you.

> **USAGE** Note that there is no common English word that can refer to both a brother and a sister. You simply have to use both words. *He has 13 brothers and sisters.* The word **sibling** exists, but it is rare and very formal.

2 N-COUNT & N-TITLE **Sister** is a title given to a woman who belongs to a religious community such as a convent. *I'm Sister Agnes.* **3** N-COUNT & N-TITLE In Britain, a **sister** is a senior female nurse who supervises a hospital ward. *Sister Middleton followed the coffee trolley.* **4** N-COUNT You might use **sister** to describe a woman who belongs to the same race, religion, country, or organization as you, or who has ideas that are similar to yours. *...our Jewish brothers and sisters in New York.*

'sister-in-law, sisters-in-law. N-COUNT Your **sister-in-law** is the sister of your husband or wife, or the woman who is married to your brother.

☆ **sit** /sɪt/ **sits, sitting, sat.** **1** VERB If you **are sitting** somewhere, for example in a chair, your weight is supported by your buttocks rather than your feet. *He was unable to sit still.* **2** VERB When you **sit** somewhere, you lower your body until you are sitting on something. *He set the cases against a wall and sat on them.* **3** VERB If you **sit** someone somewhere, you tell them to sit there or put them in a sitting position. *He used to sit me on his lap.* **4** VERB If you **sit on** a committee, you are a member of it. **5** VERB In British English, if you **sit** an examination, you do it. In American English, you **take** an examination. ● See note at **exam**. **6** VERB When a parliament, law court, or other official body **is sitting**, it is officially carrying out its work. [FORMAL] **7** PHRASE If you **sit tight**, you remain where you are and do not take any action. *Sit tight. I'll be right back.* ● to **sit on the fence**: see **fence**.

▸ **sit around** (BRIT also **sit about**). PHR-VERB If you **sit around** or **sit about**, you spend time doing nothing useful. [INFORMAL] *Eve isn't the type to sit around doing nothing.*

▸ **sit back.** PHR-VERB If you **sit back** while something is happening, you relax and do not become involved in it. *Get everyone talking and then sit back and enjoy the conversation.*

▸ **sit in on.** PHR-VERB If you **sit in on** a meeting or lesson, you are present while it is taking place but do not take part in it. *Will they permit you to sit in on a few classes?*

▸ **sit on.** PHR-VERB If you say that someone **is sitting on** something, you mean that they are deliberately not dealing with it or not revealing it to others. *He had been sitting on the document for at least two months.*

▸ **sit out.** PHR-VERB If you **sit** something **out**, you wait for it to finish, without taking any action. *He can afford to sit out the property slump.*

▸ **sit through.** PHR-VERB If you **sit through** something such as a film or lecture, you stay until it is finished, although you are not enjoying it. *I sat through a long interview with the minister for tourism.*

▸ **sit up.** **1** PHR-VERB If you **sit up**, you move into a sitting position when you have been leaning back or lying down. **2** PHR-VERB If you **sit up**, you do not go to bed although it is very late. *We sat up drinking and talking.*

☆ **site** /saɪt/ **sites, siting, sited.** **1** N-COUNT A **site** is a piece of ground that is used for a particular purpose or where a particular thing happens or is situated. *...a building site. ...the site of the worst ecological disaster on earth. ...the site of Moses' tomb.* **2** VERB If something **is sited** in a particular place or position, it is placed there. *He said chemical weapons had never been sited in Germany.* ◆ **siting** N-SING *...controls on the siting of gas storage vessels.*

'sitting-room, sitting-rooms. N-COUNT A **sitting-room** is a room in a house where people sit and relax. [BRITISH]

situated /ˈsɪtʃueɪtɪd/. ADJ If something is **situated** somewhere, it is in a particular place or position. *His hotel is situated in one of the loveliest places on the Loire.*

☆ **situation** /ˌsɪtʃuˈeɪʃən/ **situations.** **1** N-COUNT You use **situation** to refer generally to what is happening at a particular place and time, or to refer to what is happening to you. *Army officers said the situation was under control... Men are not used to coping with women as equals in a work situation... I must do what any person would do in my situation.* [2] N-COUNT The **situation** of a building or town is its surroundings. [FORMAL] *A minor disadvantage is the hotel's situation on an island.*

'**sit-up**, **sit-ups**. N-COUNT **Sit-ups** are exercises that you do by sitting up from a lying position, keeping your feet on the floor, and without using your hands.

⭐ **six** /sɪks/ **sixes**. NUM **Six** is the number 6.

'**six-pack**, **six-packs**. N-COUNT If a man has a **six-pack**, his stomach muscles are very well developed.

⭐ **sixteen** /ˌsɪks'tiːn/ **sixteens**. NUM **Sixteen** is the number 16.

⭐ **sixteenth** /ˌsɪks'tiːnθ/ **sixteenths**. [1] ORD The **sixteenth** item in a series is the one that you count as number sixteen. [2] N-COUNT A **sixteenth** is one of sixteen equal parts of something.

⭐ **sixth** /sɪksθ/ **sixths**. [1] ORD The **sixth** item in a series is the one that you count as number six. [2] N-COUNT A **sixth** is one of six equal parts of something.

'**sixth form**, **sixth forms**. N-COUNT The **sixth form** in a British school consists of the classes that pupils go into at the age of sixteen to study for 'A' Levels.

⭐ **sixtieth** /'sɪkstiəθ/. ORD The **sixtieth** item in a series is the one that you count as number sixty.

⭐ **sixty** /'sɪksti/ **sixties**. NUM **Sixty** is the number 60. For examples of how numbers such as sixty and eighty are used see **eighty**.

'**six-yard 'box**. N-SING On a football pitch, **the six-yard box** is the rectangular area marked in front of each goal.

sizable /'saɪzəbəl/. See **sizeable**.

⭐ **size** /saɪz/ **sizes**, **sizing**, **sized**. [1] N-UNCOUNT The **size** of something is how big or small it is. *The company had more than doubled in size. ...an area five times the size of Britain... Cut the chicken into bite-size pieces.* ◆ **-sized** *...a medium-sized college.* [2] N-UNCOUNT The **size** of something is the fact that it is very large. *Jack walked around the hotel and was mesmerized by its sheer size.* [3] N-COUNT A **size** is one of a series of graded measurements, especially for things such as clothes or shoes. *My sister is the same height but only a size 12.*

▸**size up**. PHR-VERB If you **size up** a person or situation, you carefully look at the person or think about the situation, so that you can decide how to act. [INFORMAL] *He spent the evening sizing me up intellectually.*

sizeable (or **sizable**) /'saɪzəbəl/. ADJ **Sizeable** means fairly large. *...a sizeable chunk of land.*

sizzle /'sɪzəl/ **sizzles**, **sizzling**, **sizzled**. VERB If something **sizzles**, it makes a hissing sound like the sound made by frying food. *The sausages and burgers sizzled.*

skate /skeɪt/ **skates**, **skating**, **skated**. [1] N-COUNT **Skates** are **ice-skates** or **roller-skates**. [2] VERB If you **skate**, you move about wearing ice-skates or roller-skates. *Dan skated up to him.* ◆ **skater**, **skaters** N-COUNT *His dream was to become a professional skater.* ◆ **skating** N-UNCOUNT *They all went skating together.*

skeletal /'skelɪtəl/. ADJ BEFORE N **Skeletal** means relating to skeletons. *...the skeletal remains of seven adults.*

skeleton /'skelɪtən/ **skeletons**. [1] N-COUNT Your **skeleton** is the framework of bones in your body. [2] ADJ BEFORE N A **skeleton** staff is the smallest number of staff necessary to run an organization.

skeptic /'skeptɪk/. See **sceptic**.

skeptical /'skeptɪkəl/. See **sceptical**.

skepticism /'skeptɪsɪzəm/. See **scepticism**.

sketch /sketʃ/ **sketches**, **sketching**, **sketched**. [1] N-COUNT A **sketch** is a drawing that is done quickly without a lot of details. *Make a rough sketch showing where the vehicles were.* [2] VERB If you **sketch** something, you make a quick rough drawing of it. *He sketched a map on the back of a menu.* [3] N-COUNT A **sketch of** an incident or person is a brief description of them without many details. *Leonard had given a brief sketch of his childhood.* [4] VERB & PHR-VERB If you **sketch** or **sketch out** a plan or incident, you briefly describe or state its main points. *I had visited him in Johannesburg and sketched what I was trying to do.* [5] N-COUNT A **sketch** is a short humorous piece of acting, usually forming part of a comedy show.

sketchy /'sketʃi/ **sketchier**, **sketchiest**. ADJ Something that is **sketchy** is incomplete and does not have many details. *Details are sketchy, but first reports say at least eight people were hit.*

skewer /'skjuːə/ **skewers**, **skewering**, **skewered**. [1] N-COUNT A **skewer** is a long metal pin which is used to hold pieces of food together during cooking. [2] VERB If you **skewer** something, you push a long, thin, pointed object through it. *He skewered one of the sausages.*

skiing

⭐ **ski** /skiː/ **skis**, **skiing**, **skied**. [1] N-COUNT **Skis** are long, flat, narrow pieces of wood, metal, or plastic that are fastened to boots so that you can move easily over snow. [2] VERB When people **ski**, they move over snow on skis. ◆ **skier**, **skiers** N-COUNT *He is an enthusiastic skier.* ◆ **skiing** N-UNCOUNT *...a* skiing holiday. [3] ADJ BEFORE N **Ski** is used to refer to things that are concerned with skiing. ...*a Swiss ski resort.* ...*ski boots.*

skid /skɪd/ **skids, skidding, skidded.** VERB & N-COUNT If a vehicle **skids**, or if it goes into a **skid**, it slides sideways or forwards in an uncontrolled way. *There was heavy snow and the plane skidded on landing.*

skilful (AM **skillful**) /'skɪlfʊl/. ADJ Someone who is **skilful** at something does it very well. *He is a particularly skilful writer.* ♦ **skilfully** ADV *He dealt skilfully with a series of demanding clients.*

⭐ **skill** /skɪl/ **skills.** [1] N-COUNT A **skill** is a type of activity or work which requires special training or knowledge. *We need to focus on the basic skills of literacy and numeracy.* [2] N-UNCOUNT **Skill** is the knowledge and ability that enables you to do something well. *I tried fishing but had no skill and no luck.*

skilled /skɪld/. [1] ADJ Someone who is **skilled** has the knowledge and ability to do something well. *A train driver is a highly skilled professional.* [2] ADJ **Skilled** work can only be done by people who have had some training.

skillful /'skɪlfʊl/. See **skilful**.

skim /skɪm/ **skims, skimming, skimmed.** [1] VERB If you **skim** something from the surface of a liquid, you remove it. *Skim the fat off the gravy.* [2] VERB If something **skims** a surface or **skims** over it, it moves quickly along just above it. *We'll watch the flying fishes skimming across the water.* [3] VERB If you **skim** a piece of writing or **skim through** it, you read through it quickly. *He skimmed the pages quickly, then read them again more carefully.*

skimpy /'skɪmpi/ **skimpier, skimpiest.** ADJ **Skimpy** means too small in size or quantity. **Skimpy** clothes reveal a lot of someone's body. ...*skimpy underwear.*

⭐ **skin** /skɪn/ **skins, skinning, skinned.** [1] N-VAR Your **skin** is the natural covering of your body. *His skin is clear and smooth.* [2] N-VAR An animal **skin** is skin which has been removed from a dead animal. *That was real crocodile skin.* [3] N-VAR The **skin** of a fruit or vegetable is its outer layer or covering. ...*banana skins.* [4] N-VAR If a **skin** forms on the surface of a liquid, a thin solid layer forms on it. *Stir the custard occasionally to prevent a skin forming.* [5] VERB If you **skin** a dead animal, you remove its skin.

skinny /'skɪni/ **skinnier, skinniest.** ADJ If you say that someone is **skinny**, you mean that they are very thin in a way you find unattractive. [INFORMAL] *She had stringy hair and skinny legs.*

skip /skɪp/ **skips, skipping, skipped.** [1] VERB & N-COUNT If you **skip** along, you move along with a series of little jumps from one foot to the other, called **skips**. *They skipped down the street...* *Anna gave a little skip of joy.* [2] VERB When someone **skips**, they jump up and down over a rope which they or other people are holding at each end and turning round and round. ♦ **skipping** N-UNCOUNT

I enjoy skipping, walking, singing and playing games. [3] VERB If you **skip** something that you usually do or that most people do, you decide not do it. *It is important not to skip meals.* [4] VERB If you **skip** a part of something you are reading or a story you are telling, you miss it out or pass over it quickly. *She reinvented her own life story, skipping over the war years.* [5] N-COUNT A **skip** is a large, open, metal container used to hold and take away rubbish. [BRITISH]

skipper /'skɪpə/ **skippers.** N-COUNT The **skipper** of a boat or of a sports team is its captain. [INFORMAL]

skirmish /'skɜːmɪʃ/ **skirmishes.** N-COUNT A **skirmish** is a short battle which is not part of a planned war strategy. *One Federal soldier was killed in the skirmish that ensued.*

skirt /skɜːt/ **skirts, skirting, skirted.** [1] N-COUNT A **skirt** is a piece of clothing worn by women and girls. It fastens at the waist and hangs down around the legs. → See picture on page 819. [2] VERB Something that **skirts** an area is situated around the edge of it. ...*the gravel path that skirted the main lawn.* [3] VERB If you **skirt** something, you go around the edge of it. *She skirted round the edge of the room to the door.* [4] VERB If you **skirt** a problem or question, you avoid dealing with it. *He skirted round his main differences with her.*

skull /skʌl/ **skulls.** N-COUNT Your **skull** is the bony part of your head which encloses your brain. *He was left with a broken arm and a fractured skull.*

⭐ **sky** /skaɪ/ **skies.** N-VAR The **sky** is the space around the earth which you can see when you stand outside and look upwards. ...*warm sunshine and clear blue skies.*

skyline /'skaɪlaɪn/ **skylines.** N-COUNT The **skyline** is the line or shape that is formed where the sky meets buildings or the land. *The village church dominates the skyline.*

skyscraper /'skaɪskreɪpə/ **skyscrapers.** N-COUNT A **skyscraper** is a very tall building in a city.

slab /slæb/ **slabs.** N-COUNT A **slab of** something is a thick flat piece of it. ...*enormous slabs of meat.* ...*huge concrete paving slabs.*

slack /slæk/ **slacker, slackest.** [1] ADJ Something that is **slack** is loose and not firmly stretched or tightly in position. ...*her rather dull, slack skin.* [2] ADJ A **slack** period is one in which there is not much activity. *Business has been a bit slack.* [3] ADJ If someone is **slack** in their work, they do not do it properly.

slacken /'slækən/ **slackens, slackening, slackened.** [1] VERB If something **slackens**, or if you **slacken** it, it becomes slower, less active, or less intense. *The wind slackened... He slackened his pace for me.* [2] VERB If your grip or a part of your body **slackens**, or if you **slacken** it, it becomes looser or more relaxed. *Muscles stretch, slacken and relax during childbirth.*

▸ **slacken off.** PHR-VERB If something **slackens off**, it becomes slower, less active, or less intense. *At about five o'clock, business slackened off.*

For a full explanation of all grammatical labels, see pages vii–x ⭐ Bank of English® frequent word

slacks /slæks/. N-PLURAL **Slacks** are casual trousers. [DATED] *She was wearing black slacks.*

slain /sleɪn/. **Slain** is the past participle of **slay**.

slam /slæm/ **slams, slamming, slammed.** [1] VERB If you **slam** a door or window, or if it **slams**, it shuts noisily and with great force. *He slammed the gate shut behind him.* [2] VERB If you **slam** something **down**, you put it there quickly and with great force. *She was outraged and slammed down the phone.* [3] VERB If one thing **slams into** another, or if it **slams against** another, it crashes into it with great force. *He was killed when his car slammed into a truck... He slammed his fist against the wall.*

slander /'slɑːndə, 'slæn-/ **slanders, slandering, slandered.** [1] N-VAR **Slander** is an untrue spoken statement about someone which is intended to damage their reputation. *He is suing his former wife for slander. ...lies, rumours and slanders.* [2] VERB If someone **slanders** you, they make untrue spoken statements about you in order to damage your reputation.

slang /slæŋ/. N-UNCOUNT **Slang** is words, expressions, and meanings that are informal and are used by people who know each other very well or who have the same interests. *... US Army slang.*

slant /slɑːnt, slænt/ **slants, slanting, slanted.** [1] VERB Something that **slants** is sloping, rather than horizontal or vertical. *The morning sun slanted through the glass roof.* [2] N-SING If something is **on a slant**, it is in a sloping position. [3] VERB If information or a system **is slanted**, it is made to show favour towards a particular group or opinion. *The programme was deliberately slanted to make the home team look good.* [4] N-SING A particular **slant** on a subject is a particular way of thinking about it, especially one that is unfair or biased. *They give a slant to every single news item that's put on the air.*

slap /slæp/ **slaps, slapping, slapped.** [1] VERB & N-COUNT If you **slap** someone, or if you give them a **slap**, you hit them with the palm of your hand. *I slapped him hard across the face.* [2] PHRASE If you describe something that someone does as **a slap in the face**, you mean that it shocks or upsets you because it shows that they do not support you or respect you. [3] VERB If you **slap** someone **on** the back, you hit them in a friendly manner on their back. [4] VERB If you **slap** something onto a surface, you put it there quickly and carelessly, often with a lot of force. *I slapped the sweets down on the table... I'll show you how to slap a bit of paint on the wall.*

slash /slæʃ/ **slashes, slashing, slashed.** [1] VERB If you **slash** something, you make a long deep cut in it. *Four cars had their tyres slashed.* [2] VERB If you **slash at** something, you quickly hit at it with something. *She slashed at me with an unpleasantly large carving-knife.* [3] VERB To **slash** something such as costs or jobs means to reduce them by a large amount. [INFORMAL]

slate /sleɪt/ **slates.** [1] N-UNCOUNT **Slate** is a dark grey rock that can be easily split into thin layers. [2] N-COUNT A **slate** is one of the small flat pieces of slate that are used for covering roofs.

slaughter /'slɔːtə/ **slaughters, slaughtering, slaughtered.** [1] VERB & N-UNCOUNT If large numbers of people or animals **are slaughtered**, they are killed in a way that is cruel, unjust, or unnecessary. **Slaughter** is the cruel, unjust, or unnecessary killing of large numbers of people or animals. *...responsible for the slaughter of innocent civilians.* [2] VERB & N-UNCOUNT To **slaughter** animals such as cows and sheep means to kill them for their meat. **Slaughter** is the killing of animals for their meat. *Commercial pigs are ready for slaughter at four to six months.* [3] See note at **kill**.

slave /sleɪv/ **slaves.** [1] N-COUNT A **slave** is a person who is owned by another person and has to work for that person without pay. [2] N-COUNT If you say that someone is a **slave to** something, you mean that they are very strongly influenced or controlled by it. *Anthony was never a slave to possessions.*

slavery /'sleɪvəri/. N-UNCOUNT **Slavery** is the system by which people are owned by other people as slaves. *...a fervent campaigner for the abolition of slavery.*

slay /sleɪ/ **slays, slaying, slew, slain.** VERB To **slay** a person or animal means to kill them. [LITERARY] *...the field where Saint George is reputed to have slain the dragon.*

sleazy /'sliːzi/ **sleazier, sleaziest.** [1] ADJ If you describe a place as **sleazy**, you dislike it because it looks dirty and not respectable. [INFORMAL] *...sleazy bars.* [2] ADJ If you describe something or someone as **sleazy**, you disapprove of them because you think they are not respectable and are rather sordid. [INFORMAL] *...sex shops and sleazy magazines.*

sled /sled/ **sleds.** N-COUNT A **sled** is the same as a **sledge**. [AMERICAN]

sledge /sledʒ/ **sledges.** N-COUNT & VERB A **sledge** is a vehicle for travelling over snow. It consists of a framework which slides on two strips of wood or metal. [BRITISH]

sleek /sliːk/ **sleeker, sleekest.** [1] ADJ **Sleek** hair or fur is smooth and shiny and looks healthy. [2] ADJ A **sleek** person looks rich and stylish. [3] ADJ **Sleek** vehicles, furniture, or other objects look smooth, shiny, and expensive.

⭐ **sleep** /sliːp/ **sleeps, sleeping, slept.** [1] N-UNCOUNT **Sleep** is the natural state of rest in which your eyes are closed, your body is inactive, and your mind does not think. *Try and get some sleep... Be quiet and go to sleep.* [2] VERB & N-COUNT When you **sleep**, you rest with your eyes closed and your mind and body inactive. A **sleep** is a period of sleeping. *She slept till noon. ...a pool surrounded by sleeping sunbathers... I think he may be ready for a sleep soon.* [3] VERB If one person **sleeps with** another, or if two people **sleep together**, they have sex. **4** VERB If a building or room **sleeps** a particular number of people, it has beds for that number of people. *The villa sleeps 10.*

USAGE There are several verbal expressions in English which refer to the moment when you start to sleep. When you go to bed at night, you normally **go to sleep** or **fall asleep**. When you **go to sleep**, it is usually a deliberate action. *He didn't want to go to sleep.* You can **fall asleep** by accident, or at a time when you should be awake. *I've seen doctors fall asleep in the operating theatre.* If you have difficulty sleeping, you can say that you cannot **get to sleep** *Sometimes the fever prevents the child from getting to sleep.*

PHRASES ● If you say that you did not **lose** any **sleep over** something, you mean that you did not worry about it at all. ● If a sick or injured animal **is put to sleep**, it is painlessly killed by a vet. ● to **sleep rough**: see **rough**.

▶ **sleep around.** PHR-VERB If you say that someone **sleeps around**, you disapprove of them because they have sex with a lot of different people. [INFORMAL]

▶ **sleep off.** PHR-VERB If you **sleep off** the effects of too much drink, food, or travelling, you recover from it by sleeping. *It's a good idea to spend the first night of your holiday sleeping off the jet lag.*

▶ **sleep through.** PHR-VERB If you **sleep through** a noise, it does not wake you up. *They had slept right through the alarm.*

sleeper /ˈsliːpə/ **sleepers. 1** N-COUNT You can use **sleeper** to indicate how well someone sleeps. For example, if someone is a light **sleeper**, they are easily woken up. *I'm a very heavy sleeper.* **2** N-COUNT A **sleeper** is a train with beds for passengers on overnight journeys. You can also refer to the beds themselves as **sleepers**. [BRITISH] *The train is air-conditioned and has first and second class sleepers.* **3** N-COUNT Railway **sleepers** are large heavy beams that support the rails of a railway track. [BRITISH]

'sleeping bag, sleeping bags. N-COUNT A **sleeping bag** is a large warm bag for sleeping in, especially when you are camping.

sleepless /ˈsliːpləs/ **1** ADJ A **sleepless** night is one during which you do not sleep. **2** ADJ Someone who is **sleepless** is unable to sleep. *She was still sitting there, grim and sleepless, when Frank arrived.* ◆ **sleeplessness** N-UNCOUNT *He continued to suffer from sleeplessness.*

sleepover /ˈsliːpəʊvə/ **sleepovers.** N-COUNT A **sleepover** is an occasion when a child stays at a friend's home for the night.

sleepy /ˈsliːpi/ **sleepier, sleepiest. 1** ADJ If you feel **sleepy**, you feel tired and ready to go to sleep. *'Are we here, love?' she said in a hoarse, sleepy voice.* ◆ **sleepily** ADV *Joanna sat up, blinking*

sleepily. 2 ADJ A **sleepy** place is very quiet and does not have much activity or excitement. *...a sleepy fishing village.*

sleet /sliːt/. N-UNCOUNT **Sleet** is rain that is partly frozen.

sleeve /sliːv/ **sleeves. 1** N-COUNT The **sleeves** of a coat, shirt, or other item of clothing are the parts that cover your arms. *...a shirt with long sleeves.* **2** PHRASE If you have something **up** your **sleeve**, you have an idea or plan which you have not told anyone about. *I still have a few tricks up my sleeve.* **3** N-COUNT In British English, a record **sleeve** is the stiff envelope in which a record is kept. The usual American word is **jacket**.

sleigh /sleɪ/ **sleighs.** N-COUNT A **sleigh** is a vehicle like a sledge which can slide over snow. Sleighs are usually pulled by horses.

slender /ˈslendə/. **1** ADJ A **slender** person is thin and graceful in an attractive way. [WRITTEN] *...a tall slender woman. ...her long slender legs.* **2** ADJ You can use **slender** to describe a situation which exists but only to a very small degree. [WRITTEN] *...the slender majority won by his government.*

slept /slept/. **Slept** is the past tense and past participle of **sleep**.

slew /sluː/. **1** **Slew** is the past tense of **slay**. **2** N-SING A **slew** of things or people is a large number of them. [AMERICAN] *They'd evidently had a slew of customers.*

★ **slice** /slaɪs/ **slices, slicing, sliced. 1** N-COUNT A **slice** of bread, meat, fruit, or other food is a thin piece that has been cut from a larger piece. *...a slice of lemon... Cut the onion halves into slices.* **2** VERB If you **slice** food, you cut it into thin pieces. *Slice the steak into long thin slices... I usually buy sliced bread.* **3** VERB If something **slices through** a substance, it moves through it quickly, like a knife. [LITERARY] *The ship sliced through the water.* **4** N-COUNT If you talk about someone getting a **slice of** something, you mean that they get a part of it. *Other ports are determined to challenge Hong Kong for a larger slice of the region's trade.*

slick /slɪk/ **slicker, slickest; slicks. 1** ADJ A **slick** performance, production, or advertisement is presented in an attractive and professional way. **2** ADJ A **slick** action is done quickly and smoothly, and without any obvious effort. **3** ADJ If you describe someone as **slick**, you dislike them because they speak easily and persuasively but are not sincere. *...slick politicians.* **4** N-COUNT A **slick** is the same as an **oil slick**.

★ **slide** /slaɪd/ **slides, sliding, slid** /slɪd/. **1** VERB When something **slides** somewhere, or when you **slide** it somewhere, it moves there smoothly over or against something else. *Tears were sliding down his cheeks... She slid the door open.* **2** VERB If you **slide** somewhere, you move there smoothly and quietly. *He slid into the driver's seat.* **3** N-COUNT A **slide** in a playground is a structure that has a steep slope for children to slide down. **4** VERB To **slide into** a particular mood, attitude, or situation

---

means to gradually start to have that mood, attitude, or situation, often without intending to. *She had slid into a depression.* **5** N-COUNT A **slide** is a small piece of photographic film which you project onto a screen so that you can see the picture.

⭐ **slight** /slaɪt/ **slighter, slightest; slights, slighting, slighted.** **1** ADJ Something that is **slight** is very small in degree or quantity. *Doctors say he has made a slight improvement... He's not the slightest bit worried.* **2** PHRASE You use **in the slightest** to emphasize a negative statement. *That doesn't interest me in the slightest.* **3** ADJ A **slight** person has a slim and delicate body. **4** VERB & N-COUNT If you **are slighted**, someone does or says something that insults you by treating you as if your views or feelings are not important. You refer to what that person does or says as a **slight**. *They felt slighted by not being adequately consulted.*

⭐ **slightly** /ˈslaɪtli/. ADV **Slightly** means to some degree but not to a very large degree. *His family then moved to a slightly larger house... You can adjust it slightly.*

⭐ **slim** /slɪm/ **slimmer, slimmest; slims, slimming, slimmed.** **1** ADJ A **slim** person has a thin nicely-shaped body. **2** VERB If you **are slimming**, you are trying to make yourself thinner and lighter by eating less food. ♦ **slimmer, slimmers** N-COUNT *...meals for slimmers.* ♦ **slimming** N-UNCOUNT *We live in a society which is obsessed with slimming.* **3** ADJ A **slim** book, wallet, or other object is thinner than usual. **4** ADJ A **slim** chance or possibility is a very small one. *The chances of a new author getting published are very slim.*
▸**slim down.** PHR-VERB If a company or other organization **slims down**, or if it **is slimmed down**, it employs fewer people, in order to save money or become more efficient.

slime /slaɪm/. N-UNCOUNT **Slime** is a thick slippery substance, for example the substance which comes from a slug.

sling /slɪŋ/ **slings, slinging, slung.** **1** VERB If you **sling** something somewhere, you throw it there carelessly. *I saw him take off his anorak and sling it into the back seat.* **2** VERB If you **sling** something over your shoulder or over something such as a chair, you hang it there loosely. *He had a small green rucksack slung over one shoulder.* **3** VERB If a rope, blanket, or other object **is slung** between two points, it is hung loosely between them. *...a hammock slung between the trees.* **4** N-COUNT A **sling** is an object made of ropes, straps, or cloth that is used for carrying things. *In many parts of Kenya, babies are carried in slings all day.* **5** N-COUNT A **sling** is a piece of cloth used to support an injured arm. It goes under someone's lower arm and is tied around their neck. *Next day she was back at work with her arm in a sling.*

⭐ **slip** /slɪp/ **slips, slipping, slipped.** **1** VERB If you **slip**, you accidentally slide and lose your balance. *I guess I must have slipped on some ice.* **2** VERB If

something **slips**, it slides out of place or out of your hand. *His glasses slipped down his nose... The hammer slipped out of her grasp.* **3** VERB If you **slip** somewhere, you go there quickly and quietly. *Amy slipped downstairs and out of the house... I slipped out of bed.* **4** VERB If you **slip** something somewhere, you put it there quickly in a way that does not attract attention. *He found a coin in his pocket and slipped it into her collecting tin.* **5** VERB If you **slip** something **to** someone, or if you **slip** someone something, you give it to them secretly. *Robert had slipped her a note in school.* **6** VERB To **slip into** a particular state or situation means to pass gradually into it, in a way that is hardly noticed. *Don't slip into the habit of sleeping late.* **7** VERB If you **slip** into or **slip** out of clothes or shoes, you put them on or take them off quickly and easily. *Laila stood up and slipped on her coat before he could assist her... I slipped off my woollen gloves.* **8** N-COUNT A **slip** is a small or unimportant mistake. **9** N-COUNT A **slip** of paper is a small piece of paper.
▸**slip up.** PHR-VERB If you **slip up**, you make a small or unimportant mistake.

slipper /ˈslɪpə/ **slippers.** N-COUNT **Slippers** are loose soft shoes that you wear in the house.
→ See picture on page 820.

slippery /ˈslɪpəri/. **1** ADJ Something that is **slippery** is smooth, wet, or greasy, making it difficult to walk on or to hold. *Motorists were warned to beware of slippery conditions.* **2** PHRASE If you say that someone is on a **slippery slope to** something bad, you mean that their behaviour or actions will inevitably lead to that condition in the near future. *It is the slippery slope to anarchy when one part of society is above the law.*

split **3**

slit **2**

slit /slɪt/ **slits, slitting, slit.** **1** VERB If you **slit** something, you make a long narrow cut in it. *He slit open the bag with a penknife... My girlfriend was threatening to slit her wrists.* **2** N-COUNT A **slit** is a long narrow cut or opening in something. *Make a slit in the stem about half an inch long... She watched them through a slit in the curtains.*

slither /ˈslɪðə/ **slithers, slithering, slithered.** VERB If you **slither** somewhere, you slide along, often in an uncontrolled way. *Robert lost his footing and slithered down the bank.*

a
b
c
d
e
f
g
h
i
j
k
l
m
n
o
p
q
r
s
t
u
v
w
x
y
z

sliver /'slɪvə/ **slivers.** N-COUNT A **sliver of** something is a small thin piece or amount of it. ...slivers of glass.

slog /slɒg/ **slogs, slogging, slogged.** [1] VERB If you **slog through** something, you work hard and steadily through it. [INFORMAL] She has slogged her way through ballet classes since the age of six. [2] N-SING If you describe a task as a **slog**, you mean that it is tiring and requires a lot of effort. [INFORMAL] [3] VERB & N-SING If you **slog** somewhere, you make a long and tiring journey there, which you can refer to as a **slog**. [INFORMAL] ...a slog through heather and bracken to the top of a hill.

slogan /'sləʊgən/ **slogans.** N-COUNT A **slogan** is a short phrase that is easy to remember and is used in advertisements and by political parties.

slop /slɒp/ **slops, slopping, slopped.** VERB If you **slop** liquid, or if it **slops**, it spills over the edge of a container in a messy way. She slopped some tea into the saucer.

slope /sləʊp/ **slopes, sloping, sloped.** [1] N-COUNT A **slope** is a surface that is at an angle, so that one end is higher than the other. The street must have been on a slope. [2] VERB If a surface **slopes**, it is at an angle, so that one end is higher than the other. The bank sloped down sharply to the river. ◆ **sloping** ADJ ...the gently sloping beach. [3] VERB If something **slopes**, it leans to the right or to the left rather than being upright. The writing sloped backwards. [4] N-SING The **slope** of something is the angle at which it slopes. ...a slope of ten degrees.

sloppy /'slɒpi/ **sloppier, sloppiest.** ADJ Something that is **sloppy** is messy and careless. [INFORMAL] He has little patience for sloppy work. ◆ **sloppiness** N-UNCOUNT ...the sloppiness of the young.

slot /slɒt/ **slots, slotting, slotted.** [1] N-COUNT A **slot** is a narrow opening in a machine or container, for example a hole that you put coins in to make a machine work. [2] VERB When something **slots into** something else, or when you **slot** it **in**, you put it into a space where it fits. The car seat belt slotted into place easily. [3] N-COUNT A **slot** in a schedule or scheme is a place in it where an activity can take place. ...her daily slot on the TV programme Hot Chefs.

slouch /slaʊtʃ/ **slouches, slouching, slouched.** VERB & N-SING If you **slouch**, or if your body is in a **slouch**, you sit, stand, or walk with your shoulders and head drooping down. → See picture on page 532. Try not to slouch when you are sitting down... He sat slouched over his coffee... He walked with a slouch.

⭐ **slow** /sləʊ/ **slower, slowest; slows, slowing, slowed.** [1] ADJ Something that is **slow** moves, happens, or is done without much speed. The traffic is heavy and slow. ...slow, regular breathing... The distribution of passports has been a slow process. ◆ **slowly** ADV Christian backed slowly away... My resentment of her slowly began to fade. ◆ **slowness** N-UNCOUNT She lowered the glass with calculated slowness. [2] VERB If something

slows, or if you **slow** it, it starts to move or happen more slowly. She slowed the car and began driving up a narrow road. [3] ADJ AFTER LINK-V If someone is **slow to** do something, they do it after a delay. The government was slow to respond to the crisis... I've been a bit slow in making up my mind. [4] ADJ If you describe a situation, place, or activity as **slow**, you mean that it is not very exciting. The island is too slow for her liking. [5] ADJ If a clock or watch is **slow**, it shows a time that is earlier than the correct time. [6] ADJ Someone who is **slow** is not very clever and takes a long time to understand things.
▶**slow down.** [1] PHR-VERB If something **slows down**, or if you **slow** it **down**, it starts to move or happen more slowly. The car slowed down... We want to slow down the process of eating. [2] PHR-VERB If someone **slows down**, they become less active. He was still taking some medication which slowed him down. ● See also **slowdown.**
▶**slow up.** PHR-VERB **Slow up** means the same as **slow down** 1. ...a new code of criminal procedure has also slowed up the system.

slowdown /'sləʊdaʊn/ **slowdowns.** N-COUNT A **slowdown** is a reduction in speed or activity. There has been a sharp slowdown in economic growth.

slow 'motion. N-UNCOUNT When film or television pictures are shown in **slow motion**, they are shown much more slowly than normal.

sludge /slʌdʒ/. N-UNCOUNT **Sludge** is thick mud.

slug /slʌg/ **slugs.** [1] N-COUNT A **slug** is a small slow-moving creature, with a long slippery body, like a snail without a shell. [2] N-COUNT A **slug** is a bullet. [AMERICAN, INFORMAL]

sluggish /'slʌgɪʃ/. ADJ Something that is **sluggish** moves or works much more slowly than normal. He felt old and sluggish.

slum /slʌm/ **slums, slumming, slummed.** [1] N-COUNT A **slum** is an area of a city where living conditions are very bad. [2] VERB If you say that someone **is slumming it** or **is slumming**, you mean they are spending time in a place or in conditions that are at a much lower social level than they are used to.

slumber /'slʌmbə/ **slumbers, slumbering, slumbered.** [1] N-VAR **Slumber** is sleep. [LITERARY] He roused his brother Charles from his slumbers. [2] VERB Someone who **is slumbering** is sleeping. [LITERARY]

'slumber ,party, slumber parties. N-COUNT A **slumber party** is an occasion when a group of young friends spend the night together at the home of one of the group.

slump /slʌmp/ **slumps, slumping, slumped.** [1] N-COUNT & VERB If there is a **slump in** something such as the value of something, or if it **slumps**, it falls suddenly and by a large amount. ...a slump in property prices... Net profits slumped by 41%. [2] N-COUNT A **slump** is a time when there is a lot of unemployment and poverty. [3] VERB If you **slump** somewhere, you fall or sit down there heavily. → See picture on page 532. She slumped into a chair.

slung /slʌŋ/. **Slung** is the past tense and past participle of **sling**.

slur /slɜː/ **slurs, slurring, slurred.** [1] N-COUNT A **slur** is an insulting remark which could damage someone's reputation. *This is yet another slur on the integrity of the Metropolitan Police.* [2] VERB If someone **slurs** their speech, they do not pronounce each word clearly, because they are drunk or sleepy. *The newscaster's speech began to slur.* ◆ **slurred** ADJ *Her words were slurred, as though she were slightly drunk.*

sly /slaɪ/ **slyer, slyest.** [1] ADJ A **sly** look, expression, or remark shows that you know something that other people do not know. *He gave me a sly, meaningful look.* ◆ **slyly** ADV *Anna grinned slyly.* [2] ADJ If you describe someone as **sly**, you mean that they are clever at deceiving people.

smack /smæk/ **smacks, smacking, smacked.** [1] VERB & N-COUNT If you **smack** someone, or if you give them a **smack**, you hit them with your hand. *She smacked me on the side of the head. ...a smack across the face.* [2] VERB If you **smack** something somewhere, you put it or throw it there so that it makes a loud sharp noise. *He took the letter out of his jacket and smacked it down on the desk.* [3] VERB If something **smacks of** something that you consider bad, it reminds you of it or is like it. *Their use of trickery smacked of deceit.*

small /smɔːl/ **smaller, smallest.** [1] ADJ Someone or something that is **small** is not large in physical size. *She is small for her age... The window was far too small for him to get through.* [2] ADJ A **small** group or quantity consists of only a few people or things. *Fairly small numbers of young people commit suicide. ...a small amount of money.* [3] ADJ A **small** child is a very young child. *What were you like when you were small?* [4] ADJ You use **small** to describe something that is not significant or great in degree. *No detail was too small to escape her attention. ...a relatively small problem.* [5] ADJ AFTER LINK-V If someone makes you look or feel **small**, they make you look or feel stupid, so that you are ashamed or humiliated. *When your children misbehave, tell them without making them feel small.* [6] N-SING The **small of** your **back** is the bottom part of your back that curves inwards slightly. [7] **small wonder:** see **wonder**.

> **USAGE** You use the adjective **small** rather than **little** to draw attention to the fact that something is small. For instance, you cannot say 'The town is little' or 'I have a very little car', but you can say '**The town is small**' or '**I have a very small car**'. **Little** is a less precise word than **small**, and may be used to suggest the speaker's feelings or attitude towards the person or thing being described. For that reason, **little** is often used after another adjective. *What a nice little house you've got here!... Shut up, you horrible little boy!*

,**small** '**print.** N-UNCOUNT The **small print** of a contract or agreement is the part of it that is written in very small print.

,**small-**'**scale.** ADJ A **small-scale** activity or organization is limited in extent. *...the small-scale production of farmhouse cheeses.*

★ **smart** /smɑːt/ **smarter, smartest; smarts, smarting, smarted.** [1] ADJ **Smart** people and things are pleasantly neat and clean in appearance. *I wore a black dress and looked very smart. ...smart new offices.* ◆ **smartly** ADV *He dressed very smartly which was important in those days.* [2] ADJ A **smart** place or event is connected with wealthy and fashionable people. *...smart London dinner parties.* [3] ADJ You can describe someone who is clever as **smart**. *He's a smart kid.* [4] VERB If a part of your body or a wound **smarts**, you feel a sharp stinging pain in it. *Her eyes were smarting from the smoke.* [5] VERB If you **are smarting from** something such as criticism or failure, you feel upset about it. *The team was still smarting from its defeat.*

smartly /'smɑːtli/. ADV If someone moves or does something **smartly**, they do it quickly and neatly. [WRITTEN] *The housekeeper moved smartly to the Vicar's desk.* ● See also **smart**.

★ **smash** /smæʃ/ **smashes, smashing, smashed.** [1] VERB If something **smashes**, or if you **smash** it, it breaks into many pieces, for example when it is hit or dropped. *Two or three glasses fell off and smashed into pieces... Someone smashed a bottle.* [2] VERB If you **smash through** a wall, gate, or door, you get through it by hitting and breaking it. *Demonstrators used trucks to smash through the gates... Soldiers smashed their way into his office.* [3] VERB If something **smashes** or **is smashed** against something solid, it moves with great force against it. *He smashed his fist into Anthony's face.* [4] N-COUNT You can refer to a car crash as a **smash**. [INFORMAL] [5] VERB To **smash** a political group or system means to deliberately destroy it. [INFORMAL] *The President said he would smash terrorism.*

▶**smash up.** PHR-VERB If you **smash** something **up**, you completely destroy it by hitting and breaking it into many pieces. *She took revenge on her ex-boyfriend by smashing up his home.*

smashing /'smæʃɪŋ/. ADJ If you describe something or someone as **smashing**, you mean that you like them very much. [BRITISH, DATED] *They are smashing people.*

smear /smɪə/ **smears, smearing, smeared.** [1] VERB If you **smear** a surface **with** a substance, or if you **smear** the substance onto the surface, you spread a layer of the substance over the surface. *My sister smeared herself with suntan oil... Smear a little olive oil over the inside of the salad bowl.* ◆ **smeared** ADJ *The other child's face was smeared with dirt.* [2] N-COUNT A **smear** is a dirty or greasy mark. [3] VERB & N-COUNT To **smear** someone means to spread unpleasant and untrue rumours or accusations about them in order to damage their reputation. A **smear** is an unpleasant and untrue rumour or accusation. ...*a smear campaign by his political opponents.*

⭐ **smell** /smel/ **smells, smelling, smelled** or **smelt.**
[1] N-COUNT The **smell of** something is a quality it has which you become aware of through your nose. ...*the smell of freshly baked bread.* ...*horrible smells.* **[2]** N-UNCOUNT Your sense of **smell** is the ability that your nose has to detect things. **[3]** VERB If something **smells of** a particular thing, it has a particular quality which you become aware of through your nose. *The room smelled of lemons... It smells delicious.* ...*a foul-smelling cloud of smoke.* **[4]** VERB If you say that something **smells,** you mean that it smells unpleasant. *Do my feet smell?* **[5]** VERB If you **smell** something, you become aware of it through your nose. *As soon as we opened the front door we could smell the gas.* **[6]** VERB If you **smell** something, you put your nose near it and breathe in, so that you can discover its smell. *I took a fresh rose out of the vase on our table, and smelled it.* **[7]** VERB If you **smell** something, you feel instinctively that it is likely to happen or be true. *He knew virtually nothing about music but he could smell a hit.*

smelly /'smeli/ **smellier, smelliest.** ADJ Something that is **smelly** has an unpleasant smell. *He had extremely smelly feet.*

smelt /smelt/ **smelts, smelting, smelted.** **[1]** **Smelt** is a past tense and past participle of **smell.** **[2]** VERB To **smelt** a substance containing metal means to process it by heating it until it melts, so that the metal is extracted and changed chemically.

⭐ **smile** /smaɪl/ **smiles, smiling, smiled.** **[1]** VERB When you **smile,** the corners of your mouth curve outwards, usually because you are pleased or amused. *He loved to make people smile... Both of them smiled at the picture.* **[2]** N-COUNT A **smile** is the expression that you have on your face when you smile. *She had a big smile on her face.* **[3]** VERB If you **smile** something, you express or say it with a smile. *'Aren't we daft?' she smiled.*

smirk /smɜːk/ **smirks, smirking, smirked.** VERB & N-COUNT If you **smirk,** or if you give a **smirk,** you smile in an unpleasant way. *Charlene smirked at Mona's outfit... 'Yeah, right,' he said with a smirk.*

smog /smɒg/. N-UNCOUNT **Smog** is a mixture of fog and smoke which occurs in some industrial cities.

⭐ **smoke** /sməʊk/ **smokes, smoking, smoked.** **[1]** N-UNCOUNT **Smoke** consists of gas and small bits of solid material that are sent into the air when something burns. ...*cigarette smoke.* **[2]** VERB If something **is smoking,** smoke is coming from it. ...*a pile of smoking rubble.* **[3]** VERB When someone **smokes** a cigarette, cigar, or pipe, they suck smoke from it into their mouth and blow it out again. If you **smoke,** you regularly smoke cigarettes, cigars, or a pipe. *He sat and smoked quietly.* ♦ **smoker, smokers** N-COUNT *He was not a heavy smoker.* ♦ **smoking** N-UNCOUNT *Smoking will not be allowed.* ...*a no-smoking area.* **[4]** VERB If fish or meat **is smoked,** it is hung over burning wood so that the smoke

preserves it and gives it a special flavour. ...*smoked salmon.*

smoky /'sməʊki/ **smokier, smokiest.** **[1]** ADJ A **smoky** place has a lot of smoke in the air. **[2]** ADJ You can use **smoky** to describe something that looks or tastes like smoke. *The tea has a distinctive smoky flavour.* ...*the smoky blue of early dawn.*

smolder /'sməʊldə/. See **smoulder.**

⭐ **smooth** /smuːð/ **smoother, smoothest; smooths, smoothing, smoothed.** **[1]** ADJ A **smooth** surface has no roughness or holes. *Use a sheet of glass, perspex, or any smooth surface.* ♦ **smoothness** N-UNCOUNT ...*the smoothness of her skin.* **[2]** ADJ A **smooth** liquid or mixture has been mixed well so that it has no lumps in it. *Blend the sauce to a smooth puree.* **[3]** ADJ A **smooth** movement or process happens or is done evenly and steadily with no sudden changes or breaks. *He turned her round in a smooth movement... Research does not continue in a smooth curve.* ♦ **smoothly** ADV *Make sure that you execute all movements smoothly.* **[4]** ADJ **Smooth** means successful and without problems. ...*her smooth transition from paramedic to hospital administrator.* ♦ **smoothly** ADV *So far, talks at GM have gone smoothly.* **[5]** ADJ If you describe a drink such as wine, whisky, or coffee as **smooth,** you mean that it is not bitter and is pleasant to drink. **[6]** ADJ If you describe a man as **smooth,** you mean that he is extremely smart, confident, and polite, often in a way that you find rather unpleasant. **[7]** VERB If you **smooth** something, or if you **smooth** it **out** or **smooth** it **down,** you move your hands over its surface to make it smooth and flat. *She stood up and smoothed down her frock... Carefully Nick smoothed a sheet of newspaper across the front of the grate.* **[8]** PHRASE If you **smooth the path** or **smooth the way** towards something, you make it easier or more likely to happen. *Their talks were aimed at smoothing the path towards a treaty.*
▸**smooth out** or **smooth over.** PHR-VERB If you **smooth out** or **smooth over** a problem or difficulty, you make it less serious and easier to deal with, especially by talking to the people concerned. *Baker was smoothing out differences with European allies.*

smother /'smʌðə/ **smothers, smothering, smothered.** **[1]** VERB If you **smother** a fire, you cover it with something in order to put it out. **[2]** VERB To **smother** someone means to kill them by covering their face with something so that they cannot breathe. **[3]** VERB To **smother** something **with** or **in** things is to cover it completely with them. *He leapt up and smothered her with kisses.* ...*scones smothered in cream and jam.* **[4]** VERB To **smother** someone means to give them too much love and protection. *He smothered his youngest daughter in love.*

smoulder (AM **smolder**) /'sməʊldə/ **smoulders, smouldering, smouldered.** **[1]** VERB If something **smoulders,** it burns slowly, producing smoke but not flames. *The remains of a fire smouldered in the* log basket. ② VERB If a feeling **smoulders** inside you, you feel it intensely but rarely show it. *Anger still smoulders about the allegations.*

smudge /smʌdʒ/ **smudges, smudging, smudged.**
① N-COUNT A **smudge** is a dirty, blurred mark.
② VERB If you **smudge** something, you make it dirty or messy by touching it. *They had to swim without smudging their make-up.*

smug /smʌg/. ADJ If you say that someone is **smug**, you are criticizing the fact they seem very pleased with how good, clever, or fortunate they are. ♦ **smugly** ADV *The Major smiled smugly and sat down.*

smuggle /'smʌgəl/ **smuggles, smuggling, smuggled.** VERB If someone **smuggles** things or people **into** a place or **out of** it, they take them there illegally or secretly. *He smuggled papers out each day and photocopied them... If you try to smuggle drugs you are stupid.* ♦ **smuggler, smugglers** N-COUNT *...drug smugglers.* ♦ **smuggling** N-UNCOUNT *...diamond smuggling.*

snack /snæk/ **snacks.** N-COUNT A **snack** is a small, quick meal, or something eaten between meals.

snag /snæg/ **snags, snagging, snagged.** ① N-COUNT A **snag** is a small problem or disadvantage. *The boy was looking for work. The only snag was that he had no transportation.* ② VERB If you **snag** part of your clothing **on** a sharp or rough object, it gets caught or torn on it. *An American submarine snagged the nets of a trawler... The tip of my shoe snagged on something.*

snail /sneɪl/ **snails.** N-COUNT A **snail** is a small animal that has a spiral shell. It moves slowly, leaving behind a trail of slime.

snake /sneɪk/ **snakes, snaking, snaked.** ① N-COUNT A **snake** is a long, thin reptile with no legs. ② VERB Something that **snakes** in a particular direction goes in that direction in a line with a lot of bends. [LITERARY] *The road snaked through forested mountains.*

⭐ **snap** /snæp/ **snaps, snapping, snapped.** ① VERB & N-SING If something **snaps**, or if you **snap** it, it breaks suddenly, usually with a sharp cracking noise called a **snap**. *The rope snapped... The brake pedal had just snapped off... The joint broke with a snap.* ② VERB & N-SING If something **snaps** into a particular position, or if you **snap** it, it moves quickly into that position with a sharp sound called a **snap**. *The bag snapped open... He snapped the cap off a beer... He shut the book with a snap.* ③ VERB If someone **snaps at** you, they speak to you in a sharp, unfriendly way. *Sorry, I didn't mean to snap at you... 'Of course I don't know her,' Roger snapped.* ④ VERB If an animal **snaps at** you, it opens and shuts its jaws quickly near you. ⑤ ADJ BEFORE N A **snap** decision or action is taken suddenly, without careful thought. *It's important not to make snap judgments.* ⑥ VERB & N-COUNT If you **snap** someone or something, or if you take a **snap** of them, you take a photograph of them. [INFORMAL] *...holiday snaps.*

▸ **snap up.** PHR-VERB If you **snap** something **up**, you buy it quickly because it is a bargain or because it is just what you want. *A chunk of Britain's rail network was snapped up by Japanese bankers.*

snapshot /'snæpʃɒt/ **snapshots.** N-COUNT A **snapshot** is a photograph that is taken quickly and casually.

snare /sneə/ **snares, snaring, snared.** ① N-COUNT A **snare** is a trap for catching birds or small animals. ② VERB To **snare** a bird or animal means to catch it using a snare. ③ VERB If someone **snares** something, they get it by using cleverness and cunning. *Most of all I want to snare a husband.*

snarl /snɑːl/ **snarls, snarling, snarled.** ① VERB & N-COUNT When an animal **snarls**, or when it gives a **snarl**, it makes a fierce, rough sound while showing its teeth. *The dogs snarled at the intruders... With a snarl, the second dog made a dive for his heel.* ② VERB If you **snarl** something, you say it in a fierce, angry way. *'Let go of me,' he snarled.*

snatch /snætʃ/ **snatches, snatching, snatched.**
① VERB If you **snatch** something, or if you **snatch at** it, you take or pull it away quickly. *Mick snatched the cards from Archie's hand.* ② VERB If you **snatch** an opportunity, you quickly make use of it. *I snatched a glance at the mirror.* ③ N-COUNT A **snatch of** a conversation or a song is a very small piece of it.

sneak /sniːk/ **sneaks, sneaking, sneaked** (AM also **snuck**). ① VERB If you **sneak** somewhere, you go there quietly on foot, trying to avoid being seen or heard. *He would sneak out of his house late at night to be with me.* ② VERB If you **sneak** something somewhere, you take it there secretly. *...kids who want to sneak drinks into dance halls.* ③ VERB If you **sneak** a look at someone or something, you secretly have a quick look at them.

sneaker /'sniːkə/ **sneakers.** N-COUNT In American English, **sneakers** are casual shoes with rubber soles used for sports. The usual British word is **trainers**. → See picture on page 820.

sneer /snɪə/ **sneers, sneering, sneered.** VERB & N-COUNT If you **sneer at** someone or something, or if you give them a **sneer**, you express your contempt for them by what you say or by the expression on your face. *It is becoming fashionable again to sneer at scientists. ...a contemptuous sneer.*

sneeze /sniːz/ **sneezes, sneezing, sneezed.** VERB & N-COUNT When you **sneeze**, you suddenly take in your breath and then blow it down your nose noisily, because you have a cold or because something has irritated your nose. This action is called a **sneeze**.

sniff /snɪf/ **sniffs, sniffing, sniffed.** ① VERB & N-COUNT When you **sniff**, or when you give a **sniff**, you breathe in air noisily through your nose, for example when you are trying not to cry, or in order to show disapproval. *She wiped her face*

a
b
c
d
e
f
g
h
i
j
k
l
m
n
o
p
q
r
s
t
u
v
w
x
y
z

A

and sniffed loudly... 'Tourists!' she sniffed. **2** VERB & N-COUNT If you **sniff** something, or if you take a **sniff** of it, you smell it by sniffing. *He sniffed the perfume she wore... She sniffed at it suspiciously.*

snigger /'snɪgə/ **sniggers, sniggering, sniggered.** VERB & N-COUNT If someone **sniggers**, or if they give a **snigger**, they laugh quietly in a way which shows lack of respect. *The tourists snigger at the locals' outdated ways.*

snip /snɪp/ **snips, snipping, snipped.** VERB If you **snip** something or if you **snip at** it, you cut part of it off with scissors or shears in a single quick action. *Jeremy snipped a length of new bandage.*

snipe /snaɪp/ **snipes, sniping, sniped.** **1** VERB If someone **snipes at** you, they criticize you, often in an unfair or unkind way. *She could not resist the temptation to snipe at her successor.* ◆ **sniping** N-UNCOUNT *Despite the sniping of critics, we still managed to double our audience.* **2** VERB To **snipe at** someone means to shoot at them from a hidden position. ◆ **sniper, snipers** N-COUNT *...a sniper's bullet.* ◆ **sniping** N-UNCOUNT *10,069 people have been killed in the shelling and sniping.*

snippet /'snɪpɪt/ **snippets.** N-COUNT A **snippet of** information or news is a small piece of it. *...intriguing snippets of evidence.*

snob /snɒb/ **snobs.** N-COUNT If you call someone a **snob**, you disapprove of them because they admire upper class people and dislike lower class people.

snobbery /'snɒbəri/. N-UNCOUNT **Snobbery** is the attitude of a snob. *There was very little snobbery or class-consciousness in the wartime navy.*

snooker /'snuːkə, AM 'snʊk-/. N-UNCOUNT **Snooker** is a game involving balls on a large table. The players use long sticks called cues to hit a white ball, and score points by knocking coloured balls into the pockets at the sides of the table.

snoop /snuːp/ **snoops, snooping, snooped.** VERB & N-COUNT If someone **snoops around** a place, or if they have a **snoop around**, they secretly look around it in order to find out things. *He was the one she'd seen snooping around Kim's hotel room.* ◆ **snooper, snoopers** N-COUNT *They raised the wall to 10m, to thwart photographers and snoopers.*

snore /snɔː/ **snores, snoring, snored.** VERB & N-COUNT When someone who is asleep **snores**, they make a loud noise, called a **snore**, each time they breathe. *His echoing snores keep me awake at night.*

snorkel /'snɔːkəl/ **snorkels, snorkelling, snorkelled** (AM **snorkeling, snorkeled**). **1** N-COUNT A **snorkel** is a tube through which a person swimming just under the surface of the sea can breathe. **2** VERB When someone **snorkels**, they swim under water using a snorkel.

snort /snɔːt/ **snorts, snorting, snorted.** VERB & N-COUNT If people or animals **snort**, or if they give a **snort**, they breathe air noisily out through their noses. People sometimes snort in order to express disapproval or amusement. *Harry snorted with laughter... He gave an exasperated snort.*

★ **snow** /snəʊ/ **snows, snowing, snowed.** **1** N-UNCOUNT **Snow** is the soft white bits of frozen water that fall from the sky in cold weather. *The ground was covered in snow.* **2** VERB When it **snows**, snow falls from the sky.

snowball /'snəʊbɔːl/ **snowballs, snowballing, snowballed.** **1** N-COUNT A **snowball** is a ball of snow. **2** VERB If something such as a campaign **snowballs**, it rapidly increases and grows. *From those early days the business has snowballed.*

snowboard /'snəʊbɔːd/ **snowboards.** N-COUNT A **snowboard** is a narrow board that you stand on in order to slide quickly down snowy slopes.

snowboarding /'snəʊbɔːdɪŋ/. N-COUNT **Snowboarding** is the sport or activity of travelling down snowy slopes using a snowboard. ◆ **snowboarder, snowboarders** N-COUNT *Experienced snowboarders can zip downhill amazingly fast.*

snowy /'snəʊi/ **snowier, snowiest.** ADJ A **snowy** place is covered in snow. A **snowy** day is a day when a lot of snow has fallen.

snub /snʌb/ **snubs, snubbing, snubbed.** VERB & N-COUNT If someone **snubs** you, or if they give you a **snub**, they insult you by ignoring you or by behaving rudely towards you. *He snubbed her in public and made her feel an idiot... This was not intended in any way as a snub to Robbie.*

snuck /snʌk/. **Snuck** is a past tense and past participle of **sneak**. [AMERICAN]

snuff /snʌf/ **snuffs, snuffing, snuffed.** N-UNCOUNT **Snuff** is powdered tobacco which people take by sniffing it up their nose.
▸ **snuff out.** PHR-VERB If someone or something **snuffs out** something such as a rebellion or disagreement, they stop it, usually in a forceful or sudden way. *Every time a new flicker of resistance appeared, the government snuffed it out.*

snug /snʌg/. **1** ADJ If you feel **snug** or if you are in a **snug** place, you are very warm and comfortable. **2** ADJ If something is a **snug** fit, it fits tightly. ◆ **snugly** ADV *The shoes fitted snugly.*

snuggle /'snʌgəl/ **snuggles, snuggling, snuggled.** VERB If you **snuggle** somewhere, you settle yourself into a warm, comfortable position, especially by moving closer to another person. *Jane snuggled up against his shoulder.*

★ **so** /səʊ/. **1** ADV You use **so** to refer back to something that has just been mentioned. *'Do you think that made much of a difference to the family?'—'I think so.'... Almost all young women who turn to prostitution do so as a means of survival.* **2** ADV You use **so** when you are saying that something which has just been said about one person or thing is also true of another one. *They had a wonderful time and so did I.* **3** CONJ You use the structures **as...so** and **just as...so** to indicate that two events or situations are similar in a particular way. *Just as society has rules, so do schools.* **4** CONJ You use **so** and **so that** to introduce the result of the situation you have just mentioned. *I was an only child, and so had no experience of large families... There was snow everywhere, so that the shape of things was difficult to identify.* [5] CONJ You use **so**, **so that**, and **so as** to introduce the reason for doing the thing you have just mentioned. *Come over here so I can see you... I was beginning to feel alarm, but kept it to myself so as not to worry our two friends.* [6] ADV You can use **so** in a conversation or an account when you are checking something, summarizing something, or moving on to a new stage. *So you're a footballer?... So that's how I knew.* [7] ADV You can use **so** to emphasize the degree or extent of something. *He was so tired that he slept for 15 hours... Her hands were so wet they kept slipping off the wheel.* [8] ADV You can use **so** to intensify the meaning of an adjective, adverb, or word such as 'much' or 'many'. *John makes me so angry... So many children cannot read or write.*

USAGE So, **very**, and **too** can all be used to intensify the meaning of an adjective, an adverb, or a word like **much** or **many**. However, they are not used in the same way. **Very** is the simplest intensifier. It has no other meaning beyond that. **So** can suggest an emotional reaction on the part of the speaker, such as pleasure, surprise, or disappointment. *John makes me so angry!... Oh thank you so much!* **So** can also refer forward to a result clause introduced by **that**. *The procession was forced to move so slowly that he arrived three hours late.* **Too** suggests an excessive or undesirable amount, often so much that a particular result does not or cannot happen. *She does wear too much make-up at times... He was too late to save her.*

---

[9] ADV You can use **so** before words such as 'much' and 'many' to indicate that there is a limit to something. *There is only so much time in the day for answering letters... Even the greatest city can support only so many lawyers.* [10] CONVENTION You say **'So?'** and **'So what?'** to indicate that you think that what someone has said is unimportant. [INFORMAL] *'My name's Bruno.'—'So?'... 'You take a chance on the weather if you holiday in the UK.'—'So what?'.* [11] **ever so**: see **ever**. ● **so far**: see **far**. ● **so long as**: see **long**. ● **so much for**: see **much**. ● **every so often**: see **often**.

PHRASES ● You use **and so on** or **and so forth** at the end of a list to indicate that there are other items that you could also mention. *...health, education, tax and so on.* ● You use **or so** when you are giving an approximate amount. *They'll be here within the next fortnight or so.* ● You use the structures **not so much** and **not so much...as** to say that something is one kind of thing rather

than another kind. *This is not so much a political battle as an economic one.*

soak /səʊk/ **soaks, soaking, soaked.** [1] VERB When you **soak** something, or when you leave it **to soak**, you put it into a liquid and leave it there. *Soak the noodles in warm water for 20 minutes... He turned off the water and left the dishes to soak.* [2] VERB When a liquid **soaks** something, it makes it very wet. *Heavy rain had soaked the road surface.* ♦ **soaked** ADJ *Her dress was soaked.* ♦ **soaking** ADJ *She was soaking wet.* [3] VERB When a liquid **soaks through** something, it passes through it. *Dark patches of sweat had soaked through the fabric.* [4] VERB & N-COUNT If someone **soaks**, or if they have a **soak**, they spend a long time in a hot bath, because they enjoy it. *I had a long soak in the bath.*
▸ **soak up.** PHR-VERB When a soft or dry substance **soaks up** a liquid, the liquid goes into the substance. *Stir until the wheat has soaked up all the water.*

so-and-'so. N-UNCOUNT You use **so-and-so** instead of a word, expression, or name when talking generally rather than giving a specific example. *Civil servants may tell ministers that so-and-so is departmental policy.*

soap /səʊp/ **soaps, soaping, soaped.** [1] N-VAR **Soap** is a substance that you use with water for washing yourself or sometimes for washing clothes. *...a bar of lavender soap. ...a large packet of soap powder.* [2] N-COUNT A **soap** is the same as a **soap opera**.

'soap opera, soap operas. N-COUNT A **soap opera** is a television drama serial about the daily lives of a group of people.

soar /sɔː/ **soars, soaring, soared.** [1] VERB If the amount or level of something **soars**, it quickly increases by a great deal. [JOURNALISM] *The price of timber has soared.* [2] VERB If something **soars** into the air, it goes quickly up into the air. [LITERARY] *...listening to the seabirds and watching them soar and dive.*

sob /sɒb/ **sobs, sobbing, sobbed.** VERB & N-COUNT If you **sob**, you cry in a noisy way. A **sob** is one of the noises that you make when you are crying. *I want to go home, she said, between sobs.* ♦ **sobbing** N-UNCOUNT *The room was silent except for her sobbing.*

sober /'səʊbə/ **sobers, sobering, sobered.** [1] ADJ When you are **sober**, you are not drunk. [2] ADJ A **sober** person is serious and thoughtful. ♦ **soberly** ADV *'There's a new development,' he said soberly.* [3] ADJ **Sober** colours and clothes are plain and dull. ♦ **soberly** ADV *...a group of soberly dressed men.*
▸ **sober up.** PHR-VERB When someone **sobers up**, they become sober after being drunk.

sobering /'səʊbərɪŋ/. ADJ You say that something is a **sobering** thought or has a **sobering** effect when a situation seems serious and makes you become serious and thoughtful. *It was a sobering experience.*

a
b
c
d
e
f
g
h
i
j
k
l
m
n
o
p
q
r
s
t
u
v
w
x
y
z

,so-'called. [1] ADJ BEFORE N You use **so-called** in front of a word to indicate that you think that the word is incorrect or misleading. ...*so-called environmentally-friendly products.* [2] ADJ BEFORE N You use **so-called** to indicate that something is generally referred to by a particular name. *She was one of the so-called Gang of Four.*

⭐ **soccer** /'sɒkə/. N-UNCOUNT In American English, **soccer** is a game played by two teams of eleven players who kick a ball around a field in an attempt to score goals. The British word is **football**. → See picture on page 270.

sociable /'səʊʃəbəl/. ADJ **Sociable** people enjoy meeting and talking to other people.

⭐ **social** /'səʊʃəl/. [1] ADJ BEFORE N **Social** means relating to society. ...*unemployment, low pay and other social problems.* ♦ **socially** ADV *It is more socially acceptable for a man to be fat.* [2] ADJ BEFORE N **Social** activities are leisure activities that involve meeting other people, as opposed to activities related to work. *We ought to organize more social events.* ♦ **socially** ADV *We have known each other socially for a long time.*

⭐ **socialist** /'səʊʃəlɪst/ **socialists.** N-COUNT & ADJ A **socialist** or a person with **socialist** beliefs believes that the state should own industries on behalf of the people and that everyone should be equal. ...*members of the ruling Socialist party.* ♦ **socialism** N-UNCOUNT ...*the contest between capitalism and socialism.*

socialize (BRIT also **socialise**) /'səʊʃəlaɪz/ **socializes, socializing, socialized.** VERB If you **socialize**, you meet other people socially. *It would give people a place to socialize with each other.*

'social life, social lives. N-COUNT Your **social life** consists of ways in which you spend time with your friends and acquaintances. *Their social life revolves around the theatre.*

,social 'science, social sciences. N-VAR **Social science** is the scientific study of society. ...*sociology and the other social sciences.*

,social se'curity. N-UNCOUNT In Britain, **social security** is money that is paid by the government to people who are unemployed, poor, or ill. The American term is **welfare**.

,social 'services. N-PLURAL **Social services** are services provided by the local authority to help people who have serious family problems or financial problems.

'social work. N-UNCOUNT **Social work** is a job which involves giving help and advice to people with serious financial problems or family problems.

'social ,worker, social workers. N-COUNT A **social worker** is a person whose job is to do social work.

⭐ **society** /sə'saɪɪti/ **societies.** [1] N-VAR **Society** consists of all the people in a country or region, considered as a group. ...*Western society... We live in a capitalist society.* [2] N-COUNT A **society** is an organization for people who have the same interest or aim. ...*the North of England Horticultural Society.* [3] N-UNCOUNT You can use

society to refer to the rich, fashionable people in a particular place who meet on social occasions. *They are well-known in society.*

sociology /,səʊsi'ɒlədʒi/. N-UNCOUNT **Sociology** is the study of society or of the way society is organized. ♦ **sociological** /,səʊsiə'lɒdʒɪkəl/ ADJ ...*sociological research.* ♦ **sociologist, sociologists** N-COUNT ...*her career as a sociologist.*

sock /sɒk/ **socks.** N-COUNT **Socks** are pieces of clothing which cover your foot and ankle and are worn inside shoes.

socket /'sɒkɪt/ **sockets.** [1] N-COUNT A **socket** is a device on a piece of electrical equipment into which you can put a plug or bulb. [2] N-COUNT In British English, a **socket** is a device or point in a wall where you can connect electrical equipment to the power supply. The American word is **outlet.** [3] N-COUNT You can refer to any hollow part or opening in a structure which another part fits into as a **socket**. *Her eyes were sunk deep into their sockets.*

soda /'səʊdə/ **sodas.** [1] N-UNCOUNT **Soda** or **soda water** is fizzy water used for mixing with alcoholic drinks or fruit juice. [2] N-VAR **Soda** is a fizzy drink. A **soda** is a bottle or glass of soda. [AMERICAN]

sodden /'sɒdən/. ADJ Something that is **sodden** is extremely wet.

sodium /'səʊdiəm/. **Sodium** is a silvery-white chemical element which combines with other chemicals.

sofa /'səʊfə/ **sofas.** N-COUNT A **sofa** is a long, comfortable seat with a back and arms, which two or three people can sit on.

⭐ **soft** /sɒft, AM sɔ:ft/ **softer, softest.** [1] ADJ Something that is **soft** is pleasant to touch, and not rough or hard. ...*warm, soft, white towels.* ♦ **softness** N-UNCOUNT *The sea air robbed her hair of its softness.* [2] ADJ Something that is **soft** changes shape or bends easily when you press it. *She lay down on the soft, comfortable bed.* ...*soft cheese.* [3] ADJ Something that is **soft** is very gentle and has no force. For example, a **soft** sound is quiet and not harsh. A **soft** colour is pleasant to look at because it is not bright. *A soft spring rain had fallen all day.* ♦ **softly** ADV *She kissed him softly.* [4] ADJ If you are **soft on** someone, you do not treat them as severely as you should do; used showing disapproval. [5] ADJ BEFORE N **Soft drugs** are illegal drugs which many people do not consider to be strong, harmful, or addictive. [6] PHRASE If you **have a soft spot for** someone, you are especially fond of them.

,soft 'drink, soft drinks. N-COUNT A **soft drink** is a cold non-alcoholic drink such as lemonade.

soften /'sɒfən, AM 'sɔ:f-/ **softens, softening, softened.** [1] VERB If something **is softened**, it becomes less hard or firm. *Fry for about 4 minutes, until the onion has softened.* [2] VERB If one thing **softens** the impact or the damaging effect of another thing, it makes it seem less severe. [3] VERB If you **soften** your position, you become more sympathetic and less hostile or critical. *His party's policy has softened a lot in recent years.*

▶**soften up.** PHR-VERB If you **soften** someone **up,** you put them into a good mood before asking them to do something. [INFORMAL] *If they'd treated you well it was just to soften you up.*

⭐ **software** /ˈsɒftweə, AM ˈsɔːf-/. N-UNCOUNT Computer programs are referred to as **software**. [COMPUTING]

soggy /ˈsɒgi/ **soggier, soggiest.** ADJ Something that is **soggy** is unpleasantly wet.

⭐ **soil** /sɔɪl/ **soils, soiling, soiled.** [1] N-UNCOUNT **Soil** is the substance on the surface of the earth in which plants grow. [2] N-UNCOUNT You can use **soil** to refer to a country's territory. *The issue of foreign troops on Turkish soil is a sensitive one.* [3] VERB If you **soil** something, you make it dirty. [FORMAL] ♦ **soiled** ADJ *...a soiled white apron.*

solace /ˈsɒlɪs/. [1] N-UNCOUNT **Solace** is a feeling of comfort that makes you feel less sad. [FORMAL] *Henry was inclined to seek solace in drink.* [2] N-SING If something is a **solace to** you, it makes you feel less sad. [FORMAL]

solar /ˈsəʊlə/. [1] ADJ **Solar** is used to describe things relating to the sun. *...a total solar eclipse.* [2] ADJ **Solar** power is obtained from the sun's light and heat.

'solar system. N-PROPER **The solar system** is the sun and all the planets that go round it.

sold /səʊld/. **Sold** is the past tense and past participle of **sell**.

⭐ **soldier** /ˈsəʊldʒə/ **soldiers.** N-COUNT A **soldier** is a person who works in an army.

sole /səʊl/ **soles.**

✅ In meaning 4, **sole** is both the singular and the plural form.

[1] ADJ BEFORE N The **sole** thing or person of a particular type is the only one of that type. *Their sole aim is to destabilize the government.* ♦ **solely** ADV *Too often we make decisions based solely upon what we see in the magazines.* [2] ADJ BEFORE N If you have **sole** charge or ownership of something, you are the only person in charge of it or who owns it. *Many women are left as the sole providers in families.* [3] N-COUNT The **sole** of your foot or **of** a shoe or sock is the underneath surface of it. *They were beaten on the soles of their feet. ...shoes with rubber soles.* [4] N-VAR A **sole** is a kind of flat fish.

solemn /ˈsɒləm/. [1] ADJ Someone or something that is **solemn** is very serious rather than cheerful or humorous. ♦ **solemnly** ADV *Her listeners nodded solemnly.* ♦ **solemnity** /səˈlemnɪti/ N-UNCOUNT *...the solemnity attached to death.* [2] ADJ A **solemn** promise or agreement is formal and sincere. *The Government seems to have made solemn commitments.* ♦ **solemnly** ADV *He solemnly swore an oath of allegiance.*

solicit /səˈlɪsɪt/ **solicits, soliciting, solicited.** [1] VERB If you **solicit** money, help, or an opinion from someone, you ask them for it. [FORMAL]

♦ **solicitation, solicitations** N-COUNT *...the solicitation of money from a foreign government.* [2] VERB When prostitutes **solicit**, they offer to have sex with people in return for money. ♦ **soliciting** N-UNCOUNT *...soliciting or loitering in the central London area.*

⭐ **solicitor** /səˈlɪsɪtə/ **solicitors.** N-COUNT In Britain, a **solicitor** is a lawyer who gives legal advice, prepares legal documents and cases, and represents clients in the lower courts of law.

⭐ **solid** /ˈsɒlɪd/ **solids.** [1] N-COUNT & ADJ A **solid**, or a **solid** substance or object, stays the same shape whether it is in a container or not. *Solids turn to liquids at certain temperatures.* [2] ADJ A **solid** object or mass does not have a space inside it, or holes or gaps in it. *...50ft of solid rock... The car park was absolutely packed solid with people.* [3] ADJ A **solid** structure is strong and is not likely to collapse or fall over. ♦ **solidly** ADV *Their house, which was solidly built, resisted the main shock.* ♦ **solidity** /səˈlɪdɪti/ N-UNCOUNT *...the solidity of walls and floors.* [4] ADJ If you describe someone as **solid**, you mean they are very reliable and respectable. ♦ **solidly** ADV *Graham is so solidly consistent.* ♦ **solidity** N-UNCOUNT *He had the proverbial solidity of the English.* [5] ADJ **Solid** evidence or information is reliable because it is based on facts. **Solid** advice or work is useful and reliable. *All I am looking for is a good solid performance.* ♦ **solidly** ADV *She's played solidly throughout the spring.* [6] ADJ If you do something for a **solid** period of time, you do it without any pause or interruption throughout that time. *We had worked together for two solid years.* ♦ **solidly** ADV *For the next two hours they worked solidly on his new song.*

solidarity /ˌsɒlɪˈdærɪti/. N-UNCOUNT If a group of people show **solidarity**, they show complete unity and support for each other, especially in political or international affairs.

solidify /səˈlɪdɪfaɪ/ **solidifies, solidifying, solidified.** VERB When a liquid **solidifies**, it changes into a solid.

solitary /ˈsɒlɪtri, AM -teri/. [1] ADJ BEFORE N A **solitary** activity is one that you do alone. *His evenings were spent in solitary drinking.* [2] ADJ A person or animal that is **solitary** spends a lot of time alone. [3] ADJ BEFORE N A **solitary** person or object is alone and has no others nearby.

solitude /ˈsɒlɪtjuːd, AM -tuːd/. N-UNCOUNT **Solitude** is the state of being alone, especially when this is peaceful and pleasant. *Imagine long golden beaches where you can wander in solitude.*

solo /ˈsəʊləʊ/ **solos.** N-COUNT & ADJ & ADV A **solo**, or a **solo** performance, especially of a piece of music, is a performance done by one person. You can also say that someone does something **solo** when they do it on their own. *He had just completed his final solo album.*

soloist /ˈsəʊləʊɪst/ **soloists.** N-COUNT A **soloist** is a person who performs a solo, usually a piece of music.

a
b
c
d
e
f
g
h
i
j
k
l
m
n
o
p
q
r
s
t
u
v
w
x
y
z

soluble /'sɒljʊbəl/. ADJ A substance that is **soluble** will dissolve in a liquid.

★ **solution** /sə'luːʃən/ **solutions.** [1] N-COUNT A **solution to** a problem is a way of dealing with it so that the difficulty is removed. ...*a peaceful solution to the conflict.* [2] N-COUNT The **solution to** a riddle or a puzzle is the answer to it. [3] N-COUNT A **solution** is a liquid in which a solid substance has been dissolved.

★ **solve** /sɒlv/ **solves, solving, solved.** VERB If you **solve** a problem or a question, you find a solution or an answer to it. *Their domestic reforms did precisely nothing to solve the problem of unemployment.*

solvent /'sɒlvənt/ **solvents.** [1] ADJ If a person or a company is **solvent**, they have enough money to pay all their debts. [2] N-VAR A **solvent** is a liquid that can dissolve other substances.

sombre (AM **somber**) /'sɒmbə/. [1] ADJ If someone is **sombre**, they are serious, sad, or pessimistic. ♦ **sombrely** ADV *'All the same, I wish he'd come back,' Martha said sombrely.* [2] ADJ **Sombre** colours and places are dark and dull.

★ **some** /səm, STRONG sʌm/. [1] DET & PRON You use **some** to refer to a quantity of something or to a number of people or things, when you are not stating the quantity or number precisely. *He went to fetch some books... This year all the apples are red. My niece and nephew are going to pick some.*

> **USAGE** You use **not any** instead of **some** in negative sentences. *There isn't any money.* You only use **some** in questions when you expect the answer yes. *Did you buy some wine?* Otherwise you say **any**. *Did you buy any wine?*

[2] DET You can use **some** to emphasize that an amount or number is fairly large. For example, if an activity takes **some** time, it takes quite a lot of time. [3] QUANT If you refer to **some** of the people or things in a group, you mean a few of them but not all of them. If you refer to **some of** a particular thing, you mean a part of it but not all of it. *Spoon some of the sauce into a bowl... When the chicken is cooked I'll freeze some.* [4] DET If you refer to **some** person or thing, you are referring to that person or thing vaguely, without stating precisely which one you mean. *If you are worried about some aspect of your child's health, call us.* [5] ADV You can use **some** in front of a number to indicate that it is approximate. *I have kept birds for some 30 years.*

★ **somebody** /'sʌmbədi, AM -baːdi/. **Somebody** means the same as **someone**.

> **USAGE** You use **not anybody** instead of **somebody** in negative sentences. *There isn't anybody here.* You only use **somebody** in questions when you expect the answer yes. *Is somebody there?* Otherwise you say **anybody**. *Is anybody there?*

★ **somehow** /'sʌmhaʊ/. ADV You use **somehow** to say that you do not know or cannot say how something was done or will be done. *Somehow I knew he would tell me the truth.*

★ **someone** /'sʌmwʌn/ (or **somebody** /'sʌmbədi, AM -baːdi/). [1] PRON You use **someone** or **somebody** to refer to a person without saying exactly who you mean. *I need someone to help me.* [2] PRON If you say that a person is **someone** or **somebody** in a particular kind of work or in a particular place, you mean that they are considered to be important in that kind of work or in that place. *He was somebody in the law division.*

> **USAGE** You use **not anyone** instead of **someone** in negative sentences. *There isn't anyone here.* You only use **someone** in questions when you expect the answer yes. *Is someone there?* Otherwise you say **anyone**. *Is anyone there?*

someplace /'sʌmpleɪs/. ADV **Someplace** means the same as **somewhere**. [AMERICAN, INFORMAL] *The Simpsons lived over around Coyote Canyon someplace.*

★ **something** /'sʌmθɪŋ/. [1] PRON You use **something** to refer to a thing, situation, event, or idea, without saying exactly what it is. *He realized right away that there was something wrong... People are always out in their cars, watching television or busy doing something else.*

> **USAGE** You use **not anything** instead of **something** in negative sentences. *There isn't anything here.* You only use **something** in questions when you expect the answer yes. *Is something wrong?* Otherwise you say **anything**. *Is anything wrong?*

[2] PRON You can use **something** in expressions like **'that's something'** when you think that a situation is not very good but is better than it might have been. *Well, at least he was in town. That was something.* [3] PRON If you say that a thing is **something of** a disappointment, you mean that it is quite disappointing. If you say that a person is **something of** an artist, you mean that they are quite good at art. *She received something of a surprise when Robert said that he was coming to New York.* [4] PRON If you say that there is **something in** an idea or suggestion, you mean that it is quite good and should be considered seriously. *Could there be something in what he said?* ● **something like:** see **like**.

sometime /'sʌmtaɪm/. ADV You use **sometime** to refer to a time in the future or the past that is unknown or that has not yet been decided. *Why don't you come and see me sometime.*

★ **sometimes** /'sʌmtaɪmz/. ADV You use **sometimes** to say that something happens on some occasions. *You must have noticed how tired he sometimes looks.*

⭐ **somewhat** /'sʌmwɒt/. ADV You use **somewhat** to indicate that something is the case to a limited extent or degree. *Conditions in the village had improved somewhat since January.*

⭐ **somewhere** /'sʌmweə/. [1] ADV You use **somewhere** to refer to a place without saying exactly where you mean. *I needed somewhere to live in London.* [2] ADV You use **somewhere** when giving an approximate amount, number, or time. *Caray is somewhere between 73 and 80 years of age.* [3] PHRASE If you say that you **are getting somewhere**, you mean that you are making progress towards achieving something. *At last they were agreeing, at last they were getting somewhere.*

> **USAGE** You use **not anywhere** instead of **somewhere** in negative sentences. *He isn't going anywhere.* You only use **somewhere** in questions when you expect the answer yes. *Are you going somewhere tonight?* Otherwise you say **anywhere**. *Are you going anywhere tonight?*

⭐ **son** /sʌn/ **sons.** N-COUNT A person's **son** is their male child.

sonata /sə'nɑːtə/ **sonatas.** N-COUNT A **sonata** is a piece of classical music written for a single instrument, or for one instrument and a piano.

⭐ **song** /sɒŋ, AM sɔːŋ/ **songs.** [1] N-COUNT A **song** is a piece of music which consists of words and music sung together. *...a love song.* [2] N-UNCOUNT **Song** is the art of singing. *...dance, music, mime and song.* [3] N-VAR A bird's **song** is the pleasant musical sounds that it makes.

sonic /'sɒnɪk/. ADJ BEFORE N **Sonic** is used to describe things related to sound. *...the sonic boom from a supersonic aeroplane.*

'**son-in-law, sons-in-law.** N-COUNT A person's **son-in-law** is the husband of their daughter.

sonnet /'sɒnɪt/ **sonnets.** N-COUNT A **sonnet** is a poem with 14 lines. Each line has 14 syllables, and the poem has a fixed pattern of rhymes.

⭐ **soon** /suːn/ **sooner, soonest.** [1] ADV If something is going to happen **soon**, it will happen after a short time. *This chance has come sooner than I expected... The kidnapper is a man we must catch and the sooner the better.* [2] ADV If something happened **soon** after a particular time or event, it happened a short time after it. *Soon afterwards he separated from his wife.*

PHRASES ● If you say that something happens **as soon as** something else happens, you mean that it happens immediately after the other thing. *You'll never guess what happened as soon as I left my room.* ● If you say that something will happen **sooner or later**, you mean that it will happen, though it might take a long time. ● If you say that **no sooner** has one thing happened **than**

another thing happens, you mean that the second thing happens immediately after the first thing. *No sooner had he arrived in Rome than he was kidnapped.* ● If you say that you **would sooner** do something, you mean that you would prefer to do it. *I'd sooner not talk about it.*

soot /sʊt/. N-UNCOUNT **Soot** is black powder which rises in the smoke from a fire and collects on the inside of chimneys.

soothe /suːð/ **soothes, soothing, soothed.** [1] VERB If you **soothe** someone who is angry or upset, you make them calmer. *He would take her in his arms and soothe her.* ◆ **soothing** ADJ *...some gentle, soothing music.* [2] VERB Something that **soothes** pain makes it less severe. ◆ **soothing** ADJ *Cold tea is very soothing for burns.*

⭐ **sophisticated** /sə'fɪstɪkeɪtɪd/. [1] ADJ A **sophisticated** person is at ease in social situations and knows about culture, fashion, and other matters that are considered socially important. [2] ADJ A **sophisticated** machine or method of doing something contains more advanced features than other things of the same type. *...a large and sophisticated new British telescope.*

sophistication /sə,fɪstɪ'keɪʃən/. N-UNCOUNT **Sophistication** is the quality of being sophisticated.

soprano /sə'prɑːnəʊ, -'præn-/ **sopranos.** N-COUNT A **soprano** is a woman, girl, or boy with a high singing voice.

sordid /'sɔːdɪd/. [1] ADJ If you describe someone's behaviour as **sordid**, you mean that is immoral or dishonest. *I don't want to hear the sordid details of your relationship.* [2] ADJ If you describe a place as **sordid**, you mean that it is dirty, unpleasant, or depressing. *...the attic windows of their sordid little rooms.*

sore /sɔː/ **sores.** [1] ADJ If part of your body is **sore**, it causes you pain and discomfort. *...a sore throat.* [2] N-COUNT A **sore** is a painful spot on your body where the skin is infected.

sorely /'sɔːli/. ADV **Sorely** is used to emphasize that a feeling such as disappointment or need is very strong. *He will be sorely missed.*

sorrow /'sɒrəʊ/. N-UNCOUNT **Sorrow** is a feeling of deep sadness or regret. *It was a time of great sorrow.*

sorrows /'sɒrəʊz/. N-PLURAL **Sorrows** are events or situations that cause deep sadness. *...the joys and sorrows of everyday living.*

⭐ **sorry** /'sɒri/ **sorrier, sorriest.** [1] CONVENTION You say '**Sorry**' or '**I'm sorry**' as a way of expressing your disappointment or sadness that something you have done or have told someone has caused them hurt or trouble. *Sorry I took so long... I'm really sorry if I said anything wrong... I'm sorry to have to tell you that your son is dead... She was very sorry about all the trouble she'd caused.* [2] ADJ AFTER LINK-V If you feel **sorry for** someone who is unhappy or in an unpleasant situation, you feel sympathy and sadness for them. *I am*

a
b
c
d
e
f
g
h
i
j
k
l
m
n
o
p
q
r
s
t
u
v
w
x
y
z

very sorry for the family. **3** ADJ BEFORE N If someone or something is in a **sorry** condition, they are in a bad condition, mentally or physically. *She is a sorry sight.* **4** CONVENTION You say **'Sorry?'** when you have not heard what someone has said and you want them to repeat it.

⭐ **sort** /sɔːt/ **sorts, sorting, sorted. 1** N-COUNT A particular **sort** of something is one of its different kinds or types. *What sort of school did you go to?* **2** N-SING You describe someone as a particular **sort** when you are describing their character. *He seemed to be just the right sort for the job.* **3** VERB If you **sort** things, you arrange them into different groups or places. *The students are sorted into three ability groups... He unlatched the box and sorted through the papers.*
  PHRASES ● You use **sort of** when you want to say that your description of something is not very precise. *In the end, she sort of pushed it.* ● If you describe something as a particular thing **of sorts**, you are suggesting that its quality or standard is poor. *He made a living of sorts selling pancakes from a van.*
  ▶**sort out. 1** PHR-VERB If you **sort out** a group of things, you organize or tidy them. *...trying to sort out fact from fiction.* **2** PHR-VERB If you **sort out** a problem, you solve it. *When we reported a fault, it was sorted out within 3 hours.*

sortie /'sɔːti/ **sorties. 1** N-COUNT A **sortie** is a brief trip away from your home base, especially a trip to an unfamiliar place. [FORMAL] *From here we plan several sorties into the countryside.* **2** N-COUNT You refer to a brief raid by a military force into their enemy's territory as a **sortie**.

soufflé (or **souffle**) /'suːfleɪ, AM suːˈfleɪ/ **soufflés.** N-VAR A **soufflé** is a light food made from a mixture of beaten egg whites and other ingredients that are baked in the oven.

sought /sɔːt/. **Sought** is the past tense and past participle of **seek**.

'**sought-after.** ADJ Something that is **sought-after** is in great demand, usually because it is rare or of very good quality. *...the most sought-after prize in world sport.*

⭐ **soul** /səʊl/ **souls. 1** N-COUNT A person's **soul** is the spiritual part of them which some people believe continues existing after their body is dead. *...mourning the souls of the people killed in the blast.* **2** N-COUNT You can refer to your mind, character, thoughts, and feelings as your **soul**. *I will put my heart and soul into the job.* **3** N-SING You use **soul** in negative statements to mean nobody at all. *I've never harmed a soul.*
4 N-UNCOUNT **Soul** or **soul music** is a type of pop music performed mainly by black American musicians.

⭐ **sound** /saʊnd/ **sounds, sounding, sounded; sounder, soundest. 1** N-COUNT A **sound** is something that you hear. *Liza was so frightened she couldn't make a sound. ...the sounds of children playing.*
2 N-UNCOUNT **Sound** is what you hear when vibrations travel through air or water. *...twice the*

speed of sound. **3** VERB If something such as a bell **sounds**, or if you **sound** it, it makes a noise. *He sounded his horn in frustration.* **4** LINK-VERB When you are describing a noise, you can talk about the way it **sounds**. *They heard what sounded like a huge explosion.* **5** LINK-VERB When you talk about the way someone **sounds**, you are describing the impression you have of them when they speak. *She sounded a bit worried.*
6 LINK-VERB & N-SING You can give your opinion about something you have just read or heard by talking about the way it **sounds**, or talking about the **sound** of it. *It sounds like a wonderful idea.*
7 ADJ You can describe a building or part of someone's mind or body as **sound** when it is in good condition. *His body was still sound.* **8** ADJ If something such as advice is **sound**, it is reliable and sensible. **9** PHRASE If you are **sound asleep**, you are sleeping deeply.
  ▶**sound out.** PHR-VERB If you **sound** someone **out**, you question them to find out their opinion. *We told the company management to sound out the views of the employees.*

soundcard /'saʊndkɑːd/ **soundcards.** N-COUNT A **soundcard** is a piece of equipment which can be put into a computer so that the computer can produce music or other sounds. [COMPUTING]

soundly /'saʊndli/. **1** ADV If someone is **soundly** defeated, they are defeated thoroughly. **2** ADV If a decision, opinion, or statement is **soundly** based, there are sensible or reliable reasons behind it. **3** ADV If you sleep **soundly**, you sleep deeply.

soundtrack /'saʊndtræk/ **soundtracks.** N-COUNT The **soundtrack** of a film is its sound, speech, and especially the music.

soup /suːp/ **soups.** N-VAR **Soup** is liquid food made by cooking meat, fish, or vegetables in water.

sour /saʊə/ **sours, souring, soured. 1** ADJ Something that is **sour** has a sharp taste like the taste of a lemon. *The stewed apple was sour.* **2** ADJ **Sour** milk has an unpleasant taste because it is no longer fresh. **3** ADJ If you say that someone is **sour**, you think they are bad-tempered and unfriendly. *He gave Lane a sour look.* ◆ **sourly** ADV *Digby smiled sourly. 'Politics isn't pleasant to explain.'* **4** ADJ If a situation or relationship goes **sour**, it stops being enjoyable or satisfactory. *Palestine's dream of new democracy has quickly turned sour.* **5** VERB If a friendship or attitude **sours**, or if something **sours** it, it becomes less friendly or hopeful. *Her mood soured a little.*

⭐ **source** /sɔːs/ **sources. 1** N-COUNT The **source of** something is the person, place, or thing which you get it from, or where it comes from. *...renewable sources of energy. ...tourism, which is a major source of income for the city.* **2** N-COUNT A **source** is a person or book that provides information for a news story or for a piece of research. *Military sources say the boat was* *heading south.* **3** N-SING The **source** of a river or stream is the place where it begins.

⭐ **south** /saʊθ/. **1** N-SING The **south** is the direction on your right when you are looking towards the place where the sun rises. *...warm breezes from the south.* **2** N-SING & ADJ The **south** of a place, or the **south** part of a place, is the part which is towards the south. *...holidays in the south of France. ...the south side of the gorge.* **3** ADV **South** means towards the south, or positioned to the south of a place or thing. *Troops had moved south... The hurricane hit Florida just south of Miami.* **4** ADJ A **south** wind blows from the south.

⭐ **south-'east**. **1** N-SING The **south-east** is the direction halfway between south and east. *Look roughly to the south-east.* **2** N-SING & ADJ The **south-east** of a place, or the **south-east** part of a place, is the part which is towards the south-east. *...a suburb seven miles south-east of Havana. ...south-east London.* **3** ADV **South-east** means towards the south-east, or positioned to the south-east of a place or thing. *The monsoon should move south-east by late tomorrow.* **4** ADJ A **south-east** wind blows from the south-east.

south-'eastern. ADJ **South-eastern** means in or from the south-east of a region or country. *...the south-eastern edge of the United States.*

southerly /'sʌðəli/. **1** ADJ A **southerly** point, area, or direction is to the south or towards the south. *...the most southerly areas of Zimbabwe. ...a southerly direction.* **2** ADJ A **southerly** wind blows from the south.

⭐ **southern** /'sʌðən/. ADJ **Southern** means in or from the south of a region or country. *He comes not from Southern China, but from northern Thailand.*

southerner /'sʌðənə/ **southerners**. N-COUNT A **southerner** is a person who was born in or who lives in the southern part of a place or country. *Bob Wilson is a southerner, from Texas.*

southward /'saʊθwəd/ (or **southwards** /'saʊθwədz/). ADV & ADJ **Southward** or **southwards** means towards the south. *They drove southward. ...the southward drift of the oil slick.*

⭐ **south-'west**. **1** N-SING The **south-west** is the direction halfway between south and west. *Turn to the south-west to see the expanse of Lucy Bay.* **2** N-SING & ADJ The **south-west** of a place, or the **south-west** part of a place, is the part which is towards the south-west. *...the mountains in the south-west of the USA. ...the South-west tip of Grenada.* **3** ADV **South-west** means towards the south-west, or positioned to the south-west of a place or thing. *Go south-west until you reach the cliff.* **4** ADJ A **south-west** wind blows from the south-west.

south-'western. ADJ **South-western** means in or from the south-west of a region or country. *...south-western France.*

souvenir /ˌsuːvə'nɪə, AM 'suːvənɪr/ **souvenirs**. N-COUNT A **souvenir** is something which you buy or keep to remind you of a holiday, place, or event. *...a souvenir of the summer of 1992.*

sovereign /'sɒvrɪn/ **sovereigns**. **1** ADJ A **sovereign** state or country is independent and not under the authority of any other country. **2** ADJ **Sovereign** is used to describe the person or institution that has the highest power in a country. *...Nigeria's sovereign body.* **3** N-COUNT A **sovereign** is a king, queen, or other royal ruler.

sovereignty /'sɒvrɪnti/. N-UNCOUNT **Sovereignty** is the power that a country has to govern itself or to govern other countries. *...the reversion of Hong Kong to Chinese sovereignty.*

sow, **sows**, **sowing**, **sowed**, **sown**. **1** VERB /səʊ/ If you **sow** seeds, you plant them in the ground. **2** VERB If someone **sows** an undesirable feeling or situation, they cause it to begin and develop. *He cleverly sowed doubts in the minds of his rivals.* **3** N-COUNT /saʊ/. A **sow** is an adult female pig.

spa /spɑː/ **spas**. N-COUNT A **spa** is a place where water with minerals in it bubbles out of the ground.

⭐ **space** /speɪs/ **spaces**, **spacing**, **spaced**. **1** N-VAR You use **space** to refer to an area of any size that is empty or available. *...cutting down yet more trees to make space for houses... List in the spaces below the specific changes you have made.*

> **USAGE** You should use **space** or **room** to refer to an open or empty area. You do not use **place** as an uncount noun in this sense. **Room** is more likely to be used when you are talking about space inside an enclosed area. *There's not enough room in the bathroom for both of us... Leave plenty of space between you and the car in front.*

2 N-SING A **space** of time is a period of time. *I have known dramatic changes occur in the space of a few minutes.* **3** VERB & PHR-VERB If you **space** a series of things, or if you **space** them **out**, you arrange them so that they have gaps between them. *Women once again are having fewer children and spacing them further apart... He talks quite slowly and spaces his words out.* **4** N-UNCOUNT **Space** is the vast area that lies beyond the Earth's atmosphere and surrounds the stars and planets. *...launching satellites into space.* ● See also **spacing**.

spacecraft /'speɪskrɑːft, -kræft/.

> ✓ **Spacecraft** is both the singular and the plural form.

N-COUNT A **spacecraft** is a rocket or other vehicle that can travel in space.

spaceship /'speɪsʃɪp/ **spaceships**. N-COUNT A **spaceship** is the same as a **spacecraft**.

'**space station**, **space stations**. N-COUNT A **space station** is an object which is sent into space and

a b c d e f g h i j k l m n o p q r **s** t u v w x y z

A
B
C
D
E
F
G
H
I
J
K
L
M
N
O
P
Q
R
S
T
U
V
W
X
Y
Z

then goes around the earth, and is used as a base by astronauts.

spacing /'speɪsɪŋ/. N-UNCOUNT **Spacing** refers to the way that typing or printing is arranged on a page. *Write clearly in double spacing.* ● See also **space**.

spacious /'speɪʃəs/. ADJ A **spacious** room or other place is large, so that you can move around freely in it. *...spacious air-conditioned offices.*

spade /speɪd/ **spades.** ☐ N-COUNT A **spade** is a tool used for digging, with a flat metal blade and a long handle. → See picture on page 832. ☐ N-UNCOUNT **Spades** is one of the four suits in a pack of playing cards. Each card in the suit is called a **spade** and is marked with one or more black symbols: ♠.

spaghetti /spə'geti/. N-UNCOUNT **Spaghetti** is a type of pasta which looks like long pieces of string.

spam /spæm/ **spams.** N-VAR **Spam** is unwanted e-mail that is sent to a large number of people, usually as advertising. [COMPUTING]

span /spæn/ **spans, spanning, spanned.** ☐ N-COUNT A **span** is a period of time between two dates or events during which something exists, functions, or happens. *The batteries had a life span of six hours.* ☐ N-COUNT Your **concentration span** or your **attention span** is the length of time you are able to concentrate on something or be interested in it. ☐ VERB If something **spans** a long period of time, it lasts throughout that period of time or relates to the whole of it. *His professional career spanned 16 years.* ☐ N-COUNT The **span** of something that extends or is spread out sideways is its width. *It is a very pretty butterfly, with a 2 inch wing span.* ☐ VERB A bridge or other structure that **spans** something such as a river stretches right across it.

spank /spæŋk/ **spanks, spanking, spanked.** VERB If someone **spanks** a child, they punish them by hitting them on the bottom several times.

spanner /'spænə/ **spanners.** N-COUNT In British English, a **spanner** is a metal tool used for tightening a nut. The American word is **wrench**. → See picture on page 833.

spar /spɑː/ **spars, sparring, sparred.** ☐ VERB When boxers **spar**, they box using fairly gentle blows instead of hitting their opponent hard, for example in training. *He could not get anyone to spar with Tyson.* ☐ VERB If you **spar with** someone, you argue with them but not in an aggressive or serious way. *He sparred with his friend Jesse Jackson over political tactics.*

⭐ **spare** /speə/ **spares, sparing, spared.** ☐ ADJ & N-COUNT **Spare** things or **spares** are the same as things that you are already using that you are keeping ready in case others are needed. *Don't forget to take a few spare batteries. ...two discs, with one as a spare.* ☐ ADJ You use **spare** to describe something that is not being used by anyone, and is therefore available for someone to use. *They don't have a lot of spare cash. ...the spare*

bedroom. ☐ PHRASE If you have something such as time, money, or space **to spare**, you have some extra that you have not used or which you do not need. *You got here with ninety seconds to spare.* ☐ VERB If you **spare** time or another resource for a particular purpose, you make it available for that purpose. *Miss Jackson could only spare 35 minutes for our meeting.* ☐ VERB To **spare** someone an unpleasant experience means to prevent them from having it. *Spare them the pain of discovering the real facts... Northern Somalia was largely spared from the famine.*

spare 'part, spare parts. N-COUNT **Spare parts** are parts that you can buy separately to replace old or broken parts in a piece of equipment.

spare 'time. N-UNCOUNT Your **spare time** is the time during which you do not have to work when you can do whatever you like. *In her spare time she read books.*

sparing /'speərɪŋ/. ADJ If you are **sparing with** something, you use it or give it in very small quantities. *I've not been sparing with the garlic.* ◆ **sparingly** ADV *Medication is used sparingly.*

⭐ **spark** /spɑːk/ **sparks, sparking, sparked.** ☐ N-COUNT A **spark** is a tiny bright piece of burning material that flies up from something that is burning. ☐ N-COUNT A **spark** is a flash of light caused by electricity. ☐ N-COUNT A **spark of** a quality or feeling, especially a desirable one, is a small but noticeable amount of it. *His music lacked that vital spark of imagination.* ☐ VERB & PHR-VERB If one thing **sparks** another, or if one thing **sparks off** another, the first thing causes the second thing to start happening. *...a political crisis sparked off by religious violence.*

sparkle /'spɑːkəl/ **sparkles, sparkling, sparkled.** VERB & N-UNCOUNT If something **sparkles**, or if it has **sparkle**, it is clear and bright and shines with a lot of very small points of light. *In the marina yachts sparkle in the sunshine. ...the sparkle of coloured glass.*

sparkling /'spɑːklɪŋ/. ADJ **Sparkling** drinks are slightly fizzy. *...a glass of sparkling wine.*

sparrow /'spærəʊ/ **sparrows.** N-COUNT A **sparrow** is a small brown bird that is common in Britain.

sparse /spɑːs/. ADJ Something that is **sparse** is small in number or amount and spread out over an area. *...rock fields with sparse vegetation... Traffic was sparse on the highway.* ◆ **sparsely** ADV *...the sparsely populated interior region.*

spartan /'spɑːtən/. ADJ A **spartan** place or way of life is very simple or strict, with no luxuries. *Felicity's bedroom was spartan but functional.*

spasm /'spæzəm/ **spasms.** N-VAR A **spasm** is a sudden tightening of your muscles, which you cannot control. *A lack of magnesium causes muscles to go into spasm.*

spat /spæt/. **Spat** is the past tense and past participle of **spit**.

spate /speɪt/. N-COUNT A **spate of** things, especially unpleasant things, is a large number of them that happen or appear within a short period of time. ...*the recent spate of attacks on horses.*

spatial /'speɪʃəl/. ADJ BEFORE N **Spatial** is used to describe things relating to size, area, or position. ...*the intensity and spatial distribution of rainfall.* ♦ **spatially** ADV ...*jobs that are more spatially dispersed throughout the country.*

spatter /'spætə/ **spatters, spattering, spattered.** VERB If a liquid **spatters** a surface, or if it **is spattered** there, drops of it fall on the surface. *Turn the fish, being careful not to spatter any hot butter on yourself.* ♦ **-spattered** ...*the blood-spattered body.*

⭐ **speak** /spiːk/ **speaks, speaking, spoke, spoken.** ① VERB When you **speak**, you use your voice in order to say something. *He tried to speak, but she interrupted him. ...as I spoke these idiotic words.* ♦ **speaker, speakers** N-COUNT ...*responses made after the speaker has stopped talking.* ② VERB If you **speak for** a group of people, you make their views and demands known, or represent them. *It was the job of the Church to speak for the underprivileged.* ③ VERB If you **speak** a foreign language, you know it and can use it. *He doesn't speak English.* ♦ **speaker** N-COUNT *A fifth of the population are Russian speakers.* ④ VERB If two people **are not speaking**, they no longer talk to each other because they have quarrelled. *He is not speaking to his mother because of her friendship with his ex-wife.* ⑤ VERB If you **speak well of** someone or **speak highly of** someone, you say good things about them. If you **speak ill of** someone, you criticize them. ⑥ VERB You use **speaking** in expressions such as **generally speaking** and **technically speaking** to indicate the way in which your statement is true or relevant. *Politically speaking, do you think that these moves have been effective?* PHRASES ● You can say '**speaking as** a parent' or '**speaking as** a teacher', for example, to indicate that the opinion you are giving is based on your experience as a parent or as a teacher. ● If something **speaks for itself**, its meaning or qualities are obvious and do not need to be explained or pointed out. ● You can say **speaking of** something that has just been mentioned as a way of introducing a new topic which has some connection with that thing. *Drop hints for Christmas presents! And speaking of presents, we have 100 exclusive fragrance collections to give away.* ● Nothing **to speak of** means hardly anything or only unimportant things. *They have no weaponry to speak of.* ● You say **so to speak** to indicate that what you are saying is not literally true. *The five countries have now all passed, so to speak, their entry test.*
▸ **speak out.** PHR-VERB If you **speak out** in favour of something or against something, you say publicly that you think it is good or bad. *She continued to speak out at rallies around the country.*
▸ **speak up.** PHR-VERB If you ask someone to **speak up**, you are asking them to speak more loudly.

> **USAGE** There are some differences in the way the verbs **speak** and **talk** are used. When you **speak**, you could, for example, be addressing someone or making a speech. **Talk** is more likely to be used when you are referring to a conversation or discussion. *I talked about it with my family at dinner... Sometimes we'd talk all night.* **Talk** can also be used to emphasize the activity of saying things, rather than the words that are spoken. *She thought I talked too much.*

-speak /-spiːk/. **-speak** is used to form nouns which refer to the kind of language used by a particular person or by people involved in a particular activity. ...*a classic example of management-speak.*

⭐ **speaker** /'spiːkə/ **speakers.** ① N-COUNT A **speaker** is a person who makes a speech. *Bruce Wyatt will be the guest speaker at next month's meeting.* ② N-COUNT A **speaker** is a piece of equipment, for example part of a radio or hi-fi system, through which sound comes out. ③ See also **speak.**

spear /spɪə/ **spears, spearing, speared.** ① N-COUNT A **spear** is a weapon consisting of a long pole with a sharp point. ② VERB If you **spear** something, you push or throw a pointed object into it.

spearhead /'spɪəhed/ **spearheads, spearheading, spearheaded.** VERB & N-COUNT If someone **spearheads** a campaign, or if they are involved in the **spearhead** of it, they lead it. [JOURNALISM] ...*spearheading a national campaign against bullying.*

specs /speks/. N-PLURAL A pair of **specs** is a pair of glasses. [INFORMAL]

⭐ **special** /'speʃəl/. ① ADJ Someone or something that is **special** is different from normal, often in a way that makes it better or more important than other things. *You're very special to me, darling. ...a special variety of strawberry.* ② ADJ BEFORE N **Special** means relating to one particular person, group, or place. *Every anxious person will have his or her own special problems.*

special ef'fect, special effects. N-COUNT In film, **special effects** are unusual pictures or sounds that are created by using special techniques.

specialise. See **specialize.**

⭐ **specialist** /'speʃəlɪst/ **specialists.** N-COUNT A **specialist** is a person who has a particular skill or knows a lot about a particular subject. ...*health specialist Professor John Brimley Evans.*

speciality /speʃi'ælɪti/ **specialities.** ① N-COUNT Someone's **speciality** is the kind of work they do best or the subject they know most about. *His speciality was the history of Germany.* ② N-COUNT In British English, a **speciality** of a place is a special food or product that is always very good

a
b
c
d
e
f
g
h
i
j
k
l
m
n
o
p
q
r
s
t
u
v
w
x
y
z

there. The usual American word is **specialty**. *These potato dumplings are a speciality of northern Italy.*

★ **specialize** (BRIT also **specialise**) /'speʃəlaɪz/ **specializes, specializing, specialized.** VERB If you **specialize in** an area of study or a type of work, you know a lot about it and spend a lot of your time and attention on it. ♦ **specialization** N-UNCOUNT ...*specialization in particular products.*

specialized (BRIT also **specialised**) /'speʃəlaɪzd/. ADJ Someone or something that is **specialized** is trained or developed for a particular purpose. ...*specialized training in teaching reading.*

specially /'speʃəli/. 1 ADV If something has been done **specially** for a particular person or purpose, it has been done only for that person or purpose. ...*a soap specially designed for sensitive skins.* 2 ADV **Specially** is used to mean more than usually or more than other things. [INFORMAL] *What was specially enjoyable about that job?*

specialty /'speʃəlti/ **specialties.** N-COUNT A **specialty** is the same as a **speciality**. [AMERICAN]

★ **species** /'spiːʃiːz/

> ✓ **Species** is both the singular and the plural form.

N-COUNT A **species** is a class of plants or animals whose members have the same characteristics and are able to breed with each other.

★ **specific** /spɪ'sɪfɪk/. 1 ADJ BEFORE N You use **specific** to emphasize that you are talking about a particular thing or subject. *Massage may help to increase blood flow to specific areas of the body.* 2 ADJ If someone is **specific**, they give a description that is precise and exact. You can also use **specific** to describe their description. 3 ADJ Something that is **specific to** a particular thing is connected with that thing only. ...*financial problems specific to students.* ♦ **-specific** *Most studies of trade have been country-specific.* 4 See also **specifics**.

★ **specifically** /spɪ'sɪfɪkli/. 1 ADV You use **specifically** to emphasize that a subject is being considered separately from other subjects. ...*the first nursing home designed specifically for people with AIDS.* 2 ADV You use **specifically** to add something more precise or exact to what you have already said. *Death frightens me, specifically my own death.* 3 ADV You use **specifically** to indicate that you are stating or describing something precisely. *I asked her to repeat specifically the words that Patti had used.*

specification /,spesɪfɪ'keɪʃən/ **specifications.** N-COUNT A **specification** is a requirement which is clearly stated, for example about the necessary features in the design of something. *Handmade jewellery can be produced to your specifications.*

specifics /spɪ'sɪfɪks/. N-PLURAL The **specifics** of a subject are the details of it that need to be considered. *I don't know the specifics of your problem.*

specify /'spesɪfaɪ/ **specifies, specifying, specified.** VERB If you **specify** something, you state it precisely. *One rule specifies that learner drivers must be supervised by adults.*

specimen /'spesɪmɪn/ **specimens.** N-COUNT A **specimen** of something is an example or small amount of it which gives an idea of the whole. *Applicants have to submit a specimen of handwriting.*

speck /spek/ **specks.** N-COUNT A **speck** is a very small stain or mark, or a very small piece of something. *He brushed a speck of dust off his shoes.*

spectacle /'spektəkəl/ **spectacles.** 1 N-PLURAL Someone's **spectacles** are their glasses. [FORMAL] ...*a pair of spectacles.* 2 N-COUNT A **spectacle** is an interesting or impressive sight or event. *Mahoney stared in astonishment at the spectacle before him.*

★ **spectacular** /spek'tækjʊlə/ **spectaculars.** 1 ADJ Something that is **spectacular** is very impressive or dramatic. ♦ **spectacularly** ADV *Many of her movies had been spectacularly successful.* 2 N-COUNT A **spectacular** is a grand and impressive show or performance. ...*one of the world's great sporting spectaculars.*

spectator /spek'teɪtə, AM 'spekteɪtər/ **spectators.** N-COUNT A **spectator** is someone who watches something, especially a sporting event.

spectre (AM **specter**) /'spektə/ **spectres.** N-COUNT You talk about **the spectre of** something unpleasant when you are frightened that it might occur. *This has raised the spectre of a full-scale war.*

spectrum /'spektrəm/ **spectra** or **spectrums.** 1 N-SING **The spectrum** is the range of different colours produced when light passes through an object called a prism or through a drop of water. 2 N-COUNT A **spectrum** is a range of a particular type of thing. *The term 'special needs' covers a wide spectrum of problems.*

★ **speculate** /'spekjʊleɪt/ **speculates, speculating, speculated.** 1 VERB If you **speculate** about something, you guess about its nature or identity, or about what might happen. *The reader can speculate what will happen next.* ♦ **speculation, speculations** N-VAR ...*speculation over the future of the economy.* 2 VERB When people **speculate** financially, they buy property or shares in the hope of being able to sell them at a profit. ♦ **speculator, speculators** N-COUNT ...*a Florida real-estate speculator.*

speculative /'spekjʊlətɪv, AM -leɪt-/. ADJ A **speculative** statement or opinion is based on guesses rather than knowledge. ...*speculative stories about the mysterious disappearance.*

sped /sped/. **Sped** is a past tense and past participle of **speed**.

★ **speech** /spiːtʃ/ **speeches.** 1 N-UNCOUNT **Speech** is the ability to speak or the act of speaking. ...*the development of speech in children.* 2 N-SING Your **speech** is the way in which you speak. *His speech*

became increasingly thick and nasal. [3] N-UNCOUNT
Speech is spoken language. *...the way common letter clusters are usually pronounced in speech.* [4] N-COUNT A **speech** is a formal talk given to an audience.

speechless /'spiːtʃləs/. ADJ If you are **speechless**, you are temporarily unable to speak, usually because something has shocked you. *Alex was almost speechless with rage.*

⭐ **speed** /spiːd/ **speeds, speeding, sped.**

✓ For the phrasal verb, the past tense and past participle is **speeded**.

[1] N-VAR The **speed** of something is the rate at which it moves, happens, or is done. *He drove off at high speed... Each learner can proceed at his own speed.* [2] N-UNCOUNT **Speed** is very fast movement. *Speed is the essential ingredient of all athletics.* [3] VERB To **speed** somewhere means to move or travel there quickly. *Trains will speed through the Channel Tunnel at 186mph.* [4] VERB A motorist who **is speeding** is driving a vehicle faster than the legal speed limit. ◆ **speeding** N-UNCOUNT *He was fined for speeding.*
▸ **speed up.** PHR-VERB When something **speeds up**, it moves, happens, or is done more quickly. *I had already taken steps to speed up a solution to the problem.*

'**speed limit, speed limits.** N-COUNT The **speed limit** on a road is the maximum speed at which you are legally allowed to drive.

speedy /'spiːdi/ **speedier, speediest.** ADJ A **speedy** process, event, or action happens or is done very quickly. *We wish Bill a very speedy recovery.*
◆ **speedily** ADV *Deal speedily and efficiently with everyday cleaning tasks.*

⭐ **spell** /spel/ **spells, spelling, spelled** (BRIT also **spelt**). [1] VERB & PHR-VERB When you **spell** a word, or when you **spell** it **out**, you write or speak each letter in the word in the correct order. *How do you spell 'potato'?... If I don't know a word, I ask them to spell it out for me.* [2] VERB If something **spells** a particular result, it suggests that this will be the result. *...situations which are likely to spell disaster.* [3] N-COUNT A **spell** of an activity or type of weather is a short period of it. *...a long spell of dry weather. ...a brief spell teaching religious education.* [4] N-COUNT A **spell** is a situation in which events are controlled by a magical power. *They say she died after a witch cast a spell on her.*
▸ **spell out.** [1] PHR-VERB When you **spell** something **out**, you explain it in detail. *Be assertive and spell out exactly how you feel.* [2] See **spell** 1.

spellcheck /'speltʃek/ **spellchecks, spellchecking, spellchecked.** VERB If you **spellcheck** something you have written on a computer, you use a special program to check for spelling mistakes. [COMPUTING] *This model allows you to spellcheck over 100,000 different words.*

spellchecker /'speltʃekə/ **spellcheckers.** N-COUNT A **spellchecker** is a special program on a computer which you can use to check for spelling mistakes. [COMPUTING]

spelling /'spelɪŋ/ **spellings.** [1] N-COUNT The **spelling** of a word is the correct sequence of letters in it. [2] N-UNCOUNT **Spelling** is the ability to spell words in the correct way. It is also an attempt to spell a word in the correct way. *His spelling is very bad.*

spelt /spelt/. **Spelt** is a past tense and past participle form of **spell**. [BRITISH]

⭐ **spend** /spend/ **spends, spending, spent.** [1] VERB When you **spend** money, you pay money for things you want. *Every three months I spend a hundred pounds on clothes.* [2] VERB If you **spend** time or energy doing something, you use your time or effort doing it. If you **spend** time in a place, you stay there for a period of time. *She had spent 29 years as a nurse... We spent the night in a hotel.*

spent /spent/. [1] **Spent** is the past tense and past participle of **spend**. [2] ADJ **Spent** substances or containers have been used and cannot be used again. *Radioactive waste is simply spent fuel.*

sperm /spɜːm/.

✓ In meaning 1, the plural is **sperm** or **sperms**.

[1] N-COUNT A **sperm** is a cell produced in the sex organs of a male animal which can enter a female animal's egg and fertilize it. [2] N-UNCOUNT **Sperm** is the liquid that contains sperm when it is produced.

spew /spjuː/ **spews, spewing, spewed.** VERB When things **spew** from a place, they come out in large quantities. *Leaking oil spewed from the tanker.*

sphere /sfɪə/. [1] N-COUNT A **sphere** is an object that is perfectly round in shape like a ball. → See picture on page 829. [2] N-COUNT A **sphere of** activity or interest is a particular area of activity or interest. *...nurses working in all spheres of the health service.*

spice /spaɪs/ **spices.** N-VAR A **spice** is a part of a plant, or a powder made from that part, which you put in food to give it flavour.

spiced /spaɪst/. ADJ When food is **spiced**, it has had spices or other strong-tasting foods added to it.

spicy /'spaɪsi/ **spicier, spiciest.** ADJ **Spicy** food is strongly flavoured with spices.

spider /'spaɪdə/ **spiders.** N-COUNT A **spider** is a small creature with eight legs.

spike /spaɪk/ **spikes.** [1] N-COUNT A **spike** is a long piece of metal with a sharp point. *...a 15-foot wall topped with iron spikes.* [2] N-COUNT Some long pointed objects can be referred to as **spikes**. *Her hair stood out in spikes.*

spiked /spaɪkt/. ADJ **Spiked** things have spikes or a spike on them. *...huge iron spiked gates.*

spiky /'spaɪki/ **spikier, spikiest.** ADJ Something that is **spiky** has sharp points. → See picture on page 526. *...tall, spiky evergreen trees.*

spill /spɪl/ **spills, spilling, spilled** (BRIT also **spilt** /spɪlt/). [1] VERB If you **spill** a liquid, it accidentally flows over the edge of its container. *I almost*

a
b
c
d
e
f
g
h
i
j
k
l
m
n
o
p
q
r
s
t
u
v
w
x
y
z

spilled my drink... Don't spill water on your suit. [2] VERB If people or things **spill** out of a place, they come out in large numbers. *The crowd spilled out into the street.*

⭐ **spin** /spɪn/ **spins, spinning, spun.** [1] VERB If something or someone **spins**, or if you **spin** them, they turn quickly around a central point. *He spun around, looking guilty... Ella spun the wheel and turned on to Main Street.* [2] VERB When someone **spins**, they make thread by twisting together pieces of a fibre. *...machinery for spinning cotton.* [3] VERB If someone **spins** a story, they give you an account of something that is untrue or only partly true.
▶ **spin out.** PHR-VERB If you **spin** something **out**, you make it last longer than it normally would. *He deliberately spun out his speech.*

spinach /'spɪnɪdʒ, -ɪtʃ/. N-UNCOUNT **Spinach** is a vegetable with large green leaves.

spinal /'spaɪnəl/. ADJ BEFORE N **Spinal** means relating to your spine. *...spinal injuries.*

spine /spaɪn/ **spines.** N-COUNT Your **spine** is the row of bones down your back.

'**spin-off, spin-offs.** [1] N-COUNT A **spin-off** is something useful that unexpectedly happens as a result of trying to achieve something else. *...commercial spin-offs from its research.* [2] N-COUNT A **spin-off** is a book, film, or television series that is derived from something similar that is already successful.

spiral /'spaɪərəl/ **spirals, spiralling, spiralled** (AM **spiraling spiraled).** [1] N-COUNT & ADJ BEFORE N A **spiral** is a shape which winds round and round, with each curve above or outside the previous one. **Spiral** things are in the shape of a spiral. *...the spiral staircase.* [2] VERB If something **spirals** somewhere, it grows or moves in a spiral curve. *Dense smoke spiralled upwards from the ground.* [3] VERB If an amount or level **spirals** upwards or downwards, it rises or falls quickly and at an increasing rate. You can refer this kind of change in a level or amount as a particular kind of **spiral**. *Her drug habit was spiralling out of control. ...oil's upward price spiral.*

spire

spire /spaɪə/ **spires.** N-COUNT The **spire** of a church is a tall cone-shaped structure on top of a tower.

⭐ **spirit** /'spɪrɪt/ **spirits, spiriting, spirited.** [1] N-SING Your **spirit** is the part of you that is not physical and that is connected with your deepest thoughts and feelings. *Marian retains a restless, youthful spirit.* [2] N-COUNT A person's **spirit** is a part of them that is not physical and that is believed to remain alive after their death. [3] N-COUNT A **spirit** is a ghost or supernatural being. [4] N-UNCOUNT **Spirit** is courage, determination, and energy that someone shows during difficult times. *Everyone who knew her admired her spirit.* [5] N-PLURAL You can refer to your **spirits** when saying how happy or unhappy you are. For example, if your spirits are high, you are happy. *A bit of exercise will help lift his spirits.* [6] N-SING The **spirit** in which you do something is the attitude you have when you are doing it. *They approached the talks in a conciliatory spirit.* [7] N-SING The **spirit** of something such as a law or an agreement is the way that it was intended to be interpreted or applied. *The requirement for work permits violates the spirit of the 1950 treaty.* [8] VERB If someone or something **is spirited away**, they are taken from a place quickly and secretly without anyone noticing. [9] N-PLURAL In British English, **spirits** are strong alcoholic drinks such as whisky and gin. The American word is **liquor.**

spirited /'spɪrɪtɪd/. ADJ **Spirited** means showing great energy, confidence, or courage. *Dr Lawrence gave a spirited defence of her position.*

⭐ **spiritual** /'spɪrɪtʃuəl/. [1] ADJ **Spiritual** means relating to people's deepest thoughts and beliefs, rather than to their bodies and physical surroundings. ◆ **spiritually** ADV *We were physically and spiritually exhausted.*
◆ **spirituality** /ˌspɪrɪtʃuˈælɪti/ N-UNCOUNT *...the peaceful spirituality of Japanese culture.* [2] ADJ **Spiritual** means relating to people's religious beliefs. *...the spiritual leader of Ireland's Catholics.*

spit /spɪt/ **spits, spitting, spat** (AM also **spit**). [1] N-UNCOUNT **Spit** is the watery liquid produced in your mouth. [2] VERB If someone **spits**, they force an amount of spit out of their mouth. If you **spit** liquid or food somewhere, you force a small amount of it out of your mouth. *They spat at me and taunted me... Spit out that gum.*

⭐ **spite** /spaɪt/. [1] PREP You use **in spite of** to introduce a fact which makes the rest of the statement you are making seem surprising. *He hired her in spite of the fact that she had never sung on stage.* [2] PREP If you do something **in spite of yourself**, you do it although you did not really intend to or expect to. *'What's Tony's reaction to all this?' Amy asked, laughing in spite of herself.* [3] VERB & N-UNCOUNT If you do something to **spite** someone, or if you do it **out of spite**, you do it because you want to hurt or upset them. *Just to spite Loren again, Shannon kissed Pitt.*

⭐ **splash** /splæʃ/ **splashes, splashing, splashed.** [1] VERB & N-SING If you **splash** around in water, you hit or disturb the water in a noisy way. A **splash** is the sound made when something hits or falls into water. *Players spent most of their time splashing through puddles... It hit the water with a huge splash.* ② VERB & N-COUNT If you **splash** a liquid somewhere or if it **splashes**, it hits someone or something and scatters in a lot of small drops. A **splash of** liquid is a quantity of it that hits something in this way. *Tears splashed into her hands.* ③ PHRASE If you **make a splash**, you become noticed or become popular because of something that you have done. [INFORMAL]

▶ **splash out.** PHR-VERB If you **splash out on** something, especially on a luxury, you buy it even though it costs a lot of money. [BRITISH, INFORMAL] *He wanted to splash out on a new car.*

splatter /'splætə/ **splatters, splattering, splattered.** VERB If a liquid **splatters** on something or **is splattered** on it, it drops or is thrown over it. *The men were splattered with beer.*

splendid /'splendɪd/. ① ADJ If you say that something is **splendid**, you mean that it is very good. [DATED] *What a splendid idea!* ◆ **splendidly** ADV *We get along splendidly.* ② ADJ If you describe a building or work of art as **splendid**, you mean that it is beautiful and impressive. *...a splendid Victorian mansion.* ◆ **splendidly** ADV *Nigel's book is splendidly illustrated.*

splendour (AM **splendor**) /'splendə/ **splendours.** N-VAR The **splendour** of something is its beautiful and impressive appearance or features. *...the splendour of the palace of Versailles.*

splinter /'splɪntə/ **splinters, splintering, splintered.** ① N-COUNT A **splinter** is a very thin sharp piece of wood or glass which has broken off from a larger piece. ② VERB If something **splinters** or **is splintered**, it breaks into splinters. *The stone rocketed into the glass, splintering it.*

⭐ **split** /splɪt/ **splits, splitting, split.** ① VERB If something **splits**, or if you **split** it, it is divided into two or more parts. *In a severe gale the ship split in two. ...uniting families split by the Korean war.* ② VERB & N-COUNT If an organization **splits**, or if it **is split**, one group of members disagrees strongly with the other members, and may form a group of their own. You also refer to a disagreement of this kind as a **split**. *Women priests are accused of splitting the church.* ③ VERB If something such as wood or a piece of clothing **splits**, or if it **is split**, a long crack or tear appears in it. → See picture on page 655. *I'd split the trousers I had on.* ④ VERB If two or more people **split** something, they share it between them. *I was happy to split the profits with them.*

▶ **split up.** ① PHR-VERB If two people **split up**, they end their relationship or marriage. *I split up with my boyfriend last year.* ② PHR-VERB If a group of people **split up**, they go away in different directions. *We had decided to split up in an attempt to get more done.* ③ PHR-VERB If you **split** something **up**, you divide it into a number of separate sections. *He split up the company.*

,**split** '**second.** N-SING A **split second** is a very

short period of time. *I had to make a split-second decision.*

splutter /'splʌtə/ **splutters, spluttering, spluttered.** ① VERB If someone **splutters**, they make spitting sounds and have difficulty speaking clearly, often because they are embarrassed or angry. *'I don't understand,' spluttered Jack.* ② VERB If something **splutters**, it makes a series of short sharp sounds. *The flame spluttered and went out.*

spoil /spɔɪl/ **spoils, spoiling, spoiled** (BRIT also **spoilt** /spɔɪlt/). ① VERB If you **spoil** something, you prevent it from being successful or satisfactory. *It's important not to let mistakes spoil your life.* ② VERB If you say that someone **spoils** their children, you mean that they give their children everything they want and that this has a bad effect on their character. ◆ **spoilt** or **spoiled** ADJ *A spoilt child is rarely popular with other children.* ③ VERB If you **spoil yourself**, or if you **spoil** someone you love, you give yourself or them something nice as a treat, or you do something special for them. ④ N-PLURAL The **spoils of** something are things that people get as a result of winning a battle or of doing something successfully. *...the spoils of war.*

spoke /spəʊk/ **spokes.** ① **Spoke** is the past tense of **speak**. ② N-COUNT The **spokes** of a wheel are the bars that join the outer ring to the centre.

spoken /'spəʊkən/. **Spoken** is the past participle of **speak**.

⭐ **spokesman** /'spəʊksmən/ **spokesmen.** N-COUNT A **spokesman** is a male spokesperson.

spokesperson /'spəʊkspɜːsən/ **spokespersons.** N-COUNT A **spokesperson** is a person who speaks as the representative of a group or organization.

spokeswoman /'spəʊkswʊmən/ **spokeswomen.** N-COUNT A **spokeswoman** is a female spokesperson.

sponge /spʌndʒ/ **sponges, sponging, sponged.** ① N-UNCOUNT **Sponge** is a very light absorbent substance with lots of little holes in it. Sponge can be either man-made or natural and is capable of absorbing a lot of water or of acting as an insulating material. ② N-COUNT A **sponge** is a piece of sponge that you use for washing yourself or for cleaning things. ③ VERB If you **sponge** something, you wipe it with a wet sponge. *Gently sponge your face.* ④ N-VAR A **sponge** is a light cake or pudding made from flour, eggs, sugar, and sometimes fat. *...chocolate sponge cake.*

▶ **sponge off** or **sponge on.** PHR-VERB If you say that someone **sponges off** other people or **sponges on** them, you disapprove of them because they get money from others, rather than trying to support themselves. [INFORMAL]

⭐ **sponsor** /'spɒnsə/ **sponsors, sponsoring, sponsored.** ① VERB If an organization **sponsors** something such as an event, it pays some or all of the expenses connected with it, often in order to get publicity for itself. ② VERB In Britain, if you **sponsor** someone who is doing something to

a
b
c
d
e
f
g
h
i
j
k
l
m
n
o
p
q
r
s
t
u
v
w
x
y
z

raise money for charity, you give them a sum of money for the charity if they succeed in doing it. **3** VERB If you **sponsor** a proposal, you officially put it forward and support it. *The resolution was sponsored by 13 nations.* **4** N-COUNT A **sponsor** is a person or organization that sponsors something or someone.

sponsorship /'spɒnsəʃɪp/. N-UNCOUNT **Sponsorship** is financial support given by a sponsor. *...skiers in need of sponsorship.*

spontaneity /ˌspɒntə'neɪɪti/. N-UNCOUNT **Spontaneity** is spontaneous, natural behaviour. *He had the spontaneity of a child.*

spontaneous /spɒn'teɪniəs/. **1** ADJ **Spontaneous** acts are not planned or arranged, but are done because someone suddenly wants to do them. *I joined in the spontaneous applause.* ♦ **spontaneously** ADV *He was never spontaneously warm or friendly towards us.* **2** ADJ A **spontaneous** event happens because of processes within something, rather than being caused by things outside it. *...a spontaneous explosion.* ♦ **spontaneously** ADV *These images surface spontaneously in dreams.*

spooky /'spuːki/ **spookier, spookiest.** ADJ If something is **spooky**, it has a frightening and unnatural atmosphere. [INFORMAL] *It's really spooky out here.*

spool /spuːl/ **spools.** N-COUNT A **spool** is a round object in a machine such as a sewing machine or film projector onto which thread, tape, or film is wound.

spoon /spuːn/ **spoons, spooning, spooned.** **1** N-COUNT A **spoon** is an implement used for eating, stirring, and serving food. It is shaped like a small shallow bowl with a long handle. → See picture on page 825. **2** VERB If you **spoon** food somewhere, you put it there using a spoon. *Spoon the sauce over the meat.*

sporadic /spə'rædɪk/. ADJ **Sporadic** events happen at irregular intervals. ♦ **sporadically** ADV *Fighting has occurred sporadically since 1988.*

spore /spɔː/ **spores.** N-COUNT **Spores** are cells produced by fungi such as mushrooms, which can develop into new fungi. [TECHNICAL]

⭐ **sport** /spɔːt/ **sports, sporting, sported.** **1** N-VAR **Sports** are games and other competitive activities which need physical effort and skill. *She excels at sport.* → See pictures on pages 830 and 831. **2** VERB If you say that someone **is sporting** something such as a distinctive item of clothing, you mean that they are wearing it. *He sported a collarless jacket with black panels.*

sporting /'spɔːtɪŋ/. ADJ BEFORE N **Sporting** means relating to sport or used for sport. *...sporting events.*

sportsman /'spɔːtsmən/ **sportsmen.** N-COUNT A **sportsman** is a man who takes part in sports.

sportswoman /'spɔːtswʊmən/ **sportswomen.** N-COUNT A **sportswoman** is a woman who takes part in sports.

sporty /'spɔːti/ **sportier, sportiest.** ADJ A **sporty** person enjoys playing sport.

⭐ **spot** /spɒt/ **spots, spotting, spotted.** **1** N-COUNT **Spots** are small, round, coloured areas on a surface. *The swimsuit comes in navy with white spots.* **2** N-COUNT **Spots** on a person's skin are small lumps or marks. **3** N-COUNT A **spot of** a substance is a small amount of it. *Spots of rain had begun to fall.* **4** N-COUNT You can refer to a particular place as a **spot**. *...the island's top tourist spots.* **5** VERB If you **spot** something or someone, you notice them. *Smoke was spotted coming up the stairs.*

PHRASES ● If you are **on the spot**, you are at the actual place where something is happening. *Troops are on the spot and protecting civilians.* ● If you do something **on the spot**, you do it immediately. *He was sacked on the spot.* ● If you **put** someone **on the spot**, you force them to make a difficult decision or answer a difficult question. ● to **have a soft spot for** someone: see **soft**.

spotlight /'spɒtlaɪt/ **spotlights, spotlighting, spotlighted.** **1** N-COUNT A **spotlight** is a powerful light, used for example in a theatre, which can be directed so that it lights up a small area. **2** VERB To **spotlight** a particular problem or situation means to make people notice it and think about it. *The budget crisis also spotlighted a weakening American economy.*

spouse /spaʊs/ **spouses.** N-COUNT Someone's **spouse** is the person they are married to. [FORMAL]

spout /spaʊt/ **spouts, spouting, spouted.** **1** VERB If something **spouts** liquid or fire, or if liquid or fire **spouts** out of something, it comes out very quickly with a lot of force. *...a fountain that spouts water 40 feet into the air.* **2** VERB If you say that someone **spouts** something, you disapprove of them because they say something which you think is wrong or insincere. *He accused Mr Brown of spouting nonsense.* **3** N-COUNT The **spout** of a kettle or teapot is the tube that the liquid comes out of.

sprain /spreɪn/ **sprains, spraining, sprained.** **1** VERB If you **sprain** your ankle or wrist, you accidentally damage it by twisting it, for example when you fall. *...a badly sprained ankle.* **2** N-COUNT A **sprain** is the injury caused by spraining a joint.

sprang /spræŋ/. **Sprang** is the past tense of **spring**.

sprawl /sprɔːl/ **sprawls, sprawling, sprawled.** **1** VERB If you **sprawl** somewhere, you sit or lie down with your legs and arms spread out in a careless way. *I tripped the guy so he sprawled on the ground.* **2** VERB & N-UNCOUNT If a place **sprawls** over a large area of land, it completely covers that area. You can refer to this area as a **sprawl**. *...Dublin's urban sprawl.*

⭐ **spray** /spreɪ/ **sprays, spraying, sprayed.** **1** N-UNCOUNT **Spray** consists of a lot of small drops of water which are being splashed or forced into the air. *...the spray from the waterfall.* **2** VERB If you

spray drops of a liquid or small pieces of something somewhere, or if they **spray** somewhere, they cover a place or shower someone. *He sprayed aftershave on his cheeks... The bullet slammed into the ceiling, spraying them with bits of plaster.* [3] N-VAR A **spray** is a liquid kept under pressure in a container, which you can force out in very small drops. *...a can of insect spray.*

⭐ **spread** /spred/ **spreads, spreading.** [1] VERB If you **spread** something somewhere, you open it out or arrange it over a place or surface, so that all of it can be seen or used easily. *She spread a towel on the sand and lay on it.* [2] VERB If you **spread** your hands, arms, or legs, you move them far apart. *Sitting on the floor, spread your legs as far as they will go.* [3] VERB If you **spread** a substance on a surface, you put a thin layer of the substance over the surface. *Spread the bread with the cheese.* [4] N-VAR A **spread** is a soft food which is put on bread. *...a salad roll with low fat spread.* [5] VERB If something **spreads**, or if it **is spread** by people, it gradually reaches or affects a larger and larger area or more and more people. *Cholera is not spreading as quickly as it did in the past.* [6] N-SING **The spread** of something is its increasing presence or occurrence. *...the spread of modern technology.* [7] VERB If something **is spread over** a period of time, it is organized so that it takes place at regular intervals over that period. *The course is spread over a five week period.* [8] N-SING A **spread of** ideas, interests, or activities is a wide variety of them. *We have an enormous spread of industries.*
▸**spread out.** [1] PHR-VERB If people, animals, or vehicles **spread out**, they move apart from each other. [2] PHR-VERB If you **spread** something **out**, you arrange it over a surface, so that all of it can be seen or used easily. *Tom was spreading out a map of Scandinavia on the bed.* [3] PHR-VERB If you **spread out**, you relax by sitting or lying with your legs and arms stretched far apart.

spree /spriː/ **sprees.** N-COUNT If you go on something such as a spending **spree**, you do something such as spend money in an excessive way. *...an all-day drinking spree.*

sprig /sprɪɡ/ **sprigs.** N-COUNT A **sprig** is a small twig or stem with leaves on it which has been picked from a bush or plant.

⭐ **spring** /sprɪŋ/ **springs, springing, sprang, sprung.** [1] N-VAR **Spring** is the season between winter and summer. In the spring the weather starts to get warmer and plants begin to grow. → See Reference Page on Times and Dates. [2] N-COUNT A **spring** is a coil of wire which returns to its original shape after it is pressed or pulled. [3] N-COUNT A **spring** is a place where water comes up through the ground. *...the hot springs of Banyas de Sant Loan.* [4] VERB When a person or animal **springs**, they move suddenly upwards or forwards. *He sprang to his feet.* [5] VERB If something **springs** in a particular direction, it moves there suddenly and quickly. *The lid of the*

boot sprang open. [6] VERB If one thing **springs from** another, the first thing is the result of the second. *His anger sprang from his suffering at the loss of wife.* [7] VERB If you **spring** some news or an event on someone, you tell them something that they did not expect to hear, without warning them. *The Congress Party sprang a surprise yesterday by strongly opposing the bill.* [8] PHRASE If a boat or container **springs a leak**, liquid starts coming in or out through a hole or crack. *A tanker carrying propane gas sprang a leak.*
▸**spring up.** PHR-VERB If something **springs up**, it suddenly appears or comes into existence. *Arts centres sprang up all over the country.*

sprinkle /ˈsprɪŋkəl/ **sprinkles, sprinkling, sprinkled.** VERB If you **sprinkle** a thing **with** a substance, you scatter the substance over it. *Sprinkle the meat with salt... He sprinkled sand on the fire.*

sprint /sprɪnt/ **sprints, sprinting, sprinted.** [1] N-COUNT A **sprint** is a short fast race. *...the 100-metres sprint.* [2] VERB & N-SING If you **sprint** somewhere, or if you break into a **sprint**, you run as fast as you can over a short distance. *Sergeant Horne sprinted to the car.* ♦ **sprinter, sprinters** N-COUNT *...Europe's top sprinter.*

sprout /spraʊt/ **sprouts, sprouting, sprouted.** [1] VERB When plants, vegetables, or seeds **sprout**, they produce new shoots or leaves. *It only takes a few days for beans to sprout.* [2] VERB When leaves, shoots, or plants **sprout** somewhere, they grow there. *Leaf-shoots were beginning to sprout on the hawthorn.* [3] N-COUNT **Sprouts** are the same as **Brussels sprouts.**

spruce /spruːs/ **spruces, sprucing, spruced.**

☑ **Spruce** can also be used as the plural form.

N-VAR A **spruce** is a kind of evergreen tree. **Spruce** is the wood of this tree.
▸**spruce up.** PHR-VERB If something **is spruced up**, its appearance is improved. *We spruced ourselves up a bit and went out for dinner.*

sprung /sprʌŋ/. **Sprung** is the past participle of **spring**.

spun /spʌn/. **Spun** is the past tense and past participle of **spin**.

⭐ **spur** /spɜː/ **spurs, spurring, spurred.** [1] VERB & PHR-VERB If something **spurs** you **to** do something, or if something **spurs** you **on** to do it, it encourages you to do it. *It's the money that spurs them to do it... I know people want me to lose but that only spurs me on.* [2] N-SING Something that acts as a **spur** encourages someone to do something or makes something happen faster or sooner. *...a belief in competition as a spur to efficiency.* [3] PHRASE If you do something **on the spur of the moment**, you do it suddenly, without planning it. *They admitted they had stolen a vehicle on the spur of the moment.* [4] N-COUNT **Spurs** are sharp metal points attached to the heels of a rider's boots and used to make the horse go faster.

spurious /ˈspjʊəriəs/. ADJ A **spurious** claim or argument seems to be correct or genuine, but is

a
b
c
d
e
f
g
h
i
j
k
l
m
n
o
p
q
r
s
t
u
v
w
x
y
z

really false or dishonest; used showing disapproval. *He was arrested in 1979 on spurious corruption charges.*

spurn /spɜːn/ **spurns, spurning, spurned.** VERB If you **spurn** something, you refuse to accept it. [FORMAL] *He spurned the advice of management consultants. ...a spurned lover.*

spurt /spɜːt/ **spurts, spurting, spurted.** ☐1 VERB & N-COUNT If something **spurts** liquid or fire, or if liquid or fire **spurts** from somewhere or something, it comes out quickly in a thin powerful stream called a **spurt**. *I saw flames spurt from the roof... A spurt of diesel came from one valve.* ☐2 N-COUNT A **spurt of** activity or emotion is a sudden brief period of it. *A spurt of anger flashed through me.* ☐3 VERB & N-COUNT If someone or something **spurts** somewhere, or if they move there with a **spurt**, they suddenly increase their speed for a short while in order to get there. *The back wheels spun and the van spurted up the last few feet. ...at the end when the athlete puts on a spurt.*

spy /spaɪ/ **spies, spying, spied.** ☐1 N-COUNT A **spy** is a person whose job is to find out secret information about another country or organization. ☐2 VERB Someone who **spies** for a country or organization tries to find out secret information for them about other countries or organizations. *The agent spied for East Germany for more than twenty years.* ♦ **spying** N-UNCOUNT *...a ten-year sentence for spying.* ☐3 VERB If you **spy on** someone, you watch them secretly. *He spied on her while pretending to work on the shrubs.* ☐4 VERB If you **spy** someone or something, you notice them. [LITERARY] *He spied an old friend.*

sq. sq is used as a written abbreviation for **square** when you are giving the measurement of an area. *...25,500 sq ft.*

squabble /ˈskwɒbəl/ **squabbles, squabbling, squabbled.** VERB & N-COUNT When people **squabble**, or when they have a **squabble**, they quarrel about something unimportant. *The children were squabbling over the remote control.*

☆ **squad** /skwɒd/ **squads.** ☐1 N-COUNT A **squad** is a section of a police force that is responsible for dealing with a particular type of crime. *...the fraud squad.* ☐2 N-COUNT A **squad** is a group of players from which a sports team will be chosen. ☐3 N-COUNT A **squad of** soldiers is a small group of them.

squadron /ˈskwɒdrən/ **squadrons.** N-COUNT A **squadron** is a section of one of the armed forces, especially the air force.

squalid /ˈskwɒlɪd/. ☐1 ADJ A **squalid** place is dirty, untidy, and in bad condition. *...living in squalid conditions.* ☐2 ADJ If you describe an activity as **squalid**, you think that it is unpleasant and perhaps dishonest. *...the squalid pursuit of profit.*

squalor /ˈskwɒlə/. N-UNCOUNT You can refer to squalid conditions or surroundings as **squalor**. *He was out of work and living in squalor.*

squander /ˈskwɒndə/ **squanders, squandering, squandered.** VERB If you **squander** money, resources, or opportunities, you waste them. *They squander money on lottery tickets.*

☆ **square** /skweə/ **squares, squaring, squared.** ☐1 N-COUNT A **square** is a shape with four sides of the same length and four corners that are all right angles. → See picture on page 829. ☐2 ADJ If something is **square**, it has a shape similar to a square. *...a square table.* ☐3 N-COUNT In a town or city, a **square** is a flat open place, often in the shape of a square. ☐4 ADJ BEFORE N **Square** is used before units of length when mentioning the area of something. For example, if a rectangle is three metres long and two metres wide, its area is six square metres. ☐5 VERB To **square** a number means to multiply it by itself. ☐6 N-COUNT The **square of** a number is the number produced when you multiply that number by itself. ☐7 VERB If two different situations or ideas **square with** each other, they can be accepted together or they seem compatible. *That explanation squares with the facts.*

squarely /ˈskweəli/. ☐1 ADV **Squarely** means directly and in the middle, rather than indirectly or at an angle. *I kept the gun aimed squarely at his eyes.* ☐2 ADV If you face something **squarely**, you face it directly, without trying to avoid it.

squash /skwɒʃ/ **squashes, squashing, squashed.** ☐1 VERB If someone or something **is squashed**, they are pressed or crushed with such force that they become injured or lose their shape. *She made clay models and squashed them flat again.* ☐2 ADJ AFTER LINK-V If people or things are **squashed into** a place, they are put into a place where there is not enough room for them to be. *There were 2000 people squashed into her recent show.* ☐3 N-UNCOUNT **Squash** is a game in which two players hit a small rubber ball against the walls of a court using rackets.

squat /skwɒt/ **squats, squatting, squatted.** ☐1 VERB & PHR-VERB If you **squat**, or if you **squat down**, you lower yourself towards the ground, balancing on your feet with your legs bent. → See picture on page 532. *He came over and squatted on his heels, looking up at the boys.* ☐2 ADJ If you describe someone or something as **squat**, you mean they are short and thick, usually in an unattractive way. *...squat stone houses.* ☐3 VERB People who **squat** occupy an unused building or unused land illegally. ☐4 N-COUNT A **squat** is an empty building that people are living in illegally.

squatter /ˈskwɒtə/ **squatters.** N-COUNT A **squatter** is someone who occupies an unused building or unused land illegally.

squeak /skwiːk/ **squeaks, squeaking, squeaked.** VERB & N-COUNT If something or someone **squeaks**, they make a short, high-pitched sound called a **squeak**. *The door squeaked open.*

squeal /skwiːl/ squeals, squealing, squealed. VERB &
N-COUNT If someone or something **squeals**, they
make a long high-pitched sound called a **squeal**.
...a squeal of brakes.

⭐ **squeeze** /skwiːz/ squeezes, squeezing, squeezed.
[1] VERB & N-COUNT If you **squeeze** something soft
or flexible, or if you give it a **squeeze**, you press it
firmly from two sides. Dip the bread briefly in
water, then squeeze it dry. [2] VERB If you **squeeze**
a liquid or a soft substance out of an object, you
get the liquid or substance out by pressing the
object. Joe squeezed some detergent over the
dishes. [3] VERB If you **squeeze** someone or
something somewhere, or if they **squeeze** there,
they manage to get through or into a small
space. ...youngsters who can squeeze through tiny
windows.

squid /skwɪd/ squids.

✅ **Squid** can also be used as the plural form.

N-VAR A **squid** is a sea creature with a long soft
body and many tentacles. **Squid** is pieces of this
creature eaten as food.

squint /skwɪnt/ squints, squinting, squinted. [1] VERB
If you **squint at** something, you look at it with
your eyes partly closed. The girl squinted at the
photograph... He squinted his eyes and looked at
the floor. [2] N-COUNT If someone has a **squint**,
their eyes look in different directions from each
other.

squirm /skwɜːm/ squirms, squirming, squirmed. VERB
If you **squirm**, you wriggle, for example because
you are nervous or uncomfortable. We'll make
him squirm.

squirrel /ˈskwɪrəl, AM ˈskwɜːrəl/ squirrels.
N-COUNT A **squirrel** is a small furry wild animal
with a long bushy tail. → See picture on page
815.

squirt /skwɜːt/ squirts, squirting, squirted. VERB &
N-COUNT If you **squirt** liquid somewhere, or if the
liquid **squirts** somewhere, it is forced through a
narrow opening so that it comes out in a thin fast
stream called a **squirt**. It just needs a little squirt
of oil.

St.

✅ The plural for meaning 2 is **SS**.

[1] **St** is a written abbreviation for **Street**. ...116
Princess St. [2] **St** is a written abbreviation for
Saint. ...St Thomas.

stab /stæb/ stabs, stabbing, stabbed. [1] VERB If
someone **stabs** another person, they push a knife
into their body. Stephen was stabbed to death.
[2] VERB If you **stab** something or if you **stab** at it,
you push at it with your finger or with something
pointed. He stabbed at Frank with his finger.
[3] N-COUNT If you have a **stab** at something, you
try to do it. [INFORMAL] I thought I'd take a stab at
snowboarding. [4] N-SING You can refer to a
sudden, usually unpleasant feeling as a **stab of**
that feeling. [LITERARY] She felt a stab of pity for him.

stabbing /ˈstæbɪŋ/ stabbings. [1] N-COUNT A
stabbing is an incident in which someone stabs

someone else with a knife. [2] ADJ BEFORE N A
stabbing pain is a sudden sharp pain.

stabilize (BRIT also **stabilise**) /ˈsteɪbɪlaɪz/
stabilizes, stabilizing, stabilized. VERB If something
stabilizes, or if someone or something **stabilizes**
it, it becomes stable. Although her illness is
serious, her condition is beginning to stabilize.
♦ **stabilization** N-UNCOUNT ...the stabilisation of
property prices.

⭐ **stable** /ˈsteɪbəl/ stabler, stablest; stables, stabling,
stabled. [1] ADJ If something is **stable**, it is not
likely to change or come to an end suddenly.
♦ **stability** /stəˈbɪlɪti/ N-UNCOUNT ...a time of
political stability. [2] ADJ If an object is **stable**, it is
firmly fixed in position and is not likely to move
or fall. [3] N-COUNT A **stable** or **stables** is a
building in which horses are kept. [4] VERB When
horses are **stabled**, they are put into a stable.

stack /stæk/ stacks, stacking, stacked. [1] N-COUNT A
stack of things is a neat pile of them. There were
stacks of books on the bedside table.

> **USAGE** A **stack** of things is usually tidy,
> and often consists of flat objects placed
> directly on top of each other. ...a neat
> stack of dishes. A **heap** of things is usually
> untidy, and often has the shape of a hill or
> mound. Now, the house is a heap of
> rubble. A **pile** can be tidy or untidy. ...a
> neat pile of clothes.

[2] VERB & PHR-VERB If you **stack** a number of
things, or if you **stack** them **up**, you arrange
them in neat piles. He ordered them to stack up
pillows behind his back. [3] N-PLURAL **Stacks of**
something means a lot of it. [INFORMAL] You'll have
stacks of money. [4] PHRASE When **the odds are
stacked against** someone, they are unlikely to
succeed because the conditions are not
favourable. The odds are stacked against civilians
getting a fair trial.

⭐ **stadium** /ˈsteɪdiəm/ stadiums (or stadia /ˈsteɪdiə/).
N-COUNT A **stadium** is a large sports ground with
rows of seats all round it.

⭐ **staff** /stɑːf, stæf/ staffs, staffed. [1] N-COUNT The
staff of an organization are the people who work
for it. **Staff** can take the singular or plural form of
the verb. The staff were very good. [2] PASSIVE-VERB
If an organization **is staffed** by particular people,
they are the people who work for it. They are
staffed by volunteers. ♦ **staffed** ADJ ...poorly
staffed hotels.

staffing /ˈstɑːfɪŋ, ˈstæf-/. N-UNCOUNT **Staffing**
refers to the number of workers employed to
work in a particular organization or building.
Staffing levels in prisons are too low.

stag /stæg/ stags. N-COUNT A **stag** is an adult male
deer.

⭐ **stage** /steɪdʒ/ stages, staging, staged. [1] N-COUNT A
stage of an activity, process, or period is one part
of it. ...the final stage of a world tour. [2] N-COUNT
In a theatre, the **stage** is an area where actors or

a
b
c
d
e
f
g
h
i
j
k
l
m
n
o
p
q
r
s
t
u
v
w
x
y
z

A
B
C
D
E
F
G
H
I
J
K
L
M
N
O
P
Q
R
S
T
U
V
W
X
Y
Z

entertainers perform. *I went on stage and did my show.* ☐3 N-SING You can refer to performing and the production of plays in a theatre as **the stage**. *He was the first comedian I ever saw on the stage.* ☐4 VERB If someone **stages** a play or other show, they organize and present a performance of it. ☐5 VERB To **stage** an event or ceremony means to organize it. *The conference is staging a debate on constitutional reform.* ☐6 to **set the stage**: see **set**.

stagger /'stægə/ **staggers, staggering, staggered.** ☐1 VERB If you **stagger**, you walk very unsteadily, for example because you are ill or drunk. *She staggered back to the hospital.* ☐2 VERB If something **staggers** you, it surprises you very much. ♦ **staggered** ADJ AFTER LINK-V *I'm absolutely staggered at the verdict.* ☐3 VERB To **stagger** things means to arrange them so that they do not all happen at the same time.

staggering /'stægərɪŋ/. ADJ Something that is **staggering** is very surprising. *...a staggering £25,000-a-week.* ♦ **staggeringly** ADV *The South Pole expedition proved to be staggeringly successful.*

stagnant /'stægnənt/. ☐1 ADJ If something such as a business or society is **stagnant**, there is little activity or change; used showing disapproval. *He is seeking advice on how to revive the stagnant economy.* ☐2 ADJ **Stagnant** water is not flowing, and is therefore often dirty and unhealthy.

stagnate /stæg'neɪt, AM 'stægneɪt/ **stagnates, stagnating, stagnated.** VERB If something such as a business or society **stagnates**, it becomes inactive or does not change; used showing disapproval. ♦ **stagnation** N-UNCOUNT *...the stagnation of the steel industry.*

staid /steɪd/. ADJ If you say that someone or something is **staid**, you mean that they are serious, dull, and rather old-fashioned. *...the traditionally staid image of golf.*

stain /steɪn/ **stains, staining, stained.** ☐1 N-COUNT A **stain** is a mark on something that is difficult to remove. *...grass stains.* ☐2 VERB If a liquid **stains** something, the thing becomes coloured or marked by the liquid. ♦ **stained** ADJ *His clothing was stained with mud.* ♦ **-stained** *...ink-stained fingers.*

stained 'glass. N-UNCOUNT **Stained glass** consists of pieces of glass of different colours used to make decorative windows or other objects.

stainless steel /ˌsteɪnləs 'stiːl/. N-UNCOUNT **Stainless steel** is a metal which does not rust, made from steel and chromium.

stair /steə/ **stairs.** ☐1 N-PLURAL **Stairs** are a set of steps inside a building which go from one floor to another. *We walked up a flight of stairs.* ☐2 N-COUNT A **stair** is one of the steps in a flight of stairs. *Terry was sitting on the bottom stair.*

staircase /'steəkeɪs/ **staircases.** N-COUNT A **staircase** is a set of stairs inside a house.

stairway /'steəweɪ/ **stairways.** N-COUNT A **stairway** is a flight of steps, inside or outside a building.

★ **stake** /steɪk/ **stakes, staking, staked.** ☐1 PHRASE If something is **at stake**, it is being risked and might be lost or damaged if you are not successful. *The tension was naturally high for a game with so much at stake.* ☐2 N-PLURAL The **stakes** involved in a risky action or a contest are the things that can be gained or lost. *The players knew exactly how high the stakes were.* ☐3 VERB If you **stake** something such as your money or your reputation **on** the result of something, you risk your money or reputation on it. *He again staked his reputation on getting the treaty through.* ☐4 N-COUNT If you have a **stake in** something, its success matters to you, for example because you own part of it. *...investors who want a more direct stake in overseas companies.* ☐5 N-COUNT A **stake** is a pointed wooden post in the ground. ● to **stake** your **claim**: see **claim**.

stale /steɪl/. ☐1 ADJ **Stale** food or air is no longer fresh. ☐2 ADJ AFTER LINK-V If you feel **stale**, you have no new ideas or enthusiasm for what you are doing.

stalemate /'steɪlmeɪt/ **stalemates.** N-VAR **Stalemate** is a situation in which neither side in an argument or contest can make progress. *The war had reached a stalemate.*

stalk /stɔːk/ **stalks, stalking, stalked.** ☐1 N-COUNT The **stalk** of a flower, leaf, or fruit is the thin part that joins it to the plant or tree. ☐2 VERB If you **stalk** a person or a wild animal, you follow them quietly and secretly in order to catch them or observe them. *The hunters stalked their prey.* ☐3 VERB If you **stalk** somewhere, you walk there in a stiff, proud, or angry way. *He got up and stalked up and down the flat.* ☐4 VERB If someone **stalks** someone else, they keep following them or contacting them in a frightening way. *Even after their divorce he continued to stalk and threaten her.* ♦ **stalker, stalkers** N-COUNT *A stalker can terrify you with obscene letters.*

stall /stɔːl/ **stalls, stalling, stalled.** ☐1 VERB If a process **stalls**, or if someone or something **stalls** it, the process stops but may continue at a later time. *Continental's managers had a good reason to stall the negotiations.* ☐2 VERB If you **stall** someone, you deliberately prevent them from doing something until later, for example by talking to them. *Brian stalled the man until the police arrived.* ☐3 VERB If you **stall**, you try to avoid doing something until later. *Thomas had spent all week stalling over his decision.* ☐4 VERB If a vehicle **stalls**, or if you accidentally **stall** it, the engine stops suddenly. ☐5 N-COUNT A **stall** is a large table on which you put goods that you want to sell, or information that you want to give people. *...market stalls selling local fruits.* ☐6 N-PLURAL The **stalls** in a theatre or concert hall are the seats on the ground floor in front of the stage. [BRITISH]

stallion /'stæliən/ **stallions.** N-COUNT A **stallion** is a male horse.

stalwart /'stɔːlwət/ **stalwarts.** N-COUNT & ADJ A **stalwart**, or someone who is **stalwart**, is a loyal and hard-working employee or supporter. ...*my stalwart bodyguard.*

stamina /'stæminə/. N-UNCOUNT **Stamina** is the physical or mental energy needed to do a tiring activity for a long time. *You have to have a lot of stamina to be a top-class dancer.*

stammer /'stæmə/ **stammers, stammering, stammered.** VERB & N-COUNT If someone **stammers**, or if they have a **stammer**, they speak with difficulty, hesitating and repeating words or sounds. *He turned white and began to stammer.* ♦ **stammering** N-UNCOUNT ...*a speech therapist specialising in stammering.*

⭐ **stamp** /stæmp/ **stamps, stamping, stamped.** 1 N-COUNT A **stamp** or a **postage stamp** is a small piece of paper which you stick on an envelope or parcel, to show that you have paid the cost of posting it. 2 N-COUNT A **stamp** is a small block of wood or metal with words or a design on it. You press it onto an ink pad and then onto a document in order to produce a mark on the document. The mark is also called a **stamp**. 3 VERB If you **stamp** a mark or word on an object, you press the mark or word onto the object, using a stamp. *He examined his passport and stamped it.* 4 VERB If you **stamp**, or if you **stamp** your foot, you put your foot down very hard on the ground, for example because you are angry. *His foot stamped down on the accelerator.* 5 See also **rubber stamp**.
▶ **stamp out.** PHR-VERB If you **stamp** something **out**, you put an end to it. ...*new laws to stamp out sexual discrimination at work.*

,**stamped addressed 'envelope.** See **sae**.

stampede /stæm'piːd/ **stampedes, stampeding, stampeded.** VERB & N-COUNT If a group of people or animals **stampede**, or if there is a **stampede**, they run in a wild, uncontrolled way. *There was a stampede for the exit.*

stance /stæns/ **stances.** 1 N-COUNT Your **stance on** a particular matter is your attitude to it. ...*the Catholic Church's stance on contraception.* 2 N-COUNT Your **stance** is the way that you are standing. [FORMAL] *Take a comfortably wide stance and flex your knees a little.*

⭐ **stand** /stænd/ **stands, standing, stood.** 1 VERB & PHR-VERB When you **are standing**, or when you are **standing up**, your body is upright, your legs are straight, and your weight is supported by your feet. *They told me to stand still.* ...*a shop assistant who has to stand up all day.* 2 VERB & PHR-VERB When someone who is sitting **stands**, or when they **stand up**, they change their position so that they are upright and on their feet. *When I walked in, they all stood up.* 3 VERB If you **stand** back, you move a short distance sideways or backwards, so that you are standing in a different place. *I stood aside to let her pass.* 4 VERB If

something such as a building **stands** somewhere, it is upright in that position. [WRITTEN] *The house stands alone on top of a small hill.* 5 VERB If you **stand** something somewhere, you put it there in an upright position. *Stand the plant in the open in a sunny, sheltered place.* 6 N-COUNT If you **make a stand**, or if you **take a stand**, you do something or say something in order to make it clear what your attitude to a particular thing is. *He felt the need to make a stand against racism.* 7 VERB If you ask someone where they **stand on** an issue, you want to know their attitude or view on it. *Where do you stand on feminism?* 8 VERB If a law, decision, or offer **stands**, it still exists and has not been changed or cancelled. *Although exceptions could be made, the rule still stands.* 9 VERB If something that can be measured **stands at** a particular level, it is at that level. *The inflation rate now stands at 3.6 per cent.* 10 VERB If something can **stand** a situation or a test, it is good enough or strong enough to cope with it. *The economy would not stand another rise in interest rates.* 11 VERB If you cannot **stand** someone or something, you hate them. *He cannot stand his boss... You eat like a pig. I can't stand looking at you.* 12 VERB If you **stand to** gain something, you are likely to gain it. *His shops stand to lose millions of pounds.* 13 VERB In British English, if you **stand** in an election, you are a candidate in it. The American word is **run**. *She is to stand as a Member of the European Parliament.* 14 N-COUNT A **stand** is a small shop or stall, outdoors or in a large public building. ...*a newspaper stand.* 15 N-COUNT A **stand** is an object or piece of furniture that is designed for supporting or holding a particular kind of thing. ...*a hat stand.* ...*a music stand.*

PHRASES ● You can describe someone's final attempt to defend themselves before they are defeated as their **last stand**. *So is this really the last stand of the private investor?* ● See also **standing**. ● to **stand a chance**: see **chance**. ● to **stand firm**: see **firm**. ● to **stand on** your own **two feet**: see **foot**. ● to **stand trial**: see **trial**. ● to **stand** your **ground**: see **ground**. ● to **stand** someone **in good stead**: see **stead**.
▶ **stand aside.** See **stand down**.
▶ **stand by.** 1 PHR-VERB If you **are standing by**, you are ready and waiting to provide help or to take action. *Warships are standing by to evacuate their citizens if necessary.* 2 PHR-VERB If you **stand by** and let something bad happen, you do not do anything to stop it; used showing disapproval. *We cannot stand by and watch people starve.* ● See also **standby**.
▶ **stand down.** PHR-VERB If someone **stands down**, or if someone **stands aside**, they resign from an important job. *He stood down as chairman last January.*
▶ **stand for.** 1 PHR-VERB If letters **stand for** particular words, they are an abbreviation for those words. *AIDS stands for Acquired Immune Deficiency Syndrome.* 2 PHR-VERB The ideas or attitudes that someone or something **stands for**

a
b
c
d
e
f
g
h
i
j
k
l
m
n
o
p
q
r
s
t
u
v
w
x
y
z

are the ones that they support or represent. *He hates us and everything we stand for.* **3** PHR-VERB If you will not **stand for** something, you will not allow it to happen or continue. *It's outrageous, and we won't stand for it any more.*

▸**stand in.** PHR-VERB If you **stand in for** someone, you take their place or do their job, because they are ill or away. *He will stand in for Mr Goh when he is abroad.* ● See also **stand-in.**

▸**stand out.** PHR-VERB If something **stands out**, it can be clearly noticed or is clearly better or more important than other similar things. *The dark silhouette of the castle ruins stood out boldly against the fading light... He played the violin, and he stood out from all the other musicians.*

▸**stand up.** PHR-VERB If something such as a claim or a piece of evidence **stands up**, it is accepted as true or satisfactory after being carefully examined. *How well does this thesis stand up to close examination?* ● See also **stand** 1, 2, **stand-up.**

▸**stand up for.** PHR-VERB If you **stand up for** someone or something, you defend them openly; used showing approval. *Don't be afraid to stand up for yourself.*

▸**stand up to.** **1** PHR-VERB If something **stands up to** rough treatment, it remains almost undamaged. *Is this building going to stand up to the strongest gales?* **2** PHR-VERB If you **stand up to** someone more powerful than you are, you defend yourself against their attacks or demands.

⭐ **standard** /ˈstændəd/ **standards.** **1** N-COUNT A **standard** is a level of quality or achievement, especially a level that is thought to be acceptable. *...new national standards for hospital cleanliness.* **2** N-PLURAL **Standards** are moral principles which affect people's attitudes and behaviour. *...the decline of moral standards.* **3** ADJ **Standard** means usual and normal. *Everyone wore suits, which is standard practice.*

standardize (BRIT also **standardise**) /ˈstændədaɪz/ **standardizes, standardizing, standardized.** VERB To **standardize** things means to change them so that they all have the same features. ◆ **standardization** N-UNCOUNT *...the need for standardisation of working hours in Community countries.*

standard of ˈ**living, standards of living.** N-COUNT Your **standard of living** is the level of comfort and wealth which you have.

standby /ˈstændbaɪ/ **standbys.** **1** N-COUNT A **standby** is someone or something that is always ready to be used if they are needed. *We simply selected a standby from our second team.* **2** PHRASE If someone or something is **on standby**, they are ready to be used if they are needed. **3** ADJ BEFORE N A **standby** ticket for something such as the theatre or a plane journey is a cheap ticket that you buy just before the performance starts or the plane takes off, if there are still some seats left. *...standby flights from New York.*

ˈ**stand-in, stand-ins.** N-COUNT A **stand-in** is a person who takes someone else's place because the other person is ill or away.

standing /ˈstændɪŋ/ **1** N-UNCOUNT Someone's **standing** is their status or reputation. *...an artist of international standing.* **2** ADJ BEFORE N You use **standing** to describe something which is permanently in existence. *Elizabeth had a standing invitation to stay with her.* ● See also **stand, long-standing.**

ˈ**stand-off, stand-offs.** N-COUNT A **stand-off** is a situation in which neither of two opposing groups will make a move until the other one does something, so nothing can happen until one of them gives way.

standpoint /ˈstændpɔɪnt/ **standpoints.** N-COUNT If you look at an event, situation, or idea from a particular **standpoint**, you look at it in a particular way. *From a military standpoint, the situation is under control.*

standstill /ˈstændstɪl/. N-SING If movement or an activity comes to a **standstill**, it stops completely. *The country was brought to a standstill by public sector strikes.*

ˈ**stand-up** (also **standup**). **1** ADJ & N-UNCOUNT A **stand-up** comedian stands alone in front of an audience and tells jokes. **Stand-up** is stand-up comedy. **2** ADJ BEFORE N If people have a **stand-up** fight or argument, they hit or shout at each other violently.

stank /stæŋk/. **Stank** is the past tense of **stink**.

staple /ˈsteɪpəl/ **staples, stapling, stapled.** **1** ADJ BEFORE N A **staple** food, product, or activity is one that is basic and important in people's everyday lives. *Rice is the staple food of more than half the world's population.* **2** N-COUNT **Staples** are small pieces of wire, used for holding sheets of paper together firmly. **3** VERB If you **staple** something, you fasten it to something else using staples.

⭐ **star** /stɑː/ **stars, starring, starred.** **1** N-COUNT A **star** is a large ball of burning gas in space. Stars appear to us as small points of light in the sky on clear nights. **2** N-COUNT You can refer to a shape or an object as a **star** when it has four or more points sticking out of it in a regular pattern. → See picture on page 829. **3** N-COUNT Famous actors, musicians, and sports players are often referred to as **stars.** **4** VERB If an actor or actress **stars in** a play or film, he or she has one of the most important parts in it. You can also say that a play or film **stars** a famous actor or actress. *He's starred in dozens of films.* **5** N-PLURAL Your horoscope is sometimes referred to as your **stars.** [INFORMAL] *My stars said I would find love.*

starboard /ˈstɑːbəd/. ADJ The **starboard** side of a ship is the right side when you are facing the front.

starch /stɑːtʃ/ **starches.** **1** N-VAR **Starch** is a carbohydrate found in foods such as bread, potatoes, and rice. **2** N-UNCOUNT **Starch** is a substance used for stiffening cloth.

stardom /ˈstɑːdəm/. N-UNCOUNT **Stardom** is the state of being very famous, usually as an actor, musician, or sports player. *She shot to stardom on Broadway.*

stare /steə/ **stares, staring, stared.** VERB & N-UNCOUNT If you **stare at** someone or something, or if you give someone or something a **stare**, you look at them for a long time. *Tamara stared at him in disbelief... Hlasek gave him a long, cold stare.*

> **USAGE** The verbs **stare** and **gaze** are both used to talk about looking at something for a long time. If you **stare at** something or someone, it is often because you think they are strange or shocking. *Various families came out and stared at us.* If you **gaze at** something, it is often because you think it is marvellous or impressive. *A fresh-faced little girl gazes in wonder at the bright fairground lights.*

stark /stɑːk/ **starker, starkest.** [1] ADJ **Stark** choices or statements are harsh and unpleasant. *He issued a stark warning to Washington.* ◆ **starkly** ADV *The point is a starkly simple one.* [2] PHRASE If two things are **in stark contrast** to one another, they are very different from each other.

start /stɑːt/ **starts, starting, started.** [1] VERB & N-COUNT If you **start to** do something, or if you make a **start** on it, you do something you were not doing before. *I started to tidy up... The boy started crying... After several starts, she read the report properly.* [2] VERB & N-SING When something **starts**, or when someone **starts** it, it takes place or begins to exist from a particular time. You can also refer to **the start of** something. *The meeting starts at 10.30... We have started a campaign for better nursery services... ...shortly before the start of the war... She demanded to know why she had not been told from the start.* [3] VERB & PHR-VERB If someone **started** or **started off** as a particular thing, their first job was as that thing. *Mr. Dambar had started off as an assistant.* [4] VERB & PHR-VERB If you **start** an engine or car, or if you **start** it **up**, it begins to work. *The engine of the seaplane started up... The car won't start.* [5] N-COUNT A **start** is a sudden jerky movement your body makes because you are surprised or frightened. *Sylvia woke with a start.*

PHRASES ● You use **for a start** or **to start with** to introduce the first of a number of things or reasons that you want to mention or could mention. *For a start, the beach is dreadful.* ● If you **get off to a good start**, you are successful in the early stages of doing something. If you **get off to a bad start**, you are not successful in the early stages of doing something. *Rescue efforts got off to a slow start.* ● See also **head start**. ● to **get off to a flying start**: see **fly**.

▶**start off.** PHR-VERB If you **start off by** doing something, you do it as the first part of an activity. *I started off by setting out the facts.* ● See also **start** 3.

▶**start on.** PHR-VERB If you **start on** something

that needs to be done, you begin doing it. *No need for you to start on the washing-up yet.*

▶**start out.** [1] PHR-VERB If someone or something **starts out as** a particular thing, they are that thing at the beginning although they change later. *What started out as fun quickly became hard work.* [2] PHR-VERB If you **start out by** doing something, you do it at the beginning of an activity or process. *I started out by bringing up my children strictly.*

▶**start over.** PHR-VERB If you **start over**, or if you **start** something **over**, you begin something again from the beginning. [AMERICAN] *Okay, let's start over.*

▶**start up.** PHR-VERB If you **start up** something such as a new business, you create it or cause it to start. *You could start up your own newspaper.* ● See also **start** 4.

starter /ˈstɑːtə/ **starters.** [1] N-COUNT A **starter** is a small quantity of food served as the first course of a meal. [2] N-COUNT The **starter** of a car is a device that starts the engine. [3] PHRASE You use **for starters** when you mention something to indicate that it is the first item or point in a series. *What do Diana Ross and Judi Dench have in common? For starters, they both sing.*

'starting point, starting points. N-COUNT Something that is a **starting point for** a discussion or process can be used to begin it or act as a basis for it. *These proposals represent a realistic starting point for negotiation.*

startle /ˈstɑːtəl/ **startles, startling, startled.** VERB If something sudden and unexpected **startles** you, it surprises you and frightens you slightly. *The sound of his voice startled her.* ◆ **startled** ADJ *Martha gave her a startled look.*

startling /ˈstɑːtlɪŋ/. ADJ Something that is **startling** is so unexpected or remarkable that people are surprised by it. *There were some startling successes.*

starve /stɑːv/ **starves, starving, starved.** [1] VERB If people **starve**, they suffer greatly from lack of food which sometimes leads to their death. ◆ **starvation** /stɑːˈveɪʃən/ N-UNCOUNT *Up to four million people face starvation.* [2] VERB To **starve** someone means to not give them any food. *Judy decided I was starving myself.* [3] VERB If someone or something **is starved of** something they need, they are suffering because they are not getting enough of it. *...a childhood which was starved of affection.*

starving /ˈstɑːvɪŋ/. ADJ AFTER LINK-V If you say you are **starving**, you mean you are very hungry. [INFORMAL]

stash /stæʃ/ **stashes, stashing, stashed.** [1] VERB If you **stash** something valuable in a secret place, you store it there to keep it safe. *...the bottle of whiskey that we had stashed behind the bookcase.* [2] N-COUNT You can refer to something you have stashed as a **stash of** something. [INFORMAL] *A large stash of drugs had been found aboard the yacht.*

a
b
c
d
e
f
g
h
i
j
k
l
m
n
o
p
q
r
s
t
u
v
w
x
y
z

★ **state** /steɪt/ **states, stating, stated.** ☐1 N-COUNT You can refer to countries as **states**, particularly when you are discussing politics. *...the policy process in the modern capitalist state.* ● See note at **country.** ☐2 ADJ BEFORE N A **state** occasion is a formal one involving the head of a country. *...a state visit to India.* ☐3 N-COUNT Some large countries such as the USA are divided into smaller areas called **states.** ☐4 N-PROPER The USA is sometimes referred to as **the States.** [INFORMAL] ☐5 N-SING You can refer to the government of a country as **the state.** *...the state social-security system.* ☐6 VERB If you **state** something, you say or write it in a formal or definite way. *Please state your name.* ☐7 N-COUNT When you talk about the **state of** someone or something, you are referring to the condition they are in or what they are like at a particular time. *I was then in a state of clinical depression.*

stately /'steɪtli/. ADJ Something or someone that is **stately** is impressive because they look very graceful and dignified.

★ **statement** /'steɪtmənt/ **statements.** ☐1 N-COUNT A **statement** is something that you say or write which gives information in a formal or definite way. *Her husband made a formal statement to the police... The statement by the military denied any involvement.* ☐2 N-COUNT A **statement** is a printed document showing all the money paid into and taken out of a bank or building society account.

state of af'fairs. N-SING If you refer to a particular **state of affairs**, you mean the general situation and circumstances connected with someone or something. *...a more democratic, and modern, state of affairs.*

'state of mind, states of mind. N-COUNT Your **state of mind** is your mood or mental state at a particular time. *He's thought to be in a disturbed state of mind.*

,state-of-the-'art. ADJ If you describe something as **state-of-the-art**, you mean that it is the best available because it has been made using the most modern techniques and technology. *...state-of-the-art technology.*

statesman /'steɪtsmən/ **statesmen.** N-COUNT A **statesman** is an important and experienced politician, especially one who is widely known and respected.

static /'stætɪk/. ☐1 ADJ Something that is **static** does not move or change. *Property prices remained static between February and April.* ☐2 N-UNCOUNT **Static** or **static electricity** is electricity which is caused by friction and which collects in things such as your body or metal objects. ☐3 N-UNCOUNT If there is **static** on the radio or television, you hear loud crackling noises.

★ **station** /'steɪʃən/ **stations, stationing, stationed.** ☐1 N-COUNT A **station** is a building by a railway line where a train stops. ☐2 N-COUNT A **bus station** or **coach station** is a place where buses or coaches start a journey. ● See also **police station.**

☐3 N-COUNT If you talk about a particular radio or television **station**, you are referring to the programmes broadcast by a particular radio or television company. *...an independent local radio station.* ☐4 VERB If soldiers or officials **are stationed** somewhere, they are sent there to do a job or to work for a period of time. *...United States military personnel stationed in the Philippines.*

stationary /'steɪʃənri, AM -neri/. ADJ Something that is **stationary** is not moving.

> **USAGE** You should take care not to confuse the words **stationary**, which is always an adjective and means 'not moving', and **stationery**, meaning 'paper products'.

stationery /'steɪʃənri, AM -neri/. N-UNCOUNT **Stationery** is paper, envelopes, and writing equipment.

★ **statistic** /stə'tɪstɪk/ **statistics.** ☐1 N-COUNT **Statistics** are facts obtained from analyzing information that is expressed in numbers. *Official statistics show real wages declining by 24%.* ♦ **statistical** ADJ *...statistical proof.* ♦ **statistically** ADV *The results are not statistically significant.* ☐2 N-UNCOUNT **Statistics** is a branch of mathematics concerned with the study of information that is expressed in numbers.

statue /'stætʃuː/ **statues.** N-COUNT A **statue** is a large sculpture of a person or an animal, made of stone, bronze, or some other hard material.

stature /'stætʃə/. ☐1 N-UNCOUNT Someone's **stature** is their height. *She was a little short in stature.* ☐2 N-UNCOUNT Someone's **stature** is their importance and reputation. *It's good to see an actor of the stature of Tom Courtney on an Edinburgh stage.*

★ **status** /'steɪtəs/. ☐1 N-UNCOUNT Your **status** is your social or professional position. *The status of children in society has long been underestimated.* ☐2 N-UNCOUNT **Status** is the prestige and importance that someone or something has in the eyes of other people. *He has risen to gain the status of a national hero... Men's work was given more status.* ☐3 N-UNCOUNT **Status** is an official classification which gives a person, organization, or country certain rights or advantages. *The personal allowance depends on your age and marital status.*

status quo /,steɪtəs 'kwəʊ/. N-SING **The status quo** is the situation that exists at a particular time. [FORMAL] *The federation voted to maintain the status quo.*

statute /'stætʃuːt/ **statutes.** N-COUNT A **statute** is a rule or law which has been formally written down.

statutory /'stætʃʊtəri, AM -tɔːri/. ADJ **Statutory** means relating to rules or laws which have been formally written down. [FORMAL] *We had a statutory duty to report to Parliament.*

staunch /stɔːntʃ/ **stauncher, staunchest.** ADJ A **staunch** supporter of someone or something supports them very strongly and loyally.
♦ **staunchly** ADV *She was staunchly anti-abortion.*

stave /steɪv/ **staves, staving, staved.** PHR-VERB If you **stave off** something bad, you succeed in stopping it happening for a while. *...a last-minute bid to stave off defeat.*

⬛ **stay** /steɪ/ **stays, staying, stayed.** **1** VERB If you **stay** in a place or position, you continue to be there and do not leave. *She stayed at home to raise her children... Stay away from the rocks.* **2** VERB If you **stay** in a town or hotel, or at someone's house, you live there for a short time. *We stayed the night in a little hotel.* **3** N-COUNT The time you spend in a place is referred to as your **stay** there. *He had a short stay in hospital.* **4** LINK-VERB If someone or something **stays** in a particular condition or situation, they continue to be in it. *The company was struggling to stay ahead of its rivals... Nothing stays the same for long.* **5** VERB If you **stay out of** something or **stay away from** it, you do not get involved in it. *He warned young people to stay away from drugs.*
PHRASES ● If you say that something is **here to stay**, you mean that people have accepted it and it has become a part of everyday life. *Satellite TV is here to stay.* ● If you **stay put**, you remain somewhere. *He is very happy to stay put in Lyon.*
▸**stay in.** PHR-VERB If you **stay in**, you remain at home during the evening and do not go out.
▸**stay on.** PHR-VERB If you **stay on** somewhere, you remain there after other people have left or after the time when you were going to leave. *He had managed to arrange to stay on in Adelaide.*
▸**stay out.** PHR-VERB If you **stay out**, you remain away from home at night. *I met some friends and stayed out until eleven or twelve.*
▸**stay up.** PHR-VERB If you **stay up**, you remain out of bed at a later time than normal. *I used to stay up late with my mom and watch movies.*

stead /sted/. PHRASE If something will **stand you in good stead**, it will be useful to you in the future. *My years of teaching stood me in good stead.*

steadfast /ˈstedfɑːst, -fæst/. ADJ If you are **steadfast in** your beliefs or opinions, you are convinced that they are right and you refuse to change them; used showing approval. *He remained steadfast in his belief that he had done the right thing.* ♦ **steadfastly** ADV *She steadfastly refused to look his way.*

⬛ **steady** /ˈstedi/ **steadier, steadiest; steadies, steadying, steadied.** **1** ADJ Something that is **steady** continues or develops gradually without any interruptions and is unlikely to change suddenly. *They were forecasting a steady rise in sales... I want to find a steady job.* ♦ **steadily** ADV *Relax as much as possible and keep breathing steadily.* **2** ADJ If an object is **steady**, it is firm and does not move about. *Hold the camera steady.* **3** ADJ A **steady** look or voice is calm and controlled.

♦ **steadily** ADV *He moved back a little and stared steadily at Elaine.* **4** VERB If you **steady** something, or if it **steadies**, it stops shaking or moving about. *She placed her hands on the controls again and steadied the plane.* **5** VERB If you **steady yourself**, you control your voice or expression, so that people will think that you are calm. *Somehow she steadied herself.*

steak /steɪk/ **steaks.** **1** N-VAR **Steak** is beef without much fat on it. **2** N-COUNT A fish **steak** is a large flat piece of fish.

⭐ **steal** /stiːl/ **steals, stealing, stole, stolen.** **1** VERB If you **steal** something from someone, you take it away from them without their permission and without intending to return it. *He was accused of stealing a small boy's bicycle... We have now found the stolen car.* ♦ **stealing** N-UNCOUNT *She has since been jailed for six months for stealing.* **2** VERB If you **steal** somewhere, you move there quietly and cautiously. *They can steal away at night and join us.*

stealth /stelθ/. N-UNCOUNT If you do something with **stealth**, you do it in a slow, quiet, and secretive way. *Reform has proceeded by stealth.*

⭐ **steam** /stiːm/ **steams, steaming, steamed.** **1** N-UNCOUNT **Steam** is the hot mist that forms when water boils. **Steam** vehicles and machines are powered by steam. *...steam trains.* **2** VERB If something **steams**, it gives off steam. *The kettle began to steam.* **3** VERB If you **steam** food, you cook it in steam. *Boil or steam the rice.* ● See note at **cook**. **4** PHRASE If you **run out of steam**, you stop doing something because you have no more energy or enthusiasm left. [INFORMAL]

steamer

steamer /ˈstiːmə/ **steamers.** **1** N-COUNT A **steamer** is a ship that is powered by steam. **2** N-COUNT A **steamer** is a special saucepan used for steaming food such as vegetables and fish.

steamy /ˈstiːmi/ **steamier, steamiest.** **1** ADJ A **steamy** place is very hot and humid, usually because it is full of steam. *...a steamy kitchen.* **2** ADJ **Steamy** means erotic or passionate. [INFORMAL] *...steamy sex scenes.*

⭐ **steel** /stiːl/ **steels, steeling, steeled.** **1** N-UNCOUNT **Steel** is a very strong metal made mainly from iron. ● See also **stainless steel**. **2** VERB If you **steel yourself**, you prepare to deal with

a
b
c
d
e
f
g
h
i
j
k
l
m
n
o
p
q
r
s
t
u
v
w
x
y
z

something unpleasant. *I had been steeling myself for something like this.*

steely /'sti:li/. **1** ADJ You use **steely** to describe something that has a hard, greyish colour. *...the steely grey light.* **2** ADJ **Steely** is used to describe someone who is hard, strong, and determined. *Their indecision has been replaced by confidence and steely determination.*

steep /sti:p/ **steeper, steepest. 1** ADJ A **steep** slope rises at a very sharp angle and is difficult to go up. ♦ **steeply** ADV *The ground rose steeply.* **2** ADJ A **steep** increase is very big. ♦ **steeply** ADV *Unemployment is rising steeply.*

steeped /sti:pt/. ADJ AFTER LINK-V If a place or person is **steeped in** a quality or characteristic, they are surrounded by it or deeply influenced by it. *The castle is steeped in history.*

steer /stɪə/ **steers, steering, steered. 1** VERB When you **steer** a car, boat, or plane, you control it so that it goes in the direction you want. *She would often let me steer the car along our driveway.* **2** VERB If you **steer** someone in a particular direction, you guide them there. *I steered him towards the door.* **3** PHRASE If you **steer clear of** someone or something, you deliberately avoid them. *The rabbis try to steer clear of political questions.*

'steering wheel, steering wheels. N-COUNT The **steering wheel** in a vehicle is the wheel which the driver holds to steer the vehicle.

★ **stem** /stem/ **stems, stemming, stemmed. 1** N-COUNT The **stem** of a plant is the thin upright part on which the flowers and leaves grow. **2** N-COUNT The **stem** of a glass or vase is the long thin part which connects the bowl to the base. **3** VERB If you **stem** something that is spreading from one place to another, you stop it spreading. [FORMAL] *The authorities seem powerless to stem the rising tide of violence.* **4** VERB If a condition or problem **stems from** something, that is what originally caused it. *Most of her problems stemmed from her childhood.*

stench /stentʃ/ **stenches.** N-COUNT A **stench** is a strong, unpleasant smell. *...the stench of decaying fish.*

stencil /'stensəl/ **stencils, stencilling, stencilled** (AM **stenciling, stenciled**). **1** N-COUNT A **stencil** is a piece of paper, plastic, or metal with a design cut out of it. You place the stencil on a surface and create a design by putting ink or paint over the cut area. **2** VERB If you **stencil** letters or designs, you print them using a stencil.

★ **step** /step/ **steps, stepping, stepped. 1** N-COUNT A **step** is the movement made by lifting your foot and putting it down in a different place. *I took another step back... He heard steps in the corridor.* **2** VERB If you **step on** something or **step** in a particular direction, you put your foot on the thing or move your foot in that direction. *He stepped on glass and cut his foot... Doug stepped sideways.* **3** N-COUNT A **step** is one of a series of actions that you take in order to achieve

something. *He greeted the agreement as the first step towards peace.* **4** N-COUNT A **step** is a raised flat surface, often one of a series, on which you put your feet in order to walk up or down to a different level. *He sat down on the bottom step of the stairs.*

PHRASES ● If you stay **one step ahead** of someone or something, you manage to achieve more than they do or avoid competition or danger from them. *The Opposition, using last-minute knowledge, has managed to keep one step ahead.* ● If people are **in step with** each other, their ideas or opinions are the same. If they are **out of step** with each other, their ideas or opinions are different. *Britain is out of step with the rest of Europe on this matter.* ● If you do something **step by step**, you do it by progressing gradually from one stage to the next. *The king took the boy, step by step, through everything that had happened.*

▸**step aside.** See **step down**.

▸**step back.** PHR-VERB If you **step back from** a situation, you think about it in a fresh and detached way. *It was necessary to step back from the project and look at it as a whole.*

▸**step down.** PHR-VERB If you **step down** or **step aside**, you resign from an important job or position. *Judge Ito said that if his wife was called as a witness, he would step down as trial judge.*

▸**step in.** PHR-VERB If you **step in**, you get involved in a difficult situation, in order to help. *President Bush had to step in to settle the dispute.*

▸**step up.** PHR-VERB If you **step up** something, you increase it. *The Japanese then stepped up their campaign against the guerrillas.*

stepfather (or **step-father**) /'stepfɑːðə/ **stepfathers.** N-COUNT Your **stepfather** is the man who has married your mother after the death or divorce of your father.

stepmother (or **step-mother**) /'stepmʌðə/ **stepmothers.** N-COUNT Your **stepmother** is the woman who has married your father after the death or divorce of your mother.

'stepping stone, stepping stones. 1 N-COUNT A **stepping stone** is a job or event that helps you to make progress, especially in your career. *Many students now see university as a stepping stone to a good job.* **2** N-COUNT **Stepping stones** are a line of stones which you can walk on in order to cross a shallow stream or river.

stereo /'steriəʊ/ **stereos. 1** ADJ **Stereo** is used to describe a recording or a system of playing music in which the sound is directed through two speakers. *...a stereo cassette player.* **2** N-COUNT A **stereo** is a record player with two speakers.

stereotype /'steriətaip/ **stereotypes, stereotyping, stereotyped. 1** N-COUNT A **stereotype** is a fixed general image or set of characteristics that a lot of people believe represent a particular type of person or thing. *...the stereotype of the polite, industrious Japanese.* **2** VERB If someone **is stereotyped** as something, people form a fixed general image of them, so that it is assumed that they will behave in a particular way. ...*the way women are stereotyped in a lot of films.*

sterile /'steraɪl, AM -rəl/. **1** ADJ Something that is **sterile** is completely clean and free of germs. ...*a sterile needle.* ◆ **sterility** /stə'rɪlɪti/ N-UNCOUNT ...*the antiseptic sterility of the hospital.* **2** ADJ A person or animal that is **sterile** is unable to have or produce babies. ◆ **sterility** N-UNCOUNT *This disease causes sterility.* **3** ADJ A **sterile** situation is lacking in energy and new ideas. *Too much time has been wasted in sterile debate.* ◆ **sterility** N-UNCOUNT *They are quitting in disgust at the sterility of politics.*

sterilize (BRIT also **sterilise**) /'sterɪlaɪz/ **sterilizes, sterilizing, sterilized.** **1** VERB If you **sterilize** a thing or place, you make it completely clean and free from germs. *Sterilize a large needle by boiling it.* **2** VERB If a person or an animal **is sterilized,** they have an operation that makes it impossible for them to have or produce babies. ◆ **sterilization, sterilizations** N-VAR ...*the decision to have a sterilization.*

⭐ **sterling** /'stɜːlɪŋ/. **1** N-UNCOUNT **Sterling** is the money system of Great Britain. **2** ADJ If you describe someone's work or character as **sterling,** you mean it is excellent. [FORMAL] *Those are sterling qualities to be admired in anyone.*

stern /stɜːn/ **sterner, sternest; sterns.** **1** ADJ Someone or something that is **stern** is very serious and strict. ...*a stern warning.* ◆ **sternly** ADV *'We will take the necessary steps,' she said sternly.* **2** N-COUNT The **stern** of a boat is the back part of it.

steroid /'steroɪd, AM 'stɪr-/ **steroids.** N-COUNT A **steroid** is a type of chemical substance which occurs naturally in the body, and can also be made artificially.

stew /stjuː, AM stuː/ **stews, stewing, stewed.** **1** N-VAR A **stew** is a meal made by cooking meat and vegetables in liquid at a low temperature. ...*beef stew.* **2** VERB If you **stew** meat, vegetables, or fruit, you cook them slowly in liquid.

steward /'stjuːəd, AM 'stuː-/ **stewards.** **1** N-COUNT A **steward** is a man whose job is to look after passengers on a ship, plane, or train. **2** N-COUNT A **steward** is someone who helps to organize a race, march, or other public event.

stewardess /ˌstjuːə'des, ˌstuː-/ **stewardesses.** N-COUNT A **stewardess** is a woman whose job is to look after passengers on a ship, plane, or train.

stick 1 noun uses

⭐ **stick** /stɪk/ **sticks.** **1** N-COUNT A **stick** is a thin branch which has fallen off a tree. ...*bundles of dried sticks.* **2** N-COUNT A **stick** is a long thin piece of wood which is used for a particular purpose. ...*a walking stick.* ...*a hockey stick.* **3** N-COUNT A **stick of** something is a long thin piece of it. ...*a stick of celery.* ...*a stick of dynamite.*

stick 2 verb uses

⭐ **stick** /stɪk/ **sticks, sticking, stuck.** **1** VERB If you **stick** something somewhere, you put it there in a rather casual way. [INFORMAL] *He folded the papers and stuck them in his desk drawer.* **2** VERB If you **stick** a pointed object in something, you push it in. *The doctor stuck the needle in Joe's arm.* **3** VERB If you **stick** one thing to another, you attach it using glue, sticky tape, or another sticky substance. *I was going to stick a notice on the window saying 'Tickets For The Court'.* **4** VERB If something **sticks** somewhere, it becomes attached or fixed in one position and cannot be moved. *It stops the rice sticking to the pan.* **5** PHRASE If someone in an unpleasant or difficult situation **sticks it out,** they do not leave or give up. *I really didn't like New York, but I wanted to stick it out a little bit longer.* **6** See also **stuck.**

▶**stick around.** PHR-VERB If you **stick around,** you stay where you are. [INFORMAL] *I didn't stick around long enough to find out.*

▶**stick by.** PHR-VERB If you **stick by** someone, you continue to help or support them. ...*friends who stuck by me during the difficult times.*

▶**stick out.** PHR-VERB If something **sticks out,** or if you **stick** it **out,** it extends beyond something else. ...*a nozzle sticking out of the front grill... Eve stuck her head out the window.* ● See also **stick** 5.

▶**stick to.** **1** PHR-VERB If you **stick to** something, you stay close to it or with it and do not change to something else. *Stick to the main road... I think he had better stick to acting.* **2** PHR-VERB If you **stick to** a promise or agreement, you do what you said you would do.

▶**stick together.** PHR-VERB If people **stick together,** they stay with each other and support each other's interest. *If we all stick together, we ought to be okay.*

▶**stick up.** **1** PHR-VERB If you **stick up** a picture or a notice, you fix it to a wall. **2** PHR-VERB If something **sticks up,** it points upwards. *His hair stuck up.*

▶**stick up for.** PHR-VERB If you **stick up for** someone or something, you support or defend them forcefully. *Why do you always stick up for her?*

▶**stick with.** PHR-VERB If you **stick with** someone or something, you stay with them and do not change to something else. *If you're in a job that keeps you busy, stick with it.*

sticker /'stɪkə/ **stickers.** N-COUNT A **sticker** is a small piece of paper or plastic with writing or a picture on it, that you can stick onto a surface.

'stick insect, stick insects. N-COUNT A **stick insect** is an insect with a long thin body and legs. → See picture on page 824.

sticky /'stɪki/ **stickier, stickiest.** **1** ADJ A **sticky** substance can stick to other things. **Sticky** things are covered with a sticky substance. ...*sticky paper.* **2** ADJ **Sticky** weather is unpleasantly hot and damp. ...*an uncomfortably sticky day.* **3** ADJ A **sticky** situation is difficult or embarrassing. [INFORMAL] *Her research was going through a sticky patch.*

stiff /stɪf/ **stiffer, stiffest.** **1** ADJ Something that is **stiff** is firm and does not bend easily. *His*

gaberdine trousers were brand new and stiff.
♦ **stiffly** ADV *Moira sat stiffly upright in her straight-backed chair.* [2] ADJ Something such as a drawer or door that is **stiff** does not move as easily as it should. *The gears were too stiff.* [3] ADJ If you are **stiff**, your muscles or joints ache when you move. ♦ **stiffly** ADV *He climbed stiffly from the car.* ♦ **stiffness** N-UNCOUNT *...pain and stiffness in the neck.* [4] ADJ **Stiff** behaviour is rather formal and not relaxed. *She looked at him with a stiff smile.* ♦ **stiffly** ADV *...a stiffly worded letter.* [5] ADJ **Stiff** means difficult or severe. *...stiff anti-drugs laws.* [6] ADJ BEFORE N A **stiff** drink is a large amount of a strong alcoholic drink. *...a stiff whisky.* [7] ADJ A **stiff** wind blows quite strongly. [8] ADV If you are bored **stiff**, worried **stiff**, or scared **stiff**, you are extremely bored, worried, or scared. [INFORMAL] [9] **stiff upper lip**: see **lip**.

stiffen /'stɪfən/ **stiffens, stiffening, stiffened.** [1] VERB If you **stiffen**, you stop moving and become very tense, for example because you are afraid or angry. *His father's face stiffened with dismay.* [2] VERB & PHR-VERB If your muscles or joints **stiffen**, or if they **stiffen up**, they become difficult to bend or move. *My elbow was starting to stiffen up where I'd landed on it.* [3] VERB If attitudes or behaviour **stiffen**, they become stronger or more severe, and less likely to be changed. *Canada has recently stiffened its immigration rules.* [4] VERB When something such as cloth **is stiffened**, it is made firm. *...paper that had been stiffened with a kind of paste.*

stifle /'staɪfəl/ **stifles, stifling, stifled.** VERB To **stifle** something means to stop it happening or continuing. *Ed stifled a yawn and looked at his watch... Regulations on children stifled all their creativity.*

stifling /'staɪfəlɪŋ/. [1] ADJ **Stifling** heat is so intense that it makes you feel uncomfortable. [2] ADJ If a situation is **stifling**, it makes you feel uncomfortable because you cannot do what you want. *Life at home with her parents and two sisters was stifling.*

stigma /'stɪgmə/ **stigmas.** N-VAR If you say that something has a **stigma** attached to it, you mean that people consider it to be unacceptable or a disgrace, and you think this is unfair. *...the stigma attached to mental illness.*

stigmatize (BRIT also **stigmatise**)
/'stɪgmətaɪz/ **stigmatizes, stigmatizing, stigmatized.** VERB If someone or something **is stigmatized**, they are unfairly regarded by many people as unacceptable or disgraceful.

stiletto /stɪ'letəʊ/ **stilettos.** N-COUNT **Stilettos** are women's shoes that have high, very narrow heels.

still 1 adverb uses

⭐ **still** /stɪl/. [1] ADV If a situation that used to exist **still** exists, it has continued and exists now. *I still dream of home... Brian's toe is still badly swollen.* [2] ADV If something that has not yet happened could **still** happen, it is possible that it will happen. *We could still make it, but we won't get*

there till three. [3] ADV You use **still** to emphasize that something remains the case or is true. *Despite the ruling, Boreham was still found guilty.* [4] ADV You use **still** before saying something that shows that you think what has just been said or mentioned is not important or is not worth worrying about. *'Any idea who is going to be here this weekend?'—'No. Still, who cares?'* [5] ADV You use **still** in expressions such as **still further**, **still another**, and **still more** to show that you find the number or quantity of things you are referring to surprising or excessive. *There are clouds forecast for tomorrow and they could delay the flight still further.* [6] ADV You use **still** with words such as 'better' or 'more' to indicate that something has even more of a quality than something else. *Pizza may be good for you, but spaghetti sauce is better still.*

still 2 not moving

⭐ **still** /stɪl/ **stiller, stillest.** [1] ADJ If you stay **still**, you stay in the same position without moving. *He played the tape through once, then sat very still for several minutes.* [2] ADJ If something is **still**, there is no movement or activity there. *The night air was very still.* ♦ **stillness** N-UNCOUNT *...the beauty and stillness of the forest.*

,**still 'life**, **still lifes.** N-VAR A **still life** is a painting or drawing of an arrangement of objects such as flowers or fruit. **Still life** is this type of painting or drawing.

stimulant /'stɪmjʊlənt/ **stimulants.** N-COUNT A **stimulant** is a drug that increases your heart rate and makes you less likely to sleep.

⭐ **stimulate** /'stɪmjʊleɪt/ **stimulates, stimulating, stimulated.** [1] VERB To **stimulate** something means to encourage it to begin or develop further. *These businesses stimulate the creation of local jobs.* [2] VERB If you **are stimulated** by something, it makes you feel full of ideas and enthusiasm. ♦ **stimulating** ADJ *It is a complex yet stimulating book.* ♦ **stimulation** N-UNCOUNT *...the mental stimulation of a challenging job.* [3] VERB If something **stimulates** a part of a person's body, it causes it to move or function automatically. ♦ **stimulation** N-UNCOUNT *...electrical stimulation of the brain.*

stimulus /'stɪmjʊləs/ **stimuli** /'stɪmjʊlaɪ/. N-VAR A **stimulus** is something that encourages activity in people or things. *Headaches can be triggered by a vast range of stimuli.*

sting /stɪŋ/ **stings, stinging, stung.** [1] VERB If an insect or plant **stings** you, it pricks your skin, usually with poison, so that you feel a sharp pain.

> **USAGE** Note that wasps and bees **sting** you, but animals, snakes, and mosquitoes **bite** you.

[2] N-COUNT The **sting** of an insect is the part that stings you. [3] VERB & N-SING If a part of your body **stings**, or if you feel a **sting**, you feel a sharp pain there. *His cheeks were stinging from the icy wind.*

4 VERB If someone's remarks **sting** you, they upset and annoy you. *Some of the criticism has stung him.* ♦ **stinging** ADJ *...a stinging attack on the government.*

stink /stɪŋk/ **stinks, stinking, stank, stunk.** **1** VERB & N-SING If something **stinks**, it smells extremely unpleasant. A **stink** is a very unpleasant smell. *The place stinks of fried onions.* **2** VERB If you say that something **stinks**, you mean that it involves ideas, feelings, or practices that you do not like. [INFORMAL] *They have done something very bad. It's illegal, it stinks.*

stint /stɪnt/ **stints.** N-COUNT A **stint** is a period of time spent doing a particular job or activity. *...a five-year stint in Hong Kong.*

stipulate /'stɪpjʊleɪt/ **stipulates, stipulating, stipulated.** VERB If you **stipulate** that something must be done, you say clearly that it must be done. *The company's rules stipulate that board members must retire at 75.* ♦ **stipulation, stipulations** N-COUNT *Clifford's only stipulation is that his clients obey his advice.*

⭐ **stir** /stɜː/ **stirs, stirring, stirred.** **1** VERB When you **stir** a liquid, you mix it inside a container using something such as a spoon. *There was Mrs Bellingham, stirring sugar into her tea.* **2** VERB If you **stir**, you move slightly, for example because you are uncomfortable or beginning to wake up. [WRITTEN] *Eileen shook him, and he started to stir.* **3** VERB If something **stirs** you or **stirs** an emotion in you, it makes you react with a strong emotion. [WRITTEN] *Amy remembered the anger he had stirred in her.* **4** N-SING If an event causes a **stir**, it causes great excitement, shock, or anger. *His film has caused a stir in America.* **5** See also **stirring.**
▸ **stir up.** **1** PHR-VERB If something **stirs up** dust or mud, it causes it to move around. *They saw first a cloud of dust and then the car that was stirring it up.* **2** PHR-VERB If you **stir up** a particular mood or situation, usually a bad one, you cause it. *As usual, Harriet is trying to stir up trouble.*

stirring /'stɜːrɪŋ/ **stirrings.** **1** ADJ A **stirring** event, performance, or account of something makes people very excited or enthusiastic. *The Prime Minister made a stirring speech.* **2** N-COUNT When there is a **stirring** of emotion, people begin to feel it. *...the first stirrings of a sense of guilt.*

stitch /stɪtʃ/ **stitches, stitching, stitched.** **1** VERB If you **stitch** cloth, you use a needle and thread to join two pieces together or to make a decoration. *Fold the fabric and stitch the two layers together.* **2** N-COUNT **Stitches** are the short pieces of thread that have been sewn in a piece of cloth. **3** N-COUNT A **stitch** is a loop made by one turn of wool around a knitting needle. **4** VERB & PHR-VERB When doctors **stitch** a wound, or when they **stitch** it **up**, they use a special needle and thread to sew the skin together. *Dr Armonson stitched up her wrist wounds.* **5** N-COUNT A **stitch** is a piece of thread that has been used to stitch a wound. *He*

had six stitches in a head wound. **6** N-SING A **stitch** is a sharp pain in your side, usually caused by laughing a lot or running.

⭐ **stock** /stɒk/ **stocks, stocking, stocked.** **1** N-VAR **Stocks** are shares in the ownership of a company. A company's **stock** consists of all the shares that people have bought in it. *...the buying and selling of stocks.* **2** VERB A shop that **stocks** particular goods keeps a supply of them to sell. *The inn gift shop stocks quality Indian crafts.* **3** N-UNCOUNT A shop's **stock** is the total amount of goods which it has available to sell. **4** N-COUNT A **stock of** things is a supply of them. *...stocks of paper and printing ink.* **5** N-VAR **Stock** is a liquid made by boiling meat, bones, or vegetables with water.

PHRASES ● If goods are **in stock**, a shop has them available to sell. If they are **out of stock**, it does not. ● If you **take stock**, you pause and think about a situation before deciding what to do next. *It was time to take stock of the situation.*
▸ **stock up.** PHR-VERB If you **stock up with** something or **stock up on** it, you buy a lot of it, in case you cannot get it later. *The authorities have urged people to stock up on fuel.*

stockbroker /'stɒkbrəʊkə/ **stockbrokers.** N-COUNT A **stockbroker** is someone whose profession is buying and selling stocks and shares for clients.

stockbroking /'stɒkbrəʊkɪŋ/. N-UNCOUNT **Stockbroking** is the professional activity of buying and selling stocks and shares for clients.

⭐ **'stock exchange, stock exchanges.** N-COUNT A **stock exchange** is a place where people buy and sell stocks and shares.

stockholder /'stɒkhəʊldə/ **stockholders.** N-COUNT In American English, a **stockholder** is a person who owns shares in a company. The usual British word is **shareholder.**

stocking /'stɒkɪŋ/ **stockings.** N-COUNT **Stockings** are items of women's clothing which fit closely over their feet and legs. Stockings are usually made of nylon or silk and are held in place by suspenders. *...a pair of silk stockings.*

stockist /'stɒkɪst/ **stockists.** N-COUNT A **stockist** of a particular brand or type of goods is a person or shop that sells it. [BRITISH] *Take it to your nearest Kodak Photo CD stockist.*

⭐ **'stock market, stock markets.** N-COUNT The **stock market** consists of the activity of buying stocks and shares, and the people and institutions that organize it.

stockpile /'stɒkpaɪl/ **stockpiles, stockpiling, stockpiled.** **1** VERB If people **stockpile** things, they store large quantities of them for future use. *People are stockpiling food for the coming winter.* **2** N-COUNT A **stockpile** is a large store of something. *...stockpiles of chemical weapons.*

stocky /'stɒki/ **stockier, stockiest.** ADJ A **stocky** person has a body that is broad, solid, and short.

stoke /stəʊk/ **stokes, stoking, stoked.** **1** VERB & PHR-VERB If you **stoke** a fire, or if you **stoke** it **up**, you put more fuel onto it. *He stoked up the fire in*

a b c d e f g h i j k l m n o p q r **s** t u v w x y z

the hearth. 2 VERB & PHR-VERB If you **stoke** something such as a feeling, or if you **stoke** it **up**, you cause it to be felt more strongly. *These demands are helping to stoke fears of civil war.*

stole /stəʊl/. **Stole** is the past tense of **steal**.

stolen /ˈstəʊlən/. **Stolen** is the past participle of **steal**.

★ **stomach** /ˈstʌmək/ **stomachs, stomaching, stomached.** 1 N-COUNT Your **stomach** is the organ inside your body where food is digested. *My stomach is completely full.* 2 N-COUNT You can refer to the front part of your body below your waist as your **stomach**. → See picture on page 822. *The children lay down on their stomachs.* 3 VERB If you cannot **stomach** something, you strongly dislike it and cannot accept it. *He could not stomach violence.*

stomp /stɒmp/ **stomps, stomping, stomped.** VERB If you **stomp** somewhere, you walk there with heavy steps, often because you are angry. *He stomped out of the room.*

★ **stone** /stəʊn/ **stones, stoning, stoned.**

☑ In meaning 5, **stone** is both the singular and the plural form.

1 N-VAR **Stone** is a hard solid substance found in the ground and often used for building. *He could not tell whether the floor was wood or stone.* 2 N-COUNT A **stone** is a small piece of rock. *He removed a stone from his shoe.* 3 VERB If people **stone** someone or something, they throw stones at them. *Youths burned cars and stoned police.* 4 N-COUNT In British English, the **stone** in a fruit such as a peach or plum is the large seed in the middle of it. The usual American word is **pit**. 5 N-COUNT A **stone** is a measurement of a person's weight, equal to 14 pounds or 6.35 kilograms. [BRITISH] *I weighed around 16 stone.* ● See note at **weight**. 6 N-COUNT You can refer to a jewel as a **stone**. *...a diamond ring with three stones.* 7 PHRASE If you say that one place is **a stone's throw** from another, you mean that the places are close to each other.

'**Stone Age.** N-PROPER **The Stone Age** is a very early period of human history, when people used tools and weapons made of stone, not metal.

stony /ˈstəʊni/ **stonier, stoniest.** 1 ADJ **Stony** ground is rough and contains a lot of stones. 2 ADJ If someone's expression or behaviour is **stony**, they show no friendliness or sympathy. *He drove us home in stony silence.*

stood /stʊd/. **Stood** is the past tense and past participle of **stand**.

stool /stuːl/ **stools.** N-COUNT A **stool** is a seat with legs but no support for your back or arms.

stoop /stuːp/ **stoops, stooping, stooped.** 1 VERB & N-SING If you **stoop**, or if you have a **stoop**, you stand or walk with your shoulders bent forwards. *He was a tall, thin fellow with a slight stoop.* 2 VERB If you **stoop**, **stoop down**, or **stoop over**, you bend your body forwards and downwards. *Stooping down, he picked up a big stone.* 3 VERB If you say that someone **stoops to**

doing something, you are criticizing them because they do something wrong or immoral that they would not normally do. *He never stooped to personal abuse... How could anyone stoop so low?*

★ **stop** /stɒp/ **stops, stopping, stopped.** 1 VERB If you **stop** doing something that you have been doing, you no longer do it. *He can't stop thinking about it... Does either of the parties want to stop the fighting?... I stopped to read the notices on the bulletin board.* 2 VERB & PHRASE If you **stop** something, or if you **put a stop to** it, you prevent it from happening or continuing. *He tried to stop the show before it could open... She really would have liked to stop us seeing each other... Motherhood won't stop me from pursuing my acting career... His daughter should have stood up and put a stop to all these rumours.* 3 VERB If an activity or process **stops**, it comes to an end. *The rain had stopped... The system overheated and filming had to stop.* 4 VERB If something such as a machine **stops**, it is no longer moving or working. *The clock had stopped at 2.12 a.m... Arnold stopped the engine and got out of the car.* 5 VERB & N-SING When a moving person or vehicle **stops**, or when they come to **a stop**, they no longer move. *The car failed to stop at an army checkpoint... The event literally stopped the traffic... He slowed the car almost to a stop.* 6 VERB & PHR-VERB If you **stop** or **stop off** somewhere on a journey, you stay there for a short while before continuing. *The president stopped off in Poland on his way to Munich.* 7 N-COUNT A **stop** is a place where buses or trains regularly stop so that people can get on and off. 8 to **stop dead**: see **dead**. ● to **stop short of**: see **short**.

> USAGE When an action comes to an end or stops, you say that someone **stops doing** it. *She stopped reading and closed the book.* However, if you say that someone **stops to do** something, you mean that they interrupt their movement or another activity in order to do that thing. *I stopped to read the notices on the bulletin board.*

▸ **stop by.** PHR-VERB If you **stop by** somewhere, you make a short visit to a person or place. [INFORMAL] *Perhaps I'll stop by the hospital.*

stoppage /ˈstɒpɪdʒ/ **stoppages.** N-COUNT When there is a **stoppage**, people stop working because of a disagreement with their employers.

storage /ˈstɔːrɪdʒ/. N-UNCOUNT **Storage** is the process of keeping something in a particular place until it is needed. *Some of the space will it be used for storage.*

★ **store** /stɔː/ **stores, storing, stored.** 1 N-COUNT A **store** is a shop. In British English, **store** is used mainly to refer to a large shop selling a variety of goods, but in American English, a **store** can be any shop. **2** VERB & PHR-VERB To **store** something or to **store** it **away** means to keep it in a place until it is needed. *The information can be stored in a computer... He simply stored the tapes away.* **3** N-COUNT A **store of** something is a supply of it kept in a place until it is needed. *I have a store of food and water here.* **4** N-VAR A **store** is a place where things are kept while they are not being used. *...a grain store.* **5** PHRASE If something is **in store** for you, it is going to happen at some time in the future. *Off we went into the night, not knowing what lay in store.* **6** See also **department store**.

▸**store away.** See **store** 2.

▸**store up.** PHR-VERB If you **store** something **up**, you keep it until you think that the time is right to use it. *Investors were storing up a lot of cash in anticipation of disaster.*

storey (AM **story**) /'stɔːri/ **storeys.** N-COUNT The **storeys** of a building are its floors or levels. *...a modern three-storey building.*

⭐ **storm** /stɔːm/ **storms, storming, stormed.** **1** N-COUNT A **storm** is very bad weather, with heavy rain, strong winds, and often thunder and lightning. **2** N-COUNT If something causes a **storm**, it causes an angry or excited reaction from a large number of people. *The announcement provoked an immediate storm of protest.* **3** VERB If you **storm into** or **out of** a place, you enter or leave it quickly and noisily, because you are angry. *After a bit of an argument, he stormed out.* **4** VERB If a place that is being defended **is stormed**, a group of people attack it, usually in order to get inside it. *The refugees decided to storm the embassy.* ♦ **storming** N-UNCOUNT *...the storming of the Bastille.* **5** PHRASE If someone or something **takes** a place **by storm**, they are extremely successful there. *Kenya's long distance runners have taken the athletics world by storm.*

stormy /'stɔːmi/ **stormier, stormiest.** **1** ADJ If there is **stormy** weather, there is a strong wind and heavy rain. **2** ADJ A **stormy** situation involves a lot of angry argument or criticism. *Their working relationship was stormy at times.*

⭐ **story** /'stɔːri/ **stories.** **1** N-COUNT A **story** is a description of imaginary people and events, which is written or told in order to entertain. *I shall tell you a story about four little rabbits.* **2** N-COUNT A **story** is a description or account of things that have happened. *...the story of the women's movement in Ireland.* **3** N-COUNT A news **story** is a piece of news in a newspaper or in a news broadcast. **4** See also **storey**.

PHRASES ● You use **a different story** to refer to a situation, usually a bad one, which exists in one set of circumstances when you have mentioned that it does not exist in another set of circumstances. *Where Marcella lives, the rents are fairly cheap, but a little further north it's a different story.* ● If you say it's **the same old story** or **the old story**, you mean that something unpleasant or undesirable seems to happen again and again. *It's the same old story. They want one person to do*

three people's jobs. ● If you say that something is **only part of the story** or is **not the whole story**, you mean that the explanation or information given is not enough for a situation to be fully understood. *This may be true but it is only part of the story.* ● If someone tells you their **side of the story**, they tell you why they behaved in a particular way and why they think they were right, when other people think that person behaved wrongly. *He had already made up his mind before even hearing her side of the story.*

stout /staʊt/ **stouter, stoutest.** **1** ADJ A **stout** person is rather fat. **2** ADJ **Stout** shoes, branches, or other objects are thick and strong. **3** ADJ If you use **stout** to describe someone's actions, attitudes, or beliefs, you approve of them because they are strong and determined. ♦ **stoutly** ADV *She stoutly defended her husband.*

stove /stəʊv/ **stoves.** N-COUNT A **stove** is a piece of equipment for heating a room or cooking. *She put the kettle on the gas stove.*

stow /stəʊ/ **stows, stowing, stowed.** VERB & PHR-VERB If you **stow** something somewhere, or if you **stow** it **away**, you put it carefully somewhere until it is needed. *I helped her stow her bags in the boot of the car.*

straddle /'strædəl/ **straddles, straddling, straddled.** **1** VERB If you **straddle** something, you put or have one leg on either side of it. *He sat down, straddling the chair.* **2** VERB If something such as a bridge or town **straddles** a river, road, or border, it stretches across it or exists on both sides of it. *...the Rumaila oilfield, which straddles the border between Kuwait and Iraq.* **3** VERB Someone or something that **straddles** different periods, groups, or fields of activity exists in, belongs to, or takes elements from them all. *He straddles two cultures, having been brought up in Britain and later converted to Islam.*

⭐ **straight** /streɪt/ **straighter, straightest.** **1** ADJ & ADV If something is **straight**, it continues in one direction or line and does not bend or curve. *Keep the boat in a straight line... She looked straight at me... He couldn't walk straight.* **2** ADV If you go **straight** to a place, you go there immediately. *We went straight to the experts for advice... We'll go to a meeting in Birmingham and come straight back.* **3** ADJ BEFORE N A **straight** choice or a **straight** fight involves only two people or things. *It's a straight choice between low-paid jobs and no jobs.* **4** ADJ & ADV If you are **straight** with someone, you speak to them honestly and frankly. *Can't you give me a straight answer?... What if they were to tell you straight that they have used an illegal drug?* **5** PHRASE If you **get** something **straight**, you make sure that you understand it properly or that someone else does. *You need to get your facts straight... Let's get things straight. I didn't lunch with her.* **6 a straight face**: see **face**. ● to **set the record straight**: see **record**.

,**straight a**'**way** (or **straightaway**). ADV If you do something **straight away**, you do it

A
B
C
D
E
F
G
H
I
J
K
L
M
N
O
P
Q
R
S
T
U
V
W
X
Y
Z

immediately. *I knew straight away he was different.*

straighten /'streɪtən/ **straightens, straightening, straightened.** [1] VERB & PHR-VERB If you **straighten** something, or if you **straighten** it **out**, it becomes straight rather than having bends or curls in it, or being in the wrong position. *She sipped her coffee and straightened a picture on the wall... I had my Afro hair straightened... The road twisted its way up the mountain then straightened out.* [2] VERB & PHR-VERB If you are bending and you then **straighten** or **straighten up**, you make your body straight and upright. *I straightened until rock bumped my head... He straightened up and looked around.*

▶**straighten out.** [1] PHR-VERB If you **straighten out** a confused situation, you succeed in dealing with it or getting it properly organized. *...an appointment with him to straighten out a couple of things.* [2] See **straighten** 1.

straightforward /ˌstreɪt'fɔːwəd/. [1] ADJ If something is **straightforward**, it is not complicated to do or understand. *Disposable nappies are fairly straightforward to put on... The question seemed straightforward enough.* ♦ **straightforwardly** ADV *Acid rain is not straightforwardly attributable to the burning of coal.* [2] ADJ If you describe a person or their behaviour as **straightforward**, you approve of them because they are honest and direct, and do not try to hide their feelings. ♦ **straightforwardly** ADV *His daughter says straightforwardly that he was not good enough.*

⭐ **strain** /streɪn/ **strains, straining, strained.** [1] N-VAR If **strain** is put on a person or organization, they have to do more than they are really able to do. *The prison service is already under considerable strain. ...the stresses and strains of a busy and demanding career.* [2] N-UNCOUNT **Strain** is an injury to a muscle in your body, caused by using it too much or twisting it awkwardly. *Avoid muscle strain by warming up.* [3] VERB To **strain** something means to make it do more than it is really able to do. *The volume of scheduled flights is straining the air traffic control system.* [4] VERB If you **strain** a muscle, you injure it by using it suddenly or too much. [5] VERB If you **strain to** do something, you make a great effort to do it. *Several thousand supporters strained to catch a glimpse of the new president.* [6] VERB When you **strain** food, you separate the liquid part of it from the solid parts by sieving it.

strained /streɪnd/. [1] ADJ If someone's appearance, voice, or behaviour is **strained**, they seem worried and nervous. *His laughter seemed a little strained.* [2] ADJ If relations between people are **strained**, their relationship has become difficult because they no longer like or trust each other.

strait /streɪt/ **straits.** [1] N-COUNT You can refer to a narrow strip of sea which joins two large areas of sea as a **strait** or **the straits**. [2] N-PLURAL If someone is **in dire straits** or **in desperate**

straits, they are in a very difficult situation. *The company's closure has left many small businessmen in desperate financial straits.*

strand /strænd/ **strands, stranding, stranded.** [1] N-COUNT A **strand of** thread, wire, or hair is a thin piece of it. [2] N-COUNT A **strand of** a plan, theory, or story is one aspect of it. *He's trying to bring together various strands of radical philosophic thought.* [3] VERB If you **are stranded**, you are prevented from leaving a place, for example because of bad weather. *Hundreds of motorists are preparing to spend a second night stranded in their cars.*

⭐ **strange** /streɪndʒ/ **stranger, strangest.** [1] ADJ **Strange** means unusual or unexpected. *I had a strange dream... There was something strange about the flickering blue light.* ♦ **strangely** ADV *The hut suddenly seemed strangely silent... Strangely, the race didn't start until 8.15pm.* ♦ **strangeness** N-UNCOUNT *There was a strangeness in her manner.* [2] ADJ BEFORE N A **strange** person or place is one that you do not know. *I ended up alone in a strange city.*

stranger /'streɪndʒə/ **strangers.** [1] N-COUNT A **stranger** is someone you have not met before or do not know at all. If two people are **strangers**, they have never met or do not know each other at all. *Telling a complete stranger about your life is difficult.* [2] N-COUNT If you are a **stranger** in a place, you do not know the place at all. If you are a **stranger to** something, you have had no experience of it or do not understand it. *I'm a stranger here... He is no stranger to controversy.*

USAGE You do not use **stranger** to talk about someone who comes from a country which is not your own. You can refer to him or her as a **foreigner**, but this word can sound rather rude. It is better to talk about **someone from abroad**.

---

strangle /'stræŋgəl/ **strangles, strangling, strangled.** [1] VERB To **strangle** someone means to kill them by tightly squeezing their throat. [2] VERB To **strangle** something means to prevent it from developing or succeeding. *The country's economic plight is strangling its scientific institutions.*

stranglehold /'stræŋgəlhəʊld/ **strangleholds.** N-COUNT To have a **stranglehold** on something means to have control over it and prevent it being free or developing. *The troops are tightening their stranglehold on the city... It took the country over 40 years to break the stranglehold of the old system.*

strap /stræp/ **straps, strapping, strapped.** [1] N-COUNT A **strap** is a narrow piece of leather, cloth, or other material. Straps are used to carry things or hold them in place. *...the strap of her beach bag... I undid my watch strap.* [2] VERB If you **strap** something somewhere, you fasten it there with a strap.

strata /ˈstrɑːtə, AM ˈstreɪtə/. **Strata** is the plural of **stratum**.

⭐ **strategic** /strəˈtiːdʒɪk/. [1] ADJ **Strategic** means relating to the most important, general aspects of something such as a military operation or political policy. ...*a strategic plan for reducing infant mortality.* ♦ **strategically** ADV ...*strategically important roads.* [2] ADJ **Strategic** weapons are very powerful, long-range weapons, and the decision to use them can be made only by a political leader. [3] ADJ If you put something in a **strategic** position, you place it cleverly in a position where it will be most useful or have the most effect. ♦ **strategically** ADV ...*a strategically placed chair.*

strategist /ˈstrætədʒɪst/ **strategists.** N-COUNT A **strategist** is someone who is skilled in planning the best way to achieve something, especially in war.

⭐ **strategy** /ˈstrætədʒi/ **strategies.** [1] N-VAR A **strategy** is a general plan or set of plans intended to achieve something, especially over a long period. [2] N-UNCOUNT **Strategy** is the art of planning the best way to achieve something, especially in war. ...*military strategy.*

stratum /ˈstrɑːtəm, AM ˈstreɪtəm/ **strata.** N-COUNT A **stratum of** society is a group of people in it who are similar in their social class. [FORMAL] ...*the lower strata of American society.*

straw /strɔː/ **straws.** [1] N-UNCOUNT **Straw** is the dried yellowish stalks from crops such as wheat or barley. [2] N-COUNT A **straw** is a thin tube of paper or plastic, which you use to suck a drink into your mouth. [3] PHRASE If you say that an event is **the last straw**, you mean that it is the latest in a series of unpleasant events, and makes you feel that you cannot tolerate a situation any longer.

strawberry /ˈstrɔːbri, AM -beri/ **strawberries.** N-COUNT A **strawberry** is a small red fruit with tiny seeds in its skin. → See picture on page 821.

stray /streɪ/ **strays, straying, strayed.** [1] VERB If someone **strays** somewhere, they wander away from where they should be. *Tourists often get lost and stray into dangerous areas.* [2] ADJ BEFORE N & N-COUNT A **stray** dog or cat has wandered away from its owner's home. A **stray** is a stray dog or cat. [3] VERB If your mind or your eyes **stray**, you do not concentrate on or look at one particular subject, but start thinking about or looking at other things. *She could not keep her eyes from straying towards him.* [4] ADJ BEFORE N **Stray** things have become separated from other similar things. ...*a stray lock of hair.*

streak /striːk/ **streaks, streaking, streaked.** [1] N-COUNT A **streak** is a long narrow stripe or mark on something. *A streak of orange smoke shot up into the sky.* [2] VERB If something **streaks** a surface, it makes streaks on it. *His face was pale and streaked with dirt.* [3] N-COUNT If someone has a **streak of** a particular type of behaviour, they sometimes behave in that way. *There is a streak of*

madness in us both. [4] VERB To **streak** somewhere means to move there very quickly. *A meteorite streaked across the sky.*

⭐ **stream** /striːm/ **streams, streaming, streamed.** [1] N-COUNT A **stream** is a small narrow river. [2] N-COUNT A **stream of** things is a large number of them occurring one after another. ...*a never-ending stream of jokes... We had a constant stream of visitors.* [3] VERB If a mass of people, liquid, or light **streams** somewhere, it enters or moves there in large amounts. *Refugees have been streaming into Travnik for months... Tears streamed down their faces.*

streamline /ˈstriːmlaɪn/ **streamlines, streamlining, streamlined.** VERB To **streamline** an organization or process means to make it more efficient by removing unnecessary parts of it. *They have streamlined application procedures.* ♦ **streamlined** ADJ ...*the streamlined organisations of the future.*

streamlined /ˈstriːmlaɪnd/. ADJ A **streamlined** object or animal has a shape that allows it to move quickly or efficiently through air or water.

⭐ **street** /striːt/ **streets.** [1] N-COUNT A **street** is a road in a town or village, usually with houses along it. *He walked briskly down the street.* ...*activities to keep young people off the streets.* [2] N-COUNT You can use **the street** or **the streets** when talking about activities that happen out of doors in a town rather than in a building. *Changing money on the street is illegal. ...street theatre.* [3] PHRASE If you talk about **the man in the street**, you mean ordinary people in general. *What does all this mean for the man in the street?*

streetcar /ˈstriːtkɑː/ **streetcars.** N-COUNT In American English, a **streetcar** is an electric vehicle for carrying people which travels on rails in the streets of a town. The British word is **tram**.

'street crime. N-UNCOUNT **Street crime** refers to crimes such as vandalism, car theft and mugging.

⭐ **strength** /streŋθ/ **strengths.** [1] N-UNCOUNT Your **strength** is the physical energy that you have, which gives you the ability to do things such as lift heavy objects. *He threw it forward with all his strength... You don't need strength to take part in this sport.* [2] N-UNCOUNT Someone's **strength** in a difficult situation is their courage and determination. *Something gave me the strength to overcome the difficulty... She had often displayed great strength of character.* [3] N-VAR Someone's **strengths** are the qualities and abilities that they have which are an advantage to them, or which make them successful. *Take into account your own strengths and weaknesses... The novel's greatest strength is its portrayal of daily life.* [4] N-UNCOUNT The **strength** of an object or material is its ability to be treated roughly or to support heavy weights. *He checked the strength of the cables.* [5] N-UNCOUNT The **strength** of a person, organization, or country is the power and influence that they have because they are successful. [6] N-UNCOUNT If you refer to **the strength of** a feeling, opinion, or belief, you are

⭐ Bank of English® frequent word   For a full explanation of all grammatical labels, see pages vii–x

a b c d e f g h i j k l m n o p q r s t u v w x y z

talking about how deeply it is felt or believed by people, or how much they are influenced by it. *He was surprised at the strength of his own feeling.* **7** N-UNCOUNT The **strength** of a group of people is the total number of people in it. *...elite forces, comprising about one-tenth of the strength of the army.*

PHRASES ● If a person or organization **goes from strength to strength**, they become more and more successful or confident. ● If one thing is done **on the strength of** another, it is done because of the influence of that other thing. *On the strength of those grades, he won a scholarship to Syracuse University.*

⭐ **strengthen** /'streŋθən/ **strengthens, strengthening, strengthened.** VERB To **strengthen** something means to make it stronger. *Cycling strengthens all the muscles of the body.*

strenuous /'strenjʊəs/. ADJ A **strenuous** action or activity involves a lot of effort or energy. *Avoid strenuous exercise in the evening... She made strenuous efforts to pay off her debts.* ♦ **strenuously** ADV *The former ambassador has strenuously denied the allegations.*

⭐ **stress** /stres/ **stresses, stressing, stressed.** **1** VERB & N-UNCOUNT If you **stress** a point, or if you lay **stress on** it, you emphasize it because you think it is important. *Sir Colin was keen to stress that the technology division was doing particularly well. ...the military's stress on tradition and continuity.* **2** N-VAR If you feel under **stress**, you feel worried and tense because of difficulties in your life. *She was suffering from stress. ...the stresses of modern living.* **3** N-VAR **Stresses** are strong physical pressures applied to an object. *Earthquakes happen when stresses in rock are suddenly released as the rocks fracture.* **4** VERB & N-VAR If you **stress** a word or part of a word when you say it, you put emphasis called **stress** on it, so that it sounds slightly louder. *The stress falls on the last syllable.*

stressed /strest/. ADJ If you feel **stressed**, you feel tension and anxiety because of difficulties in your life.

stressful /'stresfʊl/. ADJ A **stressful** situation or experience causes someone to feel stress.

⭐ **stretch** /stretʃ/ **stretches, stretching, stretched.** **1** VERB Something that **stretches** over an area or distance covers or exists in the whole of that area or distance. *Vast forests stretched the length of the valley... The procession stretched for several miles.* **2** N-COUNT A **stretch of** land or water is a length or area of it. **3** VERB When you **stretch**, or when you **stretch** your arms or legs, you put your arms or legs out straight and tighten your muscles. *He yawned and stretched.* **4** N-COUNT A **stretch of** time is a period of time. *...an 18-month stretch in the army.* **5** VERB When something soft or elastic **stretches**, or when it **is stretched**, it becomes longer or bigger as well as thinner, usually because it is pulled. *The cables are designed not to stretch.* **6** VERB If something **stretches** your money or resources, it uses them up so you have

hardly enough for your needs. ♦ **stretched** ADJ *...the company's stretched finances.*

▸**stretch out.** **1** PHR-VERB If you **stretch out**, or if you **stretch yourself out**, you lie with your legs and body in a straight line. *I stretched out in the bottom of the boat and closed my eyes.* **2** PHR-VERB If you **stretch out** a part of your body, you hold it out straight. *He was about to stretch out his hand to grab me.*

stretcher /'stretʃə/ **stretchers.** N-COUNT A **stretcher** is a long piece of canvas with a pole along each side, which is used to carry an injured person.

strewn /struːn/. ADJ If a place is **strewn with** things, they are scattered everywhere in it. *The room was strewn with books. ...the rock-strewn hillside.*

stricken /'strɪkən/. ADJ If a person or place is **stricken by** something such as an unpleasant feeling, illness, or natural disaster, they are severely affected by it. *...a family stricken by cancer. ...the drought-stricken region of Tigray.*

⭐ **strict** /strɪkt/ **stricter, strictest.** **1** ADJ A **strict** rule or order is very precise or severe and must be obeyed absolutely. *She gave me strict instructions not to say anything.* ♦ **strictly** ADV *The acceptance of new members is strictly controlled.* **2** ADJ A **strict** person does not tolerate behaviour which is not polite or obedient, especially from children. *My parents were very strict.* ♦ **strictly** ADV *My own mother was brought up very strictly.* **3** ADJ BEFORE N The **strict** meaning of something is its precise meaning. *It's not quite peace in the strictest sense of the word, rather the absence of war.* ♦ **strictly** ADV *Actually, that is not strictly true... Strictly speaking, it is not one house at all, but three houses joined together.* **4** ADJ BEFORE N You use **strict** to describe someone who never does things that are against their beliefs. For example, a **strict** vegetarian never eats meat.

strictly /'strɪktli/. ADV You use **strictly** to emphasize that something is of one particular type, or intended for one particular thing or person, rather than any other. *He seemed fond of her in a strictly professional way... Early horse racing in Virginia was strictly for aristocrats.*

stride /straɪd/ **strides, striding, strode.** **1** VERB If you **stride** somewhere, you walk there with quick long steps. *He turned abruptly and strode off down the corridor.* **2** N-COUNT A **stride** is a long step which you take when you are walking or running. **3** N-COUNT If you **make strides** in something that you are doing, you make rapid progress in it. *The country has made enormous strides politically.* **4** PHRASE In British English, if you **take** a difficult situation **in your stride**, you deal with it calmly and easily. The American expression is **take** something **in stride**. *She has learned to take criticism in her stride.*

strident /'straɪdənt/. **1** ADJ If you use **strident** to describe someone or the way they express themselves, you disapprove of the noticeable or

A B C D E F G H I J K L M N O P Q R S T U V W X Y Z

persistent way that they make their feelings or opinions known. ...*the unnecessarily strident tone of the President's remarks.* [2] ADJ A **strident** voice or sound is loud and unpleasant.

strife /straɪf/. N-UNCOUNT **Strife** is strong disagreement or fighting. *Money is a major cause of strife in many marriages.*

⭐ **strike** /straɪk/ **strikes, striking, struck.** [1] N-COUNT & VERB When workers go **on strike**, or when they **strike**, they stop working for a period of time, usually to try to get better pay or conditions. *Staff at the hospital went on strike in protest at the incidents... They shouldn't be striking for more money.* ♦ **striker, strikers** N-COUNT *The strikers want higher wages.* [2] VERB If you **strike** someone or something, you deliberately hit them. [FORMAL] *She took two quick steps forward and struck him across the mouth.* [3] VERB If something that is falling or moving **strikes** something, it hits it. [FORMAL] *His head struck the bottom when he dived into the 6ft end of the pool.* [4] VERB To **strike** someone or something means to attack them or to affect them, quickly and violently. *The killer says he will strike again... A powerful earthquake struck the Italian island of Sicily.* [5] N-COUNT A military **strike** is a military attack. [6] VERB If an idea or thought **strikes** you, it suddenly comes into your mind. *It suddenly struck me that I was wasting my time.* [7] VERB If something **strikes** you **as** being a particular thing, it gives you the impression of being that thing. *He struck me as a very serious but friendly person.* [8] PASSIVE-VERB If you **are struck** by something, you think it is very impressive, noticeable, or interesting. *She was struck by his energy.* [9] VERB You can use **strike** to indicate that you arrive at an agreement, decision, or situation. *You have to strike a balance between sleep and homework... I was struck dumb by this and had to think it over for a moment.* [10] VERB If something **strikes** fear or terror into people, it makes them very frightened or anxious. [11] VERB When a clock **strikes**, its bells make a sound to indicate what the time is. *The clock struck nine.* [12] VERB If you **strike** a match, you make it produce a flame by moving it quickly against something rough. [13] VERB To **strike** oil or gold means to discover it in the ground as a result of mining or drilling.
▶ **strike down.** PHR-VERB If someone **is struck down**, especially by an illness, they are killed or severely harmed. [WRITTEN] *Frank had been struck down by a massive heart attack.*
▶ **strike off.** PHR-VERB If a doctor or lawyer **is struck off**, their name is removed from the official register and they are not allowed to practise their profession.
▶ **strike out.** [1] PHR-VERB If you **strike out** in a particular direction, you start travelling in that direction. *They left the car and struck out along the muddy track.* [2] PHR-VERB If you **strike out**, you begin to do something different, often

because you want to become more independent. *She wanted me to strike out on my own.*
▶ **strike up.** PHR-VERB When you **strike up** a conversation or friendship, you begin it.

striker /ˈstraɪkə/ **strikers.** N-COUNT In football and some other team sports, a **striker** is a player whose main job is to attack and score goals.

⭐ **striking** /ˈstraɪkɪŋ/. [1] ADJ Something that is **striking** is very noticeable or unusual. *He bears a striking resemblance to Lenin.* ♦ **strikingly** ADV *The men really were strikingly similar.* [2] ADJ A **striking** person is very attractive. ...*the striking blond actor.* ♦ **strikingly** ADV ...*a strikingly handsome man.*

⭐ **string** /strɪŋ/ **strings, stringing, strung.** [1] N-VAR **String** is thin rope made of twisted threads, used for tying things together or tying up parcels. [2] N-COUNT A **string of** things is a number of them on a piece of string, thread, or wire. *She wore a string of pearls.* [3] N-COUNT A **string of** places or objects is a number of them that form a line. ...*a string of villages.* [4] N-COUNT The **strings** on a musical instrument such as a violin or guitar are thin pieces of tightly-stretched wire or nylon. [5] N-PLURAL The **strings** are the section of an orchestra which consists of instruments played with a bow. [6] VERB If you **string** something somewhere, you hang it up between two or more objects. *He had strung a banner across the wall.* [7] PHRASE If something is offered to you **with no strings attached**, it is offered without any special conditions. *Aid should be given to developing countries with no strings attached.*
▶ **string along.** PHR-VERB If you **string** someone **along**, you deceive them by letting them believe that you have the same desires, beliefs, or hopes as them. [INFORMAL] *She took advantage of him, stringing him along for years even after they were divorced.*
▶ **string together.** PHR-VERB If you **string** things **together**, you make them into one thing by adding them to each other, one at a time. *The speaker strung together a series of jokes.*

stringent /ˈstrɪndʒənt/. ADJ **Stringent** laws, rules, or conditions are severe or are strictly controlled. [FORMAL] ...*stringent controls on the possession of weapons.*

⭐ **strip** /strɪp/ **strips, stripping, stripped.** [1] N-COUNT A **strip of** something is a long narrow piece of it. *The simplest rag-rugs are made with strips of fabric.* [2] N-COUNT A **strip** of land or water is a long narrow area of it. [3] VERB If you **strip**, or if someone **strips** you, your clothes are removed from your body. *Women residents stripped naked in protest.* [4] VERB If someone **is stripped**, their clothes are taken off by another person, for example in order to search for hidden or illegal things. [5] VERB To **strip** someone **of** their property, rights, or titles means to take those things away from them. *The soldiers have stripped the civilians of their passports.* [6] VERB To **strip** something means to remove everything that covers it. *I stripped the beds and vacuumed the* carpets. **7** N-COUNT In a newspaper or magazine, a **comic strip** is a series of drawings which tell a story.

▶**strip away.** PHR-VERB To **strip away** something misleading or unnecessary means to remove it completely, so that people can see what is important or true. *Strip away the disputes about terminology, and most theories about these diseases look very similar.*

▶**strip off.** PHR-VERB If you **strip off**, or if you **strip** your clothes **off**, you take off your clothes. *He stripped off his wet clothes and stepped into the shower.*

stripe /straɪp/ **stripes.** N-COUNT A **stripe** is a long line which is a different colour from the areas next to it. *The walls in the front bedroom are painted with broad, pale blue and white stripes.* → See picture on page 829.

striped /straɪpt/. ADJ Something that is **striped** has stripes on it. *...striped wallpaper.*

stripper /'strɪpə/ **strippers.** N-COUNT A **stripper** is a person who earns money by taking off their clothes slowly and in a sexy way to music. *...a male stripper.*

strive /straɪv/ **strives, striving, strove** (or **strived**) **striven** (or **strived**). VERB If you **strive for** something or **strive to** do something, you make a great effort to get or do it. *The school strives to treat pupils as individuals.*

strode /strəʊd/. **Strode** is the past tense of **stride.**

⭐ **stroke** /strəʊk/ **strokes, stroking, stroked.** **1** VERB If you **stroke** someone or something, you move your hand slowly and gently over them. *He held her quietly, his hand stroking her hair.* **2** N-COUNT If someone has a **stroke**, a blood vessel in their brain bursts or gets blocked, which may kill them or cause one side of their body to be paralysed. **3** N-COUNT The **strokes** of a pen or brush are the movements or marks you make with it when you are writing or painting. *...short, upward strokes of the pencil.* **4** N-COUNT When you are swimming or rowing, your **strokes** are the repeated movements you make with your arms or the oars. *I turned and swam a few strokes further out to sea.* **5** N-COUNT A swimming **stroke** is a particular style or method of swimming. **6** N-COUNT In sports such as tennis, cricket, and golf, a **stroke** is the action of hitting the ball. **7** N-COUNT The **strokes** of a clock are the sounds that indicate each hour. *On the stroke of 12, fireworks suddenly exploded.* **8** N-SING A **stroke of** luck is something lucky that suddenly happens. *It didn't rain, which turned out to be a stroke of luck.* **9** PHRASE If something happens **at a stroke** or **in one stroke**, it happens suddenly and completely because of one single action. *How can Britain reduce its prison population in one stroke?*

stroll /strəʊl/ **strolls, strolling, strolled.** VERB & N-COUNT If you **stroll** somewhere, or if you go for a **stroll**, you walk in a slow relaxed way. *After dinner, I took a stroll round the city.*

stroller /'strəʊlə/ **strollers.** N-COUNT In American English, a **stroller** is a small chair on wheels, in which a baby or small child can sit and be wheeled around. The British word is **pushchair**.

⭐ **strong** /strɒŋ, AM strɔːŋ/ **stronger, strongest.** **1** ADJ A **strong** person is healthy with good muscles. *I'm not strong enough to carry him... His strong hand eased the bag from her.* **2** ADJ **Strong** objects or materials are not easily broken. *The vacuum flask has a strong casing, which won't crack or chip.* ◆ **strongly** ADV *The fence was very strongly built.* **3** ADJ Someone who is **strong** is confident and determined. *She had a strong and supportive sister.* **4** ADJ If you have **strong** opinions on something or express them using **strong** words, you have extreme or very definite opinions which you are willing to express or defend. *I am a strong supporter of the NHS.* ◆ **strongly** ADV *I would strongly advise against it.* **5** ADJ **Strong** action is firm and severe. *The government has said it will take strong action against any further strikes.* **6** ADJ **Strong** means great in degree or intensity. *He was surprised that his answer should have caused such a strong reaction.* ◆ **strongly** ADV *He is strongly influenced by Spanish painters.* **7** ADJ **Strong** is used to describe people or things that have all the qualities that make them likely to be successful. *She was a strong contender for Britain's Olympic team... He would have a strong case for arguing that he was unlikely to receive a fair trial.* **8** ADJ BEFORE N Your **strong** points are the things you are good at. *Discretion is not Jeremy's strong point.* **9** ADJ You use **strong** to say how many people there are in a group. For example, a group that is twenty **strong** has twenty people in it. **10** ADJ **Strong** drinks, chemicals, or drugs contain a lot of a particular substance. *...strong liquor.* **11** ADJ A **strong** colour, flavour, smell, sound, or light is intense and easily noticed. *The wine goes with strong and mild cheese alike.* ◆ **strongly** ADV *He leaned over her, smelling strongly of sweat.* **12** PHRASE If someone or something is still **going strong**, they are still alive, in good condition, or popular after a long time.

stronghold /'strɒŋhəʊld, AM 'strɔːŋ-/ **strongholds.** N-COUNT If a place is a **stronghold of** an attitude or belief, many people there have this attitude or belief. *...Europe's last stronghold of male dominance.*

strove /strəʊv/. **Strove** is a past tense of **strive.**

struck /strʌk/. **Struck** is the past tense and past participle of **strike.**

structural /'strʌktʃərəl/. ADJ **Structural** means relating to or affecting the structure of something. *...structural alterations made to the house.* ◆ **structurally** ADV *When we bought the house, it was structurally sound.*

⭐ **structure** /'strʌktʃə/ **structures, structuring, structured.** **1** N-VAR The **structure of** something is the way in which it is made, built, or organized. *...the structure of French education.* **2** N-COUNT A

structure is something that is built from or consists of parts connected together in an ordered way. *The house was a handsome four-story brick structure.* [3] VERB If you **structure** something, you arrange it in an organized pattern or system. *By structuring the course this way, we're forced to produce companies think is valuable.* ♦ **structured** ADJ ...*a much more structured training programme.*

⭐ **struggle** /'strʌɡəl/ **struggles, struggling, struggled.** [1] VERB If you **struggle to** do something difficult, you try hard to do it. *Those who have lost their jobs struggle to pay their supermarket bills.* [2] N-VAR A **struggle** is an attempt to obtain something or to defeat someone who is denying you something. *Life became a struggle for survival. ...a power struggle.* [3] VERB If you **struggle** when you are being held, you twist and turn your body in order to try to get free. *I struggled, but he was a tall man.* [4] VERB & N-COUNT If two people **struggle with** each other, or if they are in a **struggle**, they fight. *He died in a struggle with prison officers.* [5] VERB If you **struggle to** move yourself or **to** move a heavy object, you manage to do it with great difficulty. *He was struggling to free himself... I struggled with my bags.* [6] N-SING An action or activity that is **a struggle** is very difficult for you to do. *Losing weight was a terrible struggle.*

strum /strʌm/ **strums, strumming, strummed.** VERB If you **strum** a guitar, you play it by moving your fingers up and down across the strings.

strung /strʌŋ/. **Strung** is the past tense and past participle of **string**.

strut /strʌt/ **struts, strutting, strutted.** [1] VERB Someone who **struts** walks in a proud way, with their head high and their chest out; used showing disapproval. *He struts around town like he owns the place.* [2] N-COUNT A **strut** is a piece of wood or metal which strengthens or supports a building or structure.

stub /stʌb/ **stubs, stubbing, stubbed.** [1] N-COUNT The **stub** of a cigarette or a pencil is the short piece which remains when the rest has been used. *...an ashtray of cigarette stubs.* [2] N-COUNT The **stub** of a cheque or ticket is the small part that you keep. [3] VERB If you **stub** your **toe**, you hurt it by accidentally kicking something.
▶**stub out.** PHR-VERB When someone **stubs out** a cigarette, they put it out by pressing it against something hard.

stubble /'stʌbəl/. [1] N-UNCOUNT **Stubble** consists of the short stalks which are left in fields after corn or wheat has been harvested. [2] N-UNCOUNT The very short hairs on a man's face when he has not shaved recently are referred to as **stubble**. *He scratched at the stubble on his jaw.*

stubborn /'stʌbən/. [1] ADJ A **stubborn** person is determined to do what they want and refuses to change their mind. *...his stubborn resistance to anything new.* ♦ **stubbornly** ADV *He stubbornly refused to tell her how he had come to be in such a state.* ♦ **stubbornness** N-UNCOUNT *His refusal to*

talk was simple stubbornness. [2] ADJ A **stubborn** stain is difficult to remove. *This treatment removes the most stubborn stains.*

stuck /stʌk/. [1] **Stuck** is the past tense and past participle of **stick**. [2] ADJ AFTER LINK-V If something is **stuck** in a particular position, it is fixed there and cannot move. *The tanker is stuck fast on the rocks.* [3] ADJ AFTER LINK-V If you are **stuck** in a place or in an unpleasant situation, you want to get away from it, but are unable to. *He was stuck in a line of slow-moving traffic.* [4] ADJ AFTER LINK-V If you **get stuck** when you are trying to do something, you are unable to continue doing it because it is too difficult. *They will be there to help if you get stuck.*

stud /stʌd/ **studs.** [1] N-COUNT **Studs** are small pieces of metal which are attached to a surface for decoration. *...a canary yellow jacket with gold studs.* [2] N-COUNT **Studs** are small round earrings attached to a bar which goes through your ear. [3] N-UNCOUNT Horses or other animals that are kept for **stud** are kept to be used for breeding.

studded /'stʌdɪd/. ADJ Something that is **studded** is decorated with studs. *...a beautiful gold bracelet studded with diamonds.*

⭐ **student** /'stjuːdənt, 'stuː-/ **students.** N-COUNT A **student** is a person who is studying at a university, college, or school. *...art students.*

⭐ **studio** /'stjuːdiəʊ, 'stuː-/ **studios.** [1] N-COUNT A **studio** is a room where a designer, painter, or photographer works. *...Giorgio Armani at work in his studio.* [2] N-COUNT A **studio** is a room where radio or television programmes, records, or films are made. *...a recording studio.*

⭐ **study** /'stʌdi/ **studies, studying, studied.** [1] VERB & N-VAR If you **study**, or if you do a course of **study**, you spend time learning about a particular subject or subjects. *Kids would rather play than study... He studied History and Economics... It enabled students to devote more time to their studies.* [2] N-COUNT A **study of** a subject is a piece of research on it. *...the first study of English children's attitudes.* [3] N-PLURAL **Studies** are educational subjects. *...a business studies course.* [4] VERB If you **study** something, you look at it or consider it carefully. *He studied her face for a moment.* [5] N-COUNT A **study** in a house is a room used for reading, writing, and studying. [6] See also **case study**.

⭐ **stuff** /stʌf/ **stuffs, stuffing, stuffed.** [1] N-UNCOUNT You can use **stuff** to refer to things in a general way, without mentioning the things themselves by name. *Don't tell me you still believe in all that stuff? ...a place to buy computer stuff... He pointed to a duffle bag. 'That's my stuff.'* [2] VERB If you **stuff** something somewhere, you push it there quickly and roughly. *I stuffed my hands in my pockets.* [3] VERB If you **stuff** a container or space **with** something, you fill it with something or with a quantity of things until it is full. *...wallets stuffed with dollars.* [4] VERB If you **stuff** a bird such as a chicken, or a vegetable such as a pepper, you put a mixture of food inside it before cooking it. [5] VERB If a dead animal **is stuffed**, it is filled with a substance so that it can be preserved and displayed.

stuffing /'stʌfɪŋ/ **stuffings.** [1] N-VAR **Stuffing** is a mixture of food that is put inside a bird such as a chicken before it is cooked. [2] N-UNCOUNT **Stuffing** is material that is put inside cushions or soft toys to fill them and make them firm.

stuffy /'stʌfi/ **stuffier, stuffiest.** [1] ADJ If you describe a person or institution as **stuffy**, you are criticizing them for being formal and old-fashioned. [INFORMAL] *Why were grown-ups always so stuffy and slow to recognize good ideas?* [2] ADJ If a place is **stuffy**, it is unpleasantly warm and there is not enough fresh air. *...that stuffy, overheated apartment.*

stumble /'stʌmbəl/ **stumbles, stumbling, stumbled.** [1] VERB If you **stumble**, you nearly fall while walking or running. *I stumbled sideways before landing flat on my back.* [2] VERB If you **stumble** while speaking, you make a mistake, and have to pause before saying the words properly. *She stumbled slightly over her words sometimes.*
▸**stumble across** or **stumble on.** PHR-VERB If you **stumble across** something, or if you **stumble on** something, you discover it unexpectedly. *You may be fortunate enough to stumble across a village fiesta.*

'stumbling block, stumbling blocks. N-COUNT A **stumbling block** is a problem which stops you from achieving something. *This issue has turned out to be the main stumbling block to convening the peace conference.*

stump /stʌmp/ **stumps, stumping, stumped.** [1] N-COUNT A **stump** is a small part of something that remains when the rest of it has been removed or broken off. *...a tree stump.* [2] VERB If a question or problem **stumps** you, you cannot think of any solution or answer to it.
▸**stump up.** PHR-VERB If you **stump up** a sum of money, you pay the money that is required for something, often reluctantly. [BRITISH, INFORMAL] *Customers do not have to stump up any cash for at least four weeks.*

stun /stʌn/ **stuns, stunning, stunned.** [1] VERB If you **are stunned** by something, you are shocked or astonished by it and are therefore unable to speak or do anything. *Many cinema-goers were stunned by the film's violent and tragic end.*
♦ **stunned** ADJ *When they told me she had gone missing I was totally stunned.* [2] VERB If a blow on the head **stuns** you, it makes you unconscious or confused and unsteady. ● See also **stunning**.

stung /stʌŋ/. **Stung** is the past tense and past participle of **sting**.

stunk /stʌŋk/. **Stunk** is the past participle of **stink**.

stunning /'stʌnɪŋ/. ADJ A **stunning** person or thing is extremely beautiful or impressive. *...how the top supermodels manage to look stunning. ...a stunning display of fireworks.* ♦ **stunningly** ADV *...stunningly beautiful countryside.*

stunt /stʌnt/ **stunts, stunting, stunted.** [1] N-COUNT A **stunt** is something interesting that someone does to get attention or publicity. *...turning her wedding into a publicity stunt.* [2] N-COUNT A **stunt** is a dangerous and exciting piece of action in a film. *The team will perform daily stunts including ramp-to-ramp jumps.* [3] VERB If something **stunts** the growth or development of a person or thing, it prevents them from growing or developing normally. *...a bone disease that stunted her growth. ...The blackthorns were so stunted they looked like plants rather than bushes.*

★ **stupid** /'stjuːpɪd, AM 'stuː-/ **stupider, stupidest.** [1] ADJ If you say that someone or something is **stupid**, you mean that they show a lack of good judgement or intelligence and they are not at all sensible. *How could I have been so stupid?... I made a stupid mistake.* ♦ **stupidly** ADV *We had stupidly been looking at the wrong column of figures.* ♦ **stupidity** /stjuː'pɪdɪti, AM stuː-/ **stupidities** N-VAR *I stared at him, astonished by his stupidity.* [2] ADJ You say that something is **stupid** to indicate that you do not like it or that it annoys you. [INFORMAL] *Friendship is much more important to me than a stupid old ring!*

sturdy /'stɜːdi/ **sturdier, sturdiest.** ADJ Someone or something that is **sturdy** looks strong and is unlikely to be easily injured or damaged. *She was a short, sturdy woman.* ♦ **sturdily** ADV *...a tall, sturdily-built man.*

stutter /'stʌtə/ **stutters, stuttering, stuttered.** VERB & N-COUNT If someone **stutters**, or if they have a **stutter**, they have difficulty speaking because they keep repeating the first sound of a word. *He spoke with a pronounced stutter.* ♦ **stuttering** N-UNCOUNT *Gerard had suffered in school with his stuttering and stammering.*

★ **style** /staɪl/ **styles, styling, styled.** [1] N-COUNT The **style** of something is the general way it is done or presented. *Kenny's writing style is clear and straightforward. ...American-style management.* [2] N-UNCOUNT If places or people have **style**, they are smart and elegant. *Bournemouth, you have to admit, has style.* [3] N-VAR The **style** of a product is its design. *Several styles of hat were available... Each design is very different in style... Guests have been asked to dress 1920s-style.* [4] VERB If something such as a car or someone's hair **is styled** in a particular way, it is designed or shaped in that way. *His thick blond hair had just been styled before his trip. ...classically styled clothes.*

stylish /'staɪlɪʃ/. ADJ Someone or something that is **stylish** is smart, elegant, and fashionable. *...the stylish shops of Buchanan Street.* ♦ **stylishly** ADV *...stylishly dressed middle-aged women.*

stylistic /staɪ'lɪstɪk/. ADJ **Stylistic** describes things relating to the methods and techniques used in creating a piece of writing, music, or art. ♦ **stylistically** ADV *Stylistically, this book is a very different one from Remains of The Day.*

stylized (BRIT also **stylised**) /'staɪlaɪzd/. ADJ Something that is **stylized** uses various artistic conventions in order to create an effect. ...*highly stylised furniture designs.*

suave /swɑːv/ **suaver, suavest.** ADJ If you describe a man as **suave**, you think he is charming, polite, and elegant, but not sincere.

sub /sʌb/ **subs.** ① N-COUNT In team games such as football, a **sub** is a player who is brought into a match to replace another player. [BRITISH] *Connell joined Hegarty on the subs' bench.* ② N-COUNT A **sub** is a **submarine**. [INFORMAL]

subcommittee (or **sub-committee**) /'sʌbkəmɪti/ **subcommittees.** N-COUNT A **subcommittee** is a small committee made up of members of a larger committee.

subconscious /ˌsʌb'kɒnʃəs/. ① N-SING Your **subconscious** is the part of your mind that can influence you even though you are not aware of it. *The memory of it all was locked deep in my subconscious.* ② ADJ A **subconscious** feeling or action exists in or is influenced by your subconscious. ...*a subconscious cry for affection.*
♦ **subconsciously** ADV *Subconsciously I had known that I would not be in personal danger.*

subculture /'sʌbkʌltʃə/ **subcultures.** N-COUNT A **subculture** consists of the ideas, art, and way of life of a particular group within a society, which are different from those of the rest of the society. ...*the violent subculture of London youth gangs.*

subdivision /ˌsʌbdɪ'vɪʒən/ **subdivisions.** N-COUNT ① A **subdivision** is an area or section which is a part of a larger area or section. *Months are a conventional subdivision of the year.* ② N-COUNT A **subdivision** is an area of land for building houses on. [AMERICAN] ...*a 400-home subdivision.*

subdue /səb'djuː, AM -'duː/ **subdues, subduing, subdued.** VERB If soldiers or the police **subdue** a group of people, they defeat them or bring them under control by using force. *They have not been able to subdue the rebels.*

subdued /səb'djuːd, AM -'duːd/. ① ADJ Someone who is **subdued** is quiet, often because they are sad. *The audience are strangely subdued, clapping politely after each song.* ② ADJ **Subdued** lights, feelings, sounds, or colours are not very noticeable. ...*a night-club atmosphere with subdued lighting.*

⭐ **subject, subjects, subjecting, subjected.** ① N-COUNT /'sʌbdʒɪkt/ The **subject of** a conversation, letter, or book is the person or thing that is being discussed or written about. *We got on to the subject of relationships... Their epic fight is the subject of a new film... He's now the subject of an official inquiry.* ② N-COUNT A **subject** is an area of knowledge that is studied at school, college, or university. *Mathematics was voted their favourite subject.* ③ N-COUNT In grammar, the **subject** of a clause is the noun group which refers to the person or thing that does the action expressed by the verb. For example, in 'My cat keeps catching birds', 'my cat' is the subject. ④ ADJ

AFTER LINK-V If someone or something is **subject to** something, they are affected, or likely to be affected, by it. *Prices may be subject to alteration.* ⑤ PREP If an event will take place **subject to** a condition, it will take place only if that condition exists. *Tickets for both offers, subject to availability, can be collected from the information desk.* ⑥ N-COUNT The people who live in or belong to a particular country, usually one ruled by a monarch, are the **subjects** of that monarch or country. ...*British subjects.* ⑦ VERB /səb'dʒekt/ If you **subject** someone **to** something unpleasant, you make them experience it. ...*the man who had subjected her to four years of beatings.*

subjective /səb'dʒektɪv/. ADJ Something that is **subjective** is based on personal opinions and feelings. *Taste in art is a subjective matter.*
♦ **subjectively** ADV *She subjectively rated herself a winner.* ♦ **subjectivity** N-UNCOUNT ...*the film-maker's subjectivity.*

'subject matter. N-UNCOUNT The **subject matter** of a conversation, book, or film is the thing, person, or idea that is being discussed, written about, or shown. *Artists were given greater freedom in their choice of subject matter.*

subjunctive /səb'dʒʌŋktɪv/. N-SING In English, a clause expressing a wish or suggestion can be put in **the subjunctive**, or in **the subjunctive mood**, by using the base form of a verb or 'were'. An example is 'He asked that they all be removed'.

sublime /sə'blaɪm/. ADJ & N-SING If you describe something as **sublime**, or as **the sublime**, you mean that it has a wonderful quality that affects you deeply. [LITERARY] *She elevated every rare small success to the sublime.*

submarine /ˌsʌbmə'riːn/ **submarines.** N-COUNT A **submarine** is a ship that can travel below the surface of the sea.

submerge /səb'mɜːdʒ/ **submerges, submerging, submerged.** ① VERB If something **submerges**, it goes below the surface of the water. *The river burst its banks, submerging an entire village.* ② VERB If you **submerge yourself in** an activity, you give all your attention to it. *Vicky tried to submerge herself in her work.*

submission /səb'mɪʃən/. ① N-UNCOUNT **Submission** is a state in which people accept that they are under the control of someone else. *Singapore island was being bombed, shelled, and starved into submission.* ② N-UNCOUNT The **submission of** a proposal or application is the act of sending it to someone, so they can decide whether to accept it or not. [FORMAL]

submissive /səb'mɪsɪv/. ADJ If you are **submissive**, you behave in a quiet obedient way.
♦ **submissively** ADV *The troops submissively lay down their weapons.*

submit /səb'mɪt/ **submits, submitting, submitted.** ① VERB If you **submit to** something, you accept it reluctantly, for example because you are not powerful enough to resist it. *Mrs. Jones submitted*

A
B
C
D
E
F
G
H
I
J
K
L
M
N
O
P
Q
R
S
T
U
V
W
X
Y
Z

to an operation on her right knee. ② VERB If you **submit** a proposal or application to someone, you send it to them so they can decide whether to accept it or not. *Head teachers yesterday submitted a claim for a 9 per cent pay rise.*

subordinate, subordinates, subordinating, subordinated. ① N-COUNT /sə'bɔːdɪnət/ Your **subordinate** is someone who is in a less important position than you in the organization that you both work for. ② ADJ Something or someone who is **subordinate** to something or someone else is considered to be less important than the other thing or person. *Science became subordinate to technology... Women were regarded as subordinate to free men.* ③ VERB /sə'bɔːdɪneɪt/ If you **subordinate** one thing **to** another, you treat it as less important than the other thing. *...subordinating Spain to wider American defence needs.* ♦ **subordination** N-UNCOUNT *...governmental subordination to the president.*

sub,ordinate 'clause, subordinate clauses. N-COUNT A **subordinate clause** is a clause in a sentence which adds to the information given in the main clause. It cannot usually stand alone as a sentence.

subscribe /səb'skraɪb/ **subscribes, subscribing, subscribed.** ① VERB If you **subscribe to** an opinion or belief, you are one of a number of people who have this opinion or belief. *Most scientists subscribe to the idea that salt increases water retention.* ② VERB If you **subscribe to** a service, magazine, or organization, you pay money regularly to receive the service or magazine, or to belong to or support the organization. *...computer-users who subscribe to the Internet.* ♦ **subscriber, subscribers** N-COUNT *I have been a subscriber to Railway Magazine for many years.*

subscription /səb'skrɪpʃən/ **subscriptions.** N-COUNT A **subscription** is an amount of money that you pay regularly to receive a service or magazine, or to belong to or support an organization.

⭐ **subsequent** /'sʌbsɪkwənt/. ADJ BEFORE N **Subsequent** means existing or happening after the time or event that has just been referred to. *The book was banned in the US, as were two subsequent books.* ♦ **subsequently** ADV *He was born in Hong Kong where he subsequently practised as a lawyer.*

subservient /səb'sɜːviənt/. ① ADJ If you are **subservient**, you do whatever someone wants you to do. *Verbal abuse was used to keep the women subservient.* ♦ **subservience** N-UNCOUNT *...obedience and subservience to authority.* ② ADJ AFTER LINK-V If you treat one thing as **subservient to** another, you treat it as less important than the other thing. *...the philosophy that the weak should be subservient to the strong.*

subside /səb'saɪd/ **subsides, subsiding, subsided.** ① VERB If a feeling or sound **subsides**, it becomes less strong or loud. *Catherine's sobs finally subsided.* ② VERB If the ground or a

building **is subsiding**, it is sinking to a lower level.

subsidiary /səb'sɪdiəri, AM -dieri/ **subsidiaries.** ① N-COUNT A **subsidiary** is a company which is part of a larger and more important company. *...British Asia Airways, a subsidiary of British Airways.* ② ADJ If something is **subsidiary**, it is less important than something else with which it is connected. *All the undergraduates take two subjects for their honours degree, and two subsidiary subjects.*

subsidize (BRIT also **subsidise**) /'sʌbsɪdaɪz/ **subsidizes, subsidizing, subsidized.** VERB If an authority **subsidizes** something, they pay part of the cost of it. *Governments have subsidized the housing of middle and upper-income groups.* ♦ **subsidized** ADJ *...Scotland's subsidised theatre.*

⭐ **subsidy** /'sʌbsɪdi/ **subsidies.** N-VAR A **subsidy** is money paid by an authority in order to help an industry or business, or to pay for a public service. *...farming subsidies.*

subsistence /səb'sɪstəns/. N-UNCOUNT **Subsistence** is the condition of only having just enough food or money to stay alive.

⭐ **substance** /'sʌbstəns/ **substances.** ① N-COUNT A **substance** is a solid, powder, liquid, or gas. *...a crumbly black substance that smells like fresh soil.* ② N-UNCOUNT **Substance** is the quality of being important or significant. [FORMAL] *Why do we chatter so wittily but say nothing of any substance?* ③ N-SING **The substance of** what someone says or writes is the main thing that they are trying to say. ④ N-UNCOUNT If you say that something has no **substance**, you mean that it is not true. [FORMAL] *There is no substance in any of these allegations.*

⭐ **substantial** /səb'stænʃəl/. ① ADJ **Substantial** means large in amount or degree. *That is a very substantial improvement.* ♦ **substantially** ADV *Firms still expect to cut jobs substantially in the months ahead.* ② ADJ A **substantial** building is large and strongly built. *...a substantial late Victorian house.*

substantially /səb'stænʃəli/. ① ADV If something is **substantially** correct, it is generally correct. [FORMAL] *He checked the details given and found them substantially correct.* ② See also **substantial**.

substantiate /səb'stænʃieɪt/ **substantiates, substantiating, substantiated.** VERB To **substantiate** a statement or a story means to supply evidence proving that it is true. [FORMAL] *There is little scientific evidence to substantiate the claims.*

substantive /səb'stæntɪv/. ADJ **Substantive** issues, questions, or talks are meaningful and important. [FORMAL] *They are prepared to discuss substantive issues tomorrow.*

⭐ **substitute** /'sʌbstɪtjuːt, AM -tuːt/ **substitutes, substituting, substituted.** ① VERB If you **substitute** one thing **for** another, you use it instead of the other thing. *Would phone conversations substitute for cosy chats over lunch?* ♦ **substitution,**

substitutions N-VAR ...*a straight substitution of carob for chocolate.* [2] N-COUNT A **substitute** is something or someone that you use instead of something or someone else. *Reduced-calorie cheese is a great substitute for cream cheese.*

subterranean /ˌsʌbtəˈreɪniən/. ADJ A **subterranean** river or tunnel is underground. [FORMAL]

subtle /ˈsʌtəl/ **subtler, subtlest.** [1] ADJ Something **subtle** is not immediately obvious or noticeable. ...*the slow and subtle changes that take place in all living things.* ♦ **subtly** ADV *The truth is subtly different.* [2] ADJ **Subtle** smells, tastes, sounds, or colours are pleasantly complex and delicate. ♦ **subtly** ADV ...*subtly coloured rugs.*

subtlety /ˈsʌtəlti/ **subtleties.** [1] N-COUNT **Subtleties** are very small details or differences which are not obvious. ...*the subtleties of human behaviour.* [2] N-UNCOUNT **Subtlety** is the quality of not being immediately obvious or noticeable. *African dance is vigorous, but full of subtlety.* [3] N-UNCOUNT **Subtlety** is the ability to use indirect methods to achieve something. *They had obviously been hoping to approach the topic with more subtlety.*

subtract /səbˈtrækt/ **subtracts, subtracting, subtracted.** VERB If you **subtract** one number **from** another, you take the first number away from the second. ♦ **subtraction, subtractions** N-VAR *She's ready to learn simple addition and subtraction.*

suburb /ˈsʌbɜːb/ **suburbs.** N-COUNT The **suburbs** of a city are the areas on the edge of it where people live.

suburban /səˈbɜːbən/. [1] ADJ BEFORE N **Suburban** means relating to a suburb. ...*a suburban shopping centre in Sydney.* [2] ADJ If you describe something as **suburban**, you mean that it is dull and conventional. *His clothes are conservative and suburban.*

suburbia /səˈbɜːbiə/. N-UNCOUNT **Suburbia** is sometimes used to refer to the suburbs of cities and large towns considered as a whole. ...*bright summer mornings in leafy suburbia.*

subversion /səbˈvɜːʃən, AM -ʒən/. N-UNCOUNT **Subversion** is the attempt to weaken or destroy a political system or a government. *He was arrested in parliament on charges of subversion.*

subversive /səbˈvɜːsɪv/ **subversives.** [1] ADJ Something that is **subversive** is intended to weaken or destroy a political system or government. *The play was promptly banned as subversive.* [2] N-COUNT **Subversives** are people who attempt to weaken or to destroy a political system or government.

subvert /səbˈvɜːt/ **subverts, subverting, subverted.** VERB To **subvert** something means to destroy its power and influence. [FORMAL] ...*an alleged plot to subvert the state.*

subway /ˈsʌbweɪ/ **subways.** [1] N-COUNT In British English, a **subway** is a passage for pedestrians underneath a busy road. The American word is

underpass. [2] N-COUNT In American English, a **subway** is an underground railway. The British word is **underground.**

★ **succeed** /səkˈsiːd/ **succeeds, succeeding, succeeded.** [1] VERB To **succeed** means to achieve the result that you wanted or to perform in a satisfactory way. *We have succeeded in persuading cinemas to show the video.* ...*the skills and qualities needed to succeed.* [2] VERB If you **succeed** another person, you take over their job or position when they leave. *Prince Rainier III succeeded to the throne on 9 May 1949.*

★ **success** /səkˈses/ **successes.** N-UNCOUNT **Success** is the achievement of something you have wanted to achieve. *Work was the key to success... Most of the cast was amazed by the play's success.*

★ **successful** /səkˈsesfʊl/. ADJ Someone or something that is **successful** achieves a desired result or performs in a satisfactory way. *How successful will this new treatment be?... She is a successful lawyer.* ♦ **successfully** ADV *The doctors have successfully concluded preliminary tests.*

succession /səkˈseʃən/ **successions.** [1] N-COUNT A **succession of** things of the same kind is a number of them that exist or happen one after the other. *Adams took a succession of jobs. ...scoring three goals in quick succession.* [2] N-UNCOUNT **Succession** is the act or right of being the next person to have a particular job or position. *She is now seventh in line of succession to the throne.*

successive /səkˈsesɪv/. ADJ **Successive** means happening or existing one after another without a break. *Jackson was the winner for a second successive year.*

successor /səkˈsesə/ **successors.** N-COUNT Someone's **successor** is the person who takes their job after they have left.

suc'cess story, success stories. N-COUNT Someone or something that is a **success story** is very successful, often unexpectedly or in spite of unfavourable conditions.

succinct /səkˈsɪŋkt/. ADJ Something that is **succinct** expresses facts or ideas clearly and in few words; used showing approval. ♦ **succinctly** ADV *Readers are told succinctly what they need to know.*

succulent /ˈsʌkjʊlənt/. ADJ **Succulent** food is juicy and delicious. ...*succulent vegetables and well-fried chips.*

succumb /səˈkʌm/ **succumbs, succumbing, succumbed.** VERB If you **succumb to** persuasion or desire, you are unable to resist it. *Don't succumb to the temptation to have just one cigarette.*

★ **such** /sʌtʃ/. [1] PREDET & DET & PRON You use **such** to refer to the person or thing you have just mentioned or to something similar. *How can we make sense of such a story as this?... There have been previous attempts at coups. We regard such methods as entirely unacceptable... We are scared* because we are being watched – such is the atmosphere in Pristina.

> **USAGE** Such is followed by **a** when the noun is something that can be counted. ...*such a pleasant surprise.* It is not followed by **a** when the noun is plural or something that cannot be counted. ...*such beautiful women.* ...*such power.*
> You do not use **such** when you are talking about something that is present, or about the place where you are. You need to use the phrases **like that** or **like this**. For example, if you are admiring someone's watch, you do not say 'I'd like such a watch'. You say **'I'd like a watch like that'**. Similarly, you do not say about the town where you are living 'There's not much to do in such a town'. You say **'There's not much to do in a town like this'**. Such in other contexts is quite formal.

2 PREDET & DET You use **such** to emphasize the degree or extent of something. *It was such a pleasant surprise... One will never understand why these political issues can acquire such force.* PHRASES ● You use **such as** or **such...as** to introduce one or more examples of something. ...*serious offences, such as assault.* ...*such careers as teaching, nursing, hairdressing and catering.* ● You use **such...that** when saying what the result or consequence of something is. *He was in such a hurry that he almost pushed me over on the stairs... He could put an idea in such a way that Alan would believe it was his own.* ● You use **such as it is** to indicate that something is not very good, important, or useful. ...*the British Women's Movement, such as it is these days.* ● You use **as such** with a negative to indicate that a word or expression is not a very accurate description of the actual situation. *I am not a learner as such – I used to ride a bike years ago.* ● You use **as such** after a noun to indicate that you are considering that thing on its own, separately from other things or factors. *Mr Simon said he was not against taxes as such.* ● You use **such and such** to refer to something without being specific. *I said, 'Well what time'll I get to Leeds?' and he said such and such a time.*

suck /sʌk/ **sucks, sucking, sucked.** **1** VERB If you **suck** something, you hold it in your mouth and pull at it with the muscles in your cheeks and tongue, for example in order to get liquid out of it. *You may prefer to give her a dummy to suck instead... He sucked on his cigarette.* **2** VERB If something **sucks** a liquid, gas, or object in a particular direction, it draws it there with a powerful force. ...*a simple air pump that continuously sucks in the air.*

sucker /'sʌkə/ **suckers.** **1** N-COUNT If you call someone a **sucker**, you mean that it is easy to cheat or fool them. [INFORMAL] **2** N-COUNT If you describe someone as a **sucker for** something,

you mean that they find it very difficult to resist it. [INFORMAL] *I'm such a sucker for romance.* **3** N-COUNT On a plant, a **sucker** is a new growth that is sent out from the base of the plant or from its root.

⭐ **sudden** /'sʌdən/. **1** ADJ Something that is **sudden** happens quickly and unexpectedly. ...*the sudden death of her father.* ◆ **suddenly** ADV ...*David's account of why he had suddenly left London.* ◆ **suddenness** N-UNCOUNT *The enemy seemed stunned by the suddenness of the attack.* **2** PHRASE If something happens **all of a sudden**, it happens quickly and unexpectedly. *All of a sudden she fell silent.*

sue /suː/ **sues, suing, sued.** VERB If you **sue** someone, you start a legal case against them to claim money from them because they have harmed you in some way. *She threatened to sue him for unfair dismissal... If I were her, I'd sue.*

suede /sweɪd/. N-UNCOUNT **Suede** is thin soft leather with a slightly rough surface.

⭐ **suffer** /'sʌfə/ **suffers, suffering, suffered.** **1** VERB If you **suffer** pain or an illness, or if you **suffer from** a pain or illness, you are badly affected by it. *She began to suffer stomach cramps... Many team members suffered from diarrhoea.* ◆ **sufferer, sufferers** N-COUNT ...*arthritis sufferers.* **2** VERB If you **suffer** something bad, you are in a situation in which something painful, harmful, or very unpleasant happens to you. ...*the possibility that they could suffer complete defeat.* **3** VERB If you **suffer**, you are badly affected by an unfavourable event or situation. *It is the poor who have suffered most from food shortages.* **4** VERB If something **suffers**, it becomes worse in quality or condition as a result of neglect or an unfavourable situation. *I'm not surprised that your studies are suffering.*

suffering /'sʌfərɪŋ/ **sufferings.** N-VAR **Suffering** is serious pain which someone feels in their body or their mind. *He wanted to die in order to put an end to his suffering.*

suffice /sə'faɪs/ **suffices, sufficing, sufficed.** VERB If something will **suffice**, it will be enough to achieve a purpose or to fulfil a need. [FORMAL] *You don't even have to do it in person; a polite letter will suffice.*

⭐ **sufficient** /sə'fɪʃənt/. **1** ADJ If something is **sufficient** for a particular purpose, there is as much of it as is necessary. *His savings were not sufficient to cover the cost.* ◆ **sufficiently** ADV *It was many months before I had sufficiently recovered to move about.* **2** ADJ BEFORE N If something is a **sufficient** cause or condition for something to happen, it can happen. [FORMAL] *Discipline is a necessary, but certainly not a sufficient condition for learning to take place.*

suffix /'sʌfɪks/ **suffixes.** N-COUNT A **suffix** is a letter or group of letters added to the end of a word in order to form a different word, often of a different word class.

suffocate /'sʌfəkeɪt/ **suffocates, suffocating, suffocated.** VERB If someone **suffocates**, or is

suffocated, they die because there is no air for them to breathe. ✦ **suffocation** N-UNCOUNT *Many of the victims died of suffocation.*

⭐ **sugar** /'ʃʊgə/ **sugars.** 1 N-UNCOUNT **Sugar** is a sweet substance, often in the form of white or brown crystals, used to sweeten food and drink. 2 N-COUNT If someone takes **sugar** in their tea or coffee, they have one or more small spoonfuls of sugar in it. *How many sugars do you take?*

⭐ **suggest** /sə'dʒest, AM səg'dʒ-/ **suggests, suggesting, suggested.** 1 VERB If you **suggest** something, you put forward a plan or idea for someone to consider. *I suggested we walk to the park... I suggested that we should charter a boat... I suggested to Mike that we go out for a meal.*

> **USAGE** Note that **suggest** cannot usually be followed directly by a noun or pronoun referring to a person. You generally have to put the preposition **to** in front of it. You do not 'suggest someone something', you '**suggest something to someone**'. *John Caskey first suggested this idea to me.* Nor do you 'suggest someone to do something'. You '**suggest that someone does something**'. A subjunctive is sometimes used in the 'that' clause. *Beatrice suggested that he spend the summer at their place.*

2 VERB If you **suggest** that something is the case, you say something which you believe is the case. *I'm not suggesting that is what is happening.* 3 VERB If one thing **suggests** another, it implies it or makes you think that it is the case. *Earlier reports suggested that a meeting would take place on Sunday.*

⭐ **suggestion** /sə'dʒestʃən, AM səg'dʒ-/ **suggestions.** 1 N-COUNT If you make a **suggestion**, you put forward an idea or plan for someone to think about. *John made some suggestions for improvements.* 2 N-COUNT A **suggestion** is something that someone says which implies that something is the case. *There are suggestions that jealousy drove her to murder.* 3 N-SING If there is a **suggestion** of something, there is a slight sign of it. *...that fashionably faint suggestion of a tan.* 4 N-UNCOUNT **Suggestion** means giving people a particular idea by associating it with other ideas. *...the power of suggestion.*

suggestive /sə'dʒestɪv, AM səg'dʒ-/ 1 ADJ AFTER LINK-V If one thing is **suggestive of** another, it gives a hint of it or reminds you of it. *...long, curving nails suggestive of animal claws.* 2 ADJ **Suggestive** remarks cause people to think about sex, often in a way that makes them feel uncomfortable. ✦ **suggestively** ADV *She winked at him suggestively.*

suicidal /ˌsuːɪ'saɪdəl/ 1 ADJ People who are **suicidal** want to kill themselves. 2 ADJ If you describe an action or behaviour as **suicidal**, you

mean that it is very dangerous. *It would have been suicidal to attempt the descent in the dark.*

⭐ **suicide** /'suːɪsaɪd/ **suicides.** 1 N-VAR People who commit **suicide** deliberately kill themselves. *...a growing number of suicides in the community.* 2 ADJ BEFORE N The people involved in a **suicide** attack, mission, or bombing do not expect to survive. *...a suicide bomber.*

⭐ **suit** /suːt/ **suits, suiting, suited.** 1 N-COUNT A **suit** is a matching jacket and trousers, or a matching jacket and skirt. → See picture on page 820. 2 N-COUNT A **suit** can be a piece of clothing worn for a particular activity. *...bathing suits.* 3 VERB If a piece of clothing or a particular style or colour **suits** you, it makes you look attractive. 4 VERB If you say that something **suits** you, you mean that it is convenient, acceptable, or appropriate for you. *Would nine o'clock suit you?* 5 N-COUNT In a court of law, a **suit** is a legal action taken by one person against another. 6 N-COUNT A **suit** is one of the four types of card in a set of playing cards. These are hearts, diamonds, clubs, and spades. 7 PHRASE If people **follow suit**, they do what someone else has just done. *Efforts to persuade the remainder to follow suit have continued.* 8 See also **suited**.

> **USAGE** You do not use the verb **suit** if clothes are simply the right size for you. The verb you need is **fit**. *Even the smallest size doesn't fit him... The gloves didn't fit.*
> You can say that something **suits** a person or place if it looks attractive on that person or in that place. However, you cannot usually say that one colour, pattern, or object **suits** another. The verb you need is **match**. *She wears a straw hat with a yellow ribbon to match her yellow cheesecloth dress... His clothes don't quite match.*

⭐ **suitable** /'suːtəbəl/ ADJ Someone or something that is **suitable for** a particular purpose or occasion is right or acceptable for it. *She had no other dress suitable for the occasion. ...a suitable venue.* ✦ **suitability** N-UNCOUNT *...information on the suitability of a product for use in the home.* ✦ **suitably** ADV *...suitably qualified staff.*

suitcase /'suːtkeɪs/ **suitcases.** N-COUNT A **suitcase** is a case for carrying your clothes when you are travelling.

suite /swiːt/ **suites.** 1 N-COUNT A **suite** is a set of rooms in a hotel or other building. *...a new suite of offices.* 2 N-COUNT A **suite** is a set of matching furniture. 3 N-COUNT A bathroom **suite** is a matching bath, basin, and toilet.

suited /'suːtɪd/ ADJ AFTER LINK-V If something or someone is **suited** to a particular purpose or person, they are right or appropriate for that purpose or person. *Satellites are uniquely suited to*

a b c d e f g h i j k l m n o p q r s t u v w x y z

⭐ Bank of English® frequent word   For a full explanation of all grammatical labels, see pages vii–x

provide this information... As a couple they seemed ideally suited.

suitor /'suːtə/ **suitors.** N-COUNT A woman's **suitor** is a man who wants to marry her. [DATED]

sulfur /'sʌlfə/. See **sulphur**.

sulk /sʌlk/ **sulks, sulking, sulked.** VERB & N-COUNT If you **sulk**, or if you go into a **sulk**, you are silent and bad-tempered for a while because you are annoyed. If I ever beat him at anything, he'd go off and have a sulk.

sullen /'sʌlən/. ADJ A **sullen** person is bad-tempered and does not speak much. ♦ **sullenly** ADV 'I've never seen it before,' Harry said sullenly.

sulphur (AM **sulfur**) /'sʌlfə/. N-UNCOUNT **Sulphur** is a yellow chemical which has a strong unpleasant smell.

sultan /'sʌltən/ **sultans.** N-COUNT A **sultan** is a ruler in some Muslim countries.

sultry /'sʌltri/ **sultrier, sultriest.** [1] ADJ **Sultry** weather is hot and humid. [2] ADJ A **sultry** woman is attractive in a way that suggests hidden passion. [WRITTEN]

⭐ **sum** /sʌm/ **sums, summing, summed.** [1] N-COUNT A **sum** of money is an amount of it. ...the relatively modest sum of £50,000. ● See also **lump sum**. [2] N-COUNT A **sum** is a simple calculation in arithmetic. I can't do my sums. [3] N-SING In mathematics, **the sum of** two numbers is the number that is obtained when they are added together. The sum of all the angles of a triangle is 180 degrees. [4] PHRASE You use **in sum** to introduce a statement that briefly describes a situation. [FORMAL] In sum, all is proceeding as expected.

▸ **sum up.** [1] PHR-VERB If you **sum up** or **sum** something **up**, you briefly describe the main features of something. Well, to sum up, what is the message that you are trying to get across?... The atmosphere is best summed up as being peaceful. [2] See also **summing up**.

summarize (BRIT also **summarise**) /'sʌməraɪz/ **summarizes, summarizing, summarized.** VERB If you **summarize** something, you give a brief description of its main points. The article can be summarized in three sentences... To summarise, this is a clever approach to a common problem.

summary /'sʌməri/ **summaries.** [1] N-COUNT A **summary** is a short account of something giving the main points but not the details. ...a summary of the report. [2] ADJ BEFORE N **Summary** actions are done without delay and without careful consideration. [FORMAL] ...reports of summary executions. ♦ **summarily** /'sʌmeərili/ ADV Several detainees had been summarily executed.

⭐ **summer** /'sʌmə/ **summers.** N-VAR **Summer** is the season between spring and autumn. In summer the weather is usually warm or hot. → See Reference Page on Times and Dates.

'**summer camp, summer camps.** N-COUNT In the United States, a **summer camp** is a place in the country where children can stay during the school summer holidays.

summertime (or **summer time**) /'sʌmətaɪm/. N-UNCOUNT **Summertime** is the period of time during which summer lasts. It's a very beautiful place in the summertime.

,**summing 'up, summings up.** N-COUNT In a court of law, the **summing up** is a summary of all the evidence that has been presented at the trial.

⭐ **summit** /'sʌmɪt/ **summits.** [1] N-COUNT A **summit** is a meeting between the leaders of two or more countries to discuss important matters. ...last month's Arab summit in Baghdad. [2] N-COUNT The **summit** of a mountain is the top of it.

summon /'sʌmən/ **summons, summoning, summoned.** [1] VERB If you **summon** someone, you order them to come to you. The Chief summoned me downstairs. [2] VERB & PHR-VERB If you **summon** the courage, energy, or strength **to** do something, or if you **summon** it **up**, you make a great effort to do it. It took her a full month to summon the courage to tell her mother.

summons /'sʌmənz/ **summonses, summonsing, summonsed.** [1] N-COUNT A **summons** is an order to come and see someone. I received a summons to the Palace. [2] N-COUNT & VERB If someone receives a **summons**, or if they **are summonsed**, they are officially ordered to appear in a court of law. She was summonsed to appear before the magistrates.

sumptuous /'sʌmptʃuəs/. ADJ Something that is **sumptuous** is magnificent and obviously expensive. ...a variety of sumptuous fabrics.

⭐ **sun** /sʌn/ **suns.** [1] N-SING **The sun** is the ball of fire in the sky that the Earth goes round, and that gives us heat and light. The sun was low in the sky. [2] N-UNCOUNT You refer to the light and heat that reach us from the sun as **the sun**. How pleasant it would be to sit in the sun. ...environmental hazards such as wind and sun.

sunbathe /'sʌnbeɪθ/ **sunbathes, sunbathing, sunbathed.** VERB When people **sunbathe**, they sit or lie in a place where the sun shines on them, in order to get a suntan. ♦ **sunbathing** N-UNCOUNT ...a huge deck space for sunbathing.

sunburn /'sʌnbɜːn/. N-UNCOUNT If someone has **sunburn**, their skin is red and sore because they have spent too much time in the sun.

⭐ **Sunday** /'sʌndeɪ, -di/ **Sundays.** N-VAR **Sunday** is the day after Saturday and before Monday. → See Reference Page on Times and Dates.

sundry /'sʌndri/. [1] ADJ If you refer to **sundry** people or things, you mean several people or things of various sorts. [FORMAL] ...scientists, business people, and sundry others. [2] PHRASE **All and sundry** means everyone. I made tea for all and sundry at the office.

sunflower /'sʌnflaʊə/ **sunflowers.** N-COUNT A **sunflower** is a tall plant with large yellow flowers.

sung /sʌŋ/. **Sung** is the past participle of **sing**.

sunglasses /'sʌnɡlɑːsɪz, -ɡlæs-/. N-PLURAL **Sunglasses** are spectacles with dark lenses to protect your eyes from bright sunlight. A pair of designer sunglasses.

sunk /sʌŋk/. **Sunk** is the past participle of **sink**.

sunken /'sʌŋkən/. **1** ADJ BEFORE N **Sunken** ships have sunk to the bottom of a sea, ocean, or lake. ...*the sunken sailing-boat.* **2** ADJ BEFORE N **Sunken** gardens, roads, or other features are below the level of their surrounding area. *The room was dominated by a sunken bath.* **3** ADJ **Sunken** eyes or cheeks curve inwards and make you look thin and unwell. *Her eyes were sunken and black-ringed.*

sunlight /'sʌnlaɪt/. N-UNCOUNT **Sunlight** is the light that comes from the sun. *The calm sea glistened in the sunlight.* ...*a ray of sunlight.*

sunny /'sʌni/ **sunnier, sunniest.** **1** ADJ When it is **sunny**, the sun is shining brightly. ...*a warm, sunny day.* **2** ADJ **Sunny** places are brightly lit by the sun. ...*a sunny windowsill.*

sunrise /'sʌnraɪz/ **sunrises.** **1** N-UNCOUNT **Sunrise** is the time in the morning when the sun first appears. *The rain began before sunrise.* **2** N-COUNT A **sunrise** is the colours and light that you see in the sky when the sun first appears. *There was a spectacular sunrise yesterday.*

sunscreen /'sʌnskriːn/ **sunscreens.** N-VAR A **sunscreen** is a cream that protects your skin from the sun's rays in hot weather.

sunset /'sʌnset/ **sunsets.** **1** N-UNCOUNT **Sunset** is the time in the evening when the sun disappears from the sky. *The fast is broken at sunset.* **2** N-COUNT A **sunset** is the colours and light that you see in the sky when the sun disappears in the evening. *There was a red sunset over Paris.*

sunshine /'sʌnʃaɪn/. N-UNCOUNT **Sunshine** is the light and heat that comes from the sun. *The bay glittered in the sunshine.*

suntan /'sʌntæn/ **suntans.** **1** N-COUNT If you have a **suntan**, the sun has turned your skin an attractive brown colour. **2** ADJ BEFORE N **Suntan** lotion, oil, or cream protects your skin from the sun.

⭐ **super** /'suːpə/. ADJ **Super** means very nice or good. [BRITISH, INFORMAL] *We had a super time.*

⭐ **superb** /suː'pɜːb/. ADJ If something is **superb**, it is very good indeed. ...*a superb staircase made from oak.* ♦ **superbly** ADV *The orchestra played superbly.*

superficial /ˌsuːpə'fɪʃəl/. **1** ADJ If you describe someone as **superficial**, you disapprove of them because they do not think deeply, and have little understanding of anything serious or important. ...*someone boring, superficial and overly macho.* ♦ **superficiality** /ˌsuːpəfɪʃi'ælɪti/ N-UNCOUNT ...*the superficiality of the music industry.* **2** ADJ If you describe something such as an action, feeling, or relationship as **superficial**, you mean that it includes only the simplest and most obvious aspects of that thing. ...*a superficial knowledge of music.* ♦ **superficiality** N-UNCOUNT ...*the superficiality of the judgements we make when we first meet people.* ♦ **superficially** ADV *The film touches on these difficult questions, but only superficially.* **3** ADJ **Superficial** injuries are

not very serious, and affect only the surface of the body. You can also describe damage to an object as **superficial**. ...*four superficial wounds to his chest... The explosion caused superficial damage.*

superfluous /suː'pɜːfluəs/. ADJ Something that is **superfluous** is unnecessary or is no longer needed. *Further comment was superfluous.*

superimpose /ˌsuːpərɪm'pəʊz/ **superimposes, superimposing, superimposed.** VERB If one image is **superimposed on** or **over** another, it is put on top of it so that you can see the second image through it. *The features of different faces were superimposed over one another.*

superintendent /ˌsuːpərɪn'tendənt/ **superintendents.** N-COUNT & N-TITLE In British English, a **superintendent** is a senior police officer of the rank above an inspector. In the United States, a **superintendent** is the head of a police department. ...*Superintendent Appleby.*

⭐ **superior** /suː'pɪəriə/ **superiors.** **1** ADJ You use **superior** to describe someone or something that is better than other similar people or things. ...*a woman greatly superior to her husband in education and sensitivity. ...superior quality coffee.* ♦ **superiority** /suːˌpɪəri'ɒrɪti, AM -'ɔːrɪti/ N-UNCOUNT ...*the technical superiority of laser discs over tape.* **2** ADJ A **superior** person or thing has more authority or importance than another person or thing in the same organization or system. ...*negotiations between the mutineers and their superior officers.* **3** N-COUNT Your **superior** in an organization that you work for is a person who has a higher rank than you. **4** ADJ If you describe someone as **superior**, you disapprove of them because they behave as if they are better or more important than other people. *Finch gave a superior smile.*

superlative /suː'pɜːlətɪv/ **superlatives.** N-COUNT & ADJ In grammar, the **superlative** or the **superlative** form of an adjective or adverb is the form that indicates that something has more of a quality than anything else. For example, 'biggest' is the superlative form of 'big'. Compare **comparative**.

supermarket /'suːpəmɑːkɪt/ **supermarkets.** N-COUNT A **supermarket** is a large shop which sells all kinds of food and some household goods.

supermodel /'suːpəmɒdəl/ **supermodels.** N-COUNT A **supermodel** is a fashion model who is famous all over the world.

supernatural /ˌsuːpə'nætʃrəl/. ADJ & N-SING **Supernatural** creatures, forces, and events are believed by some people to exist or happen, although they are impossible according to scientific laws. You can refer to these things generally as **the supernatural**. ...*evil spirits who looked like humans and possessed supernatural powers.*

superpower /'suːpəpaʊə/ **superpowers.** N-COUNT A **superpower** is a very powerful and influential

a
b
c
d
e
f
g
h
i
j
k
l
m
n
o
p
q
r
s
t
u
v
w
x
y
z

supersede /ˌsuːpə'siːd/ **supersedes, superseding, superseded.** VERB If something **is superseded** by something newer, it is replaced because it has become old-fashioned or unacceptable. *Hand tools are relics of the past that have now been superseded by the machine.*

supersonic /ˌsuːpə'sɒnɪk/. ADJ BEFORE N **Supersonic** aircraft travel faster than the speed of sound.

superstar /'suːpəstɑː/ **superstars.** N-COUNT A **superstar** is a very famous entertainer or sports player. [INFORMAL] *...a Hollywood superstar.*

superstition /ˌsuːpə'stɪʃən/ **superstitions.** N-VAR **Superstition** is belief in things that are not real or possible, for example magic. *Westerners, too, have their superstitions about numbers.*

superstitious /ˌsuːpə'stɪʃəs/. ADJ People who are **superstitious** believe in things that are not real or possible, for example magic. *Jean was extremely superstitious and believed the colour green brought bad luck.*

supervise /'suːpəvaɪz/ **supervises, supervising, supervised.** VERB If you **supervise** an activity or a person, you make sure that the activity is done correctly or that the person is behaving correctly. *I supervise the packing of all mail orders.*
♦ **supervision** /ˌsuːpə'vɪʒən/ N-UNCOUNT *A toddler requires close supervision.* ♦ **supervisor, supervisors** N-COUNT *...a supervisor at a factory.*

supervisory /ˌsuːpə'vaɪzəri/. ADJ BEFORE N **Supervisory** means concerned with the supervision of people or activities. *...supervisory staff.*

supper /'sʌpə/ **suppers.** [1] N-VAR Some people refer to the main meal eaten in the early part of the evening as **supper.** *He invited me to supper.* [2] N-VAR **Supper** is a simple meal eaten just before you go to bed at night. [BRITISH] [3] See note at **meal.**

supplant /sə'plɑːnt, -'plænt/ **supplants, supplanting, supplanted.** VERB If one thing **supplants** another, it takes its place. [FORMAL] *By the 1930s the wristwatch had almost completely supplanted the pocket watch.*

supple /'sʌpəl/. [1] ADJ A **supple** object or material bends or changes shape easily without cracking or breaking. *...supple leather driving gloves.* [2] ADJ A **supple** person can move and bend their body very easily.

supplement /'sʌplɪmənt/ **supplements, supplementing, supplemented.** [1] VERB If you **supplement** something, you add something to it in order to improve it. *I suggest supplementing your diet with vitamins E and A.* [2] N-COUNT A **supplement** is something which is added to another thing in order to improve it. *...a supplement to their basic pension.*

supplementary /ˌsʌplɪ'mentri/, AM -teri/. ADJ **Supplementary** things are added to something in order to improve it. *...whether or not we need to take supplementary vitamins.*

supplier /sə'plaɪə/ **suppliers.** N-COUNT A **supplier** is a person or company that provides you with goods or equipment. *...one of the UK's biggest food suppliers.*

⭐ **supply** /sə'plaɪ/ **supplies, supplying, supplied.**
[1] VERB If you **supply** someone **with** something, you provide them with it. *...a pipeline which will supply the city with gas. ...an agreement not to produce or supply chemical weapons.* [2] N-PLURAL You can use **supplies** to refer to food, equipment, and other essential things that people need, especially when these are provided in large quantities. *...food and gasoline supplies.* [3] N-VAR A **supply of** something is an amount of it which is available for use. If something is **in short supply**, there is very little of it available. *The brain requires a constant supply of oxygen.* [4] N-UNCOUNT **Supply** is the quantity of goods and services that can be made available for people to buy. *Prices change according to supply and demand.*

⭐ **support** /sə'pɔːt/ **supports, supporting, supported.**
[1] VERB & N-UNCOUNT If you **support** someone or their aims, or if you give them your **support**, you agree with them, and perhaps try to help them because you want them to succeed. *He thanked everyone who had supported the strike... Only 60 clubs pledged their support for the scheme.*
♦ **supporter, supporters** N-COUNT *...supporters of the former President.* [2] N-UNCOUNT If you give **support** to someone during a difficult time, you are kind to them and help them. *...mentally ill people in need of support.* [3] VERB & N-UNCOUNT If you **support** someone, or if you give them financial **support**, you provide them with money or the things that they need. *He has a wife and two young children to support.* [4] VERB & N-UNCOUNT If a fact **supports** a statement or a theory, or if it provides **support** for it, it helps to show that it is true or correct. *History offers some support for this view.* [5] VERB If you **support** a sports team, you want them to win and perhaps go regularly to their games. ♦ **supporter** N-COUNT *I'm a Liverpool supporter.* [6] VERB If something **supports** an object, it is underneath the object and holding it up. *...the thick wooden posts that supported the ceiling.* [7] N-COUNT A **support** is a bar or other object that supports something. [8] VERB & N-UNCOUNT If something **supports** you, or if it provides you with **support**, it prevents you from falling because you are holding onto it or leaning on it. *Alice was leaning against him as if for support.*

> **USAGE** If you dislike something very much or get very annoyed by it, you do not say 'I can't support it'. You say **'I can't bear it'** or **'I can't stand it'.** *She can't bear the new Labour government... I cannot stand going shopping.*

supportive /sə'pɔːtɪv/. ADJ If you are **supportive**, you are kind and helpful to someone at a difficult time in their life.

⭐ **suppose** /sə'pəʊz/ **supposes, supposing, supposed.** ① VERB You use **suppose** or **supposing** when you are considering a possible situation or action and trying to think what effects it would have. *Suppose someone gave you an egg and asked you to describe exactly what was inside... Supposing it wasn't the wind that had thrown the door open?* ② VERB If you **suppose** that something is true, you believe that it is probably true. *I supposed you would have a meal somewhere with Rachel.*

> **USAGE** Note that when you are using the verb **suppose** with a **that** clause in order to state a negative opinion or belief, you normally make **suppose** negative, rather than the verb in the **that** clause. For instance, it is more usual to say **'I don't suppose he ever saw it'** than 'I suppose he didn't ever see it'. The same pattern applies to other verbs with a similar meaning, such as **believe, consider** and **think**. *He didn't believe she could do it... I don't consider that you kept your promise... I don't think he saw me.*

③ PHRASE You can say **I suppose** before stating something that you believe to be true, or something that you think you should do, when you want to express slight uncertainty or reluctance about it. [SPOKEN] *'What would you tell them?'—'The truth, I suppose.'... I suppose I'd better do some homework... 'Is that the right way up?'— 'Yeah. I suppose so.'*

⭐ **supposed.** ① ADJ /sə'pəʊzd, sə'pəʊst/ If you say that something is **supposed to** happen, you mean that it is planned or expected. Sometimes this use suggests that the thing does not really happen in this way. *Public spending is supposed to fall, not rise, in the next few years... The first debate was supposed to have been held on Tuesday.* ② ADJ If you say that something is **supposed to** be true, you mean that people say it is true but you do not know for certain that it is true. *'The Whipping Block' has never been published, but it's supposed to be a really good poem.* ③ ADJ BEFORE N /sə'pəʊzɪd/ You can use **supposed** when you want to suggest that the following word or description is misleading, or when it is not definitely known to be true. *She had long suspected him and her supposed friend Michelle of being lovers.* ♦ **supposedly** ADV *Thirty eight women have died while taking these supposedly safer pills.*

suppress /sə'pres/ **suppresses, suppressing, suppressed.** ① VERB If someone in authority **suppresses** an activity, they prevent it from continuing, by using force or making it illegal. *The movement was suppressed by army troops.* ♦ **suppression** /sə'preʃən/ N-UNCOUNT *...the suppression of human rights.* ② VERB If a natural function or reaction of your body **is suppressed**, it is stopped, for example by drugs or illness. ③ VERB If you **suppress** your feelings or reactions, you do not express them, even though you might want to. *I had a lot of suppressed anger.* ♦ **suppression** N-UNCOUNT *A mother's suppression of her own feelings can cause problems.* ④ VERB If someone **suppresses** a piece of information, they prevent other people from learning it. ♦ **suppression** N-UNCOUNT *...the deliberate suppression of information.*

supremacy /suː'preməsi/. N-UNCOUNT If one group of people has **supremacy over** another group, they are more powerful. *The president has been able to assert his ultimate supremacy over the prime minister.*

⭐ **supreme** /suː'priːm/. ① ADJ BEFORE N **Supreme** is used in a title to indicate that a person or group is at the highest level of an organization or system. *...NATO's Supreme Commander in Europe. ...the Supreme Court.* ② ADJ You use **supreme** to emphasize the greatness of a quality or thing. *Her approval was of supreme importance.* ♦ **supremely** ADV *We are supremely confident because we have the right mixture of skills and experience.*

⭐ **sure** /ʃʊə/ **surer, surest.** ① ADJ AFTER LINK-V If you are **sure** that something is true, you are certain that it is true. If you are not **sure about** something, you do not know for certain what the true situation is. *He was not even sure that he should have been teaching... It is impossible to be sure about the value of land.* ② ADJ AFTER LINK-V If someone is **sure of** getting something, they will certainly get it. *Neither can be sure of success.* ③ ADJ AFTER LINK-V If you say that something is **sure to** happen, you are emphasizing your belief that it will happen. *Kids are sure to love crawling through the tunnel.* ④ ADJ **Sure** is used to emphasize that something such as a sign or ability is reliable or accurate. *Sharpe's leg and shoulder began to ache, a sure sign of rain... She has a sure grasp of social issues.* ⑤ CONVENTION **Sure** is a way of saying 'yes' or 'all right'. [INFORMAL] *'He rang you?'—'Sure. Last night.'.*
  PHRASES ● You say **sure enough**, especially when telling a story, to confirm that something you thought was true or would happen was really true or actually happened. *I called the hotel and asked them to check the room. Sure enough, they had found the ticket in the blankets.* ● If you say that something is **for sure**, or that you know it **for sure**, you mean that it is definitely true. *One thing is for sure: they will not be calling him James.* ● If you **make sure** that something is done, you take action so that it is done. *Make sure that you follow the instructions carefully.* ● If you **make sure** that something is the way that you want or expect it to be, you check that it is that way. *He looked in the bathroom to make sure that he was alone.* ● If you are **sure of yourself**, you are very confident about your own abilities or opinions.

a
b
c
d
e
f
g
h
i
j
k
l
m
n
o
p
q
r
s
t
u
v
w
x
y
z

★ **surely** /'ʃʊəli/. [1] ADV You use **surely** to emphasize that you think something should be true, and you would be surprised if it was not true. *You surely haven't forgotten Dr Walters?* [2] PHRASE If you say that something is happening **slowly but surely**, you mean that it is happening gradually but it is definitely happening.

surf /sɜːf/ **surfs, surfing, surfed.** [1] N-UNCOUNT **Surf** is the mass of white foam formed by waves as they fall on the shore. [2] VERB If you **surf**, you ride on big waves on a special board. ♦ **surfer, surfers** N-COUNT *...fanatical surfers who travel the world looking for the perfect wave.* ♦ **surfing** N-UNCOUNT *The best time for surfing in Waikiki is in January.* [3] VERB If you **surf** the Internet, you move from place to place on the Internet. ♦ **surfer** N-COUNT *...programs and games for net surfers to download.*

★ **surface** /'sɜːfɪs/ **surfaces, surfacing, surfaced.** [1] N-COUNT The **surface** of something is the top part of it or the outside of it. *...tiny little waves on the surface of the water... Its total surface area was seven thousand square feet.* [2] VERB If someone or something under water **surfaces**, they come up to the surface of the water. *He surfaced, gasping for air.* [3] N-SING **The surface** of a situation is what can be seen easily rather than what is not immediately obvious. *Back in Britain, things appear, on the surface, simpler... It's brought to the surface a much wider controversy.*

surge /sɜːdʒ/ **surges, surging, surged.** [1] N-COUNT & VERB If there is a **surge** in the level or rate of something, or if the level or rate of something **surges**, there is a sudden large increase in it. *The shares surged from 43p to 163p earlier this year.* [2] N-COUNT If you feel a **surge of** a particular emotion or feeling, you experience it suddenly and powerfully. *McKee felt a sudden surge of hope.* [3] N-COUNT & VERB If there is a **surge of** a physical force such as water or electricity, or if it **surges**, there is a sudden powerful movement of it. *Thousands of volts surged through his car.* [4] VERB If people **surge** forward, they move forward suddenly and powerfully, usually in a crowd. *The crowd surged into the station.*

surgeon /'sɜːdʒən/ **surgeons.** N-COUNT A **surgeon** is a doctor who performs surgery.

★ **surgery** /'sɜːdʒəri/ **surgeries.** [1] N-UNCOUNT **Surgery** is medical treatment which involves cutting open a person's body in order to repair or remove a diseased or damaged part. *Robson had had emergency surgery to remove a cancerous growth.* [2] N-COUNT A **surgery** is the room or house where a doctor or dentist works. [BRITISH] [3] N-VAR A doctor's or dentist's **surgery** is the period of time each day when he or she sees patients at his or her surgery. [BRITISH] *Bring him along to the morning surgery.* [4] See also **plastic surgery**.

surgical /'sɜːdʒɪkəl/. ADJ BEFORE N **Surgical** means relating to surgery. *...surgical instruments. ...a surgical operation.* ♦ **surgically** ADV *Some cysts do need to be surgically removed.*

surmise /sə'maɪz/ **surmises, surmising, surmised.** VERB If you **surmise** that something is true, you guess from the information available that it is true, but you do not know for certain. [FORMAL] *There's so little to go on, we can only surmise what happened.*

surname /'sɜːneɪm/ **surnames.** N-COUNT Your **surname** is the name that you share with other members of your family.

surpass /sə'pɑːs, -'pæs/ **surpasses, surpassing, surpassed.** VERB If one person or thing **surpasses** another, the first is better than, or has more of a particular quality than, the second. [FORMAL] *He was determined to surpass the achievements of his older brothers.*

★ **surplus** /'sɜːpləs/ **surpluses.** [1] N-VAR & ADJ If there is a **surplus of** something, there is more than is needed. **Surplus** things are not needed because there are already enough of them. *Germany suffers from a surplus of teachers... Few people have large sums of surplus cash.* [2] N-COUNT A **surplus** refers to a situation in which a person or organization receives more than it spends. For example, if a country has a trade **surplus**, it exports more than it imports.

★ **surprise** /sə'praɪz/ **surprises, surprising, surprised.** [1] N-COUNT & ADJ BEFORE N A **surprise** or a **surprise** event or fact is an unexpected event or fact. *His success came as a surprise to many people... I have a surprise for you: We are moving to Switzerland!... Baxter arrived here this afternoon, on a surprise visit.* [2] N-UNCOUNT **Surprise** is the feeling that you have when something unexpected happens. *They looked at her in surprise... To my surprise, I found I liked it.* [3] VERB If something **surprises** you, it gives you a feeling of surprise. *It surprised me that a driver of Alain's experience should make those mistakes.*

★ **surprised** /sə'praɪzd/. ADJ If you are **surprised at** something, you have a feeling of surprise, because it is unexpected or unusual. *She was surprised at what happened... Chang seemed surprised to find the big living-room empty.*

★ **surprising** /sə'praɪzɪŋ/. ADJ Something that is **surprising** is unexpected or unusual and makes you feel surprised. *It is not surprising that children learn to read at different rates.* ♦ **surprisingly** ADV *Her voice was surprisingly good.*

surreal /sə'riːəl/. ADJ If you describe something as **surreal**, you mean that it is very strange and like a dream. *There is a surreal quality to this part of the rainforest.*

★ **surrender** /sə'rendə/ **surrenders, surrendering, surrendered.** [1] VERB & N-VAR If you **surrender**, you stop fighting or resisting someone or something and agree that you have been beaten. **Surrender** is the act of surrendering. *He surrendered to American troops. ...after the Japanese surrender in 1945.* [2] VERB & N-UNCOUNT If you **surrender** something you would rather keep, you give it up or let someone else have it, often after a struggle. **Surrender** is the act of surrendering something.

Nadja had to fill out forms surrendering all rights to her property. ...the deadline for the surrender of weapons.

surrogate /ˈsʌrəgeɪt, AM ˈsɜːr-/ **surrogates**. ADJ BEFORE N & N-COUNT You use **surrogate** to describe a person or thing that acts as a substitute for someone or something else. He had been a wonderful friend to all of us; a surrogate father... Arms control should not be made into a surrogate for peace.

⭐ **surround** /səˈraʊnd/ **surrounds, surrounding, surrounded**. [1] VERB If something or someone **is surrounded** by something, that thing is situated all around them. ...the fluid that surrounds the brain. ...in the surrounding hills. [2] VERB If you **are surrounded** by people such as soldiers or police, they spread out so that they are in positions all the way around you. He tried to run away but gave up when he found himself surrounded. [3] VERB The circumstances, feelings, or ideas which **surround** something are those that are closely associated with it. Controversy surrounds the cause of his death. [4] VERB If you **surround yourself with** certain people or things, you make sure that you have a lot of them near you all the time. He surrounded himself with admirers... They love being surrounded by familiar possessions.

surroundings /səˈraʊndɪŋz/. N-PLURAL The place where someone or something is can be referred to as their **surroundings**. ...a peaceful holiday home in beautiful surroundings.

surveillance /səˈveɪləns/. N-UNCOUNT **Surveillance** is the careful watching of someone, especially by the police or army. The police kept Golding under surveillance.

⭐ **survey, surveys, surveying, surveyed**; verb /səˈveɪ/, noun /ˈsɜːveɪ/. [1] VERB & N-COUNT To **survey** people or organizations, or to make a **survey** of them, means to try to find out information about their opinions or behaviour by asking them questions. A survey showed people were confused about what they should eat. [2] VERB If you **survey** something, you look at or consider the whole of it carefully. He pushed himself to his feet and surveyed the room. [3] VERB & N-COUNT To **survey** a building or area of land, or to do a **survey** of it, means to examine it and measure it, usually in order to make a map of it. ...the geological survey of India. ◆ **surveyor, surveyors** N-COUNT ...the surveyor's maps. [4] VERB & N-COUNT If someone **surveys** a house, or if they do a **survey** of it, they examine it carefully and report on its structure. ...a structural survey undertaken by a qualified surveyor. ◆ **surveyor** N-COUNT Our surveyor warned us that the house needed totally rebuilding.

⭐ **survival** /səˈvaɪvəl/. N-UNCOUNT **Survival** is the fact of continuing to live or exist in spite of great danger or difficulty. An animal's sense of smell is still crucial to its survival. ...companies which have been struggling for survival.

⭐ **survive** /səˈvaɪv/ **survives, surviving, survived**. [1] VERB If someone **survives** in a dangerous situation, they do not die. Drugs that dissolve blood clots can help people survive heart attacks. ◆ **survivor, survivors** N-COUNT There were no survivors of the plane crash. [2] VERB If you **survive** in difficult circumstances, you manage to continue in spite of them. ...people who are struggling to survive without jobs... When the market economy is introduced, many factories will not survive. ◆ **survivor** N-COUNT ...female survivors of domestic violence. [3] VERB If you **survive** someone, you continue to live after they have died. Most women will survive their spouses.

susceptible /səˈseptɪbəl/. [1] ADJ AFTER LINK-V If you are **susceptible to** something or someone, you are likely to be influenced by them. Young people are the most susceptible to advertisements. [2] ADJ AFTER LINK-V If you are **susceptible to** a disease or injury, you are likely to be affected by it. [3] ADJ BEFORE N A **susceptible** person is very easily influenced emotionally.

⭐ **suspect, suspects, suspecting, suspected**. [1] VERB /səˈspekt/ If you say that you **suspect** that something is true, you mean that you believe it is probably true, but you want to make it sound less strong or direct. I suspect they were right... Do women really share such stupid jokes? We suspect not. [2] VERB If you **suspect** that something dishonest or unpleasant has been done, you believe that it has probably been done. He suspected that the woman staying in the flat above was using heroin. [3] N-COUNT /ˈsʌspekt/ A **suspect** is a person who the police think may be guilty of a crime. [4] ADJ If something is **suspect**, it cannot be trusted or regarded as genuine. The whole affair has been highly suspect.

⭐ **suspend** /səˈspend/ **suspends, suspending, suspended**. [1] VERB If you **suspend** something, you delay or stop it for a while. The union suspended strike action this week. [2] VERB If someone **is suspended** from their job, they are prevented from doing it for a fixed period of time, usually as a punishment. Julie was suspended from her job shortly after the incident. [3] VERB If something is **suspended** from a high place, it is hung from that place. ...a map of Europe suspended from the ceiling.

suspenders /səˈspendəz/. N-PLURAL In American English, **suspenders** are a pair of straps that go over someone's shoulders and are fastened to their trousers at the front and at the back to prevent the trousers from falling down. The British word is **braces**.

suspense /səˈspens/. N-UNCOUNT **Suspense** is a state of excitement or anxiety about something that is going to happen very soon. There was genuine suspense before Green was named the winner.

suspension /səˈspenʃən/ **suspensions**. [1] N-UNCOUNT The **suspension of** something is the act of delaying or stopping it for a while. ...the suspension of flights between London and

a
b
c
d
e
f
g
h
i
j
k
l
m
n
o
p
q
r
s
t
u
v
w
x
y
z

Manchester. **2** N-VAR Someone's **suspension** is their removal from a job for a period of time, usually as a punishment. ...*a two-year suspension following a positive drug test.* **3** N-UNCOUNT A vehicle's **suspension** consists of the springs and other devices, which give a smooth ride over bumps in the road.

⭐ **suspicion** /sə'spɪʃən/ **suspicions. 1** N-VAR **Suspicion** is a belief or feeling that someone has committed a crime or done something wrong. *He was arrested on suspicion of drunk driving.* **2** N-VAR If there is **suspicion** of someone or something, people do not trust them or consider them to be reliable. *I was always regarded in the Army with a certain amount of suspicion.* **3** N-COUNT A **suspicion** is a feeling that something is probably true or is likely to happen. *I had a sneaking suspicion she was enjoying herself.*

suspicious /sə'spɪʃəs/. **1** ADJ If you are **suspicious of** someone or something, you do not trust them. *He was suspicious of all journalists.* ♦ **suspiciously** ADV *'What's the matter with you?'* Jake asked suspiciously. **2** ADJ If you describe someone or something as **suspicious**, you mean that there is some aspect of them which makes you think that they are involved in a crime or a dishonest activity. *Police last night found a suspicious package.* ♦ **suspiciously** ADV ...*suspiciously large sums of money.*

⭐ **sustain** /sə'steɪn/ **sustains, sustaining, sustained. 1** VERB If you **sustain** something, you continue it or maintain it for a period of time. ...*how to get enough food to sustain life.* **2** VERB If you **sustain** something such as a defeat, loss, or injury, it happens to you. [FORMAL] *He had sustained a cut on his left eyebrow.* **3** VERB If something **sustains** you, it supports you by giving you help, strength, or encouragement. [FORMAL] *He'll have lots of great memories to sustain him when he's away.*

sustainable /sə'steɪnəbəl/. ADJ A **sustainable** plan, method, or system can be continued at the same pace or level of activity without harming its efficiency and the people affected by it. ...*an efficient and sustainable transport system.*

swab /swɒb/ **swabs.** N-COUNT A **swab** is a small piece of cotton wool used for cleaning a wound.

swagger /'swægə/ **swaggers, swaggering, swaggered.** VERB & N-SING If you **swagger**, or if you walk with a **swagger**, you walk in a proud way, holding your body upright and swinging your hips. *He swaggered confidently up to the bar.*

swallow /'swɒləʊ/ **swallows, swallowing, swallowed. 1** VERB & N-COUNT When you **swallow** something, or when you take a **swallow**, you cause something to go from your mouth down into your stomach. *You are asked to swallow a capsule containing vitamin B... Jan lifted her glass and took a quick swallow.* **2** VERB If someone **swallows** a story or a statement, they believe it completely. *I too found this story a little hard to swallow.* **3** VERB If you **swallow** your feelings, you do not express them, although you want to very much.

Gordon has swallowed the anger he felt. **4** N-COUNT A **swallow** is a small bird with pointed wings and a forked tail.

swam /swæm/. **Swam** is the past tense of **swim.**

swamp /swɒmp/ **swamps, swamping, swamped. 1** N-VAR A **swamp** is an area of wet land with wild plants growing in it. **2** VERB If something **swamps** a place or object, it fills it with water. *The Ventura river burst its banks, swamping a mobile home park.* **3** VERB If you **are swamped** by things or people, you have more of them than you can deal with. *The railway station was swamped with thousands of families.*

swan /swɒn/ **swans.** N-COUNT A **swan** is a large white bird with a long neck that lives on rivers and lakes.

swap (or **swop**) /swɒp/ **swaps, swapping, swapped. 1** VERB & N-COUNT If you **swap** something **with** someone, or if you do a **swap**, you give it to them and receive something else in exchange. *I wouldn't swap jobs with her... Next week they will swap places. ...if she ever fancies a job swap.* **2** VERB If you **swap** one thing **for** another, you remove the first thing and replace it with the second. *He'd swapped his overalls for a suit and tie.* **3** VERB When you **swap** stories or opinions with someone, you tell each other stories or give each other your opinions. *They all sat together at table, laughing and swapping stories.*

swarm /swɔːm/ **swarms, swarming, swarmed. 1** N-COUNT A **swarm of** bees or other insects is a large group of them flying together. **2** VERB When bees or other insects **swarm**, they move or fly in a large group. **3** VERB When people **swarm** somewhere, they move there quickly in a large group. *People swarmed to the shops, buying up everything in sight.* **4** VERB If a place **is swarming with** people, it is full of people moving about in a busy way. *Within minutes the area was swarming with officers.* **5** N-COUNT A **swarm of** people is a large group of them moving about quickly.

swat /swɒt/ **swats, swatting, swatted.** VERB If you **swat** an insect, you hit it with a quick, swinging movement.

swathe (or **swath**) /sweɪð, AM swɑːð/ **swathes, swathing, swathed. 1** N-COUNT A **swathe of** land is a long strip of land. *The army took over another swathe of territory.* **2** VERB To **swathe** someone or something **in** cloth means to wrap them in it completely. *She swathed her enormous body in thin black fabrics.*

sway /sweɪ/ **sways, swaying, swayed. 1** VERB When people or things **sway**, they lean or swing slowly from one side to the other. *The people swayed back and forth.* **2** VERB If you **are swayed** by someone or something, you are influenced by them. *Don't ever be swayed by fashion.* **3** PHRASE If someone or something **holds sway**, they have great power or influence over a particular place or activity. ...*ideas that held sway for centuries.*

swear /sweə/ **swears, swearing, swore, sworn.** **1** VERB
If someone **swears**, they use language that is
considered to be rude or offensive. *They swore at
them and ran off.* **2** VERB If you **swear to** do
something, you solemnly promise that you will
do it. *We have sworn to fight cruelty... Alan swore
that he would do everything in his power to help
us... He swore allegiance to the U.S. government.*
3 VERB If you **swear** that something is true, or if
you say that you can **swear** to it, you say very
firmly that it is true. *I swear I've told you all I know.*
4 VERB If someone **is sworn to** secrecy or
silence, they promise another person that they
will not reveal a secret. *She was bursting to
announce the news but was sworn to secrecy.*
5 See also **sworn**.
▶**swear by.** PHR-VERB If you **swear by**
something, you believe that it can be relied on to
have a particular effect. *Many people swear by
vitamin C's ability to ward off colds.*
▶**swear in.** PHR-VERB When someone **is sworn
in**, they solemnly promise to fulfil the duties of a
new job or appointment.

sweat /swet/ **sweats, sweating, sweated.**
1 N-UNCOUNT **Sweat** is the salty colourless liquid
which comes through your skin when you are
hot, ill, or afraid. *He wiped the sweat off his face.*
2 VERB When you **sweat**, sweat comes through
your skin. ♦ **sweating** N-UNCOUNT ...*symptoms
such as sweating, irritability, anxiety and
depression.* **3** PHRASE If someone is **in a sweat** or
in a cold sweat, they are sweating a lot,
especially because they are afraid or ill. *The very
thought brought me out in a cold sweat.*

sweater /swetə/ **sweaters.** N-COUNT A **sweater** is
a warm knitted piece of clothing which covers
the upper part of your body and your arms.

sweatshirt /swetʃɜːt/ **sweatshirts.** N-COUNT A
sweatshirt is a loose warm piece of casual
clothing, usually made of thick cotton, which
covers the upper part of your body and your
arms. → See picture on page 819.

sweaty /sweti/ **sweatier, sweatiest.** ADJ If your
clothing or body is **sweaty**, it is soaked or
covered with sweat.

★ **sweep** /swiːp/ **sweeps, sweeping, swept.** **1** VERB If
you **sweep** an area of ground, you push dirt or
rubbish off it with a broom. *She was in the kitchen
sweeping crumbs into a dust pan.* **2** VERB If you
sweep things off something, you push them off
with a quick smooth movement of your arm. *She
swept the cards from the table.* **3** VERB If a strong
force **sweeps** you along, it moves you quickly
along. ...*landslides that buried homes and swept
cars into the sea.* **4** VERB If events or ideas
sweep through a place, they spread quickly
through it. *A flu epidemic is sweeping through
Moscow.* ...*the wave of patriotism sweeping the
country.* **5** VERB To **sweep** something **away** or
aside means to remove it quickly and
completely. *In times of war, governments often
sweep human rights aside.* **6** VERB If your gaze or
a light **sweeps** an area, it moves over it.

Helicopters with searchlights swept the park.
7 PHRASE If someone **sweeps** something bad or
wrong **under the carpet**, they try to prevent
people from hearing about it.
▶**sweep up.** PHR-VERB If you **sweep up** dirt or
rubbish, you push it together with a brush and
then remove it. *Get a broom and sweep up that
glass.*

sweeping /swiːpɪŋ/. **1** ADJ If someone makes
a **sweeping** statement or generalization, they
make a firm definite statement although they
have not considered the relevant facts or details
carefully; used showing disapproval. *You can't
make sweeping generalizations about youngsters
of today.* **2** ADJ **Sweeping** changes or reforms
are large in scale and have very important or
significant results.

★ **sweet** /swiːt/ **sweeter, sweetest; sweets.** **1** ADJ
Sweet food or drink contains a lot of sugar. ...*a
mug of sweet tea.* ♦ **sweetness** N-UNCOUNT
Florida oranges have a natural sweetness.
2 N-COUNT In British English, **sweets** are sweet
things such as toffees, chocolates, or mints. In
American English, **sweets** are referred to as
candy. **3** N-COUNT A **sweet** is something sweet,
such as fruit or a pudding, that you eat at the end
of a meal. [BRITISH] **4** ADJ A **sweet** smell is pleasant
and fragrant. ...*the sweet smell of her shampoo.*
5 ADJ A **sweet** sound is pleasant, smooth, and
gentle. ...*the sweet sounds of Mozart.* ♦ **sweetly**
ADV *He sang much more sweetly than he has
before.* **6** ADJ If you describe something as
sweet, you mean that it gives you great pleasure
and satisfaction. [WRITTEN] *There are few things
quite as sweet as revenge.* **7** ADJ If you describe
someone as **sweet**, you mean that they are
pleasant, kind, and gentle towards other people.
How sweet of you to think of me! ♦ **sweetly** ADV *I
just smiled sweetly.* **8** ADJ If you describe a small
person or thing as **sweet**, you mean that they are
attractive in a child-like way. [INFORMAL] ...*a sweet
little baby girl.*

sweetcorn /swiːtkɔːn/. N-UNCOUNT **Sweetcorn**
consists of the yellow seeds of the maize plant,
which are eaten as a vegetable.

sweeten /swiːtən/ **sweetens, sweetening,
sweetened.** VERB If you **sweeten** food or drink, you
add sugar, honey, or another sweet substance to
it.

sweetener /swiːtənə/ **sweeteners.** N-VAR A
sweetener is an artificial substance that can be
used instead of sugar.

sweetheart /swiːthɑːt/ **sweethearts.** **1** N-VOC
You call someone **sweetheart** if you are very
fond of them. *Happy birthday, sweetheart.*
2 N-COUNT Your **sweetheart** is your boyfriend or
girlfriend. [DATED]

swell /swel/ **swells, swelling, swelled, swollen.**

✓ The forms **swelled** and **swollen** are both
used as the past participle.

1 VERB If the amount or size of something
swells, it becomes larger than it was before. *His*

a
b
c
d
e
f
g
h
i
j
k
l
m
n
o
p
q
r
s
t
u
v
w
x
y
z

bank balance has swelled by £222,000... Women continue to swell the ranks of teachers. [2] VERB & PHR-VERB If something such as a part of your body **swells**, or if it **swells up**, it becomes larger and rounder than normal. The limbs swell to an enormous size... The glands in the neck swell up. [3] VERB If you **swell with** a feeling, you are suddenly full of that feeling. [LITERARY] She could see her two sons swell with pride. [4] See also **swollen**.

swelling /'swelɪŋ/ **swellings.** N-VAR A **swelling** is a raised curved shape on the surface of your body which appears as a result of an injury or an illness. ...painful swellings of the big toe joint... The cyst was causing swelling.

sweltering /'sweltərɪŋ/. ADJ If the weather is **sweltering**, it is very hot. In LA it's sweltering – 98 degrees in the shade. ...a day of sweltering heat.

swept /swept/. **Swept** is the past tense and past participle of **sweep**.

swerve /swɜːv/ **swerves, swerving, swerved.** VERB & N-COUNT If a vehicle or other moving thing **swerves**, it suddenly changes direction, often in order to avoid colliding with something else. This movement is called a **swerve**. Her car swerved off the road... Ned swerved the truck... He swung the car to the left and that swerve saved Malone's life.

swift /swɪft/ **swifter, swiftest.** [1] ADJ A **swift** event or process happens very quickly or without delay. The police were swift to act... We wish him a swift recovery. ♦ **swiftly** ADV ...the police failed to act swiftly enough. ♦ **swiftness** N-UNCOUNT ...the secrecy and swiftness of the invasion. [2] ADJ Something that is **swift** moves very quickly. With a swift movement, she reached into the cot.

⭐ **swim** /swɪm/ **swims, swimming, swam, swum.** [1] VERB & N-SING When you **swim**, or when you go for a **swim**, you move through water by making movements with your arms and legs. I swim a mile a day... When can we go for a swim? ♦ **swimmer, swimmers** N-COUNT I'm a good swimmer. [2] VERB If objects **swim**, they seem to be moving backwards and forwards, usually because you are ill. He felt too hot, he couldn't breathe, the room swam. [3] VERB If your head **is swimming**, you feel dizzy.

swimming /'swɪmɪŋ/. N-UNCOUNT **Swimming** is the activity of swimming, especially as a sport or for pleasure. It was too chilly for swimming... I now go swimming five times a week.

'**swimming pool, swimming pools.** N-COUNT A **swimming pool** is a place that has been built for people to swim in. It consists of a large hole that has been tiled and filled with water.

swimsuit /'swɪmsuːt/ **swimsuits.** N-COUNT A **swimsuit** is a piece of clothing that is worn for swimming, especially by women and girls.

swindle /'swɪndəl/ **swindles, swindling, swindled.** VERB & N-COUNT If someone **swindles** a person or an organization, or if someone is involved in a **swindle**, they deceive the person or organization in order to get money from them. A City

businessman swindled investors out of millions of pounds. ...a tax swindle. ♦ **swindler, swindlers** N-COUNT ...an insurance swindler.

⭐ **swing** /swɪŋ/ **swings, swinging, swung.** [1] VERB & N-COUNT If something **swings**, or if you **swing** it, it moves backwards and forwards or from side to side from a fixed point, once or several times. You can refer to this movement as a **swing**. The pendulum slowly started to swing... She was swinging a bottle of wine by its neck... Roy swung his legs carefully off the couch. ...walking with a slight swing to her hips. [2] VERB If a vehicle **swings** in a particular direction, or if a driver **swings** his or her vehicle in a particular direction, he or she turns it suddenly in that direction. He got into Margie's car and swung out onto the road... He swung the car off the road. [3] VERB & N-COUNT If you **swing at** someone or something, or if you take a **swing at** them, you try to hit them. I picked up his baseball bat and swung at the man's head... I often want to take a swing at someone. [4] N-COUNT A **swing** is a seat hanging by two ropes or chains from a metal frame or tree. You can sit on the seat and move backwards and forwards through the air. [5] VERB & N-COUNT If people's opinions, attitudes, or feelings **swing**, or if there is a **swing** in them, they change significantly. The mood amongst Tory MPs seems to be swinging away from their leader. ...violent mood swings. [6] PHRASE If something is **in full swing**, it is operating fully and is no longer in its early stages. The international rugby season is in full swing.

swipe /swaɪp/ **swipes, swiping, swiped.** VERB & N-COUNT If you **swipe at** a person or thing, or if you take a **swipe at** them, you try to hit them, making a swinging movement with your arm. She swiped at Rusty as though he was a fly... She took a casual swipe at the nettles.

'**swipe card, swipe cards.** N-COUNT A **swipe card** is a plastic card with a magnetic strip on it containing information that can be read by a machine.

swirl /swɜːl/ **swirls, swirling, swirled.** [1] VERB If you **swirl** something liquid or flowing, or if it **swirls**, it moves round and round quickly. She swirled the ice-cold liquid around her mouth... The black water swirled around his legs. [2] N-COUNT A **swirl** is a pattern made by moving something round and round quickly. ...small swirls of chocolate cream.

swish /swɪʃ/ **swishes, swishing, swished.** VERB & N-COUNT If something **swishes**, it moves quickly through the air, making a soft sound. This action is called a **swish**. A car swished by... She turned with a swish of her skirt.

⭐ **switch** /swɪtʃ/ **switches, switching, switched.** [1] N-COUNT A **switch** is a small control for an electrical device which you use to turn the device on or off. ...a light switch. [2] VERB & N-COUNT If you **switch to** something different, for example to a different system, task, or subject of conversation, or if there is a **switch to** it, you change to it from what you were doing or saying before. The law would encourage companies to switch from coal to cleaner fuels... A friend spurred Chris into switching jobs... New technology made a switch to oil possible. **3** VERB If you **switch** two things, you replace one with the other. The ballot boxes have been switched.

▸**switch off.** **1** PHR-VERB If you **switch off** an electrical device, you stop it working by operating a switch. The driver dipped the headlights and then switched them off. **2** PHR-VERB If you **switch off**, you stop paying attention to something. [INFORMAL] You've got so many things to think about that it's difficult to switch off.

▸**switch on.** PHR-VERB If you **switch on** an electrical device, you make it start working by operating a switch. He pointed the light at his feet and tried to switch it on.

switchboard /'swɪtʃbɔːd/ **switchboards.** N-COUNT A **switchboard** is a place in a large office or business where all the telephone calls are connected. He asked to be connected to the central switchboard.

swivel /'swɪvəl/ **swivels, swivelling, swivelled** (AM **swiveling, swiveled**). VERB If someone or something **swivels**, or if you **swivel** them, they turn around a central point so that they are facing in a different direction. He swivelled round to face Sarah... She swivelled her chair round.

swollen /'swəʊlən/. **1** **Swollen** is a past participle of **swell**. **2** ADJ If a part of your body is **swollen**, it is larger and rounder than normal, usually as a result of injury or illness. Her glands were swollen and painful.

swoon /swuːn/ **swoons, swooning, swooned.** VERB If you **swoon**, you are strongly affected by your feelings for someone you love or admire very much. Virtually every woman in the '20s swooned over Valentino.

swoop /swuːp/ **swoops, swooping, swooped.** **1** VERB & N-COUNT If police or soldiers **swoop on** a place, or if they carry out a **swoop on** a place, they go there suddenly and quickly, usually in order to arrest someone or to attack the place. The drugs squad swooped and discovered 240 kilograms of cannabis. ...a swoop on a German lorry. **2** VERB When a bird or aeroplane **swoops**, it suddenly moves downwards through the air in a smooth curving movement. More than 20 helicopters began swooping in low.

swop /swɒp/. See **swap**.

sword /sɔːd/ **swords.** N-COUNT A **sword** is a weapon with a handle and a long blade.

swore /swɔː/. **Swore** is the past tense of **swear**.

sworn /swɔːn/. **1** **Sworn** is the past participle of **swear**. **2** ADJ BEFORE N If you make a **sworn** statement or declaration, you swear that everything that you have said in it is true. ...sworn legal statements.

swum /swʌm/. **Swum** is the past participle of **swim**.

swung /swʌŋ/. **Swung** is the past tense and past participle of **swing**.

syllable /'sɪləbəl/ **syllables.** N-COUNT A **syllable** is a part of a word that contains a single vowel-sound and that is pronounced as a unit. For example, 'book' has one syllable, and 'reading' has two syllables.

syllabus /'sɪləbəs/ **syllabuses.** N-COUNT You can refer to the subjects that are studied in a particular course as the **syllabus**. ...the history syllabus.

⭐ **symbol** /'sɪmbəl/ **symbols.** **1** N-COUNT Something that is a **symbol of** a society or aspect of life seems to represent it because it is typical of it. To them, the monarchy is the special symbol of nationhood. **2** N-COUNT A **symbol of** something such as an idea is a shape or design that is used to represent it. I frequently use sunflowers as symbols of strength. **3** N-COUNT A **symbol for** an item in a calculation or formula is a number, letter, or shape that represents the item. What's the chemical symbol for mercury?

symbolic /sɪm'bɒlɪk/. **1** ADJ If you describe an event, action, or procedure as **symbolic**, you mean that it represents an important change, although it has little practical effect. The President's visit is loaded with symbolic significance. ♦ **symbolically** ADV It was a simple enough gesture, but symbolically important. **2** ADJ **Symbolic** is used to describe things involving or relating to symbols. ...symbolic representations of landscape. ♦ **symbolism** /'sɪmbəlɪzəm/ N-UNCOUNT ...a film much praised for its visual symbolism.

symbolize (BRIT also **symbolise**) /'sɪmbəlaɪz/ **symbolizes, symbolizing, symbolized.** VERB If one thing **symbolizes** another, it is used or regarded as a symbol of it. The fall of the Berlin Wall symbolised the end of the Cold War.

symmetrical /sɪ'metrɪkəl/. ADJ If something is **symmetrical**, it has two halves which are exactly the same, except that one half is the mirror image of the other. ...rows of perfectly symmetrical windows. ♦ **symmetrically** ADV The hors d'oeuvres were arranged symmetrically on two plates.

symmetry /'sɪmɪtri/ **symmetries.** N-VAR Something that has **symmetry** is symmetrical in shape, design, or structure. ...the incredible beauty and symmetry of a snowflake.

sympathetic /ˌsɪmpə'θetɪk/. **1** ADJ If you are **sympathetic to** someone who has had a misfortune, you are kind to them and show that you understand how they are feeling. She was very sympathetic to the problems of adult students. ...a sympathetic friend. ♦ **sympathetically** ADV She nodded sympathetically. **2** ADJ If you are **sympathetic to** a proposal or action, you approve of it and are willing to support it. The London galleries are sympathetic to new ideas.

sympathize (BRIT also **sympathise**) /'sɪmpəθaɪz/ **sympathizes, sympathizing, sympathized.**

a
b
c
d
e
f
g
h
i
j
k
l
m
n
o
p
q
r
s
t
u
v
w
x
y
z

sympathy

712

1 VERB If you **sympathize with** someone who has had a misfortune, you show that you are sorry for them. *Anyone who has been in a troubled relationship will sympathise with Sue... He would sympathize but he wouldn't understand.* **2** VERB If you **sympathize with** someone's feelings, you understand them and are not critical of them. *He liked Max, and sympathized with his ambitions.* **3** VERB If you **sympathize with** a person or group, you approve of their actions or proposals. *Most of the people living there sympathized with the guerrillas.* ♦ **sympathizer, sympathizers** N-COUNT *...a large group of Nazi sympathisers.*

⭐ **sympathy** /'sɪmpəθi/ **sympathies. 1** N-UNCOUNT If you have **sympathy for** someone who has had a misfortune, you are sorry for them, and show this in the way you behave towards them. *We expressed our sympathy for her loss... I have had very little help from doctors and no sympathy whatsoever.* **2** N-VAR If you have **sympathy with** someone's ideas or opinions, you agree with them. *I have some sympathy with this point of view.* **3** N-UNCOUNT If you take some action **in sympathy with** someone else, you do it in order to show that you support them. *A few players grumbled in sympathy with each other.*

symphony /'sɪmfəni/ **symphonies.** N-COUNT A **symphony** is a piece of music written to be played by an orchestra, usually in four parts.

'symphony orchestra, symphony orchestras. N-COUNT A **symphony orchestra** is a large orchestra that plays classical music.

symposium /sɪm'pəʊziəm/ **symposiums.** N-COUNT A **symposium** is a conference in which experts or scholars discuss a particular subject.

⭐ **symptom** /'sɪmptəm/ **symptoms. 1** N-COUNT A **symptom** of an illness is something wrong with your body that is a sign of the illness. *...patients with flu symptoms.* **2** N-COUNT A **symptom of** a bad situation is something that happens which is considered to be a sign of this situation. *Your problem with keeping boyfriends is just a symptom of a larger problem.*

symptomatic /ˌsɪmptə'mætɪk/. ADJ AFTER LINK-V If something is **symptomatic of** something else, especially something bad, it is a sign of it. [FORMAL] *The city's problems are symptomatic of the crisis that is spreading throughout the country.*

synagogue /'sɪnəgɒg/ **synagogues.** N-COUNT A **synagogue** is a building where Jewish people worship.

synchronize (BRIT also **synchronise**) /'sɪŋkrənaɪz/ **synchronizes, synchronizing, synchronized.** VERB If you **synchronize** two activities, processes, or movements, you cause them to happen at the same time and speed as each other. *It was virtually impossible to synchronise our lives so as to take holidays and weekends together.*

syndicate /'sɪndɪkət/ **syndicates.** N-COUNT A **syndicate** is an association of people or organizations that is formed for business

purposes or to carry out a project. *...a major crime syndicate.*

syndrome /'sɪndrəʊm/ **syndromes. 1** N-COUNT A **syndrome** is a medical condition that is characterized by a particular group of symptoms. *...sudden infant death syndrome.* **2** N-COUNT You can refer to an undesirable condition that is characterized by a particular type of activity or behaviour as a **syndrome**. *Scientists call this the 'it won't affect me' syndrome.*

synonym /'sɪnənɪm/ **synonyms.** N-COUNT A **synonym** is a word or expression which means the same as another one.

synonymous /sɪ'nɒnɪməs/. **1** ADJ **Synonymous** words or expressions have the same meaning as each other. **2** ADJ If you say that one thing is **synonymous with** another, you mean that the two things are very closely associated with each other. *Paris has always been synonymous with elegance.*

synthesis /'sɪnθɪsɪs/ **syntheses** /'sɪnθɪsiːz/. N-COUNT A **synthesis of** different ideas or styles is a mixture or combination of them. [FORMAL] *...her synthesis of feminism and socialism.*

synthesize (BRIT also **synthesise**) /'sɪnθɪsaɪz/ **synthesizes, synthesizing, synthesized.** VERB If you **synthesize** different ideas, facts, or experiences, you combine them to develop a single idea or impression. [FORMAL] *The movement synthesised elements of modern art that hadn't been brought together before.*

synthetic /sɪn'θetɪk/. ADJ **Synthetic** products are made from chemicals or artificial substances rather than from natural ones. *...synthetic rubber.*

syphon /'saɪfən/ **syphons.** See **siphon.**

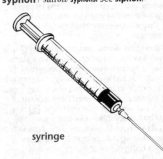

syringe

syringe /sɪ'rɪndʒ/ **syringes.** N-COUNT A **syringe** is a small tube with a fine hollow needle, used for injecting drugs or for taking blood from someone's body.

syrup /'sɪrəp/ **syrups.** N-VAR **Syrup** is a sweet liquid made by cooking sugar with water or fruit juice.

⭐ **system** /'sɪstəm/ **systems. 1** N-COUNT A **system** is a way of working, organizing, or doing something which follows a fixed plan or set of rules. *...the present system of funding for higher* *education.* 2 N-COUNT You use **system** to refer to a set of equipment, parts, or devices. *...powerful computer systems.. ...a central heating system. ...the body's digestive system.* 3 N-COUNT You use **system** to refer to a whole institution or aspect of society that is organized in a particular way. *...the British legal system. ...Australia's road and rail system.* 4 N-COUNT A **system** is a set of rules, especially in mathematics or science, which is used to count or measure things. *...the decimal system of metric weights.* 5 N-SING People sometimes refer to the government or administration of a country as **the system**. *These feelings are likely to make people attempt to overthrow the system.* 6 See also **immune system**, **nervous system**, **solar system**.

systematic /ˌsɪstə'mætɪk/. ADJ Something that is done in a **systematic** way is done according to a fixed plan, in a thorough and efficient way. *They commenced a systematic search.*
♦ **systematically** ADV *The army has systematically violated human rights.*

systemic /sɪ'stiːmɪk/. ADJ **Systemic** means affecting the whole of a system or organism. [FORMAL] *The economy is locked in a systemic crisis.*

T t

tab /tæb/ **tabs**. N-COUNT A **tab** is a small piece of cloth or paper that is attached to something, usually with information about that thing written on it.
PHRASES ● If someone **keeps tabs on** you, they make sure that they always know where you are and what you are doing, often in order to control you. [INFORMAL] ● If you **pick up the tab**, you pay a bill on behalf of a group of people or provide the money that is needed for something.

⭐ **table** /'teɪbəl/ **tables, tabling, tabled**. 1 N-COUNT A **table** is a piece of furniture with a flat top that you put things on or sit at. *...the kitchen table.* 2 N-COUNT A **table** is a set of facts or figures arranged in columns and rows. 3 PHRASE If you **turn the tables on** someone who is causing you problems, you change the situation completely so that you cause problems for them instead. 4 VERB If someone **tables** a proposal, they say formally that they want it to be discussed at a meeting. [BRITISH] *They've tabled a motion criticising the Government.*

tablecloth /'teɪbəlklɒθ, AM -klɔːθ/ **tablecloths**. N-COUNT A **tablecloth** is a cloth used to cover a table.

tablespoon /'teɪbəlspuːn/ **tablespoons**. N-COUNT A **tablespoon** is a fairly large spoon used for serving food and in cookery.

tablet /'tæblət/ **tablets**. N-COUNT A **tablet** is a small, solid, round mass of medicine which you swallow. *I take herbal sleeping tablets.*

tabloid /'tæblɔɪd/ **tabloids**. N-COUNT A **tabloid** is a newspaper with small pages, short articles, and lots of photographs.

taboo /tæ'buː/ **taboos**. N-COUNT & ADJ If there is a **taboo** on a subject or activity, or if it is **taboo**, it is a social custom to avoid doing that activity or talking about that subject, because people find it embarrassing or offensive. *Addiction remains something of a taboo... Cancer is a taboo subject.*

tacit /'tæsɪt/. ADJ If someone gives their **tacit** agreement or approval, they agree to something or approve it without actually saying so. *He gave tacit support to terrorists.* ♦ **tacitly** ADV *He tacitly admitted that they had breached regulations.*

tack /tæk/ **tacks, tacking, tacked**. 1 N-COUNT A **tack** is a short nail with a broad flat head. 2 VERB If you **tack** something to a surface, you pin it there with tacks. *He had tacked this note to her door.* 3 N-UNCOUNT If you change **tack** or try a different **tack**, you try a different method for dealing with a situation. *This report takes a different tack from the 20 that have come before.*
►**tack on**. PHR-VERB If you say that something **is tacked on to** something else, you think that it is added in a hurried and unsatisfactory way. *The child-care bill is to be tacked on to the budget plan.*

⭐ **tackle** /'tækəl/ **tackles, tackling, tackled**. 1 VERB If you **tackle** a difficult task, you start dealing with it in a determined way. *Drastic measures are needed to tackle the crisis.* 2 VERB & N-COUNT If you **tackle** someone in a game such as football, you try to take the ball away from them. This action is called a **tackle**. 3 VERB If you **tackle** someone about a difficult matter, you speak to them frankly about it, usually in order to get something changed or done. 4 N-UNCOUNT **Tackle** is the equipment that you need for an activity, especially fishing.

tacky /'tæki/ **tackier, tackiest**. ADJ If you describe something as **tacky**, you dislike it because it is cheap and badly made or vulgar. [INFORMAL] *...tacky red sunglasses.*

tact /tækt/. N-UNCOUNT **Tact** is the ability to avoid upsetting or offending people by being careful not to say or do things that would hurt their feelings. *He has handled the affair with great tact.*

tactful /'tæktfʊl/. ADJ If you describe someone as **tactful**, you approve of them because they are careful not to say or do anything that would offend or upset other people. *Sorry, that wasn't a very tactful question, was it?* ♦ **tactfully** ADV *Alex tactfully refrained from further comment.*

⭐ **tactic** /'tæktɪk/ **tactics**. N-COUNT **Tactics** are the methods that you choose in order to achieve what you want. *...delaying tactics.*

tactical /'tæktɪkəl/. 1 ADJ A **tactical** action or plan is intended to help someone achieve what they want in the future, rather than immediately.

a
b
c
d
e
f
g
h
i
j
k
l
m
n
o
p
q
r
s
t
u
v
w
x
y
z

The forces made a tactical withdrawal from the area. ♦ **tactically** ADV Many will vote tactically for the party that has the best possibility of beating the government. [2] ADJ **Tactical** means relating to tactics. He's made a tactical error.

tag /tæg/ **tags, tagging, tagged.** [1] N-COUNT A **tag** is a small piece of card or cloth which is attached to an object and has information about that object on it. ...baggage tags. [2] VERB If you **tag** something, you attach something to it or mark it so that it can be identified later.

▶**tag along.** PHR-VERB If you **tag along with** someone, you go with them, especially because you are interested in what they are doing. He said we could tag along with them.

tail /teɪl/ **tails, tailing, tailed.** [1] N-COUNT The **tail** of an animal is the part extending beyond the end of its body. [2] N-COUNT You can use **tail** to refer to the end or back of something, especially something long and thin. ...the tail of the plane. [3] VERB To **tail** someone means to follow close behind them and watch what they do. [INFORMAL] He trusted her so little that he had her tailed.

▶**tail off.** PHR-VERB If something **tails off**, it gradually becomes less, and perhaps ends completely. Last year, economic growth tailed off to below four percent.

tailor /ˈteɪlə/ **tailors, tailoring, tailored.** [1] N-COUNT A **tailor** is a person who makes clothes, especially for men. [2] VERB If you **tailor** something such as a plan or system to someone's needs or purposes, you make it suitable for them by changing the details of it. ...scripts tailored to American comedy audiences.

tailor-'made. ADJ Something that is **tailor-made for** a person or purpose is very suitable or was specially designed for them. These questions were tailor-made for Professor Posner.

taint /teɪnt/ **taints, tainting, tainted.** [1] VERB If you say that something or someone **is tainted** by something undesirable or corrupt, you mean that their status or reputation is harmed by it. ...a series of political scandals that has tainted the political stars of a generation. ♦ **tainted** ADJ ...tainted evidence. [2] N-SING A **taint** is an undesirable quality in something which spoils it. Her party never shook off the taint of corruption.

take 1 used with nouns describing actions

take /teɪk/ **takes, taking, took, taken.** [1] VERB You can use **take** to say that someone does something. For example, you can say '**he took a look**' instead of 'he looked'. She was too tired to take a shower... Betty took a photograph of us. [2] VERB You can use **take** with nouns instead of using a more specific and often more formal verb. For example, you can say '**he took control**' instead of 'he assumed control'. The Patriotic Front took power after a three-month civil war.

take 2 other verb and noun senses

take /teɪk/ **takes, taking, took, taken.** [1] VERB If you **take** something, you reach for it and hold it. Let me take your coat... Opening a drawer, she took

out a letter. [2] VERB If you **take** something with you when you go somewhere, you carry it with you. I'll take these papers home and read them. [3] VERB If you **take** something from its owner, you steal it. [4] VERB If a person, vehicle, or path **takes** someone somewhere, they transport or lead them there. She took me to a Mexican restaurant. [5] VERB To **take** something or someone means to win or capture them from an enemy or opponent. Marines went in, taking 15 prisoners. [6] VERB If you **take** something that is offered to you, you accept it. When I took the job I thought I could change the system. [7] VERB If you **take** a road or route, you choose to travel along it. Take the Chester Road to the outskirts of town. [8] VERB If you **take** a car, train, bus, or plane, you use it to go from one place to another. She took the train to New York. [9] VERB If you **take** a particular size in shoes or clothes, that size fits you. 47 per cent of women in the UK take a size 16 or above. [10] VERB If someone **takes** a drug or medicine, they swallow it. [11] VERB If you **take** an event or piece of news well or badly, you react to it well or badly. No one took my messages seriously. [12] VERB If something **takes** a certain amount of time, you need that amount of time in order to do it. The sauce takes 25 minutes to prepare. [13] VERB If something **takes** a particular quality or thing, it requires it. Walking across the room took all her strength. [14] VERB If you cannot **take** something unpleasant, you cannot bear it. Don't ever ask me to look after those kids again. I just can't take it! [15] VERB If you **take** a subject or course at school or university, you choose to study it. Students are allowed to take European history and American history. [16] VERB If you **take** an exam, you do it or take part in it. ● See note at **exam**. [17] VERB The teacher who **takes** a class for a subject teaches the class that subject. [BRITISH]

USAGE Take and bring are both used to talk about carrying something or accompanying someone somewhere, but **take** is to suggest movement away from the speaker and **bring** is used to suggest movement towards the speaker. We could not bring it here because it is rather heavy... Anna took the book to bed with her. In the first sentence, bring suggests that we are coming to the same place as the speaker, that is, the speaker is here too. In the second sentence, took suggests that Anna moved away from the speaker when she went to bed, or alternatively that the speaker is merely reporting something that he or she was not involved in.
The difference between **bring** and **take** is equivalent to that between **come** and **go**. Bring and come suggest movement towards the speaker, while **take** and **go** suggest movement away.

take 3 phrases

take /teɪk/ takes, taking, took, taken.

PHRASES ● You can say **'I take it'** to someone in order to confirm that you have understood their meaning or understood a situation. *I take it that neither of you reads 'The Times'.* ● If you say to someone **'take it or leave it'**, you are telling them that they can accept something or not accept it, but that you are not prepared to discuss any other alternatives.

take 4 phrasal verbs

★ **take** /teɪk/ takes, taking, took, taken.

▸**take after.** PHR-VERB If you **take after** a member of your family, you look or behave like them. *He takes after his dad.*

▸**take apart.** PHR-VERB If you **take** something **apart**, you separate it into its different parts.

▸**take away.** [1] PHR-VERB If you **take** something **away from** someone, you remove it from them. *'Give me the knife,' he said softly, 'or I'll take it away from you.'* [2] See also **takeaway**.

▸**take back.** [1] PHR-VERB If you **take** something **back**, you return it. *I once took back a pair of shoes that fell apart after a week.* [2] PHR-VERB If you **take back** something that you said, you admit that it was wrong. *Take back what you said about Jeremy!*

▸**take down.** [1] PHR-VERB When people **take down** a structure, they separate it into pieces and remove it. *The Canadian army took down the barricades.* [2] PHR-VERB If you **take down** information, you write it down. *I took down his comments in shorthand.*

▸**take in.** [1] PHR-VERB If you **take** someone **in**, you allow them to stay in your house or country, especially when they are homeless or in trouble. *The monastery has taken in 26 refugees.* [2] PHR-VERB If you **are taken in** by someone or something, you are deceived or fooled by them. *He is a real charmer who totally took me in.* [3] PHR-VERB If you **take** something **in**, you pay attention to it and understand it when you hear or read it. *Robert took it all in without needing second explanations.*

▸**take off.** [1] PHR-VERB When an aircraft **takes off**, it leaves the ground and starts flying. ● See also **takeoff**. [2] PHR-VERB If you **take off** something that you are wearing, you move it off your body. *She took off her spectacles.* ● See note at **wear**. [3] PHR-VERB If you **take** time **off**, you do not go to work. *She took two days off work.*

▸**take on.** [1] PHR-VERB If you **take on** a job or responsibility, you accept it. *Don't take on more responsibilities than you can handle.* [2] PHR-VERB If you **take on** someone more powerful than you, you fight them or compete against them. [3] PHR-VERB If you **take** someone **on**, you give them a job. *The party has been taking on staff.* [4] PHR-VERB If something **takes on** a new appearance or quality, it develops that appearance or quality. *His writing took on a feverish intensity.*

▸**take out.** [1] PHR-VERB If you **take out** something such as a loan or insurance policy, a company agrees to let you have it. [2] PHR-VERB If you **take** someone **out**, you take them to an enjoyable place, and you pay for both of you. *Rachel took me out to lunch.* [3] PHR-VERB If you **take** your unhappiness or anger **out on** someone, you behave in an unpleasant way towards them, even though it is not their fault that you feel upset. *Just because you've had a bad day at work, there's no need to take it out on us.* [4] See also **takeout**.

▸**take over.** [1] PHR-VERB To **take over** something such as a company or country means to gain control of it. *A British newspaper says British Airways plan to take over Trans World Airways.* ● See also **takeover**. [2] PHR-VERB If you **take over** a job, or if you **take over**, you start doing the job after someone else has stopped doing it. *In 1966, Pastor Albertz took over from him as governing mayor.*

▸**take to.** [1] PHR-VERB If you **take to** someone or something, you like them immediately. *My wife Caroline and I immediately took to Alan.* [2] PHR-VERB If you **take to** doing something, you begin to do it regularly. *They had taken to wandering through the streets.*

▸**take up.** [1] PHR-VERB If you **take up** an activity or job, you start doing it. *He left a job in the City to take up farming.* [2] PHR-VERB If you **take** someone **up on** an offer that they have made, you accept their offer. *Since she'd offered to babysit, I took her up on it.* [3] PHR-VERB If you **take up** a matter, you start to deal with it or discuss how you are going to deal with it. *Dr Mahathir intends to take up the proposal with the prime minister.*

▸**take upon.** PHR-VERB If you **take it upon yourself to** do something, you do it even though it is not your duty. *Knox had taken it upon himself to choose the wine.*

takeaway /ˈteɪkəweɪ/ takeaways. N-COUNT In British English, a **takeaway** is a shop or restaurant which sells hot food to be eaten elsewhere. A meal that you buy there is also called a **takeaway**. The American word is **takeout**.

taken /ˈteɪkən/. [1] **Taken** is the past participle of **take**. [2] ADJ AFTER LINK-V If you are **taken with** something or someone, you find them attractive and interesting. *She seems very taken with the idea.*

takeoff /ˈteɪkɒf, AM -ɔːf/ takeoffs. N-VAR **Takeoff** is the beginning of a flight, when an aircraft leaves the ground. *The commuter plane was waiting for takeoff.*

takeout /ˈteɪkaʊt/ takeouts. See **takeaway**.

★ **takeover** /ˈteɪkəʊvə/ takeovers. [1] N-VAR A **takeover** is the act of gaining control of a company by buying a majority of its shares. *...the proposed takeover of Midland Bank.* [2] N-COUNT A **takeover** is the act of taking control of a country,

a
b
c
d
e
f
g
h
i
j
k
l
m
n
o
p
q
r
s
t
u
v
w
x
y
z

political party, or movement by force. *There's been a military takeover of some kind.*

taker /'teɪkə/ **takers.** N-COUNT If there are no **takers** or few **takers** for an offer or challenge, hardly anyone is willing to accept it.

takings /'teɪkɪŋz/. N-PLURAL The **takings** of a business such as a shop or cinema consist of the amount of money it gets from selling its goods or tickets during a certain period. [BRITISH]

⭐ **tale** /teɪl/ **tales.** **1** N-COUNT A **tale** is a story, especially one involving adventure or magic. **2** N-COUNT You can refer to an interesting, exciting, or dramatic account of a real event as a **tale**. *...tales of horror and loss resulting from Monday's earthquake.* **3** See also **fairy tale**.

⭐ **talent** /'tælənt/ **talents.** N-VAR **Talent** is the natural ability to do something well. *Both her children have a talent for music... It is important to use people's talents to the full.*

talented /'tæləntɪd/. ADJ Someone who is **talented** has a natural ability to do something well. *Howard is a talented pianist.*

talisman /'tælɪzmən/ **talismans.** N-COUNT A **talisman** is an object which you believe has magic powers to protect you or bring you luck.

⭐ **talk** /tɔːk/ **talks, talking, talked.** **1** VERB & N-VAR When you **talk**, you say things to someone. **Talk** is the things you say. *They were talking about American food... A teacher reprimanded a girl for talking in class... We had a long talk about her father.* **2** VERB & N-COUNT If you **talk**, or if you give a **talk on** or **about** something, you make an informal speech about it. *He intends to talk to young people about the dangers of AIDS.* **3** VERB & N-PLURAL When different sides in a dispute or negotiation **talk**, or when they have **talks**, they have formal discussions. *The two sides still aren't prepared to talk to each other. ...peace talks.* **4** VERB If someone **talks** when they are being held by police or soldiers, they reveal important or secret information, usually unwillingly. **5** VERB If you **talk** politics or sport, for example, you discuss it. *...middle-aged men talking business.*

USAGE There are some differences in the way the verbs **talk** and **speak** are used. **Talk** is more likely to be used when you are referring to a conversation or discussion. *I talked about it with my family at dinner... Sometimes we'd talk all night.* **Talk** can also be used to emphasize the activity of saying things, rather than the words that are spoken. *She thought I talked too much.* When you **speak** however, you could, for example, be addressing someone or making a speech.

▶**talk down.** PHR-VERB If someone **talks** something **down**, they reduce its value or importance by saying bad things about it. *Businessmen are tired of politicians talking the economy down.*

▶**talk into.** PHR-VERB If you **talk** someone **into** doing something, they persuade them to do it.

▶**talk out of.** PHR-VERB If you **talk** someone **out of** doing something, you persuade them not to do it.

▶**talk over.** PHR-VERB If you **talk** something **over**, you discuss it thoroughly and honestly. *He always talked things over with his friends.*

▶**talk through.** PHR-VERB To **talk through** a problem is the same as to **talk** it **over**. *That's how we cope, by talking things through.*

▶**talk up.** PHR-VERB If someone **talks up** a particular thing, they increase its value, success, or importance by saying exaggerated things about it. *Politicians accuse the media of talking up the possibility of a riot.*

⭐ **tall** /tɔːl/ **taller, tallest.** **1** ADJ Someone or something that is **tall** is above average height. → See picture on page 324. *He was very tall.* **2** ADJ You use **tall** to ask or talk about the height of someone or something. *How tall are you?... I'm only 5ft tall.* **3** PHRASE If something is **a tall order**, it is very difficult. *Financing your studies may seem like a tall order.* **4** See note at **high**.

tally /'tæli/ **tallies, tallying, tallied.** **1** N-COUNT A **tally** is a record of amounts or numbers which you keep changing and adding to as the activity which affects it progresses. *The final tally was 817 votes for her and 731 for Mr Lee.* **2** VERB If two numbers or statements **tally**, they agree with each other or are exactly the same. *This description didn't seem to tally with what we saw.*

tame /teɪm/ **tamer, tamest; tames, taming, tamed.** **1** ADJ A **tame** animal or bird is not afraid of humans. **2** ADJ If you say that something or someone is **tame**, you are criticizing them for being weak and boring. *Some of today's political demonstrations look rather tame.* ♦ **tamely** ADV *He tamely did what someone else told him.* **3** VERB If someone **tames** a wild animal or a wild bird, they train it not to be afraid of humans.

tamper /'tæmpə/ **tampers, tampering, tampered.** VERB If someone **tampers with** something, they interfere with it or try to change it when they have no right to do so. *He found his computer had been tampered with.* ♦ **tampering** N-UNCOUNT *The phone lines also have a security code to prevent tampering.*

tampon /'tæmpɒn/ **tampons.** N-COUNT A **tampon** is a firm piece of cotton wool that a woman puts inside her vagina when she has a period, in order to absorb the blood.

tan /tæn/ **tans, tanning, tanned.** **1** N-COUNT If you have a **tan**, your skin has become darker than

usual because you have been in the sun.
[2] VERB If a part of your body **tans**, your skin becomes darker than usual because you spend time in the sun. ♦ **tanned** ADJ *He is very tanned.*

tandem /'tændəm/ **tandems.** [1] N-COUNT A **tandem** is a bicycle designed for two riders. → See picture on page 817. [2] PHRASE If two things happen or are done **in tandem**, they happen or are done together.

tangible /'tændʒɪbəl/. ADJ If something is **tangible**, it is clear enough to be easily seen, felt, or noticed. *...tangible evidence that the economy is starting to recover.*

tangle /'tæŋgəl/ **tangles, tangling, tangled.**
[1] N-COUNT A **tangle of** something is a mass of it twisted together in a confusing manner. *...a tangle of wires.* [2] VERB & PHR-VERB If something **is tangled**, or if it **is tangled up**, it becomes twisted into a confusing mass that is difficult to separate into its original form. *Animals get tangled in fishing nets and drown.*

⭐ **tank** /tæŋk/ **tanks.** [1] N-COUNT A **tank** is a large container for holding liquid or gas. *...a tank full of goldfish.* [2] N-COUNT A **tank** is a military vehicle covered with armour and equipped with guns or rockets.

tanker /'tæŋkə/ **tankers.** N-COUNT A **tanker** is a ship or truck used for transporting large quantities of gas or liquid, especially oil.

tanned /tænd/. See **tan**.

tantalize (BRIT also **tantalise**) /'tæntəlaɪz/ **tantalizes, tantalizing, tantalized.** VERB If something or someone **tantalizes** you, they make you feel hopeful and excited about something, usually before disappointing you. *...the dreams of democracy that have so tantalized them.*
♦ **tantalizing** ADJ *...a tantalising aroma of roast beef.*

tantamount /'tæntəmaʊnt/. ADJ AFTER LINK-V If you say that one thing is **tantamount to** a second, more serious thing, you are emphasizing how bad or unfortunate the first thing is by saying it is almost the same as the second. [FORMAL] *Slowing down can seem tantamount to admitting you're weak.*

tantrum /'tæntrəm/ **tantrums.** N-COUNT If a child has a **tantrum**, it suddenly loses its temper in a noisy and uncontrolled way.

⭐ **tap** /tæp/ **taps, tapping, tapped.** [1] N-COUNT A **tap** is a device that controls the flow of a liquid or gas from a pipe or container. *She turned on the tap and splashed her face with cold water.* [2] VERB & N-COUNT If you **tap** something, or if you **tap on** it, you hit it with a quick light blow or a series of quick light blows. This kind of blow is called a **tap**. *O'Leary tapped the pavement with his foot... A tap on the door interrupted him.* [3] VERB If you **tap** a resource, you make use of it. *Hydro-electric power taps the energy of river water.* [4] VERB & N-COUNT If someone **taps** your telephone, they attach a special device called a **tap** to the line so

that they can secretly listen to your conversations.

⭐ **tape** /teɪp/ **tapes, taping, taped.** [1] N-UNCOUNT **Tape** is a narrow plastic strip covered with a magnetic substance. It is used to record sounds, pictures, and computer information. *Many students declined to be interviewed on tape.* [2] N-COUNT A **tape** is a cassette with magnetic tape wound round it. [3] VERB If you **tape** music, sounds, or television pictures, you record them using a tape recorder or a video recorder. ♦ **taping, tapings** N-VAR *...an unauthorized taping.* [4] N-VAR A **tape** is a strip of cloth used to tie things together or to identify who a piece of clothing belongs to. *...name tapes.* [5] N-UNCOUNT **Tape** is a sticky strip of plastic used for sticking things together. *...adhesive tape.* [6] VERB If you **tape** one thing to another, you attach it using sticky tape. *The envelope was taped shut.* ● See also **red tape**.
▸ **tape up.** PHR-VERB If you **tape** something **up**, you fasten tape around it firmly, in order to protect it or hold it in a fixed position.

'tape measure, tape measures. N-COUNT A **tape measure** is a strip of metal, plastic, or cloth with marks on it, used for measuring.

taper /'teɪpə/ **tapers, tapering, tapered.** VERB If something **tapers**, or if you **taper** it, it gradually becomes thinner at one end. *...a beard that tapered to a sharp point.* ♦ **tapered** ADJ *...the elegantly tapered legs of the dressing-table.*
▸ **taper off.** PHR-VERB If something **tapers off**, it gradually reduces in amount, number, or size. *The storm is expected to taper off today.*

'tape recorder, tape recorders. N-COUNT A **tape recorder** is a machine used for recording and playing music, speech, or other sounds.

tapestry /'tæpɪstri/ **tapestries.** N-VAR A **tapestry** is a piece of heavy, good quality cloth with a picture or pattern sewn on it.

tar /tɑː/. N-UNCOUNT **Tar** is a thick, black, sticky substance used in making roads.

⭐ **target** /'tɑːgɪt/ **targets, targeting, targeted.**
[1] N-COUNT A **target** is something that someone is trying to hit with a weapon or other object. *Both his kicks missed the target... The mine could be a prime target for guerilla attack.* [2] VERB If someone **targets** someone or something, they decide to attack or criticize them. *He targets the economy as the root cause of the deteriorating law and order situation.* [3] N-COUNT The **target of** an attack or a criticism is the person or thing being attacked or criticized. *They have been the target of racist abuse.* [4] N-COUNT A **target** is a result that you are trying to achieve. *...the park's annual target of 11 million visitors.* [5] PHRASE If someone or something is **on target**, they are making good progress and are likely to achieve the result that is wanted. [6] VERB If you **target** a particular group of people, you try to appeal to those people or affect them. *The union was particularly keen to target young people.*

⭐ Bank of English® frequent word   For a full explanation of all grammatical labels, see pages vii-x

a
b
c
d
e
f
g
h
i
j
k
l
m
n
o
p
q
r
s
t
u
v
w
x
y
z

tariff /'tærɪf/ **tariffs.** [1] N-COUNT A **tariff** is a tax on goods coming into a country. [2] N-COUNT A **tariff** is the rate at which you are charged for something. [BRITISH]

tarmac /'tɑːmæk/. N-UNCOUNT **Tarmac** is a material used for making road surfaces, consisting of crushed stones mixed with tar. **Tarmac** is a trademark. [BRITISH]

tarnish /'tɑːnɪʃ/ **tarnishes, tarnishing, tarnished.** [1] VERB If something **tarnishes** a person's reputation, it damages it and causes people to lose respect for that person. ♦ **tarnished** ADJ *He wants to improve his tarnished image.* [2] VERB If metal **tarnishes**, or if something **tarnishes** it, it becomes stained and loses its brightness. ♦ **tarnished** ADJ *...tarnished brass.*

tart /tɑːt/ **tarts.** [1] N-VAR A **tart** is a shallow pastry case with a filling of sweet food or fruit. *...jam tarts.* [2] ADJ If something such as fruit is **tart**, it has a sharp slightly bitter taste.

tartan /'tɑːtən/. ADJ **Tartan** cloth, which traditionally comes from Scotland, has different coloured stripes crossing each other. → See picture on page 829.

★ **task** /tɑːsk, tæsk/ **tasks.** N-COUNT A **task** is an activity or piece of work which you have to do. *Walker had the unenviable task of breaking the bad news to Hill... ...administrative tasks.*

★ **taste** /teɪst/ **tastes, tasting, tasted.** [1] N-UNCOUNT Your sense of **taste** is your ability to recognize the flavour of things with your tongue. [2] N-COUNT The **taste** of something is the flavour that it has, for example whether it is sweet or salty. *I like the taste of wine.* [3] VERB If food or drink **tastes of** something, it has that particular flavour. *I drank a cup of tea that tasted of diesel... The pizza tastes delicious.* [4] VERB & N-SING If you **taste** some food or drink, or if you have a **taste of** it, you try a small amount of it in order to see what its flavour and texture is like. [5] VERB If you can **taste** something that you are eating or drinking, you are aware of its flavour. *You can taste the chilli in the dish.* [6] VERB & N-SING If you **taste** something such as a way of life or a pleasure, or if you have a **taste of** it, you experience it for a short period of time. [7] N-SING If you have a **taste for** something, you enjoy it. *That gave me a taste for reading.* [8] N-UNCOUNT & N-PLURAL A person's **taste** is their choice in the things that they like or buy, for example their clothes, possessions, or favourite music. *There was music for all ages and all tastes.* [9] PHRASE If you say that something that is said or done is **in bad taste** or **in poor taste**, you mean that it is offensive, often because it concerns death or sex and is inappropriate for the situation.

tasteful /'teɪstful/. ADJ If you describe something as **tasteful**, you mean that it is attractive and elegant. *...a tasteful linen suit.* ♦ **tastefully** ADV *...a large and tastefully decorated home.*

tasteless /'teɪstləs/. [1] ADJ If you describe something as **tasteless**, you mean that it is vulgar and unattractive. [2] ADJ If you describe something such as a remark or joke as **tasteless**, you mean that it is offensive. [3] ADJ If you describe food or drink as **tasteless**, you mean that it has very little or no flavour.

tasty /'teɪsti/ **tastier, tastiest.** ADJ If you say that food, especially savoury food, is **tasty**, you mean that it has a pleasant and fairly strong flavour which makes it good to eat.

tattered /'tætəd/. ADJ If something such as clothing is **tattered**, it is torn or crumpled, especially because it is old and has been used a lot.

tatters /'tætəz/. [1] N-PLURAL Clothes that are **in tatters** are badly torn in several places. [2] N-PLURAL If you say that something such as a plan or relationship is **in tatters**, you are emphasizing that it is weak and has suffered a lot of damage.

tattoo /tæ'tuː/ **tattoos, tattooing, tattooed.** [1] N-COUNT A **tattoo** is a design on someone's skin, made by pricking little holes and filling them with coloured dye. [2] VERB If someone **tattoos** you, they draw a design on your skin by pricking little holes and filling them with coloured dye. *He had the words 'Angie loves Ian' tattooed on his left shin.*

taught /tɔːt/. **Taught** is the past tense and past participle of **teach**.

taunt /tɔːnt/ **taunts, taunting, taunted.** [1] VERB If someone **taunts** you, they try to upset or annoy you by saying unkind or insulting things to you, especially about your weaknesses or failures. [2] N-COUNT A **taunt** is an unkind or insulting comment that is intended to upset or annoy you. *...racist taunts.*

taut /tɔːt/ **tauter, tautest.** ADJ Something that is **taut** is stretched very tight.

★ **tax** /tæks/ **taxes, taxing, taxed.** [1] N-VAR **Tax** is an amount of money that you have to pay to the government so that it can pay for public services. *...the basic rate of income tax.* [2] VERB When a person or company **is taxed**, they have to pay a part of their income or profits to the government. When goods **are taxed**, a percentage of their price has to be paid to the government. *Biscuits and ice cream are taxed at 11 percent.* [3] VERB If something **taxes** your strength, your patience, or your resources, it uses nearly all of them, so that you have great difficulty in carrying out what you are trying to do. [4] See also **taxing**.

taxable /'tæksəbəl/. ADJ **Taxable** income is income on which you have to pay tax.

taxation /tæk'seɪʃən/. [1] N-UNCOUNT **Taxation** is the system by which a government takes money from people so that it can use it to pay for public services. [2] N-UNCOUNT **Taxation** is the amount of money that people have to pay in taxes. *The result will be higher taxation.*

,tax-'free. ADJ Tax-free is used to describe income on which you do not have to pay tax. ...*a tax-free savings plan.*

taxi /'tæksi/ taxis, taxiing, taxied. [1] N-COUNT A taxi is a car driven by a person whose job is to take people where they want to go in return for money. → See picture on page 835. [2] VERB When an aircraft taxis along the ground, it moves slowly along it before taking off or after landing.

taxing /'tæksɪŋ/. ADJ A taxing task or problem requires a lot of mental or physical effort.

taxpayer /'tækspeɪə/ taxpayers. N-COUNT Taxpayers are people who pay a percentage of their income to the government as tax.

TB /,ti: 'bi:/. TB is a very serious infectious disease that affects someone's lungs and other parts of their body. TB is an abbreviation for 'tuberculosis'.

⭐ tea /ti:/ teas. [1] N-VAR Tea is a drink made by pouring boiling water on the chopped dried leaves of a plant called the tea bush. A cup of tea can be referred to as a tea. *Would you like a cup of tea?* [2] N-VAR Tea is the chopped dried leaves that you use to make tea. ...*a packet of tea.* [3] N-VAR Drinks such as mint tea are made by pouring boiling water on the dried leaves of the particular plant or flower. ...*herbal teas.* [4] N-VAR Tea is a meal some people eat in the late afternoon, especially in Britain. It consists of food such as sandwiches and cakes, with tea to drink. [5] N-VAR Some people refer to the main meal that they eat in the early part of the evening as tea. [BRITISH] [6] See note at **meal**.

⭐ teach /ti:tʃ/ teaches, teaching, taught. [1] VERB If you teach someone something, you give them instructions so that they know about it or know how to do it. *George had taught him how to ride a horse... She taught Julie to read.* [2] VERB To teach someone something means to show them how to think, feel, or act in a new or different way. *We have to teach drivers to respect pedestrians and cyclists.* [3] VERB If you teach, your job is to help students to learn about a subject by explaining it or showing them how to do it. *Ingrid is currently teaching Mathematics at Shimla Public School.* ◆ **teacher, teachers** N-COUNT ...*her chemistry teacher.* ◆ **teaching** N-UNCOUNT ...*the teaching of English in schools.* [4] to teach someone a **lesson**: see **lesson**.

⭐ teaching /'ti:tʃɪŋ/ teachings. N-COUNT The teachings of a particular person, school of thought, or religion are all the ideas and principles that they teach.

teak /ti:k/. N-UNCOUNT Teak is a very hard wood.

⭐ team /ti:m/ teams, teaming, teamed. [1] N-COUNT A team is a group of people who play together against another group in a sport or game. Team can take the singular or plural form of the verb. *The team is close to bottom of the League.* [2] N-COUNT You can refer to any group of people who work together as a team. Team can take the singular or plural form of the verb. ...*a team of doctors.*

▶team up. PHR-VERB If you team up with someone, you join them in order to work together for a particular purpose. *Elton teamed up with Eric Clapton to make the record... A friend suggested that we team up for a working holiday in Europe.*

'team-mate, team-mates. N-COUNT In a game or sport, your team-mates are the other members of your team.

teamwork /'ti:mwɜ:k/. N-UNCOUNT Teamwork is the ability that a group of people have to work well together.

teapot /'ti:pɒt/ teapots. N-COUNT A teapot is a container with a lid, a handle, and a spout, used for making and serving tea.

tear 1 crying

⭐ tear /tɪə/ tears. [1] N-COUNT Tears are the drops of liquid that come out of your eyes when you are crying. [2] N-PLURAL You can use tears in expressions such as in tears, burst into tears, and close to tears to indicate that someone is crying or is almost crying. *He was in floods of tears.*

tear 2 damaging or moving

⭐ tear /teə/ tears, tearing, tore, torn. [1] VERB & N-COUNT If you tear something such as paper or cloth, you pull it into two pieces or you pull it so that a hole appears in it. A tear in something is a hole that has been made in it. *Mary Ann tore the edge off her napkin... He took a small notebook from his jacket pocket and tore out a page... Nancy quickly tore open the envelope... I peered through a tear in the van's curtains.* [2] VERB To tear something from somewhere means to remove it violently. *She tore the windscreen wipers from his car.* [3] VERB If you tear somewhere, you move there very quickly, often in an uncontrolled or dangerous way. *The door flew open and Miranda tore into the room.* [4] See also **wear and tear**.

▶tear apart. PHR-VERB If something tears people apart, it causes them to quarrel or to leave each other. *The quarrel tore the party apart.*

▶tear away. PHR-VERB If you tear someone away from a place or activity, you force them to leave the place or stop doing the activity, even though they want to remain there or carry on. *She couldn't tear herself away from the radio.*

▶tear down. PHR-VERB If you tear something down, you destroy it or remove it completely. *They tore the school down some years later.*

▶tear off. PHR-VERB If you tear off your clothes, you take them off quickly in a rough way.

▶tear up. PHR-VERB If you tear up a piece of paper, you tear it into a lot of small pieces. *Don't you dare tear up her ticket. ...a torn up old photograph.*

tearful /'tɪəfʊl/. ADJ If someone is tearful, their face or voice shows signs that they have been crying or that they want to cry.

tear gas /'tɪə gæs/. N-UNCOUNT **Tear gas** is a gas that causes your eyes to sting and fill with tears. It is used by the police to control violent crowds.

tease /tiːz/ **teases, teasing, teased.** VERB To **tease** someone means to laugh at them or make jokes about them in order to embarrass, annoy, or upset them. *'You must be expecting a young man,' she teased.*

teaspoon /'tiːspuːn/ **teaspoons.** [1] N-COUNT A **teaspoon** is a small spoon that you use to put sugar into tea or coffee. [2] N-COUNT A **teaspoon of** food or liquid is the amount that a teaspoon will hold. *He wants three teaspoons of sugar in his coffee.*

⭐ **technical** /'teknɪkəl/. [1] ADJ **Technical** means involving the sorts of machines, processes, and materials used in industry, transport, and communications. *A number of technical problems will have to be solved. ...jobs that require technical knowledge.* [2] ADJ You use **technical** to describe the practical skills and methods used to do an activity such as an art, a craft, or a sport. *Their technical ability is exceptional.* ◆ **technically** ADV *While Sade's voice isn't technically brilliant it has a quality which is unmistakable.* [3] ADJ **Technical** language involves using special words to describe the details of a specialized activity. *...a technical term.*

technicality /,teknɪ'kælɪti/ **technicalities.** [1] N-PLURAL The **technicalities of** a process or activity are the detailed methods used to do it. *...the technicalities of classroom teaching.* [2] N-COUNT A **technicality** is a point based on a strict interpretation of a law or a set of rules. *The earlier verdict was overturned on a legal technicality.*

technically /'teknɪkli/. ADV If something is **technically** true or possible, it is true or possible according to a strict interpretation of the facts, laws, or rules, but may not be important or relevant in a particular situation. *Technically, the two sides have been in a state of war ever since 1949.*

technician /tek'nɪʃən/ **technicians.** N-COUNT A **technician** is someone whose job involves skilled practical work with scientific equipment, for example in a laboratory.

⭐ **technique** /tek'niːk/ **techniques.** [1] N-COUNT A **technique** is a particular method of doing an activity, usually a method that involves practical skills. *...the techniques of modern agriculture.* [2] N-UNCOUNT **Technique** is skill and ability in an artistic, sporting, or other practical activity that is developed through training and practice. *...the band's lack of technique.*

⭐ **technology** /tek'nɒlədʒi/ **technologies.** N-VAR **Technology** refers to things which are the result of scientific knowledge being used for practical purposes. *...the rapid development of technology. ...the moral issues posed by new technologies.* ◆ **technological** /,teknə'lɒdʒəkəl/ ADJ BEFORE N *...an era of very rapid technological change.*

◆ **technologically** /,teknə'lɒdʒɪkli/ ADV *...technologically advanced aircraft.*

teddy /'tedi/ **teddies.** N-COUNT A **teddy** or a **teddy bear** is a soft toy that looks like a bear.

tedious /'tiːdiəs/. ADJ If you describe something such as a job or a situation as **tedious**, you mean it is boring and frustrating. ◆ **tediously** ADV *These introductory chapters are tediously repetitive.*

teem /tiːm/ **teems, teeming, teemed.** VERB If a place **is teeming with** people, there are a lot of people moving around in it. *The area is teeming with tourists. ...the teeming streets of Calcutta.*

teen /tiːn/ **teens.** [1] N-PLURAL If you are **in** your **teens**, you are between thirteen and nineteen years old. *I first met John in my late teens.* [2] ADJ BEFORE N **Teen** is used to describe films, magazines, music, or activities that are aimed at or done by teenagers. *...a teen movie.*

teenage /'tiːneɪdʒ/. ADJ BEFORE N **Teenage** children are aged between thirteen and nineteen years old. *Almost one in four teenage girls now smoke. ...'Smash Hits', a teenage magazine.*

⭐ **teenager** /'tiːneɪdʒə/ **teenagers.** N-COUNT A **teenager** is someone between thirteen and nineteen years of age.

teeter /'tiːtə/ **teeters, teetering, teetered.** [1] VERB **Teeter** is used in expressions such as **teeter on the brink** to emphasize that something seems to be in a very unstable situation or position. *His voice teetered on the edge of hysteria.* [2] VERB If someone or something **teeters**, they shake in an unsteady way, and seem to be about to lose their balance and fall over. *He watched the cup teeter on the edge before it fell.*

teeth /tiːθ/. **Teeth** is the plural of **tooth**.

TEFL /'tefəl/. N-UNCOUNT **TEFL** is the teaching of English to people whose first language is not English, especially people from a country where English is not spoken. **TEFL** is an abbreviation for 'teaching English as a foreign language'.

telecommunications /,telɪkəmjuːnɪ'keɪʃənz/. N-UNCOUNT **Telecommunications** is the technology of sending signals and messages over long distances using electronic equipment, for example by radio and telephone.

telegram /'telɪgræm/ **telegrams.** N-COUNT A **telegram** is a message that is sent by electricity or radio and then printed and delivered to someone's home or office.

telemarketing /'telɪ,mɑːkɪtɪŋ/. N-UNCOUNT **Telemarketing** is the selling of a company's products or services by telephone.

telepathy /tɪ'lepəθi/. N-UNCOUNT **Telepathy** is the direct communication of thoughts and feelings between people's minds, without the need to use speech or writing. ◆ **telepathic** /,telɪ'pæθɪk/ ADJ *They had a telepathic understanding.*

⭐ **telephone** /'telɪfəʊn/ **telephones, telephoning, telephoned.** ① N-UNCOUNT **The telephone** is an electrical system used to talk to someone in another place by dialling a number on a piece of equipment and speaking into it. *She was wanted on the telephone... He made a telephone call to his wife.* ② N-COUNT A **telephone** is the piece of equipment used to talk to someone by telephone. *He got up and answered the telephone.* ③ VERB If you **telephone** someone, you dial their telephone number and speak to them by telephone. *They usually telephone first to see if she is at home.*

PHRASES ● If you are **on the telephone**, you are speaking to someone by telephone. *Linda remained on the telephone to the police for three hours.* ● If someone is **on the telephone**, they have a telephone in their house or office which is connected to the rest of the telephone system. *He's not on the telephone.*

'**telephone box, telephone boxes.** N-COUNT In British English, a **telephone box** is a small shelter in the street in which there is a public telephone. The American term is **phone booth**.

telesales /'telɪseɪlz/. N-UNCOUNT **Telesales** means the same as **telemarketing**.

telescope /'telɪskəʊp/ **telescopes.** N-COUNT A **telescope** is an instrument shaped like a tube. It has lenses inside it that make distant things seem larger and nearer when you look through it.

televise /'telɪvaɪz/ **televises, televising, televised.** VERB If an event **is televised**, it is filmed and shown on television.

⭐ **television** /'telɪvɪʒən, -'vɪʒ-/ **televisions.** ① N-COUNT A **television** or a **television set** is a piece of electrical equipment consisting of a box with a glass screen on which you can watch programmes with pictures and sounds. ② N-UNCOUNT **Television** is the system of sending pictures and sounds by electrical signals over a distance so that people can receive them on a television set. *Toy manufacturers began promoting some of their products on television.*

⭐ **tell** /tel/ **tells, telling, told.** ① VERB If you **tell** someone something, you give them information. *They told us the dreadful news... John just told me that your birthday is on the same day as mine... I had told people what he had been doing.* ② VERB If you **tell** someone **to** do something, you order, instruct, or advise them to do it. *A passer-by told the driver to move his car.* ③ VERB If facts or events **tell** you something, they reveal certain information to you through ways other than speech. *The facts tell us that this is not true... The photographs tell a different story.* ④ VERB If you can **tell** what is happening or what is true, you are able to judge correctly what is happening or what is true. *You never can tell what life is going to bring you... You can tell he's joking.* ⑤ VERB If an unpleasant or tiring experience begins to **tell**, it begins to have a serious effect. *The strains*

of office are beginning to tell on the prime minister.

> **USAGE** Note that the verb **tell** is usually followed by a direct object indicating the person who is being addressed. *He told Alison he was suffering from leukaemia... What did she tell you?* 'What did she tell to you?' is wrong. With the verb **say**, however, if you want to mention the person who is being addressed, you should use the preposition **to**. 'What did she say you?' is wrong. '**What did she say to you?**' is correct.
> **Tell** is used to report information that is given to someone. *The manufacturer told me that the product did not contain corn.* **Tell** can also be used with a 'to' infinitive to report an order or instruction. *My mother told me to shut up and eat my dinner.* **Say** is the most general verb for reporting the words that someone speaks.

▸**tell apart.** PHR-VERB If you cannot **tell** people or things **apart**, you are not able to recognize the differences between them and cannot therefore identify them individually. *I can tell only tell Mark and Dave apart by the colour of their shoes!*
▸**tell off.** PHR-VERB If you **tell** someone **off**, you speak to them angrily or seriously because they have done something wrong. *I'm always being told off for being so awkward.*

telling /'telɪŋ/. ① ADJ If something is **telling**, it shows the true nature of a person or situation. *How a man shaves may be a telling clue to his age.* ◆ **tellingly** ADV *Tellingly, fewer than 1.1 percent have university qualifications.* ② PHRASE You use **there's no telling** to introduce a statement when you want to say that it is impossible to know what will happen in a situation. *There's no telling how long the talks could drag on.*

telly /'teli/ **tellies.** N-VAR **Telly** means the same as **television**. [INFORMAL, BRITISH] *I've seen him on the telly.*

temper /'tempə/ **tempers, tempering, tempered.** ① N-VAR If you say that someone has a **temper**, you mean that they become angry very easily. *I hope he can control his temper.* ② PHRASE If you **lose** your **temper**, you become very angry. ③ N-VAR If someone is **in** a particular type of **temper**, that is the way they are feeling. *Lee stormed off the field in a furious temper.* ④ VERB To **temper** something means to make it less extreme. [FORMAL] *He had to learn to temper his enthusiasm.*

temperament /'temprəmənt/ **temperaments.** N-VAR Your **temperament** is your basic nature, especially as it is shown in the way that you react to situations or to people. *His impulsive temperament regularly got him into difficulties.*

temperamental /ˌtemprə'mentəl/. ① ADJ If you say that someone is **temperamental**, you are

a b c d e f g h i j k l m n o p q r s t u v w x y z

criticizing them for having moods that change often and suddenly. ...*a man given to temperamental outbursts.* [2] ADJ If you describe something such as a machine or car as **temperamental**, you mean that it often does not work properly. *Old cars can be temperamental.*

temperate /'tempərɪt/. ADJ A **temperate** climate or place is one that is never extremely hot or extremely cold.

⭐ **temperature** /'temprətʃə/ **temperatures.** [1] N-VAR The **temperature** of something is how hot or cold it is. *Winter closes in and the temperature drops below freezing.* [2] N-COUNT Your **temperature** is the temperature of your body. *His temperature continued to rise.*
PHRASES ● If someone **takes** your **temperature**, they use a thermometer to measure your temperature. ● If you **have a temperature**, your temperature is higher than it usually is and you feel ill.

USAGE In Britain, two different scales are commonly used for measuring temperature. On the **Celsius** (formerly **Centigrade**) scale, water freezes at zero degrees and boils at 100 degrees. On the **Fahrenheit** scale, water freezes at 32 degrees and boils at 212 degrees. Celsius is the scale which is officially used for talking about the weather. Fahrenheit is considered more old-fashioned, but is still widely used. If you want to emphasize how cold it is, you are more likely to use Celsius, as the numbers are lower. Conversely, if you want to emphasize how warm it is, you are more likely to use Fahrenheit. The first of the following examples shows a temperature in Celsius and the second shows a temperature in Fahrenheit. *The temperature has been down to minus seven... With temperatures in the 70s, sun lovers have been flocking to resorts.* In the United States, the Fahrenheit scale is almost always used.

---

template /'templeɪt, AM -plɪt/ **templates.** N-COUNT A **template** is a thin piece of metal or plastic which is cut into a particular shape. It is used to help you cut wood, paper, metal, or other materials accurately, or to reproduce the same shape many times.

⭐ **temple** /'tempəl/ **temples.** [1] N-COUNT A **temple** is a building used for the worship of a god or gods, especially in the Buddhist and Hindu religions. [2] N-COUNT Your **temples** are the flat parts on each side of the front part of your head, near your forehead.

tempo /'tempəʊ/ **tempos.** [1] N-SING The **tempo** of an event is the speed at which it happens. *He was dissatisfied with the tempo of political change.* [2] N-VAR The **tempo** of a piece of music is the speed at which it is played.

temporal /'tempərəl/. ADJ BEFORE N **Temporal** powers or matters relate to ordinary institutions and activities rather than to religious or spiritual ones. [FORMAL] ...*the spiritual and temporal leader of the people.*

⭐ **temporary** /'tempərəri, AM -reri/. ADJ Something that is **temporary** lasts for only a limited time. *His job here is only temporary.* ...*a temporary loss of memory.* ◆ **temporarily** ADV *Checkpoints between the two zones were temporarily closed.*

tempt /tempt/ **tempts, tempting, tempted.** VERB Something that **tempts** you attracts you and makes you want it, even though it may be wrong or harmful. *Children not attending schools may be tempted into crime... Don't let credit tempt you to buy something you can't afford.* ◆ **tempting** ADJ ...*Raoul's tempting offer of the Palm Beach trip.*

temptation /temp'teɪʃən/ **temptations.** N-VAR **Temptation** is the state you are in when you want to do or have something, although you know it might be wrong or harmful. *Will they be able to resist the temptation to buy?*

tempted /'temptɪd/. ADJ AFTER LINK-V If you say that you are **tempted to** do something, you mean that you would like to do it. *I'm very tempted to sell my house.*

⭐ **ten** /ten/ **tens.** NUM **Ten** is the number 10.

tenacious /tɪ'neɪʃəs/. ADJ A **tenacious** person is very determined and does not give up easily. ...*a tenacious and persistent interviewer.* ◆ **tenaciously** ADV *In spite of his illness, he clung tenaciously to his job.*

tenacity /tɪ'næsɪti/. N-UNCOUNT If you have **tenacity**, you are very determined and do not give up easily. *Hard work and sheer tenacity are crucial to career success.*

tenancy /'tenənsi/ **tenancies.** N-VAR **Tenancy** is the use that you have of land or property belonging to someone else, for which you pay rent. *His father took over the tenancy of the farm.*

tenant /'tenənt/ **tenants.** N-COUNT A **tenant** is someone who pays rent for the place they live in, or for land or buildings that they use.

⭐ **tend** /tend/ **tends, tending, tended.** [1] VERB If something **tends to** happen, it usually happens or it happens often. *I tend to forget things.* [2] VERB If someone or something **tends towards** a particular characteristic, they often display that characteristic. *The local cuisine tends towards boiled meat dishes.* [3] VERB If you **tend** someone or something, or **tend to** them, you do what is necessary to keep them in a good condition. [FORMAL] *He tends the flower beds and evergreens.*

⭐ **tendency** /'tendənsi/ **tendencies.** N-COUNT A **tendency** is a worrying or unpleasant habit or action that keeps occurring. *Her suicidal tendencies continued... Shetland jumpers have a tendency to be annoyingly itchy.*

tender /'tendə/ **tenders, tendering, tendered.** [1] ADJ A **tender** person expresses gentle and caring feelings. ◆ **tenderly** ADV *Mr. White tenderly embraced his wife.* ◆ **tenderness** N-UNCOUNT *She* smiled, politely rather than with tenderness. **2** ADJ BEFORE N If someone is at a **tender** age, they are young and inexperienced. **3** ADJ Meat or other food that is **tender** is easy to cut or chew. **4** ADJ If a part of your body is **tender**, it is sensitive and painful when it is touched. **5** VERB & N-VAR If a company **tenders for** something, or if they put in a **tender for** it, it makes a formal offer to supply goods or do a job for a particular price. **6** VERB If you **tender** something such as a suggestion or money, you formally offer or present it. [FORMAL] *She quickly tendered her resignation.*

tendon /'tendən/ **tendons.** N-COUNT A **tendon** is a strong cord of tissue in your body joining a muscle to a bone.

tenement /'tenəmənt/ **tenements.** N-COUNT A **tenement** is a large old terraced building divided into a lot of flats, also called **tenements**.

tenet /'tenɪt/ **tenets.** N-COUNT The **tenets** of a theory or belief are the principles on which it is based. [FORMAL] *Non-violence and patience are the central tenets of their faith.*

tennis

⭐ **tennis** /'tenɪs/. N-UNCOUNT **Tennis** is a game played by two or four players on a rectangular court with a net across the middle. The players use rackets to hit a ball over the net.

tenor /'tenə/ **tenors.** **1** N-COUNT A **tenor** is a male singer with a fairly high voice. **2** ADJ A **tenor** musical instrument has a range of notes of fairly low pitch. **3** N-SING The **tenor of** something is the general meaning or mood that it expresses. [FORMAL] *The whole tenor of discussions has changed.*

tense /tens/ **tenses, tensing, tensed.** **1** ADJ If you are **tense**, you are worried and nervous, and cannot relax. *Never had she seen him so tense.* **2** ADJ If your body is **tense**, muscles are tight and not relaxed. **3** VERB & PHR-VERB If your muscles **tense**, or if they **tense up**, they become tight and stiff, often because you are anxious or frightened. *Jane tensed her muscles to stop them from shaking.* **4** N-VAR The **tense** of a verb is the form which shows whether you are referring to past, present, or future time.

⭐ **tension** /'tenʃən/ **tensions.** **1** N-VAR **Tension** is a feeling of fear or nervousness produced before a difficult, dangerous, or important event. The

tension between the two countries is likely to remain. **2** N-UNCOUNT **Tension** is a feeling of worry and nervousness which makes it difficult for you to relax. *Laughing has actually been shown to relieve tension.* **3** N-UNCOUNT The **tension** in a rope or wire is how tightly it is stretched.

tent /tent/ **tents.** N-COUNT A **tent** is a shelter made of canvas or nylon and held up by poles and ropes, used mainly by people who are camping.

tentacle /'tentəkəl/ **tentacles.** N-COUNT The **tentacles** of an animal such as an octopus are the long thin parts used for feeling, holding things, and moving.

tentative /'tentətɪv/. **1** ADJ **Tentative** agreements or plans are not definite or certain, but have been made as a first step. *...a tentative agreement to hold a preparatory conference.* **2** ADJ If someone is **tentative**, they are cautious and not very confident because they are uncertain or afraid. *She did not return his tentative smile.* ◆ **tentatively** ADV *I tentatively suggested an alternative route.*

⭐ **tenth** /tenθ/. ORD The **tenth** item in a series is the one that you count as number ten.

tenuous /'tenjʊəs/. ADJ If you describe something such as a connection, a reason, or someone's position as **tenuous**, you mean that it is very uncertain or weak. *This decision puts the President in a somewhat tenuous position.*

tenure /'tenjə/. **1** N-UNCOUNT **Tenure** is the legal right to live in a place or to use land or buildings for a period of time. **2** N-UNCOUNT **Tenure** is the period of time during which someone holds an important job. *...during his tenure as foreign minister.*

tepid /'tepɪd/. **1** ADJ A **tepid** liquid is slightly warm. **2** ADJ If you describe a feeling or reaction as **tepid**, you mean that it lacks enthusiasm or liveliness. *...tepid applause.*

⭐ **term** /tɜːm/ **terms, terming, termed.** **1** PHRASE If you talk about something **in** particular **terms**, or **in terms of** a particular thing, you are specifying which aspect of it you are discussing. *The video explains in simple terms how the new tax works... Our goods compete in terms of product quality.* **2** N-COUNT A **term** is a word or expression with a specific meaning. *Myocardial infarction is the medical term for a heart attack.* **3** VERB If you say that something **is termed** a particular thing, you mean that that is what people call it or that is their opinion of it. *He termed the war a humanitarian nightmare.* **4** N-VAR A **term** is one of the periods of time that a school, college, or university year is divided into. *...the last day of term.* **5** N-COUNT A **term** is a period of time that someone spends doing a particular job or in a particular place. *Felipe Gonzalez won a fourth term of office. ...a seven-year prison term.* **6** N-PLURAL The **terms** of an agreement or arrangement are the conditions that have been accepted by the people involved in it.

PHRASES ● If you **come to terms with** something difficult or unpleasant, you learn to accept it. *It was hard to come to terms with her death.* ● If two people are treated **on equal terms** or **on the same terms**, neither of them has an advantage over the other. ● If two people are **on good terms** or **on friendly terms**, they are friendly with each other. ● You use the expressions **in the long term, in the short term,** and **in the medium term** to talk about what will happen over that period of time. *In the long term the company hopes to open in Moscow.* ● If you say you are **thinking in terms of** doing something or **talking in terms of** doing it, you mean that you are considering it. *United should be thinking in terms of winning the European Cup.* ● a **contradiction in terms**: see **contradiction.** ● **in real terms**: see **real.** ● **in no uncertain terms**: see **uncertain.**

terminal /'tɜːmɪnəl/ **terminals.** ☐ ADJ A **terminal** illness or disease cannot be cured and eventually causes death. ◆ **terminally** ADV *The patient is terminally ill.* ☐ N-COUNT A **terminal** is a place where vehicles, passengers, or goods begin or end a journey. ☐ N-COUNT A computer **terminal** is a piece of equipment consisting of a keyboard and a screen connected to a computer. [COMPUTING]

terminate /'tɜːmɪneɪt/ **terminates, terminating, terminated.** ☐ VERB When something **terminates,** or when you **terminate** it, it ends completely. [FORMAL] *His contract terminates at the season's end.* ◆ **termination** N-UNCOUNT *...the abrupt termination of trade.* ☐ VERB When a train or bus **terminates** somewhere, it ends its journey there.

terminology /ˌtɜːmɪ'nɒlədʒi/ **terminologies.** N-VAR The **terminology** of a subject is the set of special words and expressions used in connection with it. *...football terminology.*

termite /'tɜːmaɪt/ **termites.** N-COUNT **Termites** are small white insects that eat wood.

terrace /'terɪs/ **terraces.** ☐ N-COUNT A **terrace** is a row of similar houses joined together by their side walls. [BRITISH] ☐ N-COUNT A **terrace** is a flat area of stone or grass next to a building where people can sit. *...a garden terrace.* ☐ N-COUNT **Terraces** are a series of flat areas of ground built like steps on a hillside so that crops can be grown there.

terraced house

,terraced 'house, **terraced houses.** ADJ A **terraced house** or a **terrace house** is one of a row of similar houses joined together by their side walls. [BRITISH]

terracotta /ˌterə'kɒtə/. N-UNCOUNT **Terracotta** is a brownish-red clay that has been baked but not glazed and that is used for making things such as flower pots and tiles.

terrain /tə'reɪn/. N-UNCOUNT The **terrain** in an area is the type of land that is there. *...rugged mountainous terrain.*

★ **terrible** /'terɪbəl/. ☐ ADJ **Terrible** means extremely bad. *Her French is terrible.* ◆ **terribly** ADV *My son has suffered terribly.* ☐ ADJ BEFORE N You use **terrible** to emphasize the great extent or degree of something. *Her death is a terrible waste.* ◆ **terribly** ADV *I'm terribly sorry to bother you.*

terrific /tə'rɪfɪk/. ☐ ADJ If you describe something or someone as **terrific,** you are very pleased with them or very impressed by them. [INFORMAL] *You look terrific, Ann.* ☐ ADJ BEFORE N **Terrific** means very great in amount, degree, or intensity. *There was a terrific bang.*

terrify /'terɪfaɪ/ **terrifies, terrifying, terrified.** VERB If something **terrifies** you, it makes you feel extremely frightened. *The idea of death terrified me.* ◆ **terrified** ADJ *He was terrified of heights.*

terrifying /'terɪfaɪɪŋ/. ADJ If something is **terrifying,** it makes you very frightened. *Crime is increasing at a terrifying rate.*

territorial /ˌterɪ'tɔːriəl/. ADJ **Territorial** means concerned with the ownership of a particular area of land or water. *Argentina feels very strongly about its territorial claims to Antarctica.*

★ **territory** /'terətri, AM -tɔːri/ **territories.** ☐ N-VAR **Territory** is land which is controlled by a particular country or ruler. *The government denies that any of its territory is under rebel control.* ☐ N-UNCOUNT You can use **territory** to refer to an area of knowledge or experience. *...on their own familiar territory of trade.* ☐ N-UNCOUNT **Territory** is land with a particular character. *...mountainous territory.*

terror /'terə/ **terrors.** ☐ N-VAR **Terror** is very great fear. *I shook with terror... He had a real terror of facing people.* ☐ **reign of terror**: see **reign.**

★ **terrorist** /'terərɪst/ **terrorists.** N-COUNT A **terrorist** is a person who uses violence in order to achieve political aims. *...terrorist attacks.* ◆ **terrorism** N-UNCOUNT *...indiscriminate acts of terrorism.*

terrorize (BRIT also **terrorise**) /'terəraɪz/ **terrorizes, terrorizing, terrorized.** VERB If someone **terrorizes** you, they frighten you by making it seem likely that they will attack you. *...pensioners terrorised by anonymous telephone calls.*

terse /tɜːs/. ADJ A **terse** comment or statement is brief and unfriendly. ◆ **tersely** ADV *'It's too late,' he said tersely.*

tertiary /'tɜːʃəri, AM -ʃieri/. ADJ BEFORE N **Tertiary** education is education at university or college level.

⭐ **test** /test/ **tests, testing, tested.** ☐1 VERB & N-COUNT
When you **test** something, or when you conduct
a **test** on it, you try using it in order to find out
what it is, what condition it is in, or how well it
works. *...travelling to Holland to test a British-built
boat. ...the banning of nuclear tests.* ☐2 VERB &
N-COUNT If you **test** someone, or if you give them
a **test**, you ask them questions to find out how
much they know about something. *...an
arithmetic test.* ☐3 N-COUNT If an event or situation
is a **test of** a person or thing, it reveals their
qualities or effectiveness. *The test of any civilised
society is how it treats its minorities.* ☐4 VERB If you
are tested for a particular disease or medical
condition, you are examined in order to find out
whether you have that disease or condition. *My
doctor wants me to be tested for diabetes.*
☐5 N-COUNT A medical **test** is an examination of
your body in order to check that you are healthy.
☐6 PHRASE If you **put** something **to the test**, you
find out how useful or effective it is by using it.
*Ramsay's comic skills were first put to the test on
the big screen.*

testament /'testəmənt/ **testaments.** N-VAR If one
thing is a **testament to** another thing, it shows
that the other thing exists or is true. [FORMAL] *That
he has recovered so swiftly is a testament to his will
power.*

,test 'case, test cases. N-COUNT A **test case** is a
legal case which becomes an example for
deciding other similar cases.

testicle /'testɪkəl/ **testicles.** N-COUNT A man's
testicles are the two sex glands that produce
sperm.

testify /'testɪfaɪ/ **testifies, testifying, testified.**
☐1 VERB When someone **testifies** in a court of
law, they give a statement of what they saw
someone do or what they know of a situation,
after having promised to tell the truth. ☐2 VERB If
one thing **testifies to** another, it supports the
belief that the second thing is true. [FORMAL]
Cathedrals testify to every stage of the city's history.

testimonial /,testɪ'məʊniəl/ **testimonials.**
N-COUNT A **testimonial** is a written statement
about a person's character and abilities, often
written by their employer.

testimony /'testɪməni, AM -məʊni/ **testimonies.**
☐1 N-VAR In a court of law, someone's **testimony**
is a formal statement that they make about what
they saw someone do or what they know of a
situation, after having promised to tell the truth.
☐2 N-UNCOUNT If one thing is **testimony to**
another, it shows that the second thing has a
particular quality. *The environmental movement is
testimony to the feelings of support for nature.*

testosterone /te'stɒstərəʊn/. N-UNCOUNT
Testosterone is a hormone found in higher
levels in men than in women.

tether /'teðə/ **tethers, tethering, tethered.** ☐1 PHRASE
If you are **at the end of** your **tether**, you are so
worried or tired because of your problems that
you feel you cannot cope. ☐2 VERB If you **tether**
an animal or object **to** something, you attach it
there with a rope or chain.

⭐ **text** /tekst/ **texts, texting, texted.** ☐1 N-VAR **Text** is
any written material. *A CD-ROM can store more
than 250,000 pages of typed text.* ☐2 N-COUNT A
text is a book or other piece of writing, especially
one connected with science or education. *His
early plays are set texts in universities.* ☐3 N-COUNT
A **text** is the same as a **text message**. *He'd sent
me about 20 texts.* ☐4 VERB If you **text** someone,
you send them a text message on a mobile
telephone. *Mary texted me when she got home.*

textbook /'tekstbʊk/ **textbooks.** N-COUNT A
textbook is a book about a particular subject
that is intended for students.

textile /'tekstaɪl/ **textiles.** ☐1 N-COUNT **Textiles** are
types of woven cloth. ☐2 N-PLURAL **Textiles** are
the industries concerned with making cloth.
75,000 jobs will be lost in textiles and clothing.

texting /'tekstɪŋ/. N-UNCOUNT **Texting** means
the same as **text messaging**.

'text ,message, text messages. N-COUNT A **text
message** is a message that you send using a
mobile phone.

'text ,messaging. N-UNCOUNT **Text
messaging** is the sending of written messages
using a mobile phone.

texture /'tekstʃə/ **textures.** N-VAR The **texture** of
something is the way that it feels when you
touch it. *Her skin is pale, the texture of fine wax.*

⭐ **than** /ðən, STRONG ðæn/. PREP & CONJ You use
than to link two parts of a comparison or
contrast. *...a package smaller than a cigarette
box... It contains less than 1 per cent fat... He could
have helped her more than he did... It was more a
formality than a genuine partnership.* ● **less than:**
see **less.** ● **more than:** see **more.** ● **more often
than not:** see **often.** ● **other than:** see **other.**
● **rather than:** see **rather.**

⭐ **thank** /θæŋk/ **thanks, thanking, thanked.**
☐1 CONVENTION You say **thank you** or, more
informally, **thanks** to express your gratitude or
acknowledgement when someone does
something for you or gives you something. *Thank
you for your call... Thanks for the information...
'Would you like a cigarette?' – 'No thank you.'* ☐2 VERB
& N-PLURAL When you **thank** someone, or when you
give them your **thanks**, you express your gratitude
to them for something. *I thanked them for their long
and loyal service... They accepted their certificates
with words of thanks.* ☐3 CONVENTION You can use
thank you to say firmly that you do not want
someone's help or to tell them that you do not
like the way they are behaving towards you. *I can
stir my own tea, thank you.*
　　PHRASES ● You say **'Thank God', 'Thank
Goodness'**, or **'Thank heavens'** when you are
very relieved about something. *Thank heavens we
have you here.* ● If something happens **thanks to**
someone or something, they are responsible for
it or caused it to happen. *Thanks to recent
research, effective treatments are available.*

a
b
c
d
e
f
g
h
i
j
k
l
m
n
o
p
q
r
s
t
u
v
w
x
y
z

thankful /'θæŋkfʊl/. ADJ When you are **thankful**, you feel happy and relieved that something has happened. *I'm just thankful that I've got a job.* ♦ **thankfully** ADV *Simon thankfully slipped off his uniform and relaxed.*

thankfully /'θæŋkfʊli/. ADV You use **thankfully** to express approval and relief about a statement that you are making. *Thankfully, he had not been injured.*

thanks /θæŋks/. See **thank**.

Thanksgiving /ˌθæŋks'gɪvɪŋ/. N-UNCOUNT In the United States, **Thanksgiving** or **Thanksgiving Day** is a public holiday on the fourth Thursday in November.

that 1 demonstrative uses

⭐ **that** /ðæt/. **1** PRON & DET You use **that** to refer back to an idea, situation, or period of time that you have referred to previously. *You particularly wanted to talk to me. Why was that?... 'I've never been to Paris.'—'That's a pity.'... She returned to work later that week.* **2** DET & PRON You use **that** when you are referring to someone or something which is a distance away from you, especially when you indicate or point to them. *You see that man over there?... What's that you're writing?... That looks heavy.* **3** ADV If something is not **that** bad, funny, or expensive, for example, it is not as bad, funny, or expensive as it might be or as has been suggested. *Do I look that stupid?*

PHRASES ● You use **that is** or **that is to say** to indicate that you are about to explain something more clearly, more specifically, or in more detail. *...random genetic change – that is, mutations.*
● You use **that's that** or **that's it** to indicate that there is nothing more to be done or said, or that the end has been reached. *I'm staying here, and that's that... When he left the office, that was it, the workday was over.* ● See also **those**. ● **this and that**: see **this**.

that 2 conjunction and relative pronoun uses

⭐ **that** /ðət, STRONG ðæt/. **1** CONJ You use **that** after many verbs, nouns, and adjectives to introduce a clause. *He said that he did not want to be seen. ...breaking the news that your marriage is over... It's obvious that you need more time.* **2** PRON You use **that** immediately after a noun to introduce a clause which gives more information about the noun. *...a car that won't start. ...a man that Maddock had known for nearly 20 years.* **3** CONJ You use **that** after expressions with 'so' and 'such' in order to introduce the result or effect of something. *She came towards me so quickly that she knocked a chair over.*

thatched /θætʃd/. ADJ A **thatched** house has a roof made of straw or reeds.

that's /ðæts/. **That's** is a spoken form of 'that is'.

thaw /θɔː/ **thaws, thawing, thawed. 1** VERB When something frozen **thaws**, or when you **thaw** it, it melts. *It's so cold the snow doesn't get a chance to thaw... Always thaw frozen pastry thoroughly.* **2** N-COUNT A **thaw** is a period of warmer weather

when the snow and ice melt. **3** VERB & N-SING If something **thaws** relations between people, or if there is a **thaw** in relations, people become friendly again after a period of tension. *It took up to Christmas for political relations to thaw.*

⭐ **the.**

✓ **The** is usually pronounced /ðə/ before a consonant and /ði/ before a vowel, but pronounced /ðiː/ when you are emphasizing it.

1 DET **The** is the definite article. You use **the** at the beginning of noun groups to refer to someone or something when they are generally known about or when it is clear which particular person or thing you are referring to. *Amy sat outside in the sun... Who was that on the phone?... I patted him on the head.* **2** DET You can use **the** in front of a singular noun to refer to all people or things of that type. *The computer has made considerable strides in recent years.* **3** DET You use **the** in front of an adjective when you are referring to a particular thing that is described by that adjective. *He's wishing for the impossible.* **4** DET You can use **the** in front of adjectives and plural nouns to refer to all people of a particular type or nationality, or to a couple or family with a particular name. *...care for the elderly... The Germans and the French both have identity-card systems.* **5** DET You use **the** in front of numbers that refer to days and dates. *The meeting should take place on the fifth of May. ...how bad things were in the thirties.* **6** DET You use **the** in front of superlative adjectives and adverbs. *Brisk daily walks are still the best exercise.* **7** DET You use **the** in front of two comparative adjectives or adverbs to describe how one amount or quality changes in relation to another. *The more confidence you build up in yourself, the greater are your chances of success.* **8** DET **The** is used in rates, prices, and measurements to refer to a single unit, which is related or compared to a number of units of a different kind. *The exchange rate would soon be $2 to the pound.*

⭐ **theatre** (AM **theater**) /'θɪətə/ **theatres.**
1 N-COUNT A **theatre** is a building with a stage on which plays and other entertainments are performed. *We went to the theatre.* **2** N-UNCOUNT **Theatre** is entertainment involving the performance of plays. *...theatre for children.* **3** N-COUNT In American English, a **theater** or a **movie theater** is a place where people go to watch films. The British word is **cinema**. **4** N-COUNT In a hospital, a **theatre** is a room where surgeons carry out operations.

theatrical /θi'ætrɪkəl/. **1** ADJ BEFORE N **Theatrical** means relating to the theatre. *...outstanding British theatrical performances.* **2** ADJ **Theatrical** behaviour is deliberately exaggerated and unnatural. *...her big, theatrical gestures.* ♦ **theatrically** /θi'ætrɪkli/ ADV *He looked theatrically at his watch.*

theft /θeft/ **thefts.** N-VAR **Theft** is the criminal act of stealing. ...*the theft of classified documents from a car.*

★ **their** /ðeə/. **1** DET You use **their** to indicate that something belongs or relates to the group of people, animals, or things you are talking about. *Janis and Kurt have announced their engagement... The trees shed their leaves.* **2** DET You use **their** instead of 'his or her' to indicate that something belongs or relates to a person without saying whether that person is a man or a woman. Some people think this use is incorrect. *...anyone looking for an adequate income for their investments.*

theirs /ðeəz/. **1** PRON You use **theirs** to indicate that something belongs or relates to the group of people, animals, or things that you are talking about. *...at the table next to theirs... Theirs had been a happy and satisfactory marriage.* **2** PRON You use **theirs** instead of 'his or hers' to indicate that something belongs or relates to a person without saying whether that person is a man or a woman. Some people think this use is incorrect. *I don't know whose handkerchief it is. Somebody must have left theirs.*

★ **them** /ðəm, STRONG ðem/. **1** PRON **Them** is used as the object of a verb or preposition. You use **them** to refer to a group of people, animals, or things. *The Beatles – I never get tired of listening to them... His dark socks, I could see, had a stripe on them.* **2** PRON You use **them** instead of 'him or her' to refer to a person without saying whether that person is a man or a woman. Some people think this use is incorrect. *It takes great courage to face your child and tell them the truth.*

★ **theme** /θiːm/ **themes.** N-COUNT A **theme** in a piece of writing, a discussion, or a work of art is an important idea or subject that runs through it. *The book's central theme is power.*

★ **themselves** /ðəmˈselvz/. **1** PRON You use **themselves** to refer to people, animals, or things when the object of a verb or preposition refers to the same people or things as the subject of the verb. *They all seemed to be enjoying themselves... The men talked amongst themselves.* **2** PRON You use **themselves** to emphasize the people or things that you are referring to. **Themselves** is also sometimes used instead of 'them' as the object of a verb or preposition. *The islands themselves are largely uninhabitable. ...men and women who are in the same position as themselves.* **3** PRON You use **themselves** instead of 'himself or herself' to refer back to the person who is the subject of sentence without saying whether it is a man or a woman. Some people think this use is incorrect. *What can a patient with emphysema do to help themselves?*

★ **then** /ðen/. **1** ADV **Then** means at a particular time in the past or in the future. *Things were simpler, clearer then... Since then, Knowles has published around 50 titles... I'm coming up on Friday so I can drop it off then.* **2** ADV You use **then** to say that one thing happens after another, or is after another on a list. *He thought a bit and*

then answered... *He'll speak first, then Robert's mother, then me.* **3** ADV You use **then** to introduce a summary or conclusion to what you have just said, or to end a conversation. *By 1931, then, France alone in Europe was a country of massive immigration... He stood up. 'That's settled then.'... Bye bye then.* **4** ADV You use **then** with words like 'now', 'well', and 'okay', to introduce a new topic or a new point of view. *Well then, I'll put the kettle on.* **5** ADV You use **then** to introduce the second part of a sentence which begins with 'if'. The first part of the sentence describes a possible situation, and **then** introduces the result of the situation. *If the answer is 'yes', then we must decide on an appropriate course of action.* **6** ADV You use **then** at the beginning of a sentence or after 'and' or 'but' to introduce a comment or an extra piece of information. *He sounded sincere, but then, he always did.* **7** **now and then**: see **now**. ● **there and then**: see **there**.

theologian /ˌθiːəˈləʊdʒən/ **theologians.** N-COUNT A **theologian** is someone who studies religion and the nature of God.

theology /θiˈɒlədʒi/. N-UNCOUNT **Theology** is the study of religion and the nature of God. ♦ **theological** /ˌθiːəˈlɒdʒɪkəl/ ADJ *...a theological college.*

theoretical /ˌθiːəˈretɪkəl/. ADJ **Theoretical** means based on or using the ideas and abstract principles of a subject, rather than the practical aspects of it. *...a lecturer in theoretical physics.*

theoretically /ˌθiːəˈretɪkəli/. ADV You use **theoretically** to say that although something is supposed to be true or to exist in the way stated, it may not in fact be true or exist in that way. *Theoretically, the price is supposed to be marked... No one believes it will happen. But it is theoretically possible.*

theorize (BRIT also **theorise**) /ˈθiːəraɪz/ **theorizes, theorizing, theorized.** VERB If you **theorize** that something is true, or if you **theorize about** something, you develop a set of abstract ideas about it in order to explain it. *By studying the way people behave, we can theorize about what is going on in their mind.* ♦ **theorist, theorists** N-COUNT *...the leading theorist of the French Communist Party.*

★ **theory** /ˈθiːəri/ **theories.** **1** N-COUNT A **theory** is a formal idea or set of ideas intended to explain something. *...Darwin's theory of evolution.* **2** N-COUNT If you have a **theory** about something, you have your own opinion about it which you cannot prove but which you think is true. *My theory is that male fashion designers really don't like women.* **3** N-UNCOUNT The **theory of** a practical subject or skill is the set of rules and principles that form the basis of it. *...the theory and practice of sustainable agriculture.* **4** PHRASE You use **in theory** to say that although something is supposed to be true or to happen in the way stated, it may not in fact be true or

a
b
c
d
e
f
g
h
i
j
k
l
m
n
o
p
q
r
s
t
u
v
w
x
y
z

happen in that way. *In theory I'm on call day and night.*

therapeutic /ˌθerəˈpjuːtɪk/. **1** ADJ If something is **therapeutic**, it helps you to feel happier and more relaxed. *Day-dreaming is very therapeutic.* **2** ADJ **Therapeutic** treatment is designed to treat a disease or to improve a person's health. [TECHNICAL] *...therapeutic drugs.*

therapist /ˈθerəpɪst/ **therapists.** N-COUNT A **therapist** is a person skilled in a type of therapy.

★ **therapy** /ˈθerəpi/. N-UNCOUNT **Therapy** is the treatment of mental or physical illness without the use of drugs or operations. *...group therapy sessions for men who batter their wives.*

★ **there.**

☑ **There** is pronounced /ðə/, STRONG ðeə/ for meanings 1 and 2, and /ðeə/ for all other meanings.

1 PRON You use **there** as the subject of the verb 'be' to say that something exists or does not exist, or to draw attention to it. *There must be an option other than war... There's no way we can afford to buy a house... There are no cars on some of the islands.*

USAGE **There** is normally followed by a plural form of the verb **be** when it is used to introduce a count noun in the plural. *There were policemen everywhere.* However, when it introduces a series of nouns in the singular, linked by **and**, a singular form of the verb **be** is normally used. *There is a time and a place for everything... There was a street fair and an old-fashioned brass band.* Do not confuse the spelling of **there** with **their** as a possessive pronoun.

2 ADV If something is **there**, it exists or is available. *The group of old buildings by the main road is still there today... The book is there for people to read.* **3** ADV You use **there** to refer to a place that has already been mentioned. *Durrell was born in India in 1912; the families of both his parents had lived there for generations.* **4** ADV You say **there** to indicate a place that you are pointing to or looking at. *The toilets are over there... Where did I put it? – Oh there it is.* **5** ADV You use **there** when speaking on the telephone to ask if someone is available to speak to you. *Hello, is Gordon there please?* **6** ADV You use **there** to refer to a point that someone has made in a conversation. *I think you're right there John.* **7** ADV You use **there** to refer to a stage that has been reached in an activity or process. *We are making further investigations and will take the matter from there.* **8** ADV You can use **there** in expressions such as **there you go** or **there we are** when accepting that an unsatisfactory situation cannot be changed. [SPOKEN] *It's the wages that count. Not over-generous, but there you are.* **9** ADV You can use **there** in expressions such

as **there you go** and **there we are** when emphasizing that something proves that you were right. [SPOKEN] *'There you are, you see!' she exclaimed. 'I knew you'd say that!'*

PHRASES ● You use **there again** to introduce an extra piece of information which either contradicts what has been said or gives an alternative to it. *You may strike lucky and find a sympathetic and helpful clerk, but, there again, you might not.* ● If something happens **there and then** or **then and there**, it happens immediately. ● You say **'there you are'** or **'there you go'** when you are offering something to someone. *There you are, Lennie, you take the nice biscuit.*

thereafter /ˌðeərˈɑːftə, -ˈæftə/. ADV **Thereafter** means after the event or date mentioned. [FORMAL] *In 1954 he met, and shortly thereafter married, Simone Forti.*

thereby /ˌðeəˈbaɪ/. ADV You use **thereby** to introduce a result of the event or action just mentioned. [FORMAL] *Our bodies can sweat, thereby losing heat by evaporation.*

★ **therefore** /ˈðeəfɔː/. ADV You use **therefore** to introduce a logical result or conclusion. *The process is said to be much quicker and therefore cheaper.*

therein /ˌðeərˈɪn/. **1** ADV **Therein** means in the place just mentioned. [FORMAL] *...the documents, or the information contained therein.* **2** ADV When you say **therein** lies a situation or problem, you mean that an existing situation has caused that situation or problem. [FORMAL, DATED] *Santa Maria di Castellabate is barely mentioned in guidebooks; therein lies its charm.*

thermal /ˈθɜːməl/. **1** ADJ BEFORE N **Thermal** means relating to heat or caused by heat. *...thermal power stations.* **2** ADJ BEFORE N **Thermal** clothes are specially designed to keep you warm. *...thermal underwear.*

thermometer /θəˈmɒmɪtə/ **thermometers.** N-COUNT A **thermometer** is an instrument for measuring the temperature of a room or of a person's body.

★ **these** /ðiːz/. **1** DET & PRON You use **these** to refer to people or things that have been mentioned. *Switch to an interest-paying current account. Most banks and larger building societies now offer these accounts... Please bring with you any drugs that you are taking. These must be handed to the sister.* **2** DET & PRON You use **these** to introduce people or things that you are going to talk about. *If you're converting your loft, these addresses will be useful... These are some of the things you can do.* **3** DET People use **these** to introduce people or things into a story. [INFORMAL, SPOKEN] *I was on my own and these fellows came along.* **4** PRON You use **these** when you are identifying someone or asking about their identity. *These are my children.* **5** DET & PRON You use **these** to refer to people or things that are near you, especially when you touch them or point to them. *These scissors are awfully heavy... These are the only tapes we have.* **6** PHRASE If you say that **these days** something happens, you mean that at the present time it happens, in contrast to in the past. *Living in Bootham these days can be depressing.*

thesis /ˈθiːsɪs/ **theses** /ˈθiːsiːz/. [1] N-COUNT A **thesis** is an idea or theory that is expressed as a statement and discussed in a logical way. [2] N-COUNT A **thesis** is a long piece of writing based on your own ideas and research that you do as part of a university degree.

⭐ **they** /ðeɪ/. [1] PRON You use **they** to refer to a group of people, animals, or things. *The two men were far more alike than they would ever admit.* [2] PRON You use **they** instead of 'he or she' to refer to a person without saying whether that person is a man or a woman. Some people think this use is incorrect. *The teacher is not responsible for the student's success or failure. They are only there to help the student learn.* [3] PRON You use **they** in expressions such as 'they say' or 'they call it' when you want to refer vaguely to what people in general say, think, or do. *They say there's plenty of opportunities.*

they'd /ðeɪd/. **They'd** is the usual spoken form of 'they had', especially when 'had' is an auxiliary verb. **They'd** is also a spoken form of 'they would'. *They'd both lived in this road all their lives... He agreed that they'd visit her.*

they'll /ðeɪəl/. **They'll** is the usual spoken form of 'they will'.

they're /ðeə, ðeɪə/. **They're** is the usual spoken form of 'they are'.

they've /ðeɪv/. **They've** is the usual spoken form of 'they have', especially when 'have' is an auxiliary verb. *They've gone out.*

⭐ **thick** /θɪk/ **thicker, thickest.** [1] ADJ Something that is **thick** has a large distance between its two opposite surfaces. *...a thick stone wall.* ♦ **thickly** ADV *Slice the meat thickly.* [2] ADJ You can use **thick** to talk or ask about how wide or deep something is. *The folder was two inches thick... How thick are these walls? ...a plant with a brown root as thick as a finger.* ♦ **thickness, thicknesses** N-VAR *The size of the fish will determine the thickness of the steaks.* [3] ADJ If something that consists of several things is **thick**, it has a large number of them very close together. *...our father's thick, wavy hair.* ♦ **thickly** ADV *The trees grew thickly here by the river.* [4] ADJ **Thick** smoke, fog, or cloud is difficult to see through. [5] ADJ **Thick** liquids are fairly stiff and solid and do not flow easily. *They had to battle through thick mud.* [6] ADJ If you describe someone as **thick**, you think that they are stupid. [INFORMAL, BRITISH] PHRASES ● If things happen **thick and fast**, they happen very quickly and in large numbers. *The rumours have been coming thick and fast.* ● If you are **in the thick of** an activity or situation, you are very involved in it. *The AWPA ran into political trouble and Naomi was in the thick of it.*

thicken /ˈθɪkən/ **thickens, thickening, thickened.** VERB If something **thickens**, or if you **thicken** it, it

becomes thicker. *The crowds around him began to thicken... Thicken the sauce by adding the cream.*

thief /θiːf/ **thieves.** N-COUNT A **thief** is a person who steals something from another person.

thigh /θaɪ/ **thighs.** N-COUNT Your **thighs** are the top parts of your legs, between your knees and your hips. → See picture on page 822.

⭐ **thin** /θɪn/ **thinner, thinnest; thins, thinning, thinned.** [1] ADJ If something is **thin**, there is a small distance between its two opposite surfaces. *...a thin cable... The material was too thin.* ♦ **thinly** ADV *Peel and thinly slice the onion.* [2] ADJ A **thin** person or animal has no extra fat on their body. [3] ADJ **Thin** liquids are weak and watery. [4] VERB & PHR-VERB If something **thins** or **thins out**, it becomes less crowded because people or things have been removed from it. *By midnight the crowd had thinned... As soon as seedlings are large enough to handle, start thinning them out.* [5] PHRASE If you say that people or things are **thin on the ground**, you mean that there are not very many of them and so they are hard to find. *Good managers are often thin on the ground.*

⭐ **thing** /θɪŋ/ **things.** [1] N-COUNT You use **thing** as a substitute for another word when you are unable to be more precise, or you do not need or want to be more precise. *What's that thing in the middle of the fountain? ...iron and silicon and things like that... Getting drunk is a thing all young men do.* [2] N-SING **Thing** is often used instead of the pronouns 'anything', or 'everything' in order to emphasize what you are saying. *Don't you worry about a thing.* [3] N-COUNT A **thing** is a physical object that is considered as having no life of its own. *It's not a thing, Beauchamp. It's a human being!* [4] N-COUNT You can call a person or an animal a particular **thing** when you are expressing your feelings towards them. [INFORMAL] *Oh you lucky thing!* [5] N-PLURAL Your **things** are your clothes or possessions. *Sara told him to take all his things and not to return.* [6] N-PLURAL **Things** can refer to life in general and the way it affects you. *How are things going?*

PHRASES ● If you do something **first thing**, you do it at the beginning of the day, before you do anything else. If you do it **last thing**, you do it at the end of the day. *I always do it last thing on a Saturday.* ● If you **have a thing about** someone or something, you have very strong positive or negative feelings about them. [INFORMAL] *He's got this thing about ties.* ● You say **for one thing** when you give only one reason for something, but want to indicate that there are other reasons. *She was unable to sell it, because for one thing its size was awkward.* ● If you **do** your **own thing**, you live or behave in the way you want to, without paying attention to convention or depending on other people. ● You can say **'The thing is'** to introduce an explanation or opinion relating to something that has just been said. *I'm getting a grant for a speech therapy course. But the thing is, I don't know whether I want to do it any more.*

⭐ **Bank of English® frequent word**   For a full explanation of all grammatical labels, see pages vii-x

a
b
c
d
e
f
g
h
i
j
k
l
m
n
o
p
q
r
s
t
u
v
w
x
y
z

★ **think** /θɪŋk/ **thinks, thinking, thought.** 1 VERB If you **think** that something is the case, you have the opinion that it is the case. *I certainly think there should be a ban on tobacco advertising... What do you think of my theory?* ♦ **thinking** N-UNCOUNT *...his thinking on welfare provisions.* 2 VERB If you **think** that something is true or will happen, you have the impression that it is true or will happen, although you are not certain of the facts. *Nora thought he was seventeen years old... The storm is thought to be responsible for as many as four deaths.*

USAGE Note that when you are using the verb **think** with a **that** clause in order to state a negative opinion or belief, you normally make **think** negative, rather than the verb in the **that** clause. For instance, it is more usual to say '**I don't think he saw me**' than 'I think he didn't see me'. The same pattern applies to other verbs with a similar meaning, such as **believe**, **consider**, and **suppose**. *He didn't believe she could do it... I don't consider that you kept your promise... I don't suppose he ever saw it.*

3 VERB If you **think** a lot of someone or something, you admire them. *People at the club think very highly of him.* 4 VERB & N-SING When you **think about** ideas or problems, or when you have **a think about** them, you make a mental effort to consider them or solve them. *She closed her eyes for a moment, trying to think... I'll have a think about that.* ♦ **thinking** N-UNCOUNT *...quick thinking.* 5 VERB When you **think of** something, you remember it or it comes into your mind. *Nobody could think of anything to say... I was trying to think what else we had to do.* 6 VERB When you **are thinking** something, you have words or ideas in your mind without saying them out loud. *I remember thinking how lovely he looked.* 7 VERB If you **are thinking of** doing something, you are considering doing it. *Martin was thinking of taking legal action against Zuckerman.* 8 See also **thought**.

PHRASES • You can use '**I think**' as a way of being polite when you are explaining or suggesting something, giving your opinion, or responding to an offer. *I think he means 'at' rather than 'to'... 'Would you like to do that another time.'—'Yes I think so.'* • If you say that someone would **think nothing of** doing something difficult or strange, you mean that they would do it and not think that it was difficult or strange at all. *I thought nothing of betting £1,000 on a horse.*

▸**think back.** PHR-VERB If you **think back**, you remember things that happened in the past. *I thought back to the time in 1975 when my son was desperately ill.*

▸**think over.** PHR-VERB If you **think** something **over**, you consider it carefully before making a decision.

▸**think through.** PHR-VERB If you **think** a problem or situation **through**, you consider it thoroughly. *I didn't think through the consequences of promotion.*

▸**think up.** PHR-VERB If you **think** something **up**, for example an idea or plan, you invent it using mental effort. *Julian has been thinking up new ways of raising money.*

thinker /ˈθɪŋkə/ **thinkers.** N-COUNT A **thinker** is a person who spends a lot of time thinking deeply about important things, especially a philosopher who is famous for thinking of new ideas.

★ **thinking** /ˈθɪŋkɪŋ/. See **think**. • See also **wishful thinking**.

★ **third** /θɜːd/ **thirds.** 1 ORD The **third** item in a series is the one that you count as number three. 2 N-COUNT A **third** is one of three equal parts of something.

thirdly /ˈθɜːdli/. ADV You use **thirdly** when you are about to mention the third thing in a series of items. *First of all, there are not many of them, and secondly, they have little money and, thirdly, they have few big businesses.*

‚third 'party, **third parties.** N-COUNT A **third party** is someone who is not one of the two main people or groups involved in a business or legal matter, but who becomes involved in a minor way.

★ ‚Third 'World. N-PROPER The countries of Africa, Asia, and South America are sometimes referred to as **the Third World**.

thirst /θɜːst/ **thirsts.** 1 N-VAR **Thirst** is the feeling that you want to drink something. *Drink water to quench your thirst.* 2 N-UNCOUNT **Thirst** is the condition of not having enough to drink. *They died of thirst.* 3 N-SING A **thirst for** something is a very strong desire for it. *Children show a real thirst for learning.*

thirsty /ˈθɜːsti/. ADJ If you are **thirsty**, you feel a need to drink something.

★ **thirteen** /ˌθɜːˈtiːn/. NUM **Thirteen** is the number 13.

★ **thirteenth** /ˌθɜːˈtiːnθ/. ORD The **thirteenth** item in a series is the one that you count as number thirteen.

★ **thirtieth** /ˈθɜːtiəθ/. ORD The **thirtieth** item in a series is the one that you count as number thirty.

★ **thirty** /ˈθɜːti/ **thirties.** NUM **Thirty** is the number 30. For examples of how numbers such as thirty and eighty are used see **eighty**.

★ **this** /ðɪs/. 1 DET & PRON You use **this** to refer to a person or thing that has been mentioned. *President Clinton had long prepared for this challenge... I had been on many film sets, but never one like this.* 2 PRON & DET You use **this** to introduce someone or something that you are going to talk about. *This is what I will do. I will telephone Anna and explain... This report is from our Jerusalem correspondent, Gerald Butt.* 3 PRON & DET You use **this** to refer to a person or thing that is near you now, or to the present time. When there are two or more people or things near you, **this** refers to the nearest one. *Is this what you were looking for?... This is my colleague, Mr Arnold Landon... This place is run like a hotel.* **4** PRON You use **this** when you refer to a situation which is happening or has just happened and which you feel involved in. *Tim, this is awful... Is this what you want to do with the rest of your life?* **5** DET You use **this** to refer to the next occurrence of a particular day, month, season, or festival. *...this Sunday's 7.45 performance... We're getting married this June.* **6** PRON You use **this** in order to say who you are when you are speaking on the telephone, radio, or television. *'Hello, is this Mr Brown?'—'Yeah, who's this?'* **7** PHRASE You can refer to a variety of things that you are doing or talking about as **this and that** or **this, that and the other**. *'And what are you doing now?'—'Oh, you know, this and that.'*

thorn /θɔːn/ **thorns.** N-COUNT **Thorns** are the sharp points on some plants and trees.

thorny /'θɔːni/. **1** ADJ A **thorny** plant or tree is covered with thorns. **2** ADJ A **thorny** problem or question is difficult to deal with.

⭐ **thorough** /'θʌrə, AM 'θɜːrəʊ/. **1** ADJ A **thorough** action is done very carefully and methodically. *We are making a thorough investigation.* ♦ **thoroughly** ADV *Food that is being offered hot must be reheated thoroughly.* ♦ **thoroughness** N-UNCOUNT *...the fairness and thoroughness of the disciplinary process.* **2** ADJ Someone who is **thorough** does things in a careful and methodical way. ♦ **thoroughness** N-UNCOUNT *His thoroughness and attention to detail is legendary.* **3** ADJ You can use **thorough** for emphasis. *The management has got itself into a thorough mess.* ♦ **thoroughly** ADV *I thoroughly enjoy your programme.*

⭐ **those** /ðəʊz/. **1** DET & PRON You use **those** to refer to people, things, or situations which have already been mentioned. *Most of those crimes are committed by boys... Waterfalls never fail to attract and those at the Falls of Clyde are no exception.* **2** DET & PRON You use **those** when you are referring to people or things that are a distance away from you in position or time, often when you indicate or point to them. *What are those buildings?... Those are nice shoes.* **3** PRON You use **those** to mean 'people'. *He caused much anguish to those around him.*

⭐ **though** /ðəʊ/. **1** CONJ & ADV You use **though** to introduce a fact or comment which contrasts with something else that is being said, or makes it seem surprising. *Gaelic has been a dying language for many years, though children are nowadays taught it in school... I like him. Though he makes me angry sometimes.* **2** **as though**: see **as**.

⭐ **thought** /θɔːt/ **thoughts.** **1** **Thought** is the past tense and past participle of **think**. **2** N-COUNT A **thought** is an idea or opinion. *The thought of someone suffering through a mistake of mine makes me shiver... ...his thoughts on love and*

fatherhood. **3** N-UNCOUNT **Thought** is the activity of thinking, especially deeply, logically, or with concentration. *After much thought I decided to end my marriage.* **4** N-UNCOUNT **Thought** is the group of ideas and beliefs or way of thinking which belongs, for example, to a particular religion or political party. *This school of thought argues that depression is best treated by drugs.* **5** See also **second thoughts**.

thoughtful /'θɔːtfʊl/. **1** ADJ If you are **thoughtful**, you are quiet and serious because you are thinking about something. ♦ **thoughtfully** ADV *Daniel nodded thoughtfully.* **2** ADJ If you describe someone as **thoughtful**, you approve of them because they remember what other people want, need, or feel, and try not to upset them. ♦ **thoughtfully** ADV *...the bottle of wine he had thoughtfully purchased for the celebrations.*

thoughtless /'θɔːtləs/. ADJ If you describe someone as **thoughtless**, you are critical of them because they forget or ignore other people's wants, needs, or feelings. ♦ **thoughtlessly** ADV *They thoughtlessly planned a picnic without him.*

⭐ **thousand** /'θaʊzənd/ **thousands.** **1** NUM A **thousand** or **one thousand** is the number 1,000. **2** N-PLURAL & PRON If you refer to **thousands of** things or people, you are emphasizing that there are very many of them. **Thousands** means very many. *I must have driven past that place thousands of times.*

thousandth /'θaʊzənθ/. ORD The **thousandth** item in a series is the one you count as number one thousand.

thrash /θræʃ/ **thrashes, thrashing, thrashed.** **1** VERB If one player or team **thrashes** another in a game or contest, they defeat them easily. [INFORMAL] ♦ **thrashing, thrashings** N-COUNT *...his team's 5-0 thrashing of the home team.* **2** VERB If someone **thrashes** you, they hit you several times as a punishment. ♦ **thrashing** N-COUNT *If Sarah caught her, she would get a thrashing.* **3** VERB If someone **thrashes about**, they move in a wild or violent way, often hitting against something. *Jimmy collapsed on the floor, thrashing his legs about.*

▸ **thrash out.** PHR-VERB If people **thrash out** something such as a problem or a plan, they discuss it in detail until a solution is reached. *...a sincere effort by two people to thrash out differences.*

thread /θred/ **threads, threading, threaded.** **1** N-VAR & VERB **Thread** or a **thread** is a long, thin piece of cotton, silk, nylon, or wool. When you **thread** a needle, you put a piece of thread through the hole in the top of the needle. **2** VERB If you **thread** small objects such as beads onto a string, you join them together by pushing the string through them. **3** N-COUNT The **thread** on a screw, or on something such as a lid, is the raised spiral line of metal or plastic around it which allows it to be fixed in place by twisting. **4** N-COUNT The **thread** of a story or a situation is an aspect of it

⭐ Bank of English® frequent word   For a full explanation of all grammatical labels, see pages vii–x

that connects all the different parts together. *He lost the thread of Wan Da's narrative.* **5** VERB If you **thread** your **way** through a group of people or things, you move through it carefully. *Anna threaded her way through the crowded room.*

⭐ **threat** /θret/ **threats.** **1** N-VAR A **threat to** someone or something is a danger that something unpleasant might happen to them. A **threat** is also the cause of this danger. *Some couples see single women as a threat to their relationships. ...small projects under threat from spending cuts.* **2** N-SING A **threat** is a statement by someone that they will do something unpleasant, especially if you do not do what they want. *He may be forced to carry out his threat to resign.*

⭐ **threaten** /'θretən/ **threatens, threatening, threatened.** **1** VERB If someone **threatens to** do something unpleasant to you, or if they **threaten** you, they say or imply that they will do something unpleasant to you, especially if you do not do what they want. ♦ **threatening** ADJ *...a threatening phone call.* **2** VERB If something **threatens** people or things, it is likely to harm them. *30 percent of reptiles, birds, and fish are currently threatened with extinction.* **3** VERB If something unpleasant **threatens** to happen, it seems likely to happen. *The fighting is threatening to turn into full-scale war.*

⭐ **three** /θriː/ **threes.** NUM **Three** is the number 3.

ˌ**three-diˈmensional.** ADJ A **three-dimensional** object is solid rather than flat, because it can be measured in three dimensions, usually the height, depth, and width.

ˌ**three-ˈquarters.** QUANT **Three-quarters** is an amount that is three out of four equal parts of something. *Three-quarters of the country's workers took part in the strike... Road deaths have increased by three-quarters.*

threshold /'θreʃhəʊld/ **thresholds.** **1** N-COUNT The **threshold** of a building or room is the floor in the doorway, or the doorway itself. **2** N-COUNT A **threshold** is an amount, level, or limit on a scale. *She has a low threshold of boredom.* **3** PHRASE If you are **on the threshold of** something exciting or new, you are about to experience it. *We are on the threshold of a new era in astronomy.*

threw /θruː/. **Threw** is the past tense of **throw**.

thrift /θrɪft/ **thrifts.** **1** N-UNCOUNT **Thrift** is the quality and practice of being careful with money and not wasting things. **2** N-COUNT In the United States, a **thrift** is a kind of savings bank.

thrill /θrɪl/ **thrills, thrilling, thrilled.** VERB & N-COUNT If something **thrills** you, or if something gives you a **thrill**, it gives you a feeling of great pleasure or excitement. *I can still remember the thrill of not knowing what I would get on Christmas morning.*

thrilled /θrɪld/. ADJ AFTER LINK-V If you are **thrilled** about something, you are pleased and excited about it. *I was so thrilled to get a good report.*

thriller /'θrɪlə/ **thrillers.** N-COUNT A **thriller** is a book, film, or play that tells an exciting story about something such as criminal activities or spying.

thrilling /'θrɪlɪŋ/. ADJ Something that is **thrilling** is very exciting and enjoyable. *...a thrilling adventure movie.*

thrive /θraɪv/ **thrives, thriving, thrived.** VERB If someone or something **thrives**, they do well and are successful, healthy, or strong. *...a thriving business... He thrived on such adversity.*

⭐ **throat** /θrəʊt/ **throats.** **1** N-COUNT Your **throat** is the back of your mouth and the top part of the tubes that go down into your stomach and your lungs. **2** N-COUNT Your **throat** is the front part of your neck. → See picture on page 823. **3** PHRASE If you **clear** your **throat**, you cough once in order to make it easier to speak or to attract people's attention.

throb /θrɒb/ **throbs, throbbing, throbbed.** **1** VERB & N-SING If a part of your body **throbs**, you feel a series of strong and usually painful beats there. You can refer to this feeling as a **throb**. *...the throbbing pain in her ankle.* **2** VERB & N-SING If something **throbs**, it vibrates and makes a rhythmic noise, called a **throb**. [LITERARY] *The music throbbed hypnotically.*

throne /θrəʊn/ **thrones.** **1** N-COUNT A **throne** is an ornate chair used by a king, queen, or emperor on important occasions. **2** N-SING You can talk about **the throne** as a way of referring to the position of being king, queen, or emperor. *...the heir to the throne.*

throng /θrɒŋ, AM θrɔːŋ/ **throngs, thronging, thronged.** **1** N-COUNT A **throng** is a large crowd of people. **2** VERB When people **throng** somewhere, they go there in great numbers. ♦ **thronged** ADJ AFTER LINK-V *The streets are thronged with people.*

throttle /'θrɒtəl/ **throttles, throttling, throttled.** **1** VERB To **throttle** someone means to kill or injure them by holding them tightly by the throat so that they cannot breathe. **2** N-COUNT The **throttle** of a motor vehicle or aircraft is a device that controls the quantity of fuel entering the engine and is used to control the vehicle's speed.

⭐ **through** /θruː/. **1** PREP & ADV To move, cut, or travel **through** something, means to move, cut, or travel from one side or end to the other. *Go straight through that door under the EXIT sign... He went straight through to the kitchen... The exhaust pipe had been cut through.* **2** PREP If you can see, hear, or feel something **through** a particular thing, that thing is between you and the thing you can see, hear, or feel. *They could hear music pulsing through the walls of the house.* **3** PREP & ADV If something happens **through** a period of time, it happens from the beginning until the end. *...hard work right through to the summer.* **4** PREP If you go **through** a particular experience or event, you experience it. *We have been going through a bad time.* **5** ADJ AFTER LINK-V If you are

through with something or if it is **through**, you have finished doing it and will never do it again. If you are **through with** someone, you do not want to have anything to do with them again. *I'm through with women.* **6** PREP If something happens because of something else, you can say that it happens **through** it. *Geoff had to retire early through ill health.* **7** PREP & ADV If someone gets **through** an examination or a round of a competition, they succeed or win. **8** PREP If you go **through** or look **through** a list of things, you deal with them one after another. *Try working through the opening exercises in this chapter.*

⭐ **throughout** /θruːˈaʊt/. **1** PREP & ADV If something happens **throughout** a particular period of time, it happens during the whole of that period. *The school runs cookery and sewing courses throughout the year... It was an absorbing contest throughout.* **2** PREP & ADV If something happens or exists **throughout** a place, it happens or exists in all parts of it. *The route is well signposted throughout.*

⭐ **throw** /θrəʊ/ **throws, throwing, threw, thrown.**
1 VERB If you **throw** an object that you are holding, you move your hand quickly and let go of the object, so that it moves through the air. *He spent hours throwing a tennis ball against a wall... He threw Brian a rope.* **2** VERB To **throw** something into a place or position means to cause it to fall there. *Fox threw his coat on the nearest chair... He threw me to the ground.* **3** VERB If you **throw** a part of your body somewhere, you move it there suddenly and with a lot of force. *She threw her hands into the air... He threw himself on his bed.* **4** VERB If a horse **throws** its rider, it makes the rider fall off. **5** VERB If a person or thing **is thrown** into an unpleasant situation or state, something causes them to be in it. *Abidjan was thrown into turmoil because of a protest by taxi drivers.* **6** VERB If you **throw yourself**, your energy, or your money into a particular job or activity, you become involved in it very enthusiastically. **7** VERB If someone **throws** a fit or tantrum, they are suddenly very angry and start to behave in an uncontrolled way. **8** VERB When someone **throws** a party, they organize one. [INFORMAL] **9** VERB If something such as a remark or an experience **throws** you, it confuses you because it is unexpected. *That reporter really threw me.*
▸**throw away.** **1** PHR-VERB If you **throw away** or **throw out** something you do not want, you get rid of it. *I never throw anything away.* **2** PHR-VERB If you **throw away** something good that you have, you waste it. *Failing to tackle the deficit would be throwing away an opportunity.*
▸**throw in.** PHR-VERB If someone who is selling or offering something **throws** something in when they sell or offer it, they add it to what they are selling or offering for no extra charge. *...a weekend break in Paris—with free beer thrown in.*
▸**throw off.** PHR-VERB If you **throw off** something that is restricting you or making you

unhappy, you get rid of it. *Resorts need to throw off their outdated image.*
▸**throw out. 1** See **throw away** 1. **2** PHR-VERB If you **throw** someone **out**, you force them to leave. *I wanted to kill him, but instead I just threw him out of the house.* **3** PHR-VERB If a court or committee **throws out** a case, proposal, or request, they reject it.
▸**throw up.** PHR-VERB To **throw up** means to vomit. [INFORMAL]

thrown /θrəʊn/. **Thrown** is the past participle of **throw**.

thrush /θrʌʃ/ **thrushes.** N-COUNT A **thrush** is a small brown bird with small marks on its chest.

thrust /θrʌst/ **thrusts, thrusting, thrust.** **1** VERB & N-COUNT If you **thrust** something somewhere, or if you make a **thrust** with it, you push or move it there quickly with a lot of force. *They thrust him into the back of a jeep. ...knife thrusts.* **2** N-SING The **thrust of** an activity or idea is the main or essential things it involves. *The main thrust of the research will be the study of the early Universe.*

thud /θʌd/ **thuds, thudding, thudded.** N-COUNT & VERB A **thud** is a dull sound, usually made by a solid, heavy object hitting something soft. If something **thuds** somewhere, it makes this sound as it hits it. *She tripped and fell with a sickening thud... She ran up the stairs, her bare feet thudding on the wood.*

thug /θʌg/ **thugs.** N-COUNT If you refer to someone as a **thug**, you disapprove of them and think they are violent or a criminal.

thumb /θʌm/ **thumbs, thumbing, thumbed.** N-COUNT Your **thumb** is the short, thick digit on the side of your hand next to your first finger. → See picture on page 823.
▸**thumb through.** PHR-VERB If you **thumb through** a book or magazine, you glance at each page quickly rather than reading them carefully.

thump /θʌmp/ **thumps, thumping, thumped.** **1** VERB & N-COUNT If you **thump** someone or something, or if you give them a **thump**, you hit them hard with your fist. *I'll thump you... I heard you thumping on the door... He felt a thump on his shoulder.* **2** VERB & N-COUNT If you **thump** something somewhere, or if it **thumps** there, it hits something else with a loud, dull sound called a **thump**. *He thumped the can down on the table.* **3** VERB When your heart **thumps**, it beats strongly and quickly, usually because you are afraid or excited.

thunder /ˈθʌndə/ **thunders, thundering, thundered.** **1** N-UNCOUNT & VERB **Thunder** is the loud noise that you hear from the sky after a flash of lightning. When it **thunders**, you hear thunder. **2** N-UNCOUNT & VERB The **thunder** of something such as traffic is the loud, deep, continuous noise it makes. If something **thunders**, it makes this noise. *...the thunder of the sea on the rocks.*

thunderous /ˈθʌndərəs/. ADJ A **thunderous** noise is very loud and deep. *They greeted him with thunderous applause.*

thunderstorm /'θʌndəstɔːm/ **thunderstorms.**
N-COUNT A **thunderstorm** is a storm in which
there is thunder, lightning, and heavy rain.

⭐ **Thursday** /'θɜːzdeɪ, -di/ **Thursdays.** N-VAR
Thursday is the day after Wednesday and before
Friday. → See Reference Page on Times and
Dates.

⭐ **thus** /ðʌs/. **1** ADV You use **thus** to introduce
the consequence or conclusion of something that
you have just mentioned. [FORMAL] *Neither of them
thought of turning on the lunch-time news. Thus
Caroline didn't hear of John's death until Peter
telephoned... Some people will be more capable
and thus better paid than others.* **2** ADV If you say
that something is **thus** or happens **thus**, you
mean that it is, or happens, as you describe.
[FORMAL] *Joanna was pouring the drink. While she
was thus engaged, Charles sat on one of the bar-
stools.*

thwart /θwɔːt/ **thwarts, thwarting, thwarted.** VERB If
you **thwart** someone or **thwart** their plans, you
prevent them from doing or getting what they
want. *The security forces were doing all they could
to thwart terrorists.*

thyme /taɪm/. N-UNCOUNT **Thyme** is a type of
herb.

tick /tɪk/ **ticks, ticking, ticked.** **1** N-COUNT In British
English, a **tick** is a written mark like a V with the
right side extended. You use it to show that
something is correct or has been dealt with. The
usual American word is **check**. *Place a tick in the
appropriate box.* **2** VERB If you **tick** something
that is written on a piece of paper, you put a tick
next to it. *Please tick this box if you do not wish to
receive such mailings.* **3** VERB & N-COUNT When a
clock or watch **ticks**, it makes a regular series of
short sounds as it works. The **tick** of a clock is this
series of short sounds. ♦ **ticking** N-UNCOUNT *...the
endless ticking of clocks.* **4** VERB If you talk about
what makes someone **tick**, you are talking about
the reasons for their character and behaviour.
[INFORMAL] *Their parents simply don't understand
what makes them tick.*

▶**tick away** or **tick by.** PHR-VERB If you say that
the clock or time is **ticking away** or **ticking by**,
you mean that time is passing, especially when
there is something urgent that needs to be done
or when someone is waiting for something to
happen.

▶**tick off.** **1** PHR-VERB If you **tick off** an item on
a list, you put a tick by it to show that it has been
dealt with. **2** PHR-VERB If you **tick** someone **off**,
you speak to them angrily because they have
done something wrong. [INFORMAL] *Harry will be
ticked off for being careless.* ♦ **ticking off, tickings
off** N-COUNT *They got a ticking off from the police.*

▶**tick over.** PHR-VERB Something that is **ticking
over** is working or operating steadily, but not
producing very much or making much progress.
*Zambia will be able to afford enough imports to
keep the economy ticking over.*

⭐ **ticket** /'tɪkɪt/ **tickets.** **1** N-COUNT A **ticket** is an
official piece of paper or card which shows that

you have paid for a journey or have paid to enter
a place of entertainment. ● See also **season
ticket.** **2** N-COUNT If you get a **ticket**, you are
given a piece of paper which orders you to pay a
fine or to appear in court because you have
committed a driving or parking offence. *...the
money she owed on an unpaid parking ticket.*

tickle /'tɪkəl/ **tickles, tickling, tickled.** **1** VERB When
you **tickle** someone, you move your fingers
lightly over their body, often in order to make
them laugh. **2** VERB If something **tickles**, it
causes an irritating feeling by lightly touching a
part of your body. *A beard doesn't scratch, it just
tickles.*

tidal /'taɪdəl/. ADJ **Tidal** means relating to or
produced by tides. *...tidal energy.*

'tidal wave, **tidal waves.** **1** N-COUNT A **tidal wave**
is a very large wave, often caused by an
earthquake. **2** N-COUNT A **tidal wave of**
emotions, things, or people is a very large
number of them all occurring at the same time. *A
tidal wave of refugees was sweeping across Europe.*

⭐ **tide** /taɪd/ **tides, tiding, tided.** **1** N-COUNT The **tide** is
the regular change in the level of the sea on the
shore. *The tide was going out.* **2** N-COUNT The **tide
of** opinion or fashion is what the majority of
people think or do at a particular time. *The tide of
opinion seems overwhelmingly in his favour.*

▶**tide over.** PHR-VERB If someone or something
tides you **over**, they help you to get through a
period when you are having difficulties,
especially by providing you with money. *He can
fall back on odd jobs to tide him over.*

tidy /'taɪdi/ **tidier, tidiest; tidies, tidying, tidied.** **1** ADJ
Something that is **tidy** is neat and arranged in an
orderly way. *...a tidy desk.* ♦ **tidily** ADV *...books
and magazines stacked tidily on shelves.*
♦ **tidiness** N-UNCOUNT *...the tidiness of his Swiss
apartment.* **2** ADJ **Tidy** people keep their things
tidy. *She's obsessively tidy.* ♦ **tidiness** N-UNCOUNT
I'm very impressed by your tidiness. **3** VERB When
you **tidy** a place, you make it neat by putting
things in their proper places. *He tidied his garage.*
4 ADJ BEFORE N A **tidy** amount of money is a
large amount. [INFORMAL] *He has made a tidy profit.*

▶**tidy away.** PHR-VERB When you **tidy** something
away, you put it in a cupboard or drawer so that
it is not in the way. *McMinn tidied away the
glasses and tea-cups.*

▶**tidy up.** PHR-VERB When you **tidy up** or **tidy** a
place **up**, you put things back in their proper
places so that everything is neat. *Kelly spent an
hour tidying things up around the shop.*

⭐ **tie** /taɪ/ **ties, tying, tied.** **1** VERB & PHR-VERB If you **tie**
two things together, or if you **tie** them **up**, you
fasten them together with a knot. *They tied the
ends of the bags securely... He tied up the bag and
took it outside.* **2** VERB & PHR-VERB If you **tie**
someone or something in a place or position, or
if you **tie** them **up**, you put them in that place or
position and fasten them there using rope or
string. *He tied her hands behind her back... He had
tied the dog to one of the trees.* **3** VERB If you **tie**

a piece of string or cloth around something, you put a piece of string or cloth around it and fasten the ends together in a knot or bow. *Roll the meat and tie it with string.* [4] VERB If you **tie** something in a knot or bow, you fasten the ends together in a knot or bow. *She tied a knot in the ribbon.*

[5] N-COUNT A **tie** is a long narrow piece of cloth that is worn round the neck under a shirt collar and tied in a knot at the front. → See picture on page 820. [6] VERB If one thing **is tied to** another, the two things have a close connection or link. *Their bonuses are tied to the company's profits.*

[7] N-COUNT **Ties** are the connections you have with people or a place. *France's close ties with the Arab world.* [8] VERB & N-COUNT If two people **tie** in a competition or game, or if there is a **tie** between them, they have the same number of points or the same degree of success. *Ronan Rafferty had tied with Frank Nobilo... The first game ended in a tie.*

▶ **tie up.** See **tie** 1 and 2.

tier /tɪə/ **tiers.** N-COUNT A **tier** is a row or layer of something that has other layers above or below it. *...the auditorium with the tiers of seats around and above it.*

tiger /'taɪgə/ **tigers.** N-COUNT A **tiger** is a large fierce animal belonging to the cat family. Tigers are orange with black stripes. → See picture on page 816.

★ **tight** /taɪt/ **tighter, tightest; tights.** [1] ADJ **Tight** clothes or shoes fit very closely. *...her tight black jeans.* ◆ **tightly** ADV *He buttoned his collar tightly round his thick neck.* [2] ADV & ADJ If you hold someone or something **tight**, you hold them firmly. *Hold on tight!... He kept a tight hold of her arm.* ◆ **tightly** ADV *She climbed back into bed and wrapped her arms tightly round her body.* [3] ADJ **Tight** controls or rules are very strict. ◆ **tightly** ADV *The internal media was tightly controlled by the government during the war.* [4] ADJ Skin, cloth, or string that is **tight** is stretched or pulled so that it is smooth or straight. ◆ **tightly** ADV *Her sallow skin was drawn tightly across the bones of her face.* [5] ADJ **Tight** is used to describe an amount of something or a group of things that is closely packed together. *She curled up in a tight ball.* ◆ **tightly** ADV *Many animals travel in tightly packed lorries.* [6] ADJ A **tight** schedule or budget allows very little time or money for unexpected events or expenses. *Financially, things are a bit tight.* ◆ **to sit tight:** see **sit.**

tighten /'taɪtən/ **tightens, tightening, tightened.** [1] VERB If you **tighten** your grip on something, or if your grip on something **tightens**, you hold it more firmly or securely. *I could feel him tighten his hold on the stick.* [2] VERB If you **tighten** a rope or chain, or if a rope or chain **tightens**, it stretches until it is straight. [3] VERB & PHR-VERB When you **tighten** a screw, nut, or other device, or when you **tighten** it **up**, you turn it or move it so that it is more firmly in place or holds something more firmly. *I used my thumbnail to tighten the screw... It's important to tighten up the wheels properly.*

[4] VERB To **tighten** rules or controls means to make them stricter. *...an attempt by anti-abortionists to tighten the rules. ...his plans to tighten his grip on the machinery of central government.* [5] **to tighten** your **belt:** see **belt.**

tights /taɪts/. N-PLURAL **Tights** are a piece of clothing made of thin material such as nylon that covers your hips and each of your legs and feet separately. *...a new pair of tights.*

tile /taɪl/ **tiles.** N-VAR **Tiles** are flat square pieces of baked clay, carpet, cork, or other substance, which are fixed as a covering onto a floor, wall, or roof.

tiled /taɪld/. ADJ A **tiled** surface is covered with tiles. *...the hard tiled floor.*

★ **till** /tɪl/ **tills.** [1] PREP & CONJ **Till** is often used instead of **until.** *They had to wait till Monday... They slept till the alarm bleeper woke them.* [2] N-COUNT In a shop or other place of business, a **till** is a counter or cash register where money is kept, and where customers pay for what they have bought. [BRITISH]

tilt /tɪlt/ **tilts, tilting, tilted.** VERB If you **tilt** an object, or if it **tilts**, you change its position so that one end or side is higher than the other. *Leonard tilted his chair back on two legs and stretched his long body.*

timber /'tɪmbə/. N-UNCOUNT In British English, **timber** is wood used for building houses and making furniture. The American word is **lumber**. *...a single-storey timber building.*

★ **time** /taɪm/ **times, timing, timed.** [1] N-UNCOUNT **Time** is what we measure in minutes, hours, days, and years. → See Reference Page on Times and Dates. *...a two-week period of time... Time passed, and still Ma did not appear... Religion has changed over time.* [2] N-SING You use **time** to ask or talk about a specific point in the day, which can be stated in hours and minutes and is shown on clocks. → See Reference Page on Telling the Time. *'What time is it?'—'Eight o'clock.'... He asked me the time.* [3] N-COUNT The **time** when something happens is the point in the day when it happens or is supposed to happen. *Departure times are 0815 from St Quay, and 1815 from St Helier.* [4] N-UNCOUNT & PHRASE You use **time** to refer to the period that someone spends doing something or when something has been happening. If something happens **all the time**, it happens continually. *Adam spent a lot of time in his grandfather's office... I haven't got much time... We can't be together all the time.* [5] N-SING If you say that something happens for **a time**, you mean that it happens for a fairly long period of time. *He stayed for quite a time.* [6] N-COUNT You use **time** or **times** to talk about a period of time. *We were in the same college, which was male-only at that time... During the time I was married I tried to be the perfect wife... Homes are more affordable than at any time in the past five years. ...one of the most severe recessions in modern times.* [7] N-COUNT When you describe the **time** that you had on a particular occasion or during a

a
b
c
d
e
f
g
h
i
j
k
l
m
n
o
p
q
r
s
t
u
v
w
x
y
z

particular part of your life, you are describing the sort of experience that you had then. *I had a great time while the kids were away.* [8] N-UNCOUNT If you say it is **time for** something, you mean that this thing ought to happen or be done now. *It was time for him to go to work... This was no time to make a speech.* [9] N-COUNT When you talk about a **time** when something happens, you are referring to a specific occasion when it happens. *The last time I saw her was about sixteen years ago.* [10] N-COUNT You use **time** after numbers to say how often something happens. *It was her job to make tea three times a day... How many times has your mother told you?*

> **USAGE** You do not say 'one time a year' or 'two times a year'; you say **'once a year'** or **'twice a year'**. You also do not say 'two times as much'; you say **'twice as much'**.

[11] N-PLURAL You use **times** after numbers when comparing one thing to another and saying, for example, how much bigger, smaller, better, or worse it is. *...an area five times the size of Britain.* [12] VERB You use **times** in arithmetic to link numbers or amounts that are multiplied together. *Four times six is 24.* [13] VERB If you **time** something, you plan or decide to do it or cause it to happen at a particular time. *We had timed our visit for March 7... He had timed his intervention well.* [14] VERB If you **time** an action or activity, you measure how long it lasts. *He timed each performance with a stop-watch.* [15] See also **timing**.

PHRASES • If you say it is **about time** that something was done, or that it is **high time** that something was done, you are emphasizing that it should be done now, and really should have happened or been done sooner. *It's about time he learnt to behave properly.* • If someone is **ahead of** their **time** or **before** their **time**, they have new ideas a long time before other people start to think in the same way. • If you say that someone or something is, for example, the best writer **of all time**, or the most successful film **of all time**, you mean that they are the best or most successful that there has ever been. • If something is the case **for the time being**, it is the case, but only until something else becomes possible or happens. *The situation is calm for the time being.* • If you are **in time for** a particular event, or if you are **on time**, you are not late. *I arrived just in time for my flight... Their planes usually arrive on time.* • If something will happen **in time**, it will happen eventually. *He would sort out his own problems, in time.* • If you say that something will happen, for example, **in** a week's **time**, you mean that it will happen a week from now. • **Once upon a time** is used at the beginning of children's stories to indicate that something happened or existed a long time ago or in an imaginary world. *'Once upon a time,' he*

began, 'there was a man who had everything.'* • If you say that something was the case **at one time**, you mean that it was the case during a particular period in the past. *At one time 400 men, women and children lived in the village.* • You use **at the same time** to introduce a statement that contrasts with the previous statement. *I was afraid of her, but at the same time I really liked her.* • If you **take** your **time** doing something, you do it slowly and do not hurry. • If you say that something will **take time**, you mean that it will take a long time. *Change will come, but it will take time.* • If you do something **from time to time**, you do it occasionally. • See also **timing**. • **time and again**: see **again**.

'time-honoured. ADJ BEFORE N A **time-honoured** tradition or way of doing something is one that has been used and appreciated for a very long time. *The beer is brewed in the time-honoured way.*

timeless /'taɪmləs/. ADJ If you describe something as **timeless**, you mean that it is so good or beautiful that it cannot be affected by changes in society or fashion. *There is a timeless quality to his best work.*

timely /'taɪmli/. ADJ If you describe an event as **timely**, you mean that it happens at exactly the right moment. *Disaster was only averted by the timely arrival of the maintenance man.*

timetable /'taɪmteɪbəl/ **timetables.** [1] N-COUNT A **timetable** is a plan of the times when particular events are to take place. *Don't you realize we're working to a timetable?* [2] N-COUNT A **timetable** is a list of the times when trains, boats, buses, or aeroplanes arrive at or depart from a place.

timid /'tɪmɪd/. ADJ **Timid** people are shy, nervous, and have no courage or self-confidence. ◆ **timidly** ADV *The little boy stepped forward timidly.* ◆ **timidity** /tɪ'mɪdɪti/ N-UNCOUNT *She doesn't ridicule my timidity.*

timing /'taɪmɪŋ/. [1] N-UNCOUNT **Timing** is the skill or action of judging the right moment in a situation or activity at which to do something. *His photo is a wonderful happy moment caught with perfect timing.* [2] N-UNCOUNT You can refer to the time at which something happens or is planned to happen as its **timing**. *The timing of the minister's visit could detract from the goodwill it's supposed to generate.* • See also **time**.

tin /tɪn/ **tins.** [1] N-UNCOUNT **Tin** is a soft silvery-white metal. [2] N-COUNT In British English, a **tin** is a sealed metal container filled with food. The usual American word is **can**. *...a tin of tomatoes.* [3] N-COUNT A **tin** is a metal container with a lid. *Store the cookies in an airtight tin.* [4] N-COUNT A baking **tin** is a metal container used for baking things such as cakes and bread in an oven.

tinge /tɪndʒ/ **tinges.** N-COUNT A **tinge** of a colour, feeling, or quality is a small amount of it. *His skin had an unhealthy greyish tinge. ...a tinge of guilt.*

tinged /tɪndʒd/. ADJ If something is **tinged with** a colour, feeling, or quality, it has a small amount of that colour, feeling, or quality in it. *Her homecoming was tinged with sadness.* ◆ **-tinged** *...pink-tinged flowers.*

tingle /'tɪŋɡəl/ **tingles, tingling, tingled.** ☐1 VERB When a part of your body **tingles**, you feel a slight prickly sensation there. ◆ **tingling** N-UNCOUNT *A sensation of burning or tingling may be experienced in the hands.* ☐2 VERB & N-COUNT If you **tingle with** a feeling such as excitement, or if you feel a **tingle of** that feeling, you feel it very strongly. *When I look over and see Terry I tingle all over. ...a sudden tingle of excitement.*

tinker /'tɪŋkə/ **tinkers, tinkering, tinkered.** VERB If you **tinker with** something, you make some small alterations to it in order to repair or improve it. *They tinkered with the engine.*

tinned /tɪnd/. ADJ In British English, **tinned** food has been preserved by being sealed in a tin. The usual American word is **canned**. *...tinned fish.*

tint /tɪnt/ **tints, tinted, tinting.** ☐1 N-COUNT A **tint** is a small amount of a colour. *...the unusual green tint of these glass bottles.* ☐2 VERB If something **is tinted**, it has a small amount of a particular colour or dye in it. *Eyebrows can be tinted with the same dye.* ◆ **-tinted** *The General wore green-tinted glasses.*

⭐ **tiny** /'taɪni/ **tinier, tiniest.** ADJ Someone or something that is **tiny** is extremely small. *Though she was tiny, she had a very loud voice.*

⭐ **tip** /tɪp/ **tips, tipping, tipped.** ☐1 N-COUNT The **tip of** something long and narrow is the end of it. *...the tips of his fingers. ...the southern tip of Florida.* ☐2 PHRASE If you say that a problem is **the tip of the iceberg**, you mean that it is one small part of a much larger problem. *The above complaints are, I suspect, just the tip of the iceberg.* ☐3 VERB If an object or part of your body **tips**, or if you **tip** it, it moves into a sloping position with one end or side higher than the other. *She had to tip her head back to see him.* ☐4 VERB If you **tip** something somewhere, you pour it there. *Tip the vegetables into a bowl... Tip away the salt and wipe the pan.* ☐5 N-COUNT A **tip** is a place where rubbish is left. [BRITISH] ☐6 N-COUNT & VERB If you give someone such as a waiter a **tip**, or if you **tip** them, you give them some money for their services. *She tipped the barmen 10 dollars.* ☐7 N-COUNT A **tip** is a useful piece of advice. *A good tip is to buy the most expensive lens you can afford.* ☐8 VERB If a person **is tipped to** do something or **is tipped for** success at something, experts or journalists believe that they will do that thing or achieve that success. *He is tipped to be the country's next foreign minister.*

▶**tip off.** PHR-VERB If someone **tips** you **off**, they give you information about something that has happened or is going to happen. ◆ **tip-off, tip-offs** N-COUNT *The man was arrested at his home after a tip-off to police.*

▶**tip over.** PHR-VERB If something **tips over**, it falls over or turns over.

tiptoe /'tɪptəʊ/ **tiptoes, tiptoeing, tiptoed.** VERB & PHRASE If you **tiptoe** somewhere, or if you walk somewhere **on tiptoe**, you walk there very quietly without putting your heels on the floor. *She slipped out of bed and tiptoed to the window.*

tirade /taɪ'reɪd/ **tirades.** N-COUNT A **tirade** is a long angry speech criticizing someone or something.

tire /taɪə/ **tires, tiring, tired.** ☐1 VERB & PHR-VERB If something **tires** you, or if it **tires** you **out**, it uses a lot of your energy, leaving you very tired and needing to rest. *The oppressive afternoon heat had quite tired him out.* ☐2 VERB If you **tire of** something, you become bored with it. *He would never tire of international cricket.* ☐3 See also **tyre**.

⭐ **tired** /taɪəd/. ☐1 ADJ If you are **tired**, you feel that you want to rest or sleep. *She was too tired to take a shower.* ◆ **tiredness** N-UNCOUNT *He felt half dead with tiredness.* ☐2 ADJ AFTER LINK-V If you are **tired of** something, you do not want it to continue because you are bored with it. *I was tired of being a bookkeeper.*

tireless /'taɪələs/. ADJ If you describe someone or their efforts as **tireless**, you approve of the fact that they put a lot of hard work into something, and refuse to give up. ◆ **tirelessly** ADV *He worked tirelessly for the cause of health and safety.*

tiresome /'taɪəsəm/. ADJ If you describe someone or something as **tiresome**, you mean that you find them irritating or boring. *...the tiresome old lady next door.*

tiring /'taɪərɪŋ/. ADJ If you describe something as **tiring**, you mean that it makes you tired so that you want to rest or sleep. *Travelling is tiring. ...a long and tiring day.*

⭐ **tissue** /'tɪʃuː, 'tɪsjuː/ **tissues.** ☐1 N-VAR In animals and plants, **tissue** consists of cells that are similar in appearance and function. *...muscle tissue.* ☐2 N-UNCOUNT **Tissue** or **tissue paper** is thin paper used for wrapping things that are easily damaged. ☐3 N-COUNT A **tissue** is a piece of thin soft paper that you use as a handkerchief.

titillate /'tɪtɪleɪt/ **titillates, titillating, titillated.** VERB If something **titillates** someone, it pleases and excites them, especially in a sexual way. ◆ **titillating** ADJ *...titillating gossip.* ◆ **titillation** N-UNCOUNT *People buy sex manuals for titillation, they don't buy them for ideas.*

⭐ **title** /'taɪtəl/ **titles.** ☐1 N-COUNT The **title** of a book, play, film, or piece of music is its name. ☐2 N-COUNT Someone's **title** is a word such as 'Lord' or 'Mrs' that is used before their name to show their status or profession. *She has been awarded the title Professor.* ☐3 N-COUNT A **title** in a sports competition is the position of champion. *He has retained his title as world chess champion.*

titled /'taɪtəld/. ADJ Someone who is **titled** has a name such as 'Lord', 'Lady', 'Sir', or 'Princess'

a
b
c
d
e
f
g
h
i
j
k
l
m
n
o
p
q
r
s
t
u
v
w
x
y
z

before their own name showing that they are a member of the aristocracy. ...*a titled lady*.

to 1 preposition and adverb uses

★ **to**.

> ✓ **To** is usually pronounced /tə/ before a consonant and /tʊ/ before a vowel, but pronounced /tuː/ when you are emphasizing it.

1 PREP You use **to** when indicating the place that someone or something visits, moves towards, or points at. *Ramsay made a second visit to Italy... She went to the window and looked out... He pointed to a chair.* **2** PREP If you go to an event, you go where it is taking place. *We went to a party at the leisure centre.* **3** PHRASE If someone moves **to and fro**, they move repeatedly from one place to another and back again. *She stood up and began to pace to and fro.* **4** PREP If something is attached **to** something larger or fixed **to** it, the two things are joined together. *There was a piece of cloth tied to the dog's collar.* **5** PREP You use **to** when indicating the position of something. For example, if something is **to** your left, it is nearer your left side than your right. *Atlanta was only an hour's drive to the north.* **6** PREP When you give something **to** someone, they receive it. **7** PREP You use **to** to indicate who or what an action or a feeling is directed towards. *...troops loyal to the government. ...repairs to the house.* **8** PREP You use **to** when indicating someone's reaction to something. *To his surprise, the bedroom door was locked.* **9** PREP You use **to** when indicating the person whose opinion you are stating. *It was clear to me that he respected his boss.* **10** PREP You use **to** when indicating the state that someone or something gradually starts to be in. *...an old ranch house that has been converted to a nature centre. ...a return to active politics.* **11** PREP You use **to** when indicating the last thing in a range of things. *I read everything from fiction to history and science.* **12** PREP You use **to** when you are stating a time. For example, 'five to eight' means five minutes before eight o'clock. → See Reference Pages on Times and Dates and Telling the Time. **13** PREP You use **to** in ratios and rates. *...a mixture of one part milk to two parts water.* **14** ADV If you push a door **to**, you close it but do not shut it completely. *He slipped out, pulling the door to.*

to 2 used before the base form of a verb

★ **to**.

> ✓ **To** is pronounced /tə/ before a consonant and /tʊ/ before a vowel.

1 You use **to** with an infinitive when indicating the purpose of an action. *...programs set up to save animals.* **2** You use **to** with an infinitive when commenting on your attitude or intention in making a statement. *I'm disappointed, to be honest.* **3** You use **to** with an infinitive in various other constructions when talking about an action or state. *The management wanted to know... Nuclear plants are expensive to build. ...advice*

about how to do her job... *The Foreign Minister is to visit China.*

toad /təʊd/ **toads.** N-COUNT A **toad** is an animal like a frog, but with a drier skin.

toast /təʊst/ **toasts, toasting, toasted. 1** N-UNCOUNT **Toast** is slices of bread heated until they are brown and crisp. *...a piece of toast.* **2** VERB When you **toast** bread, you heat it so that it becomes brown and crisp. ● See note at **cook**. **3** N-COUNT & VERB When you drink a **toast to** someone, or when you **toast** them, you wish them success or good health, and then drink some alcoholic drink.

toaster /ˈtəʊstə/ **toasters.** N-COUNT A **toaster** is a piece of electric equipment used to toast bread.

tobacco /təˈbækəʊ/ **tobaccos.** N-VAR **Tobacco** is the dried leaves of a plant which people smoke in pipes, cigars, and cigarettes.

★ **today** /təˈdeɪ/. **1** ADV & N-UNCOUNT **Today** means the day on which you are speaking or writing. *How are you feeling today?... Today is Friday.* **2** ADV & N-UNCOUNT You can refer to the present period of history as **today**. *The United States is in a serious recession today. ...the Africa of today.*

toddler /ˈtɒdlə/ **toddlers.** N-COUNT A **toddler** is a young child who has only just learnt to walk.

toe /təʊ/ **toes, toeing, toed. 1** N-COUNT Your **toes** are the five movable parts at the end of each foot. → See picture on page 822. **2** N-COUNT The **toe** of a shoe or sock is the part that covers the end of your foot. **3** PHRASE If you **toe the line**, you behave in the way that people in authority expect you to. *...politicians that wouldn't toe the party line.*

toenail /ˈtəʊneɪl/ **toenails.** N-COUNT Your **toenails** are the thin hard areas at the end of each of your toes. → See picture on page 822.

toffee /ˈtɒfi, AM ˈtɔːfi/ **toffees.** N-VAR A **toffee** is a sweet made by boiling sugar and butter together with water.

★ **together** /təˈgeðə/. **1** ADV If people do something **together**, they do it with each other. *We went on long bicycle rides together... They all live together in a three-bedroom house... Together they swam to the ship.* **2** ADV If two things happen **together**, they happen at the same time. *Three horses crossed the finish line together.* **3** ADV If things are joined **together**, they are joined to each other so that they touch or form one whole. *Mix the ingredients together thoroughly... She clasped her hands together on her lap.* **4** ADV If things or people are situated **together**, they are in the same place and very near to each other. *The trees grew close together... We gathered our things together.* **5** ADV You use **together** when you are adding two or more amounts or things to each other in order to consider a total amount or effect. *The two main opposition parties together won 29.8 per cent.* **6** PREP **Together with** something means as well as that thing. *Return the completed questionnaire, together with your cheque for £60.*

toil /tɔɪl/ **toils, toiling, toiled.** VERB & N-UNCOUNT If you say that people **toil**, or if you describe their work as **toil**, you mean that they work hard doing unpleasant or tiring tasks. [LITERARY] *Workers toiled long hours... Hours of toil paid off in the end.*

toilet /'tɔɪlət/ **toilets.** ⒈ N-COUNT A **toilet** is a large bowl connected to the drains which you use when you want to get rid of urine or faeces from your body. *She flushed the toilet and went back in the bedroom.* ⒉ N-COUNT In British English, a **toilet** is a small room containing a toilet. The American word is **bathroom**.

'toilet paper. N-UNCOUNT **Toilet paper** is paper that you use to clean yourself after getting rid of urine or faeces from your body.

toiletries /'tɔɪlətriz/. N-PLURAL **Toiletries** are things that you use when cleaning or taking care of your body, such as soap and toothpaste.

token /'təʊkən/ **tokens.** ⒈ N-COUNT A **token** is a piece of paper, plastic, or metal which can be used instead of money. *...£10 book tokens. ...subway tokens.* ⒉ N-COUNT If you give something to someone as a **token of** your feelings for them, you give it as a way of expressing those feelings. *The ring was given as a token of love.* ⒊ ADJ BEFORE N You use **token** to describe things or actions which show your intentions or feelings but are small or unimportant. *...token gestures of force.* ⒋ PHRASE You use **by the same token** to introduce a statement that you think is true for the same reasons that were given for a previous statement. *If you give up exercise, your muscles shrink and fat increases. By the same token, if you expend more energy you will lose fat.*

told /təʊld/. ⒈ **Told** is the past tense and past participle of **tell**. ⒉ PHRASE You can use **all told** to indicate a summary, generalization, or total. *All told, he went to 14 different schools.*

tolerable /'tɒlərəbəl/. ADJ If something is **tolerable**, it is acceptable or bearable, but not pleasant or good. *The pain was tolerable.* ♦ **tolerably** ADV *Their captors treated them tolerably well.*

tolerant /'tɒlərənt/. ADJ If you are **tolerant**, you let other people say and do what they like, even if you do not agree with it or approve of it. *People are becoming more tolerant of homosexuals.* ♦ **tolerance** N-UNCOUNT *...religious tolerance.*

tolerate /'tɒləreɪt/ **tolerates, tolerating, tolerated.** ⒈ VERB If you **tolerate** things that you do not agree with or approve of, you allow them to exist or happen. *We will not tolerate such behaviour.* ⒉ VERB If you can **tolerate** something unpleasant or painful, you are able to bear it. *Women tolerate pain better than men.*

toll /təʊl/ **tolls, tolling, tolled.** ⒈ VERB When a bell **tolls**, it rings slowly and repeatedly, often as a sign that someone has died. ⒉ N-COUNT A **toll** is a sum of money that you have to pay in order to use a particular bridge or road. ⒊ PHRASE If

something **takes a toll** or **takes its toll**, it has a bad effect on someone or something, or causes a lot of suffering. *Winter takes its toll on your health.* ⒋ See also **death toll**.

tomato /tə'mɑːtəʊ, AM -'meɪ-/ **tomatoes.** N-VAR A **tomato** is a small, soft, red vegetable that is used in cooking or eaten raw. → See picture on page 836.

tomb /tuːm/ **tombs.** N-COUNT A **tomb** is a stone structure containing the body of a dead person.

tombstone /'tuːmstəʊn/ **tombstones.** N-COUNT A **tombstone** is a large flat piece of stone on someone's grave, with their name written on it.

⭐ **tomorrow** /tə'mɒrəʊ, AM -'mɔːr-/. ⒈ ADV & N-UNCOUNT **Tomorrow** refers to the day after today. *The results will be announced tomorrow... Tomorrow is her thirteenth birthday.* ⒉ ADV & N-UNCOUNT You can refer to the future as **tomorrow**. *What is education going to look like tomorrow? ...tomorrow's computer industry.*

⭐ **ton** /tʌn/ **tons.** ⒈ N-COUNT A non-metric **ton** is a unit of weight equal to 2,240 pounds in Britain and 2,000 pounds in the United States. ⒉ N-COUNT A metric **ton** is a unit of weight equal to 1,000 kilograms.

⭐ **tone** /təʊn/ **tones, toning, toned.** ⒈ N-COUNT The **tone** of a sound is its particular quality. *They began speaking in low tones. ...the clear tone of the bell.* ⒉ N-COUNT Someone's **tone** is a quality in their voice which shows what they are feeling or thinking. *I still didn't like his tone of voice... Her tone implied that her patience was limited.* ⒊ N-UNCOUNT The **tone** of a speech or piece of writing is its style and the feelings expressed in it. *The tone of the letter was very friendly... His comments to reporters were conciliatory in tone.* ⒋ VERB & PHR-VERB Something that **tones** or **tones up** your body makes it firm and strong. *The massage tones up the child's muscles.*
▸ **tone down.** PHR-VERB If you **tone down** something that you have written or said, you make it less forceful, severe, or offensive. *It would help if you toned down your language.*

tongue /tʌŋ/ **tongues.** ⒈ N-COUNT Your **tongue** is the soft movable part inside your mouth that you use for tasting, licking, and speaking. → See picture on page 823. ⒉ N-COUNT A **tongue** is a language. [LITERARY] *English is not her native tongue.* ⒊ PHRASE A **tongue-in-cheek** remark is made as a joke, and is not serious or sincere. ⒋ to **bite** your **tongue**: see **bite**.

tonic /'tɒnɪk/ **tonics.** ⒈ N-VAR **Tonic** or **tonic water** is a colourless, fizzy drink that has a slightly bitter flavour. *...a gin and tonic.* ⒉ N-COUNT You can refer to anything that makes you feel stronger or more cheerful as a **tonic**. *Seeing Marcus at that moment was a great tonic.*

⭐ **tonight** /tə'naɪt/. ADV & N-UNCOUNT **Tonight** refers to the evening or night that will come at the end of today. *What are you doing tonight?... Tonight is the opening night of the opera.*

tonne /tʌn/ **tonnes.** N-COUNT A **tonne** is a unit of weight equal to 1,000 kilograms.

a
b
c
d
e
f
g
h
i
j
k
l
m
n
o
p
q
r
s
t
u
v
w
x
y
z

too /tuː/. [1] ADV You use **too** after mentioning another person, thing, or aspect that a previous statement applies to or includes. *'Nice to talk to you.'—'Nice to talk to you too.'... 'I've got a great feeling about it.'—'Me too.'... Depression may be expressed physically too... He doesn't want to see me. I, too, have been afraid to talk to him.* [2] ADV You use **too** after adding a piece of information or a comment to a statement, in order to emphasize it. *We did learn to read, and quickly too... 'That money's mine.'—'Of course it is, and quite right too.'* [3] ADV You use **too** to indicate that there is more of a thing or quality than is desirable or acceptable. *Eggs shouldn't be kept in the fridge, it's too cold... She was drinking too much... We have too much to do today.* [4] ADV You can use **too** to make a negative opinion politer or more cautious. *Americans are never too keen to leave their beloved country... I wasn't too happy with what I'd written so far.* [5] **too bad**: see **bad**.
● **none too**: see **none**.

PHRASES ● You use **all too** or **only too** to emphasize that something happens to a greater degree than is pleasant or desirable. *She remembered it all too well... The letter spoke only too clearly of his anxiety for her.*

> **USAGE Too** can be used to intensify the meaning of an adjective, an adverb, or a word like **much** or **many**. **Too**, however, also suggests an excessive or undesirable amount, often so much that a particular result does not or cannot happen. *She does wear too much make-up at times... He was too late to save her.*
> **Too** is not generally used to modify an adjective inside a noun group. For instance, you cannot say 'the too heavy boxes' or 'too expensive jewellery'. There is one exception to this rule, which is when the noun group begins with **a** or **an**. Notice the word order in the following examples. *...if the products have been stored at too high a temperature... He found it too good an opportunity to miss... It was too long a drive for one day.*

took /tʊk/. **Took** is the past tense of **take**.

★ **tool** /tuːl/**tools**. [1] N-COUNT A **tool** is any instrument or simple piece of equipment, for example a hammer or a knife, that you hold in your hands and use to do a particular kind of work. → See pictures on pages 832 and 833. [2] N-COUNT You can refer to anything that you use for a particular purpose as a particular type of **tool**. *The video has become an invaluable teaching tool.*

toolbar /'tuːlbɑː/**toolbars**. N-COUNT A **toolbar** is a strip across a computer screen containing pictures which represent different computer functions. [COMPUTING]

★ **tooth** /tuːθ/**teeth**. [1] N-COUNT Your **teeth** are the hard, white objects in your mouth that you use for biting and chewing. → See picture on page

823. [2] N-PLURAL The **teeth** of a comb, saw, or zip are the parts that stick out in a row. [3] **to grit your teeth**: see **grit**.

toothbrush /'tuːθbrʌʃ/**toothbrushes**. N-COUNT A **toothbrush** is a small brush used for cleaning your teeth.

toothpaste /'tuːθpeɪst/**toothpastes**. N-VAR **Toothpaste** is a thick substance which you use to clean your teeth.

★ **top** /tɒp/**tops, topping, topped**. [1] N-COUNT The **top** of something is its highest point or part. *I waited at the top of the stairs... Don't fill it up to the top.* [2] ADJ BEFORE N The **top** thing or layer in a series of things or layers is the highest one. *Our new flat was on the top floor.* [3] PHRASE If one thing is **on top of** another, it is on its highest part. *...the fairy on top of the Christmas tree. ...hot chocolate with whipped cream on top.* [4] N-COUNT The **top** of a bottle, jar, or tube is its cap or lid. [5] ADJ BEFORE N You can use **top** to describe the highest level of a scale or measurement. *The vehicles have a top speed of 80 kilometres per hour.* [6] ADJ N-SING If someone is **top of** a table or league, or if they are **at the top of** it, their performance is better than that of all the other people involved. *She came top in French and second in maths... The United States will be at the top of the medal table.* [7] N-SING & ADJ BEFORE N If someone is at **the top of** an organization or career, they are among the most senior, important, or successful people in it. You can also refer to the **top** people in an organization or career. *...the men at the top of the company... He has got to the top on natural talent. ...a top model.* [8] See also **topped**.

PHRASES ● **On top of** other things means in addition to them. *An extra 700 jobs are being cut on top of the 2,000 that were lost last year.* ● If you are **on top of** a task, you are dealing with it successfully. ● If you say that something is **over the top**, you mean that it is unacceptable because it is too extreme. [BRITISH, INFORMAL] *Her paintings are over the top.*

▸ **top up.** PHR-VERB If you **top up** a container, you fill it again when it has been partly emptied. *He topped her glass up.*

,**top 'class.** ADJ **Top class** means amongst the finest of its kind. *...a top class dancer.*

topic /'tɒpɪk/**topics**. N-COUNT A **topic** is a particular subject that you write about or discuss. *The weather is a constant topic of conversation in Britain.*

topical /'tɒpɪkəl/. ADJ **Topical** means relating to events that are happening at the time when you are speaking or writing. *The magazine's aim is to discuss topical issues.*

topless /'tɒpləs/. ADJ If a woman goes **topless**, she does not wear anything to cover her breasts. *...a topless dancer.*

topped /tɒpt/. ADJ If something is **topped by** or **with** another thing, the other thing is on top of it. *...hot scones topped with fresh cream.*

topple /'tɒpəl/**topples, toppling, toppled**. [1] VERB If someone or something **topples** somewhere, or if they **topple over**, they become unsteady and fall over. *His foot slipped and he toppled into the boat head first.* [2] VERB To **topple** a government or leader means to cause them to lose power. [JOURNALISM] *...the revolution which toppled the regime.*

,**top 'secret.** ADJ **Top secret** information or activity is intended to be kept completely secret. *...a top-secret military mission.*

torch /tɔːtʃ/ **torches.** [1] N-COUNT In British English, a **torch** is a small, battery-powered electric light which you carry in your hand. The American word is **flashlight.** [2] N-COUNT A **torch** is a long stick with burning material at one end, used to provide light or to set things on fire.

tore /tɔː/. **Tore** is the past tense of **tear.**

torment, torments, tormenting, tormented. [1] N-VAR /'tɔːment/ **Torment** is extreme suffering, usually mental suffering. *He spent years in torment going from psychiatrist to psychiatrist. ...the torments of being a writer.* [2] VERB /tɔː'ment/ If something **torments** you, it causes you extreme mental suffering. *He had lain awake all night, tormented by jealousy.* [3] VERB To **torment** a person or animal means to annoy them in a playful, rather cruel way, for your own amusement.

torn /tɔːn/. **Torn** is the past participle of **tear.**

tornado /tɔː'neɪdəʊ/ **tornadoes** or **tornados.** N-COUNT A **tornado** is a violent storm with strong circular winds.

torpedo /tɔː'piːdəʊ/ **torpedoes, torpedoing, torpedoed.** [1] N-COUNT A **torpedo** is a bomb shaped like a tube that travels underwater. [2] VERB If a ship **is torpedoed**, it is hit, and usually sunk, by a torpedo.

torrent /'tɒrənt, AM 'tɔːr-/ **torrents.** [1] N-COUNT A **torrent** is a lot of water falling or flowing rapidly or violently. *Torrents of water gushed into the reservoir... The rain came down in torrents.* [2] N-COUNT A **torrent of** abuse or questions is a lot of insults or questions directed continuously at someone.

torrential /tə'renʃəl, AM tɔːr-/. ADJ **Torrential** rain falls very fast and very heavily.

torso /'tɔːsəʊ/ **torsos.** N-COUNT Your **torso** is the main part of your body, excluding your head, arms, and legs. [FORMAL]

tortoise /'tɔːtəs/ **tortoises.** N-COUNT A **tortoise** is a slow-moving animal with a shell into which it can pull its head and legs for protection.

tortuous /'tɔːtʃʊəs/. [1] ADJ A **tortuous** road is full of bends and twists. [FORMAL] [2] ADJ A **tortuous** process is long and complicated. [FORMAL]

★ **torture** /'tɔːtʃə/ **tortures, torturing, tortured.** VERB & N-VAR If someone **is tortured**, or if they are subjected to **torture**, another person deliberately causes them great pain, in order to punish them or make them reveal information. *Many died under torture, others committed suicide. ...a medieval torture.*

Tory /'tɔːri/ **Tories.** ADJ & N-COUNT In Britain, a **Tory** politician or voter is a member of or votes for the

Conservative Party. A **Tory** is a member of or votes for the Conservative Party.

toss /tɒs, AM tɔːs/ **tosses, tossing, tossed.** [1] VERB If you **toss** something somewhere, you throw it there lightly and carelessly. *She tossed his suitcase onto one of the beds... He tossed Malone a can of beer.* [2] VERB If you **toss** your head, you move it backwards quickly and suddenly, often as a way of expressing anger or contempt. [3] VERB & N-COUNT In sports and informal situations, if you decide something by **tossing** a coin, or by **the toss of** a coin, you spin a coin into the air and guess which side of the coin will face upwards when it lands. [4] VERB If something such as the wind or sea **tosses** an object, it causes it to move from side to side or up and down. *The seas grew turbulent, tossing the small boat like a cork.*

★ **total** /'təʊtəl/ **totals, totalling, totalled** (AM **totaling, totaled).** [1] N-COUNT & ADJ BEFORE N A **total** is the number that you get when you add several numbers together or when you count how many things there are in a group. *The companies have a total of 1,776 employees... The total cost of the project would be more than $240 million.* [2] PHRASE If there are a number of things **in total**, there are that number of them when you count or add them all together. *I was with my husband for eight years in total.* [3] VERB If several numbers **total** a certain figure, that is the figure you get when all the numbers are added together. *They will compete for prizes totalling nearly £3000.* [4] ADJ **Total** means complete. *I have total confidence that things will change.*
♦ **totally** ADV *...something totally different... The fire totally destroyed the top floor.*

totalitarian /ˌtəʊtælɪ'teəriən/. ADJ A **totalitarian** political system is one in which one political party controls everything and does not allow any other parties to exist.

totter /'tɒtə/ **totters, tottering, tottered.** VERB When someone **totters** somewhere, they walk there in an unsteady way.

★ **touch** /tʌtʃ/ **touches, touching, touched.** [1] VERB & N-SING If you **touch** something, or if you give it a **touch**, you put your fingers or hand on it. *Kate leaned forward and touched his hand reassuringly... Don't touch that chair. ...a gentle touch on the hand.* [2] VERB When two things **touch**, or when one thing **touches** another, their surfaces come into contact with each other. *Their knees were touching... Annie lowered her legs, until her feet touched the floor.* [3] N-UNCOUNT Your sense of **touch** is your ability to tell what something is like when you feel it with your hands. *The wine should feel decidedly cold to the touch.* [4] VERB If you **touch on** a particular subject, you mention it briefly. [5] VERB If something that someone says or does **touches** you, it affects you emotionally, often because that person is suffering or is being very kind.
♦ **touched** ADJ AFTER LINK-V *He was touched that we came.* ♦ **touching** ADJ *...a touching tale of love and romance.* [6] N-COUNT A **touch** is a detail

which is added to something to improve it. *They called the event 'a tribute to heroes', which was a nice touch.* [7] N-UNCOUNT If you are **in touch with** someone, you write, phone, or visit each other regularly. *We will be in touch with you shortly... We have to keep in touch by phone.*

PHRASES • If you say that something is **touch and go**, you mean that it is uncertain whether it will happen or succeed. *It was touch and go whether we'd go bankrupt.* • If you are **in touch with** a subject or situation, you know the latest information about it. If you are **out of touch with** it, your knowledge of it is out of date.

▸**touch down.** PHR-VERB When an aircraft **touches down**, it lands.

'**touch-screen, touch-screens.** N-COUNT A **touch-screen** is a computer screen that allows the user to give commands to the computer by touching parts of the screen rather than by using the keyboard or mouse.

touchy /'tʌtʃi/ **touchier, touchiest.** [1] ADJ **Touchy** people are easily upset or irritated. [2] ADJ A **touchy** subject is one that needs to be dealt with carefully, because it might upset or offend people.

★ **tough** /tʌf/ **tougher, toughest.** [1] ADJ A **tough** person has a strong character and can tolerate difficulty or hardship. ♦ **toughness** N-UNCOUNT *Mrs Potter has won a reputation for toughness and determination.* [2] ADJ A **tough** substance is strong, and difficult to break or cut. *...dark brown beans with a rather tough outer skin.* [3] ADJ A **tough** task or way of life is difficult or full of hardship. *She had a pretty tough childhood.*

toughen /'tʌfən/ **toughens, toughening, toughened.** [1] VERB If you **toughen** something, or if it **toughens**, you make it stronger so that it will not break easily. *...toughened glass.* [2] VERB & PHR-VERB If an experience **toughens** you, or if it **toughens** you **up**, it makes you stronger in character. *He thinks boxing is good for kids, that it toughens them up.*

★ **tour** /tʊə/ **tours, touring, toured.** [1] VERB & N-VAR When people such as musicians, politicians, or theatre companies **tour**, or when they go **on tour**, they go to several different places, stopping to meet people or perform. *He toured for nearly two years... The band will go on tour... Their British tour was a virtual sell-out.* [2] N-COUNT A **tour** is a trip or journey to an interesting place or around several interesting places. [3] VERB If you **tour** a place, you go on a journey or trip round it.

tourism /'tʊərizəm/. N-UNCOUNT **Tourism** is the business of providing services for people on holiday.

★ **tourist** /'tʊərist/ **tourists.** N-COUNT A **tourist** is a person who is visiting a place for pleasure, especially when they are on holiday.

★ **tournament** /'tʊənəmənt/ **tournaments.** N-COUNT A **tournament** is a sports competition in which players who win a match continue to play further matches until just one person or team is left.

tout /taʊt/ **touts, touting, touted.** [1] VERB If

someone **touts** something, they try to sell it or convince people that it is good; used showing disapproval. *The product is touted as being completely natural.* [2] VERB If someone **touts for** business or custom, they try to obtain it. [BRITISH] [3] N-COUNT A **tout** is someone who unofficially sells tickets outside a sports ground or theatre, often for more than their original value. [BRITISH]

tow /təʊ/ **tows, towing, towed.** [1] VERB If one vehicle **tows** another, the first vehicle pulls the second along behind it. *They threatened to tow away my car.* [2] PHRASE If you have someone **in tow**, they are following you closely because you are looking after them or you are leading them somewhere. [INFORMAL] *There she was on my doorstep with child in tow.*

★ **towards** /tə'wɔːdz, AM tɔːrdz/.

> ✔ The form **toward** is also used and is the more usual form in American English.

[1] PREP If you move or look **towards** something or someone, you move or look in their direction. *Caroline leant across the table towards him.* [2] PREP If people move **towards** a particular situation, that situation becomes nearer in time or more likely to happen. *She also began moving toward a different life-style.* [3] PREP If you have a particular attitude **towards** something or someone, you feel like that about them. *Not everyone in the world will be kind and caring towards you.* [4] PREP If something happens **towards** a particular time, it happens just before that time. *The Channel tunnel was due to open towards the end of 1993.* [5] PREP If something is **towards** part of a place or thing, it is near that part. *...towards the top of the hill.* [6] PREP If you give money **towards** something, you give it to help pay for that thing. *He gave them £50,000 towards a house.*

towel /taʊəl/ **towels, towelling, towelled** (AM **toweling, toweled**). [1] N-COUNT A **towel** is a piece of thick, soft cloth that you use to dry yourself with. [2] VERB If you **towel** something, you dry it with a towel. *I towelled myself dry.* [3] PHRASE If you **throw in the towel**, you stop trying to do something because you realize that you cannot succeed.

tower [1]

★ **tower** /taʊə/ **towers, towering, towered.** [1] N-COUNT A **tower** is a tall narrow structure, that is often part of a church or castle. [2] VERB Someone or something that **towers over** surrounding people or things is a lot taller than they are.

towering /ˈtaʊərɪŋ/ ADJ BEFORE N If you describe something such as a mountain or cliff as **towering**, you mean that it is very high and therefore impressive. [LITERARY]

⭐ **town** /taʊn/ **towns.** **1** N-COUNT A **town** is a place with many streets and buildings where people live and work. **2** N-UNCOUNT You use **town** in order to refer to the town where you live. *She left town.*

,**town 'hall** (or **Town Hall**) **town halls.** N-COUNT The **town hall** in a town is a large building owned and used by the town council, often as its headquarters.

township /ˈtaʊnʃɪp/ **townships.** N-COUNT In South Africa, a **township** was a town where only black people lived.

toxic /ˈtɒksɪk/. ADJ A **toxic** substance is poisonous. ♦ **toxicity** /tɒkˈsɪsɪti/ **toxicities** N-VAR ...*data on the toxicity of chemicals.*

⭐ **toy** /tɔɪ/ **toys, toying, toyed.** N-COUNT A **toy** is an object that children play with, for example a doll or a model car.
▸**toy with.** **1** PHR-VERB If you **toy with** an idea, you consider it casually, without making any decisions about it. **2** PHR-VERB If you **toy with** an object or with your food, you keep moving it around but do not use it properly or eat it, especially because you are thinking about something else.

⭐ **trace** /treɪs/ **traces, tracing, traced.** **1** VERB If you **trace** someone or something, you find them after looking for them. *They traced the van to a New Jersey car rental agency.* **2** VERB & PHR-VERB If you **trace** the origin or development of something, or if you **trace** it **back**, you find out or describe how it started or developed. *He can trace his jealousy back to when he was age two.* **3** VERB If you **trace** a picture, you copy it by covering it with a piece of transparent paper and drawing over the lines underneath. **4** N-COUNT A **trace** is a sign which shows that someone or something has been in a place. ...*traces of chemicals in food and water.*

⭐ **track** /træk/ **tracks, tracking, tracked.** **1** N-COUNT A **track** is a narrow road or path. **2** N-COUNT A **track** is a piece of ground that is used for races. **3** N-COUNT Railway **tracks** are the rails that a train travels along. **4** N-PLURAL Animal **tracks** are the footprints that animals make. **5** VERB If you **track** animals or people, you try to find them by following their footprints or other signs.
PHRASES ● If a place is **off the beaten track**, it is in a quiet and isolated area. ● If you **keep track of** a situation or a person, you have accurate information about them all the time. If you **lose track of** them, you no longer know where they are or what is happening. *It's so easy to lose track of who's playing who and when.* ● If you are **on the right track**, you are acting or progressing in a way that is likely to result in success.

▸**track down.** PHR-VERB If you **track down** someone or something, you find them after a long and difficult search. *It took two years to track him down.*

,**track 'record, track records.** N-COUNT If you talk about the **track record** of a person, company, or product, you are referring to their past achievements or failures.

tracksuit /ˈtræksuːt/ **tracksuits.** N-COUNT A **tracksuit** is a loose, warm suit consisting of trousers and a sweatshirt, worn mainly when exercising.

tractor

tractor /ˈtræktə/ **tractors.** N-COUNT A **tractor** is a farm vehicle that is used for pulling farm machinery.

⭐ **trade** /treɪd/ **trades, trading, traded.** VERB & N-UNCOUNT When people or countries **trade**, they buy, sell, or exchange goods or services. This activity is called **trade**. *Texas has a long history of trade with Mexico.* ♦ **trading** N-UNCOUNT ...*trading on the stock exchange.*

trademark /ˈtreɪdmɑːk/ **trademarks.** N-COUNT A **trademark** is a name or symbol that a company uses on its products and that cannot legally be used by another company.

⭐ **trader** /ˈtreɪdə/ **traders.** N-COUNT A **trader** is a person whose job is to trade in goods or stocks.

,**trade 'union** (or **trades union**) **trade unions.** N-COUNT A **trade union** is an organization formed by workers in order to represent their rights and interests to their employers.

,**trade 'unionist** (or **trades unionist**) **trade unionists.** N-COUNT A **trade unionist** is an active member of a trade union.

⭐ **tradition** /trəˈdɪʃən/ **traditions.** N-VAR A **tradition** is a custom or belief that has existed for a long time. ...*the rich traditions of Afro-Cuban music.*
♦ **traditional** ADJ ...*traditional teaching methods.*
♦ **traditionally** ADV *Married women have traditionally been treated as dependent on their husbands.*

⭐ **traffic** /ˈtræfɪk/ **traffics, trafficking, trafficked.**
1 N-UNCOUNT **Traffic** refers to all the vehicles that are moving along the roads in an area. *Traffic was unusually light for that time of day.* **2** N-UNCOUNT **Traffic** refers to the movement of ships, trains, or

a b c d e f g h i j k l m n o p q r s t u v w x y z

aircraft between one place and another. *Air traffic had returned to normal.* ③ VERB & N-UNCOUNT If someone **traffics in** illegal or stolen goods, or if they are involved in the **traffic** of such goods, they buy and sell them illegally. *Traffic in illicit drugs was now worth some $500 thousand million a year.* ◆ **trafficking** N-UNCOUNT *...charges of drug trafficking.* ◆ **trafficker, traffickers** N-COUNT *Mexican police have arrested a powerful drug trafficker.*

'traffic circle, traffic circles. N-COUNT In American English, a **traffic circle** is a circle at a place where several roads meet. The British word is **roundabout**.

'traffic jam, traffic jams. N-COUNT A **traffic jam** is a long line of vehicles that cannot move because there is too much traffic, or because the road is blocked.

'traffic light, traffic lights. N-COUNT **Traffic lights** are the coloured lights at road junctions which control the flow of traffic.

⭐ **tragedy** /ˈtrædʒɪdi/ **tragedies.** ① N-VAR A **tragedy** is an extremely sad event or situation. *They have suffered an enormous personal tragedy.* ② N-VAR **Tragedy** is a type of serious drama, usually ending in the death of the main character.

tragic /ˈtrædʒɪk/. ① ADJ Something that is **tragic** is extremely sad, usually because it involves death or suffering. *It was just a tragic accident.* ◆ **tragically** /ˈtrædʒɪkli/ ADV *He died tragically young.* ② ADJ BEFORE N **Tragic** is used to refer to literary tragedy. *...Shakespearian tragic heroes.*

⭐ **trail** /treɪl/ **trails, trailing, trailed.** ① N-COUNT A **trail** is a rough path across open country or through forests. ② N-COUNT A **trail** is a series of marks or other signs left by someone or something as they move along. *He left a trail of clues at the scenes of his crimes.* ③ PHRASE If you are **on the trail of** a person or thing, you are trying to find them. *...on the trail of the world's most ruthless terrorist.* ④ VERB If you **trail** someone or something, you follow them secretly. *I trailed her to a shop in Kensington.* ⑤ VERB If you **trail** something, it hangs down loosely behind you as you move along. *He let his fingers trail in the water.* ⑥ VERB If someone **trails** somewhere, they move there slowly and without enthusiasm. *He trailed through the wet Manhattan streets.* ⑦ VERB In a contest, if someone **is trailing**, they are behind their opponents. *They trailed by nine points to six at half-time.*

▶ **trail away** or **trail off.** PHR-VERB If a speaker's voice **trails off** or **trails away**, their voice becomes quieter and they hesitate until they stop speaking completely.

trailer /ˈtreɪlə/ **trailers.** ① N-COUNT A **trailer** is a vehicle without an engine which is pulled by a car or lorry. In American English, a **trailer** is also the same as a **caravan**. ② N-COUNT A **trailer** for a film or television programme is a set of short extracts which are shown to advertise it.

'trailer park (or **trailer court**) **trailer parks.** N-COUNT In American English, a **trailer park** is an area where people can pay to park their trailers and live in them. The usual British term is **caravan site**.

⭐ **train** /treɪn/ **trains, training, trained.** ① N-COUNT A **train** is a number of carriages or trucks pulled by a railway engine. → See picture on page 835. *He arrived in Shenyang by train.* ② N-COUNT A **train of thought** or a **train of events** is a connected series of thoughts or events. *He lost his train of thought for a moment.* ③ VERB If you **train** to do something, or if someone **trains** you **to** do it, they teach you the skills that you need in order to do it. *Stavros was training to be a priest... They train teachers in counselling skills... I'm a trained nurse.* ◆ **-trained** *...an American-trained lawyer.* ◆ **trainer, trainers** N-COUNT *...teacher trainers.* ◆ **training** N-UNCOUNT *Kennedy had no formal training as a decorator.* ④ VERB If you **train for** an activity such as a race, or if someone **trains** you **for** it, you prepare for it by doing particular physical exercises. ◆ **trainer** N-COUNT *She went to the gym with her trainer.* ◆ **training** N-UNCOUNT *He will soon be back in training for next year's National.* ⑤ VERB If you **train** something such as a gun, a camera, or a light **on** someone or something, you keep it pointing steadily towards them. *She trained her binoculars on the horizon.*

trainee /treɪˈniː/ **trainees.** N-COUNT A **trainee** is a junior employee who is being taught how to do a job.

trainer /ˈtreɪnə/ **trainers.** N-COUNT In British English, **trainers** are shoes with rubber soles used for sports. The usual American word is **sneakers**. → See picture on page 820.

trainspotter /ˈtreɪnspɒtə/ **trainspotters.** ① N-COUNT A **trainspotter** is someone who is very interested in trains and spends time going to stations and recording the numbers of the trains that they see. [BRITISH] ② N-COUNT A **trainspotter** is someone whom other people think is boring because they want to know every detail about a particular subject; used showing disapproval. [BRITISH]

trainspotting /ˈtreɪnspɒtɪŋ/. N-UNCOUNT **Trainspotting** is the hobby of going to railway stations and recording the numbers of the trains that you see. [BRITISH]

trait /treɪt, treɪ/ **traits.** N-COUNT A **trait** is a characteristic, quality, or tendency that someone or something has. *Creativity is a human trait.*

traitor /ˈtreɪtə/ **traitors.** N-COUNT A **traitor** is someone who betrays their country or a group of which they are a member by helping their enemies.

tram /træm/ **trams.** N-COUNT In British English, a **tram** is a public transport vehicle, usually powered by electricity, which travels along rails laid in the surface of a street. The usual American word is **streetcar**. → See picture on page 835.

tramp /træmp/ **tramps, tramping, tramped.**
1 N-COUNT A **tramp** is a person with no home or job who travels around and gets money by doing occasional work or by begging. **2** VERB If you **tramp** somewhere, you walk with slow heavy footsteps, for a long time. *She spent all day yesterday tramping the streets.*

trample /'træmpəl/ **tramples, trampling, trampled.**
1 VERB To **trample on** someone's rights or values means to deliberately ignore or disregard them. *Diplomats denounced the leaders for trampling on their citizens' civil rights.* **2** VERB If someone **is trampled**, they are injured or killed by being trodden on by animals or people. **3** VERB If you **trample on** something, you tread heavily on it and damage it. *They don't want people trampling on the grass.*

trance /trɑːns, træns/ **trances.** N-COUNT If someone is **in a trance**, they seem to be asleep, but they can see and hear things and respond to commands.

tranquil /'træŋkwɪl/. ADJ **Tranquil** means calm and peaceful. ◆ **tranquillity** N-UNCOUNT *He enjoyed the tranquillity of village life.*

tranquillize (BRIT also **tranquillise,** AM also **tranquilize**) /'træŋkwɪlaɪz/ **tranquillizes, tranquillizing, tranquillized.** VERB To **tranquillize** a person or an animal means to make them become calm, sleepy, or unconscious by means of a drug.

tranquillizer (BRIT also **tranquilliser,** AM also **tranquilizer**) /'træŋkwɪlaɪzə/ **tranquillizers.** N-COUNT A **tranquillizer** is a drug that is used to tranquillize people or animals.

⭐ **transaction** /træn'zækʃən/ **transactions.** N-COUNT A **transaction** is a business deal.

transatlantic /,trænzət'læntɪk/. **1** ADJ BEFORE N **Transatlantic** flights or signals go across the Atlantic Ocean, usually between the United States and Britain. *Many transatlantic flights land there.* **2** ADJ BEFORE N **Transatlantic** is used to refer to something that happens, exists, or originates in the United States. [BRITISH] *...transatlantic fashions.*

transcend /træn'send/ **transcends, transcending, transcended.** VERB Something that **transcends** normal limits or boundaries goes beyond them, because it is more significant than them. *Human rights transcend age, class and race.*

transcribe /træn'skraɪb/ **transcribes, transcribing, transcribed.** VERB If you **transcribe** something that is spoken or written, you write it down, copy it, or change it into a different form of writing.

transcript /'trænskrɪpt/ **transcripts.** N-COUNT A **transcript of** something that is spoken is a written copy of it.

⭐ **transfer, transfers, transferring, transferred;** verb /træns'fɜː/, noun /'trænsfɜː/. **1** VERB & N-VAR If you **transfer** something or someone **from** one place **to** another, they go from the first place to the second. The **transfer of** something or someone is the act of transferring them. *He wants to transfer some money to her account... Arrange for the transfer of medical records to your new doctor.* **2** VERB & N-VAR If you **are transferred** to a different place or job, or if you get a **transfer,** you move to a different place or job within the same organization. *Two senior members of staff had been transferred.*

⭐ **transform** /træns'fɔːm/ **transforms, transforming, transformed.** VERB To **transform** someone or something means to change them completely. *...transforming them from a guerrilla force into a regular army.* ◆ **transformation** /,trænsfə'meɪʃən/ **transformations** N-VAR *...the transformation of an attic into a study.*

transfusion /træns'fjuːʒən/ **transfusions.** N-COUNT A blood **transfusion** is a process in which blood is injected into the body of a person who is badly injured or ill.

transient /'trænziənt, AM -nʃənt/ **transients.** **1** ADJ Something that is **transient** does not last very long or is constantly changing. [FORMAL] *In most cases, pain is transient.* ◆ **transience** /'trænziəns AM -nʃənt/ N-UNCOUNT *There is a sense of transience about her.* **2** N-COUNT **Transients** are people who stay in a place for only a short time and do not have a fixed home. [FORMAL]

transistor /træn'zɪstə/ **transistors.** **1** N-COUNT A **transistor** is a small electronic component in something such as a television or radio, which is used to amplify or control electronic signals. **2** N-COUNT A **transistor** or a **transistor radio** is a small portable radio. [DATED]

transit /'trænzɪt/. **1** N-UNCOUNT & PHRASE **Transit** is the carrying of goods or people by vehicle from one place to another. People or things that are **in transit** are travelling or being taken from one place to another. *...goods lost in transit.* **2** ADJ BEFORE N A **transit** area or building is a place where people wait or where goods are kept between different stages of a journey. *...a transit lounge at Moscow airport.* **3** N-UNCOUNT In American English, a **transit** system is a system for moving people or goods from one place to another, for example on buses or trains. The usual British word is **transport.** *...the Chicago Transit Authority.*

⭐ **transition** /træn'zɪʃən/ **transitions.** N-VAR **Transition** is the process in which something changes from one state to another. ◆ **transitional** ADJ *...the transitional stage between the old and new methods.*

transitive /'trænzɪtɪv/. ADJ A **transitive** verb has an object.

translate /trænz'leɪt/ **translates, translating, translated.** **1** VERB If something that someone has said or written **is translated,** it is said or written again in a different language. *Martin Luther translated the Bible into German.* ◆ **translation** N-UNCOUNT *The papers have been sent to Saudi Arabia for translation.* ◆ **translator, translators** N-COUNT *To work as a translator, you need fluency in at least one foreign language.* **2** VERB To

a b c d e f g h i j k l m n o p q r s **t** u v w x y z

A **translate** one thing **into** another means to convert it into something else. *Your decision must be translated into specific, concrete actions.*

B **translation** /trænz'leɪʃən/ **translations.** N-COUNT A **translation** is a piece of writing or speech that has been translated from a different language.

C **translucent** /trænz'luːsənt/. ADJ If a material is **translucent**, some light can pass through it. *...translucent plastic sheeting.*

D **transmission** /trænz'mɪʃən/ **transmissions.**
E ☐1 N-UNCOUNT The **transmission** of something involves passing or sending it to a different place or person. *...the fax machine and other forms of electronic data transmission.* ☐2 N-UNCOUNT The
F **transmission** of television or radio programmes is the broadcasting of them. ☐3 N-COUNT A
G **transmission** is a television or radio broadcast. ☐4 N-VAR A vehicle's **transmission** is the system of gears by which the power from the engine
H reaches and turns the wheels.

transmit /trænz'mɪt/ **transmits, transmitting,**
I **transmitted.** ☐1 VERB When a message or electronic signal **is transmitted**, it is sent by wires, radio waves, or satellite. *This is currently the most*
J *efficient way to transmit certain types of data like electronic mail.* ☐2 VERB To **transmit** something to
K a different place or person means to pass or send it to the place or person. [FORMAL] *...transmitting the infection through operations.*

L **transmitter** /trænz'mɪtə/ **transmitters.** N-COUNT A **transmitter** is a piece of equipment used for broadcasting television or radio programmes.

M **transparency** /træns'pærənsi, AM -'per-/
N **transparencies.** ☐1 N-COUNT A **transparency** is a small piece of photographic film in a frame which
O can be projected onto a screen. ☐2 N-UNCOUNT **Transparency** is the quality that an object or substance has if you can see through it.
P
transparent /træns'pærənt, AM -'per-/. ☐1 ADJ
Q If an object or substance is **transparent**, you can see through it. *...a sheet of transparent plastic.* ☐2 ADJ If a situation, system, or activity is
R **transparent**, it is easily understood or recognized. ♦ **transparently** ADV *He had been*
S *transparently honest with her.*

transpire /træn'spaɪə/ **transpires, transpiring,**
T **transpired.** ☐1 VERB When it **transpires** that something is the case, people discover that it is the case. [FORMAL] *It transpired that there was*
U *something wrong with the roof.* ☐2 VERB When something **transpires**, it happens. [FORMAL]
V
transplant, transplants, transplanting, transplanted.
☐1 N-VAR /'trænsplɑːnt, -plænt/ A **transplant** is a
W surgical operation in which a part of a person's body is replaced because it is diseased. *...a heart*
X *transplant.* ☐2 VERB /træns'plɑːnt, -'plænt/ To **transplant** someone or something means to move them to a different place. *Marriage had*
Y *transplanted Rebecca from London to Manchester.*

Z ☆ **transport, transports, transporting, transported.**
☐1 N-UNCOUNT /'trænspɔːt/ **Transport** refers to any type of vehicle that you can travel in. → See

pictures on pages 834 and 835. *Have you got your own transport?. ...public transport.*
☐2 N-UNCOUNT **Transport** is the moving of goods or people from one place to another. *The transport of soldiers and equipment is now complete.* ☐3 VERB /træns'pɔːt/ When goods or people **are transported from** one place **to** another, they are moved there.

transportation /ˌtrænspɔː'teɪʃən/. N-UNCOUNT **Transportation** is the same as **transport**. [AMERICAN]

☆ **trap** /træp/ **traps, trapping, trapped.** ☐1 N-COUNT & VERB A **trap** is a device for catching animals. If you **trap** animals, you catch them using a trap.
☐2 VERB & N-COUNT If someone **traps** you, they trick you so that you do or say something which you did not want to. A **trap** is a trick that is intended to catch or deceive someone. *Were you trying to trap her into making some admission?*
☐3 VERB If you **are trapped** somewhere, something falls onto you or blocks your way, preventing you from moving. *His car pushed another vehicle forward, trapping a young boy.*

trapped /træpt/. ADJ If you feel **trapped**, you are in an unpleasant situation in which you lack freedom, and you feel you cannot escape from it. *Gordon found himself trapped in a dead-end job.*

trappings /'træpɪŋz/. N-PLURAL The **trappings** of power or wealth are the extra things, such as decorations and luxury items, that go with it; used showing disapproval.

trash /træʃ/. N-UNCOUNT In American English, **trash** consists of unwanted things or waste material such as old food. The British word is **rubbish**.

> **USAGE** In American English, the words **trash** and **garbage** are most commonly used to refer to waste material that is thrown away. *...the smell of rotting garbage... She threw the bottle into the trash.* In British English, **rubbish** is the usual word. **Garbage** and **trash** are sometimes used in British English, but only informally and metaphorically. *I don't have to listen to this garbage... The book was trash.*

trauma /'trɔːmə, AM 'traʊmə/ **traumas.** N-VAR **Trauma** is a very severe shock or very upsetting experience, which may cause psychological damage. *...the trauma of divorce.*

traumatic /trɔː'mætɪk, AM traʊ-/. ADJ A **traumatic** experience is very shocking or upsetting, and may cause psychological damage.

☆ **travel** /'trævəl/ **travels, travelling, travelled (AM traveling, traveled).** ☐1 VERB If you **travel**, you go from one place to another, often to a place that is far away. *Students often travel hundreds of miles to get here.* ☐2 N-UNCOUNT **Travel** is the act of travelling. *Information on travel in New Zealand is available at the hotel.* ☐3 N-PLURAL Someone's

travels are the journeys they make to places a long way from their home. *He also collects things for the house on his travels abroad.* [4] VERB When light, sound, or news from one place reaches another, you say that it **travels** to the other place. *When sound travels through water, strange things can happen.*

USAGE The noun **travel** is used to talk about the general activity of travelling. It is either uncount or plural. You cannot say 'a travel'. If you want to talk about a particular instance of someone going somewhere, you should refer to it as a **journey**. *...a journey by train from Berlin.* You should use **trip** to refer to the whole business of going somewhere, staying there and returning. *He suggested I cancel my trip to China.* **Voyage** is a more literary word, and is used only when you are talking about travelling by ship or spacecraft.

'travel agent, travel agents. [1] N-COUNT A **travel agent** or **travel agent's** is a shop where you can arrange a holiday or journey. [2] N-COUNT A **travel agent** is a person or business that arranges holidays and journeys.

⭐ **traveller** (AM **traveler**) /'trævələ/ **travellers.** N-COUNT A **traveller** is a person who is making a journey or who travels a lot.

'traveller's cheque (AM **traveler's check**) **traveller's cheques.** N-COUNT **Traveller's cheques** are special cheques that you can exchange for local currency when you are abroad.

traverse /'trævɜːs, trə'vɜːs/ **traverses, traversing, traversed.** VERB If someone or something **traverses** an area of land or water, they go across it. [FORMAL] *...the muddy path that traversed the meadow.*

travesty /'trævəsti/ **travesties.** N-COUNT If you describe something as a **travesty of** something else, you mean that it is a very bad representation of the other thing. *They issued a statement calling the judgment a 'travesty of justice'.*

trawler

trawler /'trɔːlə/ **trawlers.** N-COUNT A **trawler** is a fishing boat with large nets that are dragged along the bottom of the sea.

tray /treɪ/ **trays.** N-COUNT A **tray** is a flat piece of wood, plastic, or metal that has raised edges and that is used for carrying food or drinks.

treacherous /'tretʃərəs/. [1] ADJ If you describe someone as **treacherous**, you think they are likely to betray you. [FORMAL] [2] ADJ If you say that something is **treacherous**, you mean that it is dangerous and unpredictable. *Blizzards had made the roads treacherous.*

treachery /'tretʃəri/. N-UNCOUNT **Treachery** is behaviour in which someone betrays their country or betrays a person who trusts them. [FORMAL]

tread /tred/ **treads, treading, trod, trodden.** [1] VERB If you **tread on** something, you put your foot on it when you are walking or standing. *Oh, sorry, I didn't mean to tread on your foot.* [2] VERB If you **tread** in a particular way, you walk that way. [LITERARY] *He trod softly up the stairs.* [3] N-SING Someone's **tread** is the sound made by their feet as they walk. [WRITTEN] *She had heard the creak of his heavy tread.* [4] VERB If you **tread** carefully, you behave with caution. [5] N-COUNT The **tread** of a tyre is the pattern of grooves on it.

treadmill /'tredmɪl/ **treadmills.** N-COUNT You can refer to a task or a job as a **treadmill** when you have to keep doing it although it is unpleasant.

treason /'triːzən/. N-UNCOUNT **Treason** is the crime of betraying your country.

treasure /'treʒə/ **treasures, treasuring, treasured.** [1] N-UNCOUNT In children's stories, **treasure** is a collection of valuable old objects, such as gold coins and jewels. [2] N-COUNT **Treasures** are valuable objects, especially works of art and items of historical value. *...stolen art treasures.* [3] VERB If you **treasure** something that you have, you keep it carefully because it gives you great pleasure and you think it is very special. *She treasures her memories of those joyous days.*
♦ **treasured** ADJ BEFORE N *...my most treasured possessions.*

treasurer /'treʒərə/ **treasurers.** N-COUNT The **treasurer** of a society or organization is the person in charge of its finances.

Treasury /'treʒəri/. N-PROPER In Britain, the United States, and some other countries, **the Treasury** is the government department that deals with the country's finances.

⭐ **treat** /triːt/ **treats, treating, treated.** [1] VERB If you **treat** someone or something in a particular way, you behave towards them in that way. *Stop treating me like a child... All faiths should be treated with respect.* [2] VERB When a doctor **treats** a patient or an illness, he or she tries to make the patient well again. *The boy was treated for a minor head wound.* [3] VERB If something **is treated with** a particular substance, the substance is put onto or into it, for example in order to clean it. *If you use timber it is vital to have* it treated with preservative. [4] N-COUNT & VERB If you give someone a **treat**, or if you **treat** them, you buy or arrange something special for them which they will enjoy. *Sometimes as a special treat my grandfather took me to the docks... Go on, treat yourself to a new dress.*

⭐ **treatment** /ˈtriːtmənt/ **treatments.** [1] N-VAR **Treatment** is medical attention given to a sick or injured person or animal. *There are two standard treatments for this disease.* [2] N-UNCOUNT Your **treatment** of someone is the way you behave towards them. *Ginny's rage at his treatment of Chris... We don't want any special treatment.*

⭐ **treaty** /ˈtriːti/ **treaties.** N-COUNT A **treaty** is a written agreement between countries.

treble /ˈtrebəl/ **trebles, trebling, trebled.** VERB If something **trebles**, or if you **treble** it, it becomes three times greater in number or amount. *The number of claims has almost trebled this year.*

⭐ **tree** /triː/ **trees.** N-COUNT A **tree** is a tall plant with a hard trunk, branches, and leaves.

trek /trek/ **treks, trekking, trekked.** VERB & N-COUNT If you **trek** somewhere, or if you go on a **trek**, you go on a long journey across difficult terrain, usually on foot. *...trekking through the jungles.*

tremble /ˈtrembəl/ **trembles, trembling, trembled.** [1] VERB If you **tremble**, you shake slightly, usually because you are frightened or cold. *I was trembling with fear.* [2] VERB If something **trembles**, it shakes slightly. [LITERARY] *He felt the earth tremble under him.*

⭐ **tremendous** /trɪˈmendəs/. [1] ADJ You use **tremendous** to emphasize how strong a feeling or quality is, or how large an amount is. *I felt a tremendous pressure on my chest. ...a tremendous amount of information.* ♦ **tremendously** ADV *I enjoyed it tremendously.* [2] ADJ You can describe someone or something as **tremendous** when you think they are very impressive.

tremor /ˈtremə/ **tremors.** [1] N-COUNT A **tremor** is a small earthquake. [2] N-COUNT A **tremor** is a shaking of your body or voice that you cannot control. *Winslow felt a little tremor of excitement.*

trench /trentʃ/ **trenches.** N-COUNT A **trench** is a long narrow channel dug in the ground.

⭐ **trend** /trend/ **trends.** N-COUNT A **trend** is a change towards something different. *...the growing trend towards overseas investment.*

trendy /ˈtrendi/ **trendier, trendiest.** ADJ If you say that something or someone is **trendy**, you mean that they are very fashionable and modern. [INFORMAL] *...a trendy London restaurant.*

trepidation /ˌtrepɪˈdeɪʃən/. N-UNCOUNT **Trepidation** is fear or anxiety about something that you are going to do or experience. [FORMAL] *They will await the outcome with some trepidation.*

trespass /ˈtrespəs/ **trespasses, trespassing, trespassed.** VERB If you **trespass on** someone's land, you go onto it without their permission.

⭐ **trial** /ˈtraɪəl/ **trials.** [1] N-VAR & PHRASE A **trial** is the legal process in which a judge and jury listen to evidence and decide whether a person is guilty

of a crime. You say that the person being judged is **on trial** or that they **stand trial**. *New evidence showed the police lied at the trial.* [2] N-VAR & PHRASE A **trial** is an act of testing something or someone to see how well they perform a task. You say that the thing or person being tested is **on trial**. *The vaccine is about to go on trial in the US.* [3] PHRASE If you do something **by trial and error**, you try different ways of doing it until you find the best one.

triangle /ˈtraɪæŋgəl/ **triangles.** N-COUNT A **triangle** is a shape with three straight sides. → See picture on page 829. ♦ **triangular** /traɪˈæŋgjʊlə/ ADJ *...the triangular frame.*

tribe /traɪb/ **tribes.** N-COUNT **Tribe** is sometimes used to refer to a group of people of the same race, language, and customs, especially in a developing country. Some people disapprove of this use. **Tribe** can take the singular or plural form of the verb. *...the Xhosa tribe.* ♦ **tribal** /ˈtraɪbəl/ ADJ *...tribal lands.*

tribulation /ˌtrɪbjʊˈleɪʃən/ **tribulations.** N-VAR You can refer to the suffering or difficulty that you experience in a particular situation as **tribulations**. [FORMAL] *...the trials and tribulations of everyday life.*

tribunal /traɪˈbjuːnəl/ **tribunals.** N-COUNT A **tribunal** is a special court or committee that is appointed to deal with particular problems. **Tribunal** can take the singular or plural form of the verb. *...an industrial tribunal.*

tribute /ˈtrɪbjuːt/ **tributes.** [1] N-VAR A **tribute** is something that you say or do to show your admiration and respect for someone. *He paid tribute to the organising committee.* [2] N-SING If one thing is a **tribute** to another, it is the result of the other thing and shows how good it is. *Their success is a tribute to their discipline.*

⭐ **trick** /trɪk/ **tricks, tricking, tricked.** [1] VERB & N-COUNT If someone **tricks** you, or if they **play a trick on** you, they deceive you, often in order to make you do something. *His family tricked him into going to Pakistan.* [2] N-COUNT A **trick** is a clever or skilful action that someone does in order to entertain people. *...card tricks.* [3] N-COUNT A **trick** is a special way of doing something. *There is a trick to installing it properly.* [4] PHRASE If something **does the trick**, it achieves what you wanted. [INFORMAL] *Sometimes a few choice words will do the trick.*

trickle /ˈtrɪkəl/ **trickles, trickling, trickled.** [1] VERB & N-COUNT If a liquid **trickles** somewhere, or if there is a **trickle** of it, it flows slowly in a thin stream. *A tear trickled down the old man's cheek. ...a trickle of water.* [2] VERB & N-COUNT If people or things **trickle** somewhere, or if there is a **trickle of** them to that place, they move there slowly in small amounts. *A trickle of refugees began to flee the country.*

tricky /ˈtrɪki/ **trickier, trickiest.** ADJ A **tricky** task or problem is difficult to deal with.

tried /traɪd/. **Tried** is the past tense and past participle of **try**.

trifle /ˈtraɪfəl/ **trifles.** ☐1 PHRASE You can use **a trifle** to mean slightly. *He seemed a trifle annoyed.* ☐2 N-COUNT **Trifles** are things that are not considered important. *He didn't waste himself over trifles.* ☐3 N-VAR **Trifle** is a cold dessert made of layers of sponge cake, fruit, jelly, and custard.

⭐ **trigger** /ˈtrɪɡə/ **triggers, triggering, triggered.** ☐1 N-COUNT The **trigger** of a gun is the small lever which you pull to fire it. ☐2 VERB To **trigger** a bomb or system means to cause it to work. *The thieves must have deliberately triggered the alarm.* ☐3 VERB & PHR-VERB If something **triggers** an event, or if it **triggers off** an event, it causes the event to happen. *It is still not clear what events triggered off the demonstrations.* ☐4 N-COUNT If something acts as a **trigger for** another thing, the first thing causes the second thing to begin. *Stress may act as a trigger for these illnesses.*

trillion /ˈtrɪljən/. NUM A **trillion** is a million million.

trilogy /ˈtrɪlədʒi/ **trilogies.** N-COUNT A **trilogy** is a series of three books, plays, or films with the same characters or subject.

trim /trɪm/ **trimmer, trimmest; trims, trimming, trimmed.** ☐1 ADJ Something that is **trim** is neat and attractive. *The neighbours' gardens were trim and neat.* ☐2 ADJ If someone has a **trim** figure, they are slim. *...a trim woman in her forties.* ☐3 VERB & N-COUNT If you **trim** something, or if you give it a **trim**, you cut off small amounts of it to make it look neater. *His hair needed a trim.* ☐4 VERB If something such as a piece of clothing **is trimmed with** a type of material or design, it is decorated with it, usually along its edges. *...an ivory dress trimmed with blue bows.* ☐5 N-VAR The **trim** on something such as a piece of clothing is a decoration along its edges in a different colour or material. *...black leather boots with fur trim.*

trimming /ˈtrɪmɪŋ/ **trimmings.** ☐1 N-VAR The **trimming** on something such as a piece of clothing is the decoration along its edges in a different colour or material. *...the lace trimming on her satin nightgown.* ☐2 N-PLURAL **Trimmings** are extra things that can be added to something or included in something. *...turkey with all the trimmings.*

trio /ˈtriːəʊ/ **trios.** N-COUNT A **trio** is a group of three people, especially musicians or singers.

⭐ **trip** /trɪp/ **trips, tripping, tripped.** ☐1 N-COUNT A **trip** is a journey that you make to a place and back again. *We went out on a day trip. ...a business trip.* ● See also **round trip.** ☐2 N-COUNT A **trip** is an imaginary experience caused by taking drugs. [INFORMAL] ☐3 VERB If you **trip** when you are walking, or if you **trip up**, you knock your foot against something and fall over. *He was just coming down the ramp when he tripped up.* ☐4 VERB & PHR-VERB If you **trip** someone who is walking, or if you **trip** them **up**, you put your foot or something else in front of them so that they

knock their own foot against it and fall. ☐5 N-COUNT If you say that someone is, for example, on a power **trip**, a guilt **trip**, of a nostalgia **trip**, you mean that their behaviour is motivated by power, guilt, or nostalgia. [INFORMAL] *The biggest power trip must be the private plane.*

triple /ˈtrɪpəl/ **triples, tripling, tripled.** ☐1 ADJ BEFORE N **Triple** means consisting of three things or parts. *...a triple somersault.* ☐2 VERB If something **triples**, or if you **triple** it, it becomes three times greater in size or number. *The Exhibition has tripled in size from last year.*

triplet /ˈtrɪplət/ **triplets.** N-COUNT **Triplets** are three children born at the same time to the same mother.

tripod /ˈtraɪpɒd/ **tripods.** N-COUNT A **tripod** is a stand with three legs, used to support something such as a camera.

⭐ **triumph** /ˈtraɪʌmf/ **triumphs, triumphing, triumphed.** ☐1 N-VAR A **triumph** is a great success or achievement. *The building is a triumph of modern design.* ☐2 N-UNCOUNT **Triumph** is a feeling of great satisfaction when you win or achieve something. *Any feeling of triumph will be short-lived.* ☐3 VERB If you **triumph**, you win a victory or succeed in overcoming something. *The film is about good triumphing over evil.*

triumphant /traɪˈʌmfənt/. ADJ If you are **triumphant**, you feel very happy because you have won a victory or achieved something. ♦ **triumphantly** ADV *They marched triumphantly into the capital.*

trivia /ˈtrɪviə/. N-UNCOUNT **Trivia** consists of unimportant facts or details. *The two men chatted about such trivia as their favourite kinds of food.*

trivial /ˈtrɪviəl/. ADJ If you describe something as **trivial**, you think that it is unimportant and not serious. *...trivial details.*

triviality /ˌtrɪviˈæliti/ **trivialities.** N-VAR If you refer to something as a **triviality**, you think it is unimportant.

trod /trɒd/. **Trod** is the past tense of **tread**.

trodden /ˈtrɒdən/. **Trodden** is the past participle of **tread**.

trolley /ˈtrɒli/ **trolleys.** ☐1 N-COUNT A **trolley** is a small cart on wheels that you use to carry things such as shopping or luggage. [BRITISH] *...supermarket trolleys.* ☐2 N-COUNT A **trolley** is a small table on wheels on which food and drinks can be carried. [BRITISH] ☐3 N-COUNT In American English, a **trolley** is an electric vehicle which travels on rails along a street. The British word is **tram**.

trombone /trɒmˈbəʊn/ **trombones.** N-COUNT A **trombone** is a brass musical instrument which you play by blowing into it and sliding part of it backwards and forwards. → See picture on page 827.

⭐ **troop** /truːp/ **troops, trooping, trooped.** ☐1 N-PLURAL **Troops** are soldiers. *...more than 35,000 troops from a dozen countries.* ☐2 N-COUNT A **troop** is a group of soldiers within a cavalry or armoured regiment. ☐3 VERB If people **troop** somewhere,

a
b
c
d
e
f
g
h
i
j
k
l
m
n
o
p
q
r
s
t
u
v
w
x
y
z

they walk there in a group. *They all trooped back to the house.*

trooper /'tru:pə/ **troopers.** [1] N-COUNT A **trooper** is a soldier of low rank in the cavalry or in an armoured regiment in the army. [2] N-COUNT In the United States, a **trooper** is a police officer in a state police force.

trophy /'trəʊfi/ **trophies.** N-COUNT A **trophy** is a prize such as a cup, given to the winner of a competition.

tropical /'trɒpɪkəl/. ADJ **Tropical** means belonging to or typical of the tropics. *...tropical diseases. ...tropical weather.*

tropics /'trɒpɪks/. N-PLURAL The **tropics** are the hottest parts of the world, near the equator.

trot /trɒt/ **trots, trotting, trotted.** [1] VERB & N-SING When an animal such as a horse **trots**, or when it breaks into a **trot**, it moves fairly fast, taking quick small steps. *Pete got on his horse and started trotting across the field.* [2] VERB If you **trot** somewhere, you move fairly fast, taking small quick steps. *I trotted down the steps.* [3] PHRASE If several things happen **on the trot**, they happen one after the other, without a break. [INFORMAL] *She lost five games on the trot.*

▶**trot out.** PHR-VERB If you say that someone **is trotting out** old ideas or information, you mean that they are repeating them in a boring way.

⭐ **trouble** /'trʌbəl/ **troubles, troubling, troubled.** [1] N-VAR You can refer to problems or difficulties as **trouble**. *I had trouble parking. ...financial troubles.* [2] N-SING If you say that one aspect of a situation is **the trouble**, you mean that it is the aspect which is causing problems. *The trouble is that these restrictions have remained.* [3] VERB If something **troubles** you, it makes you feel worried. *He was troubled by the lifestyle of his son.* ♦ **troubling** ADJ *...troubling chest pains.* [4] N-UNCOUNT If you have back **trouble**, for example, there is something wrong with your back. [5] N-UNCOUNT If there is **trouble**, people are quarrelling or fighting. *...fans who make trouble during the World Cup.*

PHRASES ● If someone is **in trouble**, they have broken a rule or law and are likely to be punished by someone in authority. *He was in trouble with his teachers.* ● If you **take the trouble to** do something, you do it although it requires some time or effort.

troubled /'trʌbəld/. ADJ **Troubled** means worried or full of problems. *Rose sounded deeply troubled. ...this troubled country.*

troublemaker /'trʌbəlmeɪkə/ **troublemakers.** N-COUNT A **troublemaker** is someone who causes trouble.

troublesome /'trʌbəlsəm/. ADJ Someone or something that is **troublesome** causes problems or difficulties. *...a troublesome back injury.*

trough /trɒf, AM trɔ:f/ **troughs.** [1] N-COUNT A **trough** is a long container from which farm animals drink or eat. [2] N-COUNT A **trough** is a low point in a pattern that has regular high and low

points. *American bank shares have risen by 60% since their trough last October.*

troupe /tru:p/ **troupes.** N-COUNT A **troupe** is a group of actors, singers, or dancers who work together.

trousers /'traʊzəz/.

✓ The form **trouser** is used as a modifier.

N-PLURAL In British English, **trousers** are a piece of clothing that you wear over your body from the waist downwards, and that cover each leg separately. You can also say **a pair of trousers**. The usual American word is **pants**. → See picture on page 820. *...a blue blouse and white trousers... Alexander rolled up his trouser legs.*

trout /traʊt/ **trouts.** N-VAR A **trout** is a kind of fish that lives in rivers and streams. **Trout** is the flesh of this fish eaten as food.

truant /'tru:ənt/ **truants.** [1] N-COUNT A **truant** is a child who stays away from school without permission. [2] PHRASE If children **play truant**, they stay away from school without permission.

truce /tru:s/ **truces.** N-COUNT A **truce** is an agreement between two people or groups to stop fighting or quarrelling for a short time.

⭐ **truck** /trʌk/ **trucks.** [1] N-COUNT In American English a **truck** is a large vehicle that is used to transport goods by road. The usual British word is **lorry**. → See picture on page 834. [2] N-COUNT A **truck** is an open vehicle used for carrying goods on a railway. [BRITISH]

trudge /trʌdʒ/ **trudges, trudging, trudged.** VERB & N-SING If you **trudge** somewhere, you walk there with slow heavy steps. This way of walking is called a **trudge**. *...the long trudge home.*

⭐ **true** /tru:/ **truer, truest.** [1] ADJ If something is **true**, it is based on facts and is not invented or imagined. *He said it was true that a collision had happened... The film is based on a true story.* [2] ADJ BEFORE N **True** means real, genuine, or typical. *This country professes to be a true democracy... The true cost often differs from that.*

PHRASES ● If a dream, wish, or prediction **comes true**, it actually happens. ● If a general statement **holds true** in particular circumstances, or if your previous statement **holds true** in different circumstances, it is true or valid in those circumstances. *The nearer the cinema, the worse the restaurant. This rule holds true across most of London.*

⭐ **truly** /'tru:li/. [1] ADV **Truly** means completely and genuinely. *Not all doctors truly understand the reproductive cycle... Believe me, Susan, I am truly sorry.* [2] ADV You can use **truly** in order to emphasize your description of something. *They were truly appalling.* [3] ADV You can use **truly** to emphasize that what you are saying is true. *I do not expect a war between my country and yours. Truly I do not.* [4] CONVENTION You can write **Yours truly** before your signature at the end of a letter to someone you do not know very well. [5] **well and truly**: see **well**.

trump /trʌmp/ **trumps.** **1** N-UNCOUNT In a game of cards, **trumps** is the suit which is chosen to have the highest value in a particular game. **2** PHRASE Your **trump card** is the most powerful thing that you can use or do to gain an advantage. *The Ten took their appeal to the Supreme Court; this, they believed, would be their trump card.*

trumpet /'trʌmpɪt/ **trumpets.** N-COUNT A **trumpet** is a brass wind instrument. → See picture on page 827.

trumpeter /'trʌmpɪtə/ **trumpeters.** N-COUNT A **trumpeter** is someone who plays a trumpet.

trundle /'trʌndəl/ **trundles, trundling, trundled.** **1** VERB If a vehicle **trundles** somewhere, it moves there slowly. *The train eventually trundled in at 7.54.* **2** VERB If you **trundle** something somewhere, especially an object with wheels, you move or roll it along slowly. *The old man lifted the barrow and trundled it away.*

trunk /trʌŋk/ **trunks.** **1** N-COUNT The **trunk** of a tree is the large main stem from which the branches grow. **2** N-COUNT A **trunk** is a large strong case or box used for storing things or for taking on a journey. **3** N-COUNT An elephant's **trunk** is its long nose. **4** N-COUNT In American English, the **trunk** of a car is a covered space at the back or front that is used for luggage. The usual British word is **boot**.

trust /trʌst/ **trusts, trusting, trusted.** **1** VERB & N-UNCOUNT If you **trust** someone, or if you have **trust in** them, you believe that they are honest and will not deliberately do anything to harm you. *The president can't be trusted... He destroyed my trust in men... You've betrayed their trust.* **2** VERB If you **trust** someone **to** do something, you believe that they will do it. *I knew I could trust him to meet a tight deadline.* **3** VERB If you **trust** someone **with** something, you allow them to look after it or deal with it. *I'd trust him with my life.* **4** N-UNCOUNT **Trust** is responsibility that you are given to deal with important, valuable, or secret things. *...a position of trust which was generously paid.* **5** VERB If you do not **trust** something, you feel that it is not safe or reliable. *He didn't trust his legs to hold him up.* **6** VERB If you **trust** someone's judgment or advice, you believe that it is good or right. **7** N-COUNT A **trust** is a financial arrangement in which an organization keeps and invests money for someone. *They've set up a trust fund for their son... The money will be put in trust until she is 18.*

trustee /trʌ'stiː/ **trustees.** N-COUNT A **trustee** is someone with legal control of money or property that is kept or invested for another person.

trusting /'trʌstɪŋ/. ADJ A **trusting** person believes that people are honest and sincere and do not intend to harm him or her.

trustworthy /'trʌstwɜːði/. ADJ A **trustworthy** person is reliable, responsible, and can be trusted completely.

truth /truːθ/ **truths.** **1** N-UNCOUNT The **truth** about something is all the facts about it, rather than things that are imagined or invented. *In the town very few know the whole truth... I want you to tell me the truth.* **2** N-UNCOUNT If you say that there is some **truth** in a statement or story, you mean that it is true, or partly true. *The criticisms have at least an element of truth.* **3** N-COUNT A **truth** is something that is generally accepted to be true. *...universal truths.*

truthful /'truːθfʊl/. ADJ If a person or their comments are **truthful**, they are honest and do not tell any lies. ♦ **truthfully** ADV *I answered all their questions truthfully.* ♦ **truthfulness** N-UNCOUNT *...qualities such as honesty and truthfulness.*

try /traɪ/ **tries, trying, tried.** **1** VERB & N-COUNT If you **try to** do something, or if you have a **try** at doing something, you make an effort to do it. *I tried hard to persuade him to stay... I must try and see him... I tried calling him when I got here but he wasn't at home... After a few tries Patrick had given up.* **2** VERB & N-COUNT If you **try** something new or different, or if you give it a **try**, you use it or do it in order to find out how useful, effective, or enjoyable it is. *You could try a little cheese melted on the top.* **3** VERB If you **try** a particular place or person, you go to that place or person because you think they may be able to provide you with what you want. *Have you tried the local music shops?* **4** VERB When a person **is tried**, they appear in court and are found innocent or guilty after the judge and jury have heard the evidence. **5** N-COUNT In the game of rugby, a **try** is the action of scoring by putting the ball down behind the goal line of the opposing team. **6** to **try** your **hand**: see **hand**. ● to **try** your **luck**: see **luck**.

USAGE **Try and** is often used instead of **try to** in spoken English, but you should avoid it in writing. *Just try and stop me!* Notice also the difference between **try to** and **try** with the -ing form of the verb. **Try to** means 'attempt to', whereas **try** with the -ing form of the verb is used for making suggestions. *I'm going to try to open a jammed door... Try opening the windows to freshen the air.*

▶**try on.** PHR-VERB If you **try on** a piece of clothing, you put it on to see if it fits you or if it looks nice.
▶**try out.** PHR-VERB If you **try** something **out**, you test it in order to find out how useful or effective it is. *London Transport hopes to try out the system in September.*

trying /'traɪɪŋ/. ADJ Someone or something that is **trying** is difficult to deal with and makes you feel impatient or annoyed. *The whole business has been very trying.*

'T-shirt (or **tee-shirt**) **T-shirts.** N-COUNT A **T-shirt** is a cotton shirt with short sleeves and no collar or buttons. → See picture on page 819.

tub /tʌb/ **tubs.** [1] N-COUNT A **tub** is a deep container of any size. ...*four tubs of ice cream.* [2] N-COUNT In American English, a **tub** is a container which you fill with water and sit in while you wash your body. The British word is **bath**.

⭐ **tube** /tjuːb, AM tuːb/ **tubes.** [1] N-COUNT A **tube** is a long hollow cylinder. *He is fed by a tube that enters his nose.* [2] N-COUNT A **tube** of paste is a long thin container which you squeeze in order to force the paste out. ...*a tube of toothpaste.* [3] N-SING **The Tube** is the underground railway system in London. [BRITISH] *He travelled by tube.*

tuberculosis /tjuːˌbɜːkjʊˈləʊsɪs, AM tuː-/. N-UNCOUNT **Tuberculosis**, or **TB**, is a serious infectious disease that affects the lungs.

tubing /'tjuːbɪŋ, AM 'tuː-/. N-UNCOUNT **Tubing** is plastic, rubber, or other material made in the shape of a tube.

tuck /tʌk/ **tucks, tucking, tucked.** VERB If you **tuck** something somewhere, you put it there so that it is safe, comfortable, or neat. *He tried to tuck his flapping shirt inside his trousers.*

▸**tuck away.** [1] PHR-VERB If you **tuck away** something such as money, you store it in a safe place. *I tucked the box away in the linen drawer.* [2] PHR-VERB If someone or something **is tucked away**, they are well hidden in a quiet place where very few people go. *His home in Bexley is tucked away in a miniature forest.*

▸**tuck in.** [1] PHR-VERB If you **tuck in** a piece of material, you secure it in position by placing the edge of it behind or under something else. *Tuck the sheets in firmly... Straighten your cap and tuck your shirt in.* [2] PHR-VERB If you **tuck** a child **in** bed, or if you **tuck** them **in**, you make them comfortable by straightening the sheets and blankets and pushing the loose ends under the mattress.

▸**tuck into** or **tuck in.** PHR-VERB If someone **tucks into** a meal, or if they **tuck in**, they start eating enthusiastically or hungrily. [BRITISH, INFORMAL] *Tuck in while it's hot.*

⭐ **Tuesday** /'tjuːzdeɪ, -di, AM 'tuːz-/ **Tuesdays.** N-VAR **Tuesday** is the day after Monday and before Wednesday. → See Reference Page on Times and Dates.

tug /tʌg/ **tugs, tugging, tugged.** [1] VERB & N-COUNT If you **tug** something, if you **tug at** it, or if you give it a **tug**, you give it a quick pull. *Anna tugged at Martha's arm. 'Look,' she said.* [2] N-COUNT A **tug** is a small powerful boat which pulls large ships, usually when they come into a port.

tuition /tjuˈɪʃən, AM tuː-/. N-UNCOUNT If you are given **tuition** in a particular subject, you are taught about that subject, especially on your own or in a small group. *I've seriously been considering having private tuition.*

tulip /'tjuːlɪp, AM 'tuː-/ **tulips.** N-COUNT **Tulips** are garden flowers that grow in the spring.

tumble /'tʌmbəl/ **tumbles, tumbling, tumbled.** VERB & N-COUNT If someone or something **tumbles**, or if they take a **tumble**, they fall with a rolling or bouncing movement. *The gun tumbled out of his hand... He injured his ribs in a tumble from his horse.*

tummy /'tʌmi/ **tummies.** N-COUNT Your **tummy** is your stomach. [INFORMAL]

tumour (AM **tumor**) /'tjuːmə, AM 'tuː-/ **tumours.** N-COUNT A **tumour** is a mass of diseased or abnormal cells that has grown in someone's body.

tumultuous /tjuːˈmʌltʃʊəs, AM tuː-/. [1] ADJ **Tumultuous** feelings or events are very exciting or confusing. ...*the tumultuous changes in Eastern Europe.* [2] ADJ A **tumultuous** reaction to something is very noisy, because the people involved are very happy or excited. ...*tumultuous applause.*

tuna /'tjuːnə, AM 'tuːnə/.

✓ The plural is **tuna** or **tunas**.

N-VAR A **tuna** or a **tuna fish** is a large fish that lives in warm seas. **Tuna** or **tuna fish** is the flesh of this fish eaten as food.

⭐ **tune** /tjuːn, AM tuːn/ **tunes, tuning, tuned.** [1] N-COUNT A **tune** is a series of musical notes that is pleasant to listen to. ...*a merry little tune.* [2] VERB When someone **tunes** or **tunes up** a musical instrument, they adjust it so that it produces the right notes. [3] VERB If your radio or television **is tuned to** a particular broadcasting station, you are listening to or watching the programmes being broadcast on that station.
PHRASES ● A person or musical instrument that is **in tune** produces exactly the right notes. ● If you say that someone **has changed** their **tune**, you are criticizing them because they have changed their opinion or way of doing things. ● **To the tune of** a particular amount means to the extent of that amount. *The family suddenly found itself in debt to the tune of some $5,000.*

▸**tune in.** PHR-VERB If you **tune in to** a particular television or radio station or programme, you watch or listen to it.

tunic /'tjuːnɪk, AM 'tuː-/ **tunics.** N-COUNT A **tunic** is a loose garment that is worn on the top part of your body.

⭐ **tunnel** /'tʌnəl/ **tunnels, tunnelling, tunnelled** (AM **tunneling, tunneled**). [1] N-COUNT A **tunnel** is a long passage which has been made under the ground, usually through a hill or under the sea. [2] VERB To **tunnel** somewhere means to make a tunnel there. *The rebels tunnelled out of a maximum security jail.*

turbine /'tɜːbaɪn, AM -bɪn/ **turbines.** N-COUNT A **turbine** is a machine or engine which uses a stream of air, gas, water, or steam to turn a wheel and produce power.

turbulent /'tɜːbjʊlənt/. [1] ADJ A **turbulent** time, place, or relationship is one in which there is a lot of change and confusion. ...*six turbulent years of rows and reconciliations.* ◆ **turbulence**

/'tɜːbjʊləns/ N-UNCOUNT ...*a region often beset by political turbulence.* **2** ADJ **Turbulent** water or air contains strong currents which change direction suddenly. ◆ **turbulence** N-UNCOUNT *His plane encountered strong turbulence.*

turf /tɜːf/ **turfs, turfing, turfed.** N-UNCOUNT **Turf** is short, thick, even grass.
▸**turf out.** PHR-VERB If someone **is turfed out of** a place or position, they are forced to leave. [BRITISH, INFORMAL] *She should have been turfed out of her job years ago.*

turkey /'tɜːki/ **turkeys.** **1** N-COUNT A **turkey** is a large bird that is kept on a farm for its meat. **2** N-UNCOUNT **Turkey** is the meat of a turkey eaten as food.

turmoil /'tɜːmɔɪl/. N-UNCOUNT **Turmoil** is a state of confusion or great anxiety. ...*the political turmoil of 1989... Her marriage was in turmoil.*

turn 1 to change in direction or nature

⭐ **turn** /tɜːn/ **turns, turning, turned.** **1** VERB To **turn** means to move in a different direction or to move into a different position. **Turn around** or **turn round** means the same as **turn.** *He turned his head left and right... She had turned the bedside chair to face the door.* **2** VERB & N-COUNT When you **turn** in a particular direction, you change the direction in which you are moving or travelling. A **turn** is a change of direction. *Now turn right to follow West Ferry Road... You can't do a right-hand turn here.* ● See also **turning.** **3** VERB If you **turn to** a particular page in a book, you open it at that page. **4** VERB If you **turn** your attention or thoughts **to** a particular person or thing, you start thinking about them or discussing them. *We turn now to the British news.* **5** VERB If you **turn to** someone, you ask for their help or advice. *There was no one to turn to.* **6** VERB When something **turns into** something else, or when you **turn** it **into** something else, it becomes something different. *The government plans to turn the country into a one-party-state.* **7** N-COUNT If a situation or trend takes a particular kind of **turn**, it changes so that it starts developing in a different or opposite way. ...*the latest turn in the fighting.* **8** to **turn** your **back**: see **back.** ● to **turn the tables:** see **table.**

turn 2 your time or occasion to do something

⭐ **turn** /tɜːn/ **turns.** N-COUNT If it is your **turn to** do something, you now have the right or duty to do it, when other people have done it before you or will do it after you. *Tonight it's my turn to cook.*
PHRASES ● You use **in turn** to refer to actions or events that are in a sequence one after the other, for example because one causes the other. *Cuba buys rice from China which in turn purchases sugar from the island.* ● If two or more people **take turns to** do something or **take it in turns to** do it, they do it one after the other several times, rather than doing it together.

turn 3 phrasal verbs

⭐ **turn** /tɜːn/ **turns, turning, turned.**

▸**turn against.** PHR-VERB If you **turn against** someone or something, or if something **turns** you **against** them, you stop supporting them, trusting them, or liking them. *Working with the police has turned me against the use of violent scenes as entertainment.*
▸**turn around** or **turn round.** **1** See **turn 1.** **2** PHR-VERB If you **turn** something **around**, or if it **turns around**, it is moved so that it faces the opposite direction. *I turned the car around and headed south.*
▸**turn away.** PHR-VERB If you **turn** someone **away**, you reject them or send them away. *Hard times are forcing many community colleges to turn away students.*
▸**turn back.** PHR-VERB If you **turn back**, or if someone **turns** you **back** when you are going somewhere, you change direction and go towards where you started from. *Police attempted to turn back protesters.*
▸**turn down.** **1** PHR-VERB If you **turn down** a person or their request or offer, you refuse their request or offer. *After careful consideration I turned the invitation down.* **2** PHR-VERB When you **turn down** a radio, heater, or other piece of equipment, you reduce the amount of sound or heat being produced, by adjusting the controls. *He kept turning the central heating down.*
▸**turn off.** **1** PHR-VERB If you **turn off** the road or path you are going along, you start going along a different road or path which leads away from it. *Turn off at the sign to Walton.* **2** PHR-VERB When you **turn off** a piece of equipment or a supply of something, you stop heat, sound, or water being produced by adjusting the controls. *The light's a bit too harsh. You can turn it off.*
▸**turn on.** **1** PHR-VERB When you **turn on** a piece of equipment or a supply of something, you cause heat, sound, or water to be produced by adjusting the controls. *She asked them why they hadn't turned the lights on.* **2** PHR-VERB If someone **turns on** you, they attack you or speak angrily to you.
▸**turn out.** **1** PHR-VERB If something **turns out** a particular way, it happens in that way or has the result or degree of success indicated. *I was positive things were going to turn out fine.* **2** PHR-VERB If something **turns out** to be a particular thing, it is discovered to be that thing. *It turned out that I knew the person who got shot.* **3** PHR-VERB When you **turn out** something such as a light or gas, you move the device that controls it so that it stops giving out light or heat. *Turn the lights out.* **4** PHR-VERB If people **turn out** for a particular event or activity, they go and take part in it or watch it. **5** See also **turnout.**
▸**turn over.** **1** PHR-VERB If you **turn** something **over**, or if it **turns over**, it is moved so that the top part is now facing downwards. *I don't suppose you thought to turn over the tape, did you?* **2** PHR-VERB If you **turn** something **over** in your mind, you think carefully about it. **3** PHR-VERB If you **turn** something **over to** someone, you give it to them when they ask for

⭐ Bank of English® frequent word For a full explanation of all grammatical labels, see pages vii-x

it, because they have a right to it. *I would turn the evidence over to the police.* 4 See also **turnover**.

▸ **turn round.** See **turn around**.

▸ **turn up.** 1 PHR-VERB If you say that someone or something **turns up**, you mean that they arrive, often unexpectedly or after you have been waiting a long time. *This is similar to waiting for a bus that never turns up.* 2 PHR-VERB When you **turn up** a radio, heater, or other piece of equipment, you increase the amount of sound, heat, or power being produced. *I turned the volume up.*

turning /'tɜːnɪŋ/ **turnings.** N-COUNT If you take a particular **turning**, you go along a road which leads away from the side of another road. *Take the next turning on the right.* ● See also **turn**.

'turning point, turning points. N-COUNT A **turning point** is a time at which an important change takes place which affects the future of a person or thing. *Hungary's opening of the border was a turning point for the refugees.*

turnip /'tɜːnɪp/ **turnips.** N-VAR A **turnip** is a round vegetable with a green and white skin. → See picture on page 836.

turnout (or **turn-out**) /'tɜːnaʊt/ **turnouts.** N-COUNT The **turnout** at an event is the number of people who go to it. *It was a marvellous afternoon with a huge turnout of people.*

turnover /'tɜːnəʊvə/. 1 N-UNCOUNT The **turnover** of a company is the value of goods or services sold during a particular period of time. *The zoo has an annual turnover of £7 million.* 2 N-UNCOUNT The **turnover** of people in an organization is the rate at which people leave and are replaced. *Short-term contracts increase staff turnover.*

turquoise /'tɜːkwɔɪz/ **turquoises.** ADJ & N-VAR Something that is **turquoise** is greenish-blue in colour. *I glanced out at the turquoise sea.*

turtle /'tɜːtəl/ **turtles.** N-COUNT A **turtle** is a large reptile with a thick shell which lives in the sea.

tusk /tʌsk/ **tusks.** N-COUNT The **tusks** of an elephant or wild boar are its two very long pointed teeth.

tussle /'tʌsəl/ **tussles, tussling, tussled.** VERB & N-COUNT If one person **tussles with** another, or if they **tussle**, they grab hold of and struggle with each other. A **tussle** is a struggle in which people grab hold of each other.

tutor /'tjuːtə, AM 'tuːt-/ **tutors, tutoring, tutored.** 1 N-COUNT A **tutor** is a teacher at a British university or college. 2 N-COUNT A **tutor** is someone who gives private lessons to a pupil or a small group of pupils. 3 VERB If someone **tutors** a person or subject, they teach that person or subject. *She was tutored at home by her parents... He still tutors medical students in anatomy.*

tutorial /tjuː'tɔːriəl, AM 'tuːt-/ **tutorials.** N-COUNT In a university or college, a **tutorial** is a regular meeting between a tutor and one or several students, for discussion of a subject that is being studied.

tuxedo /tʌk'siːdəʊ/ **tuxedos.** N-COUNT A **tuxedo** is a black or white jacket worn by men for formal social events.

⭐ **TV** /,tiː 'viː/ **TVs.** N-VAR **TV** means the same as **television**. *I prefer going to the cinema to watching TV. ...a brand-new TV.*

tweed /twiːd/ **tweeds.** N-VAR **Tweed** is a thick woollen cloth, often woven from different coloured threads.

⭐ **twelfth** /twelfθ/ **twelfths.** 1 ORD The **twelfth** item in a series is the one that you count as number twelve. 2 N-COUNT A **twelfth** is one of twelve equal parts of something.

⭐ **twelve** /twelv/ **twelves.** NUM **Twelve** is the number 12.

⭐ **twentieth** /'twentiəθ/. ORD The **twentieth** item in a series is the one that you count as number twenty.

⭐ **twenty** /'twenti/ **twenties.** NUM **Twenty** is the number 20. For examples of how numbers such as twenty and eighty are used see **eighty**.

24-7 (or **twenty-four seven**) /,twentifɔː'sevən/. ADV & ADJ If something happens **24-7**, it happens all the time without ever stopping. **24-7** means twenty-four hours a day, seven days a week. [AMERICAN, INFORMAL] *I feel like sleeping 24-7. ...a 24-7 radio station.*

⭐ **twice** /twaɪs/. 1 ADV If something happens **twice**, it happens two times. *I've visited Africa twice... Try to do this exercise at least twice a day.* 2 ADV & PREDET If one thing is, for example, **twice as** big or old **as** another thing, or if it is **twice** the size or age **of** another thing, it is two times as big or old as the other thing. *It took us nearly twice as long to return to the station as it had to come from it... Unemployment in Northern Ireland is twice the national average.*

twig /twɪg/ **twigs.** N-COUNT A **twig** is a very small thin branch of a tree or bush.

twilight /'twaɪlaɪt/. 1 N-UNCOUNT **Twilight** is the time after sunset when it is just getting dark. *They returned at twilight.* 2 N-UNCOUNT **Twilight** is the dim light that there is outside just after sunset. *...the deepening autumn twilight.*

⭐ **twin** /twɪn/ **twins.** 1 N-COUNT If two people are **twins**, they have the same mother and were born on the same day. *...her twin sister.* 2 ADJ BEFORE N **Twin** is used to describe a pair of things that look the same and are close together. *...the twin towers of a new office development. ...the world's largest twin-engined aircraft.*

twinkle /'twɪŋkəl/ **twinkles, twinkling, twinkled.** 1 VERB If a star or a light **twinkles**, it shines with an unsteady light which rapidly and constantly changes from bright to faint. 2 VERB & N-SING If you say that someone's eyes **twinkle**, or that there is a **twinkle** in their eye, you mean that their face expresses good humour, amusement, or mischief.

twirl /twɜːl/ **twirls, twirling, twirled.** 1 VERB If you **twirl** something, or if it **twirls**, it turns round and round with a smooth fairly fast movement. *Bonnie twirled her empty glass in her fingers.*

2 VERB If you **twirl**, you move round and round rapidly, for example when you are dancing. *She bounded out of bed, startling Boris, and twirled around the room on her toes.*

⭐ **twist** /twɪst/ **twists, twisting, twisted.** **1** VERB If you **twist** something, you turn it to make a spiral shape, for example by turning the two ends of it in opposite directions. *Her hands began to twist the handles of the bag... She twisted her hair into a bun.* **2** VERB If you **twist** something, especially a part of your body, or if it **twists**, it moves into a strange, uncomfortable, or distorted shape or position. *He twisted her arms behind her back. ...the twisted wreckage of a train.* **3** VERB If you **twist** part of your body such as your head or your shoulders, you turn that part while keeping the rest of your body still. *She twisted her head sideways... Susan twisted round in her seat.* **4** VERB If you **twist** a part of your body such as your ankle or your wrist, you injure it by turning it too sharply or in an unusual direction. *I twisted my knee last year playing tennis.* **5** VERB If you **twist** something, you turn it so that it moves around in a circular direction. *He takes out a jar and twists the lid off.* **6** VERB If someone **twists** what you say, they repeat it in a way that changes its meaning, in order to harm you or benefit themselves. *You're twisting my words around.* **7** N-COUNT A **twist** in something is an unexpected and significant development. *The long-running battle took a new twist last night.*

twisted /ˈtwɪstɪd/. ADJ If you describe a person as **twisted**, you dislike them because you think they are strange in an unpleasant way.

twister /ˈtwɪstə/ **twisters.** N-COUNT A **twister** is the same as a **tornado**. [AMERICAN]

twitch /twɪtʃ/ **twitches, twitching, twitched.** VERB & N-COUNT If a part of your body **twitches**, it makes a little jerking movement, called a **twitch**. *He saw the corners of Alex's mouth twitch... He developed a nervous twitch.*

⭐ **two** /tuː/ **twos.** NUM **Two** is the number 2.

‚**two-'thirds** (or **two thirds**). QUANT **Two-thirds** is an amount that is two out of three equal parts of something. *Two-thirds of families in Britain already own their homes. ...a treaty to cut their nuclear arsenals by two-thirds.*

‚**two-'way.** ADJ **Two-way** means moving or working in two opposite directions. *The bridge is now open to two-way traffic... We all carry two-way radios.*

tycoon /taɪˈkuːn/ **tycoons.** N-COUNT A **tycoon** is a person who is successful in business and so has become rich and powerful.

type 1 sort or kind

⭐ **type** /taɪp/ **types.** **1** N-COUNT A **type of** something is a group of those things that have particular features in common. *...several types of lettuce... In 1990, 25% of households were of this type.* **2** N-COUNT If you refer to a particular thing or person as a **type of** something more general, you are considering that thing or person as an example of that more general group. *Have you*

done this type of work before?... I am a very determined type of person.* **3** N-COUNT If you refer to a person as a particular **type**, you mean that they have that particular appearance, character, or type of behaviour. *I was rather an outdoor type... She was certainly not the type to murder her husband.*

type 2 writing and printing

⭐ **type** /taɪp/ **types, typing, typed.** VERB If you **type** something, you use a typewriter or word processor to write it. *I had never really learnt to type properly.* ♦ **typing** N-UNCOUNT *He learnt shorthand and typing.*

▸**type in** or **type into.** PHR-VERB If you **type** information **into** a computer or **type** it **in**, you press keys on the keyboard so that the computer stores or processes the information.

▸**type up.** PHR-VERB If you **type up** a handwritten text, you produce a typed copy of it.

typewriter /ˈtaɪpraɪtə/ **typewriters.** N-COUNT A **typewriter** is a machine with keys which are pressed in order to print letters, numbers, or other characters onto paper.

typhoon /taɪˈfuːn/ **typhoons.** N-COUNT A **typhoon** is a very violent tropical storm.

⭐ **typical** /ˈtɪpɪkəl/. **1** ADJ You use **typical** to describe someone or something that shows the most usual characteristics of a particular type of person or thing, and is therefore a good example of that type. *Aaron was brought up as a typical American child... A typical day begins at 8.30.* **2** ADJ If a particular action or feature is **typical of** someone or something, it shows their usual qualities or characteristics. *This is not typical of Chinese, but is a feature of the Thai language.*

typically /ˈtɪpɪkəli/. **1** ADV You use **typically** to say that something usually happens in the way that you are describing it. *The day typically begins with exercises and swimming.* **2** ADV You use **typically** to say that something shows all the most usual characteristics of a particular type of person or thing. *Ashley's pretty bedroom looks typically English.* **3** ADV You use **typically** to indicate that someone has behaved in the way that they normally do. *Typically, he took the setback in good humour.*

typify /ˈtɪpɪfaɪ/ **typifies, typifying, typified.** VERB To **typify** something means to be a typical example of it. *The design typifies Ercol's furniture: elegant and substantial.*

typist /ˈtaɪpɪst/ **typists.** N-COUNT A **typist** is someone who works in an office typing letters and other documents.

tyranny /ˈtɪrəni/. N-UNCOUNT **Tyranny** is cruel and unjust rule by a person or small group of people.

tyrant /ˈtaɪərənt/ **tyrants.** N-COUNT A **tyrant** is someone who treats the people they have authority over in a cruel and unfair way.

tyre (AM **tire**) /taɪə/ **tyres.** N-COUNT A **tyre** is a thick ring of rubber filled with air and fitted round the wheel of a vehicle.

a
b
c
d
e
f
g
h
i
j
k
l
m
n
o
p
q
r
s
t
u
v
w
x
y
z

U u

ubiquitous /juː'bɪkwɪtəs/. ADJ If you describe something as **ubiquitous**, you mean that it seems to be everywhere at the same time. *The video camcorder has become ubiquitous.*

ugly /'ʌgli/ **uglier, ugliest.** [1] ADJ If you say that someone or something is **ugly**, you mean that they are unattractive and unpleasant to look at. ♦ **ugliness** N-UNCOUNT *...the raw ugliness of his native city.* [2] ADJ If you refer to a situation as **ugly**, you mean that it is very unpleasant, usually because it involves violence. *There have been some ugly scenes.*

ulcer /'ʌlsə/ **ulcers.** N-COUNT An **ulcer** is a sore area on or inside a part of your body which is very painful and may bleed.

⭐ **ultimate** /'ʌltɪmət/. [1] ADJ BEFORE N You use **ultimate** to describe the final result or the original cause of a long series of events. *It is still not possible to predict the ultimate outcome.* [2] ADJ BEFORE N You use **ultimate** to describe the most important or extreme thing of a particular kind. *The ultimate authority remained the presidency... The death penalty would be the ultimate abuse of human rights.* [3] PHRASE The **ultimate in** something is the best or most advanced thing of its kind. *This hotel is the ultimate in luxury.*

⭐ **ultimately** /'ʌltɪmətli/. [1] ADV **Ultimately** means finally, after a long series of events. *That struggle will ultimately succeed.* [2] ADV You use **ultimately** to emphasize that what you are saying is the most important point in a discussion. *Ultimately, the problem lies with employers.*

ultimatum /ˌʌltɪ'meɪtəm/ **ultimatums.** N-COUNT An **ultimatum** is a warning that unless someone acts in a particular way within a particular time limit, action will be taken against them. *Workers have issued an ultimatum to the government.*

ultrasound /'ʌltrəsaʊnd/ **ultrasounds.** [1] N-UNCOUNT **Ultrasound** refers to sound waves which travel at such a high frequency that they cannot be heard by humans. [2] N-COUNT An **ultrasound** or an **ultrasound scan** is a medical test in which ultrasound waves are used to form a picture of the inside of someone's body.

ultraviolet /ˌʌltrə'vaɪələt/. ADJ **Ultraviolet** light or radiation causes your skin to darken after you have been in sunlight.

umbrella /ʌm'brelə/ **umbrellas.** [1] N-COUNT An **umbrella** is an object which you use to protect yourself from the rain or hot sun. It consists of a long stick with a folding frame covered in cloth. → See picture on page 819. [2] N-SING **Umbrella** refers to a single idea or group that includes a lot of different ideas or groups. *Does coincidence come under the umbrella of the paranormal? ...an*

umbrella group of several human rights organisations.

umpire /'ʌmpaɪə/ **umpires, umpiring, umpired.** [1] N-COUNT An **umpire** is a person whose job is to make sure that a sports match or contest is played fairly and that the rules are not broken. [2] VERB If you **umpire** a game, you are its umpire.

⭐ **unable** /ʌn'eɪbəl/. ADJ If you are **unable to** do something, it is impossible for you to do it. *I was unable to accept the invitation... Mary felt herself blushing and unable to meet her eyes.*

unacceptable /ˌʌnək'septəbəl/. ADJ If you describe something as **unacceptable**, you strongly disapprove of it or object to it and feel that it should not be allowed to happen or continue. *It is totally unacceptable for children to swear.*

unaffected /ˌʌnə'fektɪd/. [1] ADJ AFTER LINK-V If someone or something is **unaffected by** an event, they are not changed by it in any way. *She seemed totally unaffected by what she'd drunk.* [2] ADJ If you describe someone as **unaffected**, you approve of them because they are natural and genuine in their behaviour.

unanimity /ˌjuːnə'nɪmɪti/. N-UNCOUNT When there is **unanimity** among a group of people, they all agree about something.

unanimous /juː'nænɪməs/. ADJ When a group of people or their opinion is **unanimous**, they all agree about something. ♦ **unanimously** ADV *Its executive committee voted unanimously to reject the proposals.*

unannounced /ˌʌnə'naʊnst/. ADJ If someone arrives or does something **unannounced**, they do it unexpectedly and without anyone having being told about it beforehand. *He had just arrived unannounced from South America.*

unanswered /ʌn'ɑːnsəd, -'æns-/. ADJ Something such as a question or letter that is **unanswered** has not been answered. *Some of the most important questions remain unanswered.*

unarmed /ˌʌn'ɑːmd/. ADJ If a person or vehicle is **unarmed**, they are not carrying any weapons.

unashamed /ˌʌnə'ʃeɪmd/. ADJ If you describe someone's behaviour or attitude as **unashamed**, you mean that they are open and honest about things that other people might find embarrassing or shocking. ♦ **unashamedly** ADV *...an unashamedly traditional view.*

unattractive /ˌʌnə'træktɪv/. [1] ADJ **Unattractive** people and things are unpleasant in their appearance. [2] ADJ If you describe something as **unattractive**, you mean that people do not like it and do not want to be involved with it. *The market is still unattractive to many insurers.*

unauthorized (BRIT also **unauthorised**) /ˌʌnˈɔːθəraɪzd/. ADJ If something is **unauthorized**, it has been produced or is happening without official permission. ...*a new unauthorized biography of the Russian President.*

unavailable /ˌʌnəˈveɪləbəl/. ADJ When things or people are **unavailable**, you cannot obtain them, meet them, or talk to them. *Mr Hicks is out of the country and so unavailable for comment.*

unavoidable /ˌʌnəˈvɔɪdəbəl/. ADJ If something bad is **unavoidable**, it cannot be avoided or prevented. *The job losses were unavoidable.*

unaware /ˌʌnəˈweə/. ADJ AFTER LINK-V If you are **unaware of** something, you do not know about it. *Many people are unaware of just how much drink they consume... She was unaware that she was being filmed.*

unbalanced /ˌʌnˈbælənst/. [1] ADJ If you describe someone as **unbalanced**, you mean that they appear to be very disturbed or upset, and perhaps slightly mad. *He was shown to be mentally unbalanced.* [2] ADJ If you describe something such as a report or argument as **unbalanced**, you think that it is unfair or inaccurate because it emphasizes some things and ignores others.

unbearable /ˌʌnˈbeərəbəl/. ADJ If you describe something as **unbearable**, you mean that it is so unpleasant, painful, or upsetting that you feel unable to accept it or deal with it. *War has made life almost unbearable for the civilians.* ♦ **unbearably** ADV *It had become unbearably hot.*

unbeatable /ˌʌnˈbiːtəbəl/. ADJ If you describe something as **unbeatable**, you mean that it is the best thing of its kind. *These resorts, like Magaluf and Arenal, remain unbeatable in terms of price.*

unbeaten /ˌʌnˈbiːtən/. ADJ In sport, if a person or their performance is **unbeaten**, nobody has ever beaten them. *He's unbeaten in 20 fights.*

unbelievable /ˌʌnbɪˈliːvəbəl/. [1] ADJ If you say that something is **unbelievable**, you are emphasizing that it is very extreme, impressive, or shocking. *The pressure they put us under there was unbelievable... It was an unbelievable moment when Chris won... I find it unbelievable that people can accept this sort of behaviour.* ♦ **unbelievably** ADV *What you did was unbelievably stupid.* [2] ADJ If an idea or theory is **unbelievable**, it is so unlikely or so illogical that you cannot believe it. *I know it sounds unbelievable but I never wanted to cheat.* ♦ **unbelievably** ADV *Lainey was, unbelievably, pregnant again.*

unborn /ˌʌnˈbɔːn/. ADJ & N-PLURAL An **unborn** child is still inside its mother's womb or is going to be born in the future. **The unborn** are children who are not born yet. *They will affect generations of Britons still unborn.*

unbroken /ˌʌnˈbrəʊkən/. ADJ If something is **unbroken**, it is continuous or complete. ...*an unbroken run of 38 match wins... We've had ten days of almost unbroken sunshine.*

uncanny /ˌʌnˈkæni/. ADJ If something is **uncanny**, it is strange and difficult to explain. *I had this uncanny feeling that I was seeing the future.* ♦ **uncannily** ADV *The night was uncannily still.*

uncertain /ˌʌnˈsɜːtən/. [1] ADJ If you are **uncertain about** something, you do not know what to do. *He was uncertain about his brother's intentions... They were baffled and uncertain how to proceed.* ♦ **uncertainly** ADV *He entered the hallway and stood uncertainly.* [2] ADJ If something is **uncertain**, it is not known or not definite. *It's uncertain whether they will accept the plan.* [3] PHRASE If you say that someone tells a person something **in no uncertain terms**, you are emphasizing that they say it firmly and clearly so that there is no doubt about what they mean.

uncertainty /ˌʌnˈsɜːtənti/ **uncertainties**. N-VAR **Uncertainty** is a state of doubt about the future or about what is the right thing to do. ...*the uncertainties concerning the future funding of the company.*

unchallenged /ˌʌnˈtʃælɪndʒd/. ADJ When something is **unchallenged**, people accept it without questioning whether it is right or wrong. *This new research has not gone unchallenged.*

unchanged /ˌʌnˈtʃeɪndʒd/. ADJ Something that is **unchanged** has stayed the same during a period of time. *Prices have remained virtually unchanged.*

uncharacteristic /ˌʌnkærɪktəˈrɪstɪk/. ADJ If an action or mood is **uncharacteristic of** someone, it is not their usual type of behaviour. *It was uncharacteristic of her father to disappear like this... She made an uncharacteristic error of judgement.* ♦ **uncharacteristically** ADV *Owen has been uncharacteristically silent.*

unchecked /ˌʌnˈtʃekt/. ADJ If something undesirable is left **unchecked**, it keeps growing without anyone trying to stop it. ...*the corruption which flourished unchecked.*

⭐ **uncle** /ˈʌŋkəl/ **uncles**. N-COUNT Your **uncle** is the brother of your mother or father, or the husband of your aunt.

unclear /ˌʌnˈklɪə/. [1] ADJ If something is **unclear**, it is not known or not certain. *It is unclear how much support they have.* [2] ADJ AFTER LINK-V If you are **unclear about** something, you do not understand it properly or are not sure about it. *He is still unclear about his own future.*

uncomfortable /ˌʌnˈkʌmftəbəl/. [1] ADJ If you are **uncomfortable**, you are not physically relaxed, and feel slight pain or discomfort. ♦ **uncomfortably** ADV *He awoke to find himself lying uncomfortably on a pile of firewood.* [2] ADJ If you are **uncomfortable**, you are slightly worried or embarrassed, and not relaxed and confident. ♦ **uncomfortably** ADV *Dr Wilding pulled uncomfortably at his tie.* [3] ADJ Something that is **uncomfortable** makes you feel slight pain or

a
b
c
d
e
f
g
h
i
j
k
l
m
n
o
p
q
r
s
t
u
v
w
x
y
z

A
B
C
D
E
F
G
H
I
J
K
L
M
N
O
P
Q
R
S
T
U
V
W
X
Y
Z

physical discomfort when you experience it or use it. ...*an uncomfortable chair.*

uncomplicated /ˌʌnˈkɒmplɪkeɪtɪd/. ADJ **Uncomplicated** things are simple and straightforward. ...*his uncomplicated sense of humour.*

uncompromising /ˌʌnˈkɒmprəmaɪzɪŋ/. ADJ If you describe someone as **uncompromising**, you mean that they are determined not to change their opinions or aims in any way. ...*a tough and uncompromising politician.*

unconcerned /ˌʌnkənˈsɜːnd/. ADJ If someone is **unconcerned about** something, they are not interested in it or not worried about it. *Sue is unconcerned about her health.*

unconditional /ˌʌnkənˈdɪʃənəl/. ADJ Something that is **unconditional** is done or given to someone freely, without anything being required in return. *Children need unconditional love.* ♦ **unconditionally** ADV *The hostages were released unconditionally.*

unconfirmed /ˌʌnkənˈfɜːmd/. ADJ If a report or rumour is **unconfirmed**, there is not yet any definite proof that it is true.

unconnected /ˌʌnkəˈnektɪd/. ADJ If two things are **unconnected with** each other, they are not related to each other in any way. ...*personal problems unconnected with her marriage... I can't believe that those two murders are unconnected.*

unconscious /ʌnˈkɒnʃəs/. **1** ADJ Someone who is **unconscious** is in a state similar to sleep, as a result of a shock, accident, or injury. *He was dragged from his van and beaten unconscious.* ♦ **unconsciousness** N-UNCOUNT *He slipped into unconsciousness.* **2** ADJ If you are **unconscious of** something, you are unaware of it. Similarly, if feelings or attitudes are **unconscious**, you are unaware of them. *Mr Battersby was apparently quite unconscious of their presence. ...an unconscious hatred for men.* ♦ **unconsciously** ADV *Bob stared at it, unconsciously holding his breath.* **3** N-SING In psychology, **the unconscious** is the part of your mind which contains feelings and ideas that you do not know about or cannot control.

unconstitutional /ˌʌnkɒnstɪˈtjuːʃənəl, AM -ˈtuː-/. ADJ Something that is **unconstitutional** is against the rules of an organization or political system. *The Moldavian parliament has declared the elections unconstitutional.*

uncontrollable /ˌʌnkənˈtrəʊləbəl/. ADJ If something such as an emotion is **uncontrollable**, you can do nothing to prevent it or control it. *He burst into uncontrollable laughter.* ♦ **uncontrollably** ADV *I started shaking uncontrollably.*

uncontrolled /ˌʌnkənˈtrəʊld/. ADJ If something such as a feeling or activity is **uncontrolled**, no attempt is made to stop or restrain it. ...*the dangers of uncontrolled economic growth.*

unconventional /ˌʌnkənˈvenʃənəl/. ADJ If someone is **unconventional**, they do not behave in the same way as most other people in their society. *He had rather unconventional work habits, preferring to work through the night.*

unconvincing /ˌʌnkənˈvɪnsɪŋ/. ADJ If you describe a statement, argument, or explanation as **unconvincing**, you do not believe it is true or valid. *The reasons given were unconvincing.* ♦ **unconvincingly** ADV *'It is doing me no harm,' he said, unconvincingly.*

uncount noun /ˌʌnkaʊnt ˈnaʊn/ **uncount nouns.** N-COUNT An **uncount noun** is a noun such as 'gold' or 'information' which has only one form and can be used without a determiner.

uncover /ʌnˈkʌvə/ **uncovers, uncovering, uncovered.** **1** VERB If you **uncover** something secret, you find out about it. *Auditors said they had uncovered evidence of widespread fraud.* **2** VERB To **uncover** something means to remove a cover from it.

undaunted /ʌnˈdɔːntɪd/. ADJ If you are **undaunted**, you are confident about dealing with something that would frighten or worry most people. *He seems undaunted by such setbacks.*

undecided /ˌʌndɪˈsaɪdɪd/. ADJ If you are **undecided** about something, you have not yet made a decision about it. *She was still undecided as to what career she wanted to pursue.*

undemocratic /ˌʌndeməˈkrætɪk/. ADJ In an **undemocratic** system, decisions are made by a small number of powerful people without consulting all the people who are affected; used showing disapproval.

undeniable /ˌʌndɪˈnaɪəbəl/. ADJ If something is **undeniable**, it is definitely true or definitely exists. *Her charm is undeniable.* ♦ **undeniably** ADV *Bringing up a baby is undeniably hard work.*

⭐ **under** /ˈʌndə/. **1** PREP If something is **under** something else, it is directly below or beneath it. ...*a labyrinth of tunnels under the ground... He'd been held under the water and drowned... I had my head under the blanket... A river boat passed under the bridge.* **2** PREP & ADV If something or someone is **under** a particular age or amount, they are less than that age or amount. *Expenditure this year should be just under 15 billion pounds. ...a film for very young viewers – aged, say, six and under.* **3** PREP If something happens **under** particular circumstances or conditions, it happens when those circumstances or conditions exist. *Under normal circumstances, these three men would probably never have met... They had to be able to work under pressure... Under current laws, charges must be laid by the alleged victim.* **4** PREP If people live or work **under** a particular person, that person is their ruler, boss, or teacher. ...*the Baltic Republics, forcibly incorporated into the Soviet Union under Stalin... I am the new manager and you will be working under me. ...the artists who had studied under Beuys.* **5** PREP If you do something **under** a particular name, you use that name instead of your real name. *Mrs Coke is a novelist, writing under the name Claire Hunter... The patient was registered under a false name.*

6 PREP You use **under** to say which section of a list, book, or system something is classified in. *This study is described under 'General Diseases of the Eye'... 'Where would it be?'—'Filed under C, second drawer down.'*

underclass /'ʌndəklɑːs, -klæs/ **underclasses.** N-COUNT The **underclass** consists of people who are poor, and who have little chance of improving their situation.

undercover /ˌʌndə'kʌvə/. ADJ **Undercover** work involves secretly obtaining information for the government or the police. *...an undercover operation designed to catch drug smugglers.*

undercurrent /'ʌndəkʌrənt, -kɜːr-/ **undercurrents.** N-COUNT If there is an **undercurrent of** a feeling, the feeling exists in a weak form, and may become powerful later. *...a growing undercurrent of fear.*

undercut /ˌʌndə'kʌt/ **undercuts, undercutting, undercut.** VERB If a business **undercuts** its competitors or their prices, it sells a product more cheaply than its competitors.

underdeveloped /ˌʌndədɪ'veləpt/. ADJ An **underdeveloped** country does not have modern industries and usually has a low standard of living. Some people prefer to use the term **developing**.

underdog /'ʌndədɒg, AM -dɔːg/ **underdogs.** N-COUNT The **underdog** in a contest is the person who seems least likely to succeed or win.

underestimate /ˌʌndər'estɪmeɪt/ **underestimates, underestimating, underestimated.**
1 VERB If you **underestimate** something, you do not realize how large it is or will be. *They had underestimated how much tax would be demanded.* **2** VERB If you **underestimate** someone, you do not realize what they are capable of doing. *Opponents make the mistake of underestimating him.*

undergo /ˌʌndə'gəʊ/ **undergoes, undergoing, underwent, undergone.** VERB If you **undergo** something necessary or unpleasant, it happens to you. *New recruits have been undergoing training... He recently underwent brain surgery.*

undergraduate /ˌʌndə'grædʒuət/ **undergraduates.** N-COUNT An **undergraduate** is a student at a university or college who is studying for his or her first degree. *...a 21-year-old history undergraduate.*

underground; adverb /ˌʌndə'graʊnd/; noun and adjective /'ʌndəgraʊnd/. **1** ADV & ADJ BEFORE N Something that is **underground** is below the surface of the ground. *The plane hit so hard that one engine was buried 16 feet underground. ...an underground car park.* **2** N-SING In British English, **the underground** in a city is the railway system in which electric trains travel below the ground in tunnels. The American word is **subway**. **3** ADJ

BEFORE N **Underground** political activities take place secretly, and are directed against the government. *...the underground Kashmir Liberation Front.*

undergrowth /'ʌndəgrəʊθ/. N-UNCOUNT **Undergrowth** consists of bushes and plants growing closely together under trees. [BRITISH] *He pushed his way through the undergrowth.*

underlie /ˌʌndə'laɪ/ **underlies, underlying, underlay, underlain.** VERB If something **underlies** a feeling or situation, it is the cause or basis of it. *Try to figure out what feeling underlies your anger.*

underline /ˌʌndə'laɪn/ **underlines, underlining, underlined.** **1** VERB In British English, if a person or event **underlines** something, they draw attention to it and emphasize its importance. The American word is **underscore**. *The Second World War underlined the importance of science and technology.* **2** VERB In British English, if you **underline** a word or sentence, you draw a line underneath it. The American word is **underscore**.

underlying /ˌʌndə'laɪɪŋ/. ADJ BEFORE N The **underlying** aspects of an event or situation are the aspects that are not obvious but that have great significance or effect. *To stop a problem you have to understand its underlying causes.*

★ **undermine** /ˌʌndə'maɪn/ **undermines, undermining, undermined.** VERB To **undermine** a feeling or a system means to make it less certain or less secure. *The conversations were designed to undermine her authority.*

underneath /ˌʌndə'niːθ/. **1** PREP & ADV If one thing is **underneath** another, it is directly below or beneath it. *We all dived underneath the tables... Pull back a bit of this carpet to see what's underneath.* **2** ADV & N-SING The part of something which is **underneath** is the part which normally touches the ground or faces towards the ground. **The underneath of** something is the part which is underneath. *Check the actual construction of the chair by looking underneath... I know what the underneath of a car looks like.* **3** ADV & PREP You use **underneath** when you are talking about feelings and emotions that people do not show in their behaviour. *Underneath, Sofia was deeply committed to her husband... Underneath her calm exterior was a growing sense of panic.*

underpants /'ʌndəpænts/. N-PLURAL **Underpants** are a piece of underwear with two holes for your legs and elastic around the waist. In British English, **underpants** refers only to men's underwear. In American English it refers to both men's and women's underwear.

underrate /ˌʌndə'reɪt/ **underrates, underrating, underrated.** VERB If you **underrate** someone, you do not realize how clever, able, or important they are. ◆ **underrated** ADJ *He is a very underrated poet.*

underscore /ˌʌndə'skɔː/ **underscores, underscoring, underscored.** **1** VERB In American English, if a person or an event **underscores** something, they draw attention to it and

a b c d e f g h i j k l m n o p q r s t u v w x y z

emphasize its importance. The British word is **underline**. *The recent violence in Los Angeles underscores how real the problems are.* [2] VERB In American English, if you **underscore** a word or a sentence, you draw a line underneath it. The British word is **underline**.

underside /ˈʌndəsaɪd/ **undersides.** N-COUNT The **underside of** something is the part of it which normally faces towards the ground.

★ **understand** /ˌʌndəˈstænd/ **understands, understanding, understood.** [1] VERB If you **understand** someone, or if you **understand** what they are saying, you know what they mean. *I don't understand what you are talking about... She could barely understand a word of English.* [2] VERB To **understand** someone means to know how they feel and why they behave in the way that they do. *My husband and I understand each other very well.* [3] VERB You say that you **understand** something when you know why or how it happens. *They are too young to understand what is going on.* [4] VERB If you say that you **understand** that something is the case, you mean that you think it is the case because you have heard or read that it is. [FORMAL] *I understand that he's just taken early retirement... He was understood to be reluctant to take over.*

understandable /ˌʌndəˈstændəbəl/. ADJ If you describe someone's behaviour or feelings as **understandable**, you mean that they have reacted to a situation in a natural way or in the way you would expect. *It is understandable that Mr Khan should want something to be done.* ♦ **understandably** ADV *Most organizations are, quite understandably, suspicious of new ideas.*

★ **understanding** /ˌʌndəˈstændɪŋ/ **understandings.** [1] N-SING & N-UNCOUNT If you have an **understanding of** something, you know how it works or what it means. *They have to have a basic understanding of computers... Mr Smith seems to have little understanding of the procedures.* [2] ADJ If you are **understanding** towards someone, you are kind and forgiving. *Fortunately for John, he had an understanding wife.* [3] N-UNCOUNT If there is **understanding** between people, they are friendly towards each other and trust each other. *...a foundation which works to promote understanding between Muslims, Christians and Jews.* [4] N-COUNT An **understanding** is an informal agreement about something. *We had an understanding that we'd talk in the summer... He left half the shares to Grandma on the understanding that she'd leave hers to Mum.*

understate /ˌʌndəˈsteɪt/ **understates, understating, understated.** VERB If you **understate** something, you describe it in a way that suggests that it is less important or serious than it really is. *The figures probably understate the extent of the epidemic.*

understated /ˌʌndəˈsteɪtɪd/. ADJ BEFORE N If you describe a style, colour, or effect as **understated**, you like it because it is not obvious. *...understated elegance.*

understatement /ˈʌndəsteɪtmənt/ **understatements.** N-VAR An **understatement** is a statement which does not fully express the extent to which something is true. *To say I'm disappointed is an understatement.*

understood /ˌʌndəˈstʊd/. **Understood** is the past tense and past participle of **understand**.

undertake /ˌʌndəˈteɪk/ **undertakes, undertaking, undertook, undertaken.** [1] VERB When you **undertake** a task or job, you start doing it and accept responsibility for it. [FORMAL] *She undertook a major reorganization of the legal department.* ♦ **undertaking, undertakings** N-COUNT *Organizing the show has been a massive undertaking.* [2] VERB If you **undertake to** do something, you promise that you will do it. [FORMAL] *He undertook to edit the text himself.* ♦ **undertaking** N-COUNT *Frank would have to give an undertaking to be a responsible parent.*

undertaker /ˈʌndəteɪkə/ **undertakers.** N-COUNT In British English, an **undertaker** is a person whose job is to deal with the bodies of people who have died and to arrange funerals. The American word is **mortician**.

undertook /ˌʌndəˈtʊk/. **Undertook** is the past tense of **undertake**.

undervalue /ˌʌndəˈvæljuː/ **undervalues, undervaluing, undervalued.** VERB If you **undervalue** something, you fail to recognize how valuable or important it is. *We must never undervalue freedom.*

underwater /ˌʌndəˈwɔːtə/. ADV & ADJ BEFORE N Something that exists or happens **underwater** exists or happens below the surface of the sea, a river, or a lake. *Some stretches of beach are completely underwater. ...underwater photography.*

underway /ˌʌndəˈweɪ/. ADJ AFTER LINK-V If an activity gets **underway**, it starts. If an activity is **underway**, it has already started. *An investigation is underway.*

underwear /ˈʌndəweə/. N-UNCOUNT **Underwear** is clothing which you wear next to your skin under your other clothes.

underwent /ˌʌndəˈwent/. **Underwent** is the past tense of **undergo**.

underworld /ˈʌndəwɜːld/. N-SING The **underworld** consists of organized crime and the people involved in it. *...a wealthy businessman with underworld connections.*

underwrite /ˌʌndəˈraɪt/ **underwrites, underwriting, underwrote, underwritten.** VERB When an insurance company or other organization **underwrites** an activity or **underwrites** the cost of it, they agree to provide any money that is needed to cover losses or buy special equipment, often for an agreed fee. [TECHNICAL]

undesirable /ˌʌndɪˈzaɪərəbəl/. ADJ If you describe something or someone as **undesirable**, you think they will have harmful effects. *There can be undesirable side-effects... It is clearly undesirable that people should be exposed to this.*

undid /ʌnˈdɪd/. **Undid** is the past tense of **undo**.

undisclosed /ˌʌndɪsˈkləʊzd/. ADJ **Undisclosed** information has not been revealed to the public. *She was paid an undisclosed sum in damages.*

undisputed /ˌʌndɪˈspjuːtɪd/. ADJ If you describe something as **undisputed**, you mean that everyone accepts that it exists or is true. *Japan is now the undisputed champion of consumer electronics.*

undisturbed /ˌʌndɪˈstɜːbd/. [1] ADJ Something that remains **undisturbed** has not been touched, moved, or changed. *The desk looked undisturbed.* [2] ADJ If you are **undisturbed** in something that you are doing, you are able to continue doing it and are not affected by something that is happening. *He was able to work undisturbed.*

undo /ʌnˈduː/. **undoes, undoing, undid, undone.** [1] VERB If you **undo** something, you unfasten, loosen, or untie it. *She undid the buttons of her jacket... Her hair had come undone.* [2] VERB To **undo** something that has been done means to reverse its effect. *It would be difficult to undo the damage.*

undoing /ʌnˈduːɪŋ/. N-SING If you say that something is someone's **undoing**, you mean that it is the cause of their failure. *His lack of experience may prove to be his undoing.*

undoubted /ʌnˈdaʊtɪd/. ADJ You can use **undoubted** to emphasize that something exists or is true. *The event was an undoubted success.* ♦ **undoubtedly** ADV *He is undoubtedly a highly talented player.*

undress /ʌnˈdres/. **undresses, undressing, undressed.** VERB When you **undress**, you take off your clothes. If you **undress** someone, you take off their clothes. ♦ **undressed** ADJ *He got undressed in the bathroom.* ● See note at **wear**.

undue /ʌnˈdjuː, AM -ˈduː/. ADJ BEFORE N If you describe something bad as **undue**, you mean that it is greater or more extreme than you think is reasonable. *This would help the families to survive the drought without undue suffering.* ♦ **unduly** ADV *He appealed to firms not to increase their prices unduly.*

undulating /ˈʌndʒʊleɪtɪŋ/. ADJ **Undulating** means having gentle curves or slopes, or moving gently and slowly up and down or from side to side. [LITERARY] *...gently undulating hills.*

unearth /ʌnˈɜːθ/. **unearths, unearthing, unearthed.** VERB If someone **unearths** something hidden or secret, they discover it. *Investigators have unearthed evidence of systematic fraud.*

unease /ʌnˈiːz/. N-UNCOUNT If you have a feeling of **unease**, you feel that something is wrong and you are anxious or uncomfortable about it. *The atmosphere was one of unease.*

uneasy /ʌnˈiːzi/. [1] ADJ If you are **uneasy**, you feel that something is wrong and you are anxious or uncomfortable about it. *Richard was uneasy about how best to approach his elderly mother.* ♦ **uneasily** ADV *Meg shifted uneasily on her chair.*

♦ **uneasiness** N-UNCOUNT *I felt a great uneasiness about meeting her again.* [2] ADJ If you describe a situation or relationship as **uneasy**, you mean that is not settled and may not last. *An uneasy calm has settled over Los Angeles.* ♦ **uneasily** ADV *...a country whose component parts fit uneasily together.*

unemployed /ˌʌnɪmˈplɔɪd/. ADJ & N-PLURAL Someone who is **unemployed** does not have a job although they want one. **The unemployed** are people who are unemployed.

★ **unemployment** /ˌʌnɪmˈplɔɪmənt/. N-UNCOUNT **Unemployment** is the fact that people who want jobs cannot get them. *...the highest unemployment rate in western Europe.*

unequivocal /ˌʌnɪˈkwɪvəkəl/. ADJ If you describe someone's attitude as **unequivocal**, you mean that it is very clear and firm. [FORMAL] *The message to him was unequivocal: 'Get out'.* ♦ **unequivocally** ADV *He stated unequivocally that the French forces were ready to go to war.*

unethical /ʌnˈeθɪkəl/. ADJ If you describe someone's behaviour as **unethical**, you think it is morally wrong. [FORMAL] *It is unethical to sell properties at clearly inflated prices.*

uneven /ʌnˈiːvən/. [1] ADJ An **uneven** surface is not level or smooth. *...the uneven surface of the car park.* [2] ADJ Something that is **uneven** is not regular or consistent. *Her breathing was uneven.*

★ **unexpected** /ˌʌnɪkˈspektɪd/. ADJ Something that is **unexpected** surprises you because you did not think it was likely to happen. *His death was totally unexpected.* ♦ **unexpectedly** ADV *Mr Kirk had unexpectedly strong support.*

unexplained /ˌʌnɪkˈspleɪnd/. ADJ If something is **unexplained**, the reason for it or the cause of it is unclear or is not known. *...the unexplained death of an opposition leader.*

★ **unfair** /ʌnˈfeə/. ADJ Something that is **unfair** is not right or not just. *It was unfair that he should suffer so much. ...unfair dismissal.* ♦ **unfairly** ADV *She claims she was unfairly dismissed.* ♦ **unfairness** N-UNCOUNT *He raged at the unfairness of life.*

unfaithful /ʌnˈfeɪθfʊl/. ADJ If someone is **unfaithful** to their lover or to the person they are married to, they have a sexual relationship with someone else. *James had been unfaithful to her many times. ...her unfaithful husband.*

unfamiliar /ˌʌnfəˈmɪliə/. ADJ If something is **unfamiliar to** you, or if you are **unfamiliar with** it, you know very little about it and have not seen or experienced it before. *She speaks no Japanese and is unfamiliar with Japanese culture.*

unfashionable /ʌnˈfæʃənəbəl/. ADJ If something is **unfashionable**, it is not approved of or done by most people. *Wearing fur has become deeply unfashionable.*

unfavourable (AM **unfavorable**) /ʌnˈfeɪvərəbəl/. [1] ADJ **Unfavourable** conditions or circumstances cause problems and reduce the chance of success. *...unfavourable*

a
b
c
d
e
f
g
h
i
j
k
l
m
n
o
p
q
r
s
t
u
v
w
x
y
z

conditions for the development of British industry. **2** ADJ If you have an **unfavourable** reaction to something, you do not like it. ♦ **unfavourably** ADV I was forever being compared to her unfavourably.

unfettered /ˌʌnˈfetəd/. ADJ **Unfettered** activities are not restricted in any way. [FORMAL] Unfettered free trade is an ideal, never achieved.

unfinished /ˌʌnˈfɪnɪʃt/. ADJ If something is **unfinished**, it has not been completed. ...Jane Austen's unfinished novel.

unfit /ˌʌnˈfɪt/. **1** ADJ If you are **unfit**, your body is not in good condition because you have not been taking regular exercise. **2** ADJ If someone or something is **unfit for** a particular purpose, they are not suitable or not of a good enough quality. He declared her mentally unfit for duty... The wine was unfit for human consumption.

unfold /ˌʌnˈfəʊld/ **unfolds, unfolding, unfolded.** **1** VERB When a situation or story **unfolds**, it develops and becomes known or understood. The facts started to unfold before them. **2** VERB If someone **unfolds** something which has been folded or if it **unfolds**, it is opened out and becomes flat. He quickly unfolded the blankets.

unforeseen /ˌʌnfəˈsiːn/. ADJ An **unforeseen** event happens unexpectedly. Her office was shut due to unforeseen circumstances.

unforgettable /ˌʌnfəˈgetəbəl/. ADJ If something is **unforgettable**, it is so impressive that you are likely to remember it for a long time. A visit to the Museum is an unforgettable experience.

unfortunate /ˌʌnˈfɔːtʃʊnət/. **1** ADJ If you say that someone is **unfortunate**, you mean that something unpleasant or unlucky has happened to them. He was one of those unfortunate people who put on weight very easily. **2** ADJ If you say that something that has happened is **unfortunate**, you mean that it is a pity that it happened. He described the alleged plot as a 'very unfortunate incident'.

⭐ **unfortunately** /ˌʌnˈfɔːtʃʊnətli/. ADV You can use **unfortunately** to express regret about what you are saying. Unfortunately, my time is limited... Unfortunately for us, he is panicking.

unfounded /ˌʌnˈfaʊndɪd/. ADJ If you say that a belief is **unfounded**, you mean that it is wrong, and is not based on facts or evidence. There were unfounded rumours of alcohol abuse.

unfriendly /ˌʌnˈfrendli/. ADJ If you describe someone as **unfriendly**, you mean that they behave in an unkind or hostile way. His manner was unfriendly.

unfulfilled /ˌʌnfʊlˈfɪld/. **1** ADJ You say that a hope is **unfulfilled** when the thing that you hoped for has not happened. Do you have any unfulfilled ambitions? **2** ADJ If someone feels **unfulfilled**, they feel dissatisfied with life or with their achievements.

unfurl /ˌʌnˈfɜːl/ **unfurls, unfurling, unfurled.** VERB If you **unfurl** something such as a flag or umbrella,

or if it **unfurls**, you unroll or unfold it so that it is flat or open and can be seen or used. Anti-nuclear protesters unfurled a banner.

⭐ **unhappy** /ʌnˈhæpi/ **unhappier, unhappiest.** **1** ADJ If you are **unhappy**, you are sad and depressed. ♦ **unhappily** ADV ...an unhappily married woman. ♦ **unhappiness** N-UNCOUNT There was a lot of unhappiness in my adolescence. **2** ADJ AFTER LINK-V If you are **unhappy** about something, you are not pleased with it or not satisfied with it. Republicans are unhappy that the government isn't doing more. ♦ **unhappiness** N-UNCOUNT ...his unhappiness with the government's decision. **3** ADJ BEFORE N An **unhappy** situation is not satisfactory or desirable. This event is a symptom of the unhappy state of British politics.

unharmed /ˌʌnˈhɑːmd/. ADJ If someone or something is **unharmed** after an accident or violent incident, they are not hurt or damaged in any way. His eleven year old daughter was unharmed in the attack.

unhealthy /ʌnˈhelθi/ **unhealthier, unhealthiest.** **1** ADJ Something that is **unhealthy** is likely to cause illness or poor health. ...unhealthy foods such as hamburger and chips. **2** ADJ If you are **unhealthy**, you are not very fit or well.

unheard of /ˌʌnˈhɜːd ɒv/. PHR You can say that an event or situation is **unheard of** when it never happens, or has never happened before. My mother was a career woman, which was unheard of in those days.

unhelpful /ˌʌnˈhelpfʊl/. ADJ If you say that someone or something is **unhelpful**, you mean that they do not help you or improve a situation, and may even make things worse. The criticism is both unfair and unhelpful.

unhurt /ˌʌnˈhɜːt/. ADJ If someone who has been attacked, or involved in an accident, is **unhurt**, they are not injured. The lorry driver escaped unhurt, but a pedestrian was injured.

⭐ **unidentified** /ˌʌnaɪˈdentɪfaɪd/. ADJ If you describe someone or something as **unidentified**, you mean that nobody knows who or what they are. He was shot this morning by unidentified intruders.

unification /ˌjuːnɪfɪˈkeɪʃən/. N-UNCOUNT **Unification** is the process by which two or more countries join together and become one country.

⭐ **uniform** /ˈjuːnɪfɔːm/ **uniforms.** **1** N-VAR A **uniform** is a special set of clothes which some people wear to work in, and which some children wear at school. Philippe was in uniform. **2** ADJ If something is **uniform**, it does not vary, but is even and regular throughout. Chips should be cut into uniform size. ♦ **uniformity** /ˌjuːnɪˈfɔːmɪti/ N-UNCOUNT ...uniformity of color. ♦ **uniformly** ADV Microwaves heat water uniformly. **3** ADJ If you describe a number of things as **uniform**, you mean that they are all the same. Along each wall stretched uniform green metal filing cabinets. ♦ **uniformity** N-UNCOUNT ...the dull uniformity of the houses.

uniformed /'juːnɪfɔːmd/. ADJ **Uniformed** people such as police officers are wearing a uniform while doing their job.

unify /'juːnɪfaɪ/ **unifies, unifying, unified.** VERB If someone **unifies** different things or parts, they are brought together to form one thing. *He had unified the party.* ♦ **unified** ADJ *...a unified system of taxation.*

unilateral /ˌjuːnɪ'lætərəl/. ADJ A **unilateral** decision or action is taken by only one of the groups or countries involved in a particular situation, without the agreement of the others. *...unilateral nuclear disarmament.*

unimaginable /ˌʌnɪ'mædʒɪnəbəl/. ADJ If you describe something as **unimaginable**, you are emphasizing that it is difficult to imagine or understand properly, because it is not part of people's normal experience. *...unimaginable horrors.* ♦ **unimaginably** /ˌʌnɪ'mædʒɪnəbli/ ADV *Conditions are unimaginably bad.*

unimportant /ˌʌnɪm'pɔːtənt/. ADJ If you describe something or someone as **unimportant**, you mean that they do not have much effect or value, and are therefore not worth considering.

unimpressed /ˌʌnɪm'prest/. ADJ AFTER LINK-V If you are **unimpressed by** something or someone, you do not think they are particularly good or important.

uninhibited /ˌʌnɪn'hɪbɪtɪd/. ADJ If you describe a person as **uninhibited**, you mean that they express their opinions and feelings openly, and behave as they want to, without worrying what other people think.

uninstall /ˌʌnɪn'stɔːl/ **uninstalls, uninstalling, uninstalled.** VERB If you **uninstall** a computer program, you remove it permanently from your computer. [COMPUTING]

unintentional /ˌʌnɪn'tenʃənəl/. ADJ Something that is **unintentional** is not done deliberately, but happens by accident. ♦ **unintentionally** ADV *...an unintentionally funny adaptation of 'Dracula'.*

uninterrupted /ˌʌnɪntə'rʌptɪd/. ADJ If something is **uninterrupted**, it continues without any breaks or interruptions. *This enables the healing process to continue uninterrupted.*

⭐ **union** /'juːnjən/ **unions.** [1] N-COUNT A **union** is the same as a **trade union.** [2] N-UNCOUNT When the **union** of two or more things occurs, they are joined together and become one thing. *Britain should move towards closer union with our economic partners.*

unionist /'juːnjənɪst/ **unionists.** N-COUNT A **unionist** is someone who believes in the set of political principles based on the idea that two or more political or national units should be joined or remain together.

⭐ **unique** /juː'niːk/. [1] ADJ Something that is **unique**, is the only one of its kind. *Each person's signature is unique.* ♦ **uniquely** ADV *The Antarctic is a uniquely fragile environment.* ♦ **uniqueness** N-UNCOUNT *...the uniqueness of China's own*

experience. [2] ADJ AFTER LINK-V If something is **unique to** one thing or person, it concerns or belongs only to that thing or person. *This creature is unique to Borneo.* ♦ **uniquely** ADV *The problem isn't uniquely American.* [3] ADJ Some people use **unique** to mean very unusual and special. *Kauffman was a woman of unique talent.* ♦ **uniquely** ADV *...this uniquely beautiful city.*

unison /'juːnɪsən, -zən/. PHRASE If a group of people do something **in unison**, they all do it together at the same time.

⭐ **unit** /'juːnɪt/ **units.** [1] N-COUNT If you consider something as a **unit**, you consider it as a single complete thing. *...the basic family unit.* [2] N-COUNT A **unit** is a group of people who work together at a specific job, often in a particular place. *...the health services research unit.* [3] N-COUNT A **unit** is a small machine which has a particular function, often part of a larger machine. *The unit plugs into any TV set.* [4] N-COUNT A **unit** of measurement is a fixed, standard length, quantity, or weight. The litre, the centimetre, and the ounce are all units.

unite /juː'naɪt/ **unites, uniting, united.** VERB If a group of people or things **unite**, or if someone or something **unites** them, they join together and act as a group. *Only the president can unite the people.*

⭐ **united** /juː'naɪtɪd/. [1] ADJ When people are **united** about something, they agree about it and act together. *Every party is united on the need for parliamentary democracy.* [2] ADJ **United** is used to describe a country which has been formed from two or more countries or states. *...a united Germany.*

⭐ **U,nited 'Nations.** N-PROPER The United **Nations** is a worldwide organization which most countries belong to. Its role is to encourage international peace, cooperation, and friendship.

⭐ **unity** /'juːnɪti/. [1] N-UNCOUNT **Unity** is the state of different areas or groups being joined together to form a single country or organization. *...European economic unity.* [2] N-UNCOUNT When there is **unity**, people are in agreement and act together for a common purpose. *The choice was meant to create an impression of party unity.*

⭐ **universal** /ˌjuːnɪ'vɜːsəl/. ADJ Something that is **universal** relates to everyone in the world or to everyone in a particular group or society. *...universal health care.* ♦ **universally** ADV *...a universally accepted point of view.*

⭐ **universe** /'juːnɪvɜːs/ **universes.** N-COUNT The **universe** is the whole of space, and all the stars, planets, and other forms of matter and energy in it.

⭐ **university** /ˌjuːnɪ'vɜːsɪti/ **universities.** N-VAR A **university** is an institution where students study for degrees and where academic research is done. *They want their daughter to go to university.*

unjust /ˌʌn'dʒʌst/. ADJ If you describe an action, system, or law as **unjust**, you think that it treats a person or group badly in a way that they

a
b
c
d
e
f
g
h
i
j
k
l
m
n
o
p
q
r
s
t
u
v
w
x
y
z

do not deserve. ♦ **unjustly** ADV *She was unjustly accused of stealing money.*

unjustified /ˌʌnˈdʒʌstɪfaɪd/. ADJ If you describe a belief or action as **unjustified**, you think that there is no good reason for having it or doing it. *...totally unjustified allegations.*

unkind /ʌnˈkaɪnd/ **unkinder, unkindest.** ADJ If someone is **unkind**, they behave in an unpleasant, unfriendly, or slightly cruel way. *I think it's very unkind of you to make up stories about him... No one has an unkind word to say about him.* ♦ **unkindly** ADV *Several viewers commented unkindly on her costume.* ♦ **unkindness** N-UNCOUNT *He realized the unkindness of the remark.*

⭐ **unknown** /ˌʌnˈnəʊn/ **unknowns.** **1** ADJ & N-COUNT If something or someone is **unknown to** you, you do not know what or who they are. An **unknown** is something that is unknown. *An unknown number of demonstrators were arrested. ...a man unknown to me... The length of the war is one of the biggest unknowns.* **2** ADJ & N-COUNT An **unknown** person is not famous or publicly recognized. You can refer to a person like this as an **unknown**. *A group of complete unknowns had established a wholly original form of humour.* **3** N-SING **The unknown** refers generally to things or places that people do not know about or understand. *Fear of the unknown is what brings out prejudice.*

unlawful /ˌʌnˈlɔːfʊl/. ADJ If something is **unlawful**, the law does not allow you to do it. [FORMAL] *...employees who believe their dismissal was unlawful.* ♦ **unlawfully** ADV *The government acted unlawfully in imposing the restrictions.*

unleaded /ˌʌnˈledɪd/. ADJ & N-UNCOUNT **Unleaded** fuels contain a reduced amount of lead in order to reduce the pollution caused when they are burned. You can refer to such fuels as **unleaded**. *All its V8 engines will run happily on unleaded.*

unleash /ʌnˈliːʃ/ **unleashes, unleashing, unleashed.** VERB If you say that someone or something **unleashes** a powerful movement or feeling, you mean that it starts suddenly and has an immediate strong effect. *Food rationing will unleash a new stream of refugees.*

⭐ **unless** /ʌnˈles/. CONJ You use **unless** to introduce the only circumstances in which an event you are mentioning will not take place or in which a statement you are making is not true. *I'm not happy unless I ride or drive every day.*

⭐ **unlike** /ʌnˈlaɪk/. **1** PREP If one thing is **unlike** another thing, the two things have different features from each other. *This was a foreign country, so unlike San Jose.* **2** PREP You can use **unlike** to contrast two people or things and show how they are different. *Unlike aerobics, walking entails no expensive fees for classes or clubs.* **3** PREP If you describe something that someone has done as **unlike** them, you mean

that it is not typical of their normal behaviour. *It was so unlike him to say something like that.*

⭐ **unlikely** /ʌnˈlaɪkli/ **unlikeliest.** **1** ADJ If you say that something is **unlikely to** happen or **unlikely to** be true, you believe that it will not happen or that it is not true, although you are not completely sure. *He is unlikely to arrive before Sunday... In the unlikely event of anybody phoning, could you just scribble a message down?* **2** ADJ BEFORE N If you describe someone or something as **unlikely**, you mean it is surprising that they have a particular role or have done a particular thing. *Bespectacled Potter, a yoga fanatic, looks an unlikely drugs dealer.*

unlimited /ʌnˈlɪmɪtɪd/. ADJ If there is an **unlimited** quantity of something, you can have as much of it as you want. *You'll also have unlimited access to the swimming pool.*

unload /ˌʌnˈləʊd/ **unloads, unloading, unloaded.** VERB If you **unload** goods from a vehicle, or if you **unload** a vehicle, you remove the goods from the vehicle. *...a petrol tanker which was unloading at a power station.*

unlock /ˌʌnˈlɒk/ **unlocks, unlocking, unlocked.** VERB If you **unlock** something such as a door, a room, or a container, you open it using a key. *He unlocked the car and threw the coat on to the back seat... Who left this door unlocked?*

unlucky /ʌnˈlʌki/. **1** ADJ If you are **unlucky**, you have bad luck. *They were unlucky not to reach the World Cup Final.* **2** ADJ **Unlucky** is used to describe something that is thought to cause bad luck. *Sixteen is her unlucky number.*

unmarked /ˌʌnˈmɑːkt/. **1** ADJ Something that is **unmarked** has no marks of damage or injury on it. *Her shoes are still white and unmarked.* **2** ADJ Something that is **unmarked** has no signs on it which identify what it is or whose it is. *...an unmarked police car.*

unmistakable (or **unmistakeable**) /ˌʌnmɪsˈteɪkəbəl/. ADJ If you describe something as **unmistakable**, you mean that it is so obvious that it cannot be mistaken for anything else. *He didn't give his name, but the voice was unmistakable.* ♦ **unmistakably** ADV *The name was unmistakably French.*

unmoved /ˌʌnˈmuːvd/. ADJ AFTER LINK-V If you are **unmoved by** something, you are not emotionally affected by it.

unnamed /ˌʌnˈneɪmd/. ADJ **Unnamed** people or things are talked about but their names are not mentioned. *The cash comes from an unnamed source.*

unnatural /ʌnˈnætʃərəl/. **1** ADJ If you describe something as **unnatural**, you mean that it is strange and often frightening, because it is different from what you normally expect. *The aircraft rose with unnatural speed.* ♦ **unnaturally** ADV *The house was unnaturally silent.* **2** ADJ If you describe someone's behaviour as **unnatural**, you mean that it does not seem normal or spontaneous. *She gave him a bright,*

determined smile which seemed unnatural.
♦ **unnaturally** ADV *Try to avoid shouting or speaking unnaturally.*

unnecessary /ʌn'nesəsri, AM -seri/. ADJ If you describe something as **unnecessary**, you mean that it is not needed or does not have to be done. *He accused Diana of making an unnecessary fuss.* ♦ **unnecessarily** ADV *I didn't want to upset my husband or my daughter unnecessarily.*

unnerve /ʌn'nɜːv/ **unnerves, unnerving, unnerved.** VERB If something **unnerves** you, it frightens, worries, or startles you. *The news about Dermot had unnerved me.* ♦ **unnerving** /ʌn'nɜːvɪŋ/ ADJ *He has always found flying to be an unnerving experience.*

unnoticed /ʌn'nəʊtɪst/. ADJ If something happens or passes **unnoticed**, it is not seen or noticed by anyone. *I tried to slip up the stairs unnoticed.*

unobtrusive /ˌʌnəb'truːsɪv/. ADJ If you describe something or someone as **unobtrusive**, you mean that they are not easily noticed or do not draw attention to themselves. [FORMAL] *He managed the factory with unobtrusive efficiency.*
♦ **unobtrusively** ADV *They slipped away unobtrusively.*

unofficial /ˌʌnə'fɪʃəl/. ADJ An **unofficial** action is not authorized, approved, or organized by a person in authority. *...an unofficial strike.*
♦ **unofficially** ADV *The replica is unofficially valued at nearly £500.*

unorthodox /ʌn'ɔːθədɒks/. ADJ If you describe someone's behaviour, beliefs, or customs as **unorthodox**, you mean that they are different from what is generally accepted. *...his unorthodox management style.*

unpack /ˌʌn'pæk/ **unpacks, unpacking, unpacked.** VERB When you **unpack** a suitcase, box, or bag, or when you **unpack** the things inside it, you take the things out of it. *When I'd unpacked I went and tapped on his door.*

unpaid /ˌʌn'peɪd/. [1] ADJ BEFORE N If you do **unpaid** work, you do a job without receiving any money for it. [2] ADJ **Unpaid** taxes or bills have not been paid yet.

unpalatable /ʌn'pælɪtəbəl/. ADJ If you describe an idea as **unpalatable**, you mean that you find it unpleasant and difficult to accept. [FORMAL] *I began to learn the unpalatable truth about John.*

unparalleled /ʌn'pærəleld/. ADJ If you describe something as **unparalleled**, you are emphasizing that it is, for example, bigger, better, or worse than anything else of its kind. *The country is facing a crisis unparalleled since the Second World War.*

unpleasant /ʌn'plezənt/. [1] ADJ If something is **unpleasant**, it gives you bad feelings, for example by making you feel upset or uncomfortable. *The symptoms can be uncomfortable, unpleasant and serious.*
♦ **unpleasantly** ADV *The smell was unpleasantly*

strong. [2] ADJ An **unpleasant** person is unfriendly and rude. ♦ **unpleasantly** ADV *Melissa laughed unpleasantly.*

unplug /ˌʌn'plʌg/ **unplugs, unplugging, unplugged.** VERB If you **unplug** a piece of electrical equipment, you take its plug out of the socket.

unpopular /ˌʌn'pɒpjʊlə/. ADJ If something or someone is **unpopular**, most people do not like them. *He had been unpopular at school.*
♦ **unpopularity** N-UNCOUNT *...the unpopularity of the new tax.*

unprecedented /ʌn'presɪdentɪd/. [1] ADJ If something is **unprecedented**, it has never happened before. *Such policies would require unprecedented cooperation between nations.* [2] ADJ If you describe something as **unprecedented**, you are emphasizing that it is very great in quality, amount, or scale. *...an unprecedented success.*

unpredictable /ˌʌnprɪ'dɪktəbəl/. ADJ If someone or something is **unpredictable**, you cannot tell what they are going to do or how they are going to behave. *...Britain's notoriously unpredictable weather.* ♦ **unpredictability** N-UNCOUNT *...his unpredictability and his tendency to make scandalous remarks.*

unprepared /ˌʌnprɪ'peəd/. [1] ADJ If you are **unprepared for** something, you are not ready for it, and are therefore surprised or at a disadvantage when it happens. *She was totally unprepared for the shattering news.* [2] ADJ If you are **unprepared to** do something, you are not willing to do it. *He was unprepared to co-operate.*

unproductive /ˌʌnprə'dʌktɪv/. ADJ Something that is **unproductive** does not produce anything useful. *...unproductive land. ...a busy but unproductive night.*

unprofitable /ʌn'prɒfɪtəbəl/. ADJ An industry, company, or product that is **unprofitable** does not make enough profit.

unprotected /ˌʌnprə'tektɪd/. [1] ADJ An **unprotected** person or place is not looked after or defended, and so they may be harmed or attacked. *Two-dozen soldiers raced down the hillside toward the unprotected camp.* [2] ADJ If something is **unprotected**, it is not covered or treated with anything, and so it may easily be damaged. *If we are unprotected from the sun for long enough, our skin will burn.*

unpublished /ˌʌn'pʌblɪʃt/. ADJ An **unpublished** book, letter, or report has never been published.

unqualified /ˌʌn'kwɒlɪfaɪd/. [1] ADJ If you are **unqualified**, you do not have any qualifications, or do not have the right qualifications for a particular job. [2] ADJ **Unqualified** means total, unlimited, and complete. *The event was an unqualified success.*

unquestionable /ʌn'kwestʃənəbəl/. ADJ If you describe something as **unquestionable**, you are emphasizing that it is so obviously true or real that nobody can doubt it. *His loyalty and*

a
b
c
d
e
f
g
h
i
j
k
l
m
n
o
p
q
r
s
t
u
v
w
x
y
z

devotion to the King were unquestionable.
♦ **unquestionably** ADV *The next two years were unquestionably the happiest of his life.*

unravel /ʌn'rævəl/ **unravels, unravelling, unravelled** (AM **unraveling, unraveled**). VERB If you **unravel** a mystery or puzzle, or if it **unravels**, it gradually becomes clearer and you can work out the answer to it. *Carter was still trying to unravel the truth of the woman's story.*

unreal /ˌʌn'riːl/. ADJ AFTER LINK-V If you say that a situation is **unreal**, you mean that it is so strange that you find it difficult to believe it is happening. ♦ **unreality** /ˌʌnri'æliti/ N-UNCOUNT *The rest of the weekend had a strange air of unreality.*

unrealistic /ˌʌnriə'lɪstɪk/. ADJ If you say that someone is being **unrealistic**, you mean that they do not recognize the truth about a situation, especially about the difficulties involved. *...their unrealistic expectations of parenthood.*

unreasonable /ʌn'riːzənəbəl/. **1** ADJ If you say that someone is being **unreasonable**, you mean that they are behaving in a way that is not fair or sensible. ♦ **unreasonably** ADV *We unreasonably expect near perfect behaviour from our children.* **2** ADJ An **unreasonable** decision, action, price, or amount seems unfair and difficult to justify. ♦ **unreasonably** ADV *The banks' charges are unreasonably high.*

unrelated /ˌʌnri'leɪtɪd/. ADJ If one thing is **unrelated to** another, there is no connection between them. *My line of work is unrelated to politics... Two of them died from apparently unrelated causes.*

unrelenting /ˌʌnri'lentɪŋ/. **1** ADJ If you describe someone's behaviour as **unrelenting**, you mean that they are continuing to do something in a very determined way. *She established her authority with unrelenting thoroughness.* **2** ADJ If you describe something unpleasant as **unrelenting**, you mean that it is continuing without stopping. *...the unrelenting pressures of his job.*

unreliable /ˌʌnri'laɪəbəl/. ADJ If you describe a person, machine, or method as **unreliable**, you mean that you cannot trust them to do or provide what you want. *The car was horribly slow and unreliable.*

unremarkable /ˌʌnri'mɑːkəbəl/. ADJ If you describe someone or something as **unremarkable**, you mean that they do not have many exciting, original, or attractive qualities. *...a tall, lean man, with an unremarkable face.*

unrepentant /ˌʌnri'pentənt/. ADJ If you are **unrepentant**, you are not ashamed of your beliefs or actions. *Pamela was unrepentant about her strong language.*

unresolved /ˌʌnri'zɒlvd/. ADJ If a problem or difficulty is **unresolved**, no satisfactory solution has been found to it. [FORMAL]

unrest /ʌn'rest/. N-UNCOUNT If there is **unrest** in a particular place or society, people are expressing anger and dissatisfaction, often by demonstrating or rioting. [JOURNALISM] *There is growing unrest among students in several major cities.*

unrestricted /ˌʌnri'strɪktɪd/. ADJ If an activity is **unrestricted**, you are free to do it in the way that you want, without being limited by any rules.

unrivalled (AM **unrivaled**) /ʌn'raɪvəld/. ADJ If you describe something as **unrivalled**, you are emphasizing that it is better than anything else of the same kind. *...an unrivalled knowledge of south Arabian society.*

unruly /ʌn'ruːli/. **1** ADJ If you describe people as **unruly**, you mean that they behave badly and are difficult to control. **2** ADJ **Unruly** hair is difficult to keep tidy.

unsafe /ʌn'seɪf/. **1** ADJ If a building, machine, activity, or area is **unsafe**, it is dangerous. *Critics claim the trucks are unsafe.* **2** ADJ AFTER LINK-V If you are **unsafe**, you are in danger of being harmed. *I felt very unsafe.*

unsatisfactory /ˌʌnsætɪs'fæktəri/. ADJ If you describe something as **unsatisfactory**, you mean that it is not as good as it should be, and cannot be considered acceptable. *...questions to which he received unsatisfactory answers.*

unsavoury (AM **unsavory**) /ʌn'seɪvəri/. ADJ If you describe someone or something as **unsavoury**, you mean that you find them unpleasant or morally unacceptable. *Mr King had written a string of unsavoury reports.*

unscathed /ʌn'skeɪðd/. ADJ If you are **unscathed** after a dangerous experience, you have not been injured or harmed by it.

unscrupulous /ʌn'skruːpjʊləs/. ADJ If you describe a person as **unscrupulous**, you are critical of the fact that they are prepared to act in a dishonest or immoral way in order to get what they want.

unseeded /ʌn'siːdɪd/. ADJ In sports competitions such as tennis or badminton, an **unseeded** player is someone who has not been ranked amongst the top players by the tournament's organizers.

unseen /ˌʌn'siːn/. ADJ You use **unseen** to describe things that you cannot see or have not seen. *There was barely time for the two boys to escape unseen. ...a spectacular ballroom, unseen by the public for over 30 years.*

unsettled /ʌn'setəld/. **1** ADJ In an **unsettled** situation, there is a lot of uncertainty about what will happen. *...Britain's unsettled political scene.* **2** ADJ AFTER LINK-V If you are **unsettled**, you cannot concentrate on anything, because you are worried. *To tell the truth, I'm a bit unsettled tonight.*

unsettling /ʌn'setəlɪŋ/. ADJ If you describe something as **unsettling**, you mean that it causes you to feel restless or rather worried. *His sense of humour was really unsettling.*

unsightly /ʌnˈsaɪtli/. ADJ If you describe something as **unsightly**, you mean that it is unattractive to look at. ...*an unsightly hole in the garden.*

unskilled /ˌʌnˈskɪld/. [1] ADJ People who are **unskilled** do not have any special training for a job. ...*work as an unskilled labourer.* [2] ADJ **Unskilled** work does not require any special training. ...*low-paid, unskilled jobs.*

unsolicited /ˌʌnsəˈlɪsɪtɪd/. ADJ Something that is **unsolicited** is given without being asked for and may not have been wanted. ...*unsolicited advice.*

unsolved /ˌʌnˈsɒlvd/. ADJ An **unsolved** problem or mystery has never been solved.

unspeakable /ʌnˈspiːkəbəl/. ADJ If you describe something as **unspeakable**, you are emphasizing that it is extremely unpleasant. ...*unspeakable horrors.* ♦ **unspeakably** /ʌnˈspiːkəbli/ ADV *unspeakably boring.*

unspecified /ʌnˈspesɪfaɪd/. ADJ You say that something is **unspecified** when you are not told exactly what it is. *He was arrested on unspecified charges.*

unspoiled /ˌʌnˈspɔɪld/ (BRIT also **unspoilt** /ˌʌnˈspɔɪlt/). ADJ If you describe a place as **unspoiled**, you think it is beautiful because it has not been changed or built on for a long time.

unspoken /ˌʌnˈspəʊkən/. ADJ If your thoughts or feelings are **unspoken**, you do not speak about them.

unstable /ˌʌnˈsteɪbəl/. [1] ADJ You can describe something as **unstable** if it is likely to change suddenly, especially if this creates difficulty. *The situation is unstable and potentially dangerous.* [2] ADJ **Unstable** objects are likely to move or fall. ...*unstable rock formations.* [3] ADJ If people are **unstable**, their emotions and behaviour keep changing because their minds are disturbed. *He was emotionally unstable.*

unsteady /ʌnˈstedi/. [1] ADJ If you are **unsteady**, you have difficulty doing something because you cannot completely control your body. *The boy was very unsteady and had staggered around when he got up.* ♦ **unsteadily** ADV *She pulled herself unsteadily from the bed.* [2] ADJ If you describe something as **unsteady**, you mean that it is not regular or stable. *His voice was unsteady and only just audible.* [3] ADJ **Unsteady** objects are not held, fixed, or balanced securely. ...*a slightly unsteady item of furniture.*

unsubscribe /ˌʌnsəbˈskraɪb/ **unsubscribes, unsubscribing, unsubscribed.** VERB If you **unsubscribe** from an online service, you send a message saying that you no longer wish to receive that service. [COMPUTING]

unsubstantiated /ˌʌnsəbˈstænʃieɪtɪd/. ADJ An **unsubstantiated** statement or story has not been proved true.

unsuccessful /ˌʌnsəkˈsesfʊl/. [1] ADJ Something that is **unsuccessful** does not achieve what it was intended to achieve. ...*a second unsuccessful operation on his knee.* ♦ **unsuccessfully** ADV *He has been trying unsuccessfully to sell the business.* [2] ADJ Someone who is **unsuccessful** does not achieve what they intended to achieve. *He and his friend Boris were unsuccessful in getting a job.*

unsuitable /ˌʌnˈsuːtəbəl/. ADJ Someone or something that is **unsuitable** for a particular purpose or situation does not have the right qualities for it. *Amy's shoes were unsuitable for walking.*

unsure /ˌʌnˈʃʊə/. [1] ADJ If you are **unsure of yourself**, you lack confidence. *He made her feel hot, and awkward, and unsure of herself.* [2] ADJ AFTER LINK-V If you are **unsure about** something, you feel uncertain about it. *Fifty-two per cent were unsure about the idea.*

unsuspecting /ˌʌnsəˈspektɪŋ/. ADJ You can use **unsuspecting** to describe someone who is not aware of something that is happening or going to happen. ...*his unsuspecting victim.*

unsympathetic /ˌʌnsɪmpəˈθetɪk/. [1] ADJ If someone is **unsympathetic**, they are not kind or helpful to a person in difficulties. *Her husband was unsympathetic and she felt she had no one to turn to.* [2] ADJ An **unsympathetic** person is unpleasant and difficult to like. ...*a very unsympathetic main character.*

untenable /ˌʌnˈtenəbəl/. ADJ An argument or position that is **untenable** cannot be defended successfully against criticism or attack. *He claimed the charges against him were untenable.*

unthinkable /ʌnˈθɪŋkəbəl/. [1] ADJ & N-SING If you say that something is **unthinkable**, you mean that it cannot possibly be accepted or imagined as a possibility. **The unthinkable** is something that is unthinkable. *Any thought of splitting up the company was unthinkable... The unthinkable had happened – a power failure.* [2] ADJ You can use **unthinkable** to describe a situation or event which is extremely unpleasant to imagine or remember. *This place is going to be unthinkable without you.*

untidy /ʌnˈtaɪdi/ **untidier, untidiest.** [1] ADJ Something that is **untidy** is messy, and not neatly arranged. *Clothes were thrown in the luggage in an untidy heap.* ♦ **untidily** ADV *Her long hair tumbles untidily around her shoulders.* [2] ADJ If you describe a person as **untidy**, you mean that they do not care about whether things are neat and well arranged.

untie /ˌʌnˈtaɪ/ **unties, untying, untied.** [1] VERB If you **untie** something that is tied to another thing, or if you **untie** two things that are tied together, you remove the string or rope that holds them. *Just untie my hands.* [2] VERB If you **untie** something such as string or rope, you undo the knot in it.

⭐ **until** /ʌnˈtɪl/. [1] PREP & CONJ If something happens **until** a particular time, it happens during the period before that time and stops at that time. *I waited until it got dark.* [2] PREP & CONJ

a
b
c
d
e
f
g
h
i
j
k
l
m
n
o
p
q
r
s
t
u
v
w
x
y
z

untold

If something does not happen **until** a particular time, it does not happen before that time and only happens after it. *The traffic laws don't take effect until the end of the year.*

> **USAGE** Note that you only use **until** or **till** when you are talking about time. You do not use these words to talk about place or position. Instead, you should use **as far as** or **up to**. *Then you'll be riding with us as far as the village?... We walked up to where his bicycle was.*

untold /ˌʌnˈtəʊld/. **1** ADJ BEFORE N You can use **untold** to emphasize how unpleasant something is. *This might do untold damage to her health.* **2** ADJ BEFORE N You can use **untold** to emphasize that an amount or quantity is very large, especially when you are not sure how large it is. *An Olympic gold medal can lead to untold riches for an athlete.*

untouched /ˌʌnˈtʌtʃt/. **1** ADJ Something that is **untouched** has not been changed or damaged in any way. *The western part of the island is still untouched by tourism... There was one building that remained untouched.* **2** ADJ If food or drink is **untouched**, none of it has been eaten or drunk. *The coffee was untouched.*

untrained /ˌʌnˈtreɪnd/. **1** ADJ Someone who is **untrained** has not been taught the skills that they need for a particular job. **2** ADJ You use **untrained** with words like 'eye' and 'ear' to describe how something seems to someone who is not an expert. *They don't look very different to the untrained eye.*

untreated /ˌʌnˈtriːtɪd/. **1** ADJ If an injury or illness is left **untreated**, it is not given medical treatment. **2** ADJ **Untreated** materials, water, or chemicals are harmful and have not been made safe.

untrue /ˌʌnˈtruː/. ADJ Something that is **untrue** is not true. *Such remarks are both offensive and untrue.*

unused. **1** ADJ /ʌnˈjuːzd/ Something that is **unused** has not been used or is not being used at the moment. *Any unused land should return to farm land.* **2** ADJ AFTER LINK-V /ʌnˈjuːst/ If you are **unused to** something, you have not often done it or experienced it. *He was unused to having his speeches interrupted.*

⭐ **unusual** /ʌnˈjuːʒəl/. ADJ If something is **unusual**, it does not happen very often or you do not see it or hear it very often. *It's very unusual for him to make a mistake. ...rare and unusual plants.* ♦ **unusually** ADV *...an unusually harsh winter.*

unveil /ʌnˈveɪl/ **unveils, unveiling, unveiled. 1** VERB If someone **unveils** something such as a new statue or painting, they draw back the curtain which is covering it, in a special ceremony. **2** VERB If you **unveil** something that has been kept secret, you make it known to the public. *The company unveiled plans to open 100 new stores.*

unwanted /ˌʌnˈwɒntɪd/. ADJ You say that something is **unwanted** when someone does not want it. *...unwanted pregnancies... Every year thousands of unwanted animals are abandoned.*

unwarranted /ʌnˈwɒrəntɪd, AM -ˈwɔːr-/. ADJ Something that is **unwarranted** is not justified or deserved. [FORMAL] *He accused the police of using unwarranted brutality.*

unwelcome /ʌnˈwelkəm/. **1** ADJ An **unwelcome** experience is one that you do not like and did not want. *The media has brought more unwelcome attention to the Royal Family.* **2** ADJ If a visitor is **unwelcome**, you did not want them to come. *She was, quite deliberately, making him feel unwelcome.*

unwell /ˌʌnˈwel/. ADJ AFTER LINK-V If you are **unwell**, you are ill. *Mrs Potter was too unwell to go with him.*

unwieldy /ʌnˈwiːldi/. **1** ADJ An **unwieldy** object is difficult to move or carry because it is big or heavy. **2** ADJ An **unwieldy** system does not work well because it is too large or is badly organized. *...France's unwieldy welfare system.*

unwilling /ˌʌnˈwɪlɪŋ/. ADJ If you are **unwilling to** do something, you do not want to do it. *He was unwilling to discuss the matter.*
♦ **unwillingly** ADV *Unwillingly, she moved aside.*
♦ **unwillingness** N-UNCOUNT *...the unwillingness of banks to grant loans.*

unwind /ˌʌnˈwaɪnd/ **unwinds, unwinding, unwound. 1** VERB When you **unwind** after working hard, you relax. *It is the perfect place to unwind.* **2** VERB If you **unwind** something that is wrapped round something else, you undo it or straighten it out.

unwise /ˌʌnˈwaɪz/. ADJ Something that is **unwise** is foolish. *It would be unwise to expect too much.* ♦ **unwisely** ADV *She had acted unwisely.*

unwitting /ʌnˈwɪtɪŋ/. ADJ If you describe a person or their actions as **unwitting**, you mean that the person does something or is involved in something without realizing it. *It had been an unwitting blunder on Blair's part.* ♦ **unwittingly** ADV *...a woman who had unwittingly bought a stolen car.*

unworkable /ˌʌnˈwɜːkəbəl/. ADJ If an idea or plan is **unworkable**, it cannot succeed. *This proposal would be unworkable.*

unworthy /ʌnˈwɜːði/. **1** ADJ If someone is **unworthy of** something, they do not deserve it. [LITERARY] *She felt unworthy of any respect.* **2** ADJ If you say that an action is **unworthy of** someone, you mean that it is not a nice thing to do and someone with their reputation or position should not do it. *His accusations are unworthy of a prime minister.*

unwound /ˌʌnˈwaʊnd/. **Unwound** is the past tense and past participle of **unwind**.

unwrap /ˌʌnˈræp/ **unwraps, unwrapping, unwrapped.** VERB When you **unwrap** something, you take off the paper or covering that is around it.

unwritten /ˌʌnˈrɪtən/. ADJ **Unwritten** things

have not been printed or written down. *The book he had meant to write remained unwritten.*

unzip /ˌʌnˈzɪp/ **unzips, unzipping, unzipped.** 1 VERB To **unzip** something such as an item of clothing or bag means to unfasten its zip. *She unzipped her coat.* 2 VERB To **unzip** a computer file means to open a file that has been compressed. [COMPUTING] *Unzip the icons into a sub-directory.*

up 1 preposition, adverb, and adjective uses

⭐ **up** /ʌp/ **ups.** 1 PREP & ADV **Up** means towards a higher place, or in a higher place. *I ran up the stairs... The Newton Hotel is halfway up a steep hill... He put his hand up.* 2 ADV If someone stands **up**, they move so that they are standing. *He got up and went out into the foyer.* 3 ADV **Up** means in the north or towards the north. *Mark was travelling up to London by train.* 4 PREP If you go **up** something such as a road or river, you go along it. *A line of tanks came up the road.* 5 ADV If you go **up to** something or someone, you move to the place where they are and stop there. *The girl ran up to the car... A boy of about ten came up on roller skates.* 6 ADJ AFTER LINK-V If you are **up**, you are not in bed. *He was up at 6am.* 7 ADV If an amount goes **up**, it increases. If an amount of something is **up**, it is at a higher level than it was. *They recently put my rent up.* 8 ADJ AFTER LINK-V If a period of time is **up**, it has come to an end. *When the six weeks were up, everybody was sad that she had to leave.*

PHRASES ● If you move **up and down**, you move repeatedly in one direction and then in the opposite direction. *Her son started to jump up and down... I strolled up and down thoughtfully before calling a taxi.* ● If you have **ups and downs**, you experience a mixture of good things and bad things. *Every relationship has a lot of ups and downs.* ● If you are **up against** something, you have a difficult situation or problem to deal with. *They were up against a good team but did very well.* ● If someone or something is **up for** discussion, election, or review, they are about to be considered or judged. *The whole question of school curriculum is up for discussion.* ● You use **up to** to say how large something can be or what level it has reached. *...up to twenty thousand students... It could be up to two years before the process is complete.* ● If you do not feel **up to** doing something, you do not feel well enough to do it. ● If you say that it is **up to** someone to do a particular thing, you mean that it is their responsibility to do it. *It is up to you to tell them.* ● If something happens **up to** or **up until** a particular time, it happens until that time. *Please feel free to call me any time up until half past nine.*

up 2 verb uses

up /ʌp/ **ups, upping, upped.** VERB If you **up** something such as the amount of money you are offering for something, you increase it. *We are talking about upping everybody's pay.*

ˌ**up-and-ˈcoming.** ADJ BEFORE N **Up-and-coming** people are likely to be successful in the future.

upbeat /ˈʌpbiːt/. ADJ If you describe someone as **upbeat**, you mean they are cheerful and optimistic about a situation. [INFORMAL] *Ann was in an upbeat mood.*

upbringing /ˈʌpbrɪŋɪŋ/. N-UNCOUNT Your **upbringing** is the way your parents treat you and the things that they teach you. *Her son had a good upbringing.*

update,updates, updating, updated. 1 VERB /ʌpˈdeɪt/ If you **update** something, you make it more modern, usually by adding newer parts to it. *...an updated edition of the book.* 2 N-COUNT /ˈʌpdeɪt/ An **update** is a news item which has been rewritten so that it includes the latest developments in a situation.

ˌ**up ˈfront** (or **upfront**). 1 ADV If a payment is made **up front**, it is made in advance , so that the person being paid can be sure that they will be paid. *Some companies charge a fee up front.* 2 ADJ If you are **up front about** something, you act openly or publicly so that people know what you are doing or what you believe. *I'm very upfront about being happily married.*

upgrade /ˌʌpˈɡreɪd/ **upgrades, upgrading, upgraded.** VERB & N-COUNT To **upgrade** something, or to give it an **upgrade**, means to change it so that it is more important or better. *...upgraded catering facilities. ...an upgrade of the sports facilities.*

upheaval /ʌpˈhiːvəl/ **upheavals.** N-VAR An **upheaval** is a big change which causes a lot of trouble and confusion. *Algeria has been going through political upheaval for the past two months.*

upheld /ʌpˈheld/. **Upheld** is the past tense and past participle of **uphold**.

uphill /ˌʌpˈhɪl/. 1 ADV & ADJ If you go **uphill**, you go up a slope. *We walked uphill in single file. ...a long, uphill journey.* 2 ADJ BEFORE N If you refer to something as an **uphill** struggle, you mean that it requires a great deal of effort and determination.

uphold /ʌpˈhəʊld/ **upholds, upholding, upheld.** VERB If you **uphold** a law, principle, or decision, you support and maintain it.

upholstery /ʌpˈhəʊlstəri/. N-UNCOUNT **Upholstery** is the soft covering on chairs and sofas that makes them comfortable.

upkeep /ˈʌpkiːp/. 1 N-UNCOUNT The **upkeep** of a building or place is the continual process of keeping it in good condition. *The maintenance department is responsible for the general upkeep of the park.* 2 N-UNCOUNT The **upkeep** of a group of people or services is the process of providing them with the things that they need. *He offered to pay £100 a month towards his son's upkeep.*

uplifting /ʌpˈlɪftɪŋ/. ADJ If something is **uplifting**, it makes you feel cheerful and happy. *...a very uplifting experience.*

upmarket /ˌʌpˈmɑːkɪt/. ADJ **Upmarket** places or products are intended to appeal to people with sophisticated and expensive tastes. [BRITISH] *...an upmarket hotel.*

a b c d e f g h i j k l m n o p q r s t u v w x y z

A

B

C

D

E

F

G

H

I

J

K

L

M

N

O

P

Q

R

S

T

U

V

W

X

Y

Z

⭐ **upon** /ə'pɒn/. **1** PREP If one thing is **upon** another, it is on it. [FORMAL] *He set the tray upon the table... I imagined the eyes of the others in the room upon me.* **2** PREP You use **upon** when mentioning an event that is followed immediately by another. *Upon leaving the club, he collapsed.* **3** PREP You use **upon** between two occurrences of the same noun in order to say that there are large numbers of the thing mentioned. *...row upon row of women.* **4** PREP If an event is **upon** you, it is just about to happen. *The football season is upon us.*

⭐ **upper** /'ʌpə/. **1** ADJ You use **upper** to describe something that is above something else. *...a smart restaurant on the upper floor.* **2** ADJ The **upper** part of something is the higher part. *...the upper rungs of the ladder.* **3** PHRASE If you have **the upper hand** in a situation, you have more power than the other people involved and can make decisions about what happens.

,**upper 'class, upper classes.** N-COUNT & ADJ The **upper class** or **the upper classes** are the group of people in a society who own the most property and have the highest social status. You say people like this are **upper class**. *...wealthy, upper class families.*

upright /'ʌpraɪt/. **1** ADJ If you are sitting or standing **upright**, you have your back straight and are not bending or lying down. *The wind was so strong I couldn't stand upright.* **2** ADJ You can describe people as **upright** when they are careful to follow acceptable rules of behaviour and behave in a moral way. *...an upright citizen.*

uprising /'ʌpraɪzɪŋ/ **uprisings.** N-COUNT When there is an **uprising**, a group of people start fighting against the people who are in power in their country.

uproar /'ʌprɔː/. **1** N-UNCOUNT & N-SING An **uproar** is a lot of shouting and noise because people are very angry or upset about something. **2** N-UNCOUNT & N-SING An **uproar** is a lot of public criticism and debate about something that has made people angry. *...last year's uproar over school spending cuts.*

uproot /ʌp'ruːt/ **uproots, uprooting, uprooted.** **1** VERB If you **uproot yourself**, or if you **are uprooted**, you leave or are made to leave a place where you have lived for a long time. *He was not prepared to uproot his family from the Midlands.* **2** VERB If someone **uproots** a tree or plant, or if the wind **uproots** it, it is pulled out of the ground.

⭐ **upset, upsets, upsetting, upset;** verb and adjective /ʌp'set/, noun /'ʌpset/. **1** ADJ If you are **upset**, you are unhappy or disappointed because something unpleasant has happened. *They are terribly upset by the break-up of their parents' marriage.* **2** VERB If something **upsets** you, it makes you feel worried or unhappy. *I'm sorry if I've upset you.* ◆ **upsetting** ADJ *The whole incident was very upsetting.* **3** VERB If events **upset** something such as a procedure or a state of affairs, they cause it to go wrong. *Political problems could upset agreements between*

Moscow and Kabul. **4** N-COUNT & ADJ BEFORE N If you have a **stomach upset**, or if you have an **upset stomach**, you have a slight illness in your stomach caused by an infection or by something that you have eaten.

upside down (or **upside-down**) /,ʌpsaɪd 'daʊn/. **1** ADV & ADJ If something has been put **upside down**, it has been turned round so that the part that is usually lowest is above the part that is usually highest. *The painting was hung upside down. ...an upside-down map of Britain.* **2** PHRASE If you **turn** a place **upside down**, you move everything around and make it untidy, because you are looking for something.

upstage /,ʌp'steɪdʒ/ **upstages, upstaging, upstaged.** VERB To **upstage** someone is to draw attention away from them by being more attractive or interesting.

upstairs /,ʌp'steəz/. **1** ADV If you go **upstairs** in a building, you go up a staircase towards a higher floor. *Maureen ran upstairs to her bedroom.* **2** ADV & ADJ If something or someone is **upstairs** in a building, they are on a floor that is higher than the ground floor. *There is another bar upstairs. ...the upstairs apartment.* **3** N-SING The **upstairs** of a building is the floor or floors that are higher than the ground floor.

upstart /'ʌpstɑːt/ **upstarts.** N-COUNT You can refer to someone as an **upstart** when they behave as if they are important, but you think that they are too new in a place or job to be treated as important.

upstream /,ʌp'striːm/. ADV & ADJ Something that is moving **upstream** is moving along a river towards the source of the river. Something that is **upstream** is towards the source of a river. *He lives about 60 miles upstream from Oahe.*

upsurge /'ʌpsɜːdʒ/. N-SING If there is an **upsurge in** something, there is a sudden large increase in it. [FORMAL] *...the upsurge in oil prices.*

uptight /,ʌp'taɪt/. ADJ If someone is **uptight**, they are very tense, because they are worried or annoyed about something. [INFORMAL]

,**up-to-'date** (or **up to date**). **1** ADJ If something is **up-to-date**, it is the newest thing of its kind. *...Germany's most up to date electric power station.* **2** ADJ If you are **up-to-date with** something, you have the latest information about it.

uptown /,ʌp'taʊn/. ADV & ADJ BEFORE N If you go **uptown**, or go to a place **uptown**, you go away from the centre of a town or city towards one of its suburbs. [AMERICAN] *Susan continued to live uptown. ...uptown New Orleans.*

upturn /'ʌptɜːn/ **upturns.** N-COUNT If there is an **upturn in** the economy or in a company or industry, it becomes more successful.

upwards /'ʌpwədz/.

✓ In British English, **upwards** is an adverb and **upward** is an adjective. In formal British English and in American English, **upward** is both an adjective and an adverb.

1 ADV & ADJ BEFORE N If you move or look **upwards**, you move or look up towards a higher place. *They climbed upward along the steep cliffs surrounding the village... Lie face upwards with a cushion under your head... She started once again on the steep upward climb.* **2** ADV If an amount or rate moves **upwards**, it increases. *The share price is likely to leap upwards.* **3** PREP A quantity that is **upwards of** a particular number is more than that number. *...projects worth upwards of 200 million pounds.*

uranium /jʊˈreɪniəm/. N-UNCOUNT **Uranium** is a radioactive metal that is used to produce nuclear energy and weapons.

⭐ **urban** /ˈɜːbən/. ADJ **Urban** means belonging to, or relating to, a town or city. *...densely populated urban areas.*

⭐ **urge** /ɜːdʒ/ **urges, urging, urged.** **1** VERB If you **urge** someone **to** do something, you try hard to persuade them to do it. *He had urged her to come to Ireland... 'Now read,' I urged.* **2** N-COUNT If you have an **urge to** do or have something, you have a strong wish to do or have it. *The urge to have children was beginning to take over her life. ...his urge for revenge.*

▸ **urge on.** PHR-VERB If you **urge** someone **on**, you encourage them to do something. *Urged on by his strong-willed mother, he set out to become a doctor.*

⭐ **urgent** /ˈɜːdʒənt/. **1** ADJ If something is **urgent**, it needs to be dealt with as soon as possible. *...an urgent need for food and water... He had urgent business in New York.* ♦ **urgency** N-UNCOUNT *It is a matter of utmost urgency.* ♦ **urgently** ADV *An alternative road is urgently needed.* **2** ADJ If you speak in an **urgent** way, you show that you are anxious for people to notice something or do something. ♦ **urgency** N-UNCOUNT *She was surprised at the urgency in his voice.* ♦ **urgently** ADV *'Are you still there?' Jerrold asked urgently.*

urinate /ˈjʊərɪneɪt/ **urinates, urinating, urinated.** VERB When you **urinate**, you get rid of urine from your body.

urine /ˈjʊərɪn/. N-UNCOUNT **Urine** is the liquid that you get rid of from your body when you go to the toilet.

URL /ˌjuː ɑː ˈel/ **URLs.** N-COUNT A **URL** is an address that shows where a particular page can be found on the World Wide Web. **URL** is an abbreviation for 'Uniform Resource Locator'. [COMPUTING] *The URL of the Lonely Planet travel centre is http://www.lonelyplanet.com.*

urn /ɜːn/ **urns.** **1** N-COUNT An **urn** is a container like a large vase, especially one in which the ashes of a cremated person are kept. **2** N-COUNT An **urn** is a metal container used for making a large quantity of tea or coffee and keeping it hot.

⭐ **us** /əs, STRONG ʌs/. PRON A speaker or writer uses **us** to refer to a group of people which includes himself or herself. *Neither of us forgot about it... He told us we had to leave Delhi by 7am.*

usable /ˈjuːzəbəl/. ADJ If something is **usable**, it is in a good enough state or condition to be used. *There is very little usable land left.*

usage /ˈjuːsɪdʒ/. **1** N-UNCOUNT **Usage** is the way in which words are actually used in particular contexts, especially with regard to their meanings. *...an Australian Guide to Modern English Usage.* **2** N-UNCOUNT **Usage** is the degree to which something is used or the way in which it is used. *The motor wore out because of constant usage.*

use 1 verb uses

⭐ **use** /juːz/ **uses, using, used.** **1** VERB If you **use** a particular thing, you do something with it in order to do a job or to achieve something. *May I use your phone?... Use a very sharp knife to cut the beef... He had never used violence.* **2** VERB & PHR-VERB If you **use** a supply of something, or if you **use** it **up**, you finish it so that none of it is left. *It isn't them who use up the world's resources.* **3** VERB If you **use** a particular word or expression, you say or write it. **4** VERB If you say that someone **uses** people, you disapprove of them because they are only interested in other people when they can benefit from them.

use 2 noun uses

⭐ **use** /juːs/ **uses.** **1** N-UNCOUNT Your **use of** something is the action or fact of your using it. *...the use of any artificial drugs. ...microcomputers and their use in classrooms.* **2** N-VAR If something has a particular **use**, it is intended for a particular purpose. *Infrared detectors have many uses... They both loved the fabric, but couldn't find a use for it.* **3** N-UNCOUNT If you have the **use of** something, you have the permission or ability to use it. *They had regular use of a car... Crippled by polio in 1921, he had lost the use of his legs.* **4** N-COUNT A **use** of a word is a particular meaning that it has or a particular way in which it can be used.

PHRASES ● If something such as a technique, building, or machine is **in use**, it is used regularly. If it has gone **out of use**, it is no longer used regularly. ● If you **make use of** something, you do something with it in order to do a job or achieve something. *I shall make use of this time to see to the washing.* ● You use expressions such as **it's no use**, **there's no use** and **what's the use** to indicate that an action will not achieve anything. *It's no use arguing with a drunk.*

used 1 modal uses and phrases

⭐ **used** /juːst/. **1** MODAL If something **used to** be done or **used to** be the case, it was done regularly in the past or was the case in the past. *People used to come and visit him every day... The gallery in north London used to be a warehouse.* **2** PHRASE If you **are used to** something, you are familiar with it because you have done it or experienced it many times before. If you **get**

a
b
c
d
e
f
g
h
i
j
k
l
m
n
o
p
q
r
s
t
u
v
w
x
y
z

A B C D E F G H I J K L M N O P Q R S T U V W X Y Z

used to something, you become familiar with it. *I'm used to having my sleep interrupted.*

used 2 adjective uses

used /juːzd/. **1** ADJ A **used** handkerchief, glass, or other object is dirty or spoiled because it has been used. **2** ADJ A **used** car has already had one or more owners.

⭐ **useful** /ˈjuːsfʊl/. **1** ADJ If something is **useful**, you can use it to do something or to help you. *...useful information.* ◆ **usefully** ADV *...the problems to which computers could be usefully applied.* ◆ **usefulness** N-UNCOUNT *...the usefulness of his work.* **2** PHRASE If an object or skill **comes in useful**, it can help you achieve something in a particular situation.

useless /ˈjuːsləs/. **1** ADJ If something is **useless**, you cannot use it. *Their money was useless in this country.* **2** ADJ If a course of action is **useless**, it does not achieve anything. *She knew it was useless to protest.* **3** ADJ If you say that someone or something is **useless**, you mean that they are no good at all. [INFORMAL] *He was useless at any game with a ball.*

⭐ **user** /ˈjuːzə/ **users.** N-COUNT The **users** of a product, machine, service, or place are the people who use it. *Beach users have complained that the bikes are noisy.*

user-'friendly. ADJ If you describe something such as a machine or system as **user-friendly**, you mean that it is well designed and easy to use.

usher /ˈʌʃə/ **ushers, ushering, ushered.** **1** VERB If you **usher** someone somewhere, you show them where they should go, often by going with them. *I ushered him into the office.* **2** N-COUNT An **usher** is a person who shows people where they are going to sit, for example at a wedding or concert. ▸**usher in.** PHR-VERB If a person or event **ushers in** an important change, they help make it happen. [JOURNALISM] *...a unique opportunity to usher in a new era of stability in Europe.*

⭐ **usual** /ˈjuːʒʊəl/. ADJ **Usual** is used to describe what happens or what is done most often in a particular situation. *An officer was asking the usual questions... The winter has been colder than usual... It is usual to tip waiters.*

PHRASES ● You use **as usual** to indicate that you are describing something that normally happens or that is normally the case. *As usual when he was nervous, his stomach began to rumble.* ● If something happens **as usual**, it happens in the way that it normally does. *When somebody died everything went on as usual.*

⭐ **usually** /ˈjuːʒʊəli/. ADV If something **usually** happens, it is the thing that most often happens in a particular situation. *We usually eat in here.*

usurp /juːˈzɜːp/ **usurps, usurping, usurped.** VERB If you say that someone **usurps** a job, role, title, or position, you mean that they take it from someone when they have no right to do this. [FORMAL]

utensil /juːˈtensəl/ **utensils.** N-COUNT **Utensils** are

tools or other objects that you use when you are cooking or doing other tasks in your home. → See pictures on page 825. *...aluminium cooking utensils.*

uterus /ˈjuːtərəs/ **uteruses.** N-COUNT A woman's **uterus** is her womb. [TECHNICAL]

utilise /ˈjuːtɪlaɪz/. See **utilize**.

utilitarian /ˌjuːtɪlɪˈteəriən/. ADJ **Utilitarian** objects and buildings are designed to be useful rather than beautiful.

utility /juːˈtɪlɪti/ **utilities.** **1** N-COUNT A **utility** is an important service such as water, electricity, or gas that is provided for everyone, and that everyone pays for. **2** N-UNCOUNT The **utility** of something is its usefulness. [FORMAL] *He inwardly questioned the utility of his work.*

utilize (BRIT also **utilise**) /ˈjuːtɪlaɪz/ **utilizes, utilizing, utilized.** VERB If you **utilize** something, you use it. [FORMAL] *...ways in which her skill and experience could be utilized.* ◆ **utilization** N-UNCOUNT *...the utilisation of human resources.*

utmost /ˈʌtməʊst/. **1** ADJ BEFORE N You can use **utmost** to emphasize the importance or seriousness of something or to emphasize the way that it is done. [FORMAL] *I have a matter of the utmost urgency to discuss with you... Utmost care must be taken not to spill any of the contents.* **2** N-SING If you say that you are doing your **utmost to** do something, you are emphasizing that you are trying as hard as you can to do it. *He will try his utmost to help them.*

utopia /juːˈtəʊpiə/ **utopias.** N-VAR If you refer to an imaginary situation as a **utopia**, you mean that it is one in which society is perfect and everyone is happy, but which you feel is not possible.

utopian /juːˈtəʊpiən/. ADJ If you describe a plan or idea as **utopian**, you are criticizing it because it is unrealistic and shows a belief that things can be improved much more than is possible.

utter /ˈʌtə/ **utters, uttering, uttered.** **1** VERB If someone **utters** sounds or words, they say them. [LITERARY] *They departed without uttering a word.* **2** ADJ BEFORE N You use **utter** to emphasize the great degree or amount of something bad. *This is utter nonsense. ...this utter lack of responsibility.*

utterance /ˈʌtərəns/ **utterances.** N-COUNT Someone's **utterances** are the things that they say. [FORMAL] *...the Queen's public utterances.*

utterly /ˈʌtəli/. ADV You use **utterly** to emphasize the great degree or amount of something bad. *The new laws coming in are utterly ridiculous.*

'U-turn, U-turns. **1** N-COUNT If you make a **U-turn** when you are driving or cycling, you turn in a half circle in one movement, so that you are then going in the opposite direction. **2** N-COUNT When a government does a **U-turn**, it abandons a policy and does something completely different.

V v

V, v /viː/. **V** or **v** is an abbreviation of **versus**. It is used to indicate that two teams are competing against each other. ...*Newcastle United v Leicester City.*

vacancy /'veɪkənsi/ **vacancies.** **1** N-COUNT A **vacancy** is a job or position which has not been filled. *We have a vacancy for an editorial assistant.* **2** N-COUNT If there are **vacancies** at a hotel, there are rooms still available for people to stay in.

vacant /'veɪkənt/. **1** ADJ If something is **vacant**, it is not being used by anyone. ...*a vacant seat.* **2** ADJ If a job or position is **vacant**, it has not yet been filled, and people can apply for it. *The post has been vacant since June.* **3** ADJ A **vacant** look suggests that someone does not understand or that they are not concentrating. ♦ **vacantly** ADV *He looked vacantly out of the window.*

vacate /veɪ'keɪt, AM 'veɪkeɪt/ **vacates, vacating, vacated.** VERB If you **vacate** a place or a job, you leave it and make it available for other people. [FORMAL] *He vacated the flat and went to stay with an uncle.*

vacation /və'keɪʃən, AM veɪ-/ **vacations.** **1** N-VAR In American English, a **vacation** is a period of time when you are not working and are away from home for relaxation. The British word is **holiday**. *We went on vacation to Puerto Rico.* **2** N-COUNT A **vacation** is a period of the year when universities or colleges are officially closed. *During his summer vacation he visited Russia.*

vaccinate /'væksɪneɪt/ **vaccinates, vaccinating, vaccinated.** VERB If a person or animal is **vaccinated**, they are given a vaccine, usually by injection, to prevent them from getting a disease. *Have you had your child vaccinated against whooping cough?* ♦ **vaccination, vaccinations** N-VAR *Consider getting a vaccination.*

vaccine /'væksiːn, AM væk'siːn/ **vaccines.** N-VAR A **vaccine** is a substance containing the germs that cause a disease. It is given to people to prevent them getting the disease.

vacuum /'vækjuːm, -juːəm/ **vacuums, vacuuming, vacuumed.** **1** N-COUNT If someone or something creates a **vacuum**, they leave a place or position which then needs to be filled by someone or something else. *The collapse of the army left a vacuum in the area.* **2** N-COUNT A **vacuum** is a space that contains no air or other gas. **3** VERB If you **vacuum** something, you clean it using a vacuum cleaner.

'vacuum cleaner, vacuum cleaners. N-COUNT A **vacuum cleaner** or a **vacuum** is an electric machine which sucks up dust and dirt from floors and carpets.

vagary /'veɪgəri/ **vagaries.** N-COUNT The **vagaries of** something are the unexpected and unpredictable changes in it. [FORMAL] ...*the vagaries of the weather.*

vagina /və'dʒaɪnə/ **vaginas.** N-COUNT A woman's **vagina** is the passage connecting her outer sex organs to her womb. ♦ **vaginal** ADJ BEFORE N ...*vaginal infections.*

vague /veɪg/ **vaguer, vaguest.** **1** ADJ If something is **vague**, it is not clear, distinct, or definite. You can also say that someone is **vague** about something. *The description was pretty vague... They have only a vague idea of the amount of water available.* ♦ **vaguely** ADV *Judith could vaguely remember her mother lying on the sofa.* **2** ADJ If you describe someone as **vague**, you mean that they do not seem to be thinking clearly. ♦ **vaguely** ADV *He looked vaguely around the room.* **3** ADJ A **vague** shape or outline is not clear or easy to see.

vaguely /'veɪgli/. ADV **Vaguely** means to a small degree. *The voice on the line was vaguely familiar to me.*

vain /veɪn/ **vainer, vainest.** **1** ADJ BEFORE N & PHRASE A **vain** attempt to do something does not succeed. If you do something **in vain**, what you do has no effect. *He searched everywhere in the vain hope that he had simply mislaid it... It became obvious that all her complaints were in vain.* ♦ **vainly** ADV *He hunted vainly through his pockets for a piece of paper.* **2** ADJ If you describe someone as **vain**, you disapprove of them because they are too proud of their appearance.

valiant /'væliənt/. ADJ **Valiant** means very brave. ♦ **valiantly** ADV *They have fought valiantly to defend her freedom.*

valid /'vælɪd/. **1** ADJ A **valid** reason or argument is logical and reasonable, and therefore worth taking seriously. *He recognized the valid points that both sides were making.* ♦ **validity** /və'lɪdɪti/ N-UNCOUNT *This argument has lost much of its validity.* **2** ADJ If a ticket or document is **valid**, it can be used and will be accepted by people in authority. *You will need a valid passport.*

validate /'vælɪdeɪt/ **validates, validating, validated.** VERB To **validate** a statement or claim means to prove that it is true or correct. *This discovery seems to validate the claims of popular astrology.* ♦ **validation, validations** N-VAR *There had been no recent assessment or validation of the allegations.*

 valley /'væli/ **valleys.** N-COUNT A **valley** is a low area of land between hills, often with a river flowing through it.

 valuable /'væljuəbəl/. **1** ADJ Something that is **valuable** is very useful. ...*the valuable contribution of ambulancemen to patient care.* **2** ADJ **Valuable** objects are worth a lot of money. ...*valuable books.*

A

valuables /'væljuəbəlz/. N-PLURAL **Valuables** are things that you own that are worth a lot of money, especially small objects such as jewellery.

B

valuation /ˌvæljʊ'eɪʃən/ **valuations.** N-VAR A **valuation** is a judgement about how much money something is worth. ...*an independent valuation of the company.*

C

⭐ **value** /'vælju:/ **values, valuing, valued.**
1 N-UNCOUNT The **value** of something such as a quality or a method is its importance or usefulness. *The value of this work experience should not be underestimated.* **2** VERB If you **value** someone or something, you think that they are important and you appreciate them. *She genuinely values his opinion.* **3** N-VAR The **value** of something is the amount of money it is worth. *The company's market value rose to $5.5 billion... Italy's currency went down in value by 3.5 per cent. ...land of little value.* **4** VERB When experts **value** something, they decide how much money it is worth. ...*cocaine valued at around $53 million.* **5** N-UNCOUNT A thing's **value** is its worth in relation to the money that it costs. *Scottish salmon is excellent value for money.* **6** N-PLURAL The **values** of a person or group are their moral principles and beliefs. ...*traditional family values.* **7** See also **face value.**

D

E

F

G

valve /vælv/ **valves.** N-COUNT A **valve** is a device which controls the flow of a gas or liquid, for example in a pipe or tube.

H

vampire /'væmpaɪə/ **vampires.** N-COUNT In horror stories, **vampires** are creature who come out of their graves at night and suck the blood of living people.

I

J

⭐ **van** /væn/ **vans.** N-COUNT A **van** is a medium-sized road vehicle that is used for carrying goods. → See picture on page 834.

K

vandal /'vændəl/ **vandals.** N-COUNT A **vandal** is someone who deliberately damages things, especially public property.

L

vandalism /'vændəlɪzəm/. N-UNCOUNT **Vandalism** is the deliberate damaging of things, especially public property.

M

vandalize (BRIT also **vandalise**) /'vændəlaɪz/ **vandalizes, vandalizing, vandalized.** VERB If something **is vandalized** by someone, they deliberately damage it. *The walls had been horribly vandalized with spray paint.*

N

O

vanguard /'vænɡɑːd/. N-SING If someone is **in the vanguard of** something such as a revolution or an area of research, they are involved in the most advanced part of it.

P

Q

vanilla /və'nɪlə/. N-UNCOUNT **Vanilla** is a flavouring used in ice cream and other sweet food.

R

S

vanish /'vænɪʃ/ **vanishes, vanishing, vanished.** VERB If someone or something **vanishes**, they disappear suddenly or cease to exist altogether. *Anne vanished from outside her home last Wednesday. ...endangered animals and those species which have vanished.*

T

U

V

W

X

Y

Z

vanity /'vænɪti/. N-UNCOUNT If you refer to someone's **vanity**, you disapprove of them because they are too interested in their own appearance, or in other good qualities they believe they possess. *With my usual vanity, I thought he might be falling in love with me.*

vantage point /'vɑːntɪdʒ pɔɪnt, 'vænt-/ **vantage points.** N-COUNT A **vantage point** is a place from which you can see a lot of things. *From a concealed vantage point, he saw a car arrive.*

vapour (AM **vapor**) /'veɪpə/ **vapours.** N-VAR **Vapour** consists of tiny drops of water or other liquids in the air, which appear as mist.

variable /'veəriəbəl/ **variables.** **1** ADJ Something that is **variable** is likely to change at any time. *The potassium content of foodstuffs is very variable.* ♦ **variability** N-UNCOUNT ...*the variability in the climate.* **2** N-COUNT A **variable** is a factor in a situation that can change. *The major economic variables are not under control.*

variance /'veəriəns/. PHRASE If one thing is **at variance with** another, the two things seem to contradict each other. [FORMAL] *Many of his statements were at variance with the facts.*

variant /'veəriənt/ **variants.** N-COUNT A **variant of** something has a different form from the usual one. ...*a variant of the zebra... Many words have variant spellings.*

variation /ˌveəri'eɪʃən/ **variations.** **1** N-COUNT A **variation on** something is the same thing presented in a different form. ...*this delicious variation on an omelette.* **2** N-VAR A **variation** is a difference in a level, amount, or quantity. ...*a wide variation in the prices charged for canteen food.*

varied /'veərid/. ADJ Something that is **varied** consists of things of different types, sizes, or qualities. *It is essential that your diet is varied and balanced.* ● See also **vary.**

⭐ **variety** /və'raɪɪti/ **varieties.** **1** N-UNCOUNT If something has **variety**, it consists of things which are different from each other. *Susan's idea of freedom was to have variety in her life style.* **2** N-SING A **variety of** things is a number of different kinds or examples of the same thing. *Hampstead has a variety of good shops and supermarkets.* **3** N-COUNT A **variety of** something is a type of it. *She has 12 varieties of old-fashioned roses.*

⭐ **various** /'veəriəs/. ADJ If you say that there are **various** things, you mean there are several different things of the type mentioned. *Various countries will be putting forward ideas... The joys of gardening are many and various.*

variously /'veəriəsli/. ADV You can use **variously** to introduce a number of different ways in which something is described. *He is variously described as a designer, a stylist, and a photographer.*

varnish /'vɑːnɪʃ/ **varnishes, varnishing, varnished.** **1** N-VAR **Varnish** is an oily liquid which is painted onto wood to give it a hard, clear, shiny surface.

2 VERB If you **varnish** something, you paint it with varnish.

⭐ **vary** /'veəri/ **varies, varying, varied.** **1** VERB If things **vary**, they are different in size, amount, or degree. *As they're handmade, each one varies slightly... The amount of sleep we need varies from person to person.* **2** VERB If something **varies**, or if you **vary** it, it becomes different or it changes. *The cost of the alcohol duty varies according to the amount of wine in the bottle.* **3** See also **varied**.

vase /vɑːz, AM veɪs/ **vases.** N-COUNT A **vase** is a jar used for holding cut flowers or as an ornament.

⭐ **vast** /vɑːst, væst/. ADJ Something that is **vast** is extremely large. *...vast stretches of land.*

vastly /'vɑːstli, 'væst-/. ADV **Vastly** means to an extremely great degree or extent. *...two vastly different accounts of what happened.*

vault /vɔːlt/ **vaults, vaulting, vaulted.** **1** N-COUNT A **vault** is a secure room where money and other valuable things can be kept safely. *...bank vaults.* **2** N-COUNT A **vault** is a room underneath a church or in a cemetery where people are buried. **3** N-COUNT A **vault** is an arched roof or ceiling. **4** VERB If you **vault** something or **vault over** it, you jump over it, putting one or both of your hands on it. *He could easily vault the wall.*

VCR /ˌviː siː 'ɑː/ **VCRs.** N-COUNT A **VCR** is a machine that can be used to record television programmes or films onto video tapes. **VCR** is an abbreviation for 'video cassette recorder'.

VDU /ˌviː diː 'juː/ **VDUs.** N-COUNT A **VDU** is a machine with a screen which is used to display information from a computer. **VDU** is an abbreviation for 'visual display unit'. [COMPUTING]

veal /viːl/. N-UNCOUNT **Veal** is meat from a calf.

veer /vɪə/ **veers, veering, veered.** VERB If something **veers** in a particular direction, it suddenly moves in that direction. *The plane veered off the runway.*

⭐ **vegetable** /'vedʒtəbəl/ **vegetables.** N-COUNT **Vegetables** are edible plants such as cabbages, potatoes, and onions.

vegetarian /ˌvedʒɪ'teəriən/ **vegetarians.** N-COUNT & ADJ A **vegetarian** is someone who does not eat meat or fish. *...a strict vegetarian diet.*

vegetation /ˌvedʒɪ'teɪʃən/ N-UNCOUNT **Vegetation** is plants, trees and flowers. [FORMAL]

vehement /'viːəmənt/. ADJ **Vehement** feelings and opinions are strongly held and forcefully expressed. ♦ **vehemence** N-UNCOUNT *He spoke with more vehemence than he had intended.* ♦ **vehemently** ADV *Krabbe has always vehemently denied using drugs.*

⭐ **vehicle** /'viːɪkəl/ **vehicles.** **1** N-COUNT A **vehicle** is a machine with an engine, for example a car, that carries people or things from place to place. **2** N-COUNT You can use **vehicle** to refer to something that you use in order to achieve a particular purpose. *Her art became a vehicle for her political beliefs.*

veil /veɪl/ **veils.** **1** N-COUNT A **veil** is a piece of thin soft cloth that women sometimes wear over their heads and which can also cover their face.

2 N-COUNT You can refer to something that hides a situation or activity as a **veil**. *...the chilling facts behind this veil of silence.*

veiled /veɪld/. **1** ADJ BEFORE N A **veiled** comment is expressed in a disguised form rather than directly and openly. *This last clause is a thinly-veiled threat.* **2** ADJ A **veiled** person is wearing a veil.

vein /veɪn/ **veins.** **1** N-COUNT Your **veins** are the tubes in your body through which your blood flows towards your heart. **2** N-COUNT The **veins** on a leaf are the thin lines on it. **3** N-UNCOUNT Something that is written or spoken **in** a particular **vein** is written or spoken in that style or mood. *The girl now replies in similar vein.*

velocity /vɪ'lɒsɪti/ **velocities.** N-VAR **Velocity** is the speed at which something moves. [TECHNICAL]

velvet /'velvɪt/. N-UNCOUNT **Velvet** is a soft fabric with a thick layer of short cut threads on one side.

vendetta /ven'detə/ **vendettas.** N-VAR If one person has a **vendetta against** another, the first person wants revenge for something the second person did to them in the past.

vendor /'vendə/ **vendors.** N-COUNT A **vendor** is someone who sells things such as newspapers or hamburgers from a small stall or cart. *...ice-cream vendors.*

veneer /vɪ'nɪə/. N-SING If you refer to the pleasant way that someone behaves or that something appears as a **veneer**, you are critical of them because you believe that their true nature is unpleasant, and this is being hidden. *He was able to fool the world with his veneer of education.*

venerable /'venərəbəl/. **1** ADJ **Venerable** people deserve respect because they are old and wise. **2** ADJ **Venerable** things are impressive because they are old and historically important. *...venerable institutions like the Theatre National de l'Odeon.*

vengeance /'vendʒəns/. **1** N-UNCOUNT **Vengeance** is the act of harming someone because they have harmed you. *He swore vengeance on everyone involved in the murder.* **2** PHRASE If you say that something happens **with a vengeance**, you are emphasizing that it happens to a great extent. *It began to rain again with a vengeance.*

venison /'venɪzən/. N-UNCOUNT **Venison** is the meat of a deer eaten as food.

venom /'venəm/. **1** N-UNCOUNT **Venom** is a feeling of great bitterness or anger towards someone. *There was no mistaking the venom in his voice.* **2** N-UNCOUNT The **venom** of certain snakes, spiders, or other creatures is the poison that they inject into animals, insects, or people when they bite or sting them.

vent /vent/ **vents, venting, vented.** **1** N-COUNT A **vent** is a hole in something which allows air to come in and smoke, gas, or smells to go out. *There was a small air vent in the ceiling.* **2** VERB If

a
b
c
d
e
f
g
h
i
j
k
l
m
n
o
p
q
r
s
t
u
v
w
x
y
z

you **vent** your feelings, you express them forcefully. *The rioters were prevented from venting their anger on the police.*

ventilate /'ventɪleɪt/ **ventilates, ventilating, ventilated.** VERB If you **ventilate** a room or building, you allow fresh air to get into it. *...badly ventilated rooms.* ♦ **ventilation** N-UNCOUNT *The only ventilation comes from tiny sliding windows.*

★ **venture** /'ventʃə/ **ventures, venturing, ventured.** [1] N-COUNT A **venture** is a new project or activity which is exciting and difficult because it involves the risk of failure. *...his latest writing venture.* [2] VERB If you **venture into** an activity, you do something that involves the risk of failure because it is new and different. *He enjoyed little success when he ventured into business.* [3] VERB If you **venture** somewhere, you go there, although it might be dangerous. *People are afraid to venture out for fear of sniper attacks.*

★ **venue** /'venjuː/ **venues.** N-COUNT The **venue** for an event or activity is the place where it will happen. *The Embassy was the venue for a New Year's Eve party.*

veranda (or **verandah**) /və'rændə/ **verandas.** N-COUNT A **veranda** is a platform with a roof along the outside wall of a house.

verb /vɜːb/ **verbs.** N-COUNT A **verb** is a word such as 'sing' or 'feel' which is used to say what someone or something does or what happens to them, or to give information about them.

verbal /'vɜːbəl/. [1] ADJ You use **verbal** to indicate that something is expressed in speech rather than in writing or action. *We have a verbal agreement with her.* ♦ **verbally** ADV *Twins often have difficulty expressing themselves verbally.* [2] ADJ You use **verbal** to indicate that something is connected with words and the use of words. *Wayne has great verbal dexterity.*

★ **verdict** /'vɜːdɪkt/ **verdicts.** [1] N-COUNT In a law court, a **verdict** is the decision that is given by the jury or judge at the end of a trial. *The jury returned a unanimous guilty verdict.* [2] N-COUNT Someone's **verdict on** something is their opinion of it, after thinking about it or investigating it. *The critics were too quick to give their verdict on us.*

verge /vɜːdʒ/ **verges, verging, verged.** [1] PHRASE If you are **on the verge of** something, you are about to do it or it is about to happen. *Carole was on the verge of tears.* [2] N-COUNT The **verge** of a road is the narrow strip of grassy ground at the side. [BRITISH]
▶ **verge on.** PHR-VERB If someone or something **verges on** a particular state or quality, they are almost the same as that state or quality. *...a fury that verged on madness.*

verify /'verɪfaɪ/ **verifies, verifying, verified.** VERB If you **verify** something, you check or confirm that it is true. *A clerk simply verifies that the payment and invoice amounts match.* ♦ **verification** /,verɪfɪ'keɪʃən/ N-UNCOUNT *...the agency's verification procedures.*

veritable /'verɪtəbəl/. ADJ You can use **veritable** to emphasize the size or nature of something. *...a veritable feast of pre-match entertainment.*

vernacular /və'nækjʊlə/ **vernaculars.** N-COUNT **The vernacular** is the language or dialect that is most widely spoken by ordinary people in a region or country. *...books or plays written in the vernacular.*

versatile /'vɜːsətaɪl, AM -təl/. [1] ADJ If you say that a person is **versatile**, you approve of them because they have many different skills. *...one of the game's most versatile athletes.* ♦ **versatility** /,vɜːsə'tɪlɪti/ N-UNCOUNT *...her incredible versatility as an actress.* [2] ADJ A **versatile** activity, material, or machine can be used for many different purposes. *Never before has computing been so versatile.* ♦ **versatility** N-UNCOUNT *Velvet is not known for its versatility.*

verse /vɜːs/ **verses.** [1] N-UNCOUNT **Verse** is writing arranged in lines which have rhythm and which often rhyme at the end. *I have been moved to write a few lines of verse.* [2] N-COUNT A **verse** is one of the parts into which a poem, a song, or a chapter of the Bible or Koran is divided.

★ **version** /'vɜːʃən, -ʒən/ **versions.** [1] N-COUNT A **version** of something is a form of it in which some details are different from earlier or later forms. *...an updated version of his book.* [2] N-COUNT Someone's **version of** an event is their personal account of it.

versus /'vɜːsəs/. [1] PREP You use **versus** to say that two ideas or things are opposed. *...the debate about bottle-feeding versus breastfeeding.* [2] PREP **Versus** is used to indicate that two people or teams are competing against each other in a sporting event. *...the winning goal in a Scotland versus England game.*

vertebra /'vɜːtɪbrə/ **vertebrae** /'vɜːtɪbreɪ/. N-COUNT **Vertebrae** are the small circular bones that form your backbone.

vertical /'vɜːtɪkəl/. ADJ Something that is **vertical** stands or points straight upwards. *...a vertical wall of rock.* ♦ **vertically** ADV *Cut each bulb in half vertically.*

★ **very** /'veri/. [1] ADV **Very** is used to give emphasis to an adjective or adverb. *The problem and the answer are very simple... Thank you very much.* [2] ADJ BEFORE N You use **very** with certain nouns in order to specify an extreme position or extreme point in time. *I turned to the very end of the book, to read the final words... He was wrong from the very beginning.* [3] ADJ BEFORE N You use **very** with nouns to emphasize that something is exactly the right one or exactly the same one. *She died in this very house.* [4] CONVENTION **Very well** is used to say that you agree to do something or you accept someone's answer, even though you might not be completely satisfied with it. *'I know that as well as you do.'—'Very well, we won't argue about it.'* [5] PHRASE The expression **very much so** is an emphatic way of answering 'yes' to something or saying that it is true or correct. *'Are you enjoying your holiday?'—'Very much so.'*.

USAGE Very, **so**, and **too** can all be used to intensify the meaning of an adjective, an adverb, or a word like **much** or **many**. However, they are not used in the same way. **Very** is the simplest intensifier. It has no other meaning beyond that. **So** can suggest an emotional reaction on the part of the speaker, such as pleasure, surprise, or disappointment. *John makes me so angry!... Oh thank you so much!* **So** can also refer forward to a result clause introduced by **that**. *The procession was forced to move so slowly that he arrived three hours late.* **Too** suggests an excessive or undesirable amount, often so much that a particular result does not or cannot happen. *She does wear too much make-up at times... He was too late to save her.*

⭐ **vessel** /'vesəl/ **vessels.** [1] N-COUNT A **vessel** is a ship or a large boat. [FORMAL] *...a New Zealand navy vessel.* [2] N-COUNT A **vessel** is a bowl or other container in which liquid is kept. [FORMAL] *...storage vessels.* [3] See also **blood vessel**.

vest /vest/ **vests, vesting, vested.** [1] N-COUNT A **vest** is a piece of underwear which is worn to keep the top part of your body warm. [BRITISH] [2] N-COUNT In American English, a **vest** is a sleeveless piece of clothing with buttons which people usually wear over a shirt. The British word is **waistcoat**. → See picture on page 820. [3] VERB If something **is vested in** you, or if you **are vested with** it, it is given to you as a right or responsibility. [FORMAL] *The mass media have been vested with significant power.*

vested 'interest, vested interests. N-COUNT If you have a **vested interest in** something, you have a very strong reason for acting in a particular way, for example to protect your money or reputation. *The administration has no vested interest in proving public schools good or bad.*

vestige /'vestɪdʒ/ **vestiges.** N-COUNT The **vestiges of** something are the small parts that still remain after most of it has gone. *...the last vestige of a UN force that once numbered more than 30,000.*

vet /vet/ **vets, vetting, vetted.** [1] N-COUNT A **vet** is someone who is qualified to treat sick or injured animals. [BRITISH] [2] VERB If someone or something **is vetted**, that person or thing is checked carefully to make sure that they reach certain standards, particularly standards of morality or trust. [BRITISH] *He had not been allowed to read any book until his mother had vetted it.* ◆ **vetting** N-UNCOUNT *...the procedure for carrying out security vetting.*

⭐ **veteran** /'vetərən/ **veterans.** [1] N-COUNT A **veteran** is someone who has served in the armed forces of their country, especially during a war.

[2] N-COUNT A **veteran** is someone who has been involved in a particular activity for a long time. *...Tony Benn, the veteran Labour MP and former Cabinet minister.*

veterinary /'vetərənəri, AM -neri/. ADJ BEFORE N **Veterinary** is used to describe the work of a person whose job is to treat sick or injured animals, or to describe the medical treatment of animals. *...a veterinary examination.*

veto /'viːtəʊ/ **vetoes, vetoing, vetoed.** [1] VERB & N-COUNT If someone in authority **vetoes** something, or if they put a **veto** on it, they forbid it, or stop it being put into action. *The President vetoed the economic package passed by Congress... The veto was a calculated political risk.* [2] N-UNCOUNT **Veto** is the right that someone in authority has to forbid something. *...the President's power of veto.*

vex /veks/ **vexes, vexing, vexed.** VERB If someone or something **vexes** you, they make you feel annoyed. *Everything about her vexed him.* ◆ **vexed** ADJ *Farmers and industrialists alike are vexed and blame the government.* ◆ **vexing** ADJ *There remains, however, another and more vexing problem.*

⭐ **via** /'vaɪə, 'viːə/. [1] PREP If you go somewhere **via** a particular place, you go through that place on the way to your destination. *Mr Baker will return home via Britain and France.* [2] PREP If you do something **via** a particular means or person, you do it by making use of that means or person. *...the technology to allow relief workers to contact the outside world via satellite.*

viable /'vaɪəbəl/. ADJ Something that is **viable** is capable of doing what it is intended to do. *Cash alone will not make Eastern Europe's banks viable.* ◆ **viability** N-UNCOUNT *...the shaky financial viability of the nuclear industry.*

vibrant /'vaɪbrənt/. [1] ADJ Something or someone that is **vibrant** is full of energy and enthusiasm. *...her vibrant personality.* ◆ **vibrancy** N-UNCOUNT *She was a woman with extraordinary vibrancy.* [2] ADJ **Vibrant** colours are very bright and clear. *The grass was a vibrant green.* ◆ **vibrantly** ADV *...vibrantly coloured rugs.*

vibrate /vaɪ'breɪt, AM 'vaɪbreɪt/ **vibrates, vibrating, vibrated.** VERB If something **vibrates**, or if you **vibrate** it, it shakes with repeated small quick movements. *The noise vibrated the table.* ◆ **vibration, vibrations** N-VAR *The vibrations of the vehicles rattled the shop windows.*

vicar /'vɪkə/ **vicars.** N-COUNT A **vicar** is a priest in the Church of England.

⭐ **vice** /vaɪs/ **vices.**

✅ The spelling **vise** is used in American English for meaning 3.

---

[1] N-COUNT A **vice** is a habit which is regarded as a weakness in someone's character, but not usually as a serious fault. *I spend too much on clothes, that's my only vice.* [2] N-UNCOUNT **Vice** refers to criminal activities connected with pornography or prostitution. [3] N-COUNT A **vice** or

a b c d e f g h i j k l m n o p q r s t u **v** w x y z

vise is a tool with a pair of jaws that hold an object tightly while you do work on it.

vice versa /ˌvaɪsə ˈvɜːsə/. PHRASE **Vice versa** is used to indicate that the reverse of what you have said is also true. For example, 'Women may bring their husbands with them, and vice versa' means that men may also bring their wives with them.

vicinity /vɪˈsɪnɪti/. N-SING If something is **in the vicinity** of a place, it is in the nearby area. *There were a hundred hotels in the vicinity of the station.*

vicious /ˈvɪʃəs/. ☐ ADJ A **vicious** person is violent and cruel. ♦ **viciously** ADV *She had been viciously attacked with a hammer.* ♦ **viciousness** N-UNCOUNT ...*the intensity and viciousness of these attacks.* ☐ ADJ A **vicious** remark is cruel and intended to upset someone. ♦ **viciously** ADV *'He deserved to die,' said Penelope viciously.*

vicious 'circle. N-SING A **vicious circle** is a problem or difficult situation that has the effect of creating new problems which then cause the original problem or situation to occur again.

⭐ **victim** /ˈvɪktɪm/ **victims.** N-COUNT A **victim** is someone who has been hurt or killed by someone or something. ...*the victims of violent crime.*

⭐ **victimize** (BRIT also **victimise**) /ˈvɪktɪmaɪz/ **victimizes, victimizing, victimized.** VERB If someone **is victimized**, they are deliberately treated unfairly. *The students had been victimized because they'd voiced opposition to the government.* ♦ **victimization** N-UNCOUNT ...*society's cruel victimization of women.*

victor /ˈvɪktə/ **victors.** N-COUNT The **victor** in a contest or battle is the person who wins. [LITERARY]

Victorian /vɪkˈtɔːriən/ **Victorians.** ☐ ADJ **Victorian** means belonging to, connected with, or typical of Britain in the middle and last parts of the 19th century, during the reign of Queen Victoria. ...*a lovely old Victorian house.* ☐ ADJ You can use **Victorian** to describe people who have old-fashioned qualities, especially in relation to discipline and morals. *Victorian values are much misunderstood.* ☐ N-COUNT The **Victorians** were the people who lived in the reign of Queen Victoria.

victorious /vɪkˈtɔːriəs/. ADJ You use **victorious** to describe someone who has won a victory in a struggle, war, or competition. ...*a member of the victorious British team.*

⭐ **victory** /ˈvɪktəri/ **victories.** N-VAR A **victory** is a success in a war or a competition. *The New Democracy party has claimed victory.*

⭐ **video** /ˈvɪdiəʊ/ **videos, videoing, videoed.** ☐ N-COUNT A **video** is a film or television programme recorded on videotape. ☐ N-UNCOUNT **Video** is the recording and showing of films and events, using a video recorder, videotapes, and a television set. *She has watched the race on video.* ☐ N-COUNT A **video** is the same as a **VCR**. ☐ VERB If you **video** something, you record it on

magnetic tape, either by using a video recorder or a camera.

'video game, video games. N-COUNT A **video game** is a computer game that you play on your television or on a similar device.

'video recorder, video recorders. N-COUNT A **video recorder** or a **video cassette recorder** is the same as a **VCR**.

videotape /ˈvɪdiəʊteɪp/ **videotapes.** N-VAR **Videotape** is magnetic tape that is used to record pictures and sounds which can be shown on television.

vie /vaɪ/ **vies, vying, vied.** VERB If one person **vies with** another **to** do something, or if they **vie to** do it, they both try hard to do it sooner or better than the other person. [FORMAL] *The brothers vied with each other to offer their help.*

view 1 opinions

⭐ **view** /vjuː/ **views, viewing, viewed.** ☐ N-COUNT Your **views on** something are the opinions or beliefs that you have about it. *We have similar views on the matter... I take the view that she should be stopped as soon as possible... In my view things won't change.* ☐ N-SING Your **view of** a particular subject is the way that you understand and think about it. ...*a Christian-centred view of religion.* ● See also **point of view**. ☐ VERB If you **view** something in a particular way, you think of it in that way. *We would view favourably any sensible suggestion.* ☐ PREP You use **in view of** when you are taking into consideration facts that have just been mentioned or are just about to be mentioned. *She has to be extra careful in view of her past medical history.* ☐ PHRASE If you do something **with a view to** a particular result, you do it to achieve that result. *He has called a meeting of all parties tomorrow, with a view to forming a national reconciliation government.*

view 2 being able to see things

⭐ **view** /vjuː/ **views, viewing, viewed.** ☐ N-COUNT The **view** from a particular place is everything you can see from that place, especially when it is considered to be beautiful. ☐ N-SING If you have a **view** of something, you can see it. *He stopped in the doorway, blocking her view.* ☐ N-UNCOUNT You use **view** in expressions to do with being able to see something. For example, if something is **in view**, you can see it. If something is **in full view of everyone**, everyone can see it. *A group of riders came into view.* ☐ VERB If you **view** something, you inspect it or look at it for a particular purpose. [FORMAL] *Check out the motor museum and view the classic cars.* ☐ PHRASE If something such as a work or art is **on view**, it is being exhibited in public.

viewer /ˈvjuːə/ **viewers.** N-COUNT **Viewers** are people who watch television.

viewpoint /ˈvjuːpɔɪnt/ **viewpoints.** N-COUNT Someone's **viewpoint** is the way they think about things in general or about a particular thing. *The novel is shown entirely from the girl's viewpoint.*

vigil /'vɪdʒɪl/ **vigils.** N-COUNT A **vigil** is a period of time when people remain quietly in a place, especially at night, for example because they are praying or are making a political protest. *Protesters are holding a twenty-four hour vigil.*

vigilant /'vɪdʒɪlənt/. ADJ Someone who is **vigilant** gives careful attention to a particular problem or situation and concentrates on noticing any danger or trouble that there might be. *Inspector Murphy warned the public to be vigilant and report anything suspicious.*
♦ **vigilance** /'vɪdʒɪləns/ N-UNCOUNT *Drugs are a problem that requires constant vigilance.*

vigilante /,vɪdʒɪ'lænti/ **vigilantes.** N-COUNT **Vigilantes** are people who organize themselves into an unofficial group to protect their community and to catch and punish criminals.

vigor. See **vigour**.

vigorous /'vɪgərəs/. ADJ **Vigorous** actions involve using a lot of energy and enthusiasm. *...the benefits of vigorous exercise.* ♦ **vigorously** ADV *He shook his head vigorously... The police vigorously denied that excessive force had been used.*

vigour (AM **vigor**) /'vɪgə/. N-UNCOUNT **Vigour** is physical or mental energy and enthusiasm. *The election was fought with vigour.*

vile /vaɪl/ **viler, vilest.** ADJ If you say that someone or something is **vile**, you mean that they are extremely unpleasant.

villa /'vɪlə/ **villas.** N-COUNT A **villa** is a fairly large house, especially one that is used for holidays in Mediterranean countries.

⭐ **village** /'vɪlɪdʒ/ **villages.** N-COUNT A **village** consists of a group of houses, together with other buildings such as a church and school, in a country area.

villager /'vɪlɪdʒə/ **villagers.** N-COUNT You refer to the people who live in a village as the **villagers**.

villain /'vɪlən/ **villains.** N-COUNT A **villain** is someone who deliberately harms other people or breaks the law in order to get what he or she wants.

vindicate /'vɪndɪkeɪt/ **vindicates, vindicating, vindicated.** VERB If a person **is vindicated**, they are proved to be correct, after people have said that they were wrong. [FORMAL] *The director said he had been vindicated by the experts' report.*
♦ **vindication, vindications** N-VAR *He called the success a vindication of his party's free-market economic policy.*

vindictive /vɪn'dɪktɪv/. ADJ Someone who is **vindictive** deliberately tries to upset or cause trouble for people who they think have done them harm. ♦ **vindictiveness** N-UNCOUNT *He is letting vindictiveness get in the way of his judgment.*

vine /vaɪn/ **vines.** N-COUNT A **vine** is a climbing or trailing plant, especially one which produces grapes.

vinegar /'vɪnɪgə/. N-UNCOUNT **Vinegar** is a sharp-tasting liquid, usually made from sour wine

or malt, which is used to make things such as salad dressing.

vineyard /'vɪnjəd/ **vineyards.** N-COUNT A **vineyard** is an area of land where grape vines are grown in order to produce wine.

vintage /'vɪntɪdʒ/ **vintages.** ① N-COUNT The **vintage** of a good quality wine is the year and place that it was made. ② ADJ BEFORE N **Vintage** wine is good quality wine that has been stored for several years in order to improve its quality. ③ ADJ BEFORE N **Vintage** cars or aeroplanes are old but are admired because they are considered to be the best of their kind.

vinyl /'vaɪnɪl/. N-UNCOUNT **Vinyl** is a strong plastic used for making things such as floor coverings and furniture.

viola /vi'əʊlə/ **violas.** N-COUNT A **viola** is a musical instrument which looks like a violin but is slightly larger.

⭐ **violate** /'vaɪəleɪt/ **violates, violating, violated.** ① VERB If someone **violates** an agreement, law, or promise, they break it. *They violated the ceasefire agreement.* ♦ **violation, violations** N-VAR *To deprive the boy of his education is a violation of state law.* ② VERB If you **violate** someone's privacy or peace, you disturb it. [FORMAL] ③ VERB If someone **violates** a special place, for example a tomb, they damage it or treat it without respect. ♦ **violation** N-VAR *...the violation of the graves.*

⭐ **violence** /'vaɪələns/. ① N-UNCOUNT **Violence** is behaviour which is intended to hurt or kill people. *Twenty people were killed in the violence.* ② N-UNCOUNT If you do or say something with **violence**, you use a lot of force and energy in doing or saying it, often because you are angry. [LITERARY] *The violence in her tone gave Alistair a shock.*

⭐ **violent** /'vaɪələnt/. ① ADJ If someone is **violent**, or if they do something which is **violent**, they use physical force or weapons to hurt or kill other people. *A quarter of current inmates have committed violent crimes.* ♦ **violently** ADV *Some opposition activists have been violently attacked.* ② ADJ A **violent** event happens suddenly and with great force. *A violent impact hurtled her forward.* ♦ **violently** ADV *A nearby volcano erupted violently.* ③ ADJ If you describe something as **violent**, you mean that it is said, done, or felt with great force and energy. *He had violent stomach pains.* ♦ **violently** ADV *Other experts violently disagree.*

violet /'vaɪəlɪt/ **violets.** ① N-COUNT A **violet** is a small purple or white flower that blooms in the spring. ② ADJ & N-UNCOUNT Something that is **violet** is bluish-purple.

violin /,vaɪə'lɪn/ **violins.** N-COUNT A **violin** is a musical instrument with four strings stretched over a shaped hollow box. You hold a violin under your chin and play it with a bow. → See picture on page 827. ♦ **violinist** /,vaɪə'lɪnɪst/ **violinists** N-COUNT *...the famous jazz violinist.*

a
b
c
d
e
f
g
h
i
j
k
l
m
n
o
p
q
r
s
t
u
v
w
x
y
z

VIP /ˌviː ˈpiː/ **VIPs.** N-COUNT A **VIP** is someone who is given better treatment than ordinary people because he or she is famous or important. **VIP** is an abbreviation for 'very important person'.

virgin /ˈvɜːdʒɪn/ **virgins.** ⓵ N-COUNT A **virgin** is someone who has never had sex. ♦ **virginity** /vəˈdʒɪnɪti/ N-UNCOUNT She lost her virginity when she was 20. ⓶ ADJ You use **virgin** to describe something such as land that has never been used or spoiled. ...a sloping field of virgin snow.

virile /ˈvɪraɪl, AM -rəl/. ADJ If you describe a man as **virile**, you mean he has the qualities that a man is traditionally expected to have, such as strength and sexuality. ♦ **virility** /vɪˈrɪlɪti/ N-UNCOUNT Children are also considered to be proof of a man's virility.

virtual /ˈvɜːtʃuəl/. ⓵ ADJ BEFORE N You can use **virtual** to indicate that something is so nearly true that for most purposes it can be regarded as being true. ...the virtual banning of religion. ⓶ ADJ BEFORE N **Virtual** objects and activities are generated by a computer to simulate real objects and activities. [COMPUTING] ...a virtual shopping centre. ♦ **virtually** ADV Virtually all cooking was done over coal-fired ranges.

ˌvirtual reˈality. N-UNCOUNT **Virtual reality** is an environment which is produced by a computer and seems very like reality to the person experiencing it. [COMPUTING]

virtue /ˈvɜːtʃuː/ **virtues.** ⓵ N-UNCOUNT **Virtue** is thinking and doing what is right, and avoiding what is wrong. ⓶ N-COUNT A **virtue** is a good quality or way of behaving. His virtue is patience. ⓷ N-VAR The **virtue** of something is an advantage or benefit that it has, especially in comparison with something else. Its other great virtue, of course, is its hard-wearing quality. ⓸ PREP You use **by virtue of** to explain why something happens or is true. [FORMAL] Mr Olaechea has British residency by virtue of his marriage.

virtuoso /ˌvɜːtʃuˈəʊzəʊ/ **virtuosos** (or **virtuosi** /ˌvɜːtʃuˈəʊzi/). ⓵ N-COUNT A **virtuoso** is someone who is exceptionally good at playing a musical instrument. ⓶ ADJ A **virtuoso** performance or display shows exceptional skill.

virtuous /ˈvɜːtʃuəs/. ⓵ ADJ A **virtuous** person behaves in a moral and correct way. ...virtuous people who obey the rules and are nice to others. ⓶ ADJ If you describe someone as **virtuous**, you mean that they feel very pleased with their own good behaviour; often used showing disapproval. I cleaned the flat, which left me feeling virtuous. ♦ **virtuously** ADV 'I've already done that,' said Ronnie virtuously.

virulent /ˈvɪrʊlənt/. ⓵ ADJ **Virulent** feelings or actions are extremely bitter and hostile. Now he faces virulent attacks from the Italian media. ♦ **virulently** ADV The talk was virulently hostile. ♦ **virulence** N-UNCOUNT The virulence of the café owner's anger had appalled her. ⓶ ADJ A **virulent** disease or poison is extremely powerful and dangerous. ♦ **virulence** N-UNCOUNT ...the virulence of the epidemic.

★ **virus** /ˈvaɪərəs/ **viruses.** ⓵ N-COUNT A **virus** is a kind of germ that can cause disease. ⓶ N-COUNT In computer technology, a **virus** is a program that introduces itself into a system, altering or destroying the information stored there. [COMPUTING]

visa /ˈviːzə/ **visas.** N-COUNT A **visa** is an official document or a stamp put in your passport which allows you to enter or leave a particular country.

vise /vaɪs/. See **vice**.

visibility /ˌvɪzɪˈbɪlɪti/. N-UNCOUNT **Visibility** is how far or how clearly you can see in particular weather conditions. Visibility was poor.

★ **visible** /ˈvɪzɪbəl/. ⓵ ADJ If an object is **visible**, it can be seen. The mainland is clearly visible from their island. ⓶ ADJ You use **visible** to describe something or someone that people notice or recognize. He was making a visible effort to control himself. ♦ **visibly** ADV They emerged visibly distressed.

★ **vision** /ˈvɪʒən/ **visions.** ⓵ N-COUNT Your **vision** of a future situation or society is what you imagine or hope it would be like, if things were very different from the way they are now. I have a vision of a society that is free of exploitation and injustice. ⓶ N-UNCOUNT Your **vision** is your ability to see clearly with your eyes. ...loss of vision.

visionary /ˈvɪʒənri, AM -neri/ **visionaries.** ⓵ N-COUNT A **visionary** is someone who has strong original ideas about how things might be different in the future, especially about how things might be improved. ⓶ ADJ You use **visionary** to describe the strong original ideas of a visionary. ...visionary architecture.

★ **visit** /ˈvɪzɪt/ **visits, visiting, visited.** ⓵ VERB & N-COUNT If you **visit** someone, or if you **pay** them a **visit**, you go to see them and spend time with them. Bill would visit on weekends. ⓶ VERB & N-COUNT If you **visit** a place, or if you make a **visit to** a place, you go to see it. ...the Pope's visit to Canada. ▸**visit with.** PHR-VERB If you **visit with** someone, you go to see them and spend time with them. [AMERICAN] I visited with him in San Francisco.

★ **visitor** /ˈvɪzɪtə/ **visitors.** N-COUNT A **visitor** is someone who is visiting a person or place.

vista /ˈvɪstə/ **vistas.** ⓵ N-COUNT A **vista** is a view, especially a beautiful view from a high place. I looked out on a crowded vista of hills and rooftops. ⓶ N-COUNT A **vista** is a vision of a situation or of a range of possibilities. ...a vista of a future without hope.

visual /ˈvɪʒuəl/. ADJ **Visual** means relating to sight, or to things that you can see. Watching TV requires the processing of visual images. ...careers in the visual arts. ♦ **visually** ADV ...visually impaired children.

visualize (BRIT also **visualise**) /ˈvɪʒuəlaɪz/ **visualizes, visualizing, visualized.** VERB If you **visualize** something, you imagine what it is like by forming a mental picture of it. He could not visualize her as *old... It was hard to visualize how it could have been done.*

⭐ **vital** /ˈvaɪtəl/. **1** ADJ If something is **vital**, it is necessary or very important. *It is vital that action is taken quickly. ...vital information.* ♦ **vitally** ADV *Lesley's career in the church is vitally important to her.* **2** ADJ **Vital** people, organizations, or activities are very energetic and full of life. *He was a vital and witty man.*

vitality /vaɪˈtælɪti/. N-UNCOUNT If someone or something has **vitality**, they have great energy and liveliness. *He had enormous vitality. ...the financial vitality of the corporation.*

⭐ **vitamin** /ˈvɪtəmɪn, AM ˈvaɪt-/ **vitamins**. N-COUNT **Vitamins** are organic substances in food which you need in order to remain healthy. *...vitamin D. ...vitamin supplements.*

vivid /ˈvɪvɪd/. **1** ADJ **Vivid** memories and descriptions are very clear and detailed. *...a very vivid dream.* ♦ **vividly** ADV *I remember the phone call vividly.* **2** ADJ Something that is **vivid** is very bright in colour. *...a vivid blue sky.* ♦ **vividly** ADV *...vividly coloured birds.*

vocabulary /vəʊˈkæbjʊləri, AM -leri/ **vocabularies**. **1** N-VAR Your **vocabulary** is the total number of words you know in a particular language. *...people with a limited vocabulary.* **2** N-SING The **vocabulary** of a language is all the words in it. *...a new word in the German vocabulary.*

vocal /ˈvəʊkəl/. **1** ADJ You say that people are **vocal** when they speak forcefully and with feeling about something. *She continued to be very vocal in opposing his business.* **2** ADJ BEFORE N **Vocal** means involving the use of the human voice, especially in singing.

vocalist /ˈvəʊkəlɪst/ **vocalists**. N-COUNT A **vocalist** is a singer who sings with a pop group. *...the band's lead vocalist.*

vocals /ˈvəʊkəlz/. N-PLURAL In a pop song, the **vocals** are the singing, in contrast to the playing of instruments.

vocation /vəʊˈkeɪʃən/ **vocations**. N-VAR If you have a **vocation**, you have a strong feeling that you are especially suited to a particular job or role in life. You can also call your job a **vocation** if you feel like this about it. *He found his vocation early: poetry and classical scholarship.*

vocational /vəʊˈkeɪʃənəl/. ADJ **Vocational** training and skills are the training and skills needed for a particular job or profession. *...newer universities offering more vocational courses.*

vociferous /vəˈsɪfərəs, AM vəʊs-/. ADJ If you describe someone as **vociferous**, you mean that they speak with great energy and determination, because they want their views to be heard. [FORMAL] *He was a vociferous opponent of Conservatism.* ♦ **vociferously** ADV *The Prime Minister has campaigned vociferously for this result.*

vodka /ˈvɒdkə/ **vodkas**. N-VAR **Vodka** is a strong clear alcoholic drink.

vogue /vəʊg/. **1** N-SING If there is a **vogue for** something, it is very popular and fashionable. *...the vogue for so-called health teas.* **2** PHRASE If something is **in vogue**, is very popular and fashionable. If it **comes into vogue**, it becomes very popular and fashionable.

⭐ **voice** /vɔɪs/ **voices, voicing, voiced**. **1** N-COUNT When someone speaks or sings, you hear their **voice**. *'The police are here,' she said in a low voice.* **2** N-COUNT You can use **voice** to refer to someone's opinion on a particular topic. *There were no dissenting voices.* **3** N-SING If you have a **voice in** something, you have the right to express an opinion on it. *But your partners will have no voice in how you operate your company.* **4** VERB If you **voice** an opinion or an emotion, you say what you think or feel. *Some scientists have voiced concern that the disease could be passed on to humans.* **5** N-SING In grammar, if a verb is in **the active voice**, the person who performs the action is the subject of the verb. If a verb is in **the passive voice**, the thing or person affected by the action is the subject of the verb.

void /vɔɪd/ **voids**. **1** N-COUNT If you describe a situation or a feeling as a **void**, you mean that it seems empty because there is nothing

volleyball

interesting or worthwhile about it. *His sudden death left a very deep void in my life.* **2** N-COUNT You can describe a large or frightening space as a **void**. *The ship moved silently through the black void.* **3** ADJ AFTER LINK-V Something that is **void** is officially considered to have no value or authority. *The vote was declared void.*

volatile /'vɒlətaɪl, AM -təl/. **1** ADJ A **volatile** situation is likely to change suddenly and unexpectedly. *Armed soldiers guard the streets in this volatile atmosphere.* **2** ADJ A **volatile** person is someone whose moods or attitudes change quickly and frequently.

volcanic /vɒl'kænɪk/. ADJ **Volcanic** means coming from or created by volcanoes. *St Vincent is a lush, volcanic island.*

volcano /vɒl'keɪnəʊ/ **volcanoes.** N-COUNT A **volcano** is a mountain from which hot melted rock, gas, steam and ash sometimes burst. *The volcano erupted last year killing about 600 people.*

volley /'vɒli/ **volleys, volleying, volleyed.** **1** N-COUNT A **volley of** gunfire is a lot of bullets that are fired at the same time. *A volley of shots rang out.* **2** VERB & N-COUNT In sports such as tennis and football, if someone **volleys**, they hit or kick the ball it before it touches the ground. A **volley** is a shot like this. *He volleyed the ball into the net.*

volleyball /'vɒlibɔːl/. N-UNCOUNT **Volleyball** is a sport in which two teams use their hands to hit a large ball over a high net. → See picture on page 781.

volt /vəʊlt/ **volts.** N-COUNT A **volt** is a unit used to measure the force of an electric current.

voltage /'vəʊltɪdʒ/ **voltages.** N-VAR The **voltage** of an electrical current is its force measured in volts. *...high-voltage power lines.*

★ **volume** /'vɒljuːm/ **volumes.** **1** N-COUNT The **volume** of something is the amount of it that there is. *The volume of sales has increased slightly. ...the sheer volume of traffic.* **2** N-COUNT The **volume** of an object is the amount of space that it contains or occupies. *When egg whites are beaten they can rise to seven or eight times their original volume.* **3** N-COUNT A **volume** is one book in a series of books. *...the first volume of his autobiography.* **4** N-UNCOUNT The **volume** of a radio, TV, or sound system is how loud it is. *He turned down the volume.*

★ **voluntary** /'vɒləntri, AM -teri/. **1** ADJ **Voluntary** is used to describe actions and activities that you do because you choose them, rather than because you have to do them. *...classes where attendance is voluntary.* ◆ **voluntarily** ADV *He asked people to surrender their firearms voluntarily.* **2** ADJ **Voluntary** work is work which people do not get paid for, but which they do to help an organization such as a charity. **3** ADJ BEFORE N A **voluntary** organization, for example a charity, is controlled by the people who have chosen to work for it, often without being paid.

★ **volunteer** /ˌvɒlən'tɪə/ **volunteers, volunteering, volunteered.** **1** N-COUNT A **volunteer** is someone who does work without being paid for it, especially for an organization such as a charity. *She now helps in a local school as a volunteer.* **2** N-COUNT A **volunteer** is someone who offers to do a particular task without being forced to do it. *What I want now is two volunteers to come down to the front.* **3** N-COUNT A **volunteer** is someone who chooses to join the armed forces, especially in wartime, as opposed to someone who is forced to join by law. **4** VERB If you **volunteer to** do something, you offer to do it without being forced to do it. *Mary volunteered to clean up the kitchen... He volunteered for overseas service.* **5** VERB If you **volunteer** information, you tell someone something without being asked. [FORMAL] *No one volunteered any further information... 'They were both great supporters of Franco,' Ryle volunteered.*

vomit /'vɒmɪt/ **vomits, vomiting, vomited.** **1** VERB If you **vomit**, food and drink comes back up from your stomach and out through your mouth. **2** N-UNCOUNT **Vomit** is partly digested food and drink that comes out of someone's mouth when they vomit.

voracious /və'reɪʃəs, AM vɔːr-/. ADJ If you describe a person, or their appetite for something, as **voracious**, you mean that they want a lot of it. [FORMAL] *She was a voracious reader.*

★ **vote** /vəʊt/ **votes, voting, voted.** **1** N-COUNT A **vote** is a choice made by a particular person or group in a meeting or an election. *He walked to the local polling centre to cast his vote... Mr Reynolds was re-elected by 102 votes to 60... They took a vote and decided not to do it.* **2** N-SING **The vote** is the total number of votes or voters in an election, or the number of votes received or cast by a particular group. *The vote was overwhelmingly in favour of the Democratic Party. ...a huge majority of the white male vote.* **3** N-SING If you have **the vote** in an election, or have **a vote** in a meeting, you have the legal right to indicate your choice. *In Italy women did not get the vote until 1945.* **4** VERB When you **vote**, you indicate your choice officially at a meeting or in an election, for example by raising your hand or writing on a piece of paper. *Who are you going to vote for?... Recently the parliament voted to allow greater political and religious freedoms.* ◆ **voting** N-UNCOUNT *Voting began about two hours ago.* ◆ **voter, voters** N-COUNT *Nearly a third of the voters were either still undecided or said they would abstain.*

voucher /'vaʊtʃə/ **vouchers.** N-COUNT A **voucher** is a piece of paper that can be used instead of money to pay for something. *...a voucher for a pair of cinema tickets.*

vow /vaʊ/ **vows, vowing, vowed.** **1** VERB If you **vow to** do something, you make a solemn promise or decision that you will do it. *She vowed to avenge his death... I solemnly vowed that some day I would return to live in Europe... 'I'll kill him,' she* vowed. [2] N-COUNT A **vow** is a solemn promise. *I made a silent vow to be more careful in the future... I took my marriage vows and kept them.*

vowel /vaʊəl/ **vowels.** N-COUNT A **vowel** is a sound such as the ones represented in writing by the letters 'a', 'e' 'i', 'o' and 'u', which you pronounce with your mouth open, allowing the air to flow through it.

voyage /ˈvɔɪɪdʒ/ **voyages.** N-COUNT A **voyage** is a long journey on a ship or in a spacecraft. [LITERARY] *...Columbus's voyage to the West Indies.* ● See note at **travel**.

vs. vs. is an written abbreviation for **versus**. *What happened in the Broncos vs. Canberra game?*

vulgar /ˈvʌlgə/ [1] ADJ If you describe something as **vulgar**, you think it is in bad taste or of poor artistic quality. *I think it's a very vulgar house. ...vulgar consumerism.* ◆ **vulgarity** N-UNCOUNT *I hate the vulgarity of this room.* [2] ADJ If you describe someone or something as **vulgar**, you dislike them because they use bad language, or because they refer to sex or the body in an

unpleasant way. *'Don't be vulgar,' she reprimanded. ...vulgar jokes.* ◆ **vulgarity** N-UNCOUNT *It's his vulgarity that I can't take.*

⭐ **vulnerable** /ˈvʌlnərəbəl/ [1] ADJ If someone or something is **vulnerable to** something, they have some weakness or disadvantage which makes them more likely to be harmed or affected by that thing. *People with high blood pressure are especially vulnerable to diabetes. ...attacks on vulnerable targets.* ◆ **vulnerability** /ˌvʌlnərəˈbɪlɪti/ N-UNCOUNT *...anxieties about the country's vulnerability to invasion.* [2] ADJ A **vulnerable** person is weak and without protection, with the result that they are easily hurt physically or emotionally. *Old people are particularly vulnerable members of our society.* ◆ **vulnerability** N-UNCOUNT *...the special emotional vulnerability of childhood.*

vulture /ˈvʌltʃə/ **vultures.** N-COUNT A **vulture** is a large bird which lives in hot countries and eats the flesh of dead animals.

vying /ˈvaɪɪŋ/. **Vying** is the present participle of **vie**.

W w

wacky (or **whacky**) /ˈwæki/ **wackier, wackiest.** ADJ If you describe something or someone as **wacky**, you mean that they are eccentric, unusual, and often funny. [INFORMAL] *...a wacky new television comedy series.*

wad /wɒd/ **wads.** N-COUNT A **wad of** something such as paper or banknotes is a thick, tightly packed bundle of it.

wade /weɪd/ **wades, wading, waded.** VERB If you **wade** through mud or water, you walk through it with difficulty.
▶**wade in** or **wade into.** PHR-VERB If someone **wades in**, or if they **wade into** something, they intervene in something in a very determined and forceful way, often without thinking about the consequences. *They don't just listen sympathetically. They wade in with remarks like, 'If I were you...'*
▶**wade through.** PHR-VERB If you **wade through** a difficult book or document, you spend a lot of time and effort reading it. *Managers have no time to wade through the reports.*

wafer /ˈweɪfə/ **wafers.** N-COUNT A **wafer** is a thin crisp biscuit, often eaten with ice cream.

waffle /ˈwɒfəl/ **waffles, waffling, waffled.** [1] VERB & N-UNCOUNT If someone **waffles**, they talk or write a lot without saying anything clear or important. You can call what they say or write **waffle**. *We had 15 seconds of comment and 15 minutes of waffle.* [2] N-COUNT A **waffle** is a type of thick pancake.

waft /wɒft, wæft/ **wafts, wafting, wafted.** [1] VERB If sounds or scents **waft** through the air, or if something **wafts** them, they move gently through the air. *A slight breeze rose, wafting the*

heavy scent of flowers past her. [2] N-COUNT You can call a sound or scent which has been carried on the air a **waft**. *A waft of perfume drifted into Ingrid's nostrils.*

wag /wæg/ **wags, wagging, wagged.** [1] VERB When a dog **wags** its tail, or when its tail **wags**, its tail moves repeatedly from side to side. [2] VERB If you **wag** your finger, you shake it repeatedly and quickly from side to side, usually because you are telling someone off.

⭐ **wage** /weɪdʒ/ **wages, waging, waged.** [1] N-COUNT Someone's **wages** are the amount of money that is regularly paid to them for the work that they do. *His wages have gone up.*

USAGE **Pay** is a general word which you can use to refer to the money you get from your employer for doing your job. Manual workers are paid **wages**, or **a wage**. The plural is more common than the singular, especially when you are talking about the actual cash that someone receives. *Every week he handed all his wages in cash to his wife.* Wages are usually paid, and quoted, as an hourly or a weekly sum. *...a starting wage of five dollars an hour.* Professional people and office workers receive a **salary**, which is paid monthly. However, when talking about someone's salary, you usually give the annual figure. *I'm paid a salary of £15,000 a year.* Your **income** consists of all the money you receive from all sources, including your pay.

---

a
b
c
d
e
f
g
h
i
j
k
l
m
n
o
p
q
r
s
t
u
v
w
x
y
z

2 VERB To **wage** a campaign or war means to start it and carry it on over a period of time. *Peter waged a 17-month legal battle to fight the move.*

wager /'weɪdʒə/ **wagers, wagering, wagered.** VERB & N-COUNT If you **wager on** the result of a horse race, football match, or other event, or if you have a **wager on** it, you bet money on the result.

wagon (BRIT also **waggon**) /'wægən/ **wagons.** N-COUNT A **wagon** is a strong vehicle with four wheels which is used for carrying heavy loads, and which is usually pulled by a horse or tractor.

wail /weɪl/ **wails, wailing, wailed.** **1** VERB & N-COUNT If you **wail**, or if you let out a **wail**, you cry loudly. *'Now look what you've done!' Shirley wailed... Alice let out a wail of terror.* **2** VERB & N-COUNT If something such as a siren **wails**, or if it makes a **wail**, it makes long, high-pitched, piercing sounds. *...the wail of sirens.*

waist /weɪst/ **waists.** **1** N-COUNT Your **waist** is the middle part of your body, above your hips. → See picture on page 822. **2** N-COUNT The **waist** of a garment such as a dress or pair of trousers is the part of it which covers the middle part of your body.

waistcoat /'weɪstkəʊt, 'weskət/ **waistcoats.** N-COUNT In British English, a **waistcoat** is a sleeveless piece of clothing with buttons, usually worn over a shirt. The American word is **vest**. → See picture on page 820.

⭐ **wait** /weɪt/ **waits, waiting, waited.** **1** VERB If you **wait**, you spend some time, usually doing very little, before something happens. *Stop waiting for things to happen. Make them happen... I waited to see how she responded... We will have to wait a week or so before we know whether the operation is a success.* ♦ **waiting** ADJ *She headed toward the waiting car.* **2** N-COUNT A **wait** is a period of time in which you do very little, before something happens. *...the four-hour wait for the organizers to declare the result.* **3** VERB If something **is waiting for** you, it is ready for you to use, have, or do. *When we came home we had a meal waiting for us.* **4** VERB If you say that something **can wait**, you mean that it can be dealt with later. *I want to talk to you, but it can wait.* **5** VERB **Wait** is used in expressions such as **wait a minute** and **wait a moment** to interrupt someone when they are speaking, for example because you object to what they are saying or because you want them to repeat something. **6** VERB If you **can't wait** to do something, or **can hardly wait** to do it, you are very excited about it and eager to do it. [SPOKEN]

▸ **wait around** or **wait about** PHR-VERB If you **wait around**, or if you **wait about**, you stay in the same place, usually doing very little, because you cannot act before something happens or before someone arrives. *The attacker may have been waiting around for an opportunity to strike.*

waiter /'weɪtə/ **waiters.** N-COUNT A **waiter** is a man who serves food and drink in a restaurant.

'waiting list, waiting lists. N-COUNT A **waiting list** is a list of people who have asked for something which cannot be given to them immediately, for example medical treatment or housing, and who must therefore wait until it is available. *There were 20,000 people on the waiting list for a new home.*

'waiting-room, waiting-rooms. N-COUNT A **waiting-room** is a room in a place such as a railway station or a doctor's surgery, where people can sit and wait.

waitress /'weɪtrəs/ **waitresses.** N-COUNT A **waitress** is a woman whose job is to serve food and drink in a restaurant.

waive /weɪv/ **waives, waiving, waived.** **1** VERB If you **waive** your right to something, for example legal representation, or if someone else **waives** it, you no longer have the right to receive it. **2** VERB If someone **waives** a rule, they decide not to enforce it. *The art gallery waives admission charges on Sundays.*

waiver /'weɪvə/ **waivers.** N-COUNT A **waiver** is an agreement by a person, government, or organization to give up a right or claim or to not enforce a particular rule or law. *Non-members do not qualify for the tax waiver.*

⭐ **wake** /weɪk/ **wakes, waking, woke, woken.**

✓ The form **waked** is used in American English for the past tense.

1 VERB & PHR-VERB When you **wake**, or when you **wake up**, you become conscious again after being asleep. *She woke to find her dark room lit by flashing lights... At dawn I woke him up and said we were leaving.* **2** N-COUNT A **wake** is a gathering of people who have collected together to mourn someone's death. **3** N-COUNT The **wake** of a boat is the track of waves that it makes behind it as it moves through the water.

PHRASES ● If one thing follows **in the wake of** another, it happens after the other thing is over, often as a result of it. *The governor has enjoyed a huge surge in the polls in the wake of last week's convention.* ● If you leave something **in** your **wake**, you leave it behind you as you go. *Adam stumbles on, leaving a trail of devastation in his wake.*

▸ **wake up. 1** See **wake** 1. **2** PHR-VERB If you **wake up to** something, you become aware of it. *People should wake up to the fact that people with disabilities have got a vote as well.*

⭐ **walk** /wɔːk/ **walks, walking, walked.** **1** VERB & N-SING When you **walk**, or when you move at a **walk**, you move along by putting one foot in front of the other on the ground. *They would stop the car and walk a few steps... When I was your age I walked five miles to school... She slowed to a steady walk.* **2** N-COUNT A **walk** is an outing made by walking. *He often took long walks in the hills.* **3** N-SING A **walk** of a particular distance is the distance which a person has to walk to get somewhere. *The hotel is a short walk from the Empire State Building.* **4** VERB If you **walk** someone somewhere, you walk there with them. *I walked her to the car.* **5** VERB If you **walk** your dog, you take it for a walk in order to keep it healthy.

►**walk off with.** **1** PHR-VERB If someone **walks off with** something that does not belong to them, they take it without permission. [INFORMAL] **2** PHR-VERB If you **walk off with** something such as a prize, you win it very easily. [JOURNALISM]

►**walk out.** **1** PHR-VERB If you **walk out of** a meeting, performance, or unpleasant situation, you leave it suddenly, usually to show that you are angry or bored. *Several councillors walked out of the meeting in protest.* ♦ **walkout** /'wɔːkaʊt/ **walkouts** N-COUNT *This protest included a staged walkout by the U.S. representative.* **2** PHR-VERB If someone **walks out on** their family or their partner, they leave them suddenly. **3** PHR-VERB If workers **walk out**, they go on strike. ♦ **walkout** N-COUNT *County public works employees staged a one-day walkout today.*

walker /'wɔːkə/ **walkers.** N-COUNT A **walker** is a person who walks, especially in the countryside for pleasure.

walking /'wɔːkɪŋ/ N-UNCOUNT **Walking** is the activity of going for walks in the country. *I've started to do a lot of walking and cycling.*

walk of ˈlife, walks of life. N-COUNT The **walk of life** that you come from is the position that you have in society and the kind of job you have. *...people from all walks of life.*

walkway /'wɔːkweɪ/ **walkways.** N-COUNT A **walkway** is a path or passage for pedestrians, especially one which is raised above the ground.

★ **wall** /wɔːl/ **walls.** **1** N-COUNT A **wall** is one of the vertical sides of a building or room. *...the bedroom walls.* **2** N-COUNT A **wall** is a long narrow vertical structure made of stone or brick that surrounds or divides an area of land. *He climbed over a garden wall to steal apples.* **3** N-COUNT The **wall** of something hollow is its side. *...the stomach wall.*

walled /wɔːld/ ADJ A **walled** area of land is surrounded by a wall. *...a walled rose garden.*

wallet /'wɒlɪt/ **wallets.** N-COUNT A **wallet** is a small flat folded case where you can keep banknotes and credit cards.

wallow /'wɒləʊ/ **wallows, wallowing, wallowed.** **1** VERB If you say that someone **is wallowing in** an unpleasant situation or feeling, you are criticizing them for being deliberately unhappy. *He was drunk, wallowing in self-pity.* **2** VERB When an animal **wallows** in mud or water, it lies or rolls about in it slowly.

wallpaper /'wɔːlpeɪpə/ **wallpapers, wallpapering, wallpapered.** **1** N-VAR **Wallpaper** is thick coloured or patterned paper that is used to decorate the walls of rooms. **2** VERB If someone **wallpapers** a room, they cover the walls with wallpaper. **3** N-UNCOUNT **Wallpaper** is the background on a computer screen. [COMPUTING]

walnut /'wɔːlnʌt/ **walnuts.** N-COUNT **Walnuts** are light brown edible nuts which have a wrinkled

shape and a very hard round shell.

waltz /wɔːlts/ **waltzes, waltzing, waltzed.** **1** N-COUNT A **waltz** is a piece of music with a rhythm of three beats in each bar, which people can dance to. **2** N-COUNT & VERB When two people do a **waltz**, or when they **waltz**, they dance a waltz together. **3** VERB If you **waltz** into a place, you enter in a quick confident way that makes other people notice you. [INFORMAL] *Suddenly this guy waltzed in, and asked for my autograph.*

wander /'wɒndə/ **wanders, wandering, wandered.** **1** VERB & N-SING If you **wander** around a place, or if you take a **wander** round it, you walk around in a casual way. *I was perfectly happy simply to wander the streets every now and then... A wander around any market will reveal stalls piled high with vegetables.* **2** VERB If a person or animal **wanders** from a place where they are supposed to stay, they move away from the place without going in a particular direction. *He has wandered off somewhere.* **3** VERB If your mind **wanders** or your thoughts **wander**, you stop concentrating on something and start thinking about other things.

wane /weɪn/ **wanes, waning, waned.** **1** VERB If a condition, attitude, or emotion **wanes**, it becomes weaker, often so that it eventually disappears. *His interest in these sports began to wane.* ♦ **waning** ADJ *...her mother's waning strength.* **2** PHRASE If a condition, attitude, or emotion is **on the wane**, it is becoming weaker. *The party's influence was clearly on the wane.*

★ **want** /wɒnt/ **wants, wanting, wanted.** **1** VERB If you **want** something, you feel a desire or a need for it. *I want a drink... People wanted to know who this talented designer was... He wanted his power recognised... Do you want another cup of coffee?* **2** VERB If you say that something **wants** doing, you think that it needs to be done. [INFORMAL] *The windows wanted cleaning.* **3** VERB If you tell someone that they **want to** do a particular thing, you are advising them to do it. [INFORMAL] *You want to be careful what you say.* **4** VERB If someone **is wanted** by the police, the police are searching for them. ♦ **wanted** ADJ BEFORE N *He is one of the most wanted criminals in Europe.* **5** N-SING A **want of** something is a lack of it. [FORMAL] *The men were daily becoming weaker from want of rest.*

PHRASES ● You say **if you want** when you are making or agreeing to an offer or suggestion in a casual way. *You're welcome to stay the night if you want.* ● If you do something **for want of** something else, you do it because the other thing is not available or not possible. *Many had gone into teaching for want of anything better to do.*

wanting /'wɒntɪŋ/. ADJ If you find something **wanting**, or if it proves **wanting**, it is not as good as you think it should be. *He analysed his game and found it wanting.*

WAP /wæp/. N-UNCOUNT **WAP** is a system which allows devices such as mobile phones to connect

a
b
c
d
e
f
g
h
i
j
k
l
m
n
o
p
q
r
s
t
u
v
w
x
y
z

to the Internet. **WAP** is an abbreviation for 'Wireless Application Protocol'. [COMPUTING]

⭐ **war** /wɔː/ **wars.** **1** N-VAR A **war** is a period of fighting between countries. *They've been at war for the last fifteen years.* **2** N-VAR **War** is intense economic competition between countries or organizations. *...a trade war.* **3** See also **civil war.** **4** PHRASE If two people, countries, or organizations have a **war of words**, they criticize each other because they strongly disagree about something. [JOURNALISM]

ward /wɔːd/ **wards, warding, warded.** **1** N-COUNT A **ward** is a room in a hospital which has beds for many people, often people who need similar treatment. **2** N-COUNT A **ward** is a district which forms part of a political constituency or local council. **3** N-COUNT Someone's **ward** is a child who they are responsible for as their appointed guardian.

▸**ward off.** PHR-VERB To **ward off** a danger or illness means to do something to prevent it from affecting you or harming you. *...urgent measures to ward off the threat of starvation.*

warden /'wɔːdən/ **wardens.** **1** N-COUNT A **warden** is an official who is responsible for a particular place or thing, and for making sure that certain laws are obeyed. *...a safari park warden.* **2** N-COUNT In British English, a **warden** is someone who works in a prison supervising the prisoners. The American word is **guard.**

warder /'wɔːdə/ **warders.** N-COUNT A **warder** is the same as a prison **warden.** [BRITISH]

wardrobe /'wɔːdrəʊb/ **wardrobes.** **1** N-COUNT A **wardrobe** is a tall cupboard in which you hang your clothes. **2** N-COUNT Someone's **wardrobe** is the total collection of clothes that they own. *She asked her friend for advice on building up her wardrobe.*

ware /weə/ **wares.** **1** **Ware** is used to form nouns that refer to objects that are made of a particular material, or that are used for a particular purpose. *...porcelain cooking ware.* **2** N-PLURAL Someone's **wares** are the things that they sell, usually in the street or in a market. [DATED]

warehouse /'weəhaʊs/ **warehouses.** N-COUNT A **warehouse** is a large building where raw materials or manufactured goods are stored.

warfare /'wɔːfeə/. N-UNCOUNT **Warfare** is the activity of fighting a war. *...the threat of chemical warfare.*

warhead /'wɔːhed/ **warheads.** N-COUNT A **warhead** is the front end of a bomb or missile, where the explosives are carried.

⭐ **warm** /wɔːm/ **warmer, warmest; warms, warming, warmed.** **1** ADJ Something that is **warm** has some heat but not enough to be hot. *Because it was warm, David wore only a white cotton shirt. ...warm water.* ● See note at **hot.** **2** ADJ **Warm** clothes and blankets are made of a material such as wool which protects you from the cold. ◆ **warmly** ADV *Remember to wrap up warmly on cold days.* **3** ADJ A **warm** person is friendly and

affectionate. ◆ **warmly** ADV *He greeted me warmly.* **4** VERB If you **warm** a part of your body, or if something hot **warms** it, it stops feeling cold and starts to feel hotter. *She went to warm her hands by the log fire.* **5** VERB If you **warm to** a person or an idea, you become fonder of the person or more interested in the idea. *Those who got to know him better warmed to his openness and honesty.*

▸**warm up.** **1** PHR-VERB If you **warm** something **up,** or if it **warms up,** it gets hotter. *Have you warmed the potato up, Mum?... The weather had warmed up.* **2** PHR-VERB If you **warm up** for an event such as a race, you prepare yourself for it by doing exercises or by practising just before it starts. ◆ **warm-up, warm-ups** N-COUNT *The exercises can be fun and a good warm-up for the latter part of the programme.* **3** PHR-VERB When an engine **warms up,** it becomes ready for use a little while after being switched on or started. *We spent a frustrating five minutes while the pilot warmed up the engines.*

warmth /wɔːmθ/. **1** N-UNCOUNT The **warmth** of something is the heat that it has or produces. *...the warmth of the fire.* **2** N-UNCOUNT The **warmth** of something such as a garment or blanket is the protection that it gives you against the cold. **3** N-UNCOUNT Someone who has **warmth** is friendly and enthusiastic in their behaviour towards others.

⭐ **warn** /wɔːn/ **warns, warning, warned.** **1** VERB If you **warn** someone about a possible danger or problem, you tell them about it so that they are aware of it. *United Nations officials warn of epidemics and famine... When I had my first baby friends warned me that children were expensive.* **2** VERB If you **warn** someone **not to** do something, you advise them not to do it in order to avoid possible danger or punishment. *Mrs Blount warned me not to interfere... 'Don't do anything yet,' he warned... Officials warned people against eating or picking mushrooms.*

⭐ **warning** /'wɔːnɪŋ/ **warnings.** N-VAR A **warning** is something which is said or written to tell people of a possible danger, problem, or other unpleasant thing that might happen. *The police have issued a warning to parents that he could be anywhere in Britain by now... The soldiers opened fire without warning.*

warp /wɔːp/ **warps, warping, warped.** **1** VERB If something **warps** or **is warped,** it becomes damaged by bending or curving, often because of the effect of heat or water. *The wood had started to warp.* ◆ **warped** ADJ *The door was warped.* **2** VERB If something **warps** someone's character or mind, it damages them or influences them in a bad way. ◆ **warped** ADJ *...the sort of appalling deed which is committed by the warped mind.*

warrant /'wɒrənt, AM 'wɔːr-/ **warrants, warranting, warranted.** **1** VERB If something **warrants** a particular action, it makes the action seem necessary or appropriate. *The allegations are*

warrant N-COUNT A **warrant** is an official document signed by a judge or magistrate, which gives the police special permission to do something such as arrest someone or search their house.

serious enough to warrant an investigation. 2 N-COUNT A **warrant** is an official document signed by a judge or magistrate, which gives the police special permission to do something such as arrest someone or search their house.

warranty /'wɒrənti, AM 'wɔːr-/ **warranties.** N-COUNT A **warranty** is a written guarantee which enables you to get a product repaired or replaced free of charge within a certain period of time. *The equipment is still under warranty.*

warrior /'wɒrɪə, AM 'wɔːr-/ **warriors.** N-COUNT A **warrior** is a fighter or soldier, especially one in former times who was very brave and experienced in fighting.

warship /'wɔːʃɪp/ **warships.** N-COUNT A **warship** is a ship with guns that is used for fighting in wars.

wart /wɔːt/ **warts.** N-COUNT A **wart** is a small lump which grows on your skin and which is usually caused by a virus.

wartime /'wɔːtaɪm/. N-UNCOUNT **Wartime** is a period of time when there is a war. ...his wartime experiences in France.

wary /'weəri/. ADJ If you are **wary of** someone or something, you are cautious because you do not know much about them and you believe they may be dangerous or cause problems. *She warned them to be wary of strangers... They were very wary about giving him a contract.* ◆ **warily** ADV *She studied me warily.*

was /wəz, STRONG wɒz, AM wʌz/. **Was** is the first and third person singular of the past tense of **be**.

⭐ **wash** /wɒʃ/ **washes, washing, washed.** 1 VERB & N-COUNT If you **wash** something, or if you give it a **wash**, you clean it using water and soap or detergent. *It took a long time to wash the mud out of his hair... Rub down the door and wash off the dust... That coat could do with a wash.* 2 VERB & N-COUNT If you **wash**, or if you **have a wash**, you clean part of your body using soap and water. *She washed her face with cold water... You are going to have your dinner, get washed, and go to bed... She had a wash and changed her clothes.* 3 N-SING **The wash** is all the clothes, sheets and other things that are washed together at one time. *His grey socks were in the wash.* 4 VERB If a sea or river or something carried by a sea or river **washes** somewhere or **is washed** there, it flows there gently. *The force of the water washed him back into the cave.* 5 to **wash** your **hands** of something: see **hand**. ● See also **washing**.
▶ **wash away.** PHR-VERB If rain or floods **wash away** something, they destroy it and carry it away. *Flood waters washed away one of the main bridges.*
▶ **wash down.** PHR-VERB If you **wash** something **down with** a drink, you swallow it and then drink the drink, for example to make it easier to swallow or digest. ...a massive beef sandwich washed down with a bottle of beer.
▶ **wash up.** 1 PHR-VERB If you **wash up**, you wash the pans, plates, cups, and cutlery which have been used in cooking and eating a meal.

[BRITISH] *I bet you make breakfast and wash up their plates, too.* 2 PHR-VERB If something **is washed up** on a piece of land, it is carried there by a river or the sea and left there. 3 See also **washing-up**.

washable /'wɒʃəbəl/. ADJ **Washable** clothes or materials can be washed without being damaged. ...washable vinyl.

washbasin (or **wash basin**) /'wɒʃbeɪsən/ **washbasins.** N-COUNT A **washbasin** is a large bowl for washing your hands and face. It is usually fixed to a wall, with taps for hot and cold water.

washer /'wɒʃə/ **washers.** 1 N-COUNT A **washer** is a thin flat ring made of metal or plastic, which is placed over a bolt before the nut is screwed on. 2 N-COUNT A **washer** is the same as a **washing machine**. [INFORMAL]

washing /'wɒʃɪŋ/. N-UNCOUNT **Washing** is clothes, sheets, and other things that need to be washed, are being washed, or have just been washed. *They were anxious to bring the washing in before it rained.*

'**washing machine, washing machines.** N-COUNT A **washing machine** is a machine that you use to wash clothes in.

,**washing-'up.** N-UNCOUNT To **do the washing-up** means to wash the pans, plates, cups, and cutlery which have been used in cooking and eating a meal. [BRITISH]

wasn't /'wɒzənt, AM 'wʌz-/. In informal English, **wasn't** is the usual spoken form of 'was not'.

wasp /wɒsp/ **wasps.** N-COUNT A **wasp** is a small insect with a painful sting. It has yellow and black stripes across its body. → See picture on page 824.

⭐ **waste** /weɪst/ **wastes, wasting, wasted.** 1 VERB & N-SING If you **waste** something such as time, money, or energy, you use too much of it doing something that is not important or necessary, or is unlikely to succeed. You can say that doing this is a **waste of** time, money, or energy. *The last thing she wanted to do was waste time looking at old cars... I resolved not to waste money on a hotel... It was just a waste of government money... I thought it was a waste of time moaning about it.* 2 VERB If you **waste** an opportunity, you do not take advantage of it when it is available. 3 N-UNCOUNT & N-PLURAL **Waste** or **wastes** is material which has been used and is no longer wanted, for example because the valuable or useful part has been removed. ...industrial waste. 4 ADJ **Waste** land is land which is not used or looked after by anyone. 5 N-PLURAL **Wastes** are a large area of land, for example a desert, in which there are very few people, plants, or animals. ...the barren wastes of the Sahara.
▶ **waste away.** PHR-VERB If someone **wastes away**, they become extremely thin and weak because they are ill or are not eating properly.

wasteful /'weɪstfʊl/. ADJ Action that is **wasteful** uses too much of something valuable

A B C D E F G H I J K L M N O P Q R S T U V W X Y Z

such as time, money, or energy. *This kind of training is ineffective, and wasteful of scarce resources.*

wasteland /'weɪstlænd/ **wastelands.** N-VAR A **wasteland** is an area of land which cannot be used, for example because it is infertile or because it has been misused by people.

watch 1 looking and paying attention

⭐ **watch** /wɒtʃ/ **watches, watching, watched.** [1] VERB If you **watch** someone or something, you look at them, usually for a period of time. *Two girls stood chewing slowly, watching the ambulance... They had been sitting watching television.* [2] VERB If you **watch** a situation, you pay attention to it or you are aware of it, but are not participating in it. *Human rights groups have been closely watching the case.* [3] VERB If you tell someone to **watch** a particular person or thing, you are warning them to be careful that the person or thing does not get out of control or do something unpleasant. *You really ought to watch these quiet types.*

USAGE If you want to say that someone is paying attention to something they can see, you say that they **are watching it** or **are looking at it.** In general, you **watch** something that is moving or changing, while you **look at** something that is not moving. *He watched Blake run down the stairs... I asked him to look at the picture above his bed.* You use **see** to talk about things that you are aware of because a visual impression reaches your eyes. You often use **can** in this case. *I can see the fax here on the desk.*

PHRASES ● You say **'watch it'** in order to warn someone to be careful. [INFORMAL] ● If someone **keeps watch**, they look around all the time, usually when other people are asleep, so that they can warn the others of danger or an attack. ● If you **keep watch on** events or a situation, you pay attention to what is happening, so that you can take action at the right moment.

▸ **watch for** or **watch out for.** PHR-VERB If you **watch for** something, or if you **watch out for** it, you pay attention so that you notice it, either because you do not want to miss it or because you want to avoid it. *We'll be watching for any developments... Watch out for hidden sugar in food by reading the nutrition label carefully.*

▸ **watch out.** PHR-VERB If you tell someone to **watch out**, you are warning them to be careful, because something unpleasant might happen to them or they might get into difficulties. *You have to watch out because there are land mines all over the place.*

▸ **watch out for.** See **watch for.**

watch 2 instrument that tells the time

⭐ **watch** /wɒtʃ/ **watches.** N-COUNT A **watch** is a small clock which you wear on a strap on your wrist or on a chain.

watchdog /'wɒtʃdɒg, AM -dɔ:g/ **watchdogs.** N-COUNT A **watchdog** is a person or committee whose job is to make sure that companies do not act illegally or irresponsibly. *...the head of Britain's gas industry watchdog.*

watchful /'wɒtʃfʊl/. ADJ Someone who is **watchful** is careful to notice everything that is happening. *They had been alert and watchful, but had seen nothing suspicious.*

⭐ **water** /'wɔ:tə/ **waters, watering, watered.** [1] N-UNCOUNT **Water** is a clear thin liquid that has no colour or taste when it is pure. It falls from clouds as rain. *Get me a glass of water.* [2] N-UNCOUNT & N-PLURAL When people are talking about a large area of water, for example a lake or sea, they sometimes call it **the water** or **the waters**. *Monique ran down to the water's edge. ...the calm waters of Cowes Harbour.* [3] N-PLURAL A country's **waters** consist of the area of sea which is near it and which is regarded as belonging to it. *...ferries operating in British waters.* [4] VERB If you **water** plants, you pour water into the soil to help them to grow. [5] VERB If your eyes **are watering**, you have tears in them because they are sore or because you are upset. [6] VERB If you say that your mouth **is watering**, you mean that you can smell or see some appetizing food.

▸ **water down.** PHR-VERB If something, especially a proposal, speech, or statement **is watered down**, it is made much weaker and less forceful or less controversial.

watercolour (AM **watercolor**) /'wɔ:təkʌlə/ **watercolours.** [1] N-PLURAL **Watercolours** are coloured paints, used for painting pictures, which you apply with a wet brush or dissolve in water first. [2] N-COUNT A **watercolour** is a picture which has been painted using watercolours.

waterfall /'wɔ:təfɔ:l/ **waterfalls.** N-COUNT A **waterfall** is a place where water flows over the edge of a steep cliff and falls into a pool below.

waterfront /'wɔ:təfrʌnt/ **waterfronts.** N-COUNT A **waterfront** is a street or piece of land which is next to an area of water, for example a harbour or the sea. *...a two-bedroom apartment on the waterfront.*

waterproof /'wɔ:təpru:f/. ADJ Something that is **waterproof** does not let water pass through it. *...waterproof clothing.*

watershed /'wɔ:təʃed/ **watersheds.** N-COUNT If something such as an event is a **watershed** in the history or development of something, it is very important because it represents the beginning of a new stage in it. *The election of Mary Robinson in 1990 was a watershed in Irish politics.*

watertight /'wɔ:tətaɪt/. [1] ADJ Something that is **watertight** does not allow water to pass through it, for example because it is tightly sealed. *The batteries are safely enclosed in a watertight compartment.* **2** ADJ A **watertight** case or agreement is one that nobody can disprove or find fault with. *The police had a watertight case.*

waterway /ˈwɔːtəweɪ/ **waterways.** N-COUNT A **waterway** is a canal, river, or narrow channel of sea which ships or boats can sail along.

watery /ˈwɔːtəri/. **1** ADJ Something that is **watery** is weak or pale. *A watery light began to show through the branches.* **2** ADJ **Watery** food or drink contains too much water or is thin and tasteless like water. *...a plateful of watery soup.* **3** ADJ Something that is **watery** contains, resembles, or consists of water. *Emma's eyes went red and watery.*

watt /wɒt/ **watts.** N-COUNT A **watt** is a unit of measurement of electrical power. *...a 100-watt light-bulb.*

⭐ **wave** /weɪv/ **waves, waving, waved.** **1** VERB & N-COUNT If you **wave** or **wave** your hand, or if you give a **wave**, you move your hand from side to side in the air, usually in order to say hello or goodbye to someone. *He smiled and waved to journalists... Paddy spotted Mary Ann and gave her a cheery wave.* **2** VERB If you **wave** someone somewhere, you make a movement with your hand to indicate that they should move in a particular direction. *Leshka waved him away with a show of irritation.* **3** VERB If you **wave** something, you hold it up and move it rapidly from side to side. *More than 4000 people waved flags and sang nationalist songs.* **4** N-COUNT A **wave** is a raised mass of water on the sea or a lake, caused by the wind or the tide. **5** N-COUNT A **wave** is a sudden increase in a particular feeling, activity, or type of behaviour, especially an undesirable or unpleasant one. *...the current wave of violence... The loneliness and grief comes in waves.* **6** N-COUNT **Wave** is used to refer to the way in which things such as sound, light, and radio signals travel. *Radio waves have a certain frequency.* **7** See also **new wave**, **shock wave**, **tidal wave**.

wavelength /ˈweɪvleŋθ/ **wavelengths.** **1** N-COUNT A **wavelength** is the distance between the same point on consecutive cycles of a wave of energy such as light or sound. *Blue light has a shorter wavelength than red.* **2** N-COUNT A **wavelength** is the size of radio wave which a particular radio station uses to broadcast its programmes. **3** PHRASE If two people are **on the same wavelength**, they find it easy to understand each other and they tend to agree, because they share similar interests or opinions.

waver /ˈweɪvə/ **wavers, wavering, wavered.** **1** VERB If you **waver**, you are uncertain or indecisive about something. *Some military commanders wavered over whether to support the coup.* **2** VERB If something **wavers**, it shakes with very slight movements or changes. *The shadows of the dancers wavered continually.*

wavy /ˈweɪvi/ **wavier, waviest.** ADJ **Wavy** hair is not straight or curly, but curves slightly. → See picture on page 312.

wax /wæks/. N-UNCOUNT **Wax** is a solid, slightly shiny substance made of fat or oil which is used to make candles and polish.

⭐ **way** /weɪ/ **ways.** **1** N-COUNT If you refer to a **way** of doing something, you are referring to how you can do it, for example the method you can use to achieve it. *Another way of making new friends is to go to an evening class... I can't think of a worse way to spend my time.* **2** N-COUNT You can refer to the **way** that an action is done to indicate the quality that it has. *She smiled in a friendly way.* **3** N-PLURAL The **ways** of a particular person or group of people are their customs or their usual behaviour. *I won't alter my ways because I'm under pressure.* **4** N-COUNT If a general statement or description is true **in** a particular **way**, that is a particular manner or form that it takes in a specific case. *She was afraid in a way that was quite new to her... In some ways, the official opening is a formality.* **5** N-SING The **way** you feel about something is your attitude to it or your opinion about it. *I'm terribly sorry, I had no idea you felt that way.* **6** N-COUNT **The way** to a particular place is the route that you must take in order to get there. *Does anybody know the way to the bathroom?... We'll go out the back way... This is the way in.* **7** N-SING You use **way** to indicate the direction or position of something. *As he strode into the kitchen, he passed Pop coming the other way... Turn the cake the right way up.* **8** N-SING If someone or something is **in the way**, they prevent you from moving freely or from seeing clearly. *I couldn't see it because a truck was in the way... Get out of my way!* **9** N-SING You use **way** in expressions such as **push** your **way** and **make** your **way** to indicate movement or progression, especially when this is difficult or slow. *He elbowed his way to the bar... Fergus sat at the desk working his way through a mass of papers.* **10** N-SING You use **way** in expressions such as **a long way** and **a little way** to say how far away something is. *We've a fair way to go yet.* **11** N-SING You use **way** in expressions such as **all the way**, **most of the way**, and **half the way** to refer to the extent to which an action has been completed. *When was the last time you listened to an album all the way through?* **12** ADV You can use **way** to emphasize, for example, that something is a great distance away or is very much below or above a particular level or amount. *Way down in the valley to the west is the town of Freiburg... I have to decide my plan way in advance.*

PHRASES ● If an object that is supporting something **gives way**, it breaks or collapses. *He fell when a ledge gave way beneath him.* ● If you **give way to** someone or something that you have been resisting, you stop resisting and allow yourself to be persuaded or controlled by them. *The President has given way to pressure from the*

a b c d e f g h i j k l m n o p q r s t u v w x y z

hardliners. • If a moving person or a vehicle or its driver **gives way**, they slow down or stop in order to allow other people or vehicles to pass in front of them. [BRITISH] • If you **lose** your **way**, you become lost when you are trying to go somewhere. • If one person or thing **makes way for** another, the first is replaced by the second. *The building will be demolished in January to make way for new offices.* • If you **go out of** your **way to** do something, you make a special effort to do it. *She went out of her way to make him feel at home.* • If you **keep out of** someone's **way**, you avoid them. • When something **is out of the way**, it is over or you have dealt with it. *The plan has to remain confidential at least until the local elections are out of the way.* • If an activity or plan is **under way**, it has begun and is now taking place. *Peace talks are under way.* • If someone **gets** their **way** or **has** their **way**, nobody stops them doing what they want to do. You can also say that someone **gets** their **own way** or **has** their **own way**. *As long as she got her own way, she could be a delightful child.* • If someone says that you **can't have it both ways**, they mean that you have to choose between two things and cannot do or have them both. • If you say that someone or something **has a way of** doing a particular thing, you mean they often do it. *Bosses have a way of always finding out about such things.* • You say **by the way** when you add something to what you have said, especially something that you have just thought of. [SPOKEN] *By the way, how is your back?* • You use **in a way** to indicate that your statement is true to some extent or in one respect. *In a way, I suppose I'm frightened of failing.*

,**way of ˈlife, ways of life.** N-COUNT Someone's **way of life** consists of their habits and their daily activities.

wayward /ˈweɪwəd/. ADJ A **wayward** person is likely to change suddenly, and is therefore difficult to control.

⭐ **we** /wɪ, STRONG wiː/. PRON **We** is used as the subject of a verb. A speaker or writer uses **we** to refer to a group of people which includes himself or herself. *We ordered another bottle of champagne... We students outnumbered our teachers.*

⭐ **weak** /wiːk/ **weaker, weakest.** 1 ADJ If someone is **weak**, they do not have very much strength or energy. ◆ **weakly** ADV *Sharon shook her head weakly.* ◆ **weakness** N-UNCOUNT *Symptoms of infection include weakness, nausea and vomiting.* 2 ADJ Something that is **weak** is not strong or good, and is likely to break or fail. *Ron has weak eyesight... She had a weak heart.* 3 ADJ If you describe someone as **weak**, you mean that they are not very confident or determined, so that they are often frightened or worried, or easily influenced by other people. ◆ **weakness** N-UNCOUNT *Many people felt that admitting to stress was a sign of weakness.* 4 ADJ If something

such as an argument or case is **weak**, it is not convincing or there is little evidence to support it. *The evidence against him was weak.* 5 ADJ A **weak** drink, chemical, or drug contains very little of a particular substance, for example because it has been diluted with a lot of water. *...a cup of weak tea.*

⭐ **weaken** /ˈwiːkən/ **weakens, weakening, weakened.** 1 VERB To **weaken** something means to make it less strong or less powerful. *The recession has weakened so many firms that many can no longer survive... Family structures are weakening and breaking up.* 2 VERB If someone **weakens**, they become less certain about a decision they have made. *Jennie weakened, and finally relented... The verdict hasn't weakened his resolve to fight the charges against him.*

weakness /ˈwiːknəs/ **weaknesses** 1 N-COUNT If you have a **weakness for** something, you like it very much. *Stephen had a weakness for cats.* 2 See also **weak**.

⭐ **wealth** /welθ/. 1 N-UNCOUNT **Wealth** is a large amount of money or property owned by someone, or the possession of it. *His own wealth grew.* 2 N-SING A **wealth of** something means a very large amount of it. [LITERARY] *The city boasts a wealth of beautiful churches.*

wealthy /ˈwelθi/ **wealthier, wealthiest.** ADJ & N-PLURAL **Wealthy** people have a large amount of money or property. You can call people like this **the wealthy.**

wean /wiːn/ **weans, weaning, weaned.** 1 VERB When a mother **weans** her baby, she stops feeding it with milk from her breast and starts giving it other food. 2 VERB If you **wean** someone **off** a bad habit, you gradually make them stop doing it or liking it. *...a programme to wean addicts off drugs.*

⭐ **weapon** /ˈwepən/ **weapons.** N-COUNT A **weapon** is an object such as a gun, knife, or missile... *armed with makeshift weapons.*

weaponry /ˈwepənri/. N-UNCOUNT **Weaponry** is all the weapons that a group or country has or that are available to it.

⭐ **wear** /weə/ **wears, wearing, wore, worn.** 1 VERB When you **wear** clothes, shoes, or jewellery, you have them on your body. *He was wearing a brown uniform.* 2 VERB If you **wear** your hair in a particular way, it is cut or styled in that way. *She wore her hair in a long braid.* 3 N-UNCOUNT You can use **wear** to refer to clothes that are suitable for a particular time or occasion. *...an extensive range of beach wear.* 4 N-UNCOUNT **Wear** is the amount or type of use that something has over a period of time. *You'll get more wear out of a hat if you choose one in a neutral colour.* 5 VERB & N-UNCOUNT If something **wears**, or if it shows signs of **wear**, it becomes thinner or weaker from constant use. *Your horse needs new shoes if the shoe has worn thin or smooth. ...a large, well-*

upholstered armchair which showed signs of wear.
6 See also **worn**.

USAGE After you get up in the morning, you **get dressed**, or you **dress**, by **putting on** your clothes. *He put on his shoes and socks.* Small children and sick people may be unable to **dress themselves**, so someone else has to **dress** them.

When you **are dressed**, you **are wearing** your clothes, or you **have** them **on**. *Edith had her hat on... They ought to stop walking round the house with nothing on.* During the day you might want to **get changed**, or to **change**, or to **change** your clothes. *She returned having changed from trousers and a pullover into a short-sleeved blouse and a skirt... Adams changed his shirt a couple of times a day.*

Before you go to bed, you **get undressed**, or you **undress**, by **taking off** your clothes. *He won't take his clothes off in front of me.*

See also the note at **clothes**.

▸**wear away.** PHR-VERB If you **wear** something **away**, it becomes thin and eventually disappears because it is used a lot or rubbed a lot. *The softer rock wears away.*
▸**wear down.** **1** PHR-VERB If you **wear** something **down**, it becomes flatter or smoother as a result of constantly rubbing against something else. **2** PHR-VERB If someone **wears** you **down**, they weaken you by continually attacking or criticizing you, or by trying to persuade you to do something. *They hoped the waiting would wear down my resistance.*
▸**wear off.** PHR-VERB If a feeling or sensation **wears off**, it slowly disappears. *Now that the initial shock was wearing off, he was in pain.*
▸**wear out.** **1** PHR-VERB When something **wears out**, it is used so much that it becomes thin or weak and cannot be used any more. *He wore out his shoes wandering around Mexico City.* ● See also **worn-out**. **2** PHR-VERB If something **wears** you **out**, it makes you feel extremely tired. [INFORMAL]

weary /ˈwɪəri/ **wearier, weariest; wearies, wearying, wearied.** **1** ADJ If you are **weary**, you are very tired. ♦ **wearily** ADV *I sighed wearily.*
♦ **weariness** N-UNCOUNT *Despite his weariness, Brand mustered a wan smile.* **2** VERB & ADJ AFTER LINK-V If you **weary** of something, or if you are **weary of** it, you become tired of it. *He had wearied of teaching in state universities... She was weary of being alone.*

⭐ **weather** /ˈweðə/ **weathers, weathering, weathered.** **1** N-UNCOUNT The **weather** is the condition of the atmosphere in an area at a particular time, for example, whether it is raining, hot, or windy. *The weather was bad. ...cold weather.* **2** VERB If

something such as rock or wood **weathers**, it changes colour or shape as a result of the effects of wind, sun, rain, or frost. **3** VERB If you **weather** a difficult time, you survive it. *The company has weathered the recession.*

weave /wiːv/ **weaves, weaving, wove, woven.**

✓ The form **weaved** is used for the past tense and past participle for meaning 3.

1 VERB If you **weave** cloth, you make it by crossing threads over and under each other using a machine called a loom. ♦ **weaver, weavers** N-COUNT *...a linen weaver from Ireland.*
♦ **weaving** N-UNCOUNT *I studied weaving.*
2 N-COUNT The **weave** of a cloth is the way in which the threads are arranged. *Fabrics with a close weave.* **3** VERB If you **weave** your **way** somewhere, you move between and around things as you go there.

web /web/ **webs.** **1** N-COUNT A spider's **web** is the thin net which it makes from the sticky substance it produces in its body. **2** N-COUNT A **web** is a complicated pattern of connections or relationships, often considered as an obstacle or a danger. *They accused him of weaving a web of lies and deceit.* **3** See also **World-Wide Web**.

webcam (or **Webcam**) /ˈwebkæm/ **webcams.** N-COUNT A **webcam** is a video camera that takes pictures which can be viewed on a website. [COMPUTING]

webcast (or **Webcast**) /ˈwebkɑːst, -kæst/ **webcasts.** N-COUNT A **webcast** is an event such as a concert which you can watch on the Internet. [COMPUTING]

webmaster (or **Webmaster**) /ˈwebmɑːstə, -mæs-/ **webmasters.** N-COUNT A **webmaster** is someone who is in charge of a website, especially someone who does that as their job. [COMPUTING]

web page (or **Web page**) **web pages.** N-COUNT A **web page** is a set of data or information which is designed to be viewed as part of a website. [COMPUTING]

⭐ **website** (also **Web site** or **web site**) /ˈwebsaɪt/ **websites.** N-COUNT A **website** is a set of data and information about a particular subject which is available on the Internet. [COMPUTING]

webspace /ˈwebspeɪs/ N-UNCOUNT **Webspace** is computer memory that you can use to create web pages. [COMPUTING]

wed /wed/ **weds, wedded.**

✓ The form **wed** is used in the present tense and is the past tense. The past participle can be either **wed** or **wedded**.

VERB If one person **weds** another or if two people **wed**, they get married. [JOURNALISM]

we'd /wɪd, wiːd/ **We'd** is the usual spoken form of 'we would' or 'we had', especially when 'had' is an auxiliary verb. *I don't know how we'd have managed without her!*

⭐ **wedding** /ˈwedɪŋ/ **weddings.** N-COUNT A **wedding** is a marriage ceremony and the celebration that often takes place afterwards.

wedge /wedʒ/ **wedges, wedging, wedged.**
1 N-COUNT A **wedge** is an object with one pointed edge and one thick edge, which you put under a door to keep it firmly in position. **2** VERB If you **wedge** something such as a door or window, you keep it firmly in position by pushing a wedge or a similar object between it and the surface next to it. *We slammed the gate after them, wedging it shut with planks.* **3** VERB If you **wedge** something somewhere, you fit it there tightly. *Wedge the plug into the hole.* **4** PHRASE If someone **drives a wedge between** two people who are close, they cause ill feelings between them in order to weaken their relationship.

⭐ **Wednesday** /'wenzdeɪ, -di/ **Wednesdays.** N-VAR **Wednesday** is the day after Tuesday and before Thursday. → See Reference Page on Times and Dates.

wee /wiː/. ADJ **Wee** means small or little; used especially in Scotland. *...a wee child.*

weed /wiːd/ **weeds, weeding, weeded.** **1** N-COUNT A **weed** is a wild plant growing where it is not wanted, for example in a garden. **2** VERB If you **weed** an area, you remove the weeds from it. *The Hodges are busy weeding and planting.*
▸**weed out.** PHR-VERB If you **weed out** things or people that are not wanted in a group, you find them and get rid of them. *He is keen to weed out the many applicants he believes may be frauds.*

⭐ **week** /wiːk/ **weeks.** **1** N-VAR A **week** is a period of seven days, which is often considered to start on Monday and end on Sunday. → See Reference Page on Times and Dates. *I had a letter from my mother last week... Her mother stayed for another two weeks.* **2** N-COUNT Your working **week** is the hours that you spend at work during a week. *...workers on a three-day week because of the slump.* **3** N-SING **The week** is the part of the week that does not include Saturday and Sunday. *...looking after the children during the week.*

weekday /'wiːkdeɪ/ **weekdays.** N-COUNT A **weekday** is any day of the week except Saturday and Sunday.

⭐ **weekend** /ˌwiːk'end/ **weekends.** N-COUNT A **weekend** is Saturday and Sunday. *I'll phone you at the weekend.*

⭐ **weekly** /'wiːkli/ **weeklies.** **1** ADJ BEFORE N & ADV **Weekly** is used to describe something that happens or appears once a week. *...a weekly newspaper... The group meets weekly.* **2** N-COUNT A **weekly** is a newspaper or magazine that is published once a week.

weep /wiːp/ **weeps, weeping, wept.** VERB & N-SING If someone **weeps** or if they have a **weep**, they cry. *She wept tears of joy... There are times when I sit down and have a good weep.*

⭐ **weigh** /weɪ/ **weighs, weighing, weighed.** **1** VERB If someone or something **weighs** a particular amount, that is how heavy they are. *He weighs 19 stone.* **2** VERB If you **weigh** someone or something, you measure how heavy they are. **3** VERB & PHR-VERB If you **weigh** the facts about a

situation, or if you **weigh** them **up**, you consider them very carefully before you decide or say anything. *She weighed her options... 'I've been weighing up all the alternatives.'* **4** VERB If a problem **weighs on** you, it makes you worried or unhappy. *The separation weighed on both of them.*
▸**weigh down.** **1** PHR-VERB If something that you are wearing or carrying **weighs** you **down**, it stops you moving easily because it is heavy. *...soldiers weighed down by their heavy packs.* **2** PHR-VERB If you **are weighed down** by something, it makes you very worried or causes you great problems. *...countries that are weighed down by the burden of overseas debt.*

⭐ **weight** /weɪt/ **weights, weighting, weighted.** **1** N-VAR The **weight** of a person or thing is how heavy they are, measured in units such as kilos or pounds. *What is your height and weight?... This reduced the weight of the load.*

> **USAGE** In British English, a person's weight is normally measured in **stones** and **pounds**. A **stone** is equivalent to 14 pounds, or 6.35 kilograms. When you are mentioning someone's weight, you often omit the word **pounds**. **Stone** usually has a singular form although its meaning is plural. *Jodie confessed she now weighed 9 stone 12.*
> In American English, only **pounds** are used. *I weigh 110 pounds.*

2 N-COUNT **Weights** are metal objects which weigh a known amount. *I was in the gym lifting weights.* **3** N-COUNT You can refer to a heavy object as a **weight**. *Straining to lift heavy weights can lead to a rise in blood pressure.* **4** N-SING If you feel a **weight** on you, you have a worrying problem or responsibility. *A great weight lifted from me... I feel a much greater weight of responsibility in my current job.*
PHRASES ● If someone is not **pulling** their **weight**, they are not working as hard as everyone else who is involved in the same task. ● If you **throw** your **weight behind** a person or a plan, you use all your influence and do everything you can to support them.
▸**weight down.** PHR-VERB If you **weight** something **down**, you put something heavy on it or in it, often so that it cannot move easily.

weighted /'weɪtɪd/. ADJ A system that is **weighted** in favour of a person or group is organized so that this person or group has an advantage. *The peace process is so heavily weighted against them that it will never achieve results.*

weightlifting (or **weight-lifting**) /'weɪtˌlɪftɪŋ/. N-UNCOUNT **Weightlifting** is a sport in which the competitor who can lift the heaviest weight wins.

'weight ˌtraining. N-UNCOUNT **Weight training** is a kind of exercise in which people lift or push heavy weights with their arms and legs.

well

weighty /'weɪti/ **weightier, weightiest. ADJ** Weighty issues seem serious or important. [FORMAL] *Surely such weighty matters merit a higher level of debate?*

weir /wɪə/ **weirs. N-COUNT** A **weir** is a low dam built across a river to control the flow of water.

weird /wɪəd/ **weirder, weirdest. ADJ** Weird means strange and peculiar. *It must be really weird to be rich.* ◆ **weirdly** ADV ...*men who dressed weirdly.*

★ **welcome** /'welkəm/ **welcomes, welcoming, welcomed.** ⬚1⬚ VERB & N-COUNT If you **welcome** someone or if you give them a **welcome**, you greet them in a friendly way when they arrive. *She was there to welcome him home from war... There would be a fantastic welcome awaiting him.* ⬚2⬚ CONVENTION You say **'Welcome'** to someone who has just arrived. *Welcome to Washington... Welcome back, Deborah – It's good to have you here.* ⬚3⬚ ADJ If you say that someone is **welcome** in a particular place, you are encouraging them to go there by assuring them that they will be accepted. *New members are always welcome.* ⬚4⬚ PHRASE If you **make** someone **welcome** or **make** them **feel welcome**, you make them feel happy and accepted in a new place. ⬚5⬚ VERB & ADJ If you **welcome** an action or decision, or if you say it is **welcome**, you approve of it and support it. *The leadership issued a statement welcoming the coup... This was certainly a welcome change of fortune.* ⬚6⬚ ADJ AFTER LINK-V If you tell someone that they are **welcome to** do something, you are encouraging them to do it. *...a conservatory which guests are welcome to use.* ⬚7⬚ CONVENTION You can acknowledge someone's thanks by saying **'You're welcome'**. *'Thank you for the information.'—'You're welcome.'*

weld /weld/ **welds, welding, welded.** ⬚1⬚ VERB If you **weld** one piece of metal to another, you join them by heating their edges and putting them together so that they cool and harden into one piece. ⬚2⬚ N-COUNT A **weld** is a join where two pieces of metal have been welded together.

★ **welfare** /'welfeə/ ⬚1⬚ N-UNCOUNT The **welfare** of a person or group is their health, comfort, and prosperity. *I do not think he is considering Emma's welfare.* ⬚2⬚ ADJ **Welfare** services are provided to help with people's living conditions and financial problems. *He has urged complete reform of the welfare system.* ⬚3⬚ N-UNCOUNT In American English, **welfare** is money that is paid by the government to people who are unemployed, poor, or ill. The British term is **social security**.

welfare 'state. N-SING In Britain and some other countries, the **welfare state** is a system in which the government uses money collected from taxes to provides social services such as health and education and gives money to people when they are unable to work.

well 1 discourse uses

★ **well** /wel/.

☑ **Well** is used mainly in spoken English.

⬚1⬚ ADV You say **well** to indicate that you are about to say something else, especially when you are hesitating, when you are trying to make your statement less strong, when you are about to correct a statement, or when you are changing the topic. *Well, I thought she was a bit unfair about me... There was a note. Well, not really a note.* ⬚2⬚ CONVENTION You say **oh well** to indicate that you accept a situation or that someone else should accept it, even though you or they are not very happy about it. *Oh well, it could be worse.* ● **very well**: see **very**.

well 2 adverb uses

★ **well** /wel/ **better, best.** ⬚1⬚ ADV If you do something **well**, you do it to a high standard or to a great extent. *All the Indian batsmen played well... He speaks English better than I do... People live longer nowadays, and they are better educated... I don't really know her very well.* ⬚2⬚ ADV If you do something **well**, you do it thoroughly and completely. *Mix all the ingredients well.* ⬚3⬚ ADV You use **well** to ask or talk about the extent or standard of something. *How well do you remember your mother, Franzi?... He wasn't dressed any better than me.* ⬚4⬚ ADV You use **well** in front of prepositions and a few adjectives in order to emphasize them. For example, if you say that one thing happened **well before** another, you mean that it happened a long time before it. *Franklin did not turn up until well after midnight... The show is well worth a visit.* ⬚5⬚ ADV You use **well** after verbs such as 'may' and 'could' when you are saying what you think is likely to happen. *The murderer may well come from the estate.*

well 3 phrases

★ **well** /wel/.

PHRASES ● If one thing is involved and another thing is involved **as well**, the second thing is also involved. *It is most often diagnosed in women in their thirties and forties, although I've seen it in many younger women, as well.* ● If one thing is involved **as well as** another, the first thing is involved in addition to the second. *Jim Morrison was a poet as well as a singer.* ● If you say that something that has happened **is just as well**, you mean that it is fortunate that it happened in the way it did. *Judging from everything you've said, it was just as well she wasn't there.* ● If you say that you **might as well** do something, or that you **may as well** do it, you mean that you will do it although you do not have a strong desire to do it and may even feel slightly reluctant about it. *Anyway, you're here; you might as well stay.* ● If you say that something is **well and truly** over, you are emphasizing that it is completely finished or gone. *The war is well and truly over.*

well 4 adjective use

★ **well** /wel/. ADJ If you are **well**, you are healthy and not ill. *I'm not very well today.*

well 5 noun uses

well /wel/ **wells.** ⬚1⬚ N-COUNT A **well** is a hole in the

a
b
c
d
e
f
g
h
i
j
k
l
m
n
o
p
q
r
s
t
u
v
w
x
y
z

ground from which a supply of water is extracted. **2** N-COUNT A **well** is an oil well.

well ⑥ verb use

well /wel/. **wells, welling, welled.** VERB & PHR-VERB If tears **well** in your eyes, or if they **well up** in your eyes, they come to the surface. *Tears well up in her eyes when she recalls the tragic loss.*

we'll /wɪl, STRONG wiːl/. **We'll** is the usual spoken form of 'we shall' or 'we will'. *Whatever you want to chat about, we'll do it tonight.*

,**well-'balanced.** **1** ADJ Someone who is **well-balanced** is sensible and does not have many emotional problems. **2** ADJ If you describe something that is made up of several parts as **well-balanced**, you mean that there is a good mixture of each part. *...a well-balanced diet.*

'**well-being** (or **wellbeing**). N-UNCOUNT Someone's **well-being** is their health and happiness. *Singing can create a sense of wellbeing.*

,**well 'done.** **1** CONVENTION You say '**Well done**' to indicate that you are pleased that someone has got something right or done something good. **2** ADJ If meat is **well done**, it has been cooked thoroughly.

,**well-'dressed.** ADJ Someone who is **well-dressed** is wearing smart or elegant clothes.

,**well-es'tablished.** ADJ If something is **well-established**, it has existed for quite a long time and is successful. *...well-established companies.*

,**well-in'formed.** ADJ Someone who is **well-informed** knows a lot about many different subjects or about one particular subject.

,**well-in'tentioned.** ADJ **Well-intentioned** means the same as **well-meaning**.

★ ,**well-'known.** ADJ Something or someone that is **well-known** is famous or familiar. *She was a very well-known author.* ● See note at **famous**.

,**well-'meaning.** ADJ Someone who is **well-meaning** tries to be helpful, but is usually unsuccessful or causes unfortunate results.

,**well-'off.** ADJ Someone who is **well-off** is rich enough to be able to do and buy most of the things that they want.

,**well-'paid.** ADJ If you say that a person or their job is **well-paid**, you mean that they receive a lot of money for the work that they do.

,**well-to-'do.** ADJ **Well-to-do** means the same as **well-off**.

went /went/. **Went** is the past tense of **go**.

wept /wept/. **Wept** is the past tense and past participle of **weep**.

were /wə, STRONG wɜː/. **1** **Were** is the plural and the second person singular of the past tense of **be**. **2** **Were** is sometimes used instead of 'was' in certain structures, for example in conditional clauses or after the verb 'wish'. [FORMAL] *If she were to marry, her husband would have to live at Park Villa... Jerry wished he were back in Washington.*

we're /wɪə/. **We're** is the usual spoken form of 'we are'. *I'm married, but we're separated.*

weren't /wɜːnt/. **Weren't** is the usual spoken form of 'were not'. *We weren't totally happy with the way things sounded.*

★ **west** /west/. **1** N-SING **The west** is the direction in which you look to see the sun set. **2** N-SING & ADJ **The west of** a place, or the **west** part of a place, is the part which is towards the west. *...a house in the west of the city... He's from the west coast of Africa.* **3** ADV **West** means towards the west, or positioned to the west of a place or thing. *We'll drive west to Kanchanaburi... The plan is to build a huge new film studio just west of London.* **4** ADJ A **west** wind blows from the west. **5** N-SING **The West** is used to refer to the United States, Canada, and the countries of Western, Northern, and Southern Europe.

westerly /'westəli/. **1** ADJ A **westerly** point, area, or direction is to the west or towards the west. *They set out in a westerly direction along the riverbank.* **2** ADJ A **westerly** wind blows from the west.

★ **western** /'westən/ **westerns.** **1** ADJ **Western** means in or from the west of a region or country. **2** ADJ **Western** means coming from or associated with the societies of the United States, Canada, and the countries of Western, Northern, and Southern Europe. **3** N-COUNT A **western** is a film or book about the life of cowboys.

westerner /'westənə/ **westerners.** N-COUNT A **westerner** is a person who was born in or who lives in the United States, Canada, or Western, Northern, or Southern Europe.

westward /'westwəd/ (or **westwards**) /'westwədz/. ADV & ADJ **Westward** or **westwards** means towards the west. *...the settlers who moved westwards in the 19th century. ...the one-hour westward flight over the Andes to Lima.*

★ **wet** /wet/ **wetter, wettest; wets, wetting, wetted.**

> ✓ The forms **wet** and **wetted** are both used as the past tense and past participle of the verb.

1 ADJ If something is **wet**, it is covered in water or another liquid. *My gloves were soaking wet.* **2** VERB To **wet** something means to cause it to have water or another liquid on it. *For the best results wet the hair and work the shampoo well into the scalp.* **3** ADJ When the weather is **wet**, it is raining. *It was very wet and windy the day I drove over to Milland.* **4** ADJ If something such as paint or cement is **wet**, it is not yet dry. **5** VERB If someone **wets** their bed or clothes, or if they **wet themselves**, they urinate in their bed or clothes because they cannot control their bladder.

wetland /'wetlænd/ **wetlands.** N-VAR A **wetland** is an area of very wet muddy land with wild plants growing in it. You can also refer to a wetland as **wetlands**. *...a scheme that aims to protect the wilderness of the wetlands.*

we've /wɪv, STRONG wiːv/. **We've** is the usual spoken form of 'we have', especially when 'have' is an auxiliary verb. *'Hello, I don't think we've met,' Robert introduced himself.*

For a full explanation of all grammatical labels, see pages vii-x   ★ Bank of English® frequent word

whack /wæk/ **whacks, whacking, whacked.** VERB If you **whack** someone or something, you hit them hard. [INFORMAL] *Someone whacked him on the head.*

whacky. See **wacky.**

whale /weɪl/ **whales.** N-COUNT A **whale** is a very large sea mammal.

whaling /'weɪlɪŋ/. N-UNCOUNT **Whaling** is the activity of hunting and killing whales. *...commercial whaling in Antarctica.*

wharf /wɔːf/ **wharves.** N-COUNT A **wharf** is a platform by a river or the sea where ships can be tied up.

⭐ **what** /wɒt/. **1** PRON & DET You use **what** in questions when you are asking for information. *What do you want?... 'Indeed it has.'—'What?'... Hey! What are you doing? ...What kind of poetry does he like?* **2** CONJ & DET You use **what** after certain words, especially verbs and adjectives, when you are referring to a situation that is unknown or has not been specified. *I want to know what happened to Norman... She turned scarlet from embarrassment, once she realized what she had done.* **3** CONJ You use **what** at the beginning of a clause in structures where you are changing the order of the information to give special emphasis to something. *What she does possess is the ability to get straight to the core of a problem.* **4** CONJ & DET You use **what** to indicate that you are talking about the whole of an amount. *He drinks what is left in his glass as if it were water... They had had to use what money they had.* **5** PREDET & DET You use **what** to express your opinion of something, for example when you are surprised by it. *What a horrible thing to do... What ugly things; throw them away.* **6** CONVENTION You say **'What?'** when you want someone to repeat something because you did not hear it properly. 'What' is not as polite as 'pardon' or 'sorry'. *'They could paint this place,' she said. 'What?' he asked.* **7** CONVENTION You can say **'What'** to express surprise or disbelief. *'We've got the car that killed Myra Moss.'—'What!'*

PHRASES ● You use **what about** when you are making a suggestion or offer. *What about a cup of tea?* ● You use **what if** at the beginning of a question about the consequences of something, especially something undesirable. *What if this doesn't work out?* ● If you know **what's what**, you know the important things that need to be known about a situation. ● You say **what with** to introduce the reasons for a situation, especially an undesirable one. *Maybe they are tired, what with all the sleep they're losing.* ● **what's more**: see **more.**

⭐ **whatever** /wɒt'evə/. **1** CONJ & DET You use **whatever** to refer to anything or everything of a particular type. *Franklin was free to do pretty much whatever he pleased... Whatever doubts he might have had about Ingrid were all over now.* **2** CONJ You use **whatever** when you are indicating that you do not know the precise

identity, meaning, or value of the thing just mentioned. *'I love you,' he said.—'Whatever that means,' she said.* **3** CONJ You use **whatever** to say that something is the case in all circumstances. *We shall love you whatever happens... People will judge you whatever you do.* **4** ADV You use **whatever** after a noun group to emphasize a negative statement. *I have nothing whatever to say.* **5** ADV You use **whatever** to ask in an emphatic way about something which you are surprised about. *Whatever is the matter with you both?*

what's /wɒts/. **What's** is the usual spoken form of 'what is' or 'what has', especially when 'has' is an auxiliary verb.

whatsoever /,wɒtsəu'evə/. ADV You use **whatsoever** after a noun group in order to emphasize a negative statement. *My school did nothing whatsoever in the way of athletics.*

wheat /wiːt/. N-UNCOUNT **Wheat** is a cereal crop grown for its grain, which is ground into flour to make bread.

⭐ **wheel** /wiːl/ **wheels, wheeling, wheeled.** **1** N-COUNT A **wheel** is a circular object which turns round on a rod attached to its centre. Wheels are fixed underneath vehicles so that they can move along. *The car wheels spun and slipped on some oil.* **2** N-COUNT A **wheel** is the same as a **steering wheel.** **3** VERB If you **wheel** an object that has wheels somewhere, you push it along. *He wheeled his bike into the alley.* **4** VERB If you **wheel around**, you turn round suddenly. *He wheeled around to face her.*

wheelchair /'wiːltʃeə/ **wheelchairs.** N-COUNT A **wheelchair** is a chair with wheels that sick or disabled people use in order to move about.

wheeze /wiːz/ **wheezes, wheezing, wheezed.** VERB If you **wheeze**, you breathe with difficulty, making a hissing or whistling sound.

⭐ **when** /wen/. **1** ADV You use **when** to ask questions about the time at which things happen. *When did you get married?... 'I'll be there this afternoon.'—'When?'* **2** CONJ You use **when** to introduce a clause where you refer to the time at which something happens. *I asked him when he'd be back to pick me up... I don't know when the decision was made... When I met the Gills, I had been gardening for nearly ten years... She remembered clearly that day when she'd gone exploring the rockpools.* **3** CONJ You use **when** to introduce the reason for an opinion or question. *How can you understand, when you don't have kids?* **4** CONJ You use **when** in order to introduce a fact or comment which makes the other part of the sentence rather surprising or unlikely. *The temperature sensor is making the computer think the engine is cold when, in fact, it's hot.*

⭐ **whenever** /wen'evə/. CONJ You use **whenever** to refer to any time or every time that something happens or is true. *She always called at the vicarage whenever she was in the area... Avoid processed foods whenever possible.*

⭐ Bank of English® frequent word　　　For a full explanation of all grammatical labels, see pages vii–x

where /weə/. **1** ADV You use **where** to ask questions about the place something is in, or is coming from or going to. *Where did you meet him?... 'You'll never believe where Julie and I are going.'—'Where?'* **2** CONJ & PRON You use **where** to specify or refer to the place in which something is situated or happens. *People began looking across to see where the noise was coming from... He knew where Henry Carter had gone... Conditions which apply to your flight are available at the travel agency where you book your holiday.* **3** CONJ & PRON & ADV You use **where** when you are referring to or asking about a situation, a stage in something, or an aspect of something. *It's not hard to see where she got her feelings about herself... The government is at a stage where it is willing to talk... Where will it all end?* **4** CONJ **Where** is used to introduce a clause which contrasts with what is said in the main clause. *Sometimes a teacher will be listened to, where a parent might not.*

whereabouts. **1** N-SING /ˈweərəbaʊts/ The **whereabouts** of a person or thing is the place where they are. *...a map showing the whereabouts of local castles.* **2** ADV /ˌweərə'baʊts/ You use **whereabouts** in questions when you are asking precisely where something is. *Whereabouts in Liverpool are you from?*

whereas /weər'æz/. CONJ You use **whereas** to introduce a comment which contrasts with what is said in the main clause. *She shows her feelings, whereas I don't.*

whereby /weə'baɪ/. PRON A system or action **whereby** something happens is one that makes that thing happen. [FORMAL] *...a deal whereby the union will receive nearly a million pounds.*

wherein /weər'ɪn/. **1** PRON **Wherein** means in which place. [FORMAL] *...a little room wherein are five cubicles.* **2** ADV & CONJ **Wherein** means in which part or respect. [FORMAL] *Wherein lies the truth?... It is difficult to know wherein Mr Ritchie hoped to find salvation for his country.*

whereupon /ˌweərə'pɒn/. CONJ You use **whereupon** to say that one thing happens immediately after another thing and usually as a result of it. [FORMAL] *'Well, get on with it then,' said Dobson, whereupon Davies started to explain.*

wherever /weər'evə/. **1** CONJ You use **wherever** to say that something happens or is true in any place or situation. *Some people enjoy themselves wherever they are.* **2** CONJ You use **wherever** to indicate that you do not know where a place or person is. *'Till we meet again, wherever that is,' said the chairman.*

whether /'weðə/. **1** CONJ You use **whether** to talk about a choice or doubt between two or more alternatives. *They now have two weeks to decide whether or not to buy.* **2** CONJ You use **whether** to say that something is true in any of the circumstances you mention. *We're in this together, whether we like it or not.*

which /wɪtʃ/. **1** PRON & DET You use **which** to ask questions when there are two or more possible answers or alternatives. *Which is your cabin ?... Which woman or man do you most admire?* **2** DET & PRON You use **which** to refer to a choice between two or more possible answers or alternatives. *I wanted to know which school it was you went to... There are so many diets on the market, how do you know which to choose?* **3** PRON You use **which** at the beginning of a relative clause that specifies the thing you are talking about or that gives more information about it. *Soldiers opened fire on a car which failed to stop at an army checkpoint.* **4** PRON & DET You use **which** to refer back to what has just been said. *They ran out of drink. Which actually didn't bother me because I wasn't drinking... It could be a sign she has an infection, in which case she needs to see a doctor.*

whichever /wɪtʃ'evə/. **1** DET & CONJ You use **whichever** to indicate that it does not matter which of the possible alternatives happens or is chosen. *Whichever way you look at it, nuclear power is the energy of the future... We will gladly exchange your goods, or refund your money, whichever you prefer.* **2** DET & CONJ You use **whichever** to specify which of a number of possibilities is the right one or the one you mean. *...learning to relax by whichever method suits you best... Fishing is from 6 am to dusk or 10.30pm, whichever is sooner.*

whiff /wɪf/ **whiffs.** **1** N-COUNT If there is a **whiff of** something, there is a faint smell of it. *He caught a whiff of her perfume.* **2** N-COUNT A **whiff of** something bad or harmful is a slight sign of it. *Just a whiff of a scandal would destroy us.*

while /waɪl/ **whiles, whiling, whiled.** **1** CONJ If one thing happens **while** another thing is happening, the two things happen at the same time. *I sat on the settee to unwrap the package while he stood by... Her parents could help with child care while she works.* **2** CONJ You use **while** to introduce a clause which contrasts with the other part of the sentence. *The first two services are free, while the third costs £35.00.* **3** CONJ You use **while** in a clause to say that although something is the case, it does not affect the truth of the other part of the sentence. *While the news, so far, has been good, there may be days ahead when it is bad.* **4** N-SING A **while** is a period of time. *They walked on in silence for a while... He was married a little while ago.* • to be **worth** your **while**: see **worth**. PHRASES • You use **all the while** in order to say that something happens continually or that it happens throughout the time when something else is happening. *All the while the people at the next table watched me eat.* • If something happens **once in a while**, it happens occasionally.
▸**while away.** PHR-VERB If you **while away** the time in a particular way, you spend time in that way because you are waiting for something or

because you have nothing else to do. *They whiled away the hours telling stories.*

⭐ **whilst** /waɪlst/. CONJ **Whilst** means the same as **while** when it is used as a conjunction. [BRITISH, FORMAL] *The girls met four years ago whilst singing backing vocals for local Birmingham bands.*

whim /wɪm/ **whims**. N-VAR A **whim** is a sudden desire to do or have something without any particular reason. *We decided, more or less on a whim, to sail to Morocco.*

whimper /'wɪmpə/ **whimpers, whimpering, whimpered**. VERB & N-COUNT If someone **whimpers**, they make quiet unhappy or frightened sounds called **whimpers**, as if they are about to start crying. *She lay at the bottom of the stairs, whimpering in pain... David's crying subsided to a whimper.*

whimsical /'wɪmzɪkəl/. ADJ Something that is **whimsical** is unusual and slightly playful, and is not trying to make a serious point. *...his gentle and whimsical humour.*

whine /waɪn/ **whines, whining, whined**. [1] VERB & N-COUNT If something or someone **whines**, they make a long, high-pitched noise called a **whine**, which often sounds sad or unpleasant. *The dog started to whine with impatience. ...the whine of air-raid sirens.* [2] VERB If someone **whines about** something, they complain about it in an annoying way.

whinge /wɪndʒ/ **whinges, whingeing, whinged**. VERB & N-COUNT If you say that someone **is whingeing** or having a **whinge**, you mean that they are complaining in an annoying way about something unimportant. [BRITISH, INFORMAL]

⭐ **whip** /wɪp/ **whips, whipping, whipped**. [1] N-COUNT A **whip** is a long thin piece of leather or rope fastened to a handle. It is used for hitting animals or people. [2] VERB If someone **whips** an animal or person, they hit them with a whip. ♦ **whipping, whippings** N-COUNT *He threatened to give her a whipping.* [3] VERB If you **whip** something **out** or **whip** something **off**, you take it out or take it off very quickly and suddenly. *Bob whipped out his notebook... She whipped off her skis and charged up the hill.* [4] VERB If you **whip** cream or eggs, you stir them very quickly to make them thick or stiff. *...whipped cream.*
▸ **whip up**. PHR-VERB If someone **whips up** an emotion such as hatred, they deliberately cause and encourage people to feel that emotion. *He accused politicians of whipping up anti-foreign sentiments.*

whir /wɜː/. See **whirr**.

whirl /wɜːl/ **whirls, whirling, whirled**. [1] VERB If something or someone **whirls around** or if you **whirl** them **around** they move round or turn round very quickly. *He whirled around and began to run back down the alley. ...whirling snow.* [2] N-COUNT You can refer to a lot of intense activity as a **whirl** of activity.

whirlwind /'wɜːlwɪnd/ **whirlwinds**. N-COUNT A **whirlwind** is a tall column of air which spins round and round very fast and moves across the land or sea.

whirr (or **whir**) /wɜː/ **whirrs, whirring, whirred**. VERB & N-COUNT If something such as a machine **whirrs**, it makes a series of low sounds so quickly that they seem like one continuous sound. This sound is called a **whirr**. *...the constant whirr of his electric fan.*

whisk /wɪsk/ **whisks, whisking, whisked**. [1] VERB If you **whisk** someone or something somewhere, you take them there quickly. *I was whisked away in a police car.* [2] VERB If you **whisk** eggs or cream, you stir air into them very fast. [3] N-COUNT A **whisk** is a kitchen tool used for whisking eggs or cream. ➔ See picture on page 825.

whisker /'wɪskə/ **whiskers**. N-COUNT The **whiskers** of an animal such as a cat or mouse are the long stiff hairs that grow near its mouth.

whiskey /'wɪski/ **whiskeys**. N-VAR **Whiskey** is whisky made in Ireland or the United States.

whisky /'wɪski/ **whiskies**. N-VAR **Whisky** is a strong alcoholic drink made, especially in Scotland, from grain such as barley or rye.

⭐ **whisper** /'wɪspə/ **whispers, whispering, whispered**. VERB & N-COUNT If you **whisper** something, or if you say it in a **whisper**, you say it very quietly, using only your breath and not your voice. *'Keep your voice down,' I whispered... He whispered the message to David... They spoke in whispers.*

whistle /'wɪsəl/ **whistles, whistling, whistled**. [1] VERB When you **whistle**, you make sounds by forcing your breath out between your lips or teeth. *He whistled a tune... He whistled, surprised but not shocked.* [2] VERB If something such as a train or a kettle **whistles**, it makes a loud, high sound. *Somewhere a train whistled.* [3] VERB If something such as the wind or a bullet **whistles** somewhere, it moves there, making a high loud sound. *As I stood up a bullet whistled past my back.* [4] N-COUNT A **whistle** is a small metal tube which you blow in order to produce a loud sound and attract someone's attention.

'whistle-blowing. N-UNCOUNT **Whistle-blowing** is the act of telling the authorities or the public that the organization you are working for is doing something immoral or illegal.

⭐ **white** /waɪt/ **whiter, whitest; whites**. [1] ADJ & N-VAR Something that is **white** is the colour of snow or milk. [2] ADJ & N-COUNT A **white** person has a pale skin and belongs to a race of European origin. **Whites** are white people. *He was white, with brown shoulder-length hair. ...a law that has kept blacks and whites apart.* [3] ADJ **White** wine is wine of a pale yellowish colour. [4] ADJ **White** coffee contains milk or cream. [BRITISH] [5] N-VAR The **white** of an egg is the transparent liquid surrounding the yolk. [6] N-COUNT The **white** of your eye is the white part of your eyeball.

,white-'collar. ADJ BEFORE N **White-collar** workers work in offices rather than doing manual work in industry.

⭐ Bank of English® frequent word   For a full explanation of all grammatical labels, see pages vii–x

A B C D E F G H I J K L M N O P Q R S T U V W X Y Z

'**White House.** N-PROPER **The White House** is the official home in Washington DC of the President of the United States. You can also use **White House** to refer to the President of the United States and his or her officials.

whitewash /'waɪtwɒʃ/. **1** N-UNCOUNT **Whitewash** is a mixture of lime or chalk and water used for painting walls white. **2** N-SING A **whitewash** is an attempt to hide the unpleasant facts about something from the public in order to make a situation look less serious than it really is. *He has described the investigation as a whitewash.*

whittle /'wɪtəl/**whittles, whittling, whittled.** ►**whittle away** or **whittle down.** PHR-VERB To **whittle** something **away** or to **whittle** it **down** means to make it smaller or less effective. *He had whittled eight interviewees down to two.*

whizz /wɪz/ **whizzes, whizzing, whizzed.** VERB If something **whizzes** somewhere, it moves there very fast. [INFORMAL] *Stewart felt a bottle whizz past his head.*

⭐ **who** /huː/. **1** PRON You use **who** when asking questions about the name or identity of a person or group of people. *Who's there?... Who did you ask?... Who do you work for?... 'You reminded me of somebody.'—'Who?'* **2** CONJ You use **who** to introduce a clause where you talk about the identity of a person or a group of people. *I was suddenly curious and asked who she was... They haven't found out who did it.* **3** PRON You use **who** at the beginning of a relative clause when specifying the person or group of people you are talking about or when giving more information about them. *The woman, who needs constant attention, is cared for by relatives... The hijacker gave himself up to police, who are now questioning him.*

USAGE **Who** is now commonly used as the object where in the past it was only considered correct to use **whom**. **Who**, however, cannot be used directly after a preposition; for example, you cannot say 'the woman to who I spoke'. Instead you can say '**the woman to whom I spoke**' or '**the woman I spoke to**'. There are some types of sentence, for example when you are talking about quantities, in which **who** cannot be used: *...twenty masked prisoners, many of whom are armed with makeshift weapons.*

who'd /huːd/. **Who'd** is the usual spoken form of 'who had', especially when 'had' is an auxiliary verb. **Who'd** is also a spoken form of 'who would'.

whoever /huː'evə/. **1** PRON You use **whoever** to refer to someone when their identity is not yet known. *Whoever was responsible for this crime is a very dangerous man... Whoever wins this year is going to be famous for life.* **2** CONJ You use **whoever** to indicate that the actual identity of

the person who does something will not affect a situation. *You can have whoever you like to visit you... Everybody who goes into this region, whoever they are, is at risk of being taken hostage.*

⭐ **whole** /həʊl/. **1** QUANT If you refer to **the whole of** something, you mean all of it. *I was cold throughout the whole of my body... We spent the whole summer in Italy.* **2** N-SING A **whole** is a single thing which contains several different parts. *The group's various businesses do not yet form a coherent whole.* **3** ADJ If something is **whole**, it is in one piece and is not broken or damaged. *Much of the temple was ruined, but the front was whole... He plucked an ice cube from the glass and swallowed it whole.* **4** ADJ BEFORE N You use **whole** to emphasize what you are saying. [INFORMAL] *...a whole new way of doing business... There's a whole group of friends he doesn't want you to meet.*

PHRASES ● If you refer to something **as a whole**, you are referring to it generally and as a single unit. *In rural India as a whole, 80% of women are illiterate.* ● You say **on the whole** to indicate that what you are saying is only true in general and may not be true in every case. *The wines they make are, on the whole, of a high standard.*

USAGE **Whole** is often used to mean the same as **all**, but when used in front of plurals **whole** and **all** have different meanings. For example, if you say '**Whole buildings have been destroyed**', you mean that some buildings have been destroyed completely. If you say '**All the buildings have been destroyed**', you mean that every building has been destroyed.

wholehearted /,həʊl'hɑːtɪd/. ADJ If you support something or agree to something in a **wholehearted** way, you support or agree to it enthusiastically and completely. *He has my wholehearted support.* ♦ **wholeheartedly** ADV *I agree wholeheartedly with you.*

wholesale /'həʊseɪl/. **1** ADJ & ADV **Wholesale** goods or goods that are bought **wholesale** are bought cheaply in large quantities and then sold again to shops. *...the decline in wholesale prices over the past three months... Each tablet is sold wholesale for just 2p or 3p.* **2** ADJ BEFORE N & ADV You use **wholesale** to describe something undesirable or unpleasant that is done to an excessive extent. *...a campaign to stop the wholesale destruction of villages.*

wholesaler /'həʊseɪlə/**wholesalers.** N-COUNT A **wholesaler** is a person whose business is buying large quantities of goods and selling them in smaller amounts to shops.

wholesome /'həʊlsəm/. **1** ADJ If you describe something as **wholesome**, you approve of it because you think it will have a positive influence on people, especially because it does not involve anything sexually immoral. *...good, wholesome fun.* [2] ADJ If you describe food as **wholesome**, you approve of it because you think it is good for your health.

who'll /'hu:l/. **Who'll** is a spoken form of 'who will' or 'who shall'.

wholly /'həʊlli/. ADV **Wholly** means completely. *This is a wholly new approach.*

⭐ **whom** /hu:m/.

> ✒ **Whom** is used in formal or written English instead of 'who' when it is the object of a verb or preposition.

[1] PRON You use **whom** in questions when you ask about the name or identity of a person or group of people. *'I want to send a telegram.' 'Fine, to whom?'... Whom did he expect to answer his phone?* [2] CONJ You use **whom** to introduce a clause where you talk about the name or identity of a person or a group of people. *He asked whom I'd told about his having been away... They have a free hand to appoint whom they like.* [3] PRON You use **whom** at the beginning of a relative clause when specifying the person or people you are talking about, or when giving more information about them. *One writer in whom I had taken an interest was Immanuel Velikovsky... The Homewood residents whom I knew had little money and little free time.* [4] See note at **who**.

whoop /wu:p, AM hu:p/**whoops, whooping, whooped.** VERB & N-COUNT If you **whoop**, or if you let out a **whoop**, you shout loudly in a very happy or excited way. [WRITTEN] *Harry whooped with delight. ...loud whoops and yells.*

whore /hɔ:/ **whores.** N-COUNT A **whore** is the same as a **prostitute**.

who're /'hu:ə/. **Who're** is a spoken form of 'who are'.

who's /hu:z/. **Who's** is the usual spoken form of 'who is' or 'who has', especially when 'has' is an auxiliary verb.

⭐ **whose** /hu:z/. [1] PRON You use **whose** at the beginning of a relative clause to indicate that something belongs to or is associated with the person or thing mentioned in the previous clause. *I saw a man shouting at a driver whose car was blocking the street.* [2] PRON & DET You use **whose** in questions to ask about the person or thing that something belongs to or is associated with. *Whose was the better performance?... Whose is this?... Whose daughter is she?* [3] DET & CONJ You use **whose** to introduce a clause where you talk about the person or thing that something belongs to or is associated with. *I can't remember whose idea it was for us to meet again... It doesn't matter whose it is.*

who've /hu:v/. **Who've** is the usual spoken form of 'who have,' especially when 'have' is an auxiliary verb.

⭐ **why** /waɪ/. [1] ADV You use **why** when asking questions about the reason for something. *Why hasn't he brought the whisky?... 'I just want to see him.'—'Why?'... Why should I leave?* [2] CONJ & ADV

You use **why** at the beginning of a clause in which you talk about the reason for something. *Experts wonder why the US government is not taking similarly strong actions... I don't know why... Here's why.* [3] ADV You use **why** with 'not' to introduce a suggestion in the form of a question. *Why not give Claire a call?... Why don't we talk it through?* [4] CONVENTION You say **why not** in order to agree with what someone has suggested. *'Want to spend the afternoon with me?'—'Why not?'*

wicked /'wɪkɪd/. [1] ADJ You use **wicked** to describe someone or something that is very bad in a way that is deliberately harmful to people. *She described the shooting as a wicked attack.*
♦ **wickedness** N-UNCOUNT *...the wickedness of nuclear weapons.* [2] ADJ If you describe someone or something as **wicked**, you mean that they are mischievous in a way that you find enjoyable. *She had a wicked sense of humour.* ♦ **wickedly** ADV *...a wickedly funny parody.*

wicker /'wɪkə/. N-UNCOUNT **Wicker** is material made by weaving canes or twigs together, which is used to make baskets and furniture.

⭐ **wide** /waɪd/ **wider, widest.** [1] ADJ Something that is **wide** measures a large distance from one side to the other. *...a wide-brimmed sunhat... Wreckage was scattered over a wide area.* [2] ADV If you open or spread something **wide**, you open or spread it to its fullest extent. *Open your mouth wide... 'It was huge,' he announced, spreading his arms wide.* [3] ADJ You use **wide** to talk or ask about how much something measures from one side or edge to the other. *The road is only one track wide. ...a desk that was almost as wide as the room.* [4] ADJ You use **wide** to describe something that includes a large number of different things or people. *...a wide choice of hotels. ...a wide range of topics... The case has attracted wide publicity.* ♦ **widely** ADV *He published widely in scientific journals.* [5] ADJ BEFORE N **Wider** is used to describe something relating to the most important or general parts of a situation rather than the details. *He emphasised the wider issue of superpower cooperation.* [6] ADJ A **wide** shot or punch does not hit its target. *Nearly half the missiles landed wide.* [7] **far and wide**: see **far**. ♦ **wide of the mark**: see **mark**.

¹**wide-eyed.** [1] ADJ If you describe someone as **wide-eyed**, you mean that they seem inexperienced, and perhaps lack common sense. *...a wide-eyed boy ready to explore.* [2] ADJ & ADV If someone is **wide-eyed**, their eyes are more open than usual, especially because they are surprised or frightened. *...an expression of wide-eyed amazement... Trevor was staring wide-eyed at me.*

widen /'waɪdən/ **widens, widening, widened.** [1] VERB If you **widen** something, or if it **widens**, it becomes bigger from one side or edge to the other. *The river widens considerably as it begins to turn east.* [2] VERB If something **widens**, or if you **widen** it, it becomes greater in range, size, or variety or affects a larger number of people or

a b c d e f g h i j k l m n o p q r s t u v **w** x y z

things. *The search for my brother widened... Newspapers enjoyed a widening circle of readers.*

wide-'ranging. ADJ If something is **wide-ranging**, it affects or deals with a great variety of different things. *...a wide-ranging debate.*

widescreen /'waɪdskriːn/. ADJ A **widescreen** television has a screen that is wide in relation to its height.

⭐ **widespread** /'waɪdspred/. ADJ Something that is **widespread** exists or happens over a large area or to a very great extent. *Food shortages are widespread.*

widow /'wɪdəʊ/ **widows.** N-COUNT A **widow** is a woman whose husband has died.

widowed /'wɪdəʊd/. ADJ If someone **is widowed**, their husband or wife has died.

widower /'wɪdəʊə/ **widowers.** N-COUNT A **widower** is a man whose wife has died.

width /wɪdθ/ **widths.** N-VAR The **width** of something is the distance that it measures from one side to the other. *Measure the full width of the window... The road was reduced to 18ft in width.*

wield /wiːld/ **wields, wielding, wielded.** ⊡ VERB If you **wield** a weapon or tool, you carry it and use it. *...a gang member wielding a knife.* ⊡ VERB If someone **wields** power, they have it and are able to use it.

⭐ **wife** /waɪf/ **wives.** N-COUNT A man's **wife** is the woman he is married to.

wig /wɪg/ **wigs.** N-COUNT A **wig** is a mass of false hair which is worn on your head.

wiggle /'wɪgəl/ **wiggles, wiggling, wiggled.** VERB & N-COUNT If you **wiggle** something, or if it **wiggles**, it moves around with small, quick movements, called **wiggles**. *Your baby will try to shuffle or wiggle along the floor. ...a wiggle of the hips.*

⭐ **wild** /waɪld/ **wilder, wildest; wilds.** ⊡ ADJ **Wild** animals and plants live or grow in natural surroundings and are not looked after by people. ⊡ ADJ **Wild** land is natural and not cultivated. *...forests and other wild areas.* ⊡ N-PLURAL The **wilds** are remote areas, far away from towns. ⊡ ADJ **Wild** behaviour is uncontrolled, excited, or energetic. *As George himself came on stage they went wild.* ♦ **wildly** ADV *The crowd clapped wildly.* ⊡ ADJ BEFORE N A **wild** idea or guess is unusual or made without much thought. ♦ **wildly** ADV *'Thirteen?' he guessed wildly.* ⊡ PHRASE If something or someone **runs wild**, they behave in a natural, free or uncontrolled way. *Molly has let that girl run wild.*

wilderness /'wɪldənəs/ **wildernesses.** N-COUNT A **wilderness** is an area of natural land which is not cultivated. *...one of the largest wilderness areas in North America.*

wildlife /'waɪldlaɪf/. N-UNCOUNT You can use **wildlife** to refer to animals and other living things that live in the wild. *Pets or wildlife could be affected by the pesticides.*

wildly /'waɪldli/. ADV You use **wildly** to emphasize the degree, amount, or intensity of

something. *The community and police have wildly different stories of what happened... The island's hotels vary wildly.* ● See also **wild**.

wilful (AM **willful**) /'wɪlfʊl/. ⊡ ADJ BEFORE N **Wilful** actions or attitudes are done or expressed deliberately, especially with the intention of hurting someone. *Wilful neglect of our manufacturing industry has caused this problem.* ♦ **wilfully** ADV *...claims that the Front has wilfully perverted democracy.* ⊡ ADJ A **wilful** person is obstinate and determined to get what they want. *He is a wilful and rather spiteful young man.*

will 1 modal verb uses

⭐ **will** /wɪl/.

☑ The usual spoken form of **will not** is **won't**.

⊡ MODAL You use **will** to indicate that you hope, think, or have evidence that something is going to happen in the future. *70 per cent of airports in the Far East will have to be upgraded... Will you ever feel at home here?* ⊡ MODAL You use **will** to talk about someone's intention to do something. *'Dinner's ready.'—Thanks, Carrie, but we'll have a drink first.'... What will you do next?... Will you be remaining in the city?* ⊡ MODAL You use **will** to say that someone or something is able to do something in the future. *How will I recognize you?* ⊡ MODAL You use **will** when making offers, invitations, or requests. *Will you stay for supper?... Won't you sit down?* ⊡ MODAL You use **will** to say that someone is willing to do something. You use **will not** or **won't** to indicate that someone refuses to do something. *All right, I'll forgive you... I'll answer the phone... If you won't let me pay for a taxi, then at least allow me to lend you something.*

will 2 wanting something to happen

⭐ **will** /wɪl/ **wills, willing, willed.** ⊡ N-VAR **Will** is the determination to do something. *He was said to have lost his will to live... It's a constant battle of wills with your children.* ● See also **free will**. ⊡ N-SING If something is **the will of** a person or group of people with authority, they want it to happen. *He has submitted himself to the will of God... Democracy responds and adjusts to the will of the people.* ⊡ VERB If you **will** something **to** happen, you try to make it happen using mental rather than physical effort. *I looked at the telephone, willing it to ring.* ⊡ N-COUNT A **will** is a legal document stating what you want to happen to your money and property when you die. ⊡ PHRASE If you can do something **at will**, you can do it whenever you want. *...scientists who can adjust their experiments at will.*

willful. See **wilful.**

⭐ **willing** /'wɪlɪŋ/. ⊡ ADJ If someone is **willing to** do something, they do not mind doing it or have no objection to doing it. ♦ **willingly** ADV *I am glad you have come here so willingly.* ♦ **willingness** N-UNCOUNT *I had to prove my willingness to work hard.* ⊡ ADJ If you describe someone as **willing**, you mean that they are eager and enthusiastic. *He was a natural and willing pupil.*

willow /ˈwɪləʊ/ **willows.** N-COUNT A **willow** is a tree with long narrow leaves and branches that hang down.

willpower (also **will-power** or **will power**) /ˈwɪlpaʊə/. N-UNCOUNT **Willpower** is a very strong determination to do something. *His attempts to stop smoking by willpower alone failed.*

wilt /wɪlt/ **wilts, wilting, wilted.** VERB If a plant **wilts**, it gradually bends downwards and becomes weak, because it needs more water or is dying.

wily /ˈwaɪli/ **wilier, wiliest.** ADJ **Wily** people are clever and cunning. *...the wily old general.*

wimp /wɪmp/ **wimps.** N-COUNT If you call someone a **wimp**, you disapprove of them because they lack confidence or determination, or because they are often afraid of things. [INFORMAL]

⭐ **win** /wɪn/ **wins, winning, won.** 1 VERB & N-COUNT If you **win** a fight, game, or argument, you defeat your opponent, or you do better than everyone else involved. You can also talk about a **win**. *I don't think they'll win the election... Sanchez Vicario won 2-6, 6-4, 6-3. ...eight games without a win.* 2 VERB If you **win** a prize or medal, you get it because you have defeated everyone else in a competition, or you have been very successful at something. *The first correct entry wins the prize... He won a silver medal at the 1994 World Championships.* 3 VERB If you **win** something that you want or need, you succeed in getting it. *British Aerospace has won an order worth $340 million.* 4 See also **winning**.
▸ **win over** or **win round.** PHR-VERB If you **win** someone **over** or **win round**, you persuade them to support you or agree with you. *Not all my staff agree but I am winning them over.*

wince /wɪns/ **winces, wincing, winced.** VERB & N-COUNT If you **wince**, or if you give a **wince**, the muscles of your face tighten suddenly because you are in pain or have experienced something unpleasant. *Just reading about it makes you wince.*

winch /wɪntʃ/ **winches, winching, winched.** 1 N-COUNT A **winch** is a machine for lifting heavy objects. It consists of a cylinder around which a rope or chain is wound. 2 VERB If you **winch** an object or person somewhere, you lift or lower them using a winch.

wind 1 air

⭐ **wind** /wɪnd/ **winds, winding, winded.** 1 N-VAR A **wind** is a current of air moving across the earth's surface. *There was a strong wind blowing... A gust of wind had blown the pot over.* 2 VERB If you **are winded** by something such as a blow, you have difficulty breathing for a short time. *The cow stamped on his side, winding him.* 3 N-UNCOUNT **Wind** is the air that you sometimes swallow with food or drink, or gas that is produced in your intestines, which causes an uncomfortable feeling.

wind 2 turning or wrapping

⭐ **wind** /waɪnd/ **winds, winding, wound.** 1 VERB If a road, river, or line of people **winds** in a particular direction, it goes in that direction with a lot of

bends or twists in it. *The convoy wound its way through the West Bank.* 2 VERB When you **wind** something **around** something else, you wrap it round it several times. *She wound the bandage around his knee.* 3 VERB When you **wind** a mechanical device, for example a watch, you turn a key or handle on it round and round in order to make it operate.
▸ **wind down.** PHR-VERB If someone **winds down** a business or activity, they gradually reduce the amount of work that is done or the number of people that are involved. *Aid workers have already begun winding down their operation.*
▸ **wind up.** PHR-VERB If someone **winds up** a business or activity, they close it down or finish it. *Could we wind up this meeting as quickly as possible?*

windfall /ˈwɪndfɔːl/ **windfalls.** N-COUNT A **windfall** is a sum of money that you receive unexpectedly.

windmill /ˈwɪndmɪl/ **windmills.** N-COUNT A **windmill** is a tall building with sails which turn as the wind blows. Windmills are used to grind grain or pump water.

⭐ **window** /ˈwɪndəʊ/ **windows.** 1 N-COUNT A **window** is a space in the wall of a building or in the side of a vehicle, which has glass in it so that light can pass through and people can see in or out. *He looked out of the window. It was a lovely day.* 2 N-COUNT On a computer screen, a **window** is one of the work areas that the screen can be divided into. [COMPUTING]

windscreen /ˈwɪndskriːn/ **windscreens.** N-COUNT In British English, the **windscreen** of a car or other vehicle is the glass window at the front through which the driver looks. The usual American word is **windshield**.

windshield /ˈwɪndʃiːld/ **windshields.** See **windscreen**.

windy /ˈwɪndi/ **windier, windiest.** ADJ If it is **windy**, the wind is blowing a lot.

⭐ **wine** /waɪn/ **wines.** N-VAR **Wine** is an alcoholic drink, usually made from grapes.

'wine bar, wine bars. N-COUNT A **wine bar** is a place where people can buy and drink wine, and sometimes eat food as well.

⭐ **wing** /wɪŋ/ **wings.** 1 N-COUNT The **wings** of a bird or insect are the parts of its body that it uses for flying. 2 N-COUNT The **wings** of an aeroplane are the long flat parts at each side which support it while it is flying. 3 N-COUNT A **wing** of a building is a part of it which sticks out from the main part. *...the east wing of the palace.* 4 N-COUNT A **wing** of an organization is a group within it which has a particular function or has particular beliefs. *...the military wing of the African National Congress.* ● See also **left-wing, right-wing.** 5 N-COUNT The **wings** of a car are the parts around the wheels. [BRITISH] 6 N-PLURAL In a theatre, **the wings** are the sides of the stage which are hidden from the audience by curtains or scenery.

winged /wɪŋd/. ADJ A **winged** insect or other creature has wings.

A
B

wink /wɪŋk/ **winks, winking, winked.** VERB & N-COUNT
If you **wink at** someone, or if you give them a
wink, you look towards them and close one eye
very briefly, usually as a signal that something is
a joke or a secret.

C ★ **winner** /'wɪnə/ **winners.** N-COUNT The **winner** of a
prize, race, or competition is the person, animal,
or thing that wins it.

D ★ **winning** /'wɪnɪŋ/ **winnings.** [1] ADJ BEFORE N You
can use **winning** to describe a person or thing
E that wins something such as a competition,
game, or election. ...*the winning goal.* [2] ADJ
F BEFORE N **Winning** is used to describe actions or
qualities that please people and make them feel
friendly towards you. ...*his winning personality.*
G **winnings** /'wɪnɪŋz/. N-PLURAL You can refer to
the money that someone wins in a competition
H or by gambling as their **winnings**.

★ **winter** /'wɪntə/ **winters.** N-VAR **Winter** is the
I season between autumn and spring. In winter
the weather is usually cold. → See Reference
J Page on Times and Dates.

★ **wipe** /waɪp/ **wipes, wiping, wiped.** [1] VERB & N-COUNT
K If you **wipe** something, or if you give it a **wipe**,
you rub its surface to remove dirt or liquid from
L it. *He began to wipe the basin clean... Lainey wiped
her hands on the towel... I'm going to give the toys
a good wipe.* [2] VERB If you **wipe** dirt or liquid
M from something, you remove it, for example by
using a cloth or your hand. *Nancy wiped the
N sweat from her face.*
▸**wipe out.** PHR-VERB To **wipe out** a place or a
group of people or animals means to destroy it
O completely. ...*the epidemic that wiped out
thousands of seals in Europe.*

P ★ **wire** /waɪə/ **wires, wiring, wired.** [1] N-VAR A **wire** is a
long thin piece of metal that is used to fasten
Q things or to carry electric current. ...*fine copper
wire.* [2] See also **barbed wire.**
R ▸**wire up.** PHR-VERB If you **wire up** something
such as a building or piece of equipment, you
install or connect wires inside it so that electricity
S or signals can pass into or through it. *I even wired
up the alarm system.*

T **wireless** /'waɪələs/ **wirelesses.** [1] ADJ **Wireless**
technology uses radio waves rather than
electricity and therefore does not require any
U wires. ...*the fast-growing wireless communication
market.* [2] N-COUNT A **wireless** is a radio. [DATED]

V **wiring** /'waɪərɪŋ/. N-UNCOUNT The **wiring** in a
building or machine is the system of wires that
supply electricity to the different parts of it.

wiry /'waɪəri/ **wirier, wiriest.** [1] ADJ Someone who
W is **wiry** is rather thin but is also strong. [2] ADJ
Something such as hair or grass that is **wiry** is
X stiff and rough to touch.

wisdom /'wɪzdəm/. [1] N-UNCOUNT **Wisdom** is
Y the ability to use your experience and knowledge
to make sensible decisions and judgments. ...*the
patience and wisdom that comes from old age.*
Z [2] N-SING If you talk about **the wisdom of** an
action or decision, you are talking about how

sensible it is. *I have grave doubts about the
wisdom of resuming nuclear tests.*

★ **wise** /waɪz/ **wiser, wisest.** ADJ A **wise** person is able
to use their experience and knowledge to make
sensible decisions and judgments. *He has made a
wise choice of publisher.* ♦ **wisely** ADV *They've
invested their money wisely.*

★ **wish** /wɪʃ/ **wishes, wishing, wished.** [1] N-COUNT A
wish is a desire for something. *Her wish is to be in
films.* [2] VERB If you **wish to** do something, you
want to do it. [FORMAL] *I wish to leave a message.*
[3] VERB If you **wish** that something were the
case, you would like it to be the case, even
though it is impossible or unlikely. *I wish I could
paint like that.* [4] VERB & N-COUNT If you **wish for**
something, or if you make a **wish**, you express
the desire for something silently to yourself. In
fairy stories, when someone wishes for
something, it often happens by magic. *What did
you wish for?* [5] VERB If you **wish** someone
something such as luck or happiness, you express
the hope that they will be lucky or happy. *I wish
you both a very good journey.* [6] N-PLURAL If you
express your good **wishes** towards someone, you
are politely expressing your friendly feelings
towards them and your hope that they will be
successful or happy. *Please give him my best
wishes.*

,**wishful 'thinking.** N-UNCOUNT If a hope or
wish is **wishful thinking**, it is unlikely to come
true. *It is wishful thinking to expect deeper change
under his leadership.*

wistful /'wɪstfʊl/. ADJ If someone is **wistful**,
they are sad because they want something and
know they cannot have it. *He looked a little
wistful.* ♦ **wistfully** ADV *'I wish I had a little
brother,' said Daphne wistfully.*

wit /wɪt/ **wits.** [1] N-UNCOUNT **Wit** is the ability to
use words or ideas in an amusing and clever way.
He writes beautifully and with great wit.
[2] N-PLURAL You can refer to someone's ability to
think quickly in a difficult situation as their **wits**.
She'd better learn to keep her wits about her.

witch /wɪtʃ/ **witches.** N-COUNT A **witch** is a woman
who is believed to have magic powers, especially
evil ones.

witchcraft /'wɪtʃkrɑːft, -kræft/. N-UNCOUNT
Witchcraft is the use of magic powers, especially
evil ones.

'**witch-hunt, witch-hunts.** N-COUNT A **witch-hunt**
is an attempt to find and punish a particular
group of people who are being blamed for
something, often simply because of their
opinions and not because they have actually
done anything wrong; used showing disapproval.

★ **with** /wɪð, wɪθ/. [1] PREP If one thing or person
is **with** another, they are together in one place.
*She is currently staying with her father... He walked
with her to the front door.* [2] PREP If you discuss
something **with** someone, or if you fight or argue
with someone, you are both involved in a
discussion, fight, or argument. *We didn't even*

discuss it with each other... I must have been arguing with him for fifteen minutes... The war with Spain was over. **3** PREP If you do something **with** a particular tool, object, or substance, you do it using that tool or object. Wipe the mushrooms with a damp cloth... She had never been allowed to eat with her fingers. **4** PREP If someone stands or goes somewhere **with** something, they are carrying it. A man came round with a tray of chocolates. **5** PREP Someone or something **with** a particular feature or possession has that feature or possession. She was six feet tall with red hair. ...a single-storey house with a flat roof. **6** PREP If something is filled or covered **with** a substance or **with** things, it has that substance or those things in it or on it. His legs were caked with dried mud. **7** PREP You use **with** to indicate what a state, quality, or action relates to, involves, or affects. He still has a serious problem with money... Depression lowers the human ability to cope with disease. **8** PREP You use **with** when indicating the way something is done or the feeling that someone has when they do something. He listened with great care... He agreed, but with reluctance. **9** PREP You use **with** when indicating a sound, gesture, or facial expression that is made at the same time as an action. 'Broken again,' Jane said with a sigh... The front door closed with a crash. **10** PREP You use **with** to indicate the feeling that makes someone behave in a particular way. Gil was white and trembling with anger. **11** PREP You use **with** when mentioning the position or appearance of someone or something at the time that they do something, or what someone else is doing at that time. Joanne stood with her hands on the sink, staring out the window... She walked back to the bus stop, with him following. **12** PREP You use **with** to introduce a current situation that is a factor affecting another situation. With all the night school courses available, there is no excuse for not getting some sort of training.

⭐ **withdraw** /wɪðˈdrɔː/ **withdraws, withdrawing, withdrew, withdrawn. 1** VERB If you **withdraw** something from a place, you remove it or take it away. [FORMAL] He reached into his pocket and withdrew a sheet of notepaper. **2** VERB When troops **withdraw**, or when someone **withdraws** them, they leave the place where they are fighting or where they are based and return nearer home. **3** VERB If you **withdraw** money from a bank account, you take it out of that account. He withdrew £750 from his account. **4** VERB If you **withdraw from** an activity or organization, you stop taking part in it. They threatened to withdraw from the talks. **5** VERB If you **withdraw** a remark or statement you have made, you say that you want people to ignore it. [FORMAL] I demand that the Prime Minister withdraw that totally offensive remark.

⭐ **withdrawal** /wɪðˈdrɔːəl/ **withdrawals. 1** N-VAR The **withdrawal of** something is the act or process of removing it or ending it. [FORMAL] ...the

withdrawal of American troops from South Vietnam. **2** N-UNCOUNT Someone's **withdrawal** from an activity or an organization is their decision to stop taking part in it. ...his withdrawal from government in 1946. **3** N-COUNT If you make a **withdrawal** from your bank account, you take money out of it. **4** N-UNCOUNT **Withdrawal** is the period during which someone feels ill after they have stopped taking a drug which they were addicted to. ...vitamins to help addicts overcome the first stages of withdrawal. **5** N-UNCOUNT **Withdrawal** is behaviour in which someone prefers to be alone and does not want to talk to other people. Her periods of withdrawal and mental illness increased.

withdrawn /wɪðˈdrɔːn/. **1** **Withdrawn** is the past participle of **withdraw**. **2** ADJ AFTER LINK-V Someone who is **withdrawn** is quiet and shy.

withdrew /wɪðˈdruː/. **Withdrew** is the past tense of **withdraw**.

wither /ˈwɪðə/ **withers, withering, withered. 1** VERB If something **withers away**, it becomes weaker until it no longer exists or is no longer effective. The Party still predicts that ultimately religion will wither away. **2** VERB If a plant **withers**, or if something **withers** it, it shrinks, dries up, or dies.

withered /ˈwɪðəd/. ADJ If a person or a part of their body is **withered**, their skin is very wrinkled and dry, and looks old. ...a withered old man.

withhold /wɪðˈhəʊld/ **withholds, withholding, withheld.** VERB If you **withhold** something that someone wants, you do not let them have it. [FORMAL] The Council gave no reason for withholding these particular documents.

⭐ **within** /wɪˈðɪn/. **1** PREP & ADV If something is **within** a place, area, or object, it is inside it or surrounded by it. [FORMAL] ...one of the quiet villages within the Forest of Dean... A small voice called from within. 'Yes, just coming.' **2** PREP & ADV Something that happens or exists **within** a society, organization, or system, happens or exists inside it or to something that is part of it. ...the motives that attract people to work within a social service... Why not join the enemy and destroy it from within? **3** PREP & ADV If you have a feeling, you can say that it is **within** you. [LITERARY] She could almost feel fresh life and hope rising within her. ...a profound sense of loneliness deep within. **4** PREP If something is **within** a particular limit, it does not go beyond that limit. The film will be finished within its budget. **5** PREP If you are **within** a particular distance of a place, you are less than that distance from it. The man was within a few feet of him... It was within easy walking distance of the hotel. **6** PREP **Within** a particular length of time means before that length of time has passed. And within twenty-four hours I'd got the money. **7** PREP If something is **within sight, within earshot,** or **within reach,** you can see it, hear it, or reach it.

⭐ **without** /wɪˈðaʊt/. **1** PREP You use **without** to indicate that someone or something does not have or use the thing mentioned. *I don't like myself without a beard. ...a meal without barbecue sauce.* [2] PREP If one thing happens **without** another thing, or if you do something **without** doing something else, the second thing does not happen or occur. *They worked without a break until about eight... Alex had done this without consulting her.* [3] PREP If you do something **without** a particular feeling, you do not have that feeling when you do it. *'Hello' he said without surprise.* [4] PREP If you do something **without** someone else, they are not with you when you do it. *We never go anywhere without you.*

withstand /wɪð'stænd/ **withstands, withstanding, withstood** /wɪð'stʊd/. VERB To **withstand** a force or action means to survive it or not to give in to it. [FORMAL] *The buildings should withstand the severest earthquake.*

⭐ **witness** /'wɪtnəs/ **witnesses, witnessing, witnessed.**
[1] N-COUNT A **witness to** an event such as an accident or crime is a person who saw it. [2] VERB & PHRASE If you **witness** something, or if you **are witness to** it, you see it happen. *Anyone who witnessed the attack should call the police.* [3] N-COUNT A **witness** is someone who appears in a court of law to say what they know about a crime or other event. *Eleven witnesses will be called to testify.* [4] N-COUNT A **witness** is someone who writes their name on a document that you have signed, to confirm that it really is your signature. [5] VERB If someone **witnesses** your signature, they write their name after it, to confirm that it really is your signature. [6] PHRASE If something or someone **bears witness to** something else, they show or say that it exists or happened. [FORMAL] *Many of these poems bear witness to his years spent in India.*

witty /'wɪti/ **wittier, wittiest.** ADJ Someone or something that is **witty** is amusing in a clever way. *His plays were very good, very witty.*

wives /waɪvz/. **Wives** is the plural of **wife**.

wizard /'wɪzəd/ **wizards.** [1] N-COUNT In legends and fairy stories, a **wizard** is a man who has magic powers. [2] N-COUNT If you say that someone is a **wizard** at a particular kind of activity, you mean that they are very good at it. *...a financial wizard.* [3] N-COUNT A **wizard** is a computer program that guides you through the stages of a particular task. [COMPUTING]

wobble /'wɒbəl/ **wobbles, wobbling, wobbled.** VERB If someone or something **wobbles**, they make small movements from side to side, for example because they are unsteady.

wobbly /'wɒbli/ **wobblier, wobbliest.** [1] ADJ If something is **wobbly**, it moves unsteadily from side to side. *I was sitting on a wobbly plastic chair.* [2] ADJ If you feel **wobbly**, or if your legs feel **wobbly**, you feel weak and have difficulty standing up, especially because you are afraid, ill, or exhausted.

woe /wəʊ/ **woes.** [1] N-UNCOUNT **Woe** is very great sadness. [LITERARY] *He listened to my tale of woe.*

[2] N-PLURAL You can refer to someone's problems or misfortunes as their **woes**. [WRITTEN]

woeful /'wəʊfʊl/. ADJ You can use **woeful** to emphasize that something is very bad or undesirable. *...the woeful state of the economy.*
♦ **woefully** ADV *Public expenditure on the arts is woefully inadequate.*

woke /wəʊk/. **Woke** is the past tense of **wake**.

woken /'wəʊkən/. **Woken** is the past participle of **wake**.

wolf /wʊlf/ **wolves, wolfs, wolfing, wolfed.** [1] N-COUNT A **wolf** is a wild animal that looks like a large dog. [2] VERB & PHR-VERB If someone **wolfs** their food, or if they **wolf** it **down**, they eat it all very quickly and greedily. [INFORMAL] *He wolfed down a sandwich.*

⭐ **woman** /'wʊmən/ **women.** N-COUNT A **woman** is an adult female human being.

womanhood /'wʊmənhʊd/. N-UNCOUNT **Womanhood** is the state of being a woman rather than a girl, or the period of a woman's adult life. *...young girls approaching womanhood.*

womb /wuːm/ **wombs.** N-COUNT A woman's **womb** is the part inside her body where a baby grows before it is born.

women /'wɪmɪn/. **Women** is the plural of **woman**.

won /wʌn/. **Won** is the past tense and past participle of **win**.

⭐ **wonder** /'wʌndə/ **wonders, wondering, wondered.**
[1] VERB If you **wonder** about something, you think about it and try to guess or understand more about it. *I wondered what that noise was... 'Why does she want to get in there?' Pete wondered.* [2] VERB If you **wonder at** something, you are surprised and amazed about it. *He liked to sit and wonder at all that had happened.* [3] N-SING If you say that it is a **wonder** that something happened, you mean that it is very surprising that it happened. *It's a wonder that it took almost ten years.* [4] N-UNCOUNT **Wonder** is a feeling of surprise and amazement. *'That's right!' Bobby exclaimed in wonder.* [5] N-COUNT A **wonder** is something remarkable that people admire. *...the wonders of space and space exploration.*
PHRASES ● If you say '**no wonder**', '**little wonder**', or '**small wonder**', you mean that you are not surprised by something that has happened. *No wonder my brother wasn't feeling well.* ● If you say that something or someone **works wonders** or **does wonders**, you mean that they have a very good effect on something. *A few moments of relaxation can work wonders.*

⭐ **wonderful** /'wʌndəfʊl/. ADJ If you describe something or someone as **wonderful**, you think they are extremely good. *The cold, misty air felt wonderful on his face... It's wonderful to see you.*
♦ **wonderfully** ADV *It works wonderfully well.*

won't /wəʊnt/. **Won't** is the usual spoken form of 'will not'.

woo /wuː/ **woos, wooing, wooed.** [1] VERB If you **woo** people, you try to get them to help or support you. *They wooed customers by offering low interest* rates. **2** VERB If a man **woos** a woman, he spends time with her and tries to persuade her to marry him. [DATED]

★ **wood** /wʊd/**woods.** **1** N-VAR **Wood** is the material which forms the trunks and branches of trees. *Their dishes were made of wood.* **2** N-COUNT A **wood** is a large area of trees growing near each other. You can refer to one or several of these areas as **woods**. *...a walk in the woods.*

wooded /'wʊdɪd/. ADJ A **wooded** area is covered in trees. *...a wooded valley.*

★ **wooden** /'wʊdən/. ADJ A **wooden** object is made of wood. *...faded wooden floorboards.*

woodland /'wʊdlənd/**woodlands.** N-VAR **Woodland** is land covered with trees.

woodwork /'wʊdwɜːk/. **1** N-UNCOUNT You can refer to the doors and other wooden parts of a house as the **woodwork**. *...fresh paint on the woodwork.* **2** N-UNCOUNT **Woodwork** is the activity or skill of making things out of wood.

wool /wʊl/**wools.** **1** N-UNCOUNT **Wool** is the hair that grows on sheep and on some other animals. **2** N-VAR **Wool** is a material made from animal's wool. It is used for making clothes, blankets, and carpets. **3** See also **cotton wool**.

woollen (AM **woolen**) /'wʊlən/. ADJ **Woollen** clothes are made from wool. *...woollen socks.*

woolly (AM **wooly**) /'wʊli/**woollier, woolliest.** **1** ADJ Something that is **woolly** is made of wool or looks like wool. *He wore a woolly hat.* **2** ADJ If you describe people or their ideas as **woolly**, you are criticizing them for being inconsistent or confused. *He abhors woolly thinking.*

★ **word** /wɜːd/**words, wording, worded.** **1** N-COUNT A **word** is a single unit of language in writing or speech. In English, a word has a space on either side of it when it is written. *The words stood out clearly.* **2** N-SING If you have **a word with** someone, you have a short conversation with them, usually in private. [SPOKEN] *It's time you had a word with him... Could I have a quiet word?* **3** N-COUNT If you offer someone a **word of** warning, advice, or praise, you warn, advise, or praise them. *May I say a word of thanks to all the people who sent letters.* **4** N-SING If you say that someone does not hear, understand, or say **a word**, you are emphasizing that they hear, understand, or say nothing at all. *Not a word was spoken.* **5** N-UNCOUNT If there is **word** of something, people receive news or information about it. *There is no word from the authorities on the attack.* **6** N-SING If you give your **word**, you promise to do something. *...an adult who gave his word the boy would be supervised.* **7** VERB To **word** something in a particular way means to choose or use particular words to express it. *If I had written the letter, I might have worded it differently.* ♦ **-worded** *...a carefully-worded speech.*

PHRASES ● If one person **has words with** another, they have a serious discussion or argument, especially because one has complained about the other's behaviour. *We had*

words and she stormed out. ● You say **in a word** to indicate that you are summarizing what you have just been saying. *Victor, in a word, got increasingly fed up.* ● If you **have the last word** in an argument, you make the comment that finishes it and defeats the other person. ● You say **in other words** when introducing a simpler or clearer explanation of something that has just been said. *The mobile library services have been reorganised – in other words, they visit fewer places.* ● If you say that someone has said something, but **not in so many words**, you mean that they said it or expressed it, but in an indirect way. *'And has she agreed to go?'—'Not in so many words. But I read her thoughts.'* ● If you repeat something **word for word**, you repeat it exactly as it was originally said or written. *I don't try to memorize speeches word for word.*

wording /'wɜːdɪŋ/. N-UNCOUNT The **wording** of a piece of writing or a speech is the words that are used in it, especially when these are chosen to have a particular effect. *The wording is so vague that no one actually knows what it means.*

,**word 'processing.** N-UNCOUNT **Word processing** is the work or skill of producing printed material using a word processor. [COMPUTING]

,**word 'processor, word processors.** N-COUNT A **word processor** is a computer which is used to produce printed material such as letters and books. [COMPUTING]

wore /wɔː/. **Wore** is the past tense of **wear**.

★ **work** /wɜːk/**works, working, worked.** **1** VERB People who **work** have a job, usually one which they are paid to do. *Weiner works for the US Department of Transport... He worked as a bricklayer's mate.* **2** N-UNCOUNT People who have **work**, or who are **in work**, have a job, usually one which they are paid to do. *Fewer people are in work... I was out of work... What kind of work do you do?* **3** VERB When you **work**, you do tasks which your job involves, or a task that needs to be done. *We work really hard and we get the lowest pay. ...people like me who were working 24 hours a day to survive.*

USAGE The verb **work** has a different meaning in the continuous tenses than it does in the simple tenses. You use the continuous tenses, with the '-ing' form, to talk about a temporary job, but the simple tenses to talk about a permanent job. For example, if you say '**I'm working in London**', this suggests that the situation is temporary, and you may soon move to a different place. If you say '**I work in London**', this suggests that London is your permanent place of work.
The verb **live** behaves in a similar way. You use the continous tenses, with the '-ing' form, to talk about a temporary home, but the simple tenses to talk about a permanent home.

a
b
c
d
e
f
g
h
i
j
k
l
m
n
o
p
q
r
s
t
u
v
w
x
y
z

4 N-UNCOUNT **Work** consists of the tasks which your job involves, or any tasks which need to be done. *I've got work to do... There have been days when I have finished work at 2pm.* **5** N-UNCOUNT **Work** is the place where you do your job. *Many people travel to work by car.* **6** N-COUNT A **work** is something such as a painting, book, or piece of music. *...the complete works of Shakespeare.* **7** VERB If a machine or piece of equipment **works**, it operates and performs its function. *The pump doesn't work and we have no running water.* **8** VERB If an idea, method, or system **works**, it is successful. *95 per cent of these diets do not work... A methodical approach works best.* **9** VERB If you **work** a machine or piece of equipment, you operate it. *Many adults still depend on their children to work the video.* **10** See also **working**, **social work**.

PHRASES ● If you **work** your **way** somewhere, you move or progress there slowly, and with a lot of effort or work. *Many personnel managers started as secretaries or personnel assistants and worked their way up.* ● If you say that you will **have** your **work cut out to** do something, you mean that it will be a very difficult task. *He will have his work cut out to get into the team.*

▶**work into.** PHR-VERB If you **work** one substance **into** another or **work** it **in**, you add it to the other substance and mix the two together thoroughly. *Gradually pour the liquid into the flour, working it in carefully with a wooden spoon.*

▶**work off.** PHR-VERB If you **work off** energy or anger, you get rid of it by doing something that requires a lot of physical effort. *If I've had a bad day I'll work it off by cooking.*

▶**work out.** **1** PHR-VERB If you **work out** a solution to a problem or mystery, you find the solution by thinking or talking about it. *Negotiators are due to meet later today to work out a compromise.* **2** PHR-VERB If something **works out** at a particular amount, it is calculated to be that amount. *It will probably work out cheaper to hire a van and move your own things.* **3** PHR-VERB If a situation **works out**, it happens or progresses in a satisfactory way. *The deal just isn't working out the way we were promised.* **4** PHR-VERB If you **work out**, you go through a physical exercise routine. ● See also **workout**.

▶**work up.** **1** PHR-VERB If you **work yourself up**, you make yourself very upset or angry about something. *She worked herself up into a bit of a state.* ◆ **worked up** ADJ AFTER LINK-V *Steve shouted at her. He was really worked up now.* **2** PHR-VERB If you **work up** the enthusiasm or courage **to** do something, you gradually make yourself feel it. *She had never worked up the nerve to tell anyone.*

workable /'wɜːkəbəl/. ADJ A **workable** idea or system is realistic and practical, and likely to be effective.

★ **worker** /'wɜːkə/ **workers.** **1** N-COUNT **Workers** are people who are employed in industry or business

and who are not managers. **2** N-COUNT You can use **worker** to say how well or badly someone works. *He is a hard worker.*

workforce /'wɜːkfɔːs/ **workforces.** **1** N-COUNT The **workforce** is the total number of people in a country or region who are physically able to do a job and are available for work. **2** N-COUNT The **workforce** is the total number of people who are employed by a particular company.

★ **working** /'wɜːkɪŋ/ **workings.** **1** ADJ BEFORE N **Working** people have jobs which they are paid to do. *Like working women anywhere, Asian women are buying convenience foods.* **2** ADJ BEFORE N A **working** day or week is the number of hours that you work during a day or a week. *...a shorter, more flexible working week.* **3** ADJ BEFORE N If you have a **working** knowledge of a subject, you have a useful but not very thorough knowledge of it. **4** N-PLURAL The **workings** of a piece of equipment, an organization, or a system are the ways in which it operates. ● **in working order**: see **order**. **5** See also **work**.

,**working 'class, working classes.** N-COUNT & ADJ The **working class** or **working classes** are the people in a society who do not own much property, who have low social status, and whose work involves physical skills rather than intellectual skills. You can also say that someone is from a **working class** background.

workload /'wɜːkləʊd/ **workloads.** N-COUNT Your **workload** is the amount of work that you have to do. *Wilson has had a heavy workload this season.*

workman /'wɜːkmən/ **workmen.** N-COUNT A **workman** is a man who works with his hands, for example a builder or plumber.

,**work of 'art, works of art.** **1** N-COUNT A **work of art** is a painting or piece of sculpture of high quality. **2** N-COUNT You can refer to something that has been skilfully produced as a **work of art**. *The chocolate-and-brandy fig cake was a real work of art.*

workout /'wɜːkaʊt/ **workouts.** N-COUNT A **workout** is a period of physical exercise or training. *...a 35-minute aerobic workout.*

workplace /'wɜːkpleɪs/ **workplaces.** N-COUNT Your **workplace** is the place where you work. *...the difficulties facing women in the workplace.*

workshop /'wɜːkʃɒp/ **workshops.** **1** N-COUNT A **workshop** is a room or building containing tools or machinery for making or repairing things. **2** N-COUNT A **workshop** is a period of discussion or practical work on a particular subject in which a group of people share their knowledge and experience. *...a writers' workshop.*

workstation /'wɜːksteɪʃən/ **workstations.** N-COUNT A **workstation** is a computer. [COMPUTING]

★ **world** /wɜːld/ **worlds.** **1** N-SING The **world** is the planet that we live on. *It's a beautiful part of the* world... More than anything, I'd like to drive around the world. [2] N-COUNT A **world** is a planet. ...the possibility of life on other worlds. [3] ADJ BEFORE N You can use **world** to describe someone or something that is one of the most important or significant of its kind on earth. China has once again emerged as a world power. ...a world authority on heart-diseases. [4] N-COUNT Someone's **world** is the life they lead, the people they have contact with, and the things they experience. I lost my job and it was like my world collapsed. [5] N-SING You can use **world** to refer to a particular field of activity, and the people involved in it. ...the latest news from the world of finance. [6] N-SING You can use **world** to refer to a particular group of living things, for example **the animal world**, **the plant world**, and **the insect world**.

PHRASES ● **The world over** means throughout the world. Some problems are the same the world over. ● If you say that someone has **the best of both worlds**, you mean that they have the benefits of two things and none of the disadvantages. Her living room provides the best of both worlds, with an office at one end and comfortable sofas at the other. ● You can use **the outside world** to refer to all the people who do not live in a particular place or who are not involved in a particular situation. For many, the post office is the only link with the outside world.

,world-'class. ADJ A **world-class** competitor in a sporting event is one of the best in the world at what they do. [JOURNALISM]

,world-'famous. ADJ Someone or something that is **world-famous** is known about by people all over the world. ...the world-famous Oxford Street.

worldly /'wɜːldli/ **worldlier, worldiest.** [1] ADJ **Worldly** is used to talk about the ordinary things of life, especially things like possessions, rather than spiritual things. [LITERARY] Neither parent had left much in the way of worldly goods behind them. [2] ADJ Someone who is **worldly** is experienced, practical, and knowledgeable about life.

,world 'view, **world views.** N-COUNT A person's **world view** is the way they see and understand the world, especially regarding issues such as politics, philosophy, and religion.

★ ,world 'war, **world wars.** N-VAR A **world war** is a war involving countries from all over the world.

★ worldwide /,wɜːld'waɪd/. ADJ & ADV **Worldwide** means happening throughout the world. Today, doctors are fearing a worldwide epidemic... His books have sold more than 20 million copies worldwide.

,World-Wide 'Web. N-PROPER The **World-Wide Web** is a system which links documents and pictures into an information database that is stored in computers in many different parts of the world and which can be accessed with a single program. **The World-Wide Web** is often abbreviated to **the Web**.

worm /wɜːm/ **worms, worming, wormed.** [1] N-COUNT A **worm** is a small thin animal without bones or legs which lives in the soil. [2] N-PLURAL If animals or people have **worms**, worms are living as parasites in their intestines. [3] VERB If you **worm** an animal, you give it medicine in order to kill the worms that are living in its intestines. [4] VERB If you **worm** your **way** somewhere, you move there slowly and with difficulty.

worn /wɔːn/. [1] **Worn** is the past participle of **wear**. [2] ADJ **Worn** things are damaged or thin because they are old and have been used a lot. ...a worn blue carpet. [3] ADJ AFTER LINK-V If someone looks **worn,** they look old and tired.

,worn-'out. [1] ADJ **Worn-out** things are too old, damaged, or thin from use to be used any more. ...his worn-out shoes. [2] ADJ If you are **worn-out,** you are extremely tired.

★ worry /'wʌri, AM 'wɜːri/ **worries, worrying, worried.** [1] VERB If you **worry,** you keep thinking about a problem or about something unpleasant that might happen. Don't worry, your luggage will come on afterwards by taxi... I worry about her constantly. ◆ **worried** ADJ I'm worried about what is going to happen if we get in the same situation again. [2] VERB If someone or something **worries** you, they cause you to worry. 'Why didn't you tell us?'—'I didn't want to worry you.' [3] N-UNCOUNT **Worry** is the state or feeling of anxiety and unhappiness caused by the problems that you have or by thinking about unpleasant things that might happen. His last years were overshadowed by financial worry. [4] N-COUNT A **worry** is a problem that you keep thinking about and that makes you unhappy. My main worry was that Madeleine Johnson would still be there.

worrying /'wʌriɪŋ, AM 'wɜːriɪŋ/. ADJ If something is **worrying,** it causes people to worry. This is a very worrying incident.

worse /wɜːs/. **Worse** is the comparative of **bad** and **badly**.

PHRASES ● If a situation **goes from bad to worse,** it becomes even more unpleasant or unsatisfactory. ● If a situation changes **for the worse,** it becomes more unpleasant or more difficult. ● If you tell someone that they **could do worse than** do a particular thing, you are advising them that it would be quite a good thing to do. Scientists in search of a challenging career could do worse than consider forensic science.

worsen /'wɜːsən/ **worsens, worsening, worsened.** VERB If a situation **worsens,** or if something **worsens** it, it becomes more difficult, unpleasant, or unacceptable. The security forces had to intervene to prevent the situation worsening... These options would actually worsen the economy.

a b c d e f g h i j k l m n o p q r s t u v w x y z

worship /'wɜːʃɪp/ **worships, worshipping, worshipped** (AM **worshiping, worshiped**). **1** VERB & N-UNCOUNT To **worship** God or a god means to show your respect to God or a god, for example by saying prayers. The act of showing respect in this way is called **worship**. ...*Jews worshipping at the Wailing Wall.* ...*places of worship.* ♦ **worshipper, worshippers** N-COUNT *The mosque will hold 1,000 worshippers.* **2** VERB If you **worship** someone or something, you love them or admire them very much. *He worships his father.*

worst /wɜːst/. **1** **Worst** is the superlative of **bad** and **badly**. **2** N-SING **The worst** is the most unpleasant or unfavourable thing that could happen or does happen. *The country had come through the worst of the recession.*
PHRASES ● You use **at worst** when considering a situation in the most unfavourable or most pessimistic way. *At best Nella would be an invalid; at worst she would die.* ● If someone is **at their worst**, they are behaving as unpleasantly or doing something as unsuccessfully as it is possible for them to do. *This was their mother at her worst.*

worth /wɜːθ/. **1** PREP If something is **worth** an amount of money, it can be sold for that amount or has that value. *These books might be worth £80 or £90 or more to a collector.* **2** **Worth** combines with amounts of money, so that when you talk about a particular amount of money's **worth of** something, you mean the quantity of it that you can buy for that amount of money. *I went and bought about six dollars' worth of potato chips.* **3** N-UNCOUNT Someone's **worth** is their value, usefulness, or importance. ...*highly skilled people who had already proven their worth to their companies.* **4** PREP You use **worth** to say that something is so enjoyable or useful that it is a good thing to do or have. *This restaurant is well worth a visit... He's decided to get a look at the house and see if it might be worth buying.* **5** PHRASE If an action or activity is **worth** your **while**, it will be helpful or useful to you. *It might be worth your while to go to court and ask for the agreement to be changed.*

worthless /'wɜːθləs/. ADJ Something that is **worthless** is of no real use or value. ...*a worthless piece of old junk.*

worthwhile /ˌwɜːθ'waɪl/. ADJ If something is **worthwhile**, it is enjoyable or useful, and worth the time, money, or effort spent on it. ...*a worthwhile movie that was compelling enough to watch again... It might be worthwhile to consider your attitude to an insurance policy.*

worthy /'wɜːði/ **worthier, worthiest.** ADJ If someone or something is **worthy of** something, they deserve it because they have the qualities or abilities required. [FORMAL] *The bank might think you're worthy of a loan... Agassi was a worthy winner.*

⭐ **would** /wəd STRONG wʊd/.

✓ In spoken English, **would** is often abbreviated to **'d**.

1 MODAL You use **would** when you are saying what someone believed, hoped, or expected to happen or be the case. *Would he always be like this?... A report yesterday that said British unemployment would continue to rise.* **2** MODAL You use **would** when you are referring to the result or effect of a possible situation. *It would be fun to be taken to fabulous restaurants.* **3** MODAL You use **would** to say that someone was willing to do something. You use **would not** to indicate that someone refused to do something. *She indicated that she would help her husband... He wouldn't say where he had picked up the information.* **4** MODAL You use **would**, especially with verbs such as 'like', 'love', and 'wish' when saying that someone wants to do or have something or wants something to happen. *She asked me what I would like to do... Ideally, she would love to become pregnant again... Anne wouldn't mind going to Italy or France to live.* **5** MODAL You use **would** in polite questions and requests. *Would you like a drink?... Do you think it would be all right if I smoked?* **6** MODAL You say that someone **would** do something when it is or was typical of them. *I was amazed, during a 'Women In Rock' debate, to be told, 'Well, you would say that: you're a man.'... Sunday mornings my mother would bake. I'd stand by the fridge and help.* **7** MODAL You use **would** or **would have** to express your opinion about something that you think is true. *I think you'd agree he's a very respected columnist... I would have thought it a proper job for the Army to fight rebellion.* **8** MODAL If you talk about what **would have** happened if a possible event had occurred, you are talking about the result or effect of that event. *My daughter would have been 17 this week if she had lived.* **9** MODAL If you say that someone **would have** liked or preferred something, you mean that they wanted to do it or have it but were unable to. *I would have liked a bit more time.*

'would-be. ADJ BEFORE N You use **would-be** to describe what someone wants to do or become. For example, if someone is a **would-be** writer, they want to become a writer.

wouldn't /'wʊdənt/. **Wouldn't** is the usual spoken form of 'would not'.

would've /wʊdəv/. **Would've** is a spoken form of 'would have', especially when 'have' is an auxiliary verb.

⭐ **wound, wounds, wounding, wounded.** **1** /waʊnd/. **Wound** is the past tense and past participle of **wind 2.** **2** N-COUNT /wuːnd/ A **wound** is an injury to your body, especially a cut or hole caused by a gun, knife, or similar weapon. **3** VERB If a weapon or something sharp **wounds** you, it injures your body. *A bomb exploded in a hotel, killing six people and wounding another five... Helicopters flew the two wounded men out.* **4** VERB If you **are wounded** by what someone says or does, they make you feel hurt and upset.

> **USAGE** Note that when someone is hurt accidentally, for example in a car crash or when they are playing sport, you do not say that they **are wounded** or that they receive a **wound**. You say that they **are injured** or that they receive an **injury**. In more formal English, **injury** can also be an uncount noun. *A man and his baby were injured in the explosion... Many of the deaths that occur in cycling are due to head injuries... Two teenagers escaped serious injury when their car rolled down an embankment.* **Wound** is normally restricted to soldiers who are injured in battle, or to deliberate acts of violence against a particular person. *...stab wounds.*

wound up /waʊnd 'ʌp/. ADJ If someone is **wound up**, they are very tense and nervous or angry. [INFORMAL]

wove /wəʊv/. **Wove** is the past tense of **weave**.

woven /'wəʊvən/. **Woven** is the past participle of **weave**.

wow /waʊ/. EXCLAM You can say **'wow'** when you are very impressed, surprised, or pleased. [INFORMAL] *Wow, this is so exciting.*

wrangle /'ræŋgəl/ **wrangles, wrangling, wrangled.** VERB & N-COUNT If two people **are wrangling over** something, or if they are involved in a **wrangle over** it, they are arguing about it for a long time about it. *...diplomatic wrangles over how to mark the occasion.* ♦ **wrangling, wranglings** N-VAR *Their decision follows months of wrangling.*

⭐ **wrap** /ræp/ **wraps, wrapping, wrapped.** 1 VERB & PHR-VERB If you **wrap** something, or if you **wrap** it **up**, you fold paper or cloth tightly round it to cover it. *Diana is taking the opportunity to wrap up the family presents.* 2 VERB If you **wrap** something such as a piece of paper or cloth **around** another thing, you put it around it. *She wrapped a handkerchief around her bleeding palm.* 3 VERB If you **wrap** your arms, fingers, or legs **around** something, you put them tightly around it. *He wrapped his arms around her and held her for half a minute.* 4 See also **wrapping**. ▸**wrap up.** 1 PHR-VERB If you **wrap up**, you put warm clothes on. *It can be breezy, so wrap up well.* 2 PHR-VERB If you **wrap up** something such as a job or an agreement, you complete it in a satisfactory way. *The deal was wrapped up in just 24 hours.* 3 See also **wrap** 1.

wrapped 'up. ADJ AFTER LINK-V If someone is **wrapped up** in something or someone, they spend nearly all their time thinking about them, so that they forget about other things which may be important. *They were totally wrapped up in their own problems.*

wrapper /'ræpə/ **wrappers.** N-COUNT A **wrapper** is

a piece of paper, plastic, or foil which covers and protects something that you buy, especially food.

wrapping /'ræpɪŋ/ **wrappings.** N-VAR **Wrapping** is something such as paper or plastic which is used to cover and protect something. *I tore off the wrapping and opened the box.*

wrath /rɒθ, AM ræθ/. N-UNCOUNT **Wrath** means anger. [LITERARY]

wreak /riːk/ **wreaks, wreaking, wreaked** or **wrought.** 1 VERB Something or someone that **wreaks** havoc or destruction causes a great amount of disorder or damage. [JOURNALISM] *Torrential rain wreaked havoc on the Gold Coast yesterday.* 2 VERB If you **wreak** revenge or vengeance on someone, you do something to harm them, because they have harmed you. [LITERARY] 3 See also **wrought**.

wreath /riːθ/ **wreaths.** N-COUNT A **wreath** is a ring of flowers and leaves which is put onto a grave as a sign of remembrance for the dead person.

wreck /rek/ **wrecks, wrecking, wrecked.** 1 VERB To **wreck** something means to completely destroy or ruin it. *Twenty-one people were killed and 50 houses wrecked. ...the injuries which nearly wrecked his career.* 2 N-COUNT A **wreck** is something such as ship, car, plane, or building which has been destroyed, usually in an accident.

wreckage /'rekɪdʒ/. N-UNCOUNT When a plane, car, or building has been destroyed, you can refer to what remains as the **wreckage**.

wren /ren/ **wrens.** N-COUNT A **wren** is a very small brown bird.

wrench /rentʃ/ **wrenches, wrenching, wrenched.** 1 VERB If you **wrench** something, usually something that is in a fixed position, you pull or twist it violently. *He felt two men wrench the suitcase from his hand... She wrenched herself from his grasp.* 2 VERB If you **wrench** a limb or one of your joints, you twist and injure it. 3 N-SING If you say that leaving someone or something is **a wrench**, you feel very sad about it. 4 N-COUNT A **wrench** is an adjustable metal tool used for tightening or loosening nuts and bolts. → See picture on page 833.

wrestle /'resəl/ **wrestles, wrestling, wrestled.** 1 VERB If you **wrestle with** a difficult problem or situation, you try to solve it. 2 VERB If you **wrestle with** someone, you fight them by forcing them into painful positions or throwing them to the ground, rather than by hitting them. Some people wrestle as a sport.

wrestler /'reslə/ **wrestlers.** N-COUNT A **wrestler** is someone who wrestles as a sport.

wrestling /'reslɪŋ/. N-UNCOUNT **Wrestling** is a sport in which two people wrestle and try to throw each other to the ground.

wretched /'retʃɪd/. 1 ADJ You describe someone as **wretched** when you feel sorry for them because they are in an unpleasant situation or have suffered unpleasant experiences. [FORMAL] *...wretched people who had to sell or starve.* 2 ADJ If you describe something or someone as

a
b
c
d
e
f
g
h
i
j
k
l
m
n
o
p
q
r
s
t
u
v
w
x
y
z

⭐ Bank of English® frequent word   For a full explanation of all grammatical labels, see pages vii-x

wretched, you think that they are very bad. [SPOKEN] *The pay has always been wretched... Wretched woman, he thought, why the hell can't she wait?*

wriggle /ˈrɪgəl/ **wriggles, wriggling, wriggled.** VERB If you **wriggle**, or if you **wriggle** a part of your body, you twist and turn your body with quick movements. *Janey wriggled out of her father's arms... She pulled off her shoes and stockings and wriggled her toes.*

▸ **wriggle out of.** PHR-VERB If you **wriggle out of** doing something that you do not want to do, you manage to avoid doing it. [INFORMAL] *I had wriggled out of the washing up.*

wring /rɪŋ/ **wrings, wringing, wrung.** VERB If you **wring** something **out of** someone, you manage to make them give it to you even though they do not want to.

▸ **wring out.** PHR-VERB When you **wring out** a wet cloth or a wet piece of clothing, you squeeze the water out of it by twisting it strongly.

wrinkle /ˈrɪŋkəl/ **wrinkles, wrinkling, wrinkled.** [1] N-COUNT **Wrinkles** are lines which form on someone's face as they grow old. [2] VERB When you **wrinkle** your nose or forehead, or when it **wrinkles**, you tighten the muscles in your face so that the skin folds. *Jack wrinkled his nose at that distasteful thought.*

wrinkled /ˈrɪŋkəld/. [1] ADJ Someone who has **wrinkled** skin has a lot of wrinkles. *...the old man's wrinkled face.* [2] ADJ **Wrinkled** clothes have lots of small untidy folds or lines in them. *His white uniform was dirty and wrinkled.*

wrist /rɪst/ **wrists.** N-COUNT Your **wrist** is the part of your body between your hand and arm which bends when you move your hand. → See picture on page 823.

writ /rɪt/ **writs.** N-COUNT A **writ** is a legal document that orders a person to do a particular thing.

★ **write** /raɪt/ **writes, writing, wrote, written.** [1] VERB When you **write** something on a surface, you use something such as a pen or pencil to produce words, letters, or numbers on it. *They were still trying to teach her to read and write... She took a card out and wrote an address on it.* [2] VERB If you **write** something such as a book, a poem, or a piece of music, you create it and record it on paper or perhaps on a computer. *She writes for many papers, including the Sunday Times.* [3] VERB When you **write to** someone, or when you **write** them a letter, you give them information, ask them something, or express your feelings in a letter. In American English, you can also **write** someone. *She had written him a note a couple of weeks earlier... The next day I wrote a letter to the manager.* [4] VERB & PHR-VERB When someone **writes** something such as a cheque, receipt, or prescription, or when they **write** it **out**, they put the necessary information on it and usually sign it. *I'll write you a cheque in a moment... Get my wife to write you out a receipt before you leave.* [5] See also **writing, written.**

▸ **write down.** PHR-VERB When you **write** something **down**, you record it on a piece of paper using a pen or pencil. *I did write down what I thought was good about the course.*

▸ **write in.** PHR-VERB If you **write in to** an organization, you send them a letter. *...another thing you might like to write in to this programme about.*

▸ **write into.** PHR-VERB If a rule or detail **is written into** a law or agreement, it is included in it when the law or agreement is made.

▸ **write off.** [1] PHR-VERB If you **write off to** a company or organization, you send them a letter asking for something. *He wrote off to the New Zealand Government for these pamphlets.* [2] PHR-VERB If you **write off** an amount of money you have lost, you accept that you will never get it back. *He had long since written off the money.* [3] PHR-VERB If you **write** someone or something **off**, you decide that they are unimportant or useless and that they are not worth further serious attention. *He is fed up with people writing him off because of his age.* [4] PHR-VERB If someone **writes off** a vehicle, they have a crash in it and it is so badly damaged that it is not worth repairing. *One of Pete's friends wrote his car off there.* [5] See also **write-off.**

▸ **write out.** See **write** 4.

▸ **write up.** PHR-VERB If you **write up** something that has been done or said, you record it on paper in a neat and complete form, usually using notes that you have made. *Mr Sadler conducted interviews, and his girlfriend wrote them up.*

'write-off, write-offs. N-COUNT If a vehicle is a **write-off**, it is so badly damaged in an accident that it is not worth repairing.

★ **writer** /ˈraɪtə/ **writers.** [1] N-COUNT A **writer** is a person whose job is writing books, stories, or articles. [2] N-COUNT The **writer** of a story or other piece of writing is the person who wrote it.

writhe /raɪð/ **writhes, writhing, writhed.** VERB If you **writhe**, you twist and turn your body violently backwards and forwards, usually because you are in great pain.

★ **writing** /ˈraɪtɪŋ/ **writings.** [1] N-UNCOUNT **Writing** is something that has been written or printed. *Joe tried to read the writing on the opposite page... If you have a complaint about your holiday, please inform us in writing.* [2] N-UNCOUNT You can refer to any piece of written work as **writing**, especially when you are considering the style of language used in it. *It was such a brilliant piece of writing.* [3] N-UNCOUNT **Writing** is the activity of writing, especially of writing books for money. [4] N-UNCOUNT Your **writing** is the way the words that you write down look when you see them on paper. *It was a little difficult to read your writing.*

★ **written** /ˈrɪtən/. [1] **Written** is the past participle of **write.** [2] ADJ A **written** test or piece of work is one which involves writing rather than doing something practical or giving spoken answers. [3] ADJ BEFORE N A **written** agreement or law has been officially written down. *We're waiting for written confirmation from the Americans.*

⭐ **wrong** /rɒŋ, AM rɔːŋ/ **wrongs, wronging, wronged.** 1 ADJ AFTER LINK-V If you say that there is something **wrong**, you mean that there is something unsatisfactory about the situation, person, or thing you are talking about. *Pain is the body's way of telling us that something is wrong. ...a relationship that felt wrong from the start... What's wrong with him?* 2 ADJ BEFORE N & ADV **Wrong** means not correct or not suitable. *The wrong man had been punished... I really made the wrong decision there... You've done it wrong.* ♦ **wrongly** ADV *She was wrongly blamed for breaking a vase.* 3 ADJ AFTER LINK-V If you are **wrong about** something, what you say or think about it is not correct. *I was wrong about it being a casual meeting.* ♦ **wrongly** ADV *People believed (wrongly) that the disease could be transmitted in saliva.* 4 ADJ AFTER LINK-V If you say that something someone does is **wrong**, you mean that it is bad or immoral. *She was wrong to leave her child alone... We don't consider we did anything wrong.* 5 N-UNCOUNT **Wrong** is used to refer to actions that are bad or immoral. *Johnson didn't seem to be able to tell the difference between right and wrong.* 6 N-COUNT A **wrong** is an unjust action or situation. *We too should be compensated financially for the terrible wrongs done to us.* 7 VERB If someone **wrongs** you, they treat you in an unfair way. [LITERARY]
PHRASES ● If something **goes wrong**, it stops working or is no longer successful. *Something* went wrong with the lift. ...when my marriage started to go wrong. ● If someone who is involved in an argument or dispute is **in the wrong**, they have behaved in a way which is morally or legally wrong.

wrongdoing /ˈrɒŋduːɪŋ, AM ˈrɔːŋ-/ **wrongdoings.** N-VAR **Wrongdoing** is behaviour that is illegal or immoral. *The bank has denied any wrongdoing.*

wrote /rəʊt/. **Wrote** is the past tense of **write**.

wrought /rɔːt/. 1 VERB If something **has wrought** a change, it has caused it. [LITERARY] *Events in Paris wrought a change in British opinion towards France.* 2 **Wrought** is a past tense and past participle of **wreak**.

wrung /rʌŋ/. **Wrung** is the past tense and past participle of **wring**.

wry /raɪ/. ADJ If someone responds to a bad or difficult situation with a **wry** remark or facial expression, it shows that they find a bad or difficult situation slightly amusing or ironic. *There is a wry sense of humour in his work.* ♦ **wryly** ADV *She turned and smiled wryly.*

wuss /wʊs/ **wusses.** N-COUNT If you call someone a **wuss**, you are criticizing them for being afraid; used showing disapproval. [SPOKEN, INFORMAL]

⭐ **WWW** /ˌdʌbljuː dʌblju: ˈdʌblju:/. **WWW** is an abbreviation for 'World-Wide Web'. It appears at the beginning of website addresses in the form **www**. [COMPUTING] *Check out our website at www.cobuild.collins.co.uk.*

Xx Yy Zz

xenophobia /ˌzenəˈfəʊbiə/. N-UNCOUNT **Xenophobia** is fear or strong dislike of people from other countries. ♦ **xenophobic** ADJ *The man was obsessively xenophobic.*

Xerox /ˈzɪərɒks/ **Xeroxes, Xeroxing, Xeroxed.** 1 N-COUNT A **Xerox** is a machine that can make copies of pieces of paper which have writing or other marks on them. **Xerox** is a trademark. 2 VERB & N-COUNT If you **Xerox** a document, or if you make a **Xerox** of it, you make a copy of it using a Xerox machine.

'**X-ray, X-rays, X-raying, X-rayed.** 1 N-COUNT An **X-ray** is a type of radiation that can pass through most solid materials. X-rays are used by doctors to examine the bones or organs inside your body, and at airports to see inside people's luggage. 2 N-COUNT An **X-ray** is a picture made by sending X-rays through something. 3 VERB If someone or something **is X-rayed**, an x-ray picture is taken of them.

⭐ **yacht** /jɒt/ **yachts.** N-COUNT A **yacht** is a large boat with sails or a motor, used for racing or for pleasure trips.

yachting /ˈjɒtɪŋ/. N-UNCOUNT **Yachting** is the sport or activity of sailing a yacht.

yank /jæŋk/ **yanks, yanking, yanked.** VERB & N-COUNT If you **yank** something somewhere, or if you give it a **yank**, you pull it suddenly with a lot of force. *She yanked open the drawer... Grabbing his ponytail, Shirley gave it a yank.*

yacht

⭐ **yard** /jɑːd/ **yards.** 1 N-COUNT A **yard** is a unit of length equal to 36 inches or approximately 91.4 centimetres. 2 N-COUNT A **yard** is a flat area of concrete or stone that is next to a building and often has a wall around it. ③ N-COUNT You can refer to a large open area where a particular type of work is done as a **yard**. *...a ship repair yard.* ④ N-COUNT In American English, a **yard** is an area of land next to a house, with plants, trees, and grass. The usual British word is **garden**.

yardstick /'jɑːdstɪk/ **yardsticks.** N-COUNT If you use someone or something as a **yardstick**, you use them as a standard for comparison when you are judging other people or things. *The best yardstick was to measure traffic against the 1990 figures.*

yarn /jɑːn/ **yarns.** ① N-VAR **Yarn** is thread that is used for knitting or making cloth. ② N-COUNT A **yarn** is a story that someone tells, often with invented details which make it more interesting.

yawn /jɔːn/ **yawns, yawning, yawned.** ① VERB & N-COUNT When you **yawn**, you open your mouth wide and breathe in more air than usual, often when you are tired. A **yawn** is an act of yawning. *Rosanna stifled a huge yawn.* ② VERB A gap or opening that **yawns** is large and wide, and often frightening. [LITERARY] *Liddie's doorway yawned blackly open.*

yd, yds. N-COUNT **yd** is a written abbreviation for **yard**. *...200 yds further on.*

★ **yeah** /jeə/. CONVENTION **Yeah** is used in written English to represent the way yes is pronounced in informal speech. *'Bring us something to drink.'—'Yeah, yeah.'*

★ **year** /jɪə/ **years.** ① N-COUNT A **year** is a period of twelve months, beginning on the first of January and ending on the thirty-first of December. → See Reference Page on Times and Dates. ② N-COUNT A **year** is any period of twelve months. *The museums attract more than two and a half million visitors a year.* ③ N-COUNT A period of the year which is connected with schools or business can be called a school **year** or a business **year**. ④ N-PLURAL You can use **years** to emphasize that you are referring to a very long time. *I haven't laughed so much in years.* ⑤ PHRASE If something happens **all year round**, it happens continually throughout the year. ⑥ See also **New Year**.

yearly /'jɪəli/. ① ADJ BEFORE N & ADV A **yearly** event happens once a year or every year. *...their yearly meeting in London... Clients normally pay fees in advance, monthly, quarterly, or yearly.* ② ADJ BEFORE N & ADV You use **yearly** to describe something such as an amount that relates to a period of one year. *...a yearly budget for health care... Novello says college students will spend $4.2 billion yearly on alcoholic beverages.*

yearn /jɜːn/ **yearns, yearning, yearned.** VERB If someone **yearns for** something, they want it very much. *He yearned for freedom... I yearned to be a movie actor.* ♦ **yearning, yearnings** N-VAR *...a yearning for a child of my own.*

-year-old, -year-olds. -year-old combines with numbers to form adjectives and nouns that indicate the age of people or things. *She has a six-year-old daughter called Ceri. ...a ski school for 3- to 6-year-olds.*

yeast /jiːst/ **yeasts.** N-VAR **Yeast** is a kind of fungus which is used to make bread rise, and in making alcoholic drinks such as beer.

yell /jel/ **yells, yelling, yelled.** VERB & N-COUNT If you **yell** or **yell out**, or if you give a **yell**, you shout loudly, usually because you are excited, angry, or in pain. *I'm sorry I yelled at you last night... He let out a yell.*

★ **yellow** /'jeləʊ/ **yellows, yellowing, yellowed.** ① ADJ & N-VAR Something that is **yellow** is the colour of lemons or egg yolks. *...the soft yellows of the desert sands.* ② VERB If something **yellows**, it becomes yellow in colour, often because it is old.

,**yellow 'card, yellow cards.** N-COUNT In football or rugby, the **yellow card** is a card that the referee shows to a player to warn them that if they break the rules again they will have to leave the pitch.

yen /jen/.

> ✓ **Yen** is both the singular and the plural form.

N-COUNT The **yen** is the unit of currency used in Japan.

★ **yes** /jes/. ① CONVENTION You use **yes** to give a positive response to a question, or when you are saying that something is true, accepting an offer or request, or giving permission. *'Are you a friend of Nick's?'—'Yes.'... 'That's a type of whitefly, is it?'—'Yes, it is a whitefly.'... 'Can I ask you something?'—'Yes, of course.'* ② CONVENTION You can use **yes** when contradicting something that someone says. *'I don't know what you're talking about.'—'Yes, you do.'*

★ **yesterday** /'jestədeɪ, -di/. ADV & N-UNCOUNT You use **yesterday** to refer to the day before today. *She left yesterday. ...yesterday's meeting.*

★ **yet** /jet/. ① ADV You use **yet** in negative statements to indicate that something has not happened up to the present time, although it probably will happen. You also use **yet** in questions to ask if something has happened up to the present time. *No decision has yet been made... He had asked around and learned that Billy was not yet here... Have you got satellite TV yet?*

> **USAGE** In British English, **yet** and **already** are usually used with the present perfect tense. *Have they said sorry or not yet?... I have already started knitting baby clothes.* In American English, a past tense is commonly used. *I didn't get any sleep yet... She already told the neighbors not to come.* This usage is becoming more common in British English.

② ADV If you say that something should not or cannot be done **yet**, you mean that it should not or cannot be done now, although it will have to be done at a later time. *Don't get up yet.* ③ ADV You use **yet** to say that there is still a possibility that something will happen. *A negotiated* settlement might yet be possible. **4** ADV You use **yet** after an expression referring to a period of time, when you want to say how much longer a situation will continue. *Unemployment will go on rising for some time yet.* **5** ADV If you say that you have **yet to** do something, you mean that you have never done it. *He has been nominated three times for the Oscar but has yet to win.* **6** CONJ You can use **yet** to introduce a fact which seems rather surprising after the previous fact you have just mentioned. *I don't eat much, yet I am a size 16.* **7** ADV You can use **yet** to emphasize a word, especially when you are saying that something is surprising because it is more extreme than previous things of its kind, or a further case of them. *I saw yet another doctor.*

⭐ **yield** /jiːld/ **yields, yielding, yielded.** **1** VERB If you **yield** to someone or something, you stop resisting them. *She yielded to pressure and gave her fee to charity... Gessler was the first to yield, announcing his resignation in January.* **2** VERB If you **yield** something that you have control of or responsibility for, you allow someone else to have control or responsibility. *The President is now under pressure to yield power to the republics.* **3** VERB If something **yields**, it breaks or moves position because pressure has been put on it. *He reached the massive door of the barn and pushed. It yielded.* **4** VERB & N-COUNT When something **yields** an amount of something such as food or money, it produces that amount. The amount produced is called a **yield**. *The vineyard yields 200 tonnes of grapes annually... A yield of more than 7 per cent is expected from the shares.*

yoga /ˈjəʊgə/. N-UNCOUNT **Yoga** is a type of exercise in which you move your body into various positions in order to become more fit or flexible, to improve your breathing, and to relax your mind.

yogurt (or **yoghurt**) /ˈjɒgət, AM ˈjəʊ-/ **yogurts.** N-VAR **Yoghurt** is a slightly sour thick liquid made by adding bacteria to milk. A **yogurt** is a small pot of yogurt.

yoke /jəʊk/ **yokes, yoking, yoked.** **1** N-SING If you say that people are under **the yoke of** something or someone bad, you mean they are forced to live in a difficult or unhappy state because of that thing or person. [LITERARY] *People are still suffering under the yoke of slavery.* **2** VERB If two or more people or things **are yoked** together, they are forced to be closely linked with each other. *The pact signed in 1965 yoked Ontario into the United States economy.*

yolk /jəʊk/ **yolks.** N-VAR The **yolk** of an egg is the yellow part in the middle.

⭐ **you** /juː/. **1** PRON A speaker or writer uses **you** to refer to the person or people that he or she is speaking to. *When I saw you across the room I knew I'd met you before.* **2** PRON A speaker or writer sometimes uses **you** to refer to people in general. *In those days you did what you were told.*

you'd /juːd/. **You'd** is the usual spoken form of 'you had', especially when 'had' is an auxiliary

verb. **You'd** is also a spoken form of 'you would'. *I think you'd better tell us why you're asking these questions.*

you'll /juːl/. **You'll** is the usual spoken form of 'you will'.

⭐ **young** /jʌŋ/ **younger** /ˈjʌŋgə/ **youngest** /ˈjʌŋgəst/. **1** ADJ & N-PLURAL A **young** person, animal, or plant has not lived or existed for long and is not yet mature. You can refer to people who are young as **the young**. *...his younger brother.* **2** N-PLURAL The **young** of an animal are its babies.

⭐ **youngster** /ˈjʌŋstə/ **youngsters.** N-COUNT Young people, especially children, are sometimes referred to as **youngsters**.

⭐ **your** /jɔː, jʊə/. **1** DET A speaker or writer uses **your** to indicate that something belongs or relates to the person or people that he or she is talking or writing to. *Emma, I trust your opinion a great deal... I left all of your messages on your desk.* **2** DET A speaker or writer sometimes uses **your** to indicate that something belongs or relates to people in general. *Pain-killers are very useful in small amounts to bring your temperature down.*

you're /jɔː, jʊə/. **You're** is the usual spoken form of 'you are'.

⭐ **yours** /jɔːz, jʊəz/. **1** PRON A speaker or writer uses **yours** to refer to something that belongs or relates to the person or people that he or she is talking or writing to. *I'll take my coat upstairs. Shall I take yours, Roberta?... I believe Paul was a friend of yours.* **2** CONVENTION People write **Yours, Yours sincerely,** or **Yours faithfully** at the end of a letter before they sign their name. *With best regards, Yours, George... Yours faithfully, Michael Moore, London Business School.*

⭐ **yourself** /jɔːˈself, jʊə-/ **yourselves.** **1** PRON A speaker or writer uses **yourself** to refer to the person that he or she is talking or writing to. **Yourself** is used when the object of a verb or preposition refers to the same person as the subject of the verb. *Treat yourselves to a glass of wine to help you relax.* **2** PRON You use **yourself** to emphasize the person that you are referring to. *They mean to share the business between them, after you yourself are gone.*

⭐ **youth** /juːθ/ **youths** /juːðz/. **1** N-UNCOUNT Someone's **youth** is the period of their life when they are a child, before they are a fully mature adult. *In my youth my ambition had been to be an inventor.* **2** N-UNCOUNT **Youth** is the quality or state of being young and perhaps immature or inexperienced. *The team is now a good mixture of experience and youth.* **3** N-COUNT Journalists often refer to young men as **youths**. *...gangs of youths who broke windows and looted shops.* **4** N-PLURAL **The youth** are young people considered as a group. *He represents the opinions of the youth of today.*

youthful /ˈjuːθfʊl/. ADJ Someone who is **youthful** behaves as if they are young or younger than they really are. *I'm a very youthful 50.*

a b c d e f g h i j k l m n o p q r s t u v w x y z

you've /juːv/. **You've** is the usual spoken form of 'you have', especially when 'have' is an auxiliary verb.

yr, yrs. N-COUNT **Yr** is a written abbreviation for **year**.

yuppie /'jʌpi/ **yuppies.** N-COUNT A **yuppie** is a young middle-class person with a well-paid job, who likes to have an expensive lifestyle; used showing disapproval.

zap /zæp/ **zaps, zapping, zapped.** VERB To **zap** someone or something means to kill, destroy, or hit them, usually using a gun, spray, or laser. [INFORMAL] *A guard zapped him with the stun gun.*

zeal /ziːl/. N-UNCOUNT **Zeal** is great enthusiasm, especially in connection with work, religion, or politics. *Mr Lopez approached his task with religious zeal.*

zealous /'zeləs/. ADJ Someone who is **zealous** spends a lot of time or energy supporting something that they believe in very strongly, especially a political or religious ideal.
♦ **zealously** ADV *Details of the group's past activities were zealously guarded.*

zebra /'zebrə, 'ziː-/.

☑ The plural can be **zebra** or **zebras**.

N-COUNT A **zebra** is an African wild horse which has black and white stripes. → See picture on page 816.

zero /'zɪərəʊ/ **zeros** or **zeroes.** ☐1 NUM **Zero** is the number 0. ☐2 N-UNCOUNT **Zero** is freezing point on the Centigrade scale. It is often written as 0° C. *...thirty degrees below zero.* ☐3 ADJ You can use **zero** to say that there is none at all of the thing mentioned. *His chances are zero.*

> **USAGE** As a number, **zero** is used mainly in scientific contexts, or when you want to be precise. In spoken British English, **nought** is much more common. *The acceleration is so extreme, from nought to 60 in a fraction of one second.* However, when you are stating a telephone number, you say **o** (/əʊ/). In some sports contexts, especially football scores, **nil** is used. *England beat Poland two-nil at Wembley.* In tennis, **love** is the usual word. *He won the first set and took a two-games-to-love lead in the second.*

zest /zest/. ☐1 N-UNCOUNT **Zest** is a feeling of pleasure and enthusiasm. *...a lovable girl with a zest for life.* ☐2 N-UNCOUNT **Zest** is a quality in an activity or situation which you find exciting. *Live interviews add zest and a touch of the unexpected to any piece of research.*

zigzag (or **zig-zag**) /'zɪgzæg/ **zigzags, zigzagging, zigzagged.** ☐1 N-COUNT A **zigzag** is a line with a series of angles in it, like a continuous series of 'W's. ☐2 VERB If you **zigzag**, you move forward by going at an angle first to one side then to the other. *He zigzagged his way across the field.*

zinc /zɪŋk/. N-UNCOUNT **Zinc** is a bluish-white metal which is used to make other metals such as brass or to cover other metals such as iron to stop them rusting.

zip /zɪp/ **zips, zipping, zipped.** ☐1 N-COUNT In British English, a **zip** is a device used to open and close parts of clothes and bags. It consists of two rows of metal or plastic teeth which separate or fasten together as you pull a small tag along them. The usual American word is **zipper**. → See picture on page 249. ☐2 VERB & PHR-VERB When you **zip** something, or when you **zip up** something, you close it using a zip. *He zipped up his jeans.*

zipper /'zɪpə/ **zippers.** N-COUNT A **zipper** is the same as a **zip**. [AMERICAN]

zodiac /'zəʊdiæk/. N-SING The **zodiac** is a diagram used by astrologers to represent the positions of the planets and stars. It is divided into twelve sections, each with a special name and symbol.

⭐ **zone** /zəʊn/ **zones, zoning, zoned.** ☐1 N-COUNT A **zone** is an area that has particular features or characteristics. *The area has been declared a disaster zone.* ☐2 VERB If an area of land **is zoned**, it is formally set aside for a particular purpose. *The land was not zoned for commercial purposes.*
♦ **zoning** N-UNCOUNT *...the use of zoning to preserve agricultural land.*

zoo /zuː/ **zoos.** N-COUNT A **zoo** is a park where live animals are kept so that people can look at them.

zoology /zuː'ɒlədʒi, zəʊ-/. N-UNCOUNT **Zoology** is the scientific study of animals. *...the Cambridge Museum of Zoology.* ♦ **zoological** ADJ BEFORE N *...zoological specimens.* ♦ **zoologist, zoologists** N-COUNT *...a renowned zoologist and writer.*

zoom /zuːm/ **zooms, zooming, zoomed.** VERB If you **zoom** somewhere, you go there very quickly. *We zoomed through the gallery.* [INFORMAL]
▸ **zoom in.** PHR-VERB If a camera **zooms in on** something that is being filmed or photographed, it gives a close-up picture of it. *...a tracking system which can follow a burglar round a building and zoom in on his face.*

zucchini /zuː'kiːni/.

☑ The plural can be **zucchini** or **zucchinis**.

N-VAR In American English, **zucchini** are long thin green vegetables of the marrow family. The British word is **courgette**. → See picture on page 836.

Animals

goat

hedgehog

duck

goose

badger

pig

bull

cow

horse

donkey

squirrel

sheep

dogs (*pl*)

cats (*pl*)

hen

chick

Animals

panda

camel

zebra

elephant

lion

tiger

leopard

giraffe

monkey

rhinocerous

chimpanzee

gorilla

Bikes

moped

scooter

motorcycle/motorbike/bike

bicycle/bike

child's scooter

tandem

Boats

barge

dinghy

liner

lifeboat

steamer

trawler

yacht

Clothes

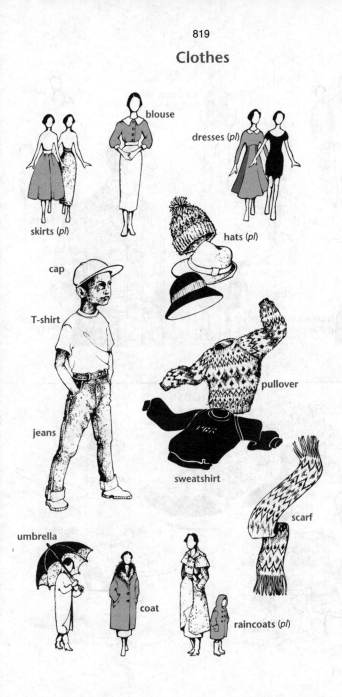

skirts (pl)

blouse

dresses (pl)

hats (pl)

cap

T-shirt

pullover

jeans

sweatshirt

scarf

umbrella

coat

raincoats (pl)

Clothes

suits (*pl*)

tie

waistcoat [BRIT]/
vest [AM]

collar

lapels (*pl*)

shirts (*pl*)

trousers [BRIT]/
pants [AM]

jacket

Shoes

sneaker [AM]

trainer [BRIT]

sandals (*pl*)

slippers (*pl*)

boots (*pl*)

shoes (*pl*)

Fruit

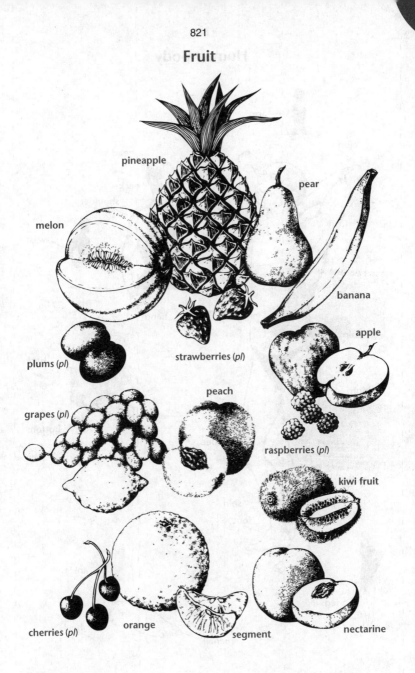

pineapple

pear

melon

banana

apple

plums (*pl*)

strawberries (*pl*)

grapes (*pl*)

peach

raspberries (*pl*)

kiwi fruit

cherries (*pl*)

orange

segment

nectarine

Human Body

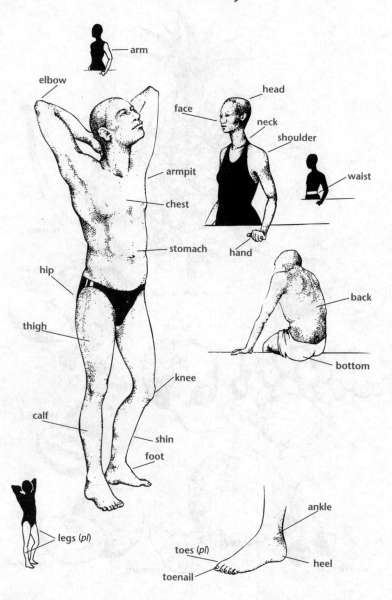

arm

elbow

head

face

neck

shoulder

armpit

chest

waist

stomach

hand

hip

back

thigh

bottom

knee

calf

shin

foot

legs (*pl*)

ankle

toes (*pl*)

toenail

heel

Human Body

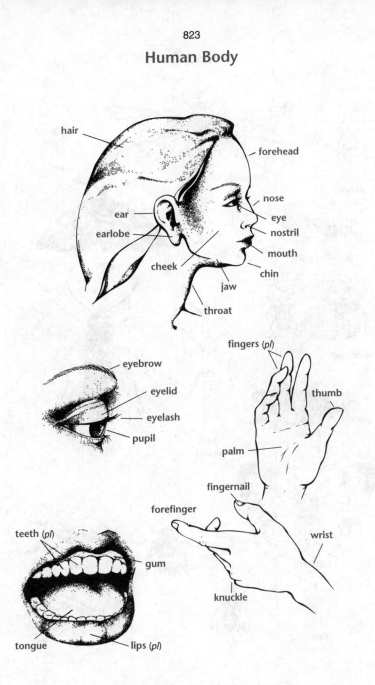

hair

forehead

nose

eye

nostril

ear

earlobe

mouth

chin

cheek

jaw

throat

fingers (*pl*)

eyebrow

thumb

eyelid

eyelash

pupil

palm

fingernail

forefinger

teeth (*pl*)

wrist

gum

knuckle

tongue

lips (*pl*)

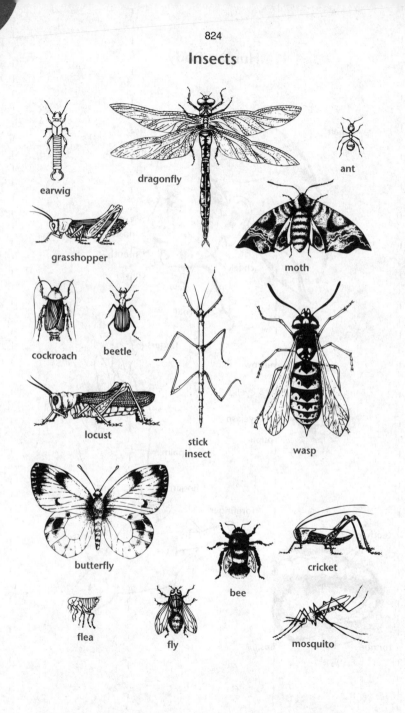

Insects

earwig

dragonfly

ant

grasshopper

moth

cockroach

beetle

locust

stick insect

wasp

butterfly

cricket

bee

flea

fly

mosquito

Kitchen Utensils

whisk

fork

spoon

knives (*pl*)

saucepan

bowl

frying pan

grater

corkscrew

funnel

tin opener

sieve

scissors

Lines

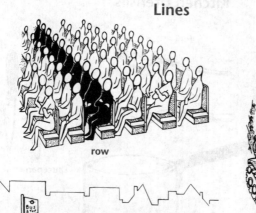

row

queue [BRIT]/**line** [AM]

column

procession

parade

Musical Instruments

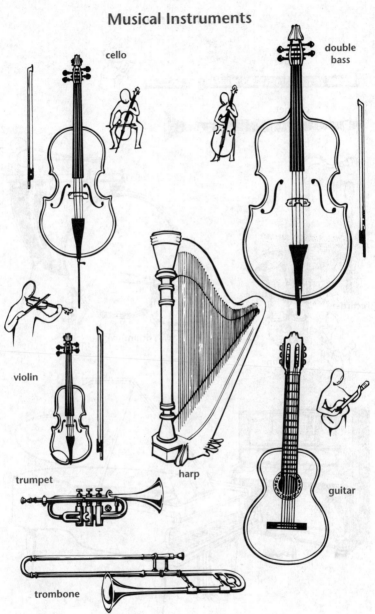

cello

double bass

violin

harp

trumpet

guitar

trombone

Musical Instruments

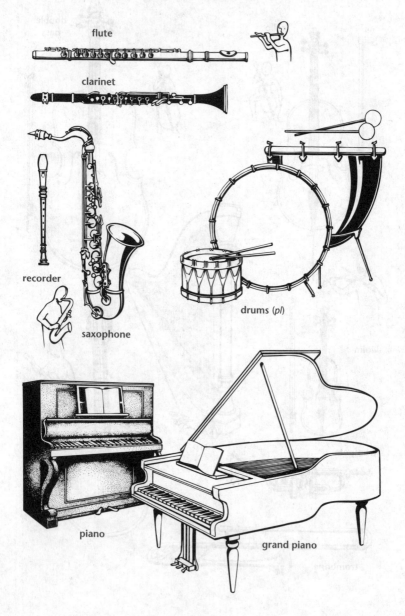

flute

clarinet

recorder

saxophone

drums (*pl*)

piano

grand piano

Shapes and Patterns

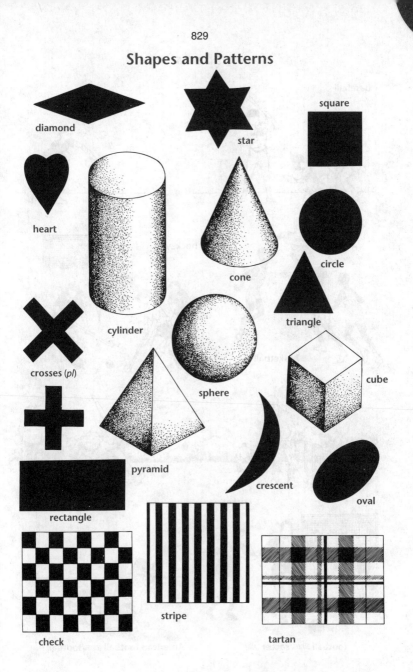

diamond

star

square

heart

cylinder

cone

circle

crosses (pl)

sphere

triangle

pyramid

cube

crescent

oval

rectangle

stripe

check

tartan

Sports

baseball

hockey

basketball

cricket

football [BRIT]/soccer [AM]

American football [BRIT]/football [AM]

Sports

ice-skating

netball

rugby

polo

skiing

tennis

volleyball

Tools

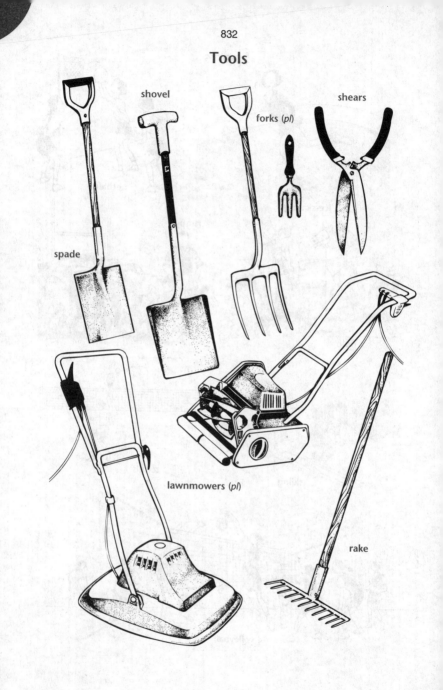

shovel

forks (*pl*)

shears

spade

lawnmowers (*pl*)

rake

Tools

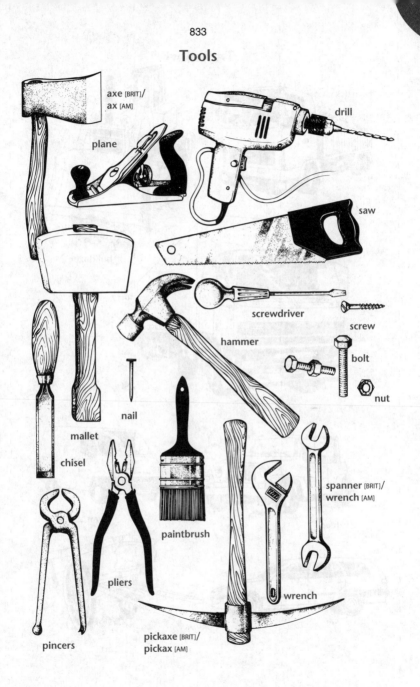

Transport

truck

bulldozer

lorry [BRIT]/truck [AM]

Jeep

van

car

cart

Transport

minibus

bus

coach

taxi

tram [BRIT] / streetcar [AM]

train

Vegetables

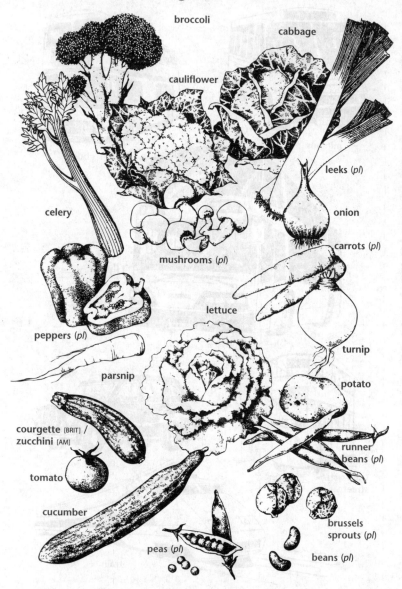

broccoli

cabbage

cauliflower

leeks (*pl*)

celery

onion

carrots (*pl*)

mushrooms (*pl*)

lettuce

turnip

peppers (*pl*)

potato

parsnip

courgette [BRIT] / zucchini [AM]

runner beans (*pl*)

tomato

cucumber

brussels sprouts (*pl*)

peas (*pl*)

beans (*pl*)

ENGLISH GRAMMAR GUIDE

CONTENTS

Clauses and sentences

Main points

Simple sentences have one clause.

Clauses usually consist of a noun group as the subject, and a verb group.

Clauses can also have another noun group as the object or complement.

Clauses can have an adverbial, also called an adjunct.

Changing the order of the words in a clause can change its meaning.

Compound sentences consist of two or more main clauses. Complex sentences always include a subordinate clause, as well as one or more main clauses.

---

1 A simple sentence has one clause, beginning with a noun group called the subject. The subject is the person or thing that the sentence is about. This is followed by a verb group, which tells you what the subject is doing, or describes the subject's situation.

> *I waited.*
> *The girl screamed.*

2 The verb group may be followed by another noun group, which is called the object. The object is the person or thing affected by the action or situation.

> *He opened <u>the car door.</u>*
> *She married <u>a young engineer.</u>*

After link verbs like 'be', 'become', 'feel', and 'seem', the verb group may be followed by a noun group or an adjective, called a complement. The complement tells you more about the subject.

> *She was <u>a doctor.</u>*
> *He was <u>angry.</u>*

3 The verb group, the object, or the complement can be followed by an adverb or a prepositional phrase, called an adverbial. The adverbial tells you more about the action or situation, for example how, when, or where it happens. Adverbials are also called adjuncts.

> *They shouted <u>loudly.</u>*
> *She won the competition <u>last week.</u>*
> *He was a policeman <u>in Birmingham.</u>*

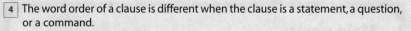
4 The word order of a clause is different when the clause is a statement, a question, or a command.

> *He speaks* English very well. (statement)
> *Did she win* at the Olympics? (question)
> *Stop* her. (command)

Note that the subject is omitted in commands, so the verb comes first.

5 A compound sentence has two or more main clauses: that is, clauses which are equally important. You join them with 'and', 'but', or 'or'.

> He met Jane at the station <u>and</u> went shopping.
> I wanted to go <u>but</u> I felt too ill.
> You can come now <u>or</u> you can meet us there later.

Note that the order of the two clauses can change the meaning of the sentence.

> He went shopping <u>and</u> met Jane at the station.

If the subject of both clauses is the same, you usually omit the subject in the second clause.

> I wanted to go <u>but felt</u> too ill.

6 A complex sentence contains a subordinate clause and at least one main clause. A subordinate clause gives information about a main clause, and is introduced by a conjunction such as 'because', 'if', 'that', or a 'wh'-word. Subordinate clauses can come before, after, or inside the main clause.

> <u>When he stopped,</u> no one said anything.
> <u>If you want,</u> I'll teach you.
> They were going by car <u>because it was more comfortable.</u>
> I told him <u>that nothing was going to happen to me.</u>
> The car <u>that I drove</u> was a Ford.
> The man <u>who came into the room</u> was small.

The noun group

Main points

Noun groups can be the subject, object, or complement of a verb, or the object of a preposition.

Noun groups can be nouns on their own, but often include other words such as determiners, numbers, and adjectives.

Noun groups can also be pronouns.

Singular noun groups take singular verbs, plural noun groups take plural verbs.

---

1 Noun groups are used to say which people or things you are talking about. They can be the subject or object of a verb.

> *<u>Strawberries</u> are very expensive now.*
> *Keith likes <u>strawberries</u>.*

A noun group can also be the complement of a link verb such as 'be', 'become', 'feel', or 'seem'.

> *She became <u>champion</u> in 1964*
> *He seemed <u>a nice man.</u>*

A noun group can be used after a preposition, and is often called the object of the preposition.

> *I saw him in <u>town.</u>*
> *She was very ill for <u>six months.</u>*

2 A noun group can be a noun on its own, but it often includes other words. A noun group can have a determiner such as 'the' or 'a'. You put determiners at the beginning of the noun group.

> *<u>The girls</u> were not in <u>the house.</u>*
> *He was eating <u>an apple.</u>*

3 A noun group can include an adjective. You usually put the adjective in front of the noun.

> *He was using <u>blue ink.</u>*
> *I like living in <u>a big city.</u>*

Sometimes you can use another noun in front of the noun.

> *I like <u>chocolate cake.</u>*
> *She wanted a job in <u>the oil industry.</u>*

A noun with 's (apostrophe s) is used in front of another noun to show who or what something belongs to or is connected with.

4

The noun group

> *I held <u>Sheila's hand</u> very tightly.*
> *He pressed a button on <u>the ship's radio.</u>*

4 A noun group can also have an adverbial, a relative clause, or a 'to'-infinitive clause after it, which makes it more precise.

> *I spoke to <u>a girl in a dark grey dress.</u>*
> *She wrote to <u>the man who employed me.</u>*
> *I was trying to think of <u>a way to stop him.</u>*

A common adverbial used after a noun is a prepositional phrase beginning with 'of'.

> *He tied the rope to <u>a large block of stone.</u>*
> *<u>The front door of the house</u> was wide open.*
> *I hated <u>the idea of leaving him alone.</u>*

Participles and some adjectives can also be used after a noun.
➤ See Units 31 and 94.

> *She pointed to <u>the three cards lying on the table.</u>*
> *He is <u>the only man available.</u>*

5 Numbers come after determiners and before adjectives.

> *I had to pay <u>a thousand dollars.</u>*
> *<u>Three tall men</u> came out of the shed.*

6 A noun group can also be a pronoun. You often use a pronoun when you are referring back to a person or thing that you have already mentioned.

> *I've got <u>two boys</u>, and <u>they</u> both enjoy playing football.*

You also use a pronoun when you do not know who the person or thing is, or do not want to be precise.

> *<u>Someone</u> is coming to mend it tomorrow.*

7 A noun group can refer to one or more people or things. Many nouns have a singular form referring to one person or thing, and a plural form referring to more than one person or thing. ➤ See Unit 13.

> *<u>My dog</u> never bites people.*
> *She likes <u>dogs.</u>*

Similarly, different pronouns are used in the singular and in the plural.

> *<u>I</u> am going home now.*
> *<u>We</u> want more money.*

When a singular noun group is the subject, it takes a singular verb. When a plural noun group is the subject, it takes a plural verb.

> *<u>His son plays</u> football for the school.*
> *<u>Her letters are</u> always very short.*

The verb group

Main points

In a clause, the verb group usually comes after the subject and always has a main verb.

The main verb has several different forms.

Verb groups can also include one or two auxiliaries, or a modal, or a modal and one or two auxiliaries.

The verb group changes in negative clauses and questions.

Some verb groups are followed by an adverbial, a complement, an object, or two objects.

1 The verb group in a clause is used to say what is happening in an action or situation. You usually put the verb group immediately after the subject. The verb group always includes a main verb.

> I <u>waited.</u>
> They <u>killed</u> the elephants.

2 Regular verbs have four forms: the base form, the third person singular form of the present simple, the '-ing' form or present participle, and the '-ed' form used for the past simple and for the past participle.

ask	asks	asking	asked
dance	dances	dancing	danced
reach	reaches	reaching	reached
try	tries	trying	tried
dip	dips	dipping	dipped

Irregular verbs may have three forms, four forms, or five forms.
Note that 'be' has eight forms.

cost	costs	costing		
think	thinks	thinking	thought	
swim	swims	swimming	swam	swum
be	am/is/are	being	was/were	been

➤ See pages 216–217 for details of verb forms.

3 The main verb can have one or two auxiliaries in front of it.

> I <u>had met</u> him in Zermatt.
> The car <u>was being repaired.</u>

6

The verb group

The main verb can have a modal in front of it.

> You <u>can go</u> now.
> I <u>would like</u> to ask you a question.

The main verb can have a modal and one or two auxiliaries in front of it.

> I <u>could have spent</u> the whole year on it.
> She <u>would have been delighted</u> to see you.

4 In negative clauses, you have to use a modal or auxiliary and put 'not' after the first word of the verb group.

> He <u>does not speak</u> English very well.
> I <u>was not smiling.</u>
> It <u>could not have been</u> wrong.

Note that you often use short forms rather than 'not'.

> I <u>didn't</u> know that.
> He <u>couldn't</u> see it.

5 In 'yes/no' questions, you have to put an auxiliary or modal first, then the subject, then the rest of the verb group.

> <u>Did</u> you <u>meet</u> George?
> <u>Couldn't</u> you <u>have been</u> a bit quieter?

In 'wh'-questions, you put the 'wh'-word first. If the 'wh'-word is the subject, you put the verb group next.

> Which <u>came</u> first?
> Who <u>could have done</u> it?

If the 'wh'-word is the object or an adverbial, you must use an auxiliary or modal next, then the subject, then the rest of the verb group.

> What <u>did</u> you <u>do?</u>
> Where <u>could</u> she <u>be going?</u>

6 Some verb groups have an object or two objects after them.
➤ See Units 51 and 52.

> He closed <u>the door.</u>
> She sends <u>you her love.</u>

Verb groups involving link verbs, such as 'be', have a complement after them.
➤ See Unit 73.

> They were <u>sailors.</u>
> She felt <u>happy.</u>

Some verb groups have an adverbial after them.

> We walked <u>through the park.</u>
> She put the letter <u>on the table.</u>

The imperative and 'let'

Main points

The imperative is the same as the base form of a verb.

You form a negative imperative with 'do not', 'don't', or 'never'.

You use the imperative to ask or tell someone to do something, or to give advice, warnings, or instructions on how to do something.

You use 'let' when you are offering to do something, making suggestions, or telling someone to do something.

1 The imperative is the same as the base form of a verb. You do not use a pronoun in front of it.

> _Come_ to my place.
> _Start_ when you hear the bell.

2 You form a negative imperative by putting 'do not', 'don't', or 'never' in front of the verb.

> _Do not write_ in this book.
> _Don't go_ so fast.
> _Never open_ the front door to strangers.

3 You use the imperative when you are:

- asking or telling someone to do something

> _Pass_ the salt.
> _Hurry up!_

- giving someone advice or a warning

> _Mind_ your head.
> _Take_ care!

- giving someone instructions on how to do something

> _Put_ this bit over here, so it fits into that hole.
> _Turn_ right off Broadway into Caxton Street.

4 When you want to make an imperative more polite or more emphatic, you can put 'do' in front of it.

> _Do have_ a chocolate biscuit.
> _Do stop_ crying.
> _Do be_ careful.

The imperative and 'let'

5 The imperative is also used in written instructions on how to do something, for example on notices and packets of food, and in books.

> *To report faults, <u>dial</u> 6666.*
> *<u>Store</u> in a dry place.*
> *<u>Fry</u> the chopped onion and pepper in the oil.*

Note that written instructions usually have to be short. This means that words such as 'the' are often omitted.

> *Wear rubber gloves.*
> *Turn off switch.*
> *Wipe bulb.*

Written imperatives are also used to give warnings.

> *<u>Reduce</u> speed now.*

6 You use 'let me' followed by the base form of a verb when you are offering to do something for someone.

> *<u>Let me</u> take your coat.*
> *<u>Let me</u> give you a few details.*

7 You use 'let's' followed by the base form of a verb when you are suggesting what you and someone else should do.

> *<u>Let's go</u> outside.*
> *<u>Let's look</u> at our map.*

Note that the form 'let us' is only used in formal or written English.

> *<u>Let us</u> consider a very simple example.*

You put 'do' before 'let's' when you are very keen to do something.

> *<u>Do let's</u> get a taxi.*

The negative of 'let's' is 'let's not' or 'don't let's'.

> *<u>Let's not</u> talk about that.*
> *<u>Don't let's</u> actually write it in the book.*

8 You use 'let' followed by a noun group and the base form of a verb when you are telling someone to do something or to allow someone else to do it.

> *<u>Let</u> me see it.*
> *<u>Let</u> Philip have a look at it.*

Questions

Main points

In most questions the first verb comes before the subject.

'Yes/no'-questions begin with an auxiliary or a modal.

'Wh'-questions begin with a 'wh'-word.

1 Questions which can be answered 'yes' or 'no' are called 'yes/no'-questions.

> *'Are you ready?'* – *'Yes.'*
> *'Have you read this magazine?'* – *'No.'*

If the verb group has more than one word, the first word comes at the beginning of the sentence, before the subject. The rest of the verb group comes after the subject.

> <u>*Is he*</u> *coming?*
> <u>*Can John*</u> *swim?*
> <u>*Will you*</u> *have finished by lunchtime?*
> <u>*Couldn't you*</u> *have been a bit quieter?*
> <u>*Has he*</u> *been working?*

2 If the verb group consists of only a main verb, you use the auxiliary 'do', 'does', or 'did' at the beginning of the sentence, before the subject. After the subject you use the base form of the verb.

> <u>*Do the British*</u> *take sport seriously?*
> <u>*Does that*</u> *sound like anyone you know?*
> <u>*Did he*</u> *go to the fair?*

Note that when the main verb is 'do', you still have to add 'do', 'does', or 'did' before the subject.

> <u>*Do they*</u> *do the work themselves?*
> <u>*Did you*</u> *do an 'O' Level in German?*

3 If the main verb is 'have', you usually put 'do', 'does', or 'did' before the subject.

> <u>*Does anyone have*</u> *a question?*
> <u>*Did you have*</u> *a good flight?*

When 'have' means 'own' or 'possess', you can put it before the subject, without using 'do', 'does', or 'did', but this is less common.

> <u>*Has he*</u> *any idea what it's like?*

Questions

4 If the main verb is the present simple or past simple of 'be', you put the verb at the beginning of the sentence, before the subject.

> <u>Are you</u> ready?
> <u>Was it</u> lonely without us?

5 When you want someone to give you more information than just 'yes' or 'no', you ask a 'wh'-question, which begins with a 'wh'-word:

what	when	where	which	who	whom
whose	why	how			

Note that 'whom' is only used in formal English.

6 When a 'wh'-word is the subject of a question, the 'wh'-word comes first, then the verb group. You do not add 'do', 'does', or 'did' as an auxiliary.

> <u>What</u> happened?
> <u>Which</u> is the best restaurant?
> <u>Who</u> could have done it?

7 When a 'wh'-word is the object of a verb or preposition, the 'wh'-word comes first, then you follow the rules for 'yes/no'-questions, adding 'do', 'does', or 'did' where necessary.

> <u>How many</u> are there?
> <u>Which</u> do you like best?

If there is a preposition, it comes at the end. However, you always put the preposition before 'whom'.

> <u>What</u>'s this <u>for</u>?
> <u>With whom</u> were you talking?

Note that you follow the same rules as for 'wh'-words as objects when the question begins with 'when', 'where', 'why', or 'how'.

> <u>When</u> would you be coming down?
> <u>Why</u> did you do it?
> <u>Where</u> did you get that <u>from</u>?

8 You can also use 'what', 'which', 'whose', 'how many', and 'how much' with a noun.

> <u>Whose idea</u> was it?
> <u>How much money</u> have we got in the bank?

You can use 'which', 'how many', and 'how much' with 'of' and a noun group.

> <u>Which of</u> the suggested answers was the correct one?
> <u>How many of</u> them bothered to come?

➤ See Unit 6 for more information on 'wh'-words.

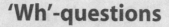
'Wh'-questions

Main points

You use 'who', 'whom', and 'whose' to ask about people, and 'which' to ask about people or things.

You use 'what' to ask about things, and 'what for' to ask about reasons and purposes.

You use 'how' to ask about the way something happens.

You use 'when' to ask about times, 'why' to ask about reasons, and 'where' to ask about places and directions.

1 You use 'who', 'whom', or 'whose' in questions about people. 'Who' is used to ask questions about the subject or object of the verb, or about the object of a preposition.

> _Who_ discovered this?
> _Who_ did he marry?
> _Who_ did you dance with?

In formal English, 'whom' is used as the object of a verb or preposition. The preposition always comes in front of 'whom'.

> _Whom_ did you see?
> _For whom_ were they supposed to do it?

You use 'whose' to ask which person something belongs to or is related to. 'Whose' can be the subject or the object.

> _Whose_ is nearer?
> _Whose_ did you prefer, hers or mine?

2 You use 'which' to ask about one person or thing, out of a number of people or things. 'Which' can be the subject or object.

> _Which_ is your son?
> _Which_ does she want?

3 You use 'what' to ask about things, for example about actions and events. 'What' can be the subject or object.

> _What_ has happened to him?
> _What_ is he selling?
> _What_ will you talk about?

'Wh'-questions

You use 'what…for' to ask about the reason for an action, or the purpose of an object.

> *<u>What</u> are you going there <u>for</u>?*
> *<u>What</u> are those lights <u>for</u>?*

4 You use 'how' to ask about the way in which something happens or is done.

> *<u>How</u> did you know we were coming?*
> *<u>How</u> are you going to get home?*

You also use 'how' to ask about the way a person or thing feels or looks.

> *'<u>How</u> are you?' – 'Well, <u>how</u> do I look?'*

5 'How' is also used:

• with adjectives to ask about the degree of quality that someone or something has

> *<u>How good</u> are you at Maths?*
> *<u>How hot</u> shall I make the curry?*

• with adjectives such as 'big', 'old', and 'far' to ask about size, age, and distance

> *<u>How old</u> are your children?*
> *<u>How far</u> is it to Montreal from here?*

Note that you do not normally use 'How small', 'How young', or 'How near'.

• with adverbs such as 'long' and 'often' to ask about time, or 'well' to ask about abilities

> *<u>How long</u> have you lived here?*
> *<u>How well</u> can you read?*

• with 'many' and 'much' to ask about the number or amount of something

> *<u>How many</u> were there?*
> *<u>How much</u> did he tell you?*

6 You use 'when' to ask about points in time or periods of time, 'why' to ask about the reason for an action, and 'where' to ask about place and direction.

> *<u>When</u> are you coming home?*
> *<u>When</u> were you in London?*
> *<u>Why</u> are you here?*
> *<u>Where</u> is the station?*
> *<u>Where</u> are you going?*

You can also ask about direction using 'which direction…in' or 'which way'.

> *<u>Which direction</u> did he go <u>in</u>?*
> *<u>Which way</u> did he go?*

Question tags: forms

Main points

You add a question tag to a statement to turn it into a question.

A question tag consists of a verb and a pronoun. The verb in a question tag is always an auxiliary, a modal, or a form of the main verb 'be'.

With a positive statement, you usually use a negative question tag containing a short form ending in '-n't'.

With a negative statement, you always use a positive question tag.

---

1 A question tag is a short phrase that is added to the end of a statement to turn it into a 'yes/no'-question. You use question tags when you want to ask someone to confirm or disagree with what you are saying, or when you want to sound more polite. Question tags are rarely used in formal written English.

> *He's very friendly, <u>isn't he?</u>*
> *You haven't seen it before, <u>have you?</u>*

2 You form a question tag by using an auxiliary, a modal, or a form of the main verb 'be', followed by a pronoun. The pronoun refers to the subject of the statement.

> *David's school is quite nice, <u>isn't it?</u>*
> *She made a remarkable recovery, <u>didn't she?</u>*

3 If the statement contains an auxiliary or modal, the same auxiliary or modal is used in the question tag.

> *Jill<u>'s</u> coming tomorrow, <u>isn</u>'t she?*
> *You <u>didn</u>'t know I was an artist, <u>did</u> you?*
> *You<u>'ve</u> never been to Benidorm, <u>have</u> you?*
> *You <u>will</u> stay in touch, <u>won</u>'t you?*

4 If the statement does not contain an auxiliary, a modal, or 'be' as a main verb, you use 'do', 'does', or 'did' in the question tag.

> *You <u>like</u> it here, <u>do</u>n't you?*
> *Sally still <u>works</u> there, <u>does</u>n't she?*
> *He <u>played</u> for Ireland, <u>did</u>n't he?*

5 If the statement contains the present simple or past simple of 'be' as a main verb, the same form of the verb 'be' is used in the question tag.

> *It <u>is</u> quite warm, <u>isn</u>'t it?*
> *They <u>were</u> really rude, <u>were</u>n't they?*

Question tags: forms

6 If the statement contains the simple present or simple past of 'have' as a main verb, you usually use 'do', 'does', or 'did' in the question tag.

> He <u>has</u> a problem, <u>doesn't</u> he?

You can also use the same form of 'have' in the question tag, but this is not very common.

> She <u>has</u> a large house, <u>hasn't</u> she?

7 With a positive statement you normally use a negative question tag, formed by adding '-n't' to the verb.

> You <u>like</u> Ralph a lot, <u>don't</u> you?
> They <u>are</u> beautiful, <u>aren't</u> they?

Note that the negative question tag with 'I' is 'aren't'.

> <u>I'm</u> a fool, <u>aren't I</u>?

8 With a negative statement you always use a positive question tag.

> It <u>doesn't</u> work, <u>does</u> it?
> You <u>won't</u> tell anyone else, <u>will</u> you?

Question tags: uses

Main points

You can use negative statements with positive question tags to make requests.

You use positive statements with positive question tags to show reactions.

You use some question tags to make imperatives more polite.

---

1 You can use a negative statement and a positive question tag to ask people for things, or to ask for help or information.

> You *wouldn't* sell it to me, *would* you?
> You *won't* tell anyone else this, *will* you?

2 When you want to show your reaction to what someone has just said, for example by expressing interest, surprise, doubt, or anger, you use a positive statement with a positive question tag.

> You've been to North America before, *have you?*
> You *fell* on your back, *did you?*
> I borrowed your car last night. – Oh, you *did, did you?*

3 When you use an imperative, you can be more polite by adding one of the following question tags.

will you	won't you	would you

> *See* that she gets safely back, *won't you?*
> *Look* at that, *would you?*

When you use a negative imperative, you can only use 'will you' as a question tag.

> *Don't* tell Howard, *will you?*

'Will you' and 'won't you' can also be used to emphasize anger or impatience. 'Can't you' is also used in this way.

> Oh, hurry up, *will you!*
> For goodness sake be quiet, *can't you!*

4 You use the question tag 'shall we' when you make a suggestion using 'let's'.

> *Let's* forget it, *shall we?*

You use the question tag 'shall I' after 'I'll'.

> *I'll* tell you, *shall I?*

Question tags: uses

5 You use 'they' in question tags after 'anybody', 'anyone', 'everybody', 'everyone', 'nobody', 'no one', 'somebody' or 'someone'.

> _Everyone_ will be leaving on Friday, won't _they?_
> _Nobody_ had bothered to plant new ones, had _they?_

You use 'it' in question tags after 'anything', 'everything', 'nothing', or 'something'.

> _Nothing_ matters now, does _it?_
> _Something_ should be done, shouldn't _it?_

You use 'there' in question tags after 'there is', 'there are', 'there was', or 'there were'.

> _There's_ a new course out now, isn't _there?_

6 When you are replying to a question tag, your answer refers to the statement, not the question tag.

If you want to confirm a positive statement, you say 'yes'. For example, if you have finished a piece of work and someone says to you 'You've finished that, haven't you?', the answer is 'yes'.

> 'It _became_ stronger, didn't it?' – '_Yes,_ it did.'

If you want to disagree with a positive statement, you say 'no'. For example, if you have not finished your work and someone says 'You've finished that, haven't you?', the answer is 'no'.

> You've just _seen_ a performance of the play, haven't you? – _No,_ not yet.

If you want to confirm a negative statement, you say 'no'. For example, if you have not finished your work and someone says 'You haven't finished that, have you?', the answer is 'no'.

> 'You _didn't know_ that, did you?' – '_No._'

If you want to disagree with a negative statement, you say 'yes'. For example, if you have finished a piece of work and someone says 'You haven't finished that, have you?', the answer is 'yes'.

> 'You _haven't been_ there, have you?' – '_Yes,_ I have.'

Indirect questions

Main points

You use indirect questions to ask for information or help.
In indirect questions, the subject of the question comes before the verb.
You can use 'if' or 'whether' in indirect questions.

1 When you ask someone for information, you can use an indirect question beginning with a phrase such as 'Could you tell me…' or 'Do you know…'.

> *Could you tell me* how far it is to the bank?
> *Do you know* where Jane is?

2 When you want to ask someone politely to do something, you can use an indirect question after 'I wonder'.

> *I wonder* if you can help me.

You also use 'I wonder' followed by an indirect question to indicate what you are thinking about.

> *I wonder* what she'll look like.
> *I wonder* which hotel it was.

3 In indirect questions, the subject of the question comes before the verb, just as it does in affirmative sentences.

> *Do you know where <u>Jane is?</u>*
> *I wonder if <u>you can help.</u>*
> *She asked me why <u>I was late.</u>*

4 You do not normally use the auxiliary 'do' in indirect questions.

> *Can you remember when <u>they open</u> on Sundays?*
> *I wonder what <u>he feels</u> about it.*

The auxiliary 'do' can be used in indirect questions, but only for emphasis, or to make a contrast with something that has already been said. It is not put before the subject as in direct questions.

> *I wonder if he <u>does</u> do anything.*

Indirect questions

5 You use 'if' or 'whether' to introduce indirect questions.

I wonder <u>if</u> you'd give the children a bath?
I'm writing to ask <u>whether</u> you would care to come and visit us.

'Whether' is used especially when there is a choice of possibilities.

I wonder <u>whether</u> it is the police or just a neighbour.
I wonder <u>whether</u> that's good for him or not.

Note that you can put 'or not' immediately after 'whether', but not immediately after 'if'.

I wonder <u>whether</u> or not we are so different from our ancestors.

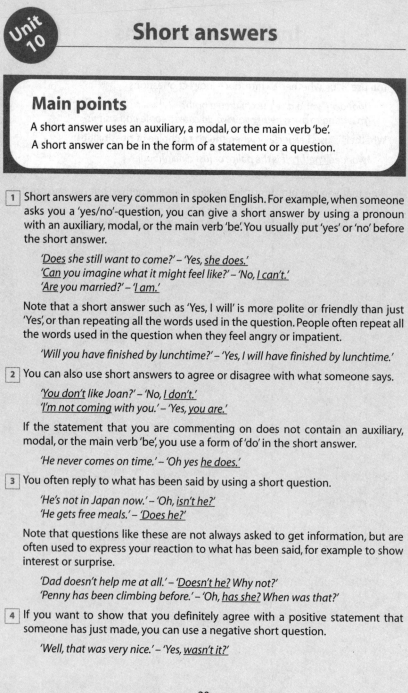

Short answers

Main points

A short answer uses an auxiliary, a modal, or the main verb 'be'.

A short answer can be in the form of a statement or a question.

---

1 Short answers are very common in spoken English. For example, when someone asks you a 'yes/no'-question, you can give a short answer by using a pronoun with an auxiliary, modal, or the main verb 'be'. You usually put 'yes' or 'no' before the short answer.

> '<u>Does</u> she still want to come?' – 'Yes, <u>she does.</u>'
> '<u>Can</u> you imagine what it might feel like?' – 'No, <u>I can't.</u>'
> '<u>Are</u> you married?' – '<u>I am.</u>'

Note that a short answer such as 'Yes, I will' is more polite or friendly than just 'Yes', or than repeating all the words used in the question. People often repeat all the words used in the question when they feel angry or impatient.

> 'Will you have finished by lunchtime?' – 'Yes, I will have finished by lunchtime.'

2 You can also use short answers to agree or disagree with what someone says.

> '<u>You don't</u> like Joan?' – 'No, <u>I don't.</u>'
> '<u>I'm not coming</u> with you.' – 'Yes, <u>you are.</u>'

If the statement that you are commenting on does not contain an auxiliary, modal, or the main verb 'be', you use a form of 'do' in the short answer.

> 'He never comes on time.' – 'Oh yes <u>he does.</u>'

3 You often reply to what has been said by using a short question.

> 'He's not in Japan now.' – 'Oh, <u>isn't he?</u>'
> 'He gets free meals.' – '<u>Does he?</u>'

Note that questions like these are not always asked to get information, but are often used to express your reaction to what has been said, for example to show interest or surprise.

> 'Dad doesn't help me at all.' – '<u>Doesn't he?</u> Why not?'
> 'Penny has been climbing before.' – 'Oh, <u>has she?</u> When was that?'

4 If you want to show that you definitely agree with a positive statement that someone has just made, you can use a negative short question.

> 'Well, that was very nice.' – 'Yes, <u>wasn't it?</u>'

Short answers

5 When you want to ask for more information, you can use a 'wh'-word on its own or with a noun as a short answer.

> 'He saw a snake.' – *'Where?'*
> 'He knew my cousin.' – *'Which cousin?'*

You can also use 'Which one' and 'Which ones'.

> 'Can you pass me the cup?' – *'Which one?'*

6 Sometimes a statement about one person also applies to another person. When this is the case, you can use a short answer with 'so' for positive statements, and with 'neither' or 'nor' for negative statements, using the same verb that was used in the statement.

You use 'so', 'neither', or 'nor' with an auxiliary, modal, or the main verb 'be'. The verb comes before the subject.

> 'You were different then.' – *'So were you.'*
> 'I don't normally drink at lunch.' – *'Neither do I.'*
> 'I can't do it.' – *'Nor can I.'*

You can use 'not either' instead of 'neither', in which case the verb comes after the subject.

> 'He doesn't understand.' – *'We don't either.'*

7 You often use 'so' in short answers after verbs such as 'think', 'hope', 'expect', 'imagine', and 'suppose', when you think that the answer to the question is 'yes'.

> 'You'll be home at six?' – *'I hope so.'*
> 'So it was worth doing?' – *'I suppose so.'*

You use 'I'm afraid so' when you are sorry that the answer is 'yes'.

> 'Is it raining?' – *'I'm afraid so.'*

With 'suppose', 'think', 'imagine', or 'expect' in short answers, you also form negatives with 'so'.

> 'Will I see you again?' – *'I don't suppose so.'*
> 'Is Barry Knight a golfer?' – 'No, *I don't think so.'*

However, you say 'I hope not' and 'I'm afraid not'.

> 'It isn't empty, is it?' – *'I hope not.'*

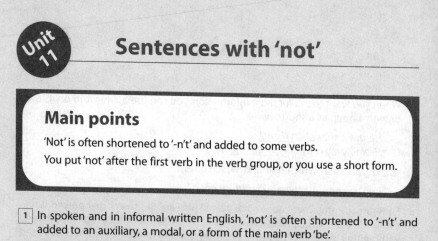

Sentences with 'not'

Unit 11

Main points

'Not' is often shortened to '-n't' and added to some verbs.

You put 'not' after the first verb in the verb group, or you use a short form.

---

1 In spoken and in informal written English, 'not' is often shortened to '-n't' and added to an auxiliary, a modal, or a form of the main verb 'be'.

> I _haven't_ heard from her recently.
> I _wasn't_ angry.

Here is a list of short forms.

isn't	haven't	don't	can't	shan't	daren't
aren't	hasn't	doesn't	couldn't	shouldn't	needn't
wasn't	hadn't	didn't	mightn't	won't	
weren't			mustn't	wouldn't	
			oughtn't		

If the verb is already shortened, you cannot add '-n't'.

> It'_s not_ easy.
> I'_ve not_ had time.

You cannot add '-n't' to 'am'. You use 'I'm not'.

> I'_m not_ excited.

2 If the verb group has more than one word, you put 'not' after the first word, or you use a short form.

> I _was not_ smiling.
> He _hadn't_ attended many meetings.
> They _might not_ notice.
> I _haven't_ been playing football recently.

3 If the sentence only contains a main verb other than 'be', you use the auxiliary 'do'.

You use 'do not', 'does not', 'did not', or a short form, followed by the base form of the main verb.

> They _do not need_ to talk.
> He _does not speak_ English very well.
> I _didn't know_ that.

22

Sentences with 'not'

Unit 11

Note that if the main verb is 'do', you still use a form of 'do' as an auxiliary.

They <u>didn't do</u> anything about it.

4 If the main verb is the present or past simple of 'be', you put 'not' immediately after it, or you use a short form.

It <u>is not</u> difficult to understand.
It'<u>s not</u> the same, is it?
He <u>wasn't</u> a bad actor actually.

5 If the main verb is 'have', you usually use a form of 'do' as an auxiliary.

They <u>don't have</u> any money.

You can also use a short form, or you can put 'not' after the verb but this is not very common.

He <u>hadn't</u> enough money.

6 You can put 'not' in front of an '-ing' form or a 'to'-infinitive.

We stood there, <u>not knowing</u> what to do.
Try <u>not to worry.</u>

7 In negative questions, you use a short form.

Why <u>didn't</u> she win at the Olympics?
<u>Hasn't</u> he put on weight?
<u>Aren't</u> you bored?

8 You can use a negative question:

- to express your feelings, for example to show that you are surprised or disappointed

Hasn't he done it yet?

- in exclamations

Isn't the weather awful!

- when you think you know something and you just want someone to agree with you

'Aren't you Joanne's brother?' – 'Yes, I am.'

9 Note the meaning of 'yes' and 'no' in answers to negative questions.

<u>Isn't</u> Tracey going to get a bit bored in Birmingham?'
– 'Yes.' (She is going to get bored.)
– 'No.' (She is not going to get bored.)

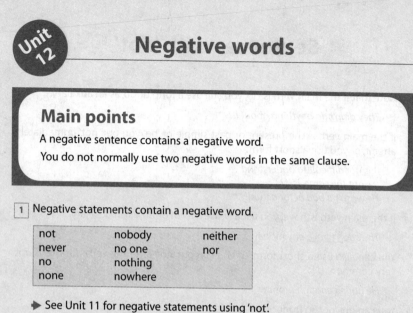

Unit 12

Negative words

Main points

A negative sentence contains a negative word.
You do not normally use two negative words in the same clause.

---

1 Negative statements contain a negative word.

not	nobody	neither
never	no one	nor
no	nothing	
none	nowhere	

▶ See Unit 11 for negative statements using 'not'.

2 You use 'never' to say that something was not the case at any time, or will not be the case at any time.

If the verb group has more than one word, you put 'never' after the first word.

  I've never had such a horrible meal.
  He could never trust her again.

3 If the only verb in the sentence is the present simple or past simple of any main verb except 'be', you put 'never' before the verb.

  She never goes abroad.
  He never went to university.

If the only verb in the sentence is the simple present or simple past of the main verb 'be', you normally put 'never' after the verb.

  He's never late.
  There were never any people in the house.

You can also use 'never' at the beginning of an imperative sentence.

  Never walk alone late at night.

4 You use 'no' before a noun to say that something does not exist or is not available.

  He has given no reason for his decision.
  The island has no trees at all.

Note that if there is another negative word in the clause, you use 'any', not 'no'.

  It won't do any good.

Negative words

5 You use 'none' or 'none of' to say that there is not even one thing or person, or not even a small amount of something.

> *You can't go to a college here because there are <u>none</u> in this area.*
> *'Where's the coffee?' – 'There's <u>none</u> left.'*
> *<u>None of</u> us understood the play.*

➤ See Unit 27 for more information on 'none' and 'none of'.

6 You also use 'nobody', 'no one', 'nothing', and 'nowhere' in negative statements. You use 'nobody' or 'no one' to talk about people.

> *<u>Nobody</u> in her house knows any English.*
> *<u>No one</u> knew.*

'No one' can also be written 'no-one'.

> *There's <u>no-one</u> here.*

You use 'nothing' to talk about things.

> *There's <u>nothing</u> you can do.*

You use 'nowhere' to talk about places.

> *There's almost <u>nowhere</u> left to go.*

➤ See Unit 21 for more information about these words.

7 You do not normally use two negative words in the same clause. For example, you do not say 'Nobody could see nothing'. You say 'Nobody could see anything'.

You use 'anything', 'anyone', 'anybody', and 'anywhere' instead of 'nothing', 'no one', 'nobody', and 'nowhere' when the clause already contains a negative word.

> *<u>No-one</u> can find Howard or Barbara <u>anywhere.</u>*
> *I could <u>never</u> discuss <u>anything</u> with them.*

8 The only negative words that are often used together in the same clause are 'neither' and 'nor'.

You use 'neither' and 'nor' together to say that two alternatives are not possible, not likely, or not true.

> *<u>Neither</u> Margaret <u>nor</u> John was there.*
> *They had <u>neither</u> food <u>nor</u> money.*

Count nouns

Main points

Count nouns have two forms, singular and plural.

They can be used with numbers.

Singular count nouns always take a determiner.

Plural count nouns do not need a determiner.

Singular count nouns take a singular verb and plural count nouns take a plural verb.

In English, some things are thought of as individual items that can be counted directly. The nouns which refer to these countable things are called count nouns. Most nouns in English are count nouns.

➤ See Unit 15 for information on uncount nouns.

1 Count nouns have two forms. The singular form refers to one thing or person.

> …a _book_ … …the _teacher._

The plural form refers to more than one thing or person.

> … _books_ … …some _teachers._

2 You add '-s' to form the plural of most nouns.

book	→	books	school	→	schools

You add '-es' to nouns ending in '-ss', '-ch', '-s', '-sh', or '-x'.

class	→	classes	watch	→	watches
gas	→	gases	dish	→	dishes
fox	→	foxes			

Some nouns ending in '-o' add '-s', and some add '-es'.

photo	→	photos	piano	→	pianos
hero	→	heroes	potato	→	potatoes

Nouns ending in a consonant and '-y' change to '-ies'.

country	→	countries	lady	→	ladies
party	→	parties	victory	→	victories

Count nouns

Nouns ending in a vowel and '-y' add an '-s'.

boy	→ boys	day	→ days
key	→ keys	valley	→ valleys

Some common nouns have irregular plurals.

child	→ children	foot	→ feet
man	→ men	mouse	→ mice
tooth	→ teeth	woman	→ women

⊖ WARNING: Some nouns that end in '-s' are uncount nouns, for example 'athletics' and 'physics'. ➤ See Unit 15.

3 Count nouns can be used with numbers.

… _one_ table…   … _two_ cats…   … _three hundred_ pounds.

4 Singular count nouns cannot be used alone, but always take a determiner such as 'a', 'another', 'every', or 'the'.

We've killed _a_ pig.
He was eating _another_ apple.
I parked _the_ car over there.

5 Plural count nouns can be used with or without a determiner. They do not take a determiner when they refer to things or people in general.

Does the hotel have _large rooms?_
The film is not suitable for _children._

Plural count nouns do take a determiner when they refer precisely to particular things or people.

Our computers are very expensive.
These cakes are delicious.

➤ See Unit 23 for more information on determiners.

6 When a count noun is the subject of a verb, a singular count noun takes a singular verb.

My _son likes_ playing football.
The _address_ on the letter _was_ wrong.

A plural count noun takes a plural verb.

Bigger _cars cost_ more.
I thought more _people were_ coming.

➤ See also Unit 14 on collective nouns.

Singular and plural

Main points

Singular nouns are used only in the singular, always with a determiner.

Plural nouns are used only in the plural, some with a determiner.

Collective nouns can be used with singular or plural verbs.

1 Some nouns are used in particular meanings in the singular with a determiner, like count nouns, but are not used in the plural with that meaning. They are often called 'singular nouns'.

Some of these nouns are normally used with 'the' because they refer to things that are unique.

air	country	countryside	dark	daytime	end	future	ground
moon	past	sea		seaside	sky	sun	wind	world

The sun was shining.
I am scared of *the dark.*

Other singular nouns are normally used with 'a' because they refer to things that we usually talk about one at a time.

bath	chance	drink	fight	go	jog	move	rest
ride	run	shower	smoke	snooze	start	walk	wash

I went upstairs and had *a wash.*
Why don't we go outside for *a smoke?*

2 Some nouns are used in particular meanings in the plural with or without determiners, like count nouns, but are not used in the singular with that meaning. They are often called 'plural nouns'.

His *clothes* looked terribly dirty.
Troops are being sent in today.

Some of these nouns are always used with determiners.

activities	authorities	feelings	likes	pictures	sights	travels

I went to *the pictures* with Tina.
You hurt *his feelings.*

Singular and plural

Some are usually used without determiners.

airs	expenses	goods	refreshments	riches

> *Refreshments are available inside.*
> *They have agreed to pay for travel and expenses.*

⊖ WARNING: 'Police' is a plural noun, but does not end in '-s'.

> *The police were informed immediately.*

3 A small group of plural nouns refer to single items that have two linked parts. They refer to tools that people use or things that people wear.

binoculars	pincers	pliers	scales	scissors	shears	tweezers
glasses	jeans	knickers	pants	pyjamas	shorts	tights
trousers						

> *She was wearing brown trousers.*   *These scissors are sharp.*

You can use 'a pair of' to make it clear you are talking about one item, or a number with 'pairs of' when you are talking about several items.

> *I was sent out to buy a pair of scissors.*
> *Liza had given me three pairs of jeans.*

Note that you also use 'a pair of' with words such as 'gloves', 'shoes', and 'socks' that you often talk about in twos.

4 With some nouns that refer to a group of people or things, the same form can be used with singular or plural verbs, because you can think of the group as a unit or as individuals. Similarly, you can use singular or plural pronouns to refer back to them. These nouns are often called 'collective nouns'.

army	audience	committee	company	crew	data	enemy
family	flock	gang	government	group	herd	media
navy	press	public	staff	team		

> *Our little group is complete again.*   *Our family isn't poor any more.*
> *The largest group are the boys.*   *My family are perfectly normal.*

The names of many organizations and sports teams are also collective nouns, but are normally used with plural verbs in spoken English.

> *The BBC is showing the programme on Saturday.*
> *The BBC are planning to use the new satellite.*
> *Liverpool is leading 1-0.*
> *Liverpool are attacking again.*

Uncount nouns

Main points

Uncount nouns have only one form, and take a singular verb.

They are not used with 'a', or with numbers.

Some nouns can be both uncount nouns and count nouns.

---

1 English speakers think that some things cannot be counted directly. The nouns which refer to these uncountable things are called uncount nouns. Uncount nouns often refer to:

substances:	coal food ice iron rice steel water
human qualities:	courage cruelty honesty patience
feelings:	anger happiness joy pride relief respect
activities:	aid help sleep travel work
abstract ideas:	beauty death freedom fun life luck

> The donkey needed <u>food</u> and <u>water.</u>
> Soon, they lost <u>patience</u> and sent me to Durban.
> I was greeted with shouts of <u>joy.</u>
> All prices include <u>travel</u> to and from London.
> We talked for hours about <u>freedom.</u>

➤ See Unit 13 for information on count nouns.

2 Uncount nouns have only one form. They do not have a plural form.

> I needed <u>help</u> with my homework.
> The children had great <u>fun</u> playing with the puppets.

⊖ WARNING: Some nouns which are uncount nouns in English have plurals in other languages.

advice	baggage	equipment	furniture	homework
information	knowledge	luggage	machinery	money
news	traffic			

> We want to spend more <u>money</u> on roads.
> Soldiers carried so much <u>equipment</u> that they were barely able to move.

Uncount nouns

3 Some uncount nouns end in '-s' and therefore look like plural count nouns. They usually refer to:

subjects of study:	mathematics physics
activities:	athletics gymnastics
games:	cards darts
illnesses:	measles mumps

Mathematics is too difficult for me.
Measles is in most cases a harmless illness.

4 When an uncount noun is the subject of a verb, it takes a singular verb.

Electricity is dangerous.
Food was very expensive in those days.

5 Uncount nouns are not used with 'a'.

They resent having to pay money to people like me.
My father started work when he was ten.

Uncount nouns are used with 'the' when they refer to something that is specified or known.

I am interested in the education of young children.
She buried the money that Hilary had given her.

6 Uncount nouns are not used with numbers. However, you can often refer to a quantity of something which is expressed by an uncount noun, by using a word like 'some'. ➤ See Unit 23.

Please buy some bread when you go to town.
Let me give you some advice.

Some uncount nouns that refer to food or drink can be count nouns when they refer to quantities of the food or drink.

Do you like coffee? (uncount)   *We asked for two coffees.* (count)

Uncount nouns are often used with expressions such as 'a loaf of', 'packets of', or 'a piece of', to talk about a quantity or an item. 'A bit of' is common in spoken English.

I bought two loaves of bread yesterday.
He gave me a very good piece of advice.
They own a bit of land near Cambridge.

7 Some nouns are uncount nouns when they refer to something in general and count nouns when they refer to a particular instance of something.

Victory was now assured. (uncount)
In 1960, the party won a convincing victory. (count)

Personal pronouns

Unit 16

Main points

You use personal pronouns to refer back to something or someone that has already been mentioned.

You also use personal pronouns to refer to people and things directly.

There are two sets of personal pronouns: subject pronouns and object pronouns.

You can use 'you' and 'they' to refer to people in general.

1 When something or someone has already been mentioned, you refer to them again by using a pronoun.

> *John took <u>the book</u> and opened <u>it.</u>*
> *He rang <u>Mary</u> and invited <u>her</u> to dinner.*
> *'Have you been to <u>London</u> ?' – 'Yes, <u>it</u> was very crowded.'*
> *<u>My father</u> is fat – <u>he</u> weighs over fifteen stone.*

In English, 'he' and 'she' normally refer to people, occasionally to animals, but very rarely to things.

2 You use a pronoun to refer directly to people or things that are present or are involved in the situation you are in.

> *Where shall <u>we</u> meet, Sally?*
> *<u>I</u> do the washing; <u>he</u> does the cooking; <u>we</u> share the washing-up.*
> *Send <u>us</u> a card so <u>we</u>'ll know where <u>you</u> are.*

3 There are two sets of personal pronouns, subject pronouns and object pronouns. You use subject pronouns as the subject of a verb.

I	you	he	she	it	we	they

Note that 'you' is used for the singular and plural form.

> *<u>We</u> are going there later.*
> *<u>I</u> don't know what to do.*

4 You use object pronouns as the direct or indirect object of a verb.

me	you	him	her	it	us	them

Note that 'you' is used for the singular and plural form.

> *The nurse washed <u>me</u> with cold water.*
> *The ball hit <u>her</u> in the face.*
> *John showed <u>him</u> the book.*
> *Can you give <u>me</u> some more cake?*

Note that, in modern English, you use object pronouns rather than subject pronouns after the verb 'be'.

> *'Who is it?' – 'It<u>'s me.</u>'*
> *There <u>was</u> only John, Baz, and <u>me</u> in the room.*

You also use object pronouns as the object of a preposition.

> *We were all sitting in a cafe <u>with him.</u>*
> *Did you give it <u>to them?</u>*

5 You can use 'you' and 'they' to talk about people in general.

> *<u>You</u> have to drive on the other side of the road on the continent.*
> *<u>They</u> say she's very clever.*

6 You can use 'it' as an impersonal subject in general statements which refer to the time, the date, or the weather.
➡ See Unit 17.

> *'What time is <u>it</u>?' '<u>It</u>'s half past three.'*
> *<u>It</u> is January 19th.*
> *<u>It</u> is rainy and cold.*

You can also use 'it' as the subject or object in general statements about a situation.

> *<u>It</u> is too far to walk.*
> *I like <u>it</u> here. Can we stay a bit longer?*

7 A singular pronoun usually refers back to a singular noun group, and a plural pronoun to a plural noun group. However, you can use plural pronouns to refer back to:

- indefinite pronouns, even though they are always followed by a singular verb

> *If <u>anybody comes,</u> tell <u>them</u> I'm not in.*

- collective nouns, even when you have used a singular verb

> *His <u>family was</u> waiting in the next room, but <u>they</u> had not yet been informed.*

Impersonal subject 'it'

Main points

You use impersonal 'it' as the subject of a sentence to introduce new information.

You use 'it' to talk about the time or the date.

You use 'it' to talk about the weather.

You use 'it' to express opinions about places, situations, and events.

'It' is often used with the passive of reporting verbs to express general beliefs and opinions.

---

1 'It' is a pronoun. As a personal pronoun it refers back to something that has already been mentioned.

> *They learn to speak <u>English</u> before they learn to read <u>it</u>.*
> *<u>Maybe he changed his mind,</u> but I doubt <u>it</u>.*

You can also use 'it' as the subject of a sentence when it does not refer back to anything that has already been mentioned. This impersonal use of 'it' introduces new information, and is used particularly to talk about times, dates, the weather, and personal opinions.

2 You use impersonal 'it' with a form of 'be' to talk about the time or the date.

> *<u>It is</u> nearly one o'clock.*
> *<u>It's</u> the sixth of April today.*

3 You use impersonal 'it' with verbs which refer to the weather:

drizzle	hail	pour	rain	sleet	snow	thunder

> *<u>It's</u> still <u>raining</u>.*
> *<u>It snowed</u> steadily through the night.*
> *<u>It was pouring</u> with rain.*

You can describe the weather by using 'it' followed by 'be' and an adjective with or without a noun.

> *It's a lovely day.*
> *It was very bright.*

Impersonal subject 'it'

You can describe a change in the weather by using 'it' followed by 'get' and an adjective.

> *It was getting cold.*
> *It's getting dark.*

4 You use impersonal 'it', followed by a form of 'be' and an adjective or noun group, to express your opinion about a place, a situation, or an event. The adjective or noun group can be followed by an adverbial or by an '-ing' clause, a 'to'-infinitive clause, or a 'that'-clause.

> *It was terribly <u>cold in the trucks.</u>*
> *<u>It's fun working</u> for him.*
> *<u>It was a pleasure to be</u> there.*
> *<u>It's strange that</u> it hasn't been noticed before.*

5 You use 'it' followed by a verb such as 'interest', 'please', 'surprise', or 'upset' which indicates someone's reaction to a fact, situation, or event. The verb is followed by a noun group, and a 'that'-clause or a 'to'-infinitive clause.

> *<u>It pleases me that</u> he should want to talk about his work.*
> *<u>It surprised him to realize</u> that he hadn't thought about them until now.*

6 You can also use 'it' with the passive of a reporting verb and a 'that'-clause when you want to suggest that an opinion or belief is shared by many people. This use is particularly common in news reports, for example in newspapers, on the radio, or on television.

> *<u>It was said that</u> he could speak their language.*
> *Nowadays <u>it is believed that</u> the size is unimportant.*
> *<u>It is thought that</u> about a million puppies are born each year.*

Note that the passive of reporting verbs can also be used without impersonal 'it' to express general opinions.

> *<u>The factories were said to be</u> much worse.*
> *<u>They are believed to be</u> dangerous.*

➤ See Units 76 and 77 for more information on reporting verbs.

Impersonal subject 'there'

Main points

You use 'there' followed by a form of 'be' and a noun group to introduce new information.

You use 'there' with a singular or plural verb, depending on whether the following noun is singular or plural.

You can also use 'there' with modals.

---

1 'There' is often an adverb of place.

> *Are you comfortable <u>there?</u>*
> *The book is <u>there</u> on the table.*

You can also use 'there' as the impersonal subject of a sentence when it does not refer to a place. In this case you use 'there' to introduce new information and to focus upon it. After 'there' you use a form of 'be' and a noun group.

> <u>*There is work*</u> *to be done.*
> <u>*There will be a party*</u> *tonight.*
> <u>*There was no damage.*</u>
> <u>*There have been two telephone calls.*</u>

Note that the impersonal subject 'there' is often pronounced without stress, whereas the adverb is almost always stressed.

2 You use 'there' as the impersonal subject to talk about:

- the existence or presence of someone or something

> *There are two people who might know what happened.*
> *There are many possibilities.*
> *There is plenty of bread.*

- something that happens

> *There was a general election that year.*
> *There's a meeting every week.*
> *There was a fierce battle.*

- a number or amount

> *There are forty of us, I think.*
> *There is a great deal of anger about his decision.*
> *There were a lot of people camped there.*

Impersonal subject 'there'

3 When the noun group after the verb is plural, you use a plural verb.

> *There are many reasons* for this.
> *There were two men* in the room.

You also use a plural verb before phrases such as 'a number (of)', 'a lot (of)', and 'a few (of)'.

> *There were a lot of* people camped there.
> *There are* only *a few* left.

4 When the noun group after the verb is singular or uncountable, you use a singular verb.

> *There is one point* we must add here.
> *There isn't enough room* in here.

You also use a singular verb when you are mentioning more than one person or thing and the first noun after the verb is singular or uncountable.

> *There was a man* and a woman.
> *There was a sofa* and two chairs.

5 You can also use 'there' with a modal, followed by 'be' or 'have been'.

> *There could be* a problem.
> *There should be* a change in government.
> *There can't have been* anybody outside.
> *There must have been* some mistake.

6 In spoken and informal written English, short forms of 'be' or a modal are normally used after 'there'.

> *There's* no danger.
> *There'll* always *be* a future for music.
> I knew *there'd be* trouble.
> *There's been* quite a lot of research into it.
> I didn't even know *there'd been* a murder.

7 You can also use 'there' with 'appear' or 'seem', followed by 'to be' or 'to have been'.

> *There appears to be* a vast amount of confusion on this point.
> *There don't seem to be* many people on campus.
> *There seems to have been* some carelessness.

Demonstrative pronouns

Main points

You use the demonstrative pronouns 'this', 'that', 'these', and 'those' when you are pointing to physical objects or identifying people.

You use 'one' or 'ones' instead of a noun that has been mentioned or is known.

1 You use the demonstrative pronouns 'this', 'that', 'these', and 'those' when you are pointing to physical objects. 'This' and 'these' refer to things near you, 'that' and 'those' refer to things farther away.

> _This_ is a list of rules.
> 'I brought you _these_.' Adam held out a bag of grapes.
> _That_ looks interesting.
> _Those_ are mine.

You can also use 'this', 'that', 'these', and 'those' as determiners in front of nouns.
➤ See Unit 23.

> _This book_ was a present from my mother.
> When did you buy _that hat_?

2 You use 'this', 'that', 'these', and 'those' when you are identifying or introducing people, or asking who they are.

> Who's _this_?
> _These_ are my children, Susan and Paul.
> Was _that_ Patrick on the phone?

3 You use 'this', 'that', 'these', and 'those' to refer back to things that have already been mentioned.

> _That_ was an interesting word you used just now.
> More money is being pumped into the education system, and we assume _this_ will continue.
> 'Let's go to the cinema.' – '_That's_ a good idea.'
> _These_ are not easy questions to answer.

You also use 'this' and 'these' to refer forward to things you are going to mention.

> _This_ is what I want to say: it wasn't my idea.
> _These_ are the topics we will be looking at next week: how the accident happened, whether it could have been avoided, and who was to blame.
> _This_ is the important point: you must never see her again.

Demonstrative pronouns

4 You use 'one' or 'ones' instead of a noun that has already been mentioned or is known in the situation, usually when you are adding information or contrasting two things of the same kind.

> *My car is the blue one.*
> *Don't you have one with buttons instead of a zip?*
> *Are the new curtains longer than the old ones?*

You can use 'which one' or 'which ones' in questions.

> *Which one do you prefer?*
> *Which ones were damaged?*

You can say 'this one', 'that one', 'these ones', and 'those ones'.

> *I like this one better.*
> *We'll have those ones, thank you.*

You can use 'each one' or 'one each', but note that there is a difference in meaning. In the following examples, 'each one' means 'each brother' but 'one each' means 'one for each child'.

> *I've got three brothers and each one lives in a different country.*
> *I bought the children one each.*

5 In formal English, people sometimes use 'one' to refer to people in general.

> *One has to think of the practical side of things.*
> *One never knows what to say in such situations.*

6 There are several other types of pronoun, which are dealt with in other units.

▶ See Unit 22 for information on possessive pronouns.

▶ See Unit 6 for information on 'who', 'whom', 'whose', 'which', and 'what' as interrogative pronouns.

▶ See Units 92 and 93 for information on 'that', 'which', 'who', 'whom', and 'whose' as relative pronouns.

Most determiners, except 'the', 'a', 'an', 'every', 'no', and the possessives, are also pronouns.

▶ See Units 27 to 30.

Reflexive pronouns

Main points

Reflexive pronouns can be direct or indirect objects.

Most transitive verbs can take a reflexive pronoun as object.

Reflexive pronouns can be the object of a preposition.

Reflexive pronouns can emphasize a noun or pronoun.

---

1 The reflexive pronouns are:

singular:	myself yourself himself herself itself
plural:	ourselves yourselves themselves

Note that, unlike 'you' and 'your', there are two forms for the second person: 'yourself' in the singular and 'yourselves' in the plural.

2 You use reflexive pronouns as the direct or indirect object of the verb when you want to say that the object is the same person or thing as the subject of the verb in the same clause.

For example, 'John taught himself' means that John did the teaching and was also the person who was taught, and 'Ann poured herself a drink' means that Ann did the pouring and was also the person that the drink was poured for.

> _She_ stretched _herself_ out on the sofa.
> _The men_ formed _themselves_ into a line.
> _He_ should give _himself_ more time.

Note that although the subject 'you' is omitted in imperatives, you can still use 'yourself' or 'yourselves'.

> _Here's the money, go and buy yourself an ice cream._

3 Most transitive verbs can take a reflexive pronoun.

> I _blame myself_ for not paying attention.
> He _introduced himself_ to me.

⊖ WARNING: Verbs which describe actions that people normally do to themselves do not take reflexive pronouns in English, although they do in some other languages.

> I usually _shave_ before breakfast.
> She _washed_ very quickly and rushed downstairs.

➤ See Unit 53 for more information.

Reflexive pronouns

4 You use a reflexive pronoun as the object of a preposition when the object of the preposition refers to the same person or thing as the subject of the verb in the same clause.

> *I was thoroughly ashamed of myself.*
> *They are making fools of themselves.*
> *Tell me about yourself.*

Note that you use personal pronouns, not reflexive pronouns, when referring to places and after 'with' meaning 'accompanied by'.

> *You should have your notes in front of you.*
> *He would have to bring Judy with him.*

5 You use reflexive pronouns after nouns or pronouns to emphasize the person or thing that you are referring to.

> *The town itself was so small that it didn't have a bank.*
> *I myself have never read the book.*

6 You use a reflexive pronoun at the end of a clause to emphasize that someone did something without any help from anyone else.

> *She had printed the card herself.*
> *I'll take it down to the police station myself.*
> *Did you make these yourself?*

7 You use reflexive pronouns with 'by' to say:

● that someone does something without any help from other people

> *…when babies start eating their meals by themselves.*
> *She was certain she could manage by herself.*

● that someone is alone

> *He went off to sit by himself.*
> *I was there for about six months by myself.*

You can also use 'on my own', 'on your own', and so on, to say that someone is alone or does something without any help.

> *We were in the park on our own.*
> *They managed to reach the village on their own.*

You can use 'all' for emphasis.

> *Did you put those shelves up all by yourself?*
> *We can't solve this problem all on our own.*

⊖ WARNING:'One another' and 'each other' are not reflexive pronouns.

➤ See Unit 54 for more information on 'one another' and 'each other'.

Indefinite pronouns

Main points

Indefinite pronouns refer to people or things without saying exactly who or what they are.

When an indefinite pronoun is the subject, it always takes a singular verb.

You often use a plural pronoun to refer back to an indefinite pronoun.

---

1 The indefinite pronouns are:

anybody	everybody	nobody	somebody
anyone	everyone	no one	someone
anything	everything	nothing	something

Note that 'no one' is written as two words, or sometimes with a hyphen: 'no-one'.

2 You use indefinite pronouns when you want to refer to people or things without saying exactly who or what they are. The pronouns ending in '-body' and '-one' refer to people, and those ending in '-thing' refer to things.

I was there for over an hour before <u>anybody</u> came.
It had to be <u>someone</u> with a car.
Jane said <u>nothing</u> for a moment.

3 When an indefinite pronoun is the subject, it always takes a singular verb, even when it refers to more than one person or thing.

<u>*Everyone knows*</u> *that.*
<u>*Everything was*</u> *fine.*
<u>*Is anybody*</u> *there?*

When you refer back to indefinite pronouns, you use plural pronouns or possessives, and a plural verb.

Ask <u>anyone</u>. <u>They</u>'ll tell you.
Has <u>everyone</u> eaten as much as <u>they</u> want?
You can't tell <u>somebody</u> why <u>they</u>'ve failed.

⊖ WARNING: Some speakers prefer to use singular pronouns. They prefer to say 'You can't tell somebody why he or she has failed'.

Indefinite pronouns

4 You can add apostrophe s ('s) to indefinite pronouns that refer to people.

> *She was given a room in <u>someone's</u> studio.*
> *That was <u>nobody's</u> business but mine.*

⊖ WARNING: You do not usually add apostrophe s ('s) to indefinite pronouns that refer to things. You do not say 'something's value', you say 'the value of something'.

5 You use indefinite pronouns beginning with 'some-' in:

- affirmative clauses

> *<u>Somebody</u> shouted.*
> *I want to introduce you to <u>someone.</u>*

- questions expecting the answer 'yes'

> *Would you like <u>something</u> to drink?*
> *Can you get <u>someone</u> to do it?*

6 You use indefinite pronouns beginning with 'any-':

- as the subject or object in statements

> *<u>Anyone</u> knows that you need a licence.*
> *You still haven't told me <u>anything.</u>*

You do not use them as the subject of a negative statement. You do not say 'Anybody can't come in'.

- in both affirmative and negative questions

> *Does <u>anybody</u> agree with me?*
> *Won't <u>anyone</u> help me?*

7 If you use an indefinite pronoun beginning with 'no-', you must not use another negative word in the same clause. You do not say 'There wasn't nothing'.

> *There was <u>nothing</u> you could do.*
> *<u>Nobody</u> left, <u>nobody</u> went away.*

8 You use the indefinite adverbs 'anywhere', 'everywhere', 'nowhere', and 'somewhere' to talk about places in a general way. 'Nowhere' makes a clause negative.

> *I thought I'd seen you <u>somewhere.</u>*
> *No-one can find Howard or Barbara <u>anywhere.</u>*
> *There was <u>nowhere</u> to hide.*

9 You can use 'else' after indefinite pronouns and adverbs to refer to people, things, or places other than those that have been mentioned.

> *<u>Everyone else</u> is downstairs.*
> *I don't like it here. Let's go <u>somewhere else.</u>*

Possession

Main points

Possessives and possessive pronouns are used to say that one person or thing belongs to another or is connected with another.

You use apostrophe s ('s) to say who something belongs to.

You use phrases with 'of' to say that one person or thing belongs to another or is connected with another.

---

1 You use possessives to say that a person or thing belongs to another person or thing or is connected with them. The possessives are sometimes called 'possessive adjectives'.

my	your	his	her	its	our	their

Note that 'your' is both singular and plural.

> *I'd been waiting a long time to park <u>my car.</u>*
> *They took off <u>their shoes.</u>*

⊖ WARNING: The possessive 'its' is not spelled with an apostrophe. The form 'it's' with an apostrophe is the short form for 'it is' or 'it has'.

2 You put numbers and adjectives after the possessive and in front of the noun.

> *<u>Their two small children</u> were playing outside.*
> *She got a bicycle on <u>her sixth birthday.</u>*

3 You use a possessive pronoun when you want to refer to a person or thing and to say who that person or thing belongs to or is connected with. The possessive pronouns are:

mine	yours	his	hers	ours	theirs

Note that 'yours' is both singular and plural.

> *Is that coffee <u>yours</u> or <u>mine ?</u>*
> *It was his fault, not <u>theirs.</u>*

⊖ WARNING: There is no possessive pronoun 'its'.

4 You can also say who or what something belongs to or is connected with by using a noun with apostrophe s ('s). For example, if John owns a motorbike, you can refer to it as 'John's motorbike'.

Possession

Sylvia put her hand on <u>John's</u> arm.
I like the <u>car's</u> design.

You add apostrophe s ('s) to singular nouns and irregular plural nouns, usually referring to people rather than things.

I wore a pair of my <u>sister's</u> boots.
<u>Children's</u> birthday parties can be boring.

With plural nouns ending in '-s' you only add the apostrophe (').

It is not his <u>parents'</u> problem.

You add apostrophe s ('s) to people's names, even when they end in '-s'.

Could you give me <u>Charles's</u> address?

Note that when you use two or more names linked by 'and', you put the apostrophe s ('s) after the last name.

They have bought <u>Sue and Tim's</u> car.

5 When you want to refer to someone's home, or to some common shops and places of work, you can use apostrophe s ('s) after a name or noun on its own.

He's round at <u>David's.</u>
He bought it at the <u>chemist's.</u>
She must go to the <u>doctor's.</u>

6 You can also use apostrophe s ('s) with some expressions of time to identify something, or to say how much time is involved.

Did you see the cartoon in <u>yesterday's</u> newspaper?
They have four <u>weeks'</u> holiday per year.

7 You can use a prepositional phrase beginning with 'of' to say that one person or thing belongs to or is connected with another.

She is the mother <u>of the boy</u> who lives next door.
Ellen aimlessly turned the pages <u>of her magazine.</u>

After 'of' you can use a possessive pronoun, or a noun or name with apostrophe s ('s).

He was an old friend <u>of mine.</u>
That word was a favourite <u>of your father's.</u>
She's a friend <u>of Stephen's.</u>

8 You can add 'own' after a possessive, or a noun or name with apostrophe s ('s), for emphasis.

<u>My own</u> view is that there are no serious problems.
The <u>professor's own</u> answer may be unacceptable.

Determiners

Main points

Determiners are used at the beginning of noun groups.

You use specific determiners when people know exactly which things or people you are talking about.

You use general determiners to talk about people or things without saying exactly who or what they are.

---

1 When you use a determiner, you put it at the beginning of a noun group, in front of numbers or adjectives.

> *I met the two Swedish girls in London.*
> *Our main bedroom is through there.*
> *Have you got another red card?*
> *Several young boys were waiting.*

2 When the people or things that you are talking about have already been mentioned, or the people you are talking to know exactly which ones you mean, you use a specific determiner.

> *The man began to run towards the boy.*
> *Young people don't like these operas.*
> *Her face was very red.*

The specific determiners are:

the definite article:	the
demonstratives:	this that these those
possessives:	my your his her its our their

Note that 'your' is used both for the singular and plural possessive.

➤ See Unit 19 for 'this', 'that', 'these', and 'those' as pronouns.

3 When you are mentioning people or things for the first time, or talking about them generally without saying exactly which ones you mean, you use a general determiner.

> *There was a man in the lift.*
> *We went to an art exhibition.*
> *You can stop at any time you like.*
> *There were several reasons for this.*

Determiners

The general determiners are:

a	all	an	another	any	both	each
either	enough	every	few	fewer	less	little
many	more	most	much	neither	no	other
several	some					

4 Each general determiner is used with particular types of noun, such as:

- singular count nouns

a	an	another	any	each	either	every	neither	no

I got a postcard from Susan.   *He opened another shop.*
Any big tin container will do.

- plural count nouns

all	any	both	enough	few	fewer	many
more	most	no	other	several	some	

There were few doctors available.   *Several projects were postponed.*
He spoke many different languages.

- uncount nouns

all	any	enough	less	little	more	most
much	no	some				

There was little applause.   *He did not speak much English.*
We need more information

⊖ WARNING: The following general determiners can never be used with uncount nouns.

a	an	another	both	each	either	every
few	many	neither	several			

5 Most of the determiners are also pronouns, except 'the', 'a', 'an', 'every', 'no' and the possessives.

I saw several in the woods last night.   *There is enough for all of us.*
Have you got any that I could borrow?

You use 'one' as a pronoun instead of 'a' or 'an', 'none' instead of 'no', and 'each' instead of 'every'.

Have you got one?   *There are none left.*
Each has a separate box and number.

Main uses of 'the'

Main points

You can use 'the' in front of any noun.

You use 'the' when the person you are talking to knows which person or thing you mean.

You use 'the' when you are referring back to someone or something.

You use 'the' when you are specifying which person or thing you are talking about.

You use 'the' when you are referring to something that is unique.

You use 'the' when you want to use one thing as an example to say something about all things of the same type.

1 'The' is called the definite article, and is the commonest determiner. You use 'the' when the person you are talking to knows which person or thing you mean. You can use 'the' in front of any noun, whether it is a singular count noun, an uncount noun, or a plural count noun.

> *She dropped _the can._*
> *I remembered _the fun_ I had with them.*
> *_The girls_ were not at home.*

2 You use 'the' with a noun when you are referring back to someone or something that has already been mentioned.

> *I called for _a waiter_ ... ... _The waiter_ with a moustache came.*
> *I have bought _a house_ in Wales... ... _The house_ is in an agricultural area.*

3 You use 'the' with a noun and a qualifier, such as a prepositional phrase or a relative clause, when you are specifying which person or thing you are talking about.

> *I've no idea about _the geography of Scotland._*
> *_The book that I recommended_ now costs over three pounds.*

4 You use 'the' with a noun when you are referring to something of which there is only one in the world.

> *They all sat in _the sun._*
> *We have landed men on _the moon._*
> *_The sky_ was a brilliant blue.*

Main uses of 'the'

You also use 'the' when you are referring to something of which there is only one in a particular place.

> *Mrs Robertson heard that <u>the church</u> had been bombed.*
> *He decided to put some words on <u>the blackboard.</u>*

5 You can use 'the' with a singular count noun when you want to make a general statement about all things of that type. For example, if you say 'The whale is the largest mammal in the world', you mean all whales, not one particular whale.

> <u>The computer</u> *allows us to deal with a lot of data very quickly.*
> *My father's favourite flower is <u>the rose.</u>*

6 You can use 'the' with a singular count noun when you are referring to a system or service. For example, you can use 'the phone' to refer to a telephone system and 'the bus' to refer to a bus service.

> *I don't like using <u>the phone.</u>*
> *How long does it take on <u>the train?</u>*

7 You can use 'the' with the name of a musical instrument when you are talking about someone's ability to play the instrument.

> *'You play <u>the guitar,</u> I see,' said Simon.*
> *Geoff plays <u>the piano</u> very well.*

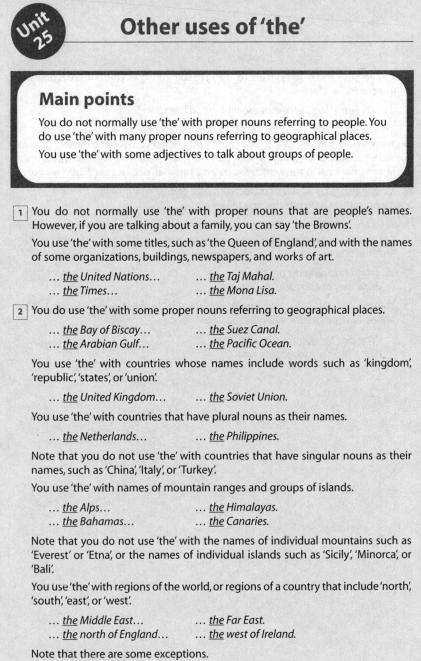

Other uses of 'the'

Main points

You do not normally use 'the' with proper nouns referring to people. You do use 'the' with many proper nouns referring to geographical places.

You use 'the' with some adjectives to talk about groups of people.

1 You do not normally use 'the' with proper nouns that are people's names. However, if you are talking about a family, you can say 'the Browns'.

You use 'the' with some titles, such as 'the Queen of England', and with the names of some organizations, buildings, newspapers, and works of art.

> ... _the_ United Nations...   ... _the_ Taj Mahal.
> ... _the_ Times...   ... _the_ Mona Lisa.

2 You do use 'the' with some proper nouns referring to geographical places.

> ... _the_ Bay of Biscay...   ... _the_ Suez Canal.
> ... _the_ Arabian Gulf...   ... _the_ Pacific Ocean.

You use 'the' with countries whose names include words such as 'kingdom', 'republic', 'states', or 'union'.

> ... _the_ United Kingdom...   ... _the_ Soviet Union.

You use 'the' with countries that have plural nouns as their names.

> ... _the_ Netherlands...   ... _the_ Philippines.

Note that you do not use 'the' with countries that have singular nouns as their names, such as 'China', 'Italy', or 'Turkey'.

You use 'the' with names of mountain ranges and groups of islands.

> ... _the_ Alps...   ... _the_ Himalayas.
> ... _the_ Bahamas...   ... _the_ Canaries.

Note that you do not use 'the' with the names of individual mountains such as 'Everest' or 'Etna', or the names of individual islands such as 'Sicily', 'Minorca', or 'Bali'.

You use 'the' with regions of the world, or regions of a country that include 'north', 'south', 'east', or 'west'.

> ... _the_ Middle East...   ... _the_ Far East.
> ... _the_ north of England...   ... _the_ west of Ireland.

Note that there are some exceptions.

> ...North America...   ...South-East Asia.

Other uses of 'the'

You do not use 'the' with 'northern', 'southern', 'eastern', or 'western' and a singular name.

… <u>northern</u> England…   *… <u>western Africa.</u>*

You use 'the' with the names of areas of water such as seas, oceans, rivers, canals, gulfs, and straits.

… <u>the</u> Mediterranean Sea…   *… <u>the</u> Atlantic Ocean.*
… <u>the</u> river Ganges…   *… <u>the</u> Panama Canal.*
… <u>the</u> Gulf of Mexico…   *… <u>the</u> straits of Gibraltar.*

Note that you do not use 'the' with lakes.

…Lake Geneva…   *…Lake Superior.*

Note that you do not use 'the' with continents, cities, streets, or addresses.

…Asia…   *…Tokyo.*
…Oxford Street…   *…15 Park Street.*

3 You use 'the' with adjectives such as 'rich', 'poor', 'young', 'old', and 'unemployed' to talk about a general group of people. You do not need a noun.

Only <u>the rich</u> could afford his firm's products.
They were discussing the problem of <u>the unemployed.</u>

When you use 'the' with an adjective as the subject of a verb, you use a plural verb.

In the cities <u>the poor are</u> as badly off as they were in the villages.

4 You use 'the' with some nationality adjectives to talk about the people who live in a country.

They will be increasingly dependent on the support of <u>the French.</u>
<u>The Spanish</u> claimed that the money had not been paid.

With other nationalities, you use a plural noun.

…Germans…   *…the Americans.*

When you use 'the' with a nationality adjective as the subject of a verb, you use a plural verb.

<u>The British are</u> worried.

5 You use 'the' with superlatives.

He was <u>the cleverest</u> man I ever knew.
He was <u>the youngest.</u>
His shoulders hurt <u>the worst.</u>
It was <u>the most exciting</u> summer of their lives.

'A' and 'an'

Main points

You only use 'a' or 'an' with singular count nouns.
You use 'a' or 'an' to talk about a person or thing for the first time.

1 You only use 'a' or 'an' with singular count nouns. 'A' and 'an' are called the indefinite article.

> I got *a postcard* from Susan.
> He was eating *an apple.*

Remember that you use 'a' in front of a word that begins with a consonant sound even if the first letter is a vowel, for example 'a piece, a university, a European language'. You use 'an' in front of a word that begins with a vowel sound even if the first letter is a consonant, for example 'an exercise, an idea, an honest man'.

2 You use 'a' or 'an' when you are talking about a person or thing for the first time.

> She picked up *a book.*
> After weeks of looking, we eventually bought *a house.*
> *A colleague* and I got some money to do research on rats.

Note that the second time you refer to the same person or thing, you use 'the'.

> She picked up *a book* ... ... *The book* was lying on the table.
> After weeks of looking, we bought *a house* ... ... *The house* was in a village.

3 After the verb 'be' or another link verb, you can use 'a' or 'an' with an adjective and a noun to give more information about someone or something.

> His brother was *a sensitive child.*
> He seemed *a worried man.*
> It was *a really beautiful house.*

You can also use 'a' or 'an' with a noun followed by a qualifier, such as a prepositional phrase or a relative clause, when you want to give more information about someone or something.

> The information was contained in *an article on biology.*
> I chose *a picture that reminded me of my own country.*

'A' and 'an'

4 You use 'a' or 'an' after the verb 'be' or another link verb when you are saying what someone is or what job they have.

> *He became <u>a school teacher.</u>*
> *She is <u>a model</u> and <u>an artist.</u>*

5 You use 'a' or 'an' to mean 'one' with some numbers. You can use 'a' or 'an' with nouns that refer to whole numbers, fractions, money, weights, or measures.

a hundred	a quarter	a pound	a kilo
a thousand	a half	a dollar	a litre

6 You do not use 'a' or 'an' with uncount nouns or plural count nouns. You do not need to use a determiner at all with plural count nouns, but you can use the determiners 'any', 'a few', 'many', 'several', or 'some'.

> *I love <u>dogs.</u>*
> *Do you have <u>any dogs?</u>*
> *Many adults don't listen to <u>children.</u>*
> *I have <u>some children</u> like that in my class.*

Note that if you do not use a determiner with a plural count noun, you are often making a general statement about people or things of that type. For example, if you say 'I love dogs', you mean all dogs. However, if you say 'There are eggs in the kitchen', you mean there are some eggs. If you do use a determiner, you mean a number of people or things but not all of them, without saying exactly how many.

> *I have <u>some friends</u> coming for dinner.*
> *He has bought <u>some plants</u> for the house.*
> *I have <u>some important things</u> to tell them.*

All, most, no, one

Main points

You use 'all' with plural count nouns and uncount nouns. You use 'all' to talk about every person or thing in the world, or in the group you are talking about.

You use 'most' with plural count nouns and uncount nouns. You use 'most' to talk about nearly all of a number of people or things, or nearly all of a quantity of something.

You use 'no' with singular and plural count nouns and uncount nouns. You use 'no' to say that something does not exist or is not present.

1 You use 'all' with plural count nouns and uncount nouns to talk about every person or thing in the world or in the group that you are talking about.

> *All children should complete the primary course.*
> *All important decisions were taken by the government.*
> *He soon lost all hope of becoming a rock star.*
> *All luggage will be searched.*

2 You use 'most' with plural count nouns and uncount nouns to talk about nearly all of a number of people or things, or nearly all of a quantity of something.

> *The method was suitable for most purposes.*
> *Most good drivers stop at zebra crossings.*
> *Most milk is still delivered to people's houses.*
> *He ignored most advice, and did what he thought best.*

3 You use 'no' with singular count nouns, plural count nouns, and uncount nouns to say that something does not exist or is not present.

> *There was no chair for me to sit on.*
> *They had no immediate plans to change house.*
> *No money was available for the operation.*

Note that if there is another word in the clause that makes it negative, you use 'any', not 'no'.

> *It hasn't made any difference.*
> *He will never do any work for me again.*

4 'All' and 'most' are also pronouns, so you can say 'all of' and 'most of'. 'No' is not a pronoun, so you must say 'none of'.

> He spent <u>all of the money</u> on a new car.
> <u>Most of my friends</u> live in London.
> <u>None of those farmers</u> had ever driven a tractor.

Note that you use 'all of', 'most of', and 'none of' with an object pronoun.

> <u>All of us</u> were sleeping.
> I had seen <u>most of them</u> before.
> <u>None of them</u> came to the party.

Note that if the clause is already negative, you use 'any of', not 'none of'.

> I had<u>n't</u> eaten <u>any of</u> the biscuits.

When 'none of' is followed by a plural noun or pronoun, the verb is usually plural, but can be singular.

> <u>None of us are</u> the same.
> <u>None of them has</u> lasted very long.

5 You can use 'all the' with a plural count noun or an uncount noun. There is no difference in meaning between 'all the' and 'all of the'.

> <u>All the girls</u> think it's great.
> <u>All the best jokes</u> came at the end of the programme.
> Thank you for <u>all the help</u> you gave me.

⊖ WARNING: You cannot say 'most the' or 'none the'. You must say 'most of the' or 'none of the'.

6 You can use 'all' after a noun or pronoun to emphasize that the noun or pronoun refers to everyone or everything that has been mentioned or is involved.

Note that you can use 'all' to emphasize the subject or the object.

> <u>The band all</u> live together in the same house.
> I enjoyed <u>it all.</u>

Both, either, neither

Main points

You use 'both', 'either', and 'neither' to talk about two people or things that have been mentioned or are known to the hearer.

You use 'both' with plural nouns, and 'either' and 'neither' with singular nouns.

You use 'both of', 'either of', and 'neither of' with plural nouns or pronouns.

1 You use 'both', 'either', and 'neither' when you are saying something about two people or things that have been mentioned, or are known to the person you are talking to.

There were excellent performances from <u>both actresses.</u>
Denis held his cocoa in <u>both hands.</u>
No argument could move <u>either man</u> from this decision.
<u>Neither report</u> mentioned the Americans.

2 You use 'both' when you think of the two people or things as a group. You use 'both' with a plural noun.

<u>Both children</u> were happy with their presents.
<u>Both policies</u> make good sense.

3 You use 'either' when you think of the two people or things as individuals. You use 'either' with a singular noun.

<u>Either way</u> is acceptable.
She could not see <u>either man.</u>

4 You use 'neither' when you are thinking of the two people or things as individuals and you are making a negative statement about them. You use 'neither' with a singular noun.

In reality, <u>neither party</u> was enthusiastic.
<u>Neither man</u> knew what he was doing.

5 You can use 'both' with a specific determiner such as 'the', 'these', or 'my'.

<u>Both the young men</u> agreed to come.
<u>Both these books</u> have been recommended to us.
<u>Both her parents</u> were dead.

⊖ WARNING: You cannot use 'either' or 'neither' with a specific determiner.

Both, either, neither

6 You can use 'both of', 'either of', or 'neither of' with a plural noun or pronoun.

Note that when 'both of', 'either of', and 'neither of' are followed by a noun rather than a pronoun, you must use a specific determiner such as 'the', 'these', or 'her' before the noun.

> <u>Both of these restaurants</u> are excellent.
> <u>Either of them</u> could have done the job.
> <u>Neither of our boys</u> was involved.

Note that 'neither of' is normally used with a singular verb but it can be used with a plural verb.

> Neither of us <u>was having</u> any luck.
> Neither of the children <u>were</u> there.

7 Remember that you can also use 'both', 'either', and 'neither' as conjunctions. You use 'both...and' to give two alternatives and say that each of them is possible or true.

> I am looking for opportunities <u>both</u> in this country <u>and</u> abroad.
> <u>Both</u> I <u>and</u> my wife were surprised to see you there.

You use 'either...or' to give two alternatives and say that only one of them is possible or true.

> You can have <u>either</u> fruit <u>or</u> ice cream.
> I was expecting you <u>either</u> today <u>or</u> tomorrow.
> You <u>either</u> love him <u>or</u> hate him.

You also use 'neither...nor' to give two alternatives and say that each of them is not possible or is not true.

> <u>Neither</u> Margaret <u>nor</u> John was there.
> He did it <u>neither</u> quickly <u>nor</u> well.

Unit 29

Quantity 1

Main points

You use 'much' and 'little' with uncount nouns to talk about a quantity of something.

You use 'many' and 'few' with plural nouns to talk about a number of people or things.

You use 'much' in negative sentences and questions, and 'a lot of' or 'plenty of' rather than 'much' in affirmative sentences.

You use 'more' and 'less' with uncount nouns, and 'more' and 'fewer' with plural count nouns.

---

1 You use 'much' to talk about a large quantity of something, and 'little' to talk about a small quantity of something. You only use 'much' and 'little' with uncount nouns.

> I haven't got <u>much time.</u>
> We've made <u>little progress.</u>

2 You use 'many' to talk about a large number of people or things, and 'few' to talk about a small number of people or things. You can only use 'many' and 'few' with plural count nouns.

> He wrote <u>many novels.</u>
> There were <u>few visitors</u> to our house.

3 You normally use 'much' in negative sentences and questions.

> He did <u>not</u> speak <u>much</u> English.
> Why have<u>n't</u> I given <u>much</u> attention to this problem?

In affirmative sentences you do not use 'much', you use 'a lot of', 'lots of', or 'plenty of' instead. You can use them with both uncount nouns and plural nouns.

> He demanded <u>a lot of attention.</u>
> I make <u>a lot of mistakes.</u>
> They spent <u>lots of time</u> on the project.
> He remembered a large room with <u>lots of windows.</u>
> I've got <u>plenty of money.</u>
> There are always <u>plenty of jobs</u> to be done.

Note that you can use 'so much' and 'too much' in affirmative sentences.

> She spends <u>so much time</u> here.
> There is <u>too much chance</u> of error.

Quantity 1

4 You use 'so much' to emphasize that a large quantity of something is involved.

> *I have so much work to do.*
> *They have so much money and we have so little.*

You use 'too much' and 'too many' to say that the quantity of something, or the number of people or things, is larger than is reasonable or necessary.

> *He has too much work.*
> *Too many people still smoke.*

You use 'very many' to emphasize that a large number of people or things are involved.

> *Very many old people live alone.*

Note that 'very much' is used with nouns and verbs.

> *There isn't very much time.*
> *I liked it very much.*

5 You use 'few' and 'little' to emphasize that only a small quantity of something or a small number of people or things are involved. They can be used with 'very' for greater emphasis.

> *The town has few monuments.*
> *I have little time for anything but work.*
> *Very few cars had reversing lights.*
> *I had very little money left.*

Note that 'a few' and 'a little' just indicate that a quantity or number is small.

> *He spread a little honey on a slice of bread.*
> *I usually do a few jobs for him in the house.*

6 You use 'more' with uncount nouns and plural count nouns to refer to a quantity of something or a number of people or things that is greater than another quantity or number.

> *His visit might do more harm than good.*
> *He does more hours than I do.*

You use 'less' with uncount nouns to refer to an amount of something that is smaller than another amount.

> *The poor have less access to education.*
> *This machinery uses less energy.*

You use 'fewer', or 'less' in informal English, with plural nouns to refer to a number of people or things that is smaller than another number.

> *There are fewer trees here.*
> *They have sold less computers this year.*

59

Quantity 2

Main points

You use 'some' to talk about a quantity or number without being precise.

You use 'any' to talk about a quantity or number that may or may not exist.

You use 'another', or 'another' and a number, to talk about additional people or things.

You use 'each' and 'every' to talk about all the members of a group of people or things.

1 You use 'some' with uncount nouns and plural nouns to talk about a quantity of something or a number of people or things without being precise.

> I have left <u>some food</u> for you in the fridge.
> <u>Some trains</u> are running late.

You normally use 'some' in affirmative sentences.

> There's <u>some chocolate cake</u> over there.
> I had <u>some good ideas.</u>

You use 'some' in questions when you expect the answer to be 'yes', for example in offers or requests.

> Would you like <u>some coffee?</u>
> Could you give me <u>some examples?</u>

You can use 'some' with a singular noun when you do not know which person or thing is involved, or you think it does not matter.

> <u>Some</u> man phoned, but didn't leave his number.
> Is there <u>some</u> problem?

2 You use 'any' in front of plural and uncount nouns to talk about a quantity of something that may or may not exist. You normally use 'any' in questions and negative sentences.

> Are there <u>any jobs</u> men can do but women can't?
> It hasn't made <u>any difference.</u>

You use 'any' with a singular noun to emphasize that it does not matter which person or thing is involved.

> <u>Any</u> container will do.

You can use 'no' with an affirmative verb instead of 'not any'.

> There weren't <u>any tomatoes</u> left.
> There <u>were no tomatoes</u> left.

60

Quantity 2

You can also use 'not' and 'any', or 'no', with a comparative.

> *Her house wasn't any better than ours.*
> *Her house was no better than ours.*

3 You use 'another' with singular nouns to talk about an additional person or thing.

> *Could I have another cup of coffee?*
> *He opened another shop last month.*

You can also use 'another' with a number and a plural noun to talk about more people or things.

> *Another four years passed before we met again.*
> *I've got another three books to read.*

You use 'other' with plural nouns and 'the other' with singular or plural nouns.

> *I've got other things to think about.*
> *The other man has gone.*
> *The other European countries have a beaten us.*

4 You use 'each' or 'every' with a singular noun to talk about all the members of a group of people or things. You use 'each' when you are thinking about the members as individuals, and 'every' when you are making a general statement about all of them.

> *Each county is subdivided into several districts.*
> *Each applicant has five choices.*
> *Every child would have milk every day.*
> *She spoke to every person at that party.*

You can modify 'every' but not 'each'.

> *He spoke to them nearly every day.*
> *We went out almost every evening.*

5 You can use 'some of', 'any of', or 'each of', and a noun group to talk about a number of people or things in a group of people or things.

> *Some of the information has already been analysed.*
> *It was more expensive than any of the other magazines.*
> *He gave each of us advice about our present goals.*

You can use 'each of' and a plural noun group but 'every' must be followed by 'one of'.

> *Each of the drawings is different.*
> *Every one of them is given a financial target.*

Note that you can also use 'each' with 'one of'.

> *This view of poverty influences each one of us.*

Position of adjectives

Main points

There are two main positions for adjectives: in front of a noun, or as the complement of a link verb.

Most adjectives can be used in either of these positions, but some adjectives can only be used in one.

1 Most adjectives can be used in a noun group, after determiners and numbers if there are any, in front of the noun.

> He had a <u>beautiful smile.</u>
> She bought a loaf of <u>white bread.</u>
> There was no <u>clear evidence.</u>

2 Most adjectives can also be used after a link verb such as 'be', 'become', or 'feel'.

> I'<u>m cold.</u>
> I <u>felt angry.</u>
> Nobody <u>seemed amused.</u>

3 Some adjectives are normally used only after a link verb.

afraid	alive	alone	asleep	aware	content	due
glad	ill	ready	sorry	sure	unable	well

For example, you can say 'She was glad', but you do not talk about 'a glad woman'.

> I wanted to <u>be alone.</u>
> We were <u>getting ready</u> for bed.
> I'<u>m</u> not quite <u>sure.</u>
> He didn't know whether to <u>feel glad</u> or <u>sorry.</u>

4 Some adjectives are normally used only in front of a noun.

eastern	northern	southern	western	atomic
countless	digital	existing	indoor	introductory
maximum	neighbouring	occasional	outdoor	

For example, you talk about 'an atomic bomb', but you do not say 'The bomb was atomic'.

> He sent <u>countless letters</u> to the newspapers.
> This book includes a good <u>introductory chapter</u> on forests.

5 When you use an adjective to emphasize a strong feeling or opinion, it always comes in front of a noun.

absolute	complete	entire	outright	perfect	positive
pure	real	total	true	utter	

> *Some of it was <u>absolute rubbish.</u>*
> *He made me feel like a <u>complete idiot.</u>*

6 Some adjectives that describe size or age can come after a noun group consisting of a number or determiner and a noun that indicates the unit of measurement.

deep	high	long	old	tall	thick	wide

> *He was about <u>six feet tall.</u>*
> *The water was <u>several metres deep.</u>*
> *The baby is <u>nine months old.</u>*

Note that you do not say 'two pounds heavy', you say 'two pounds in weight'.

7 A few adjectives are used alone after a noun.

designate	elect	galore	incarnate

> *She was now the <u>president elect.</u>*
> *There are empty <u>houses galore.</u>*

8 A few adjectives have a different meaning depending on whether they come in front of or after a noun.

concerned	involved	present	proper	responsible

For example, 'the concerned mother' means a mother who is worried, but 'the mother concerned' means the mother who has been mentioned.

> *It's one of those incredibly <u>involved stories.</u>*
> *The <u>people involved</u> are all doctors.*
> *I'm worried about the <u>present situation.</u>*
> *Of the 18 <u>people present,</u> I knew only one.*
> *Her parents were trying to act in a <u>responsible manner.</u>*
> *We do not know the <u>person responsible</u> for his death.*

Order of adjectives

Main points

You put opinion adjectives in front of descriptive adjectives.

You put general opinion adjectives in front of specific opinion adjectives.

You can sometimes vary the order of adjectives.

If you use two or more descriptive adjectives, you put them in a particular order.

If you use a noun in front of another noun, you put any adjectives in front of the first noun.

1 You often want to add more information to a noun than you can with one adjective. In theory, you can use the adjectives in any order, depending on the quality you want to emphasize. In practice, however, there is a normal order.

When you use two or more adjectives in front of a noun, you usually put an adjective that expresses your opinion in front of an adjective that just describes something.

> You live in a <u>nice big</u> house.
> He is a <u>naughty little</u> boy.
> She was wearing a <u>beautiful pink</u> suit.

2 When you use more than one adjective to express your opinion, an adjective with a more general meaning such as 'good', 'bad', 'nice', or 'lovely' usually comes before an adjective with a more specific meaning such as 'comfortable', 'clean', or 'dirty'.

> I sat in a <u>lovely comfortable</u> armchair in the corner.
> He put on a <u>nice clean</u> shirt.
> It was a <u>horrible dirty</u> room.

3 You can use adjectives to describe various qualities of people or things. For example, you might want to indicate their size, their shape, or the country they come from.

Descriptive adjectives belong to six main types, but you are unlikely ever to use all six types in the same noun group. If you did, you would normally put them in the following order:

size	age	shape	colour	nationality	material

Order of adjectives

This means that if you want to use an 'age' adjective and a 'nationality' adjective, you put the 'age' adjective first.

> *We met some <u>young Chinese</u> girls.*

Similarly, a 'shape' adjective normally comes before a 'colour' adjective.

> *He had <u>round black</u> eyes.*

Other combinations of adjectives follow the same order.
Note that 'material' means any substance, not only cloth.

> *There was a <u>large round wooden</u> table in the room.*
> *The man was carrying a <u>small black plastic</u> bag.*

4 You usually put comparative and superlative adjectives in front of other adjectives.

> *Some of the <u>better English</u> actors have gone to live in Hollywood.*
> *These are the <u>highest monthly</u> figures on record.*

5 When you use a noun in front of another noun, you never put adjectives between them. You put any adjectives in front of the first noun.

> *He works in the <u>French</u> film industry.*
> *He receives a <u>large weekly</u> cash payment.*

6 When you use two adjectives as the complement of a link verb, you use a conjunction such as 'and' to link them. With three or more adjectives, you link the last two with a conjunction, and put commas after the others.

> *The day was <u>hot and dusty.</u>*
> *The room was <u>large but square.</u>*
> *The house was <u>old, damp and smelly.</u>*
> *We felt <u>hot, tired and thirsty.</u>*

Adjective + 'to' or 'that'

Main points

Adjectives used after link verbs are often followed by 'to'-infinitive clauses or 'that'-clauses.

Some adjectives are always followed by 'to'-infinitive clauses.

You often use 'to'-infinitive clauses or 'that'-clauses after adjectives to express feelings or opinions.

You often use 'to'-infinitive clauses after adjectives when the subject is impersonal 'it'.

1 After link verbs, you often use adjectives that describe how someone feels about an action or situation. With some adjectives, you can add a 'to'-infinitive clause or a 'that'-clause to say what the action or situation is.

afraid	anxious	ashamed	disappointed	frightened
glad	happy	pleased	proud	sad
surprised	unhappy			

If the subject is the same in both clauses, you usually use a 'to'-infinitive clause. If the subject is different, you must use a 'that'-clause.

I was <u>happy to see</u> them again.
He was <u>happy that</u> they were coming to the party.

You often use a 'to'-infinitive clause when talking about future time in relation to the main clause.

I am <u>afraid to go</u> home.
He was <u>anxious to leave</u> before it got dark.

You often use a 'that'-clause when talking about present or past time in relation to the main clause.

He was <u>anxious that</u> the passport was missing.
They were <u>afraid that</u> I might have talked to the police.

2 You often use 'sorry' with a 'that'-clause. Note that 'that' is often omitted.

I'm very <u>sorry that</u> I can't join you.
I'm <u>sorry</u> I'm so late.

Adjective + 'to' or 'that'

3 Some adjectives are not usually used alone, but have a 'to'-infinitive clause after them to say what action or situation the adjective relates to.

able	apt	bound	due	inclined	liable
likely	prepared	ready	unlikely	unwilling	willing

> They were <u>unable to help</u> her.
> They were not <u>likely to forget</u> it.
> I am <u>willing to try.</u>
> I'm <u>prepared to say</u> I was wrong.

4 When you want to express an opinion about someone or something, you often use an adjective followed by a 'to'-infinitive clause.

difficult	easy	impossible	possible	right	wrong

> She had been <u>easy to deceive.</u>
> The windows will be almost <u>impossible to open.</u>
> Am I <u>wrong to stay</u> here?

Note that in the first two examples, the subject of the main clause is the object of the 'to'-infinitive clause. In the third example, the subject is the same in both clauses.

5 With some adjectives, you use a 'that'-clause to express an opinion about someone or something.

awful	bad	essential	extraordinary	funny	good
important	interesting	obvious	sad	true	

> I was <u>sad that</u> people had reacted in this way.
> It is <u>extraordinary that</u> we should ever have met!

6 You can also use adjectives with 'to'-infinitive clauses after 'it' as the impersonal subject. You use the preposition 'of' or 'for' to indicate the person or thing that the adjective relates to.

> It was <u>easy to find</u> the path.
> It was <u>good of John to help</u> me.
> It was <u>difficult for her to find</u> a job.

➤ See Unit 17 for 'it' as impersonal subject.

➤ See Unit 47 for more information about adjectives followed by 'of' or 'for'.

'-ing' and '-ed' adjectives

Main points

Many adjectives ending in '-ing' describe the effect that something has on someone's feelings.

Some adjectives ending in '-ing' describe a process or state that continues over a period of time.

Many adjectives ending in '-ed' describe people's feelings.

---

1 You use many '-ing' adjectives to describe the effect that something has on your feelings, or on the feelings of people in general. For example, if you talk about 'a surprising number', you mean that the number surprises you.

alarming	amazing	annoying	astonishing	boring
charming	confusing	convincing	depressing	disappointing
embarrassing	exciting	frightening	interesting	shocking
surprising	terrifying	tiring	worrying	welcoming

> He lives in a <u>charming</u> house just outside the town.
> She always has a warm <u>welcoming</u> smile.

Most '-ing' adjectives have a related transitive verb.

➤ See Unit 51 for information on transitive verbs.

2 You use some '-ing' adjectives to describe something that continues over a period of time.

ageing	booming	decreasing	dying	existing
increasing	living	remaining		

> Britain is an <u>ageing</u> society.
> <u>Increasing</u> prices are making food very expensive.

These adjectives have related intransitive verbs.

➤ See Unit 51 for information on intransitive verbs.

3 Many '-ed' adjectives describe people's feelings. They have the same form as the past participle of a transitive verb and have a passive meaning. For example, 'a frightened person' is a person who has been frightened by something.

alarmed	amused	astonished	bored	delighted
depressed	disappointed	excited	frightened	interested
satisfied	shocked	surprised	tired	worried

> She looks <u>alarmed</u> about something.
> A <u>bored</u> student complained to his teacher.
> She had big blue <u>frightened</u> eyes.

Note that the past participles of irregular verbs do not end in '-ed', but can be used as adjectives. ▶ See pages 216–217 for a list of irregular past participles.

> The bird had a <u>broken</u> wing.
> His coat was dirty and <u>torn.</u>

4 Like other adjectives, '-ing' and '-ed' adjectives can be:

● used in front of a noun

> They still show <u>amazing</u> loyalty to their parents.
> This is the most <u>terrifying</u> tale ever written.
> I was thanked by the <u>satisfied</u> customer.
> The <u>worried</u> authorities cancelled the match.

● used after link verbs

> It's <u>amazing</u> what they can do.
> The present situation is <u>terrifying.</u>
> He felt <u>satisfied</u> with all the work he had done.
> My husband was <u>worried.</u>

● modified by adverbials such as 'quite', 'really', and 'very'

> The film was <u>quite boring.</u>
> There is nothing <u>very surprising</u> in this.
> She was <u>quite astonished</u> at his behaviour.
> He was a <u>very disappointed</u> young man.

● used in the comparative and superlative

> His argument was <u>more convincing</u> than mine.
> He became even <u>more depressed</u> after she died.
> This is one of <u>the most boring books</u> I've ever read.
> She was <u>the most interested</u> in going to the cinema.

5 A small number of '-ed' adjectives are normally only used after link verbs such as 'be', 'become', or 'feel'. They are related to transitive verbs, and are often followed by a prepositional phrase, a 'to'-infinitive clause, or a 'that'-clause.

convinced	delighted	finished	interested	involved	pleased
prepared	scared	thrilled	tired	touched	

> The Brazilians are <u>pleased</u> with the results.
> He was always <u>prepared</u> to account for his actions.
> She was <u>scared</u> that they would find her.

Comparison: basic forms

Main points

You add '-er' for the comparative and '-est' for the superlative of one-syllable adjectives and adverbs.

You use '-er' and '-est' with some two-syllable adjectives.

You use 'more' for the comparative and 'most' for the superlative of most two-syllable adjectives, all longer adjectives, and adverbs ending in '-ly'.

Some common adjectives and adverbs have irregular forms.

---

1 You add '-er' for the comparative form and '-est' for the superlative form of one-syllable adjectives and adverbs. If they end in '-e', you add '-r' and '-st'.

cheap	→	cheaper	→	cheapest
safe	→	safer	→	safest

close	cold	fast	hard	large	light	nice
poor	quick	rough	small	weak	wide	young

They worked <u>harder.</u>
I've found a <u>nicer</u> hotel.

If they end in a single vowel and consonant (except '-w'), double the consonant.

big	→	bigger	→	biggest

fat	hot	sad	thin	wet

The day grew <u>hotter.</u>
Henry was the <u>biggest</u> of them.

2 With two-syllable adjectives and adverbs ending in a consonant and '-y', you change the '-y' to '-i' and add '-er' and '-est'.

happy	→	happier	→	happiest

angry	busy	dirty	easy	friendly
funny	heavy	lucky	silly	tiny

It couldn't be <u>easier.</u>
That is the <u>funniest</u> bit of the film.

Comparison: basic forms

3 You use 'more' for the comparative and 'most' for the superlative of most two-syllable adjectives, all longer adjectives, and adverbs ending in '-ly'.

careful	→	more careful	→	most careful
beautiful	→	more beautiful	→	most beautiful
seriously	→	more seriously	→	most seriously

> Be _more careful_ next time.
> They are the _most beautiful_ gardens in the world.
> It affected Clive _most seriously._

Note that for 'early' as an adjective or adverb, you use 'earlier' and 'earliest', not 'more' and 'most'.

4 With some common two-syllable adjectives and adverbs you can either add '-er' and '-est', or use 'more' and 'most'.

common	cruel	gentle	handsome	likely
narrow	pleasant	polite	simple	stupid

Note that 'clever' and 'quiet' only add '-er' and '-est'.

> It was _quieter_ outside.   He was the _cleverest_ man I ever knew.

5 You normally use 'the' with superlative adjectives in front of a noun, but you can omit 'the' after a link verb.

> It was _the happiest_ day of my life.   I was _happiest_ when I was on my own.

⊖ WARNING: When 'most' is used without 'the' in front of adjectives and adverbs, it often means almost the same as 'very'.

> This book was _most interesting._   I object _most strongly._

6 A few common adjectives and adverbs have irregular comparative and superlative forms.

good/well	→	better	→	best
bad/badly	→	worse	→	worst
far	→	farther/further	→	farthest/furthest
old	→	older/elder	→	oldest/eldest

> She would ask him when she knew him _better._
> She sat near the _furthest_ window.

Note that you use 'elder' or 'eldest' to say which brother, sister, or child in a family you mean.

> Our _eldest_ daughter couldn't come.

Comparison: uses

Main points

Comparative adjectives are used to compare people or things.

Superlative adjectives are used to say that one person or thing has more of a quality than others in a group or others of that kind.

Comparative adverbs are used in the same way as adjectives.

---

1 You use comparative adjectives to compare one person or thing with another, or with the same person or thing at another time. After a comparative adjective, you often use 'than'.

> She was much <u>older than</u> me.
> I am <u>happier than</u> I have ever been.

2 You use a superlative to say that one person or thing has more of a quality than others in a group or others of that kind.

> Tokyo is Japan's <u>largest city.</u>
> He was <u>the tallest person</u> there.

3 You can use comparative and superlative adjectives in front of a noun.

> I was <u>a better writer</u> than he was.
> He had <u>more important things</u> to do.
> It was <u>the quickest route</u> from Rome to Naples.

You can also use comparative and superlative adjectives after link verbs.

> My brother is <u>younger</u> than me.
> He feels <u>more content</u> now.
> The sergeant was <u>the tallest.</u>
> This book was <u>the most interesting.</u>

4 You can use adverbs of degree in front of comparative adjectives.

a bit	far	a great/good deal	a little	a lot	much
rather	slightly				

> This car's <u>a bit more expensive.</u>
> Now I feel <u>a great deal more confident.</u>
> It's <u>a rather more complicated</u> story than that.

Comparison: uses

You can also use adverbs of degree such as 'by far', 'easily', 'much', or 'quite' in front of 'the' and superlative adjectives.

> It was _by far the worst hospital_ I had ever seen.
> She was _easily the most intelligent person_ in the class.

Note that you can put 'very' between 'the' and a superlative adjective ending in '-est'.

> It was of _the very highest quality._

5 When you want to say that one situation depends on another, you can use 'the' and a comparative followed by 'the' and another comparative.

> _The smaller_ it is, _the cheaper_ it is to post.
> _The larger_ the organisation is, _the greater_ the problem of administration becomes.

When you want to say that something increases or decreases, you can use two comparatives linked by 'and'.

> It's getting _harder and harder_ to find a job.
> Cars are becoming _more and more expensive._

6 After a superlative adjective, you can use a prepositional phrase to specify the group you are talking about.

> Henry was _the biggest of them._
> These cakes are probably _the best in the world._
> He was _the most dangerous man_ in _the country._

7 You use the same structures in comparisons using adverbs as those given for adjectives:

- 'than' after comparative adverbs

> Prices have been rising _faster than_ incomes.

- 'the' and a comparative adverb followed by 'the' and another comparative adverb

> _The quicker_ we finish, _the sooner_ we will go home.

- two comparative adverbs linked by 'and'

> He sounded _worse and worse._
> He drove _faster and faster_ till we told him to stop.

Other ways of comparing

Main points

This includes words like: 'as…as', 'the same (as)' and 'like'.

You use 'as…as…' to compare people or things.

You can also compare people or things by using 'the same (as)'.

You can also compare people or things by using a link verb and a phrase beginning with 'like'.

---

1 You use 'as…as…' to compare people or things that are similar in some way. You use 'as' and an adjective or adverb, followed by 'as' and a noun group, an adverbial, or a clause.

> You're <u>as bad as your sister.</u>
> The airport was <u>as crowded as ever.</u>
> I am <u>as good as she is.</u>
> Let us examine it <u>as carefully as we can.</u>

2 You can make a negative comparison using 'not as…as…' or 'not so…as…'.

> The food <u>wasn't as</u> good <u>as</u> yesterday.
> They are <u>not as</u> clever <u>as</u> they appear to be.
> He is <u>not so</u> old <u>as</u> I thought.

3 You can use the adverbs 'almost', 'just', 'nearly', or 'quite' in front of 'as…as…'.

> He was <u>almost as</u> fast <u>as</u> his brother.
> Mary was <u>just as</u> pale <u>as</u> before.
> She was <u>nearly as</u> tall <u>as</u> he was.

In a negative comparison, you can use 'not nearly' or 'not quite' before 'as…as…'.

> This is <u>not nearly as</u> complicated <u>as</u> it sounds.
> The hotel was <u>not quite as</u> good <u>as</u> they expected.

4 When you want to say that one thing is very similar to something else, you can use 'the same as' followed by a noun group, an adverbial, or a clause.

> Your bag is <u>the same as</u> mine.
> I said <u>the same as</u> always.
> She looked <u>the same as</u> she did yesterday.

Other ways of comparing

If people or things are very similar or identical, you can also say that they are 'the same'.

> *Teenage fashions are <u>the same</u> all over the world.*
> *The initial stage of learning English is <u>the same</u> for many students.*

You can use some adverbs in front of 'the same as' or 'the same'.

almost	exactly	just	more or less
much	nearly	roughly	virtually

> *He did <u>exactly the same as</u> John did.*
> *You two look <u>almost the same.</u>*

You can use 'the same' in front of a noun group, with or without 'as' after the noun group.

> *They reached almost <u>the same height.</u>*
> *It was painted <u>the same colour as</u> the wall.*

5 You can also compare people or things by using a link verb such as 'be', 'feel', 'look', or 'seem' and a phrase beginning with 'like'.

> *It <u>was like</u> a dream.*
> *He still <u>feels like</u> a child.*
> *He <u>looked like</u> an actor.*
> *The houses <u>seemed like</u> mansions.*

You can use some adverbs in front of 'like'.

a bit	a little	exactly	just	least	less
more	most	quite	rather	somewhat	very

> *He looks <u>just like</u> a baby.*
> *Of all his children, she was the one <u>most like</u> me.*

6 If the noun group after 'as' or 'like' in any of these structures is a pronoun, you use an object pronoun or possessive pronoun.

> *Jane was as clever as <u>him.</u>*
> *His car is the same as <u>mine.</u>*

7 You can also use 'less' and 'least' to make comparisons with the opposite meaning to 'more' and 'most'.

> *They were <u>less fortunate</u> than us.*
> *He was <u>the least skilled</u> of the workers.*
> *We see him <u>less frequently</u> than we used to.*

Adverbials

Main points

Adverbials are usually adverbs, adverb phrases, or prepositional phrases.

Adverbials of manner, place, and time are used to say how, where, or when something happens.

Adverbials usually come after the verb, or after the object if there is one.

The usual order of adverbials is manner, then place, then time.

1 An adverbial is often one word, an adverb.

> Sit there _quietly,_ and listen to this music.

However, an adverbial can also be a group of words:

- an adverb phrase

> He did not play _well enough_ to win.

- a prepositional phrase

> The children were playing _in the park._

- a noun group, usually a time expression

> Come and see me _next week._

2 You use an adverbial of manner to describe the way in which something happens or is done.

> They looked _anxiously_ at each other.
> She listened _with great patience_ as he told his story.

You use an adverbial of place to say where something happens.

> A plane flew _overhead._
> No birds or animals came _near the body._

You use an adverbial of time to say when something happens.

> She will be here _soon._
> He was born _on 3 April 1925._

3 You normally put adverbials of manner, place, and time after the main verb.

> She sang _beautifully._
> The book was lying _on the table._
> The car broke down _yesterday._

Adverbials

If the verb has an object, you put the adverbial after the object.

> *I did learn to play a few tunes <u>very badly</u>.*
> *Thomas made his decision <u>immediately</u>.*
> *He took the glasses <u>to the kitchen</u>.*

If you are using more than one of these adverbials in a clause, the usual order is manner, then place, then time.

> *They were sitting <u>quite happily</u> <u>in the car</u>.* (manner, place)
> *She spoke <u>very well</u> <u>at the village hall</u> <u>last night</u>.* (manner, place, time)

4 You usually put adverbials of frequency, probability, and duration in front of the main verb.

> *She <u>occasionally comes</u> to my house.*
> *You have <u>very probably heard</u> the news by now.*
> *They had <u>already given</u> me the money.*

A few adverbs of degree also usually come in front of the main verb.

> *She <u>really enjoyed</u> the party.*

5 When you want to focus on an adverbial, you can do this by putting it in a different place in the clause:

● you can put an adverbial at the beginning of a clause, usually for emphasis

> *<u>Slowly</u>, he opened his eyes.*
> *<u>In September</u> I travelled to California.*
> *<u>Next to the coffee machine</u> stood a pile of cups.*

Note that after adverbials of place, as in the last example, the verb can come in front of the subject.

● you can sometimes put adverbs and adverb phrases in front of the main verb for emphasis, but not prepositional phrases or noun groups

> *He <u>deliberately</u> chose it because it was cheap.*
> *I <u>very much</u> wanted to go with them.*

● you can change the order of adverbials of manner, place, and time when you want to change the emphasis

> *They were sitting <u>in the car</u> <u>quite happily</u>.* (place, manner)
> *<u>At the meeting</u> <u>last night</u>, she spoke <u>very well</u>.* (place, time, manner)

Adverbials of manner

Main points

Most adverbs of manner are formed by adding '-ly' to an adjective, but sometimes other spelling changes are needed.

You cannot form adverbs from adjectives that end in '-ly'.

Some adverbs have the same form as adjectives.

You do not use adverbs after link verbs, you use adjectives.

Adverbials of manner are sometimes prepositional phrases or noun groups.

1 Adverbs of manner are often formed by adding '-ly' to an adjective.

| Adjectives: | bad | beautiful | careful | quick | quiet | soft |
| Adverbs: | badly | beautifully | carefully | quickly | quietly | softly |

2 Adverbs formed in this way usually have a similar meaning to the adjective.

> She is as clever as she is <u>beautiful.</u>
> He talked so politely and danced so <u>beautifully.</u>
> 'We must not talk. We must be <u>quiet,</u>' said Sita.
> She wanted to sit <u>quietly,</u> to relax.

3 There are sometimes changes in spelling when an adverb is formed from an adjective.

'-le' changes to '-ly':	gentle	→	gently
'-y' changes to '-ily':	easy	→	easily
'-ic' changes to '-ically':	automatic	→	automatically
'-ue' changes to '-uly':	true	→	truly
'-ll' changes to '-lly':	full	→	fully

Note that 'public' changes to 'publicly', not 'publically'.

⊖ WARNING: You cannot form adverbs from adjectives that already end in '-ly'. For example, you cannot say 'He smiled at me friendlily'. You can sometimes use a prepositional phrase instead: 'He smiled at me in a friendly way'.

Adverbials of manner

4 Some adverbs of manner have the same form as adjectives and have similar meanings, for example 'fast', 'hard', and 'late'.

> *I've always been interested in <u>fast</u> cars.* (adjective)
> *The driver was driving too <u>fast.</u>* (adverb)

Note that 'hardly' and 'lately' are not adverbs of manner and have different meanings from the adjectives 'hard' and 'late'.

> *It was a <u>hard</u> decision to make.*
> *I <u>hardly</u> had any time to talk to her.*
> *The train was <u>late</u> as usual.*
> *Have you seen John <u>lately?</u>*

5 The adverb of manner related to the adjective 'good' is 'well'.

> *He is a <u>good</u> dancer.*
> *He dances <u>well.</u>*

Note that 'well' can sometimes be an adjective when it refers to someone's health.

> *'How are you?' – 'I am very <u>well,</u> thank you.'*

6 You do not use adverbs after link verbs such as 'be', 'become', 'feel', 'get', 'look', and 'seem'. You use an adjective after these verbs. For example, you do not say 'Sue felt happily'. You say 'Sue felt happy'.

➤ See Unit 73 for more information on link verbs.

7 You do not often use prepositional phrases or noun groups as adverbials of manner. However, you occasionally need to use them, for example when there is no adverb form available. The prepositional phrases and noun groups usually include a noun such as 'way', 'fashion', or 'manner', or a noun that refers to someone's voice.

> *She asked me <u>in such a nice manner</u> that I couldn't refuse.*
> *He did it <u>the right way.</u>*
> *They spoke <u>in angry tones.</u>*

Prepositional phrases with 'like' are also used as adverbials of manner.

> *I slept <u>like a baby.</u>*
> *He drove <u>like a madman.</u>*

Adverbials of time

Main points

Adverbials of time can be time expressions such as 'last night'.

Adverbials of time can be prepositional phrases with 'at', 'in', or 'on'.

'For' refers to a period of time in the past, present, or future.

'Since' refers to a point in past time.

---

1 You use adverbials of time to say when something happens. You often use noun groups called time expressions as adverbials of time.

yesterday	today	tomorrow	last night
last year	next Saturday	next week	the day after tomorrow
the other day			

Note that you do not use the prepositions 'at', 'in', or 'on' with time expressions.

> *One of my children wrote to me <u>today.</u>*   *So, you're coming back <u>next week?</u>*

You often use time expressions with verbs in the present tense to talk about the future.

> *The plane leaves <u>tomorrow morning.</u>*   *They're coming <u>next week.</u>*

2 You can use prepositional phrases as adverbials of time:

- 'at' is used with:

clock times:	at eight o'clock, at three fifteen
religious festivals:	at Christmas, at Easter
mealtimes:	at breakfast, at lunchtimes
specific periods:	at night, at the weekend, at weekends, at half-term

- 'in' is used with:

seasons:	in autumn, in the spring
years and centuries:	in 1985, in the year 2000, in the nineteenth century
months:	in July, in December
parts of the day:	in the morning, in the evenings

Note that you also use 'in' to say that something will happen during or after a period of time in the future.

> *I think we'll find out <u>in</u> the next few days.*

● 'on' is used with:

days:	on Monday, on Tuesday morning, on Sunday evenings
special days:	on Christmas Day, on my birthday, on his wedding anniversary
dates:	on the twentieth of July, on June 21st

3 You use 'for' with verbs in any tense to say how long something continues to happen.

> *He is in Italy for a month.*   *I remained silent for a long time.*
> *I will be in London for three months.*

⊖ WARNING: You do not use 'during' to say how long something continues to happen. You cannot say 'I went there during three weeks'.

4 You use 'since' with a verb in the present perfect or past perfect tense to say when something started to happen.

> *Marilyn has lived in Paris since 1984.*
> *I had eaten nothing since breakfast.*

5 You can use many other prepositional phrases as adverbials of time. You use:

● 'during' and 'over' for a period of time in which something happens

> *I saw him twice during the holidays.*   *Will you stay here over Christmas?*

● 'from…to/till/until' and 'between…and' for the beginning and end of a period of time

> *The building is closed from April to May.*
> *She worked from four o'clock till ten o'clock.*
> *Can you take the test between now and June?*

● 'by' when you mean 'not later than'

> *By eleven o'clock, Brody was back in his office.*
> *Can we get this finished by tomorrow?*

● 'before' and 'after'

> *I saw him before the match.*   *She left the house after ten o'clock.*

'Since', 'till', 'until', 'after', and 'before' can also be conjunctions with time clauses.

➤ See Unit 96.

> *I've been wearing glasses since I was three.*

6 You use the adverb 'ago' with the past simple to say how long before the time of speaking something happened. You always put 'ago' after the period of time.

> *We saw him about a month ago.*   *John's wife died five years ago.*

⊖ WARNING: You do not use 'ago' with the present perfect tense. You cannot say 'We have gone to Spain two years ago'.

Frequency and probability

Main points

This includes words like: 'always', 'ever', 'never', 'perhaps', 'possibly' and 'probably'.

Adverbials of frequency are used to say how often something happens.

Adverbials of probability are used to say how sure you are about something.

These adverbials usually come before the main verb, but they come after 'be' as a main verb.

---

1 You use adverbials of frequency to say how often something happens.

a lot	always	ever	frequently	hardly ever	never
normally	occasionally	often	rarely	sometimes	usually

> We _often_ swam in the sea.
> She _never_ comes to my parties.

2 You use adverbials of probability to say how sure you are about something.

certainly	definitely	maybe	obviously
perhaps	possibly	probably	really

> I _definitely_ saw her yesterday.
> The driver _probably_ knows the quickest route.

3 You usually put adverbials of frequency and probability before the main verb and after an auxiliary or a modal.

> He _sometimes works_ downstairs in the kitchen.
> You _are definitely wasting_ your time.
> I _have never had_ such a horrible meal!
> I _shall never forget_ this day.

Note that you usually put them after 'be' as a main verb.

> He _is always_ careful with his money.
> You _are probably_ right.

'Perhaps' usually comes at the beginning of the sentence.

> _Perhaps_ the beaches are cleaner in the north.
> _Perhaps_ you need a membership card to get in.

Frequency and probability

'A lot' always comes after the main verb.

I go swimming __a lot__ in the summer.

4 'Never' is a negative adverb.

She __never__ goes abroad.
I've __never__ been to Europe.

You normally use 'ever' in questions, negative sentences, and 'if'-clauses.

Have you __ever__ been to a football match?
Don't __ever__ do that again!
If you __ever__ need anything, just call me.

Note that you can sometimes use 'ever' in affirmative sentences, for example after a superlative.

She is the __best__ dancer I have __ever__ seen.

You use 'hardly ever' in affirmative sentences to mean almost never.

We __hardly ever__ meet.

Adverbials of duration

Main points

'Already' is used to say that something has happened earlier than expected.

'Still' is used to say that something continues to happen until a particular time.

'Yet' is used to say that something has not happened before a particular time.

'Any longer', 'any more', 'no longer', and 'no more' are used to say that something has stopped happening.

1 You use adverbials of duration to say that an event or situation is continuing, stopping, or is not happening at the moment.

> She _still_ lives in London.
> I couldn't stand it _any more._
> It isn't dark _yet._

2 You use 'already' to say that something has happened sooner than it was expected to happen. You put 'already' in front of the main verb.

> He had _already bought_ the cups and saucers.
> I've _already seen_ them.
> The guests were _already coming_ in.

You put 'already' after 'be' as a main verb.

> Julie was _already_ in bed.

You can also use 'already' to emphasize that something is the case, for example when someone else does not know or is not sure.

> I am _already_ aware of that problem.

You do not normally use 'already' in negative statements, but you can use it in negative 'if'-clauses.

> Show it to him _if he hasn't already seen it._

You can put 'already' at the beginning or end of a clause for emphasis.

> _Already_ he was calculating the profit he could make.
> I've done it _already._

Adverbials of duration

3 You use 'still' to say that a situation continues to exist up to a particular time in the past, present, or future. You put 'still' in front of the main verb.

We <u>were still waiting</u> for the election results.
My family <u>still live</u> in India.
You <u>will still get</u> tickets, if you hurry.

You put 'still' after 'be' as a main verb.

Martin's mother died, but his father <u>is still</u> alive.

You can use 'still' after the subject and before the verb group in negative sentences to express surprise or impatience.

You <u>still</u> haven't given us the keys.
He <u>still</u> didn't say a word.
It was after midnight, and he <u>still</u> wouldn't leave.

Remember that you can use 'still' at the beginning of a clause with a similar meaning to 'after all' or 'nevertheless'.

<u>Still,</u> he is my brother, so I'll have to help him.
<u>Still,</u> it's not too bad. We didn't lose all the money.

4 You use 'yet' at the end of negative sentences and questions to say that something has not happened or had not happened up to a particular time, but is or was expected to happen later.

We haven't got the tickets <u>yet.</u>
Have you joined the swimming club <u>yet?</u>
They hadn't seen the baby <u>yet.</u>

Remember that 'yet' can also be used at the beginning of a clause with a similar meaning to 'but'.

I don't miss her, <u>yet</u> I do often wonder where she went.
They know they won't win. <u>Yet</u> they keep on trying.

5 You use 'any longer' and 'any more' at the end of negative clauses to say that a past situation has ended and does not exist now or will not exist in the future.

I wanted the job, but I couldn't wait <u>any longer.</u>
He's not going to play <u>any more.</u>

In formal English, you can use an affirmative clause with 'no longer' and 'no more'. You can put them at the end of the clause, or in front of the main verb.

He could stand the pain <u>no more.</u>
He <u>no longer</u> wanted to buy it.

Adverbials of degree

Main points

Adverbs of degree usually modify verbs.

Some adverbs of degree can modify adjectives, other adverbs, or clauses.

---

1 You use adverbs of degree to modify verbs. They make the verb stronger or weaker.

> I _totally disagree._   I can _nearly swim._

2 Some adverbs can come in front of a main verb, after a main verb, or after the object if there is one.

badly	completely	greatly	seriously	strongly	totally

> Mr Brooke _strongly_ criticized the Bank of England.
> I disagree _completely_ with John Taylor.
> That argument doesn't convince me _totally._

Some adverbs are mostly used in front of the verb.

almost	largely	nearly	really	quite

> He _almost_ crashed into a lorry.

Note that 'really' is used at the beginning of a clause to express surprise, and at the end of a clause as an adverb of manner.

> _Really,_ I didn't know that!   He wanted it _really,_ but was too shy to ask.

'A lot' and 'very much' come after the main verb if there is no object, or after the object.

> She helped _a lot._   We liked him _very much._

'Very much' can come after the subject and in front of verbs like 'want', 'prefer', and 'enjoy'.

> I _very much_ wanted to take it with me.

3 Some adverbs of degree go in front of adjectives or other adverbs and modify them.

awfully	extremely	fairly	pretty	quite	rather	really	very

> ...a _fairly large_ office, with filing space.

Note that you can use 'rather' before or after 'a' or 'an' followed by an adjective and a noun.

> *Seaford is <u>rather a</u> pleasant town.* *It is <u>a rather</u> complicated story.*

When 'quite' means 'fairly', you put it in front of 'a' or 'an' followed by an adjective and a noun.

> *My father gave me <u>quite a large sum</u> of money.*

However, when 'quite' means 'extremely', you can put it after 'a'. You can say 'a quite enormous sum'.

4 | You use some adverbs of degree to modify clauses and prepositional phrases.

entirely	just	largely	mainly	partly	simply

> *Are you saying that <u>simply because I am here?</u>*
> *I don't think it's worth going <u>just for a day.</u>*

5 | You use 'so' and 'such' to emphasize a quality that someone or something has. 'So' can be followed by an adjective, an adverb, or a noun group beginning with 'many', 'much', 'few', or 'little'.

> *John is <u>so interesting</u> to talk to.* *Science is changing <u>so rapidly.</u>*
> *I want to do <u>so many</u> different things.*

'Such' is followed by a singular noun group with 'a', or a plural noun group.

> *There was <u>such a noise</u> we couldn't hear.* *They said <u>such nasty things.</u>*

⊖ WARNING: 'So' is never followed by a singular noun group with 'a' or a plural noun group.

6 | You use 'too' when you mean 'more than is necessary' or 'more than is good'. You can use 'too' before adjectives and adverbs, and before 'many', 'much', 'few', or 'little'.

> *The prices are <u>too high.</u>* *I've been paying <u>too much</u> tax.*

You use 'enough' after adjectives and adverbs.

> *I waited until my daughter was <u>old enough</u> to read.*
> *He didn't work <u>quickly enough.</u>*

Note that 'enough' is also a determiner.

> *We've got <u>enough money</u> to buy that car now.*

7 | You use emphasizing adverbs to modify adjectives such as 'astonishing', 'furious', and 'wonderful', which express extreme qualities.

absolutely	completely	entirely	perfectly	purely	quite
really	simply	totally	utterly		

> *I think he's <u>absolutely wonderful.</u>*

Place and direction

Main points

This includes words like: 'above', 'below', 'down', 'from', 'to', 'towards' and 'up'.

You normally use prepositional phrases to say where a person or thing is, or the direction they are moving in.

You can also use adverbs and adverb phrases for place and direction.

Many words are both prepositions and adverbs.

1 You use prepositions to talk about the place where someone or something is. Prepositions are always followed by a noun group, which is called the object of the preposition.

above	among	at	behind	below		beneath	beside
between	in	inside	near	on		opposite	outside
over	round	through	under	underneath			

He stood *near* the door.
Two minutes later we were safely *inside* the taxi.

Note that some prepositions consist of more than one word.

in between	in front of	next to	on top of

There was a man standing *in front of* me.
The books were piled *on top of* each other.

2 You can also use prepositions to talk about the direction that someone or something is moving in, or the place that someone or something is moving towards.

across	along	back to	down	into	onto	out of
past	round	through	to	towards	up	

They dived *into* the water.
She turned and rushed *out of* the room.

3 Many prepositions can be used both for place and direction.

The bank is just *across* the High Street. (place)
I walked *across* the room. (direction)
We live in the house *over* the road. (place)
I stole his keys and escaped *over* the wall. (direction)

Place and direction

4 You can also use adverbs and adverb phrases for place and direction.

abroad	away	downstairs	downwards	here	indoors
outdoors	there	underground	upstairs	anywhere	everywhere
nowhere	somewhere				

> Sheila was <u>here</u> a moment ago.
> Can't you go <u>upstairs</u> and turn the bedroom light off?

Note that a few noun groups can also be used as adverbials of place or direction.

> Steve lives <u>next door</u> at number 23.
> I thought we went <u>the other way</u> last time.

5 Many words can be used as prepositions and as adverbs, with no difference in meaning. Remember that prepositions have noun groups as objects, but adverbs do not.

> Did he fall <u>down the stairs?</u>
> Please do sit <u>down.</u>
> I looked <u>underneath the bed,</u> but the box had gone!
> Always put a sheet of paper <u>underneath.</u>

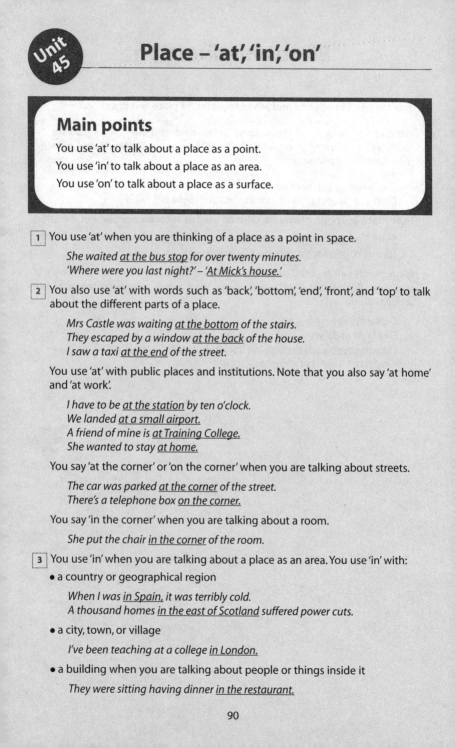

Place – 'at', 'in', 'on'

Main points

You use 'at' to talk about a place as a point.

You use 'in' to talk about a place as an area.

You use 'on' to talk about a place as a surface.

1. You use 'at' when you are thinking of a place as a point in space.

> She waited _at the bus stop_ for over twenty minutes.
> 'Where were you last night?' – '_At Mick's house._'

2. You also use 'at' with words such as 'back', 'bottom', 'end', 'front', and 'top' to talk about the different parts of a place.

> Mrs Castle was waiting _at the bottom_ of the stairs.
> They escaped by a window _at the back_ of the house.
> I saw a taxi _at the end_ of the street.

You use 'at' with public places and institutions. Note that you also say 'at home' and 'at work'.

> I have to be _at the station_ by ten o'clock.
> We landed _at a small airport._
> A friend of mine is _at Training College._
> She wanted to stay _at home._

You say 'at the corner' or 'on the corner' when you are talking about streets.

> The car was parked _at the corner_ of the street.
> There's a telephone box _on the corner._

You say 'in the corner' when you are talking about a room.

> She put the chair _in the corner_ of the room.

3. You use 'in' when you are talking about a place as an area. You use 'in' with:

- a country or geographical region

> When I was _in Spain,_ it was terribly cold.
> A thousand homes _in the east of Scotland_ suffered power cuts.

- a city, town, or village

> I've been teaching at a college _in London._

- a building when you are talking about people or things inside it

> They were sitting having dinner _in the restaurant._

Place – 'at', 'in', 'on'

You also use 'in' with containers of any kind when talking about things inside them.

> *She kept the cards <u>in a little box.</u>*

4 Compare the use of 'at' and 'in' in these examples.

> *I had a hard day <u>at the office.</u>* ('at' emphasizes the office as a public place or institution)
> *I left my coat behind <u>in the office.</u>* ('in' emphasizes the office as a building)
> *There's a good film <u>at the cinema.</u>* ('at' emphasizes the cinema as a public place)
> *It was very cold <u>in the cinema.</u>* ('in' emphasizes the cinema as a building.)

5 When talking about addresses, you use 'at' when you give the house number, and 'in' when you just give the name of the street.

> *They used to live <u>at 5, Weston Road.</u>*
> *She got a job <u>in Oxford Street.</u>*

Note that American English uses 'on': 'He lived on Penn Street.'

You use 'at' when you are talking about someone's house.

> *I'll see you <u>at Fred's house.</u>*

6 You use 'on' when you are talking about a place as a surface. You can also use 'on top of'.

> *I sat down <u>on the sofa.</u>*
> *She put her keys <u>on top of the television.</u>*

You also use 'on' when you are thinking of a place as a point on a line, such as a road, a railway line, a river, or a coastline.

> *Scrabster is <u>on the north coast.</u>*
> *Oxford is <u>on the A34</u> between Birmingham and London.*

➤ See Unit 40 for information on 'at', 'in', and 'on' in adverbials of time.

Transport prepositions

Main points

This includes phrases like: 'by bus', 'in a car', 'on the plane', and 'off the train'.

You can use 'by' with most forms of transport.

You use 'in', 'into', and 'out of' with cars.

You normally use 'on', 'onto', and 'off' with other forms of transport.

1 When you talk about the type of vehicle or transport you use to travel somewhere, you use 'by'.

by bus	by bicycle	by car	by coach	by plane	by train

She had come _by car_ with her husband and her four children.
I left Walsall in the afternoon and went _by bus and train_ to Nottingham.

⊖ WARNING: If you want to say you walk somewhere, you say you go 'on foot'. You do not say 'by foot'.

Marie decided to continue _on foot._

2 You use 'in', 'into', and 'out of' when you are talking about cars, vans, lorries, taxis, and ambulances.

I followed them _in my car._
The carpets had to be collected _in a van._
Mr Ward happened to be getting _into his lorry._
She was carried _out of the ambulance_ and up the steps.

3 You use 'on', 'onto', and 'off' when you are talking about other forms of transport, such as buses, coaches, trains, ships, and planes.

Why don't you come _on the train_ with me to New York?
Peter Hurd was already _on the plane_ from California.
The last thing he wanted was to spend ten days _on a boat_ with Hooper.
He jumped back _onto the old bus,_ now nearly empty.
Mr Bixby stepped _off the train_ and walked quickly to the exit.

You can use 'in', 'into', and 'out of' with these other forms of transport, usually when you are focusing on the physical position or movement of the person, rather than stating what form of transport they are using.

> *The passengers <u>in the plane</u> were beginning to panic.*
> *He got back <u>into the train</u> quickly, before Batt could stop him.*
> *We jumped <u>out of the bus</u> and ran into the nearest shop.*

Adjective + preposition

Main points

Some adjectives used after link verbs can be used alone or followed by a prepositional phrase.

Some adjectives must be followed by particular prepositions.

Some adjectives can be followed by different prepositions to introduce different types of information.

1. When you use an adjective after a link verb, you can often use the adjective on its own or followed by a prepositional phrase.
   ➤ See Unit 33 for other patterns.

   He was <u>afraid</u>.
   He was <u>afraid of</u> his enemies.

2. Some adjectives cannot be used alone after a link verb. If they are followed by a prepositional phrase, it must have a particular preposition:

aware of	accustomed to	unaware of	unaccustomed to
fond of	used to		

   I've always been terribly <u>fond of</u> you.
   He is <u>unaccustomed to</u> the heat.

3. Some adjectives can be used alone, or followed by a particular preposition:

   • used alone, or with 'of' to specify the cause of a feeling

afraid	ashamed	convinced	critical	envious	frightened
jealous	proud	scared	suspicious	terrified	tired

   They may feel <u>jealous of</u> your success.
   I was <u>terrified of</u> her.

   • used alone, or with 'of' to specify the person who has a quality

brave	careless	clever	generous	good	intelligent
kind	nice	polite	sensible	silly	stupid
thoughtful	unkind	unreasonable	wrong		

   That was <u>clever of</u> you!
   I turned the job down, which was <u>stupid of</u> me.

Adjective + preposition

- used alone or used with 'to', usually referring to:

similarity:	close equal identical related similar
marriage:	married engaged
loyalty:	dedicated devoted loyal
rank:	junior senior

My problems are very <u>similar to</u> yours.   *He was <u>dedicated to</u> his job.*

- used alone, or followed by 'with' to specify the cause of a feeling

bored	content	displeased	dissatisfied	impatient
impressed	pleased	satisfied		

I could never be <u>bored with</u> football.   *He was <u>pleased with</u> her.*

- used alone, or with 'at', usually referring to:

strong reactions:	alarmed amazed astonished shocked surprised
ability:	bad excellent good hopeless useless

He was <u>shocked at</u> the hatred they had known.
She had always been <u>good at</u> languages.

- used alone, or with 'for' to specify the person or thing that a quality relates to

common	difficult	easy	essential	important
necessary	possible	unnecessary	unusual	usual

It's <u>difficult for young people</u> on their own.
It was <u>unusual for them</u> to go away at the weekend.

4 Some adjectives can be used alone, or used with different prepositions.

- used alone, with an impersonal subject and 'of' and the subject of the action, or with a personal subject and 'to' and the object of the action.

cruel	friendly	generous	good	kind	mean
nasty	nice	polite	rude	unfriendly	unkind

It was <u>rude of</u> him to leave so suddenly.
She was <u>rude to</u> him for no reason.

- used alone, with 'about' to specify a thing or 'with' to specify a person

angry	annoyed	delighted	disappointed
fed up	furious	happy	upset

She was still <u>angry about</u> the result.
They're getting pretty <u>fed up with</u> him.

Noun + preposition

Main points

'Of' can be used to add many different types of information, 'with' is used to specify a quality or possession.

Some nouns are always followed by particular prepositions.

1 You can give more information about a noun by adding a prepositional phrase after it.

> Four men <u>on holiday</u> were in the car.
> A sound <u>behind him</u> made him turn.

2 You often use the preposition 'of' after a noun to add various kinds of information. For example, you can use 'of' to indicate:

● what something is made of or consists of

> ...a wall <u>of stone.</u>
> A feeling <u>of panic</u> was rising in him.

● what the subject matter of speech, writing, or a picture is

> She gave a brief account <u>of her interview.</u>
> There was a picture <u>of them both</u> in the paper.

● what a person or thing belongs to or is connected with

> She was the daughter <u>of the village priest.</u>
> The boys sat on the floor <u>of the living room.</u>

● what qualities a person or thing has

> She was a woman <u>of energy and ambition.</u>
> They faced problems <u>of great complexity.</u>

3 After nouns referring to actions, you use 'of' to indicate the subject or object of the action.

> ...the arrival <u>of the police.</u>
> ...the destruction <u>of their city.</u>

After nouns referring to people who perform an action, you use 'of' to say what the action involves or is aimed at.

> ...supporters <u>of the hunger strike.</u>
> ...a student <u>of English.</u>

Note that you often use two nouns, rather than a noun and a prepositional phrase. For example, you say 'bank robbers', not 'robbers of the bank'.

Noun + preposition

4 After nouns referring to measurement, you use 'of' to give the exact figure.

> …*an average annual temperature <u>of 20 degrees.</u>*
> …*a speed <u>of 25 kilometres an hour.</u>*

You can use 'of' after a noun to give someone's age.

> *Jonathan was a child <u>of seven</u> when it happened.*

5 You use 'with' after a noun to say that a person or thing has a particular quality, feature, or possession.

> …*a girl <u>with red hair.</u>*
> …*the man <u>with the gun.</u>*

Note that you use 'in' after a noun to say what someone is wearing.

> …*a grey-haired man <u>in a raincoat.</u>*
> …*the man <u>in dark glasses.</u>*

6 Some nouns are usually followed by a particular preposition. Here are some examples of:

● nouns followed by 'to'

alternative	answer	approach	attitude	introduction
invitation	reaction	reference	resistance	return

> *This was my first real <u>introduction to</u> Africa.*

● nouns followed by 'for'

admiration	desire	dislike	need	reason	respect
responsibility	search	substitute	taste	thirst	

> *Their <u>need for</u> money is growing fast.*

● nouns followed by 'on'

agreement	attack	comment	effect	tax

> *She had a dreadful <u>effect on</u> me.*

● nouns followed by 'with' or 'between'

connection	contact	link	relationship

> *His illness had some <u>connection with</u> his diet.*

● nouns followed by 'in'

decrease	difficulty	fall	increase	rise

> *They demanded a large <u>increase in</u> wages.*

Verb + preposition

Main points

Some verbs do not take an object and are normally followed by a preposition.

Some verbs take an object followed by a particular preposition.

Some verbs can take either an object or a preposition.

---

1 Many verbs that are used without an object are normally followed by a prepositional phrase. Some verbs take a particular preposition:

belong to	consist of	hint at	hope for	insist on	lead to
listen to	pay for	qualify for	refer to	relate to	sympathize with

The land <u>belongs to</u> a rich family.
She then <u>referred to</u> the Minister's report.

2 With other verbs that are used without an object, the choice of a different preposition may alter the meaning of the clause.

agree on/with	appeal for/to	apologize for/to	conform to/with
result from/in	suffer from/with		

They <u>agreed on</u> a plan of action.
You <u>agreed with</u> me that we should buy a car.
His failure <u>resulted from</u> lack of attention to details.
The match <u>resulted in</u> a draw.

3 With verbs that are used without an object, different prepositions are used to introduce different types of information.

• 'about' indicates the subject matter

care	complain	dream	explain	hear	know	speak	talk
think	write						

We will always <u>care about</u> freedom.
Tonight I'm going to <u>talk about</u> engines.

• 'at' indicates direction

glance	glare	grin	laugh	look	shout	smile	stare

I don't know why he was <u>laughing at</u> that joke.
'Hey!' she <u>shouted at</u> him.

Verb + preposition

- 'for' indicates purpose or reason

apologize	apply	ask	look	wait

> *He wanted to <u>apologize for</u> being late.*
> *I'm going to <u>wait for</u> the next bus.*

- 'into' indicates the object involved in a collision

bump	crash	drive	run

> *His car <u>crashed into</u> the wall.*
> *She <u>drove into</u> the back of a lorry.*

- 'of' indicates facts or information

hear	know	speak	talk	think

> *I've <u>heard of</u> him but I don't know who he is.*
> *Do you <u>know of</u> the new plans for the sports centre?*

- 'on' indicates confidence or certainty

count	depend	plan	rely

> *You can <u>count on</u> me.*
> *You can <u>rely on</u> him to be polite.*

- 'to' indicates the listener or reader

complain	explain	listen	say	speak	talk	write

> *They <u>complained to</u> me about the noise.*
> *Mary turned her head to <u>speak to</u> him.*

- 'with' indicates someone whose opinion is the same or different

agree	argue	disagree	side

> *Do you <u>agree with</u> me about this?*
> *The daughters <u>sided with</u> their mothers.*

4 Some verbs have an object, but are also followed by a preposition.

> *The police <u>accused</u> him <u>of</u> murder.*
> *They <u>borrowed</u> some money <u>from</u> the bank.*

Some verbs can take either an object or a prepositional phrase with no change in meaning.

> *He had to fight <u>them</u>.*   *He was fighting <u>against history</u>.*

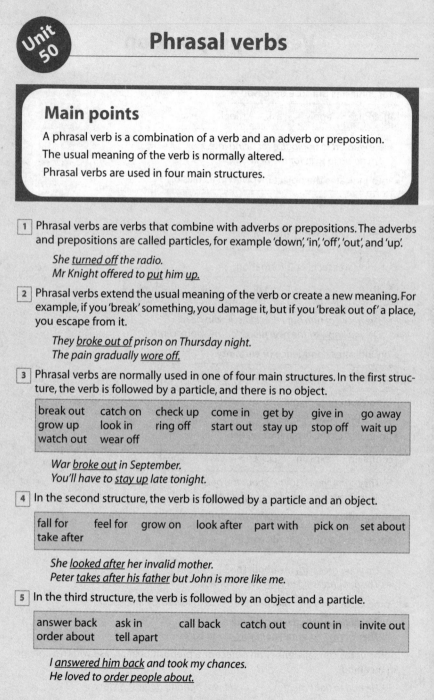

Phrasal verbs

Main points

A phrasal verb is a combination of a verb and an adverb or preposition.

The usual meaning of the verb is normally altered.

Phrasal verbs are used in four main structures.

1 Phrasal verbs are verbs that combine with adverbs or prepositions. The adverbs and prepositions are called particles, for example 'down', 'in', 'off', 'out', and 'up'.

> She <u>turned off</u> the radio.
> Mr Knight offered to <u>put</u> him <u>up.</u>

2 Phrasal verbs extend the usual meaning of the verb or create a new meaning. For example, if you 'break' something, you damage it, but if you 'break out of' a place, you escape from it.

> They <u>broke out of</u> prison on Thursday night.
> The pain gradually <u>wore off.</u>

3 Phrasal verbs are normally used in one of four main structures. In the first structure, the verb is followed by a particle, and there is no object.

break out	catch on	check up	come in	get by	give in	go away
grow up	look in	ring off	start out	stay up	stop off	wait up
watch out	wear off					

> War <u>broke out</u> in September.
> You'll have to <u>stay up</u> late tonight.

4 In the second structure, the verb is followed by a particle and an object.

| fall for | feel for | grow on | look after | part with | pick on | set about |
| take after | | | | | | |

> She <u>looked after</u> her invalid mother.
> Peter <u>takes after his father</u> but John is more like me.

5 In the third structure, the verb is followed by an object and a particle.

| answer back | ask in | call back | catch out | count in | invite out |
| order about | tell apart | | | | |

> I <u>answered him back</u> and took my chances.
> He loved to <u>order people about.</u>

Phrasal verbs

6 Some phrasal verbs can be used in both the second structure and the third structure: verb followed by a particle and an object, or verb followed by an object and a particle.

add on	bring up	call up	fold up	hand over	
knock over	point out	pull down	put away	put up	
rub out	sort out	take up	tear up	throw away	try out

> *It took ages to <u>clean up the mess.</u>*
> *It took ages to <u>clean the mess up.</u>*
> *There was such a mess. It took ages to <u>clean it up.</u>*

⊖ WARNING: If the object is a pronoun, it must go in front of the particle. You cannot say 'He cleaned up it'.

7 In the fourth structure, the verb is followed by a particle and a preposition with an object.

break out of	catch up with	come down with	get on with
go down with	keep on at	look forward to	make off with
miss out on	play around with	put up with	run away with
stick up for	talk down to	walk out on	

> *You go on ahead. I'll <u>catch up with</u> you later.*
> *Children have to learn to <u>stick up for</u> themselves.*

8 A very few verbs are used in the structure: verb followed by an object, a particle, and a preposition with its object.

do out of	let in for	put down to	put up to
take out on	talk out of		

> *I'll <u>take you up on</u> that generous invitation.*
> *Kroop tried to <u>talk her out of</u> it.*

Verbs and objects

Main points

Intransitive verbs do not have an object.

Transitive verbs have an object.

Some verbs can be used with or without an object, depending on the situation or their meaning.

1 Many verbs do not normally have an object. They are called 'intransitive' verbs. They often refer to:

existence:	appear die disappear happen live remain
the human body:	ache bleed blush faint shiver smile
human noises:	cough cry laugh scream snore speak yawn
light, smell, vibration:	glow shine sparkle stink throb vibrate
position, movement:	arrive come depart fall flow go kneel run sit sleep stand swim wait walk work

An awful thing <u>has happened.</u>
The girl <u>screamed.</u>
I <u>waited.</u>

Note that intransitive verbs cannot be used in the passive.

2 Many verbs normally have an object. These verbs are called 'transitive' verbs. They are often connected with:

physical objects:	build buy carry catch cover cut destroy hit own remove sell use waste wear
senses:	feel hear see smell taste touch
feelings:	admire enjoy fear frighten hate like love need prefer surprise trust want
facts, ideas:	accept believe correct discuss expect express forget include know mean remember report
people:	address blame comfort contact convince defy kill persuade please tease thank warn

He <u>hit the ball</u> really hard.   *Did you <u>see the rainbow?</u>*
They both <u>enjoyed the film.</u>   *She <u>reported the accident</u> to the police.*
Don't <u>blame me.</u>

Verbs and objects

Note that transitive verbs can be used in the passive.

They <u>were blamed</u> for everything.

⊖ WARNING: 'Have' is a transitive verb, but cannot be used in the passive. You can say 'I have a car' but not 'A car is had by me'.

3 Often, the people you are talking to know what the object is because of the situation, or because it has already been mentioned. In this case you can omit the object, even though the verb is transitive.

accept	answer	change	choose	clean	cook
draw	drive	eat	explain	forget	help
iron	know	learn	leave	paint	park
phone	read	remember	ride	sing	steal
study	type	understand	wash	watch	write

I don't own a car. I can't <u>drive.</u>
You don't <u>smoke,</u> do you?
I asked a question and George <u>answered.</u>
Both dresses are beautiful. It's difficult to <u>choose.</u>

4 Many verbs have more than one meaning, and are transitive in one meaning and intransitive in another meaning. For example, the verb 'run' is intransitive when you use it to mean 'move quickly' but transitive when you use it to mean 'manage or operate'.

call	fit	lose	manage	miss	move
play	run	show	spread		

The hare <u>runs</u> at enormous speed.
She <u>runs a hotel.</u>
She <u>moved</u> gracefully.
The whole incident <u>had moved her</u> profoundly.

5 A few verbs are normally intransitive, but can be used with an object that is closely related to the verb.

dance (a dance)	die (a death)	dream (a dream)	laugh (a laugh)
live (a life)	sigh (a sigh)	smile (a smile)	

Steve <u>smiled his thin, cruel smile.</u>
He appears to have <u>lived the life of any other rich gentleman.</u>
I once <u>dreamed a very nice dream.</u>

Verbs with two objects

Main points

Some verbs have two objects, a direct object and an indirect object.

The indirect object can be used without a preposition, or after 'to' or 'for'.

1 Some verbs have two objects after them, a direct object and an indirect object. For example, in the sentence 'I gave John the book', 'the book' is the direct object. 'John' is the indirect object. Verbs that have two objects are sometimes called 'ditransitive' verbs or 'double-transitive' verbs.

> His uncle had <u>given</u> him books on India.
> She <u>sends</u> you her love.
> I <u>passed</u> him the cup.

2 When the indirect object is a pronoun, or another short noun group such as a noun with 'the', you put the indirect object in front of the direct object.

> Dad gave <u>me</u> a car.
> You promised <u>the lad</u> a job.
> He had lent <u>my cousin</u> the money.
> She bought <u>Dave and me</u> an ice cream.

3 You can also use the prepositions 'to' and 'for' to introduce the indirect object. If you do this, you put the preposition and indirect object after the direct object.

> He handed his room key <u>to the receptionist.</u>
> Bill saved a piece of cake <u>for the children.</u>

When the indirect object consists of several words, you normally use a preposition to introduce it.

> She taught physics and chemistry <u>to pupils at the local school.</u>
> I made that lamp <u>for a seventy-year-old woman.</u>

You often use a preposition when you want to emphasize the indirect object.

> Did you really buy that <u>for me?</u>

4 With some verbs you can only use 'for', not 'to', to introduce the indirect object.

| book | buy | cook | cut | find | keep |
| make | paint | pour | prepare | save | win |

Verbs with two objects

They booked a place <u>for me.</u>
He had found some old clothes <u>for the beggar.</u>
They bought a present <u>for the teacher.</u>
She painted a picture <u>for her father.</u>

5 With some verbs you normally use 'to' to introduce the indirect object.

give	lend	offer	pass	pay	post	promise	read
sell	send	show	teach	tell			

I had lent my bicycle <u>to a friend.</u>
Ralph passed a message <u>to Jack.</u>
They say they posted the letter <u>to me</u> last week.
He sold it <u>to me.</u>

Note that you can use 'for' with these verbs, but it has a different meaning. 'For' indicates that one person does something on behalf of another person, so that the other person does not have to do it.

His mother paid the bill <u>for him.</u>
If you're going out, can you post this <u>for me,</u> please?

Reflexive verbs

Main points

Transitive verbs are used with a reflexive pronoun to indicate that the object is the same as the subject, for example: 'I hurt myself'.

Some verbs which do not normally have a person as the object can have reflexive pronouns as the object.

---

1 You use a reflexive pronoun after a transitive verb to indicate that the object is the same as the subject.

> He blamed <u>himself</u> for his friend's death.
> I taught <u>myself</u> French.

➤ See Unit 20 for more information on reflexive pronouns.

2 In theory, most transitive verbs can be used with a reflexive pronoun. However, you often use reflexive pronouns with the following verbs.

| amuse | blame | cut | dry | help | hurt | introduce |
| kill | prepare | repeat | restrict | satisfy | teach | |

> Sam <u>amused himself</u> by throwing branches into the fire.
> 'Can I borrow a pencil?' – 'Yes, <u>help yourself.</u>'
> <u>Prepare yourself</u> for a shock.
> He <u>introduced himself</u> to me.

3 Verbs like 'dress', 'shave', and 'wash', which describe actions that people do to themselves, do not usually take reflexive pronouns in English, although they do in some other languages. With these verbs, reflexive pronouns are only used for emphasis.

> I usually <u>shave</u> before breakfast.
> He prefers to <u>shave himself,</u> even with that broken arm.
> She <u>washed</u> very quickly and rushed downstairs.
> Children were encouraged to <u>wash themselves.</u>

4 'Behave' does not normally take an object at all, but can take a reflexive pronoun as object.

> If they don't <u>behave,</u> send them to bed.
> He is old enough to <u>behave himself.</u>

Reflexive verbs

5 Some verbs do not normally have a person as object, because they describe actions that you do not do to other people. However, these verbs can have reflexive pronouns as object, because you can do these actions to yourself.

apply	compose	distance	enjoy	excel	exert	express	strain

I really <u>enjoyed</u> the party.
Just go out there and <u>enjoy yourself.</u>
She <u>expressed</u> surprise at the news.
Professor Dale <u>expressed himself</u> very forcibly.

6 When 'busy' and 'content' are used as verbs, they always take a reflexive pronoun as their direct object. They are therefore true 'reflexive verbs'.

He had <u>busied himself</u> in the laboratory.
I had to <u>content myself</u> with watching the little moving lights.

Reciprocal verbs

Main points

Some verbs describe two people or two groups of people doing the same thing to each other, for example: 'We met', 'I met you', 'We met each other'.

You use 'each other' or 'one another' for emphasis.

With some verbs, you use 'each other' or 'one another' after 'with'.

---

1 Some verbs refer to actions that involve two people or two groups of people doing the same thing to each other. These verbs are sometimes called 'reciprocal' verbs.

> *We met in Delhi.*
> *Jane and Sarah told me that they met you.*
> *They met each other for the first time last week.*

2 The two people or groups of people involved in the action are often mentioned as the plural subject of the verb, and the verb does not have an object. For example, 'John and Mary argued' means that John argued with Mary and Mary argued with John.

| argue | clash | coincide | combine | compete |
| fight | kiss | marry | match | meet |

> *The pair of you have argued about that for years.*
> *We competed furiously.*
> *Their children are always fighting.*
> *They kissed.*

3 When you want to emphasize that both people or groups of people are equally involved, you can use the pronouns 'each other' or 'one another' as the object of the verb. Verbs that refer to actions in which there is physical contact between people are often used with 'each other' or 'one another'.

| cuddle | embrace | fight | hug | kiss | touch |

> *We embraced each other.*
> *They fought one another desperately for it.*
> *They kissed each other in greeting.*
> *It was the first time they had touched one another.*

Reciprocal verbs

4 Some verbs do not take an object, so you use a preposition before 'each other' or 'one another'.

> *They <u>parted from each other</u> after only two weeks.*
> *We <u>talk to one another</u> as often as possible.*

5 With some verbs you have a choice of preposition before 'each other' or 'one another'. For example, you can 'fight with' one another or 'fight against' one another.

with/against:	compete fight
with/from:	part
with/to:	correspond relate talk

> *Many countries are <u>competing with each other</u>.*
> *Did you <u>compete against each other</u> in yesterday's race?*
> *Stephen and I <u>parted with one another</u> on good terms.*
> *They <u>parted from one another</u> quite suddenly.*

6 With some verbs, you can only use 'with' before 'each other' or 'one another'.

Note that most of these verbs refer to people talking or working together.

| agree | argue | clash | collide |
| communicate | co-operate | disagree | quarrel |

> *We do <u>agree with each other</u> sometimes.*
> *Have they <u>communicated with each other</u> since then?*
> *The two lorries <u>collided with one another</u> on the motorway.*

7 If you want to focus on one of the people involved, you make them the subject of the verb and make the other person the object.

> *<u>She</u> married <u>a young engineer</u>.*
> *<u>You</u> could meet <u>me</u> at the restaurant.*

If the verb cannot take an object, you mention the other person after a preposition.

> *Youths clashed <u>with police</u> in Belfast.*
> *She was always quarrelling <u>with him</u>.*

Ergative verbs

Main points

Ergative verbs are both transitive and intransitive. The object of the transitive use is the subject of the intransitive use, for example: 'I opened the door'; 'The door opened'.

A few verbs are only ergative with particular nouns.

A few of these verbs need an adverbial when they are used without an object.

1 Some verbs can be used as transitive verbs to focus on the person who performs an action, and as intransitive verbs to focus on the thing affected by the action.

> When <u>I opened the door,</u> there was Laverne.
> Suddenly <u>the door opened.</u>

Note that the object of the transitive verb, in this case 'the door', is the subject of the intransitive verb. Verbs like these are called 'ergative' verbs.

2 Ergative verbs often refer to:

● changes

begin	break	change	crack	dry	end	finish
grow	improve	increase	slow	start	stop	tear

> I <u>broke</u> the glass.
> The glass <u>broke</u> all over the floor.
> The driver <u>stopped</u> the car.
> A big car <u>stopped.</u>

● cooking

bake	boil	cook	defrost	fry	melt	roast	simmer

> I'<u>ve boiled</u> an egg.
> The porridge <u>is boiling.</u>
> I'<u>m cooking</u> spaghetti.
> The rice <u>is cooking.</u>

● position or movement

balance	close	drop	move	open
rest	rock	shake	stand	turn

Ergative verbs

She <u>rested</u> her head on his shoulder.
Her head <u>rested</u> on the table.
An explosion <u>shook</u> the hotel.
The whole room <u>shook.</u>

● vehicles

back	crash	drive	fly	reverse	run	sail

He <u>had crashed</u> the car twice.
Her car <u>crashed</u> into a tree.
She <u>sailed</u> her yacht round the world.
The ship <u>sailed</u> on Monday.

3 Some verbs can be used in these two ways only with a small set of nouns. For example, you can say 'He fired a gun' or 'The gun fired'. You can do the same with other words referring to types of gun, 'cannon', 'pistol', or 'rifle'. However, although you can say 'He fired a bullet', you cannot say 'The bullet fired'.

catch:	belt, cloth, clothing, dress, shirt, trousers
fire:	cannon, gun, pistol, rifle
play:	guitar, music, piano, violin
ring:	alarm, bell
show:	anger, disappointment, emotions, fear, joy
sound:	alarm, bell, horn

I <u>caught</u> my dress on the fence.
My tights <u>caught</u> on a nail.
A car <u>was sounding</u> its horn.
A horn <u>sounded</u> in the night.

4 A few verbs can be used in both ways, but need an adverbial when they are used without an object.

clean	freeze	handle	mark	polish	sell	stain	wash

He <u>sells</u> books.
This book <u>is selling well.</u>
She <u>had handled</u> a machine gun.
This car <u>handles very nicely.</u>

Common verb + noun patterns

Main points

Examples are: 'have a bath'; 'give a shout'; 'make promises'; 'take care'.

Common verbs are often used with nouns to describe actions.

You use 'have' with nouns referring to eating, drinking, talking, and washing.

You use 'give' with nouns referring to noises, hitting, and talking.

You use 'make' with nouns referring to talking, plans, and travelling.

---

1 When you want to talk about actions, you often use common verbs with nouns as their object. The nouns describe the action. For example, if you say 'I had a shower', the noun tells you what the action was. The common verbs have very little meaning.

> I _had a nice rest._   She _made a remark_ about the weather.

The nouns often have related verbs that do not take an object.

> Helen went upstairs to _rest._   I _remarked_ that it would be better if I came.

2 Different verbs are used with different nouns.

You use 'have' with nouns referring to:

meals:	breakfast dinner drink lunch meal taste tea
talking:	chat conversation discussion talk
washing:	bath shower wash
relaxation:	break holiday rest
disagreement:	argument fight quarrel trouble

> We usually _have lunch_ at one o'clock.
> He was _having his first holiday_ for five years.

3 You use 'give' with nouns referring to:

human noises:	cry gasp giggle groan laugh scream shout sigh whistle yell
facial expressions:	grin smile
hitting:	kick punch push slap
talking:	advice answer example information interview lecture news report speech talk warning

> Mr Sutton _gave a shout_ of triumph.
> She _gave a long lecture_ about Roosevelt.

112

Common verb + noun patterns

4 You use 'make' with nouns referring to:

talking and sounds:	comment enquiry noise point promise remark sound speech suggestion
plans:	arrangement choice decision plan
travelling:	journey tour trip visit

> He _made the shortest speech_ I've ever heard.
> In 1978 he _made his first visit_ to Australia.

5 You use 'take' with these nouns:

care	chance	charge	decision	interest	offence
photograph	responsibility	risk	time	trouble	turns

> He was _taking no chances._
> She was prepared to _take great risks._

6 You use 'go' and 'come' with '-ing' nouns referring to sports and outdoor activities.

> She _goes climbing_ in her holidays.
> Every morning, he _goes jogging_ with Tommy.

Note that you can also use 'go for' and 'come for' with 'a jog', 'a run', 'a swim', 'a walk'.

> They _went for a run_ before breakfast.

7 You use 'do' with '-ing' nouns referring to jobs connected with the home, and nouns referring generally to work.

> He wants to _do the cooking._
> He _does all the shopping_ and I _do the washing._
> The man who _did the job_ had ten years' training.
> He has to get up early and _do a hard day's work._

'Do' is often used instead of more specific verbs. For example, you can say 'Have you done your teeth?' instead of 'Have you brushed your teeth?'

> Do I need to _do my hair?_

Auxiliary verbs

Main points

The auxiliaries 'be', 'have', and 'do' are used in forming tenses, negatives, and questions.

The auxiliary 'be' is used in forming the continuous tenses and the passive.

The auxiliary 'have' is used in forming the perfect tenses.

The auxiliary 'do' is used in making negative and question forms from sentences that have a verb in a simple tense.

1 The auxiliary verbs are 'be', 'have', and 'do'. They are used with a main verb to form tenses, negatives, and questions.

> He _is_ planning to get married soon.
> I _haven't_ seen Peter since last night.
> Which doctor _do_ you want to see?

2 'Be' as an auxiliary is used:

- with the '-ing' form of the main verb to form continuous tenses

> He _is_ living in Germany.
> They _were_ going to phone you.

- with the past participle of the main verb to form the passive

> These cars _are_ made in Japan.
> The walls of her flat _were_ covered with posters.

3 You use 'have' as an auxiliary with the past participle to form the perfect tenses.

> I _have_ changed my mind.
> I wish you _had_ met Guy.

The present perfect continuous, the past perfect continuous, and the perfect tenses in the passive, are formed using both 'have' and 'be'.

> He _has been_ working very hard recently.
> She did not know how long she _had been_ lying there.
> The guest-room window _has been_ mended.
> They _had been_ taught by a young teacher.

Auxiliary verbs

4 'Be' and 'have' are also used as auxiliaries in negative sentences and questions in continuous and perfect tenses, and in the passive.

He __isn't__ going.
__Hasn't__ she seen it yet?
__Was__ it written in English?

You use 'do' as an auxiliary to make negative and question forms from sentences that have a verb in the present simple or past simple.

He __doesn't__ think he can come to the party.
__Do__ you like her new haircut?
She __didn't__ buy the house.
__Didn't__ he get the job?

Note that you can use 'do' as a main verb with the auxiliary 'do'.

He __didn't do__ his homework.
__Do__ they __do__ the work themselves?

You can also use the auxiliary 'do' with 'have' as a main verb.

He __doesn't have__ any money.
__Does__ anyone __have__ a question?

You only use 'do' in affirmative sentences for emphasis or contrast.

I __do__ feel sorry for Roger.

● WARNING: You never use the auxiliary 'do' with 'be' except in the imperative.

__Don't be__ stupid!
__Do be__ a good boy and sit still.

5 Some grammars include modals among the auxiliary verbs. When there is a modal in the verb group, it is always the first word in the verb group, and comes before the auxiliaries 'be' and 'have'.

She __might be__ going to Switzerland for Christmas.
I __would have__ liked to have seen her.

Note that you never use the auxiliary 'do' with a modal.

➤ See Units 79-91 for more information on modals.

The present tenses

Main points

There are four present tenses – present simple ('I walk'), present continuous ('I am walking'), present perfect ('I have walked'), and present perfect continuous ('I have been walking').

All the present tenses are used to refer to a time which includes the present.

Present tenses can also be used for predictions made in the present about future events.

1 | There are four tenses which begin with a verb in the present tense. They are the present simple, the present continuous, the present perfect, and the present perfect continuous. These are the present tenses.

2 | The present simple and the present continuous are used with reference to present time. If you are talking about the general present, or about a regular or habitual action, you use the present simple.

George <u>lives</u> in Birmingham.
They often <u>phone</u> my mother in London.

If you are talking about something in the present situation, you use the present continuous.

He'<u>s playing</u> tennis at the University.
I'<u>m cooking</u> the dinner.

The present continuous is often used to refer to a temporary situation.

She'<u>s living</u> in a flat at present.

3 | You use the present perfect or the present perfect continuous when you are concerned with the present effects of something which happened at a time in the past, or which started in the past but is still continuing.

<u>Have</u> you <u>seen</u> the film at the Odeon?
We'<u>ve been waiting</u> here since before two o'clock.

4 | If you are talking about something which is scheduled or timetabled to happen in the future, you can use the present simple tense.

The next train <u>leaves</u> at two fifteen in the morning.
It'<u>s</u> Tuesday tomorrow.

The present tenses

5 If you are talking about something which has been arranged for the future, you can use the present continuous. When you use the present continuous like this, there is nearly always a time adverbial like 'tomorrow', 'next week', or 'later' in the clause.

> We're going on holiday with my parents this year.
> The Browns are having a party next week.

6 It is only in the main clauses that the choice of tense can be related to a particular time. In subordinate clauses, for example in 'if'– clauses, time clauses, and defining relative clauses, present tenses often refer to a future time in relation to the time in the main clause.

> You can go at five if you have finished.
> Let's have a drink before we start.
> We'll save some food for anyone who arrives late.

7 The present simple tense normally has no auxiliary verb, but questions and negative sentences are formed with the auxiliary 'do'.

> Do you live round here?
> Does your husband do most of the cooking?
> They don't often phone during the week.
> She doesn't like being late if she can help it.

The past tenses

Main points

There are four past tenses – past simple ('I walked'), past continuous ('I was walking'), past perfect ('I had walked'), and past perfect continuous ('I had been walking').

All the past tenses are used to refer to past time.

The past tenses are often used as polite forms.

The past tenses have special meanings in conditional clauses and when referring to imaginary situations.

1 There are four tenses which begin with a verb in the past tense. They are the past simple, the past continuous, the past perfect, and the past perfect continuous. These are the past tenses. They are used to refer to past time, and also to refer to imaginary situations, and to express politeness.

2 The past simple and the past continuous are used with reference to past time. You use the past simple for events which happened in the past.

> I _woke_ up early and _got_ out of bed.

If you are talking about the general past, or about regular or habitual actions in the past, you also use the past simple.

> She _lived_ just outside London.
> We often _saw_ his dog sitting outside his house.

If you are talking about something which continued to happen before and after a particular time in the past, you use the past continuous.

> They _were sitting_ in the kitchen, when they heard the explosion.
> Jack arrived while the children _were having_ their bath.

The past continuous is often used to refer to a temporary situation.

> He _was working_ at home at the time.
> Bill _was using_ my office until I came back from America.

3 You use the past perfect and past perfect continuous tenses when you are talking about the past and you are concerned with something which happened at an earlier time, or which had started at an earlier time but was still continuing.

> I _had heard_ it was a good film so we decided to go and see it.
> It was getting late. I _had been waiting_ there since two o'clock.

The past tenses

4 You sometimes use a past tense rather than a present tense when you want to be more polite. For example, in the following pairs of sentences, the second one is more polite.

> <u>Do</u> you <u>want</u> to see me now?
> <u>Did</u> you <u>want</u> to see me now?
> I <u>wonder</u> if you can help me.
> I <u>was wondering</u> if you could help me.

5 The past tenses have special meanings in conditional clauses and when referring to hypothetical and imaginary situations, for example after 'I wish' or 'What if…?'. You use the past simple and past continuous for something that you think is unlikely to happen.

> If they <u>saw</u> the mess, they would be very angry.
> We would tell you if we <u>were selling</u> the house.

You use the past perfect and past perfect continuous when you are talking about something which could have happened in the past, but which did not actually happen.

> If I <u>had known</u> that you were coming, I would have told Jim.
> They wouldn't have gone to bed if they <u>had been expecting</u> you to arrive.

The continuous tenses

Main points

Continuous tenses describe actions which continue to happen before and after a particular time.

Continuous tenses can also indicate duration and change.

1 You use a continuous tense to indicate that an action continues to happen before and after a particular time, without stopping. You use the present continuous for actions which continue to happen before and after the moment of speaking.

> I'm looking at the photographs my brother sent me.
> They're having a meeting.

2 When you are talking about two actions in the present tense, you use the present continuous for an action that continues to happen before and after another action that interrupts it. You use the present simple for the other action.

> The phone always rings when I'm having a bath.
> Friends always talk to me when I'm trying to study.

3 When you are talking about the past, you use the past continuous for actions that continued to happen before and after another action, or before and after a particular time. This is often called the 'interrupted past'. You use the past simple for the other action.

> He was watching television when the doorbell rang.
> It was 6 o'clock. The train was nearing London.

⊖ WARNING: If two things happened one after another, you use two verbs in the past simple tense.

> As soon as he saw me, he waved.

4 You can use continuous forms with modals in all their usual meanings.

➤ See Units 79 to 91 for more information on modals.

> What could he be thinking of?
> They might be telling lies.

5 You use continuous tenses to express duration, when you want to emphasize how long something has been happening or will happen for.

> We _had been living_ in Athens for five years.
> They'_ll be staying_ with us for a couple of weeks.
> He _has been building up_ the business all his life.
> By 1992, he _will have been working_ for ten years.

Note that you do not have to use continuous tenses for duration.

> We _had lived_ in Africa for five years.
> He _worked_ for us for ten years.

6 You use continuous tenses to describe a state or situation that is temporary.

> I'_m living_ in London at the moment.
> He'_ll be working_ nights next week.
> She'_s spending_ the summer in Europe.

7 You use continuous tenses to show that something is changing, developing, or progressing.

> Her English _was improving._
> The children _are growing up_ quickly.
> The video industry _has been developing_ rapidly.

8 As a general rule, verbs which refer to actions that require a deliberate effort can be used in continuous tenses, verbs which refer to actions that do not require a deliberate effort are not used in continuous tenses.

> I _think_ it's going to rain. ('think' = 'believe'. Believing does not require deliberate effort)
> Please be quiet. I'_m thinking._ ('think' = 'try to solve a problem'. Trying to solve a problem does require deliberate effort)

However, many verbs are not normally used in the continuous tenses. These include verbs that refer to thinking, liking and disliking, appearance, possession, and perception.

▶ See Unit 62 for lists of these verbs.

Unit 61

The perfect tenses

Main points

You use the present perfect ('I have walked') to relate the past to the present.

You use the past perfect ('I had walked') to talk about a situation that occurred before a particular time in the past.

---

1 You use the present perfect tense when you are concerned with the present effects of something which happened at an indefinite time in the past.

> I'm afraid I've forgotten my book.
> Have you heard from Jill recently?

Sometimes, the present effects are important because they are very recent.

> Karen has just passed her exams.

You also use the present perfect when you are thinking of a time which started in the past and is still continuing.

> Have you really lived here for ten years?
> He has worked here since 1987.

You also use the present perfect in time clauses, when you are talking about something which will be done at some time in the future.

> Tell me when you have finished.
> I'll write to you as soon as I have heard from Jenny.

2 When you want to emphasize the fact that a recent event continued to happen for some time, you use the present perfect continuous.

> She's been crying.
> I've been working hard all day.

3 You use the past perfect tense when you are looking back from a point in past time, and you are concerned with the effects of something which happened at an earlier time in the past.

> I apologized because I had forgotten my book.
> He felt much happier once he had found a new job.
> They would have come if we had invited them.

You also use the past perfect when you are thinking of a time which had started earlier in the past but was still continuing.

> I was about twenty. I had been studying French for a couple of years.
> He hated games and had always managed to avoid children's parties.

122

The perfect tenses

4 You use the future perfect tense when you are looking back from a point in the future and you are talking about something which will have happened at a time between now and that future point.

> *In another two years, you <u>will have left</u> school.*
> *Take these tablets, and in twenty-four hours the pain <u>will have gone.</u>*

You also use the future perfect when you are looking back from the present and guessing that an action will be finished.

> *I'm sure they <u>will have arrived</u> home by now.*
> *It's too late to ring Don. He <u>will have left</u> the house by now.*

5 You can also use other modals with 'have', when you are looking back from a point in time at something which you think may have happened at an earlier time.

> *I <u>might have finished</u> work by then.*
> *He <u>should have arrived</u> in Paris by the time we phone.*

➤ For more information on modals with 'have', see Units 79 to 91.

Talking about the present

Main points

For the general present, general truths, and habitual actions, you use the present simple ('I walk').

For something which is happening now, or for temporary situations, you use the present continuous ('I am walking').

1. If you are talking about the present in general, you normally use the present simple tense. You use the present simple for talking about the general present including the present moment.

   My dad <u>works</u> in Saudi Arabia.
   He <u>lives</u> in the French Alps near the Swiss border.

2. If you are talking about general truths, you use the present simple.

   Water <u>boils</u> at 100 degrees centigrade.
   Love <u>makes</u> the world go round.
   The bus <u>takes</u> longer than the train.

3. If you are talking about regular or habitual actions, you use the present simple.

   <u>Do</u> you <u>eat</u> meat?
   I <u>get</u> up early and <u>eat</u> my breakfast in bed.
   I <u>pay</u> the milkman on Fridays.

4. If you are talking about something which is regarded as temporary, you use the present continuous.

   Do you know if she'<u>s</u> still <u>playing</u> tennis these days?
   I'<u>m working</u> as a British Council officer.

5. If you are talking about something which is happening now, you normally use the present continuous tense.

   We'<u>re having</u> a meeting. Come and join in.
   Wait a moment. I'<u>m listening</u> to the news.

6. There are a number of verbs which are used in the present simple tense even when you are talking about the present moment. These verbs are not normally used in the present continuous or the other continuous tenses.

Talking about the present

These verbs usually refer to:

thinking:	believe forget imagine know realize recognize suppose think understand want wish
liking and disliking:	admire dislike hate like love prefer
appearance:	appear look like resemble seem
possession:	belong to contain have include own possess
perception:	hear see smell taste
being:	be consist of exist

> I *believe* he was not to blame.
> She *hates* going to parties.
> Our neighbours *have* two cars.

Note that you normally use verbs of perception with the modal 'can', rather than using the present simple tense.

> I *can smell* gas.

Some other common verbs are not normally used in the present continuous or the other continuous tenses.

concern	deserve	fit	interest	involve	matter
mean	satisfy	surprise			

> What *do* you *mean*?

⊖ WARNING: Some of the verbs listed above can be used in continuous tenses in other meanings. For example, 'have' referring to possession is not used in continuous tenses. You do not say 'I am having a car'. But note the following examples.

> We*'re having* a party tomorrow.
> He*'s having* problems with his car.
> She*'s having* a shower.

Talking about the past

Main points

For actions, situations, or regular events in the past, you use the past simple ('I walked'). For regular events in the past, you can also use 'would' or 'used to'.

For events that happened before and after a time in the past, and for temporary situations, you use the past continuous ('I was walking').

For present effects of past situations, you use the present perfect ('I have walked'), and for past effects of earlier events you use the past perfect ('I had walked').

For future in the past, you use 'would', 'was/were going to', or the past continuous ('I was walking').

1 When you want to talk about an event that occurred at a particular time in the past, you use the past simple.

   The Prime Minister <u>flew</u> into New York yesterday.
   The new term <u>started</u> last week.

You also use the past simple to talk about a situation that existed over a period of time in the past.

   We <u>spent</u> most of our time at home last winter.
   They <u>earned</u> their money quickly that year.

2 When you want to talk about something which took place regularly in the past, you use the past simple.

   They <u>went</u> for picnics most weekends.
   We usually <u>spent</u> the winter at Aunt Meg's house.

   ⊖ WARNING: The past simple always refers to a time in the past. A time reference is necessary to say what time in the past you are referring to. The time reference can be established in an earlier sentence or by another speaker, but it must be established.

When you want to talk about something which occurred regularly in the past, you can use 'would' or 'used to' instead of the past simple.

   We <u>would</u> normally <u>spend</u> the winter in Miami.
   People <u>used to believe</u> that the world was flat.

   ⊖ WARNING: You do not normally use 'would' with this meaning with verbs which are not used in the continuous tenses.

   ▶ For a list of these verbs, see Unit 62.

126

Talking about the past

3 When you want to talk about something which continued to happen before and after a given time in the past, you use the past continuous.

> I hurt myself when I <u>was mending</u> my bike.
> It was midnight. She <u>was driving</u> home.

You also use the past continuous to talk about a temporary state of affairs in the past.

> Our team <u>were losing</u> 2-1 at the time.
> We <u>were staying</u> with friends in Italy.

▶ For more information on continuous tenses, see Unit 60.

4 When you are concerned with the present effects or future effects of something which happened at an indefinite time in the past, you use the present perfect.

> I'm afraid I<u>'ve forgotten</u> my book, so I don't know.
> <u>Have</u> you <u>heard</u> from Jill recently? How is she?

You also use the present perfect when you are thinking of a time which started in the past and still continues.

> <u>Have</u> you ever <u>stolen</u> anything? (= at any time up to the present)
> He <u>has been</u> here since six o'clock. (= and he is still here)

5 When you are looking back from a point in past time, and you are concerned with the effects of something which happened at an earlier time in the past, you use the past perfect.

> I apologized because I <u>had left</u> my wallet at home.
> They would have come if we <u>had invited</u> them.

6 When you want to talk about the future from a point of view in past time, you can use 'would', 'was / were going to', or the past continuous.

> He thought to himself how wonderful it <u>would taste.</u>
> Her daughter <u>was going to</u> do the cooking.
> Mike <u>was taking</u> his test the week after.

'Will' and 'going to'

Main points

When you are making predictions about the future or talking about future intentions, you can use either 'will' ('I will walk') or 'going to' ('I am going to walk').

For promises and offers relating to the future, you use 'will' ('I will walk').

For future events based on arrangements, you use the future continuous ('I will be walking').

For events that will happen before a time in the future, you use the future perfect ('I will have walked').

1 You cannot talk about the future with as much certainty as you can about the present or the past. You are usually talking about what you think might happen or what you intend to happen. This is why you often use modals. Although most modals can be used with future reference, you most often use the modal 'will' to talk about the future.

> Nancy <u>will arrange</u> it.
> When <u>will</u> I <u>see</u> them?

2 When you are making predictions about the future that are based on general beliefs, opinions, or attitudes, you use 'will'.

> The weather tomorrow <u>will be</u> warm and sunny.
> I'm sure you <u>will enjoy</u> your visit to the zoo.

This use of 'will' is common in sentences with conditional clauses.

> You'<u>ll be</u> late, if you don't hurry.

When you are using facts or events in the present situation as evidence for a prediction, you can use 'going to'.

> It'<u>s going to rain</u>. (I can see black clouds)
> I'<u>m going to be</u> late. (I have missed my train)

3 When you are talking about your own intentions, you use 'will' or 'going to'.

> I'<u>ll ring you</u> tonight.
> I'<u>m going to stay</u> at home today.

When you are saying what someone else has decided to do, you use 'going to'.

> They'<u>re going to have</u> a party.

'Will' and 'going to'

⊖ WARNING: You do not normally use 'going to' with the verb 'go'. You usually just say 'I'm going' rather than 'I'm going to go'.

> *'What <u>are you going to do</u> this weekend?' – 'I'<u>m going</u> to the cinema.'*

When you are announcing a decision you have just made or are about to make, you use 'will'.

> *I'm tired. I think I'<u>ll go</u> to bed.*

4 In promises and offers relating to the future, you often use 'will' with the meaning 'be willing to'.

> *I'<u>ll do</u> what I can.*
> *I'<u>ll help</u> with the washing-up.*

Note that you can use 'will' with this meaning in an 'if'-clause.

> *I'll put you through, if you'<u>ll hang on</u> for a minute. (= if you are willing to hang on for a minute)*

⊖ WARNING: Remember that you do not normally use 'will' in 'if'-clauses.

▶ See Unit 66 for more information on 'if'-clauses.

> *If you <u>do</u> that, you will be wasting your time.*
> *The children will call out if they <u>think</u> he is wrong.*

5 When you want to say that something will happen because arrangements have been made, you use the future continuous tense.

> *I'<u>ll be seeing</u> them when I've finished with you.*
> *I'<u>ll be waiting</u> for you outside.*
> *She'<u>ll be appearing</u> at the Royal Festival Hall.*

6 When you want to talk about something that has not happened yet but will happen before a particular time in the future, you use the future perfect tense.

> *By the time we phone he'<u>ll</u> already <u>have started.</u>*
> *By 2010, he <u>will have worked</u> for twelve years.*

Present tenses for future

Main points

When you are talking about the future in relation to official timetables or the calendar, you use the present simple ('I walk').

When talking about people's plans and arrangements for the future, you use the present continuous ('I am walking').

In 'if'-clauses, time clauses, and defining relative clauses, you can use the present simple ('I walk') to refer to the future.

1 When you are talking about something in the future which is based on an official timetable or calendar, you use the present simple tense. You usually put a time adverbial in these sentences.

> My last train _leaves_ Euston _at 11.30._
> The UN General Assembly _opens_ in New York _this month._
> Our next lesson _is on Thursday._
> We _set off early tomorrow morning._

2 In statements about fixed dates, you normally use the present simple.

> Tomorrow _is_ Tuesday.
> It_'s_ my birthday next month.
> Monday _is_ the seventeenth of July.

3 When you want to talk about people's plans or arrangements for the future, you use the present continuous tense.

> I_'m meeting_ Bill next week.
> They_'re getting married_ in June.

4 You often talk about the future using the present tense of verbs such as 'hope', 'expect', 'intend', and 'want' with a 'to'-infinitive clause, especially when you want to indicate your uncertainty about what will actually happen.

> We _hope to see_ you soon.
> Bill _expects to be_ back at work tomorrow.

After the verb 'hope', you often use the present simple to refer to the future.

> I hope you _enjoy_ your holiday.

Present tenses for future

5 In subordinate clauses, the relationships between tense and time are different. In 'if'-clauses and time clauses, you normally use the present simple for future reference.

> *If he <u>comes</u>, I'll let you know.*
> *Please start when you <u>are</u> ready.*
> *We won't start until everyone <u>arrives</u>.*
> *Lock the door after you finally <u>leave</u>.*

6 In defining relative clauses, you normally use the present simple, not 'will', to refer to the future.

> *Any decision <u>that you make</u> will need her approval.*
> *Give my love to any friends <u>you meet</u>.*
> *There is a silver cup for the runner <u>who finishes first</u>.*

7 If you want to show that a condition has to be the case before an action can be carried out, you use the present perfect for future events.

> *We won't start until everyone <u>has arrived</u>.*
> *I'll let you know when I <u>have arranged</u> everything.*

Conditionals using 'if'

Main points

You use conditional clauses to talk about a possible situation and its results.

Conditional clauses can begin with 'if'.

A conditional clause needs a main clause to make a complete sentence. The conditional clause can come before or after the main clause.

1 You use conditional clauses to talk about a situation that might possibly happen and to say what its results might be.

You use 'if' to mention events and situations that happen often, that may happen in the future, that could have happened in the past but did not happen, or that are unlikely to happen at all.

> _If_ the light comes on, the battery is OK.
> I'll call you _if_ I need you.
> _If_ I had known, I'd have told you.
> _If_ she asked me, I'd help her.

2 When you are talking about something that is generally true or happens often, you use a present or present perfect tense in the main clause and the conditional clause.

> If they _lose_ weight during an illness, they soon _regain_ it afterwards.
> If an advertisement _does not tell_ the truth, the advertiser _is committing_ an offence.
> If the baby _is crying,_ it _is_ probably hungry.
> If they _have lost_ any money, they _report_ it to me.

⊖ WARNING: You do not use the present continuous in both clauses. You do not say 'If they are losing money, they are getting angry.'

3 When you use a conditional clause with a present or present perfect tense, you often use an imperative in the main clause.

> _Wake_ me _up_ if you're worried.
> If he has finished, _ask_ him to leave quietly.
> If you are very early, _don't expect_ them to be ready.

4 When you are talking about something which may possibly happen in the future, you use a present or present perfect tense in the conditional clause, and the simple future in the main clause.

> If I _marry_ Celia, we _will need_ the money.
> If you _are going_ to America, you _will need_ a visa.
> If he _has done_ the windows, he _will want_ his money.

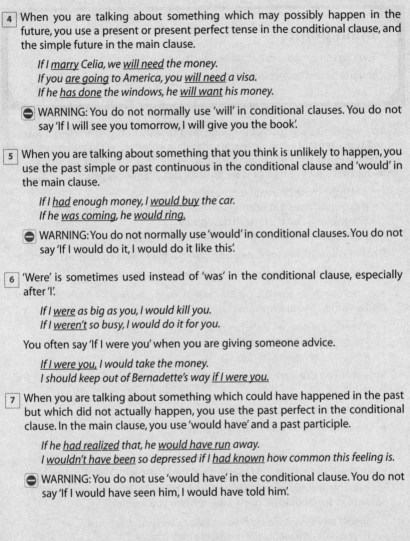 WARNING: You do not normally use 'will' in conditional clauses. You do not say 'If I will see you tomorrow, I will give you the book'.

5 When you are talking about something that you think is unlikely to happen, you use the past simple or past continuous in the conditional clause and 'would' in the main clause.

> If I _had_ enough money, I _would buy_ the car.
> If he _was coming_, he _would ring._

WARNING: You do not normally use 'would' in conditional clauses. You do not say 'If I would do it, I would do it like this'.

6 'Were' is sometimes used instead of 'was' in the conditional clause, especially after 'I'.

> If I _were_ as big as you, I would kill you.
> If I _weren't_ so busy, I would do it for you.

You often say 'If I were you' when you are giving someone advice.

> _If I were you,_ I would take the money.
> I should keep out of Bernadette's way _if I were you._

7 When you are talking about something which could have happened in the past but which did not actually happen, you use the past perfect in the conditional clause. In the main clause, you use 'would have' and a past participle.

> If he _had realized_ that, he _would have run_ away.
> I _wouldn't have been_ so depressed if I _had known_ how common this feeling is.

WARNING: You do not use 'would have' in the conditional clause. You do not say 'If I would have seen him, I would have told him'.

'If' with modals; 'unless'

Main points

You can use a modal in a conditional clause.

You use 'unless' to mention an exception to what you are saying.

---

1 You sometimes use modals in conditional clauses. In the main clause, you can still use a present tense for events that happen often, 'will' for events that are quite likely in the future, 'would' for an event that is unlikely to happen, and 'would have' for events that were possible but did not happen.

> If he <u>can't</u> come, he usually phones me.
> If they <u>must</u> have it today, they will have to come back at five o'clock.
> If I <u>could</u> only find the time, I'd do it gladly.
> If you <u>could</u> have seen him, you would have laughed too.

'Should' is sometimes used in conditional clauses to express greater uncertainty.

> If any visitors <u>should</u> come, I'll say you aren't here.

2 You can use other modals besides 'will', 'would' and 'would have' in the main clause with their usual meanings.

> She <u>might</u> phone me, if she has time.
> You <u>could</u> come, if you wanted to.
> If he sees you leaving, he <u>may</u> cry.

Note that you can have modals in both clauses: the main clause and the conditional clause.

> If he <u>can't</u> come, he <u>will</u> phone.

➤ See Units 79 to 91 for more information.

3 In formal English, if the first verb in a conditional clause is 'had', 'should', or 'were', you can put the verb at the beginning of the clause and omit 'if'.

For example, instead of saying 'If he should come, I will tell him you are sick', it is possible to say 'Should he come, I will tell him you are sick'.

> <u>Should</u> ministers decide to hold an inquiry, we would welcome it.
> <u>Were</u> it all true, it would still not excuse their actions.
> <u>Had</u> I known, I would not have done it.

'If' with modals; 'unless'

4 When you want to mention an exception to what you are saying, you use a conditional clause beginning with 'unless'.

> *You will fail your exams.*
> *You will fail your exams <u>unless you work harder.</u>*

Note that you can often use 'if...not' instead of 'unless'.

> *You will fail your exams <u>if</u> you do <u>not</u> work harder.*

When you use 'unless', you use the same tenses that you use with 'if'.

> *She <u>spends</u> Sundays in the garden unless the weather <u>is</u> awful.*
> *We usually <u>walk,</u> unless we'<u>re going</u> shopping.*
> *He <u>will</u> not <u>let</u> you go unless he <u>is forced</u> to do so.*
> *You <u>wouldn't believe</u> it, unless you <u>saw</u> it.*

5 'If' and 'unless' are not the only ways of beginning conditional clauses. You can also use 'as long as', 'only if', 'provided', 'provided that', 'providing', 'providing that', or 'so long as'. These expressions are all used to indicate that one thing only happens or is true if another thing happens or is true.

> *We were all right <u>as long as</u> we kept our heads down.*
> *I will come <u>only if</u> nothing is said to the press.*
> *She was prepared to come, <u>provided that</u> she could bring her daughter.*
> *<u>Providing</u> they remained at a safe distance, we would be all right.*
> *Detergent cannot harm a fabric, <u>so long as</u> it has been properly dissolved.*

I wish, if only, ...as if...

Main points

You use 'I wish' and 'If only' to talk about wishes and regrets.

You use '...as if...' and '...as though...' to show that information in a manner clause is not or might not be true.

1 You can express what you want to happen now by using 'I wish' or 'If only' followed by a past simple verb.

> *I wish he wasn't here.*
> *If only she had a car.*

Note that in formal English, you sometimes use 'were' instead of 'was' in sentences like these.

> *I often wish that I were really wealthy.*

When you want to express regret about past events, you use the past perfect.

> *I wish I hadn't married him.*

When you want to say that you wish that someone was able to do something, you use 'could'.

> *If only they could come with us!*

When you want to say that you wish that someone was willing to do something, you use 'would'.

> *If only they would realise how stupid they've been.*

2 When you want to indicate that the information in a manner clause might not be true, or is definitely not true, you use 'as if' or 'as though'.

> *She reacted as if she didn't know about the race.*
> *She acts as though she owns the place.*

After 'as if' or 'as though', you often use a past tense even when you are talking about the present, to emphasize that the information in the manner clause is not true. In formal English, you use 'were' instead of 'was'.

> *Presidents can't dispose of companies as if people didn't exist.*
> *She treats him as though he was her own son.*
> *He looked at me as though I were mad.*

I wish, if only, …as if…

3 You can also use 'as if' or 'as though' to say how someone or something feels, looks, or sounds.

> She felt <u>as if</u> she had a fever.
> He looked <u>as if</u> he hadn't slept very much.
> Mary sounded <u>as though</u> she had just run all the way.

You can also use 'it looks' and 'it sounds' with 'as if' and 'as though'.

> It looks to me <u>as if</u> he wrote down some notes.
> It sounds to me <u>as though</u> he's just being awkward.

4 When the subject of the manner clause and the main clause are the same, you can often use a participle in the manner clause and omit the subject and the verb 'be'.

> He ran off to the house <u>as if escaping</u>.
> He shook his head <u>as though dazzled</u> by his own vision.

You can also use 'as if' or 'as though' with a 'to'-infinitive clause.

> <u>As if to remind</u> him, the church clock struck eleven.

5 In informal speech, people often use 'like' instead of 'as if' or 'as' to say how a person feels, looks, or sounds. Some speakers of English think that this use of 'like' is incorrect.

> He felt <u>like</u> he'd won the pools.
> You look <u>like</u> you've seen a ghost.
> You talk just <u>like</u> my father does.

You can also use 'like' in prepositional phrases to say how someone does something.

> He was sleeping <u>like a baby.</u>
> I behaved <u>like an idiot</u>, and I'm sorry.

Verbs with '-ing' clauses

Main points

Many verbs are followed by an '-ing' clause.

Some verbs are followed by an object and an '-ing' clause that describes what the object is doing.

1 Many verbs are followed by an '-ing' clause. The subject of the verb is also the subject of the '-ing' clause. The '-ing' clause begins with an '-ing' form. The most common of these verbs are:

• verbs of saying and thinking

admit	consider	deny	describe	imagine	mention
recall	suggest				

> He *denied taking* drugs.
> I *suggested meeting* her for a coffee.

Note that all of these verbs except for 'describe' can also be followed by a 'that'-clause. ➤ See Unit 76.

> He *denied that* he was involved.

• verbs of liking and disliking

adore	detest	dislike	dread	enjoy	fancy
like	love	mind	resent		

> Will they *enjoy using* it?
> I *don't mind telling* you.

'Like' and 'love' can also be followed by a 'to'-infinitive clause. ➤ See Unit 71.

• other common verbs

avoid	commence	delay	finish	involve	keep
miss	postpone	practise	resist	risk	stop

> I've just *finished reading* that book.
> *Avoid giving* any unnecessary information.

• common phrasal verbs

burst out	carry on	end up	give up	go round	keep on
put off	set about				

Verbs with '-ing' clauses

She <u>carried on reading.</u>
They <u>kept on walking</u> for a while.

Note that some common phrases can be followed by an '-ing' clause.

can't help	can't stand	feel like

I <u>can't help worrying.</u>

2 After the verbs and phrases mentioned above, you can also use 'being' followed by a past participle.

They enjoy <u>being praised.</u>
I dislike <u>being interrupted.</u>

After some verbs of saying and thinking, you can use 'having' followed by a past participle.

admit	deny	mention	recall

Michael <u>denied having seen</u> him.

3 'Come' and 'go' are used with '-ing' clauses to describe the way that a person or thing moves.

They both <u>came running out.</u>
It <u>went sliding</u> across the road out of control.

'Go' and 'come' are also used with '-ing' nouns to talk about sports and outdoor activities. ➔ See Unit 56.

Did you say they might <u>go camping?</u>

4 Some verbs can be followed by an object and an '-ing' clause. The object of the verb is the subject of the '-ing' clause.

catch	find	imagine	leave	prevent	stop	watch

It is hard <u>to imagine him existing</u> without it.
He <u>left them making</u> their calculations.

Note that 'prevent' and 'stop' are often used with 'from' in front of the '-ing' clause.

I wanted to <u>prevent him from seeing</u> that.

Most verbs of perception can be followed by an object and an '-ing' clause or a base form. ➔ See Unit 72.

I <u>saw him riding</u> a bicycle.
I <u>saw a policeman walk over</u> to one of them.

➔ See also Unit 94 for '-ing' clauses after nouns.

139

Infinitives

Main points

Some verbs are followed by a 'to'-infinitive clause. Others are followed by an object and a 'to'-infinitive clause.

Some verbs are followed by a 'wh'-word and a 'to'-infinitive clause. Others are followed by an object, a 'wh'-word, and a 'to'-infinitive clause.

Nouns are followed by 'to'-infinitive clauses that indicate the aim, purpose or necessity of something, or that give extra information.

1 Some verbs are followed by a 'to'-infinitive clause. The subject of the verb is also the subject of the 'to'-infinitive clause.

● verbs of saying and thinking

| agree | choose | decide | expect | hope | intend | learn | mean | offer |
| plan | promise | refuse |

She had agreed to let us use her flat.
I decided not to go out for the evening.

● other verbs

| fail | manage | pretend | tend | want |

England failed to win a place in the finals.

2 Some verbs are followed by an object and a 'to'-infinitive clause. The object of the verb is the subject of the 'to'-infinitive clause.

● verbs of saying and thinking

| advise | ask | encourage | expect | invite | order | persuade |
| remind | teach | tell |

I asked her to explain.
They advised us not to wait around too long.

Infinitives

● other verbs

allow	force	get	help	want

> *I could <u>get someone else to do</u> it.*
> *I <u>didn't want him to go</u>.*

Note that 'help' can also be followed by an object and a base form.

> *I <u>helped him fix</u> it.*

⊖ WARNING: You do not use 'want' with a 'that'-clause. You do not say 'I want that you do something'.

3 Some verbs are followed by 'for' and an object, then a 'to'-infinitive clause. The object of 'for' is the subject of the 'to'-infinitive clause.

appeal	arrange	ask	long	pay	wait	wish

> *Could you <u>arrange for a taxi to collect</u> us?*
> *I <u>waited for him to speak</u>.*

4 Some link verbs, and 'pretend' are followed by 'to be' and an '-ing' form for continuing actions, and by 'to have' and a past participle for finished actions.

➤ See also Unit 73.

> *We <u>pretended to be looking</u> inside.*
> *I <u>don't appear to have written down</u> his name.*

5 Some verbs are normally used in the passive when they are followed by a 'to'-infinitive clause.

believe	consider	feel	find	know	report	say	think
understand							

> *He <u>is said to have died</u> a natural death.*
> *<u>Is</u> it <u>thought to be</u> a good thing?*

6 Some verbs are followed by a 'wh'-word and a 'to'-infinitive clause. These include:

ask	decide	explain	forget	imagine
know	learn	remember	understand	wonder

I <u>didn't know what to call</u> him.
She <u>had forgotten how to ride</u> a bicycle.

Some verbs are followed by an object, then a 'wh'-word and a 'to'-infinitive clause.

ask	remind	show	teach	tell

I <u>asked him what to do.</u>
Who will <u>show him how to use</u> it?

Some verbs only take 'to'-infinitive clauses to express purpose.
▶ See Unit 97.

The captain <u>stopped to reload</u> the gun.
He <u>went to get</u> some fresh milk.

7 You use a 'to'-infinitive clause after a noun to indicate the aim of an action or the purpose of a physical object.

We arranged a meeting <u>to discuss the new rules.</u>
He had nothing <u>to write with.</u>

You also use a 'to'-infinitive clause after a noun to say that something needs to be done.

I gave him several things <u>to mend.</u>
'What's this?' – 'A list of things <u>to remember.</u>'

8 You use a 'to'-infinitive clause after a noun group that includes an ordinal number, a superlative, or a word like 'next', 'last', or 'only'.

She was the <u>first</u> woman <u>to be elected to the council.</u>
Mr Holmes was <u>the oldest</u> person <u>to be chosen.</u>
The <u>only</u> person <u>to speak</u> was James.

9 You use a 'to'-infinitive clause after abstract nouns to give more specific information about them.

All it takes is <u>a willingness to learn.</u>
He'd lost <u>the ability to communicate</u> with people.

Infinitives (cont.)

The following abstract nouns are often followed by a 'to'-infinitive clause:

ability	attempt	chance	desire	failure
inability	need	opportunity	unwillingness	willingness

Note that the verbs or adjectives which are related to these nouns can also be followed by a 'to'-infinitive clause. For example, you can say 'I attempted to find them', and 'He was willing to learn'.

➤ See Unit 95 for information on nouns that are related to reporting verbs and can be followed by a 'to'-infinitive clause.

Verb + 'to' or '-ing'

Main points

Some verbs take a 'to'-infinitive clause or an '-ing' clause with little difference in meaning. Others take a 'to'-infinitive or '-ing' clause, but the meaning is different.

---

1 The following verbs can be followed by a 'to'-infinitive clause or an '-ing' clause, with little difference in meaning.

attempt	begin	bother	continue	fear	hate	love	prefer
start	try						

> It _started raining._
> A very cold wind _had started to blow._
> The captain _didn't bother answering._
> I _didn't bother to answer._

Note that if these verbs are used in a continuous tense, they are followed by a 'to'-infinitive clause.

> The company _is beginning to export_ to the West.
> We _are continuing to make_ good progress.

After 'begin', 'continue', and 'start', you use a 'to'-infinitive clause with the verbs 'understand', 'know', and 'realize'.

> I _began to understand_ her a bit better.

2 You can often use 'like' with a 'to'-infinitive or an '-ing' clause with little difference in meaning.

> I _like to fish._
> I _like fishing._

However, there is sometimes a difference. You can use 'like' followed by a 'to'-infinitive clause to say that you think something is a good idea, or the right thing to do. You cannot use an '-ing' clause with this meaning.

> They _like to interview_ you first.
> I _didn't like to ask_ him.

Verb + 'to' or '-ing'

3 After 'remember', 'forget', and 'regret', you use an '-ing' clause if you are referring to an event after it has happened.

> I *remember discussing* it once before.
> I'll never *forget going out* with my old aunt.
> She did not *regret accepting* his offer.

You use a 'to'-infinitive clause after 'remember' and 'forget' if you are referring to an event before it happens.

> I must *remember to send* a gift for her child.
> Don't *forget to send in* your entries.

After 'regret', in formal English, you use a 'to'-infinitive clause with these verbs to say that you are sorry about what you are saying or doing now:

announce	inform	learn	say	see	tell

> I *regret to say* that it was all burned up.

4 If you 'try to do' something, you make an effort to do it. If you 'try doing' something, you do it as an experiment, for example to see if you like it or if it is effective.

> I *tried to explain.*
> *Have* you *tried painting* it?

5 If you 'go on doing' something, you continue to do it. If you 'go on to do' something, you do it after you have finished doing something else.

> I *went on writing.*
> He later *went on to form* a computer company.

6 If you 'are used to doing' something, you are accustomed to doing it. If you 'used to do' something, you did it regularly in the past, but you no longer do it now.

> We *are used to working* together.
> I *used to live* in this street.

7 After 'need', you use a 'to'-infinitive clause if the subject of 'need' is also the subject of the 'to'-infinitive clause. You use an '-ing' form if the subject of 'need' is the object of the '-ing' clause.

> We *need to ask* certain questions.
> It *needs cutting.*

Verbs with other clauses

Main points

'Make' and 'let' can be followed by an object and a base form.

Some verbs of perception can be followed by an object and an '-ing' clause, or an object and a base form.

'Have' and 'get' can be followed by an object and a past participle.

'Dare' is followed by a 'to'-infinitive clause or a base form.

1 You can use an object and a base form after 'make' to say that one person causes another person to do something, or after 'let' to say they allow them to do something.

> My father <u>made me go</u> for the interview.
> Jenny <u>let him talk.</u>

2 Some verbs of perception are used with an object and an '-ing' clause if an action is unfinished or continues over a period of time, and with an object and a base form if the action is finished.

feel	hear	see	watch

> He <u>heard a distant voice shouting.</u>
> Dr Hochstadt <u>heard her gasp.</u>

You normally use an '-ing' clause after 'notice', 'observe', 'smell', and 'understand'.

> I could <u>smell Chinese vegetables cooking.</u>
> We can <u>understand them wanting</u> to go.

3 You can use an object and a past participle after 'have' or 'get', when you want to say that someone arranges for something to be done. 'Have' is slightly more formal.

> We'<u>ve</u> just <u>had the house decorated.</u>
> We must <u>get the car repaired.</u>

You also use 'have' and 'get' with an object and a past participle to say that something happens to someone, especially if it is unpleasant.

> She <u>had her purse stolen.</u>
> He <u>got his car broken into</u> at the weekend.

Verbs with other clauses

4 You use 'have' followed by an object and an '-ing' clause, or an object and a past participle, when you want to say that someone causes something to happen, either intentionally or unintentionally.

> Alan <u>had me looking</u> for that book all day.
> He <u>had me</u> utterly <u>confused.</u>

5 You use 'want' and 'would like' with an object and a past participle to indicate that you want something to be done.

> I <u>want the work finished</u> by January 1st.
> How <u>would</u> you <u>like your hair cut,</u> sir?

6 'Dare' can be followed by a 'to'-infinitive clause or a base form in negative or interrogative sentences:

- when there is an auxiliary or modal in front of 'dare'

> He <u>did</u> not <u>dare to walk</u> to the village.
> What bank <u>would dare offer</u> such terms?

- when you use the form 'dares' or 'dared' (but not 'dares not' or 'dared not')

> No one <u>dares disturb</u> him.
> No other manager <u>dared to compete.</u>

You must use a base form in:
- negative or interrogative sentences without an auxiliary or modal before 'dare'

> I <u>daren't ring</u> Jeremy again.
> Nobody <u>dare disturb</u> him.
> <u>Dare</u> she <u>go in?</u>

- negative sentences with 'dares not' or 'dared not'

> He <u>dares not risk</u> it.
> Sonny <u>dared not disobey.</u>

Note that the phrase 'how dare you' is always followed by a base form.

> How <u>dare</u> you <u>speak</u> to me like that?

'Dare' is rarely used in affirmative sentences.

Link verbs

Main points

Link verbs are used to join the subject with a complement.

Link verbs can have adjectives, noun groups, or 'to'-infinitive clauses as complements.

You can use 'it' and 'there' as impersonal subjects with link verbs.

---

1 A small but important group of verbs are followed by a complement rather than an object. The complement tells you more about the subject. Verbs that take complements are called 'link' verbs.

appear	be	become	feel	get	go	grow
keep	look	prove	remain	seem	smell	sound
stay	taste	turn				

> I *am* proud of these people.
> She *was getting* too old to play tennis.
> They *looked* all right to me.

2 Link verbs often have adjectives as complements describing the subject.

> We *felt* very happy.
> He *was* the tallest in the room.

➤ See Units 31 to 33 and Unit 47 for more information about adjectives after link verbs.

3 You can use link verbs with noun groups as complements to give your opinion about the subject.

> He's not <u>the right man for it.</u>
> She seemed <u>an ideal person to look after them.</u>

You also use noun groups as complements after 'be', 'become', and 'remain' to specify the subject.

> He became <u>a geologist.</u>
> Promises by MPs remained just <u>promises.</u>
> This one is <u>yours.</u>

Note that you use object pronouns after 'be'.

> It's <u>me</u> again.

148

4 | Some link verbs can have 'to'-infinitive clauses as complements.

appear	get	grow	look	prove	seem

> *He appears to have taken my keys.*
> *She seemed to like me.*

These verbs, and 'remain', can also be followed by 'to be' and a complement.

> *Mary seemed to be asleep.*
> *His new job proved to be a challenge.*

5 | You can use 'it' and 'there' as impersonal subjects with link verbs.

> *It seems silly not to tell him.*
> *There appears to have been a mistake.*

➡ See Units 17 and 18 for more information.

You can use 'be' with some abstract nouns as the subject, followed by a 'that'-clause or a 'to'-infinitive clause as the complement.

advice	agreement	answer	decision	idea	plan	problem
solution						

> *The answer is that they are not interested in it.*
> *The idea was to spend more money on training.*

Some can only have a 'that'-clause.

conclusion	explanation	fact	feeling	reason	report
thought	understanding				

> *The fact is that I can't go to the party.*

Reporting the past

Main points

A report structure is used to report what people say or think.

You use the present tense of the reporting verb when you are reporting something that someone says or thinks at the time you are speaking.

You often use past tenses in report structures because a reported clause usually reports something that was said or believed in the past.

1. You use a report structure to report what people say or think. A report structure consists of two parts. One part is the reporting clause, which contains the reporting verb.

> <u>I told him</u> nothing was going to happen to me.
> <u>I agreed</u> that he should do it.

The other part is the reported clause.

> He felt <u>that he had to do something.</u>
> Henry said <u>he wanted to go home.</u>

➤ See Units 75-77 for more information on report structures.

2. For the verb in the reporting clause, you choose a tense that is appropriate at the time you are speaking.

Because reports are usually about something that was said or believed in the past, both the reporting verb and the verb in the reported clause are often in a past tense.

> Mrs Kaur <u>announced</u> that the lecture <u>had begun.</u>
> At the time we <u>thought</u> that he <u>was</u> mad.

3. Although you normally use past tenses in reports about the past, you can use a present tense in the reported clause if what you are saying is important in the present, for example:

- because you want to emphasize that it is still true

> <u>Did</u> you <u>tell</u> him that this young woman <u>is looking</u> for a job?

- because you want to give advice or a warning, or make a suggestion for the present or future

> I <u>told</u> you they <u>have</u> this class on Friday afternoon, so you should have come a bit earlier.

4 You use a present tense for the reporting verb when you are reporting:

- what someone says or thinks at the time you are speaking

    She <u>says</u> she wants to see you this afternoon.
    I <u>think</u> there's something wrong.

Note that, as in the last example, it may be your own thoughts that you are reporting.

- what someone often says

    He <u>says</u> that no one understands him.

- what someone has said in the past, if what they said is still true

    My doctor <u>says</u> it's nothing to worry about.

5 If you are predicting what people will say or think, you use a future tense for the reporting verb.

    No doubt he <u>will claim</u> that his car broke down.
    They <u>will think</u> we are making a fuss.

6 You very rarely try to report the exact words of a statement. You usually give a summary of what was said. For example, John might say:

'I tried to phone you about six times yesterday. I let the phone ring for ages but there was no answer. I couldn't get through at all so I finally gave up.'

You would probably report this as:

John said he tried to phone several times yesterday, but he couldn't get through.

7 When you are telling a story of your own, or one that you have heard from someone else, direct speech simply becomes part of the narrative.

In this extract a taxi driver picks up a passenger:

    'What part of London are you headed for?' I asked him.
    'I'm going to Epsom for the races. It's Derby day today.'
    'So it is,' I said. 'I wish I were going with you. I love betting on horses.'

You might report this as part of the narrative without reporting verbs:

My passenger was going to Epsom to see the Derby, and I wanted to go with him.

Reported questions

> ## Main points
>
> You use reported questions to talk about a question that someone else has asked.
>
> In reported questions, the subject of the question comes before the verb.
>
> You use 'if' or 'whether' in reported 'yes/no'-questions.

1 When you are talking about a question that someone has asked, you use a reported question.

> She asked me <u>why I was so late.</u>
> He wanted to know <u>where I was going.</u>
> I demanded to know <u>what was going on.</u>
> I asked her <u>if I could help her.</u>
> I asked her <u>whether there was anything wrong.</u>

In formal and written English, 'enquire' (also spelled 'inquire') is often used instead of 'ask'.

> Wilkie had enquired <u>if she did a lot of acting.</u>
> He inquired <u>whether he could see her.</u>

2 When you are reporting a question, the verb in the reported clause is often in a past tense. This is because you are often talking about the past when you are reporting someone else's words.

> She <u>asked</u> me why I <u>was</u> so late.
> Pat <u>asked</u> him if she <u>had hurt</u> him.

However, you can use a present or future tense if the question you are reporting relates to the present or future.

> Mark <u>was asking</u> if you'<u>re enjoying</u> your new job.
> They <u>asked</u> if you'<u>ll be</u> there tomorrow night.

3 In reported questions, the subject of the question comes before the verb, just as it does in affirmative sentences.

> She asked me why <u>I was late.</u>
> I asked what <u>he was doing.</u>

4 You do not normally use the auxiliary 'do' in reported questions.

> She asked him if <u>his parents spoke</u> French.
> They asked us what <u>we thought.</u>

Reported questions

The auxiliary 'do' can be used in reported questions, but only for emphasis, or to make a contrast with something that has already been said. It is not put before the subject as in direct questions.

> *She asked me whether I really <u>did</u> mean it.*
> *I told him I didn't like classical music. He asked me what kind of music I <u>did</u> like.*

5 You use 'if' or 'whether' to introduce reported 'yes/no'-questions.

> *I asked him <u>if</u> he was on holiday.*
> *She hugged him and asked him <u>whether</u> he was all right.*
> *I asked him <u>whether</u> he was single.*

'Whether' is used especially when there is a choice of possibilities.

> *I was asked <u>whether</u> I wanted to stay at a hotel <u>or</u> at his home.*
> *They asked <u>whether</u> Tim was <u>or</u> was <u>not</u> in the team.*
> *I asked him <u>whether</u> he loved me or not.*

Note that you can put 'or not' immediately after 'whether', but not immediately after 'if'.

> *The police didn't ask <u>whether or not</u> they were in.*

▶ See Units 74, 76, and 77 for more information on reporting.

Reporting: 'that'-clauses

Main points

You usually use your own words to report what someone said, rather than repeating their exact words.

Report structures contain a reporting clause first, then a reported clause.

When you are reporting a statement, the reported clause is a 'that'-clause.

You must mention the hearer with 'tell'. You need not mention the hearer with 'say'.

1 When you are reporting what someone said, you do not usually repeat their exact words, you use your own words in a report structure.

> *Jim said he wanted to go home.*

Jim's actual words might have been 'It's time I went' or 'I must go'.

Report structures contain two clauses. The first clause is the reporting clause, which contains a reporting verb such as 'say', 'tell', or 'ask'.

> <u>She said</u> that she'd been to Belgium.
> <u>The man in the shop told me</u> how much it would cost.

You often use verbs that refer to people's thoughts and feelings to report what people say. If someone says 'I am wrong', you might report this as 'He felt that he was wrong'. ► See Unit 77 for more information.

2 The second clause in a report structure is the reported clause, which contains the information that you are reporting. The reported clause can be a 'that'-clause, a 'to'-infinitive clause, an 'if'-clause, or a 'wh'-word clause.

> She said <u>that she didn't know.</u>
> He told me <u>to do it.</u>
> Mary asked <u>if she could stay with us.</u>
> She asked <u>where he'd gone.</u>

3 If you want to report a statement, you use a 'that'-clause after a verb such as 'say'.

admit	agree	answer	argue	claim	complain	decide
deny	explain	insist	mention	promise	reply	say
warn						

> He <u>said that</u> he would go.
> I <u>replied that</u> I had not read it yet.

Reporting: 'that'-clauses

You often omit 'that' from the 'that'-clause, but not after 'answer', 'argue', 'explain', or 'reply'.

> *They <u>said</u> I had to see a doctor first.*
> *He <u>answered that</u> the price would be three pounds.*

You often mention the hearer after the preposition 'to' with the following verbs.

admit	announce	complain	explain	mention	say	suggest

> *He <u>complained to me</u> that you were rude.*

4 'Tell' and some other reporting verbs are also used with a 'that'-clause, but with these verbs you have to mention the hearer as the object of the verb.

convince	inform	notify	persuade	reassure	remind	tell

> *He <u>told me</u> that he was a farmer.*
> *I <u>informed her</u> that I could not come.*

The word 'that' is often omitted after 'tell'.

> *I <u>told them</u> you were at the dentist.*

You can also mention the hearer as the object of the verb with 'promise' and 'warn'.

> *I <u>promised her</u> that I wouldn't be late.*

5 Note the differences between 'say' and 'tell'. You cannot use 'say' with the hearer as the object of the verb. You cannot say 'I said them you had gone'. You cannot use 'tell' without the hearer as the object of the verb. You cannot say 'I told that you had gone'. You cannot use 'tell' with 'to' and the hearer. You cannot say 'I told to them you had gone'.

6 The reporting verbs that have the hearer as object, such as 'tell', can be used in the passive.

> *She <u>was told</u> that there were no tickets left.*

Most reporting verbs that do not need the hearer as object, such as 'say', can be used in the passive with impersonal 'it' as subject, but not 'answer', 'complain', 'insist', 'promise', 'reply', or 'warn'.

> *It <u>was said</u> that the money had been stolen.*

➤ See also Units 74 and 77.

Other report structures

Main points

When reporting an order, a request, or a piece of advice, the reported clause is a 'to'-infinitive clause, used after an object.

When reporting a question, the reported clause is an 'if'-clause or a 'wh'-word clause.

Many reporting verbs refer to people's thoughts and feelings.

---

1 If you want to report an order, a request, or a piece of advice, you use a 'to'-infinitive clause after a reporting verb such as 'tell', 'ask', or 'advise'. You mention the hearer as the object of the verb, before the 'to'-infinitive clause.

advise	ask	beg	command	forbid	instruct
invite	order	persuade	remind	tell	warn

> Johnson _told her to wake_ him _up._
> He _ordered me to fetch_ the books.
> He _asked her to marry_ him.
> He _advised me to buy_ it.

If the order, request, or advice is negative, you put 'not' before the 'to'-infinitive.

> He had ordered his officers _not to use_ weapons.
> She asked her staff _not to discuss_ it publicly.
> Doctors advised him _not to play_ for three weeks.

If the subject of the 'to'-infinitive clause is the same as the subject of the main verb, you can use 'ask' or 'beg' to report a request without mentioning the hearer.

> I _asked to see_ the manager.
> Both men _begged not to be named._

2 If you want to report a question, you use a verb such as 'ask' followed by an 'if'-clause or a 'wh'-word clause.

> I _asked if_ I could stay with them.
> They _wondered whether_ the time was right.
> He _asked_ me _where_ I was going.
> She _inquired how_ Ibrahim was getting on.

Other report structures

Note that in reported questions, the subject of the question comes before the verb, just as it does in affirmative sentences.

➤ See Unit 75.

3 Many reporting verbs refer to people's thoughts and feelings but are often used to report what people say. For example, if someone says 'I must go', you might report this as 'She wanted to go' or 'She thought she should go'.

Some of these verbs are followed by:

● a 'that'-clause

accept	believe	consider	fear	feel	guess
imagine	know	suppose	think	understand	worry

> We both <u>knew</u> that the town was cut off.
> I had always <u>believed</u> that I would see him again.

● a 'to'-infinitive clause

intend	plan	want

> He doesn't <u>want</u> to get up.

● a 'that'-clause or a 'to'-infinitive clause

agree	decide	expect	forget	hope
prefer	regret	remember	wish	

> She <u>hoped she wasn't going to cry.</u>
> They are in love and <u>wish to marry.</u>

'Expect' and 'prefer' can also be followed by an object and a 'to'-infinitive.

> I'm sure she <u>doesn't expect you to take</u> the plane.
> The headmaster <u>prefers them to act</u> plays they have written themselves.

4 A speaker's exact words are more often used in stories than in ordinary conversation.

> 'I knew I'd seen you,' I said.
> 'Only one,' replied the Englishman.
> 'Let's go and have a look at the swimming pool,' she suggested.

157

The passive voice

Main points

You use the passive voice to focus on the person or thing affected by an action.

You form the passive by using a form of 'be' and a past participle.

Only verbs that have an object can have a passive form. With verbs that can have two objects, either object can be the subject of the passive.

1 When you want to talk about the person or thing that performs an action, you use the active voice.

> Mr Smith <u>locks</u> the gate at 6 o'clock every night.
> The storm <u>destroyed</u> dozens of trees.

When you want to focus on the person or thing that is affected by an action, rather than the person or thing that performs the action, you use the passive voice.

> The gate <u>is locked</u> at 6 o'clock every night.
> Dozens of trees <u>were destroyed.</u>

2 The passive is formed with a form of the auxiliary 'be', followed by the past participle of a main verb.

> Two new stores <u>were opened</u> this year.
> The room <u>had been cleaned.</u>

Continuous passive tenses are formed with a form of the auxiliary 'be' followed by 'being' and the past participle of a main verb.

> Jobs <u>are</u> still <u>being lost.</u>
> It <u>was being done</u> without his knowledge.

3 After modals you use the base form 'be' followed by the past participle of a main verb.

> What <u>can be done?</u>
> We <u>won't be beaten.</u>

When you are talking about the past, you use a modal with 'have been' followed by the past participle of a main verb.

> He <u>may have been given</u> the car.
> He <u>couldn't have been told</u> by Jimmy.

4 You form passive infinitives by using 'to be' or 'to have been' followed by the past participle of a main verb.

> *He wanted <u>to be forgiven.</u>*
> *The car was reported <u>to have been stolen.</u>*

5 In informal English, 'get' is sometimes used instead of 'be' to form the passive.

> *Our car <u>gets cleaned</u> every weekend.*
> *He <u>got killed</u> in a plane crash.*

6 When you use the passive, you often do not mention the person or thing that performs the action at all. This may be because you do not know or do not want to say who it is, or because it does not matter.

> *Her boyfriend <u>was shot</u> in the chest.*
> *Your application <u>was rejected.</u>*
> *Such items should <u>be</u> carefully <u>packed</u> in tea chests.*

7 If you are using the passive and you do want to mention the person or thing that performs the action, you use 'by'.

> *He had been poisoned <u>by</u> his girlfriend.*
> *He was brought up <u>by</u> an aunt.*

You use 'with' to talk about something that is used to perform the action.

> *A circle was drawn in the dirt <u>with</u> a stick.*
> *He was killed <u>with</u> a knife.*

8 Only verbs that usually have an object can have a passive form. You can say 'people spend money' or 'money is spent'.

> *An enormous amount of money <u>is spent</u> on beer.*
> *The food <u>is sold</u> at local markets.*

With verbs which can have two objects, you can form two different passive sentences. For example, you can say 'The secretary was given the key' or 'The key was given to the secretary'.

> *They <u>were offered</u> a new flat.*
> *The books <u>will be sent</u> to you.*

➤ See Unit 52 for more information on verbs that can have two objects.

Introduction to modals

> ## Main points
>
> The modal verbs are: 'can', 'could', 'may', 'might', 'must', 'ought', 'shall', 'should', 'will', and 'would'
>
> Modals are always the first word in a verb group.
>
> All modals except for 'ought' are followed by the base form of a verb.
>
> 'Ought' is followed by a 'to'-infinitive.
>
> Modals have only one form.

Modals can be used for various different purposes. These are explained in Units 80-91.

1 Modals are always the first word in a verb group. All modals except for 'ought' are followed by the base form of a verb.

> I _must leave_ fairly soon.
> I think it _will look_ rather nice.
> Things _might have been_ so different.
> People _may be watching._

2 'Ought' is always followed by a 'to'-infinitive.

> She _ought to go_ straight back to England.
> Sam _ought to have realized_ how dangerous it was.
> You _ought to be doing_ this.

3 Modals have only one form. There is no '-s' form for the third person singular of the present tense, and there are no '-ing' or '-ed' forms.

> There's nothing _I can_ do about it.
> I'm sure _he can_ do it.

4 Modals do not normally indicate the time when something happens. There are, however, a few exceptions.

'Shall' and 'will' often indicate a future event or situation.

> I _shall_ do what you suggested.
> He _will_ not return for many hours.

'Could' is used as the past form of 'can' to express ability. 'Would' is used as the past form of 'will' to express the future.

> When I was young, I _could_ run for miles.
> He remembered that he _would_ see his mother the next day.

5 In spoken English and informal written English, 'shall' and 'will' are shortened to '-'ll', and 'would' to '-'d', and added to a pronoun.

> *I'll see you tomorrow.*
> *I hope you'll agree.*
> *Posy said she'd love to stay.*

'Shall', 'will', and 'would' are never shortened if they come at the end of a sentence.

> *Paul said he would come, and I hope he will.*

In spoken English, you can also add '-'ll' and '-'d' to nouns.

> *My car'll be outside.*
> *The headmaster'd be furious.*

⊖ WARNING: Remember that '-d' is also the short form of the auxiliary 'had'.

> *I'd heard it many times.*

Modals – negation, questions

Main points

You use negative words with modals to make negative clauses.

Modals go in front of the subject in questions.

You never use two modals together.

---

1 To make a clause negative, you put a negative word immediately after the modal.

> You <u>must not</u> worry.
> I <u>can never</u> remember his name.
> He <u>ought not</u> to have done that.

'Can not' is always written as one word, 'cannot'.

> I <u>cannot</u> go back.

However, if 'can' is followed by 'not only', 'can' and 'not' are not joined.

> We <u>can not only</u> book your flight for you, but also advise you about hotels.

2 In spoken English and informal written English, 'not' is often shortened to '-n't' and added to the modal. The following modals are often shortened in this way:

could not:	couldn't
should not:	shouldn't
must not:	mustn't
would not:	wouldn't

> We <u>couldn't</u> leave the farm.
> You <u>mustn't</u> talk about Ron like that.

Note the following irregular short forms:

shall not:	shan't
will not:	won't
cannot:	can't

> I <u>shan't</u> let you go.
> <u>Won't</u> you change your mind?
> We <u>can't</u> stop now.

'Might not' and 'ought not' are sometimes shortened to 'mightn't' and 'oughtn't'.

Note that 'may not' is very rarely shortened to 'mayn't' in modern English.

Modals – negation, questions

3 To make a question, you put the modal in front of the subject.

> *Could you give me an example?*
> *Will you be coming in later?*
> *Shall I shut the door?*

Modals are also used in question tags.

➤ See Units 7 and 8 for more information.

4 You never use two modals together. For example, you cannot say 'He will can come'. Instead you can say 'He will be able to come'.

> *I shall have to go.*
> *Your husband might have to give up work.*

5 Instead of using modals, you can often use other verbs and expressions to make requests, offers, or suggestions, to express wishes or intentions, or to show that you are being polite.

For example, 'be able to' is used instead of 'can', 'be likely to' is used instead of 'might', and 'have to' is used instead of 'must'.

> *All members are able to claim expenses.*
> *I think that we are likely to see more of this.*

These expressions are also used after modals.

> *I really thought I wouldn't be able to visit you this week.*

6 'Dare' and 'need' sometimes behave like modals.

➤ See Unit 72 for information on 'dare' and Units 71 and 90 for information on 'need'.

Possibility

Main points

You use 'can' to say that something is possible.

You use 'could', 'might', and 'may' to indicate that you are not certain whether something is possible, but you think it is.

1 When you want to say that something is possible, you use 'can'.

> *Cooking <u>can</u> be a real pleasure.*
> *In some cases this <u>can</u> cause difficulty.*

You use 'cannot' or 'can't' to say that something is not possible.

> *This <u>cannot</u> be the answer.*
> *You <u>can't</u> be serious.*

2 When you want to indicate that you are not certain whether something is possible, but you think it is, you use 'could', 'might', or 'may'. There is no important difference in meaning between these modals, but 'may' is slightly more formal.

> *That <u>could</u> be one reason.*
> *He <u>might</u> come.*
> *They <u>may</u> help us.*

You can also use 'might not' or 'may not' in this way.

> *He <u>might not</u> be in England at all.*
> *They <u>may not</u> get a house with central heating.*

Note that 'could not' normally refers to ability in the past.

➤ See Unit 83.

3 When there is a possibility that something happened in the past, but you are not certain if it actually happened, you use 'could have', 'may have', or 'might have', followed by a past participle.

> *It <u>could have been</u> tomato soup.*
> *You <u>may have noticed</u> this advertisement.*

You can also use 'might not have' or 'may not have' in this way.

> *He <u>might not have seen</u> me.*
> *They <u>may not have done</u> it.*

You use 'could not have' when you want to indicate that it is not possible that something happened.

> *He didn't have a boat, so he <u>couldn't have rowed</u> away.*
> *It <u>couldn't have been</u> wrong.*

You also use 'could have' to say that there was a possibility of something happening in the past, but it did not happen.

> *It <u>could have been</u> awful. (But it wasn't awful.)*
> *You <u>could have got</u> a job last year. (But you didn't get a job.)*

4 You also use 'might have' or 'could have' followed by a past participle to say that if a particular thing had happened, then there was a possibility of something else happening.

> *She said it <u>might have been</u> all right, if the weather had been good.*
> *(But the weather wasn't good, so it wasn't all right.)*
> *If I'd been there, I <u>could have helped</u> you. (But I wasn't there, so I couldn't help you.)*

5 'Be able to', 'not be able to', and 'be unable to' are sometimes used instead of 'can' and 'cannot', for example after another modal, or when you want to use a 'to'-infinitive, an '-ing' form, or a past participle.

> *When <u>will I be able to</u> pick them up?*
> *He had <u>been unable to</u> get a ticket.*

6 You use 'used to be able to' to say that something was possible in the past, but is not possible now.

> *Everyone <u>used to be able to</u> have free eye tests.*
> *You <u>used to be able to</u> buy cigarettes in packs of five.*

7 Note that you also use 'could' followed by a negative word and the comparative form of an adjective to emphasize a quality that someone or something has. For example, if you say 'I couldn't be happier', you mean that you are very happy indeed and cannot imagine being happier than you are now.

> *You <u>couldn't</u> be <u>more wrong</u>.*
> *He <u>could hardly</u> have felt <u>more ashamed</u> of himself.*

Probability and certainty

Main points

You use 'must', 'ought', 'should', or 'will' to express probability or certainty.

You use 'cannot' or 'can't' as the negative of 'must', rather than 'must not' or 'mustn't', to say that something is not probable or is not certain.

1 When you want to say that something is probably true or that it will probably happen, you use 'should' or 'ought'. 'Should' is followed by the base form of a verb. 'Ought' is followed by a 'to'-infinitive.

> We <u>should</u> arrive by dinner time.
> She <u>ought</u> to know.

When you want to say that you think something is probably not true or that it will probably not happen, you use 'should not' or 'ought not'.

> There <u>shouldn't</u> be any problem.
> That <u>ought not</u> to be too difficult.

2 When you want to say that you are fairly sure that something has happened, you use 'should have' or 'ought to have', followed by a past participle.

> You <u>should have</u> heard by now that I'm O.K.
> They <u>ought to have</u> arrived yesterday.

When you want to say that you do not think that something has happened, you use 'should not have' or 'ought not to have', followed by a past participle.

> You <u>shouldn't have</u> had any difficulty in getting there.
> This <u>ought not to have</u> been a problem.

3 You also use 'should have' or 'ought to have' to say that you expected something to happen, but that it did not happen.

> Yesterday <u>should have been</u> the start of the soccer season.
> She <u>ought to have been</u> home by now.

Note that you do not normally use the negative forms with this meaning.

4 When you are fairly sure that something is the case, you use 'must'.

> Oh, you <u>must</u> be Sylvia's husband.
> He <u>must</u> know something about it.

Probability and certainty

If you are fairly sure that something is not the case, you use 'cannot' or 'can't'.

> This <u>cannot</u> be the whole story.
> He <u>can't</u> be very old – he's about 25, isn't he?

⊖ WARNING: You do not use 'must not' or 'mustn't' with this meaning.

5 When you want to say that you are almost certain that something has happened, you use 'must have', followed by a past participle.

> This article <u>must have been</u> written by a woman.
> We <u>must have taken</u> the wrong road.

To say that you do not think that something has happened, you use 'can't have', followed by a past participle.

> You <u>can't have forgotten</u> me.
> He <u>can't have said</u> that.

6 You use 'will' or '-'ll' to say that something is certain to happen in the future.

> People <u>will</u> always say the things you want to hear.
> They<u>'ll</u> manage.

You use 'will not' or 'won't' to say that something is certain not to happen.

> You <u>won't</u> get much sympathy from them.

7 There are several ways of talking about probability and certainty without using modals. For example, you can use:

- 'bound to' followed by the base form of a verb

> It was <u>bound to</u> happen.
> You're <u>bound to</u> make a mistake.

- an adjective such as 'certain', 'likely', 'sure', or 'unlikely', followed by a 'to'-infinitive clause or a 'that'-clause

> They were <u>certain</u> that you were defeated.
> I am not <u>likely</u> to forget it.

➤ See Unit 33 for more information on these adjectives.

Ability

Main points

You use 'can' to talk about ability in the present and in the future.

You use 'could' to talk about ability in the past.

You use 'be able to' to talk about ability in the present, future, and past.

1 You use 'can' to say that someone has the ability to do something.

> You <u>can</u> all read and write.
> Anybody <u>can</u> become a qualified teacher.

You use 'cannot' or 'can't' to say that they do not have the ability to do something.

> He <u>cannot</u> dance.

2 When you want to talk about someone's ability in the past as a result of a skill they had or did not have, you use 'could', 'could not', or 'couldn't'.

> He <u>could</u> run faster than anyone else.
> A lot of them <u>couldn't</u> read or write.

3 You also use 'be able to', 'not be able to', and 'be unable to' to talk about someone's ability to do something, but 'can' and 'could' are more common.

> She <u>was able to</u> tie her own shoelaces.
> They <u>are not able to</u> run very fast.
> Many people <u>were unable to</u> read or write.

4 You use 'was able to' and 'were able to' to say that someone managed to do something in a particular situation in the past.

> After treatment he <u>was able to</u> return to work.
> The farmers <u>were able to</u> pay the new wages.
> We <u>were able to</u> find time to discuss it.

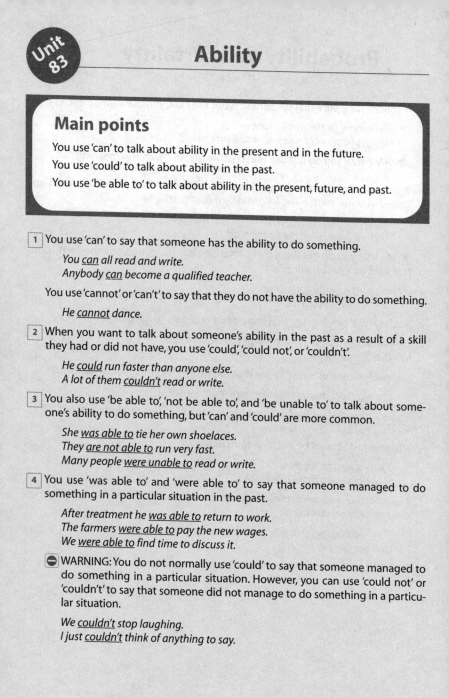 WARNING: You do not normally use 'could' to say that someone managed to do something in a particular situation. However, you can use 'could not' or 'couldn't' to say that someone did not manage to do something in a particular situation.

> We <u>couldn't</u> stop laughing.
> I just <u>couldn't</u> think of anything to say.

5 When you want to say that someone had the ability to do something in the past, but did not do it, you use 'could have' followed by a past participle.

> You _could have given_ it all to me.
> You know, she _could have done_ French.

You often use this form when you want to express disapproval about something that was not done.

> You _could have been_ a little bit tidier.
> You _could have told_ me!

6 You use 'could not have' or 'couldn't have' followed by a past participle to say that it is not possible that someone had the ability to do something.

> I _couldn't have gone_ with you, because I was in London at the time.
> She _couldn't have taken_ the car, because Jim was using it.

7 In most cases, you can choose to use 'can' or 'be able to'. However, you sometimes have to use 'be able to'. You have to use 'be able to' if you are using another modal, or if you want to use an '-ing' form, a past participle, or a 'to'-infinitive.

> Nobody else _will be able to_ read it.
> …the satisfaction of _being able to_ do the job.
> I don't think I'd have _been able to_ get an answer.
> You're foolish to expect _to be able to_ do that.

8 You also use 'can' or 'could' with verbs such as 'see', 'hear', and 'smell' to say that someone is or was aware of something through one of their senses.

> I _can smell_ gas.
> I _can't see_ her.
> I _could see_ a few stars in the sky.
> There was such a noise we _couldn't hear._

Permission

Main points

You use 'can' or 'be allowed to' to talk about whether someone has permission to do something or not.

You usually use 'can' to give someone permission to do something.

You usually use 'can' or 'could' to ask for permission to do something.

1 You use 'can' to say that someone is allowed to do something. You use 'cannot' or 'can't' to say that they are not allowed to do it.

> Students <u>can</u> take a year away from university.
> Children <u>cannot</u> bathe except in the presence of two lifesavers.

You use 'could' to say that someone was allowed to do something in the past. You use 'could not' or 'couldn't' to say that they were not allowed to do it.

> We <u>could</u> go to any part of the island we wanted.
> Both students and staff <u>could</u> use the swimming pool.
> We <u>couldn't</u> go into the library after 5 pm.

2 You also use 'be allowed to' when you are talking about permission, but not when you are asking for it or giving it.

> When Mr Wilt asks for a solicitor he will <u>be allowed to</u> see one.
> It was only after several months that I <u>was allowed to</u> visit her.
> You<u>'re</u> not <u>allowed to</u> use calculators in exams.

3 In more formal situations, 'may' is used to say that someone is allowed to do something, and 'may not' is used to say that they are not allowed to do it.

> They <u>may</u> do exactly as they like.
> The retailer <u>may not</u> sell that book below the publisher's price.

4 When you want to give someone permission to do something, you use 'can'.

> You <u>can</u> borrow that pen if you want to.
> You <u>can</u> go off duty now.
> She <u>can</u> go with you.

'May' is also used to give permission, but this is more formal.

> You <u>may</u> speak.
> You <u>may</u> leave as soon as you have finished.

Permission

5 When you want to refuse someone permission to do something, you use 'cannot', 'can't', 'will not', 'won't', 'shall not', or 'shan't'.

> *'Can I have some sweets?' – 'No, you <u>can't!</u>'*
> *'I'll just go upstairs.' – 'You <u>will not!</u>'*
> *You <u>shan't</u> leave without my permission.*

6 When you are asking for permission to do something, you use 'can' or 'could'. If you ask in a very simple and direct way, you use 'can'.

> *<u>Can</u> I ask a question?*
> *<u>Can</u> we have something to wipe our hands on please?*

'Could' is more polite than 'can'.

> *<u>Could</u> I just interrupt a minute?*
> *<u>Could</u> we put this fire on?*

'May' is also used to ask permission, but this is more formal.

> *<u>May</u> I have a cigarette?*

'Might' is rather old-fashioned and is not often used in modern English in this way.

> *<u>Might</u> I inquire if you are the owner?*

7 You have to use 'be allowed to' instead of a modal if you are using another modal, or if you want to use an '-ing' form, a past participle, or a 'to'-infinitive.

> *Teachers <u>will be allowed to</u> decide for themselves.*
> *I am strongly in favour of people <u>being allowed to</u> put on plays.*
> *They have not <u>been allowed to</u> come.*
> *We were going <u>to be allowed to</u> travel on the trains.*

Instructions and requests

Main points

You use 'Could you' to tell someone politely to do something.

Imperatives are not very polite.

You also use 'Could you' to ask someone politely for help.

You use 'I would like', 'Would you mind', 'Do you think you could', and 'I wonder if you could' to make requests.

1 When you want to tell someone to do something, you can use 'Could you', 'Will you', and 'Would you'. 'Could you' is very polite.

> _Could you_ make out her bill, please?
> _Could you_ just switch on the light behind you?

'Will you' and 'Would you' are normally used by people in authority. 'Would you' is more polite than 'Will you'.

> _Would you_ tell her that Adrian phoned?
> _Will you_ please leave the room?

Note that although these sentences look like questions ('Will you', not 'You will'), they are not really questions.

2 If someone in authority wants to tell someone to do something, they sometimes say 'I would like you to do this' or 'I'd like you to do this'.

> Penelope, I _would like_ you to get us the files.
> I'_d like_ you to finish this work by Thursday.

3 You can use an imperative to tell someone to do something, but this is not very polite.

> _Stop_ her.
> _Go_ away, all of you.

However, imperatives are commonly used when talking to people you know very well.

> _Come_ here, love.
> _Sit down_ and let me get you a drink.

You often use imperatives in situations of danger or urgency.

> _Look out!_ There's a car coming.
> _Put_ it _away_ before Mum sees you.

Instructions and requests

4 When you want to ask someone to help you, you use 'Could you', 'Would you', 'Can you', or 'Will you'. 'Could you' and 'Would you' are used in formal situations, or when you want to be very polite, for example because you are asking for something that requires a lot of effort. 'Could you' is more polite than 'Would you'.

> _Could you_ show me how to do this?
> _Would you_ do me a favour?

'Will you' and 'Can you' are used in informal situations, especially when you are not asking for something that requires a lot of effort.

> _Will you_ post this for me on your way to work?
> _Can you_ make me a copy of that?

5 You also use 'I would like' or 'I'd like', followed by a 'to'-infinitive or a noun group, to make a request.

> _I would like_ to ask you one question.
> _I'd like_ steak and chips, please.

6 You can also make a request by using:

- 'Would you mind', followed by an '-ing' form

> _Would you mind_ doing the washing up?
> _Would you mind_ waiting a moment?

- 'Do you think you could', followed by the base form of a verb

> _Do you think you could_ help me?

- 'I wonder if you could', followed by the base form of a verb

> _I wonder if you could_ look after my cat for me while I'm away?

Suggestions

Main points

You use 'could', 'couldn't', or 'shall' to make a suggestion.

You use 'Shall we' to suggest doing something with someone.

You use 'You might like' or 'You might want' to make polite suggestions.

You use 'may as well' or 'might as well' to suggest a sensible action.

You use 'What about', 'Let's', 'Why don't', and 'Why not' to make suggestions.

---

1 You use 'could' to suggest doing something.

> *You <u>could</u> phone her.*
> *She <u>could</u> go into research.*
> *We <u>could</u> go on Friday.*

You also use 'couldn't' in a question to suggest doing something.

> *<u>Couldn't</u> you just build some more factories?*
> *<u>Couldn't</u> we do it at the weekend?*

2 You use 'Shall we' to suggest doing something with somebody else.

> *<u>Shall we</u> go and see a film?*
> *<u>Shall we</u> talk about something different now?*

You use 'Shall I' to suggest doing something yourself.

> *<u>Shall I</u> contact the Chairman?*

3 You use 'You might', followed by a verb meaning 'like' or 'want', to make a suggestion in a very polite way.

> *I thought perhaps <u>you might like</u> to come along with me.*
> *<u>You might want</u> to try another shop.*

You can also do this using 'It might be', followed by a noun group or an adjective, and a 'to'-infinitive.

> *I think <u>it might be a good idea</u> to stop recording now.*
> *<u>It might be wise</u> to get a new car.*

4 You use 'may as well' or 'might as well' to suggest doing something, but only because it seems the sensible thing to do, or because there is no reason not to do it.

> *You <u>may as well</u> open them all.*
> *He <u>might as well</u> take the car.*

Suggestions

5 You can also make a suggestion by using:

- 'What about' or 'How about' followed by an '-ing' form

    What about going to Judy's?
    How about using my car?

- 'Let's' followed by the base form of a verb

    Let's go outside.

- 'Why don't I', 'Why don't you' or 'Why don't we' followed by the base form of a verb

    Why don't I pick you _up_ at seven?
    Why don't you write to her yourself?
    Why don't we just give them what they want?

- 'Why not' followed by the base form of a verb

    Why not bring him along?
    Why not try both?

Offers and invitations

Main points

You use 'Would you like' to offer something to someone or to invite them to do something.

You use 'Can I', 'Could I', and 'Shall I' when you offer to help someone.

1 When you are offering something to someone, or inviting them to do something, you use 'Would you like'.

> *Would you like* a drink?
> *Would you like* to come for a meal?

You can use 'Will you' to offer something to someone you know quite well, or to give an invitation in a fairly informal way.

> *Will you* have another biscuit, Dave?
> *Will you* come to my party on Saturday?

2 You use 'Can I' or 'Could I' when you are offering to do something for someone. 'Could I' is more polite.

> *Can I* help you with the dishes?
> *Could I* help you carry those bags?

You also use 'Shall I' when you are offering to do something, especially if you are fairly sure that your offer will be accepted.

> *Shall I* shut the door?
> *Shall I* spell that for you?

3 You use 'I can' or 'I could' to make an offer when you want to say that you are able to help someone.

> I have a car. *I can* take Daisy to the station.
> *I could* pay some of the rent.

4 You also use 'I'll' to offer to do something.

> *I'll* give them a ring if you like.
> *I'll* show you the hotel.

5 You use 'You must' if you want to invite someone very persuasively to do something.

> *You must* come round for a meal some time.
> *You must* come and visit me.

Offers and invitations

6 There are other ways of making offers and giving invitations without using modals. For example, you can use 'Let me' when offering to help someone.

> <u>Let me</u> take you to your room.
> <u>Let me</u> drive you to London.

You can make an offer or give an invitation in a more informal way by using an imperative sentence, when it is clear that you are not giving an order.

> <u>Have</u> a cigar.
> <u>Come</u> to my place.

You can add emphasis by putting 'do' in front of the verb.

> <u>Do have</u> a chocolate biscuit.
> <u>Do help</u> yourselves.

You can also give an invitation by using 'Why don't you' or 'How about'.

> <u>Why don't you</u> come to lunch tomorrow?
> <u>How about</u> coming with us to the party?

Wants and wishes

Main points

You use 'would like' to say what you want.

You use 'wouldn't like' to say what you do not want.

You use 'would rather' or 'would sooner' to say what you prefer.

You also use 'wouldn't mind' to say what you want.

1 You can say what someone wants by using 'would like' followed by a 'to'-infinitive or a noun group.

> I _would like_ to know the date of the next meeting.
> John _would like_ his book back.

When the subject is a pronoun, you often use the short form '-'d' instead of 'would'.

> I'_d like_ more information about the work you do.
> We'_d like_ seats in the non-smoking section, please.

In spoken English, you can also use the short form '-'d' instead of 'would' when the subject is a noun.

> Sally'_d like_ to go to the circus.

2 You can say what someone does not want by using 'would not like' or 'wouldn't like'.

> I _would not like_ to see it.
> They _wouldn't like_ that.

3 You use 'would like' followed by 'to have' and a past participle to say that some-one wishes now that something had happened in the past, but that it did not happen.

> I _would like to have felt_ more relaxed.
> She'_d like to have heard_ me first.

You use 'would have liked', followed by a 'to'-infinitive or a noun group, to say that someone wanted something to happen, but it did not happen.

> Perhaps he _would have liked_ to be a teacher.
> I _would have liked_ more ice cream.

Note the difference. 'Would like to have' refers to present wishes about past events. 'Would have liked' refers to past wishes about past events.

4 You can also use 'would hate', 'would love', or 'would prefer', followed by a 'to'-infinitive or a noun group.

> I _would hate_ to move to another house now.
> I _would prefer_ a cup of coffee.

Note that 'would enjoy' is followed by a noun group or an '-ing' form, not by a 'to'-infinitive.

> I _would enjoy a bath_ before we go.
> I _would enjoy seeing_ him again.

5 You can use 'would rather' or 'would sooner' followed by the base form of a verb to say that someone prefers one situation to another.

> He'_d rather_ be playing golf.
> I'_d sooner_ walk than take the bus.

6 You use 'I wouldn't mind', followed by an '-ing' form or a noun group, to say that you would like to do or have something.

> I _wouldn't mind_ being the manager of a store.
> I _wouldn't mind_ a cup of tea.

Obligation and necessity 1

Main points

You use 'have to', 'must', and 'mustn't' to talk about obligation and necessity in the present and future.

You use 'had to' to talk about obligation and necessity in the past.

You use the auxiliary 'do' with 'have to' to make questions.

You use 'have got to' in informal English.

1 When you want to say that someone has an obligation to do something, or that it is necessary for them to do it, you use 'must' or 'have to'.

> You _must_ come to the meeting tomorrow.
> The plants _must_ have plenty of sunshine.
> I enjoy parties, unless I _have to_ make a speech.
> He _has to_ travel to find work.

2 There is sometimes a difference between 'must' and 'have to'. When you are stating your own opinion that something is an obligation or a necessity, you normally use 'must'.

> I _must_ be very careful not to upset him.
> We _must_ eat before we go.
> He _must_ stop working so hard.

When you are giving information about what someone else considers to be an obligation or a necessity, you normally use 'have to'.

> They _have to_ pay the bill by Thursday.
> She _has to_ go now.

Note that you normally use 'have to' for things that happen repeatedly, especially with adverbs of frequency such as 'often', 'always', and 'regularly'.

> I always _have to_ do the shopping.
> You often _have to_ wait a long time for a bus.

3 You use 'must not' or 'mustn't' to say that it is important that something is not done or does not happen.

> You _must not_ talk about politics.
> They _mustn't_ find out that I came here.

Note that 'must not' does not mean the same as 'not have to'. If you 'must not' do something, it is important that you do not do it.

If you 'do not have to' do something, it is not necessary for you to do it, but you can do it if you want.

⊖ WARNING: You only use 'must' for obligation and necessity in the present and the future. When you want to talk about obligation and necessity in the past, you use 'had to' rather than 'must'.

> *She <u>had to</u> catch the six o'clock train.*
> *I <u>had to</u> wear a suit.*

4 You use 'do', 'does', or 'did' when you want to make a question using 'have to' and 'not have to'.

> *How often <u>do</u> you <u>have to</u> buy petrol for the car?*
> *<u>Does</u> he <u>have to</u> take so long to get ready?*
> *What <u>did</u> you <u>have to</u> do?*
> *<u>Don't</u> you <u>have to</u> be there at one o'clock?*

⊖ WARNING: You do not normally form questions like these by putting a form of 'have' before the subject. For example, you do not normally say 'How often have you to buy petrol?'

5 In informal English, you can use 'have got to' instead of 'have to'.

> *You'<u>ve</u> just <u>got to</u> make sure you tell him.*
> *She'<u>s got to</u> see the doctor.*
> *<u>Have</u> you <u>got to</u> go so soon?*

⊖ WARNING: You normally use 'had to', not 'had got to', for the past.

> *He <u>had to</u> know.*
> *I <u>had to</u> lend him some money.*

6 You can only use 'have to', not 'must', if you are using another modal, or if you want to use an '-ing' form, a past participle, or a 'to'-infinitive.

> *They <u>may have to</u> be paid by cheque.*
> *She grumbled a lot about <u>having to</u> stay abroad.*
> *I would have <u>had to</u> go through London.*
> *He doesn't like <u>to have to</u> do the same job every day.*

Obligation and necessity 2

Main points

You use 'need to' to talk about necessity.

You use 'don't have to', 'don't need to', 'haven't got to', or 'needn't' to say that it is not necessary to do something.

You use 'needn't' to give someone permission not to do something.

You use 'need not have', 'needn't have', 'didn't need to', or 'didn't have to' to say that it was not necessary to do something in the past.

1 You can use 'need to' to talk about the necessity of doing something.

You might <u>need to</u> see a doctor.
A number of questions <u>need to</u> be asked.

2 You use 'don't have to' when there is no obligation or necessity to do something.

Many women <u>don't have to</u> work.
You <u>don't have to</u> learn any new typing skills.

You can also use 'don't need to', 'haven't got to', or 'needn't' to say that there is no obligation or necessity to do something.

You <u>don't need to</u> buy anything.
I <u>haven't got to</u> go to work today.
I can pick John up. You <u>needn't</u> bother.

3 You also use 'needn't' when you are giving someone permission not to do something.

You <u>needn't</u> say anything if you don't want to.
You <u>needn't</u> stay any longer tonight.

4 You use 'need not have' or 'needn't have' and a past participle to say that someone did something which was not necessary. You are often implying that the person did not know at the time that their action was not necessary.

I <u>needn't have</u> waited until the game began.
Nell <u>needn't have</u> worked.
They <u>needn't have</u> worried about Reagan.

Obligation and necessity 2

5 You use 'didn't need to' to say that something was not necessary, and that it was known at the time that the action was not necessary. You do not know if the action was done, unless you are given more information.

> *They <u>didn't need</u> to talk about it.*
> *I <u>didn't need</u> to worry.*

6 You also use 'didn't have to' to say that it was not necessary to do something.

> *He <u>didn't have to</u> speak.*
> *Bill and I <u>didn't have to</u> pay.*

7 You cannot use 'must' to refer to the past, so when you want to say that it was important that something did not happen or was not done, you use other expressions.

You can say 'It was important not to', or use phrases like 'had to make sure' or 'had to make certain' in a negative sentence.

> *It was <u>important</u> not to take the game too seriously.*
> *It was <u>necessary</u> that no one was aware of being watched.*
> *You <u>had to make sure</u> that you didn't spend too much.*
> *We <u>had to</u> do our best to <u>make certain</u> that it wasn't out of date.*

Mild obligation and advice

Main points

You use 'should' and 'ought' to talk about mild obligation.

You use 'should have' and 'ought to have' to say that there was a mild obligation to do something in the past, but it was not done.

You can also use 'had better' to talk about mild obligation.

1. You can use 'should' and 'ought' to talk about a mild obligation to do something. When you use 'should' and 'ought', you are saying that the feeling of obligation is not as strong as when you use 'must'.

'Should' and 'ought' are very common in spoken English.

'Should' is followed by the base form of a verb, but 'ought' is followed by a 'to'-infinitive.

When you want to say that there is a mild obligation not to do something, you use 'should not', 'shouldn't', 'ought not', or 'oughtn't'.

2. You use 'should' and 'ought' in three main ways:

- when you are talking about what is a good thing to do, or the right thing to do.

  We <u>should</u> send her a postcard.
  We <u>shouldn't</u> spend all the money.
  He <u>ought</u> to come more often.
  You <u>ought not</u> to see him again.

- when you are trying to advise someone about what to do or what not to do.

  You <u>should</u> claim your pension 3-4 months before you retire.
  You <u>shouldn't</u> use a detergent.
  You <u>ought</u> to get a new TV.
  You <u>oughtn't</u> to marry him.

- when you are giving or asking for an opinion about a situation. You often use 'I think', 'I don't think', or 'Do you think' to start the sentence.

  I think that we <u>should</u> be paid more.
  I don't think we <u>ought</u> to grumble.
  Do you think he <u>ought not</u> to go?
  What do you think we <u>should</u> do?

Mild obligation and advice

3 You use 'should have' or 'ought to have' and a past participle to say that there was a mild obligation to do something in the past, but that it was not done. For example, if you say 'I should have given him the money yesterday', you mean that you had a mild obligation to give him the money yesterday, but you did not give it to him.

> *I <u>should have</u> finished my drink and gone home.*
> *You <u>should have</u> realised that he was joking.*
> *We <u>ought to have</u> stayed in tonight.*
> *They <u>ought to have</u> taken a taxi.*

You use 'should not have' or 'ought not to have' and a past participle to say that it was important not to do something in the past, but that it was done. For example, if you say 'I should not have left the door open', you mean that it was important that you did not leave the door open, but you did leave it open.

> *I <u>should not have</u> said that.*
> *You <u>shouldn't have</u> given him the money.*
> *They <u>ought not to have</u> told him.*
> *She <u>oughtn't to have</u> sold the ring.*

4 You use 'had better' followed by a base form to indicate mild obligation to do something in a particular situation. You also use 'had better' when giving advice or when giving your opinion about something. The negative is 'had better not'.

> *I think I <u>had better</u> show this to you now.*
> *You'<u>d better</u> go tomorrow.*
> *I'<u>d better not</u> look at this.*

⊖ WARNING: The correct form is always 'had better' (not 'have better'). You do not use 'had better' to talk about mild obligation in the past, even though it looks like a past form.

Defining relative clauses

Main points

You use defining relative clauses to say exactly which person or thing you are talking about.

Defining relative clauses are usually introduced by a relative pronoun such as 'that', 'which', 'who', 'whom', or 'whose'.

A defining relative clause comes immediately after noun, and needs a main clause to make a complete sentence.

1 You use defining relative clauses to give information that helps to identify the person or thing you are talking about.

The man <u>who you met yesterday</u> was my brother.
The car <u>which crashed into me</u> belonged to Paul.

When you are talking about people, you use 'that' or 'who' in the relative clause.

He was the man <u>that</u> bought my house.
You are the only person here <u>who</u> knows me.

When you are talking about things, you use 'that' or 'which' in the relative clause.

There was ice cream <u>that</u> Mum had made herself.
I will tell you the first thing <u>which</u> I can remember.

2 'That', 'who', or 'which' can be:

• the subject of the verb in the relative clause

The thing <u>that</u> really surprised me was his attitude.
The woman <u>who</u> lives next door is very friendly.
The car <u>which</u> caused the accident drove off.

• the object of the verb in the relative clause

The thing <u>that</u> I really liked about it was its size.
The woman <u>who</u> you met yesterday lives next door.
The car <u>which</u> I wanted to buy was not for sale.

In formal English, 'whom' is used instead of 'who' as the object of the verb in the relative clause.

She was a woman <u>whom</u> I greatly respected.

Defining relative clauses

3 You can leave out 'that', 'who', or 'which' when they are the object of the verb in the relative clause.

> *The woman you met yesterday lives next door.*
> *The car I wanted to buy was not for sale.*
> *The thing I really liked about it was its size.*

> ⊖ WARNING: You cannot leave out 'that', 'who', or 'which' when they are the subject of the verb in the relative clause. For example, you say 'The woman who lives next door is very friendly'. You do not say 'The woman lives next door is very friendly'.

4 A relative pronoun in a relative clause can be the object of a preposition. Usually the preposition goes at the end of the clause.

> *I wanted to do the job <u>which</u> I'd been training <u>for.</u>*
> *The house <u>that</u> we lived <u>in</u> was huge.*

You can often omit a relative pronoun that is the object of a preposition.

> *Angela was the only person <u>I could talk to.</u>*
> *She's the girl <u>I sang the song for.</u>*

The preposition always goes in front of 'whom', and in front of 'which' in formal English.

> *These are the people <u>to whom</u> Catherine was referring.*
> *He was asking questions <u>to which</u> there were no answers.*

5 You use 'whose' in relative clauses to indicate who something belongs to or relates to. You normally use 'whose' for people, not for things.

> *A child <u>whose</u> mother had left him was crying loudly.*
> *We have only told the people <u>whose</u> work is relevant to this project.*

6 You can use 'when', 'where', and 'why' in defining relative clauses after certain nouns. You use 'when' after 'time' or time words such as 'day' or 'year'. You use 'where' after 'place' or place words such as 'room' or 'street'. You use 'why' after 'reason'.

> *There had been <u>a time when</u> she hated all men.*
> *This is <u>the year when</u> profits should increase.*
> *He showed me <u>the place where</u> they work.*
> *That was <u>the room where</u> I did my homework.*
> *There are several <u>reasons why</u> we can't do that.*

Non-defining clauses

Main points

You use non-defining relative clauses to give extra information about the person or thing you are talking about.

Non-defining relative clauses must be introduced by a relative pronoun such as 'which', 'who', 'whom', or 'whose'.

A non-defining relative clause comes immediately after a noun and needs a main clause to make a complete sentence.

1. You use non-defining relative clauses to give extra information about the person or thing you are talking about. The information is not needed to identify that person or thing.

> Professor Marvin, <u>who was always early,</u> was there already.

'Who was always early' gives extra information about Professor Marvin. This is a non-defining relative clause, because it is not needed to identify the person you are talking about. We already know that you are talking about Professor Marvin.

Note that in written English, a non-defining relative clause is usually separated from the main clause by a comma, or by two commas.

> I went to the cinema with Mary, who I think you met.
> British Rail, which has launched an enquiry, said one coach was badly damaged.

2. You always start a non-defining relative clause with a relative pronoun. When you are talking about people, you use 'who'. 'Who' can be the subject or object of a non-defining relative clause.

> Heath Robinson, <u>who</u> died in 1944, was a graphic artist and cartoonist.
> I was in the same group as Janice, <u>who</u> I like a lot.

In formal English, 'whom' is sometimes used instead of 'who' as the object of a non-defining relative clause.

> She was engaged to a sailor, <u>whom</u> she had met at Dartmouth.

3. When you are talking about things, you use 'which' as the subject or object of a non-defining relative clause.

> I am teaching at the Selly Oak centre, <u>which</u> is just over the road.
> He was a man of considerable inherited wealth, <u>which</u> he ultimately spent on his experiments.

WARNING: You do not normally use 'that' in non-defining relative clauses.

4 You can also use a non-defining relative clause beginning with 'which' to say something about the whole situation described in a main clause.

> *I never met Brando again, <u>which</u> was a pity.*
> *She was a little tense, <u>which</u> was understandable.*
> *Small computers need only small amounts of power, <u>which</u> means that they will run on small batteries.*

5 When you are talking about a group of people or things and then want to say something about only some of them, you can use one of the following expressions:

many of which	many of whom	none of which	none of whom
one of which	one of whom	some of which	some of whom

> *They were all friends, <u>many of whom</u> had known each other for years.*
> *He talked about several very interesting people, <u>some of whom</u> he was still in contact with.*

6 You can use 'when' and 'where' in non-defining relative clauses after expressions of time or place.

> *This happened in 1957, <u>when</u> I was still a baby.*
> *She has just come back from a holiday in Crete, <u>where</u> Alex and I went last year.*

Participle clauses

Main points

Nouns are followed by '-ing' clauses that say what a person or thing is doing.

Nouns are followed by '-ed' clauses that show that a person or thing has been affected or caused by an action.

1. You can often give more information about a noun, or an indefinite pronoun such as 'someone' or 'something', by adding a clause beginning with an '-ing' form, an '-ed' form, or a 'to'-infinitive.

> He gestured towards <u>the box lying on the table.</u>
> I think <u>the idea suggested by Tim</u> is the best one.
> She wanted <u>someone to talk to.</u>

2. You use an '-ing' clause after a noun to say what someone or something is doing or was doing at a particular time.

> The young girl <u>sitting opposite him</u> was his daughter.
> Most of the people <u>strolling in the park</u> were teenagers.

3. You can also use an '-ing' clause after a noun to say what a person or thing does generally, rather than at a particular time.

> Problems <u>facing parents</u> should be discussed.
> The men <u>working there</u> were not very friendly.

4. You often use an '-ing' clause after a noun which is the object of a verb of perception, such as 'see', 'hear', or 'feel'.

➤ See also Unit 72.

> Suddenly we saw Amy <u>walking down the path.</u>
> He heard a distant voice <u>shouting.</u>
> I could feel something <u>touching my face and neck,</u> something ice-cold.

Participle clauses

5 You use an '-ed' clause after a noun to show that someone or something has been affected or caused by an action.

> *He was the new minister <u>appointed by the President.</u>*
> *The man <u>injured in the accident</u> was taken to hospital.*

Remember that not all verbs have regular '-ed' forms.

> *A story <u>written by a young girl</u> won the competition.*
> *She was wearing a dress <u>bought in Paris.</u>*

Adding to a noun group

Main points

Some adjectives can be used after nouns.
You can use relative clauses after nouns.
Adverbials of place and time can come after nouns.
A noun can be followed by another noun group.
You can use 'that'-clauses after some nouns.

1 You can use some adjectives after a noun to give more information about it, but the adjectives are usually followed by a prepositional phrase, a 'to'-infinitive clause, or an adverbial.

> This is a warning to people <u>eager for a quick profit.</u>
> These are the weapons <u>likely to be used.</u>
> For a list of the facilities <u>available here,</u> ask the secretary.
> You must talk to the people <u>concerned.</u>

▶ See Unit 31 for more information on adjectives used after nouns.

2 When you want to give more precise information about the person or thing you are talking about, you can use a defining relative clause after the noun.

> The man <u>who had done it</u> was arrested.
> There are a lot of things <u>that are wrong.</u>
> Nearly all the people <u>I used to know</u> have gone.

Note that you can also use defining relative clauses after indefinite pronouns such as 'someone' or 'something'.

> I'm talking about somebody <u>who is really ill.</u>

▶ See Unit 92 for more information on defining relative clauses.

3 You can use an adverbial of place or time after a noun.

> People <u>everywhere</u> are becoming more selfish.
> This is a reflection of life <u>today.</u>

4 You can add a second noun group after a noun. The second noun group gives you more precise information about the first noun.

> Her mother, <u>a Canadian,</u> died when she was six.

Adding to a noun group

Note that the second noun group is separated by commas from the rest of the clause.

5 Nouns such as 'advice', 'hope', and 'wish', which refer to what someone says or thinks, can be followed by a 'that'-clause. Here are some examples:

advice	agreement	belief	claim	conclusion	decision
feeling	hope	promise	threat	warning	wish

It is my firm <u>belief that</u> more women should stand for Parliament.
I had a <u>feeling that</u> no-one thought I was good enough.

Note that all these nouns are related to reporting verbs, which also take a 'that'-clause. For example, 'information' is related to 'inform', and 'decision' is related to 'decide'.

Some of these nouns can also be followed by a 'to'-infinitive clause.

agreement	decision	hope	order	promise	threat
warning	wish				

The <u>decision to go</u> had not been an easy one.
I reminded Barnaby of his <u>promise to buy his son a horse.</u>

6 A few other nouns can be followed by a 'that'-clause.

advantage	confidence	danger	effect	evidence	fact
idea	impression	news	opinion	possibility	view

He didn't want her to get the <u>idea that</u> he was rich.
I had no <u>evidence that</u> Jed was the killer.
He couldn't believe the <u>news that</u> his house had just burned down.

Note that when a noun group is the object of a verb, it may be followed by different structures.

➤ See Units 69 to 72 for more information.

Main points

You use time clauses to say when something happens.

Time clauses can refer to the past, present, or future.

Time clauses are introduced by words such as 'after', 'when', or 'while'.

A time clause needs a main clause to make a complete sentence. The time clause can come before or after the main clause.

1 You use time clauses to say when something happens. The verb in the time clause can be in a present or a past tense.

> *I look after the children <u>while</u> she <u>goes</u> to London.*
> *I haven't given him a thing to eat <u>since</u> he <u>arrived.</u>*

⊖ WARNING: You never use a future tense in a time clause. You use one of the present tenses instead.

> *Let me stay here <u>till</u> Jeannie <u>comes</u> to bed.*
> *I'll do it <u>when</u> I<u>'ve finished</u> writing this letter.*

2 When you want to say that two events happen at the same time, you use a time clause with 'as', 'when', or 'while'.

> *We arrived <u>as they were leaving.</u>*

Sometimes the two events happen together for a period of time.

> *She wept bitterly <u>as she told her story.</u>*

Sometimes one event interrupts another event.

> *He was having his dinner <u>when</u> the telephone rang.*
> *John will arrive <u>while</u> we are watching the film.*

Note that you often use a continuous tense for the interrupted action.
▶ See Unit 60.

3 When you want to say that one event happens before or after another event, you use a time clause with 'after', 'as soon as', 'before', or 'when'.

> *<u>As soon as</u> we get tickets, we'll send them to you.*
> *Can I see you <u>before</u> you go, Helen?*
> *<u>When</u> he had finished reading, he looked up.*

Note that you use the past perfect to indicate an event that happened before another event in the past.

Time clauses

4 When you want to mention a situation which started in the past and continued until a later time, you use a time clause with 'since' or 'ever since'. You use a past simple or a past perfect in the time clause, and a past perfect in the main clause.

> He hadn't cried <u>since he was</u> a boy of ten.
> Janine had been busy <u>ever since she had heard</u> the news.
> I'<u>d wanted</u> to come ever since I was a child.

If the situation started in the past and still continues now, you use a past simple in the time clause, and a present perfect in the main clause.

> I've been in politics <u>since I was</u> at university.
> Ever since you arrived <u>you've been causing</u> trouble.

Note that after impersonal 'it' and a time expression, if the main clause is in the present tense, you use 'since' with a past simple.

> It <u>is</u> two weeks now since I <u>wrote</u> to you.

If the main clause is in the past tense, you use 'since' with a past perfect.

> It <u>was</u> nearly seven years since I'<u>d seen</u> Toby.

➤ For 'since' as a preposition, see Unit 40.

5 When you want to talk about when a situation ends, you use a time clause with 'till' or 'until' and a present or past tense.

> We'll support them <u>till they find</u> work.
> I stayed there talking to them <u>until I saw</u> Sam.
> She waited <u>until he had gone.</u>

6 When you want to say that something happens before or at a particular time, you use a time clause with 'by the time' or 'by which time'.

> <u>By the time</u> I went to bed, I was exhausted.
> He came back later, <u>by which time</u> they <u>had gone.</u>

7 In written or formal English, if the subject of the main clause and the time clause are the same, you sometimes omit the subject in the time clause and use a participle as the verb.

> I read the book <u>before going</u> to see the film.
> The car was stolen <u>while parked</u> in a London street.

Purpose and reason clauses

Main points

Purpose clauses are introduced by conjunctions such as 'so', 'so as to', 'so that', 'in order to' or 'in order that'.

Reason clauses are introduced by conjunctions such as 'as', 'because', or 'in case'.

A purpose or reason clause needs a main clause to make a complete sentence.

A purpose clause usually comes after a main clause. A reason clause can come before or after a main clause.

1 You use a purpose clause when you are saying what someone's intention is when they do something. The most common type of purpose clause is a 'to'-infinitive clause.

> *The children sleep together <u>to keep</u> warm.*
> *They locked the door <u>to stop</u> us from getting in.*

Instead of using an ordinary 'to'-infinitive, you often use 'in order to' or 'so as to' with an infinitive.

> *He was giving up his job <u>in order to stay</u> at home.*
> *I keep the window open, <u>so as to let</u> fresh air in.*

To make a purpose clause negative, you have to use 'in order not to' or 'so as not to' with an infinitive.

> *I would have to give myself something to do <u>in order not to</u> be bored.*
> *They went on foot, <u>so as not to</u> be heard.*

Another way of making purpose clauses negative is by using 'to avoid' with an '-ing' form or a noun group.

> *I had to turn away <u>to avoid letting</u> him see my smile.*
> *They drove through town <u>to avoid the motorway.</u>*

2 Another type of purpose clause begins with 'in order that', 'so', or 'so that'. These clauses usually contain a modal.

When the main clause refers to the present, you usually use 'can', 'may', 'will', or 'shall' in the purpose clause.

> *Any holes should be fenced <u>so that</u> people <u>can't</u> fall down them.*
> *I have drawn a diagram <u>so that</u> my explanation <u>will</u> be clearer.*

Purpose and reason clauses

When the main clause refers to the past, you usually use 'could', 'might', 'should', or 'would' in the purpose clause.

> *She said she wanted tea ready at six <u>so</u> she <u>could</u> be out by eight.*
> *Someone lifted Philip onto his shoulder <u>so that</u> he <u>might</u> see the procession.*

You use 'in order that', 'so', and 'so that', when the subject of the purpose clause is different from the subject of the main clause. For example, you say 'I've underlined it so that it will be easier.' You do not say 'I've underlined it to be easier.'

3 You can also talk about the purpose of an action by using a prepositional phrase introduced by 'for'.

> *She went out <u>for a run.</u>*
> *They said they did it <u>for fun.</u>*
> *I usually check, just <u>for safety's sake.</u>*

4 You use a reason clause when you want to explain why someone does something or why it happens. When you are simply giving the reason for something, you use 'because', 'since', or 'as'.

> *I couldn't see Helen's expression, <u>because</u> her head was turned.*
> *<u>Since</u> it was Saturday, he stayed in bed.*
> *<u>As</u> he had been up since 4 am, he was very tired.*

You can also use 'why' and a reported question to talk about the reason for an action.

▶ See Unit 75.

> *I asked him <u>why</u> he had come.*

5 When you are talking about a possible situation which explains the reason why someone does something, you use 'in case' or 'just in case'.

> *I've got the key <u>in case</u> we want to go inside.*
> *I am here <u>just in case</u> anything unusual happens.*

⊖ WARNING: You do not use a future tense after 'in case'. You do not say 'I'll stay behind in case she'll arrive later'.

Result clauses

Main points

You use result clauses to talk about the result of an action or situation.

Result clauses are introduced by conjunctions such as 'so', 'so…(that)', or 'such…(that)'.

A result clause needs a main clause to make a complete sentence. The result clause always comes after the main clause.

1 You use 'so' and 'so that' to say what the result of an action or situation is.

He speaks very little English, <u>so</u> I talked to him through an interpreter.
My suitcase had become damaged on the journey home, <u>so that</u> the lid would not stay closed.

2 You also use 'so…that' or 'such…that' to talk about the result of an action or situation.

He dressed <u>so</u> quickly <u>that</u> he put his boots on the wrong feet.
She got <u>such</u> a shock <u>that</u> she dropped the bag.

'That' is often omitted.

They were <u>so</u> surprised they didn't try to stop him.
They got <u>such</u> a fright they ran away again.

3 You only use 'such' before a noun, with or without an adjective.

They obeyed him with <u>such willingness</u> that the strike went on for over a year.
Sometimes they say <u>such stupid things</u> that I don't even bother to listen.

If the noun is a singular count noun, you put 'a' or 'an' in front of it.

I was in <u>such a panic</u> that I didn't know it was him.

Note that you only use 'so' before an adjective or an adverb.

It all sounded <u>so crazy</u> that I laughed out loud.
They worked <u>so quickly</u> that there was no time for talking.

4 When you want to say that a situation does not happen because someone or something has an excessive amount of a quality, you use 'too' with an adjective and a 'to'-infinitive. For example, if you say 'They were too tired to walk', you mean that they did not walk because they were too tired.

He was <u>too proud to apologise.</u>
She was <u>too weak to lift</u> me.

Result clauses

You also use 'too' with an adverb and a 'to'-infinitive.

> *They had been walking <u>too silently to be heard.</u>*
> *She spoke <u>too quickly</u> for me <u>to understand.</u>*

5 When you want to say that a situation happens or is possible because someone or something has a sufficient amount of a quality, you use 'enough' after adjectives and adverbs, followed by a 'to'-infinitive.

> *He was <u>old enough to understand.</u>*
> *I could see <u>well enough to know</u> we were losing.*

You normally put 'enough' in front of a noun, not after it.

> *I don't think I've got <u>enough information to speak</u> confidently.*

6 You also use 'and as a result', 'and so', or 'and therefore' to talk about the result of an action or situation.

> *He had been ill for six months, <u>and as a result</u> had lost his job.*
> *She was having great difficulty getting her car out, <u>and so</u> I had to move my car to let her out.*
> *We have a growing population <u>and therefore</u> we need more and more food.*

You can also put 'therefore' after the subject of the clause. For example, you can say 'We have a growing population and we therefore need more food'.

'As a result' and 'therefore' can also be used at the beginning of a separate sentence.

> *In a group, they are not so frightened. <u>As a result,</u> patients reveal their problems more easily.*
> *He lacks money to invest in improving his tools. <u>Therefore</u> he is poor.*

Contrast clauses

Main points

These are clauses introduced by 'although', 'in spite of' and 'though'.

You use contrast clauses when you want to make two statements, and one statement makes the other seem surprising.

Contrast clauses are introduced by conjunctions such as 'although', 'in spite of', or 'though'.

A contrast clause needs a main clause to make a complete sentence. The contrast clause can come before or after the main clause.

1 When you simply want to contrast two statements, you use 'although', 'though' or 'even though'.

Although he was late, he stopped to buy a sandwich.
Though he has lived for years in London, he writes in German.
I used to love listening to her, even though I could only understand about half of what she said.

Sometimes you use words like 'still', 'nevertheless', or 'just the same' in the main clause to add emphasis to the contrast.

Although I was shocked, I still couldn't blame him.
Although his company is profitable, it nevertheless needs to face up to some serious problems.
Although she hated them, she agreed to help them just the same.

When the subject of the contrast clause and the main clause are the same, you can often omit the subject and the verb 'be' in the contrast clause.

Although poor, we still have our pride. (Although we are poor…)
Though dying of cancer, he painted every day. (Though he was dying of cancer…)

2 Another way of making a contrast is to use 'despite' or 'in spite of', followed by a noun group.

Despite the difference in their ages they were close friends.
In spite of poor health, my father was always cheerful.

⊜ WARNING: You say 'in spite of' but 'despite' without 'of'.

3 You can also use an '-ing' form after 'despite' or 'in spite of'.

> *Despite working hard, I failed my exams.*
> *Conservative MPs are against tax rises, in spite of wanting lower inflation.*

4 You can also use 'despite the fact that' or 'in spite of the fact that', followed by a clause.

> *Despite the fact that it sounds like science fiction, most of it is*
> *technically possible at this moment.*
> *They ignored this order, in spite of the fact that they would probably*
> *get into trouble.*

It is possible to omit 'that', especially in spoken English.

> *He insisted on playing, in spite of the fact he had a bad cold.*

Manner clauses

Main points

You use manner clauses to talk about how something is done.

Manner clauses are introduced by conjunctions such as 'as', 'as if', 'as though', or 'like'.

A manner clause needs a main clause to make a complete sentence. The manner clause always comes after the main clause.

---

1 When you want to say how someone does something, or how something is done, you use 'as'.

> He behaves <u>as</u> he does, because his father was really cruel to him.
> The bricks are still made <u>as</u> they were in Roman times.

You often use 'just', 'exactly', or 'precisely' in front of 'as' for emphasis.

> It swims on the sea floor <u>just as</u> its ancestors did.
> I like the freedom to plan my day <u>exactly as</u> I want.
> Everything was going <u>precisely as</u> she had planned.

2 When you want to indicate that the information in the manner clause might not be true, or is definitely not true, you use 'as if' or 'as though'.

> Almost <u>as if</u> she'd read his thought, she straightened her back and returned to her seat.
> Just act <u>as though</u> everything's normal.

After 'as if' or 'as though', you often use a past tense even when you are talking about the present, to emphasize that the infomation in the manner clause is not true. In formal English, you use 'were' instead of 'was'.

> You talk about him <u>as if</u> he <u>were</u> dead.
> It is Malcolm's 37th birthday, but he and his mother both behave <u>as if</u> he <u>were</u> 7.

➤ See also Unit 68 for more information on '…as if…' and '…as though…'

3 You also use 'the way (that)', 'in a way (that)', or 'in the way (that)' to talk about how someone does something, or how something is done.

> I was never allowed to sing <u>the way</u> I wanted to.
> They did it <u>in a way that</u> I had never seen before.
> We make it move <u>in the way that</u> we want it to.

Manner clauses

4 You can use 'how' in questions and reported questions to talk about the method used to do something, and sometimes to indicate your surprise that it was possible to do it.

> *'How* did he get in?' – 'He broke a window.'
> *I wondered* <u>how</u> *he could afford a new car.*

Sometimes, you can use 'how' to talk about the manner in which someone does something.

> *I watched* <u>how</u> *he did it, then tried to copy him.*
> *Tell me* <u>how</u> *he reacted when he saw you.*

Changing sentence focus

Main points

You can sometimes change the focus of a sentence by moving part of the sentence to the front.

You can also change the focus of a sentence by using an expression such as 'The fact is', 'The thing is', or 'The problem is'.

You can also use impersonal 'it' to change the focus of a sentence.

---

1 In most affirmative clauses, the subject of the verb comes first.

> _They_ went to Australia in 1956.
> _I've_ no idea who it was.

However, when you want to emphasize another part of the sentence, you can put that part first instead.

> _In 1956_ they went to Australia.
> _Who it was_ I've no idea.

2 One common way of giving emphasis is by placing an adverbial at the beginning of the sentence.

> _At eight o'clock_ I went down for my breakfast.
> _For years_ I'd had to hide what I was thinking.

Note that after adverbials of place and negative adverbials, you normally put the subject after the verb.

> She rang the bell for Sylvia. In _came a girl_ she had not seen before.
> On no account _must they_ be let in.

After adverbials of place, you can also put the subject before the verb. You must do so, if the subject is a pronoun.

> The door opened and _in she came._
> He'd chosen Japan, so _off we went_ to the Japanese Embassy.

3 When you want to say that you do not know something, you can put a reported question at the beginning of the sentence.

> _What I'm going to do next_ I don't quite know.
> _How he managed_ I can't imagine.

Changing sentence focus

4 Another way of focusing on information is to use a structure which introduces what you want to say by using 'the' and a noun, followed by 'is'. The nouns most commonly used in this way are:

| answer | conclusion | fact | point | problem | question | rule |
| solution | thing | | trouble | truth | | |

The second part of the sentence is usually a 'that'-clause or a 'wh'-clause, although it can also be a 'to'-infinitive clause or a noun group.

> *The problem is* that she can't cook.
> *The thing is,* how are we going to get her out?
> *The solution is* to adopt the policy which will produce the greatest benefits.
> *The answer is* planning, timing, and, above all, practical experience.

It is also common to use a whole sentence to introduce information in following sentences.

▶ See Unit 102 for more information.

5 You can also focus on information by using impersonal 'it', followed by 'be', a noun group, and a relative clause.

The noun group can be the subject or object of the relative clause.

> *It was Ted who* broke the news to me.
> *It is* usually *the other vehicle that* suffers most.
> *It's money that* they want.
> *It was me* Dookie wanted.

There are many other ways of focusing on information:

> *Ted was the one who broke the news to me.*
> *Money is what we want.*
> *What we want is money.*

6 You can also focus on the information given in the other parts of a clause, or a whole clause, using impersonal 'it'. In this case, the second part of the sentence is a 'that'-clause.

> *It was from Francis that she first heard the news.*
> *It was meeting Peter that really started me off on this new line of work.*
> *Perhaps it's because he's a misfit that I get along with him.*

205

Cohesion

Main points

You can use pronouns and determiners to refer back to something that has already been mentioned.

You use coordinating conjunctions to link clauses.

1 When you speak or write, you usually need to make some connection with other things that you are saying or writing. The most common way of doing this is by referring back to something that has already been mentioned.

2 One way of referring back to something is to use a personal pronoun such as 'she', 'it', or 'them', or a possessive pronoun such as 'mine' or 'hers'.

> _My father_ is fat. _He_ weighs over fifteen stone.
> _Mary_ came in. _She_ was a good-looking woman.
> 'Have you been to _London_ ?' – 'Yes, _it_ was very crowded.'
> 'Have you heard of _David Lodge_ ?' – 'Yes, I've just read a novel of _his._'
> 'Would you mind moving _your car_, please?' – 'It's not _mine._'

3 You can also use a specific determiner such as 'the' or 'his' in front of a noun to refer back to something.

> A _man_ and a _woman_ were walking up the hill. _The_ man wore shorts, a T-shirt, and basketball sneakers. _The_ woman wore a print dress.
> 'Thanks,' said Brody. He put the telephone down, turned out the light in _his_ office, and walked out to _his_ car.

4 The demonstratives 'this', 'that', 'these' and 'those' are also used to refer back to a thing or fact that has just been mentioned.

> In 1973 he went on a _caravan holiday_. At the beginning of _this_ holiday he began to experience pain in his chest.
> There's a lot of _material_ there. You can use some of _that._

5 The following general determiners can also be used to refer back to something:

another	both	each	either	every	neither	other

> Five _officials_ were sacked. _Another_ four were arrested.
> There are more than two hundred and fifty _species of shark,_ and _every_ one is different.

Cohesion

6 Another common way of making connections in spoken or written English is by using one of the following coordinating conjunctions:

and	but	nor	or	so	then	yet

> *Anna had to go into town <u>and</u> she wanted to go to Bride Street.*
> *I asked if I could borrow her bicycle <u>but</u> she refused.*
> *He was only a boy then, <u>yet</u> he was not afraid.*

You can use a coordinating conjunction to link clauses that have the same subject. When you link clauses which have the same subject, you do not always need to repeat the subject in the second clause.

> *She was born in Budapest <u>and</u> raised in Manhattan.*
> *He didn't yell <u>or</u> scream.*
> *When she saw Morris she went pale, <u>then</u> blushed.*

7 Most subordinating conjunctions can also be used to link sentences together, rather than to link a subordinate clause with a main clause in the same sentence.

> *'When will you do it?' – '<u>When</u> I get time.'*
> *'Can I borrow your car?' – '<u>So long as</u> you drive carefully.'*
> *We send that by airmail. <u>Therefore</u>, it's away on Thursday and our client gets it on Monday.*

8 When people are speaking or writing, they often use words that refer back to similar words, or words that refer back to a whole sentence or paragraph.

> *Everything was <u>quiet</u>. Everywhere there was the <u>silence</u> of the winter night.*
> *'<u>What are you going to do?</u>' – 'That's a good <u>question</u>.'*

GLOSSARY OF GRAMMAR TERMS

abstract noun a noun used to refer to a quality, idea, feeling, or experience, rather than a physical object; EG *size, reason, joy.* → See Units 15, 70, 73

active voice verb groups such as 'gives', 'took', 'has made', which are used when the subject of the verb is the person or thing doing the action or responsible for it. Compare with **passive voice.** → See Unit 78

adjective a word used to tell you more about a person or thing, such as their appearance, colour, size, or other qualities; EG *...a pretty blue dress.* → See Units 31-36, 47

adjunct another name for **adverbial.**

adverb a word that gives more information about when, how, where, or in what circumstances something happens; EG *quickly, now.* → See Units 21, 36-44, 95

adverbial an adverb, or an adverb phrase, prepositional phrase, or noun group which does the same job as an adverb, giving more information about when, how, where, or in what circumstances something happens; EG *then, very quickly, in the street, the next day.* → See Units 38-46

adverbial of degree an adverbial which indicates the amount or extent of a feeling or quality; EG *She felt extremely tired.* → See Unit 43

adverbial of duration an adverbial which indicates how long something continues or lasts; EG *He lived in London for six years.* → See Unit 42

adverbial of frequency an adverbial which indicates how often something happens; EG *She sometimes goes to the cinema.* → See Unit 41

adverbial of manner an adverbial which indicates the way in which something happens or is done; EG *She watched carefully.* → See Unit 39

adverbial of place an adverbial which gives more information about position or direction; EG *They are upstairs... Move closer.* → See Unit 44-45

adverbial of probability an adverbial which gives more information about how sure you are about something; EG *I've probably lost it.* → See Unit 41

adverbial of time an adverbial which gives more information about when something happens; EG *I saw her yesterday.* → See Unit 40

adverb phrase two adverbs used together; EG *She spoke very quietly... He did not play well enough to win.* → See Unit 38

affirmative a clause or sentence in the affirmative is one which does not contain a negative word such as 'not' and which is not a question. → See Units 21, 29-30, 41-42

apostrophe s an ending ('s) added to a noun to indicate possession; EG *...Harriet's daughter... the professor's husband... the Managing Director's secretary.* → See Units 21-22

article see **definite article, indefinite article.**

auxiliary another name for **auxiliary verb.**

auxiliary verb one of the verbs 'be', 'have', and 'do' when they are used with a main verb to form tenses, negatives, and questions. Some grammars include modals in the group of auxiliary verbs. → See Units 3, 5, 7, 9-11, **57**

base form the form of a verb without any endings added to it, which is used in the 'to'-infinitive and for the imperative; EG *walk, go, have, be.* The base form is the form you look up in a dictionary. → See Units 3, 72, 79

cardinal number a number used in counting; EG *one, seven, nineteen.* → See Units 2, 13, 23, 26, 30-31

clause a group of words containing a verb. See also **main clause** and **subordinate clause**. → See Unit 1

collective noun a noun that refers to a group of people or things, which can be used with a singular or plural verb; EG *committee, team, family.*
→ See Unit 14

comparative an adjective or adverb with '-er' on the end or 'more' in front of it; EG *slower, more important, more carefully.* → See Units 35-36

complement a noun group or adjective, which comes after a link verb such as 'be', and gives more information about the subject of the clause; EG *She is a teacher... She is tired.* → See Units 1-3, 73

complex sentence a sentence consisting of a main clause and a subordinate clause; EG *She wasn't thinking very quickly because she was tired.* → See Unit 1

compound sentence a sentence consisting of two or more main clauses linked by 'and', 'or' or 'but'; EG *They picked her up and took her into the house.* → See Unit 1

conditional clause a subordinate clause, usually starting with 'if' or 'unless', which is used to talk about possible situations and their results; EG *They would be rich if they had taken my advice... We'll go to the park, unless it rains.* → See Units 66-67

conjunction a word such as 'and', 'because', or 'nor', that links two clauses, groups, or words. → See Units 1, 97, 102

continuous tense a tense which contains a form of the verb 'be' and a present participle; EG *She was laughing... They had been playing badminton.* See **tense**. → See Unit 60

contrast clause a subordinate clause, usually introduced by 'although' or 'in spite of the fact that', which contrasts with a main clause; EG *Although I like*

her, I find her hard to talk to.
→ See Unit 99

coordinating conjunction a conjunction such as 'and', 'but', or 'or', which links two main clauses.
→ See Unit 102

countable noun another name for **count noun.**

count noun a noun which has both singular and plural forms; EG *dog/dogs, foot/feet lemon/lemons.* → See Units 13, 24, 26-27, 29-30

declarative another name for **affirmative.**

defining relative clause a relative clause which identifies the person or thing that is being talked about; EG *...the lady **who lives next door** ...I wrote down everything **that she said.***
→ See Unit 92

definite article the determiner 'the'.
→ See Units 24-25

delexical verb a common verb such as 'give', 'have', 'make', or 'take', which has very little meaning in itself and is used with a noun as object that describes the action; EG *She **gave** a small cry... I've just **had** a bath.*
→ See Unit 56

demonstrative one of the words 'this', 'that', these', and 'those'; EG *...**this** woman. ...**that** tree... **That** looks interesting... **This** is fun.* → See Unit 19

descriptive adjective an adjective which describes a person or thing, for example indicating their size, age, shape, or colour, rather than expressing your opinion of that person or thing. Compare with **opinion adjective**.
→ See Unit 32

determiner one of a group of words including 'the', 'a', 'some', and 'my', which are used at the beginning of a noun group. → See Units 2, 13-14, 23-30

direct object a noun group referring to the person or thing affected by an action, in a clause with a verb in the active voice; EG *She wrote her name... I shut the windows.* → See Units 16, 20, 51-53

direct speech the actual words spoken by someone. → See Units 74-77

ditransitive verb another name for a verb with two objects, such as 'give', 'take', or 'sell'; EG *She gave me a kiss.* → See Unit 52

double-transitive verb another name for a verb with two objects. → See Unit 52

-ed' adjective an adjective which has the same form as the '-ed' form of a regular verb, or the past participle of an irregular verb; EG *...boiled potatoes. ...a broken wing.* → See Unit 34

'-ed' form the form of a regular verb used for the past simple and for the past participle. → See Units 3, 57, 94

ellipsis the leaving out of words when they are obvious from the context.

emphasizing adverb an adverb such as 'absolutely' or 'utterly', which modifies adjectives that express extreme qualities, such as 'astonishing' and 'wonderful'; EG *You were absolutely wonderful.* → See Unit 43

ergative verb a verb which is both transitive and intransitive in the same meaning. The object of the transitive use is the subject of the intransitive use; EG *He boiled a kettle... The kettle boiled.* → See Unit 55

first person see **person**.

future tense see **tense**.

gerund another name for the '-ing' form when it is used as a noun. → See Units 69, 71-72

'if'-clause see **conditional clause**.

imperative the form of a verb used when giving orders and commands, which is the same as its base form; EG *Come here... Take two tablets every four hours... Enjoy yourself.* → See Units 4, 8, 12, 66

impersonal 'it' 'it' used as an impersonal subject to introduce new information; EG *It's raining ... It's ten o'clock.* → See Units 16-17, 33, 47, 73, 76, 96, 101

indefinite adverb a small group of adverbs including 'anywhere' and 'somewhere' which are used to indicate place in a general way. → See Unit 21

indefinite article the determiners 'a' and 'an'. → See Unit 26

indefinite pronoun a small group of pronouns including 'someone' and 'anything' which are used to refer to people or things without saying exactly who or what they are. → See Units 21, 94-95

indirect object an object used with verbs that take two objects. For example, in 'I gave him the pen' and 'I gave the pen to him', 'him' is the indirect object and 'pen' is the direct object. Compare with **direct object**. → See Units 16, 20, 52

indirect question a question used to ask for information or help; EG *Do you know where Jane is?... I wonder which hotel it was.* → See Unit 9

indirect speech the words you use to report what someone has said, rather than using their actual words. Also called **reported speech**. → See Units 74-77

infinitive the base form of a verb; EG *I wanted to go... She helped me dig the garden.* → See Units 11, 33-34, 65, 70, 73, 76-77, 79, 82, 91, 95, 97-98

'-ing' adjective an adjective which has the same form as the present participle of a verb; EG *...a smiling face ...a winning streak.* → See Unit 34

'-ing' form a verb form ending in '-ing' which is used to form verb tenses, and as an adjective or a noun. Also called the **present participle**. → See Units 3, 34, 69, 71-72, 94

interrogative pronoun one of the pronouns 'who', 'whose', 'whom', 'what', and 'which', when they are used to ask questions. → See Unit 6

interrogative sentence a sentence in the form of a question. → See Unit 5

intransitive verb a verb which does not take an object; EG *She arrived... I was yawning.* → See Unit 51

irregular verb a verb that has three forms or five forms, or whose forms do not follow the normal rules. → See Unit 3 and appendix of verb tables

link verb a verb which takes a complement rather than an object; EG *be, become, seem, appear.* → See Unit 73

main clause a clause which does not depend on another clause, and is not part of another clause. → See Unit 1

main verb all verbs which are not auxiliaries or modals. → See Units 3, 5, 57

manner clause a subordinate clause which describes the way in which something is done, usually introduced with 'as' or 'like'; EG *She talks like her mother used to.* → See Units 68, 100

modal a verb such as 'can', 'might', or 'will', which is always the first word in a verb group and is followed by the base form of a verb. Modals are used to express requests, offers, suggestions, wishes, intentions, politeness, possibility, probability, certainty, obligation, and so on. → See Units 7-8, 18, 60-61, 64, 67, **79-91**, 97

mood the mood of a clause is the way in which the verb forms are used to show whether the clause is a statement, command, or question.

negative a negative clause, question, sentence, or statement is one which has a negative word such as 'not', and indicates the absence or opposite of something, or is used to say that something is not the case; EG *I don't*

know you... I'll never forget. Compare with **positive.** → See Units 4, **11-12**, 57, 80

negative word a word such as 'never', 'no', 'not', 'nothing', or 'nowhere', which makes a clause, question, sentence, or statement negative. → See Units 3-4, 7-8, 10-**12**, 21, 23, 27, 30, 80

non-defining relative clause a relative clause which gives more information about someone or something, but which is not needed to identify them because we already know who or what they are; EG *That's Mary, who was at university with me.* Compare with **defining relative clause.** → See Unit 93

non-finite clause a 'to'-infinitive clause, '-ed' clause, or '-ing' clause. → See Units 69-73, 94

noun a word which refers to people, things, ideas, feelings, or qualities; EG *woman, Harry, guilt.* → See Units 2, **13-15**, 23-31, 48, 56, 94-95

noun group a group of words which acts as the subject, complement, or object of a verb, or as the object of a preposition. → See Units 1-**2**, 38-40, 44

object a noun group which refers to a person or thing that is affected by the action described by a verb. Compare with **subject.** Prepositions also have noun groups as objects. → See Units 16, 20, **51-56**

object pronoun one of a set of pronouns including 'me', 'him', and 'them', which are used as the object of a verb or preposition. Object pronouns are also used as complements after 'be'; EG *I hit him... It's me.* → See Unit 16

opinion adjective an adjective which you use to express your opinion of a person or thing, rather than just describing them. Compare with **descriptive adjective.** → See Unit 32

ordinal number a number used to indicate where something comes in an order or sequence; EG *first, fifth, tenth, hundredth.*

participle a verb form used for making different tenses. Verbs have two participles, a present participle and a past participle. → See Units 3, 34, 57, 69, 71-72, 94

particle an adverb or preposition which combines with verbs to form phrasal verbs. → See Unit 50

passive voice verb groups such as 'was given', 'were taken', 'had been made', which are used when the subject of the verb is the person or thing that is affected by the action. Compare with **active voice**. → See Units 70, **78**

past form the form of a verb, often ending in '-ed', which is used for the past simple tense. → See Units 3, 59

past participle a verb form which is used to form perfect tenses and passives. Some past participles are also used as adjectives; EG *watched, broken, swum.* → See Units 3, 57, 70, 94

past tense see **tense**.

perfect tense see **tense**.

person one of the three classes of people who can be involved in something that is said. The person or people who are speaking or writing are called the first person ('I', 'we'). The person or people who are listening or reading are called the second person ('you'). The person, people or things that are being talked about are called the third person ('he', 'she', 'it', 'they').

personal pronoun one of the group of words including 'I', 'you', and 'me', which are used to refer back to yourself, the people you are talking to, or the people or things you are talking about. See also **object pronoun** and **subject pronoun**. → See Units **16**, 102

phrasal verb a combination of a verb and a particle, which together have a

different meaning to the verb on its own; EG *back down, hand over, look forward to.* → See Units **50**, 69

plural the form of a count noun or verb, which is used to refer to or talk about more than one person or thing; EG *Dogs have ears... The women were outside.* → See Units 2, 13-14

plural noun a noun which is normally used only in the plural form; EG *trousers, scissors.* → See Unit 14

positive a positive clause, question, sentence, or statement is one which does not contain a negative word such as 'not'. Compare with **negative**. → See Units 21, 29-30, 41-42

possessive one of the determiners 'my', 'your', 'his', 'her', 'its', 'our', or 'their', which is used to show that one person or thing belongs to another; EG *...your car.* → See Units **22**-23

possessive adjective another name for **possessive**.

possessive pronoun one of the pronouns 'mine', 'yours', 'hers', 'his', 'ours', or 'theirs'. → See Units **22**, 37

preposition a word such as 'by', 'with' or 'from', which is always followed by a noun group. → See Units 5, 16, 20, **44-50**, 52, 54, 92

prepositional phrase a structure consisting of a preposition followed by a noun group as its object; EG *on the table, by the sea.* → See Units 22, 34, 36, 38-40, 43, 46-49, 97

present participle see **'-ing' form**.

present tense see **tense**.

progressive tense another name for **continuous tense**. → See Unit 60

pronoun a word which you use instead of a noun, when you do not need or want to name someone or something directly; EG *it, you, none.* → See Units 6, **16-17**, **19-22**, 37, 92-95, 102

proper noun a noun which is the name of a particular person, place, organization, or building. Proper nouns are always written with a capital letter; EG *Nigel, Edinburgh, the United Nations, Christmas.* → See Unit 25

purpose clause a subordinate clause which is used to talk about the intention that someone has when they do something; EG *I came here **in order to ask you out to dinner.*** → See Unit 97

qualifier a word or group of words, such as an adjective, prepositional phrase, or relative clause, which comes after a noun and gives more information about it; EG *...the person involved. ...a book **with a blue cover.** ...the shop **that I went into.*** → See Units 22, 92-94

question a sentence which normally has the verb in front of the subject, and which is used to ask someone about something; EG *Have you any money?* → See Units **5-10**, 11, 58, 75, 80

question tag an auxiliary or modal with a pronoun, which is used to turn a statement into a question; EG *He's very friendly, **isn't he?** ...I can come, **can't I?*** → See Units 7-8

reason clause a subordinate clause, usually introduced by 'because', 'since', or 'as', which is used to explain why something happens or is done; EG *Since you're here, we'll start.* → See Unit 97

reciprocal verb a verb which describes an action which involves two people doing the same thing to each other; EG *I **met** you at the dance... We've **met** one another before... They **met** in the street.* → See Unit 54

reflexive pronoun a pronoun ending in '-self' or '-selves', such as 'myself' or 'themselves', which you use as the object of a verb when you want to say that the object is the same person or thing as the subject of the verb in the same clause; EG *He hurt **himself.*** → See Unit 20

reflexive verb a verb which is normally used with a reflexive pronoun as object; EG *He **contented himself** with the thought that he had the only set of keys.* → See Unit 53

regular verb a verb that has four forms, and follows the normal rules. → See Unit 3

relative clause a subordinate clause which gives more information about someone or something mentioned in the main clause. See also **defining relative clause** and **non-defining relative clause**. → See Units **92-93**, 95

relative pronoun 'that' or a 'wh'-word such as 'who' or 'which', when it is used to introduce a relative clause; EG *...the girl **who** was carrying the bag.* → See Units 92-93

reported clause the clause in a report structure which indicates what someone has said; EG *She said **that I couldn't see her.*** → See Units 74-77

reported question a question which is reported using a report structure rather than the exact words used by the speaker. See also **indirect question**. → See Unit 75

reported speech the words you use to report what someone has said, rather than using their actual words. Also called **indirect speech**. → See Units 74-77

reporting clause the clause in a report structure which contains the reporting verb. → See Units 74, 76

reporting verb a verb which describes what people say or think; EG *suggest, say, wonder.* → See Units 74, 76-77

report structure a structure which is used to report what someone says or thinks, rather than repeating their exact words; EG *She told me she'd be late.* → See Units 74-77

result clause a subordinate clause introduced by 'so', 'so...that', or 'such...(that)', which indicates the result of an action or situation;

213

EG *I don't think there's any more news, so I'll finish.* → See Unit 98

second person see **person**.

semi-modal a term used by some grammars to refer to the verbs 'dare', 'need', and 'used to', which behave like modals in some structures.
→ See Units 63, 72, 90

sentence a group of words which express a statement, question, or command. A sentence usually has a verb and a subject, and may be a simple sentence with one clause, or a compound or complex sentence with two or more clauses. In writing, a sentence has a capital letter at the beginning and a full stop, question mark, or exclamation mark at the end.
→ See Units 1, 66, 92-93, 96-102

short form a form in which one or more letters are omitted and two words are joined together, for example an auxiliary or modal and 'not', or a subject pronoun and an auxiliary or modal; EG *aren't, couldn't, he'd, I'm, it's, she's.* → See Unit 11

simple tense a present or past tense formed without using an auxiliary verb; EG *...I wait. ...she sang.* See **tense**. → See Units 58-63, 65

singular the form of a count noun or verb which is used to refer to or talk about one person or thing; EG *A dog was in the back of the car... That woman is my mother.* → See Units 13-14

singular noun a noun which is normally used only in the singular form; EG *the sun, a bath.* → See Unit 14

strong verb another name for **irregular verb**.

subject the noun group in a clause that refers to the person or thing who does the action expressed by the verb; EG *We were going shopping.* → See Units 1, 3, 5, 9-10, 13, 15-18, 21, 25, 38, 53, 55, 69-71, 75-77, 80, 102

subject pronoun one of the set of pronouns including 'I', 'she', and 'they', which are used as the subject of a verb. → See Unit 16

subordinate clause a clause which must be used with a main clause and is not usually used alone, for example a time clause, conditional clause, relative clause, or result clause, and which begins with a subordinating conjunction such as 'because' or 'while'. → See Units 1, 66-68, 92-93, 96-100, 102

subordinating conjunction a conjunction such as 'although', 'as if', 'because' or 'while', which you use to begin a subordinate clause.
→ See Unit 102

superlative an adjective or adverb with '-est' on the end or 'most' in front of it; EG *thinnest, quickest, most beautiful.*
→ See Units 32, **35-36**, 70

tag question a statement to which a question tag has been added; EG *She's quiet, isn't she?* → See Units 7-8

tense the form of a verb which shows whether you are referring to the past, present, or future. → See Units 57-65

future 'will' or 'shall' with the base form of the verb, used to refer to future events; EG *She **will come** tomorrow.* → See Unit 64

future continuous 'will' or 'shall' with 'be' and a present participle, used to refer to future events; EG *She **will be going** soon.* → See Units 60, 64

future perfect 'will' or 'shall' with 'have' and a past participle, used to refer to future events; EG *I **shall have finished** by tomorrow.* → See Units 61, 64

future perfect continuous 'will' or 'shall' with 'have been' and a present participle, used to refer to future events; EG *I **will have been walking** for three hours by then.* → See Units 60-61, 64

past simple the past form of a verb, used to refer to past events; EG *They waited.* → See Units 59, 63, 74

past continuous 'was' or 'were' with a present participle, usually used to refer to past events; EG *They **were** worrying about it yesterday.* → See Units 59-60, 63

past perfect 'had' with a past participle, used to refer to past events; EG *She **had finished.*** → See Units 59, 61, 63

past perfect continuous 'had been' with a present participle, used to refer to past events; EG *He **had been waiting** for hours.* → See Units 59-61, 63

present simple the base form and the third person singular form of a verb, usually used to refer to present events; EG *I **like** bananas... My sister **hates** them.* → See Units 58, 62, 65, 74

present continuous the present simple of 'be' with a present participle, usually used to refer to present events; EG *Things **are improving.*** → See Units 58, 60, 62, 65

present perfect 'have' or 'has' with a past participle, used to refer to past events which exist in the present; EG *She **has loved** him for ten years.* → See Units 58, 61, 63, 65

present perfect continuous 'have been' or 'has been' with a present participle, used to refer to past events which continue in the present; EG *We **have been sitting** here for hours.* → See Units 58, 60-61, 63

'that'-clause a clause starting with 'that', used mainly when reporting what someone has said; EG *She said that she'd wash up for me.* → See Units 33-34, 76-77, 95

third person see **person**.

time clause a subordinate clause which indicates the time of an event; EG *I'll phone you **when I get back.*** → See Unit 96

time expression a noun group used as an adverbial of time; EG *last night,*

the day after tomorrow, the next time. → See Unit 40

'to'-infinitive the base form of a verb preceded by 'to'; EG *to go, to have, to jump.* → See Units 11, 33-34, 65, 70-73, 76-77, 79, 82, 91, 95, 97-98

transitive verb a verb which takes an object; EG *She's **wasting** her money.* → See Unit 51

uncount noun a noun which has only one form, takes a singular verb, and is not used with 'a' or numbers. Uncount nouns often refer to substances, qualities, feelings, activities, and abstract ideas; EG *coal, courage, anger, help, fun.* → See Units **15**, 24, 27, 29-30

verb a word which is used with a subject to say what someone or something does, or what happens to them; EG *sing, spill, die.* → See Units 3-4, 10, 49-65, 69-78

verb group a main verb, or a main verb with one or more auxiliaries, a modal, or a modal and an auxiliary, which is used with a subject to say what someone does, or what happens to them; EG *I'll show them... She's been sick.* → See Units 1, **3**, 5, 11-12, 57, 79

'wh'-question a question which expects the answer to give more information than just 'yes' or 'no'; EG *What happened next?... Where did he go?* Compare with **'yes/no'-question**. → See Units 5-**6**, 9, 75

'wh'-word one of a group of words starting with 'wh-', such as 'what', 'when' or 'who', which are used in 'wh'-questions. 'How' is also called a 'wh'-word because it behaves like the other 'wh'-words. → See Units 5-**6**, 70, 75, 77, 92-93

'yes/no'-question a question which can be answered by just 'yes' or 'no', without giving any more information; EG *Would you like some more tea?* Compare with **'wh'-question**. → See Units 5, 7, 10, 75

IRREGULAR VERBS

INFINITIVE	PAST FORM (PRETERITE)	PAST PARTICIPLE	INFINITIVE	PAST FORM (PRETERITE)	PAST PARTICIPLE
arise	arose	arisen	eat	ate	eaten
awake	awoke	awoken	fall	fell	fallen
be	was, were	been	feed	fed	fed
beat	beat	beaten	feel	felt	felt
become	became	become	fight	fought	fought
begin	began	begun	find	found	found
bend	bent	bent	fly	flew	flown
bet	bet	bet	forbid	forbade	forbidden
bind	bound	bound	forget	forgot	forgotten
bite	bit	bitten	freeze	froze	frozen
bleed	bled	bled	get	got	got, (AM) gotten
blow	blew	blown			
break	broke	broken	give	gave	given
bring	brought	brought	go	went	gone
build	built	built	grind	ground	ground
burn	burned or burnt	burned or burnt	grow	grew	grown
			hang	hung or hanged	hung or hanged
burst	burst	burst			
buy	bought	bought	have	had	had
can¹	could	–	hear	heard	heard
cast	cast	cast	hide	hid	hidden
catch	caught	caught	hit	hit	hit
choose	chose	chosen	hold	held	held
cling	clung	clung	hurt	hurt	hurt
come	came	come	keep	kept	kept
cost	cost or costed	cost or costed	kneel	knelt or kneeled	knelt or kneeled
creep	crept	crept	know	knew	known
cut	cut	cut	lay	laid	laid
deal	dealt	dealt	lead¹	led	led
dig	dug	dug	lean	leaned or leant	leaned or leant
dive	dived, (AM) dove	dived	leap	leaped or leapt	leaped or leapt
do	did	done			
draw	drew	drawn	learn	learned or learnt	learned or learnt
dream	dreamed or dreamt	dreamed or dreamt	leave	left	left
			lend	lent	lent
drink	drank	drunk	let	let	let
drive	drove	driven			

INFINITIVE	PAST FORM (PRETERITE)	PAST PARTICIPLE	INFINITIVE	PAST FORM (PRETERITE)	PAST PARTICIPLE
lie[1]	lay	lain	speak	spoke	spoken
light	lit *or* lighted	lit *or* lighted	speed	speeded *or* sped	speeded *or* sped
lose	lost	lost	spell	spelled *or* spelt	spelled *or* spelt
make	made	made			
may	might	–	spend	spent	spent
mean[1]	meant	meant	spill	spilled *or* spilt	spilled *or* spilt
meet	met	met			
pay	paid	paid	spit	spat, *(AM)* spit	spat, *(AM)* spit
put	put	put			
quit	quit	quit	spoil	spoiled *or* spoilt	spoiled *or* spoilt
read	read	read			
rid	rid	rid	spread	spread	spread
ride	rode	ridden	spring	sprang	sprung
ring[1]	rang	rung	stand	stood	stood
rise	rose	risen	steal	stole	stolen
run	ran	run	stick[2]	stuck	stuck
say	said	said	sting	stung	stung
see	saw	seen	stink	stank	stunk
seek	sought	sought	strike	struck	struck *or* stricken
sell	sold	sold			
send	sent	sent	swear	swore	sworn
set[2]	set	set	sweep	swept	swept
shake	shook	shaken	swell	swelled	swollen
shed	shed	shed	swim	swam	swum
shine	shone *or* shined	shone *or* shined	swing	swung	swung
			take	took	taken
shoe	shod	shod	teach	taught	taught
shoot	shot	shot	tear[2]	tore	torn
show	showed	shown	tell	told	told
shrink	shrank	shrunk	think	thought	thought
shut	shut	shut	throw	threw	thrown
sing	sang	sung	wake	woke, *(AM)* waked	woken
sink	sank	sunk			
sit	sat	sat	wear	wore	worn
sleep	slept	slept	weep	wept	wept
slide	slid	slid	win	won	won
smell	smelled *or* smelt	smelled *or* smelt	wind[2]	wound	wound
			write	wrote	written

PREFIXES AND SUFFIXES

Prefixes are beginnings of words, which have a regular and predictable meaning, and can be added to words to make a new word. Suffixes are word endings which can be added to words, usually to make a new word with a similar meaning but different part of speech.

Listed here are the most frequent prefixes, followed by the most frequent suffixes.

Prefixes

a- forms adjectives which have 'not', 'without', or 'opposite' in their meaning. For example, *atypical* behaviour is not typical of someone.

anti- forms nouns and adjectives which refer to some sort of opposition. For example, an *anti-government* demonstration is a demonstration against the government.

auto- forms words which refer to someone doing something to, for, or about themselves. For example, your *autobiography* is an account of your life, which you write yourself.

bi- forms nouns and adjectives which have 'two' as part of their meaning. For example, if someone is *bilingual*, they speak two languages.

bi- also forms adjectives and adverbs which refer to something happening twice in a period of time, or once in two consecutive periods of time. A *bimonthly* event happens twice a month, or once every two months.

co- forms verbs and nouns which refer to people sharing things or doing things together. For example, if two people *co-write* a book, they write it together. The *co-author* of a book is one of the people who has written it.

counter- forms words which refer to actions or activities that oppose another action or activity. For example, a *counter-measure* is an action you take to weaken the effect of another action or situation.

de- is added to some verbs to make verbs which mean the opposite. For example, to *deactivate* a mechanism means to switch it off so that it cannot work.

dis- can be added to some words to form words which have the opposite meaning. For example, if someone is *dishonest*, they are not honest.

eco- forms nouns and adjectives which refer to something related to the environment. For example, *eco-friendly* products do not harm the environment.

ex- forms words which refer to people who are no longer a particular thing. For example, an *ex-policeman* is someone who is no longer a policeman.

extra- forms adjectives which refer to something being outside or beyond something else. For example, Britain's *extra-European* commitments are its commitments outside of Europe.

extra- also forms adjectives which refer to something having a large amount of a particular quality. For example, if something is *extra-strong*, it is very strong.

hyper- forms adjectives which refer to people or things which have a large amount of, or too much of a particular quality. For example, *hyperinflation* is very extreme inflation.

il-, im-, in-, and **ir-** can be added to some words to form words which have the opposite meaning. For example, if an activity is *illegal*, it is not legal. If someone is *impatient*, they are not patient.

inter- forms adjectives which refer to things that move, exist, or happen between two or more people or things. For example, *inter-city* trains travel between cities.

ir-. See il-.

kilo- forms words which refer to things which have a thousand parts. For example, a *kilometre* is a thousand metres.

mal- forms words which refer to things that are bad or unpleasant, or that are unsuccessful or imperfect. For example, if a machine *malfunctions*, it does not work properly.

mega- forms words which refer to units which are a million times bigger. For example, a *megawatt* is a million watts.

micro- forms nouns which have 'small' as part of their meaning. For example, a *micro-organism* is a very small living thing that you cannot see with the naked eye.

mid- forms nouns and adjectives which refer to the middle part of a particular period of time, or the middle part of a particular place. For example, *mid-June* is the middle of June.

milli- forms nouns which refer to units which are a thousand times smaller. For example, a *millimetre* is a thousandth of a metre.

mini- forms nouns which refer to things which are a smaller version of something else. For example, a *minibus* is a small bus.

mis- forms verbs and nouns which refer to something being done badly or wrongly. For example, if you *miscalculate* a figure, you wrongly calculate it.

mono- forms nouns and adjectives which have 'one' or 'single' as part of their meaning. For example, *monogamy* is the custom of being married to only one person.

multi- forms adjectives which refer to something that consists of many things of a particular kind. For example, a *multi-coloured* object has many different colours.

neo- forms nouns and adjectives which refer to modern versions of styles and political groups of the past. For example, *neo-classical* architecture is based on ancient Greek or Roman architecture.

non- forms nouns and adjectives which refer to people or things that do not have a particular quality or characteristic. For example, a *non-smoker* does not smoke. A *non-fatal* accident is not fatal.

non- also forms nouns which refer to situations where a particular action has not taken place. For example,

someone's *non-attendance* at a meeting is the fact of their not having attended the meeting.

out- forms verbs which refer to an action as being done better by one person than by another. For example, if you can *outswim* someone, you can swim further or faster than they can.

over- forms words which refer to a quality or action that exists or is done to too great an extent. For example, if someone is being *over-cautious*, they are being too cautious.

part- forms words which refer to something that is partly but not completely a particular thing. For example, *part-baked bread* is only partly baked.

poly- forms nouns and adjectives which have 'many' as part of their meaning. For example, a *polysyllabic* word contains many syllables.

post- forms words that refer to something that takes place after a particular date, period, or event. For example, a *post-Christmas* sale takes place just after Christmas.

pre- forms words that refer to something that takes place before a particular date, period, or event. For example, a *pre-election* rally takes place just before an election.

pro- forms adjectives which refer to people who strongly support a particular person or thing. For example, if you are *pro-democracy*, you support democracy.

pseudo- forms nouns and adjectives which refer to something which is not really what it seems or claims to be. For example, a *pseudo-science* is something that claims to be a science, but is not.

re- forms verbs and nouns which refer to an action or process being repeated. For example, if you *re-read* something, you read it again.

semi- forms nouns and adjectives which refer to people and things that are partly, but not completely, in a particular state. For example, if you are *semi-conscious*, you are partly, but not wholly, conscious.

sub- forms nouns which refer to things that are part of a larger thing. For example, a *subcommittee* is a small committee made up of members of a larger committee.

sub- also forms adjectives which refer to people or things that are inferior. For example, *substandard* living conditions are inferior to normal living conditions.

super- forms nouns and adjectives which refer to people and things that are larger, better, or more advanced than others. For example, a *super-fit* athlete is extremely fit, and a *supertanker* is a very large tanker.

tri- forms nouns and adjectives which have 'three' as part of their meaning. For example, a *tricycle* is a cycle with three wheels.

ultra- forms adjectives which refer to people and things that possess a quality to a very large degree. For example, an *ultra-light* fabric is extremely light.

un- can be added to some words to form words which have the opposite meaning. For example, if something is *unacceptable*, it is not acceptable.

under- forms words which refer to an amount or value being too low or not enough. For example, if someone is *underweight*, their weight is lower than it should be.

Suffixes

-ability and -ibility replace '-able' and '-ible' at the end of adjectives to form nouns which refer to a particular state or quality. For example, *reliability* is the state or quality of being reliable.

-able forms adjectives which indicate what someone or something can have done to them. For example, if something is *readable*, it can be read.

-al forms adjectives which indicate what something is connected with. For example, *environmental* problems are problems connected with the environment.

-ally is added to adjectives ending in '-ic' to form adverbs which indicate how something is done or what something relates to. For example, if something is done *enthusiastically*, it is done in an enthusiastic way.

-ance and -ence form nouns which refer to a particular action, state, or quality. For example, *brilliance* is the state or quality of being brilliant, and *reappearance* is the action of reappearing.

-ation, -ication, -sion and -tion form nouns which refer to a state or process, or to an instance of that process. For example, the *protection* of the environment is the process of protecting it.

-cy forms nouns which refer to a particular state or quality. For example, *accuracy* is the state or quality of being accurate.

-ed is added to verbs to make the past tense and past participle. Past participle forms are often used as adjectives which indicate that something has been affected in some way. For example, *cooked* food is food that has been cooked.

-ence. See -ance.

-er and -or form nouns which refer to a person who performs a particular action, often because it is their job. For example, a *teacher* is someone who teaches.

-er and -or also form nouns which refer to tools and machines that perform a particular action. For example, a *mixer* is a machine that mixes things.

-ful forms nouns which refer to the amount of a substance that something contains or can contain. For example, a *handful* of sand is the amount of sand that you can hold in your hand.

-ful also forms adjectives which indicate that something has a particular quality. For example, something that is *beautiful* has the quality of beauty.

-ibility. See -ability.

-ic forms adjectives which indicate that something or someone is connected with a particular thing. For example, *photographic* equipment is equipment connected with photography.

-ical forms adjectives which indicate what something is connected with. For example, a *geographical* term is a term that is used in geography.

-ication. See **-ation.**

-ing is added to verbs to make the **-ing** form, or present participle. Present participle forms are often used as adjectives describing a person or thing who is doing something. For example, a *sleeping* baby is a baby that is sleeping and an *amusing* joke is a joke that amuses people. Present participle forms are also used as nouns which refer to activities. For example, if you say you like *dancing*, you mean that you like to dance.

-ish forms adjectives which indicate that someone or something has a quality to a small extent. For example, if you say that something is *largish*, you mean it is fairly large, and something that is *yellowish* is slightly yellow in colour.

-ish also forms words that indicate that a particular time or age mentioned is approximate. For example, if someone is *fortyish*, they are about forty years old.

-ism forms nouns which refer to particular beliefs, or to behaviour based on these beliefs. For example, *professionalism* is behaviour that is professional and *racism* is the beliefs and behaviour of a racist.

-ist replaces '-ism' at the end of nouns to form nouns and adjectives. The nouns refer to the people who have particular beliefs. For example, a *fascist* is someone who supports *fascism*. The adjectives indicate that something is related to or is based on particular beliefs.

-ist also forms nouns which refer to people who do a particular kind of work. For example, a *geologist* is someone who works in the field of geology.

-ist also forms nouns which refer to people who play a particular musical instrument, often as their job. For example, a *violinist* is someone who plays the violin.

-ity forms nouns which refer to a particular state or quality. For example, *solidity* is the state or quality of being solid.

-less forms adjectives which indicate that someone or something does not have a particular thing. For example, someone who is *childless* does not have any children.

-ly forms adverbs which indicate how something is done. For example, if someone whistles *cheerfully*, they whistle in a cheerful way.

-ment forms nouns which refer to the process of making or doing something, or to the result of this process. For example, *assessment* is the process of assessing something and the judgment made as a result of assessing it.

-ness forms nouns which refer to a particular state or quality. For example, *gentleness* is the state or quality of being gentle.

-or. See **-er.**

-ous forms adjectives which indicate that someone or something has a particular quality. For example, someone who is *courageous* shows courage.

-sion, -tion. See **-ation.**

-y forms adjectives which indicate that something is full of something else or is covered in it. For example, if something is *dirty*, it is covered with dirt.

-y also forms adjectives which mean that something is like something else. For example, if something tastes *chocolatey*, it tastes like chocolate, although it is not actually chocolate.

PRONUNCIATION

IPA Symbols

VOWEL SOUNDS		CONSONANT SOUNDS	
ɑː	calm, ah	b	bed, rub
æ	act, mass	d	done, red
aɪ	dive, cry	f	fit, if
aɪə	fire, tyre	g	good, dog
aʊ	out, down	h	hat, horse
aʊə	flour, sour	j	yellow, you
e	met, lend, pen	k	king, lick
eɪ	say, weight	l	lip, bill
eə	fair, care	m	mat, ram
ɪ	fit, win	n	not, tin
iː	seem, me	p	pay, lip
ɪə	near, beard	r	run, read
ɒ	lot, spot	s	soon, bus
əʊ	note, coat	t	talk, bet
ɔː	claw, faun	v	van, love
ɔɪ	boy, joint	w	win, wool
ʊ	could, stood	x	loch
uː	you, choose	z	zoo, buzz
ʊə	lure, pure	ʃ	ship, wish
ɜː	turn, third	ʒ	measure, leisure
ʌ	fund, must	ŋ	sing, working
ə	*the first vowel in* about	tʃ	cheap, witch
i	*the second vowel in* very	θ	thin, myth
		ð	then, bathe
		dʒ	joy, bridge

Notes

In this dictionary the International Phonetic Alphabet (IPA) is used to show how the words are pronounced. The symbols used in the International Phonetic Alphabet are shown in the table above. Primary and secondary stress are shown by marks above and below the line, in front of the stressed syllable. For example, in the word 'abbreviation', represented /əˌbriːviˈeɪʃən/, the second syllable has secondary stress and the fourth syllable has primary stress.

Compound words, that is words which are made up of more than one word with either a space or a hyphen between them, are not usually given pronunciations. Pronunciations for the individual words that make up the compounds can be found at their entries at other parts of the dictionary. However, compound words are given stress markers.

Where appropriate, American pronunciations are given immediately after the British English pronunciations and are preceded by the abbreviation AM.

/ɑː/ or /æ/
A number of words are shown in the dictionary with alternative pronunciations with /ɑː/ and /æ/, such as 'path' /pɑːθ, pæθ/. In this case, /pɑːθ/ is the standard British pronunciation. However, in many other accents of English, including standard American English, the pronunciation is /pæθ/.